COMBAT FLEETS OF THE WORLD 1986/87

Their Ships, Aircraft, and Armament

Edited by
JEAN LABAYLE COUHAT

English language version prepared by
A. D. BAKER III

This guide was first published in 1897 by Captain de Balincourt, French Navy. It was continued from 1928 to 1943 by Captain Vincent-Bréchignac, French Navy, and from 1943 to 1974 by Henri Le Masson.

NAVAL INSTITUTE PRESS
Annapolis, Maryland

WORKS BY JEAN LABAYLE COUHAT

- *French Warships of World War I* } Published by Ian Allan, London. Sold in France by Éditions
- *French Warships of World War II* } Maritimes et d'Outre-Mer
- Articles for *"La Revue Maritime," "Marine," "Revue de Défense Nationale,"* and *"Armées d'aujourdhui"*
- Monographs on the French, American, British, and Soviet navies, published by Éditions Ozanne. These works are all out of print.
- *Flottes de Combat 1974* in collaboration with H. Le Masson
- *Flottes de Combat 1976*
- *Flottes de Combat 1978*
- *Flottes de Combat 1980*
- *Flottes de Combat 1982*
- *Flottes de Combat 1984*
- *Combat Fleets of the World 1976/77 Their Ships, Aircraft, and Armament*
- *Combat Fleets of the World 1978/79 Their Ships, Aircraft, and Armament*
- *Combat Fleets of the World 1980/81 Their Ships, Aircraft, and Armament*
- *Combat Fleets of the World 1982/83 Their Ships, Aircraft, and Armament*
- *Combat Fleets of the World 1984/85 Their Ships, Aircraft, and Armament*

} Published in the United States, Canada, and Great Britain under the auspices of the U.S. Naval Institute

First published in 1986 by
Arms and Armour Press Limited,
2-6 Hampstead High Street,
London NW3 1QQ.

Distributed in Australia by
Capricorn Link (Australia) Pty. Ltd.,
P.O. Box 665,
Lane Cove, New South Wales 2066,
Australia.

Published in the U.S.A. by
Naval Institute Press,
United States Naval Institute
Annapolis, Maryland 21402.

Printed in the United States of America.

British Library Cataloguing in Publication Data:

Combat fleets of the world.
1986/87
1. Warships — Handbooks, manuals, etc.
I. Labayle Couhat, Jean II. Baker, A.D.
(Arthur Davidson) III. Flottes de combat
English
623.8′25′0212 V750

ISBN 0-85368-860-5

CONTENTS

TERMS AND ABBREVIATIONS

Most ships' characteristics are given in the following sample:

	Bldr	Laid down	L	In serv.
D 602 SUFFREN	Lorient	12-62	15-5-65	1967

D: 5,090 tons (6,090 fl) **S:** 34 kts
Dim: 157.6 (148.0 pp) × 15.54 × 7.25 (max.)
A: 1/Masurca system (II × 1) — 4/MM 38 Exocet — 2/100-mm, Model 1953 (I × 2) — 4/20-mm AA (I × 4) — 1/Malafon system (13 missiles) — 2/ catapults for L-5 torpedoes (10 torpedoes)
Electron Equipt: Radar: 1/DRBI-23, 1/DRBV-50, 2/DRBR-51, 1/DRBC-32A, 1/DRBN-32
Sonar: 1/DUBV-23, 1/DUBV-43 — SENIT-1,2 Syllex systems
M: 2 Rateau double-reduction GT; 2 props; 72,500 hp
Boilers: 4 multitube, automatic-control; 45 kg/cm², 450°C
Electric: 3,440 kw (2 × 1,000-kw turbogenerators, 3 × 480-kw diesel alternators)
Range: 2,000/30; 2,400/29; 5,100/18
Man: 23 officers, 164 petty officers, 168 men

Ships' hull numbers and names are in capitals and small capitals. Hull dimensions are in meters, calibers in millimeters, speeds in knots, ranges in nautical miles; speeds and ranges of aircraft are in kilometers/hour and kilometers, unless otherwise indicated.

D: Displacement. In most cases, standard displacement, as defined by the Treaty of Washington (1922), is given. Where possible, full load (fl) is given; otherwise, normal (avg) displacement or trial displacement is given. In the case of most submarines, two displacements are given: the first figure is surfaced displacement; the second is submerged displacement. When available, the figure for standard displacement precedes the surfaced and submerged figures.

S: Speed. This is given in knots and generally refers to maximum speed; in some cases trial speed is given. For submarines, surfaced speed is given first and is followed by submerged speed.

Dim: Hull dimensions are given as follows: length overall × beam × draft (full load, unless otherwise stated). Length between perpendiculars is given as "pp"; length at the waterline as "wl." In cases where two figures are given for one of the dimensions, e.g., the beam of the flight deck and of the hull of an aircraft carrier, the hull measurement is given as "hull."

A: Armament. Number of guns/bore diameter; or number of torpedo tubes or launchers with diameter. Figures in parentheses show the number of mounts and whether they are single, double, triple, etc.; e.g., (III × 2) indicates two triple mounts.

M: Machinery. Geared turbine is shown as GT; in some cases, the type or manufacturer of turbine is given, e.g., Parsons, etc. COSAG, CODAG/ CODOG, COGAG/COGOG are used when such combinations of machinery have to be shown. "Props" indicates propellers. "CP" indicates controllable-pitch.

Boilers: In most cases, number and type are shown. Steam pressure is expressed in kilograms/square centimeter and steam superheat in degrees centigrade.

Electric: Electric generating power, in kilowatts (kw) or kilovolt-Amperes (kVA).

Armor: Armor protection, thickness given in millimeters.

Range: Cited in nautical miles at a given speed.

Man: Ship's company. Where not broken down into "officers" and "men" (i.e., noncommissioned personnel), a total complement figure is given as "tot."

Dates: Dates are given in the following sequence: day-month-year.

A	Armament
AA	Antiaircraft
A & C, AT & Ch	Shipbuilding yard *(Atelier & Chantiers)*
AAW	Anti-war warfare
ADAWS	Action Data Automation Weapon System
AEW	Airborne early warning
ARM	Anti-radiation missile
ASM	Anti-ship missile
Ast Nav	Shipyard *(Astilleros Navales)*
ASW	Antisubmarine warfare
Author.	Authorized
avg	Average, normal
BB	Boatbuilding
Bldr	Builder
BPDMS	Basic Point Defense Missile System
BW	Boat Works
BY	Boat Yard
CAAIS	Computer-Assisted Action Information System
CH, Ch Nav	Builder, shipyard *(Chantier, Chantier Navals)*
CIWS	Close-In Weapon System (U.S.)
CN, Cant Nav	Naval shipyard *(Cantière Navale)*
COD	Carrier Onboard Delivery
COGAG/CODAG/COSAG/ COGOG/CODOG	Combined propulsive machinery systems, gas turbine, diesel, steam. *CO* means *combined, A* means *and, O* means *or.* For example, CODOG means *combined diesel or gas turbine*
CP	Controllable-pitch
D	Displacement
d.c.	Depth charge
d.c.t.	Depth-charge thrower
DD, DDM	Dry dock, dry dock company (Dutch)
DECM	Deceptive Electronic Countermeasures
Dim	Dimensions
DP	Dual-purpose
DSRV	Deep Submergence Rescue Vessel
dwt	Deadweight tonnage
ECM	Electronic countermeasures
ECCM	Electronic counter-countermeasures
Electron Equipt	Electronic equipment
ELINT	Electronic intelligence
Eng	Engineering
E/O	Electro-Optical
ESM	Electronic support measures (i.e., passive EW)
EW	Electronic Warfare
FF, FFG	Frigate, guided-missile frigate
f.c.s.	Fire-control system
fl	Full load
freq.	Frequency
FRAM	Fleet Rehabilitation and Modernization (U.S.)
fwd	Forward
G.E.	General Electric Company
GFCS	Gunfire-control system
G.M.	General Motors Corp.
grt	Gross registered tons
GT	Geared turbine
GWS	Guided Weapon System (U.K.)
HF	High frequency
HMDY	Her Majesty's Dockyard
H.S.A.	Hollandse Signaal Apparaaten
hp	Horsepower
IFF	Identification Friend or Foe
kg	Kilogram
Kon. Mij.	Royal Company (Dutch)
kt	Kiloton
kts	Knots
kVA	Kilovolt-ampere
kw	Kilowatt
L	Launched
LAMPS	Light Airborne Multi-Purpose System (U.S.N. helicopter)
LF	Low frequency
loa	Length overall
LRMP	Long-Range Maritime Patrol (U.S.)
M	Machinery
MAD	Magnetic Anomaly Detection
Man	Manpower on board ship, crew, ship's company
MAP	Military Assistance Program (U.S. and allies)
MCM	Mine Countermeasures
MF	Medium frequency
mg	Machine gun
mm	Millimeters
MSC	Military Sealift Command
MTU	Motoren and Turbinen Union
N.B.	New Brunswick
NBC	Nuclear, biological, and chemical
NDY	Naval dockyard
n.m.	Nautical miles
nrt	Net registered tons
N.S.	Nova Scotia
NTDS	Naval Tactical Data System
NY	Navy Yard
oa	Overall
PADLOC	Passive/Active Detection and Location
PDMS	Point-Defense Missile System
pp	Between perpendiculars
PUFFS	Passive Underwater Fire-Control System
RAS	Replenishment-At-Sea
RDY	Royal dockyard
RL	Rocket launcher
rpm	Revolutions per minute or rounds per minute
S	Speed
SAM	Surface-to-air missile
SAR	Search and rescue
SB	Shipbuilding
S.F.C.N.	Société Française de Construction Navale
SINS	Ship's Inertial Navigation System
SLBM	Submarine-Launched Ballistic Missile

SLEP	Service Life Extension Program
SSBN	Nuclear-powered fleet ballistic-missile submarine
SSM	Surface-to-surface missile
STIR	Separate Track and Illumination Radar
SURTASS	Surface Towed Array Surveillance System
SY	Shipyard
syst	System
TACAN	Tactical Air Navigation beacon
TACTASS	Tactical Towed Acoustic Sensor System
TASS	Towed Array Surveillance System
TT	Torpedo tubes/launchers
tot.	Total
VDS	Variable-depth sonar
VLS	Vertical-Launch System
Wks	Works
wl	Waterline

CONVERSION TABLES

♦ METERS (m.) to FEET (ft.)
based on 1 inch = 25.4 millimeters

m	0	1	2	3	4	5	6	7	8	9
	ft.	ft.	ft.	ft.	ft.	ft.	ft.	ft.	ft.	ft.
—	—	3.28084	6.5617	9.8425	13.1234	16.4042	19.6850	22.9659	26.2467	29.5276
10	32.8084	36.0892	39.3701	42.6509	45.9317	49.2126	52.493	55.774	59.005	62.336
20	65.617	68.898	72.178	75.459	78.740	82.021	85.302	88.583	91.863	95.144
30	98.425	101.706	104.987	108.268	111.549	114.829	118.110	121.391	124.672	127.953
40	131.234	134.514	137.795	141.076	144.357	147.638	150.919	154.199	157.480	160.761
50	164.042	167.323	170.604	173.884	177.165	180.446	183.727	187.008	190.289	193.570
60	196.850	200.131	203.412	206.693	209.974	213.255	216.535	219.816	223.097	226.378
70	229.659	232.940	236.220	239.501	242.782	246.063	249.344	252.625	255.905	259.186
80	262.467	265.748	269.029	272.310	275.590	278.871	282.152	285.433	288.714	291.995
90	295.276	298.556	301.837	305.118	308.399	311.680	314.961	318.241	321.522	324.803
100	328.084	331.365	334.646	337.926	341.207	344.488	347.769	351.050	354.331	357.611
10	360.892	364.173	367.454	370.735	374.016	377.296	380.577	383.858	387.139	390.420
20	393.701	396.982	400.262	403.543	406.824	410.105	413.386	416.667	419.947	423.228
30	426.509	429.790	433.071	436.352	439.632	442.913	446.194	449.475	452.756	456.037
40	459.317	462.598	465.879	469.160	472.441	475.722	479.002	482.283	485.564	488.845
50	492.126	495.407	498.688	501.97	505.25	508.53	511.81	515.09	518.37	521.65
60	524.93	528.22	531.50	534.78	538.06	541.34	544.62	547.90	551.18	554.46
70	557.74	561.02	564.30	567.59	570.87	574.15	577.43	580.71	583.99	587.27
80	590.55	593.83	597.11	600.39	603.67	606.96	610.24	613.52	616.80	620.08
90	623.36	626.64	629.92	633.20	636.48	639.76	643.04	646.33	649.61	652.89
200	656.17	659.45	662.73	666.01	669.29	672.57	675.85	679.13	682.41	685.70
10	688.98	692.26	695.54	698.82	702.10	705.38	708.66	711.94	715.22	718.50
20	721.78	725.07	728.35	731.63	734.91	738.19	741.47	744.75	748.03	751.31
30	754.59	757.87	761.15	764.44	767.72	771.00	774.28	777.56	780.84	784.12
40	747.40	790.68	793.96	797.24	800.52	803.81	807.09	810.37	813.65	816.93
50	820.21	823.49	826.77	830.05	833.33	836.61	839.89	843.18	846.46	849.74
60	853.02	856.30	859.58	862.86	866.14	869.42	872.70	875.98	879.26	882.55
70	885.83	889.11	892.39	895.67	898.95	902.23	905.51	908.79	912.07	915.35
80	918.63	921.92	925.20	928.48	931.76	935.04	938.32	941.60	944.88	948.16
90	951.44	954.72	958.00	961.29	964.57	967.85	971.13	974.41	977.69	980.97
300	984.25	987.53	990.81	994.09	997.38	1000.66	1003.94	1007.22	1010.50	1013.78
10	1017.06	1020.34	1023.62	1026.90	1030.18	1033.46	1036.75	1040.03	1043.31	1046.59
20	1049.87	1053.15	1056.43	1059.71	1062.99	1066.27	1069.55	1072.83	1076.12	1079.40
30	1082.68	1085.96	1089.24	1092.52	1095.80	1099.08	1102.36	1105.64	1108.92	1112.20
40	1115.49	1118.77	1122.05	1125.33	1128.61	1131.89	1135.17	1138.45	1141.73	1145.01
50	1118.29	1151.57	1154.86	1158.14	1161.42	1164.70	1167.98	1171.26	1174.54	1177.82

♦ MILLIMETERS (mm.) to INCHES (in.)
based on 1 inch = 25.4 millimeters

mm	0	1	2	3	4	5	6	7	8	9
	in.	in.	in.	in.	in.	in.	in.	in.	in.	in.
—	—	0.03937	0.07874	0.11811	0.15748	0.19685	0.23622	0.27559	0.31496	0.35433
10	0.39370	0.43307	0.47244	0.51181	0.55118	0.59055	0.62992	0.66929	0.70866	0.74803
20	0.78740	0.82677	0.86614	0.90551	0.94488	0.98425	1.02362	1.06299	1.10236	1.14173
30	1.18110	1.22047	1.25984	1.29921	1.33858	1.37795	1.41732	1.45669	1.49606	1.53543
40	1.57480	1.61417	1.65354	1.69291	1.73228	1.77165	1.81102	1.85039	1.88976	1.92913
50	1.96850	2.00787	2.04724	2.08661	2.12598	2.16535	2.20472	2.24409	2.28346	2.32283
60	2.36220	2.40157	2.44094	2.48031	2.51969	2.55906	2.59843	2.63780	2.67717	2.71654
70	2.75591	2.79528	2.83465	2.87402	2.91339	2.95276	2.99213	3.03150	3.07087	3.11024
80	3.14961	3.18898	3.22835	3.26772	3.30709	3.34646	3.38583	3.42520	3.46457	3.50394
90	3.54331	3.58268	3.62205	3.66142	3.70079	3.74016	3.77953	3.81890	3.85827	3.89764
100	3.93701									

CONVERSION FACTORS

Meter	Yard	Foot	Inch	Centimeter	Millimeter
1	1.093 61	3.280 84	39.370 1	100	1 000
0.914 4	1	3	36	91.44	914.4
0.304 8	0.333 333	1	12	30.48	304.8
0.254	0.027 777 8	0.083 333	1	2.54	25.4 j
0.01	0.010 936 1	0.032 808 4	0.398 701	1	10
0.001	0.001 093 61	0.003 280 84	0.039 370 4	0.1	1

Nautical mile		Statute mile		Meters
1	=	1.151 52	=	1 853.18

♦ Boiler working pressure

Kilogram per square centimeter (atmosphere)		*Pounds per square inch*
1	equivalent →	14.223 3
0.070 307	← equivalent	1

♦ Conversion for Fahrenheit and centigrade scales

1 degree centigrade = 1.8 degrees Fahrenheit
1 degree Fahrenheit = 5/9 degree centigrade
t °F = 5/9(t − 32)°C.
t °C = (1.8 t + 32)°F.

♦ Weights

1 kilogram = 2.204 62 *pounds* (av)
1 *pound* = 0.453 592
1 ton (metric) = 0.984 21 *ton*
1 *ton* = 1.016 05 *metric ton*

♦ Power

1 (CV) = 0.986 32 *horsepower* (HP) 0.735 88 kilowatt (Greenwich) (75 kgm s)
1 *horsepower* (HP) = 1.013 87 (CV) 0.746 08 kilowatt (Greenwich)

PREFACE TO THE ENGLISH LANGUAGE EDITION

This year's edition of *Combat Fleets* comes in a new format to improve ease of handling, keep production costs within bounds, and, frankly, to ease the strain on the bindings. The same column width has been retained, so that the photography remains as large as possible. Even so, the book has grown again, both a testament to the over 7,000 photographs that were forwarded by contributors from around the world for illustration or research purposes and because of the continued proliferation of new naval and quasi-naval ships and aircraft.

The 1986/87 *Combat Fleets* adds descriptions of the forces of half-a-dozen "fleets" that have sprung into existence over the last two years. Well over 80 percent of the photos are new, and the total has reached over 3,000. New line drawings by Robert Dumas, Louis Gassier, and myself have been added. Every effort has been made to make the book an accurate reflection of the fleets of the world on 1 January 1986, although it must be recognized that the developments of the last few months of 1985 will not have been reported in their entirety prior to the closing of the main text pages. Therefore, an addenda with both photos and text is attached.

Users are directed to the Terms and Abbreviations sections on the previous pages; a short study will assist in understanding the condensed data format used in the book. Conversion tables between the English system and the metric sytem employed here are also given. One deviation has been made from the metric system, however: Because so many of the users are U.S. citizens, *displacements for U.S. Navy ships have been retained in long tons of 2,240 lbs.* For those seeking to make comparisons between a U.S. Navy ship and, say, a similar Soviet vessel, it will be necessary to convert the U.S. displacement to metric by multiplying by 1.01605 or by converting the metric displacement to English long tons by multiplying it by 0.98421. The volume concludes with an index to all ship names (and also class names for the navies of the People's Republic of China and the U.S.S.R.) used in the book. Major naval weapons systems, sensors, and aircraft are described at the beginning of each country-of-origin entry.

To avoid offense to any of the large number of contributors of information and photography to *Combat Fleets,* they will all be listed together alphabetically in the succeeding paragraph. However, Leo and Linda Van Ginderen, of Antwerp, Belgium, must be given special mention. The majority of the new photos in *Combat Fleets* 1986/87 come from their vast and constantly updated collection, and they have been incredibly generous in sharing their materials and knowledge. *Combat Fleets* would have been impossible to produce without them.

Others too have helped, some through prompt answers to a single request for photography or data and others through regular submissions and lengthy correspondence: CAPT Kendall Allen, USNR; Dr. Giorgio Arra; CDR James Auer, USN; CDR Jim Baskerville, USN; Juan M. Blanco Traba, Empresa Nacional Bazán; Larry C. Booda, editor, *Undersea Technology;* Charlotte Bordelon, Bollinger Machine Shop and Shipyard, Inc.; John Bouvia; Ralph H. Brandt, president, Unitrag, Ltd.; Mary Breig, editor, *Fleet News,* Canadian Coast Guard; Robert C. Carlisle (and associates Domingo Cruz, JOC Dave Kronberger, USN, and Pat Toombs), Still Photos Branch, U.S. Navy Office of Information; Raymond Cheung, London correspondent, *Defense Technology;* Walter Cloots; Bill Cooper, Pacer Systems, Inc.; Robert Cressman; Mike Curtin, director, Hampton Roads Naval Museum; Peter B. Dakan and Ross Dessert, Boeing Marine Systems; Göran Damström, Wärtsilä, Helsinki Shipyard; Gary Davies, Maritime Photographic; Wilhelm Donko, correspondent on the U.S. Navy; Ann J. Dowdy, Swiftships, Inc., who graciously prepared special data sheets; Charles Dragonette; Leslie M. Dury, correspondent on Royal Navy and European developments; Dipl.-Ing. Hartmut Ehlers, correspondent on Turkey, Africa, and other areas, and photographer; Ron Elias, photographer, Ingalls Shipbuilding; Gordon Falt, Bath Iron Works; John R. Forster, Lantana Boatyard, Inc.; Dr. Norman Friedman, consummate expert on naval systems; Roger J.L. Fry; Ross Gillett, editor, *The Navy,* photographer and correspondent on the Royal Australian navy; T. K. Glenn, R.C.A. Government and Commercial Systems, Missile and Surface Radar Division; Louis R. Grainger, Military Sealift Command; CDR Alvin H. Grobmeier, USN (Ret.); Gilbert Gyssels, prolific photographer; Charles Haberlein; LT(JG) James V. Hardy, USN, VF-111; René Hieronymus; Dr. Dan Hightower, NOSC, Hawaii; CDR H. Wyman Howard, USN; Kohji Ishiwata, editor, *Ships of the World;* John Jedrlinic; Vic Jeffery, Command Public Relations Officer, R.A.N., Rockingham; Florian Jentsch; John Jordan; B. R. Kellum, General Dynamics, Electric Boat Division; Teddy Kilbourne, Ingalls Shipbuilding; Dane Konop, National Oceanic and Atmospheric Administration (NOAA); Gerhard Koop, photographer and correspondent on the *Bundesmarine;* Jürg Kürsener; Annikki Laaksonen, Rauma-Repola OY, Uusikaupunki Shipyard; Dr. Roger L. Levin, president, MAR Inc.; Michel Louagie, photographer; Patty M. Maddocks, photo librarian, U.S. Naval Institute; Bill Malacrida, Swiftships, Inc.; Charles W. Mann, MonArk Boat Co.; Peter J. Mantle, Lockheed Marine Systems Group; Paul J. Martineau, Ingalls Shipbuilding; Roy T. McMillan, Todd Shipyards Corp.; Ron E. McWilliams, Boeing Marine Systems; Edward A. Michalski, director, Audiovisual Div., DDI, Office of the Assistant Secretary of Defense (Public Affairs); Ted Minter, correspondent on the U.S. Navy; Ray E. Nichols, Tacoma Boatbuilding Co.; Jurrien S. Noot; Debbie Nye, Robert E. Direcktor, Inc.; Antony Preston, naval editor, *Jane's Defense Weekly;* Norman Polmar, editor, *Ships and Aircraft of the U.S. Fleet* and *Guide to the Soviet Navy;* Rudolph Putz, Tacoma Boatbuilding Co.; Fred H. Rainbow, editor, U.S. Naval Institute *Proceedings;* John C. Reilly; Bram Risseeuw, correspondent on South American and European navies; Dr. Stephen S. Roberts; LCDR Mark L. Rosenthal, USN; Al Ross II; Ray Saenz, Defense Systems Division, General Electric Co.; Carol St. John, MonArk Boat Co.; Dr. Robert L. Scheina, historian, U.S. Coast Guard, photographer and expert on South American navies; Howard W. Serig, Jr., for the superb color photograph on our dust jacket; CDR W. F. Shepherd, USN; Rev. Albert T. Tappman; Clive and Sue Taylor, photographers; Tacy Cook Telego, Military Sealift Command; Dipl.-Ing. Stefan Terzibaschitsch, photographer and Europe's leading expert on the U.S. Navy; Christophe Van Oyen; Michael Wake, editor, *The Naval Architect;* Armin Wetterhahn, author (with Siegfried Breyer) of *Handbuch der Warschauer-Pakt-Flotten;* Mark Willis, Maritime Photographic; Christopher C. Wright III, editor, *Warship International;* Jürgen Zeitlhofer; and many others, who might prefer to remain anonymous. To any whose letters have gone unacknowledged, my deepest apologies.

Especial appreciation is due to Jean Labayle Couhat, editor and compiler of *Les Flottes de Combat,* upon which this English-language version is closely based. M. Labayle Couhat has rapidly and thoroughly checked the proof pages for this edition and made many invaluable last-minute additions, corrections, and deletions, as well as supplying unique photos that arrived too late for inclusion in the French edition. M. Labayle Couhat remains the indisputable dean of naval reference compilers.

The sources of information for this publication are many and varied, official and unofficial. Particularly valuable have been the following periodicals: *Air International, Alle Hens, Aviation Week, Combat Craft, Flight, International Defense Review, Jane's Defence Weekly, Marine Rundschau, Maritime Defense, Navy International, Pacific Defense Reporter, Royal Navy News Ships Monthly, Ships of the World, Soldat und Technik, Surface Warfare,* and *Warship International.* Our sister references *Jane's Fighting Ships* and *Weyers Flottentaschenbuch,* edited by John E. Moore and Gerhard Albrecht, respectively, were frequently consulted, as well.

My boundless gratitude goes to my Naval Institute colleague, Carol Swartz, senior manuscript editor of the Naval Institute Press, who kept track of the 90-lb. manuscript and mountains of photos while rendering decypherable thousands of tiny entries written between the lines and down the sides of the manuscript pages. Carol graciously coped with dozens of notes with late changes and fielded innumerable telephoned addenda; she is the real "editor" of this work. Beverly S. Baum and Moira M. Megargee again brought the whole together through expert production, and the people at Progressive Typographers, Inc., of Emigsville, Pennsylvania, made the whole thing readable and, we hope, pleasing to the eye. And for all her expert, but tedious, work on the index, I thank Marge Whittington. The late Mary Veronica Amoss once again translated M. Labayle Couhat's introduction with speed and fidelity. Thomas F. Epley, director of the Naval Institute Press, and Lionel Leventhal of Arms and Armour Press kept me at this lengthy and complex project and had faith in the outcome. Finally, I cannot express enough my gratitude to my wife Anne-marie and my daughter, Alexandra, for their assistance, patience, and support through many months of evening and weekend labor.

Combat Fleets appears on a two-year cycle, but the work of the editors is never-ending. Any user who has information to update or correct a photograph to contribute for use in preparing the next 1988/89 edition is encouraged to contact the editors via the Naval Institute Press, Annapolis, Md. 21402. Dates and locations for all photographs are desirable, and all material used will be credited to the contributors. *Your* assistance in making *Combat Fleets* as accurate, thorough, and timely as possible is, once again, urgently solicited.

A. D. Baker III
1-1-86

PREFACE TO THE FRENCH EDITION

This 1986 edition of *Flottes de Combat* is the last to appear under my name alone. I have reached an age where I want to prepare a successor. Hence, I have asked my friend, Reserve Sr. Lieutenant Bernard Prézelin, who has been helping me correct the proofs of this work, to collaborate on the 1988 edition, which we will sign together. It will be time to entrust him solely or to his directed team with this nearly century-old document. Monsieur Prézelin is completely competent to be my successor: he has youthful enthusiasm, love of the navy, a tireless scholarship, the genius for details, and the critical spirit needed for creating a document of this importance.

Since Admiral de Joybert, then CNO, asked me in 1974 to replace the late lamented Henri le Masson, I have strived to improve the work in each edition, and I have had the satisfaction of seeing it adopted by the Americans. The American edition, entitled *Combat Fleets of the World,* is published under the auspices of the U.S. Naval Institute in Annapolis. Translated, adapted, and completed by Mr. A. D. Baker III and the Naval Institute staff, it appears a few months after the French work, and I have had the pleasure of noting that the two editions have in turn benefited from reciprocal data, and that a good harmony has always reigned between the responsible Americans and myself. I hope this will hold true with my successor. As in each new edition, there are noteworthy improvements: notably, enhancement from over 700 photos and data, plus new diagrams by M. L. Gassier for Soviet ships, and by M. Robert Dumas for units of the other navies.

As with the preceding editions, the present one owes an enormous debt to all those who furnished data and photos.

My gratitude goes especially to:

—the officers of the Naval Etat-Major in Paris, who always gave us friendly advice and assistance;

—the captain and personnel of the Armed Forces Public Relations service (Naval Section);

—my friend, Capitaine de Vaisseau Croullebois, director of the excellent periodical *Cols Bleu (Blue Jacket),* whose assignment regrettably ends next January;

—the reconnaissance flotillas of Naval aviation;

—defense Attachés and naval attachés accredited in Paris;

—the various foreign admiralties that consented to answer my questions, as well as the Soavaernets Taktikskole of Copenhagen.

I must also mention the authors of analogous works published abroad: Captain John Moore of *Jane's Fighting Ships,* M. Gerhard Albrecht of *Weyers Flotten Taschenbuch,* and M. Giorgio Giorgerini of the Italian *Almanacco Navale.*

Many shipyards and industrial companies furnished copious documentation, and especially in France, the Thomson-CSF; in Great Britain, Brooke Marine, Vosper Thornycroft, Vickers and Yarrow; Ingalls and Bath Iron Works in the United States; Karlskronavarvet in Sweden.

As usual, I received a flood of information and photos from the following persons, to whom my warmest thanks go for the indebtedness of *Flottes de Combat:* Messrs. Carlo Martinelli, Giorgio Arra, Gerhard Koop, Hannsjörg Kowark, Norman Polmar, author of the recent and remarkable 13th edition of the famous "The Ships and Aircraft of the U.S. Fleet," and also Messrs. Maurice Voss, Peter Voss, Pradignac and Léo, J. Taibo, Stephan Terzibaschitsch, and Wilhelm Donko.

I also thank M. Kohji Ishiwata, director of the periodical *Ships of the World,* who gave me nearly all the photos in the chapter on the Japanese Navy.

J.LC.
15-09-85

THE FOUR MAJOR NAVIES

"In the year 2000, the space above the oceans will be very much in use. It has nothing to do with its own importance: the sea will remain indispensable for transportation, for the launching of military power, and as the impregnable hiding place for ballistic-missile submarines."

—Admiral Yves Leenherdt
Chief of the Naval General Staff
Défense Nationale, August 1985

There are two events that will affect naval strategy and tactics to some degree: the generalized use of outer space by surveillance and telecommunications satellites, and the so-called cruise missile.

A surveillance satellite might be geographically stationary, but most of them are not. There are two types of such satellites: one is optical and the other works by radar. The former travels at a high speed, around 25,000 km an hour, and being something like a telescope, it allows what is happening on earth to be observed; but it has a narrow field of vision (only about 60 km). An hour and a half later after the first pass, it passes again some 1,500 km from the area that it previously flew over. If, on its first passage, it saw a ship or naval force, the chances are that the second time it passes it will see nothing, because the ship or naval force will have moved on, leaving no trace upon the sea. Furthermore, to see anything, it must have good visibility, and that is relatively rare, because more than 70 percent of the time maritime skies are filled with clouds.

The radar surveillance satellite, which is not affected by clouds, may be of greater interest. Passing over at an altitude of 250 to 850 km, its field of observation is broader than that of the optical satellite. Therefore, it can be useful in observing any maritime area that is considered essential. It is very expensive, however, because it requires a miniature and dependable nuclear reactor to provide the power to make the radar work. In this area, the Soviets seem to be somewhat in advance of the Americans. They are already doing tests, which became known when one of their satellites came down in the far north of Canada some years ago. At the time of the Falklands War, it is thought that they launched a radar satellite to survey the zone of operations, but perhaps owing to the reactor's malfunction or for some other reason, the system did not work. It is likely that future research will be directed towards perfecting radar surveillance satellites. But when the number of satellites that would be required to observe the seas and oceans, which occupy seven tenths of the surface of earth, is considered, their use will undoubtedly be limited.

The surveillance satellite, whether optical or radar, cannot now be any more than marginally useful in the conduct of naval operations, and probably won't be for a long time. On the other hand, it can be very useful in observing what is taking place on land. It can photograph a specific objective, record a concentration of troops or vehicles, and count the number of ships at a naval base that appear available or unavailable. It can see that treaties concerning strategic armaments are being respected (the SALT agreements), follow naval construction in a dockyard, watch the progress being made, and determine its characteristics (a case in point being the Soviet aircraft carriers in the yard at Nikolayev). And it can pinpoint transmitting installations, radar, and missile silos, etc., of the adversary. Very soon, the French civilian satellite SPOT will be making pictures of the land and will, as has recently been said, have a naval "interest."

The conflict in the Falklands War brought into public view military interest in telecommunications relay satellites. They had been around for some time, but it was their military application in that conflict that made clear all the advantages that were to be gained by a navy that could afford them for its operational missions. The only operational British telecommunications satellite, *Skynet,* which was unstable in orbit, did not cover the area of the Falklands, and to compensate for that handicap the Royal Navy, at its headquarters in Northwood, did not have the means of transmission needed to control and command a combined fleet sent so far away. It is thanks to the use of American satellites, the civilian MARISAT and the military *FleetSatCom* and DSCS, that the British were able to keep in touch with their forces more than 11,000 km from home by encrypted communications. Thus Admiral Woodward, the commander of the forces on the spot, was able at all times to keep informed about the progress of diplomatic negotiations, receive all the military information that he needed for the success of his mission, and make known his own needs. Without the help of the American satellites, the British government and high command would certainly have faced much more difficulty in the management of that crisis. Until now, the commander of a naval force operating far from home, who was inadequately or not at all in touch by radio with his superior authorities, could not possibly keep informed about the general situation.[1] Thanks to the telecommunications satellite, he can now, wherever he might be and in complete security, be in almost instantaneous contact with the authorities on land and can benefit from all the information that they have been able to procure by other means. It is now possible, while remaining on the spot, if the political-strategic context so permits, to see his operational responsibility more clearly. The telecommunications relay satellite has therefore become of vital interest, especially in the handling of those crises that, due to the present world situation, threaten at any moment. The Americans understand the situation so well that, with Milstar, they are bringing into being an

[1] Information with regard to the general situation must not be confused with tactical information, the latter being in the hands of the naval force: ships, airplanes, helicopters, etc.

interforces system of telecommunications with higher performance, more dependability, and more security than its predecessors.

The best indication of the importance that the U.S. Navy attaches to the use of space in all its forms is the recent creation of the Naval Space Warfare Systems Command. This organization, headed by a rear admiral, will deal primarily with everything that concerns space technology, while an operational command, the Naval Space Command, also headed by a rear admiral, is responsible for supplying the forces at sea with information. As everyone knows, the USSR is also extremely interested in space, and, as stated above, has taken the lead in the area of radar observation satellites.[2] England, with its Skynet-IV and associated SCOT-1A, will also improve its long-distance transmissions. The French Navy, in turn, has entered the era of spatial communications by putting Telecom satellites and the interforces Syracuse into orbit. This system, which will be completely operational in 1986, will consist of three stationary stations, nine heavy mobile stations, three light stations, and eleven naval stations to be installed in major warships. The use of mobile stations, which are more difficult to track than stationary ones, guarantees the security of the system in a sudden attack. Unfortunately, the Syracuse system covers only one part of the terrestrial globe and cannot communicate with submarines. It must, therefore, be perfected, and other satellites must be launched to extend its areas of coverage. In a few years, the use of higher frequencies will increase the capacity of these new satellites.

Satellites, for observation and, especially, for telecommunications, have a tremendous future, but because of their expense, only the great powers, or an association of such, will be in a financial position to bring such programs into being.

Finally, it must be remembered that satellites with a low orbit, such as those for optical surveillance and with radar, even though militarily valuable, are no less vulnerable by reason of lack of structural strength than they are unchangeable in their trajectory. This is certainly the explanation for the efforts being made by the Russians and Americans to solve this problem and then to develop systems that could destroy these satellites or make them harmless. For this reason, the classic means of observation for navies—embarked aircraft patrols—must not be abandoned but continued. As of now, the geographically stationary orbit telecommunications satellite is not very vulnerable, but one day it may be. For very long distance transmissions, it is necessary to continually improve HF communications, making them ever more responsive, dependable, and secure, and to develop, as the Americans are doing, mobile LF and VLF systems that can be reconstituted after aggression.

The cruise missile is a subsonic, long-range weapon that has the characteristic of being able to change its course over the whole length of its trajectory at a very low altitude. This should not be confused with aerodynamic missiles, which have been in service in the Soviet Navy for a long time and have a flight profile of the type low-high-low.

The Americans were the first to study and perfect a weapon of the cruise missile type, the Tomahawk. Considering the number of missiles the U.S. Navy is expected to acquire (nearly 4,000 for the navy alone) and their price, it is obvious that the Americans attach great importance to this system and believe in its effectiveness. There are several versions of the Tomahawk, the three main ones being the TLAM-N, the TLAM-C, and the TASM-C.*

The first two are for attacks on land targets. Thanks to a special device, the missiles fly over water at an average height of 100 m, following the profile of the earth. Tomahawk can be detected when in flight above the sea, but because of its low altitude, it is almost undetectable during passage over land. The TLAM-N can carry its military nuclear charge up to 2,500 km; the TLAM-C has a conventional military charge of about 500 kg, and its range is about 1,250 km. With their SS-N-21, the Soviets have a system analogous to the TLAM-N.

The TASM-C is an antiship missile whose maximum practical range is in the neighborhood of 460 km. It carries a conventional military charge. The Soviet Navy does not yet have this capability in its SS-N-21.

As of now, the various versions of the Tomahawk can be fired from armored watertight containers on surface ships and from the torpedo tubes of nuclear-attack submarines. Ultimately, they will also be fired from vertical launchers installed in surface ships and nuclear attack submarines.

If the use of the cruise missile against a fixed target on land has been resolved, its use against moving naval targets more than 400 km distant is more difficult. As is the case with any weapon fired beyond the horizon, it is necessary first to designate and identify the objective. This can be done by a forward observer, a submarine, an aircraft, or a surveillance satellite. The target's location must be continuously maintained because the target has moved during the flight of the missile, which is relatively slow. When the missile arrives within range, its automatic target detector goes into action and leads it to a target, but this must be the one originally aimed at, and the missile must not be misled by enemy countermeasures; everything, therefore, depends on the automatic homing system's ability to discriminate between various targets and on its effectiveness in resisting countermeasures. This type of missile is visible during its passage above the water, especially if a far-away warning plane as efficient as the American E-2C Hawkeye is embarked, and it can be lured away, as has just been said, or destroyed during its final approach. Finally, its most serious deficiency is that, once fired, it cannot be brought back on board, as can an assault plane, to start the attack anew; it is, then, essential that it arrives at its target, otherwise its launching is of no use. Fired from land, the cruise missile can prevent entry to certain areas (narrow seas, straits, etc.) by any ships or surface formations, but it can not prevent a submarine, carrying missiles of this type, from getting in and launching missiles such as the American TLAM-N or TLAM-C or the Soviet SS-N-21 against land targets. The antiship cruise missile, operating *alone* or in small numbers, is not that final weapon that some people, here or there, have said or written.

Used *en masse,* the antiship cruise missile could be formidable, because it has the potential to saturate the defense. The same is true of the Soviet long-range aerodynamic missiles launched by surface ships and submarines (SS-N-12, SS-N-19) or by bombers with a long range of action (AS-4, AS-6). Faced with a saturating threat of this order, most western ships would probably be sunk. Many of them have only short-range surface-to-air systems mounted in six or eight launchers whose non-automatic reloading takes time. So much labor is involved that these systems can launch, only in the best of instances, six or eight missiles, after which, while they are being reloaded, the ship is hopelessly vulnerable to the arrival of new assailants.[3] This is why, before the saturating threat of the cruise missile and antiship missiles in general was realized it was considered sufficient to make up for this handicap by adding more surface-to-air missiles, doubling, for example, the number of mounts (as in the case of the British Type-22 frigates) or by completing the defense of these ships with artillery systems and with electronic countermeasures. The Soviets, aware of the Tomahawk threat, soon understood that they must increase the number of short-range missiles on board their most valuable ships. To avoid the complexity of automatic-reloading systems, they were the first to deploy vertical-launching missiles; for example, there are facilities for adding 96 such missiles of the SA-N-9 type to the aircraft carrier *Novorossiysk* and 128 to the nuclear cruiser *Frunze,* although neither ship yet has an operational system.

Indeed, the SA-N-9 system probably is not capable of intercepting missiles flying close to the ground, but such cruise missiles will not be a reality tomorrow. The U.S. Navy is somewhat behind in imitating the Soviets: all of its future combat ships and many of the destroyers slated for refits will have vertical launchers. The British also have adopted a 32-missile, vertical-launch version of Sea Wolf for their future Type-23 frigates. For the 1990s, the French Navy is developing a similar system, the SAAM, and its future nuclear aircraft carrier will carry launching silos for this new surface-to-air weapon, a short-range missile that will be capable of intercepting a cruise missile as well as other weapons traveling close to the surface. Obviously, these new armament systems must have mechanisms that allow them to fire on several targets at a time, and ships must have more and more efficient countermeasures of other types installed.

It should also be noted that there is again interest in small-caliber quick-firing artillery as the last chance against an antiship missile. The British have reinforced the defense of their ships with everything available. Having acquired some Goalkeepers from the Netherlands, they have also adopted the American Mk 15 CIWS, Vulcan/Phalanx and have gone so far as to have installed light machine guns along the hand-rails of some of their ships. The Americans are planning to upgrade the performance of the Mk 15 CIWS Phalanx, not only against missiles traveling just above the water but also against those weapons that make high-angle diving attacks.

After these observations on navies and space and the threat created by the cruise missile, this introduction will now turn to its objective, a description of the evolution of the four largest navies.

U.S. NAVY

Since the 1984–85 edition of *Combat Fleets* was issued, 3 *Ohio*-class SSBNs, each one carrying 24 missiles, have joined the fleet: the *Henry M. Jackson, Alabama,* and *Alaska.* These three submarines, like their predecessors, the *Ohio, Michigan, Florida,* and *Georgia,* are based at Bangor, Washington, on the West Coast of the United States, whereas those of the *Lafayette*-class are deployed and based on the Atlantic at Charleston, South Carolina, and Holy Loch, Scotland. Six *Ohios* are under construction, ordered, or authorized, while five more, at the rate of one per year, are planned in the 1987–1991 program. On 25 January 1986, when the *Alaska* joined the service, the naval component of the American deterrence force totaled 37 SSBNs with 768 SLBMs* with multiple, independent warheads (MIRV):

7 *Ohio* × 24 Trident 1 missiles (8 Type W76 MIRV)	= 168 SLBM, 1,344 MIRV
12 Lafayette × 16 Trident 1 missiles (8 Type W76 MIRV)	= 192 SLBM, 1,536 MIRV
18 Lafayette × 16 Poseidon missiles (14 Type W68 MIRV)	= 288 SLBM, 4,032 MIRV
Total:	768 SLBM, 6,912 MIRV

The Soviet Navy faces these 37 American SSBNs with 77 strategic submarines (63 of them nuclear-powered), but it must be pointed out that only 24 of them have MIRV-type missiles. Details of these submarines can be found in the section on the Soviet Navy in this book.

The SALT II agreement on the limitation of strategic arms places at 1,200, whether SLBM or ICBM, the total number of MIRV vectors that each of these two nations is authorized to possess. If, to the 768 SLBMs cited above, are added the 550 Minuteman III (3 MIRV), it appears that the Americans are on the high side of the number authorized. On the Soviet side, the smaller number of this type of SLBM is compensated by their greater number of missiles with a single warhead and of multiple-warhead ICBMs (SS-17, -18, and -19). The SALT II agreement was signed in 1975 by President Ford, but has never been ratified by the American Senate. President Reagan, therefore, is not obliged to respect it. Nevertheless, to prove his goodwill, he has decided to respect the spirit rather than the letter of the agreement. That is why he ordered the disarming of the SSBN 635 *Sam Rayburn* (16 Poseidons) before the seventh *Ohio* (the *Alaska*) went into service, and her sisters *Andrew Jackson* (SSBN 619) and *Nathan Hale* (SSBN 623) will be deactivated in April 1986 to compensate for the commencement of sea trials by the *Nevada* (SSBN 733). It is probable that, unless a new agreement is signed, he or his successor will do the same thing every time a new *Ohio* joins the fleet, and will play the same game with the number of ICBMs to be maintained in service.

[2] Particularly in ensuring the target location for aerodynamic missiles with great range (for example, the SS-N-12 and SS-N-19); this is possible only if a very complex, dependable, and precise system of transmissions in data is available.

* TLAM-N = Tomahawk Land Missile Attack Nuclear
TLAM-C = Tomahawk Land Missile Attack Conventional
TASM-C = Tomahawk Anti-Ship Missile Conventional

[3] The French Navy, with its Crotale EDIR, has a very effective system against low-flying missiles.

* Sea-launched ballistic missiles.

The U.S. Navy has 97 nuclear attack submarines (SSN). In that category, the *Los Angeles*-class continues to hold high priority. At the time of this writing, 33 of the class are in service, and 19 more are in different stages of construction, are ordered or authorized. The program for 1987–1991 allows for 14 more. The *Los Angeles* class has begun being equipped with the Tomahawk in both its anti-land target and antiship versions. Beginning with SSN 721, the *Chicago,* this weapon will also be fired from underwater by twelve vertical launchers situated forward in the boat as well as from torpedo tubes, as it was in the earlier boats. Equipped with this missile, with the most elaborate version of the Mk-48 torpedo, and soon with the Submarine Standoff weapon that will replace the obsolescent Subroc, plus a very sophisticated, multifunctional sonar, the *Los Angeles* class probably has no equal in the world, even among the most recent Soviet achievements. One of its principal missions is to chase and destroy enemy SSNs and SSBNs. Nevertheless, research for accurate target discrimination is becoming more and more intensive. The need to be ever more quiet for protection against enemy antisubmarine weapons, and to put in operation state-of-the-art armament and equipment, will force the U.S. Navy, as it has the Soviets, along the route of big-tonnage SSNs. The submerged displacement of the *Los Angeles* class is less than 7,000 tons; that of future SSNs will exceed 9,000 tons. Research on these boats is well along, and the first unit will be in the 1989 budget and will lead the thirty or so replacing the *Sturgeon*-class SSNs, whose life, while awaiting the new submarines, will be, thanks to well-programmed alterations, prolonged to 30 years before they are condemned. As far as the future SSNs are concerned, it is reasonable to suppose that the building of the prototype, provisionally christened the SSN 21 (nuclear attack submarine of the twenty-first century) will take at least five years.

Thorough study of the Falklands War demonstrated that the U.S. Navy was right in insisting that the building of big nuclear aircraft carriers should not be abandoned. In this opinion, the navy has received the firm support of the Secretary of Defense, the Secretary of the Navy, and of President Reagan, in opposition to the campaign against these ships that has arisen in some of the press and even in some high circles in defense.

There are fourteen aircraft carriers in service, four of them nuclear powered (the *Enterprise* and three of the *Nimitz* class). Two improved *Nimitz*-class carriers, the CVN 71 *Theodore Roosevelt* and CVN 72 *Abraham Lincoln,* are in the yard, while a third unit of this class, the CVN 73 *George Washington,* will have her keel laid in 1986. The *Theodore Roosevelt,* which has been afloat since 3 November 1984, is proceeding very rapidly and the ship is to be commissioned in October 1986, probably joining the fleet in the autumn of 1987.

Parallel with this new construction, the Service Life Extension Program (SLEP), which aims at prolonging the life of ships in service by some fifteen years, is going ahead on schedule. It has been completed in the conventional carriers *Saratoga* and *Forrestal,* is now proceeding in the *Independence,* and is programmed for the *Kitty Hawk* and the *Constellation.* The term *aircraft carriers* refers to ships with embarked aircraft. These planes should be just as, if not more, sophisticated as those to which they would be opposed in case of conflict, hence the priority accorded the all-weather F-14 Tomcat fighter and the F/A-18 Hornet fighter bomber. These planes are already in service in numerous squadrons, and the production of several hundred of them is proceeding to augment and replenish embarked aircraft.

The Falklands affair made it evident that these aircraft must have at their disposal a long-distance alert system to prepare them to meet in time any aerial or long-range missile threat, whether the latter be fired from a submarine, a surface ship, or from the land. With its E-2C Hawkeye, the U.S. Navy has an excellent plane that it will continue to build in small numbers and to improve.

Among the other combat ships, the battleship *Iowa* was returned to service in the spring of 1984. She is based on the Atlantic, while the *New Jersey,* having completed a visit to the Mediterranean, has reached the Pacific. The alterations to the *Missouri,* although they did not appear in the 1985 budget, will be pursued thanks to some budgetary maneuvering; those of the *Wisconsin* are written into the 1986 budget. These four battleships are excellent platforms for the Tomahawk (32 weapons in each ship), are well protected, and their powerful gun armament can be very useful, although that was not totally proven in Lebanon, in a conflict that involved a secondary nation with a maritime border.

As to cruisers whose mission is antiair, the navy does not plan to build more than the 27 CG 47-class ships incorporating the Aegis system. This number of units seems adequate for escorting aircraft carriers and battleship battle groups, and furthermore their mission could be equally well fulfilled by the future *Arleigh Burke* class of big destroyers. Four cruisers with Aegis are now in service, the *Ticonderoga* (CG 47), the *Yorktown* (CG 48), the *Vincennes* (CG 49) and the *Valley Forge* (CG 50), and six others are on the ways, one of which, the *Bunker Hill* (CG 52) is the first American surface combat ship to have vertical launchers. Five more are on order. In comparison with the CG 47, these later cruisers will benefit from improvements in the program aimed at increasing their antisubmarine capacity (particularly the Sea Hawk helicopter and the very-low-frequency SQR-19 towed array sonar) and from the offensive weapon Tomahawk. With the Aegis system, they can simultaneously follow 256 targets and deal with 18 of them. The *Arleigh Burke* (DDG 51), the first of a series of very big destroyers, was ordered recently, and 17 more with a lighter version of the original Aegis are in the 1987–1991 program. The DDG 51 will also incorporate technical innovations, particularly in the areas of naval architecture and propulsion, and will, when all is said and done, be a mini-*Ticonderoga.* Considered by many too sophisticated and therefore very expensive, it is quite possible that the navy will be obliged to revise downward the number of these ships it wants to build, maybe to far less than the announced sixty.

The 31 *Spruance*-class destroyers, although of very recent construction (the last one went into service on 5 March 1983), will, in successive stages, be given alterations with a view toward improving their armament and antisubmarine equipment, their AA and anti-missile defense, and giving them more potential offensive with the Tomahawk. Seven of those to be modernized will be given two quadruple mounts for the Tomahawk, but the rest of them will have vertical launching pads, which will allow 29 cruise missiles to be embarked, almost as many as in an *Iowa,* or a mixture of that weapon and the future, long-range antisubmarine weapon that is due to replace the present Asroc. These alterations will not present too many problems, because there is plenty of space in these ships — their designers and the Navy Department having had the wisdom at the time the project was defined to foresee alterations halfway through the ships' lives.

As to frigates, the FFG 7 program is going ahead. All that remains is to put in service the final five of the fifty-one units; except for one, they will join the fleet this year. For the moment at least, the U.S. Navy does not foresee the building of any more frigates, but the author would not be surprised to learn that when opposition to the cost of the DDG 51 arises, the navy has renewed its interest in a new type of intermediate ship between the DDG 51 and the FFG 7 that would be suitable for carrying out missions that do not need such responsive armament and equipment.

The minesweeper program is now in its completion phase, although it has experienced numerous frustrating delays. Later units of both the oceangoing *Avenger* class and the coastal *Cardinal* class will have a mine-hunting sonar designed by the French firm Thomson-CSF.

The U.S. Navy is determined to modernize its amphibious fleet. It plans to build up to eleven large LHDs, retaining at the same time the efficient *Tarawa*-class amphibious assault ships, which were built several years ago, and the *Austin*-class transports. The LHDs will displace over 40,000 tons, full load, and will do 24 knots. Equipped with protection, sheltering three LCAC-type amphibious craft, and with a flight deck big enough to maneuver numerous helicopters and/or planes with short takeoffs and landings, such as the AV-8B Harrier, it will transport a large contingent of Marines, close to 2,000 men. The prototype of the class, the *Wasp,* is already building. On the other hand, the U.S. Navy will not build more *Whidbey Island*-class LSDs than the eight already ordered or authorized. In their place, it will build a new class of LSD based on the *Whidbey Island,* but with greater cargo capacity at the cost of a smaller docking well. The navy has also launched a big program of amphibious vehicles that operate on an air cushion, the LCAC, in effect, to modernize its LCU-type landing craft force.[4] Finally, as it is doing for the aircraft carriers, it plans a SLEP program of modernizing all the *Austin*-class amphibious ships in service to prolong their existence.

The logistic support fleet, not only that of the U.S. Navy but also of the Military Sealift Command, will be modernized and strengthened. What is called the Afloat Prepositioning Force, which embarks on a permanent basis material and equipment for the U.S. Marines, is proceeding rapidly. To replace the variety of units that were bought for this purpose, it will soon comprise thirteen large ships, new or converted, which will be able to store in their holds the equipment, armament, and munitions necessary to maintain three Marine Amphibious Brigades of 15,500 men each for a long time. By the end of 1985, the eight 55,355-ton container ships with a speed of 33 knots, which the U.S. Navy bought from Sea Land and modified to service the Rapid Deployment Force, were all operational. Based at American ports, half on the East Coast and half on the West Coast, they will be prepared to get underway with a minimum of delay.

Priority in the areas of arms and equipment for the U.S. Navy will continue to be:

— Telecommunications and space armament
— The strategic missile Trident-2 (D5) which is scheduled to replace Trident-1 in the *Ohio*-class SSBNs
— The Tomahawk
— Passive underwater detection, particularly toward sonar with very low frequency, an area where the Soviets may be catching up with the Americans
— Systematic research aimed at reducing noise created by submarines and surface ships
— An antisubmarine weapon with great range and change of environment to replace Subroc in nuclear attack submarines
— An antisubmarine rocket to succeed Asroc on surface ships. The search for a weapon common to these ships and to SSNs has been abandoned as too complicated
— Improvement in the performances of antisubmarine torpedoes (MK-48 ADCAP, MK-50, etc.)
— The Aegis system
— Aerial defense and anti-missile systems;
— Better protection against smoke, toxic gas, etc., a lesson learned in the Falklands War
— Greater protection of ships against light projectiles and the shock effect of a nuclear explosion
— In new or converted ships, the replacement, if possible, of superstructures made of aluminum, which is too fragile and too vulnerable, with steel superstructures, etc.

Finally, the U.S. Navy will continue to allot prime importance to all forms of electronic warfare, particularly for countering the saturating threat of the cruise missile, for it is obvious that the Soviet Navy is making a tremendous effort to catch up with the American Navy in that area.

This brief summary on the U.S. Navy and its evolution shows clearly that America must always retain its maritime superiority over the USSR, a proof *sine qua non,* according to one of the most recent chiefs of naval operations, Admiral Hayward, of a judicious and efficacious strategy.

SOVIET NAVY

The Soviet Navy never ceases to strengthen itself, more in quality than in numbers. After difficulties at the onset, the building of the enormous Typhoon-class SSBNs seems now to have achieved its rhythm, with one of them going into service every year. Four of these submarines have now been completed. Although it was expected following the completion of the Delta-III program, it was surprising to learn from U.S. sources that

[4] With the LCAC, it is possible to launch waves of assault troops beyond the range of hostile coastal radars and to create, thanks to their speed of 42 knots, the effect of surprise.

the fifteenth boat of the series, now referred to as Delta-IV, was a different version and would be equipped with a new type of strategic missile, the SS-N-23, which, in still another surprise, employs liquid fuel propulsion, where it was thought that after the SS-N-20 went into service in the Typhoons, the Soviet Navy had decided to adopt solid fuel for the propulsion of its ballistic missiles. This three-stage SS-N-23 is probably no more than an improvement of the two-stage SS-N-18, giving the Delta-IV greater range and, more important, a number of miniaturized MIRV heads. It is said that eventually the SS-N-23 will replace the SS-N-18 in the Delta-III submarines, which makes it appear that its dimensions are probably identical with the latter, that its installation in SSBNs was foreseen a long time ago, and, therefore, when it was being built, it was adapted to the launching tubes. If that is not the case, installation of the SS-N-23 could require extensive alterations to the Delta-IIIs and put them out of commission for a long time. Whatever the case, the Americans estimate that this Delta-IV, at least four of which will be built, is intended to break through the arctic icecap and come to the surface to fire its weapons.

In order to meet the demands of the agreements on strategic arms, the Soviets are continuing to disarm their Yankee-class SSBNs, at least as strategic submarines: fewer than 22 of them remain in service. The rest have been or will be converted to nuclear attack submarines (SSN or SSGN).

In short, the naval component of the Soviet deterrent force today is composed of 63 submarines with a total of 948 ballistic missiles:

4 Typhoon × 20 SS-N-20 missiles = 80 ballistic missiles (MIRV)
1 Delta-IV × 16 SS-N-23 missiles = 16 ballistic missiles (MIRV)
14 Delta-III × 16 SS-N-18 missiles = 224 ballistic missiles (MIRV)
4 Delta-II × 16 SS-N-8 missiles = 64 ballistic missiles
18 Delta-I × 12 SS-N-8 missiles = 216 ballistic missiles
1 Yankee-II × 12 SS-N-17 missiles = 12 ballistic missiles
21 Yankee × 16 SS-N-6 missiles = 336 ballistic missiles

The Soviet Navy has 125 nuclear attack submarines, 49 of them equipped with aerodynamic missiles. In this category, the building of Oscar-class SSGNs (14,500 tons submerged) is still underway: two are in service, a third is undergoing trials, and others are under construction. They carry 24 long-range SS-N-19 missiles. Since the last edition of this book, three types of big nuclear-powered attack submarines have joined the fleet: the Mike, the Sierra, and the Akula. The Mike, which displaces 9,700 tons submerged, has a titanium hull and two high-powered reactors, doubtless operated by liquid metal instead of pressurized water. They are considered the successors to the fast Alfa, whose construction was discontinued after the first seven (one since dismantled), doubtless because they are too small and do not carry enough armament. The Sierra also has a titanium hull and an advanced type of water-pressurized reactor. It displaces 7,550 tons submerged and is believed to be the successor to the Victor-I-class SSN, which went into service between 1968 and 1975. About twenty of these will probably be built.

The Akula, built in the yard at Komsomolsk on the Amur River in the Far East, is very much like the Sierra, but what its exact role is is not clear. Whatever the case, these new submarines have 650-mm and 533-mm torpedo tubes, a direction-changing antisubmarine weapon, and, certainly, as far as the Mike, Sierra, and Victor-III—perhaps also the Akula—carry nuclear SS-N-21 cruise missiles, whose mission is to attack land targets, like the American Tomahawk. All these SSNs, as well as the 18 Victor-IIIs, have up-to-date sonars, including very low frequencies towed passive arrays. The reactors and the main propulsion systems of these boats are now dependable, which was not the case with the first generation of SSNs, and the ruggedness of these submarines has been demonstrated when they were frequently in trouble in recent years. Their large volume of surrounding ballast tankage constitutes an effective protection and is a valuable safeguard against sinking in case of collision.

Building of the Kilo-class conventional attack submarines is being maintained at the rate of 4 or 5 a year, at least some of which are for export.

From the above, it can be concluded that, on the material level, the Soviet submarine force continues to improve. Soviet submarines also are very enterprising, and have no hesitation in approaching a merchant ship or warship, and leaving the scene, as happened on 21 March 1984, when an incident, such as a collision, might occur.

In other categories of significant warships, few units have joined the fleet since the 1984 edition of this book: the nuclear cruiser *Frunze,* three large *Udaloy*-class destroyers, two more *Sovremennyys*, and two Krivak-class frigates, which are equipped with a helicopter and have been transferred to the KGB's fleet. The *Frunze,* compared with her sister ship, the *Kirov,* has many improvements, particularly in antiair and antimissile defense.

The rather slow rate of building destroyers is not surprising, because they are large and complex ships with a wide range of armament and equipment:

Under construction or fitting out there are:

—A 65,000-ton nuclear-powered aircraft carrier
—The VTOL carrier *Baku* (originally thought to be named *Kharkov*)
—A third *Kirov*-class guided-missile cruiser
—Two *Slava*-class missile cruisers
—Three or four *Udaloy*- and *Sovremennyy*-class destroyers, and at least one Krivak-III-class helicopter frigate

The nuclear aircraft carrier ordered from the Nosenko Yard in Nikolayev is proceeding so fast that her sea trials scheduled for 1989 might be advanced by a year. It is too soon to know whether this is an aircraft carrier with catapults and arresting gear or a ship for short take-off-and-landing aircraft. Whichever is the case, when the ship joins the fleet, it will not mean any more than that the Soviet Navy has embarked aviation worthy of that name. Having no experience in this area, there is no reason why it should devote less time than do Western navies to adopt a satisfactory doctrine for the use of aircraft carriers and of embarked aviation.

The sortie into the Black Sea of the *Baku,* fourth and last of the VTOL carriers, which has been expected for a long time, was delayed because of significant changes to her armament and equipment by comparison with her predecessors.

When the nuclear aircraft carrier goes into service, the Soviet Navy, along with its two or three *Kirovs*, will be able to take pride in having a nuclear-propulsion task group. It would be logical for this formation to be attached to the Pacific Fleet, as much to increase its offensive ability against land in the event of a confrontation with China and, if that should be the case, for long deployment in the Indian Ocean. The presence of this task force in the Pacific, which may be the precursor of others, is not yet any more than a far-off prospect, but it could encourage the U.S. Navy to downgrade its Atlantic Fleet in favor of its Pacific Fleet. If that should be the case, it would reduce the pressure that the former exerts on the Soviet Arctic Fleet, whose main mission seems always to be defensive, as was shown by the big air/naval maneuvers that took place in the North Atlantic in July 1985.

In matters of weapons and equipment, the Soviet Navy continues to make progress. As has already been said, its most recent submarines now have modern, multi-function sonars, including towed, very low frequency antennas. A new 650-mm wake-homing torpedo is now in service; it has a conventional military or nuclear charge and its range is around 100 km. The SS-N-16, which is the newest antisubmarine weapon that can be used in any environment (sea-air-land), is probably also launched via the 650-mm torpedo tubes.

New search and weapon-guidance radars, doubtless more efficient and sophisticated than their predecessors, have been seen on board the newest ships, including phased-array prototypes, prefiguring those that are to be installed in future ships. More than ever before, the Soviets are interested in electronic warfare: their big modern surface ships are now loaded with passive EW equipment, more and more efficient chaff-launching systems, and IR alert systems.

In connection with strategic missiles, it was noted above that the SS-N-23 continues the Soviet use of liquid-fueled rocket propulsion for submarine-launched ballistic missiles, when it had been thought that the Soviets would abandon that means of propulsion, which Western navies have always refused to adopt because of its intrinsic vulnerability. A new, short-range surface-to-air missile, the SA-N-9, more sophisticated than the SA-N-4, which has been in service for nearly two decades, is almost operational: so far as can be discovered, it does not seem that this new system would be able to intercept a low-flying missile like the Exocet. Like the SA-N-6 surface-to-air missiles that are carried by the *Kirov*- and *Slava*-class cruisers, the SA-N-9 is launched vertically.

Recently, the foreign technical press has written of a Soviet organization called Spetsnaz. A branch of the GRU (the Soviet military intelligence service), Spetsnaz consists of small groups of commandos, from six to ten men, who are highly trained not only to carry out attacks on important enemy military installations (for example, radio stations, munition depots, combustible storage, oil pipelines), but also to pinpoint and physically eliminate responsible enemy politicians and high military authorities. Spetsnaz has four naval brigades, probably one for each fleet, each one consisting of a general staff, a section especially chosen to deal with enemy naval authorities, a possible fleet of midget submarines, three underwater demolition battalions, a battalion of parachutists, a communications company, and several units for logistic support. In time of war, the first priority of the naval commandos of Spetsnaz will be at SSBN and SSN bases, as well as in communications and command installations. This kind of activity, which can be compared with terrorism, like the increasing below-nuclear threats that are now being made by countries friendly to the USSR, should restore a certain reality to the use of clandestine support and command organizations.

During the past two years, a slow but continual growth has been observed in the Pacific Fleet, which now includes two *Kiev*-class VTOL carriers, the *Minsk* and the *Novorossiysk.* The Black Sea fleet continues to provide the surface-ship squadron that the Soviets deploy in the Mediterranean, while Mediterranean-deployed submarines come primarily from the Northern Fleet. This squadron, called the Sovmedron by NATO, with its surface ships, submarines, and the support of long-range aviation based on the shores of the Black Sea, presents a decided threat in the Mediterranean. However, the importance of this Sovmedron should not be exaggerated. In general—and from a permanent point of view—it consists only of a relatively light surface force: five or six destroyers or cruisers, frigates, or corvettes and the usual intelligence collectors (AGI). The most formidable part of the force, and the most to be feared, are the five or six conventional and nuclear submarines from the Northern Fleet that remain on fairly long deployment in this theater. Making very few calls in friendly ports, these submarines, as much to rest their crews as to keep their maintenance up-to-date, spend most of their time alongside a supply or repair ship in one of the anchorages that the Sovmedron frequents.

It must also not be forgotten that this squadron is completely "homeless" in the Mediterranean, because it does not have a single naval base of its own. That is not to say that it has no facilities here and there that it can make use of, notably at Tivat in Yugoslavia for its submarines, which somewhat compensates for this handicap. Its activities are, in general, on a small scale. Once or twice a year, for example when a new ship comes out of a yard on the Black Sea or when the Soviet Navy is engaging in a large-scale exercise, the navy is reinforced by several large ships such as VTOL carriers and missile cruisers, but their stay in the Mediterranean does not last long.

Indeed, it appears that the Sovmedron has two main missions:

—To hamper the freedom of action of Western fleets, particularly that of the U.S. Sixth Fleet, but also that of the French Squadron, which, with its two aircraft carriers *Clemenceau* and *Foch,* is the most powerful surface force in the theater, after that of the United States.
—To support by its presence the states with which the Soviet Union has friendly relations, and also to support discreetly the movements of terrorists or others whose objective is to upset established order and hinder the interests of the West. But it has to be careful not to allow an ill-thought-out, badly prepared, or inopportune action to unleash stronger reactions than foreseen.

In October 1977, the use of the U.S. Sixth Fleet and the Soviet squadron *(Eskadra)* as tools in the management of the Yom Kippur crisis, was a determining factor in the outcome of that crisis. Because of a mutual respect between the ships of both nations, no incident occurred, but several actions, whose objective was to improve the outcome in the interests of the powers concerned, did: the delivery to Israel of aircraft, by way of the

American aircraft carriers, and the transfer of Soviet material to the Arab States with the aid of the squadron's amphibious ships. Throughout the affair, the naval forces showed their ability to manage a crisis, but the warning was clear, and at any moment a very serious Soviet-American incident could have produced extreme consequences. Therefore, it is probably to control more directly another possible crisis than to produce eventual military actions that the Soviet Mediterranean *Eskhadra,* until that time a quasi-independent force, was put under the orders of the Soviet officer commanding the Southwest theater.

Paradoxical as it may seem to the reader, the author is of the opinion that the presence of a Soviet naval force, at least at its present level, contributes to the maintenance of a degree of equilibrium in this high-risk area. In this small theatre of operations, which could tomorrow become a real trap for surface forces threatened by long-range aircraft and their missiles, SSNs, and other SSGNs—and tomorrow perhaps by cruise missiles based around its shores—it would seem that the simultaneous departure of big-ship forces, Soviet as well as American, could be the precursor of great danger. Also, it is not unreasonable to think that as long as the 6th Fleet and the Soviet Mediterranean squadron stay there, a crisis in the Mediterranean, no matter how serious, could eventually be overcome.

ROYAL NAVY

The Chevaline modernization program of the four *Resolution*-class ballistic-missile submarines will be completed this year (1986) when the *Repulse* re-enters service. This very important program has replaced the three *Polaris* nuclear-warhead re-entry vehicles with six warheads, each with more maneuverability and a greater ability to penetrate. These missiles have been re-engineered, and advantage was taken of this conversion to improve the navigation and tactical armament of their launching submarines. It is worth remembering that the *Resolution* class is the only potential dissuasion force of the United Kingdom, which has put them at the disposal of NATO, the British government having at all times the right to withdraw them if, in its opinion, the greater interest of the country requires it. The Chevaline conversion of the *Resolutions* will permit their existence and credibility to be prolonged until the four ballistic-missile submarines armed with the American Trident-II, which are scheduled to replace them, begin to enter service in the mid-1990s. In spite of its past and present critics, some of them even in the Conservative Party, the Trident program now seems to be sailing before the wind, but, because of its mounting cost, it has been decided to spread it out over 20 years instead of the 15 originally foreseen. The prototype of the PWR-2 reactor that is to be installed in these SSBNs, and also in new SSNs, is under construction and is expected to be in operation in 1987 or 1988. By comparison with the reactors now in service, the PWR-2 will have a power output and length of life 50 percent higher. The first SSBN of this generation might be laid down next year in the Vickers shipyards.

As of now, the Royal Navy has 14 SSNs, three of them of the new *Trafalgar* class; a fourth unit of the class will commission during 1986. The principal mission of these submarines is identical to that of their American counterparts: to hunt and destroy Soviet SSBNs and SSNs and to sink big surface ships. The *Trafalgar*-class boats are considered quieter than their predecessors of the *Swiftsure* and *Valiant* classes.

The *Upholder,* first of a series of eight to ten conventional torpedo attack submarines with very high performance, has been ordered, but although it was anticipated that one would go into construction every year, the 1985–1986 White Paper on defense made no mention of future orders. In connection with these boats, it is worth mentioning that they are to be equipped with an active-passive sonar derived from Thomson-CSF's Eledone.

The *Ark Royal,* third and last of the *Invincible*-class V/STOL aircraft carriers, went into service in November 1985, but will not be truly operational until this year. With the three *Invincibles*, the Royal Navy will have two active carriers with the third in reserve or undergoing repair. The *Invincible* will be the first to undergo repair, particularly to correct her propulsion machinery, which vibrates when she is making more than 21 knots.

The Royal Navy has 52 destroyers and frigates. Eight big Type 22 (Batch 2 and Batch 3) frigates are in the yards or on order, and the prototype Type 23-class frigate is also on order. It is envisaged that at least eight ships of this latter class will be built. The Type 23 has an original propulsion system consisting of four diesel generator sets driving two electric motors for silent operation in antisubmarine operations, and also two gas turbines for higher speeds. The Type 23 will deploy the forthcoming Anglo-Italian EH-101 helicopter. Counting the new ships and those that will be taken out of service, it can be estimated that by the latter half of the next decade, the Royal Navy will have 46 relatively modern antiair and antisubmarine ships (6 *Amazons*, 14 *Sheffields*, 14 Type 22, and 12 Type 23).

Modernization of the Royal Navy's minehunter force is progressing according to plan. There is not much to be said about this program except that its single-role minehunter will have a sonar and a system of minehunting that seems to be less up-to-date than those of the so-called "Tripartite" ships designed together by Belgium, France, and the Netherlands.

In the area of fleet logistic support, the Royal Navy will replace its Royal Fleet Auxiliary *Tidespring* and *Olna* classes of fleet oilers, which are now more than 20 years old, with big replenishment ships (fuel, food, spare parts, ammunition), six of which are expected to be built. The ships will have a landing deck and a hangar with space for several helicopters. In this connection, it should be noted that with the *Hermes* out of service and the amphibious assault ship *Fearless* in reserve, the Royal Navy now has very few ships that can launch assault helicopters with a minimum of delay: the amphibious landing ship *Intrepid* with two Sea Kings and the auxiliary helicopter support ship *Reliant* with five of the same type of helicopter. To make up for this handicap, the Royal Navy is counting on the conversion of the civilian container ship *Contender Bezant* into the auxiliary helicopter carrier *Argus.*

To the great regret of the British armament industry, the Royal Navy has adopted the American Harpoon missile and the Mk 15 CIWS (Vulcan/Phalanx) point-defense gun system. The Type 22 Batch-3 and the Type 23 frigates will carry the Harpoon. The explanation for this choice is that the Royal Navy's attack submarines already carry the Sub-Harpoon. The Mk 15 CIWS was chosen because there is no analogous British system.

A new heavy torpedo, the Spearfish, is being developed for submarines. It is intended to replace the Mk 24 Tigerfish. The light antisubmarine Stingray is now operational, beginning to succeed the American Mk 46.

The Royal Navy has made some headway in making up for its slowness of the last few years in submarine detection. It now has the Type 2016 and its successor, the Type 2050 low-frequency sonar; and very low frequency, passive, towed linear array sonars, some of them for surface ships and some for submarines, are serving with the fleet.

To conclude this review of the Royal Navy and its evolution, something must be said about the Fleet Air Arm. Recently ordered were 9 Sea Harriers which, together with those in service or on order, will bring the number of these aircraft ordered to 53. The new units are intended to have Blue Vixen radar to replace the Blue Fox, which demonstrated some deficiencies in operation. For air defense, they will use four American air-to-air AMRAAM missiles and two Sidewinders; for assault, two air-to-sea British Sea Eagles will be carried.

To compensate for the lack of an embarked long-distance early-warning plane, whose lack was very much felt in the Falklands, the Royal Navy has installed in eight Sea King helicopters the Searchwater radar, with which the Nimrods of the RAF are equipped. In spite of its known performance, this radar is a makeshift solution for the inability to embark in the VTOL carriers of the *Invincible* class a true early-warning plane, such as the U.S. Navy's E-2C Hawkeye. Modernization of the 34 Nimrod planes belonging to the Maritime Group of the RFA (Royal Fleet Auxiliary) has been completed; it consists of an in-flight replenishing system, Sidewinder missiles for self-defense, and improved avionics.

FRENCH NAVY

There are two significant dates for the French Navy to remember: 4 August 1984, when, with the entry into orbit of the TELECOM 1A, it entered the era of space communication, and 25 May 1985 when *L'Inflexible,* its first ballistic-missile submarine equipped with a multi-warhead strategic missile, left base at Isle Longue on its first operational patrol. But this is only a stage, because *Le Tonnant* and *Le Foudroyant* at Cherbourg and *L'Indomitable* and *Le Terrible* at Brest will be converted on the model of *L'Invincible* and will be back-fitted to carry an improved M4 missile, with which it will be possible to reach objectives more than 5,000 km away.

When conversions are completed around 1992, the French Navy will have available 80 M4 or modernized M4 SLBMs, with a total of 480 individual warheads. Its ability to respond to a nuclear aggression will be three times stronger than it is today, and the first new-generation ballistic-missile submarine will probably go into service in 1994. The keel of this 15,000-ton boat, whose plans are well along, will be laid in 1988 at Cherbourg in a new yard specially designed for the building of SSBNs and SSNs. Clearly, the characteristics of this SSBN (depth, quietness, equipment, etc.) will be better than those of *L'Inflexible* and of other submarines of the first generation.

The nuclear attack submarine *Saphir* went into service on 6 July 1984, and the third boat of this class, the *Casabianca,* is on her sea trials. The authorization to lay down the first nuclear aircraft carrier should be signed in 1986. The aircraft carrier *Clemenceau* went to be refitted in September 1985 at Toulon: she will have her antiair and antimissile defense strengthened (Crotale EDIR surface-to-air missiles and Sagaie countermeasures for both medium and long range). A year later the *Foch* will commence the same modernization.

The *Jean de Vienne,* a Type C-70 antisubmarine guided-missile destroyer, joined the Mediterranean squadron in the spring of 1984, the *Primauguet* is on trials, and *La Motte-Piquett* is building at Lorient. The seventh of this class will be fitted out at Brest before being towed to Lorient for completion. The *Cassard,* first of the antiair version of these destroyers, went into the water on 11 November 1985.

The *Foudre,* the first of three big landing ships, which was included in the 1984–1988 program, will start building at Brest in 1986.

In the autumn of that same year, the logistic fleet will be reinforced with the fourth *Durance*-class fleet oiler. Thanks to these ships, the French Navy will have a fleet of modern oilers, something it has lacked for several years.

In the area of weapons and equipment, the SM 39 submarine-launched missile system is now operational, and the same is the case for the most sophisticated version of the MM 40 Exocet. The performance of low-frequency hull-mounted and towed sonars has been or will be improved. For submarine detection, the French Navy is also interested in very low frequency, towed, passive linear sonar, which will be installed in several ships. To evaluate the new towed array and ASW equipment (especially the new Murène torpedo), it has been decided to convert the frigate *Commandant Rivière* into an experimental ship.

In naval aviation, two flotillas of Super-Étendard planes are now equipped to carry the nuclear tactical weapon AN 52 and will be made capable of launching the medium-range air-to-ground missile ASMP. For maritime patrol, the first two of sixteen Atlantique Mk 2 aircraft provided for in the 1984–88 program have been ordered.

Jean LaBayle Couhat
October 1985

ALBANIA

People's Socialist Republic of Albania

PERSONNEL: 3,000 men, with about 300 Coast Guard troops

MERCHANT MARINE (1984): 20 ships — 56,133 grt

Neither the U.S.S.R. nor China is now supporting Albania, and the material condition of the ships listed below must be suffering. All Soviet equipment transferred prior to 1961.

◆ **3 Soviet Whiskey-class submarines**

D: 1,050/1,350 tons **S:** 17/13.5 kts **Dim:** 76.0 × 6.3 × 4.8
A: 6/533-mm TT (4 fwd, 2 aft) — 12 torpedoes or 24 mines
Electron Equipt: Radar: 1/Snoop Plate
M: 2 Type 37-D, 2,000-hp diesels, electric motors; 2 props; 2,500 hp
Range: 6,000/5 (snorkel) **Endurance:** 40-45 days **Man:** 50 tot.

REMARKS: All reported out of service in 1980, but may be repairable.

◆ **4 Soviet Kronshtadt-class patrol boats**

D: 300 tons (330 fl) **S:** 18 kts **Dim:** 52.1 × 6.5 × 2.2
A: 1/85-mm DP — 2/37-mm AA (I × 2) — 6/12.7-mm mg (II × 3) — 2/d.c.t. — 2/d.c. rack — 2/RBU-900 ASW RL — mines
M: 3 Type 9-D diesels; 3 props; 3,300 hp **Range:** 3,500/14 **Fuel:** 20 tons
Man: 40 tot.

◆ **6 Chinese Shanghai-II-class patrol boats**

D: 122.5 tons (135 fl) **S:** 28 kts **Dim:** 38.78 × 5.41 × 1.55 (props)
A: 4/37-mm AA (II × 2) — 4/25-mm AA (II × 2)
Electron Equipt: Radar: 1/Pot Head
M: 2/1,200-hp diesels, 2/910-hp diesels; 4 props; 4,220-hp **Man:** 38 tot.
Electric: 39 kw **Endurance:** 7 days **Range:** 750/16.5

REMARKS: Transferred 1974-75; probably operational.

◆ **30 Chinese Huchuan-class hydrofoil torpedo boats**

Huchuan-class hydrofoil torpedo boat 1976

D: 39 tons (45.8 fl) **S:** 50 kts **Dim:** 22.30 × 3.80 (6.26 over fenders) × 1.15
A: 2/533-mm TT — 4/14.5-mm mg (II × 2)
Electron Equipt: Radar: 1/Skin Head
M: 3 M50-F4 diesels; 3 props; 3,600 hp
Electric: 5.6 kw **Range:** 500/30 **Man:** 11 tot.

REMARKS: Bow foils only; stern planes on surface. Transferred 1974-75.

◆ **2 Soviet T-43-class ocean minesweepers**

D: 500 tons (570 fl) **S:** 14 kts **Dim:** 58.0 × 8.6 × 2.3 (3.5 sonar)
A: 4/37-mm AA (II × 2) — 8/12.7-mm mg (II × 4) — 2/d.c.t. — mines
Electron Equipt: Radar: 1/Ball End — Sonar: Tamir-11
M: 2 Type 9-D diesels; 2 props; 2,200 hp **Range:** 3,200/10

◆ **6 Soviet T-301-class coastal minesweepers**

D: 145.8 tons (160 fl) **S:** 12.5 kts **Dim:** 38.0 × 5.1 × 1.6
A: 1/45-mm AA — 4/12.7-mm mg (II × 2) — mines
M: 3 6-cyl. diesels; 3 props; 1,440 hp **Range:** 2,500/8 **Man:** 32 tot.

◆ **1 Soviet Khobi-class small oiler**

PATOS (ex-Sov. *Linda*)

D: 1,525 tons (fl) **S:** 12 kts **Dim:** 62.0 × 10.0 × 4.4
M: 2 diesels; 2 props; 1,600 hp

REMARKS: Transferred 2-59. 795 grt. Sister *Semani* is civil.

◆ **1 Soviet Toplivo-I-class fuel lighter** — 450 tons (fl)

◆ **1 Soviet Sekstan-class degaussing tender**

D: 280 tons (345 fl) **S:** 10 kts **Dim:** 40.8 × 12.0 × . . .
M: 1 diesel; 1 prop; 400 hp **Man:** 24 tot.

◆ **2 Soviet Tuger-class coastal tugs**

MUJOULQINAKU N. . .

D: 300 tons (fl) **S:** 12 kts **Dim:** 30.7 × 7.7 × 2.3
M: 1 set reciprocating steam; 1 prop; 500 hp
Boilers: 2

◆ **1 Soviet Nyryat-1-class diving tender**

D: 120 tons (fl) **S:** 12 kts **Dim:** 29.0 × 5.0 × 1.7
M: 1 diesel; 1 prop; 450 hp **Range:** 1,600/10

◆ **4 Soviet Poluchat-I-class torpedo retrievers**

SKENDERBEU + 3 others

D: 90 tons (fl) **S:** 18 kts **Dim:** 29.6 × 5.8 × 1.5
A: 2/14.5-mm mg (II × 1) **M:** 2 M50 diesels; 2 props; 2,400 hp
Range: 450/17; 900/10 **Man:** 20 tot.

◆ **2 Soviet Shalanda-class cargo lighters**

◆ **1 Soviet Duna-class power barge**

ALGERIA

Democratic and Popular Republic of Algeria

PERSONNEL (1984): 3,800 men with about 300 to 350 officers, not necessarily on full-time active duty with the navy.

MERCHANT MARINE (1984): 147 ships — 1,372,245 grt
(tankers: 21 — 596,225 grt)

NAVAL AVIATION: The Algerian Air Force uses 3 Fokker F-27 (Maritime) Mk 400 and 2 Beech Super King Air 200 patrol aircraft for maritime surveillance.

SUBMARINES

◆ **2 Soviet Romeo class** Bldr: Baltic SY, Leningrad (In serv. 1957-60)

D: 1,330/1,700 tons **S:** 15.5/13 kts **Dim:** 77.0 × 6.7 × 4.9
A: 8/533-mm TT (6 fwd, 2 aft) — 14 torpedoes or 28 mines
Electron Equipt: Radar: 1/Snoop Plate — EW: 1/Stop Light
Sonar: 1/med. freq.; passive array
M: 2 Type 37 D diesels; electric motors; 2 props; 3,000 hp(sub.)
Endurance: 45 days **Range:** 7,000/5 **Man:** 56 tot.

REMARKS: On 5-year loan; 1 transferred early 1982, second in 2-83. Diving depth, 270-300 meters. One has lower portion of forward edge of sail projecting forward.

FRIGATES

◆ **3 Soviet Koni class** Bldr: Zelenodolsk SY

901 MOURAD RAÏS (In serv. 20-12-80) 902 RAÏS KELLIK (In serv. 24-3-82)
903 RAÏS KORFO (In serv. 10-84)

Raïs Kellik French Navy, 1980

D: 1,900 tons (fl) **S:** 27 kts **Dim:** 95.0 × 12.8 × 4.2 (hull)
A: 1/SAN-4 SAM syst. (II × 1; 20 missiles) — 4/76.2-mm DP (II × 2) — 4/30-mm AA (II × 2) — 2/RBU-6000 — 2/d.c. racks — mines
Electron Equipt: Radar: 1/Strut Curve, 1/Don-2, 1/Pop Group, 1/Hawk Screech, 1/Drum Tilt
IFF: 2/Square Head, 1/High Pole B (Salt Pot C on 902)
EW: 2/Watch Dog passive — 1/Cross Loop A (D/F), 2/chaff RL(XVI × 2)
M: CODAG: 1/15,000-hp gas turbine, 2/7,500 hp diesels, 3 props; 30,000 hp **Range:** 1,800/14
Man: 130 tot.

REMARKS: In service dates reflect delivery dates. Have two chaff launchers, deckhouse abaft stack, unlike earlier examples. D.C. racks bolt to mine rails.

GUIDED-MISSILE CORVETTES

Raïs Ali (803) VP-23, U.S. Navy, 5-82

◆ **3 (+1) Soviet Nanuchka-II-class** Bldr: Petrovskiy SY, Leningrad

801 Raïs Hamidou 802 Salah Raïs 803 Raïs Ali

Raïs Hamidou (801) French Navy, 1980

D: 770 tons (fl) **S:** 30 kts **Dim:** 59.3 × 12.6 × 2.4
A: 4/SS-N-2C (II × 2)—1/SA-N-4 SAM syst. (II × 1; 20 missiles)—2/57-mm DP (II × 1)
Electron Equipt: Radar: 1/Mius, 1/Square Tie, 1/Pop Group, 1/Muff Cob
EW: 1/Bell Tap, 1/Cross Loop (D/F), 2/chaff RL (XVIX2)
IFF: 2/Square Head, 1/Salt Pot B
M: 3 M507 diesels; 3 props; 24,000 hp **Range:** 900/30; 2,500/12 **Man:** 60 tot.

Remarks: 801 arrived in Algeria 4-7-80, 802 in 2-81, 803 in 5-82. A fourth is on order. The Square Tie radar antenna is mounted within the Band Stand radome atop the bridge. Contract to reengine with MTU diesels signed 5-83.

GUIDED-MISSILE PATROL BOATS

◆ **9 Soviet Osa-II-class**

644 645 646 647 648 649 650 651 974

D: 215 tons (240 fl) **S:** 36 kts **Dim:** 39.0 × 7.7 × 1.9
A: 4/SS-N-2B Styx SSM (I × 4)—4/30-mm AA (II × 2)
Electron Equipt: Radar: 1/Square Tie, 1/Drum Tilt
IFF: 2/Square Head, 1/High Pole B
M: 3 M504 diesels; 3 props; 15,000 hp
Range: 430/34; 790/20 **Man:** 30 tot.

Remarks: Transferred 1976-78, except 974: 12-80. Contract for replacement of engines by MTU diesels discussed 1983.

◆ **2 Soviet Osa-I class**

641 642

D: 175 tons (210 fl) **S:** 36 kts **Dim:** 39.0 × 7.7 × 1.8
A: 4/SS-N-2A Styx SSM (I × 4)—4/30-mm AA (II × 2)
Electron Equipt: Radar: 1/Square Tie, 1/Drum Tilt
IFF: 2/Square Head, 1/High Pole B
M: 3 M503A diesels; 3 props; 12,000 hp **Man:** 30 tot.

Remarks: Transferred 1967. No. 643 lost in explosion, 1981.

Note: Six Soviet Komar-class missile boats, transferred 1966, are believed no longer operational.

PATROL BOATS

◆ **1 (+ . . .) Bulgarian design** Bldr: Mers-el-Kebir SY

N. . . (In serv. 1985)

D: 500 tons (fl) **S:** 35 kts **Dim:** 54.0 × . . . × . . .
A: 1/76-mm Oto Melara DP—2/40-mm Breda AA (II × 1)
Electron Equipt: Radar: . . .
M: 3 MTU 20V 538 series diesels; 3 props; 12-15,000 hp
Range: . . . / . . . **Man:** . . .

Remarks: Ordered 7-83; first unit said to have been launched by 11-84.

Note: Six Soviet SO-1-class patrol boats, transferred 1965-67, have been discarded.

MINE WARFARE SHIPS

◆ **2 Soviet T-43-class ocean minesweepers** (transferred 1968)

M 521 M 522

D: 500 tons (570 fl) **S:** 14 kts **Dim:** 58.0 × 8.4 × 2.3
A: 4/37-mm AA (II × 2)—8/12.7-mm mg (II × 4)—2/d.c.t.—mines
M: 2 Type 9 D diesels; 2 props; 2,200 hp **Range:** 3,200/10

Remarks: Replacement by European-built ships planned. Both reported to be non-operational by 1985.

AMPHIBIOUS WARFARE SHIPS

◆ **2 British Brooke Marine design landing ships**

	Bldr	Laid down	L	In serv.
472 Kalaat Beni Hammed	Brooke Marine, Lowestoft	. . .	18-5-83	4-83
473 Kalaat Beni Rached	Vosper-Thornycroft, Woolston	20-12-82	15-5-84	10-84

Kalaat Beni Rached (473) Walles Foto, 9-84

Kalaat Beni Hammed (472)—note articulated bow ramp
L. & L. Van Ginderen, 1984

D: 2,130 tons (fl) **S:** 16 kts **Dim:** 93.0 (80.00 pp) × 15.0 × 2.5
A: 2/40-mm Breda AA (II × 1)—2/20-mm AA (I × 2)
Electron Equipt: Radar: 1/Decca TM 1229, 1/Marconi S800
M: 2 MTU 12V7763 TB92 diesels; 2 props; 6,000 hp
Range: 3,000/12 **Endurance:** 28 days(10 with troops)
Man: 81 tot. + 240 troops

Remarks: 472 ordered 10-81; 473 sub-contracted to Vosper-Thornycroft 18-10-82. Naja optronic gun director. Helicopter deck aft. Pontoon sections stowed on deck forward. The vehicle deck is 75 m long by 7.4 m wide and is served by a 30 m by 7 m hatch. The bow ramp extends to 18 m and is 4-5 m wide, while the stern ramp measures 5 m by

AMPHIBIOUS WARFARE SHIPS *(continued)*

4 m. The traveling crane has a 16-ton capacity. Minimum beaching gradient is 1:40. Can carry 650 tons of cargo, but beaching limit is 450.

◆ **1 Soviet Polnocny-A-class medium landing ship**

471 N. . .

471 1982

D: 770 tons (fl) **S:** 18 kts **Dim:** 73.0 × 8.6 × 2.0
A: 2/30-mm AA (II × 1)—2/140-mm barrage RL (XVIII × 2)
Electron Equipt: Radar: 1/Don-2, 1/Drum Tilt
IFF: 1/Square Head, 1/High Pole A
M: 2 diesels; 2 props; 5,000 hp **Range:** 1,500/14 **Man:** 40 tot.

REMARKS: Transferred 9-76.

MISCELLANEOUS

◆ **1 Soviet Poluchat-1-class torpedo retriever**

A 641

D: 90 tons (fl) **S:** 18 kts **Dim:** 29.6 × 5.8 × 1.5
M: 2 M50 diesels; 2 props; 2,400 hp **Man:** 20 tot.

◆ **1 Soviet Nyryat-1-class diving tender**

D: 120 tons (fl) **S:** 12 kts **Dim:** 29.0 × 5.0 × 1.7
M: 1 diesel; 1 prop; 450 hp **Range:** 1,600/10

◆ **1 tug/diving tender** (purchased 1965)

VP 650 YAVDEZAN

◆ **1 survey craft** Bldr: Matsukara, Hirao, Japan

A 673 EL IDRISSI (L: 17-4-80) **D:** 250 tons

COAST GUARD

◆ **3 (+3) British Brooke Marine 37.5-meter design patrol boats** Bldr: 341, 342: Brooke Marine, Lowestoft; others: ONCN/CNE, Mers-el-Kebir

341 EL YAKEDH (In serv. 12-82)	344 N. . . (In serv. 2-85)
342 EL MORAKEB (In serv. 4-83)	345 N. . . (In serv. 1985)
343 N. . . (In serv. 5-84)	346 N. . . (In serv. 1985)

D: 166 tons (250 fl) **S:** 27 kts **Dim:** 37.50 (34.74 pp) × 6.86 × 1.78
A: 1/76-mm OTO Melara DP—2/14.5-mm Soviet mg(I × 2)
Electron Equipt: Radar: 1/Decca 1226
M: 2 MTU 12V538 TB92 diesels; 2 props; 6,000 hp
Range: 2,500/15 **Man:** 3 officers, 24 men

El Yakedh (341) French Navy, 9-84

El Morakeb (342) Skyfotos, 1983

REMARKS: Also known as "Kebir" class. Program replaced indigenous missile boat in 1981. First Algerian-built unit planned for 10-83 delivery. Laurence Scott optronic GFCS. Planned Soviet twin 30-mm AA aft not mounted on first two, but may replace 76-mm on others.

◆ **6 Mangusta-class patrol boats** Bldr: Baglietto, Italy (In serv. 1977-78)

323 OMBRINE	324 DORADE	331 REQUIN
332 ESPADON	333 MARSOUIN	334 MURENE

D: 91 tons (fl) **S:** 32 kts **Dim:** 30.0 × 5.84 × 2.1
A: 2/25-mm AA (II × 2)—2/23-mm AA (II × 1)
Electron Equipt: Radar: 1/3RM 20 SMA
M: 3 diesels; 3 props; 4,050 hp **Range:** 800/24; 1,400/12.5
Man: 3 officers, 11 men

Requin (now renumbered and armed) C. Martinelli, 1977

◆ **0 (+3) P-1200-class patrol boats** Bldr: Watercraft, Shoreham, U.K.

D: 38.5 tons (fl) **S:** 35 kts **Dim:** 20.80 (18.00 wl) × 5.79 × 1.52
A: 1/20-mm AA—2/7.72-mm mg
Electron Equipt: Radar: 1/nav.
M: 2 M.A.N. D2540 diesels; 2 props; 1,300 hp **Range:** 600/21
Man: 11

REMARKS: Ordered 12-84. Glass-reinforced plastic construction. Also ordered were two Type 802, 8-m habor patrol craft with twin Volvo AQAD40 inboard/outboard engines.

◆ **10 Type 20-GC-class patrol craft** Bldr: Baglietto, Italy (In serv. 8-76 to 12-76)

100 112 113 114 221 222 235 236 237 325

Baglietto—20-GC class C. Martinelli, 1977

ALGERIA *(continued)*
COAST GUARD *(continued)*

D: 44 tons (fl) **S:** 36 kts **Dim:** 20.4 × 5.2 × 1.7 **A:** 1/20-mm AA
M: 2 CRM 18DS diesels; 2 props; 2,700 hp **Range:** 445/20 **Man:** 11 tot.

◆ **12 18-ton patrol craft** Bldr: ONCN/CNE, Mers-el-Kebir (In serv. 1982-83)

◆ **2 small fisheries protection craft**

Djebel Antar Djebel Handa

ANGOLA

People's Republic of Angola

Personnel: (1984): about 1,500 total

Merchant Marine (1984): 87 ships—97,283 grt (tankers: 3—2,052 grt)

Naval Aviation: One Fokker F-27 Maritime patrol aircraft.

Note: The ex-Portuguese craft were located in Angola in 1975 and were transferred on independence.

GUIDED-MISSILE PATROL BOATS

◆ **6 Soviet Osa-II class**

D: 215 tons (245 fl) **S:** 36 kts **Dim:** 39.0 × 7.7 × 1.8
A: 4/SS-N-2 *Styx* (I × 4)—4/30-mm (II × 2) **Man:** 30 tot.
Electron Equipt: Radar: 1/Square Tie, 1/Drum Tilt
IFF: 2/Square Head, 1/High Pole B
M: 3 Type M504 diesels; 3 props; 15,000 hp **Range:** 430/34; 790/20

Remarks: Delivered in pairs, 10-82, 12-82, and 11-83 by RO/FLO cargo ship *Stakhanovets Petrash.*

TORPEDO BOATS

◆ **4 Soviet Shershen class**

D: 150 tons (180 fl) **S:** 45 kts **Dim:** 34.0 × 7.2 × 1.5
A: 4/30-mm AA (II × 2)—4/533-mm TT
Electron Equipt: Radar: 1/Pot Drum, 1/Drum Tilt
IFF: 1/Square Head, 1/High Pole A
M: 3 M503A diesels; 3 props; 12,000 hp **Range:** 450/34; 700/20

Remarks: Delivered 12-77 to 11-79. Unlike many recent transfers of this class, all retained torpedo tubes.

PATROL BOATS

◆ **2 Soviet Zhuk class** (transferred 23-1-77)

D: 50 tons (60 fl) **S:** 34 kts **Dim:** 26.0 × 4.9 × 1.5
A: 4/14.5-mm mg (II × 2) **M:** 2 M50 diesels; 2 props; 2,400 hp

◆ **2 Soviet Poluchat-I class** (transferred 12-79)

D: 90 tons (fl) **S:** 18 kts **Dim:** 29.6 × 5.8 × 1.5 **Range:** 450/17; 900/10
A: 2/14.5-mm mg (II × 1) **M:** 2 M50 diesels; 2 props; 2,400 hp **Man:** 20 tot.

◆ **5 Portuguese Argos class** Bldr: Castelo SY

(P 375, P 1130: Alfeite Navy Yd, Lisbon) In serv. 1963-65

P 361 (ex-*Lira*) P 375 (ex-*Escorpido*) P 1130 (ex-*Centauro*)
P 362 (ex-*Orion*) P 379 (ex-*Pegaso*)

D: 180 tons (210 fl) **S:** 18 kts **Dim:** 41.6 × 6.2 × 2.2 **Fuel:** 16 tons
A: 2/40-mm AA (I × 2) **M:** 2 Maybach diesels; 2 props; 2,000 hp **Man:** 24 tot.

Remarks: Two others, *Argos* and *Dragao,* transferred for cannibalization.

◆ **1 Portuguese Jupiter class** Bldr: Mondego SY (In serv. 1965)

P 1133 (ex-*Venus*)

D: 32 tons (43.5 fl) **S:** 20 kts **Dim:** 20.7 × 5.0 × 1.3 **A:** 1/20-mm AA
M: 2 Cummins diesels; 2 props; 1,270 hp

◆ **5 Portuguese Bellatrix class** Bldr: Bayerische Schiffsbaugesellschaft, West Germany (In serv. 1961-62)

P 366 (ex-*Espiga*) P 368 (ex-*Pollux*) P 378 (ex-*Rigel*)
P 367 (ex-*Fomelhaut*) P 377 (ex-*Altair*)

D: 23 tons (27.6 fl) **S:** 15 kts **Dim:** 20.5 × 4.6 × 1.2
A: 1/20-mm AA—1/37-mm RL (atop 20-mm AA)
M: 2 Cummins diesels; 2 props; 470 hp **Man:** 7 tot.

AMPHIBIOUS WARFARE SHIPS

◆ **2 commercial-design vehicle landing craft** Bldr: Scheepswerf Ton Bodewes, Franeker, Neth. (In serv. 1979)

47 10 Diciembre 48 11 Noviembre

D: 850 (fl) **S:** 10 kts **Dim:** 53.0 (pp) × 11.5 × 2.2
M: 2 Caterpillar diesels; 2 props; . . . hp

Remarks: 446 grt/575 dwt. May be engaged in civil cargo-carrying tasks.

◆ **3 Soviet Polnocny-B-class medium landing ships** Bldr: Polnocny SY, Gdansk, Poland

D: 800 tons (fl) **S:** 19 kts **Dim:** 74.0 × 8.6 × 2.0
A: 2/30-mm AA (II × 1)—2/140-mm barrage RL (XVIII × 2)
Electron Equipt: Radar: 1/Don 2, 1/Drum Tilt
IFF: 1/Square Head
M: 2 diesels; 2 props; 5,000 hp **Range:** 1,500/14 **Man:** 40 tot.

Remarks: First transferred 16-12-77, second 16-12-78, third 1-12-79.

◆ **1 Portuguese Alfange-class medium landing ship** Bldr: Mondego SY (In serv. 1965)

N . . . . (ex-*Alfange*)

D: 500 tons (fl) **S:** 11 kts **Dim:** 57.0 × 11.8 × 1.9 **A:** 2/20-mm AA
M: 2 diesels; 2 props; 1,000 hp **Range:** 1,500/9 **Man:** 14 tot. + 35 troops

Remarks: A second unit was not placed in service. Design based on British LCT (4) class of World War II.

◆ **5 Soviet T-4-class landing craft** (Transferred 1976)

D: 70 tons (fl) **S:** 10 kts **Dim:** 19.0 × 4.3 × 1.0
M: 2 diesels; 2 props, 600 hp **Man:** 5 tot.

◆ **Up to 9 Portuguese LDM-400-class landing craft**

D: 56 tons (fl) **S:** 9 kts **Dim:** 17.0 × 5.0 × 1.2 **A:** 1/20-mm AA
M: 2 Cummins diesels; 2 props; 450 hp

ANTIGUA-BARBUDA

Merchant Marine (1984): 3 ships—559 grt

COAST GUARD

◆ **1 U.S. 65-ft Commercial Cruiser-class patrol craft** Bldr: Swiftships, Inc., Morgan City, Louisiana

P-01 Liberta (In serv. 30-4-84)

Liberta (P-01) Swiftships, 1984

D: . . . tons **S:** 23 kts **Dim:** 19.96 × 5.59 × 1.52
A: 1/12.7-mm mg **Electron Equipt:** Radar: 1/Raytheon 1210
M: 2 G.M. 12V71 TI diesels; 2 props; 1,350 hp
Electric: 20 kw **Range:** 500/18 **Man:** 6 tot.

Remarks: Aluminum construction. U.S. Grant-Aid.

ARGENTINA

Argentine Republic

Personnel 1985: 23,400 men, including 2,300 officers and 3,000 Marines

Merchant Marine 1984: 530 ships — 2,422,111 grt (tankers: 74 — 883,227 grt)

Note: Fiscal constraints have forced cutting new programs, the disposal of older ships, the reduction of manpower by 7,500 (including 500 officers and 3,000 Marines), and a severe restriction in annual steaming days.

Naval Aviation: In 1985, the aircraft for shipboard service included: 14 Super Étendard (4 in storage, remainder now flown from land), 6 A-4Q Skyhawk fighter-bombers, and 6 S-2E and 3 S-2A Tracker ASW aircraft. Helicopters: 5 Sikorsky SH-3D, 2 WG-13 Mk 23 Lynx, 6 Hughes 500M Cayuse, 2 Sikorsky S-61NR, and 8 Alouette-III.

For land-based duties: 3 Aeromacchi MB-339AA and 8 MB-326GB attack/trainers; 3 Fokker F-28-3000, 1 BAe 125 Series 400A, 5 Lockheed L-188 Electra, and 2 Short Skyvan transports; 8 Beech Super King Air 200, 5 Beech B80 Queen Air, and 3 Fairchild Porter light transports; 11 Beech T-34 C-1 trainers; and 2 Puma helicopters.

Orders for 4 additional Lynx helicopters have been canceled by Great Britain. Because it has proven difficult to operate the super Étendard on the small, slow *Veinticinco de Mayo,* 12 ex-Israeli A-4E Skyhawks were ordered in 12-84. 12 ex-Brazilian Air Force EMB-326GB Xavante were purchased late in 1982, and 7 Electra transports intended for conversion to maritime patrol/ASW aircraft in 2-83: 2 with APS-20 radar and Exocet launch capability, 2 with maritime search radars, intercept gear and chaff, and 3 for survey and transport duties.

Super Étendard 3-A-204, one of two aircraft in the attack on HMS *Sheffield* R. Scheina, 1982

Warships In Service Or Under Construction As Of 1 January 1986

	L	Tons Std.	Main Armament
◆ **4 (+2) submarines**			
2(+2) German TR-1700	1980-82	1,750	6/533-mm TT
2 German 209	1972-73	980	8/533-mm TT
◆ **1 aircraft carrier**			
Veinticinco de Mayo	1943	15,892	9/40-mm AA 19 aircraft
◆ **2 destroyers**			
2 Sheffield	1972-74	3,150	4 Exocet, 1 Sea Dart SAM, 1/114-mm DP, 1 ASW helicopter
◆ **9 (+4) frigates**			
4 MEKO 360	1981-82	2,900	8 Exocet, Albatros, 1/127-mm DP, 2 helicopter
1 (+5) MEKO 140	1982-. . .	1,200	4 Exocet, 1/76-mm DP, helicopter
3 A-69	1977-80	1,170	4 Exocet, 1/100-mm DP
◆ **2 corvettes**			
2 Achomawi	1944-45	1,235	4/40-mm AA

◆ **6 patrol boats**

◆ **6 minesweeper/minehunters**

◆ **1 landing ship**

AIRCRAFT CARRIER

Note: A 30,000-ton replacement for *Veinticino de Mayo* is planned, finances permitting.

◆ **1 British Colossus-class**

	Bldr	Laid down	L	In serv.
Veinticinco de Mayo (ex-*Karel Dorman,* ex-*Venerable*)	Cammell Laird	3-12-42	30-12-43	17-1-45

D: 15,892 tons (19,896 fl) **S:** 24.5 kts (limited to 18.0)
Dim: 212.67 (192.04 pp) × 24.49 (40.66 flight deck) × 7.5
A: 9/40-mm AA (I × 10) — 10 A-4E Skyhawk, 5 S-2E Tracker, 2 SH-3D helo
Electron Equipt: Radar: Dutch 2/LW-02, 1/SGR-109 (height-finding), 1/SGR-105 (DA-05), 1/SGR-103 (ZW-01), 1/SMA MM/SPN-720 air control — TACAN: URN-20

Veinticinco De Mayo R. Scheina, 1982

M: 2 sets Parsons GT; 2 props; 40,000 hp **Electric:** 2,500 kw
Boilers: 4 Admiralty 3-drum type; 30.23 kg/cm² (since refit), 371° C
Fuel: 3,200 tons **Range:** 6,200/23; 12,000/14 **Man:** 1,509 tot.

Remarks: Purchased by The Netherlands from the British Navy in 1948. Rebuilt from 1955 to 1958 by Wilton-Fijenoord; 165.80 meters angled flight deck, steam catapult, mirror optical landing equipment, new antiaircraft guns, and new radar equipment of Dutch conception and construction. Modified for service in the tropics. Partially air-conditioned. In 1967 new boilers were installed from the British aircraft carrier *Leviathan,* which was never completed. Purchased in 1968 by Argentina and again refitted, recommissioning 22-8-69. She is equipped with the British C.A.A.I.S. data display system, compatible with the ADAWS-4 data system on the *Sheffield*-class destroyers. 1980 refit enlarged flight deck to permit deck-parking three additional aircraft. Altered 1982-83 to permit operating Super Étendard fighter/bombers; 1/40-mm AA removed. Super Étendards replaced by Skyhawks, 1985. Persistent engineering problems. Planned to replace by 1992.

SUBMARINES

◆ **1 (+3) TR-1700-class diesel-electric attack submarines**

	Bldr	Laid down	L	In serv.
S 33 Santa Cruz	Thyssen Noordseewerke, Emden	6-12-80	28-9-82	14-12-84
S 34 San Juan	Thyssen Noordseewerke, Emden	18-3-82	20-6-83	. . .-85
S 35 N.	Manuel Domecq Garcia, Buenos Aires	14-10-83	. . .	. . .
S 36 N.	Manuel Domecq Garcia, Buenos Aires	. . .	. . .	. . .

Santa Cruz (S 33) — on trials Thyssen, 1984

D: 1,770 tons (2,150 surf./2,364 sub. fl)
S: 25 kts (sub) — 13 snorkel, 15 kts (surf)
Dim: 66.00 × 7.30 × 6.50
Range: 20/25, 50/20, 110/15, 460/6 sub. — 12,000/8 surf.
A: 6/533-mm TT, 22 SST-4 wire-guided torpedoes
M: Diesel-electric: 4/MTU 16V652 MB80 1,100 kw generator sets; 1 6,600-kw motor; 1 prop, 8,970 hp (8,000 sust.)
Fuel: 314 tons **Endurance:** 30 days **Man:** 30 tot.

Remarks: Ordered 30-11-77. Originally only the first to be build in Germany. Two smaller Type TR-1400 replaced by 2 TR-1700 in the 2-82 change to order. However, late in 1984, first Argentine-built unit reportedly for sale, indicating only two German-built units may serve in Argentine Navy, last two probably canceled. In addition, delivery of S 34 was delayed through 9-85 or later for lack of payments. 300-m depth. Battery has eight groups of 120 cells, 5,858 amp/10 hr. H.S.A. SINBADS weapons control system, SAGEM plotting table. Pressure hull 48.0 m long. Torpedoes auto-reload in 50 seconds.

SUBMARINES *(continued)*

San Juan (S 34) Thyssen, 1984

◆ German Type 209 class diesel-electric coastal submarines

	Bldr	Laid down	L	In serv.
S 31 Salta	Howaldtswerke, Kiel	3-4-70	9-11-72	7-3-74
S 32 San Luis	Howaldtswerke, Kiel	1-10-70	3-4-73	24-5-74

Salta Argentine Navy, 1982

D: 980 tons standard, 1,105, surfaced, 1,230 submerged
Dim: 55.9 × 6.20 × 5.50 **S:** 23 max. submerged, 12 snorkel; 11 surf.
A: 8/533-mm TT (14 German SST-4 and U.S. Mk 37 torpedoes)
M: 4 MTU 12V493 TY60, 600-hp diesels, 4/405-kw generators, Siemens electric motor; 1 prop; 5,000 hp
Endurance: 40 days **Fuel:** 63 tons
Range: 230/8; 400/4 submerged; 6,000/8 snorkel
Man: 5 officers, 26 men

Remarks: Built in four sections at Kiel and assembled at the Navy Yard in Rio Santiago. *San Luis* fired 6 torpedoes, without success, in the Falklands War; *Salta* did not take part. H.S.A. M8 fire-control system.

DESTROYERS

◆ 2 British Sheffield-class guided-missile destroyers

	Bldr	Laid down	L	In serv.
D 1 Hercules	Vickers, Barrow	1971	24-10-72	10-5-76
D 2 Santisima Trinidad	Ast. Nav., Rio Santiago	2-72	9-11-74	-81

D: 3,150 tons (4,100 fl) **S:** 28 kts **Dim:** 125.0 (119.5pp) × 14.34 × 4.2 (hull)
A: 4/Exocet MM 38 SSM (I × 4) — 1/Sea Dart Mk 30 Mod. 2 SAM syst. (II × 1, 20 missiles) — 1/114-mm DP Mk 8 — 2/20-mm AA — 1/WG 13 Lynx helicopter — 6/324-mm ASW TT (III × 2)
Electron Equipt: Radar: 1/965M, 1/992Q, 2/909, 1/1006
Sonar: 1/184M, 1/162M — EW: intercept array
M: COGOG 2 Olympus TM 3B gas turbines, 27,200 hp each for boost; 2 Tyne RM 1A gas turbines, 4,100 hp each for cruising; 2 CP, 5-bladed props
Electric: 4,000 kw **Range:** 4,000/18 **Man:** 270 tot.

Hercules (D 1) Argentine Navy, 1984

Santisima Trinidad — Exocet has replaced boats L. & L. Van Ginderen, 4-81

Remarks: Ordered 18-5-70. D 2 was sabotaged on 22-8-75 and was delayed, running initial trials on 7-3-80. D 1, refitted 1980, had MM 38 Exocet missiles added atop the hangar; these were relocated in place of the boats abreast the stack in both, early 1982, when EW gear was also fitted. Have ADAWS-4 data system. Both reported to be for sale in 9-84, due to inability to obtain spares from Britain.

Note: Ex-U.S. *Gearing*-class destroyer *Comodoro Py* (D 27, ex-*Perkins,* DD 877) stricken 1984. Ex-U.S. *Allen M. Sumner*-class destroyers *Bouchard* (D 26, ex-*Borie,* DD 704) and *Piedrabuena* (D 29, ex-*Collett,* DD 730) stricken 1984-85; sister *Segui* (D 25, ex-*Hank,* DD 702) stricken 1983.

FRIGATES

◆ 4 MEKO-360 H2 Class Bldr: Blohm + Voss, Hamburg

	Laid down	L	In serv.
D 10 Almirante Brown	8-9-80	28-3-81	2-2-83
D 11 La Argentina	31-3-81	25-9-81	19-7-83
D 12 Heroina	24-8-81	17-2-82	7-11-83
D 13 Sarandi	9-3-82	31-8-82	27-4-84

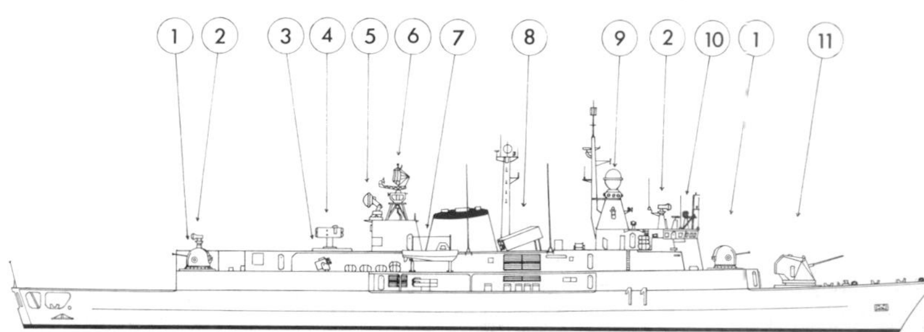

1. Twin 40-mm AA 2. LIROD radar/optronic director 3. SCLAR chaff/flare rocket launcher 4. Albatros SAM launcher 5. STIR missile director 6. DA-08 long-range radar antenna 7. triple ASW torpedo tubes 8. quadruple MM 40 Exocet ramps (under shield) 9. WM-25 track-while-scan radar 10. ZW-06 navigational radar 11. 127-mm dual-purpose gunmount

FRIGATES *(continued)*

Sarandi (D 13) P. Voss, 5-84

La Argentina (D 11) G. Gyssels, 6-83

Almirante Brown (D 10) French Navy, 2-83

D: 2,900 tons (3,360 fl) **S:** 30.5 kts
Dim: 125.9(119.0 pp) × 15.0 × 4.32(5.80 sonar)
A: 8/MM 40 Exocet SSM (IV × 2)—1 Albatros SAM syst. (VIII × 1; 24 Aspide missiles)—1/27-mm OTO Melara DP—8/40-mm Breda AA (II × 4)—6/324-mm ILAS-3 ASW TT (III × 2; 18 torp.)—2/helicopters (10 ASW torp.)
Electron Equipt: Radar: 1/H.S.A. ZW-06, 1/H.S.A. DA-08A, 1/H.S.A. WM 25, 1/STIR, 2/H.S.A. LIROD
Sonar: Krupp Atlas 80, hull-mounted
EW: AEG-Telefunken syst., 2/SCLAR chaff (XX × 2)
M: COGOG: 2 Olympus TM 3B gas turbines, 25,800 hp each; 2 Tyne RM 1C, 5,100 hp each for cruise; 2 Escher-Wyss CP props; 51,600 hp max.
Electric: 2,600 kw (2/940-kw sets, 2/360 kw) **Range:** 4,500/18
Man: 26 officers, 84 petty officers, 90 men

Almirante Brown and La Argentina on trials Schulz-Alex/Blohm + Voss, 1983

Remarks: Considered to be destroyers by Argentine Navy. Ordered 11-12-78 as a class of *six,* four of which were to be built in Argentina, but altered to four when MEKO-140-series frigate program was introduced. Albatros system has a 16-missile Aspide SAM rapid-reload magazine nearby. SEWACO weapons data/control system. The two H.S.A. LIROD radar/optronic GFCS each control two twin 40-mm AA, for which 10,752 rounds can be carried. Graseby G1738 towed torpedo decoy system. Four Lynx helicopters for these ships canceled by U.K., 1982. The MEKO concept calls for modularized weapons and electronics systems, to permit rapid modernization and repair. Nigeria's *Aradu* is very similar.

◆ **1 (+5) MEKO 140 A16 class** Bldr: AFNE, Rio Santiago, Ensenada

	Laid down	L	In serv.
P 4 Espora	10-3-80	23-1-82	. .1985
P 5 Rosales	7-1-81	4-3-83	. . .
P 6 Spiro	1-4-82	24-6-83	. . .
P 7 Parker	9-2-82	31-3-84	. . .
P 8 Robinson	6-6-83	11-84	. . .
P 9 Seaver	1-12-83	. . .	. . .

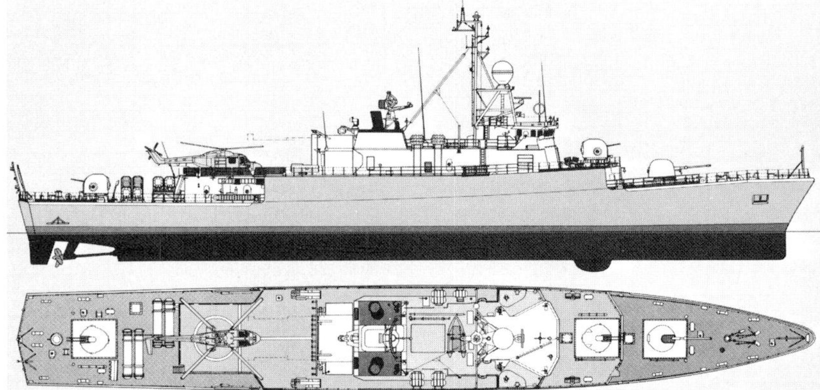
MEKO 140 A 16 class with hangar Blohm + Voss

Espora (P 4) on trials Blohm + Voss, 1984

D: 1,560 tons (1,790 fl) **S:** 27 kts **Dim:** 91.2 (86.4 pp) × 11.0 × 3.33 (hull)
A: 4/MM 38 Exocet SSM (II × 2)—1/76-mm DP OTO Melara—4/40-mm AA Breda (II × 2), 2/12.7-mm mg (I × 2)—6/324-mm ASW TT (III × 2)—1/helo
Electron Equipt: Radar: 1/Decca TM 1226, 1/H.S.A. DA-05/2, 1/H.S.A. WM-28, 2/H.S.A. LIROD
Sonar: 1/ASO-4
EW: RDC-2ABC and RCM-2 systems, 2/Dagaie chaff RL
M: 2 SEMT-Pielstick 16 PC2-5V400 diesels; 2/5-bladed props; 22,600 hp
Electric: 1,410 kVA (3 × 470 kVA diesel sets) **Range:** 4,000/18
Fuel: 230 tons **Man:** 11 officers, 46 petty officers, 36 men

Remarks: All reported to be available for sale, late 1984. Ordered 8-79. Blohm + Voss design, based on Portuguese *João Coutinho* class. Have fin stabilizers. LIROD radar/electro-optical system controls 40-mm AA. Carry Whitehead A244S ASW torpedoes. To carry 5 tons aviation fuel, 70 tons fresh water. HSA DAISY data system. Telescoping helo hangar on P7–P9 only.

Espora (P 4)—on trials (no-hangar version) Blohm + Voss, 1984

FRIGATES *(continued)*

◆ **3 French type A-69 class** Bldr: Lorient DY

	Laid down	L	In serv.
P 1 Drummond (ex-*Good Hope,* F 432)	12-3-76	5-3-77	10-78
P 2 Guerrico (ex-*Transvaal,* F 102)	1-10-76	9-77	10-78
P 3 Granville	end-78	28-6-80	22-6-81

Granville (P 3) Argentine Navy, 1984

D: 1,100 tons (1,250 fl) **S:** 24 kts
Dim: 80.5 (76.0 pp) × 10.3 × 3.0 (5.2 sonar)
A: 4/MM 38 Exocet (II × 2)—1/100-mm DP mod. 1968—2/40-mm AA (II × 1)—2/20-mm AA (I × 2)—6/324-mm ASW TT (III × 2)
Electron Equipt: Radar: 1/Decca 1226, 1/DRBV-51A, 1/DRBC-32C
Sonar: Diodon
M: 2 SEMT-Pielstick 12 PC 2 diesels; 2 CP props; 11,000 hp **Electric:** 840 kw
Range: 3,000/18; 4,500/15 **Man:** 5 officers, 79 men

Remarks: The first two were originally ordered by South Africa, but delivery was embargoed. Purchased by Argentina, 25-9-78 to augment fleet in case of war with Chile. Armament and some electronic gear differ from French Navy version. P 3 has Breda twin 40-mm AA controlled by a CSEE Naja optronic GFCS; the others have older Bofors L60 mountings. P 3 has Dagaie chaff system. P 2 damaged on 7-4-82 during the invasion of South Georgia; repaired.

CORVETTES

◆ **2 U.S. Achomawi class** Bldr: Charleston SB & DD Co.

	Laid down	L	In serv.
A 1 Comandante General Irigoyen (ex-*Cahuilla,* ATF 152)	16-6-44	2-11-44	10-3-45
A 3 Francisco De Churruca (ex-*Luiseno,* AFT 156)	7-11-44	17-3-45	16-6-45

Comandante General Irigoyen (A 1) R. Scheina, 1980

D: 1,235 tons (1,675 fl) **S:** 16.5 kts **Dim:** 62.48 (59.44 wl) × 11.73 × 4.67
A: 4/40-mm AA (II × 2, I × 2)—2/20-mm AA (I × 2)
M: 4 G.M. 12-278A diesels, electric drive; 1 prop; 3,000 hp
Fuel: 363 tons **Electric:** 400 kw **Range:** 7,000/15; 15,000/8 **Man:** 85 tot.

Remarks: A 1 transferred 1961 as an ocean tug; rerated a patrol ship in 1966. A 3 purchased 1-7-75. Retain tug and salvage facilities. A 3: 2/40-mm AA (II × 1) only.

Note: Three ex-U.S. *Sotoyomo*-class seagoing tugs used as patrol vessels have been stricken: *Yamona* (A 6, ex-*Maricopa,* ATA 146) and *Alfarez Sobral* (A 9, ex-*Catawba,* ATA 210) in 1984, and *Comodoro Somellera* (A 10, ex-*Salish,* ATA 187) in 1985.

PATROL BOATS

◆ **2 Intrepida class** (Lürssen TNC 45 design)

	Bldr	L	In serv.
ELPR 1 Intrepida	Lürssen, Bremen-Vegesack	12-12-74	20-7-74
ELPR 2 Indomita	Lürssen, Bremen-Vegesack	8-4-74	12-74

Intrepida (ELPR 1) Argentine Navy, 1984

D: 240 tons (265 fl) **S:** 37.8 kts **Dim:** 44.9 (42.3 pp) × 7.4 × 2.28 (prop.)
A: 1/76-mm DP OTO Melara—2/40-mm wire-guided TT (German SST-4 torp.)
Electron Equipt: Radar: 1/Decca 101, 1/HSA WM22
M: 4 MTU MD 872 diesels; 4 props; 14,400 hp **Electric:** 330 kw
Range: 640/36; 1,700/16 **Man:** 5 officers, 37 men

Remarks: Anti-rolling stabilizers. Plans canceled to acquire two more. Have passive threat-warning intercept gear.

◆ **4 Israeli Dabur class** Bldr: Israeli Aircraft Industries, Israel (In serv. 1978)

P 61 Baradero P 62 Barranqueras P 63 Clorinda
P 64 Concepcion Del Uruguay

D: 26.8 tons (34.2 fl) **S:** 22 kts **Dim:** 19.8 × 5.4 × 1.75
A: 2/20-mm AA (I × 2)—4/12.7-mm mg (II × 2)
Electron Equipt: Radar: Decca 101
M: 2 G.M. 12V-71T diesels; 2 props; 1,200 hp **Range:** 700/16 **Man:** 8 tot.

MINE WARFARE SHIPS

◆ **6 British "Ton"-class minesweepers/minehunters**

	L		L
M 1 Neuquen (ex-*Hickleton*)	26-1-55	M 4 Tierra Del Fuego (ex-*Bevington*)	17-3-53
M 2 Rio Negro (ex-*Tarlton*)	10-11-54	M 5 Chaco (ex-*Rennington*)	27-11-58
M 3 Chubut (ex-*Santon*)	18-8-55	M 6 Formosa (ex-*Ilmington*)	8-3-54

Three Argentine "Tons"; minehunter at left L. & L. Van Ginderen, 4-84

D: 370 tons (425 fl) **S:** 15 kts **Dim:** 46.33 (42.68 pp) × 8.76 × 2.50
A: 1/40-mm AA **Electron Equipt:** Radar: Type 978
M: 2 Paxman Deltic 18A-7A diesels; 2 props; 3,000 hp **Fuel:** 45 tons
Range: 2,300/13; 3,000/8 **Man:** 27 tot. (M 5, M 6: 36 tot.)

Remarks: M 5 and M 6 refitted as minehunters in 1968, with Plessey Type 193M sonar. The others may retain Mirrlees JVSS-12 diesels, totaling 2,500 hp. In poor condition, may soon be stricken.

AMPHIBIOUS WARFARE SHIPS

◆ **1 new-construction tank landing ship** Bldr: Hyundai SY, South Korea

	Laid down	L	In serv.
N.	. . .	. . .	. . .

D: 2,000 tons light (3,770 fl) **S:** 15 kts **Dim:** 100.0 (96.1 pp) × 15.4 × 4.2 max.
A: 3/40-mm AA (I × 3)—2/20-mm AA (I × 2)
Electron Equipt: Radar: 1/navigational

AMPHIBIOUS WARFARE SHIPS *(continued)*

M: 2 diesels; 2 props; 7,600 hp (6,860 sust.) **Electric:** 750 kw
Range: 7,500/13 **Man:** 13 officers, 104 men + 200 troops

Remarks: Ordered 1982. Max. cargo: 1,300 tons; beaching load: 690 tons. Can carry 17 battle tanks. Platform for 2 helicopters. Davits for 4 LCVP landing craft.

Note: May have been canceled.

◆ **1 Modified U.S. DeSoto County-class tank landing ship**

	Bldr	L	In serv.
Q 42 Cabo San Antonio	AFNE, Rio Santiago	1968	2-11-78

Cabo San Antonio (Q 42) Argentine Navy, 1983

D: 4,300 tons (8,000 fl) **S:** 16 kts **Dim:** 134.72 (129.8 wl) × 18.9 × 5.5
A: 12/40-mm AA (IV × 3)—2/20-mm AA (I × 2)
Electron Equipt: Radar: 1 navigational, 1/AWS-1
M: 6 diesels; 2 CP props; 13,700 hp **Electric:** 900 kw **Man:** 124 tot.

Remarks: Differs from U.S. Navy version primarily in armament and in having a 60-ton Stülcken heavy-lift kingpost set amidships. Carries 4 LCVP. Tank deck 88-m long can stow 23 medium tanks. 700 troops can be carried. Three U.S. Mk 51 Mod. 2 optical GFCS.

◆ **4 U.S. LCM(6)-class landing craft (In serv. 6-71)**

EDM 1 EDM 2 EDM 3 EDM 4

D: 24 tons (56 fl) **S:** 10 kts **Dim:** 17.07 × 4.37 × 1.17 (aft)
A: 2/12.7-mm mg **M:** 2 Gray Marine 64 HN9 diesels; 2 props; 330-450 hp
Range: 130/10 **Cargo:** 30 tons

◆ **8 U.S. LCVP-class landing craft**

EDVP 30–37

D: 13 tons (fl) **S:** 9 kts **Dim:** 10.90 × 3.21 × 1.04 (aft)
M: 1 Gray Marine 64 HN9 diesel; 225 hp **Range:** 110/9

Remarks: It is not known whether the above list includes the four LCVP carried by *Cabo San Antonio.* Cargo: 36 troops or 3.5 tons. Five others discarded post-1982.

HYDROGRAPHIC SHIPS

◆ **1 Puerto Deseado class**

	Bldr	Laid down	L	In serv.
Q 20 Puerto Deseado	Astarsa, San Fernando	17-3-76	4-12-77	26-2-79 (trials)

Puerto Deseado (Q 20) nested with Comodoro Rivadavia (Q 11), Cormoran (Q 15), and Petrel (Q 16) R. Scheina, 1982

D: 2,133 tons **S:** 15 kts **Dim:** 70.81 (67.0 pp) × 13.2 × 4.5
M: 2 Fiat-GMT diesels; 2 props; 2,700 hp **Electric:** 1,280 kVA
Range: 12,000/12 **Man:** 12 officers, 53 men, 9 scientists, 10 technicians

Remarks: Used for hydrometeorological reporting. Four Hewlett-Packard 2108-A computers for data analysis/storage. Has seismic, gravimetric, and magnetometer equipment. Omega- and NAVSAT-equipped. Has geology laboratory. Ice-reinforced. The previously listed *Alvaro Alberto,* completed 1983, is subordinate to the Ministry of Marine, as is the *Capitan Oca Balda* (598 dwt), completed 1983.

◆ **1 Comodoro Rivadavia class**
Bldr: Mestrina, el Tigre (L: 29-11-73, in serv. 6-12-76)

Q 11 Comodoro Rivadavia

D: 655 tons (830 fl) **S:** 12 kts **Dim:** 52.2 × 8.8 × 2.6 **Man:** 27 tot.
M: 2 Werkspoor Stork RHO-218K diesels; 1,160 hp **Range:** 6,000/12

◆ **2 inshore survey craft** Bldr: Cadenazzi, el Tigre (In serv. 1965)

Q 16 Petrel

D: 52 tons (fl) **S:** 9 kts **Dim:** 19.7 × 4.5 × 1.7
M: 2 diesels; . . . props; 340 hp **Man:** 9 tot.

Q 15 Cormoran Bldr: AFNE, Rio Santiago (In serv. 20-2-64)

D: 82 tons (102 fl) **S:** 11 kts **Dim:** 25.3 × 5.0 × 1.8
M: 2 diesels; 2 props; 440 hp **Man:** 19 tot.

ICEBREAKER

◆ **1 antarctic support** Bldr: Wärtsilä, Helsinki, Finland

	Laid down	L	In serv.
Q 5 Almirante Irizar	4-7-77	3-2-78	15-12-78

Almirante Irizar (Q 5)—red hull and stack, white superstructure Wärtsilä, 1978

D: 11,811 (14,900 fl) **S:** 16.5 kts **Dim:** 119.3 × 25.0 × 9.5
A: 2/40-mm AA (1 × 2) **Electric:** 2,640 kw **Man:** 123 crew plus 100 scientists
Electron Equipt: Radar: 1 Plessey AWS-2, 2/navigational
M: Diesel-electric; 4 SEMT-Pielstick 8 PC 2.5 L/400 diesels; 2 Stromberg motors; 2 props; 16,200 hp

Remarks: Ordered 17-12-75. Canadian RAST helicopter downhaul winch system, 2 helicopters. Wärtsilä bubbler system to keep ice from hull bottom. Sixty-ton towing winch. Two 16-ton cranes. Used as a hospital ship during Falklands War. May be transferred to civil control.

AUXILIARY SHIPS

◆ **1 antarctic supply ship** Bldr: Principe & Menghe SY, Maciel Isl.

	Laid down	L	In serv.
Q 6 Bahia Paraiso	27-2-79	3-7-80	11-12-81

D: 9,200 tons (fl) **S:** 18 kts **Dim:** 130.7 (120.0 pp) × 19.5 × 7.0 **A:** None
M: 2 diesels; 2 CP props; 15,000 hp **Fuel:** 300 tons **Man:** 180 tot.

Bahia Paraiso—as a hospital ship during Falklands War Argentine Navy, 1982

AUXILIARY SHIPS *(continued)*

REMARKS: To carry up to 82 passengers or 252 troops, 3,500m³ dry and 250m³ refrigerated stores, plus 1,200 tons cargo fuel. Two helicopters plus hangar. Icebreaking hull form. Used as hospital ship during Falklands War.

◆ **3 "Costa Sur"-class transports** Bldr: Principe & Menghe SY, Maciel Isl.

	Laid down	L	In serv.
B 3 Canal Beagle	10-1-77	14-10-77	28-4-78
B 4 Bahia San Blas	11-4-77	29-4-78	27-11-78
B 5 Cabo De Hornos (ex-*Bahia Camarones*)	29-4-78	4-11-78	18-7-79

Cabo de Hornos (B 5) L. & L. Van Ginderen, 11-82

D: 7,640 tons (fl) **S:** 15 kts **Dim:** 119.9 × 17.5 × 6.4 **A:** None
M: 2 AFNE-Sulzer diesels; 2 props; 6,400 hp

REMARKS: To supply remote stations. 4,600 grt/5,800 dwt. 9,700 cubic meters cargo. Also carry passengers and cargo in commercial service.

NOTE: The ex-U.S. *Klickitat*-class tanker *Punta Delgada* (B16, ex-*Sugarland,* ex-*Nanticoke,* AOG 66) was stricken in 1983. The replenishment oiler *Punta Medanos* (B 18) was stricken 1984. The Argentine Navy employs the state-owned commercial tankers *Puerto Rosales* and *Campo Duran* for occasional underway replenishment duties.

◆ **1 coastal tanker** Bldr: Puerto Belgrano SY

B 12 Punta Alta (In serv. 1938)

Punta Alta (B 12) L. & L. Van Ginderen, 4-84

D: 1,900 tons (fl) **S:** 8 kts **Dim:** 64.0 × 10.3 × 3.8
M: 1 set reciprocating steam; 1,850 hp **Fuel:** 146 tons
Man: 40 tot.

REMARKS: 800 dwt. Used primarily for harbor storage service at Puerto Belgrano.

◆ **1 lighthouse supply ship** Bldr: Wheeler SB Co., Freeport, N.Y.

B 7 San Julian (ex-U.S. Army FS 281, L:1-45)

D: 900 tons (fl) **S:** 12 kts **Dim:** 53.49 (49.99 pp) × 9.75 × 3.05
M: 2 G.M. 6-278A diesels; 2 props; 1,000 hp **Fuel:** 57 tons
Range: 4,300/9.5 **Man:** 30 tot.

REMARKS: Purchased after WW II. Reported stricken early 1980s, but retained for lighthouse and navigational aid/buoy-lending services. Cargo: 595 m³.

◆ **2 auxiliary ocean tugs** Bldr: Ast. Vicente Forte, Buenos Aires

R 2 Querandi (In serv: 22-8-78) R 3 Tehuelche (In serv: 2-11-78)

D: 370 tons (fl) **S:** 12 kts **Dim:** 33.6 × 8.4 × 3.0
M: 2 M.A.N. 6V 23.5/33 diesels; 1,200 hp **Range:** 1,200/12 **Man:** 30 tot.

NOTE: The ex-U.S. *Sotoyomo*-class auxiliary ocean tugs *Chiriguano* (A 7, ex-ATA 227) and *Sanaviron* (A 8, ex-ATA 228) were stricken in 1984 and 1985, respectively.

San Julian (B 7) L. & L. Van Ginderen, 8-84

Querandi (R 2) R. Scheina, 1980

◆ **1 training ship** Bldr: Union Naval de la Levante, Valencia, Spain

Q 31 Piloto Alsina (ex-*Ciudad de Formosa*) (In serv. 1963)

D: 2,800 tons (fl) **S:** 14 kts **Dim:** 105.60 (99.98 pp) × 17.89 × 2.52
M: 3 Maquinista-Burmeister & Wain 8-cyl. diesels: 1 prop; 4,800 hp
Electric: 480 kw **Fuel:** 224 tons

REMARKS: Former passenger/cargo ferry purchased and commissioned 17-3-81 for training duties. 3,986 grt/720 dwt.

◆ **1 sail-training vessel**

	Bld	L	In serv.
Q 2 Libertad	AFNE, Rio Santiago	30-5-56	1962

Libertad (Q 2) J.-C. Bellonne, 9-84

AUXILIARY SHIPS *(continued)*

D: 3,025 tons (3,625 fl) **S:** 12 kts **Dim:** 94.25 (79.9 pp) × 13.75 × 6.75
M: Diesels; 2 props; 2,400 hp **Range:** 12,000 **Man:** 222 men and 140 cadets.

REMARKS: World's largest active sailing ship. Armament removed.

◆ **5 small sail-training yachts**

Q 73 ITATI II Bldr: Cadenazzi SY, 1979 **D:** 80 tons (fl) **S:** 15 kts

Q 25 FORTUNA-I Bldr: Tandanor, Buenos Aires **D:** 17 tons
Q 26 FORTUNA II Bldr: Tandanor, Buenos Aires **D:** 31.5 tons
Q 72 TEQUARA
Q . . ADHARA

YARD AND SERVICE CRAFT

◆ **6 U.S. YTL-422-class small harbor tugs (1944-45)**

R 5 MOCOVI (ex-YTL 441) R 6 CALCHAQUI (ex-YTL 445)
R 10 CHULUPI (ex-YTL 426) R 16 CAPAYAN (ex-YTL 443)
R 18 CHIQUILLAN (ex-YTL 444) R 19 MORCOYAN (ex-YTL 448)

Bldrs: R 5, 16, 18: Robt. Jacobs, City Isl., NY; R 6, 19: H.C. Grebe Co; R 10: Everett Pacific BY, Everett, Wash.

Mocovi (R 5) L. & L. Van Ginderen, 4-81

D: 70 tons (80 fl) **S:** 10 kts **Dim:** 20.16 × 5.18 × 2.44
M: 1 Hoover-Owens-Rentschler diesel; 300 hp **Electric:** 40 kw
Fuel: 7 tons **Man:** 5 tot.

REMARKS: R 16, 18, 19 leased 3-65, others 3-69; purchased outright 16-6-77.

NOTE: The *Pehuenche*-class harbor tugs *Pehuenche* (R 29) and *Tonocote* (R 30) were stricken 1984.

◆ **4 floating dry docks**

Y 1 (ex-U.S.ARD 23): 3,500-ton capacity; 14.9 × 24.7 × 1.73 (light) (In serv. 1944)
Y 2: 1,500-ton capacity; 91.5 × 18.3 (In serv. 1913)
Y 3, Y 4: 750-ton capacity; 65.8 × 14
A: 12,000-ton capacity; 172.5 × 26 (In serv. 1958)
B: 2,800-ton capacity; 110.0 × 18.0 (In serv. 1956)
C: 1,000-ton capacity; 75.0 × 15.7

◆ **4 floating cranes**

NOTE: The former sail training ship *Presidente Sarmiento* (1898) and the sail corvette *Uruguay* (1874) are maintained by the Navy as museums at Buenos Aires.

PREFECTURA NAVAL ARGENTINA
(COAST GUARD)

NOTE: Ships and craft painted white. Attached aircraft include 2 Puma helicopters and several Short Skyvan transports. The *Prefectura Naval* was transferred from naval control to the Ministry of Defense in 10-84.

PATROL SHIPS AND BOATS

◆ **5 "Halcon"-class ocean patrol ships** Bldr: Bazán, El Ferrol, Spain

	Laid down	L	In serv.
GC 24 DOCTOR MANUEL MANTILLA	16-2-81	29-6-81	15-5-82
GC 25 AZOPARDO	1-4-81	14-10-81	1-83
GC 26 THOMPSON	6-81	7-12-81	20-6-83
GC 27 PREFECTO FIQUE	9-81	24-2-82	29-7-83
GC 28 PREFECTO DERBES	11-81	16-6-82	16-11-83

D: 767 tons normal (900 fl) **S:** 21.5 kts **Dim:** 67.0 (63.0 pp) × 10.0 × 3.06
A: 1/40-mm AA Breda-Bofors—1 Alouette-III helo
Electron Equipt: Radar: 1 Decca AC 1226 **Electric:** 710 kw
M: 2 Bazán-MTU 16V956 TB91 diesels; 2 props; 9,000 hp (7,500 sust.)
Range: 5,000/18 **Man:** 9 officers/24 men/4 cadets

REMARKS: Ordered 3-79 to patrol 200-nautical-mile economic zone. Endurance 20 days. Carry 144 rounds 40-mm. Same class built for Mexico. Helicopters, when aboard, would be on loan from Navy.

Doctor Manuel Mantilla (GC 24) Bazán, 1982

◆ **1 former whaler, used for ocean patrol** (In serv. 1958; purchased 1975)

GC 13 DELFIN

D: 1,000 tons **S:** 15 kts **Dim:** 60.0 × 9.0 × 4.7 **A:** 1/40-mm AA
M: Diesel; 2,300 hp **Man:** 32 tot.

◆ **1 Modified Dorado class** Bldr: Puerto Belgrano Naval Base

GC 45 ROBALO (In serv. 1942)

D: 215 tons (fl) **S:** 12 kts **Dim:** 35.0 × 4.0 × 1.9
M: 2 G.M. diesels; 2 props; 900 hp **Man:** 10

◆ **2 Dorado class** Bldr: Rio Santiago Navy Base

GC 34 DORADO (In serv. 1939) GC 43 MANDUBI (In serv. 1940)

D: 208 tons (fl) **S:** 11 kts **Dim:** 33.2 × 4.0 × 1.9
M: 2 G.M. diesels; 2 props; 880 hp **Man:** 10

REMARKS: GC 34 used on pilot ship duties. Both possibly stricken.

PATROL CRAFT

◆ **17 Z-28 class** Bldr: Blohm + Voss, Hamburg (All in serv. 9-79/1-80)

GC 64 MAR DEL PLATA GC 73 CABO CORRIENTES
GC 65 MARTIN GARCIA GC 74 QUEQUEN
GC 66 RIO LUJAN GC 75 BAHIA BLANCA
GC 67 RIO URUGUAY GC 76 INGENIERO WHITE
GC 68 RIO PARAGUAY GC 77 GOLFO SAN MATIAS
GC 69 RIO PARANA GC 79 RIO DESEADO
GC 70 RIO PLATA GC 80 USHUAIA
GC 71 LA PLATA GC 81 CANAL DE BEAGLE
GC 72 BUENOS AIRES

Buenos Aires (GC 72) R. Scheina, 9-82

D: 81 tons (fl) **S:** 22 kts **Dim:** 27.65 (26.0) × 5.30 × 1.65
A: 1/20-mm AA—2/7.62-mm mg (I × 2)
M: 2 MTU 8V331 TC92 diesels; 2 props; 2,100 hp (1,770 sust.)
Electric: 90 kVA **Range:** 780/18; 1,200/12 **Man:** 15-23 tot.

REMARKS: Ordered 24-11-78. Fin stabilizers fitted. During the Falklands War, *Madryn* (GC 78) and *Rio Iguaza* (GC 83) were lost, and *Islas Malvinas* (GC 82) was captured and renamed *Tiger Bay* by British forces. Not all units have the 20-mm gun.

◆ **3 Lynch-class** Bldr: AFNE, Rio Santiago (In serv. 1964-67)

GC 21 LYNCH GC 22 TOLL GC 23 EREZCANO

D: 100 tons (117 fl) **S:** 22 kts **Dim:** 27.44 × 5.80 × 1.85
A: 1/20-mm AA **M:** 2 Maybach diesels; 2 props; 2,700 hp **Man:** 16 tot.

◆ **14 patrol craft** Bldr: Cadenazzi SY, Tigre, 1978-79

GC 48 through GC 61

D: 13 tons **S:** 25 kts **Dim:** 12.54 × 3.57 × 1.1 **A:** 1 mg
M: 2 G.M. diesels; 2 props; 560 hp

FRIGATES *(continued)*

15 CIWS—6/324-mm ASW TT Mk 32 for Mk 46 torpedoes (III × 2)—2 helicopters (see remarks)
Electron Equipt: Radar: 1/SPS-55, 1/SPS-49(V)2, 1/Mk 92, 1/SPG-60 STIR
Sonar: 1/SQS-56—EW: SLQ-32(V)2, Mk 36 SRBOC (VI × 2)
TACAN: URN-25
M: 2 G.E. LM 2500 gas turbines; 1 CP prop; 41,000 hp; 2/350-hp aux. propulsors
Electric: 3,000 kw **Fuel:** 587 tons (plus 64 tons helo fuel)
Range: 4,200/20; 5,000/18 **Man:** 226 tot.

REMARKS: First two ordered 27-2-76 in lieu of Australian DDL design. The third was ordered 23-1-79 and the fourth on 28-4-80. In 1980 two were authorized for construction in Australia, and it was announced that four more would be ordered later. The first two Australian built ships were ordered 12-10-83. Two drop-down, diesel-electric driven propellers are located forward beneath the hull for emergency propulsion and maneuvering. Crew larger than in U.S. sisters. (F 04 arrived Australia 25-10-85.

The selection of the Sikorsky S-70B2 helicopter for these ships will require that the first three be lengthened and have fin stabilization systems added at Garden Island Dockyard; F 01-F 04 will all require the RAST helicopter down-haul and traversing system to be added. During 1984-88 an Écureuil light liaison helicopter is being carried. The S-70B2 will be able to carry two anti-ship missiles (Penguin Mk 2 Mod. 7 or Sea Skua).

The Australian-built units will have Mulloka sonars in place of SQS-56, an Australian-developed towed-array sonar, the Winnan countermeasures system, with Hoveroc decoys, and, possibly, box-launcher-mounted Ikara ASW missiles. F 01 and 02 had their two Mk 24 target designators atop the pilothouse and EW systems added after delivery; their Mk 15 Vulcan-Phalanx Close-in Weapons Systems were ordered during 1984. All carry the SLQ-25 towed torpedo decoy.

NOTE: Four additional frigates are needed to replace the remaining "River"-class units. Originally, it had been intended that these would be additional Australian-built examples of the *Oliver Hazard Perry* class, but various possibilities remained under review during 1985.

◆ **5 "River"-class frigates**

	Bldr	Laid down	L	In serv.
DE 46 PARRAMATTA	Cockatoo D. & Eng. Co.	3-1-57	31-1-59	4-7-61
DE 48 STUART	Cockatoo D. & Eng. Co.	20-3-59	8-4-61	28-6-63
DE 49 DERWENT	Williamstown Nav. DY	18-8-65	16-12-67	20-1-70
DE 50 SWAN	Williamstown Nav. DY	18-8-65	16-12-67	20-1-70
DE 53 TORRENS	Cockatoo D. & Eng. Co.	18-8-65	28-9-68	19-1-71

Stuart (DE 48)—as modernized LSPH S. Given, R.A.N., 4-84

Parramatta (F 46)—with new stack, LW-02 radar antenna lowered, triple ASW TT, etc. G. Gyssels, 12-82

Torrens (DE 53) ABPH E. Pitman, R.A.N., 6-83

Swan (DE 50)—recess for Ikara on starboard side ABPH E. Pitman, R.A.N., 6-83

D: 2,100 tons (2,750 fl) **S:** 30 kts **Dim:** 112.75 (109.75 pp) × 12.5 × 3.9
A: 2/114-mm DP Mk 6(II × 1)—1/Sea Cat/SAM syst. (IV × 1, 24 missiles)—1/Ikara ASW missile launcher—6/324-mm Mk 32 ASW TT (III × 2; not in DE 50, 53)—DE 50, 53 only: 1/Limbo Mk 10 ASW Mortar (III × 1)
Electron Equipt: Radar: 1/978, 1/LW-02, 1/WM 22, 1/Ikara control, DE 50, 53: 1/M 45 also
Sonar: 1/Mulloka, 1/162, 1/170 (DE 50 and DE 53 only)
EW: intercept arrays (not in DE 46)
M: 2 sets GT; 2 props; 34,000 hp **Fuel:** 400 tons
Electric: 1,140 kw (DE 46: 1,500 kw) **Man:** 13 officers, 238 men
Boilers: 2 Babcock & Wilcox, 38.7 kg/cm², 450°C **Range:** 4,500/12

REMARKS: Sister *Yarra* (DE 45) was stricken 22-11-85. Improved versions of the British *Rothesay* class. Profiles of the DE 50 and DE 53 differ from those of other three, resembling more the British *Leander* class. DE 46, DE 48, and DE 49 give an extensive mid-life overhaul, receiving two triple Mk 32 ASW torpedo tubes in place of the Limbo mortar, Mulloka sonar in place of part of their original suits, H.S.A. M 22 gunfire-control systems with optronic back-up director, having their boilers converted to use diesel fuel, and having their accommodations improved; DE 46 completed 8-81, DE 48 on 29-7-83, and DE 49 began work in 7-81 for completion 12-85. DE 50 and DE 51 are now to receive only normal refits and will not be modernized; DE 50 is to become training ship in 1990. The Ikara missile carries a U.S. Mk 46 ASW torpedo as its payload. Variable-depth sonars have been removed, where fitted. Sea Cat has optical GWS 20 system in early units, HSA M4 radar director (M 45 radar) in DE 50, 53.

PATROL BOATS

Note: Tenders were let to 13 firms during 9-84 for design and ultimate construction of a "Pacific Patrol Boat" on behalf of Papua New Guinea, the Soloman Islands, Tonga, Vanuatu and Western Samoa.

◆ **15 Fremantle class** Bldr: North Queensland Eng. and Agents, Cairns (P 203: Brooke Marine, Lowestoft)

	L	In serv.		L.	In serv.
P 203 FREMANTLE	15-2-79	8-10-79	P 211 BENDIGO	9-4-83	28-5-83
P 204 WARRNAMBOOL	25-10-80	14-3-81	P 212 GAWLER	9-7-83	30-8-83
P 205 TOWNSVILLE	16-5-81	18-7-81	P 213 GERALDTON	22-10-83	10-12-83
P 206 WOLLONGONG	17-10-81	28-11-81	P 214 DUBBO	21-1-84	10-3-84
P 207 LAUNCETON	23-1-82	1-3-82	P 215 GEELONG	14-4-84	2-6-84
P 208 WHYALLA	22-5-82	3-7-82	P 216 GLADSTONE	28-7-84	8-9-84
P 209 IPSWICH	25-9-82	13-11-82	P 217 BUNBURY	3-11-84	15-12-84
P 210 CESSNOCK	15-1-83	5-3-83			

Gladstone (P 216) L. & L. Van Ginderen, 12-84

D: 200 tons (230 fl) **S:** 30 kts **Dim:** 42.0 × 7.15 × 1.8
A: 1/40-mm AA—1/81-mm mortar—2/12.7-mm mg (II × 2)
Electron Equipt: Radar: 1/Kelvin-Hughes 1006
M: 2 MTU MD 16V538 TB91 diesels; 2 CP props; 7,200 hp—1 Dorman 12JTM diesel; 1 prop; . . . hp for cruising
Range: 1,450/28; 4,800/8 **Man:** 3 officers/19 men

REMARKS: Brooke Marine PCF-420 design. Ordered 9-77. Five more (*Ballarat, Mildura, Armidale, Bundaberg, Pirie*) authorized 1980, but canceled 1982. P 203 was built as pattern craft. The 40-mm AA was to be replaced with newer weapons, but will now be retained for reasons of economy. P 203: 26 tons overweight (246 fl), later reduced to 20

PATROL BOATS *(continued)*

Bunbury (P 217) LSPH E. Pitman, R.A.N., 2-85

tons; all later units will be 10 tons over original 220-tons design fl. Addition of a lightweight SAM system, possibly the Swedish RBS-70, under study 1985. P 206 aground 6-85, later salved.

◆ **5 Attack-class coastal-patrol boats** Bldr: Evans Deakin, Ltd. (except P 83, P 99, P 101: Walkers, Ltd.) — * Reserve crews

	Laid down	L	In serv.
P 82 Adroit*	8-67	3-2-68	17-8-68
P 83 Advance*	3-67	16-8-67	24-1-68
P 87 Ardent	10-67	27-4-68	26-10-68
P 91 Aware*	7-67	7-10-67	21-6-68
P 101 Bayonet*	10-68	6-11-68	22-2-69

Advance (P 83) — used for reserve training R. Gillett, 11-84

D: 146 tons (fl) **S:** 24 kts **Dim:** 32.76 (30.48 pp) × 6.2 × 1.9
A: 1/40-mm Mk 7 AA — 2/7.62-mm machine guns **Radar:** 1/Decca RM 916
M: 2 Davey-Paxman Ventura 16 YJCM diesels; 2 props; 3,500 hp (2,460 sust.)
Range: 1,220/13 **Man:** 3 officers, 19 men

Remarks: Steel hull; light-alloy superstructure; air-conditioned. P 91 is unarmed. Sisters P 84 *Aitape,* P 92 *Ladava,* P 93 *Lae,* P 94 *Madang,* P 85 *Samarai* transferred to Papua New Guinea in 1974. P 86 *Archer* and P 95 *Bandolier* sold in 1973 to Indonesia and transferred in 1973 and 1974, respectively. P 88 *Arrow* sank 25-12-74 in Cyclone Tracey. Transferred to Indonesia were *Barricade* (P 98) on 22-4-82, *Bombard* (P 99) on 11-83, and *Acute* (P 81) on 6-5-83. *Barbette* (P 97) stricken 15-6-84, *Buccaneer* (P 100) stricken 27-7-84, *Attack* (P 90) stricken 21-2-85, for transfer to Indonesia 24-5-85; P 97 transferred to Indonesia 22-2-85, P 100 in 5-85, and P 90 in 1-86. *Assail* (P 89) stricken 18-10-85.

MINE WARFARE SHIPS

◆ **0 (+2 + 4) "Bay"-class catamaran minehunters** Bldr: Carrington Slipway, Tomago

	Laid down	L	In serv
MHCAT 01 Rushcutter	31-5-84	3-85	3-86
MHCAT 02 Shoalwater	3-85	. . .	11-86

D: 100 tons (170 fl) **S:** 10 kts **Dim:** 31.0 (28.0 wl) × 9.0 × 2.0
A: 2/12.7-mm mg (I × 2) — 2/PAP-104 disposal vehicles
Electron Equipt: Radar: 1/Kelvin-Hughes Type 1006(4)
Sonar: Krupp Atlas DSQS-11H
M: 2 SACM-Poyaud 325 hp diesels, electric drive; 2 Schöttel props; 180 hp
Range: 1,200/10 **Man:** 2 officers, 12 men

Remarks: Ordered late 1981. Glass-reinforced plastic construction. If first pair successful, plan construction of four (originally to have been six) more, beginning in mid-1988, for delivery by mid-91. Sonar transducer beneath port hull. Sonar/mine-

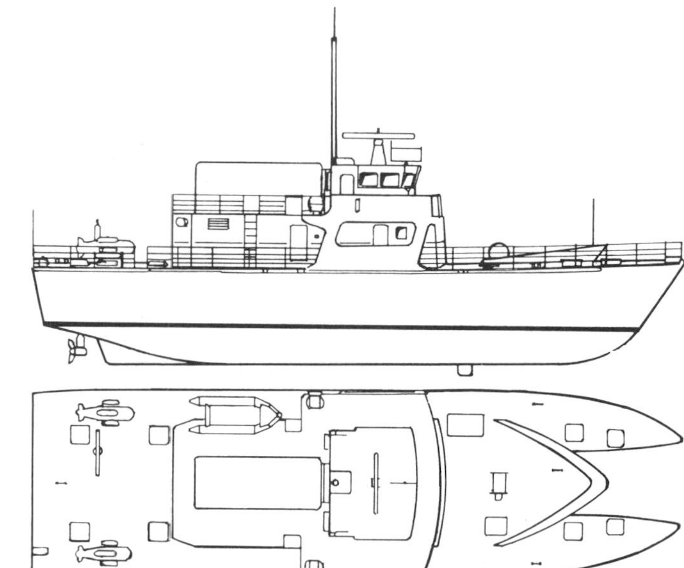

MHCAT — minehunting catamaran A.D. Baker III, 1-82

counter measures control room in dismountable deckhouse. Main engines drive propulsion generators *and* ships service generators.

◆ **1 British "Ton"-class coastal minehunter**

	Bldr	Laid down	L	In serv.
M 1121 Curlew (ex-*Chediston*)	Montrose SY	30-4-53	6-10-53	28-9-54

D: 375 tons (445 fl) **S:** 15 kts **Dim:** 46.33 (42.68 pp) × 8.76 × 2.50
A: Removed
Electron Equipt: Radar: 1/978 — Sonar: 193
M: Napier Deltic 18A-7A diesels; 2 props; 3,000 hp **Fuel:** 45 tons
Range: 2,300/13; 3,500/8 **Man:** 3 officers, 35 men

Remarks: Bought in 1962 during refit 26-6-67 to 13-12-68 after refitting. Air-conditioned and stabilized. M 1121 equipped as minehunter, with type 193 sonar and four divers, only 1/40-mm AA. Proposal to replace these two survivors of a group of six ex-RN minesweepers with a new class of two oceangoing minehunters in the mid-1980s deferred for lack of funds. Sisters *Snipe* (M 1102) stricken 3-6-83, *Ibis* (M 1183) stricken 4-5-84. *Curlew* is due for disposal in 1986-87, and plans for acquiring further seagoing minehunters have been shelved.

Curlew (M 1121) R. Gillett, 11-84

AMPHIBIOUS WARFARE SHIPS

◆ **1 modified British Sir Bedivere class**

	Bldr	Laid down	L	In serv.
L 50 Tobruk	Carrington Skipways, Tomago	7-2-79	1-3-80	23-4-81

Tobruk (L 50) — with Army pontoon section stowed on hull side
ABPH E. Pitman, 9-83

AMPHIBIOUS WAREFARE SHIPS *(continued)*

Tobruk (L 50)—showing stern ramp L. & L. Van Ginderen, 2-83

D: 3,400 tons (6,000 fl) **S:** 17 kts **Dim:** 129.5 × 19.6 × 4.3
A: 2/40-mm AA (I × 2)
Electron Equipt: Radar: 1/Decca RM 916, 1/Decca 1226
M: 2 Mirrlees-Blackstone KDM8 diesels; 2 props; 9,600 hp
Electric: 1,990 kw **Man:** approx. 18 officers, 50 men

Remarks: Announced 8-76 as a replacement for the *Sydney.* Can carry Wessex Mk 31B troop helicopters operating from platform amidships and aft, and can carry 300-500 troops, Leopard tanks, and other military vehicles. Bow and stern ramps fitted. Two LCVP carried. Can carry two LCM 8 on deck. Two 4.5-ton cranes fwd.; 60-ton heavy lift boom before bridge.

◆ **6 Balikpapan-class utility landing craft** Bldr: Walkers Ltd., Maryborough

L 126 Balikpapan (L: 15-8-71)
L 127 Brunei (L: 15-10-71)
L 128 Labuan (L: 29-12-71)
L 129 Tarakan (L: 16-3-72)
L 130 Wewak (L: 18-5-72)
L 133 Betano (L: 5-12-72)

Betano (L 133) L. & L. Van Ginderen, 9-84

Balikpapan (L 126) L. & L. Van Ginderen, 9-84

D: 316 tons (503 fl) **S:** 10 kts **Dim:** 44.5 × 10.1 × 1.9
A: 2/7.62-mm mg (I × 2) **M:** 2 G.M. 6-71 diesels; 2 props; 675 hp
Electron Equipt: Radar: 1/Decca RM 916
Range: 3,000/10 **Man:** 2 officers, 11 men

Remarks: In service 1971-74. *Salamaua* (L 131) and *Buna* (L 132) were transferred to Papua New Guinea in 1974. Can carry three Leopard tanks. Originally Army-subordinated. L 127 and L 133 used in inshore survey work. L 128 is used for Reserve training. L 130 placed in storage ashore after decommissioning 16-8-85.

HYDROGRAPHIC SHIPS

◆ **1 Cook class**

	Bldr	Laid down	L	In serv.
A 291 Cook	Williamstown Nav. DY	30-9-74	27-8-77	28-10-80

Cook (A 291) LSPH E. Pitman, R.A.N., 3-85

D: 1,910 tons (2,550 fl) **S:** 17 kts **Dim:** 96.6 (91.2 pp) × 13.41 × 4.6
Electron Equipt: Radar: 1/Decca TM 829—Sonar: 1/Simrad SU-2
M: 4 Caterpillar D398TA diesels; 2 props; 3,400 hp **Fuel:** 640 tons
Range: 11,000/14 **Man:** 137 crew, 13 scientists

Remarks: Intended for oceanographic research and hydrographic survey. Carries one inshore survey launch. Survey equipment includes Decca Hi-Fix 6, Mini-Ranger MRS3, Atlas DESC-10 echo-sounder, and Harris narrow-beam echo-sounders. Unsatisfactory design not fully operational until mid-82.

◆ **1 Moresby class**

	Bldr	Laid down	L	In serv.
A 573 Moresby	State DY, Newcastle, NSW	1-7-62	7-9-63	6-3-64

Moresby (A 573) ABPH E. Pitman, R.A.N., 1982

D: 1,714 tons (2,340 fl) **S:** 19 kts **Dim:** 95.7 (86.7 pp) × 12.8 × 4.6
Electron Equipt: Radar: 1/Decca TM 829—Sonar: 1/Simrad SU-2
M: Diesel-electric propulsion: 3/1,330-hp diesels; 3 CSVM generator sets, each 1,330 kw/800 rpm; 2 electric motors, 2 props; 5,000 hp
Man: 13 officers, 133 men

Remarks: A small helicopter can be carried. Ship is air-conditioned. 2/40-mm AA removed, exhaust pipe added on foredeck, stack heightened 1973-74. Three inshore survey launches carried.

◆ **1 Flinders class**

	Bldr	Laid down	L	In serv.
A 312 Flinders	Williamstown Nav. DY	11-6-71	29-7-72	27-4-73

D: 765 tons (fl) **S:** 13.5 kts **Dim:** 49.1 × 10.05 × 3.7
Electron Equipt: Radar: Decca TM 829—Sonar: Simrad SU-2
M: 2 Paxman Ventura diesels; 2 props; 1,680 hp **Range:** 5,000/9
Man: 4 officers, 34 men

Remarks: Similar to the Philippine ship *Atyimba.* Replaced the *Paluma,* stricken in 1974. Operates along Barrier Reef. Received new survey launch in 1982.

Note: The oceanographic research ship *Kimbla* (AGOR 314), a former net tender, was placed in storage 15-2-85. Planned replacement by civil *Cape Pillar* not pursued.

HYDROGRAPHIC SHIPS *(continued)*

Flinders (A 312) R.A.N., 1980

◆ **0 (+4) inshore survey boats** (In serv. 1987-88)

A. . . N. . . A. . . N. . . A. . . N. . . A. . . N. . .

D: 120 tons (fl) **S:** . . . **Dim:** 29.0 × 6.0 × 2.0
M: Diesels; 2 props; . . . hp **Range:** 1,800/. . .
Man: 1 officer, 9 men

REMARKS: Programmed construction.

AUXILIARIES

◆ **0 (+1) modified French Durance-class replenishment oilers**

	Bldr	Laid down	L	In serv.
AOR 304. . . SUCCESS	Vickers, Cockatoo DY	9-8-80	3-3-84	1986

Success (AOR 304)—at launch LSPH P. Simpson, R.A.N., 3-84

D: 17,993 tons (fl) **S:** 18 kts **Dim:** 157.3 (149.0 pp) × 21.2 × 10.8
A: 3/40-mm AA (I × 3)—4/12.7-mm mg (I × 4) **Fuel:** 750 tons
Electronic Equipt: Radar: . . .
M: 2 SEMT-Pielstick 16 PC 2.5 diesels; 1 CP prop; 20,000 hp **Electric:** 5440 kw
Range: 9,000/15 **Man:** 16 officers, 12 CPO, 22 PO, 127 men

REMARKS: First unit ordered 9-79 from design prepared by DTCN, France. Second proposed 1980, but will not be built. To carry 8,220 tons distillate fuel, 1,131 tons aviation fuel, 170 tons munitions, 183 tons provisions, 259 tons water, and 45 tons of spare parts. Will carry 2 stores-handling land craft in davits and will be able to refuel three ships simultaneously. Helicopter platform. Construction progress slow and costs tripled. Scheduled to commence trials late 11-85.

NOTE: The replenishment oiler *Supply* (AO 195, ex-*Tide Austral*) was decommissioned for disposal 11-85.

◆ **1 destroyer tender** Bldr: Cockatoo D & E, Sydney

	Laid down	L	In serv.
AD 215 STALWART	6-64	7-10-66	4-2-68

Stalwart (AD 215) L. & L. Van Ginderen, 2-83

D: 10,000 tons (15,500 fl) **S:** 20 kts **Dim:** 157.12 (143.25 pp) × 20.57 × 9.0
A: 4/40-mm AA (II × 2) **Electric:** 3,200 kw
Electron Equipt: Radar: 1/978, 1/293 Q
M: 2 Scott-Sulzer 6 cyl. Mk RD 68 diesels; 2 props, 14,400 hp
Range: 12,000/12 **Man:** 396 tot.

REMARKS: Helicopter platform and hangar for two Wessex or one Sea King. Workshops and foundry (400 m^2); boiler shop (100 m^2); electric shop; electronic shop (300 m^2); mechanical workshop (500 m^2); and shops for precision equipment and plastic-boat repairs. Four 3-ton and two 6-ton cranes. Carries spare missiles for destroyers and frigates. Acts as R.A.N. Fleet Flagship.

◆ **1 training ship**

	Bldr	Laid down	L	In serv.
AGT 203 JERVIS BAY (ex-*Australian Trader*)	State DY, Newcastle	18-8-67	17-2-69	17-6-69

Jervis Bay (AGT 203) L. & L. Van Ginderen, 10-84

D: 8,915 tons (fl) **S:** 17 kts **Dim:** 135.7 (123.5 pp) × 21.5 × 6.1
A: None **Electron Equipt:** Radar: 1/Decca RM916, 1/Kelvin-Hughes 1006
Fuel: 820 tons **Electric:** 2000 kw
M: 2 Crossley-Pielstick 16 PC 2V 400 diesels; 2 props; 13,000 hp
Man: 111 crew plus 40 trainees

REMARKS: A former roll-on/roll-off cargo ferry converted to a training ship to replace the destroyer *Duchess.* Commissioned 25-8-77. Name commemorates a Royal Navy armed merchant cruiser of World War II. Can also serve as a transport and vehicle cargo ship. Operates with destroyer *Vampire* as a training squadron. U.S. WSC-3 SATCOMM gear added 1984.

◆ **1 modified Daring-class destroyer**

	Bldr	Laid down	L	In serv.
D 11 VAMPIRE	Cockatoo D. & Eng. Co.	1-7-52	27-10-56	28-6-59

Vampire (D 11) L. & L. Van Ginderen, 2-84

D: 2,800 tons (3,670 fl) **S:** 30 kts **Dim:** 118.87 (111.55 pp) × 13.1 × 5.1
A: 6/114-mm DP Mk 6 (II × 3)—2/40-mm AA (I × 2)
Electron Equipt: Radar: 1/LW-02, 1/8GR-301A, 2/HSA M22
EW: UA-8/9, FH-12

AUXILIARIES *(continued)*

M: Parsons GT; 2 props; 54,000 hp **Boilers:** 2 Foster-Wheeler
Fuel: 584 tons **Range:** 3,700/20 **Man:** 321 tot.

Remarks: Completed modernization in 1971 with Dutch fire-control and air-search radars. Refit commenced 3-81 for further service as a training ship; two twin 40-mm AA, Limbo ASW mortar, and sonars removed. Scheduled for retention until 1990, when she is to be replaced by the frigate *Swan* (DE 50).

◆ **2 general-purpose tenders** Bldr: Walkers, Ltd, Maryborough

	Laid down	L	In serv.
AG 244 Banks	11-58	15-12-59	16-2-60
AG 247 Bass	11-58	26-3-60	15-11-60

Banks (AG 244) R. Gillett, 2-83

D: 207 tons (255 fl) **S:** 10 kts **Dim:** 30.8 (27.5 pp) × 6.7 × 2.5
M: Diesels; 2 props; . . . hp **Man:** 2 officers, 12 men

Remarks: AG 247 was originally equipped as a hydrographic ship and AG 244 for fisheries protection, but both were used primarily for reserve training until 1983. AG 247: 260 tons fl. AG 247 to Darwin 11-85 for reserve training.

◆ **5 small training yachts** Bldr: Swarbrick Bros., Osbourne Park, West Australia (In serv. 1984)

3807 Alexander of Cresswell
3808 Friendship of Leeuwin
3809 Lady Perhyn of Nirimba
3810 Charlotte of Cerberus
3811 Scarborough of Cerberus

D: 4.35 tons (fl) **S:** . . . **Dim:** 11.10 × 3.20 × 1.95
M: 1 Yanmar diesel; 22 hp **Man:** 8 to 10

Remarks: Many other small sailboats are also used for training.

Note: Four new 30-m training craft were proposed in 1978, but none have been ordered.

YARD AND SERVICE CRAFT

◆ **2 British "Ham"-class diving tenders, former inshore minesweepers**
Bldr: J. Samuel White, Cowes

DTV 1001 Seal (ex-*Wintringham*) (L: 24-5-55)
DTV 1002 Porpoise (ex-*Neasham*) (L: 14-3-55)

Seal (DTV 1001) L. & L. Van Ginderen, 3-84

D: 120 tons (159 fl) **S:** 14 kts **Dim:** 32.43 (30.48 pp) × 6.45 × 1.75
M: 2 Paxman YHAXM diesels; 2 props; 1,100 hp **Fuel:** 15 tons
Range: 2,000/9 **Man:** 7 crew + 14 divers

Remarks: Transferred in 1966, but not converted until 12-68 (*Seal*) and 1973. Assigned to the school of diving and underwater demolition in Sydney. Can support fourteen divers. Sister *Popham* (Y 299) sold 1974. Large deckhouse replaced sweep winch and cable reel.

◆ **1 coastal tug** Bldr: Australian SB Industries, South Coogee, West Australia

	Laid down	L	In serv.
OT 2601 Tammar	20-4-83	10-3-84	15-3-84

Tammar (OT 2601) LSPH S. Given, R.A.N., 3-84

D: 265 tons (300 fl) **S:** 11.5 kts **Dim:** 25.68 (23.63 pp) × 8.42 × 2.00
Electron Equipt: Radar: 1/Furuno navigational
M: 2 G.M. 16 V149 TI diesels; . . . props; 2,560 hp
Range: 1400/10 **Man:** 6 tot.

Remarks: Ordered 30-3-83 for use at HMAS *Sterling,* Cockburn Sound. 160 grt. Bollard pull 40 tons.

◆ **1 medium harbor tug** Bldr: Shoreline Eng., Portland, Victoria

OT 1801 Quokka (L: 10-83)

Quokka (OT 1801) LSPH S. Given, R.A.N., 3-84

D: 110 tons (fl) **S:** 9 kts **Dim:** 18.17 (16.84 pp) × 5.91 × 2.55
Electron Equipt: Radar: 1/Furuno navigational
M: 2 G.M. 8 V53 diesels; 633 hp

Remarks: Used at Cockburn Sound, West Australia. Bollard pull 8.5 tons

◆ **3 501-class harbor tugs** Bldr: Stannard Bros., Sydney (504: Perrin Eng., Brisbane)

HTS 501 Bronzewing (In serv. 12-68) HTS 502 Currawong (In serv. 1969)
HTS 504 Mollymawk (In serv. 1972)

D: 34 tons (47.5 fl) **S:** 9 kts **Dim:** 19.4 × 4.6 × . . .
M: 2 G.M. diesels; 2 props; 340 hp **Range:** 710/9.5 **Man:** 3 tot.

Remarks: Sister 503 to Papua New Guinea 1974. Civilian-manned. Named 1983.

YARD AND SERVICE CRAFT *(continued)*

Mollymawk (HTS 504) R. Gillett, 8-82

◆ **2 wooden-hulled harbor tugs** (In serv. 1946)

TB 9 SARDIUS AT 1536

D: 60 tons (fl) **S:** 8 kts **Dim:** 13.7 × 4.6 × 2.0
M: 1 Hercules diesel; 240 hp **Range:** 500/8 **Man:** 4 tot.

REMARKS: TB 9 to be retained into 1990s; AT 1536 laid up 1983.

◆ **3 torpedo-recovery craft** Bldr: Williamstown DY (In serv. 1970-71)

TRV 801 TAILOR TRV 802 TREVALLY TRV 803 TUNA

Tuna (TRV 803) G. Gyssels, 11-82

D: 91.6 tons **S:** 13 kts **Dim:** 27.0 × 6.4 × 1.4
M: 3 G.M. 6-71 diesels; 3 props; 684 hp **Range:** 500/8 **Man:** 1 officer, 8 men

REMARKS: TRV 802 previously used as a diving tender. All named 1982

NOTE: The torpedo recovery launch *Bincleaves* (TRB 586) was stricken in 1985.

◆ **1 Seaward Defense Boat general-purpose tender**

	Bldr	In serv.
SDB 1325	E. Jack, Launceton, Tasmania	4-11-83

SDB 1325 LSPH S. Given, R.A.N., 2-83

D: 47 tons (58 fl) **S:** 12 kts **Dim:** 24.4 × 4.9 × 1.3
M: 2 Buda diesels; 2 props; 390 hp **Range:** 2,000/10 **Man:** 2 officers, 10 men

REMARKS: Last of 28 lengthened versions of the British "72-ft. HDML." Wooden hull.

NOTE: Water tender/cargo lighter/training ships *Gayundah* (MRL 253), MWL 254, and MWL 257 were stricken late in 1982; along with the General-Purpose Vessel GPV 958 and the tank-cleaning vessel TCV *Colac*.

◆ **4 liquid-cargo lighters** Bldr: Williamston DY

WFL 8001 WARRIGAL (In serv. 10-84) WFL 8003 WOMBAT (In serv. 10-2-83)
WFL 8002 WALLABY (In serv. 3-2-83) WFL 8004 WYULDA (In serv. 10-84)

Wallaby (WFL 8002) R. Gillett, 1984

D: 265 tons light (1,206 fl) **S:** 9 kts **Dim:** 38.0 × 10.2 × 3.98
M: 2 G.E.C. diesels; 1 Harbourmaster outdrive prop fwd., 1 aft; 564 hp
Range: 100/9 **Man:** 5 tot.

REMARKS: Cargo: 564 tons diesel fuel, 107 tons feedwater, 104 tons distilled water, 93 tons waste, and 73 tons ballast. Civilian manned. Replaced fuel oil barges OFL 1201-1204, 1207, 1208 in 1984. Known as WFL, Water Fuel Lighters.

◆ **3 stores lighters** Bldr: Cockatoo DY, Sydney

CSL 01 WATTLE (In serv. 15-8-72) CSL 02 BORONIA (In serv. 25-9-72)
CSL 03 TELOPEA (In serv. 31-10-72)

CSL 01—with 100-ton concrete ammunition barge CAL 10012, one of 6 sisters, alongside R. Gillett, 8-82

D: 145.1 tons (fl) **S:** 8 kts **Dim:** 23.7 × 9.75 × 2.0
M: 2 G.M. 671 diesels; 2 props; 600 hp **Range:** 320/8 **Man:** 4 (civil.)

REMARKS: Catamarans. One 3-ton electric crane. Based on AWL 304 design, but with pilothouse aft.

◆ **1 aircraft lighter** Bldr: Cockatoo DY, Sydney

AWL 304 (In serv. 16-1-67)

D: 175 tons (fl) **S:** 8.8 kts **Dim:** 23.7 × 9.75 × 2.0
M: 2 G.M. diesels; 2 props; . . . hp **Man:** 3 (civil.)

REMARKS: Built 1967 to carry 2 Skyhawk or 1 Tracker to service the *Melbourne*. Similar to CSL 01 class, but with A-frame aft and low pilothouse forward, to port. Now used as a general stores lighter and cable layer.

◆ **2 Harbor Personnel Launches** Bldr: Bertram, U.S.A. (In serv. 1966)

38101 38102

D: 12 tons (fl) **S:** 22 kts **Dim:** 11.5 × 3.9 × . . .
M: 2 G.M. 8V53M diesels; 2 props; 500 hp **Range:** 200/22 **Man:** 2 tot.

REMARKS: Originally purchased as air-sea rescue boats.

YARD AND SERVICE CRAFT *(continued)*

◆ **15 Navy workboats** Bldr: North Queensland Engineers, Cairns

NWB 1280-1294 (In serv. 1980-81)

NWB 1282 L. & L. Van Ginderen, 2-82

D: 12.5 tons **S:** 12 kts **Dim:** 12.0 × . . . × . . . **M:** 2 diesels; 2 props; . . . hp

Remarks: Army operates 7 additional. Some (including NWB 1288) are configured as diving tenders. Aluminum construction.

◆ **38 wooden-hulled workboats** (In serv. 1944-46)

AWB 404, 411, 413, 416-424, 426, 428, 430, 433-436, 440-442, 444, 445, 1658, 4001-4003, 4006, 4007, 4010, 4011

AWB 430 R. Gillett, 8-82

D: 10 tons light (22 fl) **S:** 8 kts **Dim:** 12.2 × 3.81 × 1.37
M: 1 Gray Marine 64 HN 9 diesel; 175 hp **Range:** 600/8

Remarks: Superstructures vary. Some have unofficial names (AWB 420, *Amethyst*).

Other self-propelled service craft include:
1 10.6-m Fast Motor Boat: FMB 3501
10 10.0-m Fast Utility Boats: FUB 3310-3319
1 7.9-m Fast Utility Boat: FUB 2603
7 10.0-m Harbor Personnel Boats: HPB 3350-3356
1 9.1-m Harbor Personnel Boat: HPB 30102
7 7.9-m Harbor Personnel Boat: HPB 2620-2626
1 7.6-m Harbor Personnel Boat: HPB 25101
20 Light Utility Boats in 3 types: LUB 20 . . . series
4 Firefish Radio Controlled Surface Targets: RCST 02-05
10 10.0-m Sea Boats: SB 3330-3339
2 Survey Motor Boats: SMB 3401 (*Fantome*), 3405
1 training yacht: *Franklin*
1 7.9-m workboat: WB 2601

Other non-self-propelled service craft include:
8 300-ton Concrete Ammunition Lighters: CAL 201-206, 208, 209
8 100-ton Concrete Ammunition Lighters: CAL 101, 102, 10010-10015
8 50-ton Concrete Ammunition Lighters: CAL 501-504, 508, 5010-5012
4 Container Pontoons: 1-4
1 Deperming Lighter: DGL 1
3 Dry Dock Caissons: DCI 1, 2; DC 219
21 60-ton Flat-Top Lighters: FTL 60101-60121
1 Flat Top Lighter: FTL 764
1 1,000-ton capacity Floating Dock: FD 1002

ROYAL AUSTRALIAN ARMY CORPS OF ENGINEERS

Personnel: Approx. 300

◆ **16 U.S. LCM (8)-class landing craft** Bldrs: AB 1050-1061: North Queensland Engineers, Cairns; others: Dillingham SY, Fremantle (In serv. 1967)

AB 1050-1053, 1055, 1056, 1058-1067

AB 1051—green-painted L. & L. Van Ginderen, 9-84

D: 34 tons light (116 fl) **S:** 12 kts (9 loaded) **Dim:** 22.70 × 6.41 × 1.37
M: 2 G.M. 12V71 diesels; 2 props; 600 hp **Range:** 200/9
Man: 5 tot.

Remarks: Cargo: 55 tons. Some kept in land storage. Sister AB 1057 transferred to Tonga in 1982; AB 1054 stricken 1984. LCVPs 752, 755-757: stricken 1984. The Army plans to replace the LCMs with a larger type of utility landing craft.

◆ **2 harbor tugs** (In serv. 1963)

AT 2700 Joe Mann AT 2701 The Luke

Joe Mann (AT 2700)—with an NLE (Naval Lighterage Equipment) pontoon R. Gillett, 8-82

D: 54.5 tons (60 fl) **S:** 10 kts **Dim:** 17.06 × 5.20 × 1.60
M: 2 G.M. 6-71 diesels; 1 prop; 333 hp **Man:** 3 tot.
Range: 5,700/8

Remarks: AT 2700 based at Sydney, AT 2701 at Brisbane. AT 2701 has smaller pilothouse. Both fitted for firefighting.

◆ **2 NLE (Naval Lighterage Equipment) self-propelled pontoons**

201 Casper 202 Pollux

D: 32.6 tons **S:** 4 kts **Dim:** 25.5 × 6.4 × . . .
M: 2 portable diesel outdrives

AUSTRALIA *(continued)*
ROYAL AUSTRALIAN ARMY CORPS OF ENGINEERS *(continued)*

◆ **7 Navy workboats** Bldr: North Queensland Engineers, Cairns

AM 417-423 (In serv. 1979-80)

AM 417—with portable cover over passenger deck R. Gillett, 1984

Remarks: Data as for naval version. Crew: 2.

◆ **2 Sharkcat launches** Bldr: Shark Cat, Queensland

AM 215 AM 216 (In serv. 1980)

Remarks: Glass-reinforced plastic, 60-knot, radar-equipped catamarans, for landing craft command and control. **D:** About 4 tons. Several sisters are operated by the RAAF Marine Section.

◆ **2 diving tender/survey craft** (In serv. 1979)

AB 251 African Queen AB 252

Note: Also in service are over 70 U.S. Army-design LARC 5, 5-ton amphibious lighters and a variety of river-crossing craft and small assault boats.

AUSTRIA

Republic of Austria

Austrian Army Danube Flotilla

Personnel: 1 officer, 26 men

Merchant Marine (1984): 26 ships—129,186 grt

◆ **2 patrol craft for the Danube** Bldr: Korneuberg Werft AG

	Laid down	L	In serv.
A 604 Niederösterreich	31-3-69	26-7-69	16-4-70

Niederösterreich (A 604)

D: 73 tons (fl) **S:** 22 kts **Dim:** 29.67 × 5.41 × 1.1
A: 1/20-mm AA—2/12.7-mm mg—2/7.62-mm mg—1/84-mm mortar
M: 2 MWM V-16 diesels; 1,620 hp **Fuel:** 9.3 tons
Range: 900/. . . **Man:** 1 officer, 11 men

A 601 Oberst Brecht Bldr: Korneuberg Werft AG (In serv. 14-1-58)

D: 10 tons **S:** 14 kts **Dim:** 12.30 × 2.51 × 0.75
A: 1/12.7-mm mg—1/84-mm mortar
M: 2 Graf & Stift 6-cyl. diesels; 290 hp
Range: 160/10 **Man:** 5 tot.

◆ **10 U.S.-built M-3-class launches** (4 M-3B in serv. 1965, 6 M-3D in serv. 1976)

D: 2.9-3.2 tons **S:** 18 kts **Dim:** 8.25 × 2.5 × 1.0
M: 2 G.M. gasoline/diesel engines; 176 hp **Man:** 3 tot.

◆ **several motorized pontoons**

D: 8.5 to 40 tons fl **Dim:** 19.0 × 17.0 (some: 30.0) × 0.7

M-3D launch 1983

THE BAHAMAS

Commonwealth of the Bahamas

Merchant Marine (1984): 103 ships—3,191,971 grt (tankers: 37—2,732,335 grt)

POLICE MARINE DIVISION

◆ **0 (+3) "Protector" class** Bldr: Fairey Marine, Cowes, U.K.

P 03 N. . . (In serv. 4-86) P 04 N. . . (In serv. 8-86)
P 04 N. . . (In serv. 6-86)

Protector class Fairey Marine, 1984

D: 100 tons (fl) **S:** 30 kts **Dim:** 33.00 (28.96 wl) × 6.73 × 1.95 (props)
A: 1/20-mm AA—2/7.62 mm mg **Electron Equipt:** Radar: 1/Furuno FR-701
M: 3 G.M. Detroit Diesel 16 V149 TIB diesels; 3 props; 5,400 hp
Range: 300/24; 600/14 **Man:** 17 crew + 8 spare **Fuel:** 16 tons

Remarks: Ordered 1985 for delivery spring 1986 to end-1986. Steel construction.

◆ **1 103-foot patrol boat** Bldr: Vosper Thornycroft

	Laid down	L	In serv.
P 01 Marlin	22-11-76	20-6-77	23-5-78

Marlin (P 01) Vosper, 1978

THE BAHAMAS *(continued)*
POLICE MARINE DIVISION *(continued)*

D: 100 tons (125 fl) **S:** 24 kts **Dim:** 31.5 × 5.9 × 1.6
A: 1/20-mm AA **M:** 2 Paxman Ventura diesels; 2 props; 2,900 hp
Range: 2,000/13 **Man:** 3 officers, 16 men

Remarks: Fin stabilizers, steel hulls. Two 50-mm flare launchers. Sister *Flamingo* sunk 11-5-80 by Cuban MiG-21 aircraft.

◆ **5 Keith Nelson patrol craft** Bldr: Vosper-Thornycroft. First four in serv. 5-3-71, last three 10-12-77

P 22 Andros P 25 Exuma P 27 Inagua
P 23 Eleuthera P 26 Abaco

D: 30 tons (37 fl) **S:** 19.5 kts **Dim:** 18.29 (17.07 pp) × 5.03 × 1.53
A: 2/7.62-mm mg (I × 2) **Electron Equipt:** Radar: 1/Decca 110
M: 2 Caterpillar 3408 TA diesels; 2 props; 950 hp
Fuel: 4 tons **Electric:** 29 kVA
Range: 650/16 **Man:** 11 tot.

Remarks: Fiberglass construction, air-conditioned. First unit, *Acklins* (P 21) destroyed by fire, 1980. *San Salvador* (P 24) stricken 1982.

◆ **4 small patrol craft** Bldr: Phoenix Marine, Florida, U.S.A.

P 30, P 31 (In serv. 6-81) P 32, P 33 (In serv. 12-81)

D: 8 tons (fl) **S:** 24 kts **Dim:** 8.8 × 3.0 × 0.7
A: 2/7.62-mm mg (I × 2) **Range:** 350/21
M: 2 Volvo TAMD 40 diesel outdrives; . . . hp **Man:** 4 tot.

Remarks: Glass-reinforced plastic construction.

◆ **1 support craft, former fishing boat** (Purchased 21-10-81)

AO 2 Fort Charlotte (ex-. . .)

D: 150 tons (fl) **S:** 12 kts **Dim:** 45.1 × 6.1 × 2.1
A: 2/7.62-mm mg (I × 2) **Range:** 3,500/12
M: 1 G.M. Detroit Diesel 16-71 diesel; 1 prop; 800 hp **Man:** 16 tot.

Remarks: Used for constabulary transport and supply.

◆ **1 support craft, former fishing boat** (Purchased 6-8-80)

AO 1 Fort Montague (ex-. . .)

D: 90 tons (fl) **S:** 10 kts **Dim:** 28.6 × 7.0 × 1.8
A: 2/7.62-mm mg (I × 2) **Range:** 3,000/10
M: 1 G.M. 12-71 diesel; 1 prop; . . . hp **Man:** 16 tot.

Note: 1 Fairey "Spear" patrol craft reported delivered 1985.

BAHRAIN

State of Bahrain

Merchant Marine (1984): 72 ships — 44,470 grt (tankers: 5 — 2,896 grt)

DEFENSE FORCES

Personnel (1984): 300

CORVETTES

◆ **0 (+2) Type 62-001** Bldr: Lürssen, Vegesack, West Germany

	Laid down	L	In serv.
. . . N. . .	. . .	1985	. . .
. . . N. . .	. . .	. . .	. . .

D: Approx. 600 tons (fl) **S:** 30+ kts **Dim:** 62.95 × 9.30 × . . .
A: 4/MM 40 Exocet SSM — 1/76-mm OTO Melara Compact DP — 2/40-mm AA (II × 1) — 2/20-mm AA (I × 2) — 1/. . . helicopter
Electron Equipt: Radar: . . . — EW: . . .
M: . . . diesels; 2 props; . . . hp **Range:** 4,000/. . .

Remarks: Contract announced 5-85. The raised helicopter pad incorporates an elevator to lower the helicopter to a hangar below. Eight air-to-surface missiles for the helicopter are to be carried. See drawing in addenda.

PATROL BOATS

◆ **2 (+2) TNC 45-class guided-missile boats** Bldr: Lürssen, Vegesack, West Germany

20 Ahmed Al Fateh (In serv. 5-2-84) 21 Al Jaberi (In serv. 5-84)

D: 203 tons light (259 fl) **S:** 40.5 kts
Dim: 44.9 (42.3 fl) × 7.3 × 2.05 (2.31 props)
A: 4/MM 40 Exocet SSM (II × 2) — 1/76-mm OTO Melara DP — 2/40-mm Breda AA (II × 1) — 2/12.7-mm M3 mg (I × 2)

Ahmed al Fateh (20) P. Voss, 28-8-83

Electron Equipt: Radar: 1/Decca. . . nav.; 1/. . . search radar; 1/PEAB 9 LV223 f.c.s.
EW: Decca RDL-2 ABC passive warning, 1/Dagaie chaff RL (X × 1)
M: 4 MTU 16V538 TB92 diesels; 4 props; 15,600 hp (13,460 sust.)
Electric: 405 kVA **Range:** 500/38.5; 1,500/16 **Man:** 6 officers, 30 men

Remarks: Ordered 1979; very similar to TNC 45 class for the United Arab Emirates. Panda backup director for 40-mm guns. Carry 250 rds 76-mm, 1,800 rds. 40-mm, 6,000 rds. 12.7-mm ammunition. Two additional ordered 1985. Fuel: 45 tons.

◆ **2 FPB 38-class patrol boats** Bldr: Lürssen, Vegesack

	L	In serv.		L	In serv.
10 Al Riffa	4-81	3-3-82	11 Hawar	. . .	3-3-82

Al Riffa (10) and Hawar (11) L. & L. Van Ginderen, 8-81

D: 188 tons normal (205 fl) **S:** 34 kts **Dim:** 38.5 (36.0 pp) × 7.0 × 2.2 (props)
A: 2/40-mm AA Breda AA (II × 1) — 2/mine rails
Electron Equipt: Radar: 1/Decca . . . nav.; 1/9GR 600 **Electric:** 130 kVA
M: 2 MTU diesels; 2 props; 9,000 hp
Range: 550/31.5; 1,100/16 **Man:** 3 officers, 24 men

Remarks: Ordered 1979. 2/3-pdr. saluting cannon. CSEE Lynx optical GFCS. 57-mm flare rocket/chaff launcher abaft mast.

◆ **2 65-ft Commercial Cruiser class** Bldr: Swiftships, Morgan City, LA, U.S.A. (In serv. 4-82)

30 Al Jasrah 31 Al Jarim

Al Jarim (31) with Al Jasrah (30) Swiftships, Inc., 4-82

BAHRAIN *(continued)*
PATROL BOATS *(continued)*

D: 33 tons (fl) **S:** 30 kts **Dim:** 19.17 × 5.56 × 1.98
A: 1/12.7-mm mg **Electron Equipt:** Radar: 1/Decca 110
M: 2 G.M. 12V71 TI diesels; 2 props; 1,200 hp **Range:** 1,200/18

Remarks: Aluminum construction.

MINISTRY OF THE INTERIOR
COAST GUARD

PATROL BOATS AND CRAFT

◆ **1 30-meter Wasp class** Bldr: Souter, Cowes, U.K.

N. . . (In serv. 8-85)

30-meter Wasp for Bahrain Souter, 1985

D: 10.5 tons (fl) **S:** 23.6 kts **Dim:** 30.0 (26.75 wl) × 6.40 × 1.60
A: 1/20-mm AA, 1/7.62-mm mg
M: 2 G.M. 16V149 TI diesels; 2 props; 3,100 hp **Fuel:** 17 tons
Electric: 47 kVA **Range:** 500/22; 1,000/12 **Man:** 16 tot.

Remarks: Enlarged version of standard 20-m Wasp, ordered 3-8-84. Glass-reinforced plastic construction. A VIP lounge is built over the stern. Outfitted as a yacht.

◆ **2 20-meter Wasp class fiberglass-hulled** Bldr: Souter, Cowes, U.K. (Ord. 1-83; in serv. 1983)

Bahrain 4 Bahrain 5

D: 34 tons (fl) **S:** 21 kts **Dim:** 20.0 (16.0 wl) × 5.0 × 1.5
A: 2/7.62-mm mg (I × 2)
M: 2 G.M. 12V71 TI diesels; 2 props; 1,200 hp **Man:** 8 tot.

◆ **3 11-Meter Wasp class fiberglass-hulled** Bldr: Souter, Cowes, U.K. (Ord. 20-8-82; in serv. 1983)

Sahem 1 Sahem 2 Sahem 3

D: 7.25 tons (fl) **S:** 24 kts **Dim:** 11.0 × 3.2 × 0.56
A: 1/7.62-mm mg **M:** 2 Perkins TV8.450 diesels; 2 waterjets; 612 hp

◆ **4 Sword class fiberglass-hulled** Bldr: Fairey Marine, Cowes, U.K.

Saif 1 Saif 2 Saif 3 Saif 4 (In serv. 1980)

D: 15.2 tons **S:** 28 kts **Dim:** 13.7 × 4.1 × 1.32
M: 2 G.M. 8V71 TI diesels; 2 props; 850 hp **Range:** 500/. . . **Man:** 6 tot.

◆ **3 patrol craft** Bldr: Vosper, Singapore (In serv. 1977)

Al Bayneh Junnan Quaimas

D: 6.3 tons (fl) **S:** 27 kts **Dim:** 11.1 × 3.3 × 0.9
M: 1 Sabre diesel; 210 hp

◆ **3 Tracker-class** Bldr: Fairey Maine, U.K.

Bahrain 1 (In serv. 1975) Bahrain 2 (In serv. 1980) Bahrain 3 (In serv. 1980)

D: 26 tons (fl) **S:** 28 kts **Dim:** 19.6 × 4.9 × 1.5 **A:** 1/20-mm AA
M: 2 G.M. diesels; 2 props; 1,120 hp **Range:** 500

◆ **2 Spear-class fiberglass-hulled** Bldr: Fairey Marine, U.K. (In serv. 1975)

Sahem 4 5 Khataf

D: 4.5 tons (10 fl) **S:** 26 kts **Dim:** 9.1 × 2.75 × 0.84
A: 2/7.62-mm mg **M:** 2 Perkins diesels; 2 props; 290 hp
Range: 220/26 **Man:** 3 tot.

◆ **3 27-foot** Bldr: Cheverton, Cowes, U.K. (In serv. 1977)

15 Noon 16 Askar 17 Suwad

D: 3.3 tons **S:** 15 kts **Dim:** 8.23 × 2.44 × 0.81
M: 2 diesels; 1 prop; 150 hp

◆ **1 50-foot** Bldr: Cheverton, Cowes, U.K. (In serv. 1976)

6 Mashtan

D: 9 tons **S:** 22 kts **Dim:** 15.2 × 4.3 × 1.4
M: 2 G.M. 8V TI diesels; 2 props; 900 hp **Range:** 660/12

◆ **1 utility landing craft** Bldr: Swiftships, Inc., Morgan City, Louisiana (In serv. 15-11-82)

Ajirah

Ajirah Swiftships, 11-82

D: 428 tons (fl) **S:** 12 kts **Dim:** 39.62 × 10.97 × 1.30
A: None **Electron Equipt:** Radar: 1/Decca . . . nav.
M: 2 G.M. Detroit Diesel 16V71N diesels; 2 props; . . . hp
Fuel: 20 tons **Range:** 1,500/10 **Man:** 2 officers, 6 men

Remarks: Aluminum construction. Cargo: vehicles, supplies, up to 100 tons cargo fuel and 88 tons water. Bow ramp. 15-ton crane. Turning radius: 77 m. Two sisters in Venezuelan Navy.

MISCELLANEOUS

◆ **1 Loadmaster II-class landing craft** Bldr: Fairey Marine, Cowes, U.K. (In serv. 1981)

40 Safra II

D: 150 tons (fl) **S:** 8 kts **Dim:** 22.5 × 7.5 × 1.2
M: 2 G.M. 8V92N diesels; 2 props; 776 hp **Range:** 500/. . . **Man:** 6 tot.

◆ **1 Loadmaster-class landing craft** Bldr: Cheverton, Cowes, U.K. (In serv. 1976)

7 Safra I

D: 90 tons (fl) **S:** 10 kts **Dim:** 18.23 × 6.1 × 1.0
M: 2 diesels; 2 props; 240 hp **Range:** 600/9 **Man:** 13 tot.

Remarks: Can carry 40 tons of vehicles or dry cargo, or 60 tons of liquid cargo.

◆ **10 wooden motor dhows for logistics and patrol duties**

◆ **1 utility hovercraft** Bldr: Tropimere, U.K. (In serv. 1977)

D: 4.23 tons (fl) **S:** 45 kts **Dim:** 8.9 × 4.5 × 3.6 high

◆ **1 tug** (In serv. 1981)

N. . . . . . .

D: 12 tons (fl) **S:** . . . kts **Dim:** 11.0 × . . . × . . .
M: 1 G.M. 6V71 diesel; 300 hp

BANGLADESH

People's Republic of Bangladesh

Personnel (1985): 7,500 men (600 officers)

Merchant Marine (1984): 248 ships — 366,858 grt (tankers: 43 — 50,643 grt)

Note: Reports that Bangladesh had received a Chinese-built Romeo-class submarine and that five more are on order are the result of confusion over translation errors made on press reports of the arrival of the submarine chaser *Durjoy.*

FRIGATES

◆ **2 British Leopard-class (Type 41) frigates**

	Bldr	Laid down	L	In serv.
F 15 Abu Bakr (ex-*Lynx,* f 27)	John Brown, Clydebank	13-8-53	12-1-55	14-3-57
F 17 Ali Haider (ex.-*Jaguar,* F37)	Wm. Denny, Dumbarton	2-11-53	30-7-57	12-12-59

FRIGATES *(continued)*

Abu Bakr (F 15) 1982

D: 2,300 tons (2,520 fl) **S:** 23 kts **Dim:** 103.63 (100.58 pp) × 12.19 × 4.8 (fl)
A: 4/114-mm Mk 6 DP (II × 2)—1/40-mm Mk 9 AA
Electron Equipt: Radar: 1/965, 1/978, 1/993, 1/275 fire-control
M: 8 Admiralty 16 VVS ASR 1 diesels; 2 CP props; 12,400 hp
Electric: 1,500 kw **Fuel:** 230 tons
Range: 2,300/23; 7,500/16 **Man:** 10 officers, 200 men

Remarks: F 17 purchased 6-7-78; arrived Bangladesh 11-78 after overhaul. F 15 purchased 12-3-82, commissioned 19-3-82. Squid ASW mortar and sonars removed while in Royal Navy. Fin stabilizers. 1/Mk 6 GFCS with Type 275 radar for 114-mm guns; 40-mm, local control only.

◆ **1 ex-British Salisbury-class (Type 61) aircraft direction frigate**

	Bldr	Laid down	L	In serv.
F 16 Umar Farooq (ex-*Llandaff,* F 61)	Hawthorn Leslie	27-8-53	30-11-55	11-4-58

Umar Farooq (F 16) 1979

D: 2,170 tons (2,408 fl) **S:** 24 kts **Dim:** 103.6 (100.58 pp) × 12.19 × 4.8
A: 2/114-mm Mk 6 Dp (II × 1)—2/40-mm Mk 5AA (II × 1)—1/Mk 4 Squid ASW mortar (III × 1)
Electron Equipt: Radar: 1/985, 1/993, 1/277Q, 1/982, 1/975, 1/275
Sonar: 1/174, 1/170B
M: 8 Admiralty 16 VVS ASR 1 diesels; 2 props; 12,400 hp
Range: 2,300/24; 7,500/16 **Man:** 14 officers, 223 men

Remarks: Transferred 10-12-76. Mk 6 GFCS for 114-mm mount.

PATROL BOATS AND CRAFT

◆ **4 Chinese Hoku-class guided-missile patrol boats**

P 8111 Duranta P 8112 Durbar P 8113 Duruedya P 8114 Durdam

D: 68 tons (79 fl) **S:** 38 kts **Dim:** 27.0 × 6.3 × 1.8 (1.3 hull)
A: 2 CSS-N-1 SSM (I × 2)—2/25-mm AA (II × 1)
Electron Equipt: Radar: 1/Square Tie **Electric:** 65 Kw
M: 4 M-50F-4 diesels; 4 props; 4,800 hp **Range:** 520/26 **Man:** 17 tot.

Remarks: First two delivered 6-4-83; others in 10-83. Steel construction. Have 5-day endurance.

◆ **2 fisheries protection patrol boats** Bldr: Vosper Pty, Tanjong Rhu, Singapore

P 316 Megna (L: 19-1-84) P 317 Jamuna (L: 19-3-84)

Megna (P 316)—fitting out 1984

D: 410 (fl) **S:** 20 kts **Dim:** 46.5 × 7.5 × 2.0 (hull)
A: 2/7.62-mm mg (I × 2) **Range:** 2,000/16 **Man:** 44
Electron Equipt: Radar: 1/Decca 1229
M: 2 Paxman Valenta 12 CM diesels; 2 props; 6,000 hp

Remarks: Operated for the Ministry of Agriculture by the Navy for 200-nautical-mile economic zone patrol.

◆ **4 (+ 2) Chinese Hainan-class submarine chasers**

P 801 Durjoy (In serv. 10-9-82)
P 802 N. . . (In serv. 8-84)
P 803 N. . . (In serv. 8-84)
P 804 N. . . (In serv. 8-84)
P 805 N. . .
P 806 N. . .

D: 375 tons normal (400 fl) **S:** 30.5 kts **Dim:** 58.77 × 7.20 × 2.20 (hull)
A: 4/57-mm AA (II × 2)—4/25-mm AA (II × 2)—4/RBU-1200 ASWRL (V × 4)—2/BMB-2 d.c. mortars—2/d.c. racks—mines
Electron Equipt: Radar: 1/Pot Head—Sonar: 1/Tamir-11
M: 4 diesels; 4 props; 8,800 hp **Man:** 70 tot.

Remarks: Delivery date for last two uncertain.

◆ **4 Soviet P-4-class torpedo boats** (In serv. mid-1950s)

T 8221 T 8222 T 8223 T 8224

D: 19.3 tons (22.4 fl) **S:** 55 kts **Dim:** 19.3 × 3.7 × 1.0
A: 2/14.5-mm mg (II × 1)—2/450-mm TT **Man:** 12 tot.
Electron Equipt: Radar: 1/Skin Head **M:** 2 M50 diesels; 2 props; 2,400 hp

Remarks: Delivered from China 6-4-83 along with the two Hoku-class missile boats. Aluminum construction. Thoroughly obsolescent.

◆ **1 Japanese-built patrol boat**

	Bldr	L	In serv.
Shamjala	Sumidagawa, Tokyo	2-7-81	1982

D: 160 tons (fl) **S:** 26.5 kts **Dim:** 30.0 × . . . × . . . **A:** . . .
M: 2 diesels; 2 props; . . .hp

Remarks: Apparently a variant of the Japanese Maritime Safety Agency's *Akagi* (130-ton) class. Six patrol boats of this size were planned, but further orders did not materialize.

◆ **2 ex-Yugoslav Kraljevica-class patrol boats**

P 301 Karnaphuli (ex-Yugoslav PBR 502) P 302 Tistna (ex-Yugoslav PBR 505)

Tistna (P 302) 1976

D: 190 tons (202 fl) **S:** 18 kts **Dim:** 41.0 × 6.3 × 2.2
A: 2/40-mm AA (I × 2)—4/20-mm AA (I × 4)—2/Mk 6 d.c. throwers—2/d.c. racks—2/128-mm RL (V × 2)
Electron Equipt: Radar: 1/Decca 45—Sonar: QCU-2 **Range:** 1,000/12
M: 2 M.A.N. W8V 30/38 diesels; 2 props; 3,300 hp
Man: 4 officers, 40 men

Remarks: Transferred 6-6-75.

◆ **8 Chinese Shanghai-II-class patrol boats**

101 Shaheed Daulat
102 Shaheed Farid
103 Shaheed Mohibullah
104 Shaheed Akhtaruddin
105 Towheed
106 Towfiq
107 Tamjeed
108 Tanveer

Shaheed Farid (102) and sister 1980

BANGLADESH *(continued)*

D: 122 tons (135 fl) **S:** 28.5 kts **Dim:** 38.78 × 5.41 × 1.55 (max.)
A: 4/37-mm AA (II × 2)—4/25-mm AA (II × 2) **Man:** 36 tot.
Electron Equipt: Radar: 1/Pot Head **Electric:** 39 kw
M: 2 M50F-4/1,200-hp and 2/910-hp diesels; 4 props; 4,220 hp **Range:** 750/16.5

REMARKS: 101-104 delivered 6-7-80. 105-108 delivered 5-82. Two earlier units, delivered 1974, now stricken.

◆ **1 salvaged Pakistani patrol boat** Bldr: Brooke Marine, Lowestoft, U.K.

P 201 BISHKALI (ex-*Jessore*)—In serv. 20-5-65

D: 115 tons (143 fl) **S:** 24 kts **Dim:** 32.62 (30.48 pp) × 6.10 × 1.55 **Man:** 30
A: 2/40-mm AA (I × 2) **M:** 2 MTU 12V538 diesels; 2 props; 3,400 hp

REMARKS: Sunk in 1971 War of Independence; salvaged and repaired, Khulna SY; recommissioned 23-11-78.

◆ **2 Ajay-class patrol boats** Bldr: Hooghly D & E, Calcutta (In serv. 1-62)

P 201 PADMA (ex-*Akshay,* P 3136) P 202 SURMA (ex-*Ajay,* P 3135)

D: 120 tons (151 fl) **S:** 18 kts **Dim:** 35.75 (33.52 pp) × 6.1 × 1.9
A: 8/20-mm AA (IV × 2)
M: 2 Paxman YHAXM diesels; 2 props; 1,000 hp—1 Foden FD-6 cruise diesel; 100 hp **Range:** 500/12; 1,000/8 **Man:** 3 officers, 32 men

REMARKS: Indian version of British "Ford" class, donated and commissioned 12-4-73 and 26-7-74, respectively. Recently rearmed with Yugoslav weapons.

◆ **5 river patrol boats** Bldr: DEW Narayengonj, Dacca

P 101 PAENA (6-72) P 103 PATUAKHALI (11-74) P 105 RANGAMATI (6-77)
P 102 NOAKAHLI (7-72) P 104 BOGRA (6-77)

D: 69.5 tons (fl) **S:** 10 kts **Dim:** 22.9 × 6.1 × 1.9 **A:** 1/40-mm AA
M: 2 Cummins diesels; 2 props **Range:** 700/8 **Man:** 3 officers, 30 men

REMARKS: Last two differ in configuration, gun forward. More may be built.

AUXILIARIES

◆ **1 small underway-replenishment ship** Bldr: . . .

A 515 KHANJAHAN ALI

D: 2,900 tons (fl) **S:** . . . **Dim:** 76.1 × 11.4 × 5.3
M: 1 6-cyl. diesel; 1 prop; 1,350 hp

REMARKS: Transferred 1983 from state-owned shipping line and equipped for underway refueling. 1,342 grt.

◆ **1 transport, former passenger/cargo ship** Bldr: Ch. & At. de St. Nazaire (Penhöet), France (In serv. 1953)

A 504 SHAHEED SALAHUDDIN (ex-*Hizbal Bahr,* ex-*Eastern Queen,* ex-*General Mangan*)

D: 8,800 light (14,800 fl) **S:** 16 kts **Dim:** 162.01 × 19.72 × 6.94
M: 2 Penhöet/Burmeister & Wain 9-62 BTF-115 diesels; 2 props; 9,600 hp
Electric: 1,500 kw **Fuel:** 1,045 tons **Range:** 9,750/13
Man: 25 officers, 125 men

REMARKS: 11,684 grt/6,383 nrt/5,882 dwt. Purchased 18-2-81 from Bangladesh Shipping Corp. and commissioned 10-4-81. Mostly used as a stationary barracks.

◆ **1 small repair ship**

A. . . SHAHAYAK

REMARKS: Former riverine passenger ship, 55-m. overall. Purchased, re-engined, and commissioned as a tender in 1978.

◆ **1 training ship** Bldr: Atlantic SB, Montreal, Canada (1957)

A 601 SHAHEED RUHUL AMIN (ex-*Anticosti,* Canadian merchant)

D: 710 tons (fl) **S:** 11.5 kts **Dim:** 47.5 × 11.1 × 3.1 **A:** 1/40-mm AA
M: 1 Caterpillar diesel **Range:** 4,000/10 **Man:** 8 officers, 72 men

REMARKS: Transferred 1972 from relief agency; recommissioned after conversion, 10-12-74.

◆ **1 floating drydock** Bldr: Tito SY, Trogir, Yugoslavia

A 701 SUNDARBAN (In serv. 15-8-80)

Lift capacity: 3,500 tons **Dim:** 117.0 × 27.6 × 0.3 loaded.

REMARKS: Self-docking type with 7 sectional pontoons. 17.6-m between dock walls, which are 101.4-m long.

◆ **1 Chinese Dinghai-class seagoing tug** Bldr: Wuhu SY

A 721 KHADEM (In serv. 1984)

D: 1,472 tons (fl) **S:** . . . **Dim:** 60.22 × 11.60 × 4.44
A: 4/14.5-mm mg (II × 2) **Electron Equipt:** Radar: 2/ . . . nav.
M: 2 diesels; 2 props; 2,640 hp **Man:** 4 officers, 28 men
Range: 7,200/ . . .

REMARKS: 980.28 grt. See photo in addenda.

BARBADOS

COAST GUARD

PERSONNEL (1985): 92 (11 officers, 81 men); to increase to 120

MERCHANT MARINE (1984): 35 ships—8,414 grt

◆ **1 patrol boat** Bldr: Brooke Marine, Lowestoft, U.K.

	L	In serv.
P 01 TRIDENT	14-4-81	11-81

Trident (P 01) Brooke Marine, 1981

D: 165 tons (200 fl) **S:** 25 kts **Dim:** 37.50 × 6.86 × 1.78
A:: 1/40-mm AA—1/20-mm AA **Man::** 25 tot.
Electron Equipt: Radar: 1/Decca TM 1226
M: 2 Paxman Valenta 12 RP 200 diesels; 2 props; 4,000 hp **Range:** 3,000/12

◆ **2 converted shrimp boats** Bldr: Desco Marine

P 02 ENTERPRISE (In serv. 8-81) P 03 EXCELLENCE (In serv. 7-1-82)

D: 130 tons (fl) **S:** 12 kts **Dim:** 22.8 × 6.2 × 1.8
A: 1/20-mm AA **M:** 1 Caterpillar diesel; . . . hp **Man:** 2 officers, 8 men

REMARKS: Wooden-hulled craft, converted for use as seagoing patrol boats by Swan Hunter, Trinidad.

◆ **1 Halmatic 20-meter Guardian-class police patrol craft** Bldr: Aquarius Boat, U.K.

P 04 GEORGE FERGUSON (In serv. 12-74)

D: 30 tons (fl) **S:** 24 kts **Dim:** 20.0 × 5.25 × 1.5
M: 2 G.M. 12V71 TI diesels; 2 props; 1,300 hp **Range:** 650/12 **Man:** 11 tot.

REMARKS: Fiberglass hull. Can carry 2/7.62-mm mg.

◆ **2 Halmatic 12-meter Guardian-class police patrol craft** Bldr: Aquarius Boat, U.K. (In serv. 12-73 to 2-74)

P 05 COMMANDER MARSHALL P 06 J. T. C. Ramsay

D: 11.5 tons **S:** 21 kts **Dim:** 12.0 × 3.7 × 1.0
M: 2 Caterpillar Mk 334 TA diesels; 2 props; 580 hp **Man:** 4 tot.

REMARKS: Like P 04, used for search and rescue. Can carry 1/7.62-mm mg. Glass-reinforced plastic hull from Halmatic.

BELGIUM

Kingdom of Belgium

PERSONNEL (1985): 300 officers, 4,191 men (including 1,116 draftees)

MERCHANT MARINE (1984): 338 ships—2,406,714 grt (tankers: 21—469,781 grt)

NAVAL AVIATION: Three Alouette-IIIB helicopters.

FRIGATES

◆ **4 Wielingen class, Type E 71**

	Bldr	Laid down	L	In serv.
F 910 WIELINGEN	Boëlwerf, Temse	5-3-74	30-3-76	20-1-78
F 911 WESTDIEP	Cockerill, Hoboken	2-9-74	8-12-75	20-1-78
F 912 WANDELAAR	Boëlwerf, Temse	5-3-75	21-6-77	27-10-78
F 913 WESTHINDER	Cockerill, Hoboken	8-12-75	31-1-77	27-10-78

FRIGATES *(continued)*

Westdiep (F 911) L. & L. Van Ginderen, 7-84

Wielingen (F 910) L. & L. Van Ginderen, 11-84

D: 1,880 tons (2,283 fl) **S:** 28 kts on gas turbine
Dim: 106.38 (103 pp) × 12.3 × 5.3 (over sonar)
A: 4 MM 38 (II × 2) Exocet—1/100-mm DP—1/NATO Sea Sparrow SAM syst 8 missiles)—1/375-mm Bofors ASW RL (II × 1)—2 launching racks for L-5 ASW torpedoes
Electron Equipt: Radar: 1/Raytheon TM 1645/9X, 1/DA-05, 1/H.S.A. WM-25
Sonar: 1/SQS-505A
EW: Elcos-1 intercept—2/Mk 36 SRBOC chaff (VI × 2)
M: CODOG: 2 Cockerill CO-240V-12 diesels, each 3,000 hp; 1 Rolls-Royce Olympus TM 3B gas turbine, 28,000 hp; 2 CP props
Fuel: 250 tons diesel **Electric:** 2,000 kw
Range: 4,500/18; 6,000/16 **Man:** 15 officers, 145 men

Remarks: Vosper fin stabilizers. 15 knots max. on one diesel, 20 knots on two. Belgian-Dutch automatic surface- and air-search radar system, including fire control and SEWACO-IV automatic tactical data system. Two Panda optical gun directors. The ASW rocket launcher carries six 103-mm rocket flare rails. U.S. SLQ-25 NIXIE ASW decoys. Planned to add 30-mm Goalkeeper AA system, probably in place of other armament.

PATROL CRAFT

◆ **2 Leie-class river gunboats** Bldr: Hitzler, Regensburg

P 902 Liberation (In serv. 4-8-54) P 903 Meuse (In serv. 20-8-53)

Meuse (P 903) L. & L. Van Ginderen, 9-85

D: 25 tons (27.5 fl) **S:** 19 kts **Dim:** 23.25 × 3.8 × 0.9
A: 2/12.7-mm mg (I × 2) **M:** 2 MWM diesels; 2 props; 440 hp
Man: 1 officer, 6 men

Remarks: P 902 is 26 meters in length, 4 meters in beam, 30 tons (fl). Sisters *Rupel* (P 907, ex-*Tresignies*) and *Ourthe* (P 908) were sold 8-9-83; *Leie* (P 901) and *Semois* (P 906) were sold 21-2-85; *Sambre* (P 904) was donated to the Sea Scouts, and *Schelde* (P 905) given to a museum in 1984.

MINE WARFARE SHIPS

A consortium of Boëlwerf, Beliard Mercantile, and ACEC has been formed to study a minehunter design to follow the "Tripartite" program.

◆ **1 (+9) Tripartite class minehunters** Bldr: Béliard, Ostend and Antwerp

	Laid down	L	In serv.
M 915 Aster	24-2-83	26-6-84	-85
M 916 Bellis	7-83	19-2-85	1986
M 917 Crocus	12-83	10-85	. . .
M 918 Dianthus	5-84	. . .	. . .
M 919 Fuchsia	10-84	. . .	. . .
M 920 Iris	. . .	. . .	. . .
M 921 Lobelia	. . .	. . .	. . .
M 922 Myosotis	. . .	. . .	. . .
M 923 Narcis	. . .	. . .	. . .
M 924 Primula	. . .	. . .	. . .

Aster (M 915)—en route to fitting-out yard L. & L. Van Ginderen, 6-84

D: 511 tons (595 fl) **S:** 15 kts **Dim:** 51.6 (47.1 pp) × 8.96 × 2.49 (hull)
A: 1/20-mm AA **Electron Equipt:** Radar: Decca 1229—Sonar: DUBM-21B
M: 1 Brons/Werkspoor A-RUB 215X 12 diesel; 1 CP prop; 1,900 hp (1,200 rpm); 2 120-hp maneuvering props (active rudder); bow-thruster
Electric: 880 kw **Range:** 3,000/12 **Man:** 34 tot. (49 accommodations)

Remarks: Same as French *Eridan* and Dutch *Alkmaar* classes. Original construction consortium, Polyship, dissolved. Ships reordered 12-2-81 from Béliard; hulls launched at Ostend and fitted out by Béliard Mercantile at Rupelmonde, Antwerp. Three Astazou-IV, 320-kw gas-turbine generators; 1 140-kw diesel set. Two PAP-104 remote-controlled mine locators; automatic pilot; automatic track-plotter; TORAN and Sydelis navigation systems; conventional wire sweep also. Glass-reinforced-plastic construction. To replace MSO and MSC classes.

◆ **6 U.S. Dash-class oceangoing minesweeper/minehunters**

	L	In serv.
M 902 Van Haverbeke (ex-MSO 522)	29-10-59	7-11-60
M 903 A. F. Dufour (ex-*Lagen*, ex-MSO 498)	13-8-54	27-9-55
M 904 De Brouwer (ex-*Nansen*, ex-MSO 499)	15-10-54	1-11-55
M 906 Breydel (ex-AM 504)	25-3-55	24-1-56
M 908 Georges Truffaut (ex-AM 515)	1-11-55	21-9-56
M 909 Francois Bovesse (ex-AM 516)	28-2-56	21-12-56

Bldrs: M 902: Peterson Bldrs, Sturgeon Bay, Wisc.; M 903, 904: Bellingham BY, Bellingham, Wash.; M 906: Tacoma BY, Tacoma, Wash.; M 908, 909: Tampa SB, Tampa, Fla.

Breydel (M 906) G. Gyssels, 1-85

D: 720 tons (780 fl) **S:** 14 kts
Dim: 52.42 (50.3 pp) × 10.97 × 4.20 **A:** 2/12.7-mm mg (II × 1, not in M 906)
Electron Equipt: Radar: 1/Decca 1229—Sonar: SQQ-14
M: 4 G.M. 8-268A diesels; 2 CP props; 1,520 hp **Fuel:** 53 tons diesel
Range: 3,000/10; 2,400/12 **Man:** 5 officers, 67 men

Remarks: Transferred 1955-60, except M 903 and M 904 transferred from Norway in 1966. Equipped as minehunters, with PAP-104 remote-control minehunting submersibles. Wooden hulls. *Artevelde* (M 907) stricken 1-2-85.

MINE WARFARE SHIPS *(continued)*

◆ **5 U.S. Adjutant-class coastal minesweepers** Bldr: Béliard, Ostend (M 928: Boëlwerf, Temse)

	L	In serv.		L	In serv.
M 928 Stavelot	26-3-55	1-7-55	M 932 Nieupoort	12-3-55	9-1-56
M 929 Heist	. . .	4-4-56	M 933 Koksisde	4-6-55	29-11-55
M 930 Rochefort	5-6-54	28-11-55			

Rochefort (M 930) M. Louagie, 2-85

Heist (M 929)—restored as a minesweeper L. & L. Van Ginderen, 9-85

D: 330 tons (390 fl) **S:** 13.5/12 kts **Dim:** 44.0 (42.1 pp) × 8.3 × 2.6
A: 1/40-mm AA
Electron Equipt: Radar: 1/Decca 1229—Sonar: AN/UQS-1
M: 2 G.M. 8-268A diesels; 2 props; 880 hp **Fuel:** 40 tons
Range: 2,700/10.5 **Man:** 4 officers, 17 petty officers, 19 men

Remarks: M 928, stricken 1979, restored to service 1982-83. M 929, converted to degaussing tender (A 964) in 1978, restored as a minesweeper 6-85. Two minehunter conversions, *Verriers* (M 934, ex-U.S. AMS 259) and *Veurne* (M 935, ex-U.S. AMS 260) stricken 6-85. M 932 has a lengthened forward deckhouse.

◆ **12 Herstal-class inshore minesweepers** Bldr: Mercantile Marine Yd., Kruibeke

	L	In serv.		L	In serv.
M 473 Lokeren	18-5-57	8-8-58	M 479 Huy	17-11-56	14-10-57
M 474 Turnhout	7-9-57	29-9-58	M 480 Seraing	16-3-57	24-3-58
M 475 Tongeren	16-11-57	9-12-58	M 482 Vise	7-9-57	11-9-58
M 476 Merksem	5-4-58	6-2-59	M 483 Ougrée	16-11-57	10-11-58
M 477 Oudenaerde	3-5-58	25-4-59	M 484 Dinant	5-4-58	14-1-59
M 478 Herstal	6-8-56	14-10-57	M 485 Andenne	3-5-58	20-4-59

Vise (M 482) L. & L. Van Ginderen, 5-85

D: 160 tons (190 fl) **S:** 15 kts **Dim:** 34.5 (32.5 pp) × 6.7 × 2.1
A: 2/12.7-mm mg (II × 1) **Electron Equipt:** Radar: 1/Decca 1229
M: 2 Fiat-Mercedes Benz MB 820 diesels; 2 props; 1,260 hp
Fuel: 24 tons **Range:** 2,300/10 **Man:** 1 officer, 7 petty officers, 9 men

Remarks: Wooden hulls. Intended to sweep the Schelde River. Fitted for magnetic, acoustic, and mechanical sweeping to a depth of 4.50 to 10 m. M 471, 472, 478 were designated RDS-Ready Duty Ship, sweep gear removed, deckhouse in place of cable reel, and pollution cleanup gear and special cranes added aft; M 471, 478 restored as minesweepers, 1983, while *Kortijk* (M 472) has been altered to serve as a research ship. Modified version of British "-ham" class. M 478 to M 485, built with U.S funds, are ex-U.S. MSI 90-97. Sister *Hasselt* (M 471) scheduled to strike early 1986.

AUXILIARIES

◆ **2 "command and logistics support ships" for mine countermeasures**

	Bldr	Laid down	L	In serv.
A 961 Zinnia	Cockerill (Hoboken)	8-11-66	6-5-67	5-9-67

Zinnia (A 961) G. Gyssels, 5-83

D: 1,705 tons (2,685 fl) **S:** 18 kts (20 on trials)
Dim: 99.5 (94.2 wl) × 14.0 × 3.6 **Range:** 14,000/12.5
A: 3/40-mm (I × 3)—1/Alouette-IIIB helicopter
Electron Equipt: Radar: 2/Decca navigational
M: 2 Cockerill-Ougrée V 12 TR 240 CO diesels; 1 CP prop; 5,000 hp
Fuel: 150 m³ diesel; 300 m³ for supply to minesweepers—500 tons total
Man: 13 officers, 46 petty officers, 64 men

Remarks: Fin stabilizers, telescoping helicopter hangar.

	Bldr	Laid down	L	In serv.
A 960 Godetia	Boëlwerf, Temse	15-2-65	7-12-65	23-5-66

Godetia (A 960) L. & L. Van Ginderen, 4-84

Godetia (A960) L. & L. Van Ginderen, 4-84

AUXILIARIES *(continued)*

D: 1,700 tons (2,500 fl) **S:** 18 kts **Dim:** 91.83 (87.85 pp) × 14.0 × 3.5
A: 1/40-mm AA **Electron Equipt:** Radar: 2/nav.
M: 4 ACEC-M.A.N. diesels; 2 CP props; 5,400 hp
Fuel: 294 tons **Range:** 2,250/15; 8,700/12
Man: 10 officers, 37 petty officers, 48 men

REMARKS: 15 knots on one diesel. Passive tank stabilization. Protected closed-circuit ventilation. Can accommodate oceanographic research personnel and has space for laboratory. Minesweeping cables are stowed on reels on the helicopter deck, which has been extended aft to continue to permit one Alouette-III to land. 8/12.7-mm mg (II × 4) removed 1983; quickly remountable.

◆ **1 new-construction oceanographic research ship**

	Bldr	Laid down	L	In serv.
A. 962 BELGICA	Boëlwerf, Temse	17-10-83	6-1-84	5-7-84

D: 835 tons (fl) **S:** 12 kts **Dim:** 50.90 (44.95 pp) × 10.00 × 4.40
M: 1 ABC 6M DZC-1000-150 diesel; 1 Kort-nozzle prop; 1,570 hp **Fuel:** 158 tons
Electron Equipt: Radar: 1/Decca . . . nav.
Electric: 640 kw **Range:** 20,000/12 **Man:** 15 crew + 11 scientists

Belgica (A 962) L. & L. Van Ginderen, 9-84

Belgica (A 962) L. & L. Van Ginderen, 6-84

REMARKS: For use in North and Irish Seas or for fisheries or hydrographic research. Can carry two laboratory containers on deck. 150-hp thrusters fore and aft. Very bluff hull lines, bulbous bow.

Kortrijk (M 472) G. Gyssels, 4-84

◆ **1 converted Herstal-class minesweeper**

	Bldr	L	In serv.
M 472 KORTRIJK	Mercantile Marine, Kruibeke	5-57	13-6-58

REMARKS: Data as for *Herstal* class. Used for oceanographic research in place of the stricken *Mechelen* (A 962); had been used as a pollution clearance ship.

◆ **1 U.S. Adjutant-class former minesweeper** Bldr: Boëlwerf, Temse

	In serv.
A 963 SPA (ex-M 927) — Missile/munitions transport for frigates	1-1-56

Spa (A 963) L. & L. Van Ginderen, 10-84

REMARKS: Data as for minesweeper sisters.

◆ **1 oceanographic research and sail-training craft**

	Bldr	Laid down	L	In serv.
A 958 ZENOBE GRAMME	Boëlwerf, Temse	7-10-60	23-10-61	1962

Zenobe Gramme (A 958) L. & L. Van Ginderen, 3-84

D: 149 tons **S:** 10 kts **Dim:** 28.15 (23.10 wl) × 6.85 × 2.64
M: 1 MWM 518A diesel; 232 hp **Man:** 14 tot.

REMARKS: Fitted out as Bermudian ketch (240m³ sail area).

◆ **1 seagoing tug** Bldr: Ch. Navals & Atelier Const. de Hemixem

A 954 ZEEMEEUW (In serv. 1971)

D: 400 tons (fl) **S:** 10 kts **Dim:** 27.94 (26.60 pp) × 7.29 × 3.37
M: 2 ABC 6-cyl. diesels; 2 props. . . . hp **Electric:** 96 kw **Man:** . . .

REMARKS: 146 grt/24 nrt. Acquired from another Belgian government agency, 1982. Based at Zeebrugge and used on pollution control duties.

BELGIUM *(continued)*
AUXILIARIES *(continued)*

Zeemeeuw (A 954) L. & L. Van Ginderen, 2-83

◆ **2 seagoing tugs** Bldr: H. Bodewes, Millengen a/d Ryn (In serv. 1960)

A 950 Valcke (ex-*Astronoom*, ex-*Schouwenbank*)
A 998 Ekster (ex-*Astrodom*, ex-*Steenbank*)

Valcke (A 950) L. & L. Van Ginderen, 9-84

D: 420 tons (fl) **S:** 13 kts **Dim:** 30.08 × 7.55 × 2.99
Electron Equipt: Radar: 1/Decca 1229
M: 24-cycle, single-acting 8-cyl. diesels, electric drive; 1 prop; 1,250 hp

Remarks: 183 grt. Purchased 1980 from A. Smit. Based at Zeebrugge on pollution-control duties. A 950 in collision 1985, out of service for many months.

YARD AND SERVICE CRAFT

Note: The small harbor tug *Hommel* (A 951) had been stricken by mid-1985.

◆ **2 Bij-class small harbor tugs**

	Bldr	In serv.
A 953 Bij	Akerboom, Lisse	1959
A 956 Krekel	Rupelmonde SY	1961

Krekel (A 956) L. & L. Van Ginderen, 3-82

D: 60 tons (71 fl) **S:** 10 kts **Dim:** 17.65 (16.0) × 5.2 × 2.0
M: 2 MWM RHS 518A diesels; 2 Voith-Schneider vertical cycloidal props; 300 hp

◆ **1 small fireboat tug** A 959 Mier Bldr: Liège SY (1962): 12.5 m o.a., 17.5 tons, 90 hp

◆ **1 personnel launch** Spin (1958)—32 tons, 14.6 m., 1 diesel; Voith-Schneider prop; 250 hp; 8 kts—can also be used as a tug.

Note: Fuel barges FN 4, 5, 6 stricken 1983, as was diving tender ZM4.

Spin G. Gyssels, 10-81

BELIZE

Personnel (1985): 33 total

Merchant Marine (1984): 3 ships—620 grt

Aviation: 2 Pilatus—Britten-Norman BN 2B Defender.

◆ **2 20-meter Wasp class patrol craft** Bldr: Souter, Cowes, U.K. (In serv. 19-9-84)

PB 01 Dangriga PB 02 Toledo

Dangriga (PB 01) L. Dury, 8-83

D: 36.25 tons (fl) **S:** 23 kts **Dim:** 20.00 (16.00 pp) × 5.00 × 1.50
A: 1/12.7-mm mg—4/7.72-mm mg (I × 4) **Electron Equipt:** Radar: . . .
M: 2 G.M. 16V71 TI diesels; 2 props; 2,400 hp **Man:** 2 officers, 6 men
Range: 430/18

Remarks: Glass-reinforced plastic construction. Completed 8-84, not commissioned in-country until 19-9-84.

◆ **1 patrol craft** Bldr: Brooke Marine, Lowestoft, U.K. (In serv. 1982)

PBM 02 Belmopan

D: 15 tons (fl) **S:** 22 kts **Dim:** 12.2 × 3.6 × 0.6 **A:** 3 mg (I × 3)
M: 2 Caterpillar diesels; 2 props; 370 hp

Remarks: Sister *Belize* (PBM 01) deleted 1982.

BENIN

People's Republic of Benin

Personnel: About 100

Merchant Marine (1984): 13 ships—4,604 grt

Four Zhuk in the port of Cotonou 1-84

◆ **2 ex-North Korean, Soviet P 4-class torpedo boats** (transferred 1979)

D: 19.3 tons (22.4 fl) **S:** 54 kts **Dim:** 19.3 × 3.7 × 1.0
A: 2/14.5-mm mg (II × 1)
Electron Equipt: Radar: 1/. . . nav. **M:** 2 M50 diesels; 2 props; 2,400 hp

Remarks: Aluminum-construction hydroplanes. May in fact be newer craft of similar design to P 4 from North Korea. Torpedo tubes removed.

◆ **5 Soviet Zhuk-class patrol craft**

D: 60 tons (fl) **S:** 34 kts **Dim:** 24.0 × 5.0 × 1.5 (props)
A: 4/14.5-mm mg (II × 2) **M:** 2 M50 diesels; 2 props; 2,400 hp
Electron Equipt: Radar: 1/spin Trough

Remarks: Transferred: 2 in 1979, 2 in 5-80, 1 in 9-80.

BERMUDA

The Crown Colony of Bermuda

Merchant Marine (1984): 76 ships—822,123 grt (8 tankers—230,105 grt)

BERMUDIAN POLICE

◆ **1 sport cruiser** Bldr: Harris Boat, Newburyport, Mass., U.S.A.

Blue Heron (In serv. 22-5-78)

D: 7 tons **S:** . . . **Dim:** 10.9 × . . . × . . .
M: 2 G.M. diesels; 2 props; 260 hp **Man:** 3

◆ **2 small craft** Bldr: Mako Marine, Florida, U.S.A.

Heron II (In serv. 7-81) Heron III (In serv. 4-78)

Remarks: 7.1 and 6.7 m overall, about 1 ton, powered by one 235-hp Evinrude outboard each. Patrol craft *Heron I* and *White Heron* stricken 1983. New patrol craft acquisitions are planned.

BOLIVIA

Republic of Bolivia

Personnel (1985): 4,000 including 600 Almirante Grau Battalion marines

Merchant Marine (1984): 2 ships—14,913 grt

Note: The Bolivian River and Lake Force was retitled the Bolivian Navy on 1-1-82.

Naval Aviation: 1 Cessna U206 and 3 Cessna 402C light transports.

◆ **1 seagoing cargo ship** Bldr: Fairfield, U.K., 1951

Libertador Bolívar (ex-*Simon Bolívar*, ex-*Ciudad de Barquisimeto*)

D: 9,000 tons **S:** 14.5 kts **Dim:** 128.3 (120.4 pp) × 16.76 × 6.7
M: 1 Doxford diesel; 4,350 hp **Range:** 7,000/14

Remarks: Donated by Venezuela, 1977. Home-ported in Argentina. Used to generate revenue and for training in preparation for possible ceding to Bolivia of a "corridor to the sea" between Peru and Chile. 4,214 grt/6,390 dwt/2,352 nrt.

◆ **7 river patrol craft/transports**

MO 1 Almirante Grau, 52 tons
MO 2 Nicolas Suarez, 26 tons
MO 3 Mariscal Santa Cruz, 52 tons
MO 4 Presidente Busch, 52 tons
MO 5 Comandante Arandia, 82 tons
MO 6 Topater
MO 8 Coronel Eduardo Avaroa, 82 tons

Remarks: Iron- or wooden-hulled, raftlike craft with high superstructures and speeds of 8-10 knots.

◆ **1 U.S. design river patrol boat** Bldr: Hope/Progressive SB, Houma, La.

PR 51 Santa Cruz de la Sierra (In serv. 1985)

D: . . . **S:** . . . **Dim:** 20.42 × . . . × . . .
A: 1/20-mm AA **Electron Equipt:** Radar: 1/Furuno nav.
M: 2 G.M. diesels; 2 props; . . . hp **Man:** 10 tot.

Remarks: Aluminum hull. See photo in addenda.

◆ **1 or more Brown-class patrol launches** (In serv. 1978- . . .)

Almirante Guillermo Brown

D: 4 tons **S:** 12 kts **Dim:** 7.0 × 2.3 × 1.0
M: 1 Ford Penta diesel; 116 hp **Man:** 12 tot.

◆ **2 ex-U.S. PBR Mk-II patrol boats** (Transferred 1974)

D: 8.9 tons **S:** 24 kts **Dim:** 9.73 × 3.53 × 0.81
A: 3/12.7-mm mg (II × 1, I × 1)—1/60-mm mortar
Electron Equipt: Radar: 1/Raytheon 1900
M: 2 G.M. 6V53N diesels; 2 water jets; 430 hp **Range:** 150/23 **Man:** 4 tot.

◆ **24 miscellaneous Lake Titicaca and river service launches** (several oar-propelled)

◆ **2 hospital launches**

Julian Apaza Bruno Racua

Remarks: Launched 1977-78; 17 tons. *Apaza* a gift of the USA.

BRAZIL

Federative Republic of Brazil

Personnel (1985): 6,285 officers, 44,000 men (including 14,000 marines in the Fuzileiros Navais and reservists).

Merchant Marine (1984): 706 ships—5,721,821 grt (tankers: 86—2,794,500 grt)

Naval Aviation: Uses 4 SH-3D and 4 SH-3H Sea King, 9 Westland Wasp HAS.1 (UH-2), 17 Bell 206B JetRanger II (SAH-11) helicopters, 9 Westland Mk 21 Lynx (to be equipped with Sea Skua missiles), 11 AS 350 Esquilo (UH-12), and 3 AS-330 Super Puma. In 3-85, 16 used Bell 206Bs were ordered in the U.S. in lieu of purchasing a planned 15 AS 332F Super Puma with AM-39 missiles. Plans to acquire A-4 Skyhawk aircraft have been canceled.

The Air Force makes available to the Navy: 3 RC-130E Hercules, and 12 EMB Bandeirante in a sea-surveillance version. Eight Grumman S-2E Tracker aircraft are available for use on *Minas Gerais,* and 5 S-2A are used for training and transport. To support the Navy, the Air Force also operates 2 Piper/Embraer Seneca II and 4 Neiva T-25 Universal aircraft. The Air Force Coastal Command also has 6 Puma helicopters for search-and-rescue purposes.

Weapons and Sensors: Avibrás Indústria Aerospacial is developing the Barracuda anti-ship missile. The SM-70 version will be quadruple-mounted on trucks for coastal defeuse, and the MM-70 is for shipboard use. Range: 70-km. Length: 5-m.

Warships In Service Or Under Construction As Of 1 January 1986

	L	Tons	Main armament
◆ **1 light aircraft carrier (ASW)**			
Minas Gerais	1944	15,890	10/40-mm AA, 18-22 aircraft
◆ **7 (+3) submarines**			
0 (+3) Type 1400	1986-	1,400	8/533-mm TT
3 Oberon	1971-75	1,610	8/533-mm TT
2 GUPPY III	1945	1,650	10/533-mm TT
2 GUPPY II	1944-45	1,517	10/533-mm TT

WARSHIPS *(continued)*

◆ **7 destroyers**

2 Gearing, FRAM I	1944-45	2,425	2/127-mm DP, 6 ASW TT ASROC
4 Allen M. Sumner, FRAM II	1944	2,200	6/127-mm DP, 6 ASW TT
1 Allen M Sumner	1944	2,200	6/127-mm DP, 1 Sea Cat SAM,6 ASW TT

◆ **6 (+4) frigates**

0 (+4) new construction	1985-	1,600	4 Exocet, 1/114-mm DP, 6 ASW TT, 1 helicopter
4 Niteroi	1974-75	3,200	1/114-mm DP, 2/40-mm AA, 1 Branik system, 2 Sea Cat systems, 1 Bofors ASW RL, 6 ASW TT, 1 helicopter
2 Constitucão	1976-77	3,200	2/114-mm DP, 2/40-mm AA, 4 Exocet, 2 Sea Cat systems, 1 Bofors ASW RL, 6 ASW TT, 1 helicopter

◆ **12 corvettes**

9 Imperial Marinheiro	1954-55	911	1/76.2-mm DP
3 Sotoyomo	1945	570	2/20-mm AA

◆ **6 patrol boats**

◆ **7 (+2) river patrol ships**

◆ **6 mine warfare ships**

◆ **2 amphibious warfare ships**

LIGHT AIRCRAFT CARRIER (ASW)

Note: Long-range plans call for replacing *Minas Gerais* with one or two small carriers. Although it was announced in 1984 that the first of these would be operational in 1990, this seems very unlikely. The aircraft to be carried *may* include a navalized version of the Embraer AMX fighter project. Plans to acquire A-4 Skyhawks as an interim jet aircraft have been shelved.

◆ **1 British Colossus class**

	Bldr	Laid down	L	In serv.
A 11 Minas Gerais (ex-*Venegeance*)	Swan Hunter, Wallsend-on-Tyne	16-11-42	23-3-44	15-1-45

D: 15,890 tons (19,890 fl) **S:** 24 kts
Dim: 211.25 × 36.44 (24.50 hull) × 7.15
A: 10/40-mm AA (IV × 2, II × 1) — 6-8/S-2E aircraft — 4-6/SH-3, 2/SAH-11, 3/UH-12 helicopters
Electron Equipt: Radar: 1/SPS-40B, 1/SPS-4, 1/Raytheon 1402, 2/SPG-34 fire control — EW: SLR-2
M: Parsons GT; 2 props; 42,000 hp
Boilers: 4 Admiralty 3-drum; 28 kg/cm², 371°C **Fuel:** 3,200 tons
Electric: 2,500 kw **Range:** 12,000/14; 6,200/23
Man: 1,000 ship's company plus 300 aviation personnel

Minas Gerais (A 11) U.S. Navy, 1985

Minas Gerais (A 11) U.S. Navy, 1985

Minas Gerais (A 11) 1985

Remarks: Purchased from Great Britain in 12-56; refitted in Rotterdam, completing in 1960 with new weapons, steam catapult, angled flight deck (8.5°), mirror optical landing equipment, new radars, and 2 new elevators. GFCS for the 40-mm AA include 2 Mk 63 (with SPG-34 radar on the quadruple mounts) and 1 Mk 51 Mod. 2. Hangar 135.6 × 15.8 × 5.3 high; 2 elevators 13.7 × 10.4. Catapult can launch 15-ton aircraft. In refit 1976-81. A data link system for cooperation with the *Niteroi* class has been installed, and U.S. SPS-40B radar has replaced SPS-12. Plans to purchase 12 A-4 Skyhawk fighter-bombers for use from this ship were announced in 1984 and canceled early in 1985. The SPS-8B height-finding radar was removed during 1984.

SUBMARINES

Note: On 29-11-84 the Navy announced plans to build a 2,200-ton "NAC-1" class submarine of Brazilian design following the construction of the two IKL Type 1400 submarines in Brazil. Long-range plans also call for construction of nuclear-powered submarines.

◆ **0 (+3 + 2) West German Type 1400 class**

	Bldr	Laid down	L	In serv.
S . . . Tupi	Howaldtswerke, Kiel	8-3-85	1986	1988
S . . . Tamoyo	Howaldtswerke, Kiel	. . .	. . .	1989
S . . . Timbyra	Ast. Ilha das Cobras, Rio	. . .	. . .	. . .

D: 1,400 tons surf., 1,900 sub. **S:** 21.5 sub. **Dim:** 61.0 × 6.2 × 5.5
A: 8/533-mm TT fwd. — 16 Mk 24 Mod. 1 Tigerfish torpedoes
Electron Equipt: Radar: . . .
Sonar: Krupp-Atlas CSV-83/1
EW: Thomson-CSF DR-4000
M: 4 MTU 12V493 TY60, 600 bhp diesels, 4 AEG 420-kw generators, electric drive; 1 prop; 5,000 hp
Range: 8,200/8 snorkel; 50/16, 400/4 submerged **Fuel:** 118 tons **Man:** 30 tot.

Remarks: The largest version of the Type 209 yet ordered; order placed 8-82. Will have Ferranti KAFS action data system, 2 Kollmorgan periscopes, Sperry MK 29 Mod. 2 Ships Inertial Guidance System (SINS). Can make 25 knots for brief period. Diving depth: 250 m.

◆ **3 British Oberon class**

	Bldr	Laid down	L	In serv.
S 20 Humaita	Vickers-Barrow	3-11-70	5-10-71	18-6-73
S 21 Tonelero	Vickers-Barrow	18-21-70	22-11-72	8-9-78
S 22 Riachuelo	Vickers-Barrow	26-5-73	6-9-75	12-3-77

Riachuelo (S 22) L. & L. Van Ginderen, 7-77

D: 1,610 tons standard, 2,030 surf., 2,400 sub.
S: 17.5/15 kts **Dim:** 89.9 × 8.07 × 5.48
A: 6/533-mm TT forward (18 U.K. Mk 8 and Mk 24 and U.S. Mk 37 torpedoes)
Electron Equipt: Sonar: 1/187, 1/2007, DUUG-1, AUUD-1
M: 2 Admiralty Standard Range 16 VVS-ASR1 diesels; 2 electric generators, each 1,280 kw; 2 electric motors; 2 props; 6,000 hp
Range: 11,000/11 snorkel **Endurance:** 56 days **Man:** 5 officers, 57 men

SUBMARINES *(continued)*

REMARKS: S 21 several years late entering active service due to a fire on board during construction. Batteries made up of 224 elements in two sections, with a 7,240-ampere capacity for five hours. "One-man control" system for immersion and diving. Digital tactical data system. Satellite navigation receiver installed. Two short torpedo tubes aft are no longer used.

◆ 2 ex-U.S. GUPPY III class

	Bldr	Laid down	L	In serv.
S 15 GOIÁS (ex-*Trumpetfish,* SS 425)	Cramp S.B.	23-8-43	13-5-45	29-1-46
S 16 AMAZONAS (ex-*Greenfish,* SS 351)	Electric Boat Co.	29-1-44	21-12-45	7-6-46

Goiás (S 15) 1975

D: 1,650 tons standard, 1,975 surf., 2,540 sub. **S:** 20/13-15 kts
Dim: 99.4 × 8.2 × 5.2 **A:** 10/533-mm TTs, 6 fwd, 4 aft (24 torpedoes)
Electron Equipt: Radar: 1/SS-2A — Sonar: BQG-4 PUFFS, BQR-2B
M: Diesel-electric propulsion; 4 diesel generator sets (6,400 hp); 2 electric motors (5,400 hp)
Range: 12,000/10 surf., 95/5 sub. **Man:** 86 tot.

REMARKS: S 15 purchased 17-10-73, S 16 on 19-12-73. S 15 converted to GUPPY-II in 1948, lengthened to GUPPY III in 1962; S 16 to GUPPY II 1948, GUPPY III in 1961. S 15 has Fairbanks-Morse 38D 8⅛-10 diesels, S 16 has G.M. 16-278A. Two 126-cell batteries.

◆ 2 ex-U.S. GUPPY II class

	Bldr	Laid down	L	In serv.
S 12 BAHIA (ex-*Sea Leopard,* SS 483)	Portsmouth NSY	7-11-44	2-3-45	11-6-45
S 14 CEARA (ex-*Amberjack,* SS 522)	Boston NSY	8-2-44	15-12-44	4-3-46

D: 1,517 tons standard, 1,950 surf., 2,540 sub. **S:** 18/13-15 kts
Dim: 93.8 × 8.2 × 5.2 **A:** 10/533-mm TT, 6 fwd, 4 aft (24 torpedoes)
Electron Equipt: Radar: 1/SS-2A — Sonar: BQR-2B, BQS-4
M: Diesel-electric propulsion; 3 Fairbanks-Morse 38D 8⅛-10 generator groups; 2 electric motors; 2 props; 4,800/5,400 hp
Fuel: 330 tons diesel **Range:** 10,000/10 surf., 95/5 sub. **Man:** 86 tot.

REMARKS: Purchased 27-3-73 and 17-10-73. One generator set removed on conversion. Two 126-cell batteries. Converted from fleet submarines 1947-49. S 14 has auxiliary rudder atop hull. Sisters *Rio Grande do Sul* (S 11, ex-*Grampus,* SS 523) and *Rio de Janeiro* (S 13, ex-*Odax,* SS 484) stricken 1978: *Guanabara* (S 10, ex-*Dogfish,* SS 350) stricken late 1983.

DESTROYERS

◆ 2 ex-U.S. Gearing class, FRAM I

	Bldr	Laid down	L	In serv.
D 25 MARCILIO DIAZ (ex-*Henry W. Tucker,* DDR 875)	Consolidated Steel Corp	29-5-44	8-11-44	10-3-45
D 26 MARIZ E. BARROS (ex-*Brinkley Bass,* DD 887)	Consolidated Steel Corp	20-6-44	26-5-45	1-10-45

Marcilio Diaz (D 25) G. Gyssels, 1981

D: 2,425 tons (3,600 fl) **S:** 30 kts
Dim: 119.17 × 12.52 × 4.61 (6.4 over sonar)
A: 4/127-mm (II × 2) — 1/ASROC ASW syst. (VIII × 1; 12 total missiles) — 6/324-mm Mk 32 ASW TT (III × 2) — 1/Wasp helicopter
Electron Equipt: Radar: 1/SPS-10, 1/SPS-40, 1/Mk 25 fire control
Sonar: 1/SQS-23 — EW: WLR-1, ULQ-6
M: 2 sets GT; 2 props, 60,000 hp
Boilers: 4 Babcock & Wilcox, 43.3 kg, 454°C **Electric:** 1,200 kw
Fuel: 750 tons **Range:** 2,400/25; 4,800/15 **Man:** 14 officers, 260 men

REMARKS: Purchased 3-12-73 and reached Brazil in 6-74. Mk 37 GFCS. Former DASH drone ASW helicopter hangar used for Westland Wasp.

◆ 5 ex-U.S. Allen M. Sumner class

	Bldr	Laid down	L	In serv.
D 34 MATO GROSSO (ex-*Compton,* DD 705)	Federal SB, Kearny	28-3-44	17-9-44	4-11-44
D 35 SERGIPE (ex-*James C. Owens,* DD 776)	Bethlehem, San Pedro	9-4-44	1-10-44	17-2-45
D 36 ALAGAOS (ex-*Buck,* DD 761)	Bethlehem, San Fran.	1-2-44	11-3-44	28-6-46
D 37 RIO GRANDE DO NORTE (ex-*Strong,* DD 758)	Bethlehem, San Fran.	25-7-43	23-4-44	8-3-45
D 38 ESPIRITO SANTO (ex-*Lowry,* DD 770)	Bethlehem, San Pedro	1-8-43	6-2-44	28-7-44

Rio Grande do Norte (D 37) U.S. Navy, 1985

Mato Grosso (D 34) — with Sea Cat SAM system aft 1975

D: 2,200 tons (3,320 fl) **S:** 30 kts **Dim:** 114.75 × 12.45 × 5.8
A: 6/127-mm (II × 3) — (D 34 only; 1/quadruple Sea Cat SAM) — 2/Hedgehog ASW RL (XXIV × 2) — 6/324-mm Mk 32 ASW TT (III × 2) — 1/Wasp helicopter (not on D34)
Electron Equipt: Radar: 1/SPS-10, 1/SPS-40 (D 34: 1/SPS-6, D 38; 1/SPS-29), 1 Mk 25 fire-control — EW: WRL-1 or 3 intercept
Sonar: 1/SQS-44 (D 34: SQS-31); D 35 also: SQA-10 VDS
M: 2 sets GT; 2 props; 60,000 hp
Boilers: 4 Babcock & Wilcox, 43.3 kg/cm², 454°C **Fuel:** 460 tons
Electric: 1,200 kw **Range:** 1,260/30; 4,600/15 **Man:** 15 officers, 260 men

REMARKS: All except D 34 had FRAM II modernization. D 34 transferred 27-9-72, the others in 1973. Mk 37 GFCS. Sea Cat system added in D 34 uses M 20 optical director. D 38 has ULQ-6 jamming gear. D 35 collided with a merchant ship 11-84, out of service for 8-mos. or more.

◆ 3 ex-U.S. Fletcher class

	Bldr	Laid down	L	In serv.
D 31 PIAUI (ex-*Lewis Hancock,* DD 675)	Federal SB & DD	31-3-43	1-8-43	29-9-43
D 32 SANTA CATARINA (ex-*Irwin,* DD 794)	Bethlehem, San Pedro	2-5-43	31-10-43	14-2-44
D 33 MARANHÃO (ex-*Shields,* DD 596)	Puget Sound B & DD	10-8-44	29-4-44	8-2-45

D: 2,050 tons (2,850 fl) **S:** 33 kts **Dim:** 114.85 × 12.03 × 5.5
A: 5/127-mm DP (I × 5) — 10/40-mm AA (IV × 2, II × 2 — D 33: none)
Electron Equipt: Radar: 1/SPS-10, 1/SPS-66, 1/Mk 25 fire-control
M: 2 sets GT; 2 props; 60,000 hp **Electric:** 880 kw
Boilers: 4 Babcock & Wilcox, 43.3 kg/cm², 454°C **Fuel:** 450 tons
Range: 1,260/30; 3,600/14 **Man:** 15 officers, 247 men

DESTROYERS *(continued)*

Piaui (D 31) L. & L. Van Ginderen, 5-83

Remarks: D 31 transferred on loan under Mutual Aid Agreement on 2-8-67, D 32 on 10-5-68. D 33 purchased 1-7-72; the other two were bought outright on 11-4-73. ASW armament and sonar were to have been deleted and the ships used for 200-nm Economic Zone patrol, but were placed in Special Reserve in 1983 with quintuple 533-mm TT mount, 2 Hedgehog ASW spigot mortars and a d.c. rack still aboard. Unlikely now to see further service. Mk 37 GFCS for 127-mm, 3 Mk 5/mod. 1 GFCS for 40-mm.

FRIGATES

◆ **0 (+4) new-construction ocean patrol frigates** Bldr: First two: Ast. Ilha das Cobras, Rio; others: Caneco, . . .

	Laid down	L	In serv.
V28 Inhaúma	23-9-83	-85	6-87
V29 Jaceguary	5-10-84	6-86	4-88
V30 Frontin	. . .	. . .	. . .
V31 Julio de Noronha	. . .	. . .	. . .

Inhaúma (V 28)—artist's impression 1985

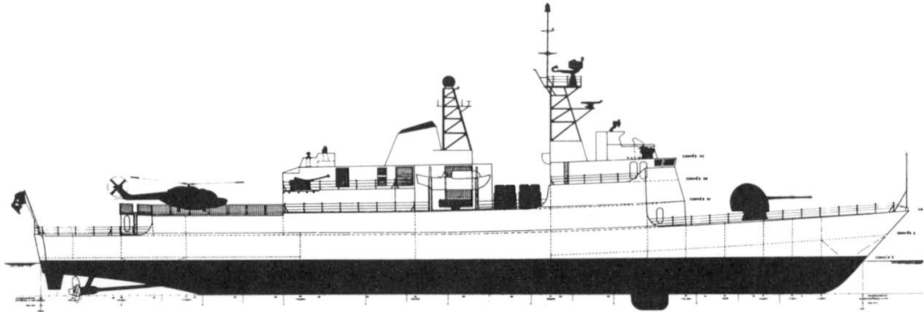

New ocean patrol frigate

D: 1,600 tons (1,900 fl) **S:** 26 kts **Dim:** 95.77 (90.00 pp) × 11.40 × 3.64
A: 4/MM 38 Exocet SSM—1/114-mm Vickers Mk 8 DP—2/40-mm Bofors L 70 AA (I × 2)—6/324-mm ASW TT for Mk 46 torpedoes (III × 2)—1/Lynx helicopter
Electron Equipt: Radar: 1/navigational, 1/Plessey AWS-4, 1/Orion RTN-10X
Sonar: Krupp-Atlas. ASO-4-2
EW: . . . passive, 2/Plessey Shield chaff RL (VI × 2)
M: CODOG: 1 G.E. LM-2500 gas turbine, 27,000 hp; 2 MTU 16V956 TB91 diesels, 7,880 hp; 2 CP props
Range: 4,000/15. **Man:** 16 officers, 31 petty officers, 73 men

Remarks: Originally to have been a program of 12 smaller "corvettes," intended for Coast Guard service. Four were authorized 11-81, with the possibility of more later, and the first two were ordered 15-2-82. Will have Ferranti CAAIS 2-50 (Computer-Assisted Information System). The projected 6th through 12th ships are to carry the Brazilian-designed Barracuda SSM in place of Exocet and will also have eight Avibras SS-1-N SAMs.

◆ **6 British Vosper Thornycroft Mk 10 class**

ASW:	Bldr	Laid down	L	In serv.
F 40 Niteroi	Thornycroft, Woolston	8-6-72	8-2-74	20-11-76
F 41 Defensora	Thornycroft, Woolston	14-12-75	27-3-75	5-3-77
F 44 Independencia	Ast. Ilha das Cobras, Rio	11-6-72	2-9-74	3-9-79
F 45 União	Ast. Ilha das Cobras, Rio	11-6-72	14-3-75	12-9-80
General-purpose:				
F 42 Constitucão	Thornycroft, Woolston	13-3-74	15-4-76	31-3-78
F 43 Liberal	Thronycroft, Woolston	2-5-75	7-2-77	18-11-78

Constitucão (F 42)—general-purpose version Vosper, 1979

Liberal (F 43)—general-purpose version L. & L. Van Ginderen, 7-85

Independencia (F 44)—ASW version U.S. Navy, 1983

D: 3,200 tons (3,800 fl)
S: 30.5 kts (28 cruising on gas turbines, 22 on diesels)
Dim: 129.24 (121.92 pp) × 13.52 × 4.20 (5.94 sonar)
A: ASW type: 1/114-mm Mk 8 Vickers automatic DP—2/40-mm Bofors AA (I × 2)—2/Sea Cat SAM systems (III × 2)—Branik ASW system—1/375-mm, Bofors ASW RL (II × 1)—6/324-mm ASW TT (III × 2)—1/Lynx helicopter—1/d.c. rack (5 charges)
General-purpose type: similar but without the Branik system and with a second 114-mm Mk 8 aft and 4 launchers (II × 2) for the MM 38 Exocet SSM system
Electron Equipt: Radar: 1/Plessey AWS-2 air search, 1/H.S.A. ZW-06, 2/Orion RTN-10 X f.c.—1/Ikara tracker (not in F 42, 43)
Sonar: 1/EDO 610 E; ASW ships also have 1/EDO 700 E VDS
EW: Decca RDL-2/3 intercept—2/Plessey Shield RL (VI × 2)
M: CODOG: 2 Rolls-Royce Olympus TM3B gas turbines, 28,000 hp each; 4 MTU 16V956 TB91 diesels, 3,940 hp each; 2 Escher-Wyss CP props; 56,000 hp max.
Endurance: 45 days **Electric:** 4,500 kw **Fuel:** 480 tons
Range: 1,300/29; 5,300/17 **Man:** 21 officers, 180 men

Remarks: Ordered 20-9-70. Fitted with retractable fin stabilizers. Branik is the name of the system devised for handling the Australian Ikara ASW missile in these ships. All have CAAIS action data system (Ferranti 1600B computers) and are equipped with Decca EW gear. The Brazilian-built units experienced considerable delays in fitting out. Plessey Shield decoy launchers were ordered for these ships in 1984.

CORVETTES

◆ **9 Imperial Marinheiro class** Bldr: L. Smit, Kinderdijk, Netherlands

	L	In serv.
V 15 Imperial Marinheiro	24-11-54	8-6-55
V 16 Iguatemi	1954	17-9-55
V 18 Forte De Coimbra	11-6-54	26-7-55
V 19 Caboclo	28-8-54	4-55
V 20 Angostura	1955	1955
V 21 Bahiana	11-54	26-6-55
V 22 Mearim	8-54	3-8-55
V 23 Purus	6-11-54	4-55
V 24 Solimões	24-11-54	1955

CORVETTES *(continued)*

Imperial Marinheiro (V 15) 1971

D: 911 tons (960 fl) **S:** 15 kts **Dim:** 55.72 × 9.55 × 3.6
A: 1/76.2-mm DP—4/20-mm AA (I × 4)
M: 2 Sulzer diesels; 2 props; 2,160 hp **Fuel:** 135 tons diesel **Man:** 60 tot.

REMARKS: Oceangoing tug design. Were intended to be convertible for minesweeping or minelaying. V 15 is used as a submarine tender. Officially designated "vedettes" and used in district patrols and in support of the 200-mile economic zone. Sister *Iparanga* (V 17) stricken 1983.

◆ **3 U.S. Sotoyomo class**—former auxiliary ocean tugs Bldr: Gulfport Boiler & Welding Works, Port Arthur, Texas

	Laid down	L	In serv.
R 21 TRITÃO (ex-ATA 234)	3-3-45	7-5-45	11-12-45
R 22 TRIDENTE (ex-ATA 235)	21-3-45	19-5-45	3-12-45
R 23 TRIUNFO (ex-ATA 236)	10-4-45	6-6-45	3-12-45

D: 570 tons (835 fl) **S:** 13 kts **Dim:** 43.59 (41.00 pp) × 10.31 × 4.01
A: 2/20-mm AA (I × 2)
M: 2 G.M. 12-278A diesels, electric drive; 1 prop; 1,500 hp
Electric: 120 kw **Fuel:** 171 tons **Range:** 16,500/8 **Man:** 49 tot.

REMARKS: Purchased 16-3-47 (R 23: 22-4-47). Now used to patrol 200-n.m. economic zone; armament possibly enhanced. To be replaced by three oilfield supply tugs purchased while building, 1985.

PATROL BOATS AND CRAFT

◆ **6 Piratini-class patrol boats** Bldr: Ast. Ilha das Cobras, Rio

	In serv.		In serv.
P 10 PIRATINI (ex-PGM 109)	30-11-70	P 13 Parati (ex-PGM 119)	7-71
P 11 PIRAJÁ (ex-PGM 110)	1-71	P 14 PENEDO (ex-PGM 120)	9-71
P 12 PAMPEIRO (ex-PGM 118)	3-71	P 15 POTI (ex-PGM 121)	10-71

Penedo (P 14) 1985

D: 105 tons (fl) **S:** 18.0 kts (15.5 sust.) **Dim:** 28.95 × 6.1 × 1.55
A: 1/81-mm mortar with 12.7-mm mg atop—2/12.7-mm mg (I × 2)
M: 4 Cummins VT-12M diesels; 2 props; 1,100 hp
Electric: 40 kw **Range:** 1,000/15; 1,700/12 **Man:** 2 officers, 14 men

REMARKS: These patrol craft are based on the 95-foot WPBs of the U.S. Coast Guard and were funded by the U.S.

◆ **10 or more U.S. Swift Mk I patrol craft**

R 61, R 62, R 63, R 64, etc.

D: 22.5 tons (fl) **S:** 22 kts **Dim:** 15.3 × 4.55 × 1.1 **A:** 1/12.7-mm mg
M: 2 G.M. 12V71 TI diesels; 2 props; 850 hp
Range: 400/22 **Man:** 6 tot.

REMARKS: Employed by naval police and port captains. Six ordered 16-1-81 from DM-Commercio, Importacão & Maintencão de Producto Nauticas. Earlier units built in U.S., transferred under AID program.

RIVER PATROL SHIPS

◆ **0 (+3) new-construction river patrol ships**

	Bldr.	Laid down	L	In serv.
P. . . PORTO ESPERANCA	Ars. de Marinha, Rio	14-1-85	. . .	. . .
P. . . N. . .	. . .	1986	. . .	. . .
P. . . N. . .	. . .	1987	. . .	. . .

D: 270 tons (380 fl) **S:** 12 kts **Dim:** 49.33 (45.57 pp) × 8.45 × 1.40
A: . . . **M:** 2 diesels; 2 props; . . . hp
Man: 8 officers, 54 men

REMARKS: Replaces program for ships named *Cascaval* and *Jararaca*, announced 1981. All for use on Paraguay River; second two to build at private yards. Will have a helo deck and can carry 2 LCVP.

◆ **3 Roraima class** Bldr: MacLaren, Niteroi

	L	In serv.		L	In serv.
P 30 RORAIMA	9-11-72	21-2-75	P 32 AMAPA	9-3-73	1-76
P 31 RONDÔNIA	10-1-73	3-12-75			

Rondônia (P 31) Brazilian Navy, 1983

Amapa (P 32) 1985

D: 340 tons (365 fl) **S:** 14.5 kts **Dim:** 46.3 × 8.45 × 1.37
A: 1/40-mm AA—6/12.7-mm mg (I × 6)—2/81-mm mortars
Electron Equipt: 3/navigational radars
M: 2 M.A.N. V6V16/18 TL diesels; 2 props; 1,824 hp
Range: 6,000/11 **Man:** 9 officers, 54 men

REMARKS: In Amazon Flotilla. Carry one LCVP.

◆ **2 Pedro Teixeira class**—

	Bldr	L	In serv.
P 20 PEDRO TEIXEIRA	Ilha das Cobras, Rio	11-6-72	17-12-73
P 21 RAPOSO TAVARES	Ilha das Cobras, Rio	11-6-72	17-12-73

Pedro Teixeira (P 20)—note hangar offset to starboard 1985

D: 690 tons (fl) **S:** 16 kts **Dim:** 63.55 × 9.71 × 1.70
A: 1/40-mm AA—6/12.7-mm mg (I × 6)—2/81-mm mortars—1/SAH-11 helicopter
Electron Equipt: Radar: 2/navigational
M: 2 MEP-M.A.N. V6V16/18 TLS diesels; 2 props; 3,840 hp
Range: 6,800/10 **Man:** 6 officers, 72 men

◆ **1 old river monitor**

	Bldr	Laid down	L	In serv.
U 17 PARNAIBA	Arsenal de Marinha, Rio	11-6-36	2-9-37	11-37

RIVER PATROL SHIPS *(continued)*

Parnaiba (U 17) 1976

D: 620 tons (720 fl) **S:** 12 kts **Dim:** 55.0 × 10.1 × 1.6
A: 1/76.2-mm DP—2/47-mm—2/40-mm AA (I × 2)—6/20-mm AA (I × 6)
M: 2 sets triple-expansion reciprocating steam; 2 props; 1,300 hp
Boilers: 2/3-drum **Fuel:** 90 tons **Range:** 1,350/10 **Man:** 90 tot.

Remarks: In Mato Grosso Flotilla. Was to be replaced by *Cascavel* and *Jararaca.*

MINE WARFARE SHIPS

Note: Two mine countermeasures ships were reported ordered 7-83 from Verolme Estaleiros Reunidos do Brazil. No further data available.

◆ **6 German Schütze-class (Type 340a) patrol minesweepers** Bldr: Abeking and Rasmussen, Lemwerde, West Germany

	L	In serv.		L	In serv.
M 15 Aratu	27-5-70	5-5-71	M 18 Aracatuba	1971	13-12-72
M 16 Anhatomirim	4-11-70	30-11-71	M 19 Abrolhos	7-5-74	16-4-75
M 17 Atalaia	14-4-71	13-12-72	M 20 Albardão	9-74	21-7-75

Anhatomirim 1972

D: 241 tons (280 fl) **S:** 24 kts **Dim:** 47.44 × 7.16 × 2.4 **A:** 1/40-mm AA
M: 4 Maybach diesels; 2 Escher-Wyss vertical cycloidal props; 4,500 hp
Electric: 120 kw plus 340 kw sweep generator **Fuel:** 22 tons
Range: 710/20 **Man:** 39 tot.

Remarks: Four ordered 4-69, two 11-73. Fitted for magnetic, mechanical, and acoustic minesweeping. Wooden hulls. A new series of minesweepers is planned.

AMPHIBIOUS WARFARE SHIPS

Note: Long-range plans call for acquisition of two new landing ships to replace those listed.

◆ **1 U.S. De Soto County-class tank landing ship** Bldr: Avondale, New Orleans

	L	In serv.
G 26 Duque de Caxias (ex-*Grant County,* LST 1174)	12-10-56	8-11-57

D: 4,164 tons (7,800 fl) **S:** 16 kts **Dim:** 135.7 (129.8 wl) × 18.9 × 5.3
A: 2/76.2-mm DP (II × 1) **Electron Equipt:** Radar: 1/SPS-21
M: 4 Fairbanks-Morse 38D 8⅛ × 12 diesels; 2 CP props; 13,900 hp
Electric: 900 kw **Range:** 13,000/10 **Man:** 11 officers, 164 men

Remarks: Transferred 15-1-73; purchased 12-17-78. Can carry 700 men. Air-conditioned. Tank deck 88-m long. Four LCVP in davits; can carry four causeways (pontoon sections). Platform for helicpter. Stülcken 60-ton lift gear reported added forward in place of 4/76.2-mm. Mk 51 Mod. 2 GFCS for guns.

◆ **1 U.S. LST 542-class tank landing ship** Bldr: Bethlehem, Hingham, Mass.

	Laid down	L	In serv.
G 28 Garcia D'Avila (ex-*Outagamie County,* LST 1073)	20-2-45	22-3-45	17-4-45

D: 1,490 tons light (4,100 fl) **S:** 11.6 kts **Dim:** 100.0 × 15.25 × 4.29
A: 8/40-mm AA (II × 2, I × 4)
M: 2 G.M. 2-278A diesels; 2 props; 1,700 hp **Electric:** 300 kw

Remarks: Loaned 25-5-71; purchased 1-12-73. Beaching displacement: 2,336 tons. Carries 2 LCVP.

◆ **3 U.S. LCU 1610-type landing craft** Bldr: Navy Yard, Rio, 1974-78

L 10 Guarapari L 11 Timbau L 12 Camboriu

Guarapari (L 10) 1978

D: 200 tons (396 fl) **S:** 11 kts **Dim:** 41.0 × 8.42 × 2.0
A: 3/12.7-mm mg.
M: 2 G.M. 12V71 diesels; 2 props; 1,000 hp **Range:** 1,200/8

Remarks: Typed EDCG—"Embarcaçao de Desembarque de Carga Generales." Can carry 172 tons cargo. The uncompleted *Tramandai* (L 13) was scrapped in 1983.

◆ **28 LCVP** Built in Japan, 1959-60

◆ **15 EDVP** Built in Brazil, 1971

Dim: 11.0 × 3.2 × 0.6 (fwd), 1.0 (aft) **M:** Brazilian Scania diesel

Remarks: Glass-reinforced plastic construction. Can carry 36 men with full pack or one jeep with trailer and 17 men or 1/105-mm howitzer or an anti-tank gun and 18 men. At least one U.S. LCM (6) design landing craft is also in service.

HYDROGRAPHIC AND OCEANOGRAPHIC SHIPS

◆ **1 U.S. Robert D. Conrad-class oceanographic ship** Bldr: Marietta Co., Pt. Pleasant, West Virginia (In serv. 8-2-65)

H 41 Almirante Camara (ex-*Sands,* T-AGOR 6)

Almirante Camara (H 41) 1974

D: 1,020 tons (1,370 fl) **S:** 13.5 kts
Dim: 63.7 (59.7 pp) × 12.2 × 4.9 mean
Electron Equipt: Radar: 1/RCA CRM-N1A-75
M: 2 Caterpillar D-378 diesels, electric drive; 1 prop; 1,000 hp
Electric: 850 kw (plus 620 kw) **Fuel:** 211 tons **Range:** 10,000/12
Man: 8 officers, 18 men, 15 oceanographers

Remarks: Loaned 1-7-74. An auxiliary 620-hp gas turbine powers a small electric maneuvering propeller for stationkeeping purposes at extremely low rpm; also has bowthruster. Has echo-sounders capable of measuring 11,000-meter depths.

◆ **1 Antarctic exploration support ship** Bldr: Aalborg Vaerft, Denmark (In serv. 10-57)

H 42 Barão de Teffé (ex-*Thala Dan*)

D: . . . **S:** 12 kts **Dim:** 75.14 (65.54 pp) × 13.77 × . . .
M: 1 Burmeister & Wain 7-cyl. diesel; 1 CP prop; 1,970 hp
Electric: 680 kw **Fuel:** 457 tons **Man:** 50 tot.

Remarks: 2,183 grt/2,164 dwt. Purchased 5-82 from J. Lauritzen in lieu of the Royal Navy ice patrol ship, *Endurance.* Conversion completed 8-82 as antarctic support ship, including helicopter deck over stern (added overall length not included above). Ice-reinforced-hulled former cargo ship.

◆ **2 Sirius class**

	Bldr	Laid down	L	In serv.
H 21 Sirius	Ishikawajima, Tokyo	12-56	30-7-57	1-1-58
H 22 Canopus	Ishikawajima, Tokyo	12-56	20-11-57	15-3-58

HYDROGRAPHIC AND OCEANOGRAPHIC SHIPS *(continued)*

Canopus (H 22)

D: 1,463 tons (1,900 fl) **S:** 15 kts **Dim:** 77.9 × 12.03 × 3.7
M: 2 Sulzer 7T6-36 diesels; 2 CP props; 2,700 hp **Range:** 12,000/11
Fuel: 343 tons **Man:** 102 tot.

Remarks: 1 SAH-11 helicopter, 1 LCVP, 3 small survey craft. Fully equipped. Armament removed.

◆ **6 wooden-hulled hydrographic boats** Bldr: Bormann, Rio de Janeiro

	In serv.		In serv.
H 11 Paraibano	10-68	H 15 Itacurussá	3-71
H 12 Rio Branco	10-68	H 16 Camocim	1971
H 14 Nogueira Da Gama (ex-*Jaceguai*)	3-71	H 17 Caravelas	1971

Nogueira da Gama (H 14) 1971

D: 32 tons (50 fl) **S:** 11 kts **Dim:** 16.0 × 4.6 × 1.3
M: 2 G.M. 6-71 diesels; 2 props; 330 hp **Range:** 600/11 **Man:** 2 officers, 9 men

Remarks: In Amazon Flotilla.

◆ **1 former sail-training ship**

	Bldr	L	In serv.
H 10 Almirante Saldanha	Vickers, Barrow	19-12-33	6-34

Almirante Saldanha (H 10) 1975

D: 3,325 tons (3,825 fl) **S:** 11 kts **Dim:** 93.6 × 15.8 × 5.5
M: 1 Sulzer diesel; 1 CP prop; 1,400 hp **Range:** 12,000/10
Fuel: 390 tons **Electric:** 550 kw **Man:** 210 tot.

Remarks: Former 4-masted schooner, refit completed in 7-61 as an oceanographic research ship and for training. Refitted again for zooplankton research, completed 6-80; received NAVSAT and Omega navigation systems, new current and salinity meter systems.

◆ **3 Argus-class coastal survey ships**

	Bldr	L	In serv.
H 31 Argus	Ars. de Marinha, Rio	6-12-57	29-1-59
H 32 Orion	Ars. de Marinha, Rio	5-2-58	11-6-59
H 33 Taurus	Ars. de Marinha, Rio	7-1-58	23-4-59

D: 250 tons (350 fl) **S:** 15 kts **Dim:** 44.67 (41.14 pp) × 6.50 × 2.80
M: 2 Caterpillar DT 379 diesels; 2 props; 1,200 hp **Fuel:** 35 tons
Range: 3,000/. . . **Endurance:** 20 days **Man:** 34 tot.

Remarks: Based on the Portuguese *Azevia*-class gunboat. H 32 modernized in 1973/74, with new propulsion machinery, auxiliaries, and electronic equipment.

Taurus (H 33) 1985

◆ **1 fisheries research oceanographic ship** Bldr: INACE, Fortaleza

U 15 Suboficial Oliveira (In serv. 22-5-81)

D: 108 tons (120 fl) **Dim:** 35.5 × 6.7 × . . .
M: 2 diesels; . . . props; 740 hp **Range:** 1400/8 **Man:** 10 tot.

Remarks: For use by the Naval Research Institute in "Capo Frio Project" for shrimp cultivation.

AUXILIARY SHIPS

◆ **1 cadet training ship, modified Mk 10 frigate**

	Bldr:	Laid down	L	In serv.
U 30 Brasil	Ast. Ilha das Cobras, Rio	18-9-81	23-9-83	1987

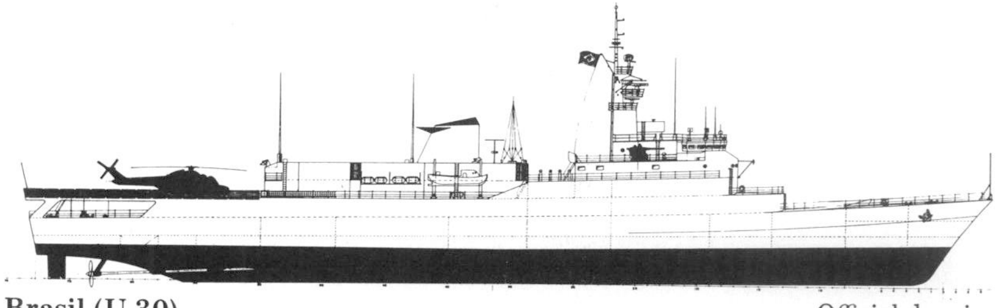
Brasil (U 30) Official drawing

D: 2,380 tons (3,400 fl) **S:** 18 kts **Dim:** 131.25 × 13.52 × 4.21 mean (fl)
A: 2/40-mm Bofors L70 AA (I × 2)—1/Lynx helicopter
Electron Equipt: Radar: 2/navigational
M: 2 Ishikawajima Brazil-Pielstick 6 PC. 2 L400 diesels; 2 props; 7,800 hp
Range: 7,000/15 **Man:** 26 officers, 69 petty officers, 120 men, 200 cadets

Remarks: Uses hull of the Mk 10 frigate design, but has less powerful plant and simpler weapons and electronics. Electro-optical GFCS only. Fin stabilizers. Will replace *Custódio de Mello* (U 26) for training cadets from Naval and Merchant Marine Academies. Master CIC with 3 satellite training CICs, navigational training compartment for 40 trainees, 2 other classrooms. A planned 76-mm OTO Melara Compact mount forward has not been installed.

◆ **4 Custódio de Mello class transports** (1 used as training ship)

	Bldr	Laid down	L	In serv.
U 26 Custódio de Mello	Ishikawajima, Tokyo	12-53	10-6-54	1-12-54
G 16 Barroso Pereira	Ishikawajima, Tokyo	12-53	7-8-54	1-12-54
G 21 Ary Parreiras	Ishikawajima, Tokyo	12-55	24-8-56	29-12-56
G 22 Soares Dutra	Ishikawajima, Tokyo	12-55	13-12-56	23-3-57

Custódio de Mello (U 26) G. Gyssels, 6-84

D: 4,800 tons (8,600 fl) **S:** 16 kts **Dim:** 119.2 (110.4 pp) × 16.0 × 6.1
A: 2/76.2-mm DP (I × 2)—2/20-mm AA (I × 2)—U 26: 4/76.2-mm DP (I × 4)
Electron Equipt: Radar: U 26: 1/navigational, 1/SPS-4—others: 2/navigational
M: GT; 2 props; 4,800 hp **Boilers:** 2 Foster-Wheeler; 350°C **Fuel:** 880 tons
Man: 118 tot. Can carry 1,972 troops (497 normal)

Remarks: 4,200 dwt/4,879 grt. Living spaces mechanically ventilated and partially air-conditioned. *Custódio de Mello,* used as training ship, is to be replaced by *Brasil* (U 30). Others have a helicopter platform aft, can carry 497 troops, and are occasionally used in commercial service; all have 425m³ refrigerated cargo space.

AUXILIARY SHIPS *(continued)*

◆ **1 U.S. Aristaeus-class small repair ship** Bldr: Maryland DD, Baltimore

	Laid down	L	In serv.
G 24 Belmonte (ex-*Helios*, ARB 12, ex-LST 1127)	23-11-44	14-2-45	26-2-45

Belmonte (G 24)

D: 2,030 tons (4,100 fl) **S:** 9 kts **Dim:** 100.0 (96.3 wl) × 15.25 × 3.36
A: 8/40-mm AA (IV × 2) **M:** 2 G.M. 12-567A diesels; 2 props; 1,800 hp
Electric: 600 kw **Fuel:** 584 tons **Range:** 6,000/9

Remarks: 1-62; purchased 28-12-67. 1/60-ton winch crane, 2/10-ton booms. Used mainly as a transport.

◆ **0 (+2) fleet supply ships** Bldr: Lenin SY, Gdansk, Poland (In serv. 1971)

G 29 Almirante Gastão Motta (ex-*Itatiuga*) N. . . (ex-*Itacpuca*)

D: approx. 12,000 tons (fl) **S:** 20.5 kts **Dim:** 161.02 (150.02 pp) × 22.99 × 9.72
A: . . . **Electron Equipt:** Radar: . . .
M: 1 Sulzer diesel; 1 prop; 18,400 hp
Man: 25 officers, 36 petty officers, 153 men

Remarks: Cargo vessel purchased 1984 from Lloydd Brasileiro Steamship Co. Under conversion 1985–. . . at Rio de Janeiro Naval Arsenal to act as fleet supply ship to replace *Marajo* (G 27). Will carry cargo fuel and water, as well as ammunition for underway transfer. Helicopter deck and facilities for two Sea King. Extensive medical and dental facilities. Total accommodations: 214. Second unit purchased 5-85.

◆ **1 fleet replenishment oiler** Bldr: Ishikawajima do Brasil, Rio

	Laid down	L	In serv.
G 27 Marajo	13-12-66	31-1-68	22-10-68

Marajo (G 27) U.S. Navy, 1985

D: 16,000 tons (fl) **S:** 13.6 kts **Dim:** 137.1 (127.69 pp) × 19.22 × 7.35
M: 1 Sulzer GRD 68 diesel; 8,000 hp **Cargo capacity:** 7,200 tons
Fuel: 700 tons **Electric:** 1,200 kw **Range:** 9,200/14.5 **Man:** 80 tot.

Remarks: 6,600 grt/11,119 dwt. Two liquid replenishment stations per side.

◆ **1 river oiler**

G 17 Potengi Bldr: Papendrecht, Holland (L: 16-3-38)

D: 600 tons **S:** 10 kts **Dim:** 54.5 × 7.5 × 1.8
M: 2 diesels; 2 props; 550 hp **Range:** 600/8 **Man:** 20 tot.

Remarks: In Mato Grosso Flotilla. **Cargo capacity:** 450 tons

◆ **1 U.S. Penguin-class submarine rescue ship**

	Bldr	Laid down	L	In serv.
K 10 Gastão Moutinho (ex-*Skylark*, ASR 20; ex-*Yustaga*, ATF 165)	Charleston SB & DD	23-7-45	19-3-46	19-7-46

Gastão Moutinho (K 10)

D: 1,780 tons (2,140 fl) **S:** 14.5 kts
Dim: 62.48 (59.44 wl) × 11.96 × 4.72 **A:** 2/20-mm AA (I × 2)
Radar: 1/SPS-5 **M:** 4 G.M. 12-278A diesels; electric drive; 1 prop; 3,000 hp
Electric: 400 kw **Fuel:** 301 tons **Range:** 15,000/8

Remarks: Begun as an *Achomawi*-class fleet tug. Purchased 30-6-73. Has rescue bell, salvage equipment, pumps, 4 pontoons, etc. Often employed as a hydrographic survey ship and as a diving tender.

◆ **2 oceangoing tugs** Bldr: Sumitomo Heavy Industries, Japan (Both L: 1976)

R 24 Almirante Guilhem (ex-. . .)
R 25 Almirante Guillobel (ex-. . .)

D: 2,400 tons (fl) **S:** 14 kts **Dim:** 63.15 × 13.40 × 4.50 **A:** . . .
M: 2 G.M. 20-645 ET diesels; 2 CP props; 7,200 hp **Electric:** 550 kw
Fuel: 670 tons **Man:** 40 tot.

Remarks: Purchased 1980 from Superpesa Maritime Transport, Ltd., and commissioned 22-1-81. Former oilfield supply tugs. 84 ton bollard pull. 525-hp bow-thruster.

◆ **1 lighthouse and buoy tender**

	Bldr	Laid down	L	In serv.
H 34 Graça Aranha	Elbin, Niteroi	end 1970	23-6-74	9-9-76

Graça Aranha (H 34) 1976

D: 1,253 tons (2,300 fl) **S:** 13 kts **Dim:** 75.57 × 13.0 × 3.71
M: Diesel; 1 CP prop; 2,000 hp; 1 bow-thruster **Man:** 101 tot.

Remarks: Telescoping helicopter hangar for one SAH-11. Two LCVP carried as supply lighters.

YARD AND SERVICE CRAFT

◆ **1 large yard tug**

R 14 Laurindo Pitta Bldr: Vickers, 1910, rebuilt 1969

D: 514 tons **S:** 11 kts **Dim:** 39.04 × 7.77 × 4.6
M: 2 sets reciprocating steam; 2 props; . . . hp **Man:** 33 tot.

◆ **4 Comandante Marriog-class yard tugs** Bldr: Turn-Ship Ltd., U.S.A. (In serv. 1981)

R 14 Comandante Didier R 17 Tenente Magalhaes
R 15 Comandante Marriog R 18 Cabo Schram

D: 115 tons (fl) **S:** 10 kts **Dim:** 19.8 × 7.0 × 2.0
M: 2 G.M. diesels; . . . props; 900 hp **Man:** 6 tot.

◆ **6 yard tugs** Bldr: Holland Nautic Yard, Haarlem (In serv. 1953)

R 31 Audaz R 33 Guarani R 35 Passo De Patria
R 32 Centauro R 34 Lamego R 36 Voluntario

D: 220 tons (fl) **S:** 11 kts **Dim:** 27.6 × 7.2 × 3.1
M: 1 Krupp Womag diesel; 765 hp **Man:** 12 tot.

◆ **3 Isaias de Noronha-class tugs** (1972-74)

R. . . Isaias De Noronha R. . . D.N.O.G.
R. . . Teniente Lahmeyer

D: 200 tons (fl) **Dim:** 47.0 × . . . × . . .

Remarks: Latter pair reported as only 100 tons, 32.0 m o.a.

◆ **1 personnel and stores transport** Bldr: Embrasa, Itajai, Santa Caterina (L: 29-8-74)

R 47 Sargento Borges

D: 108.5 tons **S:** 10 kts **Dim:** 28.0 × 6.5 × 1.5
M: 2 diesels; 2 props; 480 hp **Cargo:** 106 passengers **Range:** 400/10

◆ **4 Rio Pardo-class harbor passenger ferries** Bldr: Inconav Niteroi Shipbuilders (In serv. 1975-76)

U 40 Rio Pardo U 42 Rio Chui
U 41 Rio Negro U 43 Rio Oiapoque

YARD AND SERVICE CRAFT *(continued)*

D: 150 tons **S:** 14 kts **Dim:** 35.38 × 6.5 × 1.9
M: 2 diesels; 2 props; 1,096 hp **Cargo:** 400 passengers

◆ **6 Rio Doce-class river transports** Bldr: G. deVries Leutsch, Amsterdam (In serv. 1956)

U 20 Rio Doce | U 22 Rio Formoso | U 24 Rio Turvo
U 21 Rio Das Contas | U 23 Rio Real | U 25 Rio Verde

D: 150 tons (200 fl) **S:** 14 kts **Dim:** 36.6 × 6.5 × 2.1
M: 2 Sulzer diesels; 2 props; 450 hp **Cargo:** 600 passengers
Range: 700/14 **Man:** 10 tot.

◆ **7 Anchova-class personnel launches** Bldr: Brazil (1965-67)

R 54 Anchova | R 55 Arenque | R 56 Atum | R 57 Acará
R 58 Agulha | R 59 Aruana | R 60 Argentina

D: 11 tons (13 fl) **S:** 25 kts **Dim:** 13.0 × 3.8 × 1.2
M: 2 diesels; 280 hp **Cargo:** 12 passengers **Range:** 400/20 **Man:** 3 tot.

◆ **1 command ship**

G 15 Paraguassu (ex-*Guarapuava*)

D: 285 tons **S:** 12 kts **Dim:** 40.0 × 7.0 × 1.2
M: Diesel; 1 prop **Range:** 2,500/10

Remarks: Former river transport ship, bought in 1971, refitted for the Mato Grosso Flotilla, and used as a river buoy tender and flagship.

◆ **1 river transport/despatch boat for the Mato Grosso Flotilla**

G. . . Piraim (In serv. 1982)

D: 91.5 tons (fl) **S:** 7 kts **Dim:** 25.0 × . . . × 0.97
M: 2 MWM diesels; 2 props; 400 hp **Range:** 700/7
Electric: 60 kVA **Man:** 2 officers, 13 men, 2 civil pilots

◆ **2 small service transports**

Tenente Fabio Tenente Raul

D: 55 tons **S:** 10 kts **Dim:** 20.28 × 5.1 × 1.2 **M:** Diesel; 135 hp
Cargo capacity: 22 tons **Range:** 350

◆ **5 munitions lighters**

São Francisco Dos Santos (1964), Ubirajara Dos Santos (1968), Operatĩo Luis Leal (1968), Miguel Dos Santos (1968), Aprendiz Lédio Conceição (1968)

Remarks: Last two for torpedoes.

◆ **1 yard oiler** (purchased 1973)

R 11 Martins De Oliviera (ex-*Gastão Moutinho*)

D: 588 tons **S:** 10.3 kts **Dim:** 49.4 × 7.0 × 2.4

◆ **1 yard oiler:** Anita Garibaldi — no data

◆ **2 water tankers** (L; 1957)

R 43 Paulo Afonso R 42 Itapura

D: 485.3 tons **Dim:** 42.8 × 7.0 × 2.5 **M:** 1 diesel **Cargo:** 389 tons

◆ **3 miscellaneous small water tankers**

R 38 Doctor Gondim R 40 Guairia R 41 Iguaçu

Iguaçu (R 41) G. Gyssels, 1981

◆ **5 Commandante Varella class navigational aid tenders**

	Bldr:	Laid down	L	In serv.
H 18 Comandante Varella	Ast. Ilha das Cobras, Rio	1-8-78	18-9-81	30-9-82
H 19 Comandante Menhaes	Sao João de Nilo SY	. . .	. . .	. . .
H 20 Tenente Castelho	Sao João de Nilo SY	. . .	. . .	. . .
H. . . Tenente Boanerges	Sao João de Nilo SY	. . .	. . .	1985
H 26 Faroleiro Mario Seixax	. . .	. . .	. . .	. . .

Comandante Varella (H 18) 1985

D: 300 tons light (440 fl) **S:** 12 kts **Dim:** 37.51 (34.5 pp) × 8.60 × 2.56
M: 2 8-cyl. diesels; 2 props; 1,300 hp **Range:** 2,880/12 **Man:** 22 tot.

◆ **8 130-ton navigational aid tenders**

H 13 Mestro João Dos Santos | H 30 Faroleiro Nascimento
H 24 Castelhanos | H. . . Cabo Branco
H 27 Faroleiro Areas | H. . . Cabo Callanhar
H 28 Faroleiro Santana | H. . . Cabo Frio

Remarks: No data available. Also in use are H 21 *Sirius* and captured U.S. fishing poachers *Sea Horse* and *Condor.*

◆ **2 river hospital shops** Bldr: Naval Arsenal, Rio de Janeiro

	Laid down	L	In serv.
U 18 Oswaldo Cruz	1981	11-7-83	31-5-84
U 19 Carlos Chagas	1982	16-4-84	12-84

D: 500 tons (fl) **S:** 9 kts **Dim:** 47.18 (45.0 pp) × 8.45 × 1.75
M: 2 diesels; 2 props; 714 hp **Range:** 4,000/9
Electric: 420 kVA **Man:** 4 officers, 21 men, 6 doctor/dentists, 15 health personnel

Remarks: Intended to serve in Amazon Flotilla with the similar *Roraima*-class gunboats. Helo deck for one AS 350. Two sickbays (6 total beds), operating theater, two clinics, dental laboratory, x-ray facilities.

◆ **3 Voga Picada-class training craft** Bldr: CARBRASMAR, Rio de Janeiro (All in serv. 17-1-84)

U 31 Voga Picada U 32 Rosca Fina U 33 Leva Ariba

Rosca Fina (U 32) 1985

D: 50 tons (fl) **S:** 11 kts **Dim:** 18.60 × 4.70 × 1.20
M: 1 M.W.M. diesel; 1 prop; 650 hp **Range:** 200/11
Man: 5 crew + 11 trainees

◆ **3 Aspirante Nascimento-class training craft** Bldr: Embrassa Itajai, Santa Catarina (In serv. 1980-81)

U 10 Aspirante Nascimento U 11 Guardia Marinha Jansen
U 12 Guardia Marinha Brito

Aspirante Nascimento (U 10) 1985

BRAZIL *(continued)*
YARD AND SERVICE CRAFT *(continued)*

D: 130 tons (fl) **S:** 10 kts **Dim:** 28.0 (25.0 pp) × 6.50 × 1.80
A: 1/12.7-mm mg **M:** 2 M.W.M. D232V12 diesels; 2 props; 650 hp **Range:** 700/10
Man: 2 officers, 10 men, 24 midshipmen

Remarks: Used for navigation and seamanship training at the Naval Academy. Also used for training are sail yacht *Cisne Branco* and ex-U.S. fishing boat *Night Hawk.*

FLOATING DRY DOCKS

◆ **1 U.S. AFDL 34 class** Bldr: V.P. Loftis (In serv. 10-44)

G 27 Cidade De Natal (ex-U.S. AFDL 39, ex-ARDC 6)

Lift capacity: 2,800 tons **Dim:** 118.6 × 25.6 × 2.84 (light)

Remarks: Loaned 10-11-66; purchased 28-12-77. Concrete construction. 17.7-m clear width inside, 105.2-m length on blocks.

◆ **1 U.S. AFDL 1 class** Bldr: Chicago Bridge & Iron, Cal. (In serv. 12-43)

G 26 Almirante Jeronimo Goncalves (ex-*Goiaz,* ex-AFDL 4, ex-AFD 4)

Lift capacity: 1,000 tons **Dim:** 60.96 × 19.51 × 1.04 (light)

Remarks: Loaned 10-11-66; purchased 28-7-77. Steel construction. 13.7-m clear width inside, 56.4-m length on blocks.

◆ **1 U.S. ARD 12 class** Bldr: Pacific Bridge, Alameda, Cal. (In serv. 11-43)

G 25 Afonso Pena (ex-*Ceara,* ex-ARD 14)

Lift capacity: 3,500 tons **Dim:** 149.86 × 24.69 × 1.73 (light)

Remarks: Loaned 1963; purchased 28-12-77. Steel construction, pointed ship-type bow. 18.0-m clear with inside, 118.6-m length on blocks.

◆ **1 U.S. dry dock companion craft** Bldr: Bushell Lyons Ironwks, Tampa, Fla. (In serv. 22-3-45)

. . . (ex-YFN 903)

D: 170 tons (590 fl) **Dim:** 33.53 × 10.36 × 2.74

Remarks: Converted non-self-propelled cargo barge. Loaned 1963; purchased 28-12-77.

BRUNEI DARUSSALEM

Personnel: (1985): 446 (including 42 officers and "Special Boat Squadron" of 6 officers) and 114 men for river duties

Merchant Marine (1984): 2 ships—853 grt

◆ **3 guided-missile patrol boats** Bldr: Vosper Thornycroft, Singapore

	L	In serv.
P 02 Waspada	3-8-77	7-78
P 03 Pejuang	3-78	1979
P 04 Seteria	22-6-78	1979

D: 150 tons (fl) **S:** 32 kts **Dim:** 36.88 (33.53 pp) × 7.16 × 1.8
A: 2/MM 38 Exocet SSM—2/30-mm AA (II × 1)—2/7.62-mm mg (I × 2)
Electron Equipt: Radar: 1/Decca AC 1229—EW: Decca RDL intercept
M: 2 MTU 20V538 TB91 diesels; 2 props; 9,000 hp (7,500 sust.)
Fuel: 16 tons **Range:** 1,200/14 **Man:** 4 officers, 20 men

Waspada (P 02) G. Arra, 1984

Seteria (P 04)—note different bridge G. Arra, 1984

Remarks: P 02 has enclosed upper bridge (open on other two) and facilities for training. All have Sperry Sea Archer fire control system and two 50-mm rocket-flare launchers. The 30-mm mount is BMARC/Oerlikon GCM-BO1

◆ **3 patrol craft** Bldr: Vosper, Singapore

N. . . . . . . N. . . . . . . N. . . . . . .

D: 35 tons (fl) **S:** 25 kts **Dim:** 25.24 × 5.8 × 1.60
A: 2/20-mm AA (II × 1)—2/7.62-mm mg
M: 2 diesels; 2 CP props; 3,072 hp (plus 1/200-hp cruise diesel, 8 kts)
Man: 5 officers, 8 men

Remarks: Built on speculation 1979, purchased 1980. Steel hull, aluminum superstructure. Replace *Masna* (P 11), *Saleha* (P 12), and *Norain* (P 13), discarded 1978-79.

◆ **3 Periwa-class patrol craft**

	Bldr	L	In serv.
P 14 Periwa	Vosper, Singapore	5-74	9-9-74
P 15 Pemburu	Vosper, Singapore	30-1-75	17-6-75
P 16 Penyarang	Vosper, Singapore	20-3-75	24-6-75

Periwa (P 14) 1974

D: 30 tons (38.5 fl) **S:** 32 kts **Dim:** 21.7 × 6.1 × 1.2
A: 2/20-mm AA (I × 2)—2/7.62-mm mg
Electron Equipt: Radar: Decca RM 916 (P 14, 15: Decca 1216A)
M: 2 MTU 12V331 TC81 diesels; 2,700 hp **Range:** 600/20; 1,000/16

◆ **3 Bendahara-class river patrol craft**

P 21 Bendahara P 23 Kemaindera P 22 Maharajalela

D: 10 tons (fl) **S:** 20 kts **Dim:** 14.1 × 3.6 × 0.9
A: 2/7.62-mm mg **Electron Equipt:** Radar: Decca RM 616
M: 2 6-71 G.M. diesels; 334 hp **Range:** 200/18 **Man:** 6 tot.

◆ **2 Loadmaster-class landing craft** Bldr: Cheverton, Cowes, U.K.

L 31 Damuan (5-76) L 32 Puni (2-77)

D: 64.3 tons (light) **S:** 8.5 kts **Dim:** 22.86 × 6.1 × 1.07
Electron Equipt: Radar: Decca RM 1216
M: 2 G.M. 6-71 diesels; 2 props; 348 hp **Cargo:** 30 tons
Range: 300/8.5; 1,000/6 **Man:** 8 tot.

Remarks: L 31: 19.8-m overall, 60-tons light.

◆ **3 FPB 512-class landing craft** Bldr: Rotork, U.K.

S 24 (In serv. 11-80) S 25 (In serv. 5-81) S 26 (In serv. 5-81)

D: 8.8 tons (fl) **S:** 27 kts **Dim:** 12.7 × 3.2 × . . .
A: 3/7.62-mm mg (I × 3) **Electron Equipt:** Radar: 1/Decca 060 **Range:** 100/12
M: 2 Ford Mermaid diesels; 2 Castoldi waterjets; 430 hp **Man:** 3 tot.

Remarks: Glass-reinforced plastic hulls, bow ramps. For patrol and transport duties.

BRUNEI DARUSSALEM *(continued)*

◆ **25 small armed river craft for the Special Boat Squadron**

A: 1/7.62-mm mg **M:** 100 hp

◆ **3 support tenders** Bldr: Cheverton, Cowes, U.K. (In serv. 1982)

BURONG NURI N. . .

D: 23 tons (fl) **S:** 12 kts **Dim:** 17.0 × 4.3 × . . .
M: 2 G.M. diesels, 2 props; 400 hp

REMARKS: Used as tugs, target tugs, diving tenders or for anti-pollution duties. Glass-reinforced plastic construction.

MARINE POLICE

◆ **4 patrol craft** Bldr: Vosper Thornycroft, Singapore, 1978-80

TENANG ABADI N. . . . . . . N. . . . . . .

D: 14 tons (fl) **S:** 28 kts **Dim:** 18.0 × 4.88 × 0.79 **A:** Machine guns
M: 2 MTU diesels; 2 water jets

REMARKS: Glass-reinforced plastic hulls. The second pair was ordered early in 1979.

BULGARIA

People's Republic of Bulgaria

PERSONNEL: approx. 4,000 men

MERCHANT MARINE (1984): 197 ships—1,282,962 grt (tankers: 18—311,735 grt)

SUBMARINES

◆ **2 Soviet Romeo class**

13 SLAVA 14 POBIEDA

D: 1,330/1,700 tons **S:** 15.5/13 kts **Dim:** 77.0 × 6.7 × 4.9
A: 8/533-mm TT (6 fwd, 2 aft)—14 torpedoes or 24 mines
Electron Equipt: Radar: 1/Snoop Plate—Sonar: MF active; passive array
M: 2/2,000-hp diesels; electric drive; 3,000 hp **Range:** 7,000/5 (snorkel)
Endurance: 45 days **Man:** 60 tot.

REMARKS: Transferred 1971-72. Replaced two Whiskey class with same names. Can dive to 300 meters.

FRIGATES

◆ **2 Soviet Riga class**—Transferred 1957 and 1958

15 DRUZKIY 16 SMELYY

D: 1,260 tons (1,480 fl) **S:** 30 kts **Dim:** 91.0 × 10.2 × 3.2 (4.4 sonar)
A: 3/100-mm DP—3/533-mm TT—2/RBU-1200 ASW RL (V × 2)—1/MBU-600 Hedgehog
Electron Equipt: Radar: 1/Slim Net, 1/Neptune, 1/Sun Visor—IFF: 2/Square Head, 1/High Pole
Sonar: 1/MF hull-mounted—EW: 2/Watch Dog intercept
M: 2 sets GT; 2 props; 20,000 hp **Boilers:** 2; 27 kg/cm², 360°C
Range: 550/28; 2,000/13 **Electric:** 450 kw **Fuel:** 230 tons **Man:** 180 tot.

CORVETTES

◆ **3 Soviet Poti class**—Transferred 12-75 (In serv. 1961-68)

41 N. . . 42 N. . . 43 N. . .

D: 400 tons (fl) **S:** 38 kts **Dim:** 59.4 × 7.9 × 2.0 (mean hull)
A: 2/57-mm AA (II × 1)—2/RBU-6000 rocket launchers—4/400-mm ASW TT
Electron Equipt: Radar: 1/Spin Trough, 1/Strut Curve, 1/Muff Cob
IFF: 2/Square Head, 1/High Pole B
Sonar: 1 high frequency—EW: 2 Watch Dog
M: CODAG: 2 M503A diesels of 4,000 hp each plus 2 gas turbines of 20,000 hp each; 2 props plus waterjet thrust
Range: 520/37; 4,500/10 **Man:** . . .

REMARKS: One is named *Khabri.*

GUIDED-MISSILE, PATROL, AND TORPEDO BOATS

◆ **3 Soviet Osa-II-class guided-missile patrol boats**—Transferred 1978, 1982

101 111 . . .

D: 190 tons (240 fl) **S:** 35 kts **Dim:** 38.6 × 7.6 × 2.0 mean
A: 4/SS-N-2B Styx—4/30-mm AA (II × 2) **Man:** 30 tot.
Electron Equipt: Radar: 1/Square Tie, 1/Drum Tilt—IFF: 2/Square Head, 1/High Pole B
M: 3 Type M504 diesels; 3 props; 15,000 hp **Range:** 500/34; 750/25

◆ **3 Soviet Osa-I-class guided-missile patrol boats**—Transferred 1970-71.

103 112 113

D: 175 tons (215 fl) **S:** 36 kts **Dim:** 38.6 × 7.6 × 1.8
A: 4/SS-N-2A Styx—4/30-mm (II × 2) **Man:** 30 tot.
Electron Equipt: Radar: 1/Square Tie, 1/Drum Tilt—IFF: 2/Square Head, 1/High Pole B
M: 2 Type M503A diesels; 3 props; 12,000 hp **Range:** 500/34; 750/25

◆ **7 Soviet Shershen-class torpedo boats**—Transferred 1970

D: 150 tons (170 fl) **S:** 45 kts **Dim:** 34.7 × 6.7 × 1.5
A: 4/533-mm TT—4/30-mm AA (II × 2) **Man:** 20 tot.
Electron Equipt: Radar: 1/Drum, 1/Drum Tilt
M: 3 Type M503A diesels; 3 props; 12,000 hp **Range:** 460/42; 850/30

◆ **6 Soviet SO-1 class**—Transferred 1963

44 45 46 . . . .

D: 190 tons (215 fl) **S:** 28 kts **Dim:** 42.0 × 6.1 × 1.9 (3.2 over sonar)
A: 4/25-mm AA (II × 2)—4/RBU-1200 ASW RL (V × 4)—2/d.c. rack—mines
Electron Equipt: Radar: 1/Pot Head—IFF: 1/Dead Duck, 1/High Pole
M: 3 Type 40D diesels; 3 props; 7,500 hp **Range:** 340/28; 1,900/16 **Man:** 30 tot.

◆ **6 Soviet Zhuk-class patrol boats**—Transferred 1980-81

511-516

D: 60 tons (fl) **S:** 34 kts **Dim:** 24.0 × 5.0 × 1.8 (props)
A: 4/14.5-mm mg (II × 2) **Man:** 12 tot.
M: 2 Type M50F diesels; 2 props; 2,400 hp **Range:** 700/30; 1,100/15

MINE WARFARE SHIPS

◆ **4 Soviet Vanya-class minesweepers**—Transferred 1971-72

D: 220 tons (245 fl) **S:** 16 kts **Dim:** 40.2 × 7.9 × 1.7
A: 2/30-mm AA (II × 1)
Electron Equipt: Radar: 1/Don-2—IFF; 1/Square Head, 1/High Pole B
M: 2 diesels; 2 props; 2,200 hp **Range:** 10/2,400 **Man:** 30 tot.

◆ **2 Soviet T-43-class minesweepers**

D: 500 tons (570 fl) **S:** 15 kts **Dim:** 58.0 × 8.4 × 2.3
A: 4/37-mm AA (II × 2)—8/14.5-mm AA (II × 4)—mines **Man:** 65 tot.
Electron Equipt: Radar: 1/Ball End, 1/Neptune
IFF: 1/Square Head, 1/High Pole A
M: 2 Type 9D diesels; 2 props; 2,200 hp **Range:** 2,000/14; 3,200/10

REMARKS: Transferred 1953. The two Bulgarian T 43s are early versions of the class with flush bridge faces. They are the only known units of that configuration with tripod, rather than pole, masts. One is named *Vukov Klanac.*

◆ **4 Soviet Yevgenya-class inshore minesweepers**—Transferred 1977-. . .

D: 80 tons (90 fl) **S:** 11 kts **Dim:** 26.2 × 6.1 × 1.5 **A:** 2/14.5-mm AA (II × 1)
Electron Equipt: Radar: 1/Spin Trough—IFF: 1/High Pole B
M: 2 diesels; 2 props; 600 hp **Range:** 300/10 **Man:** 12 tot.

REMARKS: Plastic hull. Equipped with towed television minehunting and marking system effective to 30-meter depths. Probably replaced PO 2 class. Pendant numbers sighted include 51 and 52.

AMPHIBIOUS WARFARE SHIPS

◆ **23 Soviet Vydra-class landing craft**—Transferred 1970-79

D: 600 fl **S:** 11 kts **Dim:** 54.9 × 7.6 × 2.0
Electron Equipt: Radar: 1/Spin Trough **M:** 2 diesels; 2 props; 1,040 hp
Range: 2,700/10 **Cargo:** 220 tons

AUXILIARIES AND SERVICE CRAFT

◆ **1 Mesar-class replenishment oiler** Bldr: Bulgaria (In serv. 1980)

11 ANLENE

Anlene (AOR 11) 6-80

BULGARIA *(continued)*
AUXILIARIES AND SERVICE CRAFT *(continued)*

D: 3,500 (fl) **S:** 20 kts **Dim:** 97.5 × 13.2 × 5.0
A: 4/30-mm AA (II × 2) **M:** 2 diesels; 2 props; 12,000 hp

Remarks: Deployed to Mediterranean 1980 with the two Rigas. Over-the-stern underway refueling; also has dry stores cargo. Unusually fine hull lines for an oiler.

◆ **1 Soviet Moma-class survey ship/buoy tender** Bldr: Poland (1977)

D: 1,260 tons (1,540 fl) **S:** 17 kts **Dim:** 73.3 × 10.8 × 3.8
Electron Equipt: Radar: 2/Don-2—IFF: 1/High Pole A
M: 2 Sgoda-Sulzer 6 TD 48 diesels; 2 CP props; 3,600 hp
Endurance: 35 days **Range:** 8,700/11 **Man:** 56 tot.

◆ **1 East German Type-700 salvage tug**—Transferred 4-64

Jupiter

D: 700 tons (792 fl) **S:** 13 kts **Dim:** 44.7 × 10.7 × 3.9
M: 2 diesels; 2 props; 1,680 hp **Range:** 4,000/12 **Man:** 39 tot.

◆ **1 inshore survey craft:** (In serv. 1973)

General Vladimir Zaimov—**D:** 600 tons (fl), 48.0 m o.a., 12 kts.

◆ **1 small degaussing tender**—No. 317

◆ **3 Type 024 yard oilers** (In serv. 1956)

D: 450 tons (fl) **S:** 9 kts **Dim:** 46.0 × 6.1 × 2.5

◆ **2 small tugs**

◆ **2 diving tenders**—Nos. 333 and 337

◆ **6 torpedo retrievers**

◆ **6 barracks barges**

◆ **2 fireboats**

FRONTIER POLICE

The Bulgarian Frontier Police operate 12 ex-naval PO 2-class launches and 2 25-knot patrol craft.

BURMA

The Socialist Republic of the Union of Burma

Personnel: approx. 7,000, including reserves and naval infantry

Merchant Marine (1984): 105 ships—108,384 grt (tankers: 5—3,435 grt)

CORVETTES

◆ **1 U.S. PCE 827 class** Bldr: Willamette Iron & Steel, Portland, Ore.

	Laid down	L	In serv.
41 Yan Taing Aung (ex-*Farmington,* PCR 894)	7-12-42	15-5-43	10-8-44

D: 640 tons (903 fl) **S:** 15 kts **Dim:** 56.24 (54.86 wl) × 10.08 × 2.87 (hull)
A: 1/76.2-mm DP Mk 26—6.40-mm AA (II × 3)—8/20-mm AA (II × 4)—1/Mk 10 Hedgehog—2/Mk 6 d.c. launcher—2/d.c. rack
Electron Equipt: Radar: 1/SPS-5
Sonar: 1/QCU-2
M: 2 G.M. 12-567A diesels; 2 props; 1,800 hp **Electric:** 240 kw
Fuel: 125 tons **Range:** 9,000/10 **Man:** 100 tot.

Remarks: Transferred 18-6-55.

◆ **1 U.S. Admirable-class former fleet minesweeper** Bldr: Willamette Iron & Steel, Portland, Ore.

	Laid down	L	In serv.
42 Yan Gyi Aung (ex-*Creddock,* MSF 356)	10-11-43	22-7-44	18-12-45

D: 650 tons (905 fl) **S:** 14 kts **Dim:** 56.24 (54.86) × 10.08 × 2.87 (hull)
A: 1/76.2-mm DP Mk 26—2/40-mm AA (II × 1)—4/20-mm AA (II × 2)—1/Mk 10 hedgehog—2/Mk 6 d.c. launcher—2/d.c. rack
Electron Equipt: Radar: 1/SPS-5
Sonar: QCU-2
M: 2 Busch-Sulzer Type 539 diesels; 2 props; 1,710 hp
Electric: 280 kw **Fuel:** 140 tons **Range:** 9,300/10 **Man:** 100 tot.

Remarks: Minesweeping gear removed prior to transfer 21-3-67.

PATROL BOATS

◆ **2 (+2) PGM 412 class** Bldr: Burma Naval Dockyard, Rangoon

PGM 412 (In serv. 1983) PGM. . . (In serv. 1984) PGM. . . PGM. . .

D: 128 tons (fl) **S:** 16 kts **Dim:** 33.5 × 6.7 × 2.0
A: 2/40-mm AA (I × 2) **Range:** 1,400/14
Man: 17 tot.
M: 2 Deutz SBA 16MB216 LLKR diesels; 2 props; 2,720 hp

◆ **6 U.S. PGM 43 class** Bldrs: 401-404: Marinette Marine, Marinette, Wisc.; 405, 406: Peterson Bldrs, Sturgeon Bay, Wisc.

	In serv.		In serv.
401 (ex-PGM 43)	8-59	404 (ex-PGM 46)	9-59
402 (ex-PGM 44)	8-59	405 (ex-PGM 51)	6-61
403 (ex-PGM 45)	9-59	406 (ex-PGM 52)	6-61

D: 100 tons (141 fl) **S:** 17 kts **Dim:** 30.81 × 6.45 × 2.30
A: 1/40-mm AA—4/20-mm AA (II × 2)—2 mg (I × 2)
Electron Equipt: Radar: EDO 320 (405, 406: Raytheon 1500)
M: 8 G.M. 6-71 diesels; 2 props; 2,040 hp **Fuel:** 16 tons
Range: 1,000/16 **Man:** 17 tot.

Note: The last two U.S. Coast Guard 83-ft design patrol boats, PGM 102 and 110, were discarded 1984-85; PGM 102, 103, 105, 106, and 108 were stricken in 1983.

RIVERINE PATROL VESSELS

◆ **2 improved 301 class** Bldr: Similak, Burma (In serv. 1967)

Y 311 Y 312

D: 250 tons **S:** 14 kts **Dim:** 37.0 × 7.3 × 1.1
A: 2/40-mm AA (I × 2)—2/20-mm AA (I × 2)
M: 2 Mercedes-Benz diesels; 2 props; 1,000 hp

◆ **2 Nawarat class** Bldr: Dawbon DY, Rangoon (In serv. 1961)

Nawarat Nagakyay

Nawarat

D: 400 tons (450 fl) **S:** 12 kts **Dim:** 49.7 × 8.23 × . . .
A: 2/25-pounder guns (Army ordinance)—2/40-mm AA
M: 2 Paxman-Ricardo diesels; 2 props; 1,160 hp **Man:** 43 tot.

◆ **10 Y 301 class** Bldr: Uljanik, Pula, Yugoslavia (In serv. 1957-60)

Y 301–Y 310

Y 301 class

D: 120 tons **S:** 13 kts **Dim:** 32.0 × 7.25 × 0.8
A: 2/40-mm AA (I × 2)—2/20-mm AA (I × 2)
M: 2 Mercedes-Benz diesels; 2 props; 1,100 hp **Man:** 29 tot.

◆ **6 U.S. PBR Mk II-class patrol craft** Bldr: Uniflite, Bellingham, Washington (In serv. 1978)

PBR 211–216

D: 8.9 tons (fl) **S:** 24 kts **Dim:** 9.73 × 3.53 × 0.81
A: 3/12.7-mm mg (II × 1, I × 1)—1/60-mm mortar
Electron Equipt: Radar: 1/Raytheon 1900
M: 2 G.M. GV53N diesels; 2 water jets; 430 hp
Range: 150/23 **Man:** 4-5 tot.

AUXILIARIES

◆ **10 30- to-40-ton river boats** Bldr: Burma (In serv. 1951-52)

◆ **25 30- to-40-ton river boats** Bldr: Yugoslavia (In serv. 1965)

BURMA *(continued)*
AUXILIARIES *(continued)*

◆ **1 hydrographic survey ship** Bldr: Tito SY, Belgrade, Yugoslavia

Thu Tay Thi (In serv. 1965)

Thu Tay Thi

D: 1,100 tons (1,271 fl) **S:** 15 kts **Dim:** 62.21 (56.80 pp) × 11.00 × 3.60
M: 2 MB820 Db diesels; 2 props; 1,710 hp **Man:** 99 tot.

Remarks: Helicopter platform. Carries 2 inshore survey craft. Can be armed with 1/40-mm AA, 2/20-mm AA (I × 2).

◆ **1 inshore survey boat** Bldr: Netherlands (In serv. 1957)

Yay Bo **D:** 108 tons **Man:** 25 tot.

◆ **4 landing craft** Bldr: Yokohama Yacht, Japan (L: 3-69)

Aiyar Maung	Aiyar Mai
Aiyar Min Thar	Aiyar Min Tha Mee

Aiyar Maung Yokohama Yacht, 1969

D: 250 tons (fl) **S:** 10 kts **Dim:** 38.25 × 9.14 × 1.4
M: 2 Kubota diesels; 2 props; 560 hp **Cargo:** 100 tons **Man:** 10 tot.

◆ **2 landing craft** Bldr: Yokohama Yacht, Japan (In serv. 1978)

Sinde Htonbo

D: 220 tons (fl) **S:** 10 kts **Dim:** 29.5 × 6.72 × 1.4
M: 2 Kubota diesels; 2 props; 300 hp **Cargo:** 50 tons, 30 passengers

◆ **1 U.S. LCU 1610-class utility landing craft** Bldr: Southern SB, U.S.

Aiyar Lulin (ex-U.S. LCU 1626)

D: 190 tons (390 fl) **S:** 11 kts **Dim:** 41.0 × 9.0 × 2.0
A: 2/20-mm AA (I × 2) **M:** 4 G.M. 6-71 diesels; 2 props; 1,200 hp

Remarks: Used as a transport. Transferred on completion, 6-67.

◆ **1 diving and repair tender** Bldr: Japan (In serv. 1967)

Yan Long Aung **D:** 520 tons

Remarks: Formerly a torpedo retriever and torpedo boat tender.

PEOPLE'S PEARL AND FISHERIES MINISTRY

◆ **3 Danish "Osprey"-class fisheries protection ships**

	Bldr	In serv.
In Daw	Frederikshavn SY	5-80
In Ma	Frederikshavn SY	25-3-82
In Ya	Frederikshavn SY	25-3-82

D: 385 tons (505 fl) **S:** 20 kts
Dim: 49.95 (45.80 pp) × 10.5 (8.8 wl) × 2.75
A: 2/40-mm AA (II × 1)—1/20-mm AA **Electric:** 359 kVA
M: 2 Burmeister & Wain "Alpha" 16V23L-VO diesels; 2 CP props; 4,640 hp
Range: 4,500/16 **Man:** 15 or more tot.

Remarks: Sister to Danish *Havornen,* armed in Burma. Helicopter hangar and flight deck aft. Rescue launch recessed into inclined ramp at stern. Second pair arrived in Burma 24-5-82.

◆ **3 "Swift"-class fisheries patrol boats** Bldr: Vosper, Singapore (1980-81)

421 422 423

D: 96 tons (fl) **S:** 27 kts **Dim:** 32.3 × 7.2 × . . .
A: 2/40-mm AA (I × 2)—2/20-mm AA (I × 2)—2/7.62-mm mg
M: 2 MTU 12V331 TC81 diesels; 2 props; . . . hp **Range:** 1,800/24
Man: 15 tot.

◆ **6 "Carpentaria"-class fisheries patrol boats** Bldr: deHavilland, Australia (1979-80)

Burmese "Carpentaria"-class patrol boat on trials G. Gyssels, 1980

D: 27 tons (fl) **S:** 27 kts **Dim:** 16.0 × 5.0 × 1.2
A: 2/7.62-mm mg (I × 2) **Electron Equipt:** Radar: 1/Decca 110
M: 2 G.M. 12V71 TI diesels; 2 props; 1,120 hp **Range:** 700/22
Man: 8 tot.

Remarks: Ordered 12-78. Sisters in Indonesian and Solomon Islands forces. Aluminum construction.

CAMEROON

United Republic of Cameroon

Personnel (1985): 350 total

Merchant Marine (1984): 48 ships—74,373 grt

Naval Aviation: One Dornier 128-6 Maritime Patrol aircraft with MEL Marec radar ordered 1983.

GUIDED-MISSILE PATROL BOATS

◆ **1 French P 48S class** Bldr: Soc. Française Contructions Navales (SFCN), Villeneuve-la-Garenne

	Laid down	L	In serv.
Bakassi	12-81	22-10-82	8-10-83

Bakassi SFCN, 1983

CAMEROON *(continued)*
GUIDED-MISSILE PATROL BOATS *(continued)*

D: 270 tons (308 fl) **S:** 26 kts **Dim:** 50.0 (47.0 pp) × 7.45 × 2.35
A: 8/MM 40 Exocet (IV × 2)—2/40-mm AA (I × 2)
Electron Equipt: Radar: 1/Decca TM1229C, 1/Decca RM1230
M: 2 SACM 195V16 CZSHR diesels; 2 props; 6,400 hp **Electric:** 280 kw
Range: 2,000/16 **Man:** 6 officers, 21 petty officers, 12 men

Remarks: Ordered 14-12-80; enlarged version of P 48 class. Two CSEE Naja optronic sights for 40-mm AA, with RADOP ranging system using the navigation radars. Racal CANE 100 (Command and Navigation Equipment) fitted.

PATROL BOATS

◆ **1 French P 48 class** Bldr: SFCN, Villeneuve-la-Garenne

	Laid down	L	In serv.
L'Audacieux	10-2-75	31-10-75	11-5-76

L'Audacieux

D: 250 tons (fl) **S:** 18.5 kts **Dim:** 47.5 (45.5 pp) × 7.1 × 2.5
A: 2/40-mm AA (I × 2) **M:** 2 MGO AGO V12 CZSHR diesels; 2 props; 4,200 hp
Electric: 100 kw **Range:** 2,000/15 **Man:** 4 officers, 30 men

◆ **2 Chinese Shanghai-II class**—Transferred 7-76

101 Cap Cameroon 102 Man o'War Bay

D: 122 tons (135 fl) **S:** 28.5 kts **Dim:** 38.78 × 5.41 × 1.55
A: 4/37-mm AA (II × 2)—4/25-mm AA (II × 2)
Electron Equipt: Radar: 1/Pot Head **Endurance:** 7 days
M: 2 M50F diesels of 1,200 hp, 2 12D6 diesels of 910 hp; 4 props; 4,220 hp
Range: 750/165 **Electric:** 39 kw **Man:** 25 tot.

PATROL CRAFT

◆ **2 small coastal surveillance craft**

Le Valeureux Bldr: Chantiers Navals de l'Estérel, Nice (In serv. 19-11-70)

Le Valeureux Estérel, 1970

D: 45 tons **S:** 25 kts **Dim:** 26.8 × 4.97 × 1.55 **A:** 2/20-mm AA
M: 2 G.M. 12V71 diesels; 2 props; 960 hp **Man:** 1 officer, 8 men

Quartier Maître Alfred Motto Bldr: A.C.R.E., Libreville, Gabon (In serv. 12-11-73)

D: 96 tons (fl) **S:** 15.5 kts **Dim:** 29.1 × 6.2 × 1.85 (aft)
A: 2/20-mm AA—2 mg **M:** 2 Baudoin diesels; 2 props; 1,290 hp
Man: 2 officers, 15 men

AMPHIBIOUS WARFARE CRAFT

◆ **1 LCM** Bldr: Carena, Abidjan, Ivory Coast (In serv. 1973)

D: 57 tons (fl) **S:** 9 kts **Dim:** 17.5 × 4.28 × 1.3
M: 2 Baudoin diesels; 490 hp

◆ **5 LCVP-type landing craft** Bldr: A.C.R.E., Libreville, Gabon

Souellaba Indépendance Reunification Manoka Machtigal

D: 11 tons **S:** 10 kts

SERVICE CRAFT

◆ **2 10-ton harbor launches**

Sanaga Bimbia

◆ **6 FAC 408-class Seatrucks** Bldr: Rotork Marine, Poole, U.K. (In serv. 1978)

D: 2 tons **S:** 10 to 35 kts **Dim:** 7.37 × 2.74 × . . .
M: 1 or 2 inboard/outboard motors

Remarks: For patrolling rivers and lagoons. Two similar 12-m craft were delivered 1-82 by Tanguy Marine, France, along with one 17-m "Seatruck."

Note: Customs or police forces also operate 12 Type 650 and 800 launches of 3.5 tons delivered 1977-1982 by Chantiers Plascoa, Cannes.

CANADA

The Canadian Armed Forces are completely unified. There are six operational commands: Mobile Command, Maritime Command, Air Transport Command, Air Defense Command, Training Command, and Material Command. The Maritime Command is in charge of the naval ships, the ship-based aircraft, and all of the units of the former Maritime Air Command (RCAF). Its principal role is ASW, but it can also be called upon to transport men and equipment for the Mobile Command. The new government elected in 1984 has promised to once again separate the three services.

Personnel (1984): about 18,450 men active, plus 3,000 in the Naval Reserve, and 7,400 civil employees.

Merchant Marine: (1984): 1,310 ships—3,449,496 grt (tankers: 62—439,130 grt)

Naval Aviation: Made up of ship-based ASW helicopters, maritime patrol aircraft, and ASW aircraft, formerly carrier-based but now maintained at land bases.

Primary strength as follows:

—32 ASW CHSS 2 (CH-124A) Sea King helicopters (*see* U.S.A. section), armed with Mk 44 or Mk 46 torpedoes and AQS-13 sonar. Several are used in logistics service aboard the replenishment oilers. All are based on the East Coast, at Shearwater, Nova Scotia. Problems with stress cracking kept many grounded during 1982, now corrected. Being fitted with Emerson *Calypso* acoustic processors.

Canada signed a contract on 25-7-76 with Lockheed for the manufacture of 18 CP-140 Aurora maritime patrol aircraft, based on the U.S. Navy's P-3 Orion. The first plane was delivered 28-5-80, with the remaining arriving by 3-81. The Canadian version of the plane is fitted not only for reconnaissance, ASW, and electronic warfare, but also for detecting atmospheric and maritime pollution and for analyzing oil spills at sea. It has a crew of twelve. The Aurora has the Orion's A-NEW system, based on the miniaturized Univac ASQ-114 computer, which can store 65,000 words of 30 bits and has a retrieval time of 4 microseconds. There are 36 launching chutes for dropping active and passive sonobuoys and racks for 120 reserve sonobuoys. Other principal systems are: 2ASN-84 inertial navigation computers; Doppler radar; tactical recorder flight-control director; tactical data link system; FLIR (Forward-Looking Infrared); SLAR (Side-Looking Airborne Radar) antennas; detectors for lasers; a low-light television pod.

CP-140 Aurora, number 140101 1980

—15 CS-2F Tracker former carrier-based ASW aircraft, now used as land-based maritime surveillance aircraft, with additional fuel in the former weapons bay. Omega navigation systems were added during 1979-80, and a wing-mounted camera pod is installed. Twelve are based at Shearwater, Nova Scotia, while the 3 Pacific Coast units also perform ship target service duties, along with several CT-33A Silver Star jet trainers. Some 8-12 Canadian Challenger 600/601 corporate jets were ordered 1985 to supply naval and land forces with EW training.

Warships in Service As Of 1 January 1984

	L	Tons	Main armament
◆ **3 submarines**			
3 Oberon	1964-66	2,070 (surf.)	8/533-mm TT

WARSHIPS *(continued)*

◆ **4 destroyers**

4 Iroquois	1970-71	3,551	1/127-mm DP, 2 Can. Sea Sparrow, ASW weapons, 2 Sea King helicopters

◆ **16 (+6) frigates**

0 (+6) Halifax	. . .	3,471	8/Harpoon, Sea Sparrow SAM, 1/57-mm DP, ASW weapons, 1 helicopter
2 Annapolis	1961-63	2,400	2/76.2-mm DP, ASW weapons, 1 Sea King helicopter
4 Mackenzie	1961-62	2,380	4/76.2-mm DP, ASW weapons
4 Restigouche	1954-57	2,390	2/76.2-mm DP, ASROC, other ASW weapons
6 St. Laurent	1952-56	2,260	2/76.2-mm DP, ASW weapons, 1 Sea King helicopter

WEAPONS AND SYSTEMS

A. MISSILES

◆ **Surface-to-air missiles.** The Canadian Navy has adopted the short-range surface-to-air NATO Sea Sparrow for its four *Iroquois*-class destroyers. The missile is designed to attack aircraft or missiles flying at a low altitude or at a transonic speed. Its characteristics are:

Length: 3.660 m. **Diameter:** 0.200 m.
Wingspan: .020 m. **Weight:** 204 kg.
Speed: Mach 3.5. **Practical antiaircraft range:** 8,000 to 10,000 m.

The launching system, on the *Iroquois* class, designed by Raytheon Canada, is made up of two loaders and two launchers. The launchers are fixed one to port and one to starboard, perpendicular to the axis of the ship. They are retractable, can be trained and elevated, and are housed in the structure forward of the bridge. Each launcher has four missiles ready to be fired. A new Raytheon vertical-launch system for Sea Sparrow underwent trials aboard *Huron* in 2-81 at Roosevelt Roads, Puerto Rico, and will be used on the *Halifax* class.

Canada is purchasing the U.S. Harpoon missile for use by CP-140 Aurora aircraft, submarines, and surface ships. In 1984, 34 RGM-84D shipboard versions were ordered.

B. GUNS

The following guns are currently in use:

57-mm Bofors SAK Mk 2. Single mount, to be used on the *Halifax* class. *See* Swedish section for data.

76.2-mm Mk 22. Twin DP (U.S. Mk 34 mount) mounted behind a g.r.p. spray shield.
Length: 50 calibers. **Muzzle velocity:** 822 m/s.
Maximum firing rate: 50 rounds per minute per barrel.
Arc of elevation: 115° to +85°.
Maximum effective antiaircraft range: 4,000 to 5,000 m.
Fitted on the *St. Laurent, Restigouche, Mackenzie,* and *Annapolis* class of frigates.

76.2-mm Mk 6. Twin barrel, automatic (British model).
Length: 70 calibers. **Muzzle velocity:** . . . m/s. **Maximum firing rate:** 60 rounds per minute per barrel.
Maximum effective antiaircraft range: 5,000 m.
Installed forward on the *Restigouche* and *Mackenzie* classes of frigates.

127-mm OTO-Melara (*see* Italy section)
Installed on the *Iroquois*-class destroyers.

C. ASW WEAPONS

◆ **Depth-charge and torpedo launchers**

—British Mk 10 Limbo triple-barreled mortar on destroyers and frigates.
—U.S. ASROC on 4 *Restigouche*-class frigates.
—U.S. Mk 32 ASW triple torpedo tubes on all destroyers and frigates.

◆ **Torpedoes**

—U.S. Mk 44 and 46 ASW torpedoes aboard ships, and on Sea King helicopters and maritime patrol aircraft.
—U.S. Mk 37 aboard submarines, in Northrop NT37C improved version.
—U.S. Mk 48 mod. 4 on submarines; 48 ordered 1985

D. ELECTRONICS

◆ **Radars:**

—SPS-12 long-range air search.
—SPS-49(v), U.S. (Raytheon) 2-D air-search radar on *Halifax* class.
—SPS-501 long-range air search (version of Dutch LWO-3) installed in *Iroquois*-class destroyers. Uses LWO-3 antenna, SPS-12 transmitter.
—SPS-503, Canadian-made radar using the Plessey AWS-4's antenna, for 8 modernized frigates.
—SPS-10 and Sperry Mk 2 navigation/surface search.
—SPQ-2D combination search (Italian radar) installed in the *Iroquois* class.
—Sea Giraffe HC 150, Ericsson surface search on the *Halifax* class.

◆ **Sonars:**

—SQS-501 for detection of submarines lying on the sea bottom.
—SQS-503 hull-mounted MF.
—SQS-504 towed MF, Type 503 transducer.
—SQS-505 hull-mounted LF installed in the *Iroquois* and *Halifax* classes.
—SQS-505 towed LF installed in the *Iroquois* class (SQA-502 hoist). SQS-505 TASP with digital acoustic processing and SHINPADS display tested in an *Iroquois*-class ship in 1984.
—SQR-501 CANTASS towed passive linear hydrophone array for the *Halifax* class; uses "wet end" of U.S. AN/SQR-18A system with Canadian receiver/processor.

SUBMARINES

Note: In 1985-86, the Canadian Government is studying proposals from France, Italy, the Netherlands, the U.K., Sweden, and two from West Germany for replacement submarines for the *Oberon* class. The requirement is initially for four submarines, and an 8- or 12-boat fleet is also being looked at. Some or all may be built in Canada. Armament will include Sub-Harpoon missiles and U.S. Mk 48 torpedoes; low manning levels, quiet operation, and long endurance are required. The first submarines would replace the *Oberons* as they are stricken 1992-94.

◆ **3 British Oberon class**

	Bldr	Laid down	L	In serv.
SS 72 Ojibwa (ex-*Onyx*)	H.M. DY, Chatham	27-9-62	29-2-64	23-9-65
SS 73 Onandaga	H.M. DY, Chatham	18-6-64	25-9-65	22-6-67
SS 74 Okanagan	H.M. DY, Chatham	25-3-65	17-9-66	22-6-68

Ojibwa (SS 72)—after modernization L. & L. Van Ginderen, 12-82

D: 1,610/2,070/2,410 tons **Dim:** 17.5/15 kts
Dim: 89.92(87.45 pp) × 8.07 × 5.48
A: 8/533-mm TT (6 fwd, 2 aft)—22 NT37C torpedoes—see remarks
Electron Equipt: Radar: 1/1006
Sonar: British: 1/2007, 1/Krupp-Atlas CSU3-41
M: 2 Admiralty Standard Range 16VVS-AS21 diesels, diesel-electric drive; 2 props; 6,000 hp

Remarks: The *Ojibwa* was begun under the name of *Onyx* for the Royal Navy and transferred while still under construction. The living spaces have been modified for Canadian weather conditions. Being modernized under "SOUP" (Submarine Operational Update Program), beginning in 1980 with SS 72; getting Singer-Librascope Mk 1 Mod. 0 fire-control system using Sperry UYK-20 computer and new sonar suit with the Krupp-Atlas CSU3-41 active-passive system for the passive array, and an active transducer in the sail replacing the original Type 187, 197, and 719 sets. The Type 2007 long-range passive search array will be retained. Able to employ U.S. Mk 48 torpedoes and Sub-Harpoon missiles. SS 72 completed 6-82, SS 73 in 1984, and SS 74 in 1986. Two Thorn-EMI Pertel low light-level t.v. periscopes in each. The aft tubes can only be employed for NT37C torpedoes.

DESTROYERS

◆ **4 Iroquois DDH 280 class**

	Bldr	Laid down	L	In serv.
DDH 280 Iroquois	Marine Industries, Sorel	15-1-69	28-11-70	29-7-72
DDH 281 Huron	Marine Industries, Sorel	15-1-69	3-4-71	16-12-72
DDH 282 Athabascan	Davie S.B., Lauzon	1-6-69	27-11-70	30-11-72
DDH 283 Algonquin	Davie S.B., Lauzon	1-9-69	23-4-71	30-9-73

Iroquois (DDH 280)—with new TACAN G. Gyssels, 3-85

DESTROYERS *(continued)*

Iroquois (DDH 280) G. Gyssels, 3-85

Huron (DDH 281) G. Arra, 1984

D: 3,551 tons (4,200 fl) **S:** 30/29 kts
Dim: 128.92 (121.31 pp) × 15.24 × 4.42
A: 2/Canadian Sea Sparrow SAM syst. (IV × 2; 32 AIM-7E missiles)—1/127-mm OTO Melara DP—1/Mk 10 Limbo ASW mortar (III × 1)—6/324-mm Mk 32 TT (III × 2)—2/Sea King ASW helicopters.
Electron Equipt: Radar: 1/navigational, 1/SP-501, 1/SPQ-2D; 2/WM-22 dir.
Sonar: 1/SQS-505, 1/SQS-505(VDS), 1/SQS-501
EW: WLR-1, ULQ-6 jammer—1/6-rail flare and chaff RL—2/Knebworth/Corvus chaff RL (VIII × 2)—TACAN: URN-20 (DDH 280: URN-25)
M: COGOG: 2 FT 4A2 Pratt & Whitney gas turbines, 25,000 hp each, 2 Solar Mk FT 12H gas turbines, 3,700 hp each; 2 five-bladed CP props; 50,000 hp
Electric: 2,750 kw **Range:** 4,500/20 **Man:** 27 officers, 258 men

Remarks: Two paired stacks, angled to avoid corrosion of the antennas by stack gases. Bear Trap positive-control helicopter landing system. Passive-tank anti-rolling system fitted to improve stability at low speeds. *Huron* tested the Raytheon vertical-launch Sea Sparrow SAM system in 2-81. U.S. WSC-3 SATCOMM capability added 1982; 2 OE-82 antennas. Have H.S.A. ASWDS computerized data display system. DDH 283 tested the AN/SAR-8 IRSTD (Infrared Search and Target Designation) system atop her pilothouse in 1984.

Modernization Notes: These ships are being updated under the TRUMP (Tribal Update and Modernization Program) under a design prepared by Litton Systems Canada. The first will commence reconstruction at Davie SB, Lauzon, Que., late in 1986, completing in 1988, and the last (DDH 281) will complete by 5-91. ASW systems are to be basically unchanged, except for removal of the Limbo mortar. The U.S. Mk 41 VLS (Vertical Launch System) for 32 Standard SM 2 Block II SAMS will replace the 127-mm forward, while an OTO Melara 76-mm DP gun will be installed in the former Sea Sparrow magazine area. A Mk 15 CIWS (Vulcan-Phalanx) will be placed atop the hangar, and ASW torpedo stowage and handling will be improved. The 76-mm gun and Standard missiles will be controlled by a single H.S.A. STIR 1.8 fire-control illuminator/tracker. The LW-08 long-range air-search radar will be retained, supplemented by a DA-06 medium-range radar atop the mast. Harpoon anti-ship missiles are no longer planned to be carried. Plessey's Shield decoy RL (VI × 2) will replace Knebworth-Corvus, and the CANEWS EW system (with Ramses jammer) will replace WLR-1. The SHINPADS command and control system will be added, as will the U.S. SLQ-25 Nixie torpedo decoy.

The cruise turbines will be replaced by two G.M. Allison 570KF gas turbines, each generating 6,394 shp, and the twin stacks will be integrated into a single, larger structure; yet to be decided is whether the boost engines will be replaced with G.E. LM-2500 gas turbines. A new 1,000-kw diesel generator will be fitted. An inertial navigation system is planned.

Iroquois (DDH 280) after modernization Litton Canada, 1985

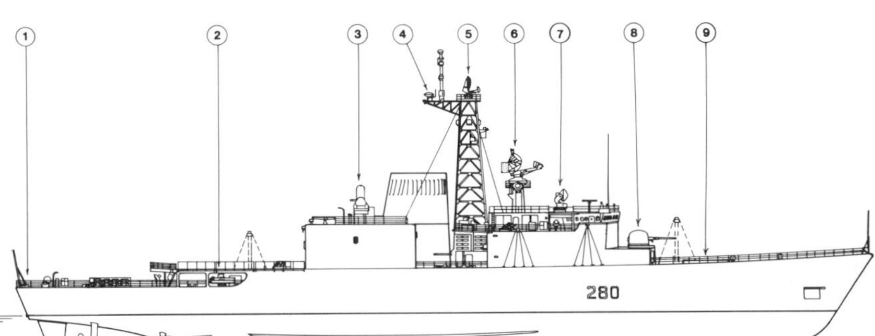

Iroquois as modernized A.D. Baker III, 6-85
1. VDS housing 2. Triple Mk 32 ASW TT 3. Mk 15 CIWS 20-mm gatling AA 4. URN-25 TACAN 5. DA-08 radar 6. LW-08 long-range search radar 7. STIR 1.8 fire-control tracker/illuminator radar 8. 76-mm OTO Melara Compact DP 9. Standard SM-2 VLS launcher Ex-41

FRIGATES

◆ 0 (+6 +6) Halifax, or "City" class

	Bldrs	Laid down	L	In serv.
FFH 330 Halifax	St. Johns SB, New Brunswick	7-85	. . .	11-89
FFH 331 Vancouver	Marine Ind., Sorel, Que.	. . .	. . .	9-90
FFH 332 Ville de Quebec	St. Johns SB, New Brunswick	. . .	. . .	9-90
FFH 333 Toronto	Marine Ind., Sorel, Que.*	. . .	. . .	3-91
FFH 334 Regina	St. Johns SB, New Brunswick, Que.	. . .	. . .	3-91
FFH 335 Calgary	Marine Ind., Sorel, Que.*	. . .	. . .	3-92

* To fit out at Versatile Vickers, Montreal

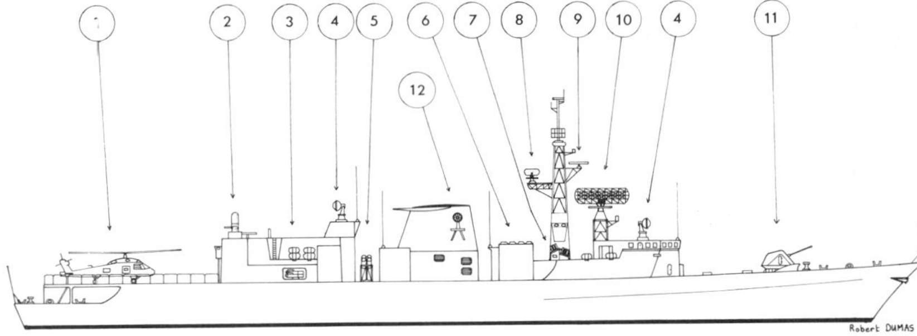

1. Sea Hawk helicopter 2. Mk 15 CIWS 3. helicopter hangar 4. STIR weapon-control radars 5. Harpoon anti-ship missiles (IV × 2) 6. Sea Sparrow vertical launchers 7. Shield decoy RL 8. Sea Giraffe radar 9. 1629C navigational radar 10. SPS-49 long-range air-search radar 11. 57-mm SAK Mk 2 DP mount 12. OF-82 SATCOMM antennas

D: 3,471 tons (4, 254 fl) **S:** 29.2 kts (27 sust.)
Dim: 133.50(124.50 pp) × 14.80 × 4.64 (mean)
A: 8/Harpoon SSM (IV × 2)—Sea Sparrow VLS syst. (VIII × 4)—1/57-mm Bofors SAK Mk 2 DP—1/20-mm Mk 15 CIWS—6/324-mm Mk 32 ASW TT(III × 2)—1/SH-60B Sea Hawk helicopter
Electron Equipt: Radar: 1/Raytheon 1629C nav., 1/Ericsson Sea Giraffe 150 HC search, 1/SPS-49 long-range air search, 2 H.S.A. STIR f.c.
Sonar: SQS-505 hull-mounted, SQR-501 CANTASS towed array
EW: Ramses jammer, M.E.L. CANEWS intercept, 4/Shield RL (VI × 4)—TACAN: URN-25
M: CODOG: 2 G.E. LM-2500 gas turbines/1 S.E.M.T.-Pielstick 20PA6-V280-BTC diesel (11,780 hp); 2 CP props; 50,000 hp
Electric: 4,880 kVA(4 M.W.M. TBO-602 V-16K diesel generator sets)
Fuel: 479 tons **Range:** 4,500/20 **Man:** 180 tot.(225 accommodations)

FRIGATES *(continued)*

REMARKS: First six ordered 29-7-83 from consortium of St. Johns Shipbuilding and Dry Dock, Paramax Electronics, and Sperry. Announced 19-11-84 that a second group of six are to be built. FFH 330 was to have been laid down 12-84, but program (first announced 22-12-77!) continues to experience design delays.

Helicopter to be employed not yet firm, may not be SH-60B. Will have *Bear Trap* helicopter recovery system. Fin stabilizers. The U.S./Canadian AN/SAR-8 IRSTD(Infrared Search and Target Designation) system is to be carried. SQR-501 CANTASS towed tactical passive hydrophone system uses the "wet end" of the U.S. SQR-18A TACTASS. Originally were to have only two 8-cell Sea Sparrow VLS, but this was doubled by 1984. Will have AN/SLQ-25 Nixie towed torpedo decoys and a bubbler noise-reduction system. The SHINPADS (Shipboard Integrated Processing And Display System) data system will be fitted.

Halifax (FFH 330)—official model R.C.N., 1984

Halifax (FFH 330)—artist's rendering R.C.N., 1984

NOTE: A "Destroyer Life Extension Program" (DELEX) was approved 7-8-80. All 16 older frigates are receiving: ADLIPS (Automated Data Link Processing System), hull and machinery overhaul and repair, new underwater telephones, the Mk 12 IFF system, secure UHF communications, and a new navigational radar. Additional features are being added to the various ships in proportion to their future value, with $22 million per ship being spent on the 1964-vintage *Annapolis* class, down to only $5 million for the *St. Laurent*-class ships, which, as the oldest, are the first to be worked on. Individual class DELEX features are listed in the Remarks sections.

◆ **2 Annapolis class**

	Bldr	Laid down	L	In serv.
DDE 265 ANNAPOLIS	Halifax Shipyards Ltd	7-60	27-4-63	19-12-64
DDE 266 NIPIGON	Marine Industries, Sorel	4-60	10-12-61	30-5-64

D: 2,400 tons (3,000 fl) **S:** 28 kts **Dim:** 113.1 × 12.8 × 4.4
A: 2/76.2-mm DP Mk 33 (II × 1)—1/Mk 10 Limbo mortar (III × 2)—6/324-mm ASW TT (III × 2) Mk 32—1/Sea King helicopter
Electron Equipt: Radar: 1/nav. 1/SPS-503, 1/SPS-10, 1/fire control
Sonar: 1/SQS-505, 1/SQS-504 VDS, 1/SQS-501
EW: CANEWS intercept, 4/Mk 36 SRBOC RL(VI × 4)—TACAN: URN-20

Annapolis (DDE 265)—prior to refit G. Arra, 3-84

M: 2 sets English-Electric GT; 2 props; 30,000 hp
Boilers: 2 Babcock & Wilcox; 43.3 kg/cm², 454°C **Electric:** 1,400 kw
Range: 4,750/14 **Man:** 18 officers, 210 men

REMARKS: Have Litton CCS-280 data system. Under DELEX will receive SPS-503 (CMR-1820) air-search radar with Plessey AWS-4 antenna, new EW system, fire-control syst., and navigational radar; SQS-503 sonar replaced by SQS-505. SLQ-25 Nixie torpedo decoys added. Refits scheduled to commence: DDE 265 in 1984, 266 in 1985. Both on East Coast. To remain in service until 1994-96.

◆ **4 Mackenzie-class frigates**

	Bldr	Laid down	L	In serv.
DDE 261 MACKENZIE	Canadian-Vickers	15-12-58	25-5-61	6-10-62
DDE 262 SASKATCHEWAN	Victoria Machinery	16-7-59	1-2-61	16-2-63
DDE 263 YUKON	Burrard, Vancouver	25-10-59	27-7-61	25-5-63
DDE 264 QU'APPELLE	Davie S.B., Lauzon	14-1-60	2-5-62	14-19-63

Saskatchewan (DDE 262)—with new navigation radar
Cdr. G. Eldridge, R.C.N., 1983

Qu'appelle (DDE 264)—Mk 33, 76.2-mm/50-cal. forward
L. & L. Van Ginderen, 10-82

D: 2,380 tons (2,890 fl) **S:** 28 kts **Dim:** 111.5 × 12.8 × 4.1
A: 4/76.2-mm DP (II × 2—see remarks)—2/Mk 10 Limbo mortars (III × 2)—6/324-mm ASW TT Mk 32 (III × 2)
Electron Equipt: Radar: 1/SPS-12, 1/SPS-10, 1/Sperry Mk 2, 1/SPG-48, 1/SPG-34
Sonar: 1/SQS-503, 1/SQS-501—EW: WLR-1
M: 2 sets English-Electric GT; 2 props; 30,000 hp
Boilers: 2 Babcock & Wilcox; 43 kg/cm², 454°C **Range:** 4,750/14
Man: 11 officers, 199 men

REMARKS: All employed in the Pacific. U.S. Mk 69 gunfire control forward, Mk 63 aft. DDE 264 has had British Mk 6, 76.2-mm/70-cal. gun mount forward replaced by U.S. Mk 34, 76.2-mm/50-cal. mount, which is mounted aft on all. Under DELEX are receiving SQS-505 in place of SQS-503, a new navigational radar in place of Mk 2, and the SLQ-25 Nixie torpedo decoy. Will remain in service until 1990-93. Refit of DDE 264 completed 1-84; DDE 263 scheduled to complete 1-85, DDE 262 in 1-86 and DDE 261 in 1987, all by Burrard Yarrows, Victoria.

FRIGATES *(continued)*

◆ **4 modified Restigouche-class ASW frigates**

	Bldr	Laid down	L	In serv.
DDE 236 Gatineau	Davie SB, Lauzon	30-4-53	3-6-57	17-2-59
DDE 257 Restigouche	Canadian-Vickers	15-7-53	22-11-54	7-6-58
DDE 258 Kootenay	Burrard, Vancouver	21-8-52	15-6-54	7-3-59
DDE 259 Terra Nova	Victoria Machinery	14-11-52	21-6-55	6-6-59

Terra Nova (DDE 259)—pre-modernization G. Arra, 1983

Kootenay (DDE 258)—post-DELEX modernization G. Arra, 1983

D: 2,390 tons (2,900 fl) **S:** 28 kts **Dim:** 113.1 × 12.8 × 4.3
A: 2/76.2-mm DP Mk 6 (II × 1) fwd—1/ASROC syst. (VIII × 1, 8 reloads)—1/Mk 10 Limbo mortar (III × 1) (DDE 258, 259: 6/324-mm ASW TT (III × 2)
Electron Equipt: Radar: 1/nav., 1/SPS-503, 1/SPS-10, 1/fire control
Sonar: 1/SQS-501, 1/SQS-503, 1/SQS-505(VDS)
EW: CANEWS passive, ULQ-6 jammer, 4 Mk 36 SRBOC RL (VI × 4)
M: 2 sets English-Electric GT; 2 props; 30,000 hp
Boilers: 2 Babcock & Wilcox, 43.3 kg/cm², 454°C **Electric:** 1,800 kw
Range: 4,750/14 **Man:** 13 officers, 201 men

Remarks: All on Pacific Coast. Reconstruction with lengthened hull for VDS and ASROC in place of aft 76.2-mm mount and one Limbo completed 1968-73. U.S. Mk 69 fire-control system. Unmodified sisters *Chaudière, Columbia,* and *St. Croix* were reduced to disposal reserve in 1974, although *Columbia* remains in use as a stationary training ship at Esquimault. DDE 258 completed DELEX modernization 11-83, DDE 259 in 1984. SPS-503 radar replaced SPS-12, a new navigational radar was added, U.S. WSC-3 SATCOMM gear (two OE-82 antennas) was added, MK 32 ASW TT replaced the Knebworth/Corvus chaff RL on the upper deck aft and four Mk 137 launchers for the U.S. Mk 36 SRBOC chaff system replaced the flare rocket launcher atop the ASROC reload magazine. The GFCS was updated, data link capability improved, SLQ-25 Nixie torpedo decoys added, and a 400-kw generator was added. Data in listing are for ships post-DELEX; to be retained to 1994-96.

◆ **6 St. Laurent-class helicopter frigates**

	Bldr	Laid down	L	In serv.
DDE 206 Saguenay	Halifax Shipyards	4-4-51	30-7-53	15-12-56
DDE 207 Skeena	Burrard, Vancouver	1-6-51	19-8-52	30-3-57
DDE 229 Ottawa	Canadian-Vickers	8-6-51	29-4-53	10-11-56
DDE 230 Margaree	Halifax Shipyards	12-9-51	29-3-56	5-10-57
DDE 233 Fraser	Burrard, Vancouver	11-12-51	19-2-53	28-6-57
DDE 234 Assiniboine	Marine Industries, Sorel	19-5-52	12-2-54	16-8-56

Fraser (DDE 233)—post-DELEX—TACAN on lattice
L. & L. Van Ginderen, 7-84

Ottawa (DDE 229)—post-DELEX L. & L. Van Ginderen, 8-85

D: 2,260 tons (2,860 fl) **S:** 28 kts **Dim:** 111.5 × 12.8 × 4.2
A: 2/76.2-mm DP Mk 33—1/Mk 10 Limbo mortar (III × 1)—6/324-mm Mk 32 ASW TT (III × 2)—1/Sea King helicopter
Electron Equipt: Radar: 1/SPS-12, 1/SPS-10, 1 navigational, 1/SPG-48 f.c.
Sonar: 1/SQS-503, 1/SQS-501, 1/SQS-504 VDS
EW: WLR-1—TACAN: URN-20
M: 2 sets English-Electric GT; 2 props; 30,000 hp
Boilers: 2 Babcock & Wilcox; 43.3 kg/cm², 454°C
Electric: 1,400 kw **Range:** 4,750/14 **Man:** 18 officers, 210 men

Remarks: *St. Laurent* (DDE 205) stricken in 1974. *Fraser,* which was completed by Yarrow, Ltd., has a lattice mast between her funnels to support the TACAN dome; the others carry their TACAN atop a pole mast. Nos. 207, 229, and 233 given major overhauls 1977-78. DELEX overhaul begun 1980 on 207, 229, 230, and 233; DDE 206, 230, 234 refitted 9-7-84 to 8-85: no major updates. Scheduled for retirement 1987-90.

OCEANOGRAPHIC AND HYDROGRAPHIC SHIPS

◆ **2 oceanographic research ships**

	Bldr	Laid down	L	In serv.
AGOR 172 Quest	Burrard DD, Vancouver	1967	9-7-68	21-8-69

Quest (AGOR 172) L. & L. Van Ginderen, 7-81

D: 2,130 tons (fl) **S:** 15 kts **Dim:** 77.2 (71.62 pp) × 12.8 × 4.6
Electron Equipt: Radar: 1/Decca 838, 1/Decca 929 **Fuel:** 256 tons
Range: 10,000/12 **Man:** 37 tot.

Remarks: A modification of the *Endeavour* (AGOR 171) with the same machinery. Can carry a small helicopter. See remarks on the *Endeavour.*

	Bldr	L	In serv.
AGOR 171 Endeavour	Yarrow, Ltd., Victoria	17-8-61	9-3-65

D: 1,560 tons (fl) **S:** 16 kts **Dim:** 71.85 (65.53 wl) × 11.73 × 4.0
M: 2 Fairbanks-Morse 38D8⅛, 9-cylinder diesels, G.E. electric drive; 2 props; 2,960 hp

OCEANOGRAPHIC AND HYDROGRAPHIC SHIPS *(continued)*

Endeavour (AGOR 171) 1985

Electron Equipt: Radar: 1/Decca 838, 1/Decca 929 **Fuel:** 256 tons
Range: 10,000/12 **Man:** 37 crew plus 14 scientists

Remarks: (for both ships): Reinforced hulls for navigation in icefields. Two electro-hydraulic 5- and 9-ton cranes. Bulbous bows. Anti-rolling and anti-pitching devices. Civilian crews.

◆ **1 former minelayer**

	Bldr	Laid down	L	In serv.
AGOR 114 Bluethroat	Geo. T. Davie, Lauzon	31-10-52	15-9-55	28-11-55

Bluethroat (AGOR 114) L. & L. Van Ginderen, 1985

D: 785 tons (870 fl) **S:** 13 kts **Dim:** 47.0 × 9.9 × 3.0
M: 2 diesels; 2 props; 1,200 hp **Man:** 27 tot.

Remarks: Completed as a mine and magnetic loop layer; redesignated a cable layer in 1959 and as a research ship in 1964.

◆ **1 ex-Royal Canadian Mounted Police patrol boat** Bldr: Canadian SB & Eng. Co.

AGOR 140 Fort Steele (L: 18-7-59, in serv. 11-59)

Fort Steele (AGOR 140) L. & L. Van Ginderen, 10-82

D: 85 tons (110 fl) **S:** 18 kts **Dim:** 35.97 × 6.4 × 2.1
M: Paxman Ventura 12 YJCM diesels; 2 CP props; 2,800 hp
Range: 1,200/16 **Man:** 16 tot.

Remarks: Taken over 1973. Although designated a research ship, primarily acts as training ship for Reserves at Halifax. Originally had Napier Deltic diesels.

DEEP SUBMERGENCE EXPERIMENTAL SHIP

◆ **1 former Italian stern-haul trawler** Bldr: Marelli, Italy (L: . . .)

ASXL 20 Cormorant (ex-*Aspa Quarto*) (In serv. 10-11-78)

Cormorant (ASXL 20) 1978

D: 2,350 tons (fl) **S:** 15 kts **Dim:** 74.6 (72.0 pp) × 11.9 × 5.3
Electron Equipt: Radar: 1/Decca TM 1229, 1/RM 1229
M: 3 Marelli-Deutz ACR 12456 CV, 950 hp diesels, electric drive; 1 CP prop; 2,100 hp
Electric: 730 kVA + 250 kw **Range:** 11,800/15; 13,000/12

Remarks: Ex-Italian stern haul trawler bought in 1975 and adapted to handle and service the SDL-1 submersible, which can dive to 600 m. A large hangar for SDL-2 and a gallows crane have been built on the stern. The ship can also support conventional and saturation divers and has extensive compressor facilities, decompression chambers, etc. Numerous specialized echo-sounders fitted.

REPLENISHMENT OILERS

◆ **2 Protecteur-class multi-purpose underway replenishment ships**

	Bldr	Laid down	L	In serv.
AOR 509 Protecteur	St. John SB & DD (NB)	17-10-67	18-7-68	30-8-69
AOR 510 Preserver	St. John SB & DD (NB)	17-10-67	29-5-69	30-7-70

Preserver (AOR 510) L. & L. Van Ginderen, 3-84

D: 8,380 tons light (24,700 fl) **S:** 21 kts
Dim: 172.0 (166.42 pp) × 23.16 × 9.15
A: guns: see remarks — 3/Sea King helicopters
Electron Equipt: Radar: 1/Decca . . . , 1/Decca TM 969 — TACAN: URN-20
Sonar: 1/SQS-505
M: 1 set Canadian G.E. GT; 1 prop; 21,000 hp **Boilers:** 2 **Electric:** 3,500 kw
Cargo capacity: 13,250 tons, with 12,000 tons of distillate fuel, 600 tons of diesel oil, 400 tons of jet fuel, frozen and dry foods, spare parts, munitions, etc.
Range: 4,100/20; 7,500/11.5 **Man:** 15 officers, 212 men, 57 passengers

Remarks: Four replenishment-at-sea stations, one elevator abaft the navigation bridge, two 15-ton cranes on the afterdeck. One bow-thruster. Daily fresh-water distillation capacity is 80 tons. Twin 76.2-mm gunmount, formerly carried at the extreme bow, was removed in both in 1983; locally controlled, it was of little use and had several times been washed overboard. Can be used to carry military vehicles and troops for commando purposes. Carry four LCVPs. Both operate in the Atlantic.

◆ **1 Provider-class multi-purpose underway replenishment ship**

	Bldr	Laid down	L	In serv.
AOR 508 Provider	Davie SB, Lauzon	1-5-61	5-7-62	28-9-63

D: 7,300 tons (22,000 fl) **S:** 20 kts
Dim: 168.0 (159.4 pp) × 23.17 × 9.15 **M:** GT; 1 prop; 21,000 hp
Boilers: 2 **Fuel:** 1,200 tons **Range:** 5,000/20
Electric: 2,140 kw **Man:** 15 officers, 151 men

Remarks: 14,054 grt. Platform and hangar for two Sea King helicopters. Can carry 12,000 tons of distillate fuel, 1,200 tons of diesel, 1,000 tons of aviation gas, 250 tons of provisions, munitions, and various spare parts. Operates in the Pacific. Refitted 1982.

REPLENISHMENT OILERS *(continued)*

Provider (AOR 508) G. Arra, 1982

SMALL OILERS

◆ **1 "Dun" class** Bldr: Canadian Bridge Co., Walkerville, Ont.

	Laid down	L	In serv.
AOTL 502 Dundurn	27-1-43	18-9-43	25-11-43

D: 950 tons (1,500 fl) **S:** 10 kts **Dim:** 54.5 × 9.8 × 3.9
M: 1 Fairbanks-Morse diesel; 1 prop; 700 hp **Man:** 24 tot.

Remarks: Sister *Dundalk* (AOTL 501) stricken 17-2-82. Cargo: 792 tons liquid, 25 tons dry.

REPAIR SHIP

◆ **1 "Park"-class dépôt repair ship** Bldr: Burrard DD, Vancouver

	Laid down	L	In serv.
ARE 100 Cape Breton (ex-*Flamborough Head*)	5-7-44	7-10-44	25-4-45

D: 8,450 tons (11,270 fl) **S:** 11 kts **Dim:** 134.6 (129.4) × 17.4 × 6.96
M: 1 set triple-expansion, reciprocating; 2,500 hp
Boilers: 2 Foster-Wheeler 17.6 kg/cm², 316°C **Fuel:** 709 tons
Range: 5,000/9

Remarks: Purchased from the Royal Navy in 1951. Used as training ship 1953-58. Refitted 1958-59. Equipped for pierside service at Esquimault and not expected ever to steam again. Sister *Cape Scott* (ARE 101) discarded in 1977.

RESERVE TRAINING SHIPS AND CRAFT

Note: In addition to the ships and craft listed below, the four *Mackenzie*-class frigates are used primarily for training, and the research ship *Fort Steele* is used to train Reserves. The units below retain hull numbers associated with their former functions.

The *Bay* and *Porte* classes are planned to be replaced by a new class of 46-m, 484-ton "coastal class" units that can be converted to mine countermeasures vessels through the addition of portable modules. The smaller training craft are to be replaced by 30-m, 244-ton "harbor class" craft with a diving tender capability. The first 10 of these ships were to be requested in 1985-86.

◆ **6 Bay-class former minesweepers**

	Bldr	Laid down	L	In serv.
PFL 159 Fundy	Davie S.B., Lauzon	3-55	14-6-56	27-11-56
PFL 160 Chignecto	Davie S.B., Lauzon	10-55	26-2-57	1-8-57
PFL 161 Thunder	Port Arthur S.B., Ont.	9-55	27-10-56	3-10-57
PFL 162 Cowichan	Yarrows Ltd., Victoria	7-56	26-2-57	19-12-57
PFL 163 Miramichi	Victoria Machinery	2-56	22-2-57	28-10-57
PFL 164 Chaleur	Marine Industries, Sorel	2-56	17-11-56	12-9-57

Thunder (PFL 161) 1985

D: 370 tons (415 fl) **S:** 15 kts **Dim:** 50.0 (46.05 pp) × 9.21 × 2.8
Electron Equipt: Radar: 1/Sperry Mk 2 **Electric:** 690 kw
M: 2 12-278A G.M. diesels; 2 props; 2,500 hp
Fuel: 53 tons **Range:** 4,500/11 **Man:** 3 officers, 35 men

Remarks: Reclassified as patrol escorts in 1972 and used for training reserve personnel. They took the names of minesweepers transferred to France in 1954. The *Gaspé* (143), *Comox* (146), *Ungava* (148), and *Trinity* (157) were transferred to Turkey in 1958. Hull of composite construction. One 40-mm AA removed.

◆ **5 Porte class** Bldrs: 180, 183: Davie, Lauzon; 184: Victoria Mach. & DD; 185: Burrard DD; 186: Pictou Foundry

	In serv.
YMG 180 Porte St. Jean	4-6-52
YMG 183 Porte St. Louis	28-8-52
YMG 184 Porte De La Reine	19-9-52
YMG 185 Porte Quebec	28-8-52
YMG 186 Porte Dauphine	10-12-52

Porte St. Louis (YMG 183) L. & L. Van Ginderen, 10-84

D: 300 tons (429 fl) **S:** 12 kts **Dim:** 38.0 × 8.5 × 3.9
M: 1 Fairbanks-Morse 6-cyl. diesel, electric drive; 1 prop; 600 hp
Fuel: 47 tons **Range:** 4,100/10 **Min:** 3 officers, 20 men

Remarks: Launched 1950-52. Built as auxiliary minesweepers and net tenders.

◆ **5 former Mounted Police patrol craft** (In serv. 1957-59)

PB 191 Adversus, PB 192 Detector, PB 193 Captor, PB 194 Acadian, PB 195 Sidney

Captor (PB 193) L. & L. Van Ginderen, 9-81

D: 48 tons **S:** 12 kts **Dim:** 19.8 × 4.6 × 1.2
M: 1 Cummins diesel; 410 hp **Range:** 1,000/10.5

◆ **1 former Mounted Police patrol craft** Bldr: Smith & Rhulorel, Lunenburg, N.S.

PB 196 Nicholson (In serv. 1968)

D: 85 tons (fl) **S:** 16 kts **Dim:** 36.0 × 6.4 × 2.1
M: 2 Paxman YJCM diesels; 2 CP props; 2,800 hp **Range:** 900/13
Man: 18 tot.

◆ **5 Ville-class former tugs** Bldr: Russell Bros., 1944

YTL 582 Burrard (ex-*Lawrenceville*), YTL 586 Queensville, YTL 587 Plainsville, YTL 588 Youville, YTL 589 Loganville

D: 25 tons **S:** . . . **Dim:** 12.2 × 3.2 × 1.5 **M:** 1 diesel; 150 hp

◆ **3 miscellaneous reserve training craft**

YAG 116 (18 tons) YFL 104 (102 tons) YDT 2 (70 tons)

◆ **1 sailing ketch for cadet training**

YAC 3 Oriole — Based at Esquimault

SEAGOING TUGS

◆ **2 Saint-class oceangoing tugs** Bldr: St. John DD

ATA 531 Saint Anthony (In serv. 22-2-57) ATA 532 Saint Charles (In serv. 7-6-57)

Saint Charles (ATA 532) L. & L. Van Ginderen, 4-82

D: 840 tons (1,017 fl) **S:** 14 kts **Dim:** 46.2 (40.7 pp) × 10.0 × 5.2
M: 1 Fairbanks-Morse diesel; 1 prop; 1,920 hp **Man:** 21 tot.

YARD AND SERVICE CRAFT

◆ **5 Glen-class harbor tugs** (In serv. 1975-77)

Bldrs: 640, 641: Yarrow, Esquimault; others: Georgetown SY, Prince Edward Isl.

YTB 640 Glendyne YTB 642 Glenevis YTB 644 Glenside
YTB 641 Glendale YTB 643 Glenbrook

Glenbrook (YTB 643) L. & L. Van Ginderen, 5-82

D: 255 tons (400 fl) **S:** 11.5 kts **Dim:** 28.2 × 8.5 × 3.8
M: 2 Ruston AP-3 diesels; 2 vertical cycloidal props; 1,750 hp **Man:** 6 tot.

◆ **5 new Ville-class harbor tugs** Bldr: YTL 590,591: Vito Steel & Barge Co.; others: Georgetown SY, Prince Edward Isl. (In serv. 1974)

YTL 590 Lawrenceville YTL 592 Listerville YTL 594 Marysville
YTL 591 Parksville YTL 593 Merrickville

D: 70 tons (fl) **S:** 9.8 kts **Dim:** 13.6 × 4.5 × 2.4
M: 1 diesel; 370 hp **Man:** 3 tot.

◆ **1 Wood-class harbor tug** Bldr: Falconer Marine (In serv. 1944)

YTL 553 Wildwood

D: 65 tons (fl) **S:** 10 kts **Dim:** 18.3 × 4.9 × 1.5
M: 1 diesel; 250 hp **Man:** 3 tot.

DIVING TENDERS

◆ **3 steel-hulled** Bldr: Ferguson, Pictou, N.S. (In serv. 1962-63)

YDT 10 YDT 11 YDT 12

D: 70 tons (132 fl) **S:** 11 kts **Dim:** 38.3 × 8.0 × . . .
M: 1 G.M. 6-71 diesel; 228 hp

YDT 12 1980

◆ **3 wooden-hulled**

YDT 6 YDT 8 YDT 9

D: 70 tons (fl) **Dim:** 22.9 × 5.6 × . . . **M:** 2 G.M. diesels; 2 props; 330 hp

Remarks: YDT 6 has a larger after deckhouse.

YDT 8 at Halifax G. Gyssels, 1984

FIREBOATS

◆ **2 130-ton**

YFB 561 Firebird YFB 562 Firebrand

Firebird (YFB 561) L. & L. Van Ginderen, 8-79

◆ **2 48-ton**

YFB 556 Fire Tug 1 YFB 557 Fire Tug

TORPEDO RETRIEVERS

Note: The first of a new class of 30-m, 215-ton torpedo retriever "range vessels" was to be requested in 1985-86 to replace the craft below.

◆ **2 Songhee class** Bldr: Falconer Marine (In serv. 1944)

YPT 1 Songhee YPT 120 Nimpkish

D: 162 tons (fl) **Dim:** 22.8 × . . . × . . . **M:** 2 diesels; 2 props; 400 hp

MISCELLANEOUS SERVICE CRAFT

◆ Approximately 12 self-propelled units in the categories of fuel-oil lighter, water tanker, degaussing tender, water tender, floating crane, etc., plus a number of non-self-propelled cargo and fuel barges, power barges, sludge-removal craft, etc.

Self-propelled lighter YFNL 220 L. & L. Van Ginderen, 11-81

Support barge YRC 62 L. & L. Van Ginderen, 5-82

COAST GUARD

Created in 1972 from a number of government agencies, the Canadian Coast Guard is a civilian organization in the Federal Transportation Ministry. It mans some 150 ships, 20 icebreakers, and 34 helicopters.

Canadian icebreakers and major service ships are broken down into the following categories:

Type	Designation	Ice-thickness	No. in service
1500	Polar Icebreaker	3-m	0
1400	Sub-Polar Icebreaker	1.6-m	0
1300	Heavy Gulf Icebreaker	1.2-m	1
1200	River Icebreaker	0.7-m	7(+1)
1100	Light Icebreaker/Navaids Tender	20-40-ton*	11(+6)
1050	Navaids Tender	15-ton*	0(+2)
1000	Ice-Strengthened Navaids Tender	10-20-ton*	13
900	Small Ice-Strengthened Navaids Tender	5-10-tons*	5
800	Small Navaids Tender	2-5-ton*	7
700	Special River Navaids Tender	5-10-ton*	5
600	Large Search & Rescue Cutter	—	6
500	Intermediate Search & Rescue Cutter	—	1
400	Small Search & Rescue Cutter	—	10
300	Search & Rescue Lifeboat	—	16
200	Small Search & Rescue Cutter	—	0
100	Small Search & rescue Craft	—	9

* Buoy derrick capacity

Aviation: The Canadian Coast Guard operates one Douglas DC-3 transport and 28 helicopters: 1 Sikorsky S-61N, 3 Alouette-III, 5 Bell 212, 10 Bell 206B, 7 Bell 206L, and 2 MBB BO-105CBS.

POLAR ICEBREAKERS (Type 1500)

◆ 0 (+1) Polar 8 Project Bldr: . . .

N. . . (In serv. mid-1990s)

Polar 8—artist's impression Official, 1984

D: 37,738 tons (fl) **S:** 15 kts **Dim:** 194.0 × 32.3 × 12.2
M: CODAGE: 2 gas turbines, 4 diesel generator sets; 3 props; 100,000 hp
Range: 30,000/. . . **Man:** 175 tot.

Remarks: Design project assigned to Burrard-Yarrows SB, but St. Johns also bidding to build. Funding still delays this oft-postponed project to build the world's most powerful icebreaker. Intended to break 2.45-in ice in continuous steaming or up to 20-in ice by ramming.

HEAVY GULF ICEBREAKERS (Type 1300)

◆ 1 turbo-electric drive

	Bldr	L	In serv.
Louis S. St. Laurent	Canadian Vickers, Montreal	3-6-66	8-69

Louis S. St. Laurent L. & L. Van Ginderen, 3-82

D: 14,509 tons (fl) **S:** 17.7 kts **Dim:** 111.70 (101.80 pp) × 24.38 × 9.45
Electron Equipt: Radar: 2/Kelvin-Hughes 14-12, 1/Kelvin-Hughes 14-9
M: 3 sets GT, electric drive; 3 props; 24,000 hp
Electric: 4,300 kw **Boilers:** 4 Babcock & Wilcox; 42.2 kg/cm², 449°C
Fuel: 3,632 tons **Range:** 16,000/13 **Man:** 81 tot.

Remarks: 10,907 grt. Accommodations for 216 total. Two helicopters with hangar below flight deck served by an elevator. Flume passive stabilization tanks. Carries two 15.2-m stores landing craft. Operates off Maritime Provinces. Serious fire 3-82.

RIVER ICEBREAKERS (Type 1200)

◆ 0 (+ 1) new construction Bldr: Burrard Yarrows, . . .

	Region	L	In serv.
N. . .	. . .	. . .	7-87

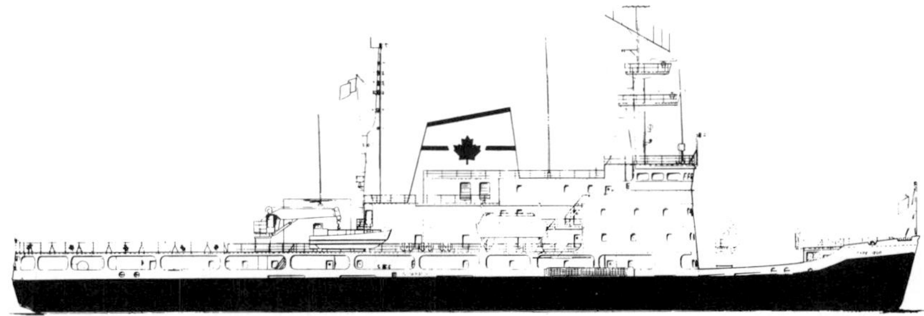

New Type 1200 icebreaker Burrard Yarrows Corp.

D: 8,290 tons (fl) **S:** 16.5 **Dim:** 99.80 × 19.70 × 7.24
Electron Equipt: Radar: 2/nav.
M: Diesel-electric, 2 props; 16,000 hp
Fuel: . . . **Range:** 15,000/13.5 **Man:** 72 tot. accommodations

Remarks: Ordered 25-5-84. Design based on *Pierre Radisson* class. 5,910 grt. Will be based on Atlantic Coast.

◆ 3 Pierre Radisson river icebreakers

	Bldr	Region	L	In serv.
Pierre Radisson	Burrard DD, Vancouver	Laurentian	3-6-77	1978
Sir John Franklin	Burrard DD, Vancouver	Newfoundland	10-3-78	1980
Des Groseilliers	Port Weller DD, Ont.	Laurentian	20-2-82	7-8-82

D: 6,400 tons (7,721 fl) **S:** 16.2 kts **Dim:** 98.15 (87.90 pp) × 19.50 × 7.16
Electron Equipt: Radar: 1/TR-611-1, 1/TR-311-S1 **Electric:** 2,250 kw
M: Diesel-electric: 6 Montreal Loco MLW 251V-16F diesels (17,580 hp total); 6 G.E.C. alternators (11,100 kw); 2 G.E.C. motors; 2 props; 13,600 hp
Fuel: 2,215 tons **Range:** 15,000/13.5 **Man:** 55 tot. (76 accomm.)

Remarks: 5,910 grt/2,820 dwt; 440 m³ cargo capacity. *Franklin:* 6,100 grt, range: 16,500/135. Bow-thruster-equipped. Telescopic hangar and flight deck for one Bell-212 helicopter. Passive-tank stabilization. Used on St. Lawrence River and Great Lakes in winter, in Arctic in summer. Third unit ordered 1981.

RIVER ICEBREAKERS *(continued)*

Des Groseilliers L. & L. Van Ginderen, 6-84

◆ **1 river icebreaker**

NORMAN MCLEOD ROGERS Bldr: Vickers, Montreal (In serv. 6-69)

Norman McLeod Rogers L. & L. Van Ginderen, 4-82

D: 6,506 tons (fl) **S:** 16.5 kts **Dim:** 89.92 (81.10 pp) × 19.05 × 6.10
Electron Equipt: Radar: 2/Kelvin-Hughes 14/12
M: CODAG: 4 Fairbanks-Morse 12-cyl., 2,000-hp diesels; 2 G.E. W-41G, 4,400-hp gas turbines; electric drive; 2 props; 13,200 hp
Electric: 1,615 kw **Fuel:** 1,095 tons **Range:** 12,000/12
Cargo: 900 tons **Man:** 55 tot.

REMARKS: 4,179 grt/2,320 dwt. Also navigation tender. One helicopter, telescoping hangar. Operates in Laurentian Region.

◆ **1 cable-laying river icebreaker** Bldr: Vickers, Montreal

JOHN CABOT (In serv. 31-5-65)

John Cabot 1969

D: 4,180 tons light (6,502 fl) **S:** 15 kts **Dim:** 95.50 (84.13 pp) × 18.29 × 6.73
Electron Equipt: Radar: 1/Decca 969, 1/Decca 2400
M: 4 Fairbanks-Morse 38D8-12 diesels, electric drive; 2 props; 9,000 hp
Electric: 1,060 kw **Fuel:** 719 tons
Range: 10,000/12 **Man:** 79 tot.

REMARKS: 5,097 grt/2,220 dwt. Carries 400 miles of cable in 3 tanks. Flume passive stabilization and heeling tanks, telescoping helo hangar, 1,000 hp bow-thruster, 70-ton towing winch (50-ton bollard pull). Operates in Newfoundland Region.

◆ **1 river icebreaker** Bldr: Davie SB, Lauzon, Que.

JOHN A. MACDONALD (In serv. 9-60)

D: 9,307 tons (fl) **S:** 15.5 kts **Dim:** 96.01 (88.40 pp) × 21.30 × 8.58
M: 9 Fairbanks-Morse 38D8⅛ diesels, electric drive; 3 props; 15,000 hp
Fuel: 2,245 tons **Range:** 20,000/10 **Man:** 80 tot.

REMARKS: 6,186 grt/3,380 dwt. Three helicopters, fixed hangar. 221-m³ cargo space. Four stores landing craft. Operates in Maritime Provinces Region.

John A. MacDonald L. & L. Van Ginderen, 10-82

◆ **1 river icebreaker** Bldr: Marine Ind., Sorel, Que.

	Laid down	L	In serv.
LABRADOR	18-11-49	14-12-51	8-7-54

D: 3,500 tons (7,051 fl) **S:** 16 kts **Dim:** 81.99 (76.2 pp) × 19.44 × 9.30
M: 6 Fairbanks-Morse 38D8⅛ diesels, electric drive; 2 props; 10,000 hp
Fuel: 2,641 tons **Range:** 23,000/12 **Man:** 85 tot.

REMARKS: 3,823 grt. Patterned on U.S. Coast Guard "Wind" class. Transferred from Canadian Navy 2-58. Heeling tanks, telescoping helicopter hangar. Operates in Maritime Region.

LIGHT ICEBREAKER/NAVIGATIONAL AIDS TENDERS (Type 1100)

◆ **0 (+ 6) new construction**

	Bldr	Laid down	L	In serv.
MARTHA L. BLACK	Burrard Yarrows, Vancouver, B.C.	3-84	. . .	2-86
GEORGE R. PEARKES	Burrard Yarrows, Victoria, B.C.	3-84	. . .	5-86
ANN HARVEY	Halifax SY	1984	. . .	10-86
SIR WILLIAM ALEXANDER	Marine Industries, Sorel, Que.	. . .	. . .	9-86
EDWARD CORNWALLIS	Marine Industries, Sorel, Que.	. . .	. . .	12-86
SIR WILFRID LAURIER	Collingwood SY, . . .	. . .	. . .	7-86

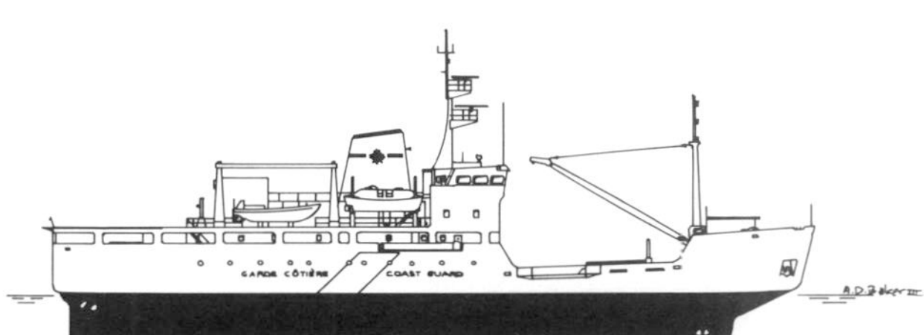

Type 1100 icebreaker A.D. Baker III

D: 3,140 tons light (4,662 fl) **S:** 15.3 kts **Dim:** 83.00 (75.00 pp) × 16.20 × 5.75
Electron Equipt: Radars: 2/nav.
M: Diesel-electric: 3 Bombardier/Alco 12V-251 diesels (2,950-hp each) 3 Can. G.E. generators, 2,000 kw each, 2 Can. G.E. motors; 2 props; 8,000 hp—bow-thruster
Fuel: 693 tons **Range:** 6,500 + /15 **Man:** 44 (+ 6 spare accom.)

REMARKS: 1,950 grt/1,522 dwt. Will carry one Bell 212 helicopter. Cargo capacity is 400 tons in forward hold, 50 tons aft. Carry 670 tons water ballast. Construction of pair assigned to Marine Industries delayed by strike.

◆ GRIFFON Bldr: Davie SB, Lauzon, Que (In serv. 12-70)

Griffon L. & L. Van Ginderen, 8-78

LIGHT ICEBREAKERS/NAVIGATIONAL AIDS TENDERS *(continued)*

D: 2,959 tons (fl) **S:** 14.0 kts **Dim:** 71.32 × 14.94 × 4.73
Electron Equipt: Radar: 2/Kelvin-Hughes 14-12 **Electric:** 422 kw
M: 4 Fairbanks-Morse 38D8⅛-8 diesels, electric drive; 2 props; 4,000 hp
Fuel: 345 tons **Range:** 5,500/11 **Man:** 38 tot.

REMARKS: 160-ton cargo capacity. Flume passive tank stabilization. Helicopter landing platform, no hangar; 10- and 20-ton buoy derricks. Plans were announced during 1982 to order two similar ships. Operates in Central Region (Great Lakes).

◆ J.E. BERNIER Bldr: Davie SB, Lauzon, Que (In serv. 8-67)

J. E. Bernier—with hangar extended L. & L. Van Ginderen, 12-84

D: 3,150 tons (fl) **S:** 13.5 kts **Dim:** 70.48 (64.62 pp) × 14.94 × 4.91
Electron Equipt: Radar: Kelvin-Hughes; 1/14-12, 1/14-9
M: 2 diesels, electric drive; 2 props; 4,250 hp **Fuel:** 450 tons
Range: 8,000/11 **Man:** 37 tot.

REMARKS: Similar to *Griffon* and *Montcalm* class, but thinner plating. Has telescoping helo hangar. Flume passive stabilization tanks. Operates in Laurentian Region.

◆ NARWHAL Bldr: Canadian Vickers, Montreal (In serv. 7-63)

D: 2,222 tons (fl) **S:** 12 kts **Dim:** 76.66 (69.80 pp) × 12.80 × 3.75
M: 2 Cooper-Bessemer direct-drive diesels, fluid couplings; 2 props; 2,000 hp
Electric: 796 kw **Fuel:** 399 tons
Range: 9,200/11 **Man:** 35 tot.

REMARKS: 2,064 grt/697 dwt. Originally typed "Depot Ship/Lighthouse and Buoy Tender; and intended for summer use as an Arctic supply ship carrying 60 stevedores, 20 stores landing craft crew, and 20 administrators. During rest of year, based at Dartmouth, N.S. Has 40-ton buoy derrick. Mid-life refit at Halifax Shipyard, 1984-85: helicopter deck and telescoping hangar added, new engines.

◆ WOLFE Bldr: Canadian Vickers, Montreal (In serv. 11-59)

Wolfe—note telescoping hangar and stores landing craft 1969

D: 2,207 tons (fl) **S:** 13 kts **Dim:** 76.94 (67.16 pp) × 14.71 × 4.98
M: 2 sets 4-cylinder, triple-expansion reciprocating steam; 2 props; 4,000 hp
Boilers: 2 Babcock & Wilcox; 16.5 kg/cm², 288°C
Fuel: 997 tons **Range:** 6,000/10 **Man:** 43 tot.

REMARKS: Longer version of *Montcalm:* 2,022 grt. Operates in Western Region. Two 9.1-m landing craft, telescoping helo hangar, 25-ton buoy boom.

◆ CAMSELL Bldr: Burrard DD, Vancouver (In serv. 10-59)

D: 3,150 tons (fl) **S:** 13.5 kts **Dim:** 68.15 (61.53 pp) × 14.63 × 4.88
M: 2 diesels, electric drive; 2 props; 4,250 hp **Fuel:** 536 tons
Range: 12,000/11 **Man:** 42 tot.

REMARKS: 2,022 grt. Based at Vancouver, B.C. Used in lighthouse supply work. Telescoping helicopter hangar.

◆ ALEXANDER HENRY Bldr: Port Arthur SB, Port Arthur, Ont. (In serv. 7-59)

Alexander Henry L. & L. Van Ginderen, 7-84

D: 3,195 tons (fl) **S:** 13 kts **Dim:** 64.01 × 13.26 × 5.86
M: Diesels, electric drive; 2 props; 3,550 hp **Fuel:** 387 tons
Range: 6,000/12 **Man:** 34 tot.

REMARKS: 1,674 grt. Based on Lake Ontario at Parry Sound. Has two 9.1-m stores landing craft, helicopter deck but no hangar; 20-ton derrick.

◆ SIR HUMPHREY GILBERT Bldr: Davie SB, Lauzon, Que (In serv. 6-59)

D: 3,053 tons (fl) **S:** 13 kts **Dim:** 67.06 (61.53 pp) × 14.63 × 4.98
M: 2 diesels, electric drive; 4,250 hp **Fuel:** 552 tons
Range: 10,000/11 **Man:** 40 tot.

REMARKS: 1,931 grt. Home-ported at Quebec City. 25-ton buoy derrick. Telescoping helicopter hangar. No landing craft. Refitted 1984 at Halifax SY, with new bow, Wärtsilä bubbler system.

◆ SIR WILLIAM ALEXANDER Bldr: Halifax SY (In serv. 6-59)

Sir William Alexander—hangar extended L. & L. Van Ginderen, 12-82

D: 3,607 tons **S:** 13.5 kts **Dim:** 83.06 × 13.72 × 5.33
M: 2 diesels, electric drive; 2 props; 4,250 hp **Fuel:** 563 tons
Range: 12,000/12.5 **Man:** 41 tot.

REMARKS: 2,154 grt/1,610 dwt. Based at Dartmouth, Nova Scotia. Carries two 9.1-m stores landing craft. Helo deck, no hangar. 20-ton buoy boom.

◆ MONTCALM Bldr: Davie SB, Lauzon, Que. (In serv. 7-3-57)

D: 2,094 tons **S:** 13 kts **Dim:** 67.16 × 14.71 × 4.98
M: 2 sets Vickers-Skinner Uniflow 4-cyl., triple-expansion reciprocating steam; 2 props; 4,000 hp
Boilers: 2 Babcock & Wilcox; 16.5 kg/cm², 288°C **Fuel:** 571 tons
Range: 4,000/10 **Man:** 45 tot.

REMARKS: 2,017 grt. Based at Quebec City. Telescoping helicopter hangar, two 9.1-m stores landing craft, 25-ton buoy derrick.

◆ WALTER E. FOSTER Bldr: Canadian Vickers, Montreal (In serv. 12-54)

D: 2,907 tons (fl) **S:** 12.5 kts **Dim:** 69.85 × 12.95 × 5.03
M: 2 sets Vickers-Skinner Uniflow 4-cyl., triple-expansion reciprocating steam; 2 props; 2,000 hp
Boilers: 2 **Fuel:** 482 tons **Range:** 3,000/11 **Man:** 43 tot.

REMARKS: 1,672 grt. Based at St. John, Newfoundland. No helo facilities.

◆ EDWARD CORNWALLIS Bldr: Canadian Vickers, Montreal (In serv. 12-49)

LIGHT ICEBREAKERS/NAVIGATIONAL AIDS TENDERS *(continued)*

Walter E. Foster 1969

Edward Cornwallis L. & L. Van Ginderen, 3-80

D: 3,996 tons (fl) **S:** 13.5 kts **Dim:** 78.94 (73.15 pp) × 13.26 × 5.51
M: 2 sets Vickers-Skinner Uniflow 4-cyl., triple-expansion reciprocating; 2 props; 2,800 hp
Boilers: 2, Scotch **Fuel:** 589 tons **Range:** 7,500/12.5 **Man:** 43 tot.

REMARKS: 1,965 grt/1,800 dwt. In reserve at Dartmouth, N.S. since 1969, but was reactivated 1980 with helicopter deck replacing cargo facilities aft. To scrap 1986.

NAVIGATIONAL AIDS TENDERS (Type 1050)

◆ **2 Samuel Risley class**

	Bldr	L	In serv.
SAMUEL RISLEY	VITO Corp., Vancouver	. . .	4-85
EARL GREY	Ferguson Ind., Pictou, N.S.	. . .	12-85

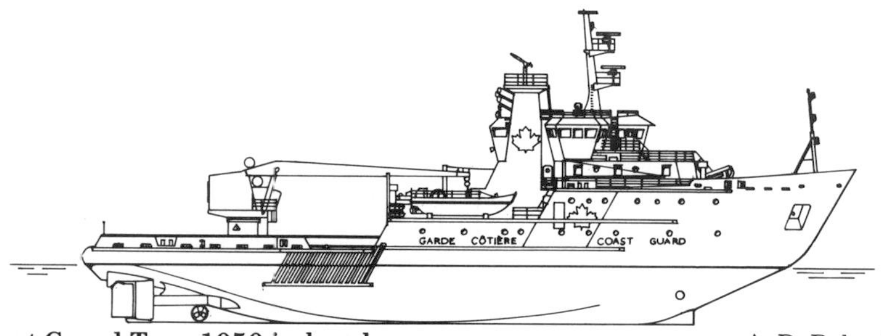

Coast Guard Type 1050 icebreaker A. D. Baker III

D: 2,935 tons (fl) **S:** 12 kts **Dim:** 69.73 × 13.70 × 5.20
Electron Equipt: Radar
M: 4 Bombardier/Wärtsilä diesels; 2 Kort nozzle CP props; 8,800 hp — 750-hp bow-thruster — 400-hp stern-thruster
Fuel: . . . tons **Range:** . . . **Man:** 31

REMARKS: Design based on offshore supply vessel technology. Able to break 0.6 m ice. Computerized directional control. Buoy crane capacity 15 ton at 8.0 m radius/8.5 tons at 20 m. Two fire monitors produce 600 m³/hr to 75 m range

ICE-STRENGTHENED NAVIGATIONAL AIDS TENDERS (Type 1000)

◆ **2 Provo Wallis class** Bldr: Marine Industries, Sorel, Que.

PROVO WALLIS (In serv. 10-69) BARTLETT (In serv. 12-69)

D: 1,722 tons (fl) **S:** 12.5 kts **Dim:** 57.68 × 12.95 × 3.66
Electron Equipt: Radar: 2/Kelvin-Hughes 14-12
M: 2 direct-drive diesels; 2 CP props; 1,760 hp **Fuel:** 102 tons
Range: 3,300/11 **Man:** 29 tot.

REMARKS: 1,313 grt. Carry one 9.1-m landing craft. Have 15-ton derrick. *P. Wallis* based at St. John's, *Bartlett* at Dartmouth, N.S. *P. Wallis* crew: 30 tot.

Provo Wallis L. & L. Van Ginderen, 7-77

◆ TRACY Bldr: Port Weller DD, Ltd. (In serv. 17-4-68)

Tracy L. & L. Van Ginderen, 1-84

D: 1,320 tons (fl) **S:** 13 kts **Dim:** 55.17 (50.29 pp) × 11.58 × 3.66
Electron Equipt: Radar: 1/Kelvin-Hughes 14-12 **Electric:** 402 kw
M: 2 Fairbanks-Morse 38D8⅛-8 diesels, electric drive; 2 props; 2,000 hp
Fuel: 131 tons **Range:** 5,000/11.5 **Man:** 30 tot.

REMARKS: 960 grt. Based at Sorel, Quebec.

◆ MONTMAGNY Bldr: Russell Bros., Owen Sound, Ont. (In serv. 5-63)

Montmagny L. & L. Van Ginderen, 12-81

D: 625 tons (fl) **S:** 12 kts **Dim:** 45.11 × 8.84 × 2.59
M: 2 Werkspoor diesels; 2 props; 1,048 hp **Fuel:** 48 tons
Range: 4,000/10 **Man:** 22 tot.

REMARKS: 497 grt. Based at Sorel, Quebec. One 7-ton derrick.

◆ NICOLET Bldr: Collingwood SY, Collingwood, Ont. (In serv. 12-66)

D: 901 tons (fl) **S:** 13 kts **Dim:** 51.74 × 11.10 × 3.05
Electron Equipt: Radar: 1/Kelvin-Hughes 14-9
M: 2 diesels; 2 props; 1,350 hp **Fuel:** 76 tons
Range: 3,000/10 **Man:** 26 tot.

REMARKS: 887 grt. Based at Sorel, Que., for use as a hydraulic survey and soundings ship on the St. Lawrence Ship Channel. An updated *Beauport.*

ICE-STRENGTHENED NAVIGATIONAL AIDS TENDERS *(continued)*

Nicolet L. & L. Van Ginderen, 6-84

◆ SIMCOE Bldr: Canadian Vickers, Montreal (In serv. 1962)

D: 1,392 tons (fl) **S:** 13 kts **Dim:** 54.62 × 11.58 × 3.83
M: 2 diesels, electric drive; 2 props; 2,000 hp **Fuel:** 156 tons
Range: 5,000/10 **Man:** 34 tot.

REMARKS: 961 grt. Based on Lake Ontario at Prescott.

◆ THOMAS CARLTON Bldr: St. John's DD (In serv. 1960)

D: 1,636 tons (fl) **S:** 12 kts **Dim:** 50.84 × 12.83 × 4.15
M: 2 diesels, electric drive; 2 props; 2,900 hp **Fuel:** 178 tons
Range: 2,200/11 **Man:** 38 tot.

REMARKS: 1,217-grt. Home-ported at St. John, New Brunswick. Helicopter platform, no hangar; has 20-ton buoy derrick.

◆ BEAUPORT Bldr: Davie SB, Lauzon, Que. (In serv. 1960)

Beauport—broad bow, like Nicolet L. & L. Van Ginderen, 7-82

D: 789 tons (fl) **S:** 13 kts **Dim:** 51.05 × 10.36 × 2.74
Electron Equipt: Radar: 1/LN-47 **M:** 2 diesels; 2 props; 1,280 hp
Fuel: 63 tons **Range:** 3,000/10 **Man:** 26 tot.

REMARKS: 813 grt. Based at Sorel, Que., as a hydraulic survey and soundings ship on the St. Lawrence Ship Channel. 8-ton electric buoy crane.

◆ SIMON FRASER Bldr: Burrard DD, Vancouver (In serv. 2-60)

Simon Fraser L. & L. Van Ginderen, 12-79

D: 1,375 tons (fl) **S:** 13.5 kts **Dim:** 62.26 × 12.80 × 4.27
M: 2 diesels, electric drive; 2 props; 2,900 hp **Fuel:** 178 tons
Range: 5,000/10 **Man:** 38 tot.

REMARKS: 1,352 grt. Based at Quebec City. Helicopter deck and telescoping hangar. Very similar to *Tupper.* Refitted at Versatile Vickers SY, Montreal, 1985

◆ TUPPER Bldr: Marine Ind., Sorel, Que. (In serv. 12-59)

D: 1,380 tons (fl) **S:** 13.5 kts **Dim:** 62.36 × 12.80 × 4.23
M: 2 diesels, electric drive; 2 props; 2,900 hp **Fuel:** 206 tons
Range: 5,000/11 **Man:** 37 tot.

REMARKS: 1,358 grt. Based at Charlottetown, Prince Edward Isl. Helicopter deck, no hangar. 15-ton buoy derrick.

◆ MONTMORENCY Bldr: Davie SB, Lauzon, Que. (In serv. 8-57)

D: 980 tons (fl) **S:** 12 kts **Dim:** 50.14 × 9.75 × 3.35
M: 2 diesels; 2 props; 1,200 hp **Fuel:** 142 tons
Range: 3,500/11 **Man:** 30 tot.

REMARKS: 751 grt. Operates on Lake Huron, from Parry Sound. 12-ton buoy derrick.

◆ **2 Alexander McKenzie class** Bldr: Burrard DD, Vancouver, B.C.

ALEXANDER MCKENZIE (In serv. 1950) SIR JAMES DOUGLAS (In serv. 11-56)

D: 768 tons (fl) **S:** 11.5 kts **Dim:** 46.00 × 9.22 × 3.17
M: 2 diesels; 2 props; 1,000 hp **Fuel:** 86 tons
Range: 6,000/10.5 **Man:** 29 tot.

REMARKS: *McKenzie:* 560 grt; based at Dartmouth, N.S., since 1982. *Douglas:* 564 grt; based at Prince Rupert, British Columbia. 10-ton buoy boom. *Douglas* is 45.87 o.a. by 9.45 beam; range: 5,500/10.5 on 89 tons fuel. Both soon to be stricken.

SMALL ICE-STRENGTHENED NAVIGATIONAL AIDS TENDERS (Type 900)

◆ NAMAO Bldr: Riverton Boatwks, Manitoba (In serv. 1975)

D: 386 tons (fl) **S:** 12 kts **Dim:** 33.53 × 8.53 × 2.13
M: 2 diesels; 2 props; 1,350 hp **Fuel:** 34.5 tons **Range:** 2,000/11
Man: 10 tot.

REMARKS: Employed as buoy tender on Lake Winnepeg.

◆ ROBERT FOULIS Bldr: St. John DD, N.B. (In serv. 24-11-69)

D: 332 tons (fl) **S:** 11 kts **Dim:** 31.70 × 7.62 × 2.44
M: 2 diesels; 2 props; 960 hp **Fuel:** 21 tons **Range:** 1,500/10 **Man:** 12 tot.

REMARKS: 258 grt. Employed on St. John River, New Brunswick.

◆ KENOKI Bldr: Erieu Dry Dock, Frien, Ont. (In serv. 5-64)

Kenoki—with pilings retracted 1969

D: 274 tons (438 fl) **S:** 10.5 kts **Dim:** 33.22 × 9.75 × 1.85
Electron Equipt: Radar: 1/Kelvin-Hughes 14-9 **M:** 2 diesels; 2 props; 800 hp
Fuel: 40 tons **Range:** 1,000/10 **Man:** 12 tot.

REMARKS: 310 grt. Barge-like hull with four hydraulic pilings for precise positioning while working as a shallow-water buoy tender. Two 5-ton cranes. Based at Prescott, Ont.

◆ SKIDEGATE Bldr: Burrard Dry Dock, Vancouver, B.C. (In serv. 4-64)

Skidegate 1969

SMALL ICE-STRENGTHENED NAVIGATIONAL AIDS TENDERS *(continued)*

D: 203 tons (fl) **S:** 11.5 kts **Dim:** 26.59 × 6.73 × 2.44
M: 2 Cummins V-12 diesels; 2 props; 680 hp **Fuel:** 22 tons
Range: 2,350/10 **Man:** 11 tot.

REMARKS: 136 grt. Based at Prince Rupert, B.C.

◆ VERENDRYE Bldr: Davie SB, Lauzon, Que. (In serv. 10-59)

D: 406 tons (fl) **S:** 10 kts **Dim:** 36.40 × 7.95 × 3.05
M: 2 diesels; 2 props; 760 hp **Fuel:** 28 tons **Range:** 2,000/9.5 **Man:** 20 tot.

REMARKS: 297 grt. Based at Sorel, Que., for use on St. Lawrence Ship Channel. 6-ton electrohydraulic buoy crane.

SMALL NAVIGATIONAL AIDS TENDERS (type 800)

◆ **2 Partridge Island class** Bldr: Breton Industrial, Hawkesbury, N.S.

PARTRIDGE ISLAND (In serv. 6-85) ÎLE DES BARQUES (In serv. 1985)

D: . . . **S:** . . . **Dim:** . . . × . . . × . . .
M: Diesels; . . . props; . . . hp **Man:** . . . tot.

REMARKS: *Partridge Island* based at St. John Newf.; *Île des Barques* operates in the Laurentian Region.

◆ **2 Cove Isle class** Bldr: Canadian Dredge & Dock, Kingston, Ont.

COVE ISLE (In serv. 1980) GULL ISLE (In serv. 1980)

D: 116 tons (fl) **S:** 10 kts **Dim:** 20.00 × 6.00 × 1.35
M: 2 diesels; 2 props; 470 hp **Range:** 2,500/8 **Man:** 5 tot.
Fuel: 20.5 tons

REMARKS: Both operate on Great Lakes, in Central Region.

◆ F. G. OSBOURNE (In serv. 1974)—workboat

D: . . . tons **S:** 8 kts **Dim:** 15.85 × 5.18 × 1.22
M: Diesels; . . . hp **Man:** 4 tot.

◆ JEAN BOURDON Bldr: Kingston SY, Ont. (In serv. 5-68)

Jean Bourdon L. & L. Van Ginderen, 7-82

D: 84 tons (fl) **S:** 10.5 kts **Dim:** 20.60 × 6.10 × 1.67
Electron Equipt: Radar: 1/Raytheon 1405A
M: 2 diesels; 2 props; 340 hp **Electric:** 30 kw **Fuel:** 4.8 tons
Range: 750/10 **Man:** 4 tot.

REMARKS: 82.2 grt. For hydrographic survey work on the St. Lawrence Ship Channel; based at Sorel, Que.

◆ NOMAD V (In serv. 1966)

D: . . . tons **S:** 7 kts **Dim:** 12.80 × 4.27 × 1.22 **M:** Diesels; . . . hp

◆ NOKOMIS Bldr: Lunenberg Foundry (In serv. 1957)

D: 65 tons (fl) **S:** 9.5 kts **Dim:** 20.24 × 5.33 × 2.16
M: 1 diesel; 120 hp **Fuel:** 4.1 tons **Range:** 650/9 **Man:** 4 tot.

REMARKS: 64 grt. Based at Parry Sound, Lake Huron.

◆ BARGE 501 (In serv. . . .)

D: 56 tons (fl) **S:** 10 kts **Dim:** 17.07 × 4.37 × 1.17
M: 2 Gray Marine 64 HN9 diesels; 2 props; 330 hp
Range: 130/10 **Man:** 4 tot.

REMARKS: Former U.S. Navy LCM (6) landing craft, used on Great Lakes for survey work. Was offered for sale in 1982, but was still on official list 9-84.

SPECIAL RIVER NAVIGATIONAL AIDS TENDERS (Type 700)

NOTE: All below serve in the Western Region, mostly on the Mackenzie River, Northwest Territories.

◆ DUMIT Bldr: Allied SB, Vancouver, B.C. (In serv. 7-79)

D: 628 tons (fl) **S:** 12 kts **Dim:** 48.80 × 12.20 × 1.64
M: Diesel-electric; . . . props; 1,140 hp
Fuel: 175 tons **Range:** 9,000/10 **Man:** 10 tot.

◆ NAHIDIK Bldr: Allied SB, Vancouver, B.C. (In serv. 1974)

D: 1,122 tons (fl) **S:** 14 kts **Dim:** 53.35 × 15.24 × 1.98
M: Diesel electric: 2 diesels; 2 props; 4,360 hp
Fuel: 331 tons **Range:** 1,000/11 **Man:** 15 tot.

◆ TEMBAH Bldr: Allied SB, Vancouver (In serv. 9-63)

D: 181 tons (fl) **S:** 13 kts **Dim:** 37.51 × 7.92 × 0.91
M: 2 diesels; 2 props; 680 hp **Fuel:** 21 tons **Range:** 1,000/11 **Man:** 9 tot.

◆ ECKALOO Bldr: Allied SB, Vancouver, B.C. (In serv. 1961)

D: 135 tons (fl) **S:** 10 kts **Dim:** 25.26 × 6.71 × 1.22
M: 2 diesels; 2 props; 600 hp **Fuel:** 17.3 tons **Range:** 600/9.5 **Man:** 9 tot.

◆ **1 Dumit class** Bldr: Allied SB, Vancouver, B.C. (In serv. 1958)

MISKANAW (operates on the Hay River)

D: 99.6 tons (fl) **S:** 10 kts **Dim:** 19.51 × 5.97 × 1.22
M: 2 diesels; 2 props; 300 hp **Fuel:** 9.9 tons **Range:** 300/9.5 **Man:** 9 tot.

LARGE SEARCH AND RESCUE CUTTERS (Type 600)

◆ **1 modified offshore anchor-handling vessel** Bldr: Marystown SY, Marystown, N.S.

	Laid down	L	In serv.
MARY HICHENS (ex-*Beau Bois*)	23-5-83	5-11-83	31-3-84

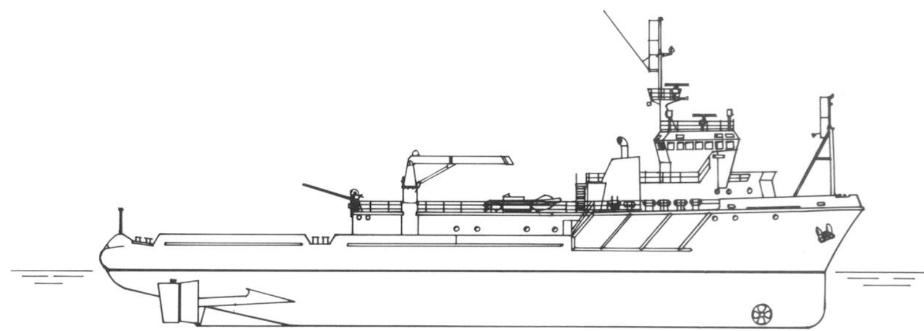

Mary Hitchens

D: 3,262 tons (fl) **S:** 15 kts **Dim:** 64.40 (56.40 pp) × 13.80 × 5.91
M: 2 B & W Alpha 14-U28L-VO diesels; 2 Kort-nozzle CP props; 7,420 hp—bow-thruster
Fuel: . . . tons **Range:** 8,000/15
Man: 7 officers, 2 cadets, 10 men, and up to 85 survivors

REMARKS: Ulstein Type 704 oilfield supply-tug design purchased on completion. Based at Dartmouth, N.S. Carries 8,000 liters foam concentrate and fire monitors. Can pump 5,000 lit./min. Two 6.7-m rigid inflatable rescue boats. Tank stabilization.

◆ **1 former oilfield supply tug** Bldr: Bel-Aire SY, North Vancouver, B.C. (In serv. 1972)

GEORGES A. DARBY (ex-. . .)

D: 2,204 tons (fl) **Dim:** 56.08 × 13.72 × 4.72
M: 2 Ruston diesels; 2 props; 4,380 hp **Range:** 6,500/11.5 **Man:** 16 tot.

REMARKS: Purchased 1-82 and refitted for Coast Guard at Vancouver for Pacific service. 885 grt. Similar to *Grenfell.*

◆ **2 former oilfield supply ships** Bldr: Bel-Aire SY, North Vancouver, B.C.

GRENFELL (ex-M/V *Baffin Service,* ex-*Nordic V*) (In serv. 8-73)
JACKMAN (ex-M/V *Hudson Service,* ex-*Nordic IV*) (In serv. 8-73)

Grenfell L. & L. Van Ginderen, 1981

LARGE SEARCH AND RESCUE CUTTERS *(continued)*

D: 2,106 tons (fl) **S:** 13 kts **Dim:** 56.10 (51.94 pp) × 13.70 × 4.42
M: 4 G.M. 16-565C diesels; 2 props; 6,400 hp **Electric:** 360 kw
Fuel: 587 tons **Range:** 6,500/12 **Man:** 16 tot.

REMARKS: 877 grt/452 dwt. Acquired from Nordic Offshore Services in 1979 and based at St. Johns, Newfoundland. Typical oilfield supply tugs with long, low, open cleared fantail. Main engines built 1950, rebuilt in 1972 for shipboard use. Ice-strengthened hulls. *Grenfell:* 2,113 tons, 457 tons fuel

◆ ALERT Bldr: Davie SB, Lauzon, Que. (In serv. 20-11-69)

Alert L. & L. Van Ginderen, 12-82

D: 2,164 tons (fl) **S:** 18.7 kts **Dim:** 71.40 × 12.12 × 4.94
M: 2 diesels; electric drive; 2 props; 9,716 hp **Range:** 6,000/14.5
Fuel: 275 tons **Man:** 38 tot.

REMARKS: 1,752 grt. Was to have been a class of six. Telescoping hangar for helicopter. Operates in Atlantic.

NOTE: Type 600 rescue cutler *Daring* (ex-R.C.M.P. *Wood*) was stricken 1985, having been replaced by *Mary Hichens.*

INTERMEDIATE SEARCH AND RESCUE CUTTERS (Type 500)

◆ VILLE MARIE Bldr: Russell-Hipwell Eng., Owen Sound, Ont. (In serv. 1960)

Ville Marie L. & L. Van Ginderen, 6-84

D: 518 tons (fl) **S:** 13.5 kts **Dim:** 40.92 × 8.71 × 2.24
M: 2 diesels; 2 props; 1,000 hp **Fuel:** 50 tons **Range:** 1,000/13 **Man:** 23 tot.

REMARKS: 390 grt. Also used as soundings boat for St. Lawrence Ship Channel, based at Sorel, Que.

SMALL SEARCH AND RESCUE CUTTERS (Type 400)

◆ **1 or more new construction**

REMARKS: No data available, except that they have Kevlar plastic hulls, and one will operate in the Central Region (Great Lakes).

◆ **4 Point Henry class** Bldr: Breton Industry & Machinery, Point Hawkesbury, N.S.

CG 123 POINT HENRY CG 125 POINT RACE
CG 124 ÎLE ROUGE CG 126 CAPE HURD

D: 77 tons (97 fl) **S:** 24 kts **Dim:** 21.30 × 5.50 × 1.70
M: 2 MTU 8V396 TC2 diesels; 2 props; 1,300 hp
Fuel: 7 tons **Range:** 1,000/12 **Man:** 5 tot.

REMARKS: CG 123, 125 proceeded from Nova Scotia to the Pacific Coast under own power. CG 126 based in Central Region, CG 124 in Laurentian Region. First two completed 1980, other pair 4-82.

◆ **3 R class, based on U.S. Coast Guard 95-ft. design**

	Bldr	In serv.
CG 140 RACER	Yarrow, Esquimault, B.C.	1963
CG 143 READY	Burrard DD, Vancouver, B.C.	1963
CG 145 RIDER	Victoria Mach Dépôt, Victoria, B.C.	1962

Rally (CG 141) outboard Rapid (CG 142) L. & L. Van Ginderen, 10-82

D: 105 tons (fl) **S:** 20 kts **Dim:** 29.03 (27.34 pp) × 6.10 × 1.96
M: 4 Cummins VT-12-M-700 diesels; 2 props; 2,400 hp
Electric: 76 kw **Fuel:** 12 tons **Range:** 1,050/16; 1,500/12.5 **Man:** 12 tot.

REMARKS: CG 145 was taken over from the Bureau of Fisheries in 1969. CG 143 is in reserve. Sisters *Rally* (CG 141), *Rapid* (CG 142) and *Relay* (CG 144) stricken 1983.

◆ **3 S class—for Great Lakes service**

	Bldr	In serv.
SPUME	Grew Ltd., Penatanguishene, Ont.	11-63
SPRAY	J. J. Taylor & Son, Toronto, Ont.	1964
SPINDRIFT	Cliff Richardson BY, Medford, Ont.	1964

Spindrift 1969

D: 57 tons (fl) **S:** 14 kts **Dim:** 21.88 × 5.11 × 1.40
M: 2 diesels; 2 props; 1,050 hp
Fuel: 5.3 tons **Range:** 500/13.5 **Man:** 4 tot.

SEARCH AND RESCUE LIFEBOATS (Type 300)

◆ **16 U.S. Coast Guard 44-ft. motor lifeboat class**

	In serv.	Region		In serv.	Region
CG 101 SOURIS	1967	Mar.	CG 109 THUNDER BAY	1974	Cent.
CG 102 WESTPORT	1969	Mar.	CG 114 BURGEO	1973	Newf.
CG 103 BICKERTON	1969	West.	CG 115 SHIPPEGAN	1975	Mar.
CG 104 BAMFIELD	1970	West.	CG 116 CLARK'S HARBOUR	1975	Mar.
CG 105 TOFINO	1970	West.	CG 117 SAMBRO	1975	Mar.
CG 106 BULL HARBOUR	1970	West.	CG 118 LOUISBURG	1975	Mar.
CG 107 BURIN	1974	Newf.	CG 140 PORT MOUTON	1982	Mar.
CG 108 TOBERMORY	1974	Central	CG 141 CAP AUX MEULES	1982	Mar.

D: 17.9 tons (fl) **S:** 14 kts **Dim:** 13.45 × 3.86 × 1.01
Electron Equipt: Radar: 1/Raytheon 1900
M: 2 G.M. 6-71 diesels; 2 props; 360 hp (294 hp sust.) **Range:** 150/10.5
Fuel: 1.2 tons **Man:** 3 tot.

REMARKS: First unit built U.S.C.G. Yard, Curtis Bay, Md. in 1967, remainder built in Canada, CG 140 and 141 by Georgetown SY, Prince Edward Isl. CG 107 and later are 485 hp.

SMALL RESCUE CRAFT (Type 100)

◆ **8 miscellaneous**

	In serv.	Region		In serv.	Region
RELITE	1967	West	CG 121 SORA	1968	Cent.
SWIFT	1981	West	CG 122 GANGES	1976	West
CG 119 GREBE	1973	Cent.	CG 156 OSPREY	1982	West
CG 120 TEAL	1972	Cent.	CG 157 BITTERN	1982	Cent.

AIR CUSHION VEHICLES

◆ **2 British Hovercraft SRN-6 class**

CG 045 CG 039

◆ **1 British Hovercraft SRN-5 class**

CG 021

◆ **1 Bell Voyager class**

DEPARTMENT OF FISHERIES AND OCEANS

FISHERIES PATROL SHIPS

◆ **1 seagoing patrol ship** Bldr: West Coast Manly SY, Vancouver, B.L.

	Laid down	L	In serv.
Leonard J. Cowley	15-1-84	24-10-84	4-85

D: 1,470 tons light (2,080 fl) **S:** 12.25 kts
Dim: 72.00 (67.60 pp) × 14.00 × 4.50 (4.90 max.)
M: 2 Nohab Polar F312A diesels; 1 Kort-nozzle CP prop; 3,140 hp
Fuel: 400 tons **Range:** 12,000/12 **Man:** 30 crew + 10 spare

Remarks: 1,730 grt. Helo deck. Bow-thruster. For Pacific Region. Ordered 8-11-83.

◆ **1 research vessel** Bldr: Bel-Aire SY, Vancouver

	Laid down	L	In serv.
John P. Tully	30-1-84	27-10-84	5-85

D: 2,200 tons (fl) **S:** 14 kts **Dim:** 68.90 (60.00 pp) × 14.00 × 4.50
M: 2 Deutz SBV-628 diesels; 1 CP prop; 3,120 hp
Fuel: 400 tons **Range:** 12,000/12 **Man:** 25 crew + 15 scientists

Remarks: 1,750 grt. For oceanographic/fisheries research and hydrographic survey.

◆ **1 aluminum construction** Bldr: John Manly SY, Vancouver

James Sinclair (In serv. 4-81) — Pacific Region

James Sinclair 1981

D: . . . **S:** 16.5 kts **Dim:** 37.8 × 8.4 × . . .
M: 2 MTU 12V538 TB91 diesels; 2 props; 4,600 hp
Electron Equipt: Radar: 2/Sperry navigational

◆ **1 seagoing patrol ship** Bldr: Marystown SY, Newfoundland

Cygnus (In serv. 1981) — Newfoundland Region

Cygnus 1981

D: 1,461 tons (fl) **S:** 16 kts **Dim:** 62.5 × 12.2 × . . .
M: 2 Nohab diesels; 1 prop; . . . hp

◆ **1 seagoing patrol ship** Bldr: . . .

Cape Rodger (In serv. 1977) — Maritime Region

D: 1,255 tons **S:** . . . **Dim:** 87.3 × 15.2 × . . .
M: Diesels; . . . props; . . . hp

◆ **2 fisheries research boats** Bldr: Ferguson, Pictou (In serv. 1981)

Alfred Needler Wilfred Templeman

Remarks: 50 m. o.a.; no other data available. One based at Halifax, the other at St. Johns, Newfoundland.

◆ **2 Louisbourg class patrol/survey ships** Bldr: . . . (In serv. 1977)

Louisbourg Louis M. Laurier (ex-*Cape Harrison*)

Louisbourg L. & L. Van Ginderen, 10-82

D: 450 tons (fl) **S:** 20 kts **Dim:** 38.1 (36.6 pp) × 8.2 × 2.5
M: 2 MTU 12V538 TB91 diesels; 2 props; 4,500 hp

Remarks: *Louisbourg* patrols the Maritime Provinces region, *Laurier* was renamed 1984 after conversion as a survey boat by Breton Industrial & Marine, Port Hawkesbury, N.S.

◆ **1 seagoing patrol ship** Bldr: Yarrow, Esquimault

Tanu (In serv. 7-9-68) — Pacific Region

D: 880 tons (925 fl) **S:** 15 kts **Dim:** 54.69 (50.06 pp) × 32.00 × 3.35 mean
M: 2 Fairbanks-Morse 38D8⅛ × 8 diesels; 1 CP prop; 2,400 hp
Range: 5,000/12 **Electric:** 500 kw **Man:** 34 tot.

Remarks: Has 125 hp Pleuger active rudder. Aluminum superstructure. Similar to *Chebucto.*

◆ **1 seagoing patrol ship** Bldr: Ferguson, Pictou, N.S.

Chebucto (In serv. 1966) — Maritime Region

Chebucto — gun no longer carried L. & L. Van Ginderen, 11-71

D: 865 tons normal **S:** 15 kts **Dim:** 54.6 × 9.45 × . . .
M: 2 Fairbanks-Morse 38D8⅛ × 8 diesels; 1 CP prop; 2,560 hp
Range: 6,000/12 **Electric:** 300 kw **Man:** 35 tot.

PATROL BOATS

The units below run from 40-ft. (12.2 m) to 116-ft (35.5 m) in length and are listed in descending length.

	Displacement	Length		Beam	Year	Region
Golden Bay	136 grt	30.5	×	5.4	1975	Que.
. . .	148 grt	25	×	. . .	1984	. . .
Cumella	80	23.17	×	5.1	1983	. . .
Groswater Bay	80	23.17	×	5.1	1984	. . .
Cratena	94	20.9	×	4.8	1953	Mar.
Sooke Post	59 grt	20.7	×	5.2	1973	Pac.
Goose Bay	44	20.1	×	4.8	1968	Newfdl.
Hawke Bay	44	20.1	×	4.8	1965	Newfdl.
Pistolet Bay	44	20.1	×	4.8	1966	Newfdl.

CANADA *(continued)*
PATROL BOATS *(continued)*

Burin Bay	44	20.1 × 4.8	1967	Newfdl.
Atlin Post	57 grt	19.8 × 5.2	1975	Pac.
Kitimat II	57 grt	19.8 × 5.2	1974	Pac.
Comox Post	57 grt	19.8 × 5.2	1975	Pac.
Chilco Post	57 grt	19.2 × 5.2	1975	Pac.
Gander Bay	44	18.6 × 4.9	1969	Newfdl.
Garia Bay	49	18.6 × 5.8	1961	Newfdl.
Badger Bay	42	17.4 × 4.7	1954	Newfdl.
Baso Reef	48 grt	17.1 × 5.1	1984	Pac.
Cutter Rock	36 grt	16.1 × 4.3	1967	Pac.
Christie Bay I	35	15.8 × . . .	1972	West.
Stuart Post	37 grt	15.8 × 4.6	1973	Pac.
Babine Post	37 grt	15.8 × 4.6	1972	Pac.
North Rock	31 grt	15.2 × 4.6	1975	Pac.
Surge Rock	33 grt	14.6 × 4.3	1964	Pac.
Boltenia	29 grt	14.6 × 3.7	1951	Newfdl.
Bonilla Rock	41 grt	14.6 × 4.6	1971	Pac.
Lomond	24 grt	14.3 × 4.3	1959	Newfdl.
Beaver Rock	31 grt	14.3 × 4.3	1961	Pac.
Pillar Rock	31 grt	14.3 × 4.3	1961	Pac.
Falcon Rock	28 grt	14.3 × 5.8	1960	Pac.
Buctouche Light	20 grt	14.0 × 4.0	1963	Mar.
Temple Rock	23 grt	13.4 × 3.6	1960	Pac.
11A-6538	36	13.1 × 4.0	1969	Mar.
11A-6539	36	13.1 × 4.0	1969	Mar.
Seal Rock	24 grt	13.1 × 3.6	1959	Pac.
. . .	9.25 grt	12.8 × 3.9	1984	Mar.
Rustico Light	17 grt	12.8 × 4.0	1965	Mar.
11A-6204	45	12.8 × 4.0	1969	Mar.
11A-6206	45	12.8 × 4.0	1969	Mar.
11A-5831	46	12.8 × 4.0	1968	Mar.
11A-5832	46	12.8 × 4.0	1968	Mar.
Marilla	10 grt	12.8 × . . .	1955	West.
1B-1284	. . .	12.8 × 4.6	1975	Mar.
1B-1452	45	12.8 × 4.0	1979	Mar.
Brama	20 grt	12.5 × 3.7	1955	Pac.
Gavia	17 grt	12.5 × 3.4	1955	Pac.
Walker Rock	15 grt	12.2 × 4.0	1976	Pac.
Star Rock	18 grt	12.2 × 3.4	1957	Pac.
7C-109	30	12.2 × 3.4	1966	Mar.
17A-601	23	12.5 × 4.0	1976	Mar.

Regions: Pac.—Pacific; Que.—Quebec; Mar.—Maritimes; Newfdl.—Newfoundland; West.—Western

PATROL CRAFT

The craft listed below by region are all less than 40-ft (12.2 m) in length. There are, in addition, some 500 craft of 20-ft (6.1 m) or less in service. Maritimes: *La Bradelle, Johnny Hoe,* 11A-5743, 11A-5830, 20A-1138, 20A-1139, 20A-1141, 20A-1142, 20A-1152, 20A-1153—Western Region: *Sangstercraft*—Pacific: *FD202, Petrel Rock, Anchor Rock, Babine River, Canoe Rock, Crescent Rock, Gale Rock, Bertram, Beluga, Gull Rock, Heron Rock, Legace Bay, Little Atlin, Little Brama, Little Crescent, Little Falcon, Little Nahmint, Little Pillar, Little River, Little Rock, Mission Jet, Nimpkish, RD 105, Roanna, Tatchie River, Vancouver Sport Fishing, Vedder Rock, Warrior Rock, 13K49012, 13K56195, 13K76101, 13K76026, 13K76149.*

Note: The Canadian Department of Energy, Mines and Resources operates a number of oceangoing survey and oceanographic research ships which, for reasons of space, cannot be listed here.

CAPE VERDE ISLANDS

Republic of Cape Verde

Personnel: . . .

Merchant Marine (1984): 24 ships—13,690 grt

PATROL BOATS

◆ **2 Soviet Shershen-class former torpedo boats**

451 452

D: 180 tons (fl) **S:** 45 kts **Dim:** 34.0 × 7.2 × 1.5
A: 4/30-mm AA (II × 2) **Electron Equipt:** Radar: 1/Pot Head, 1/Drum Tilt
M: 3 M-503A diesels; 3 props; 12,000 hp **Range:** 450/34, 700/20

Remarks: Transferred 3-, and 7-79. Torpedo tubes removed prior to transfer.

◆ **1 Soviet Zhuk class**—transferred 1980

D: 60 tons (fl) **S:** 34 kts **Dim:** 24.0 × 5.0 × 1.8 **A:** 4/14.5-mm mg (II × 2)
Electron Equipt: Radar: 1/Spin Trough **M:** 2 M50 diesels; 2 props; 2,400 hp

◆ **1 Soviet Kameuka class survey ship** Bldr: Gdansk SY, Poland

A 450 5th July (In serv. 1968-72)

5th July (A 450)—with two Shershen astern 1982

D: 703 tons (fl) **S:** 13.7 kts **Dim:** 53.5 × 9.1 × 2.6
Electron Equipt: Radar: 1/Don-2 **Range:** 4,000/10
M: 2 diesels; 2 CP props; 1,765 hp **Man:** 40 tot.

Remarks: Transferred 1980 for use as a training ship. Also capable of acting as a navigational buoy tender. One 5-ton crane.

◆ **1 oceanographic and fisheries research ship**

N. . . (ex-*Fengur*)

D: . . . **S:** . . . **Dim:** 27.3 × 7.4 × . . .
M: Diesels; . . . hp

Remarks: Transferred 6-5-84 by Icelandic Government. 140 grt/60 dwt.

CHILE

Republic of Chile

Personnel (1984): 22,261 total (2,049 officers; 18,175 men; 2,037 naval infantry). Civil Service personnel number about 6,600.

Merchant Marine (1984): 219 ships—472,934 grt (tankers: 7—186,700 grt)

Naval Aviation: The naval air arm has 25 aircraft (6 Embraer 111 Bandeirante and 3 Embraer 110 Bandeirante maritime surveillance aircraft, 10 Pilatus PC-7 trainers, and 6 Casa 212 Aviocar) and 19 helicopters (10 Alouette-III, 6 Bell 206A JetRanger, and 3 AS.332 Super Puma). The principal air base is at El Belloto, near Valparaiso.

SUBMARINES

◆ **2 IKL Type 1300** Bldr: Howaldtswerke, Kiel, West Germ:

	Laid down	L	In serv.
S 20 Thomson	1-11-80	28-2-82	31-8-84
S 21 Simpson	15-1-81	29-7-83	12-84

Simpson (S 21) P. Voss, 7-84

Thomson (S 20) HDW, 1984

SUBMARINES *(continued)*

D: 1,285 tons surf./1,390 submerged. **S:** 10/22 kts
Dim: 61.00 × 6.20 × 5.50 (surf.)
A: 8/533-mm TT fwd. (16 tot. torpedoes)
Electron Equipt: Radar: 1/Calypso II
Sonar: . . .
M: 4 MTU 12V-493 AZ-80 diesels; 4/450-kw AEG generators; 1 Siemens electric motor; 5,000 hp
Fuel: 110 tons **Range:** 400/4; 16/21.5 sub; 8,200/8 snorkel
Endurance: 50 days **Man:** 5 officers, 26 men

REMARKS: Ordered 12-80; construction encountered political opposition in West Germany. Utilized components from canceled Iranian order. Maximum snorkel speed is 12 kts. S 21, damaged in collision 29-3-84 on trials, was completed 18-9-84. S 20 was completed 7-5-84. Have larger casing than earlier IKL-designed submarines.

◆ **2 British Oberon class**

	Bldr	Laid down	L	In serv.
S 22 O'BRIEN	Scott Lithgow	17-1-71	21-12-72	4-76
S 23 HYATT	Scott Lithgow	16-1-72	26-9-73	27-9-76

O'Brien (S 22) G. Arra, 1977

D: 1,650/2,070/2,450 tons **S:** 15/17.5 kts **Dim:** 89.92 (87.45 pp) × 8.07 × 5.48
A: 8/533-mm TT (6 fwd, 2 aft)—22 torpedoes
Electron Equipt: Radar: 1/1006—Sonar: 1/2007, 1/187, 1/197, 1/719
M: 2 1,840 hp Admiralty Standard Range 16 VVS-AS21 diesels, diesel-electric drive; 2 props; 6,000 hp
Man: 65 tot.

REMARKS: Delivery of these submarines was a year late because of a number of malfunctions in the electrical equipment. The after two "short" torpedo tubes were for countermeasures weapons and may no longer be in use.

NOTE: U.S. *Brooklyn*-class cruisers *O'Higgins* (02, ex-*Brooklyn,* CL 40) and *Chacabuco* (03, ex-*Prat,* ex-*Nashville,* CL 43) were stricken in 1984. Ex-Swedish cruiser *Almirante Latorre* (ex-*Göta Lejon*) decommissioned 9-84.

DESTROYERS

◆ **2 British "County"-class guided-missile destroyers**

	Bldr	Laid down	L	In serv.
11 CAPITAN PRAT (ex-*Norfolk*)	Swan Hunter, Wallsend-on Tyne	15-3-66	16-11-67	7-3-70
12 ALMIRANTE COCHRANE (ex-*Antrim*)	Fairfield SB & Eng., Govan	20-1-66	19-10-67	14-7-70

Almirante Cochrane (12) L. & L. Van Ginderen, 8-84

Capitan Prat (11)—with Exocet missiles Chilean Navy, 1984

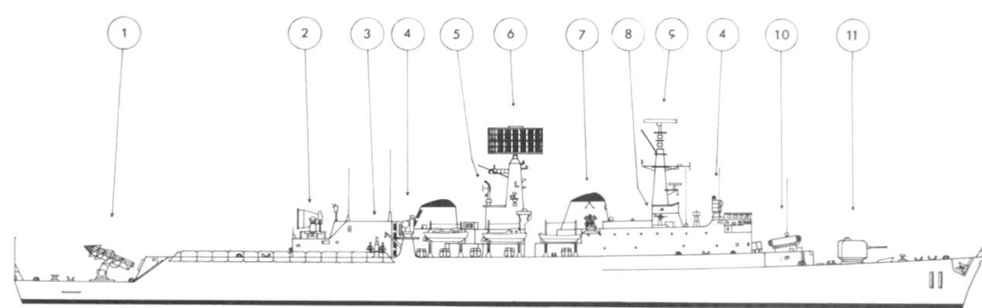

Capitan Prat (11): 1. Sea Slug launcher 2. Type 901 radar director 3. Sea Cat launcher 4. MRS. 3 radar director for Sea Cat 5. Type 278 height-finding radar 6. Type 965M air early-warning radar 7. Knebworth/Corvus chaff RL 8. 20-mm AA 9. Type 9920 search radar 10. Exocet launchers 11. 114-mm Mk 6 gunmounts

D: 5,440 tons (6,200 fl) **S:** 32.5 kts (30 sust.)
Dim: 158.55 (153.9 pp) × 16.46 × 6.3 (max.)
A: 4/MM 38 Exocet—1/Sea Slug Mk 2 syst. (II × 1, 30 missiles)—2/Sea Cat GWS 22 Syst. (IV × 2, . . . missiles)—2/114-mm Mk 6 DP (II × 1)—2/20-mm AA (I × 2)—1/helicopter
Electron Equipt: Radar: 1/978, 1/965M, 1/992Q, 1/277, 1/901, 1/903, 2/904
Sonar: 1/184, 1/162
EW: UA-8/9 passive, jammers, 2 Knebworth/Corvus chaff RL (VIII × 2)
M: COSAG: 2 sets A.E.I. GT (15,000 hp each) and 4 English Electric G6 gas turbines (7,500 hp each); 2 props; 60,000 hp
Boilers: 2 Babcock & Wilcox; 49.2 kg/cm², 510°C **Fuel:** 600 tons
Electric: 4,750 kw **Range:** 3,500/28 **Man:** 33 officers, 438 men

REMARKS: *Prat* purchased by Chile, left U.K. 17-2-82, transferred 6-4-82 in Chile; *Cochrane* purchased 22-6-84, commissioned 25-6-84. Four pair fin stabilizers. Twin rudders. Sea Slug magazine runs 80-m long through ship, with two parallel rows of 15 missiles. Exocet missiles not aboard at time of transfer, and SCOT SATCOMM equipment deleted. Have ADAWS-1 data system. See also notes under class entry in Great Britain section.

◆ **2 Almirante Williams class**

	Bldr	Laid down	L	In serv.
D 18 ALMIRANTE RIVEROS	Vickers-Armstrong	12-4-57	12-12-58	31-12-60
D 19 ALMIRANTE WILLIAMS	Vickers-Armstrong	20-6-56	5-5-58	26-3-60

Almirante Riveros (D 18) Chilean Navy, 11-83

D: 2,730 tons (3,300 fl) **S:** 34.5 kts **Dim:** 122.5 (113.99 pp) × 13.1 × 3.9
A: 4/MM 38 Exocet—2/Sea Cat SAM systems (IV × 2)—4/102-mm DP (I × 4)—4/40-mm AA (I × 4)—6/324-mm Mk 32 ASW TT (III × 2)—2/Squid ASW mortars (III × 2)
Electron Equipt: Radar: 1/Decca 629, 1 Plessey AWS-1, 1 Marconi SNW-10, 1/SWW-20, 2/SGR-102, 2/SNG-20
Sonar: 1/164B—EW: WLR-1 intercept
M: 2 sets Parsons-Pamatreda GT; 2 props; 50,000 hp
Boilers: 4 Babcock & Wilcox; 43.3 kg/cm², 454°C **Range:** 7,800
Man: 17 officers, 249 men

REMARKS: Refitted in Great Britain, D 18 in 1973-75 and D 19 in 1971-74. Dutch M-4 radar directors for Sea Cat. Exocet replaced four 533-mm TT (IV × 1); 2 Exocet removed from each and placed on *Allen M. Sumner* class, 1980. The 114-mm guns are unique to this class; gunhouse weight is 26 tons, muzzle velocity is 900 m/sec., firing rate is 46 rpm, range is 18,500 m, and maximum altitude is 12,000 m.

◆ **2 U.S. Allen M. Sumner FRAM II class**

	Bldr	Laid down	L	In serv.
D 16 MINISTRO ZENTENO (ex-*Charles S. Sperry,* DD 697)	Federal SB & DD, Kearny, N.J.	19-10-43	30-9-44	26-12-44
D 17 MINISTRO PORTALES (ex-*Douglas H. Fox,* DD 779)	Todd Pacific SY, Tacoma, Wash.	31-1-44	13-3-44	17-5-44

D: 2,200 tons (3,300 fl) **S:** 30 kts **Dim:** 114.75 × 12.45 × 5.8 (sonar)
A: 2/MM 38 Exocet—6/127-mm DP 38-cal. (II × 3)—2/40-mm AA (I × 2)—2/20-mm AA (I × 2)—6/324-mm Mk 32 ASW TT (III × 2)—2/Hedgehogs—1 SH-57A helicopter
Electron Equipt: Radar: 1/SPS-40 (D 17) or SPS-29 (D 16), 1/SPS-10, 1/Mk 25
Sonar: 1/SQS-40—ECM: WLR-1
M: 2 sets GT; 2 props; 60,000 hp

DESTROYERS *(continued)*

Ministro Zenteno (D 16)—with added AA guns U.S. Navy, 1982

Boilers: 4 Foster-Wheeler and Babcock & Wilcox; 43.3 kg/cm², 454°C
Fuel: 650 tons **Range:** 1,260/30; 4,600/15 **Man:** 14 officers, 260 men

REMARKS: Purchased 8-1-74. VDS removed 1980; 2 Exocet SSM from *Williams* class mounted on 01 deck between stacks. By 1982, the Exocet missiles appear to have been removed, and 40-mm AA guns have been added at the forward corners of the helicopter platform. Mk 37 GFCS.

FRIGATES

◆ **2 British Leander class**

	Bldr	Laid down	L	In serv.
PF 06 CONDELL	Yarrow & Co	5-6-71	12-6-72	21-12-73
PF 07 LYNCH	Yarrow & Co	6-12-72	6-12-73	25-5-74

Condell (PF 06)—in camouflage paint Chilean Navy, 1983

Lynch (Pf 07) U.S. Navy, 1985

D: 2,500 tons (2,962 fl) **S:** 27 kts **Dim:** 113.38 (109.73 pp) × 13.12 × 5.49 (fl)
A: 4/MM 38 Exocet—2/114-mm Mk VI DP (II × 1)—1/Sea Cat SAM system (IV × 1; 16 missiles)—2/20-mm AA (I × 2)—6/324-mm ASW TT (III × 2)—1 helicopter
Electron Equipt: Radar: 1/978, 1/965, 1/992 Q, 1/903, 1/904
Sonar: 1/177, 1/170B, 1/162—EW:UA-8/9 intercept, 2/Knebworth/Corvus chaff RL (VIII × 2)
M: 2 sets GT; 2 props; 30,000 hp
Boilers: 2 Babcock & Wilcox; 38.7 kg/cm², 450°C **Electric:** 2,500 kw
Fuel: 500 tons **Range:** 4,500/12 **Man:** 263 tot.

REMARKS: Ordered 14-1-70. GWS 22 FCS for Sea Cat, MRS 3 GFCS for 114-mm. Exocet missiles at stern in lieu of Limbo ASW mortar. The Chilean Navy has expressed a desire to purchase two ex-RN units of this class, when available.

NOTE: The last of the U.S. *Charles Lawrence*-class frigates (ex-ADP fast transports), *Virgilio Uribe* (ex-*Daniel Griffin,* APO 38, ex-DE 54), was stricken 1984.

CORVETTES

◆ **1 U.S. Abnaki-class former fleet tug** Bldr: Charleston SB & DD Co., S.C.

	Laid down	L	In serv.
63 SERGENTE ALDEA (ex-*Arikara,* ATF 98)	28-11-42	22-4-43	15-11-43

Sergente Aldea (63) Chilean Navy

D: 1,235 tons (1,675 fl) **S:** 15 kts
Dim: 62.48 (59.44 wl) × 11.73 × 4.67 **A:** 1/76.2-mm DP Mk 26—2/20-mm AA
Electron Equipt: Radar: 1/SPS-5
M: Diesel-electric: 4 Busch-Sulzer BS539 diesels; 1 prop; 3,000 hp
Electric: 400 kw **Fuel:** 363 tons **Range:** 7,000/15; 15,000/8 **Man:** 85 tot.

REMARKS: Transferred 1-7-71 on lease.

◆ **2 U.S. Sotoyomo-class former auxiliary ocean tugs** Bldr: Levingston, SB, Orange, Texas

	Laid down	L	In serv.
60 LIENTUR (ex-ATA 177)	27-4-44	5-6-44	2-9-44
62 LAUTARO (ex-ATA 122)	19-10-42	27-11-42	10-6-43

Lautaro (62) Chilean Navy

D: 534 tons (835 fl) **S:** 13 kts **Dim:** 43.59 (41.00 pp) × 10.31 × 4.01
A: 1/76.2-mm DP Mk 26—4/20-mm AA (II × 2)
Electron Equipt: Radar: 1/Decca 505
M: 2 G.M. 12-278A diesels, electric drive; 2 props; 1,500 hp
Electric: 90-120 kw **Fuel:** 171 tons **Range:** 16,500/18 **Man:** 46 tot.

REMARKS: Purchased 9-47.

GUIDED-MISSILE BOATS

◆ **3 (+2) Israeli Reshev (Sa'ar IV) class** Bldr: Israeli SY, Haifa

	L	In serv.	Transferred
. . . CASMA (ex-*Romach*)	1-74	3-74	12-79
. . . CHIPANA (ex-*Keshet*)	23-8-73	10-73	1-81
. . . N. . . (ex-*Reshev*)	19-2-73	4-73	2-84
. . . N. . . (ex-. . .)	. . .	. . .	. . .
. . . N. . . (ex-. . .)	. . .	. . .	. . .

GUIDED-MISSILE BOATS *(continued)*

D: 415 tons (450 fl) **S:** 32 kts **Dim:** 58.10 × 7.60 × 2.40
A: 6/Gabriel SSM (I × 6)—2/76-mm DP OTO Melara (I × 2)—2/20-mm AA (I × 2)—2/12.7-mm mg (I × 2)
Electron Equipt: Radar: 1/Neptune, 1/EL/M-2221 f.c. (Orion)
EW: passive syst.—4 large/72 small chaff RL
M: 4 MTU MD 871 diesels; 4 props; 14,000 hp **Range:** 1,500/30; 4,000/17
Man: 45 tot.

REMARKS: Harpoon SSM removed prior to transfer. Transfer of *Reshev* and two scheduled for 1985 uncertain.

TORPEDO BOATS

◆ **4 Guacolda (Lürssen 36-m design) class** Bldr: Bazán, Cadiz, Spain (In serv. 1965-66)

81 FRESIA 82 GUACOLDA 83 QUIDORA 84 TEHUALDA

Guacolda class Chilean Navy, 1985

D: 134 tons (fl) **S:** 30 kts **Dim:** 36.2 (34.0 wl) × 5.6 × 1.68
A: 2/40-mm AA—4/533-mm TT (British Mk IV)
Electron Equipt: Radar: 1/Decca 505
M: 2 Mercedes-Benz MB839Bb diesels; 2 props; 4,800 hp
Electric: 90 kVA **Range:** 1,500/15 **Man:** 20 tot.

PATROL BOATS

◆ **1 U.S. PC 1638-class submarine chaser** Bldr: ASMAR, Talcahuano

	In serv.
P 37 PAPUDO (ex-U.S. PC 1646)	27-11-71

Papudo (P 37) 1977

D: 313 tons (417 fl) **S:** 20 kts **Dim:** 52.9 × 7.0 × 3.1
A: 1/40-mm AA—4/20-mm AA (II × 2)—1/trainable Mk 15 Hedgehog—4/Mk 6 d.c. throwers—1 d.c. rack
M: 2 G.M. 16-567 diesels; 2 props; 2,800 hp **Fuel:** 60 tons **Range:** 5,000/10
Man: 69 tot.

REMARKS: The construction of two additional units of this class, to be named *Abtao* (P 36) and *Pisaqua* (P 38), was canceled.

◆ **2 small trawler-type** Bldr: ASMAR, Talcahuano, 1966-67

PC 75 MARINERO FUENTALBAS PC 76 CABO ODGER

D: 215 tons **S:** 9 kts **Dim:** 24.4 × 6.4 × 2.75 **A:** 1/20-mm AA
M: 1 Cummins diesel; 340 hp **Range:** 2,600/9

REMARKS: Purchased 1966.

◆ **2 patrol launches** Bldr: MacLaren, Niteroi, Brazil (In serv. 11-82)

ONA YAGAN

D: 14 tons (fl) **S:** 19 kts **Dim:** 13.2 × 3.6 × 1.1
A: . . . **M:** 2 MTU GV 331 TC82 diesels; 2 props; 1,320 hp

REMARKS: Built as compensation for the late delivery of "Anchova"-class patrol boats for the Chilean Coast Guard. One based at Puerto Montt, the other at Chiloe.

HYDROGRAPHIC SURVEY AND RESEARCH SHIPS

◆ **1 U.S. Cherokee-class former fleet tug** Bldr: Commercial Iron Wks, Portland, Ore.

	Laid down	L	In serv.
AGS 64 YELCHO (ex-USS *Tekesta*, ATF 93)	7-9-42	20-3-43	16-8-43

Yelcho (AGS 64) 1970

D: 1,235 tons (1,675 fl) **S:** 15 kts **Dim:** 62.48 (59.44 wl) × 11.73 × 4.67
A: 1/76.2-mm Mk 26 DP—2/20-mm AA **Electric:** 260 kw
M: 4 G.M. 12-278 diesels, electric drive; 1 prop; 3,000 hp
Fuel: 363 tons **Range:** 7,000/15; 15,000/8 **Man:** 5 officers, 59 men

REMARKS: Used for oceanographic research. Loaned 15-5-60. Carries survey launch on fantail.

◆ **1 Antarctic patrol, transport, and research ship**

	Bldr	Laid down	L	In serv.
AP 45 PILOTO PARDO	Haarlemsche Scheepsbouw	1957	1958	8-58

Piloto Pardo (AP 45) 1977

D: 1,250 tons (2,545 fl) **S:** 14 kts **Dim:** 83.0 × 11.9 × 7.4 (fl)
M: Diesel-electric propulsion; 1 prop; 2,000 hp **Range:** 6,000/10
Man: 44 crew, 24 passengers

REMARKS: Armament removed; can carry 2 Bell 47-G helicopters.

AUXILIARY SHIPS AND SERVICE CRAFT

◆ **1 U.K. "Later Tide"-class replenishment oiler** Bldr: Hawthorn Leslie, Hebburn-on-Tyne

	Laid down	L	In serv.
AO 52 ALMIRANTE MONTT (ex-*Tidepool*)	4-12-61	11-12-62	28-6-63

Almirante Montt (AO 52) as Tidepool L. & L. Van Ginderen, 7-81

D: 8,531 tons light (27,400 fl) **S:** 18.3 kts
Dim: 177.60 (167.65 pp) × 21.64 × 9.75
Electron Equipt: Radar: 1/Kelvin-Hughes 14/12, 1 Kelvin-Hughes 14/16
M: 1 set Pametrada GT; 1 prop; 15,000 hp
Boilers: 2 Babcock & Wilcox, 60 kg/cm², 510°C **Man:** 110 tot.

REMARKS: Sold to Chile and was to have been transferred 2-4-82 at Valparaiso; repossessed because of Argentine invasion of Falklands, returned and commissioned in Chilean Navy 8-82. 14,130 grt/18,900 dwt. Cargo: Approx. 18,000 tons liquid. Hangar and flight deck for one large helicopter.

AUXILIARY SHIPS AND SERVICE CRAFT *(continued)*

◆ **1 replenishment oiler** Bldr: Burmeister & Wain, Copenhagen

	L	In serv.
AO 53 Araucano	21-6-66	10-1-67

Araucano (AO 53) 1977

D: 23,000 tons (fl) **S:** 17 kts **Dim:** 160.93 × 21.95 × 8.8 **A:** Removed
M: Burmeister & Wain diesel, type 62 VT 2 BF 140, 9-cyl.; 1 prop; 10,800 hp
Range: 12,000/14.5

Remarks: Can replenish two ships at sea simultaneously. Carries 21,126 cu. meters liquid and 1,444 cu. meters dry cargo. Can carry 8/40-mm AA (II × 4).

Note: The U.S. *Patapsco*-class tanker *Beagle* (AOG 54, ex-*Genesee,* AOG 8) was stricken in 1983.

◆ **1 small tanker** Bldr: Marco SY, Iquique (In serv. 1966)

AO 55 Guardian Brito (ex-*Silvia*)

D: 482 tons (fl) **S:** 10 kts **Dim:** 39.60 × 7.44 × 3.30 (max.)
M: MWM diesel; . . . hp **Range:** 3,000/8 **Man:** 1 officer, 7 men

Remarks: Acquired 13-1-83 from the Ultramar Co. Based at Punta Arena. Also in service is *Aquila* (AO 48); see addenda.

◆ **2 (+1) French BATRAL-class landing ship/transports** Bldr: ASMAR, Talcahuano

	L	In serv.		L	In serv.
R 91 Maipo	26-9-81	12-82	R 93 Chacabuco	16-7-85	1986
R 92 Rancagua	26-3-82	1-7-83	R 94 N. . .	. . .	. . .

Maipo (R 91) Chilean Navy, 12-82

D: 770 tons (1,330 fl) **S:** 16 kts (13 sustained)
Dim: 80.0 (68.0 pp) × 13.0 × 3.0 (max.) **A:** 2/20-mm AA (I × 2)
M: 2 SACM V-12 diesels; 2 props; 3,600 hp **Range:** 4,500/13 **Man:** 40 tot.

Remarks: Constructed with French technical assistance. Cargo: 350 tons. Bow ramp, helicopter platform. Can carry 138 troops.

◆ **1 transport, former passenger-cargo ship** Bldr: Aalborg Vaerft, 1953

AP 47 Aquiles (ex-Danish *Tjaldur*)

Aquiles (AP 47) Chilean Navy, 1983

D: 3,400 tons (fl) **S:** 16 kts **Dim:** 87.8 (82.0 pp) × 13.42 × 5.2
A: 2/40-mm AA (I × 2) — 2/20-mm AA (I × 2)
M: 1 Burmeister & Wain diesel; 1 prop; 3,600 hp
Range: 5,500/16 **Man:** 32 crew, 447 troops

Remarks: Former mixed-cargo ship purchased in 1967. 2,660 grt/1,395 dwt.

Note: U.S. LST 542-class former tank-landing ship *Comandante Hemmerdinger* (AP 88, ex-*New London County,* T-LST 1066) was stricken in 1982.

◆ **2 Orompello-class landing ships**

AP 94 Orompello Bldr: Dade DD Co., Miami, Fla. (In serv. 15-9-64)
AP 95 Elicura Bldr: ASMAR, Talcahuano (In serv. 10-12-63)

D: 290 tons (750 fl) **S:** 12 kts **Dim:** 43.9 (42.05 pp) × 10.3 × 6.9
A: 3/20-mm AA **Electron Equipt:** Radar: 1 Raytheon 1500B
Electric: 120 kw **M:** 2 Cummins VT-17-700M diesels; 2 props; 900 hp
Fuel: 71 tons **Range:** 2,900/10.5 **Cargo:** 350 tons **Man:** 20 tot.

◆ **1 Meteoro-class coastal ferry** Bldr: ASMAR, Talcahuano

AP 110 Meteoro (In serv. 1967)

D: 205 tons (fl) **S:** 8 kts **Dim:** 24.4 × 6.7 × . . . **M:** Diesel
Man: 220 passengers

Remarks: Sister *Grumete Perez Huemel* (AF 112) has been stricken.

◆ **1 submarine tender** Bldr: Orenst & Koppel, Germany (In serv. 1966)

70 Angamos (ex-*Puerto Montt,* ex-Danish *Kobenhavn*)

D: 3,560 tons **S:** 16 kts **Dim:** 93.92 × 16.2 × 4.5
M: 2 Lind-Pielstick V-8 diesels; 2 props; 6,500 hp

Remarks: Former car and passenger ferry, purchased 4-77 and in service in 1979. Now fitted with workshops, spare parts stores, ammunition and torpedo magazines. 4,616 grt. Also used as a transport.

◆ **1 sail-training ship**

	Bldr	L	In serv.
BE 43 Esmeralda (ex-*Don Juan de Austria*)	Bazán, Cadiz	12-5-53	9-54

Esmeralda (BE 43) Chilean Navy

D: 3,673 tons **S:** 11 kts **Dim:** 94.1 × 13.1 × 8.7
A: 4/47-mm saluting **M:** Fiat diesel; 1,400 hp **Range:** 8,000/8
Man: 271 crew, 80 midshipmen

Remarks: Four-masted schooner, ordered by Spain, sold to Chile in 1953. Similar to the Spanish *Juan Sebastian de Elcano.* Refitted in South Africa, 1977. The small yacht *Blanco Estella* (14 crew) is also used for training.

◆ **1 buoy tender and lighthouse-servicing ship**

ATA 73 Colo Colo Bldr: Bow, McLachlan, Paisley, U.K. (In serv. 1929)

D: 790 tons **S:** 11 kts **Dim:** 41.38 × 8.72 × 4.07
M: 1 set triple-expansion, reciprocating; 1 prop; 1,050 hp **Boilers:** 2
Fuel: 155 tons

◆ **1 tug**

YT 115 Galvez Bldr: Southern Shipbuilders, U.K. (In serv. 1975)

D: 112 grt **S:** . . . **Dim:** 25.5 × 7.3 × 2.8

Note: Tugs *Reyes* (YT 120) and *Cortez* (YT 128) were stricken 1983.

◆ **1 10,000-ton capacity floating dry dock** Bldr: ASMAR, Talcahuano

Valparaiso III (L: 8-10-83)

D: 4,150 tons (light) **Dim:** 167.0 × 33.0 (26.1 interior width) × 3.95

Remarks: Built for shipyard, rather than naval service, but available to the Navy.

◆ **2 U.S. ARD 24-class floating dry docks** (In serv. 1944)

131 Ingeniero Mery (ex-ARD 25) 132 Mutilla (ex-ARD 32)

Capacity: 3,500 tons **Dim:** 149.86 × 24.69 × 1.73 (light)

Remarks: 131 leased 15-12-60; 132 transferred 20-8-73. Both at Talcahuano. Dock inside dimensions: 118.6-m on blocks, 18.0-m clear width, 6.3-m draft over blocks. Bow end pointed.

◆ **1 small floating dry dock** (In serv. 1908)

Manterola

Capacity: 1,000 tons **Dim:** 66.0 × 12.8 × . . .

CHILE *(continued)*

CHILEAN COAST GUARD

PATROL CRAFT

◆ **10 "Anchova"-class patrol craft** Bldr: MacLaren, Niteroi, Brazil (In serv. 1980-82)

GC 1801 Pillan	GC 1805 Corcovado	GC 1808 Osorno
GC 1802 Troncador	GC 1806 Llaina	GC 1809 Choshuenco
GC 1803 Rano-Kau	GC 1807 Antuco	GC 1810 Copahue
GC 1804 Villarrica		

D: 31 tons (43 fl) **S:** 25 kts **Dim:** 18.60 × 5.25 × 1.62
A: 2/20-mm AA (I × 2)—2/d.c. racks **Electron Equipt:** Radar: 1/Decca 110
M: 2 MTU 8V331 TC 81 diesels; 2 props; 1,800 hp
Range: 700/15 **Electric:** 10 kw

Remarks: Ordered 1977. Wooden construction. Named for volcanoes ("Anchova" is the builder's class name). Last pair delivered 16-11-82.

◆ **1 hospital craft** Bldr: ASMAR, Talcahuano (In serv. 1964)

Cirujano Videla

D: 140 tons (fl) **S:** 14 kts **Dim:** 31.0 × 6.5 × 2.0
M: 2 Cummins VT-12-700M diesels; 2 props; 1,400 hp **Electric:** 60 kw

Remarks: Modified U.S. PGM 59 gunboat design, with enlarged superstructure. Originally used by Navy for civil assistance programs but later transferred to Coast Guard for same function.

◆ **13 search-and-rescue craft** Bldr: ASENAV, Valdivia (In serv. 1981-84)

LPM 1901-1913

D: 14 tons (fl) **S:** 18 kts **Dim:** 13.3 × 3.5 × 1.0
M: 2 MTU 6V331 TC92 diesels; 2 props; 1,320 hp

Remarks: Names include: *Aquila, Arica, Calle-Calle, Corrae, Punta Gruesa.*

◆ **1 service launch for search and rescue at Easter Island**

Kimitahi (In serv. 1981)—**D:** 14 tons **S:** 17 kts.

CHINA

People's Republic of China

Personnel: 126,000 men in the following categories:
Regular naval: 36,000 afloat/32,000 ashore
Naval air arm: 30,000, Marine Corps: 28,000. There are also about 1,000,000 paramilitary personnel in the Naval Militia.

Merchant Marine (1984): 1,262 ships—9,300,358 grt (tankers: 136 ships—1,343,220 grt)

Note: This does not include the large number of ships involved only in coastal trade.

Naval Aviation: The naval air arm, which is under the control of the navy, consists of about 850 aircraft, including 600 Fagot, Fantan-A (50), Farmer (300), and Fresco fighters, 150 Badger, Bat, and Beagle light bombers, and about 60 transports, 20 Madge (Be-6) seaplanes, and 40 Mi-4 (H 4) Hound and 6 French-supplied Super Frelon helicopters. Its principal mission is defense of the coast and of naval surface forces near the coast. A few of the aircraft are believed to be equipped for minelaying. Control of naval aircraft is integrated with the continental air-defense system. The Badger bombers are being equipped with C 801 (Styx-copy) anti-ship missiles; these are also land-launched from tracked vehicles. These missiles are 7.381-m long, travel at Mach 0.9, and have a 95–100-km range.

Warships In Service Or Under Construction As Of 1 January 1986

	L	Tons (Surfaced)	Main armament
◆ **114 (+. . .) submarines**			
2 (+2) Xia	1981	. . .	12 CSS-NX-3, TT
3 (+1) Han	1971-83	. . .	TT
1 Golf	1964	2,300	3 ballistic missiles, 10/533-mm TT
3 Ming	1975-82	1,500	8/533-mm TT
84 Romeo	1964 on	1,330	8/533-mm TT
21 Whiskey	1960-64	1,050	6/533-mm TT
◆ **19 destroyers**		Tons	
15 Luda	1970-83	3,960	4/130-mm, 6 Styx
4 Gordyy	1938-40	1,660	4/130-mm, 4 Styx
◆ **28 frigates**			
0 (+2) . . .	1986?	. . .	. . .
17 Jianghu	1974-84	1,600	2/100-mm, 4 Styx
2 Jiangdong	1972-75	1,800	4/100-mm, 2 SAM
5 Jiangnan	1966-68	1,400	3/100-mm
4 Riga	1953-56	1,420	3/100-mm, 2 Styx

◆ **190-195 guided-missile patrol boats**

◆ **230 torpedo boats**

◆ **500+ patrol boats and craft**

◆ **115-120 minesweepers**

◆ **500+ amphibious ships and craft**

WEAPONS AND SENSORS

China at present manufactures nearly all of its own weapons and sensors, although most designs are based directly on Soviet or Western designs. Two versions of the Soviet SS-N-2a Styx are in use, the Hai Ying-2 (also known as the CSS-N-1) and a lengthened version known in the West as the CSS-N-2 and employed only on the Luda-class destroyers. A smaller, rocket-powered anti-ship missile was shown to the public in 9-84. China's only naval surface-to-air missile, intended for the two Jiangdong-class frigates, has been in development since the 1960s and may finally have entered service in 1983-84. Guns are all based on Soviet models, but China has developed unique naval mountings, including a twin 57-mm weapon and a side-by-side twin 14.5-mm mg mount also used by the Romanian Navy. The ASW rocket launcher used on the Luda-class destroyers is a 12-tubed, Chinese-designed version of the Soviet RBU-1200, with a range of 1,200 m. A Chinese ASW torpedo has been in development since the 1970s, but China was attempting in 1985 to obtain a license to build the U.S. Mk 46.

Radars are, with a few exceptions, known by their Western nicknames:

Name	Origin	Band	Function
Ball End	U.S.S.R.	E/F	Surface search
Bean Sticks	China	S	Early warning
Eye Shield	China	E/F	Surface search (Chinese name: MX-902)
Fin Curve	U.K.	I	Nav. (Decca 707 copy)
Fog Lamp	China	H/I	SAM f.c.
Neptun	U.S.S.R.	I	Nav.
Pot Head	U.S.S.R.	I	Nav./surface search
Rice Lamp	China	I	Gun control
Rice Screen	China	?	3-D air search
Skin Head	U.S.S.R.	I	Surface search
Slim Net	U.S.S.R.	E/F	Air/surface search
Square Tie	U.S.S.R	. . .	Surface search (Chinese name: Type 331)
Sun Visor	U.S.S.R.	I	Gun f.c.
Type 756	China	S	Nav.

IFF systems have only come into general use since the early 1980s and are still not universally fitted. The equipment includes the Soviet Square Head interrogation antenna and the High Pole A transponder. Sonars are of Soviet design.

CLASS NAMES AND PENDANTS

The class names used below are generally those assigned by Western intelligence services; the Chinese Navy uses a numbered system, for which few of the designations are known.

For combatants, three-digit hull numbers are assigned: 100—destroyers; 200, 300, 400—submarines; 500—frigates; 600 and 700—coastal patrol/subchasers; 800—mine warfare; 900—amphibious warfare. Small combatants have a four-digit pendant, the first number of which signifies area subordination. Auxiliaries have three-digit numbers preceded by a letter signifying function:

B—Cable layer	Q—Crane
C—Icebreaker	S—Research ship
E—Diving tender	T—Tug (all types)
H—Buoy tender	U—Repair
J—Salvage and rescue (submarine-associated)	W—Dredge
K—Hydrographic survey	X—Liquid cargo
L—Dry cargo/stores	Y—Dry cargo/transport

In addition, the numerous ships subordinated to the various districts of the Maritime Border Defense Force have four-digit pendants preceded by a letter signifying the district; known prefixes include "S" for Shenyang, "N" for Nanjing (commonly seen in the Shanghai area), and "G" for Guangzhou.

BALLISTIC MISSILE SUBMARINES

◆ **2 (+2) Xia class** Bldr: Huludao SY (In serv. 1986-87-. . .)

406 (L: 4-81) . . . (L: 1982)

D: 7,000 tons submerged **S:** 20 kts sub. **Dim:** 120.0 × 10.0 × . . .
A: 12 CSS-NX-3 strategic missiles—. . . /TT
M: 1 pressurized water nuclear reactor, turbo-electric drive; 1 prop; . . . hp

Remarks: The first "Xia" (western nickname)-class submarine was launched in 4-81 from the same facility that builds the Han-class nuclear-powered attack submarine—

BALLISTIC MISSILE SUBMARINES *(continued)*

Huludao shipyard, 200 km northeast of Peking in Liao Ning province. At least two additional units are expected. The first CSS-NX-3 submerged launch took place on 12-10-82 to a range of 1,600 km from the Golf-class trials submarine. The missile is believed to have 2 solid-propulsion stages and to have a range of 1,500 n.m. (2,795 km).

◆ **1 Soviet Golf Class**

D: 2,300/2,700 tons **S:** 12 kts submerged **Dim:** 100.0 × 8.5 × 6.6
A: 3 ballistic missiles—10/533-mm TT (6 fwd, 4 aft)
M: 3 diesels, electric drive; 3 props; 6,000 hp **Range:** 9,000/5

Remarks: Plans furnished by the Soviet Union at a time when relations between the two countries were good. Launched first Chinese SLBM on 12-10-82.

SUBMARINES

◆ **3 (+1) Han class, nuclear**

	Bldr	Laid down	L	In serv.
401	Huludao SY	1965-68	1972	1974
402	Huludao SY	. . .	1977	1980
403	Huludao SY	. . .	1983	21-9-84
. . .	Huludao SY	. . .	. . .	. . .

D: 4,500 tons submerged **S:** 25 kts surf./30 kts sub. **Dim:** 90.0 × 8.0 × . . .
A: . . . /TT
M: 1 pressurized water nuclear reactor, turbo-electric drive; 1 prop (?); . . . hp

Remarks: The trials series for the first unit were very protracted. The class is believed to be intended to consist of 4 units.

◆ **3 Ming class** Bldr: . . .

D: 1,500/1,900 tons **S:** 17/15 kts **Dim:** 76.0 × 6.7 × 5.0
A: 6/533-mm TT **M:** Diesel-electric; 1 prop

Remarks: First two launched 1975; third launched 1982. Evidently a Chinese design derived from the Romeo.

◆ **84 Soviet Romeo class** Bldrs: Wuzhang, Guangzhou, Jiangnan, and Huludao shipyards (In serv. 1960-1982)

Romeo 267 R. Gillett, 9-84

Romeo 260 5-84

D: 1,319/1,712 tons **S:** 15.2/13 kts **Dim:** 76.60 × 6.70 × 4.95
A: 8/533-mm TT (6 fwd/2aft)—14 torpedoes or 28 mines
Electron Equipt: Radar: 1/Snoop Plate—Sonar: Tamir-5L active, Feniks passive
M: Diesel-electric: 2 diesels, 2,000 hp each; 2 props; 2,700 HP—2 electric creep motors: 100 hp
Endurance: 60 days, 224-cell battery: 6,000 Amp Hr.
Range: 14,000/9 surf.; 350/9 sub. **Man:** 53 men

Remarks: Diving depth: 270 meters. Foreign transfers include 7 to North Korea between 1973 and 1975, 4 to Egypt in 1982-83.

◆ **21 Soviet Whiskey class** Bldr: 15 at Jiangnan SY, 6 at Wuzhang, SY

D: 1,050/1,350 tons **S:** 17/13.5 **Dim:** 76.0 × 6.3 × 4.8
A: 6/533-mm TT (4 fwd, 2 aft)—12 torpedoes or 24 mines
Electron Equipt: Radar: 1/Snoop Plate—Sonar: Tamir-5L active; . . . passive
M: Diesel-electric: 2 Type 37D diesels; 2,000 hp each; 2,500 hp
Range: 8,300/8 snorkel

Remarks: A few were delivered by the U.S.S.R., the others were built in China (1960-64), probably at the Jiangnan Shipyard near Shanghai. Several retain a twin 25-mm AA in a semi-enclosed mount at the base of the forward end of the sail. About 6 are believed to be in reserve or in reduced commission for training.

DESTROYERS

◆ **15 Luda class** Bldr: Luda SY, Guangzhou SY, and Zhonghua SY, Shanghai (In serv., 1972-1984)

105, 106, 107, 108, 109, 110, 111, 131, 132, 133, 161, 162, 163, 164, 165

Luda 132—with 8/57-mm AA, two f.c. radars R.N.Z.N., 1980

Luda 110—with 8/37-mm AA R. Gillett, 9-84

D: 3,960 tons (fl) **S:** 32 kts **Dim:** 131.0 × 12.7 × 4.8
A: 6/CSS-N-2 Styx SSM (III × 2)—4/130-mm DP (II × 2)—8/57-mm or 37-mm AA (II × 4)—4/25-mm AA (II × 2)—2 12-tubed ASW RL—4/BMB-2 d.c. mortars—2/d.c. racks—mines
Electron Equipt: Radar: 1/Fin Curve or Type 756 navigational, 1/Eye Shield (MX-902) short-range air-search, 1 Bean Sticks or Pea Sticks (antenna variant) long-range air-search, 1/Square Tie, 1/Sun Visor (not on all) 2/Rice Lamp for 57-mm f.c. (not on all)
Sonar: . . . EW: 2/Watch Dog
IFF: 3/Square Head interrogators, 1/High Pole A transponder
M: 2 sets GT; 2 props; 60,000 hp **Boilers:** 4 **Range:** 4,000/15 **Man:** 300 tot.

Remarks: Superficially resembles Soviet Kotlin, but is larger and has a flat transom stern, larger superstructure, etc. Some systems of Soviet design; the ASW rocket launchers are derived from the Soviet RBU-1200 design, but have more tubes. Equipment varies greatly from ship to ship, with only a small number having fire-control radar systems, even on the Soviet Wasp Head 130-mm GFCS. The SSM used is derived from the Soviet SS-N-2 Styx, but is longer. One ship of this class (probably 160) lost 8-78 near Zanjiang through explosion. All equipped for underway fuelling.

Ludas 105, 108, and 132 are the only units confirmed to mount twin 57-mm vice 37-mm AA; they also carry the Rice Lamp AA fire-control radars not mounted on the others. Pea Sticks long-range air search is carried by 107, 131, and 162; the remainder have Bean Sticks. Sun Visor fire-control radars are mounted on the Wasp Head directors for the 130-mm DP guns only on 105, 108, 131, 161, and 162. Plans to modernize these basically excellent platforms with British equipment fell through in 1983. In 1985 it was announced that U.S. MK15 CIWS (Vulcan/Phalaux) would be added, along with U.S. Mk 46 ASW torpedoes and, possibly, ASW helicopters (Kaman SH-2F Lamps I) in a few.

◆ **4 Soviet Gordyy-class**

	Bldr	L	In serv.
101 Anshan (ex-*Razyaschiy*)	Dalzavod SY, Vladivostok	1938	1940
102 Zhangzhun (ex-*Reshitel'nyy*, ex-*Pritkiy*)	Dalzavod SY, Vladivostok	1939	1941
103 Ji Lin (ex-*Retivyy*)	Komsomolsk SY	1940	1941
104 Fu Zhun (ex-*Rezkiy*, ex-*Pospenshnyy*)	Komsomolsk SY	1939	1942

D: 1,657 tons (2,039 fl) **S:** 38 kts when built, certainly much less today
Dim: 112.86 × 10.20 × 3.8 **Range:** 800/38; 2,600/20 **Man:** 197 tot.
A: 4/HY-2 SSM (II × 2)—4/130-mm (I × 4)—8/37-mm AA (II × 4)—mines
Electron Equipt: Radar: 1/Fin Curve, 1/Square Tie—Sonar: none
M: 2 sets GT; 2 props; 48,000 hp **Boilers:** 3 **Fuel:** 500 tons

Remarks: All assembled in Far East from prefabrications by 61 Kommuna SY, Nikolayev. Transferred by the U.S.S.R., two in 12-54, the others in 7-55. The SSM, derived from the Soviet SS-N-2 Styx, replaced 6/533-mm TT (III × 2) between 1972 and 1974. No ASW armament.

FRIGATES

◆ **0 (+2 + . . .) new construction** Bldr: Jiangnan SY, Shanghai

REMARKS: A new class of frigates with CODOG propulsion systems incorporating the LM-2500 gas turbine was commenced in 1984-85. Armament will include the French 100-mm Compact DP gun and the U.S. Mk 15 CIWS. A displacement of "2,000 tons" is reported.

◆ **17 Jianghu class, guided-missile** Bldr: Hudong SY, Shanghai (1975-84)

509-516, 518, 521, 524-527, 533, 534, 551

Jianghu 512—rectangular stack, single 100-mm mounts, no Eye Shield radar 1983

Jianghu 533—with twin 100-mm mounts, Eye Shield radar, and rounded stack Chinese Navy, 1984

D: 1,586 tons (1,900 fl) **S:** 25.5 kts **Dim:** 103.2 × 10.2 × 3.05 (hull)
A: 4/HY-2 Styx SSM (II × 2)—2/100-mm DP—12/37-mm AA (II × 6)—2 or 4/RBU 1200 (V × 2 or 4)—4/BMB-2 d.c. mortars—2/d.c. racks—mines (533, 534 have 2 twin 100, only 4 twin 37-mm)
Electron Equipt: Radar: 1/Eye Shield (MX-902) air search, 1/Square Tie f.c., 1/Type 756 navigational
Sonar: 1/medium freq.—EW: None
IFF: 2/Square Head, 1/High Pole A
M: 2/SEMT-Pielstick diesels; 2 props; 16,000 hp **Range:** 4,000/15; 1,750/25
Endurance: 15 days **Man:** 195 tot.

REMARKS: First launched 1975. A variation of the Jiantung class with SSM vice SAM. Have only an optical rangefinder for 100-mm fire control.

Early units (509-516 had bow bulwarks and a rectangular stack. Later ships have a rounded stack, while 533 and 534, with twin 100-mm gunmounts, omitted the bow bulwarks and deleted two of the twin 37-mm AA mounts to save top weight. Most have only 2 RBU-1200 ASW RL, while 515, 516, and units in the S 21 series have 4 RBU-1200. Two with twin 57-mm AA vice 100-mm guns were delivered to Egypt 1984-85.

◆ **2 Jiangdong-class guided missile** Bldr: Hudong SY, Shanghai

531 ZHONGDONG (In serv. 1972) 535 N. . . (In serv. 1975)

Zhongdong (531)—with two Gordyy-class destroyers in the background 1982

Zhongdong (531)—with new radars installed 1983

D: 1,568 tons (1,900 fl) **S:** 25.5 kts **Dim:** 103.2 × 10.2 × 3.05 (hull)
A: 2/SAM systems—4/100-mm DP (II × 2)—8/37-mm AA (II × 4)—2/RBU-1200 (V × 2)—2/BMB-2 d.c. mortars—2/d.c. racks
Electron Equipt: Radar: 1/Type 756 nav., 1/Rice Screen, 2/Fog Lamp, 1/Rice Lamp, 1/Sun Visor
Sonar: 1/MF hull-mounted—EW: None
IFF: 1/High Pole A transponder
M: 2 SEMT-Pielstick diesels; 2 props; 16,000 hp **Range:** 4,000/15; 1,750/25
Endurance: 15 days **Man:** 195 tot.

REMARKS: SAM systems, of Chinese design, may recently have achieved operational status. A Fog Lamp missile f.c. radar is now mounted on the foremast, with a second aft. A Rice Screen phased-array 3-D air-search radar antenna surmounts the foremast, and a Rice Lamp gun f.c. radar is atop the aftermast.

Jianghu 514 R. Gillett, 9-84

FRIGATES *(continued)*

◆ **5 Jiangnan class** Bldr: Shantou SY and Jiangnan SY, Shanghai (In serv. 1964-68)

501 502 503 504 508

Jiangnan-class frigate 504 U.S. Navy, 1983

D: 1,400 tons (fl) **S:** 28 kts **Dim:** 92.0 × 10.2 × 3.0 (hull)
A: 3.100-mm (I × 3, 1 fwd, 2 aft)—8/37-mm AA (II × 4)—4/14.5-mm mg (II × 2)—2/RBU-1200 (V × 2)—4/BMB-2 d.c. mortars—2/d.c. racks—mines
Electron Equipt: Radar: 1/Fin Curve nav.—Sonar: MF hull-mounted
M: 2 diesels; 2 props; 16,000 hp

REMARKS: Chinese version of the Soviet Riga class, with diesel propulsion. One built at Shanghai 1968, the others at Shantou. Lack sensors and radar f.c., but do have optical director for 100-mm guns.

◆ **4 Soviet Riga class**

	Bldr	L	In serv.
505 GUIYANG	Hudong SY, Shanghai	26-9-56	1958
506 KUNMING	Guangzhou SY	1957	1959
507 CHENGDU	Hudong SY, Shanghai	28-4-56	1958
509 GUILIN	Guangzhou SY	1957	1959

Kunming (506) 1980

Chengdu (507) 1982

D: 1,280 tons (1,510 fl) **S:** 28 kts **Dim:** 91.0 × 10.2 × 3.2
A: 2/SSM (II × 1)—3/100-mm DP (I × 3)—4/37-mm AA (II × 2)—4/14.5-mm mg (II × 2)—4/BMB-2 d.c. mortars—2/d.c. racks—mines
Electron Equipt: Radar: 1/Type 756 nav. 1/Slim Net, 1/Square Tie, 1/Sun Visor
Sonar: MF hull-mounted—EW: None
IFF; 2/Square Head, 1/High Pole A
M: 2 sets GT; 2 props; 20,000 hp **Boilers:** 2: 27 kg/cm², 360°C **Fuel:** 230 tons
Electric: 450 kw **Range:** 550/28; 2,000/13 **Man:** 175 tot.

REMARKS: Twin, trainable CSS-N-1 Styx launcher replaced torpedo tube mount during early 1970s. Very limited endurance.

CORVETTES

NOTE: Some of the following ships, acquired in 1949 following the departure of Kuomintang forces, may have been stricken in recent years.

◆ **1 Japanese Ukuru class** Bldr: Hitachi, Kanagawa

	L	In serv.
HUI AN (ex-*Shisaka*)	31-10-44	7-45

D: 940 tons (1,020 fl) **S:** 19.5 kts **Dim:** 78.6 × 9.1 × 3.0
A: 12/37-mm AA (II × 3, I × 6)—2/BMB-2 d.c. mortars—2/d.c. racks—mines
M: 2 diesels; 2 props; 4,200 hp **Range:** 5,000/16 **Man:** 150 tot.

REMARKS: Reengined and rearmed with Soviet guns during 1950s. Again rearmed late 1970s, when twin 37-mm AA replaced three single 100-mm mounts, and ASW ordnance was added.

◆ **up to 5 Japanese Kaibokan Type D class**

	Bldr	Laid down	L	In serv.
WU JANG (ex-CD 14)	Yokosuka NY	5-10-43	25-1-44	27-3-44
JANGSHA (ex-CD 118)	Ishikawajima, Tokyo	8-6-44	20-11-44	27-12-44
DUNGAN (ex-CD 192)	Mitsubishi, Nagasaki	5-12-44	30-1-45	28-2-45
JIAN (ex-CD 194)	Mitsubishi, Nagasaki	18-12-44	15-2-45	15-3-45
SHIAN (ex-CD 198)	Mitsubishi, Nagasaki	17-1-45	26-2-45	31-3-45

Japanese Kaibokan Type D in Chinese service

D: 740 tons (940 fl) **S:** 17 kts **Dim:** 69.5 × 8.6 × 3.0
A: 2/100-mm DP (I × 2)—6/37-mm AA (II × 2, I × 2)—mines
M: 1 set GT; 1 prop; 2,500 hp
Boilers: 2 Kampon **Range:** 4,500/14 **Man:** 150 tot.

REMARKS: Some have probably been discarded. Very lightly built. Rearmed in 1950s: some had 2 U.S. 76.2-mm Mk 26 DP. No ASW armament. Only two or three remain.

◆ **1 Japanese Etorufu class** Bldr: Uraga DY, Tokyo

	L	In serv.
JANGBEI (ex-*Oki*)	20-12-42	31-3-43

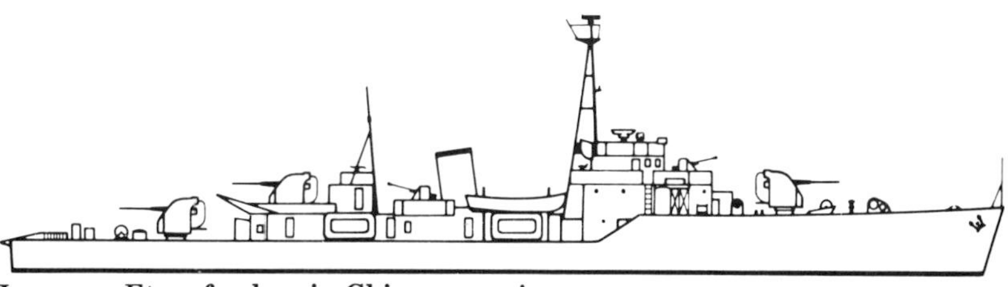

Japanese Etorufu class in Chinese service

D: 860 tons (1, 020 fl) **S:** 19 kts **Dim:** 77.7 × 8.8 × 3.0
A: 3/100-mm DP (I × 3)—3/37-mm AA—mines
M: 2 diesels; 2 props; 4,200 hp
Range: 8,000/16 **Man:** 150 tot.

REMARKS: Rearmed with Soviet weapons during late 1950s. No ASW capability.

◆ **1 Australian Bathurst-class former minesweeper** Bldr: Cockatoo DY & Eng., Sydney

	Laid down	L	In serv.
LOYANG (ex-merc. *Cheung Hing,* ex-Aust. *Bendigo*)	12-8-40	1-3-41	10-5-41

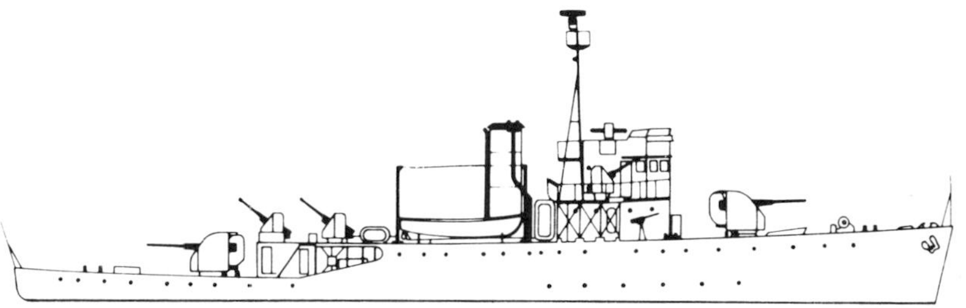

Australian Bathurst class in Chinese service

D: 733 tons **S:** 15 kts **Dim:** 56.59 × 9.47 × 3.20
A: 2/100-mm DP (I × 2)—5/37-mm AA (I × 5)—2/14.5-mm mg (I × 2)
M: 2 sets triple-expansion reciprocating steam; 2 props; 1,800 hp
Boilers: 2/Yarrow 3-drum **Fuel:** 153 tons **Range:** 1,730/14; 2,640/10
Man: 100 tot.

◆ **1 Japanese Hashidate-class former river gunboat**

	Bldr	L	In serv.
NANJANG (ex-*Uji*)	Sakurajima, Osaka	29-9-40	30-4-41

CORVETTES *(continued)*

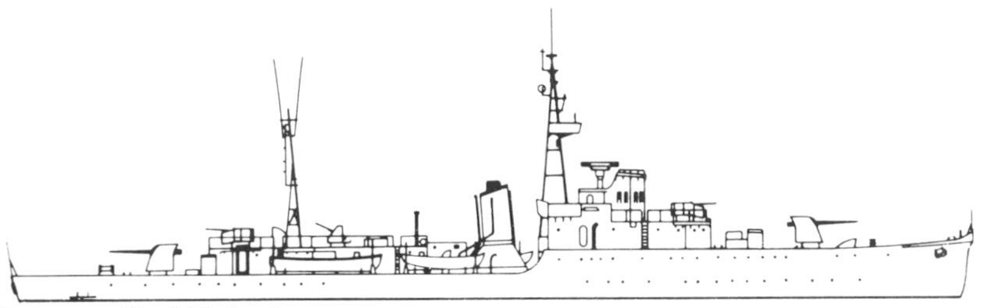

Japanese Hashidate class

D: 999 tons light (1,200 fl) **S:** 19 kts **Dim:** 79.2 × 9.7 × 2.4
A: 2/130-mm (I × 2)—5/37-mm AA (II × 2, I × 1)—mines
M: 2 sets GT; 2 props; 4,600 hp **Boilers:** 2 Kampon
Range: 3,400/14 **Man:** 170 tot.

REMARKS: Sunk twice during World War II. Rearmed with Soviet guns during mid-1950s; 130-mm guns same as on *Gordyy*-class destroyers.

GUIDED-MISSILE PATROL BOATS

◆ **0 (+16) H-3 project** Bldr: . . .

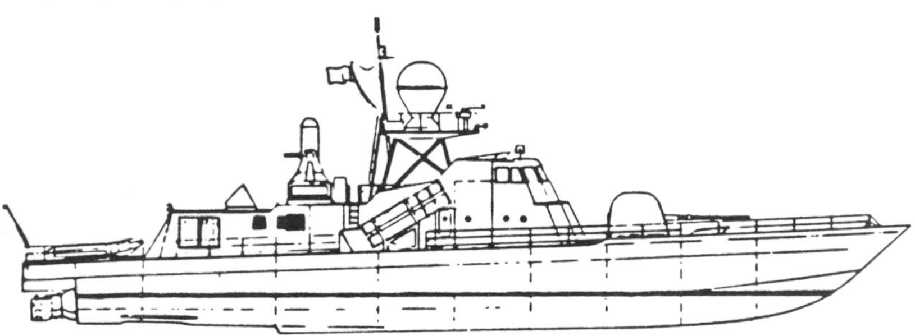

H-3 notional configuration H-3 R & D Group, 1985

D: 239 tons (fl) **S:** 50+ kts **Dim:** 47.0 × 7.5 × 1.9
A: 4/SSM—1/76-mm OTO Melara DP—1/20-mm Mk 15 CIWS
Electron Equipt: Radar: 1/nav., 1/H.S.A. WM-25 series
M: 3 G.M. Allison 570kF gas turbines; 3 KaMeWa waterjets; 19,182 hp

REMARKS: Aluminum construction project, designed by Edward Heinemann, of Douglas Aircraft fame, with Nickum & Spaulding Associates. Armament and electronics listed are provisional; a newly noted Chinese SSM of MM 40 Exocet dimensions may be intended. Prototype may be built in U.S., with up to 15 production versions to be built in China.

◆ **1 Hola class** (In serv. 1970)

D: 300 tons **S:** . . . kts **Dim:** 43.0 × . . . × . . .
A: 2/HY-2 SSM (I × 2)—2/37-mm AA (II × 2)

REMARKS: An enlarged version of Osa-I, and at one time equipped with a large radome. Apparently unsuccessful. Two additional SSM also removed by 1980s.

◆ **120 Huangfeng (Soviet Osa-I) class** Bldr: Jiangnan SY, Shanghai, 1960-

No. 3115, with radome aft and 30-mm AA R. Gillett, 9-84

D: 175 tons, 186.5 normal (205 fl) **S:** 35 kts **Dim:** 38.75 × 7.60 × 1.7 (mean)
A: 4/HY-2 Styx SSM—4/25-mm or 30-mm AA (II × 2)
Electron Equipt: Radar: 1/Square Tie—IFF: 2/Square Head, 1/High Pole A
M: 3 M503A diesels; 3 props; 12,000 hp
Electric: 65 kw **Range:** 800/30 **Man:** 28 tot.

REMARKS: At least four were transferred by the U.S.S.R. circa 1960 and have 4/30-mm AA (II × 2) but no Drum Tilt gun fire-control radar. Most Chinese-built units had two twin 25-mm AA until early 1980s, when increasing numbers with a Chinese-built version of the Soviet AK-230, 30-mm AA began to appear; more recently, several have had a radome installed aft for a probable f.c. radar for the 30-mm AA. The 1980s have also seen the introduction of IFF equipment. Considerable numbers of the craft have been seen in an incomplete state in the Shanghai area in recent years, and not all of the listed total are operational.

No. 3113, with 25-mm AA, no IFF or gun f.c. radar Chinese Navy, 1979

No. 5102, with 30-mm AA, but no radome aft R. Gillett, 9-84

◆ **70-75 Hoku class**

Hoku-class, guided-missile patrol boat—with Homa hydrofoil variant inboard 1978

D: 68 tons (74 normal/79.19 fl) **S:** 38 kts
Dim: 27.0 × 6.30 × 1.8 (1.295 mean hull)
A: 2/HY-2 Styx SSM—2/25-mm AA (II × 1)
Electron Equipt: Radar: 1/Square Tie **M:** 4 M50 diesels; 4 props; 4,800 hp
Electric: 65 kw **Endurance:** 5 days **Range:** 520/26 **Man:** 17 tot.

REMARKS: Steel-hulled improvement on Komar. Also referred to as "Hegu"class. A slightly longer variant, with hydrofoils and a second 25-mm AA mount aft, is nicknamed "Homa" and apparently appeared in only a single, unsuccessful, prototype form.

TORPEDO BOATS

◆ **120 Huchuan-class hydrofoils** Bldr: Hudong SY, Shanghai (In serv. 1966-1980)

D: 39 tons (45.8 fl) **S:** 50 kts **Dim:** 22.50 × 3.80 (6.26 over foils) × 1.146
A: 2/533-mm TT—4/14.5-mm mg(II × 2)
Electron Equipt: Radar: 1/Type 756
M: 3 M50 diesels; 3 props; 3,600 hp **Electric:** 5.6 kw
Range: 500/30 **Man:** 11 tot.

REMARKS: Identical to the hydrofoils delivered to Albania, Pakistan, and Tanzania. Also built in Romania. Not all units have the foils fitted; no foils aft, as stern planes on surface. In most, both gunmounts are aft, but in a few, one mount is forward. Some have Skin Head radar, while later ships have a Type 756 slotted-waveguide radar antenna.

TORPEDO BOATS *(continued)*

Chinese Huchuan class—unit in foreground (3214) has no hydrofoils; craft in background to left does

◆ **60 Soviet P 6-class wooden-hulled** Bldr: China, 1960s

D: 56 tons (66.5 fl) **S:** 43 kts **Dim:** 25.3 × 6.1 × 1.7
A: 2/533-mm TT—4.25-mm AA (II × 2)
Electron Equipt: Radar: 1/Skin Head
M: 4 M50 diesels; 4 props; 4,800 hp **Man:** 20 tot.

REMARKS: Beginning to be retired.

◆ **50 Soviet P 4-class aluminum-hulled hydroplanes (1950s)**

D: 19.3 tons (22.4 fl) **S:** 55 kts **Dim:** 19.3 × 3.7 × 1.0
A: 2/14.5-mm mg (II × 1)—2/450-mm TT **Man:** 12 tot.
Electron Equipt: Radar: 1/Skin Head **M:** 2 M50 diesels; 2 props; 2,400 hp

REMARKS: Majority believed to be in reserve. Four transferred to Bangladesh, 1983.

PATROL BOATS

◆ **40-45 Hainan class** (In serv. 1964-. . .)

Hainan-class patrol boat 642 R. Gillett, 9-84

D: 375 tons (400 fl) **S:** 30.5 kts **Dim:** 58.77 × 7.20 × 2.20 (hull)
A: 4/57-mm AA (II × 2)—4/25-mm AA (II × 2)—4/RBU-1200 (V × 4)—2/BMB-2 d.c. mortars—2/d.c. racks—mines
Electron Equipt: Radar: 1/Pot Head—IFF; 1/High Pole A transponder
M: 4 diesels; 4 props; 8,800 hp
Range: 2,000/14 **Man:** 70 tot.

REMARKS: Hull numbers in 600s and 800s. Early units had 2/76.2-mm DP U.S. Mk 26 vice 4/57-mm AA and Skin Head radars. Two were transferred to Pakistan, 1976, and two more in 1980; eight delivered to Egypt 1983-85.

NOTE: An enlarged version of Hainan, nicknamed the Haiju class has been reported. On an overall length of 64 m, the armament is 2/57-mm AA (II), 4/30-mm AA (II × 2), 4/RBU-1200 ASW RL (V × 4). No confirmation available.

Hainan-class patrol boat 687 R. Gillett, 9-84

◆ **20 Soviet Kronshtadt class** (In serv. 1956-57)

Chinese Kronshtadt No. 275 1970

D: 300 tons (330 fl) **S:** 18 kts **Dim:** 52.1 × 6.5 × 2.2
A: 1/85-mm DP—2/37-mm AA—6/14.5-mm mg (II × 3)—2/BMB-1 d.c. projectors—2/d.c. racks. Some: 2/RBU-1200 ASW RL (V × 2)
Electron Equipt: Radar: 1/Ball End **M:** 3 diesels; 3 props; 3,300 hp
Fuel: 20 tons **Range:** 3,500/14 **Man:** 50 tot.

REMARKS: Six could have been delivered by the U.S.S.R., the other built in Shanghai and Canton. Other information indicates that only two were built in China, the balance in the Soviet Union. Hull numbers in 600s.

◆ **325-330 Shanghai-II class** (In serv. 1962-. . .)

Shanghai-II—late version R. Gillett, 9-84

Shanghai-II class—early version with squared-off bridge 1976

D: 122.5 tons (134.8 fl) **S:** 28.5 kts **Dim:** 38.78 × 5.41 × 1.49 (hull; 1.554 full load)
A: 4/37-mm AA (II × 2)—4/25-mm AA (II × 2)—depth charges—mines. Some: 2/81-mm recoilless rifles (II × 1)
Electron Equipt: Radar: Pot Head or Skin Head
M: 2 M50F-4, 1,200-hp, and 2/12D6, 910-hp diesels; 4 props; 4,220 hp
Endurance: 7 days **Electric:** 39 kw **Range:** 750/16.5 **Man:** 36 tot.

REMARKS: Still being constructed. A large number have been transferred to foreign navies. Very unsophisticated and sparsely equipped. Shanghai-I class was smaller and had 2/57-mm (II × 1) forward; a few of the 12 built 1959-60 may remain in service: 125 tons (fl); 36.0 × 5.5 × 1.4; propulsion as for Shanghai-II.

PATROL BOATS *(continued)*

◆ **25 Shantou class** (In serv. 1955-60)

Shantou class—with recoilless rifle on bow

D: 80 tons (fl) **S:** 28 kts **Dim:** 25.1 × 6.0 × 1.8
A: 4/37-mm AA (II × 2)—2/14.5-mm mg (I × 2)—1/81-mm recoilless rifle
Electron Equipt: Radar: 1/Skin Head
M: 2 Type 3D12, 300-hp diesels; 2 M50, 1,200-hp diesels; 4 props; 3,000 hp

REMARKS: Formerly nicknamed the "Swatow" class. Similar to P 6, but broader and with a steel hull.

PATROL CRAFT

◆ **. . . 25-meter class** Bldr: . . . (In serv. 1980s)

D: 53.5 tons normal (55.77 fl) **S:** 38 kts **Dim:** 25.0 × 5.0 × . . .
A: 4/25-mm AA (II × 2) **Electron Equipt:** Radar: 1/Pot Head
M: 3 M50-series diesels; 3 props; 3,600 hp **Electric:** 12 kw
Endurance: 5-7 days **Range:** 300/27; 490/. . . **Man:** 20 tot.

REMARKS: Official data for a class of patrol craft that has yet to receive a Western nickname. Apparently a production successor to the Beihai class.

◆ **30 Beihai-class patrol craft** Bldr: . . . (1960s)

Beihai class 1966

D: 80 tons (fl) **S:** 18 kts **Dim:** 27.5 × 5.5 × 1.6
A: 4/25-mm AA (II × 2) **M:** 3 diesels; 3 props; 900 hp

REMARKS: Majority subordinated to Naval Militia of the various "Military Maritime Districts."

◆ **15 Huangpu-class patrol craft** Bldr: . . . (In serv. 1970s)

REMARKS: Data as for Beihai class, except A: 4/14.5-mm mg (II × 2). Have low superstructure fore and aft, providing additional accommodations for police or troops.

◆ **40 Yulin-class patrol craft** Bldr: . . . (In serv. 1964-68)

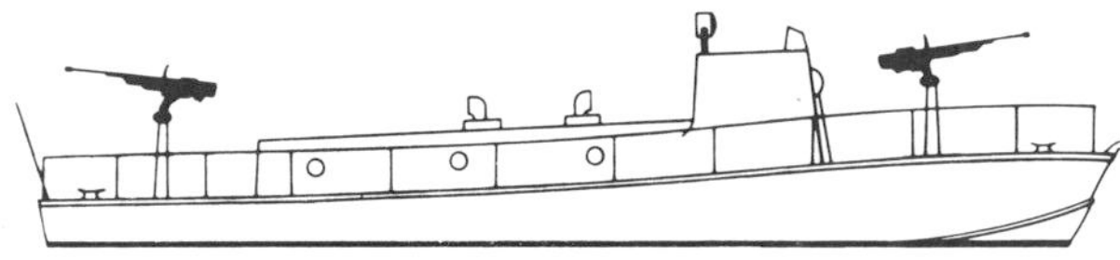

Yulin class

D: 9.8 tons (fl) **S:** 20 kts **Dim:** 13.0 × 2.9 × 1.1
A: 2/12.7-mm mg (I × 2) **M:** 1 diesel; 1 prop; 300 hp

REMARKS: Craft of this class also transferred to Kampuchea, Congo, and Tanzania.

◆ **1 or more Yingkou-class patrol craft** Bldr: . . . (In serv. 1960-65)

D: 40 tons (fl) **S:** 18 kts **Dim:** 20.0 × . . . × . . . **A:** 2/12.7-mm mg
M: 2 diesels; 2 props; 600 hp

REMARKS: Subordinated to "Military Maritime District" in South China militia.

◆ **several hundred armed fishing trawlers**

REMARKS: Many Chinese fishing trawlers are armed with 1 or 2/12.7-mm mg and perform dual service as fisheries patrol craft and fishing trawlers. There are several classes of these Militia-subordinated, steel-hulled, single-screwed craft displacing 200–450 tons (fl).

Yingkou class 1967

Chinese armed fishing trawler T 710 1973

Customs Patrol 301 at Shanghai R. Gillett, 9-84

The above craft, armed with 4/14.5-mm mg (II × 2), is one of a number operated by customs and piloting agencies. This particular unit displaces 245 tons (fl), has a max. speed of 28 knots (27 continuous), an endurance of 2,000 n.m. at 16 kts, and has dimensions of 44.50 × 7.00 × 1.85.

MINE WARFARE SHIPS

◆ **23 Soviet T-43-class fleet minesweepers** Bldrs: Wuzhang SY, Guangzhous SY (In serv. 1956-1970s)

Chinese T-43-class minesweeper 853 R. Gillett, 9-84

D: 500 tons (590 fl) **S:** 14 kts **Dim:** 60.0 × 8.6 × 2.16
A: 4/37-mm AA (II × 2)—4/25-mm AA (II × 2)—4/12.7-mm mg (II × 2)—2/d.c. projectors—mines
Electron Equipt: Radar: 1/Ball End—IFF: 1/Square Head, 1/High Pole A
M: 2/Type 9D diesels; 2 props; 2,200 hp
Fuel: 70 tons **Electric:** 550 kw **Range:** 3,200/10 **Man:** 65-80 tot.

REMARKS: A few shorter-hulled, 58-meter, 570-ton units were transferred from the U.S.S.R.; the majority are long-hulled ships and were built in China. Several were built or converted as surveying ships and civilian research ships. At least one minesweeper has an 85-mm DP gun forward. Current hull numbers in the 800s.

MINE WARFARE SHIPS *(continued)*

◆ **up to 80 auxiliary minesweepers converted from fishing boats**

Auxiliary minesweepers—subordinated to the Shanghai area Military Maritime District. Sometimes referred to as the Lien Yun class, these ships displace about 400 tons, are armed with 12.7-mm machine guns, and are based on a steel-hulled trawler design. 1970

◆ **20 Fushun-class coastal minesweepers**—derived from Shanghai II gunboat design—see patrol boat entry for characteristics.

◆ **. . . Type 312 drone minesweepers** (In serv. late 1960s-. . .)

Type 312 drone minesweeper Chinese Navy, 1984

D: 46.95 tons (fl) **S:** 2 kts **Dim:** 20.94 × 4.20 × 1.30
M: 1 Type 3D12 diesel; 1 CP prop; 300 hp

Remarks: Normally operated by radio control to a range of 3 n.m., but can be manned. Electric propulsion for sweeping at 1 to 5 kts. Diesel generator amidships powers integral electromagnet for magnetic sweeping and a noisemaker for actuating acoustic mines. All equipment shock-mounted. Laser precision navigation system. Officially stated not to be good sea boats; large numbers have been built, however.

AMPHIBIOUS WARFARE SHIPS

◆ **3 Yukan-class landing ships** Bldr: Zhonghua SY, Shanghai (In serv. 1978-80)

927 934 937

Yukan No. 927 and a sister R. Gillett, 9-84

D: 3,400 (5,00 fl) **S:** 17 kts **Dim:** 120.0 × 15.0 × 3.7
A: 8/57-mm AA (II × 4)—8/25-mm AA (II × 4) **M:** Diesels; 2 props; . . . hp
Electron Equipt: Radar: 2/nav.—IFF: 1/High Pole A

Remarks: Evidently built to replace aging World War II-built U.S. LSTs, these ships are larger and considerably faster than their predecessors. Carry two U.S.-design LCVPs. Bow and stern ramps.

Yukan No. 927 and a sister—note lowered stern ramp R. Gillett, 9-84

◆ **15 ex-U.S. LST 1- and LST 542-class tank landing ships** (In serv. 1943-45)

LST 1 class—76.2-mm gun on bow, old pendant number 1970

D: 1,625 tons (4,080 fl) **S:** 11 kts **Dim:** 99.98 × 15.24 × 4.36
A: 2-3/76.2-mm DP (II)—6-8/37-mm AA (II)
M: 2 G.M. 12-278A or 12-567A diesels; 2 props; 1,800 hp

Remarks: Cargo capacity: 2,100 tons. Some are immobile as accommodations ships or tenders for submarines. Most rearmed during late 1950s with U.S. 76.2-mm guns and Soviet twin 37-mm AA.

◆ **4 (+ . . .) Yudao-class medium landing ships** (In serv. 1980-. . .)

D: 1,000 tons (fl) **S:** . . . **Dim:** 65.0 × . . . × . . .
A: 8/25-mm AA (II × 4) **M:** Diesels

Remarks: Smaller, but apparently faster than the Yu Ling class. Probably intended as replacements for World War II-era U.S. LSM 1 class. Resemble a smaller version of the LST 1 design.

◆ **15 ex-U.S. LSM 1-class medium landing ships** (In serv. 1944-45)

LSM-1-class 936, showing mine port aft R. Gillett, 9-84

D: 743 tons (1,095 fl) **S:** 12.5 kts **Dim:** 62.03 × 10.52 × 2.54
A: 6/37-mm AA (II × 3)—4/25-mm AA (II × 2)—mines
Electron Equipt: Radar: 1/Fin Curve
M: 2 Fairbanks-Morse 38D8⅛-10 or G.M. 16-278A diesels; 2 props; 2,800 hp
Range: 2,500/12

Remarks: Rearmed with Soviet weapons late 1950s. Most have two mine-laying ports in the stern. Several have superstructure built over the open tank deck.

◆ **1 or more Yuling-class utility landing craft** (In serv. 1971-75)

D: 600 tons (fl) **S:** 12 kts **Dim:** 50.0 × 7.0 × 2.0
A: 8/14.5-mm mg (II × 4) **Electron Equipt:** Radar: 1/Type 756 nav.
M: 2 diesels; 2 props; . . . hp

AMPHIBIOUS WARFARE SHIPS *(continued)*

Yuling class N 1122 of the Nanjing Maritime Border Defense force 1983

◆ **6-8 U.S. LCT (6)-class utility landing craft** (In serv. 1943-45)

U.S. LCT (6)-class landing craft Y 698 R. Gillett, 9-84

D: 143 tons (309 fl) **S:** 10 kts **Dim:** 36.3 × 9.6 × 1.2
A: 4/145-mm mg (I × 4)
M: 3 G.M. 6-71 diesels; 3 props; 675 hp **Range:** 1,200/7

Remarks: Acquired 1949. Cargo: 150 tons. Sterns since enclosed and pilothouses greatly enlarged. Several LCT (5) of similar design may also survive. Now considered to be "transports" and have "Y"-series pendants.

◆ **300 Yunnan-class landing craft** Bldr: Huangzhou SY (In serv. 1968-72)

Yunnan class No. 5561 R. Gillett, 9-84

D: 133.2 tons (fl) **S:** 10.5 kts **Dim:** 27.50 (24.07 pp) × 5.40 × 1.40
A: 2-4/14.5-mm mg (I or II × 2) **M:** 2 diesels; 2 props; 600 hp
Range: 500/10 **Man:** 6 tot.

Remarks: Cargo: 46 tons (1 tank). Cargo deck 15.0 × 4.0 m

◆ **40-50 Yuchin-class landing craft** (In serv. 1962-72)

Yuchin class No. N 3015 of the Nanjing Maritime Border Defense Force R. Gillett, 9-84

D: 60 tons light (110 fl) **S:** 9 kts **Dim:** 24.0 × 5.1 × 1.2
A: 2/14.5-mm mg (I × 2) **M:** 2 diesels; 2 props; 600 hp

◆ **20-30 Yuchai-class landing craft** (In serv. 1960s)

Yuchai class Y 761 R. Gillett, 9-84

D: 70 tons (fl) **S:** 10 kts **Dim:** 20.0 × 4.3 × 1.0
A: 4/14.5-mm mg (II × 2) **M:** 2 diesels; 2 props; 600 hp

Remarks: Some, including unit shown above, have "Y"-pendants, indicating service as "transports" rather than as landing craft *per se.*

◆ **approx. 50 copies U.S. LCM(6)-class landing craft** (In serv. 1950s-1960s)

D: 24 tons (56 fl) **S:** 9 kts **Dim:** 17.0 × 4.4 × 1.2
A: 2/12.7-mm mg (I × 2) **M:** 2 diesels; 2 props; 300 hp

◆ **1 Dagu-A-class air-cushion landing craft prototype**

Dagu-A air-cushion vehicle—note bow door 1981

D: 61 tons (fl) **S:** 55 kts **Dim:** 27.2 × 13.8 × 9.6 (high)
M: 2 turboprop propulsion engines; 1 gas turbine lift engine, geared also to 2 auxiliary propellers

Remarks: Cargo: 16.8 tons. Designed by Shanghai SB Research and Development Institute. The function of the small airscrews amidships is uncertain; they may aid in maneuvering. There are six centrifugal lift-fans. Appears to be an engineering prototype rather than an operational combatant. Other hovercraft designs reported include the Payi and Jingsah designs, both smaller than the Dagu-A.

AUXILIARY SHIPS

There is no comprehensive information on the Chinese fleet's logistic support, but China has designated and built large numbers of auxiliary vessels, running the spectrum of logistics support, repair, hydrographic survey, and research types, including a great many tugs and small oilers.

ICEBREAKERS

◆ **2 Haiping class** Bldr: Jiu Shin SY, Shanghai

Haiping 101 (L: 26-12-69) Haiping 102 (L: 1972)

D: 3,200 tons **S:** 16 kts **Dim:** 84.0 × 15.0 × 5.0
A: 8/37-mm AA (II × 4)—8/25-mm AA (II × 4)
M: 2 diesels; 2 props; 5,200 hp

Remarks: Differ in details of superstructure. Can also be used as ocean tugs.

HYDROGRAPHIC SURVEY SHIPS

◆ **1 Kanzhu class** (In serv. 1973)

K 420

Kanzhu class No. K 420 1975

HYDROGRAPHIC SURVEY SHIPS *(continued)*

D: 1,000 tons (fl) **S:** 20 kts **Dim:** 65.0 × 9.0 × 3.0
A: 4/37-mm AA (II × 2)—4/25-mm AA (II × 2)—4/14.5-mm mg (II × 2)
M: 4 diesels; 2 props; 4,400 hp **Man:** 120 tot.

REMARKS: Operates in South China waters.

◆ **3 Yanlai class** (In serv. early 1970s)

K 629 K 512 K . . .

D: 1,100 tons (fl) **S:** 16 kts **Dim:** 72.0 × 9.8 × 3.0
A: 4/37-mm AA (II × 2)—4/25-mm AA (II × 2)
M: 2 diesels; 2 props; 2,200 hp

REMARKS: Funnel amidships; large crane aft.

◆ **2 Modified T-43-class minesweepers** (In serv. late 1960s)

T-43-class research ship S 994 R. Gillett, 9-84

D: 500 tons (590 fl) **S:** 14 kts **Dim:** 60.0 × 8.6 × 2.16
A: 2/37-mm AA (II × 1)—4/14.5-mm AA (II × 2)
Electron Equipt: Radar: 1/Fin Curve **Range:** 3,200/10
M: 2 Type 9D diesels; 2 props; 2,200 hp **Fuel:** 70 tons

REMARKS: "S" pendant indicates research role, rather than hydrographic survey. Extended after deckhouse, no minesweeping equipment. Four-point mooring capability.

◆ **2 Hace-class coastal survey ships** (In serv. 1960s)

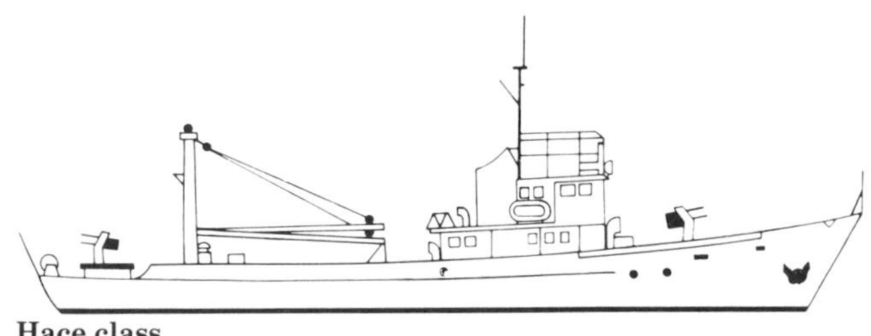

Hace class

D: 400 tons **S:** 12 kts **Dim:** 38.0 × 7.6 × 3.4 **A:** 4/14.5-mm mg (II × 2)
M: 1 diesel; 1 prop; 400 hp

REMARKS: Design derived from that of a coastal cargo ship.

◆ **1 British "Flower"-class former corvette**

	Bldr	L	In serv.
N. . . . . . . (ex-*Clover*)	Fleming & Ferguson, U.K.	30-1-41	31-5-41

D: 1,060 tons (1,340 fl) **S:** 16 kts **Dim:** 62.48 × 10.23 × 4.80 **A:** . . .
M: 1 set 4-cyl., triple-expansion reciprocating steam; 1 prop; 1,750 hp
Boilers: 2 Admiralty 3-drum **Fuel:** 230 tons **Range:** 3,100/15; 5,000/10

REMARKS: Used as a corvette until early 1970s; one sister scrapped at that time.

◆ **1 Yanlun class** (In serv. 1965)—no data available

◆ **up to 10 additional naval survey ships**

OCEANOGRAPHIC SURVEY SHIPS

◆ **2 Haiyang class** (In serv. 1972-73)

HAIYANG 01 HAIYANG 02

D: 3,295 tons **S:** 20 kts **Dim:** 104.0 × 13.8 × 5.0
A: 6/37-mm AA (II × 3) **M:** 2 diesels; 2 props; 9,000 hp

REMARKS: Resemble passenger liners; white-painted.

◆ **3 Shukuang class** (In serv. late 1960s)

SHUKUANG 01 SHUKUANG 02 SHUKUANG 03

D: 500 tons (590 fl) **S:** 14 kts **Dim:** 60.0 × 8.4 × 2.15
A: 1/37-mm AA **M:** 2 diesels; 2 props; 2,200 hp
Range: 3,200/10

REMARKS: Design closely derived from T-43-class minesweeper. White-painted. There is also *Shukuang* 04, a more modern-appearing ship about the same size.

◆ **2 Shihjian class** Bldr: Hutung SY, Shanghai (In serv. 1968-69)

SHIHJIAN N. . . . . . .

D: 2,955 tons **S:** 16.2 kts **Dim:** 94.73 (87.00 pp) × 14.04 × 4.75
A: 8/14.5-mm mg (II × 4) **Electric:** 1,065 kw
M: 2 Type 6 ESD(2) 48/82 diesels; 2 props; 4,000 hp **Range:** 7,500/14.5

REMARKS: 2,500 grt/1,000 dwt. Enlarged version of *Dong Fang Hong* class.

◆ **2 Dong Fang Hong class** Bldr: Hutung SY, Shanghai (In serv. 1964-66)

N. . . . . . . DONG FANG HONG

Dong Fang Hong 1978

D: 2,900 tons **S:** 14 kts **Dim:** 86.00 × 11.50 × 4.75 **A:** None
M: 2 diesels; 2 props; 4,000 hp

NOTE: Subordinated to the Shandong Oceanographic College. There are also large numbers of civilian-agency-subordinated research vessels for oil exploration, fisheries research, etc.

EXPERIMENTAL SHIPS

◆ **2 Yuanwang-class satellite and missile tracking ships** Bldr: Hutung SY, Shanghai (In serv. 1980)

YUANWANG 1 YUANWANG 2

Yuanwang 2 R.N.Z.N., 1980

D: 17,100 tons (21,000 fl) **S:** 20 kts **Dim:** 190.0 × 22.6 × 7.5
M: 1 diesels; 1 prop; . . . hp

REMARKS: First observed during the 5-80 Chinese ICBM tests in the Central Pacific. Have one large parabolic tracking antenna, two log-periodic HF ("fish-spine") antennas, several precision theodolite optical tracking stations, and two smaller missile-tracking radars, as well as positions for later installation of equipment. Large helicopter deck, but no hangar. Have a bow-thruster and retractable fin stabilizers.

NOTE: The Xiang Yang Hong ("East is Red"—the title of the Chinese national anthem)—series ships are mainly disparate in size and characteristics; all are capable of a variety of experimental duties (including general oceanography), particularly in support of missile and satellite research and hydrometerology. All are under the general subordination of the Academy of Sciences.

◆ **1 new-construction research ship** (In serv. 1982)

XIANG YANG HONG 16

D: 4,000 tons (fl) **S:** . . . **Dim:** . . . × . . . × . . .

REMARKS: Operated for the East China Branch of the National Bureau of Oceanography, for biological and mineral bottom sampling. Possibly a sister to *Xiang Yang Hong 9.*

EXPERIMENTAL SHIPS *(continued)*

◆ **1 Xiang Yang Hong 10 class** Bldr: Hutung SY, Shanghai (In serv. 1980)

XIANG YANG HONG 10

Xiang Yang Hong 10—Super Frélon helicopter on deck aft R.N.Z.N., 1980

D: 10,975 tons **S:** 20 kts **Dim:** 156.2 × 20.6 × 6.8
M: 2 diesels; 2 props; . . . hp

REMARKS: Operated by the East China Sea Branch, State Oceanographic Bureau. Uses same hull and propulsion as the Dajiang-class submarine tenders, but has twin, side-by-side funnels and hangar space for only one French Super Frélon helicopter; the crane forward is smaller, and the kingposts abaft the stacks and the heavy foremast support large log-periodic HF antennas. Has retractable fin stabilizers. Departed for 150-day Antarctic expedition 20-11-84.

◆ **1 Xiang Yang Hong 9 class** Bldr: Hutung SY, Shanghai (In serv. 1979)

XIANG YANG HONG 9

Xiang Yang Hong 9 U.S. Navy, 1982

D: 4,400 tons **S:** . . . kts **Dim:** 110.0 × . . . × . . . **M:** Diesels; 4,000 hp
Range: 11,000/. . . **Man:** 145 tot.

◆ **1 Polish Francesco Nullo-class (Type B-41)**—former cargo ship
Bldr: Paris Commune SY, Gdynia, Poland (In serv. 1967)

XIANG YANG HONG 5 (ex-*Chang Niy*)

Xiang Yang Hong 5 R.N.Z.N., 1980

D: 14,500 tons (fl) **S:** 16 kts **Dim:** 152.6 (141.6 pp) × 19.5 × 8.75
M: 1 Ciegielski-Sulzer 6RD68 diesel; 1 prop; 7,200 hp **Range:** 15,000/16

REMARKS: Extensively rebuilt as a hydrometeorological-research and radiosonde-balloon tracking ship at Canton in 1970-72, and altered again after 1976, with a two-level superstructure replacing the after two hatches. Has one large log-periodic HF antenna forward. One of her four Chinese-operated merchant sisters briefly served as an unaltered support ship as *Xiang Yang Hong 10* in the late 1970s (not the same ship as the new unit above).

◆ **1 Xiang Yang Hong 2 class** (In serv. 1971)

XIANG YANG HONG 2

D: 1,000 tons (fl) **S:** . . . kts **Dim:** 72.5 × 8.7 × . . .
M: 2 diesels; 2 props; . . . hp

◆ **3 Xiang Yang Hong 1 class** (In serv. 1972-74)

XIANG YANG HONG 1 XIANG YANG HONG 4 XIANG YANG HONG 6

Xiang Yang Hong 6 U.S. Navy, 1979

D: Approx. 1,000 tons (fl) **S:** . . . kts **Dim:** 67.0 × 10.0 × . . .
M: 2 diesels; 2 props; . . . hp

REMARKS: Carried 2/37-mm AA (II × 1), 8/14.5-mm mg (II × 4) as completed.

SUBMARINE SUPPORT SHIPS

NOTE: A new submarine tender was officially reported completed 1985; no data available.

◆ **3 Dajiang class** Bldr: Hudong SY, Shanghai (In serv. 1978-80)

J 302 R 327 (ex-J 506) J 121

J 302—note rescue submersible on deck beside crane R. Gillett, 9-84

R 327—note 2 Super Frélon helicopters (old number) R.N.Z.N., 1980

D: 10,975 tons (fl) **S:** 20 kts **Dim:** 156.2 × 20.6 × 6.8 **A:** None
A: None **Electron Equipt:** Radar: 2/Fin Curve, 1/Eye Shield (MX-902)
M: 2 diesels; 2 props; . . . hp

REMARKS: Carry two French Super Frélon heavy helicopters in a double hangar. J 301 differs in not having the deep recesses at the stern (evidently intended to permit a 4-point moor). The huge crane forward tends two trainable cradles just forward of the bridge; the cradles are semicircular in section and support salvage-and-rescue submersibles. The ships share the hull and propulsion of the research ship *Xiang Yang Hong 10* and probably also have fin stabilizers. Former J 506 transferred to Academy of Sciences, 1983, and renumbered R 327; large log-periodic antenna added.

◆ **1 Dalang class** Bldr: Guangzhou SY (In serv. 1975)

J 503

D: 4,000 tons (fl) **S:** 16 kts **Dim:** 130.0 × 14.0 × 4.0
A: 8/37-mm AA (II × 4)—4/14.5-mm mg (II × 2)
M: 2 diesels; 2 props; 4,000 hp

REMARKS: Primarily intended for general salvage and towing duties in support of submarines.

SUBMARINE SUPPORT SHIPS *(continued)*

No. J 503—Dalang class 1980

◆ **1 Dazhi class** Bldr: Hudong SY, Shanghai (In serv. mid-1960s)

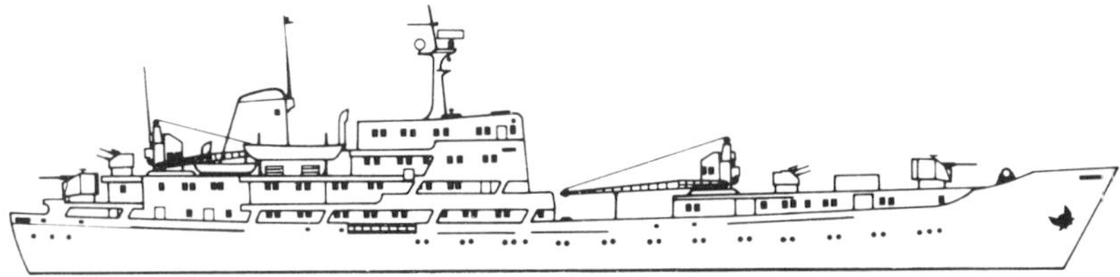

Dazhi class

D: 5,800 tons (fl) **S:** 14 kts **Dim:** 106.7 × 15.3 × 6.1
A: 4/37-mm AA (II × 2)—8/25-mm AA (II × 4)
M: 1 diesel; 1 prop; . . . hp

◆ **1 Hudong class** Bldr: Hudong SY, Shanghai (In serv. 1969)

J 301

Hudong-class submarine tender J 301 R. Gillett, 9-84

D: 5,000 tons (fl) **S:** . . . kts **Dim:** 95.0 × 17.0 × 4.5
A: 4/37-mm AA (II × 2)—4/14.5-mm mg (II × 2) **M:** 1 diesel; 1 prop; . . . hp
Electron Equipt: Radar: 1/Fin Curve

Remarks: Has large gantry over stern for lowering a submarine rescue chamber.

Note: There are several other small submarine support classes, including the 1,100-ton Dazhou class (J 502, J 504) and the 2,800-ton, 82-meter Dadong class (J 304, . . .).

REPAIR SHIPS

◆ **1 Romanian Galati class** Bldr: Galati SY (In serv. early 1970s)

D: 5,200 tons (fl) **S:** 12.5 kts **Dim:** 100.60 (93.70 pp) × 13.92 × 6.60 **A:** . . .
M: 1 Sulzer 5TAD56 diesel; 1 prop; . . . hp **Electric:** 345 kw
Fuel: 250 tons **Range:** 5,000/12.5

Remarks: Converted from a cargo ship, with minimal external alterations. Of nine sisters purchased by China, two others serve the navy as cargo ships.

◆ **1 U.S. Achelous class** Bldr: Kaiser Co., Vancouver, Wash.

	Laid down	L	In serv.
Takushan (ex-*Hsing An*, ex-*Achilles*, ARL 41, ex-LST 455)	3-8-42	17-10-42	30-1-43

Takushan (U 891) R. Gillett, 9-84

D: 4,100 tons (fl) **S:** 11 kts **Dim:** 99.98 × 15.24 × 3.40
A: 12/37-mm AA (II × 6) **M:** 2 G.M. 12-567A diesels; 2 props; 1,800 hp
Electric: 350 kw **Range:** 9,000/9 **Man:** 290 tot.

Remarks: Acquired 1949. Has 60-ton A-frame gantry, plus several cranes. Generally immobile at Shanghai. Bow doors still functional.

CABLE SHIPS/BUOY TENDERS

◆ **4 or more . . . class** Bldr: Chunghua SY, Shanghai (In serv. late 1970s)

B 873 H 263 N 2304 . . .

Cable layer B 873 with Yuchai LCM alongside—note fixed gantry aft
R. Gillett, 9-84

Buoy tender H 263—note lack of bow sheaves, buoy crane, and handling deck, with reinforced hull sides R. Gillett, 9-84

Cable layer N 2304—note quadrantial gantry aft R. Gillett, 9-84

D: 1,550 tons (fl) **S:** 14 kts (sust.)
Dim: 71.40 (63.00 pp) × 10.50 × 3.60
A: 4/37-mm AA (II × 2)—4/14.5-mm mg *or* 8/14.5-mm mg (II × 2) *or* none
M: 2 Type 8300Z diesels; 2 props; 2,200 hp **Electron Equipt:** Radar: 1/Fin Curve

Remarks: Design built for both military and civil use. Cable tank has 187-m³ capacity; ship can lay cable up to 100-mm thick. Those with "B" pendants serve as cable layers; those with "H" pendants are used as mooring buoy tenders. Several ("N" pendants) also serve the Nanjing Maritime Border Defense Force.

REPLENISHMENT OILERS

◆ **3 Fuqing class** Bldr: Dalien SY (In serv. 1980-82)

X 575 X 615 X 950

D: 21,740 tons (fl) **S:** 18.6 kts **Dim:** 160.8 × 21.8 × 9.4 **A:** None
Electron Equipt: Radar: 2/Fin Curve—IFF: 1/High Pole A
Electric: 2,480 kw **M:** 1/Burmeister & Wain diesel; 1 prop; 13,000 hp
Range: 15,000/14 **Man:** 26 officers, 120 men

Remarks: Equipment similar to U.S. Navy transfer systems. Two liquid replenishment stations per side, with constant-tension solid transfer stations each side just forward

REPLENISHMENT OILERS *(continued)*

X 615 (composite photo)—note gun positions abreast streamlined stack and on forecastle U.S. Navy, 1980

X 950—rectangular stack, no armament positions U.S. Navy, 5-83

of the stack. Helo deck, but no hangar. Provision for four twin 37-mm AA gunmounts. X 615 has a rounded stack and a higher aft superstructure than X 950. Both have 4 small electric cranes for stores handling. Carry 11,000 tons fuel oil, 1,000 tons diesel fuel, 200 tons feedwater, 200 tons potable water.

TRANSPORT OILERS

◆ **2 or more new construction** (In serv. 1981-. . .)

X 620 X 621

D: 4,940 tons (fl) **S:** 14 kts **Dim:** 101.0 (92.0 pp) × 13.8 × 5.5
M: 1 diesel; 1 prop; 2,600 hp **Range:** 2,400/14

Remarks: 3,318.5 dwt. Cargo: 3,002 tons fuel oil (4,240 m³). Most are for commercial service, but two also employed by the navy.

◆ **6 or more Fulin class** Bldr: Hudong SY, Shanghai (In serv. 1972)

D: 2,200 tons (fl) **S:** 10 kts **Dim:** 66.0 × 10.0 × 4.0
A: 4/25-mm AA (II × 2) **Electron Equipt:** Radar: 1/Fin Curve
M: 1 diesel; 1 prop; 600 hp **Range:** 1,500/8 **Man:** 30 tot.

Remarks: Part of a series of 20, most of which went into merchant service. Several reported to have a single underway replenishment rig. At least one (N 1104) is subordinated to the Nanjing Maritime Border Defense Force. Resemble an enlarged Fuzhou.

◆ **14 or more Fuzhou class** Bldr: Hudong SY, Shanghai (In serv. 1964-70)

Fuzhou class N 1101 of the Nanjing Maritime Border Defense Force R. Gillett, 9-84

D: 1,200 tons (fl) **S:** 10-12 kts **Dim:** 60.0 (55.0 pp) × 9.0 × 3.5
A: 4.25-mm AA (II × 2)—4/14.5-mm mg (II × 2)
Electron Equipt: Radar: 1/Fin Curve or Type 756
M: 1 diesel; 1 prop; 600 hp **Man:** 30 tot.

Remarks: Cargo: 600 tons. Five also built in a water-tanker version. Many of the oilers are subordinated to Maritime Border Defense Force. Some are not armed.

◆ **5 Leizhou class** (In serv. early 1960s)

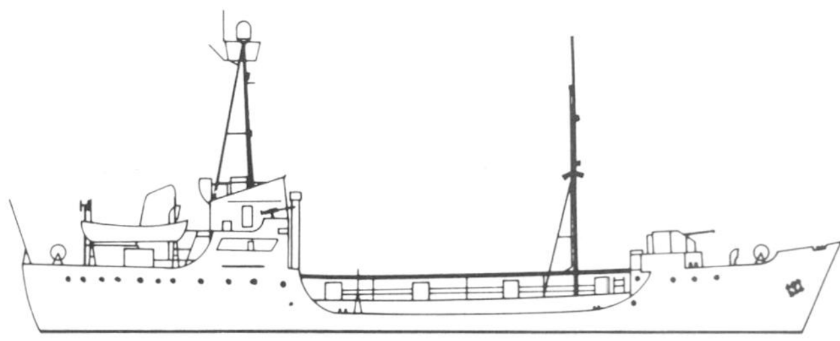

Leizhou transport oiler

D: 900 tons **S:** 10-12 kts **Dim:** 53.0 (48.0 pp) × 9.8 × 3.0
A: 4/37-mm AA (II × 2)—2/12.7-mm mg (I × 2) **M:** 1 diesel; 1 prop; 600 hp
Man: 30 tot.

Remarks: Four also built in a water-tanker version, and another was built as a cargo ship (Y 737) with a single kingpost and two cargo holds amidships.

◆ **2 U.S. Mettawee-class former gasoline tankers** (In serv. 1943-44)

D: 700 tons (2,200 fl) **S:** 14 kts **Dim:** 67.21 (64.77 pp) × 11.28 × 3.99
A: 1/37-mm AA—4/14.5-mm mg (II × 2)
M: 1 Fairbanks-Morse 37E16 diesel, 1 prop; 800 hp **Fuel:** 29 tons
Electric: 155 kw

◆ **1 Japanese 2 TM class** Bldr: Mitsubishi, Nagasaki (In serv. 1944)

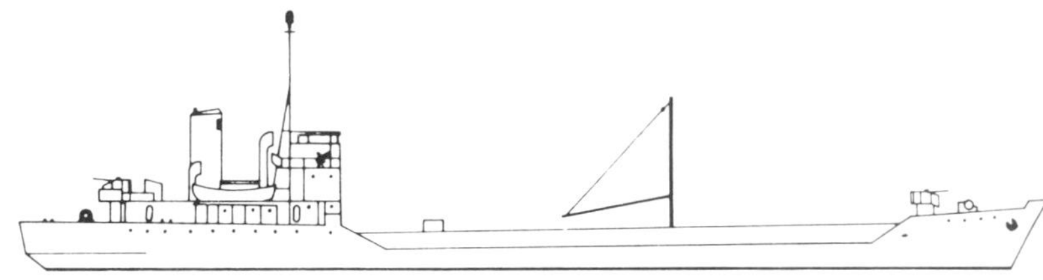

2 TM class

D: 2,935 tons (4,750 fl) **S:** 11.5 kts **Dim:** 98.8 (93.0 pp) × 13.8 × 6.0
A: 4/37-mm AA (II × 2)—4/14.5-mm mg (II × 2)
M: 1 set GT; 1 prop; 1,100 hp **Boilers:** 2 watertube **Range:** 5,000/11

Remarks: No compound curves to hull. Acquired 1949.

WATER TANKERS

◆ **5 Fuzhou class** Bldr: Hudong SY, Shanghai (In serv. 1964-70)

Fuzhou-class water or gasoline tanker X 629—no armament R. Gillett, 9-84

Remarks: Data generally as for transport oiler version. Armament distributed differently and lack raised cargo expansion tank top amidships. Formerly armed with 4/25-mm AA (II × 2)—4/14.5-mm mg (II × 2).

◆ **4 Leizhou class** (In serv. early 1960s)

Remarks: Appearance similar to transport oiler version, but lack raised tank top in well-deck area.

◆ **. . . harbor oilers** (In serv. . . .)

Two small liquid cargo transports subordinated to the Nanjing District of the Maritime Border Defense Force. Capacity is about 50-70 tons. The total number of craft of this design and the Western nickname are unavailable.

WATER TANKERS *(continued)*

Harbor Tanker N 1143 and a sister R. Gillett, 9-84

TRANSPORTS

◆ **4 Qiongsha Class** Bldr: Guangzhou SY (In serv. 1980-. . .)

Y 832 Y. . . Y. . . Y. . .

Qiongsha-class transport Y 832 U.S. Navy, 5-83

D: 2,150 tons (fl) **S:** 16.2 kts **Dim:** 86.0 (76.0 pp) × 13.4 × 3.9
A: 8/14.5-mm mg (II × 4) **Electron Equipt:** Radar: 2/Fin Curve
M: 3 8NVD48A-2U diesels; 3 props; 3,960 hp
Fuel: 195 tons **Electric:** 575 kw **Man:** 59 tot.

REMARKS: Built for South Seas Fleet service. Carry about 400 troops. Cargo holds fore and aft, each tended by two 1-ton derricks, can hold 350 tons.

CARGO SHIPS

◆ **1 or more . . . class** (In serv. 1980)

Cargo ship L 201 1980

REMARKS: A cargo ship of about 1,000 dwt, armed with 2/37-mm AA (II × 1) and 4/14.5-mm mg (II × 2) and equipped with a Fin Curve navigational radar. Three holds, served by two electrohydraulic cranes. Class name not available.

◆ **3 or more Hongoi 081 class** Bldr: . . . (In serv. 1970s)

Y 443 Y 755 Y 756

D: 1,950 tons (fl) **S:** 10-12 kts **Dim:** 62.0 (58.0 wl) × 12.0 × 4.5
A: 4/25-mm AA **M:** 1 diesel; . . . hp

REMARKS: 875 grt/1,100 dwt. Sisters in commercial service.

◆ **2 Romanian Galati class** (In serv. early 1970s)

REMARKS: Characteristics as for the repair-ship version described earlier.

◆ **1 Zhandou 59 class** (In serv. 1959-65)

D: 4,735 tons (fl) **S:** 12.5 kts **Dim:** 99.4 × 13.0 × 5.5 **A:** None
M: 1 diesel; 1 prop; . . . hp **Man:** 50 tot.

REMARKS: 2,798 grt/3,200 dwt. One of a class of 20 built for merchant marine service; two were combined to produce an oil-drilling platform in the mid-1970s.

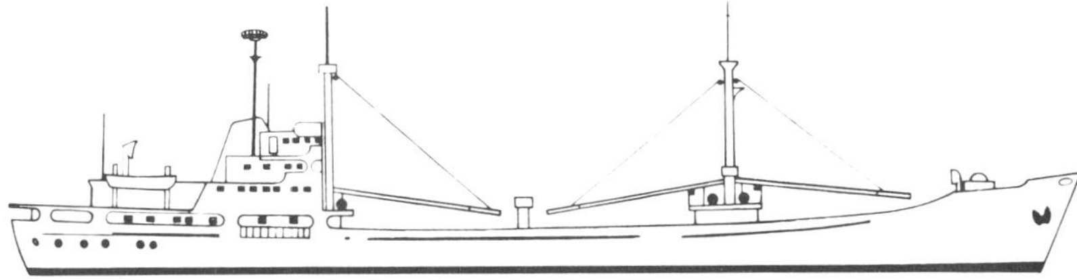

Zhandou 59 class

◆ **3 Danlin class** (In serv. mid-1960s)

L 202 L 591 L 790

Danlin class L 202 R. Gillett, 9-84

D: 1,150 tons (fl) **S:** 10-12 kts **Dim:** 60.0 × 9.1 × 3.5
A: 2/37-mm AA (I × 2)
M: 1 diesel; 1 prop; 600 hp **Cargo:** About 600 tons

◆ **1 or more U.S. Army FS-331 class** (In serv. 1943-44)

FS-331-class cargo ship in Chinese service (old number) 1970

D: 465 tons (935 fl) **S:** 13.5 kts **Dim:** 53.49 (49.99 pp) × 9.75 × 3.05
A: Varies. Typical: 4/25-mm AA (II × 2)
M: 2 G.M. 6-278A diesels; 2 props; 1,000 hp **Fuel:** 57 tons
Range: 3,000/12.5; 4,300/9.5 **Man:** 30 tot.

REMARKS: Survivor(s) of a group of six or more acquired 1949. Cargo: 595 m^3.

Small cargo transport N 1127 R. Gillett, 9-84

REMARKS: One of a number of units of this design (including N 1121 and N 3215), most of which seem to be subordinated to the Maritime Border Defense Force districts of about 450 tons (fl) displacement, they have a single cargo hold amidships, are equipped with a Type 756 navigational radar, and are armed with two twin side-by-side 14.5-mm mg mounts. Maximum speed is about 9 kts on a single 300-hp diesel.

SEAGOING TUGS

◆ **1 or more new-construction naval seagoing salvage tugs** Bldr: Dalien SY (In serv. . . .)

D: 5,279 tons (fl) **S:** 19 kts **Dim:** 102.2 (92.0 pp) × 16.0 × 6.5
M: 2 Burmeister & Wain/Dalien 8S50LU diesels; 2 CP props; 13,600 hp
Man: 50 tot.

SEAGOING TUGS *(continued)*

REMARKS: Construction announced 1980; may be intended for civil subordination. 106-ton bollard pull. Equipped with 450-hp bow-thruster, firefighting cannon, pumps, divers' support gear, etc.

◆ **3 or more Hujia-class seagoing** Bldr: . . . (In serv. 1980s)

T 155 T 867 T. . .

Hujia-class tug T 867 R. Gillett, 9-84

D: 750 tons (fl) **S:** 13.5 kts **Dim:** 49.0 (44.5 pp) × 9.5 × 3.7 **A:** . . .
M: 2 LVP 24 diesels; 2 CP props; 1,800 hp **Fuel:** 135 tons
Electric: 336 kVA **Range:** 2,200/13.5; 1,100/9 (towing)

◆ **2 Tuzhong class salvage tugs** Bldr: Zhonghua SY, Shanghai (In serv. late 1970s)

T 164 T 710

Tuzhong-class salvage tug T 710 1980

D: 3,600 tons (fl) **S:** 18.5 kts **Dim:** 84.90 (77.00 pp) × 14.00 × 5.50
A: None **M:** 2/9 ESDZ 43/82B diesels; 2 CP props; 9,000 hp
Range: 18,000/. . . **Electron Equipt:** Radar: 1/Fin Curve, 1/Square Tie

REMARKS: Powerful salvage tug equipped for firefighting, emergency repairs, and with high-capacity pumps. Has 35-ton-capacity towing winch. T 710 has Square Tie missile fire-control radar on foremast, possibly for weapons trials purposes. There is provision for mounting at least two twin 37-mm AA.

◆ **3 Dinghai class** Bldr: Wuhu SY (In serv. late 1970s)

Dinghai-class tug T 837 R. Gillett, 9-84

D: 1,472 tons (fl) **S:** . . . kts **Dim:** 60.22 × 11.60 × 4.44 **A:** . . .
M: 2 diesels; 2 props; 2,460 hp **Range:** 7,200/. . .

REMARKS: Also built for civil use. 980.28 grt. 25-ton-capacity towing winch. Equipped for firefighting. One transferred to Bangladesh Navy, 1984.

◆ **3 Yanting class—D:** 450 tons—trawler-type hull

◆ **3 FT 14-class converted trawlers—D:** 400 tons (fl)

◆ **16 Soviet Gromovoy class** Bldr: China (early 1960s)

Gromovoy-class tug T 802, outboard two T-43-class minesweepers R. Gillett, 9-84

D: 900 tons (fl) **S:** 11 kts **Dim:** 45.7 (41.5 pp) × 9.45 × 4.6
A: 2/12.7-mm mg (I × 2) **M:** 2 diesels; 2 props; 1,200 hp

REMARKS: Soviet commercial tug design, built under license.

◆ **4 Soviet Roslavl class** Bldr: See remarks (In serv. 1958-64)

D: 750 tons (fl) **S:** 11 kts **Dim:** 44.5 × 9.5 × 3.5
M: 2 diesels, electric drive; 2 props; 1,200 hp

REMARKS: One transferred from the U.S.S.R.; the other built circa 1964-65 in China.

◆ **2 U.S. Sotoyomo class** (In serv. 1943-45)

D: 435 tons (835 fl) **S:** 13 kts **Dim:** 43.59 (40.74 wl) × 10.31 × 4.01 **A:** . . .
M: 2 G.M. 12-278A diesels, electric drive; 1 prop; 1,500 hp
Fuel: 158 tons **Electric:** 120 kw **Man:** 50 tot.

REMARKS: Acquired 1949. Former U.S. names unknown.

◆ **2 U.S. Army "254-design" class** (In serv. early 1940s)

U.S. Army 254-design tug T 800 R. Gillett, 9-84

D: 600 tons (967 fl) **S:** 12 kts **Dim:** 45.4 (42.7 pp) × 10.1 × 5.33
M: 1 set Skinner Uniflow 53CYRS triple-expansion reciprocating steam; 1 prop; 1,200 hp
Boilers: 2/14 kg/cm² **Fuel:** 325 tons **Range:** 4,200/8

REMARKS: Acquired 1949. Former U.S. LT numbers unkown. Wooden hulls.

YARD AND SERVICE CRAFT

There are a reported 380 units in this category, but the true total number is probably far larger and would include yard oilers, tugs, barges, floating dry docks, dredges, and the like. No details are available.

Two Chinese Navy harbor tugs R. Gillett, 9-84

COLOMBIA

Republic of Colombia

PERSONNEL: (1984): 9,700 total, including 2,500 marines

MERCHANT MARINE (1984): 82 ships—373,828 grt (tankers: 6 ships—30,744 grt)

SUBMARINES

◆ **2 German Type 209 Mod. 1 class**

	Bldr	L	In serv.
SS 28 PIJAO	Howaldtswerke, Kiel	10-4-74	17-4-75
SS 29 TAYRONA	Howaldtswerke, Kiel	16-7-74	18-7-75

Tayrona (S 29) G. Gyssels, 10-81

D: 990 tons std./1,180 surf./1,290 sub. **S:** 11/22 kts
Dim: 56.10 × 6.20 × 5.50 (surf.)
A: 8/533-mm TT fwd (6 reloads)
Electron Equipt: Radar: 1/Calypso II
Sonar: Krupp-Atlas active/passive.
M: 4 MTU 12V493 TY60 diesels, 600 hp each; 4 A.E.G. 405-kw generators; 1 Siemens motor, 5,000 hp
Fuel: 100 tons **Endurance:** 30 days **Range:** 8,000/8 (snorkel)
Man: 5 officers, 26 men

REMARKS: Have H.S.A. Mk 8 torpedo f.c.s.

◆ **2 Italian S.X. 506 midgets** Bldr: Cosmos, Livorno, Italy (1972-74)

SS 20 INTREPIDO SS 21 INDOMABLE

D: 58/70 tons **S:** 8.5 kts **Dim:** 23.0 × 2.0 × 4.0
Cargo capacity: 2,050 kg of explosives; 8 frogmen fully equipped; 2 submarine vehicles (for the frogmen) supported by a fixed system on lower part of the hull, one on each side.
Range: 1,200/7 **Man:** 5 tot.

REMARKS: Similar submarines have been bought by the Pakistani and Taiwanese navies. Sisters *Roncador* (SS 23) and *Quita Sueno* (SS 24) are no longer in service.

FRIGATES

◆ **4 FS 1500 class** Bldr: Howaldtswerke, Kiel, W. Germany

	Laid down	L	In serv.
51 ALMIRANTE PADILLA	3-81	8-1-82	31-10-83
52 CALDAS	1981	14-6-82	14-2-84
53 ANTIOQUIA	22-6-81	28-8-82	30-4-84
54 INDEPENDIENTE	22-6-81	21-1-83	27-7-84

D: 1,600 tons (1,850 fl) **S:** 27 kts **Dim:** 95.3 (90.0 pp) × 11.3 × 3.5 (hull)
A: 8/MM-40 Exocet SSM—1/76-mm OTO Melara DP—2/40-mm Breda AA (II × 1)—4/30-mm Emerlec AA (II × 2)—6/324-mm Mk 32 ASW TT (III × 2)—1/BO-105 helicopter
Electron Equipt: Radar: 1/navigational, 1/Sea Tiger air search, 1/Castor IIB f.c.
Sonar: Krupp Atlas ASO4-2—EW: Scimitar jammer; Phoenix-II, SUSIE passive; 2/Dagaie chaff RL
M: 4 MTU 20V1163 TB82 diesels; 2 CP props; 23,000 hp (21,000 sust.)
Fuel: 200 tons **Range:** 5,000/14 **Electric:** 2,120 kw **Man:** 92 tot.

REMARKS: Ordered 1980, with the first originally scheduled for delivery 20-7-82. Fin stabilizers, helicopter hangar. Engines are a new model not previously installed in a ship. Thomson CSF Vega II f.c.s. for the 76-mm gun, 2 Canopus optronic directors. Torpedo tubes, Exocet, 30-mm AA, and Dagaie chaff not yet mounted at time of commissioning. Either the Israeli Barak or French 4-cell Crotale SAM system is planned for later installation.

Independiente (54) HDW, 1984

Almirante Padilla (51)—with 8 MM 40 Exocet added R. Scheina, 7-84

NOTE: The two destroyers of the Halland class, *Veinte de Julio* (D 05) and *Siete de Agosto* (D 06) were to be disposed of 1983-84 upon arrival of the FS 1500-class frigates. The destroyer *Santander* (D 03, ex-U.S. *Waldron,* DD 699) was stricken in 1984, as was the frigate *Boyaca* (D 07, ex-U.S. *Hartley,* DE 1029)

CORVETTES

◆ **4 U.S. Cherokee- and Abnaki-class* former fleet tugs** Bldr: Charleston SB & DD Co.

	Laid down	L	In serv.
RM 72 PEDRO DE HEREDIA (ex-*Choctaw,* ATF 70)	4-4-42	18-10-42	21-4-43
RM 73 SEBASTIAN DE BELALCAZAR (ex-*Carib,* ATF 82)	7-9-42	7-2-43	24-7-43
RM 74 RODRIGO DE BASTEDAS (ex-*Hidatsa,* ATF 102)*	8-8-43	29-12-43	25-4-44
RM 76 BAHIA SOLANO (ex-*Jacarilla,* ATF 104)*	25-8-43	25-2-44	26-6-44

Pedro de Heredia (RM 72) L. & L. Van Ginderen, 11-81

D: 1,235 tons (1,675 fl) **S:** 16.5 kts **Dim:** 62.48 × 11.73 × 4.67
A: 1/76.2-mm DP
M: 4 G.M. 12-278 diesels (ex-ATF 102, ex-ATF 104: 4 Busch-Sulzer B5-539 diesels, electric drive); 1 prop; 3,000 hp
Electric: 300 kw **Range:** 15,000/8 **Man:** 75 tot.

REMARKS: RM 76, 73, 74 reactivated from U.S. Maritime Commission reserve fleet and transferred 15-3-79 for use as patrol and rescue ships. RM 72 transferred 1961; purchased 31-3-78; possibly stricken 1985.

PATROL BOATS

◆ **2 U.S. Asheville class**

	Bldr	Laid down	L	In serv.
P 111 Quito Sueño (ex-*Tacoma,* PG 92)	Tacoma Boat, Tacoma, Wash.	24-7-67	13-4-68	14-7-69
P 112 Albuquerque (ex-*Welch,* PG 93)	Peterson, Sturgeon Bay, Wisc.	8-8-67	25-7-68	8-9-69

Albuquerque (P 112) W. Donko, 7-83

D: 225 tons (245 fl) **S:** 40 kts (16 cruising)
Dim: 50.14 (46.94 wl) × 7.28 × 2.9
A: 1/76.2-mm 50 DP Mk 34—4/12.7-mm mg (II × 2)
Electron Equipt: Radar: 1/LN-66, 1/SPG-50 **Electric:** 100 kw
M: CODOG: 1 G.E. 7LM-1500-PE 102 gas turbines; 13,300 hp (12,500 sust.) 2 Cummins VT 12-875M diesels, 1,650 hp (1,450 sust.); 2 CP props

Remarks: Leased 16-5-83, towed to Jonathan Corp., Norfolk, Va., for reactivation. Used on anti-drug patrol. Mk 63 GFCS for 76.2-mm gun. Offer of two more not taken up due to difficulty of maintaining engineering plant.

◆ **6 miscellaneous captured drug runners**

. . . Turbu, . . . Tolu, . . . Serranilla, . . . Teniente De Navio Jose Maria Palas, . . . Teniente De Navio Alejandro Bal Domero Salgado, . . . Teniente Primo Alcala

Remarks: Characteristic unknown; placed in service 1981 to help combat drug traffic in the Caribbean. Most are ex-drug runners. *Rigel,* a former trawler used in this service, was lost 15-8-82.

RIVER PATROL BOATS AND CRAFT

◆ **2 Rio Hacha class** Bldr: Unial Barranquilla (In serv. 1955)

CF 35 Rio Hacha CF 37 Arauca

Arauca (CF 37)

D: 170 tons (184 fl) **S:** 13 kts **Dim:** 47.25 × 8.23 × 1.0
A: 2/76.2-mm DP (I × 2)—4/20-mm AA (I × 4)
M: 2 Caterpillar diesels; 2 props; 800 hp **Range:** 1,000/12 **Man:** 27-43 tot.

Remarks: Sister *Leticia* disarmed and equipped as a hospital boat.

◆ **CF 33 Cartagena** Bldr: Yarrow, Glasgow (In serv. 1930)

D: 142 tons **S:** 15.5 kts **Dim:** 41.9 × 7.16 × 0.8
A: 2/76.2-mm—1/20-mm AA—4/7.7-mm mg **Range:** 2,100/15 **Man:** 39 tot.
M: 2 Gardner diesels; 2 props (in tunnels); 600 hp **Fuel:** 24 tons

Remarks: Principal parts of the ship protected against small arms.

Cartagena (CF 33)

OCEANOGRAPHIC RESEARCH SHIPS

◆ **2 Malpelo class** Bldr: Martin Jansen, Leer, W. Germany

BO 155 Providencia (In serv. 5-81) BO 156 Malpelo (In serv. 4-81)

Malpelo (BO 156) 1983

D: 1,090 tons (fl) **S:** 13 kts **Dim:** 50.3 (44.0 pp) × 10.0 × 4.0
M: 2 M.A.N. 6-cyl. diesels; 1 Kort-nozzle prop; 1,570 hp
Range: 16,000/11.5 **Man:** 9 officers, 18 men, 6 scientists

Remarks: Delivered 1981 for DIMAR (Dirección General Maritima Portuario), one for geophysical research, one for fisheries. White-painted. Naval manned. Bow-thruster, flapped Becker rudder. Prime contractor: Ferrostaal, Kiel. Both commissioned 24-7-81.

◆ **1 U.S. PCE 821-class former ASW escort** Bldr: Pullman Standard Car Co., Chicago

	Laid down	L	In serv.
BO 151 San Andres (ex-*Rockville,* PCER 851)	18-10-43	22-2-44	15-5-44

San Andres (BO 151) 1976

D: 674 tons (858 fl) **S:** 15 kts **Dim:** 56.23 × 10.05 × 3.0 **Electric:** 180 kw
M: 2 G.M. 12-567A diesels; 2 props; 1,800 hp **Man:** 60 tot.

Remarks: Purchased 5-6-69 and then converted. Possibly stricken.

◆ **1 U.S. former refrigerated stores lighter** Bldr: Niagara SB, Buffalo, N.Y.

BO 153 Quindio (ex-U.S. YFR 433) (In serv. 11-11-43)

D: 380 tons (600 fl) **Dim:** 40.4 × 9.10 × 2.5 **M:** 1 Union diesel; 600 hp
Man: 17 tot.

Remarks: Leased 7-64; purchased 31-3-78.

AUXILIARY SHIPS

◆ **1 U.S. Patapsco-class tanker, former gasoline tanker**

	Bldr	Laid down	L	In serv.
BT 67 Tumaco (ex-U.S. *Chewaucan,* AOG 50)	Cargill, Inc. Savage, Minn.	23-12-43	22-7-44	19-2-45

D: 4,570 tons (fl) **S:** 14 kts **Dim:** 94.7 (89.0 pp) × 14.78 × 4.9
A: 2/76.2-mm DP (I × 2) **M:** 2 G.M. 16-278A diesels; 2 props; 3,300 hp
Range: 8,350/11.5 **Man:** 45 tot.

COLOMBIA *(continued)*
AUXILIARY SHIPS *(continued)*

Tumaco (BT 67) 1976

REMARKS: Purchased 1-7-75. Foremast deleted, small lattice mast stepped for navigational radar. Cargo: 2,575 tons. Retains one Mk 52 radar GFCS (with Mk 26 radar) and one Mk 51 GFCS.

◆ **1 small transport/cargo ship** Bldr: Sander, Delfzijl, Netherlands (In serv. 1953)

TM 43 CIUDAD DE QUIBDO (ex-M/V *Shamrock*)

D: 633 tons **S:** 11 kts **Dim:** 50.3 × 7.2 × 2.8
M: 1 M.A.N. diesel; 1 prop; 390 hp **Fuel:** 32 tons
Man: 11 tot.

REMARKS: Purchased 1953.

◆ **2 hospital boats**

BD 36 LETICIA Former river patrol boat, see under *Rio Hacha* class. Has 6 beds, surgery facilities, etc.

BD 33 SOCORRO Bldr: Cartagena Naval DY, 1956

D: 70 tons **S:** 9 kts **Dim:** 25.0 × 5.5 × 0.75 **M:** 2 G.M. diesels; 270 hp
Man: 10 tot.

REMARKS: Originally fitted to carry 56 troops on the rivers, now used for surgery.

TUGS

◆ **1 U.S. Sotoyomo-class auxiliary ocean tug** Bldr: Levingston SY, Orange, Texas

	Laid down	L	In serv.
RM 75 BAHIA UTRIA (ex-*Koka,* ATA 185)	5-8-44	11-9-44	17-11-44

D: 534 tons (835 fl) **S:** 13 kts **Dim:** 43.6 × 10.3 × 4.0
A: 1/76.2-mm DP Mk 26 **Electric:** 120 kw
M: 2 G.M. 12-278A diesels, electric drive; 1 prop; 1,500 hp **Range:** 8,000/8

REMARKS: Transferred 1-7-71. Sister *Bahia Honda* lost 2-75.

◆ **1 ex-U.S. small harbor tug** Bldr: Henry C. Grebe (In serv. 2-9-43)

RM 73 TENIENTE RICARDO SORZANO (ex-YTL 231)

D: 70 tons (80 fl) **S:** 9 kts **Dim:** 20.2 × 5.2 × 1.5 **Electric:** 15 kw
M: 1 Cooper-Bessemer diesel; 240 hp **Fuel:** 7 tons

REMARKS: Loaned 1963; purchased 31-3-78.

◆ **1 old harbor tug** (L: 1928)—possibly stricken

RM 71 ANDAGOYA

D: 117 grt **S:** 12 kts **Dim:** 28.0 × 6.1 × 3.0 **M:** 1 diesel; 400 hp

◆ **6 Capitan Castro class**—for river use

RR 81 CAPITAN CASTRO
RR 82 CANDIDO LEGUIZAMO
RR 84 CAPITAN ALVARO RUIS
RR 86 CAPITAN RIGOBERTO GIRALDO
RR 87 CAPITAN VLADIMIR VALEK
RR 88 TENIENTE LUIS BERNAL

D: 50 tons **S:** 10 kts **Dim:** 20.0 × 4.25 × 0.75 **M:** 2 G.M. diesels; 260 hp

◆ **1 floating dry dock for river force use**

JAIME ARIAS—D: 700 tons (fl) Capacity: 165 tons

◆ **1 school sailing ship** Bldr: Celaya, Bilbao, Spain (In serv. 7-9-68)

GLORIA

D: 1,300 tons (fl) **S:** 10.5 kts (on diesel) **Dim:** 64.7 × 10.6 × 6.6
M: 1 diesel; 500 hp **Sail areas:** 1,400 m² (bark-rigged)

COAST GUARD
(Cuerpo del Guardacosta)

Established 1981. The surviving craft of the former customs service fleet have been refitted and incorporated. A major function is anti-drug patrol.

Gloria G. Gyssels, 7-85

PATROL BOATS

◆ **2 U.S. 105-ft. Commercial Cruiser class** Bldr: Swiftships Inc., Berwick, La.

AN 101 OLAYA HERRERA (In serv. 16-10-81)
AN 102 RAFAEL DEL CASTILLO Y RADA (In serv. 2-83)

Rafael del Castillo y Rada (102) 1983

D: 103 tons (fl) **S:** 25 kts **Dim:** 31.5 × 6.6 × 2.1
A: 1/40-mm AA—2/12.7-mm mg
M: 2 MTU 12V331 TC92 diesels; 2 props; 7,000 hp **Range:** 1,600/25; 2,400/15
Electric: 113 kw **Man:** 3 officers, 16 men

◆ **2 Jorge Soto del Corval class** Bldr: Rauma Repola SY, Rauma, Finland (In serv. 1971)

A 208 CARLOS ALBAN A 209 NITO RESTREPO

D: 100 tons (130 fl) **S:** 18 kts **Dim:** 34.0 × 6.0 × 1.9 **A:** 1/20-mm AA
M: 2 MTU diesels; 2 CP props; 2,500 hp

REMARKS: A 208 recommissioned 1980, A 209 in 1981. Sister *J.S. del Corval* hulked.

◆ **1 Pedro Gaul class** Bldr: F. Schürenstedt, Bardenfleth, W. Germany

A 206 CARLOS E. RESTREPO (In serv. 1964)

D: 85 tons (fl) **S:** 26 kts **Dim:** 34.7 × 5.5 × 1.8 **A:** 1/20-mm AA
M: 2 Maybach 12-cyl. diesels; 2 props; 2,500 hp

REMARKS: Sisters *Pedro Gaul* (AN 204) and *Estaban Jaramillo* (A 205) hulked. A 206 recommissioned 1981.

COMOROS

Republic of the Comoros

MERCHANT MARINE (1984): 2 ships—977 grt

PATROL CRAFT

◆ **2 Japanese Yamayuri class** Bldr: Ishihara, Takasago (In serv. 10-81)

KASTHALA NTRINGHUI

D: 27 tons (40.3 fl) **S:** 20.7 kts **Dim:** 18.0 × 4.3 × 0.82 (1.1 prop) **A:** . . .
M: 2 Type RD 10T diesels; 2 props; 900 hp **Man:** 6 tot.

REMARKS: Identical to craft in the Japanese Maritime Safety Agency.

COMOROS *(continued)*

AUXILIARIES

◆ **1 former French transport** Bldr: Toulon DY (In serv. 1957)

VILLE DE NIMACHOVA (ex-*Issole*)

D: 600 tons (fl) **S:** 12 kts **Dim:** 49.0 × 7.0 × 2.2
M: 2 diesels; 2 props; 1,000 hp **Fuel:** 36 tons **Range:** 2,600/10.8

REMARKS: Stricken from French Navy and acquired by Comoros in 1981. Former "regional transport" with bow doors and beaching ramp for vehicle cargo. Cargo: 240 tons plus 60 tons on deck.

◆ **1 British LCT(8)-class tank-landing ship** (In serv. 1945)

N. . . . . . . (ex-Fr. LCT 9061, ex-Br. *Buttress,* LCT(8) 4099)

L 9061 C. Limonier, 1975

D: 657 tons (1,000 fl) **S:** 12 kts **Dim:** 70.48 × 11.9 × 1.8
A: 2/20-mm AA (I × 2)—1/120-mm mortar, Army model
M: 4 Paxman diesels; 2 props; 1,840 hp **Man:** 29 tot.

REMARKS: Bought 7-65 by France, transferred by France, 1976.

CONGO

People's Republic of the Congo

PERSONNEL (1984): 250 total

MERCHANT MARINE (1984): 21 ships—8,458 grt

COASTAL NAVY

The naval forces are divided into coastal navy and the river navy. Plans to acquire three additional seagoing patrol boats were in hand during 1985; under consideration are three 357-ton Spanish "Cormoran"-class gunboats.

◆ **3 Spanish "Piraña"-class patrol boats** Bldr: Bazán, Cadiz—ordered 1980

	In serv.
P 601 MARIEN NGOUABI (ex-*L'Intrépide*)	10-11-82
P 602 LES TROIS GLORIEUSES (ex-*Le Vaillant*)	1-83
P 603 LES MALOANGO (ex-*Le Terrible*)	3-83

Marien Ngouabi (P 601) Bazán, 1983

D: 125 tons (138 fl) **S:** 25 **Dim:** 32.70 (30.60 pp) × 6.15 × 1.55
A: 1/40-mm—1/20-mm AA—2/12.7-mm mg (I × 2)
Electron Equipt: Radar: 1/Raytheon RM 1220/6 × 8
M: 2 M.A.N./Bazan V8V 16/8TLS diesels; 2 props; 3,200 hp
Electric: 210 kw **Range:** 1,100/17 **Man:** 3 officers, 16 men

REMARKS: CSEE Panda optronic GFCS. Renamed on delivery; arrived in Congo 1-6-83; by 8-84 badly needed overhaul, which began at builders in 1985.

◆ **6 Soviet Zhuk-class patrol boats (3 transferred 1982, 3 in 2-84)**

V 301 V 302 V 303 V 304 V 305 V 306

D: 48 tons (60 fl) **S:** 34 kts **Dim:** 24.0 × 5.0 × 1.2 (1.8 props)
A: 4/14.5-mm mg (II × 2) **Fuel:** 10 tons **Man:** 12 tot.
M: 2 M50F-4 diesels; 2 props; 2,400 hp **Range:** 700/28; 1,100/15

◆ **1 Soviet Shershen-class former torpedo boat**

D: 150 tons (170 fl) **S:** 45 kts **Dim:** 34.7 × 6.7 × 1.5
A: 4/30-mm AA (II × 2) **Electron Equipt:** Radar: 1/Pot Drum, 1/Drum Tilt
M: 3 M503A diesels; 3 props; 12,000 hp **Range:** 460/42; 850/30

REMARKS: Transferred 1979; torpedo tubes removed prior to delivery.

◆ **3 ex-Chinese Shanghai-II-class patrol boats** (Transferred 3-75)

P 401 P 402 P 403

D: 122.5 tons (135 fl) **S:** 28.5 kts **Dim:** 38.78 × 5.41 × 1.55
A: 4/37-mm AA (II × 2)—4/25-mm AA (II × 2)
Electron Equipt: Radar: 1/Pot Head
M: 2 M50F-4, 1,200 hp and 2/12D6 diesels; 4 props; 4,220 hp **Man:** 36 tot.
Endurance: 7 days **Electric:** 39 kw **Range:** 750/16.5

RIVER NAVY

◆ **2 13-m and 2 11.4-m Arcor (France)-built patrol craft** (In serv. 1982)

◆ **4 ex-Chinese Yu Lin-class patrol craft** (Transferred 1966)

D: 9.8 tons (fl) **S:** 25 kts **Dim:** 13.0 × 2.9 × 1.1 **A:** 1/12.7-mm mg
M: 1 diesel; 1 prop; 300 hp

◆ **2 locally built small craft**

◆ **10 outboard-powered small craft**

COSTA RICA

Republic of Costa Rica

PERSONNEL: 100 men

MERCHANT MARINE (1984): 27 ships—19,750 grt

PATROL BOATS

◆ **1 105-foot Commercial Cruiser class** Bldr: Swiftships, Morgan City, Louisiana

FP 1055 ISLA DEL COCO

Isla del Coco (FP 1055) Swiftships, 4-85

D: 118 tons (fl) **S:** 36 kts **Dim:** 31.73 × 7.1 × 2.16
A: 2/12.7-mm mg (I × 2)
M: 3 MTU 12V331 TC92 diesels; 3 props; 10,500 hp **Range:** 1,200/18
Man: 21 tot.

REMARKS: Refitted 1984 to 3-85 by builders.

COSTA RICA *(continued)*
PATROL BOATS *(continued)*

◆ **5 65-foot Commercial Cruiser class** Bldr: Swiftships, Morgan City, Louisiana (In serv. 1978)

FP 657 FP 658 FP 659 FP 660 FP 661

D: 33 tons (fl) **S:** 32 kts **Dim:** 19.77 × 5.56 × 1.98
A: 2/12.7 mm mg (I × 2)
M: 2 MTU 8V331 diesels; 2 props; 1,400 hp **Range:** 1,200/18

REMARKS: See photo of FP 657, refitted 1985, in addenda. In 1985 Swiftships was also building two 34-ft and one 42-ft patrol craft for Costa Rica.

CUBA

Republic of Cuba

PERSONNEL: Approx. 9,000 men, including 1,000 naval infantry

MERCHANT MARINE (1984): 418 ships—959,171 grt (tankers: 19—70,474 grt)

SUBMARINES

◆ **3 Soviet Foxtrot class**

D: 1,900/2,400 tons **S:** 16/15.5 kts **Dim:** 91.5 × 7.5 × 6.0
A: 10/533-mm TT (6 fwd, 4 aft)—22 torpedoes or 44 mines
M: 3/2,000 hp diesels, 3 electric motors; 3 props; 5,300 hp **Endurance:** 70 days
Range: 11,000/8 snorkel **Man:** 78 tot.

REMARKS: Transferred 1-79, 1-80, and 2-84. A non-operational Whiskey-class submarine was transferred 4-79 for use as a battery-charging barge.

FRIGATES

◆ **2 Soviet Koni class** Bldr: Zelenodolsk SY

356 MARIEL . . . N. . .

Mariel (356) U.S. Navy, 7-84

D: 1,900 tons (fl) **S:** 27 kts **Dim:** 95.0 × 12.8 × 4.2 (4.4 hull)
A: 1/SAN-4 SAM syst. (II × 1; 20 missiles)—4/76.2-mm DP (II × 2)—4/30-mm AA (II × 2)—2/RBU-6000—mines
Electron Equipt: Radar: 1/Strut Curve, 1/Don-2, 1/Pop Group, 1/Hawk Screech, 1/Drum Tilt—IFF: 2/Square Head, 1/High Pole A
Sonar: 1/MF, hull-mounted
EW: 2 Watch Dog, 2/chaff RL (XVI × 2)
M: CODAG: 1 gas turbine, 2 diesels; 3 props; 30,000 hp
Range: 1,800/14 **Man:** 120 tot.

REMARKS: *Mariel* delivered 23-9-81; second unit arrived 2-84. Like the Algerian units, have a continuous deckhouse amidships.

GUIDED-MISSILE PATROL BOATS

◆ **13 Soviet Osa-II class**

Cuban Osa-II—note man with SA-7 Grail missile amidships U.S. Navy, 7-84

D: 190 tons (240 fl) **S:** 35 kts **Dim:** 38.6 × 7.6 × 2.0
A: 4/SS-N-2 Styx (I × 4)—4/30-mm AA (II × 2)
Electron Equipt: Radar: 1/Square Tie, 1/Drum Tilt
IFF: 2/Square Head, 1/High Pole A
M: 3 M504 diesels; 3 props; 15,000 hp **Range:** 500/34; 750/25 **Man:** 30 tot.

REMARKS: Transferred: 2 in 1977, 3 in 1978, 2 in 1979, 2 in 11-81, 2 in 1-82, 2 in 2-82. Carry SA-7 Grail (Strela) surface-to-air missiles in hand-held launchers.

◆ **5 Soviet Osa-I class**

D: 175 tons (210 fl) **S:** 36 kts **Dim:** 38.6 × 7.6 × 1.8
A: 4/SS-N-2 Styx (I × 4)—4/30-mm AA (II × 2)
Electron Equipt: Radar: 1/Square Tie, 1/Drum Tilt
IFF: 2/Square Head, 1/High Pole A
M: 3 M503A diesels; 3 props; 12,000 hp **Range:** 500/34; 750/25 **Man:** 30 tot.

REMARKS: Two were delivered in 1972, two in 1973, and two in 1974; one deleted in 1981.

NOTE: All remaining Soviet Komar-class guided-missile boats were inoperable or had been disposed of by 1985.

◆ **4 Soviet S.O.-1 class**

Cuban S.O.-1 U.S. Navy, 1972

D: 190 tons (215 fl) **S:** 28 kts **Dim:** 42.0 × 6.1 × 1.9
A: 4/25-mm AA (II × 2)—4/RBU-1200 ASW RL—2/d.c. racks (24 d.c.)
Electron Equipt: Radar: 1/Pot Head **M:** 3 Type 40D diesels; 3 props; 7,500 hp
Range: 340/28; 1,900/7 **Man:** 30 tot.

REMARKS: Six were transferred in 1964 and six in 1967. Three additional believed discarded by 1983 and an additional 5 by 1985.

NOTE: The four remaining Kronshtadt-class patrol boats had been discarded by 1985.

◆ **21 Soviet Zhuk class**

Cuban Navy Zhuk patrol boat U.S. Navy, 7-84

D: 48 tons (60 fl) **S:** 34 kts **Dim:** 24.0 × 5.0 × 1.2 (1.8 props)
A: 4/14.5-mm mg (II × 2) **Fuel:** 10 tons **Man:** 12 tot.
M: 2 M50 F-4 diesels; 2 props; 2,400 hp **Range:** 700/28; 1,100/15

REMARKS: Transferred 1 in 12-71, 1 in 7-74, 4 in 10-75, 2 in 12-76, 4 in 1977-79, 6 in 1980 (including 3 in 12-80), and 3 in 1984. One or more additional 1984 transfers passed onto Nicaragua.

TORPEDO BOATS

◆ **9 Soviet Turya-class semi-hydrofoils**

D: 215 tons (250 fl) **S:** 40 kts
Dim: 39.0 × 7.6 (12.5 over foils) × 2.0 (4.0 over foils)

TORPEDO BOATS *(continued)*

Cuban Navy Turya 193 U.S. Navy, 7-84

A: 2/57-mm AA aft (II × 1)—2/25-mm AA (II × 1)—4/533-mm TT (I × 4)
Electron Equipt: Radar: 1/Pot Drum, 1/Muff Cob
IFF: 1/Square Head, 1/High Pole B
M: 3 M504 diesels; 3 props; 15,000 hp **Range:** 400/38; 650/25 **Man:** 24 tot.

REMARKS: First two delivered 2-79, the first foreign transfer of this class; 2 in 2-80, 2 in 1-81, 2 in 1-83, and 1 in 11-83. ASW capability omitted. Semi-retractable forward hydrofoils; stern planes on surface. Uses Osa-II hull and propulsion. Hand-held SA-7 Grail ("Sa-N-5") surface-to-air missiles were carried by mid-1984.

◆ **6 Soviet P 6 class**

D: 56 tons (66.5 fl) **S:** 43 kts **Dim:** 25.3 × 6.1 × 1.7
A: 4/25-mm AA (II × 2)—2/533-mm TT—d.c.
Electron Equipt: Radar: 1/Skip Head
M: 4 M50 diesels; 4 props; 4,800 hp **Range:** 450/30 **Man:** 12 tot.

REMARKS: Built post-1955. Delivered in 1962. Wooden hulls. Possibly no longer operational.

◆ **6 Soviet P 4 class**

Cuban P 4 U.S. Navy

D: 19.3 tons (22.4 fl) **S:** 55 kts **Dim:** 19.3 × 3.7 × 1.0
A: 2/14.5-mm mg (aft)—2/450-mm TT **Electron Equipt:** Radar: 1/Skin Head
M: 2 M50 diesels; 2 props; 2,400 hp **Man:** 12 tot.

REMARKS: Pre-1955. Delivered 1962-64. Aluminum, stepped-hydroplane hulls. Probably in poor condition. Half or more of the original dozen had been discarded by 1985.

MINE WARFARE SHIPS

3 Soviet Sonya-class coastal minesweepers

D: 380 tons (450 fl) **S:** 14 kts **Dim:** 48.8 × 8.8 × 2.1
A: 2/30-mm AA (II × 1)—2/25-mm AA (II × 1)
Electron Equipt: Radar: 1/Spin Trough
IFF: 1/High Pole B, 1/Square Head
M: 2 diesels; 2 props; 2,400 hp **Range:** 1,600/14; 3,000/10 **Man:** 40 tot.

REMARKS: Delivered 8-80, 10-80, and 1-85—all by tow. Wooden hulls, sheathed in glass-reinforced plastic.

Cuban Sonya under tow on delivery voyage 1980

◆ **9 Soviet Yevgenya-class inshore minesweepers** Bldr: Srednyy Neva SY, Kolpind

D: 80 tons (90 fl) **S:** 11 kts **Dim:** 26.2 × 6.1 × 1.5 **A:** 2/25-mm AA (II × 1)
Electron Equipt: Radar: 1/Spin Trough—IFF; 1/High Pole B
M: 2 diesels; 600 hp **Range:** 300/10 **Man:** 12 tot.

REMARKS: Two transferred 1978, two in 1979, two in 12-80, 1 in 11-82, and 2 in 11-84; two others, delivered 9-84, were transferred to Nicaragua. Equipped to search for mines in depths of up to 30 m using towed television, marker buoys, and standard wire cable gear. Glass-reinforced-plastic construction.

AMPHIBIOUS WARFARE SHIPS AND CRAFT

◆ **2 Soviet Polnocny B class** Bldr: Polnocny SY, Gdansk (In serv. circa 1968)

Polnocny B under tow to Cuba Skyfotos, 10-82

D: 800 tons (fl) **S:** 19 kts **Dim:** 74.0 × 8.6 × 2.0 (aft)
A: 4/30-mm AA (II × 2)—2/140-mm artillery RL (XVIII × 2)
Electron Equipt: Radar: 1/Spin Trough, 1/Drum Tilt
IFF: 1/Square Head, 1/High Pole B
M: 2 diesels; 2 props; 5,000 hp **Range:** 900/18; 1,500/14
Man: 30 tot. plus 200 troops

REMARKS: The first, wearing transfer pendant, arrived in 9-82; the second, number 442, arrived 4-12-82. These particular units are configured for troop carrying, as evidenced by the large number (23) of 10-man life rafts carried. Cargo: 180 tons (5 tanks).

◆ **7 Soviet T-4-class landing craft** (In serv. 1950s-1970s)

D: 70 tons (fl) **S:** 10 kts **Dim:** 19.0 × 4.3 × 1.0
M: 2 diesels; 2 props; 600 hp **Man:** 5 tot.

REMARKS: Transferred 1967-74. Used as utility lighters.

HYDROGRAPHIC SURVEY SHIPS

◆ **1 Soviet Biya class** Bldr: Gdansk, Poland (1972-76)

H 103 GUAMA (ex-GS 186)

D: 750 tons (fl) **S:** 13 kts **Dim:** 55.0 × 9.2 × 2.6
Electron Equipt: Radar: 1/Don-2 **M:** 2 diesels; 2 CP props; 1,200 hp
Range: 4,700/11 **Man:** 25 tot.

REMARKS: Transferred 11-80. Carries one survey launch. Also useful as a buoy tender; one 5-ton crane.

◆ **1 converted trawler**

H 101 SIBONEY **D:** 600 tons

REMARKS: Built in Spain, 1972. Also used for training.

◆ **6 Soviet Nyryat-1 class.**

H 91 H 92 H 93 H 94 H 95 H 96

D: 120 tons (fl) **S:** 12 kts **Dim:** 29.0 × 5.0 × 1.7
M: 1 diesel; 2 props; 450 hp **Radar:** 1/Spin Trough **Range:** 1,600/10
Man: 15 tot.

CUBA *(continued)*
HYDROGRAPHIC SURVEY SHIPS *(continued)*

Remarks: Date of transfer not known. Known in U.S.S.R. as GPB 480 class. Same class, with different equipment, also used as diving tenders.

AUXILIARIES

◆ **1 cargo ship:** Arenal (1965) 763 grt. Acquired 12-82. No other data available.

◆ **1 Soviet Pelym-class degaussing tender**

Pelym-class degaussing tender en route Cuba 2-82

D: 1,300 tons (fl) **S:** 16 kts **Dim:** 65.5 × 11.6 × 3.4
A: None **Electron Equipt:** Radar: 1/Don-2
M: 2 diesels; 2 props; . . . hp **Range:** 4,500/12 **Man:** 70 tot.

Remarks: Arrived in Cuba 2-82 under tow. Probably intended to support the Foxtrot-class submarines.

◆ **1 intelligence collector, former fishing boat** Bldr: Sociedad Española de Construcción Naval, Bilbao (In serv. 1967)

Isla de la Juventud (ex-*Arminza*)

Isla de la Juventud U.S. Navy, 7-84

D: 1,556 grt **S:** 13 kts **Dim:** 70.0 × 12.6 × 5.4
M: 1 MWM diesel; 1 prop; 2,200 hp

Remarks: Equipped with a variety of electronic collection antennas. Converted around 1980.

◆ **1 yacht**

Granma

Remarks: Small cabin cruiser in which Fidel Castro returned to Cuba in 1956. Maintained by the navy as a museum.

◆ **3 small service launches** Bldr: U.S.A. (In serv. 1949)

A 1 A 2 A 3

D: 58 tons **Dim:** 22.50 × 4.6 × 1.6
M: 2 Gray Marine diesels; 2 props; 225 hp

◆ **1 Soviet Okhtenskiy-class seagoing tug** (In serv. 1960s)

Caribe

D: 700 tons (950 fl) **S:** 13.3 kts **Dim:** 47.3 × 10.3 × 5.5
M: 2 diesels; 1 prop; 1,500 hp **Range:** 7,800/7 **Man:** 40 tot.

Remarks: Transferred 1976.

◆ **2 Soviet Yelva-class diving tenders**

D: 295 tons (fl) **S:** 12.4 kts **Dim:** 40.9 × 8.0 × 2.1
M: 2 3D12A diesels; 2 props; 600 hp **Radar:** 1/Spin Trough

Remarks: Transferred 1978. Can support 7 divers to 60-m depths.

◆ **1 or more Soviet Poluchat-I-class torpedo retrievers**

Cuban Navy Poluchat-I 1983

D: 90 tons (fl) **S:** 18 kts **Dim:** 29.6 × 6.1 × 1.9
A: 4/14.5-mm mg (II × 2)
Electron Equipt: Radar: 1/Spin Trough—IFF: 1/High Pole A
M: 2 M50-F1 diesels; 2 props; 1,800 hp
Range: 450/17; 900/10 **Man:** 20 tot.

Remarks: Transfer date uncertain. Equipped for patrol boat duties as well as for retrieving torpedoes via a stern ramp.

◆ **1 Soviet Whiskey-class battery-charging barge**

D: 1,050 tons **Dim:** 75.0 × 6.3 × 4.8
Electric: 3,500 kw

Remarks: Former submarine, transferred under tow 4-79 with propellers removed, torpedo tubes sealed, and periscopes removed, for use as a charging station for the Foxtrot-class submarines.

COAST GUARD

◆ **7 craft**

GF 528 GF 725 GF 825 GF 720 Similar to 40-foot U.S. Coast Guard small craft

GF 101 GF 102 GF 701 Similar to U.S. Coast Guard small craft

Remarks: Assigned to the Department of the Interior. Hull numbers painted in red to distinguish these boats from naval ships.

◆ **1 patrol craft**

Guanabacoa Bldr: Cadiz, Spain (L: . . .)

S: 22 kts

◆ **6 fast launches** Bldr: Spain, 1971-72

Camilo Cienfuegos Maceo Marti
Escambray Cuartel Moncada Finlay

Remarks: No other information available.

CYPRUS

Republic of Cyprus

Merchant Marine (1984): 737 ships—6,727,887 grt (tankers: 79—3,348,388 grt)

Two Agusta-Bell 47G helicopters are assigned coastal patrol duties.

◆ **2 patrol boats** Bldr: Ch. Navals de l'Estérel, Cannes

Aphrodite (In serv. 12-82) Salamis (In serv. 24-5-83)

D: 96 tons (fl) **S:** 32 kts **Dim:** 32.1 × 6.45 × 1.9
A: 1/40-mm AA—1/20-mm AA
M: 2 MTU diesels; 2 props; 4,000 hp **Range:** 1,500/15

Remarks: Wooden construction. First unit ordered 9-81. *Salamis* powered by SACM diesels producing 4,640 hp.

DENMARK

Kingdom of Denmark

Personnel (1984): 5,800 men (1,300 officers, 3,200 enlisted, 1,300 conscripts), plus 2,600 civilians. There are 10,000 Naval Reservists and 5,200 members of the Home Guard.

Merchant Marine (1984): 1,101 ships—5,211,262 grt
(tankers: 66 ships—2,557,088 grt)

Naval Aviation: Eight Mk 80 Lynx helicopters, the first of which was delivered 15-5-80. The Air force took delivery of three U.S. Gulfstream G III Maritime Patrol Aircraft during 1981-82.

Danish Westland Mk 80 Lynx Danish Navy

SUBMARINES

Note: Financial restrictions having precluded the desired construction of six German Type 210 submarines to replace the current generation, the Danish Government first sought to lease German Navy Type 206 units. Rebuffed at this, it turned to Norway, where negotiations for the purchase of three Kobben-class submarines were underway in 1985 (data in Norwegian section).

◆ **2 German Type 205**

	Bldr	Laid down	L	In serv.
S 320 Narhvalen	RDY Copenhagen	16-2-65	10-9-68	27-2-70
S 321 Nordkaperen	RDY Copenhagen	20-1-66	18-12-69	22-12-70

Narhvalen (S 320) L. & L. Van Ginderen, 6-85

D: 370 light/430 surf./480 tons **S:** 10/17 kts **Dim:** 45.41 × 4.60 × 3.80 (surf.)
A: 8/533-mm TT fwd **Man:** 22 tot.
Electron Equipt: Radar: 1/Thomson-CSF Calypso
Sonar: 1/SRS-M1H, 1/GHG AN5039A1
M: 2 MTU 820 Db, 600-hp diesels; 2/405-kw generators, 1/2,300 hp motor

Remarks: Modeled on the German Type 205 and Norwegian Type 207 (*Kobben* class).

◆ **2 Delfinen class**

	Bldr	Laid down	L	In serv.
S 327 Spaekhuggeren	RDY Copenhagen	1-12-54	20-2-57	27-6-59
S 329 Springeren	RDY Copenhagen	3-1-61	26-4-63	22-10-64

Spaekhuggeren (S 327) L. & L. Van Ginderen, 4-84

D: 595/643 tons **S:** 13/12 kts **Dim:** 54.0 × 4.7 × 3.8
A: 4/533-mm TT fwd
M: Burmeister & Wain 12-cyl. diesels, 2 motors; 2 props; 1,200 hp
Range: 4,000/8.5 **Man:** 33 tot.

Remarks: S 329 built with U.S. "Offshore" funds, as U.S. SS 554. Diving depth: 100-m. Sister *Tumleren* (S 328) stricken 8-81, and *Delfinen* (S 326) was decommissioned 1983 and stricken 1985.

FRIGATES

◆ **2 Peder Skram class**

	Bldr	Laid down	L	In serv.
F 352 Peder Skram	Helsingør Vaerft	25-9-64	20-5-65	30-6-66
F 353 Herluf Trolle	Helsingør Vaerft	18-12-64	8-9-65	16-4-67

Peder Skram (F 352) 1980

Herluf Trolle (F 353)—with 5 Harpoon aboard L. & L. Van Ginderen, 5-84

D: 2,030 tons (2,720 fl) **S:** 28 kts (16.5 diesel)
Dim: 112.5 (108.0 pp) × 12.0 × 3.6
A: 8/Harpoon SSM (IV × 2)—1 NATO Sea Sparrow SAM system (VIII × 1)—2/127-mm 38-cal. DP, U.S. Mk 30 (II × 1)—4/40-mm AA (I × 4)—4/533-mm TT (I × 4)—1 d.c. rack
Electron Equipt: Radar: 1 Skanter 009, 1/CWS-2, 1/CWS-3, 3 M-46 fire-control, 1/Mk 91 Mod. 1 fire-control (2 radar directors)
Sonar: 1 Plessey PMS 26—EW: Decca Racal Cutlass intercept
M: CODOG propulsion: 2 G.M. 16-567D diesels (4,800 hp); 2 Pratt & Whitney PWA GG 4A-3 gas turbines (44,000 hp); 2 CP props
Man: 200 tot.

Remarks: Danish design, built with U.S. "Offshore" funds. Speed with diesels: 16 knots. There are two radar directors for the Mk 91 Mod. 1 Sea Sparrow system, which, along with Harpoon, was added 1977-79, as was the CEPLO computerized tactical data system. The torpedo tubes fire Swedish Type 61 wire-guided torpedoes. Plessey AWS-4 will replace one of the search radars. F 353 had a serious engine-room fire, 15-7-82, recommissioning after repairs in 10-83.

Note: Plans call for replacing these ships in the 1990s with two "Standard-flex 2,000" frigates.

◆ **3 Nils Juel (Type KV 72) class** Bldr: Aalborg Vaerft

	Laid down	L	In serv.
F 354 Nils Juel	20-10-76	27-9-78	22-8-80
F 355 Olfert Fischer	6-12-78	15-1-80	16-10-81
F 356 Peter Tordenskjold	3-12-79	2-81	2-4-82

D: 1,100 tons (1,320 fl) **S:** 30 kts (20 on a diesel)
Dim: 84.0 (80.0 pp) × 10.3 × 3.1
A: 8/Harpoon SSM (IV × 2)—1 NATO Sea Sparrow SAM (VIII × 1)—1/76-mm OTO Melara Compact DP—1 d.c. rack
Electron Equipt: Radar: 1/Plessey AWS-5, 2 Skanter 009, 1 Phillips 3-cm, 1 Phillips 9 LV 200 GFCS (with Type 771 low-light t.v. tracker), 1/Mk 91 Mod. 1 MFCS (2 dir.)
Sonar: Plessey PMS-26
EW: Decca-Racal Cutlass passive
M: CODOG: 1 G.E. LM-2500 gas turbine (26,600 hp), 1 MTU 20V-956 TB82 diesel (4,800 hp); 2 CP props
Range: 800/28; 2,500/18 **Electric:** 1,500 kw (3,500-kw diesel sets)
Fuel: 130 tons **Man:** 18 officers, 9 CPO, 63 men

Remarks: Ordered 5-12-75. Planned ASW torpedo system not installed. Two Breda SCLAR chaff/flare RL not yet added. NATO Sea Sparrow system, with no reloads,

FRIGATES *(continued)*

Nils Juel (F 354)—with 6 Harpoon aboard   L. & L. Van Ginderen, 4-85

Olfert Fischer (F 355)   Official, 1982

has two radar directors. DataSAAB CEPLO data system. F 355 commissioning delayed by fire 5-81. Planned to receive U.S. RAM (Rolling Airframe Missile) SAM system, using two lightweight, 8–10-missile launchers per ship.

FISHERIES PROTECTION FRIGATES

◆ **1 modified Hvidbjørnen class**   Bldr: Aalborg Vaerft

	Laid down	L	In serv.
F 340 Beskyterren	15-12-74	27-5-75	27-2-76

Beskyterren (F 340)—with Lynx on deck   Danish Navy, 1983

D: 1,970 tons (fl) **S:** 18 kts **Dim:** 74.4 × 11.8 × 4.5
A: 1/76.2-mm DP—1/Lynx helicopter **Man:** 60 tot.
Electron Equipt: Radar: 1/CWS-1, 1/Skanter 009
Sonar: 1/Plessey PMS-26
M: 4 Burmeister & Wain Alpha diesels; 1 CP prop; 7,440 hp **Range:** 6,000/13 (one engine)

Remarks: Serves as a fisheries-protection ship. An OTO Melara Compact 76-mm gun was to have been fitted. Plessey AWS-6 to replace CWS-1 radar.

◆ **4 Hvidbjørnen class**

	Bldr	Laid down	L	In serv.
F 348 Hvidbjørnen	Aarhus Flydedok	6-61	23-11-61	12-62
F 349 Vaedderen	Aalborg SY	10-61	6-4-62	3-63
F 350 Ingolf	Svendborg Skibsvaerft	12-61	27-7-62	6-63
F 351 Fylla	Aalborg SY	6-62	18-12-62	7-63

D: 1,345 tons (1,650 fl) **S:** 18 kts **Dim:** 72.6 × 11.6 × 4.9
A: 1/76.2-mm DP—1/Lynx helicopter **Man:** 10 officers, 60 men

Ingolf (F 350)   L. & L. Van Ginderen, 7-85

Electron Equipt: Radar: 1/CWS-1, 1/Skanter 009
Sonar: 1 Plessey PMS-46
M: 4 G.M. 16-567C diesels; 1 CP prop; 6,400 hp **Range:** 6,000/13

Remarks: Reinforced bow. F 350, used for hydrographic surveying, has no gun or helicopter, but carries four 13-meter SKA-1-class survey launches on her flight deck. Plessey AWS-6 to replace CWS-1 radar. These ships may be discarded, pending a 1985 survey of Denmark's fishing industry.

GUIDED-MISSILE BOATS

◆ **10 Willemoes class**   Bldr: Frederikshavn SY

	In serv.		In serv.
P 540 Bille	10-76	P 545 Norby	22-11-77
P 541 Bredal	21-1-77	P 546 Rodsteen	16-2-78
P 542 Hammer	1-4-77	P 547 Sehested	19-5-78
P 543 Huitfeldt	15-6-77	P 548 Suenson	10-8-78
P 544 Krieger	22-9-77	P 549 Willemoes	7-10-76

Rodsteen (P 546)—empty racks for 4 Harpoon SSM   L. & L. Van Ginderen, 6-85

Suenson (P 548)—no EW dome atop mast   L. & L. Van Ginderen, 6-85

D: 232 tons (265 fl) **S:** 40 kts (36 normal)—diesels: 12 kts
Dim: 46.1 (42.4 pp) × 7.4 × 2.1 (2.7 over props)
A: 4/Harpoon SSM—1/76-mm OTO Melara Compact—2/533-mm TT

GUIDED-MISSILE BOATS *(continued)*

Electron Equipt: Radar: 1/9GA-208, 1/NWS-3, 1/9LV 200 fire-control
M: CODOG: 3 Rolls-Royce Proteus 52M/544 gas turbines; 2 G.M. 8V-71 diesels; 3 Liaan CP props; 12,750/800 hp
Electric: 420 kw **Range:** 400/36 **Man:** 5 officers, 21 men

REMARKS: Based on the Swedish Lürssen-designed Spica class and ordered in 1972. The torpedoes are Swedish Type 61s, wire-guided, with a range of 20,000 meters. Endurance is normally 36 hours. Two triple 103-mm flare rocket rails on pilothouse sides. Decca-Racal Cutlass intercept system ordered 1980 for all. Have TORCI torpedo f.c.s. and CEPLO tactical data system. Normally operate with only two Harpoon aboard. Can carry 20 mines in lieu of SSM and torpedoes or 6 torpedo tubes and no SSM.

TORPEDO BOATS

◆ **6 Søløven class**

	Bldr	Laid down	L	In serv.
P 510 Søløven	Vosper, Portsmouth	8-62	19-4-63	12-2-65
P 511 Søridderen	Vosper, Portsmouth	10-62	22-8-63	10-2-65
P 512 Søbjørnen	RDY Copenhagen	7-63	19-8-64	9-65
P 513 Søhesten	RDY Copenhagen	8-63	31-3-65	6-66
P 514 Søhunden	RDY Copenhagen	2-64	12-1-66	1-67
P 515 Søulven	RDY Copenhagen	6-64	27-4-66	3-67

Søløven (P 510)—with 1/40-mm, 4 TT, 1/20-mm L. & L. Van Ginderen, 6-85

D: 95 tons (114 fl) **S:** 50 kts (10 on diesel)
Dim: 30.26 (27.44 pp) × 7.3 × 2.15
A: 1 or 2/40-mm AA (I × 2)—2 or 4/533-mm TT
Electron Equipt: Radar: 1/NWS-1
M: Rolls-Royce Marine Proteus gas turbines; 3 props; 10,500 hp (12,750 max); 2 G.M. 6V-71 diesels, 530 hp, for cruising
Man: 4 officers, 22 men

REMARKS: A modification of the British Brave class. All normally in reserve. Four 50-mm flare RL on fwd 40-mm shield. P 510 was built as PT 821 with U.S. funds. Four of these craft were to be refitted, the other two discarded, in 1984-85; they will receive RADAMEC Type 409 optronic gun directors. Can be configured with 2/40-mm and 2 TT or 1/40-mm and 4 TT. A 20-mm AA can be carried aft.

PATROL BOATS

◆ **0 (+6 + 10) "Standard-flex 300"-class multifunction** Bldr: Aaborg Vaerft

	Laid down	L	In serv.
P. . . N. . .	. . .	. . .	1987
P. . . N. . .	. . .	. . .	. . .
P. . . N. . .	. . .	. . .	. . .
P. . . N. . .	. . .	. . .	. . .
P. . . N. . .	. . .	. . .	. . .
P. . . N. . .	. . .	. . .	. . .

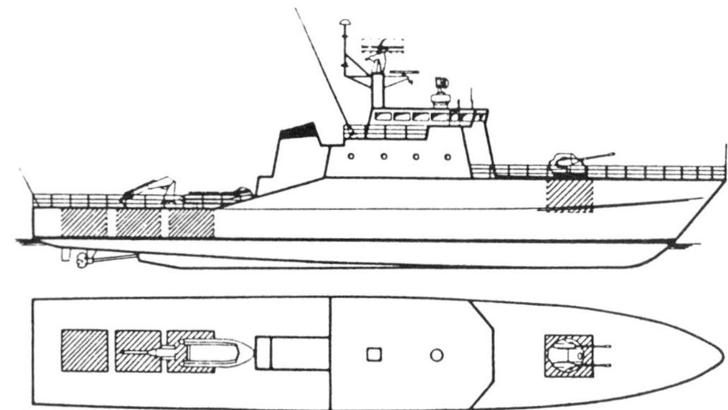
Standard-flex 300 in patrol-boat configuration (Shaded areas show interchangeable mission module locations)

D: 320 tons **S:** 35 kts gas turbine/20 diesel/6 electric
Dim: 44.0 × 8.5 × . . .
A: Patrol boat: 2/30-mm AA
Torpedo boat: 1/76-mm OTO Melara DP, Harpoon SSM, 2/533 mm TT, SAM syst.
Minelayer: 1/20-mm AA, SAM syst.
Minesweeper: 2/30-mm AA
Electron Equipt: Radar: 1/nav., 1/9GA-208, 1/9LV-200
Sonar: . . . EW: . . .
M: CODAG: 1 gas turbine, 2 diesels; 3 props; . . . hp—electric drive for minesweeping/laying—bow-thruster
Man: 15–17 tot. (28 accom.) **Range:** . . .

REMARKS: Glass-reinforced plastic construction concept intended to replace *Daphne*-class patrol boats, existing minesweepers, and the *Søløven*-class torpedo boats. First six approved for construction 1984, with first, perhaps optimistically, scheduled for delivery in 1986. As patrol boats (the initial configuration) will carry a twin AA mount forward and a rigid inflatable inspection boat aft; as torpedo boats will carry a 76-mm gun forward with missiles and torpedo tubes aft; as a minelayer will carry an undetermined SAM system forward, a light AA aft, mine rails, and a crane; in mine countermeasures configuration, will have a twin AA forward, sweep gear aft, and a SAM system. All configurations are intended to be interchangable, using modular, plug-in equipment. First unit ordered 7-85 to a Karlskronavarvet design.

◆ **3 Agdlek class for fisheries protection** Bldr: Svendborg Vaerft

	In serv.
Y 386 Agdlek	12-3-74
Y 387 Agpa	14-5-74
Y 388 Tulugaq	26-6-79

Tulugaq (Y 388) 1979

D: 330 tons (fl) **S:** 12 kts **Dim:** 31.4 × 7.7 × 3.3 **A:** 2/20-mm AA (I × 2)
Electron Equipt: Radar: 2/Terma 20T48 (NWS-3)
M: 1 Burmeister & Wain Alpha diesel; 800 hp **Man:** 15 tot.

REMARKS: For fisheries patrol service in Greenland waters. Can carry two survey launches. Y 388 has only one radar, is .3-m longer, and can make 14 kts.

◆ **9 Barsø class** Bldr: Svendborg

Y 300 Barsø	Y 302 Romsø	Y 304 Thurø	Y 306 Farø	Y 308 Romø
Y 301 Drejø	Y 303 Samsø	Y 305 Vejrø	Y 307 Laesø	

Farø (Y 306)—note trawl boards aft L. & L. Van Ginderen, 1981

PATROL BOATS *(continued)*

D: 155 tons (fl) **S:** 11 kts **Dim:** 25.5 × 6.0 × 2.8 **A:** 2/20-mm AA (I × 2)
Electron Equipt: Radar: 1/Terma 20T48 (NWS-3) **M:** 1 diesel; 1 prop; 385 hp

REMARKS: The first six were completed in 1969 and the last three 1972-73. For fisheries protection duties.

◆ **2 Maagen-class fisheries patrol boats** Bldr: Helsingør (In serv. 5-60)

Y 384 MAAGEN Y 385 MALLEMUKKEN

Maagen (Y 384)—with auxiliary sails set Danish Navy, 1983

D: 175 tons (190 fl) **S:** 10 kts **Dim:** 27.0 × 7.2 × 2.75
A: 2/20-mm AA (I × 2)
Electron Equipt: Radar: 1/Terma 20T48 (NWS-3), 1/Skanter 009
M: Diesel; 1 prop; 350 hp

REMARKS: Based in Greenland.

◆ **8 Daphne-class antisubmarine patrol boats** Bldr: RDY, Copenhagen

	Laid down	L	In serv.
P 530 DAPHNE	4-60	10-11-60	19-12-61
P 531 DRYADEN	7-60	1-3-61	4-4-62
P 533 HAVFRUEN	3-61	4-10-61	20-12-62
P 534 NAJADEN	9-61	20-6-62	26-4-63
P 535 NYMFEN	4-62	1-11-62	4-10-63
P 536 NEPTUN	9-62	29-5-63	18-12-63
P 537 RAN	12-62	10-7-63	15-5-64
P 538 ROTA	6-63	26-11-63	20-1-65

Dryaden (P 531) Danish Navy, 1983

D: 150 tons (170 fl) **S:** 20 kts **Dim:** 38.0 × 6.75 × 2.0
A: 1/40-mm AA—2 d.c. projectors—2 d.c. racks **Man:** 23 tot.
Electron Equipt: Radar: 1/NWS-3—Sonar: Plessey PMS 26
M: 2 Maybach diesels, 1,300 hp, and 1 Foden cruise FD-6 diesel, 100 hp; 3 props

REMARKS: P 530, P 534, and P 536, which were paid for with U.S. "Offshore" funds as PGM 47, PGM 49, and PGM 50, are now completely disarmed. *Havmanden* (P 532) was struck in 1978; others may follow soon. Will be the first class to be replaced by the "Standard-flex 300" units.

PATROL CRAFT

◆ **3 Y 377 class** Bldr: Botved (In serv. 1975)

Y 377 Y 378 Y 379

D: 9 tons (fl) **S:** 27 kts **Dim:** 9.8 × 3.3 × 0.9
Electron Equipt: Radar: 1/NWS-3
M: 2 Volvo Penta inboard/outboard diesels; 2 props; 600 hp

◆ **2 Y 375 class** Bldr: Botved (In serv. 1974)

Y 375 Y 376

Y 376 1978

D: 12 tons (fl) **S:** 26 kts **Dim:** 13.3 × 4.5 × 1.1
Electron Equipt: Radar: 1/NWS-3 **M:** 2 diesels; 2 props; 680 hp

PATROL CRAFT MANNED BY THE HOME GUARD

◆ **6 MHV 20 class** Bldr: Ejvinds, Plastikbodevaerft Svendborg (In serv. 1974-81)

MHV 20 MHV 21 MHV 22 MHV 23 MHV 24 MHV 25

MHV 25 H. Ehlers, 4-85

D: 60 tons (fl) **S:** 15 kts **Dim:** 16.5 × 4.2 × 2.0 **A:** 1/12.7-mm mg
M: 2 MTU diesels; 2 props; 500 hp **Radar:** 1/NWS-3

REMARKS: Additional units of these craft were intended to replace the older MHV units, but no further units were authorized. Glass-reinforced plastic hulls.

◆ **7 MHV-90 class** (In serv. 1974-75)

MHV 90 MHV 91 MHV 92 MHV 93 MHV 94 MHV 95 MHV 96

D: 85 tons (130 fl) **S:** 10.7 kts **Dim:** 19.8 × 5.7 × 1.6 **A:** 1/20-mm AA
M: 1 Burmeister & Wain diesel; 400 hp **Radar:** 1/NWS-3

◆ **3 MHV 70 class** Bldr: Navy Yard, Copenhagen (In serv. 1958)

MHV 70 MHV 71 MHV 72

D: 78 tons (130 fl) **S:** 10 kts **Dim:** 20.1 × 5.1 × 2.5 **A:** 1/20-mm AA aft
Electron Equipt: Radar: 1/NWS-3 **M:** 1 diesel; 200 hp

PATROL CRAFT MANNED BY THE HOME GUARD *(continued)*

MHV 95 H. Ehlers, 4-85

MHV 71—with new, enlarged pilothouse Danish Navy, 1983

◆ **6 MHV 80 class** (In serv. 1941)

MHV 81 (ex-Askø)	MHV 83 (ex-Manø)	MHV 85 (ex-Hjortø)
MHV 82 (ex-Enø)	MHV 84 (ex-Baagø)	MHV 86 (ex-Lyø)

MHV 84 H. Ehlers, 4-85

D: 74 tons **S:** 11 kts **Dim:** 24.4 × 4.9 × 1.6 **A:** 1/20-mm AA
Electron Equipt: Radar: 1/NWS-3 **M:** 1 diesel; 350 hp

Remarks: In Home Guard service 1958. Former inshore minesweepers. Wooden hulls. The gun mount is not normally aboard.

◆ **31 smaller craft, including:**

MHV 1, MHV 3 through MHV 15; MHV 51, MHV 52, MHV 54, MHV 56 through 64, MHV 65 through 68, MHV 74, 75. Small, wooden-hulled fishing boat designs. Most have an NWS-3 radar. No fixed armament.

MHV 60 H. Ehlers, 4-85

MINE WARFARE SHIPS

◆ **4 Falster-class minelayers**

	Bldr	Laid down	L	In serv.
N 80 Falster	Nakskov Skibsvaerft	4-62	19-9-62	7-11-63
N 81 Fyen	Frederikshavn Vaerft	4-62	3-10-62	18-9-63
N 82 Møen	Frederikshavn Vaerft	10-62	6-6-63	20-4-64
N 83 Sjaelland	Nakskov Skibsvaerft	1-63	14-6-63	7-7-64

Sjaelland (N 83) L. & L. Van Ginderen, 4-84

Møen (N 82) Netherlands Navy, 1984

D: 1,880 tons (fl) **S:** 16.5 kts **Dim:** 77.0 (72.5 pp) × 12.8 × 3.4
A: 4/76.2-mm DP U.S. Mk 33 (II × 2)—400 mines (4 minelaying tracks)
Electron Equipt: Radar: 1/CWS-2, 1/NWS-2, 1/NWS-3, 1/M-46
M: 2 G.M. 16-567D3 diesels; 2 CP props; 4,800 hp **Fuel:** 130 tons
Man: 10 officers, 108 men

Remarks: NATO design. The Turkish ship *Nusret* is identical. N 82 is training ship for naval cadets. N 83 converted to submarine tender in 1976, to replace *Henrik Gerner* (can still lay mines). N 80 and N 82 built with U.S. "Offshore" funds as MMC 14 and MMC 15. Have 2/57-mm multiple chaff launchers. All to be refitted for service through 2000.

MINE WARFARE SHIPS *(continued)*

◆ **2 Lindormen-class coastal minelayers** Bldr: Svendborg

	Laid down	L	In serv.
N 43 Lindormen	20-1-77	7-6-77	26-10-77
N 44 Loussen	2-77	9-9-77	30-1-78

Loussen (N 44) Maritime Photographic, 5-85

D: 575 tons (fl) **S:** 14 kts **Dim:** 43.3 (40.0 pp) × 9.0 × 2.65
A: 2/20-mm AA (I × 2) — 50 to 60 mines **Electron Equipt:** Radar: 1/NWS-3
M: 2 Wichmann 7AX diesels; 2 props; 4,200 hp **Electric:** 192 kw
Man: 27 tot.

Remarks: Built to replace the *Lougen* class. 20-mm AA not always mounted. Controlled minefield planters.

Note: The minelayer *Langeland*, in reserve since 1982, was stricken 1985.

◆ **6 ex-U.S. Adjutant- and Redwing*-class coastal minesweepers**

	Bldr	In serv.
M 572 Alssund (ex-MSC 128)*	Hiltebrand DD, Kingston, NY	5-4-55
M 573 Egernsund (ex-MSC 129)*	Hiltebrand DD, Kingston, NY	3-8-55
M 574 Grønsund (ex-MSC 256)	Stephen Bros. SY	21-9-56
M 575 Guldborgsund (ex-MSC 257)	Stephen Bros. SY	11-11-56
M 577 Ulvsund (ex-MSC 263)	Harbor BY, Terminal Isl., Cal.	20-9-56
M 578 Vilsund (ex-MSC 264)	Harbor BY, Terminal Isl., Cal.	15-11-56

Guldborgsund (M 575) — survey ship mode M. Willis, 5-85

D: 350 tons (376 fl) **S:** 13 kts (8 sweeping)
Dim: 43.89 (41.50 pp) × 7.95 × 2.55 **A:** 1/40-mm AA
Electron Equipt: Radar: 1/NWS-3 — Sonar: 1/UQS-1 **Man:** 38 tot.
M: 2 G.M. 8-268A diesels; 2 props; 1,000 hp **Fuel:** 40 tons **Range:** 2,500/10

Remarks: Hull entirely of wood. The first two are 405 tons (fl); they have davits abreast the stack to handle noise makers. M 575 has a charthouse between the stack and bridge so that she can act as a survey ship; she still has minesweeping equipment. *Aarøsund* (M 571) stricken 1981, and *Omøsund* (M 576) placed in reserve for use as cannibalization spares. In 3-83 it was announced that three of these ships will be modernized.

AUXILIARY SHIPS

◆ **4 SKA 11-class inshore survey launches** (In serv. 1958-68)

SKA 11 SKA 12 SKA 13 SKA 14

D: 52 tons (fl) **S:** 12 kts **Dim:** 20.0 × 5.2 × 2.1
M: 1 G.M. diesel; 540 hp

Remarks: Stationed in Greenland.

◆ **4 inshore survey launches** (In serv. 1958-68)

SKA 5 SKA 6 SKA 7 SKA 8

SKA 7 S Terzibaschitsch, 6-84

D: 27 tons **S:** 9 kts **Dim:** 13.0 × . . . × . . . **Man:** 6 tot.
M: 1 diesel; . . . hp **Electron Equipt:** Radar: 1/Skanter 009

Remarks: Minesweeper *Gulborgsund* and frigate *Ingolf* also used in survey work, the latter being able to transport four of this class.

◆ **2 U.S. YO 65-class coastal oilers** Bldr: Jeffersonville Boat & Machine, Indiana

	Laid down	L	In serv.
A 568 Rimfaxe (ex-YO 226)	21-4-45	20-7-45	22-10-45
A 569 Skinfaxe (ex-YO 229)	25-5-45	28-8-45	7-12-45

Skinfaxe (A 569) D. Koop, 5-84

D: 440 tons (1,390 fl) **S:** 10 kts **Dim:** 53.0 × 9.75 × 4.0 **A:** 1/20-mm AA
Electron Equipt: Radar: 1/NWS-3 **Electric:** 40 kw **Man:** 23 tot.
M: 1 G.M. 8-278A diesel; 1 prop; 640 hp **Fuel:** 25 tons **Range:** 2,000/8

Remarks: Transferred 2-8-62. Cargo: 900 tons.

◆ **1 torpedo transport/retriever**

A 558 Sleipner

Sleipner (A 558) 1980

AUXILIARY SHIPS *(continued)*

D: 150 tons (fl) **S:** 9 kts **Dim:** 30.0 × . . . × . . .
Electron Equipt: Radar: 1/NWS-3 **M:** 1 diesel; . . . hp

REMARKS: Former coastal cargo ship.

◆ **1 small torpedo retriever**

TO 9 MUNIN—no data available

◆ **1 royal yacht** Bldr: Royal DY, Copenhagen

	L	In serv.
A 540 DANNEBROG	10-10-31	1932

Dannebrog (A 540) 1980

D: 1,130 tons **S:** 14 kts **Dim:** 74.9 × 10.4 × 3.7
Electron Equipt: Radar: 1/Skanter 009 **Electric:** 507 kVA
M: 2 Burmeister & Wain Alpha 6 T23L-KVO diesels; 2 CP props; 1,600 hp

REMARKS: Re-engined, new electrical generating plant winter 1980-81. Does not wear pendant number assigned.

MINISTRY OF FISHERIES

◆ **1 "Osprey" FV 710-class fisheries patrol ship** Bldr: Frederikshavn SY (In serv. 7-79)

HAVØRNEN

Havørnen 1983

D: 320 tons (506 fl) **S:** 18 kts **Dim:** 49.98 (45.8 pp) × 10.50 × 2.75
Electron Equipt: Radar: 2/Furuno FRM-64
M: 2 Burmeister & Wain Alpha 16V23L-VO diesels; 2 CP props; 4,640 hp
Range: 4,500/16 **Man:** 15 tot. (accommodations for 35)

REMARKS: Has flight deck for one Lynx or Alouette-III helicopter and a stern ramp for a 6.5-m rubber inspection dinghy. Built to mercantile specifications, a modified British "Osprey" design.

◆ **1 fisheries research ship** Bldr: Dannebrog, Aarhus

DANA (In serv. 1982)

D: 2,483 grt **S:** 15.5 kts **Dim:** 78.43 × 14.7 × . . .
M: 2 diesels; 1 CP prop; 4,600 hp **Man:** 27 crew, plus 12 scientists

◆ **1 fisheries oceanographic ship** (In serv. 1960)

SENS VAEVER

D: 280 tons (fl) **S:** 11.5 kts **Dim:** 30.53 × 6.35 × 3.15
M: 1 Burmeister & Wain 406 VD diesel; 1 prop; 420 hp **Fuel:** 20 tons
Range: 2,600/9 **Man:** 10 tot.

◆ **2 Nordsøen-class salvage & rescue tugs** Bldr: Frederikshavn DY (In serv. 1968)

NORDYLLAND NORDSØEN

D: 900 tons (fl) **S:** 14.5 kts **Dim:** 52.35 (45.75 pp) × 10.00 × 3.35
M: 2 Burmeister & Wain 8-23MTBF-308G diesels; 1 CP prop; 1,960 hp
Electric: 472 kw **Man:** 12 tot.

MINISTRY OF TRADE AND SHIPPING

ICEBREAKERS

NOTE: Danish icebreakers all civilian-manned and are subordinate to the Ministry of Trade and Shipping. During summer months they are maintained by the Danish Navy at Frederikshavn.

◆ **1 new construction** Bldr: Svendborg (L: 6-80)

THORBJORN

Thorbjørn H. Ehlers, 4-85

D: 2,250 tons (fl) **S:** 16.5 kts **Dim:** 67.5 × 15.3 × 4.70
M: 4 Burmeister & Wain Alpha diesels, electric drive; 2 props; 6,800 hp

REMARKS: Can be used for hydrographic surveys by the Navy when not needed for icebreaking, and can also act as a tug.

◆ **2 Danbjørn class** Bldr: Lindø Vaerft, Odense

DANBJØRN (In serv. 1965) ISBJØRN (In serv. 1966)

Danbjørn Danish Navy

D: 3,685 tons (fl) **S:** 14 kts **Dim:** 76.8 × 16.8 × 6.0
M: Diesel-electric; 2 props; 11,880 hp **Man:** 34 tot.

◆ **1 Elbjørn class** Bldr: Frederikshavn Vaerft (In serv. 1953)

ELBJØRN

D: 898 tons (1,400 fl) **S:** 12 kts **Dim:** 47.0 × 12.1 × 4.35
M: Diesel electric; 2 props; 3,600 hp

REMARKS: Used by Danish Navy for survey work in the summer.

DENMARK *(continued)*
ICEBREAKERS *(continued)*

Elbjørn Danish Navy

MINISTRY OF THE ENVIRONMENT
(These units are manned by naval and civil personnel)

POLLUTION CONTROL SHIPS AND CRAFT

◆ **2 Gunnar Thorson class** Bldr: Ørnskov SY, Frederikshavn

Gunnar Thorson (In serv. 8-5-81) Gunnar Seidenfaden (In serv. 2-7-81)

Gunnar Thorson Danish Navy, 1981

D: 672 tons (750 fl) **S:** 14.5 kts **Dim:** 55.6 (47.9 pp) × 12.3 × 3.9
M: 2 Burmeister & Wain Alpha 8V-23L-VO diesels; 2 CP props; 2,320 hp

◆ **2 "Sea Truck" design**

	Bldr	In serv.
Mette Miljo	Carl B. Hoffman SY, Esbjerg	22-2-80
Marie Miljo	Søren Larsen SY, Nykøbing Mors	22-2-80

Mette Miljo H. Ehlers, 4-85

D: 157 tons **S:** 10 kts **Dim:** 29.8 × 8.0 × 1.6
M: 2 Grenaa diesels; 2 props; . . . hp **Man:** 8 tot.

◆ **2 Miljo 101 class** Bldr: Eljvinds, Svendborg

Miljo 101 (In serv. 1-11-77) Miljo 102 (In serv. 1-12-77)

Miljo 101 Danish Navy, 1982

D: 16 tons **S:** 15 kts **Dim:** 16.2 × 4.2 × . . .
M: 1 MWM TBD 232 V12 diesel; 1 prop; 454 hp
Range: 350/8 **Man:** 3 tot.

Remarks: Glass-reinforced plastic construction. Carry spill containment gear.

DJIBOUTI

Republic of Djibouti

Merchant Marine (1984): 7 ships—3,108 grt

◆ **2 glass-reinforced plastic patrol craft** Bldr: Plascoa, France

N. . . (In serv. 3-85) N. . . (In serv. 10-85)

D: 30 tons (light) **S:** . . . **Dim:** 23.0 × 5.5 × 1.5
A: 1/20-mm AA **M:** 2 diesels; 2 props; . . . hp
Range: 1,000/. . . **Man:** 15 tot.

Remarks: Ordered 10-84.

◆ **1 ex-French patrol craft** Bldr: Tecimar (In serv. 1974)

D: 30 tons (fl) **S:** 25 kts **Dim:** 13.3 × 4.1 × 1.1
A: 1/12.7-mm and 1/7.5-mm mg **M:** 2 G.M. 6V71 diesels; 2 props; 240 hp

Remarks: Transferred 1977 from the French colonial police at Djibouti. Glass-reinforced plastic construction.

DOMINICA

Merchant Marine (1984): 3 ships—890 grt

COAST GUARD

◆ **1 U.S. 65-ft commercial cruiser-class patrol boat** Bldr: Swiftships, Inc., Morgan City, Louisiana, U.S.A.

P-04 Melville (In serv. 2-5-84)

D: 34 tons (fl) **S:** 23 kts **Dim:** 19.96 × 5.58 × 1.52
A: Small arms **Electron Equipt:** Radar: 1/Raytheon 1210
M: 2 G.M. 12V71 TI diesels; 2 props; 1,350 hp
Range: 500/18 **Electric:** 20 kw **Man:** 6 tot.

Remarks: One of three sisters presented to Caribbean Island republics by the U.S. government, the others going to Antigua-Barbuda and St. Lucia. Aluminum construction. Blue hull, white upperworks.

DOMINICAN REPUBLIC

Personnel (1984): 370 officers and 3,630 men

Merchant Marine (1984): 37 ships—37,192 grt (tanker: 2 ships—1,492 grt)

FRIGATE

◆ **1 Canadian "River" class**

	Bldr	L	In serv.
451 Mella (ex-*Presidente Trujillo*, ex-*Carlplace*)	Davie, S.B., Lauzon, Quebec	6-7-44	13-12-44

Mella (F 451) 1981

D: 1,445 tons (2,300 fl) **S:** 19 kts **Dim:** 92.35 × 11.45 × 4.3
A: 1/76.2-mm DP—2/40-mm AA (II × 1)—4/20-mm AA—2/47-mm saluting guns
Electron Equipt: Radar: 1/SPS-64
M: 2 sets triple-expansion; 2 props; 5,500 hp **Boilers:** 2 (3-drum)
Fuel: 645 tons **Range:** 7,700/12 **Man:** 15 officers, 135 men

Remarks: Bought in 1947. Serves as fleet flagship and as a training ship; can carry 50 cadets.

CORVETTES

◆ **3 ex-U.S. Cohoes-class former net tenders**

	Bldr	L	In serv.
P 207 Cambiaso (ex-*Etlah*, AN 79)	Marietta Mfg., W. Va.	16-12-44	16-4-45
P 208 Separación (ex-*Passaconaway*, AN 86)	Marine Iron & Ry, Duluth	30-6-44	27-4-45
P 209 Calderas (ex-*Passaic*, AN 87)	Leatham B. Smith, Wisc.	29-6-44	6-3-45

D: 650 tons (785 fl) **S:** 12.3 kts **Dim:** 51.36 (44.5 pp) × 10.31 × 3.3
A: 2/76.2-mm DP (I × 2)—3/20-mm AA (I × 3)
Electron Equipt: Radar: 1/SPS-64 **Fuel:** 88 tons **Man:** 48 tot.
M: Diesel-electric: 2 Busch-Sulzer B5-539 diesels, 1 motor; 1 prop; 1,200 hp
Electric: 120 kw

Remarks: Recommissioned from the U.S. Maritime Commission's reserve fleet, where they had been laid up since 1963, and transferred 9-76. Despite low speed and general unsuitability, they are employed as patrol ships and tugs. Also used in general support, navigational tender, and hydrographic survey duties. P 207 and P 208 have had the net tender "horns" at the bow removed and a new, curved stem added; they also received a second 76.2-mm gun on the forecastle.

◆ **2 ex-U.S. Admirable-class former minesweepers** Bldr: Associated SB, Seattle, Wash.

	Laid down	L	In serv.
BM 454 Prestol Botello (ex-*Sepcración*, ex-*Skirmish*, MSF 303)	8-4-43	16-8-43	30-6-44
BM 455 Tortugero (ex-*Signet*, MSF 302)	8-4-43	16-8-43	20-8-44

D: 600 tons (903 fl) **S:** 15 kts **Dim:** 54.24 × 10.06 × 4.4
A: 1/76.2-mm DP—2/40-mm AA (I × 2)—6/20-mm AA (I × 6)
Electron Equipt: Radar: 1/SPS-69
M: 2 Cooper-Bessemer GSB-8 diesels; 2 props; 1,710 hp **Electric:** 240 kw
Fuel: 260 tons **Range:** 5,600/9 **Man:** 100 tot.

Remarks: Transferred in 1-66. BN 454 renamed 1976. All minesweeping equipment and ASW armament removed from both.

PATROL BOATS AND CRAFT

◆ **2 110-ft Commercial Cruiser class** Bldr: Swiftships, Inc., Morgan City, Louisiana

GC 108 Canopus (In serv. 6-84) GC 109 Orion (In serv. 8-84)

Orion (GC 109) Swiftships, 8-84

D: 93.5 tons (fl) **S:** 23 kts (20 sust.) **Dim:** 33.53 × 7.32 × 1.83
A: . . . **Electron Equipt:** Radar:. . .
M: 3 G. M. 12V92 TI diesels; 3 props; 2,700 hp
Electric: . . . **Range:** 1,500/12 **Man:** . . .

Remarks: Aluminum construction.

Note: The proposed acquisition of three ex-U.S. Navy "Osprey"-class fast patrol boats, PTF 23, 24, and 26, did not take place, due to the condition of the craft.

◆ **1 ex-U.S. PGM 71 class** Bldr: Peterson SB, Sturgeon Bay, Wisc.

GC 102 Betelgeuse (ex-PGM 77)

D: 130 tons (145.5 fl) **S:** 16 kts **Dim:** 30.8 (30.2 pp) × 6.4 × 1.85
A: 1/20-mm AA—2/12.7-mm mg (I × 2)
M: 2 Caterpillar D-348TA diesels; 2 props; 1,450 hp **Range:** 1,000/12
Man: 20 tot.

Remarks: Transferred 14-1-66. One of many gunboats of this class transferred to smaller navies by the United States. Re-engined and armament reduced, 1980.

◆ **3 ex-U.S. Coast Guard Argo class**

	Bldr	L	In serv.
P 204 Independencia (ex-*Icarus*, WPC 110)	Bath Iron Wks., Bath, Me.	19-3-32	1-4-32
P 205 Libertad (ex-*Rafael*, *Atoa*, ex-*Thetis*, WPC 115)	Bath Iron Wks.,	9-11-31	1-12-31
P 206 Restauración (ex-*Galatea*, WPC 108)	John H. Mathis, Camden, N.J.	16-12-32	3-2-33

D: 235 tons (350 fl) **S:** 14 kts **Dim:** 50.29 (49.00 pp) × 7.70 × 3.05 max.
A: 1/76.2-mm DP—1/40-mm AA—1/20-mm AA
M: 2 diesels; 2 props; 1,280 hp **Fuel:** 25 tons diesel
Range: 1,300/15 **Man:** 40 tot.

Remarks: Stricken from U.S. Coast Guard: P 204 on 21-10-46, P 205 on 1-7-47, and P 206 on 15-3-48, and sold to the Dominican Republic on 1-7-48. Re-engined during late 1960s-early 1970s.

◆ **1 former U.S. Army aircraft-rescue launch**

GC 105 Capitan Alsina (L: 1944)

D: 100 tons (fl) **S:** 17 kts **Dim:** 31.5 × 5.8 × 1.75 **A:** 2/20-mm AA (I × 2)
M: 2 G.M. diesels; 2 props; 1,000 hp **Man:** 20 tot.

Remarks: Wooden hull. Used as Naval Academy training craft, refitted 1977.

◆ **4 U.S. 85-ft Commercial Cruiser-class patrol craft** Bldr: Sewart Seacraft, Berwick, La.

	In serv.		In serv.
GC 104 Aldebarán	1972	GC 106 Bellatrix	1967
GC 103 Procion	1967	GC 108 Capella	1968

Capella (GC 108) L. & L. Van Ginderen, 3-84

D: 60 tons (fl) **S:** 21.7 kts **Dim:** 25.9 × 5.7 × 2.1 **A:** 3/12.7-mm mg (I × 3)
M: 2 G.M. 16V71N diesels; 2 props; 1,400 hp **Range:** 800/20 **Man:** 9 tot.

DOMINICAN REPUBLIC *(continued)*
PATROL BOATS AND CRAFT *(continued)*

◆ **1 former U.S. 63-ft aircraft-rescue launch** (In serv. 1953)

GC 101 Rigel

D: 27 tons (fl) **S:** 18.5 kts **Dim:** 19.3 × 4.7 × 1.2 **A:** 2/12.7-mm mg
M: 2 G.M. 6V71 diesels; 2 props; 800 hp **Range:** 450/15 **Man:** 9 tot.

◆ **4 small patrol craft** Bldr: Dominican NY (In serv. 1975)

BA 3 Carite BA 6 Atón BA 9 Picúa BA 15 Jurel

D: 30 tons (fl) **S:** 12 kts **Dim:** 12.7 × 4.0 × 1.8 **A:** 1/76.2-mm mg
M: 2 G.M. diesels; 200 hp

Remarks: Have auxiliary sail power. Sisters *Albacora* and *Bonito* discarded.

AUXILIARY SHIPS

◆ **1 converted U.S. LSM 1-class cargo carrier** Bldr: Brown Bros., Houston, Tex.

	Laid down	L	In serv.
BDM 301 Sirio (ex-LSM 483)	17-2-45	10-3-45	13-4-45

D: 734 tons (1,100 fl) **S:** 12 kts **Dim:** 62.8 × 10.4 × 2.1 **Man:** 30 tot.
M: 2 G.M. 16-278A diesels; 2,800 hp **Electric:** 240 kw **Fuel:** 164 tons

Remarks: Transferred 3-58. Decked over, bow doors plated up, bridge re-sited on centerline, 1970.

◆ **1 utility landing craft** Bldr: Dominican NY (In serv. 1958)

LDM 302 Samana

D: 128 tons (310 fl) **S:** 8/7 kts **Dim:** 36.4 × 11.0 × 1.15 **A:** 1/12.7-mm mg
M: 3 G.M. 64HN9 diesels; 3 props; 450 hp **Fuel:** 80 tons **Man:** 17 tot.

Remarks: U.S. LCT(5) design, used for logistics duties. Sister *Enriquillo* discarded 1979.

◆ **1 small buoy tender**

BA 10 Neptuno (ex-*Toro*) Bldr: J. H. Mathis, U.S.A., 1954

D: 72.2 tons (fl) **S:** 10 kts **Dim:** 19.5 × 5.7 × 2.4 **M:** 1 G.M. diesel; 225 hp
Man: 7 tot.

◆ **1 former 110-ft U.S. Coast Guard buoy tender**

	Bldr	Laid down	In serv.
FB 1 Capotillo (ex-*Camelia,* WAGL 206)	Racine Boat Co., Muskegon, Mich.	18-10-09	13-7-11

D: 327 tons (377 fl) **S:** 10 kts **Dim:** 33.53 × 7.32 × 2.44
M: 2 diesels; 2 props; 220 hp **Range:** 1,700/9; 2,100/7 **Man:** 23 tot.

Remarks: Stricken from U.S. Coast Guard 18-8-47 and purchased 29-12-47 by the Dominican Republic. Re-engined and rehabilitated early 1970s.

◆ **2 small oilers** Bldr: Ira S. Bushey, Brooklyn, N.Y.

	Laid down	L	In serv.
BT 4 Capitan W. Arvelo (ex-U.S. YO 213)	3-2-45	21-6-45	8-11-45
BT 5 Capitan Beotegui (ex-U.S. YO 215)	23-4-45	30-8-45	17-12-45

D: 1,076 tons (fl) **S:** 8 kts **Dim:** 47.6 × 9.3 × 4.0 **A:** 2/20-mm AA (I × 2)
M: 1 Union diesel; 1 prop; 525 hp **Cargo:** 6,071 barrels fuel
Man: 25 tot.

Remarks: Both were loaned 4-64; lease extended 31-12-80. Smaller than standard U.S. YO-65-class yard oiler.

◆ **1 small survey ship, converted sport-fishing boat**

BA 8 Atlantida

D: . . . **S:** . . . **Dim:** 12.1 × 3.6 × 1.8
M: 2 G.M. 4-71 diesels; 2 props; 300 hp

◆ **1 U.S. Cherokee-class fleet tug** Bldr: Charleston SB & DD, S. Carolina

	Laid down	L	In serv.
RM 21 Macorix (ex-*Kiowa,* ATF 72)	22-6-42	5-11-42	7-6-43

D: 1,235 tons (1,675 fl) **S:** 15 kts **Dim:** 62.48 (59.44 wl) × 11.73 × 4.67
A: 1/76.2-mm DP—2/20-mm AA (I × 2) **Electron Equipt:** Radar: 1/SPS-5D
M: 4 G.M. 12-278 diesels, electric drive; 1 prop; 3,000 hp
Electric: 260 kw **Fuel:** 295 tons **Man:** 85 tot.

Remarks: Transferred 16-10-72; lease extended 31-12-80. Has what appear to be multiple mg mounts abreast after tripod mast.

◆ **2 U.S. Sotoyomo-class auxiliary ocean tugs**

	Bldr	Laid down	L	In serv.
RM 18 Caonabo (ex-*Sagamore,* ATA 208)	Gulfport Boiler, Port Arthur, Tex.	27-11-44	19-1-45	19-3-45
RM 22 Enriquillo (ex-*Stallion,* ATA 193)	Levingston SB, Orange, Tex.	26-10-44	24-11-44	1-2-45

Caonaba (RM 18) 1981

D: 534 tons (860 fl) **S:** 13 kts **Dim:** 43.59 × 10.31 × 3.96
A: 1/76-mm DP—2/20-mm AA (I × 2) **Electron Equipt:** Radar: 1/nav.
M: 2 G.M. 12-278A diesels, electric drive; 1 prop; 1,500 hp **Electric:** 120 kw
Fuel: 160 tons **Range:** 8,000/8 **Man:** 45 tot.

Remarks: RM 18 leased 1-2-72, extended 31-12-80. RM 22 purchased 30-10-80.

◆ **2 Hercules-class harbor tugs** Bldr: Dominican NY (In serv. 1960)

RP 12 Hercules RP 13 Guacanagarix

D: 200 tons (fl) **S:** . . . kts **Dim:** 21.4 × 4.8 × 2.7
M: 1 Caterpillar diesel; 1 prop; 500 hp **Man:** 8 tot.

◆ **1 former landing craft**

RDM 303 Ocoa Bldr: U.S.A.

D: 50 tons (fl) **S:** 9 kts **Dim:** 17.1 × 4.3 × 1.2
M: 2 G.M. 6-71 diesels; 2 props; 450 hp **Range:** 130/9

Remarks: Modified as a tug about 1976. Retains bow ramp.

◆ **3 small harbor tugs**

RP 20 Isabela RP 19 Calderas RP 22 Puerto hermoso—no data

◆ **1 U.S. YTL 422-class small tug** Bldr: Robt. Jacob, City Isl., NY

RP 16 Bohechio (ex-*Mercedes,* ex-YTL 600) (In serv. 25-7-45)

D: 70 tons (80 fl) **S:** 10 kts **Dim:** 20.1 × 5.5 × 2.4
M: 1 Hoover-Owens-Rentschler diesel; 1 prop; 375 hp **Fuel:** 7 tons

Remarks: Transferred 1-71.

TRAINING CRAFT

◆ **1 sail-training ship for Naval Academy** (In serv. 1979)

BA 7 Nube Del Mar (ex-*Catuan*)

D: 40 tons (fl) **S:** 12 kts **Dim:** 12.8 × 3.6 × . . .
M: 1 Volvo Penta 21A diesel; 1 prop; 75 hp

◆ **1 training launch (In serv. . . .)**

BA. . . Duarte

D: 60 tons (fl) **S:** . . . kts **Dim:** 22.9 × 5.7 × 2.1
M: 1 G.M. 6-71 diesel; 1 prop; 325 hp **Man:** 30 tot.

◆ **2 small fishing boats** (In serv. 1979)

BA 11 Alto Velo BA 12 Saona

ECUADOR

Republic of Ecuador

Personnel (1984): 3,800 total

Merchant Marine (1984): 135 ships—411,641 grt (tankers: 26 ships—166,943)

Naval Aviation: A small detachment with three French Alouette-III helicopters, three Israeli Arava light transports, two Cessna T-37, two T-41, one Cessna 320, one Cessna 177, three Beech T-34C-1 trainers and one Beech Super King Air light transport.

SUBMARINES

◆ **2 German Type 209 (IK 79)** Bldr: Howaldtswerke, Kiel

	Laid down	L	In serv.
S 11 Shryi	5-8-74	6-10-76	6-11-77
S 12 Huancavilca	20-1-75	15-3-77	16-3-78

Huancavilca (S 12) P. Voss, 4-84

D: 1,285 tons surf./1,390 sub. **S:** 21.4 kts (1 hr.) **Dim:** 59.50 × 6.20 × 5.50
A: 8/533-mm TT (fwd.)—14 torpedoes **Fuel:** 110 tons
Electron Equipt: Radar: 1 Thomson-CSF Calypso
Sonar: 1/Atlas A526 passive, 1/CSUAN 407 A9 active, 1/DUUX-2
M: 4 MTU 12V493 TY60 diesels, 4 Siemens 405 kw generators, electric drive: 1 Siemens motor; 1 prop; 5,000 hp
Endurance: 45 days **Range:** 400/4 sub.; 8,400/8 snorkel
Man: 5 officers, 26 men

Remarks: Ordered 1974. Hollandse Signaal M8 torpedo f.c.s. S 12 commenced a refit at her builders, 4-84.

DESTROYER

◆ **1 U.S. Gearing FRAM-I class**

	Bldr	Laid down	L	In serv.
DD 01 Presidente Eloy Alfaro (ex-*Holder,* DD 819)	Consolidated Steel, Orange, Tex.	23-4-45	25-8-45	18-5-46

Presidente Eloy Alfaro (DD 01) J. Jedrlinic, 1980

D: 2,425 tons (3,500 fl) **S:** 30 kts **Dim:** 119.1 × 12.4 × 5.8
A: 4/127-mm DP (II × 2)—6/324-mm Mk 32 ASW TT (III × 2)—1/helicopter
Electron Equipt: Radar: 1/LN-66, 1/SPS-10, 1/SPS-40, 1/Mk 25 fire-control
Sonar: SQS-23—EW: WLR-1
M: 2 sets GT; 2 props; 60,000 hp
Boilers: 4 Babcock & Wilcox; 43.3 kg/cm², 454°C **Electric:** 1,200 kw
Fuel: 650 tons **Range:** 2,400/25, 4,800/15 **Man:** 270 tot.

Remarks: Transferred by sale on 1-9-78, the *Alfaro* began overhaul in the U.S. 8-78; arrived in Ecuador mid-1980. ASROC deleted. Mk 37 GFCS. Transfer of sister *Southerland* (DD 743) was canceled.

FRIGATE

◆ **1 U.S. Charles Lawrence-class fast transport**

	Bldr	Laid down	L	In serv.
DD 03 Moran Valverde (ex-*26 de Julio,* ex-*Enright,* APD 66)	Phila. Navy Yd	22-2-43	29-5-43	21-9-43

Moran Valverde (DD 03) U.S. Navy, 1974

D: 1,400 tons (2,130 fl) **S:** 23 kts **Dim:** 93.27 × 11.27 × 4.7
A: 1/127-mm DP—6/40-mm AA (II × 3)—2 d.c. racks
Electron Equipt: Radar: 1/SPS-6, 1/navigational
M: G.E. turbo-electric drive; 2 props; 12,000 hp **Electric:** 680 kw
Boilers: 2 Foster-Wheeler "D" Express; 30.6 kg/cm², 399°C **Fuel:** 350 tons
Range: 2,000/23; 5,000/15 **Man:** 212 tot.

Remarks: Transferred 7-67. Could carry 162 troops when in U.S. Navy. Davits can handle four LCPR/LCVP, but carries only two to reduce top weight. Has a raised helicopter deck over the stern area.

CORVETTES

◆ **6 Italian modified Wadi M'ragh class**

	Bldr	Laid down	L	In serv.
CM 11 Esmeraldas	CNR, Muggiano	27-9-79	5-10-80	7-8-82
CM 12 Manabi	CNR, Ancona	1-2-80	5-2-81	21-6-83
CM 13 Los Rios	CNR, Muggiano	1-9-79	28-2-81	1-10-83
CM 14 El Oro	CNR, Ancona	1-3-80	5-2-81	10-12-83
CM 15 Galapagos	CNR, Muggiano	20-10-80	5-7-81	26-5-84
CM 16 Loja	CNR, Ancona	6-2-81	27-2-82	26-5-84

Esmeraldas (CM 11) CNR, 1982

D: 620 tons (700 fl) **S:** 37 kts **Dim:** 62.3 (57.8 pp) × 9.3 × 2.8
A: 6/MM 40 Exocet SSM (III × 2)—1 Albatros SAM system (IV × 1; Aspide missiles)—1/76-mm OTO Melara DP—2/40-mm Breda AA (II × 1)—6/324-mm ILAS-3 ASW TT (III × 2)
Electron Equipt: Radar: 1/Decca TM1226, 1/RAN-10S, 1/Orion 10X, 1/Orion 20 X
Sonar: Diodon—EW: Gamma syst., 1/SCLAR chaff RL
M: 4 MTU 20V956 TB92 diesels; 4 props; 24,400 hp (20,400 sust.)
Electric: 750 kw **Fuel:** 126 tons
Range: 1,200/31; 4,000/18 **Man:** 51 tot.

CORVETTES *(continued)*

Manabi (CM 12) U.S. Navy, 1985

El Oro (CM 14) U.S. Navy, 1985

Remarks: Ordered 1978 from CNR del Tirreno. More powerful engines than earlier units of class, helicopter platform added. Selenia IPN-10 data system, with NA 21 mod. 0 radar f.c.s. and two CO3 directors for guns and SAM system. Have a helicopter platform, but no aircraft have been acquired, and there is no hangar.

GUIDED-MISSILE PATROL BOATS

◆ **3 Quito class** Bldr: Lürssen, Vegesack, West Germany

	L	In serv.
LM 31 Quito	20-11-75	13-7-76
LM 32 Guayaquil	5-4-76	22-12-77
LM 33 Cuenca	12-76	17-7-77

Quito (LM 31) G. Koop, 1976

D: 250 tons (265 fl) **S:** 35 kts **Dim:** 47.0 × 7.0 × 2.4
A: 4/MM 38 Exocet SSM (II × 2)—1/76-mm OTO Melara—2/35-mm AA (II × 1)
Electron Equipt: Radar: 1/Decca TM1226, 1/Thomson-CSF Triton, 1/Thomson-CFS Pollux f.c.
M: 4 MTU 16V538 diesels; 4 props; 14,000 hp **Electric:** 330 kw
Fuel: 39 tons **Range:** 600/30 **Man:** 34 tot.

Remarks: Carry 250 rounds of 76-mm and 1,100 rounds of 35-mm ammunition. Thomson-CSF Vega fire control system.

◆ **3 Manta class** Bldr: Lürssen, Vegesack, W. Germany

LM 24 Manta (In serv. 11-6-71) LM 25 Tulcan (In serv. 2-4-71) LM 27 Nueva Rocafuerte (ex-*Tena*) (In serv. 23-6-71)

Manta (LM 24) U.S. Navy, 1981

D: 119 tons (134 fl) **S:** 35 kts **Dim:** 36.2 × 5.8 × 1.7
A: 4/Gabriel II SSM (I × 4)—2/30-mm AA Emerlec (II × 1)
Electron Equipt: Radar: 1/navigational, 1/Thomson-CSF Pollux
M: 2 Mercedes-Benz diesels; 3 props; 9,000 hp **Fuel:** 21 tons
Range: 700/30; 1,500/15 **Man:** 19 tot.

Remarks: Similar to Chilean *Guacolda* class, but faster. New guns added 1979; Gabriel missiles and Thomson-CSF Vega fire control system (without Triton search radar) replaced 2/533-mm TT 1980-81.

PATROL CRAFT

◆ **3 Port Director class** Bldr: Halter, New Orleans, 1976

Comandancia De Balao
Comandancia De Guayaquil
Comandancia De Salinas

D: 34 tons (fl) **S:** 25 kts **Dim:** 19.66 × 5.18 × 1.24 **A:** . . .
M: 2 G.M. 12V71 TI diesels; 2 props; 960 hp

◆ **3 LPI class** Bldr: F. Schürenstedt, Bardenfleth, W. Germany (In serv. 1954-55)

LC 81 Baba Hoyo (ex-*10 de Agosto*)
LC 82 Pichincha (ex-*9 de Octubre*)
LC 83 Portoviejo (ex-*3 de Noviembre*)

D: 45 tons (64 fl) **S:** 20 kts **Dim:** 23.4 × 4.6 × 1.8 **A:** 1 or 2 mg
M: 2 Böhn & Kahler diesels; 2 props; 1,200 hp **Range:** 556/16 **Man:** 9 tot.

◆ **2 ex-U.S. Coast Guard utility boats**—transferred 1971

UT 111 Rio Napo UT 112 Isla Puna

D: 10.6 tons **S:** 19 kts **Dim:** 12.27 × 3.45 × 1.0 **A:** . . .
M: 2 G.M. diesels; 2 props; 380 hp **Range:** 280/18 **Man:** 4-5 tot.

AMPHIBIOUS WARFARE SHIPS

◆ **1 ex-U.S. LST 542-class tank landing ship** Bldr: Chicago Bridge & Iron

	Laid down	L	In serv.
T 55 Hualcopo (ex-*Summit County,* LST 1148)	15-2-45	23-5-45	1-6-45

D: 1,650 tons (4,080 fl) **S:** 11.6 kts **Dim:** 100.04 × 15.24 × 4.3
A: 8/40-mm (II × 2, I × 4) **M:** 2 G.M. 12-567A diesels; 2 props; 1,700 hp
Electric: 300 kw **Range:** 7,200/10 **Man:** 119 tot.

Remarks: Bought 2-77. Used as transport; has ice-reinforced waterline.

◆ **1 ex-U.S. LSM 1-class medium landing ships** Bldr: Charleston NY, S.C.

	Laid down	L	In serv.
T 52 Tarqui (ex-LSM 555)	3-3-45	22-3-45	24-9-45

D: 513 tons (1,095 fl) **S:** 12.5 kts **Dim:** 62.0 × 10.5 × 2.2
A: 2/40-mm AA (II × 1) **M:** 2 G.M. 16-278A diesels; 2 props; 2,800 hp
Range: 2,500/12 **Man:** 60 tot.

Remarks: Built 1945, transferred 11-58. Used as transports. Sister *Jambeli* (T 51, ex-LSM 539) stricken 1983.

◆ **6 "Sea Trucks"** Bldr: Rotork, U.K. (In serv. 1979)

LF 91 LF 92 LF 93 LF 94 LF 95 LF 96

D: 5 tons (9 fl) **S:** 26 kts (light) **Dim:** 12.65 × 3.20 × . . .
M: 2 Volvo AQD 40A diesels; 2 outdrive props; 240 hp **Cargo:** 4 tons

ECUADOR *(continued)*

AUXILIARY SHIPS

◆ **1 oceanographic research ship** Bldr: Ishikawajima Harima, Tokyo (In serv. 21-10-81)

HI 92 ORION (ex-*Dometer*)

Orion (HI 92) Ishikawajima Harima, 1981

D: 1,105 grt **S:** 12.6 kts **Dim:** 70.17 (64.20 pp) × 10.70 × 3.6 (5.40 max.)
Electron Equipt: Radar: 2/Decca 1226 **Electric:** 700 kw
M: 3 G.M. 16V92 TI diesels, electric drive (2 motors); 1 prop; 950 hp
Range: 6,000/12 **Man:** 6 officers, 25 men, 19 scientists

REMARKS: *Dometer* was delivery name, changed to *Orion* on arrival for commissioning. Equipped to conduct physical and biological oceanography, geophysical research, and hydrographic surveys.

◆ **1 inshore oceanographic research craft**

O 112 RIGEL Bldr: Halter Marine, New Orleans (In serv. 1975)

D: 50 tons **Man:** 10 tot.

◆ **1 ex-U.S. Army FS 381-class small cargo ship** Bldr: Higgins, New Orleans (In serv. 1944)

T 12 CALICUCHIMA (ex-FS 525)

D: 650 tons (930 fl) **S:** 11.5 kts **Dim:** 54.86 (52.37 pp) × 9.75 × 3.05
M: 2 G.M. 6-278A diesels; 2 props; 1,000 hp **Fuel:** 100 tons
Range: 4,000/11 **Man:** 30 tot.

REMARKS: Used to supply the Galápagos Islands. Leased 8-4-63; purchased 30-8-78.

◆ **1 ex-U.S. small water tanker**

T 41 ATALHUAPA (ex-YW 131) Bldr: Leatham D. Smith, Wisc. (In serv. 17-9-45)

D: 440 tons (1,390 fl) **S:** 7 kts **Dim:** 53.1 × 9.8 × 4.6
M: 1 G.M. diesel; 1 prop; 640 hp **Fuel:** 25 tons **Man:** 20 tot.

REMARKS: Transferred 2-5-63; purchased 1-12-77. Cargo: 930 tons water.

◆ **2 U.S. Abnaki- and Achomawi-class fleet tugs** Bldr: Charleston SB & DD, Charleston, S.C.

	Laid down	L	In serv.
R 101 CAYAMBE (ex-*Los Rios,* ex-*Cusabo,* ex-ATF 155)	18-9-44	26-2-45	19-5-45
R 105 CHIMBORAZO (ex-*Chowanoc,* ATF 100)	24-4-43	20-8-43	21-2-44

Cayambe—now new number 1966

D: 1,235 tons (1,675 fl) **S:** 16.5 kts **Dim:** 62.48 (59.44 wl) × 11.73 × 4.67
A: 1/76.2-mm DP—2/40-mm AA (I × 2)—2/20-mm AA (I × 2)
Electron Equipt: Radar: 1/Decca 916
M: 4 G.M. 12-278A diesels, electric drive; 1 prop; 3,000 hp **Electric:** 400 kw
Fuel: 376 tons **Range:** 16,000/8; 7,000/15 **Man:** 85 tot.

REMARKS: R 105: **A:** 2/12.7-mm mg; **M:** 4 Busch-Sulzer B5-539 diesels; pipe *vice* stack. *Cayambe* leased 2-11-60, purchased 30-8-78. *Chimborazo* purchased 1-10-77.

◆ **1 medium harbor tug** (In serv. 1952)

R 102 SANGAY (ex-*Losa*)

D: 295 tons (390 fl) **S:** 12 kts **Dim:** 32.6 × 7.9 × 4.25
M: 1 Fairbanks-Morse diesel; 1 prop; . . . hp

REMARKS: Bought 1964.

◆ **1 former U.S. Army tug** Bldr: Equitable Bldg. (In serv. 1945)

R 103 COTOPAXI (ex-*R. T. Ellis*)

D: 150 tons **S:** 9 kts **Dim:** 25.0 × 6.62 × 2.9 **M:** Diesel; 1 prop; 650 hp

REMARKS: Bought 1947.

◆ **2 small tugs**

R. . . TUNGURAHUA R 104 ANTIZANA—no data

◆ **1 sail-training bark** Bldr: Ast. Celaya SY, Bilbao, Spain

	L	In serv.
BE 01 GUAYAS	23-9-76	23-7-77

D: 934 grt **S:** 10.5 kts **Dim:** 76.2 × 10.6 × 4.2
M: 1 G.M. 12V-149 diesel; 1 prop; 700 hp

◆ **1 repair barge**

BT 62 PUTAMAYO (ex-YR 340) Bldr: New York Navy Yard, 1944

D: 520 tons (770 fl) **Dim:** 45.7 × 10.4 × 1.8 **Electric:** 330 kw

REMARKS: Transferred 7-62; purchased 1-12-77.

◆ **1 ex-U.S. auxiliary repair dock** (In serv. 1944)

DF 121 AMAZONAS (ex-ARD 17)

Capacity: 3,500 tons **Dim:** 149.9 × 24.7 × 1.7 (light)

REMARKS: Transferred 7-1-61. Pointed bow. Length over blocks: 118.6 m; 18.0 clear width. Dry dock companion craft YFND 20 leased 2-11-61 to support.

COAST GUARD
Established 1980

PERSONNEL (1982): 13 officers, 257 enlisted men

◆ **14 U.S. Baycraft 40-ft. patrol craft** (In serv. 1979-80)

REMARKS: Fiberglass hulls; modified sport-fishing boat design. No other data available. The two U.S. PGM 71-class patrol boats *Veinticinco de Julio* (ex-*Quito,* ex-PGM 75) and *Diez de Agosto* (ex-*Guayaquil,* ex-PGM 76) were stricken in 1983.

EGYPT

Arab Republic of Egypt

PERSONNEL (1985): Approx. 30,000 total

MERCHANT MARINE (1984): 330 ships—778,591 grt
(tankers: 41 ships—104.030 grt)

NAVAL AVIATION: The Navy operates 18 Westland Sea King Mk 47 helicopters and 12 Aerospatiale SA 342 L Gazelle helicopters; another 12 Gazelles are on order. The Sea Kings are to be fitted to guide Otomat anti-ship missiles, and the Gazelles can carry AS.12 wire-guided missiles.

COAST DEFENSES: The Navy is responsible for coastal defenses. Fifty Coast Defense, truck-mounted versions of the Otomat missile were purchased 1983. Targeting will be performed by land-based Sea King helicopters. Some Soviet Samlet coast-defense missiles remain in service also.

SUBMARINES

◆ **8 Soviet and Chinese Romeo class**

4 Soviet-built: 834, 837, 840, 843
4 Chinese-built: 831, 842, 852, . . .

D: 1,330/1,700 tons **S:** 15.2/13 kts **Dim:** 77.60 × 6.70 × 4.95
A: 8/533-mm TT (6 fwd, 2 aft)—14 torpedoes or 28 mines
Electron Equipt: Radar: 1/Snoop Plate—Sonar: Hercules (Chinese units: Tamir-5L active, Feniks)
M: Diesel-electric, 2 Type 37D diesels, 2,000 hp each; 2 props; 2,700 hp—2/50-hp creep motors

SUBMARINES *(continued)*

Chinese-built Romeo 831 1984

Endurance: 60 days **Range:** 350/4 sub.; 14,000/9 surf.; 7,000/5 snorkel)
Man: 56 tot.

REMARKS: The Soviet-built units were transferred—5 in 1966, 1 in 1969, and began refitting with European equipment in 1981. They had been constructed between 1957 and 1960 at Baltic Shipyard, Leningrad; two Soviet-built units have been discarded. Two units, launched in 1980, were delivered from China on 28-3-83; delivered 10-83; the second Chinese pair were delivered 3-1-84 and commissioned 21-5-84. The Chinese-built units have sonar domes atop their bows and displace 1,319 tons surfaced/ 1,712 tons submerged. All have 224 battery cells, producing 6,000 amp/hr. Operating depth is 270 m (300 max.). The Soviet-built units are to be updated by Thyssen Nordseewerke, under a contract signed 1984.

◆ **3 Soviet Whiskey class**

810 816 819

Egyptian Whiskey (old number) L. & L. Van Ginderen, 1980

D: 1,050/1,350 tons **S:** 17/16 kts **Dim:** 75.0 × 6.3 × 4.8
A: 6/533-mm TT (4 fwd, 2 aft)—12 torpedoes or 28 mines
Electron Equipt: Radar: 1/Snoop Plate
Sonar: Hercules, passive array
M: 2 Type 37D diesels; 2,000 hp each; 2 electric motors; 2 props; 2,500 hp
Endurance: 40-45 days **Range:** 6,000/5 (snorkel) **Man:** 50 tot.

REMARKS: Survivors of six transferred from 6-57 to 8-62. Reported in poor condition. In refit 1978-79; were to get British electronic intercept equipment.

DESTROYER

◆ **1 British "Z" class**

	Bldr	Laid down	L	In serv.
921 EL FATEH (ex-*Zenith*, ex-*Wessex*)	Wm. Denny, Dumbarton, Scotland	19-5-42	5-6-44	22-12-44

El Fateh (921) L. & L. Van Ginderen, 5-85

D: 1,730 tons (2,575 fl) **S:** 31 kts **Dim:** 110.6 × 10.9 × 5.2
A: 4/102-mm DP (I × 4)—6/40-mm AA (II × 1, I × 4)—8/533-mm TT—4/d.c. projectors
Electron Equipt: Radar: 1/Decca 916, 1/Marconi SNW-10, 1/Type 275 f.c.
M: 2 sets GT; 2 props; 40,000 hp **Boilers:** 2 Admiralty 3-drum
Fuel: 580 tons **Range:** 2,800/20 **Man:** 250 tot.

REMARKS: Purchased 1955, refitted 1956 and again in 1964.

NOTE: Of the four Soviet-built Skoryy-class destroyers, *Al Zaffer* and *Suez* were discarded 1984, and *6 October* and *Damiet* were to have been stricken by end-1985.

FRIGATES

◆ **2 Chinese Jianghu class** Bldr: Jiangnan SY, Shanghai

951 NAJIM AL ZAFIR (In serv. 27-10-84) 952 EL NASSER (In serv. 16-4-85)

Najim al Zafir (951) 10-84

El Nasser (952)—shortly prior to delivery R. Gillett, 9-84

D: 1,568 tons (1,900 fl) **S:** 25.5 kts **Dim:** 103.2 × 10.2 × 3.05 (hull)
A: 4/HY-2 Styx SSM (II × 2)—4/57-mm AA (II × 2)—12/37-mm AA (II × 6)—4/RBU-1200 ASW RL (V × 4)—4/BMB-2 d.c. mortars—2/d.c. racks—mines
Electron Equipt: Radar: 1/Type 756, 1/Eye Shield, 1/Square Tie
Sonar: MF, hull-mounted
EW: None—IFF: 2/Square Head, 1/High Pole A
M: 2 SEMT-Pielstick diesels; 2 props; 16,000 hp
Range: 1,750/25; 4,000/15 **Endurance:** 15 days **Man:** 195 tot.

REMARKS: Ordered 1982. 951 completed 7-84, arriving in Egypt in 10-84. 952 completed 12-84, arriving in Egypt 3-85. There are plans to update the armament suits and sensors. Differ from Chinese Navy units in having twin 57-mm guns vice single or twin 100-mm mounts fore and aft, and in having an enclosed housing for the optical rangefinder atop the bridge. There is no radar fire-control equipment for the eight gunmounts, all of which are locally controlled via on-mount sights.

◆ **2 Spanish Descubierta class** Bldr: Bazán, Cartagena

	Laid down	L	In serv.
936 EL SUEZ (ex-*Centinela*)	31-10-78	6-10-79	21-5-84
941 EL ABOUKIR (ex-*Serviola*)	28-2-79	20-12-79	27-10-84

D: 1,363 tons (1,575 fl) **S:** 26 kts **Dim:** 88.88 (85.80 pp) × 10.40 × 3.70
A: 8/Harpoon SSM (IV × 2)—1/Mk 29 SAM launcher (VIII; 24 NATO Sea Sparrow missiles)—1/76-mm OTO Melara Compact—2/40-mm AA (I × 2)—1/375-mm Bofors ASW RL (II × 1)—6/324-mm Mk 32 ASW TT (III × 2, Stingray torpedoes)
Electron Equipt: Radar: 1/HSA ZW-06/Z, 1/HSA DA-05/2, 1/HSA WM-25 f.c.
Sonar: Raytheon 1160B hull-mounted, Raytheon 1167 VDS
EW: Elettronica Beta intercept
M: 4 MTU-Bazán 16 MA656 TB91 diesels; 2 CP props; 18,000 hp
Electric: 1,810 kw **Fuel:** 250 tons **Range:** 6,000/18
Man: 10 officers, 106 men (146 accom.)

FRIGATES *(continued)*

El Aboukir (941)—fitting out; note VDS position aft L. & L. Van Ginderen, 10-84

El Aboukir (941)—fitting out L. & L. Van Ginderen, 10-84

REMARKS: Originally ordered 25-5-76 for the Spanish Navy, but sold 1982. 936 completed 28-2-84 and 941 on 6-9-84. Have fin stabilizers, plus U.S. "Prairie/Masker" bubble system to reduce sound radiation below the waterline. Carry 600 rds 76-mm ammunition. H.S.A. SEWACO weapons control system. The U.S. supplied the Harpoon missiles in 1984.

NOTE: British *Black Swan*-class frigate *Tarik* (ex-*El Malek Farouk*, ex-*Whimbrel*) and British Hunt I-class frigate *Port Said* (ex-*Mohammed Ali el Kebit*, ex-*Cottesmore*), are inoperable hulks used for accommodations at pierside.

GUIDED-MISSILE PATROL BOATS

NOTE: Still planned is the acquisition of a further six Western-designed guided-missile patrol boats. A repeat of the *Ramadan* class, Spain's Bazán "Cormoran" design, and a 61-m, 465-ton, 38-kt. PSSM-200 design from Tacoma Boatyard, Tacoma, Washington are leading contenders; the latter would have 8/Harpoon, a 76-mm OTO Melara compact, and a 30-mm gatling gun. Funds to order these ships are expected to become available in 1988.

◆ **6 Chinese Hoku class** Bldr: . . . (In serv. 27-10-84)

401 402 403 404 405 406

D: 68 tons, 73.88 normal (79.19 fl) **S:** 38 kts
Dim: 27.0 × 6.30 × 1.8 (1.295 hull)
A: 2/HY-2 Styx SSM (I × 2)—2/25-mm AA (II × 1)
Electron Equipt: Radar: 1/Square Tie
M: 4 M50F-4 diesels; 4 props; 4,800 hp **Electric:** 65 kw
Endurance: 5 days **Range:** 520/26 **Man:** 17 tot.

REMARKS: Delivered 9-84 and commissioned together the following month; did not have missiles aboard during public display. Steel construction.

◆ **6 Ramadan class** Bldr: Vosper Thornycroft, Portchester, U.K.

	Laid down	L	In serv.
561 RAMADAN	22-9-78	6-9-79	20-7-81
562 EL KADESSEYA	23-2-79	31-1-80	15-9-81
563 KHYBER	23-4-79	19-2-80	6-4-82
564 EL YARMOUK	15-5-79	12-6-80	18-5-82
565 BADR	29-9-79	17-6-81	17-6-82
566 HETTEIN	29-2-80	25-11-80	28-10-82

El Kadesseya (562)—old number L. & L. Van Ginderen, 6-82

El Yarmouk (561)—old number L. & L. Van Ginderen, 6-82

D: 262 tons (312 fl) **S:** 35 kts **Dim:** 52.0 (48.0 pp) × 7.6 × 2.0 (hull)
A: 4/Otomat SSM (II × 2)—1/76-mm OTO Melara Compact DP—2/40-mm Breda AA (II × 1)
Electron Equipt: Radar: Marconi: 1/S820, 1/S810, 2/ST802
EW: Decca-Racal Cutlass and MEL Matilda passive, Decca-Racal Cygnus jammer, Mel Protean chaff RL (VI × 2)
M: 4 MTU 20V538 TB91 diesels; 4 props; 16,000 hp **Fuel:** 43 tons
Electric: 420 kw **Range:** 2,000/15 **Man:** 31 tot.

REMARKS: Ordered 4-9-77. Have Marconi Sapphire fire control system with two ST 802 radar/t.v. directors, two Lawrence Scott optical directors. Ferranti CAAIS automated data system. First pair arrived Egypt 13-11-81, second 23-7-82, third in 12-82.

◆ **6 6 October class** Bldr: Egypt/Vosper Thornycroft (In serv. 1980-81)

783 785 787 789 790 791

6 October class (791)—Otomat racks empty L. & L. Van Ginderen, 7-82

D: 71 tons (82 fl) **S:** 40 kts **Dim:** 25.3 × 6.0 × 1.8
A: 2/Otomat SSM—4/30-mm AA Type A32 (II × 2)
Electron Equipt: Radar: Marconi: 1/S810, 1/ST802
EW: MEL Matilda passive, MEL Protean chaff RL (VI × 2)
M: 4 CRM 18V-12D/55 YE diesels; 4 props; 5,400 hp **Range:** 400/30
Man: 20 tot.

GUIDED-MISSILE PATROL BOATS *(continued)*

Remarks: Wooden hulls, built at Alexandria DY, Egypt, 1969-75. Completed by Vosper Thornycroft at Portchester, Portsmouth 1979-81, with Italian-French missiles and British guns; diesels are Italian. Basic design is that of the Soviet Komar class. Uses Marconi Sapphire radar/t.v. fire control system. 791 was lost overboard during delivery 16-12-80, salvaged, returned to U.K. 30-6-81, and completed repairs 13-8-82.

◆ 7 ex-Soviet Osa-I class

631 633 635 637 639 641 643

Egyptian Osa-I 1975

D: 175 tons (215 fl) **S:** 35 kts **Dim:** 38.6 × 7.6 × 1.8
A: 4/SS-N-2A Styx SSM (I × 4) — 1/SA-7 Grail position — 4/30-mm AA (II × 2)
Electron Equipt: Radar: 1/Square Tie, 1/Drum Tilt, 1/Decca 916 — IFF: 2/Square Head, 1/High Pole A
M: 3 M503A diesels; 3 props; 12,000 hp **Range:** 500/34; 750/25

Remarks: Transferred 1966. Reported being refitted with 3 MTU diesels. All carry shoulder-launched SA-7 Grail (SA-N-5) SAMs, launched from a tub amidships. Passive warning equipment now fitted.

PATROL BOATS

◆ 8 Chinese Hainan class

	In serv.		In serv.
. . . Nour	23-10-83	. . . N. . .	21-5-84
. . . Al Hadi	23-10-83	. . . N. . .	6-84
. . . N. . .	21-5-84	. . . N. . .	6-84
. . . N. . .	21-5-84	. . . N. . .	6-84

D: 375 tons normal (400 fl) **S:** 30.5 kts **Dim:** 58.77 × 7.20 × 2.20 (hull)
A: 4/57-mm AA (II × 2) — 4/25-mm AA (II × 2) — 4/RBU-1200 ASW RL (V × 4) — 2/BMB-2 d.c. mortars — 2/d.c. racks — mines
Electron Equipt: Radar: 1/Pot Head **Range:** 2,000/14
M: 4 diesels; 4 props; 8,800 hp **Man:** 70 tot.

Remarks: First pair arrived 10-83, next three in 2-84, and final trio in 6-84. All were delivered aboard the Chinese float-on cargo ship *Shamekou.*

◆ 4 Chinese Shanghai-II class

Egyptian Navy Shanghai-II 1984

D: 122.5 tons normal (134.8 fl) **S:** 28.5 kts **Dim:** 38.78 × 5.41 × 1.55
A: 4/37-mm AA (II × 2) — 4/25-mm AA (II × 2)
Electron Equipt: Radar: 1/Pot Head
M: 2 M50F-4, 1,200-hp diesels; 2/12D6, 910 hp diesels; 4 props; 4,220 hp
Electric: 39 kw **Range:** 750/16.5 **Man:** 36 tot. **Endurance:** 7 days

Remarks: Transferred 1984 with transfer numbers E 601–604. Do not have depth charges, as on Chinese Navy examples.

Note: The Hainans and the Shanghai IIs essentially replaced the 12 Soviet S.O.-1-class submarine chasers delivered 1962-63, although up to 6 may be retained in reserve status.

TORPEDO BOATS

◆ 6 Soviet Shershen class

310 321 332 343 354 365

Shershen 343 — with 122-mm rocket launchers, Grail tub abaft Drum Tilt

D: 150 tons (180 fl) **S:** 45 kts **Dim:** 34.0 × 7.2 × 1.5
A: 4/30-mm AA (II × 2) — 4/533-mm TT (I × 4) or 2/122-mm RL (XX × 2)
Electron Equipt: 1/Square Tie, 1/Drum Tilt
M: 3 M503A diesels; 3 props; 12,000 hp

Remarks: Transferred 1967-68. Three are armed with two 20-tubed 122-mm artillery rocket launchers instead of torpedoes. Most carry shoulder-launched SA-7 Grail (SA-N-5) missiles as well. All P-6-class torpedo boats discarded by 1985.

MINE WARFARE SHIPS

◆ 0 (+2) Tripartite-class minehunters
Bldr: Van der Giessen do Noord, the Netherlands

Remarks: Ordered 6-3-85; see Netherlands section for data.

◆ 4 ex-Soviet Yurka-class minesweepers

530 Assuan 533 Guizan 536 Qena 539 Suhag

D: 400 tons (460 fl) **S:** 16 kts **Dim:** 52.0 × 9.3 × 2.0
A: 4/30-mm AA (II × 2) — 10 mines **Electron Equipt:** Radar: 1/Don-2
M: 2 diesels; 2 props; 4,000 hp **Range:** 2,000/14; 3,200/10

Remarks: Delivered new 1969. Do not have Drum Tilt radar fire-control system. Low-magnetic alloy steel construction.

Note: The six T-43-class minesweepers have been retired, and at least one has been used as a missile target.

◆ 2 Soviet T-301-class minesweepers (In serv. circa 1950)

El Fayoud El Manufieh

D: 145.8 tons (160 fl) **S:** 12.5 kts **Dim:** 38.0 × 5.1 × 1.6
A: 2/45-mm — 2/12.7-mm mg **M:** 3 6-cyl. diesels; 3 props; 1,440 hp
Fuel: 20 tons **Range:** 2,500/8

Remarks: Transferred 1962-63. No radars. Used in harbor service only.

AMPHIBIOUS WARFARE SHIPS

◆ 3 Soviet Polnocny A-class LSM
Bldr: Polnocny SY, Gdansk, Poland

D: 770 tons (fl) **S:** 19 kts **Dim:** 73.0 × 8.6 × 2.0
A: 2/30-mm AA (II × 1) — 2/140-mm artillery RL (XVIII × 2)
Electron Equipt: Radar: 1/Don-2, 1/Drum Tilt
M: 2 Type 40D diesels; 2 props; 4,000 hp
Range: 900/18; 1,500/14 **Man:** 40 tot.

Remarks: Transferred 1974. Cargo: 3 tanks or 180 tons.

◆ 9 ex-Soviet Vydra-class LCUs

Egyptian Vydra with rocket launchers 1976

D: 425 tons (600 fl) **S:** 11 kts **Dim:** 54.9 × 7.6 × 2.0
A: 4/40-mm AA (II × 2) — 8/15-tubed artillery RL — see remarks

AMPHIBIOUS WARFARE SHIPS *(continued)*

Electron Equipt: Radar: 1/Spin Trough removed **M:** 2 diesels; 2 props; 800 hp
Range: 2,700/10 **Man:** 20, plus 200 troops

REMARKS: Transferred 1967-69. Armament now removed. Some had 37-mm AA vice 40-mm. Cargo: 200 tons.

◆ **5 ex-Soviet SMB-I-class LCUs**

D: 180 tons (335 fl) **S:** 10 kts **Dim:** 48.2 × 6.5 × 2.0
Electron Equipt: Radar: none **M:** 2 diesels; 2 props; 600 hp
Range: 400/8 **Man:** 16 tot.

REMARKS: Transferred 1965. Cargo: 180 tons.

◆ **8 U.S. "Seafox"-class swimmer delivery craft** Bldr: Uniflite, Bellingham, Wash.

D: 11.3 tons (fl) **S:** 30+ kts **Dim:** 11.0 × 3.0 × 0.84
A: Small arms **Electron Equipt:** Radar: 1/LN-66
M: 2 G.M. 6V92 TA diesels; 2 props; 900 hp **Man:** 3 tot.

REMARKS: Ordered 1982. Glass-reinforced plastic construction.

◆ **10 to 12 small landing craft of various origins**

AUXILIARY SHIPS

◆ **8 Soviet Toplivo-2-class coastal tankers** Bldr: Alexandria SY, Egypt

D: 466 tons (1,180 fl) **S:** 10 kts **Dim:** 54.26 (49.40 pp) × 9.40 × 3.10 (3.40 max.)
Electron Equipt: Radar: 1/Spin Trough
M: 1 Russkiy Dizel 6 DR 30/50-5-2 diesel; 1 prop; 600 hp **Electric:** 250 kw
Fuel: 19 tons **Range:** 1,500/10 **Man:** . . . tot.

REMARKS: 308 grt/508 dwt. Part of a series of 26 ordered in Egypt for the U.S.S.R. prior to that country's expulsion. Cargo: 606m³ (500 tons diesel oil).

◆ **4 Soviet Okhtenskiy-class tugs**

AL ISKANDARANI EL MAKS
EL AGAMI EL DIKHILA

D: 700 tons (950 fl) **S:** 13.3 kts **Dim:** 47.3 × 10.3 × 5.5
Electron Equipt: Radar: 1/Don-2 or Spin Trough
M: 2 diesels, electric drive; 1 prop; 1,500 hp **Range:** 7,800/7 **Man:** 40 tot.

REMARKS: Two transferred 1966; two assembled in Egypt.

◆ **1 British "River"-class former frigate**

	Bldr	Laid down	L	In serv.
511 RACHID (ex-*Spey*)	Smith's Dock Co., Ltd.	7-41	18-21-41	3-42

Rachid (511) 1978

D: 1,460 tons (2,175 fl) **S:** 19 kts **Dim:** 91.85 × 11.17 × 4.34 (fl)
A: 1/102-mm—4/40-mm AA (II × 2)—1/SA-N-5 Grail SAM system
M: Triple-expansion; 2 props; 5,500 hp **Boilers:** 2 **Fuel:** 640 tons
Range: 7,700/12; 5,000/16 **Man:** 110 tot.

REMARKS: Bought in 12-49. Used as a submarine tender.

◆ **2 Soviet Nyryat-I-class diving tenders**

D: 120 tons (fl) **S:** 12 kts **Dim:** 29.0 × 5.0 × 1.7
Electron Equipt: Radar: 1/Spin Trough **M:** 1 diesel; 1 prop; 450 hp
Range: 1,600/10 **Man:** 15 tot.

REMARKS: Transferred 1964.

◆ **2 Soviet Poluchat-I-class torpedo retrievers**

D: 80 tons (90 fl) **S:** 18 kts **Dim:** 29.6 × 5.8 × 1.5
Electron Equipt: Radar: 1/Spin Trough
M: 2 M50 diesels; 2 props; 2,400 hp **Range:** 450/17; 900/10 **Man:** 20 tot.

◆ **2 Soviet PO-2-class general-purpose launches**

D: 50 tons (fl) **S:** 9 kts **Dim:** 21.0 × . . . × . . .
M: 1 diesel; 1 prop; 150 hp

◆ **1 Soviet Sekstan-class degaussing tender**

D: 408 tons (fl) **S:** 10.5 kts **Dim:** 41.0 × 9.3 × 4.2
M: 1 diesel; 1 prop; 400 hp **Range:** 1,200/10

REMARKS: Wooden construction.

TRAINING SHIPS

◆ **1 former yacht** Bldr: Samuda, Scotland (In serv. 1865)

EL HORRIA (ex-*Mahroussa*)

El Horria G. Garier, 1976

D: 4,561 tons (fl) **S:** 16 kts **Dim:** 145.6 (121.9 pp) × 13.0 × 5.3
A: Several mg **M:** 3 sets GT; 3 props; 5,500 hp

REMARKS: World's oldest active naval ship; carried President Sadat in naval review, 12-80. Used as a training ship.

◆ **1 navigational training ship for the Naval Academy**

EL KOUSSER **D:** 1,000 tons

◆ **1 former yacht, attached to the Naval Academy**

INTISAR **D:** 500 tons

COAST GUARD

The Coast Guard is a branch of the naval service in Egypt

PATROL BOATS

◆ **3 (+6) U.S. Commercial Cruiser design** Bldr: (1st 3) Swiftships, Inc., Morgan City, La.; others: . . . SY, Egypt. (In serv.: first 3: 16-4-85, others: 1986)

335–343

Egyptian Coast Guard patrol boats Swiftships, 1985

D: 102 tons (fl) **S:** 27 kts **Dim:** 28.30 × 5.66 × 1.60
A: . . . **Electron Equipt:** Radar: . . .
M: 2 MTU 12V331 TC92 diesels; 2 props; 2,660 hp
Range: 1,000/12 **Fuel:** 11.7 tons **Man:** 2 officers, 12 men

REMARKS: Ordered 11-83. First 3 built in U.S., remainder assembled in Egypt from U.S.-supplied components. Aluminum construction.

◆ **0 (+6) Timsah-II class** Bldr: Timsah SY, Ismailia (In serv. . . .)

D: 99 tons **S:** 24 kts **Dim:** 29.0 × 5.2 × 1.48
A: 2/20-mm Oerlikon GAM-BO1 AA (I × 2)
Electron Equipt: Radar: . . .
M: 2 MTU 12V331 TC92 diesels; 2 props; 2,660 hp
Range: 600/. . . **Fuel:** 10 tons **Man:** 13 tot.

REMARKS: Revised version of Timsah class, with different engines, waterline exhausts vice stack. Ordered 1-85.

◆ **12 Timsah class** Bldr: Timsah SY, Alexandria (In serv. 1981-84, 1986–)

D: 100 tons (fl) **S:** 25 kts **Dim:** 29.0 × 5.2 × 1.48
A: 2/30-mm Oerlikon A 32 AA (II × 1)—1/20-mm AA
M: 2 MTU 8V331 diesels; 2 props; 2,960 hp
Fuel: 10 tons **Range:** 600/. . . **Man:** 13 tot.

REMARKS: Based on *Nisr*-class design. First unit laid down 1-1-80, launched 11-81, delivered 12-81.

EGYPT *(continued)*
PATROL BOATS *(continued)*

Timsah-class unit at launch 1983

◆ **3 Nisr class** Bldr: de Castro BY, Port Said (In serv. 1963)

NIMR NISR THAR

D: 110 tons (fl) **S:** . . . **Dim:** 31.0 × 5.2 × 1.5 **A:** 1/20-mm AA
M: 2 Maybach diesels; 2 props; . . . hp

PATROL CRAFT

◆ **4 small patrol craft** Bldr: Canal Naval Const., Port Fuad, Egypt

D: 10 tons **S:** . . . **Dim:** . . . × . . . × . . . **M:** 1 Thornycroft diesel

REMARKS: Ordered 12-12-83. No further data available.

◆ **6 MV70 class** Bldr: Crestitalia, Ameglia (La Spezia), Italy

D: 33 tons (41.5 fl) **S:** 34 kts **Dim:** 21.0 × 5.2 × 0.9
A: 2/30-mm Oerlikon A32 (II × 1)—1/20-mm AA—2/12.7-mm mg
M: 2 MTU 12V331 TC92 diesels; 2 props; 2,800 hp **Range:** 500/3

REMARKS: Fiberglass hulls.

◆ **30 DC-35 class** Bldr: Dawncraft, Wroxham, U.K. (In serv. 1977)

D: 4 tons (fl) **S:** 25 kts **Dim:** 10.7 × 3.5 × 0.8
M: 2 Perkins T6-354 diesels; 2 props; 390 hp **Man:** 4 tot.

REMARKS: Fiberglass hulled. For harbor police duties.

◆ **20 28-ft. "Enforcer" class** Bldr: Bertram Yacht, Miami, Fla. (In serv. 1973)

D: 8 tons (fl) **S:** 24 kts **Dim:** 8.5 × . . . × . . .
A: 2/12.7-mm mg (I × 2) **M:** 2 diesels; 2 props; 300 hp

REMARKS: Formerly naval, had 4/122-mm RL on sides of hull. Fiberglass construction.

NOTE: The Customs Service received twelve 19.8-m Sea Spectre-class patrol craft in 1980-81.

EL SALVADOR

Republic of El Salvador

PERSONNEL: 130 officers and men plus 500-man Marine battalion

MERCHANT MARINE (1984): 11 ships—3,501 grt

PATROL CRAFT

◆ **1 U.S. 77-ft Commercial Cruiser** Bldr: Swiftships, Inc., Morgan City, La. (In serv. 6-85)

GC 11

D: 48 tons (fl) **S:** 26 kts **Dim:** 23.47 × 6.10 × 1.52
A: 1/25-mm U.S. Mk 88—2/12.7-mm mg (I × 2)
Electron Equipt: Radar: . . . **Range:** . . .
M: 3 G.M. 12V71 TI diesels; 3 props; 1,200 hp

REMARKS: Aluminum construction. See photo in addenda.

◆ **3 aluminum-hulled** Bldr: Camcraft, Crown Pt., Louisiana

GC 6 (In serv. 10-75) GC 7 (In serv. 12-75) GC 8 (In serv. 11-75)

D: 100 tons (fl) **S:** 25 kts **Dim:** 30.5 × 6.4 × 1.5 **A:** 3/12.7-mm mg (I × 3)
M: 3 G.M. 12V71 TI diesels; 3 props; 1,200 hp **Range:** 780/24 **Man:** 10 tot.

◆ **1 U.S. 65-ft Commercial Cruiser class** Bldr: Sewart Seacraft, Berwick, Louisiana (In serv. 9-67)

GC 5

D: 33 tons (fl) **S:** 25 kts **Dim:** 19.8 × 4.9 × 1.5 **A:** 3/12.7-mm mg (I × 3)
M: 3 G.M. 8V71 diesels; 3 props; 1,590 hp

REMARKS: Overhauled, redelivered 1-2-85 by builder.

◆ **25 small launches with outboard motors**

EQUATORIAL GUINEA

Republic of Equatorial Guinea

PERSONNEL: (1985): approx. 60 tot.

MERCHANT MARINE (1984): 2 ships—6,412 grt

◆ **4 patrol boats**—ordered 9-82 from Ast. Celayo, Bilbao, Spain; no data available.

◆ **2 small patrol craft**

NOTE: The Soviet P-6-class torpedo boat and Poluchat-I-class patrol boat formerly listed were out of service by 1985.

ETHIOPIA

PERSONNEL: 1,500 men including 250 officers

MERCHANT MARINE (1984): 21 ships—30,008 grt (tankers: 2 ships—3,368 grt)

NAVAL AVIATION: Still in service may be 4 DHC Otter and 3 DHC Twin Otter light transports, and 6 UH-1 Huey helicopters.

FRIGATES

◆ **2 Soviet Petya-II class**

F 1616 (In serv. 20-7-83) F 1617 (In serv. 20-3-84)

D: 950 tons light, 1,020 tons std. (1160 fl) **S:** 29 kts (16 on diesel)
Dim: 81.8 (78.00 pp) × 9.20 × 2.97
A: 4/76.2-mm DP (II × 2)—2/RBU-6000 ASWRL (XII × 2)—10/400-mm ASW TT (V × 2)—2/d.c. racks—mines
Electron Equipt: Radar: 1/Don-2, 1/Strat Curve, 1/Hawk Screech
Sonar: 1/HF hull-mounted
EW: 2/Watch Dog intercept—IFF: High Pole B
M: CODAG: 2/15,000-hp gas turbines, 1 Type 61-V3, 6,000-hp diesel; 3 props (CP on centerline); 36,000 hp—2 active rudders; 100 hp
Range: 450/29; 1,800/16 (diesel); 4,800/10 **Man:** 8 off., 84 crew

REMARKS: In service dates above are those of arrival at Massawa. Believed to be standard Petya-IIs, i.e., not "export model" with 3/533-mm TT and 4/RBU-2500. Hawk Screech gunfire control radar has two associated target designators on the open bridge.

GUIDED-MISSILE PATROL BOATS

◆ **4 Soviet Osa-II class**

FMB 160 FMB 161 FMB 162 FMB 163

D: 210 tons (240 fl) **S:** 35 kts **Dim:** 38.6 × 7.6 × 2.0
A: 4/SS-N-2B Styx SSM—4/30-mm AA (II × 2)
Electron Equipt: Radar: 1/Square Tie, 1/Drum Tilt
IFF; 2/Square Head, 1/High Pole B
M: 3 M504 diesels; 3 props; 15,000 hp **Range:** 500/34; 750/25 **Man:** 30 tot.

REMARKS: First unit transferred 1978, second 10-80, third 13-1-81, the fourth in 1982.

TORPEDO BOATS

◆ **2 Soviet MOL class**

FTB 110 FTB 111

D: 175 tons (220 fl) **S:** 36 kts **Dim:** 38.6 × 7.6 × 1.9
A: 4/533-mm TT (I × 4)—4/30-mm AA (II × 2)
Electron Equipt: Radar: 1/Pot Head, 1/Drum Tilt
IFF: 1/Square Head, 1/High Pole B
M: 3 M503A diesels; 3 props; 12,000 hp **Man:** 30 tot.

REMARKS: Transferred 1978.

ETHIOPIA *(continued)*

PATROL BOATS

◆ **2 Soviet Zhuk class**—transferred 10-82

PC 16 PC 17

D: 48 tons (60 fl) **S:** 34 kts **Dim:** 24.0 × 5.0 × 1.8 (props)
A: 4/14.5-mm (II × 2) **Electron Equipt:** Radar: 1/Spin Trough
M: 2 M50F-4 diesels; 2 props; 2,400 hp

◆ **3 aluminum-hulled boats** Bldr: Swiftships, Morgan City, Louisiana

P 201 P 203 P 204

P 203—with 23-mm AA 1978

D: 118 tons (fl) **S:** 32 kts **Dim:** 31.73 × 7.1 × 2.16
A: 4/30-mm Emerlec AA (II × 2) **Electron Equipt:** Radar: Decca RM 916
M: 2 MTU MB 16V538 TB90 diesels; 2 props; 7,000 hp
Range: 1,200/18 **Man:** 21 tot.

REMARKS: Ordered 1976, delivered 4-77; two additional units were canceled by the U.S. arms embargo. P 203 and P 204 have four 23-mm AA (II × 2) and two 12.7-mm machine guns (II × 1). P 202 lost 1984.

◆ **1 ex-U.S. Coast Guard Cape design** Bldr: Peterson Bldrs, Sturgeon Bay, Wisc. (In serv. 5-62)

PC 15 (ex-U.S. PGM 58)

PC 14 (since discarded)

D: 80 tons (105 fl) **S:** 18 kts **Dim:** 28.95 × 6.1 × 1.55
A: 1/40-mm AA—1/20-mm AA
M: 4 Cummins VT-12M700 diesels; 2 props; 2,200 hp **Electric:** 40 kw
Fuel: 12 tons **Range:** 460/20; 1,500/10 **Man:** 15 tot.

REMARKS: PC 11 lost in action, 4-77. PC 12-14 discarded 1984.

◆ **1 ex-Dutch Wildervank-class former minesweeper**

MS 41 (ex-M 829 *Elst*)

D: 373 tons (417 fl) **S:** 14 kts **Dim:** 46.62 × 8.75 × 2.28
A: 2/40-mm AA (I × 2) **Electron Equipt:** Radar: 1/ZW-04
M: 2 Werkspoor diesels; 2 props; 2,500 hp **Range:** 2,500/10 **Man:** 40 tot.

REMARKS: Launched 21-3-56; bought in 1970. All minesweeping gear removed. Wooden construction.

PATROL CRAFT

◆ **4 aluminum-hulled craft** Bldr: Sewart Seacraft, Berwick, La. (In serv. 1965-67)

GB 21 GB 22 GB 23 GB 24 (ex-*John, Caroline, Patrick, Jacqueline*)

D: 15 tons (fl) **S:** 20 kts **Dim:** 13.1 × 3.9 × 0.9 **A:** 2/12.7-mm mg
M: 2 G.M. 6-71 diesels; 2 props; 500 hp **Man:** 7 tot.

AMPHIBIOUS SHIPS

◆ **2 Soviet Polnocny-B class** Bldr: Polnocny SY, Gdansk, Poland

LTC 1037 LTC 1038

D: 800 tons (fl) **S:** 19 kts **Dim:** 74.0 × 8.6 × 2.0
A: 4.30-mm AA—2/140-mm RL (XVIII × 2)
Electron Equipt: Radar: 1/Spin Trough, 1/ Drum Tilt
IFF: 1/Square Head, 1/High Pole
M: 2 diesels; 2 props; 4,000 hp **Range:** 900/18; 1,500/14 **Man:** 40 tot.

REMARKS: Transferred 11-81 and 1-83. Cargo: 180 tons.

◆ **2 French EDIC-class LCU** Bldr: SFCN, Villeneuve la Garonne (L: 5-77)

LTC 1035 LTC 1036

D: 250 tons (670 fl) **S:** 8 kts **Dim:** 59.0 × 11.95 × 1.3
A: 2/20-mm AA (I × 2) **M:** 2 MGO diesels; 2 props; 1,000 hp
Range: 1,800/8 **Man:** 1 officer, 15 men

REMARKS: Cargo: 11 trucks or 5 light armored vehicles.

◆ **6 Soviet T-4 class landing craft**

D: 70 tons (fl) **S:** 10 kts **Dim:** 19.0 × 4.3 × 1.0
M: 2 diesels; 2 props; 600 hp **Man:** 5 tot.

REMARKS: Four transferred 1977-78, two in 1984.

TRAINING SHIP

◆ **1 U.S. Barnegat-class former seaplane tender**

	Bldr	Laid down	L	In serv.
A 01 ETHIOPIA (ex-*Orca,* AVP 49)	Lake Washington SY	13-7-42	4-10-42	23-1-44

D: 1,766 tons (2,800 fl) **S:** 17 kts **Dim:** 94.7 (91.5 pp) × 12.52 × 3.65
A: 1/127-mm DP—5/40-mm AA (II × 2, I × 1)
Electron Equipt: Radar: 1/SPS-12, 1/navigational, 1/Mk 26
M: 4 Fairbanks-Morse 38D8 ⅛ × 10 diesels; 2 props; 6,000 hp
Electric: 600 kw **Range:** 15,000/12 **Man:** 215 tot.

REMARKS: Transferred in 1-62. Had Mk 52 radar GFCS for 127-mm gun.

NOTE: Also in service are a tug, AO 2, and a small service launch, TR 74.

FIJI

Dominion of Fiji

PERSONNEL (1984): 145 men (26 officers)

MERCHANT MARINE (1984): 56 ships—29,216 grt (6 tankers—4,933 grt)

PATROL BOATS

◆ **0 (+6) patrol boats** Bldr: Government Yard, Suva

D: . . . **S:** 18 kts **Dim:** 33.0 × . . . × . . .
A: . . .
M: . . .

◆ **0 (+4) Australia . . . class**

◆ **3 ex-U.S. Redwing-class minesweepers** Bldr: Bellingham SY, Washington

	In serv.
204 KIKAU (ex-*Woodpecker,* MSC 209)	3-2-56
205 KULA (ex-*Vireo,* MSC 205)	7-6-55
206 KIRO (ex-*Warbler,* MSC 206)	23-7-55

Kula (205)—with Bell 222 helicopter 9-84

D: 370 tons (fl) **S:** 13 kts **Dim:** 43.9 × 8.5 × 2.6
A: 1/20-mm AA—2/12.7-mm mg
M: 2 G.M. 8-268A diesels; 2 props; 880 hp **Range:** 2,500/10 **Man:** 39 tot.

REMARKS: The first two were transferred 10-75, the third 6-76. All minesweeping gear removed. *Kula* has a small flight deck built over the fantail for one Bell 222 helicopter.

NOTE: Auxiliaries *Ruve* and *Latui* are described in the addenda.

FINLAND

Republic of Finland

The naval force, limited by the Treaty of Paris to 10,000 tons and 4,500 men, is a separate establishment under the orders of the chief of the armed forces. Submarines and torpedo boats are excluded from the fleet, and there is no naval aviation. A Fokker F-27 MK 400M Maritime Patrol aircraft was delivered to the Air Force 31-1-84.

PERSONNEL (1985): about 2,500, including 200 officers and 600 Frontier Guards

MERCHANT MARINE (1984): 332 ships—2,168,471 grt (tankers: 42 ships—997,130 grt)

WEAPONS

The *Turunmaa*-class corvettes and the minelayer *Pohjanmaa* have a single-barrel automatic Bofors 120-mm gun with the following characteristics:

weight without munitions: 28.5 tons
length: 46 calibers
muzzle velocity: 800 m/sec
training speed: 40°/sec
elevation speed: 30°/sec
arc of elevation: −10° to +80
maximum rate of fire: 80 rounds/min
projectile weight: 35 kg
maximum effective range, surface fire: 12,000 m

The other major weapons employed are Soviet SS-N-2 Styx missiles, Bofors 40-mm L70 AA guns, Soviet twin 30-mm AA guns, and 23-mm AA in twin mountings. Swedish RBS-15 anti-ship missiles were ordered in 1983 to equip the *Helsinki* class.

CORVETTES

◆ **2 Turunmaa class**

	Bldr	Laid down	L	In serv.
03 TURUNMAA	Wärtsilä, Helsinki	3-67	11-7-67	29-8-68
04 KARJALA	Wärtsilä, Helsinki	3-67	16-8-67	21-10-68

Karjala (04) Finnish Navy, 1984

D: 605 tons (770 fl) **S:** 35 kts **Dim:** 74.1 × 7.8 × 2.83
A: 1/120-mm Bofors DP—2/40-mm AA (I × 2)—2/12.7-mm mg (I × 2)—2/RBU-1200 ASW RL (V × 2)—2/d.c. racks
Electron Equipt: Radar: 1/H.S.A. M22, 1/navigational
M: CODOG propulsion: 1 Bristol-Siddeley Olympus TM3B, 22,000-hp gas turbine; 3 Mercedes-Benz 1,100-hp diesels; 3 CP props
Electric: 880 kVA **Fuel:** 120 tons **Range:** 2,500/14 **Man:** 70 tot.

REMARKS: Flush-deck hull, closed bridge, sharp profile. Cruises on the diesels (3 × 1,100 hp) at 17 knots. Ka-Me-Wa controllable-pitch propellers. Have Vosper fin stabilizers. Soviet ASW rocket launchers are behind doors in main-deck superstructure, abreast the mast; the d.c. racks are internal, at the stern. Six 103-mm flare Rl rails on 120-mm mount. 9LV 200 t.v./IR director added on mast, 1978. Both in refit 1984-85; to recevied Data Saab EOS-400 optronic f.c.s.

GUIDED-MISSILE PATROL BOATS

◆ **1 (+3 +6) Helsinki (PB 80) class** Bldr: Wärtsilä, Helsinki

	Laid down	L	In serv. (scheduled)
60 HELSINKI	3-9-80	5-11-80	1-9-81
61 TURKU	1-84	1985	1-10-85
62 N.	. . .	. . .	1-10-85
63 N.	. . .	. . .	1-6-86

D: 250 tons (280 fl) **S:** 30 kts **Dim:** 45.0 × 8.9 × 3.0 (props)
A: 4/RBS-15 SSM (II × 2)—1/57-mm Bofors Mk 1 DP—4/23-mm AA (II × 2)
Electron Equipt: Radar: 1/navigational, 1/9GA208, 1/9L V225 f.c.
Sonar: Simrad SS 304
M: 3 MTU 16V538 TB92 diesels; 3 props; 12,000 hp
Range: . . . **Man:** 30 tot.

REMARKS: Prototype ordered 5-10-78. Three additional ordered 13-1-83; six more planned. Aluminum hull. *Helsinki* has only one twin 23-mm AA mount.

Helsinki (60)—on trials Finnish Navy, 1983

◆ **4 Soviet Osa-II class**

11 TUIMA 12 TUISKU 14 TUULI 15 TYRSKY

Tyrsky (15) Finnish Navy, 1984

D: 210 tons (240 fl) **S:** 35 kts **Dim:** 38.6 × 7.6 × 2.0
A: 4/SS-N-2B Styx—4/30-mm AA (II × 2)
Electron Equipt: Radar: 1/Square Tie, 1/Drum Tilt, 1/navigational
M: 3 M504 diesels; 3 props; 15,000 hp **Range:** 500/34; 750/25
Man: 30 tot.

REMARKS: Transferred in 1975. Some Western electronic equipment has been added, including a navigational radar. Engines reported to be unreliable.

◆ **Sea-sled hull type** Bldr: Reposaaren Konepaja, Pori

	Laid down	L	In serv.
16 ISKU	11-68	4-12-69	1970

Isku (16) 1979

D: 115 tons (140 fl) **S:** 15 kts **Dim:** 26.35 × 8.70 × 2.00
A: 4/SS-N-2A Styx (I × 4)—2/30-mm AA (II × 1)
Electron Equipt: Radar: 1/navigational, 1/Square Tie
M: 4 Soviet M50-series diesels; 4 props; 4,800 hp **Man:** 25 tot.

REMARKS: Barge-like hull, designed for more powerful propulsion plant. Used primarily for training.

PATROL BOATS

◆ **1 prototype** Bldr: Fiskar's Turan, Veneveistamo SY/Laivateollisuus

33 HURJA

D: 54 tons (60 fl) **S:** 42 kts **Dim:** 21.7 × 5.0 × . . . **A:** . . .
M: Diesels; waterjets; . . . hp

REMARKS: Glass-reinforced plastic prototype hull delivered 1-7-80 to Laivateollisuus for fitting out. This class was intended to replace at least seven of the Nuoli class during the 1980s, but no further orders have materialized.

PATROL BOATS *(continued)*

◆ **6 Nuoli class** Bldr: Laivateollisuus, Turku (In serv. 1961-66)

	In serv.		In serv.
35 Nuoli 5	6-7-62	41 Nuoli 11	5-5-64
38 Nuoli 8	10-10-62	42 Nuoli 12	30-11-64
40 Nuoli 10	5-5-64	43 Nuoli 13	12-10-66

Nuoli 5 (35) Finnish Navy, 1983

D: 40 tons (64 fl) **S:** 40 kts **Dim:** 22.0 × 6.65 × 1.5
A: 1/40-mm AA—1/20-mm AA **Electron Equipt:** Radar: Decca 707
M: 3 Soviet M50 diesels; 3,600 hp **Man:** 15 tot.

Remarks: Nuoli 10-13 have a lower superstructure. Sisters *Nuoli-1-3, 6,* and *9* discarded by 1984; survivors to be modernized.

◆ **3 Ruissalo class** Bldr: Laivateollisuus, Turku

	L	In serv.
53 Ruissalo	16-6-59	11-8-59
54 Raisio	2-7-59	12-9-59
55 Röytta	2-6-59	14-10-59

◆ **2 Rihtniemi class** Bldr: Rauma-Repola, Rauma

51 Rihtniemi	1956	21-2-57
52 Rymattlya	1956	20-5-57

Ruissalo (53) Finnish Navy, 1979

D: 115 tons (135 fl) **S:** 18 kts **Dim:** 34.0 × 6.0 × 1.8
A: 4/23-mm AA (II × 2)—2/RBU-1200 ASW RL (V × 2)—mines
M: 2 Mercedes-Benz diesels; 2 CP props; 2,500 hp **Man:** 20 tot.

Remarks: *Ruissalo* and *Rihtniemi* classes are former convertible minesweeper/gunboats, modernized 1977-80. 51 and 52 originally only 31 meters overall and are 5.7 meters in beam. All five now have bow bulwarks.

MINE WARFARE SHIPS

◆ **1 minelayer/training ship** Bldr: Wärtsilä, Helsinki

	Laid down	L	In serv.
01 Pohjanmaa	5-78	28-8-78	8-6-79

Pohjanmaa (01) Finnish Navy, 1983

D: 1,100 tons (fl) **S:** 20 kts **Dim:** 78.3 × 11.6 × 3.0
A: 1/120-mm Bofors DP—2/40-mm AA (I × 2)—8/23-mm AA (II × 4)—2/RBU-1200 ASW RL (II × 2)—mines
Electron Equipt: Radar: 1/navigational, 1/H.S.A. DA 05 air search, 1/9GA 208, 1/9LV100
Sonar: 2 sets
M: 2 Wärtsilä-Vasa 16V22 diesels; 2 CP prop; 5,800 hp
Electric: 1,040 kVA **Range:** 3,500/17 **Man:** 80 crew plus 70 cadets

Remarks: Training facilities fitted in portable containers mounted on the two internal mine rails, easily removable if the ship is required for combat. Bow-thruster. Six 102-mm flare RL rails mounted on 120-mm mount.

◆ **1 Soviet Riga-class former frigate** (In serv. circa 1957)

02 Hameenmaa

Hameenma (02) L. & L. Van Ginderen, 9-83

D: 1,282 tons (1510 fl) **S:** 30 kts **Dim:** 91.0 (87.0 pp) × 10.2 × 3.2
A: 2/100-mm DP (I × 2)—2/40-mm Bofors AA (I × 2)—2/30-mm AA (II × 2)—4/BMB-2 d.c. mortars—2/d.c. racks—2 mine rails
Electron Equipt: Radar: 1/Decca navigational, 1/Slim Net, 1/Sun Visor B
M: 2 sets GT; 2 props; 20,000 hp **Boilers:** 2: 27 kg/cm², 360°C
Electric: 450 kw **Range:** 550/28; 2,000/13 **Fuel:** 229 tons **Man:** 175 tot.

Remarks: Transferred 1964. Sister *Uusimaa* stricken 1980 for spares and *Hameenmaa* redesignated as a minelayer, with torpedo tubes, after 100-mm gun and some ASW equipment deleted. Twin 30-mm AA mount at extreme bow. Wasp Head director with Sun Visor B radar for 100-mm fire control.

◆ **1 coastal minelayer** Bldr: Valmet Oy, Helsinki (L: 16-3-57)

05 Keihassalmi

Keihassalmi (05) L. & L. Van Ginderen, 1982

D: 290 tons (360 fl) **S:** 15 kts **Dim:** 56.0 × 7.7 × 2.0
A: 4/30-mm AA (II × 2)—2/20-mm AA (I × 2)—100 mines
Electron Equipt: Radar: 1/navigational, 1/Drum Tilt
M: 2 Wärtsilä diesels; 2 props; 2,000 hp **Man:** 60 tot.

Remarks: Given Soviet guns 1972, Drum Tilt f.c. radar 1976.

MINE WARFARE SHIPS *(continued)*

◆ **6 Kuha-class inshore minesweepers** Bldr: Laivateollisuus, Turku

	In serv.		In serv.		In serv.
KUHA 21	28-6-74	KUHA 23	-75	KUHA 25	17-6-75
KUHA 22	-74	KUHA 24	7-3-75	KUHA 26	13-11-75

Kuha 22—now has twin 23-mm AA aft, 12.7-mm mg fwd 1974

D: 90 tons (fl) **S:** 12 kts **Dim:** 26.6 × 6.9 × 2.0
A: 2/23-mm AA (II × 1)—1/12.7-mm mg **Man:** 2 officers, 12 men
M: 2 Cummins NT-380M diesels; 2 outboard-drive props; 600 hp

REMARKS: Glass-reinforced plastic hulls. Plans for eight additional canceled. Engines, flexibly mounted, drive rudder/propellers through hydrostatic transmissions. Can tow Type F-82 electrode sweep while also controlling a *Kiskii* drone with a similar sweep deployed.

◆ **7 Kiskii-class drone minesweepers** Bldr: Fiskars Turun, Turku

	Laid down	L	In serv.
521 KISKII 1	. . .	. . .	1983
522 KISKII 2	20-1-83	21-10-83	4-11-83
523 KISKII 3	14-2-83	10-11-83	28-11-83
524 KISKII 4	5-4-83	28-11-83	12-12-83
525 KISKII 5	16-5-83	2-5-84	24-5-83
526 KISKII 6	29-8-83	9-5-84	24-5-83
527 KISKII 7	12-9-83	10-5-84	24-5-83

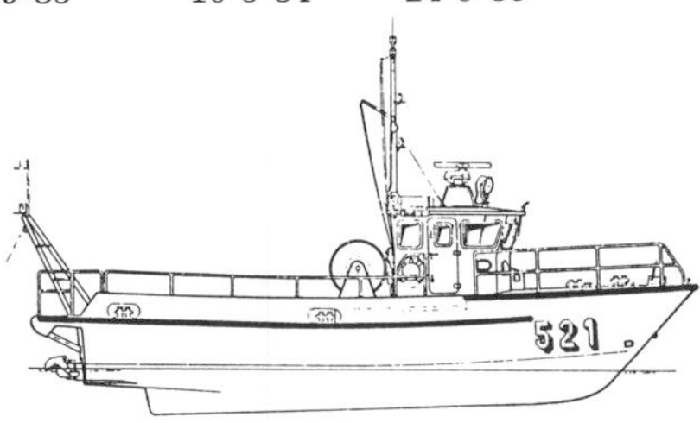

Kiskii class Finnish Navy, 1983

D: 17 tons (20 fl) **S:** 11 kts **Dim:** 15.18 × 4.10 × 1.20
A: 1/20-mm AA **Range:** 250/10 **Man:** 4 tot.
M: 2 Valmet 611 CSMP diesels; 2 Hamilton waterjets; 340 hp

REMARKS: Can be operated by crews or under remote control by Kuha-class inshore minesweepers. Glass-reinforced plastic construction. Tow a Type F-82 electrode sweep to counter magnetic mines and can also counter acoustic mines. *Kiskii 1* was a trials prototype.

NOTE: Two small non-self-propelled minelaying barges were ordered from Lehtinen Sy, Rauma, in 12-84.

AMPHIBIOUS WARFARE SHIPS

◆ **4 landing craft/patrol boats** Bldr: 2 by Hollming, 2 by Rauma-Repola

D: 28 tons (38 fl) **S:** 24 kts **Dim:** 20.50 × 5.90 × 1.00
A: 1/20-mm AA—mines **Range:** 240/24 **Man:** 4 tot.
M: 2 Wizeman-MTU diesels; 2 KaMeWa waterjets; 1,100 hp

REMARKS: Ordered 17-1-83; laid down 8/9-83.

◆ **3 Kampela-class utility landing craft** Bldr: Enso-Gutzeit, Savonlinna

KAMPELA 1 (In serv. 29-7-76) KAMPELA 2 (In serv. 21-10-76)
KAMPELA 3 (In serv. 23-10-79)

D: 90 tons (260 fl) **S:** 9 kts **Dim:** 32.5 × 8.0 × 1.5 **Man:** 10 tot.
A: A9/23-mm AA (II × 2)—mines **M:** 2 Scania diesels; 2 props; 460 hp

REMARKS: *Kampela* 3 built by Finnmekano, Teija.

◆ **6 Kala-class utility landing craft** Bldr: Rauma-Repola, Rauma (In serv. 1956-59)

KALA 1—KALA 6

D: 60 tons (200 fl) **S:** 9 kts **Dim:** 27.0 × 8.0 × 1.8 **Man:** 10 tot.
A: 1/20-mm AA—34 mines **M:** 2 Valmet diesels; 2 props; 360 hp

Kampela class Finnish Navy, 1984

◆ **5 Kave-class landing craft** Bldr: Hollming, Rauma (In serv. 1956-60)

KAVE 1 KAVE 2 KAVE 3 KAVE 4 KAVE 6

D: 27 tons (60 fl) **S:** 9 kts **Dim:** 18.0 × 5.0 × 1.3 **A:** 1/20-mm AA
M: 2 Valmet diesels; 2 props; 360 hp **Man:** 3 tot.

REMARKS: *Kave* 1 built by Haminen Konepaja Oy.

AUXILIARY SHIPS

Note: A new naval tug was ordered 12-84 from Lehtinen SY, Rauma; no data available.

◆ **1 pollution cleanup ship** Bldr: Laivateollisuus, Turku

99 HYLSE (In serv. 3-6-81)

D: 1,500 (fl) **S:** 7 kts **Dim:** 49.9 × 12.5 × 3.0
M: 2 Saab-Scania DSI-14 diesels; 2 retractable, steerable props; 680 hp

REMARKS: Owned by Board of Navigation, operated by Navy, with civilian crew. Has bow ramp on rectangular hull and can be used to transport 100 tons of deck cargo. Storage tanks can hold 550 m^3 of recovered seawater/oil slurry and 850 m^3 recovered oil. One 10-m and one 13-m oil-skimming boats carried.

◆ **1 missile patrol boat tender** Bldr: Wärtsilä, Helsinki

90 LOUHI (ex-*Sisu*)(L: 24-9-38)

Louhi (90) 1979

D: 2,075 tons **S:** 16 kts **Dim:** 64.1 × 14.2 × 5.1 **A:** 4/37-mm AA (II × 2)
M: 2 Atlas diesels, electric drive; 2 props; 4,000 hp **Man:** 100 tot.

REMARKS: Former icebreaker, converted 1975 as tender to missile boats. Refitted 1979; received AA guns from Riga-class frigate.

◆ **1 cable ship** Bldr: Rauma-Repola (L: 15-12-65)

PUTSAARI

D: 430 tons (fl) **S:** 10 kts **Dim:** 45.5 × 8.9 × 2.3
M: 1 Wärtsilä diesel; 1 prop; 450 hp **Man:** 20 tot.

◆ **1 salvage tender**

220 PARAINEN (ex-*Pellinki*, ex-*Meteor*)

Parainen (220) 1978

AUXILIARY SHIPS *(continued)*

D: 700 tons **S:** 12 kts **Dim:** . . . × . . . × . . . **M:** Diesels

Remarks: 352 grt. Purchased 1978. Former rescue tug, has diving and fire-fighting facilities.

◆ **1 modified Valas-class diving tender** Bldr: Hollming SY, Rauma

. . . Mersu (In serv. 10-80)

D: 300 tons (fl) **S:** 12 kts **Dim:** 30.65 × 8.1 × 3.4
A: 2/23-mm AA (II × 1)—1/12.7-mm mg
M: 1 Wärtsilä Vasa 22 diesel; 1 prop; 1,450 hp **Man:** 1 officer, 6 crew; 20 divers

Remarks: Can also be used to transport 300 personnel. Appearance generally as the *Valas* class.

◆ **4 Valas-class general-service tenders** Bldr: Hollming Oy, Rauma (In serv. 1979-81)

220 Valas 221 Vahakari 222 Vaarlehti 223 Vänö

Vahakari (221) 1980

D: 100 tons (275 fl) **S:** 12 kts **Dim:** 30.65 × 7.85 × 3.40
A: 2/23-mm AA (II × 1)—1/12.7-mm mg—20 mines
M: 1 Wärsilä Vasa 22 diesel; 1 prop; 1,300 hp **Man:** 11 tot.

Remarks: Ordered 1978. Can break .4-meter ice. Carry 30 tons of cargo or 150 passengers. Stern ramp for vehicle-loading or minelaying.

◆ **3 Pukkio-class general-service tenders** Bldr: Valmet, Turku (In serv. 1947-48)

Pansio Porkkala Pyharanta

D: 162 tons **S:** 10 kts **Dim:** 28.5 × 6.0 × 2.7
A: 1/40-mm AA—1/20-mm AA—20 mines **M:** 1 Wärtsilä diesel; 1 prop; 300 hp
Man: 10 tot.

Remarks: Used as tugs, transports, minelayers, and patrol boats.

◆ **6 Hauki-class personnel transports** Bldr: 1-3: Linnan Telakka, Turku; 4-6: Valmet, Kolka (In serv. 1978-80)

Hankoniemi (334) 1980

D: 46 tons (fl) **S:** 10 kts **Dim:** 14.4 × 4.6 × 2.2
M: 2 Valmet 611 CSM diesels; 1 prop; 280 hp **Man:** 2 tot.

Remarks: Cargo: 45 personnel or 6 tons supplies. Can break .2-meter ice. Operated for the Coast Artillery.

◆ **2 Lohi-class personnel transports** Bldr: Savonlinna SY (In serv. 7-9-84)

Lohi Lohm

D: 28 tons (38 fl) **S:** 24 kts **Dim:** 20.50 × 5.90 × 1.00
A: 1/20-mm AA—mines
M: 2 Wizeman-Mercedes Benz diesels; 2 KaMeWa waterjets; 1,000 hp
Range: 240/24 **Man:** . . .

Remarks: Have a near-vertical bow door and ramp for landing personnel embarked. Ordered 17-1-83 and laid down 8-83 and 9-83. Aluminum construction. Used as VIP transports, patrol hospital launches, etc.

◆ **1 presidential yacht** Bldr: Uusikaupanki SY (In serv. 5-84)

Kultaranta VII

D: 15 tons (fl) **S:** 25 kts **Dim:** 12.5 × 4.0 × 1.4 **M:** 2 diesels; 2 props; 700 hp

Remarks: Described as a "communications ship" and used is a presidential yacht in summer and for search and rescue and medical transport in winter.

◆ **6 Ahven-class training tenders** Bldr: Valmet, Kotka

A1 Ahven A2 N. . . . . . . A3 N. . . . . . . A4 N. . . . . . . A5 N. . . . . . . A6 N. . . . . . .

D: . . . **S:** . . . **Dim:** 10.3 × 3.2 × . . .
M: 1 Valmet 611 diesel; . . . hp

Remarks: Glass-reinforced plastic construction. First unit delivered 1980. Intended as tugs, buoy tenders, and navigational training craft.

◆ **57 (+12) service launches, K, Y, L, YM, and H and new construction**

D: 2 to 34 tons **S:** 7 to 10 kts

Remarks: For local transport, primarily in support of Coast Artillery. Four 9-ton launches were ordered 12-84 from Unden Kaupungin SY, Uusikaupunki, and 8- to 10-ton launches were ordered from Valkoisen SY, Paimio.

Coast Artillery service launch 1982

COAST GUARD

Operated by the Ministry of the Interior. All ships now have black hull with a red-white-red diagonal stripe, as on U.S. Coast Guard ships. Upperworks are white.

Aviation: Three Soviet Mi-8 helicopters were purchased 12-80 for search-and-rescue duties.

PATROL BOATS ("Outer Sea Patrol Ships")

◆ **0 (+1) improved Turva class** Bldr: Rauma-Repola SY, Uusikaupunki

N. . . (In serv. . . .)

D: 700 tons **S:** 16 kts **Dim:** 49.00 (43.80 pp) × 10.00 × 4.60
A: 1/20-mm AA **Electron Equipt:** Radar: . . .
M: 2 Wärtsilä-Vasa 8- R22 diesels; 2 props; 3,200 hp

Remarks: Ordered 12-12-84.

◆ **1 new construction** Bldr: Hollming, Rauma

N. . .

D: 250 tons(270 fl) **S:** 20 kts **Dim:** 43.80 (38.50 pp) × 8.80 × 2.20
A: . . .
M: 2 MTU 16V536 TB93 diesels; 2 KaMeWa waterjets; 7,500 hp

Remarks: Ordered 21-11-84. Aluminum construction.

PATROL BOATS *(continued)*

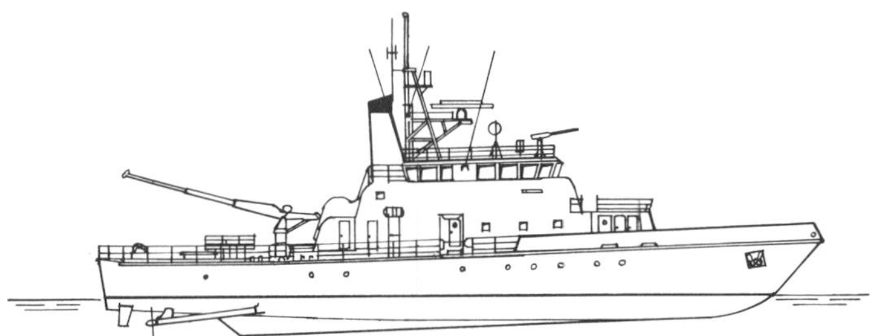

New 270-ton Coast Guard cutter A.D. Baker III, 5-85

◆ **1 improved Valpas class** Bldr: Laivateollisuus, Turku

TURVA (In serv. 15-12-77)

Turva L. & L. Van Ginderen, 1984

D: 550 tons **S:** 16 kts **Dim:** 48.5 × 8.6 × 3.9 **A:** 1/20-mm AA
M: 2 Wärtsilä diesels; 1 prop; 2,000 hp

REMARKS: Ordered 24-6-75. An improved *Valpas,* similar in appearance.

◆ **1 Valpas class** Bldr: Laivateollisuus, Turku

	Laid down	L	In serv.
VALPAS	20-5-70	22-12-70	21-7-71

Valpas 1974

D: 545 tons **S:** 15 kts **Dim:** 48.3 × 8.7 × 4.0 **A:** 1/20-mm AA
M: 1 Werkspoor TMABS-398 diesel; 1 CP prop; 2,000 hp **Man:** 22 tot.

REMARKS: Ice-strengthened, equipped with sonar.

◆ **1 Viima class** Bldr: Laivateollisuus, Turku

	L	In serv.
VIIMA	20-7-64	12-10-64

D: 135 tons **S:** 23 kts **Dim:** 35.7 × 6.6 × 2.0 **A:** 1/20-mm AA
M: 3 Maybach diesels; 3 CP props; 4,050 hp **Man:** 12 tot.

REMARKS: A variant of the Finnish Navy *Ruissalo* class.

◆ **1 Silma class** Bldr: Laivateollisuus, Turku

	Laid down	L	In serv.
SILMA	30-8-62	23-3-63	19-8-63

D: 530 tons **S:** 15 kts **Dim:** 48.3 × 8.3 × 4.3 **A:** 1/20-mm AA
M: 1 Werkspoor diesel; 1 prop; 1,800 hp **Man:** 22 tot.

◆ **1 Uisko class** Bldr: Valmet, Helsinki (In serv. 1959)

UISKO

D: 370 tons **S:** 15 kts **Dim:** 43.4 × 7.3 × 3.83 **A:** 1/20-mm AA
M: 1 Werkspoor diesel; 1 prop; 1,800 hp **Man:** 20 tot.

◆ **1 (+6) Lokki class** Bldr: Valmet-Laivateollisuus, Turku

LOKKI (In serv. 27-11-81)

Lokki Liavateollisuus, 1981

D: 53 tons (60 fl) **S:** 25 kts **Dim:** 26.8 × 5.2 × . . . **A:** . . .
M: MTU 8V396 TC83 diesels; 2 props; 2,040 hp **Electric:** 30 kw **Man:** 8 tot.

REMARKS: Aluminum construction. Prototype ordered 17-5-80. To replace *Koskelo* class. No further orders as of mid-1985.

◆ **8 Koskelo class** Bldr: Valmet, Helsinki (In serv. 1955-60)

KAAKKURI	KOSKELO	KUOVI	TAVI
KIISLA	KUIKKA	KURKI	TELKKÄ

D: 75 tons (97 fl) **S:** 23 kts **Dim:** 29.42 × 5.02 × 1.5 **A:** 1/20-mm AA
M: Mercedes-Benz diesels; 2 props; 2,700 hp **Man:** 11 tot.

REMARKS: All but one (used as a replacement for the training ship *Eckero*) are to be discarded on completion of units of the new *Lokki* class. All modernized and re-engine 1970-74 by Laivateollisuus, Turku.

SERVICE CRAFT

◆ **98 small craft, Series RV, NV, and PV**

D: 1.1 to 20 tons **S:** Most, 9 to 13 kts **Dim:** 8 to 14 overall

REMARKS: The newest are RV 37 to RV 39, delivered 1978 by Hollming.

D: 20 tons **S:** 12 kts **Dim:** 14.3 × 3.5 × . . . **M:** 1 MTU diesel; 300 hp

ICEBREAKERS (Under Board of Navigation)

◆ **D (+1 +1) new construction** Bldr: Wärtsilä, Helsinki

KARHU II (In serv. 1986)

Karhu II—artist's impression Hwänolä/Wärtsilä, 1984

D: . . . **S:** . . . **Dim:** 99.0 × 24.20 × 8.00
M: 4 Wärtsilä Vasa 16V32 diesels (7,425 hp each); Kymi-Stromberg a.c. cyclo-converters, 3 props; 17,700 hp.

REMARKS: Ordered 29-3-84. Will have 2 transverse thrusters, bow propeller, Wärtsilä "bubbler" system. A second unit is planned.

FINLAND *(continued)*
ICEBREAKERS *(continued)*

◆ **2 Urho class** Bldr: Wärtsilä, Helsinki

URHO (In serv. 5-3-75) SISU (In serv. 28-1-76)

Urho Wärtsilä, 1975

D: 7,960 tons (9,500 fl) **S:** 18 kts **Dim:** 104.6 × 23.8 × 8.3
M: 5 SEMT-Pielstick 5,000-hp diesels, electric drive; 4 props; 22,000 hp

REMARKS: Sisters to Swedish *Atle* class. One helicopter. Two props forward, two aft.

◆ **3 Tarmo class** Bldr: Wärtsilä, Helsinki

TARMO VARMA APU

Varma Wärtsilä

D: 4,890 tons **S:** 17 kts **Dim:** 85.7 × 21.7 × 6.8
M: 4 Sulzer diesels, electric drive; 4 props; 10,000 hp

REMARKS: In service 1963, 1968, and 1970, respectively. Two props forward, two aft.

◆ **2 Karhu class** Bldr: Wärtsilä, Helsinki

MURTJALA SAMPO

D: 3,540 tons **S:** 16 kts **Dim:** 74.2 × 17.4 × 6.4
M: Diesel-electric; 4 props (2 fwd), 7,500 hp

REMARKS: In service 1959 and 1960, respectively. Sister *Hansa* is owned by West Germany (in serv. 25-11-66), has a Finnish crew, and summers in Finnish waters. Sister *Korhu* was to be discarded on completion of *Karhu II.*

◆ **1 Voima class** Bldr: Wärtsilä, Helsinki (In serv. 1954)

VOIMA

D: 4,415 tons **S:** 16.5 kts **Dim:** 83.6 × 19.4 × 6.8
M: 6 Wärtsilä Vasa 16V22 diesels (17,460 hp), electric drive; 4 props; 14,000 hp

REMARKS: Reconstructed and re-engined 1978-79 by Wärtsilä; expected to serve until 1994.

NOTE: The Board of Navigation also owns the pollution-control ship *Hylse* (99), operated by the navy; see entry on navy pages.

Voima 1979

FRANCE

French Republic

PERSONNEL (1985): 67,040 men and women on active duty, including 4,458 officers, 28,951 chief petty officers and petty officers, and 33.631 other enlisted personnel. Also on duty are 2,952 members of the Gendarmerie Marine.

NAVAL AVIATION: In service are 27 F-8E Crusader interceptors, 70 Super Étendard fighter-bombers, 13 Étendard IVP photoreconnaissance aircraft, 32 Atlantic Mk 1 and 5 Gardian patrol aircraft, 18 Super Frélon, and 38 WG-13 Lynx helicopters, and 188 service and training aircraft and helicopters. See aviation section after aircraft carriers for additional details.

MERCHANT MARINE (1984): 1,174 ships—8,945,046 grt (tankers: 94 ships—5,336,202 grt)

WARSHIPS IN SERVICE OR UNDER CONSTRUCTION AS OF 1 JANUARY 1986

	L	Tons	Main armament
◆ **3 aircraft carriers**			
2 CLEMENCEAU (fixed-wing)	1957-60	22,000	8/100-mm DP, 40 aircraft
1 JEANNE D'ARC (helicopter)	1961	10,000	4/100-mm DP, 6/MM 38 Exocet, 8 heavy helicopters
◆ **24 (+3) submarines**			
1 L'INFLEXIBLE (nuclear)	1982	8,000	16 missiles, 4 TT
5 LE REDOUTABLE (nuclear)	1967-77	8,000	16 missiles, 4 TT
1 GYMNOTE	1964	3,000	2 missiles
2 (+3) RUBIS (nuclear)	1979-. . .	2,265	4 TT
4 AGOSTA	1974-76	1,200	4 TT
9 DAPHNE	1959-67	700	12 TT
2 NARVAL	1954-58	1,320	6 TT
◆ **1 guided-missile cruiser**			
1 COLBERT	1956	8,500	1 Masurca, 4/MM38, 2/100-mm DP, 12/57-mm AA
◆ **16 (+7)destroyers**			
0(+4) C 70 AA	1984-90	4,000	Mk 13 launcher, 8/MM 40, 2/100-mm DP, 2 TT
4 (+3) GEORGES LEYGUES	1975-	3,800	1/100-mm DP, 4/MM 38, 2 TT 2 WG 13 Lynx helicopters
3 TOURVILLE	1972-74	4,800	1 Malafon, 6/MM 38, 1 Crotale, 2/100-mm DP, 2 TT, 2 WG 13 Lynx helicopters
2 SUFFREN	1965-66	5,090	1 Masurca, 2/100-mm DP, 1 Malafon, 4/MM 38
1 ACONIT	1970	3,500	8/MM 40, 2/100-mm DP, 1 Malafon, ASW mortar, 2 TT
1 LA GALISSONNIÈRE	1960	2,750	2/100-mm DP, 1 Malafon, 1 helicopter
1 DUPERRÉ	1956	2,750	1/100-mm DP, 4/MM 38
2 D'ESTRÉES	1954	2,750	2/100-mm DP, 1 Malafon, ASW weapons

WARSHIPS *(continued)*

2 Kersaint	1954	2,750	1 SM-1MR, 6/57-mm AA, 1 ASW RL, 6 TT

◆ **25 frigates**

17 D'Estienne D'Orves	1973-80	1,100	1/100-mm DP, 2/MM 38, 1 ASW rocket launcher, 4 TT
1 Balny	1962	1,750	2/100-mm DP, 1 ASW mortar, 6 TT
7 Commandant Rivière	1958-63	1,750	4/MM 38, 2/100-mm DP, 1 ASW mortar, 6 TT

◆ **19 (+4) patrol boats and craft**

6 (+4) P 400	1984-	320	1/40-mm AA
4 Trident	1976	115	1/40-mm 6/SS 12 SSM
1 Sterne	1979	270	2 mg
1 La Combattante	1963	180	2/40-mm AA, 4/SS 12 SSM
1 Mercure	1957	365	2/20-mm AA
1 Sirius	1954-57	400	1/40-mm AA, 1 or 2/20-mm
4 "ham"	1954-55	140	1/20-mm AA
1 trawler type	1965	1,800	1/40-mm AA

◆ **25 (+5) minehunters and minesweepers**

5 (+5) Tripartite (minehunters)	1979-. . .	500	1/20-mm AA
5 Circé (minehunters)	1970-72	460	1/20-mm AA
10 U.S. MSO (5 minehunters)	1953-56	700	1/40-mm AA
5 Sirius	1955-56	400	1 or 2/20-mm AA

◆ **18 (+1) amphibious warfare ships**

0 (+1) TCD 90	1968	9300	2 Sadral, 1/40-mm AA
2 Ouragan	1963-67	5,800	4/40-mm AA
3 Argens	1958-60	1,750	3/40-mm AA
4 Champlain (Batral)	1973-82	750	2/40-mm AA
9 EDIC	1958-69	250	2/20-mm AA

1984-88 Program

	Orders		Deliveries	
Program	1984-85	1986-88	1984-88	Post-1988
Nuclear-powered aircraft carriers		1		1
Destroyers, frigates, and corvettes		3 FL 25	2 C70 ASW (#5 & 6) 1 C70 AA (#1)	1 C70 ASW (#7) 3 C70 AA 3 FL 25
Nuclear-powered attack submarines	1 (#6)	2 (#7, 8)	3 (#2, 3, 4)	4 (#5-8)
Mine countermeasures ships	2 exp* 4†	5‡	8 Tripartite 2 exp.* 4†	1 Tripartite 5‡
Patrol boats	4 P400		10 P400	
Replenishment ships		1 *Durance* (#5) 1 AFS	1 *Durance* (#4)	1 *Durance* (#5) 1 AFS
Landing ships	1 LSD	2 (#2 & 3)		3 (LSD 1-3)
Atlantic Mk 2 patrol aircraft	2	14		16

*Mine warfare experimental ships
†Mine disposal diver support ships
‡900-ton oceangoing minehunters, able to sweep to 300 m depths.
Note: Nuclear-powered attack submarines 2-5 are of the *Rubis* class; 6-8 are of the "Post-*Rubis*" class

WEAPONS AND SYSTEMS

A. MISSILES

◆ **strategic ballistic**

M 20

This missile, which has replaced the M 2, has two stages, is aerodynamically unstable, and has the following characteristics:

Total height	10.40 m	Launch	compressed air
Height 1st stage	5.20 m	Launch weight	20 tons
Height 2nd stage	2.60 m	Max. range	3,000 km
Diameter	1.50 m		

Solid propulsion system:

fuel mass	10 tons, 1st stage 6 tons, 2nd stage
thrust	45 tons, 1st stage 32 tons, 2nd stage
burn duration	50 sec., 1st stage 52 sec., 2nd stage

The thermonuclear warhead is in the megaton range and has been especially "hardened" to facilitate penetration and to counter nuclear anti-missile defenses.

M 4, Improved M 4

This missile entered service in 1985 aboard *L'Inflexible* and has three stages. Characteristics include:

Total height	11.05 m	Launch	powder charge
Diameter	1.93 m	Launch weight	around 36 tons
		Max. range	4,000 km (M 4B: 5,000)

Solid propulsion system:

fuel mass	20 tons, 1st stage; 8 tons, 2nd stage; 1.5 tons, 3rd stage
thrust	70 tons, 1st stage; 30 tons, 2nd stage; 7 tons, 3rd stage
burn duration	65 sec., 1st stage; 75 sec., 2nd stage; 45 sec., 3rd stage

The payload will be 6 warheads of around 150 KT, of great precision and with improved penetration over the already excellent M 20. The launch interval will be shorter between missiles than with the M 20 and will be capable of being carried out at greater depths. The first at-sea firings took place in early 3-82, from *Gymnote.* M 4 will be backfitted into all earlier submarines except *Le Redoutable* by 1992. To effect installation, it will not be necessary to replace the existing missile tubes. The M 4 has 6 TN-70 warheads, which spread over a 150- × 350-km area at a range of 4,000 km; The Improved M 4 uses the TN-71 reentry vehicle to a range of 5,000 km.

M 5

A new weapon being developed for the "second generation" ballistic-missile submarines. To have a range of 6,000 km (3,240 n.m.), with multiple independently targeted warheads (MIRV).

◆ **surface-to-air**

Masurca

A medium-range missile (30 nautical-mile range, intercept between 100 ft and 75,000 ft) launched by a solid-propellant booster, which in a few seconds brings it to a speed close to Mach 3; a slower-burning solid propellant maintains this speed throughout the flight. The missile and booster together are 8.6 m long and weight 2,098 kg. Other characteristics are:

	Missile	Booster
Length	5.38 m	3.32 m
Diameter	0.406 m	0.57 m
Span of fins	—	1.5 m
Weight	950.0 kg	1,148.0 kg
Warhead	100.0 kg	—

Mod. 3, a semiactive homing missile, is the only one now in service. It follows a trajectory determined by proportional navigation, keeping its antenna pointed at the target, which is illuminated by the launching ship's radar transmitter.

Masurca, which is installed in the *Suffren*-class guided-missile destroyers and in the guided-missile cruiser *Colbert,* consists of (1) a target-designator and weapon-assignment console, including a computer, which uses the shipboard search radar and the Senit automatic tactical data system, and (2) two guidance systems, each with: DRBR 51 tracking radar, a director carrying the rear-reference beam and illumination beam for the control system, an illumination beam, a twin launcher, storage and maintenance facilities, including two horizontal ready-service drums containing 18 missiles in addition to reserve missiles in the magazines, and IFF and control equipment.

The Masurca systems aboard *Colbert* and the *Suffren* class were modernized 1983-85 to keep the system up-to-date to the end of its expected service life (1995).

Standard SM-1 MR

A one-stage U.S.-designed-and-manufactured missile with solid fuel. Characteristics:

Length: 4.60 m	Guidance: semiactive homing, proximity fuze
Diameter: .41 m	Range: 50,000 m, max.
Weight: 590 kg	Interception altitude: 60 ft to 80,000 ft

The complete system consists of, in addition to the missile:

1 single Mk 13 launcher, 1 vertical stowage-loader containing 40 missiles, various computers, SPS 39B height-finding radar, and 2 SPG 51C tracking radars.

SM-1 MR is mounted on T-47-type destroyers modified for Tartar and will be installed in the C-70 AAW-type destroyers, which will have the DRBJ 11B height-finding radar. It has replaced the earlier Tartar ITR and SM-1A in French naval service.

Crotale

A French Air Force missile adapted for naval use. Electronics are by Thomson-CSF and the missile by Matra. Characteristics for the R440N missile are:

Length: 2.930 m

MISSILES *(continued)*

Diameter: 0.156 m
Span: cruciform (0.54 m with fins extended), antipitching canards forward
Weight: 85.1 kg
Range: 8,000 m
Interception altitudes: 150 ft to 12,000 ft
Warhead: 14 kg
Guidance: beam-riding, then detonation by infrared fuze incorporated in the missile
Launcher: octuple

Crotale is installed on the F 67 and C 70 types of destroyers. It is used with DRBV 51C radar and has a Thomson tracking radar in the KU band. Eighteen reload missiles are carried in the magazine. The prototype was installed in the test ship *Ile d'Oléron* in May 1977, while the first operational installation was aboard *Georges Leygues* in 1978.

Crotale is being updated to enable it to handle Mach. 2.0 targets at altitudes down to 4 m. The missiles, named Crotale EDIR *(Écartometrie Différentielle Infra Rouge),* are being equipped with a new proximity fuze, and an infrared tracker is being added to the launcher/director; range is increased to 13,000 m. Will be carried by *Clemenceau* and *Foch* and by the 7th C 70-class ASW destroyer and will be backfitted in earlier Crotale ships beginning in 1986.

SADRAL (System d'Auto Défense Rapprocheé Anti-aérienne Leger)

A contract has been given to Matra to develop a new short-range lightweight surface-to-air missile, the SATCP *(Surface-Air, á Trés Courte Portie).* The system will have an automatic director and IR homing, with laser-backup proximity and impact fuzing. The missile itself, to be called "Mistral," will have:

Length: 1.80 m — Warhead: 3 kg, tungsten ball
Diameter: 0.90 m — Range: under 500 to around 6,000 m, at altitudes down to 3m.
Weight: 17 kg
Speed: Mach 2.7

The missiles will be installed in a 6-missile, rapid-reload, lightweight launcher. The system should be operational about 1988 in the antiaircraft destroyers of the C 70 AAW type.

Matra is also offering the vertically launched SAMAT system in several versions. SAMAT 1 and 2 would use the *Mica* missile body, derived from the *Magic*-successor air-to-air missile. SAMAT 1 would have IR homing, a range of 4 km, and is intended to supplement Crotale. SAMAT 2 would have active radar terminal homing, a range of 10–11 km, and is intended to replace Crotale. SAMAT 3 would use a ramjet sustainer motor for longer ranges and would have the SAMAT 2 seeker.

Aerospatiale is developing the SAN (Surface-Air Naval) missile system for deployment about 1995. It will have a 5–7-km range and use an I/J-band radar control system.

◆ Surface-to-surface

MM 38 Exocet Manufacturer: S.N.I.A.S. (Aerospatiale)

A homing missile with solid-fuel propulsion. Characteristics:
Weight: 700 kg, approx. (explosive charge: more than 150 kg)
Speed: Mach 1 — Diameter: 0.35 m
Range: 37 km, min — Wingspan: 1.00 m
Length: 5.20 m — Cylindrical body with a pointed nose, cruciform wings with arrow shape.

The fire-control solution requires a fix on the target provided by the surface radar of the firing ship and uses the necessary equipment for launching the missile and determining the correct range and height bearing of the target.

The missile is launched at a slight elevation (about 15°). After the boost phase, it reaches its flight altitude and is stabilized at between 3 and 15 meters. Altitude is maintained by a radar altimeter.

During the first part of the flight, the missile is automatically guided by an inertial system that has received the azimuth of the target. When within a certain distance from the target, an automatic homing radar begins to seek the target, picks it up and directs the missile. Great effort has been made to protect the missile from countermeasures during this phase. A new "Super ADAC" seeker, with improved anti-jamming features is offered for backfit to earlier missiles.

Detonation takes place upon impact or by pseudo-proximity fuze, according to interception conditions, size of the target ship, and the condition of the sea.

SM 39 Exocet

A submarine torpedo-tube-launched version of the Exocet concept, SM 39 began in 1981 aboard the *Narval*-class submarine *Requin.* It will have a range of 50 km. The missile is 4.7-m long by 350 mm in diameter and weights 650 kg. With its solid-fueled launch/ejection capsule, the missile is 5.8 m long, weights 1,350 kg, and fits within a 533-mm torpedo tube. The system operational 1985 on *Saphir.*

MM 40 Exocet

An offshoot of the MM 38 and the AM 39 and also built by S.N.I.A.S., the MM 40 is an over-the-horizon missile whose range will be adapted to radar performance, but it will be able to use fire-control data relayed by an outside source. Instead of the usual metal launcher, it has a fiberglass, cylindrical one, which, because it is lighter and has less fittings, increases firepower by allowing more missiles to be carried.

It has been proposed to equip the future C 70 ASW-type guided-missile destroyers with eight launchers each (four per side) for MM 40, and the *Montcalm* will be the first ship to have it. In older ships with box launchers for MM 38 Exocet missiles, the old launchers will be retained, with one MM 40 in each box.

Length: 5.80 m — Weight: 850 kg
Diameter: 0.35 m — Speed: Mach .95
Wingspan: 1.135 m — Range: 65 km

SS 12 M Manufacturer: Aerospatiale

Wire-guided, solid-fueled missile. Characteristics:
Length: 1.870 m — Weight: 75 kg (upon firing)
Diameter: 0.210 m — Warhead: 30 kg (about)
Wingspan: 0.650 — Range: 5,500 m
No longer used on French Navy ships but is used by foreign fleets.

B. AVIATION MISSILES

◆ Air-to-ground

ANS (Anti-navire Supersonique)

A new project, succeeding the ASMP project *(Air-Surface á Moyenne Porte)* and intended for use by Super Étendard carrier-based and Tornado land-based aircraft. A surface-to-surface version is projected. Being developed jointly by Aerospatiale and Messerschmidt-Bölkow-Blohm for service introduction in the late 1980s.

Length: 5.38 m — Weight: . . .
Diameter: 0.35 m — Range: 50–100 km
Wingspan: 0.956 m — Speed: Mach 2.4

ANS will fit in the MM 40 Exocet launch tube for shipboard use. For use by helicopters, Atlantic II patrol airplanes, and West German Tornado fighter-bombers, it will employ two boosters.

AM 39 Manufacturer: Aerospatiale

This is the air-to-sea version of the MM 38. After being launched, it has the same flight characteristics as the MM 38.
Length: 4.633 m
Diameter: 0.348 m
Wingspan: 1.004 m
Weight: 650 kg (before launching)
Range: 50–70 km, according to altitude and speed at launch
Radar: Active home-seeking head (EMD)

Operational since 1978, AM 39 is known as a "fire and forget" missile because it permits an aircraft that has fired to renew its attack or to seek a new target. It will be used with the Atlantique Mk 2 patrol aircraft and the Super Étendard aircraft. It is equally suitable for use by such medium-weight helicopters as the Super Frélon.

AS 11 Builder: Aerospatiale

A wire-guided system with optical alignment on the target. Used for training by CM 175 aircraft.
Length: 1.210 m — Wingspan: 0.50 m
Diameter: 0.164 m — Weight: 29.900 kg

AS 12 Builder: Aerospatiale

A wire-guided system with optical alignment on the target. Used by WG-13 Lynx helicopter.
Length: 1.870 m — Wingspan: 0.650 m
Diameter: 0.210 m — Weight: 75 kg
Range: Maximum 7,500 to 8,000 m; minimum 1,500 m

AS 15 TT Builder: Aerospatiale

Length: 2.16 m — Range: 15 km
Weight: 96 kg
For use by light helicopters (Dauphin, Lynx); developed under the Saudi Arabian "Sawari" program. First production deliveries 3-85.

AS 20 Builder: Aerospatiale

Length: 2.60 m — Weight: 140 kg
Diameter: 0.25 m — Guidance: radio command
Wingspan: 0.80 m — Range: 4,000 m to 8,000 m
Used in firing training for the AS 30.

AS 30 Builder: Aerospatiale

System developed for firing from a maneuvering aircraft at middle, low, or very low altitude. Used by the Super Étendard.
Length: 3.785 m — Wingspan: 1.000 m
Diameter: 0.342 m — Total weight: 528 kg
Range: maximum 9 to 12,000 m; minimum 1,500 m
Guidance: radio command

AS 37 Martel Builders: Matra and Hawker Siddeley Dynamics

Two types, television and anti-radar. Only the latter is used in the French Navy.
Length: 4.122 m — Total weight: 531 m
Diameter: 0.40 m — Range: over 20,000 m
Wingspan: 1.192 m
Passive homing head (EMD); the missile homes on the radar emissions of the enemy vessel. Immediately after being fired, the missile is on its own, permitting the aircraft to depart or evade. Used with Atlantic Mk 1 aircraft.

AVIATION MISSILES *(continued)*

◆ **Air-to-air**

R 530 Builder: Matra

There are two versions of this missile: infrared (IR) and radar-homing (EMD).
Length: IR type: 3.198 m; EMD type: 3.284 m
Diamter: 0.263 m
Wingspan: 1.103 m
Weight: IR type: 193.5 kg, EMD type: 192 kg
Range: maximum 10,000 m: minimum 5,000 m
Guidance: Semi-passive-homing (MD) or infrared-homing

Sidewinder

The French Navy uses this air-to-air American missile (*see* U.S.A. section).

Magic Builder: Matra

Length: 2.900 m
Diameter: 0.157 m
Wingspan: 0.660 m
Weight: 89 kg
Range: 300/8,000 m
Guidance: Infrared-homing

C. GUNS

100-mm Compact (Usinor/Creusot-Loire)

Single-barrel automatic, for export only.
Weight of mount: 17.3 tons
Length of barrel: 55 calibers
Range: 17,200 m
Muzzle-velocity: 870m/sec.
Max. effective range for surface fire: 12,000 m
Max. effective range for autiaircraft fire: 6,000 m
Max. rate of fire: 90 max., or 20 or 45 rpm
Arc of elevation: −15° to +80°
Max. speed: training 50°/sec, elevation, 33°/sec

Most installations have a 42-round magazine, while those for Malaysia had 90-round magazines. Used by Saudi Arabian frigates; two sold to China.

100-mm, Models 1953 and 1968

Single-barrel automatic, for use against aircraft, surface vessels, or land targets. Model 1968 is a lighter version of Model 1953. The ammunition is the same. Characteristics of Model 1968:
Weight of mount: 22 tons
Length of barrel: 55 calibers
Range at 40° elevation: 17,000 m
Maximum effective range for surface fire: 15,000 m
Maximum effective range for antiaircraft fire: 8,000 m
Maximum rate of fire: 60 rounds/minute (78 rds/min in recent models)
Arc of elevation: −15° to +80°
Maximum speed: training, 40°/sec, elevation, 25°/sec

Model 1953 uses an analog fire-control system with electro-mechanical and electronic equipment for the fire-control solution. The director can be operated in optical and radar modes. Used in *Jeanne d'Arc,* the *Suffren* class, *La Galissonière, Surcouf* T-47 ASW destroyers, and the *Cdt. Rivière* class.

Model 1968 used a digital fire-control system, with central units, and memory disks or magnetic tape for data storage. Light radar gun director. Optical direction equipment can be added. Used in the *Colbert, Tourville* class, *Georges Leygues* class, *Aconit, Duperré,* and A-69 class.

57-mm Model 1951

Twin-barrel automatic:
Length of barrel: 60 calibers
Muzzle velocity: 865 m/sec
Maximum range: 13,000 m
Effective antiaircraft range: 5,000 m
Maximum rate of fire: 60 rounds/min per barrel
Arc of elevation: −8° to 90°
Maximum rate of fire: 60 rounds per minute, per barrel

30-mm

Single-barrel automatic:
Length: 2.440 m
Weight: 4 tons
Muzzle velocity: 1,000 m/sec
Maximum effective range: 2,800 m
Maximum rate of fire: 650 rounds per minute

Used only on the frigates *Balny, Enseigne de Vaisseau Henry, Protet,* and *Victor Schoelcher.*

Also in service are typical 40-mm guns based on Bofors designs and 20-mm guns of Oerlikon design.

A new 20-mm mounting has been designed by DCAN for the GIAT CN-MIT-20F2 gun, which has a 650-720 rd/min firing rate. Two 150-round magazines are carried on the mount. Weight: 322 kg empty. Length: 2.6 m.

D. ANTISUBMARINE WEAPONS

Malafon

A glider that carries L-4 torpedoes and is launched with the assistance of a double booster. It is stabilized by automatic pilot and guided by radio command.
Glider: speed, 230 m/sec; range, 12,000 m
Missile: length, 6.15 m; diameter, 0.65 m; span, 3.30 m; weight, including torpedo, 1,500 kg

The Malafon, initially built by Latécoère in partnership with St. Trôpez, is installed in the two *Suffren*-class destroyers, *La Galissonnière,* the Type T-47 ASW conversions, the *Aconit,* and the *Tourville*-class destroyers.

A successor to Malafon is planned, using the Murène homing torpedo as a payload.

Malafon on launcher M. Louagie, 6-84

375-mm Rocket Launchers, Models 1964 or 1972

Sextuple mount. Automatic loading in vertical position. Firing rate, 1 rocket/second. Range: 1,600 m. Time or proximity fuze. Based on Bofors quadruple mounting. Normally has six illumination-flare rocket rails mounted also.

Automatic-loading 305-mm ASW and bombardment mortar—with flare rails

305-mm Mortar

Quadruple mount; automatic loading. ASW projectile weight: 230 kg; range: 400 to 3,000 m. Can also fire a 100-kg projectile against land targets; range: 6,000 m. Normally has four illumination-flare rocket rails mounted on the face of the rotating housing. Used only on the *Commandant Rivière* class (removed from *Aconit*).

E. TORPEDOES

◆ **For surface ships:**

	Weight in kg	Diameter in mm	Speed in kts
L 3	900	550	25
L 4	500	533	30
L 5, Mod. 1 and Mod. 4	1,000	533	35

◆ **For submarines**

	Weight in kg	Diameter in mm	Speed in kts
Z 13	1,700	550	30
E 12	1,600	550	25
E 14	900	550	25
L 5, Mod. 3	1,300	533	35
F 17 Mod. 1	1,300	533	35
F 17 Mod. 2(Murène)	1,320	533	35

TORPEDOES *(continued)*

◆ **For aircraft**

In addition to the U.S. Mk 46 torpedo, French naval aircraft use the **L 4** torpedo.

NOTE: The new F 17P (F 17 Mod. 2) Murène general-purpose wire-guided ASW torpedo entered service in 1985. 5.62 m long, it weights 250 kg and used a silver-zinc battery. Range is 20–30 km.

F. SONARS

◆ **For surface ships**

	Type	Frequency	Average range
DUBA 1	Hull	HF	2,500 m
DUBA 3	Hull	HF	3,000 m
DUBV 24	Hull	LF	6,000 m
DUBV 23	Bow	LF	*see* Remarks
DUBV 24C	Hull	MF	*see* Remarks
DUBV 43	Towed	LF	*see* Remarks
DUBA 25	Hull	MF (9 kHz)	*see* Remarks
DUBA 26	Hull	MF	*see* Remarks
DUBM 20	Hull—on *Circé*-class minehunters		
DUBM 21	Hull—on new Tripartite and modernized MSO minehunters		
DUBM 41	Towed—on modernized MSO; sidescan minehunting		
DSBV 61	A towed passive linear array system, VLF		
Diodon	A 12 kHz hull-mounted sonar developed for export. Is also available in 11 and 13 kHz models.		
SQS-505	Hull—Canadian set on aircraft carriers		
SQS-17	U.S. mid-frequency set on *Cdt. Rivière* class		

DUBV 43 VDS fish and hoist gear on Aconit (D 609) S. Terzibaschitsch, 6-82

REMARKS: DUBV 23 and DUBV 43 are used simultaneously and, under normal sound-propagation conditions, achieve ranges of 8,000 and 10,000 meters; the DUBV-43C operates at depths of up to 700 m; when used with DUBV-43C, hull-mounted sonar becomes DUBV-24. In certain bathymetric conditions, the range is 20,000 meters. DUBA 25 is a new sonar designed for the A-69 class and the C 70 AA destroyers. The DUBM-41B can be towed at 10 kts and covers a 400-m swath, compared to the 4-kt/50-m capability of the DUBM 41.

◆ **For submarines**

Listening devices, active-passive sonars, and underwater telephone equipment, including:

DUUA 1	On the *Narval* and unmodernized *Daphne* classes, and *Agosta:* active
DUUA 2	On modernized *Daphne, Agosta,* and *Rubis* classes (DUUA 2B in latter): active
DSUV 2	Hydrophone array on *Narval* and *Daphne* classes
DSUV 22	Hydrophone array on the *Rubis* class
DUUV 23	Panoramic passive array on the ballistic-missile submarines
DSUX 21	Multifunction system for *L'Inflexible* and earlier missile submarines

◆ **For helicopters**

	Frequency	Remark
AQS-13	HF	U.S. sonar
DUAV 4	HF	In the WG-13 Lynx

G. COMBAT INFORMATION SYSTEMS SENIT

This system serves four principal purposes:

It establishes the combat situation from the manual collection of information derived from detection equipment on board and from the automatic or manual collection of information from external sources.

It disseminates the above data to the ship and to other vessels by automatic means (Links 11 and 14).

It assists in decision making.

It transmits to the target-designation console all the information it requires.

The several versions of the SENIT are similar in general concept but differ in construction and programming in order to ensure fulfillment of the various missions assigned to each type of ship.

SENIT 1: A system with one or two computers. Installed in the *Suffren,* the *Duquesne,* and the *Colbert.*

SENIT 2: A single-computer system. Installed in the T-47 type *Kersaint*-class destroyers, as well as in the *Duperré,* which uses a version with two computers.

SENIT 3: A central system consisting of two computers and two memory banks, the entire group designed for the control of various weapons (guns, Malafon ASW system, torpedoes). Installed in the *Aconit,* and the three *Tourville*-class ships.

The above three systems are based on equipment of U.S. origin, some built in France under license.

SENIT 4: A system conceived by the French Navy's programming center and designed around the French Iris N 55 computer. Fitted in the *Georges Leygues* class.

SENIT 5: Also designed by the French Navy's programming center, this system will be fitted on small ships. It uses the French M 15 minicomputer.

SENIT 6: Another system designed by the French Navy's programming center. It will equip the future C-70 AAW version of the *Georges Leygues* class. It combines a number of M 15 computers and a new generation of display devices particularly adapted for command purposes.

DLT D3

All submarines subsequent to the *Narval* class use the Direction de Lancement Torpilles DLT D3. There are three identical data displays for current and historical target data, and the system can be used to launch torpedoes and missiles.

H. RADARS

◆ **Air search**

DRBV 20C:	Metric, long-range. Mounted on aircraft carriers and *Colbert.*
DRBV 22A:	Mounted in T-47 ASW version destroyers, frigates, *Duperré, Aconit,* and *La Galissonière.* L-band (23 cm).
DRBV 22C:	*Ile d'Oléron.*
DRBV 22D:	*Jeanne d'Arc, Henri Poincaré.*
DRBV 22E:	*Rance.*
DRBV-23B:	On aircraft carriers
DRBV 23C:	Mounted in *Colbert.*
DRBV 26:	Mounted in the *Tourville* and first 4 *Georges Leygues* class and aboard AA destroyers. 150-n.m. range. Commercial name: Jupiter.
DRBV 27:	New radar in development for the new carriers.

◆ **Height-finding/three-dimensional**

DRBI 10:	Mounted in aircraft carriers, *Colbert, Ile d'Oléron.* "Nodding"-type antenna with "Robinson" feed.
DRBI 23:	Mounted in the *Duquesne* and *Suffren;* monopulse.
SPS-39B:	American radar. Mounted on Standard-equipped T-47-class destroyers.
DRBJ 11B:	Pulse-coded radar for the C-70 AAW-class guided-missile destroyers and the new nuclear-powered carriers.

◆ **Surface and low-altitude air search**

DRBV 15:	Pulse-doppler design, with pulse-compression and frequency agility, intended to replace the DRBV 51. Commercial name: Sea Tiger. Replaced DRBV 13 in *Aconit* and will replace DRBV 50 in the *Suffren* class, in the carrier *Jeanne d'Arc,* and in the final three C 70 ASW destroyers.
DRBV 31:	Mounted on the Standard-equipped T-47-class destroyers.
DRBV 50:	Mounted on aircraft carriers, *Jeanne d'Arc,* T-47 ASW destroyers, the *Rhin, Ile d'Oléron, Colbert,* and *La Galissonnière.*
DRBV 51A:	Mounted on A-69 class and the *Duperré.*
DRBV 51B:	Mounted on the *Georges Leygues* class.
DRBV 51C:	Mounted on the *Tourville* class.

◆ **Navigational**

Decca RM 416, 1229, etc.: Commercial radars used on smaller units.
DRBN 32: French Navy designator for Decca 1226 navigational radar.

◆ **Fire-control**

DRBC 31:	For the 57-mm guns of the *Colbert* and T-47 Tartar destroyers.
DRBC 32A:	For the 100-mm guns on ASW-modified T-47-class destroyers, some frigates, the *Jeanne d'Arc, Clemenceau,* and *La Galissonnière.*
DRBC 32B:	For 100-mm guns on the *Aconit.*
DRBC 32C:	Mounted on the *Colbert,* carriers, and the A69 class.
DRBC 32D:	Mounted on the *Tourville* class.
DRBC 32E:	Mounted on the A-69-class corvettes. X-band.
DRBC 33:	A monopulse, frequency-agile system in development for the C 70 AA class and for backfit on the *Suffren* class.
SPG-51C:	U.S. tracking radar used with the Standard system on the T-47-type AAW destroyers.
DRBC 51:	Tracking radar for the Masurca on the *Colbert, Suffren,* and *Duquesne.* C-band (5-cm) tracker, 7-cm command signal.

Also in use is the DIBV Vampir, an infrared detection and fire-control system built by Thomson-CSF.

I. COUNTERMEASURES

The French navy uses the eight-barreled Syllex chaff launcher (a version of the British Knebworth/Corvus), which is being replaced by the Sagaie, a long-range system. Smaller ships will receive the Dagaie system, and some major classes will get both. Both Sagaie and Dagaie are fired automatically by the electronic intercept system. Sagaie has a range of 8 km for chaff or 3 km for chaff/IR deception rounds.

Electronics countermeasures systems in use include:
Intercept systems: ARBR/ARBA 10C, ARBR 10F, ARBR 16, ARBR 17
Jammers: ARBB 32, ARBB 33

J. COMMUNICATIONS

Recent construction or recently modified major ships are receiving radome-mounted antennas for the Syracuse satellite communications transmission system. The system will be fully operational in 1987. Syracuse operates at 7-8 gHz and transmission rate is 2400 bit voice/75-baud telemetry per sec.

To ensure communications with submerged ballistic-missile submarines, the ELF Astarte system is being developed, with a transmitter at Rosnay. Also being developed is an airborne system using U.S. VLF equipment mounted in four Transall aircraft.

NUCLEAR-POWERED AIRCRAFT CARRIER

◆ **0 (+1) Richelieu class** Bldr: Brest Naval Arsenal

	Laid down	L	In serv.
R. . . RICHELIEU	6-88	. . .	1996

D: 34,000 tons (39,680 fl) **S:** 27 kts at 38,060 tons
Dim: 261.50 (238.00 wl) × 61.00 (31.50 wl) × 8.45
A: 35 to 40 aircraft (including fixed-wing fighters and helicopters)—56 SAAM vertical-launch SAM (VIII × 7)—3/Sadral point-defense SAM (VI × 3)—possible 8/20-mm AA (I × 8)
Electron Equipt: Radar: 2/Decca nav., 1/DRBJ 11B, 1/DRBV 15, 1/DRBV 27, EW: ARBR 17, ARBB 33, 4/Sagaie RL
IR: DIBV 10 *Vampir*
M: 2 131-megawatt, type K15 pressurized-water reactor plants; double-reduction geared steam turbines; 2 4-bladed props; 83,000 hp
Electric: 13,100 kw (4/2,000-kw and 6/850-kw turbo alternators)
Man: 1,150 total ship's crew, plus 550 air group personnel (1,850 total accomm.)

REMARKS: General: This ship represents an expansion on the abortive PH 74/PH 75 nuclear carrier program of the 1970s and is intended as replacement for *Clemenceau,* which will be 35 years old when the "PAN" (Porte-Avions Nuclear) enters service. A second unit to replace *Foch* falls outside the current 1984-88 planning program and would complete around 2000. Will be named *Richelieu.*

Hull: Design based on *Clemenceau,* but with more robust construction and protection systems. Fin stabilizers will be installed.

Aviation installations: The flight deck will be 261.5 m long, with a 195-m 8.3-degree angled deck portion. Maximum flight deck width is 60 m for an area of 12,300 m². There will be two U.S. Type C13 steam catapults, one on the angled deck and the other on the port side of the bow, an arrangement that emphasizes parking arrangements over an ability to launch and land simultaneously. There will be two 50-ton deck-edge elevators, both to starboard amidships. The nuclear propulsion arrangement allows the island to be mounted much farther forward than is standard practice, ahead of both elevators, and permits more efficient deck utilization. The 138-m long by 29-m broad by 6.1-m high (4,600 m²) hangar will be lower than on the *Clemenceau* class, but considerably larger in area and better protected. The second ship may substitute a ski-jump takeoff ramp for the bow catapult if V/STOL aircraft are carried. The initial combat aircraft will be the Super Étendard, but a new fighter bomber, the ACM *(Avion de Combat Maritime)* may be developed to replace the Super Étendard in the later 1990s. Aviation fuel capacity: 3,000 m³; munitions magazines: 4,900 m³.

Propulsion: The plant will be located in five compartments.

Electronics: Will have the SENIT-6 data system. There will be a rocket-launched torpedo decoy system.

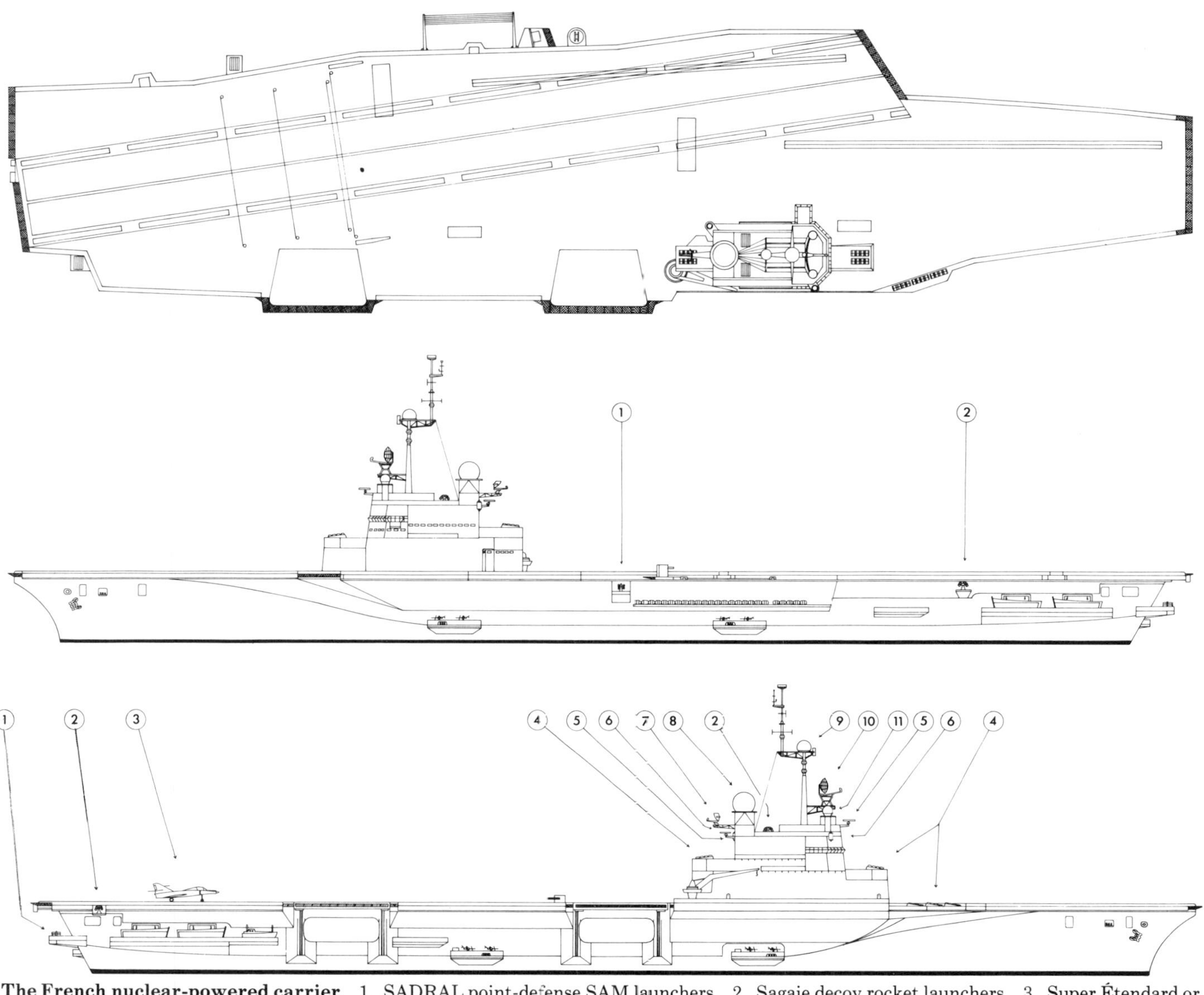

The French nuclear-powered carrier 1. SADRAL point-defense SAM launchers 2. Sagaie decoy rocket launchers 3. Super Étendard or successor fighter-bomber 4. SAAM vertical-launch SAM groups 5. Decca nav. radars 6. EW antenna arrays 7. DRBV 15 radar 8. DRBJ 11B radar 9. TACAN 10. DRBV 27 radar 11. Syracuse SATCOMM antenna radomes

AIRCRAFT CARRIERS

◆ **2 Clemenceau class**

	Budget	Bldr	Laid down	L	In serv.
R 98 Clemenceau	1953	Brest Arsenal	11-55	21-12-57	22-11-61
R 99 Foch	1955	Ch. Atlantique	2-57	28-7-60	15-7-63

D: 22,000 tons (27,307 mean, 32,700 fl)
S: 32 kts **Range:** 4,800/23; 7,500/18
Dim: 265.0 (238.0 pp) × 31.72 beam × 51.2 flight deck × 7.8 light draft × 8.6 fl
A: R 98: 2/Crotale EDIR SAM syst. (VIII × 2; 36 missiles)—4/100-mm Model 1953 DP
R 99: 8/100-mm Model 1953 DP
Both: 16/Super Étendard, 10/F-8E Crusader, 3/Étendard IVP, 7/Alizé, 2 or more/helicopters
Electron Equipt: R 98: Radar: 1/Decca 1226, 1/DRBV 23B, 1/DRBV 15, 2/DRBI 10, 2/DRBC 32C, 1/NRBA 51
EW: ARBR 16, ARBX 10B, 2/Sagaie RL
Sonar: SQS-503—TACAN: SRN-6
R 99: Radar: 1/Decca 1226, 1/DRBV 20C, 1/DRBV 23B, 2/DRBI 10, 1/DRBV 50, 1/NRBA 50, 2/DRBC 31C, 2/DRBC 32C
EW:. . .
Sonar: SQS-503—TACAN:SRN-6
M: 2 sets Parsons GT; 2 props; 126,000 hp **Electric:** 14,000 kw
Boilers: 6; 45 kg/cm², 450°C **Fuel:** 3,720 tons **Endurance:** 60 days
Armor: Reinforced flight deck, armored bulkheads in engine room and magazines, reinforced-steel bridge superstructure
Man: Peacetime: As aircraft carriers: 64 officers, 476 petty officers, 798 other enlisted. Total: 1,338 men
As helicopter carriers: 45 officers, 392 petty officers, 547 other enlisted. Total: 984

Remarks: Flight deck 257 m in length; deck angled at 8°, 165.5 × 29.5; deck forward of the angled deck: 93 × 28; width of the deck abreast the island: 35. Hangar dimensions, 180 × 22 to 24 × 7 (height). Two elevators 16 m long, 11 m in width, one forward on the main flight deck, one slightly abaft the island, able to raise a 15-ton aircraft 8.50 m in 9 seconds. Two 50-meter Mitchell-Brown type BS5 steam catapults, able to launch 15/20-ton aircraft at 110 knots, one forward, another on the angled deck. New catapult mechanisms installed in the mid-1980s. Optical-mirror landing equipment of French manufacture.

The propulsion machinery was built by the Chantiers de l'Atlantique. Living spaces are air-conditioned. Medium-sized island with three bridges: flag, navigation, aviation. Communication systems, especially with fighter aircraft, are a significant aspect of the ships' capabilities.

The *Foch,* built in a special dry dock at St. Nazaire, was towed to Brest for the installation of her armament.

Aviation fuel: 1,800 m³ of jet fuel and 109 m³ of aviation gasoline carried by the *Foch;* 1,200 m³ of jet fuel and 400 m³ of aviation gasoline by the *Clemenceau.*

Between September 1977 and November 1978, *Clemenceau* underwent a significant refit in the Toulon dockyard. The work consisted of a general overhaul of her installations and living spaces, modernization of the flight deck, reinforcement of the arrest-

Foch (R 99)—with Syracuse SATCOMM system Pradignac & Leo, 1984

Foch (R 99) Pradignac & Leo, 1984

Foch (R 99) L. & L. Van Ginderen, 1983

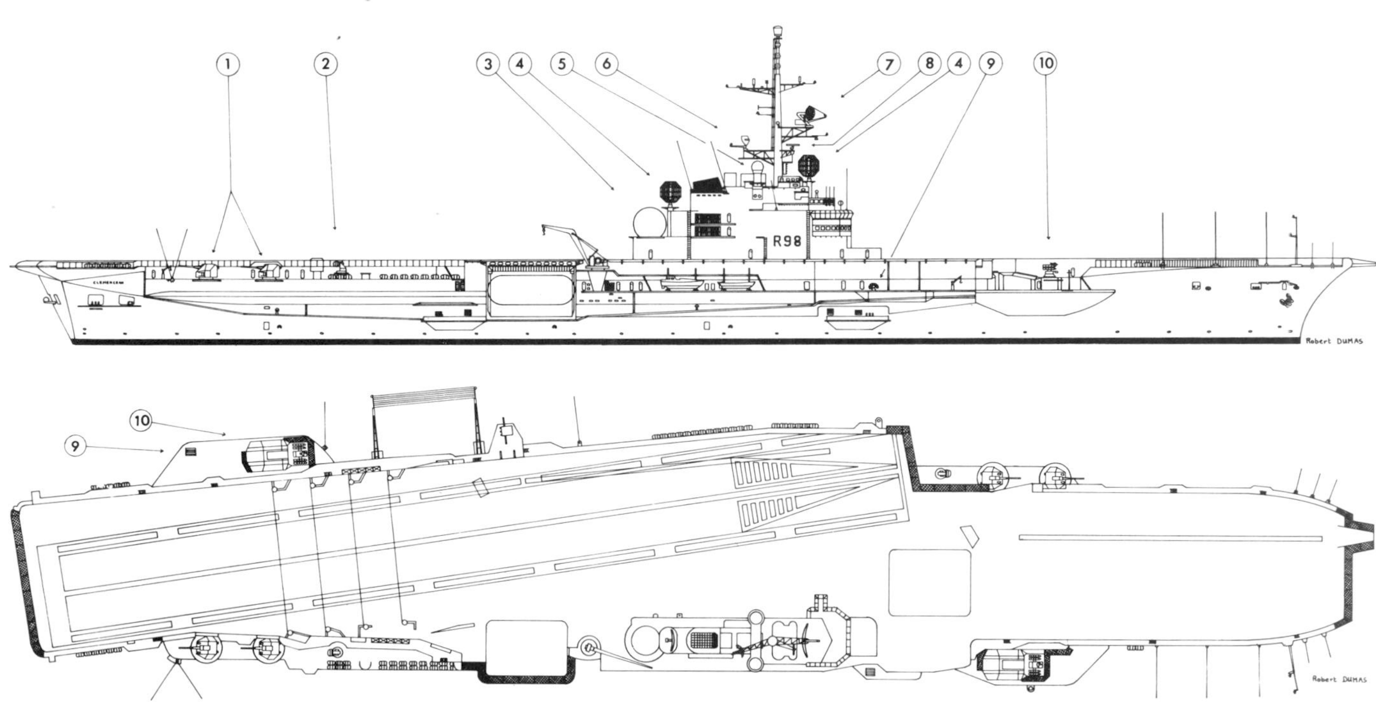

Clemenceau (R 98) 1. 100-mm Model 1953 DP 2. DRBC 32C f.c. radar directors 3. NRBA 51 aircraft landing-aid radar 4. DRBI 10 height-finding radar 5. Syracuse SATCOMM antenna radomes 6. DRBV 15 search radar 7. DRBV 23B early-warning radar 8. Decca 1226 nav. radar 9. Sagaie decoy RL 10. Crotale EDIR SAM launchers

AIRCRAFT CARRIERS *(continued)*

ing gear, strengthening of the catapults, machinery overhaul, and the addition of two auxiliary boilers. Her electronic systems were modernized, and she was given the SENIT 2 combat data system removed from the inactivated destroyer *Jaurreguiberry*. On the *Clemenceau*, this system has three main functions: establishment of a situation based on information from external sources (land-based radars, aircraft, ships); dissemination of those data to the ship and to other ships; and assistance in decision making. The ship was equipped with a closed-circuit television system that displays needed information in interested parts of the ship: flight-deck control, the combat operations center, the ready rooms, the air operations office. To operate the Super Étendard, the *Clemenceau* has been fitted with a central inertial guidance system that transfers information to the inertial guidance system in each plane. Her magazines have been modified to carry AN-52 tactical nuclear weapons. The *Foch* underwent a similar overhaul 15-7-80 to 4-12-81, receiving SENIT 2 from the inactivated destroyer *Tartu*.

Clemenceau is in refit 9-85 to 9-86 to improve sensor and defensive systems, including the substitution of two Crotale EDIR systems for four of the 100-mm guns. *Foch* will be modernized to a similar standard beginning in 1987. Both received Syracuse SATCOMM systems during refits ending in 1984.

◆ **1 helicopter-carrier and cadet training ship**

	Budget	Bldr	Laid down	L	In serv.
R 97 JEANNE D'ARC (ex-*La Résolue*)	1957	Brest Ars.	7-7-60	30-9-61	30-6-64

Jeanne d'Arc (R 97)—at end of refit Pradignac & Leo, 26-4-84

Jeanne d'Arc (R 97) Pradignac & Leo, 26-4-84

D: 10,000 tons (12,365 fl) **S:** 26.5 kts (cruising)
Dim: 182.0 (172.0 wl) × 24.0 × 22.0(wl) × 6.6 (7.3 aft)
A: 6/MM 38 Exocet—4/100-mm DP Model 1953 (I × 4)—8 helicopters (*see* Remarks)
Electron Equipt: Radar: 1/DRBV 22D, 1/DRBV 50, 1/DRBN 32, 3/DRBC 32A
Sonar: SQS-503—TACAN: SRN-6
EW: 2 Syllex RL (VIII × 2)
M: 2 sets Rateau-Bretagne GT; 2 props; 40,000 hp **Electric:** 4,400 kw
Boilers: 4 asymmetric, multitube, 45 kg/cm²—superheat 450°C
Fuel: 1,360 tons **Range:** 3,000/26.5; 3,750/25; 5,500/20; 6,800/16
Man: Ships company: 31 officers, 182 petty officers, 414 other enlisted

REMARKS: Replaced the former cruiser *Jeanne d'Arc* as a training ship for officer cadets; when on this mission, she carries only four Super Frélon heavy helicopters. In wartime, she would be used for ASW missions, amphibious assault, or as a troop transport. The number of heavy helicopters embarked can be quickly augmented by simple structural changes.

Aviation facilities include: a 62 × 21-m flight deck aft of the island structure, which permits the simultaneous takeoff of two Super Frélon helicopters, while two machines can be stationed forward of the takeoff area and two others astern, one on each side of the elevator. An elevator (12-ton capacity) is located at the after end of the flight deck.

The hangar deck can, if some of the living quarters used by midshipmen are removed, accommodate eight helicopters. At the after end of the hangar deck there are machine shops for maintenance and repair, including helicopter electronic equipment and an area for inspection. The compartments for handling weapons and ammunition (torpedoes, missiles, etc.) are there also.

In addition to the navigation bridge, the superstructure contains a helicopter-control bridge, a modular-type information-and-operations center, and a combined control center for amphibious operations. Two LCVP landing craft are carried.

The engineering spaces are divided into two compartments, each with two boilers and a turbine, separated by a bulkhead.

The *Jeanne d'Arc* was in refit during 1983-84; the DRBI 10 height-finding radar was removed. The SENIT-2 data system is now to be installed in 1989-90.

NAVAL AVIATION

The Naval Air establishment is made up of combatant flotillas, maintenance squadrons or sections, bases, schools, and the special services necessary to ensure the efficient operation of the flight components.

Administration is handled by the Aeronautical Division of the Naval General Staff and the Central Service Branch of Naval Air, both headed by flag officers. Operational and training matters are directed by the Navy Staff, whose various bureaus include aviation officers.

Primary training in fixed-wing planes is provided by the Air Force; helicopter pilots are given initial training by the Army as well as the Air Force. Specialization of pilots in multi-engine aircraft or in carrier-based fixed-wing and rotary aircraft is provided by Naval Air. The latter also trains navigators and maintenance crews at the Naval Air School, Rochefort.

The combat flotillas are:

(a) those embarked which, flying from aircraft carriers or helicopter carriers, carry out intercept, attack, reconnaissance, or CAP missions and engage in antisubmarine warfare;

(b) maritime patrol flotillas and antisubmarine warfare flotillas that are land-based.

The service support squadrons and sections have various missions: schools, training exercises, transportation, logistical support for seagoing forces, experimental and salvage operations.

Authority over embarked flotillas and squadrons is assigned to a rear admiral, commander, aircraft carriers and seagoing aviation (ALPA).

Maritime patrol squadrons are commanded by a rear admiral (ALPATMAR).

Shore-based flotillas, squadrons, and sections are commanded by the Préfets Maritimes (Naval District Commandants) through the regional aviation commanders.

Bases: Nîmes-Garon, Saint-Mandrier (helicopters), Saint-Raphaël (experimental station), Hyères, Cuers (maintenance), Ajaccio-Aspretto (training), Lorient-Lann Bihoué, Lanvéoc-Poulmic (helicopters), Landivisiau.

For training, the French Navy uses at its schools Étendard IVM, Alizé, Nord 262, C-47, CM-175, Alouette-II, and Rallye 880 aircraft. Support organizations employ MS 760, Nord 262, Rallye 880, C-47, C-54, CM-175, Falcon 10, and Piper Navajo aircraft and Alouette-II, Alouette-III, Lynx, and Super Frélon helicopters. A total of 71 Super Étendard attack aircraft were ordered; all were operational by 1982; but 5 were loaned to Iraq in 9-83 and returned in 9-85, and one has been lost.

Super Étendard J. M. Guhl, 1984

Super Étendard—with AM-39 missile

NAVAL AVIATION *(continued)*

FIRST-LINE OPERATIONAL COMBAT ORGANIZATIONS

Flotilla	Subordination	Bases	Equipment	Missions
4 F	ALPA	Lann-Bihoué	**8 Alizé**	ASW/AEW
6 F	ALPA	Nîmes-Garons	**8 Alizé**	ASW/AEW
11 F	ALPA	Landivisiau	**12 Super Étendard**	Attack
12 F	ALPA	Landivisiau	**12 Crusader (F-8E)**	Interception
14 F	ALPA	Landivisiau	**14 Super Étendard**	Attack
16 F	ALPA	Landivisiau	**8 Étendard IV P**	Reconnaissance
17 F	ALPA	Hyères	**12 Super Étendard**	Attack
21 F	ALPATMAR	Nîmes-Garons	**7 Atlantic Mk 1**	Maritime patrol
22 F	ALPATMAR	Nîmes-Garons	**7 Atlantic Mk 1**	Maritime patrol
23 F	ALPATMAR	Lann-Bihoué	**7 Atlantic Mk 1**	Maritime patrol
24 F	ALPATMAR	Lann-Bihoué	**7 Atlantic Mk 1**	Maritime patrol
31 F	ALPA	St. Mandrier	**12 WG-13 Lynx**	ASW
32 F	ALPA	Lanvéoc-Poulmic	**5 Super Frélon**	ASW & troop transport
33 F	ALPA	St. Mandrier	**7 Super Frélon**	Troop transport
34 F	ALPA	Lanvéoc-Poulmic	**9 WG-13 Lynx**	ASW
35 F	ALPA	*Jeanne d'Arc* or Lanvéoc-Poulmic	**2 WG-13 Lynx** **4 Alouette-III**	
12 S	ALPATMAR	Faaa, Tahiti	**3 Gardian**	Maritime patrol
4 S	ALPATMAR	Tontouta, New Caledonia	**2 Gardian**	Maritime patrol

A new ACM *(Avion de Combat Marine)* fighter-bomber to replace the Super Étendard in the late 1990s is in the planning stages. A flight-demonstrator prototype, the Rafale (ACX)is expected to fly in 1986, powered by two G.E. F404 engines; the production aircraft would be powered by two SNECMA M88 engines of 7,500-lb thrust each.

A total of 42 Atlantique MK 2 patrol aircraft are planned, 16 in the 1984-88 Plan. The prototype was completed in mid-1981, but the first production aircraft is not expected to fly before 1988.

Étendard-IVM—now used only for training

F-SE Crusader

Alizé

Gardian (Falcon 20) French Navy, 1984

Super Frélon

Alouette-III

Atlantique Mk 2 prototype

WG-13 Lynx

NAVAL AVIATION *(continued)*

Atlantic Mk 1

Xingu multi-engine trainer French Navy, 1983

Type	Mission	Wingspan	Length	Height	Weight (max.) kilos	Engine	Max. speed in Mach or in knots	Maximum ceiling	Range	Weapons	Remarks
◆ **SHIP-BASED PLANES**											
CRUSADER F8-E (FN) (Ling-Temco-Vought)	All-weather interceptor	10.72	16.61	4.80	13,000	1 J57 P20 *A* Pratt & Whitney turbojet with after-burner	Mach 1.8	50,000 ft	1,500 miles 2 hr 30 min	4/20-mm guns, M 530 air-to-air missiles	(1) 2 Flotilles are modified to carry the ANT 52 nuclear bomb. (2) 28 to 34 Alizé aircraft were modernized 1980-84 with Iguane radar, Omega radio-navigation equipment, and ARAR 12-A intercept gear. (3) Can be outfitted with a small photo pod for reconnaissance missions. The Atlantique Mk 2, which will enter service in 1989, will have the same airframe, engines, and characteristics as the Mk I but its weapon system will be entirely new, built around a Type 15 M digital tactical computer. It will be able to transport 3 tons of weapons, e.g., 4 Martel under the wings or 2 AM 39 inboard. 32 aircraft will be procured. (4) Localization, classification and attack of contacts picked up by an antisubmarine ship. Carries DUAV-4 dipping sonar. (5) Detection, identification, and neutralization of small surface vessels with weak antiaircraft defense. 4 equipped with MAD for ASW.
SUPER-ÉTENDARD (Dassault) (1)	Fleet air defense attack,	9.60	14.35	3.85	11,900	1 8 K 50 SNECMA turbojet developing 5 tons of thrust	Mach 1 at 11,000 m; Mach 0.97 at low altitude			2/30-mm guns, bombs, rockets, or one AM 39	
Étendard-IVP (Dassault)	Photo-reconnaissance	9.60	14.50	3.85	10,200	1 SNECMA Atar 8 turbojet	Mach 1.3	35,000 ft	750 miles 1 hr 45 or 2 hr 15 with supplemental reserve tank	100-mm rockets, 68-mm rockets, photo-flash bombs flash bombs	
Alizé (BR 1050) (Bréguet) (2)	AEW, ASW	15.60	13.66	5	8,200	1 Rools-Royce Dart 21 turboprop (1,925 hp + 230 kt of thrust)	240 kts	11,000 ft	685 miles 3 hr 45	Air-to-surface missiles, Mk 46 torpedoes, 100-mm rockets, ASW depth charges 50 to 250 kg bombs, acoustic buoys, mortar-type projectiles	
◆ **LAND-BASED PLANES**											
Gardian (Bréguet)	Maritime surveillance, search & rescue	16.3	17.15	5.32	15,200	2 Garrett ATF3 turbo jets	Mach 0.86	42,000 ft	2,200 n. miles 5 hr 30 min	Varan radar, ventral chuté to launch rescue gear	
Atlantic Mk 1 (Br 1150) (Bréguet) (3)	Patrol, ASW (2)	36.30	31.75	11.33	43,500	2 Rolls-Royce Tyne 20 turboprops, 6,000 hp each	300 kts	30,000 ft	4,300 miles 17 hr	Air-to-surface missiles, L 4 or Mk 46 torpedoes, ASW depth charges, sonobuoys, mortar-type projectiles (ASW), photo-flash bombs	
◆ **HELICOPTERS**											
Super Frélon (S.N.I.A.S.)	ASW (2 used as transports)	18.90 (rotor diameter)	23	6.35	13,000	3 C3 Turboméca III turboshafts, each with 1,500 hp	145 kts	10,000 ft	420 miles 3 hr 30 min	Mk 46 ASW torpedoes	
Lynx (WG-13) (Westland S.N.I.A.S.) (4)	ASW (3) and surface attack aircraft (4)	12.80 (rotor diameter)	15.2	3.20	4,150	2 BS 360 Rolls-Royce Gem turboshafts, of 900 or 750 hp each	150 kts	12,000 ft	1 hr 30, half hovering, half in flight 2 hr 30 min with 3 men and 4 missiles	Mk 46 torpedoes, air-to-surface missiles	
Alouette-III (S.N.I.A.S.) (5)	ASW (6)	11.02 (rotor diameter)	12.8	3.0	2,200	1 Turbomeca Astazou turboshaft, 870 hp	110 kts	10,000 ft	325 miles 2 hr 30 min	Mk 46 torpedoes	

Note: Other aircraft in service include Nord 262, PA-31, 5 Falcon 10 Sea, 8 MS 760, 6 Rallye 800, Alouette-II, C-47, 12 CM 175 Magister, and 6 CAP 10 for training and support duties. 16 Embraer Xingu were delivered 1982-83 from Brazil to replace the Nord 262 as a multi-engine trainer.

BALLISTIC-MISSILE SUBMARINES

General Note for Submarines: Names and pendant numbers ceased to be displayed on 1-1-83, to augment security.

Note: The seventh SNLE *(Sous-marin nucléaire Lance Engins)* has been delayed somewhat from the schedule originally announced by President Mitterand on 24-7-81. The 14-15,000-ton ship is now scheduled to be laid down at DCAN, Cherbourg, at the end of 1988, for an operational date of 1994. The ship will be powered by a new nuclear-propulsion plant, the 131-megawatt K15, also to be used in the new nuclear-powered aircraft carriers.

◆ 1 L'Inflexible class

	Bldr	Laid down	L	In serv.
S 615 L'Inflexible	DCAN, Cherbourg	27-3-80	23-6-82	1-4-85

D: 8,080/8,920 tons **S:** over 20 kts (sub.) **Dim:** 128.70 × 10.60 × 10.00
A: 16/M 4 ballistic missiles—4/533-mm TT fwd (12 torpedoes or SM 39 missiles)
Electron Equipt: Radar: DRUA 33—EW: radar detector
Sonar: DSUX 21 multifunction, DUUX5
M: 1 pressurized-water reactor, 2 steam turbines; turbo-reduction drive; 1 prop; 16,000 hp—electric emergency propulsion with 5,000 n.m. range
Man: 2 crews in rotation, each of 15 officers, 120 men

Remarks: Ordered 9-78, *L'Inflexible* has most characteristics in common with the five preceding SSBNs of *Le Redoutable* class, but takes advantage of many technological advances in propulsion, sonar systems, navigation systems, etc., and is able to dive 100 m deeper. The ship will be equipped from the outset with the M 4 missile, which will have six TN-70 Multiple Independent Re-entry Vehicle (MIRV) warheads. Sail planes higher on more streamlined sail than in *Le Redoutable* class.

BALLISTIC-MISSILE SUBMARINES *(continued)*

L'Inflexible (S 615) J. Biaugeaud, 1985

L'Inflexible (S 615) J. Biaugeaud, 1985

◆ **5 nuclear-powered Le Redoutable class** Bldr: DCAN, Cherbourg

	Laid down	L	Trials	In serv.
S 611 Le Redoutable	11-64	29-3-67	7-69	1-12-71
S 612 Le Terrible	22-6-67	12-12-69	1971	1-1-73
S 610 Le Foudroyant	12-12-69	4-12-71	5-73	6-6-74
S 613 L'Indomitable	4-12-71	17-9-74	12-75	23-12-76
S 614 Le Tonnant	10-74	17-9-77	4-79	3-4-80

Le Terrible (S 612) E.C.P.A., 1978

Le Foudroyant (A 610) L. & L. Van Ginderen, 2-83

D: 8,000/9,000 tons **S:** 20 kts, max. **Dim:** 128.0 × 10.6 × 10.0
A: 16 M 20 ballistic missiles—4/550-mm TT fwd (18 L 5 and F 17 torpedoes)
Electron Equipt: Radar: 1/DRUA 33—EW: radar detector
Sonar: 1/DUUV-23, 1/DUUX-2
M: Principal: 1 pressurized water reactor, 2 steam turbines with 1 set turboreduction gears; 1 prop; 16,000 hp
Secondary: 1 electric motor driven by batteries powered by 1 SEMT-Pielstick 16 PA4, 850-kw diesel generator set (sufficient fuel for 5,000 n.m.)
Man: Twin crews of 15 officers and 120 men for each ship, manning in rotation

Remarks: *Le Redoutable* (authorized in March 1963) and other submarines of this class are the principal elements of the French naval deterrent. They can dive more than 200 meters. All, with the exception of *Le Redoutable,* will be back-fitted to carry the M 4 missile. The substitution will not require replacing the existing missile tubes. The sonar suit will be upgraded by the installation of DSUX-21, and other equipment will be modernized. S 614 began modernization 1-2-85 at Cherbourg.

◆ **1 experimental ballistic-missile submarine (non-nuclear)**

	Bldr	Laid down	L	In serv.
S 655 Gymnote	DCAN, Cherbourg	17-3-63	17-3-64	17-10-66

Gymnote J.-C. Bellonne, 1977

D: 3,000 tons std., 3,250 surfaced (fl) **S:** 11/10 kts **Dim:** 84.0 × 10.6 × 7.6
M: 4 sets 620-kw diesel generators; 2 electric motors; 2 props; 2,600 hp
Man: 8 officers, 38 petty officers, 45 other enlisted

Remarks: Used for testing missiles designed for the SSBNs. Has two vertical missile-launching tubes to port. Bow diving planes do not retract. Noncombatant. Currently involved in M 4 developmental trials. The pressure hull was laid down in 1958 for a nuclear-powered attack submarine that was canceled in 1959. To be stricken 1986.

NUCLEAR-POWERED ATTACK SUBMARINES

◆ **0 (+1 + 2) "Post-Rubis" class** Bldr: Cherboug Arsenal

	Laid down	L	Trials	In serv.
S 605 N. . .	. . .	. . .	. . .	. . .
S 6. . . N. . .	. . .	. . .	. . .	. . .
S. . . N. . .	. . .	. . .	. . .	. . .

D: . . . **S:** . . . **Dim:** . . . × . . . × . . .
A: . . .
Electron Equipt: . . .
M: 1 48-megawatt natural circulation, pressurized water reactor; 2 turboalternator sets; 1 electric motor; 1 prop; 9,500 hp—emergency backup system: 200 kw
Endurance: 90 days **Man:** . . .

Remarks: S 605 ordered 17-10-84. Will employ all improved, body-of-revolution hull form. Will have two crews, improved combat data, sensor, and communications systems. Second and third to order 1986, 1988.

NUCLEAR-POWERED ATTACK SUBMARINES *(continued)*

◆ **2 (+2) Rubis class, Type SNA 72** Bldr: DCAN, Cherbourg

	Laid down	L	Trials	In serv.
S 601 RUBIS (ex-*Provence*)	11-12-76	7-7-79	1-4-81	23-2-83
S 602 SAPHIR (ex-*Bretagne*)	1-9-79	1-9-81	1-7-83	6-7-84
S 603 CASABIANCA	9-81	22-12-84	4-86	4-87
S 604 N	10-82	. . .	10-87	11-88
S 605 N	11-10-84	. . .	10-89	10-90

Saphir (S 602) G. Gyssels, 2-85

Saphir (S 602) J. Pradignac, 5-85

D: 2,265 std. 2,385 surf. 2,670 tons sub. **S:** 25 kts **Dim:** 72.10 × 7.60 × 6.40
A: 4/533-mm TT fwd (14 torpedoes, SM 39 missiles, or mines)
Electron Equipt: Radar: 1/DRUA 33—EW: ARUR, ARUD
Sonar: 1/DSUV 22, 1/DUUA 2B, 1/DUUX 2
M: Principal: 1 48-megawatt pressurized water reactor; two turbo alternator sets; 1 electric motor; 1 prop; 9,500 hp
Secondary: 1 electric motor driven by batteries powered by 1 SEMT-Pielstick 16PA4, 85C-kw diesel generator set
Endurance: 45 days **Man:** 9 officers, 35 chief petty officers, 22 other enlisted

REMARKS: Names for the first two changed 11-80. Fire-control, torpedo-launching, and submarine-detection systems are the same as for the *Agosta* class. *Rubis* was financed under the Third Military Equipment Plan. The second through the fourth came under the Fourth Plan (1977-82). *Saphir* was ordered under the 1977 budget, the third under the 1979 budget, and the fourth in 1981. *Rubis's* reactor became operational (went critical) early 2-81, and trials started 6-81. S 602 the first to carry the SM 39 Exocet missile. All have the Pivair optronic periscope and employ the SADE automated combat data system. Diving depth: 300 m.

ATTACK SUBMARINES

◆ **4 Agosta class** Bldr: Cherbourg Arsenal

	Laid down	L	In serv.
S 620 AGOSTA	10-11-72	19-10-74	28-7-77
S 621 BÉVÉZIERS	17-5-73	14-6-75	27-9-77
S 622 LA PRAYA	1974	15-5-76	9-3-78
S 623 OUESSANT	1974	23-10-76	27-7-78

D: 1,230/1,490/1,740 tons (fl) **S:** 12.5 kts/20.5 kts for 5 min., 17.5 kts for 1 hr.
Dim: 67.57 × 6.8 × 5.4
A: 4/550-mm TT fwd—20 L 5 Mod. 3 and F 17 torpedoes (rapid loading)
Electron Equipt: Radar: 1/DRUA 33—EW: ARUR, ARUD
Sonar: 1/DUUA 1D, 1/DUUA 2A, 1/DUUA 2D, 1/DSUV 22, 1/DUUX 2A
M: 2 SEMT-Pielstick 320-16 PA 4 185 diesel generator sets (850 kw each); 1 × 3,500-kw propulsion motor; 1 prop; 4,600 hp (1 × 23-hp creep motor)
Fuel: 185 tons **Endurance:** 45 days **Man:** 7 officers, 47 men
Range: 7,000/10 (snorkel); 178/3.5 (creep motor), 7,900/. . . surf. (1 engine)

REMARKS: Oceangoing submarines, authorized in the 1970-75 program. Weapons and equipment similar to the refitted *Daphné* class. DLA D3 fire control centralized in one computer bank. Air-conditioned. Retractable deck fittings on hull exterior. Advanced techniques for quiet operations both inboard and outboard. The torpedo tubes accept torpedoes of either 550-mm or 533-mm diameter. S 621 used in SM 39 Exocet trials. 320-cell battery with twice the capacity of the *Daphné* class. Diving depth 300 m. To be equipped to fire SM 39 guided missiles. Spain built four of this class of submarine, and Pakistan has two—from an embargoed South African order.

Bévéziers (S 621) L. & L. Van Ginderen, 1-85

La Praya (S 622) Pradignac & Leo, 6-84

◆ **9 Daphné class**

	Budget	Bldr	Laid down	L	In serv.
S 641 DAPHNÉ	1955	Dubigeon, Nantes	3-58	20-6-59	1-6-64
S 642 DIANE	1955	Dubigeon, Nantes	7-58	4-10-60	20-6-64
S 643 DORIS	1955	Cherbourg Ars.	1-9-58	14-5-60	26-8-64
S 645 FLORE	1956	Cherbourg Ars.	1-9-58	21-12-60	21-5-64
S 646 GALATÉE	1956	Cherbourg Ars.	1-9-58	22-9-61	25-7-64
S 648 JUNON	1960	Cherbourg Ars.	7-61	11-5-64	25-2-66
S 649 VÉNUS	1960	Cherbourg Ars.	8-61	24-9-64	1-1-66
S 650 PSYCHÉ	1964	Brest Arsenal	5-65	28-6-67	1-7-69
S 651 SIRÈNE	1964	Brest Arsenal	5-65	28-6-67	1-3-70

Doris (S 643) M. Bar, 6-84

Diane (S 642) Maritime Photographic, 10-85

D: 700 std./869 surf./1,043 sub. tons **S:** 13.5/16 kts **Dim:** 57.75 × 6.76 × 5.25 (max.)
A: 12/550-mm TT, 8 fwd, 4 aft (no reloads)
Electron Equipt: Radar: 1/Calypso II
Sonar: 1/DUUA 2B, 1/DSUV 2, 1/DUUX 2
M: 2 SEMT-Pielstick/Jeumont-Schneider 450-kw diesel generator sets; 2 × 1,000 hp (1,300 for a brief period) electric motors; 2 props—*see* Remarks
Range: 4,300/7.5 (snorkel) **Man:** 6 officers, 39 men

REMARKS: Development of the *Aréthuse* class. Very quiet when submerged. Modernized, beginning in 1971, with special attention given to detection equipment and weapons. S 650 and S 651 were the last modernized, in 1981. S 641, not fully modernized, does not have the large bow sonar dome. Can submerge to 300 meters. Have DLT D3 torpedo fire-control system. The first seven have Type 12 PA1 diesels, while S 650 and S 651 use Type 12 PA4-135. This class of submarine has been purchased by the following countries: Portugal, four in 1964; Pakistan, four in 1966, South Africa, three in 1967. Spain has built four with French technical assistance. One Portuguese unit was sold to Pakistan in 1976. S 651 flooded and sank 11-10-72 but was salvaged; sisters *Minerve* (S 647) and *Eurydice* (S 644) lost 27-1-68 and 4-3-70. Six will reportedly strike by 1988.

ATTACK SUBMARINES *(continued)*

◆ 2 Narval class

	Budget	Bldr	Laid down	L	In serv.
S 633 Dauphin	1950	Cherbourg Ars.	5-52	17-9-55	1-8-58
S 638 Morse	1954	Seine Maritime	2-56	10-12-58	2-5-60

D: 1,320/1,635/1,910 tons **S:** 15/18 kts **Dim:** 77.63 × 7.82 × 5.40
A: 6/550-mm TT fwd — 20 torpedoes
Electron Equipt: Radar: 1/search, 1/attack
Sonar: DUUA 1, DSUV 2, DUUX 2
M: 3 SEMT-Pielstick 12 PA4 motor generator sets; 2 electric motors; 2 props; 3,000 hp (2 × 40-hp creep motors)
Endurance: 45 days **Range:** 15,000/8 (snorkel) **Man:** 7 officers, 57 men

Remarks: Rebuilt from 1966 to 1970; re-engined, with complete modernization of detection devices and weapons. Separate fixed-pitch bow planes are extended to rise or descend. *Requin,* modified 1980 for trials with the SM 39 submerged-launch missile, discarded 11-85. *Marsouin* (S 632) decommissioned 8-11-82 for cannibalization; *Narval* (S 631), which had a special swimmer-delivery vehicle housing on deck aft, stricken spring 1983. S 638 to strike 1986. S 633 is used in trials of materials and equipment for future submarines.

GUIDED-MISSILE CRUISER

	Budget	Bldr	Laid down	L	In serv.
C 611 Colbert	1953	Brest	12-53	24-3-56	5-5-59

D: 8,500 tons (11,300 fl) **S:** 31.5 kts
Dim: 180.80 (175.00 pp) × 20.20 (19.70 wl) × 7.90 (max.)
A: 4/MM 38 Exocet — 1/Masurca SAM syst. (II × 1, 48 missiles) — 2/100-mm DP, Model 1968 (I × 2) — 12/57-mm AA (II × 6)
Electron Equipt: Radar: 1/DRBN 32, 1/DRBV 50, 1/DRBV 23C, 1/DRBV 20C, 2/DRBR 51, 1/DRBR 32C, 2/DRBC 31, 1/DRBI 10D
EW: ARBB 31, ARBB 32, ARBR 10F, 2/Syllex countermeasures RL — TACAN: URN-20
M: 2 sets C.E.M. Parsons GT; 2 props; 86,000 hp **Electric:** 4,920 kw
Boilers: 4 asymmetric, multitube; 45 kg/cm², 450°C **Range:** 4,000/25
Man: 25 officers, 208 petty officers, 329 men
Armor: Deck: 50 mm, Belt: 50 to 80 mm

Colbert (C 611) J. Pradignac, 1984

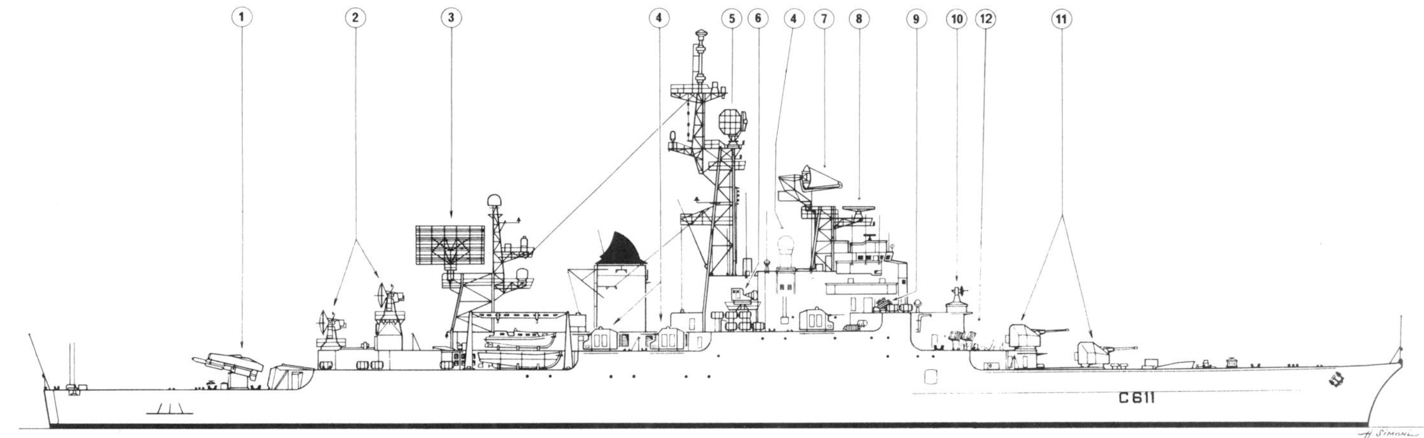

Colbert 1. Masurca twin launcher 2. DRBR 51 Masurca tracker/illuminator radars 3. DRBV 20C early-warning radar 4. twin 57-mm AA mounts 5. DRBI 10D height-finding radar 6. DRBC 31 radar director for 57-mm AA 7. DRBV 23C stabilized air-search radar 8. DRBV 50 surface/air-search radar 9. Syllex chaff RL (VIII × 2) 10. DRBC 32C radar director for 100-mm guns 11. 10-mm Model 1968 dual-purpose guns 12. MM 38 Exocet launch cells (Note that the forward arrow marked "4" points to the Syracuse SATCOMM antenna radome rather than the forwardmost 57-mm AA mount.)

Colbert (C 611) J.-C. Bellonne, 12-82

GUIDED-MISSILE CRUISER *(continued)*

Remarks: Converted into a surface-to-air guided-missile cruiser between 4-70 and 10-72. The SENIT 1 tactical data system enables real-time control of the surface and air situation at the center of a widely dispersed formation, making this an excellent command ship, able also to coordinate the air defense of the formation. The ship can be used as a command post for an interservice operation overseas. During the 1970-72 refit the bridge superstructure was rebuilt, the electronic equipment for command and control was modernized, the electric power increased, and living spaces were improved, including air-conditioning. Four MM 38 Exocet anti-ship missiles were installed in 1980. In addition to the two DRBR 31 radar directors for the 57-mm AA guns, there are also four lead-computing visual directors. Machinery and boilers are installed in two separate compartments, each with two boilers and a turbine, separated by an 18-meter-long watertight compartment. Refitted 9-81 to 11-82, during which the Syracuse satellite communications system was fitted and the Masurca system updated. Scheduled for disposal in 1997.

GUIDED-MISSILE DESTROYERS

◆ 0 (+4) Cassard (C 70 AA) class

	Bldr	Laid down	L	In serv.
D 614 Cassard	DCAN, Lorient	3-9-82	6-2-85	3-88
D. . . Jean Bart	DCAN, Lorient	5-84	1986	3-90
D. . . Courbet	DCAN, Lorient	5-86	1989	1991
D. . . N.	DCAN, Lorient	5-87	. . .	1992-3

D: 3,820 tons (4,340 fl) **S:** 29.6 kts **Dim:** 139.00 (129.00 pp) × 14.00 × 5.50
A: 8/MM40 SSM—1/Mk 13 launcher (40 Standard SM-1 MR missiles)—2/SADRAL systems (VI × 2)—1/100-mm DP—2/20-mm AA (I × 2)—2 fixed catapults for Type L-5 ASW torpedoes (10 torpedoes)—1/light helicopter
Electron Equipt: Radar: 2/Decca 1229, 1/DRBJ 11B, 1/DRBV 26, 2 SPG-51C, 1/DRBC 33
Sonar: 1/DUBA 25A—IR: DIBV 10 Vampir
EW: ARBB 33, ARBR 17, 2 Dagaie and 2 Sagaie countermeasures RL
M: 4 SEMT-Pielstick 18 PA 6 BTC diesels; 2 props; 42,300 hp
Electric: 3,400 kw **Fuel:** 600 tons **Range:** 4,800/24; 8,000/17
Man: 12 officers, 124 petty officers, 105 men (251 accomm.)

Remarks: 1977-82 program; the first was authorized under the 1978 budget, the second under the 1979 budget, and the third and fourth in 1983.

The Mk 13 launchers and missile fire-control systems are being taken from the four *Kersaint* (converted T-47)-class destroyers. The design has been recast, with a second 100-mm mount aft being replaced by a helicopter shelter for a small, AS.15 missile-equipped helicopter, flanked on either side by launchers for SADRAL system short-range point-defense missiles. After the second unit, the forward Model 1968 100-mm gun will be replaced by the new "Compact" model. The space beneath the helicopter deck may eventually accommodate the DSBV 61 towed linear passive hydrophone array. The ships will have the SENIT 6 digital data system, and the new DRBC 33 radar fire-control director will be aided by a Piranha III t.v./laser attachment. Also installed will be 2 CSEE Lynx and 2 Naja optronic directors. A SAMAHE deck traversing system will be fitted for the helicopter. Provision has been made for installing the DSBV 61 towed passive linear hydrophone array. The Model 1968 gun will have a 78 rd/min firing capability.

◆ 4 (+3) Georges Leygues (C 70 ASW) class   Bldr: Brest Arsenal

	Laid down	L	In serv.
D 640 Georges Leygues	16-9-74	17-12-76	10-12-79
D 641 Dupleix	17-10-75	2-12-78	16-6-81
D 642 Montcalm	5-12-75	31-5-80	28-5-82
D 643 Jean De Vienne	26-10-79	17-11-81	25-5-84
D 644 Primauguet	19-11-81	17-3-84	1987
D 645 La Motte-Picquet	9-2-82	6-2-85	1988
D 646 N.	2-84	. . .	1990

D: 3,830 tons (4,170 fl) **S:** 30 kts (GT), 21 kts (diesels)
Dim: 139.00 (129.00 pp) × 14.00 × 4.10 (hull); 5.73 (props); 5.50 (sonar)
A: 4/MM 38 Exocet (D 642 and later: 4 or 8 MM 40)—1/Crotale system (VIII × 1; 26 missiles)—1/100-mm DP, Model 1968—2/20-mm AA (I × 2)—2 catapults for L-5 ASW torpedoes (10 torpedoes)—2/WG-13 Lynx helicopters
Electron Equipt: D 640–643: Radar: 2/DRBN 32 (Decca 1226), DRBV 26, DRBV 516C, 1/DRBC 32D
Sonar: DUBV 23 hull-mounted; DUBV 43B VDS
EW: ARBR 16, ARBR 11B (D/F), ARBB 32, 2/Syllex (D 643: Dagaie) countermeasures RL
D 644–646: Radar: 2/DRBN 32 (Decca RM 1226), DRBV 15A, 1/DRBC 33 with optronics
Sonar: DUBV 24C hull-mounted, DUBV 43B VDS, DSBV 61 towed array
EW: ARBR 17, HF monitoring syst, 2/Dagaie RL
M: CODOG: 2 Rolls-Royce Olympus TM3B gas turbines; 2 SEMT-Pielstick 16 PA 6 CV 280 diesels; 2 CP props; 52,000 hp (gas turbine), 10,400 hp (diesel)
Electric: 3,400 kw (4 × 850-kw alternator sets) **Fuel:** 600 tons distillate
Range: 1,000/30; 9,500/17 diesels
Man: Peacetime: 18 officers, 127 petty officers, 83 men (accommodations for 250 total)

Remarks: Units 6 and 7 built at Brest and fitted out at Lorient Dockyard. Main propulsion and auxiliary equipment is divided among four compartments from forward to aft: forward auxiliary room, turbine room, diesel room with the reduction gears, and after auxiliary room. On diesel power and with the DUBV 43 sonar in the water, maximum speed is 19 knots. Centralized control of the propulsion machinery from the bridge greatly reduces the engineering staff required (3 officers, 23 petty officers, 24 men).

As in the *De Grasse,* much attention has been given to habitability, which caused the addition of 5 meters of length and 150 tons to the original plans. Denny Brown automatic stabilizers fitted. Have SENIT 4 data system. Dagaie rocket launchers

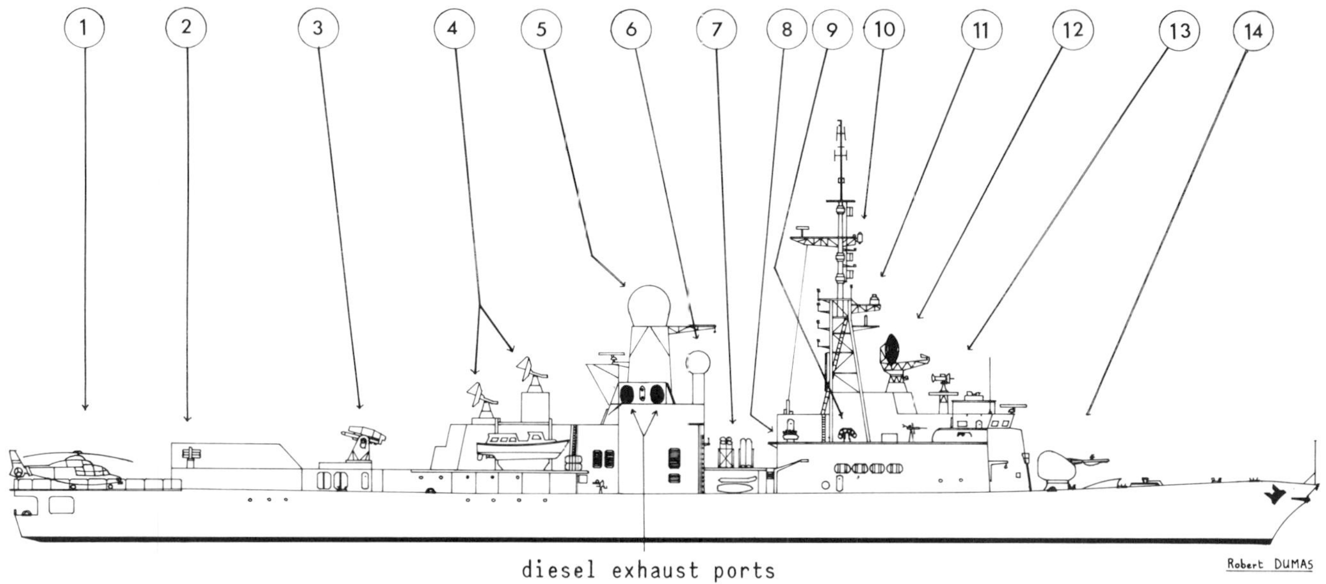

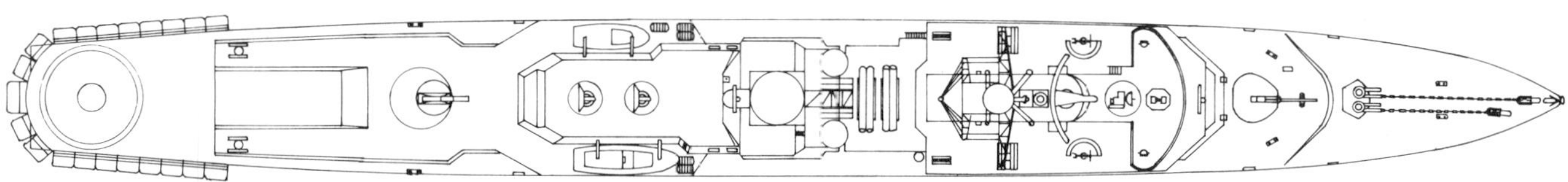

C 70 AA class 1. small helicopter 2. SADRAL launcher (VI × 2) 3. Mk 13 missile launcher for Standard SM-1 MR 4. SPG-51C tracker/illuminator radars 5. DRBJ 11B 3-D radar 6. Syracuse SATCOMM antennas 7. MM 40 Exocet launch cells 8. Dagaie countermeasures launcher 9. Sagaie countermeasures launcher 10. DIBV 10 Vampir IR system 11. ARBR 17 EW antenna 12. DRBV 26 radar 13. DRBC 33 f.c. radar director 14. 100-mm DP

GUIDED-MISSILE DESTROYERS *(continued)*

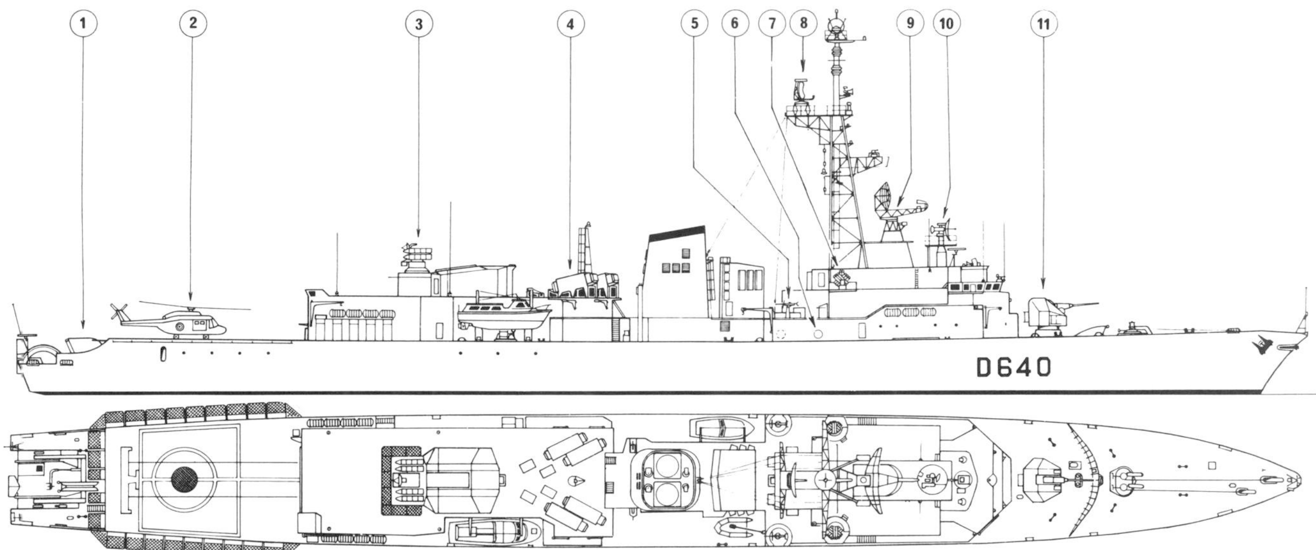

Georges Leygues 1. DUBV 43 sonar 2. WG-13 Lynx helicopter 3. Crotale launcher 4. Exocet launchers 5. 20-mm AA 6. ASW torpedo catapults 7. Syllex system 8. DRBV 51C radar 9. DRBV 26 radar 10. DRBC 32D radar 11. 100-mm gunmount, Model 1968

Primaguet (D 644)—on trials; note higher bridge 16 Flot., French Navy, 7-85

Georges Leygues (D 640)—with Syracuse L. & L. Van Ginderen, 3-85

replace Sagaie in D 643 and later ships. *Montcalm* carries 4/MM 40 SSM now, but this may later be doubled. Have 1 CSEE Panda optronic backup director for the 100-mm gun. The helicopters can be used for ASW with Mk 46 torpedoes or Mk 54 depth bombs or for anti-ship duties with AS-12 missiles.

The final three have a modified sensor suit and the pilothouse placed one deck higher. D 640–643 will eventually have their sonar suits updated to match the others, but will retain the original radars. Beginning with D 694, the Crotale EDIR SAM system is installed. All have the SENIT 4 combat data system and Syracuse SATCOMM equipment. The DIBV 10 *Vampir* IR system is to be added.

Dupleix (D 641) J. Pradignac, 5-85

◆ **3 Tourville class, Type F 67, ex-C 67A** Bldr: Lorient Arsenal

	Budget	Laid down	L	In serv.
D 610 Tourville	1967	3-70	13-5-72	21-6-74
D 611 Duguay Trouin	1967	1-71	1-6-73	17-9-75
D 612 De Grasse	1970	1972	30-11-74	1-10-77

D: 4,800 tons (5,800 fl) **S:** 32 kts
Dim: 152.75 (142.0 pp) × 15.3 × 5.7 (hull) (6.48 props)
A: 6/MM 38 Exocet—1/Crotale syst. (VIII × 1, 26 missiles)—2/100-mm DP, Model 1968 (I × 2)—2/20-mm AA (I × 2)—1/Malafon ASW syst. (13 missiles)—2/catapults for L-5 antisubmarine torpedoes (10 torpedoes—2/WG-13 Lynx helicopters
Electron Equipt: Radar: 2 DRBN 32 (Decca 1226), 1/DRBV 26, 1/DRBV 51B, 1/DRBC 32D
Sonar: 1/DUBV 23, 1/DUBV 43
EW: ARBB 32, ARBR 16, 2/Syllex countermeasures RL
M: 2 sets Rateau double-reduction GT; 2 props; 54,400 hp
Electric: 4,440 kw (2 × 1,500-kw turbogenerators, 3 × 480-kw diesel alternators)
Boilers: 4 asymmetric, multitube, automatic-control; 45 kg/cm², 450°C
Range: 1,900/30; 4,500/18 **Man:** 17 officers, 122 petty officers, 143 men

Remarks: SENIT 3 data system fitted. *Duguay Trouin* was equipped with the Crotale antiaircraft missile system during 1979, *Tourville* in 1980 and *De Grasse* in 1981. In preparation for Crotale, the third 100-mm gunmount atop the helicopter hangar on *Tourville* and *Duguay Trouin* was removed; it was never carried by *De Grasse.* During her Crotale installation refit, the *Tourville* had her boilers converted to burn distillate fuel, which has been burned by *De Grasse* from the outset. Fin stabilizers are fitted. These ships, particularly *De Grasse,* have a very high standard of habitability and seakeeping qualities on a par with those of the *Suffren* class. The Syllex countermeasures launchers are to be replaced by 2 Dagaie systems and the Crotale EDIR missile substituted about 1990.

GUIDED-MISSILE DESTROYERS *(continued)*

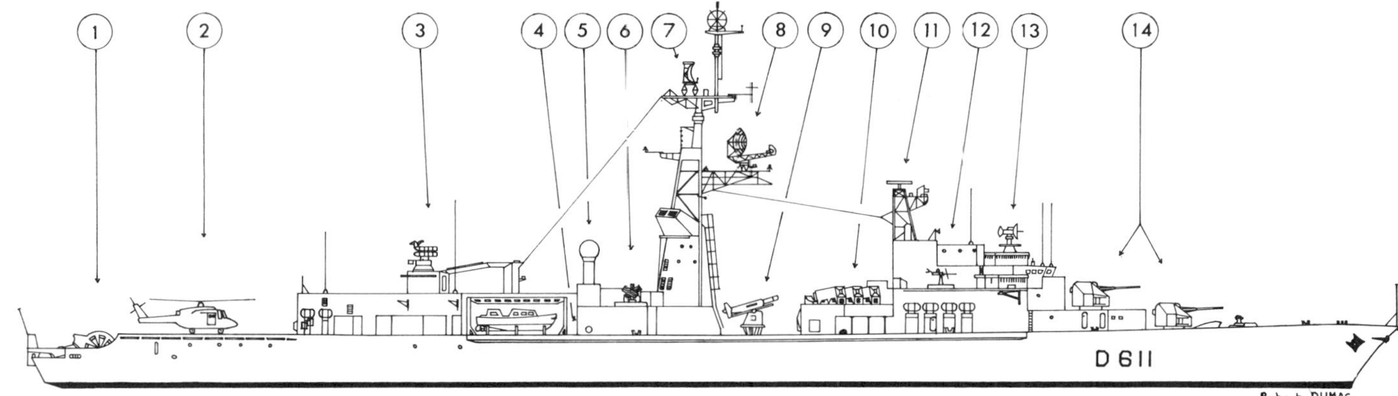

Duguay Trouin (D 611) 1. DUBV 43 VDS 2. WG-13 Lynx helicopter 3. Crotale SAM system 4. catapults for L5 ASW torpedoes 5. Syracuse SATCOMM antenna radomes 6. Syllex chaff rocket launcher 7. DRBV 51B search radar 8. DRBV 26 early-warning radar 9. Malafon ASW system 10. MM 38 Exocet launchers 11. Decca 1226 nav. radar 12. 20-mm AA 13. DRBC 32D f.c. radar director 14. 100-mm Model 1968 DP

Duguay Trouin (D 611)—with Syracuse aft 16 Flot., French Navy, 1985

Tourville (D 610) J. Goss, 11-81

De Grasse (D 612) J. Pradignac, 1984

◆ **2 Suffren class**

	Bldr	Budget	Laid down	L	In serv.
D 602 Suffren	Lorient Ars.	1960	12-62	15-5-65	20-7-67
D 603 Duquesne	Brest Ars.	1960	11-64	11-2-66	1-4-70

D: 5,090 tons (6,090 fl) **S:** 34 kts
Dim: 157.60 (148.00 pp) × 15.54 × 7.25 (max.)
A: 1/Masurca SAM syst. (II × 1; 48 missiles)—4/MM 38 Exocet SSM—2/100-mm, Model 1953 (I × 2)—4/20-mm AA (I × 4)—1/Malafon ASW syst. (13 missiles)—2/catapults for L-5 torpedoes (10 torpedoes)

Suffren (D 602)—with Syracuse added Pradignac & Leo, 9-84

Suffren (D 602) Pradignac & Leo, 6-84

GUIDED-MISSILE DESTROYERS *(continued)*

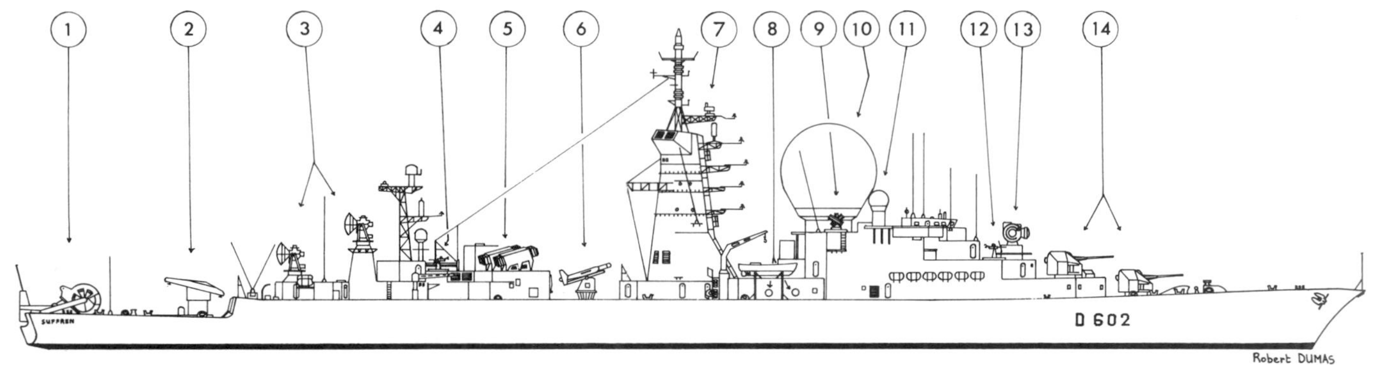

Suffren (D 602) 1. DUBV 43 VDS 2. Masurca twin SAM launcher 3. DRBR 51 f.c. radar directors 4. 20-mm AA 5. MM 38 Exocet launchers 6. Malafon ASW system 7. DRBV 50 search radar 8. catapults for L5 ASW torpedoes 9. Syllex chaff launcher 10. radome over DRBI 23 3-D radar 11. Syracuse SATCOMM antenna radomes 12. 20-mm AA 13. DRBC 32A f.c. radar director 14. 100-mm Model 1953 DP

Duquesne (D 603) G. Gyssels, 6-83

Suffren (D 602) Pradignac & Leo, 6-84

Electron Equipt: Radar: 1/DRBN 32, 1/DRBI 23, 1/DRBV 50, 2/DRBR 51, 1/DRBC 32A
Sonar: 1/DUBV 23, 1/DUBV 43—TACAN: URN-20
EW: ARBB 31, ARBB 32, 2 Syllex countermeasures RL
M: 2 sets Rateau double-reduction GT; 2 props; 72,500 hp
Electric: 3,440 kw (2 × 1,000-kw turbogenerators, 3 × 480-kw diesel alternators)
Boilers: 4 multitube, automatic-control; 45 kg/cm², 450°C
Range: 2,000/30; 2,400/29; 5,100/18
Man: 23 officers, 164 petty officers, 168 men

REMARKS: Built under the 1960-65 plan, these ships are extremely seaworthy; they roll and pitch only slightly and vibrate very little. Three pairs of nonretractable, anti-rolling stabilizers. Living and operating spaces are air-conditioned. SENIT 1 data system fitted. A new gunfire-control radar with Piranha III optronic attachment is to be installed in place of DRBC 32A in 1987. Two Dagaie and two Sagaie countermeasures launchers will replace Syllex.

◆ **1 C 65 class**

	Bldr	Laid down	L	In serv.
D 609 ACONIT	Lorient Ars.	1967	7-3-70	30-3-73

Aconit (D 609) Maritime Photographic, 9-85

D: 3,500 tons (3,840 fl) **S:** 27 kts **Dim:** 127.0 × 13.4 × 4.05 (5.8 props)
A: 8/MM 40 Exocet SSM (IV × 2)—2/100-mm DP, Model 1968 (I × 2)—1/Malafon ASW system (13 missiles)—2/catapults for L-5 ASW torpedoes (10 torpedoes)
Electron Equipt: Radar: 1/DRBN 32, 1/DRBV 15, 1/DRBV 22A, 1/DRBC 32B
Sonar: 1/DUBV 23, 1/DUBV 43 VDS
EW: ARBB 32, ARBR 16, 2/Syllex countermeasures RL
M: 1 set Rateau double-reduction GT; 1 prop; 28,650 hp (31,500 hp for short periods)
Boilers: 2 asymmetric, multitube, automatic-control; 45 kg/cm², 450°C
Electric: 2,960 kw **Range:** 1,600/27; 5,000/18
Man: 15 officers, 103 petty officers, 114 men

REMARKS: One computer controls the SENIT 3 data system functions and the weapons. Propulsion machinery is very compact and produced 31,500 hp on trials. Equipped with fin stabilizers. During a major refit in 1984-85 she received 8/MM 40 Exocet in place of the 305-mm mortar and DRBV 15 in place of DRBV 13.

◆ **1 T-56 class, ASW**

	Bldr	Laid down	L	In serv.
D 638 LA GALISSONNIÈRE	Lorient Ars.	11-58	12-3-60	9-7-62

D: 2,750 tons (3,740 fl) **S:** 34 kts (32 fl)
Dim: 132.80 × 12.70 × 5.40 (fwd) 5.90 (props)
A: 2/100-mm DP, Model 1953 (I × 2)—1/Malafon ASW syst. (13 missiles)—6/550-mm TT (III × 2) for L-3 torpedoes—1/Alouette-III ASW helicopter
Electron Equipt: Radar: 1/DRBN 32, 1/DRBV 22A, 1/DRBV 50, 1/DRBC 32A
Sonar: 1/DUBV 23, 1/DUBV 43 VDS—TACAN: URN 20
EW: ARBR/ARBA 10C

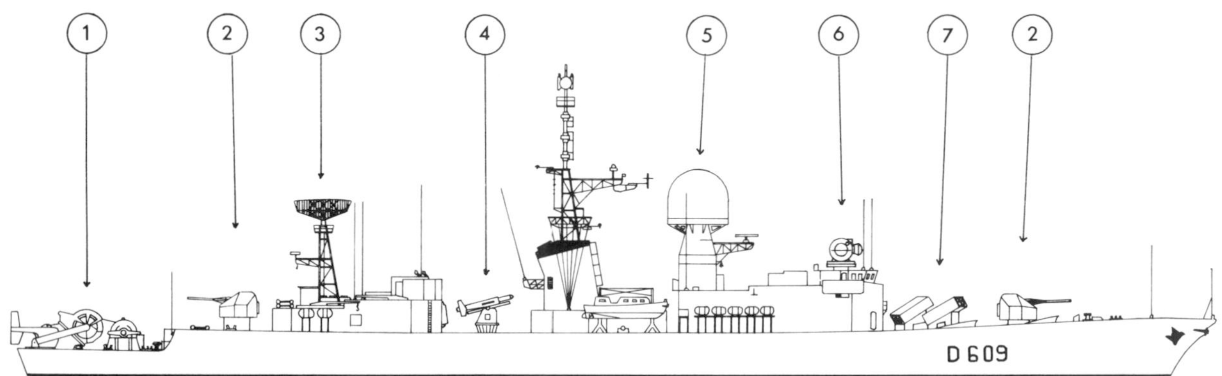

Provisional view of Aconit as modernized 1. DUBV 43 sonar 2. 100-mm DP mounts 3. DRBV 22A radar 4. Malafon launcher 5. DRBV 15 radar 6. 100-mm gun director with DRBC 32B radar 7. MM 40 Exocet launch cells

GUIDED-MISSILE DESTROYERS *(continued)*

La Galissonnière (D 638)—with hangar opened to create a flight deck
L. & L. Van Ginderen, 6-84

La Galissonnière—with hangar open G. Gyssels, 6-84

M: 2 sets Rateau GT; 2 props; 63,000 hp
Boilers: 4 ACB-Indret; 35 kg/cm², 385°C **Fuel:** 800 tons
Range: 1,500/30; 5,000/18
Man: Peacetime: 15 officers, 92 petty officers, 165 men

REMARKS: Formerly an experimental vessel for ASW sonar, with two bow-mounted sonars. A quadruple 305-mm ASW mortar and six torpedo tubes (III × 2) have been removed. The hangar unfolds to become the helicopter flight deck. Due for disposal in 1990.

◆ **1 modified T-53 class, ASW**

	Bldr	Laid down	L	In serv.
D 633 DUPERRÉ	Lorient Ars.	11-54	23-6-56	8-10-57

Duperré (D 633) 16 Flot., French Navy, 1980

Duperré (D 633) Skyfotos, 7-83

D: 2,750 tons (3,740 fl) **S:** 34 kts (32 fl) **Dim:** 132.8 × 12.7 × 5.9 (props)
A: 4/MM 38 Exocet—1/100-mm DP, Model 1968—2/20-mm AA (I × 2)—2/catapults for L-5 torpedoes (8 torpedoes)—1/WG-13 Lynx helicopter
Electron Equipt: Radar: 2/DRBN 32, 1/DRBV 22A, 1/DRBV 51, 1/DRBC 32C,
Sonar: 1/DUBV 23, 1/DUBV 43 VDS
EW: ARBR 16, 2/Syllex countermeasures RL
M: 2 sets Rateau GT; 2 props; 64,000 hp **Electric:** 1,640 kw
Boilers: 4/ACB-Indret; 35 kg/cm², 385°C **Fuel:** 800 tons
Range: 1,500/30; 5,000/18
Man: Peacetime: 15 officers, 102 petty officers, 142 men

REMARKS: From 1967 to 1971, the *Duperré* was unarmed and was used for towed-sonar research, using the huge array later mounted in the auxiliary *Aunis.* Reconverted at Brest from 1972 to 21-5-74, as the final step in the long evolution of the T-47, *Surcouf*-class destroyer design. The hangar is fixed and has maintenance facilities, and the flight deck has a harpoon helicopter-recovery system similar to that on the *Tourville* and *Georges Leygues* classes. SENIT 2 data system fitted. The ship ran aground 13-4-78 and was badly damaged, but was repaired using components cannibalized from the inactivated *La Bourdonnais,* recommissioning 2-80. Flagship for destroyer squadron in the Atlantic; now due for disposal 1990.

◆ **2 D'Estrées class, converted Type T-47, ASW**

	Bldr	Laid down	L	In serv.
D 627 MAILLE BRÉZÉ	Lorient Ars.	10-53	26-9-54	4-5-57
D 628 VAUQUELIN	Lorient Ars.	3-54	26-9-54	3-11-56

Maille Brézé (D 627) L. & L. Van Ginderen, 11-84

Maille Brézé (D 627) L. & L. Van Ginderen, 11-84

D: 2,750 tons (3,740 fl) **S:** 32 kts **Dim:** 132.5 × 12.72 × 5.9 (props)
A: 2/100-mm DP, Model 1953 (I × 2)—2/20-mm AA (I × 2)—1/Malafon ASW syst. (13 missiles)—1/375-mm Bofors ASW RL (VI × 1)—6 TT (III × 2) for L-3 ASW torpedoes
Electron Equipt: Radar: 1/DRBN 32, 1/DRBV 22A, 1/DRBV 50, 2/DRBC 32A
Sonar: 1/DUBV 23, 1/DUBV 43 VDS
TACAN: URN 20 or . . .—EW: ARBR/ARBA 10C
M: 2 sets Rateau GT; 2 props; 63,000 hp **Electric:** 1,440 kw
Boilers: 4/ACB-Indret; 35 kg/cm², 385°C **Fuel:** 800 tons
Range: 1,500/30; 5,000/18
Man: Peacetime: 15 officers, 103 petty officers, 151 men

REMARKS: ASW conversions completed between 1-68 and 1-71: weapon system renewed, living spaces air-conditioned, electrical system and safety installations completely redesigned. These ships do not have the SENIT system. The *D'Estrées* has carried the British SCOT satellite-communications system as an experiment. A new, smaller TACAN is fitted in the D 628. Sisters *Casabianca* (D 631) stricken 1984, *D'Estrées* (D 629) and *Guépratte* (D 632) in 1985; the other two are to strike by 1988.

◆ **2 Kersaint class, converted Type T-47**

	Bldr	Laid down	L	In serv.
D 625 DUPETIT THOUARS	Brest Ars.	3-51	4-3-54	15-9-56
D 630 DU CHAYLA	Brest Ars.	7-53	27-11-54	4-6-57

GUIDED-MISSILE DESTROYERS *(continued)*

Du Chayla (D 630) L. & L. Van Ginderen, 6-84

D: 2,750 tons (3,850 fl) **S:** 32 kts (at 3,800 tons)
Dim: 128.50 × 12.96 × 5.00 (6.30 sonar)
A: 1/Mk 13 launcher (40 Standard SM-1 MR missiles)—6/57-mm AA (II × 3) — 1/375-mm ASW RL (VI × 1) Model 1954—6/550-mm TT (III × 2) for L-3 ASW torpedoes
Electron Equipt: Radar: 1/DRBV 22A, 1/SPS-39 B, 1/DRBV 31, 2/SPG-51B, 1/DRBC 31
Sonar: 1/DUBA 1, 1/DUBV 24
EW: ARBR/ARBA 10C—TACAN: URN 20
M: 2 sets Rateau GT; 2 props; 63,000 hp **Electric:** 1,600 kw
Boilers: 4 ACB-Indret; 35 kg/cm², 385°C
Range: 1,200/32; 3,500/20; 4,100/14
Man: Peacetime: 15 officers, 87 petty officers, 173 men

Remarks: Converted to carry U.S. Tartar missile system, 1961-65. DRBV 20 air-search radar replaced by later DRBV 22A. Sisters *Bouvet* (D 624) and *Kersaint* (D 622) stricken 1-1-82 and 1-12-83, respectively, to provide missile systems for the 1st and 2nd C-70AA-class destroyers under construction. D 625 to strike 1987 and D 630 in 1988 for the same purpose. Have SENIT 2 data system.

FRIGATES

◆ 0 (+3) FL 25 class

	Bldr	Laid down	L	In serv.
F. . . N. . .	. . .	. . .	. . .	. . .
F. . . N. . .	. . .	. . .	. . .	. . .
F. . . N. . .	. . .	. . .	. . .	. . .

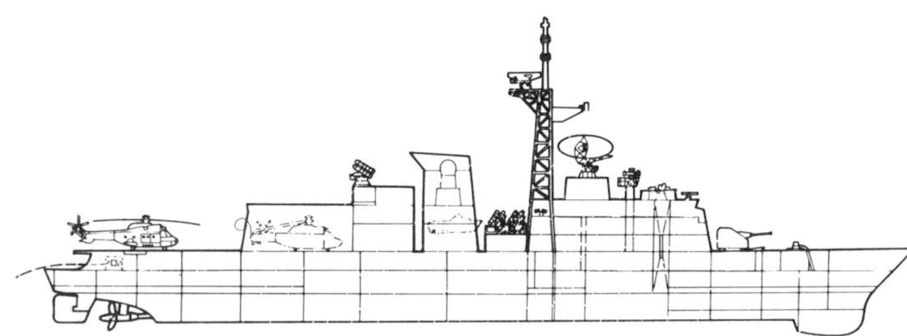

FL 25 class—provisional layout French Navy, 1984

D: 3,000 tons (mean trials) **S:** 26 kt. **Dim:** 113.0 pp × 13.0 × 3.90 (hull)
A: 8/MM 40 Exocet (IV × 2)—1/Crotale EDIR SAM syst. (VIII × 1; . . . missiles)—2/Sadral SAM syst. (VI × 2; . . . Mistral missiles)—1/100-mm Compact DP—2/20-mm AA (I × 2)—2/catapults for F17 ASW torpedoes (18 tot.)—1/helicopter (AS.15 and/or AM 39 Exocet ASM)
Electron Equipt: Radar: 1/Decca 1226, 1/DRBV 15 (Sea Tiger), 1/DRBV 26 (Jupiter II), 1/DRBC-33, 1/Crotale control
Sonar: . . . hull-mounted, DSBV 61 TASS
EW: ARBR 17 intercept, 2 ARBB 33 jammer, 2 Sagaie chaff RL (VI × 2), 2 Dagaie chaff R2
M: CODELOD: 4 SEMT-Pielstick 16 PA6 BTC diesels; 2 props; 32,500 hp (2 electric motors for speeds up to 12 kts)
Electric: . . . **Range:** 7,000/15 **Man:** 156 crew + 24 troops

Remarks: Intended to begin replacement of the *Cdt. Rivière* class, hence envisioned use of Super Puma helicopter to carry troops as well as for surveillance, torpedo-dropping, and anti-ship duties. Will have *Syracuse* SATCOMM equipment and the DIBV 10 *Vampir* IR surveillance device. Torpedo complement listed is for ship and helo launch. Fixed-pitch props. Steel superstructure. Data above are provisional.

◆ 17 D'Estienne D'Orves class, Type A-69 Bldr: Lorient Arsenal

	Laid down	L	In serv.
F 781 D'Estienne D'Orves	1-9-72	1-6-73	10-9-76
F 782 Amyot D'Inville	9-73	30-11-74	13-10-76
F 783 Drogou	10-73	30-11-74	30-9-76
F 784 Détroyat	12-74	31-1-76	4-5-77
F 785 Jean Moulin	15-1-75	31-1-76	11-5-77
F 786 Quartier-Maître Anquetil	1-8-75	7-8-76	4-2-78
F 787 Commandant De Pimodan	1-9-75	7-8-76	20-5-78
F 788 Second Maître Le Bihan	1-11-76	13-8-77	7-7-79
F 789 Lieutenant De Vaisseau Le Henaff	3-77	16-9-78	13-2-80
F 790 Lieutenant De Vaisseau Lavallée	11-11-77	29-5-79	16-8-80
F 791 Commandant L'Herminier	7-5-79	7-3-81	1985
F 792 Premier Maître L'Her	15-12-78	28-6-80	15-12-81
F 793 Commandant Blaison	15-11-79	7-3-81	28-4-82
F 794 Enseigne De Vaisseau Jacoubet	4-79	26-9-81	23-10-82
F 795 Commandant Ducuing	1-10-80	26-9-81	17-3-83
F 796 Commandant Birot	23-3-81	22-5-82	14-3-84
F 797 Commandant Bouan	12-10-81	23-4-83	19-6-84

Commandant de Pimodan (F 787)—with MM 38 Exocet J. Pradignac, 6-85

Commandant Blaison (F 793)—with MM 40 Exocet J. Pradignac, 1985

Jean Moulin (F 785)—without Exocet L. & L. Van Ginderen, 12-84

FRIGATES *(continued)*

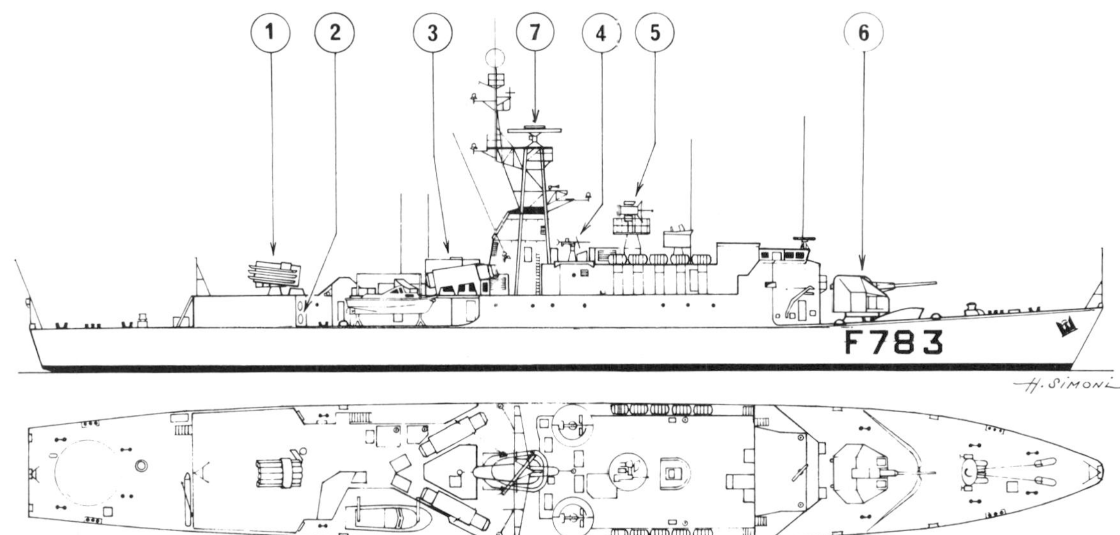

Drogu 1. Sextuple Bofors ASW rocket launcher, Model 1954 2. ASW torpedo tubes 3. Exocet launchers 4. 20-mm AA gunmounts 5. DRBC 32E fire-control radar 6. 100-mm DP gunmount, Model 1968 7. DRBV 51A search radar

Commandant Birot (F 796)—with MM 38 Exocet, Dagaie Pradignac & Leo, 1984

D: 1,100 tons (1,250 fl) **S:** 24 kts
Dim: 80.0 (76.0 pp) × 10.3 × 3.0 (5.3 sonar)
A: F 781, 783, 785, 786, 787, 796, 797: 2/MM 38 Exocet (I × 2); F 792—795: 2/MM 38 Exocet (II × 1)—1/100-mm DP, Model 1968—2/20-mm AA (I × 2)—1/375-mm ASW rocket launcher (VI × 1)—4/TT for L-3 and L-5 ASW torpedoes
Electron Equipt: Radar: 1/DRBN 32, 1/DRBV 51A, 1/DRBC 32E
Sonar: 1/DUBA 25
EW: ARBR 16, 2/Dagaie RL (in final 7 ships)
M: 2 SEMT-Pielstick 12 PC 2 diesels; 2 CP props; 11,000 hp
Electric: 840 kw **Endurance:** 15 days **Range:** 4,500/15
Man: 7 officers, 42 petty officers, 56 men

REMARKS: Very economical and seaworthy ships designed for coastal antisubmarine warfare, but available for scouting missions, instruction, and showing the flag. Can carry a troop detachment of one officer and seventeen men. The control system for the 100-mm gun consists of a DRBC 32E monopulse, X-band radar, and a semi-analog, semi-digital computer; it also has an optical sight. F 781, F 783, F 786, and F 787 of the Mediterranean Squadron have 2/MM 38 Exocet. All have fin stabilizers. Stacks and masts were modified from the *Jean Moulin* (F 785) onward; the heightened stack is being backfitted in earlier units. Plans to add a helicopter facility to F 793 and F 794 were abandoned. F 791 has 2 SEMT-Pielstick 12 PA 6 BTC diesels totaling 14,400 hp, with infrared signature suppression features; protracted trials delayed commissioning. The original *Lieutenant de Vaisseau Le Henaff* and *Commandant L'Herminier* were completed to a slightly modified design for South Africa and then sold to Argentina, which also ordered an additional unit.

◆ **1 Modified Commandant Rivière class**

	Bldr	Laid down	L	In serv.
F 729 BALNY	Lorient Ars.	3-60	17-3-62	1-2-70

D: 1,750 tons (2,230 fl) **S:** 26 kts **Dim:** 102.7 (98.0 pp) × 11.8 × 5.0 (prop)
A: 2/100-mm DP, Model 1953 (I × 2)—2/30-mm AA (I × 2)—1/305-mm ASW mortar (IV × 1)—6/TT for L-3 ASW torpedoes (III × 2)
Electron Equipt: Radar: DRBN 32, 1/DRBV 22A, 1/DRBC 32C
Sonar: 1/DUBA 3, 1/SQS 17—EW: ARBR 16
M: CODAG: 1 Turbomeca M 38 gas turbine (11,500 hp), 2 AGO V-16 diesels (3,600 hp each); 1 CP prop; 18,700 hp
Electric: 1,280 kw **Range:** 13,000/10
Man: 9 officers, 67 petty officers, 93 men

Balny (F 729) 1975

REMARKS: Allocated for trials in 1964 with the French Navy's first combined gas-turbine *and* diesel plant (CODAG). The gas turbine is a version of the Atar-8 turbojet used in the Étendard fighter, reduced in rate from 15,000 shp to 11,500 hp. Both diesels and the gas turbine can be clutched together to drive the single propeller, which is 3.6 meters in diameter and extends 1 meter beneath the keel. The compactness of the *Balny's* propulsion plant compared with that of the all-diesel plants in her half-sisters of the *Commandant Rivière* class permits her to carry approximately 100 more tons of fuel, which accounts for her great endurance on diesels alone. Because one of her 100-mm guns is mounted atop the lengthened after superstructure, it has not been possible to install Exocet anti-ship missiles.

◆ **7 Commandant Rivière class** Bldr: Lorient Arsenal

	Laid down	L	In serv.
F 725 VICTOR SCHOELCHER	10-57	11-10-58	15-10-62
F 726 COMMANDANT BORY	3-58	11-10-58	5-3-64
F 727 AMIRAL CHARNER	11-58	12-3-60	14-12-62
F 728 DOUDART DE LAGRÉE	3-60	15-4-61	1-5-63
F 740 COMMANDANT BOURDAIS	4-59	15-4-61	10-3-63
F 748 PROTET	9-61	7-12-62	1-5-64
F 749 ENSEIGNE DE VAISSEAU HENRY	9-62	14-12-63	1-1-65

D: 1,750 tons (2,070 normal, 2,230 fl) **S:** 26 kts (26.6 on trials)
Dim: 102.7 (98.0 pp) × 11.8 × 4.35 (max.)
A: 4/MM 38 Exocet—2/100-mm DP, Model 1963 (I × 2)—2/30- or 40-mm AA—1/305-mm ASW mortar (IV × 1)—6/TT L-3 ASW torpedoes (III × 2)
Electron Equipt: Radar: 1/DRBN 32, 1/DRBV 22A, 1/DRBC 32C
Sonar: 1/DUBA 3, 1/SQS-17
EW: ARBR 16, 2/Dagaie countermeasures RL
M: 4 SEMT-Pielstick 12 PC-series diesels; 2 props; 16,000 hp
Electric: 1,280 kw **Fuel:** 210 tons **Range:** 2,300/26; 7,500/16.5
Endurance: 45 days **Man:** 9 officers, 66 petty officers, 91 men

Victor Schoelcher (F 725) J.-C. Bellonne, 1983

FRIGATES *(continued)*

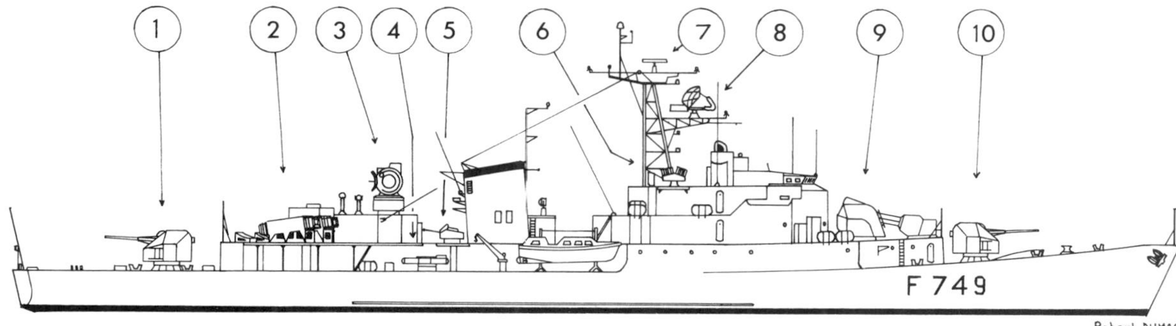

Enseigne De Vaisseau Henry 1. After 100-mm Model 1953 DP 2. MM 38 Exocet launchers 3. DRBC 32C f.c. radar director 4. ASW TT 5. 40-mm AA 6. Dagaie decoy RL 7. DRBN 32 (Decca RM 1226) nav. radar 8. DRBV 22A air-search radar 9. 305-mm quadruple mortar 10. forward 100-mm DP

Amiral Charner (F 727) LSPH S. Given, R.A.N., 1984

Protet (F 748)—30-mm AA and Dagaie G. Gyssels, 6-82

REMARKS: Designed for escort duty in various climates; air-conditioned. Can embark a flag officer and staff or an 80-man commando unit. F 726 originally had free-piston generators driving turbines, but these were replaced with a standard diesel plant in 1974-75. Beginning in the mid-1970s, four Exocet missiles replaced a 100-mm gun atop the after superstructure. F 728 replaced *Forbin* as cadet training ship in 1981. F 726 was the first ship to carry the Dagaie countermeasures rocket-launching system. F 725, F 748, and F 749 have 30-mm AA, the others have 40-mm AA. Sister *Commandant Rivière* (F 733) rerated as an auxiliary and converted 1985 as sonar trials ship.

PATROL BOATS

◆ **6 (+4) P 400 (Super PATRA) class** Bldr: CMN, Cherbourg

	Laid down	L	In serv.	Op. Area
P 682 L'Audacieuse	11-4-83	21-3-84	21-3-85	Indian Ocean
P 683 La Boudeuse	15-6-83	21-5-84	. . .	Nouméa
P 684 La Capricieuse	12-4-83	31-10-84	. . .	Papeete
P 685 La Fougeuse	25-11-83	17-12-84	. . .	Indian Ocean
P 686 La Glorieuse	21-2-84	25-1-85	. . .	Papeete
P 687 La Gracieuse	26-4-84	26-3-85	. . .	Papeete
P 688 La Moqueuse	4-10-84	. . .	. . .	Fr. Guyana
P 689 La Railleuse	27-12-84	. . .	. . .	Fr. Guyana
P 690 La Rieuse	14-3-85	. . .	. . .	Cherbourg
P 691 La Tapageuse	6-85	. . .	. . .	Cherbourg

L'Audacieuse (P 682) French Navy, 1984

D: 371.5 tons (414 fl) **S:** 24 kts **Dim:** 54.50 (50.0) × 8.0 (7.7 wl) × 2.54 (1.9 hull)
A: 1/40-mm AA—1/20-mm AA—1/7.62-mm mg
Electron Equipt: Radar: 1/DRBN 32 (Decca 1226)
M: 2 Alsthom/SEMT-Pielstick 16 PA 4V200 VGDS diesels; 2 props; 8,000 hp
Electric: 360 kw **Range:** 4,000/15 **Endurance:** 15 days
Man: 3 officers, 22 men + 23 passengers **Fuel:** 73 tons

REMARKS: First six ordered 5-82, remainder on 6-3-84. Four were originally to have been part of the *Force de Service Public* (Public Service Force) under the designation SP 400 class; they were to have had firefighting, search-and rescue, and antipollution equipment. All will now be identical. Last two to relieve *Glaive* (P 671) and *Pertuisane* (P 673) on Atlantic Coast. Carry 840 rds. 40-mm and 2,100 rds. 20-mm ammunition; equipped for later addition of two Exocet missiles and a fire-control radar. Maximum permissible displacement is 446 tons. P 686 carried small variable-depth sonar for trials in 1985.

◆ **4 Trident ("PATRA") class**

	Bldr	L	In serv.
P 670 Trident	Auroux, Arcachon	31-5-76	17-12-76
P 671 Glaive	Auroux, Arcachon	25-8-76	3-77
P 672 Épée	C.N.M. Cherbourg	31-3-76	9-10-76
P 673 Pertuisane	C.N.M. Cherbourg	2-6-76	20-1-77

Glaive (P 671) G. Gyssels, 2-85

Pertuisane (P 673) L. & L. Van Ginderen, 5-85

PATROL BOATS *(continued)*

D: 115 tons (148 fl) **S:** 28 kts **Dim:** 40.70 (38.5 wl) × 5.90 × 1.55
A: 1/40-mm AA—2/12.7-mm mg (I × 2)
Electron Equipt: Radar: 1/DRBN 32 (Decca 1226)
M: 2 AGO 195 V 12 CZSHR diesels; 2 CP props; 5,000 hp (4,400 sust.)
Electric: 120 kw **Range:** 750/20; 1,500/15; 1,750/10
Man: 2 officers, 5 petty officers, 12 men

REMARKS: Thirty were planned, then fourteen, but only four were finally built. Two sisters have been built for the Ivory Coast, and another, initially commissioned as *Rapière* (P 674) in the French Navy, was sold to Mauritania in 1982. *Epée* and *Trident* are stationed overseas, other two serve Gendarmerie Maritime. Carry 500 rounds of 40-mm, 2,000 rounds 12.7-mm ammunition. Six SS-12 wire-guided missile launchers atop the superstructure have been replaced by a single 12.7-mm mg.

◆ **1 Sterne class** Bldr: A & C. de la Perrière, Lorient

	Laid down	L	In serv.
P 680 STERNE	18-5-79	31-10-79	18-7-80

Sterne (P 680) LV (R) B. Prézelin, French Navy, 3-84

D: 270 tons (380 fl) **S:** 20 kts **Dim:** 49.00 (43.60 pp) × 7.50 × 2.80
A: 2/12.7-mm mg (I × 2) **Electron Equipt:** Radar: 1/DRBN-32, 1/Decca. . . .
M: 2 SACM V12 CZSHR diesels; 2 props; 4,200 hp **Electric:** 160 kw
Endurance: 15 days **Range:** 1,500/19; 4,900/12 **Man:** 16 tot.

REMARKS: Constructed to merchant marine specifications for fisheries patrol duties within the 200-nautical-mile economic zone, including rescue services. Equipped with a large infirmary. Passive tank stabilization system. Can patrol at speeds up to 6.5 knots on an electrohydraulic drive system connected to the starboard propeller. Two rubber inspection dinghies are carried. Accommodations for 23 persons.

◆ **1 former stern-haul trawler** Bldr: Le Trait (1965-67)

P 681 ALBATROS (ex-*Nevé*) (In serv. 23-3-84)

Albatros (P 681) J.-C. Bellonne, 1-84

D: 1,800 tons (2,800 fl) **S:** 15 kts **Dim:** 85.0 (75.0 pp) × 13.5 × 6.0
A: 1/40-mm AA—2/12.7-mm mg (I × 2) **Electron Equipt:** Radar: 2/navigational
M: Diesel-electric drive; 1 prop, 2,200 hp
Range: 12,000/15 **Man:** 6 officers, 20 petty officers, 16 men + 15 passengers

REMARKS: Purchased 1982 from Société Naval Caenaise for use in Antarctic area fisheries patrol duties, off Kerguelen, Crozet, St. Paul, and Amsterdam islands. Based at La Réunion.

◆ **1 Combattante-I class**

	Bldr	Laid down	L	In serv.
P 730 LA COMBATTANTE	CMN, Cherbourg	4-62	20-6-63	1-3-64

La Combattante (P 730) L. & L. Van Ginderen, 2-85

D: 180 tons (202 fl) **S:** 23 kts **Dim:** 45.0 × 7.35 × 2.45 (fl)
A: 1/40-mm AA—2/12.7-mm mg (I × 2)
M: 2 SEMT-Pielstick 8 PA4 200 VGDS diesels; 2 CP props; 3,600 hp
Electric: 120 kw **Range:** 2,000/12
Man: 3 officers, 22 men

REMARKS: Antimagnetic, laminated wood and plastic hull. Re-engined 1978. Launcher for 4 SS-12 wire-guided missiles removed. Formerly based at Tahiti; now operates in Mediterranean for the *Gendarmarie Maritime.*

◆ **1 Type DB-1 former minesweeper** Bldr: Const. Méc. de Normandie, Cherbourg

	Laid down	L	In serv.
P 765 MERCURE	1-55	21-2-57	20-12-58

Mercure (P 765) LV (R) B. Prézelin, French Navy, 11-84

D: 365 tons (400 fl) **S:** 15 kts **Dim:** 44.35 (42.0 pp) × 8.27 × 4.04
A: 2/20-mm AA (II × 1) **Electron Equipt:** Radar: 1/DRBN 32
M: 2 MGO diesels; 2 Ka-Me-Wa CP props; 5,000 hp **Range:** 6,200/10
Man: 5 officers, 14 petty officers, 18 men

REMARKS: The *Mercure* was converted to a fisheries-protection ship, re-entering service 22-12-80. Minesweeeping equipment removed. Insulated against cold climate. Habitability modernized. Carries two 6-man rubber inspection boats with 20-hp motors. Physician and dentist carried; accommodations for 44 personnel. Former pendant number M 765. Construction financed by U.S. as MSC 254. Six sisters built for West Germany have since been transferred to Turkey.

NOTE: The four Canadian "Bay"-class former minesweepers operated as colonial gunboats were stricken during 1985-86: *La Lorientaise* (P 652), *La Dunkerquoise* (P 653), *La Dieppoise* (P 655) and *La Paimpolaise* (P 657), as was the former *Sirius*-class minesweeper, *Canopus* (P 659).

◆ **4 British "Ham"-class ex-minesweepers**

	Bldr	In serv.
P 661 JASMIN (ex-*Stedham*)	Blackmore, Bideford	5-11-55
P 662 PETUNIA (ex-*Pineham*)	McLean, Renfrew	1956
P 742 PAQUERETTE (ex-*Kingham*)	J. S. White	14-8-54
P 784 GÉRANIUM (ex-*Tibenham*)	McGruer	23-7-55

Jasmin (P 661) LV (R) B. Prézelin, 3-85

PATROL BOATS *(continued)*

D: 140 tons (170 fl) **S:** 14 kts **Dim:** 33.43 × 6.45 × 1.7 **A:** 1/20-mm AA
M: 2 Paxman YHAXM diesels; 2 props; 550 hp **Fuel:** 15 tons
Endurance: 4 days **Man:** 1 officer, 10 petty officers, 2 men

REMARKS: Except for the *Petunia* (P 662), which is used by the Navy as a buoy tender and patrol boat, all are manned by the Gendarmerie. Built with U.S. Offshore Procurement funds as USN MSI 86, MSI 87, MSI 82, and MSI 84, respectively. Sister *Jonquille* (P 787) stricken 1984, *Violette* (P 788) in 1985; P 662 to discard 1986.

PATROL CRAFT

◆ **4 P 778 class** Bldr: CMN, Cherbourg (In serv. 1974)

P 778 P 779 P 780 *(Karukera)* P 781 *(Gugane)*

D: 20 tons (30 fl) **S:** 25 kts **Dim:** 24.9 × 5.3 × . . . **A:** 1/12.7-mm mg
M: 2 diesels; 2 props; . . . hp

REMARKS: *P 778* at Papeete, *P 779* at La Réunion, *P 780* at Cayenne, *P 781* at Pointe á Pitre. Manned by Gendarmerie Marine. Names in parentheses are unofficial. P 778 to be stricken 1986.

◆ **2 Volte 43 class** Bldr: Tecimar (In serv. 1975)

P 772 P 774

P 772 Tecimar, 1974

D: 14 tons **S:** 21 kts **Dim:** 13.30 × 3.90 × 1.10
A: 1/12.7-mm mg—1/7.62-mm mg **M:** 2 G.M. 8V71 diesels; 2 props; 670 hp
Electron Equipt: Radar: 1/Decca 1229 **Range:** 400/20 **Man:** 4 tot.

REMARKS: Hull molded of glass-reinforced plastic. Manned by the Gendarmerie, P 772 and 774 at Brest. P 771 transferred to Djibouti, P 770 stricken.

MINE WARFARE SHIPS

NOTE: The tender *Loire* (A 615) is, in effect, a mine-countermeasures support ship. However, because she has an auxiliary "A" pendant, and for convenience, she is listed with her *Rhin*-class sisters under Support Tenders.

◆ **0 (+5) seagoing minehunter/minesweepers**

	Bldr	Laid down	L	In serv.
M. . . N. . .	. . .	. . .	. . .	1990
M. . . N. . .	. . .	. . .	. . .	. . .
M. . . N. . .	. . .	. . .	. . .	. . .
M. . . N. . .	. . .	. . .	. . .	. . .
M. . . N. . .	. . .	. . .	. . .	. . .

D: 800 to 1,000 tons (fl) **S:** . . . **Dim:** . . . × . . . × . . .
A: . . . **Electron Equipt:** Radar: . . .
Sonar: towed DUBM 41C
M: Diesels; 2 props; . . . hp **Man:** . . .

REMARKS: Typed BAMO—*Bâtiment Antimines Oceaniques.* Designed by GESMA mine-warfare center. Glass-reinforced plastic construction. First five replace original last five ships in Tripartite program; five others may order in 1990s. Will carry a remote-controlled minehunting device with sonar and t.v. sensors.

◆ **5 (+5) Tripartite-class minehunters** Bldr: Lorient Arsenal

	Laid down	L	In serv.
M 641 ERIDAN	20-12-77	2-2-79	16-4-84
M 642 CASSIOPÉE	26-3-79	28-9-81	5-5-84
M 643 ANDROMÈDE	6-3-80	22-5-82	19-10-84
M 644 PÉGASE	22-10-80	23-4-83	30-5-85
M 645 ORION	17-8-81	6-2-85	1985
M 646 CROIX DU SUD	22-4-82	6-2-85	1986
M 647 AIGLE	. . .	. . .	1987
M 648 LYRE	14-10-83	. . .	1987
M 649 PERSÉE	30-10-84	. . .	1988
M 650 SAGITTAIRE	. . .	. . .	1988

Cassiopée (M 642) LV (R) B. Prézelin, French Navy, 4-85

Eridan (M 641) 16 Flot., French Navy, 1982

D: 500 tons (562 fl) **S:** 15 kts on main engine, 7 kts while hunting
Dim: 51.6 (47.1 pp) × 8.96 × 2.49 (hull) 2.64 (max.)
A: 1/20-mm AA—2/12.7-mm mg (I × 2)—2/PAP-104 remote-control mine-locators
Electron Equipt: Radar: 1/Decca 1229, 1/automatic track-plotter with numerical calculator, automatic pilot, Toran and Syledis radio navigation systems, Decca HiFix
Sonar: DUBM 21B
M: 1 Brons-Werkspoor A-RUB 215 × 12 diesel; 1 CP prop; 1,900 hp 2 electric maneuvering props, 120 hp each; bow-thruster
Electric: 750 kw **Range:** 3,000/12 **Man:** 5 officers, 29 petty officers, 21 men

REMARKS: Hull built of glass-reinforced polyester plastic. Program well behind schedule; last five canceled in favor of a larger design. Will have one mechanical drag sweep. France, Belgium, and The Netherlands are cooperating in building these ships for the requirements of the three countries. French examples are rated at a heavier displacement, (562 fl vice 544), with 595 tons given as limiting displacement. Have the EVEC 20 automatic plotting table and other precision navigation equipment. In 1985 began to receive the AP-4 acoustic sweep.

◆ **5 Circé-class minehunters** Bldr: Const. Méc. de Normandie, Cherbourg

	Laid down	L	In serv.
M 712 CYBÈLE	15-9-70	2-3-72	28-9-72
M 713 CALLIOPE	4-4-70	20-10-71	28-9-72
M 714 CLIO	4-9-69	10-6-71	18-5-72
M 715 CIRCÉ	30-1-69	15-12-70	18-5-72
M 716 CÉRÈS	2-2-71	10-8-72	8-3-73

Calliope (M 713) L. & L. Van Ginderen, 6-85

MINE WARFARE SHIPS *(continued)*

Circé (M 715) G. Gyssels, 2-85

Cybèle (M 712) LV (R) B. Prézelin, 4-85

D: 460 tons (495 fl) **S:** 15 kts **Dim:** 50.9 (46.5 pp) × 8.9 × 3.6 (max.)
A: 1/20-mm AA—2 PAP-104 remote control mine-locators
Electron Equipt: Radar: Decca 1229—Sonar: DUBM 20 (minehunting)
M: 1 MTU diesel; 1 prop; 1,800 hp
Range: 3,000/12 **Man:** Peacetime: 4 officers, 19 petty officers, 24 men

REMARKS: Designed for the detection and destruction of mines laid as deep as 60 meters. Hull made of laminated wood. Stress is on anti-magnetism and silence. Two independent propulsion systems, one for navigation, the other for minesweeping, both with remote control. Special rudders with small propellers mounted at the base of the rudder's after end and powered by a 260-hp electric motor, giving a speed of 7 knots and permitting exceptional maneuverability. Mines are destroyed either by divers (six in each crew) or by the PAP-104 *(poisson auto-propulsé)* wire-guided sled device, which is 2.7 meters long, 1.1 meters in diameter, weighs 700 kg, is moved by two electric motors that drive it at 6 knots for a distance of up to 500 meters, and has a television camera that displays an image of the mine. It can deposit its explosive charge of 100 kg near the mine. When the sled has been recovered, the charge is detonated by ultrasonic waves. These ships do not have minesweeping gear. *Cérès* carried the prototype EVEC automatic plotting table, now aboard all. All to receive updated DUBM 20A sonar with coherent processing feature during mid-1980s refits.

◆ **5 ex-U.S. Agile class, converted to minehunters** Bldr: Bellingham Shipyard, Bellingham, Washington

	In serv.	Converted
M 615 CANTHO (ex-MSO 476)	14-10-55	1-9-78
M 616 DOMPAIRE (ex-MSO 454)	21-5-55	14-4-77
M 617 GARIGLIANO (ex-MSO 452)	30-10-54	18-9-79
M 618 MYTHO (ex-MSO 475)	21-5-55	7-4-78
M 619 VINH-LONG (ex-MSO 477)	14-10-55	10-4-78

D: 700 tons (780 fl) **S:** 13.5 kts (14 kts on trials) **Dim:** 50.29 × 10.67 × 3.15
A: 1/40-mm AA—2/PAP-104 remote-control mine-locators
Electron Equipt: Radar: 1/Decca 1229
Sonar: DUBM 21
M: 2 G.M. 8-278A diesels; 2 CP props; 1,600 hp; bow-thruster
Range: 3,000/10 **Man:** Peacetime: 4 officers, 22 petty officers, 28 men

REMARKS: Modified as minehunters 1976-79. Mechanical minesweeping capability retained. All have new bridge superstructure. Have EVEC 11 automatic plotting tables.

Dompaire (M 616) G. Gyssels, 2-85

◆ **5 ex-U.S. Agile-class ocean minesweepers**

	Bldr	In serv.
M 610 OUISTREHAM (ex-MSO 513)	Peterson Bldrs., Sturgeon Bay, Wisc.	8-56
M 612 ALENÇON (ex-MSO 453)	Bellingham SY, Wash.	6-54
M 613 BERNEVAL (ex-MSO 450)	Bellingham SY, Wash.	12-53
M 620 BERLAIMONT (ex-MSO 500)	Bellingham SY, Wash.	1-56
M 623 BACCARAT (ex-MSO 505)	Tacoma Boat, Wash.	3-56

Alençon (M 612)—short stack L. & L. Van Ginderen, 6-85

Berlaimont (M 620)—tall stack M. Louagie, 1-85

D: 700 tons (780 fl) **S:** 13.5 kts (14 kts on trials) **Dim:** 50.29 × 10.67 × 3.15
A: 1/40-mm AA **Electron Equipt:** Radar: Decca 1229—Sonar: DUBM 41B
M: 2 G.M. 8-268A diesels; 2 CP props; 1,600 hp **Fuel:** 47 tons
Range: 3,000/10 **Man:** 5 officers, 53 men

REMARKS: Conversion of these ships to minehunters was canceled. However, they began receiving the new DUBM 41B sonar in 1978. M 620 recommissioned 3-80, M 613 in 7-80, M 612 in 1-81, and M 610 on 1-7-81. M 612 and M 613 have short stacks. Sister *Narvik* (M 609) was reclassified A 769 1-1-76 as a trials ship for the AP-4 acoustic sweep and the DUBM 21 sonar—*see* Experimental Ships.

MINE WARFARE SHIPS *(continued)*

◆ **5 Sirius-class coastal minesweepers** Bldr: CMN, Cherbourg

	L	In serv.
M 737 CAPRICORNE	8-8-56	11-7-58
M 749 PHÉNIX	23-5-55	21-12-56
M 755 CAPELLA	6-10-55	1-5-56
M 756 CÉPHÉE	3-1-56	11-6-56
M 757 VERSEAU	26-4-56	10-9-56

Verseau (M 757) L. & L. Van Ginderen, 9-84

D: 400 tons (440 fl) **S:** 15 kts (11.5 kts when sweeping)
Dim: 46.4 (42.7 pp) × 8.55 × 2.5 **A:** 1/20-mm AA
Electron Equipt: Radar: 1/DRBN 31
M: 2 SEMT-Pielstick 16 PA1-175 diesels; 2 props; 1,600 hp **Fuel:** 48 tons
Range: 3,000/10 **Man:** 3 officers, 35 men

REMARKS: French-built versions of the British "Ton" class. Engines built by S.G.C.M. Hull laminated wood and light aluminum alloy. Keel and stem in heavy wood. Have gear for sweeping mechanical, magnetic, and acoustic mines. The *Capricorne* (M 737) has greater degaussing capability than the others. All have one diesel sweep-generator (500 hp). *Aries* (M 758) was loaned to Morocco in 1975. *Bételgeuse* (A 747) was reclassified 1-5-77 as an experimental ship and used for trials with the DUBM 41 sonar and its computer. M 749 through M 757 were financed under the U.S. Offshore Procurement program as MSC 232 to MSC 235. To be stricken 1988-89.

AMPHIBIOUS WARFARE SHIPS

◆ **0 (+1 + 2) TCD 90 dock landing ships**

	Bldr	Laid down	L	In serv.
L 9011 FOUDRE	Brest Ars.	1986	late 1987	1990
L 9012 N. . .	. . .	. . .	. . .	1992
L 9013 N. . .	. . .	. . .	. . .	1993

D: 9,300 tons (11,800 fl) **S:** 21 kts **Dim:** 168.00 (160.00 pp) × 23.50 (22.00 wl) × 5.2 (9.10 flooded)
A: 2/SADRAL SAM syst (VI × 2, . . Mistral missiles)—1/40-mm AA—2/20-mm AA (I × 2)—4/Super Puma or Puma helicopter
Electron Equipt: Radar: 2/Decca . . . 1/*Rodeo* (French Army radar)
EW: . . . intercept;
M: 2 SEMT-Pielstick 16 PC 2.5-V400 diesels; 2 CP props; 20,000 hp cont.
Electric: 4,250 kw **Range:** 11,000/15 **Fuel:** . . .
Man: 210 crew + 350 passengers or 1,200 troops (470 extra emergency)

REMARKS: TCD = *Transport de Chalands de Débarquement* intended to carry one mechanized, 350-man regiment plus 1,080 tons combat vehicles and cargo for the Rapid Action Force; will also be able to act as logistics support ships. Docking well for 2 CDIC (EDIC replacement) or 10 CTM landing craft or one P 400 patrol boat: 1,740 m². Helo platform 1,080 m² with two spots, plus third spot on rolling dock-well cover; hangar for 4 helicopters. Vehicle cargo area of 1,360 m² can be extended by using dock floor; 60-ton elevation connects dock floor and cargo decks. Side loading doors. Will have Syracuse SATCOMM system. Propulsion plant same as in *Meuse*-class replenishment ships.
First ordered 5-11-84; others to order 1986, 1988.

NOTE: A smaller dock landing ship, ordered 12-83 to support the Pacific nuclear-weapons testing facility, is described in the auxiliary pages with other ships subordinated to the same agency.

◆ **2 Ouragan-class dock landing ships**

	Budget	Bldr	Laid down	L	In serv.
L 9021 OURAGAN	1960	Brest Ars.	6-62	9-11-63	1-6-65
L 9022 ORAGE	(22-7-65)	Brest Ars.	6-66	22-4-67	1-3-68

Ouragan (L 9021) L. & L. Van Ginderen, 11-83

Orage (L 9022) U.S. Navy, 8-82

D: 5,800 tons (8,500 fl) **S:** 17.3 kts
Dim: 149.0 (144.5 pp) × 21.5 × 5.4 (8.7 max.)
A: 4/40-mm AA (I × 4)—2/120-mm mortars (on L 9021 only)
Electron Equipt: Radar: 1/DRBN 32—Sonar: 1/SQS-17 on L 9021
M: 2 SEMT-Pielstick diesels; 2 CP props; 8,640 hp **Electric:** 2,650 kw
Range: 4,000/15 **Man:** 10 officers, 66 petty officers, 135 men

REMARKS: Bridge to starboard of permanent helicopter deck. L 9022 is assigned to the Pacific Test Center and acts as transport to and from France, as well as floating headquarters, employing a modular structure within the well deck. Both have repair facilities. Can carry 349 troops, including 14 officers, or 470 troops for a short distance. A 120-meter-long well with a 14-by-5.5-meter stern gate can be submerged by 3 meters. When ships are ballasted down, displacement reaches 14,400 tons. Movement of the sluices and valves is automatic, using pumps (3,000 m³/h) controlled from a central position. A removable deck in six sections covers 36 meters of the after part of the well and allows the landing and takeoff of heavy helicopters. A 90-meter-long temporary deck in 15 sections can be used to stow cargo or vehicles, but its use reduces

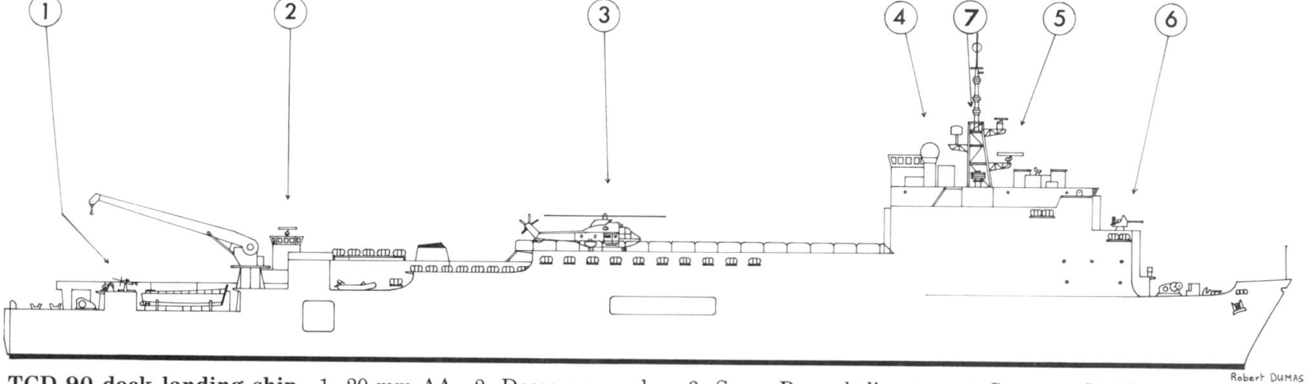

TCD 90 dock landing ship 1. 20-mm AA 2. Decca nav. radar 3. Super Puma helicopter 4. Syracuse SATCOMM antenna radomes 5. Decca nav. radar 6. 40-mm AA 7. SADRAL point-defense SAM system

AMPHIBIOUS WARFARE SHIPS *(continued)*

the number of landing craft that can be carried, because the well is then diminished by half.

If used as transports, they can embark either two EDIC landing craft for infantry and tanks, carrying 11 light tanks or trucks, or 18 LCM Mk 6 with tanks or vehicles and, in addition, heavy helicopters on a landing platform. If used as cargo-carriers, they can embark 1,500 tons of material. Lifting equipment includes two 35-ton cranes. A combined command center permits the simultaneous direction of helicopter and amphibious operations. To be discarded in 1990 and 1993, respectively.

◆ **3 Argens-class tank landing ships**

	Bldr	Laid down	L	In serv.
L 9004 Bidassoa (BDC-5)	Seine Maritime	1-60	30-12-60	7-61
L 9007 Trieux (BDC-1)	A.C. de Bretagne	12-57	6-12-58	18-3-60
L 9008 Dives (BDC-4)	Seine Maritime	5-59	29-6-60	14-4-61

Bidassoa (L 9004) G. Gyssels, 10-83

D: 1,400 tons 1,750 (av), 4,225 (fl) **S:** 11 kts
Dim: 102.12 (96.6 pp) × 15.54 × 3.2
A: 3/40-mm AA (I × 3) — 1/120-mm mortar **Man:** 6 officers, 69 men
Electron Equipt: Radar: DRBN 32
M: 2 SEMT-Pielstick 16 PA1 diesels; 2 props; 2,000 hp **Range:** 18,500/10

Remarks: Design derived from U.S. LST 1 class. Can carry 1,800 tons of cargo, 4 LCVP landing craft, and a maximum of 807 passengers (normally 170 troops). MacGregor-type loading hatches. *Trieux* modified with a hangar for two Alouette-III helicopters. The mortar is mounted at the bow. Sisters *Blavet* (L 9009) and *Argens* (L 9003) stricken 1985; L 9004, 9008 to strike 1986.

◆ **4 Champlain-class medium landing ships** Bldrs: L 9030, 9031: Brest Arsenal; others: At. Francais de Pouest, Grand-Querilly

	Laid down	L	In serv.
L 9030 Champlain	1973	17-11-73	5-10-74
L 9031 Francis Garnier	1973	17-11-73	21-6-74
L 9032 Dumont D'Urville	4-81	27-11-81	5-2-83
L 9033 Jacques Cartier	10-81	28-4-82	23-9-83

D: 750 tons (1,330 fl; L 9032, 9033: 1,386 fl) **S:** 16 kts (13 cruising)
Dim: 80.0 (68.0 pp) × 13.0 × 3.0 (2.50 hull) **Electric:** 360 kw
A: L 9030, 9031: 2/40-mm AA (I × 2) — 2/81-mm mortars (I × 2) — 2/12.7-mm mg — L 9032, 9033: 2/20-mm AA (I × 2) — 2/81-mm mortars (I × 2) — 2/12.7-mm mg
Electron Equipt: Radar: 1/DRBN 32
M: 2 SACM V-12 diesels; 2 CP props; 3,600 hp **Range:** 3,500/13
Man: 3 officers, 15 petty officers, 26 enlisted

Remarks: Bow-door design, embarkation ramp and helicopter platform aft. Cargo: 350 tons. Living quarters for a landing team (5 officers, 15 noncommissioned officers, 118 men) and its 12 vehicles, including Leopard armored personnel carriers. L 9032 and L 9033 are able to transport 180 men; they have a 40-ton capacity bow ramp, improved accommodations, and carry 1 LCVP and 1 LCP landing craft. Their superstructure is one deck higher, and they can carry a 330-ton-vehicle cargo for beaching and 208 tons of potable water. All have a helicopter deck for one Alouette-III. A sister ship has been built for Gabon.

Jacques Cartier (L 9033) 16 Flot., French Navy, 1984

Francis Garnier (L 9031) L. & L. Van Ginderen, 3-84

◆ **0 (+. . .) CDIC-class tank landing craft**

Remarks: CDIC = *Chalands de de'barqucment d'infantrie et de chars.* A project design to replace the EDICs, with substantially similar characteristics.

◆ **9 EDIC-class tank landing craft**

	L		L		L
L 9091	7-1-58	L 9096	11-10-58	L 9073	1968
L 9093	17-4-58	L 9070	30-3-67	L 9074	22-7-69
L 9094	24-7-58	L 9072	1968	L 9083	1964

L 9094 G. Gyssels, 11-82

D: 250 tons (670 fl) **S:** 8 kts **Dim:** 59.0 × 11.95 × 1.3 (1.62 fl)
A: 2/20-mm AA (I × 2) **M:** 2 MGO diesels; 2 props; 1,000 hp
Range: 1,800/8 **Man:** 5 petty officers, 12 men

Remarks: EDIC = *Engins de débarquement pour infanterie et chars.* L 9082 and L 9083: 310 tons (685 fl). Can carry 11 trucks or 5 LVTs. Two each can be carried aboard the *Ouragan* and the *Orage.* L 9095 transferred to Senegal, 1-7-74. L 9071 stricken 19-4-77, L 9092 and L 9082 stricken 1981. L 9084 reclassified BAME (repair barge). L 9096 was loaned to Lebanon 7-11-83 and returned in 1-85: l 9073, L 9091 and L 9093 are to be stricken during 1986.

◆ **21 repeat U.S. LCM (8)-class landing craft** Bldr: CMN, Cherbourg (CTM 4, 5, 11: C.N. Auroux, Arcachon)

	In serv.		In serv.		In serv.		In serv.
CTM 1	19-10-82	CTM 5	21-12-82	CTM 9	25-5-83	CTM 13	11-4-84
CTM 2	27-10-82	CTM 6	16-2-83	CTM 10	22-6-83	CTM 14	8-8-84
CTM 3	12-82	CTM 7	3-83	CTM 11	20-7-83	CTM 15	25-10-84
CTM 4	2-12-82	CTM 8	1983	CTM 12	11-8-83	CTM 16–21	1985

D: 48 tons (150 fl) **S:** 9.5 kts **Dim:** 23.80 × 6.35 × 1.25
M: 2 Poyaud 520 V8 diesels; 2 props; 480 hp
Range: 380/8.0 **Fuel:** 3.4 tons **Man:** 6 tot.

Remarks: Repeat version of earlier CTM 1–16. Cargo capacity: 90 tons. A small navigational radar is fitted.

AMPHIBIOUS WARFARE SHIPS *(continued)*

CTM 18 LV (R) B. Prézelin, French Navy, 4-85

◆ **6 U.S. LCM (3) class**

LCM 1035	LCM 1036	LCM 1055
LCM 1056	LCM 1057	LCM 1058

L 1055 G. Gyssels, 6-82

D: 26 tons (52 fl) **S:** 8 kts **Dim:** 15.25 × 4.3 × 1.2
M: 2 Gray Marine 64 HN9 diesels; 2 props; 450 hp **Cargo:** 30 tons

REMARKS: Transferred 6-58, except for LCM 1057 and 1058, built at La Réunion and delivered 3-83 for local service at Mayotte Naval Base. LCM 1031, 1045, 1052, 1074, and 1076 stricken 1984-85.

EXPERIMENTAL SHIPS

NOTE: For smaller experimental trials tenders (under 300 tons), see Miscellaneous Service Craft entry at end of France section.

◆ **0 (+1) Mine countermeasure experimental ship**

	Bldr	Laid down	L	In serv.
A 785 NÉREIDE	Lorient Ars.	. . .	. . .	1986-88

D: 720 tons, (1,000 fl) **S:** 15 kts **Dim:** 56.50 (51.70 pp) × 11.00 × 3.63
A: . . .
Electron Equipt: Radar: . . .—Sonar: . . .
M: 2 SACM MGO 175-V12-RVR diesels; 2 CP props; 2,500 hp

REMARKS: Typed BEGM—*Bâtiment d'Expérimentation de la Guerre des Mines.* Ordered 11-10-84. Uses same hull and machinery as the new hydrographic survey ships. A second unit was in the 1984-88 Plan; possibly canceled.

◆ **1 missile-range tracking ship** Bldr: Cantieri Riuniti de Adriatico, Monfalcone, Italy

	L	In serv.
A 603 HENRI POINCARÉ (ex-*Maina Morasso*)	10-60	1-3-68

Henri Poincaré (A 603) DCAN, 1974

D: 22,640 tons (23,430 fl) **S:** 15 kts **Dim:** 180.00 (160.00 pp) × 22.20 × 9.40
A: 2/20-mm AA **Electron Equipt:** Radar: 1/DRBV 22D, 2/Gascogne, 1/Savoie
M: 1 set Parsons GT; 1 prop; 10,000 hp; bow-thruster **Electric:** 7,355 kw
Boilers: 2 Foster-Wheeler; 48 kg/cm², 445°C **Range:** 11,800/13.5
Man: 22 officers, 144 petty officers, 159 men, and several civilian technicians

REMARKS: Flagship of Group M (the Naval Test and Measurement Group), which makes at-sea tests, takes measurements, and conducts experiments, as requested by the Navy or any other organization, civilian or military. The chief mission of the *Henri Poincaré* is to measure the trajectory of ballistic missiles (MSBS and SSBS) fired from the experimental station at Landes or from missile-carrying nuclear submarines and to compute their flight characteristics, especially from re-entry to impact. Her secondary mission is to assist the flag officer in controlling the naval and air elements in the test area, particularly recovery and security.

A former Italian tanker, the ship was entirely rebuilt by DCAN at Brest between 1964 and 1967, during which time she was given three radars for tracking and trajectory-measuring in ballistic tests and a sonar dome. She also has: an automatic tracking station; celestial position-fixing equipment; a camera-equipped theodolite; infrared equipment; a Transit navigational system; aerological, meteorological, and oceanographic equipment; excellent communications equipment; a programming and transcribing center for all experiments and installations; and a platform and hangar for two heavy or five light helicopters. Refitted 1-8-79 to 1-6-80, with 2 Gascogne tracking radars in place of original 2 Bearn, as well as other alterations. Received Syracuse SATCOMM system in 1983.

◆ **1 Commandante Rivière-class sonar trials ship, former frigate**

	Laid down	L	In serv.
A 753 COMMANDANTE RIVIÈRE (ex-F 733)	4-57	11-10-58	4-12-62

D: 2,100 tons (fl) **S:** 16 kts **Dim:** 103.00 × 12.52 (11.8 wl) × . . .
A: 1/40-mm AA—2/12.7-mm mg (I × 2)
Electron Equipt: Radar: 1/Decca 1226, 1/DRBV-22A
Sonar: DSBV 61 towed passive array; DUBV 43B VDS
M: 4 SEMT-Pielstick 12 PC-series diesels; 2 props; 16,000 hp
Man: 9 officers, 14 chief petty officers, 34 petty officers, 58 men + 37 technicians
Electric: 1,280 kw **Fuel:** . . . **Range:** . . .

REMARKS: Converted during 1985 as replacement for the former frigate *L'Agenais* (A 784) in towed sonar array trials. The 100-mm guns, MM 38 Exocet missiles were removed, and a 40-mm AA replaced the 305-mm ASW mortar. A new, broader stern of about 20-m length replaced the original and supports the DUBV 43 variable-depth sonar hoist equipment removed from the stricken destroyer *Casabianca* (D 631). The original hull-mounted SQS-17 sonar has been replaced, possibly by DUBV 24. Original 26-kt speed either reduced or restricted. Intended to test interface between hull-mounted, VDS, and passive linear towed hydrophone array sonars. To recommission 1-86.

◆ **1 guided-missile trials ship** Bldr: A. G. Weser, Bremen

	L	In serv.
A 610 ILE D'OLÉRON (ex-*Lazarettschiff München,* ex-*Sperrbrecher 32,* ex-*Mur*)	1939	29-8-45 (French Navy)

Ile d'Oléron G. Gyssels, 6-83

D: 5,500 tons (6,500 fl) **S:** 14.5 kts **Dim:** 115.05 (107.00 pp) × 15.24 × 6.50
A: 1/Crotale syst. (VIII × 1)—. . ./MM 40 Exocet
Electron Equipt: Radar: 1/DRBN 32, 1/DRBV 22C, 1/DRBV 50, 1/DRBI 10
M: 2 M.A.N. 6-cyl. diesels; 1 prop; 3,500 hp **Electric:** 1,240 kw
Fuel: 340 tons **Range:** 5,900/14; 7,200/19
Man: 9 officers, 46 petty officers, 113 men

REMARKS: Taken from the Germans as a prize of war and used as a transport until converted, 1957-58, to an experimental ship for missiles. Besides the radars listed, she carries guidance radars for the systems under test. Used for MM 38 Exocet trials and, since 1977, for Crotale. Trials with MM 40 Exocet began 2-80. Helicopter deck aft.

◆ **1 electronics experimental ship**

	Bldr	L	In serv.
A 644 BERRY (ex-*Medoc*)	Roland Werft, Bremen	10-9-58	26-11-64

Berry (A 644) G. Gyssels, 6-85

EXPERIMENTAL SHIPS *(continued)*

D: 1,150 tons (2,700 fl) **S:** 15 kts **Dim:** 86.7 (78.5 pp) × 11.6 × 4.6
A: 2/20-mm AA (I × 2) **M:** 2 MWM diesels; 1 prop; 2,400 hp
Range: 7,000/15

REMARKS: An ex-stores ship, converted 1976-77 at Toulon and recommissioned 2-77. Used for trials with electronic-warfare equipment. Painted white. Former sister *Aunis,* a sonar-trials ship, was stricken 1-7-81.

◆ **1 ex-U.S. Agile-class ocean minesweeper** Bldr: Peterson Builders, Sturgeon Bay, Wisc. In serv. 3-2-57

A 769 NARVIK (ex-M 609, ex-MSO 512)

Narvik (A 769) LV (R) B. Prézelin, French Navy, 6-85

REMARKS: Since recommissioning 1-1-76, conducts experiments with the AP-4 acoustic sweep and the DUBM 21 series. For data, see ex-U.S. *Agile* class under Mine Warfare Ships. Retains 1/40-mm AA.

NOTE: The *Sirius*-class mine-countermeasures trials ship *Bételgeuse* (A 747) was stricken 1982, and the U.S. *Adjutant*-class trials minelayer *Jacinthe* (A 680) was stricken 15-1-82.

◆ **1 underwater-research ship**

	Budget	Bldr	Laid down	L	In serv.
A 646 TRITON	1967	Lorient Ars.	1967	7-3-70	20-1-72

Triton (A 646) G. Gyssels, 6-85

D: 1,410 tons (1,510 fl) **S:** 13 kts **Dim:** 74.00 (68.00 pp) × 11.85 × 3.65
M: 2 MGO V-12 ASHR diesels, electric drive; aft: 1/Voith-Schneider 30 G cycloidal propeller; 880 hp; forward: 2 electric motors, 1/Voith-Schneider 26 G cycloidal propeller; 530 hp
Electric: 640 kw **Range:** 4,000/13
Man: Ship's company: 4 officers, 44 men; divers: 5 officers, 12 men

REMARKS: Assigned to GISMER (Groupe d'Intervention sous la Mer) for deep-sea diving and observation. Has a decompression chamber, laboratories, television, navigational radar, sonar for deep-water area search, etc. Helicopter platform. Good maneuverability at very slow speeds; capable of remaining positioned above a point 300 meters deep. Can be used in submarine-rescue operations. Her 15-ton crane can lower and raise: (a) a 13.5-ton tethered bell that can be sunk to 250 meters and can carry two four-man diving teams; (b) the two-man submarine *Griffon,* which is capable of diving to 600 meters for underwater exploration; (c) diving devices, sleds (troika, automatically guided). The *Griffon* has a manipulator arm, and other characteristics are:

D: 14.2 to 16.7 tons **Dim:** 7.8 × 2.3 × 3.1 (height) **M:** 1 electric motor
Range: 24 hours/4 kts

NOTE: The *Chamois*-class local support tender *Isard* is also subordinated to GISMER and supports the ERIC *(Engin de Recherche et d'Intervention par Cable)* wire-guided submersible. For data, see the *Chamois* class under Miscellaneous Auxiliary Ships. The submersible craft-support ship *Gustave Zedé* (A 759; ex-*Marcel le Bihan, ex-German Grief)* was stricken during 1984.

◆ **1 ASW weapons-trials support tender**

	Bldr	L	In serv.
A 743 DENTI	DCAN, Toulon	7-10-75	15-7-76

Denti (A 743) G. Gyssels, 6-83

D: 170 tons (fl) **S:** 12 kts **Dim:** 34.70 (30.00 pp) × 6.60 × 2.27
Electron Equipt: Radar: 1/Decca . . .
M: 2 Baudouin DP 8 diesels; 2 props; 960 hp
Range: 800/12 **Man:**

REMARKS: Employed by DCAN Toulon in support of weapons trials. Essentially a recovery craft, with an overhead rail gantry aft. Carries divers also.

OCEANOGRAPHIC RESEARCH SHIPS

◆ **1 expeditionary ship**

	Bldr	Laid down	L	In serv.
A 757 D'ENTRECASTEAUX	Brest	7-69	30-5-70	10-10-70

D'Entrecasteaux (A 757) Skyfotos, 3-82

D'Entrecasteaux (A 757) L. & L. Van Ginderen, 5-82

D: 2,058 tons (2,440 fl) **S:** 15 kts **Dim:** 89.0 × 12.0 × 3.9
Electron Equipt: Radar: 2/DRBN 32
M: 2 diesel engines, electric drive; 2 CP props; 2,720 hp; for extremely slow maneuvering: 2 retractable Schöttel propellers, 1 fwd, 1 aft
Range: 10,000/12
Man: 6 officers, 73 men, up to 38 Hydrographic Service scientists and technicians

REMARKS: For oceanographic research and hydrographic duties. Has a dynamic mooring/maneuvering system permitting station-keeping in 5,000-m depths. Can take

OCEANOGRAPHIC RESEARCH SHIPS *(continued)*

soundings and surveys to a depth of 6,000 meters. Helicopter platform and hangar (Alouette-III helicopter). Electrohydraulic oceanographic equipment cranes, one landing craft, three hydrographic launches, hull-mounted scanning sonar. Painted white.

◆ **1 underwater archeological research ship**

	Bldr	L
A 789 Archéonaute	Auroux, Arcachon	25-8-67

Archéonaute (A 789) J.-C. Bellonne, 1972

D: 100 tons (120 fl) **S:** 12 kts **Dim:** 29.3 × 6.0 × 1.7
M: 2 Baudouin diesels; 2 CP props; 600 hp
Man: 2 officers, 4 men, 3 scientific research personnel, 6 divers

Remarks: Ordered by the Office of Cultural Affairs, manned by Navy personnel. Laboratory and workshops, decompression chamber, underwater television.

HYDROGRAPHIC SURVEY SHIPS

◆ **0 (+4) new construction** Bldr: Lorient Arsenal

	Laid down	L	In serv.
A 791 La Pérouse	1985	. . .	. . .
A 792 Borda	1985	. . .	. . .
A 793 La Place	. . .	. . .	. . .
A 794 Arago	. . .	. . .	. . .

D: 720 tons light (1,000 fl) **S:** 15 kts **Dim:** 56.50 (51.70 pp) × 11.00 × 2.60
M: 2 S.A.C.M. MGO Type 175 V 16SHR diesels; 1 CP prop; 2,200 hp—plus a 200-hp swivelling propulsor
Range: 6,000/12 **Man:** 29 crew + 11 hydrographic survey party

Remarks: First two ordered 24-7-84. This program replaces the one 2,000-ton Type BH1 and two 800-ton Type BH2 described in the previous edition. The ships will carry the Thomson-CSF TSM 5425 wreck-identification sonar. They will replace four older coastal survey ships. A near-sister will serve as a mine-warfare trials ship.

◆ **2 converted ex-trawlers** Bldr: Gdynia, Poland

	L	In serv. with French Navy
A 756 L'Espérance (ex-*Jacques Coeur*)	1962	12-7-69
A 766 L'Estafette (ex-*Jacques Cartier*)	1962	16-11-72

L'Espérance (A 756) L. & L. Van Ginderen, 12-84

D: 900 tons (1,300 fl) **S:** 13.5 kts **Dim:** 63.45 (59.75 pp) × 9.82 × 5.85 (fl)
M: 2 M.A.N. diesels; 1 prop; 1,870 hp **Range:** 7,500/13
Man: 3 officers, 11 petty officers, 29 enlisted

Remarks: Former oceangoing fishing trawlers, purchased 1968-69. Carry one survey launch. Large oceanographic winch on stern, articulated crane amidships. Painted white.

	Bldr	L	In serv.
A 758 La Recherche (ex-*Guyane*)	Ziegler, Dunkerque	4-51	19-3-62 (in French Navy)

La Recherche (A 758) C. Martinelli, 1981

D: 810 tons (910 fl) **S:** 13.5 kts **Dim:** 67.5 (62 pp) × 10.4 × 4.5
M: 1 Werkspoor MABS 398 diesel; 1 prop; 1,535 hp
Range: 3,100/10 **Man:** 2 officers, 10 petty officers, 26 men

Remarks: Operated for the French Overseas Ministry. Bought in 1960. Hull bulged for improved stability. Carries two inshore survey launches. Painted white.

◆ **2 Astrolabe-class survey ships**

	Bldr	Laid down	L	In serv.
A 780 Astrolabe	Seine Maritime	1962	27-5-63	7-64
A 781 Boussole	Seine Maritime	6-62	11-4-63	7-64

Astrolabe (A 780) Skyfotos, 9-82

D: 330 tons (440 fl) **S:** 12.5 kts **Dim:** 42.7 (36.65 pp) × 8.45 × 2.9
M: 2 Baudouin DV 8 diesels; 1 CP prop; 800 hp
Range: 4,000/12 **Man:** 1 officer, 32 men

Remarks: Air-conditioned. Carry two 8.8-m Type VH8 survey launches equipped with the *Trident* radiolocation system; they are later to be fitted with TORAN. Painted white. Formerly had "P"-series pendants, and A 780 at one time carried 1/40-mm AA, 2/12.7-mm mg.

◆ **1 inshore survey ship**

	Bldr	L	In serv. (French Navy)
A 794 Corail (ex-*Marc Joly*)	Thuin, Belgium	1967	11-4-75

Corail (A 794) 1975

HYDROGRAPHIC SURVEY SHIPS *(continued)*

D: 54.78 tons (light) **S:** 10.3 kts **Dim:** 17.8 × 4.92 × 1.83
M: 1 Caterpillar diesel; 1 prop; 250 hp **Man:** 7 tot.

Remarks: Ex-fishing boat, operates in the Pacific. Painted white.

SUPPORT TENDERS

◆ 1 multi-purpose repair ship

	Budget	Bldr	Laid down	L	In serv.
A 620 Jules Verne (ex-*Achéron*)	1961	Brest Ars.	1969	30-5-70	1-6-76

Jules Verne (A 620) J.-C. Bellonne, 1982

D: 6,485 tons (10,250 fl) **S:** 18 kts **Dim:** 147.0 × 21.56 × 6.5
A: 2/40-mm AA (I × 2) **M:** 2 SEMT-Pielstick T2 PC diesels; 1 prop; 11,200 hp
Electric: 3,800 kw **Range:** 9,500/18
Man: 16 officers, 150 petty officers, 116 men

Remarks: Six years after being launched as an ammunition ship, the uncompleted *Jules Verne* was converted to a floating workshop to provide support to a force of from three to six surface warships. Has significant capabilities for both regular maintenance and battle-damage repair: mechanical, engine, electrical, sheet-metal, electronic workshops, etc. She carries a stock of torpedoes and other munitions. Has a platform and hangar for two Alouette-III helicopters. Operates in support of the Indian Ocean Flotilla.

◆ 5 Rhin class Bldr: Lorient Arsenal (differences as noted)

	Budget	Purpose	Laid down	L	In serv.
A 615 Loire	1962	Minesweepers	9-7-65	1-10-66	10-10-67
A 621 Rhin	1959	Electronics	24-4-61	17-3-62	1-3-64
A 622 Rhône	1960	Submarines	23-2-62	8-12-62	1-12-64

Loire (A 615)—helicopter hangar, 3 radars, IFF interrogator
L. & L. Van Ginderen, 5-85

Rhône (A 622)—helo deck, no hangar (A 615 similar) L. & L. Van Ginderen, 1-85

D: 2,075 tons (2,445 fl) **S:** 16.5 kts **Dim:** 101.05 (92.05 pp) × 13.1 × 3.65
A: 3/40-mm AA (I × 3) **Electron Equipt:** Radar: 2/DRBN 32
M: 2 SEMT-Pielstick 16 PA 2V diesels; 1 prop; 3,200 hp
Electric: 920 kw **Range:** 13,000/13
Man: A 621, 622: 6 officers, 42 petty officers, 76 men (A 615: 9 officers, 131 men)

	Budget	Purpose	Laid down	L	In serv.
A 618 Rance	1964	Experimental	8-64	5-5-65	5-2-66

Rance (A 618) G. Gyssels, 6-82

A: None **Electron Equipt:** Radar: 1/DRBN 32, 1/DRBV 22E
EW: ARBR/ARBA 10
M: SEMT-Pielstick 12 PA 4 diesels; 3,600 hp
Man: 10 officers, 39 petty officers, 69 men

	Budget	Purpose	Bldr	Laid down	L	In serv.
A 617 Garonne	1964	Repair	Lorient	11-63	8-8-64	9-65

Garonne (A 617) J.-C. Bellonne, 1977

D: 2,320 tons **S:** 15 kts **Dim:** 101.5 (92.05 pp) × 13.8 × 3.7
A: 1/40-mm AA—2/20-mm AA **Electron Equipt:** Radar: 1/DRBN 32
M: 2 SEMT-Pielstick 12 PA 4 diesels; 1 prop; 3,600 hp **Range:** 13,000/13
Man: 6 officers, 39 petty officers, 69 men

Remarks: *Rhin* has 1,700 m³ of store rooms and 700 m³ of workshops, many air-conditioned. She has a hangar and flight deck for one helicopter, which is equipped to serve minesweepers with spare sweep gear, cable, and repairs. *Rhône* is fitted to service submarines; helicopter deck but no hangar. *Loire* has a helicopter deck and hangar. All have one 5-ton crane with a 12-meter reach. The profile of the *Rance* is different from that of the other ships of this group; an additional deck has been fitted between her navigating bridge and her stack. She has a laboratory, radioactive decontamination stations, and carries up to three Alouette helicopters, using both the stern and her hangar roof as landing platforms. *Garonne* was designed for overseas service. She has metalworking and carpentry shops, an extra deck with lower overhead, and a 30-ton crane mounted in the center of her fantail; no helicopter facilities.

Note: BAME 9084, the former EDIC-class landing craft L 9084, altered as an electronics repair craft and stationed at Mayotte, the Comoros, has been stricken. BAME = *Batiment-Annexe-Électronique.*

FLEET REPLENISHMENT SHIPS

◆ 3 (+1) Durance-class fleet oilers Bldr: Brest Arsenal

	Laid down	L	In serv.
A 629 Durance	10-12-73	6-9-75	1-12-76
A 607 Meuse	2-6-77	2-12-78	2-8-80
A 608 Var	12-78	9-5-81	29-1-83
A 630 Marne	4-8-82	6-2-85	10-86

D: 7,600 tons (17,800 fl) **S:** 20 kts
Dim: 157.3 (149.0 pp) × 21.2 × 8.65 (10.8 fl)
A: 1/40-mm AA—2/20-mm AA (I × 2)—A 629: 2/40-mm AA (I × 2)—no 20-mm
M: 2 SEMT-Pielstick 16 PC 2.5 V400 diesels; 2 CP props; 20,000 hp
Electric: 5,400 kw **Fuel:** 750 tons **Range:** 9,000/15
Man: 8 officers, 62 petty officers, 89 men (*Var:* 10 officers, 62 p.o., 90 men)

Remarks: Two dual solids/liquids underway-replenishment stations per side. Can supply two ships alongside and one astern. *Durance:* 7,500 tons fuel oil, 1,500 tons diesel fuel, 500 tons JP-5, 130 tons distilled water, 170 tons fresh provisions, 150 tons munitions, 50 tons spare parts; *Meuse:* 5,090 tons fuel oil, 4,014 tons diesel, 1,140 tons JP-5, 250 tons distilled water, 180 tons provisions, 122 tons munitions, and 45 tons spare parts. *Var* and No. 4: 5,090 tons fuel oil, 3,310 tons diesel, 1,090 tons JP-5,260 tons distilled water, 170 tons ammunition, 180 tons provisions, 15 tons spares. Hangar

FLEET REPLENISHMENT SHIPS *(continued)*

Durance (A 629)—tank deck plated in at sides P. Voss, 10-83

Meuse (A 607)—tank deck open-sided Pradignac & Leo, 6-84

Var (A 608)—Syracuse SATCOMM antennas atop bridge 16 Flot., French Navy, 1983

for one Alouette-III (*Var:* Lynx) and flight deck for larger helicopters. Superstructure before the bridge one deck higher in *Meuse.* In *Meuse* the 40-mm AA is aft; in *Var* it is forward. *Var* and Marne are equipped as flagships for a major area commander and can accommodate 257 persons. The forward superstructure block is extended aft by 8 meters to provide increased staff accommodations, and the two beam-mounted stores cranes immediately abaft the bridge are replaced by a single, centerline crane; the Syracuse SATCOMM system is fitted. The fifth ship l'Atlantique, which will resemble A 608 and A 630, was ordered 3-84 from CNM, La Seyne, for an undisclosed foreign customer; laid down 3-5-85. A fifth for the French Navy was to be ordered in 1986 under the 1984-88 Plan. A near sister is building in Australia for the R.A.N.

TRANSPORT OILERS

◆ **0 (+1) chartered freighting tanker** Bldr: Ch. de l'Atlantique, St. Nazaire

	Laid down	L	In serv.
N. . .	. . .	. . .	. . .

Remarks: A 32,000 deadweight ton freighting tanker was ordered 20-3-85 as a replacement for *Port Vendres.* The ship will be chartered from the owners, SOCATRA, Bordeaux, and SOFLUMAR, Paris, and is intended to operate between the Persian Gulf and La Réunion. There will be one underway replenishment station per side.

◆ **1 chartered tanker** Bldr: Brodogradilište, Uljanik, Yugoslavia

Port Vendres (ex-*Mont-Agel,* ex-*Wiiri*) (L: 17-2-73; in serv. 3-73)

Port Vendres LV (R) B. Prézelin, French Navy, 6-85

D: Approx. 31,000 tons (fl) **S:** 15.5 kts
Dim: 175.10 (163.20 pp) × 25.05 × 9.68
M: 1 Burmeister & Wain 6K74EF diesel; 1 prop; 10,600 hp
Electric: 1,544 kw **Man:** 27 tot.

Remarks: 15,285 grt/25,253 dwt. Chartered 4-8-82 and to be returned to owners by 1988. Cargo capacity 32,088 m³ liquid. Has a 1,200-hp KaMeWa tunnel bow-thruster. Can refuel over the stern.

◆ **2 Punaruu class** Bldr: Trosik Verkstad, Brevek, Norway

	In serv. (French Navy)
A 625 Papenoo (ex-*Bow Queen*)	9-11-71
A 632 Punaruu (ex-*Bow Cecil*)	16-11-71

Papenoo (A 625) French Navy, 1983

D: 1,195 tons light (4,050 fl) **S:** 13 kts **Dim:** 83.00 (70.70 pp) × 13.85 × 5.50
Electron Equipt: Radar: 1/Decca RM 316
M: 2 Normo LSMC-8 diesels; 1 CP prop; 2,050 hp **Electric:** 290 kw
Fuel: 174 tons **Range:** 8,000/11.5 **Man:** 2 officers, 20 men

Remarks: 1,119 grt, 2,889 dwt. Former Norwegian solvent tankers purchased at the end of 1969. Highly automated ships. Capacity: 2,554 m³. Ten washable "inox" cargo tanks that can accept any liquid. Astern fueling capability. Bow-thruster equipped (530 kw). Operate primarily in the Pacific

LIGHT-FUELS TANKER

	Bldr	Laid down	L	In serv.
A 619 Aber Wrach	CNM, Cherbourg	11-62	11-63	27-3-66

Aber Wrach (A 619) L. & L. Van Ginderen, 1984

D: 1,220 tons (3,500 fl) **S:** 12 kts **Dim:** 86.55 (80.0 pp) × 12.2 × 4.8
A: 1/40-mm AA **M:** 1 SEMT-Pielstick 6 PL diesel; 1 CP prop; 2,000 hp
Electron Equipt: Radar: 1/DRBN 32—EW: ARBR/ARBA 10
Range: 5,000/12 **Man:** 3 officers, 45 men

Remarks: Cargo capacity: 2,200 tons. Carries diesel oil, jet fuel, and gasoline in point-to-point service. Capable of astern underway fueling, or anchored alongside.

SUPPORT SHIPS FOR NUCLEAR WEAPONS TESTING

Note: The seven ships described below were financed by and are operated for DIRCEN — Direction des centres d'expérimentation nuclear—the French nuclear-weapon testing agency, in support of activities at Muraroa in the South Pacific. They are manned by the French Navy.

◆ **0 (+1) BTMS small dock landing ship**

	Bldr	Laid down	L	In serv.
A. . . N. . .	Dubigeon, Nantes	11-84	12-85	10-87

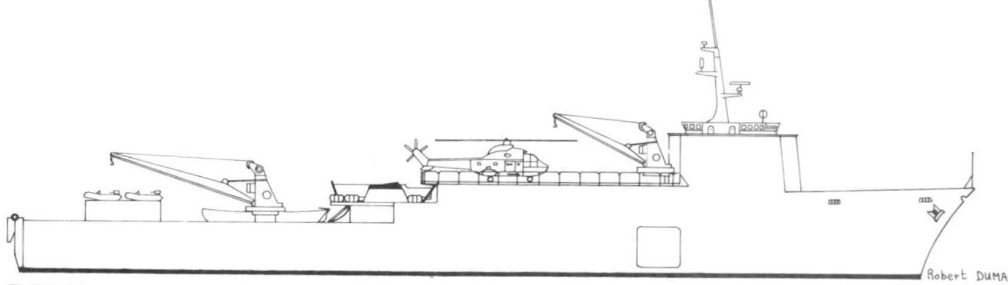

BTMS

SUPPORT SHIPS FOR NUCLEAR WEAPONS TESTING *(continued)*

D: 4,200 tons (4,880 fl) **S:** 15 kts **Dim:** 113.50 (105.00 pp) × 17.00 × 4.24
A: . . . —2/Super Puma helicopters
Electron Equipt: Radar: 1/navigational
M: 2 SACM MGO 195 V12 RVR diesels; 2 CP props; 4,800 hp—side-thruster
Electric: 1,600 kw **Range:** 6,000/12 **Fuel:** . . .
Endurance: 30 days **Man:** 6 officers, 17 petty officers, 29 enlisted + 50 passengers

REMARKS: BTMS = *Bâtiment de Transport Moyen et de Soutien,* intended for Directorate of Nuclear Experimentation for use between Papeete and the Muraroa test center. Miniature LSD-design, with 78.0 × 11.8-m docking well aft for one EDIC landing craft. Cargo capacity: 1,100 tons. Can load vehicles via stern dock door/ramp and starboard side ramp. No hangar. Ordered 12-83. Other reports indicate keel not to be laid until 1986.

NOTE: The following six ships were originally ordered to support *Force de Surface à Missions Civiles* (Civil Missions Surface Force) duties on the Atlantic coast of France.

◆ **2 Type RR 4000 class tug/supply vessels** Bldr: Breheret, Conéron, Nantes

	L	In serv.		L	In serv.
A 634 RARI	16-4-84	2-85	A 635 REVI	15-5-84	3-85

Rari (A 634) LV (R) B. Prézelin, French Navy, 7-84

D: 900 tons light (1,450 fl) **S:** 14.5 kts **Dim:** 51.00 (49.50 wl) × 12.60 × 4.00
Electron Equipt: Radar: 1/Decca . . . nav. **Range:** 5,000/12
M: 2 SACM Type 195 V12 RVR; 2 CP props; 4,000 hp **Man:** 2 officers, 18 men

REMARKS: Can carry 18 passengers. Bollard pull: 47 tons. Two 2.5-ton thrust side-thrusters. Have a 14-ton crane aft, plus a quadrantial gantry at the extreme stern. Two water cannons for firefighting. Can carry fuel cargo.

◆ **1 Type RR 2000 (Modified Chamois) class**

	Bldr	Laid down	L	In serv.
A 633 TAAPE	de la Perrière, Lorient	22-10-82	14-4-83	30-6-83

Taape (A 633) BAN Lanveoc-Poulmic, French Navy, 1984

D: 383 tons (505 fl) **S:** 14.2 kts **Dim:** 41.02 (38.50 pp) × 7.5 × 3.18
M: 2 SACM M60 V16 ASHR diesels; 2 CP Kort-nozzle props; 2,200 hp
Range: 7,200/12 **Man:** 2 officers, 18 men

REMARKS: A variation of the FISH-class design also used in the *Chamois*-class tenders. 24.8 bollard pull. Can carry 100 tons of cargo on the long, open afterdeck. Transported to Muraroa in the landing ship *Orage* in 4-84.

◆ **3 seagoing tugs** Bldr: SFCN, Villeneuve-la-Garenne

	Laid down	L	In serv.
A 636 MAITO	24-6-83	6-1-84	27-2-84
A 637 MAROA	30-8-83	20-1-84	30-3-84
A 638 MANINI	11-84	-85	-85

Maroa (A 637) 1984

D: 250 tons (278 fl) **S:** 11 kts **Dim:** 27.60 (24.50 wl) × 8.90 × 3.50
M: 2 SACM Type 175 6L RUR diesels; 2 Voith-Schneider vertical cycloidal props; 1,280 hp
Range: 1,200/11 **Man:** 6 tot. + 4 passengers.

REMARKS: For service at Muraroa. Bollard pull: 12 tons. Have a firefighting water cannon.

MISCELLANEOUS AUXILIARY SHIPS

◆ **6 (+2 + 2) Chamois-class local support or diving tenders** Bldr: Ch. de la Perrière, Lorient

	Laid down	L	In serv.
A 767 CHAMOIS	. . .	30-4-76	24-9-76
A 768 ELAN	16-3-77	28-7-77	7-4-78
A 774 CHEVREUIL	15-9-76	8-5-77	7-10-77
A 775 GAZELLE	30-12-76	7-6-77	13-1-78
A 776 ISARD	2-11-77	2-5-78	15-12-78
A 779 TAPATAI (ex-*Silver Fish*)	. . .	1971	27-3-81
A 611 VULCAIN	. . .	. . .	1986
A 612 PLUTON	. . .	. . .	. . .
A 613 ACHÉRON	. . .	. . .	. . .
A 614 STYX	. . .	. . .	1988

Chevreuil (A 774)—stern gantry dismounted L. & L. Van Ginderen, 8-84

Isard (A 776)—white-painted divers' support ship M. Bar, 1979

D: 305 tons light (505 fl) **S:** 14.5 kts **Dim:** 41.5 (36.96 pp) × 7.5 × 3.18
M: 2 SACM MGO V16 AFHR diesels; 2 CP Kort-nozzle props; 2,200 hp
Range: 7,200/12 **Man:** 2 officers, 16 petty officers, 2 men

REMARKS: Except for a 5.6-ton crane, the first four are identical to the 14 merchant FISH class designed for the supply of petroleum platforms. Hydraulic 50-ton stern

MISCELLANEOUS AUXILIARY SHIPS *(continued)*

crane mounted on A 767, A 774. All but A 776 can carry 100 tons dry cargo on deck or 125 tons fuel and 40 tons water (or 65 tons fuel/125 tons water). A 768 and A 775 primarily used as water tankers. Can be used for coastal towing and cleaning up oil spills. Two rudders and an 80-hp bow-thruster. After winch with 28-ton bollard pull. Can be used as transports for 28 passengers, as minelayers, or as torpedo retrievers. *Isard* is equipped as a divers' support ship and tender for the ERIC wire-guided submersible (2 tons, 4 m overall, 600 m diving depth). She has a ULISM decompression chamber capable of simulating pressures to a water depth of 150 m. She also has a longer aft structure, supporting divers' rubber dinghys and a small helicopter deck; the ship is subordinated to GISMER. A 779, a former merchant unit of this class, was purchased at Noumea in 1979 and commissioned for service in support of the Pacific Test Center.

The first two of four additional units, intended to replace the U.S. MSC class mine-clearance, diver-support ships, were ordered 11-10-84. They will resemble *Isard* (A 776) and will have a 13.7-kt speed.

NET TENDERS

◆ **1 seagoing net tender**

	Bldr	Laid down	L	In serv.
A 731 Tianée	Brest Ars.	1-4-73	1-11-73	8-7-75

Tianée (A 731) 1974

D: 842 tons (905 fl) **S:** 12 kts **Dim:** 54.3 × 10.6 × . . .
M: 2/480-kw diesel generator sets, 1/880-kw electric motor; 1 prop; 1,200 hp
Range: 5,200/12 **Man:** 1 officer, 12 petty officers, 24 men

Remarks: Living quarters air-conditioned, transverse bow-thruster. Used primarily as a mooring-buoy tender. Stationed at Papeete.

◆ **5 U.S. AN 93 class**

	Bldr	L	In serv.
A 760 Cigale (ex-AN 98)	A.C. de la Rochelle-Pallice	23-9-54	24-6-55
A 761 Criquet (ex-AN 96)	A.C. Seine Maritime	3-6-54	25-3-55
A 762 Fourmi (ex-AN 97)	A.C. Seine Maritime	6-7-54	24-6-55
A 763 Grillon (ex-AN 95	Penhoët	18-2-54	25-3-55
A 764 Scarabée (ex-AN 94)	Penhoët	21-11-53	15-2-55

Scarabée (A 764) L. & L. Van Ginderen, 8-84

D: 770 tons (850 fl) **Dim:** 46.28 (44.5 pp) × 10.2 × 3.2
A: 1/40-mm AA—4/20-mm (I × 4) AA
Electron Equipt: Radar: 1/Decca . . . nav.
M: 2 SEMT-Pielstick PA-1 diesels, electric drive; 1 prop; 1,600 hp
Fuel: 125 m³ diesel oil **Range:** 5,200/12
Man: 1 officer, 36 men

Remarks: U.S. "Offshore" mutual assistance. One sister built for Spain, two others built in Italy. Used as mooring-buoy and salvage tenders, except A 760, used as a torpedo retriever with no armament (A 764 also unarmed).

◆ **3 La Prudente-class port netlayers**

	Bldr	L	In serv.
Y 749 La Prudente	A.C. de la Manche	13-5-68	27-7-69
Y 750 La Persévérante	A.D. de la Rochelle-Pallice	14-5-68	3-3-69
Y 751 La Fidèle	A.C. de la Manche	26-8-68	10-6-69

Persévérante (Y 750) G. Gyssels, 7-82

D: 446 tons (626 fl) **S:** 10 kts **Dim:** 43.5 (42.0 pp) × 10.0 × 2.8
M: 2 Baudouin diesels, electric drive; 1 prop; 620 hp **Electric:** 440 kw
Range: 4,000/10 **Man:** 1 officer, 8 petty officers, 21 men

Remarks: Used as mooring-buoy tenders. Lifting power via pivoting gantry forward: 25 tons.

◆ **1 new-construction small mooring-buoy tender** Bldr: IMC, Rochefort sur Mer

Y. . . Telenn Mor (In serv. 1985)

D: . . . **S:** . . . **Dim:** . . . × . . . × . . .
M: 2 diesels; 2 props; 900 hp

Remarks: No other data yet available.

◆ **1 Tupa class** (In serv. 16-3-74)

Y 667 Tupa

Tupa (Y 667) French Navy, 1983

D: 292 tons light **S:** 6 kts **Dim:** 28.5 × 8.3 × 0.85
M: 1 diesel; 1 prop; 210 hp

Remarks: Based at Muraroa. Used as a mooring-buoy tender.

◆ **1 Calmar class** (In serv. 12-8-70)

Y 698 Calmar

D: 270 tons light **S:** 9.5 kts **Dim:** . . . × . . . × . . .
M: 1 Baudoin diesel; 1 prop; . . . hp

Remarks: Based at Lorient. Used as a mooring-buoy tender.

DIVING TENDERS

◆ **1 base tender**

	Bldr	L	In serv.
A 722 Poseidon	SIGNAV, St.-Malo	5-12-74	14-1-77

D: 200 tons (220 fl) **S:** 13 kts **Dim:** 40.5 (38.5 pp) × 7.2 × 2.2
M: 1 diesel; 600 hp **Endurance:** 8 days **Man:** 42 tot.

Remarks: Used for training combat frogmen. Based at Toulon.

DIVING TENDERS *(continued)*

Poseidon (A 722) J.-C. Bellonne, 1977

◆ **4 ex-U.S. Adjutant-class former coastal minesweepers**

	Bldr	In serv.
A 701 Ajonc (ex-M 667, ex-MSC 71)	F. L. Sample, Maine	26-2-54
M 711 Gardenia (ex-M 676, ex-MSC 114)	Tacoma Boat, Wash.	30-8-54
A 723 Liseron (ex-M 683, ex-MSC 98)	Tacoma Boat, Wash.	1-1-55
M 770 Magnolia (ex-M 685, ex-MSC 87)	Stephen Bros.	30-10-54

Liseron (A 723) L. & L. Van Ginderen, 6-85

D: 300 tons (372 fl) **S:** 13 kts **Dim:** 4.30 (41.5 pp) × 7.95 × 2.55
Electron Equipt: Radar: 1/Decca 1229
M: 2 G.M. 8-268A diesels; 2 props; 1,200 hp **Fuel:** 40 tons
Range: 2,500/10 **Man:** 3 officers, 9 petty officers, 20 men

Remarks: *Ajonc* (A 701) is a tender to the French Navy's diving school (PLONGECO) at St. Mandrier; the others support mine-demolition divers. A deckhouse has replaced the minesweeping winch, and the forward superstructure has been enlarged. Wooden construction. To be replaced 1986-88 by four new modified *Chamois*-class units.

Note: U.K. "Ham"-class diving tender *Myosotis* (A 710, ex-*Riplingham*) was stricken 1985.

TORPEDO RECOVERY SHIPS

Note: The net tender *Cigale* (A 760) is also used as a torpedo retriever, and some of the tenders of the *Chamois* class can be employed as such.

◆ **1 former tuna-fishing boat**

A 699 Pélican (ex-*Kerfany*) Bldr: Avondale, U.S.A., 1951

D: 362 tons (425 fl) **S:** 11 kts **Dim:** 37.0 × 8.55 × 4.0
M: 1 Burmeister & Wain diesel; 1 prop; 650 hp **Man:** 5 petty officers, 14 men

Remarks: Purchased 1965. 550-mm torpedo tube at stern.

◆ **2 small torpedo retrievers for use at the St. Tropez trials center**

Pégase Bldr: SFCN (In serv. 1975)—880-hp catamaran with one 550-mm torpedo tube aft

Sambracite (In serv. 1974)

Pélican (A 699) G. Gyssels, 6-82

COASTAL TRANSPORTS

◆ **9 Ariel class** Bldr: A: SFCN, Franco-Belge; B: DCAN, Brest

	Bldr	L		Bldr	L
Y 604 Ariel	A	27-4-63	Y 700 Néréide	B	17-2-77
Y 613 Faune	A	8-9-71	Y 701 Ondine	B	4-10-79
Y 622 Dryade	A	1973	Y 702 Naiade	B	4-10-79
Y 661 Korrigan	A	6-3-64	Y 741 Elfe	A	14-4-70
Y 696 Alphée	A	10-6-69			

Ariel (Y 604) J.-C. Bellonne, 1983

D: 195 tons (225 fl) **S:** 15 kts **Dim:** 40.5 × 7.45 × 3.3
M: 2 MGO (1,640 hp) or Poyaud (1,730 hp) diesels; 2 props
Man: 9 tot., 400 passengers (250 seated)

Remarks: Can carry 400 passengers (250 seated). All based at Brest, except *Ariel* and *Naiade* at Toulon.

◆ **1 small personnel transport:** Treberon (In serv. 26-11-79)—at Brest

◆ **3 Merlin class (In serv. 6-68)**

Bldrs: Y 735 and Y 736: C.N. Franco-Belges; Y 671: A du Mourillon

Y 735 Merlin Y 736 Mélusine Y 671 Morgane

Morgane (Y 671) G. Arra, 1982

D: 170 tons **S:** 11 kts **Dim:** 31.5 × 7.06 × 2.4
M: MGO diesels; 2 props; 960 hp **Man:** 400 passengers

Remarks: All based at Toulon.

COASTAL TRANSPORTS *(continued)*

◆ **1 Sylphe class** Bldr: C.N. Franco-Belges (In serv. 1960)

Y 710 Sylphe

Sylphe (Y 710) 1976

D: 142 tons (189 fl) **S:** 12 kts **Dim:** 38.5 (36.75 pp) × 6.9 × 2.5
M: 1 MGO diesel; 1 prop; 425 hp **Man:** 9 tot.

Remarks: Has operated from Brest since 1981.

SALVAGE AND RESCUE TUGS

Note: The French government leased four powerful salvage tugs as a result of the *Amoco Cadiz* disaster; the fourth, *Abeille Normandie* has been returned to its owners. All are owned by the PROGEMAR consortium.

◆ **2 Abeille Flandre class** Bldr: Ulstein Hatlo A/S, Ulsteinvick, Norway

Abeille Flandre (In serv. 1978) (ex-*Neptun Suecia*)
Abeille Landuedoc (In serv. 1978)

Abeille Flandre L. & L. Van Ginderen, 12-81

D: . . . **S:** 17 kts **Dim:** 63.40 (58.60 pp) × 14.74 × 6.90 **Fuel:** 1,450 tons
M: 4/8-cyl. Atlas diesels; 2 CP props; 23,000 hp **Electric:** 1,280 kw

Remarks: 1,577 grt. *A. Flandre* at Brest, *A. Languedoc* at Cherbourg. Ice-strengthened; have bow-thrusters.

◆ **1 Abeille Normandie class** Bldr: Beliard-Murdoch, Ostend

Abeille Provence (In serv. 1978)

Abeille Provence G. Gyssels, 1980

D: . . . **S:** 16 kts **Dim:** 66.76 (61.02 pp) × 13.01 × 5.70
M: 2/20-cyl. SACM diesels; 2 CP props; 16,000 hp **Electric:** 1,600 kw
Fuel: 1,079 tons

Remarks: 1,401 grt. Ice-strengthened, equipped for salvage and firefighting. 120-ton bollard pull. Two 550-hp bow-thrusters. Based at Toulon.

SEAGOING TUGS

◆ **3 Tenace class**

	Bldr	L	In serv.
A 664 Malabar	Oelkers, Hamburg	16-4-75	3-2-76
A 669 Tenace	Oelkers, Hamburg	12-71	15-11-73
A 674 Centaure	de la Rochelle-Pallice	8-1-74	15-11-74

Malabar (A 664) M. Louagie, 6-85

D: 970 tons (1,440 fl) **S:** 13.5 kts **Dim:** 51.0 × 11.5 × 5.7
M: 2 diesels; 1 prop; 4,600 hp **Fuel:** 500 tons **Range:** 9,500/13
Man: 4 officers, 30 petty officers, 24 men

Remarks: Bollard-pull capacity; 60 tons. Living quarters air-conditioned. All based at Brest. A 664 employed as fisheries protection ship 15-9-80 to 6-11-80.

Note: Ex-U.S. Navy seagoing tug *Hippopotame* (A 660, ex-*Utrecht,* ex-ATR 47) stricken early 1986.

COASTAL TUGS

◆ **0 (+14 . . .) new construction** Bldr: C.N. LaManche, Dieppe

A. . . N. . . (In serv. . . .)

D: . . . **S:** 12.75 kts **Dim:** 29.55 × 9.00 × 3.7
M: 1 SACM AGO 195 V12 RVR diesel; 1 prop; 2,000 hp

Remarks: Ordered 10-84. Program not confirmed; data provisional.

◆ **3 Belier class** Bldr: Cherbourg Arsenal

	L	In serv.
A 695 Belier	4-12-79	25-7-80
A 696 Buffle	18-1-80	19-7-80
A 697 Bison	20-11-80	16-4-81

Bison (A 697) G. Gyssels, 1981

D: 500 tons (800 fl) **S:** 11 kts **Dim:** 32.0 × 8.8 × . . .
M: 2 SACM AGO 195 V8 CSHR diesels, electric drive; 2 Voith-Schneider vertical cycloidal props; 2,600 hp
Man: 1 officer, 7 petty officers, 4 men

Remarks: Based at Toulon. Bollard pull: 25 tons. Have two firefighting monitors atop bridge.

COASTAL TUGS *(continued)*

◆ 11 Actif group

	Bldr	D: light/fl	In serv.
A 667 Hercule	Franco-Belges	194/240	21-3-60
A 671 Le Fort	FCG, Bordeaux	248/311	12-7-71
A 672 Utile	FCG, Bordeaux	226/288	8-4-71
A 673 Lutteur	. . .	226/288	19-7-63
A 685 Robuste	Franco-Belges	194/239	4-4-60
A 686 Actif	FCM, Le Havre	226/288	11-7-63
A 687 Laborieux	FCM, Le Havre	226/287	14-8-63
A 688 Valeureux	Franco-Belges	196/247	17-10-60
A 692 Travailleur	FCM, Le Havre	226/288	11-7-63
A 693 Acharné	La Perrière, Lorient	218/293	5-7-74
A 694 Efficace	La Perrière, Lorient	230/. . .	17-10-74

Travailleur (A 692) J. Pradignac, 3-85

D: See name list **S:** 11.8 kts **Dim:** 28.3 (25.3 pp) × 7.9 × 4.3
M: 1 MGO ASHR diesel; 1,100 to 1,450 hp **Range:** 2,400/1

Remarks: Bollard pull: 17 tons. Similar, but not identical, ships. *Courageux* (A 706) stricken 1980.

HARBOR TUGS

◆ 20 pusher tugs Bldr: La Perrière, Lorient (In serv. 1976-1983)

P. 1–P. 20

P. 7—24-ton pusher tug G. Gyssels, 6-83

D: 24 tons (fl) **S:** 9.2 kts **Dim:** 11.50 (11.25 wl) × 4.30 × 1.45
M: 2 Poyaud 520 V8M diesels; 2 props; 440 hp **Fuel:** 1.7 tons
Range: 191/9.1, 560/8 **Man:** 2 tot.

Remarks: For dockyard use. Primarily for pushing, but have 4.1-ton bollard pull. No names or NATO pendant numbers assigned.

Note: The tugs listed below have two-letter contractions of names on bows instead of official pendant numbers.

◆ 2 Bonite class Bldr: SFCN, Châlon-sur-Seine

Y 634 Rouget (In serv. 1974) Y 630 Bonite (In serv. 1975)

D: 93 tons (fl) **S:** 11 kts **M:** 380 hp

Remarks: Bollard-pull capacity: 7 tons.

Bonite (Y 630) J.-C. Bellonne, 1975

◆ 28 Acajou class (alphabetical listing; pendant numbers not borne)

Y 601 Acajou	Y 618 Èrable	Y 638 Marronier	Y 740 Papayer
Y 607 Balsa	Y 635 Equeurdreville	Y 668 Mélèze	Y 688 Peuplier
Y 623 Charme	Y 644 Frêne	Y 669 Merisier	Y 689 Pin
Y 620 Chataigner	Y 654 Hêtre	Y 739 Noyer	Y 695 Platane
Y 624 Chêne	Y 655 Hevea	Y 682 Okoumé	Y 720 Santal
Y 629 Cormier	Y 663 Latanier	Y 719 Olivier	Y 708 Saule
Y 717 Ébène	Y 666 Manguier	Y 686 Palétuvier	Y 704 Sycomore

Manguier (Y 666) G. Gyssels, 1981

D: 105 tons (fl) **S:** 11 kts **Dim:** 21.0 × 6.9 × 3.2 **M:** 1 diesel; 700 hp

Remarks: Bollard-pull capacity: 10 tons. *Bouleau* (Y 612) stricken 1980.

◆ 29 Oiseau class (alphabetical listing, pendant numbers not borne)

Y 602 Aigrette	Y 723 Engoulevent	Y 725 Marabout	Y 691 Pinson
Y 720 Alouette	Y 687 Fauvette	Y 675 Martin Pêcheur	Y 694 Pivert
Y 730 Ara	Y 748 Gelinotte	Y 636 Martinet	Y 724 Sarcelle
Y 611 Bengali	Y 648 Goeland	Y 670 Merle	Y 726 Toucan
Y 625 Cigogne	Y 728 Grand Duc	Y 621 Mésange	Y 722 Vanneau
Y 628 Colibri	Y 653 Héron	Y 673 Moineau	
Y 632 Cygne	Y 747 Loriot	Y 617 Mouette	
Y 729 Eider	Y 727 Macreuse	Y 687 Passereau	

Bengali (Y 611) DCAN, 1975

D: 200 tons (fl) **S:** 9 kts **Dim:** 18.4 × 5.7 × 2.5
M: 1 Poyaud diesel; 250 hp **Range:** 1,700/9

Remarks: Bollard-pull capacity: 3.5 tons. *Ibis* (Y 658) on loan to Senegal.

TRAINING SHIPS AND CRAFT

Note: In addition to the designated ships and craft below, the French Navy operates a number of other units primarily in training roles. These include the helicopter carrier *Jeanne d'Arc* (R 97), frigate *Doudart de Lagrée* (F 728), and the diving tenders *Poseidon* (A 722) and *Ajonc* (A 701).

◆ 8 Léopard class

	Bldr	Laid down	L	In serv.
A 748 Léopard	de la Manche, St.-Malo	6-4-81	4-6-81	4-12-82
A 749 Panthère	de la Manche, St.-Malo	9-6-81	3-9-81	4-12-82
A 750 Jaguar	de la Manche, St.-Malo	27-9-81	29-10-81	18-12-82
A 751 Lynx	La Perrière, Lorient	23-7-81	27-2-82	18-12-82
A 752 Guépard	de la Manche, St.-Malo	11-10-82	1-12-82	1-7-83
A 753 Chacal	de la Manche, St.-Malo	11-10-82	11-2-83	10-9-83
A 754 Tigre	La Perrière, Lorient	16-4-82	8-10-82	1-7-83
A 755 Lion	La Perrière, Lorient	21-2-82	13-12-82	10-9-83

TRAINING SHIPS AND CRAFT *(continued)*

Chacal (A 753) Pradignac & Leo, 4-84

D: 463 tons (fl) **S:** 15 kts **Dim:** 43.00 (40.15 pp) × 8.30 × 3.21
A: 2/20-mm AA (I × 2) **Electron Equipt:** Radar: 1/Decca . . .
M: 2 SACM 75 V16 ASHR diesels; 2 props; 2,200 hp **Range:** 4,100/12
Man: 1 officer, 13 men, plus 17 trainees and 4 instructors

Remarks: First four authorized 1980, second group 1981. Replaced the minesweepers of the U.S. *Adjutant* class in training duties. Also for patrol use if required.

◆ **2 ex-trawlers**

A 772 Engageante (ex-*Cayolle*) A 773 Vigilante (ex-*Iseran*)

Vigilante (A 773) L. & L. Van Ginderen, 11-82

D: 286 tons fl (156 grt) **S:** 11 kts **Dim:** 30.0 (25.0 pp) × 6.7 × 3.8 (aft)
Electron Equipt: Radar: 1/Decca . . . **M:** 1 Deutz diesel; 1 prop; 560 hp

Remarks: Built 1964; purchased 1975. Used by petty officers' navigation school.

◆ **2 tenders** Bldr: Bayonne (In serv. 1971)

Y 706 Chimère Y 711 Farfadet

Farfadet (Y 711) Pradignac & Leo, 1983

D: 100 tons **S:** 11 kts **M:** 1 diesel; 200 hp

Remarks: Used by the Naval Academy for training in maneuvering.

◆ **2 British "Ham"-class former inshore minesweepers**

	In serv.
A 735 Hibiscus (ex-*Sparham*, ex-MSI 85)	9-55
A 736 Dahlia (ex-*Whippinham*, ex-MSI 88)	9-55

Hibiscus (A 735) L. & L. Van Ginderen, 3-85

D: 140 tons (170 fl) **S:** 14 kts **Dim:** 32.43 × 6.45 × 1.70
A: 1/20-mm AA **Electron Equipt:** Radar: 1/Decca 1229
M: 2 Paxham YHAXM diesels; 2 props; 550 hp **Endurance:** 4 days
Fuel: 15 tons **Range:** 2,350/9 **Man:** 2 officers, 10 men

Remarks: Wooden-hulled. Built in Great Britain with U.S. Offshore Procurement funds. Used as general-purpose tenders and training craft at Cherbourg. Sisters *Tulipe* (A 737, ex-*Frettenham*, ex-MSI 75), *Capucine* (A 738, ex-*Petersham*, ex-MSI 78), *Oeillet* (ex-*Isham*, ex-MSI 79) and *Hortensia* (ex-*Mileham*, ex-MSI 76) stricken 1985; other pair to strike 1986.

◆ **2 auxiliary barkentines** Bldr: Chantiers de Normandie, Fécamp (In serv. 1932)

A 649 L'Étoile A 650 La Belle Poule

La Belle Poule (A 650) 1974

D: 225 tons (275 fl) **S:** 6 kts **Dim:** 32.25 × 7.0 × 3.2
M: Sulzer diesel; 125 hp

Remarks: Assigned to the Naval Academy.

◆ **1 sail-training yawl** (L: 1932)

A 653 La Grande Hermine (ex-*La Route Est Belle*, ex-*Menestrel*)

Remarks: Fourteen-meter yawl purchased in 1964 for the reserve officers' school. D: 7 tons (13 fl).

◆ **1 sail-training craft** Bldr: C.N. de Vendée (l: 1927)

A 652 Mutin

D: 40 tons (55 fl) **S:** . . . **Dim:** 33.0 (22.0 hull) × 6.5 × 3.2 (1.5 fwd)
M: 1 Baudouin 6-cyl. diesel; 1 prop; 112 hp

Remarks: Assigned to the annex of the Seamanship School. 240m^3 sail area.

MISCELLANEOUS SERVICE CRAFT

◆ **2 weapons range safety patrol boats** Bldrs: C.N. de L'Estérel

	L	In serv.
A 712 Athos	20-11-79	22-11-79
A 713 Aramis	9-9-80	22-9-80

MISCELLANEOUS SERVICE CRAFT *(continued)*

Athos (A 712) L. & L. Van Gindere, 9-83

D: 80 tons (99.5 fl) **S:** 28 kts **Dim:** 32.1 × 6.5 × 1.9
A: 1/20-mm AA **Electron Equipt:** Radar: 1/Decca . . .
M: 2 SACM diesels; 2 props; 4,640 hp **Range:** 1,500/15
Man: 1 officer, 6 petty officers, 10-11 men (including 6 divers)

REMARKS: Operate at the Landes Test Center, both as range-safety craft and for weapons-recovery duties. Wooden hulls.

◆ **1 trials support tender**

DCAN 164 MÉROU

Mérou—with bow doors open G. Gyssels, 7-82

REMARKS: A diving tender with bow-door arrangement. Based at Toulon and civilian-operated.

◆ **1 range safety patrol craft**

A 702 GIRELLE

Girelle (A 702) E.C.P.A., 1976

D: . . . **S:** . . . **M:** . . .

REMARKS: Wooden construction. Operates from St. Raphaël.

◆ **1 range safety patrol boat** Bldr: C.N. de L'Esterel (in serv. 14-2-74)

A 714 TOURMALINE

Tourmaline (A 714) 1974

D: 37 tons (45 fl) **S:** 15 kts **Dim:** 26.8 × 4.97 × 1.53
M: 2 diesels; 2 props; 480 hp

REMARKS: Wooden construction. Can carry 1/20-mm AA.

◆ **6 fireboats**

Y 745 AIGUIÈRE Y 618 CASCADE Y 746 EMBRUN
Y 645 GAVE Y 646 GEYSER Y 684 OUED

Aiguière (A 745)—red-painted, no pendant number L. & L. Van Ginderen, 4-82

D: 70 tons (85 fl) **S:** 11.3 kts **Dim:** 23.8 × 5.3 × 1.7
M: 2 Poyaud 6 PZM diesels; 2 props; 405 hp

◆ **1 degaussing (deperming) tender**

Y 732

Y 732 DCAN, 1970

D: 260 tons **S:** 10 kts **Dim:** 38.2 × 4.3 × 2.4
M: 1 diesel; 1 prop; 375 hp **Man:** 5 tot.

◆ **1 radiological monitoring ship** (In serv. 1969)

Y 743 PALANGRIN

D: 44 tons **S:** 9 kts **M:** 1/220-hp diesel

Palangrin (Y 743) Pradignac & Leo, 1984

◆ **18 motor lighters, converted from LCM (3)-class landing craft**

CHA 1, 2, 6, 7, 8, 9, 13, 14, 15, 16, 17, 18, 19, 22, 23, 24, 25, 26

D: 20 tons (50 fl) **S:** 7 kts **Dim:** 15.2 × 4.4 × 1.6
M: 1 diesel; 100 hp (CHA 1, CHA 6: 115 hp)

◆ **18 water lighters**

1 to 18

FRANCE *(continued)*
MISCELLANEOUS SERVICE CRAFT *(continued)*

CHA 13 L. & L. Van Ginderen, 8-84

D: . . . **S:** 9 kts **Dim:** . . . × . . . × . . . **M:** 1 diesel; 430 hp

Remarks: Nos. 5 and 6 in Tahiti, No. 2 at Brest, Nos. 1 and 11 at Toulon, No. 12 at Lorient, others at the CEP (Centre d'Expérimentation Pacifique).

◆ **4 water lighters for SSBNs**

1 2 3 4

D: 44 tons light **S:** 6 kts **Dim:** . . . × . . . × . . . **M:** 1 diesel; 496 hp

Remarks: Two at Brest, two at Cherbourg.

GABON

Gabonese Republic

Personnel (1984): approx. 300

Merchant Marine (1982): 20 ships—97,267 grt (tankers: 2 ships—74,471 grt)

Naval Aviation: One Embraer EMB 111 Bandeirante maritime patrol aircraft is operated by the Air Force.

PATROL BOATS AND CRAFT

◆ **0 (+2) French "Super PATRA" class** Bldr: CMN, Cherbourg

N. . . N. . .

D: 371.5 tons light (422.5 fl) **S:** 24 kts
Dim: 54.50 (50.0 pp) × 8.0 (7.7 wl) × 2.54 (2.08 hull)
A: One unit: 1/57-mm Bofors SAK 57 Mk 2—1/20-mm Oerlikon AA; other: 2/20-mm Oerlikon AA (I × 2)
Electron Equipt: 1/Decca-Racal 1226
M: 2 SEMT-Pielstick 16PA4V200 VGDS diesels; 2 CP props; 8,000 hp
Electric: 360 kw **Fuel:** 73 tons **Range:** 4,000/15
Endurance: 15 days **Man:** 3 officers, 22 men + 23 passengers

Remarks: Reported ordered 11-84. Limiting displacement 446 tons. Carries 840 rds 40-mm, 2,100 rds 20-mm ammunition. Can carry two MM 40 Exocet SSM. For search-and-rescue use, carries inflatable launch and can accommodate 23 rescued personnel. Have two contraband storerooms. Engines to be built by Uni-Diesel.

◆ **1 wooden-hulled** Bldr: de l'Estérel, Cannes (In serv. 12-1-78)

GC 05 General Nazaire Boulingui Kounba (ex-*President el Haj Omar Bongo*)

General Nazaire Boulingui Kounba d l'Estérel, 1977

D: 100 tons (fl) **S:** 32 kts **Dim:** 42.0 × 7.8 × 1.9
A: 4/SS-12M SSM (II × 2)—1/40-mm Bofors AA—1/20-mm AA
Electron Equipt: Radar: Decca RM 1226
M: 3 SACM AGO 195 12CSNR diesels; 3 props; 5,400 hp
Fuel: 28.4 tons **Range:** 1,000/18 **Man:** 3 officers, 20 men

Remarks: Wire-guided, optically aimed anti-ship missiles. Reported re-engined at Port-Gentil, completing early 1985; the original 3 MTU 16V538 TB91 diesels produced 40 kts on 10,500 hp.

◆ **2 N'Golo class** Bldr: Intermarine, Sarzana, Italy

GC 04 N'Golo (In serv. 1981)

N'Golo (GC 04)—the first; the second is identical Intermarine, 1978

D: 65 tons (88 fl) **S:** 43 kts **Dim:** 27.3 × 6.8 × 2.1
A: 1/40-mm AA—2/20-mm AA **Electron Equipt:** Radar: 1/Decca RM 916
M: 2 MTU diesels; 2 props; 7,000 hp **Man:** 13 tot.

Remarks: Replaces the original *N'Golo,* which was destroyed by fire 13-3-80. This design uses the largest glass-reinforced plastic hull of any high-speed craft in the world.

◆ **1 U.S. aluminum-hulled design** Bldr: Swiftships, Morgan City, La. (In serv. 2-76)

GC 03 N'Guene

D: 118 tons (fl) **S:** 27 kts **Dim:** 32.17 (29.18 pp) × 2.3 (props)
A: 2/40-mm AA (I × 2)—2/20-mm AA (I × 2)—2/12.7-mm mg (I × 2)
Electron Equipt: Radar: Decca RM 916 **Range:** 825/25 **Man:** 21 tot.
M: 3 G.M. 16V149 TE diesels; 3 props; 4,800 hp **Electric:** 80 kw

◆ **1 32-m wooden-hulled** Bldr: de l'Estérel, Cannes (In serv. 3-72)

GC 02 Colonel Djoué Dabany (ex-*President Albert Bernard Bongo*)

Colonel Djoué Dabany (GC 02) de l'Estérel, 1972

D: 80 tons **S:** 30 kts **Dim:** 32.0 × 5.8 × 1.5 **A:** 2/20-mm AA (I × 2)
M: 2 MTU diesels; 2,700 hp **Man:** 17 tot.

◆ **1 Gabonese design** Bldr: Libreville DY, Gabon (In serv. 16-1-68)

GC 01 President Léon M'Ba

D: 85 tons **S:** 12.5 kts **Dim:** 28.0 × 6.2 × 1.54
A: 1/75-mm recoilless rifle—1/12.7-mm mg **Man:** 1 officer, 15 men
M: 2 Baudoin diesels; 2 props; 540 hp **Range:** 1,000/12

AMPHIBIOUS WARFARE SHIPS AND CRAFT

◆ **1 French Champlain-class landing ship** Bldr: Atelier Français de l'Ouest, Grand Quevilly, Rouen, France

	Laid down	L	In serv.
LO 5 President El Hadj Omar Bongo	7-3-83	16-4-84	24-10-84

D: 770 tons (1,336 fl) **S:** 16 kts **Dim:** 80.0 × 13.0 × 2.40
A: 2/40-mm AA (I × 2)—1/81-mm mortar—2/12.7-mm mg (I × 2)
Electron Equipt: Radar: 1/DRBN-32 (Decca 1226)
M: 2 SACM 195V12 diesels; 2 CP props; 3,600 hp
Range: 4,500/13 **Man:** 47

Remarks: Purchase announced 28-2-84. Capacity: 340 tons stores, plus 138 troops and 7 combat vehicles. Helicopter platform aft. Carries one LCVP and one personnel landing craft.

◆ **1 transport** Bldr: DCAN, Dakar (In serv. 11-5-76)

GC. . . Manga

D: 152 tons **S:** 9 kts **Dim:** 24.0 × 6.4 × 1.3 **A:** 2/12.7-mm mg

GABON *(continued)*
AMPHIBIOUS WARFARE SHIPS AND CRAFTS *(continued)*

Electron Equipt: Radar: Decca 101
M: 2 Poyaud V8-520 diesels; 2 props; 480 hp **Man:** 10 tot.

Remarks: Landing craft design, equipped with bow ramp.

◆ **2 harbor launches** Bldr: Tanguy Marine, Le Havre (In serv. 1985)

D: 2.5 tons (7.5 fl) **S:** . . . **Dim:** 12.00 × 2.95 × 0.30
M: 2 Volvo Penta AQAD-40B diesel outdrives; 165 hp

Remarks: One unit is only 10.00 m o.a., 2.25 tons (6.25 fl). Ordered 10-84.

COAST GUARD

◆ **2 harbor patrol craft** Bldr: La Manche, Dieppe (In serv. 24-11-77)

Ndjole Omboué

D: 18 tons (fl) **S:** 10 kts **Dim:** 12.4 × 3.7 × 0.9 **M:** 1 diesel; 1 prop; 170 hp

◆ **1 Arcoa 960 launch**—S: 25 kts

◆ **6 Arcoa launches**—S: 15 kts

◆ **1 buoy tender** Bldr: La Manche, Dieppe (In serv. 24-11-77)

N'Gombe

D: 60 tons (fl) **S:** 10 kts **Dim:** 17.0 × 4.5 × 1.3
M: 1 Baudoin DNP-6 diesel; 1 prop; 215 hp

THE GAMBIA

Republic of the Gambia

Note: The "unification" of the Gambia with Senegal on 1-2-82 was supposed to have unified the armed forces of both countries, but this has not yet occurred to any appreciable extent.

Merchant Marine (1984): 7 ships—3,290 grt

PATROL CRAFT

◆ **3 Tracker Mk-2 class** Bldr: Fairey Marine, U.K. (In serv. 1977-78)

P 2 Jato P 3 Challenge P 4 Champion

D: 31.5 tons (fl) **S:** 29 kts **Dim:** 19.25 × 4.98 × 1.45
A: 1/20-mm AA—2/7.62-mm mg
M: 2 G.M. 12V-71 TI diesels; 2 props; 1,290 hp
Range: 650/20 **Man:** 11 tot.

◆ **1 Lance class** Bldr: Fairey Marine, U.K. (In serv. 28-10-76)

P 1 Sea Dog

D: 17 tons (fl) **S:** 24 kts **Dim:** 14.81 × 4.76 × 1.3
A: 1/20-mm AA—3/7.62-mm mg (I × 3)
M: 2 G.M. 8V-71 TI diesels; 2 props; 850 hp **Range:** 500/15
Man: 6 crew plus 10-man boarding party

◆ **1 Keith Nelson 75-foot class** Bldr: Camper & Nicholson, U.K. (In serv. 1974)

Mansa Kila IV

D: 70 tons (fl) **S:** 24.5 kts **Dim:** 22.9 × 6.0 × 1.6 **A:** 2/20-mm AA (I × 2)
M: 2 diesels; 2 props; 1,840 hp **Range:** 800/20 **Man:** 11 men

GERMANY (EAST)

German Democratic Republic

Personnel: 14,600 total, including approx. 3,000 Frontier Guards personnel and 400 in naval aviation.

Merchant Marine (1984): 409 ships—1,421,714 grt (tankers: 13 ships—73,994 grt)

Naval Aviation: Helicopters in naval service included 8 Mi-14 Haze-A for land-based ASW, and 13 Mi-8 Hip-F and 7 Mi-8 Hip-C transport helicopters.

Weapons and Systems: Nearly all of Soviet design. *See* U.S.S.R. section for details.

Warships In Service Or Under Construction As Of 1 January 1986

	L	Std. Tons	Main armament
◆ **2 frigates**			
2 Koni	1977-78	1,500	1/SA-N-4, 4/76.2-mm, 4/30-mm, 2 ASW RL
◆ **17 corvettes**			
17 Parchim	1980-82	960	2/57-mm AA, 4 ASW TT, 2 ASW RL
◆ **64 missile and torpedo boats**			
2(+. . .) Tarantul I	1984	480	4 Styx, 1/76-mm AA
15 Osa-I	1964-	175	4 Styx, 4/30-mm AA
17 Shershen	1966-	150	4/30-mm AA, 4/533-mm TT
30 Libelle	1975-79	20	2/533-mm TT
◆ **45 minesweepers**			
45 Kondor I, II	1968-79	22/310	2 or 6/25-mm AA
◆ **12 landing ships**			

Note: Ships and craft in auxiliary status have pendant numbers beginning with a letter denoting the general function:

- A: Salvage ships and tugs
- B: Torpedo retrievers
- C: Liquid cargo carriers
- D: Ships and craft of the SHD
- E: Dry cargo carriers
- F: Fireboats (*Feurluschboot*)
- G: Coastal Border Brigade (GBK—*Grenzbrigade Küste*) units
- H: Miscellaneous units
- K: Diving tenders
- S: Training units (*Schulschiff*)
- U: Air/Sea rescue units
- V: Experimental units (*Versuch*)

Navigational service and hydrographic survey units are operated by the civilian-manned Naval Hydrographic Service (SHD-*Seehydrographischen Dienst*): The ships wear "SHD" on a band on their stacks and do not carry pendant numbers; they do display their names.

FRIGATES

◆ **2 Soviet Koni class** Bldr: Zelenodolsk SY

141 Rostock (In serv. 25-7-78) 142 Berlin (In serv. 10-5-79)

Rostock (141) M.O.D., Bonn, 5-83

Berlin (142) M.O.D., Bonn, 5-84

D: 1,500 tons (1,900 fl) **S:** 27 kts **Dim:** 95.0 × 12.8 × 4.2 (hull)
A: 1/SA-N-4 SAM system (II × 1, 20 missiles)—4/76.2-mm DP (II × 2)—4/30-mm AA (II × 2)—2/RBU-6000 ASW RL (XII × 2)—2/d.c. racks (24 d.c.)—20 mines
Electron Equipt: Radar: 1/TSR-333, 1/Strut Curve, 1/Pop Group, 1/Hawk Screech, 1/Drum Tilt
Sonar: med.-freq., hull-mounted
IFF: 2/Square Head, 1/High Pole-A
EW: 2/Watch Dog
M: CODAG: 1 15,000-hp gas turbine; 2 diesels; 3 props; 30,000 hp
Range: 1,800/14 **Man:** 130 tot.

Remarks: TSR-333 substituted for Don-2. No chaff RL, unlike units delivered more recently. Depth-charge racks bolt to mine rails.

CORVETTES

◆ **17 Parchim class** Bldr: Peenewerft, Wolgast (In serv. 1981-85)

	In serv.		In serv.
241 Lübz	9-4-81	232 Ribnitz-Damgarten	1982*
242 Parchim	3-9-81	233 Teterow	1984*
243 Bützow	1981	234 N.	1984
244 Bad Doberan	1981	235 N.	1984
221 Perleberg	1981	211 N.	1984
222 Wismar	1982	212 N.	1985
223 Waren	1982	213 Gädebusch	6-85*
224 Güstrow	1982*	214 Bergen	7-85*
231 Ludwigslust	1982*		

* Name/number correlation tentative

Lübz (241) M.O.D., Bonn, 7-81

Ribnitz-Damgarten (232) M.O.D., Bonn, 7-84

Teterow (233) M.O.D., Bonn, 3-84

D: 960 tons (1,200 fl) **S:** 25 kts **Dim:** 72.5 × 9.4 × 3.5 (max.)
A: 2/57-mm AA (II × 1) — 2/30-mm AA (II × 1) — 2/SA-N-5 SAM systems (IV × 2) — 4/400-mm ASW TT (I × 4) — 2/RBU-6000 ASW RL (XII × 2) — 2/d.c. racks — mines
Electron Equipt: Radar: 1/TSR-333, 1/Strut Curve, 1/Muff Cob
Sonar: MF hull-mounted; high-freq. dipping sonar
IFF: 1/High Pole-B
EW: 2/Watch Dog, 2/chaff RL (XVI × 2)
M: 2 diesels; 2 props; 12,000 hp **Man:** 60 tot.

Remarks: Two began trials 1980, 4 in 1981, 2 in 1982, 4 in 1983. Intended to replace the Hai-III class. Previously referred to by NATO as the "Bal-Com-4" and by the press as the "Koralle" class. Helicopter dipping sonar deploys through door on starboard side of main deck superstructure. D.C. racks exit through doors in stern.

Note: The last four of 12 Hai-III-class corvettes, *Gadebusch, Grevesmühlen, Pirna,* and *Ribnitz-Damgarten,* were stricken 1984-85.

GUIDED-MISSILE CORVETTES

◆ **2 (+ . . .) Soviet Tarantul-I class** Bldr: Petrovskiy SY, Leningrad

813 Albin Köbis (In serv. 9-84) . . . N. . . (In serv. 2-85)

D: 480 tons (540 fl) **S:** 35 kts
Dim: 56.60 (52.50 pp) × 10.50 max. (9.4 wl) × 2.50
A: 4/SS-N-2C Styx SSM (II × 2) — 1/76.2-mm DP — 1/SA-N-5 SAM syst. (IV × 2; . . . SA-7 Grail missiles) — 2/30-mm, 6-barreled gatling AA (I × 2)
Electron Equipt: Radar: 1/Krivach (or TSR-333) nav., 1/Plank Shave missile targetting, 1/Bass Tilt gun f.c.
EW: 4/intercept antenna, 2 decoy RL (XVI × 2)
IFF: 1/Square Head, 1/High Pole-B
M: CODOG/COGOG: 2 probable NK-12MV gas turbines (12,000 hp each), 1 or 2 diesel or gas turbine cruise engines (approx. 2-3,000 hp each); probable 2 props
Range: . . . **Man:** 50 tot.

Remarks: Export version of Tarantul design, with simplified electronics. May be intended to replace the aged Osa-Is. The main propulsion gas turbines exhaust through the transom stern, adding their residual thrust to the power. The cruise engine(s) exhaust through a small stack. The SA-N-5 launcher is on the stern, flanked by the two decoy rocket launchers.

GUIDED-MISSILE PATROL BOATS

◆ **15 Soviet Osa-I-class missile boats** Bldr: U.S.S.R.

711 Albert Gast	734 Paul Eisenschneider
712 Friedrich Schulze	735 Otto Tost
713 N. . .	751 Paul Wiekzorek
714 Max Reichpietsch	752 Rudolf Egelhofer
715 Heinrich Dorrenbach	753 Richard Sorge
731 Walter Krämer	754 Fritz Gast
732 Karl Meseberg	755 Joseph Schares
733 August Lüttgens	

Shershen-class Joseph Roemer (852) to stern of Osa-I Rudolf Egelhofer (752) M.O.D., Bonn

D: 185 tons (215 fl) **S:** 35 kts **Dim:** 38.6 × 7.6 × 1.8
A: 4/Styx (SS-N-2) — 4/30-mm AA (II × 2)
Electron Equipt: Radar: 1/Square Tie, 1/Drum Tilt
IFF: 2/Square Head, 1/High Pole-A
M: 3 M503A diesels; 3 props; 12,000 hp **Range:** 500/34; 750/25 **Man:** 30 tot.

Remarks: Transferred 1966. Until 1981-82, boats 711–714 bore "S"-series training squadron pendants. Nearing end of useful lives.

TORPEDO BOATS

◆ **18 Soviet Shershen-class torpedo boats** Bldr: U.S.S.R.

811 Max Hoop	832 Erich Kuttner	853 Heinz Biemler
812 Willi Bäntsch	833 Artur Becker	854 Heinz Kapelle
813 Arvid Harnack	834 Fritz Heckert	855 Adam Kuckhoff
814 Bernard Bästlein	835 Ernst Schneller	S 816 Rudolf Breitscheid
815 Fritz Behn	851 Edgar André	S 836 Bruno Kühn
831 Wilhelm Florin	852 Joseph Roemer	S 856 Ernst Grube

Erich Kuttner (832) M.O.D., Bonn, 1980

D: 150 tons (170 fl) **S:** 45 kts **Dim:** 34.7 × 6.7 × 1.5
A: 4/Styx (SS-N-2) — 4/30-mm AA (II × 2)

TORPEDO BOATS *(continued)*

Electron Equipt: Radar: 1/Pot Drum, 1/Drum Tilt
IFF: 1/Square Head, 1/High Pole-A
M: 3 M503A diesels; 3 props; 12,000 hp **Range:** 460/42; 850/30

REMARKS: Transferred 1968-76. No d.c. racks, unlike Soviet Navy units. Nearing end of useful lives.

◆ **30 Libelle-class light torpedo boats** Bldr: East Germany (In serv. 1975-78)

911-915, 921-925, 931-935, 941-945, 951-955, 991-995

Libelle class No. 995 M.O.D., Bonn, 1975

Libelle class No. 993 M.O.D., Bonn, 1976

D: 30 tons (fl) **S:** 50 kts **Dim:** 19.6 × 4.5 × 2.0
A: 2/533-mm TT—2/23-mm AA (II × 1) **Electron Equipt:** Radar: 1/TSR-333
M: 3 M50F-4 diesels; 3 props; 3,600 hp **Man:** 10 tot.

REMARKS: Can quickly convert to commando/frogman carriers. Torpedoes discharged over stern; short tubes on deck eject buoys containing wire payout canisters for torpedo guidance. Names reported: *Fritz Globig, Karl Baier.* One additional unit is used as a trials craft (V87).

PATROL CRAFT

◆ **10 Bremse class**

G 30 to G 39

Bremse class No. G 39 1978

D: 25 tons **S:** 14 kts **Dim:** 23.0 × 5.0 × 1.1 **A:** Small arms
M: 2 diesels; 2 props; 600 hp **Electron Equipt:** Radar: 1/TSR-333

REMARKS: Built early 1970s. Operated by the Border Guard on rivers and inland waterways. The Border Guard also has a number of smaller craft.

MINE WARFARE SHIPS

◆ **27 Kondor-II-class patrol minesweepers** Bldr: Peenewerft, Wolgast (In serv. 1971-78)

311 Uranienburg	324 Röbel	341 Eilensburg
312 Genthin	325 Rathenow	342 Boltenhagen
313 Zerbst	326 Neuruppin	343 Bernau
314 Bitterfeld	331 Klütz	344 Meiningen
315 Rosslau	332 Torgau	345 Riesa
316 Dessau	333 Tangerhütte	346 Strassburg
321 Kyritz	334 Poessnick	351 . . .
322 Guben	335 Altenburg	352 . . .
323 Timendorf	336 Freiberg	353 . . .

Rathenow (325) L. & L. Van Ginderen, 1984

Zerbst (313) M.O.D., Bonn, 6-84

D: 260 tons (310 fl) **S:** 17 kts **Dim:** 55.0 × 7.0 × 2.4
A: 6/25-mm AA (II × 3)—mines **Electron Equipt:** Radar: 1/TSR-333
M: 2 Type 40D diesels; 2 CP props; 5,000 hp **Man:** 40 tot.

REMARKS: Typed "High Seas Minesweepers" by the East German Navy. Those units with a deckhouse aft (including 313–315, 321, 325, and 332) carry within them the cable reel/winch for the Type 1-Ss/e "Fernräumgerat" (a magnetic minesweeping array) added since 1982. All may carry a small sonar. Three, with "S" pendants, served as training ships. Three additional units are trials craft.

◆ **18 Kondor-I-class inshore minesweepers, used as patrol boats**
Bldr: Peenewerft, Wolgast (In serv. 1968-70)

G 411 Stendal	G 421 Ahrenskoop	G 441 Anklam
G 412 Bergen	G 422 Zwickau	G 442 Ueckermünde
G 413 Greifswald	G 423 Prerow	G 443 Rerik
G 414 Pasewalk	G 424 Graal-Müritz	G 444 Weisswasser
G 415 Prenzlau	G 425 Zingst	G 445 Neustrelitz
G 416 Meissen	G 426 Witte	G 446 Demmin

Neustrelitz (G 445) M.O.D., Bonn, 6-84

MINE WARFARE SHIPS *(continued)*

D: 225 tons (275 fl) **S:** 17 kts **Dim:** 52.0 × 7.0 × 2.4
A: 2/25-mm AA (II × 1)—mines **Electron Equipt:** Radar: 1/TSR-333
M: 2 Type 40D diesels; 2 CP props; 5,000 hp **Man:** 30 tot.

REMARKS: Typed "Coastal Minesweeper" by East Germany. Attached to Border Guard as patrol boats, but retain minesweeping gear. Three served as training units, with "S" numbers until early 1980s: 814–816. Two have been converted as torpedo-recovery craft; two others, *Komet* and *Meteor,* altered as intelligence collectors; another is the state yacht *Ostseeland;* V 85 is a trials craft; *Ernst Thaelmann* was converted to a youth-training ship in 1977.

AMPHIBIOUS SHIPS AND CRAFT

◆ **12 Frosch-class landing ships** Bldr: Peenewerft, Wolgast (In serv. 1976-79)

611 EBERSWALDE-FINOW	615 EISENHÜTTENSTADT	633 HETTSTEDT
612 HOYERSWERDA	616 GRIMMEN	634 COTTBUS
613 LÜBBEN	631 SCHWERIN	635 ANKLAM
614 NEUBRANDENBURG	632 FRANKFURT/ODER	636 SCHWEDT

Eisenhüttenstadt (615)—with two 40-tubed, 122-mm artillery RL 1980

Hoyerswerda (612)—note mine rails aft L. & L. Van Ginderen, 10-83

D: 1,900 tons (fl) **S:** 16 kts **Dim:** 98.0 × 12.5 × 2.8
A: 4/57-mm AA (II × 2)—4/30-mm (II × 2)—2/122-mm artillery RL (XL × 2)—mines
Electron Equipt: Radar: 1/Strut Curve, 1/Muff Cob, 1/TSR-333—IFF: 1/High Pole-B
M: 2 Type 40D diesels; 2 props; 5,000 hp

REMARKS: Cargo capacity 400 to 600 tons or 11 tanks and a company of troops. Similar in general form to Soviet Ropucha class, but smaller and with a blunter bow, heavier armament, etc. Two 40-tubed rocket launchers of the type carried by the Soviet ship *Ivan Rogov* are mounted forward of the bridge. Two additional units have been completed as Frosch-II-class supply ships—see under Auxiliaries.

INTELLIGENCE COLLECTION SHIPS

◆ **2 modified Kondor-I class** Bldr: Peenewerft, Wolgast (In serv. 1968-70)

KOMET (ex-. . .) METEOR (ex-. . .)

Komet L. & L. Van Ginderen, 4-81

REMARKS: No armament. Collection antennas added; data otherwise as for Kondor-I-class minesweepers.

◆ **1 Okean-class trawler** (In serv. 1958)

HYDROGRAPH

Hydrograph 1976

D: 1,050 tons (fl) **S:** 11 kts **Dim:** 54.2 × 9.3 × 3.6
Electron Equipt: Radar: 1/TSR-333
M: 1 8NVD48 diesel; 1 prop; 800 hp **Range:** 9,400/11 **Man:** 32 tot.

REMARKS: Former trawler equipped with signal collection devices.

NOTE: *Darss*-class D 41, *Jasmund,* is probably an intelligence ship also.

HYDROGRAPHIC SURVEY SHIPS

Note: All survey ships and buoy tenders are operated under SHD, the Naval Hydrographic Service, and are civilian-manned. The ships display their names and do not carry pendant numbers.

◆ **1 Soviet Finik class** Bldr: Polnocny SY, Gdansk, Poland (In serv. 12-80)

DORNBUSCH

D: 1,200 tons (fl) **S:** 13 kts **Dim:** 61.30 × 11.80 (10.80 wl) × 3.27
Electron Equipt: Radar: 2/Don-2—IFF: 1/High Pole-B
M: 2 Cegielski-Sulzer diesels; 2 CP props; 1,920 hp (plus two 75-kw electric motors for quiet, 6-kt. operations)
Electric: 675 kVA **Endurance:** 15 days **Range:** 3,000/13
Man: 5 officers, 23 men

REMARKS: Replaced a navigational buoy tender/light cable layer of the same name. Intended for navigational buoy tending and hydrographic survey, for which 4 echo-sounders are fitted. Bow-thruster of 176 hp.

◆ **1 modified Kondor-II class**

KARL FRIEDRICH GAUSS

REMARKS: Since 1978. No armament; white-painted. Data as for Kondor-II-class minesweepers. Has more extensive superstructure, twin kingposts aft for handling boats, buoys, etc.

◆ **1 Soviet Kamenka class** Bldr: Szczecin SY, Poland (In serv. 1972)

BUK

Buk 1983

D: 703 tons (fl) **S:** 13.7 kts **Dim:** 53.5 × 9.1 × 2.6
M: 2 Zgoda-Sulzer diesels; 2 CP props; 1,765 hp **Range:** 4,000/10

REMARKS: Buoy tender and survey ship; one 5-ton crane.

◆ **3 Arkona class** (In serv. 1965-70)

ARKONA DARSSER ORT STUBBENKAMMER

D: 55 tons **S:** 10 kts **M:** Diesel

REMARKS: Also act as navigational buoy tenders.

◆ **8 Breitling-class buoy tenders** (In serv. 1971-72)

BREITLING, ESPER ORT, GOLWITZ, GRASS ORT, LANDTIEFF, PALMER ORT, RAMZOW, ROSEN ORT

D: 158 tons (320 fl) **S:** 11.5 kts **Dim:** 29.6 × 6.2 × 1.9
M: 1 diesel; 1 prop; 580 hp

HYDROGRAPHIC SURVEY SHIPS *(continued)*

Breitling—note "SHD" logo on kingpost-stack 1983

EXPERIMENTAL SHIPS V = *Versuch* (Research)

◆ **1 ex-civilian research ship** (In serv. late 1950s)

V 84 Rügen (ex-V 71, ex-*Meteor*)

Rügen (V 84)—with old number 1976

D: 700 tons **S:** 10 kts **Dim:** 50.8 × 3.8 × 3.4 **Range:** 7,900/9 **Man:** 30 tot.
Electron Equipt: Radar: 1/TSR-333 **M:** 1 diesel; 1 prop; 540 hp

Remarks: Built as a fishing boat.

◆ **1 Libelle-class torpedo boat** (In serv. 1975)

V 87

Note: Believed to have been the *Libelle*-class prototype; see data on earlier page.

◆ **3 Kondor-II-class minesweepers** (In serv. 1971-78)

V 381 Pritzwark V 382 Wittstock V 383 Schönebeck

Schönebeck (V 383)—note deckhouse aft 1978

Remarks: Involved in trials of new mine-countermeasures equipment, including the 1-Ss/e array for the Kondor-II class. Data otherwise as for minesweeper-designated sisters.

◆ **1 Kondor-I-class minesweeper** (In serv. 1968-70)

V 85N. . . . . . . (ex-V 31)

Remarks: Data as for standard minesweeper/gunboat version. Possible name: *Eisleben.*

AMPHIBIOUS WARFARE SUPPORT SHIPS

◆ **2 Frosch-II class** Bldr: Peenewerft, Wolgast (1980)

E 35 Nordperd E 36 Südperd

D: 2,000 tons (fl) **S:** 16 kts **Dim:** 98.0 × 12.5 × 2.8
A: 4/57-mm AA (II × 2)—4/25-mm AA (II × 2)—mines

Nordperd (E 35)—note 2 twin 25-mm AA at bow M.O.D., Bonn, 1984

Electron Equipt: Radar: 1/TSR-333, 1/Strut Curve, 1/Muff Cob
IFF: 1/Square Head, 1/High Pole-A
M: 2 Type 40D diesels; 2 props; 5,000 hp **Man:** 120 tot.

Remarks: Differ from Frosch-I in having a large crane amidships and two cargo hatches, and in having 25-mm (mounted right forward to cover the beach) in place of 30-mm AA. Although they have an auxiliary-series pendant number, the bow ramp is retained to permit a beaching capability, and they presumably can be used as assault landing ships if needed. Believed to carry munitions, at least in peacetime.

STORES SHIPS

◆ **7 (+?) Darss class** Bldr: Neptunwerft, Rostock (In serv. 1982-84)

E 11 Monchgut E 61 Wittow V 86 Werdau
E 12 Graniz E . . . Kühlung D 41 Jasmund (In serv. 6-85)
E 41 Darss E . . . N. . .

Darss (E 41) M.O.D., Bonn, 8-83

D: 1,500 tons (fl) **S:** 12-14 kts **Dim:** 68.5(62.0 pp) × 10.0 × 3.5
A: Provision for 6/25-mm AA (II × 3)
Electron Equipt: Radar: 1/TSR-333—IFF: 1/High Pole-B
M: 1 diesel; 1 prop; 1,600 hp **Man:** 60 tot.

Remarks: E 41 launched 27-7-82. Cargo: Approx. 650 tons missiles, ammunition, dry stores, etc., plus about 200 tons cargo fuel. Intended for dead-in-the-water replenishment at sea, as indicated by the heavy rubbing strakes on the hull sides and the 12 rubber fenders carried. Can refuel two ships simultaneously over stern. Crane between the two holds is the same 15–25-ton model used on the Frosch-II class. "V" pendant for *Werdau* indicates trials employment. D 41 is equipped as an intelligence collector, no crane, 5-m radome abaft stack.

OILERS

◆ **1 Soviet Baskunchak class** Bldr: Kamysh Burun SY, Kerch' (In serv. 1964-68)

C 42 Usedom (ex-C27)

Usedom (C 42) 1982

D: 2,940 tons **S:** 13.2 kts **Dim:** 83.6 (74.0 pp) × 12.0 × 4.6
Electron Equipt: Radar: 1/TSR-333
M: 1/8DR43/61 VI diesel; 1 prop; 2,000 hp **Electric:** 325 kw **Fuel:** 124 tons
Range: 5,000/12.6 **Man:** 30 tot.

Remarks: 1,770 grt/1,660 dwt. Cargo: 1,490 tons (9,993 barrels fuel oil). Has provision for mounting 4/25-mm AA (II × 2), one mount forward, one aft.

OILERS *(continued)*

◆ **3 Hiddensee class** Bldr: Peenewerft, Wolgast (In serv. 1960-61)

C 24 HIDDENSEE C 43 POEL C 61 RIEMS

Poel (C 43) L. & L. Van Ginderen, 9-83

D: 1,450 tons (fl) **S:** 12 kts **Dim:** 53.7 × 9.0 × 4.5
Electron Equipt: Radar: 1/TSR-333 **M:** 2 diesels; 1,400 hp **Man:** 26 tot.

REMARKS: Laid down during World War II. *Sahel* in French Navy was a sister. Cargo: 650 tons. Provision for 4/25-mm AA (II × 2), one mount forward, one aft. C 24 re-engined and partially automated in 1984, reducing crew to 12 total.

NOTE: The surviving "Kümo"-series support ships, *Ruden* and *Vilm,* were stricken 1983-84.

TRAINING SHIPS S = *Schulschiff* (Schoolship)

◆ **1 Polish Wodnik class** Bldr: Gdansk SY (In serv. 6-7-76)

S 61 WILHELM PIECK

Wilhelm Pieck (S 61)—at Piraeus, Greece L. & L. Van Ginderen, 1984

D: 1,800 tons (fl) **S:** 17 kts **Dim:** 73.0 × 12.0 × 4.0
A: 4/30-mm AA (II × 2)—4/25-mm AA (II × 2)
Electron Equipt: Radar: 2/TSR-333, 1/Drum Tilt **Man:** 80 tot.
M: 2 Cegielski-Sulzer 6 TD48 diesels; 2 props; 3,600 hp **Electric:** 530 kw

REMARKS: In service 6-7-76. Sister to *Wodnik* and *Gryf* in Polish Navy and *Oka* and *Luga* in Soviet Navy. Design developed from that of the Soviet Moma-class surveying ships.

SALVAGE SHIP

◆ **1 Polish Piast class** Bldr: Gdansk SY, 1977

A 46 OTTO VON GUERICKE

Otto Von Guericke M.O.D., Bonn, 1983

D: 1,560 tons (1,732 fl) **S:** 16.5 kts **Dim:** 73.2 × 10.0 × 4.0
M: 2 Cegielski-Sulzer 6DT48 diesels; 2 props; 3,600 hp **Range:** 3,000/12
Electron Equipt: Radar: 1/TSR-333 **A:** 8/25-mm AA (II × 4)

REMARKS: Sister to Polish *Piast* and *Lech.* Armed 1983. Has diving bell. Built on Soviet Moma-class survey-ship hull and propulsion plant.

AIR/SEA RESCUE SHIP

◆ **1 converted Havel-class fishing trawler** (In serv. 1971)

U 33 HUGO ECKENER

Hugo Eckener (U 33) 1977

D: 384 tons (488 fl) **S:** 10.6 kts **Dim:** 37.66 (32.95 pp) × 8.20 × 3.63 max.
M: 1 type 8 NVD36A1 diesel; 578 hp **Electric:** 280 kw **Man:** 20 tot.
Range: 6,500/10 **Electron Equipt:** Radar: 1/TSR-333

MISCELLANEOUS SHIPS

◆ **2 Kondor-I-class torpedo retriever/target ships**

B 82 LIBBEN (ex-B 74, ex-B 62) B 81 N. . . (ex-B 73)

Libben (B 62)—old number 1980

REMARKS: Converted Kondor-I-class minesweepers, which they basically resemble. No armament. Ramp at stern for torpedo recovery. Radar reflector array on mast, below TSR-333 radar. See data under minesweepers.

◆ **1 yacht** (In serv. circa 1970)

OSTSEELAND

REMARKS: Kondor-I minesweeper hull; large, rakish superstructure. Used by head of state.

NOTE: Original state yacht *Ostseeland,* renamed *Ostseeland II* by 1981, may still be in service.

◆ **several small diving tenders**

◆ **up to 11 Jugend-class barracks barges** Bldr: Peenewerft, Wolgast (In serv. 1961-64)

D: 1,800 tons (fl) **S:** 70.0 × 12.2 × 2.4

REMARKS: Accommodations for 300. Provision for 4/25-mm AA (II × 2)

◆ **1 small cable tender**

FREESENDORF Built 1963

MISCELLANEOUS SHIPS *(continued)*

◆ **1 Soviet Type KM U1 tug** (In serv. 1983)

A 16

D: 300 tons (fl) **S:** 11 kts **Dim:** 29.3 × 8.2 (wl) × 3.7(moulded depth)
M: 2 6-cyl. diesels; 1 CP prop; 1,200 hp

◆ **1 Soviet Prometey class** (Type KM U1) **tug** Bldr: Gorokhovets SY, U.S.S.R.

A 16 (In serv. 1983)

D: 319 tons (fl) **S:** 12 kts **Dim:** 29.8 (28.2pp) × 8.3 × 3.2
M: 2 Type 6D30/50-4 diesels; 2 Kort-nozzle CP props; 1,200 hp
Range: 1,800/12 **Electric:** 50 kw **Man:** 3-5 tot.

Remarks: Has ice-strengthened hull, 14-ton bollard pull. Over 100 sisters built in U.S.S.R. since 1971.

◆ **1 Type 700 seagoing tug (also salvage tug)** Bldr: Peenewerft, Wolgast (In serv. 1964)

A 14 Thale

Thale (A 14) 1978

D: 700 tons (792 fl) **S:** 12.8 kts **Dim:** 44.7 × 10.7 × 3.9
Electron Equipt: Radar: 1/TSR-333 **Range:** 4,000/12
M: 2 diesels; 2 props; 1,680 hp **Man:** 6 officers, 33 men

Remarks: 505 grt. Sister to Bulgarian *Jupiter.* Bollard pull: 16 tons. Provision made for 2/25-mm AA (II × 2).

◆ **7 Type 270 harbor tugs** Bldr: Peenewerft, Wolgast (In serv. 1959-60)

A 11 Peene A 13 Belt A 23 Elbe
A 12 Spee A 22 Havel A 71 Oder A 72 Erich Krenkel

Elbe (A 23) 1980

D: 270 tons **S:** 12 kts **Dim:** 30.0 × 5.5 × 2.5
M: 2 Buckau-Wolf GNVD26A diesels; 1 prop; 550 hp **Man:** 12 tot.

Remarks: Provision for 2/25-mm AA (II × 1)

◆ **6 Ibis-class fireboats** Bldr: Volkswerft, Berlin (In serv. 1959-60)

F 31 F 32 F 45 F 46 F 82 F 83

Ibis class F 46 L. & L. Van Ginderen, 1980

D: 124 tons **S:** 12 kts **Dim:** 32.3 (29.3 pp) × 5.9 ×1.6
M: 2 Buckau-Wolf 6NVD26A diesels; 1 prop; 540 hp
Man: 3 officers, 10 men

Remarks: Three fire monitors. Can also act as tugs. Three sisters built for Egypt, 1961.

◆ **5 Gustav Koenigs-class harbor fuel lighters** Bldr: VEB, Rosslau/Elbe

C 16 C 17 C 25 C 76 C 77

SOCIETY FOR SPORTS AND MECHANICS

The Naval College of this paramilitary youth organization maintains a number of craft for training, the largest of which is the *Ernst Thaelmann.*

◆ **1 converted Kondor-I-class minesweeper**

Ernst Thaelmann

Remarks: Conversion completed 19-8-77. Superstructure enlarged; carries 10 crew and 28 trainees.

◆ **1 sail-training ship** Bldr: Warnowerft, Warnow (In serv. 1951)

Wilhelm Pieck

Wilhelm Pieck 1978

D: . . . **S:** 8 kts (on diesel) **Dim:** 41.0 × 7.7 × 5.5
M: 1 diesel; 100 hp **Fuel:** 16 tons
Man: 13 crew plus 24 trainees

GERMANY-GERMAN DEMOCRATIC REPUBLIC *(continued)*
SOCIETY FOR SPORTS AND MECHANICS *(continued)*

◆ **There are also a number of small craft used for youth training, including: . . . MAB-14 class** Bldr: Berliner Yachtwerft (In serv. 1979-. . .)

D: 18-24 tons (fl) **S:** . . . **Dim:** 14.55 (13.13 wl) × 3.97 × 1.05
M: 1 Type 6VD15.4/12-1 diesel; 1 prop; 140 hp

GERMANY (WEST)

Federal Republic of Germany

Personnel: approx. 38,500 men (including 5,600 officers and 6,700 naval aviation personnel)

Merchant Marine (1984): 1,813 ships—6,242,467 grt
(tankers: 130 ships—1,743,558 grt)

Ships In Service, Under Construction, Or Ordered
As Of 1 January 1986

	L	Tons	Main armament
◆ **24 submarines**			
18 Type 206	1972-74	450	8/533-mm TT
6 Type 205	1961-68	370	8/533-mm TT
◆ **7 destroyers**			
3 Charles F. Adams	1967-69	3,370	1/Tartar, 2/127-mm DP, 1/ASROC
4 Hamburg	1960-63	3,400	4/MM 38, 3/100-mm, 8/40-mm AA, 4/ASW TT
◆ **9 frigates**			
6 Type 122	1979-82	2,900	8/Harpoon, 1/Sea Sparrow, 1/76-mm, 4/ASW TT, 2/helicopters
3 Köln	1958-62	1,750	2/100-mm DP, 6/40-mm AA, 2/ASW RL, 4/ASW TT
◆ **5 corvettes**			
5 Thetis	1960-62	604	2/40-mm AA, 1/ASW RL, 4/ASW TT
◆ **40 guided-missile boats**			
10 Type 143A	1981-83	300	4/MM 38, 1/76-mm DP, 1/RAM system, mines
10 Type 143	1973-76	295	4/MM 38, 2/76-mm DP, 2/533-mm TT
20 Type 148	1972-75	234	4/MM 38, 1/76-mm DP, 1/40-mm AA
◆ **64 (+10 +20) minesweepers/minehunters**			

Naval Aviation:

1 squadron of Starfighter (45F-104 G and 11 TF-1046 2-seat) all-weather interceptor attack and one squadron of 26 (RF-104G) reconnaissance airplanes. All are to be replaced 1986-87. Characteristics are:
- Length: 16.61 meters
- Wingspan: 6.68 meters
- Takeoff weight: 9,900 kg
- Motor: 1 G.E. J79 SE 11A turbojet, 7,170 kg thrust
- Max. speed: Mach 2
- Altitude: 50,000 feet
- Range: 250 to 600 nautical miles, depending on equipment
- Weapons: 4,000 kg maximum (bombs, rockets, Kormoran ASM, etc.)

1 squadron of 19 Bréguet Atlantic-1150 aircraft, of which 5 have been modified for electronic warfare. The ASW aircraft underwent modernization in 1981-83.

1 squadron of 22 Mk 43 Sea King helicopters for search-and-rescue operations. The Sea Kings are being upgraded to permit carrying 4 Sea Skua anti-ship missiles, a Sea Spray Mk 3 search radar, electronic intercept gear, chaff, and a computer data system. The first two were to have completed by 1984 and all by 1988, but delays have moved initial redeliveries to 1987.

On 7-4-76 the German government decided to begin construction of 112 MRCA Tornado variable-geometry fighter-bombers for the Navy. The first four entered service in 7-82 and 47 were operational by 7-84. Characteristics are:
- Length: 17.2 meters
- Wingspan: 13.90 meters max./8.40 meters min.
- Maximum takeoff weight: 26,000 kg
- Maximum speed: Mach 2.2
- Ceiling: 15,200 m
- Weapons: 4 Kormoran ASM or 10 Mk 83 or Mk 82 bombs or 8 BL 755 cluster bombs—plus 2 AIM 9 Sidewinder and a 23-mm gun

Deliveries were scheduled for: 1 in 1981, 26 in 1982, 22 in 1983, 32 in 1986, 16 in 1987, and 15 in 1988, but total production may cease at 95.

Tornado 1982

Twelve Westland/Bréguet WG-13 Lynx Mk 88 ASW helicopters were bought for the new Type 122 frigates. The Bendix DAQS-18 dipping sonar is employed. First 4 delivered 1981, 8 in 1982, and 4 in 1983. Two more ordered 11-84 for delivery 1986.

There are also 20 Dornier DO-28D-2 liaison aircraft, an HFB 32 ECM aircraft, a small number of Piaggio P 149D basic trainers, and 4 IAI Westwind target tugs.

Lynx Mk 88 of the West German Navy P. Voss, 8-84

WEAPONS AND SYSTEMS

With a few exceptions, such as torpedoes, West German ships have weapons and systems of foreign origin.

(A) MISSILES

◆ **Surface-to-air**

Standard Tartar SM-1 MR on board the 3 *Charles F. Adams*-class destroyers

In conjunction with the U.S.A., the General Dynamics RIM-116A RAM (Rolling Airframe Missile) is being developed as a close-in defense weapon. The system will carry 21 missiles per EX-31 launcher. A total of 63 launchers are programmed for purchase.

◆ **Surface-to-surface**

MM 38 Exocet on board *Hamburg*-class destroyers and Types 143A, 143, and 148 guided-missile patrol boats. The U.S. Harpoon (RGM-84A) is carried by the Type 122 frigates and by refitted units of the *Charles F. Adams*-class destroyers. The Anglo-French ANS missile will replace both MM 38 Exocet and the Kormoran air-launched SSM from the mid-1990s.

◆ **Air-to-surface**

Kormoran missiles, carried by F-104 and Tornado aircraft. Kormoran II, with a new digital radar seeker from Thomson-CSF, will enter service about 1989.

(B) GUNS

Automatic 127-mm U.S. Mk 42 Mod. 10 on *Adams*-class destroyers

French Model 1953 100-mm dual-purpose on *Hamburg*-class destroyers, *Köln*-class frigates, *Rhein*-class tenders, and the training ship *Deutschland*

OTO Melara Compact 76-mm guns on board Types 143, 143A, and 148 guided-missile patrol boats

40-mm (70-caliber) Bofors, in single or twin mounts on many types of ships. Replaced by open Breda mountings in combatants

20-mm Oerlikon and Rheinmetall

(C) ANTISUBMARINE WARFARE

◆ **Rocket launchers**

Quadruple 375-mm Bofors, automatically loaded in a vertical position

The U.S. ASROC system, with a Mk 112 octuple launcher for missiles having a Mk 46 ASW torpedo payload

◆ **Torpedoes**

U.S. Mk 37 Mod. 0 on submarines (possibly no longer in use)

ANTISUBMARINE WARFARE *(continued)*

U.S. Mk 44 and Mk 46 on *Charles F. Adams*-class destroyers, Type 122 frigates, and Bréguet Atlantic-1150 ASW patrol aircraft

Wire-guided "Seeal (SST-4)" type (20,000 m range) on Type 143 missile boats, and submarines

Wire-guided "Seeschlange" type on Type 206 submarines; range; 10,000 m

(D) ELECTRONICS

In addition to the U.S. radars mounted in the *Charles F. Adams*-class destroyers, the West German Navy uses the following Dutch radars (Hollandse Signaal-apparaaten):

LW-02 long-range air search (Band D)
SGR-105 multi-purpose search (Band E-F)
SGR-103 surface search (Band I)
Band X for 100-mm and 40-mm fire control

Type 148 missile patrol boats have a Thomson-CSF Triton target-designation radar and Vega fire-control system with Pollux radar.

Type 143 missile patrol boats carry the AGIS fire-control system combined with Dutch H.S.A. WM 27 M radar. AGIS has two UNIVAC computers, one for fire control and the other for real-time threat-processing. WM 27 has two antennas within its dome, one for search and one for tracking. An automatic data link permits AGIS to relay information with other units of the Type 143, *Charles F. Adams*-class, and with future combatants destined for service with the fleet operating from Glücksberg-Meierwik. The *Adams*-class destroyers are receiving the Lockheed-built Mk 86 gun-fire-control system, with SPQ-9 and SPG-60 radar. As a countermeasure system, the Breda SCLAR chaff rocket launcher (20 tubes) has been adopted. (U.S. Mk 36 Super RBOC on the *Adams* class).

Aside from the SQS-23 on the *Adams* class, sonars are of West German origin.

SUBMARINES

◆ **0 (+12 +6) Type 211** Bldr: . . .

D: 1,040 tons surf./1,300 sub. **S:** 11/23 kts
Dim: 59.00 × 5.40 × 4.50 (surf.)
A: 8/533-mm TT—(14 Seeal-3 ASW and DM2A3 torpedoes)
Electron Equipt: Radar: . . . —Sonar: Krupp-Atlas. . .
M: 2 MTU 16V396 SB83, 1,260-bhp diesels; 2/870-kw generators; electric drive; 1 prop; 6,000 hp **Fuel:** 100 tons
Range: 5,000/8 snorkel **Endurance:** 40 days **Man:** 20 tot.

REMARKS: Six of this general type ordered from Thyssen Nordseewerke for Norway as the "Type 210," for delivery beginning 1989. Diving depth 250 m. In German Navy will replace Type 205 and some Type 206, with first 9 delivering 1990-93, the rest by 1997. To use a Norwegian-developed, Kongsberg MSI-90U fire control system. Program remained in concept planning through mid-1985.

◆ **18 Type 206** Bldrs: (A)—Howaldtswerke-Deutsche Werft, Kiel; (B)—Rheinstahl Nordseewerke, Emden

	Bldr	Laid down	L	In serv.
S 192 U 13	A	24-11-69	28-9-71	19-4-73
S 193 U 14	B	10-9-70	1-2-72	19-4-73
S 194 U 15	A	29-5-70	15-6-72	17-4-74
S 195 U 16	B	22-4-71	29-8-72	9-11-73
S 196 U 17	A	19-10-70	10-10-72	28-11-73
S 197 U 18	B	28-7-71	31-10-72	19-12-73
S 198 U 19	A	14-1-71	15-12-72	9-11-73
S 199 U 20	B	15-2-72	16-1-73	24-5-74
S 170 U 21	A	14-4-71	9-3-73	16-8-74
S 171 U 22	B	3-5-72	27-3-73	26-7-74
S 172 U 23	B	21-8-72	22-5-73	2-5-75
S 173 U 24	B	10-7-72	26-6-73	16-10-74
S 174 U 25	A	6-10-71	23-5-73	14-6-74
S 175 U 26	B	17-11-72	20-11-73	13-3-75
S 176 U 27	A	11-1-72	21-8-73	16-10-74
S 177 U 28	B	26-1-72	22-1-74	18-12-74
S 178 U 29	A	29-2-72	5-11-73	27-11-74
S 179 U 30	B	27-4-73	26-3-74	13-3-75

U 20 (S 199) L. & L. Van Ginderen, 5-84

U 15 (S 194) P. Voss, 4-84

D: 450 tons surf./500 tons sub. **S:** 10 surf./17 kts sub. (5 snorkel)
Dim: 48.6 × 4.6 × 4.3
A: 8/533-mm TT—(16 torpedoes)—24 mines in external container
Electron Equipt: Radar: 1/Thomson-CSF Calypso
Sonar: 1/WSU AN 410A4, 1/GHG AN 5039A1, 1/DBQS-21D, 1/DUUX-2
M: 2 MTU 12V493AZ diesels; 600 hp each, 2/405-kw generators; 1/2,300-hp electric motor
Range: 4,500/5 (snorkel); 200/5 submerged **Man:** 4 officers, 18 men

REMARKS: *U 13* to *U 24* authorized in 1969, *U 25* to *U 30* in 2-70. An external "mine-belt" container has been developed for these submarines to permit them to carry a full complement of torpedoes plus 24 mines. Three batteries, 92 cells each. Now have H.S.A. Mk 8; new Krupp-Atlas control systems are to be installed in 12 of the 18 by HDW, with recommissionings now delayed to 1989-91. Modernized units to be typed 206A.

◆ **6 Type 205** Bldr: Howaldtswerke, Kiel

	Laid down	L	In serv.
S 180 U 1	1-2-65	17-2-67	6-6-67
S 181 U 2	1-9-64	15-7-66	11-10-66
S 188 U 9	10-12-64	20-10-66	11-4-67
S 189 U 10	15-7-65	5-6-67	28-11-67
S 190 U 11	1-4-66	9-2-68	21-6-68
S 191 U 12	1-9-66	10-9-68	14-1-69

U 9 (S 188) L. & L. Van Ginderen, 5-84

U 10 (S 189) Marineamt, 1981

D: 419 tons surf./450 sub. **S:** 10 surf./17 kts sub. **Dim:** 43.5 × 4.6 × 3.8
A: 8/533-mm TT
Electron Equipt: Radar: 1/Thomson-CSF Calypso
Sonar: 1/SRS-M1H, 1/GHG AN5039A1
M: 2 MTU 12V493AZ, 600-hp diesels, 2/405-kw generators, 1/2,300-hp electric motor
Man: 4 officers, 17 men

SUBMARINES *(continued)*

REMARKS: *U 10* is 43.8-m overall; *U 11, 12:* 45.8-m overall. Diving depth: 150M. The poor quality of the antimagnetic steel used in the first six of this class caused serious pitting, which made it necessary to rebuild the *U 1* and *U 2* (originally launched 21-10-61 and 25-1-62) with regular steel. Beginning with the *U 9,* laid down in 1964, these submarines were built with a new antimagnetic steel. Have H.S.A. Mk 8 torpedo f.c.s. The *U 3* was stricken in 1968, the *U 4* and *U 8* in 1974, the *U 5* in 1975, and the *U 6* and *U 7* in 1974.

GUIDED-MISSILE DESTROYERS

◆ **3 U.S. Charles F. Adams (Type 103B) class** Bldr: Bath Iron Works, Bath, Maine

	Laid down	L	In serv.
D 185 LÜTJENS (ex-DDG 28)	1-3-66	11-8-67	22-3-69
D 186 MÖLDERS (ex-DDG 29)	12-4-66	13-4-68	20-9-69
D 187 ROMMEL (ex-DDG 30)	22-8-67	1-2-69	2-5-70

Mölders (D 186)—as modernized L. & L. Van Ginderen, 5-84

Lütjens (D 185)—prior to modernization L. & L. Van Ginderen, 7-84

D: 3,550 tons (4,720 fl) **S:** 35 kts **Dim:** 134.4 (128.1 pp) × 14.38 × 6.4 (max)
A: 1/Tartar Mk 13 missile launcher (40 Harpoon and Standard SM-1 MR missiles)—2/127-mm Mk 42 DP (I × 2)—6/324-mm Mk 32 ASW TT (III × 2)—1 Mk 112 ASROC ASW RL (VIII × 1)
Electron Equipt: Radar: 1/SPS-40, 1/SPS-10, 1/SPS-52, 1/Kelvin-Hughes 14/9, 2/SPG-51C, SPQ-9, 1/SPG-60
Sonar: 1/SQS-23—EW: FL-1800, 2/Mk 36 RBOC chaff—TACAN: URN-20
M: GT; 2 props; 70,000 hp **Electric:** 3,000 kw
Boilers: 4 Combustion Engineering, 84 kg/cm² pressure, superheat 500°C
Fuel: 950 tons **Range:** 1600/30; 4,030/18 **Man:** 21 officers, 319 men

REMARKS: Authorized 1964. They differ in several ways, especially in profile, from the *Charles F. Adams* design, on which they are based. Installation of the SM-1 MR system and digitalization of some computer equipment was completed 1981-82. All three were further modernized, with most of the improvements originally planned for the U.S. Navy units of the class: the Mk 13 missile system was revised to permit carrying Harpoon anti-ship missiles, the Mk 68 gunfire control system was replaced by the Mk 86 GFCS with SPQ-9 and SPG-60 radars (the latter permitting a third SAM fire control channel as well), the U.S. SYS-1 computerized data systems, the Mk 36 Super RBOC chaff system, and the substitution of the German FL-1800 EW system for WLR-6. D 185 began modernization 5-4-82 at Howaldtswerke, completing 29-3-84. D 186 refitted 12-83 to 7-85, and D 187 4-85 to 12-86. Have Satir-1 NTDS data link.

Rommel (D 187)—as modernized L. & L. Van Ginderen, 9-85

◆ **4 Hamburg class (Type 101B)** Bldr: H. C. Stülcken, Hamburg

	Laid down	L	In serv.
D 181 HAMBURG	29-1-59	26-3-60	23-3-64
D 182 SCHLESWIG-HOLSTEIN	20-8-59	20-8-60	12-10-64
D 183 BAYERN	14-9-60	14-8-62	6-7-65
D 184 HESSEN	15-2-61	4-5-63	8-10-68

Hamburg (D 181) G. Gyssels, 3-85

Bayern (D 183) P. Voss, 10-84

D: 3,500 tons (4,700 fl) **S:** 35 kts **Dim:** 133.7 (128.0 pp) × 13.4 × 5.2 (max.)
A: 4/MM 38 Exocet SSM—3/100-mm Mod. 1953 DP (I × 3)—8/40-mm Breda AA (II × 4)—4/533-mm ASW TT—2/375-mm Bofors ASW RL (IV × 2)—2/d.c. racks (12 d.c.)—60–80 mines
Electron Equipt: Radar: 1/Kelvin-Hughes 14/9, 1/DA-08, 1/LW-04, 1/SGR-103—3/M45
Sonar: 1/Atlas ELAC 1BV med. freq.
EW: WLR-6, 2/SCLAR chaff RL
M: 2 sets GT; 2 props; 68,000 hp **Boilers:** 4/59 kg/cm², 465°C **Fuel:** 810 tons
Electric: 5,400 kw **Range:** 920/34; 3,400/18 **Man:** 270 tot.

REMARKS: Between the beginning of 1975 and the end of 1977, refitted with 4/MM 38 to replace mount C, in the following order: D 184, D 181, D 182, and D 183. Five fixed anti-ship torpedo tubes (3 in bows, 2 aft) removed, 40-mm replaced by later model, new air-search radar. There are three H.S.A. M4 radar directors for the 100-mm guns. The d.c. racks are bolted to the mine rails. Further modernization, beginning with D 184, is planned, including the installation of 2/21-missile EX-31 launchers for the RAM SAM system, and a new computer data system.

GUIDED-MISSILE FRIGATES

◆ **0 (+6) Type 124 class**

Remarks: In project definition through the end of 1985 was a program for six new guided-missile frigates, to be based in part on the successful Type 122 design. A delay may permit adopting features of the "Nato Frigate." The ships will rationally replace the four *Hamburg*-class destroyers and the three remaining *Köln*-class frigates in the 1990s. They are intended to be delivered in 1993-96.

◆ **6 (+2) Bremen (Type 122) class**

	Bldr	Laid down	L	In serv.
F 207 BREMEN	Bremer-Vulkan	9-7-79	27-9-79	7-5-82
F 208 NIEDERSACHSEN	AG Weser, Bremen	9-11-79	9-6-80	15-10-82
F 209 RHEINLAND-PFALZ	Blohm + Voss, Hamburg	25-9-79	3-9-80	9-5-83
F 210 EMDEN	Nordseewerke, Emden	23-6-80	17-12-80	9-10-83
F 211 KÖLN	Blohm + Voss, Hamburg	16-6-80	29-5-81	19-10-84
F 212 KARLSRUHE	Howaldtswerke, Kiel	10-3-81	8-1-82	19-4-84
F. . . AUGSBURG	Thyssen, Emden	. . .	. . .	. . .
F. . . LÜBECK	Bremer Vulcan	. . .	. . .	. . .

GUIDED MISSILE FRIGATES *(continued)*

Niedersachsen (F 208)—with 2 Lynx on deck G. Gyssels, 2-85

Bremen (F 207) P. Voss, 8-83

Rheinland-Pfalz (F 209) L. & L. Van Ginderen, 4-85

Karlsruhe (F 212) P. Voss, 4-84

D: 2,930 tons (3,780 fl) **S:** 30 kts
Dim: 130.0 (121.8 wl) × 14.4 × 4.26 (6.0 sonar)
A: 8/Harpoon SSM (IV × 2)—1/NATO Sea Sparrow SAM system (VIII × 1, Mk 29 launcher, 24 RIM-7M missiles)—1/76-mm OTO Melara DP—4/324-mm Mk 32 ASW TT (I × 4)—2/Lynx Mk 88 ASW helicopters
Electron Equipt: Radar: 1/3RM20, 1/DA-08, 1/WM-25, 1/STIR
Sonar: 1/DSQS-21B(Z) (bow-mounted)
EW: FL 1800S intercept array (7.5-17 GHz), Mk 36 Super RBOC chaff RL (VI × 4)
M: CODOG: 2 G.E.-Fiat LM 2500 GT (50,000 hp); 2 MTU 20V956 TB92 diesels (10,400 hp); 2/5-bladed Escher-Wyss CP props
Electric: 3,000 kw (4/750-kw diesel sets) **Range:** 5,700/17 **Fuel:** 610 tons
Man: 21 officers, 160 men (plus 6-officer/12-man air complement)

Remarks: Germanized version of Dutch *Kortenaer* class. Ordered 7-77; two additional canceled. The helicopters will be equipped with DAQS-13D dipping sonar. Two RAM point-defense SAM launchers are to be added atop the hangar. Fin stabilizers fitted. Have SATIR tactical data sysem, Canadian Bear Trap helicopter landing system, and H.S.A. Vesta helicopter transponder. Fitted with U.S. Prarie/Masker bubbler system to reduce radiated noise, fin stabilizers, a citadel nuclear-biological-gas protection system, and the U.S. SLQ-25 Nixie towed torpedo decoy. F 212 has a revised engine air intake system. Carry 16 torpedoes for helos, 8 for tubes. Construction of two additional units was approved by the government 7-85.

FRIGATES

◆ **3 Köln class (Type 120)** Bldr: H. C. Stülcken, Hamburg

	Laid down	L	In serv.
F 222 Augsburg	29-10-58	15-8-59	7-4-62
F 224 Lübeck	28-10-59	23-7-60	6-7-63
F 225 Braunschweig	28-7-60	3-2-62	16-6-64

Augsberg (F 222) L. & L. Van Ginderen, 5-85

D: 2,425 tons (2,970 fl) **S:** 30 kts (20 on diesels)
Dim: 109.83 (105.0 pp) × 10.5 × 4.61 (fl)
A: 2/100-mm Mod. 1953 DP (I × 2)—6/40-mm AA (II × 2, I × 2)—2/375-mm Bofors ASW RL (IV × 2; 70 rockets)—4/533-mm ASW TT (I × 4)—2/d.c. racks (12 d.c.)—82 mines
Electron Equipt: Radar: 1/DA-02, 1/SGR-103, 1/Kelvin-Hughes 14/9, 2/M 44 fire-control, 1/M 45 fire-control
Sonar: 1/PAE/CWE MF hull-mounted—EW: . . . intercept
M: CODAG: 4 M.A.N. V-16-cylinder diesels (each 3,000 hp); 2 Brown-Boveri gas turbines (each 13,000 hp); 2 CP props; 36,000 hp
Electric: 2,700 kw **Fuel:** 361 tons **Range:** 900/30; 2,910/22
Man: 17 officers, 193 men

Remarks: The rocket-launcher magazines carry 72 projectiles. Two diesels and one gas turbine on each of the two shafts. Made 33 knots on trials. Three sisters disposed of: *Köln* (F 220) on 17-12-82 for static training at the Naval Technical School; *Karlsrühe* (F 223) on 27-12-82, to Turkey 28-3-83; and *Emden* (F 221) on 23-9-83 for transfer to Turkey late 1983. The three survivors are to be retained into the mid-1990s. F 225 heavily damaged in collision with HMS *Plymouth,* 11-4-84.

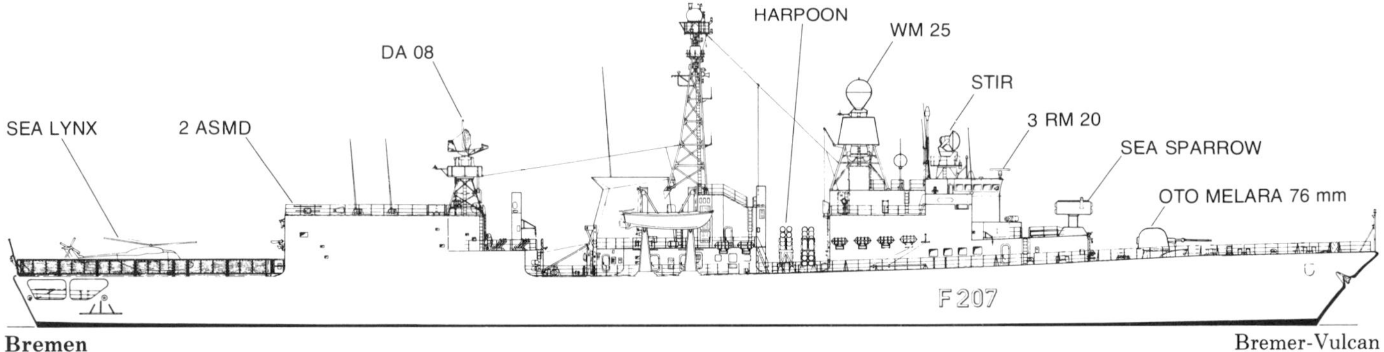

Bremen Bremer-Vulcan

CORVETTES

◆ **0 (+3) Type 423**

Remarks: Programmed class for delivery 1990-93 to replace the *Thetis* (Type 420) class. No data available; program probably canceled or deferred.

◆ **5 Thetis class (Type 420)** Bldr: Roland Werft, Bremen-Hemelingen

	Laid down	L	In serv.
P 6052 Thetis	19-6-59	22-3-60	1-7-61
P 6053 Hermes	8-10-59	9-8-60	16-12-61
P 6054 Najade	22-3-60	6-12-60	12-5-62
P 6055 Triton	15-8-60	5-8-61	10-11-62
P 6056 Theseus	1-7-61	20-3-62	15-8-63

Thetis (P 6052) G. Gyssels, 1985

Triton (P 6055) Marineamt, 5-84

D: 575 tons (658 fl) **S:** 23.5 kts **Dim:** 69.78 (65.5 pp) × 8.2 × 2.65
A: 2/40-mm AA (II × 1)—1/Bofors 375-mm ASW RL (IV × 1)—4/533-mm ASW TT (I × 4)—2/d.c. racks (12/d.c.)—mines
Electron Equipt: Radar: 1/Kelvin-Hughes 14/9, 1/TRS-N
Sonar: ELAC 1BV—EW: . . . intercept
M: 2 M.A.N. V84V diesels; 2 props; 6,800 hp **Electric:** 540 kw
Range: 2,760/15 **Man:** 5 officers, 43 men **Fuel:** 78 tons

Remarks: Former torpedo-recovery boats, well designed for operations in the Belts and the Baltic. Have H.S.A. Mk 9 torpedo f.c.s. and an optical lead-computing gun f.c.s. P 6054 has forward superstructure extended toward bow to accommodate a medical facility. Carry 20 ASW RL projectiles.

GUIDED-MISSILE PATROL BOATS

◆ **10 Type 143A** Bldrs: A: Lürssen, Vegesack; B: Kröger, Rendsburg

		Laid down	L	In serv.
P 6121 S71 Gepard	A	11-7-79	25-9-81	7-12-82
P 6122 S72 Puma	A	17-12-79	8-2-82	24-2-83
P 6123 S73 Hermelin	B	1-2-80	8-12-81	28-4-83
P 6124 S74 Nerz	A	24-7-80	18-8-82	14-7-83
P 6125 S75 Zobel	B	3-7-80	30-6-82	29-9-83
P 6126 S76 Frettchen	A	22-12-80	26-1-83	15-12-83
P 6127 S77 Dachs	B	9-3-80	14-12-82	1-3-84
P 6128 S78 Ozelot	A	25-6-81	7-6-83	3-5-84
P 6129 S79 Wiesel	A	5-10-80	8-8-83	12-7-84
P 6130 S80 Hyäne	A	7-12-81	5-10-83	13-11-84

D: 300 tons (390.6 fl) **S:** 36 kts (32 fl)
Dim: 57.6 (54.4 pp) × 7.76 × 2.99 (2.56 hull)
A: 4/MM 38 Exocet—provision for 1/RAM ASMD (XXI × 1, RIM-116A missiles)—1/76-mm OTO Melara DP—mines
Electron Equipt: Radar: 1/3RM 20, 1/H.S.A. WM-27—EW: FL 1800 intercept, chaff

Dachs (P 6127) G. Koop, 5-84

S 76 Frettchen (P 6126) L. & L. Van Ginderen, 4-85

M: 4 MTU 16V956 SB80 diesels; 4 props; 16,000 hp **Electric:** 540 kw
Fuel: 116 tons **Range:** 600/30; 2,600/16 **Man:** 4 officers, 18 p.o., 12 men

Remarks: Ordered 1978. A repeat Type 143 with the much-delayed RAM point-defense SAM system intended to replace the after 76-mm gun, and mine rails in place of the wire-guided torpedoes. Wood-planked hull on steel frame. Have AGIS integrated data system. Lack after optical GFCS found on Type 143/143B. Constitute the 7th Fast Patrol Boat Squadron. RAM to become operational circa 1987-88.

◆ **10 Type 143/143B** Bldrs: A: Lürssen, Vegesack; B: Kröger, Rendsburg

	Bldr	Laid down	L	In serv.
P 6111 S61 Albatros	A	4-5-72	22-10-73	1-11-76
P 6112 S62 Falke	A	25-10-72	21-3-74	13-4-76
P 6113 S63 Geier	A	14-2-73	18-9-74	2-6-76
P 6114 S64 Bussard	A	4-7-73	14-4-75	14-8-76
P 6115 S65 Sperber	B	18-1-73	15-1-74	27-9-76
P 6116 S66 Grief	A	12-12-73	4-9-75	25-11-76
P 6117 S67 Kondor	B	19-6-73	6-3-75	17-12-76
P 6118 S68 Seeadler	A	12-6-74	17-11-75	28-3-77
P 6119 S69 Habicht	B	25-1-74	5-6-75	23-12-77
P 6120 S70 Kormoran	A	26-11-74	14-4-76	29-7-77

D: 300 tons (393 fl) **S:** 36 kts (32 fl)
Dim: 57.6 (54.4 pp) × 7.76 × 2.82 (2.56 hull)
A: 4/MM 38 Exocet—2/76-mm OTO Melara AA (I × 2)—2/533-mm TT (aft-launching, for Seeal wire-guided torpedoes)
Electron Equipt: Radar: 1/3RM 20, 1/H.S.A. WM-27—EW: . . . intercept, chaff
M: 4 MTU 16V956 TB91 diesels; 4 props; 16,000 hp **Electric:** 540 kw
Fuel: 116 tons **Range:** 600/30; 2,600/16 **Man:** 4 officers, 18 p.o., 12 men

Remarks: Wood-planked hull on steel frame. To be refitted to Type 143A standard, except that the torpedo tubes will be retained, thus becoming Type 143B. There is a secondary OGR-7/3 optical f.c.s. for the aft 76-mm gun. PG 119 carried a *mockup* RAM launcher aft during 1983. EW equipment is less elaborate than on the Type 143A; both classes have a chaff-dispensing mast abaft the mainmast central leg.

S 67 Kondor (P 6117) L. & L. Van Ginderen, 5-85

GUIDED-MISSILE PATROL BOATS *(continued)*

S 66 Grief (P 6116) L. & L. Van Ginderen, 5-85

◆ **20 Type 148, steel-hulled** Bldrs: A: Constructions Mécaniques de Normandie, Cherbourg; B: Lürssen, Vegesack

	Bldr	Laid down	L	In serv.
P 6141 S41 Tiger	A	11-10-71	27-9-72	30-10-72
P 6142 S42 Iltis	A	2-2-72	12-12-72	8-1-73
P 6143 S43 Luchs	A	23-3-72	7-3-73	9-4-73
P 6144 S44 Marder	A	15-4-72	5-5-73	14-7-73
P 6145 S45 Leopard	A	13-9-72	3-7-73	21-8-73
P 6146 S46 Fuchs	B	10-3-72	21-5-73	17-10-73
P 6147 S47 Jaguar	A	29-11-72	20-9-73	13-11-73
P 6148 S48 Löwe	B	10-7-72	10-9-73	9-1-74
P 6149 S49 Wolf	A	23-1-73	11-1-74	26-2-74
P 6150 S50 Panther	B	30-9-72	10-12-73	27-3-74
P 6151 S51 Häher	A	5-4-73	26-4-74	12-6-74
P 6152 S52 Storch	B	12-3-73	25-3-74	17-7-74
P 6153 S53 Pelikan	A	11-9-73	4-7-74	24-9-74
P 6154 S54 Elster	B	29-6-73	8-7-74	14-11-74
P 6155 S55 Alk	A	9-4-74	15-11-74	7-1-75
P 6156 S56 Dommel	B	13-12-73	30-10-74	12-2-75
P 6157 S57 Weihe	A	2-7-74	13-2-75	3-4-75
P 6158 S58 Pinguin	B	11-3-74	26-2-75	22-5-75
P 6159 S59 Reiher	A	8-11-74	15-5-75	24-6-75
P 6160 S60 Kranich	B	9-5-74	26-5-75	6-8-75

D: 234 tons (264 fl) **S:** 35.8 kts **Dim:** 47.0 (45.9 pp) × 7.1 × 2.66 (fl)
A: 4/MM 38 Exocet—1/76-mm DP OTO Melara (fwd)—1/40-mm Bofors AA (aft)—8 mines in place of the 40-mm AA
Electron Equipt: Radar: 1/3RM 20 navigation, 1/Triton, 1/Pollux
M: 4 MTU MD 872 16-cyl. diesels; 4 props; 14,400 hp (12,000 sust.)
Electric: 270 kw **Range:** 570/30; 1,600/15 **Fuel:** 39 tons
Man: 4 officers, 15 p.o., 18 men

Remarks: All hulls fitted out at Cherbourg. Ordered 18-12-70, as CMN's type *Combattante II* A4L. Steel construction. Thomson-CSF Vega fire-control system with Pollux radar; Triton is used for target designation. P 6152 has Triton II search radar and Castor II fire-control radar, the latter with a Piranha optronic attachment. Another ship conducted trials with the CSEE Naja optronic and CSEE Panda optical directors during the 1982-83. All have the Palis (Passive-Active-Link) system for data sharing and can use NATO LINK 11. P 6159 has an enclosed Mauser 40-mm gun mounting.

S 56 Dommel (P 6156) P. Voss, 9-84

S 52 Storch (P 6152)—with new radars L. & L. Van Ginderen, 6-83

Note: The 10 Zobel (Type 142)-class torpedo boats have been disposed of: *Zobel* (P 6092) on 7-9-82; *Hermelin* (P 6095) on 12-1-83; *Nerz* (P 6096) on 8-7-82; *Puma* (P 6097) on 17-12-81; *Gerpard* (P 6098) on 9-11-82; *Dachs* (P 6094) on 2-12-83; *Frettchen* (P 6100) on 9-8-83; *Ozelot* (P 6101) on 10-1-84; *Wiesel* (P 6093) on 6-4-84; and Hyäne (P 6099) on 5-6-84. P 6093, 6101, 6099 to Turkey on 8-10-84, and 6098, 6094, and 6100 on 14-5-84. P 6092 sold to builders, Lürssenwerft 28-12-83; P 6096 used for Type 343 minesweeper equipment trials; P 6095 is to be used as a missile target, and P 6097 is a static training hulk at the Naval Technical School.

MINE WARFARE SHIPS

◆ **0 (+12) Type 355 pressure-mine sweepers**

Remarks: Remains a project to design a ship capable of detecting and disposing of the "unsweepable" pressured mine. If successful, may be build during 1990s.

◆ **0 (+10 + 10) Type 332 coastal minehunters** Bldr: . . .

◆ **0 (+10) Type 343 minesweepers** Bldr: 4 by Lürssen, Vegesack; 3 by Abeking & Rasmussen, Lemwerde; 3 by Krögerwerft, Rendsburg (In serv. 1988-90)

	Bldr	Laid down	L	In serv.
M . . . N . . .	. . .	. . .	. . .	1988
M . . . N . . .	. . .	. . .	. . .	. . .
M . . . N . . .	. . .	. . .	. . .	. . .
M . . . N . . .	. . .	. . .	. . .	. . .
M . . . N . . .	. . .	. . .	. . .	. . .
M . . . N . . .	. . .	. . .	. . .	. . .
M . . . N . . .	. . .	. . .	. . .	. . .
M . . . N . . .	. . .	. . .	. . .	. . .
M . . . N . . .	. . .	. . .	. . .	. . .
M . . . N . . .	. . .	. . .	. . .	1990

Type 343 minesweeper—artist's impression 1984

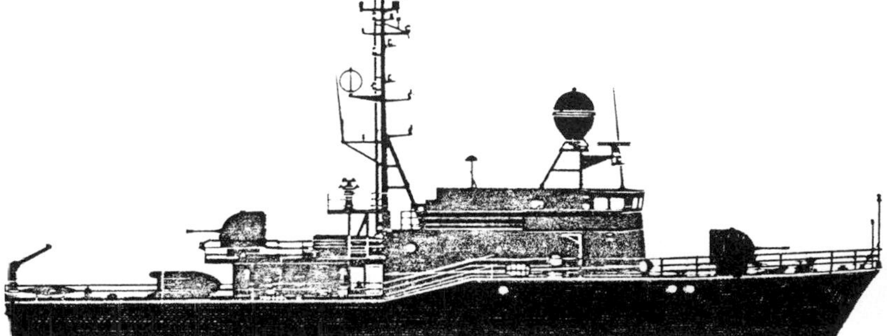

Type 343 class 1983

MINE WARFARE SHIPS *(continued)*

D: 570-590 tons (fl) **S:** 21 kts **Dim:** 54.0 (51.0 pp) × 9.2 × 2.5
A: 2/40-mm AA (I × 2)—mines
Electron Equipt: Radar: 1/nav., 1/H.S.A. WM 27/28
Sonar: DSQS-11
EW: intercept array, 1 decoy RL, 2 infrared decoy projectors
M: 2 MTU diesels; 2 CP props; . . . hp **Electric:** 3 generators/. . . kw
Range: . . ./. . . **Man:** 37 tot.

REMARKS: Messerschmidt-Bölkow-Blohm (MBB) was selected as prime contractor 10-1-85, with initial orders for the 10 Type 343 non-magnetic steel-hulled minehunter/minesweepers expected spring 1985. Characteristics not fully determined. The Type 343s will be configured for mechanical, acoustic, and magnetic minesweeping to replace Type 340/341 (Schütze)-class patrol minesweepers. The later two series of Type 332-class minehunters will be very similar, except for carrying remote-controlled minehunting submersibles; initial orders were to come in 1987, and the final 10 Type 332 may have controls for "Toika"-type drones. May carry RAM launcher in place of aft 40-mm AA.

◆ **6 Type 351 drone minesweeper-control ships** Bldr: Burmester, Bremen

	L	In serv.	Conversion completed
M 1073 SCHLESWIG	2-10-57	30-10-58	19-3-81
M 1076 PADERBORN	5-12-57	16-12-58	17-9-81
M 1079 DÜREN	12-6-58	22-4-59	7-11-83
M 1081 KONSTANZ	30-9-58	23-7-59	24-5-82
M 1082 WOLFSBURG	10-12-58	8-10-59	4-3-82
M 1083 ULM	10-2-59	7-11-59	11-11-81

Schleswig (M 1073) L. & L. Van Ginderen, 8-85

D: 488 tons (fl) **S:** 16.5 kts **Dim:** 47.5 × 8.5 × 2.75 **A:** 1/40-mm AA
Electron Equipt: Radar: 1/TRS-N—Sonar: DSQS-11A
M: 2 MD 871 UM/1D diesels; 2 CP props; 3,300 hp **Range:** 2,200/16
Man: 44 tot.

REMARKS: Type 320 minesweepers, each converted to control three F-1 "Troika" drone magnetic/acoustic/mechanical minesweepers. Also carry and tow an Oropesa sweep rig and stow numerous channel-marking ("Dan") buoys.

◆ **18 Type HL 351 "Troika" drones** Bldr: MAK, Kiel

	In serv.		In serv.		In serv.
SEEHUND 1	1-8-80	SEEHUND 7	17-9-81	SEEHUND 13	1-9-82
SEEHUND 2	1-8-80	SEEHUND 8	17-9-81	SEEHUND 14	1-9-82
SEEHUND 3	1-8-80	SEEHUND 9	17-9-81	SEEHUND 15	1-9-82
SEEHUND 4	17-7-81	SEEHUND 10	11-11-81	SEEHUND 16	13-5-82
SEEHUND 5	17-7-81	SEEHUND 11	11-11-81	SEEHUND 17	13-5-82
SEEHUND 6	17-7-81	SEEHUND 12	11-11-81	SEEHUND 18	13-5-82

Seehund 5 G. Gyssels, 8-84

D: 91 tons (96.5 fl) **S:** 9.4 kts **Dim:** 24.92 × 4.46 × 1.8 **A:** None
M: 1 MWM TRHS 518A diesel; Schöttel prop; 445 hp **Electric:** 208 kw
Range: 520/8.8 **Man:** 3 tot.

REMARKS: Ordered 1977, to operate three-apiece with the Type-351 control ships. Essentially remote-controlled, self-propelled magnetic minesweeping solenoids with all machinery highly shock-protected. Also able to carry two Type SDG-21 Oropesa mechanical minesweeping gear. Dates given are completions; were originally commissioned in groups of three on same date as Type 351 control ships were recommissioned (see above).

◆ **3 HFG F-1 "Troika" trials craft** Bldr: Ottenser Eisenwerke, Hamburg

SEEKUH 1 (L: . . .) SEEKUH 2 (L: 24-3-66) SEEKUH 3 (L: 24-3-66)

"Seekuh" trials craft 1977

D: 104 tons (181 fl) **S:** . . . kts **Dim:** 27.0 × 3.53 × 2.30 hull/3.01 max.
A: None
M: 2 MWM 8-cyl. diesels, electric drive; 1 Schöttel prop/rudder; 700 hp
Electric: 176 kw **Man:** 3 tot.

REMARKS: Prototypes for "Troika" concept involved in an extraordinarily protracted trial period. *Seekuh 1* (ex-Y 1677) is 23.8 m o.a., 90 tons, 290 hp. Earlier concept trials craft *Walross* (Y 1676) now stricken. All worked with small minesweeper *Niobe.*

◆ **12 Type 331 A* and 331 B minehunters** Bldr: Burmester, Bremen

	L	In serv.		L	In serv.
M 1070 GÖTTINGEN	1-4-57	31-5-58	M 1078 CUXHAVEN	11-3-58	11-3-59
M 1071 KOBLENZ	6-5-57	8-7-58	M 1080 MARBURG	4-8-58	11-6-59
M 1072 LINDAU	16-2-57	24-4-58	M 1084 FLENSBURG*	7-4-59	3-12-59
M 1074 TÜBINGEN	12-8-57	25-9-58	M 1085 MINDEN	9-6-59	22-1-60
M 1075 WETZLAR	24-6-57	20-8-58	M 1086 FULDA*	19-8-59	5-3-60
M 1077 WEILHEIM	4-2-59	28-1-59	M 1087 VÖLKLINGEN	20-10-59	21-5-60

Flensburg (M 1084)—Type 331A, with Kelvin-Hughes radar—note auxiliary propulsors raised at stern G. Gyssels, 7-84

Weilheim (M 1077)—Type 331B, with TRS-N radar G. Gyssels, 1-85

D: 388 tons (402 fl) **S:** 17 kts **Dim:** 47.45 × 8.5 × 3.68 (sonar down)
A: 1/40-mm AA
Electron Equipt: Radar: 1/TRS-N or Kelvin-Hughes 14/9
Sonar: DSQS-11 (Type 331A: Plessey 193M Mk 20G)
M: 2 Maybach diesels; 2 CP props; 3,340 hp **Electric:** 220 kw
Range: 1,400/16; 3,950/9 **Man:** 46 tot.

REMARKS: All are conversions from the Type 320, *Lindau*-class, wooden-hulled minesweepers. The Type 331As were converted 1968-72, the Type 331Bs in 1975-79. None

MINE WARFARE SHIPS *(continued)*

have mechanical sweep gear. Minehunting speed is 6 kts, on two 50-kw electric motors. Six divers and 2 French PAP-104 remote-controlled minehunting devices are carried.

◆ **21 Type 340 and Type 341 patrol minesweepers** Bldr: Abeking & Rasmussen, Lemwerde (except: Schürenstedt, Bardenfleth: M 1064, 1065, 1092, 1094; Schlichting, Travemünde: M 1067, 1090, 1095)

	L	In serv.		L	In serv.
Type 340			M 1064 Deneb	11-9-61	7-12-61
M 1051 Castor	12-7-62	11-12-62	M 1065 Jupiter	15-2-61	30-5-61
M 1054 Pollux	15-9-60	28-4-61	M 1067 Atair	20-4-61	27-9-61
M 1055 Sirius	15-3-61	5-10-61	M 1069 Wega	10-10-62	8-4-63
M 1056 Rigel	2-4-62	19-9-62	M 1090 Perseus	22-9-60	16-3-61
M 1057 Regulus	18-12-61	20-6-62	M 1092 Pluto	9-8-60	19-12-60
M 1058 Mars	1-12-60	18-7-61	M 1093 Neptun	9-6-60	29-9-60
M 1059 Spica	25-5-60	10-5-61	M 1094 Widder	12-3-59	26-9-60
M 1060 Skorpion	21-5-63	9-10-63	M 1095 Herkules	25-8-60	9-12-60
Type 341			M 1096 Fische	14-7-59	12-1-60
M 1062 Schütze	20-5-58	14-4-59	M 1097 Gemma	6-10-59	5-7-60
M 1063 Waage	9-4-59	19-3-62			

Skorpion (M 1060)—Type 340 G. Gyssels, 8-83

Perseus (M 1090)—Type 341 G. Gyssels, 9-84

D: 241 tons (280 fl) **S:** 24.6 kts **Dim:** 47.44 × 7.2 (6.96 wl) × 2.4
A: 1/40-mm AA (*see* Remarks) **Electron Equipt:** Radar: 1/TRS-N
M: Maybach or Mercedes-Benz diesels; 2 Escher-Wyss cycloidal props; 4,000/4,200 hp
Electric: 120 kw plus 340-kw sweep generator **Fuel:** 22 tons
Range: 640/22; 1,000/18 **Man:** 39 tot.

Remarks: Multi-purpose ships that can be employed as minesweepers, coastal patrol craft (2/40-mm AA), and minelayers (2 mine rails), the minesweeping gear to be removed in the latter two instances. Have appeared only in the minesweeper configuration for many years. *Stier* (former M 1061), used as a submarine-rescue ship, has been given a new hull number and disarmed; decompression chamber in new stern deckhouse. Eight with Mercedes-Benz diesels are Type 340; the remainder, with Maybach diesels, are Type 341. Sisters *Capella* (ex-M 1098), *Krebs* (ex-M 1052), *Orion* (ex-M 1053), *Steinback* (ex-M 1091), and *Uranus* (ex-M 1099) have been operated by the *Deutscher Marinebund* youth organization since the mid-1970s; *Algol* (ex-M 1068) is used by the naval damage control school, and *Mira* (ex-M 1050), formerly used by the Naval Technical School, was sold for scrap in 1984.

◆ **10 Type 394 inshore minesweepers** Bldr: Krögerwerft, Rendsburg

	L	In serv.		L	In serv.
M 2658 Frauenlob	26-2-65	27-9-66	M 2663 Minerva	25-8-66	16-6-67
M 2659 Nautilus	19-5-65	26-10-66	M 2664 Diana	13-12-66	21-9-67
M 2660 Gerion	19-6-65	17-2-67	M 2665 Loreley	14-3-67	29-3-68
M 2661 Medusa	25-1-66	17-2-67	M 2666 Atlantis	20-6-67	29-3-68
M 2662 Undine	16-5-66	20-3-67	M 2667 Acheron	11-10-67	10-2-68

D: 238 tons (246 fl) **S:** 14.3 kts **Dim:** 38.01 × 8.03 × 2.1
A: 1/40-mm AA
Electron Equipt: Radar: 1/TRS-N
M: 2 Mercedes-Benz MB 820 Db diesels; 2 props; 2,000 hp
Electric: 554 kw **Fuel:** 30 tons **Range:** 648/14; 1,770/7
Man: 4 officers, 20 men

Remarks: Wooden construction. Differ from Type 393 in having a 260-kw diesel sweep current generator. Formerly had "Y,"- and earlier "W,"-series pendants.

Undine (M 2662) M. Louagie, 6-84

◆ **8 Type 393 inshore minesweepers** Bldr: Krögerwerft, Rendsburg

	L	In serv.		L	In serv.
M 2650 Ariadne	23-4-60	23-10-61	M 2654 Nymphe	20-9-62	8-5-63
M 2651 Freya	25-6-60	6-1-62	M 2655 Nixe	3-12-62	20-6-63
M 2652 Vineta	17-9-60	9-4-62	M 2656 Amazone	27-2-63	4-9-63
M 2653 Herta	18-2-61	7-6-62	M 2657 Gazelle	14-8-63	9-12-63

Nixe (M 2655) L. & L. Van Ginderen, 5-83

D: 199-205 tons light (252 fl) **S:** 14.3 kts **Dim:** 38.01 × 8.03 × 1.99
A: 1/40-mm AA **Electron Equipt:** Radar: 1/TRS-N
M: 2 Mercedes-Benz MB 820 Db diesels; 2 props; 2,000 hp **Electric:** 554 kw
Fuel: 30 tons **Range:** 830/12 **Man:** 4 officers, 20 men

Remarks: Similar to Type 394, but have a 260-kw gas turbine sweep current generator.

AMPHIBIOUS WARFARE CRAFT

◆ **22 Type 520 utility landing craft** Bldr: Howaldtswerke, Hamburg, 1965-66 (launch dates in parentheses)

L 760 Flunder (6-1-66)
L 761 Karpfen (5-1-66)
L 762 Lachs (17-2-66)
L 763 Plötze (16-2-66)
L 764 Rochen (18-3-66)
L 765 Schlei (17-5-66)
L 766 Stör (18-5-66)
L 767 Tümmler (14-6-66)
L 768 Wels (15-6-66)
L 769 Zander (13-7-66)
L 788 Butt (28-3-65)
L 789 Brasse (28-3-65)
L 790 Barbe (26-11-65)
L 791 Delphin (25-11-65)
L 792 Dorsch (17-3-66)
L 793 Felchen (19-4-66)
L 794 Forelle (20-4-66)
L 795 Inger (14-7-66)
L 796 Makrele (22-8-66)
L 797 Müräne (23-8-66)
L 798 Renke (22-9-66)
L 799 Salm (23-9-66)

Barbe (L 790) L. & L. Van Ginderen, 6-85

AMPHIBIOUS WARFARE CRAFT *(continued)*

D: 166 tons (403 fl) **S:** 11 kts **Dim:** 40.04 (36.7 pp) × 8.8 × 1.6 (2.1 max.)
A: 2/20-mm Rheinmetall Rh 202 AA (II × 1) **Range:** 1,200/11
Electron Equipt: Radar: 1/Kelvin-Hughes 14/9
M: 2 MWM 12-cyl. diesels; 2 props; 1,200 hp **Electric:** 130 kVA
Man: 17 tot.

REMARKS: Design based on the American LCU 1646 class. *Renke* (L 798) and *Salm* (L 799) in reserve; *Inger* (L 795) used for reserve training. Cargo: 237 tons max.; 141.6 normal.

◆ **21 Type 521 landing craft** Bldr: Rheinwerft, Walsum (LCM 1, 2: Blohm + Voss, Hamburg) (In serv. 1964-67)

LCM 1–16; LCM 18–20; LCM 27; LCM 28

LCM 16 L. & L. Van Ginderen, 10-83

D: 116 tons (168 fl) **S:** 10.6 kts **Dim:** 23.56 × 6.40 × 1.46
M: 2 MWM 8-cyl. diesels; 2 props; 684 hp **Range:** 690/10; 1,430/7 **Man:** 7 tot.

REMARKS: Design based on U.S. LCM (8). LCM 1 to LCM 8 are in reserve. LCM 11–20 have a 20-kw diesel generator and a 2-ton cargo boom; they can be used to carry up to 18 torpedoes. Cargo: 60 tons or 50 troops. During 1981, six were reclassified as auxiliaries; LCM 21 as A 1423, and LCM 22–26 as A 1430-A 1434.

AUXILIARY SHIPS

HYDROGRAPHIC SURVEY SHIP

◆ **1 Type 750** Bldr: J. R. Köser Norderwerft, Hamburg

	Laid down	L	In serv.
A 1452 PLANET (ex-Y 843)	30-4-64	23-9-65	15-4-67

Planet—pendant A 1452 not painted on G. Koop, 1977

D: 1,513 tons (1,917 fl) **S:** 13.9 kts **Dim:** 80.43 (74.0 pp) × 12.60 × 3.97
M: 4 MWM 12-cyl., 850-hp diesels, electric drive; 1 prop; 1,390 hp
Electric: 650 kw **Range:** 9,300/13.4 **Man:** 39 crew plus 13 scientists

REMARKS: Operated for the Ministry of Communications by a civilian crew. Hangar for one helicopter. Capable of conducting geophysical, meteorological, biological, chemistry, and hydrographic research. Denny-Brown stabilizers, 125-hp Pleuger active rudder and bow-thruster fitted. Main engines provide 560 kw of the electrical power. Painted white, with buff stack and mast.

SUPPORT TENDERS

◆ **10 Rhein-class Types 401, 402, and 403**

(a) Type 401, for missile boats

	Bldr	L	In serv.
A 58 RHEIN	Schlieker, Hamburg	10-12-59	6-11-61
A 61 ELBE	Schlieker, Hamburg	5-5-60	17-4-62
A 63 MAIN	Lindenauwerft, Kiel	23-7-60	29-6-63
A 66 NECKAR	Lürssen, Vegesack	26-6-61	7-12-63
A 68 WERRA	Lindenauwerft, Kiel	26-3-63	2-9-64
A 69 DONAU	Schlichting, Travemünde	26-11-60	23-5-64

(b) Type 402, for mine-countermeasures ships

A 65 SAAR	Norderwerft, Hamburg	11-3-61	11-5-63
A 67 MOSEL	Schlieker, Hamburg	15-12-60	8-6-63

(c) Type 403, for submarines

A 55 LAHN	Flenderwerke, Lübeck	21-11-61	24-3-64
A 56 LECH	Flenderwerke, Lübeck	4-5-62	8-12-64

Elbe (A 61)—Type 401 small combatant tender L. & L. Van Ginderen, 4-85

Lahn (A 55)—Type 403 submarine tender S. Terzibaschitsch, 6-84

Saar (A 65)—Type 402 minecraft tender L. & L. Van Ginderen, 6-85

D: (a): 2,370 tons (3,000 fl); (b): 2,330 tons (3,000 fl); (c) 2,400 tons (2,956 fl)
S: 20 kts (trials, 22) **Dim:** 98.2 × 11.83 × 5.20
A: 2/100-mm AA (I × 2) (not in A 55, A 56)—4/40-mm AA (I × 4, except II × 2 in A 55 and A 56)—mines
Electron Equipt: Radar: 1/Kelvin-Hughes 14/9, 1/SGR-105, 1/SGR-103, 2/Mk 45 fire control; A 55 and A 56: 14/9 and SGR-103 only
M: 6 Maybach diesels (Mercedes-Benz 839Db in A 54-56, 65, 67); 2 props; 11,400 hp
Electric: 2,250 kw **Fuel:** 334 tons **Range:** 2,500/16
Man: 98 tot. (space for 40 officers, 40 petty officers, 130 nonrated men)

REMARKS: Slight variations in length: Type 402 are 98.5 m o.a., Type 403 are 98.6 m o.a. Type 401 have one crane to port, Type 402 have two side by side farther aft. A 54, A 55, A 56, A 65, A 67 have electric drive; the others have diesel-reduction drive, CP props. Tenders carry 200 tons of fuel oil, 40 reserve torpedoes; A 55, A 56, and A 58 have an additional 200 tons of stores; A 66, A 68, and A 69 can be used as training ships. *Weser* (A 62) and *Ruhr* (A 64) transferred to the Greek and Turkish navies in 1975 and 1976, respectively. *Isar* (A 54), long in reserve, was transferred to Turkey 30-9-82 and delivered under tow. Two of the combatant-tender version are to be re-equipped to support the new Type-143A missile boats as Type-401D tenders. Type 401 and 402 have two M4 radar GFCS. The Type 401 and 402 units are scheduled to receive the RAM point-defense missile system.

UNDERWAY REPLENISHMENT SHIPS

NOTE: These ships are grouped together here because, despite their dissimilar functions, they are variations on the same basic design.

◆ 8 Type 701A, Type 701C, and 701E supply ships

	Bldr	Laid down	L	In serv.
(a) Type 701A				
A 1411 LÜNEBURG	Flensburger SY	8-7-64	3-5-65	31-1-66
A 1416 NIENBURG	Flensburger SY	16-11-65	28-7-66	1-8-68
A 1417 OFFENBURG	Blohm + Voss, Hamburg	1966	10-9-66	27-5-68
(b) Type 701C				
A 1412 COBURG	Flensburger SY	9-4-65	15-12-65	9-7-68
A 1414 GLÜCKSBURG	Flensburger SY	18-8-65	3-5-66	9-7-68
A 1415 SAARBURG	Blohm + Voss, Hamburg	1-3-66	15-7-66	30-7-58
A 1418 MEERSBURG	Flensburger SY	5-8-65	22-3-66	25-6-68
(c) Type 701E				
A 1413 FREIBURG	Blohm + Voss, Hamburg	1965	15-4-66	27-5-68

Lüneburg (A 1411)—Type 701A P. Voss, 10-84

Meersburg (A 1418)—Type 701C L. & L. Van Ginderen, 6-83

Freiburg (A 1413)—Type 701E—note helo deck P. Voss, 9-84

D: Type 701A: 1,896 tons light (3,483 fl); Type 701C: 3,709 tons (fl); Type 701E: 3,900 tons (fl) **S:** 17 kts
Dim: 104.15 (98.00 pp) × 13.2 × 4.2 (Type 701C: 114.9 overall; Type 701E: 118.3 overall)
A: 4/40-mm AA (II × 2) in preservation (fwd. mount active in A 1415)
M: 2 Maybach MD 872 diesels; 2 CP props; 5,600 hp **Electric:** 1,935 kw
Range: 3,000/17; 3,200/14 **Man:** 82 tot.

REMARKS: Originally configured to carry more than 1,100 tons of cargo, including 640 tons fuel, 205 tons ammunition, 100 tons spare parts (10,000 separate items), and 131 tons fresh water, plus 267m³ refrigerated stores. A 1415 lengthened 11.5 meters in 1974-75 to carry spare Exocet missiles and other supplies for the new Type-143 and Type-148 classes; stowage for spare parts increased to 30,000 items, with inventory management by the Nixdorf computer system. A 1412, A 1414, A 1418 also converted to Type 702C standard, 1975-77. A 1413, converted 1981-84 to support Type-122 frigates, is equipped with helicopter facilities to permit vertical replenishment, 9 spare Harpoon missiles and repair facilities for Mk 88 Lynx helicopters. A 1412 has a bow-thruster. All are equipped with fin stabilizers, one 3-ton and two 2-ton cranes.

◆ 2 Type 760 ammunition ships

Bldr: Orenstein & Koppel, Lübeck

	Laid down	L	In serv.
A 1435 WESTERWALD	3-11-65	25-2-66	11-2-67
A 1436 ODENWALD	3-11-65	5-5-66	23-3-67

Odenwald (A 1436) L. & L. Van Ginderen, 10-82

D: 3,460 tons (4,014 fl) **S:** 17 kts **Dim:** 105.3 × 14.0 × 4.6
A: 4/40-mm AA (II × 2) in preservation
M: 2 Maybach MD 872 diesels; 2 CP props; 5,600 hp **Electric:** 1,285 kw
Range: 3,500/17 **Man:** 60 tot. (A 1436: 45 tot.)

REMARKS: Similar to Type 701, but carry only ammunition. A 1436 had the forward 40-mm AA mount removed 1981. Cargo: 1,080 tons.

◆ 2 Type 762 mine-supply ships

Bldr: Blohm + Voss, Hamburg

	Laid down	L	In serv.
A 1437 SACHSENWALD	1-8-66	10-12-66	20-8-69
A 1438 STEIGERWALD	9-5-66	10-3-67	20-8-69

Steigerwald (A 1438) M. Louagie, 6-84

D: 2,962 tons (3,380 fl) **S:** 17 kts **Dim:** 110.7 × 13.9 × 3.79
A: 4/40-mm AA (II × 2)—mines
M: 2 Maybach MD 872 diesels; 2 CP props; 5,600 hp **Electric:** 1,300 kw
Range: 3,500/17 **Man:** 65 tot.

REMARKS: The designation "supply ships" is something of a euphemism, since these ships have four mine ports at the stern and are actually minelayers, capable of carrying 668 to 1,048 mines, depending on type. Construction of a torpedo-transport version was canceled.

REPAIR SHIPS

◆ 2 Type 726, former U.S. Aristaeus class

	Bldr	L	In serv.
A 512 ODIN (ex-*Ulysses,* ARB 9)	Bethlehem, Hingham	2-12-44	27-12-44
A 513 WOTAN (ex-*Diomedes,* ARB 11)	Chicago Bridge & Iron	11-11-44	23-1-45

Wotan (A 513) P. Voss, 9-83

D: 3,435 tons (3,455 fl) **S:** 11 kts **Dim:** 101.0 × 15.28 × 2.80
M: 2 G.M. 12-278A (A 513: 12-567A) diesels; 2 props; 1,800 hp
Fuel: 438 tons **Range:** 13,200/11 **Man:** 143 tot. (civilian personnel)

REMARKS: Modified former LST 967 and LST 1119, respectively, transferred in 6-61. A 10-ton traveling crane moves on rails between the bridge and the forward sheer. Have accommodations for 187.

REPLENISHMENT OILERS

◆ **2 Type 704 former merchant tankers**

	Bldr	L	In serv.
A 1443 RHÖN (ex-*Okene*)	Kröger, Rendsburg	23-8-74	5-9-77
A 1442 SPESSART (ex-*Okapi*)	Kröger, Rendsburg	13-2-75	23-9-77

Spessart (A 1442) L. & L. Van Ginderen, 3-85

D: 14,260 tons (fl); 6,209 grt/10,950 dwt **S:** 16 kts **Dim:** 130.2 × 19.3 × 8.20
M: 1 MAK 12-cyl. diesel; CP prop; 8,000 hp **Electric:** 2,000 kw **Man:** 42 tot.

REMARKS: 6,200 grt. Converted while building. Purchased from Bulk Acid Carriers, Monrovia, in 1976. Fitted with one underway-replenishment station per side. Cargo: 9,500 m³ distillate fuel, 1,650 m³ fuel oil, 400 m³ water. Replenishment facilities are to be upgraded.

◆ **4 Type 703** Bldr: Lindenauwerft, Kiel

	Laid down	L	In serv.
A 1424 WALCHENSEE	12-10-64	10-7-65	29-6-66
A 1425 AMMERSEE	28-3-66	9-7-66	2-3-67
A 1426 TEGERNSEE	21-4-66	22-10-66	23-3-67
A 1427 WESTENSEE	28-10-66	8-4-67	6-10-67

Tegernsee (A 1426) P. Voss, 8-84

D: 2,174 tons (fl) **S:** 12.5 kts **Dim:** 71.9 × 11.2 × 4.28
M: 2 MWM 12-cyl. diesels; 1 CP prop; 1,200 hp **Electric:** 635 kw
Cargo capacity: 1,130 m³ **Range:** 3,250/12 **Man:** 21 tot.

◆ **1 Type 763 former merchant tanker** Bldr: Lindenauwerft, Kiel

	Laid down	L	In serv.
A 1407 WITTENSEE (ex-*Sioux*)	15-2-58	23-9-58	5-12-58

Wittensee (A 1407) 1975

D: 1,237 tons (1,854 fl) **S:** 12 kts **Dim:** 67.45 × 9.84 × 4.25
M: 1 MAK 6-cyl. diesel; 1,250 hp **Electric:** 216 kw **Cargo:** 1,238 tons
Range: 6,240/12 **Man:** 21 tot. (civilian crew) **Cargo capacity:** 1,250 m³

REMARKS: Purchased 26-3-59. Sister *Bodensee* transferred to Turkey 8-77. 998 grt.

◆ **1 Type 766 former merchant tanker** Bldr: Norderwerft, Hamburg

	Laid down	L	In serv.
A 1429 EIFEL (ex-*Friedrich Jung*)	5-11-57	2-4-58	26-7-58

D: 6,720 tons (fl) **S:** 13 kts **Dim:** 101.76 × 14.43 × 7.1
M: 2 M.A.N. 8-cyl. diesels; 1 prop; 3,360 hp **Electric:** 760 kVA
Cargo: 6,500 m³ **Range:** 7,300/12 **Man:** 40 tot.

REMARKS: 3,444 grt. Purchased and commissioned 27-5-63. Equipped for underway replenishment. One fueling station per side, plus over-the-stern capability.

Eifel (A 1429) P. Voss, 9-82

◆ **1 Type 766 former merchant tanker** Bldr: Norderwerft, Hamburg

	Laid down	L	In serv.
A 1428 HARZ (ex-*Claere Jung*)	31-3-53	2-9-53	26-11-53

Harz (A 1428) L. & L. Van Ginderen, 5-83

D: 5,380 tons (fl) **S:** 12 kts **Dim:** 92.40 × 13.60 × 6.70
M: 2 OEW 8-cyl. diesels; 1 prop; 2,520 hp **Electric:** 380 kVA
Cargo: 5,000 m³ **Range:** 7,200/11 **Man:** 28 tot.

REMARKS: 2,800 grt. Purchased and commissioned 27-5-63. Equipped for underway replenishment, one station per side.

INTELLIGENCE COLLECTORS

◆ **2 Type-442B converted trawlers** Bldr: Unterweser, Bremerhaven

	L	In serv.	Conv.
A 50 ALSTER (ex-*Mellum*)	21-11-60	21-3-61	19-10-71
A 53 OKER (ex-*Hoheweg*)	29-8-60	19-10-60	11-2-72

Alster (A 50) L. & L. Van Ginderen, 8-82

D: 1,187 tons (1,497 fl) **S:** 15 kts **Dim:** 72.83 (68.35 pp) × 10.50 × 5.60
M: 1 Klöckner-Humboldt-Deutz 8-cyl., 1,800-hp diesel, electric drive; 1 KHD 8-cyl. auxiliary propulsion diesel, 400-hp electric drive; 1 prop

REMARKS: Two Type-423 replacements planned, with a third ship to be built in the 1990s; will be of about 300 tons, with a crew of 40.

◆ **1 Type-740 converted inshore minesweeper** Bldr: Abeking & Rasmussen, Lemwerde

	Laid down	L	In serv.
Y 836 HOLNIS	15-8-64	20-5-65	31-3-66

D: 150 tons (180 fl) **S:** 16.5 kts **Dim:** 36.87 × 7.40 × 1.80
M: 2 Mercedes-Benz MB 820Db diesels; 2 props; 2,000 hp
Electric: 380 kw **Fuel:** 13 tons **Man:** 27 tot.

INTELLIGENCE COLLECTORS *(continued)*

Holnis (Y 836) L. & L. Van Ginderen, 1980

REMARKS: Wooden construction, prototype of a class of 20 Type-390 inshore minesweepers, the other 19 of which were canceled. Altered circa 1968 as an intelligence collector.

◆ **1 Type-422A converted tug** Bldr: Akers Mek., Oslo

	L	In serv.
A 52 OSTE (ex-USN *Puddefjord,* ex-Ger. *Puddefjord*)	21-10-42	1943

Oste (A 52) G. Koop, 1978

D: 690 tons (940 fl) **S:** 11 kts **Dim:** 49.39 (45.00 pp) × 9.10 × 5.70
M: 2/5-cyl. Akers diesels; 1 prop; 1,600 hp **Electric:** 360 kw **Man:** 45 tot.

REMARKS: Served U.S. Navy 1946-57. Commissioned in German Navy 21-1-57 as a tender (Type 419). Converted for use as an intelligence collector circa 1968.

SEAGOING TUGS

◆ **3 Baltrum (Type 722) class** Bldr: Schichau, Bremerhaven

	Laid down	L	In serv.
A 1451 WANGEROOGE	1-10-65	4-7-66	9-4-68
A 1452 SPIEKEROOGE	20-11-65	26-9-66	14-8-68
A 1455 NORDERNEY	29-5-67	28-2-68	15-10-70

Spiekerooge (A 1452) S. Terzibaschitsch, 6-84

D: 854 tons (1,039 fl) **S:** 13.6 kts **Dim:** 51.78 × 12.11 × 4.2
A: 1/40-mm AA (preserved)
M: 4 MWM 16-cyl. diesels, electric drive; 2 props; 2,400 hp
Electric: 540 kw **Range:** 5,000/10 **Man:** 31 tot.

REMARKS: A 1451 is used at Cuxhaven in survival training for aircrew. Also employed as salvage tugs and port icebreakers. Sister *Baltrum* has been used as a diving-training tender since 1974; *Juist* and *Langeoog* were reconfigured for training duties during 1977-78; see page 171.

◆ **2 Helgoland (Type 720)-class salvage tugs** Bldr: Schichau, Bremerhaven

	Laid down	L	In serv.
A 1457 HELGOLAND	24-7-64	9-4-65	8-3-66
A 1458 FEHMARN	23-4-65	25-11-65	1-2-67

Helgoland (A 1457) L. & L. Van Ginderen, 10-82

D: 1,304 tons (1,558 fl) **S:** 16.6 kts **Dim:** 67.9 × 12.74 × 4.20
A: 2/40-mm AA (II × 1)—in preservation
M: 4 MWM 12-cyl. diesels, electric drive; 2 props; 3,300 hp
Electric: 1,065 kw **Range:** 6,400/16 **Man:** 34 tot.

REMARKS: *Fehmarn* serves as a tender to the submarine training establishment. Equipped to serve as mine planters, if required.

◆ **2 Eisvogel (Type 721)-class icebreaking tugs** Bldr: Hitzler, Lauenburg

	Laid down	L	In serv.
A 1401 EISVOGEL	10-3-59	28-4-60	11-3-61
A 1402 EISBÄR	12-5-59	9-6-60	1-11-61

Eisbär (A 1402) P. Voss, 2-84

D: 496 tons (641 fl) **S:** 13 kts **Dim:** 37.8 × 9.7 × 4.2
Electron Equipt: Radar: 1/Kelvin-Hughes 14/9
M: 2 Maybach 12-cyl. diesels; 2 CP props; 2,400 hp **Electric:** 180 kw
Range: 2,000/12 **Man:** 16 tot.

REMARKS: Provision for 1/40-mm AA aft.

EXPERIMENTAL SHIP

◆ **1 Type-421 former corvette** Bldr: Atlaswerke, Bremen

	Laid down	L	In serv.
A 1449 HANS BÜRKNER	12-10-60	6-6-61	18-5-63

D: 983 tons (1,348 fl) **S:** 24 kts **Dim:** 80.6 × 9.42 × 3.50
A: 1/375-mm Bofors 4-barreled ASW RL (*see* Remarks)
M: 4 M.A.N. 16-cyl. diesels; 2 CP props; 13,600 hp **Electric:** 520 kVA
Range: 2,180/15 **Man:** 50 tot.

REMARKS: Employed as an ASW trials ship. Has recently carried a small variable-depth sonar. Position for two 40-mm AA (II × 1) retained, and has previously carried two 533-mm ASW torpedo tubes. Fitted with mine rails.

EXPERIMENTAL SHIP *(continued)*

Hans Bürkner (A 1449) S. Terzibaschitsch, 6-83

TRAINING SHIPS

◆ **1 Type-440 cruiser type**

	Bldr	Laid down	L	In serv.
A 59 DEUTSCHLAND	Nobiskrug, Rendsburg	17-9-59	5-11-60	25-5-63

Deutschland (A 59) G. Koop, 9-84

D: 4,880 tons (5,684 fl) **S:** 22 kts (18 cruising) **Range:** 6,000/17
Dim: 138.2 (130.0 pp) × 16.0 × 5.0 **Man:** 33 officers, 521 men (250 cadets)
A: 4/100-mm AA (I × 4)—8/40-mm AA (II × 2, 1 × 4)—4/533-mm ASW TT—2/375-mm Bofors ASW RL (IV × 2)
Electron Equipt: Radar: 1/LW-08, 1/SGR-114, 1/SGR-105, 1/SGR-103, 4/M 45 f.c.—Sonar: 1/ELAC 1BV (med. freq.)
M: 4/2,000-hp Maybach diesels; 1 set Wahodag 8,000-hp GT; 3 props (2 CP); 16,000 hp
Boilers: 2 Wahodag, 450°C **Electric:** 1,500 kw **Fuel:** 640 tons

REMARKS: Quarters for 7 instructors and 250 cadets. Can be used as a minelayer. Two Mercedes-Benz diesels replaced by Maybach engines in 1979.

◆ **1 Type-441 sail-training ship** Bldr: Blohm + Voss, Hamburg

	Laid down	L	In serv.
A 60 GORCH FOCK	24-2-58	23-8-58	17-12-58

Gorch Fock—pendant number, A 60, not painted on L. & L. Van Ginderen, 5-83

D: 1,819 tons (2,005 fl) **S:** 10 kts (15 kts under sail)
Dim: 89.32 (81.44 hull, 70.20 pp) × 12.02 × 5.25
M: 1 M.A.N. 6-cyl. diesel; 1 prop; 890 hp **Electric:** 266 kw
Range: 1,100/10 **Man:** 74 tot. plus 200 cadets

REMARKS: 1,904 m² sail area. Carries 350 tons permanent ballast. Has made 296 nautical miles progress in one day.

YARD AND SERVICE CRAFT
HARBOR TUGS

◆ **3 Heppens (Type 724)-class tugs** Bldr: Schichau, Bremerhaven

	Laid down	L	In serv.
Y 1680 NEUENDE	29-12-70	2-6-71	27-10-71
Y 1681 HEPPENS	19-3-71	15-9-71	17-12-71
Y 1682 ELLERBEK	29-12-70	2-6-71	26-11-71

Ellerbek (Y 1682) L. & L. Van Ginderen, 5-82

D: 232 tons (319 fl) **S:** 12 kts **Dim:** 26.6 × 7.4 × 2.6
M: 1 MWM 8-cyl. diesel; 800 hp **Electric:** 120 kw **Man:** 6 tot.

◆ **4 Sylt (Type 724)-class tugs** Bldr: Schichau, Bremerhaven

	L	In serv.		L	In serv.
Y 820 SYLT	29-4-61	5-7-62	Y 822 AMRUM	6-10-61	25-1-63
Y 821 FÖHR	13-5-61	11-10-62	Y 823 NEUWERK	12-10-61	5-4-63

Neuwerk (Y 823) S. Terzibaschitsch, 1980

D: 266 tons (282 fl) **S:** 12 kts **Dim:** 30.2 × 7.9 × 4.0
M: 1 MAK 8-cyl. diesel; 1,000 hp **Range:** 1,775/12 **Man:** 10 tot.

◆ **8 Lütje Hörn (Type 723) class**

	L		L
Y 812 LUTJE HÖRN	9-5-58	Y 816 VOGELSAND	12-1-59
Y 813 MELLUM	23-10-58	Y 817 NORDSTRAND	17-4-58
Y 814 KNECHTSAND	3-12-58	Y 818 TRISCHEN	27-2-59
Y 815 SCHARNHORN	9-5-58	Y 819 LANGENESS	7-4-59

D: 52.2 tons (57.5 fl) **S:** 10 kts **Dim:** 15.2 × 5.06 × 2.2
M: 2 Deutz 8-cyl. diesels; 2 Voith-Schneider cycloidal props; 340 hp
Range: 550/9 **Man:** 4 tot.

◆ **3 miscellaneous tugs**

Y 886: 41 tons; 24.11 × 4.3 × 1.5; 1/MWM diesel; 320 hp
Y 883, Y 884: 43 tons; 22.1 × 3.8 × 1.5; 1 Deutz diesel; 250 hp

YARD AND SERVICE CRAFT HARBOR TUGS *(continued)*

Vogelsand (Y 816)—Lütje Hörn class L. & L. Van Ginderen, 5-83

WATER TANKERS

◆ **4 FW 1 (Type 705) class**

	Bldr	Laid down	L	In serv.
Y 864 FW 1	Schichau, Bremerhaven	5-4-63	22-7-63	30-11-63
Y 867 FW 4	Jadewerft, Wilhelmshaven	14-6-63	14-3-64	28-7-64
Y 868 FW 5	Ranke, Hamburg	26-7-63	26-11-63	21-2-64
Y 869 FW 6	Ranke, Hamburg	4-11-63	25-2-64	19-6-64

FW 5 (Y 868) L. & L. Van Ginderen, 1984

D: 598 tons (647 fl) **S:** 9.5 kts **Dim:** 44.03 (41.1 pp) × 7.80 × 2.63
M: 1 MWM 12-cyl. diesel; 230 hp **Electric:** 130 kVA **Fuel:** 15 tons
Range: 2,150/9 **Man:** 12 tot.

REMARKS: Cargo: 343 tons. Sister FW 2 to Turkey in 1975, FW 3 to Greece in 1976. FW 6 is in reserve.

TORPEDO-RECOVERY BOATS

◆ **9 TF 1 (Type 430) class** Bldr: Burmester, Bremen and Schweers, Bardenfleth

	L		L		L
Y 851 TF 1	13-10-65	Y 854 TF 4	21-10-65	Y 872 TF 106	10-6-66
Y 852 TF 2	22-9-65	Y 855 TF 5	28-2-66	Y 873 TF 107	13-9-65
Y 853 TF 3	13-10-65	Y 856 TF 5	4-5-66	Y 874 TF 108	22-9-65

TF 2 (Y 952) L. & L. Van Ginderen, 5-84

D: 56 tons (63.5 fl) **S:** 17 kts **Dim:** 25.22 × 5.40 × 1.60
M: 1 MWM 12-cyl. diesel; 1 prop; 1,000 hp **Man:** 6 tot.

◆ **1 TF 104 (Type 438) class** Bldr: Kröger, Warnemünde

Y 886 TF 104 (ex-*Süderoog*) (In serv. 1-10-59)

D: 41 tons **S:** . . . kts **Dim:** 24.05 × 4.60 × 1.50
M: 1 MWM 8-cyl. diesel; 320 hp

◆ **2 miscellaneous torpedo-recovery craft:** Y 883, Y 884

AIR-SEA RESCUE CRAFT

◆ **5 KW 15 (Type 369) class**

	Bldr	L
Y 827 KW 15 (ex-BG 1, ex-KW 15, ex-H 15, ex-U.S.N. 57)	Schweers, Bardenfleth	6-10-52
Y 830 KW 16 (ex-BG 2, ex-KW 16, ex-H 16, ex-U.S.N. 54)	Lürssen, Vegesack	1952
Y 832 KW 18 (ex-H 18, ex)U.S.N. 55)	Abeking & Rasmussen	17-11-51
Y 845 KW 17 (ex-BG 3, ex-KW 17, ex-H 17, ex-U.S.N. 58)	Schürenstedt	27-3-53
Y 846 KW 20 (ex-BG 4, ex-KW 20, ex-H 20, ex-U.S.N. 56)	Lürssen, Vegesack	1953

KW 18 (Y 832) L. & L. Van Ginderen, 10-84

D: 59.5 tons (69.6 fl) **S:** 25.0 **Dim:** 28.90 × 4.70 × 1.42
Electron Equipt: Radar: 1/Kelvin-Hughes 14/9
M: 2 MTU 12-cyl. diesels; 2 props; 2,000 hp **Electric:** 10 kw **Man:** 17 tot.

REMARKS: Built as patrol boats for U.S. Navy, taken over 30-11-56. Served in Border Guard 1963-1969/70.

SUBMARINE RESCUE CRAFT

◆ **1 converted *Schütze*-class former patrol minesweeper**

	Bldr	L	In serv.
Y 849 STIER (ex-M 1092)	Abeking & Rasmussen	30-10-58	28-6-61

Stier (Y 849) L. & L. Van Ginderen, 10-79

REMARKS: Data as for Type 341 class. Retains 40-mm AA. Converted 1969. Deckhouse with decompression chamber added on fantail; also carries two rubber Gemini dinghies.

EXPERIMENTAL AND TRIALS CRAFT

◆ **1 Type 742 magnetic research ship**

	Bldr	L	In serv.
Y 841 WALTHER VON LEDEBUR	Burmester, Bremen	30-6-66	21-12-67

D: 775 tons (825 fl) **S:** 19 kts **Dim:** 63.2 × 10.6 × 3.0
M: 2 Maybach 16-cyl. diesels; 2 props; 5,200 hp **Electric:** 1,620 kw
Man: 19 crew plus technicians

EXPERIMENTAL AND TRIALS CRAFT *(continued)*

Walther Von Ledebur (Y 841) P. Voss, 6-82

REMARKS: One of the largest wooden ships built in modern times. Used in mine-warfare research and can be employed as a minesweeper. Two 600-kw sweep current generators.

◆ **2 Type 741 net tenders** Bldr: Schürenstedt K. G., Bardenfleth

	Laid down	L	In serv.
Y 837 SP 1	7-9-65	21-6-66	29-6-67
Y 838 WILHELM PULLWER (ex-SP 2)	4-10-65	16-8-66	22-12-67

Wilhelm Pullwer (Y 838) L. & L. Van Ginderen, 5-82

D: 132 tons (160 fl) **S:** 12.5 kts **Dim:** 31.54 × 7.5 × 2.2
M: 2 Mercedes-Benz 8-cyl. diesels; 2 Voith-Schneider cycloidal props; 792 hp
Electric: 120 kw **Man:** 17 crew plus trials personnel

REMARKS: Used in experimental trials. Wooden hulls.

◆ **1 Type 740 torpedo-trials ship** Bldr: AG Weser, Bremerhaven

	Laid down	L	In serv.
Y 871 HEINZ ROGGENKAMP (ex-*Greif*)	23-8-52	8-11-52	30-12-52

Heinz Roggenkamp (Y 871) L. & L. Van Ginderen, 2-75

D: 935 tons (996 fl) **S:** 12 kts **Dim:** 57.19 (51.5 pp) × 9.04 × 3.10
A: 2/533-mm torpedo tubes (1 ASW, on deck; 1 underwater)—3/324-mm Mk 32 ASW TT (III × 1) **Electric:** 192 kw **Man:** 19 crew plus trials personnel
M: 1 Klöckner-Humboldt-Deutz 8-cyl. diesel; 1 prop; 1,145 hp (800 sust.)

REMARKS: Former trawler purchased 1963; commissioned after reconstruction 25-9-64. Civilian crew.

◆ **1 weapons-trials barge** Bldr: Howaldtswerke, Kiel (In serv. 26-6-64)

Y 844 BARBARA

Barbara (Y 844)—with legs retracted L. & L. Van Ginderen, 7-79

D: 3,500 tons (fl) **Dim:** 62.1 × 24.2 × 3.0 **Electric:** 1,650 kVA

REMARKS: Non-self-propelled. Eight extending legs to anchor ship to bottom. Used to test guns. Civilian crew. Helicopter deck, 12-ton crane. Named for the patron saint of artillerists.

◆ **1 former fishing cutter** Bldr: Lürssen, Vegesack (L: 6-47)

Y 882 OTTO MEYCKE (ex-*Meteor II*)

D: 50 tons **S:** 9 kts **Dim:** 17.45 (14.95 pp) × 5.0 × 1.9
M: 1 Modag SRB55 diesel; 1 prop; 150 hp **Man:** 6 tot.

REMARKS: Wooden craft, purchased 1960; commissioned 5-8-60. Primarily a diving tender. Civilian crew. Pendant number not painted on.

◆ **1 trials tender** Bldr: Nyslands, Oslo

	Laid down	L	In serv.
Y 888 FRIEDRICH VOGE (ex-*Kurefjord*)	5-12-41	16-3-43	1-7-43

Friedrich Voge (Y 888) L. & L. Van Ginderen, 1981

D: 260 tons (298 fl) **S:** 12 kts **Dim:** 33.2 × 6.7 × 3.3
M: 1 M.A.N. 8-cyl. diesel; 550 hp **Electric:** 120 kw
Man: 14 tot. plus trials personnel

REMARKS: Acquired 1959; commissioned 20-12-59.

◆ **2 ex-U.S. YMS-class minesweepers**

	Bldr	Laid down	L	In serv.
Y 881 ADOLF BESTELMEYER (ex-BYMS 2213, ex-YMS 213)	Robt. Jacob, City Isl., N.Y.	13-6-42	13-11-42	17-6-43
Y 889 RUDOLF DIESEL (ex-BYMS 2279, ex-YMS 279)	H. C. Grebe, Chicago, Ill.	23-1-43	29-7-43	15-10-43

D: Y 881: 290 tons (360 fl); Y 889: 280 tons (310 fl) **S:** 15 kts
Dim: 42.13 (39.62 pp) × 7.47 × 2.55
M: 2 G.M. 8-268A diesels; 2 props; 1,000 hp **Electric:** 290 kw **Range:** 2,500/9
Man: 16 crew plus trials personnel

REMARKS: Operated in British Navy during World War II. Acquired 1957/1960. Wooden hulls. Both employed in mine weapons trials and have two mine rails. Sister OT 2 has been stricken.

EXPERIMENTAL AND TRIALS CRAFT *(continued)*

Adolf Bestelmeyer (Y 881) L. & L. Van Ginderen, 6-81

◆ **1 ex-U.S. YMS-class minesweeper** Bldr: Weaver Bros., Orange, Texas

	Laid down	L	In serv.
Y 877 Hans Christian Oersted (ex-*Vinstra,* ex-NYMS 247, ex-YMS 247)	27-5-42	14-10-42	13-5-43

H. C. Oersted (Y 877) P. Voss, 6-83

D: 260 tons (302 fl) **S:** 16 kts **Dim:** 41.53 (39.62 pp) × 7.52 × 2.40
M: 2 Maybach diesels, electric drive; 2 props; 1,800 hp
Electric: 120 kw (plus 680 kw from main engines)
Man: 16 crew plus trials personnel

Remarks: Operated in Norwegian Navy from completion to 1959; acquired 1960 and reconstructed and re-engined, recommissioning 12-7-62. Initially used as a degaussing tender, but since 1974 used in research.

DIVING TENDERS

◆ **3 Baltrum (Type 754)-class converted seagoing tugs** Bldr: Schichau, Bremerhaven

	Laid down	L	In serv.
Y 1661 Baltrum (ex-A 1454)	29-6-66	2-6-67	8-10-68
Y 1664 Juist (ex-A 1456)	23-9-67	15-8-68	1-10-71
Y 1665 Langeoog (ex-A 1453)	12-7-66	2-5-67	14-8-68

Baltrum (Y 1661) S. Terzibaschitsch, 1980

Remarks: Data as for seagoing tug sisters; can be armed with 1/40-mm AA. Y 1661 converted 1974, others in 1978. Used to train mine-clearance divers.

◆ **1 Type-732 small diving tender** Bldr: Burmester, Bremen

Y 1678 TB 1 (In serv. 21-6-72)

D: 70 tons **S:** 14 kts **Dim:** 27.75 × 5.77 × 1.90
M: 1 MWM 12-cyl. diesel; 950 hp **Electric:** 36 kw

Remarks: Also used for research.

◆ **1 Type-392 former inshore minesweeper** Bldr: Kröger, Rendsburg

	Laid down	L	In serv.
Y 806 Hansa (ex-W 22, ex-M 2662)	7-8-57	18-11-57	23-7-58

Hansa (Y 806) L. & L. Van Ginderen, 5-83

D: 155 tons (175 fl) **S:** 14 kts **Dim:** 35.18 × 6.84 × 1.95
M: 1 Mercedes-Benz MB 820Db diesel; 1 prop; 1,000 hp **Electric:** 180 kw
Range: 1,500/12 **Man:** 20 tot.

Remarks: Wooden hull. Converted 1968-69 as a training tender for mine-clearance divers.

MISCELLANEOUS SERVICE CRAFT

◆ **7 cargo lighters, former Type 521 landing craft** Bldr: Rheinwerft, Walsam (In serv. 1966-67)

A 1409 (ex-LCM 17)
A 1423 (ex-LCM 21)
A 1430 (ex-LCM 22)
A 1431 (ex-LCM 23)
A 1432 (ex-LCM 24)
A 1433 (ex-LCM 25)
A 1434 (ex-LCM 26)

A 1430 L. & L. Van Ginderen, 10-81

Remarks: For data, see under Type 521 landing craft. Redesignated as auxiliaries 1981.

◆ **1 Type 743 support tender** Bldr: Fritz Staack, Lübeck (In serv. 1980)

Y 1679 AM 7

AM 7 (Y 1679) P. Voss, 10-84

D: . . . **S:** . . . **Dim:** 16.3 × 4.1 × . . .
M: 1 MWM diesel; 1 prop; 180 hp

Remarks: Glass-reinforced plastic construction. Typical of the AM-series workboats: AM 1 (Y 1671), AM 3 (Y 1685), AM 4 (Y 1673), AM 5 (Y 1674), AM 6 (Y 1674), AM 8 (Y 1675), AM 9 (Y . . .), AM 11 (. . .), AM 12 (. . .). There are also 6 AK-series workboats in use.

MISCELLANEOUS SERVICE CRAFT *(continued)*

◆ **1 pollution control ship** Bldr: C. Lühring, Brake

	Laid down	L	In serv.	To Navy
Y . . . . Bottsand	14-11-83	22-9-84	26-10-84	24-1-85

Bottsand P. Voss, 10-84

D: Approx. 1,100 tons (fl) **S:** 10 kt **Dim:** 46.30 × 12.00 × 3.10
A: None **Electron Equipt:** Radar: 1 navigational
M: 2 diesels, 2 rudder-props; 1,600 hp — 2 omnidirectional bow-thrusters; 400 hp
Man: 3 officers, 3 men

Remarks: 500 grt/650 dwt. Twin hulls, hinged near the stern to open scissors-fashion to 65-deg., leaving a 42-m wide Vee opening to collect oil spills at the rate of approx. 140 m^3/hr, at a speed of 1 knot. When folded can also be used as a coastal tanker and bunkerage craft. Concept known as THOR (Twin Hull Oil Recovery), which is also the name of a smaller civil-operated prototype completed in 1983. Built for the Niedersachsen Ministry for the Environment, but turned over to the *Bundesmarine* on loan, 24-1-85. Six cargo/spill tanks totalling 790 m^3. No pendant number assigned.

◆ **2 Type-710 tank-cleaning craft** Bldr: Deutsche Werft, Hamburg

	Laid down	L	In serv.
Y 1641 Förde	12-1-67	10-3-67	14-12-67
Y 1642 Jade	18-5-67	19-7-67	6-11-67

Förde (Y 1641) L. & L. Van Ginderen, 1983

D: 1,830 tons (fl) **S:** 8 kts **Dim:** 58.46 × 10.40 × 4.1 (light)
M: 1 MWM 16-cyl. diesel; 1 prop; 390 hp **Range:** 750/8 **Man:** 16 tot.

Remarks: For steam-cleaning fuel tanks and for sludge removal. Civilian crews.

◆ **2 Type-711 self-propelled floating cranes** Bldr: Rheinwerft, Walsum

Y 875 Hiev (In serv. 2-10-62) Y 876 Griep (In serv. 15-5-63)

D: 1,830 tons (1,875 fl) **S:** 6 kts **Dim:** 52.9 × 22.0 × 2.1
M: 3 MWM 600-hp diesels, electric drive; 3 vertical cycloidal props; 1,425 hp
Electric: 358 kVA **Man:** 12 tot.

Remarks: Electric-crane capacity: 100 tons. Civilian crews.

Hiev (Y 875) L. & L. Van Ginderen, 1980

◆ **3 Type-718 battery-charging craft** Bldrs: Jadewerft, Wilhelmshaven (LP 2: Oelkers, Hamburg)

LP 1 (In serv. 18-2-64) LP 2 (In serv. 17-4-64) LP 3 (In serv. 16-9-74)

LP 2 G. Koop

D: 192 tons (234 fl) **S:** 8 kts **Dim:** 27.6 × 7.0 × 1.6
M: 1 MTU diesel; 250 hp **Electric:** 960 kw (LP 3: 1,110 kw) **Man:** 6 tot.

Remarks: Each has two 405-kw generators and one (LP 3: two) 150-kw generator for charging submarine batteries. LP 3 is 7.5 m in beam, 1.8 m draft, 267 tons (fl).

TRAINING CRAFT

Note: Also included in this category are the three *Baltrum*-class former seagoing tugs and the diving tender *Hansa* listed under diving tenders.

◆ **3 Type 945/740 training cutters** Bldr: ST 1, 2: Schipper & Goern, Lauenburg;

Y 1669 ST 1 (In serv. 1-10-75) Y 1670 ST 2 (In serv. 1-10-75)
Y 1671 AM 1 (In serv. 1-8-76)

ST 2 (Y 1670) L. & L. Van Ginderen, 10-79

TRAINING CRAFT *(continued)*

D: 18.5 tons (fl) **S:** 18.5 kts **Dim:** 15.50 (14.40 wl) × 3.14 × 1.37
Electron Equipt: Radar: 1/Kelvin-Hughes 14/9
M: 2 Klöckner-Humboldt-Deutz 6-cyl. diesels; 2 Schöttel props; 500 hp

REMARKS: Used for reservist navigational/maneuvering training. Sister AK 5(Y 1673) is used for radar trials.

◆ **1 Type-368 ketch, former patrol fishing cutter** (In serv. 1942-44?)

Y 834 NORDWIND (ex-W 43)

Nordwind (Y 834) S. Terzibaschitsch, 6-84

D: 100 tons (110 fl) **S:** 11 kts
Dim: 27.00 (24.00 hull, 21.48 pp) × 6.39 × 2.94
Electron Equipt: Radar: 1/Kelvin-Hughes 14/9
M: 1 Demag 5-cyl. diesel; 1 prop; 137 hp **Range:** 1,200/7 **Man:** 10 tot.

REMARKS: Taken over by U.S. Navy 1945; acquired 1-7-56 by German Navy. Wooden hull; 195 m² sail area. Operated for the Mürwik Naval School.

NOTE: There are also 70 smaller sail-training craft, all bearing names. Included are 26 Type-914 class, 5 m long, 10 Type-913 class, 7.64 m long, 25 Type-910 (most 10.46 m o.a.), 6 Type 911, and 1 Type 912.

ACCOMMODATIONS BARGE (Type 130)

◆ **Y 811 Knurrhahn** (ex-U.S.N. *Barge 2*) (In serv. 1916)

Knurrhahn (Y 811)—outboard *Arcona* S. Terzibaschitsch, 1980

D: 1,250 tons **Dim:** 58.94 × 11.00 × 2.60
Electric: 220 kw

REMARKS: Used by U.S. Navy 1945-55. In German naval service 16-10-55. Accommodations for 300. Also in use for accommodations are the small barges *Siebethsburg, Unke,* and *Vesta.*

NOTE: There are also a number of small personnel launches, generator craft, workboats, and freight barges in service. Some of these have Y-series pendants, while most have alphanumeric pendants denoting their functions.

FLOATING DRY DOCKS

◆ **2 Type 712** Bldr: Krupp, Rheinhausen

HEBEWERK 2 (In serv. 15-3-61) HEBEWERK A (In serv. 13-1-61)

D: 1,000 tons **Dim:** 66.01 × 21.10 × . . .

REMARKS: Serviced by 4 Type-713 "Hebeponton": 500 tons, 56 m by 14.8 m.

◆ **1 Type-714 self-propelled** Bldr: Flenderwerft, Lübeck (In serv. circa 1945)

Y 879 SCHWIMMDOCK B

D: 4,500 tons **S:** . . . **Dim:** 156.00 × 25.00 × 3.50
M: 4 MWM 16-cyl. diesels, electric drive; 2 Schottel props; 500 hp

REMARKS: In German naval service 26-10-63 at Kiel. The propellers are at the starboard forward and port aft corners.

◆ **1 Type 715** Bldr: Howaldtswerke, Hamburg (In serv. 1961)

Y 842 SCHWIMMDOCK 3

D: 8,000 tons **Dim:** 164.0 × 30.0 × 3.5

REMARKS: Seven pontoon sections.

◆ **1 Type 715** Bldr: Flenderwerke, Lübeck (In serv. 8-9-67)

DRUCKDOCK *("Dock C")*

D: . . . tons **Dim:** 93.0 × 26.5 × 3.6

The compression floating dry dock used at Kiel for testing submarine pressure-hull integrity. An entire Type 205 or 206 submarine can fit inside. In the background can be seen floating dry dock *Schwimmdock B* (Y 879).

NOTE: Type 715 small floating dry dock *Hebewerk 1* was sold 30-6-84.

COAST GUARD

NOTE: A separate paramilitary force of 1,000 men *(Bundesgrenzschutz-See).*

PATROL BOATS

◆ **8 Neustadt class** Bldrs: Lürssen, Vegesack, except B-13: Schlichting, Travemünde

	Laid down	L	In serv.
BG 11 NEUSTADT	25-11-68	27-2-69	25-11-69
BG 12 BAD BRAMSTEDT	10-1-69	2-4-69	1969
BG 13 UELZEN	17-5-69	25-7-69	24-2-70
BG 14 DUDERSTADT	21-2-69	3-6-69	1970
BG 15 ESCHWEGE	27-3-69	16-9-69	19-3-70
BG 16 ALSFELD	31-5-69	11-11-69	1970
BG 17 BAYREUTH	15-9-69	9-1-70	1970
BG 18 ROSENHEIM	8-11-69	12-3-70	11-70

Eschwege (BG 15) P. Voss, 10-84

PATROL BOATS *(continued)*

D: 191 tons (218 fl) **S:** 30 kts **Dim:** 38.50 (36.00 pp) × 7.00 × 2.15
A: 2/40-mm AA (I × 2) **Electron Equipt:** Radar: 1/Kelvin-Hughes 14/9
M: 2 Maybach 16-cyl. diesels; 2 props; 7,200 hp **Fuel:** 15 tons
Electric: 195 kVA **Range:** 450/27 **Man:** 23 tot.

Remarks: Have an additional centerline propeller for cruising, powered by a 685-hp MWM diesel. Two additional units canceled. Hulls painted blue, superstructure white.

◆ **1 tug** Bldr: Mützelbeldt-Werft, Cuxhaven (L: 29-1-76)

BG 5 Rettin

D: 99.9 grt **S:** 9 kts **Dim:** 22.5 (20.0 pp) × 6.6 × 2.9
M: 2 MWM diesels; 1 prop; 590 hp

FISHERIES PROTECTION SHIPS

Note: Operated by the Ministry of Agriculture and Fisheries. Have black hulls with "Fischereischutz" (Fisheries Protection) on sides of most, grey superstructures, buff-colored masts, and orange boats.

◆ **7 patrol ships**

Seefalke Bldr: Orenstein & Koppel (In serv. 4-8-81)

Seefalke—note folding edge to helo deck P. Voss, 24-8-82

D: 2,386 tons (fl) **S:** 20 kts **Dim:** 83.10 (76.20 pp) × 12.80 × 4.70
M: 2 MWM TBD 510 L8 diesels; 2 CP props; 8,000 hp **Man:** 29 tot.

Remarks: 1,980 grt. Equipped to operate in East Greenland Sea; fin stabilizers, elaborate navigation equipment, helicopter platform, bow-thruster.

Meerkatze Bldr: Lürssen, Vegesack (In serv. 1976)

Meerkatze P. Voss, 3-84

D: 2,386 tons **S:** 15 kts **Dim:** 76.5 × 11.8 × 5.5
M: 3 MWM diesels, electric drive; 2 props; 2,300 hp **Man:** 30 tot.

Solea Bldr: Sieghold, Bremerhaven (In serv. 1974)

D: 337 grt **S:** 12 kts **Dim:** 33.5 × 9.0 × 3.6 **M:** 1 Deutz diesel; 640 hp
Man: 11 tot.

Walther Herwig Bldr: Schlichting, Travemünde (In serv. 1972)

D: 2,500 tons **S:** 15.5 kts **Dim:** 77.0 × 14.9 × 5.2
M: 2 M.A.N. diesels; 2 props; 3,380 hp **Man:** 35 tot.

Frithjof Bldr: Schlichting, Travemünde (In serv. 1967)

D: 2,140 tons **S:** 15 kts **Dim:** 76.0 × 11.8 × 5.2
M: 3 Maybach diesels, electric drive; 2 props; 2,650 hp **Man:** 35 tot.

Anton Dohrn (ex-*Walther Herwig*) Bldr: Seebeck, Bremerhaven (In serv. 1963)

D: 1,986 grt **S:** 15 kts **Dim:** 83.0 × 12.5 × 5.2
M: Maybach diesels; 2,210 hp **Man:** 38 tot.

Solea L. & L. Van Ginderen, 10-75

Walther Herwig P. Voss, 9-83

Frithjof P. Voss, 1-85

Anton Dohrn P. Voss, 12-82

FISHERIES PROTECTION SHIPS *(continued)*

POSEIDON Bldr: Mützelfeldt, Cuxhaven (In serv. 1957)

Poseidon L. & L. Van Ginderen, 5-81

D: 934 grt **S:** 12 kts **Dim:** 58.8 × 10.2 × . . .
M: 1 Verschure diesel; 800 hp **Man:** 20 tot.

GOVERNMENT CIVIL RESEARCH SHIPS

NOTE: Operated by the German Hydrographic Institute, which is subordinate to the Ministry of Transport.

◆ **1 polar research ship and transport**

	Bldr	Laid down	L	In serv.
POLARSTERN	Howaldtswerke, Kiel	22-9-81	8-1-82	8-12-82

Polarstern P. Voss, 12-82

D: 15,000 tons (fl) **S:** 15.5 kts **Dim:** 117.55 (102.20 pp) × 25.00 × 10.50
M: 4 Deutz diesels, electric drive; 2 Kort-nozzle CP props; 21,120 hp
Electric: 5,400 kVA × 2,580 kw
Man: 36 crew, 40 scientists, 30 relief staff

REMARKS: 3,900 dwt. Built for the Alfred Wegener Institute for Polar Research, Bremerhaven. Capable of carrying 1,500 tons of liquid cargo, plus stores to support Germany's Antarctic research station; 100 tons of provisions are carried in refrigerated vans on the forecastle. Helicopter deck and hangar. Can break 2-m ice; shell plating 43.5-mm at waterline. Has bow and stern side-thrusters. INDAS V system ("Integrated Navigation system with Data Acquisition and automatic ship's Steering").

◆ **8 (+1) oceanographic and hydrographic survey ships**

METEOR II Bldr: Schlichting Werft, Travemünde (In serv. 1986)

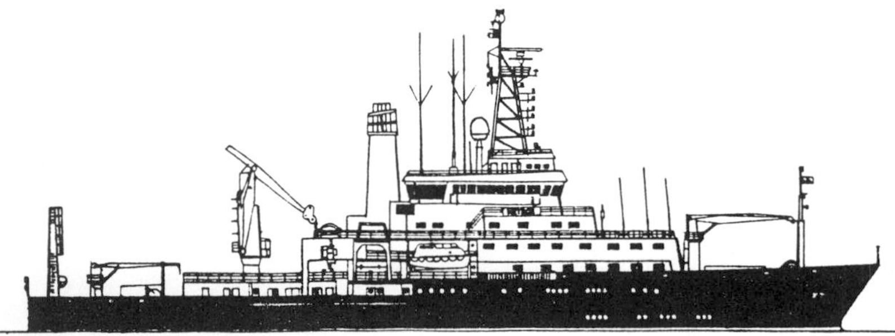

Meteor II

D: Approx. 3,500 tons (fl) **S:** 14 kts **Dim:** . . . × . . . × . . .
M: Diesel-electric; 1 prop, 4,760 hp **Range:** 10,000/. . .

REMARKS: Intended to replace *Meteor.* Has asymetrical stern form and "Grim Wheel," free-wheeling prop abaft regular propeller to improve performance by roughly 10 percent.

GAUSS Bldr: Schlichtingwerft, Travemünde (In serv. 1980)

Gauss P. Voss, 7-84

D: 1,372 tons (1,813 fl) **S:** 13.5 kts **Dim:** 68.7 (61.0 pp) × 13.0 × 4.25
Electron Equipt: Radar: 1 Raytheon 1660/12SR, 1 Raytheon RM1650/9 × R
M: 3 MAK 331 AK 800-hp diesels, electric drive; 1 prop; 1,647 hp
Electric: 220 kVA **Range:** 4,000/13.5 **Man:** 19 crew plus 12 scientists

REMARKS: Has special free-wheeling prop aft of propulsion propeller. Equipped with Becker flap-rudder, Denny-Brown fin stabilizers, and a 725-hp drop-down bow-thruster. Ships service power from main engine generators.

POSEIDON Bldr: Schichau, Unterweser (In serv. 1976)

D: 1,050 grt **S:** 15 kts **Dim:** 58.0 × 11.4 × . . . **M:** MWM diesels; 1,800 hp

VICTOR HENSEN Bldr: Schichau, Bremerhaven (L: 1975)

Victor Hensen L. & L. Van Ginderen, 8-75

D: 423 grt **S:** 12 kts **Dim:** 37.04 (33.99 pp) × 9.50 × 3.07
M: 2 MTU 6-cyl. diesels; 1 prop; . . . hp **Man:** 28 tot.

SENCKENBERG Bldr:. . . (In serv. 1976)

REMARKS: 165 grt. No other data available.

KOMET Bldr: Jadewerft, Wilhelmshaven (In serv. 1969)

Komet—note six survey launches P. Voss, 11-83

GERMANY — FEDERAL REPUBLIC OF GERMANY *(continued)*
GOVERNMENT CIVIL RESEARCH SHIPS *(continued)*

D: 1,253 grt **S:** 15 kts **Dim:** 68.0 × 11.5 × 4.0
M: 2 Maybach diesels; 1 prop; 2,650 hp **Man:** 42 tot.

METEOR Bldr: Seebeckwerft AG Weser, Bremerhaven (In serv. 1963)

Meteor L. & L. Van Ginderen, 7-81

D: 2,800 tons **S:** 14 kts **Dim:** 82.1 (77.3 pp) × 13.5 × 5.2
M: Diesel-electric; 3,765 hp **Man:** 52 crew + 24 scientists

REMARKS: To be stricken on completion of *Meteor II.* 2,615 grt.

ATAIR WEGA Bldr: Schlichting, Travemünde (In serv. 1962)

Atair Wega P. Voss, 8-83

D: 157 grt **S:** 10.5 kts **Dim:** 31.7 × 6.5 × 2.3 **M:** 1 Deutz diesel; 205 hp
Man: 13 tot.

VALDIVIA (ex-Viking Bank) Bldr: A. G. Weser, Bremerhaven (In serv. 1961)

D: 1,317 grt **S:** 13 kts **Dim:** 73.46 (63.99 pp) × 11.03 × 5.23
M: 1 M.A.N. 6L 52/74 diesel; 1 prop; 2,160 hp
Man: 24 crew plus 16 scientists

REMARKS: Purchased 1981 and converted at A. G. Weser, completing 5-82 as a submersible tender. Former stern-haul trawler. Also in government service are the research ships *Uthorn* (200 tons, 12 kts, in serv. 8-9-82) and *Bulse* (1982).

GHANA

Republic of Ghana

PERSONNEL (1984): 750 total

MERCHANT MARINE (1984): 124 ships — 186,123 grt

CORVETTES

◆ **2 Vosper Mk 1 class**

	Bldr	L	In serv.
F 17 KROMANTSE	Vosper Ltd, Portsmouth, U.K.	5-9-63	9-64
F 18 KETA	Vickers Ltd, Newcastle, U.K.	18-1-65	8-65

D: 435 tons (500 fl) **S:** 18 kts **Dim:** 53.95 (49.38 pp) × 8.7 × 3.05
A: 1/102-mm — 1/40-mm AA — 1/Squid ASW mortar (III × 1)
Electron Equipt: Radar: 1/Type 978 nav., 1/Plessey AWS-1
Sonar: 1/Type 164 (med. freq.)

Keta (F 18) G. Arra, 1975

M: 2 Bristol Siddeley-Maybach 16-cyl. diesels; 2 props; 5,720 hp
Electric: 360 kw **Fuel:** 60 tons **Range:** 1,100/18; 2,900/14
Man: 5 officers, 49 men

REMARKS: Fin stabilizers fitted. Quarters are air-conditioned. Both refitted 1974-75 and again in 1983-84.

PATROL BOATS

◆ **2 FBP 57 class** Bldr: Lürssen, Vegesack

	Laid down	L	In serv.
P 28 ACHIMOTA	1978	14-3-79	27-3-81
P 29 YOGAGA	1978	14-3-79	27-3-81

Achimota (P 28) P. Voss, 9-80

D: 380 tons (410 fl) **S:** 30 kts **Dim:** 58.10 × 7.62 × 2.83
A: 1/76-mm OTO Melara DP — 1/40-mm Bofors AA
Electron Equipt: Radar: 1/Decca 1226, 1/Thomson-CSF Canopus A
M: 3 MTU 16V538 TB91 diesels; 3 props; 10,800 hp **Man:** 40 tot.

REMARKS: Has LIOD optronic gun director atop pilothouse. Carry 250 rounds 76-mm, 750 rounds 40-mm. Carry rubber dinghy for air/sea rescue and inspection purposes.

◆ **2 FPB 45 class** Bldr: Lürssen, Vegesack

	Laid down	L	In serv.
P 26 DZATA	16-1-78	19-9-79	4-12-79
P 27 SEBO	1-78	19-9-79	2-5-80

Sebo (P 27) and Dzata (P 26) — prior to arming G. Gyssels, 1979

D: 212 tons (252 fl) **S:** 30 kts **Dim:** 44.90 (42.25 wl) × 7.00 × 2.50 (props)
A: — 2/40-mm Bofors AA (I × 20)
Electron Equipt: Radar: 1/nav.
M: 2 MTU 16V538 TB91 diesels; 2 props; 7,200 hp (6,000 sust.)
Electric: 408 kVA **Range:** 1,100/25; 2,000/15
Man: 5 officers, 30 men

REMARKS: Flare RL on sides of both 40-mm mounts. Planned Thomson-CSF Canopus-A radar not mounted.

◆ **2 Sahene class** Bldr: Ruthoff, Mainz, Germany (In serv. 1976)

P 24 SAHENE P 25 DELA

D: 160 tons (fl) **S:** 30 kts **Dim:** 35.2 × 6.5 × 1.8
A: 1/40-mm AA (with flare launchers attached)
M: 2 MTU 16V538 TB90 diesels; 2 props; 3,000 hp
Range: 1,000/30 **Man:** 32 tot.

GHANA *(continued)*
PATROL BOATS *(continued)*

Dela (P 25) 1976

REMARKS: Ordered 1973; builder went bankrupt, and four others were not delivered. Designed for rescue and fisheries protection. Rescue equipment aft.

◆ **2 British Ford class** Bldr: Yarrow, Scotstoun

P 13 ELMINA (L: 18-10-62) P 14 KOMENDA (L: 17-5-62)

D: 120 tons (160 fl) **S:** 15 kts **Dim:** 35.7 × 6.2 × 2.1
A: 1/40-mm AA—depth charges
M: 2 Paxman YHAXM diesels; 2 props; 1,100 hp **Fuel:** 23 tons
Man: 19 tot.

REMARKS: In poor condition; may no longer be in service.

GREAT BRITAIN

United Kingdom of Great Britain and Northern Ireland

PERSONNEL (1-85):

	Officers	Non-officers	Total
Royal Navy			
Men	8,900	50,500	59,400
Women	400	3,400	3,800
Royal Marines			
Men	600	6,900	7,500
Total	9,900	60,800	70,700

In addition, there were about 22,900 (300 women) Regular Reservists and 5,300 (1,200 women) Royal Naval Volunteer Reserves and 3,300 Royal Marine Reservists (of whom 1,047 are in the Volunteer & Auxiliary). There were also 2,680 members of the Royal Naval Auxiliary Service (RNAS). About 75,000 civilians are employed, including those who man the ships and craft of the Royal Fleet Auxiliary Service and the Royal Maritime Auxiliary Service. During 1985-86, Royal Naval Volunteer Reservists will rise to 7,800 total, Royal Marine Volunteer Reservists to 1,580, and the Royal Naval Auxiliary Service to 3,242 men and women.

MERCHANT MARINE (1984): 2,468 ships—15,874,062 grt (tankers: 351—7,815,777 grt)

WARSHIPS IN SERVICE, UNDER CONSTRUCTION, OR ON ORDER AS OF 1 JANUARY 1986

◆ **3 aircraft carriers**	L	Tons	Main armament
3 INVINCIBLE	1977-81	16,000	1/Sea Dart, 5/Sea Harrier, 9/Sea King
◆ **33 (+6 . . .) submarines**			
		Tons (surfaced)	
4 RESOLUTION (nuclear ballistic missile)	1966-68	7,500	16/Polaris A3, 6/533-mm TT
3 (+5) TRAFALGAR (nuclear attack)	1981-	4,200	5/533-mm TT
6 SWIFTSURE nuclear attack	1971-79	4,200	5/533-mm TT
5 VALIANT (nuclear attack)	1963-70	4,000	6/533-mm TT
0 (1 + . . .) UPHOLDER	. . .	2,160	6/533-mm TT
15 PORPOISE/OBERON	1956-66	2,030	8/533-mm TT
◆ **15 guided-missile destroyers**			
4 MANCHESTER	1980-83	3,450	1/Sea Dart, 1/114-mm DP, 1/Lynx
8 SHEFFIELD	1971-80	3,150	1/Sea Dart, 1/114-mm DP, 1/Lynx
1 BRISTOL	1969	6,100	1/Sea Dart, 1/Limbo, 1/Ikara, 1/114-mm DP
2 COUNTY	1964	5,440	1/Sea Slug, 2/Sea Cat, 2/114-mm DP, 1/Lynx
◆ **38 (+9 + . . .) frigates**			
0 (+2 + . . .) DARING	1987-	3,000	Sea Wolf, 1/114-mm AA, 8 Harpoon, 1 helo
0 (+4) CORNWALL	1984-	4,200	8 Harpoon, Sea Wolf, 1/114-mm AA, 2/Lynx
3 (+3) BOXER	1981-85	4,100	4/Exocet, 2/ Sea Wolf, 2/40-mm AA, 1/Lynx
4 BROADSWORD	1976-80	3,500	4/Exocet, 2/Sea Wolf, 2/40-mm AA, 1/Lynx
6 AMAZON	1971-75	2,750	4/MM 38 Exocet, 1/Sea Cat, 1/114-mm DP, 1/Lynx or Wasp
23 LEANDER	1961-71	2,450-650	1, 2, or 3/Sea Cat, or 1/Sea Wolf, 2/114-mm and/or 40-mm, 1/Wasp, 1/MM 38 Exocet or Ikara in 14, ASW weapons
2 ROTHESAY	1957-60	2,380	2/114-mm DP, 1/Sea Cat, 1/Wasp, 1/Limbo

◆ **43 (+3) patrol ships, boats, and craft**

◆ **40 (+8) mine warfare ships**

◆ **7 (+1) amphibious warfare ships**

WEAPONS AND SYSTEMS

A. MISSILES AND BOMBS

◆ **strategic ballistic missiles**

Trident 2D-5 Bldr: Lockheed

U. S. missile with a delivery vehicle and payload of British design and manufacture, with an independent trajectory capability (MIRV). The agreement for the acquisition of Trident was signed 14-15 July 1980. The submarines to carry Trident will not be ready until the 1990s; 80 Trident missiles are to be acquired.

Polaris A-3TK

The nuclear-powered ballistic-missile submarines of the *Resolution* class employ Polaris A-3 missiles with a payload package of entry vehicles of British design and manufacture. The payload is designated Chevaline and is composed of six 150-kT warheads with greatly improved penetration aids. Chevaline employs post-boost guidance to improve accuracy and entered service late in 1982, the missile thus being typed Polaris A-3TK.

◆ **surface-to-air missiles**
Sea Dart (GWS.30) Bldr: British Aerospace Dynamics Group

Sea Darts and launcher on Liverpool (D 92) L. & L. Van Ginderen, 11-83

Medium-range system (35 miles, interception altitudes from 100 to 60,000 ft)
Length: 4,400 m Diameter: 0.42 m Wingspan: 0.91 m Weight: 550 kg
Propulsion: solid-propellant booster, ramjet sustainer
Guidance: semi-active homing Fire control: Type 909 radar
Fitted on the *Bristol, Sheffield, Manchester,* and *Invincible* classes
Mk 30 Mod. 0 launcher on the *Bristol;* the lighter Mk 30 Mod. 2 on the *Sheffield* and *Invincible* classes. Improvements in low-altitude capability and response time are being made.

MISSILES AND BOMBS *(continued)*

Sea Slug Mk 2 Bldr: British Aerospace Dynamics Group

Short-range system (15 miles slant range, 500 to 50,000 ft)
Length: 5.94 m Wingspan: 1,420 m (1.600 with fins)
Diameter: 0.41 m Weight: 900 kg (2,000 kg with boosters)
Speed: Mach 1.8
Propulsion: solid propulsion system with four solid bosters
Fire control: Type 901, a beam-riding radar
Fitted on the "County"-class DDGs; the Mk 1 version has been retired. Now primarily to be used against surface targets.

Sea Wolf (GWS.25) Bldr: British Aerospace Dynamics Group

Short-range missile system (5,000 m)
Length: 1.9 m Wingspan: 0.45 m
Diameter: 0.3 m Weight: 82 kg
Guidance: radar
Fire control: Marconi Type 910 pulse-doppler radar, which permits control of 2-missile salvos, or by electro-optical tracker
Fitted on *Broadsword*-class frigates; being installed on some *Leander* class
Launcher contains six missiles (total weight with missiles: 3,500 kg)
Target designation is via the combined Type 967-968 radar
A vertical-launch version (GWS.26) is in development, and a new GWS.25 Mod. 3 fire-control system employing the Marconi Type 911 (ex-805SW) search-and-track radar, with DN 181 Blindfire guidance, and upgraded features to the Type 967-968 radar is now being delivered. A simplified 4-missile adaptation, using the Sea Cat quadruple launcher was being developed with government assistance in 1985.

Sea Cat (GWS.20, 22, and 24) Bldr: Short Bros. and Harland

Length: 1.47 m Wingspan: 0.65 m Range: 5,300 m (max.)
Diameter: 0.2 m Weight: 68 kg
Propulsion: 2-stage solid propellant
Guidance: GWS.22 or GWS.24 radar, or GWS.20 optical system
Launcher normally carries 4 missiles, although a 3-missile, lightweight launcher has been exported.

Javelin (GWS . . .) Bldr: Short Bros. and Harland

The Royal Navy began purchase of the hand-held Javelin (successor to Blowpipe) in 6-84 and conducted initial at-sea firings shortly thereafter in HMS *Phoebe.* Guidance is semi-autonomous, line-of-sight. The weapon will be issued to deployed units of all types for terminal defense. The Javelin missile is 1.4-m long, has a range of 4,000 m, and employs a 2-stage rocket motor. A 5-round mount is being developed.

◆ **surface-to-surface missiles**

The Royal Navy has purchased the MM 38 Exocet GWS.50 (*see* section on France). It is employed on the "County" class, the *Amazon, Broadsword,* and some units of the *Leander* class.

Two twin trailer-mounted MM 38 Exocet launchers built by Vosper Thornycroft are maintained at Gibraltar by Royal Navy personnel.

In August 1977, it was announced that the U.S. Sub-Harpoon system would be bought for use from all nuclear attack submarines. 300 have been purchased. Additional Harpoons have been procured for use on RAF Nimrod aircraft. Harpoon 1C, for surface launching, is being purchased for "Duke" and *Cornwall*-class frigates.

◆ **air-to-surface missiles**

AS 12 (*see* section on France) wire-guided is used from Wasp helicopters on frigates.

Sea Skua (CL 834) Bldr: British Aerospace Dynamics Group

Solid propellant
Length: 2.50 m Wingspan: 0.6 m
Diameter: 0.28 m Weight: 75 kg
Speed: Mach 0.8 Range: 15,000 m
Guidance: semi-active Warhead: 20 kg high explosive
Developed for use by Lynx helicopters, which can carry 2 or 4. An export surface ship version is being developed for small combatant use.

Sea Eagle (P3T) Bldr: British Aerospace Dynamics Group

Developed from the Anglo-French, television-guided Martel. Sea Eagle is intended for use as an anti-ship weapon by carrier-based Sea Harrier V/STOL aircraft as well as by land-based Tornado GR-1 and Buccaneer attack aircraft. Using active radar guidance, it employs the French Microturbo/Toulouse TRI-60 engine for propulsion. First aerial launchings took place in the spring of 1981. A Mk 2 version is not to be proceeded with.

◆ **Bombs**

500- and 1,000-lb conventional bombs are carried on *Invincible*-class carriers for use by Sea Harrier fighter bombers; nuclear bombs for these aircraft are also available, it was officially stated in 1985.

◆ **air-to-air missiles**

Sidewinder-1B (AIM-9L) Bldr: Philco-Ford

Infrared-homing, solid-fueled, Mach 2.5 lightweight weapon employed with Harrier V/STOL aircraft aboard *Invincible*-class carriers and *Hermes.*
Range: 12 nautical miles Weight: 84.4 kg Diameter: 0.127 m
Wingspan: 0.61 m Length: 2.90 m

B. GUNS

114-mm Mk 6

Double-barreled, semi-automatic, dual-purpose.
Muzzle velocity: 850 m/sec
Maximum effective range in surface fire: 17,000 m
Maximum effective range in anti-aircraft fire: 6,000 m
Rate of fire: 10-12 rounds/min/barrel
Installed on some *Leander*- and all *Rothesay*-class frigates, and on "County"-class destroyers

114-mm Mk 8

Vickers, 114-mm Mk 8 gun and Exocet launchers aboard Alacrity (F 174)
G. Arra, 1980

Single-barreled, automatic, dual-purpose; has a muzzle brake
Length of barrel: 55 calibers
Maximum effective range in surface fire: 23,000 m
Maximum effective range in anti-aircraft fire: 6,000 m
Rate of fire: 25 rounds/min
Arc of elevation: $-10° + 53°$ Shell weight: 21.0 kg
Light gunmount with glass-reinforced plastic housing
Installed on the *Bristol, Sheffield*-class destroyers, and *Amazon* and *Cornwall*-class frigates

Oto Melara 76-mm Compact

This lightweight weapon is installed in the *Peacock*-class Hong Kong patrol corvettes.

Bofors 40-mm

60-caliber guns are used on single Mk 7 and Mk 9 powered mounts and Mk 3 manual mounts; rate of fire on these obsolete weapons is only about 120 rpm.

Oerlikon 30-mm

Twin GCM-A02 mounts. Eight procured 1982 from BMARC as emergency close-defense weapons for *Sheffield*-class destroyers. Shared among class, used on units deployed to South Atlantic. Optical lead-computing sights.

Oerlikon GCM-A02 30-mm gunmount Navpic

Rarden 30-mm LS-30B

A stabilized Lawrence-Scott single mounting for the BMARC/Oerlikon 30-mm gun. Twenty-five were ordered 9-84 for the "Duke"-class frigates and to begin replacement of old 40-mm mounts. Rate of fire: 650 rpm

Goalkeeper 30-mm SGE-30

General Electric GAU-8A, 30-mm gatling gun in EX-30 mounting co-mounted with H.S.A. radar detect-and-track fire control system. Six mounts ordered 1984 for close-defense in the *Cornwall*-class frigates. See additional details in Netherlands section.

GUNS *(continued)*

Oerlikon 20-mm

Large numbers of single-barrel GAM-B01 mountings procured 1982-83 to augment close defense on a variety of classes. An 85-caliber weapon with 1,000 rpm firing rate and optical, lead-computing sight on mount.

General Dynamics Vulcan/Phalanx 20-mm

Six U.S. Mk 15 Mod.0 CIWS (Close-In Weapon System) mounts purchased 5-82 for use on the *Invincible*-class carriers. Additional mountings have since been ordered for the *Invincible* class. Uses 6-barreled G.E. Vulcan gatling gun.

20-mm

Standard Mk 4 Oerlikon single mounts and a few twin mounts, all of World War II origin, remain in many classes.

7.62-mm machine guns

Standard NATO 7.62-mm light machine guns, having been found very useful in the Falklands War for disrupting low-level air attack, have been added in considerable numbers to frigates and destroyers, using simple pintle mountings.

C. ANTISUBMARINE WEAPONS

Mk 10 Mortar (Limbo)

Triple-barreled mortar based on the Squid of World War II. Range: 700 to 1,000 m. Fitted on some *Leander* and all *Rothesay*-class frigates.

Ikara GWS 41

U.S. Mk 46 torpedo below an Australian-designed guided missile launched by a solid-fuel rocket motor
Maximum range: 18,000 m. See Australia section for further details.
Fitted on the destroyer *Bristol* and six *Leander*-class frigates.

Ikara missile and launcher aboard Galatea (F 18)—the magazine is abaft the launcher G. Arra, 1980

Mk 11 depth charge

Dropped from helicopters against shallow targets. Officially reported that there are also nuclear depth bombs for ASW.

D. TORPEDOES AND MINES

Triple STWS.1 ASW torpedo tubes on a Type 42 destroyer accommodate U.S. Mk 44 and Mk 46 or U.K.-built Stingray torpedoes. Note the swinging bulletproof plate outboard the warhead end of the tubes—another Falklands War lesson learned L. & L. Van Ginderen, 1984

U.S. Mk 44 and Mk 46 Mod. ASW torpedoes on surface ships and helicopters

The principle torpedoes of British origin are:

- the 50-year-old, straight-running Mk 8 for submarines; replaced by Sub-Harpoon in most nuclear attack submarines
- the wire-guided, submarine-launched Mk 23 for ASW, being phased out
- the wire-guided Mk 24 Tigerfish (ex-Ongar) for submarines; entered service 1979 but has not been reliable
- a new lightweight torpedo designated NST 75 11, Stingray, which entered service in 1983 for launch by helicopters and by RAF Nimrod ASW aircraft and for surface ships

Length: 2,597 m **Speed:** 45 kts
Diameter: 324 mm **Range:** 7,000 m
Weight: 266 kg **Depth:** 800 m

Stingray uses seawater-activated batteries powering an electrically driven pump-jet propulsor and employs active/passive acoustic homing.

- The heavyweight Spearfish, in development since 1981 to replace the Mk 24 Tigerfish. It has achieved over 70 kts in trials. Weighing some 2,000 kg, it is 8.5-mm long and uses a Sundstrand turbine engine; range: about 65 km. To enter service in the late 1980s.
- The Stonefish medium-depth, modular mine and Dragonfish shallow-water, anti-invasion mine with an 85 kg charge are being procured to replace earlier mines.

E. SONARS

Type 2031(1) towed passive hydrophone array winch and reel aboard Sirius (F 40) L. & L. Van Ginderen, 3-84

◆ On surface ships

No.	Type	Frequency band	Average range (above layer)
162, 162M	Sidelooking classification	High	. . .
170B	Hull, searchlight	High	2,500 m
174	Hull, searchlight	High	2,500 m
177	Hull, 360° scan	Medium	6,000 m
184	Hull, 360° scan	Medium	7,000 m
185	Underwater telephone	High	. . .
193, 193M	Minehunting	High	. . .
199*	Towed VDS	Medium	7,000 m
2008	Underwater telephone	High	. . .
2016	Hull, 360° scan	Multiple (5.5-6.5-7.5 kHz)	. . .
2031*	Towed passive array	. . .	. . .
2050	Hull, 360° scan	5.5-7.5 kHz	. . .

* 199 is the British version of the Canadian SQS-504. Two versions of the Type 2031 towed passive linear array have been developed: Type 2031(1) for use on four "Exocet *Leander*" frigates, and Type 2031(2) on the "Duke," *Boxer,* and *Cornwall* classes.

◆ On submarines

186	Passive	Low	. . .
187	Active-Passive attack	Low-Medium	. . .
2001	Active-Passive	Low	. . .
2007	Passive	Low-Medium	. . .

2020—a 360-degree coverage, low-frequency passive system for *Trafalger*-class nuclear-powered submarines; to be refitted to older classes
2023—a towed linear passive array, based on the U.S. BQR-15, for SSBNs
2024—a towed, linear passive array for use on nuclear-powered attack submarines
2040—under development for the *Upholder*-class diesel-electric submarine; based on the Thomson-CSF "Argonaute" passive system.
2046—towed array
2051—"Triton"—new Plessey suite on *Oberon*-class diesel submarines; incorporates a "clip-on" towed array and a new, streamlined bowdome.
2054—Plessey-built suite (active/passive/towed passive) for Trident ballistic-missile submarines.

SONARS *(continued)*

◆ **On helicopters**

195, 195 M	Dipping	Medium	3,000 m

F. DATA SYSTEMS

ADA (Action Data Automation):
ADAWS 1 Aerial defense system. Fitted on "County"-class destroyers
ADAWS 2 Integrated AAW and ASW defense system. Fitted on the *Bristol*
ADAWS 4 Integrated AAW and ASW defense system. Fitted on the *Sheffield*- and *Manchester*-class destroyers
ADAWS 5 Aerial and ASW defense. Fitted on the *Invincible*-class aircraft carriers
CAAIS (Computer-Assisted Action Information System)
In *Amazon*- and *Broadsword*-class frigates for tactical data-handling; linked to WSA 4 fire-control system
CACS1 (Computer-Assisted Command System)
To be employed in the *Cornwall*-class frigates. Two Ferranti FM 1600E computers, 12 Argus M700 miniprocessors

NOTE: Only the *Invincible*-class carriers and the destroyer *Bristol* have equipment compatible with the LINK 11/NTDS system of the U.S. Navy or the French Navy's SENIT system and other analogous NATO systems.

G. RADARS

◆ **Navigation**

978—(3 cm, I band)
1002—(9,650 MHz) for *Porpoise*-class submarines
1003—(. . .) in *Resolution*-, *Swiftsure*-, and *Valiant*-class submarines
1006—(9,445 MHz) in newest surface ships and submarines, navalized Kelvin-Hughes 19/9A
1007—Kelvin-Hughes Series 1600 + Red Pac, I-band (3-cm) nav. radar with manual plot, to replace Type 1006

NOTE: Auxiliaries use a number of different commercial navigational radars, primarily of Decca manufacture.

◆ **Combined air and surface search**

967/968—pulse-doppler, paired back-to-back antennas using H, G, and I-bands. Employed with GWS.25 Sea Wolf system in the *Broadsword* class. Type 967M in development, 1984.
992Q (E-F band)—stabilized medium range for low altitude air search, surface search, and target designation. To be replaced by 996/2.
993 (S-band)—short-range air-search/surface-search and target-detection radar in *Leander*- and *Rothesay*-class frigates; uses wedge-shaped "cheese" antenna
994—Plessey AWS-4; uses 993's antenna. Replacing Type 993.
996—Replacement for 992Q in older ships (996/2) and 996/1 version for Type 23 class frigates. Replaces Type 1030 STIR program. Also for target designation. Plessey to manufacture, chosen 9-83; variant of Plessey AWS-5.

◆ **Air-search, early warning**

965—Metric radar, long-range early warning. On some *Leander*-class frigates.
965M—Employs two stacked antennas from the Type 965, with an integral Mk 10 SIF IFF interrogator.
1022—Dutch H.S.A. LW-08 radar with a Marconi antenna, on *Invincible*-class, and *Manchester*- and *Sheffield*-class destroyers. Incorporates Cossor 850 IFF interrogator.

◆ **Height-finding**

277 (E-band)—controlled by ADAWS-1 computer for fire control of Sea Slug system in the "County" class.

◆ **Gun-direction**

903 (I band)—is used in all Mk 6 and Mk 5, 114-mm gun directors (MRS 3).

◆ **Missile-guidance**

901—Sea Slug system (I band)
904—MRS 3 and GWS.22 fire control for the Sea Cat
909—Sea Dart system (also 114-mm Mk 8 gun in the *Sheffield*-class destroyers)
910—Tracking radar used with the Sea Wolf (GWS.25) system
911—Marconi ST805 SW for Sea Wolf GWS.25 Mod. 3 system in *Cornwall* class; uses part of antenna array for the Dour land-based "Blindfire" radar. Also with G.W.S. 26
912—Used for Sea Cat (GWS.24) and 114-mm gun control in *Amazon*-class frigates. British designation for Selenia RTN-10X system.

◆ **For aircraft**

Sea Spray—For Lynx helicopters—surface search and target designation
Blue Fox—For Sea Harrier—a development of Sea Spray. To be replaced by Blue Vixen
Sea Searcher—For Sea King Mk 5 ASW helicopters, for use in interrogating the LAPADS sonobuoy system
Searchwater—For surface search in Nimrod patrol aircraft and air and surface search in Sea King Mk 2 AEW helicopters

H. COUNTERMEASURES

◆ **Chaff rocket launchers**

Knebworth/Corvus—an 8-tubed, 103-mm launcher in use for over a decade. Two per ship; being replaced by shield and Mk 36 Super RBOC.
Mk 36 Super RBOC—a U.S. system initially procured during the Falklands War. Uses 6-tubed, Mk 137 fixed launcher, two or four per ship. Typed "Outfit DLD."
Shield—A replacement for Knebworth/Corvus, ordered 1982. Built by Plessey. Uses 6- or 8-tubed launcher. Has infrared rounds also. Also in use are chaff rounds fired by 114-mm guns and hand-dropped chaff packets for use from helicopters.

U.S. Mk 137 sextuple decoy launcher of the Mk 36 Super RBOC system on HMS Exeter—will also fire NATO Sea Gnat decoy rounds

◆ **Electronic warfare systems**

UA-A1—"Abbeyhill", covers 1-18 GHz. Used on most modern destroyer and frigate classes. Passive intercept.
UA-8/9—older passive intercept system. 1-10 GHz
UA-13—passive array covering 12-18 GHz
RCM-3—gate-stealing jammer by Decca—being added to large surface combatants

I. COMMUNICATIONS

The Royal Navy employs the SCOT Super-High-Frequency (SHF) satellite communications system in carriers, destroyers, and frigates, although since there are not sufficient sets, only units deploying or fully operational carry the twin radomes. The carriers of the *Invincible* class and the destroyer *Bristol* also have the U.S. WSC-3 UHF SATCOMM system, with two OE-82 antennas. Royal Fleet auxiliaries, hydrographic ships, and corvettes of the "Castle" class carry the commercial MARISAT SATCOMM system. Shipboard LF/MF/HF/VHF systems are increasingly integrated and are among the best in the world; single-sideband is extensively employed.

AIRCRAFT CARRIERS

◆ **3 Invincible class**

	Bldr	Laid down	L	In serv.
R 05 INVINCIBLE	Vickers, Barrow	20-7-73	3-5-77	11-7-80
R 06 ILLUSTRIOUS	Swan Hunter, Wallsend	7-10-76	14-12-78	20-6-82
R 07 ARK ROYAL	Swan Hunter, Wallsend	14-12-78	4-6-81	1-11-85

Ark Royal (R 07)—with tug *Bustler* — Maritime Photographic, 9-85

D: 16,256 tons (19,960 fl) **S:** 28 kts
Dim: 206.6 (192.87 wl) × 31.89 (27.5 wl) × 6.4 (mean; 8.8 over sonar dome)
A: 1/Sea Dart GWS.30 Mod.2 system (II × 1; 22 missiles)—2 or 3/20-mm Mk 15 CIWS (I × 2; R 07:3)—2/20-mm AA (I × 2)—Aircraft: 5/Sea Harrier—9/Sea King Mk 2/5

AIRCRAFT CARRIERS *(continued)*

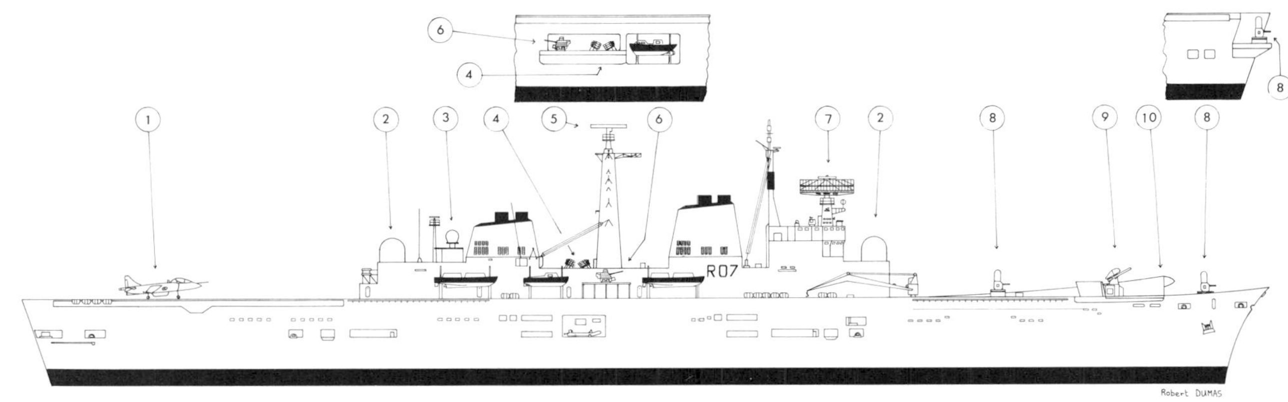

Ark Royal (R 07) 1. Sea Harrier FRS.1 2. Type 909 missile-control radar 3. SCOT SHF SATCOMM antenna 4. Shield decoy RL 5. Type 992R radar 6. Twin 30-mm Oerlikon AA 7. Type 1022 early-warning radar 8. Mk 15 CIWS, 20-mm Vulcan/Phalanx gatling AA gun 9. Sea Dart launcher 10. 12-degree "ski-jump" takeoff ramp

Illustrious (R 06) Royal Navy, 1983

Ark Royal (R 07)—without Mk 15 CIWS L. & L. Van Ginderen, 7-85

Invincible (R 05) L. & L. Van Ginderen, 11-84

Ark Royal (R 07)—on trials, incomplete, in light condition R.N. 1985

Illustrious (R 06)—with *Novorossiysk* in background 829 Squadron, 5-83

Invincible (R 05) and Ark Royal (R 07)—note difference in ski-jump angle, flight-deck length, and forecastle level PO S. Kent, R.N. 1985

Electron Equipt: Radar: 2/1006, 1/992R, 1/1022, 2/909
Sonar: 1/184, 1/762 echo-sounder, 1/185 telephone
Data system: ADAWS-5
EW: passive; 2/Knebworth/Corvus RL; Mk 36 SRBOC RL (VI × 4) (R 07: 4 Shield vice 2 Knebworth/Corvus)

M: 4 Rolls-Royce Olympus TM3B gas turbines; 2 props; 112,000 hp (94,000 sust.)
Electric: 14,000 kw **Range:** 7,000/18
Man: 131 officers, 869 men (plus 318 aircrew)

Remarks: Redesignated "ASW aircraft carriers" in 1980, previously having been, for political reasons, considered to be a type of cruiser. Although all three are to be completed, only two will be operational at any one time. *Invincible,* ordered 17-4-73 and intended for V/STOL aircraft and helicopters only, has a flight deck 183 meters long with a 7-degree "ski jump" at the forward end to assist Sea Harrier aircraft in making rolling takeoffs at full combat load. The ramp on *Ark Royal* is 12 degrees and is 12 meters longer. The 183-meter-long by 13.5-m-wide flight deck is slightly angled to port to clear the Sea Dart launcher, which is awkwardly located on the ship's centerline and has been given an elaborate blast shield to protect the aircraft aboard. The single-level hangar has three separate bays, with the amidships bay narrower to permit passage of the gas-turbine exhausts. There are two 9.7 by 16.7-m elevators. The Type 1022 long-range air-search radar uses a Marconi antenna, but has the same electronics as the H.S.A. LW-08. Four MM 38 Exocet launchers were delected from

AIRCRAFT CARRIERS *(continued)*

the design. The electrical generating plant consists of 8 General Electric 1,750-kw alternators driven by Paxman Valenta 16-RPM 200A diesels of 2,700 hp each. *Invincible* deployed with 10 Sea Harrier and 11 Sea King to the Falklands in 4-82, and the ships can accommodate up to 22 Sea King-sized helicopters (with no Sea Harriers) if required, 16 of them in the hangar. The number of Sea Harrier normally carried is to grow to 8 in 1986-88. Type 2016 sonar may be installed in *Ark Royal* and is to be backfitted in the others. Can embark 960 Marines for short periods. Type 992Q radar to be replaced by Type 996. *Ark Royal* was completed with 3 Mk 15 CIWS (Vulcan/Phalanx); the others are to be backfitted during overhauls (R 05 in 1985-86). *Ark Royal* ran first sea trials on 22-10-84; she has the CACS data system. *Ark Royal* accepted 1-7-85.

NOTE: The improved *Centaur*-class carrier *Hermes,* in reserve since 12-4-84, was stricken 1-7-85. Offered for foreign sale, the ship has been examined by the Chilean and Indian navies.

NAVAL AVIATION

The Flag Officer Naval Air Command (F.O.N.A.C.) is located at the principal naval air facility, Yeovilton, and is chiefly responsible for training and maintenance. Land-based ASW aircraft belong to the RAF and, since the reorganization of the latter, have constituted the Eighteenth, or Maritime, Group of Strike Command. While the group is part of the RAF as regards personnel and equipment, its employment is determined by the Royal Navy's commander in chief.

The Fleet Air Arm consists of:

First-line squadrons (designation characterized by a group of three figures beginning with an 8) whose missions are: attack, ASW, and helicopter assault.

Second line squadrons (designation characterized by a group of three figures beginning with a 7) that are used in schools, tests, and maintenance.

Aircraft of the Royal Navy include (as of 1-86):

		Function	Squadron Assignment
23(+24)	Sea Harrier FRS.1/2	attack/interceptor	800, 807, 899
4(+3)	Sea Harrier T.4(N)/T.4	training	899
71	Sea King HAS.2,2A	ASW, logistics	706, 810, 814, 819, 820, 824, 826
22	Sea King HAS.5	ASW	
14(+10)	Sea King HC.4	troop-carrying	707,846
8	Sea King HAS.2A(AEW)	early warning	849
56	Lynx HAS.2	ASW, attack, training	702, 815
20(+7)	Lynx HAS.3*	ASW, attack	
16(-. . .)	Wasp HAS.1†	ASW, liaison	829
19	Gazelle Mk2	liaison, training	705
12	Wessex HU.5	training, SAR, troop-carrying	707, 845, 771
16(+4)	Jetstream T.2, T.3	training	750
. . .	Canberra T.22‡	radar training	Airwork Ltd. (contractor)
19	Hunter G.A. 11‡	training	Airwork, Ltd.
1	Hunter T.7‡	training	. . .
10	Falcon 20‡	training, transport	contractor
13	Chipmunk T.10	training	Flying Grading Unit, Roborough
2	HS.125	VIP transport	RAF detachment

* Seven Lynx HAS.3 helicopters were ordered 8-85.
† Of the 40 Wasp HAS.1 remaining in 1983, a number have been retired as a result of the decline in the number of ships that require them.
‡ 10 ex-U.S. Federal Express Falcon 20 transports were leased from FR Aviation and modified to perform electronics simulation, target towing and transport duties by Falcon Jet Corp., U.S.; deliveries began 3-85 to replace the Canberra TT.18 and Hunters used in similar duties.

News aircraft include: 14 Sea Harrier FRS.1 ordered in 1983, nine Sea Harrier FRS.2 ordered in 1984 for delivery 1986-88 (to permit enlarging squadrons to 8 aircraft each), 3 Sea Harrier T.4(N) 2-seat trainers, 5 Sea King HAS.5 ordered 15-2-84, with deliveries beginning 1-85, 4 Sea King HC.4 ordered 15-2-84 for delivery beginning 8-85, 7 more ordered 2-85, and one in 6-85 for delivery 1986-88, and 4 Jetstream 31 T.3 ordered 1984 for observer training. Twelve (of 24) Wessex HU.5 were to transfer to the Royal Auxiliary Air Force in 1986. One Sea Harrier was lost 7-2-85. Six additional AEW Sea King AEW conversions were to complete by 8-85 (total 18). One Sea King lost 27-6-85.

The Royal Marines operate 12 Gazelle AH.1 and 4 Lynx AH.2 helicopters.

Royal Air Force Maritime Patrol Aircraft of No. 18 (Maritime) Group (as of 1985):

34 Nimrod MR.2	Maritime patrol	42, 120, 201, 206, 236(OCU)
65 Buccaneer S.2	Maritime strike	12, 208, 237(OCU)

Lynx HAS.2 L. & L. Van Ginderen, 7-81

Wasp HAS.1 with AS.12 missiles L. & L. Van Ginderen, 7-84

Sea Harrier FRS.1 L. & L. Van Ginderen, 7-84

Wessex HU.5 troop carrier M.O.D., 1982

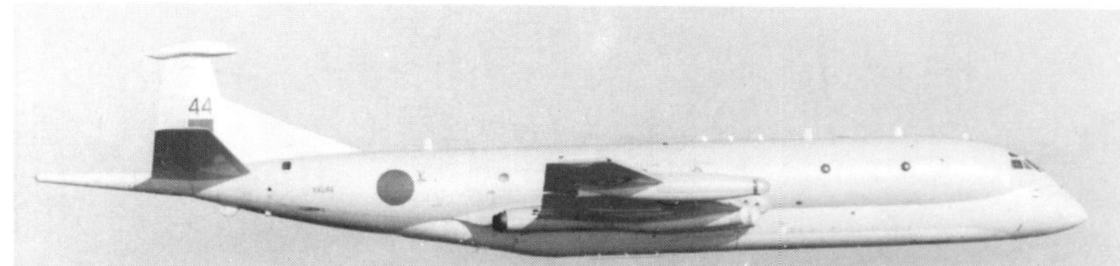
Nimrod MR.2 1981

NAVAL AVIATION *(continued)*

Sea King HAS.5 Westland, 1980

Sea King HAS.2 AEW, with Searchwater radar M.O.D., 1982

COMBAT AIRCRAFT

Type and builder	Mission	Wingspan	Length	Height	Weight	Engine	Max. speed in Mach or in knots	Practical maximum ceiling in feet	Range	Weapons	Remarks
◆ **FIXED-WING** **Sea Harrier FRS.1** (British Aerospace)	Attack fighter/ interceptor	7.6	14.5	3.71	10,500	1 Rolls-Royce Pegasus 104 vectored-thrust turbojet with 9,750 kg thrust	Mach 0.96; Mach 1.2 (diving)	50,000+	VTOL: 50 Miles STOL: 250 miles	2,270 kg, max total: 4/AIM-9L Sidewinder, 2/30-mm Aden guns, 454 kg bombs (normal load)	For the *Invincible* class.FRS.2 version to receive Blue Vixen radar, AMRAAM air-to-air missiles, and the Pegasus 105 engine. FRS.1 has Blue Fox navigation/ attack radar.
Nimrod MR.2 (British Aerospace) (RAF-operated)	ASW detection and engagement	35.30	38.63	9.08	80,510 to 87,090	4 Rolls-Royce Spey (RB 168-20) Mk 250 jet engines, 5,200-hp thrust each	450 kts	42,000	12 hrs	Bomb bay for 15-m weapons (6 torpedoes + 10 buoys) 2/Harpoon, 4 Sidewinder	Can carry nuclear depth charges. Last of 34 delivered 1985.
◆**HELICOPTERS** **Wasp HAS.1** (Westland)	ASW, antisurface	Rotor diam. 9.82	12.29	3.56	2,495	1 Rolls-Royce Numbus 503 turboshaft, 710 hp	104 kts 96 kts (cruising)	12,000	234 nm.	1-2/Mk 44 torpedo or 2/AS 12 ASM	On *Amazon, Rothesay,* and *Leander* frigates, and survey ships
Lynx HAS.2 and 3 (Westland)	ASW, anti-surface	12.80	15.16	3.60	4,763	2 Rolls-Royce Gem Z turboshafts, 750 hp each ((HAS.3: Gem 4; 1,120 hp each)	145 kts	12,000	1 hr 30 min. (half hovering, half cruising) (approx. 340 nm.)	2/Mk 44 or MK 46 torpedoes; 2-4 Sea Skua air-surface missiles	On *Sheffield, Amazon,* and *Broadsword* classes. Some to carry AN/ANS-18 dipping sonar. CTS (Central Tactical Data) system to add to HAS.3 1987-on.
Wessex HU-5 (Westland)	transport assault, SAR	17.06	20.03	4.93	5,800 (6,120 max.)	2 linked Bristol-Siddeley Gnome H 1400 turboshafts with 1,400 hp each	130 kts	6,000 hovering 14,000 cruising	3 hrs (664 nm normal)	14 troops, 2/AS 11 or 12 missiles or 2/50-mm rocket pods	Most have MIR.2 "orange-crop" ESM system.
Sea King HAS.2, 2A HC.4 HAS.5 HAS.2 (AEW)	ASW cargo troop-carrying ASW AEW	18.9	22.15		9,525	2 Rolls-Royce Gnome H 1400-1 turboshafts, 1,660 hp each driving a 5-bladed rotor and a tail rotor	122 kts	10,000	3 hr 15 min	4/Mk 44, 46 or Stingray torpedoes or 4/Mk 11 depth charges or nuclear depth charges; (HC.4: 2,727 kg stores or 22 troops)	Sea King HAS.2 and 2A have Type 195 sonar, AW 392 radar, and Marconi-Elliot AD580 doppler navigation systems. HAS.5 has Sea Searcher radar (initially: ARI 5955), LAPADS sonobuoy system. Two HAS.2A converted 1982 with Thorn-EMI Searchwater air/surface-search radar. Many now have MIR-2 "Orangecrop" EW system.
Gazelle Mk 2 (Westland/SNIAS)	reconnaissance, liason	10.5	11.97	3.18	917/975	1 Turbomeca Astazou, turboshaft, 850 hp	167 kts (140 kts cruise)	. . .	190 n.m.	rockets	Used by Royal Marines in attack/reconn. duties and by R.N. for training.
EH.101 (Agusta-Westland)	ASW	18.59	22.85 (15.85 folded)	6.5	13,000 (6,917 empty)	2 General Electric T 700-GE-401 turboshafts, 1,723 hp each	160 kts	. . .	4.5 hr. on station	4 Stingray torpedoes (2.5 hr at 100 n.m. radius); or 24 troops over 200 n.m. radius; a 4,500 kg. underslung	

COMBAT AIRCRAFT *(continued)*

Gazelle, of the Royal Marines M.O.D., 1982

Sea King HAS. Mk 2 RN, 12-84

The RAF also deploys 16 Sea King HAR.3 and 15 Wessex HC.2 SAR helicopters.

Under joint development between Westland, U.K., and Agusta, Italy, is the EH.101 helicopter, intended as replacement initially for the Sea King HAS.2 and later for the HAS.5 and HC.4. A total of 86 are planned for the Royal Navy, with the first to fly in 12-86 and production to commence in 1989. Provisional data are given in the preceding table. Earlier Sea Harrier FRS.1 are to be brought up to FRS.2 standard by substituting the Blue Vixen radar for Blue Fox and adding provision for U.S. AMRAAM air-to-air missiles (a program which may be canceled). A goal of 11 Searchwater-equipped Sea King HAS.2 conversions has been set.

BALLISTIC-MISSILE SUBMARINES

NOTE: Royal Navy submarines no longer wear hull numbers. The assigned numbers are included here for reference only.

◆ **0 (+4) Trident D5-carrying** Bldr: Vickers Shipbldg. Barrow-in-Furness

	Laid down	L	In serv.
S. . . N.	1986	. . .	1993
S. . . N.	. . .	. . .	. . .
S. . . N.	. . .	. . .	. . .
S. . . N.	. . .	. . .	. . .

D: 15,000+ tons (submerged) **S:** . . . kts **Dim:** 150.0 × 12.80 × 10.9
A: 16/Trident D5 ballistic missiles—4/553/mm TT (Sub-Harpoon and torpedoes)
Electron Equipt.: Radar: . . .
Sonar: Type 2054 suite: active, passive, intercept, towed array
M: 1 PWR 2 pressurized water reactor, steam turbines; 1 prop; 30,000 hp
Man: . . .

REMARKS: First ordered late 1985. Use of the Trident D5 missile with 8 multiple, independent re-entry vehicle (MIRV) warheads decided 3-82, necessitating use of U.S. *Ohio*-class mid-section (although it will be shorter, as eight fewer missiles will be carried). Will replace *Resolution* class and require refit only every 8-9 years.

◆ **4 Resolution class**

	Bldr	Laid down	L	In serv.
S 22 RESOLUTION	Vickers-Armstrong, Barrow	26-2-64	15-9-66	2-10-67
S 23 REPULSE	Vickers-Armstrong, Barrow	12-3-65	4-11-67	28-9-68
S 26 RENOWN	Cammell Laird, Birkenhead	25-6-64	25-2-67	15-11-68
S 27 REVENGE	Cammell Laird, Birkenhead	19-5-65	15-3-68	4-12-69

Repulse (S 23) L. & L. Van Ginderen, 10-76

Resolution (S 22) M.O.D., 1978

D: 7,500/8,400 tons **S:** 25/20 kts **Dim:** 129.54 × 10.05 × 9.15
A: 16/Polaris A3TK—6/533-mm TT (bow) **Man:** 13 Officers, 130 men
Electron Equipt: Radar: 1/1003
Sonar: 1/2001, 1/2007, 2023 towed passive array
M: 1 Rolls-Royce PWR 1 pressurized-water reactor; 1 English-Electric turbine; 1 prop; 15,000 hp

REMARKS: Characteristics are very similar to those of the U.S. *Lafayette* class, including the propulsion machinery, the launching and guidance systems, and the inertial navigation system. The original A3TK missiles were furnished by the U.S., but the 6 Cheveline MRV warheads of 150 kilotons each re-entry vehicles are of British conception and construction; introduced 1982 on S 26; S 22 (in refit 8-82 to 10-84) in 1984, and S 23 (refit 10-84 to 10-86) in 1986. Each ship has two crews, as in U.S. Navy SSBNs. Main ship's service turbo alternator produces 1,700 kw. Have diesel generator-driven electric emergency drive.

NUCLEAR-PROPELLED ATTACK SUBMARINES

◆ **3 (+3+ . . .) Trafalgar class** Bldr: Vickers, Barrow-in-Furness

	Ordered	Laid down	L	In serv.
S 107 TRAFALGAR	7-4-77	25-4-79	1-7-81	27-5-83
S 87 TURBULENT	28-7-78	8-5-80	1-12-82	28-4-84
S 88 TIRELESS	5-7-79	1981	13-7-84	5-10-85
S 90 TORBAY	26-6-81	12-82	8-3-85	1986
S 91 TRENCHANT	22-3-83	1983	. . .	1988
S 92 TALENT	10-9-84	1985	10-86	

Trafalgar (S 107) L. & L. Van Ginderen, 8-83

Trafalgar (S 107)—in dry dock, showing submerged bow planes, bow form, and sonar window L. & L. Van Ginderen, 8-84

D: 5,302 tons submerged **S:** 30 submerged **Dim:** 85.38 × 10.1 × 8.2
A: 5/533-mm TT fwd (20 Mk 24 torpedoes/Sub-Harpoon)
Electron Equipt: Radar: 1/1006—Sonar: 2001, 2020, 2024 towed array, 197, 183

NUCLEAR-PROPELLED ATTACK SUBMARINES *(continued)*

M: 1 reactor, 1 turbine; 1 shrouded pump-jet prop; 15,000 hp (1 Paxman 400-hp auxiliary propulsion diesel, electric drive)
Man: 12 officers, 86 men

Remarks: An improved version of the *Swiftsure* class. Coated with rubber compound anechoic tiles to reduce radiated and reflected noise.

◆ **6 Swiftsure class** Bldr: Vickers, Barrow-in-Furness

	Ordered	Laid down	L	In serv.
S 104 Sceptre	1-11-71	25-10-73	20-11-76	14-2-78
S 108 Sovereign	16-5-69	18-9-70	22-2-73	22-7-74
S 109 Superb	20-5-70	16-3-72	30-11-74	13-11-76
S 111 Spartan	7-2-73	26-3-76	7-4-78	22-9-79
S 112 Splendid (ex-*Severn*)	26-5-76	23-11-77	5-10-79	21-3-81
S 126 Swiftsure	3-11-67	6-6-69	7-9-71	17-4-73

Spartan (S 111) L. & L. Van Ginderen, 4-85

Sovereign (S 108) L. & L. Van Ginderen, 7-85

Sovereign (S 108) L. & L. Van Ginderen, 7-85

D: 4,000 light/4,200/4,500 tons **S:** 20/28 kts **Dim:** 82.9 × 10.12 × 8.25
A: 5/533-mm bow TT (20 Mk 8 and Mk 24 torpedoes/Sub-Harpoon)
Electron Equipt: Radar: 1/1003
Sonar: 2001 active/passive, 2007 active/passive, 2019 intercept, 2052 towed passive array, 197, 183
M: 1 reactor; 2 English Electric turbines; 1 prop; 15,000 hp (1 Paxman 400-hp auxiliary propulsion diesel, electric drive)
Man: 12 officers, 85 men

Remarks: High-performance, very quiet submarines with excellent passive sonars. Have 112-cell battery. The forward diving planes are below the surfaced waterline and retract within the outer hull. Torpedo tubes reload in 15 seconds. To receive Type 2020 sonar in place of 2007, beginning with S 109 in 1985. S 108 refitted 1983 to 24-11-84.

◆ **5 Valiant class**

	Bldr	Laid down	L	In serv.
S 46 Churchill	Vickers, Barrow	30-6-67	20-12-68	15-7-70
S 48 Conqueror	Cammell Laird	5-12-67	29-8-69	9-11-71
S 50 Courageous	Vickers, Barrow	15-5-68	7-3-70	16-10-71
S 102 Valiant	Vickers, Barrow	22-1-62	3-12-63	18-7-66
S 103 Warspite	Vickers, Barrow	10-12-63	25-9-65	18-4-67

D: 3,500/4,200/4,900 tons **S:** 20/28 kts **Dim:** 86.87 × 10.12 × 8.25
A: 6/533-mm TT fwd (26 Mk 8 and Mk 24 torpedoes/Sub-Harpoon)
Electron Equipt: Radar: 1/1003
Sonar: 2001, 2007, 197, 183, 2052 towed array
M: 1 pressurized water reactor; 2 English-Electric GT; 1 prop; 15,000 hp
Man: 13 officers, 90 men

Courageous (S 50) P. Voss, 7-84

Warspite (S 103)—off the Falklands coast L. & L. Van Ginderen, 3-84

Remarks: The propulsion plant is of entirely British design and construction. Diving depth: 300 m. Have a 112-cell emergency battery. The hull form of this class is a development of the *Dreadnought.* In 1967 the *Valiant* made a nonstop, submerged cruise from Singapore to Great Britain in 28 days (12,000 miles). S 46 completed trials with Sub-Harpoon missiles in 2-80 and was in "Long Refit" until 7-5-83. S 103 completed a "Long Refit" and refueling 10-81, S 102 in 2-80, S 103 on 27-3-82, S 48 and S 50 in 1984-85. All but S 103 eventually to get Type 2020 sonar in place of 2001.

TORPEDO ATTACK SUBMARINES

◆ **0 (+1+11) Upholder class (Type 2400)** Bldr: Vickers, Barrow-in-Furness

	Laid down	L	In serv.
S. . . Upholder	6-84	1986-87	1988

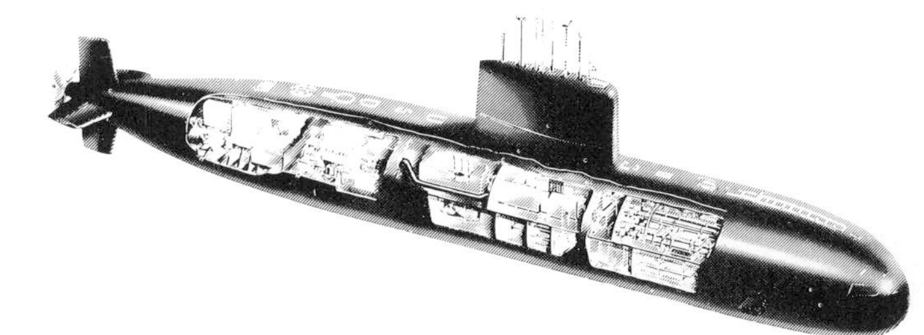

Upholder (Type 2400) Vickers, 1981

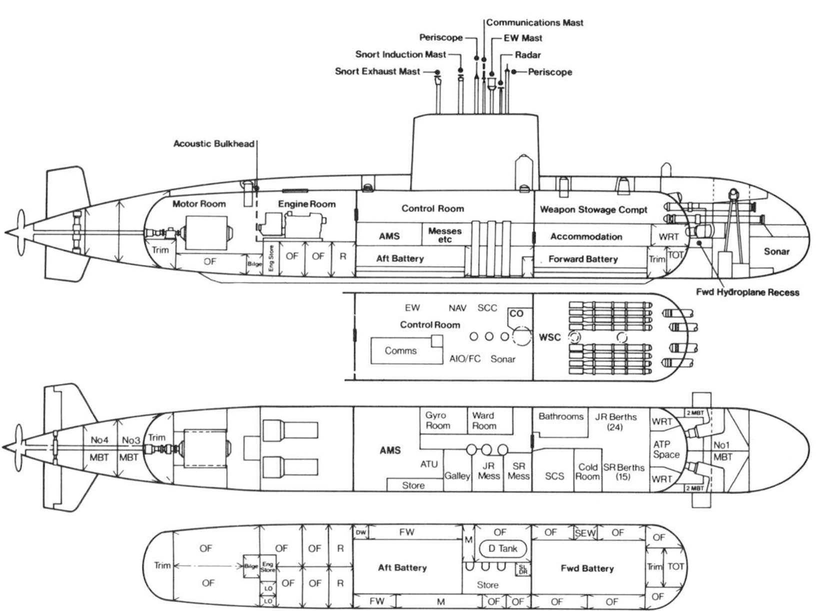

Layout of Upholder Royal Institute of Naval Architects

D: 1,870 standard/2,126 surfaced/2,362 submerged tons **S:** 12/20 kts
Dim: 70.26 (47.5 pressure hull) × 7.6 × 5.5
A: 6/522-mm TT fwd (18 tot. Mk 24 and/or Spearfish torpedoes, Sub-Harpoon)

TORPEDO ATTACK SUBMARINES *(continued)*

Electron Equipt: Radar: . . . —EW: Decca Porpoise
Sonar: Type 2040 active/passive, Micropuffs passive, 2046 towed array
M: 2 Paxman Valenta 16 RPA 200SZ 16-cyl. diesel generators, 2,035 hp each, 2 G.E.C. 2,500-kw alternators; 1/7-bladed prop; 5,400 hp
Endurance: 49 days **Fuel:** 200 tons **Range:** 8,000 (snorkel)
Man: 9 officers, 37 men

REMARKS: All to have names beginning with "U." Will be based on the Vickers commercial Type 2400 design and are intended to provide successors to the *Oberon* class. The first unit was ordered late 1983. Have 11 percent reserve buoyancy when surfaced. Two 240-cell lead-acid batteries, 6,080 Amp/hr. at one-hour rate, 8,800 Amp/hr. at five-hour rate. Barr & Stroud CK 35 search periscope with Decca EW array; CH 85 attack 'scope with infrared capability. Will be able to snorkel at 19 kts. 200-m diving depth. Two Ferranti FM 1600E computers, with Thorn E.M.T. 1553B data base. Inertial navigation system. Type 2040 sonar is a version of the Thomson-CSF Argonaute system. There will be an active sonar in the sail, while the 2040's cylindrical array will be at the bow, with intercept hydrophones arranged along the sides. The sail will have a glass-reinforced plastic skin. The fifth and later units may be of a stretched 3,000-ton surfaced displacement version to obtain longer endurance.

◆ **13 Oberon class, and 2 Porpoise class**

	Bldr	Laid down	L	In serv.
S 09 OBERON	HM Dockyard, Chatham	28-11-57	18-7-59	24-2-61
S 10 ODIN	Cammell Laird	27-4-59	4-11-60	3-5-62
S 11 ORPHEUS	Vickers-Armstrong	16-4-59	17-11-59	25-11-60
S 12 OLYMPUS	Vickers-Armstrong	4-3-60	14-6-61	7-7-62
S 13 OSIRIS	Vickers-Armstrong	26-1-62	29-11-62	11-1-64
S 14 ONSLAUGHT	HM Dockyard, Chatham	8-4-59	24-9-60	14-8-62
S 15 OTTER	Scotts SB, Greenock	14-1-60	15-5-61	20-8-62
S 16 ORACLE	Cammell Laird	26-4-60	26-9-61	14-2-63
S 17 OCELOT	HM Dockyard, Chatham	17-11-60	5-5-62	31-1-64
S 18 OTUS	Scotts, SB, Greenock	31-5-61	17-10-62	5-10-63
S 19 OPOSSUM	Cammell Laird	21-12-61	23-5-63	5-6-64
S 20 OPPORTUNE	Scotts SB, Greenock	26-10-62	14-2-64	29-12-64
S 21 ONYX	Cammell Laird	16-11-64	18-8-66	20-11-67
S 07 SEALION	Cammell Laird, Birkenhead	5-6-58	31-12-59	25-7-61
S 08 WALRUS	Scotts SB, Greenock	12-2-53	22-9-59	10-2-61

Ocelot (S 17)—standard bow dome G. Gyssels, 10-84

Opossum (S 19)—with new bow dome L. & L. Van Ginderen, 3-84

Sealion (S 07) L. & L. Van Ginderen, 8-84

D: 1,650/2,080/2,450 tons **S:** 17.5 kts **Dim:** 89.92 (87.45 pp) × 8.07 × 5.48
A: 8/533-mm TT (6 fwd, 2 short aft; 18 Mk 8 and Mk 24 torpedoes)
Electron Equipt: Radar: 1/1006 (S 07, 08: 1/1002)
Sonar: 2007, 186, 187 (S 15, S 19, S 21: 2051 in place of 2007)
M: 2/1,840-hp Admiralty Standard Range 16VVS-AS21, 1,740-hp diesels, electric drive; 2 props; 6,000 hp
Endurance: 56 days **Fuel:** 298 m³ (446 m³ emergency)
Man: 6 officers, 62 men (S 08: 65 tot., S 07: 71 tot.)

REMARKS: Conventional propulsion and hull form. Streamlined sail. Maximum depth: 200 meters. Snorkel. Air-conditioned. Excellent living spaces. Batteries with 448 total cells provide 5,300 Amp/hr. at 1-hr. rate; 7,420 Amp/hr. at 5-hr. rate. *Oberon* used in training nuclear submarine crews. *Olympus* completed a 2-year refit 7-84 with a new aluminum alloy sail and a 5-man exit chamber for Special Boat Service swimmers. The two after torpedo tubes, for Mk 23 short ASW torpedoes, are no longer used. The first *Onyx* transferred to Canada (1-64) and renamed the *Ojibwa;* another *Onyx* was built. Canada ordered three ships of this class, Australia six, Chile two, and Brazil three. The *Grampus* (S 04) of the *Porpoise* class was stricken in 1976, *Rorqual* (S 02) in 1976, *Narwhal* (S 03), *Cathelot* (S 06) in 1977, *Finwhale* (S 05) in 1978, and *Porpoise* (S 01) in 8-82. Sale of the *Cachelot* to Egypt was canceled. S 07 is used as a "padded target" for ASW weapons trials.

Nine (including S 19 in 1984, S 15, S 10, and S 21) are being modernized with the Type 2051 sonar forward and Type 2046 "clip-on" passive towed array, Ferranti-Gresham Lion Oberon Dual Guidance System (to permit firing 2 Mk 24 torpedoes at once), and MEL Manta EW intercept gear.

GUIDED-MISSILE DESTROYERS

◆ **4 Manchester class (Type 42C)**

	Bldr	Laid down	L	In serv.
D 95 MANCHESTER	Vickers, Barrow	19-5-79	24-11-80	16-12-82
D 96 GLOUCESTER	Vosper Thornycroft	26-10-79	2-11-82	9-85
D 97 EDINBURGH	Laird	8-9-80	14-4-83	18-12-85
D 98 YORK	Swan Hunter	18-1-80	21-6-82	9-8-85

York (D 98) L. & L. Van Ginderen, 7-85

Manchester (D 95)—still with Knebworth/Corvus decoy launchers
Royal Navy, 1984

Gloucester (D 96)—from astern, showing 20-mm AA abreast hangar, squarer stern than earlier Type 42 class Vosper Thornycroft, 1984

GUIDED-MISSILE DESTROYERS *(continued)*

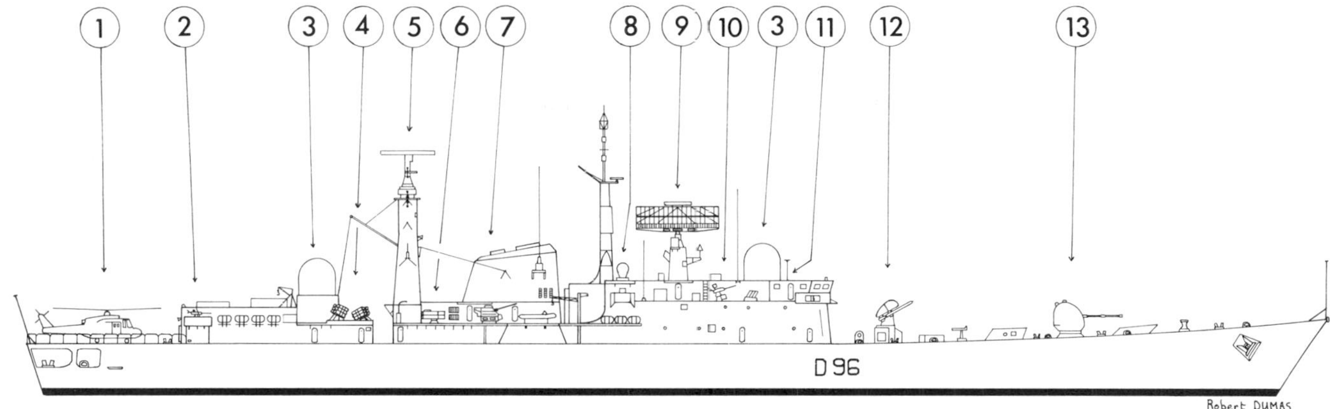

Gloucester (D 96) 1. Lynx helicopter 2. 20-mm Mk 4 AA 3. Type 909 f.c. radar 4. Shield decoy RL 5. 992Q radar 6. STWS.1 ASW TT 7. twin 30-mm Oerlikon GCM-A02 AA 8. SCOT SATCOMM antenna for Skynet 9. Type 1022 search radar 10. 20-mm GAM-B 01 AA 11. Mk 137 decoy RL for Mk 36 SRBOC system 12. Sea Dart launcher 13. 114-mm Mk 8 DP gun

D: 4,100 tons (4,775 fl) **S:** 29.5 kts (18 cruising)
Dim: 141.12 (132.3 wl) × 14.90 × 5.80 (4.20 hull)
A: 1/Sea Dart GWS.30 syst. (II × 1, 40 missiles)—1/114-mm Mk 8 DP—4/30-mm Oerlikon AA (II × 2)—4/20-mm AA (I × 4)—6/324-mm STWS.1 ASW TT (III × 2)—1/Lynx helicopter
Electron Equipt: Radar: 1/1006, 1/992Q, 1/1022, 2/909
Sonar: 1/2016 (D 95: 1/184M, 1/162M)
EW: UA-A1 passive, 2/Type 690 active, 4/Shield chaff RL (VI × 4)—D 35: 2/Knebworth/Corvus, (VIII × 2), 2/Mk 36 SRBOC (VI × 2)
M: COGOG: 2 Rolls-Royce Olympus TM3B gas turbines of 27,200 hp each for boost, 2 Rolls-Royce Tyne RM1C of 5,340 hp each for cruise; 2/5-bladed CP props; 54,400/10,680 hp
Electron Equipt: 4,000 kw (4/1,000-kw diesel sets) **Range:** 4,750/18
Fuel: 610 tons **Man:** 26 officers, 81 senior petty officers, 194 men

REMARKS: A lengthened version of the *Sheffield* class intended to provide better seaworthiness, endurance, and habitability, but having no change in armament despite the additional 16-m overall length. Have larger Sea Dart magazine. The ADAWS 7 combat data system is carried. Have LINK 11 data link system. D 95 ordered 10-11-78, D 96 on 27-3-79, and D 97 and D 104 on 25-4-79. No additional ships of this class are planned. Completion of D 97 delayed by strike at yard. D 96 delivered 16-5-85.

All are to have Type 992Q radar replaced by Type 996. The close-in AA suite is temporary, consisting of 4/20-mm AA (two each Mk 4 aft and Oerlikon GAM-B01 abreast bridge) and two twin 30-mm amidships; this *may* be replaced with Sea Wolf and/or a modern close-defense gun. D 95 has older sonar suite and earlier decoy rocket launchers aft. All have two U.S. Mk 137 chaff RL (Mk 36 Super RBOC system), which will eventually fire the NATO Sea Gnat decoy. Several 7.62-mm mg are carried, including one on each bridge wing. Active EW jammers flank the Type 1022 radar's pylon.

◆ **8 Sheffield class (Type 42)**

	Bldr	Laid down	L	In serv.
D 86 BIRMINGHAM	Cammell Laird	28-3-72	30-7-73	3-12-76
D 87 NEWCASTLE	Swan Hunter	21-2-73	24-4-75	23-3-78
D 88 GLASGOW	Swan Hunter	7-3-74	14-4-76	24-5-79
D 89 EXETER	Swan Hunter	22-7-76	25-4-78	19-9-80
D 90 SOUTHAMPTON	Vosper Thornycroft	21-10-76	29-1-79	23-7-81
D 91 NOTTINGHAM	Vosper Thornycroft	6-2-78	12-2-80	8-4-83
D 92 LIVERPOOL	Cammell Laird	5-7-78	25-9-80	9-7-82
D 108 CARDIFF	Vickers, Barrow	3-11-72	22-2-74	19-10-79

Southampton (D 90)—en route Falklands with extra AA, SCOT domes, no pendant number L. & L. Van Ginderen, 10-84

Newcastle (D 87)—refitted with Type 1022 radar; note domes off Type 909 f.c. radars L. & L. Van Ginderen, 6-84

Exeter (D 89)—EW domes on aft mast, additional AA guns not aboard L. & L. Van Ginderen, 2-84

Nottingham (D 91) L. & L. Van Ginderen, 7-85

GUIDED-MISSILE DESTROYERS *(continued)*

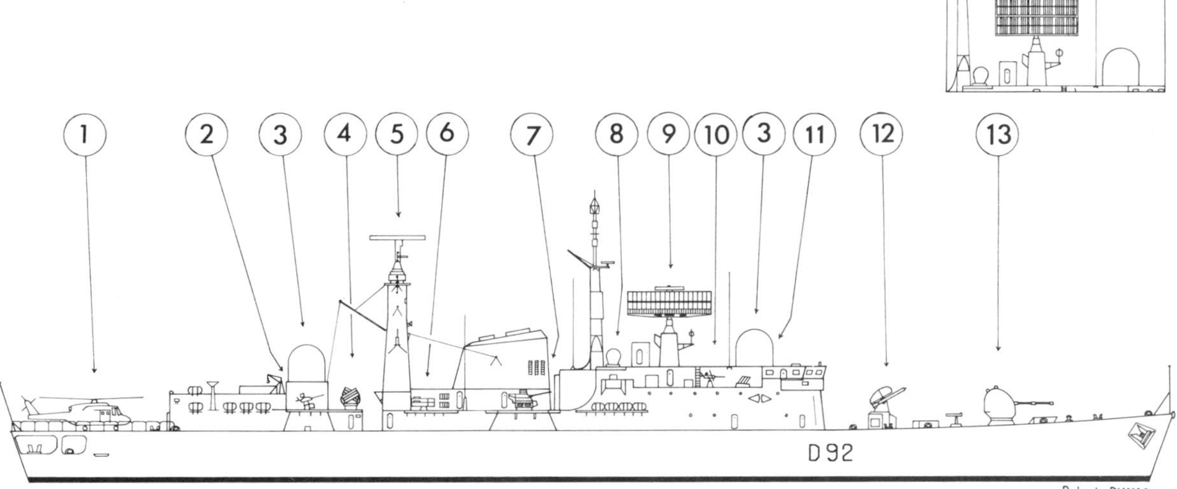

Liverpool (D 92) 1. Lynx helicopter 2. 20-mm Oerlikon GAM-B01 AA 3. Type 909 f.c. radar 4. Knebworth/Corvus chaff RL 5. Type 992Q surface/air-search radar 6. Triple STWS.1 ASW TT 7. twin 30-mm Oerlikon GCM-A02 AA 8. SCOT SATCOMM antenna for Skynet 9. Type 1022 air-search radar 10. 20-mm Mk 4 AA 11. Mk 137 decoy launcher for Mk 36 SRBOC system 12. Sea Dart launcher 13. 114-mm Mk 8 DP gun

D: 3,150 tons (4,100 fl) **S:** 28 kts (18 cruising)
Dim: 125.0 (119.5 pp) × 14.34 × 5.8 (4.2 hull)
A: 1/Sea Dart GWS.30 Mod. 2(II × 1, 20 missiles)—1/114-mm Mk 8 DP—4/30-mm Oerlikon AA (II × 2)—4/20-mm AA (I × 4)—6/324-mm STWS.1 ASW TT (III × 2)—1/Lynx helicopter—see Remarks
Electron Equipt: Radar: 1/1006, 1/1022, 1/992Q, 2/909
Sonar: 1/184M (D 88: 2016), 1/162M
EW: UA-A1 passive 2/Type 690 active (some), Knebworth/Corvus chaff RL (VIII × 2), Mk 36 SRBOC (VI × 2)
M: COGOG; 2 Rolls-Royce Olympus TM3B gas turbines, 27,200 hp each for high speed; 2 Rolls-Royce Tyne RM1A gas turbines, 4,100 hp each for cruising; 2/5-bladed CP props (D 89 and later Tyne RM1C, 5,340 hp each)
Electric: 4,000 kw (4/1,000-kw diesel sets) **Range:** 650/30; 4,500/18
Man: 26 officers, 273 men maximum (normal 250-280 tot.)

Remarks: Have ADAWS 4 tactical data system. *Cardiff,* delayed by labor problems, was completed by Swan Hunter. Completion of *Glasgow* delayed by fire 9-76. All can carry SCOT radomes for Skynet SHF satellite communications system. Very cramped ships. Helicopter used for surveillance and attack (Sea Skua missiles) as well as ASW. Have "Agouti" bubble ejector system for propellers (which rotate inwardly) to reduce cavitation noise. Two pair fin stabilizers fitted. D 89 and later had a taller mainmast and Type 1022 radar forward vice Type 965M; Type 965M was replaced in 4 early ships, beginning with D 108 and D 87 in 1984. Those same ships are updated with the ADAWS 7 data system and stack water spray equipment to reduce IR signature. In 1985 it was announced that this class would be given mid-life refits, guaranteeing longer retention; the Sea Dart system is to be improved.

Class prototype, *Sheffield* (D 80), foundered 10-5-82, having been hit by an Argentine AM 39 Exocet missile on 4-5-82. *Coventry* (D 118) was lost to bombs on 25-5-82. This class was found to be deficient in damage-control design during the Falklands War and also to be limited in sensor capability and self-defense, although the Sea Dart system functioned effectively. All will ultimately receive a new-design point-defense system.

As an interim measure, all ships have had 2/20-mm Oerlikon GAM-B01 AA mounts added on platforms abreast the after Type 909 radome, while deploying ships mount twin Oerlikon GCM-A02 30-mm mounts (on-mount sights only) on platforms that replaced the boats, abreast the stack. U.S.-supplied Mk 137 chaff rocket launchers are now mounted just abaft the pilothouse, and some ships are receiving enhanced electronic warfare suites. The Type 992Q radar is to be replaced by the new Type 996, and Type 2016 sonar is to replace the Type 184M. All receiving 2/7.62-mm mg on the bridge wings.

◆ **1 Bristol (Type 82) class**

	Bldr	Laid down	L	In serv.
D 23 Bristol	Swan Hunter	15-11-67	30-6-69	31-3-73

D: 6,100 tons (7,100 fl) **S:** 28 kts
Dim: 154.60 (149.90 wl) × 16.77 × 5.20 (6.85 over sonar)
A: 1/Sea Dart GWS.30 (II × 1, 40 missiles)—1/114-mm Mk 8 DP—4/30-mm AA (II × 2)—4/20-mm AA (I × 4)—1/Ikara GWS.40 ASW syst. (I × 1, 32 missiles)
Electron Equipt: Radar: 1/1006, 1/965M, 1/992Q, 2909, 2/Ikara control
Sonar: 1/184M, 1/162M
EW: UA-A1, Mk 36 SRBOC chaff RL (VI × 4), 2 Knebworth/Corvus chaff RL (VIII × 2)
M: COSAG; 2 A.E.I. GT (15,000 hp each) and 2 Rolls-Royce Olympus TM1A gas turbines (22,300 hp each); 2 props; 74,600 hp
Boilers: 2 Babcock & Wilcox, 49.2 kg/cm² pressure, 510°C superheat
Electric: 7,000 kw **Range:** 5,000/18 **Man:** 29 officers, 378 men

Bristol (D 23)—paying off for refit, 31-7-84 Walles Foto

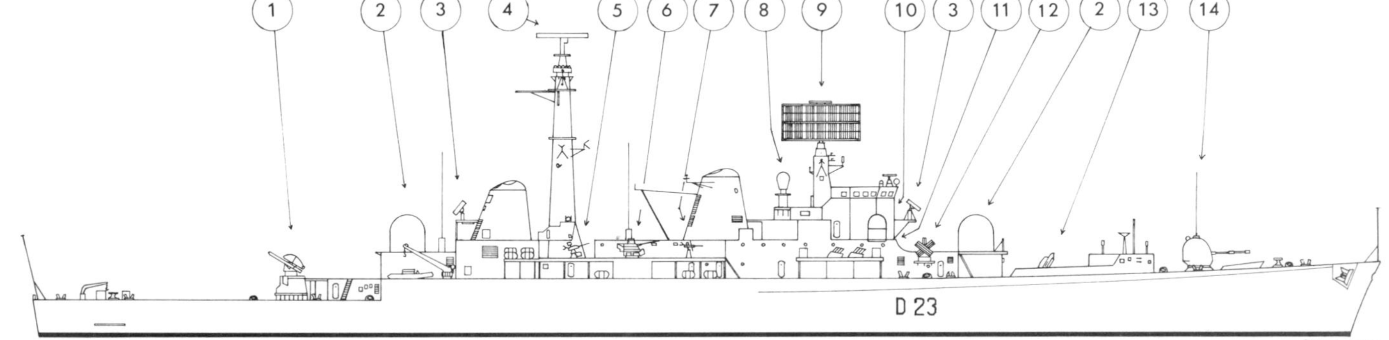

Bristol (D 23) 1. Sea Dart launcher 2. Type 909 f.c. radar 3. U.S. OE-82 antenna for WSC-3 UHF SATCOMM 4. Type 992Q radar 5. 20-mm Oerlikon GAM-B01 AA 6. twin 30-mm Oerlikon GCM-A02 AA 7. 20-mm Mk 4 AA 8. SCOT antenna for Skynet SHF SATCOMM 9. Type 965M radar 10. Ikara tracking radar 11. Mk 137 chaff RL for Mk 36 SRBOC system 12. Knebworth/Corvus chaff RL 13. Ikara launcher

GUIDED-MISSILE DESTROYERS *(continued)*

Remarks: Designed as an escort for the 50,000-ton aircraft carrier *Furious* when construction of the latter was being considered. There were to be eight in the class, but this ship, ordered in 10-66, was the only one built. Four pair fin stabilizers. Although nominally commissioned in 1973, she had not been accepted for active service by the time of her first refit in 1976-78. Equipped with the LINK 11 automated action data communications system, for the U.S. NTDS or French SENIT systems. Equipped with the ADAWS 2 data system. Designated flagship of the Third Flotilla in 1980 and given the U.S. WSC-3 satellite communications equipment. Can land a helicopter, but has no hangar. Only ship with two Ikara ASW missile-control systems; Limbo triple ASW mortar removed 1978. Generally considered an expensive failure, but is now Britain's largest non-carrier surface combatant. Was to have been stricken in 1985, but will now be retained and equipped with a new point-defense gun system. U.S. Mk 36 Super RBOC chaff, two twin Oerlikon GCM-AO2, 30-mm AA, and two Oerlikon GAM-B01, 20-mm AA added 1983. Boats removed. Had boiler explosion 17-7-84, just prior to entering refit.

◆ **2 County class**

	Bldr	Laid down	L	In serv.
D 19 Glamorgan	Fairfield, SB&E	13-9-62	9-7-64	11-10-66
D 20 Fife	Vickers-Armstrong	1-6-62	9-7-64	21-6-66

Fife (D 20)—with Sea Slug launcher replaced by deckhouse
Maritime Photographic, 9-85

Glamorgan (D 19) Gary Davies, 5-85

D: 5,440 tons (6,200 fl) **S:** 32.5 kts (30 sust.)
Dim: 158.55 (153.9 pp) × 16.46 × 6.3 (max.) **Man:** 33 officers, 438 men
A: Both: 4/MM 38 Exocet—1/Sea Slug Mk 2 system (II × 1, 30 missiles, not in D 20)—12/114-mm Mk 6 DP (II × 1)—6/324-mm ASW TT STWS.1 (III × 2)—1/Lynx helicopter—D 19 also: 2/40-mm AA (I × 2)—6/20-mm AA (II × 2, I × 2)—D 20 also: 2/Sea Cat GWS.22 systems (IV × 2)—4/20-mm Mk 4 AA (I × 4)
Electron equipt: Radar: 1/978, 1/965M, 1/992Q, 1/277, 1/901, 1/903, D 20 only: 2/904 f.c.
Sonar: 1/184M, 1/162M
EW: UA-8/9 active and passive, 2 Knebworth/Corvus chaff RL, Mk 36 SRBOC chaff RL (VI × 4)
M: COSAG; 2 sets A.E.I. GT (15,000 hp each), and 4 G 6 gas turbines (7,500 hp each); 2 props; 60,000 hp total
Electric: 4,750 kw **Fuel:** 600 tons **Range:** 3,500/28
Boilers: 2 Babcock & Wilcox; 49.21 kg/cm² pressure, 510°C superheat

Remarks: Four pairs of fin stabilizers. Twin rudders. Air-conditioned. Remote control of the boilers and engines from a command post that is completely protected from radioactive contamination. Sea Slug missile stowage extends to the midships area and is more than 80 meters long; it is inboard, along the centerline of the ship, and contains two parallel rows of 15 missiles, which are now primarily used against surface targets. Fitted with four Exocet anti-ship missiles in 1974-76. Of the Sea Slug Mk 2-equipped ships, the *Fife* (D 20), which was inactive from 9-79 as a harbor training ship, entered "Long Refit" in July 1980 and recommissioned 31-3-83, and *Glamorgan* (D 19) and *Antrim* (D 18) had their careers extended as a result of the Falklands War; *Norfolk* (D 21) was sold to Chile 17-2-82, and *Antrim* followed on 14-4-84. The helicopter can only be flown in calm seas (because of the poor hangar arrangement). Have the ADAWS 1 combat data-handling system. Each propeller is driven by one general steam turbine and two gas turbines for high speeds, and the steam turbine alone for cruising. There are 3 steam turbo alternators and 3 gas turbine generators.

Glamorgan received an accommodations deckhouse on her helicopter deck late in 1984 and is used in training. Pakistan has expressed interest in buying *Fife.* Older Sea Slug Mk 1 "County," *Kent* (D 12) was towed to Devonport Dockyard 30-10-84 to convert as accommodations hulk at Portsmouth to replace *Rame Head.* Sea Slug launcher replaced by deckhouse on D 20, 1985.

FRIGATES

◆ **0 (+2 + 7 + . . .) "Duke" (Type 23) general-purpose class**

	Bldr	Laid down	L	In serv.
F . . . Norfolk	Yarrow, Scotstoun	10-85	1987	1989
F . . . N . . .	Swan Hunter	. . .	. . .	. . .

D: 3,000 tons (3,700 fl) **S:** 28 kts (15 kts electric drive) **Dim:** 133.0 (123.0 pp) × 16.1(15.0 wl) × 4.3 (hull)
A: 8/Harpoon SSM (IV × 2)—1/Sea Wolf GWS.26 vertical launch group (32 missiles)—1/114-mm Mk 8 DP—1/30-mm Goalkeeper gatling AA—2/30-mm Rarden AA (I × 2)—4/324-mm TT (II × 2, fixed)—1/EH.101 ASW helicopter
Electron Equipt: Radar: 1/1007, 1/996 Mod. 1, 2/911 Sea Wolf control
Sonar: 1/2050, 1/2031(2) towed linear passive array
EW: UA-F1 (Decca Cutlass) passive, Decca Cygnus jammer, 4/Shield chaff RL (VI × 4)
M: CODLAG (combined Diesel-Electric and Gas Turbine): 2 Rolls-Royce SM1A Spey gas turbines (37,540 hp); 4 Paxman Valenta 12 RPM 200A diesel generator sets (5,200 kw total)—2/2,000-hp electric motors; 2 props; 41,540 hp
Range: 8,000/15 **Fuel:** 800 tons **Electric:** 5,200 kw
Man: 12 officers, 41 petty officers, 90 men

Remarks: First unit ordered 29-10-84; letter-of-intent for second signed 28-1-85. *Norfolk* was originally to have been named *Daring.* Intended as lineal replacements for the remaining *Leander*-class frigates. Prototype design assigned to Yarrow. Flush-decked hull, with large helicopter hangar, helo in-haul system, fin stabilizers. Design grew

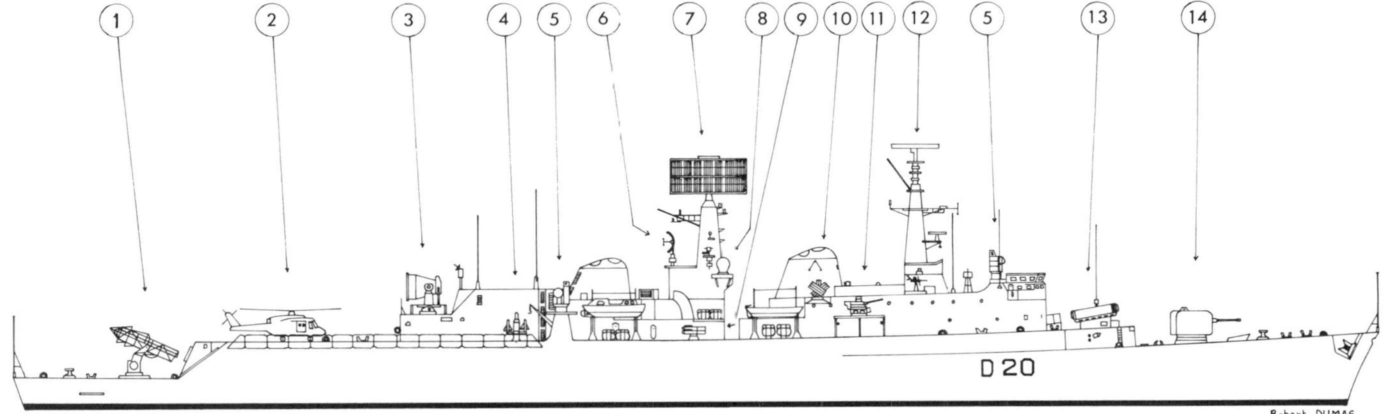

Fife (D 20) 1. Sea Slug launcher 2. Lynx helicopter 3. Type 901 Sea Slug control radar 4. Sea Cat launchers (IV × 2) 5. MRS-3 fire-control director 6. 278 height-finding radar 7. 965M early-warning radar 8. SCOT SHF SATCOMM antenna 9. STWS.1 triple ASW TT 10. Knebworth/Corvus decoy RL 11. SRBOC chaff rocket launchers (incorrectly shown as a gun) 12. Type 992Q radar 13. MM 38 Exocet launchers 14. twin 114-mm Mk 6 DP gunmount *Note:* Sea Slug launcher replaced by deckhouse, 1985.

FRIGATES *(continued)*

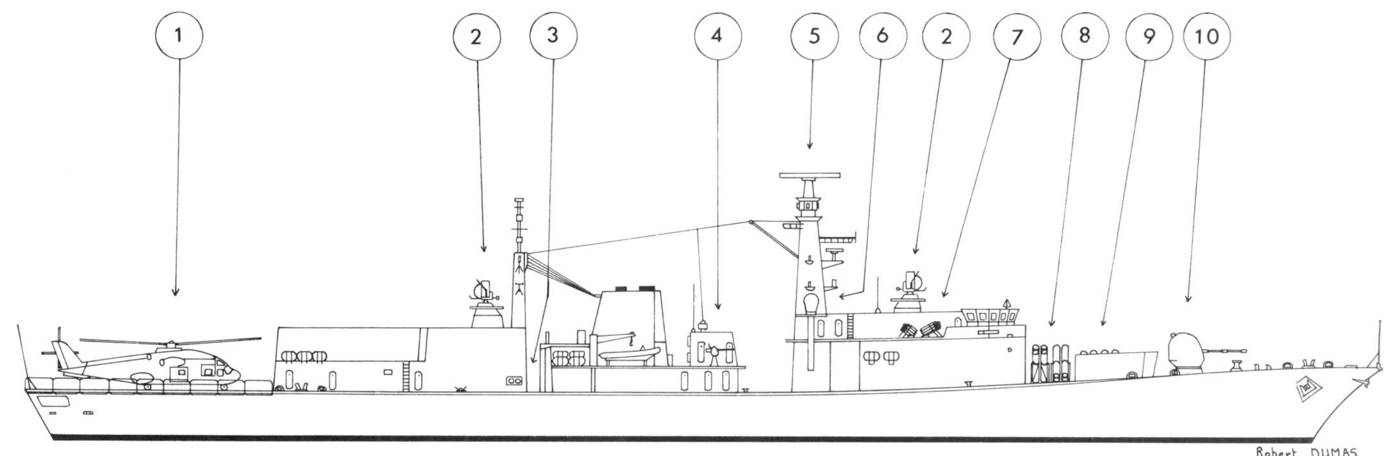

"Duke" class 1. EH.101 helicopter 2. Type 911 radar director 3. ASW TT 4. 30-mm Rarden gun 5. Type 996 radar 6. SCOT SNF SATCOMM antenna 7. Shield decoy RL 8. Harpoon SSM (IV × 2) 9. 32 vertical-launch Sea Wolf missiles 10. 114-mm Vickers Mk 8 DP gun

"Duke" class—artist's impression

considerably as a result of Falklands "Lessons-Learned." Will have first bow-mounted sonars in the Royal Navy.

The propulsion system permits running the shaft-concentric electric propulsion motors with the power from any combination of the four 1,300-kw ship's service generators; power from both the gas turbines and the electric motors can be obtained. Fixed-pitch props, with astern power available only by electric drive. Numerous improvements in damage control, as a result of Falkland War lessons. There will be accommodations for 15 officers, 57 petty officers and 105 junior ratings, but crew size may grow. Two more were to be ordered by end-1985. May carry 2 U.S. Mk 15 CIWS AA vice Goalkeeper.

◆ 0 (+4) Cornwall (Type 22 Batch 3) general-purpose class

	Bldr	Laid down	L	In serv.
F 99 CORNWALL	Yarrow, Scotstoun	12-9-83	14-10-85	1987
F. . . CUMBERLAND	Yarrow, Scotstoun	20-12-84	. . .	1988
F. . . CAMPBELLTOWN	Cammell-Laird	. . .	. . .	1989
F. . . CHATHAM	Swan-Hunter	. . .	. . .	1990

D: 4,380 tons (5,250 fl) **S:** 30 kts **Dim:** 148.00(135.65 pp) × 14.75 × 5.35 hull (6.00 max.)

A: 2/Sea Wolf GWS.25 Mod. 3 systems (VI × 2)—8/Harpoon. SSM (IV × 2)—1/114-mm Vickers Mk 8 DP—1/30-mm Goalkeeper AA gun syst.—2/30-mm LS-30B AA (I × 2)—6/324-mm STWS.2 ASW TT (III × 2)—2/Lynx (Sea Skua ASM, Stingray ASW torpedoes) or 1/EH.101 helicopters

Electron Equipt: Radar: 1/1006, 1/967/968, 2/911 f.c., 2/Goalkeeper f.c.
Sonar: Type 2050 hull-mounted, Type 2031(2) towed linear passive array
EW: UA-A1 passive, 4/Shield chaff RL (VI × 4), Mk 36, 5RBOC (VI × 2)

M: COGAG: 2 Rolls-Royce Spey SM.1A DR gas turbines (18,770 hp each) *and* 2 Rolls-Royce Tyne RM.1C gas turbines (5,340 hp each); 2 Stone Manganese CP props; 48,220 hp

Electric: 4,000 kw (4/Paxman Valenta 12PA 200CZ diesel sets) **Man:** 286 tot. (Accommodations for 320)

Range: 7,000/18 (on Tyne gas turbines) **Fuel:** 650 tons

REMARKS: Third series in the Type 22/*Broadsword*-class design, with same basic hull as Batch 2/*Boxer* class, but with a 114-mm gun on the forecastle, the anti-ship missile launchers moved to abaft the pilothouse and oriented athwartships. Will have EASAMS' Sea Archer GSA 8/GPEOD (Gun System Automation 8/General-Purpose Electro-Optical Director)T.V./IR/laser back-up directors for the 114-mm gun. The Goalkeeper gatling AA gunmount has its own integral I-band search/tracker and I/K-band tracking radars. Maximum generator output is 5,200 kw. All will have the CACS-1 Computer-Assisted Command System.

The first pair were ordered 14-12-82 and the third and fourth on 28-1-85. There are apparently to be no additional units of what is the world's largest "frigate" design.

◆ 3(+3) Boxer (Type 22 Batch 2) class ASW frigates

	Bldr:	Laid down	L	In serv.
F 92 BOXER	Yarrow, Scotstoun	5-11-79	17-6-81	14-1-84
F 93 BEAVER	Yarrow, Scotstoun	20-6-80	8-5-82	13-12-84
F 94 BRAVE	Yarrow, Scotstoun	24-5-82	19-11-83	1985
F 95 LONDON	Yarrow, Scotstoun	7-2-83	27-10-84	1986
F 96 SHEFFIELD	Swan Hunter, Wallsend	29-3-84	9-85	7-87
F 97 COVENTRY	Swan Hunter, Wallsend	29-3-84	12-85	11-87

D: 4,200 tons (4,800 fl) **S:** 30 kts (F 94 and later: 28 kts)—18 kts on cruise engines

Dim: 145.0; F 94-97: 146.5 (140.0 pp) × 14.75 × 4.3 hull (6.0 max.)

A: 4/MM 38 Exocet (I × 4)—2/Sea Wolf GWS.25 Mod.3 syst. (VI × 2)—2/40-mm Mk 7 AA (I × 2)—6/324-mm STWS.1 ASW TT (III × 2)—2/Lynx helicopters (Sea Skua ASM, Stingray torpedoes)

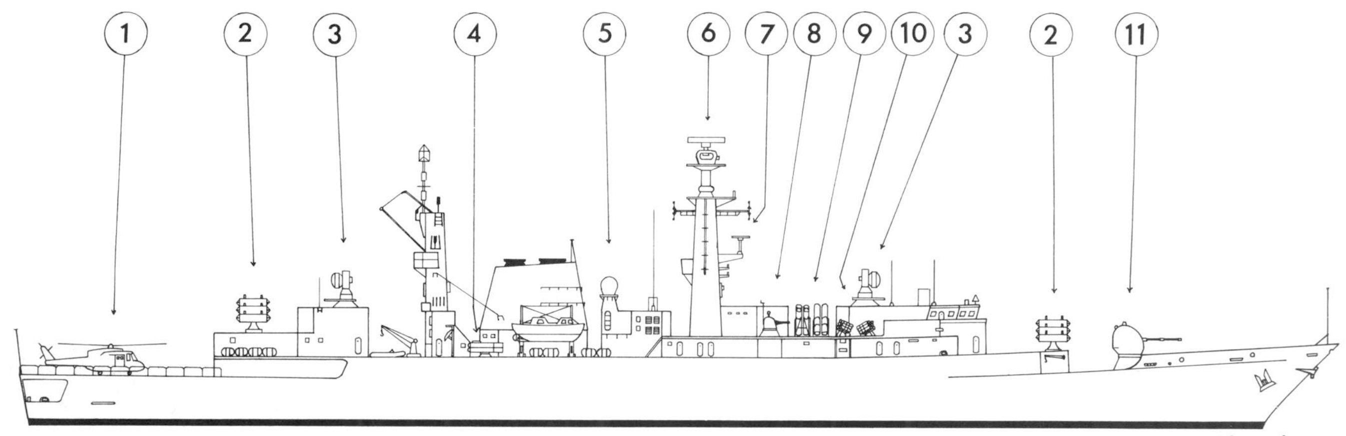

Cornwall (F 99) Type 22 Batch III 1. Lynx helicopter 2. Sea Wolf launchers 3. Type 911 missile f.c. radars 4. triple STWS.1 ASW TT 5. SCOT SHF SATCOMM radomes 6. Type 967/968 radar antenna 7. Type 1006 nav. radar 8. Goalkeeper 30-mm AA should be shown atop deckhouse 9. Harpoon SSM 10. Shield decoy RL 11. 114-mm Vickers Mk 8 DP gun

FRIGATES *(continued)*

Beaver (F 93)—with SCOT radomes aboard Walles Foto, 2-85

Beaver (F 93)—note bullnose for Type 2031(2) towed array to port on fantail L. & L. Van Ginderen, 7-84

Boxer (F 92) M.O.D., 1984

Boxer (F 92) M.O.D., 9-83

FRIGATES *(continued)*

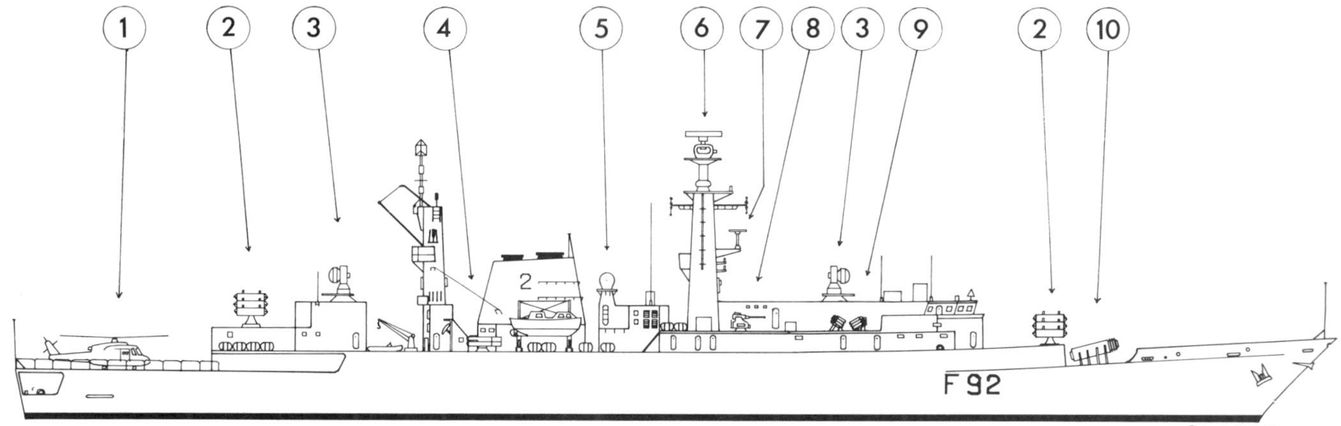

Boxer (F 92) class Batch II Type 22 1. Lynx helicopter 2. Sea Wolf launchers 3. Type 911 radar directors 4. triple STWS.1 ASW TT 5. SCOT SHF SATCOMM radome 6. Type 967/968 radar 7. Type 1006 nav. radar 8. 40-mm AA 9. Shield decoy/chaff RL 10. MM 38 Exocet SSM

Electron Equipt: Radar: 1/1006, 1/967-968, 2/910 (F 94-97: 2/911)
Sonar: Type 2016 hull-mounted, Type 2008, 1/Type 2031(2) towed linear passive array
EW: UA-A1 passive, 2/690 active, Shield decoy RL (VI × 4) chaff RL

M: F 92, F 93: COGOG: 2 Rolls-Royce Olympus TM.3B gas turbines (27,300 hp each), or 2 Rolls-Royce Tyne RM.1C gas turbines (5,340 hp each); 2 Stone Manganese CP props; 54,600 hp max.
F 95–F 97: COGAG: 2 Rolls-Royce Spey SM.1A gas turbines (18,770 hp each), or 2 Rolls-Royce Tyne RM.1C max. gas turbines (5,340 hp each); 2 CP props; 48,220 hp max. (F 94 same plant, but COGOG: 37,540 hp max.)

Range: 7,000/18 **Electric:** 4,000 kw **Fuel:** 600 tons

Man: 290 tot. (berths for 320)

Remarks: "Batch 2" employs a lengthened hull over the *Broadsword* class to improve seaworthiness, endurance, and habitability and to provide space for handling the Type 2031 towed linear passive hydrophone array. F 92 and F 93 ordered 25-4-79, F 94 (with Spey gas turbines substituted for the less-economical Olympus) ordered 27-8-81, F 95 on 23-2-82, and the other two (as Falklands war-loss replacements) on 14-12-82. To have Type 2016 hull-mounted sonar replaced by Type 2050 during first major refit. Names *Bloodhound, Boadicea,* and *Bruiser* originally selected for final three. Two 30-mm Rarden AA will replace the 40-mm AA.

Have CACS.1 data system, with 26 operators and 16 displays. F 94 is first with lightweight Marconi 805-SW (Type 911) missile directors; her hull has greater flare at the stern to permit a larger helicopter deck for the EH.101 helo, producing an overall length of 146.5 m. F 92 commissioned in 1984 for 3 years trials with the CACS.1 data system. Water-displacement fuel tanks are used, and the ships are said to have twice the range of the "Batch I" *Broadsword* class.

◆ **4 Broadsword (Type 22) class ASW frigates** Bldr: Yarrow, Scotstoun

	Ordered	Laid down	L	In serv.
F 88 Broadsword	8-2-74	7-2-75	12-5-76	3-5-79
F 89 Battleaxe	4-9-75	4-2-76	18-5-77	28-3-80
F 90 Brilliant	7-9-76	24-3-77	15-12-78	10-4-81
F 91 Brazen (ex-*Boxer*)	21-10-77	19-8-78	4-3-80	1982

Brazen (F 91)—with 20-mm AA and Mk 36 SRBOC amidships, Lynx on deck
Pradignac & Leo, 1984

Brilliant (F 90) G. Gyssels, 3-85

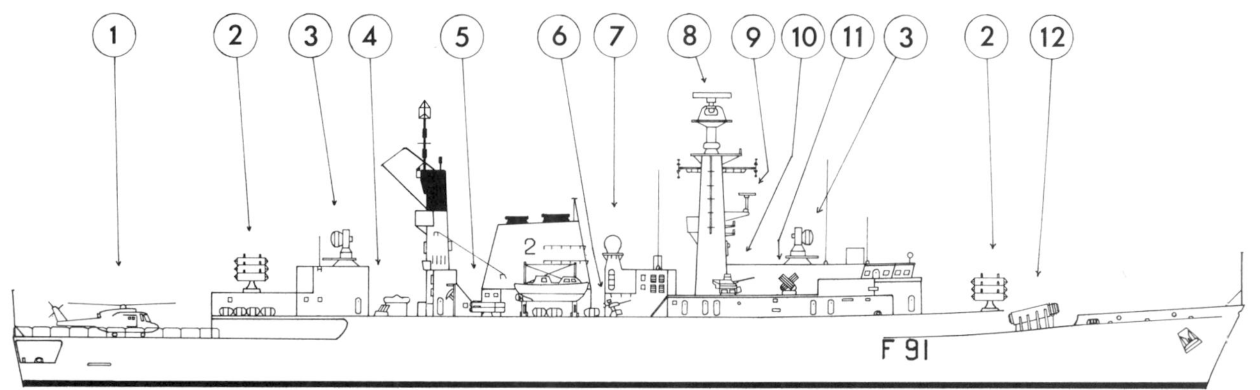

Brazen (F 91)—Type 22 Batch I 1. Lynx helicopter 2. Sea Wolf launchers 3. Type 910 radar/electro-optical directors 4. Mk 137 launchers for Mk 36 SRBOC system 5. triple STWS.1 ASW TT 6. 20-mm GAM-B01 AA 7. SCOT SHF SATCOMM radome 8. Type 967/968 radar 9. Type 1006 nav. radar 10. 40-mm AA 11. Knebworth/Corvus chaff RL 12. MM 38 Exocet launchers

FRIGATES *(continued)*

Battleaxe (F 89)—high stack L. & L. Van Ginderen, 6-84

Broadsword (F 88) J. Goss, 1984

D: 3,500 tons (4,400 fl) **S:** 29 kts (18 cruise)
Dim: 131.2 (125.0 wl) × 14.8 × 4.3 (6.0 sonar)
A: 4/MM 38 Exocet—2/Sea Wolf GWS.25 syst. (VI × 2)—2/40-mm Mk 9 AA (I × 2)—2/20-mm Oerlikon GAM-BO1 AA (I × 2; not always aboard)—6/324-mm STWS.1 ASW TT (III × 2)—1 or 2 Lynx helicopter
Electron Equipt:: Radar: 1/1006, 1/967-968, 2/910 (GWS.25)
Sonar: 1/2008, 1/2016
EW: UA-A1, passive, 2/Type 690 active Mk 36 SRBOC chaff RL (VI × 2), 2 Knebworth/Corvus chaff RL (VIII × 2)
M: COGOG; 2 Olympus TM3B gas turbines, 27,300 hp each for high speed; 2 Tyne RM1A, 4,100 hp each for cruising; 2 CP props; 54,600 hp max.
Electric: 4,000 kw (4 Paxman Ventura diesel sets; 450 v., 3 ph., 60 Hz)
Range: 4,500/18 (on Tyne); 1,200/29 (on Olympus) **Man:** 18 officers, 205 men

Remarks: Originally to have been a class of 26. Type 2016 is a multiple-frequency sonar. The Lynx can carry both ASW and antiship weapons; two were to have been carried, but only one is normally aboard. CAAIS combat data system. The 967-968 radar is a back-to-back array with track-while-scan features. Two U.S. Super RBOC chaff RL added amidships 1982-83. To be backfitted with Sea Wolf GWS.25 Mod. 3 system (Type 911 trackers) beginning in 1988 with F 88, which will also get Type 2050 sonar in place of 2016. F 89–91 have carried 2/20-mm GAM-BO1 AA amidships when on deployment. First two have higher, more elaborate stacks.

◆ **6 Amazon (Type 21) class**

	Bldr	Laid down	L	In serv.
F 169 Amazon	Vosper Thornycroft	6-11-69	26-4-71	11-5-74
F 171 Active	Vosper Thornycroft	23-7-71	23-11-72	17-6-77
F 172 Ambuscade	Yarrow, Scotstoun	1-9-71	18-1-73	5-9-75
F 173 Arrow	Yarrow, Scotstoun	28-9-72	5-2-74	29-7-76
F 174 Alacrity	Yarrow, Scotstoun	5-3-73	18-9-74	2-4-77
F 185 Avenger	Yarrow, Scotstoun	30-10-74	20-11-75	15-4-78

Avenger (F 185) (Type 21)—note ASW TT, Lynx on helo deck L. & L. Van Ginderen, 11-84

Active (F 171)—4/20-mm AA, no ASW TT Maritime Photographic, 2-85

Amazon (F 169)—with Exocet added L. & L. Van Ginderen, 5-85

Alacrity (F 174)—with Exocet, 4/20-mm AA, no ASW TT, SCOT, or UA-A1—note hull reinforcement amidships C. & S. Taylor, 1984

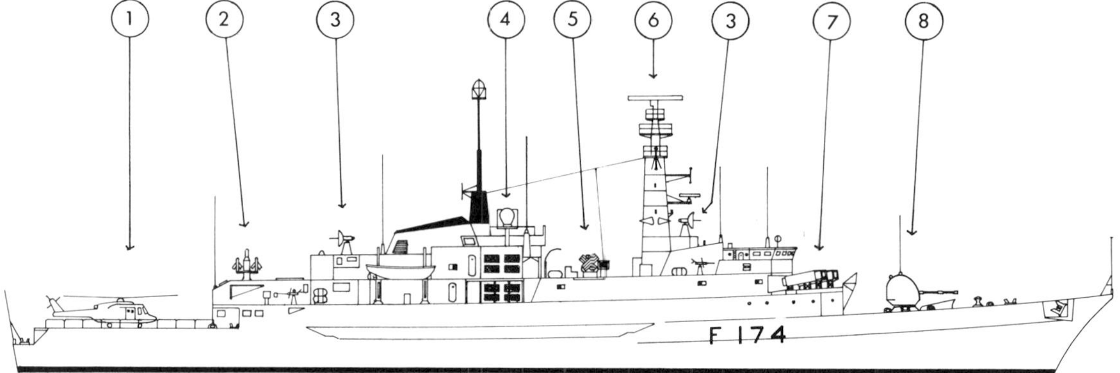

Alacrity (F 174) 1. Lynx helicopter 2. Sea Cat launcher 3. RTN-10x Orion (Type 912) radar f.c. directors 4. SCOT SHF SATCOMM radomes 5. Knebworth/Corvus chaff RL 6. Type 992Q radar 7. MM 38 Exocet launchers 8. 114-mm Vickers Mk 8 DP gun

FRIGATES *(continued)*

Avenger (F 185)—with ASW TT L. & L. Van Ginderen, 7-85

D: 2,850 tons (3,350 fl) **S:** 32 kts **Dim:** 117.04 (109.70 pp) × 12.7 × 4.6 (6.2 over sonar)
A: 4/MM 38 Exocet—1/Sea Cat GWS.24 system (IV × 1)—1/114-mm Mk 8 DP—2 or 4/20-mm Mk 4 AA (I × 2 or 4)—1/Wasp or Lynx helicopter—F 172, 184, 185 only: 6/324-mm STWS.1 ASW TT (III × 2)
Electron Equipt: Radar: 1/1006, 1/992Q, 2/912 (RTN-10X Orion)
Sonar: 1/184M, 1/162M
EW: UA-A1 passive or none, 2 Knebworth/Corvus chaff RL (VIII × 2), FH-12 HF/DF
M: COGOG; 2 Olympus TM.3B gas turbines, 25,000 hp each; 2 Tyne RM.1A gas turbines, 4,250 hp each; 2 CP props; 50,000 hp max.
Electric: 3,000 kw **Range:** 4,500/18; 1,200/30
Man: 13 officers, 164 men

Remarks: Designed jointly by Vosper Thornycroft and Yarrow. The ships have been criticized for fragility, vulnerability, and for being overloaded and top-heavy; permanent ballast had to be added, but none can carry the full originally intended weapon and sensor suite. Hulls are being strengthened, due to cracking during the Falklands War; doubler plates added amidships, beginning with F 173, completed 6-83; modifications added 100+ tons to displacement. All are based at Devonport, with F 185 as flagship. F 169, 172 did not receive Exocet until 1984-85. Ships without ASW TT have 4 single 20-mm AA.

Remote control of engine room from the bridge. Supplies on board for 60 days. Ferranti WSA 4 digital system used in fire control, employing two Selenia RTN-10X radar directors (Type 912) for both Sea Cat and the 114-mm gun; there is also a backup optical director for each. The CAAIS combat data system is a separate entity, whose data are automatically transmitted to WSA 4; both use a single FM-1600B computer. The Exocet launchers are paired, toed-in, and forward of the bridge. All can carry two SCOT radomes for the Skynet SHF communications satellite system. Four 750-kw diesel generator sets supply the 450-volt, 3-phase, 60-Hz electrical current. Type 992Q radar to be replaced by Type 996. A separate Cossor Type 1010 IFF interrogator is mounted below the Type 992Q.

Ardent (F 184) of this class was lost to multiple bomb and rocket hits 21-5-82, and *Antelope* (F 170) sank 24-5-82 after an unexploded bomb detonated, causing uncontrolled fires and eventual magazine explosions.

◆ 23 Leander class

Note: For convenience in describing the numerous appearances and functional variations in this class, they have been divided into six separate listings, in general order of construction and conversion:

◆ (a) 5 Sea Wolf antiaircraft missile conversions

	Bldr	Laid down	L	In serv.	Conv.
F 57 Andromeda	HMDY/Portsmouth	25-5-66	24-5-67	2-12-68	4-81
F 58 Hermione	Stephen/Yarrow	6-12-65	26-4-67	11-7-69	21-6-83
F 60 Jupiter	Yarrow, Scotstoun	3-10-66	4-9-67	9-8-69	21-10-83
F 71 Scylla	HMDY, Devonport	17-5-67	8-8-68	12-2-70	7-12-84
F 75 Charybdis	Harland & Wolff	27-1-67	28-2-68	2-6-69	6-8-82

Charybdis (F 75) M.O.D., 3-84

Hermione (F 58)—deckhouse on helo deck, SCOT installed, 20-mm aft L. & L. Van Ginderen, 2-85

Scylla (F 71) L. & L. Van Ginderen, 5-85

Jupiter (F 60) L. & L. Van Ginderen, 5-84

D: 2,640 tons (3,100 fl) **S:** 27 kts
Dim: 113,38 (109.73) × 13.12 × 4.60 (5.60 prop)
A: 4/MM 38 Exocet SSM (I × 4)—1/Sea Cat GWS.25 syst. (VI × 1)—2 or 3/20-mm AA (I × 2 or 3)—6/324-mm STWS.1 ASW TT (III × 2)—1/Lynx helicopter (Sea Skua ASM, Stingray torpedoes)
Electron Equipt: Radar: 1/1006, 1/967-968, 1/910
Sonar: Type 2016, Type 2008, Type 162M
EW: UA-A1 passive, 2/Type 690 jammer, 2/Knebworth/Corvus chaff RL (VIII × 2)
M: 2 sets White-English Electric GT, 2/5-bladed props; 30,000 hp
Boilers: 2 Babcock & Wilcox 3-drum; 38.7 kg/cm², 450°C
Fuel: 500 tons **Electric:** 2,500 kw **Range:** approx. 4,500/12
Man: 19 officers, 241 men

Remarks: F 58 launched by Alex Stephens, completed by Yarrow. Conversions from "Broad-beam *Leanders*" to improve warfare capabilities in all areas. Five sisters *not* converted, for economy reasons (see below). Sea Wolf, manually loaded launcher and 4 Exocet and twin 144-mm gunmount, hangar enlarged to take Lynx, sonar replaced. Limbo mortar and Type 965 radar deleted, Type 967-968 radar stepped atop new foremast, and Type 910 Sea Wolf director placed atop bridge. All have 2 Mk 4 20-mm mounts; F 58 and F 75 have a GAM-BO1, 20-mm mount to starboard at the stern. F 58 tested Thorn EMI Guardian (Type 675) jammer in 1975.

◆ (b) 4 unmodified "Broad-beamed *Leander*" general-purpose

	Bldr	Laid down	L	In serv.
F 12 Achilles	Yarrow, Scotstoun	1-12-67	21-11-68	9-7-70
F 16 Diomede	Yarrow, Scotstoun	30-1-68	15-4-69	2-4-71
F 70 Apollo	Yarrow, Scotstoun	1-5-69	15-10-70	28-5-72
F 72 Ariadne	Yarrow, Scotstoun	1-11-69	10-9-71	10-2-73

D: 2,660 tons (3,120 fl) **S:** 27 kts
Dim: 113.38 (109.73 pp) × 13.12 × 4.50 (5.49 props)
A: 2/114-mm Mk 6 DP (II × 1)—1/Sea Cat GWS.22 syst. (IV × 1)—3 or 4/20-mm AA (I × 3; F 16: II × 1, I × 2)—1/Limbo Mk 10 ASW mortar (III × 1)—1/Wasp helicopter (AS.12 ASM, Mk 44/46 torpedoes)
Electron Equipt: Radar: 1/978 or 1006, 1/993, 1/965, 1/903, 1/904
Sonar: Type 184, Type 170B, Type 162
EW: UA-8/9 passive, Type 668 or 669 active, 2/Knebworth/Corvus chaff RL (VIII × 2)—F 70, 72 also: UA-13 passive, others: FH-12 HFD/F

FRIGATES *(continued)*

Ariadne (F 72)—with UA-13 array at masthead, single 20-mm aft, Wasp on deck
L. & L. Van Ginderen, 11-84

Diomede (F 12)—FH-12 at masthead, 20-mm aft L. & L. Van Ginderen, 7-84

M: 2 sets White-English Electric GT; 2/5-bladed props; 30,000 hp
Boilers: 2 Babcock & Wilcox 3-drum; 38.7 kg/cm², 450°C
Electric: 2,500 kw **Fuel:** 500 tons **Range:** Approx. 4,500/12
Man: 19 officers, 241 men

Remarks: The newest of the Royal Navy's *Leanders,* conversion of these ships to "Sea Wolf *Leander*" configuration was canceled for reasons of economy. A fifth unmodified "Broad-beam *Leander,*" *Bacchante* (F 69), was sold to New Zealand 4-10-82. A single Oerlikon GAM-801 20-mm AA gun was mounted on the starboard side of the stern in 1982-83 in F 12, 70, and 72; F 16 received a twin 20-mm mount. F 12 entered major refit 4-6-84, F 70 on 30-7-84, and F 72 early in 1985; all are now to be retained to at least 1989. Type 994 radar may replace the Type 965 array.

◆ **(c) 4 "Exocet Leander" Batch 2TA conversions with towed arrays**

	Bldr	Laid down	L	In serv.	Conv.
F 28 Cleopatra	HMDY, Devonport	19-6-63	25-3-64	4-1-66	11-75
F 40 Sirius	HMDY, Portsmouth	9-8-63	22-9-64	15-6-66	10-77
F 42 Phoebe	Alex Stephens & Sons	3-6-63	8-7-64	15-4-66	4-77
F 56 Argonaut	Hawthorne Leslie	27-11-64	8-2-66	17-8-67	10-78

Cleopatra (F 28)—towed array without sponson, UA-13 at masthead, SCOT radomes aboard L. & L. Van Ginderen, 8-84

Sirius (F 40) G. Arra, 1984

Argonaut (F 56)—towed array sponson, FH-12 at masthead, Lynx on deck
L. & L. Van Ginderen, 12-84

D: 2,750 tons (3,300 fl) **S:** 28 kts
Dim: 113.38 (109.73 pp) × 12.50 × 5.00 (6.40 props)
A: 4/MM 38 Exocet (I × 4)—2 Sea Cat GSW.22 syst. (IV × 2—only one director)—2/20-mm Mk 4 AA (I × 2)—6/324-mm STWS.1 ASW TT (III × 2)—1/Lynx helicopter (Sea Skua ASM, Stingray torpedoes)
Electron Equipt: Radar: 1/1006, 1/993, 1/904
Sonar: Type 184M, Type 162M, Type 2031 (1) towed passive linear array
EW: UA-8/9 passive, Type 668 or 669 active, 2/Knebworth/ Corvus chaff RL (VIII × 2), also: F 28, 42: UA-13; F 40, 56: FH-12 HFD/F
M: 2 sets White-English Electric GT; 2/5-bladed props; 30,000 hp
Boilers: 2 Babcock & Wilcox 3-drum; 38.7 kg/cm², 450°C
Electric: 1,900 kw **Fuel:** 460 tons **Range:** approx. 4,000/12
Man: 20 officers, 203 men

Remarks: Original conversion completion dates in table. These four ships are Typed "Exocet *Leander* Group 2A" and have been further modified from "Exocet *Leander*" configuration by the deletion of the forward Sea Cat launcher and director, the lowering of the Exocet installation to the main deck level, the substitution of 20-mm Mk 4 AA for the 40-mm AA, the removal of the Type 965 early-warning radar (replaced by a Cossor Type 1010 IFF interrogator), and the addition o the Type 2031 (1) towed passive linear hydrophone array on the starboard quarter. F 42, completing first in 7-82, mounted 4/20-mm AA while awaiting the Type 2031 equipment; one AA gun was placed atop the former forward director platform and the other on the starboard quarter. F 28, completing reconversion in 1983, had the Type 2031, SCOT SHF SATCOMM antennas, and only 2/20-mm AA, F 56, damaged in the Falklands War, replaced *Minerva* (F 45) in the towed array conversion program, recommissioning 1984. On all but F 28, the Type 2031 (1) reel/winch is on a sponson projecting to starboard and astern, adding about 1 meter to the overall length.

◆ **(d) 3 "Exocet Leander" Batch 2B conversions**

	Bldr	Laid down	L	In serv.	Conv.
F 45 Minerva	Vickers, Armstrong	25-7-63	19-12-64	14-5-66	9-79
F 47 Danae	HMDY, Devonport	16-12-64	31-10-65	7-9-67	9-80
F 127 Penelope (ex-*Coventry*)	Vickers-Armstrong	14-3-61	17-8-62	31-10-63	1-82

Minerva (F 45) L. & L. Van Ginderen, 5-85

FRIGATES *(continued)*

Penelope (F 127) L. & L. Van Ginderen, 2-84

D: 2,650 tons (3,200 fl) **S:** 28 kts **Dim:** 113.38 (109.73 pp) × 12.50 × 4.80 (6.20 props)
A: 4/MM 38 Exocet SSM (I × 4)—3/Sea Cat GWS.22B syst. (IV × 3—2 directors)—2/40-mm AA (I × 2)—1/20-mm AA—6/324-mm STWS.1 ASW TT (III × 2)—1/Lynx helicopter (Sea Skua ASM, Stingray torpedoes)
Electron Equipt: Radar: 1/1006, 1/993, 1/965, 2/904
Sonar: Type 184M, Type 162M
EW: UA-8/9 passive, Type 668 or 669 jammer, 2/Knebworth/Corvus chaff RL (VIII × 2), Mk 36 SRBOC (VI × 2), FH-12 HFD/F
M: and Boilers: as in "Exocet Leander" Batch 2A
Electric: 1,900 kw **Fuel:** 460 tons **Range:** Approx. 4,000/12
Man: 20 officers, 203 men

Remarks: Converted from standard *Leander* configuration, except for F 127, which reconverted from Sea Wolf trials ship, recommissioning 22-1-82. Sea Cat launcher and 4 Exocet replaced twin 114-mm gun forward, single Sea Cat launcher augmented by a second launcher atop enlarged hangar, Limbo ASW mortar replaced by 2 sets ASW TT. Will not be further altered, as in Batch 2A above. F 47 has a twin 20-mm aft and 2/20-mm GAM-B01 amidships; F 127 substitutes a third GAM-B01 aft. All may receive Type 994 radar in place of Type 965. Have CAAIS combat data system. F 45 is, technically speaking, a "Batch 2A" conversion unit.

◆ **(e) 6 "Ikara Leander" conversions**

	Bldr	Laid down	L	In serv.	Conv.
F 10 Aurora	John Brown	1-6-61	28-11-62	9-4-64	3-76
F 15 Euryalus	Scotts SB&E	2-11-61	6-6-63	16-9-64	3-76
F 18 Galatea	Swan Hunter	29-12-61	23-5-63	25-4-64	9-74
F 38 Arethusa	J. Samuel White	7-9-62	5-11-63	24-11-65	4-77
F 39 Naiad	Yarrow, Scotstoun	30-10-62	4-11-63	15-3-65	7-75
F 109 Leander (ex-*Weymouth*)	Harland & Wolff	10-4-59	28-6-61	27-3-63	12-72

Arethusa (F 38)—Wasp helo on deck, SCOT radomes aboard
L. & L. Van Ginderen, 7-84

Leander (F 109) L. & L. Van Ginderen, 12-84

Euryalus (F 15)—Ikara on launcher Royal Navy, 1982

D: 2,610 tons (3,020 fl) **S:** 27 kts **Dim:** 113.38(109.73 pp) × 12.50 × 4.60 (5.70 props)
A: 2/Sea Cat GWS.22B syst. (IV × 2, 1 director)—2/40-mm AA (I × 2)—F 10, F 18: 1/20-mm AA—1/Ikara GWS.40 syst. (I × 1)—1/Limbo Mk 10 ASW mortar (III × 1)—1/Wasp helicopter (AS.12 ASM, Mk 44/46 torpedoes)
Electron Equipt: Radar: 1/1006, 1/994, 1/904, 1/Ikara tracker
Sonar: Type 170B, Type 184M, Type 162M
EW: UA-8/9 passive, Type 668/669 jammers, 2/Knebworth/Corvus chaff RL (VIII × 2)
M: 2 sets White-English Electric GT; 2/5-bladed props; 30,000 hp
Boilers: 2 Babcock & Wilcox 3-drum, 38.7 kg/cm², 450°C
Electric: 2,000 kw **Fuel:** 460 tons **Range:** approx. 4,500/12
Man: 19 officers, 238 men

Remarks: Conversions from standard *Leanders,* with the Australian ASW torpedo-carrying Ikara antisubmarine cruise-missile system replacing the twin 114-mm gun-mount, the number of Sea Cat launchers doubled, and the Type 965 radar removed (necessitating the installation of a Type 1010 IFF interrogation antenna atop the after pylon mast). Fitted for 2 SCOT antennas for the Skynet SHF SATCOMM system on platforms on the foremast. Two ships to date have had a 20-mm AA added on the starboard quarter. Retention of Limbo limits flight deck to Wasp helicopter. Sister *Dido* (F 104) sold to New Zealand, transferring 18-7-83. The *Ajax* (F 114) was stricken 31-5-85; the ship is to be used as a Harbour Training hulk at Plymouth. Have ADAWS 5 data system and LINK 10 data link. Type 994 radar (Plessey ASW.4 with Type 993's antenna retained) has replaced Type 993 in the survivors, and Type 199 VDS has been removed.

◆ **(f) 1 unmodified** ***Leander***

	Bldr	Laid down	L	In serv.
F 52 Juno	Thornycroft, Woolston	16-7-74	24-11-65	18-7-67

Juno (F 52) L. & L. Van Ginderen, 4-85

D: 2,400 tons (2,800 fl) **S:** 28 kts **Dim:** 113.38 (109.73 pp) × 12.50 × 4.40 (5.4 props)
A: 2/20-mm Mk 4 AA (I × 2)—6/324-mm STWS.1 ASW TT (III × 2)—1/Wasp helicopter
Electron Equipt: Radar: 1/1006, 1/994
Sonar: Type 184M, Type 162
EW: . . . passive, 2/Knebworth/Corvus chaff RL (VIII × 2)
M: and Boilers: as for "Ikara *Leander*" class
Electric: 1,600 kw **Fuel:** 460 tons **Range:** approx. 4,500/12
Man: 17 officers, 245 men

Remarks: *Juno* was the last unmodified early *Leander.* She entered refit 9-81 at Rosyth for conversion as a navigational training ship to replace *Torquay* in 3-84. Economics forced delay of the plan, and the ship was given a regular overhaul ending in 10-82 and placed in ready reserve; in 1984-85 the work was completed: the 114-mm mount, Limbo mortar, and Sea Cat systems removed, Type 965 radar and most EW equipment deleted; ASW TT, new navigational gear, and Type 1010 IFF interrogation added.

General Remarks: (Leander class): The design is an improvement on the *Rothesay* class, of which *Dido* (F 104), F 109, F 114, and F 127 were originally to have been members. Have twin rudders and one pair of fin stabilizers, set well aft of amidships. The "Broad-beamed *Leanders*" incorporated engineering plant improvements and

FRIGATES *(continued)*

were the first to be fitted with Sea Cat missiles on completion, earlier ships having had 2/40-mm AA (I × 2). All were intended to carry Type 199 variable-depth sonars, but these were never installed in many of the class.

NOTE: The three "Tribal"-class frigates recommissioned in 1982 for the Falklands conflict have been stricken and sold to Indonesia; *Gurkha* (F 122) and *Zulu* (F 124) decommissioned 30-3-84, and *Tartar* (F 133) on 29-3-84.

◆ **2 Rothesay class (Type 12)**

	Bldr	Laid down	L	In serv.
F 101 YARMOUTH	John Brown	29-11-57	23-3-59	26-3-60
F 107 ROTHESAY	Yarrow, Scotstoun	6-11-56	9-12-57	23-4-60

Yarmouth (F 101) Maritime Photographic, 8-85

Rothesay (F 107) L. & L. Van Ginderen, 7-85

D: 2,380 tons (2,800 fl) **S:** 26 kts
Dim: 112.78 (109.73 pp) × 12.5 × 4.50 (5.30 sonar)
A: 2/114-mm Mk 6 DP (II × 1)—2/20-mm AA (I × 2)—1/Sea Cat GWS.20 system (IV × 1)—1/Mk 10 Limbo ASW mortar (III × 1)—1/Wasp helicopter (AS.12 ASM, Mk 44/46 torpedoes)
Electron Equipt: Radar: 1/1006, 1/993, 1/903
Sonar: 1/174, 1/170B, 1/162M
EW: FH-5 HFD/F 2/Knebworth/Corvus chaff RL (VIII × 2)
M: 2 sets English Electric GT; 2 props; 30,000 hp
Electric: 1,460 kw **Boilers:** 2 Babcock & Wilcox, 38.7 kg/cm², 450°C
Fuel: 400 tons **Range:** 4,500/12
Man: 155 officers, 220 men

REMARKS: Improved version of the *Whitby* class. Original nine ships all modernized 1966-72 with Sea Cat GWS.20 system (no radar) and helicopter facility in place of one Limbo ASW mortar. MRS.3 fire-control system replaced the original Mk 6 director, and new electronics and air-conditioning were installed.

F 107 completed refit 11-84 to extend service to 1988. F 101 likely to strike 1986-87. Of seven sisters, *Brighton* (F 106) was stricken 1-81. *Falmouth* (F 113), in reserve 7-80 and stricken 12-81, was recommissioned 23-4-82 for Falklands service and was decommissioned 27-11-84 for harbor training service. *Rhyl* (F 129), on Sales List since 2-82, recommissioned 18-6-82 and was stricken 2-85. *Lowestoft* (F 103), used for trials with towed passive linear hydrophone arrays since 1978, first with DA-5 and later with Type 2031, paid off for disposal 29-3-85. *Londonderry* (F 108), a disarmed and electronics trials ship since recommissioning from conversion 11-10-79, was paid off 29-3-84 for use by HMS *Sultan* as a training hulk. *Plymouth* (F 126) was due for disposal by end-1985, and *Berwick* (F 115), placed in reserve 1-81, stricken 12-81, recommissioned 5-8-82, was stricken 17-10-85.

NOTE: The last *Whitby*-class frigate, *Torquay* (F 43), was replaced as cadet navigational and tactical training ship by *Juno* (F 52) and paid off 31-3-85.

CORVETTES

NOTE: Plans to acquire an OPV 3 (Offshore Patrol Vessel, Mk 3) design were placed in abeyance 6-85, although design work will continue. The Royal Navy may instead lease a vessel (or airship) to perform this function.

◆ **5 Peacock class** Bldr: Hall Russell, Aberdeen

	Laid down	L	In serv
P 239 PEACOCK	29-1-82	1-12-82	12-10-83
P 240 PLOVER	13-5-82	12-4-83	20-7-84
P 241 STARLING	9-9-82	7-9-83	10-8-84
P 242 SWALLOW	24-4-83	30-3-84	16-11-84
P 243 SWIFT	23-9-83	11-9-84	3-5-85

Swallow (P 242) L. & L. Van Ginderen, 11-84

Swift (P 243)—on trials Walles Foto, 3-85

D: 662 tons (fl) **S:** over 28 kts (trials)
Dim: 62.60 (60.00 pp) × 10.00 × 2.72
A: 1/76-mm OTO Melara Compact DP—4/7.62-mm mg (I × 4)
Electron Equipt: Radar: 1/1006
M: 2 APE-Crossley SEMT-Pielstick 18PA6V280 diesels; 2/3-bladed props; 14,188 hp—1/Schöttel S103 LSVEST drop-down, shrouded loiter prop; 181 hp
Range: 2,500/. . . **Fuel:** 44 tons **Electric:** 755 kw
Man: 4 officers, 6 chief petty officers, 21 men

REMARKS: Replaced the five "Ton"-class former minesweepers used for patrol duties at Hong Kong, whose government has paid 75 percent of the construction costs. Carry two Avon Sea Raider 5.4-m, 30-kt, 10-man semi-rigid rubber inspection dinghies. Some 450 rds. 76-mm ammunitions can be carried, with the gun controlled by a GSA7 Sea Archer Mk 1 electro-optical director. The auxiliary drive employs a Schöttel retractable, steerable shrouded thruster. Accommodations for 44 total. Have 2/50-mm rocket flare projectors. Maximum sustained speed: 25 kts. Two rudders. Reported to be bad rollers, with deeper bilge keels having had to be mounted. Propulsion problems occurred with P 139.

◆ **2 "Castle"-class offshore patrol vessels** Bldr: Hall Russell, Aberdeen

	Laid down	L	In serv.
P 258 LEEDS CASTLE	18-10-79	22-10-80	12-81
P 265 DUMBARTON CASTLE	25-6-80	3-6-81	12-3-82

D: 1,250 tons (1,450 fl) **S:** 20 kts **Dim:** 81.0 (75.0 pp) × 11.5 × 3.42
A: 1/40-mm AA—2/7.62-mm mg (I × 2)—mines—helicopter platform
Electron Equipt: Radar: 1/1006
M: 2 Ruston 12 RK 320DM diesels; 2 CP props; 5,640 hp (4,380 sust.)
Electric: 890 kw **Fuel:** 380 tons **Range:** 10,000/12
Man: 7 officers, 43 men (plus 25 Marine detachment as required)

REMARKS: Ordered 8-8-80, *after* both had been laid down. P 265 operated at over 2,000 tons displacement during the Falklands War. Carry acoustic and mechanical minesweeping gear as well as being able to lay mines. The helicopter deck is large enough to accommodate either Lynx or Sea King helicopter. Carry two 50-mm rocket flare launchers. Can carry 19.5 tons helicopter fuel and 30 tons of oil-spill dispersant detergent. Have Decca CANE-2 (Computer-Assisted Navigation Equipt.) NAVSAT, and Omega systems. Two Avon "Sea Raider" rubber rescue/inspection dinghies car-

CORVETTES *(continued)*

Leeds Castle (P 258)—MARISAT SATCOMM antenna fitted, inspection boat at the ready Skyfotos, 10-83

Dumbarton Castle (P 265) L. & L. Van Ginderen, 3-84

ried. Have one fire monitor and two oil-dispersing spray booms. Intended for 21-day patrols. P 258, equipped with MARISAT, conducted minelaying trials in mid-1983. P 258's 40-mm gun relocated to improve firing arcs, 1985.

◆ **7 Isles-class offshore patrol vessels** Bldr: Hall Russell, Aberdeen

	L	In serv.		L	In serv.
P 277 ANGLESEY	18-10-78	1-6-79	P 298 SHETLAND	22-11-76	14-7-77
P 278 ALDERNEY	27-2-79	6-10-79	P 299 ORKNEY	29-6-76	25-2-77
P 295 JERSEY	18-3-76	15-10-76	P 300 LINDISFARNE	1-6-77	26-1-78
P 297 GUERNSEY	17-2-77	28-10-77			

Jersey (P 295) L. & L. Van Ginderen, 2-85

Alderney (P 278) G. Gyssels, 3-84

D: 1,000 tons (1,280 fl) **S:** 16.5 kts **Dim:** 61.10 (51.97 pp) × 11.00 × 4.27
A: 1/40-mm AA Mk 3—2/7.62-mm mg (I × 2)
Electron Equipt: Radar: 1/1006—Sonar: 1/Simrad SU "Sidescan"
M: 2 Ruston 12 RK 3 CM diesels (750 rpm); 1/CP prop; 4,380 hp
Electric: 536 kw **Fuel:** 310 tons **Range:** 11,000/12
Man: 5 officers, 29 men (plus Marine detachment)

REMARKS: Near duplicates of the Scottish Department of Fisheries ships *Jura* and *Westra. Jura* (as P 296) was loaned to the Royal Navy from 1975 to 1-77 for use in patrolling offshore oil rigs and the 200-nautical-mile economic zone, the purpose for which the "Isles" class were built. First five ordered 11-2-75, other pair 21-10-77. P 277 and P 278 had fin stabilizers on completion, back-fitted in the others. Can maintain 12–15 kts in a Force 8 gale. Have Decca CANES-2 Navaid. Avon Sea Raider semi-rigid dinghies are replacing the original Geminies for inspection purposes. Carry 28.6 tons detergent (a 6-hr. supply) for oil-spill cleanup.

◆ **1 Falkland Islands support ship, former oilfield supply tug**

	Bldr	L	In serv.
P 246 SENTINEL (ex-*Seaforth Warrior,* ex-*Edda Sun*)	Husumer SY, Husumer, W. Germany	1975	27-6-75 (14-1-84 RN)

Sentinel (P 246) leaving for Falklands L. & L. Van Ginderen, 2-84

D: 1,100 tons (fl) **S:** 14 kts **Dim:** 60.50 (52.80 pp) × 13.00 × 4.50
A: 2/40-mm Mk 9 AA (I × 2)—3/7.62-mm mg (I × 3)
Electron Equipt: Radar: 2/Krupp-Atlas nav.
M: 2 MaK 12M453 A4 diesels; 2 Kort-nozzle CP props; 7,760 hp
Electric: 692 kVA **Man:** 26 tot.

REMARKS: 934 grt/733 dwt tug purchased 3-83 for service as patrol ship, supply ship, and moorings tender for duty in the Falkland Islands. Two Becker flapped rudders, 500-hp bow-thruster, 150-ton towing winch, 87-ton bollard pull. Two 50-mm rocket flare projectors, enhanced communications suite and two SeaRaider semi-rigid boats with electrohydraulic derrick added.

◆ **2 Falkland Islands support ships, former oilfield supply tugs**

	Bldr	L	In serv. (RN)
P 244 PROTECTOR (ex-*Seaforth Saga*)	Drypool Eng. & DD, Selby	7-75	22-10-83
P 245 GUARDIAN ex-*Seaforth Champion*)	Beverly SB & Eng., Beverly	1-75	22-10-83

Protector (P 244) C. & S. Taylor, 8-83

CORVETTES *(continued)*

Guardian (P 245) L. & L. Van Ginderen, 9-83

D: 1,000 tons (fl) **S:** 13.5 kts **Dim:** 58.83 × 12.04 × 4.52
A: 2/40-mm Mk 9 AA (I × 2)—3/7.62-mm mg (I × 3)
Electron Equipt: Radar: 1/. . . nav.
M: 2 British Polar U-16 diesels; 2 Kort-nozzle CP props; 6,160 hp
Man: 26 tot.

REMARKS: 802-grt oilfield tugs purchased 3-83 for use in the Falkland Islands and converted by Commercial Dry Dock Enterprises, Cardiff. Crews rotate to U.K. every six months; P 244 acts as flagship. P 246 is 58.48 m overall. Bow-thrusters in both. Two SeaRaider semi-rigid inspection boats, 2/50-mm flare launchers, and an electro-hydraulic derrick added. Can be distinguished from *Sentinel* (P 246) by greater distance between paired stacks and the pilothouse. Have two firefighting water monitors.

NOTE: The five "Ton"-class minesweepers converted as Hong Kong patrol boats have been replaced by the *Peacock* class. *Beachampton* (P 1007) was stricken 1984; *Monkton* (P 1055), *Wasperton* (P 1089), and *Yarnton* (P 1096) were placed on the Sales List 4-85, while *Wolverton* (P 1093) was stricken later in the same year.

PATROL BOATS

◆ **5 Kingfisher class** Bldr: Richard Dunston, Hessle (P 259: Fairmile Const., Berwick-on-Tweed)

	Laid down	L	In serv.
P 259 REDPOLE (ex-RAF *Sea Otter*)	. . .	. . .	1970
P 260 KINGFISHER	7-73	20-9-74	8-10-75
P 261 CYGNET	10-73	26-10-75	8-7-76
P 262 PETEREL	11-73	14-5-76	7-7-77
P 263 SANDPIPER	12-73	20-1-77	16-9-77

Peterel (P 262) L. & L. Van Ginderen, 5-85

D: 187 tons **S:** 25 kts **Dim:** 36.6 (33.8 pp) × 7.0 × 2.0
A: 1/40-mm AA—2/7.62-mm mg (I × 2)
M: 2 Paxman 16 YCJM diesels (1,500 rpm); 2 props; 4,000 hp
Range: 2,000/14 **Man:** 4 officers, 10 men

REMARKS: Unsuccessful design based on RAF *Seal*-class air-sea-rescue craft. P 259 was transferred to the RN 30-10-84 and towed to Brooke Marine, Lowestoft, 2-2-85 for refit, arming, and conversion to naval standard. A large number of additional sisters were canceled. P 262 and P 263 are used for naval officer training at Dartmouth; P 260 and P 261 were employed in patrol work in the North Sea, but have been reassigned as tenders to the mine countermeasures squadron at Rosyth. Have fin stabilizers, but evidently still have stability problems. Only P 260 has hull portholes; P 262 and P 263 have enclosed pilothouses.

PATROL CRAFT

◆ **14 P.2000 class** Bldr: Watercraft, Shoreham-by-Sea

	In serv.		In serv.
A 153 EXAMPLE	18-10-85	P 273 PURSUER	. . .
A 154 EXPLORER	. . .	P 279 BLAZER	. . .
A 163 EXPRESS	. . .	P 280 DASHER	. . .
A 167 EXPLOIT	. . . -86	P 291 PUNCHER	. . .
P 264 ARCHER	9-8-85	P 292 CHARGER	. . .
P 270 BITER	. . .	P 293 RANGER	. . .
P 272 SMITER	. . .	P 294 TRUMPETER	. . .

Example (A 153)—RNXS unit Maritime Photographic, 10-85

D: 38 tons (1/2 load) **S:** 33 kts **Dim:** 20.80 (18.00 pp) × 5.80 × 1.52
A: 1/20-mm AA (fitted for) **Electron Equipt:** Radar: 1/. . . nav.
M: 2 CV12 M800 T diesels; 2 props; 1,640 hp
Range: 620/. . . **Man:** 11 tot.

REMARKS: Glass-reinforced plastic craft ordered 7-84, primarily for peacetime training: 6 are for Royal Navy Reserve training, 4 for the Universities of Glasgow, Liverpool, Southampton, and Aberdeen, and the last 4 with "A" pendants for the Royal Naval Auxiliary Service.

◆ **5 Tracker Mk, Mk I and II class** Bldr: Fairey Allday Marine, Cowes and Hamble

	In serv.		In serv.
P 281 ATTACKER	11-3-83	P 284 HUNTER	21-3-83
P 282 CHASER	11-3-83	P 285 STRIKER	7-83
P 283 FENCER	21-3-83		

Hunter (P 284) L. & L. Van Ginderen, 8-84

D: 31 tons (34.5 fl) **S:** 21 kts **Dim:** 20.0 (19.3 pp) × 5.18 × 1.45
A: 1/20-mm AA (fitted for) **Electron Equipt:** Radar: 1/Decca 150
M: 2/G.M. 12V71 TI diesels; 2 props; 1,300 hp **Range:** 650/20
Man: 3 officers, 2 petty officers, 6 men **Electric:** 30 kw

REMARKS: Glass-reinforced plastic craft procured primarily for reserve training duties, with a wartime local patrol function. P 281 operates from HMS *Graham* for the Clyde Division, RNR: P 282 operates for the Tay Div., RNR; P 283 operates from HMS *President* for the London Div., RNR; and P 284 operates from HMS *Solent* for the London Div., RNR. P 281, built at Cowes, is a Tracker Mk I with an open lattice mast; the others, built at Hamble, have "solid" masts. Speed with engine governors lifted: 24 kts.

◆ **2 "Loyal" class** Bldr: Richard Dunston, Thorne

	In serv.
P 252 ALERT (ex-*Loyal Governor,* A 510)	1975
P 254 VIGILANT (ex-*Loyal Factor,* A 382)	1974

REMARKS: For data, see under "Loyal"-class general-purpose tenders. Operate with RN crews patrolling local waters off Ulster.

NOTE: Ex-RAF patrol boats *Sunderland* and *Stirling* acquired 8-85 for duties at Gibraltar as *Hart* (P 257) and *Cormorant* (P 256); see page 221, *Spitfire* class, for details.

MINE WARFARE SHIPS

◆ 0 (+1 + 19) "Single-Role Minehunter" (SRMH) design

	Bldr	Laid down	L	In serv.
M 132 SANDOWN	Vosper Thornycroft, Portchester	. . .	. . .	. . .

Single-Role Minehunter—artist's impression Vosper Thornycroft, 1984

D: 450 tons (fl) **S:** 15 kts **Dim:** 50.0 × 9.5 (9.0 waterline) × 2.1
A: 1/30-mm Rarden L530B AA
Electron Equipt: Radar: 1/1007—Sonar: 1/2093
M: 2 Paxman Valenta 6RP 200E diesels; 2 Voith-Schneider vertical cycloidal props; 3,000 hp—2 bow-thrusters
Electric: . . . kw (3 diesel sets) **Man:** 7 officers, 33 men
Range: . . . / . . .

REMARKS: First unit ordered 28-8-85 for a design contracted to Vosper in 1983. Glass-reinforced plastic construction. Will use electric drive for low-speed, quiet operation. Plessey's Type 2093 sonar uses a variable-depth vertical lozenge-shaped towed body lowered beneath the hull; it has search, height-finder, classification, and route survey modes. The ships will carry two Remote-Controlled Mine Disposal System Mk 2 (improved PAP 104) submersibles for identification and disposal and will carry a mine clearance diver team. Capable of dealing with mines to 200-m depths. Will replace "Ton"-class minehunters.

◆ 7 (+5) "River"-class "Extra Deep Armed Team Sweeps" (MSM/EDATS) Bldr: Richards (Shipbuilders) Ltd.; Lowestoft (L) or Great Yarmouth (G)

	Bldr.	Laid down	L	In serv.	Station
M 2003 WAVENEY (ex-*Amethyst*)	L	31-10-83	8-9-83	29-9-84	S. Wales
M 2004 CARRON	G	21-2-83	23-9-83	29-9-84	Severn
M 2005 DOVEY	G	3-3-83	1-12-83	30-3-85	Clyde
M 2006 HELFORD	G	12-10-83	16-5-84	-85	Ulster
M 2007 HUMBER	G	21-10-83	17-5-84	7-6-85	London
M 2008 BLACKWATER	G	16-1-84	29-8-84	17-6-85	RN
M 2009 ITCHEN	L	26-3-84	16-11-84	12-10-85	Solent
M 2010 HELMSDALE	L	21-5-84	11-1-85	-86	Tay
M 2011 ORWELL	G	4-6-84	7-2-85	-86	Tyne
M 2012 RIBBLE	G	17-9-84	7-5-85	-86	Mersey
M 2013 SPEY	L	12-11-84	22-5-85	-86	Forth
M 2014 ARUN	L	-85	20-8-85	-86	Sussex

Humber (M 2007) L. & L. Van Ginderen, 4-85

Dovey (M 2005) Walles Foto, 2-85

Waveney (M 2003) C. & S. Taylor, 1984

D: 770 tons (fl) **S:** 14 kts (15 on trials)
Dim: 47.60 (42.00 pp) × 10.50 × 3.10 (3.75 max.)
A: 1/40-mm Mk 3 AA—2/7.62-mm mg (I × 2)
M: 2 Ruston 6 RKCM diesels; 2 4-bladed CP props; 3,040 hp
Range: 4,500/10 **Fuel:** 88 tons **Electric:** 460 kw
Man: 7 officers, 7 petty officers, 16 men

REMARKS: 638 grt. First four ordered 27-9-83, next six in 5-83, and last two on 25-2-84, to form the 10 Mine Countermeasures Squadron. Built to commercial standards, following the design of a North Sea oilfield supply vessel. Single-compartment damage standard. Intended to work in pairs, operating the BAJ-Vickers Wire Sweep Mk 9 Team Sweep System, essentially a wire catenary stretched between the ships. Navigation gear includes 2 Kelvin Hughes MS 48 echo-sounders, Decca QM 14 (1), Decca Hifix Mk 6, and a satellite navigation receiver. All manned by Royal Naval Reserve personnel, except M 2007, used by RN for training. Announced 1985 that 12 more may be built.

◆ 9 (+4 + 2) "Hunt"-class minehunters

	Bldr	Laid down	L	In serv.
M 29 BRECON	Vosper Thornycroft	15-9-75	21-6-78	21-3-80
M 30 LEDBURY	Vosper Thornycroft	5-10-77	5-12-79	11-6-81
M 31 CATTISTOCK	Vosper Thornycroft	20-6-79	22-1-81	16-6-82
M 32 COTTESMORE	Yarrow, Scotstoun	27-9-79	9-2-82	24-6-83
M 33 BROCKLESBY	Vosper Thornycroft	8-5-80	12-1-82	3-2-83
M 34 MIDDLETON	Yarrow, Scotstoun	1-7-80	27-4-83	15-8-84
M 35 DULVERTON	Vosper Thornycroft	1-6-81	3-11-82	4-11-83
M 36 ATHERSTONE	Vosper Thornycroft	2-1-85	. . .	1986
M 37 CHIDDINGFOLD	Vosper Thornycroft	. . .	6-10-83	26-10-84
M 38 BICESTER	Vosper Thornycroft	9-1-84	4-6-85	1987
M 39 HURWORTH	Vosper Thornycroft	1-83	25-9-84	19-7-85
M 40 N.	Vosper Thornycroft	. . .	. . .	1988
M 41 N.	Vosper Thornycroft	. . .	. . .	. . .
M 42 N.	. . .	. . .	. . .	. . .
M 43 N.	. . .	. . .	. . .	. . .

D: 625 tons (725 fl) **S:** 17 kts **Dim:** 60.0 (56.6 pp) × 9.85 × 2.2
A: 1/40-mm Mk 9 AA
Electron Equipt: Radar: 1/1006—Sonar: 1/193M Mod.1
M: 2 Ruston-Paxman Deltic 9-59K diesels (1,600 rpm); 2 props; 1,900 hp (1,770 sust.); slow-speed hydraulic drive for hunting (8 kts)—bow-thruster
Electric: 1,140 kw (3 Foden FD 12 Mk 7 diesel alternators of 200 kw each for ship's service plus one 480-kw Deltic 9-55B diesel alternator for magnetic minesweeping and 1/60-kw emergency set)
Man: 6 officers, 39 men

MINE WARFARE SHIPS *(continued)*

Hurworth (M 39) L. & L. Van Ginderen, 7-85

Chiddingfold (M 37) L. & L. Van Ginderen, 7-84

Ledbury (M 30) M. Louagie, 3-85

REMARKS: Equipped for both hunting and sweeping mines. Hull constructed of glass-reinforced plastic. Carry 6 or 7 divers and 2 French PAP 104 wire-guided, remote-controlled mine locators. Have Sperry "Osborn" TA 6 acoustic, M.M. Mk 11 magnetic loop and M. Mk 3 Mod. 2 Orepesa wire sweeping gear as well. Equipped with CAAIS data system and Decca Mk 21 "Hi-Fix" navigation system. M 33 laid down *prior* to ordering on 19-6-80. Twelfth and thirteenth ordered 4-6-85.

◆ **1 prototype glass-reinforced plastic minehunter** Bldr: Vosper Thornycroft

	Ordered	L	In serv.
M 1116 WILTON	11-2-70	18-2-72	25-4-73

D: 450 tons (fl) **S:** 15 kts **Dim:** 46.33 × 8.76 × 2.6
A: 1/40-mm AA Mk 7 **M:** As for "Ton" class
Man: 5 officers, 32 men

REMARKS: First large warship with an all-glass-reinforced plastic hull. Machinery and fittings are from *Derriton,* scrapped in 1970. Two 6-tubed chaff launchers added 1984.

Wilton (M 1116) L. & L. Van Ginderen, 1-85

◆ **14 "Ton"-class minehunters**

	Bldr	Laid down	L	In serv.
M 1110 BILDESTON	J.S. Doig, Grimsby	18-5-51	9-6-52	28-4-53
M 1113 BRERETON*	Richard Ironworks	25-9-51	14-45-53	9-7-54
M 1114 BRINTON	Cook, Welton & Gemmell	30-5-51	8-8-52	4-3-54
M 1115 BRONINGTON	Cook, Welton & Gemmell	30-5-51	19-3-53	4-6-54
M 1133 BOSSINGTON	J.I. Thornycroft	1-9-54	2-12-55	11-12-56
M 1140 GAVINTON	J.S. Doig, Grimsby	29-9-52	27-7-53	12-7-54
M 1147 HUBBERSTON	Fleetlands SY, London	29-1-53	14-9-54	14-10-55
M 1151 IVESTON	Philip & Son, Dartmouth	22-10-52	1-6-54	20-6-55
M 1153 KEDLESTON*	Wm. Pickersgill & Son	26-11-52	21-12-53	2-7-55
M 1154 KELLINGTON*	Wm. Pickersgill & Son	5-1-54	12-10-54	4-11-55
M 1157 KIRKLISTON	Harland & Wolff, Belfast	2-2-53	18-2-54	21-8-54
M 1165 MAXTON	Harland & Wolff, Belfast	23-5-55	24-5-56	19-2-57
M 1166 NURTON	Harland & Wolff, Belfast	31-8-55	22-10-56	21-8-57
M 1181 SHERATON	White's SY, Southhampton	23-2-54	20-7-55	24-8-56

* Reserve Training—to be replaced by "River" class in that role.

Bossington (M 1133)—minehunter, with chaff launchers at after end of forecastle
L. & L. Van Ginderen, 11-84

◆ **9 "Ton"-class minesweepers**

	Bldr	Laid down	L	In serv.
M 1103 ALFRISTON‡	J. I. Thornycroft	16-8-51	29-4-53	16-3-54
M 1109 BICKINGTON†	White's SY, Southampton	21-9-51	14-5-53	27-5-54
M 1124 CRICHTON†	J. S. Doig, Grimsby	21-4-52	17-3-53	23-4-54
M 1125 CUXTON‡	Camper & Nicholson's	23-7-52	4-11-53	13-10-54
M 1146 HODGESTON‡	Fleetlands SY, London	22-9-52	6-4-54	17-12-54
M 1187 UPTON‡	J. I. Thornycroft	14-2-55	15-3-56	24-7-56
M 1188 WALKERTON†	J. I. Thornycroft	4-7-55	21-11-56	10-1-58
M 1200 SOBERTON†	Fleetlands SY, Gosport	11-3-55	20-11-56	17-9-57
M 1204 STUBBINGTON†	Camper & Nicholson's	26-10-54	8-8-56	30-7-57

† Coastal Division, Fisheries Protection Squadron; ‡ Reserve Training

Bickington (M 1109)—Fisheries Protection minesweeper
L. & L. Van Ginderen, 2-85

MINE WARFARE SHIPS *(continued)*

Walkerton (M 1188)—Fisheries Protection minesweeper L. & L. Van Ginderen, 1-85

D: 370 tons (425 fl) **S:** 15 kts (cruising) **Dim:** 46.33 (42.68 pp) × 8.76 × 2.50
A: 1/40-mm Mk 7 AA
Electron Equipt: Radar: 1/978—Sonar: 1/193 (hunters only)
M: 2 Paxman Deltic 18A-7A diesels; 2 props; 3,000 hp
Fuel: 43 tons (minehunters: 36 tons) **Range:** 3,000/8; 2,300/13
Man: 5 officers, 33 men (sweepers: 24 men)

Remarks: Survivors of a class of 118 completed 1952-58. All minehunters are equipped with active rudders for low-speed operations, have a Type 193 sonar, and carry mine-clearance divers. The minehunter conversions were completed 1964-69.

All have wooden hulls, sheathed with nylon below the waterline. Fin stabilizers are fitted. M 1125 was first commissioned 10-75, having gone into reserve on completion in 1953. Some (but not all) fisheries protection units have a searchlight aft.

The minehunters are being refitted for retention until the new "Single-Role Minehunters" are ready; 6-tubed chaff rocket launchers are being fitted on the forecastle, just forward of the break. Minesweepers M 1109, M 1125, M 1187, and M 1204 in refit 1984 and 1985. *Wotton* (M 1195) and *Crofton* (M 1216) decommissioned to Sales List in 1984, and *Pollington* (M 1173), *Shavington* (M 1180), and *Lewiston* (M 1208) in 1985.

Note: Trials Royal Naval Reserve Extra-Deep Armed Team Sweeps" *St. Davids* (M 07, ex-*Suffolk Monarch*) and *Venturer* (M 08, ex-*Suffolk Harvester*) were decommissioned 12-7-84 and returned to their owner. BH-N7 Wellington-class air-cushion vehicle P 235 was to be disposed of in 1985.

MINE COUNTERMEASURES SUPPORT SHIP

◆ **1 exercise minelayer and tender**

	Bldr	Laid down	L	In serv.
N 21 Abdiel	Thornycroft, Woolston	23-5-66	22-1-67	17-10-67

Abdiel (N 21)—note two mineports L. & L. Van Ginderen, 6-84

D: 1,375 tons (1,460 fl) **S:** 16 kts **Dim:** 80.42 (74.67 pp) × 11.74 × 2.85
A: 1/40-mm Mk 7 AA—44 mines **Electron Equipt:** Radar: 1/1006
M: 2 Paxman Ventura 16-YSCM diesels; 2 props; 2,690 hp **Electric:** 1,225 kw
Man: 8 officers, 90 men

Remarks: Carries and repairs spare sweeping equipment and cable. Used primarily as an exercise minelayer, using two mine ports at the stern. Gun added 1984.

Note: During the 1984 incident where the Libyan roll-on/roll-off cargo ship *Ghat* mined the Red Sea, Royal Navy minehunters *Wilton* (M 1116), *Brinton* (M 1114), *Gavinton* (M 1140) and *Kirkliston* (M 1157) were assisted in their duties by the chartered oilfield research ship *Oil Endeavor* (completed 1967 by Chantiers Navales de Ciotat as the sternhaul trawler *Marie Grace* and converted 1977). Characteristics included:

D: 2,860 tons (fl) **S:** 12 kts **Dim:** 85.20 × 16.50 × 5.62 (6.10 max.)
M: 3 M.A.N. R8V22 diesels (1,150 hp each); 2 Caterpillar D398C diesels (850 hp each); 1 Caterpillar D349 diesel (750 hp); 2 electric motors; 1 prop; 2,200 hp *and* 2 Ulstein omnidirectional thrusters of 738 hp each

Remarks: Linked generator capacity also provides 1,250-kw total load. 1,936 grt/644 nrt. Capable of 4-point moor; carries a 21-kt rescue boat. Could be chartered again if needed from owners, Ocean Inchcape, Ltd.

AMPHIBIOUS WARFARE SHIPS

ASSAULT SHIPS

Note: Landing ships and craft subordinated to the Royal Corps of Transport are covered in the Royal Army entry at the conclusion of the Great Britain section, on page 219. *Invincible*-class carriers can also carry troops.

◆ **2 Fearless class**

	Bldr	Laid down	L	In serv.
L 10 Fearless	Harland & Wolff	25-7-62	19-12-63	25-11-65
L 11 Intrepid	J. Brown (Clyde)	11-12-62	5-6-64	11-3-67

Fearless (L 10) L. & L. Van Ginderen, 11-84

Intrepid (L 11)—with armament altered L. & L. Van Ginderen, 9-85

D: 11,060 tons (12,120 fl) (16,950 tons, draft 9.15, with well deck flooded)
S: 21 kts **Dim:** 158.5 (152.4 pp) × 24.38 × 6.2
A: 4/Sea Cat GWS.20 systems (IV × 4) (L 11: IV × 2)—2/40-mm AA (I × 2)—L 11: 4/30-mm Oerlikon GCM-A02 AA (II × 2), 2/20-mm GAM-B01 AA (I × 2)
Electron Equipt: Radar: 1/978, 1/993—IFF: 1/1010 interrogator
EW: passive system, 2 Knebworth/Corvus chaff RL (VIII × 2)
M: English-Electric GT; 2 props; 22,000 hp **Electric:** 4,000 kw
Boilers: 2 Babcock & Wilcox, 38.66 kg/cm², 454°C superheat
Range: 5,000/20 **Man:** 36 officers, 520 men, 380-700 troops

Remarks: Equivalent to U.S. LPD type, and have excellent command and communication facilities for amphibious operations. CAAIS combat data system fitted. They can launch four to six assault helicopters (landing platform but no hangar). On board are four LCVP Mk 2 landing craft, which can transport 35 men or a half-ton vehicle, and four LCM (9) landing craft carrying two Chieftain tanks or four vehicles or 100 tons of supplies; four additional tanks can be carried on the tank deck. The vehicles are divided between the tank deck, a lower deck, and a half-deck reserved for jeeps. The active unit has normally been assigned as officer cadet training ship at the Royal Naval College, Dartmouth, but has been immediately available for amphibious operations as required. L 10 in reserve at Portsmouth. To be replaced in 1990s by a new LPD design. Two twin 30-mm AA replaced the after two Sea Cat launchers in L 11 1985, and two 20-mm AA were added forward.

TANK LANDING SHIPS

	Bldr	Laid down	L	In serve
L. . . SIR GALAHAD	Swan Hunter, Wallsend	12-7-85	. . .	1987

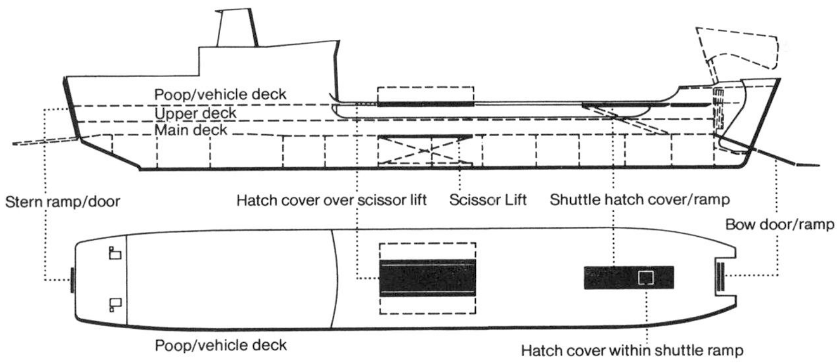

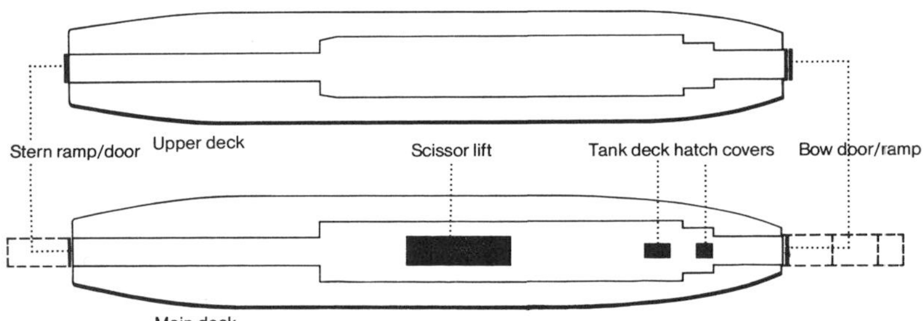

Sir Galahad—schematic of interior, showing cargo-handling arrangement
MacGregor-Navire, 1985

D: About 6,500 tons (fl) **S:** 18 kts **Dim:** 140.46 (120.00 pp) × 19.50 × 4.30
A: . . .
Electron Equipt: Radar: . . .
M: 2 Mirlees-Blackstone 9 K Major Mk 3 diesels, 2 props; 13,320 hp
Electric: 2,160 kw
Man: 51 crew, plus 339 troops

REMARKS: Ordered 6-9-84 as a replacement for ship of the same name lost in the Falkland War. Will have one 25-ton, two 20-ton, and two 8.5-ton cranes.

◆ **1 chartered merchant ship** Bldr: Trosik Verksted, Bergen, Norway

	L	In serv.
L 3522 SIR CARADOC (ex-*Gray Master*)	8-11-72	1-73

Sir Caradoc (L 3522) L. & L. Van Ginderen, 10-84

D: 5,980 tons (fl) **S:** 17.5 kts **Dim:** 124.20 (114.33) × 16.03 × 4.85
A: Removed **Electron Equipt:** Radar: 2/navigational
M: 4 Bergens-Normo LSM-9 diesels; 2 CP props; 5,040 hp
Range: 10,600/16 **Fuel:** 500 tons
Electric: 625 kw **Man:** 33 crew + 24 RFA personnel

REMARKS: 1,899 grt/3,480 dwt. Chartered 14-1-83 from Norwegian Nitre Shipping Co. and put in service 26-3-83 as replacement (with *Sir Lamorak*) for the sunken *Sir Galahad* and the damaged *Sir Tristram.* Crew augmented, armament added, and MARISAT system installed. Two 350-hp side-thrusters, bow and stern vehicle cargo ramps fitted. **A:** 2/20-mm AA removed 1984. Due to be returned to owners, 1986.

◆ **1 chartered merchant ship** Bldr: Ankerlokken Verft, Floro, Norway

	L	In serv.
L 3532 SIR LAMORAK (ex-*Lakespan Ontario,* ex-*Lady Catherine,* ex-*Lune Bridge,* ex-*Anu,* ex-*Norcliff,* ex-*Anu*)	9-5-72	7-73

D: 5,230 tons (fl) **S:** 18 kts **Dim:** 108.30 (100.00) × 20.40 × 4.95 (max)
A: None **Electron Equipt:** Radar: 2/navigational
M: 2 Lindholmen-Pielstick 8 PC 2L diesels; 2 CP props; 8,000 hp
Fuel: 600 tons

REMARKS: 1,585 grt/2,635 dwt. Chartered 14-1-83 from Cenargo Ltd. and placed in service 26-3-83 with 10 officers and 14 crewmen from the Royal Fleet Auxiliary augmenting the regular crew. Has bow and stern doors and ramps for vehicle cargo. Ice-strengthened hull. Unlike *Sir Caradoc,* was not armed. Equipped with MARISAT

Sir Lamorak (L 3532) L. & L. Van Ginderen, 6-83

SATCOMM gear. Has a 500-hp bow-thruster. Cargo bale capacity: 292,000 cu. ft. Due to be returned to owners, 1986.

◆ **5 Sir Bedivere class** (logistic lift ships in peacetime)

	Bldr	Laid down	L	In serv.
L 3004 SIR BEDIVERE	Hawthorn Leslie	10-65	20-7-66	18-5-67
L 3027 SIR GERAINT	Alexander Stephen	6-65	26-1-67	12-7-67
L 3029 SIR LANCELOT	Fairfield	3-62	25-6-63	16-1-64
L 3036 SIR PERCIVALE	Hawthorn Leslie	4-66	4-10-67	23-3-68
L 3505 SIR TRISTRAM	Hawthorn Leslie	2-66	12-12-66	14-9-67

Sir Geraint (L 3027)—guns removed, MARISAT abaft mast
L. & L. Van Ginderen, 2-85

D: 3,270 tons (5,674 fl) L 3505: 5,800 fl **S:** 17 kts **Dim:** 126.45 (L 3505: 135.37) × 17.7 × 3.8
A: Removed **Electron Equipt:** Radar: 2/navigational—2/Knebworth/Corvus chaff RL (VIII × 2)
M: 2 Mirrlees 10-ALSSDM 10-cyl. diesels; 2 props; 9,400 hp (L 3029: 2 Denny-Sulzer diesels; 9,520 hp)
Fuel: 811 tons **Range:** 8,000/15 **Man:** 18 officers, 51 men

REMARKS: In 1963 the Ministry of Transportation ordered the first of six specially designed LST-type ships for the Army, chartered in peacetime to various private maritime firms. In 1970 these ships came under the control of the Royal Fleet Auxiliary Service. Beaching cargo capacity is 340 tons. Bow and stern ramps for vehicles, interior ramps connect the two decks. Quarters for 402 men. Helicopter platform and three cranes (two 4.5, one 8.5 tons). All have MARISAT gear. L 3029 has four cranes, and is 5,550 tons full load. L 3505 badly damaged 8-6-83, but was carried home in 6-83 and repaired by Tyne Shiprepair, South Shields, 7-84 to 7-85; a new 120-ton, 8.915-m midsection being added, along with rehabilitated accommodations and helicopter deck. The others may be similarly stretched during future refits. Falklands War armament of 2/40-mm Mk 3 AA (I × 2) removed 1984. *Sir Galahad* (L 3005) was fatally damaged on 8-6-83 and was scuttled 24-6-83.

LANDING CRAFT

◆ **13 LCM (9) class** (In serv. 1963-66)

L 700–L 702 (Bldr: Brooke Marine, Lowestoft) L 710, L 711 (Bldr: J. Bolson, Poole)
L 704–L 709 (Bldr: Richard Dunston, Thorne) L 3507, L 3508 (Bldr: Vosper)

L 709—attached to *Intrepid* L. & L. Van Ginderen, 5-85

D: 75 tons (176 fl) **S:** 9 kts **Dim:** 25.7 × 6.5 × 1.7
Electron Equipt: Radar: 1/Decca 101
M: 2 Paxman YHXAM diesels; Kort-nozzle props; 624 hp **Man:** 6 tot.

LANDING CRAFT *(continued)*

Remarks: Can carry two Centurion tanks or 100 tons of cargo. All naval-manned. Can carry a Type 978 radar. *Fearless* (L 10) and *Intrepid* (L 11) can each carry four of this class. L 703 (F4-*Fearless* No. 4) lost to bomb 8-6-82.

◆ **15 LCVP MK 4 Class** Bldrs: 1 by Fairey Allday Marine, Hamble (In serv. 1982); 14 by Souter, Cowes (In serv. 18-2-85 to 9-86)

LCVP Mk 4 8404 L. & L. Van Ginderen, 7-85

LCVP Mk 4 class Souter, 1985

D: 10 tons (fl) **S:** 20 kts (16 loaded) **Dim:** 13.00 (11.90 pp) × 3.20 × 0.80
A: 2/7.62-mm mg (I × 2)
M: 2 Perkins 76-3544 diesels; 2 props; 440 hp
Range: 200/12 **Man:** 3 crew + 35 troops

Remarks: Prototype, ordered 6-2-80, is 13.50 long by 3.50 beam. Series units ordered 21-8-84. Have cargo well 8.80 × 2.13 and a cargo capacity of 5.5 tons. Aluminum construction. Replacing LCVP (1) through LCVP (3). First unit delivered 18-2-85.

◆ **3 Ferryman 18 class** Bldr: Freezer Aluminum Boats, Hayling Island (In serv. 1 on 13-8-84, 2 on 16-8-84)

D: 2.5 tons **S:** 20 kts **Dim:** 5.48 × 2.21 × 0.40
M: 1 OMC gasoline outboard; 140 hp **Cargo:** 10 troops

Remarks: New series of raider boats for Royal Marines, ordered 16-5-84. Additional aluminum and rigid inflatable raider boats of this size are also available.

◆ **26 LCVP**

LCVP (1): 102, 112, 118, 120, 123, 127, 128, 134, 136
LCVP (2): 142-149
LCVP (3): 150-158

LCVP(2) from Fearless M.O.D., 1982

D: 8.5 tons (13.5 fl) **S:** 8–10 kts **Dim:** 12.7 or 13.1 × 3.1 × 0.8
M: 2 Foden diesels; 2 props; 130 or 200 hp

Remarks: The eight LCVP (2) are carried in *Fearless* and *Intrepid.* Four fitted for mine countermeasures in the Falklands War, 5-82. All due for replacement.

◆ **3 LCP(L) (3)**

501, 503, 556

D: 6.5 tons (10 fl) **S:** 12 kts **Dim:** 11.3 × 3.4 × 1.0
M: 1 diesel; 1 prop; 225 hp

◆ **35 or more "Mexiflote" self-propelled pontoons**

A "Mexiflote" self-propelled pontoon in use during the recovery of the Falkland Islands, 6-82. Each *Sir Bedivere*-class LST can carry two of these low-freeboard craft, mounted vertically on the hull sides. Powered by 2 Sykes Marine Harbormaster F725 units: 150 hp. Sixty-seven more propulsion units ordered 1985, using Ford 2725 diesels.

AUXILIARY SHIPS

Most auxiliary and supply vessels are responsible to the Royal Fleet Auxiliary (RFA), an organization peculiar to the Royal Navy. Built to the specifications of Lloyds of London (compartmentation, security, habitability), they also meet the standards of the Shipping Naval Acts of 1911 and of the Ministry of Transportation. In 1985, it was decided to reclassify all RFA ships as "Government-Owned Vessels." Manned by the Civil Service, they fly the blue ensign of the reserve, rather than the white ensign. In addition, about 40 tugs, salvage vessels, cable layers, research vessels, etc., are assigned to the Royal Maritime Auxiliary Service (RMAS), whose personnel are also civil servants. The former Port Auxiliary Service (PAS) was absorbed by the RMAS on 1-10-76. An additional group of service craft are operated by the Royal Naval Auxiliary Service (RNXS). Ships not listed below as either RFA, RNXS, or RMAS are manned by the Royal Navy. RMAS ships have black hulls and buff upperworks, while RNXS units have black hulls and grey upperworks. They often do not display hull numbers; pendant numbers are listed hereafter in parentheses for reference only.

HYDROGRAPHIC SHIPS

Note: All Royal Navy survey ships are painted white, with buff-colored stacks and masts.

◆ **1 improved Hecla class**

	Bldr	Laid down	L	In serv.
(A 138) Herald	Robb Caledon	9-11-72	4-10-73	31-10-74

Herald—on return from Falklands deployment, gray-painted
L. & L. Van Ginderen, 2-84

D: 2,125 tons (2,945 fl) **S:** 14 kts **Dim:** 79.3 × 14.9 × 4.7
Electron Equipt: Radar: 1/1006, 1/. . . nav. **Man:** 128 tot.
M: Diesel-electric propulsion (identical to the *Hecla* class); 1 prop

Remarks: Improved version of the *Hecla* class. Carries one Wasp helicopter. Has Type 2034 Sidescan charting sonar. On ice-patrol duties, 6-83 to 2-84, gray-painted and with 2/20-mm AA. Has MARISAT. Has Type 2034 mapping sonar.

◆ **3 Hecla class**

	Bldr	Laid down	L	In serv.
(A 133) Hecla	Yarrow, Blythswood	6-5-64	21-12-64	9-9-65
(A 137) Hecate	Yarrow, Scotstoun	26-10-64	31-3-65	20-12-65
(A 144) Hydra	Yarrow, Blythswood	14-5-64	14-7-65	5-5-66

HYDROGRAPHIC SHIPS *(continued)*

Hydra—in survey colors, Wasp aft L. & L. Van Ginderen, 1-83

D: 1,915 tons (2,733 fl) **S:** 14 kts **Dim:** 79.25 (71.63 pp) × 14.94 × 4.0
M: Diesel-electric propulsion: 3 Paxman Ventura diesels (12 cyl.), each 1,280 hp; 2 electric motors; 1 prop; 2,000 hp
Fuel: 450 tons **Range:** 20,000/9; 12,000/11 **Man:** 14 officers, 104 men

REMARKS: Based on the oceanographic research vessel *Discovery.* Air-conditioned hull, reinforced against ice; bow-thruster for navigation in narrow waters. Hangar and platform for one Wasp helicopter. Excellent scientific laboratories; usually carry seven civilian scientists in addition to crew. Two survey launches. Have Type 2034 sidescan charting sonar. A 133 and A 144 were used as ambulance ships during the Falklands War, fitted with MARISAT SATCOMM gear. A 137, painted gray and armed with 2/20-mm AA and Blowpipe missiles, did a tour as ice-patrol ship in the South Atlantic 7-82 to 7-83. Have Type 2034 mapping sonars.

◆ **0 (+1) Roebuck-class coastal survey ship** Bldr: Brooke Marine, Lowestoft

	Laid down	L	In serv.
(A. . .) ROEBUCK	. . .	14-11-85	1986

D: 1,300 tons (fl) **S:** 16 kts **Dim:** 63.89 (57.60 pp) × 13.00 × 3.82
A: . . . **Electron Equipt:** Radar: . . .
M: 2 Mirrlees Blackstone ES-8 Mk 1 diesels; 2 CP props; 3,040 hp
Range: 4,000/10 **Man:** 52 tot.

REMARKS: Ordered 21-5-84 to perform hydrographic surveys in local British waters. An enlarged *Bulldog.*

◆ **4 Bulldog-class coastal survey ships** Bldr: Brooke Marine, Lowestoft

	L	In serv.
(A 317) BULLDOG	12-7-67	21-3-68
(A 319) BEAGLE (ex-*Barracuda*)	7-9-67	9-5-68
(A 320) FOX	9-11-68	11-7-68
(A 335) FAWN	29-2-68	10-9-68

Fawn L. & L. Van Ginderen, 8-84

D: 800 tons (1,088 fl) **S:** 15 kts **Dim:** 60.95 × 11.43 × 3.6
M: 4 Lister-Blackstone ERS-8-M diesels; 2 KaMeWa CP props; 2,640 hp
Electric: 720 kw **Range:** 4,600/12 **Man:** 5 officers, 34 men

REMARKS: Hulls built to commercial specifications and reinforced against ice damage. Carry one 8.7-meter survey launch. Passive tank stabilization. Decca "Hi-Fix" precision plot. Can be equipped with 2/20-mm AA on bridge wings (I × 2). Carry one 8.7-m survey boat. Have Type 2034 mapping sonars.

◆ **1 inshore survey craft** Bldr: Emsworth SY, Emsworth

	L	In serv.
(A86) GLEANER	18-10-83	5-12-84

D: 22 tons (fl) **S:** 14 kts **Dim:** 14.81 × 4.55 × 1.30
Electron Equipt: Radar: 1/Decca 110
M: 2 Rolls-Royce CG M-310 diesels; 2 props; 524 hp; 1 Perkins 4.236 M cruise diesel; 1 prop; 72 hp
Range: 450/10 **Man:** 1 officer, 4 men

Gleaner Maritime Photographic, 2-85

REMARKS: Smallest commissioned "ship" in the RN, intended for survey work in the Solent-Portsmouth area and in the Channel Islands. Glass-reinforced plastic hull by Halmatic. Speed on cruise engine: 3 to 7 kts.

NOTE: Three 9-meter survey boats ordered from Halmatic in 12-84 are intended to be carried by larger survey ships and not to operate independently:

D: 8 tons (fl) **S:** 13 kts **Dim:** 9.00 (8.25 pp) × 3.60 × 0.99
M: 2 Perkins 6.355 diesels; 2 props; 230 hp **Range:** 200/13
Man: 4 tot.

NOTE: *Echo*-class coastal survey craft *Echo* (A 70) *Enterprise* (A 71) and *Egeria* (A 72) were paid off for disposal 12-84. The similar *Woodlark* and *Waterwitch* (M 2720) were paid off 4-4-85 and 4-3-85, respectively. The cable tender *St. Margarets* (A 259) was stricken 18-12-84.

EXPERIMENTAL SHIPS

◆ **1 sonar-trials ship**

	Bldr	Laid down	L	In serv.
A 285 AURICULA	Ferguson Bros.	16-2-79	22-11-79	6-11-80

Auricula (A 285) L. & L. Van Ginderen, 3-83

D: 1,200 tons (fl) **S:** 12 kts **Dim:** 60.0 (52.0 pp) × 11.0 × 3.6
M: 2 Mirrlees-Blackstone ESL-6-MGR diesels; 2 props; 1,300 hp
Man: 7 officers, 15 men, 10 technicians

REMARKS: Ship operated by RMAS. Ordered 5-1-78. "Trials and Experimental Tender" to Admiralty Underwater Weapons Establishment, Portland; replaced *Steady.* Has a bow-thruster.

◆ **1 sonar-research ship**

	Bldr	Laid down	L	In serv.
A 367 NEWTON	Scott-Lithgow, Greenock	19-12-73	26-6-75	17-6-76

Newton (A 367) L. & L. Van Ginderen, 8-84

EXPERIMENTAL SHIPS *(continued)*

D: 3,940 tons (fl) **S:** 14 kts **Dim:** 98.6 (88.7 pp) × 16.15 × 4.7
Electron Equipt: Radar: 1/1006—Sonar: 1/182, 1/185, 1/2010, 1/2013
M: 3 Mirrlees-Blackstone EWSL-12 MA 1,450-hp diesels, electric drive; 1 Kort-nozzle prop; 2,680 hp
Electric: 2,150 kw **Fuel:** 244 tons **Range:** 5,000/9
Man: 61 men (including 12 technicians)

REMARKS: Intended for sonar-propagation trials and also fitted to lay cable over the bows. Equipped with 350-hp retractable bow-thruster and passive tank stabilization system. Propulsion plant extremely quiet, with a 300-hp electric motor for low speeds. Has four laboratories and seven special winches. Can carry and lay 400 tons of undersea cable and 361 tons cable repeaters. Navigation equipment includes SINS, satellite receivers, two optical range-finders, Decca Mk 21, and considerable other equipment. RMAS-operated. Optical rangefinder atop pilothouse.

◆ **1 torpedo-research vessel**

A 364 WHITEHEAD Bldr: Scotts SB, Greenock (L: 5-5-70)

Whitehead (A 364) 1971

D: 3,040 tons (fl) **S:** 15.5 kts **Dim:** 97.23 (88.7 pp) × 14.63 × 5.2
A: 1/533-mm TT (bow, submerged)—3/324-mm Mk 32 ASW TT (III × 1)
M: 2 Paxman 12 YLCM diesels; 1 prop; 3,400 hp
Range: 4,000/12 **Man:** 10 officers, 47 men and scientists

REMARKS: Designed not only to launch and recover exercise torpedoes but also to perform precision tracking in three dimensions, using passive hydrophone arrays, and post-firing checkout and maintenance on torpedoes. RMAS-operated.

◆ **1 sonar-research barge**

	Bldr	L	In serv.
(RDV 01) CRYSTAL	HMDY, Devonport	22-3-71	30-11-71

Crystal G. Arra, 1977

D: 3,040 tons (fl) **Dim:** 126.0 × 17.0 × 1.7 **Man:** 60 tot.

REMARKS: No propulsion plant. Assigned to test new sonars at Admiralty Underwater Weapons Establishment, Portland. RMAS-operated.

◆ **1 vertical-launch missile trials barge**

LONGBOW (ex-*Dynamic Servant,* ex-*Ocean Servant* 2) (In serv. 1976)

Longbow—trials barge for Sea Wolf VLS Y-ARD Ltd., 1984

D: 12,600 tons (fl) **S:** . . . **Dim:** 109.0 (108.0 pp) × 30.0 × . . .
A: 3/Sea Wolf VLS launchers **Electron Equipt:** Radar: 2/. . . nav., 2/911 f.c.
M: 2 Bolnes diesels; 2 Schöttel props; 1,200 hp

REMARKS: Delivered post-conversion 23-7-85. Originally chartered by British Aerospace late 1984; converted from float-on/float-off cargo barge at Govan.

REPAIR SHIP

◆ **1 former oilfield support tender** Bldr: Götaverken, Göteborg, Sweden

	L	In serv. (RN)
A 132 DILIGENCE	1981	12-3-84

Diligence (A 132) RN, 1984

D: Approx. 10,900 tons (fl) **S:** 16 kts **Dim:** 111.47 (101.30 pp) × 20.97 × 8.30
A: 4/20-mm Oerlikon GAM-B01 AA (I × 4)
Electron Equipt: Radar: 2/. . .nav.
M: 5 Nohab 16-cyl. diesels, electric drive (4 motors); CP prop; 1,800 hp—2 side-thrusters forward, 2 rotatable thrusters aft
Man: RFA: 13 officers, 29 men + 155-man naval repair party **Fuel:** 3,150 tons

REMARKS: 6,060 grt former North Sea oilfield support ship chartered during Falklands War for emergency, war-zone repairs. Purchased outright 31-10-83 and commissioned 12-3-84. Has MARISAT SATCOMM terminal, large helicopter deck (no hangar) atop massive superstructure, moon-pool for divers. Ice-strengthened hull. Cranes include four 20- to 40-ton, one 20-ton, one 15-ton and one 5-ton. Capable of firefighting, towing, and salvage. Very maneuverable; can make 6 kts sideways. Near-sister *Bar Protector* was chartered from 9-83 to 1-6-84, when relieved by *Diligence.*

ACCOMMODATIONS SHIPS

◆ **1 Head class, former repair ship**

	Bldr	Laid down	L	In serv.
A 134 RAME HEAD	Burrard, Vancouver	12-7-44	22-11-44	18-8-45

Rame Head (A 134) L. & L. Van Ginderen, 7-83

D: 9,000 tons (11,270 fl) **S:** 10 kts **Dim:** 134.6 (126.8 pp) × 17.5 × 6.9
A: Removed **M:** Triple-expansion steam; 1 prop; 2,500 hp
Boilers: 2 Foster-Wheeler, 17 kg/cm², 330°C **Fuel:** 700 tons
Electron Equipt: Radar: 1/975 **Man:** 425 tot.

REMARKS: Former escort maintenance ship employed as an accommodations ship at Portsmouth since 6-76: towed to Rosyth 13-11-84 to serve Type 42 guided-missile destroyers based there. Repair equipment maintained on board in preservation since 1972. Has one 12-ton and two 5-ton cranes. Armament removed (11 single 40-mm AA).

NOTE: The "County"-class guided-missile destroyer *Kent* (D 12) decommissioned from harbor training service 16-5-83; was recommissioned 6-8-85 as an accommodation ship for cadets.

FLEET-REPLENISHMENT SHIPS

◆ **2 Fort-class ammunition, explosives, food, and stores ships** Bldr: Scott-Lithgow, Greenock

	Laid down	L	In serv.
A 385 FORT GRANGE	9-11-73	9-12-76	6-4-78
A 386 FORT AUSTIN	9-12-75	9-3-78	11-5-79

FLEET-REPLENISHMENT SHIPS *(continued)*

Fort Austin (A 386) L. & L. Van Ginderen, 7-85

D: 22,749 tons (fl) **S:** 20 kts **Dim:** 183.8 (170.0 pp) × 24.1 × 8.6
A: 2/20-mm AA (I × 2)
Electron Equipt: Radar: Kelvin-Hughes 21/16 P
EW: 2/Knebworth/Corvus chaff RL (VIII × 2)
M: 1 Sulzer 8 RND 90 diesel; 1 prop; 23,200 hp **Electric:** 4,120 kw
Range: 10,000/20 **Man:** 140 Royal Fleet Auxiliary personnel, plus 45 naval.

Remarks: Ordered 11-71 and 4-72; 16,009 grt/8,300 dwt/6,729 nrt. In addition to the flight deck on the stern, the roof of the hangar can land helicopters. One Sea King is normally carried (although four can be accommodated), and the ships will have ASW torpedoes and other ASW stores for use if needed. Carry 3,500 tons of ammunition, food, and spares. Bow-thruster. Three sliding-stay, constant-tension, alongside-replenishment stations on each beam. Have 2/10-ton and 4/5-ton electric stores cranes. Platforms for two SCOT satellite communications radomes atop superstructure, but received MARISAT commercial system instead, and 20-mm AA were mounted on the SCOT platforms in 1982. Have Type 182 towed torpedo decoys. RFA-operated.

◆ **2 Resource-class ammunition, explosives, food, and stores ships**

	Bldr	Laid down	L	In serv.
A 480 Resource	Scotts SB, Greenock	6-64	11-2-66	18-5-67
A 486 Regent	Harland & Wolff, Belfast	9-64	9-3-66	6-6-67

Resource (A 480)—MARISAT, chaff RL added L. & L. Van Ginderen, 7-83

Regent (A 486) L. & L. Van Ginderen, 4-84

D: 22,890 tons (fl) (18,029 grt) **S:** 17 kts
Dim: 195.07 (182.88 pp) × 23.47 × 7.95
Electron Equipt: Radar: 1/Kelvin-Hughes 21/16P, 1/Kelvin-Hughes 14/12
EW: 2/Knebworth/Corvus chaff RL (VIII × 2)
M: 1 set A.E.I. GT; 1 prop; 20,000 hp **Boilers:** 2 Foster-Wheeler
Man: 119 Royal Fleet Auxiliary, 52 civilian, plus airgroup

Remarks: RFA-operated. Three sliding-stay, constant-tension, alongside-replenishment stations per side. Carry one Sea King helicopter. One to enter reserve 1984-85.

FLEET OILERS

◆ **0 (+6 + 6) new-construction replenishment ships**

	Bldr	Laid down	L	In serv.
A. . . N. . .	. . .	. . .	. . .	1990
A. . . N. . .	. . .	. . .	. . .	. . .

New Replenishment Ship—artist's rendering M.O.D., 1984

D: Approx. 40,000 (fl) **S:** 20 kts **Dim:** 202.0 (195.0 wl) × 28.0 × . . .
A: 32 Sea Wolf GWS.26 vertical-launch SAM—2/30-mm Rarden AA—3/helicopters
Electron Equipt: Radar: 1/1007, 1/. . . nav, 1/996, 2/911
EW: intercept array; Shield RL (VI × 4)
M: 2 medium-speed diesels; 2 props; . . . hp
Electric: . . . **Range:** . . .
Man: 120 RFA, 76 naval, 56 spare accom.

Remarks: Intended to carry about 70,000 barrels (12,000 m^3) liquid cargo, 5,000 m^3 munitions, and 3,000 m^3 dry stores, plus 500 m^3 refrigerated. Will replace present generation of replenishment ships. The first was expected to be ordered late in 1985. There will be two fueling stations per side, plus an astern refueling capability. One solid-replenishment station per side, plus vertical replenishment. The ships will carry ASW ordinance for their three helicopters. Will have SCOT antennas for the SHF SATCOMM Slaynet IV system.

The second series of six will be of a simplified version, primarily intended for point-to-point service as replacements for the "Leaf" series.

◆ **3 Olwen class**

	Bldr	L	In serv.
A 122 Olwen (ex-*Olynthus*)	Hawthorn Leslie	10-7-64	21-6-65
A 123 Olna	Hawthorn Leslie	28-7-75	1-4-66
A 124 Olmeda (ex-*Oleander*)	Swan Hunter	19-11-64	18-10-65

Olwen (A 122) Lts. J. Lathrop/G. Baloing, USN, 1983

Olna (A 123)—note traveling crane over flight deck L. & L. Van Ginderen, 11-84

D: 10,890 tons light (36,000 fl) **S:** 20 kts
Dim: 197.51 (185.92 pp) × 25.6 × 10.5 **A:** 2/20-mm AA (I × 2)
Electron Equipt: Radar: 1 Kelvin-Hughes 14/12, 1 Kelvin-Hughes 14/16, 1/1006
EW: 2/Knebworth/Corvus chaff RL (VIII × 2)
M: 1 set Pamatreda GT; 1 prop; 26,500 hp
Boilers: 2 Babcock & Wilcox, 60 kg/cm^2, 510°C
Man: 25 officers, 62 men, plus naval air group

Remarks: Hull reinforced against ice, living space air-conditioned, advanced automation, excellent facilities for replenishment at sea; 25,000 dwt, 18,600 grt. Helicopter platform; hangar to port recently enlarged to hold two Sea King helicopters, but normally only one is carried. Can carry 18,400 tons fuel oil, 1,720 tons diesel, 3,730 tons aircraft fuel, and 130 tons lube oil. RFA-operated. Now have MARISAT commercial communications satellite system. Chaff RL and guns added 1982.

◆ **1 later Tide class** Bldr: Hawthorn Leslie, Hebburn-on-Tyne

	Laid down	L	In serv.
A 75 Tidespring	24-7-61	3-5-62	18-1-63

FLEET OILERS *(continued)*

Tidespring (A 75) L. & L. Van Ginderen, 6-84

D: 8,531 tons light (27,400 fl) **S:** 18.3 kts
Dim: 177.6 (167.65 pp) × 21.64 × 9.75 **A:** 2/20-mm Mk 4 AA (I × 2)
Electron Equipt: Radar: 1 Kelvin-Hughes 14/12, 1 Kelvin-Hughes 14/16
EW: 2/Knebworth/Corvus Chaff RL (VIII × 2)
M: 1 set Pamatreda GT; 1 prop; 15,000 hp
Man: 30 officers, 80 men, plus air group

Remarks: RFA-operated; 18,900 dwt, 14,130 grt. As built, carried 17,400 tons fuel oil and 700 tons diesel, but with RN dependence on gas-turbine propulsion, proportions may have changed. Hangar and flight deck for 1 large helicopter. Sister *Tidepool* (A 76) sold to Chile, transferred 4-82 to Chile, repossessed for Falklands War, turned over permanently 8-82. MARISAT SATCOMM, armament, and chaff RL added 1982. Was scheduled for disposal 1984, but is being retained, completing a refit 22-12-84.

SMALL FLEET OILERS

◆ **5 Rover class** Bldr: Swan Hunter, Hebburn-on-Tyne

	L	In serv.
A 268 Green Rover	19-12-68	15-8-69
A 269 Grey Rover	17-4-69	10-4-70
A 270 Blue Rover	11-11-69	15-7-70
A 271 Gold Rover	7-3-73	22-3-74
A 273 Black Rover	30-10-73	23-8-74

Grey Rover (A 269)—chaff RL and MARISAT atop bridge
L. & L. Van Ginderen, 7-83

Blue Rover (A 270)—MARISAT fwd L. & L. Van Ginderen, 7-83

D: 4,700 tons light (11,522 fl) **S:** 19.25 kts **Dim:** 140.5 × 19.2 × 7.3
Electron Equipt: Radar: 3/Decca navigational—EW: 2/Knebworth/Corvus chaff RL (VIII × 2)
M: 2 SEMT-Pielstick 16PA 4 diesels; 1 CP prop; 15,300 hp **Electric:** 2,720 kw
Fuel: 965 tons **Range:** 15,000/15 **Man:** 16 officers, 31 men

Remarks: RFA-operated; 6,822 dwt (A 271, A 273: 6,692 dwt), 7,510 grt. Carry 6,600 tons of fuel plus water, dry stores, and provisions. Helicopter deck but no hangar. A 271 is used in supporting the training squadron at Portland. First three re-engined 1973-74. Not all carry chaff RL. Stern shapes vary, early units having two stern anchors and later units one.

SUPPORT OILERS

◆ **4 Appleleaf class** Bldr: Cammell Laird, Birkenhead

	L	In serv.
A 79 Appleleaf (ex-*Hudson Cavalier*)	24-7-75	11-79
A 81 Brambleleaf (ex-*Hudson Deep*)	22-1-76	3-80
A 109 Bayleaf (ex-*Hudson Progress*)	27-10-81	26-3-82
A 110 Orangeleaf (ex-*Balder London*)	. . .	2-5-84 (RN)

Brambleleaf (A 81) L. & L. Van Ginderen, 11-84

Bayleaf (A 109) L. & L. Van Ginderen, 5-85

D: 40,200 tons (fl) **S:** 16.4 kts **Dim:** 170.69 (163.51 pp) × 25.94 × 11.56
A: 2/20-mm AA (I × 2) **Electron Equipt:** Radar: 2/. . . nav.
M: 2 Crossley-Pielstick 14PC2V-400 diesels; 1 CP prop; 14,000 hp
Fuel: 2,498 tons **Man:** 65 tot.

Remarks: RFA-operated. A 79 chartered 1978 and refitted 12-78 to 11-79 at Wallsend Dry Docks; stack raised 3.5 m, dry cargo hold added forward, replenishment-at-sea working deck added amidships, and superstructure enlarged aft. A 81 given similar refit by Cammell Laird after charter in 1979, completing 1980. A 109, on which work had been suspended while still on the ways, was chartered 3-4-81 and similarly altered. A 110, on charter since 4-82, was purchased 26-3-84 and initially operated without replenishment equipment, receiving a similar conversion to that of her sisters in 1985 to 3-86. Average 20,440 grt, 33,750 dwt. All now have one refueling station per side, over-the-stern fueling, and MARISAT.

◆ **1 ex-Norwegian tanker** Bldr: Uddevallavarvet, Uddevalla, Sweden

	L	In serv.
A. . . Oakleaf (ex-*Oktania*)	1981	10-85 (in RFA)

D: Approx. 45,000 tons (fl) **S:** 15.75 kts **Dim:** 173.69 (168.00 wl × 32.26 × 10.22
A: . . . **Electron Equipt:** Radar: 2/. . . nav.
M: 1 Uddevalla-Burmeister & Wain 4-cyl., 2-stroke diesel; 1 CP prop; 12,250 hp
Electric: 2,472 kw **Man:** . . .

Remarks: 21,999 grt/34,800 dwt. Purchased 7-85 to replace *Plumleaf* (A 78). Ice-strengthened hull, with tunnel side-thrusters fore and aft. Cargo: 43,020 m^3.

Note: *Plumleaf* (A 78) returned to owners 1985; similar *Pearleaf* (A 77) also returned.

MISCELLANEOUS AUXILIARY SHIPS

◆ **1 helicopter support ship** Bldr: Stocznia Gdanska, Poland

	L	In serv. (RFA)
A 131 Reliant (ex-*Astronomer*)	1-77	16-11-83

D: Approx. 28,000 tons (fl) **S:** 20 kts **Dim:** 204.22 (193.81 pp) × 30.99 × 8.00
A: 4/20-mm Oerlikon GAM-B01 AA (I × 4)—5/Sea King HAS.5 helicopters
Electron Equipt: Radar: 3/nav.
EW: MEL Matilda passive, 2/Shield decoy RL (VI × 2)
M: 1 Cegielski-Sulzer 10 RND 90, 10-cyl. diesel; 1 prop; 29,000 hp (26,100 sust.)
Electric: 3,840 kw **Range:** . . . **Man:** . . .
Fuel: 3,327 tons heavy oil + 630 tons diesel + 600 tons JP-5 aircraft fuel

Remarks: 27,867 grt/23,120 dwt when chartered 4-82 as an aircraft transport and helicopter support ship for the Falklands War. At that time, a temporary hangar with standard 40-ft. containers for walls was erected forward. Purchased 26-4-83 and given further conversion, employing the 79-container module, U.S. Navy "Arapaho" helicopter support system, on loan for one year (later extended into 1986). Can carry up to 5 Sea King helicopters, with full support capability. Converted by Cammell Laird, Birkenhead. Accommodations added aft for 140 aviation personnel. Hangar measures 33 by 13 m; flight deck measures 48.66 by 29.26 m. Ship has fin stabilizers and a

MISCELLANEOUS AUXILIARY SHIPS *(continued)*

Reliant (A 131) RN, 12-83

Reliant (A 131) M.O.D., 1984

bow-thruster. Refitted again beginning 12-2-84 to correct deficiencies. 40-ton container gantry crane retained primarily as ballast, as ship is too lightly loaded.

◆ **1 helicopter training ship** Bldr: Breda SY Venice, Italy (In serv. 1981)

	In serv.
K . . . Argus (ex-*Contender Bezant*)	1986 (RN)

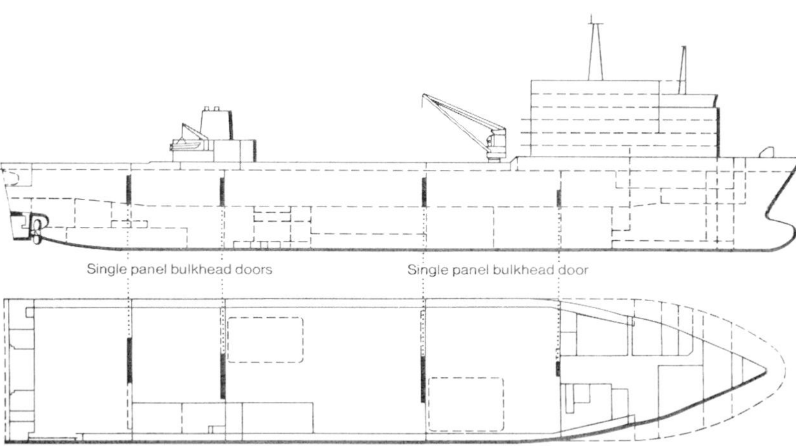

Argus—schematic of post-conversion arrangement MacGregor-Navire, 1985

D: 18,000 tons (fl) **S:** 19.25 kts **Dim:** 173.00 (160.00 pp) × 30.40 × 8.20
A: 4/20-mm Oerlikon GAM-B01 AA (I × 4)—6 Sea King helicopters (or up to 12 Sea Harrier V/STOL fighters)
Electron Equipt: Radar: . . .
EW: 4 Shield decoy RL (VI × 2)
M: 2 Linkholmen-Pielstick 18PC2.5 V400 diesels; 2 props; 21,060 hp
Range: 20,000/19 **Fuel:** 4,515 tons heavy oil/1,565 tons diesel
Electric: 3,600 kw **Man:** . . .

Remarks: Purchased 2-3-84, having been on charter since 5-82, when she was used as an aircraft transport to the Falklands. Conversion at Harland and Wolff, Belfast, to complete 1986, with vehicle cargo decks converted to a hangar and elevators added. Intended to replace *Engadine* (K 08) as helicopter training ship or to act as a transport for Harrier/Sea Harrier aircraft. Plans to purchase sister *Contender Argent* dropped late 1984. Data above pertains to ship in merchant configuration (11,445 grt); range may be reduced if fuel tankage is altered for aircraft fuel. Originally a combined container/vehicle cargo ship, with vehicle ramps to starboard at bow and stern. Will have space for 8 Sea Harriers and 3 helicopters on the hangar deck and 3 helicopters on deck, aft. There are two aircraft elevators.

◆ **1 helicopter training ship**

	Bldr	Laid down	L	In serv.
K 08 Engadine	Henry Robb Ltd.	9-8-65	16-9-66	15-12-67

Engadine (K 08)—with lengthened flight deck, MARISAT, chaff launchers
L. & L. Van Ginderen, 11-84

D: 3,875 tons light (9,105 fl) **S:** 16 kts **Dim:** 141.20 × 17.86 × 6.73
Electron Equipt: Radar: 3/nav.—EW: 12/Knebworth/Corvus chaff RL(VIII × 2)
M: 1 Sulzer 5RD68, 5-cyl. diesel; 1 prop; 5,500 hp **Electric:** 1,200 kw
Fuel: 450 tons **Man:** 61 RFA plus 14 RN (and air group: 29 officers, 84 men)

Remarks: Intended to train flight crews in ASW helicopter procedures at sea. The hangar can hold either four Wessex or two Sea King and two Wasp. A smaller hangar atop the superstructure serves a target-drone launch facility. Equipped with Denny-Brown fin stabilizers and has remote bridge control for all engineering plants. Many internal compartments are voids. RFA-operated. 6,384 grt, 4,520 dwt. Flight deck extended aft 11.9 m at Gibraltar, early 1984, to permit two Sea King on deck at once; original length 129.31 m. To be replaced by *Argus* in 1986.

◆ **1 antarctic patrol ship**

	Bldr	L	In serv.
A 171 Endurance (ex-*Anita Dan*)	Krögerwerft, Rendsburg	25-5-56	12-56

Endurance (A 171) L. & L. Van Ginderen, 5-83

D: 3,600 tons (fl) **S:** 14.5 kts **Dim:** 93.58 (82.9 pp) × 14.03 × 5.03
A: 2/20-mm Mk 4 AA (I × 2)—2/Wasp helicopters (AS.12 ASM)
Electron Equipt: Radar: 2/Decca TM 829
M: 1 Burmeister & Wain 550VTBF, 5-cyl. diesel; 1 prop; 3,220 hp (plus a bow-thruster)
Range: 12,000/14 **Man:** 13 officers, 106 men, up to 12 scientists

Remarks: Purchased 20-2-67. Hull painted red, superstructure white. Carries two Wasp helicopters and two survey launches. Converted 1967-68 by Harland & Wolff, Belfast, to support the British Antarctic Survey and act as guard ship in the Falkland Islands; 2,641 grt. MARISAT added 1978. Was to have been discarded 1982, but performed with distinction in Falklands War and will be retained. Refitted 1982 to 14-10-83.

MISCELLANEOUS AUXILIARY SHIPS *(continued)*

◆ **1 royal yacht**

	Bldr	Laid down	L	In serv.
(A 00) BRITANNIA	J. Brown (Clydebank)	7-52	16-4-53	14-1-54

Britannia L. & L. Van Ginderen, 8-84

D: 3,990 tons (4,961 fl) **S:** 21 kts **Dim:** 125.9 (115.82 pp) × 16.76 × 4.86
Electron Equipt: Radar: 2/1006 **M:** 2 sets GT; 2 props; 12,000 hp
Boilers: 2 **Fuel:** 510 tons **Range:** 3,100/20 **Man:** 21 officers, 256 men

REMARKS: 5,769 grt. Naval-manned. In wartime, would become a hospital ship (200 beds and 60 medical personnel) and have a helicopter platform. Gyrofin stabilizers. Reboilered during 1980 refit; equipped to burn distillate fuel 1984. Equipped with MARISAT 1982.

◆ **1 submarine-support ship**

A 236 WAKEFUL (ex-*Dan*, ex-*Herakles*) Bldr: Cochrane, Selkirk (In serv. 1965)

Wakeful (A 236) J. Goss, 1980

D: 900 tons (1,100 fl) **S:** 15 kts **Dim:** 44.43 (38.86 pp) × 10.7 × 4.74
Electron Equipt: Radar: 1/1006 **M:** Ruston & Hornsby 9-cyl. diesels; 1 prop; 4,750 hp **Electric:** 380 kw **Man:** 27 tot.

REMARKS: Former commercial tug, 492 grt. Purchased 1974 from Sweden to act as submarine target ship and safety vessel at Faslane; subsequently also used occasionally on fisheries patrol duties. Naval-manned. Very expensive to operate.

◆ **1 seabed operations tender**

	Bldr	Laid down	L	In serv.
K 07 CHALLENGER	Scotts SB, Govan	25-1-80	19-5-81	1984

Challenger (K 07) Walles Foto, 3-85

Challenger (K 07)—note stern gallows crane, helicopter deck abaft paired stacks
L. & L. Van Ginderen, 7-84

D: 6,500 tons (7,185 fl) **S:** 15 kts **Dim:** 134.0 (130.5 pp) × 18.0 × 5.4
Electron Equipt: Radar: 1/1006, 1/ . . . —Sonar: 1/2008, 1/2013, 1/193M
M: 5 Ruston 16 RK3CZ diesels (3,430 hp each), electric drive; 2 Voith-Schneider vertical cycloidal props aft; 10,200 hp (three bow-thrusters)
Electric: 1,500-kw harbor service **Range:** 8,000/ . . . **Man:** 186 tot.

REMARKS: Ordered 28-9-79. Royal Navy manned. Dynamic positioning system capable of maintaining a constant location in 50- to 60-kt winds, in a sea state of 5. Carries a submersible decompression chamber for 12 divers and is equipped for saturation diving. Twelve divers and their equipment are handled through a "moon-pool" amidships by a 25-ton crane, while a gallows crane on the stern will handle Towed Unmanned Submersibles (TUMS). Passive tank stabilization system. The integrated navigational system, with a GEC 4070 computer, incorporates Decca "Hi-Fix," Omega, navigational satellite reception, and a Decca radio navaid receiver. The helo platform will accept a Sea King. Completion delayed by faulty wiring. Can move at 3.5 kts sideways and can lift 25-ton objects from the bottom.

◆ **1 offshore support and salvage ship**

SEAFORTH CLANSMAN Bldr: Cochrane, Selby (In serv. 1977)

Seaforth Clansman—with new helo deck L. & L. Van Ginderen, 3-85

D: 3,320 tons (fl) **S:** 14 kts **Dim:** 78.6 (68.7 pp) × 13.7 × 5.01
M: 4 Mirrlees-Blackstone EZSL-12 diesels; 2 CP, Kort-nozzle props; 7,320 hp
Electric: 1,748 kw **Fuel:** 404 tons
Man: 46 tot. (plus 20-man naval salvage group)

REMARKS: 1,977 grt/1/180 dwt. RFA-operated; chartered 1978, extended into at least 1986. The ship was originally intended for oilfield support duties and for maintaining single-point deep moorings. Has a submersible diver's decompression chamber and a "moon-pool" opening through the keel of the ship to ensure smooth waters for diving operations. Both bow- and stern-thrusters are fitted. Has a four-point mooring system and a 30-ton capacity electrohydraulic crane to port, aft. Has no pendant number. Kingposts with four fire monitors replaced by grotesquely elevated helicopter deck during refit 5 to 7-84.

◆ **1 Falkland Islands support ship, ex-Argentine oilfield supply tug**

	Bldr	L	In serv.
. . . FALKLAND SOUND (ex-*Yehuin*, ex-*Millerntor*)	J.G. Hitzler SY, Lauenburg	1967	6-83 (RN)

D: . . . **S:** 12.5 kts **Dim:** 53.52 (49.20 pp) × 11.26 × 3.35
A: . . . **M:** 2 MTM 12-cyl. diesels; 2 CP props; 1,900 hp
Electric: 336 kw **Fuel:** 254 tons **Man:** . . .

REMARKS: 495 grt/756 dwt. Owned by Geomatter S.A., Buenos Aires, but pressed into naval use. Captured intact at the end of the Falklands War and put into service for patrol, tug, and supply duties. Initially informally named the *Black Pig* because of her black paint scheme and general appearance. Has bow-thruster.

MOORING, SALVAGE, AND NET TENDERS

◆ **2 (+1) "Sal" class** Bldr: Hall Russell, Ltd., Aberdeen

	Laid down	L	In serv.
A 185 Salmoor	19-4-84	8-5-85	11-85
A 186 Salmaster	17-9-84	12-11-85	6-86
A 187 Salmaid	29-6-84	. . .	12-85

D: 1,700 tons (fl) **S:** 15 kts **Dim:** 77.10 (65.80 pp) × 14.80 × 3.80
Electron Equipt: Radar: . . . nav.
M: 2 Ruston-Paxman 8RKC diesels; 1 CP prop; 4,000 hp
Man: 32 tot. (accommodations for 46) **Range:** . . .

Remarks: Ordered 29-1-84 as replacement for "Kin" class. Will be capable of mooring, buoy tending, salvage, diving support, and firefighting.

◆ **2 Pochard class**

	Bldr	L	In serv.
A 164 Goosander (ex-P 196)	Robb Caledon Ltd.	12-4-73	10-9-73
A 165 Pochard (ex-P 197)	Robb Caledon Ltd.	21-6-73	11-12-73

Goosander (A 164)—MARISAT added, two 40-ft. vans atop superstructure
L. & L. Van Ginderen, 9-84

D: 750 tons (1,200 fl) **S:** 10 kts **Dim:** 55.4 (48.8 pp) × 12.2 × 5.5
M: 2 Paxman RPHXM 16-cyl. diesels; 550 hp **Range:** 3,250/9.5 **Man:** 26 tot.

Remarks: RMAS-operated. All moorings, salvage, and boom vessels are multi-purpose and are capable of transporting and servicing moorings, performing salvage duties, and, in wartime, handling harbor-defense nets. Can dead-lift 200 tons over bow horns.

◆ **4 Wild Duck class**

	Bldr	L	In serv.
P 192 Mandarin	Cammell Laird	17-9-63	5-3-64
P 193 Pintail	Camell Laird	3-12-63	3-64
P 194 Garganey	Brooke Marine Ltd.	13-12-65	20-9-66
P 195 Goldeneye	Brooke Marine Ltd.	31-3-66	21-12-66

Goldeneye (P 195) L. & L. Van Ginderen, 3-83

D: 850 tons (1,300 fl) (P 192, P 193: 941/1,622 tons) **S:** 10.8 kts
Dim: 57.86 (47.24 pp) × 13.0 × 3.2 (P 192, P 193: 60.23 × 12.22 × 4.21)
M: 2 Davey-Paxman 16-cyl. diesels; 1 CP prop; 50 hp (P 192, P 193: 750 hp)
Electric: P 194, P 195: 640 kw; P 192, P 193: 405 kw **Range:** 3,000/10
Man: 7 officers, 18 men

Remarks: RMAS-operated. *Pintail* has extra accommodations for divers in deckhouse abaft stack. 200-ton deadlift capacity over bow. Retain "P" (Patrol-series) pendant numbers.

◆ **3 "Kin" class** (to be disposed of 1985-86)

	Bldr	Laid down	L	In serv.
A 232 Kingarth	Alex. Hall, Aberdeen	16-7-43	22-5-44	28-12-44
A 281 Kinbrace	Alex. Hall, Aberdeen	20-4-44	17-1-45	30-4-45
A 482 Kinloss	Alex. Hall, Aberdeen	. . .	. . .	9-7-45

Kinbrace (A 281) L. & L. Van Ginderen, 3-85

D: 950 tons (1,050 fl) **S:** 9 kts **Dim:** 54.0 × 10.6 × 3.6
M: 1 Atlas Polar M44M diesel; 630 hp **Man:** 34 tot.

Remarks: RMAS-operated; 200-ton lift. Originally had reciprocating steam engines; diesels fitted 1964-67. 775 grt, 262 dwt. Sister *Uplifter* (A 507) stricken 10-85.

Note: The Insect-class fleet tender *Scarab* is also equipped as a moorings tender (10-ton lift).

SEAGOING TUGS

◆ **3 Roysterer class** Bldr: C.D. Holmes, Hull

	L	In serv.
A 361 Roysterer	20-5-70	25-4-72
A 502 Rollicker	29-1-71	2-73
A 366 Robust	7-10-71	6-4-64

Robust (A 366) L. & L. Van Ginderen, 2-84

D: 1,630 tons (fl) **S:** 15 kts **Dim:** 54.8 (49.4 pp) × 11.6 × 5.5
M: 2 Mirrlees KMR6 diesels; 2 CP props; 4,500 hp
Range: 13,000/12 **Electron Equipt:** Radar: 2/Decca nav.
Man: 10 officers, 21 men (plus 10-man RN salvage party if needed)

Remarks: RMAS-operated; 50-ton bollard pull. Although designed for long-distance towing, have been used primarily in port service, at Devonport (A 502: Portland). Have heavy tripod mast, with after legs containing engine exhausts.

◆ **1 Typhoon class** Bldr: H. Robb, Leith

	L	In serv.
A 95 Typhoon	14-10-58	1960

D: 800 tons (1,380 fl) **S:** 17 kts **Dim:** 605. × 12.3 × 4.0
Electron Equipt: Radar: 1/978
M: 2 12-cyl. diesels; 1 CP prop; 2,750 hp

Remarks: RMAS-operated; 32-ton bollard pull. Based at Portland.

SEAGOING TUGS *(continued)*

Typhoon (A 95) L. & L. Van Ginderen, 10-82

◆ **1 Confiance class** Bldr: A. & S. Inglis, Glasgow

A 290 Confident (In serv. 1-56)

Confident (A 290) L. & L. Van Ginderen, 12-82

D: 760 tons (fl) **S:** 13 kts **Dim:** 47.2 (42.7 pp) × 10.7 × 3.4
M: 4 Paxman HAXM diesels; 2 CP props; 1,800 hp
Man: 29 tot. plus 13 salvage

Remarks: RMAS-operated. *Agile* only unit with tall mainmast. Sister *Confiance* (A 290) struck, sunk as target 22-6-84. Sisters *Agile* (A 88), *Advice* (A 89), and *Accord* (A 90) stricken 1985, with A 290 soon to follow; replaced by second flight of *Adept*-class large harbor tugs.

SERVICE CRAFT

Note: Most service craft are operated by the Royal Maritime Auxiliary Service (RMAS), a civilian organization, with some operated by the reservists of the Royal Naval Auxiliary Service (RNXS). Increasingly, pendant numbers are being displayed; in the listings below, where the numbers are not borne, they are given in parentheses.

AMMUNITION TRANSPORTS

◆ **2 Throsk class**

	Bldr	Laid down	L	In serv.
A 378 Kinterbury	Cleland SB, Wallsend	1980	8-11-80	20-1-81
A 379 Throsk	Cleland SB, Wallsend	25-8-76	31-3-77	20-9-77

Throsk (A 379) L. & L. Van Ginderen, 5-85

D: 2,193 tons (fl) **S:** 14 kts **Dim:** 70.57 (64.31 pp) × 11.9 × 4.57
M: 2 Mirrlees-Blackstone diesels; 1 prop; 3,000 hp **Range:** 1,500/14; 5,000/10
Electron Equipt: Radar: 1/Decca . . . **Man:** 10 officers, 22 men

Remarks: RMAS-operated. Two holds, two 5-ton cranes; 1,150 dwt. Two cargo holds: 750 m³ total. Can transport 760 tons in holds plus 25 tons of cargo on deck. A 378 has improved accommodations and two electric cranes; A 379 has two cargo boom cranes. Sister *St. George* (in serv. 4-81) operated by Army's Royal Corps of Transport.

DEGAUSSING TENDERS

◆ **2 Magnet class** Bldr: Clelands, Wallsend

	Laid down	L	In serv.
A 114 Magnet	3-11-78	12-7-79	15-11-79
A 115 Lodestone	22-12-78	15-11-79	4-80

Magnet (A 114) L. & L. Van Ginderen, 7-84

D: 950 grt **S:** 12 kts **Dim:** 54.8 (50.0 pp) × 11.4 × 3.0
M: 2 Mirrlees-Blackstone ESL-6-MGR diesels, electric drive; 2 props; 1,650 hp
Electric: 245 kw **Fuel:** 40 tons **Range:** 1,750/12 **Man:** 15 tot.

Remarks: Built to commercial standards. RMAS-operated. Use two 800-cell, 400-V battery banks and two variable-resistance capacitors to provide 4,000 amps DC for 40 seconds. Can deperm a 60,000-ton ship. A 115 completed a refit 21-12-84.

TORPEDO RETRIEVERS

◆ **4 Tornado class** Bldr: Hall Russell, Aberdeen

	Laid down	L	In serv.
A 140 Tornado	2-11-78	24-5-79	15-11-79
A 141 Torch	5-12-78	7-8-79	12-2-80
A 142 Tormentor	19-3-79	6-11-79	29-4-80
A 143 Toreador	14-6-79	14-2-80	1-7-80

Torch (A 141) L. & L. Van Ginderen, 4-85

D: 660 tons (698 fl) **S:** 14 kts **Dim:** 47.47 (40.0 pp) × 8.53 × 3.0
M: 2 Lister-Blackstone ESL-8-MGR diesels; 2 props; 2,200 hp
Fuel: 110 tons **Range:** 3,000/. . . **Man:** 17 tot.

Remarks: RMAS-operated.

◆ **2 Torrent class**

	Bldr	L	In serv.
A 127 Torrent	Cleland SB, Wallsend	29-3-71	10-9-71
A 128 Torrid	Cleland SB, Wallsend	7-9-71	1-72

D: 468 tons (685 fl) **S:** 11.5 kts **Dim:** 49.55 (44.2 pp) × 9,72 × 3.05
M: Paxman 16 RPHM diesel; 1 prop; 700 hp **Electric:** 300 kw **Fuel:** 49 tons
Range: 1,500/11 **Man:** 19 tot.

TORPEDO RETRIEVERS *(continued)*

Torrid (A 128) L. & L. Van Ginderen, 8-81

REMARKS: Can stow 32 torpedoes in hold and 10 on deck and perform post-firing maintenance. Stern ramp for recovery. RMAS-operated.

◆ **1 converted customs craft**

ENDEAVOR Bldr: R. Dunston, Thorne (In serv. 1966)

D: 88 tons (fl) **S:** 10.5 kts **Dim:** 23.2 × 4.4 × 2.0
M: 1 Lister-Blackstone diesel; 337 hp

REMARKS: RMAS-operated. Resembles a small tug; cannot bring recovered torpedoes aboard. Also used as range safety craft at Portland.

◆ **3 torpedo recovery launches** Bldr: R. Dunston, Thorne (In serv. 1979)

D: 15 tons **S:** 9 kts **Dim:** 13.8 × 2.98 × 0.76
M: 1 Perkins 6-354 diesel; 1 prop; 104 hp **Man:** 4 tot.

◆ **1 ex-RAF RTTL Mk 2-class former target-tow launch**

OSPREY (ex-RAF 2770) (In serv. 1940s)

Osprey L. & L. Van Ginderen, 10-82

D: 34.6 tons (fl) **S:** 30 kts **Dim:** 20.7 × 5.8 × 1.8
M: 2 Rolls-Royce Sea Griffon gasoline engines; 2 props; 2,200 hp **Man:** 9 tot.

◆ **1 ex-RAF 1300 series former air-sea rescue launch**

L 72 (ex-RAF . . .) (In serv. 1955-56)

D: 28.3 tons (fl) **S:** 13 kts **Dim:** 19.2 × 4.7 × 1.5
M: 2 Rolls-Royce C8 diesels; 2 props; 190 hp

DIVING TENDERS

◆ **5 modified Cartmel class** Bldr: Gregson, Blyth

A 308 ILCHESTER
A 309 INSTOW
A 310 INVERGORDON
A 311 IRONBRIDGE (ex-*Invergordon*)
A 318 IXWORTH

REMARKS: RMAS-operated, except A 308 and A 309, by Navy. All in service 1974, except A 310, ordered 7-80. Details and appearance as for *Cartmel*-class tenders, except for a decompression chamber on deck forward, beneath a stowage platform for a Gemini dinghy. Can be used for harbor mine clearance. Displacement is 150 tons (fl).

◆ **1 Datchet class** Bldr: Vosper, Singapore (In serv. 1968)

A 357 DATCHET

D: 70 tons (fl) **S:** 12 kts **Dim:** 22.86 × 5.79 × 1.22
Electron Equipt: Radar: 1/978
M: 2 Gray Marine diesels; 2 props; 500 hp **Range:** 500/12

REMARKS: Was RMAS, but now RN-manned; based at Plymouth.

Instow (A 309) L. & L. Van Ginderen, 7-84

Datchet (A 357) L. & L. Van Ginderen, 8-85

◆ **4 diver support craft** Bldr: Tough, Teddington (In serv. 1981-82)

D: 10 tons (fl) **S:** 8.5 kts **Dim:** 11.7 × 4.3 × 1.4
M: 1 Perkins 6-354.4 diesel; 120 hp **Man:** 2 crew, 12 divers

REMARKS: Glass-reinforced plastic construction. One unit, unofficially named *Reclaim*, is attached to HMS *Vernon*.

TRAINING CRAFT

NOTE: The five Tracker-class patrol craft delivered in 1983 and the 14 P.2000-class patrol craft ordered in 7-84 are also intended for training, as are the patrol boats *Peterel* (P 262) and *Sandpiper* (P 263), the tenders *Loyal Moderator* (A 220), *Clovelly* (A 370), *Cromarty* (A 488), and *Froxfield* (A 354) of the *Cartmel* class, and *Alnmouth* (Y 13), *Bembridge* (A 101), and *Aberdovey* (Y 10), of the *Aberdovey* class; all are described elsewhere.

Former frigates *Falmouth, Ashanti,* and *Blackpool* are employed as training hulks to train Marine Engineering Mechanics at the Harbor Training Complex, Plymouth.

◆ **4 modified "Loyal" class** Bldr: R. Dunston, Thorne

	Laid down	L	In serv.
A 92 MANLY	18-9-80	23-7-81	2-3-82
A 94 MENTOR	20-10-80	7-10-81	6-4-82
A 97 MILBROOK	30-1-81	16-12-81	24-6-82
A 107 MESSINA	7-4-81	5-3-82	1-9-82

Manly (A 92) French Navy, 6-82

TRAINING CRAFT *(continued)*

D: 128 tons (150 fl) **S:** 11.5 kts **Dim:** 24.00 × 6.40 × 2.33
Electron Equipt: Radar: 1/978 **Fuel:** 4.5 tons
M: 1 Lister-Blackstone ES4MGR diesel; 1 cycloidal prop; 330 hp
Range: 700/10 **Man:** 6 tot. (plus trainees)

REMARKS: First three serve HMS *Raleigh* training facility; last for Royal Marine training.

◆ **3 target craft, ex-side-haul trawlers** Bldr: Goole SB & Repair, Goole. (In serv. 1961)

BULLSEYE (ex-*Tokio*) MAGPIE (ex-*Honda*) TARGE (ex-*Erimo*)

Bullseye—with tug alongside L. & L. Van Ginderen, 7-85

D: 600 tons (fl) **S:** 12 kts **Dim:** 35.85 × 7.73 × 3.70
M: 1 Mirrlees 6-cyl. diesel; 1 prop; 700 hp **Fuel:** 57 tons
Man: 1 officer, 12 men

REMARKS: 273 grt/91 nrt. First two acquired 6-82 and third in 6-84 for use as radio-controlled targets at Portland. Royal Navy-manned. "T.V." on hull before name means "Target Vessel." Radar corner reflectors mounted forward, and television camera placed on stub mast forward of stack. *Magpie* is the controller unit and has a large radome atop the pilothouse.

◆ **1 navigational training tender** Bldr: Vosper (In serv. 1964)

TREVOSE

Trevose L. & L. Van Ginderen, 7-80

D: 74 tons (fl) **S:** 12 kts **Dim:** 21.9 × . . . × . . .
M: 2 diesels; 2 props; . . . hp

REMARKS: Transferred from the Royal Corps of Transport 1981 for Royal Naval Reserve training.

◆ **3 training tenders** (In serv. 1944-46)

OLIVER TWIST SMIKE URIAH HEEP

D: . . . **S:** 8 kts **Dim:** 15.2 × . . . × . . . **M:** 1 diesel; . . . hp

REMARKS: 20 grt. Wooden-hulled fishing-boat-type craft transferred from the Royal Corps of Transport in 1974-81 for use as Royal Naval Reserve training tenders.

NOTE: The last "Ford"-class Seaward Defence Boat in Royal Navy service, *Droxford* (P 3113), used in recent years for naval reserve officer training, was stricken 10-83. Stern-haul trawler *Northella,* chartered 10-83 for six months' training duties, was returned to her owners in 4-84. Oceanographic research craft *Sarsia,* chartered 3-82 for reserve officer training, was also returned. Trawler-research vessel *G.A. Reay* (999 grt, 69.15 × 12.10 × 5.07, 2,500 hp, 19.5 kts) was chartered 26-9-84, but was returned to her owners in 1985 and leased to the Indian government. *Waterwitch* (M 2720), a former inshore minesweeper of the "Ham" class later used for survey work, and from 1981 for reserve officer cadet training, was stricken 4-3-85.

Uriah Heep L. & L. Van Ginderen, 8-83

FUEL LIGHTERS

◆ **6 Oil class** Bldr: Appledore SB (All in serv. 1979)

	L		L
(Y 21) OILPRESS	10-6-68	(Y 24) OILFIELD	5-9-68
(Y 22) OILSTONE	11-7-68	(Y 25) OILBIRD	21-11-68
(Y 23) OILWELL	20-1-69	(Y 26) OILMAN	18-2-69

Oilpress (Y 21) Skyfotos, 8-82

D: 250 tons (535 fl) **S:** 10 kts **Dim:** 42.26 (39.62 pp) × 7.47 × 2.51
Electron Equipt: Radar: 1/978
M: 1 Lister-Blackstone ES-6-MGR diesel; 405 hp **Electric:** 225 kw
Fuel: 15 tons **Range:** 1,500/10 **Man:** 4 officers, 7 men

REMARKS: First three carry diesel fuel and are 247 tons (527 fl); other three carry fuel oil. RMAS-operated.

WATER LIGHTERS

◆ **7 Water class** Bldr: Drypool, Hull, except A 146: R. Dunston, Hessle

	In serv.		In serv.
Y 17 WATERFALL	1967	Y 30 WATERCOURSE	1974
Y 18 WATERSHED	1967	Y 31 WATERFOWL	25-5-74
Y 19 WATERSPOUT	1967	A 146 WATERMAN	6-78
Y 20 WATERSLIDE	1968		

Waterfowl (Y 31) L. & L. Van Ginderen, 7-84

WATER LIGHTERS *(continued)*

D: 344 tons (fl) **S:** 11 kts **Dim:** 40.02 (37.5 pp) × 7.5 × 2.44
Electron Equipt: Radar: 1/978
M: 1 Lister-Blackstone ERS-8-MGR diesel; 600 hp **Electric:** 155 kw
Range: 1,500/11 **Man:** 11 tot.

REMARKS: RMAS-operated. Built 1966-73. Carry 150 tons water cargo. Resemble "Oil" class. Y 30, Y 31, and A 146 have deckhouse over after cargo tanks, others do not.

GENERAL-PURPOSE TENDERS

◆ **7 100-foot "Insect" class** Bldr: C.D. Holmes, Beverley (In serv. 1970-73)

A 216 BEE	A 230 COCKCHAFER	A 253 LADYBIRD	A 272 SCARAB
A 229 CRICKET	A 239 GNAT	A 263 CICADA	

Ladybird (A 253) L. & L. Van Ginderen, 7-85

D: 213 tons (450 fl) **S:** 10.5 kts **Dim:** 34.06 (30.48 pp) × 8.53 × 3.2
Electron Equipt: Radar: 1/978
M: 1 Lister-Blackstone ERS-8-HGR diesel; 660 hp **Man:** 10 tot.

REMARKS: RMAS-operated; 200 tons cargo, one 3-ton crane. *Scarab,* with 5-ton winch and bow horn, is used as a moorings tender, *Gnat* and *Ladybird* transport ammunition.

◆ **8 "Loyal" class** Bldr: R. Dunston, Thorne

	In serv.		In serv.
A 157 LOYAL HELPER	1978	A 161 LOYAL MEDIATOR	1978
A 158 SUPPORTER (ex-*Loyal Supporter*)	1977	A 220 LOYAL MODERATOR	1973
		A 1770 LOYAL CHANCELLOR	1972
A 159 LOYAL WATCHER	1977	A 1771 LOYAL PROCTOR	1973
A 160 LOYAL VOLUNTEER	1977		

Loyal Mediator (A 161) L. & L. Van Ginderen, 7-83

REMARKS: RNXS-operated. Details as for *Cartmel* class, but equipped to carry up to 200 personnel in cargo hold for short distances (except *Loyal Moderator,* training craft, 12 extra berths instead). Sisters *Vigilant* (P 254, ex-*Loyal Factor,* A 382) and *Alert* (P 252, ex-*Loyal Governor,* A 510) are operated by the Royal Navy as patrol craft off Ulster. A 158 operates as a stores carrier from Belfast. Four very similar craft built as training tenders; *see* above.

◆ **32 Cartmel class** Bldr: (A): Isaac Pimblott & Sons, Northwich; (B): C.D. Holmes, Beverley; (C): John Lewis, Aberdeen; (D): R. Dunston, Thorne; (E): J. Cook, Wivenhoe

	Bldr	In serv.		Bldr	In serv.
A 350 CARTMEL	A	1968	A 381 CRICKLADE	B	1970
A 389 CLOVELLY	A	1971	A 488 CROMARTY	C	1970
A 391 CRICCIETH	A	1971	A 363 DENMEAD	B	1970
A 490 DORNOCH	C	1970	A 1769 HAMBLEDON	D	1972
A 393 DUNSTER	D	1970	A 1768 HARLECH	D	1972
A 353 ELKSTONE	E	1969	A 1776 HEADCORN	D	1972
A 277 ELSING	E	1970	A 1767 HEVER	D	1972
A 355 EPWORTH	E	1970	A 1772 HOLMWOOD	D	1973
A 274 ETTRICK	E	1970	A 1773 HORNING	D	1973
A 348 FELSTED	D	1970	A 208 LAMLASH	D	1973
A 394 FINTRY	C	1970	A 211 LECHLADE	D	1973
A 341 FOTHERBY	D	1970	A 207 LANDOVERY	D	1973
A 354 FROXFIELD	D	1970	A 83 MELTON	D	21-8-81
A 365 FULBECK	B	1969	A 84 MENAI	D	4-11-81
A 392 GLENCOE	A	1971	A 87 MEON	D	9-11-82
A 402 GRASMERE	C	1970	A 91 MILFORD	D	11-1-83

Clovelly (A 389) L. & L. Van Ginderen, 7-85

D: 143 tons (fl) **S:** 10.5 kts **Dims:** 24.38 (22.86 pp) × 6.40 × 1.98
Electron Equipt: Radar: 1/978 (not on all)
M: 1 Lister-Blackstone ERS-4-MGR diesel; 330 hp **Electric:** 106 kw
Range: 700/10 **Man:** 6 tot.

REMARKS: RMAS-operated, except *Ettrick* and *Elsing,* which are RN-manned and used for patrol at Gibraltar. Improved version of *Aberdovey* class; 25 tons cargo. First two, 5.49-meter beam. Carry stores, personnel, food. Can tow. *Clovelly, Cromarty, Froxfield, Hever,* and *Headcorn* are also used for training, and *Dornoch* and *Fotherby* have been used as diving tenders. The last four were ordered 25-2-80. Sister *Cawsand* (A 351) for sale 10-85.

◆ **8 Aberdovey class** Bldr: (A): Issac Pimblott & Sons, Northwich; (B): J. S. Doig, Grimsby

	Bldr	In serv.		Bldr	In serv.
Y 10 ABERDOVEY	A	1963	A 100 BEDDGELERT	B	1967
Y 13 ALNMOUTH	A	1966	A 101 BEMBRIDGE	B	1968
Y 14 APPLEBY	A	1967	A 103 BIBURY	B	1969
A 99 BEAULIEU	B	1966	A 104 BLAKENEY	B	1970

Bibury (A 103) L. & L. Van Ginderen, 7-83

D: 117.5 tons (fl) **S:** 10.5 kts **Dim:** 24.16 (22.86 pp) × 5.79 × 1.68
Electron Equipt: Radar: 1/978 or Decca 150
M: 1 Lister-Blackstone ER-4-MGR diesel; 225 hp **Range:** 700/10 **Man:** 6 tot.

REMARKS: RMAS-operated, except for Y 10, RNXS. Carry 25 tons cargo. *Alnmouth* and *Bembridge* used for Sea Cadet Corps training; *Aberdovey* used for training Royal Marines; *Abinger* (Y 11) attached to Aberdeen University for officer candidate training, was paid off in 1985. Sisters *Alness* (Y 12), *Ashcott* (Y 16), and *Brodick* (A 105) for sale 10-85.

GENERAL-PURPOSE TENDERS *(continued)*

◆ **1 converted ex-stern trawler** Bldr: P.K. Harris, Appledore (In serv. 1962)

A 362 DOLWEN (ex-*Hector Gull*)

Dolwen (A 362) L. & L. Van Ginderen, 1980

D: 602 tons (fl) **S:** . . . kts **Dim:** 39.65 (36.73 pp) × 9.12 × 4.40
Electron Equipt: Radar: 1/1006
M: 1 National FSSM-6 diesel; 1 CP prop; 1,160 hp

REMARKS: Gallows at stern for laying buoys; used as air bombardment safety range craft for the Royal Aircraft Establishment, Aberforth. Operated by a private contractor.

◆ **1 "Ham"-class former inshore minesweepers**

(M 2781) PORTISHAM

Portisham (M 2781) L. & L. Van Ginderen, 8-85

D: 115–120 tons (150–160 fl) **S:** 14 kts **Dim:** 32.47 × 6.10 × 1.75
Electron Equipt: Radar: 1/978 **Range:** 2,350/9
M: 2 Paxman YHAXM 12-cyl. diesels; 2 props; 1,100 hp
Electric: 108 kw **Fuel:** 15 tons **Man:** . . .

REMARKS: *Portisham*, RNXS-operated, is to be replaced in 1986 by P.2000-class training patrol boat. Built 1953-57. Carries passengers and stores. M 2726 temporarily used as an inshore survey ship, 1978-79. Sisters *Shipham* (M 2726) and *Sandringham* (M 2791) stricken 10-85.

◆ **13 motor fishing vessel tenders**

6 store carriers: MFV.7 (1943), MFV.15 (1942), MFV.96 (1944), MFV.256 (1944), MFV.740 (1945), MFV.911 (1945)
3 general-purpose: MFV.140 (1946), MFV.175 (1945), MFV.816 (1945)
4 diving tenders: MFV.119 (1944), MFV.642 (1945), MFV.775 (1945), MFV.1077 (1944)

MFV.15—stores carrier L. & L. Van Ginderen, 10-81

MFV.642—diving tender L. & L. Van Ginderen, 7-84

MFV.119—diving tender G. Gyssels, 4-83

REMARKS: Wooden-hulled fishing boats of varying characteristics. Most have "double-ended" hulls, engines and pilothouse aft.

LARGE HARBOR TUGS

◆ **7 (+2) Adept-class "Twin-Unit Tractors"** Bldr: R. Dunston, Hessle

	Laid down	L	In serv.
A 221 FORCEFUL	30-3-84	. . .	29-3-85
A 222 NIMBLE	27-4-84	21-3-85	25-6-85
A 223 POWERFUL	21-6-84	3-6-85	. . . -85
A 224 ADEPT	22-7-79	27-8-80	28-10-80
A 225 BUSTLER	28-11-79	20-2-80	15-4-81
A 226 CAPABLE	5-9-80	2-7-81	11-9-81
A 227 CAREFUL	15-1-81	12-1-82	12-3-82
A 228 FAITHFUL	30-11-84	. . .	. . .
A 231 DEXTEROUS	18-4-85	. . .	. . .

Forceful (A 221) L. & L. Van Ginderen, 7-85

D: 450 tons **S:** 12.5 kts **Dim:** 38.82 (37.00 pp) × 9.10 × 4.20 (3.40 mean)
Electron Equipt: Radar: 1/Decca . . .
M: 2 Ruston 6 RKCM diesels; 2 Voith-Schneider vertical-cycloidal props; 2,640 hp
Electric: 294 kw **Fuel:** 49 tons **Man:** 12 tot.

REMARKS: RMAS-operated. Ordered 22-2-79. 28-ton bollard pull. Also used for coastal towing. The five later units were ordered 8-2-84 to replace the *Confiance*-class seagoing tugs.

LARGE HARBOR TUGS *(continued)*

◆ **18 Dog class** Bldrs: Various (In serv. 1962-72)

(A 106) Alsatian
(A 327) Basset
(A 126) Cairn
(A 328) Collie
(A 330) Corgi
(A 129) Dalmatian
(A 155) Deerhound
(A 162) Elkhound
(A 326) Foxhound (ex-*Boxer*)
(A 169) Husky
(A 168) Labrador
(A 180) Mastiff
(A 188) Pointer
(A 182) Saluki
(A 187) Sealyham
(A 189) Setter
(A 250) Sheepdog
(A 201) Spaniel

Dalmatian (A 129)—no radar, low pilothouse L. & L. Van Ginderen, 7-83

Setter (A 189)—high pilothouse with windows, Decca radar G. Gyssels, 10-84

D: 206 tons (248 fl) **S:** 12 kts **Dim:** 28.65 (25.91 pp) × 7.72 × 3.51
Electron Equipt: Radar: 1/978
M: 2 Lister-Blackstone ERS-86-MGR diesels; 1 prop; 1,320 hp
Electric: 80 kw **Man:** 8 tot.

Remarks: RMAS-operated. 18.7-ton bollard pull. *Foxhound* renamed 22-10-77. Appearances vary, some having streamlined upper pilothouse structures, others higher pilothouses. Sister *Airedale* (A 102) sold commercially at Gibraltar, 12-84.

MEDIUM HARBOR TUGS

◆ **8 Felicity-class water tractors** Bldrs: R. Dunston, Thorne (A 148, A 152, A 196, A 198: Hancock, Pembroke)

	In serv.		In serv.
(A 112) Felicity	1968	(A 150) Genevieve	29-10-80
(A 147) Frances	5-80	(A 152) Georgina	1973
(A 148) Fiona	1973	(A 196) Gwendoline	1974
(A 149) Florence	8-8-80	(A 198) Helen	1974

D: 220 tons (fl) **S:** 10.2 kts **Dim:** 22.25 (20.73 pp) × 6.40 × 2.97 (2.10 hull)
M: 1 Lister-Blackstone ERS-8-MGR diesel; cycloidal prop; 615 hp
Fuel: 12 tons **Range:** 1,800/8 **Man:** 6 tot.

Remarks: RMAS-operated, 138 grt. 5.9 to 6.1-ton bollard pull. Final three ordered 13-12-78.

◆ **8 modified "Girl" class** Bldrs: (A): Isaac Pimblott & Sons, Northwich; (B): R. Dunston, Thorne

	Bldr	In serv.		Bldr	In serv.
(A 210) Charlotte	A	1966	(A 156) Daphne	B	1969
(A 217) Christine	A	1966	(A 252) Doris	B	1969
(A 218) Clare	A	1966	(A 173) Dorothy	B	1969
(A 145) Daisy	B	1968	(A 178) Edith	B	1969

Dorothy (A 173) L. & L. Van Ginderen, 7-84

D: 100 tons (fl) **S:** 10.5 kts **Dim:** 20.57 × 6.25 × 2.9
Electron Equipt: Radar: 1/978 or none
M: 1 Lister-Blackstone ERS-8-MGR diesel; 495 hp **Range:** 900/10 **Man:** 4 tot.

Remarks: RMAS-operated. *Clare* manned by the RN as a patrol craft at Hong Kong until 31-12-81. *Celia* (A 206) sold commercially, 1971. 50 grt; 6.5-ton bollard pull.

Frances (A 147) L. & L. Van Ginderen, 7-83

◆ **1 "Girl" class** Bldrs: (A) P.K. Harris; (B) R. Dunston, Thorne

	Bldr	In serv.
(A 121) Agnes	A	1961

D: 66.5 tons (81 fl) **S:** 10 kts **Dim:** 18.75 (17.3 pp) × 5.11 × 2.36
M: 1 Lister-Blackstone ERS-6-MGR diesel; 495 hp **Range:** 980/9.8 **Man:** 4 tot.

Remarks: RMAS-operated. 40 grt; 6.5-tons bollard pull. Sisters *Agatha* (A 116), *Alice* (A 113), *Audrey* (A 117), and *Barbara* (A 324) stricken 1982. *Betty* (A 232) was stricken 1983. *Brenda* (A 335) and *Bridget* (A 322) transferred to the Royal Corps of Transport, 19-8-83.

SMALL HARBOR TUGS

◆ **12 Triton-class water tractors** Bldr: R. Dunston, Thorne (In serv. 1972-73)

(A 181) Irene
(A 183) Isabel
(A 190) Joan
(A 193) Joyce
(A 166) Kathleen
(A 170) Kitty
(A 172) Lesley
(A 174) Lilah
(A 175) Mary
(A 199) Myrtle
(A 202) Nancy
(A 205) Norah

D: 107.5 tons (fl) **S:** 7.75 kts **Dim:** 17.65 (16.76 pp) × 5.26 × 2.8
M: 1 Lister-Blackstone ERS-4-M diesel; cycloidal prop; 330 hp
Man: 6 tot.

Remarks: RMAS-operated; 50 grt; 3-ton bollard pull. Voith vertical cycloidal prop to provide instant mobility and full power in any direction.

SMALL HARBOR TUGS *(continued)*

Lilah (A 174) and cargo barge 1109(3) L. & L. Van Ginderen, 7-84

FLOATING DRYDOCKS

Note: "AFD" indicates Admiralty Floating Dock

AFD 60 Bldr: Portsmouth Dockyard (In serv. 1966)
Capacity: 13,500 tons Dim: 149.7 × 28 (17.7 wide × 10.7 depth interior)

AFD 59 Bldr: Portsmouth Dockyard (In serv. 1960)
Capacity: 12,000 tons Dim: 148.4 × 23.5 (15.5 wide × 10.4 depth interior)

AFD 58 Bldr: Furness Shipbldg, Teeside (In serv. 1957)
Capacity: 8,000 tons Dim: 137.2 × 28.0 (18.9 wide × 6.4 depth interior)

AFD 26 Bldr: Bombay Dockyard (In serv. 1944)
Capacity: 7,750 tons Dim: 115.8 × 28.0 (15.2 wide by 5.6 depth interior)

AFD 26—with tug *Foxhound* L. & L. Van Ginderen, 9-84

Note: AFD 26 is at Rosyth, AFD 58 at Devonport, AFD 59 at Barrow-in-Furness, and AFD 60 at the Gareloch. Most Royal Navy dockings are performed at permanent, fixed dry docks at Royal Dockyards and, recently, at private repair facilities.

HARBOR SERVICE CRAFT

Note: Little information is available on the hundreds of smaller self-propelled service craft or on non-self-propelled units such as cargo, fuel, and water barges in service with the Royal Navy, Royal Dockyards, or the Royal Maritime Auxiliary Service. Some typical examples and one recent class are shown below.

◆ **7 harbor launches** Bldr: R. Dunstan, Hessle (In serv. 1981)

Harbor Service Launch 8093 Dunston, 1981

D: 40 tons (fl) **S:** 9.9 kts **Dim:** 13.90 × 4.50 × 1.21
M: 1 Dorman 8 JTM diesel; 1 prop; 270 hp **Man:** 3 tot.

Remarks: Can carry 40 passengers or act as tug; 2-ton bollard pull.

Portsmouth Dockyard service launch D 57 L. & L. Van Ginderen, 7-84

Portland-area service launch Penguin L. & L. Van Ginderen, 7-84

Power Barge M.A.C. 1002, at Portsmouth L. & L. Van Ginderen, 7-81

Harbor Launch HL 56154 at Plymouth L. & L. Van Ginderen, 7-81

MINISTRY OF DEFENCE

Note: In the wake of the hostilities following the Argentine invasion of the Falklands, the Ministry of Defence has had to maintain a sizeable fleet of chartered merchant ships to support the forces garrisoning the islands. The more important of these ships on longer-term charter or owned outright by the M.O.D. are described below.

TRANSPORTS

◆ **1 former vehicle/passenger ferry** Bldr: Cammell-Laird, Birkenhead (In serv. 12-74)

Keren (ex-*St. Edmund*)

D: Approx. 8,100 tons (fl) **S:** 21 kts **Dim:** 130.08 (119.51 pp) × 22.64 × 5.20
Electron Equipt: Radar: 2/navigational
M: 4 Stork-Werkspoor 8-cyl. diesels; 2 CP props; 20,400 hp
Electric: 2,500 kw **Man:** 14 officers, 59 crew, plus 671 passengers

TRANSPORTS *(continued)*

Keren L. & L. Van Ginderen, 6-85

Remarks: 8,987 grt/1,830 dwt. Chartered during Falklands War from Sea Link. Purchased 15-2-83. Due to labor disputes was briefly commissioned as HMS *Keren* 31-3-83 to 8-4-83. Operated by civil contractor. Used on Ascension to Port Stanley run. Helicopter deck aft, MARISAT and improved air-conditioning added. Bow-thruster. Blue hull, white upperworks, buff stack. Laid up mid-1985 at Portsmouth.

BARRACKS BARGES

◆ **2 former oilfield support barges** Bldr: Götaverken, Sweden (In serv. 1982)

Safe Dominia Safe Esperia

Remarks: 99.7-m overall. Berths for 940. Chartered 28-10-82 and 16-3-83, respectively, and carried to Falklands aboard "Flo-Flo" transports.

◆ **1 former oilfield support barge** Bldr: Dredge and Marine Ltd., Pernryn, Wales (In serv. 1977)

Pursuivant (ex-*Bargeman*)

D: . . . **Dim:** 91.98 (91.45 pp) × 28.5 × 4.85

Remarks: 4,793 grt. Purchased 1982 and converted to accommodate 800 personnel by SLP Fabricating Eng., Lowestoft; relaunched and placed in service 12-7-83.

ROYAL ARMY
ROYAL CORPS OF TRANSPORT

MEDIUM LANDING SHIPS

◆ **2 Ardennes-class logistic landing craft** Bldr: Brooke Marine, Lowestoft

	Laid down	L	In serv.
L 4001 Ardennes	27-8-75	29-7-76	1977
L 4003 Arakan	16-2-76	23-5-77	9-6-78

Ardennes (L 4001)—with deck load of containers L. & L. Van Ginderen, 2-85

D: 870 tons (1,663 fl) **S:** 10.0 kts **Dim:** 72.16 (69.95 pp) × 15.03 × 2.01
M: 2 Mirrlees-Blackstone GWSL 8-MGR 2 diesels; 2 props; 2,000 hp
Fuel: 150 tons **Range:** 2,500/10 **Man:** 4 officers, 31 men

Remarks: Replacements for the LCT(8) class, operated by the Royal Corps of Transport. Can carry 5 70-ton tanks or 24 standard 20-foot containers (254 tons) as well as 6 officers and 28 troops. No armament.

LANDING CRAFT

◆ **5 Arromanches class**

	Bldr:	L	In serv.
L 105 Arromanches	Brooke Marine, Lowestoft	6-1-81	31-7-81
L 106 Antwerp	Brooke Marine, Lowestoft	9-3-81	14-8-81
L 107 Andalsnes	James & Stone, Brightlingsea	16-3-84	22-5-84
L 108 Abbeville	James & Stone, Brightlingsea	28-8-84	9-11-84
L 109 Akyab	James & Stone, Brightlingsea	20-11-84	21-12-84

Akyab (L 109) L. & L. Van Ginderen, 3-85

D: 290 tons (fl) **S:** 9.25 kts **Dim:** 33.26 (30.00 pp) × 8.30 × 1.45 loaded
Electron Equipt: Radar: 1/Decca 110
M: 2 Doorman 8 JTCWM diesels; 2 props; 660 hp
Range: 900/9 **Fuel:** 17 tons **Man:** 6 tot.

Remarks: First two ordered 18-3-80 to begin replacement of *Avon* class. Next three ordered 31-3-83, and four more are planned. L 105 and L 106 displace 282 tons (fl) and can make 10 kts at light load; they operated in the Falklands 1982-83 and are now based at Cyprus.

◆ **8 Avon class** Bldr: Saunders-Roe, Isle of Wight (In serv. 1961-67)

RPL 03 Clyde	RPL 05 Eden	RPL 09 Itchen	RPL 11 Lodden
RPL 04 Dart	RPL 06 Forth	RPL 10 Kennet	RPL 12 Medway

Lodden (RPL 11) G. Arra, 1977

D: 61 tons (100 fl) **S:** 8 kts **Dim:** 22.0 × 6.1 × 1.7
M: 2 diesels; 2 props; 870 hp **Man:** 6 tot.

Remarks: RPL—Ramped Powered Lighter. Two-deck superstructure aft. RPL 03, 04, 09 at Hong Kong, others at Belize.

CARGO SHIP

◆ **1 Throsk class** Bldr: Appledore SB

	Laid down	L	In serv.
A 382 St. George	9-11-80	3-81	7-81

St. George (A 382) L. & L. Van Ginderen, 7-83

D: 2,193 tons (fl) **S:** 14 kts **Dim:** 70.57 (64.31 pp) × 11.90 × 4.57
M: 2 Mirrlees-Blackstone diesels; 1 prop; 3,000 hp **Range:** 1,500/14; 5,000/10
Electron Equipt: 1/1006 **Man:** 10 officers, 22 men

Remarks: Sister to RMAS-operated munitions carriers *Kinterbury* and *Throsk*, with improved accommodations. Two holds, two 5-ton cranes; 1,150 dwt. Ordered 2-10-79.

SERVICE CRAFT

◆ **2 Spitfire-class range safety boats** Bldr: James & Stone, Brightlingsea

ALFRED HERRING, V.C. (In serv. 1978) MICHAEL MURPHY, V.C. (In serv. 10-3-83)

Michael Murphy, V.C. L. & L. Van Ginderen, 3-83

D: 48 tons (60 fl) **S:** 22 kts **Dim:** 23.70 × 5.50 × 1.50
M: 2 Paxman 8YJCM4 diesels; 2 props; 2,100 hp **Man:** 9 tot.

REMARKS: Sisters to RAF target tow launches. *Herring* operates in Outer Hebrides at Royal Artillery Range, *Murphy* at Cyprus.

◆ **10 (+3) Samuel Morley, V.C.-class range safety craft** Bldrs: Morley: Fairey Marine, Hamble (except *Dalton, Masters, Hughes:* A.R.P. Whitstable); others: Halmatic, Havant.

	In serv.		In serv.
SAMUEL MORLEY, V.C.	1980	SIR WILLIAM ROE	1983
JAMES DALTON, V.C.	1981	SIR REGINALD KERR	17-3-83
RICHARD MASTERS, V.C.	1981	SIR HUMPHREY GALE	8-4-83
JOSEPH HUGHES, G.C.	1981	GEOFFREY RACKHAM, G.C.	. . .
SIR PAUL TRAVERS	20-10-82	WALTER CLEAL, G.C.	. . .
SIR CECIL SMITH	6-7-82	SIR EVAN GIBB	. . .
SIR JOHN POTTER	24-8-82		

Sir Humphrey Gale L. & L. Van Ginderen, 7-84

D: 20.6 tons (23.6 fl) **S:** 20 kts **Dim:** 14.81 × 4.65 × 1.30
M: First four: 2 Rolls-Royce C8M410 diesels; 2 props; 820 hp. Remainder: 2 Fiat 828SM diesels; 2 props; 880 hp **Range:** 320/17
Electron Equipt: Radar: 1/Decca. . . **Man:** 3 tot.

REMARKS: Glass-reinforced plastic hulls by Halmatic, Havant. *Hughes* and *Potter* based at Hong Kong. Design based on "Talisman 49" hull. Last three ordered 11-4-85

◆ **1 navigational training craft** Bldr: Richards Ironworks (In serv. 1944)

YARMOUTH NAVIGATOR

D: 140 tons **S:** 8 kts **Dim:** 29.0 × . . . × . . .

◆ **8 workboats** Bldr: Anderson, Rigden & Perkins, Whitstable

HL 1 through HL 7 (In serv. 2-3-81) HL 8 (In serv. 2-6-81)

D: 8 tons (fl) **S:** 11 kts **Dim:** 11.2 × 3.5 × . . .
M: 1 Perkins T6-354 M diesel; 129 hp **Man:** 2 tot.

REMARKS: Glass-reinforced plastic construction. Five also built for RN.

Yarmouth Navigator L. & L. Van Ginderen, 11-82

◆ **5 general-purpose workboats** (In serv. 1966-71)

WB 03 BREAM WB 04 BARBEL WB 05 ROACH WB 06 PERCH WB 07 PIKE

Roach (WB 05) Walles Foto, 7-84

D: 19 tons (fl) **S:** 8 kts **Dim:** 14.3 × . . . × . . .

◆ **5 command and control craft** (In serv. 1971)

L 01 PETREL L 02 TERN L 03 FULMAR L 04 SKUA L 05 SHEARWATER

Shearwater L. & L. Van Ginderen, 7-83

D: 12 tons (fl) **S:** 15 kts **Dim:** 12.5 × . . . × . . .

◆ **2 air-cushion vehicles** Bldr: Air Vehicles, Cowes

SH 01 (In serv. 11-5-82) SH 02 (In serv. 15-7-82)

D: 1 ton (fl) **S:** 34 kts **Dim:** 8.45 × 4.57 × 2.18 (high)
M: 1 diesel; 1 air screw; 1 lift fan; 200 hp
Crew: 1, plus 11 passengers

◆ **2 ex-Royal Navy "Girl"-class tugs** Bldr: R. Dunston, Thorne (In serv. 1963)

(A 323) BRIDGET (A 335) BRENDA

D: 66.5 tons (81 fl) **S:** 10 kts **Dim:** 18.75 (17.30 pp) × 5.11 × 2.36
M: 1 Lister-Blackstone ERS-6-MGR diesel; 1 prop; 495 hp
Range: 980/9.8 **Man:** 4 tot.

REMARKS: Transferred from Royal Navy 19-8-83. Used for handling ammunition barges at Marchwood. 6.5-ton bollard pull. Sister *Agnes* (A 121) is naval.

SERVICE CRAFT *(continued)*

Bridget (A 322) G. Arra

ROYAL AIR FORCE MARINE BRANCH

Personnel (1984): 430 RAF, 80 civilian

LONG-RANGE RECOVERY AND SUPPORT CRAFT (LRRSC)

Note: Craft have black hulls, grey upperworks, RAF roundel on hull sides and top of pilothouse. The Royal Air Force Marine Branch, established 1-4-1918, is to be disbanded 8-4-86, with afloat assets going to the other services.

◆ **2 Seal class**

	Bldr	In serv.
5000 Seal	Brooke Marine, Lowestoft	8-67
5001 Seagull	Fairmile Const., Berwich-on-Tweed	1970

Seal (5000) L. & L. Van Ginderen, 6-83

D: 159 tons (fl) **S:** 21 kts **Dim:** 36.6 (33.8 pp) × 7.0 × 2.0
Electron Equipt: Radar: 1/978
M: 2 Paxman 16 YJCM diesels; 2 props; 4,000 hp **Electric:** 110 kw
Fuel: 31 tons **Range:** 2,200/12 **Man:** 2 officers, 15 men

Remarks: Design similar to Royal Navy's *Kingfisher*-class patrol boats. Used for search-and-rescue, target towing, and recovering guided missiles and other air-dropped ordnance. Sister *Sea Otter* (5002) transferred to Royal Navy 30-10-84 and renamed *Redpole.*

RESCUE AND TARGET-TOWING LAUNCHES (RTTL)

◆ **6 Spitfire (RTTL Mk 3) class** Bldr: James & Stone, Brightlingsea

	In serv.		In serv.
4000 Spitfire	1972	4005 Hurricane	1980
4003 Halifax	1977	4006 Lancaster	1981
4004 Hampden	1980	4007 Wellington	25-5-81

D: 48 tons (60 fl) **S:** 22 kts **Dim:** 23.70 (22.15 wl) × 5.50 × 1.50
Electron Equipt: Radar: 1/Decca. . .
M: 2 Paxman 8YJCM4 diesels; 2 props; 2,000 hp **Electric:** 30 kVA
Fuel: 10 tons **Range:** 500/21; 1,000/15 **Man:** 1 officer, 8 men

Remarks: *Spitfire* is 20.6-m overall and has two side-by-side stacks; the series-construction units discharge exhaust through ports in the stern. Sisters *Sunderland* (4001) and *Stirling* (4002) to Royal Navy 8-85 as *Hart* (P 257) and *Cormorant* (P 256).

Hampden (4004) L. & L. Van Ginderen, 7-82

◆ **1 aviation trials support ship** Bldr: Hall Russell, Aberdeen (In serv. 1966)

Colonel Templar (ex-*Criscilla*)

Colonel Templar L. & L. Van Ginderen, 11-82

D: . . . **S:** . . . **Dim:** 56.6 × 11.0 × 4.1
M: 2 diesels; 1 prop; . . . hp

Remarks: 952 grt/411 nrt. Former stern-haul trawler purchased 1980 to support the Royal Aircraft Establishment, Farnborough.

◆ **5 1300-series rescue pinnaces** Bldrs: Groves & Gutteridge, Robertsons, Poole, and Dorset Yacht Co., Poole (In serv. 1955-65)

1380 1389 1390 1391 1392

Rescue Pinnace 1389 L. & L. Van Ginderen, 7-81

D: 28.3 tons (fl) **S:** 13 kts **Dim:** 19.2 × 4.7 × 1.5
M: 2 Rolls-Royce C6 diesels; 2 props; 190 hp **Man:** 5 tot.

◆ **2 1600-series range safety craft** (In serv. 1955-56)

1659 1668

D: 12 tons (fl) **S:** 16 kts **Dim:** 13.1 × 4.0 × 1.2
M: 2 Rolls-Royce C6 diesels; 2 props; 190 hp **Man:** 4 tot.

Note: The above two classes of wooden-hulled craft are to be replaced by 1986 by a new series of 8.2-m glass-reinforced plastic workboats built by Cheverton, Cowes. Five 7.3-m Cheverton-built tenders were delivered in 1981.

DEPARTMENT OF AGRICULTURE AND FISHERIES FOR SCOTLAND

AVIATION: In late 1984, a Cessna Titan with Racal ASR 360 radar and aerial cameras was purchased for surveillance, to replace a Turbine Islander chartered in 1982.

FISHERIES PROTECTION SHIPS

◆ **2 Sulisker class**

	Bldr	L	In serv.
SULISKER	Ferguson Brothers, Port Glasgow	8-80	1980
VIGILANT	Ferguson Ailsa, Port Glasgow	26-3-82	9-82

Sulisker L. & L. Van Ginderen, 2-81

D: 1,250 tons **S:** 18 kts **Dim:** 71.33 (64.00 pp) × 11.60 × 4.66
Electron Equipt: Radar: 1/Sperry Mk 3012X-59, 1/Sperry Mk 3012S-312
M: 2 Ruston 12RKCM diesels; 2 CP props; 5,640 hp **Electric:** 638 kw
Fuel: 198 tons **Range:** 7,000/14 **Man:** 8 officers, 17 men

REMARKS: Equipped with 450-hp bow-thruster, Denny-Brown fin stabilizers. 1,177 grt/337 dwt. Equipped for rescue, firefighting, and oil-spill cleanup. Elaborate navigational equipment, particularly in *Vigilant.*

◆ **2 Jura class** Bldr: Hall Russell & Co., Aberdeen

JURA (In serv. 1973) WESTRA (In serv. 1975)

Jura L. & L. Van Ginderen, 10-81

D: 778 tons (1,285 fl) **S:** 17 kts **Dim:** 59.6 × 10.7 × 4.4
M: 2 British Polar SP112VS-F diesels; 1 prop; 4,200 hp **Man:** 28 tot.

REMARKS: Design (with different engines) employed for Royal Navy's "Isles"-class offshore patrol vessels. *Jura,* chartered by Royal Navy 1973-77, had 1/40-mm AA.

◆ **2 fisheries patrol boats** Bldr: Cheverton, Cowes (In serv. 31-1-83)

MORVEN MOIDART

Moidart, home-ported at Leith L. & L. Van Ginderen, 1-84

D: 37 tons (44 fl) **S:** 24 kts **Dim:** 19.8 (17.9 pp) × 5.77 × 1.63
M: 3 G.M. 8V92 TI diesels; 3 props; 1,530 bhp **Electric:** 75 kw
Endurance: 7 days **Man:** 2 officers, 3 men

REMARKS: Glass-reinforced plastic construction. Use Murray, Cormack "North Cape 65" hulls, built at Cheverton, Newport, and fitted out at Cowes. Carry Avon Sea-Raider semi-rigid inflatable inspection dinghy.

◆ **1 fisheries patrol boat** Bldr: Osbourne, Littlehampton (In serv. 4-84)

OSPREY

D: 6.25 tons **S:** 28 kts **Dim:** 10.06 × 3.05 × 1.12
M: 2 Rolls-Royce Sabre 212 diesels; 2 props; 424 hp **Range:** 200/. . . **Man:** 3 tot.

REMARKS: Combines rigid hull with inflatable flotation/fender collar, which increases dimensions to 11.20 × 3.73 when inflated.

◆ **2 13-m patrol craft** Bldr: Cheverton, Cowes (In serv. 1981)

N. . . . . . . N. . . . . . .

◆ **1 7.9-m patrol craft** Bldr: Horne Bros. (In serv. 1981)

SKUA

NOTE: The Scottish Department of Agriculture and Fisheries also operates the research trawlers *Brenda* (460 grt, 1951), *Norma* (600 grt, 1959), *Scotia,* and *Clupea.*

Scotia L. & L. Van Ginderen, 5-82

H.M. CUSTOMS AND EXCISE MARINE DIVISION

PATROL BOATS AND CRAFT

◆ **2 33-m-class patrol boats** Bldr: Brooke Marine, Lowestoft (In serv. 1979)

SEARCHER SEEKER

Seeker L. & L. Van Ginderen, 7-84

D: 160 tons (fl) **S:** 21 kts **Dim:** 36.6 (33.8 pp) × 7.0 × 2.0
Electron Equipt: Radar: 1/978
M: 2 Paxman 16YJCM diesels; 2 props; 4,000 hp **Electric:** 110 kw
Fuel: 31 tons **Range:** 2,200/12 **Man:** . . .

REMARKS: Generally similar to RAF's *Seal* class and Royal Navy's *Kingfisher* class, but have more extensive superstructures.

◆ **6 Tracker Mk II patrol craft** Bldr: Fairey Marine, Hamble

ACTIVE ALERT CHALLENGE CHAMPION SAFEGUARD SWIFT

REMARKS: Data as for units of this class in the Royal Navy (*Attacker* class). *Alert* is a Tracker Mk I with pilothouse farther forward.

◆ **3 service launches** Bldr: Cheverton, Cowes (In serv. 8-84)

ANTELOPE AVOCET BITTERN

D: 3.75 tons (fl) **S:** 15 kts **Dim:** 8.23 × 2.74 × 0.81
M: 2 Perkins 4.236 diesels; 2 props; 140 hp **Range:** 100/13 **Man:** 2 tot.

GREAT BRITAIN *(continued)*
PATROL BOATS AND CRAFT *(continued)*

Active L. & L. Van Ginderen, 7-85

GREECE

Hellenic Republic

Personnel (1984): 19,500 men, including 2,500 officers

Merchant Marine (1984): 2,904 ships—35,058,593 grt (tankers: 413 ships —13,333,022 grt)

Naval Aviation: Greek naval aviation began in April 1975, when four Alouette-III ASW helicopters fitted with AS-12 anti-ship, wire-guided missiles went into service. Subsequently, 16 Agusta-Bell AB-212 helicopters were ordered from Italy in 1977; these are based at Eleusis, with the first two having been delivered 19-7-79. The Air Force has 14 HU-16B Grumman Albatross amphibian planes remaining for maritime reconnaissance; these carry mixed Navy/Air Force crews and are being modernized by Grumman with MEC Super Searcher radars, IFF gear, Marconi LAPADS sonobuoy signal processors, and new radars.

Greek Navy AB-212 helicopter Official

Warships In Service Or Under Construction As Of 1 January 1986

	L	Tons	Main armament
◆ **10 submarines**			
8 Type 209	1970-79	1,100	8/533-mm TT
1 Guppy III	1945	1,660	10/533-mm TT
1 Guppy II	1944	1,500	10/533-mm TT
◆ **14 destroyers**			
7 Gearing	1944-45	2,425	4-6/127-mm DP, 1/76-mm DP (in 4), ASROC (in 4), 6/ASW TT
1 Allen M. Sumner	1944	2,200	6/127-mm DP, 6/ASW TT
6 Fletcher	1942-43	2,050	4-5/127-mm DP, 6/76.2-mm DP or 10/40-mm AA, ASW weapons
◆ **7 (+4) frigates**			
0 (+4) . . .	. . .	. . .	. . .
2 Kortenaer	1979	3,000	Aspide, 2/76-mm DP, 1 helo
1 Rhein	1960	2,370	2/100-mm DP, 4/40-mm AA, mines
4 Cannon	1942-43	1,300	3/76.2-mm DP, ASW weapons

◆ **26 (+. . .) guided-missile patrol boats and torpedo boats**

◆ **7 patrol craft**

◆ **18 minesweepers**

◆ **2 minelayers**

◆ **3 amphibious-warfare ships**

SUBMARINES

◆ **8 German Type 209** Bldr: Howaldtswerke, Kiel

	Laid down	L	In serv.
S 110 Glavkos	1-9-68	15-9-70	5-11-71
S 111 Nereus	15-1-69	7-6-71	10-2-72
S 112 Triton	1-6-69	19-10-71	23-11-72
S 113 Proteus	1-10-69	1-2-72	23-11-72
S 116 Poseidon	15-4-76	21-3-78	22-3-79
S 117 Amfrititi	16-9-78	14-6-78	14-8-79
S 118 Okeanos	1-10-76	16-11-78	15-11-79
S 119 Pontos	15-1-77	22-3-79	29-4-80

Glavkos (S 110)—original version 1977

Poseidon (S 116)—second group, with higher bow 1980

D: 980/1,105/1,230 **S:** 22 kts (max. sub. for 15 min.), 12 kts, snorkel
Dim: 55.0 (116-118: 56.1) × 6.6 × 5.9
A: 8/533-mm TT fwd (+6 reserve torpedoes)
Electron Equipt: Radar: Thomson-CSF Calypso
Sonar: Atlas AN 526 passive, CSU AN 406 A9 active, DUUX-2
M: Diesel-electric propulsion; 4 MTU 12V493 TY60 diesels, each linked to an AEG generator of 420 kw; 1 Siemens motor; 1 prop; 5,000 hp
Range: 25/30; 230/8; 400/4 submerged **Man:** 5 officers, 26 men

Remarks: Diving depth 250 m. The second group of four are 56.1 m overall, 1,185 tons surfaced/1,285 tons submerged, have a higher bow, and H.S.A. SINBADS weapons control with Mk 8 torpedo f.c.s.

◆ **1 ex-U.S. GUPPY III class** Bldr: Portsmouth Naval SY, New Hampshire

	Laid down	L	In serv.
S 115 Katsonis (ex-*Remora*, SS 487)	5-3-45	12-7-45	3-1-46

Katsonis (S 115) D. Dervissis, 9-79

D: 1,660/1,975/2,540 tons **S:** 17.2/14.5 kts **Dim:** 99.52 × 8.23 × 5.18
A: 10/533-mm TT (6 fwd, 4 aft; 24 torpedoes)
Electron Equipt: Radar: 1/SS-2A
Sonar: BQG-4 (PUFFS), BQR-2B
EW: WLR-1

SUBMARINES *(continued)*

M: 4 Fairbanks-Morse 38D8⅛ 10-cyl. diesels (1,600 hp each), electric drive; 2 props; 6,400/5,480 hp
Range: 10,000-12,000/10; 95/5 submerged **Man:** 85 tot.

REMARKS: Purchased 29-10-73. GUPPY III conversion completed 1962 at Pearl Harbor SY.

◆ **1 ex-U.S. GUPPY IIA class** Bldr: Manitowoc SB, Wisconsin

	Laid down	L	In serv.
S 114 PAPANIKOLIS (ex-*Hardhead,* SS 365)	7-7-43	12-12-43	18-4-44

Papanikolis (S 114) D. Dervissis, 9-79

D: 1,517/1,870/2,440 tons **S:** 18/13.5 kts **Dim:** 93.6 × 8.2 × 5.2
A: 10/533-mm TT (6 fwd, 4 aft, 24 torpedoes)
Electron Equipt: Radar: 1/SS-2A—Sonar: BQR-2R—EW: WLR-1
M: 3 G.M. 16-278A diesels (1,600 hp each), 2 electric motors; 2 props; 3,430/5,480 hp

REMARKS: Purchased 26-7-72. The fourth diesel generator was removed to permit enlargement of the sonar compartment during GUPPY II conversion completed 1953. Two 126-cell batteries. *Triana* (S 86), ex-*Scabbardfish* (SS 397), is now used for pierside training.

DESTROYERS

◆ **6 ex-U.S. Gearing FRAM I class**

	Bldr	Laid down	L	In serv.
D 212 KANARIS (ex-*Stickell,* DD 888)	Consolidated Steel	5-1-45	16-6-45	26-9-45
D 213 KONTOURIOTIS (ex-*Rupertus,* DD 851)	Bethlehem, Quincy	2-5-45	21-9-45	8-3-46
D 214 SACHTOURIS (ex-*Arnold J. Isbell,* DD 869)	Bethlehem, Quincy	14-3-45	6-8-45	5-1-46
D 215 TOUMBAZIS (ex-*Gurke,* DD 783)	Todd SY, Seattle	1-7-44	15-4-45	5-12-45
D 216 APOSTOLIS (ex-*Charles P. Cecil,* DD 835)	Bath Iron Wks.	2-12-44	22-2-45	29-6-45
D 217 KRIEZIS (ex-*Myles C. Fox,* DD 829)	Bath Iron Wks.	14-8-44	13-1-45	20-3-45

Toumbazis (D 215) Pradignac & Leo, 1984

Sachtouris (D 214) G. Gyssels, 1985

Sachtouris (D 214) L. & L. Van Ginderen, 10-84

D: 2,425 tons (3,500 fl) **S:** 30 kts
Dim: 119.03 × 12.52 × 4.45 (6.40 over sonar)
A: 4/127-mm, 38-cal. (II × 2)—1/76-mm OTO Melara DP—1/40-mm AA—2/12.7-mm mg—1/ASROC system—6/324-mm Mk 32 ASW TT (III × 2)—1/d.c. rack
Electron Equipt: Radar: 1/navigational, 1/SPS-10, 1/SPS-40 (SPS-29 on 212, 215, 216), 1/Mk 25, 1/Orion RTN-20X
Sonar: SQS-23D—EW: WLR-1 intercept, ULQ-6 active
M: GT; 2 props; 60,000 hp **Electric:** 1,200 kw
Boilers: 4 Babcock & Wilcox; 43.3 kg/cm², 454°C superheat **Fuel:** 650 tons
Range: 2,400/25; 4,800/15 **Man:** 14 officers, 260 men

REMARKS: D 212 transferred 1-7-72; D 213 on 10-7-73 (purchased 11-7-78); D 214 on 4-12-73 (purchased 11-7-78); D 215 purchased 17-3-77; D 216 purchased 2-8-80, originally for cannibalization; and D 217 purchased 8-7-81. All have been given an Elsag NA-21 fire-control system aft, 1/76-mm OTO Melara Compact on the helicopter deck, and a 40-mm AA before the bridge; equipment for D 216 and D 217 ordered 4-85. In D 215, which was equipped as Fleet Flagship 1980-81, two of the boilers are Foster-Wheeler. The 1980-81 purchase ships had LN-66 navigational radars. Also purchased were *Corry* (DD 817) and *Dyess* (DD 880), on 8-7-81; they are being cannibalized for spares.

◆ **1 ex-U.S. Gearing DDR FRAM II class**

	Bldr	Laid down	L	In serv.
D 210 THEMISTOCLES (ex-*Frank Knox,* DD 742)	Bath Iron, Wks.	8-5-44	17-9-44	11-12-44

Themistocles (D 210) L. & L. Van Ginderen, 1980

D: 2,425 tons (3,500 fl) **S:** 30 kts
Dim: 119.03 × 12.52 × 4.45 (6.40 over sonar)
A: 6/127-mm DP (II × 3)—4/30-mm AA Emerlec (II × 2)—6/324-mm Mk 32 ASW TT (III × 2)—2 Hedgehog—1 Alouette-III ASW helicopter
Electron Equipt: Radar: 1/navigational, 1/SPS-10, 1/SPS-29, 1/Mk 25
Sonar: SQS-23, SQA-10 VDS—EW: WLR-1
M: 2 sets GT; 2 props; 60,000 hp **Electric:** 1,200 kw
Boilers: 2 Babcock & Wilcox; 43.3 kg/cm², 454°C superheat
Fuel: 650 tons **Range:** 2,400/25; 4,800/15 **Man:** 16 officers, 253 men

REMARKS: Purchased 30-1-71, having been extensively rebuilt after a grounding in 1966. Radar picket features deleted and helicopter hangar added in Greece by 1978 in place of the after 01 level deckhouse. 30-mm AA substituted for 20-mm single mounts in 1980.

◆ **1 ex-U.S. Allen M. Sumner class** Bldr: Federal SB & DD, Kearny, New Jersey

	Laid down	L	In serv.
D 211 MIAOULIS (ex-*Ingraham,* DD 694)	4-4-43	16-1-44	10-3-44

DESTROYERS *(continued)*

Miaoulis (D 211) Official

D: 2,200 tons (3,320 fl) **S:** 30 kts
Dim: 114.76 × 12.49 × 4.39 (5.79 over sonar)
A: 6/127-mm, 38-cal. DP (II × 3)—2/40-mm AA (I × 2)—6/20-mm AA (I × 6)—2 Hedgehogs—6/324-mm Mk 32 ASW TT (III × 2)—1/Alouette-III ASW helicopter
Electron Equipt: Radar: 1/navigational, 1/SPS-10, 1/SPS-40, 1/Mk 25
Sonar: SQS-29, SQA-10 VDS—EW: WLR-1
M: 2 sets GT; 2 props; 60,000 hp
Boilers: 4 Babcock & Wilcox; 43.3 kg/cm², 454°C **Fuel:** 495 tons
Range: 2,400/25; 4,800/15 **Man:** 14 officers, 260 men

Remarks: Transferred 16-7-71. Mk 37 gunfire-control system for 127-mm mounts.

◆ **6 ex-U.S. and West German Fletcher class**

	Bldr	Laid down	L	In serv.
D 06 Aspis (ex-*Conner,* DD 582)	Boston NSY	16-4-42	18-9-42	8-6-43
D 16 Velos (ex-*Charette,* DD 581)	Boston NSY	20-2-42	3-6-42	18-5-43
D 42 Kimon (ex-German Z-2, ex-*Ringgold,* DD 500)	Federal SB & DD	25-6-42	11-11-42	24-12-42
D 58 Lonchi (ex-*Hall,* DD 583)	Boston NSY	16-4-42	18-7-42	6-7-43
D 65 Nearchos (ex-German Z 3, ex-*Wadsworth,* DD 516)	Bath Iron Wks.	18-8-42	10-1-43	16-3-43
D 85 Sphendoni (ex-*Aulick,* DD 569)	Consolidated SB	14-5-41	2-3-42	27-10-42

Velos (D 16) G. Arra

Kimon (D 42)—en route Greece as Z 2 (D 171) Skyfotos, 8-81

D: 2,050 tons (2,850 fl) **S:** 32/30 kts **Dim:** 114.85 × 12.03 × 5.5
A: 4/127-mm, 38 cal. (I × 4)—6/76.2-mm DP, 50-cal. (II × 3)—5/533-mm TT (V × 1, see remarks)—6/324-mm Mk 32 ASW TT (II × 2)—2 Hedgehogs—1/d.c. rack (not in D 42, D 65)—D 42, D 65: mine rails
Electron Equipt: Radar: 1/navigational, 1/SPS-10, 1/SPS-6, 1/Mk 25, 2/Mk 34, 1/Mk 35
Sonar: SQS-4 or 29 series—EW: SLR-1 or WLR-1
M: 2 sets GT; 2 props; 60,000 hp **Electric:** 580 kw
Boilers: 4 Babcock & Wilcox; 43.3 kg/cm², 454° **Fuel:** 650 tons
Range: 1,260/30; 4,400/15 **Man:** 350 tot.

Remarks: D 06 loaned 15-9-59, D 16 on 15-6-69, D 58 on 9-2-60, and D 85 on 21-8-59; all purchased 25-4-77, along with *Thyella* (D 28, ex-*Bradford,* DD 545), stricken 2-81, and *Navarinon* (D 63, ex-*Brown,* DD 546), stricken 1981. D 65 purchased and transferred from West Germany on 30-10-80, and D 42 was purchased 9-81, originally for cannibalization. Have Mk 37 GFCS for 127-mm, Mk 56 GFCS for aft 76.2-mm, and 2 Mk 63 GFCS for amidships 76.2-mm guns. The ex-German ships had 2/533-mm ASW TT vice Mk 32 ASW TT and were equipped with mine rails; they had Kelvin-Hughes 14/9 navigational radars. Acquired for cannibalization and scrapping were ex-German Z 1 (ex-*Anthony,* DD 515) in 1979, Z 4 (ex-*Claxton,* DD 571) on 26-2-80, and Z 5 (ex-*Dyson,* DD 572) in 9-81.

FRIGATES

Note: Four frigates are to be built in Greece to replace the obsolete U.S. *Cannon*-class ships, according to official statements made in 1985. Todd Shipyards, U.S., has offered a 1,950-ton, 105-m design with 127-mm or 76-mm gun.

◆ **2 Dutch Kortenaer class** Bldr: de Schelde, Vlissingen

	Laid down	L	In serv.
F 450 Elli (ex-*Pieter Floresz*)	2-7-77	15-12-79	10-10-81
F 451 Limnos (ex-*Witte de With*)	13-6-78	27-10-79	18-9-82

Elli (F 450) L. & L. Van Ginderen, 10-81

Limnos (F 451) L. & L. Van Ginderen, 9-82

D: 3,000 tons (3,786 fl) **S:** 30 kts
Dim: 130.2 (121.8 pp) × 14.4 × 4.4 (6.0 props)
A: 8/Harpoon SSM (IV × 2)—1 Mk 29 SAM syst. (VIII × 1; 24 Aspide missiles)—2/76-mm OTO Melara DP—4/324-mm Mk 32 ASW TT (II × 2)—1/AB 212 ASW helicopter
Electron Equipt: Radar: 1/ZW-06, 1/LW-08, 1/WM-25, 1/STIR—Sonar: SQS-505
EW: Elektronica Sphinx intercept syst., 2 Knebworth/Corvus chaff RL (VIII × 2)
M: COGOG: 2 Rolls-Royce Tyne RM-1C cruise gas turbines, 4,900 hp each, 2 Rolls-Royce Olympus TM-3B gas turbines, 25,800 hp each; 2 LIPS CP props; 51,600 hp max.
Electric: 3,000 kw (4 SEMT-Pielstick PA4 diesel generator sets)
Range: 4,700/16 (on one Tyne turbine) **Man:** 17 officers, 182 men

Remarks: *Elli* was officially turned over to Greece on 26-6-81 at the commencement of sea trials, having been ordered 7-81, along with the second unit. Both were taken from production for the Dutch Navy, in order to speed delivery. Plans to build a third ship in Greece were canceled. Have Denny-Brown fin stabilizers. *Elli* had been equipped with racks to hold 8 Harpoon SSM containers (IV × 2), but these were removed prior to transfer in 1983; 32 Harpoon were ordered from the U.S. for these ships and others. One U.S. Mk 15 CIWS 20-mm gatling AA is being added for close-in defense. Hangar lengthened 2.2m to accept Italian-built helicopter vice Lynx used by Dutch Navy. Have SEWACO II combat data system. See also class notes in Netherlands section.

FRIGATES *(continued)*

◆ **1 German Rhein-class former tender** Bldr: Elsflether Werft, West Germany

	Laid down	L	In serv.
D 03 AEGEON (ex-*Weser,* A 62)	1-8-59	11-6-60	14-7-62

D: 2,370 tons (2,740 fl) **S:** 20.5 kts **Dim:** 98.18 (92.8 pp) × 11.8 × 3.9
A: 2/100-mm DP (I × 2)—4/40-mm AA (I × 4)—70 mines
Electron Equipt: Radar: 1/Kelvin-Hughes 14/9, 1/SGR-105, 1/SGR-103, 2/M 45
M: 6 Maybach 16-cyl. diesels; 2 CP props; 12,600 hp **Electric:** 2,250 kVA
Range: 2,500/16 **Man:** 110 tot.

REMARKS: Transferred 6-7-76. A small combatant tender used by Greece as a frigate. Still can act as a tender. Two Mk 2 GFCS for 100-mm DP.

◆ **4 ex-U.S. Cannon class**

	Bldr	Laid down	L	In serv.
D 01 AETOS (ex-*Ebert,* DE 768)	Tampa Shipbldg, Tampa, Florida	1-4-43	11-5-44	12-7-44
D 31 HIERAX (ex-*Slater,* DE 766)	Tampa Shipbldg, Tampa, Florida	9-3-43	13-2-44	1-5-44
D 54 LEON (ex-*Garfield Thomas,* DE 193)	Federal, Port Newark, New Jersey	23-9-43	12-12-43	24-1-44
D 67 PANTHIR (ex-*Eldridge,* DE 173)	Federal, Port Newark, New Jersey	22-2-43	25-6-43	27-8-43

Hierax (D 31) L. & L. Van Ginderen, 7-80

D: 1,300 tons (1,750 fl) **S:** 19 kts **Dim:** 93.0 (91.5 pp) × 11.17 × 3.25
A: 3/76.2-mm DP—6/40-mm AA (II × 3)—14/20-mm AA (II × 7)—6/324-mm Mk 32 ASW TT (III × 2)—1 Hedgehog—8/d.c. projectors—2/d.c. racks
Electron Equipt: Radar: 1/navigational, 1/Mk 26 f.c.
Sonar: QCU-2
M: 4 G.M. 16-278A diesels, electric drive; 2 props; 6,000 hp
Electric: 680 kw **Fuel:** 300 tons **Range:** 5,500/19; 11,500/11
Man: Peacetime: 150 men; wartime: 185 men

REMARKS: Transferred in 1951. Have Mk 52 GFCS for 76.2-mm guns (plus separate rangefinder), 3 Mk 51 Mod. 2 GFCS for 40-mm AA. Obsolete SA radar removed by 1980. Thoroughly obsolete; to be replaced by new construction.

GUIDED-MISSILE PATROL BOATS

NOTE: Three (with nine more planned) 45-m. patrol boats were reportedly ordered 1984 from Olympic marine, Lavrio. No further data available, but these apparently supercede the planned order for additional units of the Combattante III N class.

◆ **10 Combattante III N class** Bldr: (A) Hellenic SY, Skaramanga; (B) Constr. Méc. de Normandie, Cherbourg

	Bldr	L	In serv.
P 20 ANTIPLIARCHOS LASCOS	B	6-7-76	2-4-77
P 21 ANTIPLIARCHOS BLESSAS	B	10-11-76	19-7-77
P 22 ANTIPLIARCHOS TROUPAKIS	B	6-1-77	8-11-77
P 23 ANTIPLIARCHOS MYKONIOS	B	5-5-77	10-2-78
P 24 SIMAIFOROS KAVALOUTHIS	A	10-11-79	14-7-80
P 25 ANTIPLIARCHOS KOSTAKOS	A	1-3-80	9-9-80
P 26 IPOPLIARCHOS DEYIANNIS	A	14-7-80	12-80
P 27 SIMAIFOROS XENOS	A	8-9-80	31-3-81
P 28 SIMAIFOROS SIMITZOPOULOS	A	12-10-80	6-82
P 29 SIMAIFOROS STARAKIS	A	1981	12-10-81

D: 385 tons (447 fl) **S:** 36.5 kts (2nd group: 32.6)
Dim: 56.65 (53.00 pp) × 8.00 × 2.70 (props)
A: First four: 4/MM 38 Exocet SSM (II × 2)—2/76-mm OTO Melara DP (I × 2)—4/30-mm Emerlec AA (II × 2)—2/533-mm TT (2 SST-4 wire-guided torpedoes)
Later six: 6 Penguin SSM (I × 6)—2/76-mm OTO Melara Compact DP (I × 2)—4/30-mm Emerlec AA (II × 2)—2/533-mm TT (2 SST-4 torpedoes)
Electron Equipt: Radar: 1/Decca 1226, 1/Thomson-CSF Triton, 1/Thomson-CSF Castor

Simaiforos Kavalouthis (P 24)—Second Group Hellenic SY, 1981

Antipliarchos Lascos (P 20)—First Group CMN, 1976

M: First four: 4 MTU 20V538 TB92 diesels; 4 props; 20,800 hp (18,000 sust.)
Later six: 4 MTU 20V538 TB91 diesels; 4 props; 15,000 hp (13,400 sust.)
Electric: 450 kw **Range:** 800/32.5; 2,000/15 **Man:** 7 officers, 36 men

REMARKS: First four ordered 22-5-75. Second group, built in Greece, and with less expensive weapon, sensor, and propulsion systems, ordered 22-12-76. Each 76-mm gun has 350 rounds, with 80 in ready service. The Emerlec 30-mm mounts are furnished with 3,200 rounds and fire at 700 rounds/barrel/minute. Ships have excellent habitability; accommodations and operations spaces are air-conditioned. There are 3 Jeumont-Schneider 150-kw generator sets (440v., 3-ph., 60-Hz.). First group has Thomson-CSF Vega weapon control system, later ships Vega II. All have 2 CSEE Panda directors for the 30-mm AA.

◆ **4 Combattante II class** Bldr: Constr. Méc. de Normandie (CMN), Cherbourg

	L	In serv.
P 14 IPOPLIARCHOS ARLIOTIS (ex-*Evniki*)	26-4-71	4-72
P 15 IPOPLIARCHOS ANNINOS (ex-*Navsithoi*)	8-9-71	6-72
P 16 IPOPLIARCHOS KONIDIS (ex-*Kimothoi*)	20-12-71	7-72
P 17 IPOPLIARCHOS BATSIS (ex-*Kalypso*)	26-1-71	12-71

Ipopliarchos Batsis (P 17)—with old number L. & L. Van Ginderen, 1980

D: 234 tons (255 fl) **S:** 36.5 kts **Dim:** 47.0 (44.0 pp) × 7.1 × 2.5 (fl)
A: 4/MM 38 Exocet SSM (II × 2)—4/35-mm Oerlikon AA (II × 2)—2/533-mm wire-guided TT aft
Electron Equipt: Radar: 1/Decca 1226, 1/Thomson-CSF Triton, 1/Thomson-CSF Castor
M: 4 MTU MD 872 diesels; 4 props; 12,000 hp **Fuel:** 39 tons
Range: 850/25; 2,000/15 **Man:** 4 officers, 36 men

GUIDED-MISSILE PATROL BOATS *(continued)*

Remarks: Steel hull, light steel alloy superstructure. Ordered 1969. Thomson-CSF Vega weapon control system.

◆ **2 Kelefstis Stamou class** Bldr: Chantiers Navales de l'Estérel, Cannes

P 286 Kelefstis Stamou (In serv. 28-7-75)
P 287 Diopos Antoniou (In serv. 4-12-75)

Kelefstis Stamou (P 286) L. & L. Van Ginderen, 8-84

D: 80 tons (115 fl) **S:** 30 kts **Dim:** 32.0 × 5.8 × 1.5
A: 4/SS-12 wire-guided SSM—1/20-mm AA—2/12.7-mm mg (I × 2)
M: 2 MTU 12V331 TC81 diesels; 2 props; 2,700 hp **Range:** 1,500/15
Electron Equipt: Radar: 1/Decca . . . nav. **Man:** 17 tot.

Remarks: These wooden-hulled ships were ordered by Cyprus, but acquired by Greece. Pendant numbers were P 28 and P 29 until 1980.

TORPEDO BOATS

◆ **5 ex-German Type 141 class** Bldrs: (A) Lürssen, Vegesack; (B) Krögerwerft, Rendsburg

	Bldr	Laid down	L	In serv.
P 50 Esperos (ex-*Seeadler*)	A	23-9-57	1-2-58	29-8-58
P 53 Kyklon (ex-*Grief*)	A	5-2-58	28-6-58	3-3-59
P 54 Laiaps (ex-*Kondor*)	A	2-1-58	17-5-58	24-2-59
P 55 Scorpios (ex-*Kormoran*)	B	2-2-59	16-7-59	9-11-59
P 56 Tyfon (ex-*Geier*)	A	27-5-58	1-10-58	3-6-59

Kentauros (P 52)—now stricken D. Dervissis, 9-80

D: 195 tons (221 fl) **S:** 42.5 kts **Dim:** 42.62 × 7.10 × 2.39
A: 2/40-mm AA (I × 2)—4/533-mm TT (I × 4)
M: 4 Maybach 16-cyl. diesels; 4 props; 14,400 hp **Electric:** 192 kw
Range: 500/39; 1,000/32

Remarks: Transferred 1976-77. Three others, ex-*Albatros*, ex-*Bussard*, and ex-*Sperber*, were transferred to be cannibalized for spares. Wooden-planked hull skin on metal frame. *Kataigis* (P 51, ex-P 197, ex-*Falke*) stricken late 1981. *Kentauros* (P 52, ex-*Habicht*) stricken 1985.

PATROL CRAFT

◆ **3 Dilos class** Bldr: Hellenic SY, Skaramanga (In serv. 1978-80)

P 267 Dilos P 268 Lindos P 269 Knossos

D: 75 tons (86 fl) **S:** 27 kts **Dim:** 29.0 × 6.2 × 1.1
A: 2/20-mm AA (I × 2)
M: 2 MTU 12V331 TC92 diesels; 2 props; 2,700 hp **Range:** 1,600/25
Man: 15 tot.

Knossos (P 269) L. & L. Van Ginderen, 7-79

Remarks: Designed by Abeking & Rasmussen, West Germany. Used for air-sea rescue. Three each also built for Customs Service and Coast Guard.

◆ **3 Panagopoulos I class** Bldr: Hellenic SY, Skaramanga

P 61 E. Panagopoulos I (In serv. 23-6-76)
P 62 E. Panagopoulos II (In serv. 1980)
P 63 E. Panagopoulos III (In serv. 1981)

E. Panagopoulos I (P 61) D. Dervissis, 7-79

Remarks: No data available. Twin-screw diesel propulsion, armed with light mg. only. Described by builder as "pursuit vessels." Decca navigational radar.

◆ **1 Goulandris I class** Bldr: Neozioh SY, Syros

	In serv.
P 290 N.I. Goulandris II	6-6-77

N.I. Goulandris II (P 290) 1981

D: 38.5 tons **S:** 30 kts **Dim:** 24.0 × 6.2 × 1.1 **A:** 2/20-mm AA (I × 2)
M: 2 diesels; 2 props; 2,700 hp **Range:** 1,600/. . . **Man:** 10 tot.

Remarks: *N.I. Goulandris I* (P 289) blew up and sank 24-6-83.

◆ **1 ex-U.K. Scimitar-class former target boat**

	Bldr	L
P. . . Aquilon (ex-*Scimitar*, P 271)	Vosper Thornycroft, Portsmouth	4-12-69

D: 102 tons (fl) **S:** 40 kts **Dim:** 30.5 × 8.1 × 1.95
A: . . . **Electron Equipt:** Radar: 1/Decca . . . nav.
M: CODOG: 2 Rolls-Royce Proteus gas turbines (4,500 hp each) or 2 Foden diesels (180 hp each); 2 props; 9,000 hp
Range: 425/35; 1,500/21.5 **Man:** 2 officers, 10 men

Remarks: Reported purchased 4-85. Former training craft intended to simulate missile boats. Wooden construction. Of dubious utility.

MINE WARFARE SHIPS

◆ **9 U.S. Falcon (MSC 294)-class coastal minesweepers** Bldr: Peterson Bldrs, Sturgeon Bay, Wisconsin (except M 246: Tacoma Boatbldg, Tacoma, Washington)

	In serv.
M 211 Alkyon (ex-MSC 319)	3-12-68
M 213 Klio (ex-*Argo*, ex-MSC 317)	7-8-68
M 214 Avra (ex-MSC 318)	3-10-68
M 240 Pleias (ex-MSC 314)	22-6-67
M 241 Kichli (ex-MSC 308)	14-7-64
M 242 Kissa (ex-MSC 309)	1-9-64
M 246 Aigli (ex-MSC 299)	4-1-65
M 247 Dafni (ex-MSC 307)	23-9-64
M 248 Aedon (ex-MSC 310)	13-10-64

D: 300 tons (394 fl) **S:** 13 kts **Dim:** 44.32 × 8.29 × 2.55
A: 2/20-mm AA (II × 1) **M:** 2 Waukesha L-1616 diesels; 2 props; 1,200 hp
Electron Equipt: Radar: 1/. . . nav.—Sonar: UQS-1D
Fuel: 40 tons **Range:** 2,500/10 **Man:** 4 officers, 27 men

MINE WARFARE SHIPS *(continued)*

Klio (M 213) L. & L. Van Ginderen, 5-84

REMARKS: Built for Greece under the Military Aid Program; transferred on completion. Sister *Doris* (A 475, ex-M 245, ex-MSC 298) is employed as a hydrographic survey ship. Original Decca 707 radar replaced by 1984.

◆ **5 ex-Belgian U.S. Adjutant-class coastal minesweepers**
Bldrs: Consolidated SB, Morris Heights, N.Y. (M 205, M 206: Hodgdon Bros., East Boothbay, Maine)

	In serv.
M 202 ATALANTI (ex-*St. Truiden,* ex-MSC 169)	2-54
M 205 ANTIOPI (ex-*Herve,* ex-MSC 153)	3-54
M 206 PHEDRA (ex-*Malmedy,* ex-MSC 154)	5-54
M 210 THALIA (ex-*Blankenberge,* ex-MSC 170)	5-54
M 254 NIOVI (ex-*Laroche,* ex-MSC 171)	8-54

Antiopi (M 205) G. Arra, 1973

D: 330 tons (402 fl) **S:** 13 kts (8 sweeping)
Dim: 43.0 (41.50 pp) × 7.95 × 2.55 **A:** 2/20-mm AA (II × 1)
M: 2 G.M. 8-268A diesels; 2 props; 880/1,000 hp **Fuel:** 40 tons
Range: 2,500/10 **Man:** 4 officers, 27 men

REMARKS: Transferred to Belgium on completion; re-transferred to Greece 7-9-69. M 202 was configured as a hydrographic survey ship from the late 1970s to 1982.

◆ **4 ex-U.S. 50-ft-class minesweeping launches**

D: 21 tons (fl) **S:** 8 kts **Dim:** 15.20 × 4.01 × 1.31
M: 1 Navy DB diesel; 60 hp **Range:** 150/8 **Man:** 6 tot.

REMARKS: Wooden-hulled former personnel launches loaned in 1972 and purchased during 1981.

◆ **2 minelayers, former U.S. LSM 1-class landing ships** Bldr: Charleston Naval SY

	Laid down	L	In serv.
N 04 AKTION (ex-LSM 301)	18-10-44	19-11-44	1-1-45
N 05 AMVRAKIA (ex-LSM 303)	8-10-44	14-11-44	6-1-45

D: 720 tons (1,100 fl) **S:** 13 kts **Dim:** 62.0 × 10.5 × 2.4
A: 8/40-mm AA (II × 4)—6/20-mm AA (I × 6)—100 to 300 mines, depending upon type
M: 2 G.M. 16-278A diesels; 2 props; 2,800 hp **Range:** 3,500/12 **Man:** 65 tot.

Amvrakia (N 05)

REMARKS: Transferred in 1953. Four derricks, two forward and two aft, for handling mines. Two minelaying rails. Four 30-cm searchlights, 1 of 60 cm. Four Mk 51 Mod. 2 optical GFCS for the 40-mm AA. Twin rudders. Three of the same class ships were transferred to Turkey and two to Norway, who passed them on to Turkey in 1961.

AMPHIBIOUS WARFARE SHIPS

NOTE: Officially announced 1985 that five landing ships are to be built in Greece, probably to replace the U.S. LST 1/511-class ships.

◆ **1 ex-U.S. Cabildo-class dock landing ship** Bldr: Boston Naval SY

	Laid down	L	In serv.
L 153 NAFKRATOUSSA (ex-*Fort Mandan,* LSD 21)	16-12-44	6-4-45	31-10-45

D: 4,790 tons (9,375 fl) **S:** 15 kts **Dim:** 139.5 × 21.9 × 5.49
A: 8/40-mm AA (IV × 2) **Electron Equipt:** Radar: 1/SPS-5, 1/SPS-6
M: 2 sets GT; 2 props; 7,000 hp **Electric:** 600 kw
Boilers: 62/30.6 kg/cm², 393°C **Fuel:** 1,758 tons **Range:** 8,000/15
Man: 254 tot.

REMARKS: Modernized under the FRAM program and transferred 1-71. Flagship of the amphibious forces. Helicopter deck. Well deck: 103.0 × 13.3. Two 35-ton cranes. Can carry 18 LCMs, each with an LCVP nested in it. SPS-6 air-search radar recently added.

◆ **2 ex-U.S. Terrebonne Parish-class LSTs**

	Bldr	Laid down	L	In serv.
L 104 OINOUSSAI (ex-*Terrell County,* LST 1157)	Bath Iron Wks	3-3-52	6-12-52	19-3-53
L 116 KOS (ex-*Whitfield County,* LST 1169)	Christy Corp.	. . .	22-8-53	14-9-54

Kos (L 116) L. & L. Van Ginderen, 1982

D: 2,590 tons (6,225 fl) **S:** 12 kts **Dim:** 112.35 × 16.7 × 3.7
A: 6/76.2-mm AA (II × 3)—4/20-mm AA (I × 4)
Electron Equipt: Radar: 1/. . . nav., 1/SPS-10, 2/Mk 34
M: 4 G.M. diesels; 2 CP props; 6,000 hp **Man:** 115 crew, 395 troops

REMARKS: Purchased 17-3-77. Two Mk 63 GFCS.

◆ **5 ex-U.S. LST 1 and LST 511-class tank landing ships**

	Bldr	Laid down	L	In serv.
L 144 SYROS (ex-LST 325)	Philadelphia NY	10-8-42	27-10-42	1-2-43
L 154 IKARIA (ex-*Potter County,* LST 1086)	American Bridge, Ambridge, Pa.	5-12-44	28-1-45	24-2-45
L 157 RODOS (ex-*Bowman County,* LST 391)	Newport News SB & DD	14-7-42	28-10-42	3-12-42
L 171 KRITI (ex-*Page County,* LST 1076)	Bethlehem Steel, Hingham, Mass.	16-3-45	14-4-45	1-5-45
L 172 LESBOS (ex-*Boone County,* LST 389)	Newport News SB & DD	20-6-42	15-10-42	24-11-42

D: 1,653 tons (4,080 fl) **S:** 11.6 kts **Dim:** 99.98 × 15.24 × 3.4
A: 8/40-mm AA (II × 2, I × 4)—4/20-mm AA (II × 2)
Electron Equipt: Radar: 1/. . . nav.
M: 2 G.M. 12-567A (L 171: 16-278A) diesels; 1,700 hp
Electric: 300 kw **Fuel:** 569 tons **Range:** 15,000/9 **Man:** 125 tot.

REMARKS: L 144 (with reinforced waterline belt for ice operations!) was transferred 29-5-64 after a complete refit and modernization; L 154, L 157, and L 172 transferred 9-8-60; L 171 transferred 3-71 (purchased 11-7-78). All have tripod masts and carry 4 LCVP in Welin davits. Cargo: 2,100 tons

AMPHIBIOUS WARFARE SHIPS *(continued)*

Ikaria (L 154) L. & L. Van Ginderen, 1982

◆ **5 ex-U.S. LSM 1-class medium landing ships**
Bldrs: L 161, 162, 165: Brown Bros. SB, Houston; L 163: Dravo Corp, Wilmington, Del.; L 164: Charleston NSY

	Laid down	L	In serv.
L 161 Ipopliarchos Grigoropoulos (ex-LSM 45)	6-6-44	30-6-44	31-7-44
L 162 Ipopliarchos Tournas (ex-LSM 102)	23-9-44	14-10-44	9-11-44
L 163 Ipopliarchos Danioloss (ex-LSM 227)	17-7-44	9-9-44	5-10-44
L 164 Ipopliarchos Rousen (ex-LSM 399)	29-12-44	18-1-45	13-8-45
L 165 Ipopliarchos Krystallidis (ex-LSM 541)	7-7-45	18-8-45	7-12-45

Ipopliarchos Krystallidis (L 165) P. Voss, 4-83

D: 1,095 tons (fl) **S:** 12.5 kts **Dim:** 62.03 × 10.52 × 2.54
A: 2/40-mm AA (II × 1)—4/20-mm AA (I × 4)
Electron Equipt: Radar: 1/Decca . . . nav.
M: 2 Fairbanks-Morse 38D1/8-10 (L 164: G.M. 16-278A) diesels; 2 props; 2,800 hp
Electric: 240 kw **Fuel:** 161 tons **Range:** 4,900/12 **Man:** 60 tot.

Remarks: Transferred 3-11-58 (L 165: 30-10-58).

◆ **6 ex-U.S. LCU 501-class utility landing craft**

Bldrs: L 145, 146, 147: Mare Island NSY, Cal.; L 149; Missouri Valley Bridge & Iron, Leavenworth, Kan.; L 150: Pidgeon-Thomas Iron, Memphis, Tenn.; L 152: Kansas City Steel, Kansas City, Missouri

	In serv.		In serv.
L 145 Kassos (ex-LCU 1382)	30-11-44	L 149 Kythnos (ex-LCU 763)	24-12-43
L 146 Karpathos (ex-LCU 1379)	17-11-44	L 150 Sifnos (ex-LCU 677)	11-3-44
L 147 Kimonos (ex-LCU 971)	1-2-44	L 152 Skyatos (ex-LCU 827)	10-4-44

D: 143 tons (309 fl) **S:** 8 kts **Dim:** 36.3 × 9.96 × 1.14
A: 2/20-mm AA (I × 2) **M:** 3 G.M. 6-71 diesels; 675 hp **Man:** 13 tot.

Remarks: Transferred 1959-62.

◆ **2 ex-British LCT(4)-class utility landing craft** Bldrs: . . . , U.K. (In serv. 1944-45)

L 185 Kythera (ex-LCT 1198) L 189 Milos (ex-LCT 1300)

D: 280 tons light (640 fl) **S:** 9.5 kts **Dim:** 57.07 × 11.79 × 1.30 (aft)
A: 2/20-mm AA **M:** 2 Paxman diesels; 2 props; 1,000 hp
Range: 500/9.5; 3,100/7 **Man:** 12 tot.

Remarks: Transferred 1946; survivors of a group of 12. Cargo: 350 tons.

◆ **11 ex-U.S. LCM(6)-class landing craft**

D: 24 tons light (56 fl) **S:** 10 kts **Dim:** 17.07 × 4.37 × 1.17 (aft)
M: 2 Gray Marine 64HN9 diesels; 2 props; 330 hp **Range:** 130/10

Remarks: Cargo: 30 tons. Transferred: 5 in 3-56, remainder in 3-58.

◆ **7 LCVP-type landing craft** Bldr: Viking Marine, Hellas, Piraeus (In serv. 1-80)

D: 13 tons (fl) **S:** 8 kts **Dim:** 10.90 × 3.21 × 1.04 (aft)
M: 1 G.M 6-71 diesel; 200 hp

◆ **34 ex-U.S. LCVP-type landing craft**

D: 13 tons (fl) **S:** 9 kts **Dim:** 10.90 × 3.21 × 1.04 (aft)
M: 1 Gray Marine 64HN9 diesel; 225 hp **Range:** 110/9

Remarks: Carried by LSTs and the LSD. Cargo 36 troops or 3.5 tons cargo. Transferred: 10 in 11-56, 4 in 7-58, 10 in 1-62, 4 in 6-64, 3 in 10-69, and remainder in 3-71.

HYDROGRAPHIC SHIPS

◆ **1 new-construction oceanographic survey ship**
Bldr: Anastassiadis Tsortanidis, Perama

	L	In serv.
A. . . Pytheas	19-9-83	12-83

D: 670 tons (840 fl) **S:** 15 kts **Dim:** 50.00 (44.91 pp) × 9.60 × 4.22
M: 2 G.M. diesels; 2 props; 1,800 hp **Man:** 40 tot.

Remarks: Programmed 1979, ordered 5-82.

◆ **1 Naftilos class**

	Bldr	L	In serv.
A 478 Naftilos	Anastassiadis Tsortanidis, Perama	19-11-75	3-4-76

Naftilos (A 478) Greek Navy

D: 1,380 tons (1,480 fl) **S:** 15 kts **Dim:** 63.1 (56.5 pp) × 11.6 × 4.0
M: 2 Burmeister & Wain SS28LH diesels; 2 props; 2,640 hp **Man:** 57 tot.

Remarks: In service 3-4-76. Sisters *St. Lykoudis* (A 481) and *I. Theophilopoulos Karavoyiannos* (A 485) are lighthouse tenders. Helicopter landing platform.

◆ **1 modified U.S. Falcon-class coastal minesweeper**

	Bldr	In serv.
A 475 Doris (ex-M 245, ex-MSC 298)	Tacoma Boatbldg.	9-11-64

Remarks: Transferred on completion; converted late 1970s. Man: 3 officers, 32 men; other details as for minesweeper version.

◆ **2 ex-German KW1-class coastal survey ships**

A 476 Archikelefstis Maliopoulos (ex-Ger. KW 8, ex-H 8, ex-W 17)
A 477 Archikelefstis Stasis (ex-Ger. KW 2, ex-H 2, ex-W 2, ex-*Inger*, ex-*Concordia*, ex-K 613, ex-M 3253)

D: 112 tons (fl) **S:** 9 kts **Dim:** 22.30 (20.57 pp) × 6.40 × 2.75
M: 1 Demag 5-cyl. diesel; 150 hp **Electric:** 10 kVA
Range: 1,200/7 **Man:** 16 tot.

Remarks: Wooden construction, fishing-cutter hulls. Construction yard unknown; entered West German service 10-4-52. Transferred 30-8-75 as patrol boats. A 476 converted to replace sister *Anemos* (A 469), stricken 1977, while A 477 was converted in 1981 to replace the minesweeper *Atalanti* (M 202), returned to mine countermeasures duties.

AUXILIARY SHIPS

◆ **1 training ship** Bldr: Anastassiadis Tsortanidis, Perama

	Laid down	L	In serv.
A 74 Aris	10-76	4-10-78	1-81

Aris (A 74) L. & L. Van Ginderen, 8-83

AUXILIARY SHIPS *(continued)*

D: 3,100 tons (4,500 fl) **S:** 20 kts **Dim:** 100.0 (95.0 pp) × 11.0 × 4.5
A: 2/76.2-mm U.S. Mk 26 DP (I × 2)—2/40-mm AA (I × 2)—4/20-mm AA (I × 4)—1 Alouette-III helicopter
M: 2 MAK diesels; 2 props; 10,000 hp **Man:** 130 crew + 370 cadets

Remarks: Largest naval ship built in Greece. Resembles a small passenger ship and can serve as a hospital ship or transport in wartime. Completion delayed by payment dispute. Two lead-computing GFCS for the 40-mm AA.

◆ **1 yacht/training ship, ex-Canadian "River"-class frigate**

	Bldr	Laid down	L	In serv.
A. . . Argo (ex-*Christina,* ex-*Montreal,* ex-*Stormont*)	Can. Vickers, Montreal	23-12-42	12-6-43	14-11-44

D: 1,526 grt **S:** 20 kts **Dim:** 99.15 (86.59 pp) × 11.13 × 5.33 **A:** . . .
M: 2 sets 4-cyl. triple-expansion steam; 2 props; 5,500 hp **Electric:** 400 kw
Boilers: 2 water-tube, 17.6 kg/cm^2 **Range:** 7,400/15; 12,000/10
Man: . . .

Remarks: Donated 12-7-78. Former yacht of shipowner Aristotle Onassis, converted from a frigate 1951-54 by Howaldtswerke, Kiel. Used as presidential yacht.

◆ **2 personnel ferries** Bldr: Anastassiadis Tsortanidis, Perama

A 419 Pandora (In serv. 26-10-73) A 420 Pandrosos (In serv. 1-12-73)

Pandora (A 419) L. & L. Van Ginderen, 1984

D: 350 tons (390 fl) **S:** 11 kts **Dim:** 46.8 × 8.3 × 1.9
M: 2 diesels; 2 props; . . . hp

Remarks: Can carry up to 500 personnel.

◆ **1 netlayer and mooring buoy tender** Bldr: Krögerwerft, Rendsburg

A 307 Thetis (ex-U.S. AN 103) (In serv. 4-60)

Thetis (A 307) D. Dervissis, 7-79

D: 560 tons (975 fl) **S:** 12.8 kts **Dim:** 48.5 (51.7 over horns) × 10.6 × 3.7
A: 1/40-mm AA—3/20-mm AA (I × 3) **Electron Equipt:** Radar: 1/Decca 707
M: 1 M.A.N. G7V 40/60 diesel; 1 prop; 1,470 hp **Fuel:** 134 tons
Range: 6,500/10.2 **Man:** 5 officers, 45 men

Remarks: Launched 1959. Transferred 4-60. Has 152 tons water ballast. The 40-mm AA is normally not aboard; can carry 1,600 rds 40-mm, 25,200 rds 20-mm ammunition.

◆ **2 ex-U.S. Patapsco-class oilers** Bldr: Cargill SY, Savage, Minn.

	Laid down	L	In serv.
A 377 Arethousa (ex-*Natchaug,* AOG 54)	15-8-44	6-12-44	11-6-45
A 414 Ariadni (ex-*Tombigbee,* AOG 11)	23-10-42	18-11-43	13-7-44

D: 1,850 tons (4,335 fl) **S:** 13 kts **Dim:** 94.72 (89.0 pp) × 14.78 × 4.78
A: A 377:4/76.2-mm AA (I × 4)—A 414: 2/76.2-mm AA (I × 2)
Electron Equipt: Radar: 1/navigational, 1/SPS-5, 1/Mk 26
M: 2 G.M. 16-278A diesels; 2 props; 3,300 hp **Electric:** 460 kw
Fuel: 295 tons **Man:** 46 tot.

Arethousa (A 377)—note 76.2-mm gun off centerline to stbd. Official

Remarks: Former gasoline tankers. Cargo: 2,040 tons. One Mk 52 radar GFCS and one Mk 51 GFCS.

◆ **2 coastal tankers** Bldr: Kynossoura SY, Piraeus

A 416 Ouranos (In serv. 29-1-77) A 417 Hyperion (In serv. 27-2-77)

D: 1,200 tons (fl) **S:** 13 kts **Dim:** 67.7 × 10.0 × 4.7
M: 1 MWM TPD-484BU diesel; 1,750 hp

◆ **1 small harbor oiler**

A 471 Vivies

Remarks: Cargo: 187 tons; S: 11 kts.

Note: *Kronos* (A 373), built in 1943, still exists as a fuel lighter, unpowered; cargo: 110 tons.

◆ **1 ammunition ship** Bldr: Dubigeon, Nantes

	Laid down	L	In serv.
A 415 Evros (ex-German *Schwarzwald,* ex-French *Amalthée*)	30-6-55	31-1-56	7-6-56

D: 2,395 tons **S:** 15 kts **Dim:** 80.18 × 11.99 × 4.65
A: 4/40-mm AA (II × 2)
M: 1 Sulzer 6-SD-60 diesel; 3,000 hp **Electric:** 500 kw **Range:** 4,500/15
Man: 32 tot.

Remarks: Purchased 2-60 by the German Navy and converted for naval use, commissioning 11-10-61; transferred to Greece 2-6-76. 1,667 grt.

◆ **1 new-construction water tanker** Bldr: Khalkis SY

D: . . . **S:** . . . **Dim:** 67.0 × . . . × . . .
M: . . .

Remarks: 3,000 dwt. Ordered 3-85.

◆ **3 Doirani-class water lighters**

A 434 Prespa (In serv. 10-10-72) A 467 Doirani (In serv. 1972)
A 468 Kalliroe (In serv. 26-10-72)

D: 850 tons (fl) **S:** 13 kts **Dim:** 54.7 × 7.9 × 3.0
M: 1 diesel; . . . hp **Cargo:** 600 tons

Remarks: A 434 taken over from another government agency 1979. Very low freeboard.

◆ **1 ex-German FW 1-class water lighter**

	Bldr	Laid down	L	In serv.
A 433 Kerkini (ex-FW 3)	Jadewerft, Wilhelmshaven	14-6-63	15-10-63	11-5-64

Kerkini (A 433) L. & L. Van Ginderen, 12-84

AUXILIARY SHIPS *(continued)*

D: 598 tons (624 fl) **S:** 9.5 kts **Dim:** 44.03 (41.10 pp) × 7.80 × 2.63
M: 1 MWM 12-cyl. diesel; 1 prop; 230 hp **Electric:** 83 kw
Range: 2,150/9 **Man:** 12 tot.

REMARKS: Transferred 22-4-76. Cargo: 350 m³.

◆ 2 miscellaneous small water lighters

A 470 KASTORIA (In serv. . . . .) — Cargo: 520 tons
A 473 TRICHONIS (In serv. 1980) — Cargo: 650 tons

◆ 1 British Bustler-class salvage tug Bldr: Henry Robb, Leith

	Laid down	L	In serv.
A 428 ATLAS (ex-*Nisos Zakynthos*, ex-HMS *Mediator*)	18-10-43	21-6-44	8-11-44

D: 1,118 tons (1,630 fl) **S:** 16 kts **Dim:** 62.48 (59.4 pp) × 12.32 × 5.18
A: . . . **M:** 2 Atlas diesels; 2 props; 3,200 hp **Fuel:** 340 tons
Range: 3,400/11 **Man:** 42 tot.

REMARKS: Purchased from British Navy 1965 by private owner. Acquired 1-8-79 by Greek Navy and commissioned 12-79.

◆ 3 Heraklis-class coastal tugs Bldr: Anastassiadis Tsortanidis, Perama

A 423 HERAKLIS (In serv. 6-4-78) A 425 ODISSEUS (In serv. 28-6-78)
A 424 JASON (In serv. 6-3-78)

D: 345 tons **S:** 12 kts **Dim:** 30.0 × 7.9 × 3.4
M: 1 MWM diesel; 1,200 hp

◆ 6 harbor tugs

A 410 ATROMITOS } (In serv. 20-6-68) — 1,260 hp, D: 310 tons
A 411 ADAMASTOS } Dim: 30.0 × 7.9 × 3.0
A 412 AIAS (ex-U.S. *Ankachak*, YTM 767) (Transferred 1972) — 650 hp
A 421 MINOTAUROS (ex-U.S. Army ST 539) (Transferred 1962) — 650 hp
A 431 TITAN (In serv. 1962) — 240 hp
A 432 GIGAS (In serv. 26-11-61) — 1,200 hp

◆ 2 lighthouse tenders Bldr: Anastassiadis Tsortanidis, Perama

A 479 I. THEOPHILOPOULOS KARAVOYIANNOS (In serv. 2-1-76)
A 481 ST. LYKOUDIS (In serv. 17-3-76)

I. Theophilopoulos Karavoyiannos (A 479) L. & L. Van Ginderen, 12-84

D: 1,350 tons (1,450 fl) **S:** 15 kts **Dim:** 63.24 (56.50 pp) × 11.6 × 4.0
M: 1 MWM TBD-500-8UD diesel; 2,400 hp **Man:** 40 tot.

REMARKS: Near sisters to hydrographic survey ship *Naftilos*. Have a helicopter deck.

◆ 5 miscellaneous floating cranes

COAST GUARD
HARBOR CORPS

The Greek Coast Guard has some 4,000 personnel, most of whom are shore-based. There are some 80 small craft, the largest and newest of which are three units of the *Dilos*-class patrol boats, as described above. Five Cessna light aircraft are used for coastal patrol. The Greek Customs Service also operates about 20 boats in its Anti-Smuggling Flotilla.

DE 81 — *Dilos*-class patrol boat H. Ehlers, 4-84

Patrol Boat DE 52 — DE 51–55 are of the same class H. Ehlers, 5-84

8.23-m patrol craft DE 72 H. Ehlers, 5-84

Pollution-collection boat DE 24 H. Ehlers, 5-84

GRENADA

Merchant Marine (1984): 3 ships—425 grt

◆ **1 U.S. 106-ft patrol boat** Bldr: Lantana Boatyard, Florida

PB 01 Tyrrel Bay (In serv. 21-11-84)

Tyrrel Bay (PB 01) Lantana, 11-84

D: 94 tons (fl) **S:** 24 kts **Dim:** 32.31 × 6.25 × 2.13 (props)
A: 2/12.7-mm mg (I × 2)—2/7.62-mm mg (I × 2)
Electron Equipt: Radar: 1/Furuno . . . nav.
M: 3 G.M. Detroit Diesel 12V71 TI diesels; 3 props; 2,250 hp
Electric: 100 kw **Fuel:** 21 tons **Man:** 4 officers, 12 men

Remarks: Laid down 1-84 to U.S. Gov't order. Aluminum construction. Has a Magnavox MX4102 NAVSAT receiver.

◆ **1 patrol craft** Bldr: Brooke Marine, Lowestoft (In serv. 1972)

P B 2

D: 15 tons (fl) **S:** 22 kts **Dim:** 12.2 × 3.7 × 0.6 **A:** 3/7.62-mm mg (I × 3)
M: 2 Caterpillar diesels; 2 props; 740 hp

◆ **3 Spear-class patrol craft** Bldr: Fairey Marine, Hamble, U.K. (In serv. . . . ?)

D: 10 tons (fl) **S:** 26 kts **Dim:** 9.10 × 2.75 × 0.84
A: 2/7.62-mm mg (I × 2) **M:** 2 diesels; 2 props; 580 hp **Man:** 3 tot.

Note: PB 1 and the three Spear-class patrol craft were derelict at the time of the U.S. "invasion" in 1983; they have since been rehabilitated and put back in service.

GUATEMALA

Republic of Guatemala

Personnel (1984): 1000 total: 125 officers, 875 enlisted, including 700 Marines

Merchant Marine (1984): 8 ships—16,046 grt

PATROL BOATS AND CRAFT

◆ **1 U.S. Broadsword class** Bldr: Halter Marine, New Orleans, La.

P 1051 Kukulkan (In serv. 4-8-76)

D: 90.5 tons (fl) **S:** 32 kts **Dim:** 32.0 × 6.3 × 1.9
A: 1/75-mm recoilless rifle—1/81-mm mortar with a 12.7-mm mg atop it—2/12.7-mm mg (I × 2)
M: 2 G.M. 16V149 TI diesels; 3,200 hp **Electric:** 60 kw **Range:** 1,150/20
Man: 5 officers, 15 men

Kukulkan—on trials with the *Bitol* (P 655), *Picuda* (P 361), and *Barracuda* (P 362) Halter, 1976

◆ **2 U.S. 85-foot Commercial Cruiser class** Bldr: Sewart Seacraft, Berwick, La.

P 851 Utatlan (In serv. 5-67) P 852 Subteniente Osorio Saravia (In serv. 1972)

D: 50 tons **S:** 23 kts **Dim:** 25.9 × 5.8 × 1.0
A: 2/12.7-mm mg—1/81-mm recoilless rifle
M: 2 G.M. diesels; 2 props; 2,200 hp **Range:** 780/15
Man: 7 officers, 10 men

◆ **5 U.S. Cutlass class** Bldr: Halter Marine, New Orleans, La. (In serv. 1972-76)

P 651 Tecunuman P 653 Azumanche P 655 Bitol
P 652 Kaibilbalan P 654 Tzacol

D: 34 tons (fl) **S:** 25 kts **Dim:** 19.7 × 5.2 × 0.9
A: 1/12.7-mm mg—3/7.62-mm mg (I × 3) **Man:** 10 tot.
M: 2 G.M. 12V71 diesels; 2 props; 960 hp **Electric:** 20 kw **Range:** 400/15

◆ **30 river patrol craft** Bldr: Trabejos Baros SY, Guatemala (In serv. 1979)

D: . . . tons **S:** 19 or 28 kts **Dim:** 9.14 × 3.66 × 0.61
A: 2/7.62-mm mg (I × 2)
M: 1 diesel; 1 prop; 150 or 300 hp **Range:** 400-500 nm

Remarks: Wooden construction—in two series, with different engines.

AMPHIBIOUS WARFARE CRAFT

◆ **2 U.S. Machete class** Bldr: Halter Marine, New Orleans, La. (In serv. 4-8-76)

P 361 Picuda P 362 Barracuda

D: 6 tons **S:** 36 kts **Dim:** 11.0 × 4.0 × 0.76
M: 2 G.M. 6V53 PI diesels; 2 water jets; 540 hp

Remarks: Troop carriers. Square bows, aluminum construction.

◆ **1 ex-U.S. LCM (6) class**

561 Chinaltenango

D: 24 tons (56 fl) **S:** 10 kts **Dim:** 17.07 × 4.37 × 1.17 (aft)
A: 2/12.7-mm mg (I × 2)
M: 2 Gray Marine 64HN9 diesels; 2 props; 450 hp **Range:** 130/10

Remarks: Transferred in 12-65. Cargo: 30 tons.

HYDROGRAPHIC SHIP

◆ **1 new-construction coastal survey craft** (In serv. 1981)

D: . . . **S:** . . . **Dim:** 19.8 × . . . × . . .

GUINEA

Republic of Guinea

Personnel (1984): 600 total

Merchant Marine (1984): 18 ships—6,944 grt

CORVETTE

◆ **1 ex-Soviet T 58-class minesweeper**

Lamine Sadji Kaba

D: 750 tons (860 fl) **S:** 17 kts **Dim:** 70.0 × 9.1 × 2.5
A: 4/57-mm AA—2/RBU-1200 ASW RL (V × 2)—mines
Electron Equipt: Radar: 1/Don-2, 1/Muff Cob **Man:** 60 tot.
M: 2 diesels; 2 props; 4,000 hp **Range:** 2,500/13.5

GUINEA *(continued)*
CORVETTE *(continued)*

Remarks: Transferred 5-79. Unlike Soviet Navy units that were redesignated patrol ships, has had *all* mine countermeasures equipment removed, including the sweep winch.

PATROL BOATS AND CRAFT

◆ **1 U.S. 77-ft class** Bldr: Swiftships, Morgan City, La.

P 300 Vigilante (In serv. 7-85)

Vigilante (P 300) Swiftships, 6-85

D: 47.6 tons (fl) **S:** 26 kts **Dim:** 23.47 × 6.10 × 1.52
A: 2/12.7-mm mg (I × 2) **Electron Equipt:** Radar: 1/. . . nav.
M: 3 G.M. 12V71 T1 diesels; 3 props; 2,385 hp
Range: 600/18 **Man:** . . .

Remarks: Ordered 7-85. Aluminum construction.

◆ **1 U.S. 65-ft-class** Bldr: Swiftships, Inc., Morgan City, La. (In serv. 6-85)

D: 36.3 tons (fl) **S:** 24 kts **Dim:** 19.96 × 5.61 × 1.52
A: 1/12.7-mm mg—2/7.62-mm mg—1/81-mm mortar
Electron Equipt: Radar: 1/. . . nav.
M: 2 G.M. 12V71 TI diesels; 2 props; 1,590 hp
Range: 500/18 **Man:** 10 tot.

Remarks: Aluminum construction. Resembles El Salvador's GC-11 (see addenda).

◆ **2 U.S. Stinger class** Bldr: Monark, Monticello, Arkansas

P-30 P-35

Guinea's two Stinger-class patrol craft MonArk, 1985

D: 2.7 tons (fl) **S:** 35 kts **Dim:** 7.92 × 3.25 × 0.91
A: 2/12.7-mm (I × 2) **Electron Equipt:** Radar: 1/Raytheon 1200 nav.
M: 2 OMC 55 XL "Commercial" outboard motors; 310 hp **Man:** 4 tot.

Remarks: Ordered 10-84. Camouflaged in three shades of green.

◆ **2 U.S. 26-ft patrol craft** Bldr: MonArk, Monticello, Arkasas (In serv. 7-85)

A: 2/12.7-mm mg (I × 2)

◆ **6 Chinese Shanghai-II class**

P 733 P 734 P 735 P 736 P 737 P 738

D: 122.5 tons (134.8 fl) **S:** 28.5 kts **Dim:** 38.78 × 5.41 × 1.55
A: 4/37-mm AA (II × 2)—4/25-mm AA (II × 2)
Electron Equipt: Radar: 1/Pot head **Electric:** 39 kw
M: 2 M50F-4 diesels (1,200 hp each), 2 12D6 diesels (910 hp each); 4 props; 4,220 hp
Range: 750/16.5 **Endurance:** 7 days **Man:** 36 tot.

Remarks: Four transferred 1973-74, two in 1976.

◆ **3 ex-Soviet Shershen-class former torpedo boats**

D: 150 tons (170 fl) **S:** 45 kts **Dim:** 34.7 × 6.7 × 1.5
A: 4/30-mm AA (II × 2) **Range:** 460/42; 850/30
Electron Equipt: Radar: 1/Pot Drum, 1/Drum Tilt
IFF: 1/Square Head, 1/High Pole
M: 3 M503A diesels; 3 props; 12,000 hp **Man:** 24 tot.

Remarks: Two delivered 1978, one in 1979. Torpedo tubes removed prior to transfer.

◆ **1 French 28-m class** Bldr: Chantiers Navals de l'Estérel, Cannes

P 400 Almariy Bocar Biro Barry (In serv. 8-79)

D: 56 tons (fl) **S:** 35 kts **Dim:** 28.0 × 5.2 × 1.6 **A:** 1/20-mm AA
M: 2 MTU 12V331 TC82 diesels; 2 props; 2,600 hp **Range:** 750/15
Man: 12 tot.

◆ **2 ex-Soviet Poluchat-I class**

D: 70 tons (90 fl) **S:** 18 kts **Dim:** 29.6 × 5.8 × 1.5
A: 2/14.5-mm mg (II × 1) **Man:** 20 tot.
Electron Equipt: Radar: 1/Spin Trough
IFF: 1/High Pole A
M: 2 M50-series diesels; 2 props; 2,400 hp **Range:** 450/17; 900/10

GUINEA-BISSAU

Republic of Guinea-Bissau

Personnel (1984): 250 total

Merchant Marine (1984): 15 ships—3,677 grt

PATROL BOATS AND CRAFT

◆ **2 Chinese Shanghai-II class**

D: 122.5 tons **S:** 28.5 kts **Dim:** 38.78 × 5.41 × 1.55
A: 4/37-mm AA (II × 2)—4/25-mm AA (II × 2)
Electron Equipt: Radar: 1/Pot Head
M: 2 M50F4 diesels (1,200 hp each), 2 12D6 diesels (910 hp each); 4 props; 4,220 hp
Man: 36 tot. **Range:** 750/16.5 **Electric:** 39 kw **Endurance:** 7 days

Remarks: Transferred late 1983.

◆ **1 Dutch PT 1903 Mk III class** Bldr: Le Comte, Vianen, The Netherlands

Naga (In serv. 5-81)

D: 30 tons (33 fl) **S:** 30 kts **Dim:** 19.27 × 4.95 × 1.25
A: 2/12.7-mm mg (I × 2) **Range:** 1,650/17; 2,300/12 **Man:** 10 tot.
M: 2 MTU 8V331 TC92 diesels; 2 props; 1,770 hp

◆ **1 ex-Soviet Shershen-class former torpedo boat**

D: 150 tons (170 fl) **S:** 45 kts **Dim:** 34.7 × 6.7 × 1.5
A: 4/30-mm AA (II × 2) **Man:** 24 tot.
Electron Equipt: Radar: 1/Pot Drum, 1 Drum Tilt
IFF: 1/Square Head, 1/High Pole A
M: 3 M503A diesels; 3 props; 12,000 hp **Range:** 460/42; 850/30

Remarks: Transferred 12-78. Torpedo tubes removed prior to transfer.

◆ **1 ex-Soviet Poluchat-I class**

D: 70 tons (90 fl) **S:** 18 kts **Dim:** 29.6 × 5.8 × 1.5
A: 2/14.5-mm mg (II × 1) **Electron Equipt:** Radar: 1/Spin Trough
M: 2 M50-series diesels; 2 props; 2,400 hp **Range:** 450/17; 900/10
Man: 20 tot.

Remarks: Transferred 1978.

◆ **2 French Plascoa-1900 class** (In serv. . . .)

Cabo Roxo Ilha De Poilão

D: 30 tons (fl) **S:** 25 kts **Dim:** 19.0 × 5.35 × 1.2
A: 2/12.7-mm mg (I × 2) **M:** 2 G.M. diesels; 2 props; 1,050 hp
Range: 650/25; 1,500/9

GUINEA-BISSAU *(continued)*
PATROL BOATS AND CRAFT *(continued)*

◆ **3 Spanish LVC-1 class** Bldr: Aresa, Barcelona (In serv. 1979)

D: 20.8 tons (fl) **S:** 23.3 kts **Dim:** 16.00 × 4.36 × 1.30
A: 1/12.7-mm mg **M:** 2 Baudouin DNP-8 M1R diesels; 2 props; 700 hp
Range: 400/18 **Man:** 6 tot.

AUXILIARIES AND SERVICE CRAFT

◆ **1 ex-Soviet Biya-class survey ship and buoy tender** Bldr: Gdansk, Poland

D: 750 tons (fl) **S:** 13 kts **Dim:** 55.0 × 9.2 × 2.6
Electron Equipt: Radar: 1/Don-2 **M:** 2 diesels; 2 CP props; 1,200 hp
Range: 4,700/11 **Man:** 25 tot.

REMARKS: Transferred 6-78. One 5-ton buoy crane; one inshore survey launch; one 15-m² oceanographic laboratory.

◆ **2 ex-Soviet T4-class landing craft**

D: 70 tons (fl) **S:** 10 kts **Dim:** 19.0 × 4.3 × 1.0
M: 2 diesels; 2 props; 600 hp **Man:** 5 tot.

REMARKS: Employed in logistic support duties.

GUYANA

Cooperative Republic of Guyana

PERSONNEL (1984): 150 total

MERCHANT MARINE (1984): 104 ships—24,231 grt (tankers: 2 ships—933 grt)

NAVAL AVIATION: 1 Embraer EMB111 Bandeirante for coastal surveillance

◆ **2 ex-North Korean patrol boats**

D: 35 tons (fl) **S:** 40 kts **Dim:** 18.3 × 3.4 × 1.7 **A:** 2/14.5-mm mg (I × 2)
M: 2 gasoline engines; 2 props; . . . hp **Man:** 9 tot.

REMARKS: Transferred 1980.

◆ **1 103-foot British patrol boat**

	Bldr	L	In serv.
DF 1010 PECCARI	Vosper Thornycroft, Portsmouth, U.K.	26-3-76	26-1-77

D: 96 tons (109 fl) **S:** 27 kts **Dim:** 31.4 × 6.0 × 1.6
A: 2/20-mm AA (I × 2)
M: 2 Paxman Ventura 12-cyl. diesels; 2 props; 3,500 hp
Range: 1,400/14 **Man:** 22 tot.

REMARKS: A second unit was ordered in 1977, but was canceled because of lack of funds.

◆ **3 patrol boats** Bldr: Vosper Thornycroft, U.K.

JAGUAR (In serv. 28-4-71) MARGAY (In serv. 21-5-71) OCELOT (In serv. 22-6-71)

D: 10 tons **S:** 20 kts **Dim:** 14.0 × 3.4 × 2.0 **A:** 1/7.62-mm mg
M: 2 Cummins D366A diesels; 2 props; 270 hp **Range:** 150/12 **Man:** 6 tot.

REMARKS: Fiberglass hull; light-alloy superstructure.

◆ **3 45-foot boats, supplied by the U.S.**

CAMOUDIE LABANA RATTLER

◆ **2 ex-fishing boats**

EKEREKU NUMBER 2

NOTE: Guyana also received the ex-U.S. Navy tug YTM 190 and the covered barge YFN 960, both operated by the Guyana Harbor Board. The 600 grt. ramped cargo ship *Kimbla,* delivered to the Guyana government by Damen, the Netherlands, in 1981, is also non-naval.

HAITI

Republic of Haiti

PERSONNEL (1984): 40 officers, 260 men

MERCHANT MARINE (1984): 6 ships—1,762 grt

COAST GUARD

PATROL BOATS AND CRAFT

◆ **3 U.S. 65-foot Commercial Cruiser class** Bldr: Sewart, Louisiana (In serv. 1976)

MH 21 JEAN CLAUDE DUVALIER
MH 22 N. . . . . . . MH 23 N. . . . . . .

D: 33 tons (fl) **S:** 25 kts **Dim:** 21.3 × 5.2 × 1.0
A: 1/20-mm AA—2/12.7-mm mg (I × 2)
M: 3 G.M. 8V-71 diesels; 3 props; 1,590 hp

REMARKS: MH 21, cannibalized 1982 for parts, refitted for service 11-84.

◆ **9 U.S. 3812-VCF class** Bldr: MonArk, Monticello, Arkansas (In serv. 1980-81)

MH 11 LE MAROON, MH 12 OGE, MH 13 CHAVANNES, MH 14 CAPOIS LA MORT, MH 15 BAUCKMAN, MH 16 MAKANDAL, MH 17 CHARLEMAGNE PERRAULT, MH 18 SONTHONAX, MH 24 BOISROND TONNEREE

Oge (MH 12) MonArk Boat Co., 1980

D: 8.5 tons (9.0 fl) **S:** 25 kts **Dim:** 12.34 × 4.11 × . . .
A: 1/12.7-mm mg—2/7.62-mm mg (I × 2)
M: 2 G.M. 6V-71N diesels; 2 props; 480 hp **Man:** 4 tot.

◆ **1 U.S. Enforcer class** Bldr: Bertram, Miami

MH 6

Dim: 9.5 × . . . × . . . **M:** 2 Caterpillar 3160 diesels; 2 props; 420 hp

AUXILIARIES

◆ **1 U.S. Sotoyomo-class auxilliary ocean tug**

	Bldr	Laid down	L	In serv.
MH 20 HENRI CHRISTOPHE (ex-*Samoset,* ATA 180)	Levingston SB, Orange, Tx.	5-6-44	14-7-44	27-9-44

D: 689 tons (835 fl) **S:** 13 kts **Dim:** 43.6 (40.75 pp) × 10.37 × 3.65
A: 2/40-mm AA (I × 2)—2/12.7-mm mg (I × 2)
M: 2 G.M. 12-278A diesels, electric drive; 1 prop; 1,500 hp
Electric: 120 kw **Fuel:** 154 tons **Range:** 16,500/9 **Man:** 40 tot.

REMARKS: MH 20 transferred 18-9-78. One 40-mm on fantail, one forward. Transfer of sister *Keywadin* (ATA 213) for use in oceanographic research canceled 1981.

HONDURAS

Republic of Honduras

PERSONNEL: Approx. 250 total

MERCHANT MARINE (1984): 238 ships—276,736 grt (tankers: 33 ships—48,806 grt)

NAVAL AVIATION: Four Embraer EMB111 Bandeirante delivered 1983 for coastal surveillance; flown by naval crews.

PATROL BOATS AND CRAFT

◆ **2 U.S. 106-foot class** Bldr: Lantana Boatyard, Lantana, Florida

	Laid down	L	In serv.
FN 1054 TEGUCIGALPA	6-82	. . .	1983
FN 1055 COMAYAGUELA	4-83	. . .	20-5-84

HONDURAS *(continued)*
PATROL BOATS AND CRAFT *(continued)*

Comayaguela (FN 1055)—on trials Lantana Boatyard, 1984

D: 94 tons (fl) **S:** 35 (FN 1055: 33) kts **Dim:** 32.31 × 6.25 × 2.13 (props)
A: 1/20-mm Sea Vulcan gatling gun—2/12.7-mm mg (I × 2)
Electron Equipt: Radar: 1/Furuno . . . nav.
M: FN 1054: 3 G.M. Detroit Diesel 16V92 TI diesels; 3 props; 3,900 hp
FN 1055: 3 MTU 8V96 TB93 diesels; 3 props; 3,525 hp (3,000 sust.)
Electric: 100 kw **Fuel:** 21 tons **Man:** 4 officers, 12 men

Remarks: Aluminum construction. Have Magnavox MX 4102 NAVSAT receiver and two echo-sounders.

◆ **3 U.S. 105-foot class** Bldr: Swiftships, Morgan City, Louisiana

FN 1051 Guaymuras (In serv. 4-77)
FN 1052 Honduras (In serv. 3-80)
FN 1053 Hibures (In serv. 3-80)

Honduras (FN 1052) Swiftships, Inc., 3-80

D: 103 tons (fl) **S:** 32 kts **Dim:** 31.5 × 6.6 × 2.1 **A:** . . .
M: 2 MTU diesels; 2 props; 7,000 hp **Range:** 1,200/18 **Man:** 16 tot.

◆ **1 U.S. 85-foot Commercial Cruiser class** Bldr: Swiftships, Morgan City, Louisiana

FN 8502 Chamelecon (In serv. . . .)

D: 50 tons **S:** 23 kts **Dim:** 25.9 × 5.8 × 1.0
A: . . . **M:** 2 G.M. 12V71 TI diesels; 2 props; 2,200 hp **Range:** 780/15
Man: 17 tot.

◆ **5 U.S. 65-foot Commercial Cruiser class** Bldr: Swiftships, Morgan City, Louisiana

	In serv.		In serv.
FN 6501 Nacaome (ex-*Aguan*, ex-*Gral*)	12-73	FN 6504 Ulua	1980
FN 6502 Goascoran (ex-*J.T. Cabanas*)	1-74	FN 6505 Chuluteca	1980
FN 6503 Petula	1980		

D: 33 tons (fl) **S:** 25 kts **Dim:** 21.3 × 5.2
A: 2/12.7-mm mg (I × 2) **M:** 3 G.M. 8V71 diesels; 3 props; 1,590 hp
Range: 2,000/22 **Man:** 5 tot.

Remarks: First two originally ordered for Haiti and delivered to Honduras in 1977. Others, ordered 1979, have 3 MTU diesels and can make 36 kts.

◆ **2 inshore patrol craft** Bldr: Ampela Marine, Honduras (In serv. 1981-82)

FN 2501 N. . . . . . . FN 2502 N. . . . . . .

D: 3 tons (fl) **S:** 24 kts **Dim:** 7.62 × 2.74 × 0.38
A: 1/12.7-mm mg—1/7.62-mm mg
M: 1 Chrysler 6M655 TI diesel, waterjet drive; . . . hp **Range:** 250/18
Man: 4 tot.

Remarks: Built of wood and glass-reinforced plastic.

◆ **1 ex-U.S. Coast Guard Hollyhock-class buoy tender**

	Bldr	In serv.
FN . . . Hogal (ex-*Walnut*)	Moore Drydock Co., Oakland, Cal.	27-6-39

D: 825 tons (986 fl) **S:** 12 kts **Dim:** 53.4 × 10.4 × 3.7
M: 2 diesels; 2 props; 1,350 hp **Range:** 6,500/12; 10,000/7.5
Man: 40 tot.

Remarks: Transferred 1-7-82 for navigational support duties. One 20-ton buoy crane.

◆ **6 miscellaneous ex-fishing boats for logistics support**

FN 7501 Juliana FN 7503 Carmen FN 7505 Yosuro
FN 7502 San Rafael FN 7504 Mairy FN 7506 Jose Gregori

HONG KONG

British Crown Colony of Hong Kong

Merchant Marine (1984): 340 ships—5,784,336 grt (tankers: 40 ships—1,286,410 grt)

Note: In addition to the craft listed below, the Royal Navy maintains five *Peacock*-class corvettes at Hong Kong. The Royal Hong Kong Auxiliary Air Force operates one BN-42B/T Maritime Defender and 2 SA Bulldog 128 aircraft for coastal patrol, and 3 SA.365C Dauphin helicopters for rescue work.

ROYAL HONG KONG POLICE FORCE MARINE DISTRICT

Personnel (1984): 160 officers, 3,105 men

PATROL BOATS

◆ **10 (+5) King Lai class** Bldr: Chung Wah SB & Eng, Kowloon

	Laid down	L	In serv.
PL 70 King Lai	28-2-84	14-7-84	29-10-84
PL 71 King Yee	28-2-84	17-7-84	29-11-84
PL 72 King Lim	28-2-84	29-7-84	17-12-84
PL 73 King Hau	15-3-84	2-11-84	31-1-85
PL 74 King Dai	15-3-84	8-11-84	28-2-85
PL 75 King Chung	15-3-84	12-11-84	-85
PL 76 King Shun	17-8-84	26-1-85	-85
PL 77 King Tak	25-8-84	4-2-85	-85
PL 78 King Chi	17-8-84	1-2-85	-85
PL 79 King Tai	1-12-84	-85	-85
PL 80 King Kwan	1-12-84	-85	-86
PL 81 King Mei	1-12-84	-85	-86
PL 82 King Yan	3-85	-85	-86
PL 83 King Yung	3-85	-85	-86
PL 84 King Kan	3-85	-85	-86

D: 85 tons (normal) **S:** 25 kts **Dim:** 26.50 (24.27 pp) × 5.80 × 1.80
A: 1/7.62-mm mg **Electron Equipt:** Radar: 1/. . . nav.
M: 2 MTU 12V396 TC83 diesels (1,483 hp each); 1/M.A.N. MB OM-424A V-12 cruise diesel (465 hp); 2 props, 1 waterjet
Range: 600/14; 1,400/8 **Man:** 17 tot.

Remarks: PL 70–78 ordered 10-83; PL 79–81 ordered 1/12/84. Modified version of the PL 60 class; Damen Stan Patrol 2600/Chung Wah Mk 3 design. Can make up to 7 kts on the centerline waterjet. Carry an Avon SeaRaider semi-rigid inspection boat.

HONG KONG *(continued)*
PATROL BOATS *(continued)*

NOTE: These craft replace the 65-ft *Islander* (PL 6), 78-ft *Sea Horse* (PL 4), and nine 70-ft craft: *Sea Rover* (PL 26), *Sea Farer* (PL 27), *Sea Roamer* (PL 28), *Sea Rider* (PL 29), *Sea Nomad* (PL 30), *Sea Wanderer* (PL 31), *Sea Raker* (PL 32), *Sea Rescuer* (PL 33), and *Sea Ranger* (PL 34); all were stricken 1984-85, except PL 30, PL 32 in 1983. Also disposed of was the support craft *Panther* (PL 3).

◆ **2 command boats** Bldr: Hong Kong United DY (In serv. 1965)

PL 1 SEA LION PL 2 SEA TIGER

D: 222 tons (fl) **S:** 11.8 kts **Dim:** 33.9 × 7.3 × 3.2
A: 1/12.7-mm mg **M:** 2 Cummins diesels; 2 props; 674 hp **Range:** 5,200/11.8
Man: 29 tot.

◆ **10 Damen-design** Bldr: Chung Wah SB & Eng, Kowloon

	In serv.		In serv.
PL 60 N.	2-80	PL 65 CETUS	2-9-80
PL 61 PISCES	2-80	PL 66 DORADO	8-9-80
PL 62 N.	2-80	PL 57 MERCURY	26-1-82
PL 63 N.	1980	PL 58 VULCAN	22-3-82
PL 64 N.	1980	PL 59 CERES	29-3-82

PL 60 G. Arra, 1980

D: 86 tons (normal) **S:** 23 kts **Dim:** 26.2 × 5.9 × 1.80
A: 1/12.7-mm mg **Electron Equipt:** Radar: 1 Decca 150
M: 2 MTU 12V396 TC82 diesels (1,300 hp each), 1 M.A.N. D2566 cruise diesel (195 hp); 3 props (Schöttel on centerline); 2,600 hp
Range: 1,400/8 **Man:** 1 officer, 13 men

REMARKS: First unit laid down 9-79 to a Dutch design. Cruise engine provides 7-8 kt. max. speeds. PL 67–89 ordered 3-81 for logistic support duties, with same engines, but waterjet vice Schöttel propeller for cruise (2 to 7 kts): have restricted patrol range, but have a cargo hold.

◆ **7 78-foot craft** Bldr: Vosper Thornycroft, Singapore (In serv. 5-72 to 5-73)

PL 50 SEA CAT PL 53 SEA EAGLE PL 55 SEA LYNX
PL 51 SEA PUMA PL 54 SEA HAWK PL 56 SEA FALCON
PL 52 SEA LEOPARD

Sea Eagle (PL 53) G. Arra, 1980

D: 82 tons (fl) **S:** 20.7 kts **Dim:** 23.7 × 5.2 × 1.7 **A:** 1/12.7-mm mg
M: 2 Cummins diesels; 2 props; 1,500 hp **Range:** 4,000/20 **Man:** 16 tot.

◆ **7 45-foot converted wooden tugs** Bldr: Australia (In serv. 1944-45)

PL 9 SNIPE PL 11 WREN PL 14 TERN PL 16 KESTREL
PL 10 PUFFIN PL 13 GULL PL 15 CORMORANT

D: 27.7 tons **S:** 9 kts **Dim:** 13.7 × 4.6 × 2.1
A: Small arms **M:** 1 Gardner diesel **Range:** 1,700/8 **Man:** 5 tot.

Kestrel (P 16) G. Arra

◆ **3 40-foot patrol launches** Bldr: Cheoy Lee SY (In serv. 1971)

WJB 20 JETSTREAM WJB 21 SWIFTSTREAM WJB 22 TIDESTREAM

D: 17 tons **S:** 24 kts **Dim:** 12.3 × 3.5 × 0.6 **A:** Small arms
M: 2 diesels; 2 props; 740 hp **Range:** 380/24 **Man:** 5 tot.

REMARKS: To be stricken 1986.

◆ **9 30-foot Spear class** Bldr: Fairey Allday Marine, Hamble (In serv. 1981)

PL 37 to PL 45

D: 4.5 tons (fl) **S:** 28 kts **Dim:** 9.10 × 2.89 × 0.84
A: 1/7.62-mm mg **M:** 2 Perkins T6.3544 diesels; 2 props; 370 hp
Range: 250/25 **Man:** 4 tot.

REMARKS: Glass-reinforced plastic construction.

MISCELLANEOUS CRAFT

◆ **1 support launch** Bldr: Reliance Marine, Salisbury, U.K.

PL. . . N. . . . . . . (In serv. 5-82)

D: 3 tons (fl) **S:** 25 kts **Dim:** 8.8 × 2.9 × 0.76
M: 1 Volvo Penta AQAD-40/280 diesel; 155 hp **Man:** 4 tot.

◆ **1 personnel launch** Bldr: Hip Hing Cheung SY (In serv. 1975)

PL 7 DRAGON

D: 18.5 tons **S:** 23.5 kts **Dim:** 16.0 × . . . × . . .
A: Small arms **M:** 2 diesels; 2 props; 700 hp **Range:** 300/20 **Man:** 6 tot.

NOTE: The eleven PMB 35-series personnel launches were disposed of 1982-84.

HUNGARY

Hungarian People's Republic

PERSONNEL: Approx. 500 total

MERCHANT MARINE (1984): 21 ships—79,994 grt

HUNGARIAN ARMY MARITIME FORCE

◆ **1 Yugoslav Nestin-class minesweeper/patrol boat** Bldr: Brodotehnika, Belgrade

D: 66 tons (78 fl) **S:** 15 kts **Dim:** 27.00 × 6.50 × 1.15 max.
A: 5/20-mm AA (III × 1, I × 2)—24 small mines
Electron Equipt: Radar: 1/Decca 101 **Man:** 17 tot.
M: 2 diesels; 2 props; 520 hp **Range:** 860/11

REMARKS: Has 2 flare/chaff RL. Sweep gear includes PEAM magnetic/acoustic sweep, AEL-1 explosive sweep, and MDL-1 and -2 mechanical wire sweeps. Sisters in Yugoslav and Iraqi navies. Transferred circa 1982-83. There are also several other small river minesweepers.

◆ **10 river patrol craft** (In serv. early 1960s)

D: 10 tons **S:** . . . **Dim:** . . . × . . . × . . .
A: 1/14.5-mm mg **M:** 2 diesels

◆ **5 landing craft**

◆ **several small tugs**

◆ **several river transports—of up to 1,000 tons**

ICELAND

Republic of Iceland

PERSONNEL: 160 men

MERCHANT MARINE (1984): 395 ships—178,641 grt (tankers—4 ships—2,971 grt)

AVIATION: 2 Fokker F-27 Friendship patrol aircraft, 1 Hughes helicopter, and several Sikorsky S-76 helicopters (one of which was lost 6-11-83).

NOTE: All guns are "quick-firing," single-shot weapons manufactured in the mid-1890s at the Royal Dockyard, Copenhagen.

COAST GUARD

FISHERIES-PROTECTION SHIPS

◆ **2 Aegir class**

	Bldr	L	In serv.
AEGIR	Aalborg SY, Denmark	1967	1968
TYR	Dannebrog Vaerft, Aarhus, Denmark	10-10-74	15-3-78

Tyr 1975

D: 1,150 tons (1,500 fl) **S:** 20 kts **Dim:** 69.84 (62.18 pp) × 10.02 × 5.02
A: 1/57-mm (6-pdr.)
M: 2 M.A.N. R8V 40/54 diesels; 2 KaMeWa CP props; 8,600 hp
Electric: 630 kVA **Range:** 10,000/19 **Man:** 22 tot.

REMARKS: Although built ten years apart, these two ships are nearly identical. Helicopter hangar between twin stacks. Three radar sets, fish-finding sonar. 20-ton bollard-pull towing winch, passive rolling tanks. *Tyr* is 70.90 m o. a.

◆ **1 Odinn class**

	Bldr	Laid down	L	In serv.
ODINN	Aalborg SY, Denmark	1-59	9-59	1-60

D: 1,000 tons (fl) **S:** 18 kts **Dim:** 63.63 (56.61 pp) × 10.0 × 4.8
A: 1/57-mm (6-pdr.) low-angle **Range:** 10,000/18
M: 2 Burmeister & Wain diesels; 2 props; 5,050 hp **Man:** 22 tot.

REMARKS: Rebuilt in 1975 with hangar, helicopter deck, and passive antirolling tanks.

NOTE: The fisheries patrol ship *Thor* was sold to Norway early in 1984.

◆ **1 former lighthouse tender** Bldr: Bodewes, Netherlands (In serv. 1962)

ARVAKUR

D: 716 tons (fl) **S:** 12 kts **Dim:** 32.3 × 10.0 × 4.0
A: 1/12.7-mm mg **M:** 1 Deutz diesel; 1,000 hp **Man:** 12 tot.

REMARKS: Transferred to the Coast Guard in 1969.

◆ **1 Nelson 45-foot customs launch** Bldr: W. S. Souter, Cowes, U.K. (In serv. 1978)

S: 17 kts **M:** 2 Cummins V555M diesels

◆ **. . . 21-SS Smuggler-class patrol launches** Bldr: Norway, 1975

S: 36 kts **M:** Castoldi water jets

INDIA

Republic of India

PERSONNEL (1984): Approx. 47,000 total

MERCHANT MARINE (1984): 710 ships—6,414,741 grt (tankers: 70 ships—2,125,362 grt)

NAVAL AVIATION: The Navy has 14 Magic-missile-equipped Sea Harrier FRS Mk 51 V/STOL fighters, 2 Mk 60 Harrier 2-seat trainers, and 11 Bréguet Alizé fixed-wing planes, and 14 Sea King (11 Mk 42, plus 3 Mk 42A delivered 8-80) and 19 Alouette-III helicopters. Five Soviet Ka-25 Hormone-A helicopters were delivered for the newly transferred Kashin-class guided-missile destroyers. The Indian Air Force has turned over to the Navy 5 Lockheed Constellations for long-range reconnaissance, while the U.S.S.R. has delivered 3 Il-38 May aircraft. In 7-83, 12 Sea King Mk 42B helicopters, armed with Sea Eagle missiles and equipped with Sintra-Alcatel MS-12 dipping sonars, were ordered from Britain; an additional 8 were ordered in 7-85. Support aircraft include 2 Devon transports, 4 Hughes 300 helicopters, 4 Vampire T55 jet trainers, and 7 H3T 16 Kiran trainers. Twelve BN-42B/T Maritime Defender aircraft were ordered for surveillance duties in 1982. The first HAL-built Dornier 228 was delivered 7-85, and a planned 25 more equipped for coastal ASW surveillance will follow. Ten Mk 51 and one two-seat Mk 60 Harriers are on order. The U.S.S.R. is to deliver 18 Ka-27 Helix ASW helicopters and 3 Tu-142M Bear F long-range patrol aircraft, possibly beginning in 1985.

Indian Navy Il-38 May ASW aircraft U.S. Navy, 1981

WEAPONS AND SENSORS: A mixture of Western (primarily British and Dutch) and Soviet weapons and sensors, with Western designs built in India under license. U.S. Harpoon anti-ship missiles were offered in 5-85. Hindustan Aeronautics Ltd. is developing an air-to-ground missile for Air Force and Navy use; it will have a range of 100 km at Mach 4 to Mach .85 at 30,000-foot altitude and will have a 35-kg payload. An unspecified number of French MM 38 Exocet missiles were ordered during 1982, possibly as replacements for obsolescent Soviet SS-N-2a Styx weapons.

WARSHIPS IN SERVICE, UNDER CONSTRUCTION, OR PROJECTED AS OF 1 JANUARY 1986

NOTE: A new construction agreement was reached with the Soviet Union on 20-12-82. According to *Pacific Defense Reporter* magazine for 3-83, the program includes at least 16 new ships, and their completion will give India the most powerful indigenous Indian Ocean naval force. The program reportedly includes: 3 Kresta-II-class cruisers, 3 additional Kashin guided-missile destroyers, 3 or more Nanuchka or Tarantul guided-missile corvettes, 4–6 Natya minesweepers, and 3–4 Kilo-class submarines. In addition to the Soviet order, there is a vigorous domestic construction program.

	L	Tons	Main armament
◆ **1 aircraft carrier**			
1 GLORY	1945	15,700	15 aircraft
◆ **0 (+3) cruisers**			
0 (+3) KRESTA-II	. . .	6,000	. . .
◆ **8 (+7 + . . .) submarines**			
		Tons (submerged)	
0 (+3 + . . .) KILO	1985-. . .	3,000	6/533-mm TT
0 (+4) TYPE 209	1985-. . .	1,150	8/533-mm TT
8 FOXTROT	1965-. . .	2,400	10/533-mm TT
◆ **3 (+3) destroyers**			
3 (+3) KASHIN	1963-72	3,500	2/Goa SAM, 4/SS-N-2C, 2/76-mm, ASW weapons, 1 helicopter
◆ **13 (+7) frigates**			
0 (+6) PROJECT 15	. . .	4,000	. . .
2 (+1) GODVARI	1980-. . .	3,000	4/SS-N-2C, 1/SA-N-4, 4/57-mm, 1 helicopter

WARSHIPS IN SERVICE *(continued)*

6 Leander	1968-77	2,250	2/114-mm, 1 or 2/Sea Cat, 1 helicopter
3 Leopard	1957-59	2,250	2/114-mm DP, 1/Squid
2 Whitby	1958	2,144	3/SS-N-2, 2/Limbo

◆ **13 (+9) corvettes**

0 (+5 or 6) Tarantul	. . .	480	4/SS-N-2C, 1/76-mm DP
0 (+4) New Construction	. . .	900	. . .
3 Nanuchka	1977-78	600	4/SS-N-2C, 1/SA-N-4, 2/57-mm
10 Petya II	1963	950	4/76.2-mm DP, 3/533-mm TT

◆ **14 guided-missile patrol boats**

◆ **13 (+4-6) minesweepers**

◆ **8 (+ . . .) amphibious ships**

AIRCRAFT CARRIER

◆ **1 Glory class** Bldr: Vickers-Armstrong

	Laid down	L	In serv.
R 11 Vikrant (ex-*Hercules*)	14-10-43	22-9-45	4-3-61

Vikrant (R 11)—prior to recent refit

D: 15,700 tons (19,500 fl) **S:** 24 kts (fl), 17 kts cruising
Dim: 211.25 (198.0 wl) × 24.29 × 7.15
A: 7/40-mm (I × 7)—6 Sea Harrier, 9 other aircraft
Electron Equipt: Radar: 1/ZW-06, 1/DA-05, 1/LW-08
M: 2 sets Parsons GT; 2 props; 40,000 hp
Boilers: 4 Admiralty; 28 kg/cm² **Fuel:** 3,200 tons
Range: 6,200/23; 12,000/14 **Man:** Peacetime: 1,075 tot.; wartime: 1,340 tot.

Remarks: Bought in Great Britain in 1-57 while still incomplete. Air-conditioned. One hangar, two elevators, angled flight deck, steam catapult. Flight deck: 210 × 34. Modernized 1979 to 3-1-82 with new boilers, engines, new CIC, and new Dutch-design radars. Bofors L 70 single 40-mm AA in place of original British Mk 5 twin and Mk 9 single mountings. A further refit from 12-82 to 2-83 made the ship ready for its Sea Harrier complement, but did not include a planned ski-jump ramp. Catapult and arrester gear were retained to permit continued use of Alizé ASW aircraft. With the delivery of additional Sea Harriers in 1984 and later, the Alizés are moving ashore, and the long-planned ski jump is apparently being added. The ship also carries Chetak (Alouette-III) helicopters equipped for ASW and *may* carry Sea Kings, although the latter cannot be accommodated in the hangar. The ship received the IPN-10 combat data system in 1985.

Note: A 30–40,000 ton replacement for *Vikrant,* to be built in India, is under design, but would not be available until the 1990s. In 1985, the Indian Navy was discussing the purchase of the 28,700-ton HMS *Hermes.*

SUBMARINES

◆ **0 (+3 + . . .) Soviet Kilo class** Bldr: . . . (In serv. 1985-. . .)

D: 2,500/3,000 tons **S:** 12/16 kts **Dim:** 70.0 × 9.5 × . . .
A: 6/533-mm TT (fwd)—possible SAM system
M: 2 diesels, electric drive; 1 prop; 3,500-4,000 hp **Man:** 60 tot.

Remarks: Reportedly ordered 4-84. Soviet units are built at Komsomolsk-na-Amur and at Gorkiy SY. First unit was scheduled to deliver 1985. India was also reported to be discussing the acquisition of nuclear-powered submarines from the U.S.S.R. in 4-85, but acquisition in near-term is very unlikely.

◆ **0 (+4) West German Type SSK-1500**

	Bldr	Laid down	L	In serv.
S 44 N. . .	Howaldtswerke, Kiel	2-84	. . .	1986
S 45 N. . .	Mazagon DY, Bombay	6-5-84	. . .	1988
S 46 N. . .	Howaldtswerke, Kiel	. . .	. . .	. . .
S 47 N. . .	Mazagon DY, Bombay	. . .	. . .	. . .

D: 1,660 tons surf./1,860 sub. **S:** 11/21.5 kts **Dim:** 64.40 × 6.50 × 5.50
A: 8/533-mm (fwd)—14 torpedoes (tot.)
Electron Equipt: Radar: . . .
Sonar: Krupp Atlas search and attack, Alcatel DUUX-5

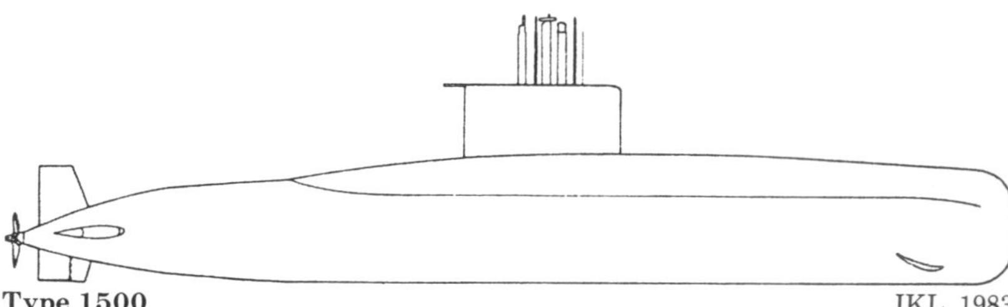

Type 1500 IKL, 1983

S 44—India's first SSK-1500, on trials J. Kürsener, 8-85

M: 4 MTU 12V493 TY60 diesels (600 hp each), 4/450-kw generators, 2 motors; 1 prop; 5,000 hp
Fuel: 118 tons **Range:** 13,000/0 (surf.); 8,200/8 (snorkel), 524/4 (sub.)
Man: 40 tot.

Remarks: Final order, signed 11-12-81, includes an option to build 2 additional units in India. A variant of the Type 209 design. Will have Singer-Librascope SFCS Mk 1 weapons control system and the Gäbler spherical escape chamber. Indian-built units reported far behind schedule in mid-85, with little accomplished.

◆ **8 Soviet Foxtrot class**

	In serv.		In serv.
S 20 Kursura	12-70	S 40 Vela	31-8-73
S 21 Karanj	10-70	S 41 Vagir	3-11-73
S 22 Kandheri	1-69	S 42 Vagli	10-8-74
S 23 Kalvari	16-7-68	S 43 Vagsheer	26-12-74

Vagli (S 42) G. Arra, 1982

Karanj (S 21) 1983

D: 1,950/2,400 tons **S:** 16/15.5 kts **Dim:** 91.5 × 7.5 × 6.0
A: 10/533-mm TT (6 fwd, 4 aft)—22 torpedoes or 44 mines
Electron Equipt: Radar: 1/Snoop Tray
Sonar: 1/MF active, passive array
M: 3 diesel generator sets (2,000 hp each), 3 motors; 3 props; 5,300 hp
Range: 11,000/8 (snorkel) **Endurance:** 70 days **Man:** 8 officers, 70 men

CRUISERS

◆ **0 (+3) Soviet Kresta-II class**

Remarks: Reportedly ordered 20-12-82. If new construction (rather than transfers from Soviet Navy inventory), will probably differ considerably from Soviet Navy units, due to the age of the Kresta-II design (mid-1960s). Since the Kresta-II building yard, Zhdanov Shipyard in Leningrad, is fully occupied with the *Sovremennyy* (a Kresta variant) and *Udaloy* programs, new Indian units would probably have to be built at 61 Kommuna Shipyard, Nikolayev. Because of the uncertainties surrounding the program, no characteristics data are given here; see U.S.S.R. section for Kresta-II. Former Royal Navy cruiser *Mysore* (ex-*Nigeria*) stricken 29-8-85.

GUIDED-MISSILE DESTROYERS

◆ **0 (+6) Project 15 class** Bldr: . . .

D: 4,500–5,000 tons (fl) **S:** . . . **Dim:** . . . × . . . × . . .
A: . . ./. . . SSM—. . ./. . . SAM
Electron Equipt: Radar: . . .
Sonar: . . .
M: CODOG

Remarks: A planned follow-on to the *Godavari* class, with Soviet ordnance, sensors, and propulsion equipment.

◆ **3 (+3) Soviet Kashin class** Bldr: 61 Kommuna SY, Nikolayev

	In serv.		In serv.		In serv.
D 51 Rajput	10-80	D 52 Rana	28-6-82	D 53 Ranjit	21-11-83
D. . . N. . .	. . .	D. . . N. . .	. . .	D. . . N. . .	. . .

D: 3,950 tons (4,950 fl) **S:** 36–39 kts **Dim:** 147.0 × 15.8 × 5.0 (hull)
A: 4/SS-N-2C SSM (I × 4)—2/SA-N-1 SAM syst. (II × 2; 44 Goa Missiles)—2/76.2-mm DP (II × 1)—8/30-mm AA (II × 4)—5/533-mm TT (V × 1)—2/RBU 6000 ASW RL (XII × 2)—1/Ka-25 Hormone-A ASW helicopter
Electron Equipt: Radar: 2/Don Kay, 1/Big Net, 1/Head Net C, 2/Peel Group, 1/Owl Screech, 2/Drum Tilt
IFF: 2/High Pole B transponders
Sonar: 1/hull-mounted med. freq., 1/med. freq. VDS
EW: 2/Watch Dog, 2 Top Hat A, 2 Top Hat B, 4/chaff RL (XVI × 4)
M: 4 gas turbines; 2 props; 94,000 hp **Range:** 1,500/35; 4,000/20 **Man:** 35 officers, 330 men

Remarks: New construction units, not conversions from former Soviet Navy units. In contrast to Soviet Navy "Modified Kashins," the SS-N-2C missiles are mounted forward and fire forward, while the after twin 76.2-mm gunmount has been omitted in favor of a hangar for the helicopter, reached by an inclined elevator/ramp. Have twin 30-mm vice 30-mm gatling guns. Program for first three was far behind delivery schedule; 3 more reported ordered 20-12-82.

Rajput (D 51) 1983

Rana (D 52) L. & L. Van Ginderen, 6-82

Ranjit (D 53) French Navy, 12-84

FRIGATES

◆ **2 (+1) Godavari class** Bldr: Mazagon Docks, Bombay

	Laid down	L	In serv.
F 51 Godavari	2-6-78	15-5-80	10-12-83
F. . . Ganga	1980	15-11-81	. . .-85
F. . . Gomati	1981	20-3-84	. . .-88

Godavari (F 51) 1984

D: 3,500 tons (4,100 fl) **S:** 27 kts **Dim:** 126.4 (123.6 pp) × 14.5 × 4.5 (hull)
A: 4/SS-N-2C SSM (I × 4)—1/SA-N-4 SAM syst. (II × 1; 20 Gecko missiles)—2/57-mm DP (II × 1)—8/30-mm AA (II × 4)—6/324-mm ASW TT (III × 2; A 184 torpedoes)—1/Sea King ASW helicopter
Electron Equipt: Radar: 1/navigational, 1/Head Net C, 1/DA-08, 1/Pop Group, 2/Drum Tilt, 1/Muff Cob
Sonar: 1 U.K. Type 184—EW: . . .
M: 2 sets GT; 2 five-bladed props; 30,000 hp **Range:** 4,500/12
Boilers: 2 Babcock & Wilcox, 3-drum; 38.7 kg/cm², 450°C
Man: 51 officers, 262 men

Remarks: Design derived from the *Leander* class, with the same propulsion plant but larger hull. Electronics and weapons systems a very diverse selection of Western

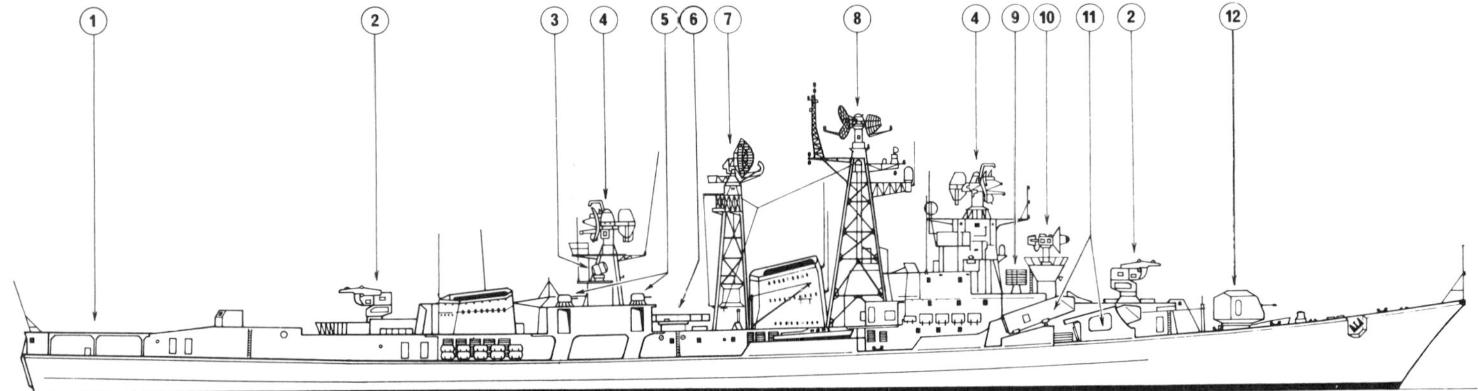

Rajput 1. Helicopter facility 2. SA-N-1 systems 3. Drum Tilt radar GFCS 4. Peel Group radar 5. Twin 30-mm AA guns 6. Torpedo tubes (V × 1) 7. Big Net radar 8. Head Net-C radar 9. RBU 6000 ASW RL 10. Owl Screech radar GFCS 11. SS-N-2C SSM 12. 76.2-mm DP (II × 1)

FRIGATES *(continued)*

European and Soviet systems. The hangar has space for a second helicopter. Have Bear Trap helicopter landing and deck traversing system. The Selenia IPN-10 combat data system is fitted.

◆ **6 British Leander class** Bldr: Mazagon Docks, Bombay

	Laid down	L	In serv.
F 33 Nilgiri	10-66	23-10-68	3-6-72
F 34 Himgiri	1967	6-5-70	23-11-74
F 35 Udaygiri	14-9-70	24-10-72	18-2-76
F 36 Dunagiri	1-73	9-3-74	5-5-77
F 41 Taragiri	1974	25-10-76	16-5-80
F 42 Vindhyagiri	1976	12-11-77	8-7-81

Udaygiri (F 35) G. Gyssels, 1977

Vindhyagiri (F 42) 1984

D: 2,250 tons (2,800 fl); later units: 3,250 tons (fl) **S:** 30 kts
Dim: 113.38 × 13.1 × 4.27 (avg.)
A: 2/114-mm DP (II × 1)—F 33: 1/Sea Cat GWS 22; Others; 2/Sea Cat with M-4 directors—1/Limbo Mk 10 ASW mortar (not on F 41 and F 42, which have 1/375-mm Bofors ASW RL (II × 1))—2/20-mm AA (I × 2)—1 Alouette-III ASW helicopter (Sea King on F 41 and F 42)—F 41, 42: 6/324-mm ILAS-3 ASW TT (III × 2; A 184 torpedoes)
Electron Equipt: Radar: F 33: 1/965, 1/993, 1/978, 2/903
F 34 on: 1/Decca navigational, 1/ZW-06, 1/LW-08, 1/M 44, 2/M 45
Sonar: 1/184 plus 1/199 VDS on F 33 and F 34; F 41, 42: Thomson-CSF hull-mounted
M: 2 sets GT; 2 five-bladed props; 30,000 hp **Electric:** 2,500 kw
Boilers: 2 Babcock & Wilcox, 3-drum; 38.7 kg/cm², 450°C **Fuel:** 500 tons
Range: Approx. 4,500/12

Remarks: The first two are very similar to British versions of the *Leander* class, but later units have been progressively improved, using H.S.A. radars and an ever-greater proportion of Indian-built components. F 41 and F 42 have very large telescoping hangars situated much nearer the stern and requiring removal of the three-barreled Limbo ASW mortar (replaced by a twin Bofors ASW RL on the forecastle); the new hangar holds a Westland Sea King ASW helicopter, and the flight deck incorporates Canadian Bear Trap haul-down gear. F 41 and F 42 also have openings in the hull sides beneath the helicopter deck at the stern. F 33 and F 34 received Type 199 variable-depth sonar; later units did not. The single Sea Cat quadruple SAM launcher in the F 33 has one MRS-3 director; later ships have two Dutch M-4 directors (with M-45 radar). F 41 and F 42 may receive SS-N-2 missiles, but are already overloaded. Later units have Decca-Racal Cutlass EW gear. All have Graseby G1738 towed torpedo decoys. F 33–36 are receiving U.S. Westinghouse sonar equipment (including VDS) in place of their original British equipment.

◆ **3 British Leopard (Type 41) class**

	Bldr	Laid down	L	In serv.
F 31 Brahmaputra (ex-*Panther*)	J. Brown, Clydebank	1956	15-3-57	28-3-58
F 37 Beas	Vickers-Armstrong	1957	9-10-58	24-5-60
F 38 Betwa	Vickers-Armstrong	1957	15-9-59	8-12-60

Brahmaputra (F 31) French Navy, 4-85

D: 2,250 tons (2,515 fl) **S:** 25 kts
Dim: 103.63 (100.58 pp) × 12.19 × 4.80 (hull)
A: 2/114-mm DP Mk 6 (II × 1)—2/40-mm AA Mk 5 (II × 1)—1/Squid ASW mortar (III × 1)
Electron Equipt: Radar: 1/293, 1/978, 1/275
Sonar: 1/177, 1/162, 1/174B
M: 8 Admiralty 16 VVS ASR1 diesels; 2 props; 12,380 hp
Electric: 1,200 kw **Range:** 7,500/15 **Man:** 240 tot.

Remarks: Beginning in 1978 with F 31, all have had their after 114-mm twin gunmounts replaced by an accommodations deckhouse to act as Cadet Training Ships. F 37 was modernized during 1980, F 38 in 1981. The 40-mm radar GFCS was removed.

◆ **2 British Whitby class**

	Bldr	Laid down	L	In serv.
F 40 Talwar	Cammell Laird	1957	18-7-58	4-60
F 43 Trishul	Harland & Wolff	1957	18-6-58	1-60

D: 2,144 tons (2,560 fl) **S:** 30 kts **Dim:** 112.7 × 12.5 × 5.4 (over sonar)
A: 3/SS-N-2 Styx SSM (I × 3)—2/40-mm AA (I × 2)—6/324-mm ILAS-3 ASW TT (III × 2)—1/Sea King helicopter
Electron Equipt: Radar: 1/293, 1/277, 1/978, 1/Square Tie
Sonar: 1/177, 1/174B, 1/162
M: 2 sets GT; 2 props; 30,000 hp **Electric:** 1,140 kw
Boilers: 2 Babcock & Wilcox; 38.7 kg/cm², 450°C **Fuel:** 370 tons
Range: 4,500/12 **Man:** 11 officers, 220 men

Remarks: Three SS-N-2 Styx launchers—removed from Osa-I-class, guided-missile patrol boats—replaced the twin 114-mm Mk 6 gunmount in these two ships. Soviet Square Tie radar associated with Styx replaced the gun director, atop the pilothouse. F 40 further refitted 1982-83 at Mazagon Dockyard, Bombay, with telescoping hangars and Canadian Bear Trap haul-down system at the expense of the two Limbo ASW mortars; modernization of F 43 reported delayed by yard problems, 7-85.

CORVETTES

◆ **0 (+4) new construction** Bldr: Mazagon Dock, Bombay

	Laid down	L	In serv.		Laid down	L	In serv.
K. . . N. . .	1-85	. . .	. . .	K. . . N. . .	. . .	. . .	. . .
K. . . N. . .	. . .	. . .	. . .	K. . . N. . .	. . .	. . .	. . .

D: 1,200 tons (fl) **S:** 27 kts **Dim:** . . . × . . . × . . .
A: . . . **Electron Equipt:** Radar: . . .
Sonar: . . .
M: 2 SEMT-Pielstick 18PA6 diesels; 2 CP props; 14,000 hp

Remarks: Ordered 12-83 to an indigenous design. No further information released.

◆ **0 (+5 or 6) Soviet Tarantul-I class** Bldr: . . .

D: 480 tons (580 fl) **S:** 36 kts **Dim:** 56.5 × 10.5 × 2.5
A: 4/SS-N-2C SSM (II × 2)—1/76.2-mm DP—1/SA-N-5 SAM syst. (IV × 1; . . . Grail missiles)—2/30-mm gatling AA (I × 2)
Electron Equipt: Radar: 1/Krivach nav., 1/Bass Tilt, 1/Plank Shave
EW: . . . —IFF: 1/High Pole, 1/Square Head
M: CODOG or COGOG: 2 NK-12MV gas turbines (12,000 hp each) two cruise gas turbines or diesels (3-4,000 hp each); 2 props
Range: . . . **Man:** . . .

Remarks: Ordered 1984 for delivery 1986-89. Uncertain whether will be built in U.S.S.R. or in India under license; early delivery date indicates at least first unit will be Soviet-built. Probably intended to replace obsolete Osa-I and II-class missile boats.

◆ **3 (+3?) Soviet Nanuchka II class** Bldr: Petrovskiy SY, Leningrad

K 71 Vijaydurg (In serv. 12-76) K 73 Hosdurg (In serv. 1-78)
K 72 Sindhurdurg (In serv. 5-77)

D: 770 tons (fl) **S:** 32 kts **Dim:** 59.3 × 12.6 × 2.4
A: 4/SS-N-2C (II × 2)—1/SA-N-4 system—2/57-mm AA (II × 1)

CORVETTES *(continued)*

Sindhurdurg (K 72) 4-79

Electron Equipt: Radar: 1/Square Tie, 1/Pop Group, 1/Muff Cob, 1/Don-2
IFF: 2/Square Head, 1/High Pole
EW: passive syst., 2 chaff RL (XVI × 2)
M: 3 Type M507 twin diesels; 3 props; 30,000 hp
Range: 900/30; 2,500/12 **Man:** 60 tot.

Remarks: Arrived in India 3-77, 8-77, and 3-78. Three or more additional units were reportedly ordered 20-12-82, but no deliveries had occurred as of 7-85. Poor sea boats. The "Band Stand" radome covers a Square Tie antenna in these export units. The diesels each are composed of two coupled M504 diesel engines.

◆ **10 Soviet Petya-II class** Bldr: U.S.S.R.

P 68 Arnala, P 69 Androth, P 73 Anjadip, P 74 Andaman, P 75 Amini, P 77 Kamorta, P 78 Kadmath, P 79 Kiltan, P 80 Kavaratti, P 81 Katchal

Andaman (P 74) G. Arra, 1982

D: 950 tons (1,150 fl) **S:** 29 kts **Dim:** 81.8 (78.0 pp) × 9.2 × 2.9 (hull)
A: 4/76.2-mm DP (II × 2)—4/RBU-2500 ASW RL (XVI × 4)—3/533-mm TT (III × 1)—2/d.c. racks—2/mine rails
Electron Equipt: Radar: 1/Don-2, 1/Slim Net, 1/Hawk Screech
Sonar: 1 Hercules med. freq.
M: CODOG: 1 Type IV3 diesel (6,000 hp), 2 gas turbines (15,000 hp each); 3 props; 36,000 hp
Range: 450/29; 4,800/10 **Man:** 98 tot.

Remarks: Transferred in 1969, 1972, and 1975. Were new-construction, export-version ships.

GUIDED-MISSILE PATROL BOATS

◆ **8 Soviet Osa-II class**

K 90 Prachand, K 91 Pralaya, K 92 Prabal, K 93 Pratap, K 94 Chamak, K 95 Chapal, K 96 Chapak, K 97 Charag

D: 215 tons (240 fl) **S:** 35 kts **Dim:** 38.6 × 7.6 × 2.0
A: 4/SS-N-2B Styx (I × 4)—4/30-mm AA (II × 2)
Electron Equipt: Radar: 1/Square Tie, 1/Drum Tilt
IFF: 2/Square Head, 1/Head Pole B
M: 3 M504 diesels; 3 props; 15,000 hp **Range:** 500/34; 750/25 **Man:** 30 tot.

Remarks: To be equipped with modern EW system. First four in service 17-2-76, second four on 5-11-76.

◆ **6 Soviet Osa-I class** (In serv. 1971)

K 82 Veer, K 83 Vidyut, K 85 Vinash, K 86 Nipat, K 88 Nirbhik, K 89 Nirghat

D: 180 tons (215 fl) **S:** 36 kts **Dim:** 38.6 × 7.6 × 1.8
A: 4/SS-N-2A Styx (I × 4)—4/30-mm AA (II × 2)
Electron Equipt: Radar: 1/Square Tie, 1/Drum Tilt
IFF: 2/Square Head, 1/High Pole B
M: 3 M503A diesels; 3 props; 12,000 hp **Range:** 500/34; 750/25 **Man:** 30 tot.

Remarks: Transferred 1971. *Vijeta* (K 84) and *Nashat* (K 87) had their missile tubes removed and three from each placed on the frigates *Talwar* (F 40) and *Trishul* (F 43). Both, however, remain in service as patrol boats.

PATROL BOATS

◆ **4 (+3) SDB Mk 3 class**

		Bldr	Laid down	L	In serv.
T58	N. . .	Garden Reach, Calcutta	17-2-83	20-12-83	1984
T. . .	N. . .	Garden Reach, Calcutta	24-3-83	20-3-84	1984
T. . .	N. . .	Goa SY	. . .	17-1-84	10-84
T. . .	N. . .	Garden Reach, Calcutta	. . .	. . .	1985
T. . .	N. . .	Garden Reach, Calcutta	. . .	. . .	. . .
T. . .	N. . .	Goa SY	. . .	. . .	. . .
T. . .	N. . .	Goa SY	. . .	. . .	. . .

D: 210 tons (fl) **S:** 34 kts **Dim:** 37.80 × . . . × 1.30 (hull)
A: 1/40-mm AA—. . .
Electron Equipt: Radar: 1/. . . nav.—Sonar: . . .
M: 2 MTU diesels; 2 props; 9,200 hp **Man:** 34 tot.

Remarks: Intended as an improved version of the SDB Mk 2 with better hull form, less rake to propeller shafts. Probably also have a centerline cruise engine. Speed also reported as 28 kts for Goa-built units.

◆ **5 SDB Mk 2 class** Bldr: Garden Reach SB & Eng., Calcutta

	L	In serv.		L	In serv.
T 51 N.	31-12-75	17-11-78	T 56 Rajtarang	2-81	1984
T 52 N.	. . .	3-9-77	T 57 Rajshree	27-5-83	1984
T 53 N.	. . .	12-4-78			

D: 160 tons (203 fl) **S:** 29 kts **Dim:** 37.50 × 7.50 × 1.75
A: 1/40-mm CT AA—2/d.c. racks (18 Mk 7 d.c.)
M: 2 Deltic (6 kts) 18-42K diesels; 2 props; 6,240 hp; 1 Kirloskar Cummins NH-220 cruise diesel, 165 hp
Electric: 220 kVA **Range:** 1,400/14 **Man:** 4 officers, 26 men

◆ **2 Soviet OSA-I class** (In serv. 1971)

. . . Vijeta (ex-K 84) . . . Nashat (ex-K 87)

Remarks: Missile tubes removed, as noted above. *Nashat* was converted to carry frogmen in 1980.

MINE WARFARE SHIPS

◆ **6 (+6) Soviet Natya class**

M 61 Pondichery, M 62 Porbandar, M 63 Bedi, M 64 Bhavnagar, M 65 Alleppy, M 66 Ratnagiri

Pondichery (M 61) 1978

D: 650 tons (750 fl) **S:** 18 kts **Dim:** 61.0 × 9.8 × 3.0
A: 4/30-mm AA (II × 2)—4/25-mm AA (II × 2)—2/RBU-1200 ASW RL (V × 2)—mines
Electron Equipt: Radar: 1/Don-2, 1/Drum Tilt—Sonar: 1/HF hull-mounted
IFF: 2/Square Head, 1/High Pole B
M: 2 diesels; 2 props; 5,000 hp **Range:** 1,800/16; 5,200/10 **Man:** 80 tot.

Remarks: Two transferred in 1978, two in 1979, and two in 1980. Differ from the units in the Soviet Navy in that they do not have a ramp at the stern. Can be used as ASW escorts. Six additional units reportedly ordered 20-17-82. Aluminum/steel alloy construction.

◆ **6 Soviet Yevgenya-class inshore minesweepers** (First 3 in serv. 15-5-83, others: 2-84)

M 83 Mahe, M 84 Malwan, M 85 Mangalore, M 86 Malpe, M 87 Mulki, M 88 Magdala

D: 80 tons (90 fl) **S:** 11 kts **Dim:** 26.2 × 6.1 × 1.5
A: 2/14.5-mm mg (II × 1) **Man:** 10 tot. **M:** 2 diesels; 2 props; 600 hp
Electron Equipt: Radar: 1/Spin Trough **Range:** 300/10

Remarks: Glass-reinforced plastic construction. Equipped for shallow-water minehunting with a towed television and marker-buoy dispenser.

◆ **4 British "Ham"-class inshore minesweepers**

	Bldr	L
M 79 Bimlipatham (ex-*Hildersham*)	Vosper, Portsmouth	5-2-54
M 80 Bassein (ex-*Littleham*)	Brooke Marine, Lowestoft	4-5-54
M 81 Bhatkal	Mazagon Docks, Bombay	5-67
M 82 Bulsar	Mazagon Docks, Bombay	17-5-69

MINE WARFARE SHIPS *(continued)*

Bhatkal (M 81)—old pendant number 1968

D: 120 tons (159 fl) **S:** 14 kts (9, sweeping)
Dim: 32.43 (30.48 pp) × 6.45 × 1.7 **A:** 1/20-mm AA
Electron Equipt: Radar: 1/978 **Man:** 2 officers, 13 men
M: 2 Paxman YHAXM diesels; 2 props; 1,000 hp **Fuel:** 25 tons

REMARKS: M 79 and M 80 were transferred in 1955. The Indian-built units have teakwood hulls but are otherwise almost identical.

AMPHIBIOUS WARFARE SHIPS

◆ **1 tank landing ship** Bldr: Garden Reach Dockyard, Calcutta

	Laid down	L	In serv.
L. . . MAGAR	. . .	7-11-84	. . .

D: 5,500 tons (fl) **S:** . . . **Dim:** . . . × . . . × . . .
A: . . . **Electron Equipt:** Radar: . . .
M: 2 SEMT-Pielstick diesels; 2 props; 8,560 hp
Range: . . . **Man:** . . .

REMARKS: Has bow doors and a helicopter deck aft. Additional units may be constructed to continue the expansion of Indian power-projection forces.

◆ **6 (+2) Soviet Polnocny-C class** Bldr: Polnocny SY, Gdansk, Poland

L 14 GHORPAD L 15 KESARI L 16 SHARDUL L 17 SHARABH
L 18 CHEETAH L 19 MAHISH L 20 N. . . L 21 N. . .

Cheetah (L 18) French Navy, 12-84

D: 1,150 (fl) **S:** 18 kts **Dim:** 81.3 × 10.1 × 2.1
A: 4/30-mm AA (II × 2)—2/140-mm rocket launchers (VIII × 2)
Electron Equipt: Radar: 1/Don-2 (Krivach in L 18)
M: 2 diesels; 2 props; 5,000 hp
Range: 900/17; 1,500/14 **Man:** 60 tot.

REMARKS: L 14 transferred in 1975, L 17 in 1976, L 18 in 12-84, L 19 in 7-85, rest by end 1986. First four do not have a helicopter platform as on other export Polnocny-Cs. Cargo: 350 tons and up to 140 troops. *Mahish* delivered 7-85.

◆ **2 Soviet Polnocny-A class** Bldr: Polnocny SY, Gdansk, Poland

L 13 GULDAR L 12 GHARIAL

D: 770 tons (fl) **S:** 19 kts **Dim:** 73.0 × 8.6 × 2.0
A: 2/25-mm AA (II × 1)—2/140-mm rocket-launchers (XVIII × 2)
Electron Equipt: Radar: 1/Don-2 **M:** 2 diesels; 2 props; 5,000 hp
Range: 900/18; 1,500/14 **Man:** 40 tot.

REMARKS: Transferred 1966. Cargo: 180 tons.

◆ **4 (+5) Vasco da Gama-class utility landing craft**

	Bldr	L	In serv.
L 34 VASCO DA GAMA	Goa SY, Goa	29-11-78	28-1-80
L 35 N.	Hooghly DY, Calcutta	16-3-80	17-12-83
L 36 N.	Goa SY, Goa	13-1-79	1-12-80
L 37 N.	Hooghly DY, Calcutta	. . .	. . .

D: 500 tons (fl) **S:** 9 kts **Dim:** 55.96 × 7.94 × 1.71 (aft)
A: 2/40-mm AA (I × 2)—mines
M: 3 Kirloskar-M.A.N. W8V 17.5/22 AMAL diesels; 3 Kort-nozzle props; 1,245 hp
Range: 1,000/8

REMARKS: Cargo: 250 tons or 120 men. Approval given to construct "five 150-man ferry craft" in 1985 probably indicates additional units of this class; third unit of second series launched 22-7-85.

HYDROGRAPHIC SURVEY SHIPS

◆ **3 (+2) Sandhayak class** Bldr: Garden Reach SB & Engineers, Calcutta

		L	In serv.		L	In serv.
J. . .	SANDHAYAK	6-4-77	26-2-81	J. . . N. . .	. . .	. . .
J. . .	NIRDESHAK	16-11-78	4-10-83	J. . . N. . .	. . .	. . .
J. . .	NIRUPAK	10-7-81	1985-86			

D: 1,200 tons (1,820 fl) **S:** 16.75 kts **Dim:** 85.77 (78.80 pp) × 12.30 × 3.34
A: 2/40-mm AA (I × 2)—1/Alouette-III helicopter
Electron Equipt: Radar: 1/Decca TM-series navigational
M: 1 GRSE-M.A.N. G8V 30/45 ATL diesel; 1 prop; 3,920 hp (plus 1 Pleuger 200-hp active rudder; 5 kts)
Fuel: 264 tons **Range:** 6,000/14 **Man:** 12 officers, 134 men

REMARKS: 2,050 grt. Telescoping hangar for one Alouette-III helicopter. Four inshore survey launches with "Hydrodist" fixing system. Have 3 precision depth-finders, Decca "Navigator," Decca "Hi-Fix," taut-wire measuring gear, and a gravimeter. Carry 169 tons water and 5 tons aviation fuel. Construction of 4th unit approved under 1985 Budget, and a sixth is planned.

◆ **1 hydrographic-survey ship**

	Bldr	L	In serv.
J 14 DARSHAK	Hindustan SY, India	2-11-59	28-12-61

Darshak (J 14) 1974

D: 2,790 tons **S:** 16 kts **Dim:** 97.3 × 14.94 × 5.8
A: 1/40-mm AA **M:** 2 diesels, electric drive; 2 props; 3,000 hp **Man:** 150 tot.

REMARKS: Carries one Alouette-III helicopter.

◆ **4 inshore-survey ships** Bldr: Goa SY, Vasco da Gama (In serv. 1984-85)

J 33 N. . . . . . . J 34 N. . . . . . . J 35 N. . . . . . . J 36 N. . . . . . .

D: 185 **S:** 12.5 kts **Dim:** 37.5 × 7.5 × 1.75
M: Diesels **Range:** 1,500/12.5

REMARKS: J 34 launched 28-5-83 and J 35 on 10-8-83. Steel-hulled. Same hulls as SDB Mk 2 patrol boat class.

◆ **2 Gaveshani-class small inshore-survey craft**

J. . . GAVESHANI J. . . N. . . . . . .

REMARKS: Launched 2-76.

AUXILIARY SHIPS

◆ **1 Soviet Ugra-class submarine tender** Bldr: U.S.S.R. (In serv. 28-12-68)

A 54 AMBA

Amba (A 54) 1968

D: 6,750 tons (9,600 fl) **S:** 20 kts **Dim:** 145.0 × 17.7 × 6.4
A: 4/76.2-mm DP (II × 2)
Electron Equipt: Radar: 1/Don-2, 1/Slim Net, 2/Hawk Screech
M: 4 diesels; 2 props; 8,000 hp **Range:** 21,000/10

REMARKS: Helicopter platform. Quarters for 750 men. Two 6-ton cranes, one 10-ton crane.

◆ **1 Soviet T 58-class submarine-rescue ship**

A 55 NISTAR

D: 930 tons (fl) **S:** 17 kts **Dim:** 71.7 × 9.1 × 2.7
Electron Equipt: Radar: 1/Don-2 **M:** 2 diesels; 2 props; 4,000 hp
Range: 2,500/12 **Man:** 60 tot.

AUXILIARY SHIPS *(continued)*

REMARKS: Built during late 1950s, transferred 1971. Two rescue chambers, port and starboard sides of the stern. Decompression chamber, diving bells.

NOTE: Two new submarine rescue ships are programmed to be built in India.

◆ **1 repair ship** Bldr: Foundation Maritime, Canada (L: 25-7-44)

A 52 DHARINI (ex-*La Petite Hermine,* ex-*Ketowna Park*)

D: 6,000 tons (fl) **S:** 9 kts **Dim:** 99.0 × 13.9 × 4.0
M: Triple-expansion reciprocating steam; 1 prop; 800 hp **Fuel:** 620 tons

REMARKS: Sold to India for cargo use, 1953; in service in Indian Navy 5-60.

◆ **1 transport** Bldr: Mazagon DY, Bombay

. . . N. . . . . . .

D: 1,800 grt **S:** 20 kts **Dim:** 74.0 (pp) × 14.4 × . . .
M: 2 diesels; 2 props; 8,000 hp

REMARKS: Ordered 3-81. No other details available.

◆ **1 hospital ship** Bldr: Hindustan SY, Calcutta

LAKSHADWEEP (L: 28-8-81)

D: . . . **S:** 12 kts **Dim:** 52.0 (46.8 pp) × 9.5 × 3.0
M: 2 diesels; 2 props; 900 hp
Man: 19 crew, plus 15 medical staff (90 hospital berths)

REMARKS: Laid down 2-81.

◆ **1 training ship** Bldr: Mazagon DY, Bombay

	Laid down	L	In serv.
TIR	. . .	15-4-83	1986

D: . . . **S:** . . . **Dim:** 107 × . . . × . . . **A:** 4 . . . **M:** Diesels

REMARKS: Ordered 1981. Intended to supplement the *Leopard* class. Carries approximately 120 cadets. Was to have completed 3-84, delayed by yard problems.

OILERS

NOTE: Construction of a new replenishment oiler was approved in the 1985 Budget.

◆ **2 Deepak class** Bldr: Bremer Vulkan Schiffbau, Bremen-Vegesack, West Germany

A 50 DEEPAK (In serv. 20-11-72) A 57 SHAKTI (In serv. 21-2-76)

Shakti (A 57)—with hangar extended 1982

D: 6,785 tons (22,000 fl) **S:** 20 kts **Dim:** 168.43 (157.50 pp) × 23.0 × 9.14
A: 3/40-mm AA (I × 3)—2/20-mm AA (I × 2) **M:** 1 set GT; 1 prop; 16,500 hp
Boilers: 2 Babcock & Wilcox **Range:** 5,500/18.5 **Man:** 169 tot.

REMARKS: 12,690 grt/15,800 dwt. Two liquid-replenishment stations per side, with British-style rigs. Telescoping hangar and flight deck for one helicopter. Carry 12,624 tons fuel oil, 1,280 tons diesel fuel, 1,495 tons aviation fuel, 812 tons fresh water, and some dry cargo.

◆ **1 former merchant tanker** Bldr: Japan (In serv. 1959)

DESH DEEP

D: 16,400 tons (fl) **S:** 13 kts **Dim:** 145.0 (135.0 pp) × 19.5 × 7.8
M: 2 Sulzer 6-cyl. diesels; 2 props; 8,200 hp **Electric:** 320 kw
Fuel: 1,056 tons **Range:** 23,000/13 **Man:** . . . tot.

REMARKS: 8,324 grt, 12,177 dwt. Taken over 1972 and operated as a freighting tanker. Cargo: 11,800 tons (100,048 m³).

TUGS

◆ **2 Gaj-class oceangoing tugs** Bldr: Garden Reach SB & Eng., Calcutta

A 51 GAJ (In serv. 20-9-73) A. . . MATANGA (L: 29-10-77; in serv. 1983)

D: 1,465 tons (1,600 fl) **S:** 15 kts **Dim:** 66.0 (60.0 pp) × 11.6 × 4.0
A: None **M:** 2 GRSE-M.A.N. G7V diesels; 2 CP props; 3,292 hp
Range: 8,000/12

REMARKS: Fitted for salvage work. 40-ton bollard pull. *Matanga* reported as 62.0 m overall by 12.3 beam, 3,920 hp.

Gaj (A 51) 1977

YARD AND SERVICE CRAFT

◆ **1 fuel lighter** Bldr: Rajabagan SY, Bombay

POSHAK (In serv. 4-82)

D: 600 tons **S:** 8 kts **Dim:** 36.3 × 7.6 × 2.4
M: 1 M.A.N. diesel; 255 hp **Cargo:** 200 tons dwt.

◆ **2 fuel lighters** Bldr: Rajabagan Yd., Bombay

PURAK (In serv. 3-6-77) PRADHAYAK (In serv. 2-78)

D: 960 tons (fl) **S:** 9 kts **Dim:** 49.7 × 8.1 × 3.0
M: 1 diesel; 1 prop; 560 hp **Cargo:** 376 tons dwt.

◆ **3 water lighters** Bldr: 1 by Rajabagan, Bombay; others: Mazagon DY, Bombay

D: 200 tons **S:** 9 kts **Dim:** 32.0 × . . . × 2.4
M: 1 diesel; 1 prop; . . . hp

◆ **1 torpedo trials and retrieval craft** Bldr: P.S. & Co., Bombay

A 71 ASTRAVAHINI (In serv. 8-9-83)

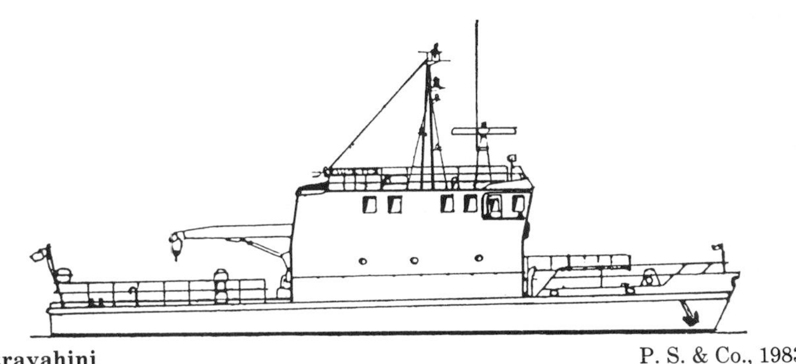

Astravahini P. S. & Co., 1983

REMARKS: No details available.

◆ **2 torpedo retrievers** Bldr: Goa SY

A 71 N. . . . . . . (In serv. 16-9-82) A 72 N. . . . . . . (L: 5-11-80)

D: 110 tons (fl) **S:** 11 kts **Dim:** 28.5 × 6.1 × 1.4
M: 1 Kirlasker-M.A.N. 12-cyl. diesel; 1 prop; 300 hp

◆ **3 diving tenders** Bldr: Cleback SY (In serv. 1979, 2-84, 8-84)

D: 36 tons (fl) **S:** 12 kts **Dim:** 14.89 (13.37 pp) × 4.40 × 1.21
M: 2 Premier Auto-Meadows diesels; 2 props; 130 hp **Fuel:** 2 tons

◆ **1 coastal tug** Bldr: Garden Reach S.B. & Eng., Calcutta

RAJAJI (In serv. 7-82)

D: 428 tons **S:** 12.5 kts **Dim:** 30.5 × 9.5 × 3.8
M: 2 Garden Reach-M.A.N. diesels; 2 Kort-nozzle props; 2,120 hp

NOTE: Construction of four new tugs was authorized under the 1985 Budget.

◆ **3 large harbor tugs** Bldr: Mazagon Dock, Bombay (In serv. 1973-74)

AJARAL ARJUN BALSHIL

◆ **1 sail-training craft** Bldr: Alcock Ashdown, Bhavnagar

VARUNA (In serv. 20-4-81) **D:** 130 tons (fl) **Dim:** 30.5 × . . . × . . .

INDIA *(continued)*
YARD AND SERVICE CRAFT *(continued)*

REMARKS: Two-masted brig for training Sea Cadets. Construction of a second sail-training ship has been proposed; to carry 90 cadets.

NOTE: There are undoubtedly a large number of other yard and service craft, for which no names or data are available.

COAST GUARD

The Coast Guard was established 1-2-77 to ensure surveillance of India's 200-nautical-mile economic zone. Commanded by an admiral, it consisted initially of ships and craft transferred from the Indian Navy. The Indian Customs Service was merged with the Coast Guard in April 1982. The name "Coast Guard" is written in large black letters on the sides of ship hulls, which are painted white.

The Coast Guard has announced that in addition to the units listed below, it plans to acquire a salvage tug of 1,570 grt, a pollution-control ship, twelve patrol aircraft, and one search-and-rescue aircraft. During 1982, two Fokker F-27 Friendship transports were transferred from Indian Airlines for patrol duties, and three Chetak (Alouette-III) helicopters were ordered. Also in service are several Cessna 182 light aircraft. Seven or more HAL-built Dornier 228 surveillance aircraft are intended for the Coast Guard, which opened its first air station in 12-85.

◆ **3 (+3) Vikram class** Bldr: Mazagon DY, Bombay

	Laid down	L	In serv.
33 VIKRAM	3-81	26-9-81	20-12-83
34 VISAYA	. . .	. . .	13-4-84
35 VEERA	. . .	30-6-84	1-85
36 N. . .	. . .	. . .	. . .
37 N. . .	. . .	. . .	. . .
38 N. . .	. . .	. . .	. . .

Vikram (33) Mazagon DY, 1983

D: 940 tons (1,100 fl) **S:** 22 kts **Dim:** 74.10 × 11.40 × 3.00 (3.48 props)
A: 1/40-mm AA—1/Chetak (Alouette-III) helicopter
Electron Equipt: Radar: 1/Decca 1230, 1/Decca . . .
M: 2 SEMT-Pielstick 16 PA6 V80 diesels; 2 CP props; 12,800 hp
Electric: 880 kw **Fuel:** 108 tons **Range:** 3,500/14
Man: 10 officers, 12 chief petty officers, 52 men

REMARKS: First 3 ordered 1979; second three ordered 1983. Have fin stabilizers, hangar for Chetak (license-built Alouette-III) helicopter. Have pollution-control equipment, diving gear, and firefighting monitors.

◆ **2 British Blackwood class former ASW frigates**

	Bldr	Laid down	L	In serv.
31 KIRPAN	Alex. Stephen, Glasgow	1957	19-8-58	7-59
32 KUTHAR	Samuel White, Cowes	1957	14-10-58	1960

Kirpan (T 31)—in naval service 1969

D: 1,180 tons (1,456 fl) **S:** 23 kts **Dim:** 94.5 (91.44 pp) × 10.05 × 4.7
A: 3/40-mm AA (I × 3)—
Electron Equipt: Radar: 2/navigational—EW: Decca-Racal Cutlass intercept
M: 1 set GT; 1 prop; 15,000 hp **Electric:** 1,108 kw
Boilers: 2 Babcock & Wilcox; 38.7 kg/cm²; 450°C **Range:** 4,500/12

REMARKS: Transferred to the Coast Guard 1-7-77. Sister *Khukri* sunk 9-12-71 by a Pakistani submarine. Sonars and two Mk 10 Limbo triple ASW mortars removed by 1983.

PATROL BOATS

◆ **1 (+2) Japanese-design** Bldr: 64: Sumidagawa SY, Tokyo; others: Garden Reach SB & Eng., Calcutta

64 JIJA BAI (In serv. 20-6-83) 65 N. . . 66 N. . . 67. . .

Jija Bai (64) Sumidigawa, 1983

D: 273 tons (fl) **S:** 25 kts (sust.) **Dim:** 44.00 × 7.40 × 1.50 (hull)
A: 1/40-mm AA **Electron Equipt:** Radar: 1/nav. **Man:** 34
M: 2 MTU 12V538 TB82 diesels; 2 props; 4,030 hp **Range:** 2,375/14

REMARKS: Same basic design as Philippine Coast Guard's *Bessang Pass* class. Two additional units authorized in 1985 Budget. The three listed as under construction were ordered in 1979 as Type 956, but may have been canceled and reordered to this design.

◆ **2 SDB Mk 2 class** Bldr: Garden Reach SB & Eng., Calcutta

	L	In serv.		L	In serv.
N. . .	. . .	23-12-80	N. . .	2-81	26-11-81

REMARKS: For specifications, see SDB Mk 2 class in naval listings, page 241.

◆ **5 Soviet Poluchat-I class**

51 PANAJI 52 PANVEL 53 PAMBAN 54 PULI 55 PULICAT

D: 80 tons (90 fl) **S:** 18 kts **Dim:** 29.57 × 6.1 × 1.9
A: 2/14.5-mm AA (II × 1) **M:** 2 M50 diesels; 2 props; 2,400 hp
Range: 460/17; 900/10 **Man:** 20 tot.

REMARKS: Transferred 1967-69.

◆ **1 British "Ford" (SDB Mk 1) class** Bldr: Hooghly Docking & Eng., Calcutta

735 ABHAY (In serv. 13-11-61)

D: 120 tons (151 fl) **S:** 18 kts **Dim:** 35.76 × 6.1 × 1.7 **A:** 1/40-mm AA
M: 2 Paxman YHAXM diesels; 2 props; 1,000 hp; 1 Foden FD-6 cruise diesel; 100 hp
Fuel: 23 tons **Range:** 500/12; 1,000/8 (cruise engine)

REMARKS: Originally a class of six: two stricken, two to Bangladesh, one to Mauritius.

◆ **8 South Korean patrol craft** Bldr: Swallow Craft, Pusan (In serv. 1983)

C01–C08

D: 32 tons (fl) **S:** 20 kts **Dim:** 20.0 × 4.7 × 1.3
A: 1/7.62-mm mg **Electron Equipt:** Radar: 1/nav.
M: 2 G.M. 12V71 TI diesels; 2 props; 1,060 hp **Range:** 500/20 **Man:** 8 tot.

◆ **. . . Norwegian SM-43 Smuggler-class launches** Bldr: GRW, India

D: . . . **S:** 36 kts **Dim:** 13.4 × . . . × . . .
M: 2 Castoldi waterjets; . . . hp **Man:** 4 tot.

REMARKS: Acquired when the Coast Guard merged with the Customs Service in 4-82. Glass-reinforced plastic construction. Original design by Båtservice, Mandal, Norway.

INDONESIA

PERSONNEL (1984): 35,800, including 5,000 Marines

MERCHANT MARINE (1984): 1,484 ships—1,856,967 grt (tankers: 162 ships—433,914 grt)

NAVAL AVIATION: The Indonesian Navy has a coastal-surveillance and logistic-support force consisting of 12 Australian N22B and 6 N22SL Searchmaster maritime surveillance aircraft, 6 C-47 Dakota transports, 3 Aero Commander light transports, and 4 CASA-212 light transports, plus 5 BO-105, 1 Alouette-III, and 10 Wasp (4 transferred 7-10-81, 6 somewhat later) helicopters. The first of 25 Nuritanio-built AS-332 Puma (NAS 132) helicopters was delivered 29-12-84, with all to deliver by 12-84; some may be fitted with AS.39 Exocet anti-ship missiles. Four older Bell Model 476 helicopters were re-engined with turbines in 1984-85. Planned is a "Naval Combat Element" of 12

NAVAL AVIATION *(continued)*

Northrop F-5E "Tiger-II" jet fighters. The Air Force has 2 Boeing 737 Surveiller long-range maritime patrol aircraft (first delivered 6-83) with "Slammer" side-look-ing radar; a third is to convert by 1987. Also used are several C-130 HMP in a surveillance role.

WARSHIPS IN SERVICE OR UNDER CONSTRUCTION AS OF 1 JANUARY 1986

	L	Tons (Surfaced)	Main armament
◆ **3 submarines**			
2 TYPE 209	1980	980	8/533-mm TT
1 WHISKEY	1958	1,050	6/533-mm TT
		Tons	
◆ **11 (+1) frigates**			
1 (+1) TRAINING FRIGATE	1980-. . .	1,850	4/Exocet, 1/57-mm DP
3 FATAHILAH	1977-79	1,160	4/Exocet, 1/120-mm DP, 1/40-mm
3 TRIBAL	1960-62	2,300	2/114 mm DP, 2/Sea Cat, ASW weapons
4 CLAUD JONES	1958-59	1,450	1 or 2/76-mm, 6/Mk 32 TT

◆ **4 guided-missile patrol boats**

◆ **22 (+. . .) patrol boats**

◆ **2 (+2) minesweepers**

◆ **11 amphibious-warfare ships**

NOTE: The names of Indonesian ships are preceded by the designation KRI (*Kapalperang Republik Indonesia,* or Warship of the Republic of Indonesia).

SUBMARINES

◆ **2 West German Type 209** Bldr: Howaldtswerke, Kiel

	Laid down	L	In serv.
401 CAKRA	25-11-77	10-9-80	18-3-81
402 NANGALA II (ex-*Candrasa*)	14-3-78	10-9-80	6-7-81

Nangala II (402) G. Gyssels, 1981

D: 980/1,150/1,440 tons **S:** 11 (snorkel)/21.5 kts
Dim: 61.00 × 6.20 × 5.50 **A:** 8/533-mm TT (fwd) — 14 total torpedoes
Electron Equipt: Radar: 1/Thompson-CSF Calypso
Sonar: 1/Atlas AN 526 passive, 1/CSU AN 407 A9 passive, DUUX-2
M: 4 MTU 12V493AZ diesels (600 hp each), 2 electric motors; 1 prop; 5,000 hp
Range: 16/21.5; 25/20; 230/8; 400/4 — 8,200/11 (snorkel)
Man: 6 officers, 28 men

REMARKS: Ordered 2-4-77. Can dive to 250 m. H.S.A. Sinbads weapons control. Ordering of a third has been postponed.

◆ **1 Soviet Whiskey class**

410 PASOPATI

Pasopati (410) 1976

D: 1,050/1,350 tons **S:** 17/16 kts **Dim:** 76.0 × 6.3 × 5.0
A: 6/533-mm TT (4 fwd, 2 aft) — 14 torpedoes or 28 mines
M: 2 diesels (4,000 hp), electric drive; 2 props; 2,500 hp
Endurance: 40 to 45 days **Range:** 6,000/5 (snorkel) **Man:** 60 tot.

REMARKS: Sister *Bramastra* (412) stricken 1981, along with *Nagabanda* (403), which had been used for dockside training. *Pasopati* has been given new batteries and was refitted for further service in 1984; now used mainly for dockside training.

FRIGATES

NOTE: Indonesia was offered the opportunity to purchase four Royal Netherlands Navy *Van Speijk*-class frigates in 5-85.

◆ **1 (+1) training frigates** Bldr: Uljanic SY, Yugoslavia

	Laid down	L	In serv.
HAJER DEWARTARA	11-5-79	11-10-80	20-8-81
N.	. . .	. . .	. . .

Hajer Dewartara (364) 10-81

D: 1,850 tons (fl) **S:** 27 kts **Dim:** 96.70 (92.00 wl) × 11.20 × 3.55
A: 4/MM 38 Exocet SSM (II × 2) — 1/57-mm Bofors — 2.20-mm AA (I × 2) — 2/ASW TT (2/SUT wire-guided torpedoes) — mines — 1 BO-105 helicopter
Electron Equipt: Radar: 1/Decca 1229, 1/H.S.A. WM-28
Sonar: PHS-32
EW: SUSIE-I system — 2/128-mm flare RL (II × 2)
M: CODOG: 1 Rolls-Royce Olympus TM-3B gas turbine, 27,250 hp; 2 MTU 16V956 TP91 diesels, 7,000 hp; 2 CP props
Fuel: 338 tons **Range:** 1,150/27 (gas turbine); 4,000/20 (diesels)
Man: 92 crew + 100 students

REMARKS: Same basic design as ship laid down in 1977 for Iraq. Ordered 14-3-78. A second was reportedly ordered 7-83. SEWACO GM 101-41 computerized data system. Fin stabilizers, 114 tons water ballast, 50 tons potable water, 7 tons helo fuel. Carries two LCVP-type landing craft. 1,000 rounds 57-mm, 3,120 rounds 20-mm ammunition. Gas turbine rated at 22,300 hp in tropics. WM-28 track-white-scan fire-control radar not fitted at time of delivery.

◆ **3 Fatahilah class** Bldr: Wilton-Fijenoord, Schiedam, The Netherlands

	Laid down	L	In serv.
361 FATAHILAH	31-1-77	22-12-77	16-7-79
362 MALAHAYATI	28-7-77	19-6-78	21-3-80
363 NALA	27-1-78	11-1-79	8-80

Malahayati (362) R. Gillett, 11-84

Nala (363) — with hangar in folded state 1980

FRIGATES *(continued)*

Malahayati (362) R. Gillett, 11-84

D: 1,160 tons (1,450 fl) **S:** 30 kts (21 diesel) **Dim:** 83.85 × 11.10 × 3.30
A: 361, 362: 4/MM 38 Exocet SSM (II × 2)—1/120-mm Bofors L-46 DP—1/40-mm Bofors L-70—2/20-mm AA (I × 2)—2/375-mm Bofors SR-375A ASW RL (II × 1)—6/324-mm Mk 32 ASW TT (III × 2); 363: 4/MM 38 Exocet (II × 2)—1/120-mm Bofors L-46 DP—2/40-mm AA (I × 2)—2/20-mm AA (I × 2)—1/BO 105 helicopter
Electron Equipt: Radar: 1/Decca AC 1229, 1/DA-05/2, 1/WM-28
Sonar: PHS-32
EW: SUSIE-I syst.—2/Knebworth/Corvus chaff RL
M: CODOG: 1 Rolls-Royce Olympus TM-3B gas turbine, 22,360 hp (tropical); 2 MTU 16V956 TB81 diesels; 800 hp; 2 CP props
Electric: 1,350 kw **Range:** 4,250/16 (diesels)
Man: 11 officers, 71 men

Remarks: Ordered 8-75. The *Nala* has a new type of helicopter deck that folds around the helicopter to form a hangar, two single 40-mm AA instead of one, and ASW torpedo tubes. DAISY computerized data system. Have an NBC warfare citadel. Living spaces air-conditioned. Fin stabilizers. Ammunition supply: 400 rounds 120-mm, 3,000 rounds 40-mm, 12 ASW torpedoes, 54 Nelli and Erica ASW rockets, 50 rounds chaff. The GFCS has a LIROD t.v./laser/infrared backup director.

◆ **3 ex-U.K. "Tribal" class**

	Bldr	Laid down	L	In serv.
331 Martha Khristina Tiyahahu (ex-*Zulu,* F 124)	Alex. Stephens & Sons	13-12-60	3-7-62	17-4-64
332 Wilhelmus Zakarias Yohannes (ex-*Gurkha,* F 122)	Thornycroft, Woolston	3-11-58	11-7-60	13-2-63
333 Hasanuddin (ex-*Tartar,* F 133)	HMDY, Devonport	22-10-59	19-9-60	26-2-62

Martha Khristina Tiyahahu (331) L. & L. Van Ginderen, 4-85

Martha Khristina Tiyahahu (331) G. Gyssels, 5-85

D: 2,300 tons (2,700 fl) **S:** 24 kts **Dim:** 109.73 (106.68 pp) × 12.95 × 3.80 (5.30 props)
A: 2/114-mm Mk 5 DP (I × 2)—2/Sea Cat GWS.21 syst. (IV × 2, 2 directors)—2/20-mm AA (I × 2)—1/Limbo Mk 10 ASW mortar (III × 2)—1/Wasp helicopter (AS.12 ASM, Mk 44/46 torpedoes)
Electron Equipt: Radar: 1/978, 1/993, 1/965, 1/903, 2/262
Sonar: Type 170B, Type 177, Type 162
EW: intercept equipt., 2/Knebworth/Corvus chaff RL (VIII × 2)
M: COSAG: 1 set Metrovik GT (15,000 hp) and 1 A.E.I. gas turbine (7,500 hp); 1/5-bladed prop; 22,500 hp
Boilers: 1 Babcock & Wilcox 3-drum; 38.7 kg/cm², 450°C
Electric: 1,450 kw **Fuel:** 400 tons **Range:** 5,300/12
Man: 13 officers, 240 men (in RN service)

Remarks: Survivors of a class of seven Royal Navy "General-Purpose" frigates, stricken 3-84 after having been recommissioned because of the Falklands War. Purchased by Indonesia 16-4-84 and towed to Vosper Thornycroft, Woolston, for overhaul/modernization during April-June 1984. 331 began post-refit trials 22-3-85 and recommissioned 2-5-85, 332 recommissioned 21-10-85. Data above as in Royal Navy service.

Twin rudders, one pair fin stabilizers. The helicopter flight deck has a small hangar beneath, into which the aircraft is lowered by elevator; the resultant hole is covered with segmented panels normally stowed beside the Limbo mortar position. MRS.3 director with Type 903 radar for the 114-m guns, two modified MRS.8 directors with Type 262 radars for the Sea Cat systems. 332 had Type 199 variable-depth sonar removed prior to transfer.

◆ **4 ex-U.S. Claud Jones class** Bldrs: 341, 343: Avondale Marine, Westwego, La.; 342, 344: American SB, Toldeo, Ohio

	L	In serv.
341 Samadikun (ex-*John R. Perry,* DE 1034)	29-7-58	5-5-59
342 Martadinata (ex-*Charles Berry,* DE 1035)	17-3-59	25-11-60
343 Monginsidi (ex-*Claud Jones,* DE 1033)	27-5-58	10-2-59
344 Ngurah Rai (ex-*McMorris,* DE 1036)	26-5-59	4-3-60

FRIGATES *(continued)*

Ngurah Rai (344) R. Gillett, 11-84

D: 1,450 tons (1,750 fl) **S:** 22 kts
Dim: 95.10 (91.75 wl) × 11.84 × 3.66 (hull)/5.50 (sonar)
A: 1 or 2/76.2-mm DP (I × 1 or 2)—0 or 2/37-mm AA (II × 1)—0 or 2/25-mm AA (II × 1)—6/324-mm ASW Mk 32 TT (III × 2)
Electron Equipt: Radar: 1/Decca 1226, 1/SPS-10, 1/SPS-6, 1/SPG-52
Sonar: SQS-42 series—EW: WLR-1 (not in 341)
M: 4 Fairbanks-Morse 38ND8⅛ diesels; 1 prop; 9,240 hp **Electric:** 600 kw
Fuel: 296 tons **Range:** 3,590/22; 10,300/9 **Man:** 15 officers, 160 men

Remarks: No. 341 was transferred on 20-2-73, No. 342 on 31-1-74, Nos. 343 and 344 on 16-12-74. Nos. 341 and 342 have a twin Soviet 37-mm AA in place of one 76.2-mm on fantail and a twin 25-mm at the forecastle break. Navigational radar added 1980-81. Have Mk 70 Mod. 2 GFCS, Mk 105 ASW FCS.

Note: The ex-Soviet Riga-class frigates *Jos Sudarso* (351) and *Lambung Manegurat* (357) were stricken 1985.

GUIDED-MISSILE PATROL BOATS

◆ **4 PSK Mk-5 class** Bldr: Korea-Tacoma SY

	In serv.		In serv.
621 Mandau	7-79	623 Badek	2-80
622 Rencong	7-79	624 Keris	2-80

Rencong (622) R. Gillett, 11-84

D: 250 tons (290 fl) **S:** 41 kts **Dim:** 53.58 × 8.00 × 1.63 (hull)
A: 4/MM 38 Exocet (II × 2)—1/57-mm Bofors AA—1/40-mm Bofors AA—2/20-mm AA (I × 2)
Electron Equipt: Radar: 1/Decca AC 1229, 1/H.S.A. WM-28
M: CODOG: 1 G.E.-Fiat LM-2500 gas turbine, 25,000 hp; 2 MTU 12V331 TC81 diesels, 1,120 hp each; 2 CP props
Fuel: 65 tons **Range:** 2,500/17 **Electric:** 400 kw **Man:** 5 officers, 34 men

Remarks: First unit laid down 5-77. Modification of U.S. *Asheville*-class design. A second group of four were not ordered as planned.

PATROL BOATS AND CRAFT

◆ **1 (+. . .) Lürssen PB 57 design** Bldr: Lürssen, Vegesack, West Germany and P.T. PAL SY, Surabaja

. . . N. . . (In serv. 1985)

D: 342 tons (399 fl) **S:** 29.5 kts **Dim:** 58.10 (54.40 wl) × 7.60 × 2.80
A: 1/76-mm OTO Melara Compact DP—1/40-mm AA
Electron Equipt: Radar: . . .
M: 3 MTU 16V956 TB92 diesels; 3 props; 11,400 hp
Electric: 405 kVA **Range:** 4,200/17 **Man:** 3 officers, 27 men

Remarks: Of two complete mid-bodies, one shipped from West Germany in 1-84 and one in 7-84, one was intended for the Navy and one for the Customs Service. Bows and sterns added at Surabaja. Three more for the Navy were planned, but construction may have been canceled; these would have been built entirely in Indonesia. Helicopter platform fitted aft.

◆ **1 (+4 + 6 + 36) Jetfoil Model 929 hydrofoils**

	Bldr	L	In serv.
Bima Samudera I	Boeing, Seattle	22-10-81	14-12-81
. . .	Boeing/P.T. PAL	1984	1987
. . .	Boeing/P.T. PAL	6-1-84	1987
. . .	Boeing/P.T. PAL	1985	1988
. . .	Boeing/P.T. PAL	1985	1988

Bima Samudera I Boeing Marine Systems, 1981

D: 115 tons (fl) **S:** 46 kts
Dim: 27.4 (foils down) × 9.1 × 1.9 (5.2 foils down, 2.0 max. foiling)
A: . . . **Electron Equipt:** Radar: 1/Decca . . .
M: 2 Allison 501-K20A gas turbines; 2 Rocketdyne R-20 waterjet pumps; 7,560 hp—2 G.M. 8V92 TI diesels; 2 props; 900 hp for hull-borne cruise
Range: 900/40; 1,500/15 **Fuel:** 33.4 tons
Man: 6 tot. plus 260 passengers

Remarks: *Bima Samudera I* was purchased by the Indonesian Agency for the Development and Application of Technology for evaluating such a craft in naval patrol, logistics support, and civil roles. Naval-manned. Delivered in-country 2-82. Has enhanced fuel tankage over standard commercial model. Aluminum construction.

The hydrofoil contract with Boeing Marine Services calls for two each of two versions of the basic Jetfoil design, with construction taking place at P.T. Pabrik Kapal (P.T.PAL), Indonesia. Another six craft are on option, and a total of 47 is foreseen. The first four were built by Boeing, Seattle, and delivered to Indonesia for fitting out. The patrol version (see illustration) may be armed with a Bofors 57-mm SAK Mk 2 DP gun and 2/12.7-mm mg and may also have two 6-tubed chaff RL and an optronic fire-control system. The troop transport version will resemble the prototype *Bima Samudera I,* with the addition of two 25-man semirigid inflatable boats slung over the stern; it will carry up to 100 troops and will be armed with a 20-mm AA and 2/12.7-mm mg (I × 2). The first production boat was laid down 10-12-83. The first two were delivered 1-85 to P.T.PAL for outfitting and completion by 1987. Numbers 3 and 4, intended as gunboats, to be shipped 3-86 and 11-86.

Indonesian patrol hydrofoil—artist's rendering Boeing Marine, 1983

PATROL BOATS AND CRAFT *(continued)*

Troop-carrying hydrofoil on trials Boeing, 1-85

◆ **4 Carpentaria class** Bldr: De Havilland Marine, Australia

	In serv.		In serv.
851 SAMADAR	8-76	855 SADARIN	12-76
854 SAWANGI	11-76	856 SALMANETI	7-77

Samadar (851) 1981

D: 27 tons (fl) **S:** 25 kts **Dim:** 15.7 × 5.0 × 1.3
A: 2/12.7-mm mg (I × 2) **Electron Equipt:** Radar: 1/Decca 110
M: 2 MTU 8V331 diesels; 2 props; 1,400 hp **Range:** 950/18 **Man:** 10 tot.

REMARKS: Grant-aid from Australia. Aluminum construction. Sisters *Sasila* (852) and *Sabola* (853) transferred to Sea Police 1981.

◆ **8 Australian Attack class**

	Bldr	L	In serv.
847 SIBARU (ex-*Bandolier*)	Walkers, Ltd.	1967	1968
848 SULIMAN (ex-*Archer*)	Walkers, Ltd.	1967	1968
857 SIGALU (ex-*Barricade*)	Evans Deakin	29-6-68	26-10-68
858 SILEA (ex-*Acute*)	Evans Deakin	29-8-67	26-4-68
8. . . SIRIBUA (ex-*Bombard*)	Walkers, Ltd.	6-7-68	5-11-68
8. . . SIADA (ex-*Barbette*)	Walkers, Ltd.	10-4-68	16-8-68
8. . . N. . . (ex-*Buccaneer*)	Evans Deakin	14-9-68	11-1-69
8. . . SIKUDA (ex-*Attack*)	Evans Deakin	8-4-67	17-11-67

Suliman (848) 10-81

D: 146 tons (fl) **S:** 21 kts **Dim:** 32.76 (30.48 pp) × 6.2 × 1.9
A: 1/40-mm AA—2/7.62-mm mg (I × 2)
Electron Equipt: Radar: 1/Decca RM 916
M: 2 Davey-Paxman Ventura 16 YJCM diesels; 3,460 hp **Fuel:** 20 tons
Range: 1,220/13 **Man:** 3 officers, 19 men

REMARKS: Light-alloys superstructure. Air-conditioned. 847 transferred 16-11-73, 848 in 1974, 857 on 22-4-82, 858 on 6-5-83, and ex-*Bombard* later in 1983. Ex-*Barbette* transferred 22-85, ex-*Buccaneer* in 1-86, and ex-*Attack* on 24-5-85.

◆ **4 ex-Yugoslav PBR-500 class**

819 KAYANG	822 DORANG
820 LEMADANG	823 TODAK

Kayang (819) 10-81

D: 190 tons (202 fl) **S:** 18 kts **Dim:** 41.0 × 6.3 × 2.2
A: 1/76.2-mm—1/40-mm AA—6/20-mm AA (II × 3)—2/Mousetrap Mk 22 ASW RL—2/d.c. projectors—2/d.c. racks
Electron Equipt: Radar: 1/Decca 45—Sonar: U.S. QCU-2
M: 2 M.A.N. W8V 30/38 diesels; 2 props; 3,300 hp **Fuel:** 15 tons
Range: 1,000/12 **Man:** 54 tot.

REMARKS: Transferred in 1959. *Krapu* (821) and *Dorang* (822) stricken 1980. Rest to strike shortly.

◆ **2 Soviet Kronshtadt class** Bldr: U.S.S.R., 1951-52

814 PANDRONG 815 SURA

Sura (815) 1978

D: 300 tons (330 fl) **S:** 18 kts **Dim:** 52.1 × 6.5 × 2.2
A: 1/85-mm—2/37-mm AA (I × 2)—6/14.5-mm—2/MBU 1200 ASW RL (V × 2)—2/d.c. projectors—2/d.c. racks—mines
M: 3 9D diesels; 3 props; 3,300 hp **Fuel:** 20 tons **Range:** 3,500/14
Man: 50 tot.

REMARKS: Transferred 1958-59 A number of others have been stricken, including *Kakap* (816) in 1981 and *Barakuda* (817) in 1985.

MINE COUNTERMEASURES SHIPS

◆ **0 (+2) Alkmaar ("Tripartite")-class minehunters** Bldr: Van der Giessen de Noord, Alblasserdam, the Netherlands

	Ordered	Laid down	L	In serv.
. . . N. . . (ex-*Zierikzee*, ex-*Veere*)	27-3-85	. . .	. . .	8-87
. . . N. . . (ex-*Vlaardingen*)	6-85	. . .	. . .	3-88

D: 510 tons (540 fl) **S:** 15 kts **Dim:** 51.5 (47.1 pp) × 8.90 × 2.45 (2.6 max.)
A: 1/20-mm AA
Electron Equipt: Radar: 1/Decca TM 1226C
Sonar: DUBM-21B
M: 1 Brons-Werkspoor A-RUB215X12 diesel; 1 CP prop; 1,900 hp—2/75-hp bow-thrusters; 2/120-hp Schöttel active rudders (7 kts)
Electric: 970 kw **Range:** 3,500/10; 3,000/12 **Man:** 45 tot.

MINE COUNTERMEASURES SHIPS *(continued)*

Remarks: Will be taken from Royal Netherlands Navy production. Glass-reinforced plastic construction. Carry two PAP-104 remote-controlled minehunting/destruction submersibles and can also tow a wire sweep. DUBM-21B can detect mines in up to 80-m depth to slant ranges of 500 m. Have three 270 gas turbines and one 160-kw diesel generator sets. Active tank stabilization. EVEC 20 plot table, autopilot, Toran and Syledis radio navaids, Decca Hi-Fix precision nav. system.

Note: A widely reported 1983 order for six Italian *Lerici*-class minehunters was not consumated.

◆ **2 ex-Soviet T-43-class minesweepers**

701 Pulau Rani 702 Pulau Ratewo

D: 500 tons (570 fl) **S:** 14 kts **Dim:** 58.0 × 8.6 × 2.3
A: 4/37-mm AA (II × 2)—8/12.7-mm mg (II × 4)—2/d.c. projectors—2/mine rails
M: 2 Type 9D diesels; 2 props; 2,200 hp **Fuel:** 70 tons **Range:** 3,200/10

Remarks: Transferred 1962-64. Used on patrol duties. Three others lost or stricken 1980-81. To be replaced by the *Alkmaar*-class units.

AMPHIBIOUS WARFARE SHIPS

◆ **6 Teluk Semangka-class landing ships** Bldr: Hyundai SY, South Korea

	In serv.		In serv.
512 Teluk Semangka	20-1-81	515 Teluk Sampit	1981
513 Teluk Penyu	20-1-81	516 Teluk Banten	1982
514 Teluk Mandar	7-81	517 Teluk Ende	2-9-82

Teluk Sampit (515) Korea Tacoma, 1981

Teluk Penyu (513) Korea Tacoma, 1981

D: 1,800 tons (3,770 fl) **S:** 15 kts **Dim:** 100.0 × 15.4 × 4.2 (3.0 mean)
A: 3/40-mm AA (I × 3)—2/20-mm AA (I × 2)
M: 2 diesels; 2 props; 6,860 hp (5,600 sust.) **Electric:** 750 kw
Range: 7,500/13 **Man:** 13 officers, 104 men, plus 202 troops

Remarks: First four ordered 6-79, two more in 6-81. Near duplicates of U.S. LST 1/542-class design. Beaching load: 690 tons (17 main battle tanks), or up to 1,800 tons max. Helicopter decks amidships and aft. Carry 2 LCVP landing craft. There is a 50-ton-capacity turntable in the tank deck and an elevator to the upper deck. 516 and 517 have a large hangar incorporated in the superstructure, the helicopter deck raised one level, the forward helicopter positions deleted, the landing craft davits moved forward of the superstructure, and increased command facilities to act as flagships; they can carry three AS.332 Super Puma helicopters.

◆ **5 ex-U.S. LST 542-class tank landing ships** Bldr: Chicago Bridge & Iron Wks., Seneca, Ill. (except 511: American Bridge, Ambridge, Pa.; 509: unknown)

	Laid down	L	In serv.
501 Teluk Langsa (ex-LST 1128)	23-11-44	19-2-45	9-3-45
504 Teluk Kau (ex-LST 652)	24-7-44	19-10-44	1-1-45
509 Teluk Ratai (ex-M/V *Inagua Shipper*, ex-LST. . .)	. . .	. . .	. . .
510 Teluk Saleh (ex-*Clarke County*, LST 601)	21-10-43	4-3-44	25-3-44
511 Teluk Bone (ex-*Iredell County*, LST 839)	25-9-44	12-11-44	6-12-44

D: 1,650 tons light (4,080 fl) **S:** 11.6 kts **Dim:** 99.98 × 15.24 × 4.29
A: 6 or 7/40-mm or 37-mm AA
M: 2 G.M. 12-567A diesels; 2 props; 1,800 hp **Electric:** 300 kw
Fuel: 590 tons
Range: 6,000/9 (loaded) **Man:** 119 crew + 264 passengers

Remarks: Transferred in 3-60, 1961, and Nos. 510 and 511 in 7-70 under the Military Assistance Program. Can carry 2,100 tons of cargo. Sisters *Teluk Bayer* and *Teluk Tomani* are in the Military Sealift Command, as is the Japanese-built near-sister *Teluk Amboina.*

HYDROGRAPHIC SHIPS

Note: The 1,000-ton hydrographic ship *Bimasakti* ordered 15-12-82 from Amels SY, Makkum, The Netherlands, is for government, not naval service:

Dim: 59.8 × 13.0 × 3.6; **M:** 2 diesels; 14 kts.

Three 36-m government research boats were ordered from La Manche, Dieppe, France.

◆ **1 Burudjulasad class** Bldr: Schlichtingwerft, Travemünde (L: 8-65; In serv. 1967)

931 Burudjulasad

Burudjulasad (931) 1981

D: 1,800 tons (2,150 fl) **S:** 19 kts **Dim:** 82.0 (78.0 pp) × 11.4 × 3.5
M: 4 M.A.N. V6V 22/30 diesels; 2 CP props; 6,400 hp **Electric:** 1,008 kw
Fuel: 600 tons **Range:** 14,500/15.7
Man: 13 officers, 88 men, 28 technicians

Remarks: Launched in 8-65. Can accommodate 28 scientists and can carry one helicopter.

◆ **1 hydrometeorological and oceanographic research ship**

Bldr: Sasebo Heavy Industries, Japan (In serv. 12-1-63)

1005 Jalanidhi

Jalanidhi (1005) 1972

D: 740 tons (985 fl) **S:** 12.7 kts **Dim:** 53.9 (48.5 pp) × 9.5 × 4.3
M: 1 M.A.N. G6V 30/42 diesel; 1,000 hp **Electric:** 261 kw **Fuel:** 165 tons
Range: 7,200/10.5

Remarks: Weather-balloon facility aft.

◆ **1 ex-Soviet PO-2-class inshore survey craft**

1008 Aries

D: 56 tons (fl) **S:** 12 kts **Dim:** 21.3 × 3.8 × 2.0
M: 1 3D12 diesel; 300 hp **Man:** 13 tot.

Remarks: Transferred in 1964.

◆ **1 hydrographic survey ship** Bldr: De Waal Scheepswerf, Nijmegen (L: 6-9-52; In serv. 7-53)

1002 Burdjamhal

D: 1,200 tons (1,500 fl) **S:** 13 kts **Dim:** 64.5 (58.5 pp) × 10.1 × 3.3
M: 2 Werkspoor TMAB-278 diesels; 2 props; 1,160 hp **Fuel:** 150 tons
Man: 90 tot.

AUXILIARY SHIPS

◆ **1 ex-Soviet Don-class submarine tender** Bldr: U.S.S.R., 1960

301 Ratulangi (ex-Sov. 441)

AUXILIARY SHIPS *(continued)*

Ratulangi (ex-441) 1979

D: 6,700 tons (fl) **S:** 21 kts **Dim:** 139.9 × 17.6 × 5.4
A: 4/100-mm DP (I × 4)—8/57-mm AA (II × 4)—8/25-mm AA (II × 4)
Electron Equipt: Radar: 1/navigational, 1/Slim Net, 1/Sun Visor A
M: 4 diesels; 2 props; 8,000 hp **Range:** 21,000/10 **Man:** 300 tot.

REMARKS: Transferred in 1962. Because of heavy armament and extensive sensors, is used for patrol duties.

◆ **1 command ship** Bldr: Ishikawajima, Japan (L: 13-6-61)

561 MULTATULI

Multatuli (561) J. Jedrlinic, 1982

D: 4,500 tons (fl) **S:** 18.5 kts **Dim:** 111.35 (103.0 pp) × 16.0 × 6.98
A: 8/37-mm AA (II × 2, I × 4)—4/14.5-mm AA (II × 2)
M: 1 Burmeister & Wain diesel; 5,500 hp **Fuel:** 1,400 tons **Range:** 6,000/16
Man: 134 tot.

REMARKS: Built as a submarine-support ship, converted as a fleet command ship in the late 1960s. Has a helicopter platform aft. Construction of two similar ships of about 10,000 tons, to carry fuel, troops, and hospital facilities, is planned.

◆ **1 ex-U.S. Achelous-class repair ship** Bldr: Chicago Bridge & Iron, Seneca, Illinois

	Laid down	L	In serv.
921 JAJA WIDJAJA (ex-*Askari,* ARL 30, ex-LST 1131)	8-12-44	2-3-45	15-3-45

Jaja Widjaja (921) 1981

D: 2,130 (3,640 fl) **S:** 11 kts **Dim:** 99.98 × 15.24 × 4.25
A: 8/40-mm AA (IV × 2) **M:** 2 G.M. 12-267A diesels; 2 props; 1,800 hp
Electric: 520 kw **Fuel:** 590 tons **Man:** 280 tot.

REMARKS: Leased 31-8-71; purchased 22-2-79. Cargo capacity: 300 tons. 60-ton lift rig.

◆ **1 replenishment oiler** Bldr: Yugoslavia, 1965

911 SORONG

D: 5,100 (dwt) **S:** 15 kts **Dim:** 112.17 × 15.4 × 6.6
A: 8/12.7-mm mg (II × 4) **M:** 1 diesel; 1 prop; . . . hp

Sorong (911) 1979

REMARKS: Cargo: 3,000 tons fuel/300 tons water. Can conduct underway replenishments.

◆ **1 ex-Soviet Khobi-class oiler**

909 PAKAN BARU

D: 1,525 tons (fl) **S:** 12.7 kts **Dim:** 67.4 (63.7 pp) × 10.0 × 4.4
M: 2 diesels; 2 props; 1,600 hp **Range:** 2,500/12.5

REMARKS: Cargo: 700 tons fuel oil.

◆ **1 sail-training ship** Bldr: Stülcken, Hamburg (L: 21-1-52)

DEWARUTJI

Dewarutji 1977

D: 810 tons (1,500 fl) **S:** 9 kts **Dim:** 58.3 (41.5 pp) × 9.5 × 4.23
M: 1 M.A.N. diesel; 575 hp **Man:** 110 men, 78 cadets

REMARKS: Sail area: 1,091 m^2.

◆ **1 ex-U.S. Cherokee-class fleet tug** Bldr: United Eng., Alameda, California

	Laid down	L	In serv.
922 RAKATA (ex-U.S. *Menominee,* ATF 73)	27-9-41	14-2-42	25-9-42

D: 1,640 tons (fl) **S:** 15 kts **Dim:** 62.5 × 11.7 × 4.7
A: 1/76.2-mm DP—2/40-mm AA (I × 2)—4/25-mm AA (II × 2)
M: 4 G.M. 12-278A diesels, electric drive; 1 prop; 3,000 hp

REMARKS: Transferred 3-61.

◆ **1 coastal tug** Bldr: P.T.PAL, Surabaja (L: 6-6-79)

D: . . . **S:** 10 kts **Dim:** 24.25 × 6.5 × . . . **M:** Diesel; 1 prop; . . . hp
Man: 10 tot.

◆ **1 coastal tug** Bldr: Ishikawajima Harima, Tokyo (L: 4-61)

934 LAMPO BATANG

D: 250 tons **S:** 11 kts **Dim:** 28.1 × 7.6 × 2.6
M: 2 M.A.N. diesels; 2 props; 600 hp **Fuel:** 18 tons **Range:** 1,000/11
Man: 13 tot.

◆ **2 Tambora-class coastal tugs** Bldr: Ishikawajima Harima. Tokyo (both L: 6-61)

935 TAMBORA 936 BROMO

D: 250 tons (fl) **S:** 10.5 kts **Dim:** 24.1 × 6.6 × 3.0
M: 2 M.A.N. diesels; 2 props; 600 hp **Fuel:** 9 tons **Range:** 690/10.5
Man: 15 tot.

MILITARY SEALIFT COMMAND (KOLINLAMIL)

Formed in 1978 to coordinate the Indonesian Navy's logistic support for its far-flung bases and outposts in the Indonesian archipelago. Some of the units have been taken over from the Indonesian Army and others from the Navy.

◆ **1 tank landing ship** Bldr: Sasebo Heavy Industries (L: 17-3-61)

9. . . TELUK AMBOINA

MILITARY SEALIFT COMMAND (KOLINLAMIL) *(continued)*

D: 4,145 tons (fl) **S:** 13 kts **Dim:** 99.9 × 15.2 × 4.6
A: 4/40-mm AA—1/37-mm AA
M: 2 M.A.N. V6V 22.30 diesels; 2 props; 3,200 hp (2,850 sust.)
Electric: 135 kw **Fuel:** 1,200 tons **Range:** 4,000/13
Man: 88 men + 212 passengers

Remarks: Built as reparations. Near duplicate of U.S. LST 542 design. Guns may have been removed. Can carry 654 tons water. Has a 30-ton crane.

◆ **2 ex-U.S. LST 542-class tank landing ships**

	Bldr	Laid down	L	In serv.
9. . . Teluk Bayer (ex-LST 616)	Chicago Bridge & Iron, Seneca, Ill.	12-2-44	12-5-44	29-5-44
9. . . Teluk Tomani (ex-LST 983)	Boston Navy Yard, Boston, Mass.	22-12-43	10-2-44	25-3-44

D: 1,650 tons (4,080 fl) **S:** 11 kts **Dim:** 99.98 × 15.24 × 4.29
A: None **M:** 2 G.M. 12-567A diesels; 2 props; 1,800 hp
Fuel: 590 tons **Range:** 6,000/9 (loaded) **Man:** 119 men + 264 passengers

Remarks: Bought since 1961. *Teluk Tomani* is used as a cattle-carrier and does not carry passengers (by mutual agreement?).

◆ **3 Krupang-class utility landing craft** Bldr: Surabaja DY

9. . . Krupang (In serv. 3-11-78) 9. . . Dili (In serv. 27-2-79) 9. . . Nusantara (In serv. 1980)

D: 400 tons (fl) **S:** 11 kts **Dim:** 42.9 (36.27 pp) × 9.14 × . . .
M: 2 diesels; 2 props; . . . hp **Range:** 700/11 **Man:** 17 tot.

Remarks: Based on U.S. LCU 1610 class. Cargo: 200 tons.

◆ **2 Amurang-class landing craft** Bldr: Korneuberg SY, Austria (In serv. 1968)

9. . . Amurang 9. . . Dore

D: 182 tons (275 fl) **S:** 8 kts **Dim:** 38.3 × 10.0 × 1.8
M: 2 diesels; 2 props; 420 hp **Man:** 17 tot.

Remarks: Sister *Banten* and one other in merchant service. 200 grt.

◆ **1 oiler** Bldr: Japan, 1965

901 Balikpapan (ex-*Komado V*)

D: 1,780 dwt **S:** 11 kts **Dim:** 69.6 × 9.6 × 4.9
M: 1 diesel; 1,300 hp **Man:** 26 tot.

Remarks: Purchased in 1977.

◆ **1 small oiler** Bldr: . . . . , Indonesia (In serv. 1979)

902 Sambu

Sambu (902)—with missile boats *Keris* (624) and *Rencong* (622) alongside
R. Gillett, 11-84

D: . . . **S:** . . . **Dim:** Approx. 70.0 × 10.0 × 4.6 m
A: 4/14.5-mm mg (II × 2) **Electron Equipt:** Radar: 1/. . . nav.
M: 1 diesel; 1 prop; . . . hp

Remarks: No further data available.

◆ **6 Hungarian Tisza-class cargo ships** Bldr: Angyalfold SY, Budapest

951 Telaud 953 Natuna 957 Karimundsa
952 Nusatelu 956 Teluk Menitawi 960 Karamaja

D: 2,000 tons (fl) **S:** 12 kts **Dim:** 74.5 (67.4 pp) × 11.3 × 4.6
A: Some ships: 4/14.5-mm mg (II × 2) **M:** 1 Lang 8-cyl. diesel; 1,000 hp
Electric: 746 kw **Fuel:** 98 tons **Range:** 4,200/10.7 **Man:** 26 tot.

Remarks: Transferred 1963-64. Taken over from the Army in 1978. Had originally been naval. 1,296 grt/1,280 dwt. Cargo: 1,100 tons.

◆ **1 former pilgrim transport** Bldr: Blohm + Voss, Hamburg (In serv. 1936)

971 Tanjung Pandan (ex-*Genung Djati*, ex-*Empire Orwell*, ex-*Empire Doon*, ex-*Pretoria*)

D: . . . **S:** . . . **Dim:** 167.6 × 22.0 × . . .
M: 8 sets GT; 4 props; . . . hp

Remarks: 17,362 grt. German liner, used as a barracks during W.W. II, to U.K. in 1945, used as a troopship, then transport for religious pilgrims. Sold to Indonesia 1962. Acquired 1981 for Kolinlamil, but has remained immobile at Tanjung Priok.

◆ **1 former passenger-cargo ship** Bldr: N.V. Scheepswerfen Machinefabrick de Merwede, Hardinxveld, the Netherlands

931 Tansung Pandan (ex-*Tjut Njak Dhien*, ex-*Prinses Irene*) (In serv. 1965)

D: . . . **S:** 16.5 kts **Dim:** 139.92 × 18.67 × 8.61
M: Diesels; 1 prop; 8,600 hp

Remarks: 8,456 grt/8,618 dwt. Purchased 1978 for use as a transport.

◆ **1 former passenger-cargo ship** Bldr: . . .

932 Tansung Oisina (ex-*Gununjati*) (In serv. . . .)

Remarks: Approx. 6–8,000 grt. Purchased 1978 for use as a transport. No further data available.

◆ **. . . coastal cargo lighters** Bldr: Fasharkan DY, Manokwari, Irian

D: . . . **S:** 8 kts **Dim:** 31.1 × 6.26 × 1.80
M: Diesels

Remarks: 200 dwt. First unit delivered 7-3-82. Others may be built.

SEA COMMUNICATIONS AGENCY

Established in 1978 to patrol Indonesia's 200-nautical-mile economic zone and to maintain navigational aids. Full name: Indonesian Directorate General of Sea Communication/Department of Transport, Communications and Tourism.

PATROL BOATS

◆ **4 Golok class** Bldr: Schlichtingwerft, Harmsdorf, W. Germany

	In serv.		In serv.
PAT 206 Golok	12-3-82	PAT 208 Pedang	12-5-82
PAT 207 Panah	12-3-82	PAT 209 Kapak	12-5-81

D: 200 tons (fl) **S:** 28 kts **Dim:** 37.50 × 7.00 × 2.00
A: 1/20-mm AA **Range:** 1,500/18 **Man:** 18 tot.
M: 2 MTU 16V652 TB61 diesels; 2 props; 4,200 hp

Remarks: Intended for search-and-rescue duties. 120^3/hr. fire pump and water monitor, rescue launch, 8-man sick bay. Hulls built by Deutsche Industrie Werke, Berlin.

◆ **5 Kujang class** Bldr: SFCN, Villeneuve-la-Garenne, France

	Laid down	L	In serv.
PAT 201 Kujang	5-80	17-10-80	19-8-81
PAT 202 Parang	7-80	18-11-80	19-8-81
PAT 203 Celurit	9-80	20-3-81	1981
PAT 204 Cundrik	7-9-80	10-11-80	1981
PAT 205 Belati	2-81	21-5-81	10-81

Parang (202) SFCN, 1981

D: 126 tons (162 fl) **S:** 28 kts
Dim: 38.32 (35.46 pp) × 6.00 × 1.78 (2.60 props) **A:** 1/20-mm AA
M: 2 S.A.C.M. AGO V12 195 CZ SHR T5; 2 props; 4,400 hp
Range: 1,500/18 **Man:** 18 tot.

Remarks: Intended for search-and-rescue duties.

◆ **6 PAT-01-class patrol craft** Bldr: Tanjung Priok SY, 1978-79

PAT 01 to PAT 06

D: 12 tons (fl) **S:** 14 kts **Dim:** 12.15 × 4.25 × 1.0
A: mg **M:** 1 Renault diesel; 260 hp

TRANSPORTS

◆ **4 Kerinci class** Bldr: Meyerwerft, Papenburg, West Germany

Kerinci (In serv. 1983) Rinjani (In serv. 10-84)
Kambuna (In serv. 8-83) Umsini (In serv. 1985)

Rinjani Meyerwerft, 1984

D: . . . **S:** 20 kts **Dim:** 144.0 (130.0 pp) × 23.4 × 5.9
M: 2 Mak 6MU601 diesels; 2 props; 17,000 hp **Electric:** 3,520 kw
Range: 5,500/20 **Man:** 119 crew + 1,596 to 1,737 passengers

Remarks: 13,861 + 13,954 grt/3,400 dwt. Intended for inter-island revenue passenger-carrying in peacetime and as military transports in time of war. Accommodations for approximately 100 first-class, 200 second, 300 third, 496 fourth-class and 500-plus economy passengers. Bow-thruster.

NAVIGATIONAL AID TENDERS

◆ **0 (+11) lighthouse and buoy tenders** Bldr: Carrington Slipway, Tomago, Australia

Remarks: Ordered 12-84. To fit out in Indonesia.

◆ **2 coastal service** Bldr: . . . , Japan (In serv. 1976)

Karakata Kumba

D: 569 grt/552 dwt **S:** 13 kts **Dim:** 50.50 (47.43 pp) × 10.00 × 3.71
M: 2 Niigata diesels; 1 prop; 850 hp

Remarks: Two more buoy tenders were ordered from Japan in 1978.

◆ **2 seagoing buoy tender/cargo ships** Bldr: . . . (In serv. 1963)

Majang Mizan

D: 2,150 tons (fl) **S:** 14 kts **Dim:** 78.0 (71.0 pp) × 13.7 × 4.0
M: 1 set 4-cyl. compound reciprocating steam; 1 prop; 1,800 hp
Boilers: Two 16 kg/cm² **Fuel:** 376 tons **Man:** 70 tot.

Remarks: 1,705 grt/1,170 dwt. Resemble small cargo ships, with bridge forward, engine aft, and holds amidships.

◆ **1 seagoing buoy tender and cable layer** Bldr: . . . , the Netherlands

Biduk (L: 30-10-51; In serv. 7-52)

D: 1,250 dwt **S:** 12 kts **Dim:** 65.0 × 12.0 × 4.5 **Boilers:** two 16-kg/cm²
M: 1 set triple-expansion reciprocating steam; 1 prop; 1,600 hp **Man:** 66 tot.

Remarks: Cable sheaves over bow. Transferred from Navy, 1978 (ex-pendant 1003).

◆ **2 split-hopper dredges** Bldr: Tanjung Priok SY, Jakarta

N. . . . . . . (In serv. 1983) N. . . . . . . (In serv. 1983)

D: 1,600 tons (fl) **S:** 10.7 kts **Dim:** . . . × . . . × 4.05 m
M: 2 Bolnes 6DNL 150 diesels; 2 CP props; 1,692 hp
Electric: 1,280 kw **Man:** 25 tot.

Remarks: 1,000 m³ capacity, able to dredge to 14 m. 272-hp bow-thruster. Built with assistance from IHC Holland. Ordered 1981, laid down 1982.

◆ **1 suction hopper dredge** Bldr: Orenstein & Koppel, Lübeck, West Germany

Irian (L: 26-6-81)

D: 9,500 tons (fl) **S:** 12 kts **Dim:** 110.0 × 18.0 × 7.1
M: 2 MWM diesels; 2 props; 7,700 hp

CUSTOMS SERVICE

Note: The Indonesian Customs Service is currently undergoing an ambitious expansion, with patrol boats and craft constructed in Western Europe and at home.

PATROL BOATS

◆ **1 (+. . .) Lürssen PB 57 design-programmed** Bldr: Lürssen, Vegesack, West Germany/P.T.PAL SY, Surabaja (In serv. 1985)

D: 342 tons (399 fl) **S:** 29.5 kts **Dim:** 58.10 (54.40 wl) × 7.60 × 2.8
A: 76-mm OTO Melara DP—1/40-mm AA **Electron Equipt:** Radar: . . .
M: 3 MTU 16V956 TB92 diesels; 3 props; 11,400 hp
Electric: 405 kVA **Range:** 4,200/17 **Man:** 3 officers, 27 men

Remarks: First unit is one of two completed mid-bodies shipped to Indonesia 1-84 and 7-84 for addition of bows and sterns at P.T.PAL, Surabaja. Plans to build three more each for the Navy and Customs Service put on hold 7-84, pending possibility of shifting production to Tanjung Priok Navy Yard. Has a small helicopter platform aft.

◆ **30 (+5) Lürssen FPB 28 class**

BC 4001 through BC 4006	Lürssen, Vegesack	4-81 to . . .-81
BC 5001 through BC 5006	Lürssen, Vegesack	. . . to . . .
BC 6001 through BC 6005	BSC, Belgium	11-81 to 8-82
BC 7001 through BC 7006	BSC, Belgium	8-2-82 to 8-82
BC 8001 through BC 8006	P.T.PAL SY, Surabaja	1-85 to . . .
BC 9001 through BC 9006	P.T.PAL SY, Surabaja	. . . to . . .

BC 4001 J. Jedrlinic, 1981

D: 61 tons (68.5 fl) **S:** 30 kts **Dim:** 28.0 (26.0 wl) × 5.4 × 1.6
A: 1/12.7-mm mg
M: BC 4001–4003 and BC 6001–6005: 2 Deutz SBA 16M 816LCK-R diesels; 2 props; 2,720 hp—others: 2 MTU diesels; 2 props; 2,620 hp
Electric: 36 kVA **Fuel:** 10 tons **Range:** 700/27.5; 1,050/17
Man: 6 officers, 13 men

Remarks: Building to replace a series of very similar craft built by Lürssen in 1962-63. A collaborative effort by Lürssen and Abeking and Rasmussen of West Germany and BSC—Belgium Shipbuilding Corp., a consortium of Fulton Marine, Ruisbrock, and Scheepswerven Van Langebrugge—delivering prefabricated sections to PAL shipyard, Surabaja, in addition to building complete boats. BC 5001–5003 rated at 30.6 kts. BC 6001 and 7001 series ordered 1980; BC 8001 and 9001 series ordered 1-81; program well behind schedule, with only two launched by 12-84.

◆ **7 BC 2001 class** Bldr: CMN, Cherbourg

	L	In serv.		L	In serv.
BC 2001	27-9-79	8-2-80	BC 2005	19-8-80	5-9-80
BC 2002	20-12-79	8-2-80	BC 2006	14-10-80	7-11-80
BC 2003	4-3-80	3-4-80	BC 2007	9-12-80	10-2-81
BC 2004	14-5-80	9-6-80			

BC 2001 J. Jedrlinic, 2-84

D: 58.5 tons (70.3 fl) **S:** 29.7 kts (at 64.4 tons)
Dim: 28.5 (26.5 wl) × 5.4 × 1.3 (1.65 props) **A:** 1/12.7-mm mg
M: 2 MTU 12V331 TC92 diesels; 2 props; 2,440 hp **Man:** . . . tot.

◆ **7 (+7) BC 3001 class** Bldr: Chantiers Navals de l'Estérel, Cannes

	In serv.		In serv.
BC 3001	9-7-79	BC 3005	22-10-80
BC 3002	24-1-80	BC 3006	22-1-81
BC 3003	24-4-80	BC 3007	3-4-81
BC 3004	12-6-80		

D: 57 tons (71 fl) **S:** 34 kts **Dim:** 28.2 × 5.2 × 1.6
A: 1/12.7-mm mg **M:** 2 MTU 12V331 TC81 diesels; 2 props; 2,700 hp
Range: 800/15 **Man:** 2 officers, 16 men

Remarks: Similar design to BC 1001 class; also built of wood. Seven more ordered 1982.

INDONESIA *(continued)*
PATROL BOATS *(continued)*

BC 3001 1983

◆ **3 BC 1001 class** Bldr: Chantiers Navals de l'Estérel, Cannes

BC 1001 (In serv. 4-75) BC 1002 (In serv. 6-75) BC 1003 (In serv. 11-75)

BC 1002 J. Jedrlinic, 5-84

D: 56 tons (fl) **S:** 34 kts **Dim:** 28.0 (26.6 wl) × 5.3 × 1.6
A: 1/12.7-mm mg **M:** 2 MTU 12V331 TC81 diesels; 2 props; 2,700 hp
Fuel: 10 tons **Range:** 750/15 **Man:** 15 tot.

◆ **up to 24 BC 401 series** Bldr: Lürssen, Vegesack (In serv. 1960-62)

Remarks: Data as for BC 4001 series, with Deutz engines. BC 401, BC 502, BC 703 and others remain in service pending completion of duplicate replacements.

MARITIME POLICE

PATROL BOATS

◆ **9 DKN 908 class** Bldr: Baglietto, Italy; Riva Trigoso, Italy (In serv. 1861-64)

DKN 908 DKN 911 DKN 914
DKN 909 DKN 912 DKN 915
DKN 910 DKN 913 DKN 916

D: 139 tons (159 fl) **S:** 21 kts **Dim:** 42.0 × 6.5 × 1.8
A: 3/20-mm AA (I × 3) **M:** 2 Maybach MD655 diesels; 2 props; . . . hp
Range: 1,500/17 **Man:** 22 tot.

◆ **10 DKN 504 class** Bldrs: DKN 504-508: Ishikawajima Harima, Tokyo; others: Uraga Dockyard, Yokosuka (In serv. 1963-64)

DKN 504 DKN 507 DKN 510 DKN 513
DKN 505 DKN 508 DKN 511
DKN 506 DKN 509 DKN 512

DKH 507 1981

D: 314 tons light (390 std., 444 fl) **S:** 15.3 kts
Dim: 48.1 (44.0 pp) × 7.5 × 2.9 **A:** 1/20-mm AA, 2/12.7-mm mg (I × 2)
M: 2 M.A.N. W8V 22/30 ALU diesels; 2 props; 1,400 hp **Electric:** 126 kw
Fuel: 41 tons **Range:** 2,700/14 **Man:** 35 tot.

Remarks: Cargo hold with 75 tons capacity.

◆ **2 Carpentaria class** Bldr: De Havilland Marine, Australia

DKN. . . (ex-*Sasila*) DKN. . . (ex-*Sabola*)

Remarks: Transferred from Indonesian Navy 1981, under which see for data.

INDONESIAN ARMY (ADRI)

At one time the Indonesian Army operated a great variety of ships, including up to 29 units in the ADRI-I series, most of which were old passenger-cargo ships acquired for use as troop transports. Most of its serviceable ships were turned over to the new Military Sealift Command in 1977 and 1978, but a new series of logistics landing craft is under construction.

◆ **28 utility landing craft** Bldr: Koja SY, Tanjung Priok (In serv. 1978-1982)

Adri XXXI to Adri LVIII

D: 580 tons (fl) **S:** 10 kts **Dim:** 42.0 (38.0 wl) × 10.7 × 1.8
M: 2 G.M. 6-71 diesels; 2 props; 680 hp **Electric:** 100 kw **Fuel:** 40 tons
Range: 1,500/10 **Man:** 15 tot.

Remarks: 300 dwt. Construction continues. Cargo: 122 tons vehicles/stores; 120 tons water. Two 150-dwt landing craft were also completed during 1980, while in 1982 the first of several 30-dwt landing craft and 180-dwt cargo lighters were acquired.

INDONESIAN AIR FORCE (AURI)

The Indonesian Air Force operates six passenger-cargo logistics ships that were completed in the mid-1960s. Of about 600 dwt, they are intended to beach and are equipped with bow doors.

IRAN

Islamic Republic of Iran

Personnel (1984): Approx. 10,000 total

Merchant Marine (1984): 306 ships—2,105,549 grt (tankers: 33 ships—944,727 grt)

Maritime Aviation: On hand before the revolution and war with Iraq were: 7 SH-3D Sea King, 7 AB-212, 5 AB-205A, 14 AB-206A, and 2 Sikorsky RH-53D helicopters; and fixed-wing assets remaining include 2 P-3F Orion long-range patrol aircraft; 4 Fokker F-27 Mk 400M Friendship transports; 4 Falcon 20 and 4 Aero Commander utility transports.

Weapons: Three Iranian destroyers use General Dynamics-developed fixed-train, elevatable box-launchers to fire U.S.-supplied Standard SM-1 MR surface-to-*air* missiles; these have a secondary anti-ship capability. Target tracking and illumination is supplied by shipboard gunnery radars. Four Vosper Mk 5 frigates carry a quintuple position, trainable launcher for Italian Sea Killer Mk 2 anti-ship missiles:

Length: 4.70 m	Range: 25 km
Diameter: 20.6 cm	Speed: 300 m/sec.
Span: 99.9 cm (cruciform)	Guidance: beam-rider/command with optical back-up
Weight: . . .	Engine: 100 kg-thrust solid-fuel with 4,400-kg thrust solid booster

Also used are Short Bros. & Harland Sea Cat short-range SAMs. Guns and torpedoes are of U.S., Italian, Swedish, and British origin. Only a dozen of U.S. Harpoon missiles were supplied, and all are believed to have been expended or are unserviceable.

Note: Although reporting on the current conflict between Iran and Iraq seems anything but accurate, the following ships appear to have been lost:
◆ 2 U.S. PF 103-class frigates, with another possibly lost in 1983
◆ 2 Combattante II-class guided-missile patrol boats (including *Peykan*)
◆ 5 patrol boats
◆ 4 mine countermeasures ships
The two Combattante II class and one of the PF 103 class were sunk by AM 39 Exocet missiles launched from Super Frélon helicopters.

Note: The U.S. *Tang*-class submarine *Kusseh* (ex-*Trout,* SS 566) was abandoned at Norfolk, Virginia, in 5-79. In 11-82 the Ayatollah Khomeini announced that he wished to renew the canceled 1978 contract for 6 West German Type 209 submarines; the West German government was still deciding its position as of 6-85.

GUIDED-MISSILE DESTROYERS

◆ **1 ex-British Battle class** Bldr: Cammell Laird, Birkenhead

	Laid down	L	In serv.
51 Artemiz (ex-*Sluys,* D 60)	24-11-43	28-2-45	30-9-46

Artemiz (D 51)—wearing old number Thornycroft, 1969

D: 2,325 tons (3,360 fl) **S:** 31 kts **Dim:** 115.32 (108.2 pp) × 12.95 × 5.2 (fl)
A: 4/Standard SM-1 MR SAM box launchers (8 missiles)—4/114-mm DP (II × 2, fwd)—4/40-mm AA (I × 4)—1/Sea Cat SAM (IV × 1)—1/Squid ASW mortar (III × 1)
Electron Equipt: Radar: 1/Decca . . . nav., 1/Plessey AWS-1 air-search, 1/Contraves Sea Hunter RTN-10X fire-control
Sonar: Plessey MS-26—EW: 1 Decca RDL-1
M: 2 sets Parsons GT; 2 props; 50,000 hp **Boilers:** 2 Admiralty 3-drum
Fuel: 680 tons **Range:** 3,200/20 **Man:** 260 tot.

Remarks: Modernized before transfer on 20-1-67. Anti-ship missiles added after refit in South Africa, 1975-76. Sea Cat system NSCS optical director only. Standard missiles are SAM version, vice SSM, using Sea Hunter for fire control. Reported sunk 1983, but appears to still exist, although only marginally operable.

◆ **2 ex-U.S. Allen M. Sumner, FRAM II, class**

	Bldr	Laid down	L	In serv.
61 Babr (ex-*Zellars,* DD 777)	Todd, Pacific	24-12-43	19-7-44	25-10-44
62 Palang (ex-*Stormes,* DD 780)	Federal SB, Kearny	25-2-44	4-11-44	27-1-45

Palang (D 62)—old number —forward box-launcher raised 1975

D: 2,200 tons (3,320 fl) **S:** 30 kts **Dim:** 114.75 × 12.45 × 5.6
A: 4/Standard SM-1 MR SAM box-launchers (8 missiles)—4/127-mm DP (II × 2)—6/324-mm Mk 32 ASW TT (III × 2)—2/Hedgehogs—1/AB-204 helicopter
Electron Equipt: Radar: 1/SPS-10, 1/SPS-29, 1/Mk 25
Sonar: 1/SQS-29—EW: WLR-1, ULQ-6
M: 2 sets GT; 2 props; 60,000 hp
Boilers: 4 Babcock & Wilcox; 43.3 kg/cm^2, 454°C **Fuel:** 650 tons
Range: 1,260/30; 4,600/14 **Man:** 14 officers, 260 men

Remarks: Purchased in 3-71 and delivered in 10-73 and 1974. The *Bordelon* (DD 881) and the *Kenneth D. Bailey* (DD 713) were transferred for cannibalization. The Standard missile launchers are on a platform between the stacks and also on the 01 level forward of the bridge. Mk 37 fire control for the 127-mm guns. VDS now removed from the *Babr.* Both believed to be inoperable.

FRIGATES

◆ **4 Saam (Vosper Mk 5) class**

	Bldr	Laid down	L	In serv.
71 Saam	Vosper Thornycroft	22-5-67	25-7-68	20-5-71
72 Zaal	Vickers, Newcastle	3-3-68	25-7-68	1-3-71
73 Rostam	Vickers, Barrow	10-12-67	4-3-69	28-2-72
74 Faramarz	Vosper Thornycroft	25-7-68	30-7-69	28-2-72

D: 1,250 tons (1,540 fl) **S:** 40/30 kts (17.5 with diesel)
Dim: 94.5 (88.4 pp) × 11.07 × 3.25
A: 1/Sea Killer SSM system (V × 1)—1/Sea Cat SAM system (III × 1) 1/114-mm DP Mk 8—2/35-mm AA (II × 1)—1/Limbo Mk 10 ASW mortar (III × 1)
Electron Equipt: Radar: 1/Plessey AWS-1 air-search, 2/Contraves Sea Hunter RTN-10X fire control
EW: Decca RDL-1 intercept

Zaal (F 72) 1977

M: CODOG: 2 Rolls-Royce Olympus TM3A gas turbines; 2 Paxman 16-cyl. Ventura diesels for cruising; 2 CP props; 46,000 hp (turbines), 3,800 hp (diesels)
Fuel: 150 tons (250 with overload) **Range:** 5,000/15
Man: 135 tot.

Remarks: Air-conditioned. Retractable fin stabilizers. All now carry Mk 8 guns in place of original Mk 6. Normally carry only 3 Sistel Sea Killer missiles. One or two believed to be operable, but status of combat systems uncertain.

◆ **1 or 2 U.S. PF 103 class** (see remarks) Bldr: Levingston SB, Orange, Texas

	Laid down	L	In serv.
81 Bayandor (ex-PF 103)	20-8-62	7-7-63	18-5-64
82 Naghdi (ex-PF 104)	12-9-62	10-10-63	22-7-64

D: 900 tons (1,135 fl) **S:** 20 kts **Dim:** 83.82 × 10.06 × 3.05 (4.27 sonar)
A: 2/76.2-mm DP (I × 2)—2/40-mm AA (II × 1)—2/23-mm AA (II × 1)—4/d.c. projectors—2/d.c. racks
Electron Equipt: Radar: 1/SPS-6, 1/Raytheon navigational, 1/Mk 34
Sonar: SQS-17A
M: 4 Fairbanks-Morse 38D8⅛-10 diesels; 2 props; 5,300 hp
Electric: 750 kw
Fuel: 110 tons **Range:** 2,400/18; 3,000/15
Man: 133 tot.

Remarks: Transferred under the Military Aid Program. Twin Soviet 23-mm AA have been added forward of the bridge in place of the single Hedgehog ASW mortar. Mk 63 GFCS for 76.2-mm guns (radar on fwd gunmount); Mk 51 Mod. 2 GFCS for 40-mm mount. Sisters *Milanian* (83, ex-PF 105) and *Kahnamuie* (84, ex-PF 106) reported lost to Iraqi forces by 1982, with a third reported lost in 1983.

PATROL BOATS

◆ **11 Combattante-II class** Bldr: Constr. Méc. de Normandie, Cherbourg

	L	In serv.		L	In serv.
P 221 Kaman	8-1-76	6-77	P 228 Gorz	28-12-77	15-9-78
P 222 Zoubin	14-4-76	6-77	P 229 Gardouneh	23-2-78	23-10-78
P 223 Khadang	15-7-76	15-3-78	P 230 Khanjar	27-4-78	1-8-81
P 225 Joshan	21-2-77	31-3-78	P 231 Neyzeh	5-7-78	1-8-81
P 226 Falakhon	2-6-77	31-3-78	P 232 Tabarzin	15-9-78	1-8-81
P 227 Shamshir	12-9-77	31-3-78			

Zoubin (P 222) CMN, 1977

Khadang (P 223)—with 4 Harpoon launchers 1978

D: 249 tons (275 fl) **S:** 36 kts **Dim:** 47.0 × 7.1 × 1.9
A: 1/76-mm OTO Melara DP—1/40-mm AA
Electron Equipt: Radar: 1/Decca 1226, 1/H.S.A. WM-28
EW: TSF TMV-433 suite: DR-2000 receiver, DALIA analyzer, Alligator 5-A jammer

PATROL BOATS *(continued)*

M: 4 MTU 16V538 TB91 diesels; 4 props; 14,400 hp **Electric:** 350 kw
Fuel: 41 ton **Range:** 700/33.7s **Man:** 31 tot.

REMARKS: Contracted 19-2-74 and 14-10-74. The last three were embargoed at Cherbourg 4-79 and released 22-6-81. P 232 captured off Spain 13-8-80 by anti-Khomeini forces but abandoned later at Toulon. P 231 and 232 had no Harpoon Tubes on delivery, and all missiles delivered by the U.S. are believed to have been expended. Two, including *Peykan* (P 224), reported lost to Iraqi forces 11-80.

◆ **1 U.S. Coast Guard Cape class** Bldr: U.S. Coast Guard, Curtis Bay, Md. (In serv. 1956-59)

P 201 KEYVAN

D: 85 tons (107 fl) **S:** 20 kts **Dim:** 29.0 × 6.2 × 2.0
A: 1/40-mm AA—2/Mk 22 Mousetrap ASW RL—2/d.c. racks
M: 4 Cummins VT-12-M700 diesels; 2 props; 2,200 hp **Electric:** 40 kw
Range: 1,500/15 **Man:** 15 tot.

REMARKS: Sisters *Mehran* (P 203) *Mahvan* (P 204) and *Tiran* (P 202) lost 1980-83, as were the three U.S. PGM 71-class patrol boats *Parvin* (P 211), *Bahram* (P 212), and *Nahid* (P 213).

MINE WARFARE SHIPS

◆ **1 ex-U.S. Falcon-class minesweeper** Bldr: Peterson (L: 1958)

301 SHAHROKH (ex-MSC 276)

D: 320 tons (378 fl) **S:** 12.5 kts (8, sweeping)
Dim: 43.0 (41.5 pp) × 7.95 × 2.55
A: 2/20-mm AA (II × 1)
Electron Equipt: Radar: 1/Decca 707 Sonar: UQS-1
M: 2 G.M. 8-268A diesels; 2 props; 890 hp **Fuel:** 27 tons
Range: 2,500/10 **Man:** 3 officers, 35 men

REMARKS: Sisters *Shabaz* lost through fire in 1975, *Simorgh* (302) and *Karkas* (303) to Iraqi forces 1980-81.

AMPHIBIOUS WARFARE SHIPS

◆ **4 (+2) Hengam-class LSTs** Bldr: Yarrow & Co., Scotstoun

	L	In serv.		L	In serv.
511 HENGAM	27-9-73	12-8-74	513 LAVAN	12-6-78	16-1-85
512 LARAK	7-5-74	12-11-74	514 TONB	6-12-79	7-85

Larak (512)—wearing old number 1976

Tonb (514)—laid up at builders L. & L. Van Ginderen, 8-82

D: 2,940 tons (fl) **S:** 14.5 kts **Dim:** 92.96 (86.87 wl) × 14.94 × 3.00 max.
A: 4/40-mm Bofors AA (I × 4) **Electron Equipt:** Radar: 1/Decca TM 1229
M: 511, 512: 4 Paxman Ventura 12 YJCM diesels; 2 CP props; 5,600 hp
513, 514: 4 MTU 12V562 TB61 diesels; 2 CP props; 5,800 hp
Range: 3,500/12 **Fuel:** 295 tons **Electric:** 1280 kw
Man: 75 crew + 168 troops

REMARKS: 513, 514, laid up since completion, were released by the British Government 5-10-84 on the excuse that they would be used in the unlikely role of hospital ships; delivered without armament. Negotiations continued into 1985 for the construction of two more, originally ordered 7-77, for which considerable material had been accumulated.

Flight deck for one Sea-King-sized helicopter aft. Cargo capacity of 600 tons on 39.6 × 8.8 × 4.5m (high) vehicle deck, with 15-m-long bow ramp. Can also carry up to 300 tons liquid cargo in lieu of some vehicle stowage. Can stow 12 Soviet T-55 or 6 British Chieftain battle tanks. Upper deck forward has a 10-ton crane to handle two Uniflote cargo lighters (LCVP) and twelve Z-boat rubber personnel landing craft. Intended for logistics support (when ten 20-ton or thirty 10-ton containers would be carried) or for amphibious assault. Magazines hold 8,000 rounds 40-mm; guns are locally controlled. 513 has an additional Decca 1216 nav. radar. 513 and 514 have a U.S. URN 25 TACAN system.

◆ **4 medium landing ships** Bldr: Ravenstein SY, Deest, Netherlands (In serv. 1-84)

21 N. . . 22 IRAN HORMUZ . . . N. . . . . . N. . .

D: . . . **S:** 9 kts **Dim:** 65.03 (58.43 pp) × 12.01 × 2.60
A: . . . **Electron Equipt:** Radar: 1/. . . nav.
M: 2 M.A.N. V12V-12.5/14 diesels; 2 props; 730 hp
Man: . . .

REMARKS: 906 grt/750 dwt. Delivered via U.K. as merchant ships, but bore naval pendants. Cargo capacity about 600 tons. Freight-barge design, with bow ramps. Second pair reported delivered in Iran 21-10-85.

HOVERCRAFT

◆ **6 BH.7 Wellington class** Bldr: British Hovercraft, Cowes, U.K. (In serv. 1970-75)

101 to 106

D: 50 to 55 tons (fl) **S:** 65 kts **Dim:** 23.9 × 13.8 × 10.36 (high)
A: Several mg **Electron Equipt:** Radar: 1/Decca 914
M: 1 Rolls-Royce Proteus 15M549 gas turbine; 1 6.4-m diameter prop; 4,250 hp
Electric: 110 kVA **Fuel:** 9 tons **Range:** 400/56

REMARKS: Four are of the logistics-support version, with a 14-ton payload. Two are of the Mk 4 version with recess for two SSM, which were not mounted. The Mk 4 uses the Gnome 15M541 engine of 4,750 hp and can carry 60 troops in side compartments as well as assault vehicles on its 56-m² cargo deck. Speed in both versions is reduced to 35 kts in a 1.4-meter sea. Overhauled at builders beginning with two in 2-84 and two more in 1985; new engines, skirts, etc.

◆ **8 SR-N6 Winchester class** Bldr: British Hovercraft (In serv. 1973-75)

01 to 08

D: 10 tons **S:** 52 kts **Dim:** 14.8 × 7.7 × 3.8 (high)
A: 1/7.6-mm mg **M:** 1 Gnome Mk 1050 gas turbine **Range:** 110/30

REMARKS: Probably inoperable.

AUXILIARY SHIPS

◆ **1 large replenishment oiler**

	Bldr	Laid down	L	In serv.
431 KHARG	Swan Hunter, Wallsend	1-76	3-2-77	25-4-80

Kharg (431) French Navy, 1985

D: 33,014 tons (fl) **S:** 21.5 kts **Dim:** 207.15 (195.00 pp) × 25.50 × 9.14
A: 2/40-mm AA (I × 2)—3 helicopters
M: 1 set Westinghouse GT; 1 prop; 26,870 hp **Electric:** 7,000 kw
Boilers: 2 Babcock & Wilcox 2-drum **Man:** 248 tot.

REMARKS: Ordered 10-74. 21,100 grt/20,000 dwt. Carries fuel and ammunition. Design is greatly modified version of the Royal Navy's *Olwen* class. Ran initial trials 11-78, but delays in fitting-out made delivery before the revolution impossible; remained at builders until released 5-10-84; ran trials again 4-9-84. Has U.S. URN-20 TACAN equipment. Delivered without armament; originally had an OTO Melara 76-mm Compact forward. One 40-mm AA was installed on the former 76-mm pedestal, the other on the helo deck—which should inhibit flight operations.

◆ **2 Bandar Abbas-class small replenishment oilers** Bldr: C. Lühring, Brake, West Germany

422 BANDAR ABBAS (L: 14-8-73) 441 BOOSHEHR (L: 22-3-74)

D: 5,000 tons (fl) **S:** 15 kts **Dim:** 108.0 × 16.6 × 4.5
A: 2/40-mm AA (I × 2)—1/helicopter **M:** 2 M.A.N. diesels; 2 props; 6,000 hp
Man: 60 tot.

AUXILIARY SHIPS *(continued)*

Booshehr (441)—composite photo G. Koop, 1974

Remarks: 3,250 dwt. Telescoping hangar. Carry fuel, food, ammunition, and spare parts. Armed after delivery. Used for patrol duties 1984-on, due to lack of operable combatants.

◆ **2 water tankers** Bldr: Mazagon Dock, Bombay, India

411 Kangan (L: 4-78) 412 Taheri (L: 17-9-78)

Kangan (411) 1979

D: 12,000 tons (fl) **S:** 12 kts **Dim:** 147.95 (140.0 pp) × 21.5 × 5.0
M: 1 M.A.N. 7L52/55A diesel; 7,385 hp

Remarks: 9,430 dwt. Intended to supply Arabian Gulf islands. Liquid cargo: 9,000 m^3.

◆ **1 U.S. 174-foot-class water tanker** Bldr: Zenith Dredge, Duluth, Minn.

	Laid down	L	In serv.
46 Lengeh (ex-U.S. YW 88)	18-3-43	18-5-43	17-10-43

D: 440 tons light (1,390 fl) **S:** 10 kts **Dim:** 53.04 × 10.01 × 4.27
M: 2 Union diesels; 2 props; 580 hp **Electric:** 80 kw **Fuel:** 25 tons
Man: 22 tot.

Remarks: Purchased in 1964. Cargo: 930 tons.

◆ **1 ex-U.S. Amphion-class repair ship** Bldr: Tampa SB, Florida

	Laid down	L	In serv.
Chah Bahar (ex-*Amphion,* AR 13)	20-9-44	15-5-45	30-1-46

D: 8,670 tons light (14,450 fl) **S:** 16 kts **Dim:** 150.0 × 21.4 × 8.4
A: 2/76.2-mm DP (I × 2) **M:** 1 set GT; 1 prop; 8,500 hp **Electric:** 3,600 kw
Boilers: 2 Foster-Wheeler "D"; 30.6 kg/cm², 382°C **Fuel:** 1,850 tons
Man: Quarters for 921 men

Remarks: Transferred in 10-71. Primarily stationary, but can steam.

◆ **1 former imperial yacht for Caspian Sea** Bldr: Boele's SW, Bolnes, The Netherlands

Chah Sevar

D: 530 tons **S:** 15 kts **Dim:** 53.0 × 7.65 × 3.2
M: 2 Stork diesels; 2 props; 1,300 hp

◆ **1 former imperial yacht for Arabian Gulf** Bldr: Burmester, W. Germany (In serv. 1970)

Kish

D: 175 tons **Dim:** 37.0 × 7.6 × 2.2 **M:** 2 MTU diesels; 2 props; 2,920 hp

YARD AND SERVICE CRAFT

◆ **2 barracks ships**

	Bldr	L	In serv.
Michelangelo	Ansaldo	9-62	. . .
Raffaello	CRDA, Monfalcone	. . .	7-7-65

D: 42,000 tons (fl) **S:** 29 kts **Dim:** 275.8 (244.0 pp) × 31.0 × 9.3
M: 4 sets GT; 4 props; 65,000 hp **Boilers:** 4 Foster-Wheeler

Remarks: Former cruise liners, purchased 12-12-76. Arrived July/August 1977 at Bandar Abbas for use as floating barracks for Iranian naval personnel and their families. Retain original names. *Raffaello* seriously damaged by Iraqi missile, 20 or 21-11-82.

◆ **2 harbor tugs**

	Bldr	L	In serv.
Hamoon	Deltawerf, Sliedrecht, Neth.	. . .	4-84
Hirmand	Damen, Hardinxveld, Neth.	1-8-84	. . .

D: 300 tons (fl) **S:** 12 kts **Dim:** 23.63 (23.53 pp) × 6.81 × 3.19
M: 2 MTU GV396 TC62 diesels; 2 props; 1,200 hp

Remarks: 122 grt.

◆ **1 ex-U.S. Army tug**

45 Bahman Shir (ex-ST 1002)

D: 150 tons

Remarks: Transferred in 1962.

◆ **2 ex-German tugs**

1 (ex-*Karl*) 2 (ex-*Ise*)

D: 134 tons

Remarks: Built in 1962-63, and transferred 17-6-74.

◆ **2 ammunition lighters** Bldr: Karachi SY & Eng. Wks. (In serv. 1978)

481 N. . . . . . . , 482 Chiroo

D: 840 grt **S:** 11 kts **Dim:** 64.0 × 10.5 × 3.2
M: 2 M.A.N. G6V-23.5/33ATL diesels; 2 props; 1,560 hp

◆ **2 water barges** Bldr: Karachi SY & Eng. Wks (In serv. 1977-78)

1701 1702

D: 1,410 grt **Dim:** 65.0 × 13.0 × 2.6

◆ **2 large fuel lighters** Bldr: Karachi SY & Eng. Wks (In serv. 1981)

1718 Dayere N. . . . . . . Daylam

D: 1,300 tons (fl) **S:** 9 kts **Dim:** 63.45 (58.48 pp) × 11.00 × 3.03
Man: 2 M.A.N. diesels; 2 props; 1,560 hp

Remarks: 933 grt/850 dwt

◆ **2 small fuel lighters** Bldr: Karachi SY & Eng. Wks. (In serv. 1981)

1703 N. . . . . . . 1704 N. . . . . . .

D: . . . **S:** . . . **Dim:** 30.51 × 9.30 × 1.83
M: 2 M.A.N. diesels; 2 props; 326 hp

Remarks: 195 grt/200 dwt.

Note: In addition to the eight units immediately above, Karachi Shipyard and Engineering Works delivered 10 other yard and service craft between 1977 and 7-81. All were designed in Great Britain. A variety of craft were built, all initially numbered 1701 through 1718. Types included a self-propelled dredge, (1711), a pontoon barge (1710), a diving tender (1705), and garbage lighter (120 m^3 hopper with compacter). Two cargo lighters were reportedly similar to the ammunition lighters described above.

◆ **1 modified U.S. 174-foot-class yard oiler** Bldr: Nav. Mec. Castellammare (In serv. 2-56)

43 Hormuz (ex-U.S. YO 247)

Hormuz (43) 1974

D: 1,400 tons (fl) **S:** 9 kts **Dim:** 54.4 × 9.8 × 4.3
A: 2/20-mm AA (I × 2) **Electron Equipt:** Radar: 1/Decca 707
M: 1 Ansaldo Q370 diesel; 600 hp **Fuel:** 25 tons

Remarks: Built under U.S. Military Aid Program. Cargo: 900 tons

◆ **1 floating dry dock** Bldr: Pacific Bridge, Alameda, Cal. (In serv. 7-44)

400 (ex-ARD 28)

D: 3,500 tons lift **Dim:** 149.8 × 25.6 × 1.7 (light)

Remarks: Transferred 1-3-77.

IRAN *(continued)*

COAST GUARD

PATROL CRAFT

◆ **up to 81 U.S. 50-ft. class** Bldr: Peterson Bldrs., Sturgeon Bay, Wisc. (In serv. 1975-78)

D: 22 tons (fl) **S:** 28 kts **Dim:** 15.24 × 4.80 × 1.9
A: 1/12.7-mm mg **Range:** 500/30
M: 2 G.M. 8V71 TI diesels; 3 props; 850 hp **Man:** 6 tot.

Remarks: Twenty were ordered in 1973 and 61 more in 1976. Shipped as kits for assembly in Iran, at Boghammar, where they were still being assembled into the 1980s. Some have probably been lost.

◆ **20 U.S. Swift Mk II class** Bldr: Peterson Bldrs., Sturgeon Bay, Wisc. (In serv. 1976-77)

1201 to 1220

D: 22 tons (fl) **S:** 26 kts **Dim:** 15.3 × 4.8 × 1.9
A: None **M:** 2 G.M. 12V71 diesels; 2 props; 900 hp **Man:** 6 tot.

Remarks: Equipped to carry extra personnel and have no fixed armament.

◆ **6 U.S. 40-foot class** Bldr: Sewart Seacraft, Louisiana (In serv. 1963)

Mahmavi-Hamaraz	Mahmavi-Vanedi	Mordarid
Mahmavi-Taheri	Mardjan	Sadaf

D: 10 tons **S:** 30 kts **Dim:** 12.2 × 3.4 × 1.1
A: 2/7.62-mm mg **M:** 2 G.M. diesels; 2 props; 600 hp

Remarks: Four given to Sudan in 1978, two stricken.

◆ **40+ U.S. Bertram Enforcer harbor patrol craft** **Dim:** 9.5 and 6.1 oa

◆ **10 Medina-class motor lifeboats** Bldr: Fairey Marine, Hamble (In serv. 1978)

1601 to 1610

D: 15.5 tons (fl) **S:** 16 kts **Dim:** 14.0 × 3.7 × 1.1
M: 2 Ford Sabre Turbo-Plus diesels; 2 props; 500 hp **Range:** 150/12
Man: 4 tot. (plus 12 passengers)

IRAQ

Republic of Iraq

Personnel (1984): about 3,000 men, including 400 officers

Merchant Marine (1984): 153 ships — 1,073,871 grt (tankers: 28 ships — 797,055 grt)

Naval Aviation: The Air Force operates eight French-supplied Super Frélon helicopters, armed with AM 39 Exocet anti-ship missiles, and in 10-83 France loaned 5 Super Étendard fighter-bombers with AM 39 missiles; returned 10-85. Some of the newly delivered 83 Mirage F.1EQ fighter-bombers also carry AM 39. Five Agusta AB 212 and an unspecified number of A 103A helicopters were ordered 1984.

Note: Losses to date during the war with Iran reportedly include:
- ◆ 4 Osa II-class guided-missile patrol boats (two to Iranian naval ships and two to aircraft)
- ◆ 6 P 6-class torpedo boats
- ◆ 1 Polnocny-C-class landing ship

◆ **2 (+2) Italian Lupo class** Bldr: CNR, Ancona (A) and Riva Trigoso (B)

	Yard	Laid down	L	In serv.
Hittin	A	31-3-82	27-7-83	3-85
Tmi Qar	A	9-82	31-3-84	-85
Al Qadissiya	B	15-4-83	. . .	. . .
Al Yarmook	A	12-3-84	18-4-85	. . .

D: 2,213 tons (2,525 fl) **S:** 35 kts (20.5 diesel)
Dim: 112.8 (106.0 pp) × 11.98 × 3.84
A: 8/Otomat Mk II SSM (I × 8) — 1/Albatros SAM syst. (VIII × 1; no reloads) — 1/127-mm DP OTO Melara — 4/40-mm AA Breda Dardo (II × 2) — 6/324-mm ASW TT (III × 2) — 2/AB 212 ASW helicopters
Electron Equipt: Radar: 1/3RM20 navigational, 1/RAN-11X surf./air search, 1/RAN-10S air search, 2/Orion RTN-10XRCT f.c., 2/Orion RTN-20X f.c.
Sonar: Edo 610E or Raytheon 1160B
EW: Lambda F passive syst. — 2/SCLAR chaff RL
M: CODOG: 2 Fiat/G.E. LM-2500 gas turbines (25,000 hp each); 2 GMT A230-20M diesels (3,900 hp each); 2 CP props
Electric: 4,000 kVA **Range:** 900/35; 3,450/20.5 **Man:** 185 tot.

Remarks: Ordered 2-81. 127-mm gun and SAM fire control by two Elsag Mk 10 Mod. 0 systems with NA-10 radar directors; 40-mm f.c. by two Dardo systems. Selenia IPN-10 combat data system. SAM system will use Aspide missiles rather than NATO Sea Sparrow. Fin stabilizers fitted. Fixed hangar, as on Venezuelan and Peruvian units of the class, to which this version will in other ways be similar. U.S. objection to the sale of major components of the LM-2500 gas turbines was overcome. *Hittin* delivered 11-84, commissioned 3-85, but had not sailed for Iraq by 6-85.

◆ **1 training frigate** Bldr: Uljanic SY, Yugoslavia

	Laid down	L	In serv.
507 Ibn Khaldum	1977	1978	21-3-80

Ibn Khaldum (507) 1980

D: 1,850 tons (fl) **S:** 26 kts **Dim:** 96.7 × 11.2 × 3.55
A: 1/57-mm Bofors SAK 57 AA — 1/40-mm AA — 8/20-mm AA (II × 4) — 1/d.c. rack
Electron Equipt: Radar: 2/navigational, 1/surface search, 1/Phillips 9LV200 Mk II f.c.
Sonar: . . .
M: CODOG: 1 Rolls-Royce Olympus TM-3B gas turbine, 22,360 hp; 2 MTU 16V956 TB61 diesels, 7,500 hp; 2 CP props
Range: 4,000/20 (diesels) **Man:** 93 men + 100 students

Remarks: Same basic design as the ship laid down in 1979 for Indonesia. To provide experience in operating larger ships for future expansion of the Iraqi fleet and has served as a transport during the Iranian war. No helicopter facilities.

GUIDED-MISSILE CORVETTES

◆ **3 (+1) modified Wadi M'ragh class** Bldr: Breda SY, Venezia: Mestre (A) or Marghera (B) yard

	Laid down	L	In serv.	Yard
211 Abdullah Ben Ari Serh	22-3-82	5-7-83	. . .	A
213 Kalid Ibn Al Walid	3-6-82	5-7-83	. . .	A
214 Sahib Ibn Ali Wakkad	17-8-82	2-12-83	. . .	B
215 Sahib Al Din Alyoobi	17-9-82	30-3-84	. . .	B

D: 600 tons (675 fl) **S:** 37.5 kts **Dim:** 62.3 (57.8 pp) × 9.3 × 2.8 (hull)
A: 6/Otomat Mk II SSM (III × 2) — 1/Albatros SAM system (IV × 1, plus 3 reload Aspide missiles) — 1/76-mm OTO Melara DP — 2/40-mm Breda Dardo AA (II × 1) — 6/324-mm ILAS-3 ASW TT (III × 2)
Electron Equipt: Radar: 1/3RM 20, 1/RAN-12 L/X, 1/Orion RTN-10X
Sonar: Diodon
EW: Electronica Gamma syst., 2/SCLAR chaff RL (XX × 2)
M: 4 MTU 20V956 TB92 diesels; 4 props; 24,400 hp (20,400 sust.)
Electric: 650 kw **Fuel:** 126 tons **Range:** 1,200/31; 4,000/18 **Man:** 51 tot.

Remarks: Ordered 2-81. Attack variant of leader version listed below. Aspide reload via manual crane. Selenia IPN-10 data system with 2 radar directors and 2 CO3 optical directors for guns. Will probably exceed 700 tons displacement by completion.

◆ **2 helicopter-equipped** Bldr: CNR, Muggiano

	Laid down	L	In serv.
F 210 Mussa Ben Mussair	15-1-82	4-12-82	8-84
F 212 Tariq Ibn Ziad	20-5-82	8-7-83	3-85

D: 610 tons (685 fl) **S:** 37.5 kts **Dim:** 62.3 (57.8 pp) × 9.3 × 2.9 (hull)
A: 2/Otomat Mk II SSM (I × 2) — 1/Albatros SAM syst. (IV × 1, plus 4 reload Aspide missiles) — 1/76-mm OTO Melara DP — 6/324-mm ILAS-3 ASW TT (III × 2) — 1/A 109A helicopter
Electron Equipt: Radar: 1/3RM 20, 1/RAN-12L/X, 1/Orion RTN-10X
Sonar: Diodon
EW: Electronica Gamma syst., 1/SCLAR chaff RL (XX × 1)

Remarks: Remaining data as per attack version above. Telescopic hangar for the helicopter.

GUIDED-MISSILE PATROL BOATS

◆ **6 Soviet Osa-II class**

D: 210 tons (240 fl) **S:** 36 kts **Dim:** 38.6 × 7.6 × 2.0
A: 4/SS-N-2B Styx (I × 4) — 4/30-mm AA (II × 2)
Electron Equipt: Radar: 1/Square Tie, 1/Drum Tilt
IFF: 2/Square Head, 1/High Pole A
M: 3 M504 diesels; 3 props; 15,000 hp **Range:** 500/34; 750/25 **Man:** 30 tot.

Remarks: Two transferred in 1974 and two in each year through 1977. Four reported lost 1980-81. Two replacements delivered 11-84.

GUIDED-MISSILE PATROL BOATS *(continued)*

◆ **4 Soviet Osa-I class**

D: 180 tons (215 fl) **S:** 36 kts **Dim:** 38.6 × 7.6 × 1.8
A: 4/SS-N-2 Styx—4/30-mm AA (II × 2)
Electron Equipt: Radar: 1/Square Tie, 1/Drum Tilt
IFF: 2/Square Head, 1/High Pole A
M: 3 M503A diesels; 3 props; 12,000 hp **Range:** 500/34; 750/25 **Man:** 30 tot.

Remarks: Two transferred 1971-72, two in 1973, and two in 1974. Of these, two have been "retired from service."

Note: Names reported for both OSA-I and OSA-II craft include: *Al Walid, Hazirani, Kanun Ath-Tani, Khalid Ibn, Nisan, Sa'd* and *Tamuz.*

TORPEDO BOATS

◆ **4 ex-Soviet P 6 class**

D: 65 tons (66.5 fl) **S:** 43 kts **Dim:** 25.3 × 6.1 × 1.7
A: 4/25-mm AA (II × 2)—2/533-mm TT (I × 2)
Electron Equipt: Radar: Pot Head
IFF: 1/Dead Duck, 1/High Pole A
M: 4 M50 diesels; 4 props; 4,800 hp **Range:** 650/26 **Man:** 2 officers, 12 men

Remarks: Two transferred 1959, four in 11-60 and six in 1-61. Six have reportedly been lost to Iranian forces, including some to Harpoon missiles. Rest probably inoperable.

PATROL BOATS AND CRAFT

◆ **3 ex-Soviet S.O.-1 class**

210 211 212

D: 190 tons (215 fl) **S:** 28 kts **Dim:** 42.0 × 6.1 × 1.9
A: 4/25-mm AA (II × 2—4/RBU-1200 ASW RL (V × 4)—2/d.c. racks—mines
Electron Equipt: Radar: 1/Pot Head
Sonar: high-frequency
M: 3 Type 40D diesels; 3 props; 7,500 hp **Range:** 340/28; 1,920/7
Man: 3 officers, 27 men

Remarks: Delivered in 1962. Probably in only marginal operating condition.

◆ **5 Soviet Zhuk class**

D: 50 tons (60 fl) **S:** 34 kts **Dim:** 24.0 × 5.0 × 1.8 (props)
A: 4/14-mm AA (II × 2) **Electron Equipt:** Radar: 1/Spin Trough
M: 2 M50 diesels; 2 props; 2,400 hp

Remarks: Transferred in 1975.

◆ **2 Soviet Poluchat-I class**

D: 80 tons (90 fl) **S:** 18 kts **Dim:** 29.6 × 6.1 × 1.9 (props)
A: 2/14.5-mm AA **Electron Equipt:** Radar: 1/Spin Trough
M: 2 M50 diesels; 2 props; 2,400 hp **Range:** 450/17; 900/10 **Man:** 20 tot.

Remarks: Transferred in 1966. May in fact be torpedo-recovery versions of the Poluchat class.

MINE WARFARE SHIPS

◆ **2 Soviet T-43-class fleet minesweepers**

465 Al Yarmouk 467 Al Kadisia

D: 500 tons (570 fl) **S:** 14 kts **Dim:** 58.0 × 8.6 × 2.3
A: 4/37-mm AA (II × 2)—8/12.7-mm mg (II × 4)—2/d.c. projectors—mines
Electron Equipt: Radar: 1/Ball End—IFF: 1/Square Head, 1/High Pole A
M: 2 Type 9D diesels; 2 props; 2,200 hp **Range:** 3,200/10

Remarks: Transferred in 1969.

◆ **3 Yevgenya-class inshore minesweepers**

D: 80 tons (90 fl) **S:** 11 kts **Dim:** 26.2 × 6.1 × 1.5 **A:** 2/25-mm AA (II × 2)
Electron Equipt: Radar: 1/Spin Trough
M: 2 diesels; 2 props; 600 hp **Range:** 300/10

Remarks: Transferred in 1975 as "oceanographic research craft." Have heavier guns than their Soviet Navy sisters.

◆ **4 Yugoslav Nestin-class river minesweepers** Bldr: Brodotehnika, Belgrade

D: 66 tons (78 fl) **S:** 15 kts **Dim:** 27.0 × 6.5 × 1.15
A: 5/20-mm AA (III × 1, I × 2)—24 mines
M: 2 diesels; 2 props; 520 hp **Range:** 860/11 **Man:** 17 tot.

Remarks: Transferred 1978-79. Have acoustic, magnetic, and mechanical sweep gear.

AMPHIBIOUS WARFARE SHIPS

◆ **3 modified roll-on/roll-off cargo ships** Bldr: Helsingor Vaerft, Denmark

	Laid down	L	In serv.
426 Al Zahraa	7-7-81	19-3-82	18-3-83
428 Khawla	19-11-81	8-82	7-83
429 Balqises	21-4-82	11-82	10-83

Al Zahraa (426) MacGregor-Navire, 1983

D: 5,800 tons (fl) **S:** 15.5 kts **Dim:** 106.0 (96.1 pp) × 18.8 × 5.25
A: . . . **M:** 2 MTU 12V1163 TB62 diesels; 2 CP props; 6,000 hp
Electric: 1,280 kw **Man:** 35 crew plus 250 troops

Remarks: 3,681 grt/3,500 dwt. Modified vehicle cargo ship design with military features. 880m² vehicle cargo space. Slewing ramp aft can handle 55-ton tanks or place tanks up to 41 tons in water. Side ramps with 50-ton capacity. Helicopter deck, 55-ton elevator to upper deck. 1,200-ton automated water ballast system.

◆ **3 Soviet Polnocny-C class** Bldr: Polnocny SY, Gdansk, Poland

D: 1,150 tons (fl) **S:** 18 kts **Dim:** 81.3 × 10.1 × 2.1
A: 4/30-mm AA (II × 2)—2/122-mm rocket launchers (XL × 2)
Electron Equipt: Radar: 1/Don-2, 1/Drum Tilt
M: 2 Type 40D diesels; 2 props; 5,000 hp **Range:** 900/17; 1,500/14

Remarks: Have a helicopter platform forward of the superstructure. Barrage rocket launchers differ from others of this class, which use 140-mm rockets. Two transferred in 1977, one in 1978, and one in 9-79. Names of first three: *Atika, Ganda,* and *Nouh.* One lost to Iranian Harpoon missiles, 1980-81.

AUXILIARY SHIPS AND CRAFT

◆ **1 Italian Stromboli-class replenishment oiler**

	Bldr	Laid down	L	In serv.
A 102 Agnadeen	Castellamare di Stabia, Naples	29-1-82	22-10-82	29-10-84

Agnadeen (A 102) C. Martinelli, 12-83

D: 8,706 tons (fl) **S:** 19.5 kts (18 sust.) **Dim:** 129.0 (118.5 pp) × 18.0 × 6.5
A: 1/76-mm OTO Melara DP
Electron Equipt: Radar: 1/3RM7-250, 1/Orion RTN-10X
M: 2 GMT A428SS diesels; 1 CP prop; 11,200 hp (9,600 sust.) **Electric:** 4,200 kw
Range: 10,000/16 **Man:** 124 tot.

Remarks: Ordered 2-81. Will probably be modified from the Italian Navy version as to cargo and equipment. Capable of serving two ships alongside while underway. Delivered 20-12-83 after fitting out at Muggiano, La Spezia. Had not sailed for Iraq as of 6-85.

◆ **1 Yugoslav Spasilac-class salvage ship** Bldr: Tito SY, Belgrade

A 51 Aka (In serv. 1978)

D: 1,590 tons (fl) **S:** 13.4 kts **Dim:** 55.50 × 12.00 × 4.34
A: 4/14.5-mm mg (II × 2) **M:** 2 diesels; 2 props; 4,340 hp **Man:** 53 tot.

IRAQ *(continued)*
AUXILIARY SHIPS AND CRAFT *(continued)*

◆ **1 transport** Bldr: Wärtsilä, Turku, Finland (In serv. 3-83)

Al Mansur

D: . . . **S:** . . . **Dim:** 121.01 (96.50 pp) × 17.53 × 5.51
A: . . .
M: 2 diesels; 2 CP props; 11,994 hp **Fuel:** 693 tons

Remarks: 7,359-grt troop transport with helicopter deck, hangar. Light armor on hull sides, bulletproof portholes.

◆ **1 presidential yacht** Bldr: Elsinore SB & Eng., Denmark

Qadissayat Saddam (L: 10-80; In serv. 1981)

Qadissayat Saddam—artist's rendering Elsinore SY, 1980

D: 1,660 tons (fl) **S:** 19.3 kts **Dim:** 82.00 × 13.00 × 3.30
M: 2 MTU 12V1163 TB82 diesels; 2 CP props; 6,000 hp
Electric: 1,095 kVA

Remarks: 2,282 grt. Can carry 56 passengers (74 additional on short cruises). Sperry retractable fin stabilizers. 300-hp bow-thruster. Helicopter deck aft above swimming pool.

◆ **1 presidential barge** Bldr: Elsinore SB & Eng., Denmark

N. . . . . . .

D: . . . **S:** . . . **Dim:** 67.0 × . . . × 1.2 **M:** . . .

Remarks: Ordered 1981. Luxurious barge-type yacht for use on the Tigris.

◆ **1 new-construction diving tender** Bldr: Gorter, The Netherlands (In serv. 10-80

N. . . . . . .

D: 200 tons (fl) **S:** 15 kts **Dim:** 28.5 (27.8 pp) × 6.4 × 1.8
M: 1 MTU 8V396 TC82 diesel; 1 prop; 870 hp

◆ **4 Soviet Nyryat-2-class diving tenders**

D: 56 tons (fl) **S:** 12 kts **Dim:** 21.3 × 3.8 × 2.0 **M:** 1 3D12 diesel; 300 hp

Remarks: May also be used as tugs.

◆ **1 Soviet Pozharney-I-class fireboat**

D: 180 tons (fl) **S:** 17 kts **Dim:** 35.0 × 6.2 × 2.0
M: 2 diesels; 2 props; 1,800 hp

◆ **1 Soviet Prometey-class tug** Bldr: Okhtenskiy SY, Leningrad

D: 319 tons (fl) **S:** 12 kts **Dim:** 29.8 (28.2 pp) × 8.3 × 3.2
M: 2 6D30/50-4 diesels; 2 Kort-nozzle props; 1,200 hp **Electric:** 50 kw
Range: 1,800/12 **Man:** 3 tot.

Remarks: Delivered mid-1970s. Has firefighting monitor.

◆ **1 new-construction floating dry dock** Bldr: Italcantiere, Trieste (In serv. 7-84)

Remarks: Ordered 2-81. 6,000-ton capacity. Still in Italy as of 6-85.

CUSTOMS SERVICE

◆ **1 yacht used as a pilot station** (In serv. 1929)

Al Thawra (ex-*Malike Aliyah*)

D: 746 tons **S:** 14 kts **M:** Diesels; 2 props; 1,800 hp

◆ **9 Tana-class pilot launches** Bldr: Kone-Jyraa Oy, Jyvasky, Finland (In serv. 1980-81)

D: . . . **S:** 33 kts **Dim:** 9.45 × 2.44 × . . .
M: 2 MTU diesels; 2 props; . . . hp

Remarks: Delivery delayed by war.

◆ **8 pilot launches** Bldr: Thornycroft, 1961-62

D: 10 tons **S:** . . . **Dim:** 11.0 × . . . × . . . **M:** 1 diesel; 125 hp

◆ **4 pilot launches** Bldr: Thornycroft

Dim: 6.4 × . . . × . . . **M:** 40 hp

◆ **6 SR. Mk 6C-class hovercraft** Bldr: British Hovercraft, Cowes

D: 17 tons **S:** 50 to 55 kts **Dim:** 18.3 × 8.5 × . . .
M: 1 Rolls-Royce Gnome gas turbine; 2 CP airscrews; 1,285 hp

Remarks: Ordered 1981. Six-ton payload; 6 to 11 hour endurance.

IRELAND

Eire

Personnel (1984): Approx. 800 active, plus 300 reserves

Merchant Marine (1984): 154 ships—221,375 grt (7 tankers—12,951 grt)

Naval Aviation: The Irish Air Force operates 3 Beech A200 Maritime Patrol Aircraft. Two longer-range maritime patrol aircraft are planned. Two Air Force-manned SA-365 Dauphin II helicopters were delivered in 1985.

FISHERIES-PROTECTION SHIPS

◆ **1 P 31 class** Bldr: Verolme DY, Cork

	Laid down	L	In serv.
P 31 Eithne	15-12-82	19-12-83	7-12-84

Eithne (P 31) Official, 1984

D: 1,760 tons (1,900 fl) **S:** 19 kts **Dim:** 81.0 × 12.0 × 4.30
A: 1/57-mm Bofors SAK 57/70 Mk 1 DP—2/20-mm Rheinmetall AA—1/SA-365 Dauphin II helicopter
Electron Equipt: Radar: 1/Decca TM 1229C, 1/Decca AC 1629C, 1/H.S.A. DA-05/4
Sonar: Plessey PMS 26L
M: 2 Ruston Paxman 12RKCM diesels; 2 CP props; 7,200 hp (6,640 sust.)
Electric: 1,625 kVA **Range:** 7,000/15 **Man:** 13 officers, 69 men, plus 4 cadets.

Remarks: P 31 ordered 23-4-82. Construction of a second unit canceled, in part because yard closed in 1983 for financial reasons. Has H.S.A. LIOD t.v./laser/IR fire-control system and 2 H.S.A. t.v./optical target designators for the 57-mm gun. Denny-Brown fin stabilizers. Considerable firefighting capability and can be replenished underway at sea. Boats include a 7.3-m crew boat, 5.5-m inspection boat, and 2 Avon Searaider semi-rigid inflatable boats with 90-hp outboard motors. Harpoon landing system for the helicopter. MEL RRB helo transponder. Carries 2 Wellop 57-mm flare RL. Has three firefighting water monitors.

◆ **3 Emer class** Bldr: Verolme, Cork

	L	In serv.
P 21 Emer	1977	18-1-78
P 22 Aoife	12-4-79	21-11-79
P 23 Aisling	3-10-79	21-5-80

D: 1,025 tons (fl) **S:** 18 kts **Dim:** 65.20 (58.50 pp) × 10.40 × 4.36
A: 1/40-mm AA—2/20-mm AA (I × 2)
Electron Equipt: Radar: 2/Decca . . .
Sonar: Simrad SU side-scan
M: 2 SEMT-Pielstick 6 PA6L-280 diesels; 1 CP prop; 4,800 hp **Fuel:** 170 tons
Range: 4,500/18; 6,750/12 **Man:** 5 officers, 41 men

Remarks: Developed version of the *Deirdre* with raised forecastle instead of bow bulwarks, to improve sea-keeping. Have advanced navigational aids, fin stabilizers. P 22 and P 23 have satellite navigation receivers, a 225-kw bow-thruster, a computerized plotting table, and a new-pattern KaMeWa propeller. Only P 23 has evaporators.

IRELAND *(continued)*
FISHERIES-PROTECTION SHIPS *(continued)*

Aoife (P 22) Verolme, 1979

◆ **1 Deirdre class** Bldr: Verolme, Cork

	L	In serv.
P 20 Deirdre	29-12-71	19-6-72

Deirdre (P 20) L. &. L. Van Ginderen, 1979

D: 980 tons (fl) **S:** 18 kts (15.5 cruising)
Dim: 62.61 (56.20 pp) × 10.40 × 4.35
A: 1/40-mm AA—2/52-mm flare launchers
M: 2 British Polar SF 112 VS-F diesels; 1 CP prop; 4,200 hp
Fuel: 150 tons **Range:** 3,000/15.5; 5,000/12 **Man:** 5 officers, 41 men

Remarks: Vosper fin stabilizers. New KaMeWa CP propeller fitted 1980.

◆ **2 ex-British "Ton"-class minesweepers**

	Bldr	In serv.
CM 10 Grainne (ex-*Oulston*)	Thornycroft	1955
CM 12 Fola (ex-*Blaxton*)	Thornycroft	1956

Grainne (CM 10) L. & L. Van Ginderen, 1983

D: 370 tons (425 fl) **S:** 15 kts **Dim:** 46.33 (42.68 pp) × 8.76 × 2.5
A: 1/40-mm AA—2/20-mm AA (II × 1)
M: 2 Mirrlees or Napier Deltic diesels; 2 props; 2,500–3,000 hp **Fuel:** 45 tons
Range: 2,300/12; 3,000/8 **Man:** 33 tot.

Remarks: Transferred in 1971. Most portable sweep gear has been landed, but winches, cable reels, and davits remain aboard. Sister *Banba* (CM 11), deactivated 1980, was stricken 1983.

AUXILIARIES AND SERVICE CRAFT

◆ **1 stores tender** Bldr: R. Dunston, U.K. 1934

John Adams

D: 94 grt **S:** 10 kts **Dim:** 25.9 × 5.6 × 2.1 **M:** 1 diesel; 216 hp

◆ **1 inshore survey launch** Bldr: Fairey Marine, Hamble (In serv. 11-78)

Hydrafix

Remarks: No data available.

◆ **1 sail-training craft** Bldr: J. Tyrell, Arklow (In serv. 7-3-81)

Asgard II

D: 120 tons (fl) **S:** . . . **Dim:** 25.6 (21.3 wl) × 6.4 × 2.9
M: 1 Kelvin 6-cyl. diesel; 1 prop; 150 hp/418.2 m² sail area **Man:** 4 crew plus 20 cadets

Remarks: Operates for both the Navy and Merchant Marine. *Tatlye,* a French-built Dufour 10.7-m sailboat, is also in service.

◆ **4 passenger and service launches**

Colleen II (In serv. 1972) Raven II (In serv. 1938)
Sir Cecil Romer (In serv. 1938) Jackdaw (In serv. 1938)

◆ **1 fuel barge**

Chowl—**D:** 100 tons **M:** 1 diesel; 50 hp

Note: In 1985, the Irish Naval Reserve (*An Slua Muiri*) operated the 13.7-m motorboat *Kathleen Roma,* bermuda ketches *Creidne* (15.8 m) and *Nancy Bet* (14.6 m), and five 5.5-m sail/oar boats.

ISRAEL

State of Israel

Personnel (1984): Active: 3,500, of whom 250 officers and 500 men are especially trained as commandos and frogmen. Reserves: 500 total.

Merchant Marine (1984): 64 ships—563,189 grt (tankers: 4 ships—991 grt)

Naval Aviation: During 1978 the Israeli Navy put into service three IAI Westwind 1124 Sea Scan maritime-reconnaissance aircraft, whose mission is to cooperate with surface forces. Range: 1,350 n.m. at 270 kts. Carry sonobuoys. AB 206 helicopters are used on the *Aliyah*-class missile boats.

WEAPONS AND SYSTEMS

The Israeli Navy uses foreign equipment, such as 76-mm OTO Melara Compact, Breda 40-mm, and Oerlikon guns, and it has perfected the Gabriel anti-ship missile systems.

Gabriel is a 400-kg, solid-propellant, surface-to-surface missile. After being fired, it climbs about 100 meters, then, at 7,500 meters from the launcher, descends slowly to an altitude of 20 meters. Optical or radar guidance is provided in azimuth, and a radio altimeter determines altitude. At a distance of 1,200 meters from the target, the missile descends to 3 meters, under either radio command or semiactive homing. The explosive charge is a 75-kg conventional warhead.

The Gabriel II carries a television camera and a transceiver for azimuth and altitude commands. The television is energized when the missile has attained a certain height and sends to the firing ship a picture of the areas that cannot be picked up by shipboard radar. The operator then can send any necessary corrections during the middle and final phases of the missile's flight, and thus find a target that cannot be seen either by the naked eye or on radar. The range of the Gabriel II is about 40,000 meters.

The Gabriel III system now entering service employs a frequency-agile, home-on-jam active radar seeker. An air-launched "Mk 3A/S" version is in development for launch from F-4, Mirage, Kfir, and A-4 Skyhawk aircraft. The sea-launched version has a range of 36,000 m at Mach .73, weighs 560 kg, and is 3.8 m long. Mk 3A/S weighs 600 kg, and has a range of 60,000 m, being launchable at 300 to 30,000-foot altitudes.

The Barak surface-to-air point-defense system, originally developed for use with an elevatable/trainable 8-cell box-launcher, will now use a 32-cell vertical launch group:

Weight: 87 kg Speed: Mach 1.8
Length: 2.5 m Guidance: Semi-active homing
Warhead: 22 kg Range: 10 km

Barak's system weight with 32 rounds requires 1.3 m² deck space plus 2 m³ belowdecks volume. The intended fire-control system employs the AMDR (Advanced Missile Detection Radar), an S-band, pulse-doppler set capable of tracking 250 Mach 0.3 to 3.0 targets. To become operational late 1980s.

Also in use are U.S.-supplied Redeye hand-held, IR-homing missiles.

The U.S. Harpoon was acquired beginning in 1978 and is used on guided-missile patrol boats in a mix with Gabriel.

Israeli Aircraft Industries and Oerlikon were cooperating in the development of a 30-mm antiaircraft gun mounting, the PCM-30. The system would replace 40-mm AA guns in earlier Israeli missile combatants, but it may have been canceled. Fourteen U.S. Vulcan/Phalanx 20-mm close-in weapon systems have been ordered for use in various units of the Sa'ar classes.

WEAPONS AND SYSTEMS *(continued)*

A Barak SAM being fired from an octuple launcher on a Reshev-class unit I.A.I., 1982

SUBMARINES

NOTE: Three new submarines, to be built with U.S. aid, are planned to replace the relatively new units below by the early 1990s. The design will probably be prepared by IKL, Lübeck, West Germany, and the ships will either be built entirely in Europe, or shipped as kits for assembly in Israel.

◆ **3 German Type 206** Bldr: Vickers, Barrow, U.K.

	Laid down	L	In serv.
GAL	1973	2-12-75	12-76
TANIN	1974	25-10-76	6-77
RAHAV	1975	1977	12-77

Gal 1982

D: 420/600 tons **Dim:** 17/11 kts **S:** 45.0 × 4.7 × 3.8
A: 8/533-mm TT, fwd 10 U.S. NT-37 torpedoes sub-Harpoon missiles
M: 2 MTU 12V493 TY60 diesels (600 hp each); AEG generators; 1 prop; 1,800 hp
Man: 22 tot.

REMARKS: Ordered in 4-72. Vickers Type 500. Carry two spare torpedoes. These submarines do *not* carry the Vickers SLAM submarine-launched antiaircraft missile systems, although provision was made for its installation. U.S. Sub-Harpoon missiles provided and fire-control systems altered, 1983.

GUIDED-MISSILE CORVETTES

◆ **0 (+5 or 6) Sa'ar V class** Bldr: . . .

D: 1,000–1,200 tons **S:** . . . **Dim:** 75.0 × . . . × . . .
A: Harpoon and Gabriel III/IV missiles — Barak SAM system (32 vertical-launch missiles) — guns — ASW torpedoes — helicopter
Electron Equipt: Radar: . . .
Sonar: . . . — EW: . . .
M: CODOG: 1 LM-2500 gas turbine, 2 . . . diesels; . . . hp
Range: . . . **Man:** . . .

REMARKS: Design, still in definition as of mid-1985, is not related to the 850-ton corvette proposed by Israeli Shipyard some years ago. Considerable U.S. technology will be incorporated, with prototype possibly to be built in U.S. Rockwell is the prime combat system integration contractor.

GUIDED-MISSILE PATROL BOATS

◆ **2 (+1) Romat class** Bldr: Israeli SY, Haifa

	L	In serv.
ROMAT	1981	10-81
KESHET	10-82	1982
N.	. . .	. . .

Keshet 1984

D: 500 tons (fl) **S:** 31 kts **Dim:** 61.7 × 7.6 × 2.4
A: 4/Harpoon SSM (II × 2) — 6/Gabriel III (I × 6) — 1/76-mm OTO Melara DP — 1/20-mm Mk 15 CIWS (Vulcan-Phalanx gatling AA) — 2/20-mm AA (I × 2) — 2/12.7-mm mg (I × 2)
Electron Equipt: Radar: 1/TH-D 1040 Neptune, 1/Orion RTN-10X
EW: MN-53 intercept system — 1/45-tube chaff RL, 4/24-tube chaff RL, 4/single chaff RL
M: 4 MTU 16V956 TB91 diesels; 4 props; 14,000 hp
Range: 1,500/30; 4,000/17
Man: 45 tot.

REMARKS: Employ the lengthened *Aliyah*-class hull, substituting additional armament for the helicopter facility. Apparently only three are to be built. Can carry up to 8 Harpoon or up to 8 Gabriel.

◆ **2 Aliyah (Sa'ar 4.5) class** Bldr: Israeli SY, Haifa

	L	In serv.
ALIYAH	10-7-80	8-80
GEOULA	10-80	31-12-80

Aliyah — with Mk 15 CIWS forward, 8 SSM 11-84

D: 500 tons (fl) **S:** 31 kts **Dim:** 61.7 × 7.6 × 2.4
A: 4/Harpoon SSM (II × 2) — 4/Gabriel SSM (I × 4) — *Aliyah*: 1/40-mm AA — 2/20-mm AA (I × 2) — 4/12.7-mm mg (I × 4) — 1 AB 206 helicopter
Electron Equipt: Radar: 1/TH-D 1040 Neptune, 1/Orion RTN-10X
EW: MN-53 intercept system — 1/45-tube chaff RL, 4/24-tube chaff RL, 4/single chaff RL
M: 4/MTU 16V956 TB91 diesels; 4 props; 14,000 hp
Range: 1,500/30; 4,000/17 **Man:** 53 tot.

REMARKS: The helicopters were intended to provide an over-the-horizon targeting capability to utilize fully the range capabilities of the Harpoon missiles, which are mounted athwartships in the gap between the fixed hangar and the bridge superstructure. Each *Aliyah* was to lead a group of missile boats. U.S. Mk 15 CIWS will replace the 40-mm mount forward.

◆ **7 Reshev (Sa'ar IV) class** Bldr: Israeli SY, Haifa

	L	In serv.		L	In serv.
KIDON	7-74	9-74	NITZAHON	10-7-78	9-78
TARSHISH	1-75	3-75	HATZMAAT	3-12-78	2-79
YAFO	2-75	4-75	MOLEDET	22-3-79	5-79
			KOMEMIYUT	19-7-79	8-80

GUIDED-MISSILE PATROL BOATS *(continued)*

A Reshev—with 4 Harpoon, 6 Gabriel, and Mk 15 CIWS forward 11-83

A Reshev—with 2 Harpoon, 6 Gabriel, two speedboats on davits, and Mk 15 CIWS 1983

D: 415 tons (450 fl) **S:** 32 kts **Dim:** 58.1 × 7.6 × 2.4
A: 2/Harpoon SSM (I or II × 2 or IV × 1)—4–6 Gabriel SSM (I)—1/76-mm OTO Melara Compact—1/20-mm Mk 15 CIWS gatling AA—2/20-mm AA (I × 2)—2/12.7-mm mg (I × 2)
Electron Equipt: Radar: 1/Thomson-CSF Neptune TH-D 1040, 1 Selenia Orion RTN-10X
EW: Elta MN-53 intercept—0 or 1/45-tube chaff RL, 4 or 6/24-tube chaff RL, 4/single chaff RL
M: 4 MTU 16V956 TB91 diesels; 4 props; 14,000 hp (10,680 sust.)
Range: 1,650/30; 4,000/17.5 **Man:** 45 tot.

Remarks: Quarters are air-conditioned. The *Tarshish* had a temporary helicopter deck in place of the after 76-mm gun for experiment with over-the-horizon targeting for Harpoon in 1979. Original missile armament was seven Gabriel. The Gabriel launchers are fixed. The 76-mm guns have been specially adapted for shore bombardment. The forward 76-mm mount was replaced by a 40-mm AA in *Nitzahon* and *Komemiyut,* pending availability of the U.S. Vulcan/Phalanx CIWS, the first of which was fitted to a *Reshev* in 2-83; all had it by 1985. Sisters *Keshet* and *Romach* were transferred to Chile 1979-80, and *Reshev* followed in 2-84, with a possible fourth to follow. Three were built in Israel for South Africa, with others built under license at Durban. The elaborate ECM/ESM system was designed by the Italian firm Elettronica.

◆ 6 Sa'ar III class Bldr: Constr. Méc. de Normandie, Cherbourg

	L		L
Sa'ar	25-11-69	Herev	20-6-69
Soufa	4-2-69	Hanit	1969
Gaasch	24-6-69	Hetz	14-12-69

Sa'ar III—with 2 Harpoon, 3 Gabriel, 1/76-mm gun French Navy, 1983

◆ 6 Sa'ar II class Bldr: Constr. Méc. de Normandie, Cherbourg

	L		L
Mivtach	11-4-67	Eilath	14-6-68
Miznag	1967	Haifa	14-6-68
Misgav	1967	Akko	1968

EDO 780 variable-depth sonar on a Sa'ar II French Navy, 1982

Miznag—Sa'ar II with 5 Gabriel, 1/40-mm AA 1978

D: 220 tons (250 fl) **S:** 40 kts **Dim:** 45.0 × 7.0 × 1.8 (2.5 fl)
A: *Sa'ar II:* 5/Gabriel SSM (III × 1, I × 2)—2/40-mm AA Breda (I × 2)—2/12.7-mm mg—*see* Remarks
Sa'ar III: 2/Harpoon SSM (I × 2)—3/Gabriel SSM (III × 1)—1/76-mm DP OTO Melara—4/12.7-mm mg (I × 4)
Electron Equipt: Radar: 1/Thomson-CSF Neptune TH-D 1040, 1/Selenia Orion RTN-10X
EW: VHFD/F and Elta MN-53 intercept gear—6/24-tube chaff RL, 4/1-tube chaff RL
M: 4 MTU MD871 diesels; 4 props; 14,000 hp **Fuel:** 30 tons
Range: 1,000/30; 1,600/20; 2,500/15 **Man:** 5 officers, 30-35 men

Remarks: Excellent sea qualities and endurance. *Sa'ar I* is the name that was used for these ships in an all-gun configuration. Four units of the *Sa'ar II* variant now carry an EDO 780 variable-depth sonar and 2/324-mm Mk 32 single ASW TT (Mk 46 torpedoes) aft and have no after gunmount. *Sa'ar III* has no ASW capability. Armaments now fairly standardized, but triple Gabriel launchers can be interchanged with the after 40-mm mountings.

GUIDED-MISSILE HYDROFOILS

◆ 3 Grumman Mk II/M 161 class

	Bldr	L	In serv.
Shimrit	Lantana BY, Lantana, Fla.	26-5-81	7-82
Livnit	Israeli SY, Haifa	1981	1983
Snapirit	Israel, SY, Haifa	. . .	6-85

Shimrit—on trials Grumman, 1981

GUIDED-MISSILE HYDROFOILS *(continued)*

Livnit, at rest, foils down, no Gabriel aboard French Navy, 11-83

D: 71 tons light (103.5 fl) **S:** 45 kts (52 designed)
Dim: 31.79 foils retracted (25.62 hull; 23.40 wl) × 12.95 (7.32 hull) × 4.75 at rest (1.93 foiling; 1.52 foils retracted)
A: 4/Harpoon SSM (II × 2)—2/Gabriel SSM (I × 2)—2/30-mm BMARC AA (II × 1)—2/12.7-mm mg (I × 2)
M: 1 Allison 501-KF gas turbine; 1 CP, 4-bladed prop; 5,400 hp—2 G.M. 6V53 diesels driving retractable 80-hp hydraulic motors for hull-borne maneuvering
Electric: 400 kw (2 Pratt & Whitney ST-6 gas turbines)
Fuel: 21 tons **Endurance:** 3 to 5 days **Range:** 750/42 foiling
Man: 15 tot.

Remarks: Ordered 1978 from Grumman, with prototype construction subcontracted to Lantana. Numerous delays in program. *Livnit* built simultaneously at Haifa. Aluminum construction. Pineapple-shaped radome conceals intercept array. Maximum speed on auxiliary system: 10 kts. Turning radius at 45 kts: 200 m. Design based on U.S. Navy's *Flagstaff* (PGH 2). *Livnit* has navigational radar atop radome, different engine air intakes. Original plans for 15 cut to 3 in 1982.

PATROL CRAFT

◆ **1 Dvora class** Bldr: Israeli Aircraft Industries, 1978

D: 47 tons (fl) **S:** 36 kts **Dim:** 21.62 × 5.49 × 0.94 (1.82 props)
A: 2/20-mm AA (I × 2)—2/12.7-mm mg **Electron Equipt:** Radar: 1/Decca 926
M: 2 MTU 12V331 TC81 diesels; 2 props; 2,720 hp
Electric: 30 kw **Range:** 700/32 **Man:** 8-10 tot.

Remarks: Privately funded prototype, acquired in 1979. The design has been offered with two Gabriel SSM and has been exported to Nicaragua, Argentina, and Chile without missiles.

◆ **37 Dabur class** Bldrs: 12 by Sewart Seacraft, U.S.A.; others by Israeli Air Industries, 1973-77

Dabur class U.S. Navy, 3-82

D: 25 tons (35 fl) **S:** 25 kts **Dim:** 19.8 × 5.8 × 0.8
A: 2/20-mm (I × 2)—2/12.7-mm mg (I × 2)
Electron Equipt: Radar: 1/Decca 101 or 926
M: 2 G.M. 12V71 TI diesels; 2 props; 960 hp
Electric: 20 kw **Range:** 1,200/17 **Man:** 1 officer, 5 men

Remarks: Quarters air-conditioned and spacious. Five given to Christian forces in Lebanon in 1976.

◆ **up to 28 Yatush class (U.S. PBR type)**

D: 6.5 tons (8.9 fl) **S:** 25 kts **Dim:** 9.73 × 3.53 × 0.81
A: 2/7.62-mm mg **M:** 2 G.M. 6V53N diesels; Jacuzzi water jets; 430 hp
Range: 150/23 **Man:** 5 tot.

Remarks: Early units built by Uniflite, Bellingham, Washington, bought in the United States in 1968, later ones built in Israel. Several may be stationed in the Red Sea. Two given to Lebanese Christians, 1975-76.

AMPHIBIOUS WARFARE SHIPS

◆ **1 former commercial landing craft** Bldr: . . . , West Germany

Bat Sheva (In serv. 1967)

Bat Sheva 1969

D: 900 tons (1,150 fl) **S:** 10 kts **Dim:** 95.1 × 11.2 × . . .
A: 4/20-mm—4/12.7-mm mg **M:** Diesels; 2 props **Man:** 26 tot.

Remarks: Bought in South Africa in 1968. Construction of two new landing ships is planned: approx. 117.0 × 17.0 × 2.2, helicopter platform, facilities for several hundred troops.

◆ **3 LCT type** Bldr: Israeli SY, Haifa (In serv. 1966-67)

Ashdod Ashkelon Ahziv

Ashdod 1971

D: 400 tons (730 fl) **S:** 10.5 kts **Dim:** 62.7 × 10.0 × 1.8
A: 2/20-mm AA (I × 2) **M:** 3 MWM diesels; 3 props; 1,900 hp
Fuel: 37 tons **Man:** 20 tot.

◆ **3 Etziongueber class** Bldr: Israeli SY, Haifa (In serv. 1965)

Etziongueber Shikmona Kessaraya

Etziongueber

D: 182 tons (230 fl) **S:** 10 kts **Dim:** 30.5 × 5.9 × 1.3
A: 2/20-mm AA (I × 2) **M:** Diesels; 2 props; 1,280 hp **Man:** 10 tot.

VARIOUS SHIPS

◆ **1 training ship**

Nogah

Remarks: Former small cargo vessel equipped as a training ship for the merchant marine.

◆ **1 small missile-boat tender**

Naharya

Remarks: Base craft for the missile craft stationed at Eilath.

◆ **1 missile-boat tender** Bldr: Todd SY, Seattle (In serv. 1976)

Ma'oz

Remarks: 4,000-ton oilfield-supply type used as a missile-boat tender in the Mediterranean.

ITALY

Italian Republic

PERSONNEL (1985): 41,900, including 5,200 officers and the San Marco (Marine) battalion

MERCHANT MARINE (1984): 1,590 ships; 9,157,867 grt (tankers: 282 ships; 4,843,042 grt)

NAVAL AVIATION: The Marinavia operates only helicopters, of which some 64 are in service: 25 SH-3D Sea King heavy ASW (now shore-based and aboard *Giuseppe Garibaldi*), 27 AB-212 light ASW helicopters for service aboard frigates and destroyers, and 12 AB-204B light ASW helicopters for training. Plans call for an eventual total of 48 AB-212 and 36 SH-3D. In 12-84, the Navy requested authorization for 22 Sea Harrier V/STOL fighter-bombers, but it faces Air Force opposition.

The Air Force conducts fixed-wing maritime ASW patrol, using 18 Bréguet Atlantics ordered in 1968 and delivered by 1973, and 8 Grumman S-2F Tracker medium-range aircraft. The Atlantics are based at Catania (No. 86 Squadron) and Cagliari/Elmas (No. 88 Squadron), and No. 87 Tracker Squadron is based at Catania. There are plans to increase the Atlantic total to 32 and to retire the Trackers.

The Bell AB-204B and AB-212 are built under license from Bell Helicopter by Agusta in Italy. Principal characteristics are:

AB-204B

Ceiling: 10,800 ft	Length: 17.4 m
Range: 2 hr 5 min without torpedoes 1 hr 15 min with torpedoes	Rotor: 14.6 m Max. weight: 4,310 kg
Armament: 2 Mk 46 or A-244 torpedoes or 4 AS-12 missiles	Motor: 1 turboshaft, 1,200 hp Max. speed: 104 kts
Electronics: ASQ-13 sonar	Cruising speed: 90 kts
Crew: 3	

AB-212

Ceiling: 5,000 ft	Length: 17.4 m
Range: 4 hr 15 min (360 nm at 100 kts)	Rotor: 14.6
Armament: 2 Mk 46 or A-244 torpedoes, depth charges, or 2 AS-12 ASM missiles	Max. weight: 5,086 kg; 3,240 light Motor: 1 turboshaft, 1,290 hp
Electronics: ASQ-13B sonar	Max. speed: 130 kts
Crew: 3	Cruising speed: 100 kts

NOTE: A new ASW helicopter, the EH-101, is being jointly developed by Agusta and Westland in Great Britain to succeed the SH-3D in the late 1980s; see page 183 for data.

WARSHIPS IN SERVICE, UNDER CONSTRUCTION, OR AUTHORIZED AS OF 1 JANUARY 1986

	L	TONS	MAIN ARMAMENT
◆ **1 helicopter carrier**			
1 GIUSEPPE GARIBALDI	1983	10,100	4/Otomat, 2/Albatros, 16/helicopters
◆ **10 (+2) submarines**			
		Tons (surfaced)	
4 (+2) NAZARIO SAURO	1976-. . .	1,456	6/533-mm TT
4 ENRICO TOTI	1967-68	535	4/533-mm TT
2 TANG	1951	2,100	8/533-mm TT
◆ **3 cruisers**			
		Tons	
1 VITTORIO VENETO	1967	7,500	1/missile launcher, 8/76.2-mm, 9/helicopters
2 ANDREA DORIA	1962-63	6,500	1/missile launcher, 8/76.2-mm, 4/helicopters
◆ **4 (+2) destroyers**			
0 (+2) ANIMOSO	1989-90	4,400	1/missile launcher, 2/127-mm, ASW weapons
2 AUDACE	1971	3,950	1/missile launcher, 2/127-mm, ASW weapons
2 IMPAVIDO	1962	3,201	1/missile launcher, 2/127-mm, ASW weapons
◆ **14 frigates**			
8 MAESTRALE	1981-	3,040	4/Otomat, 1/Sea Sparrow, 1/127-mm, ASW weapons
4 LUPO	1976-79	2,208	8/Otomat, 1/Sea Sparrow, 1/127-mm, ASW weapons
2 ALPINO	1967	2,000	6/76-mm, ASW weapons
◆ **8 (+8) Corvettes**			
0 (+8) MINERVA	. . .	. . .	4/Otomat, 1/Albatros, 1/76-mm, ASW weapons
4 PIETRO DE CRISTOFARO	1964-65	850	2/76-mm, ASW weapons
4 ALBATROS	1954	800	2/40-mm, ASW weapons

◆ **7 missile hydrofoils**

◆ **34 (+6) mine countermeasures ships**

◆ **3 (+2) amphibious ships**

WEAPONS AND SYSTEMS

A. MISSILES

◆ Surface-to-air

Standard SM-1 ER and SM-1 MR (*see* under U.S.A.)

Albatros Aspide (Italian version of the Sea Sparrow) Bldr: Selenia

Ceiling: 15 m (min.); 5,000 m (max.)	Diameter: 0.20 m
Length: 3.70 m	Weight: 204 kg
Wingspan: 1.02 m	Guidance: semiactive homing
Range: 10,000 m	

This equipment employs an octuple launcher built by OTO Melara and weighing 7 tons; elevation: 5 to +65 degrees. Controlled by NA-30 system. A quadruple launcher has been produced for use on export corvettes.

◆ Surface-to-surface

Otomat Mk 1 Bldr: OTO Melara/Matra

Length: 4,820 m	Diameter: 1,060 m (with boosters); 460 m (without boosters)
Wingspan: 1.19 m	Weight: 750 kg
Range: 60-80 km	Guidance: Thomson-CSF active homing, 3-axis

This missile flies almost at sea level after firing, climbs at a steep angle to a predetermined height, and strikes its target during descent.

Otomat Mk 2 (also known as "Teseo")

This model differs from the Mk 1 in having an Italian (SMA) active radar homing head, instead of a French one. It is also a "sea-skimmer"; that is, it flies close to the water after firing. Its explosive charge is about 200 kg and its ramjet propulsion system allows it to be used at ranges limited only by its guidance system and its target designation. Range: 150 km; speed: 300 m/sec.

Two additional projects are in development: "Briaero," a Mach 1.0 weapon with a 200–400 km range, and "Otomach," a Mach 2, turbojet-powered weapon being developed by OTO Melara and Alfa-Romeo.

◆ Air-to-surface

The French S.N.I.A.S. AS-12 wire-guided anti-shipping missile has been adopted for use by helicopters, and the Marte Mk 2 is in production for use by Sea King helicopters:

Length: 4.84 m (with 1.09m booster)	Speed: Mach 0.8
Diameter: 31.6 cm	Range: over 20 km
Span: 98.7 cm (cruciform)	Warhead: 70 kg
Weight: 340 kg	

Guidance is by gyro autopilot and radar altimeter over mid-course, with active pseudo-monopulse radar homing, using the Otomat's seeker. Fuzing is influence and impact. The airframe is that of the Sistel Sea Killer surface-launched anti-ship missile.

B. GUNS

40-mm Breda/Bofors Compact twin

Length: 70 calibers
Muzzle velocity: 1,000 m/sec.
Max. effective range, antiaircraft fire: 3,500–4,000 m
Rate of fire: 300 rounds/min/barrel
Projectile weight: 0.96 kg
Number of ready-service rounds: 444 or 736 (depending on installation)
Fire control: Dardo system (Selenia RTN-20X radar)
Impact or proximity fusing

76-mm OTO Melara

Single- or twin-barreled, automatic, for air, surface, and land targets

Length: 62 calibers
Muzzle velocity: 850 m/sec
Max. effective range, surface fire: 8,000 m
Max. effective range, antiaircraft fire: 4,000–5,000 m
Rate of fire: 60 rounds/min/barrel

GUNS *(continued)*

76-mm OTO Melara Compact

Single-barreled light antiaircraft automatic fire; entirely remote control with muzzle brake and cooling system

Length: 62 calibers
Muzzle velocity: 925 m/sec
Max. effective range, surface fire: 8,000 m
Max. effective range, antiaircraft fire: 4,000–5,000 m
Rate of fire: 85 rounds/min
Weight of mount: 7.35 tons, because of the use of light alloys and fiberglass; 80 ready-service rounds in the drum.

127-mm OTO Melara Compact

Single-barreled automatic triple-purpose, remote control

Length: 54 calibers
Muzzle velocity: 807 m/sec
Max. effective range, surface fire: 15,000 m
Max. effective range, antiaircraft fire: 7,000 m
Rate of fire: 45 rounds/ min, automatic setting
Weight of the mount: 32 tons because of the use of light alloys and a fiberglass shield. The gun has a muzzle brake; it can automatically fire 66 rounds, thanks to 3 loading drums, each with 22 rounds. Two hoists serve two loading trays with rounds coming from the magazine, and a drum may be loaded even while the gun is firing. An automatic selection system allows a choice of ammunition (antiaircraft, surface target, pyrotechnics, chaff for cluttering radar).

This equipment has also been purchased by the Canadian Navy for its *Iroquois*-class destroyers.

C. ANTISUBMARINE WEAPONS

K113 Menon mortar

The system has a single 305-mm barrel some 4.6 m long, with automatic loading. Fire control is usually directed in the underwater battery plot. The mortar is fired at a 45-degree angle, with the range fixed by a system similar to that of the no-longer-used triple-barreled Menon; firing 160-kg depth-charges round by round; gas relief valves from three powder chambers have adjustable vents; range varies from 400 to 900 m. The weapon is automatically reloaded from the magazine by hoist and a loading drum.

Torpedoes

American Mk 46 and Italian Whitehead Motofides A-244 small ASW torpedoes are used on ships (using the triple ILAS-3 tube mount, a version of the U.S. Mk 32 ASW torpedo tube set) and helicopters.

The Whitehead Motofides A-184 wire-guided torpedo uses a 533-mm carrier torpedo that ejects an A-244 passive homing torpedo; range is over 15,000 m. A-290, a 50-knot weapon using the A-244's seeker has been in development since 1981 and was to begin trials in 1984; it will use a lithium battery.

D. RADARS

The Italian Navy has used a number of American radars (SPS-6, SPS-12, SPS-52, etc.) but now primarily has a number of systems developed in Italy, including:

Type	Band	Remarks
RTN-10X Orion	I/J(X)	Gun and missile fire control (Argo system)
RTN-20X Orion	I/J(X)	With Dardo system (40-mm gun)
SPQ-2D	I/J(X)	Combined surveillance
RAN-3L	D(S)	Air search, 3-dimensional
RAN-10S	E/J (S/X)	Combined surveillance
RAN-11X	I/J(X)	Combined air/surface search
RAN-12X	I/J(X)	Combined air/surface search (in development)
RAN-20S	E/F(S)	Air search
RTN-30X	I/J(X)	Target acquisition (Albatros system)
3 RM series	I/J(X)	Navigation and surface search
MM/SPN-749(V)	I(X)	Navigation set on *Garibaldi;* 2 antennas

E. SONARS

Most of the newest equipment is American or Dutch.

	Type	Frequency		Type	Frequency
CWE 610	Hull	LF(Dutch)	SQS-10	Hull	MF
DE 1160B	Hull	MF	SQS-4	Hull	MF
DE 1164	VDS	MF	SQA-10	VDS	MF
SQS-23	Hull	MF	SQS-36	VDS	HF
SQS-29	Hull	MF	SQQ-14	Minehunting	HF
SQS-11A	Hull	MF			

F. TACTICAL INFORMATION SYSTEM

The Italian Navy has developed the SADOC system, which is compatible with the American NTDS and the French SENIT.

G. COUNTERMEASURES

A wide variety of intercept arrays, many with stabilized cylindrical radome antennas, are in use. The Breda SCLAR chaff rocket-launching system is used on frigates and larger ships; it has 20 tubes for 105-mm rockets in a trainable, elevatable launcher. A number of Wallops Barricade chaff rocket launchers were ordered 1984.

HELICOPTER CARRIER

◆ 1 Garibaldi class

	Bldr	Laid down	L	In serv.
C 551 Giuseppe Garibaldi	Italcantieri, Monfalcone	26-3-81	7-6-83	30-9-85

D: 10,100 tons (13,139 fl) **S:** 29.5 kts
Dim: 180.2 (162.8 pp) × 30.4 (23.8 wl) × 6.7
A: 4/Otomat-Teseo Mk 2 SSM (I × 4)—2/Albatros SAM (VIII × 2; 46 Aspide missiles)—6/40-mm AA Breda Dardo (II × 3)—6/324-mm ILAS-3 ASW TT (III × 2)—16/SH-3D Sea King helicopters
Electron Equipt: Radar: 1/RAN-3L, 1/RAN-20S, 1/RAN-10S, 1/SPS-702 surface search, 1/MM/SPN-749(V) navigational (2 antennas)—3/RTN-20X, 2/RTN-30X
Sonar: Raytheon DE 1160
EW: passive intercept arrays—2/SCLAR chaff RL (XX × 2)
TACAN: . . .

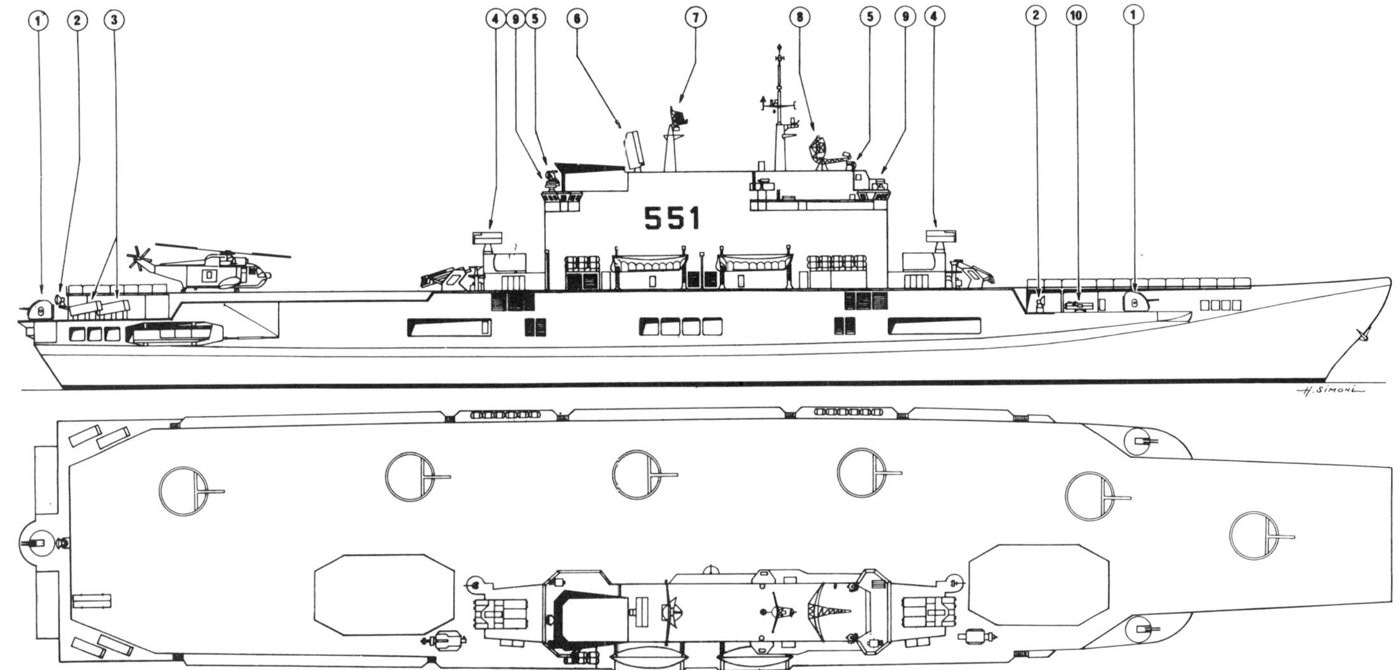

Giuseppe Garibaldi 1. Twin 40-mm AA 2. Dardo system radar (RTN-20X) 3. Otomat MK II launchers 4. Albatros SAM launchers 5. RTN-30X radar for Albatros/Aspide 6. RAN-3L 3-dimensional air-search radar 7. RAN-10S surface/air-search radar 8. RAN-20S air-search radar 9. SCLAR chaff launchers

HELICOPTER CARRIER *(continued)*

Giuseppe Garibaldi (C 551) on trials Italian Navy, 1985

M: 4 G.E./Fiat LM 2500 gas turbines; 2 CP props; 80,000 hp
Electric: 9,360 kw (6 GMT B230-12M diesel alternator sets)
Range: 7,000/20 **Man:** 560 tot. (accommodations for 825)

REMARKS: Began sea trials 1-85. The *Garibaldi* is essentially an ASW ship for helicopters, although the design would permit the handling of V/STOL aircraft as well. The flight deck is 173.8 meters long. There are two elevators, one forward of and one abaft the island. There are six flight-deck spaces for flight operations. The hangar (110 × 15 × 6 meters) can accommodate 12 Sea King, or 10 Sea Harrier and 1 Sea King, although political considerations have precluded acquisition of the "offensive" Sea Harrier to date. Steel superstructure and hull. To permit helicopter operations in heavy weather, much attention was given to stability, and the ship has two pairs of fin stabilizers; the bow has a small "ski-jump" sheer, officially to improve deck dryness. There are five decks; the flight deck; the hangar deck, which is also the main deck; and two decks and a platform deck below the hangar deck. Thirteen watertight bulkheads divide the ship into 14 sections. Has IPN-20 computerized data system, capable of handling 200 threat tracks simultaneously. Additional photo in addenda.

SUBMARINES

NOTE: Planned are 4 to 6 S-90-class submarines to replace the *Toti* and *Tang* classes. Of some 1,500–2,000 tons submerged displacement, the first is planned to be laid down in 1988 for delivery in 1993-94. Will have 22-kt submerged speed and carry 12 torpedoes (6 tubes).

◆ **4 (+2) Nazario Sauro class** Bldr: C.R.D.A., Monfalcone (last two: Italcantiere, Monfalcone)

	Laid down	L	In serv.
S 518 NAZARIO SAURO	26-6-74	9-10-76	1-3-80
S 519 CARLO FECIA DI COSSATO	15-7-76	16-11-77	1-3-80
S 520 LEONARDO DA VINCI	1-7-76	20-10-79	6-11-82
S 521 GUGLIERMO MARCONI	23-10-79	20-9-80	16-10-82
S. . . N.	. . .	1986	. . .
S. . . N.	. . .	1987	. . .

Leonardo da Vinci (S 520)—with Maestrale (F 570) in background Italian Navy, 1982

Carlo Fecia di Cossato (S 519) C. Martinelli, 3-83

D: 1,456 surf./1,641 tons sub. **S:** 14 kts surf./12 kts snorkel/20 kts sub.
Dim: 63.85 × 6.83 × . . . (12.38 keel to top of sail)
A: 6/533-mm B.512 TT fwd (12 Type A-184 torpedoes)
Electron Equipt: Radar: MM/BPS-704
Sonar: USEA/ Selenia IPD-70S system, Velox M5
M: 3 GMT A210 16M diesel generators (2,160 kw), 1 twin, 3,140-kw motor; 1 prop; 4,270 hp
Fuel: 144 tons **Endurance:** 45 days
Range: 12,500/11 surf; 7,000/12; 12,500/4 snorkel; 300+/4 sub.
Man: 6 officers, 43 men

REMARKS: First two authorized 1972; second pair ordered 12-2-76. Third pair (to have longer tubes to accommodate U.S. Harpoon missiles) ordered 7-3-83. Can travel 20 knots submerged for 1 hour, or 100 hours at 4 knots. Maximum diving depth is over 250 meters. Seven-bladed propeller. Completion of first pair delayed by need to replace original batteries. Batteries: 2 148-cell, 6,000 Amp/hr, one hour rate. Can maintain 19.3 kts for one hour submerged. Have SISU-1 fire-control system, which can track 4 targets simultaneously. Sonar system operates 200 Hz—7 kHz passive, 8–15 kHz active, and has active, passive, passive-ranging, and surveillance modes.

◆ **4 Enrico Toti class** Bldr: C.R.D.A., Monfalcone

	Laid down	L	In serv.
S 505 ATTILIO BAGNOLINI	15-4-65	28-8-67	22-6-68
S 506 ENRICO TOTI	15-4-65	12-3-67	22-1-68
S 513 ENRICO DANDOLO	10-3-67	16-12-67	29-9-68
S 514 LAZZARO MOCENIGO	12-6-67	20-4-68	11-1-69

Enrico Toti (S 506) 1978

Enrico Dandolo (S 513) G. Gyssels, 3-83

D: 535 tons surf./591 sub. **S:** 9.7 kts surf./14 sub. **Dim:** 46.20 × 4.75 × 3.99
A: 4/533-mm TT (6 A-184 torpedoes)
Electron Equipt: Radar: 1/3 RM-20/SMG
Sonar: JP-64 active, Velox passive
M: Diesel-electric propulsion: 2 Fiat/MB 820 diesels; 1 electric motor; 1 prop; 2,200 hp
Range: 7,500/4.5 **Man:** 4 officers, 22 men

REMARKS: Can make 15 kts for one hour submerged. Diving depth: 180 m.

◆ **U.S. Tang class** Bldr: Electric Boat, Groton, Connecticut

	Laid down	L	In serv.
S 515 LIVIO PIOMARTA (ex-*Trigger*, SS 564)	24-2-49	14-6-51	31-3-52
S 516 ROMEO ROMEI (ex-*Harder*, SS 568)	30-6-50	3-12-51	19-8-52

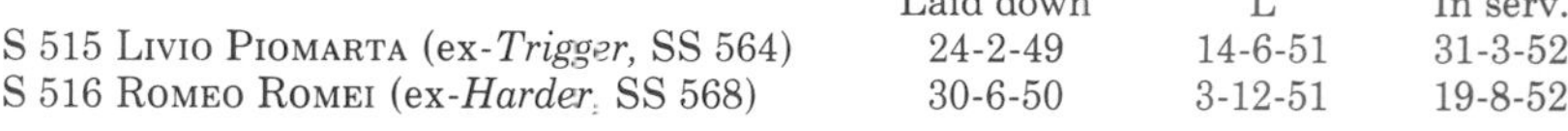

Romeo Romei (S 516) G. Arra, 1976

D: 2,100 surf./2,700 sub. tons **S:** 14 surf./14 kts sub. **Dim:** 87.5 × 8.3 × 6.2
A: 8/533-mm TT (6 long fwd, 2 short aft)
Electron Equipt: Radar: 1/BPS-12—Sonar: BQR-3, BQS-4, BQG-4

SUBMARINES *(continued)*

M: Diesel-electric propulsion: 3 Fairbanks-Morse 38ND8⅛ × 10 diesels; 2 Westinghouse motors; 2 props; 5,500 hp
Range: 7,600/15; 17/9 (sub.) **Man:** 7 officers, 71 men

REMARKS: S 515 transferred to Italy on 10-7-73; S 516 on 20-2-74. Both ships have BQG-4 "PUFFS" passive ranging sonar. Have U.S. Mk 106 Mod.14 fire-control system. Aft tubes probably no longer used.

CRUISERS

◆ **1 Vittorio Veneto class**

	Bldr	Laid down	L	In serv.
C 550 VITTORIO VENETO	Cant. Riuniti Castellammare	10-6-65	5-2-67	12-7-69

Vittorio Veneto (C 550) C. Martinelli, 1983

Vittorio Veneto (C 550) Italian Navy, 1983

Vittorio Veneto (C 550) Italian Navy, 1983

D: 7,500 tons (8,870 fl) **S:** 30.5 kts
Dim: 179.60 (170.61 pp) × 19.42 (hull) × 4.70 (7.4 max.)
A: 1/Mk 20 Mod. 7 Aster launch system (20 ASROC and 40 Standard SM-1 ER)—4/Otomat-Tesio Mk II SSM (I × 4)—8/76-mm OTO Melara DP (I × 8)—6/40-mm Breda Dardo AA (II × 3)—6/324-mm ILAS-3 ASW TT (III × 2)—6/AB-212 ASW helicopters
Electron Equipt: Radar: 1/RAN-20X, 1/SPS-52C, 1/MM/SM-702, 1/3RM-7, 2/SPG-55B, 2/RTN-10X, 3/RTN-20X—TACAN: URN-20A
Sonar: SQS-23

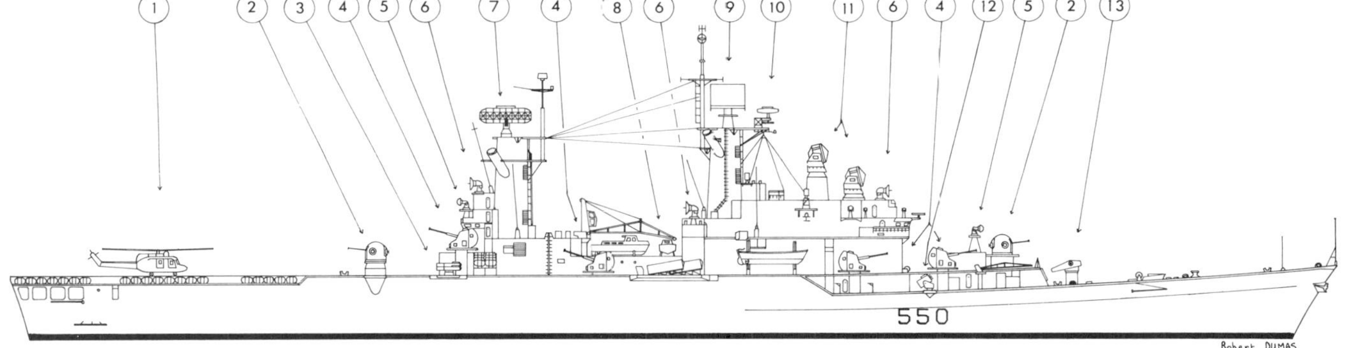

Vittorio Veneto 1. AB-212 helicopter 2. 40-mm Breda Dardo twin AA 3. ILAS-3 triple ASW TT 4. 76-mm DP 5. RTN-20X f.c. radar (for 40-mm AA) 6. RTN-20X f.c. radar (for 76-mm DP) 7. RAN-20X early-warning radar 8. Tesio/Otomat Mk 2 SSM 9. SPS-52C 3-D radar 10. MM/SM-702 surface-search radar 11. SPG-55B f.c. radar tracker illuminators (for Standard) 12. SCLAR RL 13. Mk 20 Aster launcher

CRUISERS *(continued)*

M: 2 sets Tosi GT; 2 props; 73,000 hp **Electric:** . . .
Boilers: 4 Foster-Wheeler; 43 kg/cm², 450°C **Fuel:** 1,200 tons
Range: 3,000/28; 6,000/20 **Man:** 53 officers, 504 men

REMARKS: Underwent modernization 1981-83 with 4 Otomat Mk 2 (Teseo) missiles and 3 Dardo 40-mm AA gun systems added. The radar suite was updated, the SPS-40 being replaced by the Italian RAN-20X. The flight deck (40 × 18.5) is served from a hangar immediately below by two elevators (18 × 5.3). The hangar (27.5 × 15.3) is two decks in depth. Very extensive, stabilized electronic intercept arrays. Two sets anti-rolling fin stabilizers. The Aster system can launch either ASROC ASW or Standard SM-1 ER SAM and has a total capacity of 60 missiles on three magazine drums. Beam listed does not include projections around SCLAR launchers fwd or flight deck aft.

◆ **2 Andrea Doria class**

	Bldr	Laid down	L	In serv.
C 553 ANDREA DORIA	C. Nav. Tirreno, Riva Trigoso	11-5-58	27-2-63	23-2-64
C 554 CAIO DUILIO	Navalmeccanica Castellammare	16-5-58	22-12-62	30-11-64

Andrea Doria (C 553) G. Arra, 8-84

Andrea Doria (C 553) G. Arra, 8-84

Caio Duilio (C 554) — as training cruiser P. Voss, 7-83

Caio Duilio (C 554) L. & L. Van Ginderen, 8-83

D: 6,500 tons (7,300 fl) **S:** 30 kts **Dim:** 149.3 (144.0 pp) × 17.25 × 4.96 (7.5 fl)
A: 1/Mk 10 launcher (40 Standard SM-1 ER—6 or 8/76-mm AA (I × 6 or 8)—6/324-mm ASW TT (III × 2)—3/AB-212 helicopters (C 554: 2)
Electron Equipt: Radar: 1/RAN-20S, 1/SPQ-2D, 1/SPS-52B, 2/SPG-55C, 3 or 4/RTN-10X (Argo system)
TACAN: SRN-15—Sonar: SQS-23
EW: passive arrays, 2/SCLAR chaff launchers (XX × 2)
M: 2 sets GT; 2 props; 60,000 hp **Electric:** 4,700 kw
Boilers: 4 Foster-Wheeler; 43 kg/cm², 450°C **Fuel:** 1,100 tons
Rnage: 6,000/15 **Man:** 47 officers, 437 men (C 554: 418) men

REMARKS: The flight deck is 30 × 16 meters on C 553. Hangar on main deck. Fin anti-rolling stabilizers fitted. The engineering spaces are divided into two groups, forward and aft: each has a boiler room with two boilers and a turbine compartment separated by living spaces. In each turbine space are two 1,000-kw turbo-alternators; there are also two 350-kw emergency diesel alternators. The engineering groups are automatic and remote-controlled. Listed beam does not include platforms extending from sides aft. C 554 refitted 1979-80 as training cruiser to replace *San Giorgio* (D 562). The after two 76-mm guns and the aft NA-9 gunfire control system were removed, and the hangar was converted to accommodations and classrooms; a new, lower hangar was built on abaft the old one, reducing the flight-deck length and limiting the ship to two helicopters. A small navigational radar was added atop the hangar for helicopter control.

Both received Standard SM-1 ER missiles and associated electronics during refits in the latter 1970s. Have four (C 554: 3) Argo NA-9 GFCS.

GUIDED-MISSILE DESTROYERS

◆ **0 (+2) Animoso class**

	Bldr	Laid down	L	In serv.
D 560 ANIMOSO	. . .	. . .	. . .	1991
D 561 ARDIMENTOSO	. . .	. . .	. . .	1991

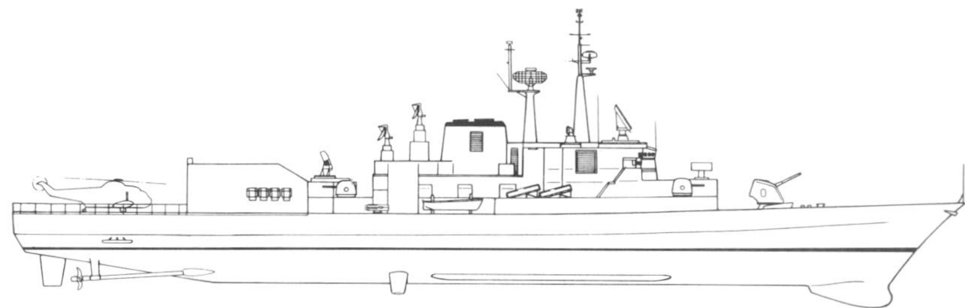

Animoso (D 560)—provisional drawing *Ships of the World,* 3-85

D: . . . tons (5,000 fl) **S:** 32 kts **Dim:** 137.0 × . . . × . . .
A: 4/Teseo-Otomat Mk II SSN—1/Mk launcher (40 Standard SM-1 MR missiles)—1/Albatros SAM syst.(VIII × 1); . . . Aspide missiles)—1/127-mm OTO Melara Compact DP—8/40-mm (II × 4) Breda Dardo AA—6/324-mm ILAS-3 ASW TT (III × 2)—2/SH-3D Sea King or EH101 helicopters
Electron Equipt: Radar: 1/RAN-20S, 1/SPS-52C, 1/surface search, 1/navigational, 2/SPG-51D, 3/GFCS
Sonar: bow-mounted array
EW: passive arrays, 2/SCLAR chaff RL (XX × 2)
M: 4 G.E./Fiat LM-2500 gas turbines; 2 props; 80,000 hp
Electric: . . . **Range:** . . . **Man:** . . .

REMARKS: Authorized 1983; several years behind schedule. May receive the OTO Melara "Super Rapid" Compact 76-mm DP vice the twin 40-mm mounts. Will replace the *Impavido* class.

◆ **2 Audace class**

	Bldr	Laid down	L	In serv.
D 550 ARDITO	Nav. Mec. Castellammare	19-7-68	27-11-71	5-12-73
D 551 AUDACE	C. Nav. del Tirreno	27-4-68	2-10-71	16-11-72

GUIDED-MISSILE DESTROYERS *(continued)*

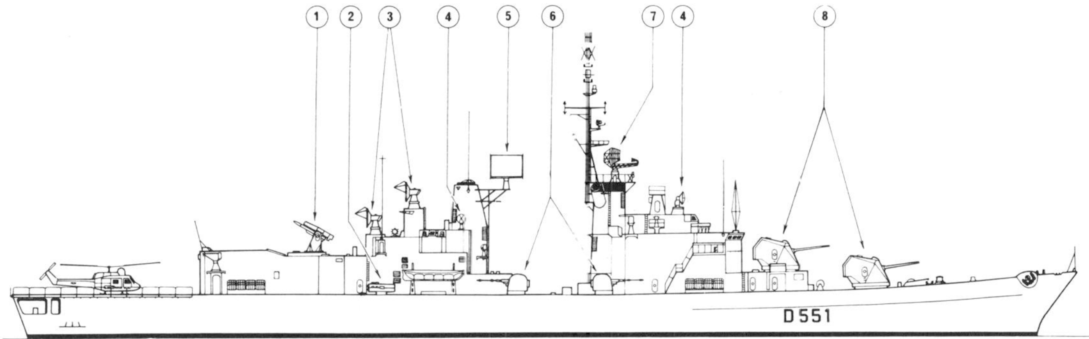

Audace (D 551) 1. Mk 13 launcher 2. Triple ASW TT 3. SPG-51B radars 4. RTN-10X fire-control radars 5. SPS-52B radar 6. 76-mm DP 7. RAN-20S radar 8. 127-mm DP H. Simoni

Audace (D 551) G. Arra, 1984

Ardito (D 550) G. Arra, 1984

Ardito (D 550)—note torpedo-tube recesses at stern L. & L. Van Ginderen, 5-84

D: 3,600 light/3,950 tons (4,559 fl) **S:** 33 kts **Dim:** 140.7 × 14.65 × 4.60 (hull)
A: 1/Mk 13 missile launcher (40 Standard SM-1 MR)—2/127-mm OTO Melara Compact DP (I × 2)—4/76-mm AA OTO Melara Compact DP (I × 4)—6/324-mm ASW TT (II × 2)—4/533-mm TT (I × 4, AS-184 wire-guided torpedoes)—2/AB-212 or 1/SH-3D Sea King ASW helicopter
Electron Equipt: Radar: 1/3 RM 20, 1/RAN-20S, 1/SPQ-2, 1/SPS-52, 2/SPG-51B, 3/RTN-10X (Argo systems)
Sonar: CWE 610
EW: passive arrays, 1/SCLAR chaff RL (XX × 2)
M: 2 sets GT; 2 props; 73,000 hp
Boilers: 4 Foster-Wheeler; 43 kg/cm², 450°C
Range: 4,000/25 **Man:** 31 officers, 350 men

Remarks: Habitability has been given much attention in the design of these very fine ships. The four single 533-mm torpedo tubes are mounted at the extreme stern, below the fantail, and launch A-184 wire-guided torpedoes aftward. Both now have RAN-20S air-search radar, replacing SPS-12 (D 550) or RAN-3 (D 551). The missile system is to be modernized. Have fin stabilizers.

◆ **2 Impavido class**

	Bldr	Laid down	L	In serv.
D 570 Impavido	C. N. del Tirreno, Riva Trigoso	10-6-57	25-5-62	16-11-63
D 571 Intrepido	Ansaldo, Livorno	16-5-59	21-10-62	18-7-64

Intrepido (D 571) L. & L. Van Ginderen, 1983

D: 3,201 tons (3,990 fl) **S:** 33.5 kts **Dim:** 131.3 × 13.65 × 4.43
A: 1/Mk 13 launcher aft (40 Standard SM-1 MR missiles)—2/127-mm 38-cal. DP (II × 1) fwd—4/76-mm DP (I × 4)—6/324-mm ASW TT (III × 2)
Electron Equipt: Radar: 1/SPS-12, /SPQ-2, 1/SPS-52B, 2/SPG-51B, 3/RTN-10X (Argo systems)
Sonar: 1/SQS-23
EW: passive arrays, 2/SCLAR chaff RL (XX × 2)
M: 2 sets Tosi GT; 2 props; 70,000 hp
Boilers: 4 Foster-Wheeler; 43 kg/cm², 450°C **Fuel:** 650 tons
Range: 3,300/20; 2,900/25; 1,500/30 **Man:** 22 officers, 318 men

Remarks: Refitted (D 571 in 1974-75, D 570 in 1976-77) with new fire control for guns and new missiles. Have fin stabilizers.

GUIDED-MISSILE FRIGATES

◆ **8 Maestrale class** Bldr: CNR, Riva Trigoso (F 571: CNR, Muggiano)

	Laid down	L	In serv.
F 570 Maestrale	8-3-78	2-2-81	7-3-82
F 571 Grecale	21-3-79	12-9-81	5-2-83
F 572 Libeccio	1-8-79	7-9-81	5-2-83
F 573 Scirocco	26-2-80	17-4-82	20-9-83
F 574 Aliseo	26-2-80	29-10-82	20-9-83

GUIDED-MISSILE FRIGATES *(continued)*

	Laid down	L	In serv.
F 575 Euro	15-4-81	25-3-83	7-4-84
F 576 Espero	1-8-82	19-11-83	4-5-85
F 577 Zeffiro	15-3-83	19-5-84	4-5-85

Grecale (F 571) C. Martinelli, 6-84

Maestrale (F 570)—showing VDS well at stern G. Gyssels, 12-82

Grecale (F 571) G. Arra, 1984

Libeccio (F 572) C. Martinelli, 10-82

D: 3,040 tons (3,200 fl) **S:** 33 kts
Dim: 122.73 (116.4 pp) × 12.88 × 4.10 (hull; 5.95 max.)
A: 4/Teseo Otomat Mk 2 SSM (I × 4)—1/Albatros SAM system (VIII × 1, 24 Aspide missiles)—1/127-mm DP OTO Melara—4/40-mm Breda Dardo AA (II × 2)—2/533-mm TT (A-184 torpedoes)—6/324-mm ILAS-3 ASW TT (III × 2)—2/AB-212 helicopters
Electron Equipt: Radar: 1/MM/SPS-702, 1/RAN-10S, 1/SPQ-2F, 1/RTN-30X (NA-30A system), 2/RTN-20X (Dardo system)
Sonar: 1/Raytheon DE 1160B, 1/Raytheon DE 1164 VDS
EW: Elettronica Newton active/passive suite, 2/SCLAR chaff launchers (XX × 2)
M: CODOG: 2 G.E./Fiat LM-2500 gas turbines, 50,000 hp; 2 GMT B 230-20 DV diesels, 10,146 hp; 2 CP props
Electric: 3,120 kw **Endurance:** 90 days **Range:** 1,500/30; 3,800/22; 6,000/15
Man: 24 officers, 200 men

Remarks: An enlarged version of *Lupo* with better seaworthiness and two helicopters at the expense of four anti-ship missiles and about 2.5 knots maximum speed. Have SADOC-2 (IPN-20) computerized data system. There is a Galileo OG-30 optronic backup director to the NA-30A GFCS system and two MM 59 optical backup directors for the 40-mm guns. Helo deck is 12 × 27 m. D 1164 is a VDS version of DE 1160 and operates on the same frequencies. The hull sonar is a commercial version of the U.S. Navy SQS-56 as used in the *Oliver Hazard Perry* (FFG 7) class. FF 576 and FF 577 ordered 10-80, 572–575 in 12-76, 576 and 577 in 10-80. Have U.S. Prairie/Masker bubbler noise-suppression system and SLQ-25 Nixie towed torpedo decoys. There are plans to lengthen the VDS tow cable from 600 m to 900 m and to attach a towed passive linear hydrophone array to the VDS fish; trials to take place with F 570.

◆ **4 Lupo class** Bldr: C. N. Riuniti, Riva Trigoso (F 567; CNR Muggiano)

	Laid down	L	In serv.
F 564 Lupo	8-10-74	29-7-76	20-9-77
F 565 Sagittario	4-2-76	22-6-77	18-11-78
F 566 Perseo	28-2-77	8-7-78	1-3-80
F 567 Orsa	1-8-77	1-3-79	1-3-80

D: 2,208 tons (2,340 trials; 2,525 fl)
Dim: 113.55 (106.00 pp) × 12.00 × 3.54 (hull)
S: 35.23 kts (trials, *Lupo*); 32 kts at 80% power; 20.3 kts on 2 diesels
A: 8/Otomat Mk 2 SSM (I × 8)—1/Nato Sea Sparrow system (VIII × 1)—1/127-mm OTO Melara DP—4/40-mm Breda AA (II × 2)—6/324-mm Mk 32 ASW TT (III × 2)—1/AB-212 helicopter
Electron Equipt: Radar: 1/3 RM 20, 1/RAN-10S combined search, 1/SPQ-2F, 1/RAN-11/LX combined search, 1/Orion RTN-10X (NA-10 mod. 2 Argo f.c. system), 1/Mk 91 mod. 1, 2/Orion RTN-20X (Dardo system)
Sonar: Raytheon 1160B
EW: active and passive systems, 2/SCLAR chaff RL (XX × 2)

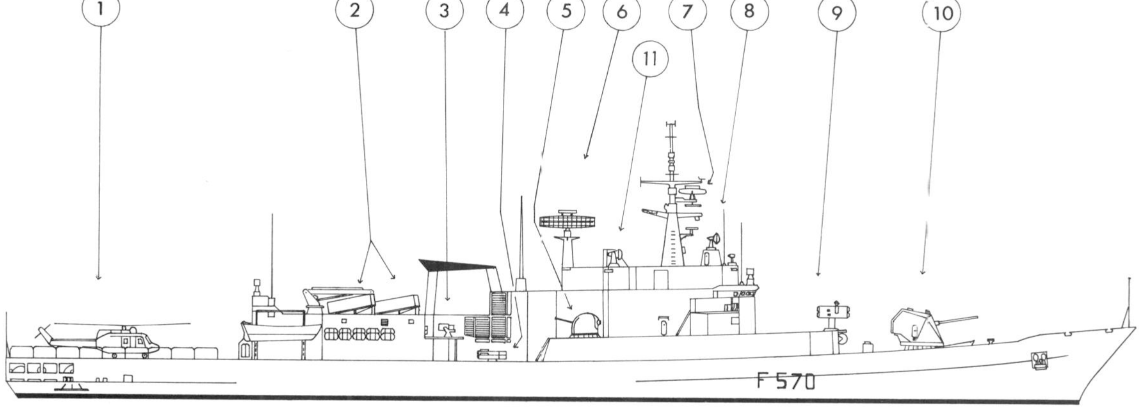

Maestrale class 1. AB-212 helicopter 2. Otomat SSM launchers 3. SCLAR chaff rocket launchers 4. ILAS-3 triple ASW TT 5. Breda Dardo twin 40-mm AA 6. RAN-10S radar antenna 7. RAN-11L/X surface-search radar antenna 8. RTN-30X gun/missile-control radar 9. Albatros launcher (VIII × 1) 10. 127-mm dual-purpose gun 11. RTN-20X radar directors

GUIDED-MISSILE FRIGATES *(continued)*

Perseo (F 566) Pradignac & Leo, 1985

Perseo (F 566) L. & L. Van Ginderen, 6-83

Sagittario (F 565) Italian Navy

M: CODOG: 2 G.E./Fiat LM-2500 gas turbines, 50,000 hp; 2 GMT A 230-20M diesels, 7,900 hp; 2 CP props
Electric: 3,120 kw (4 Fiat 236 SS diesel alternator sets)
Range: 900/35; 3,450/20 (diesels) **Man:** 17 officers, 177 men

REMARKS: Fin stabilizers. Telescopic hangar. The Otomat Mk-II (Teseo) launchers are mounted two per side abreast the hangar and two per side on the forward superstructure. The *Lupo* had her radar antennae redistributed 1978-79 and a new mast added at the after end of the stack. The SAM system uses the U.S. Mk 29 launcher and a U.S. director, rather than the later Albatros system with the similar Aspide missiles of the *Maestrale* class. The highly automated machinery plant is mounted in four compartments: auxiliaries, gas turbines, reduction gearing, and diesel alternator sets. Six ships of the same class were ordered for Venezuela, four for Peru, and four for Iraq.

FRIGATES

◆ **2 Alpino class** Bldr: C. N. del Tirreno, Riva Trigoso

	Laid down	L	In serv.
F 580 ALPINO (ex-*Circe*)	27-2-63	10-6-67	14-1-68
F 581 CARABINIERE (ex-*Climene*)	9-1-65	30-9-67	28-4-68

D: 2,000 tons (2,700 fl) **S:** 27 kts **Dim:** 113.3 (106.4 pp) × 13.3 × 3.80 (hull)
A: 6/76-mm 62-cal. DP (I × 6) — 1/305-mm Menon K113 ASW mortar (I × 1) — 6/324-mm ASW TT (III × 2) — 1/AB-212 helicopter
Electron Equipt: Radar: 1/SPS-12, 1/SPQ-2, 1/RTN-30X (NA-30 system), 3/RTN-10X (Argo systems), F 580 also: 1/MAD
Sonar: 1/SQS-43, 1/SQA-10 VDS
EW: MM/SPR-A intercept, 2/SCLAR chaff RL (XX × 2)
M: CODAG: 4 Tosi OTV-320 diesels, 4,200 hp each; 2 Tosi-Metrovik G6 gas turbines, 7,700 hp each; 2 props; 31,800 hp
Electric: 2,400 kw **Fuel:** 275 tons **Range:** 4,200/17
Man: 19 officers, 228 men

REMARKS: Fin stabilizers. Cruising, 22 knots on diesels. F 580 fitted with experimental MAD gunfire-control radar 1975.

Caribiniere (F 581) — showing VDS installation G. Arra, 1982

Carabiniere (F 581) C. Martinelli, 1981

NOTE: The last *Canopo*-class frigate, *Centauro* (F 554), was stricken during 1984. The last two *Carlo Bergamini*-class frigates, *Virgilio Fasan* (F 594) and *Carlo Margo Hini* (F 595) were to be stricken during 1985.

CORVETTES

◆ **0 (+4 + 4 + 4) Minerva class** Bldr: Italcantiere, Muggiano, and Riva Trigoso

	Bldr	Laid down	L	In serv.
F 551 MINERVA	Riva Trigoso	9-84	. . .	1986
F 552 URANIA	. . .	. . .	. . .	. . .
F 553 DANÏADE	. . .	. . .	. . .	. . .
F 554 SFINGE	. . .	. . .	. . .	. . .
F 555 DRIADE	. . .	. . .	. . .	. . .
F 556 CHIMERA	. . .	. . .	. . .	. . .
F 557 FENICE	. . .	. . .	. . .	. . .
F 558 SIBILLA	. . .	. . .	. . .	. . .

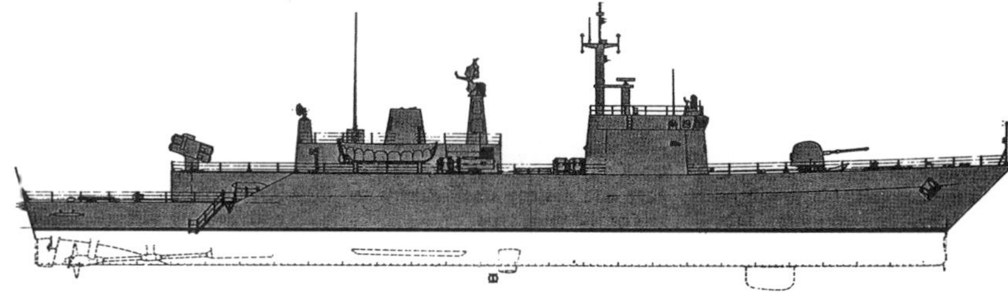

Minerva class Italian Navy, 1984

D: 1,025 tons (1,300 fl) **S:** 24-25 kts **Dim:** 87.00 (80.00 pp) × 10.30 × . . .
A: 1/Albatros SAM system (VIII × 1, 8 Aspide missiles) — 1/76-mm OTO Melara Compact DP — 6/324-mm ILAS-3 ASW TT (III × 2)
Electron Equipt: Radar: 1/MM/SPN-703 nav., 1/MM/SPS-774 combined air/surface search, 1/RTN-20X f.c. (Dardo E f.c.s.)
Sonar: 1/Raytheon DE 1167 (L/F, hull-mounted)
EW: Elettronica Newton active/passive suite, 2 Type 207/E chaff RL
M: 2 GMT BM 230.20 DVM diesels; 2 CP props; 11,000 hp
Range: 3,500/18 **Electric:** 2,600 kVa **Man:** 9 officers, 112 men

REMARKS: First four authorized 1983 to begin replacement of earlier corvettes; names for second planned group released 1985. Intended for surveillance, coastal escort, fisheries protection, training and search-and-rescue duties. Weight and space reserved for addition of Aspide reload facility, four Teseo-Otomat Mk 2 SSM, variable-depth sonar. Will have Selenia "Mini SADOC" combat data system, with two computers and three displays. Elsag NA-18 optronic GFCS for the 76-mm gun, with the Dardo E radar f.c.s. controlling the SAM system or the gun. Sonars will be the first to be built (though under license) in Italy. Fin stabilizers, satellite navigation systems fitted.

CORVETTES *(continued)*

◆ **4 Pietro de Cristofaro class**

	Bldr	Laid down	L	In serv.
F 540 Pietro de Cristofaro	C.N. del Tirreno	20-4-63	29-5-65	19-12-65
F 541 Umberto Grosso	Ansaldo, Livorno	21-10-62	12-12-64	25-4-66
F 546 Licio Visintini	C.R.D.A., Monfalcone	30-9-63	30-5-65	10-8-66
F 550 Salvatore Todaro	Ansaldo, Livorno	21-10-62	24-10-64	25-4-66

Licio Visintini (F 546) L. & L. Van Ginderen, 6-84

Salvatore Todaro (F 550) L. & L. Van Ginderen, 6-84

D: 850 tons (1,020 fl) **S:** 22 kts **Dim:** 80.37 (75.0 pp) × 10.28 × 2.80 (hull)
A: 2/76-mm DP (I × 2)—1/305-mm K113 Menon ASW mortar (I × 1)—6/324-mm ASW TT (III × 2)
Electron Equipt: Radar: 1/SPQ-2, 1/Orion RTN-10X (OG-3 system)
Sonar: 2/SQS-36 (1 hull, 1 VDS)
EW: MM/SPR-A intercept
M: 2 diesels (*see* Remarks); 2 props; 8,400 hp **Fuel:** 100 tons
Range: 4,600/18 **Man:** 7 officers, 122 men

Remarks: High-speed diesels; Fiat 3012 RSS on F 540, F 541, and F 550; Tosi on F 546, with reduction gears and Tosi-Vulcan hydraulic linkage. OG-3 gun director forward, U.S. Mk 51 director aft. The VDS uses an SQA-13 hoist. No VDS on F 540; no ASW TT on F 541.

◆ **4 Albatros class** Bldr: Nav. Mec. Castellammare di Stabia (except F 542: Breda, Marghera-Mestre, Venice)

	Laid down	L	In serv.
F 542 Aquila (ex-Dutch *Lynx*)	25-7-53	31-7-54	2-10-56
F 543 Albatros	1953	18-7-54	1-6-55
F 544 Alcione	1953	19-9-54	23-10-55
F 545 Airone	1953	21-11-54	29-12-55

D: 800 tons (950 fl) **S:** 19 kts **Dim:** 76.3 (69.49 pp) × 9.65 × 2.72 (hull)
A: 3/40-mm AA (II × 1, I × 1—except F 543: 2/40-mm II)—2/Mk 11 Hedgehog (XXIV × 2)—F 542, F 545: 6/324-mm ILAS ASW TT (III × 2)—F 542, F 545: 1/d.c. rack
Electron Equipt: Radar: 1/SPQ-2—Sonar: QCU-2
M: 2 Fiat M 409 diesels; 2 props; 5,200 hp (3,500 sust.) **Fuel:** 100 tons
Electric: 1,200 kw **Range:** 2,988/18 **Man:** 6 officers, 96 men

Remarks: Ships built with U.S. "Offshore" funds (ex-U.S. PC 1626, PC 1619, PC 1620, and PC 1921). One similar ship was delivered to The Netherlands (returned to Italy in 10-61 and commissioned 9-11-61) and four to Denmark. Originally had two 76-mm DP, two 40-mm AA (II × 1); rearmed 1963. F 543 and F 544 are equipped for minesweeping, having rubber dinghies, 2 paravanes, and equipment davits on the stern. All were to be decommissioned 1982-83, but will be retained until the *Minerva* class enters service.

Alcione (F 544) L. & L. Van Ginderen, 11-83

GUIDED-MISSILE PATROL BOATS

◆ **1 private-venture DA-360T design** Bldr: CNR, Muggiano

	Laid down	L	In serv.
Saettia	5-83	. . .	12-85

Saettia—artist's rendering CNR, 1983

D: 330 tons normal (360 fl) **S:** 40 kts (375 sust.)
Dim: 51.70 (47.20 pp) × 8.10 × . . .
A: 4/Otomat Mk 2 SSM—1/76-mm OTO Melara Compact DP—2/40-mm Breda Dardo AA (II × 1)
Electron Equipt: Radar: 1/RAN-12 L/X, 1/Orion RTN-10X f.c.
EW: Elettronica Farad A1 intercept; 2 Breda chaff RL
M: 4 MTU 16V538 TB93 diesels; 4 props; 16,560 hp sust. **Electric:** 534 kw
Range: 2,000/18 **Endurance:** 12 days **Man:** 3 officers, 28 men

Remarks: *Not* a unit of the Italian Navy. Built in hopes of sales and to test concept. Has fin stabilizers. Elsag NA 21 weapons control system with RTN-10X radar has NA 12 optronic backup director. Selenia's IPN-10 combat data system.

◆ **7 Sparviero-class hydrofoils** Bldr: CNR, Muggiano (P 420: Alinavi, La Spezia)

	Laid down	L	Delivered	In serv.
P 420 Sparviero	4-71	9-5-73	. . .	15-7-74
P 421 Nibbio	1-8-77	29-2-80	10-11-80	7-3-82
P 422 Falcone	1-10-77	27-10-80	1-3-82	7-3-82
P 423 Astore	1-7-78	20-7-81	6-8-82	5-2-83
P 424 Griffone	15-11-78	1-12-81	16-9-82	5-2-83
P 425 Gheppio	16-5-79	24-6-82	11-5-83	20-9-83
P 426 Condore	21-3-80	25-1-83	19-1-84	7-4-84

D: 63.0 tons (fl) **S:** 43 kts (heavy sea), 50 kts (calm sea)
Dim: 22.95 (24.56, foils retracted) × 7.01 (12.06 max. over foils) × 1.87 (1.45 over foils at speed, 4.37 over foils at rest)
A: 2 Otomat Mk II SSM (I × 2)—1/76-mm OTO Melara Compact
Electron Equipt: Radar: 1/3RM7-250, 1/RTN-10X (NA-10 Mod. 3 system)
M: CODOG: 1 Rolls-Royce Proteus 15 M560 gas turbine; 1 waterjet; 5,044 hp (P 420: 4,500); 1 G.M. 6V-53N diesel; 1 prop; 180 hp
Fuel: 11 tons **Range:** 1,050/8 (diesels); 400/45
Man: 2 officers, 7 men

Remarks: Prototype studied by the Alinavi Society, which was formed in 1964 by Boeing, U.S.A., the Italian government's I.R.I., and Carlo Rodriguez of Messina, builder of commercial hydrofoils. Six more (of eight planned) were ordered 1977. The three hydrofoils are raised when cruising, and the diesel engine is engaged. All-aluminum construction. Used for short-duration operations, have no berths. Design based on U.S. *Tucumcari*. F 421 onward have a later SPQ-701 surface-search radar, incorpo-

GUIDED-MISSILE PATROL BOATS *(continued)*

Griffone (P 424) C. Martinelli, 5-84

Astore (P 423) L. & L. Van Ginderen, 5-84

rating an IFF interrogator. All except P 420 have water injection to increase gas turbine power output, but they are basically underpowered. There are plans to replace the Proteus with a G.M. Allison 570 KF turbine producing 6,394 hp.

Note: The two *Freccia*-class convertible torpedo-gunboats have been stricken: *Freccia* (P 493 on 15-9-84 and *Saetta* (P 494) during 1985. *Lampo*-class torpedo boats *Lampo* (P 491) and *Baleno* (P 492) were stricken 31-3-83.

MINE WARFARE SHIPS

◆ **4 (+3 + 3) Lerici-class minehunter/minesweepers** Bldr: Intermarine, La Spezia

	Laid down	L	In serv.		Laid down	L	In serv.
M 5550 Lerici	1978	3-9-82	4-5-85	M 5555 Termoli	. . .	. . .	. . .
M 5551 Sapri	. . .	. . .	1985	M 5556 Alghero	. . .	. . .	. . .
M 5552 Milazzo	. . .	. . .	1986	M 5557 Numano	. . .	. . .	. . .
M 5553 Vieste	. . .	. . .	1986	M 5558 Crotone	. . .	. . .	. . .
M 5554 Gaeta	. . .	. . .	. . .	M 5559 Viareggio	. . .	. . .	. . .

D: 470 tons (502 fl) **S:** 15 kts **Dim:** 49.98 (45.5 pp) × 9.56 × 2.63
A: 1/20-mm AA **Electric:** 887 kVA
Range: 2,500/12; 1,500/14 **Man:** 39 tot.
Electron Equipt: Radar: 1/3ST7/DG Sonar: SQQ-14
M: 1 GMT B230-8M diesel; 1 prop; 1,840 hp (2 retractable auxiliary thrusters; 470 hp)

Remarks: First four ordered 4-78; six more, authorized 1980, will be longer and may be built at a new facility at Gaetta. Glass-reinforced, shock-resistant plastic construction throughout. Hull material 140-mm thick. To carry MIN-77 remote-controlled minehunting devices as well as conventional sweep gear. SQQ-14 is a high-frequency minehunting sonar with a retractable transducer. While minehunting, speed is 7 knots, using the two drop-down, shrouded thrusters. Carry 6–7 divers, who use CAM mine destructor charges. One Pluto remote-controlled submersible disposal and one MIN locating submersible may be carried by each ship. Range at 12 knots can be extended to 4,000 nautical miles by using the passive roll stabilization tanks to carry fuel. Four also ordered for Malaysia. Delivery of these ships has been delayed by the presence of a bridge blocking the seaward exit from the yard and by a vigorous foreign sales program that apparently takes precedence over Italian Navy requirements.

Lerici (M 5550) — on trials C. Martinelli, 10-84

Milazzo (M 5552) G. Arra, 1985

◆ **4 ex-U.S. Agile-class fleet minesweepers**

	Bldr	L	In serv.
M 5430 Salmone (ex-MSO 507)	Martinolich, San Diego	19-2-55	15-5-56
M 5431 Storione (ex-MSO 506)	Martinolich, San Diego	13-11-54	23-2-56
M 5432 Sgombro (ex-MSO 517)	Tampa Marine	1954	12-5-57
M 5433 Squalo (ex-MSO 518)	Tampa Marine	1955	20-6-57

Salmone (M 5430) L. & L. Van Ginderen, 1984

D: 665 tons (750 fl) **S:** 14 kts **Dim:** 52.27 × 10.71 × 4.0 (fl)
A: 1/40-mm AA
Electron Equipt: Radar: 1/3ST7/DG — Sonar: UQS-1
M: 2 G.M. 8-278ANW diesels; 2 CP props; 1,600 hp **Fuel:** 46 tons
Range: 3,000/10 **Man:** 7 officers, 44 men

Remarks: Had been scheduled for disposal 1982-83. Wooden construction.

MINE WARFARE SHIPS *(continued)*

◆ **21 U.S. Adjutant-class minesweepers** (9 converted as minehunters*)

	Bldr	In serv.
M 5504 Castagno (ex-MSC 74)*	H. Grebe, New York	7-8-55
M 5505 Cedro (ex-MSC 88)*	Berg SY, Wash.	9-11-53
M 5508 Frassino (ex-MSC 89)*	Berg SY, Wash.	15-2-54
M 5509 Gelso (ex-MSC 75)*	H. Grebe, New York	8-3-54
M 5510 Larice (ex-MSC 82)	Lake Union DD, Wash.	21-1-54
M 5516 Platano (ex-MSC 136)*	Bellingham BY, Wash.	16-10-54
M 5519 Mandorlo (ex-MSC 280)*	Tacoma BY, Wash.	16-12-60
M 5521 Bambu (ex-MSC 214)	CRDA, Monfalcone	8-9-56
M 5522 Ebano (ex-MSC 215)	CRDA, Monfalcone	8-11-56
M 5523 Mango (ex-MSC 216)*	CRDA, Monfalcone	5-12-56
M 5524 Mogano (ex-MSC 217)	CRDA, Monfalcone	9-1-57
M 5525 Palma (ex-MSC 238)*	CRDA, Monfalcone	28-2-57
M 5527 Sandalo (ex-MSC 240)	CRDA, Monfalcone	17-4-57
M 5531 Agave	CRDA, Monfalcone	1-2-56
M 5532 Alloro	CRDA, Monfalcone	1-2-56
M 5533 Edera	CRDA, Monfalcone	7-56
M 5535 Gelsomino	Baglietto, Varezze	5-56
M 5536 Giaggiolo	Picchiotti, Viareggio	6-56
M 5538 Loto*	Celli, Venice	21-1-56
M 5540 Timo	Costaguta, Voltri	8-56
M 5542 Vischio	C. Mediterraneo, Piera	8-56

Cedro (M 5505)—standard minehunter configuration L. & L. Van Ginderen, 5-84

Gelsomino (M 5535) L. & L. Van Ginderen, 9-84

Mandorlo (M 5519)—minehunter with unique bridge C. Martinelli, 1983

Loto (M 5538)—prototype minehunter conversion, with short forecastle L. & L. Van Ginderen, 9-84

D: 375 tons (405 fl) **S:** 12 kts **Dim:** 43.92 (42.1 pp) × 8.23 × 2.68
A: 2/20-mm AA (II × 1)
Electron Equipt: Radar: 1/3ST7/DG—(minehunters: 1/MM/SPN-703)
Sonar: UQS-1 (minehunters: SQQ-14)
M: 2 G.M. 8-268A diesels; 2 props; 1,200 hp (*see* Remarks) **Fuel:** 40 tons
Range: 2,500/10 **Man:** 2 officers, 29 men (minehunters: 3 officers, 38 men)

Remarks: M 5531 to M 5542 were built with "Offshore Procurement" funds and did not receive MSC-series hull numbers; the others were built under the U.S. Military Aid Program. M 5519 is of a later design than the others, with a lower bridge and larger stack; she was converted as a minehunter in 1975 and displaces 370 tons; her dimensions are 44.12 × 8.50 × 2.30, and her two 900-hp diesels provide a 12-kt max. speed. Eight others have since been similarly altered, with the forecastle being lengthened; they have a standard displacement of 354.5 tons and have a single 310-hp Voith-Schneider vertical cycloidal prop for minehunting. The minehunters' main engines produce 810 hp total, for 11.4 kts. The minehunters employ the Pluto remote-controlled submersible, capable of 4.5-kt speeds; the divers aboard use CAM-T destruction charges. All have wooden hulls and nonmagnetic fittings. M 5521 to M 5527 have Fiat diesels. *Mirto* (ex-M 5539) and *Pioppo* (ex-M 5515) have been converted to survey ships. *Noce* (M 5511) was stricken 30-9-83. Twelve others were discarded 1974 to 1980.

◆ **5 Aragosta-class inshore minesweepers**

	Bldr	L	In serv.
M 5450 Aragosta (ex-MSI 55)	CRDA, Monfalcone	8-56	19-7-57
M 5452 Astice (ex-MSI 61)	CRDA, Monfalcone	16-1-57	19-7-57
M 5459 Mitilo (ex-MSI 74)	Picchiotti, Viareggio	1-6-57	11-7-57
M 5463 Polipo	Costaguta, Voltri	15-6-57	10-7-57
M 5464 Porpora (ex-MSI 65)	Costaguta, Voltri	1-6-57	10-7-57

Mitilo (M 5459) L. & L. Van Ginderen, 1982

D: 120 tons (178 fl) **S:** 13.5 kts **Dim:** 32.35 × 6.47 × 2.14 **A:** None
Electron Equipt: Radar: 1/MLN-1A
M: 2 Fiat/MTU MB 820D diesels; 2 props; 1,000 hp **Electric:** 340 kw
Fuel: 15 tons **Range:** 2,000/9 **Man:** 2 officers, 13 men

Remarks: Based on British "Ham"-class design. Originally 20 in class. Built with U.S. Military Assistance Program funds. Wooden construction. Single 20-mm AA fwd removed. M 5450 has a deckhouse in place of the sweep reel and is used in support of frogmen.

AMPHIBIOUS WARFARE SHIPS

◆ **0 (+2) San Giorgio-class amphibious warfare ships**

	Bldr	Laid down	L	In serv.
L 9892 San Giorgio	CNR, Riva Trigoso	9-85	. . .	. . .
L 9893 San Marco	. . .	. . .	. . .	. . .

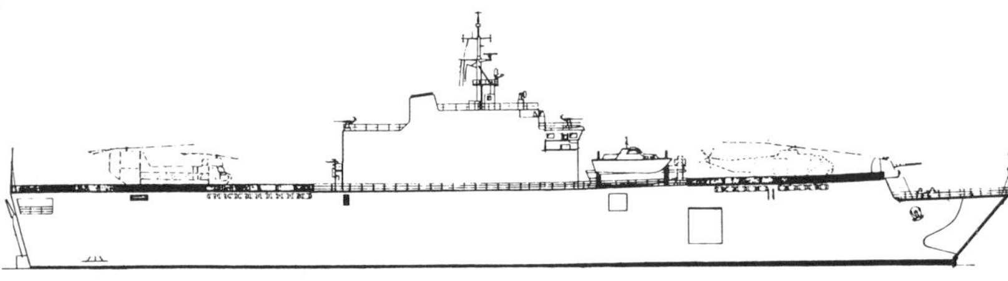

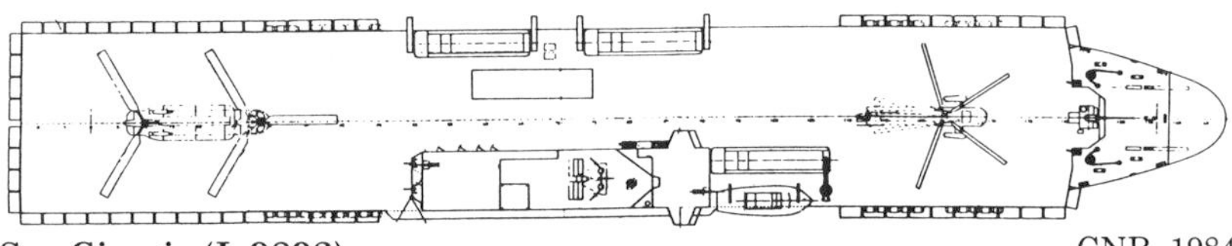

San Giorgio (L 9892) CNR, 1984

D: 7,665 tons (fl) **S:** 21 kts **Dim:** 130.00 (118.00 pp) × 20.50 × 5.00
A: 1/76-mm OTO Melara DP—2/20-mm AA (I × 2)—5/CH-47-sized helicopters
Electron Equipt: Radar: 1/. . . nav, 1/RAN-10S, 1/RTN-30X f.c.
EW: . . .— TACAN: . . .
M: 2 GMT A420.12 12-cyl., 4-stroke diesels; 2 CP props; 10,146 hp
Range: 7,500/16 **Fuel:** 400 tons **Man:** 146 crew + 400 troops

Remarks: L 9892, initially requested for 1980 Budget, was approved in 1983 and ordered 5-3-84. Second ship remains a projection, planned to be paid for with disaster relief rather than defense funds. Will be able to carry 3 LCM in docking well aft, plus 3 LCVP in davits on the flight deck. The hangar will accommodate 5 CH-47 Chinook helicopters; at its forward end is a vehicle deck that can hold up to 36 tracked vehicles, and the ship can beach and use its bow ramp to land personnel and vehicles. There will be stowage for 99 m³ refrigerated stores and 300 m³ dry stores, and the ship will carry 60 tons of aviation fuel. The 76-mm gun will not be of the Compact model, but rather an older-model weapon from a discarded frigate.

These will be versatile vessels, capable of use in amphibious assault, disaster relief, and, with Sea King or EH.101 helicopters embarked, for ASW.

◆ **2 ex-U.S. De Soto County-class LSTs**

	Bldr	L
L 9890 Grado (ex-*De Soto County,* LST 1171)	Avondale SY, New Orleans, La.	28-2-57
L 9891 Caorle (ex-*York County,* LST 1175)	Newport News SB & DD	5-9-57

Grado (L 9890) 1983

D: 4,164 tons (7,804 fl) **S:** 16 kts **Dim:** 134.7 × 18.9 × 5.5 max.
A: 6/76.2-mm 50-cal. DP (II × 3) **Electron Equipt:** Radar: 1/3 RM-20
M: 6 Fairbanks-Morse 38C8⅛ diesels; 2 CP props; 14,400 hp
Man: 13 (L 9891: 11) officers, 147 men + 550 troops

Remarks: Three Mk 51 gunfire-control systems, two forward, one aft. Carry four LCVPs each. Leased 15-7-72, purchased outright 1981. Planned for disposal on completion of *San Giorgio* and *San Marco.*

Note: The transport *Andrea Bafile* (L 9871, ex-U.S. Navy seaplane tender *St. George,* AV 16), in reserve since 1976, is reported to have been stricken in 1981.

◆ **4 U.S. LCVP class**

MTP 9748 MTP 9749 MTP 9750 MTP 9751

D: 7 tons (11 fl) **S:** 9 kts **Dim:** 10.9 × 3.2 × 1.03
M: 1 Gray Marine 64 HN9 diesel; 165 hp **Range:** 110/9

Remarks: Transferred 1953. Two stricken 1979, three in 1980, and 28 others in 1982.

HYDROGRAPHIC SHIPS

◆ **1 Ammiraglio Magnaghi class** Bldr: C. N. del Tirreno, Riva Trigoso

	Laid down	L	In serv.
A 5303 Ammiraglio Magnaghi	13-6-73	11-9-74	2-5-75

Ammiraglio Magnaghi (A 5303) L. & L. Van Ginderen, 10-84

D: 1,550 tons (1,700 fl) **S:** 17 kts **Dim:** 82.70 (76.80 pp) × 13.70 × 3.60
A: 1/40-mm—1/AB-212 helicopter **Electron Equipt:** Radar: 1/2RM-20
M: 2 GMT B306 SS diesels; 1 CP prop; 3,000 hp; 1 electric auxiliary engine; 240 hp (4 kts)
Range: 5,500/12; 4,200/16 **Man:** 15 officers, 120 men, 15 scientists.

Remarks: Equipped for survey and oceanographic studies and for search-and-rescue duties. Passive tank stabilization. Bow-thruster. Part of 1972 program. Has chemistry, physical, oceanography, photo, and hydrology labs, computerized data loggers, underwater TV.

◆ **2 ex-U.S. Adjutant-class minesweepers**

	Bldr	In serv.
A 5306 Mirto (ex-M 5539)	Breda, Marghera	4-8-56
A 5307 Pioppo (ex-M 5515, ex-MSC 135)	Bellingham SY, Washington	30-7-54

Mirto (A 5306) G. Gyssels, 9-82

Remarks: Characteristics generally as for minesweeper version; displacement: 322 tons std. Superstructure enlarged, stack raised. Both can carry two 20-mm AA (II × 1). Man: 3 officers, 31–35 men. Special survey equipment includes Elac Deneb Special scanning sonar, Atlas scanning sonar, TORAN F, Raydist, Mini Ranger III and LORAN-C. To be replaced by two new 1,000-ton ships.

REPLENISHMENT OILERS

◆ **2 Stromboli-class oilers** Bldr: C. N. del Tirreno, Riva Trigoso

	Laid down	L	In serv.
A 5327 Stromboli	1-10-73	20-2-75	31-10-75
A 5329 Vesuvio	1-7-74	4-6-77	18-11-78

Stromboli (A 5327)—with ELINT hut on helo deck Pradignac & Leo, 1985

REPLENISHMENT OILERS *(continued)*

Vesuvio (A 5329) L. & L. Van Ginderen, 1-82

D: 4,200 tons (8,706 fl) **S:** 19.5 kts
Dim: 129.0 (118.5 pp) × 18.0 × 6.5 (3.17 light)
A: 1/76-mm DP
Electron Equipt: Radar: 1/3RM7-250, 1/Orion RTN-10X
M: 2 GMT C428 SS diesels: 1 LIPS 4-bladed CP prop; 11,200 hp (9,600 sust.)
Electric: 2,350 kw **Range:** 10,000/16 **Man:** 10 officers, 114 men

Remarks: Cargo: 1,370 tons fuel oil, 2,830 tons diesel, 480 tons aviation fuel, and 200 tons miscellaneous (torpedoes, missiles, projectiles, spare parts). Capable of serving two units simultaneously alongside while underway with constant-tension fueling rigs, each capable of pumping 650 m^3/hr of fuel oil and 480 m^3/hr of diesel fuel or aviation fuel. Can also refuel over the stern at the rate of 430 m^3/hr. There are also constant-tension cargo transfer rigs on either side, each capable of transferring 1.8-ton loads, as well as two stations for lighter loads. The ships can also replenish via helicopters, although they do not have hangars. Two single 40-mm AA can be added abreast the stack. Twenty repair-party personnel can also be accommodated, and the ships can carry up to 250 passengers. NA-10 Argo GFCS. Sister built for Iraq.

EXPERIMENTAL SHIPS

◆ **1 new construction** Bldr: Picchiotti, Viareggio

A. . . N. . .

D: . . . **S:** . . . **Dim:** 45.0 × . . . × . . .
M: 2 diesels; 2 CP props; . . . hp **Man:** . . .

Remarks: Ordered 3-84; no further data available.

◆ **1 ex-landing ship** Bldr: Taranto Naval Base

	Laid down	L	In serv.
A 5314 Quarto	19-3-66	18-3-67	18-3-68

Quarto (A 5314)—bow door open Cdr. A. Fraccaroli, 1980

D: 764 tons (980 fl) **S:** 11 kts **Dim:** 66.6 × 9.55 × 1.95
A: 2/Otomat Mk 2 SSM (I × 2)—2/40-mm AA (II × 1)
Electron Equipt: Radar: 1/3ST-7, 1/SPQ-2, 1/tracking radar
M: 3 diesels; 3 props; 2,280 hp **Range:** 1,300/13 **Man:** 4 officers, 38 men

Remarks: Unsuccessful landing ship used as a trials ship since early 1970s. Blunt bow restricts speed and seaworthiness. Sisters *Marsala* (hull used as a pontoon) and *Caprara* canceled. Retains visor-type bow door.

◆ **1 converted fishing boat** Bldg: C. N. Castracani, Ancona

A 3315 Barbara

D: 185 tons (195 fl) **S:** 12 kts **Dim:** 30.50 × 6.30 × 1.50
M: 2 diesels; 2 props; 600 hp **Man:** 7 tot.

Remarks: Purchased 1975. Used for oceanographic research. Has 7.5-ton crane.

◆ **1 Aragosta-class former inshore minesweeper**

A 5305 Murena (ex- . . .)

Remarks: Characteristics generally as for minesweeper version. New superstructure, with enclosed bridge. Stern area bare.

◆ **1 former minelayer** (In serv. ca 1939-41)

GIS 61

GIS 61 C. Martinelli, 1983

D: 230 tons **S:** 7 kts **Dim:** . . . × . . . × . . .
A: 1/533-mm TT

Remarks: Used for torpedo firing trials.

SUPPORT TENDERS

◆ **1 supply ship** Bldr: Lake Washington SY, Houghton, Washington

	Laid down	L	In serv.
A 5301 Pietro Cavezzale (ex-*Oyster Bay*, AGP 6, ex-AVP 28)	17-4-42	23-5-43	17-11-43

Pietro Cavezzale (A 5301) G. Gyssels, 3-82

D: 1,766 tons (2,800 fl) **S:** 16 kts **Dim:** 94.6 × 12.58 × 3.7
A: 1/76.2-mm 50-cal. DP—2/40-mm AA (II × 1)
Electron Equipt: Radar: 1/3RM7-250, 1/SPS-6C
M: 2 Fairbanks-Morse 38D8⅛ × 10 diesels; 2 props; 6,000 hp **Electric:** 600 kw
Fuel: 400 tons **Range:** 10,000/11 **Man:** 7 officers, 105 men

Remarks: Transferred 23-10-57. Serves amphibious ships and small boats in a general support/repair tender rôle.

SALVAGE SHIPS

◆ **1 salvage ship**

	Bldr	Laid down	L	In serv.
A 5309 Anteo	C. N. Breda, Mestre	1977	11-11-78	31-7-80

D: 2,178 tons (3,070 fl) **S:** 18.3 kts **Dim:** 98.4 (93.0 pp) × 15.8 × 5.18
A: 2/20-mm AA (II × 1)—1/AB-212 helicopter
Electron Equipt: Radar: 1/3ST-7, 1/3RM-20
M: 3 GMT A-230-12V diesels (4,050 hp each), electric drive (2 motors); 1 prop; 6,000 hp (5,360 sust.)
Fuel: 270 tons **Range:** 4,000/14 **Man:** 9 officers, 104 men

Anteo (A 5309)—hangar retracted C. Martinelli, 1981

SALVAGE SHIPS *(continued)*

Salvage submersible Usel on Anteo (A 5309) A. Fraccaroli, 2-81

Remarks: Ordered 1977. Carries U.S. Navy-style submarine rescue equipment, including a McCann rescue bell capable to 150 meters, and two decompression chambers. A Type MSM-1/S, 22-ton salvage submersible named *Usel* is also carried; 9.0 × 2.5 × 2.7 meters, it can submerge to 600 meters and has a 120-hour autonomous endurance with a 4-kt max. speed. The ship supports saturation diving to 350 meters and has a 27-ton bollard pull at 10 kts. A bow-thruster is fitted.

◆ **1 U.S. AN 93-class former netlayer**

	Bldr	Laid down	L	In serv.
A 5304 Alicudi (ex-AN 99)	Ansaldo, Livorno	4-54	11-7-54	1955

Alicudi (A 5304)—with experimental radar in place of 1/20-mm AA G. Gyssels, 1985

D: 680 tons (832 fl) **S:** 14 kts **Dim:** 46.28 × 10.26 × 3.2
A: 1/40-mm AA—4/20-mm AA (I × 4) **Electron Equipt:** Radar: 1/3ST7
M: 2 Maybach MBA 6H/D650/655 diesels, electric drive; 1 prop; 1,200 hp
Fuel: 105 tons **Man:** 3 officers, 41 men

Remarks: Sister *Filicudi* (A 5305) stricken 1979. Used for salvage work and mooring-buoy laying.

◆ **1 former submarine rescue ship** Bldr: CNR, Ancona

	Laid down	L	In serv.
A 5310 Proteo (ex-*Perseo*)	1943	1944	24-8-51

Proteo (A 5310) C. Martinelli, 1981

D: 1,865 tons (2,178 fl) **S:** 16 kts **Dim:** 75.70 × 11.70 × 6.10
A: 2/20-mm AA (I × 2) **Electron Equipt:** Radar: 1/3ST-7
M: 2 Fiat diesels; 1 prop; 4,800 hp
Range: 7,500/13 **Man:** 8 officers, 106 men

Remarks: Seized by German forces after launch, towed to Trieste; returned to Ancona, and fitting out resumed 1949. Relieved by *Anteo* (A 5309) as submarine rescue ship, but is retained as an ocean tug and salvage ship. Has submersible decompression chamber, extensive divers' support equipment, and 4-point mooring capability. Refitted 1984-85 with new stack and an electrohydraulic crane.

WATER TANKERS

◆ **1 (+1) new construction** Bldr: Ferbex, Naples (L: 1984)

A. . . Tevere

D: 2,130 tons (fl) **S:** . . . **Dim:** 70.40 × 10.20 × 4.50
M: 1 GMT 420 diesel; 1 prop; . . . hp **Man:** . . .

Remarks: Two new water tankers of 1,500 tons capacity were authorized in 1982 for delivery 1983, but only one has been ordered.

◆ **1 Piave class**

	Bldr	L	In serv.
A 5354 Piave	Orlando, Livorno	18-12-71	23-5-73

Piave (A 5354) L. & L. Van Ginderen, 3-81

D: 5,003 tons (fl) **S:** 13.7 kts **Dim:** 97.8 (86.7 pp) × 13.4 × 5.9 **A:** Removed
Electron Equipt: Radar: 1/3RM-7 **M:** 2 diesels; 2,560 hp
Cargo capacity: 3,500 tons **Range:** 1,500,12 **Man:** 5 officers, 42 men

Remarks: Sister *Tevere* (A 5355) sold commercially, 1976. Formerly carried 4/40-mm AA (II × 2).

◆ **3 Basento class** Bldr: Inma, La Spezia

A 5356 Basento (In serv. 19-7-71)
A 5357 Bradano (In serv. 29-12-71)
A 5358 Brenta (In serv. 18-4-72)

Bradano (A 5357) C. Martinelli, 7-84

D: 1,930 tons (fl) **S:** 12.5 kts **Dim:** 68.65 × 10.07 × 3.90
A: Removed **Electron Equipt:** Radar: 1/3RM-7
M: 2 Fiat LA-230 diesels; 1,730 hp **Cargo Capacity:** 1,200 tons
Range: 1,650/12.5 **Man:** 2 officers, 25 men

Remarks: Can carry 2/20-mm AA (I × 2)

◆ **1 small water tanker**

A 5359 Bormida (In serv. . . .)

Bormida (A 5359) C. Martinelli

WATER TANKERS *(continued)*

D: 736 tons (fl) **S:** . . . **Dim:** 40.2 × 7.2 × 3.2
M: 1 diesel; . . . hp **Cargo:** 260 tons **Man:** 6 tot.

◆ **1 small water tanker**

A 5374 MINCIO (In serv. 1929)—645 tons; 23 men

NOTE: Ex-U.S. Army 327E-class water tankers *Adige* (A 5369), *Ticino* (A 5377), and *Tanaro* (A 5376) were scheduled to be stricken on completion of the new tanker *Tevere* in 1985. Also in service are 5 small harbor water lighters of 200 tons full load displacement: GIS 185, 500, 501, 502 and 507.

TRAINING SHIPS

NOTE: The cruiser *Ciao Duilio* (C 554) serves as a training ship also.

◆ **1 sail-training ship** Bldr: Nav. Mec. Castellammare

	Laid down	L	In serv.
A 5312 AMERIGO VESPUCCI	12-5-30	22-2-31	15-5-31

Amerigo Vespucci (A 5312) P. Voss, 8-83

D: 3,545 tons (4,186 fl) **S:** 10 kts
Dim: 101.00 over bow sprit/82.38 (70.72 pp) × 15.56 × 6.7
A: 4/40-mm AA (I × 4)—1/20-mm AA
M: 2 Tosi E6 diesels, electric drive; 1 prop; 1,900 hp
Range: 5,450/6.5 **Man:** 13 officers, 228 men, 150 cadets

REMARKS: Sail area: 3,000 m². Steel construction, including masts. Refitted 1984.

◆ **1 sail-training barkentine** Bldr: Dubigeon, France (In serv. 1920)

A 5311 PALINURO (ex-*Cdt Louis Richard*)

Palinuro (A 5311) A. Fraccaroli

D: 1,042 tons (1,341 fl) **S:** 10 kts **Dim:** 68.9 (59.0 pp) × 10.1 × 4.8
A: 2/76-mm (saluting battery) **M:** 1 M.A.N. G8V23.5/33 diesel; 450 hp
Range: 5,300/7.5 **Man:** 4 officers, 44 men

REMARKS: Former French cod-fishing craft bought in 1951, refitted and recommissioned 16-7-55. Steel hull.

◆ **1 sail-training yawl** Bldr: Costaguta, Genoa (In serv. 5-1-61)

A 5316 CORSARO II

D: 41 tons **Dim:** 20.9 × 4.7 **M:** 1 auxiliary engine; 96 hp
Man: 2 officers, 14 men

REMARKS: Based at Naval Academy, Livorno.

◆ **1 RORC-class cruising yacht** Bldr: Sangermani, Chiavari (In serv. 7-10-65)

A 5313 STELLA POLARE

D: 41 tons (47 fl) **S:** . . . **Dim:** 20.9 × 4.7 × 2.9
M: 1 Mercedes-Benz diesel; 1 prop; 96 hp **Man:** 2 officers, 4 men

REMARKS: Sail area: 197 m². Based at Naval Academy, Livorno.

◆ **1 sail-training yawl** Bldr: Baglietto (In serv. 1948)

A 5302 CAROLY

D: . . . **S:** 9 kts **Dim:** 23.75 × 4.6 × . . .
M: . . . **Man:** . . .

SERVICE CRAFT

◆ **1 yacht/ambulance craft** Bldr: Picchiotti, Viareggio

R. PAOLUCCI (In serv. 12-9-70)

D: 70 tons (fl) **S:** 21.3 kts **Dim:** 27.72 × 7.40 × . . .
M: 2 diesels; 2 props; . . . hp **Man:** 1 officer, 7 men

REMARKS: White-painted, streamlined yacht, with red crosses painted on sides.

◆ **2 diving tenders** Bldr: Crestitalia, Ameglia, La Spezia (In Serv. 5-85)

MARIO MARINO ALCIDE PEDRETTI

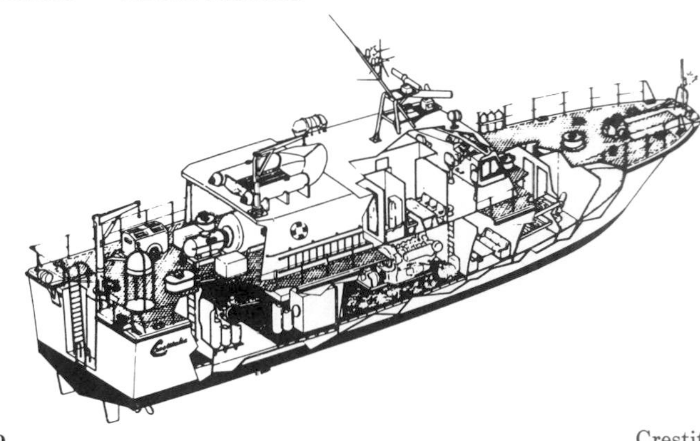

Marino Crestitalia, 1985

D: 69.5 tons (fl) **S:** 25 kts **Dim:** 26.0 × 6.9 × 1.5
M: 2 Isotta-Fraschini ID36SS12V diesels; 2 props; 3,040 hp
Range: 500/25 **Man:** . . .

REMARKS: Have 2 nav. radars, diver's decompression chambers, recovery recess with davit and divers' stage at stern. Glass-reinforced plastic construction.

◆ **4 torpedo-recovery craft** Bldr: Crestitalia, Ameglia, La Spezia (In serv. 1984)

N. . . N. . . N. . . N. . .

D: . . . **S:** 23 kts **Dim:** 11.65 × 3.9 × . . .
M: 2 diesels; 2 props; 470 hp **Range:** 250/20 **Man:** . . .

REMARKS: Can stow 3 torpedoes. Glass-reinforced plastic construction.

◆ **9 ex-British LCT(3)-class tenders** (In serv. 1943-44

A 5301 MTF 1301
A 5331 MOC 1201
A 5332 MOC 1202
A 5333 MOC 1203
A 5334 MOC 1204
A 5335 MOC 1205
A 5337 MOC 1207
A 5362 MTF 1302
A 5363 MTF 1303

MOC 1201 (A 5331)—torpedo retriever G. Arra, 1981

SERVICE CRAFT *(continued)*

MTF 1303 (A 5363) L. & L. Van Ginderen, 1980

D: MOC series: 711–752 tons (fl); MTF series: 414 tons (fl) **S:** 9 kts
Dim: 58.25 to 59.50 × 9.22 × 2.0–2.2
A: 2/20-mm AA (I × 2; not in all)
M: 2 diesels; 2 props; 1,000 hp **Man:** 1-2 officers, 20-26 men

REMARKS: MOC 1201 is used for torpedo recovery; MOC 1207 is an ammunition transport; the remainder serve as repair craft for minesweepers and small combatants. The bow door/ramp has been welded closed.

◆ **1 ex-German MFP-D cargo lighter, former landing craft** (In serv. 1942)

A 5341 MTC 1101

D: 218 tons (fl) **S:** 10 kts **Dim:** 49.8 × 6.6 × 1.12
A: 2/20-mm AA **M:** 3 Deutz diesels; 3 props; 450 hp **Range:** 540/9

REMARKS: Built 1942. Can carry 150 tons cargo; beaching capability retained. Can lay mines.

◆ **4 MZ-class cargo lighters** (In serv. 1942)

A 5344 MTC 1004 A 5345 MTC 1005 A 5346 MTC 1006
A 5350 MTC 1010

MTC 1006 (A 5346) G. Arra, 1982

D: 218 tons (fl) **S:** 10.5 kts **Dim:** 47.0 × 6.55 × 1.13
A: 2/20-mm AA **M:** 3 Deutz diesels; 3 props; 450 hp **Man:** 15-16 tot.

REMARKS: Former Italian-built landing craft. Similar to MFP-D class, but hull has sheer fore and aft. Can carry 150 tons cargo. MTC 1005 can lay mines. Sisters MTC 1007–1009 (A 5347–5350) stricken 1983.

SEAGOING TUGS

◆ **2 Atlante class** Bldr: Visitini, Donada (Both in serv. 14-8-75)

A 5317 ATLANTE A 5318 PROMETEO

Atlante (A 5317) L. & L. Van Ginderen, 9-83

D: 478 tons (750 fl) **S:** 13.5 kts **Dim:** 38.9 × 9.6 × 3.70
M: 1 Tosi QT 320/8SS diesel; 1 CP prop; 3,000 hp **Man:** 25 tot.

◆ **2 U.S. Army 293-design class**

A 5350 COLOSSO (ex-LT 214) A 5321 FORTE (ex-LT 159)

Forte (A 5321) L. & L. Van Ginderen, 9-83

D: 525 tons (835 fl) **S:** 11 kts **Dim:** 38.6 × 8.53 × 3.89
M: 2 Fairbanks-Morse 38D8⅛ diesels; 2 props; 1,690 hp
Fuel: 112 tons **Range:** 3,800/8

REMARKS: Built during World War II; transferred 1948.

◆ **1 San Giusto class** Bldr: CNR, Palermo, (In serv. 1940)

A 5326 SAN GIUSTO

San Giusto (A 5326) L. & L. Van Ginderen, 11-82

D: 370 tons (486 fl) **S:** 12 kts **Dim:** 38.7 × 7.1 × 3.8
M: Triple-expansion reciprocating steam; 900 hp

◆ **2 Gagliardo class**

	L
A 5322 GAGLIARDO	1938
A 5323 ROBUSTO	1939

Robusto (A 5323) C. Martinelli, 1980

D: 389 tons (506 fl) **S:** 8 kts **Dim:** 33.2 × 7.1 × 3.6
M: Triple-expansion reciprocating steam; 850 hp

COASTAL TUGS

◆ **4 . . . class** Bldr: C. N. Ferrari, La Spezia

	Laid down	L	In serv.
A 55 Porto Ferraio	7-84	12-84	21-7-85
A. . . N. . .	. . .	. . .	. . .
A. . . N. . .	. . .	. . .	. . .
A. . . N. . .	. . .	. . .	. . .

D: 658 tons (fl) **S:** 14 kts **Dim:** 38.95 × 9.85 × 3.76
M: 2 GMT BL230 diesels; 1 CP prop; 3,264 hp **Man:** . . .

Remarks: 45-ton bollard pull. 2/170 m³/hr water monitors, 23-ton capacity foam tank.

◆ **5 Panaria class** Bldr: DePoli SY, . . . (In serv. 1984-85)

A. . . Panaria A. . . N. . . A. . . N. . .
A. . . N. . . A. . . N. . .

D: 412 tons (fl) **S:** 11.5 kts **Dim:** 32.36 (28.00 pp) × 8.50 × 3.32
M: 1 GMT B230.8 diesel; 1 prop; 1,600 hp **Fuel:** 46 tons
Range: 1,800/11.5 **Man:** 12 tot.

Remarks: Ordered 2-6-83.

◆ **2 Ercole class** (In serv. 1971)

A 5388 Ercole A 5394 Vigoroso

D: 506 tons (fl) **S:** 8 kts **Dim:** 33.2 × 7.1 × 3.6
M: Diesels; 850 hp

Remarks: Flushed-deck diesel version of *Gagliardo* class.

◆ **2 Porto d'Ischia class** Bldr: CNR, Riva Trigoso (In serv. 1969-70)

Y 436 Porto d'Ischia Y 443 Riva Trigoso

Porto d'Ischia (Y 436) G. Arra, 1982

D: 250 tons (296 fl) **S:** 12 kts **Dim:** 25.5 × 7.1 × 3.3
M: 1 diesel; 1 CP prop; 850 hp

SMALL HARBOR TUGS

◆ **13 new construction** Bldr: (A) C. N. Vittoria, Adria; (B) C. N. Ferrari, La Spezia; (C) CINET, Malfetta

	Bldr	In serv.		Bldr	In serv.
Y 478 RP 125	A	1983	Y. . . RP 132	C	7-7-84
Y 479 RP 126	A	24-9-83	Y. . . RP 133	C	3-11-84
Y 480 RP 127	B	29-3-84	Y. . . RP 134	C	85
Y. . . RP 128	B	4-84	Y. . . RP 135	. . .	. . .
Y. . . RP 129	B	5-6-84	Y. . . RP 136	. . .	. . .
Y. . . RP 130	B	10-8-84	Y. . . RP 137	. . .	. . .
Y. . . RP 131	B	28-8-84			

D: 120 tons (fl) **S:** 9.5 kts **Dim:** 19.85 (17.00) × 5.20 × 2.10
M: 1 Fiat AIFO 828-SM diesel; 1 prop; 368 hp **Man:** 3 tot.

Remarks: First six ordered 18-8-83. 76 grt.

◆ **11 RP 113 class** Bldr: Visitini, Donada (In serv. 1978–1981)

	In serv.		In serv.
Y 463 RP 113	1978	Y 470 RP 119	1980
Y 464 RP 114	1980	Y 471 RP 120	1980
Y 465 RP 115	1980	Y 472 RP 121	1980
Y 466 RP 116	1980	Y 473 RP 122	1980
Y 468 RP 118	1980	Y 474 RP 123	1980
		Y 475 RP 124	1981

Remarks: Characteristics similar to RP 101 class below, but have a larger superstructure. RP 117 (Y 467) lost, date not available.

RP 127 C. Martinelli, 1984

◆ **12 RP-101 class** Bldr: CN Visitini-Loreo, Donado (In serv. 1972-75)

Y 403 RP 101 Y 408 RP 105 Y 456 RP 109
Y 404 RP 102 Y 410 RP 106 Y 458 RP 110
Y 406 RP 103 Y 413 RP 107 Y 460 RP 111
Y 407 RP 104 Y 452 RP 108 Y 462 RP 112

RP 110 (Y 458) C. Martinelli, 1980

D: 36 tons (75 fl) **S:** 12 kts **Dim:** 18.8 × 4.5 × 1.9
M: 1 diesel; 500 hp

Note: Earlier harbor tugs have been replaced by new construction.

MISCELLANEOUS SERVICE CRAFT

Remarks: There are a number of self-propelled and non-powered service craft in use, most with alphanumeric (non-NATO) pendant numbers denoting their functions. Insufficient information is available for a presentation in these pages.

FLOATING DRY DOCKS

◆ **13 miscellaneous**

	In serv.	Capacity		In serv.	Capacity
GO 52	1979	6,000	GO 17	1917	500
GO 51	1971	2,000	GO 11	1911	2,700
GO 23	1935	1,000	GO 10	1900	2,000
GO 22	1935	1,000	GO 8	1904	3,800
GO 20	1935	1,600	GO 5	1893	100
GO 18B	1920	600	GO 1	1942	1,000
GO 18A	1920	800			

Remarks: GO 52 is 150.5 m long by 29.6 m (21.6 m internal width).

PORT CAPTAIN CORPS
(Corpo delle Capitanere di Porto)

In operation in 1984 were some 88 large and 193 small fast patrol boats and craft, employed in port police duties. Most can carry 1 or 2/7.62-mm mg and would come under naval control in time of hostilities. Nearly all bear alphanumeric pendants in the "CP" series. Classes in use include:

CP 301, 302, 306, 308-311: 29 tons, Maierform design, 22 or 26 mo.a., 14 or 28 kt/1,000 n.m.
CP 303, 304: 18 tons, U.S. Coast Guard lifeboats, 13 mo.a. 12 kt/350 n.m.
CP 239 through CP 245: 23.5 tons
CP 246: 21.5 tons
CP 231 through CP 238: 14 tons, 13 mo.a., 24 kt/300 n.m.
CP 226 through CP 230: 18 to 20 tons
CP 601: 3 tons
CP 501, 502: 3.5 tons
CP 2046 through CP 2065: 12.4 tons, U.K. Keith Nelson
CP 1001 through CP 1006: 5.2 tons
CP 2010 through CP 2017: 10 tons, U.K. Keith Nelson, 23 kt/400 n.m.
CP 2001 through CP 2005: 9 tons, U.K. Keith Nelson, 21 kt/400 n.m.
CP 207, 222: 8 tons
CP 202, 204, 205: 8 tons
CP 2024: 15 tons, used in search-and-rescue (SAR)
CP 2032: 12 tons, used in SAR

PORT CAPTAIN CORPS *(continued)*

CP 2025 through 2031, 2033 through 2041: 11 tons, for SAR
CP 2018 through 2023: 10 tons, for SAR, U.K. Keith Nelson
CP 2006 through 2009: 11 tons, for SAR

Also in use are the tug *Audax* (78 tons), and large patrol boats *Michelle Fiorillo* (84 tons), *Bruno Gregoretti* (65 tons), and CP 313, *Dante Novaro* (57 tons; 25 kts/1,000 n.m.), 56 semi-rigid, inflatable boats (5–6 mo.a., 18–28 kt) and a number of small craft.

CP 244 (CP 239–CP 245 series) C. Martinelli, 10-82

CP 238—14-ton class L. & L. Van Ginderen, 1-81

Dante Novaro (CP 313)—25 kts, 2,400 hp 1977

CP 307—Maierform German-built lifeboat

CP 303—U.S. Coast Guard lifeboat L. & L. Van Ginderen, 1982

CP 1004 (CP 1001–1006 series) C. Martinelli, 7-84

ITALY *(continued)*
PORT CAPTAIN CORPS *(continued)*

CP 2011 (CP 2010–2017 series, built in U.K. by Keith Nelson)
C. Martinelli, 1982

CP 2021 (CP 2018–2023 series, another Keith Nelson design)
L. & L. Van Ginderen, 8-84

CUSTOMS SERVICE
(Guardia di Finanza)

The Ministry of Finance operates 157 patrol boats and 340 smaller craft under 15 administrative areas and organized into 48 squadrons. Most of the large units have 7.62- or 12.7-mm mg or 20-mm AA armament. Nearly all the larger units have names, but a complete listing is not available. The Guardia di Finanza also operates 3 Agusta A 109 and several Breda Nardi NH 500 helicopters.

PATROL BOATS AND CRAFT

◆ **2 (+3 or 4) CNL 39 class** Bldr: C. N. Liguri, Riva Trigoso (In serv. 1985)

D: 210 tons (fl) **S:** 28 kts (25 sust.) **Dim:** 40.90 × 7.60 × 2.46
A: 2/30-mm AA (II × 1)—2/7.62-mm mg (I × 2)
M: 2 CRM 18D/SS-1500 diesels; 2 props; 3,000 hp **Fuel:** 45 tons
Range: 1,000/25; 1,300/20; 3,000/15 **Man:** 22 tot.

Remarks: Two ordered 1-84; three or four more planned. Also programmed are 85 23-m "Corrubia"-class patrol boats to replace most of the units built prior to 1975; these craft will displace 55 tons, have a speed of 35 kts, and will be armed with a 30-mm Breda-Mauser AA gun.

◆ **85 Seneca class** Bldr: Crestitalia (In serv. 1983-85)

D: 8 tons **S:** 32 kts **Dim:** 11.10 × . . . × . . .
M: 2 Fiat AIFO diesels; 2 props or Castoldi waterjets; 520 hp

◆ **2 of 109 tons: G 90, G 91**—24 kts, 1/20-mm AA (In serv. 1958-59)

◆ **2 British "Dark" class** Bldr: Saunders-Roe, Beaumaris, U.K. (In serv. 1956-58)

G 80 La Spina G 81 N. . . . . . .

D: 50 tons (70 fl) **S:** 20 kts **Dim:** 21.8 (20.4 wl) × 6.0 × 1.8
A: 1/20-mm AA **Fuel:** 18 tons
M: 2 CRM 18V-12D/55 YE diesels; 2 props; 2,700 hp

Remarks: Survivors of a group of four. Re-engined during the early 1970s. Wooden planking over aluminum alloy frames in hull.

◆ **56 GC 20 class** Bldr: Baglietto, Varezze (In serv. 1970-78)

G 10 through G 66

Pizzighella (G 55)
J. Jedrlinic, 1981

D: 40 tons (48.7 fl) **S:** 34 kts **Dim:** 20.4 × 5.2 × 1.7 max.
A: 1/20-mm AA—2/7.62-mm mg **Fuel:** 6 tons
Electron Equipt: Radar: 1/SMA 3RM-20 **Range:** 450/20
M: 2 CRM 18 DS diesels; 2 props; 2,700 hp **Man:** 1 officer, 9 men

Remarks: Steel construction. Names known: *Gori, Pizzighella* (G 55), *Russo* (G 20). Ten sisters built for Algeria.

◆ **2 of 54 tons: G 70, G 71**—34 kts, 1/20-mm AA (In serv. 1966-67)

◆ **GL 432, 433:** 22.9 tons

◆ **GL 103 through 106:** 7.1 tons

◆ **GL 309 through 331:** 16.4 tons

◆ **GL 201 through 205:** 14.4 tons

Also in use are 58 craft numbered in the "V" series and ranging from 1.5 to 10.5 tons, the 28-ton patrol boat *Alberti*, the Customs Service training ship *Paolini* (G 95) of 348 tons, and the training craft *Ciorlieri*.

IVORY COAST

Republic of the Ivory Coast

Personnel (1984): 545 total (45 officers, 500 enlisted)

Merchant Marine (1984): 64 ships—143,358 grt (3 tankers—4,725 grt)

GUIDED-MISSILE PATROL BOATS

◆ **2 French Patra class** Bldr: Auroux, Arcachon

	Laid down	L	In serv.
L'Ardent	15-4-77	21-7-78	6-10-78
L'Intrepide	7-7-77	21-7-78	6-10-78

L'Ardent
Auroux, 1978

IVORY COAST *(continued)*
GUIDED-MISSILE PATROL BOATS *(continued)*

D: 125 tons (148 fl) **S:** 26.3 kts **Dim:** 40.70 (38.50 pp) × 5.90 × 1.55
A: 2/MM 40 Exocet—1/40-mm AA—1/20-mm AA—2/7.62-mm mg
Electron Equipt: Radar: 1/Decca 1226
M: 2 AGO 195 V12CZ SHR diesels; 2 CP props; 5,000 hp (4,400 sust.)
Electric: 120 kw

Remarks: Ordered 1-77 and 4-77, respectively. Exocet added 1981.

◆ **2 PR-48 class** Bldr: S.F.C.N., Villeneuve-la-Garenne

	Laid down	L	In serv.
Vigilant	2-67	23-5-67	1968
Le Valeureux	28-10-75	8-3-76	25-9-76

D: 250 tons (fl) **S:** 23 kts **Dim:** 47.5 (45.5 pp) × 7.0 × 2.25
A: 4/MM 40 Exocet—2/40-mm AA (I × 2)
M: 2 MGO diesels with Masson reduction gear; 2 props; 4,200 hp
Range: 2,000/16 **Man:** 4 officers, 30 men

Remarks: *Vigilant* refitted at Brest, France, 1981. Exocet added 1981.

AMPHIBIOUS WARFARE SHIPS

◆ **1 French BATRAL-E-class medium landing ship** Bldr: Dubigeon, Normandy

Éléphant (In serv. 2-2-77)

D: 750 tons (1,330 fl) **S:** 16 kts **Dim:** 80.0 (68.0 pp) × 13.0 × 3.0 (max.)
A: 2/40-mm AA (I × 2) **M:** 2 SACM diesels; 2 CP props; 1,800 hp
Range: 4,500/13 **Man:** 4 officers, 35 men

Remarks: Ordered 2-8-74. Similar to the French Navy's *Champlain*. Helicopter platform aft. Refitted at Brest, 1981.

◆ **10 Type 412 fast assault boats** Bldr: Rotork, U.K. (In serv. 1979-80)

D: 5.2 tons (8.9 fl) **S:** 21 kts **Dim:** 12.65 × 3.20 × . . .
M: 2 Volvo AQD 40A outdrive diesels; 2 props; 240 hp

◆ **1 Barracuda-class launch** Bldr: Halter, New Orleans, U.S.A. (In serv. 1976)

D: 6 tons (8.35 fl) **S:** 36 kts **Dim:** 11.0 × 3.8 × 0.6
M: 2 G.M. 6V-53PI diesels; 2 water jets; 540 hp **Capacity:** 20 men

◆ **2 LCVP** Bldr: Abidjan, 1970

D: 7 tons (9 fl) **S:** 9 kts **Dim:** 10.9 × 3.2 × 1.0
M: 1 Mercedes-Benz diesel

SERVICE CRAFT

◆ **1 Arcor-30 launch** Bldr: Arcor, La Teste, France (In serv. 1985)

D: 5 tons **S:** 20 kts **Dim:** 9.25 (8.30 pp) × 3.50 × 0.82
M: 2 Renault RC-160-D3 diesels; 2 props; 320 hp **Man:** 2 tot.

◆ **4 Arcor launches** Bldr: Arcor, La Teste, France (In serv. 1982)

Dim: 7.92 o.a. **M:** 2 Renault diesels

◆ **Arcor-31 launches** Bldr: Arcor, La Teste, France (In serv. 1982)

Dim: 9.45 o.a. **M:** 2 Renault diesels

JAMAICA

DEFENCE FORCE COAST GUARD

Personnel (1984): 18 officers, 150 men (plus reserves: 16 officers, 30 men)

Merchant Marine (1984): 13 ships—9,419 grt

PATROL BOATS

Note: The ordering of one 42.67-m and two 12.80-m patrol boats from Swiftships, Inc., Morgan City, La., in the U.S.A. is proposed for 1986.

◆ **1 Fort Charles class** Bldr: Teledyne Sewart, Berwick, La., (In serv. 1974)

P 7 Fort Charles

D: 103 tons (fl) **S:** 32 kts **Dim:** 31.5 × 5.7 × 2.1
A: 1/20-mm AA—2/12.7-mm mg (I × 2)
M: 2 MTU MB 16V538 TB90 diesels; 2 props; 7,000 hp
Range: 1,200/18 **Man:** 3 officers, 14 men

Remarks: Can carry 24 soldiers and serve as an 18-bed floating dispensary. Refitted 1979-81 at Jacksonville, Florida.

Fort Charles (P 7) L. & L. Van Ginderen, 1984

◆ **3 85-foot Commercial Cruiser design** Bldr: Sewart Seacraft, Berwick, La., U.S.A., 1966-67

P 4 Discovery Bay P 5 Holland Bay P 6 Manatee Bay

Manatee Bay (P 6) L. & L. Van Ginderen, 3-79

D: 60 tons **S:** 30 kts **Dim:** 25.9 × 5.68 × 1.83
A: 3/12.7-mm mg (I × 3) **M:** 3 MTU 8V331 TC81 diesels; 3 props; 3,000 hp
Fuel: 13 tons **Range:** 800/20 **Man:** 2 officers, 9 men

Remarks: Re-engined twice, most recently from 1981 to 1983, by Swiftships, Inc., more than quadrupling the original horsepower.

JAPAN

Personnel (1984): 45,200 total, plus approx. 4,300 civilian employees

Merchant Marine (1985): 10,425 ships—40,358,479 grt)
(tankers: 1,771 ships—17,520,917 grt)

The Maritime Self-Defense Force (MSDF), or Kaiso Jeitai, was created in 1954. In Article 9 of its constitution, Japan waived the right of belligerence and declared peaceful intentions. Consequently, the armed forces are designed to carry out purely defensive tasks. The duties of the MSDF involve essentially the protection of coastal traffic and of Japan's sea lines of communication, both of which are vital to the economic survival of one of the world's most industrialized nations. For some years now, however, the MSDF has tended to look more and more like an oceangoing navy, as is evidenced by the construction of more important ships.

In addition to the MSDF, Japan has a large and recently modernized Maritime Safety Agency (Kaijo Hoancho), which, in function, is roughly comparable to the U.S. Coast Guard and which, in time of war, would come under the control of the Navy. Its ships are listed at the end of this section.

Construction Programs:
1980 Budget:
2 DDG (127 *Isoyuki,* 128 *Haruyuki*), 1 frigate (228 *Yubetsu*), 1 SS (577 *Nadashio*), 2 MHC (656 *Yakushima,* 657 *Narushima*), and 3 service craft
1981 Budget:
1 DDG (171 *Hatakaze*), 2 DDG (129 *Yamayuki,* 130 *Matsuyuki*), 1 SS (578 *Hamashio*), 2 MHC (658 *Chichijima,* 659 *Toroshima*), 1 ASR (403 *Chiyoda*), and 2 service craft
1982 Budget:
3 DDG (131 . . . , 132 . . . , 133 . . .), 1 SS (579 *Akishio*), 2 MHC (660 *Hahajima,* 661 *Takashima*), and 3 service craft
1983 Budget:
1 4,500 ton DDG (172 . . .), 1 3,400-ton DDG (134 . . .), 1 SS (580 . . .), 2 MHC (662 . . . , 663 . . .), 1 8,300-ton AOE (422 . . .), 1 2,000-ton survey ship (5104 . . .), and 4 service craft

CONSTRUCTION PROGRAMS: *(continued)*

1984 Budget:
3 3,400-ton DDG (135 . . . , 136 . . . , 137 . . .), 1 SS (581 . . .), 2 MHC (664 . . . , 665 . . .), 1 8,300-ton AOE (423 . . .)
1985 Budget:
3 3,400-ton DDG (138 . . . , 139 . . . , 140 . . .), 1 SS (582 . . .), 2 MHC (666 . . . , 667 . . .), and 1 service craft
1986 Budget (Request):
1 4,500-ton DDG (173 . . .), 2 3,400-ton DDG (. . . , ...), 1 SS (583 . . .), 2 MHC (668 . . . , 669 . . .), 1 250-ton missile boat, 1 2,000-ton training ship, . . . service craft

During the period 1983–87, it had been planned to request funds to build 2 6,500-ton AEGIS DDG, 1 4,500-ton DDG, 8 3,400-ton DDG, 3 DE of 1,600 to 1,900 tons, 6 SS, 1 prototype 1,000-ton minesweeper, 12 440-ton MSG, 6 250-ton guided-missile boats, 2 submarine rescue ships (ASR), 2 8,300-ton replenishment ships, 3 3,500-ton LSTs, 3 350-ton utility landing craft, and a 2,000-ton training ship. However, financial and political constraints have deleted or deferred a number of programs, particularly the amphibious warfare units.

Naval Aviation: Naval air is an integral part of the Navy and has about 8,000 men assigned. Its headquarters are in Atsugi, and it has twelve bases along the coasts of Japan. The Air Training Command has several centers at Shimofusa. Some 20 helicopters serve on board the destroyers and frigates. As of 31 Jan. 1985, the naval air arm consisted of 212 aircraft including:
78 P-2J patrol planes
75 HSS-2 Sea King ASW helicopters
17 P-3C patrol planes
7 KV-107-II minesweeping helicopters
14 PS-2 ASW seaplanes
81 miscellaneous aircraft, including 62 KM-2 trainers

In the 1981 Budget, 6 HSS-2B, 1 S-61A rescue helicopter, 1 KM-2, and 4 TC-90 were authorized. In 1982, 7 P-3C, 1 US-1, 2 King Air TC-90, 8 SH-3B/HSS-2B, 2 OH-6D, 4 S-61A, and 2 KM-2 were approved. The 1983 Budget approved 10 P-3C, 1 US-1A, 3 King Air TC-90, 10 HSS-2B (SH-3B) Sea King, 1 S-61A, 2 OH-6D, and 2 SH-60B. The 1984 Budget approved 8 P-3C, 1 US-1A, 1 TC-90, 12 HSS-2B, 2 S-61, 3 OH-6D, 1 Learjet-U-36A, and 1 SH-60B. For 1985 10 P-3C, 1 U-36A, 10 HSS-2B, and 1 S-61A were approved. The SH-60B (S-70B) ASW helicopters are planned as prototypes and research aircraft for a Mitsubishi-built series production program to begin in 1991, substituting Japanese for U.S. electronics.

Originally set at 45, the force-level goal for P-3C long-range patrol aircraft was announced in 5-85 as 103, as the P-2J is slowly phased out; 31 P-3C will be in service by 3-87 (4 squadrons); all will be able to launch U.S. Harpoon missiles. In FY 86, 12 P-3C are to be requested. The last of 13 S-2F1 ASW aircraft was stricken 31-3-84. Three P-2Js have been converted to EP-2J ELINT collectors and 4 to UP-2J trainers; three Learjet U-36A aircraft are to replace the UP-2Js as radar and sonobuoy trainers between 10-85 and 3-87. The Shin-Meiwa PS-1 ASW seaplanes are being modernized with Litton APS-504 radars, cargo doors, cameras, and drop ports. A plan to acquire U.S. MH-53E minesweeping helicopters to replace the dwindling numbers of KV-107-IIs has been deferred for several years, but in 5-85 it was announced that a new goal of 12 had been set, and 4 are to be ordered during 1986.

P-3C Orion Kawasaki, 1982

PS-1 of the Iwakuni-based Fleet Air Wing 1982

P-2J Neptune towing target sleeve JMSDF,1984

HSS-2B Sea King JMSDF, 1984

Warships In Service And Under Construction
As Of 1 January 1986

	L	Tons (Surfaced)	Main armament
◆ **15 (+4) submarines**			
6 (+4) Yushio	1979-	2,200	6/533-mm TT
7 Uzushio	1970-75	1,850	6/533-mm TT
1 Asashio	1968	1,650	8/533-mm TT
◆ **31 (+15) destroyers**		(Std.)	
0 (+7) 3,400-ton DDG	1986-	3,400	Harpoon, Sea Sparrow, ASROC, 1/76-mm DP, ASW TT, 1 helo
0 (+3) 4,500-ton DDG	1984-	4,500	Harpoon, 1/Standard launcher, 1/127-mm, ASROC, ASW TT
7 (+5) Hatsuyuki	1980-	2,900	Harpoon missiles, Sea Sparrow, ASROC, 1/76-mm DP, ASW TT, 1/helo
2 Shirane	1978-79	5,200	2/127-mm DP, 3 helicopters
3 Tachikaze	1974-81	3,850	1/Standard launcher, 2/127-mm, ASROC, 6 TT
2 Haruna	1971-73	4,700	2/127-mm DP, 6/324-mm TT, ASROC, 3 helicopters
6 Yamagumo	1965-77	2,100	4/76-mm DP, 4/375-mm TT
3 Minegumo	1967-69	2,066	4/76-mm DP, 1 rocket launcher, 6/324-mm TT
4 Takatsuki	1966-69	3,200	2/127-mm DP, ASROC
1 Amatsukaze	1963	3,050	1/Standard launcher, 4/76-mm DP, ASROC
1 Akizuki	1959	2,300	3/127-mm AA, 4/76-mm DP
2 Ayanami	1957-60	1,700	6/76-mm DP, 4/533-mm TT
◆ **18 frigates**			
2 Yubari	1982	1,400	Harpoon missiles, 1/76-mm DP
1 Ishikari	1980-	1,200	Harpoon missiles, 1/76-mm DP
11 Chikugo	1970-76	1,470	2/76-mm DP, 2/40-mm AA, ASROC
4 Isuzu	1961-63	1,490	4/76-mm DP, ASW weapons
◆ **2 submarine chasers**			
◆ **5 torpedo boats**			
◆ **42 (+4) mine warfare ships and craft**			
◆ **8 amphibious warfare ships**			

WEAPONS AND SYSTEMS

Until the 1970s, most weapons and detection gear were of American design, built under license in Japan. However, the latest ships are being equipped with Japanese-designed, long-range, pulse-compression air-search radars and with the 76-mm OTO Melara gun. The latter is built under license. U.S. Vulcan/Phalanx 20-mm CIWS (Close-In Weapon System) and Harpoon anti-ship missiles are being procured in quantity.

In Japan, the U.S. SPS-10 radar is referred to as OPS-1, SPS-6 as OPS-15, and SPS-12 as OPS-16. Similarly, the U.S. SQS-23 sonar, when built in Japan, is referred to as the OQS-3, while the OQS-1 and -2 were license-built SQS-4/29 series equipments. The OQS-4 is an indigenous, low-frequency design, as is OQS-101.

Weapons are also produced in Japan. Mitsubishi has a license to build the U.S. Mk 46 Mod. 5 "Neartips" ASW torpedo, while the indigenously designed GRX-2 high-speed homing torpedo for submarine service and the GRX-3 short-range ASW torpedo for aircraft are in development. The U.S. Standard SM-1 MR and AIM-7E surface-to-air

WEAPONS AND SYSTEMS *(continued)*

missiles are in use, while submarines, surface ships, and aircraft are being equipped with the U.S. Harpoon anti-ship missile.

For shore defense, 56 6-tubed trucks are to be delivered beginning in 1989 to launch the Mitsubishi SSM-1 missile, powered by a turbojet:

Length: 5.0 m	Weight: 660 kg
Diameter: 35 cm	Warhead: 224 kg
Span: 1.2 m	Range: 150 km

SUBMARINES (SS)

◆ 6 (+4) Yushio class

	Bldr	Laid down	L	In serv.
573 Yushio	Mitsubishi, Kobe	3-12-76	29-3-79	26-2-80
574 Mochishio	Kawasaki, Kobe	28-4-78	12-3-80	5-3-81
575 Setoshio	Kawasaki, Kobe	28-4-79	12-2-81	17-3-82
576 Okishio	Kawasaki, Kobe	17-4-80	5-3-82	1-3-83
577 Nadashio	Mitsubishi, Kobe	16-4-81	27-1-83	6-3-84
578 Hamashio	Kawasaki, Kobe	8-4-82	1-2-84	5-3-85
579 Akishio	Mitsubishi, Kobe	15-4-83	21-1-85	3-86
580 Takeshio	Kawasaki, Kobe	3-4-84	2-86	3-87
581 N.	Mitsubishi, Kobe	11-4-85	1-87	3-88
582 N.	Kawasaki, Kobe	4-86	-88	3-89
583 N.	. . .	. . .	. . .	. . .

Okishio (SS 576) L. & L. Van Ginderen, 3-83

Nadashio (SS 577) L. & L. Van Ginderen, 8-84

D: 2,200 tons (surf.) **S:** 12/20 kts **Dim:** 76.20 × 9.9 × 7.5 **A:** 6/533-mm TT
M: 2 Kawasaki/M.A.N. V8/V24-30 AMTL, 1,700-hp diesel generator sets (2,840 kw tot.), 1 Fuji electric motor; 1 prop; 7,220 hp
Electron Equipt: Radar: ZPS-6—Sonar: SQS-36J active, ZQQ-4 passive suite
Man: 10 officers, 70 men

Remarks: Deeper-diving than the *Uzushio* class and have more modern electronic equipment. 577 and later are to be equipped with U.S. Sub-Harpoon missiles. At least 14 planned, 6 during 1983-88. Double-hull design. Plan one per year through 1988.

◆ 7 Uzushio class

	Bldr	Laid down	L	In serv.
566 Uzushio	Kawasaki, Kobe	25-9-68	11-3-70	21-1-71
567 Makishio	Mitsubishi, Kobe	21-6-69	27-2-71	2-2-72
568 Isoshio	Kawasaki, Kobe	9-7-70	18-3-72	25-11-72
569 Narushio	Mitsubishi, Kobe	8-5-71	22-11-72	28-9-73
570 Kuroshio	Kawasaki, Kobe	5-7-72	22-2-74	27-11-74
571 Takashio	Kawasaki, Kobe	6-7-73	30-6-75	30-1-76
572 Yaeshio	Kawasaki, Kobe	14-4-75	19-5-77	7-3-78

D: 1,850/3,600 tons **S:** 12/20 kts **Dim:** 72.0 × 9.9 × 7.5 **A:** 6/533-mm TT
Electron Equipt: Radar: 1/ZPS-4—Sonar: ZQQ-4 passive suite, SQS-36(J) active
M: Diesel-electric propulsion; 2 Kawasaki-M.A.N. V8/V24-30 AMTL, 1,700 hp diesels; 1 prop; 7,200 hp
Man: 10 officers, 70 men

Makishio (SS 567) L. & L. Van Ginderen, 7-84

Remarks: Tear-drop hull. Double-hull construction, bow sonar array, torpedo tubes amidships, as in modern U.S. Navy submarines. Maximum depth: 200 m.

◆ 1 Asashio class

	Bldr	Laid down	L	In serv.
565 Arashio	Mitsubishi, Kobe	5-7-67	27-10-68	25-7-69

Arashio (SS 565) *Ships of the World,* 3-84

D: 1,650 tons **S:** 14/18 kts **Dim:** 88.0 × 8.2 × 4.9
A: 8/533-mm TT (6 fwd, 2 aft: 20 torpedoes)
Electron Equipt: Radar: 1/ZPS-3—Sonar: SQS-4 active, JQS-3A, JQQ-2A passive—EW: BLR-1 intercept
M: 2 Kawasaki diesels; 2,900 hp each; 2 electric motors, 3,150 hp each; 2 props
Man: 80 tot.

Remarks: *Oshio,* built during the 1961 program and stricken 3-82, was the prototype for the other four and was considered a separate class. She had a less elaborate sonar array and a more pointed bow. *Asashio* (562) stricken early 1983, *Harushio* (563) on 30-3-84 and *Michishio* (564) on 27-3-85.

HELICOPTER-CARRYING DESTROYERS (DDH)

◆ 2 Shirane class

	Bldr	Laid down	L	In serv.
143 Shirane	Ishikawajima, Tokyo	25-2-77	18-9-78	17-3-80
144 Kurama	Ishikawajima, Tokyo	17-2-78	20-9-79	27-3-81

D: 5,200 tons (6,800 fl) **S:** 32 kts **Dim:** 158.8 × 17.5 × 5.3 (hull)
A: 2/127-mm Mk 42 DP (I × 2)—1/Mk 29 launcher (VIII × 24 Sea Sparrow)—144 only; 2/20-mm Mk 15 CIWS AA (I × 2)—1/ASROC ASW RL (VIII × 1, 16 missiles)—6/324-mm Type 68 ASW TT (III × 2)—3/HSS-2B ASW helicopters
Electron Equipt: Radar: OPS-22 nav., 1/OPS-12, 1/OPS-28, 1/WM-25 (H.S.A.), 2/GFCS-1A, 1/CCA
TACAN: URN-25
EW: NOLQ-1 passive/active, OLR-9B passive
Sonar: OQS-101 (hull), SQS-35 VDS, SQR-18A towed array
M: 2 sets GT; 2 props; 70,000 hp **Boilers:** 2; 60 kg/cm², 480°C **Man:** 370 tot.

Shirane (DDH 143)—with 2 SATCOMM radomes, no CIWS *Ships of the World,* 1984

HELICOPTER-CARRYING DESTROYERS (DDH) *(continued)*

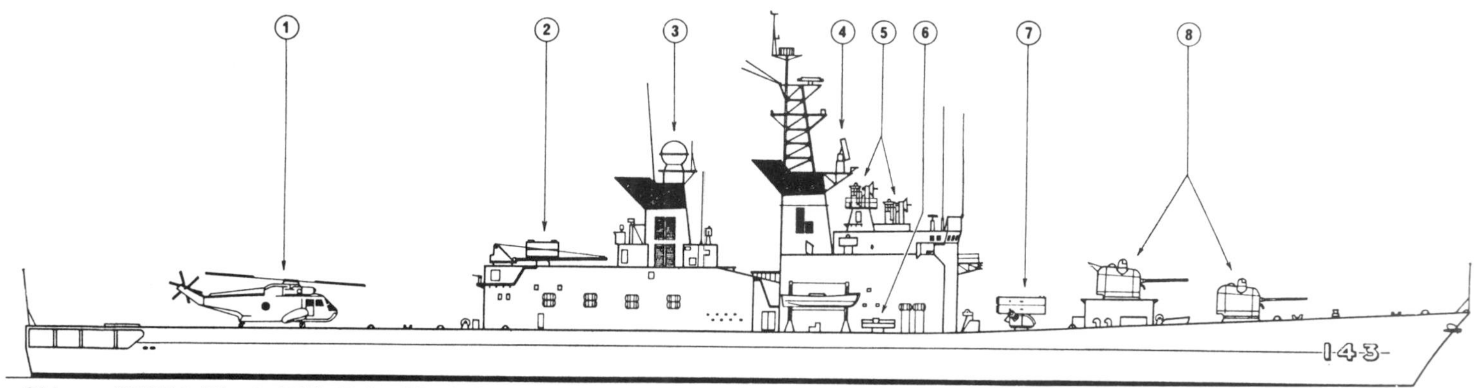

Shirane (DDH 143) 1. HSS-2B Sea King helicopter 2. Sea Sparrow Mk 29 launcher 3. WM 25 track-while-scan radar 4. OPS-12 3-dimensional air-search radar 5. GFCS-1A gunfire-control radar directors 6. Triple Mk 32 ASW torpedo tubes 7. ASROC Mk 112 ASW rocket launcher 8. Mk 42 Mod. 10 127-mm dual-purpose guns

Shirane (DDH 143) *Ships of the World,* 7-84

Kurama (DDH 144)—with 2 Mk 15 CIWS (Vulcan/Phalanx) L. & L. Van Ginderen, 10-84

Remarks: Modified *Haruna* class. Both received U.S. SQR-18A TACTASS passive towed hydrophone arrays during 1981. Have "Masker" bubble-generating system to reduce radiated noise. WM-25 controls the Sparrow missiles. Will eventually receive Harpoon missiles. Have *two* stacks, slightly staggered, compared to one on the *Haruna* class. DDH 143 still lacked Vulcan/Phalanx in late 1984. Both have TDPS-Target Data Processing System, with a U.S. UYK-20 computer and OYQ-5 display. Have LINK 11 and LINK 14 data transmission systems. A landing control radar is mounted to port of the after stack.

◆ **2 Haruna class**

	Bldr	Laid down	L	In serv.
141 Haruna	Mitsubishi, Nagasaki	19-3-70	1-2-72	22-3-73
142 Hiei	Ishikawajima-Harima	8-3-72	13-8-73	27-12-74

Haruna (DDH 141) L. & L. Van Ginderen, 7-80

Hiei (DDH 142)—with 2 SATCOMM antennas *Ships of the World,* 7-84

D: 4,700 tons (6,300 fl) **S:** 32 kts **Dim:** 153.0 × 17.5 × 5.1
A: 2/127-mm Mk 42 DP (I × 2)—6/324-mm Type 68 ASW TT (III × 2)—1/ASROC ASW system—3/HSS-2 ASW helicopters
Electron Equipt: Radar: 1/OPS-11, 1/OPS-17, 2/GFCS-1
Sonar: OQS-3—EW: OLR-9 intercept
TACAN: ORN-6
M: 2 sets GT; 2 props; 70,000 hp **Boilers:** 2; 60 kg/cm², 480°C
Man: 36 officers, 304 men

Remarks: Plan to upgrade by installing Sea Sparrow, Vulcan/Phalanx, SQS-35 VDS (for which provision was made in the design), and Harpoon; funding for DDH 141 approved FY 83, for completion 1987; funding for DDH 142 in 1984 Budget. DDH 142 received improved sonar, 1981. Have single "mack," offset to port. Had very little EW gear as built.

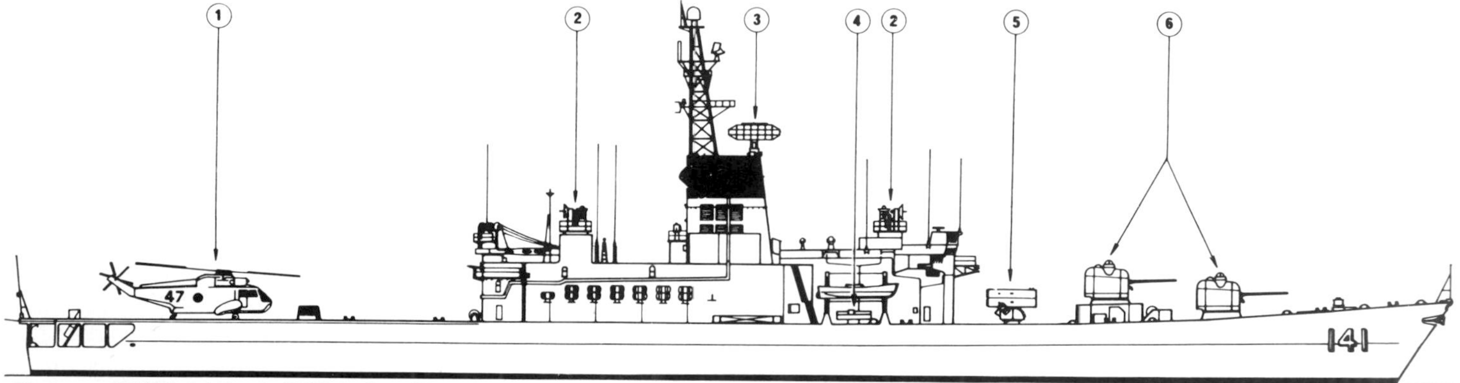

Haruna (DDH 141) 1. HSS-2 Sea King helicopter 2. GFCS-1 gunfire-control system 3. OPS-11 air-search radar 4. Mk 68 ASW TT 5. ASROC ASW rocket launcher 6. 127-mm, 54-caliber, dual-purpose guns, Mk 42 Mod. 10

GUIDED-MISSILE DESTROYERS

NOTE: A new 6,000-ton (standard displacement) guided-missile destroyer is being designed. To carry the U.S. SPY-1D AEGIS radar and Standard SM-2 MR missiles, the first of four is planned to be requested in the 1987 Budget for delivery in 1992. The others will be ordered at 2-year intervals.

◆ 0 (+7 + 3) new construction, 1983 Program (DDK)

	Bldr	Laid down	L	In serv.
134 N. . .	Ishikawajima-Harima	13-2-85	7-86	3-88
135 N. . .	Sumitomo, Uraga	1-86	9-87	1-89
136 N. . .	Mitsui, Tamano	2-86	9-87	2-89
137 N. . .	Ishikawajima-Harima	3-86	8-87	3-89
138 N. . .	. . .	. . .	. . .	. . .
139 N. . .	. . .	. . .	. . .	. . .
140 N. . .	. . .	. . .	. . .	. . .

D: 3,400 tons (4,200 fl) **S:** 30 kts **Dim:** 136.5 × 14.6 × 4.45 (mean)
A: 8/Harpoon SSM (IV × 2)—1/Mk 29 missile launcher (VIII × 1; 18 Sea Sparrow missiles)—1/76-mm OTO-Melara Compact—2/20-mm Mk 15 CIWS AA (I × 2)—1/Mk 112 ASROC ASW RL (VIII × 1; . . . rockets)—6/324-mm Type 68 ASW TT (III × 2 H.O.S. 301 for Mk 46 Mod 5 torpedoes)—1/HSS-2B helicopter

Electron Equipt: Radar: 1/OPS-28, 1/OPS-14C, 1/FCS-2-21A, 1/FCS-2-12E
Sonar: OQS-4A, SQR-18B TASS
EW: OLR-9C passive, OLR-6C active/passive, OLT-3 D/F, 2 Mk 36 SRBOC chaff RL (VI × 2)
TACAN: URN-25

M: COGAG: 4 Kawasaki-Rolls-Royce Spey SM-1A gas turbines; 2 CP props; 59,000 hp (68,400 max.)

Range: . . . **Electric:** . . . **Fuel:** . . . **Man:** 230 tot.

REMARKS: An improved *Hatsuyuki.* DD 134 ordered 29-3-84. Will have the OYQ-6 Combat Direction System, employing the U.S.-built UYK-20A computer and the Japanese OJ-194B Digital Display Indicator. The Target Designation System is designated OYQ-5. Provision will be made for the SQS-35 variable-depth sonar. U.S.-built SLQ-25 NIXIE torpedo decoys and the Prairie/Masker bubble countermeasures system will be fitted. Will have fin stabilizers, and a Beartrap/RAST-type helicopter landing and deck-handling system. DDG 135–137 in 1984 Budget, 138–140 in 1985 Budget, when one more than requested was authorized; a total of 10 is projected.

◆ 0 (+2 + 1) Hatakaze class (DDG)

	Bldr	Laid down	L	In serv.
171 HATAKAZE	Mitsubishi, Nagasaki	20-5-83	9-11-84	31-3-86
172 N.	Mitsubishi, Nagasaki	30-1-85	10-86	3-88

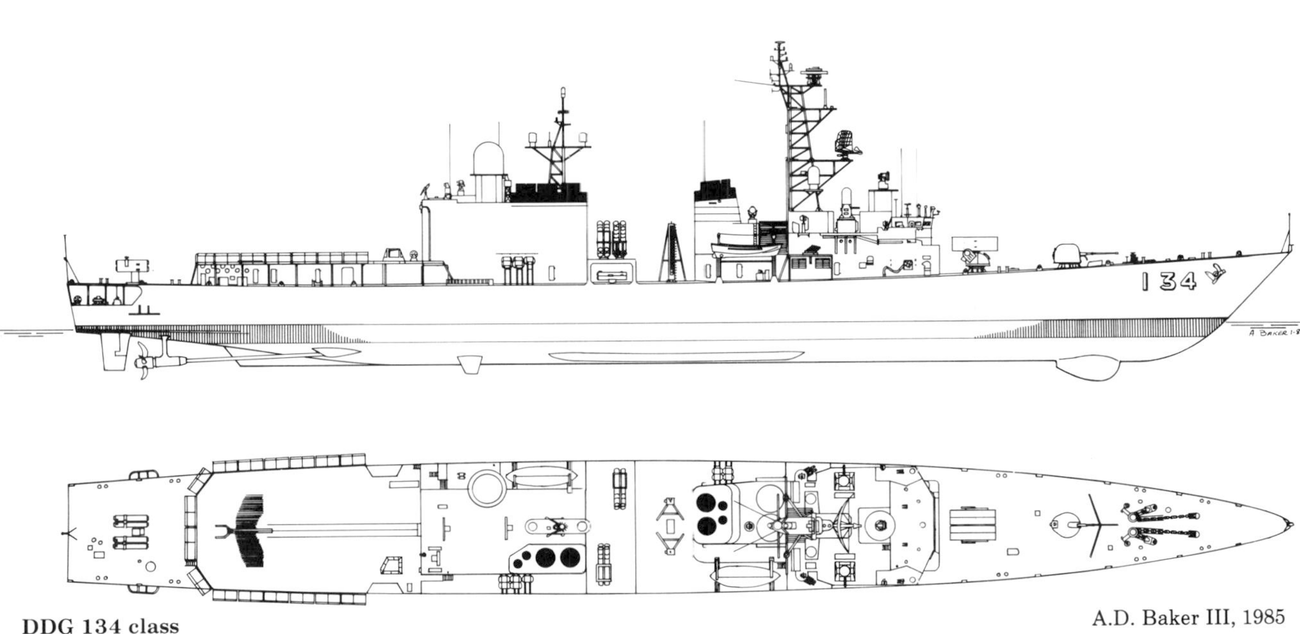

DDG 134 class — A.D. Baker III, 1985

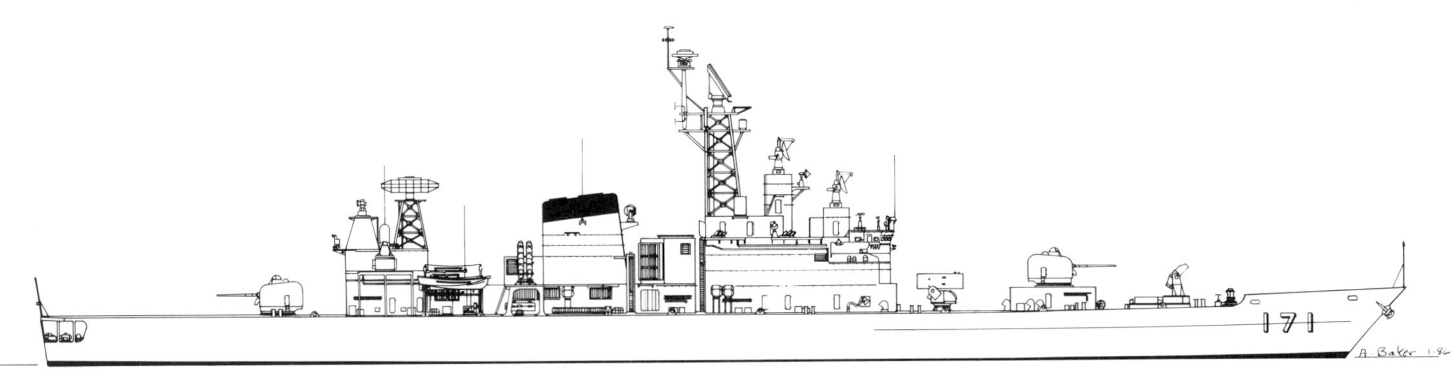

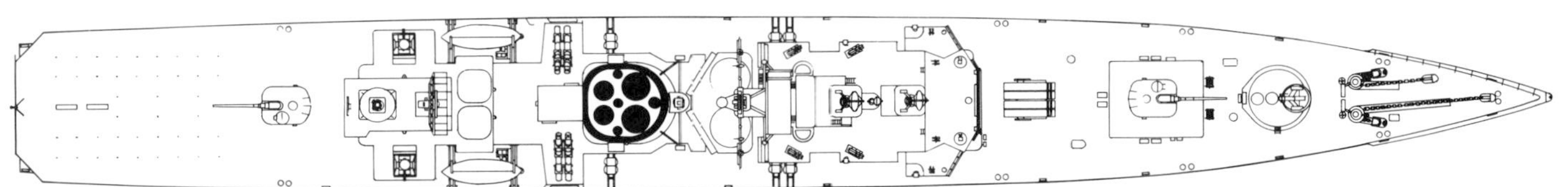

Hatakaze (DDG 171) — A.D. Baker III, 1985

GUIDED-MISSILE DESTROYERS *(continued)*

D: 4,450 tons (5,400 fl) **S:** 32 kts **Dim:** 150.0 × 16.4 × 4.80 (mean)
A: 1/Mk 13 Mod. 4 missile launcher (I × 1, 40 Standard SM-1 MR missiles)—8/Harpoon SSM (IV × 2)—2/127-mm Mk 42 DP (I × 2)—2/20-mm Vulcan/Phalanx Mk 15 Mod. 2 AA (I × 2)—1/ASROC Mk 116 ASW RL (VIII × 1)—6/324-mm Type 68 ASW TT (III × 2)—1/HSS-2B helicopter (no hangar)
Electron Equipt: Radar: 1/OPS-28, 1/OPS-11, 1/OPS-12, 2/SPG-51C, 1/GFCS-1, 1/GFCS-1A
Sonar: OQS-4—TACAN: URN-25
EW: NOLR-6C active/passive, OLR-9B passive, Mk 36 SRBOC chaff RL (VI × 4)
M: COGAG: 2 Rolls-Royce Spey SM-1A and 2 Olympus TM-3D gas turbines; 2 CP props; 72,000 hp
Range: . . . **Man:** . . .

REMARKS: Mk 13 missile launcher and one of the two 127-mm guns will be forward. No hangar for helicopter. U.S. Mk 74 Mod. 13 missile fire-control system (2/SPG-51C radar directors) for the Standard missile system. DDG 171 in 1981 Budget, 172 in 1983; 173 requested 1985 but denied. DDG 172 ordered 29-3-84.

◆ 7 (+5) Hatsuyuki class (DDK)

	Bldr	Laid down	L	In serv.
122 HATSUYUKI	Sumitomo, Uraga	14-3-79	7-11-80	23-3-82
123 SHIRAYUKI	Hitachi, Maizuru	3-12-79	4-8-81	8-2-83
124 MINEYUKI	Mitsubishi, Nagasaki	7-5-81	17-10-82	26-1-84
125 SAWAYUKI	Ishikawajima-Harima, Tokyo	22-4-81	21-6-82	15-2-84
126 HAMAYUKI	Mitsui, Tamano	4-2-81	27-5-82	18-11-83
127 ISOYUKI	Ishikawajima-Harima, Tokyo	20-4-82	19-9-83	23-1-85
128 HARUYUKI	Sumitomo, Uraga	11-3-82	6-9-83	14-3-85
129 YAMAYUKI	Hitachi, Maizura	25-2-83	10-7-84	3-86
130 MATSUYUKI	Ishikawajima-Harima, Tokyo	7-4-83	25-10-84	3-86
131 N.	Mitsui, Tamano	26-1-84	6-85	1-87
132 N.	Sumitomo, Uraga	21-12-83	8-85	2-87
133 N.	Mitsubishi, Nagasaki	8-5-84	10-85	3-87

D: DDK 122-120: 2,950 tons (3,700 fl) DDK 129-133: 3,050 tons (3,800 fl)
S: 30 kts
Dim: 131.7 (126.0 wl) × 13.7 × 4.1 (129 and later: 4.3)(hull)
A: 8/Harpoon SSM (IV × 2)—1/Mk 29 missile launcher (VIII × 1, 13 Sea Sparrow missiles)—1/76-mm DP OTO Melara Compact—2/20-mm Mk 15 CIWS AA (I × 2)—1/ASROC ASW RL (VIII × 1, 16 missiles)—6/324-mm Type 68 ASW TT (III × 2)—1/HSS-2B ASW helicopter
Electron Equipt: Radar: 1/OPS-18, 1/OPS-14B, 1/GFCS-2-21 (76-mm), 1/GFCS-2-12 (Sea Sparrow)
Sonar: OQS-4—TACAN: URN-25
EW: NOLR-6C passive, OLT-3 D/F, 2 Mk 36 SRBOC chaff RL (VI × 2)
M: COGOG: 2 Kawasaki-Rolls-Royce Olympus TM-3B gas turbines, 28,390 hp each; 2 Tyne RM-1C gas turbines, 5,340 hp each; 2 CP props; 45,000 hp (50,000 max.)
Man: 190-195 tot.

REMARKS: Have fin stabilizers, DD 122 in 1977 budget, 123 in 1978, 124-126 in 1979, 129 and 130 in 1981, and 131-133 in 1982. The Olympus engines are rated at 22,500 hp for cruise, 25,000-hp limit, while the Tyne cruise engines are rated at 4,620-hp cruise/5,000-hp max. and provide speeds up to 19.5 kts. Helicopter deck has the Canadian

Hamayuki (DDK 126) *Ships of the World,* 11-83

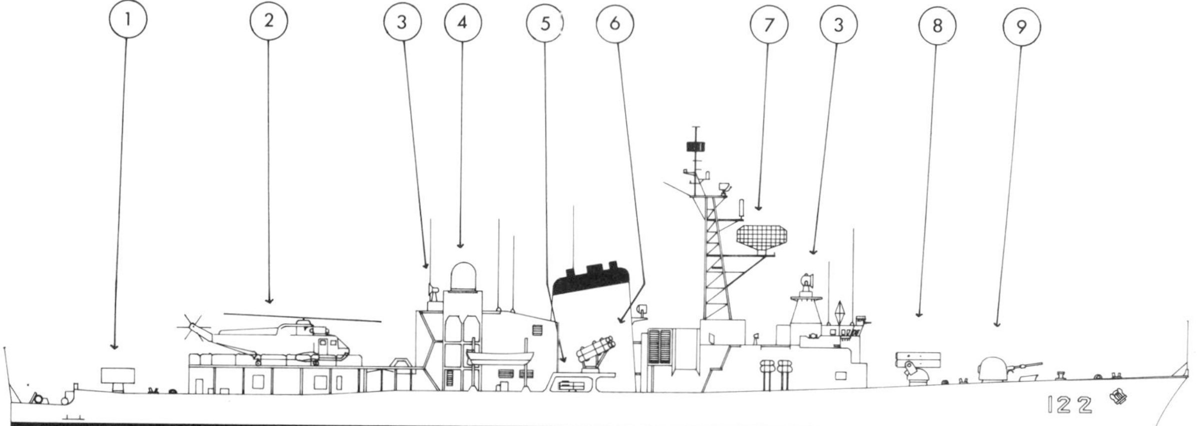

Hatsuyuki (DDG 122) 1. Mk 29 launcher for Sea Sparrow 2. HSS-2B helicopter 3. GFCS-1 or 1A fire-control radar 4. GFCS-2 antenna 5. Mk 68 ASW TT (III × 2) 6. Harpoon ASM (IV × 2) 7. OPS-14B radar antenna 8. ASROC ASW RL (VIII × 1) 9. 76-mm OTO Melara Compact dual-purpose gun

GUIDED-MISSILE DESTROYERS *(continued)*

Sawayuki (DDK 125) JMSDF, 2-84

Isoyuki (DDK 127) *Ships of the World,* 6-84

Shirayuki (DDK 123)—no Mk 15 CIWS JMSDF, 1984

Beartrap traversing/landing system. All are programmed to receive U.S. SQR-18 or 19 TACTASS towed passive linear arrays. Have TDPS—Tactical Data Processing System—with a U.S. UYK-20 computer. Have LINK 14 data relay receiver only. Stack incorporates passive infrared cooling features and a water-spray system. DDK 129 and later have steel vice aluminum superstructures. DDK 122 lacks Mk 15 CIWS and Mk 36 SRBOC chaff RL; DDK 123 lacks CIWS.

◆ **3 Tachikaze class (DDG)**

	Bldr	Laid down	L	In serv.
168 TACHIKAZE	Mitsubishi, Nagasaki	19-6-73	12-12-74	26-3-76
169 ASAKAZE	Mitsubishi, Nagasaki	27-5-76	15-10-77	27-3-79
170 SAWAKAZE	Mitsubishi, Nagasaki	14-9-79	4-6-81	30-3-83

D: 3,850 tons (4,800 fl) **S:** 32 kts **Dim:** 143.0 × 14.3 × 4.6

A: 1/Mk 13 Mod. 4 missile launcher (40 Standard SM-1 MR SAM/Harpoon SSM)—2/127-mm Mk 42 DP (I × 2)—2/20-mm Mk 15 CIWS gatling AA (I × 2)—1/ASROC Mk 116 ASW RL (VIII × 1)—6/324-mm Type 68 ASW TT (III × 2)

Asakaze (DDG 169)—with two Mk 15 CIWS *Ships of the World,* 4-85

GUIDED-MISSILE DESTROYERS *(continued)*

Sawakaze (DDG 170) *Ships of the World,* 7-84

Electron Equipt: Radar: OPS-17 (170: OPS-28), 1/OPS-11B, 1/SPS-52B, 2/SPG-51C, 1/GFCS-1A
Sonar: OQS-3 (170: OQS-4)
EW: OLT-3 system, 4/Mk 36 Mod. 2 Super RBOC chaff RL
M: 2 sets GT; 2 props; 70,000 hp **Boilers:** 2; 60 kg/cm², 480°C **Man:** 277 tot.

REMARKS: U.S. Vulcan/Phalanx gatling guns and Harpoon were added to 168 under 1981 Budget, as well as improvements to SAM system. Same improvement made to DDG 169 in 1984-85 and to DDG 170 under 1985 Budget. The SPS-52B acts as the principal air-search radar. The missile-control system is Mk 74 Mod. 13 and uses the two SPG-51C radars. The propulsion plant is identical to that of the *Haruna* class. All now can carry two SATCOMM antenna radomes atop bridge and have a LINK 14 data transmission system. The ASROC launcher has a reload magazine below the bridge.

◆ **1 Amatsukaze class (DDG)**

	Bldr	Laid down	L	In serv.
163 AMATSUKAZE	Mitsubishi, Nagasaki	29-11-62	5-10-63	15-2-65

D: 3,050 tons (4,000 fl) **S:** 33 kts **Dim:** 131.0 × 13.4 × 4.2 (mean)
A: 1/Mk 13 launcher (40 Standard SM-1 MR SAM)—4/76.2-mm 50-cal. DP Mk 33 (II × 2)—1/ASROC ASW RL (VIII × 1)—6/324-mm Type 68 ASW TT (III × 2)—2/Mk 15 trainable Hedgehog
Electron Equipt: Radar: 1/OPS-17, 1/SPS-29, 1/SPS-52, 2/SPG-51, 1/GFCS-2-21
Sonar: SQS-23—EW: OLT-1
M: 2 sets Ishikawajima-G.E. GT; 2 props; 60,000 hp **Fuel:** 900 tons
Boilers: 2 Ishikawajima-Foster-Wheeler; 38 kg/cm², 438°C **Electric:** 2,700 kw
Range: 7,000/18 **Man:** 290 tot.

REMARKS: Refitted in 1967 with ASW TT and SPS-52 radar. Crane at stern handles boats stowed in a below-decks hangar. One GFCS-2-21 radar director replaced the original two U.S. Mk 63 GFCS in 1982-83, but planned replacement of the guns by two 76-mm OTO Melara mounts and EW updates were not carried out. There are no reloads for the ASROC.

Amatsukaze (DDG 163) L. & L. Van Ginderen, 10-84

◆ **4 Takatsuki class (DD)**

	Bldr	Laid down	L	In serv.
164 TAKATSUKI	Ishikawajima, Tokyo	8-10-65	7-1-66	15-3-67
165 KIKIZUKI	Mitsubishi, Nagasaki	15-3-66	25-3-67	27-3-68
166 MOCHIZUKI	Ishikawajima, Tokyo	25-11-66	15-3-69	25-3-69
167 NAGATSUKI	Ishikawajima, Tokyo	2-3-68	19-3-69	12-2-70

Takatsuki (DD 164)—as modernized *Ships of the World,* 1985

Kikizuki (DD 165)—smooth hull sides P. Voss, 8-83

Nagatsuki (DD 167)—hull knuckle, no VDS *Ships of the World,* 11-84

D: 3,200 tons (4,500 fl) **S:** 32 kts **Dim:** 136.0 (131.0 pp) × 13.4 × 4.4 (mean)
A: 164–166: 8/Harpoon SSM (IV × 2)—1/Mk 29 SAM launcher (VIII × 1, 16 Sea Sparrow missiles)—1/127-mm Mk 42 DP—1/20-mm Mk 15 CIWS—1/ASROC Mk 116 ASW RL (VIII × 1, no reloads)—1/375-mm Bofors ASW RL (IV × 1)—6/324-mm Mk 32 ASW TT (IV × 2); 167: 2/127-mm Mk 42 DP (I × 2)—1/ASROC Mk 116 ASW RL (VIII × 1)—1/375-mm Bofors ASW RL (IV × 1)—6/324-mm ASW TT (III × 2)
Electron Equipt: Radar: 1/OPS-11B-Y, 1/OPS-17, 1/GFCS-2-12B, 1/Mk 35 (167: 2/GFCS-1)
Sonar: SQS-23 (166, 167: OQS-3), SQS-35 (J) VDS
EW: NOLR-6C (167: NOLR-1B), Mk 36 SRBOC (VI × 2, not in 167)
TACAN: 167 only: ORN-6
M: 2 sets Mitsubishi GT; 2 props; 60,000 hp
Boilers: 2 Mitsubishi-Combustion Eng.; 43 kg/cm², 454°C **Fuel:** 900 tons
Range: 7,000/20 **Man:** 270 tot.

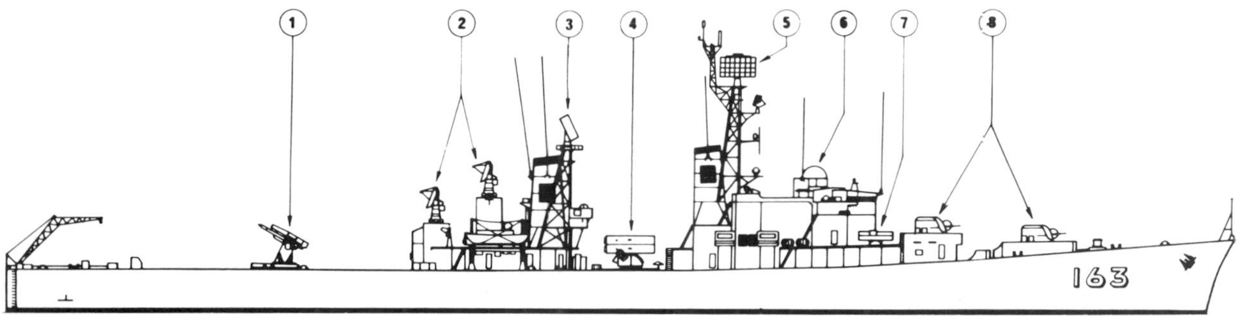

Amatsukaze (DDG 163) 1. Mk 13 missile launcher 2. SPS-51 missile-control radars 3. SPS-52-3D radar 4. ASROC ASW rocket launcher 5. SPS-29 air-search radar 6. GFCS-2-21 gunfire-control director 7. Mk 32 ASW TT 8. 76.2-mm, 50-caliber, U.S. Mk 33, dual-purpose gunmounts

GUIDED-MISSILE DESTROYERS *(continued)*

Remarks: Originally carried three U.S. DASH drone ASW helicopters, removed in 1977 and hangar not used. DD 166 and 167 have a knuckle in the hull sides forward; the earlier two do not. DD 165 has fin stabilizers. DD 164 authorized under 1981-82 Budget to receive extensive modernization completing in 10-85, DD 166 refitting under 1983-84 Budget, to complete 10-86, DD 165 authorized 1985. The DASH hangar and after 127-mm gun are to be removed. Gained will be a Mk 29 launcher aft for Sea Sparrow, 8 Harpoon missiles (IV × 2), 1/Mk 15 CIWS (Vulcan/Phalanx) gatling AA gun (only in DD 164), upgrading of the OQS-3 sonar, provision for U.S. SQR-18A TACTASS towed passive hydrophone array, replacement of the after Mk 56 GFCS with GFCS-2, substitution of the NOLR-6C EW system for the present array, addition of LINK 14 digital data link equipment, installation of the U.S. Mk 36 Super RBOC chaff launching system, installation of a MARISAT SATCOMM radome atop the after "mack," and removal of the ORN-6 TACAN where fitted; DD 166 will also receive VDS.

◆ 6 Yamagumo class (DDK)

	Bldr	Laid down	L	In serv.
113 Yamagumo	Mitsui, Tamano	23-3-64	27-2-65	29-1-66
114 Makigumo	Uraga, Yokosuka	10-6-64	26-7-65	19-3-66
115 Asagumo	Maizuru, Heavy Ind.	24-6-65	25-11-66	29-8-67
119 Aokumo	Sumitomo, Uraga	2-10-70	30-3-72	25-11-72
120 Akigumo	Sumitomo, Uraga	7-7-72	23-10-73	24-7-74
121 Yugumo	Sumitomo, Uraga	4-2-76	31-5-77	24-3-78

Makigumo (DDK 114)—raised fantail for VDS, tripod mainmast L. & L. Van Ginderen, 7-84

Yugumo (DDK 121)—lattice mainmast *Ships of the World,* 7-84

D: 2,100 tons (2,700 fl) **S:** 27 kts **Dim:** 114.9 × 11.8 × 4.0 (hull)
A: 4/76.2-mm 50-cal. DP Mk 33 (II × 2)—1/ASROC ASW RL (VIII × 1)—1/375-mm Bofors ASW RL (IV × 1)—6/324-mm Mk 116 ASW TT (III × 2)
Electron Equipt: Radar: 1/OPS-11, 1/OPS-17, 2/GFCS 1 (*see* Remarks)
Sonar: DDK 113-115: SQS-23; later: OQS-3; also SQS-35(J) VDS (not in DDK 115)
EW: NORL-1B (119-121: NOLR-5)
M: 6 Mitsubishi 12UEV 30/40N diesels; 2 props; 26,500 hp **Range:** 7,000/20
Man: 210-220 tot.

Remarks: Version of the *Minegumo* class completed with ASROC instead of DASH. DK 113-115 and 119 were given U.S. Mk 56 gun director forward (Mk 35 radar) and Mk 63 GFCS aft (Mk 34 radar on after gunmount); DDK 120 and 121 got two Japanese GFCS-1 systems instead. DDK 113 has Mitsui diesels. DDK 113 and 114 have raised sterns to house VDS; on DDK 119-121 the VDS was installed during construction, and, therefore, the stern was not raised. Final three have lattice mainmasts and a bulwark above the pilothouse.

◆ 3 Minegumo class (DDK)

	Bldr	Laid down	L	In serv.
116 Minegumo	Mitsui, Tamano	14-3-67	16-12-67	21-8-68
117 Natsugumo	Uraga, Yokosuka	26-6-67	25-7-68	25-4-69
118 Murakumo	Maizuru, Heavy Ind.	19-10-68	15-11-69	21-8-70

D: 2,100 tons (2,750 fl) **S:** 27 kts **Dim:** 114.9 × 11.8 × 4.0 (hull)
A: DDK 116, 117: 4/76.2-mm 50-cal. DP Mk 33 (II × 2); DDK 118: 1/76-mm OTO Melara Compact, 2/76.2-mm DP Mk 33 (II × 1)—1/ASROC Mk 116 ASW RL (VIII × 1, with reloads)—1/375-mm Bofors ASW RL (IV × 1)—6/324-mm Type 68 ASW TT (III × 2)

Natsugumo (DDK 117)—ASROC aft *Ships of the World,* 1984

Murakumo (DDK 118)—with OTO Melara gun and ASROC aft JMSDF, 1984

Electron Equipt: Radar: 1/OPS-11, 1/OPS-17; DDK 116: 1/Mk 35, 1/SPG-34; DDK 118: 1/GFCS-2-12, 1/GFCS-1; DDK 117: 1/GFCS-1, 1/SPG-34
Sonar: OQS-3—DDK 118: SQS-35(J) VDS also
EW: NOLR-5
M: 6 Mitsubishi 12UEV 30/40 diesels; 2 props; 26,500 hp
Range: 7,000/20 **Man:** 19 officers, 196 men

Remarks: Originally differed from the *Yamagumo* class in having a DASH drone-helicopter facility instead of ASROC, but DASH is no longer carried. In 1976, DDK 118 had an OTO Melara 76-mm gun and the prototype GFCS-2-12 radar director substituted for her after 76.2-mm twin mount and U.S. Mk 63 control system; in 1979, she received an ASROC launcher on what had been her DASH flight deck. DDK 116 and 117 received ASROC in 1982-83. DDK 116 has a U.S. Mk 56 GFCS (with Mk 35 radar) forward; the other two have a Japanese GFCS-1, and DDK 116 and 117 have a Mk 63 GFCS aft. DDK 118, with VDS, is 1.0-m longer and displaces 50 tons more.

◆ 1 Akizuki class (DD)

	Bldr	Laid down	L	In serv.
162 Teruzuki	Shin-Mitsubishi, Kobe	15-8-58	24-6-59	29-2-60

Teruzuki (DD 162) *Ships of the World,* 1983

D: 2,300 tons (3,100 fl) **S:** 32 kts **Dim:** 118.0 (115.0 pp) × 12.0 × 4.02
A: 3/127)mm 54-cal. DP Mk 39 (I × 3)—4/76.2-mm 50-cal. DP Mk 33 (II × 2)—4/533-mm TT (IV × 1)—1/375-mm Bofors ASW RL (IV × 1)—2/Mk 15 trainable Hedgehogs—6/324-mm Type 68 ASW TT (III × 2)
Electron Equipt: Radar: 1/OPS-1, 1/OPS-15, 3/Mk 34
Sonar: SQS-23, OQA-1 VDS—EW: NOLR-1
M: DD 161: 2 sets Mitsubishi-Escher-Wyss GT; DD 162: 2 sets Westinghouse GT; 2 props; 45,000 hp
Boilers: 4; 43 kg/cm², 454°C **Man:** 330 tot.

Remarks: Weapons and ASW sensors modernized in 1976-77, the Bofors ASW RL replacing a U.S. Mk 108 "Weapon Alfa," VDS being added, and SQS-23 replacing SQS-29. The 127-mm guns were removed from U.S. *Midway*-class carriers. Two U.S. Mk 57 and one Mk 63 gunfire-control systems are carried. Four reload 533-mm torpedoes can be stowed on deck. Sister *Akizuki* (DD 161) served as Fleet Flagship until 27-3-85 when reclassified as an auxiliary (ASU).

Note: All three *Murasame*-class destroyers have been reclassified as auxiliaries (ASU): *Murasame* (DD 107) and *Yudachi* (DD 108) on 30-3-84, and *Harusame* (DD 109) on 5-3-85.

◆ 2 Ayanami class (DD)

	Bldr	Laid down	L	In serv.
111 Onami	Ishikawajima, Tokyo	20-3-59	13-2-60	29-8-60
112 Makinami	Iino, Maizuru	20-3-59	25-4-60	30-10-60

GUIDED-MISSILE DESTROYERS *(continued)*

Onami (DD 111) *Ships of the World,* 1981

D: 1,700 tons (2,400 fl) **S:** 32 kts **Dim:** 109.0 × 10.7 × 3.7 (light)
A: 6/76.2-mm DP Mk 33 (II × 3)—4/533-mm TT (IV × 1)—2/Mk 15 trainable Hedgehog—6/324-mm Type 68 ASW TT (III × 2)
Electron Equipt: Radar: 1/OPS-15, 1/OPS-1, 2/Mk 34
Sonar: OQS-12 or 14; (DD 110: OQA-1 VDS also)
EW: NORL-1
M: DD 111: Hitachi-G.E. GT; DD 112: Mitsubishi-Escher-Wyss GT; 2 props; 35,000 hp
Boilers: 2; 43 kg/cm², 454°C **Range:** 6,000/18
Man: 220–230 tot.

Remarks: The boilers in DD 110 are Hitachi–Babcock & Wilcox; in DD 112: Mitsubishi. There are two U.S. Mk 63 GFCS. OPS-2 is the Japanese version of the U.S. SPS-12.

Four sisters, *Ayanami* (DD 103), *Isonami* (DD 104), *Uranami* (DD 105), and *Shikinami* (DD 106) were reclassified as auxiliaries in 1982 and are listed on later pages, as is sister *Takanami* (DD 110), reclassified 27-3-85.

FRIGATES (DE)

◆ **0 (+1 + . . .) new program**

Remarks: Funds for a new frigate of 1,600 tons standard displacement were requested in the 1984 Budget but were rejected; none was requested for 1985. The design is being further refined to about 1,900 tons. It will have CODOG propulsion, be about 110 m o.a., and may incorporate the new U.S. RAM point-defense missile system in its armament suite. One per year in the 1986 and 1987 Budgets are projected.

◆ **2 Yubari class**

	Bldr	Laid down	L	In serv.
227 Yubari	Sumitomo, Uraga	9-2-81	22-2-82	18-3-83
228 Yubetsu	Hitachi, Maizuru	14-1-82	25-1-83	3-84

Yubari (DE 227) JMSDF, 1984

Yubetsu (DE 228) *Ships of the World,* 2-84

D: 1,470 tons (1,760 fl) **S:** 25 kts **Dim:** 91.0 × 10.8 × 3.6 (hull)
A: 8/Harpoon SSM (IV × 2)—1/76-mm OTO Melara DP—1/375-mm Bofors ASW RL (IV × 1)—6/324-mm Type 68 ASW TT (III × 2)
Electron Equipt: Radar: 1/OPS-19 nav., 1/OPS-28, 1/GFCS-2-21
Sonar: OQS-4—EW: NOLQ-6C passive, OLT-3 jammer, Mk 36 SRBOC chaff RL (VI × 2)
M: CODOG: 1 Kawasaki-Rolls-Royce Olympus TM-3B gas turbine, 28,390 hp; 1 Mitsubishi 6DRV 35/44 diesel, 5,000 hp; 2 CP props
Range: . . . **Man:** 98 tot.

Remarks: An enlarged version of the *Ishikari* class, presumably as the earlier ship is too cramped for the mission requirements. Greater length permits later addition of a Vulcan/Phalanx gatling AA gun aft. DE 227 ordered under 1979 Budget, DE 228 under the 1980 Budget. A third was requested for the 1982 Budget, but was not authorized. Planned installation of a U.S. Mk 15 CIWS (Vulcan/Phalanx) aft has not occurred.

◆ **1 Ishikari class**

	Bldr	Laid down	L	In serv.
226 Ishikari	Mitsui, Tamano	17-5-79	18-3-80	30-3-81

Ishikari (DE 226)—Harpoon missiles aft L. & L. Van Ginderen, 11-84

D: 1,200 tons (1,450 fl) **S:** 25 kts **Dim:** 84.5 × 10.0 × 3.5 (mean hull)
A: 8/Harpoon SSM (IV × 2)—1/76-mm DP OTO Melara—1/375-mm Bofors ASW RL (IV × 1)—6/324-mm Type 68 ASW TT
Electron Equipt: Radar: 1/OPS-19 nav., 1/OPS-28, 1/GFCS-2-21
Sonar: OQS-4
EW: NOLQ-6C passive, OLT-3 jammer, Mk 36 SRBOC chaff RL (VI × 2)
M: CODOG: 1 Kawasaki-Rolls-Royce Olympus TM-3B gas turbine, 28,390 hp; 1 Mitsubishi 6DRV 35/44 diesel, 5,000 hp; 2 CP props
Man: 90 tot.

Remarks: Smaller, more lightly armed, faster, and with fewer sensors than the preceding *Chikugo* class. Aluminum superstructure. Either the gas turbine *or* the single diesel will drive both propellers. Ordered under 1977 program. 19 kts max. on diesel. The Combat Information Center (CIC) is below the waterline. Highly automated ship with very small crew.

◆ **11 Chikugo class**

	Bldr	Laid down	L	In serv.
215 Chikugo	Mitsui, Tamano	9-12-68	13-1-70	31-7-70
216 Ayase	Ishikawajima, Tokyo	5-12-69	16-9-70	20-7-71
217 Mikumo	Mitsui, Tamano	17-3-70	16-2-71	26-8-71
218 Tokachi	Mitsui, Tamano	11-12-70	25-11-71	17-5-72
219 Iwase	Mitsui, Tamano	6-8-71	29-6-72	12-12-72
220 Chitose	Hitachi, Maizuru	7-10-71	25-1-73	21-8-73
221 Niyodo	Mitsui, Tamano	20-9-72	28-8-73	8-2-74
222 Teshio	Hitachi, Maizuru	11-7-73	29-5-74	10-1-75
223 Yoshino	Mitsui, Tamano	28-9-73	22-8-74	6-2-75
224 Kumano	Hitachi, Maizuru	29-5-74	24-2-75	19-11-75
225 Noshiro	Mitsui, Tamano	27-1-76	23-12-76	31-8-77

Ayase (DE 216) *Ships of the World,* 1977

Noshiro (DE 225) *Ships of the World,* 1980

FRIGATES (DE) *(continued)*

D: 1,470–1,530 tons (1,700–1,800 fl) **S:** 25 kts **Dim:** 93.0 × 10.8 × 3.5 (hull)
A: 2/76.2-mm 50-cal. DP Mk 33 (II × 1)—2/40-mm AA (II × 1)—1/ASROC Mk 116 ASW RL (VIII × 1)—6/324-mm Type 68 ASW TT (III × 2)
Electron Equipt: Radar: 1/OPS-16, 1/OPS-14, 1/GFCS-1B—EW: NOLR-5
Sonar: OQS-3, SQS-35(J)(*see* Remarks)
M: 4 Mitsubishi-Burmeister & Wain UEV 30/40 or Mitsui 28VBC-38 diesels; 2 props; 16,000 hp
Range: 10,700/12; 12,000/9 **Man:** 13 officers, 152 men

Remarks: To date, SQS-35(J) towed, variable-depth sonar has been mounted in only five units; it is stowed in an open well at the stern, offset to starboard. These are the smallest ships in any navy to carry ASROC. A Mk 51 director (no radar) controls the twin 40-mm mount. DE 215 and 220 are 1,480 tons std., DE 216–219 and 221 are 1,470 tons std.; later units 1,500 tons std. DE 215, 217–219, 221, 223, 225 have the Mitsubishi diesels.

◆ **4 Isuzu class (DE)**

	Bldr	Laid down	L	In serv.
211 Isuzu	Mitsui, Tamano	16-4-60	17-1-61	29-7-61
212 Mogami	Mitsubishi, Nagasaki	4-8-60	13-3-61	28-10-61
213 Kitakami	Ishikawajima, Tokyo	7-6-62	21-6-63	27-2-64
214 Ohi	Maizuru, Heavy Ind.	10-6-62	15-6-63	22-1-64

Mogami (DE 212)—with VDS *Ships of the World,* 1983

Ohi (DE 214) *Ships of the World,* 1984

D: 1,490 tons (1,790 fl) **S:** 25 kts **Dim:** 94.0 × 10.4 × 3.5 (hull)
A: 4/76.2-mm 50-cal. DP Mk 33 (II × 2)—1/375)mm Bofors ASW RL (IV × 1) — DE 213, 214: 6/324-mm Type 68 ASW TT (III × 2)—1/d.c. projector (not on DE 212 and 213)
Electron Equipt: Radar: 1/OPS-1, 1/OPS-16, 2/Mk 34—EW: NOLR-1
Sonar: OQS-12 or -14; DE 212, 213: OQA-1 VDS also
M: Diesels; 2 props; 16,000 hp (*see* Remarks) **Man:** 180 tot.

Remarks: Each has a different diesel propulsion plant: DE 211: 4 Mitsui 35 VBU 45V; DE 212: 2 Mitsubishi UET 52/65; DE 213: 4 Mitsubishi UEV 30/40; and DE 214: 4 Mitsui 28 VBU 38. DE 212, which has only two main engines, has a smaller stack. Have two U.S. Mk 63 GFCS (Mk 34 radar on gunmounts) for the guns.

GUIDED-MISSILE PATROL BOATS

◆ **0 (+1 + 5) new construction**

	Bldr	Laid down	L	In serv.
. . . N.	. . .	. . .	. . .	1989

D: 250 tons (. . . fl) **S:** 40 kts **Dim:** . . . × . . . × . . .
A: 4/Harpoon SSM (II × 2)—1/76-mm OTO Melara DP
Electron Equipt: Radar: . . .
M: 3 Mitsubishi S20U diesels; 3 props; 18,000 hp
Man: 20 tot.

Remarks: First unit was to have been in 1983 Budget, but was postponed to 1986 to permit further design definition. Class of six planned to replace the PT 11 class. Will have conventional planing hulls. Another 12 may be built later.

PATROL BOATS (PC)

◆ **2 Mizutori class** Bldr: Sasebo Dockyard

	Laid down	L	In serv.
319 Shiratori	29-2-64	8-10-64	26-2-65
320 Hiyodori	26-2-65	29-9-65	28-2-66

Remarks: Data as for remainder of this 8-ship class, which can be found on the auxiliary pages under ASU. This pair likely to be reclassified ASU at end 3-86.

TORPEDO BOATS (PT)

◆ **5 PT 11 class** Bldr: Mitsubishi, Shimonoseki

	Laid down	L	In serv.
811 PT 11	17-3-70	10-70	23-3-71
812 PT 12	22-4-71	7-72	8-72
813 PT 13	28-3-72	7-72	12-72
814 PT 14	23-3-72	. . .	10-7-73
815 PT 15	23-4-74	. . .	8-1-75

PT 13 (813) *Ships of the World*

D: 100 tons (125 fl) **S:** 40 kts **Dim:** 35.0 × 9.2 × 1.2
A: 2/40-mm AA (I × 2)—4/533-mm TT (I × 4)
Electron Equipt: Radar: 1/OPS-13 **Man:** 26 tot.
M: CODAG: 2 Ishikawajima IM-300 gas turbines, 2 Mitsubishi 24 WZ-31MC diesels; 3 props; 11,000 hp **Range:** 300/40; 1,000/18

Remarks: Class planned for disposal commencing 3-89.

PATROL CRAFT (PB)

◆ **9 PB type** Bldr: Ishikawajima, Yokohama

PB 19 to PB 27 (PB 19–24 in serv. 31-3-72: others, 29-3-73)

D: 18 tons **S:** 20 kts **Dim:** 17.0 × 4.3 × 0.8 **A:** 1/20-mm AA (aft)
Electron Equipt: Radar: 1/OPS-29 nav. **Range:** 400/20 **Man:** 5 tot.
M: 2 Isuzu 17T-MF RCOR diesels; 2 props; 760 hp

Remarks: Fiberglass hulls. Two additional units delivered 3-79 and 28-3-80 for use as radio-controlled surface gunnery target-towing craft; 850 hp, 25 kts.

MINE WARFARE SHIPS

◆ **1 minelayer (MMC)** Bldr: Hitachi, Maizuru

	Laid down	L	In serv.
951 Souya	9-7-70	31-3-71	30-9-71

Souya (MMC 951) with minesweeper Sakate (643) JMSDF, 1984

D: 2,150 tons (3,250 fl) **S:** 18 kts **Dim:** 99.0 × 15.0 × 4.2 (hull)
A: 2/76.2-mm DP Mk 33 (II × 1)—2/20-mm AA (I × 2)—6/324-mm Mk 32 ASW TT (III × 2)—200 mines
Electron Equipt: Radar: 1/OPS-14, 1/OPS-16, 1/GFCS-1
Sonar: SQS-11A
M: 4 Kawasaki-M.A.N. V6V 22/30 ATL diesels; 2 props; 6,400 hp
Range: 7,500/14 **Man:** 185 tot.

MINE WARFARE SHIPS *(continued)*

REMARKS: Platform for KV-107-II mine-countermeasures helicopter, six mine rails, two external, four through the transom stern. Can also act as an ASW escort. Often acts as flagship for mine countermeasures forces.

◆ **1 mine-countermeasures support ship/minelayer (MST)**

	Bldr	Laid down	L	In serv.
462 HAYASE	Ishikawajima, Haruna	16-9-70	21-6-71	6-11-71

Hayase (MST 462) *Ships of the World,* 1984

D: 2,000 tons (3,050 fl) **S:** 18 kts **Dim:** 99.0 × 13.0 × 3.8
A: 2/76-mm 50-cal. DP (II × 1)—2/20-mm AA (I × 2)—6/324-mm Mk 32 ASW TT (III × 2)—200 mines
Electron Equipt: Radar: 1/OPS-17, 1/OPS-14, 1/Mk 34
Sonar: SQS-11A
M: 4 Kawasaki-M.A.N. V6V 22/30 ATL diesels; 2 props; 6,400 hp

REMARKS: The *Hayase* is similar to the *Souya* but has no forecastle, and has five mine rails exiting through the transom stern. She has a U.S. Mk 63 gun-control system. Fantail cleared as a platform for KV-107-II mine-countermeasures helicopters.

◆ **1 Kasado-class mine-countermeasures support ship (MST)**

	Bldr	L	In serv.
474 OTSU (ex-MSC 621)	Nippon Kokan, Tsurumi	5-11-64	24-2-65

Otsu (MST 474) 1981

D: 330 tons (360 fl) **S:** 14 kts **Dim:** 45.70 × 8.38 × 2.30 **A:** 1/20-mm AA
Electron Equipt: Radar: OPS-9—Sonar: ZQQ-2
M: 2 Mitsubishi YV10Z-DE diesels; 2 props; 1,200 hp **Man:** . . .

REMARKS: Reclassified 18-3-81 to replace *Kouzo* (MST 473) of the same class. Former wooden-hulled minesweeper converted to support minesweeping boats.

◆ **0 (+1 + 5) new construction deep-sea minesweepers**

	Bldr	Laid down	L	In serv.
. . . N. . .	. . .	. . .	. . .	. . .

D: 1,000 tons **S:** 18 kts **Dim:** . . . × . . . × . . .
A: . . . **Electron Equipt:** . . .
M: Diesels; . . . hp
Man: 70 tot.

REMARKS: First unit programmed for 1987 Budget, with one per year thereafter to a total of six. Intended to deploy Type S-7 deep-sea minehunting system and Type S-8 deep-sea moored minesweeping system.

◆ **0 (+2 + . . .) glass-reinforced plastic mine hunters**

	Bldr	Laid down	L	In serv.
666 N. . .	. . .	. . .	. . .	. . .
667 N. . .	. . .	. . .	. . .	. . .

D: 440 tons **S:** 14 kts **Dim:** . . . × . . . × . . .
A: 1/20-mm JM-61-MB gatling AA
Electron Equipt: Radar: 1/. . .—Sonar: . . .
M: 2 diesels; 2 CP props; 1,440 hp **Man:** . . .

REMARKS: Essentially a GRP-hulled version of the *Hatsushima* class. First two in 1985 Budget.

◆ **15 (+2) Hatsushima-class minehunter/minesweepers (MSC)**

	Bldr	Laid down	L	In serv.
649 HATSUSHIMA	Nippon Kokan, Tsurumi	6-12-77	30-10-78	30-3-79
650 NINOSHIMA	Hitachi, Kanagawa	8-5-78	9-8-79	19-12-79
651 MIYAJIMA	Nippon Kokan, Tsurumi	8-11-78	18-9-79	29-1-80
652 NENOSHIMA	Nippon Kokan, Tsurumi	4-10-79	25-7-80	25-12-80
653 UKISHIMA	Hitachi, Kanagawa	15-5-79	11-7-80	27-11-80
654 OSHIMA	Hitachi, Kanagawa	2-6-80	17-6-81	26-11-81
655 MIIJIMA	Nippon Kokan, Tsurumi	4-8-80	2-6-81	26-11-81
656 YAKUSHIMA	Nippon Kokan, Tsurumi	15-6-81	22-6-82	17-12-82
657 NARUSHIMA	Hitachi, Kanagawa	29-5-81	7-6-82	17-12-82
658 CHICHIJIMA	Hitachi, Kanagawa	2-6-82	13-7-83	16-12-83
659 TOROSHIMA	Nippon Kokan, Tsurumi	30-6-82	23-6-83	16-12-83
660 HAHAJIMA	Nippon Kokan, Tsurumi	20-5-83	27-6-84	18-12-84
661 TAKASHIMA	Hitachi, Kanagawa	7-6-83	18-6-84	18-12-84
662 NEWAJIMA	Hitachi, Kanagawa	21-5-84	6-85	12-85
663 ETAJIMA	Nippon Kokan, Tsurumi	22-5-84	6-85	12-85
664 N.	Nippon Kokan, Tsurumi	10-5-85	6-86	12-86
665 N.	Hitachi, Kanagawa	16-5-85	6-86	12-86

Toroshima (MSC 659) *Ships of the World,* 1984

Miyajima (MSC 651) L. & L. Van Ginderen, 11-84

D: 440 tons (approx 620 fl) **S:** 14 kts **Dim:** 55.0 × 9.4 × 2.4
A: 1/20-mm AA (*see* Remarks)
Electron Equipt: Radar: OPS-9—Sonar: ZQS-2B
M: 2 Mitsubishi YV12ZC-15/20 diesels; 2 CP props; 1,440 hp **Man:** 45 tot.

REMARKS: Expansion of the *Takami* design. Being equipped with Type-54 mobile mine-hunting devices, which carry and lay their own disposal charges. MSC 653 and later have a 20-mm Type JM-61-MB gatling gun AA. Wooden construction.

◆ **18 Takami-class minehunter/minesweepers**

	Bldr	L	In serv.
630 TAKAMI	Nippon, Kokan, Tsurumi	15-7-69	15-12-69
631 IOU	Hitachi, Kanagawa	12-8-69	22-1-70
632 MIYAKE	Nippon Kokan, Tsurumi	3-6-70	19-11-70
633 UTONE	Hitachi, Kanagawa	6-4-70	3-9-70
634 AWAJI	Nippon Kokan, Tsurumi	11-12-70	29-3-71
635 TOUSHI	Hitachi, Kanagawa	13-12-70	18-3-71
636 TEURI	Nippon Kokan, Tsurumi	10-71	10-3-72
637 MUROTSU	Hitachi, Kanagawa	10-71	3-3-72
638 TASHIRO	Nippon Kokan, Tsurumi	2-4-73	30-7-73
640 TAKANE	Nippon Kokan, Tsurumi	8-3-74	28-8-74
641 MUZUKI	Hitachi, Kanagawa	5-4-74	28-8-74
642 YOKOSE	Nippon Kokan, Tsurumi	21-7-75	15-12-75
643 SAKATE	Hitachi, Kanagawa	5-8-75	17-12-75
644 OUMI	Nippon Kokan, Tsurumi	28-5-76	18-11-76
645 FUKUE	Hitachi, Kanagawa	12-7-76	18-11-76
646 OKITSU	Nippon Kokan, Tsurumi	4-3-77	20-9-77
647 HASHIRA	Hitachi, Kanagawa	8-11-77	28-3-78
648 IWAI	Nippon Kokan, Tsurumi	8-11-77	28-3-78

D: 380 tons **S:** 14 kts **Dim:** 52.0 × 8.8 × 2.4 **A:** 1/20-mm AA
Electron Equipt: Radar: OPS-9—Sonar: ZQS-2
M: 2 Mitsubishi YV12ZC-15/20 diesels; 2 CP props; 1,440 hp **Man:** 45–47 tot.

MINE WARFARE SHIPS *(continued)*

Utone (MSC 633) L. & L. Van Ginderen, 5-84

REMARKS: ZQS-2 sonar is a license-built version of the British Type 193-M minehunting sonar. OPS-9 radar, used in conjunction with a Mk 20 plotter, is a Japanese version of the British Type 978. These ships are of wooden construction, and they carry four divers for mine clearance. Sister *Miyato* (MSC 639) stricken 31-3-82. Carry U.S. Mk 4 acoustic noisemaker gear and S2 wire sweep.

NOTE: The final three *Kasado*-class minesweepers, *Minase* (MSC 627), *Ibuki* (MSC 628), and *Katsura* (MSC 629) were reclassified as service craft YAS 79–81 on 26-1-84.

◆ **6 inshore minesweepers (MSB)** Bldrs: Odd-numberd craft: Hitachi, Kanagawa; even-numbered craft: Nippon Kokan, Tsurumi

	In serv.		In serv.		In serv.
MSB 707	30-3-73	MSB 709	28-3-74	MSB 711	10-5-75
MSB 708	27-3-73	MSB 710	29-3-74	MSB 712	24-4-75

MSB 709 *Ships of the World*

D: 58 tons (fl) **S:** 10 kts **Dim:** 22.5 × 5.4 × 1.1 **A:** None
M: 2 Mitsubishi 4ZV20 diesels; 2 props; 480 hp **Man:** 10 tot.

REMARKS: Wooden construction. Supported by *Otsu* (MST 474). No radar.

AMPHIBIOUS WARFARE SHIPS

NOTE: The JMSDF had planned to request two 3,500-ton tank landing ships (LST) and three 350-ton utility landing craft (LCU) during 1983-87, but these units have been thus far rejected by the government as being too construable as offensive in nature and because of fiscal constraints. As with the other JMSDF amphibious warfare ships, their primary function would be in logistic support.

◆ **3 Miura-class landing ships (LST)** Bldr: Ishikawajima Harima, Tokyo

	Laid down	L	In serv.
4151 MIURA	26-11-73	13-8-74	29-1-75
4152 OJIKA	10-6-74	2-9-75	27-3-76
4153 SATSUMA	26-5-75	12-5-76	17-2-77

Miura (LST 4151) *Ships of the World*

D: 2,000 tons (3,200 fl) **S:** 14 kts **Dim:** 98.0 (94.0 pp) × 14.0 × 3.0
A: 2/76.2-mm 50-cal. Mk 33 DP (II × 1)—2/40-mm AA (II × 1)
Electron Equipt: Radars: 1/OPS-14, 1/OPS-16, 1/GFCS-1 **Man:** 118 tot.
M: 2 Kawasaki-M.A.N. V8V 22/30 AMTL diesels; 2 props; 4,400 hp

REMARKS: Carry 180 troops, 1,800 tons cargo, LST 4153 has carried prototype OTO Melara Compact gun at bow. All have two LCVP in davits and two LCM(6) on deck, the latter served by a traveling gantry with folding rails that can be extended over the sides. GFCS-1 fwd controls 76.2-mm guns; U.S. Mk 51 Mod. 2 GFCS aft controls 40-mm mount. Tank deck can hold 10 Type 74 battle tanks.

◆ **3 Atsumi class (LSTs)** Bldr: Sasebo Heavy Industries

	Laid down	L	In serv.
4101 ATSUMI	7-12-71	13-6-72	27-11-72
4102 MOTOBU	23-4-73	3-8-73	21-12-73
4103 NEMURO	18-11-76	16-6-77	27-10-77

Nemuro (LST 4103) *Ships of the World*

D: 1,480 tons (2,400 fl) **S:** 14 kts **Dim:** 89.0 × 13.0 × 2.7
A: 4/40-mm AA (II × 2) **Electron Equipt:** Radar: 1/OPS-9
M: 2 Kawasaki-M.A.N. V8V 22/30 AMTL diesels; 2 props; 4,400 hp
Range: 4,300/12 **Man:** 100 tot.

REMARKS: Can carry 120 men and 20 vehicles or 400 tons cargo. LST 4102 and 4103 are 1,550 tons standard and have a max. speed of 13 kts. Have 2 U.S. Mk 51 Mod. 2 GFCS, two LCVP in davits, and can carry one LCVP on deck, amidships.

◆ **2 Yura-class utility landing ships (LSU)** Bldr: Sasebo Heavy Industries

	Laid down	L	In serv.
4171 YURA	23-4-80	10-8-80	27-3-81
4172 NOTO	23-4-80	1-11-80	27-3-81

Yura (LSU 4171)—gatling AA gun atop pilothouse L. & L. Van Ginderen, 8-84

D: 500 tons (590 fl) **S:** 12 kts **Dim:** 58.0 × 9.5 × 1.7 (aft)
A: 1/20-mm JM 61-MB gatling AA
M: 2 Fuji 6L 27.5X diesels; 2 CP props; 3,000 hp **Man:** 32 tot.

REMARKS: Both in 1979-80 Budget; request for a third in 1981 Budget denied. Bow doors and ramp.

◆ **15 U.S. LCM(6)-class landing craft**

D: 24 tons (56 fl) **S:** 10 kts **Dim:** 17.07 × 4.37 × 1.17 (aft)
M: 2 Yanmar diesels; 2 props; 450 hp

REMARKS: Total includes 6 units carried aboard the *Miura*-class LSTs. Built in Japan.

◆ **22 U.S. LCVP-class landing craft**

D: 13 tons (fl) **S:** 8 kts **Dim:** 10.90 × 3.21 × 1.04 (aft)
M: 1 Yanmar diesel; 1 prop; 180 hp

REMARKS: Japanese-built, most with GRP hulls. Total includes the 12-15 carried by the 6 LSTs.

HYDROGRAPHIC SHIPS

◆ **0 (+1) new construction** Bldr: Hitachi, Maizuru

	Laid down	L	In serv.
5104 Wakasa	21-8-84	21-5-85	3-86

D: 2,000 tons **S:** . . . **Dim:** . . . × . . . × . . .
A: None **M:** 2 Fuji 6 LS 27.5XF diesels; 2 CP props; 3,000 hp **Man:** . . .

Remarks: Construction authorized in 1983 budget. Ordered 29-3-84.

◆ **1 Suma class (AGS)** Bldr: Hitachi Heavy Ind., Maizuru

	Laid down	L	In serv.
5103 Suma	24-9-80	1-9-81	30-3-82

Suma (AGS 5103) *Ships of the World,* 1982

D: 1,180 tons **S:** 15 kts **Dim:** 72.0 × 12.8 × 3.4
A: None **M:** 2 Fuji 6 LS 27.5X diesels; 2 CP props; 3,000 hp **Man:** 65

Remarks: Built under 1979-80 Budget to begin replacement of the *Kusado*-class former minesweepers used as coastal survey ships. Carries one 7.9-m boat and one 11-m inshore survey launch. Passive tank stabilization, bow-thruster fitted. Operated by the "Ocean Management Group."

◆ **1 Futami class (AGS)**

	Bldr	Laid down	L	In serv.
5102 Futami	Mitsubishi, Shimonoseki	20-1-78	9-8-78	27-2-79

Futami (AGS 5102) L. & L. Van Ginderen, 6-84

D: 2,050 tons (3,000 fl) **S:** 16 kts **Dim:** 96.8 (90.0 pp) × 15.0 × 4.3
A: None **Electron Equipt:** Radar: 1/OPS-18 **Man:** 105 tot.
M: 2 Kawasaki-M.A.N. V8V 22/30 ATL diesels; 2 CP props; 4,400 hp

Remarks: Configured for both hydrographic surveying and cable-laying. Bow-thruster. Has three diesel and one gas-turbine generator sets. Carries one RCV-225 remote-controlled unmanned submersible.

◆ **1 Akashi class (AGS)**

	Bldr	Laid down	L	In serv.
5101 Akashi	Nippon Kokan, Tsurumi	21-9-68	30-5-69	25-10-69

D: 1,420 tons **S:** 16 kts **Dim:** 74.0 × 12.9 × 4.3
A: None **Electron Equipt:** Radar: OPS-9—EW: NOLR-5
M: 2 Kawasake-M.A.N. V8V 22/30 ATL diesels; 2 CP props; 3,800 hp
Range: 16,500/14 **Man:** 70 crew, 10 scientists

Remarks: Bow-thruster. Two cranes; one 5-ton and one 1-ton. Has extensive electronics intercept arrays, new radar.

◆ **1 Kasado-class converted minesweepers (MSC)** Bldr: Hitachi, Kanagawa

	Laid down	L	In serv.
5115 AGS 5 (ex-*Hario,* MSC 618)	19-3-61	10-12-61	23-3-62

D: 340 tons (355 fl) **S:** 14.5 kts **Dim:** 45.7 × 8.38 × 2.3
A: None **Electron Equipt:** Radar: OPS-4
M: 2 Mitsubishi YV10ZC diesels; 2 props; 1,200 hp **Man:** 30 tot.

Remarks: Sister AGS 1 (AGS 5111, ex-*Kasado,* MSC 604) stricken 31-3-82; AGS 2 (5112, ex-*Habuchi,* MSC 608) stricken 4-9-82, AGS 3 (5113, ex-*Tatara,* MSC 610) stricken 30-3-83, and AGS 4 (ex-*Hirado,* MSC 614) stricken 30-3-85. Appearance is virtually identical to service craft sisters typed YAS.

Akashi (AGS 5101) *Ships of the World,* 1984

EXPERIMENTAL SHIP

◆ **1 Kurihama class (AGE)**

	Bldr	Laid down	L	In serv.
6101 Kurihama	Sasebo Heavy Industries	23-3-79	20-9-79	8-4-80

Kurihama (AGE 6101) *Ships of the World*

D: 959 tons **S:** 15 kts **Dim:** 68.0 × 11.6 × 3.3
A: Various **Electron Equipt:** Radar: 1/OPS-9B
M: 2 Fuji 6S 30B diesels; 2 CP props; 2,600 hp (plus 2 electric auxiliary propulsors; 400 hp)
Man: 42 crew + 13 technicians

Remarks: For testing mines, torpedoes, and sonars. In 1979 Budget. Has Flume-type passive stabilization tanks and gas-turbine generators in superstructure. Retractable bow-thruster. Can be rigged for silent operation. Has extra accommodations for trials personnel.

CABLE-LAYER

◆ **1 Muroto class (ARC)**

	Bldr	Laid down	L	In serv.
482 Muroto	Mitsubishi, Shimonoseki	28-11-78	25-7-79	27-3-80

Muroto (AGS 482) JMSDF, 1980

D: 4,544 tons **S:** 17 kts **Dim:** 131.0 × 17.4 × 5.7
A: None **Electron Equipt:** Radar: 1/OPS-9
M: 2 Mitsubishi MTU V8V 22/30 diesels; 2 CP props; 4,400 hp **Man:** 122 tot.

Remarks: Intended to replace *Tsugaru* as naval cable layer. Able to lay cable over bow or stern at 2-6 knots. Bow-thruster. Similar to commercial *Kuroshio Maru.* Has extensive facilities for oceanographic research.

Note: The former cable-layer *Tsugaru* (ARC 481) was redesignated ASU 7001 in 1979 and is listed under training ships.

SUBMARINE RESCUE SHIPS

◆ **1 Chiyoda class (ASR)**

	Bldr	Laid down	L	In serv.
405 Chiyoda	Mitsui, Tamano	19-1-83	7-12-83	27-3-85

Chiyoda (ASR 405) *Ships of the World,* 1985

D: 3,690 tons (4,450 fl) **S:** 17 kts (16 sust.)
Dim: 112.5 (106.0 pp) × 17.6 (18.0 max.) × 4.8
A: None **Electron Equipt:** Radar: 1/OPS-16
M: 2 Mitsui 8LV42M diesels; 2 CP props; 11,500 hp
Man: 120 tot.

Remarks: in 1981 Budget as a replacement for *Chihaya.* Carries a deep-submergence rescue vehicle (DSRV) launched 15-10-84 by Kawasaki, Kobe:

D: 40 tons **S:** 4 kts **Dim:** 12.4 × 3.2 × 4.3 (high)
M: Electric motors; 40 hp **Man:** 12 passengers

The DSRV is deployed over the sides, using hoist equipment similar to that of the U.S. Navy's *Pigeon* (ASR 21) class. There is also a deep-diving rescue bell. The helicopter platform can accommodate an HSS-2 Sea King. Has bow and stern thrusters.

◆ **1 Fushimi class (ASR)**

	Bldr	Laid down	L	In serv.
402 Fushimi	Sumitomo, Uraga	5-11-68	10-9-69	10-2-70

Fushimi (ASR 402) *Ships of the World,* 1984

D: 1,430 tons **S:** 16 kts **Dim:** 76.0 × 12.5 × 3.8
Electron Equipt: Radar: OPS-9—Sonar: SQS-11A
M: 1 Kawasaki-M.A.N. V6V 22/30 ATL diesel; 1 prop; 3,000 hp **Man:** 102 tot.

Remarks: Has one rescue bell, two decompression chambers; one 12-ton crane.

Note: Submarine rescue ship *Chihaya* (ASR 401) was redesignated ASU 7011 on 27-3-85 on completion of *Chiyoda* (ASR 405).

REPLENISHMENT OILERS (AOE/AO)

◆ **0 (+1 + 1) new construction**

	Bldr	Laid down	L	In serv.
422 Towada	Hitachi, Maizuru	17-4-85	3-86	3-87
423 N.	. . .	. . .	. . .	. . .

D: 8,000 tons **S:** . . . **Dim:** . . . × . . . × . . .
A: . . . **Electron Equipt:** Radar: . . .
M: . . . **Man:** . . .

Remarks: Approved in 1984 Budget, to replace *Hamana.* Will be an all-purpose liquid and solid stores replenishment ship, like *Sagami.* Second unit proposed, for 1986 or 1987 Budget.

◆ **1 Sagami class (AOE)**

	Bldr	Laid down	L	In serv.
421 Sagami	Hitachi, Maizuru	28-9-77	4-9-78	30-3-79

D: 5,000 tons (11,600 fl) **S:** 22 kts **Dim:** 146.0 (140.0 pp) × 19.0 × 7.3
A: None **Electron Equipt:** Radar: 1/OPS-16
M: 2 Type 12 DRV diesels; 2 props; 18,600 hp **Range:** 9,500/20
Man: 130 tot.

Remarks: Has three stations per side, two for liquid transfers, one for solid. Large helicopter deck but no hangar. In addition to fuel oil, diesel fuel, and JP-5 aviation fuel, carries food and ammunition. 1975 Budget.

Sagami (AOE 421) JMSDF, 1984

◆ **1 Hamana class (AO)**

	Bldr	Laid down	L	In serv.
411 Hamana	Uraga DY	17-4-61	24-10-61	10-3-62

Hamana (AO 411) *Ships of the World,* 1984

D: 2,900 tons (7,550 fl) **S:** 16 kts **Dim:** 128.0 × 15.7 × 6.3
A: 2/40-mm AA (II × 1) **Electron Equipt:** Radar: OPS-9
M: 1 Yokohama-M.A.N. KGZ 6D/150C diesel; 1 prop; 5,000 hp **Man:** 100 tot.

Remarks: Refitted, 1978-79, with two fueling positions per side. Mk 51 Mod. 2 director for gunmount. Carries 500 tons stores for transfer via highline station forward and about 3,000 tons liquid cargo.

TRAINING SHIPS (TV)

◆ **1 Katori-class cadet-training ship (TV)**

	Bldr	Laid down	L	In serv.
3501 Katori	Ishikawajima Harima, Tokyo	8-12-67	19-11-68	10-9-69

Katori (TV 3501) Pradignac & Leo, 9-83

D: 3,372 tons (4,100 fl) **S:** 25 kts **Dim:** 127.5 (122.0 pp) × 15.0 × 4.35
A: 4/76.2-mm DP Mk 23 (II × 2)—1/375-mm Bofors ASW RL (IV × 1)—6/324-mm Mk 32 ASW TT (III × 2)
Electron Equipt: Radar: 1/SPS-12, 1/OPS-15, 1/Mk 34
Sonar: OQS-3—EW: NOLR-1B
M: 2 sets Ishikawajima GT; 2 props; 20,000 hp **Boilers:** 2 **Rage:** 7,000/18
Man: 295 crew + 165 cadets

Remarks: U.S. Mk 63 GFCS system for 76.2-mm guns. After superstructure contains an auditorium. Helicopter deck is also used for ceremonial functions and calisthenics. An Intelset satellite communication system was added in mid-1979.

◆ **2 Ayanami-class former destroyers (TV)**

	Bldr	Laid down	L	In serv.
3502 Isonami (ex-DD 104)	Mitsubishi, Kobe	14-12-56	30-9-57	14-3-58
3503 Shikinami (ex-DD 106)	Mitsui, Tamano	24-12-56	25-9-57	15-3-58

D: 1,700 tons (2,400 fl) **S:** 32 kts **Dim:** 109.0 × 10.7 × 3.7 (mean)
A: 6/76.2-mm 50-cal. U.S. Mk 33 DP (II × 3)—2/Mk 15 trainable Hedgehog ASW mortar—6/324-mm Type 68 ASW TT (III × 2)

TRAINING SHIPS (TV) *(continued)*

Isonami (TV 3502) *Ships of the World, 8-84*

Electron Equipt: Radar: 1/OPS-15, 1/OPS-2, 2/Mk 34
Sonar: OQS-12 or 14—EW: BLR-1
M: 2 sets Mitsubishi-Escher-Wyss GT; 2 props; 3,500 hp
Boilers: 2 Mitsubishi (TV 3503: Hitachi-Babcock & Wilcox); 43 kg/cm², 454°C
Range: 6,000/18 **Man:** 175 crew + 50 cadets

REMARKS: Reclassified as training ships on 30-3-83, a duty they had performed since 13-6-75, when their quadruple 533-mm anti-ship torpedo-tube mount was replaced by a classroom deckhouse and they were designated the First Training Unit. Variable-depth sonar removed from TV 3502 in 1983. There are two U.S. Mk 63 GFCS for the three gunmounts, the Mk 34 radars being mounted on two of the gunmounts. OPS-2 is the Japanese designation for the U.S. SPS-6 air-search radar.

◆ **1 Azuma-class target service ship (ATS)**

	Bldr	Laid down	L	In serv.
4201 AZUMA	Hitachi, Maizuru	15-7-68	14-4-69	26-11-69

Azuma (ATS 4201) *Ships of the World, 1983*

D: 1,950 tons (2,400 fl) **S:** 18 kts **Dim:** 98.0 (94.0 pp) × 13.0 × 3.8
A: 1/76.2-mm DP Mk 34—2/Mk 4 torpedo launchers (U.S. Mk 32 torpedoes)
Electron Equipt: Radar: 1/OPS-15, 1/SPS-40, 1/TCATS
Sonar: SQS-11A
M: 2 Kawasaki-M.A.N. V8V 23/30 ATL diesels; 2 props; 4,000 hp
Electric: 700 kw **Man:** 185 tot.

REMARKS: Has ten KD2R-5 and four BQM-34-AJ drones. Portable catapult on helicopter deck for launching. Hangar is used for drone check-out and storage. Has the only SPS-40 radar in Japanese service. TCATS (Target Control and Tracking System) radar in large radome atop bridge replaced earlier radar, 1983. Mk 51 Mod. 2 director for gun (no radar).

NOTE: A new ATS of 2,200 tons (std.), similar in configuration to *Azuma,* was requested under the 1985 Budget but not approved; a 76-mm OTO Melara Compact gun was to have been carried.

SPECIAL USE AUXILIARIES (ASU)

◆ **5 target-support craft (ASU)** Bldr: ASU 81-83: Sasebo Heavy Industries; Others: . . .

	Laid down	L	In serv.
ASU 81 (ex-YAS 101)	10-10-67	18-1-68	30-3-68
ASU 82 (ex-YAS 102)	25-9-68	20-12-68	31-3-68
ASU 83 (ex-YAS 103)	2-4-71	24-5-71	30-9-71
ASU 84 (ex-YAS 104)	4-2-72	15-6-73	19-9-73
ASU 85 (ex-YAS 105)	20-2-73	16-7-73	19-9-73

D: 490 tons (543 fl) **S:** 14.5 kts **Dim:** 51.5 × 10.0 × 2.6
Electron Equipt: Radar: OPS-10 (ASU 84: OPS-29; ASU 85: OPS-19)
M: 2 Akasaka UH-527-42 diesels; 2 props; 1,600 hp
Range: 2,500/12 **Man:** 26 men + 14 passengers

REMARKS: ASU 82 is configured as a rescue ship. The others are intended to carry, control, recover, and service up to six KD2R-5 drone target aircraft. ASU 81: 480 tons std.; ASU 85: 500 tons std. Crane and mast configurations aft differ, early units have pole and derrick, later ones have a crane, with a tripod mast stepped on the stack.

ASU 83 *Ships of the World, 1984*

◆ **1 former submarine rescue ship (ASU)**

	Bldr	Laid down	L	In serv.
7011 CHIHAYA (ex-ASR 401)	Mitsubishi, Yokohama	15-3-60	4-10-60	15-3-61

Chihaya (ASU 7011)—as ASR 401 *Ships of the World*

D: 1,340 tons (1,800 fl) **S:** 15 kts **Dim:** 73.0 × 12.0 × 3.9
Electron Equipt: Radar: OPS-4—Sonar: SQS-11A
M: 1 Yokohama-M.A.N. G6Z S170 diesel; 1 prop; 2,700 hp
Range: 5,000/12 **Man:** 90 tot.

REMARKS: Reclassified as a utility service ship on 27-3-85 after being replaced on submarine rescue duties by the new *Chiyoda* (ASR 405). Has a McCann rescue bell for six persons, 12-ton crane, four flotation pontoons, and a 4-point mooring system.

◆ **1 Akizuku-class former destroyer**

	Bldr	Laid down	L	In serv.
7010 AKIZUKI (ex-DD 161)	Mitsubishi, Nagasaki	31-7-58	26-6-59	13-2-60

Akizuki (ASU 7010)—as DD 161 *Ships of the World, 7-84*

REMARKS: Data as for sister *Teruzuki* (DD 162), except that crew has been reduced. Reclassified as ASU on 27-3-85, having served for many years as Fleet Flagship.

◆ **3 Murasame-class former destroyers (ASU)**

	Bldr	Laid down	L	In serv.
7006 MURASAME (ex-DD 107)	Mitsubishi, Nagasaki	17-12-57	31-7-58	28-2-59
7007 YUDACHI (ex-DD 108)	Ishikawajima, Tokyo	16-12-57	29-7-58	25-3-59
7008 HARUSAME (ex-DD 109)	Uraga DY, Yokosuka	17-6-58	18-6-59	15-12-59

SPECIAL USE AUXILIARIES (ASU) *(continued)*

Harusame (ASU 7008)—as DD 109 *Ships of the World,* 1983

Yudachi (ASU 7007) *Ships of the World,* 1984

D: 1,800 tons (2,400 fl) **S:** 30 kts **Dim:** 109.73 × 10.97 × 3.7 (mean)
A: 3/127-mm 54-cal. U.S. Mk 39 DP (II × 3)—4/76.2-mm 50-cal. U.S. Mk 33 DP (II × 2)—1/Mk 15 trainable Hedgehog ASW mortar (XXXIV × 1)—ASU 7008 only: 6/324-mm Type 68 ASW TT (III × 2)—others: 1/Y-gun d.c. mortar (II × 1)—1/d.c. rack
Electron Equipt: Radar: 1/OPS-15, 1/OPS-1, 1/Mk 34, 2/Mk 35
Sonar: SQS-29—EW: NORL-1B
M: 2 sets Kampon (ASU 7008: Mitsubishi-Escher-Wyss) GT; 2 props; 35,000 hp
Boilers: 2 Foster-Wheeler-D (ASU 7008: Mitsubishi); 43 kg/cm², 454°C
Range: 6,000/18 **Man:** . . .

Remarks: ASU 7006 and 7007 reclassified 30-3-84 from destroyers, ASU 7008 on 5-3-85. Hull and machinery spaces similar to those of the *Ayanami* class. Have two U.S. Mk 57 and one U.S. Mk 63 GFCS to control the five gunmounts, U.S. Mk 105 underwater battery fire-control system. OPS-1 is a Japanese equivalent to the U.S. SPS-6 air-search radar.

◆ **3 Ayanami-class former destroyers (ASU)**

	Bldr	Laid down	L	In serv.
7004 Ayanami (ex-DD 103)	Mitsubishi, Nagasaki	20-11-56	1-6-57	12-2-58
7005 Uranami (ex-DD 105)	Kawasaki, Kobe	1-2-57	29-8-57	27-2-58
7009 Takanami (ex-DD 110)	Mitsui, Maizuru	8-11-58	8-8-59	30-1-60

Uranami (ASU 7005) *Ships of the World,* 5-83

D: 1,700 tons (2,400 fl) **S:** 32 kts **Dim:** 109.0 × 10.7 × 3.7 (mean)
A: 6/76.2-mm Mk 33 DP (II × 3)—2/Mk 15 trainable Hedgehog—6/324-mm Type 68 ASW TT (III × 2)
Electron Equipt: Radar: 1/OPS-15, 1/OPS-2, 2/Mk 34
Sonar: OQS-12 or 14—EW: NORL-1B
M: 2 sets Mitsubishi-Escher-Wyss GT; 2 props; 35,000 hp
Boilers: 2 Mitsubishi (ASU 7009: Hitachi-Babcock & Wilcox); 43 kg/cm², 454°C
Range: 6,000/18 **Man:** 220–230 tot.

Remarks: ASU 7006, 7007 reclassified as utility service ships on 30-3-83, when their quadruple 533-mm TT were removed and VDS was removed from ASU 7004. ASU 7009 reclassified from DD 110 on 27-3-85 and similarly modified. There are two U.S. Mk 63 GFCS for the three gunmounts. OPS-2 is the Japanese designation for the U.S. SPS-6 radar.

Note: The two Harukaze-class former destroyers were stricken, *Harukaze* (ASU 7002, ex-DD 101) on 5-3-85, and *Yukikaze* (ASU 7003, ex-DD 102) on 27-3-85.

Takinami (ASU 7009) *Ships of the World,* 1985

◆ **1 Tsugaru class (ASU, ex-ARC)**

	Bldr	Laid down	L	In serv.
7001 Tsugaru (ex-ARC 481)	Yokohama SY	18-12-54	19-7-55	15-12-55

Tsugaru (ASU 7001) L. & L. Van Ginderen, 8-85

D: 2,150 tons **S:** 13 kts **Dim:** 103.0 × 14.6 × 4.9
A: 2/20-mm AA (I × 2) **Electron Equipt:** Radar: 1/OPS-16
M: 2 Sulzer diesels; 2 props; 3,200 hp **Man:** 103 tot.

Remarks: Originally completed as a minelayer/cable-layer; between 10-7-69 and 30-4-70 she was lengthened and the amidships part of her hull widened by 2.2 meters at Nippon Kokan, Tsurumi. Also, her cable facilities were greatly enlarged. Redesignated ASU (Auxiliary, Special Use) in 1979.

◆ **3 Mizutori-class former patrol boats (ASU)**

	Bldr	Laid down	L	In serv.
ASU 61 Otori (ex-PC 313)	Kure SY	16-12-59	27-5-60	13-10-60
ASU 62 Hatsukari (ex-PC 315)	Sasebo DY	25-1-60	24-6-60	15-11-60
ASU 63 Umidori (ex-PC 316)	Sasebo DY	15-2-62	15-10-62	30-3-63

Hatsukari (ASU 62) *Ships of the World,* 2-83

D: 420 tons (450 fl) **S:** 20 kts **Dim:** 60.00 × 7.10 × 2.35
A: 2/40-mm AA (II × 1)—1/Mk 10 Hedgehog ASW mortar (XXIV × 1)—1/d.c. rack
Electron Equipt: Radar: 1/OPS-35 or OPS-36, 1/Mk 34
Sonar: SQS-11A—EW: BLR-1
M: 2 Kawasaki-M.A.N. V8V diesels; 2 props; 3,800 hp **Fuel:** 24 tons
Range: 3,000/12 **Man:** 70 tot.

Remarks: Reclassified for training duties: ASU 61 and 62 on 31-3-82, and ASU 63 on 30-3-84. The two units of the class remaining designated PC may be retyped later as well. Mk 63 GFCS for 40-mm AA. Sisters *Kasasagi* (ASU 87, ex-PC 314), *Mizutori* (ASU 88, ex-PC 311), and *Yamadori* (ASU 90, ex-PC 312) stricken 3-85.

SPECIAL USE AUXILIARIES (ASU) *(continued)*

◆ 2 Umitaka-class former patrol boats (ASU)

	Bldr	Laid down	L	In serv.
ASU 64 WAKATAKA (ex-PC 317)	Kure SY	5-3-62	13-11-62	30-3-63
ASU 65 KUMATAKA (ex-PC 318)	Fujinagata, Osaka	20-3-63	21-10-63	25-3-64

Wakataka (ASU 64)—as PC 317 *Ships of the World,* 1985

D: 490 tons (530 fl) **S:** 20 kts **Dim:** 60.0 × 7.1 × 2.4 (hull)
A: 2/40-mm AA (II × 1)—6/324-mm Type 68 ASW TT (III × 2)—1/Mk 10 Hedgehog—1/d.c. rack
Electron Equipt: Radar: ASU 64: 1/OPS-36; ASU 65: 1/OPS-16; both: 1/Mk 34—EW: BLR-1
Sonar: SQS-11A
M: 2 Mitsui-Burmeister & Wain V8V diesels; 2 props; 4,000 hp
Fuel: 24 tons **Range:** 3,000/12 **Man:** 80 tot.

REMARKS: Reclassified 27-3-85. Mk 63 GFCS for 40-mm AA. Sister *Umitaka* (ASU 86, ex-PC 309) was stricken 20-2-85 and sister *Ootaka* (ASU 88, ex-PC 310) on 3-85.

ICEBREAKER (AGB)

◆ 1 Shirase class (AGB)

	Bldr	Laid down	L	In serv.
5002 SHIRASE	Nippon Kokan, Tsurumi	5-3-81	11-12-81	12-12-83

Shirase (AGB 5002) JMSDF, 1984

D: 11,660 tons (18,900 fl) **S:** 19 kts **Dim:** 134.0 × 28.0 × 9.2
M: 6 M.A.N.-Mitsui 12V42M diesels, electric drive; 3 props; 30,000 hp
Electron Equipt: Radar: OPS-18, OPS-22—TACAN: URN-25
Range: 25,000/15 **Man:** 37 officers, 137 men, plus 60 passengers

REMARKS: Built under 1979-80 budget to replace *Fuji* (AGB 5001). Cargo capacity: 1,000 tons. Hangar and flight deck for 2 HSS-2 and 1 OH-6 helicopters.

The icebreaker *Fuji* (AGB 5001), inactive since her final deployment in 1982-83, was stricken 11-4-84.

YACHT (ASY)

◆ 1 former ASW patrol boat, converted (ASY)

	Bldr	Laid down	L	In serv.
91 HAYABUSA (ex-PC 308)	Mitsubishi, Nagasaki	23-5-56	20-11-56	10-6-57

D: 400 tons **S:** 13 kts **Dim:** 58.0 × 7.8 × 2.2 **A:** None
M: 2 diesels; 2 props; 1,000 hp **Man:** 35 crew, plus 125 passengers

REMARKS: Unique unit, fitted with 5,000-hp gas turbine on centerline shaft, 1962-70. Rebuilt 20-11-77 to 15-4-78 at Yokohama Yacht Co. as naval yacht, with extensive superstructure added aft, new engines. Painted white.

SERVICE SHIPS AND CRAFT

NOTE: All Japanese Navy service ships and craft are listed below in the alphabetical order of the two- or three-letter designator system employed to define their functions. Self-propelled units have 2-digit hull numbers following the letter designator (as in "YO 01"). Non-self-propelled craft with the same functions have 3-digit numbers starting with "1" (as in "YO 102"). Self-propelled units that have returned to an original type designation *after* an initial type change receive 3-digit numbers beginning with "2" (as in "YG 202," ex-YO 20, ex-YG 08).

Hayabusa (ASY 91) *Ships of the World,* 1984

MINE TRIALS AND SERVICE CRAFT (YAL)

◆ 1 YAL 01 class

YAL 01 (In serv. 22-3-76)

D: 240 tons (265 fl) **S:** 12 kts **Dim:** 37.00 × 8.00 × 1.90
A: Mine rails **M:** 2 Type 64 H 19-E-4A diesels; 2 props; 800 hp **Man:** 16 tot.

◆ 3 former U.S. LCU 1466-class landing craft

YAL 02 (L: 23-1-55) YAL 03 (L: 5-1-55) YAL 04 (L: 13-12-54)

YAL 03 *Ships of the World,* 1984

D: 180 tons (347 fl) **S:** 9 kts **Dim:** 35.08 × 10.36 × 1.60 (aft)
A: 2/20-mm AA (I × 2)—mines
M: 3 Gray Marine 64YTL diesels; 3 props; 675 hp
Fuel: 11 tons **Range:** 1,200/6 **Man:** . . .

REMARKS: Three of the six-unit LCU 2001 class (ex-U.S. LCU 1602–1607), built in Japan under the Offshore Procurement Program), reconfigured to serve as exercise mine planters.

SPECIAL SERVICE CRAFT (YAS)

◆ 12 Kasado-class former coastal minesweepers

	Bldr	L	In serv.
YAS 67 MIKURA (ex-MSC 612)	Hitachi, Kanagawa	14-3-60	27-5-60
YAS 71 KARATO (ex-MSC 617)	Nippon Kokan, Tsurumi	11-12-62	23-3-63
YAS 72 MUTUSURE (ex-MSC 619)	Nippon Kokan, Tsurumi	16-12-63	24-3-64
YAS 73 CHIBURI (ex-MSC 620)	Hitachi, Kanagawa	29-11-63	25-3-64
YAS 74 KUDAKO (ex-MSC 622)	Hitachi, Kanagawa	8-12-64	24-3-65
YAS 75 RESHIRI (ex-MSC 623)	Nippon Kokan, Tsurumi	22-11-65	5-3-66
YAS 76 REBUN (ex-MSC 624)	Hitachi, Kanagawa	7-12-65	24-3-66
YAS 77 AMAMI (ex-MSC 625)	Nippon Kokan, Tsurumi	13-10-66	6-3-67
YAS 78 URUME (ex-MSC 626)	Hitachi, Kanagawa	12-11-66	30-1-67
YAS 79 MINASE (ex-MSC 627)	Nippon Kokan, Tsurumi	10-1-67	25-3-67
YAS 80 IBUKI (ex-MSC 628)	Hitachi, Kanagawa	2-12-67	27-2-68
YAS 81 KATSURA (ex-MSC 629)	Nippon Kokan, Tsurumi	18-9-67	15-2-68

D: 330–340 tons (350-360 fl) **S:** 14 kts **Dim:** 45.7 × 8.38 × 2.30
A: 1/20-mm AA **Electron Equipt:** Radar: 1/OPS-9 **Range:** 2,000/10
M: 2 Mitsubishi YV102-DE diesels; 2 props; 1,200 hp **Man:** 40 tot.

REMARKS: Majority converted to serve as mine-disposal divers' support ships. YAS 67 is tender to the Gunnery School. Wooden construction. Sister *Koshiki* (YAS 63, ex-MSC 615) stricken 1981; YAS 62 *Shisaka* and YAS 64 *Sakito* were stricken during 1982; YAS 66 *Tsukumi* and YAS 70 *Hotaka* in 3-83, YAS 65 *Kanawa* on 10-2-84, and YAS 68 *Shikine* on 30-3-84. YAS 79-81 redesignated from MSC on 21-6-84. Not all are armed.

SPECIAL SERVICE CRAFT (YAS) *(continued)*

Amami (YAS 77) *Ships of the World,* 1984

OIL SLUDGE REMOVAL CRAFT (YB)

◆ **1 YB 01-class lighter (L: 31-3-75)**

YB 01

YB 01 *Ships of the World*

D: 177 tons **S:** 9 kts **Dim:** 27.5 × 5.2 × 1.9
M: 1 diesel; 230 hp **Cargo:** 100 dwt

◆ **4 YB 101-class barges** (In serv. 1975-76)

YB 101-104

D: 100 dwt **Dim:** 17.0 × 5.2 × 2.0 **M:** Non-self-propelled

SELF-PROPELLED FLOATING CRANES (YC)

◆ **1 YC 09 class**

YC 09 (In serv. 25-2-74)

D: 260 tons **S:** 6 kts **Dim:** 26.0 × 14.0 × 0.9 **M:** 2 diesels; 2 props; 280 hp

◆ **3 YC 06 class**

YC 06 (In serv. 31-3-69) YC 07 (In serv. 28-2-70) YC 08 (In serv. 29-3-72)

D: 150 tons **S:** 5 kts **Dim:** 24.0 × 10.0 × 0.8 **M:** 2 diesels; 2 props; 240 hp

Remarks: In service 1969-72.

◆ **1 YC 05 class**

YC 05 (In serv. 27-3-67)

YC 05—pontoon hull, crawler crane *Ships of the World*

D: 110 tons **S:** 5 kts **Dim:** 22.0 × 10.0 × 0.9 **M:** 2 diesels; 180 hp

DOCKYARD SERVICE CRAFT (YD)

YD 01, 02: 0.8 tons, 7.60 × 1.90, rowboats in serv. 25-3-75; YD 03: 1.7 tons, same dimensions, in service 1978; YD 04: 0.5 tons, in serv. 25-12-79.

FIREBOAT (YE)

◆ **1 Shobo class** Bldr: Azumo, Yokosuka (In serv. 28-2-64)

YE 41 Shobo 1 (ex-*Kosuko* 6)

D: 45 tons **S:** 19 kts **Dim:** 22.9 × 5.5 × 1.0 **M:** 3 diesels; 3 props; 1,300 hp

Remarks: Employed as air/sea rescue boat and fireboat at Iwakuni Air Station for seaplanes. Three firefighting monitors. Re-engined 1977; originally made 30 kts on 2,800 hp.

COMMUNICATIONS BOATS (YF)

◆ **68 miscellaneous service boats**

YF 1029 YF 1030 (Both in serv. 1982)

D: 11 tons **S:** 18 kts **Dim:** 13.5 (12.3 pp) × 3.8 × 0.7
M: 2 Type 6BDITC-MRD diesels; 2 props; 360 hp

YF 1022 through YF 1028 (In serv. 1980)

D: 9 tons (11 fl) **S:** 14 kts **Dim:** 13.00 × 3.80 × 0.60
M: 2 Type E 120 T-MF6RE diesels; 2 props; 280 hp **Cargo:** 73 passengers

Others in service are:

	Tons	Dim:	S(kts):	Hp.
YF 1021	11	13.0 × 3.6 × 0.6	14	350
YF 2097-2101, 2103-2106, 2108, 2109	11	17.0 × 4.2 × 0.8	10	450
YF 2060-2062	11	15.0 × 3.6 × 0.6	10	160
YF 2066-2074, 2078-2081, 2083-2087, 2091, 2096, 2110, 2116	8	10.5 × 3.2 × 0.6	9	180
YF 2075	22	17.0 × 3.7 × 0.7	10	400
YF 2076, 2077	0.8	7.0 × 2.2 × 0.3	8	22
YF 2082	5	11.0 × 3.2 × 0.6	9	90
YF 2088-2090, 2092, 2095, 2111-2115, 2117-2119, 2122	5.9	11.0 × 3.2 × 0.6	10	135
YF 2120	12.6	15.0 × 3.6 × 0.7	10	230
YF 2121	33	17.0 × 4.3 × 0.7	10	480

Remarks: YF 2097 series and YF 2075 designs are essentially U.S. LCM (6) landing craft adapted as utility craft. YF 2066 series are of the U.S. LCVP design. Smaller units are of wooden or glass-reinforced plastic construction.

YF 2108—U.S. LCM(6) type *Ships of the World*

JET ENGINE FUEL CRAFT (YG)

◆ **2 YG 07-class lighters**

YG 201 (ex-YG 07; In serv. 30-3-73) YG 202 (ex-YO 20, ex-YG 08; In serv. 29-3-77)

YG 202 (as YG 08) 1977

JET ENGINE FUEL CRAFT (YG) *(continued)*

D: 270 dwt **S:** 10 kts **Dim:** 36.7 × 6.8 × 2.6
M: 1 diesel; 1 prop; 350 hp

REMARKS: YG 08 reclassified YO 20 in 1979, then again reclassified YG 202 in 1981.

CARGO CRAFT (YL)

◆ **2 YL 09-class lighters**

	Laid down	L	In serv.
YL 09	24-11-79	3-3-80	28-3-80
YL 10	. . .	17-12-82	28-2-83

YL 09 *Ships of the World,* 1980

D: 126 tons (fl) **S:** 9-10 kts **Dim:** 27.00 × 7.00 × 1.04
M: 2 Type E 120 T-MF6 RE diesels; 2 props; 560 hp **Man:** 5 tot.

REMARKS: 50 dwt. Resemble a U.S. LCM(8) and have a bow ramp, two 2-ton stores cranes.

◆ **1 YL 08-class lighter**

YL 08 (In serv. 10-3-67)

D: 50 dwt **S:** 8 kts **Dim:** 22.40 × 5.10 × 1.20 **M:** 1 diesel; 1 prop; 180 hp

◆ **4 YL 02-class lighters**

YL 03 (In serv. 31-5-54) YL 06 (In serv. 30-11-54)
YL 04 (In serv. 31-5-54) YL 07 (In serv. 30-11-54)

D: 50 dwt **S:** 8 kts **Dim:** 20.00 × 5.10 × 1.20
M: 1 diesel; 1 prop; 100 hp

◆ **1 YL 01-class lighter**

YL 01 (In serv. 30-5-53)

D: 50 dwt **S:** 7 kts **Dim:** 20.00 × 5.50 × 1.20
M: 1 diesel; 1 prop; 90 hp

◆ **1 YL 119-class barge**

YL 119 (In serv. 20-3-71)

D: 200 dwt **Dim:** 34.00 × 13.00 × 1.00

◆ **3 YL 116-class barges**

YL 116 (In serv. 21-12-63) YL 117 (In serv. 25-2-64) YL 118 (In serv. 31-3-66)

D: 100 dwt **Dim:** 21.50 × 8.40 × 1.00

◆ **2 YL 114-class barges**

YL 114 (In serv. 20-2-63) YL 115 (In serv. 12-3-63)

D: 80 dwt **Dim:** 18.40 × 7.40 × 0.90

FUEL LIGHTERS (YO)

NOTE: YO is now applied to all fuel carriers except jet fuel carriers, which are typed YG.

◆ **4 (+1) YO 21 class** Bldr: Yoshiura Shipbuilding

	Laid down	L	In serv.
YO 21	. . .	15-3-80	31-3-80
YO 22	11-11-80	26-2-81	28-2-81
YO 23	26-11-82	12-3-83	31-3-83
YO 24	4-11-83	20-1-84	29-2-84
YO 25	. . .	. . .	. . .

D: 490 tons (694 fl) **S:** 10 kts **Dim:** 45.5 × 7.8 × 2.9
M: 2 Yanmar 6 MA diesels; 2 props; 460 hp **Cargo:** 520m³

◆ **1 YO 19-class former diesel fuel lighter**

YO 19 (ex-YG 06; in serv. 20-6-63)

D: 270 dwt **S:** 9 kts **Dim:** 34.4 × 6.8 × 2.8 **M:** 2 diesels; 2 props; 330 hp

REMARKS: Reclassified under FY 1979-80. YO 290 (ex-YG 08) reclassified YG 202 in 1981.

YO 24 *Ships of the World,* 2-84

◆ **3 YO 15-class former diesel fuel lighters**

	In serv.
YO 15 (ex-YG 01)	20-5-53
YO 16 (ex-YG 02)	15-10-53
YO 18 (ex YG 04)	10-1-55

D: 100 dwt **S:** 8 kts **Dim:** 23.0 × 5.0 × 2.0 **M:** 1 diesel; 1 prop; 90 hp

REMARKS: Reclassified 1979-80. Sister YO 17 (ex-YG 03) stricken 30-3-84.

◆ **1 YO 14-class lighter**

YO 14 (In serv. 31-3-76)

D: 490 dwt. **S:** 9 kts **Dim:** 45.0 × 7.8 × 2.9 **M:** 2 diesels; 2 props; 460 hp

REMARKS: Very similar to YO 21; officially considered same class.

◆ **4 YO 10-class lighters**

YO 10 (In serv. 31-3-65) YO 12 (In serv. 21-3-67)
YO 11 (In serv. 14-3-66) YO 13 (In serv. 31-3-67)

D: 290 dwt **S:** 9 kts **Dim:** 36.5 × 6.8 × 2.6 **M:** 2 diesels; 2 props; 360 hp

◆ **3 YO 07-class lighters**

YO 07 (In serv. 28-2-63) YO 08 (In serv. 29-2-64) YO 09 (In serv. 15-3-65)

D: 490 dwt **S:** 9 kts **Dim:** 43.9 × 7.8 × 3.1 **M:** 2 diesels; 400 hp

◆ **4 YO 03-class lighters**

YO 03 (In serv. 15-4-55) YO 05 (In serv. 15-3-56)
YO 04 (In serv. 15-4-55) YO 06 (In serv. 15-3-56)

D: 300 dwt **S:** 7 kts **Dim:** 33.0 × 7.0 × 2.6
M: 2 diesels; 150 hp

◆ **1 YO 107-class barge**

YO 108 (In serv. 15-3-54)

D: 100 dwt **Dim:** 17.00 × 5.20 × 2.20

◆ **1 YO 106-class barge**

YO 106 (In serv. 20-5-53)

D: 250 dwt **Dim:** 23.00 × 7.00 × 2.50

DEBRIS CLEARANCE CRAFT (YS)

◆ **1 catamaran "sweeper boat"**

YS 01 (In serv. 30-3-79)

YS 01 *Ships of the World*

D: 80 tons **S:** 9 kts **Dim:** 22.0 × 7.80 × 1.40
M: 2 diesels; 2 props; 460 hp **Man:** 6 tot.

REMARKS: Stationed at Iwakuni Air Station seaplane base; used to clear floating debris in seaplane landing lanes and as a marker-buoy tender.

TUGS (YT)

◆ **6 (+1) YT 58-class large harbor tugs** Bldr: Yokohama Yacht

YT 58 (In serv. 31-10-78) YT 65 (In serv. 20-9-84)
YT 63 (In serv. 27-9-82) YT 66 (In serv. 30-9-85)
YT 64 (In serv. 30-9-83) YT 67 (In serv. 9-86)

YT 64 *Ships of the World*, 9-83

D: 262 tons **S:** 11 kts **Dim:** 28.40 × 8.60 × 2.50
M: 2 Niigata 6L25B diesels; 2 pivoting Korl-nozzle props; 1,800 hp

Remarks: YT 66, in 1984 Budget, ordered 17-12-84. YT 67 in 1985 Budget. Have two water cannon for firefighting.

◆ **4 YT 53-class large harbor tugs**

YT 53 (In serv. 1974) YT 56 (In serv. 13-7-76)
YT 55 (In serv. 22-8-75) YT 57 (In serv. 22-8-77)

YT 57 1977

D: 195 tons (200 fl) **S:** 11 kts **Dim:** 25.70 × 7.00 × 2.30
M: 2 Kubota M6D20BUCS diesels; 1 prop; 1,500 hp **Man:** 10 tot.

Note: The last former U.S. Navy LCM(6) landing craft used as a tug, YT 54 was stricken 30-3-84.

◆ **8 YT 35-class harbor tugs**

YT 35 (In serv. 28-2-63) YT 41 (In serv. 31-3-66) YT 46 (In serv. 29-3-67)
YT 37 (In serv. 31-3-65) YT 44 (In serv. 29-3-67) YT 48 (In serv. 31-3-68)
YT 40 (In serv. 31-3-66) YT 45 (In serv. 30-3-67)

YT 35 *Ships of the World*, 1979

D: 100 tons **S:** 10 kts **Dim:** 23.80 × 5.40 × 1.80
M: 2 diesels; 2 props; 400 hp

◆ **3 YT 60-class harbor pusher tugs** Bldr: Yokohama Yacht

YT 60 (In serv. 31-3-80) YT 62 (In serv. 16-3-81)
YT 61 (In serv. 26-3-80)

YT 61 *Ships of the World*, 1980

D: 30 tons (37 fl) **S:** 8.6 kts **Dim:** 15.50 × 4.20 × 1.50 (0.97 hull)
M: 2 Isuzu E 120-MF64A diesels; 2 cycloidal props; 380 hp

◆ **11 YT 34-class harbor pusher tugs**

YT 34 (In serv. 20-3-63) YT 42 (In serv. 31-3-65) YT 51 (In serv. 28-2-72)
YT 36 (In serv. 14-3-64) YT 43 (In serv. 29-3-66) YT 54 (In serv. 24-3-75)
YT 38 (In serv. 31-3-65) YT 47 (In serv. 20-1-67) YT 59 (In serv. 16-1-79)
YT 39 (In serv. 31-3-65) YT 49 (In serv. 5-3-68)

D: 28 tons (30 fl) **S:** 9 kts **Dim:** 14.50 × 4.00 × 1.00
M: 2 diesels; 2 props; 320 hp **Man:** 3 tot.

Remarks: Conventional tugs. Sisters YT 27 and 33 stricken 1979, and YT 32 during 1981. YT 59 displaces 30 tons std.

◆ **4 YT 25-class pusher tugs** (In serv. . . . .)

YT 25 YT 28 YT 29 YT 31

D: 26 tons **S:** 11 kts **Dim:** 14.0 × 4.0 × 1.0
M: 2 diesels; 2 props; 320 hp **Man:** 3 tot.

Remarks: Sister YT 30 discarded 30-6-84.

TRAINING TENDERS (YTE)

◆ **1 minesweeper construction experimental craft**

Bldr: Hitachi, Kanegawa

	Laid down	L	In serv.
YTE 12 Tokiwa	1980	12-1-82	12-1-83

D: 110 tons light, 142 std. (180 fl) **S:** 14 kts **Dim:** 35.0 × 7.5 × 1.5
M: 2 diesels; 2 props; 1,100 hp **Man:** 18 tot.

Remarks: Built to test glass-reinforced plastic construction techniques for building future mine countermeasures ships and for testing shock resistance and sound transmission properties. Lines based on former inshore minesweeper *Atada;* flush deck, no minesweeping gear as completed.

◆ **1 navigational training tender** Bldr: Ando Iron Works

YTE 11 (In serv. 31-3-73)

YTE 11 *Ships of the World*, 1979

D: 120 tons (170 fl) **S:** 13 kts **Dim:** 33.0 × 7.0 × 1.5
M: 2 Shinko-Zoki SG175/CM diesels; 2 props; 1,400 hp

Remarks: Based at Etajima Naval Academy to teach officer cadets ship handling and navigation. Can carry 25 cadets.

SEAPLANE BUOY TENDERS (YV)

◆ **3 YV 01 class**

YV 01 (In serv. 30-3-68) YV 02 (In serv. 28-3-69) YV 03 (In serv. 20-3-70)

YV 01 *Ships of the World*

D: 45 tons **S:** 10 kts **Dim:** 20.0 × 4.40 × 1.00 **M:** 2 diesels; 2 props; 240 hp

Remarks: Maintain seaplane fairway marker buoys.

WATER LIGHTERS (YW)

◆ **5 YW 12 class**

YW 12 (In serv. 14-3-64) YW 15 (In serv. 20-3-67)
YW 13 (In serv. 28-3-66) YW 16 (In serv. 20-3-67)
YW 14 (In serv. 30-3-66)

YW 12 *Ships of the World,* 1979

D: 160 dwt **S:** 8 kts **Dim:** 30.5 × 5.7 × 2.2 **M:** 1 diesel; 180 hp

◆ **1 YW 11 class**

YW 11 (In serv. 25-3-64)

D: 310 dwt **S:** 10 kts **Dim:** 36.7 × 6.8 × 2.8 **M:** 2 diesels; 2 props; 360 hp

◆ **1 YW 10 class**

YW 10 (In serv. 20-3-63)

D: 100 dwt **S:** 8 kts **Dim:** 23.5 × 5.1 × 1.0 **M:** 1 diesel; 160 hp

◆ **7 YW 03 class**

YW 03 (In serv. 22-3-54) YW 06 (In serv. 20-12-54) YW 09 (In serv. 20-12-54)
YW 04 (In serv. 31-3-54) YW 07 (In serv. 11-12-54)
YW 05 (In serv. 20-12-54) YW 08 (In serv. 20-12-54)

D: 150 dwt **S:** 8 kts **Dim:** 27.0 × 5.5 × 2.1 **M:** 1 diesel; 75 hp

◆ **1 YW 02 class**

YW 02 (In serv. 20-5-53)

D: 150 dwt **S:** 9 kts **Dim:** 27.0 × 5.5 × 2.1 **M:** 1 diesel; 90 hp

MOTOR BOATS (B)

◆ **12 miscellaneous**

B 4006: 8 tons — 13.00 × 3.20 × 0.50 — 14 kts (In serv. 16-3-76)
B 4007–4013: 1 ton — 5.00 × 2.10 × 0.40 — 22 kts (All in serv. 26-1-76)
B 4014–4016: 8 tons — 13.00 × 3.20 × 0.50 — 14 kts (In serv. 1978-80)
B 4017: 16 tons — 17.4 × 3.9 × 1.5 — 10 kts (In serv. 28-3-85)

Remarks: Fiberglass-hulled. B 4016 capable of 18 kts. B 4006 basically the same as B 4014–4016. B 4017 replaced the wooden-hulled B 4005 (stricken 30-3-85) and has a glass-reinforced plastic hull with pilothouse offset to port; 180 hp.

ROWING CRAFT AND SAILBOATS

64 "C" group rowing boats: C 5094–5157

D: 1.5 tons **Dim:** 9.0 × 2.5 × . . .

39 "T" group rowing punts: T 6063–6102 (T 6058–6062 stricken '85, but T 6098–6102 added 26-2-85)

D: .5 tons **Dim:** 6.0 × 1.6 × . . .

13 "Y" group sailboats: Y 7010–7022 (Y 7021, 22 added 26-2-85)

MARITIME SAFETY AGENCY

(Kaijo Hoancho)

Personnel (1984): 11,944 men (approx. 2,500 officers)

The Maritime Safety Agency, which was organized in 1948, recently underwent a massive expansion, which by 1982 made it the world's largest and best-equipped coast guard. In peacetime, it is directed by the Department of Transportation. Although most of its ships are armed, they are not considered part of the Navy; they fly only the national colors (a red disk on a white background), not the flag flown by naval ships. A stylized blue stripe has recently been added to the hull sides of larger units. In wartime, the ships would be under naval control.

Aviation: In 1985, the MSA operated 21 fixed-wing aircraft (5 YS-11A transports, 2 SC-7 Skyvan, 13 Beech 200T light transports, and 1 Cessna SA 790/185C), and 26 helicopters (22 Kawasaki-Bell 212, 4 Bell 206B, and 2 Hughes 369-HS).

HIGH-ENDURANCE HELICOPTER-CARRYING CUTTERS (PLH)

◆ **0 (+2) new construction**

	Bldr	Laid down	L	In serv.
PLH 21 Mizuho	Mitsubishi, Shimonoseki	27-7-84	5-6-85	3-86
PLH 22 N. . .	. . .	. . .	. . .	. . .

Mizuho (PLH 21) at launch *Ships of the World,* 6-85

D: 4,900 tons (5,300 fl) **S:** 23 kts **Dim:** 130.00 (123.00 wl) × 15.50 × 5.25
A: 1/35-mm Oerlikon AA — 1/20-mm JM-61-MB gatling AA — 2/Kawasaki-Bell 212 helicopters **Electron Equipt:** Radar: 3 navigational sets
M: 2 SEMT-Pielstick 14 PC 2.5V diesels; 2 CP props; 18,200 hp
Range: . . . / . . . **Electric:** 1,875 kVA **Man:** 130 tot.

Remarks: Both ordered under the 1984 program. Design is a reduced version of a 5,900-std.-ton patrol and rescue ship intended for Indian Ocean service; the new ships will operate in the Pacific and are the first MSA units to carry two helicopters. Will have a flight deck traversing system. Have a bow-thruster.

HIGH-ENDURANCE CUTTERS (PL)

◆ **6 Tsugaru class**

	Bldr	Laid down	L	In serv.
PL 02 Tsugaru	Ishikawa-Harima, Tokyo	18-4-78	6-12-78	17-4-79
PL 03 Oosumi	Mitsui, Tamano	1-9-78	1-6-79	18-10-79
PL 04 Uraga	Hitachi, Maizuru	14-3-79	12-10-79	5-3-80
PL 05 Zaō	Mitsubishi, Nagasaki	23-10-80	29-10-81	19-3-82
PL 06 Chikuzen	Kawasaki, Kobe	20-4-82	18-3-83	28-9-83
PL 07 Settsu	Sumitomo, Uraga	5-4-83	21-4-84	27-9-84

D: 3.730 tons (4.037 fl) **S:** 22 kts **Dim:** 105.4 (100.0 wl) × 14.6 × 4.8
A: 1/40-mm AA — 1/20-mm AA (not in PL 03, 04) — PL 04, 05, 06: 1/35-mm AA — all: 1/Bell 212 helicopter
M: 2 Pielstick 12PC2-5V400 diesels; 2 CP props; 15,600 hp (13,260 hp sust.)
Electric: 1,450 kVA **Fuel:** 650 tons **Range:** 5,700/18
Man: 21 officers, 7 warrant officers, 28 men, 15 spare

Settsu (PL 07) *Ships of the World,* 9-84

HIGH-ENDURANCE CUTTERS (PL) *(continued)*

Chikuzen (PL 06) *Ships of the World,* 1984

REMARKS: Have bow-thruster, 2 pair fin stabilizers, normal ship bow for operations in ice-free waters. Also have; Flume-type passive stabilization tanks in superstructure. Have 3 radars. Engines manufactured by different builders. PL 03, 04 built under 1978 program, PL 05 under 1979 program, PL 06 under 1981 program, and PL 07 under the 1983 program.

◆ **1 Soya class**

	Bldr	Laid down	L	In serv.
PL 01 SOYA	Nippon Kokan, Tsurumi	12-9-77	3-7-78	22-11-78

Soya (PL 01) *Ships of the World,* 5-85

D: 3,562 tons (4,089 fl) **S:** 21 kts **Dim:** 98.6 × 15.6 × 5.2
A: 1/40-mm AA—1/20-mm AA—1/Bell 212 helicopter
M: 2 Nippon Kokan-Pielstick 12PC2-5V400 diesels; 2 CP props; 16,000 hp (13,260 hp sust.)
Electric: 1,450 kVA **Fuel:** 650 tons **Range:** 5,700/18 **Man:** 71 tot.

REMARKS: The *Soya* was built under the 1977 program. The *Soya* has an icebreaking bow and operates in the north. Passive tank stabilization only, no bow-thruster. Four radars (one aft for helo control).

◆ **28 Shiretoko class**

	Bldr	L	In serv.
PL 101 SHIRETOKO*	Mitsui, Tamano	13-7-78	8-11-78
PL 102 ESAN	Sumitomo, Oshima	8-78	16-11-78
PL 103 WAKASA*	Kawasaki, Kobe	8-78	29-11-78
PL 104 YAHIKO	Mitsubishi, Shimonoseki	8-78	16-11-78
PL 105 MOTOBU	Sasebo Dockyard	8-78	29-11-78
PL 106 RISHIRI	Shikoku DY	27-3-79	12-9-79
PL 107 MATSUSHIMA*	Tohoku DY	11-4-79	14-9-79
PL 108 IWAKI*	Naikai, Innoshima	28-3-79	10-8-79
PL 109 SHIKINE	Usuki SY, Usuki	27-4-79	20-9-79
PL 110 SURUGA*	Kurushima DY, Onishi	20-4-79	28-9-79
PL 111 REBUN*	Narasaki SY, Muroran	6-79	21-11-79
PL 112 CHOKAI*	Nipponkai Heavy Ind., Toyama	6-79	30-11-79
PL 113 ASHIZURI*	Sanoyasu DY, Oshima	6-79	31-10-79
PL 114 OKI	Tsuneishi SY, Numakuma	6-79	16-11-79
PL 115 NOTO	Miho SY, Shimizu	7-79	30-11-79
PL 116 YONAKUNI	Hiyashigane SY, Nagasaki	6-79	31-10-79
PL 117 DAISETSU*	Hakodate DY	22-8-79	31-1-80
PL 118 SHIMOKITA	Ishikawajima, Tokyo	9-79	12-3-80
PL 119 SUZUKA	Kanasashi SY, Toyohashi	4-10-79	7-3-80
PL 120 KUNASAKI	Koyo DY, Mihara	8-10-79	29-2-80
PL 121 GENKAI*	Oshima SY, Oshima	9-79	31-1-80
PL 122 GOTO*	Onomichi SY, Onomishi	10-79	29-2-80
PL 123 KOSHIKI	Kasado DY, Kasado	9-79	25-1-80
PL 124 HATERUMA*	Osaka DY	11-79	12-3-80
PL 125 KATORI	Tohoku DY, Shiogama	5-80	17-10-80
PL 126 KUNIGAMI	Kanda SY, Kawashiri	28-3-80	21-10-80
PL 127 ETOMO*	Naikai, Innoshima	30-9-81	17-3-82
PL 128 MASHIYU	Shikoku DY, Kochi, Takamatsu	14-10-81	12-3-82

D: 974 tons (1,350-1,360 fl) **S:** 20 kts **Dim:** 77.8 (73.6 pp) × 9.6 × 3.42
A: 1/40-mm AA—1/20-mm AA—*see* Remarks

Etomo (PL 127) *Ships of the World,* 1982

Shikine (PL 109) L. & L. Van Ginderen, 5-84

M: 2 Niigata 8MA 40 or Fuji 8 S40B diesels; 2 CP props; 7,000 hp
Electric: 625 kVA **Fuel:** 191 tons **Range:** 4,406/17 **Man:** 41 tot.

REMARKS: Program helped small shipyards to stay in business. Intended to patrol the 200-nautical-mile economic zone. Starred units have Fuji 8 S40B diesels. PL 106 and later have no 20-mm AA, while PL 118, 122, 124–128 have an Oerlikon 35-mm in place of the 40-mm AA. Carry 153 tons water. Fuel capacities and endurances vary. Range greater for some: PL 127: 5,200/17. PL 120 had a serious fire 15-2-82.

◆ **2 Izu class**

	Bldr	L	In serv.
PL 31 IZU	Hitachi, Mukaishima	1-67	31-7-67
PL 32 MIURA	Maizuru DY	11-68	15-3-69

Izu (PL 31) *Ships of the World,* 1984

D: 2,081 tons (2,200 fl) **S:** 24.6 kts **Dim:** 95.5 (86.45 pp) × 11.6 × 3.8
A: 1/76.2-mm DP **M:** 2 SEMT-Pielstick 12PC2V diesels; 2 CP props; 10,400 hp
Electric: 800 kVA **Range:** 5,000/20.5; 14,500/12.7 **Man:** 72 tot.

REMARKS: Large weather radar in dome aft removed in 1978 and gun added forward.

◆ **4 Erimo class**

	Bldr	L	In serv.
PL 13 ERIMO	Hitachi, Mukaishima	14-8-65	30-11-65
PL 14 SATSUMA	Hitachi, Mukaishima	4-66	30-7-66
PL 15 DAIO	Hitachi, Maizuru	19-6-73	28-9-73
PL 16 MUROTO	Naikai, Taguma	5-8-74	30-11-74

D: 980 tons (1,009 fl) **S:** 19.5 kts **Dim:** 76.6 (73.0 pp) × 9.2 × 3.0
A: 1/76.2-mm Mk 26 DP—1/20-mm AA
M: 2 Burmeister & Wain 635V 2 BU 45 diesels; 2 props; 4,800 hp
Electric: 320 kVA **Range:** 5,000/18 **Man:** 72 tot.

REMARKS: The hull of PL 13 is reinforced against ice. PL 15 and PL 16: **D:** 1,206 tons; **Dim:** beam 9.6, draft, 3.18; **A:** 1/40-mm AA—1/20-mm AA; **M:** 7,000 hp for 20.4 kts; **Electric:** 500 kVA; **Range:** 6,600/18; **Man:** 50 tot.

HIGH-ENDURANCE CUTTERS (PL) *(continued)*

Daio (PL 15) *Ships of the World,* 1985

◆ **2 Nojima class** Bldr: Uraga Dock Co., Ltd.

	L	In serv.
PL 11 Nojima	12-2-62	30-4-62
PL 12 Ojika	. . .	10-6-63

Nojima (PL 11) L. & L. Van Ginderen, 1-83

D: 980 tons (1,009 fl) **S:** 18.1 kts **Dim:** 69.0 × 9.18 × 3.2
M: 2 Uraga-Sulzer 6 MD 42 diesels; 2 props; 3,000 hp
Electric: 310 kVA **Range:** 6,000/16.5 **Man:** 73 tot.

Remarks: Used for meteorological reporting. Passive tank stabilization.

◆ **1 Kojima-class training cutter**

	Bldr	In serv.
PL 21 Kojima	Kure DY	21-5-64

Kojima (PL 21) L. & L. Van Ginderen, 6-82

D: 1,066 tons (1,206 fl) **S:** 17.3 kts **Dim:** 69.6 × 10.3 × 3.53
A: 1/76.2-mm DP Mk 26 — 1/40-mm AA — 1/20-mm AA
M: 1 Uraga-Sulzer 7 MD 51 diesel; 1 prop; 2,600 hp
Electric: 550 kVA **Range:** 6,120/13 **Man:** 17 officers, 42 crew, 47 cadets

Remarks: Used as a training ship at Kure Academy.

MEDIUM-ENDURANCE CUTTERS (PM)

◆ **11 (+2) Teshio (500-ton) class**

	Bldr	L	In serv.
PM 01 Teshio	Shikoku DY, Kochi	30-5-80	30-9-80
PM 02 Oirase	Naikai, Takuma, Innoshima	15-5-80	29-8-80
PM 03 Echizen	Usuki Iron Wks., Usuki	2-6-80	30-9-80
PM 04 Tokachi	Narazaki, Muroran	21-11-80	24-3-81
PM 05 Hitachi	Tohoku SY, Shiogoma	15-11-80	19-3-81
PM 06 Okitsu	Usuki Iron Wks.	5-12-80	17-3-81
PM 07 Isazu	Naikai, Taguma	29-10-81	18-2-82
PM 08 Chitose	Shikoku DY, Kochi	7-7-81	17-11-82
PM 09 Kumano	Naikai, Taguma, Innoshima	8-81	10-3-83
PM 10 Sorachi	Tohoku SY, Shiogama	27-4-84	27-9-84
PM 11 N. . .	. . .	20-8-85	11-85
PM 12 N. . .	. . .	. . .	. . .
PM 13 N. . .	. . .	. . .	. . .

D: 630 tons (670 fl) **S:** 18 kts **Dim:** 67.80 (63.00 pp) × 7.90 × 2.65
A: 1/20-mm JN-61B gatling AA **Electron Equipt:** Radar: 2/JMA-159B
M: 2 Fuji 6S 32F diesels; 2 props; 3,000 hp **Electric:** 240 kVA
Endurance: 15 days **Range:** 3,200/16 **Man:** 33 tot.

Sorachi (PM 10) *Ships of the World,* 9-84

Oirase (PM 02) L. & L. Van Ginderen, 5-84

Remarks: 540 grt. Three built under 1979-80 program, three under 1980-81 program, one under 1981, 1983, and 1984 programs. Some have Arakata 6 M31 EX diesels. PM 07 also used for training and has a lengthened after deckhouse. PM 12 and 13 approved in 1985 Budget.

◆ **2 Takatori (350-ton) class**

	Bldr	L	In serv.
PM 89 Takatori	Naikai, Takuma, Innoshima	8-12-77	24-3-78
PM 94 Kumano	Naikai, Takuma, Innoshima	2-11-78	23-2-79

Kumano (PM 94) L. & L. Van Ginderen, 5-84

D: 634 tons normal **S:** 15.7 kts **Dim:** 45.70 (44.25 pp) × 9.20 × 3.88
A: None **M:** 2 Niigata 6M31EX diesels; 1 CP prop; 3,000 hp
Electric: 200 kVA **Range:** 750/15 **Man:** 34 tot.

Remarks: 469 grt. Rescue-tug types. Equipped for fire-fighting and salvage duties. Two water cannon (3,000 1./min. each). Carry an 8-m. rescue boat and a 4.6-m. speedboat.

◆ **20 Bihoro (350-ton) class**

	Bldr	In serv.
PM 73 Bihoro	Tohoku SY, Shiogama	28-2-74
PM 74 Kuma	Usuki Iron Wks., Usuki	28-2-74
PM 75 Fuji	Usuki Iron Wks., Usuki	7-2-75
PM 76 Kabashima	Usuki Iron Wks., Usuki	25-3-75
PM 77 Sado	Tohoku SY, Shiogama	1-2-75
PM 78 Ishikari	Tohoku SY, Shiogama	13-3-76
PM 79 Abakuma	Tohoku SY, Shiogama	30-1-76
PM 80 Isuzu	Nakai, Taguma	10-3-76
PM 81 Kikuchi	Usuki Iron Wks., Usuki	6-2-76
PM 82 Kuzuryu	Usuki Iron Wks., Usuki	18-3-76
PM 83 Horobetsu	Tohoku SY, Shiogama	21-1-77
PM 84 Shirakami	Tohoku SY, Shiogama	3-3-77
PM 85 Sagami	Naikai SY, Takuma	30-11-76
PM 86 Tone	Usuki Iron Wks., Usuki	30-11-76
PM 87 Yoshino	Usuki Iron Wks., Usuki	28-1-77
PM 88 Kurobe	Shikoku DY, Kochi	15-2-77

MEDIUM-ENDURANCE CUTTER (PM) *(continued)*

	Bldr	In serv.
PM 90 Chikugo	Nakai, Taguma	27-1-78
PM 91 Yamakuni	Usuki Iron Wks., Usuki	26-1-78
PM 92 Katsura	Shikoku DY, Kochi	15-2-78
PM 93 Shinano	Tohoku SY, Shiogama	23-2-78

Sado (PM 77) 1978

Kuma (PM 74) *Ships of the World,* 1984

D: 636 tons (657 fl) **S:** 18 kts **Dim:** 63.35 × 7.80 × 2.53
A: 1/20-mm AA **Electron Equipt:** Radar: 2 JMA-159B
M: 2 Niigata 6M31EX diesels; 2 CP props; 3,000 hp **Electric:** 200 kVA
Range: 3,260/16 **Man:** 34 tot.

◆ **7 Kunashiri (350-ton) class**

	Bldr	In serv.
PM 65 Kunashiri	Maizuru DY	28-3-69
PM 66 Minabe	Maizuru DY	28-3-70
PM 67 Sarobetsu	Maizuru DY	30-3-71
PM 68 Kamishima	Usuki Iron Wks., Usuki	31-1-72
PM 70 Miyake	Tohoku SY, Shiogama	25-1-73
PM 71 Awaji	Usuki Iron Wks., Usuki	25-1-73
PM 72 Yaeyama	Usuki Iron Wks., Usuki	20-12-72

Yaeyama (PM 72) *Ships of the World,* 1984

D: 498 tons (574 fl) **S:** 17.5 kts **Dim:** 58.04 × 7.38 × 2.40
A: 1/20-mm AA **M:** 2 Niigata 6MF32H diesels; 2 props; 2,600 hp
Electric: 120 kVA **Range:** 3,040/16 **Man:** 40 tot.

Remarks: PM 70 to PM 72 have 6M31EX diesels, 3,000 hp. PM 72 has controllable-pitch propellers.

◆ **5 Matsuura (350-ton) class** Bldrs: PM 60, PM 61: Osaka SB; Others: Hitachi SY, Mukaishima

	In serv.		In serv.
PM 60 Matsuura	18-3-61	PM 63 Natori	20-1-66
PM 61 Sendai	14-4-62	PM 64 Karatsu	29-3-67
PM 62 Amami	29-3-65		

D: 425 tons **S:** 16.5 kts (PM 64: 18 kts; PM 63: 16.8 kts)
Dim: 55.33 × 7.00 × 2.30 **A:** 1/20-mm AA
M: 2 Ikegai 6MSB31S diesels; 2 props; 1,400 hp (PM 63: 2 Type 6MSB31HS diesels; 1,800 hp — PM 64: 2 Type 6MA31X diesels; 2,600 hp)
Electric: 140 kVA **Range:** 3,500/12–13 **Man:** 37–40 tot.

Matsuura (PM 60) L. & L. Van Ginderen, 1981

◆ **2 Yahagi (350-ton) class**

	Bldrs	In serv.
PM 59 Horonai	Niigata SY	11-2-61
PM 69 Okinawa	Usuki Iron Wks.	8-10-69

D: 376 tons (430 fl) **S:** 15.5 kts **Dim:** 50.27 × 7.36 × 2.16
A: 1/20-mm AA **M:** 2 Ikegai 6 MSB31S diesels; 2 props; 1,400 hp
Electric: 140 kVA **Range:** 4,350/12 **Man:** 44 tot.

Remarks: PM 69 was originally built for Okinawa, transferred to MSA in 1972. Sisters *Yahagi* (PM 54) was stricken 18-1-82, *Sumida* (PM 55) and *Chitose* (PM 56) later in 1982, *Sorachi* (PM 57) on 2-8-84, and *Yubari* (PM 58) in 1985.

PATROL BOATS (PS)

◆ **2 Akagi (130-ton) class**

	Bldr	Laid down	L	In serv.
PS 101 Akagi	Sumidigawa, Tokyo	31-7-79	5-12-79	26-3-80
PS 102 Tsukuba	Sumidigawa, Tokyo	7-7-81	29-10-81	24-2-82

Tsukuba (PS 102) L. & L. Van Ginderen, 5-83

D: 127.7 tons normal **S:** 26.5 kts **Dim:** 35.0 (33.0 wl) × 6.3 × 1.3
A: 1/12.7-mm mg **M:** 2 Pielstick 16PA 4V-185 diesels; 2 props; 4,400 hp
Electric: 40 kVA **Range:** 570/20 **Man:** 12 tot.

Remarks: PS 101 in 1979 Budget, PS 102 in 1981. Glass-reinforced plastic hull; 4-day endurance. Carry a 25-man rubber rescue dinghy.

◆ **3 Bizan (130-ton) class**

	Bldr	In serv.
PS 42 Bizan	Mitsubishi, Shimonoseki	28-3-66
PS 47 Asama	Mitsubishi, Shimonoseki	31-1-69
PS 48 Shiramine	Mitsubishi, Shimonoseki	15-12-69

Shiramine (PS 48) *Ships of the World,* 1984

PATROL BOATS (PS) *(continued)*

D: 42–48 tons (83-85 fl) **S:** 21.6 kts (PS 48: 25 kts) **Dim:** 26.0 × 5.6 × 1.0
A: 1/12.7-mm mg
M: 2 Mitsubishi 12 HD 2 OMTK diesels; 2 props; 1,140 hp (PS 48: 2 MTU diesels; 2,200 hp)
Electric: 2 kw **Range:** 400/18; PS 48: 250/25 **Man:** 14 tot.

◆ **14 Hidaka (130-ton) class**

	Bldr	In serv.
PS 32 Hidaka	Azuma SY, Yokosuka	23-4-62
PS 33 Hiyama	Hitachi SY, Mukaishima	13-3-63
PS 34 Tsurugi	Hitachi, SY, Mukaishima	13-3-63
PS 35 Rokko	Shikoku DY, Shimonoseki	31-1-64
PS 36 Takanawa	Hayashigane SY, Shimonoseki	27-1-64
PS 37 Akiyoshi	Hashihama SY, Imabaki	29-2-64
PS 38 Kunimi	Hayashigane SY, Shimonoseki	15-2-65
PS 39 Takatsuki	Kurashima DY, Onishi	30-3-65
PS 41 Kamui	Hayashigame SY, Shimonoseki	15-2-66
PS 43 Ashitaka	Usuki Iron Wks., Usuki	10-2-67
PS 44 Kurama	Usuki Iron Wks., Usuki	28-2-67
PS 45 Ibuki	Usuki Iron Wks., Usuki	5-3-68
PS 46 Toumi	Usuki Iron Wks., Usuki	20-2-68
PS 49 Nobaru	Hitachi SY, Mukaishima	10-12-68

Kurama (PS 44) *Ships of the World,* 1984

D: 169 tons normal **S:** 13.7 kts **Dim:** 31.72 (30.5 wl) × 6.29 × 1.80
A: 1/12.7-mm mg (usually not mounted)
M: 1 6MSB 31S diesel; 1 prop; 700 hp **Electric:** 60 kVA
Range: 1,100/12 **Man:** 17 tot.

Remarks: PS 44 replaced in training role by *Isazu* (PM 07) on 20-4-82.

COASTAL PATROL BOATS (PC)

◆ **23 Murakomo (30-meter) class**

	Bldr	In serv.
PC 201 Murakomo	Mitsubishi, Shimonoseki	24-3-78
PC 202 Kitagumo	Hitachi, Kanagawa	17-3-78
PC 203 Yukigumo	Hitachi, Kanagawa	27-9-78
PC 204 Asagumo	Mitsubishi, Shimonoseki	21-9-78
PC 205 Hayagumo	Mitsubishi, Shimonoseki	30-1-79
PC 206 Akigumo	Hitachi, Kanagawa	28-2-79
PC 207 Yaegumo	Mitsubishi, Shimonoseki	16-3-79
PC 208 Natsugumo	Hitachi, Kanagawa	22-3-79
PC 209 Yamagiri	Hitachi, Kanagawa	29-6-79
PC 210 Kawagiri	Hitachi, Kanagawa	27-7-79
PC 211 Teruzuki	Maizuru Heavy Ind.	26-6-79
PC 212 Natsuzuki	Maizuru Heavy Ind.	26-7-79
PC 213 Miyazuki	Hitachi, Kanagawa	13-3-80
PC 214 Nijigumo	Mitsubishi, Shimonoseki	29-1-81
PC 215 Tatsugumo	Mitsubishi, Shimonoseki	19-3-81
PC 216 Hamayuki	Hitachi, Kanagawa	27-2-81
PC 217 Isonami	Mitsubishi, Shimonoseki	19-3-81
PC 218 Nagozuki	Hitachi, Kanagawa	29-1-81
PC 219 Yaezuki	Hitachi, Kanagawa	19-3-81
PC 220 Yamayuki	Hitachi, Kanagawa	16-2-82
PC 221 Komayuki	Mitsubishi, Shimonoseki	10-2-82
PC 222 Asagiri	Mitsubishi, Shimonoseki	17-2-82
PC 223 Umigiri	Hitachi, Kanagawa	23-2-83

D: 88 tons (125 fl) **S:** 31 kts **Dim:** 31.0 (28.5 pp) × 6.3 × 1.17
A: 1/12.7-mm mg **M:** 2 Ikegai MTU 16V652 TB81 diesels; 2 props; 4,800 hp
Electric: 40 kVA **Range:** 350/28 **Man:** 11 tot.

Remarks: PC 201 to PC 204 built under 1977-78 program. PC 205–208 under 1978-79, PC 209–212 under 1978-79 supplementary program, PC 213 under 1979-80 program, PC 214–219 under 1980-81 program, PC 220–221 under 1981-82.

Hamayuki L. & L. Van Ginderen, 5-84

◆ **15 (+ . . .) Akizuki (23-meter) class** Bldr: Mitsubishi, Shimonoseki (except PC 83–85: Hitachi, Kanagawa)

	In serv.
PC 64 Akizuki	28-2-74
PC 65 Shinonome	25-2-74
PC 72 Urayuki	31-5-75
PC 73 Iseyuki	31-7-75
PC 75 Hatayuki	19-3-75
PC 76 Hatagumo	21-2-76
PC 77 Hamazuki	29-11-76
PC 78 Isozuki	18-3-77
PC 79 Shimanami	23-12-77
PC 80 Yuzuki	22-3-79
PC 81 Hanayuki	27-3-81
PC 82 Awagiri	27-12-82
PC 83 Shimagiri	7-2-84
PC 84 Setogiri	22-3-85
PC 85 Hayagiri	22-2-85

Hayagiri (PC 85) *Ships of the World,* 1985

Urayuki (PC 72) L. & L. Van Ginderen, 6-84

D: 77 tons normal **S:** 22.1 kts **Dim:** 26.00 (23.00 pp) × 6.30 × 1.12
A: PC 85 only: 1/20-mm AA
M: 3 Mitsubishi 12 DM 20 MTK diesels; 3 props; 3,000 hp
Electric: 40 kVA **Range:** 290/21.5 **Man:** 10 tot.

Remarks: Superstructure on PC 83 and later differs (see photos); they also use the Mitsubishi 12V175RTC diesel of 1,000 hp.

◆ **1 Matsunami (23-meter) class** Bldr: Hitachi, Kanagawa

PC 53 Matsunami (In serv. 30-3-71)

COASTAL PATROL BOATS (PC) *(continued)*

Matsunami (PC 53) *Ships of the World,* 1984

D: 59 tons normal **S:** 20.7 kts **Dim:** 24.96 × 6.0 × 1.33
M: 2 Mercedes-Benz MB820Db diesels; 2 props; 2,200 hp; 2 DA640 cruise diesels; 180 hp
Electric: 3 kw **Range:** 270/18 **Man:** 30 tot.

Remarks: Especially configured for Emperor Hirohito for oceanographic research. Two cruise diesels can be geared to the props.

◆ 17 Shikinami (23-meter) class

	Bldr	In serv.
PC 54 Shikinami	Mitsubishi, Shimonoseki	24-2-71
PC 55 Tomonami	Mitsubishi, Shimonoseki	20-3-71
PC 56 Wakanami	Mitsubishi, Shimonoseki	30-10-71
PC 57 Isenami	Hitachi, Kanagawa	29-2-72
PC 58 Takanami	Mitsubishi, Shimonoseki	30-11-71
PC 59 Mutsuki	Hitachi, Kanagawa	18-12-72
PC 60 Mochizuki	Hitachi, Kanagawa	18-12-72
PC 61 Haruzuki	Mitsubishi, Shimonoseki	30-11-72
PC 62 Kiyozuki	Mitsubishi, Shimonoseki	18-12-72
PC 63 Urazuki	Mitsubishi, Shimonoseki	30-1-73
PC 66 Uranami	Hitachi, Kanagawa	22-12-73
PC 67 Tamanami	Mitsubishi, Shimonoseki	25-12-73
PC 68 Minegumo	Mitsubishi, Shimonoseki	30-11-73
PC 69 Kiyonami	Mitsubishi, Shimonoseki	30-10-73
PC 70 Okinami	Hitachi, Kanagawa	8-2-74
PC 71 Wakagumo	Hitachi, Kanagawa	25-3-74
PC 74 Asoyuki	Hitachi, Kanagawa	16-6-75

Haruzuki (PC 61) *Ships of the World,* 1984

D: 46 tons normal **S:** 25.8 kts **Dim:** 21.0 × 5.3 × 1.22
A: 1/12.7-mm mg (usually not mounted)
M: 12 Mercedes-Benz MB820Db diesels; 2 props; 2,200 hp **Electric:** 2 kw
Range: 240/23.8 **Man:** 10 tot.

◆ 1 Hamanami (23-meter) class Bldr: Sumidagawa, Tokyo

PC 52 Hamanami (In serv. 22-3-71)

D: 60 tons (fl) **S:** 20.9 kts **Dim:** 21.0 × 5.1 × 1.22
M: 2 Mercedes-Benz MB820Db diesels; 2 props; 2,200 hp
Electric: 2 kw **Range:** 290/20.9 **Man:** 10 tot.

Hamanami (PC 52) *Ships of the World,* 1984

◆ 1 Hamagiri (23-meter) class Bldr: Sumidagawa, Tokyo

PC 48 Hamagiri (In serv. 19-3-70)

D: 51 tons (fl) **S:** 14.6 kts **Dim:** 21.0 × 5.1 × 1.11
M: 2 Mitsubishi 12DH 20TK diesels; 2 props; 1,140 hp
Electric: 2 kw **Range:** 270/12.9 **Man:** 10 tot.

Note: The 5 *Umigiri*-class patrol boats, *Umigiri* (PC 46), *Asagiri* (PC 47), *Sagiri* (PC 49), *Setogiri* (PC 50), and *Hayagiri* (PC 51) were stricken 1982-85.

PATROL CRAFT (CL)

◆ 63 Yamayuri (15-meter) class

	Bldr	In serv.
CL 201 Yamayuri	Ishihara, Takasago	27-1-78
CL 202 Tachibana	Ishihara, Takasago	24-2-78
CL 203 Komakusa	Ishihara, Takasago	30-1-79
CL 204 Shiragiku	Ishihara, Takasago	22-2-79
CL 205 Yaguruma	Sumidagawa, Tokyo	31-7-79
CL 206 Hamanasu	Sumidagawa, Tokyo	29-9-79
CL 207 Suzuran	Sumidagawa, Tokyo	31-7-79
CL 208 Isogiku	Sumidagawa, Tokyo	12-9-79
CL 209 Isegiko	Sumidagawa, Tokyo	31-8-79
CL 210 Ayame	Yokohama Yacht	29-10-79
CL 211 Ajisai	Yokohama Yacht	26-9-79
CL 212 Himawari	Yokohama Yacht	29-10-79
CL 213 Hazakura	Yokohama Yacht	29-8-79
CL 214 Hinagiku	Ishihara, Takasago	9-7-79
CL 215 Hamagiku	Yokohama Yacht	19-9-79
CL 216 Fuyume	Ishihara, Takasago	30-7-79
CL 217 Tsubaki	Ishihara, Takasago	10-8-79
CL 218 Sazanka	Ishihara, Takasago	30-8-79
CL 219 Aoi	Sumidagawa, Tokyo	31-10-79
CL 220 Suisen	Yokohama Yacht	29-10-79
CL 221 Yaezakura	Ishihara, Takasago	25-9-79
CL 222 Akebi	Ishihara, Takasago	29-10-79
CL 223 Shirahagi	Sumidagawa, Tokyo	25-1-80
CL 224 Benibana	Sumidagawa, Tokyo	25-1-80
CL 225 Muratsubaki	Ishihara, Takasago	20-12-79
CL 226 Tsutsuji	Sumidagawa, Tokyo	22-2-80
CL 227 Ashibi	Ishihara, Takasago	20-12-79
CL 228 Satozakura	Ishihara, Takasago	26-2-80
CL 229 Yukitsubaki	Ishihara, Takasago	28-2-80
CL 230 Satsuki	Shinki	22-2-80
CL 231 Ezogiku	Yokohama Yacht	18-11-80
CL 232 Akashio	Sumidagawa, Tokyo	18-11-80
CL 233 Kozakura	Yokohama Yacht	18-11-80
CL 234 Shirame	Ishihara, Takasago	28-11-80
CL 235 Sarubia	Ishihara, Takasago	28-11-80
CL 236 Suiren	Shinki SY, Osaka	19-12-80
CL 237 Hatsugiku	Ishihara, Takasago	29-1-81
CL 238 Hamayura	Ishihara, Takasago	29-1-80
CL 239 Airisu	Yokohama Yacht	18-2-82
CL 240 Yamabuki	Sumidagawa, Tokyo	17-12-81
CL 241 Shirayuri	Nobutaka	1-2-82
CL 242 Karatachi	Ishihara, Takasago	17-12-81
CL 243 Kobai	Ishihara, Takasago	18-2-82
CL 244 Hamayūū	Ishihara, Takasago	29-1-82
CL 245 Sasayuri	Sumidagawa, Tokyo	25-1-83
CL 246 Kosumosu	Ishihara SY, Takasago	17-2-83
CL 247 Shiogiku	Sumidagawa, Tokyo	29-11-82
CL 248 Yamahagi	Yokohama Yacht	29-11-82
CL 249 Mokuren	Shinki SY, Osaka	25-1-83
CL 250 Isobuji	Ishihara, Takasago	7-3-83
CL 251 Tamatsubaki	Sumidagawa, Tokyo	26-1-84
CL 252 Yodoki	Shinki SY, Osaka	22-11-83

PATROL CRAFT (CL) *(continued)*

	Bldr	In serv.
CL 253 Iozakura	Ishihara, Takasago	25-11-83
CL 254 Himetsubaki	Ishihara, Takasago	18-1-84
CL 255 Tokikusa	Sumidagawa, Tokyo	24-2-84
CL 256 Mutsugiku	Sumidagawa, Tokyo	15-11-84
CL 257 Terugiko	Shiga, Sagai	19-12-84
CL 258 Mayazakura	Ishihara, Takasago	20-12-84
CL 259 Yamagiko	Yokohama, Yacht	22-1-85
CL 260 Tobiume	Ishihara, Takasago	24-1-85
CL 261 Kotozakura	Sumidagawa, Tokyo	28-2-85
CL 262 Minogiku	Ishihara, Takasago	14-2-85
CL 263 Kuroyuri	Yokohama Yacht	15-11-84

Mokuren (CL 249) *Ships of the World,* 1983

D: 27 tons normal (35.7 fl) **S:** 20.7 kts
Dim: 18.00 (16.60 wl) × 4.30 × 0.82 (1.10 props)
M: 2 RD10T AO6 diesels; 2 props; 900 hp **Range:** 180/19 **Man:** 6 tot.

Remarks: Three water cannon for fire-fighting. CL 251–263 have waterjets, vice propellers, and can make 21.9 kts.; their engines are type S6A-MTK (450 hp each).

◆ **4 Nogekaze class** Bldr: Sumidagawa, Tokyo

	In serv.		In serv.
CL 99 Nogekaze	10-72	CL 107 Itokaze	11-72
CL 105 Kusukaze	10-72	CL 128 Kawakaze	10-73

Itokaze (CL 107) *Ships of the World,* 1984

D: 22.5 tons normal **S:** 16.6 kts **Dim:** 16.00 × 4.10 × 0.80 (hull)
M: 2 Type UDV816 diesels; 2 props; 500 hp **Electric:** 5 kVA
Range: 160/14.7 **Man:** 6 tot.

◆ **95 Chiyokaze class**

Bldrs: Ishihara, Nobotuka, Yokohama Yacht, Sumidagawa, 1968-76

CL 44 Chiyokaze
CL 50 Suzukaze
CL 51 Urakaze
CL 53 Sugikaze
CL 54 Fujikaze
CL 55 Miyakaze
CL 57 Chinukaze
CL 59 Nachikaze
CL 65 Tomakaze
CL 66 Hibakaze
CL 67 Yurikaze
CL 68 Sumikaze
CL 69 Kashima
CL 70 Takekaze
CL 71 Kinukaze
CL 72 Shigikaze
CL 73 Uzukaze
CL 74 Akikaze
CL 75 Setokaze
CL 76 Kurekaze
CL 77 Mojikaze
CL 78 Satakaze
CL 79 Kirikaze
CL 80 Kamikaze
CL 81 Umikaze
CL 82 Yumekaze
CL 83 Makikaze
CL 84 Hakaze
CL 85 Shachikaze
CL 86 Himekaze
CL 87 Isekaze
CL 88 Komakaze
CL 89 Kishikaze
CL 90 Mayakaze
CL 91 Kikukaze
CL 92 Hirokaze
CL 93 Kibikaze
CL 94 Ashikaze
CL 95 Otokaze
CL 96 Kurikaze
CL 97 Imakaze
CL 98 Terukaze
CL 100 Tokitsukaze
CL 101 Tsukikaze
CL 102 Awakaze
CL 104 Miokaze
CL 106 Kilkaze
CL 108 Tamatsukaze
CL 109 Miyokaze
CL 110 Ayakaze
CL 111 Mitsukaze
CL 112 Hatakaze
CL 113 Numakaze
CL 114 Soyokaze
CL 115 Minekaze
CL 116 Okitsukaze
CL 117 Deigo
CL 118 Yuuna
CL 119 Adan
CL 120 Horokaze
CL 121 Somakaze
CL 122 Hatsukaze
CL 123 Sasakaze
CL 124 Hagikaze
CL 125 Tonekaze
CL 126 Shizukaze
CL 127 Murokaze
CL 129 Yamakaze
CL 130 Hikokaze
CL 131 Takakaze
CL 132 Murakaze
CL 133 Nomokaze
CL 134 Kumokaze
CL 135 Yanakaze
CL 136 Yurakaze
CL 137 Washikaze
CL 138 Kushikaze
CL 139 Hoshikaze
CL 140 Gettō
CL 141 Iwakaze
CL 142 Matsukaze
CL 143 Oitsukaze
CL 144 Arakaze
CL 145 Tanikaze
CL 146 Kochikaze
CL 147 Okikaze
CL 148 Suwakaze
CL 149 Sachikaze
CL 150 Natsukaze
CL 151 Harukaze
CL 152 Rindō
CL 153 Sawakaze
CL 154 Kaidō
CL 155 Nadeshiko
CL 156 Yamazakura

Yurikaze (CL 67) L. & L. Van Ginderen, 5-84

D: 19.5 tons normal **S:** 18.4 kts **Dim:** 15.00 × 4.10 × 0.76 (hull)
M: 2 Mitsubishi DH24MK diesels; 2 props; 500 hp **Range:** 180/16.1
Man: 6 tot.

Remarks: The *Nomakaze* (CL 103) was lost in 1978. CL 69 is named for her home port; CL 117 to CL 119 are home-ported in Okinawa.

Note: The 15 remaining craft of the *Yakaze* class, CL 42–64, were stricken 1983-85.

HYDROGRAPHIC SHIPS

◆ **1 Takuyo (2,600-ton) class** Bldr: Nippon Kokan, Tsurumi

	Laid down	L	In serv.
HL 02 Takuyo	14-4-82	24-3-83	31-8-83

Takuyo (HL 02) L. & L. Van Ginderen, 5-85

D: 2,979 tons (3,370 fl) **S:** 18.2 kts
Dim: 96.00 (90.00 wl) × 14.20 × 4.51 mean (4.91 max. over sonar)
M: 2 Fuji 6S40B diesels; 2 CP props; 5,200 hp **Electric:** 965 kVA
Range: 12,800/16.9 **Endurance:** 50 days **Man:** 39 crew + 22 survey party

Remarks: 2,481 grt. In 1981 program to replace earlier unit with same name. Has bow-thruster, side-looking, contour mapping sonars, precision echo-sounders, etc. Carries two survey launches.

◆ **1 Shoyo (1,900-ton) class** Bldr: Hitachi, Maizuru

HL 01 Shoyo (In serv. 26-2-72)

D: 2,200 tons normal **S:** 17.4 kts **Dim:** 81.70 (78.60 wl) × 12.60 × 4.20
M: 2 Fuji 12VM 32 H2F diesels; 1 prop; 4,800 hp **Electric:** 1,250 kVA
Range: 12,000/14 **Man:** 73 tot.

HYDROGRAPHIC SHIPS *(continued)*

Shoyo (HL 01) *Ships of the World*

REMARKS: 1,900 grt. Has bow-thruster.

◆ **1 Meiyo class** Bldr: Nagoya SY

HL 03 MEIYO (In serv. 15-3-63)

Meiyo (HL 03) 1975

D: 486 tons normal **S:** 12 kts **Dim:** 44.80 (40.50 pp) × 8.05 × 2.88
M: 1 Asakasa TR 655 diesel; 1 prop; 700 hp **Electric:** 140 kVA
Range: 5,280/11 **Man:** 40 tot.

COASTAL HYDROGRAPHIC SHIPS

◆ **1 Kaiyo class** Bldr: Ishikawajima Harima, Nagoya

HM 06 KAIYO (In serv. 14-5-64)

Kaiyo (HM 06) *Ships of the World,* 1984

D: 380 tons normal **S:** 12 kts **Dim:** 44.53 × 8.05 × 2.39
M: 1 Sumiyoshi Tekko S 6 NBS diesel; 1 prop; 450 hp
Electric: 90 kVA **Range:** 3,160/10 **Man:** 31 tot.

◆ **1 Tenyo class** Bldr: Yokohama Yacht

HM 05 TENYO (In serv. 31-3-61)

Tenyo (HM 05) *Ships of the World,* 1984

D: 171 tons normal **S:** 10.5 kts **Dim:** 30.20 (28.00 pp) × 5.80 × 1.96
M: 1 Mitsui MDF5-26 diesel; 1 prop; 230 hp **Electric:** 40 kVA
Range: 3,160/10.1 **Man:** 28 tot.

◆ **1 Heiyo class** Bldr: Nippon Kokan, Shimizu

HM 04 HEIYO (In serv. 22-2-55)

D: 77 tons normal **S:** 10.6 kts **Dim:** 23.30 × 4.40 × 1.45
M: 1 Yanmar 6 MSL diesel; 1 prop; 150 hp **Electric:** 12 kw
Range: 670/8.6 **Man:** 13 tot.

INSHORE HYDROGRAPHIC CRAFT

◆ **1 Kerama (15-meter) class** Bldr: Ito Tekko SY, Sasebo

HS 32 KERAMA (In serv. 28-11-73)

D: 23.2 tons normal **S:** 11 kts **Dim:** 15.0 × 4.0 × 0.86
M: 1 UDV 816 diesel; 250 hp **Range:** 450/10 **Man:** 7 tot.

REMARKS: Glass-reinforced plastic construction.

◆ **4 Akashi (15-meter) class** Bldrs: Various (In serv. 1973-77)

HS 31 AKASHI HS 33 HAYATOMO HS 34 KURIHAMA HS 35 KURUSHIMA

D: 21 tons normal **S:** 10.2 kts **Dim:** 15.0 × 4.0 × 0.84
M: 1 Nissan-MTU UD626 diesel; 180 hp **Range:** 630/9.7 **Man:** 7 tot.

REMARKS: Glass-reinforced plastic hull.

◆ **11 Hamashio class** Bldr: Nippon Hikaki, Yokosuka (In serv. 1969-72)

HS 01 HAMASHIO, HS 02 ISESHIO, HS 03 SETOSHIO, HS 04 UZUSHIO, HS 05 HAYASHIO, HS 06 ISOSHIO, HS 07 TAKASHIO, HS 08 WAKASHIO, HS 09 YUKISHIO, HS 10 OYASHIO, HS 11 KUROSHIO

Hamashio (HS 01) L. & L. Van Ginderen, 5-83

D: 6 tons normal **S:** 8.9-9.3 kts **Dim:** 10.15 × 2.65 × 0.81
M: 1 Nissan-MTU UD326 diesel; 90 hp **Range:** 343/8.5 **Man:** 7 tot.

REMARKS: Glass-reinforced plastic construction.

NAVIGATIONAL AID TENDERS

◆ **1 Tsushima class** Bldr: Mitsui, Tamano

	Laid down	L	In serv.
LL 01 TSUSHIMA	10-6-76	7-4-77	9-9-77

Tsushima (LL 01) *Ships of the World*

D: 1,865 tons normal **S:** 16 kts (17.6 trials)
Dim: 75.00 (70.00 wl) × 12.50 × 4.15
M: 1 Fuji-Sulzer 8S 40C diesel; 1 CP prop; 4,200 hp **Electric:** 900 kVA
Fuel: 477 tons **Range:** 10,000/15 **Man:** 54 tot.

REMARKS: Intended for use as a lighthouse supply ship. Has Flume-type passive stabilization tanks, bow-thruster.

NAVIGATIONAL AID TENDERS *(continued)*

◆ **3 Hokuto-class buoy tenders**

	Bldr	Laid down	L	In serv.
LL 11 Hokuto	Sasebo DY	19-10-78	20-3-79	29-6-79
LL 12 Kaio	Sasebo DY	17-7-79	20-10-79	11-3-80
LL 13 Ginga	Kawasaki, Kobe	13-6-79	16-11-79	18-3-80

Hokuto (LL 11) L. & L. Van Ginderen, 1-83

D: 620 tons light (839 fl) **S:** 13.8 kts **Dim:** 55.00 (51.00 wl) × 10.60 × 2.65
M: 2 Asakasa MH23 (LL 11: Hanshin 6L 24SH) diesels; 2 props; 1,400 hp
Electric: 300 kVA **Fuel:** 62 tons **Range:** 3,460/13
Man: 9 officers, 20 men, 2 technicians

◆ **1 (+3 + . . .) Zuiun (270-ton) class**

	Bldr	Laid down	L	In serv.
LM 101 Zuiun	Usiki Iron Wks., Usiki	19-1-83	27-4-83	27-7-83
LM 102 N. . .	. . .	. . .	. . .	. . .
LM 103 N. . .	. . .	. . .	. . .	. . .
LM 104 N. . .	. . .	. . .	. . .	. . .

Zuiun (LM 101) *Ships of the World,* 7-83

D: 370 tons normal (398 fl) **S:** 15.1 kts **Dim:** 46.00 (41.40 pp) × 7.50 × 2.23
M: 2 Mitsubishi-Akasaka MH 23-series diesels; 2 CP props; 1,300 hp
Range: 1,440/14.5 **Electric:** 120 kw **Fuel:** 34 m³ **Man:** 20 tot.

Remarks: Lighthouse service vessels. Cargo: 85 tons. One diesel is model MH23F, other is MH23. Three additional units approved in 1985 Budget.

◆ **1 Miyojo-class buoy tender** Bldr: Ishikawajima, Tokyo

LM 11 Miyojo (In serv. 25-3-74)

Miyojo (LM 11) F. Lauga, 1976

D: 248 tons (303 normal) **S:** 11 kts **Dim:** 27.0 × 12.0 × 2.58
M: 2 Niigata 6MG 16HS diesels; 2 CP props; 600 hp **Electric:** 135 kVA
Fuel: 15 tons **Range:** 1,360/10 **Man:** 18 tot.

Remarks: Has catamaran hull. Replaced a very similar ship with same name and number, which was lost in 4-72.

◆ **3 Hakuun class** Bldr: Sumidagawa, Tokyo (LM 114: Yokohama Yacht)

LM 106 Hakuun (In serv. 28-2-78) LM 107 Toun (In serv. 3-79)
LM 114 Tokuun (In serv. 23-3-82)

Hakuun (LM 106) *Ships of the World,* 1984

D: 57.6 tons (92.7 fl) **S:** 15 kts **Dim:** 24.00 (23.00 pp) × 6.00 × 1.00
Electron Equipt: Radar: 1/FRA-10 Mk III
M: 2 G.M. 12V71 TI diesels; 2 props; 1,080 hp **Electric:** 30 kVA
Range: 420/13 **Man:** 10 tot.

Remarks: Prototypes of a new class intended to replace earlier medium (LM) navigational-aid tenders.

◆ **1 Ayabane class** Bldr: Shimoda DY, Shimoda

LM 112 Ayabane (In serv. 25-12-72)

D: 187 tons normal **S:** 12.3 kts **Dim:** 32.70 × 6.5 × 1.8
M: 1 Hanshin 6 L24SH diesel; 1 prop; 500 hp **Electric:** 70 kVA
Range: 2,330/11.9 **Man:** 18 tot.

Remarks: The similar *Zuiun* (LM 101) was stricken 19-1-83.

◆ **6 (+1) 23-meter group** Bldrs: Various

	In serv.		In serv.		In serv.
LM 102 Reiun	11-71	LM 110 Seiun	3-68	LM 113 Genun	3-73
LM 105 Sekiun	3-70	LM 111 Houn	3-70	LM. . . N. . .	. . .
LM 108 Reimei	8-3-82				

Genun (LM 113) *Ships of the World,* 1984

D: 67-74 tons (normal) **S:** 9.7-10.5 kts **Dim:** 22.1 × 4.65 × 1.4
M: 1 Yanman or G.M. diesel; 120-200 hp **Range:** 760-1,060/9.5
Man: 11-12 tot.

Remarks: Minor variations but all similar. *Akatsuki* (LM 107) stricken 1979. The original LM 108, *Reimei,* completed in 1962, was replaced in 1982. *Shoun* (LM 109) stricken 1985. One approved in 1985 Budget.

NAVIGATIONAL AID TENDERS *(continued)*

◆ **12 17-meter class** Bldr: Yokohama Yacht

	In serv.		In serv.
LS 204 Hatsuhikari	3-79	LS 210 Shimahikari	17-12-79
LS 205 Nahahikari	2-79	LS 211 Akihikari	27-2-81
LS 206 Matsuhikari	3-79	LS 212 Wakahikari	5-3-82
LS 207 Michihikari	14-7-79	LS 213 Miohikari	18-3-83
LS 208 Nishihikari	14-7-79	LS 214 Urahikari	27-1-84
LS 209 Kamihikari	17-12-79	LS 215 Tamahikari	24-2-84

Kamihikari (LS 209) *Ships of the World,* 1980

D: 25 tons normal **S:** 16.3 kts **Dim:** 17.50 × 4.30 × 0.80
M: 2 E12OT-MF6R diesels; 2 props; 560 hp **Endurance:** 2 days
Range: 230/14.5 **Man:** 8 tot.

◆ **6 Urahikari (17-meter) class** Bldrs: Various (In serv. 1972-75)

LS 115 Fusahikari LS 184 Tomohikari LS 202 Takahikari
LS 156 Sekihikari LS 201 Haruhikari LS 203 Setohikari

Takahikari (LS 202) *Ships of the World,* 1984

D: 16 tons (20 fl) **S:** 17.2 kts **Dim:** 17.00 × 3.50 × . . .
M: 1 MTU UD 626 diesel; 180 hp **Range:** 320/5 **Man:** 10 tot.

◆ **5 (+3) 12-meter class** Bldr: Nippon Hikoki, Yokosuka (LS 188: Ishikawajima, Tokyo)

	In serv.		In serv.
LS 181 Keiko	29-6-79	LS 188 Taiko	24-1-85
LS 185 Shoko	26-2-79	LS . . . N . . .	. . .
LS 186 Toko	30-6-79	LS . . . N . . .	. . .
LS 187 Getsuko	30-6-79	LS . . . N . . .	. . .

D: 9.4 tons (10 fl) **S:** 15 kts **Dim:** 12.00 × 3.20 × 0.60
M: 1 diesel; 1 prop; 210 hp **Range:** 120/13.5 **Man:** 6 tot.

Remarks: LS 188 may be to a modified design. Three approved in 1985 Budget.

◆ **4 Taiko (12-meter) class** (In serv. 1970-73)

LS 122 Meiko LS 153 Suiko LS 183 Hakuko LS 219 Saiko

D: 8 tons (12 fl) **S:** 14.8 kts **Dim:** 12.0 × 3.2 × . . .
M: 1 MTU UD 626 diesel; 180 hp **Range:** 130/12.5 **Man:** 6 tot.

Remarks: Sister *Taiko* (LS 152) stricken 1-10-84; *Kyoko* (LS 151), *Myoko* (LS 171), and *Choko* (LS 218) in 1985.

◆ **11 (+5) No. 1 Kaiko (10-meter) class** Bldr: Nippon Hikoki, Yokosuka

LS 144 No. 1 Kaiko (In serv. 5-3-81)
LS 145 No. 2 Kaiko (In serv. 12-3-81)
LS 146 No. 3 Kaiko (In serv. 19-3-81)
LS 148 No. 4 Kaiko (In serv. 10-12-81)
LS 149 No. 5 Kaiko (In serv. 1982)
LS 154 No. 6 Kaiko (In serv. 1982)
LS 155 No. 7 Kaiko (In serv. 12-1-84)
LS 157 No. 8 Kaiko (In serv. 17-1-84)
LS 158 No. 9 Kaiko (In serv. 13-2-84)
LS 160 No. 10 Kaiko (In serv. 21-2-84)
LS. . . No. 11 Kaiko (In serv. . . .)
LS. . . N. . .
LS. . . N. . .
LS. . . N. . .
LS. . . N. . .
LS. . . N. . .

No. 3 Kaiko (LS 146) *Ships of the World,* 1984

D: 5.2 tons **S:** 13 kts **Dim:** 9.00 × 2.25 × . . .
M: 2 Nissan FD606 diesels; 1 prop; 230 hp **Range:** 130/12.5 **Man:** 6 tot.

Remarks: Five additional approved in 1985 Budget. Glass-reinforced plastic construction.

◆ **6 No. 1 Yoko (10-meter) class** Bldr: IHI Craft, Yokohama (In serv. 1975-79)

LS 114 No. 3 Yoko LS 182 No. 2 Yoko LS 142 No. 5 Yoko
LS 180 No. 1 Yoko LS 141 No. 4 Yoko LS 143 No. 6 Yoko

D: 3 tons (5 fl) **S:** 16.2 kts **Dim:** 7.3 × 2.45 × 0.5
M: 1 G.M. 3-53N diesel; 112 hp **Range:** 100/12 **Man:** 8 tot.

◆ **4 WAKO No. 4 class** Bldr: Yanmar Diesel, Arai

LS 123 Wako No. 4 (In serv. 31-1-74)
LS 116 Wako No. 1 (In serv. 11-10-78)
LS 117 Wako No. 2 (In serv. 11-10-78)
LS 118 Wako No. 3 (In serv. 24-3-79)

D: 2 tons **S:** 17 kts **Dim:** 6.0 × 2.4 × . . .
M: 1 gasoline engine; 115 hp **Range:** 70/17

◆ **5 TENKO No. 1 class** Bldr: Yanmar Diesel, Arai

LS 125 Tenko No. 1 (In serv. 28-7-70)
LS 102 Tenko No. 2 (In serv. 30-9-71)
LS 103 Tenko No. 3 (In serv. 30-9-71)
LS 137 Tenko No. 4 (In serv. 30-9-72)
LS 105 Tenko No. 5 (In serv. 4-12-73)

D: 0.6 tons **S:** 9 kts **Dim:** 5.6 × 1.6 × . . .
M: 1 Yanmar outboard; 12 hp **Range:** 20/9

◆ **5 EKO No. 1-class wooden launches**

LS 106 Eko No. 1 (In serv. 30-9-70)
LS 113 Eko No. 2 (In serv. 30-9-70)
LS 163 Eko No. 3 (In serv. 31-10-70)
LS 174 Eko No. 4 (In serv. 16-10-70)
LS 112 Eko No. 5 (In serv. 30-9-71)

D: 4.2 tons **S:** 6.2 kts **Dim:** 7.60 × 2.2 × . . .
M: 1 diesel; 12 hp **Range:** 80/6.2

FIREBOATS

Note: Most patrol ships, boats, and craft are fitted for fire-fighting.

◆ **5 Hiryu class** Bldr: Nippon Kokan, Yokohama (FL 05: Yokohama Yacht)

	In serv.		In serv.
FL 01 Hiryu	4-3-69	FL 04 Kairyu	18-3-77
FL 02 Shoryu	4-3-70	FL 05 Suiryu	24-3-78
FL 03 Nanryu	4-3-71		

Hiryu (FL 01) 1975

D: 199 tons (251 normal) **S:** 13.7 kts **Dim:** 27.5 × 10.4 × 2.1
M: 2 Ikegai-MTU MB820Db diesels; 2 props; 2,200 hp **Electric:** 70 kVA
Range: 400/13 **Man:** 14 tot.

FIREBOATS *(continued)*

REMARKS: Catamaran hulls. For fighting fires on board supertankers. 14.5m³ tank for fire-fighting chemicals. One 45-meter-range chemical sprayer; seven 60-meter-range water cannon.

◆ **10 Ninobiki class**

Bldrs: FM 02, FM 06, FM 08, FM 10: Sumidagawa, Tokyo: Others: Yokohama Yacht

	In serv.		In serv.
FM 01 NINOBIKI	25-2-74	FM 06 NACHI	14-2-76
FM 02 YODO	30-3-75	FM 07 KEGON	29-1-77
FM 03 OTOWA	25-12-74	FM 08 MINOO	27-1-78
FM 04 SHIRAITO	25-2-75	FM 09 RYUSEI	24-3-80
FM 05 KOTOBIKI	31-1-76	FM 10 KYOTAKI	25-3-81

Otowa (FM 03) 1975

D: 89 tons (99 normal) **S:** 13.4 kts **Dim:** 23.00 × 6.00 × 1.55
M: 1 Ikegai MTU MB820Db and 2 Nissan UDV 816 diesels; 3 props; 1,600 hp
Electric: 40 kVA **Range:** 234/13.4 **Man:** 12 tot.

REMARKS: Four fire pumps: one of 6,000 l/min., two of 3,000 l/min., and one of 2,000 l/min. Have two 750-liter and one 5,000-liter foam tanks.

ENVIRONMENTAL-PROTECTION CRAFT

◆ **1 Katsuren-class radiation monitoring craft** Bldr: Ishihara, Takasago

MS 03 KATSUREN (In serv. 13-12-75)

D: 30 tons (46 fl) **S:** 12.3 kts **Dim:** 16.50 × 5.50 × 1.10
M: 2 UDV 816 diesels; 2 props; 500 hp **Range:** 190/10.8 **Man:** 9 tot.

◆ **2 Kinagusa-class radiation monitoring craft** Bldr: Sumidagawa, Tokyo

MS 01 KINAGUSA (In serv. 25-9-70) MS 02 SAIKAI (In serv. 1-10-70)

Saikai (MS 02) *Ships of the World,* 1984

D: 16 tons (23 fl) **S:** 8.1 kts **Dim:** 10.50 × 5.00 × 0.63
M: 2 UD 326 diesels; 2 props; 180 hp **Range:** 170/7.6 **Man:** 8 tot.

◆ **1 (+ . . .) Sazankurosu-class oil-spill surveillance craft**

SS 35 SAZANKUROSU (In serv. 20-9-84)

D: 4.7 tons **S:** 25 kts **Dim:** 7.0 × 2.3 × . . .
M: 1 AQ 260A inboard/outboard motor; 130 hp
Range: . . . / . . . **Man:** . . . tot.

◆ **32 Orion-class oil-spill surveillance craft** Bldr: Yokohama Yacht and Yanmar Diesel, Arai (In serv. 1972-1979)

SS 01 ORION	SS 12 SPICA	SS 23 PERSEUS	SS 33 ALDEBARAN
SS 02 PEGASUS	SS 13 SIRIUS	SS 24 CENTAURUS	SS 34 PLEIADES
SS 04 NEPTUNE	SS 14 VEGA	SS 25 ANDROMEDA	
SS 05 JUPITER	SS 16 PROCYON	SS 26 ALTAIR	
SS 06 VENUS	SS 17 LEO	SS 27 HERCULES	
SS 07 CASSIOPEIA	SS 18 POLARIS	SS 28 GEMINI	
SS 08 PHOENIX	SS 19 RIGEL	SS 29 ARIES	
SS 09 SERPENS	SS 20 CYGNUS	SS 30 COMET	
SS 10 CARINA	SS 21 DENEB	SS 31 REGULUS	
SS 11 CAPELLA	SS 22 MERCURY	SS 32 BETELGEUSE	

Polaris (SS 18) *Ships of the World,* 1984

D: 2.1 tons (5 fl) **S:** 28.0 kts **Dim:** 5.99 × 2.44 × . . .
M: 1 AQ 200 inboard/outboard motor; 130 hp **Range:** 85/25 **Man:** 6 tot.

REMARKS: Propulsion and speeds vary: 16–28 kts from 130–210 hp.

◆ **1 Antares-class oil-spill surveillance craft** Bldr: Sajima Marina, Aburappo

SS 15 ANTARES (In serv. 1-7-75)

D: 1.6 tons **S:** 25 kts **Dim:** 5.49 × 2.41 × . . .
M: 1 Yanmar YA-19J2 diesel waterjet; 220 hp **Range:** 170/24 **Man:** 6 tot.

◆ **5 Shirasagi-class oil-spill clearance boats** Bldr: Various (In serv. 1977-79)

OR 01 SHIRASAGI	OR 03 MIZUNAGI	OR 05 ISOSHIGI
OR 02 SHIRATORI	OR 04 CHIDORI	

Shiratori (OR 02) *Ships of the World,* 1984

D: 78.5 tons (153 fl) **S:** 6.8 kts **Dim:** 22.0 × 6.4 × 0.9
M: 2 UD 626 diesels; water-jet drive; 390 hp **Range:** 160/6 **Man:** 7 tot.

◆ **3 Uraga-class oil-skimmer boats** Bldr: Lockheed, U.S.A. (In serv. 1975-76)

OS 01 TSURUMI (ex-*Uraga*) OS 02 BISAN OS 03 NARUTO

D: 11 tons (fl) **S:** 6 kts **Dim:** 8.26 × 5.00 × 0.70
M: 1 HR-6 diesel; 2 props; 90 hp **Range:** 90/4.5 **Man:** 4 tot.

◆ **18 M-101-class oil-boom-extender barges** Bldrs: Various (In serv. 1974-76)

OX 01 to OX 06, OX 08 to OX 19 (M 101 to M 119)

M 101 (OX 01) 1975

D: 48 tons **Dim:** 22.00 × 7.20 × 0.45

◆ **2 miscellaneous wooden oil-spill craft** Bldr: Eidai Sangyo (In serv. 1967)

No. 02 M 603 No. 34 M 804

D: 1.1 tons **S:** 23.4 kts **Dim:** 6.0 × 2.1 × . . .
M: 1 outboard motor; 80 hp **Range:** 80/23

JAPAN *(continued)*

TRAINING CRAFT

◆ **1 A-class** (In serv. 12-75)

Aoba

D: 15 tons **S:** 15.5 kts **Dim:** 14.0 × 3.6 × . . .
M: 1 diesel; 325 hp **Range:** 243/15.5

◆ **2 C-I class** Bldr: Yanmar Diesel, Arai (In serv. 9-75)

C-I C-II

D: 1 ton **S:** 28 kts **Dim:** 4.9 × 2.1 × . . .
M: 1 gasoline engine; 380 hp **Range:** 80/28

JORDAN

Hashemite Kingdom of Jordan

COASTAL GUARD

Personnel: 300 men, including those at the base at Aqaba and frogmen

Merchant Marine (1984): 8 ships—48,300 grt

Note: Some 3 to 6 30-meter patrol boats were reportedly ordered in Greece during 1982. Confirmation and details are lacking.

◆ **4 U.S.-supplied small craft** Bldr: Bertram, Miami

Faysal Han Hasayu Muhammed

D: 8 tons **S:** 25 tons **Dim:** 11.6 × 4.0 × 0.5
A: 1/12.7-mm mg—2/7.62-mm mg

◆ **2 U.S.-supplied small craft** Bldr: Bertram, Miami

Ali Abd Allah

D: 6.5 tons **S:** 25 kts **Dim:** 9.26 × 3.26 × 0.46
A: 1/12.7-mm mg—1/7.62-mm mg **Man:** 8 tot.

KAMPUCHEA

Democratic of Kampuchea

Merchant Marine (1980): 3 ships—3,558 grt (No recent data available)

Note: The units listed below have been delivered to forces subservient to the Vietnamese government. A few craft left behind in 1975 by fleeing forces may still exist, but no reliable details are available.

PATROL BOATS

◆ **3 Soviet Turya-class hydrofoils**

D: 215 tons (250 fl) **S:** 40 kts
Dim: 39.0 × 7.6 (12.5 over foils) × 2.0 (4.0 over foils)
A: 2/57-mm AA aft (II × 1)—2/25-mm AA fwd (II × 1)
Electron Equipt: Radar: 1/Pot Drum, 1/Muff Cob
IFF: 1/High Pole B, 1/Square Head interrogator
M: 3 M504 diesels; 3 props; 15,000 hp
Range: 400/38; 650/25 **Man:** 24 tot.

Remarks: One unit delivered 3-84, two on 23-2-85 to Kampong Song. Torpedo tubes and helicopter-type dipping sonar deleted. Fixed hydrofoils forward, with stern planing on surface. Use Osa-II hull and propulsion.

RIVER PATROL BOATS

◆ **4 Soviet Shmel class**

D: 60 tons (fl) **S:** 22 kts **Dim:** 28.3 × 4.6 × 0.9
A: 1/76.2-mm, 48-cal. gun fwd. in tank turret (with one coaxial 7.62-mm, mg)—2/25-mm AA aft (II × 1)—5/76.2-mm mg (I × 5)—1/122-mm RL (XVIII × 1)—mines
M: 2 M50-F4 diesels; 2 props; 2,400 hp **Range:** 240/20; 600/10
Man: 15-20 tot.

Remarks: Delivered 1984-85.

AMPHIBIOUS CRAFT

◆ **2 Soviet landing craft**

D: 70 tons (fl) **S:** 10 kts **Dim:** 19.0 × 4.3 × 1.0
M: 2 diesels; 2 props; 600 hp **Man:** 5 tot.

Remarks: Probable T4 class, delivered 1984-85.

KENYA

Republic of Kenya

Personnel: 350 total

Merchant Marine (1984): 25 ships—6,652 grt

GUIDED MISSILE PATROL BOATS

◆ **0 (+2) "Province" class** Bldr: Vosper-Thornycroft, Portchester, U.K.

	Laid down	L	In serv.
P. . . N. . .	11-84	. . .	1987
P. . . N. . .	11-84	. . .	1987

D: 311 tons light (363 fl) **S:** 40 kts **Dim:** 56.7 (52.0 pp) × 8.2 × 2.1
A: 4/Otomat Mk I SM (II × 2)—1/76-mm OTO Melara Compact DP—2/30-mm BMARC/Oerlikon GCM A22 AA (II × 1)
Electron Equipt: Radar: 1/Decca AC 1226, 1/Plessey AWS-4, 1/Marconi ST-802 f.c.
EW: 2 Barricade RL (IX × 2)
M: 4 Paxman Valenta 18 CM 200 diesels; 4 props; 17,900 hp (15,000 sust.)—2 electric outdrives; 160 hp
Electric: 420 kw **Fuel:** 45.5 tons **Range:** . . . **Man:** 40 tot.

Remarks: Ordered 9-84. Reported to be generally similar to craft built for Oman and Egypt.

◆ **3 32-meter class** Bldr: Brooke Marine, Lowestoft, U.K.

	L	In serv.
P 3121 Madaraka	28-175	16-6-75
P 3122 Jamhuri	14-3-75	16-6-75
P 3123 Harambee	2-5-75	28-8-75

Madaraka (P 3121)—after modernization 4-84

D: 120 tons (145 fl) **S:** 25.5 kts **Dim:** 32.6 × 6.1 × 1.7
A: 4/Gabriel SSM (I × 4)—2/30-mm AA BMARC GCM-AO AA (II × 1)
M: 2 Paxman 16-cyl. Valenta diesels; 2 props; 5,400 hp
Electron Equipt: Radar: 1/Decca 1226
Range: 2,300/12 **Man:** 3 officers, 18 men

Remarks: Ordered 10-5-73. P 3121 and 3123 received Gabriel missiles during 1982; P 3122 in 1983, with 2/40-mm AA removed.

◆ **1 37.5-meter class** Bldr: Brooke Marine, Lowestoft, U.K.

	Laid down	L	In serv.
P 3100 Mamba	17-2-72	6-11-73	7-2-74

Mamba (P 3100)—prior to modernization 1975

D: 130 tons (160 fl) **S:** 25 kts **Dim:** 37.5 × 6.86 × 1.78
A: 4/Gabriel SSM (I × 4)—2/30-mm BMARC GCM-AO AA (II × 1)

KENYA *(continued)*
GUIDED MISSILE PATROL BOATS *(continued)*

Electron Equipt: Radar: 1/Decca 1226
M: 2 Paxman 16-cyl. Valenta diesels; 2 props; 4,000 hp
Range: 3,500/13 **Man:** 3 officers, 22 men

REMARKS: Rearmed 1982, with 2/40-mm AA removed.

PATROL BOATS

◆ **3 Vosper 31-meter class** Bldr: Vosper Portsmouth, U.K.

	L	In serv.
P 3110 SIMBA	9-9-65	23-5-66
P 3112 CHUI	25-11-65	7-7-66
P 3117 NDOVU (ex-*Twigg*)	22-12-65	27-7-66

Simba (P 3110) Vosper, 1966

D: 96 tons (109 fl) **S:** 24/23 kts **Dim:** 31.25 (28.95 pp) × 5.95 × 1.65
A: 2/40-mm AA Mk 7 (I × 2) **Electron Equipt:** Radar: 1/Decca 914
M: 2 Paxman Ventura 12-cyl. diesels; 2 props; 2,900 hp **Fuel:** 14 tons
Range: 1,500/16 **Man:** 3 officers, 20 men

AUXILIARIES

◆ **1 large harbor tug** Bldr: James Lamont, Port Glasgow, U.K.

NGAMIA (In serv. 1969)

D: . . . **S:** 14 kts **Dim:** 35.3 × 9.3 × 3.9
M: Diesels; 1 prop; 1,200 hp

REMARKS: 298 grt. Transferred to Navy from Mombasa Port Authority, 1-83.

KIRIBATI

(formerly Gilbert Islands)

MERCHANT MARINE (1984): 4 ships—2,272 grt

PATROL CRAFT

◆ **1 17-meter glass-reinforced plastic patrol craft** Bldr: Cheverton, Cowes (In serv. 1980)

D: 22 tons (fl) **S:** 23.6 kts **Dim:** 17.0 × 4.5 × 1.2
A: 1/7.62-mm mg **M:** 2 G.M. 8V-71 TI diesels; 2 props; 800 hp
Range: 790/18; 1,000/12 **Man:** 7 tot.

KOREA, NORTH

Democratic People's Republic of Korea

PERSONNEL: Approximately 30,300 men, plus 40,000 reserves

MERCHANT MARINE (1984): 61 ships—459,958 grt (tankers: 4 ships—171,219 grt) (*Note:* This represents only ships engaged in international trade.)

SUBMARINES

◆ **17 Soviet Romeo class** (In serv. 1973-. . .)

D: 1,330/1,700 tons **S:** 15.2/13 kts **Dim:** 76.60 × 6.70 × 4.95
A: 8/533-mm TT (6 fwd, 2 aft)—14 torpedoes or 28 mines
Electron Equipt: Radar: 1/Snoop Plate
Sonar: Tamir-5L active, Feniks passive array
M: 2 Type 37D diesels of 2,000 hp, electric drive; 2 props; 2,700 hp—2 electric creep motors; 100 hp
Endurance: 60 days **Range:** 14,000/9 surf.; 7,500/5 snorkel; 350/. . . sub.
Man: 53 tot.

REMARKS: Seven are of Chinese construction, transferred in 1973 (two), 1974 (two), and 1975 (three). The others have been built at Mayang Do in North Korea. One lost off east coast 20-2-85. Max. diving depth: 300 m (270 normal). Batteries have 224 cells, are rated at 6,000-Amp/Hr.

◆ **4 Soviet Whiskey class**

D: 1,050/1,350 tons **S:** 16/17 kts **Dim:** 76.0 × 6.3 × 4.8
A: 6/533-mm TT (4 fwd, 2 aft)—12 torpedoes or 24 mines
Electron Equipt: Radar: 1/Snoop Plate
Sonar: Herkules, passive array
M: 2 Type 37D diesels of 2,000 hp, diesel-electric drive; 2 props; 2,500 hp
Endurance: 60 days **Range:** 4,000/5 (snorkel) **Man:** 50 tot.

REMARKS: Transferred from the U.S.S.R. during 1960s.

NOTE: Also in use are as many as 18 locally built midget submarines, intended primarily for the transport of commandos. One is reported to be 41-m. overall, but the others are probably much smaller.

FRIGATES

◆ **2 Najin class** Bldr: North Korea

3025 (In serv. 1973) 3026 (In serv. 1975)

D: 1,200 tons (1,500 fl) **S:** 25 kts **Dim:** 100.0 × 10.0 × 2.7
A: 2/SS-N-2 Styx SSM (II × 1)—2/100-mm DP (I × 2)—4/57-mm AA (II × 2)—4/25-mm AA (II × 2)—8/14.5-mm mg (II × 4)—4/d.c. projectors—30 mines
Electron Equipt: Radar: 1/Skin Head, 1/Pot Head, 1/Slim Net
Sonar: . . .
M: 2 diesels; 2 props; 15,000 hp **Range:** 4,000/14 **Man:** 155 tot.

REMARKS: Very primitive design, crude in finish and appearance. Trainable missile launcher mount (Chinese?) replaced 3/533-mm TT (III × 1) in early 1980s. Reports of two others apparently incorrect.

CORVETTES

◆ **4 Sariwan class** Bldr: North Korea, 1965

D: 475 tons **S:** 21 kts **Dim:** 62.1 × 7.3 × 2.4
A: 1/76-mm DP—2/57-mm AA (II × 2)—4/25-mm AA (II × 2)—4/d.c. projectors
M: 2 diesels; 2 props; 3,000 hp

REMARKS: Data dubious. Design based on Soviet *Tral*-class minesweeper. Possible pendant numbers: 725, 726, 727, 728.

GUIDED-MISSILE PATROL BOATS

◆ **8 (+. . .) Soju class** Bldr: North Korea

D: approx. 220 tons (fl) **S:** 34 kts **Dim:** 43.0 × . . . × . . .
A: 4/SS-N-2 Styx SSM . . .
M: 3 Type M503A diesels; 3 props; 12,000 hp
Range: . . . **Man:** . . .

REMARKS: North Korean version of Osa-I. Some reports indicate only four in service.

◆ **4 (+ . . .) So Hung class** Bldr: North Korea

D: 80 tons (fl) **S:** 40 kts **Dim:** 26.8 × 6.2 × 1.5
A: 2/SS-N-2 Styx SSM—2/25-mm AA (II × 1)
Electron Equipt: Radar: probably 1/Square Tie
M: 4 M50-F4 diesels; 4 props; 4,800 hp **Man:** 19 tot.

REMARKS: Steel-hulled version of Soviet Komar class. With only four built, may not have been successful. May use the Chaho-class patrol boat hull.

◆ **8 Soviet Osa-I class**

D: 180 tons (215 fl) **S:** 35 kts **Dim:** 38.6 × 7.6 × 1.8
A: 4/SS-N-2A Styx SSM (I × 4)—4/30-mm AA (II × 2)
Electron Equipt: Radar: 1/Square Tie, 1/Drum Tilt
IFF: 2/Square Head, 1/High Pole
M: 3 M503A diesels; 3 props; 12,000 hp **Range:** 500/34; 750/25 **Man:** 30 tot.

◆ **8 Soviet Komar class**

D: 71 tons (82 fl) **S:** 40 kts **Dim:** 25.3 × 7.0 × 1.9
A: 2/SS-N-2A Styx SSM (I × 2)—2/25-mm AA (II × 1)
Electron Equipt: Radar: 1/Square Tie **M:** 4 M50-F4 diesels; 4 props; 4,800 hp
Range: 400/30 **Man:** 18 tot.

REMARKS: Wooden construction; hull same as P 6 torpedo boat.

PATROL BOATS

◆ **7 (+. . .) Taechong class** Bldr: North Korea (In serv. 1975-. . .)

D: 140 tons (165 fl) **S:** . . . **Dim:** 44.2 × 5.5 × 2.4 (props)
A: 2/57-mm AA (II × 1)—1/37-mm AA—2/25-mm AA (II × 1)—4/14.5-mm mg (II × 2)—2/RBU-1200 ASW RL—2/d.c. racks
Electron Equipt: Radar: 1/Pot Head—Sonar: Tamir-11 (HF)
M: Diesels; . . . props; . . . hp
Range: . . . **Man:** . . .

KOREA-NORTH *(continued)*
PATROL BOATS *(continued)*

◆ **6 Chinese Hainan class**

D: 360 tons (400 fl) **S:** 30.5 kts **Dim:** 58.77 × 7.20 × 2.20
A: 4/57-mm AA (II × 2)—4/25-mm AA (II × 2)—4/RBU-1200 ASW RL (V × 4)—2/d.c. projectors—2/d.c. racks—mines
Electron Equipt: Radar: 1/Pot Head **M:** 4 Type 9D diesels; 4 props; 8,800 hp
Man: 70 tot.

Remarks: Two transferred in 1975; two in 1976; and two in 1978.

◆ **66 Chaho class** Bldr: North Korea

D: 80 tons (fl) **S:** 40 kts **Dim:** 27.7 × 6.1 × 1.8
A: 4/14.5-mm AA (II × 2)—1/200-mm artillery RL (40 tubes)
M: 4 M50 diesels; 4 props; 4,800 hp

Remarks: Based on P 6 design, but have steel hull.

◆ **45 Chong Jin and Chong Ju classes** Bldr: North Korea

Remarks: Data as for Chaho class, except armaments include: one 85-mm tank gun and four 14.5-mm antiaircraft guns (II × 2). Chong Ju variant substitutes a multiple 122-mm rocket launcher (XI × 1) for the tank turret.

◆ **15 Chinese Shanghai II class**

D: 122.5 tons (134.8 fl) **S:** 28.5 kts **Dim:** 38.78 × 5.41 × 1.55
A: 4/37-mm AA (II × 2)—4/25-mm AA (II × 2)—d.c.—mines
Electron Equipt: Radar: 1/Pot Head
M: 2 M50-F4, 1,200-hp and 2/12D6, 910-hp diesels; 4 props; 4,220 hp
Range: 750/16.5 **Electric:** 39 kw **Endurance:** 7 days **Man:** 36 tot.

Remarks: Transferred circa 1967-69.

◆ **18 Soviet S.O. 1 class**

D: 190 tons (215 fl) **S:** 28 kts **Dim:** 42.0 × 6.1 × 1.9
A: Soviet version: 4/25-mm AA (II × 2)—4/RBU-1200 ASW RL (V × 4)—2/d.c. racks—mines
North Korean version: 1/85-mm DP—2/37-mm AA (I × 2)—4/14.5-mm mg (II × 2)
Electron Equipt: Radar: 1/Pot Head or Don-2—Sonar: 1/Tamir-11(HF)
M: 3 Type 40D diesels; 3 props; 7,500 hp **Man:** 30-40 tot.

Remarks: Six transferred from U.S.S.R. in antisubmarine configuration 1957-61; remainder built in Korea for patrol purposes.

◆ **8 Chinese Shantou (Swatow) class** (In serv. early 1960s)

D: 80 tons (fl) **S:** 28 kts **Dim:** 25.1 × 6.0 × 1.8
A: 4/37-mm AA (II × 2)—2/14.5-mm mg (I × 2)
M: 4 diesels; 4 props; 3,000 hp

◆ **4 Chodo class** Bldr: North Korea (In serv. late 1950s)

D: 130 tons **S:** 24 kts **Dim:** 42.7 × 5.8 × 2.6
A: 1/76-mm DP—3/37-mm AA (I × 3)—4/25-mm AA (II × 2)
Electron Equipt: Radar: 1/Skin Head
M: 2 diesels; 2 props; 6,000 hp **Man:** 24 tot.

◆ **4 K-48 class** Bldr: North Korea (In serv. 1951-54)

D: 110 tons (fl) **S:** 24 kts **Dim:** 38.1 × 5.5 × 1.5
A: 1/76-mm DP—3/37-mm AA (I × 3)—4/14.5-mm AA (II × 2)
Electron Equipt: Radar: 1/Skin Head
M: 2 diesels; 2 props; 5,000 hp

Note: Twenty wooden-hulled Soviet-built M.O. IV-class patrol boats, built 1938-47 and transferred to North Korea in the 1950s, have been dropped from this edition as unlikely still to be operational.

TORPEDO BOATS

◆ **4 Soviet Shershen class**

D: 135 tons (170 fl) **S:** 45 kts **Dim:** 34.7 × 6.7 × 1.5
A: 4/30-mm AA (II × 2)—4/533-mm TT—2/d.c. racks (12 d.c.)
Electron Equipt: Radar: 1/Pot Drum, 1/Drum Tilt
IFF: 1/Square Head, 1/High Pole A
M: 3 M503A diesels; 3 props; 12,000 hp **Range:** 460/42; 850/30

◆ **approx. 40 Soviet P 6/North Korean Sinpo class**

D: 55 tons (66.5 fl) **S:** 43 kts **Dim:** 25.3 × 6.1 × 1.7
A: 4/25-mm AA (I × 2)—2/533-mm TT—8/d.c. in tilt racks
Electron Equipt: Radar: 1/Skin Head or Pot Head
IFF: 1/Dead Duck, 1/High Pole
M: 4 M50-F4 diesels; 4 props; 4,800 hp **Range:** 450/30

Remarks: Forty-five transferred by U.S.S.R. during early 1960s; wooden construction. A few similar Sinpo class units were built in Korea during the early 1970s. Steel construction. Some lack torpedo tubes but have additional AA guns.

◆ **12 Iwon class** Bldr: North Korea (In serv. 1970s)

D: 25 tons (fl) **S:** 45 kts **Dim:** 19.2 × 3.7 × 1.5
A: 2/25-mm AA (II × 2)—2/533-mm TT **M:** 3 diesels; 3 props; 3,600 hp

◆ **6 An Ju class** Bldr: North Korea (In serv. 1970s)

D: 35 tons (fl) **S:** 50 kts **Dim:** 19.8 × 3.7 × 1.8
A: 2/25-mm AA (II × 2)—2/533-mm TT
M: 4 M50 diesels; 4 props; 4,800 hp **Man:** 20 tot.

◆ **74 Sin Hung class** Bldr: North Korea (In serv. 1970s)

D: 25 tons (fl) **S:** 40 kts **Dim:** 18.3 × 3.4 × 1.7
A: 4/14.5-mm (II × 2)—2/450-mm TT **M:** 2 diesels; 2 props; 2,400 hp

AMPHIBIOUS CRAFT

◆ **4 Hantae-class medium landing ships** (In serv. 1980s)

Remarks: Reportedly 50-m overall and capable of carrying three tanks.

◆ **100 Nampo-class assault landing craft** Bldr: North Korea

D: 82 tons (fl) **S:** 40 kts **Dim:** 27.7 × 6.1 × 1.8 **A:** 4/14.5-mm AA (II × 2)
M: 4 M50-F4 diesels; 4 props; 4,800 hp **Range:** 375/40 **Man:** 19 tot.
Electron Equipt: Radar: 1/Pot Head

Remarks: A version of the Chaho-class gunboat with a bow ramp and troop accommodations forward.

◆ **9 Hanchon-class utility landing craft** Bldr: North Korea

Remarks: No reliable data available.

◆ **18 smaller landing craft, LCM type**

KOREA, SOUTH

Republic of Korea

Personnel: Approximately 29,000 men, plus 20,000 Marines

Merchant Marine (1984): 1,799 ships—6,771,402 grt (tankers: 137 ships—1,700,813 grt)

Naval Aviation: About a dozen land-based U.S. S-2E Tracker aircraft remain employed for surveillance and ASW. Ten or more Alouette-III helicopters are available for use on destroyers.

Note: Pendant numbers are subject to change at unspecified intervals. The numerals "0" and "4" are considered unlucky and are not used.

SUBMARINES

Remarks: A 120-ton submarine of local design was laid down during 1982 at Hyundai Shipyard. No details are available. A program to construct seagoing attack submarines of European design was officially announced as delayed for three years in late 1984; as many as a dozen had been contemplated.

◆ **5 ex-U.S. Gearing class, FRAM I**

	Bldr	Laid down	L	In serv.
919 Taejon (ex-*New*, DD 818)	Consolidated Steel, Orange, Tex.	14-4-45	18-8-45	5-4-46
921 Kuang Ju (ex-*Richard E. Kraus*, DD 849)	Consolidated Steel, Orange, Tex.	31-7-45	2-3-46	23-5-46
922 Kang Won (ex-*William R. Rush*, DD 714)	Federal SB, Newark, N.J.	19-10-44	8-7-45	21-9-45
923 Kyong Ki (ex-*Newman K. Perry*, DD 883)	Consolidated Steel, Orange, Tex.	10-10-44	17-3-45	26-7-45
925 Jeong Ju (ex-*Rogers*, DD 876	Consolidated Steel, Orange, Tex.	3-6-44	20-11-44	26-3-45

Taejon (919)—alongside Kang Won (922) L. & L. Van Ginderen, 1982

SUBMARINES *(continued)*

D: 2,425 tons (3,500 fl) **S:** 30 kts
Dim: 119.03 (116.74 wl) × 12.52 × 4.45 (6.4 sonar)
A: 919, 921, 922: 4 Harpoon SSM (II × 2)—4/127-mm DP (II × 2)—2/40-mm AA (II × 1)—4/20-mm AA (II × 2)—6/324-mm Mk 32 ASW TT (III × 2)—1/Alouette-III ASW helo
923, 925: 4/127-mm DP (IV × 2)—2/40-mm AA (II × 1)—4/20-mm AA (I × 4)—1/ASROC Mk 116 ASW RL (VIII × 1)—6/324-mm Mk 32 ASW TT
Electron Equipt: Radar: 1/SPS-10, 1/SPS-29 (919, 921: SPS-40), 1/Mk 25
Sonar: SQS-23
EW: WLR-1, 2 chaff RL—TACAN: SRN-15
M: 2 sets GT; 2 props; 60,000 hp **Electric:** 1,200 kw
Boilers: 4 Babcock & Wilcox; 39.8 kg/cm², 454°C **Fuel:** 640 tons
Range: 4,800/15; 2,400/25 **Man:** 274 tot.

REMARKS: 919, 921 were transferred 25-2-77; 922 on 1-7-79; 923 on 25-7-81; 925 on 11-8-81. Have one Mk 37 director, and 1 Mk 51 Mod. 2 for 40-mm; 40-mm AA added fwd, 20-mm AA amidships. Harpoon added 1979 on ships without ASROC. ULQ-6 ECM equipment removed.

◆ **2 ex-U.S. Gearing class, FRAM II** Bldr: Bath Iron Works

	Laid down	L	In serv.
915 CHUNG BUK (ex-*Chevalier,* DDR 805)	12-6-44	29-10-44	8-9-44
916 JEONG BUK (ex-*Everett F. Larson,* DDR 830)	4-9-44	28-1-45	6-4-45

Jeong Buk (916) J. W. Goss, 11-81

Chong Buk (915) G. Gyssels, 11-81

D: 2,400 tons (3,500 fl) **S:** 30 kts **Dim:** 119.17 × 12.45 × 5.8
A: 4/Harpoon (II × 2)—6/127-mm DP (II × 3)—2/20-mm AA (I × 2)—2/12.7-mm mg (I × 2)—6/324-mm Mk 32 ASW TT (III × 2)—2/Mk 11 Hedgehog—1/d.c. rack—1/Alouette-III helicopter
Electron Equipt: Radar: 1/SPS-10, 1/SPS-40, 1/Mk 25
Sonar: SQS-29 series—TACAN: SRN-15
EW: WLR-1, 2 chaff RL
M: 2 sets GT; 2 props; 60,000 hp **Electric:** 1,200 kw
Boilers: 4 Babcock & Wilcox; 39.8 kg/cm², 454°C **Fuel:** 640 tons
Range: 4,800/15; 2,400/25 **Man:** 14 officers, 260 men

REMARKS: Transferred on loan 5-7-72 and 30-10-72; sold outright 31-1-77. One Mk 37 director for 127-mm guns. Harpoon added 1979, flight deck widened and strengthened. The 20-mm AA are on the helicopter deckhouse. ULQ-6 ECM equipment removed.

◆ **2 ex-U.S. Allen M. Sumner class, FRAM II**

	Bldr	Laid down	L	In serv.
917 DAE GU (ex-*Wallace L. Lind,* DD 703)	Federal SB, Kearny, N.J.	19-9-43	14-6-44	8-9-44
918 INCHON (ex-*De Haven,* DD 727)	Bath Iron Works	9-8-43	9-1-44	31-3-44

D: 2,350 tons (3,320 fl) **S:** 34 kts **Dim:** 114.8 × 12.4 × 5.2
A: 4/Harpoon SSM (II × 2)—6/127-mm AA (II × 3)—4/40-mm AA (II × 2)—6/324-mm Mk 32 ASW TT (III × 2)—2/Mk 11 Hedgehogs—1/d.c. rack—1/Alouette-III helicopter
Electron Equipt: Radar: 1/SPS-10, 1/SPS-40 (918: SPS-29), 1/Mk 25
Sonar: 1/SQS-29 series, 1/SQA-10 VDS (917 only)
EW: WLR-1, 2 chaff RL
M: 2 sets G.E. GT; 2 props; 60,000 hp **Electric:** 1,200 kw
Boilers: 4 Babcock & Wilcox; 39.8 kg/cm², 454°C **Man:** 235 tot.

REMARKS: Transferred 12-73. Harpoon added 1978-79; helicopter deck and hangar enlarged to accommodate Alouette-III, 1978.

◆ **2 ex-U.S. Fletcher class**

	Bldr	Laid down	L	In serv.
911 CHUNG MU (ex-*Erben,* DD 631)	Bath Iron Works	28-10-42	21-3-43	28-5-43
913 PUSAN (ex-*Hickox,* DD 673)	Federal SB, Kearny, N.J.	12-3-43	4-7-43	10-9-43

D: 2,050 tons (2,850 fl) **S:** 35 kts **Dim:** 114.85 (wl) × 12.03 × 5.5
A: 5/127-mm 38-cal. (I × 5)—10/40-mm AA (IV × 2, II × 2)—2/Hedgehog—6/324-mm Mk 32 ASW TT (IV × 2)
Electron Equipt: Radar: 1/SPS-10, 1/SPS-6C, 1/Mk 25
Sonar: 1/SQS-4—EW: WLR-1
M: 2 sets G.E. GT; 2 props; 60,000 hp **Electric:** 540 kw
Boilers: 4 Babcock & Wilcox; 39.8 kg/cm², 454°C **Fuel:** 650 tons
Range: 4,500/12; 900/35 **Man:** 303 tot.

REMARKS: The *Chung Mu* transferred 1-5-63, the *Pusan* on 15-11-68; purchased outright 31-1-77. Have one Mk 37 director for 127-mm mount; one Mk 51 Mod. 2 director for each 40-mm mount. Sister *Seoul* (912) stricken 15-1-82.

FRIGATES

◆ **3 (+2) Ulsan class**

	Bldr	Laid down	L	In serv.
951 ULSAN	Hyundai SY, Ulsan	1-5-79	8-4-80	1-1-81
952 SEOUL	Korea SB, Pusan	1982	24-4-84	18-12-84
955 MASAN	Korea Tacoma, Masan	. . .	. . .	8-84
. . . N.	Daiwoo SY, Okpo	. . .	. . .	. . .
. . . N.	Daiwoo SY, Okpo	. . .	. . .	. . .

Ulsan (951) Hyundai, 1981

D: 1,600 tons (2,180 fl) **S:** 34 kts **Dim:** 102.0 × 11.5 × 3.6
A: 8/Harpoon SSM (IV × 2)—2/76-mm OTO Melara DP—8/30-mm Emerlec AA (II × 4)—6/324-mm Mk 32 ASW TT (III × 2)—2/d.c. racks
Electron Equipt: Radar: H.S.A. DA-05, 1/H.S.A. ZW-06, 1/H.S.A. WM 28
Sonar: 1/PHS-32—TACAN: SRN-15
EW: passive intercept, Mk 36 SRBOC (VI × 2)
M: CODOG: 2 G.E. LM 2500 gas turbines, 53,600 hp; 2 MTU 12V956 diesels, 7,200 hp; 2 CP props
Range: 4,000/18 **Electric:** 1,600 kw **Man:** 14 officers, 111 men

REMARKS: Dutch electronic equipment, including 2 H.S.A. LIOD optronic standby gun directors. Three additional ordered 1981, and a fourth in 4-84. Later units may employ twin Breda 40-mm AA in lieu of the 30-mm mounts.

FRIGATES *(continued)*

◆ **8 (+3 + . . .) An Yang Ho (KCX) class** Bldrs: (A) Korea Tacoma SB, Chinhae; (B) Hyundai SY, Ulsan; (C) Korea SB & Eng., Pusan; (D) Daewoo SY, Okpo

	Bldr	Laid down	L	In serv.
. . . An Yang Ho	A	1981	1982	12-83
. . . N. . .	B	1981	15-5-83	12-83
. . . Ma San Ho	C	1981	1982	12-83
. . . N. . .	D	. . .	19-6-83	12-83
. . . Po Hang	. . .	. . .	. . .	18-12-84
. . . Kunsan	. . .	. . .	. . .	18-12-84
. . . Kyong Nam	. . .	. . .	. . .	5-85
. . . N. . .	. . .	. . .	. . .	-85
. . . N. . .	. . .	. . .	. . .	-86
. . . N. . .	. . .	. . .	. . .	-86
. . . N. . .	. . .	. . .	. . .	. . .

Number 757 with 2 Exocet 1985

D: 900 tons (1300 fl) **S:** 25 kts **Dim:** 81.0 × 10.4 × 3.1 (2.88 hull)
A: 8/Harpoon (IV × 2) or 2/MM 38 Exocet SSM—1/76-mm OTO Melara Compact DP—4/30-mm Emerlec AA (II × 2)—6/324-mm Mk 32 ASW TT (III × 2)—d.c. racks—
Electron Equipt: Radar: 1 . . . nav., 1 H.S.A. WM-28
Sonar: 1/PHS-32—EW: 2 chaff RL
M: CODOG: 1 LM-2500 gas turbine, 27,200 hp; 2 SEMT-Pielstick 12PA6-V280 diesels; 9,600 hp; 2 CP props
Range: 4,000/15 (diesel) **Electric:** 1,200 kw **Man:** 8 officers, 79 men

Remarks: Few reliable details released. First four have Harpoon SSM, later units have Exocet. Some may be all-diesel, with four 4,170-hp MTU diesels. Korea SB, Pusan, had delivered three by 5-85. First four had gas turbine rated at 27,200 hp, later units at 27,800. An additional increment of up to 10 may be ordered. Have also been referred to as the *Donghae* class.

Note: The U.S. *Rudderow*-class frigate *Chung Nam* (827, ex-*Holt,* DE 706) was stricken during 1-84.

◆ **1 ex-U.S. Crosley-class former high-speed transport**

	Bldr	Laid down	L	In serv.
828 Che Ju (ex-*William M. Hobby,* APD 95)	Charleston Navy Yard, Charleston, S.C.	15-11-43	11-2-44	4-4-45

D: 1,650 tons (2,130 fl) **S:** 23.6 kts **Dim:** 93.13 × 11.3 × 3.2
A: 2/127-mm DP (I × 2)—6/40-mm AA (II × 3)—6/12.7-mm mg (I × 6)—1 d.c. rack
Electron Equipt: Radar: 1/SPS-5, 1/SPS-6, 1/Mk 26—Sonar: QCU-2
M: 2 sets G.E. GT, turbo-electric drive; 2 props; 12,000 hp
Boilers: 2 Foster-Wheeler "D"-express; 30.6 kg/cm², 399°C
Range: 4,800/12; 2,300/22 **Man:** 200 tot.

Remarks: Transferred on loan 6-66, and 8-67; purchased outright 15-11-74. Second 127-mm gun added aft, as on Taiwanese sisters. Have low bridge compared to ex-*Charles Lawrence* ships, below. Can still carry 160 troops; two LCVPs and two LCPLs stowed beneath quadrantal davits. One Mk 52 director for 127-mm gun; three Mk 51 Mod. 2 for 40-mm AA. Sisters *Kyong Nam* (821, ex-*Cavallaro,* APD 128) and *Ah San* (823, ex-*Harry L. Corl,* APD 825) stricken 1984. *Ung Po* (825, ex-*Julius A. Raven,* APD 110) reported stricken 1984 also.

◆ **1 ex-U.S. Charles Lawrence-class former high-speed transport**

Bldr: Charleston Navy Yard, Charleston, S.C.

	Laid down	L	In serv.
827 Jon Nam (ex-*Hayter,* APD 80)	11-8-43	11-11-43	4-4-45

Remarks: All data essentially the same as for the *Crosley* class above. Loaned in 8-67; purchased outright 15-11-74. Has high bridge as compared to the *Crosley* class. All APDs of both classes were laid down originally as DE-destroyer escorts. Sister *Kyong Puk* (826, ex-*Kephart,* APD 61) stricken 30-4-85.

GUIDED-MISSILE PATROL BOATS

◆ **8 PSMM-5 class** Bldrs: PGM 352 to 355: Tacoma Boatbuilding Co.; others: Korea Tacoma, Chinhae

	Laid down	In serv.
PGM 352 Paek Ku 52	1-75	14-3-75
PGM 353 Paek Ku 53	2-75	14-3-75
PGM 355 Paek Ku 55	. . .	1-2-76
PGM 356 Paek Ku 56	. . .	1-2-76
PGM 357 Paek Ku 57	. . .	1977
PGM 358 Paek Ku 58	. . .	1977
PGM 359 Paek Ku 59	. . .	1977
PGM 361 Paek Ku 61	. . .	1978

Paek Ku 61 (PGM 361) *Ships of the World,* 1985

D: 240 tons (268 fl) **S:** 40 kts **Dim:** 53.68 (50.30 pp) × 8.00 × 1.63
A: 4/Harpoon SSM (II × 2)—1/76-mm OTO Melara Compact DP—2/30-mm Emerlec AA (II × 1)—2/12.7-mm mg
Electron Equipt: Radar: 1/LN-66 HP, 1/SPG-50
M: 6 AVCO TF-35 gas turbines; 2 CP props; 16,800 hp
Man: 5 officers, 27 men

Remarks: Korean-built units have Westinghouse M-1200 fire-control systems, using inputs from the LN-66 HP radar and an optical director. Early ships have the U.S. Mk 63 GFCS. PGM 352–355 have 2 Standard ARM SSM launchers (each with one reload).

◆ **1 ex-U.S. Asheville class** Bldr: Tacoma Boat, Tacoma, Wash.

	L	In serv.
PGM 351 Paek Ku 51 (ex-*Benicia,* PG 96)	20-12-69	25-4-70

D: 225 tons (249 fl) **S:** 40 kts **Dim:** 50.14 × 7.28 × 2.9
A: 2/Standard ARM SSM box launchers—1/76.2-mm Mk 34 DP—1/40-mm AA—4/12.7-mm mg (II × 2)
Electron Equipt: Radar: 1/Raytheon 1645, 1/SPG-50
M: CODOG: 1 G.E. LM-1500-PE102 gas turbine, 12,500 hp; 2 Cummins VT12-875M diesels; 2 CP props; 1,450 hp
Range: 1,700/16; 390/35 **Man:** 29 tot.

Remarks: Mk 63 radar GFCS for 76.2-mm Mk 34 gun. Transferred on loan 15-10-71. One reload missile carried for each box launcher.

◆ **2 "Wildcat" type** Bldr: Korea Tacoma SB, Chinhae (In serv. 1971-72)

PKM 271 Kilurki 71 PKM 272 Kilurki 72

Kilurki 71 or 72 Korea-Tacoma

D: 120 tons (140 fl) **S:** 34/35 kts **Dim:** 32.9 × 8.0 × 1.1
A: 2/MM 38 Exocet SSM (I × 2)—1/40-mm AA—3/12.7-mm mg—2/barrage RL (IV × 2)
M: PKM 271: 2 MTU MB518D diesels; 3 props; 9,960 hp
PKM 272: 3 MTU 16V538 TB90 diesels; 3 props; 10,800 hp
Range: 1,000/20 **Man:** 4 officers, 22 men

PATROL BOATS

◆ **1 (+. . .) . . . class** Bldr: Korea Tacoma SB (In serv. 4-8-84)

D: 150 tons **S:** 37 kts **Dim:** 37.00 × 6.25 × 1.68
A: . . . **Electron Equipt:** . . .
M: . . .

REMARKS: No other details released. May be prototype for new series intended as anti-infiltration patrol boats.

◆ **32 "Sea Dolphin" type** Bldr: Korea Tacoma, Chinhae (In serv. 1970s)

PKM 211 KILURKI 11 to PKM 219 KILURKI 19
PKM 221 KILURKI 21 to PKM 229 KILURKI 29
PKM 231 KILURKI 31 to PKM 239 KILURKI 39
PKM 251 KILURKI 51 to PKM 259 KILURKI 59

"Sea Dolphin" type Korea-Tacoma

D: 113 tons (144 fl) **S:** 34 kts **Dim:** 33.1 × 6.9 × 2.45 (props)
A: 1/40-mm AA—2/30-mm Emerlec AA (II × 1)—2/20-mm AA (I × 2)—2/12.7-mm mg (I × 2)
M: 2 MTU 16V538 TB90 diesels; 2 props; 10,800 hp (9,000 sust.)
Range: 1,000/20 **Man:** 22 tot.

REMARKS: Gunboat version of the class above. In the above hull number series, the "4" numbers have been omitted.

◆ **32 PK "Schoolboy" or "Sea Hawk" class** Bldr: Korea SB & Eng.

PK 151 to PK 189 CHEBI 51 to CHEBI 89

PK 153—1/20-mm AA aft, 1/40-mm AA fwd. 1983

D: 70 tons (78 fl) **S:** 40 kts **Dim:** 25.7 × 5.4 × 1.2
A: 1/40-mm AA—1/20-mm AA—4/12.7-mm mg (II × 2)—2/7.62-mm mg (I × 2)
M: 2 MTU 16V538 TD90 diesels; 2 props; 5,200 hp **Range:** 500/20
Man: 25 tot.

REMARKS: Armament varies: recent units (and those refitted) have a Korean-designed 40-mm power-operated mount and three twin Korean-design 12.7-mm mg mounts (see photo of PK 153); early ships had a U.S. Mk 3 40-mm mount forward.

NOTE: Ex-U.S. Coast Guard "Cape"-class patrol boats PB 3, 5, 6, 8-12 stricken 1984.

MINE WARFARE SHIPS

◆ **0 (+1 + . . .) SK5000-class minehunters** Bldr: Kangnam SB

D: . . . **S:** . . . **Dim:** . . . × . . . × . . .
A: . . . **Electron Equipt:** Radar: . . . —Sonar: Plessey 193M
M: . . . diesels; 2 Voith-Schneider cycloidal props; . . . hp

REMARKS: Design based on Italian Intermarine *Lerici* design. First unit scheduled to deliver 12-86. Glass-reinforced plastic construction, with bow-thruster. Will carry Gaymarine Pluto mine-disposal vehicles and is to be equipped with Decca-Racal plotting gear. As many as 10 may ultimately be built.

◆ **5 U.S. MSC-289-class coastal minesweepers** Bldr: Peterson Bldrs., Sturgeon Bay, Wis.

	In serv.
MSC 555 NAM YANG (ex-MSC 295)	8-63
MSC 556 HA DONG (ex-MSC 296)	11-63
MSC 557 SAM KOK (ex-MSC 316)	7-68
MSC 558 YONG DONG (ex-MSC 320)	2-10-75
MSC 559 OK CHEON (ex-MSC 321)	2-10-75

Sam Kok (MSC 557)—old pendant number

D: 315 tons (380 fl) **S:** 14 kts **Dim:** 44.32 × 8.29 × 2.7
A: 2/20-mm AA (II × 1) **M:** 4 G.M. 6-71 diesels; 2 props; 1,020 hp
Electric: 1,260 kw **Fuel:** 33 tons **Man:** 40 tot.

REMARKS: Wooden construction. Built under Military Aid Program. Gas-turbine sweep generator. Lower superstructure than on the MSC 268 class, below.

◆ **3 U.S. MSC 268-class coastal minesweepers** Bldr: Harbor Boat Bldg., Terminal Isl., Cal.

	In serv.
MSC 551 KUM SAN (ex-MSC 284)	6-59
MSC 552 KO HUNG (ex-MSC 285)	8-59
MSC 553 KUM KOK (ex-MSC 286)	10-59

Kum San (MSC 551)

D: 320 tons (370 fl) **S:** 14 kts **Dim:** 43.0 (41.5 pp) × 7.95 × 2.55
A: 2/20-mm AA (II × 2) **Electron Equipt:** Radar: Decca 45—Sonar: UQS -1
M: 2 G.M. 8-268A diesels; 2 props; 1,200 hp **Fuel:** 40 tons
Range: 2,500/16 **Man:** 40 tot.

REMARKS: Built under Military Aid Program. Wooden hulls.

AMPHIBIOUS WARFARE SHIPS

◆ 8 ex-U.S. LST 1 and U.S. LST 542-class landing ships

	Bldr	L	In serv.
LST 671 Un Bong (ex-LST 1010)	Bethlehem, Fore River	29-3-44	25-4-44
LST 672 Tuk Bong (ex-LST 227)	Chicago Bridge, Seneca, Ill.	21-9-43	14-10-43
LST 673 Bi Bong (ex-LST 218)	Chicago Bridge, Seneca, Ill.	20-7-43	12-8-43
LST 675 Kae Bong (ex-LST 288)	American Bridge, Pa.	7-11-43	20-12-43
LST 676 Wee Bong (ex-*Johnson County,* LST 849)	American Bridge, Pa.	30-12-43	16-1-44
LST 677 Su Yong (ex-*Kane County,* LST 853)	Chicago Bridge, Seneca, Ill.	17-11-44	11-12-44
LST 678 Buk Han (ex-*Linn County,* LST 900)	Dravo, Pittsburgh	9-12-44	28-12-44
LST 679 Hwa San (ex-*Pender County,* LST 1080)	Bethleham, Hingham, Mass.	2-5-45	29-5-45

D: 1,653 tons (4,080 fl) **S:** 10 kts **Dim:** 100.04 × 15.24 × 4.30
A: 8/40-mm AA (II × 2, I × 4)—2/20-mm AA **Electric:** 300 kw
M: 2 G.M. 12-567A or 12-278A diesels; 2 props; 1,800 hp **Man:** 70 tot.

Remarks: Transferred 1955-58; all purchased outright 15-11-74. LST 1 class had elevators from upper deck to tank deck; later ships had a ramp.

◆ 7 ex-U.S. LSM 1-class medium landing ships

Bldr: Brown SB, Houston, Tex. (except: LSM 652: Federal SB, Newark, N.J.; LSM 661: Pullman Standard Car Co., Chicago, Ill.)

	Laid down	L	In serv.
LSM 655 Ko Mun (ex-LSM 30)	7-5-44	28-5-44	1-7-44
LSM 656 Pi An (ex-LSM 96)	15-9-44	7-10-44	28-10-44
LSM 657 Wol Mi (ex-LSM 57)	30-6-44	21-7-44	17-8-44
LSM 658 Ki Rin (ex-LSM 19)	24-4-44	14-5-44	14-6-44
LSM 659 Nung Ra (ex-LSM 84)	22-8-44	15-9-44	7-10-44
LSM 661 Sin Mi (ex-LSM 316)	6-4-44	18-6-44	21-7-44
LSM 662 Ul Rung (ex-LSM 17)	10-4-44	7-5-44	12-6-44

Ko Mun (LSM 655)—old number L. & L. Van Ginderen

D: 520 tons (1,095 fl) **S:** 13 kts **Dim:** 62.0 × 10.52 × 2.53
A: 2/40-mm AA (II × 1)—4/20-mm AA (I × 4)
Electric: 240 kw **Fuel:** 160 tons
M: 2 Fairbanks-Morse 38D8⅛ × 10 diesels; 2 props; 2,880 hp **Man:** 75 tot.

Remarks: *Pung To* has mine rails on the vehicle deck, mine-laying ports through the stern. Sisters *Tae Cho* (LSM 651, ex-U.S. LSM 546), *Tyo To* (LSM 652, ex-U.S. LSM 268), and *Ka Tok* (LSM 653, ex-U.S. LSM 462) stricken 1982. *Pung To* (ex-LSM 54), with minelaying capability stricken 1984.

Note: Ex-U.S. Navy amphibious fire-support ship *Si Hung* (ex-St. Joseph River, LSMR 527) reported stricken 1984.

◆ 6 U.S. LCU 1610-class utility landing craft Bldr: So. Korea (In serv. 1979-81)

Mulkae 72-77

D: 190 tons (390 fl) **S:** 11 kts **Dim:** 41.07 × 9.07 × 2.08
A: 4/20-mm AA (II × 2)
M: 4 G.M. 6-71 diesels; 2 Kort-nozzle props; 1,200 hp
Fuel: 13 tons **Range:** 1,200/11 **Man:** 6 tot.

Remarks: Cargo capacity: 143 tons; cargo deck 30.5 × 5.5. Copies of U.S. design with higher pilothouse; built with imported equipment.

◆ 1 LCU 501-class utility landing craft Bldr: Bison SB, Buffalo, N.Y.

Mulkae 71 (ex-U.S. LCU 531) (L: 5-9-43)

D: 309 tons (fl) **S:** 10 kts **Dim:** 36.3 × 10.0 × 1.14 **A:** 2/20-mm AA (I × 2)
M: 3 Gray Marine 6-71 diesels; 2 props; 675 hp **Man:** 12 tot.

Remarks: Transferred 1960.

◆ 10 ex-U.S. Army LCM(8)-class landing craft

D: 95-115 tons (fl) **S:** 9-12 kts **Dim:** 22.7 × 6.4 × 1.4
M: 4 G.M. 6-71 diesels; 2 props; 600 hp

Remarks: Transferred 9-78.

Note: South Korea also builds glass-reinforced plastic-hulled versions of the U.S. LCVP landing craft.

AUXILIARIES

◆ 2 ex-U.S. Tonti-class gasoline tankers Bldr: Todd SB, Houston, Tex.

		L	In serv.
AO 55 N.	(ex-*Rincon,* T-AOG 77, ex-*Tarland*)	5-1-45	10-45
AO 56 N.	(ex-*Petaluma,* T-AOG 79, ex-*Raccoon Bend*)	9-8-45	11-45

D: 2,100 tons (6,047 fl) **S:** 10 kts **Dim:** 99.1
M: 2 Nordberg diesels; 1 prop; 1,400 hp **Electric:** 515 kw
Fuel: 154 tons **Range:** 6,000/10 **Man:** 41 tot.

Remarks: 3,160 grt/3,933 dwt. Cargo 31,284 bbl. light fuels (diesel, JP-5 gasoline). Acquired from Maritime Commission by U.S. Navy 1-7-50 and 7-9-50, respectively. Leased 21-2-82. Will probably be armed.

◆ 1 ex-Norwegian oiler Bldr: Bergens Mekanske Verksteder, Norway (In serv. 1951)

AO 2 Chun Ji (ex-*Birk*)

D: 1,400 tons (4,160 fl) **S:** 12 kts **Dim:** 90.65 (84.0 pp) × 13.56 × 5.35
A: 1/40-mm AA—2/20-mm AA
M: 1 Sulzer 6 TD 48 diesel; 1 prop; 1,800 hp **Man:** 73 tot.

Remarks: Bought in 1953. The *Puchon* of the same class was lost 5-71. Can replenish alongside while underway.

◆ 2 ex-U.S. 174-foot class tankers

	Bldr	L	In serv.
YO 1 Ku Kyong (ex-YO 118)	R.T.C. SB, Camden, N.J.	6-5-44	8-8-44
YO 6 N. (ex-YO 179)	Smith SY, Pensacola, Fla.	24-11-44	26-5-45

D: 1,400 tons (fl) **S:** 7 kts **Dim:** 53.0 × 10.0 × 4.0
M: 1 Union diesel; 1 prop; 560 hp **Fuel:** 25 tons **Man:** 36 tot.

Remarks: YO 1 transferred 1946, YO 6 in 9-71. Cargo: 900 tons.

◆ 1 ex-U.S. YO 55 class tanker Bldr: R.T.C. SB, Camden, N.J.

	Laid down	L	In serv.
Hwa Chon (ex-*Derrick,* YO 59)	15-6-42	21-11-42	2-2-43

D: 800 tons (2,700 fl) **S:** 10 kts **Dim:** 71.65 × 11.3 × 4.8
M: 2 Fairbanks-Morse 37E14-5 diesels; 2 props; 1,150 hp **Electric:** 160 kw
Fuel: 105 tons **Range:** 4,600/8 **Man:** 46 tot.

Remarks: Transferred 4-55. Cargo: 1,600 tons.

Note: The last serving ex-U.S. Army FS 331-class small cargo ship, *Ma San* (AKL 909, ex-U.S. AKL 35, ex-*Lt. Thomas W. Weigle,* FS 383) was stricken during 1984.

◆ 2 ex-U.S. Diver-class salvage ships Bldr: Basalt Rock Co., Napa, Cal.

	Laid down	L	In serv.
ARS 26 Chang Won (ex-*Grasp,* ARS 24)	27-4-43	31-7-43	22-8-44
ARS 27 Gum I (ex-*Deliver,* ARS 23)	2-4-43	25-9-43	18-7-44

D: 1,530 tons (1,970 fl) **S:** 14.8 kts **Dim:** 65.1 × 12.5 × 4.0
A: 2/20-mm AA **Electron Equipt:** Radar: 1/SPS-53
M: 4 Cooper-Bessemer GSB 8 diesels; electric drive; 2 props; 2,440 hp
Electric: 460 kw **Fuel:** 300 tons
Range: 9,000/14; 20,000/7 **Man:** 83 tot.

Remarks: ARS 5 transferred 31-3-78; ARS 6 on 15-8-79, both by sale. Equipped for salvage, diver support, and towing.

◆ 2 U.S. Sotoyomo-class auxiliary tugs

	Bldr	Laid down	L	In serv.
ATA 3 Do Bang (ex-*Pinola,* ATA 206)	Gulfport Boiler Wks, Port Arthur, Tex.	26-10-44	14-12-44	10-2-45
ATA 2 Yong Mun (ex-*Keosangua,* ATA 198)	Levingston, SB, Orange, Tex.	14-12-44	17-1-45	19-3-45

D: 835 tons (fl) **S:** 13 kts **Dim:** 43.6 (40.7 pp) × 10.3 × 4.0
A: 1/76-mm Mk 22 DP—4/20-mm AA (II × 2)
M: 2 G.M. 12-278A diesels, electric drive; 1 prop; 1,500 hp
Electric: 120 kw **Fuel:** 158 tons **Man:** 45 tot.

Remarks: Transferred 2-62. ATA 3 is used in salvage work. There are also about nine harbor tugs, including YTL 13 (ex-U.S.N. YTL 550), YTL 22 (ex-Army ST 2097), YTL 23 (ex-Army ST 2099), YTL 25 (ex-Army YT 2106), YTL 26 (ex-Army ST 2065), and YTL 30 (ex-Army ST 2101). All transferred 1968-72.

Note: There are also about 35 yard and service craft.

KOREAN HYDROGRAPHIC SERVICE

Subordinate to the Ministry of Transport.

◆ 2 ex-Belgian Herstal-class inshore minesweepers

	L
Suro 5 (ex-*Temse,* ex-MSI 470)	6-8-56
Suro 6 (ex-*Tournai,* ex-MSI 481)	18-5-57

D: 160 tons (190 fl) **S:** 15 kts **Dim:** 34.5 × 6.6 × 2.1
M: 2 diesels; 2 props; 630 hp **Range:** 2,300/10 **Man:** 10 tot.

Remarks: Built in Belgium with U.S. funds. Transferred 3-70. Wooden hulls.

KOREA-SOUTH *(continued)*
KOREAN HYDROGRAPHIC SERVICE *(continued)*

◆ **1 ex-U.S. YMS-1-class minesweeper**

Suro 3 (ex-U.S. Coast Geodetic Survey *Hodgson*)

D: 289 tons (fl) **S:** 15 kts **Dim:** 44.6 × 8.1 × 3.0
M: 2 G.M. 8-268 diesels; 2 props; 1,000 hp

Remarks: Converted post–World War II as a coastal survey ship. Wooden hull. Launched 1943, transferred 1968.

◆ **3 inshore survey craft**

Suro 7, Suro 8: 30 tons
Suro 2: 145 tons

COAST GUARD

The Republic of Korea Coast Guard operates about 25 seagoing patrol boats and several hundred small craft. Several new classes have been built, in unknown numbers:

◆ **1 (or more) HDP 1000-class patrol ships** Bldr: Korea SB & Eng., Pusan

HDP 1000 class Korea SB & Eng.

D: 1,200 tons (1,450 fl) **S:** 21.5 kts **Dim:** 80.50 × 8.90 × 3.15
A: 1/40-mm Mk 3 AA—2/20-mm AA (I × 2)
Electron Equipt: Radar: 2/navigational
M: 2 SEMT-Pielstick 12 PA6-280 diesels; 2 props; 9,600 hp
Electric: . . . **Range:** 7,000/18 **Man:** 11 officers, 58 men

Remarks: A lower-powered and more lightly armed version of the *An Yang Ho*-class frigates built for the Navy. Passive-tank stabilization system. First (and possibly only) unit completed about 1982. Engines built in Japan under license.

◆ **3 "Sea Whale"-class patrol boats**

	Bldr	In serv.
505	Korea SB & Eng., Pusan	3-80
5. . .	Korea-Tacoma SY, Chinhae	5-79
5. . .	Korea-Tacoma SY, Chinhae	7-82

"Sea Whale/Sea Dragon" class Korea-Tacoma

D: 410 tons (580 fl) **S:** 24 kts **Dim:** 60.8 × 8.0 × 2.29
A: 1/40-mm AA—2/20-mm AA—2/7.62-mm mg (I × 2)
M: 2 MTU diesels; 2 props; 9,600 hp
Range: 1,500/25; 2,400/20 **Man:** 11 officers, 28 men

Remarks: Intended for rescue and inspection duties. Flume-type passive tank roll stabilization.

◆ **4 "Sea Shark"-class patrol boats** Bldr: Hyundai SB and Korea Tacoma SB.

"Sea Shark/Sea Wolf" class Hyundai

"Sea Shark/Sea Wolf" class Korea-Tacoma

D: 250 tons (280 fl) **S:** 28 kts **Dim:** 48.2 × 7.1 × 2.1 (2.5 over props)
A: 4/20-mm AA (II × 2 or II × 1, I × 2)—2/12.7-mm mg
M: 2 diesels; 2 props; 7,320 hp
Range: 3,300/15 **Man:** 5 officers, 24 men

Remarks: Some have a raised platform aft. Also offered as the "Sea Wolf" design by Korea-Tacoma SB. Range also given as 2,000 n.m. at 17 kts.

◆ . . . **"Sea Gull" class** Bldr: Korea SB & Eng.

D: 80 tons **S:** 30 kts **Dim:** 24.0 × 5.5 × . . .
A: . . . **M:** 2 diesels; 2 props; 3,920 hp
Range: 950/20 **Man:** 18 tot.

◆ . . . **"Swallow" class, glass-reinforced plastic construction**

D: 32 tons (fl) **S:** 25 tons **Dim:** 20.0 × 4.7 × 1.3
A: 1/12.7-mm mg—1/7.62-mm mg **Range:** 500/20
M: 2 G.M. 12V71 TI diesels; 2 props; 1,060 hp **Man:** 8 tot.

KUWAIT

State of Kuwait

Personnel (1984): Approx. 1,000 tot.

Merchant Marine (1984): 250 ships—2,551,074 grt (tankers: 28 ships—1,435,363 grt)

Naval Aviation: Six Aerospatiale AS.332F Super Puma helicopters armed with AM 39 Exocet missiles were ordered from France in 1983.

GUIDED-MISSILE PATROL BOATS

◆ **2 FPB 57 class** Bldr: Lürssen, Bremen-Vegesack, West Germany

	Laid down	L	In serv.
P 5702 Al Mubareki	. . .	. . .	8-83
P 5704 Sabhan	. . .	. . .	9-8-84

GUIDED-MISSILE PATROL BOATS *(continued)*

Sabhan (P 5704) French Navy, 7-84

D: 353 tons (398 fl) **S:** 36 kts **Dim:** 58.10 (54.40 wl) × 7.62 × 2.83
A: 4/MM 40 Exocet (II × 2)—1/76-mm OTO Melara DP—2/40-mm Breda AA (II × 1)—2/7.62-mm mg—mines
Electron Equipt: Radar: 1/Decca 1226, 1/9LV200 search, 1/9LV228 director, 1/Marconi S810
EW: MEL Matilda, 1/Dagaie chaff RL
M: 4 MTU 16V956 TB91 diesels; 4 props; 18,000 hp
Electric: 405 kVA **Range:** 700/35 **Man:** 4 officers, 35 men

Remarks: Ordered 1980. Function as leaders for the six TNC-45 class. Scheduled completion dates were 11-82 and 4-83. Marconi S810 search radar is in radome aft, Dagaie launcher and optical director for the 40-mm gunmount are amidships.

◆ **6 TNC-45 class** Bldr: Lürssen, Bremen-Vegesack, West Germany

	L	In serv.		L	In serv.
P 4501 Al Boom (ex-*Werjiya*)	3-82	8-82	P 4507 Al Sa'Dani (ex-*Istiqlal*)	12-82	9-8-84
P 4503 Al Betteel (ex-*Mashuwah*)	4-82	9-82	P 4509 Al Ahmadi	. . .	9-8-84
P 4505 Al Sanbouk (ex-*Jalboot*)	. . .	10-82	P 4511 Al Istiqlal (ex-*Al Mubareki*)	. . .	9-8-84

Al Ahmadi (P 4509) French Navy, 7-84

D: 231 tons (259 fl) **S:** 41.5 kts **Dim:** 44.90 (42.30 wl) × 7.00 × 2.40
A: 4/MM 40 Exocet—1/76-mm OTO Melara DP—2/40-mm Breda AA (II × 1)—2/7.62-mm mg (I × 2)
Electron Equipt: Radar: 1/Decca 1226, 1 PEAB/9LV200 search, 1 PEAB/9LV200 director
EW: MEL Matilda-intercept, 1 Dagaie chaff RL
M: 4 MTU 16V538 TB 92 diesels; 4 props; 15,600 hp (15,000 sust.)
Electric: 405 kw **Range:** 500/38.5; 1,500/16 **Man:** 5 officers, 27 men

Remarks: Ordered 1980. Carry 250 rounds 76-mm, 1,800 rounds 40-mm ammunition. Have CSEE Lynx optronic gun director for the 40-mm mount. Philips 9LV200 system for the 76-mm gun and missiles, and a flare rocket launcher amidships. First three accepted 26-4-84.

PATROL CRAFT

◆ **4 "Sea Gull" class** Bldr: Korea SB & Eng., Okpo (In serv. 1985-86)

D: 80 tons **S:** 30 kts **Dim:** 24.0 × 5.5 × . . .
A: . . . **M:** 2 diesels; 2 props; 3,920 hp
Range: 950/20 **Man:** 18 tot.

Remarks: Ordered 1985. Aluminum construction.

◆ **8 coastal patrol boats** Bldrs: Thornycroft, Woolston; first 2: Vosper Thornycroft

	L		L		L		L
Maymoon	4-68	Al Shurti	1972	Mashhoor	1969	Wathah	1970
Aman	3-68	Marzook	1969	Murshed	1970	Intisar	1972

D: 40 tons **S:** 20 kts **Dim:** 27.78 × 4.73 × 1.38
Electron Equipt: Radar: Decca 202 **Man:** 5 officers, 7 men
M: 2 Rolls-Royce 8-cyl. diesels; 2 props; 1,340 hp **Range:** 700/15

◆ **5 56-foot boats** Bldr: Vosper Thornycroft Private, Ltd., Singapore

Dastoor Kasar Qahir Sagar Salam

D: 25 tons (fl) **S:** 29-30 kts **Dim:** 17.1 × 4.9 × . . .
A: 2/7.62-mm mg (I × 2) **M:** 2 MTU 6V331 diesels; 2 props; 1,350 hp
Range: 320/20 **Man:** 2 officers, 6 men

Remarks: Steel hull, aluminum superstructure. First two ordered 9-73, in service 6-74; others ordered 1978, in service 1979.

◆ **1 U.S. Cutlass class** Bldr: Halter Marine, New Orleans, La.

Dhaher (In serv. 6-8-79)

D: 34 tons (fl) **S:** 32 kts **Dim:** 19.66 × 5.18 × 1.12
A: 2/12.7-mm mg (I × 2) **Man:** 15 tot.
M: 2 MTU 8V 331 TB92 diesels; 2 props; 1,730 hp

◆ **14 36-foot boats** Bldr: Vosper Thornycroft Private, Ltd., Singapore

Antar Al Salmi II Al Sebbah Istiqlal II
Qarah Warbah—plus 8 unnamed

Warbah Vosper, 1972

D: 6.8 tons (fl) **S:** 22 kts **Dim:** 11.1 × 3.3 × 0.6 **Man:** 4 tot.
A: 4/7.62-mm mg (II × 2) **M:** 2 Sabre 210 diesels; 2 props; 420 hp

Remarks: First four, in service 1972, and second four, in service 5-73, have no names. Wooden construction, nylon sheathed hulls.

◆ **27 Magnum Sedan class** Bldr: Magnum Marine, U.S.A.

D: . . . **S:** 60 kts **Dim:** 8.3 × 2.4 × 0.7 **Range:** 200/. . .
M: 2 Mercury Mercruiser inboard/outboard motors; 2 props; 660 hp

Remarks: High-speed craft for inshore work. Three delivered 1977, one in 1978, three in 1979. Twenty more ordered 6-84. Glass-reinforced plastic construction.

◆ **1 46-foot craft** Bldr: Thornycroft Ltd., Singapore (In serv. 1-76)

Mahroos

D: 21.5 tons (fl) **S:** 21.7 kts **Dim:** 14.1 × 4.5 × . . . **Man:** 1 officer, 4 men
A: 2/7.62-mm mg **M:** 2 Rolls-Royce C8M-410 diesels; 2 props; 780 hp

◆ **7 50-foot craft** Bldr: Thornycroft Ltd., Singapore (In serv. 1957-58)

MINE COUNTERMEASURES SHIPS

Note: Kuwait plans to add mine countermeasures units to its fleet and was holding discussions with Netherlands representatives during 11-84 over possibly ordering 4 units of the *Alkmaar* ("Tripartite") class.

AUXILIARIES

◆ **6 SR.N6 Mk 8 hovercraft** Bldr: British Hovercraft, Cowes, U.K.

D: 17 tons (fl) **S:** 50-55 kts **Dim:** 18.3 × 8.5 × . . .
M: 1 Rolls-Royce Gnome gas turbine; 1 airscrew, 1 lift fan; 1,060 hp
Range: 300 to 550 n.m./50-55 kts

Remarks: Ordered 1981. Can carry two 450-liter fuel cells on deck to increase range. Primarily for logistics support.

◆ **4 Loadmaster Mk II logistics support landing craft** Bldr: Fairey Marine, Cowes, U.K. (In serv. 1984-85)

D: 175 tons light (350 normal/420 fl) **S:** 10.5 kts (10.0 sust.)
Dim: 33.00 (30.00 pp) × 10.20 × 1.75
A: None **Electron Equipt:** Radar: 1/Decca nav.

KUWAIT *(continued)*
AUXILIARIES *(continued)*

Kuwaiti Loadmaster on trials Fairey Marine, 1984

M: 2 Caterpillar 3412 DITA (V-12) diesels; 2 Kort-nozzle props; 1,214 hp (1,010 sust.)
Range: 1,000/10 **Electric:** 72 kw **Fuel:** 30 tons **Man:** 1 officer, 6 men

Remarks: Ordered 1983. First pair completed 10-84. Cargo includes 150 tons on deck or 90 tons on deck and 60 tons liquid cargo. Can accommodate 2/60-ton tanks. Original design by Cheverton, taken over by Fairey in 1984.

◆ **3 logistics support landing craft** Bldr: Vosper Private, Ltd., Singapore (In serv. 1979-80)

Al Jahra Ceriff Hadiya

D: 320 tons (fl) **S:** 9.5 kts **Dim:** 32.3 × 7.5 × . . .
M: 2 Rolls-Royce C8M-410 diesels; 2 props; 750 hp **Range:** 1,500/9

Remarks: Unusual in having landing ramp at stern. Have full forecastle bow, low fantail like oilfield supply boats. Cargo: 170 tons, 100m² deck space. Carry 47 tons water ballast.

◆ **3 landing craft** Bldr: Vosper Thornycroft Private Ltd., Singapore

Waheed (In serv. 5-71) Regga (In serv. 5-71) Fareed (In serv. 11-75)

D: 88 tons (170 fl) **S:** 10 kts **Dim:** 27.0 × 6.9 × . . .
M: 2 Rolls-Royce C8M-410 diesels; 752 hp **Range:** 1,500/9 **Man:** 8 tot.

Remarks: Carry 40 tons deck cargo, 24.4 m³ cargo fuel, and 35.6 m³ water.

◆ **2 fireboat tugs** Bldr: Fairey Marine, Cowes, U.K. (In serv. 11-6-84)

Al Hangaf Al Mutlas

D: 67 tons (76 fl) **S:** 12 kts **Dim:** 21.00 (19.50 pp) × 5.90 × 2.15
M: 2 Caterpillar 3412 DITA (V-12) diesels; 2 props; 1,214 hp **Electric:** 72 kw

Remarks: Ordered 1983. Carry 1,000 liters firefighting foam and have a 4,500 l/min. firefighting monitor. Have 9.5-ton bollard pull. Can carry 50 deck passengers.

◆ **1 fireboat** Bldr: Vosper Thornycroft Private, Ltd., Singapore (In serv. 1978)

Waheed

D: 112.6 grt **S:** 26.6 kts **Dim:** 26.2 × 5.8 × . . .
M: 2 diesels; 2 props; 2,200 hp **Man:** 16 tot.

◆ **6 utility launches** Bldr: Fairey Marine, Cowes, U.K. (In serv. 11-6-84)

D: 3.3 tons (fl) **S:** . . . **Dim:** 8.23 × 2.74 × 0.84
M: 1 or 2 Perkins 4.236 diesel(s); 1/2 props; 72/144 hp **Man:** 3 tot.

Remarks: Four have 1 diesel, can carry 2 tons of cargo or 20 passengers. Two have 2 diesels, displace 3.8 tons, and can carry 1.5 tons cargo or 13 passengers. Glass-reinforced plastic construction. Ordered 1983.

LEBANON

Republic of Lebanon

Personnel: Approx. 200 men

Merchant Marine (1984): 251 ships—458,000 grt
(tankers: 4 ships—15,678 grt)

PATROL BOATS

Note: Semi-independent Christian forces have operated five Dabur-class patrol craft, transferred by Israel in 1976; for characteristics, see Israel section.

◆ **1 Tarablous class** Bldr: Chantiers Navals de l'Estérel, Cannes (L: 6-59)

Tarablous

Tarablous 1959

D: 105 tons (fl) **S:** 27 kts **Dim:** 38.0 × 5.5 × 1.75
A: 2/40-mm AA (I × 2) **M:** 2 Mercedes-Benz diesels; 2 props; 2,700 hp
Range: 1,500 **Man:** 3 officers, 16 men

Remarks: Wooden construction. In poor condition.

PATROL CRAFT

◆ **2 Tracker Mk II class** Fairey Allday Marine, Hamble, U.K.

N. . . . . . . (In serv. 28-1-80) N. . . . . . . (In serv. 8-2-80)

D: 31.5 tons (fl) **S:** 29 kts **Dim:** 19.25 × 4.98 × 1.45
A: . . . **M:** 2 G.M. 12V71 TI diesels; 2 props; 990 hp
Range: 650/20 **Man:** 11 tot.

Remarks: Intended primarily for customs service. One under Christian Militia control since 1983.

◆ **6 Aztec class** Bldr: Crestitalia, Ameglia, La Spezia, Italy (In serv. 1980)

CF 1001 to CF 1006

D: . . . **S:** . . . **Dim:** 9.0 × . . . × . . .
M: 2 diesels; 2 props; . . . hp

Remarks: Glass-reinforced plastic construction.

AMPHIBIOUS SHIPS

◆ **2 French EDIC-III class** Bldr: SFCN, Villeneuve-la-Garenne

Sour (In serv. 1-85) Damour (L: 11-12-84)

D: 375 tons (712 fl) **S:** 10 kts **Dim:** 59.00 (57.00 pp) × 11.90 × 1.67 (1.10 light)
A: 2/20-mm AA (I × 2)—1/81-mm mortar
Electron Equipt: Radar: 1/ . . . nav.
M: 2 SACM MGO 175-V12-A diesels; 2 props; 1,040 hp
Range: 1,800/10 **Fuel:** 35 tons **Man:** 18 crew + 33 troops

Remarks: Ordered 30-7-83 as aid from the French government. *Sour* replaced an earlier EDIC (L 9096) of the same name and loaned in 11-83. Can carry 11 trucks or 5 armored personnel carriers.

LIBERIA

Personnel (1984): 445 total

Merchant Marine (1984): 1,934 ships—62,024,700 grt
(tankers: 722 ships—41,487,497 grt)

Naval Aviation: One Cessna 337 is operated by the Coast Guard for surveillance.

COAST GUARD

PATROL CRAFT

◆ **3 CG 27 class** Bldr: Karlskrona Varvet, Sweden (In serv. 27-9-80)

8801 Master Sergeant Samuel K. Doe (ex-*Nuah River*)
8802 Albert Porte (ex-. . .)
8803 General Thomas Quiwoukpa (ex-. . .)

D: 50 tons **S:** 25 kts **Dim:** 26.72 × 5.23 × 1.13
A: 1/12.7-mm mg—2/7.62-mm mg (I × 2)
Electron Equipt: Radar: 1/Decca 1226C
M: 2 MTU 8V331 TC82 diesels; 2 props; 1,866 hp
Fuel: 11 tons **Range:** 1,000/18 **Man:** 8 tot.

Remarks: Aluminum alloy construction. Names changed due to revolution; all originally named for rivers. Same design as Swedish Coast Guard TV 102.

LIBERIA *(continued)*
PATROL CRAFT *(continued)*

Master Sergeant Samuel K. Doe (8801) 1980

◆ **2 U.S. 65-foot class** Bldr: Swiftships, Morgan City, La. (In serv. 22-7-76)

103 Cavilla 104 Mano

D: 38 tons (fl) **S:** 24 kts **Dim:** 19.8 × 5.8 × 0.8
A: 1/81-mm mortar combined with 12.7-mm mg—2/12.7-mm mg (I × 2)
M: 2 G.M. 12V71 TI diesels; 2 props; 1,920 hp
Range: 600/21.5 **Man:** 2 officers, 18 men

◆ **1 U.S. 42-foot class** Bldr: Swiftships, Morgan City, La. (In serv. 22-7-76)

101 St. Paul

D: 11 tons (12 fl) **S:** 20 kts **Dim:** 12.8 × 3.7 × 0.6
A: 2/12.7-mm mg (I × 2)
M: 2 G.M. 8V71 diesels; 2 props; 870 hp **Man:** 4 tot.

LIBYA

Socialist People's Libyan Arab Jamahiriya

Personnel: Approximately 3,000–4,000 men

Merchant Marine (1984): 105 ships—854,700 grt
(tankers: 16 ships—748,204 grt)

Naval Aviation: About 18 Soviet-supplied Mi-14 Haze, 6 French-supplied Super Frélon (with AM 39 Exocet anti-ship missiles and 25 ASW torpedoes), and 12 French Aloutte-III helicopters are in service for naval use.

SUBMARINES

Note: Two coastal submarines may have been ordered during 1982 in Yugoslavia, which has already delivered 6 *Mala*-class 2-man midget subs to Libya (2 in 1977, and 4 in 1981-82).

◆ **6 Soviet Foxtrot class** Bldr: Sudomekh SY, Leningrad

311 Al Badr 312 Al Fateh 313 Al Ahad 314 Al Mitraqah
315 Al Khyber 316 Al Hunayn

Al Ahad (313) 1978

D: 1,950/2,400 tons **S:** 18/16 kts **Dim:** 96.0 × 7.5 × 6.0
A: 10/533-mm TT (6 fwd, 4 aft)—22 torpedoes or 44 mines
Electron Equipt: Radar: Snoop Tray
Sonar: 1 med.-freq. active, passive arrays
M: 3 diesels, electric motors; 3 props; 5,300 hp **Endurance:** 70 days
Range: 11,000/8 (snorkel) **Man:** 8 officers, 70 men

Remarks: One transferred in 12-76, two in 1978, fourth commissioned 30-3-81 at Tripoli, fifth delivered 2-82, and sixth in 3-83.

FRIGATES

◆ **0 (+2) Soviet Koni class** Bldr: Zelenodolsk SY

N. . . . . . . N. . . . . . .

D: 1,900 tons (fl) **S:** 27 tons **Dim:** 95.0 × 12.8 × 4.2 (hull)
A: 1/SAN-4 system (II × 1, 20 missiles)—4/76.2-mm DP (II × 2)—4/30-mm AA (II × 2)—2/RBU-6000 ASW RL (XII × 2)—2/d.c. racks—mines
Electron Equipt: Radar: 1/Don-2, 1/Strut Curve, 1/Pop Group, 1/Hawk Screech, 1/Drum Tilt
Sonar: 1 med-freq. hull-mounted
EW: 2/Watch Dog, 1/chaff RL (XVI × 2)
M: 1 gas turbine of 15,000 hp, 2 diesels of 7,500 hp; 3 props; 30,000 hp
Range: 1,800/14

Remarks: Part of the arms package that included the 4 Nanuchka II missile corvettes. Will probably be delivered in the tropical variant with a long deckhouse amidships housing air-conditioned equipment. The depth-charge racks (10 charges each) bolt to the mine rails. Very limited endurance and obsolescent equipment limits their potential utility. Delivery still anticipated, possibly in 1986-87.

Note: A training frigate, similar to those built for Indonesia and Iraq, may have been ordered in Yugoslavia during 1982.

◆ **1 Vosper Mk 7** Bldr: Vosper Thornycroft, Woolston, U.K.

	Laid down	L	In serv.
F 211 Dat Assawari	27-9-68	9-69	1-2-73

Dat Assawari (F 211)—on trials C. Martinelli, 5-84

D: 1,325 tons (1,650 fl) **S:** 37/17 kts **Dim:** 101.6 (94.5 pp) × 11.08 × 3.36
A: 4/Otomat Mk 2 SSM (I × 4)—1/114-mm Mk 8 DP—1/Albatros Mk 2 SAM syst. (IV × 1; Aspide missiles)—2/40-mm AA (I × 2)—2/35-mm Oerlikon AA (II × 1)—6/324-mm ILAS-3 ASW TT (III × 2)
Electron Equipt: Radar: 1/RAN-10S, 1/RAN-12, 1/navigational, 2/Orion RTN-10X
Sonar: 1/Diodon (TSM 2310)
EW: Decca RDS-1, Selenia INS-1 passive, U.K. FH-12 HFD/F
M: CODOG: 2 Rolls-Royce TM 2A Olympus gas turbines, 24,000 hp each; 2 Paxman Ventura diesels, 1,900 hp each; 2 CP props
Fuel: 300 tons **Range:** 1,000/36; 5,700/17 **Man:** 132 tot.

Remarks: Began refitting in Italy, 1979; damaged by bomb 29-10-80. Ran trials in 3-83 and recommissioned 1-10-83, but did not return to Libya until 6-85. Sea Cat SAM and Limbo ASW mortar replaced by 4-cell Albatros launcher and ASW TT for A244 torpedoes. Received Selenia RAN-12L/X (IPN-10) combat data system. Otomat, new radars, sonar added. Has two NA-10 Mod. 2 gun/missile f.c.s.

CORVETTES

◆ **4 Soviet Nanuchka II class** Bldr: Petrovskiy SY, Leningrad

416 Tariq Ibn Ziyad (ex-*Ain Mara*) (In serv. 10-81)
417 N. . . . . . . (ex-*Ain al Gazala*) (In serv. 7-2-83)
418 N. . . . . . . (ex-*Ain Zaara*) (In serv. 10-83)
419 N. . . . . . . (ex-*Ain Zaquit*) (In serv. 8-85)

D: 770 tons (fl) **S:** 32 kts **Dim:** 59.3 × 12.6 × 2.4
A: 4/SS-N-2c Styx SSM (II × 2)—1/SA-N-4 system (II × 1, 20 missiles)—2/57-mm AA (II × 2)
Electron Equipt: Radar: 1/Don-2, 1/Square Tie (in Band Stand radome), 1/Pop Group, 1/Muff Cob
EW: 1/Bell Tap passive array, 2/chaff RL (XVI × 2)
M: 3 M507 diesels; 3 props; 24,000 hp **Man:** 60 tot.
Range: 900/30; 2500/12 (1 engine)

Remarks: Reason for slow delivery rate unknown. Considered to be poor sea boats by some customers, with unreliable propulsion plants (M507 is a double M503, 42-cylinder radial engine).

CORVETTES *(continued)*

Tariq Ibn Ziyad (416) U.S. Navy, 10-81

Ex-Ain Al Gazala (417) P. Voss, 1-83

◆ **4 Wadi M'ragh class** Bldr: CNR, Riva Trigoso, Italy

	L	In serv.
C 412 Assad Al Bihar (ex-*Wadi M'ragh*)	29-4-77	14-9-77
C 413 Assad Al Tougour (ex-*Wadi Majer*)	20-4-78	12-2-80
C 414 Assad Al Kalij (ex-*Wadi Mercit*)	15-12-78	28-3-81
C 415 Assad Al Hudud (ex-*Wadi Megrawa*)	21-6-79	28-3-81

Assad Al Bihar CNR, 1979

Assad Al Bihar—on trials CNR, 1979

D: 547 tons (630 fl) **S:** 34 kts **Dim:** 61.7 (57.8 pp) × 9.3 × 2.7
A: 4/Otomat Mk I SSM—1/76-mm OTO Melara DP—2/35-mm Oerlikon AA (II × 1)—6/324-mm ASW TT (III × 2)—16 mines
Electron Equipt: Radar: 1/RAN 11 L/X, 1/Decca TM 1226, 1/Orion RTN-10X
Sonar: Thomson-CSF Diodon
EW: Selenia INS-1 intercept
M: 4 MTU 16V956 TB91 diesels; 4 CP props; 16,400 hp **Electric:** 650 kw
Fuel: 126 tons **Range:** 1,400/33; 4,150/18 **Man:** 58 tot.

Remarks: Ordered in 1974. Completion delayed by prolonged trials. Have fin stabilizers, automatic degaussing system, Selenia IPN-10 combat data system, 1/NA 10 Mod. 3 GFCS, with 2C03 optical backup director. Can maintain 31.5 kts sea speed. Names changed 1981. Poorly maintained.

◆ **1 Vosper Mk 1B**

	Bldr	L	In serv.
C 411 Tobruk	Vosper, Ltd., Portsmouth	29-7-65	20-4-66

Tobruk (C 411) Shbldg. And Shipping Record, 1966

D: 440 tons (500 fl) **S:** 18 kts **Dim:** 53.95 (48.77 pp) × 8.68 × 4.0
A: 1/102-mm—4.40-mm AA (I × 4) **Range:** 2,900/14 **Man:** 5 officers, 58 men
M: 2 Paxman Ventura YJCM diesels; 2 props; 3,800 hp **Fuel:** 60 tons

Remarks: Launched in 1965. Anti-rolling devices, air-conditioned living spaces. No ASW equipment. Can be used as a yacht. Low muzzle velocity, 102-mm gun has low-angle elevation only. Refitted and modernized at Taskizak Naval Shipyard, Turkey, during 1983-84.

GUIDED-MISSILE PATROL BOATS

◆ **0 (+4) Type 400 class** Bldr: Kraljevica SY, Yugoslavia

D: 385 tons (525 fl) **S:** 34 kts **Dim:** 54.80 (51.88 pp) × 8.96 (8.16 wl) × 2.46
A: 4/SS-N-2C Styx (I × 4)—1/76-mm OTO Melara Compact DP—2/40-mm Breda Dardo AA (II × 1)—2/20-mm AA (I × 2)—2/7.62-mm mg (I × 2)
Electron Equipt: Radar: . . .
M: 4 MTU 20V538 TB92 diesels; 4 props; 1,400 hp
Range: . . . **Endurance:** 15 days **Man:** . . .

Remarks: Ordered 12-84 or 1-85. Have chaff rocket launchers on the 76-mm gunmount. Draft given is at 455-ton normal displacement.

◆ **10 French Combattante-II class** Bldr: CMN, Cherbourg

	Laid down	L	In serv.
518 Sharara (ex-*Beir Grassa*)	13-3-78	28-6-79	9-2-82
522 Shehab (ex-*Beir Gzir*)	10-6-78	22-1-80	4-3-82
524 Wahg (ex-*Beir Gtifa*)	30-1-79	20-5-80	29-5-82
526 Waheed (ex-*Beir Glulud*)	20-10-79	30-9-80	8-9-82
528 Shouaiai (ex-*Beir Algandula*)	12-9-79	14-1-81	2-11-82
532 Shoula (ex-*Beir Alkitat*)	17-12-79	3-81	29-10-82
534 Shafak (ex-*Beir Alkirim*)	11-3-80	23-6-81	17-12-82
536 Bark (ex-*Beir Alkardmen*)	9-6-80	6-10-81	11-3-83
538 Rad (ex-*Beir Alkur*)	20-10-80	30-11-81	19-5-83
542 Laheeb (ex-*Beir Alkuesat*)	20-1-81	9-1-82	29-7-83

Waheed (526) Ceclant/Premar, 4-82

GUIDED-MISSILE PATROL BOATS *(continued)*

Waheed (526)—with old name French Navy: Ceclant/Premar, 4-82

D: 258 tons (311 fl) **S:** 39 kts **Dim:** 49.0 (46.2 pp) × 7.1 × 2.4 (2.0 hull)
A: 4/Otomat SSM (II × 2)—1/76-mm OTO Melara DP—2/40-mm Breda/Bofors AA
Electron Equipt: Radar: 1/Triton search, 1/Castor tracking, 1/Vega II fire-control (all Thomson-CSF)
M: 4 MTU 20V538 TB91 diesels; 4 props; 18,000 hp **Range:** 1,600/15
Man: 8 officers, 19 men

REMARKS: Ordered 5-77. Delivery of first three embargoed 2-81 to 12-81. Names changed 1983. Delivery of final unit embargoed until 2-1-84.

◆ **12 Soviet Osa-II class**

205 AL KATUM	209 AL NABHAR	956 AL ZUARA
206 AL O'WAKH	210 AL FIKAR	. . . AL MWASH
207 AL RWAE	952 AL SAFHAA	. . . AL BTAR
208 AL BAIDA	954 AL ZAKAB	. . . AL SIDD

Libyan Osa-II 1978

NOTE: Hull numbers are in Arabic script to starboard, Western to port.

D: 210 tons (240 fl) **S:** 34 kts **Dim:** 38.6 × 7.6 × 2.0
A: 4/SS-N-2 Styx SSM (I × 4)—4/30-mm AA (II × 2)
Electron Equipt: Radar: 1/Square Tie, 1/Drum Tilt
IFF: 2/Square Head, 1/High Pole
M: 3 M504 diesels; 3 props; 15,000 hp **Range:** 500/34; 750/25 **Man:** 30 tot.

REMARKS: One transferred in 1976, four in 1977, one in 1978, three in 1979, one in 4-80, one in 5-80, and the twelfth in 7-80. Reportedly, the original order was reduced from twenty-four to twelve.

◆ **3 Sölöven class** Bldr: Vosper, Ltd, Portsmouth

	L	In serv.		L	In serv.
P 512 SUSA	31-8-67	8-68	P 514 SEBHA (ex-*Sokna*)	29-2-68	1-69
P 513 SIRTE	10-1-68	4-68			

Susa (P 512)—firing a wire-guided missile Vosper, 1968

D: 95 tons (115 lf) **S:** 50 kts **Dim:** 30.38 (27.44 pp) × 7.3 × 2.15
A: 8/SS 12 SSM (II × 4)—2/40-mm AA (I × 2)
M: CODOG: 3 Bristol-Siddeley Proteus gas turbines; 3 props; 12,750 hp; 2 G.M. 6-71 cruising diesels; 190 hp
Man: 20 tot.

REMARKS: Modeled on the Danish *Sölöven* class. All-wood construction, nylon-sheathed hull. Missiles are wire-guided and are not very accurate, particularly at high speeds.Cruise diesels are on outboard propeller shafts. Refitted in Italy 1984-85, with new engines and new electronics.

PATROL BOATS AND CRAFT

◆ **6 Yugoslav PB 90 class** Bldr: Tito Brodotekhnika SY, Belgrade (In serv. 1985-86)

D: 90 tons (fl) **S:** 27 kts **Dim:** 30.3 × 5.9 × . . .
A: 1/40-mm Bofors AA—4/20-mm AA (IV × 1)
Electron Equipt: Radar: 1/Decca 1226
M: 3 MTU diesels; 3 props; 4,350 hp **Man:** 17 tot.

REMARKS: Ordered 1984. May have a small, high-frequency sonar.

◆ **14 SAR 33-class patrol boats** Bldr: Taskizak SY, Turkey (In serv. 1982-84)

D: 150 tons (170 fl) **S:** 40 kts **Dim:** 34.5 × 8.60 × 1.85
A: 1/40-mm AA—2/12.7-mm mg (I × 2)
M: 3 SACM AGO V16CSHR; 3 CP props; 12,000 hp **Electric:** 300 kw
Fuel: 18 tons **Range:** 400/35; 1,000/. . . **Man:** 23 tot.

REMARKS: Ordered early 1980 to replace the earlier customs units in service. Wedge-shaped hull of remarkable steadiness at high speeds in heavy seas. Aluminum alloy construction. May be of a lengthened variant, 37.5 m overall. Designed by Abeking & Rasmussen, West Germany. Half reportedly delivered by end of 1983.

◆ **2 patrol boats** Bldr: Müller, Hameln, West Germany (In serv. 1-78)

JIHAD SALAM

D: 120 tons (fl) **S:** 27 kts **Dim:** 37.0 × 6.2 × . . .
A: 4/30-mm Hispano-Suiza GCM AO2 AA
M: MTU diesels; . . . props; . . . hp
Range: 1,100/27 **Man:** 21

REMARKS: Ordered for Lebanon, but when that country could not pay, sold to Libya 1-78. Transferred to Palestine Liberation Organization control in 8-81 and kept in Syria.

◆ **4 Brooke type** Bldr: Brooke Marine, Lowestoft, U.K. (In serv. 1968-70)

PC 1 ZLEITAN (ex-*Garian*)	PC 3 MERAWA
PC 2 KHAWLAN	PC 4 SABRATHA

D: 100 tons (125 fl) **S:** 23.5 kts **Dim:** 36.58 × 7.16 × 1.75
A: 1/40-mm—1/20-mm AA
M: 2 Paxman Ventura 10 YJCM diesels; 2 props; 3,600 hp
Range: 1,800/13 **Man:** 22 tot.

REMARKS: Have the same engines as the *Tobruk* and the *Zeltin.* At least one has a Soviet BM-21 multiple 122-mm rocket launcher (XX × 1) in place of the 20-mm AA gun. PC 1 renamed to commemorate former repair craft, 1982. Refitted at Taskizak Naval SY, Turkey, in 1983-84.

◆ **3 security craft** Bldr: Vosper Thornycroft, Portsmouth (In serv. 1967-69)

BENINA HOMS MISURATA

D: 100 tons **S:** 18-20 kts **Dim:** 30.5 × 6.4 × 1.7
A: 1/20-mm AA **M:** 3 Rolls-Royce diesels; 1,740 hp
Range: 1,800/14 **Man:** 15 tot.

REMARKS: Used for customs and fishery protection. Sisters *Ar Rakib, Farwa,* and *Akrama* ceded to Malta, 1978.

NOTE: Upwards of 50 radio-controlled suicide boats of Swedish and Cyprian construction are said to be in service for coast defense. No details available, except that speeds of 30 knots are attainable.

MINE WARFARE SHIPS

NOTE: Libya has laid several minefields, apparently employing the naval roll-on/roll-off cargo ship *El Timsah* and her merchant sister *Ghat,* with mine rails on the vehicle deck for the purpose.

◆ **7 (+1) Soviet Natya-class fleet minesweepers**

111 AL I'SAR (ex-*Ras el Gelais*)	119 AL. . . (ex-*Ras al Oula*)
113 AL TAYYAR (ex-*Ras Hadad*)	121 AL. . . (ex-*Ras al Dawar*)
115 AL. . . (ex-*Ras al Hamman*)	123 N. . . (ex-*Ras Massad*)
117 AL. . . (ex-*Ras al Falluga*)	125 AL. . . (ex- . . .)

D: 650 tons (750 fl) **S:** 18 kts **Dim:** 61.0 × 9.8 × 3.0
A: 4/30-mm AA (II × 2)—4/25-mm AA (II × 2)—2/RBU 1200 ASW RL (V × 2)—mines
Electron Equipt: Radar: 1/Don-2, 1/Drum Tilt
Sonar: . . .
IFF: 2/Square Head, 1/High Pole B
M: 2 diesels; 2 props; 5,000 hp **Range:** 1,600/16; 5,200/10 **Man:** 50 tot.

REMARKS: First pair delivered 3-81; second pair in 2-83; fifth on 3-9-83, the sixth during 2-84, and the seventh on 20-1-85; one more expected. Like the six built for India, they lack the ramp at the stern found on Soviet units.

MINE WARFARE SHIPS *(continued)*

ex-Ras Al Oula (119) P. Voss, 8-83

Libyan Natya No. 115 (as Ras Al Hamman) L. & L. Van Ginderen, 1-83

AMPHIBIOUS WARFARE SHIPS

◆ **3 Soviet Polnocny-C-class landing ships** Bldr: Poland

112 Ibn Al Hadrami 116 Ibn Omayar 118 Ibn El Farat

Libyan Polnocny-C class 1979

D: 1,150 tons (fl) **S:** 18 kts **Dim:** 81.3 × 10.1 × 2.1
A: 4/30-mm AA (II × 2)—2/122-mm artillery RL (XV × 2)
Electron Equipt: Radar: 1/Spin Trough, 1/Drum Tilt
M: 2 diesels; 2 props; 5,000 hp

Remarks: One transferred in 12-77 and two in 6-79. Like the Iraqi examples of this Polish-built class of medium landing ships, these export versions have a raised helicopter deck forward of the superstructure. A fourth Libyan unit, the *Ibn Al Qyis* (113), was lost on 14 or 15 September 1978 through fire at sea.

◆ **2 Ibn Ouf-class landing ships** Bldr: C.N.I.M., La Seyne

	Laid down	L	In serv.
132 Ibn Ouf	1-4-76	22-10-76	11-3-77
134 Ibn Harissa	18-4-77	18-10-77	10-3-78

Ibn Harissa (134) C. Martinelli, 1981

D: 2,800 tons (fl) **S:** 15 kts **Dim:** 100.0 × 15.65 × 2.6
A: 6/40-mm Breda AA (II × 3)—1/81-mm mortar
M: 2 SEMT-Pielstick diesels; 2 CP props; 5,340 hp
Range: 4,000/14 **Man:** 35 crew + 240 troops

Remarks: Cargo: 570 tons, including up to eleven tanks. Helicopter platform aft.

◆ **25 (+25) Turkish C 107-class large landing craft** Bldr: Taskizak SY, Istanbul, and Gölçük Naval SY

Ras El Hilel (ex-Turk Ç 132) El Kobayat (ex-Turk Ç 133)
Ibn Al Idrissi (ex-Turk Ç 130) Ibn Marwan (ex-Turk Ç 131) and 21 others

D: 280 tons (600 fl) **S:** 10 kts (8.5 loaded) **Dim:** 56.56 × 11.58 × 1.25
A: 2/20-mm AA (I × 2) **M:** 3 G.M. 6-71 TI diesels; 3 props; 900 hp
Range: 600/10; 1,100/8 **Man:** 15 tot.

Remarks: Cargo: Five heavy tanks, up to 100 troops; up to 350 tons. Design follows World War II-era British LCT(4). Cargo deck 28.5 × 7.9 m. Ordered 7-12-79, with first two taken from among ships built for Turkish Navy and delivered 7-12-79. As many as 50 may be acquired, with each Turkish yard building 25. Presumably M. Khadafi has designs on a near-neighbor's territory, as these ships are unsuitable for extended voyages. Sixteen were delivered by 4-81.

AUXILIARY SHIPS

◆ **1 support ship for small combatants**

	Bldr	Laid down	L	In serv.
711 Zeltin	Vosper Thornycroft, Woolston	1967	29-2-68	23-1-69

Zeltin (711) 1968

D: 2,200 tons (2,470 fl) **S:** 15 kts **Dim:** 98.72 (91.44 wl) × 14.64 × 3.05
A: 2/40-mm AA (I × 2)
M: 2 Paxman Ventura 16 YSCM diesels; 2 props; 3,500 hp
Electric: 800 kw **Range:** 3,000/14 **Man:** 15 officers, 86 men

Remarks: The well deck, 41 × 12, can receive small craft that draw up to 2.3 m. Hydraulically controlled stern gate. A movable crane (3-ton loading capacity) is available for the well deck, and a 9-ton crane on the port side supports the workshops.

◆ **1 ex-Italian Espresso-class roll-on/roll-off transport** Bldr: CN Luigi Orlando, Livorno (In serv. 9-71)

El Timsah (ex-*Espresso Veneto*)

D: 5,000 tons (fl) **S:** 19 kts **Dim:** 105.3 (96.5 pp) × 17.5 × 5.1
M: 2 Fiat V18 diesels; 2 CP props; 9,000 hp

Remarks: Has fin stabilizers. Used as military transport and as a minelayer. Purchased 1972; delivered 30-12-72 after refit. Berths for 100 troops. Merchant sister *Ghat* believed to have laid the 1983 Red Sea minefield.

◆ **1 Yugoslav Spasilac-class submarine rescue ship** Bldr: Tito Sy, Belgrade

722 Zlatica

D: 1,590 tons (fl) **S:** 13 kts **Dim:** 55.50 × 12.00 × 3.84 (4.34 props)
A: 4/14.5-mm mg (II × 2) **Electric:** 540 kVA
M: 2 diesels; 2 CP props; 4,340 hp **Man:** 53 tot.

Remarks: Delivered to Tripoli late in 1982. Intended to support the six Foxtrot-class submarines. Has decompression chamber, extensive diving equipment, can lay a 4-point moor, and can tow. Carries 490 tons cargo fuel.

◆ **1 small transport**

El Fateh (ex-Panamanian *Mebo II*)

D: 640 grt **S:** 10.5 kts **Dim:** 44.00 × 8.90 × 3.20
M: 2 Sulzer diesels

Remarks: Acquired 1977.

◆ **3 harbor tugs** Bldr: Jonker & Stans SY, The Netherlands (In serv. 1980)

A 33 A 34 A 35

D: 150 grt **S:** . . . **Dim:** 26.60 × 7.90 × 2.48
M: 2 diesels; 2 Voith-Schneider vertical-cycloidal props; . . . hp

Remarks: Two 17.00 × 6.25 × 2.75 harbor tugs were delivered at the same time.

LIBYA *(continued)*
AUXILIARY SHIPS *(continued)*

◆ **4 Ras El Helal-class tugs** Bldr: Mondego, Foz, Portugal

	In serv.		In serv.
Ras El Helal	22-10-77	Al Keriat	17-2-78
Al Shweiref	17-2-78	Al Tabkah	29-7-78

D: 200 grt **S:** 14 kts **Dim:** 34.8 × 9.0 × 4.0 (moulded depth)
M: 2 diesels; 2 props; 2,300 hp

◆ **1 Soviet Yelva-class diving tender**

Al Manjad (ex-VM 917)

D: 295 tons (fl) **S:** 12.4 kts **Dim:** 40.9 × 8.0 × 2.1
Electron Equipt: Radar: 1/Spin Trough
M: 2 Type 3D12 A diesels; 2 props; 600 hp

Remarks: Transferred 19-12-77. Can support seven hard-hat divers working at 60 m and has a submersible decompression chamber.

◆ **1 floating dry dock** Bldr: Blohm & Voss, Hamburg (In serv. 1984)

Capacity: 3,200 tons **Dim:** 105.20 × 26.00 × 6.40

Remarks: Ordered 20-2-84, laid down 17-4-84.

◆ **1 Soviet Poluchat-I-class torpedo retriever**

D: 90 tons (fl) **S:** 18 kts **Dim:** 29.6 × 6.1 × 1.9
A: . . . **Electron Equipt:** 2 props; 2,400 hp
Range: 450/17; 900/10 **Man:** 20 tot.

Remarks: Delivered 20-5-85 under tow by Bulgarian tug *Neptun.*

MADAGASCAR

Democratic Republic of Madagascar

Personnel: Approximately 600 men, including a 120-marine infantry company

Merchant Marine (1984): 60 ships — 77,886 grt (tankers: 6 ships — 11,412 grt)

PATROL BOAT AND CRAFT

◆ **1 French PR 48-type coastal patrol boat** Bldr: SFCN, Villeneuve-la-Garenne

	Laid down	L	In serv.
Malaika	11-66	22-3-67	12-67

D: 235 tons (250 fl) **S:** 18.5 kts **Dim:** 47.5 (45.5 pp) × 7.1 × 2.25
A: 2/40-mm AA **M:** 2 MGO diesels; 2 props; 2,400 hp
Range: 2,000/15 **Man:** 3 officers, 22 men

Remarks: Sisters with more powerful propulsion plants in the Senegalese and Tunisian navies.

◆ **1 North Korean Nampo class** (In serv. 1979-80)

D: 70 tons (fl) **S:** 40 kts **Dim:** 27.7 × 6.1 × 1.8
A: 4/14.5-mm mg (II × 2) — 1/75-mm recoilless rifle
M: 4 M50-series diesels; 4 props, 4,800 hp
Range: 375/40 **Man:** 19 tot.

Remarks: Unlike North Korean Navy version, has no bow ramp or troop accommodations, being intended for use strictly as patrol craft. Metal construction. Three sisters destroyed by typhoon during 4-84.

AMPHIBIOUS WARFARE SHIPS

◆ **1 medium landing ship**

	Bldr	Laid down	L	In serv.
Toky	Diego Suarez SY	1972	1973	10-74

D: 810 tons (avg) **S:** 13 kts **Dim:** 66.37 (56.0 pp) × 12.5 × 1.9
A: 1/76-mm — 2/20-mm AA — 1/81-mm mortar **Man:** 27 tot.
M: 2 MGO diesels; 2 props; 2,400 hp **Electric:** 240 kw **Range:** 3,000/12

Remarks: Similar to a French EDIC. Used as a transport and support ship. Forward ramp can be folded upon itself. Transport capacity: 250 tons. Quarters for 30 passengers; 120 soldiers can be carried for short distances. Financed by the French government under the Military Cooperation Pact.

TRADING SHIP

◆ **1 former trawler**

	Bldr	L
Fanantenana (ex-*Richelieu*)	A.G. Weser, Bremen	1959

D: 1,040 tons (1,200 fl) **S:** 12 kts **Dim:** 62.9 (56 pp) × 9.15 × 4.52
A: 2/40-mm AA **M:** 2 Deutz diesels ("father-mother" system); 1 prop; 1,060 + 500 hp **Man:** . . .

Remarks: 691 grt. Bought and modified, 1966-67. Can carry 300 tons of freight and up to 120 military passengers.

MARITIME POLICE

◆ **5 coast surveillance craft** Bldr: Bayerische Schiffbau, West Germany (In serv. 1962)

GC 1 Philiberi Isiranana	GC 4 Fanrosoana
GC 2 Faheleovatena	GC 5 Fahafahana
GC 3 N.	

D: 46 tons **S:** 22 kts **Dim:** 24.0 × . . . × . . .
A: 1/40-mm AA **M:** 2 diesels; 2 props; . . . hp

MALAWI

Republic of Malawi

Merchant Marine (1984): 2 ships — 1,348 grt

POLICE

PATROL CRAFT

◆ **1 for Lake Nyasa service** Bldr: SFCN, Villeneuve-la-Garenne, France (In serv. 17-12-84)

703 Chikala

Chikala (703) L. & L. Van Ginderen, 1984

D: 33 tons (36 fl) **S:** 22 kts **Dim:** 21.0 (18.5 wl) × 4.8 × 1.5
A: 1/20-mm GIAT F-2 AA **Electron Equipt:** Radar: 1/Orcca . . . nav.
M: 2 Poyaud 520-V12-M2 diesels; 2 props; 1,400 hp
Range: 650/15 **Man:** 10 tot.

Remarks: Ordered 8-11-83. Delivered in sections 10-84 and assembled in Malawi.

◆ **1 Spear class** Bldr: Fairey Marine, Hamble, U.K. (In serv. 1976)

P 702

D: 4 tons (fl) **S:** 25 kts **Dim:** 9.1 × 2.8 × 0.8
A: 2/7.62-mm mg (I × 2)
M: 2 Perkins diesels; 2 props; 290 hp **Man:** 3 tot.

Remarks: There are also as many as three additional small patrol craft on Lake Nyassa.

MALAYSIA

Note: Forces specifically assigned to the Malaysian state of Sabah are listed separately.

Personnel: Approximately 6,000 total, plus 800 reserves

Merchant Marine (1984): 429 ships — 1,664,312 grt (tankers: 67 ships — 355,153 grt)

Naval Aviation: A Naval Air Wing is to be established with 12 pilots in 5-86, to man helicopters yet to be acquired.

Note: In 1985 it was announced that submarines may be acquired.

FRIGATES

◆ **2 new construction Type 1500** Bldr: Howaldtswerke, Kiel

	Laid down	L	In serv.
F 25 Kasturi	31-1-83	14-5-83	15-8-84
F 26 Lekir	31-1-83	14-5-83	15-8-84

Kasturi (F 25) Howaldtswerke, 1984

Kasturi (F 25) L. & L. Van Ginderen, 8-84

D: 1,690 tons (1,900 fl) **S:** 28 kts **Dim:** 97.3 (91.8 pp) × 11.3 × 3.5 (hull)
A: 4/MM 38 Exocet—1/100-mm Compact DP—1/57-mm Bofors DP—4/30-mm Emerlec AA (II × 2)—1/375-mm Bofors ASW RL (II × 1)—1/light helicopter.
Electron Equipt: Radar: 1/Decca 1226 nav., 1/H.S.A. DA .08, 1/H.S.A. WM 22
Sonar: Atlas ASO 84/5
EW: "Rapids" intercept, "Scimitar" jammer; 2 Dagaie RL
M: 4 MTU 20V 1163 TB92 diesels; 2 CP props; 21,460 hp
Fuel: 200 tons **Electric:** 1,392 kVA **Range:** 3,600/18; 7,000/14 **Man:** 128 tot.

Remarks: Ordered 10-6-81. Acquisition of two more deferred. There is no hangar, only a deck for an as-yet-to-be-determined light helicopter. The 100-mm gun is of the new Creusot-Loire "Compact" model. Two H.S.A. LIOD optronic backup GFCS for the 100-mm and 57-mm guns. Both arrived in Malaysia 23-11-84. Can make 23 kts on 2 diesels. There are flare rocket launchers on the sides of the 57-mm mount. Four similar, but shorter and differently equipped sisters built for Colombia.

◆ **1 "Yarrow frigate" class**

	Bldr	Laid down	L	In serv.
F 24 Rahmat	Yarrow, Scotstoun	2-66	18-12-67	3-71

Rahmat (F 24) J. Jedrlinic, 6-83

D: 1,290 tons (1,600 fl) **S:** 27 kts (16.5 on diesels alone)
Dim: 93.97 (pl. 44 pp) × 10.36 × 3.05
A: 1/114-mm Mk 6-mm DP—3/40-mm Bofors AA (I × 3)—1/Mk 10 Limbo ASW mortar (III × 1)
Electron Equipt: Radar: 1/Decca 626, 1/H.S.A. LW 02, 1/H.S.A. M 22
Sonar: 1/170B, 1/174
M: CODOG: 1 Rolls-Royce Olympus TM-1B gas turbine, 19,500 hp; 1 Crossley-Pielstick SPC2V diesel, 3,850 hp; 2 CP Props; 22,000 hp
Electric: 2,000 kw **Range:** 1,000/27; 5,200/16.5 **Man:** 120 tot.

Remarks: Ordered 11-2-66. M 22 fire-control radar atop the mast for the 114-mm gun. The ASW mortar is covered by a hatch that serves as a platform for a light helicopter. Sea Cat SAM system and radar director replaced by a 40-mm AA gun during 1981-82 refit. Plans to replace the 114-mm mount with a French 100-mm Compact were deferred.

◆ **1 British built** Bldr: Yarrow, Scotstoun

	Laid down	L	In serv.
F 76 Hang Tuah (ex-*Mermaid*)	1965	29-12-66	16-5-73

Hang Tuah (F 76) G. Arra, 1980

D: 2,300 tons (2,520 fl) **S:** 24/23 kts **Dim:** 103.4 × 12.2 × 4.8
A: 2/102-mm Mk 19 DP—4/30-mm Emerlec AA (II × 2)—2/40-mm AA (I × 2)—1/Mk 10 Limbo ASW mortar (III × 1)
Electron Equipt: Radar: 1/Plessey AWS-1, 1/978
Sonar: 1/174, 1/170B
M: 8 16-cyl. Admiralty Standard Range-I diesels; 2 props; 14,400 hp
Fuel: 230 tons **Range:** 4,800/15 **Man:** 200-210 tot.

Remarks: Ordered for Ghana in 1964. Because of the political situation, the ship was not delivered and at the end of 1971 was purchased by the British government. Transferred to Malaysia in 5-77. Has lead-computing STD Mk 1 sight for the Mk 19 twin 102-mm mount, and no fire-control radar. Helicopter pad.

CORVETTES

◆ **2 (+1) offshore patrol vessels**

	Bldr	L	In serv.
160 Mashturi	Korea SB & Eng., Pusan	20-7-84	1-4-85
. . . N.	Malaysian SY & Eng., Johore	21-1-85	9-85
. . . N.	Malaysian SY & Eng., Johore	. . .	. . .

Mashturi (160) at launch Korea SB & Eng., 7-84

D: 1,000 tons (1,300 fl) **S:** 20 kts **Dim:** 75.0 × 10.0 × . . .
A: 1/40-mm AA—2/30-mm Emerlec AA (II × 1)
Electron Equipt: Radar: . . .
M: 2 diesels; 2 props; 6,360 hp **Range:** 5,000/20 **Man:** 76 tot.

Remarks: First two ordered 6-83. Intended to patrol the 200-n.m. economic zone. Third unit ordered 5-84.

GUIDED-MISSILE PATROL BOATS

◆ **4 Spica-M class** Bldr: Karlskrona Varvet, Sweden

	Laid down	L	In serv.
P 3511 Handalan	24-5-77	. . .	26-10-79
P 3512 Perkasa	27-6-77	. . .	26-10-79
P 3513 Pendikar	15-7-77	. . .	26-10-79
P 3514 Gempita	21-10-77	. . .	26-10-79

Handalan (P 3511) RAN, 1982

D: 240 tons (268 fl) **S:** 37.5 kts (34.5 sust.) **Dim:** 43.62 (41.00 pp) × 7.0 × 2.4 (aft)
A: 4/MM 38 Exocet SSM (II × 2)—1/57-mm Bofors DP—1/40-mm Bofors AA
Electron Equipt: Radar: 1/Decca 1226, 1/Phillips 9LV200 Mk 2 system (1 tracker, 1/9GR600 search radar)
Sonar: Simrad SU—EW: MEL SUSIE-1
M: 3 MTU 16V538 TB91 diesels; 3 props; 10,800 hp **Fuel:** 80 tons
Electric: 400 kVA **Range:** 1,850/14 **Man:** 5 officers, 34 men

Remarks: Ordered 13-8-76. Given the names of the four *Perkasa*-class torpedo/patrol boats that were stricken in 1977. Have 103-mm rocket flare launchers on the 57-mm mount and 57-mm RFL on the 40-mm mount. Can be equipped with ASW TT if required. Do *not* carry the Blowpipe SAM system offered with the original design. A planned second group of four may be ordered during 1986.

◆ **4 French Combattante-II 4AL class** Bldr: CMN, Cherbourg

	L	In serv		L	In serv.
P 3501 Perdana	31-5-72	31-12-72	P 3503 Ganas	26-10-72	28-2-73
P 3502 Serang	22-12-71	31-2-73	P 3504 Ganyang	16-3-72	20-3-73

Ganyang (P 3504)—without missiles, 40-mm gun J. Jedrlinic, 1982

D: 234 tons (265 fl) **S:** 36.5 kts **Dim:** 47.0 × 7.1 × 2.5 (fl)
A: 2/MM 38 Exocet SSM (I × 2)—1/57-mm Bofors AA—1/40-mm Bofors AA
Electron Equipt: Radar: 1 Decca 1226, 1/Triton, 1/Pollux
M: 4 MTU MB 870 diesels; 4 props; 14,000 hp **Fuel:** 39 tons
Range: 800/25 **Man:** 5 officers, 30 men

Remarks: Steel hulls. Superstructure in alloyed metal. Six 103-mm rocket flare launchers on the 57-mm mount, four 57-mm on the 40-mm mount. Thomson-CSF Vega fire-control system with Triton search radar. Pollux f.c. radar.

PATROL BOATS

◆ **6 Jerong class** Bldr: Hong Leong-Lürssen, Butterworth, Malaysia

	L	In serv.		L	In serv.
P 3505 Jerong	28-7-75	23-3-76	P 3508 Yu	17-7-76	15-11-76
P 3506 Tudak	16-3-76	16-6-76	P 3509 Baung	5-10-76	11-7-77
P 3507 Paus	2-6-76	18-8-76	P 3510 Pari	1-77	23-3-77

D: 210 tons (255 fl) **S:** 34 kts **Dim:** 44.90 × 7.00 × 2.48 (props)
A: 1/57-mm Bofors AA—1/40-mm Bofors AA
Electron Equipt: Radar: 1/Decca 1226
M: 3 MTU MB 870 diesels; 3 props; 10,800 hp **Electric:** 384 kVA
Range: 700/31.5; 2,000/15 **Man:** 5 officers, 31 men

Remarks: Lürrsen FPB 45 design. Rocket flare launchers are fitted on both gun mounts. C.S.E.E. Naja electro-optical GFCS. Fin stabilizers fitted.

Baung (P 3509) J. Jedrlinic, 1981

◆ **20 103-foot Vosper type** Bldr: Vosper Ltd., Portsmouth

Ordered in 1965:

	L		L
P 34 Kris	11-3-66	P 36 Sundang	22-5-66
P 37 Badek	8-5-66	P 38 Renchong	22-6-66
P 39 Tombak	20-6-66	P 40 Lembing	22-8-66
P 41 Serampang	15-9-66	P 42 Panah	10-10-66
P 43 Kerambit	20-11-66	P 44 Baladau	11-1-67
P 45 Kelewang	31-1-67	P 46 Rentaka	15-3-67
P 47 Sri Perlis	26-5-67	P 48 Sri Johore	21-8-67

Kerambit (P 43)—with 2/40-mm AA RAN, 1982

Ordered in March 1963:

	L		L
P 3144 Sri Sabah	30-12-63	P 3145 Sri Sarawak	20-1-64
P 3146 Sri Negri Sembilan	17-9-64		

Ordered in September 1961:

	L		L
P 3139 Sri Selangor	17-7-62	P 3142 Sri Kelantan	8-1-63
P 3143 Sri Trengganu	12-12-62		

Sri Kelantan (P 3142) J. Jedrlinic, 1983

D: 96 tons (109 fl) **S:** 27/23 kts **Dim:** 31.39 (28.95 pp) × 5.95 × 1.65
A: 1 or 2/40-mm AA (I × . . .)—2 mg **Electron Equipt:** Radar: 1/Decca 616
M: 2 Bristol-Siddeley or Maybach MD 655/18 diesels; 2 props; 3,550 hp
Range: 1,400/14 **Man:** 3 officers, 19-20 men

Remarks: Welded hulls. Vosper anti-roll stabilizers. The Malaysian prototype was delivered in February 1963 and was soon followed by many others. The middle group have greater range: 1,660/14. The class prototype, the *Sri Kegah* (P 3138), and the *Sri Pahang* (P 3141) were stricken 1976; *Sri Perek* (P 3140) foundered 1-84. Bulwark configurations vary, while early units had hull portholes. Aft 40-mm gun removed in at least three. Seventeen of the survivors had been modernized by end-1984. Sister *Sri Melaka* (P 3147, 2nd group) is detached to Sabah (see later page).

MINE WARFARE SHIPS

◆ **2 (+2) Italian Lerici-class minehunters** Bldr: Intermarine, La Spezia

	Laid down	L	In serv.
M 11 Mahamiru	. . .	4-83	25-5-84
M 12 Jerai	. . .	9-7-83	25-5-84
M 13 Ledang	. . .	. . .	-86
M 14 Kinabulu	. . .	. . .	-86

Mahamiru (M 11) and Jerai (M 12) C. Martinelli, 10-84

D: 470 tons (502 fl) **S:** 15 kts **Dim:** 49.98 (45.50 pp) × 9.56 × 2.63
A: 1/40-mm Bofors AA
Electron Equipt: Radar: 1/Decca . . . nav.—Sonar: SQQ-14
M: 2 MTU 8V396 TC82 diesels; 2 props; 1,740 hp **Electric:** 887 kVA
Fuel: 46 tons **Range:** 1,400/14; 2,500/12 **Man:** 39 tot.

Remarks: Ordered 2-81. Intended for patrol duties also. May be 1–2 meters longer than listed. Glass-reinforced plastic construction. Have different main engine, armament, and sonar than Italian Navy sisters. Two retractable auxiliary props (470 hp) used when minehunting at speeds up to 7 kts. Range at 12 kts can be extended to 4,000 n.m. by using the passive anti-rolling tanks to carry fuel. Will have two PAP-104 remote-controlled minehunting devices, good in depths up to 300 m. A chaff RL will be fitted.

AMPHIBIOUS WARFARE CRAFT

Note: In addition to these small craft, the multi-purpose ships of the *Sri Indera Sakti* class, the former U.S. Navy LSTs, and the miscellaneous utility landing craft listed under auxiliaries can be used for amphibious warfare purposes.

◆ **5 U.S. LCM(6)-class vehicle landing craft** Bldr: De Havilland Marine, Australia

LCM 1-5

D: 24 tons (56 fl) **S:** 10 kts **Dim:** 17.07 × 4.37 × 1.17
M: 2 diesels; 2 props; 330 hp **Range:** 130/10

Remarks: Transferred around 1970 from Australia. Cargo: 30 tons.

◆ **9 RCP-class personnel/vehicle landing craft** Bldr: Hong Leong-Lürssen SY, Butterworth, Malaysia (All in serv. 1974)

RCP 2 1974

D: 15 tons (30 fl) **S:** 17 kts **Dim:** 15.0 × 4.4 × . . .
A: 1/20-mm AA **M:** 2 diesels; 2 waterjets: . . . hp

Remarks: Cargo: 35 troops or one small vehicle

◆ **15 LCP-class personnel landing craft** Bldr: De Havilland Marine, Australia

LCP 1-15

D: 19 tons (fl) **S:** 16 kts **Dim:** 14.6 × 4.3 × 1.0
M: 2 Cummins diesels; 2 props; 400 hp

Remarks: Transferred 1965-66. Essentially personnel launches, with pointed bows; have light armor over pilothouse amidships. There are also several De Havilland "Titan" Mk 3 12-meter landing craft in service.

HYDROGRAPHIC SHIP

◆ **1 seagoing oceanographic research and hydrographic survey ship**

	Bldr	In serv.
A 152 Mutiara	Hong Leong-Lürssen, Butterworth, Malaysia	18-11-77

Mutiara (A 152) G. Arra, 1980

D: 1,905 tons (fl) **S:** 16 kts **Dim:** 70.0 (64.0 pp) × 13.0 × 4.0
A: 2/20-mm AA (I × 2) **M:** 1 Deutz SBA-12M-528 diesel; 1 CP prop; 2,000 hp
Range: 4,500/16 **Man:** 13 officers, 143 men

Remarks: Ordered 1975. Carries six small survey launches and has a helicopter deck. White hull, buff stack.

AUXILIARIES

◆ **3 multi-purpose support ships**

	Laid down	L	In serv.	Bldr:
A 1503 Sri Indera Sakti	15-2-80	1-7-80	24-10-80	Bremer Vulcan
A 1504 Mahawangsa	. . .	. . .	16-5-83	Korea-Tacoma, Masan
A 1505 N.	. . .	. . .	-85	Korea-Tacoma, Masan

Sri Indera Sakti (A 1503) LSPH E. Pitman, R.A.N., 11-84

D: 2,000 tons light (4,300 fl) **S:** 16.8 kts **Dim:** 100.00 (91.20 pp) × 15.00 × 4.75
A: 1/57-mm Bofors DP—2/20-mm (I × 2) **M:** 2 Deutz-KHD SBV 6M540 diesels; 2 CP props; 5,986 hp
Electric: 1,200 kw **Endurance:** 60 days **Fuel:** 1,350 tons (max.)
Range: 14,000/15 **Man:** 14 officers, 126 men, 75 passengers

Remarks: 1,800 dwt. A 1503 ordered 10-79, two more in 2-81. Intended to perform a variety of tasks, such as: provide support (including up to 1,300 tons of fuel and 200 tons water) to deployed small combatants or mine-countermeasures ships; act as a flagship; perform as a vehicle and troop transport in amphibious operations; and act as a cadet training ship. There are 1,000 m³ of cargo space for spare parts, and ten 20-ft standard cargo containers can be carried on deck amidships. Vehicle holds aft are reached by ramps on either side of the stern, which supports a helicopter deck; can carry 600 troops on the 680-m² vehicle deck. Extensive repair facilities and divers' support equipment are provided. Provisions spaces total 300 m², including 100 m³ refrigerated stores. Bow-thruster fitted, as is a 16-ton crane amidships. CSEE Naja optical GFCS. A 1504 lacks a funnel, thus effectively doubling the size of the helo deck; the second pair are configured to carry 500 tons of ammunition.

Note: The two surviving ex-U.S. LST 542-class landing ships, *Sri Banggi* (A 1501, ex-*Henry County,* LST 824) and *Rajah Jerom* (A 1502, ex-*Sedgewick County,* LST 1123) were to strike on delivery of A 1504 and A 1505.

◆ **2 utility landing craft/transports** Bldr: Penang SY, Pulau Jerejah

	L	In serv.
A. . . Lang Siput	1980	1980
A. . . Lang Tiram	25-9-80	21-10-80

D: 630 grt **S:** 9 kts **Dim:** 48.4 (45.0 pp) × 10.5 × . . .
M: 2 Caterpillar D3408 diesels; 2 props; 700 hp

AUXILIARIES *(continued)*

◆ **2 Jernih-class utility landing craft/transports** Bldr: Brooke DY, Malaysia

A. . . Jernih (In serv. 1977) A. . . Terijah (In serv. 1978)

D: 290 (fl) **S:** 8 kts **Dim:** 38.0 (35.2 pp) × . . . × 1.4
M: 2 Caterpillar D343T diesels; 2 props; 730 hp

Remarks: Capacity: 170 tons of dry cargo or 240 tons of fresh water. Intended as supply craft for Sarawak.

◆ **1 Meleban-class utility landing craft** Bldr: Brooke DY, Malaysia

A. . . Meleban (L: 15-10-77)

D: . . . **S:** 8 kts **Dim:** 50.0 (43.5 pp) × . . . × 1.37
M: 2 Caterpillar D343T diesels; 2 props; 730 hp

◆ **1 small cargo ship** (In serv. 1977)

A 301 Enterprise

◆ **1 small tanker** (In serv. 1973)

A 8 Kepah (ex-*Asiatic Supplier*)—432 grt. Purchased 1980.

◆ **1 diving tender**

	Bldr	L	In serv.
A 1109 Duyong	Kall Teck SY, Singapore	18-8-70	5-1-71

D: 140 tons (fl) **S:** 10 kts **Dim:** 33.0 × 6.3 × 1.7
A: 1/20-AA **M:** 2 Cummins diesels; 2 props; 500 hp
Man: 23 tot.

Remarks: Used as a support ship for divers. Originally configured as a torpedo retriever.

◆ **4 coastal tugs** Bldr: Penang SY, Pulau Jerejah

	L		L
Lang . . .	5-81	Lang Kangok	1982
Lang . . .	1981	Lang Hindek	1982

D: . . . **S:** 12.5 kts **Dim:** 29.0 × 7.0 × 2.0
M: 2 Ruston Paxman diesels; 2 props; 1,800 hp

◆ **3 Tunda-class harbor tugs** Bldr: Ironwood SY, Malaysia (In serv. 1978-79)

A 1 Tunda 1 A 2 Tunda 2 A 3 Tunda 3

D: 150 tons **S:** . . . **Dim:** 26.0 × . . . × . . .
M: 1 Cummins diesel; 1 prop: . . . hp

◆ **1 salvage and fire-fighting tug** (In serv. 1976)

A 4 Penyu (ex-*Salvigilant*)—Purchased 1980; 398 grt.

◆ **2 salvage and fire-fighting tugs**

A 20 Badang I A 21 Badang II—400 grt

◆ **9 miscellaneous tugs**

A 6 Sotong (ex-*Asiatic Charm*)—233 grt, blt. 1976; purchased 1980.

A 9 Siput	A 10 Teritup	A 11 Belankas
A. . . Mangkasa	A. . . Selar	A. . . Tepuruk
A. . . Kempong	A. . . Patak	

ROYAL MALAYSIAN MARINE POLICE

Note: Planned acquisitions include three 40-m patrol boats equipped with helicopter platforms and four 32-m patrol boats.

PATROL BOATS

◆ **9 Brooke Marine 29-m design** Bldr: Penang SY, Pulau Jerejah (In serv. 1982-83)

PX 28 Sangitan 8 others (PX 29–36)

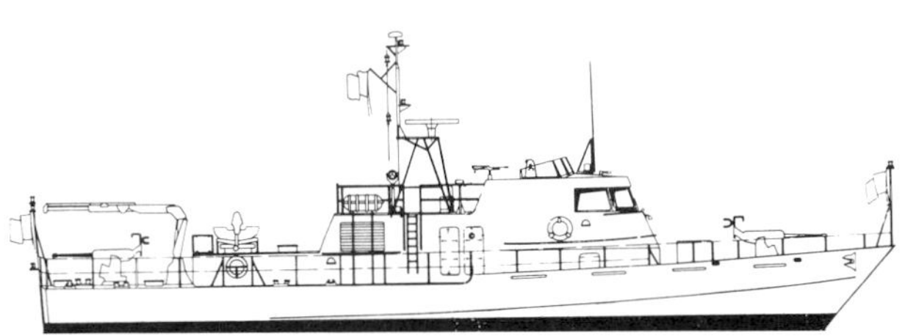

Brooke Marine 29-m design Brooke Marine

D: 114 tons **S:** 36 kts **Dim:** 29.0 (26.5 pp) × 6.0 × 1.7
A: 2/20-mm AA (I × 2)—2/7.62-mm mg (I × 2)
Electron Equipt: Radar: 1/navigational
M: 2 Paxman Valenta 16 RP 200M diesels; 2 props; 8,000 hp
Range: 1,200/24 **Man:** 4 officers, 14 men

Remarks: Ordered 1980. Status of program unavailable. Originally reported as naval, but now stated to be Marine Police-subordinated. Design evolved from the PX 26 class. Carry 2,000 rds. 20-mm ammunition.

◆ **15 PZ class** Bldr: Hong Leong-Lürrsen, Butterworth, Malaysia (In serv. 1981-1983)

PZ 10 Lang Hitan 14 others (PZ 2–15)

Lang Hitan (PZ 10) R.A.N., 1982

D: 188 tons (205 fl) **S:** 34 kts **Dim:** 38.50 (36.00 wl) × 7.00 × 2.20
A: 1/40-mm AA—1/20-mm AA—2/7.62-mm mg
M: 2 MTU 20V538 TB92 diesels; 2 props; 9,000 hp **Electric:** 130 kVA
Range: 550/31.5; 1,100/16 **Man:** 3 officers, 24 men

Remarks: Lürssen FPB 38 design. Have 2 rocket flare launchers, carry 1,000 rounds 40-mm, 2,000 rounds 20-mm.

◆ **6 PX 26 class** Bldr: Hong Leong-Lürssen, Butterworth, Malaysia (In serv. 1973-74)

PX 25 N.	PX 27 Sri Tawau	PX 29 N. . . . . . .
PX 26 Sri Kudat	PX 28 N.	PX 30 N. . . . . . .

PX 28 Brooke Marine

D: 62.5 tons **S:** 25 kts **Dim:** 28.0 × 5.4 × 1.6
A: 2/20-mm AA (I × 2) **M:** 2 MTU MB820Db diesels; 2 props; 2,460 hp
Range: 1,050/15 **Man:** 19 tot.

◆ **6 improved PX class** Bldr: Vosper Thornycroft Pty, Singapore (In serv. 1973-74)

PX 19 Alor Star	PX 21 Kuala Trengganu	PX 23 Sri Menanti
PX 20 Kota Bahru	PX 22 Johore Bahru	PX 24 Kuching

Sri Menanti (PX 23) Vosper, 1974

D: 92 tons (fl) **S:** 25 kts **Dim:** 27.3 × 5.8 × 1.5
A: 2/20-mm AA (I × 2) **M:** 2 MTU MB820Db diesels; 2 props; 2,460 hp
Range: 750/15 **Man:** 18 tot.

MALAYSIA *(continued)*
PATROL BOATS *(continued)*

◆ **16 PX class** Bldr: Vosper Thornycroft Pty, Singapore, 1963-69

PX 1 Mahkota
PX 2 Temenggong
PX 3 Hulubalang
PX 4 Maharajesetia
PX 5 Maharajelela
PX 6 Pahlawan
PX 7 Bentara
PX 8 Perwira
PX 9 Pertanda
PX 10 Shahbandar
PX 11 Sangsetia
PX 12 Laksamana
PX 13 Pekan
PX 14 Kelang
PX 15 Kuala Kangsar
PX 16 Arau

Shahbandar and Sangsetia (PX 10, PX 11) 1975

D: 85 tons (fl) **S:** 25 kts **Dim:** 26.29 × 5.7 × 1.45
A: 2/20-mm AA (I × 2)
M: 2 Mercedes-Benz MB820Db diesels; 2 props; 2,460 hp **Range:** 700/15
Man: 15 tot.

Remarks: Sisters *Sri Gumantong* (PX 17) and *Sri Labuan* (PX 18) are operated by the Sabah government

Note: The Royal Malaysian Marine Police operate a large number of smaller patrol and support craft

MALAYSIAN CUSTOMS AND EXCISE SERVICE

PATROL BOATS

◆ **6 Vosper 103-ft design** Bldr: Malaysian SY & Eng. Co.-Pasir Gudang

K 1 Bahtera Perak
K 2 Bahtera Bayu
K 3 Bahtera Hijau
K 4 Bahtera Pulai
K 5 Bahtera Jerai
K 6 Bahtera Juang

D: 100 tons (143 fl) **S:** 27 kts **Dim:** 32.40 (29.50 pp) × 7.20 × 1.80
A: 1/20-mm AA—2/7.62-mm mg (I × 2)
M: Paxman Valenta 16RP200 diesels; 2 props; 4,000 hp; 1 Cummins KTA-1550M cruise diesel; 1 prop; 575 hp
Range: 1,200/10; 2,000/8 **Fuel:** 36 tons **Man:** 26 tot.

Remarks: Ordered built under license from Vosper Pty, Singapore. First two in service 1982; last delivered 30-3-84. Generally resemble Malaysian Navy units of this design. The Customs and Excise Service also operates a number of small craft.

MALDIVE ISLANDS
Republic of the Maldives

Personnel: Approximately 150 total

Merchant Marine (1984): 32 ships—136,564 grt (tankers: 2 ships—1,377 grt)

PATROL BOATS AND CRAFT

◆ **1 20-m Tracker** Bldr: Fairey Marine, Cowes, U.K.

Remarks: Ordered 6-85.

◆ **3 9-m** Bldr: Fairey Marine, Cowes, U.K. (Ordered 6-85)

◆ **1 ex-British RTTL Mk-2-class target-towing launch**

D: 34.6 tons (fl) **S:** 30 kts **Dim:** 20.7 × 5.8 × 1.8
A: mg **M:** 2 Rolls-Royce Sea Griffon gasoline engines; 2 props; 1,100 hp
Man: 9 tot.

Remarks: Transferred in 1976 by the departing Royal Air Force.

◆ **1 ex-British 1300-class tender**

D: 28.3 tons **S:** 13 kts **Dim:** 19.2 × 4.9 × 1.5
M: 2 Rolls-Royce C6 diesels; 2 props; 190 hp **Man:** 5 tot.

Remarks: Transferred by the departing Royal Air Force. Cargo: 5 tons

◆ **3 ex-Taiwanese trawlers**

Remarks: Approximately 600 tons (fl). Fitted with 2/25-mm AA guns (II × 1) by the U.S.S.R. after confiscation for poaching in 1976.

◆ **4 ex-British 19.5-meter landing craft**

Remarks: Transferred in 1976

◆ **1 customs launch** Bldr: Fairey Marine, U.K. 1975

MALTA
Republic of Malta

Merchant Marine (1982): 93 ships—425,563 grt (tankers: 3 ships—6,973 grt)

COAST GUARD

PATROL BOATS AND CRAFT

◆ **2 ex-Yugoslav Type 131 class** Bldr: Trogir SY (In serv. 1965-68)

P 38 President Tito (ex-*Durmitor,* 138)
P 39 President Mintoff (ex-*Cer,* 139)

President Mintoff (P 39) L. & L. Van Ginderen, 7-83

D: 85 tons light (120 fl) **S:** 22 kts **Dim:** 32.0 × 5.5 × 2.5
A: 6/20-mm Hispano-Suiza HS831 AA (III × 2)
Electron Equipt: Radar: 1/Kelvin-Hughes 14/9
M: 2 MTU 820Db diesels; 2 props; 1,800 hp

Remarks: Transferred 31-3-82

◆ **2 ex-U.S. Swift-class PCF** Bldr: Sewart Seacraft, 1967

C 23 (ex-U.S. C 6823) C 24 (ex-U.S. C 6824)

C 23 P. Voss, 10-82

D: 22.5 tons (fl) **S:** 25 kts **Dim:** 15.6 × 4.12 × 1.5
A: 3/12.7-mm mg (II × 1 and 1 combined with 1/81-mm mortar)
M: 2 G.M. 12V71T diesels; 2 props; 960 hp **Endurance:** 24-36 hours
Man: 6-8 tot.

Remarks: Donated 1-71.

MALTA *(continued)*
PATROL BOATS AND CRAFT *(continued)*

◆ **2 ex-Libyan customs patrol craft** Bldr: C 31: Vosper Thornycroft, Woolston; C 32: Thornycroft, Woolston

C 28 (ex-*Ar Rakib*) C 29 (ex-*Akrama*)

C 28 L. & L. Van Ginderen, 7-83

D: 100 tons (fl) **S:** 18 kts **Dim:** 30.5 × 6.4 × 1.7
A: 1/20-mm AA **M:** 3 Rolls-Royce diesels; 3 props; 1,740 hp
Range: 1,800/14 **Man:** 15 tot.

Remarks: Transferred in 1978. C 30 (ex-*Farwa*) sank 1981.

◆ **2 British RAF RTTL Mk 2-class rescue launches**

C 68 (ex-2768) C 71 (ex-2771)

C 68 and C 71 P. Voss, 10-82

D: 34.6 tons **S:** 30 kts **Dim:** 20.7 × 5.8 × 1.8
M: 2 Rolls-Royce Sea Griffon gasoline engines; 2 props; . . . hp **Man:** 9 tot.

Remarks: Transferred early 1970s; wooden construction.

◆ **2 ex-Libyan customs launches** Bldr: Mosir SY, Trogir, Yugoslavia, 1963

C 25 (ex-*Arraid*) C 26 (ex-. . .)

C 25 P. Voss, 10-82

D: 86.2 tons (100 fl) **S:** 20 kts **Dim:** 35.0 × 5.0 × 1.7
A: 1/12.7-mm mg **M:** 2 MTU 12V493 diesels; 2 props; 1,800 hp
Range: 1,400/12 **Man:** 12 tot.

Remarks: Transferred 16-1-74.

◆ **1 ex-German customs launch**

C 27 (ex-*Brunsbuttel*) Bldr: Buschmann, Hamburg, 1953

D: 105 tons (fl) **S:** 16 kts **Dim:** 29.5 × 5.2 × 1.6
A: 1/12.7-mm mg **M:** 2 MWM TRM 134S diesels; 2 props; . . . hp
Man: 9 tot.

Remarks: Purchased in 1974.

◆ **2 small patrol craft** Bldr: Guy Coucher, France (In serv. 1979)

Aphrodite Kiklan

D: Approx. 10 tons (fl) **S:** . . . **Dim:** . . . × . . . × . . .
A: 2/7.62-mm mg (I × 2) **Electron Equipt:** Radar: 1/Decca 110
M: 2 diesels; 2 props; . . . hp

◆ **1 British RAF 1300-series pinnace general-purpose tender**

C. . .

M: 2 Rolls-Royce C6 diesels; 2 props; 190 hp **Man:** 5 tot.

Remarks: Also transferred was an RAF 1600-series range safety craft; 12 tons, 13.1 × 4.0 × 1.2, 16 kts.

MAURITANIA

Islamic Republic of Mauritania

Personnel: (1984): 320 tot.

Merchant Marine (1984): 40 ships—15,152 grt

Naval Aviation: Two Piper Cheyenne II, twin-turboprop aircraft were delivered 1981 for coastal surveillance duties. Capable of 7-hour patrols (1,525 n.m.), they have a belly-mounted Bendix RDR 1400 radar.

PATROL BOATS AND CRAFT

◆ **1 French PATRA class** Bldr: C. N. Auroux, Arcachon

	Laid down	L	In serv.
P 411 Dix Juillet (ex-*Rapière*, P 674)	15-2-81	3-6-81	1-11-81

Dix Juillet (P 411) C. N. Auroux, 1982

D: 115 tons (148 fl) **S:** 28 kts **Dim:** 40.70 (38.50 wl) × 5.90 × 1.55
A: 1/40-mm AA—1/20-mm AA—2/12.7-mm mg (I × 2)
Electron Equipt: Radar: 1/Decca 1226
M: 2 AGO 195 V12 CZSHR diesels; 2 CP props; 5,000 hp (4,400 sust.)
Electric: 120 kw **Range:** 750/20; 1,500/15 **Man:** 2 officers, 25 men

Remarks: Built on speculation, acquired by French Navy, and then sold to Mauritania, commissioning 14-5-82.

◆ **3 Spanish Barcelo class** Bldr: Bazán, San Fernando

	In serv.		In serv.		In serv.
P 362 El Viaz	12-79	P 363 El Beg	5-79	P 364 El Kenz	8-82

D: 134 tons (fl) **S:** 36.5 kts **Dim:** 36.2 × 5.8 × 1.75
A: 1/40-mm AA—2/20-mm **Electron Equipt:** Radar: 1/Raytheon 1620
M: 2 MTU MD 16V538 TB90 diesels; 6,000 hp **Electric:** 330 kVA
Fuel: 18 tons **Range:** 1,200/17 **Man:** 3 officers, 16 men

Remarks: Delivery of the first two was greatly delayed when they collided on trials, 12-78. The third unit was ordered in 1979, with delivery delayed over financial problems.

MAURITANIA *(continued)*
PATROL BOATS AND CRAFT *(continued)*

◆ **2 French 32-meter craft** Bldr: Chantiers Navals de l'Estérel, Cannes

Tichitt (In serv. 4-69) Dar El Barka (In serv. 9-69)

Tichitt L'Estérel, 1969

D: 80 tons (fl) **S:** 28 kts **Dim:** 32.0 × 5.75 × 1.7
A: 1/20-mm—1/12.7-mm mg
M: 2 Mercedes-Benz MB820Db/h diesels; 2 props; 2,700 hp
Fuel: 15 tons **Range:** 1,500/15 **Man:** 17 tot.

◆ **2 French 18-m class** Bldr: Chantiers Navals de l'Estérel, Cannes

Imag'ni (In serv. 11-65) Sloughi (In serv. 5-68)

D: 20 tons (fl) **S:** 21 kts (22.7 on trials) **Dim:** 18.15 (17.03 pp) × 4.03 × 1.1
A: 1/12.7-mm mg **M:** 2 G.M. 6-71 diesels; 2 props; 512 hp
Range: 400/15 **Man:** 8 tot.

◆ **1 service launch**

Chinguetti

MAURITIUS

Merchant Marine (1984): 18 ships—41,611 grt

PATROL BOATS

◆ **2 Soviet Zhuk class**

D: 60 tons (fl) **S:** 34 kts **Dim:** 24.0 × 5.0 × 1.8 (props)
A: 4/14.5-mm mg (II × 2) **Electron Equipt:** Radar: 1/Spin Trough
M: 2 M50 diesels; 2 props; 2,400 hp

Remarks: A gift of the Soviet Union, announced 11-82; uncertain whether delivery has taken place.

◆ **1 ex-Indian Ajay-class patrol boat** Bldr: Garden Reach DY, Calcutta, 1961

Amar

Amar 1976

D: 120 tons (160 fl) **S:** 18 kts **Dim:** 35.7 (33.52 pp) × 6.1 × 1.5
A: 1/40-mm AA
M: 2 Paxman YHAXM diesels; 2 props; 1,000 hp; 1 Foden FD 6 cruise diesel; 100 hp
Fuel: 23 tons **Range:** 1,000/8; 500/12

Remarks: Retained original name on transfer 4-74. Indian version of British "Ford"-class seaward defense boat

MEXICO

United Mexican States

Personnel (1984): 23,600 men, including 3,800 Marines

Merchant Marine (1984): 624 ships—1,489,120 grt
(tankers: 43 ships—698,625 grt)

Naval Aviation: The Mexican Navy operates 12 Grumman HU-16 Albatross amphibious patrol planes (5 of which were purchased in 1982), 1 DNC Buffalo, 1 F-27, 4 DC-3 transports, and 35 light fixed-wing aircraft, including 1 Learjet 24D, 2 T-34 Mentor and 4 Beech F-33 Bonanza trainers. Helicopters include 7 MBB BO-105S, 4 Alouette-III, 5 Hughes 269 A, 4 Bell 47G/J, and 2 Bell HU-1H, plus 10 SA 315 Lama helicopters ordered in 1982 for search-and-rescue duties. Ten Casa 212 light transports with surveillance radars were ordered 3-85 to replace the remaining HU-16s. Two locally designed Tonatiah trainers were completed in 1984 at Veracruz, with 3 more to come.

DESTROYERS

◆ **2 ex-U.S. Gearing FRAM I class** Bldr: Bethlehem Steel, Staten Island

	Laid down	L	In serv.
IE-03 Quetzalcoatl (ex-*Vogelgesang,* DD 862)	3-8-44	15-1-45	28-4-45
IE-04 Netzahualcoyotl (ex-*Steinaker,* DD 863)	1-9-44	13-2-45	26-5-45

D: 2,448 tons light (3,528 fl) **S:** 30 kts
Dim: 119.03 × 12.52 × 4.45 (6.4 sonar)
A: 4/127-mm DP (II × 2)—1/ASROC ASW RL (VIII × 1)—6/324-mm Mk 32 ASW TT (III × 2)
Electron Equipt: Radar: 1/LN-66, 1/SPS-10, 1/SPS-40B (IE-04: SPS-29)
Sonar: SQS-23—EW: WLR-1
M: 2 sets G.E. GT; 2 props; 60,000 hp **Electric:** 1,200 kw
Boilers: 4 Babcock & Wilcox; 43.3 kg/cm², 454°C **Fuel:** 650 tons

Remarks: Transferred to Mexico 24-2-82 by sale, as intended replacements for the two *Fletcher*-class destroyers. Retained ASROC launcher, usually removed in recent USN transfers.

◆ **1 ex-U.S. Fletcher class** Bldr: Consolidated Steel, Orange, Tex.

	Laid down	L	In serv.
IE-02 Cuitlahuac (ex-*John Rodgers,* DD 574)	25-7-41	7-5-42	25-1-43

Cuitlahuac (IE-02) 1983

D: 2,050 tons (2,850 fl) **S:** 30 kts **Dim:** 114.73 × 12.06 × 5.5
A: 5/127-mm Mk 30 DP (I × 5)—14/40-mm AA (IV × 2, II × 3)—5/533-mm TT (V × 1)
Electron Equipt: Radar: 1/Kelvin-Hughes 14/9, 1/Kelvin-Hughes 17/9, 1/Mk 12/22 f.c.
M: 2 sets G.E. GT; 2 props; 60,000 hp **Electric:** 590 kw
Boilers: 4 Babcock & Wilcox; 39.8 kg/cm², 454°C **Fuel:** 650 tons
Range: 4,400/15; 1,260/30 **Man:** 197 tot.

Remarks: Transferred 8-70. All ASW capability and obsolete U.S. electronics systems now deleted. Has one Mk 37 director for 127-mm guns; five Mk 51 Mod. 2 directors for 40-mm guns. Could make 35 kts when new. Sister *Cuauhtemoc* (IE-01, ex-*Harrison,* DD 573) discarded 1982.

FRIGATES

◆ **1 ex-U.S. Charles Lawrence(*) and 3 Crosley class**

		Bldr	Laid down	L	In serv.
IB-05	Tehuantepec (ex-*Joseph M. Auman,* APD 117, ex-DE 674)	Consolidated Steel, Orange, Tex.	8-11-43	5-2-44	25-4-45
IB-06	Usumacinta (ex-*Don O. Woods,* APD 118, ex-DE 721)	Consolidated Steel, Orange, Tex.	1-12-43	19-2-44	28-5-45
IB-07	Coahuila (ex-*Barber,* APD 57, ex-DE 161)*	Norfolk Navy Yd, Norfolk, Va.	27-4-43	20-5-43	10-10-43
IB-08	Chihuahua (ex-*Rednour,* APD 102, ex-DE 529)	Bethlehem SB, Hingham, Mass.	30-12-43	12-2-44	30-12-44

FRIGATES *(continued)*

Coahuila (IB-07) L. & L. Van Ginderen, 6-74

D: 1,450 tons (2,130 fl) **S:** 23 kts **Dim:** 93.26 × 11.28 × 3.83
A: 1/127-mm Mk 30 DP—6/40-mm AA (II × 3)—IB-07 also: 2/20-mm AA (I × 2)
Electron Equipt: Radar: 1/Kelvin-Hughes 14/9
M: 2 sets G.E. GT, turbo-electric drive; 2 props; 12,000 hp
Boilers: 2 "D"-Express; 30.6 kg/cm², 399°C
Fuel: 350 tons **Electric:** 680 kw **Range:** 5,000/15 **Man:** 204 tot.

REMARKS: Former high-speed transports. IB-05 and IB-06 transferred 12-63; IB-02 and IB-08, 17-2-69. Used primarily as patrol ships; no longer carry the four landing craft that were once stowed amidships. Converted to APD while being built. IB-07, with a high bridge and lattice mast aft, is a member of the *Charles Lawrence* class; the others each have a low bridge and a tripod aft to support the 10-ton-capacity cargo boom. The 127-mm gun has no director, while there are three Mk 51 Mod. 2 directors for the 40-mm antiaircraft. Two others have been lost: *California* (B-3, ex-*Belet,* APD 109) went aground 16-1-72, and *Papaloapan* (B-4, ex-*Earheart,* APD 113) in 1976.

CORVETTES

◆ **0 (+4) Aguila class**

	Bldr	Laid down	L	In serv.
GH. . . N.	Tampico NSY No. 1	11-83	. . .	1987
GH. . . N.	Salina Cruz NSY No. 8	3-84	. . .	. . .
GH. . . N.	. . .	. . .	. . .	. . .
GH. . . N.	. . .	. . .	. . .	. . .

D: 950 tons (fl) **S:** 23 kts **Dim:** 60.0 × 10.5 × . . .
A: 1/57-mm Bofors DP—1/40-mm Bofors AA—1/helicopter
M: 2 MTU 20V956 TB91 diesels; 2 props; 13,320 hp
Man: 45 total

REMARKS: A smaller variant of the Spanish-built Halcón design, with higher speed and heavier armament. Announced 23-6-83, plans called for construction of 9 units at four naval shipyards, two each at Tampico and Salina Cruz. Reduced to four units in 10-84.

◆ **6 "Halcón" class** Bldr: Bazán, San Fernando, Cadiz, Spain

	L	In serv.
GH-01 CADETE VIRGILIO URIBE	13-12-81	10-9-82
GH-02 TENIENTE JOSÉ AZUETA	29-1-82	15-10-82
GH-03 CAPITAN DE FRAGATA PEDRO SAINZ DE BARBRANDA	26-2-82	3-83
GH-04 COMODORO CARLOS CASTILIO BRETON	12-11-81	9-6-82
GH-05 VICEALMIRANTE OTHÓN P. BLANCO	26-3-82	24-2-83
GH-06 CONTRAALMIRANTE ANGEL ORTIZ MONASTERIO	23-4-82	24-3-83

Teniente José Azueta (GH-02) 10-83

D: 767 tons (910 fl) **S:** 21 kts **Dim:** 67.00 (63.00 pp) × 10.50 × 3.08
A: 1/40-mm AA—1/BO-105S helicopter
Electron Equipt: Radar: 1/Decca AC 1226—TACAN: SRN-15
M: 2 MTU 20V956 TB91 diesels; 2 props; 13,320 hp
Electric: 710 kw **Range:** 5,000/18 **Man:** 10 officers, 42 men

REMARKS: Ordered late 1980 for use in patrolling the 200-nautical-mile economic zone. Have been referred to as the "Puma" class. Generally identical to ships built for Argentina, but with more powerful engines and longer helicopter deck. Delivery of GH-04 delayed by accident; originally completed 23-10-82.

◆ **18 ex-U.S. Auk-class former fleet minesweepers**

	Bldr	L
IG-01 LEANDRO VALLE (ex-*Pioneer,* MSF 105)(1)	A	26-7-42
IG-02 GUILLERMO PRIETO (ex-*Symbol,* MSF 123)(2)	B	2-7-42
IG-03 MARIANO ESCOBEDO (ex-*Champion,* MSF 314)(3)	C	12-12-42
IG-04 PONCIANO ARRIAGA (ex-*Competent,* MSF 316)(3)	C	9-1-43
IG-05 MANUEL DOBLADO (ex-*Defense,* MSF 317)(3)	C	18-2-43
IG-06 SEBASTIAN LERDO DE TEJADA (ex-*Devastator,* MSF 318)(3)	C	19-4-43
IG-07 SANTOS DEGOLLADO (ex-*Gladiator,* MSF 319)(3)	C	7-5-43
IG-08 IGNACIO DE LA LLAVE (ex-*Spear,* MSF 322)(2)	D	25-2-43
IG-09 JUAN N. ALVAREZ (ex-*Ardent,* MSF 340)(3)	C	22-6-43
IG-10 MELCHIOR OCAMPO (ex-*Roselle,* MSF 379)(4)	E	29-8-45
IG-11 VALENTIN G. FARIAS (ex-*Starling,* MSF 64)(5)	C	15-2-42
IG-12 IGNACIO ALTAMIRANO (ex-*Sway,* MSF 120)(2)	F	29-9-42
IG-13 FRANCISCO ZARCO (ex-*Threat,* MSF 124)(2)	B	15-8-42
IG-14 IGNACIO L. VALLARTA (ex-*Velocity,* MSF 128)(2)	E	19-4-42
IG-15 JÉSUS G. ORTEGA (ex-*Chief,* MSF 315)(3)	C	5-1-43
IG-16 GUTIERRIEZ ZAMORA (ex-*Scoter,* MSF 381)(4j)	E	26-9-45
IG-18 JUAN ALDARMA (ex-*Pilot,* MSF 104)(1)	A	5-7-42
IG-19 HERMENEGILDO GALEANA (ex-*Sage,* MSF 111)(1)	G	21-11-42

Bldrs: *A,* Pennsylvania Shipyard, Beaumont, Tex.; *B,* Savannah Machine & Foundry Co., Savannah, Ga.; *C,* General Engineering and Drydock Co., Alameda, Cal.; *D* Associated Shipbuilders; *E,* Gulf Shipbuilding; *F,* J. H. Mathis, Camden, N.J.; *G,* Winslow Marine Railway and Shipbuilding, Seattle, Wash.

Ignacio L. Vallarta (IG-14)—bulwarks amidships G. Arra, 1984

D: 890 tons (1,250 fl) **S:** 17/18 kts **Dim:** 67.4 (65.5 wl) × 9.8 × 3.28
A: 1/76.2-mm Mk 22 DP—4/40-mm AA (II × 2)
Electron Equipt: Radar: 1/SPS-5 or 1/Kelvin-Hughes 14/9, 1/SO-13
M: 2 diesels, electric drive (*see* Remarks); 2 props; 2,976, 3,118, or 3,532 hp
Electric: 300-360 kw **Fuel:** 216 tons **Man:** 9 officers, 96 men

REMARKS: The numbers in parentheses after the ships' names refer to five different diesels used in propulsion plants: (1) Busch-Sulzer 539; (2) G.M. 12-278; (3) Baldwin VO-8; (4) G.M. 12-278A; (5) Alco 539. Diesels (1) and (5) produce 3,118 hp, (2) and (4) 3,532 hp, and (3) 2,976 hp.

All transferred in 1973. All minesweeping and ASW equipment removed. One other unit, *Mariano Metamoros* (ex-*Herald,* MSF 101), was converted for use as a surveying ship. Some have a small deckhouse between the stacks; some have no main deck bulwarks. New radars have been added to ships transferred without SPS-5.

◆ **16 ex-U.S. Admirable-class former fleet minesweepers**

	Bldrs	L
ID-01 DM 01 (ex-*Jubilant,* MSF 255)	American SB, Lorain, Oh.	20-2-43
ID-02 DM 02 (ex-*Hilarity,* MSF 241)	Winslow, Seattle, Wash.	30-7-44
ID-03 DM 03 (ex-*Execute,* MSF 232)	Puget Sound, Seattle, Wash.	22-1-44
ID-04 DM 04 (ex-*Specter,* MSF 306)	Associated Shipbldrs.	15-2-44
ID-05 DM 05 (ex-*Scuffle,* MSF 298)	Winslow, Seattle, Wash.	8-8-43
ID-06 DM 06 (ex-*Eager,* MSF 224)	American SB, Lorain, Oh.	10-6-44
ID-10 DM 10 (ex-*Instill,* MSF 252)	Savannah Mach., Ga.	5-3-44

CORVETTES *(continued)*

	Bldrs	L
ID-11 DM 11 (ex-*Device,* MSF 220)	Tampa SB, Fla.	21-5-44
ID-12 DM 12 (ex-*Ransom,* MSF 283)	General Eng. & DD	18-9-43
ID-13 DM 13 (ex-*Knave,* MSF 256)	American SB, Lorain, Oh.	13-3-43
ID-14 DM 14 (ex-*Rebel,* MSF 284)	General Eng. & DD	28-10-43
ID-15 DM 15 (ex-*Crag,* MSF 214)	Tampa SB, Fla.	21-3-43
ID-16 DM 16 (ex-*Dour,* MSF 223)	American SB, Lorain, Oh.	25-3-44
ID-17 DM 17 (ex-*Diploma,* MSF 221)	Tampa SB, Fla.	21-5-44
ID-18 DM 18 (ex-*Invade,* MSF 254)	Savannah Mach., Ga.	6-2-44
ID-19 DM 19 (ex-*Intrigue,* MSF 253)	Savannah Mach., Ga.	8-4-44

DM 02 (ID-02) 1975

D: 650 tons (945 fl) **S:** 15 kts **Dim:** 56.24 (54.86 wl) × 10.06 × 2.97
A: 1/76.2-mm Mk 22 DP—2/40-mm AA (I × 2)—6/20-mm AA (I × 6)
M: 2 Cooper-Bessemer GSB-8 diesels; 2 props; 1,710 hp
Electric: 240 or 280 kw **Fuel:** 138 tons **Man:** 9 officers, 86 men

REMARKS: All minesweeping and ASW equipment deleted. Three more units were scrapped, and DM 20 was converted into a hydrographic survey ship. DM 04 was transferred 2-73; all others, 1-10-62.

PATROL BOATS

◆ **31 (+4) Azteca class**

	Bldr	In serv.
P-01 ANDRES QUINTANA ROO	Ailsa	1-11-74
P-02 MATIAS DE CORDOVA	Scott	22-10-74
P-03 MIGUEL RAMOS ARIZPE	Ailsa	23-12-74
P-04 JOSÈ MARIA IZAZAGO	Ailsa	19-12-74
P-05 JUAN BAUTISTA MORALES	Scott	19-12-74
P-06 IGNACIO LOPEZ RAYON	Ailsa	19-12-74
P-07 MANUEL CRESCENCIO REJON	Ailsa	4-7-75
P-08 ANTONIO DE LA FUENTE	Ailsa	4-7-75
P-09 LEON GUZMAN	Scott	7-4-75
P-10 IGNACIO RAMIREZ	Ailsa	17-7-75
P-11 IGNACIO MARISCAL	Ailsa	23-9-75
P-12 HERIBERTO JARA CORONA	Ailsa	7-11-75
P-13 JOSÈ MARIA MATA	Lamont	13-10-75
P-14 FELIX ROMERO	Scott	23-6-75
P-15 FERNANDO LIZARDI	Ailsa	24-12-75
P-16 FRANCISCO J. MUJICA	Ailsa	21-11-75
P-17 PASTOR ROUAIX JOSÀ MARIA	Scott	7-11-75
P-18 JOSÉ MARIA DEL CASTILLO VELASCO	Lamont	14-1-75
P-19 LUIS MANUEL ROJAS	Lamont	3-4-76
P-20 JOSÈ NATIVIDAD MACIAS	Lamont	2-9-76
P-21 ESTEBAN BACA CALDERON	Lamont	18-6-76
P-22 GENERAL IGNACIO ZARAGOZA	Vera Cruz	1-6-76
P-23 TAMAULIPAS	Vera Cruz	1978
P-24 YUCATAN	Vera Cruz	1978
P-25 TABASCO	Vera Cruz	1-1-79
P-26 VERACRUZ	Vera Cruz	1-1-79
P-27 CAMPECHE	Vera Cruz	1-1-79
P-28 PUEBLA	Vera Cruz	1-1-79
P-29 MARGARITA MAZA DE JUAREZ	Salina Cruz	1-79
P-30 LEONA VICARIO	Salina Cruz	1-79
P-31 JOSEFA ORTIZ DE DOMINGUEZ	Salina Cruz	1-79
P-32 N. . .	. . .	. . .
P-33 N. . .	. . .	. . .
P-34 N. . .	. . .	. . .
P-35 N. . .	. . .	. . .

D: 115 tons (165 fl) **S:** 23 kts **Dim:** 36.50 (30.94 pp) × 8.6 × 2.0
A: 1/7.62-mm mg
M: 2 Ruston-Paxman Ventura 12-cyl. diesels; 7,200 hp **Electric:** 80 kw
Range: 2,500/12 **Man:** 2 officers, 22 men

REMARKS: Original order for 21 placed 27-3-73 with Associated British Machine Tool Makers, Ltd., which subcontracted the actual construction and assisted with the construction of another 11 in Mexico. Four additional units ordered 23-6-83.

Andres Quintana Roo (P-01)—prior to arming Ailsa Shipbldg., 1975

PATROL CRAFT

◆ **10 Olmeca class** Bldr: Acapulco NSY, Mexico (In serv. 1979-84)

D: . . . **S:** 25 kts **Dim:** 15.0 × . . . × . . .
A: 1/20-mm AA **M:** 2 Cummins VT-series diesels; 800 hp **Man:** 7 tot.

REMARKS: Glass-reinforced plastic construction. *Puebla,* the last of a first series, commissioned 22-2-83. Five additional ordered 23-6-83 and delivered by end 1984. Additional units planned.

◆ **4 Polimar class** Bldrs: Astilleros de Tampico (IF-01, IF-04); Iscacas SY, Guerrero (IF-02, IF-03)

	L		L
IF-01 POLIMAR 1	1962	IF-03 POLIMAR 3	1966
IF-02 POLIMAR 2	1966	IF-04 POLIMAR 4	1968

Polimar 1 1962

D: 57 tons (fl) **S:** 16 kts **Dim:** 20.5 × 4.5 × 1.3
A: 2/13.2-mm mg (II × 1) **M:** 2 diesels; 2 props; 450 hp

◆ **2 Azueta class** Bldr: Astilleros de Tampico

IF-06 AZUETA (L: 1959) IF-07 VILLAPANDO (L: 1960)

D: 80 tons (85 fl) **S:** 12 kts **Dim:** 26.0 × 4.9 × 2.1
A: 2/13.2-mm mg (II × 1) **M:** 2 Superior diesels; 2 props; 600 hp

RIVER PATROL CRAFT

◆ **8 AM-1 class** Bldrs: Astilleros de Tampico (4); Vera Cruz SY (4)(L: 1960-62)

AM-1 TO AM-8 (IF-11 to IF-18)

D: 37 tons (fl) **S:** 6 kts **Dim:** 17.7 × 5.0 × . . .
A: . . . **M:** Diesels

AUXILIARIES

HYDROGRAPHIC SURVEY SHIPS

◆ **1 ex-U.S. Robert D. Conrad-class oceanographic research ship**

	Bldr	L	In serv.
H-05 ALTAIR (ex-*James M. Gillis,* AGOR 4)	Christy Corp., Wisconsin	19-5-62	5-11-62

D: 1,200 tons (1,380 fl) **S:** 13.5 kts **Dim:** 63.7 × 11.4 × 6.3
Electron Equipt: Radar: 1/Raytheon TM 1600/6X; 1/TM 1660/123
M: 2 Caterpillar D-378 diesels; electric drive; 1 prop; 1,000 hp
Electric: 850 kw **Fuel:** 211 tons **Range:** 10,000/12
Man: 26 crew, 18 scientists

REMARKS: Returned to U.S. Navy by University of Miami in 1980 and laid up, until lease to Mexico on 15-6-83; Mexico bore the expense of subsequent reactivation. The large stack contains a 620-hp gas turbine generator set to drive the main shaft at speeds up to 6.5 kts for experiments requiring "quiet" sea conditions. Also has a retractable electric bow-thruster/propulsor, which can drive the ship to 4.5 kts. Refitted and recommissioned 27-11-84.

◆ **1 ex-U.S. Admirable-class former minesweeper** Bldr: Willamette Iron & Steel, Ore.

H-2 OCEANOGRAFICO (ex-DM 20, ex-*Harlequin,* MSF 365)

REMARKS: Launched 3-6-44. Data as for corvettes, except for displacement, which is approximately 900 tons (full load); no armament. Converted 1976-78.

HYDROGRAPHIC SURVEY SHIPS *(continued)*

◆ **1 ex-U.S. Auk-class former minesweeper** Bldr: General Eng. & DD, Alameda, Cal.

	Laid down	L	In serv.
H-1 Mariano Matamoros (ex-*Herald,* MSF 101)	14-3-42	4-7-42	23-3-43

Mariano Matamoros (H-1) G. Arra, 1977

Remarks: Data generally as for corvette version. Has Busch-Sulzer BS539 diesels; 3,118 hp. No armament. Large deckhouse built around after stack with a portable facility for aerological balloon-launching atop it. Oceanographic crane at stern. Radars are one SPS-5 and one Kelvin-Hughes 14/9.

Note: H-1 or H-2 was to strike when H-05 became operational.

REPAIR SHIP

◆ **1 ex-U.S. Fabius-class former aircraft repair ship**

	Bldr	L	In serv.
IA-05 General Vicente Guerrero (ex-*Megara,* ARVA 6, ex-LST 1095)	American Bridge, Pa.	25-3-45	27-6-45

General Vicente Guerrero (IA-05) L. & L. Van Ginderen, 7-84

D: 4,100 tons (fl) **S:** 11.6 kts **Dim:** 100.0 (96.3 wl) × 15.24 × 3.4
A: 8/40-mm AA (IV × 2) **M:** 2 G.M. 12-567A diesels; 2 props; 1,700 hp
Electric: 520 kw **Fuel:** 474 tons **Range:** 10,000/10 **Man:** 250 tot.

Remarks: Transferred 1-10-73. Originally intended for repairing aircraft airframes. One 10-ton boom. Two Mk 51 Mod. 2 GFCS for the 40-mm AA.

TRANSPORTS

◆ **0 (+2) new construction**

	Bldr	Laid down	L	In serv.
IA-. . . N. . .	Tampico NSY No. 1	. . .	. . .	. . .
IA-. . . N. . .	Salina Cruz NSY No. 8	. . .	. . .	. . .

Remarks: Ordered 1984 as troop transports, vehicle carriers, transports for construction materials, food, and hospital equipment and to act as floating infirmaries and civil disaster relief ships. Will replace IA-01 and IA-02. First was to complete by end 1985, but schedule does not seem to have been met.

◆ **1 Mexican built** Bldr: Ulua SY, Vera Cruz (In serv. 1959)

B-2 Zacatecas

D: 780 tons **S:** 10 kts **Dim:** 47.5 × 8.2 × 2.8
A: 1/40-mm AA—2/20-mm AA (I × 2)
M: 1 M.A.N. diesel; 1 prop; 560 hp **Man:** 13 officers, 37 men

Remarks: Was scheduled to strike at end 1985.

◆ **2 U.S. LST 542-class former landing ships**

	Bldr	L	In serv.
IA-01 Rio Panuco (ex-*Park Co.,* LST 1077)	Bethlehem Steel, Hingham, Mass.	9-3-44	31-3-44
IA-02 Manzanillo (ex-*Clearwater Co.,* LST 602)	Chicago Bridge & Iron, Seneca, Ill.	18-4-45	8-5-45

Rio Panuco (IA-01) L. & L. Van Ginderen, 3-82

D: 1,625 tons (4,100 fl) **S:** 11.6 kts **Dim:** 100.0 × 96.3 × 15.24 × 3.4
A: 8/40-mm AA (II × 2, I × 4)—IA-02: None **Electric:** 300 kw
Range: 6,000/11 **Man:** 130 men, 170 troops/passengers

Remarks: Transferred 20-9-71 and 25-2-72. Intended as disaster relief ships. IA-02 had been used in Arctic Supply by the Military Sealift Command and has two cargo kingposts, no armament, and an ice-reinforced waterline forward.

TRAINING SHIPS

◆ **1 sail-training ship** Bldr: Ast. y Talleres Celaya, Bilbao, Spain

	Laid down	L	In serv.
Cuauhtemoc	27-4-81	. . .	11-12-82

Cuauhtemoc Ingenieria Naval, 8-83

D: 1,200 tons (fl) **S:** 15 kts **Dim:** 90.0 (67.0 pp) × 10.6 × 4.2
M: 1 G.M. 12V149 diesel; 1 prop; 750 hp **Man:** 90 tot.

Remarks: Ordered 1980.

◆ **1 ex-U.S. Edsall-class training frigate** Bldr: Brown SB, Houston, Tex.

	Laid down	L	In serv.
IA-06 Manuel Azueta (ex-*Hurst,* DE 250)	27-1-43	14-4-43	30-8-43

Manuel Azueta (IA-06) L. & L. Van Ginderen, 7-81

D: 1,200 tons (1,590 fl) **S:** 21 kts **Dim:** 93.26 × 11.15 × 3.73
A: 3/76.2-mm Mk 22 DP (I × 3)—8/40-mm AA (IV × 1, II × 2)
Electron Equipt: Radar: 1/Kelvin-Hughes 14/9, 1/Kelvin-Hughes 17/9, 1/Mk 26
M: 4 Fairbanks-Morse 38D⅛, 10-cyl. diesels; 2 props; 6,000 hp
Electric: 680 kw **Fuel:** 258 tons **Range:** 13,000/12
Man: 15 officers, 201 men

Remarks: Transferred 1-10-73. Former destroyer escort. Used as training ship for the Gulf Fleet. Has one Mk 52 radar fire-control director and one Mk 51 rangefinder for the 76.2-mm guns, and three Mk 51 Mod. 2 directors for the 40-mm AA.

MEXICO *(continued)*
TRAINING SHIPS *(continued)*

◆ **1 former frigate** Bldr: Union Naval de Levante, Valencia, Spain

	Laid down	L	In serv.
IB-01 Durango	1934	28-6-35	1936

D: 1,600 tons (2,000 fl) **S:** 18 kts **Dim:** 78.2 × 11.2 × 3.1
A: 2/102-mm (I × 2)—2/57-mm (I × 2)—4/20-mm AA (II × 2)
M: 2 Enterprise DMR 38 diesels; electric drive; 2 props; 5,000 hp
Fuel: 140 tons **Range:** 3,000/12 **Man:** 24 officers, 125 men

Remarks: Originally built as an armed transport with accommodations for 20 officers, 450 men, and a number of horses. Steam turbine propulsion plant replaced 1967. Immobile as a training hulk for new recruits, but in 1982 it was announced that she was to be rehabilitated for seagoing training and VIP cruising duties.

TUGS

◆ **4 ex-U.S. Abnaki-class fleet tugs** Bldrs: IA-17, United Engineering, Alameda, Cal.; others, Charleston SB & DD, S.C.

	Laid down	L	In serv.
IA-17 Otumi (ex-*Molala,* ATF 106)	26-7-42	23-12-42	29-9-43
IA-18 Yaqui (ex-*Hitichi,* ATF 103)	24-8-43	29-1-44	27-5-44
IA-19 Seri (ex-*Abnaki,* ATF 96)	28-11-42	22-4-43	15-11-43
IA-20 Cora (ex-*Cocopa,* ATF 101)	23-5-43	5-10-43	25-3-44

D: 1,325 tons (1,675) fl) **S:** 16.5 kts **Dim:** 62.48 × 11.73 × 4.67
A: 1/76.2-mm DP **Electron Equipt:** Radar: 1/LN-66
M: 4 Busch-Sulzer BS539 diesels, electric drive; 1 prop; 3,000 hp
Electric: 400 kw **Fuel:** 304 tons **Range:** 7,000/15; 15,000/8 **Man:** 85 tot.

Remarks: IA-17 transferred 1-8-78, the others on 30-9-78. Unarmed on delivery. Used on patrol duties and as rescue tugs.

◆ **2 ex-U.S. Maritime Administration V-4 class** Bldr: Pendleton SY, New Orleans (In serv. 1943-44)

IA-12 R-2 (ex-*Montauk*) IA-13 Rf-3 (ex-*Point Vicente*)

D: 1,825 tons (fl) **S:** 14 kts **Dim:** 59.23 × 11.43 × 5.72
A: 1/76.2-mm Mk 22 DP—2/20-mm AA
M: 2 Enterprise diesels; 2 Kort-nozzle props; 2,250 hp **Fuel:** 566 tons
Range: 19,000/14 **Man:** 90 tot.

Remarks: Transferred 6-69. Sister R-4 lost in 1973; R-6 discarded in 1970. R-1 in 1978, and R-5 in 1979.

SERVICE CRAFT

◆ **2 ex-U.S. 174-foot-class harbor fuel lighters**

	Bldr	L	In serv.
IA-03 Aguascalientes (ex-YOG 6)	J. H. Mathis, Camden, N.J.	3-4-43	15-11-43
IA-04 Tlaxcala (ex-YO 107)	G. Lawley, Neponset, Mass.	3-11-43	27-11-43

D: 440 tons (1,480 fl) **S:** 8 kts **Dim:** 53.0 × 9.75 × 2.5
A: 1/20-mm AA **M:** 1 or 2 diesels; 1 prop; 500-600 hp
Man: 5 officers, 21 men

Remarks: Transferred 8-64. Cargo capacity: 980 tons (6,570 bbl).

◆ **2 yard tugs**

Pragmar Patron

Remarks: Bought in 1973.

◆ **1 ex-U.S. ARD-12-class floating dry dock**

	Bldr	In serv.
N. . . . . . . (ex-ARD 15)	Pacific Bridge, Alameda, Cal.	1-44

Lift capacity: 3,500 tons **Dim:** 149.87 × 24.69 × 1.73 (light)

Remarks: Transferred 4-71 on loan; purchased 1981.

◆ **2 ex-U.S. ARD-2-class floating dry docks** Bldr: Pacific Bridge, Alameda, Cal.

N. . . . . . . (ex-ARD 2)(In serv. 4-42) N. . . . . . . (ex-ARD-11)(In serv. 10-43)

Lift capacity: 3,500 tons **Dim:** 148.0 × 21.64 × 1.6 (light)

Remarks: Transferred 8-63 and 6-74.

◆ **1 ex-U.S. small auxiliary floating dry dock** Bldr: Doullut & Ewin, Mobile, Ala.

N. . . . . . . (ex-AFDL 28)(In serv. 8-44)

Lift capacity: 1,000 tons **Dim:** 60.96 × 19.51 × 1.04 (light)

Remarks: Transferred 1-73.

◆ **7 ex-U.S. floating cranes**

(ex-YD 156) (ex-YD 179) (ex-YD 183) (ex-YD 203)
(ex-YD 157) (ex-YD 180) (ex-YD 194)

Remarks: Transferred 1964-71; purchased 7-78 (except YD 179, 194).

◆ **1 ex-U.S. pile driver**

N. . . . . . . (ex-YPD 48)

Remarks: Transferred 8-68.

◆ **7 Class I-D oil-spill recovery boats** Bldr: Marco, Seattle, Wash. (In serv. 1982)

D: . . . **S:** 15 kts **Dim:** 11.4 × 3.08 × . . .
M: 2 G.M. 4-53 diesels; 2 outdrives; 240 hp

Remarks: Use Marco Filterbelt recovery system; speed 2 kts when operating.

MONTSERRAT

Colony of Montserrat

Merchant Marine (1984): 1 ship—711 grt

MONTSERRAT POLICE FORCE

PATROL CRAFT

◆ **1 glass-reinforced plastic-hulled** Bldr: Brooke Marine, Lowestoft, U.K.

Emerald Star (In serv. 1971)

D: 15 tons **S:** 22 kts **Dim:** 12.0 × . . . × . . .
A: 3/7.62-mm mg **Electron Equipt:** Radar: 1/Decca . . . nav.
M: 2 diesels; 2 props; 740 hp **Man:** 4 tot.

Remarks: Refitted and re-engined 1983.

MOROCCO

Kingdom of Morocco

Personnel (1984): 1,800 men, including 58 officers and 260 senior petty officers.

Merchant Marine (1984): 261 ships—433,893 grt (tankers: 18 ships—176,638 grt)

Note: Morocco is seeking to renew and expand its present forces. Discussions have been held with the Netherlands for the building of four *Fatahillah*-class light frigates and with Frederikshavn SY, Denmark, in 6-85 for the construction of one "Osprey"-class offshore patrol boat: 390 tons (fl); 20 kts; 49.98 × 10.50 × 2.70 m, powered by 2 Alpha 16V-23L-VO diesels, 4,680 hp; 1/40-mm AA, 15 crew. No firm orders are known to have been placed.

FRIGATE

◆ **1 Spanish Descubierta class** Bldr: Bazán, El Ferrol

	Laid down	L	In serv.
501 Colonel Errhamani	20-3-79	26-2-82	28-3-83

Colonel Errhamani (501) French Navy, 1983

FRIGATE *(continued)*

D: 1,270 tons (1,479 fl) **S:** 26 kts **Dim:** 88.88 (85.8 pp) × 10.4 × 3.25 (3.7 fl)
A: 4/MM 38 Exocet—1/Albatros SAM syst. (24 Aspide missiles)—1/76-mm OTO Melara DP—2/40-mm AA (I × 2)—1/375-mm Bofors ASW RL (II × 1, 24 rockets)—6/324-mm ASW TT (III × 2)
Electron Equipt: Radar: 1/DA-05, 1/ZW-06, 1/WM 25/41 (all H.S.A.)
Sonar: Raytheon DE 1160B
EW: ELT 715 intercept/jammer
M: 4 Bazán-MTU 16MA956 TB91 diesels; 2 CP props; 18,000 hp
Electric: 1,810 kw **Fuel:** 150 tons
Range: 4,000/18 (one engine) **Man:** 100 tot.

REMARKS: Ordered 14-6-77. Carries 600 rds 76-mm. Has fin stabilizers.

PATROL BOATS

◆ **4 (+3 + 3) Spanish Lazaga class** Bldr: Bazán, Cadiz

	L	In serv.
304 COMMANDANT AL KHATTABI	21-7-80	3-6-81
305 COMMANDANT BOUTOUBA	. . .	11-12-81
306 COMMANDANT EL HARTI	. . .	25-2-82
307 COMMANDANT AZOUGGARH	. . .	2-8-82

Commandant Azouggarh (307) L. & L. Van Ginderen, 12-82

D: 303 tons (420 fl) **S:** 29.6 kts **Dim:** 57.40 (54.4 pp) × 7.60 × 2.70
A: 4/Exocet SSM—1/76-mm OTO Melara DP—1/40-mm AA—2/20-mm AA (I × 2)
Electron Equipt: Radar: 1/Raytheon 1620, 1/H.S.A. WM 25
M: 2 Bazán-MTU MA16V956 TB91 diesels; 2 props; 7,780 hp
Electric: 405 kVA **Range:** 700/27; 3,000/15 **Man:** 41 tot.

REMARKS: Ordered 14-6-77. Carry 300 rds 76-mm 1,472 rds 40-mm, 3,000 rds 20-mm ammunition. Have added fuel capacity over Spanish Navy version. CSEE Naja optical director aft. Frequently carry only two MM 38. Three (+3 options) ordered 2-10-85 for offshore patrol; see addenda for details.

◆ **2 French PR-72 type** Bldr: SFCN, Villeneuve-la-Garenne

	L	In serv.		L	In serv.
302 OKBA	10-10-75	16-12-76	303 TRIKI	2-2-76	2-77

Triki (303) G. Gyssels, 10-82

D: 370 tons (440 fl) **S:** 28 kts (at 413 tons) **Dim:** 57.0 (54.0 pp) × 7.6 × 2.5
A: 1/76-mm OTO Melara DP—1/40-mm Bofors AA
M: 4 AGO 16ASHR diesels; 2 props; 11,040 hp **Electric:** 360 kw
Range: 2,500/16 **Man:** 5 officers, 48 men

REMARKS: Ordered in 6-73. Have 2 CSEE optronic gun directors.

◆ **1 Al Bachir class** Bldr: Constr. Méc. de Normandie (CMN), Cherbourg

	Laid down	L	In serv.
22 AL BACHIR	6-65	25-2-67	4-67

Al Bachir—wearing old number

D: 124.5 tons (light)(153.5 fl) **S:** 25.5 kts **Dim:** 40.6 (38.0 pp) × 6.35 × 1.4
A: 2/40-mm—2 mg **M:** 2 SEMT-Pielstick 12 PA diesels; 2 props; 3,600 hp
Fuel: 21 tons **Range:** 2,000/15 **Man:** 3 officers, 20 men

◆ **1 French Fougueux class** Bldr: Constr. Méc. de Normandie, Cherbourg

	Laid down	L	In serv.
32 LIEUTENANT RIFFI	5-63	1-3-64	5-64

D: 311 tons (374 fl) **S:** 19 kts **Dim:** 52.95 (51.82 pp) × 7.04 × 2.01
A: 2/40-mm AA **M:** 2 SEMT-Pielstick diesels; 2 CP props; 3,600 hp
Range: 2,000/15; 3,000/12 **Man:** 4 officers, 55 men

REMARKS: 1/76.2-mm gun and all ASW ordnance have been removed.

◆ **1 ex-French patrol boat** Bldr: Chantiers Navals de l'Estérel, Cannes

11 EL SABIQ (ex-P 762, ex-VC 12)(L: 13-8-57)

D: 60 tons (80 fl) **S:** 28 kts **Dim:** 31.77 × 4.7 × 1.7 **Range:** 1,500/15
A: 2/20-mm AA **M:** 2 Mercedes-Benz diesels; 2 props; 2,700 hp **Man:** 17 tot.

REMARKS: Transferred 15-11-60.

◆ **1 French Sirius-class former minesweeper** Bldr: Penhoët, St. Nazaire

51 TAWFIC (ex-*Aries,* M 758) (L: 31-3-56)

D: 365 tons light (440 fl) **S:** 15 kts **Dim:** 46.40 (42.70 pp) × 8.55 × 2.50
A: 1/40-mm AA—1/20-mm AA **Electron Equipt:** Radar: 1/DRBN-31
M: 2 SEMT-Pielstick 16 PA-1-175 diesels; 2 props; 2,000 hp
Fuel: 48 tons **Range:** 3,000/10 **Man:** 38 tot.

REMARKS: Loaned by the French Navy 28-11-74 for a period of four years, renewed 1978 and then made permanent on 30-9-80. Wood-planked hull on aluminum-alloy framing. Sweep gear removed.

PATROL CRAFT

◆ **6 French P 92 type** Bldr: CMN, Cherbourg

	L	In serv.		L	In serv.
EL WACIL	12-6-75	9-10-75	EL KHAFIR	21-1-76	16-4-76
EL JAIL	10-10-75	3-12-75	EL HARIS	31-3-76	30-6-76
EL MIKDAM	1-12-75	30-1-76	ESSAHIR	2-6-76	16-7-76

El Wacil CMN, 1975

D: 89 tons **S:** 28 kts **Dim:** 32.0 × 5.35 × 1.7 (1.42 hull)
A: 2/20-mm AA (I × 2) **Electron Equipt:** Radar: 1/Decca
M: 2 MGO 12 V BZSHR diesels; 2,700 hp **Range:** 1,200/15 **Man:** 12 tot.

REMARKS: Contract, 2-74. Laminated-wood hull. Six additional sisters were reported ordered 6-85 for the Customs Service.

AMPHIBIOUS WARFARE SHIPS

◆ **3 French Champlain-class medium landing ships** Bldr: Dubigeon, Normandy

	In serv.
402 DAOUD BEN AICHA	28-5-77
403 AHMED ES SAKALI	9-77
404 ABOU ABDALLAH EL AYACHI	12-78

D: 750 tons (1,305 fl) **S:** 16 kts **Dim:** 80.0 (68.0 pp) × 13.0 × 2.4 mean
A: 2/40-mm AA (I × 2)—2/81-mm mortars (I × 2)

MOROCCO *(continued)*
AMPHIBIOUS WARFARE SHIPS *(continued)*

Abou Abdallah El Ayachi (404) French Navy, 1984

M: 2 SACM diesels; 2 CP props; 1,800 hp
Range: 4,500/13 **Man:** 30 officers, 54 men

Remarks: Can carry 133 troops and about 12 vehicles. Helicopter platform aft.

◆ **1 French EDIC-class utility landing craft** Bldr: C. N. Franco-Belges (In serv. 1965)

401 Lieutenant Malghagh

Lieutenant Malghagh—wearing old number 1977

D: 292 tons (642 fl) **S:** 8 kts **Dim:** 59.0 × 11.95 × 1.3 (1.62 fl)
A: 2/20-mm AA (I × 2)—1/120-mm mortar (fwd)
M: 2 MGO diesels; 2 props; 1,000 hp **Range:** 1,800/8 **Man:** 16 tot.

AUXILIARIES

◆ **1 training ship**

Essaouira

D: 60 tons

Remarks: Yacht presented by Italy in 1967. Used for training watchstanders.

◆ **2 former Norwegian cargo ships**

Elaigh (ex-. . .) Ad Dakhla (ex-. . .)

D: 1,500 grt **S:** . . . **Dim:** . . . × . . . × . . .
A: 2/14.5-mm AA (II × 1) **M:** . . .

Remarks: Acquired to provide logistic support for operations along the Sahara coast. Four 5-ton cranes.

◆ **2 yachts**

Akhir (In serv. 1982)
Sequet El Hamra

◆ **1 harbor launch** Bldr: ARCOR, La Teste, France

D: 11 tons (fl) **S:** 17 kts **Dim:** 13.00 (11.30 pp) × 3.80 × 1.10
M: 1 Baudouin 12-F11-Sm diesel; 1 prop; 426 hp
Range: 400/ . . . **Man:** 4 tot.

Remarks: Ordered 1-85. Glass-reinforced plastic construction.

CUSTOMS SERVICE

◆ **0 (+6) French P92-type patrol boats** Bldr: CMN, Cherbourg

D: 89 tons **S:** 29 kts **Dim:** 32.00 (30.09 pp) × 5.35 × 1.42 (hull)
A: 2/20-mm AA **Electron Equipt:** Radar: 1/. . . **Range:** 1,200/15
M: 2 SACM MGO 175V12 BZSHR diesels; 2 props; 2,700 hp **Man:** 12 tot.

Remarks: Ordered 6-85. Wooden construction. Six sisters in Navy.

◆ **18 patrol craft** Bldr: ARCOR, La Teste, France

D: 14 tons **S:** 24 kts **Dim:** 14.20 (12.40 pp) × 4.00 × 1.20
A: 1/7.62-mm mg **M:** 2 UNI UD18-V8HS diesels; 2 props; 1,120 hp
Range: 200/. . . **Man:** . . .

Remarks: Ordered 6-85. Glass-reinforced plastic construction.

MOZAMBIQUE

People's Republic of Mozambique

Personnel (1985): Approx. 600 total

Merchant Marine (1984): 98 ships—45,753 grt (tankers: 2 ships—6,549 grt)

PATROL BOATS AND CRAFT

◆ **2 Soviet S.O.-1 class**

D: 190 tons (215 fl) **S:** 29 kts **Dim:** 42.0 × 6.1 × 1.9 (hull)
A: 4/25-mm AA (II × 2)—4/RBU-1200 ASW RL (V × 4)—2/d.c. racks (24 d.c.)—mines
Electron Equipt: Radar: 1/Pot Head—Sonar: 1/Tamir-11 (HF)
IFF: 1/Dead Duck interrogator, 1/High Pole-A transponder
M: 3 Type 40D diesels; 3 props; 7,500 hp **Range:** 340/28; 1,900/7
Man: 30 tot.

Remarks: Transferred 6-85. Built 1958-64 and hard-used, they are not likely to be of much combat value. Bad rollers and very noisy.

◆ **10 Indian-design** Bldr: Mazagon SY, Goa (In serv. 1984-85)

D: . . . **S:** 20 kts **Dim:** 18.0 × 5.0 × . . .
A: . . . **M:** 2 diesels; 2 props; 1,100 hp

Remarks: First four launched together 4-84. Can also be used for towing.

◆ **7 Soviet Zhuk class**

D: 60 tons (fl) **S:** 34 kts **Dim:** 24.0 × 5.0 × 1.8 (props)
A: 2 or 4/14.5-mm mg (II × 1 or 2) **Electron Equipt:** Radar: 1/Spin Trough
M: 2 M50 diesels; 2 props; 2,400 hp

Remarks: Transferred: 1 in -79, 2 in 10-80, 2 in 10-81, and 2 in 1982.

◆ **1 Soviet Poluchat-1 class**

D: 90 tons (fl) **S:** 18 kts **Dim:** 29.6 × 6.1 × 1.9
A: 2/14.5-mm mg (II × 1) **M:** 2 M50 diesels; 2 props; 2,400 hp
Range: 450/17; 900/10 **Man:** 20 tot.

Remarks: Transferred 1977.

◆ **2 Portuguese Jupiter class**

D: 32 tons (43.5 fl) **S:** 20 kts **Dim:** 21.5 × 5.0 × 1.3
A: 1/20-mm AA **M:** 2 Cummins diesels; 2 props; 1,270 hp **Man:** 8 tot.

Remarks: Operate on Lake Malawi (Lake Nyasa).

◆ **2 Portuguese Bellatrix class**

N. . . . . . . (ex-*Sirius*) N. . . . . . . (ex-*Vega*)

D: 23 tons **S:** 15 kts **Dim:** 20.7 × 4.6 × 1.2
A: 1/20-mm AA **Man:** 7 tot.

Remarks: Operate on Lake Malawi (Lake Nyasa).

AMPHIBIOUS WARFARE CRAFT

◆ **1 Portuguese Alfange-class landing craft**

N. . . . . . . (ex-*Cimitarra*)

D: 285 tons (635 fl) **S:** 10 kts **Dim:** 59.0 × 11.91 × 1.6
A: 2/20-mm AA (I × 2) **M:** 2 MTU MD225 diesels; 2 props; 1,000 hp
Range: 1,800/8 **Man:** 20 tot.

◆ **2 Portuguese LDM-100-class landing craft**

D: 50 tons (fl) **S:** 9 kts **Dim:** 15.25 × . . . × . . .
M: 2 G.M. diesels; 2 props; 450 hp

AUXILIARIES

◆ **2 small cargo lighters** Bldr: Mazagon SY, Goa, India

Remarks: No details available; ordered 1983.

NATO

North Atlantic Treaty Organization

NOTE: The oceanographic research ship described below is the only vessel "owned" jointly by the NATO nations. There is, however, a NATO Standing Force of frigates and destroyers, which would be augmented in time of war by warships from the major signatory nations.

◆ **1 oceanographic research ship** Bldr: CNR, Genoa

N. . . (In serv. 1986)

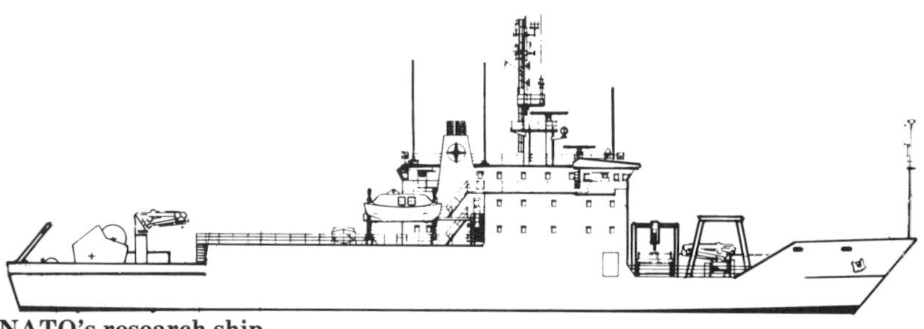

NATO's research ship

D: . . . **S:** 17 kts (16.3 sust.) **Dim:** 93.0 × 15.2 × 5.0
Electron Equipt: . . .
M: 2 GMT diesels, AEG electric drive; 2 props; 5,140 hp—450-hp electric auxiliary drive
Range: 8,000/12 **Electric:** 1,850 kw **Man:** . . .

REMARKS: Will be based at Naples and fly the Italian ensign; operated for SACLANT (Supreme Allied Commander, Atlantic). Intended for acoustic, oceanographic, and hydrographic research. Helicopter platform. Bollard pull: 20 tons.

NETHERLANDS

Kingdom of the Netherlands

PERSONNEL (1983): Approximately 16,800, including Marines, Naval Air Service, and 411 female personnel; 6,500 civilian employees

MERCHANT MARINE (1984): 1,337 ships—4,585,991 grt (tankers: 77 ships—1,180,257 grt)

NAVAL AVIATION: The Navy's aircraft are divided into four administrative groups: three maritime patrol squadrons at Valkenburg and one helicopter squadron at Dekoog. Principal types include (as of 7-83): 13 P-3C Orion (2 in storage); 6 BR-1050 Atlantique Mk 1 (grounded); 2 F-27 Maritime; and 22 WG-13 Lynx helicopters

The WG-13 Lynx are of the following subtypes: 6 UH-14A search-and-rescue, delivered in 1976; 9 SH-14B with dipping sonar, ordered in 1976; and 8 SH-14C with ASQ-81 (V)2 MAD gear, ordered in 1978.

On 8-12-78, the Dutch Navy announced that 13 Lockheed P-3C Orion would be acquired to replace the PH-2S Neptune. The first two were operational in late 1981, and the last became operational in 1984. Two Fokker F-27 Maritime were delivered 9-81 and 2-82 to replace 3 PH-2S in the Netherlands Antilles at Curaçao. Two P-3C were to be laid up to save operating funds, according to a 5-85 statement.

WARSHIPS IN SERVICE, UNDER CONSTRUCTION, OR AUTHORIZED AS OF 1 JANUARY 1986

	L	Tons (surfaced)	Main armament
◆ **7 (+3) submarines**			
2 (+3) WALRUS	1984-85	2,300	6/533-mm TT
2 ZWAARDVIS	1970-71	2,370	6/533-mm TT
3 DOLFIJN/POTVIS	1960-65	1,494	8/533-mm TT
◆ **2 destroyers**		Tons	
2 TROMP	1973-74	3,665	1/Standard, 8/Harpoon, and 1/Sea Sparrow systems, 2/120-mm DP, 6/ASW TT, 1/ASW helicopter
◆ **13–15 (+9) frigates**			
0 (+8) M CLASS	1986-	2,650	4/Harpoon and 1/Sea Sparrow systems, 1/76-mm DP, 6/ASW TT, 1/helicopter
1 (+1) JACOB VAN HEEMSKERCK	1982-83	3,000	1/Standard, 8/Harpoon, 1/Sea Sparrow, 4/ASW TT
10 KORTENAER	1976-82	3,000	2/Harpoon and 1/Sea Sparrow systems, 1 or 2/76-mm DP, 4/ASW TT, 2/helicopters
2-4 VAN SPEIJK*	1965-67	2,200	2/Harpoon, 2/Sea Cat systems, 1/76-mm DP, ASW weapons, 1/helicopter
◆ **5 patrol boats**			
◆ **22 (+6) mine warfare ships**			

* 4 for sale

WEAPONS AND SYSTEMS

A. MISSILES

◆ *surface-to-air*

U.S./SM-1 MR Standard on the *Tromp*-class destroyers and to be on the two JACOB VAN HEEMSKERCK-class frigates

U.S. RIM-7M Sea Sparrow on the *Tromp*-class destroyers and *Jacob Van Heemskerck* and the *Kortenaer*-class frigates; British Sea Cat on the *Van Speijk*-class frigates

◆ *surface-to-surface*

U.S. Harpoon on the *Tromp, Van Heemskerck, Kortenaer,* and modernized *Van Speijk* classes

B. GUNS

120-mm twin-barreled automatic in the *Tromp*-class destroyers:
Weight: 65 tons
Arc of elevation: 10° to +85°
Muzzle velocity: 850 m/sec.
Direction rate: 25°/s in train, 40°/s in elevation
Rate of fire: 45 rounds/min/barrel
Maximum effective range in surface fire: 13,000 m
Maximum effective range in antiaircraft fire: 7,000 m

76-mm OTO Melara Compact on the *Kortenaer* and *Van Speijk*-class frigates

40-mm Bofors in single Bofors L70, mountings

30-mm SGE-30 "Goalkeeper," using the U.S. General Electric GAU-8A 30-mm gatling gun and EX-30 mounting co-mounted with an H.S.A. track-while-scan radar fire-control system. The latter uses independent I-band search/acquisition and I/K-band tracking radars. The 7-barreled gatling gun has a 4,200 rd/min. maximum rate of fire, 1,190 rds are carried on-mount. Muzzle velocity is 1,021 m/sec. Total weight, with ammunition, is 6,713 kg. The frigate *Callenburgh* is the first ship to carry "Goalkeeper," which will be installed in the *Kortenaer* and *Jacob Van Heemskerck* classes.

20-mm Oerlikon AA in single World-War-II-era 70-cal. and modern 90-cal. 20 F-2 mountings

Goalkeeper Signaal-G.E.

C. ANTISUBMARINE WEAPONS

U.S. Mk 44 and Mk 46 torpedoes on ships and aircraft

U.S. Mk 37 Mod. 2, NT-37C/D and Mk 48 torpedoes on submarines. Additional Mk 48 torpedoes were ordered in 1980. U.S. Honeywell NT-37E torpedoes (reworked Mk 37) are to be acquired.

D. RADARS

All designed and manufactured by Hollandse Signaal Apparaaten (H.S.A.), a division of Phillips:

Name	Type	Band
ZW-06	Navigation/surface search	I
ZW-07	Submarine, nav./surf. search	I
LW-02/03	Long-range air-search	D
LW-04	Long-range air-search	D
LW-08*	Long-range air-search	D
DA-05, 05A	Combined surveillance	E/F
DA-08	Medium-range air-search	E/F
SPS-01	3-D air-search	F
WM-20/25	Missile- and gunfire-control	K
M-44/45	Missile- and gunfire-control	. . .
SMART†	3-D air-search	F *or* I
STIR‡	Missile- and gunfire-control	I/K
LIROD-8	radar, optronic weapon control	. . .

* An extended-range version of LW-08 is under development.
† "Signaal Multi-beam Acquisition Radar for Targeting." For the *Jacob Van Heemskerck* class and possible refit to the *Tromp* class in place of SPS-01.
‡ U.S. design, built under license. STIR = "Separate Tracking and Illumination Radar"; has 1.8- and 2.9-m-dia. parabolic dish antennas and co-mounted t.v. camera.

E. SONARS

CWE-610, LF, hull-mounted: On the *Tromp*-class destroyers, and *Van Speijk*-class frigates
SQR-18A: U.S. towed passive linear array on two *Van Speijk*-class frigates
SQS-505, MF: license-built Canadian: On the *Kortenaer*-class frigates (PQS-36)
PHS-32, MF: Export sonar, hull-mounted or VDS
PHS-36, MF: On the *Jacob Van Heemskerck* and "M"-class frigates
Type 184, MF, hull-mounted: On the *Van Speijk*-class frigates
Octopus: Active/passive submarine array on *Walrus* class, derived from French Thomson-CSF "Eledone."

F. ELECTRONIC WARFARE

In use are the "Scimitar" J-Band deception and jamming system, "RAPIDS" I-18gHz passive intercept array, and "RAMSES" I/J-Band passive and deceptive repeater equipment. Chaff rocket launchers in use are the British-designed Knebworth/Corvus, 8-tubed, 76.2-mm launcher and the U.S. Mk 36 Super RBOC system with two Hycor 6-tubed Mk 136 launchers.

G. DATA-PROCESSING

SEWACO (Sensoren Wapens Commando): built by Hollandse Signaal Apparaaten and centrally directed by a DAISY 1, 2, 3, 4, or 5 digital computer system. It exists in four versions (SEWACO I, II, III, and IV) tailored to the sensors and weapon systems of the ships that carry it.

SINBADS: Submarine tracking system. Can track 5 targets and engage 3 simultaneously.

SUBMARINES

◆ **2 (+ 2 + 1) Walrus class** Bldr: Rotterdamse Droogdok Mij, Rotterdam

	Laid down	L	Trials	In serv.
S 801 Walrus	11-10-79	28-10-85	4-87	1988
S 802 Zeeleeuw	24-9-81	7-86	2-88	1989
S. . . N. . .	. . .	. . .	1992	1992
S. . . N. . .	. . .	. . .	1992	1994
S. . . N. . .	. . .	. . .	. . .	1998

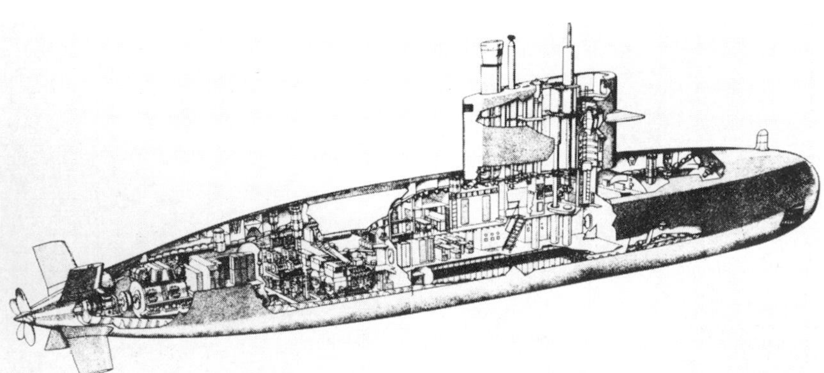

Walrus class Rhine-Schelde-Verolme, 1980

D: 1,900/2,450/2,800 tons **S:** 12/21 kts **Dim:** 67.73 × 8.40 × 7.0
A: 6/533-mm TT fwd. (20 Sub-Harpoon SSM/Mk 48 or NT.37C/O/E torpedoes/mines)
Electron Equipt: Radar: 1/ZW-07 (U.K. Decca Type 1001)
Sonar: Octopus active/passive, U.K. Type 2026 linear passive array
M: Diesel-electric: 3 SEMT-Pielstick 12 PA4V 200, 2,304 diesel generator groups; 1 Holec motor; 1 5-bladed prop; 3,950 surf./5,430 sub. hp (see Remarks)
Fuel: 310 tons **Range:** 10,000/9 (snorkel) **Man:** 7 officers, 43 men

Remarks: First two ordered 19-6-78 and 17-12-79. Second pair ordered 5-1-84. Plans to order a fifth and sixth in 1991 reduced to one in 6-85. Construction of first pair delayed by need to lengthen hull after keels laid in order to accommodate diesel generator sets. Second pair will return to use of Brons-Werkspoor 0-RUB 215X12 diesels. Propulsion plant is on resilient mountings to reduce noise emissions. Each HOLEC a.c./d.c. generator has built-in rectifiers and produces 980 kw. There are three 140-cell batteries. Endurance is 60 days. Periscope depth: 18 m. Torpedo tubes are of the "waterslug" type, capable of launching at any operational depth. Hull construction is of MAREL steel, with single-hull mid-body and double-hull ends; reserve bouyancy is 12%. Will have Gipsy data system, Sperry Mk 29 Mod. 2A inertial navigation system, NAVSAT receiver, and passive EW equipment.

◆ **2 Zwaardvis class** Bldr: Rotterdamse Droogdok Mij, Rotterdam

	Laid down	L	In serv.
S 806 Zwaardvis	7-67	2-7-70	18-2-72
S 807 Tijgerhaai	7-67	25-5-71	20-10-72

Zwaardvis (S 806) Skyfotos, 2-83

Tijgerhaai (S 807) G. Gyssels, 10-84

D: 2,350/2,408/2,640 tons **S:** 13/20 kts **Dim:** 66.92 × 8.40 × 7.10
A: 6/533-mm TT fwd — 20 torpedoes
Electron Equipt: Radar: 1/ZW-06
Sonar: . . .
M: Diesel-electric: 3 sets Werkspoor RUB 215X12, 1,400-hp diesel generators, 920 kw each; 1 3,800-kw motor; 1 5-bladed prop; 5,100 hp
Range: 10,000/9 (snorkel) **Man:** 8 officers, 59 men

Remarks: Ordered 24-12-65 and 14-7-66. Based on the U.S. Navy's *Barbel* class, which has a teardrop hull. Use of Dutch equipment necessitated modifications to the original design. The H.S.A.-M8 torpedo-firing system uses a digital computer that permits the simultaneous launching of two torpedoes, one of which may be wire-guided. For silent running, all noise-producing machinery is mounted on a false deck with spring suspension. Three 140-cell batteries. Mid-life refits planned for 1987-88.

◆ **3 Dolfijn/Potvis class**

	Bldr	Laid down	L	In serv.
S 804 Potvis	Wilton-Fijenoord	17-9-62	12-1-65	2-11-65
S 805 Tonijn	Wilton-Fijenoord	26-11-62	14-6-65	24-2-66
S 809 Zeehond	Rotterdam DDM	30-12-54	20-2-60	16-3-61

Tonijn (S 805) G. Gyssels, 9-84

SUBMARINES *(continued)*

Zeehond (S 809) L. & L. Van Ginderen, 3-85

D: 1,140/1,510/1,830 tons **S:** 14.5/17 kts **Dim:** 79.50 × 7.84 × 4.95—see Remarks
A: 8/533-mm TT (4 fwd, 4 aft) **Electron Equipt:** Radar: 1/ZW-06
M: Diesel-electric: 2 SEMT-Pielstick 12 PA4V185 diesels, 1,550 hp each; 2/920-kw electric motors; 2 props; 4,400 hp—see Remarks
Man: 8 officers, 59 men

REMARKS: S 804 and S 805 authorized in 1962, S 809 in 1949, S 809, 805: D: 1,509/1,831 tons; Dim: 78.25 × 7.80 × 4.95; 2 M.A.N. 12-V6V 22/30, 12-cylinder diesels, 1,400 hp each. The exterior hull has three parallel interior pressure cylinders, one of which is placed on top of a pair of slightly shorter ones. Diving depth: 300 m. Have two 168-cell batteries. The crew and the armament occupy the top cylinder, and the batteries and diesel engines are mounted in the other two. *Tonijn* received SEMT-Pielstick diesel generator sets during 1978; *Potvis* was given new engines in 1979. Sister *Dolfijn* (S 808) placed in reserve without refit or batteries during 1983 and was stricken 1-2-85 and sold for scrap 22-7-85. S 809 is to strike in 1986-87, S 804 in 1991, and S 805 in 1992.

GUIDED-MISSILE DESTROYERS

◆ **2 Tromp class** Bldr: Kon. Mij. de Schelde, Flushing

	Laid down	L	In serv.
F 801 TROMP	4-8-71	2-6-73	3-10-75
F 806 DE RUYTER (ex-*Heemskerck*)	22-12-71	9-3-74	3-6-76

Tromp (F 801)—with new chaff RL R. Neth. N., 1984

De Ruyter (F 806) R. Neth. N., 1982

D: 3,665 tons (4,308 fl) **S:** 28 kts (30 on trials)
Dim: 138.2 (131.0 pp) × 14.8 × 4.6 (6.6 max.)
A: 4/Harpoon missiles (II × 2)—1 Mk 13 missile launcher (I × 1, 40 SM-1 MR missiles)—1/NATO Sea Sparrow system (VII × 1, Mk 29, 60 missiles)—2/120-mm Bofors DP (II × 1)—6/324-mm Mk 32 ASW TT (III × 2)—1/Lynx ASW helicopter
Electron Equipt: Radar: 2/Decca 1226 nav., 1/SPS-01, 1/WM-25, 2/SPG-51C
Sonar: 1CWE-610, 1/162 (bottom search)
EW: Ramses active/passive array, Mk 36 SRBOC chaff syst. (VI × 4)
M: COGOG: 2 Rolls-Royce Olympus TM-3B gas turbines, 27,000 hp each; 2 Tyne RM-1C gas turbines, 4,100 hp each, for cruising (18 kts); 2 CP 4-bladed props; 54,000 hp
Electric: 4,000 kw **Fuel:** 600 tons **Range:** 5,000/18
Man: 34 officers, 271 men

REMARKS: Although the Dutch Navy designates them as frigates, these ships, by virtue of their armament and size, are more closely related to guided-missile destroyers. They have fin stabilizers, and are excellent sea boats. Equipped with an admiral's cabin and command facilities, they can act as flagships. Berthing for enlisted men is in 6-, 9-, or 12-man compartments. The propulsion machinery is arranged in three compartments, forward to aft: 2 Olympus gas turbines, 2 generator sets, and the auxiliary boilers; 2 Tyne gas turbines; 2 generator sets. The 450-V, 3-phase, 60-Hz current is produced by four groups of 1,000-kw generators, each driven by a SMIT/Paxman Valenta RP 200, 12-cylinder diesel; two sets are sufficient for full combat power. There are three auxiliary boilers for heating. Fitted with Harpoon 1977/78; normally carry only 4 (II × 2), but can carry 8 (IV × 2). SEWACO-I data system. New plastic radomes for SPS-01 radar, 1980, called "Kojack." EW system updated on *Tromp* and LINK 11 data exchange system added; F 806 to follow in 1985. Planned mid-life modernizations canceled; will now receive only an "update" late in the 1980s.

GUIDED-MISSILE FRIGATES

◆ **0 (+4 + 4) M class** Bldr: de Schelde, Vlissingen

	Laid down	L	In serv.
F 827 DE ZEVEN PROVINCEN	26-2-85	1986	1988
F 828 N. . .	6-11-85	. . .	. . .
F 829 N. . .	. . .	. . .	. . .
F 830 N. . .	. . .	. . .	. . .

D: 2,650 tons light (3,050 fl) **S:** 29 kts (20 kts on diesels)
Dim: 122.1 (114.0 pp) × 14.4 (13.1 wl) × 4.25 (6.00 sonar)
A: 4/Harpoon SSM (II × 2)—VLS Sea Sparrow SAM syst. (16 missiles)—1/76-mm OTO Melara DP—1/30-mm Goalkeeper gatling CIWS—2/20-mm AA (I × 2)—4/324-mm ASW TT (II × 2, fixed)—1/Lynx helicopter

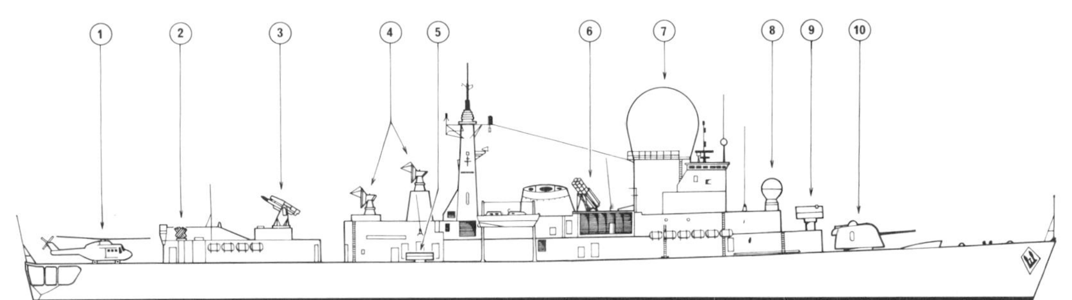

Tromp 1. Lynx helicopter 2. Two Mk 136 chaff RL 3. Mk 13 missile launcher 4. SPG-51C radars 5. Mk 32 torpedo tubes 6. Harpoon launchers 7. SPS-01 3-D radar 8. WM-25 fire-control radar 9. Sea Sparrow system 10. 120-mm gunmount

GUIDED-MISSILE FRIGATES *(continued)*

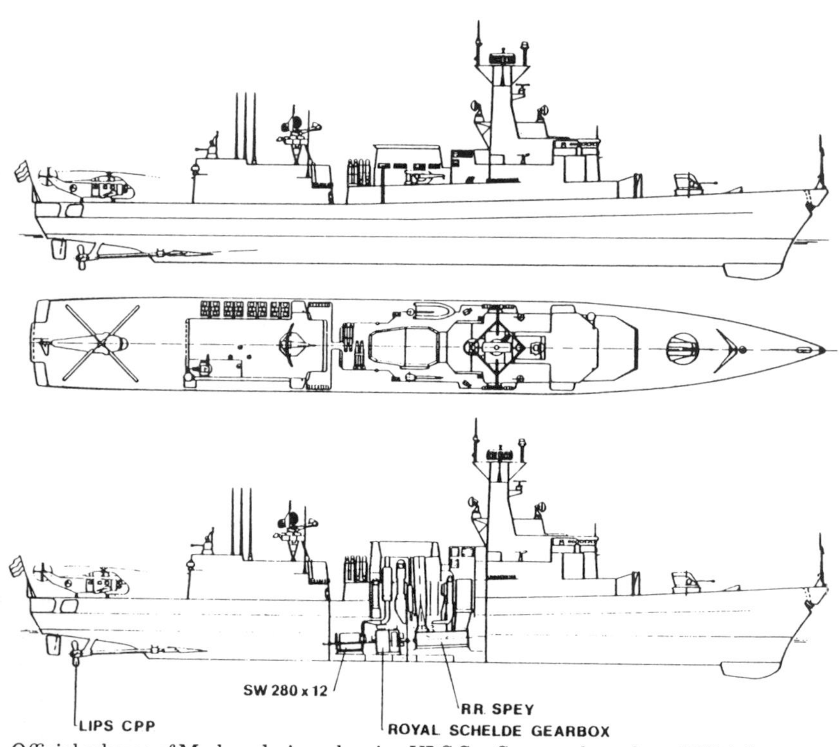

Official scheme of M-class design, showing VLS Sea Sparrow launchers (IV × 4) to port of hangar, and possible 57-mm gun installation forward

Electron Equipt: Radar: 1/Decca 1226, 1/DA-08, 1/LW-08, 1/STIR-18, 1/STIR-24, 1/Goalkeeper
Sonar: PHS-36 (SQS-509) hull-mounted, SQR-18A TASS (provision for)
EW: Ramses passive, Mk 36 SRBOC chaff RL (IV × 2)

M: CODOG: 2 Stork-Werkspoor SWD 280 V-12 cruise diesels, 4,225 hp each; 2 Rolls-Royce SM-1A Spey gas turbines; 2 CP props; 37,540 hp

Electric: 2,500 kw **Range:** 4,000/19 **Man:** 16 officers, 121 men

REMARKS: First four ordered 29-2-84, three years earlier than planned, to help shipbuilding industry. Will nominally replace "Roofdier" class, but are far more capable ships; indeed, they are little inferior to the larger *Kortenaers.* Intended for fisheries patrol and 200-nautical-mile economic zone patrol in peacetime. Accommodations for female crew members incorporated, plus bunks for 30 Marines. Endurance: 30 days.

Will have computer-controlled rudder stabilization system vice fins. Three rubber semi-rigid boats. Two diesel, two gas turbine generator sets: 600 kw each. The Bofors 57-mm SAK-57 Mk II DP gun may be substituted for the 76-mm weapon. DAISY/SEWACO data system with full LINK 10, 11, and 16 capability.

Second group of four ships ordered 29-6-85; four more planned.

◆ **1 (+1) Jacob Van Heemskerck class** Bldr: de Schelde, Vlissingen

	Laid down	L	In serv.
F 812 JACOB VAN HEEMSKERCK (ex-*Pieter Floresz*)	21-1-81	5-11-83	1-86
F 813 WITTE DE WITH	15-12-81	25-8-84	7-86

Jacob Van Heemskerck (F 812)—note ports in stern for Nixie torpedo decoy
L. & L. Van Ginderen, 8-85

Jacob Van Heemskerck (F 812) on trials L. & L. Van Ginderen, 8-85

Jacob Van Heemskerck (F 812) on trials L. & L. Van Ginderen, 8-85

D: 3,000 tons (3,750 fl) **S:** 30 kts
Dim: 130.20 (121.8 pp) × 14.40 × 4.23 (6.0 props)
A: 8 Harpoon SSM (IV × 2)—1/Mk 13 Mod. 4 launcher (I × 1, 40 SM-1 MR Standard missiles)—1/Mk 29 launcher (VIII × 1, 24 Sea Sparrow missiles)—1/30-mm Goalkeeper gatling AA—4/324-mm ASW TT (II × 2, fixed)

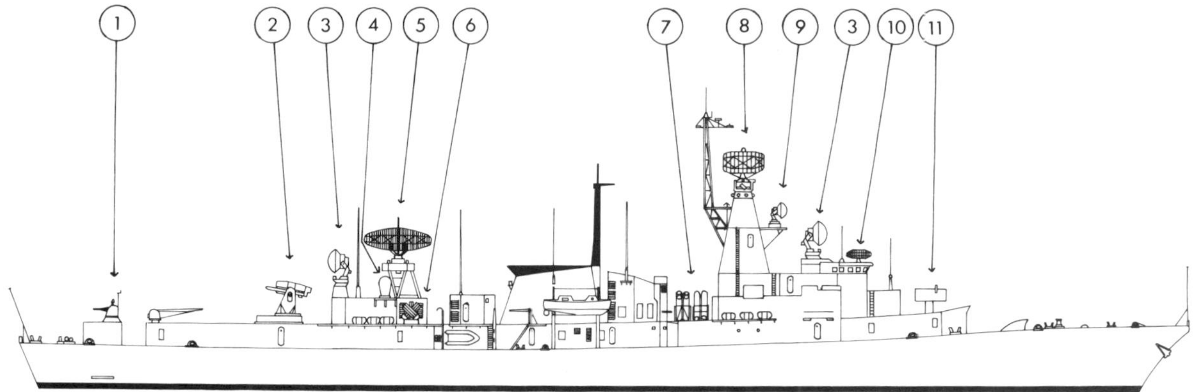

Jacob Van Heemskerck class 1. Goalkeeper 30-mm gatling AA system 2. Mk 13 Mod. 4 launcher for Standard SM-1 MR missiles 3. Modified STIR missile fire-control radars for Standard 4. Satellite communications syst. antennas 5. LW-08 long-range air-search radar 6. U.S. Super RBOC chaff launchers (VI × 4) 7. Harpoon launch cells (IV × 2) 8. DA-05 3-D radar 9. STIR fire-control radar for Sea Sparrow 10. ZW-06 navigational/surface-search radar 11. Mk 29 Sea Sparrow launcher (VIII × 1)

GUIDED-MISSILE FRIGATES *(continued)*

Electron Equipt: Radar: 1/ZW-06, 1/DA-05 or SMART, 1/LW-08, 1/STIR-18, 2/STIR-24, 1/Goalkeeper
Sonar: PHS-36 (SQS-509)
EW: Ramses passive; Mk 36 Super RBOC chaff RL (VI × 4)
M: COGOG: 2 Rolls-Royce Olympus TM-3B gas turbines, 25,800 hp each; 2 Rolls-Royce Tyne RM-1C cruise gas turbines, 4,900 hp each; 2 LIPS CP props; 51,600 hp
Electric: . . . **Range:** 4,700/16 (on 1 Tyne turbine)
Man: 176 crew plus 20 flag staff

REMARKS: Built as replacement hulls for the pair with the same pendant numbers (and original names) sold to Greece, but with the basic *Kortenaer* design modified to replace the helicopter facility with the U.S. Standard missile system. Will act as flagships, permitting the Dutch Navy to operate four escort flotillas in wartime and obviating the need for the originally planned "13th *Kortenaer.*" Have the SEWACO II data system and LINK 11 data-link capability. The DA-05 radar atop the foremast may later be replaced by H.S.A.'s new SMART (Signaal Multi-beam Acquisition Radar for Targeting), and the ships may receive the U.S. SQR-18A TACTASS towed passive hydrophone array. Have the U.S. SLQ-25 Nixie torpedo decoy system.

◆ **10 Kortenaer class** Bldrs: F 823 and F 824: Wilton-Fijenoord; others: de Schelde

	Laid down	L	In serv.
F 807 KORTENAER	8-3-75	18-12-76	26-10-78
F 808 CALLENBURGH	30-6-75	26-3-77	26-7-79
F 809 VAN KINSBERGEN	2-9-76	16-4-77	24-4-80
F 810 BANCKERT	25-2-76	30-9-78	29-10-80
F 811 PIET HEIN	28-4-77	3-6-78	14-4-81
F 816 ABRAHAM CRIJNSSEN	25-10-78	16-5-81	26-1-83
F 823 PHILIPS VAN ALMONDE	1-10-77	11-8-79	2-12-81
F 824 BLOYS VAN TRESLONG	1-5-78	15-11-80	25-11-82
F 825 JAN VAN BRAKEL	16-11-79	16-5-81	14-4-83
F 826 PIETER FLORISZ (ex-*Willem Van Der Zaan*)	15-1-80	8-5-82	1-10-83

Callenburgh (F 808)—with prototype Goalkeeper atop hangar R. Neth. N., 9-84

Jan Van Brakel (F 825) G. Gyssels, 3-85

Piet Hein (F 811) L. & L. Van Ginderen, 9-83

Kortenaer (F 807) L. & L. Van Ginderen, 5-85

D: 3,000 tons (3,786 fl) **S:** 30 kts (20, on 2 Tyne turbines)
Dim: 130.2 (121.8 pp) × 14.4 × 4.4 (6.0 props)
A: 8/Harpoon SSM (IV × 2)—1/NATO Sea Sparrow system (VIII × 1, 24 missiles, Mk 29 launcher)—1/76-mm OTO Melara DP (I × 2)—1/40-mm Bofors AA—4/324-mm Mk 32 ASW TT (II × 2)—1 or 2/WG-13 Lynx ASW helicopters

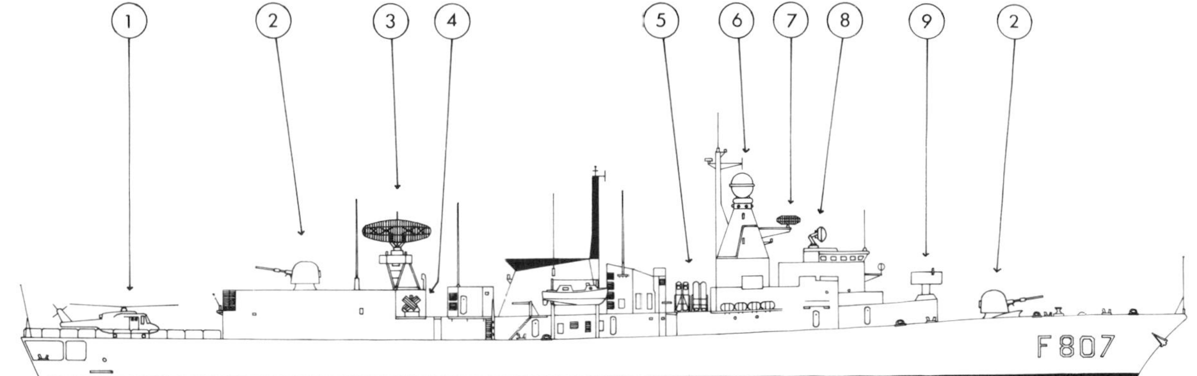

Kortenaer class 1. Lynx helicopter 2. 76-mm OTO Melara DP forward, 40-mm AA aft 3. LW-08 air-search radar 4. Knebworth/Corvus chaff RL (VIII × 2) 5. Harpoon launch cells (II × 2) 6. WM-25 track-while-scan fire-control radar 7. ZW-06 navigational/surface-search radar 8. STIR fire-control radar 9. Mk 29 Sea Sparrow launcher (VIII × 1)

GUIDED-MISSILE FRIGATES *(continued)*

Electron Equipt: Radar: 1/LW-08, 1/ZW-06, 1/WM-25, 1/STIR
Sonar: 1/SQS-505
EW: F 807-F 811: Sphinx passive system; later ships: Ramses active/passive system; all: 2/Knebworth/Corvus chaff RL (VIII × 2) or Mk 36 SRBOC (VI × 2)

M: COGOG: 2 Rolls-Royce Olympus TM-3B gas turbines, 25,800 hp each; 2 Rolls-Royce Tyne RM-1C cruise gas turbines, 4,900 hp each; 2 LIPS CP props; 51,600 hp

Electric: 3,000 kw **Range:** 4,700/16 (on 1 Tyne turbine)

Man: 18 officers, 182 men

REMARKS: F 807 to F 810 ordered 31-8-74; F 811 to F 816 ordered 28-11-74; F 823–F 826 ordered 29-12-76. The original *Pieter Florisz* (F 812) and *Witte de With* (F 813) were sold to Greece in 1981. Initially, F 807 and F 808 had two 76-mm guns, replaced by a 40-mm mount in F 807 by 1982. All are scheduled to have the 40-mm AA replaced by a 30-mm Goalkeeper gatling AA gun system; F 808 received the prototype system in 9-84 (production versions will not have the raised platform below the Goalkeeper found on F 808). In peacetime, only one Lynx helicopter is carried. Normally, only two or four Harpoon SSM (II × 2) are carried, but up to 8 can be accommodated. All ships have the Sperry Mk 29 Mod. 1 inertial navigation system.

The engineering plant is distributed in four compartments, forward to aft: auxiliaries; Olympus gas turbines; Tyne gas turbines plus reduction gears; auxiliaries. The 450-volt, 3-phase, 60-Hertz electric current is supplied by four generators driven by four SEMT-Pielstick PA4, 750-kw diesels. There are two auxiliary boilers and two evaporators.

The hull is divided by fifteen watertight bulkheads. One pair of Denny-Brown, non-retracting fin stabilizers is fitted. Particular attention has been paid to habitability.

The Mk 36 Super RBOC chaff system (2, 6-tubed Mk 136 launchers) is replacing the original Knebworth/Corvus RL. All have the SEWACO-II data system. Two of these ten units may be offered up for sale, it was announced in mid-1985.

◆ **6 (−4) Van Speijk class**

	Bldr	Laid down	L	In serv.
F 802 VAN SPEIJK*	Nederlandsche DSM	1-10-63	5-3-65	14-2-67
F 803 VAN GALEN*	Kon. Mih. de Schelde	25-7-63	19-6-65	1-3-67
F 804 TJERK HIDDES*	Nederlandsche DSM	1-6-64	17-12-65	16-8-67
F 805 VAN NES*	Kon. Mij. de Schelde	25-7-63	26-3-66	9-8-67
F 814 ISAAC SWEERS	Nederlandsche DSM	6-5-65	10-3-67	15-5-68
F 815 EVERTSEN	Kon. Mij. de Schelde	6-7-65	18-6-66	21-12-67

* For sale, as of 6-85.

Tjerk Hiddes (F 804) G. Gyssels, 4-85

Van Nes (F 805) L. & L. Van Ginderen, 6-84

Evertsen (F 815) L. & L. Van Ginderen, 5-85

Isaac Sweers (F 814)—note towed array housing Maritime Photographic, 9-85

D: 2,200 tons (2,835 fl) **S:** 28.5 kts

Dim: 113.42 (109.75 pp) × 12.48 × 4.57 (fl)

A: 2/Harpoon SSM (I × 2)—2/Sea Cat systems (IV × 2)—1/76-mm OTO Melara DP—6/324-mm Mk 32 ASW TT (III × 2)—1/Lynx ASW helicopter

Evertsen (F 815)—with SQR-18A towed linear hydrophone array aft, UA-13 EW array at masthead Skyfotos, 2-83

GUIDED-MISSILE FRIGATES *(continued)*

Electron Equipt: Radar: 1/Decca TM 1229C, 1/DA-05/2, 1/LW-03, 2/M-44 (for Sea Cat), 1/M-45 (for 76-mm)
Sonar: 1/CWE-610, 1/PDE-700 (F 814, 815; SQR-18A also)
EW: passive intercept syst., UA-13 or FH-12 intercept array, 2/Knebworth/Corvus chaff RL (VIII × 2) or Mk 36 SRBOC (VI × 2)

M: 2 sets Werkspoor-English Electric double-reduction GT; 2 props; 30,000 hp
Electric: 1,900 kw **Boilers:** 2 Babcock & Wilcox; 38.7 kg/cm², 450°C
Range: 4,500/12 **Man:** 180 tot.

Remarks: Originally similar in general to the British *Leander* class, but with broader bridge and *two* Sea Cat missile systems, each with a director. Major modernizations began 1977, during which the twin Mk 6, 114-mm gunmount was replaced by an OTO Melara 76-mm gun; the Limbo ASW mortar was deleted and two triple ASW TT added; the hangar was enlarged and made to telescope to accommodate the SH-14A or B ASW version of the Lynx helicopter; positions for Harpoon SSM canisters (normally only two carried) were added; new radars, sonars, and the SEWACO-II data system were added; and the crew requirement was reduced from 247 to 180 total. All but F 802 (which initially also had the Mk 32 ASW TT one deck higher), F 804 and F 814 have the British UA-13 passive intercept array at the masthead. Conversion dates: F 802: 24-12-76 to 3-1-78; F 803: 15-7-77 to 30-11-79; F 805: 31-3-78 to 1-8-80; F 804: 15-12-78 to 1-6-81; F 815: 18-7-79 to 26-11-82; and F 814: 1-7-80 to 28-10-83. New infrared signature suppression stack caps added. F 814 and F 815 received U.S. SQR-18A towed passive linear hydrophone array, and F 814 has SRBOC chaff RL. F 802 out of service mid-1985 with severe boiler and piping corrosion, while F 804 was also reported to have boiler problems. F 814 and F 815 are to be retained, due to their towed sonar installations; the others are available for sale.

Note: The remaining four "Roofdier" (U.S. PCE 821)-class corvettes have been decommissioned for eventual disposal: *Jaguar* (F 822) on 23-12-85, *Fret* (F 818) on 13-7-84, and *Wolf* (F 817) and *Vos* (F 820) on 1-1-85.

PATROL BOATS

◆ **5 Balder class** Bldr: Rijkswerf Willemsoord, Den Helder

	Laid down	L	In serv.
P 802 Balder (ex-SC 1627)	8-53	24-2-54	6-8-54
P 803 Bulgia (ex-SC 1628)	10-53	24-4-54	9-8-54
P 804 Freyr (ex-SC 1629)	2-54	17-7-54	1-12-54
P 805 Hadda (ex-SC 1630)	4-54	2-10-54	3-2-55
P 806 Hefring (ex-SC 1631)	8-54	1-12-54	23-3-55

Bulgia (P 803) G. Gyssels, 11-84

D: 150 tons (168 fl) **S:** 15.5 kts **Dim:** 36.35 (35.0 pp) × 6.21 × 1.8
A: 4/20-mm AA (I × 4) (2 d.c. throwers—2/d.c. racks)
Electron Equipt: Radar: 1/Kelvin Hughes 14/9
M: 2 Werkspoor RUB 1612 diesels; 2 props; 1,050 hp
Electric: 60 kw **Range:** 1,000/13 **Man:** 3 officers, 24 men

Remarks: Built with U.S. "Offshore" funds. P 803 and P 804, both active, have had their forward 40-mm U.K. "Boffin" AA mount replaced by a 20-mm AA and do not appear to carry the d.c. equipment. The three in reserve retain the 40-mm mount. All five are to be stricken by end 1987, without replacement.

MINE WARFARE SHIPS

◆ **9 (+4 + 2) Alkmaar ("Tripartite")-class minehunters** Bldr: Van der Giessen de Noord, Alblasserdam

	Ordered	Laid down	L	In serv.
M 850 Alkmaar	26-7-77	30-1-79	18-5-82	28-5-83
M 851 Delfzijl	26-7-77	29-5-80	26-2-83	17-8-83
M 852 Dordrecht	23-1-79	5-1-81	26-2-83	16-11-83
M 853 Haarlem	23-1-79	16-6-81	9-7-83	12-1-84
M 854 Harlingen	31-3-81	30-11-81	9-7-83	12-4-84
M 855 Scheveningen (ex-*Hellevoetsluis*)	31-3-81	24-5-82	2-12-83	18-7-84
M 856 Maassluis	16-12-81	7-11-82	5-5-84	12-12-84
M 857 Makkum	16-12-81	28-2-83	27-9-84	13-5-85
M 858 Middelburg	21-7-82	11-7-83	. . .	10-85
M 859 Hellevoetsluis (ex-*Scheveningen*)	21-7-82	12-12-83	. . .	3-86
M 860 Schiedam	10-12-83	3-5-84	. . .	7-86
M 861 Urk	10-12-83	1-10-84	. . .	12-86
M 864 Willemstad	3-7-84	12-85	. . .	3-88

Scheveningen (M 855) M. Louagie, 3-85

Delfzijl (M 851) M. Willis, 5-85

D: 510 tons (540 fl) **S:** 15 kts (7 kts hunting)
Dim: 51.6 (47.1 pp) × 8.96 × 2.45 (2.6 max.)
A: 1/20-mm 20F-2 AA—2/PAP-104 remote-controlled minehunting devices
Electron Equipt: Radar: 1/Decca TM 1229C
Sonar: 1/DUBM-21B—1 EVEC 20 plot table, autopilot, Toran and Syledis radio navaids, Decca HiFix precision navigation system
M: 1 Brons-Werkspoor A-RUB 215 × 12 diesel; 1 CP prop; 1,900 hp; 2/75-hp bow-thrusters; 2/120 hp Schöttel active rudders
Electric: 880 kw **Range:** 3,500/10 **Man:** 34 tot.

Remarks: Same design as "Tripartite" minehunters for France and Belgium. Hull made of a compound of glass and polyester resin. The 20-mm AA gun is not always aboard. These ships can also tow a mechanical drag sweep. The DUBM-21A sonar can detect mines in waters up to 80-m depth, at slant ranges up to 500 m. Have 3 × 270-kw gas turbine generator sets and one 160-kw diesel set. Active tank stabilization.

Note: Two, and possibly four, of the units still under construction may be sold to meet foreign sales commitments; they may not be replaced by additional units, due to severe financial constraints. Sisters *Zierikzee* (M 862, ex-*Veere*) and *Vlaardingen* (M 863) were sold 1985 to Indonesia while under construction; they will be replaced by later units in the sequence.

◆ **9 Dokkum class**

6 Coastal Minesweepers (from among the following):

M 802 Hoogezand (ex-MSC 173)	Gusto/F.A. Smulders, Schiedam	18-7-53	22-3-55	7-11-55
M 809 Naaldwijk (ex-MSC 175)	De Noord, Alblasserdam	2-11-53	1-2-55	8-12-55
M 810 Abcoude (ex-MSC 176)	Gusto/F.A. Smulders, Schiedam	10-11-53	2-9-55	18-5-56
M 812 Drachten (ex-MSC 177)	Niestern SB, Hellevoetsluis	9-12-53	24-3-55	27-1-56
M 813 Ommen (ex-MSC 178)	J. & K. Smits, Kinderdijk	22-12-53	5-4-55	19-4-56
M 815 Giethoorn (ex-MSC 179)	L. Smit & Son, Kinderdijk	22-12-53	30-3-55	29-3-56

MINE WARFARE SHIPS *(continued)*

M 817 Venlo (ex-MSC 180)	Arnhemse SB, Arnhem	10-2-54	21-5-55	26-4-56
M 823 Naarden (ex-MSC 183)	Wilton-Fijenoord, Schiedam	28-10-54	27-1-56	18-5-56
M 830 Sittard (ex-MSC 186)	Niestern SB, Hellevoetsluis	10-3-55	26-4-56	19-12-56
M 841 Gemert (ex-MSC 187)	J. & K. Smits, Kinderdijk	5-4-55	13-3-56	7-9-56

Ommen (M 813)—minesweeper, 1/20-mm AA only G. Gyssels, 1-85

3 Support Ships for Mine-demolition Divers:

M 806 Roermond (ex-MSC 174)	Wilton-Fijenoord, Schiedam	19-9-53	13-8-55	29-12-55
M 820 Woerden (ex-MSC 182)	Haarlemse SB, Haarlem	10-8-54	28-11-56	24-4-57
M 844 Rhenen (ex-MSC 189)	Arnhemse SB, Arnhem	18-4-55	31-5-56	7-12-56

Roermond (M 806)—mine clearance diver support L. & L. Van Ginderen, 9-83

D: 373 tons (453 fl) **S:** 15 kts **Dim:** 46.62 × 8.75 × 2.28
A: 1/20-mm AA
Electron Equipt: Radar: 1/Decca TM 1229C
M: 2 Fijenoord-M.A.N. V 64 diesels; 2 props; 2,500 hp
Range: 2,500/10 **Man:** 38 tot.

Remarks: Wooden construction units of same basic design as British "Ton" and French *Sirius* classes, funded by U.S. All units of the similar *Wildervank* class were disposed of by 1976. Four *Dokkums* converted to function as minehunters (with Plessey Type 193M sonar) during 1968-73 have recently been disposed of: *Dokkum* (M 801), placed in unmaintained reserve 4-83, was retrieved for use in oil fuel trials in 1984; *Drunen* (M 818) was stricken 19-4-84; *Staphorst* (M 828) was stricken 20-1-84; and *Veere* (M 842) was stricken 19-10-84.

Of the ten surviving as minesweepers, four were to be disposed of by the end of 1985, with the remainder intended to survive until 1993; sister *Hoogeveen* (M 827) was stricken 5-11-82. Three others (M 806, 820, 844) have had their sweep gear replaced by facilities for mine-disposal divers. The original 2/40-mm "Boffin" AA mounts began to be replaced by a single 20-mm Oerlikon AA forward in all from 1982 on.

Note: The entire 16-ship *Van Straelen*-class was disposed of during 1982-83, with strike dates including: *Van Straelen* (M 872) on 10-12-82, *Van Well Groeneveld* (M 875) on 25-12-82, *Bussemaker* (M 869) on 4-2-83, *Van't Hoff* (M 879) on 18-2-83, *Schuiling* (M 876) on 21-2-83, and *Houtepen* (M 882) on 4-3-83. *La Coumble* (M 870) was transferred to the Sea Scouts on 31-7-84, and Peru purchased *Van Hamel* (M 871) and *Van der Wel* (M 878) on 23-2-84 for use as survey craft; the remainder are for sale.

AMPHIBIOUS WARFARE CRAFT

◆ **6 (+6) LCA Mk 2 landing craft** Bldr: Naval Shipyard, Den Helder (In serv. 1984-85)

L 9530 L 9531 L 9532 L 9533 L 9534 L 9535

D: . . . **S:** 11 kts **Dim:** 16.0 × 4.4 × 1.3
A: 1/7.62-mm mg **Electron Equipt:** Radar: 1/Decca 110
M: 1 DAF-Turbo diesel; 1 Schöttel swivelling prop; 260 hp
Range: 220/11 **Man:** 3 Crew + 25 troops

Remarks: Glass-reinforced plastic construction, intended to replace the 10 LCA Mk 1 completed 1962-64. Were to have been 12, but only six have been ordered. L 9530 completed 10-10-84; L 9531 completed 12-84, the remainder in 1985. Can carry a Land Rover truck or BV 202 tracked snow vehicle in place of the 25 troops.

HYDROGRAPHIC SHIPS

◆ **1 Tydeman class** Bldr: B. V. De Merwede, Hardinxveld-Giessendam

	Laid down	L	In serv.
A 906 Tydeman	29-4-75	18-12-75	10-11-76

Tydeman (A 906)—white hull, buff stack, orange boats L. & L. Van Ginderen, 3-85

D: 3,000 tons (fl) **S:** 15 kts **Dim:** 90.15 × 14.43 × 4.75
M: 3 Stork-Werkspoor 8-FCHD-240 diesels, electric drive; 1 prop; 2,730 hp; 2 bow-thrusters; 1 active rudder
Electric: 1,400 kw **Range:** 10,300/13.5; 15,700/10.3
Man: 59 men, 15 civilians

Remarks: Assigned to civilian and military research. Hangar and flight deck for one small helicopter. Eight laboratories. Any two of the three main diesels power the propulsion motors, the other then provides ship's service power.

◆ **2 Blommendal class** Bldr: Boele S & M, Bolnes

	Laid down	L	In serv.
A 904 Buyskes	31-1-72	11-7-72	9-3-73
A 905 Blommendal	1-8-72	21-11-72	22-5-73

Blommendal (A 905) G. Gyssels, 3-84

D: 867 tons (1,025 fl) **S:** 14 kts **Dim:** 58.80 × 11.13 × 3.70
M: 2 Paxman 742-hp 12 RPHCZ7 diesels, Smit electric drive; 1 prop; 1,100 hp
Electric: 745 kw **Range:** 7,000/10 **Man:** 43 tot.

Remarks: Carry two survey launches and two chain-clearance drag boats. Automated data-logging system.

REPLENISHMENT SHIPS

Note: Construction of two replenishment oilers is planned, one to replace *Poolster* and the other to permit three task groups to operate independently.

◆ **1 improved Poolster class** Bldr: Verolme, Alblasserdam

	Laid down	L	In serv.
A 832 Zuiderkruis	16-7-43	15-10-74	27-6-75

D: 17,357 tons **S:** 21 kts **Dim:** 169.59 (157.00 pp) × 20.3 × 8.4 (max.)
A: 2/20-mm AA(I × 2), 1/d.c. rack (8 d.c.)

REPLENISHMENT SHIPS *(continued)*

Zuiderkruis (A 832) L. & L. Van Ginderen, 2-84

Electron Equipt: Radar: 2/Decca 1226
EW: passive syst., 2/Knebworth/Corvus chaff RL (VIII × 2)
M: 2 Werkspoor TM 410 16-cyl. diesels; 2 props; 21,000 hp **Electric:** 3,000 kw
Man: 17 officers, 26 petty officers, 130 men

Remarks: Cargo capacity: 9,000 tons fuel, 400 tons TR-5, 200 tons fresh water, spare parts, ammunition. Hangar for three Lynx helicopters. Can carry ASW torpedoes and other stores to support up to five ASW helicopters. Two fueling stations per side, amidships, and one sliding-stay, constant-tension, solid transfer station each side, forward.

◆ **1 Poolster class** Bldr: Rotterdamse Droogdok Mij., Rotterdam

	Laid down	L	In serv.
A 835 Poolster	18-9-62	16-10-63	10-9-64

Poolster (A 835) L. & L. Van Ginderen, 4-85

D: 16,836 tons (fl) **S:** 21 kts **Dim:** 168.41 (157.00 pp) × 20.33 × 8.24
A: 2/40-mm AA (I × 2)—1/d.c. rack (8 d.c.)
Electron Equipt: Radar: 1/Decca 1229, 1/Decca 2459
Sonar: 1/CWE-610
EW: passive syst., 2/Knebworth/Corvus chaff RL (VIII × 2)
M: 2 sets GT; 1 prop; 22,500 hp **Boilers:** 2 **Electric:** 2,100 kw **Man:** 200 tot.

Remarks: Cargo capacity: 10,300 tons, including 8,000 tons of fuel. Hangar for three Lynx helicopters. Also a combat supply ship capable of participating effectively in antisubmarine warfare with a hunter/killer group, thanks to her ability to handle three Lynx ASW helicopters, if required. For short distances, she can carry 300 Marines as well as her own crew. Decca 2459 dual F/I-band radar replaced DA-01 radar 1983 for trials.

TENDERS

◆ **0 (+1) new-construction torpedo-trials ship** Bldr: De Schelde, Vlissingen

	Laid down	L	In serv.
A 900 Mercuur	3-85	. . .	1987

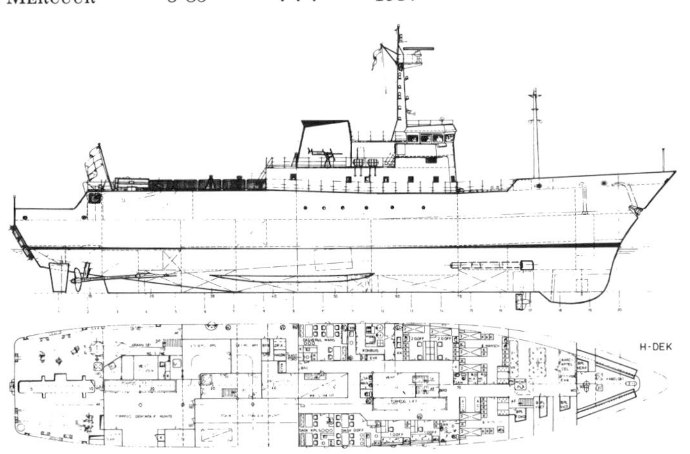

Mercuur (A 900) R. Neth. Navy, 1985

D: 1,200 tons (1,500 fl) **S:** 14 kts **Dim:** 64.85 × 12.00 × 4.30
A: 2/7.62-mm mg (I × 2)—2/533-mm TT (underwater)—mines
Electron Equipt: Radar: . . . —Sonar: . . .
M: 2 Brons-M.A.N. diesel generator sets (650 kw each); electric drive; 2 props; . . . hp—bow-thruster
Man: 4 officers, 21 men + trials personnel

Remarks: Ordered 13-6-84 to replace U.S. *Agile*-class former minesweeper of the same name as torpedo-trials ship.

◆ **1 U.S. Agile-class mine-countermeasures support ship** Bldr: Astoria Marine, Astoria, Ore.

	Laid down	L	In serv.
A 855 Onbevreesd (ex-M 885, ex-MSO 481)	8-12-52	7-11-53	21-9-54

Onbevreesd (A 855) G. Gyssels, 1981

D: 735 tons (790 fl) **S:** 15.5 kts **Dim:** 52.7 × 10.75 × 3.7
A: 1/40-mm AA—2/d.c. racks
Electron Equipt: Radar: 1/Kelvin-Hughes 14/9—Sonar: QCU-2
M: 2 G.M. 8-278A diesels; 2 CP props; 1,600 hp **Electric:** 560 kw
Fuel: 47 tons **Range:** 3,000/10 **Man:** 67 tot.

Remarks: Former ocean minesweeper. Typed "escort ship" and intended to serve as flagship for a mine-countermeasures force and to lay mines in exercises. Sister *Onversaagd* was stricken in 31-7-79, and *Onvervaard* (A 858) and *Onverdroten* (A 859) were stricken 15-5-82.

◆ **1 U.S. Agile-class torpedo-trials ship** Bldr: Peterson Bldrs., Sturgeon Bay, Wisc.

	Laid down	L	In serv.
A 856 Mercuur (ex-*Onverschrokken*, M 886, ex-MSO 483)	19-2-52	17-1-53	22-7-54

Remarks: Former ocean minesweeper. Data as for ship above, except no gun. Converted to a torpedo-trials and servicing ship in 1972; scheduled to be replaced 1986 by a new-construction torpedo retriever.

◆ **1 torpedo-trials ship** Bldr: Zaanlandse SM, Zaandam

	Laid down	L	In serv.
A 923 Van Bochove	6-12-61	20-7-62	3-8-62

Van Bochove (A 923) L. & L. Van Ginderen, 1979

D: 140.8 tons (fl) **S:** 8 kts **Dim:** 29.79 × 5.53 × 1.8
A: 2/533-mm TT (submerged, at bow)
M: 1 Kromhout diesel; 1 Schöttel prop; 140 hp **Man:** 8 tot.

TUGS

Note: Construction of two new 1,000-hp coastal tugs is planned.

◆ **2 Westgat-class coastal tugs** Bldr: Rijkswerf Willemsoord, Den Helder

	Laid down	L	In serv.
A 872 Westgat	3-4-67	22-8-67	10-1-68
A 873 Wielingen	28-8-67	6-1-68	31-5-68

D: 206 tons (fl) **S:** 12 kts **Dim:** 27.18 × 6.97 × 2.34
A: None **Electron Equipt:** 1/Kelvin-Hughes 14/9
M: 1 Bolnes diesel; 1 prop; 720 hp **Man:** 9 tot.

TUGS *(continued)*

Wielingen (A 873) L. & L. Van Ginderen, 6-84

◆ **1 Wambrau-class coastal tug** Bldr: Rijkswerf Willemsoord, Den Helder

	Laid down	L	In serv.
A 871 WAMBRAU (ex-Y 8036)	24-7-56	27-8-56	8-1-57

Wambrau (A 871) L. & L. Van Ginderen, 10-85

D: 179.4 tons (fl) **S:** 10.8 kts **Dim:** 26.38 × 6.6 × 2.45
A: None **M:** 1 Werkspoor diesel; 1 prop; 500 hp **Man:** 10 tot.

NOTE: The coastal tug *Wamandai* (A 870) was stricken at Curaçao, 1-7-85.

TRAINING SHIPS

◆ **1 former pilot ship**

	Bldr	Laid down	L	In serv.
A 903 ZEEFAKEL	J. & K. Smit, Kinderjik	28-11-49	21--7-50	16-3-51

D: 303 tons (384 fl) **S:** 12 kts **Dim:** 45.38 × 7.5 × 2.2
M: 2 Smit-M.A.N. diesels; 2 props; 640 hp **Man:** 26 tot.

REMARKS: Used for seamanship training at Den Helder.

◆ **1 sail-training ketch**

	Bldr	L	In serv.
Y 8050 URANIA (ex-*Tromp*)	Haarlemse Scheepsbouw Mij.	1929	23-4-38

D: 76.4 tons (fl) **S:** 5 kts (10 under sail) **Dim:** 23.94 × 5.29 × 3.15
M: 1 Kromhout diesel; 1 prop; 65 hp (625m² sail area) **Man:** 17 tot.

Zeefakel (A 903) P. Voss, 6-84

Urania (Y 8050) G. Arra, 1981

◆ **1 former Holland-class destroyer**

	Bldr	Laid down	L	In serv.
D 811 GELDERLAND	Wilton-Fijenoord, Schiedam	10-3-51	19-9-53	18-8-55

Gelderland (D 811)—radar antennas remounted H. Ehlers, 9-85

D: 2,215 tons (2,765 fl) **S:** 32 kts **Dim:** 111.3 × 11.33 × 3.88
A: None **M:** 2 sets Parsons GT; 2 props; 45,000 hp
Electric: 1,350 kw **Boilers:** 4 Babcock & Wilcox

REMARKS: Since 1973 used for technical training at Rotterdam and for accommodations. Does not get underway. Two twin 120-mm DP guns mounted on destroyers *Tromp* and *De Ruyter*.

NOTE: There are also 24 small sports and training sail yachts under naval control.

ACCOMMODATIONS SHIPS

◆ **1 non-self-propelled** Bldr: de Schelde, Vlissingen (In serv. 14-3-85)

A 887 Thetis

Thetis (A 887) L. & L. Van Ginderen, 3-85

D: 1,000 tons (fl) **Dim:** 68.47 (62.85 pp) × 12.82 × 1.60

Remarks: Launched 1-83. Replaced former gunboat *Soemba* (A 891) as accommodations barge at Den Oever for use by diver and frogman trainees.

◆ **1 non-self-propelled** Bldr: Voorwarts SY, Hoogezand

	Laid down	L	In serv.
A 886 Cornelius Drebbel	18-5-70	19-11-70	30-11-71

D: 775 tons (fl) **Dim:** 63.22 × 11.82 × 1.1 **Man:** 201 tot.

Remarks: Stationed at Rotterdam to serve ships in overhaul.

SERVICE CRAFT

◆ **1 fuel lighter** Bldr: H.H. Bodewes, Millingen (In serv. 1963)

Y 8536 Patria

D: 827 dwt **S:** . . . **Dim:** 61.6 × 8.1 × . . .
M: 1 Bolnes diesel; 1 prop; . . . hp **Man:** . . . tot.

Remarks: Purchased 1978. Based at Den Helder. Bow number: 611.

◆ **1 fuel barge:** Y 8538 (In serv. 1955)

◆ **1 small water tanker:** Y 8480 (In serv. 1952)

◆ **1 torpedo lighter:** Y 8512 (In serv. 1950)

◆ **2 small cargo lighters:** Y 8500 (In serv. 1953) Y 8501 (In serv. 1951)

◆ **3 personnel launches:** Y 8216, Y 8217, Y 8220 (In serv. 1951-52)

Remarks: U.S. Coast Guard 40-ft. utility boat design.

◆ **3 steam supply craft:** Y 8005 (In serv. 1937), Y 8122 (In serv. 1937), Y 8260 (In serv. 1940)

◆ **1 electrical power supply craft:** Y 8676 (In serv. 1962)

◆ **1 tank-cleaning boat:** Y 8262 (In serv. 1918)

◆ **1 hull-cleaning boat:** Y 8263 (In serv. 1967)

Y 8480—water tanker G. Koop, 9-83

Y 8676—electrical power supply craft L. & L. Van Ginderen, 10-82

Y 8500—cargo lighter L. & L. Van Ginderen, 10-81

◆ **1 Dokkum-class fuel-trials craft, former minehunter**

	Bldr	Laid down	L	In serv.
Y 8001 Dokkum (ex-M 801, ex-MSC 172)	Wilton Fijenoord, Schiedam	15-6-53	12-10-54	26-7-55

Dokkum (Y 8001) L. & L. Van Ginderen, 8-85

Remarks: Details generally as for minesweeper sisters; no armament. After having been placed in unmaintained reserve in 4-83, was reclaimed and adapted for testing fuels.

◆ **6 fast target craft** (In serv. 1982-83)

Y 8694 Y 8699–8703

Remarks: No data available.

◆ **4 Berkel-class harbor tugs** Bldr: H.H. Bodewes, Millingen

	Laid down	L	In serv.
Y 8037 Berkel	27-4-56	29-9-56	27-12-57
Y 8038 Dintel	22-5-56	17-11-56	23-1-57
Y 8039 Dommel	29-8-56	22-12-56	27-2-57
Y 8040 IJssel	17-9-56	19-1-57	20-3-57

IJssel (Y 8040) R. Neth. N., 1979

D: 163.4 tons (fl) **S:** 10.6 kts **Dim:** 25.09 × 6.27 × 2.45
M: 1 Werkspoor diesel; 1 Kort-nozzle prop; 500 hp
Man: 5 tot.

◆ **2 Bambi-class harbor tugs** Bldr: Rijkswerf Willemsoord, Den Helder

Y 8016 Bambi (L: 12-5-53) Y 8017 Dombo (L: 25-5-57)

D: 43 tons (fl) **S:** . . . kts **Dim:** 16.58 × 4.63 × 1.9
M: 1 Bolnes diesel; 1 prop; 200 hp
Man: 4 tot.

SERVICE CRAFT *(continued)*

Dombo (Y 8017) G. Koop, 9-83

◆ **1 small harbor tug** Bldr: Boot, Alphen aan den Rijn (In serv. 1942)

Y 8014 (ex-A 857, ex-RS 17, ex-OZD 4, ex-*Jade*)

D: 75 tons (fl) **S:** . . . kts **Dim:** 20.0 × 5.25 × 1.8
M: 1 diesel; 1 prop; 75 hp **Man:** 3 tot.

◆ **1 small harbor tug** Bldr: Foxhol (In serv. 1938)

Y 8028 (ex-A 868, ex-RS 28, ex-KM 15, ex-*Eems*)

Y 8028 L. & L. Van Ginderen, 1980

D: 70 tons (fl) **S:** . . . kts **Dim:** 19.5 × 5.1 × 2.3
M: 1 Bolnes diesel; 1 prop; 200 hp **Man:** 7 tot.

◆ **3 Triton-class diving tenders** Bldr: Rijkswerf Willemsoord, Den Helder

	Laid down	L	In serv.
A 848 Triton (ex-Y 8125)	3-2-64	27-2-64	5-8-64
A 849 Nautilus (ex-Y 8126)	17-3-64	1-5-64	20-4-65
A 850 Hydra (ex-Y 8127)	21-5-64	1-7-64	20-4-65

Triton (A 848) H. Ehlers, 8-85

D: 69.3 tons (fl) **S:** 9 kts **Dim:** 23.28 × 5.15 × 1.35
M: 1 Volvo Penta diesel; 1 prop; 105 hp **Man:** 8 tot.

◆ **1 training tender for divers** Bldr: Rijkswerf Willemsoord, Den Helder

	Laid down	L	In serv.
A 847 Argus (ex-Y 8124, ex-Y 8651, ex-A 950, ex-RD 10, ex-MOD IV, ex-D1)	18-5-38	6-12-38	10-5-39

D: 44.5 tons (fl) **S:** 8 kts **Dim:** 23.0 × 4.68 × 1.05
M: 1 Kromhout diesel; 1 prop; 144 hp **Man:** 8 tot.

◆ **1 floating crane:** Y 8514 (In serv. 1974)

◆ **2 floating dry docks** Y 8678 RW 22 (In serv. 1949) Y 8679 RW 60 (In serv. 1960)

◆ **1 wreck simulation craft:** Y 8690 (In serv. 1969)

◆ **18 dry-cargo barges** (In serv. 1900-1965): Y 8299, Y 8321, Y 8322, Y 8324, Y 8325, Y 8327, Y 8328, Y 8330, Y 8331, Y 8332, Y 8333, Y 8334, Y 8337, Y 8338, Y 8339, Y 8340, Y 8341, Y 8403

◆ **2 mooring pontoons:** Y 8594, Y 8595 (In serv. 1956)

◆ **3 submarine mooring pontoons:** Y 8597, Y 8598 (In serv. 1971), Y 8599 (In serv. 1977)

◆ **8 miscellaneous pontoon barges:** Y 8600, Y 8601, Y 8602, Y 8603, Y 8711, Y 8713, Y 8714, Y 8716

◆ **8 miscellaneous floats:** (In serv. 1951-53) Y 8583, Y 8584, Y 8585, Y 8586, Y 8588, Y 8589, Y 8590, Y 8592

Note: The Netherlands Pilot Service, carried in the 1980/81 edition, was transferred from nominal naval control early in 1980.

NETHERLANDS NATIONAL POLICE FORCE (MINISTRY OF JUSTICE)

Note: This organization operates about 70 patrol craft, of which only the *De Ruiter* class, listed below, is considered seagoing. A number of other jurisdictions, including the Customs Service, the Rotterdam City Police, and the Department of Communications, also operate patrol craft.

◆ **3 RP 16 class** Bldr: Schöttel, Warmond

RP 16 (In serv. 1-84) RP 20 (In serv. 7-84) RP 63 (In serv. 10-84)

RP 16 L. & L. Van Ginderen, 6-84

D: 30 tons **S:** 19 kts **Dim:** 23.50 × 5.30 × 1.60
Electron Equipt: 1/Racal Decca . . . nav.
M: 3 M.A.N. D282-ME diesels; 3 props; 1,266 hp **Man:** 6 tot.

◆ **6 15-meter class** Bldr: Schöttel, Warmond

RP 59 (In serv. 1982) RP 63 (In serv. 1984) RP 69 (In serv. 4-2-83)
RP 70 (In serv. 12-84) RP. . . RP. . .

RP 59 L. & L. Van Ginderen, 8-84

NETHERLANDS *(continued)*
NATIONAL POLICE FORCE *(continued)*

D: 17.5 tons **S:** 17 kts **Dim:** 15.36 × 3.78 × 1.25
M: RP 69: 2 DAF DKA-1160M diesels; 2 props; 440 hp; others: 1 M.A.N. D2842-ME diesel; 1 prop; 422 hp
Man: 3 or 4 tot.

◆ **3 De Ruiter class** Bldr: Schöttel, Warmond

RP 15 De Ruiter (In serv. 5-79) RP. . . N. . . . . . RP. . . N. . . . . .

D: 27 tons (fl) **S:** 18.5 kts **Dim:** 19.13 × 4.27 × 1.3
M: 2 12-cyl. diesels; 2 Schöttel vertical cycloidal props; 680 hp **Man:** 3–4 tot.

Remarks: The second and third were ordered 6-80.

◆ **3 RP 17 class** Bldr: Le Comte, Vianen, 1974

RP 17 RP 26 RP. . .

RP 17 L. & L. Van Ginderen, 6-84

D: 29 tons **S:** 15 kts **Dim:** 15.75 × 3.83 × 1.05
M: 1 MTU OM403 diesel; 1 Schöttel vertical cycloidal prop; 250 hp

◆ **7 10.8-meter class** Bldr: Le Comte, Vianen, 1970

D: 8.5 tons **S:** 14.5 kts **Dim:** 10.8 × 3.22 × 1.2
M: 1 MTU OM346 diesel; 1 Schöttel prop; 165 hp

◆ **RP 10** Bldr: Schuiten, Muiden, 1968

RP 10 L. & L. Van Ginderen, 6-82

D: 70 tons (fl) **S:** 14 kts **Dim:** 23.0 × . . . × . . .
M: 1 Bolnes GDNL diesel; 600 hp

◆ **RP 3** Bldr: Koopman, Dordrecht, 1967

D: 60 tons (fl) **S:** 12.7 kts **Dim:** 22.0 × 5.3 × 1.5
M: 2 G.M. 12V71 diesels; 2 props; 670 hp

NEW ZEALAND

Dominion of New Zealand

Personnel (1983): 2,757 total (plus 444 reserves)

Merchant Marine (1984): 118 ships—284,850 grt
(tankers: 6 ships—84,635 grt)

Naval Aviation: Eleven Wasp helicopters are available for the *Leander*-class frigates and the survey ship *Monowai.* Five Lockheed P3-B Orion patrol planes belong to the Royal New Zealand Air Force. These were modernized by Boeing over a 41-month period commencing 7-80; the first was completed 2-83. A second round of modernizations is planned to bring the aircraft up to P-3C standard. A sixth P-3B is to be purchased, plus 3 Fokker F 27 Maritime for search-and-rescue duties. The RNZAF's A-4 Skyhawks are to have a maritime attack role.

FRIGATES

◆ **2 U.K. "broad-beam Leander" class**

	Bldr	Laid down	L	In serv.
F 69 Wellington (ex-*Bacchante*)	Vickers-Armstrong, Newcastle	27-10-66	29-2-68	17-10-69
F 421 Canterbury	Yarrow, Scotstoun	12-4-69	6-5-70	22-10-71

Wellington (F 69)—prior to alterations L. & L. Van Ginderen, 10-82

Canterbury (F 421) L. & L. Van Ginderen, 2-84

D: F 69: 2,500 tons (2,962 fl); F 421: 2,470 tons (3,638 fl)
S: 28 kts (30 on trials) **Dim:** 113.38 (109.73 pp) × 13/12 × 5.49
A: 2/114-mm Mk 6 DP (II × 1)—1/Sea Cat GWS 22 syst. (IV × 1)—2/12.7-mm mg (I × 2)—1/Limbo ASW mortar (III × 1, not in F 421)—6/324-mm ASW TT (III × 2, not in F 69)—1/Wasp HAS.1 helicopter
Electron Equipt: Radar: 1/1006, 1/965, 1/993, 1/903, (F 69: RCA R76C5) for 114-mm guns, 1/904 for Sea Cat
Sonar: 1/184M, 1/162M
EW: UA-8/9 passive intercept, Type 668/669 jammer
M: 2 sets White-English Electric GT; 2/5-bladed props; 30,000 hp
Boilers: 2 Babcock & Wilcox 3-drum; 38.7 kg/cm², 450°C Superheat
Electric: 2,500 kw **Fuel:** 500 tons **Range:** Approx. 4,500/12
Man: 15 officers, 230 men

Remarks: F 69 was purchased and commissioned in the New Zealand Navy on 4-10-82, proceeding to Auckland for a refit scheduled to end in 1-85, but completion delayed. The ship's 20-mm AA and chaff RL were removed prior to transfer. The Type 199 VDS was removed and stored as a spare for *Southland.* The MRS.3 gunfire-control system was being replaced by the RCA R76C5 system in F 69. F 69 is also receiving a Marconi NTC-1 communications suite, and may get Mk 32 ASW TT removed from *Taranaki* (F 148). F 69 was transferred with a Wasp helicopter aboard. The Type 184M search sonar may be replaced with a Graseby Type 750 set.

◆ **1 U.K. Leander class**

	Bldr	Laid down	L	In serv.
F 55 Waikato	Harland & Wolff	10-1-65	18-2-65	16-9-66

FRIGATES *(continued)*

Waikato (F 55) R. Gillett, 10-34

D: 2,489 tons (2,906 fl) **S:** 28 kts
Dim: 113.38 (109.73 pp) × 12.50 × 5.49
A: 2/114-mm Mk 6 DP (II × 1) — 1/Sea Cat MRS.22 syst. (IV × 1) — 6/324-mm ASW TT (III × 2) — 1/HAS.1 Wasp helicopter
Electron Equipt: Radar: 1/978, 1/965, 1/993, 1/903, 1/904
Sonar: 1/184, 1/162B
EW: UA-8/9 intercept, FH-12 HFD/F
M: 2 sets White-English Electric GT; 2 5-bladed props; 30,000 hp
Electric: 1,900 kw
Boilers: 2 Babcock & Wilcox; 38.7 kg/cm², 450°C **Range:** 4,100/12
Fuel: 460 tons **Man:** 16 officers, 227 men

REMARKS: Originally had a Mk 10 Limbo triple ASW mortar and no ASW TT; she was refitted in 1977, when the Type 170B sonar was also removed. Became training frigate when *Otago* was stricken.

◆ **1 ex-U.K. "Ikara Leander" class**

	Bldr	Laid down	L	In serv.
F 104 SOUTHLAND (ex-*Dido*, ex-*Hastings*)	Yarrow, Scotstoun	2-12-59	22-12-61	18-9-63

Southland (F 104) — departing for refit R. N. Z. N., 1984

D: 2,450 tons (2,860 fl) **S:** 28 kts **Dim:** 113.38 (109.73 pp) × 12.50 × 5.49
A: 2/40-mm AA (I × 2) — 2/Sea Cat GWS.22 syst. (IV × 2) — 1/Ikara ASW syst. — 6/324-mm ASW TT (III × 2) — 1/HAS.1 Wasp helicopter
Electron Equipt: Radar: 1/1006, 1/994, 1/904, 1/Ikara control
Sonar: 1/184, 1/170B, 1/199VDS
EW: Argo passive intercept; Type 668/669 jammer
M: 2 sets White-English Electric GT; 2/5-bladed props; 30,000 hp
Boilers: 2 Babcock & Wilcox 3-drum; 38.7 kg/cm², 450°C Superheat
Electric: 1,600 kw **Fuel:** 460 tons **Range:** Approx. 4,100/12
Man: 19 officers, 238 men

REMARKS: Purchased and transferred to New Zealand in 18-7-83, with Wasp helicopter aboard. Commissioned 21-12-83 after refit in U.K., with Limbo ASW mortar deleted and ASW TT added, Argo EW gear installed and Type 993 radar updated to Type 994. The two Sea Cat short-range SAM launchers share a single radar director. Well-equipped for ASW, but little capability for AAW or surface warfare.

NOTE: The *Rothesay*-class frigate *Otago* (F 111) was stricken 7-11-83.

PATROL BOATS AND CRAFT

◆ **4 Pukaki-class patrol boats** Bldr: Brooke Marine, Lowestoft, U.K.

	L	In serv.
P 3568 PUKAKI	1-3-74	24-2-75
P 3569 ROTOITI	8-3-74	24-2-75
P 3570 TAUPO	25-7-74	29-7-75
P 3571 HAWEA	9-9-74	29-7-75

Rotoiti (P 3569) — with armament removed L. & L. Van Ginderen, 9-83

D: 107 tons (140 fl) **S:** 22 kts **Dim:** 32.6 × 6.1 × 1.7
A: 1/81-mm mortar combined with 12.7-mm mg — 2/12.7-mm mg (II × 1) — 2/7.62-mm mg (I × 2)
Electron Equipt: Radar: 1/Decca 916
M: 2 Ruston-Paxman 12 YCJM diesels; 2 props; 3,000 hp **Range:** 2,500/12
Man: 3 officers, 18 men

◆ **4 Moa-class training/patrol craft** Bldr: Whangarei Engineering Co., Auckland

	L	In serv.		L	In serv.
P 3553 MOA	16-7-83	19-2-84	P 3555 WAKAKURA	29-10-84	26-3-85
P 3554 KIWI	7-5-84	2-9-84	P 3556 HINAU	-85	-86

Kiwi (P 3554) L. & L. Van Ginderen, 10-84

D: 90 tons light (110.7 fl) **S:** 12 kts **Dim:** 26.82 (24.38 wl) × 6.10 × 2.18
A: 1/12.7-mm mg **Electron Equipt:** Radar: 1/. . . nav.
M: 2 Cummins KT-1150M diesels; 2 props; 730 hp **Fuel:** 11 tons
Range: 1,000/12 **Man:** 2 officers, 10 men (18 accom.)

REMARKS: Ordered 11-2-82 to replace the remaining HDML-type patrol craft. Design derived from Australian 88-ft torpedo retriever; survey craft *Takapu* and *Tarapunga* and diving tender *Manawanui* are to same basic design. The mg is not normally mounted. Based as follows for naval reserve training: *Moa* at Dunedin, *Kiwi* at Lyttleton, *Wakakura* at Wellington, and *Hinau* at Auckland.

NOTE: HDML-type training craft *Paea* (P 3552), *Kuparu* (P 3563), *Koura* (P 3564) and *Manga* (P 3567) were stricken 1984, with P 3552 the last to go, in 12-84.

SUPPLY SHIP

NOTE: Government permission was given 5-85 for the lease or purchase of a naval supply ship. No further details available.

HYDROGRAPHIC SURVEY SHIPS

◆ **1 converted passenger-cargo ship** Bldr: Grangemouth DY (L: 4-60)

A 06 Monowai (ex-*Moana Roa*)

Monowai (A 06)—white hull, buff stack L. & L. Van Ginderen, 2-84

D: 4,027 tons (fl) **S:** 13.5 kts **Dim:** 90.33 (82.30 pp) × 14.02 × 5.21
A: 2/20-mm AA (I × 2)
M: 2 Clark-Sulzer 7-cyl. diesels; 2 CP props; 3,640 hp (3,080 sust.—bow-thruster
Fuel: 300 tons **Range:** 12,000/13 **Man:** 11 officers, 115 men

Remarks: Taken over from the government-run commercial service in 1974 and converted at Scott-Lithgow, Greenock, Scotland, 9-77 to 4-10-77. Telescoping hangar fitted for one Wasp helicopter. Two 10.36-meter and one 8.84-meter survey craft carried, as well as one Rotork "Sea Truck" workboat. Decca HiFix positioning system and Omega radio navigational aids installed, as well as a navigational satellite receiver. One 4-ton crane. Side-scanning mapping sonar and other sophisticated survey equipment carried. Guns added 1980. Predecessor *Lachlan,* a former U.K. "River"-class frigate, is used as a barracks hulk.

◆ **2 inshore survey craft** Bldr: Whangarei Eng. Ltd., Auckland

	L	In serv.		L	In serv.
A 07 Takapu	5-6-80	8-7-80	A 08 Tarapunga	5-11-79	9-4-80

Takapu (A 07)—white-painted L. & L. Van Ginderen, 10-84

D: 90 tons (112.6 fl) **S:** 12 kts **Dim:** 26.82 (24.38 wl) × 6.10 × 2.18
M: 2 Cummins KT-1150M diesels; 2 props; 730 hp **Fuel:** 11 tons
Range: 1,000/12 **Man:** 2 officer, 10 men

Remarks: Ordered 30-11-77. Similar to diving tender *Manawanui*- and *Moa*-class patrol boats. Have Magnavox MX 1102 NAVSAT receiver, E.G. and G. Mk 1B sidescan sonar, Decca Trisponder position fixing, and Atlas Deso 10 echo-sounder.

OCEANOGRAPHIC RESEARCH SHIP

◆ **1 ex-U.S. Robert D. Conrad class** Bldr: Christy Corp., Sturgeon Bay, Wis.

	Laid down	L	In serv.
A 02 Tui (ex-*Charles H. Davis,* T-AGOR 5)	15-6-61	30-6-62	25-1-63

D: 1,219 tons (1,402 fl) **S:** 12 kts **Dim:** 70.0 (63.7 pp) × 11.4 × 4.7 (6.3 max.)
Electron Equipt: Radar: 1/RCA CRM-N1A-75
M: 2 Caterpillar D-378 diesels, electric; 1 prop; 1,000 hp—175-hp bow-thruster
Electric: 850 kw **Fuel:** 211 tons **Range:** 12,000/12
Man: 8 officers, 16 men, 15 scientists

Remarks: Transferred on loan 28-7-70 and commissioned 11-9-70. Was used in acoustics research for the New Zealand Defense Research Establishment, which modified the ship so that it could be used to lay and tow hydrophone arrays. Has a 620-kw gas-turbine generator to drive the prop for quiet running.

Tui (A 02)—white hull, buff stack RNZN, 1984

SERVICE CRAFT

◆ **1 harbor tug** Bldr: . . . (L: 1969)

A 10 Arataki (ex-*Aorangi*)

Arataki (with original name still visible at bow) RNZN, 11-84

D: 170 tons (fl) **S:** 12 kts **Dim:** 25.30 × 7.62 × 3.0
M: 1 Ruston 6ARM diesel; 1 prop; 1,100 hp

Remarks: Purchased 26-10-84 from Timaru Harbour Board to replace earlier tug *Arataki.* Has 16-ton bollard pull.

◆ **1 diving tender**

	Bldr	L	In serv.
Manawanui	Whangarei Eng. Ltd.	8-12-78	28-5-79

D: 90 tons (110 fl) **S:** 12 kts **Dim:** 26.82 (24.38 wl) × 6.10 × 2.20
M: 2 Cummins KT 1150M diesels; 2 props; 730 hp
Range: 1,000/12 **Man:** 16 tot.

Remarks: Other than the addition of a davit at the stern and a free-standing tripod mast, resembles the *Takapu*-class inshore survey craft.

◆ **1 workboat** Bldr: Miller & Tunnage, Port Chalmers (In serv. 1976)

Meola

D: 6 tons **S:** 9 kts **Dim:** 13.1 × . . . × . . .
M: 1 4-cyl. Gardner diesel; . . . hp

Remarks: Transferred from Ministry of Public Works 1976. Used as diving tender and general tender to naval headquarters.

◆ **1 air-support training craft** Bldr: Naval DY, HMNZS *Philomel* (In serv. 4-84)

Matua

D: 8 tons **S:** 14 kts **Dim:** 12.0 × . . . × . . .
M: 2 Perkins diesels; 2 props; . . . hp **Range:** 200/14 **Man:** 2–4 tot.

Remarks: Used for parachute recovery, helo winch training, diver support, patrol, and rescue duties at Naval Air Support Unit, Hobsonville. Plywood hull. The same organization also operates two 12.2-m, 16-kt. crash boats and two 10-m, 8-kt. personnel launches.

NICARAGUA

Republic of Nicaragua

Personnel (1985): Approximately 500 total

Merchant Marine (1984): 21 ships—19,291 grt
(tankers: 3 ships—4,398 grt)

NATIONAL GUARD (MARINE WING)

PATROL CRAFT

◆ **2 North Korean Sin Hung class**

D: 25 tons **S:** . . . **Dim:** 18.3 × 3.4 × 1.7
A: 2/14.5-mm mg (II ×1)
M: 2 M50-series diesels, 2 props; 2,400 hp

Remarks: Torpedo boats, with tubes deleted, delivered 10-83.

◆ **1 French 28.2-meter class** Bldr: C.N. de l'Estérel (In serv: 2-9-83)

GC 8 or 9 N. . . . . . .

D: 57 tons (fl) **S:** 24 kts **Dim:** 28.2 × 5.2 × 1.6
A: 2/20-mm AA (I × 2) **Range:** 800/15 **Man:** 12 tot.
M: 2 SACM AGO diesels; 2 props; 1,500 hp

Remarks: Two ordered 12-81 for Customs duties. Launched 6-9-83 and 26-5-83; delivered 24-6-83. Wooden construction. Sister *El Tayacan* lost 25-2-84 to a mine at El Bluff. Two additional *may* have been delivered 5 to 6-84.

◆ **2 Soviet Zhuk class**

GC. . . N. . . . . . . GC. . . N. . .

D: 60 tons (fl) **S:** 34 kts **Dim:** 24.0 × 5.0 × 1.8 (props)
A: 4/14.5-mm mg (II × 2) **Electron Equipt:** Radar: 1/Spin Trough
M: 2 M50 diesels; 2 props; 2,400 hp

Remarks: First unit transferred 4-82 from Algeria; second unit delivered 1984, via Cuba.

◆ **3 Israeli Dabur class** Bldr: Israeli Aircraft Industries (In serv. 5-78)

GC 10 GC 11 GC 12 GC 13

D: 25 tons (35 fl) **S:** 19.6 kts **Dim:** 19.79 × 5.40 × 1.75
A: 2/20-mm AA (I × 2) **M:** 2 G.M. 12V72 diesels; 2 props; 960 hp
Electric: 20 kw **Range:** 700/16 **Man:** 6 tot.

Remarks: One lost 4-85 to gunfire from Honduran units. Two larger *Dvora*-class patrol craft were also ordered from Israel, but their delivery was embargoed in 1979 at the request of the U.S. government.

◆ **1 U.S. 65-foot cruiser class** Bldr: Sewart Seacraft, La. (In serv. 1962)

GC 7 Rio Kuringwas

D: 60 tons **S:** 26.5 kts **Dim:** 25.9 × 5.6 × 1.8
A: 2/20-mm AA (I × 2) **M:** 3 G.M. diesels; 3 props; 2,000 hp
Range: 1,000/20 **Man:** 10 tot.

◆ **6 U.S. Hatteras-class cabin cruisers** (In serv. 1980)

Dim: 11.6 oa

MINE WARFARE CRAFT

◆ **2 Soviet Yevgenya-class inshore minesweepers** Bldr: Srednyy Neva SY, Kolpino

D: 80 tons (90 fl) **S:** 11 kts **Dim:** 26.2 × 6.1
A: 1/14.5-mm mg or 25-mm AA (II × 1)
Electron Equipt: Radar: 1/Spin Trough
M: 2 diesels; 2 props; 600 hp **Range:** 300/10 **Man:** 10 tot.

Remarks: Delivered via Cuba in 10-84. Glass-reinforced plastic construction. Can hunt for mines via television system to 30-m depths.

◆ **4 Polish K-8-class minesweeping boats** Bldr: Polnocny SY, Gdansk (In serv. 1954-59)

D: 19.4 tons (26 fl) **S:** 12 kts **Dim:** 16.9 × 3.2 × 0.8
A: 1/14.5-mm mg (II × 1) **Range:** 300/9
M: 2 3D6 diesels; 2 props; 300 hp **Man:** 6 tot.

Remarks: Transferred 11-84. Wooden construction. Tow, but do not carry, wire sweeps.

NIGERIA

Republic of Nigeria

Personnel (1985): 550 officers, 4,500 men

Merchant Marine (1984): 178 ships—442,030 grt
(tankers: 14 ships—156,558 grt)

Naval Aviation: Three Lynx Mk 89 ASW helicopters with Gem 3, 1,128-hp turbines for use aboard N.N.S. *Aradu*. Two Fokker F 27 Maritime patrol aircraft were delivered 1983-84 for coastal surveillance.

FRIGATES

◆ **1 MEKO 360-H class** Bldr: Blohm + Voss, Hamburg

	Laid down	L	In serv.
F 89 Aradu (ex-*Republic*)	2-5-79	25-1-80	22-2-82

Aradu (F 89) Ceclant/Premar II, 11-82

Aradu (F 89) Ceclant/Premar II, 11-82

D: 3,680 tons (fl) **S:** 30.5 kts
Dim: 125.9 (119.0 pp) × 15.0 (14.0 wl) × 4.32 (5.8 props)
A: 8/Otomat MK 1 SSM (I × 8)—1/127-mm OTO Melara DP—1/Albatros SAM syst., Mk 2, Mod. 9 (VIII × 1, 24 Aspide missiles)—8/40-mm Breda AA (II × 4)—6/324-mm ASW TT (III × 2, 18 torpedoes)—1/Lynx Mk 86 ASW helicopter
Electron Equipt: Radar: 1/Decca 1226, 1/Plessey AWS-5D, 1/H.S.A. WM-25, 1/H.S.A. STIR
Sonar: 1/H.S.A. PHS-32
EW: Decca RDL-2 intercept, RCM-2 jammer—2/SCLAR 105-mm chaff RL (XX × 2)
M: CODOG: 2 Rolls Royce Olympus TM-3B gas turbines, 50,000 hp; 2 MTU 20V956 TB92 diesels, 11,070 hp; 2/5-bladed CP props
Electric: 4,120 kVA **Fuel:** 440 tons **Range:** 4,500/18
Man: 26 officers, 169 men, 35 cadets

Remarks: Ordered 3-11-77. Renamed 1-11-80. Arrived at Lagos 21-12-81. Similar ships (but with COGOG propulsion, two helicopters, and different electronics) built for Argentina. Makes use of modular containers for electronics and weapon systems. Carries 460 rounds of 127-mm ammunition, 10,752 rounds of 40-mm ammunition, and 120 chaff rounds for the Elsag/Breda chaff rocket launchers, H.S.A. Vesta ASW torpedo f.c.s. Name means "Thunder."

◆ **1 training frigate**

	Bldr	Laid down	L	In serv.
F 87 Obuma (ex-*Nigeria*)	Wilton-Fijenoord, Netherlands	4-64	9-65	9-66

D: 1,724 tons (2,000 fl) **S:** 25 kts **Dim:** 109.85 (104.0 pp) × 11.3 × 3.35
A: 1/76-mm OTO Melara DP—4/40-mm AA (I × 4)

FRIGATES *(continued)*

Obuma (F 87) H. Ehlers, 6-83

Electron Equipt: Radar: 1/Plessey AWS-4, 1/navigational
Sonar: 1/162B, 1/177
M: 4 M.A.N. VV24/30B diesels; 2 props; 16,000 hp
Range: 3,500/15 **Man:** 216 tot.

REMARKS: Renamed 1981. Helicopter platform. Refit by Cammell Laird, 1970-71, and again at Schiedam, the Netherlands, in 1977. Only a simple lead-computing director is fitted for the 102-mm gunmount. Acts as training ship. Modernization, delayed since 1983, is to include replacing the 102-mm mount with an OTO Melara 76-mm Compact, an optronic f.c.s., and chaff RL. Former Squid ASW mortar deleted.

CORVETTES

◆ **2 Erin'mi class (Mk 9)** Bldr: Vosper Thornycroft, Portsmouth

	Laid down	L	In serv.
F 83 ERIN'MI	14-10-75	20-1-77	29-1-80
F 84 ENYMIRI	11-2-77	9-2-78	2-5-80

Enymiri (F 84) L. & L. Van Ginderen, 6-82

D: 850 tons (fl) **S:** 27 kts **Dim:** 69.0 (64.0 pp) × 9.6 × 3.0 (3.6 max.)
A: 1/76-mm OTO Melara DP—1/Sea Cat system (III × 1; 15 missiles)—1/40-mm Bofors AA—2/20-mm AA (I × 2)—1/375-mm Bofors ASW RL (II × 1)
Electron Equipt: Radar: 1/Decca TM 1226, 1/AWS-2, 1/H.S.A. WM-24
Sonar:1/Plessey PMS26—Decca intercept
EW: Decca "Cutlass" intercept
M: 4 MTU 20V956 TB92 diesels; 2 CP props; 20,512 hp
Electric: 889 kw **Endurance:** 10 days **Range:** 2,200/14 **Man:** 90 tot.

REMARKS: Can sustain 20 kts on two diesels. Uses three MTU 6V51 diesel generator sets of 260 kw each and one 109-kw emergency generator. Carry 750 rounds 76-mm ammunition, 24 rds. ASW rockets. Have 2/50-mm flare launchers. Funnel heightened on F 83 after initial trials. Both names are local words for "hippopotamus."

◆ **2 Dorina class (Mk 3)** Bldr: Vosper Thornycroft, Portsmouth

	Laid down	L	In serv.
F 81 DORINA	26-1-70	16-9-70	6-72
F 82 OTOBO	28-9-70	25-5-71	11-72

D: 650 tons (fl) **S:** 22 kts **Dim:** 61.57 (55.4 pp) × 7.45 × 3.35
A: 2/102-mm Mk 19 DP (II × 1)—2/40-mm Bofors AA (I × 2)—2/20-mm AA (I × 2)
Electron Equipt: Radar: 1/Decca TM 626, 1/Plessey AWS-1, 1/H.S.A. M 22
Sonar: Plessey MS 22
M: 2 M.A.N. V8V 24/30-B diesels; 2 props; 4,430 hp (3,400 sust.)
Electric: 600 kw **Fuel:** 68 tons **Range:** 3,500/14
Man: 7 officers, 13 petty officers, 46 men

Dorina (F 81)—tug alongside to starboard H. Ehlers, 12-83

REMARKS: Can carry a flag officer and his staff. Living spaces air-conditioned. Fin stabilizers. The 102-mm guns are hand-loaded. Twelve watertight compartments. Refitted 1975-76. Have sonar, but no ASW ordnance fitted.

GUIDED-MISSILE PATROL BOATS

◆ **3 Combattante-IIIB class** Bldr: CMN, Cherbourg, France

	Laid down	L	In serv.
P 181 SIRI	15-5-79	3-6-80	19-2-81
P 182 AYAM	7-9-79	10-11-80	11-6-81
P 183 EKUN	14-11-79	11-2-81	18-9-81

Siri (P 181) CMN, 1981

Ekun (P 183)—*Siri* (P 181) beyond H. Ehlers, 12-85

D: 376 tons light (430 fl) **S:** 37 kts
Dim: 56.0 (53.0 pp) × 8.16 (7.61 wl) × 2.15
A: 4/MM 38 Exocet SSM (II × 2)—1/76-mm OTO Melara DP—2/40-mm Breda AA (II × 1)—4/30-mm Emerlec AA (II × 2)
Electron Equipt: Radar: 1/Decca 1226, 1/Thomson-CSF Tritons, 1/Thomson-CSF Castor II
EW: Decca RDL intercept
M: 4 MTU 16V956 TB92 diesels; 4 props; 20,840 hp (17,320 sust.)
Range: 2,000/15 **Man:** 42 tot.

REMARKS: Ordered 11-77. Remained at Cherbourg until 9-5-82 because of payment dispute. Official commissioning date was 6-2-82 for all. Thomson-CSF Vega gun and missile f.c.s., with 2 CSEE Panda optical directors also.

◆ **3 FPB 57 class** Bldr: Lürssen, Vegesack, West Germany

	Laid down	L	In serv.
P 178 EKPE	17-2-79	17-12-79	8-80
P 179 DAMISA	17-2-79	27-3-79	4-81
P 180 AGU	17-2-79	7-11-80	4-81

D: 373 tons (436 fl) **S:** 35 kts **Dim:** 58.1 (54.4 wl) × 7.62 × 2.83 (props)
A: 4/Otomat Mk 1 (I × 4)—1/76-mm OTO Melara DP—2/40-mm Breda-Bofors (II × 1)—4/30-mm Emerlec AA (II × 2)
Electron Equipt: Radar: 1/Decca, TM 1226C, 1/H.S.A. WM-28
EW: Decca RDL intercept

GUIDED - MISSILE PATROL BOATS *(continued)*

Agu (P 180) P. Voss, 8-81

Ekpe (P 178) P. Voss, 8-81

M: 4 MTU 16V956 TB92 diesels; 4 props; 20,840 hp (17,320 sust.)
Electric: 405kVA **Range:** 1,600/32; 3,000/16 **Man:** 40 tot.

Remarks: Ordered late 1977. Sailed for Nigeria 21-8-81. Navigation systems include Decca Mk 21 "Navigator" NAVSAT receiver, Omega receiver, and Marconi "Lodestone" D/F. Made 42 kts on trials. Refitted by builders, 1983-84; P 180 badly damaged during 1984, losing 76-mm mount.

PATROL BOATS

◆ **6 65-ft Commercial Cruiser design** Bldr: Swiftships, Inc., Morgan City, La.

D: 36 tons (fl) **S:** **Dim:** 19.96 × 5.59 × 1.52
A: . . .
Electron Equipt: Radar: 1/. . . nav.
M: 2 MTU 8V396 TB93 diesels; 2 props; 1,930 hp
Range: 500/18 **Electric:** . . . **Man:** . . .

Remarks: Aluminum construction. Ordered 1985.

Note: Authority for the acquisition of up to 26 additional patrol boats to combat smuggling was given 19-4-85.

◆ **4 Makurdi class** Bldr: Brooke Marine Ltd., Lowestoft, U.K.

	L	In serv.		L	In serv.
P 167 Makurdi	21-3-74	14-8-74	P 171 Jebba	1-12-76	29-4-77
P 168 Hadejia	25-5-74	14-8-74	P 172 Oguta	17-1-77	29-4-77

Hadejia (P 168)—as rearmed Brooke Marine, 1982

D: 115 tons (143 fl) **S:** 20.5 kts **Dim:** 32.6 × 6.1 × 3.5
A: 4/30-mm Emerlec AA (II × 2) **Electron Equipt:** Radar: 1/Decca 1226
M: 2 Ruston-Paxman YJCM diesels; 2 props; 3,000 hp **Fuel:** 18 tons
Range: 2,300/12 **Man:** 4 officers, 20 men

Remarks: First two refitted by builders, 1981-82, others refitted in Nigeria; rearmed, engines overhauled. Originally had 2/40-mm AA (I × 2).

◆ **4 Argundu class** Bldr: Abeking & Rasmussen, West Germany

	L	In serv.		L	In serv.
P 165 Argundu	4-7-73	10-74	P 169 Bras	12-1-76	3-76
P 166 Yola	12-6-73	10-74	P 170 Epe	9-2-76	3-76

Yola (P 166) and Bras (P 169)—as rearmed P. Voss, 3-82

D: 90 tons **S:** 20 kts **Dim:** 32.0 (29.0 pp) × 6.0 × 1.7
A: 4/30-mm Emerlec AA (II × 2) **Electron Equipt:** Radar: 1/Decca 1229
M: 2 MTU diesels; 2 props; 2,070 hp **Range:** . . . **Man:** 25 tot.

Remarks: Refitted 1981-82 by builders; originally had 1/40-mm AA, 1/20-mm AA.

MINE COUNTERMEASURES SHIPS

◆ **0 (+2 + 2) Italian Lerici class** Bldr: Intermarine, Sarzana

	Laid down	L	In serv.
M. . . Ohue	6-84	10-85	12-87
M. . . Maraba	. . .	. . .	. . .

D: 470 tons (550 fl) **S:** 15 kts **Dim:** 49.98 (45.50 pp) × 9.56 × 2.63
A: 2/30-mm Emerlec AA (II × 1)—2/20-mm AA (I × 2)
Electron Equipt: Radar: 1/3 ST7/DG—Sonar: Thomson-CSF TSM 1022 (IBIS V)
M: 2 MTU 8V396 TC82 diesels; 2 waterjets; 1,740 hp
Electric: 887 kVA **Range:** 1,500/12 **Man:** 3 officers, 17 men

Remarks: First ship ordered 9-4-83, second in 5-84, with option for two more. Glass-reinforced plastic construction throughout. Minehunting speed is 7 kts, using the two drop-down, rotating, shrouded thrusters. Range at 12 kts can be extended to 4,000 n.m. by using the passive roll stabilization tanks as fuel tanks. Can support 6–7 mine disposal divers. Will carry two Gaymarine Pluto remote-controlled minehunting submersibles.

AMPHIBIOUS WARFARE SHIPS

◆ **2 West German Type-502 landing ships** Bldr: Howaldtswerke, Hamburg

	Laid down	L	In serv.
L 1312 Ambe	3-3-78	7-7-78	11-5-79
L 1313 Ofiom	15-9-78	7-12-78	7-79

Ambe (LST 1312) and Ofiom (L 1313) H. Ehlers, 1-85

D: 1,190 tons light (1,470 normal, 1,750 fl) **S:** 17 kts
Dim: 86.9 (74.5 pp) × 14.0 × 2.30
A: 1/40-mm AA—2/20-mm AA (I × 2) **Electron Equipt:** Radar: 1/Decca 1226
M: 2 MTU 16V956 TB92 diesels; 4 props; 7,000 hp **Electric:** 900 kw
Range: 5,000/12 **Man:** 6 officers, 53 men, plus 540 troops (1,000 for short distances)

Remarks: Cargo: 400 tons vehicles plus troops (typically: 5/40-ton tanks or 7/18-ton tanks plus 4/45-ton trucks). Articulated bow ramp, short stern ramp for loading from a pier. Can fit an 81-mm mortar forward. Each engine drives two props.

◆ **2 Oton-class landing craft** Bldr: Scheepswerf Gravel/Akerboom, Leiden, the Netherlands

	Laid down	L	In serv.
. . . Oton	9-81	22-11-81	1982
. . . Idah	1-82	8-3-82	1982

AMPHIBIOUS WARFARE SHIPS *(continued)*

D: Approx. 320 tons (fl) **S:** 10.5 kts **Dim:** 35.0 (33.3 pp) × 8.0 × 1.50
M: 2 Kelvin TBS-08 diesels; 2 props; 1,000 hp

REMARKS: 130 grt. Ordered 20-1-81. May in fact be commercial *vice* naval landing craft.

HYDROGRAPHIC SHIPS

◆ **1 British Bulldog class** Bldr: Brooke Marine Ltd., Lowestoft, U.K.

	Laid down	L	In serv.
A 498 LANA	5-4-74	4-3-76	9-76

Lana (A 498) H. Ehlers, 8-83

D: 800 tons (1,100 fl) **S:** 15 kts **Dim:** 60.95 (57.8 pp) × 11.43 × 3.7
A: 2/20-mm AA (I × 2) **Electron Equipt:** Radar: 1/Decca 1226
M: 4 Lister-Blackstone ERS-8M diesels; 2 CP props; 2,000 hp
Electric: 880 kw **Range:** 4,000/12
Man: 38 tot.

◆ **1 coastal survey craft**

	Bldr	L	In serv.
MURTULA MUHAMED	Akerboom, Leiden, Netherlands	14-8-76	28-9-76

D: 13 tons **S:** 9 kts **Dim:** 11.75 × 3.5 × 1.0
M: 1 Perkins 6-354M diesel; 1 prop; 75 hp

TRAINING SHIP

◆ **1 training ship** Bldr: Van Lent, Kaag, Netherlands (In serv. 10-5-75)

A 497 RUWAN YARO (ex-*Ogina Bereton*)

Ruwan Yaro (A 497) H. Ehlers, 12-83

D: 400 tons (fl) **S:** 17 kts **Dim:** 50.0 (44.2 pp) × 8.0 × 2.0
A: None **Electron Equipt:** Radar: 1/Decca TM 626
M: 2 Deutz SBA 12M528 diesels; 1 CP prop; 3,000 hp **Fuel:** 64 tons
Range: 3,000/15 **Man:** 31 + 11 in officers' training

REMARKS: Purchased 1976. Originally a yacht, has a glass-reinforced plastic hull and a bow-thruster.

TUGS

◆ **1 coastal tug** Bldr: Oelkers, Hamburg (In serv. 19-5-73)

A 496 RIBADU

D: 147 tons **S:** 12 kts **Dim:** 28.5 × 7.2 × 3.7 **M:** 1 diesel; 1 prop; 800 hp

◆ **2 large harbor tugs** Bldr: SY de Wiel BV, Asperen, the Netherlands

A 499 COMMANDER APAI JOE (In serv. 9-83)
A 500 COMMANDER RUDOLF (In serv. 9-84)

Commander Apai Joe (A 499) L. & L. Van Ginderen, 7-83

D: . . . **S:** . . . **Dim:** . . . × . . . × . . .
M: 2 M.A.N. diesels; 2 props; 1,510 hp

SERVICE CRAFT

◆ **3 Dutch Sea Truck tenders** Bldr: Damen, Gorinchem (In serv. 10-85)

Bldr: Damen, Gorinchem (In serv. 10-85)
P 239 P 240 P 242

D: . . . tons **S:** 20 kts **Dim:** 14.50 × 4.40 × 0.85
M: 2 MTU diesels; 2 props, 1,200 hp **Man:** 8 tot.

REMARKS: Aluminum construction, bow ramp. Can carry 1/7.632-mm mg. P. 242 used for inshore survey.

◆ **1 water lighter** WATER BARGE ONE

NOTE: There are also 44 service launches built by Fairey Marine, Hamble: 2/10-m, 22/7-m, 15/6.7-m, and 5/5.5 m. Four Cheverton 8.2-m launches are also in use.

NIGERIAN COAST GUARD

PATROL CRAFT

◆ **15 Type Mk 2 AM patrol craft** Bldr: Intermarine, La Spezia

	In serv.		In serv.		In serv.
P 200 ABEOKUTA	7-81	P 205 IKEJA	9-81	P 210 MAIDUGIRI	4-82
P 201 AKURE	7-81	P 206 ILOREN	11-81	P 211 MINNA	4-82
P 202 BAUCHI	7-81	P 207 JOS	11-81	P 212 OURERRI	4-82
P 203 BENIN CITY	7-81	P 208 KADUNA	11-81	P 213 PORT HARCOURT	4-82
P 204 ENUGU	9-81	P 209 KANO	4-82	P 214 SOKOTO	4-82

Port Harcourt (P 213) C. Martinelli, 3-82

D: 20 tons (fl) **S:** 35 kts **Dim:** 18.2 (16.5 pp) × 5.0 × 0.85
A: 1/20-mm AA—2/7.62-mm mg (I × 2)
M: 2 MTU 8V331 TB91 diesels; 2 Castoldi waterjets; 2,700 hp
Range: 300/32 **Man:** 9 tot.

REMARKS: Ordered 10-78. Glass-reinforced plastic construction.

◆ **1 "Tracker" class** Bldr: Fairey Marine, Hamble, U.K. (In serv. 2-78)

D: 31 tons (fl) **S:** 24 kts **Dim:** 19.3 × 5.0 × 1.5
A: 1/20-mm AA **M:** 2 diesels; 2 props; 1,290 hp
Range: 650/20 **Man:** 11 tot.

◆ **2 "Spear" class** Bldr: Fairey Marine, Hamble, U.K. (In serv. 1978)

D: 4.3 tons **S:** 25 kts **Dim:** 9.1 × 2.8 × 0.8

NIGERIA *(continued)*

MARINE POLICE

Note: For operations on the Niger River and Lake Chad. All craft built of glass-reinforced plastic. In addition to the craft listed below, in 4-82 it was announced that 4 13-m glass-reinforced plastic, 48 6.4-m aluminum, 34 5.5-m glass-reinforced plastic, and 30 4.9-m aluminum patrol craft and 3 4.9-m hovercraft were to be procured. Two patrol craft were ordered 5-84 from Fairey Allday Marine, U.K.

PATROL AND SERVICE CRAFT

◆ **6 14 m** Bldr: Schöttel, the Netherlands (In serv. 1982)

◆ **4 8 m** Bldr: Copeland, U.K. (In serv. 1982)

◆ **12 9.8 m** Bldr: Halmatic, Havant, U.K. (In serv. 1982-83)

D: 5.5 tons (6.5 fl) **S:** 25 kts **Dim:** 9.8 (8.8 wl) × 3.4 × 0.9
M: 2 Mermaid diesels; 2 props; 360 hp **Man:** 4-6 tot.

Remarks: Ordered 8-1-81. Glass-reinforced plastic construction.

◆ **10 Tiger-class air-cushion vehicles** Bldr: Air Vehicles, Cowes, U.K. (In serv.: 5 in 8-82; 5 in 1984-85)

D: 1 ton (fl) **S:** 34 kts **Dim:** 8.45 × 4.57 × 2.81 (high)
A: 1 diesel engine; 1 lift fan/1 prop; 200 hp **Man:** 12 tot.

◆ **2 Skima 12 hovercraft** Bldr: Pindair, U.K. (In serv. 1982)

◆ **13 Skua Q33 class** Bldr: Horne Bros., Fishbourne, U.K. (In serv. 1981-82)

D: 5 tons (fl) **S:** 30 kts **Dim:** 7.9 × 2.8 × 0.4
M: 2 Volvo Penta AQAD-40/280 diesels; 2 outdrive props; 310 hp
Man: 2–4 tot.

◆ **3 Q26-class landing craft** Bldr: Horne Bros., Fishbourne, U.K. (In serv. 1982)

D: 17 tons (fl) **S:** 35 kts **Dim:** 10.0 × 3.5 × 0.75
A: 2/7.62-mm mg (I × 2) **Man:** 2 crew, plus 24 police troops
M: 2 Sabre diesels; 2 props; 500 hp

◆ **1 P 1200 class** Bldr: Watercraft, Ltd., Shoreham, U.K. (In serv. 2-81)

D: 9.7 tons (fl) **S:** 27 kts **Dim:** 11.9 × 4.1 × 1.1
M: 2 G.M. 8V71 TI diesels; 2 props; 480 hp **Range:** 240/25

◆ **5 P 800 class** Bldr: Watercraft, Shoreham, U.K. (In serv. 12-80)

D: 3.2 tons (fl) **S:** 26 kts **Dim:** 8.0 × 2.6 × 0.8
M: 1 Volvo AQAD-40 outdrive diesel; 1 prop; 150 hp **Range:** 104/26

◆ **8 15-ton class** Bldr: Vosper Thornycroft (In serv. 1971-72)

D: 15 tons (fl) **S:** 19 kts **Dim:** 10.4 × 3.1 × 0.9
M: 2 Rolls-Royce diesels; 2 props; 290 hp

◆ **8 7-meter work boats** Bldr: Fairey Marine, Hamble, U.K. (In serv. 1982)

CUSTOMS SERVICE

◆ **1 patrol boat** Bldr: Chung Mu SY, Hong Kong

Yan-Yan (In serv. 14-9-83)

D: 100 tons (fl) **S:** 27.5 kts **Dim:** 34.0 (32.0 wl) × 6.0 × 1.34
A: . . . **M:** 2 MTU 12V396 TB93 diesels; 2 props; 3,560 hp
Fuel: 13 tons **Man:** 12 tot.

◆ **6 Watercraft 18-ton, 18-kt patrol craft** (In serv. 1982)

NORWAY

Kingdom of Norway

Personnel (1985): 8,750 men, 2,000 of whom are in the Coast Artillery

Merchant Marine (1984): 2,271 ships — 17,662 grt
(tankers: 235 ships — 11,741,315 grt)

Naval Aviation: The Norwegian Navy does not have an air arm, as such. However, two of the Air Force's formations are assigned to naval missions, usually reconnaissance and ASW patrol; a squadron of 10 Sea King Mk 43 and 20 UH-1D search-and-rescue helicopters; a group of 7 P-3B Orion patrol aircraft and 4 De Havilland Twin Otter utility aircraft. Two Boeing 737 "Surveiller" with SLAMMAR side-looking radars have been ordered for maritime patrol. In addition, 20 Bell UH-1D helicopters operate in the search-and-rescue role. The Coast Guard operates 6 WG-13 Lynx Mk 86 helicopters. The Penguin Mk 3 anti-ship missile is being acquired to permit Royal Norwegian Air Force F-16 fighters to attack ships.

P-3B Orion — Royal Norwegian Air Force Official

Sea King Mk 43 — Royal Norwegian Air Force Official

WEAPONS AND SYSTEMS

The Norwegian Navy uses mostly British, American, and Swedish weapons and systems, but it has built two systems of its own, the Terne automatic ASW defense system and the Penguin surface-to-surface missile, which are described below. Submarines are equipped with Swedish T-61 (45 kts, 20,000 m) or American NT37C (20,000 m) and Mk 37 Mod. 2 wire-guided torpedoes. Norway has also developed its own radar and electro-optical gun and missile fire-control systems. Sonars are manufactured by the Simrad Co.

Terne Mk III (ASW)

Maximum range: 900 m
1 search sonar
1 attack sonar ("Terne Mk 3" for range/depth determination)
1 computer
1 sextuple launcher mount with a rapid-reloading system.

The sextuple launcher mount weighs a little less than 3 tons. Firing is done between 45° and 75° of elevation, the latter for minimum range. Six rounds are ripple-fired at a time. Reloading is done automatically in 40 seconds, as the carriage is returned to a vertical position, in which ready-service racks reload the launchers. The rocket is 1.97 m in length, 0.2 m in diameter, 120 kg in weight (warhead: 48 kg), and has a combination timed and proximity fuse. Employed on the *Oslo* and *Sleipner* classes.

Penguin Mk 1 (Anti-ship)

Length: 2.95 m — Maximum range: 20,000 m
Wingspan: 1.4 m — Speed: Mach 0.7
Diameter: 0.28 — Guidance: infrared homing
Weight: 330 kg

The missile is protected by a fiberglass container that also serves as a launcher.

Penguin Mk 2 (Anti-ship)

Length: 2.96 m — Maximum range: 27,000 m
Wingspan: 1.42 m — Speed: Mach 0.8
Diameter: 0.28 m — Guidance: Infrared homing
Weight: 340 kg — Warhead: 120 kg Bullpup Mk 19

Note: A Mk 2 Mod. 7, helicopter-launched version is being developed for the U.S. Navy.

Penguin Mk 3 (Anti-ship, air-launched)

Length: 3.20 m — Maximum range: 40,000+ m
Wingspan: 2.00 m — Speed: Mach 0.8
Diameter: 0.28 m — Guidance: Infrared homing
Weight: 350 kg (400 with launcher) — Warhead: 120 kg

Penguin Mk 3 can be launched at altitudes of 150 to 30,000 ft.

76-mm Bofors gun

Single-barrel automatic gun mounted on the *Storm*-class patrol boats. Not intended for AA. Also used by the Singapore Navy.

Turret weight (no ammunition): 6.5 tons
Length: 50 calibers
Muzzle velocity: 825 m/sec
Rate of train: 25°/sec
Rate of elevation: 25°/sec
Rate of fire: 30 rounds/min
Cartridge weight: 11.3 kg
Shell weight: 5.9 kg
Warhead weight: 0.54 kg
Maximum range, surface mode: 8,000 m
Arc of elevation: −10° to +30°

SUBMARINES

◆ **0 (+6) German Type 210** Bldr: Thyssen Nordseewerke, Emden

	Laid down	L	In serv.
S. . . N.	. . .	. . .	3-89
S. . . N.	. . .	. . .	5-90
S. . . N.	. . .	. . .	11-90
S. . . N.	. . .	. . .	5-91
S. . . N.	. . .	. . .	11-91
S. . . N.	. . .	. . .	5-92

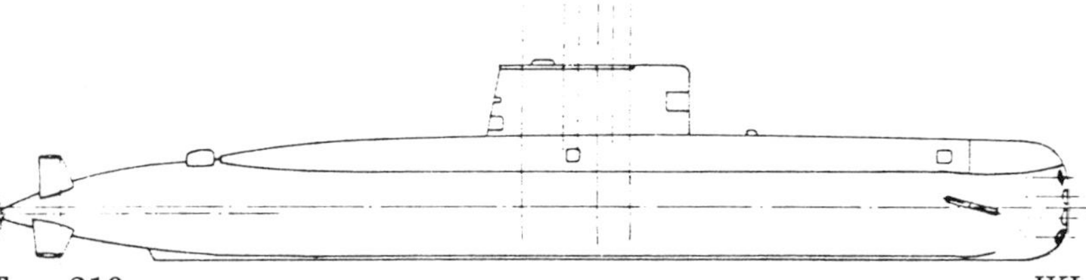

Type 210 IKL

D: 940 tons standard, 1,040 tons surf. (fl)
S: 11/23 kts **Dim:** 59.00 × 5.40 × 4.50
A: 8/533-mm TT (14 German Seeal 3, DM2A3 torpedoes)
Electron Equipt: Radar: . . . —Sonar: Krupp Atlas DBQS-21D
M: 2 MTU 16V652 MB 1,260-bhp diesels, 2/870-kw generator sets, electric drive; 1 prop; 6,000 hp
Range: 5,000/8 (snorkel) **Endurance:** 40 days
Fuel: 100 tons **Man:** 18-20 tot.

Remarks: Six ordered 30-9-82, with option to order two more, later dropped. Will have Kongsberg MSI-90U torpedo f.c.s. Diving depth: 250 m.

◆ **14 German Type 207** Bldr: Rheinstahl-Nordseewerke, Emden

	L	In serv.		L	In serv.
S 300 Ula	19-12-64	7-5-65	S 307 Stadt	10-6-66	15-11-66
S 301 Utsira	11-3-65	1-7-65	S 308 Stord	2-9-66	9-2-67
S 302 Utstein	19-5-65	9-9-65	S 309 Svenner	27-1-67	1-7-67
S 303 Utvaer	30-6-65	1-12-65	S 315 Kaura	16-10-64	5-2-65
S 304 Uthaug	8-10-65	16-2-66	S 317 Kya	20-2-64	15-6-64
S 305 Sklinna	21-1-66	17-8-66	S 318 Kobben	25-4-64	17-8-64
S 306 Skolpen	24-3-66	17-8-66	S 319 Kunna	16-7-64	1-10-64

Kobben (S 318) L. & L. Van Ginderen, 1978

D: 370/482 tons **S:** 13.5/17 kts **Dim:** 45.41 (S 309:46.41) × 4.6 × 3.80
A: 8/533-mm TT, fwd (8 Swedish Type 61 and U.S. NT37C torpedoes)
Electron Equipt: Radar: 1/Thomson-CSF Calypso—Sonar: Krupp Atlas. . .
M: 2 Mercedes-Benz MB 820Db, 600-hp diesels, 2 405-kw generators, 1 1,100-kw motor; 1 prop (2.3 m diameter); 1,700 hp
Man: 17 tot.

Remarks: Based on the West German Type 205, but deeper-diving. MSI-700 torpedo fire-control. The *Svenner* is equipped for training, has a second periscope, and is one meter longer than the others. Diving depth: 190 m. Use MSI-70U torpedo fire-control system. Six are to be modernized, to complement the new Type 210 class; three others are to be transferred to Denmark. Sister *Kinn* (S 316) stricken 1982.

GUIDED-MISSILE FRIGATES

◆ **5 Oslo class** Bldr: Marinens Hovedverft (Naval Dockyard), Horten

	Laid down	L	In serv.
F 300 Oslo	1963	17-1-64	29-1-66
F 301 Bergen	1963	23-8-65	15-5-67
F 302 Trondheim	1963	4-9-64	2-6-66
F 303 Stavanger	1964	4-2-66	1-12-67
F 304 Narvik	1964	8-1-65	30-11-66

Stavanger (F 303) L. & L. Van Ginderen, 4-85

Narvik (F 304)—with 2/20-mm AA added G. Gyssels, 3-85

D: 1,450 tons (1,850 fl) **S:** 25 kts **Dim:** 96.62 (93.87 pp) × 11.17 × 4.4
A: 6/Penguin SSM—1/NATO Sea Sparrow system (VIII × 1, 24 missiles)—4/76.2-mm DP (II × 2)—2/20-mm Rheinmetall AA (I × 2)—1/Terne-III ASW RL (VI × 1)—6/324-mm Mk 32 ASW TT (II × 2)—1/d.c. rack (6 d.c.)
Electron Equipt: Radar: 1/Decca TM 1226, 1/DRBV 22, 1/H.S.A. M 24, 1/U.S. Mk 91 Mod. 0
Sonar: 1/Terne Mk 3 attack, 1/SQS-36—EW: . . .
M: 1 set Laval-Ljungstrom PN 20 GT; 1 prop; 20,000 hp
Electric: 1,100 kw **Boilers:** 2 Babcock & Wilcox; 42.18 kg/cm², 454°C
Range: 4,500/15 **Man:** 11 officers, 19 petty officers, 120 men

Remarks: Based on the U.S. *Dealey*-class destroyer escorts, but with higher free board forward and many European subsystems. Rebuilt during the late 1970s with the Penguin anti-ship missile, NATO Sea Sparrow point-defense SAM, and ASW torpedo tubes. In the Sea Sparrow system, the Mk 91 radar director is on a pylon atop the missile-reload magazine; the launcher is a U.S. Mk 29. F 304 conducted trials during 1980 with the Raytheon C-LAS C-band acquisition radar.

Beginning in 1987, all to be modernized, with Thomson-CSF TSM 2633 (Spherion) sonar in place of the U.S. AN/SQS-36, a VDS (requiring replacement of the aft 76.2-mm gunmount with a 40-mm AA mount), digital (*vice* analog) weapons-control systems, rocket decoy system added, and habitability improvements.

CORVETTES

◆ **2 Sleipner class** Bldr: Nylands Verksted, Oslo

	L	In serv.		L	In serv.
F 310 Sleipner	9-11-63	29-4-65	F 311 Aeger	24-9-65	31-3-67

Aeger (F 311) G. Gyssels, 8-82

D: 600 tons (790 fl) **S:** 20+ kts **Dim:** 69.33 × 7.9 × 2.5
A: 1/76.2-mm Mk 34 DP—1/40-mm AA—1/Terne-III ASW RL (VI × 1)—6/324-mm Mk 32 ASW TT (III × 2)—1/d.c. rack (6 d.c.)
Electron Equipt: Radar: 1/Decca TM 1226, 1/Decca 202
Sonar: 1/Terne Mk 3 attack, 1/SQS-36
M: 4 Maybach diesels; 2 props; 9,000 hp **Man:** 61 tot.

Remarks: From the 1960 program. Now employed primarily for training. U.S. Mk 63 GFCS replaced by 2 Swedish TVT 300 optronic systems. The AN/SQS-36 sonar is to be replaced by a Thomson-CSF TSM2633 (Spherion) set.

◆ **1 former whale-catcher** Bldr: Stord Verft (L: 1951)

P 340 Vadsø

D: 600 tons (905 fl) **S:** 12 kts **Dim:** 51.0 × 9.0 × 4.1
A: 1/40-mm AA—1/d.c. rack
Electron Equipt: Radar: 1/Decca 1226, 1/Decca 202
Sonar: . . .
M: 1 M.A.K. 8M451 diesel; 1 prop; 1,400 hp **Range:** 15,000/12 **Man:** 22 tot.

Remarks: Purchased in 1976 and refitted for local patrol duties. The AA gun is mounted on what was the harpoon-gun platform at the extreme bow; the depth-charge rack is on a platform extending aft from the superstructure.

GUIDED-MISSILE PATROL BOATS

◆ **14 Hauk class** Bldrs: (A) Bergens Mekaniske Verksteder; (B) Westamarin, Alta

	Bldr	L	In serv.
P 986 Hauk	A	2-77	17-8-78
P 987 Ørn	A	2-78	19-1-79
P 988 Terne	A	5-78	13-3-79
P 989 Tjeld	A	8-78	25-5-79
P 990 Skarv	A	10-78	17-7-79
P 991 Teist	A	6-12-78	11-9-79
P 992 Jo	A	. . .	1-11-79
P 993 Lom	A	. . .	15-1-80
P 994 Stegg	A	. . .	18-3-80
P 995 Falk	A	. . .	30-4-80
P 996 Ravn	B	. . .	20-5-80
P 997 Gribb	B	. . .	10-7-80
P 998 Geir	B	. . .	16-9-80
P 999 Erle	B	. . .	10-12-80

Terne (P 988) firing Penguin Mk2 Official

Erle (P 999) G. Koop, 5-84

D: 130 tons (155 fl) **S:** 35 kts **Dim:** 36.53 × 6.3 × 1.65
A: 2-6/Penguin Mk II SSM (I × 6)—1/40-mm Bofors AA—1/20-mm Rheinmetall AA—2/533-mm TT for T-61 wire-guided torpedoes
Electron Equipt: Radar: 2/Decca TM 1226—Sonar: Simrad SQ3D/SF
M: 2 MTU 16V538 TB92 diesels; 2 props; 7,340 hp **Range:** 440/34
Man: 22 tot.

Remarks: MSI-80S fire-control system, developed by Kongsberg, uses two Decca radars plus a TVT-300 electro-optical tracker and an Ericssen laser range finder. Have 2/50-mm flare RL.

◆ **6 Snögg class** Bldr: Båtservice Verft, Mandal, 1970-71

P 980 Snögg (ex-*Lyr*)	P 982 Snarr	P 984 Kvik
P 981 Rapp	P 983 Rask	P 985 Kjapp

Snarr (P 982)—4 Penguin Mk 1 aboard J.-C. Bellonne, 1974

D: 115 tons (140 fl) **S:** 36 kts **Dim:** 36.53 × 6.3 × 1.65
A: 2-4/Penguin Mk I SSM (I × 4)—1/40-mm AA—4/533-mm TT for T-61 wire-guided torpedoes—2/d.c. racks
Electron Equipt: Radar: 1/Decca TM 626, 1/PEAB TORI fire control
M: 2 MTU 16V538 TB92 diesels; 2 props; 7,200 hp
Range: 550/36 **Man:** 3 officers, 17 men

◆ **19 Storm class** Bldrs: P 963, P 966, P 969, P 972, P 975, and P 978: Westermöen, Mandal; Others: Bergens MV

	L		L		L
P 960 Storm	19-3-63	P 967 Skudd	25-3-66	P 974 Brott	27-1-67
P 961 Blink	28-6-65	P 968 Arg	24-5-66	P 975 Odd	7-4-67
P 962 Glimt	27-9-65	P 969 Steil	20-9-66	P 977 Brask	27-5-67
P 963 Skjold	17-2-66	P 970 Brann	3-7-66	P 978 Rokk	1-6-67
P 964 Trygg	25-11-65	P 971 Tross	29-9-66	P 979 Gnist	15-8-67
P 965 Kjekk	27-1-66	P 972 Hvass	20-12-66		
P 966 Djerv	28-4-66	P 973 Traust	18-11-66		

Hvass (P 972)—6 Penguin missiles aboard G. Koop, 5-84

D: 100 tons (125 fl) **S:** 37 kts **Dim:** 36.53 × 6.3 × 1.55
A: 4-6/Penguin Mk I SSM (I × 6)—1/76-mm—1/40-mm AA
Electron Equipt: Radar: 1/Decca TM 1226, 1/H.S.A. WM-26 fire-control
M: Mayback MB 872A diesels; 2 props; 7,200 hp **Range:** 550/36
Man: 4 officers, 9 petty officers, 13 men

Remarks: Backfitted with TVT-300 electro-optical tracker and laser range finder, in a tub abaft the radar mast. Diesels are essentially the same as those in the *Hauk* and *Snögg* classes above. Two d.c. racks can be carried in lieu of the after two Penguin containers. *Pil* (P 976) reported stricken 1982.

MINE WARFARE SHIPS

◆ **2 Vidar-class minelayers** Bldr: Mjellem & Karlsen, Bergen

	Laid down	L	In serv.
N 52 Vidar	1-3-76	18-3-77	21-10-77
N 53 Vale	1-2-76	5-8-77	10-2-78

Vale (N 53) G. Koop, 4-85

D: 1,500 tons (1,722 fl) **S:** 15 kts **Dim:** 64.8 (60.0 pp) × 12.0 × 4.0
A: 2/40-mm AA (I × 2)—6/324-mm Mk 32 ASW TT (II × 2)—2/d.c. racks—320 mines
Electron Equipt: Radar: 2/Decca 1226—Sonar: Simrad SQ3D
M: 2 Wichmann 7AX diesels; 2 props; 4,200 hp **Electric:** 1,000 kw
Fuel: 247 tons **Man:** 50 tot.

Remarks: Capable of serving as minelayers (mines carried on three decks, automatic hoist, three mine-laying rails), torpedo-recovery ships, personnel and cargo transports, fisheries-protection ships, and ASW escorts. Bow-thruster fitted.

◆ **1 inshore mine-planter**

	Bldr	L
N 51 Borgen	Marinens Hovedverft, Horten	29-4-60

D: 282 tons (fl) **S:** 9 kts **Dim:** 31.28 × 8.0 × 3.35
A: 2/20-mm AA (I × 2)—2 mine rails
M: 2 G.M. 3-71 diesels; 2 Voith Schneider cycloidal props; 330 hp

Remarks: Patterned on the Swedish MUL-12 class. Designed to "plant" controlled mines by crane.

◆ **10 U.S. Falcon-class minesweepers** Bldrs: M 315, M 332, M 334: Båtservice Verft, Mandal; M 316: Skåluren, Rosendal; M 331: Forenede Båtbyggeri, Risör; M 311, M 313, M 314, M 317: Hodgdon Bros., Gowdy & Stevens, Boothbay, Maine; M 312: C. Hiltebrant DD, Kingston, New York

	In serv.
M 311 Sauda (ex-MSC 102)	25-8-53
M 312 Sira (ex-MSC 132)	28-11-55
M 313 Tana (ex-*Roeslaere,* ex-MSC 103)	9-53

MINE WARFARE SHIPS *(continued)*

M 314 Alta (ex-*Arlon,* ex-MSC 104)	10-53
M 315 Ogna	5-3-55
M 316 Vosso	16-3-55
M 317 Glomma (ex-*Bastogne,* ex-MSC 151)	12-53
M 331 Tista	27-4-55
M 332 Kvina	12-7-55
M 334 Utla	15-1-55

Tana (M 313)—minehunter, deckhouse aft L. & L. Van Ginderen, 6-81

Kvina (M 332) G. Gyssels, 7-83

D: 300 tons (372 fl) **S:** 13 kts (8, sweeping) **Dim:** 43.0 × 7.95 × 2.55
A: 2/20-mm Rheinmetall AA (I × 2)
Electron Equipt: Radar: 1/Decca 202 or 1226
Sonar: 1/UQS-1 (M 313: 1/193 M)
M: 2 G.M. 8-268A diesels; 2 props; 1,200 hp **Fuel:** 40 tons
Range: 2,500/10 **Man:** 38 tot.

Remarks: *Tana, Alta,* and *Glomma* were transferred by Belgium in 1966 in exchange for two ocean minesweepers, *Lagen* and *Namsen.* In 1977, *Tana* was converted to a prototype minehunter, with British type 193M sonar, two PAP-104 remote-controlled minehunting devices, and divers' facilities in a large deckhouse aft. She was rearmed with 2/20-mm Rheinmetall AA guns (I × 2), now backfitted into the others. At the waterline, across the stern, she has a platform for diver-recovery; this extends her overall length by more than one meter.

Note: The *Falcon* class is programmed to be replaced by a class of 8 minehunters in the late 1980s/early 1990s.

AMPHIBIOUS WARFARE SHIPS

◆ **5 Reinøysund-class utility landing craft** Bldr: Mjellem & Karlsen, Bergen (In serv. 1972-73)

L 4502 Reinøysund L 4504 Maursund L 4506 Borgsund
L 4503 Sørøysund L 4505 Rotsund

D: 596 tons (fl) **S:** 11 kts **Dim:** 51.4 × 10.3 × 1.85
A: 3/20-mm Rheinmetall (I × 3)—4/12.7-mm mg—rails for 120 mines
M: 2 MTU diesels; 2 props; . . . hp **Man:** 2 officers, 7 men

Remarks: Double-folding bow-ramp door. Cargo capacity: 5 Leopard tanks, 80–180 men. Similar to class below, but superstructure is farther forward.

◆ **2 Kvalsund-class utility landing craft** Bldr: Mjellem & Karlsen, Bergen

L 4500 Kvalsund (In serv. 6-68) L 4501 Raftsund (In serv. 3-69)

D: 590 tons (fl) **S:** 11 kts **Dim:** 50.0 × 10.2 × 1.8
A: 2/20-mm AA—rails for 120 mines
M: 2 MTU diesels; 2 props; . . . hp **Man:** 2 officers, 7 men

Remarks: Cargo capacity: 5 Leopard tanks, 80–180 men.

AUXILIARY SHIPS

Note: The 14,989 grt auto/passenger ferry *Peter Wessel* was acquired 9-85 for conversion to a casualty evacuation ship with a medical staff of 450 and facilities for 800 seriously wounded and 1,200 lightly wounded troops. Subordination of the ship not reported. A second ship may also be obtained.

◆ **1 logistic-support ship** Bldr: Horten Verft, Horten

	Laid down	L	In serv.
A 530 Horten	28-1-77	12-8-77	9-6-78

Horten (A 530) 1978

D: 2,500 tons (fl) **S:** 16.5 kts **Dim:** 87.0 (82.0 pp) × 13.7 × . . .
A: 2/40-mm AA (I × 2)—mines **Electron Equipt:** Radar: 2/Decca. . .
M: 2 Wichmann 7AX diesels; 2 props; 4,200 hp
Man: 86 tot.

Remarks: Used to support submarines and small combatants. Can accommodate up to 190 additional personnel. Helicopter deck. Bow-thruster.

◆ **1 oceanographic-research ship** Bldr: Orens MV, Trondheim (In serv. 1960)

H. U. Sverdrup (ex-U.S. AGOR 2)

D: 400 tons (fl) **S:** 11.5 kts **Dim:** 38.89 × 7.62 × 3.30
M: 1 Wichmann diesel; 1 prop; 600 hp **Electric:** 104 kw
Fuel: 65 tons **Range:** 5,000/10
Man: 10 men + 9 scientists

Remarks: 295 grt trawler hull. Operates for the Norwegian Defense Research Establishment and has a civilian crew. Purchase and outfitting financed by the U.S.A. under the Offshore Procurement Program.

◆ **1 royal yacht**

	Bldr	L
A 533 Norge (ex-*Philante*)	Camper & Nicholson's Ltd., Gosport	17-2-37

Norge (A 533) 1971

D: 1,686 tons **S:** 17 kts **Dim:** 76.27 × 8.53 × 4.65
M: 2 8-cyl. diesels; 2 props; 3,000 hp **Electric:** 300 kw
Fuel: 175 tons **Range:** 9,900/17

Remarks: Built as a yacht, then used by the Royal Navy as an ASW escort from 1940 to 1943, then as a training ship. Purchased by Norway in 1948. Displacement listed is in Thames Yacht Measurement. Can carry 50-passenger royal party.

SERVICE CRAFT

◆ **1 torpedo-recovery and oil-spill cleanup ship** Bldr: Fjellstrand, Hardinger (In serv. 10-78)

VSD 1 Vernøy

D: 150 grt **S:** 12 kts **Dim:** 31.3 × 6.67 × 2.0
M: 2 MWM diesels; 2 Schöttel props; . . . hp

SERVICE CRAFT *(continued)*

◆ **7 Torpen-class support tenders**

	Bldr	In serv.
VSD 4 Torpen	Båtservice, Mandal	12-77
ØSD 2 Wisting	Voldnes, Fosnavåg	1-78
TSD 5 Tautra	Båtservice, Mandal	2-78
NSD 35 Rotvaer	Båtservice, Mandal	3-78
RSD 23 Fjøløy	Voldnes, Fosnavåg	4-78
HSD 15 Krøttøy	Voldnes, Fosnavåg	6-78
TRSD 4 Karlsøy	P. Høivolds, Kristianstad	7-78

Torpen (VSD 4) L. & L. Van Ginderen, 9-82

D: 215 tons (300 fl) **S:** 11 kts **Dim:** 29.0 × 6.4 × 2.57
A: 1/12.7-mm mg **M:** 1 MWM TBD 601-6K diesel; 1 CP prop; 530 hp
Electron Equipt: Radar: 1/Decca 1226
Fuel: 11 tons **Range:** 1,200/11 **Man:** 6 men + 100 passengers

Remarks: Basically similar craft tailored to a variety of duties, including logistics support, ammunition transport, personnel transport, and divers' support. Cargo: 100 tons.

◆ **2 navigational training craft** Bldr: Fjellstrand, Omastrand (In serv. 1-78)

P 358 Hitra (ex-*Kvarnen,* VSD 6) P 359 Vigra (ex-*Marsteinen,* VSD 2)

Vigra (P 359) Norwegian Navy, 1982

D: 40 tons **S:** 22 kts **Dim:** 23.2 × 5.0 × 1.1 **A:** 1/12.7-mm mg
M: 2 G.M. 12V71 diesels; 2 props; 1,800 hp **Man:** 5 men + 8 cadets

Remarks: Aluminum construction. For use at the Naval Academy. Renamed and renumbered 1981.

◆ **2 tenders for combat divers** Bldr: Nielsen, Harstad (In serv. 1972)

A 531 Sarpen (ex-VDS 11, ex-SKV 11) A 532 Draug (ex-SKV 10)

D: 250 tons **S:** 12 kts **Dim:** 29.0 × 6.7 × 2.5 **M:** 1 diesel; 1 prop; 530 hp

Remarks: Renumbered 1982. Support frogmen.

Sarpen (A 531)—old number Norwegian Navy, 1981

◆ **1 harbor tug** Bldr: F. Schichau, Königsberg, Germany (In serv. 1938)

VSD 7 Samson

D: 303 grt **S:** 11 kts **Dim:** 38.7 × 8.0 × 3.25
M: 1 MWM diesel; 1 prop; 650 hp **Range:** 2,900/10

◆ **1 harbor tug** Bldr: Atlas Werke, Bremen, Germany (L: 6-2-39)

VSD 13 Ramnes (ex-German *Robbe*)

D: 101 grt **S:** 10 kts **Dim:** 24.0 × 5.70 × 2.45 **M:** 1 diesel; 250 hp

◆ **2 local patrol craft** Bldr: Fjellstrand Yacht, Omastrand

RSD23 Tarva (In serv. 1-12-74) ØSD1 Welding (In serv. 1-11-74)

D: 27.5 tons (fl) **S:** 15 kts **Dim:** 16.3 × 5.3 × 1.2
A: 1/12.7-mm mg **Electron Equipt:** Radar: 1/Decca. . .
M: 2 G.M. diesels; 2 props; 480 hp **Man:** 4 tot.

◆ **1 or more personnel launches**

SKO 122 Fuldin—No data available

Note: Other service craft, for which no data are available, include: SKV 20, *Gleodden, Varodden,* VSD 8, VSD 20, VSD 63, VSD 10, *Foracs,* Petra, SKØ 121, Fjordbåt, SKS 55, SSD 8, Akerøy, Sigurd A. (RSD 21), RØS 27, Kjeøy, VSD 3, *Torpedofisken, Arnøy,* Folden, NSD 33, NSD 81, NSD 84 and ØESD 66.

COAST GUARD (KYSTVAKT)

The Norwegian Coast Guard was established in 1976 to perform fisheries-protection duties, patrol the waters in the vicinity of offshore oil rigs, and maintain surveillance over the 200-nautical-mile economic zone. The Coast Guard operates six WG-13 Lynx Mk 86 helicopters.

PATROL SHIPS

◆ **3 Nordkapp (Type 320) class**

	Bldr	L	In serv.
W 320 Nordkapp	Bergens Mek. Verk.	14-5-80	25-4-81
W 321 Senja	Horten Verft	16-3-81	8-3-81
W 322 Andennes	Haugesund Verk.	21-3-81	30-1-82

Andennes (W 322) Norwegian Navy, 1984

PATROL SHIPS *(continued)*

Nordkapp (W 320) Norwegian Navy

D: 2,165 tons light (3,240 fl) **S:** 23 kts **Dim:** 105.00 (97.50 pp) × 13.85 × 4.55
A: 1/57-mm Bofors AA—4/20-mm Rheinmetall AA (I × 4)—6/324-mm Mk 32 ASW TT (III × 2)—1/d.c. rack (6 d.c.)—1/WG-13 Lynx helicopter
Electron Equipt: Radar: 2/Decca TM 1226, 1/Decca RM914, 1/Plessey AWS-4, 1/PEAB GLF 218 (9LV 200 Mk.2)
Sonar: 1/Simrad SS105
M: 4 Wichmann 9-AXAG diesels; 2 CP props; 14,400 hp **Electric:** 1,600 kw
Fuel: 350 tons **Range:** 7,500/15 **Man:** 42 crew + 6 helo crew (109 accomm.)

Remarks: Program delayed by design changes and lack of funding; four additional units deferred. W 322 and W 323 displace 2,854 tons full load and are not ice-strengthened, as is W 320, intended for service in Arctic waters. In time of conflict, 6 Penguin II anti-ship missiles and chaff launchers are to be added. Fin stabilized. Carry three 300-m³/hr. water cannon for firefighting and have meteorological reporting gear. The Kongsberg MSI-805 NAVKIS data system is fitted. Wartime crew: 75 total.

◆ **1 former stern-haul trawler** Bldr: Båtservice, Mandal (In serv. 5-78)

W 319 Grimsholm

Grimsholm (W 319) L. & L. Van Ginderen, 6-82

D: 1,189 grt **S:** . . . kts **Dim:** 62.71 (54.60 pp) × 11.63 × 6.43
A: 1/40-mm AA **M:** 1 MaK 9-cyl. diesel; 1 prop; 3,400 hp **Electric:** 524 kw

Remarks: Chartered 1980. Side-thrusters fore and aft.

◆ **1 former stern-haul trawler** Bldr: Brødrene Lothes, Haugesund (In serv. 7-78)

W 317 Lafjord

D: 814 grt **S:** 14.6 kts **Dim:** 55.40 × 9.81 × 6.18
A: 1/40-mm AA **M:** 1 Wichmann 7-cyl. diesel; 1 prop; 2,100 hp
Electric: 419 kw **Fuel:** 220 tons **Range:** 7,700/14.6

Remarks: Chartered 1980. Side-thrusters fore and aft.

◆ **1 former stern-haul trawler** Bldr: Smedvik, Tjørråg (In serv. 4-78)

W 315 Nordsjøbas

D: 814 grt **S:** 13.5 kts **Dim:** 52.04 (44.75 pp) × 10.01 × 6.55
A: 1/40-mm AA **Electric:** 1,088 kw **Range:** 8,300/13.5
M: 1 MaK 6-cyl. diesel; 1 prop; 2,400 hp **Fuel:** 180 tons

Remarks: Chartered 1980. Side-thrusters fore and aft.

◆ **1 former purse seiner** Bldr: Hall-Russell, Aberdeen, Scotland (In serv. 3-51)

W 312 Sørfold (ex-*Olafur Jöhannesson*, ex-*Andvan*)

D: 773 grt **S:** 12 kts **Dim:** 61.37 (55.06 pp) × 9.2 × 4.88
A: 1/40-mm AA **M:** 1 Werkspoor 8-cyl. diesel; 1 CP prop; 2,660 hp
Electric: 175 kw **Fuel:** 80 tons **Man:** . . .

Remarks: Chartered from Oddvar Jöhannesson in 1977. Side-thrusters fore and aft.

◆ **1 former trawler** Bldr: Kvina Verft/Flekkefjord MV (In serv. 11-55)

W 313 Møgsterfjord

D: 768 grt **S:** 12 kts **Dim:** 60.86 (55.01 pp) × 12.0 × 3.9
A: 1/40-mm AA **M:** 1 Wichmann 9-cyl. diesel; 1 prop; 2,500 hp
Electric: 786 kw **Man:** . . .

Remarks: Chartered from Kommandittelskapel Møgster in 1977. Bow-thruster.

◆ **1 former purse seiner** Bldr: Beliard, Crighton & Cie., France (In serv. 1955)

W 314 Stålbas (ex-*Trålbas*, ex-*Cdt. Charcot*, ex-*Jean Charcot*)

D: 498 grt **S:** . . . **Dim:** 58.76 × 9.41 × 4.51
A: 1/40-mm AA **M:** 1 Klöckner-Humboldt-Deutz 8-cyl. diesel; 1 prop; 1,500 hp
Man: . . .

Remarks: Side-thrusters fitted, fore and aft.

◆ **1 former whale-catcher** Bldr: Fredrikstad MV (In serv. 1950)

W 316 Volstad Jr. (ex-XIV)

Volstad Jr. (W 316) 1982

D: 617 grt **S:** . . . **Dim:** 51.39 (45.32 pp) × 9.05 × 5.67
A: 1/40-mm AA
M: 2 Klöchner-Humboldt-Deutz NE-66 8-cyl. diesel; 1 CP prop; 1,200 hp
Electric: 224 kw **Man:** . . .

Remarks: Chartered from Einar Volstad Partrederi in 1977. Built as a side-haul trawler, converted to a whaler in 1966, and well deck filled in.

◆ **1 former naval fisheries-protection ship**

	Bldr	L
W 300 Nornen	Mjellem & Karlsen, Bergen	20-8-62

Nornen (W 300) 1978

D: 1,060 tons (fl) **S:** 17 kts **Dim:** 61.5 × 10.0 × 3.8
A: 1/76.2-mm Mk 26 DP **M:** 4 diesels; 1 prop; 3,700 hp **Man:** 32 tot.

Remarks: Considerably altered, 1976-77: bridge enlarged, stack heightened, mast moved aft, hull side openings plated up, two new radars added, gun enclosed.

◆ **2 former naval fisheries-protection ships**

	Bldr	L
W 301 Farm (ex-A 532)	Ankerlokken Verft, Fredrikstad	22-2-62
W 302 Heimdal (ex-A 534)	Bolsones Verft, Molde	7-3-62

D: 600 grt **S:** 16.5 kts **Dim:** 54.28 (49.0 pp) × 8.2 × 3.2
A: 1/40-mm AA **M:** 2 Wichmann 9ACAT diesels; 2 CP props; 2,400 hp
Electric: 150 kVA **Man:** 29 tot.

Remarks: Modernized 1979 (W 301) and 1980 (W 302) with completely revised superstructure, new bridge resembling *Nornen's*, new armament and revised hull sides along the forecastle.

NORWAY *(continued)*
PATROL SHIPS *(continued)*

Farm (W 301) Norwegian Navy, 1984

HYDROGRAPHIC SURVEY SHIP

◆ **1 former Ministry of the Environment ship** Bldr: Mjellem & Karlsen, Bergen

Hydrograf (In serv. 12-67)

D: 302 grt **S:** 13 kts **Dim:** 38.95 (35.11 pp) × 7.83 × 2.94
A: 1/40-mm AA **M:** 1 Bergens Mek. Verk. 6-cyl. diesel; 1 prop; 780 hp
Electric: 100 kw **Fuel:** 38 tons **Range:** 3,900/13 **Man:** 3 officers, 15 men

Remarks: Now operated by the Coast Guard for the Ministry of the Environment. No pendant number. The Ministry of the Environment also operates 11 survey ships with its own personnel: *Lance* (960 tons, in serv. 1978); *Sjøvern* (215 tons, in serv. 1948); *Sjøfalk* 70 tons, in serv. 1937); *Sjøskvett* (80 tons, in serv. 1964); *Sjørokk* (75 tons, in serv. 1964); Sjødrev (80 tons, in serv. 1973); *Sjøtroll* (80 tons, in serv. 1976) and *Olijevern* 01-04 (200 tons, in serv. 1978).

OMAN

Sultanate of Oman

Personnel (1985): 2,400 total

Merchant Marine (1984): 26 ships—13,911 grt

GUIDED-MISSILE PATROL BOATS

◆ **3 "Province" class** Bldr: Vosper Thornycroft, Portchester, U.K.

	Laid down	L	In serv.
B 10 Dhofar	39-9-80	14-10-81	7-8-82
B 11 Al Sharquiyah	10-81	2-12-82	5-12-83
B 12 Al Bat'nah	9-12-81	11-82	18-1-84

D: 311 tons light (363 fl) **S:** 40 kts **Dim:** 56.7 (52.0 pp) × 8.2 × 2.1 (hull)
A: 6/MM 40 Exocet SSM (III × 2)—1/76-mm OTO Melara DP—2/40-mm Breda AA (II × 1)—2/12.7-mm mg (I × 2)
Electron Equipt: Radar: B 11: 1/Decca 1226, 1/Plessey AWS-4; others: 1/Decca TM 1226, 1/PEAB 9LV 300 syst.
EW: . . . intercept; 2 Wallops Barricade decoy RL (IX × 2)
M: 4 Paxman Valenta 18RP200 diesels; 4 props; 17,900 hp (15,000 sust.)—2/80 hp electric outdrives
Electric: 420 kw **Fuel:** 45.5 tons **Range:** 2,000/15 **Man:** 40, plus 19 trainees

Dhofar (B 10)—with AWS-4 radar, 6 SSM positions M. Louagie, 8-82

Al Bat'nah (B 12)—equipped for 8 Exocet Walles Foto, 3-84

Remarks: B 8 ordered 1980, others in 1-81. B 8 sailed for Oman 21-10-82. B 10 has the Sperry Sea Archer Mk 2 fire-control sytem, with two optical trackers. Complement includes trainees. B 9, B 10 have 8/MM 40 Exocet (IV × 2), PEAB 9LV 300 f.c.s. with I-band search radar and J-band radar/electro-optical fire-control director forward and a separate tv./IR director aft for the 40-mm AA.

◆ **1 37.5-m class** Bldr: Brooke Marine, Lowestoft, U.K.

B 2 Al Mansur (In serv. 26-3-73)

Al Mansur (B 2) 1980

D: 162 tons (184 fl) **S:** 25 kts **Dim:** 37.50 × 6.86 × 2.20
A: 2/MM 38 Exocet SSM (I × 2)—2/40-mm Breda AA (II × 1)—2/7.62-mm mg (I × 2)
Electron Equipt: Radar: 1/Decca 1229
M: 2 Paxman Ventura 16RP200 diesels; 2 props; 4,800 hp
Range: 3,250/12 **Man:** 4 officers, 28 men

Remarks: Equipped with missiles during 11-77 to 11-78 refit by builder. Have Sperry Sea Archer fire-control systems. Sister *Al Bushra* (B 1) lost overboard in Bay of Biscay 11-78 while being transported to Oman after a similar conversion, and *Al Nejah* (B 3) was stricken 1983.

PATROL BOATS

◆ **4 37.5-meter class** Bldr: Brooke Marine Ltd., Lowestoft, U.K.

	In serv.
B 4 Al Wafi	24-3-77
B 5 Al Fulk	24-3-77
B 6 Al Aul	20-7-77
B 7 Al Jabbar	6-10-77

Al Fulk (B 5) L. & L. Van Ginderen, 9-82

D: 153 tons (166 fl) **S:** 25 kts **Dim:** 37.50 × 6.86 × 1.78
A: 1/76-mm OTO Melara DP—1/20-mm AA—2/7.62-mm mg (I × 2)
Electron Equipt: Radar: 1/Decca 1226 or 1229
M: 2 Paxman Ventura 16 RP200 diesels; 2 props; 4,800 hp
Range: 3,250/12 **Man:** 3 officers, 24 men

Remarks: Carry 130 rounds 76-mm ammunition. Sperry Sea Archer fire-control system, with Lawrence Scott optical director.

PATROL CRAFT

◆ **4 25-meter class** Bldr: Vosper Pty, Singapore (In serv. 15-3-81)

B 20 Al Seeb B 21 Al Shinas B 22 Al Sadah B 23 Al Khasab

25-meter class—on trials 1980

D: 75 tons (fl) **S:** 26 kts **Dim:** 25.0 (23.0 pp) × 5.8 × 1.5
A: 1/20-mm AA—2/7.62-mm mg (I × 2)
M: 2 MTU 12V331 TC92 diesels, plus 1 Cummins N855M diesel; 3 props; 3,072 hp + 197 hp
Range: 750/14; 2,300/8 **Man:** 13 tot.

Remarks: Ordered 24-4-81. Craft completed 1980 on speculation by builder. Glass-reinforced plastic hulls. Have five spare berths. Max. speed on cruise diesel: 8 kts.

◆ **2 Tyler Vortex class** Bldr: Cheverton, Cowes (In serv. 1981)

QRB 1 QRB 2

D: 12 tons **S:** 30 kts **Dim:** 12.1 (11.5 pp) × 4.6 × . . .
A: . . . **M:** 2 Sabre 500 diesels; 2 props; 1,000 hp

Remarks: Officially typed as "Quick-reaction Boats."

AMPHIBIOUS WARFARE SHIPS AND CRAFT

◆ **1 new-construction landing ship** Bldr: Brooke Marine, Lowestoft, U.K.

	Laid down	L	In serv.
L 2 Nasr Al Bahr	. . .	16-5-84	1984

Nasr Al Bahr (L 2) Walles Foto, 3-85

D: 2,200 tons (fl) **S:** 15.5 kts **Dim:** 93.00 (80.00 pp) × 15.50 × 2.3 (mean)
A: 4/40-mm Breda AA (II × 2)—2/20-mm AA (I × 2)
Electron Equipt: Radar: 1/Decca 1226, 1/Decca 1290
EW: . . . intercept; 2 Barricade RL (IX × 2)
M: 2 Paxman Valenta 18RP200CM diesels; 2 CP props; 7,800 hp
Range: 4,000/13 **Endurance:** 28 days (10 days with troops)
Man: 13 off., 16 chief petty officers, 52 men + troops: 13 officers, 16 non-commissioned officers, 211 enlisted

Remarks: Ordered 18-3-82. A refined version of the *Al Munassir* design. Two also built for Algeria. Vehicle deck 75 m × 7.4 m, with 30-m × 7-m cargo hatch; bow ramp 18-m long by 4.5-m wide; stern ramp: 5 m by 4 m. Intended to land 450 tons cargo or seven main battle tanks on a gradient of up to 1:40. Helicopter deck for one Sea King/Commando helicopter. Traveling 16-ton crane spans cargo deck forward. Max. cargo: 650 tons. One Philips PEAB and one CSEE Lynx electro-optical gunsight; 2,000 rds 40 mm, 2,450 rds 20 mm, 244 chaff rounds.

◆ **1 for logistic support**

	Bldr	Laid down	L	In serv.
L 1 Al Munassir	Brooke Marine, Lowestoft	4-7-77	25-7-78	3-4-79

D: 2,169 tons (fl) **S:** 12 kts **Dim:** 84.0 (81.25 pp) × 15.03 × 2.15 (max.)
A: 1/76-mm OTO Melara DP—2/20-mm AA (I × 2)

Al Munassir (L 1) 1980

Electron Equipt: Radar: 1/Decca TM 1229
M: 2 Mirrlees-Blackstone ESL8MGR diesels; 2 CP props; 2,400 hp
Range: 2,500/12
Man: 9 officers, 38 men, 188 troops

Remarks: Greatly modified version of British *Ardennes* class by same builder. Cargo: 550 tons of stores or 8 heavy tanks. Has bow doors and ramp for beaching. Large helicopter deck aft can accommodate Westland Sea King or Commando helicopters and is spanned by a 16-ton-capacity traveling crane. Unusually bluff-bowed hull form. Sperry Sea Archer optical fire-control director.

◆ **3 utility landing craft** Bldr: Vosper Pty, Singapore (L: 30-6-81)

	Laid down	L	In serv.
C 8 Saba Al Bahr	. . .	30-6-81	17-9-81
C 9 Al Doghas	9-7-82	12-11-82	10-1-83
C 10 Al Temsah	8-9-82	15-12-82	12-2-83

D: 230 tons (fl) **S:** 8 kts **Dim:** 30.0 (25.6 pp) × 8.0 × 1.2
M: 2 Caterpillar 3408 TA diesels; 2 props; 1,840 hp
Range: 1,800/8 **Man:** 11 tot.

Remarks: C 8 ordered 24-4-81, C 9 and C 10 in 7-82. Cargo: 100 tons vehicles or stores, or 45 tons deck cargo plus 50 tons fresh water (plus 35 tons water ballast). C 9 and C 10 are 33 m o.a.

◆ **1 utility landing craft** Bldr: Lewis Offshore, Stornaway, Scotland (In serv. 1979)

C 7 Al Neemran

D: 85 dwt **S:** 8 kts **Dim:** 25.5 × 7.4 × 1.8 **M:** 2 diesels; . . . hp

◆ **1 75-foot Loadmaster-class landing craft** Bldr: Cheverton, Cowes, U.K. (In serv. 1-75)

C 4 Al Sansoor

D: 64 tons (130 fl) **S:** 8.75 kts **Dim:** 22.86 × 6.1 × 1.07 (max.)
M: 2 diesels; 2 props; 300 hp

Remarks: Sister *Al Doghas* (C 5) stricken 1981. The larger *Al Dhaibah* (C 6) was stricken in 1982; the smaller *Sulhafa Al Bahr* has also been discarded.

AUXILIARY SHIPS

◆ **1 training ship** Bldr: Brooke Marine, Lowestoft, U.K.

	L	In serv.
A 1 Al Mabrukah (ex-*Al Said*)	7-4-70	1971

Al Mabrukah (A 1) Walles Foto, 4-84

D: 785 tons (930 fl) **S:** 17 kts **Dim:** 54.70 × 10.70 × 3.05
A: 1/40-mm AA—2/20-mm AA (I × 2)
Electron Equipt: Radar: 1/Decca TM 1226
EW: . . . intercept, 2 Barricade RL (IX × 2)
M: 2 Paxman Ventura 12YJCM diesels; 2 props; 3,350 hp
Man: 11 officers, 23 men, 37 passengers

Remarks: Renamed and under conversion from royal yacht to fleet training ship at builders 1-83 to 4-84. Received new accommodations arrangements, communications suit, and armament; the helicopter deck was enlarged.

AUXILIARY SHIPS *(continued)*

◆ **1 supply ship**

		Bldr	L	In serv.
A 2	AL SULTANA	Conoship, Groningen, Netherlands	18-5-75	4-6-75

D: 900 tons (1,380 dwt) **S:** 11 kts **Dim:** 65.4 × 10.7 × 4.2
M: 1 Mirrlees-Blackstone diesel; 1,150 hp

REMARKS: Traveling crane serves all holds. Replaced in training rôle by *Al Mabrukah.*

◆ **1 inshore survey craft** Bldr: Watercraft, U.K. (In serv. 4-81)

H 1 AL RAHMANYAI

D: 23.6 tons (fl) **S:** 13.5 kts **Dim:** 15.5 (14.0 pp) × 4.0 × 1.25
Electron Equipt: Radar: 1/Decca 101
M: 2 Volvo TMD 120A diesels; 2 props; 520 hp
Electric: 25 kVA **Range:** 500/12

REMARKS: Glass-reinforced plastic construction. Raytheon DE 719B and Kelvin-Hughes MS 48 echo sounders, Decca DMU transponder and Sea Fix receiver, and Hewlitt-Packard 9815A data storage computer fitted.

◆ **1 sail-training craft** Bldr: Hard & MacKenzie, Buckie, Scotland (In serv. . . .)

S 1 SHABAB OMAN (ex-*Youth of Oman,* ex-*Captain Scott*)

D: 386 tons **S:** . . . **Dim:** 44.0 × 8.5 × 4.6
M: 2 diesels; 1 prop; . . . hp
Man: 5 officers, 15 men + 3 officer/instructors, 24 trainees

REMARKS: Three-masted barkentine, purchased 1977 in U.K., for training Omani youth in seamanship.

◆ **10 miscellaneous workboats** Bldr: Cheverton, Cowes, U.K.

W 4, 5, 7–11 WF 41–43 (In serv. 4-75)

D: 3.5 tons **S:** 25 kts **Dim:** 8.28 × 2.7 × 0.8 **M:** 2 diesels

ROYAL YACHT SQUADRON

◆ **1 royal yacht** Bldr: Dicchiotti, Viareggio, Italy (In serv. 1982)

AL SAID

D: 3,250 tons (fl) **S:** 18 kts **Dim:** 106.0 × 17.0 × 5.0
Electron Equipt: 1/Decca TM 1226C, 1/Decca ACS 1230C
M: 2 GMT A420-6 diesels; 2 CP props; 8,400 hp
Man: 16 officers, 140 men

REMARKS: Replaced former *Al Said* (now training ship *Al Mabrukah*). Not considered to be a naval vessel, unlike her predecessor. Helicopter pad; bow-thruster.

ROYAL OMAN POLICE

AVIATION: Two Pilantus Porter light transports for search-and-rescue duties, delivered 4-84.

◆ **1 P 2000 class** Bldr: Watercraft Ltd., Shoreham, U.K.

DHEEB AL BAHAR 1 (In serv. 12-84)

Dheeb Al Bahar Watercraft, 9-84

D: 80 tons **S:** 38 kts **Dim:** 20.80 (18.00 pp) × 5.80 × 1.50
A: 1/20-mm AA—6/7.62-mm mg (I × 6)
Electron Equipt: Radar: 1/Furuno FR-701
M: 2 MTU 12V396 TB93 diesels; 2 props; 3,920 hp (3,260 sust.)
Range: 423/35; 660/22

REMARKS: Glass-reinforced plastic construction, with aluminum superstructure. Additional units may be procured.

◆ **2 P1200 class** Bldr: Watercraft Ltd., Shoreham, U.K. (In serv. 9-84)

D: 10 tons **S:** 35 kts **Dim:** 11.90 (10.16 pp) × 4.08 × 1.06
A: 1/12.7-mm mg—6/7.62-mm mg (I × 6)
Electron Equipt: Radar: 1/. . . nav.
M: 2 M.A.N. diesels; 2 props; 1,100 hp **Range:** 300/. . . **Man:** 8 tot.

REMARKS: Ordered 7-82. Glass-reinforced plastic construction.

PATROL BOATS AND CRAFT

◆ **1 . . . class** Bldr: . . . (In serv. 1982)

HARAS 9

D: 82 tons (fl) **S:** 25 kts **Dim:** 29.9 × 5.8 × 1.2
A: 2/20-mm AA **M:** 2 MTU 12V396 diesels; 2 props; . . . hp **Man:** 13 tot.

◆ **1 Type PT 1903 Mk III patrol craft** Bldr: Le Comte, Vianen, Netherlands

HARAS 8 (In serv. 8-81)

D: 30 tons (33 fl) **S:** 30 kts **Dim:** 19.27 × 4.95 × 1.25
A: 2/12.7-mm mg (I × 2) **Range:** 1,650/17; 2,300/12
M: 2 MTU 8V331 TC92 diesels; 2 props; 1,770 hp **Man:** 10 tot.

◆ **2 CG 29 class** Bldr: Karlskrona, Sweden

HARAS 7 (In serv. 6-81) HARAS 10 (In serv. 14-4-82)

Haras 7 P. Voss, 7-81

D: 80 tons (fl) **S:** 25 kts **Dim:** 28.7 × 5.2 × 1.1
A: 2/20-mm AA (I × 2) **Electron Equipt:** Radar: 1/Decca 1226C
M: 2 MTU 8V331 IC82 diesels; 2 props; 1,866 hp

REMARKS: Aluminum construction, enlarged version of design built for Liberia.

◆ **1 CG class** Bldr: Karlskrona, Sweden (In serv. 1980)

HARAS 6

D: 53 tons (fl) **S:** 25 kts **Dim:** 24.0 × 5.5 × 1.0
A: 1/20-mm AA **Man:** 11 tot. **M:** 2 MTU 12V331 diesels; 2 props; 2,800 hp

REMARKS: Glass-reinforced plastic construction

◆ **5 Haras 1-class fiberglass-hulled** Bldr: Vosper, Singapore (In serv. 1–4; 22-12-75; 5: 11-78)

HARAS 1 HARAS 2 HARAS 3 HARAS 4 HARAS 5

Haras 1 1980

D: 45 tons (fl) **S:** 24.5 kts **Dim:** 22.9 × 6.0 × 1.5
A: 1/20-mm AA **Electron Equipt:** Radar: 1/Decca 101
M: 2 Caterpillar D348 diesels; 2 props; 1,840 hp
Range: 600/20; 1,000/11 **Man:** 11 tot.

◆ **2 small patrol craft** Bldr: Watercraft, Shoreham (In serv. 1981)

ZARA 17 ZARA 18

D: 17.25 tons (fl) **S:** 22 kts **Dim:** 13.9 (12.6 wl) × 4.3 × 1.1
M: 2 Cummins VTA-903M diesels; 2 props; 700 hp
A: 1/7.62-mm mg **Range:** 700/20 **Man:** 6 tot.

OMAN *(continued)*
PATROL BOATS AND CRAFT *(continued)*

◆ **2 landing craft** Bldr: LeComte, Vianen, the Netherlands

ZARA 20 (In serv. 1981) ZARA 22 (In serv. 1982)

D: 11 tons (23 fl) **S:** 20 kts **Dim:** 18.0 × 3.0 × 0.5
A: 2/7.62-mm mg (I × 2) **Range:** . . . **Man:** 4 tot.
M: 2 Volvo Penta AQD 70/750 diesel outdrives; 540 hp

REMARKS: *Zara 20* used as a fueling tender. *Zara 22* is 16.0-m o.a.

NOTE: Also in service are one 19-m and one 18-m tender, delivered by LeComte, Vianen, the Netherlands, in 1988, along with a 16-m craft, and an 8.2-m workboat delivered by Cheverton, Cowes, U.K., in 1983. Two 8.5-m patrol craft, powered by 2/140-hp Evinrude outboards for 40 kts, were delivered in 1985 by Gulf Craft, Ajman, United Arab Emirates.

PAKISTAN

Islamic Republic of Pakistan

PERSONNEL (1985): 1,250 officers, 14,550 men

MERCHANT MARINE (1984): 82 ships—506,586 grt (tankers: 1 ship—43,429 grt)

NAVAL AVIATION: The naval arm consists of: 3 Bréguet BR1150 Atlantic Mk 1 patrol aircraft, 6 Sea King helicopters armed with AM-39 anti-ship missiles, 4 Alouette-III helicopters, 2 Cessna liaison aircraft, and 1 Fokker F-27 transport. Plans include possible acquisition of 6 ex-RAAF P-3B Orion patrol aircraft.

SUBMARINES

◆ **2 (+2) French Agosta class** Bldr: Dubigeon, Nantes

	Laid down	L	In serv.
S 135 HASHMAT (ex-*Astrant*)	15-9-76	14-12-77	17-2-79
S 136 HURMAT (ex-*Adventurous*)	. . .	1-12-78	18-2-80

Hurmat (S 136) J.-C. Bellonne, 1980

D: 1,230/1,480/1,725 tons **S:** 12.5/20.5 kts **Dim:** 67.90 × 6.80 × 5.40
A: 4/550-mm TT, fwd (20 torpedoes and Sub-Harpoon SSM)
Electron Equipt: Radar: 1/DRUA-33
Sonar: DUUA-1D, DUUA-2A, DSUV-2H, DUUA-2B, DUUX-2A
EW: ARUR, ARUD
M: 2 SEMT-Pielstick A16 PA4 185 diesels, electric drive (1 3,500-kw motor); 1 prop; 4,600 hp; 1, 23-hp cruise motor
Fuel: 200 tons **Range:** 7,900/10 (snorkel); 178/3.5 (submerged) **Man:** 55 tot.

REMARKS: Originally ordered for South Africa, but sale canceled in 1977 by arms embargo and completion slowed. Sold to Pakistan in 11-78. Very quiet, highly automated submarines. Diving depth: 300 m. Battery capacity twice that of the *Daphné* class. Fitted for U.S. Sub-Harpoon anti-ship missiles in 1984-85. Two additional units reported ordered 1983 in Spain, but unconfirmed.

◆ **4 French Daphné class**

	Bldr	Laid down	L	In serv.
S 131 HANGOR	Naval Arsenal, Brest	1-12-67	30-6-69	12-1-70
S 132 SHUSHUK	C. N. Ciotat, Le Trait	1-12-67	30-7-69	12-1-70
S 133 MANGRO	C. N. Ciotat, Le Trait	8-7-68	7-2-70	8-8-70
S 134 GHAZI (ex-*Cachalote*)	Dubigeon, Normandy	27-10-66	16-2-68	25-1-69

D: 700 std./869 surf./1,043 sub. tons **S:** 13.5/16 kts **Dim:** 57.75 × 6.75 × 4.56
A: 12/550-mm TT (8 fwd, 4 aft), no reloads
Electron Equipt: Radar: DRUA 31
Sonar: DUUA-1 active, DSUV-1 passive
EW: ARUR, ARUD intercept
M: 2 SEMT-Pielstick 12PA4-135 450-kw diesel generator sets; 2 1,300-hp (1,000 sust.) electric motors; 2 props
Range: 4,300/7.5 (snorkel) **Man:** 5 officers, 45 men

REMARKS: S 134 purchased in 12-75 from Portugal. S 131 sank the Indian frigate *Khukri* in 1971. Diving depth: 300 m.

Ghazi (S 134) J.-C. Bellonne, 1977

◆ **2 SX-404-class midget submarines** Bldr: COSMOS, Livorno, Italy

D: 40/70 tons **S:** 11/6.5 kts **Dim:** 16.0 × 1.8 × . . .
A: 2/533-mm torpedoes in drop gear or 6-8 mines **Range:** 1,200/11 surfaced, 60/6.5 submerged **Man:** 4 tot.

REMARKS: Used for the transport of up to twelve raiders. Three discarded in 1982-83. A sixth sank 27-12-76 following an accident at sea. A number of 2-man Chariots from the same builder are also in service.

NOTE: Former ex-British "Modified *Dido*"-class cruiser *Jahangar* (C 85, ex-*Babur*, ex-HMS *Diadem*) has been an immobile training hulk and floating AA battery at Karachi since 1982.

DESTROYERS

◆ **1 (+1) ex-U.K. County class** Bldr: Swan Hunter & Wigham Richardson, Wallsend-on-Tyne, U.K.

	Laid down	L	In serv.
D 84 BABUR (ex-*London*, D 16)	26-2-60	7-12-61	4-11-63

Babur (D 84)—still with Sea Slug launcher L. & L. Van Ginderen, 6-82

D: 5,440 tons (6,200 fl) **S:** 32.5 kts (30 sust.)
Dim: 158.55 (153.90 pp) × 16.46 × 6.30 (max.)
A: 4/114-mm Mk 6 DP (II × 2)—2/Sea Cat GWS 22 systems (IV × 2)—2/20-mm AA (I × 2)—1/Alouette-III helicopter (non-ASW)
Electron Equipt: Radar: 1/978, 1/965, 1/992Q, 1/277, 1/903, 2/904
Sonar: 1/177, 1/174, 1/170B, 1/162
EW: UA-8, UA-9, 2/Knebworth/Corvus chaff RL (VIII × 2)
M: COSAG: 2 sets A.E.I. GT (15,000 hp each) and 4 G6 gas turbines (7,500 hp each); 2 props; 60,000 hp
Boilers: 2 Babcock & Wilcox; 43 kg/cm², 510°C superheat **Fuel:** 600 tons
Electric: 3,750 kw **Range:** 3,500/28 **Man:** Up to 470 tot.

REMARKS: Purchased from U.K. on 22-3-82 and commissioned 22-4-82. Replaced the former *Babur* as training cruiser. The obsolete Sea Slug Mk 1 missile launcher, with its attendant Type 901 control radar initially remained aboard but inactivated and was removed in 1984. The 114-mm guns are controlled by a single MRS.3 director with Type 903 radar. The GWS 22 Sea Cat system has two directors with Type 904 radars. The portside-opening helicopter hangar is occupied by an Alouette-III helicopter for liaison and SAR duties; thus, despite having an extensive sonar suit, the ship has no ASW ordnance. The massive 80-m-long Sea Slug magazine may be converted into cadet berthing spaces, and the helicopter facility is to be enlarged to handle a Sea King helicopter with SM-39 anti-ship missiles. In 4-84, Pakistan declared an interest in purchasing near-sister HMS *Fife*, when she is stricken from the Royal Navy.

◆ **6 ex-U.S. Gearing class, FRAM-I** Bldrs: 165, 166: Federal SB & DD Co., Newark, N.J.; 167 and 169: Bethlehem, Staten Island; 168: Todd, Seattle; 170: Consolidated Steel

	Laid down	L	In serv.
D 165 TARIQ (ex-*Wiltsie*, DD 716)	13-3-45	31-8-45	12-1-46
D 166 TAIMUR (ex-*Epperson*, DD 719)	20-6-45	29-12-45	19-3-49
D 167 TIPPU SULTAN (ex-*Damato*, DD 871)	10-5-45	21-11-45	27-4-46
D 168 TUGHRIL (ex-*Henderson*, DD 785)	27-10-44	28-5-45	4-8-45
D 169 ALAMGIR (ex-*Cone*, DD 866)	30-11-44	10-5-45	18-8-45
D 170 SHAH JAHAN (ex-*Harold J. Ellison*, DD 864)	3-10-44	14-3-45	18-12-46

D: 2,425 tons (3,460 fl) **S:** 30 kts **Dim:** 119.0 × 12.45 × 5.8 (max.)
A: 4/127-mm DP (II × 2)—4/20-mm AA (II × 2)—1/ASROC Mk 116 ASW RL (VIII × 1; 17 missiles)—6/324-mm Mk 32 ASW TT (III × 2)

DESTROYERS *(continued)*

Tippu Sultan (D 167)—prior to refit G. Gyssels, 9-81

Electron Equipt: Radar: 1/Decca 1226, 1/SPS-10B, 1/SPS-40, 1/Mk 25
Sonar: SQS-23D
EW: WLR-1, 2/Plessey Shield chaff RL (VI × 2)
M: 2 sets G.E. GT; 2 props; 60,000 hp **Electric:** 1,300 kw
Boilers: 4 Babcock & Wilcox; 39.8 kg/cm², 454°C **Fuel:** 600 tons

REMARKS: First two sold to Pakistan 29-4-77, then extensively overhauled at Puget Sound Navy Yard, 165 being completed 2-6-78, and 166 on 16-2-78. Second pair transferred 30-9-80. D 169 purchased 1-10-82. D 170 on 1-10-83. All being refitted and modernized to above standard at Karachi. The helicopter facilities are not used. Sonars are being upgraded to solid-state electronics by Raytheon, U.S.

◆ **1 ex-British Battle class**

	Bldr	Laid down	L	In serv.
D 161 BADR (ex-*Gabbard*)	Swan Hunter	2-2-44	16-3-45	10-12-46

Badr (D 161) 1974

D: 2,325 tons (3,360 fl) **S:** 31 kts **Dim:** 115.32 (108.2 pp) × 12.95 × 4.1
A: 4/114-mm DP (II × 2)—8/40-mm AA (I × 2, I × 4)—4/533-mm TT (IV × 1)—1/Mk 4 Squid ASW mortar (III × 1)
Electron Equipt: Radar: 1/975, 1/293Q, 1/Marconi SNW-10, 1/275
Sonar: 1/170, 1/174
M: 2 Parsons GT; 2 props; 50,000 hp **Boilers:** 2 Admiralty, three-drum
Fuel: 680 tons **Range:** 3,200/20 **Man:** 300 tot.

REMARKS: Transferred 29-2-56. Sister ship *Khaibar* was sunk during the Indo-Pakistani conflict, 1971. Has one radar director for the 114-mm mounts and 2 STD.1 lead-computing directors for the twin 40-mm AA. Has HFD/F array amidships. To be stricken soon.

FRIGATES

◆ **0 (+3) Modified U.K. Type 21 class**

	Bldr:	Laid down	L	In serv.
F. . . N. . .	Vosper-Thornycroft, Woolston	. . .	. . .	. . .
F. . . N. . .	Vosper-Thornycroft, Woolston	. . .	. . .	. . .
F. . . N. . .	Karachi NSY	. . .	. . .	. . .

D: 3,150 tons **S:** . . . **Dim:** 117.04 × 14.00 × 4.5 (mean hull)
A: 4–8 Harpoon SSM (II or IV × 2)—1/VLS Sea Wolf SAM system (24 missiles)—1/114-mm Mk 8 DP—1/20-mm Mk 15 CIWS AA—6/324-mm ASW TT (III × 2)—1/helicopter
Electron Equipt: Radar: 1/Decca 1226, 1/Type 996 (Plessey AWS-6), 2/Marconi 805SW f.c.
Sonar: Plessey PMS-40 hull-mounted
EW: Racal-Decca Cutlass, Racal-Decca RCM, 2 Shield RL (VI × 2)
M: COGOG: . . .
Range: . . . **Man:** . . .

REMARKS: Letter of intent signed 1985, but actual contracts not yet let, and Pakistan is still investigating other possibilities, including the Blohm + Voss MEKO concept. The Vosper-Thornycroft design is a broad-beamed version of the Type 21, *Amazon* class with updated weapons and sensors.

GUIDED-MISSILE PATROL BOATS

◆ **4 Chinese Huangfen (Soviet Osa-I) class**

P. . . N. . . P. . . N. . . P. . . N. . . P. . . N. . .

D: 186.5 tons normal (205 fl) **S:** 35 kts **Dim:** 38.75 × 7.60 × 1.70 (mean hull)
A: 4/HY-2 (CSS-N-1 Styx) SSM—4/25-mm AA (II × 2)
Electron Equipt: Radar: 1/Square Tie
M: 3 M503A diesels; 3 props; 12,000 hp **Range:** 800/30
Electric: 65 kw **Man:** 28 tot.

REMARKS: Arrived at Karachi 27-4-84 as deck cargo.

◆ **4 Chinese Hoku class**

P 1021 N. . . . . . . P 1022 N. . . . . . . P 1023 N. . . . . . . P 1023 N. . . . . . .

Hoku (P 1024) French Navy, 12-82

D: 68 tons (79 fl) **S:** 38 kts **Dim:** 27.0 × 6.3 × 1.30 mean (1.8 props)
A: 1/HY-2 (CSS-N-1 Styx) SSM (I × 2)—2/25-mm AA (II × 1)
Electron Equipt: Radar: 1/Pot Head **Electric:** 65 kw **Endurance:** 5 days
M: 4 M50-F4 diesels; 4 props; 4,800 hp **Range:** 520/26 **Man:** 20 tot.

REMARKS: Transferred: 2 in 11-81 and 2 in 2-82.

PATROL BOATS

◆ **4 Hainan class** Bldr: People's Republic of China

P 155 BALUCHISTAN P 159 SIND P 161 SARHAD P 197 PUNJAB

Baluchistan (P 155) 1978

D: 360 tons (400 fl) **S:** 30.5 kts **Dim:** 58.77 × 7.20 × 2.20 (mean hull)
A: 4/57-mm AA (II × 2)—4/25-mm AA (II × 2)—4/RBU-1200 ASW RL (V × 4)—2/d.c. throwers—2/d.c. racks—mines
Electron Equipt: Radar: 1/Pot Head—Sonar: HF, hull-mounted
M: 4 Type 9D diesels; 4 props; 8,800 hp **Range:** 1,000/10 **Man:** 60 tot.

REMARKS: First pair transferred in 1976, *Punjab* and *Sarhad* in 4-80.

◆ **8 Shanghai-II class** Bldr: People's Republic of China

P 140 LAHORE P 145 PISHIN P 149 BAHAWALPUR
P 143 MARDAN P 147 SUKKUR P 159 LARKANA
P 144 GUILGIT P 148 SEHWAN

D: 122.5 tons normal (134.8 fl) **S:** 28.5 kts **Dim:** 38.78 × 5.41 × 1.55 (hull)
A: 4/37-mm AA (II × 2)—4/25-mm AA (II × 2)—mines
Electron Equipt: Radar: 1/Pot Head

PATROL BOATS *(continued)*

Sukkur (P 147) French Navy, 1980

M: 2 M50-F4, 1,200 hp diesels, 2 12D6, 910 hp diesels; 4 props; 4,220 hp
Electric: 39 kw **Endurance:** 7 days **Man:** 36 tot. **Range:** 750/16.5

Remarks: Eight transferred in 1972, four in 1973. Very primitive ships. Sisters *Quetta* (P 141), *Bannu* (P 154), *Kalat* (P 156), and *Sahival* (P 160), officially in reserve since 1982, are no longer operable.

TORPEDO BOATS

◆ **4 Huchwan-class hydrofoils** Bldr: People's Republic of China

HDF 01 HDF 02 HDF 03 HDF 04

HDF 03—note small bow foil out of water below pendant number 1973

D: 39 tons (45 fl) **S:** 50 kts
Dim: 22.50 × 3.80 (6.26 over foils) × 1.15 (1.12 foilborne)
A: 4/14.5-mm AA (II × 2)—2/533-mm TT
Electron Equipt: Radar: 1/Skin Head **M:** 3 M50F diesels; 3 props; 3,600 hp
Range: 500/30 **Electric:** 5.6 kw **Man:** 11 tot.

Remarks: Maintained in land storage to prevent corrosion. Cruising speed: 32 kts. Foils forward only; stern planes on surface.

PATROL CRAFT

◆ **2 U.S. patrol craft** Bldr: Uniflite, Bellingham, Wash. (In serv. 1983)

D: 10.0 **S:** 16 kts **Dim:** 12.19 × . . . × . . .
A: . . . **M:** 2 G.M. 6-71N diesels; 2 waterjets; 512 hp

◆ **2 U.S. PBR Mk III patrol craft** Bldr: Uniflite, Bellingham, Wash. (In serv. 1983)

D: 8.9 tons (fl) **S:** 30 kts **Dim:** 9.73 × 3.53 × 0.81
A: 3/12.7-mm mg (II × 1, I × 1)—1/60-mm mortar
Electron Equipt: Radar: 1/Raytheon 1900
M: 2 G.M. 6V53T diesels; 2 Jacuzzi waterjets; 550 hp
Range: 150/23 **Man:** 4 tot.

Remarks: The above four glass-reinforced plastic construction craft were ordered 6-82, apparently for trials and comparison purposes.

◆ **18 MV55 class** Bldr: Crestitalia, Ameglia, Italy (In serv. 1979-80)

P 551–568

D: 22.8 tons (fl) **S:** 30 kts **Dim:** 16.5 × 5.2 × 0.88 **Man:** 5 tot.
A: 1/14.5-mm mg **M:** 2 V-6 diesels; 2 props; 1,600 hp **Range:** 425/25

Remarks: Glass-reinforced plastic construction. P 553 named *Vaqar*; others presumably also named. These craft are used for Customs duties and are not under naval control in peacetime. Twelve 19.8-m "Swallow"-class patrol craft may be built for similar duties, under license from South Korea.

MINE WARFARE SHIPS

Note: In 4-84 it was announced that 4 minehunters were to be acquired; characteristics and dates not reported.

◆ **3 ex-U.S. Falcon-class coastal minesweepers**

	Bldr	In serv.
M 160 Mahmood (ex-MSC 267)	Quincy Adams Yacht, Quincy, Mass.	4-57
M 164 Mujahid (ex-MSC 261)	Hodgdon Bros., East Boothbay, Maine	10-56
M 165 Mukhtar (ex-MSC 274)	Bellingham SY, Bellingham, Wash.	7-59

Mukhtar (M 165) 1974

D: 320 tons (372 fl) **S:** 13 kts (8, sweeping) **Dim:** 43.0 × 7.95 × 2.55
A: 4/23-mm AA ZSU-23 (IV × 1)
Electron Equipt: Radar: 1/Decca 45
Sonar: UQS-1D
M: 2 G.M. 8-268A diesels; 12 props; 1,200 hp **Range:** 2,500/10 **Man:** 39 tot.

Remarks: Wooden hulls. All built under the Military Assistance Program. *Munsif* (M 166, ex-MSC 273) stricken 1979; *Murabak* (ex-MSC 262) and MSC 289-class units *Momin* (ex-MSC 293) and *Moshal* (ex-MSC 294) stricken 1983.

AUXILIARY SHIPS

◆ **1 oceanographic research ship**

	Bldr	Laid down	L	In serv.
Behr Paima	Ishikawajima Harima, Tokyo	16-2-82	. . .	17-12-82

D: . . . **S:** 13.75 kts **Dim:** 61.0 × 11.8 × 3.7
M: 2 Daihatsu diesels; 2 props; 2,000 hp

Remarks: Ordered 15-4-81. 1,183 grt.

Note: Ex-U.K. "River"-class frigate *Zulfiquar* (F 262, ex-*Dhanush*, ex-U.K. *Deveron*, used for many years as a hydrographic survey ship, and inshore survey craft *Jatli* were stricken 1983. Transfer of the ex-U.S. Navy destroyer tender *Everglades* (AD 24) was not carried out as planned.

◆ **1 ex-U.S. T-2-class replenishment oiler** Bldr: Marinship Corp., Sausalito, Calif.

A 41 Dacca (ex-*Mission Santa Clara*, TAO 132) (In serv. 21-6-44)

Dacca (A 41)—with *Hangor* (S 131) alongside 1975

D: 5,730 tons light (22,380 fl) **S:** 15 kts **Dim:** 159.56 × 20.73 × 9.4
A: 6/40-mm AA (I × 6) **Electron Equipt:** Radar: 1/RCA CRM-NIA-75
M: 1 set G.E. GT, electric drive; 1 prop; 10,000 hp **Electric:** 1,150 kw
Boilers: 2 Combustion Engineering "D"; 42 kg/cm², 440°C **Fuel:** 1,300 tons
Man: 15 officers, 145 men

Remarks: Acquired by U.S. Navy 11-5-47. Loaned 17-1-63, after conversion to permit underway replenishment alongside, one station each side. Bought outright 31-5-74. Cargo: 15,300 tons.

◆ **1 ex-U.S. Cherokee-class ocean tug** Bldr: Commercial Iron Works, Portland, Ore.

	Laid down	L	In serv.
A 42 Madadgar (ex-*Yuma*, ATF 94)	13-2-43	17-7-43	31-8-43

D: 1,325 tons (1,675 fl) **S:** 16.5 kts **Dim:** 62.48 (59.44 pp) × 11.73 × 4.67
A: 2/40-mm AA (I × 2)—1/20-mm AA **Electron Equipt:** Radar: 1/Decca 45
M: 4 G.M. 12-278 diesels, electric drive; 1 prop; 3,000 hp **Electric:** 260 kw
Fuel: 295 tons **Man:** 85 tot.

Remarks: Employed as a salvage and rescue tug.

◆ **1 large harbor tug** Bldr: Worstd Dutmer, Meppel, Netherlands (L: 29-11-55)

A 43 Rustom

D: 530 tons (fl) **S:** 9.5 kts **Dim:** 32.0 × 9.1 × 3.3
M: 1 Crossley diesel; 1 prop; 1,000 hp **Range:** 3,000/8 **Man:** 21 tot.

◆ **2 small harbor tugs** Bldr: Costaguta-Voltz, Italy (In serv. 9-58)

Gama (ex-U.S. YTL 754) Bholu (ex-U.S. YTL 755)

Remarks: Built under the U.S. Offshore Procurement Program. 300 hp.

PAKISTAN *(continued)*
AUXILIARY SHIPS *(continued)*

Madadgar (A 42)—note 20-mm AA before bridge J.-C. Bellonne, 1977

◆ **1 small pusher tug** Bldr: Naval DY, Karachi (In serv. 11-1-83)

Goga

◆ **1 water tanker** Bldr: . . . , Trieste, Italy (In serv. 1957)

A 46 Zum Zum

D: 600 tons (1,225 fl) **S:** 8 kts **Dim:** 54.0 × 9.8 × 4.6
A: 2/20-mm AA (I × 2) **M:** 2 diesels; 2 props; 800 hp

◆ **2 logistics craft** Bldr: Le Comte, Vianen, Netherlands (In serv. 18-2-82)

D: 13 tons (fl) **S:** 21 kts **Dim:** 18.1 × 3.8 × 0.9
M: 2 Volva Penta AQAD 40 diesels; 2 outdrives; 520 hp

Remarks: Glass-reinforced plastic-hulled landing craft.

◆ **1 degaussing tender** Bldr: Karachi DY (In serv. 1979)

D: 260 tons (fl) **S:** 10 kts **Dim:** 35.22 (34.0 wl) × 7.00 × 2.4
M: 1 diesel; 1 prop; 375 hp **Man:** 5 tot.

Remarks: Built with French technical assistance and very similar in design to French Navy's Y 732. Wooden hull.

◆ **1 floating dry dock** Bldr: Karachi DY (In serv. 1981)

N. . . **Lift capacity:** 2,000 tons

◆ **1 U.S. ARD-2-class floating dry dock** Bldr: Pacific Bridge, Alameda (In serv. 4-43)

Peshawar (ex-ARD 6)

Dim: 148.03 × 21.64 × 1.6 (light) **Lift capacity:** 3,500 tons

Remarks: Transferred 6-61.

◆ **1 small floating dry dock** (In serv. 1974)

FC II **Lift capacity:** 1,200 tons

PANAMA

Republic of Panama

Personnel (1985): Approx. 500 tot.

Merchant Marine (1984): 5,499 ships—37,244,233 grt (tankers: 622 ships—10,045,086 grt)

Naval Aviation: There are no "naval" aircraft. The Air Force operates a number of aircraft with a secondary maritime patrol role, including 3 DHC Twin Otter, 3 CASA C-212, 2 Britten-Norman Islander, 2 Cessna U-17, and a Cessna 172. Helicopters include 8 Bell UH-1B, 9 UH-1H, and 4 UH-1N. Larger transports include an L-188 Electra, 4 C-47s, 1 Skyvan, and a Falcon 20 for VIP transport.

NATIONAL GUARD

PATROL BOATS AND CRAFT

◆ **2 U.S. 65-ft class** Bldr: Swiftships, Morgan City, La. (In serv. 7-82)

GC 16 Comandante Torrijas GC 17 Presidente Porras

Comandante Torrijas (GC 16) Swiftships, 7-82

D: 35 tons (fl) **S:** 21 kts **Dim:** 19.81 × 5.64 × 1.83
A: 1/12.7-mm mg **Electron Equipt:** Radar: 1/Decca 110
M: 2 G.M. 12V71 TI N75 diesels; 2 props; 1,020 hp
Electric: 40 kw **Man:** 8 tot.

Remarks: Aluminum construction.

◆ **2 103-foot boats** Bldr: Vosper Thornycroft, Portsmouth, U.K. (In serv. 3-71)

GC 10 Panquiaco (L: 22-7-70) GC 11 Ligia Elena (L: 25-8-70)

D: 96 tons (123 fl) **S:** 24 kts **Dim:** 31.25 × 6.02 × 1.98
A: 2/20-mm AA (I × 2) **Electron Equipt:** Radar: 1/Decca 916
M: 2 Paxman Ventura 12-YJCM diesels; 2 props; 2,800 hp **Electric:** 80 kVA
Man: 23 tot.

◆ **2 ex-U.S. Coast Guard 40-foot Mk 1-class utility boats** (In serv. 1950)

GC 14 Marti GC 15 Jupiter

D: 13 tons (fl) **S:** 18 kts **Dim:** 12.3 × 3.4 × 1.0
A: 1/12.7-mm mg **M:** 2 G.M. 6-71 diesels; 2 props; 300 hp
Range: 160/8 **Man:** 4 tot.

Remarks: Transferred in 1962.

◆ **2 ex-U.S. 63-foot AVR class**

GC 12 Ayanasi GC 13 Zarti

D: 35 tons (fl) **S:** 22.5 kts **Dim:** 19.3 × 4.7 × 1.0
A: 2/12.7-mm mg (I × 2) **Electron Equipt:** Radar: 1/Raytheon 1500B
M: 2 G.M. 8V-71 diesels; 2 props; 900 hp **Man:** 8 tot.

Remarks: In service in 1943 and transferred 1965-66.

AUXILIARY SHIPS AND CRAFT

◆ **1 ex-U.S. LSMR-class rocket-assault ship** Bldr: Brown SB Co., Houston

	Laid down	L	In serv.
GC 10 Tiburon (ex-*Smokey Hill River,* LSMR 531)	2-6-45	7-7-45	21-9-45

D: 2,084 tons (fl) **S:** 12 kts **Dim:** 62.87 × 10.52 × 2.18
A: None **M:** 2 G.M. 16-278A diesels; 2 props; 2,800 hp
Electric: 440 kw **Man:** . . .

Remarks: Purchased from a commercial source 14-3-75 and used for logistics-support duties. May have had bow doors added, although as completed she had none and had her well deck plated over. Cargo: approximately 400 tons.

◆ **2 logistics-support landing craft** Bldr: Ch. de la Manche, France (In serv. 1978)

GN. . . GN. . .

D: 60 tons (fl) **S:** 9 kts **Dim:** 12.6 × . . . × . . .
M: 2 SKL 8NVD26 diesels; 2 props; 400 hp

Remarks: *Not* BATRAL-class landing ships, as recorded elsewhere.

◆ **3 ex-U.S. Army LCM (8)-class landing craft**

GN 1 GN 2 GN 3

D: 115 tons (fl) **S:** 9 kts **Dim:** 22.7 × 6.4 × 1.4
A: None **M:** 4 G.M. 6-71 diesels; 2 props; 600 hp **Man:** 6 tot.

Remarks: Transferred 1972. Used for logistics-support duties. Two-level superstructure added aft.

PANAMA *(continued)*
AUXILIARY SHIPS AND CRAFT *(continued)*

◆ **1 ex-U.S. YF-852-class cargo lighter**

	Bldr	Laid down	L	In serv.
N. . . (ex-YF 886)	Defoe SB, Bay City, Michigan	13-4-45	25-5-45	4-8-45

D: 590 tons (fl) **S:** 11 kts **Dim:** 40.23 × 9.1 × 2.7
M: 2 G.M. 6-71 diesels; 2 props; 600 hp **Man:** 11 tot.

Remarks: Transferred 5-75. Cargo: 250 tons.

◆ **1 former shrimp boat,** used for logistics support

GN 8

S: 11 kts **Capacity:** 150 passengers

PAPUA NEW GUINEA

Personnel (1985): 410 total

Merchant Marine (1984): 82 ships—25,760 grt
(tankers: 6 ships—2,797 grt)

Naval Aviation: The Papua New Guinea Defense Force operates 6 Nomad N.22B light transports, 6 C-47, 1 Super King Air 200, and 1 Gulfstream II transports for coastal patrol and logistics duties.

PATROL BOATS

◆ **0 (+4) ASI 315 design** Bldr: Australian SB Ind. (WA), Pty, Ltd., South Coogie, W. Australia

	In serv.		In serv.
P. . . N. . .	1986	P. . . N. . .	. . .
P. . . N. . .	. . .	P. . . N. . .	. . .

ASI 315 design—artist's rendering Australian SB Ind., 1985

D: 165 tons (fl) **S:** 20 kts (sust.) **Dim:** 31.50 (28.60 wl) × 8.10 × 2.12
A: 1/20-mm AA—2/12.7-mm mg (I × 2)
Electron Equipt: Radar: 1/Furuno 1011
M: 2 Caterpillar 3516 diesels; 2 props; 2,400 hp (sust.)
Range: 2,500/12 **Fuel:** 33 tons **Electric:** 120 kw
Endurance: 10 days **Man:** 3 officers, 14 men

Remarks: "Pacific Patrol Boat" design winner, for Australian foreign aid program; others building for smaller island nations. Ordered late 1985.

◆ **4 ex-Australian Attack class**

	Bldr	In serv.
P 85 Samarai	Evans Deakin, Queensland	1-3-68
P 92 Ladava	Walkers, Ltd., Maryborough	21-10-68
P 93 Lae	Evans Deakin, Queensland	3-4-68
P 94 Madang	Evans Deakin, Queensland	28-11-68

D: 146 tons (fl) **S:** 21-24 kts **Dim:** 32.76 (30.48 pp) × 6.2 × 1.9
A: 1/40-mm AA—2/7.62-mm mg (I × 2)
Electron Equipt: Radar: 1/Decca RM916

Samarai (P 85) R. Gillett, 1983

M: 2 Davey-Paxman Ventura 16-YJCM diesels; 3,500 hp **Fuel:** 20 tons
Range: 1,220/13 **Man:** 18 tot.

Remarks: Transferred in 1975. *Aitape* (P 84) stricken 1981 for spares.

AMPHIBIOUS WARFARE SHIPS

◆ **4 Burfoam-class utility landing craft** Bldr: Sing Koon Seng SY, Singapore

	In serv.		In serv.
Burfoam	21-7-81	Bursea	6-4-82
Burcrest	8-9-81	Burwave	18-5-82

D: 200 tons light (725 fl) **S:** 9 kts **Dim:** 37.25 (33.50 pp) × 9.00 × . . .
M: 2 Deutz SBA-6M-816-1 LKR diesels; 2 props; 626 hp
Range: 1,870/9 **Fuel:** 160 tons **Man:** 18 tot.

Remarks: 260 grt/350 dwt. Owned by government, employed in commercial and logistics service.

◆ **2 ex-Australian Balikpapan-class utility landing craft** Bldr: Walkers, Maryborough

31 Salamaua 32 Buna

Salamaua (31) G. Gyssels, 1980

D: 310 tons (503 fl) **S:** 8 kts **Dim:** 44.5 × 12.2 × 1.9
A: 2/12.7-mm mg (I × 2) **M:** 3 G.M. 12V71 diesels; 3 props; 675 hp
Range: 1,300–2,280/10 depending on load **Man:** 2 officers, 11 men

Remarks: In service in 1972 and transferred 1975. Cargo: 140-180 tons.

◆ **7 Kokuba-class personnel landing craft** Bldr: Australia (In serv. 1975)

Kokuba Kutuba Kiaipit Kandep
Kuniawa Kiunga Kukipi

D: 12 tons (fl) **S:** 9 kts **Dim:** 12.0 × 4.0 × 1.0
M: 2 Gardner diesels; 2 props; 150 hp

◆ **1 ex-Australian tug** Bldr: Perrin, Brisbane, 1972

HTS 503

D: 47.5 tons **S:** 9 kts **Dim:** 15.4 × 4.6 × . . .
M: 2 G.M. diesels; 2 props; 340 hp **Range:** 710/9 **Man:** 3 tot.

Remarks: Transferred in 1974. Retained RAN number.

PARAGUAY

Republic of Paraguay

Personnel (1985): 2,500 total, including 500 Marines and Coast Guard

Merchant Marine (1984): 39 ships—37,799 grt
(tankers: 4 ships—3326 grt)

Naval Aviation: 4 H-13 Sioux helicopters, 2 AT-6 Texan trainers, 3 Cessna U-206, 1 Cessna 150M light utility aircraft, and 1 C-47 transport.

PARAGUAY *(continued)*

RIVER GUNBOATS

◆ **1 Brazilian Roraima class** Bldr: Ars. de Rio de Janeiro, Brazil

	Laid down	L	In serv.
P. 2 ITAIPU	3-3-83	16-3-84	2-4-85

D: 220 tons light (384 fl) **S:** 14.5 kts **Dim:** 46.3 (45.0 pp) × 8.45 × 1.42 (max)
A: 1/40-mm—6/12.7-mm mg (II × 3)—2/81-mm mortar (I × 1)
Electron Equipt: Radar: 3/navigational **Range:** 4,500/11
M: 2 M.A.N. V6V 16/18 TL diesels; 2 props; 1,824 hp
Endurance: 30 days **Man:** 63 tot.

REMARKS: Order announced 11-4-83. Has small helicopter deck.

◆ **3 ex-Argentinian Bouchard-class former ocean minesweepers**

	Bldr	L	In serv.
M. 1 NANAWA (ex-*Bouchard*)	Rio Santiago NY	20-3-36	16-5-37
M. 2 CAPITÁN MEZA (ex-*Seaver*)	Hansen & Puccini, San Fernando	2-5-37	20-5-39
M. 3 TENIENTE FARINA (ex-*Py*)	Rio Santiago NY	31-3-38	1-7-38

D: 450 tons (650 fl) **S:** 16 kts **Dim:** 59.5 × 7.3 × 2.6
A: 4/40-mm AA (II × 2)—2/12.7-mm mg—mines
M: 2 M.A.N. diesels; 2 props; 2,000 hp **Range:** 3,000/12 **Man:** 70 tot.

REMARKS: Transferred: M. 1 donated 1-64, the other two purchased on 6-3-68.

◆ **2 Paraguay class** Bldr: Odero, Genoa (In serv. 5-31)

C. 1 PARAGUAY (ex-*Comodoro Meya*) C. 2 HUMAITÁ (ex-*Capitán Cabral*)

Humaita (C.2)—in floating dry dock DF.1 1970

D: 636 tons, 745 avg. (865 fl) **S:** 17.5 kts **Dim:** 70.15 × 10.7 × 1.65
A: 4/120-mm (II × 2)—3/76.2-mm AA (I × 3)—2/40-mm AA (I × 2)—6 mines
M: 2 sets Parsons GT; 2 props; 3,800 hp **Boilers:** 2
Fuel: 170 tons **Range:** 1,700/16 **Man:** 86 tot.

◆ **1 old former tug** Bldr: Werf Conrad, Haarlem (In serv. 1908)

A. 1 CAPITÁN CABRAL (ex-*Adolfo Riquelme*)

D: 206 tons (fl) **S:** 9 kts **Dim:** 30.5 × 7.0 × 2.9
A: 1/76.2-mm—2/37-mm **M:** Reciprocating; 300 hp **Man:** 47 tot.

REMARKS: Wooden hull, used for riverine patrol on the Upper Paraña River.

PATROL CRAFT

◆ **6 small craft** Bldr: Sewart Seacraft, Berwick, La.

PT. 101 PT. 102 PT. 103 PT. 104 PT. 105 PT. 106

D: 15 tons (fl) **S:** 20 kts **Dim:** 13.1 × 3.9 × 0.9
A: 2/12.7-mm mg **M:** 2 G.M. G-71 diesels; 2 props; 500 hp **Man:** 7 tot.

REMARKS: PT. 101 and PT. 102 in service in 12-67; PT. 103, PT. 104, and PT. 105, in 9-70; and PT. 106, in 3-71.

AUXILIARY SHIPS

◆ **1 repair/headquarters ship** Bldr: Brown SB, Houston

	Laid down	L	In serv.
BC. 1 BOQUERON (ex-*Teniente Pratt Gil*, PH. 1, ex-*Corrientes*, ex-LSM 86)	22-8-44	15-9-44	13-10-44

D: 743 tons (1,095 fl) **S:** 12.6 kts **Dim:** 61.88 × 10.51 × 2.54
A: 2/40-mm AA (II × 1)
M: 2 Fairbanks-Morse 38D8⅛ × 10 diesels; 2 props; 2,800 hp
Electric: 240 kw **Man:** . . .

REMARKS: An ex-U.S. LSM-1-class landing ship donated by Argentina on 13-1-72, after conversion to a command and repair ship. Well deck plated over to create a helicopter deck aft; superstructure enlarged and moved to the centerline. Renamed 1980.

◆ **1 cargo and training ship** Bldr: Thomás Ruiz de Velasco, Bilbao, Spain (In serv. 2-68)

GUARANI

Guarani L. & L. Van Ginderen, 10-83

D: 714 grt/1,047 dwt **S:** 12.2 kts **Dim:** 73.6 × 11.9 × 3.7
M: 1 diesel; 1 prop; 1,300 hp

REMARKS: Purchased and repaired after a fire in 1974 to provide seagoing experience for naval cadets and to engage in commercial voyages to raise revenue for running the navy. Cargo: approximately 1,000 tons.

◆ **2 ex-U.S. LCU-501-class landing craft** (In serv. circa 1944-45)

BT. 1 (ex-YFB 82, ex-LCU. . .) BT. 2 (ex-YFB 86, ex-LCU. . .)

D: 143 tons (309 fl) **S:** 10 kts **Dim:** 36.3 × 9.8 × 1.2 (aft)
M: 3 Gray Marine 64YTL diesels; 3 props; 675 hp

REMARKS: Transferred in 6-70. Used for logistics duties. Cargo: 125 tons.

◆ **2 ex-U.S. 64-foot YTL-422-class tugs**

	Bldr	Laid down	L	In serv.
R. 5 (ex-YTL 211)	Robert Jacob, Inc.	26-12-41	20-6-42	21-8-42
R. 6 (ex-YTL 567)	Gunderson Bros.	5-3-45	17-8-45	30-10-45

D: 84 tons **S:** 9 kts **Dim:** 20.2 × 5.5 × 2.4
M: 1 diesel; 300 hp **Man:** 5 tot.

REMARKS: Transferred in 3-67 and 4-74.

◆ **1 ex-U.S. floating dry dock** Bldr: Doullut & Ewin, Mobile, Ala. (In serv. 6-44)

N. . . (ex-AFDL 26)

Dim: 60.96 × 19.5 × 1.04 (light)
Lifting capacity: 1,000 tons

REMARKS: Transferred in 3-65.

◆ **1 ex-U.S. floating workshop**

	Bldr	Laid down	L	In serv.
N. . . (ex-YR 37)	Mare Island Naval SY	14-12-41	12-1-42	15-5-42

D: 600 tons (fl) **Dim:** 45.72 × 10.36 × 1.8 **Electric:** 210 kw **Man:** 47 tot.

REMARKS: Transferred 3-65.

◆ **3 dredges**

D. 1 N. . . . . . . (In serv. 1907)—140 tons, 30 crew
D. 2 TENIENTE O. CARRERAS SAGUIER (In serv. 1957)—110 tons, 19 crew
RP. 1 N. . . . . . . (In serv. 1908)—107 tons, 29 crew

NOTE: Also believed in service are river transport *Presidente Stroessner* (T. 1, 150 tons, 10 kts, In serv. 1901), a 50-ton survey launch, buoy tender B. 1 (30-tons), and several small stores carriers.

PERU

Republic of Peru

PERSONNEL (1985): 2,100 officers, 19,000 men, plus 2,500 officers and men of the Naval Infantry

MERCHANT MARINE (1984): 670 ships—787,746 grt (tankers: 16 ships—167,541 grt)

NAVAL AVIATION: The air arm consists of the following helicopters and fixed-wing aircraft: 9 AM 39 Exocet SSM-equipped SH-3D Sea King, 6 Agusta-Bell AB 212, 10 Bell 206 JetRanger, 6 Bell UH-1, and 2 Alouette-III helicopters; 2 Fokker F-27 Maritime, 9 Grumman S-2 Tracker ASW aircraft, 2 DHC-6 Twin Otter floatplanes, 2 C-47 transports, 1 Piper Aztec liaison aircraft, and 6 Beech T-34C trainers.

Warships In Service And Under Construction
As Of 1 January 1986

	L	Tons (surfaced)	Main armament
◆ **12 submarines**			
6 Type 209	1973-1981	980-1,000	8/533-mm TT
4 Dos De Mayo	1953-57	825	6/533-mm TT, 1/127-mm DP (on two units)
2 GUPPY-IA	1944	1,830	10/533-mm TT
◆ **2 cruisers**		(Std)	
1 Aguirre	1950	9,850	4/152-mm DP, 6/57-mm AA, 4/40-mm AA, 3 helicopters
1 Almirante Grau	1944	9,529	8/152-mm DP, 8/57-mm AA
◆ **6 destroyers**			
6 Friesland	1954-56	2,496	4/20-mm DP, 4/40-mm AA
◆ **3 (+1) frigates**			
3 (+1) Lupo	1976-83	2,208	8/Otomat, 1/Albatros SAM system, 1/127-mm DP
◆ **6 guided-missile corvettes**			
6 PR 72	1978-79	560	4/MM 38 Exocet, 1/76-mm DP, 2/40-mm AA

SUBMARINES

◆ **6 German Type 209** Bldr: Howaldtswerke, Kiel

	L	In serv.
S 31 Casma	31-8-79	19-12-80
S 32 Antofagasta	19-12-79	14-3-80
S 33 Pisagua (ex-*Blume*)	19-5-81	8-4-82
S 34 Chipana (ex-*Pisagua*)	7-8-81	12-7-83
S 35 Islay	11-10-73	23-1-75
S 36 Arica	5-4-74	4-4-75

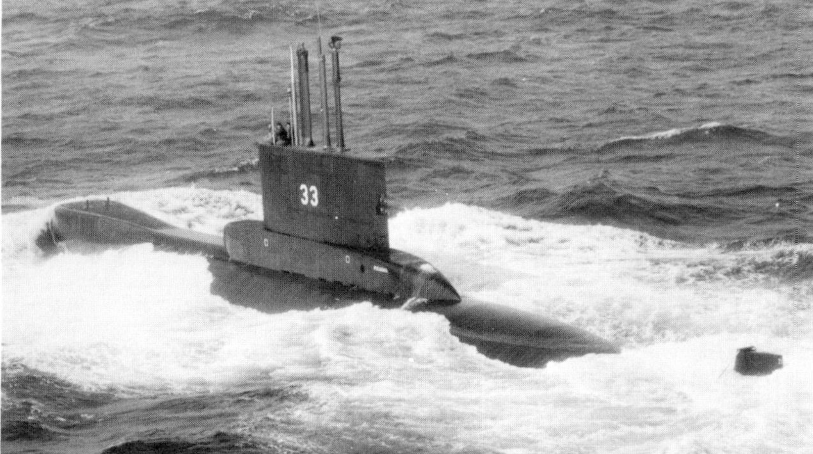

Pisagua (S 33)—bulged sonar bow Skyfotos, 9-83

Islay (P 35)—low bow L. & L. Van Ginderen, 9-83

D: 980/1,230 tons **S:** 21 kts for 5 minutes, submerged, 12 snorkel, 11 surf.
Dim: 54.40 × 6.20 × 5.50 **A:** 8/533-mm TT—(14 total SST-4 and NT37C torpedoes)
M: 4 MTU Type 12V493 TY60 diesels, each linked to a 450-kw AEG generator, 1 Siemans electric motor; 1 prop; 5,000 hp
Range: 230/8; 400/4 (sub.) **Endurance:** 40 days
Fuel: 63 tons **Man:** 5 officers, 26 men

Remarks: S 31 and S 32 were ordered 12-8-76, and two more in 3-77. S 31 and later are 56.1-m overall, 1,185 tons surfaced/1,290 tons submerged. Use H.S.A. SINBADS f.c.s. S 33 delivery delayed by collision 2-4-82. S 35 and S 36 have DUUX-2CN sonar equipment.

◆ **4 Dos de Mayo class** Bldr: General Dynamics, Groton, Conn.

	Laid down	L	In serv.
S 41 Dos De Mayo (ex-*Lobo*)	12-5-52	6-2-54	14-6-54
S 42 Abtao (ex-*Tiburon*)	12-5-52	27-10-53	20-2-54
S 43 Angamos (ex-*Atun*)	27-10-55	5-2-57	1-7-57
S 44 Iquique (ex-*Merlin*)	27-10-55	5-2-57	1-10-57

Angamos (S 43)—now has bow sonar dome

D: 825/1,400 tons **S:** 16/10 kts **Dim:** 74.1 × 6.7 × 4.2
A: S 41, S 42: 1/127-mm DP—all: 6/533-mm TT (4 fwd, 2 aft)
Electron Equipt: Radar: 1/SS-2A—Sonar: BQR-3, BQA-1A
M: 2 G.M. 12-278A diesels, 2 electric motors; 2 props; 2,400 hp
Fuel: 45 tons **Range:** 5,000/10 (snorkel) **Man:** 40 tot.

Remarks: Patterned after the U.S. *Marlin* class of 1941. These were the last U.S. submarines to be built for a foreign customer. S 41 and S 42 were refitted in 1965, S 43 and S 44 in 1968. The 127-mm gun carried by S 41 and S 42 is a 25-caliber U.S. "Wet" model and is mounted abaft the sail.

◆ **2 ex-U.S. GUPPY-IA class** Bldr: Portsmouth Naval SY, New Hampshire

	Laid down	L	In serv.
S 49 Pedrera (ex-*Sea Poacher,* SS 406)	23-2-44	20-5-44	31-7-44
S 50 Pacocha (ex-*Atule,* SS 403)	2-12-43	6-3-44	21-6-44

Peruvian submarines in silhouette—from background to foreground: *Dos de Mayo* or *Abtao* (S 41 or 42) with deck gun and bow dome; a GUPPY-1A; and a Type 209 U.S. Navy, 1982

D: 1,830/2,440 tons **S:** 17/15 kts **Dim:** 93.57 × 8.23 × 5.18
A: 10/533-mm TT (6 fwd, 4 aft)
Electron Equipt: Radar: 1/SS-2A—Sonar: BQS-4, BQR-2B
M: 4 Fairbanks-Morse 38D8⅛ diesels, 2 electric motors; 2 props; 4,610 hp
Fuel: 330 tons **Range:** 10,000/10 **Man:** 82 tot.

Remarks: Purchased in 7-74. Both were converted to GUPPY-IA configuration during 1951. They can maintain 15 kts for half an hour while submerged, 3 kts for thirty-six hours. Snorkel speed is 7.5 kts. A third submarine of this class, ex-*Tench* (SS-417), was towed out in 11-76 for cannibalization.

CRUISERS

◆ **1 ex-Dutch guided-missile cruiser** Bldr: Rotterdamse Droogdok Mij. Rotterdam

	Laid down	L	In serv.
84 Aguirre (ex-*De Zeven Provincien,* ex-*Eendracht,* ex-*Kijkduin*)	19-5-39	22-8-50	17-12-53

Aguirre (84) 1978

D: 9,850 tons (12,250 fl) **S:** 32 kts **Dim:** 185.7 (182.4 pp) × 17.25 × 6.7
A: 4/152-mm DP (II × 2)—6/57-mm AA (II × 3)—4/40-mm AA (I × 4)—2/d.c. racks (8 d.c.)—3 SH-3D Sea King helicopters
Electron Equipt: Radar: 2/Decca. . . , 1/LW-02, 1/SGR-103, 1/DA-02, 1/ZW-03, 1/M 25, 2/M 45
Sonar: CWC-10N
M: 2 sets Parsons GT; 2 props; 79,000 hp **Boilers:** 4 Yarrow-Werkspoor, three-drum
Armor: Belt: 76-102-mm; decks (2): 20-25-mm
Electric: 4,000 kw **Range:** 6,000/17 **Man:** 856 tot.

CRUISERS *(continued)*

REMARKS: Purchased in 8-76. The Terrier missile system was replaced by a hangar (20.4 × 16.5) and a helicopter platform (35.0 × 17.0) at Rotterdam. Recommissioned on 31-10-77. The helicopters carry French AM 39 Exocet anti-ship missiles. The hangar roof is also a helicopter platform. Carries 1,620 rounds 152-mm, 6,400 rds 57-mm, 8,000 rds 40-mm ammunition.

◆ **1 ex-Dutch cruiser** Bldr: Wilton-Fijenoord, Schiedam

	Laid down	L	In serv.
81 ALMIRANTE GRAU (ex-*de Ruyter,* ex-*de Zeven Provincien*)	5-9-39	24-12-44	18-11-53

Almirante Grau (81) L. & L. Van Ginderen, 3-85

Almirante Grau (81) L. & L. Van Ginderen, 3-85

D: 9,529 tons (11,850 fl) **S:** 32 kts **Dim:** 187.32 (182.4 pp) × 17.25 × 6.7
A: 8/152-mm DP (II × 4)—6/40-mm AA (I × 6)—2/d.c. racks (12 d.c.)
Electron Equipt: Radar: 1/Decca. . . , 1/LW-01, 1/LW-02, 1/SGR-105, 1/SGR-103, 1/SGR-104, 2/M 45, 4/M 44
Sonar: CWC-10N—EW: . . .
M: 2 sets Parsons GT; 2 props; 85,000 hp **Boilers:** 4 Yarrow-Werkspoor, three-drum
Armor: Belt: 76-102-mm; decks (2): 20-25-mm **Electric:** 4,000 kw
Range: 2,100/32; 6,900/12 **Man:** 49 officers, 904 men

REMARKS: Purchased 7-3-73, commissioning 23-5-73. Refitting at Amsterdamse Droogdok Maatschappij 26-3-85 to 1987; delayed by shipyard bankruptcy. Four twin Bofors 57-mm AA removed prior to arrival in Netherlands, navigational radar added atop foremast. Receiving new H.S.A. radars and fire-control systems. Carries 3,250 rds, 152-mm, 16,000 rds 40-mm ammunition. A 100-mm flare rocket launcher with 100 rds is mounted on the fantail.

DESTROYERS

◆ **6 ex-Dutch Friesland class**

	Bldr	Laid down	L	In serv.
70 COLONEL BOLOGNESI (ex-*Overijssel,* D 815)	Wilton-Fijenoord, Schiedam	15-10-53	8-7-56	4-10-57
71 CASTILLA (ex-*Utrecht,* D 817)	Kon. Mij. De Schelde, Vlissingen	15-2-54	2-6-56	1-10-57
76 CAPITÁN QUIÑONES ex-*Limburg,* D 814)	Kon. Mij. De Schelde, Vlissingen	28-11-53	5-9-55	31-10-56
77 VILLAR ex-*Amsterdam,* D 819)	Nederlandse Dok, Amsterdam	26-3-55	25-8-56	10-8-58
78 GALVEZ ex-*Groningen,* D 813)	Nederlandse Dok, Amsterdam	4-2-52	9-1-54	19-9-56
79 DIEZ CANSECO ex-*Rotterdam,* D 818)	Rotterdamse DDM, Rotterdam	7-4-54	26-1-56	28-2-57

Colonel Bolognesi (70) L. & L. Van Ginderen, 7-82

D: 2,496 tons (3,100 fl) **S:** 36 kts **Dim:** 116.0 (112.8 pp) × 11.77 × 5.2
A: 4/120-mm DP (II × 2)—4/40-mm AA (I × 4)—2/375-mm Bofors ASW RL (IV × 2)—1/d.c. rack (8 d.c.)
Electron Equipt: Radar: 1/Decca 1229, 1/LW-02, 1/DA-01, 1/ZW-06, 1/M 45
Sonar: 1/CWE-10N, 1/PAE 1N
M: 2 sets G.E. GT; 2 props; 60,000 hp
Boilers: 4 Babcock & Wilcox; 39.8 kg/cm², 454°C **Electric:** 1,350 kw
Range: 920/36; 3,300/22; 4,000/15 **Man:** 284 tot.

REMARKS: 77 transferred 19-5-80; 76 transferred 27-6-80; 78 purchased 27-8-80 and transferred 2-2-81; 79 transferred 11-7-81; 70 purchased 14-6-82. Two forward 40-mm AA removed 1965, fire control for remaining 40-mm AA removed 1977-78. Same propulsion plant as U.S. *Gearing* class. Have one 103-mm rocket flare launcher with 100 rds. Carry 1,300 rds 120-mm, 4,300 rds 40-mm, and 98 rds 375-mm ASW ammunition. Plans have been prepared to modernize two of these ships with new weapons and sensors, including Exocet missiles, in the Netherlands, beginning in 1987. Sister *Guise* (72, ex-*Drenthe,* D 816) purchased 11-7-81, stricken 8-85.

NOTE: Ex-British *Daring*-class destroyers *Palacios* (ex-*Diana*) and *Ferré* (ex-*Decoy*) were put up for sale late in 1984. Ex-Netherlands *Holland*-class destroyer *Garcia y Garcia* (75, ex-*Holland*) was decommissioned for eventual disposal during 1985.

GUIDED-MISSILE FRIGATES

◆ **3 (+1) Italian Lupo type**

	Bldrs	Laid down	L	In serv.
51 MELITON CARVAJAL	CNR, Riva Trigoso	8-10-74	17-11-76	5-2-79
52 MANUEL VILLAVICENCIO	CNR, Riva Trigoso	6-10-76	7-2-78	25-6-79
53 MONTERO	CNTR, Callao	1977	8-10-82	25-7-84
54 MARIATEGUI	CNTR, Callao	1977	8-10-84	1986

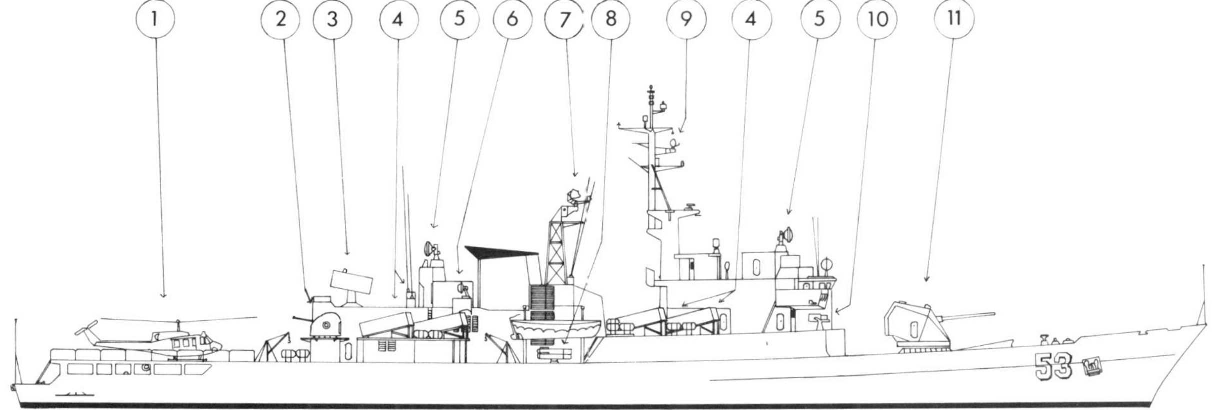

Montero 1. AB 212 helicopter 2. 40-mm Dardo AA mounts (II × 2) abreast fixed hangar 3. Albatros launcher for Aspide missiles (VIII × 1) 4. Otomat anti-ship missiles 5. RTN-30X/RTN-10X missile and gun f.c. radars 6. RTN-20X radar f.c.s. for 40-mm Dardo system 7. RAN-10S search radar 8. ILAS-3 ASW TT (III × 2) 9. RAN-11 L/X radar 10. Breda SCLAR multi-purpose rocket launchers (XX × 2) 11. OTO Melara 127-mm/54-cal. gun

GUIDED-MISSILE FRIGATES *(continued)*

Meliton Carvajal (51) U.S. Navy, 1984

Montero (53) U.S. Navy, 1984

D: 2,208 tons (2,500 fl) **S:** 32 kts **Dim:** 108.4 (106.0 pp) × 11.28 × 3.66
A: 8/Otomat Mk 2 (I × 8) — 1/127-mm OTO Melara DP — 1/Albatros SAM system (VIII × 1) — 4/40-mm Breda Dardo AA (II × 2) — 6/324-mm Mk 32 ASW TT (III × 2) — 1/AB-212 ASW helicopter
Electron Equipt: Radar: 1/3RM20, 1/RAN-10S air search, 1/RAN-11LX surface search, 1/RTN-10X, 2/RTN-20X, 1/RTN-30X
Sonar: Edo 610E
EW: passive intercept, 2/SCLAR chaff RL (XX × 2)
M: CODOG: 2 Fiat-G.E. LM-2500 gas turbines, 25,000 hp each; 2 GMT A230-20M diesels, 3,900 hp each; 2 CP props
Electric: 3,120 kw **Range:** 900/35; 3,450/20.5 (diesel)
Man: 20 officers, 165 men

Remarks: Italian technicians assisted in the building of Nos. 53 and 54 at Callao. Differ from the Italian Navy's version in having a fixed (vice telescoping) hangar and a step down to the hull at the stern; the Dardo 40-mm mounts are one deck higher, and the SAM fire-control system differs. Selenia IPN-IC data system fitted. There are no reloads for the Albatros system, which uses Aspide missiles. The helicopter provides over-the-horizon targetting and mid-course guidance for the Otomat missiles.

GUIDED-MISSILE CORVETTES

◆ **6 French PR-72-560 class**

	Bldr	L	In serv.
P 101 Velarde	Lorient DY	16-9-78	25-7-80
P 102 Santillana	SFCN	11-9-79	25-7-80
P 103 De Los Heroes	Lorient DY	20-5-79	17-11-80
P 104 Herrera	SFCN	16-2-79	26-2-81
P 105 Larrea	Lorient DY	20-5-79	16-6-81
P 106 Sanchez Carrion	SFCN	28-6-79	14-9-81

Herrera (P 104) — old number SFCN, 1981

D: 470 tons light (560 normal, 610 fl) **S:** 37 kts (34 sust.)
Dim: 64.0 (59.0 pp) × 8.35 × 2.6
A: 4/MM 38 Exocet SSM (II × 2) — 1/76-mm OTO Melara DP — 2/40-mm Breda-Bofors AA (II × 1)
Electron Equipt: Radar: 1/Decca 1226, 1/Thomson-CSF THD 1040 Triton, 1/Castor III fire control
M: 4 SACM AGO 240, V-16 diesels; 4 props; 22,000 hp **Electric:** 560 kw
Range: 1,200/30; 2,500/16 **Man:** 36 tot.

Remarks: These ships, designed by SFCN Villeneuve-la-Garonne, have been given the names of the Vosper patrol boats that were transferred to the Coast Guard. Vega weapons control system, with backup optical gun director.

RIVER GUNBOATS

◆ **1 Marañon class** Bldr: John I. Thornycroft, Woolston, U.K.

	Laid down	L	In serv.
13 Marañon	4-50	23-4-51	7-51
14 Ucayali	4-50	7-3-51	7-51

Marañon (13) 1975

D: 350 tons (365 fl) **S:** 12 kts **Dim:** 47.22 × 9.75 × 1.22
A: 2/76.2-mm DP (I × 2) — 4/20-mm (II × 2) **Man:** 4 officers, 36 men
M: 2 British Polar 441 diesels; 2 props; 800 hp **Range:** 5,000/10

Remarks: Based at Iquitos and in service on the Upper Amazon. Superstructure of aluminum alloy.

◆ **1 ex-U.S. Cannon-class former frigate** Bldr: Western Pipe & Steel Co., San Pedro, Cal.

	Laid down	L	In serv.
61 Castilla (ex-*Bangust,* DE 739)	11-2-43	6-6-43	30-10-43

D: 1,240 tons (1,900 fl) **S:** 21 kts (new) **Dim:** 93.27 (91.44 wl) × 11.15 × 3.56 (mean)
A: 3/76.2-mm Mk 26 DP (I × 3) — 6/40-mm AA (II × 4) — 10/20-mm AA (I × 10)
Electron Equipt: Radar: 1/navigational
M: 2 G.M. 16-278A diesel generator sets, electric drive; 2 props; 6,000 hp
Electric: 680 kw **Fuel:** 315 tons **Range:** 8,300/14
Man: 12 officers, 160 men

Remarks: Purchased 2/52. Employed at Iquitos on the Upper Amazon as headquarters and training ship for the Amazon Flotilla. ASW equipment and gunfire-control equipment deleted. Portholes added to hull sides fore and aft, ASW ordnance and sensors deleted. Sister *Rodriguez* (ex-*Weaver,* DE 741) is employed as an accommodations hulk for submarines at Callao.

◆ **2 Amazonas class** Bldr: Electric Boat Co., Groton, Conn. (In serv. 1934)

11 Amazonas 12 Loreto

Loreto (12) 1975

D: 250 tons **S:** 15 kts **Dim:** 46.7 × 6.7 × 1.2
A: 2/76.2-mm DP (I × 2) — 2/40-mm AA (I × 2) — 2/20-mm AA (I × 2)
M: 2 diesels; 2 props; 750 hp **Range:** 4,000/10 **Man:** 5 officers, 20 men

Remarks: Based at Iquitos on Upper Amazon.

Note: Old river gunboat *America* (15), reported nonoperational 1981, may be retained as a hulk or relic.

PATROL CRAFT

◆ **3 P-33 class** Bldr: American Shipbldg. & Designs, Miami, Fla. (In serv. 1982)

P-33 (In serv. 15-9-82) P-34 (In serv. 20-11-82) P-35 (In serv. 4-2-83)

PATROL CRAFT *(continued)*

P-33 Am. Shipbldg., 1982

D: 4.8 tons (fl) **S:** 27 kts **Dim:** 10.06 (9.19 pp) × 3.35 × 0.76
A: 1 or 2/12.7-mm mg (I × 1 or 2)
Electron Equipt: Radar: 1/Raytheon 2800 **Range:** 450/27
M: 2 Perkins ST-6-354-4M diesels; 2 props; 480 hp

Remarks: Glass-reinforced plastic construction with Kevlar armor.

AMPHIBIOUS WARFARE SHIPS

◆ **4 ex-U.S. Terrebone Parish-class tank landing ships**

	Bldr:	L	In serv.
DT 141 Paita (ex-*Walworth County,* LST 1164)	Ingalls SB, Pascagoula	18-5-53	26-10-53
DT 142 Pisco (ex-*Waldo County,* LST 1163)	Ingalls SB, Pascagoula	17-3-53	17-9-53
DT 143 Callao (ex-*Washoe County,* LST 1165)	Ingalls SB, Pascagoula	14-7-53	30-11-53
DT 144 Eten (ex-*Traverse County,* LST 1160)	Bath Iron Wks, Bath, Me.	3-10-53	19-12-53

D: 2,590 tons (6,225 fl) **S:** 13 kts **Dim:** 117.35 × 16.76 × 3.7 mean (5.18 max.)
A: . . . **Electron Equipt:** Radar: . . .
M: 4 G.M. 15-278A diesels; 2 CP props; 6,000 hp **Electric:** 600 kw
Range: 6,000/9 **Fuel:** 1,060 tons **Man:** . . .

Remarks: Leased from U.S. for five years on 7-8-84; reactivated from Maritime Administration reserve by Todd SY, San Francisco, Cal., and delivered mid-10-84. Having been in Military Sealift Command Service from 1972 until deactivated, they were unarmed at time of transfer; formerly carried 6/76.2-mm DP (II × 3), with 2 Mk 63 GFCS; were to receive some 40-mm AA after arrival in Peru. Have accommodation for 395 troops, bow ramp. Cargo: approx. 2,200 tons. All officially recommissioned 4-3-85.

Note: U.S. LST 1-class landing ships *Paita* (141, ex-*Burnett County,* LST 512) ran aground and was lost, 1983, and *Salaverry* (ex-*Iquitos,* ex-*Carelne,* ex-LST . . .) was stricken 1985. Sister *Chimbote* (142, ex-*Rawhiti,* ex-LST 283, decommissioned 3-85, exists as a storage hulk. The ex-U.S. medium landing ships *Atico* (37, ex-LSM 554) and *Lomas* (36, ex-LSM 396) were decommissioned in 3-85.

HYDROGRAPHIC SURVEY SHIPS

◆ **1 oceanographic research and survey ship** Bldr: SIMA, Callao

	Laid down	L	In serv.
Humboldt	3-1-77	13-10-78	1980

D: 1,200 tons (1,980 fl) **S:** 14 kts **Dim:** 76.0 × 12.0 × 4.4
M: 2 diesels; 2 props; 3,000 hp **Man:** 48 tot.

◆ **1 ex-U.S. Sotoyomo-class former tug** Bldr: Levingston SB, Orange, Tex.

	Laid down	L	In serv.
136 Unanue (ex-*Wateree,* ATA 174)	5-10-43	18-11-43	20-7-44

D: 534 tons (835 fl) **S:** 13 kts **Dim:** 43.59 × 10.31 × 4.01
M: 2 G.M. 12-278A diesels, electric drive; 1 prop; 1,500 hp **Electric:** 120 kw

Remarks: Sold to Peru in 11-61. Refitted 1985 with reinforced bow, improved heating, for possible Antarctic expedition 1985-86.

◆ **2 Dutch Van Straelen-class inshore survey ships, former inshore minesweepers** Bldr: De Vries-Leutsch, Amsterdam

	Laid down	L	In serv.
AEH. . . Icaro (ex-*Van Hamel,* M 871)	27-4-59	28-5-60	14-10-60
AEH. . . Melo (ex-*Van der Wel,* M 878)	30-5-60	3-5-61	6-10-61

D: 151 tons (171 fl) **S:** 13 kts **Dim:** 33.08 (30.30 wl) × 6.88 × 1.80
Electron Equipt: Radar: 1/. . . nav.
M: 2 Werkspoor diesels; 2 props; 1,100 hp

Remarks: Purchased 23-2-84 for conversion in Peru to inshore survey duties. May have received interplot 200 survey system and new engines: 2 G.M. 16V92N diesels; 1,400 hp; wooden construction.

◆ **1 inshore survey craft** Bldr: SIMA, Chimbote (In serv. 1982)

AEH 174 N. . . . . . .

D: 49 tons **S:** 13 kts **Dim:** 19.8 × 5.2 × 0.9
M: Diesels **Man:** 3 crew, plus 2 scientists

Remarks: Has a side-looking sonar for bottom mapping to 1,200-m depths.

◆ **3 inshore survey craft** (In serv. 1943)

AEH 171 Cardenas (ex-YP 99) AEH 173 N. . . . . . . (ex-YP 243)
AEH 172 N. . . . . . . (ex-YP 242)

D: 50 tons (60 fl) **S:** 12 kts **Dim:** 22.9 × 5.2 × 1.5
M: 2 Superior diesels; 2 props; 320 hp **Fuel:** 3 tons **Man:** 11 tot.

Remarks: Ex-U.S. patrol craft, purchased in 11-58.

◆ **1 river research craft** (In serv. 5-76)

N. . . . . . . **Dim:** 23.5 × . . . × . . . **Man:** 16 tot.

Remarks: Operated on the Amazon by the Navy for the Oceanographic Institute.

REPLENISHMENT OILERS

◆ **1 Talara class** Bldr: SIMA, Callao

	Laid down	L	In serv.
152 Telara	1975	9-7-76	3-77

D: 30,000 tons (fl) **S:** 16.25 kts **Dim:** 171.18 (161.55 pp) × 25.38 × 9.53
M: 1 Burmeister & Wain 6K 47EF diesel; 1 prop; 11,600 hp
Electric: 1,890 kw

Remarks: 16,633 grt, 25,648 dwt. Cargo: 35,642 m³. Sisters *Trompeteros* and *Bayovar* (transferred 1979) are operated by Petroperu, the state fuel monopoly, which transferred this ship to the Navy upon completion. One underway fueling station per side.

◆ **2 Parinas class** Bldr: SIMA, Callao

	L	In serv.
155 Parinas	12-6-67	13-6-68
156 Pimental	5-4-68	27-6-69

Parinas (155) L. & L. Van Ginderen, 6-85

D: 13,600 tons (fl) **S:** 14.25 kts **Dim:** 134.19 (124.82 pp) × 18.98 × 7.27
M: 1 Burmeister & Wain 7-cyl. diesel; 1 prop; 4,900 hp **Electric:** 464 kw
Fuel: 610 tons

Remarks: 7,121 grt, 10,140 dwt. Cargo: 13,851 m³. Normally used by Petroperu for commercial purposes, but have naval crews and can refuel ships from one rig on either beam. No. 156 had her commercial certification withdrawn 19-6-77 pending repairs.

◆ **2 Sechura class** Bldr: SIMA, Callao

	Laid down	L	In serv.
158 Zorritos	8-10-55	8-10-58	1959
159 Lobitos	1964	5-65	1966

Zorritos (158) H. Ehlers, 9-85

REPLENISHMENT OILERS *(continued)*

D: 8,700 tons (fl) **S:** 12 kts **Dim:** 116.82 (109.73 pp) × 15.91 × 6.63
M: 1 Burmeister & Wain 562-VTF-115 diesel; 1 prop; 2,400 hp
Electric: 750 kw **Fuel:** 549 tons

REMARKS: 4,297 grt, 5,732 dwt. Cargo: 7,488 m³. Sister *Sechura,* built in England 1952-55 and fully equipped for underway replenishment, was stricken in 1968. Ncs. 158 and 159 are used for commercial cargoes for Petroperu, but have one fueling station on either beam.

CARGO SHIPS

◆ **1 Ilo-class transport** Bldr: SIMA, Callao

131 ILO

Ilo (131) P. Voss, 8-84

D: 18,400 tons (fl) **S:** 15.6 kts **Dim:** 153.85 (144.53 pp) × 20.4 × 9.2
M: 1 B & W 6K 47EF diesel; 1 prop; 11,600 hp **Electric:** 1,140 kw

REMARKS: In service 15-12-71. Cargo: 13,000 tons. Sister *Rimac* is in commercial service for the state shipping company. *Ilo* is also used to carry commercial cargo.

◆ **1 ex-U.S. Bellatrix-class attack cargo ship** Bldr: Tampa SB, Tampa, Fla.

	L	In serv.
31 INDEPENDENCIA (ex-*Bellatrix,* AKA 3, ex-*Raven,* AK 20)	16-4-41	16-2-42

Independencia (31) J.-C. Bellonne, 2-83

D: 6,200 tons (14,225 fl) **S:** 15 kts **Dim:** 140.0 × 19.2 × 7.95
A: 1/127-mm DP—4/76.2-mm 50-cal. DP (I × 4)—10/20-mm AA (I × 10)
Electron Equipt: Radar: 1/SPS-6, 1/Decca . . . , 1/Mk 26
M: 1 Nordberg TSM diesel; 1 prop; 6,000 hp **Range:** 18,000/14
Man: 19 officers, 220 men

REMARKS: Former U.S. C2-T-class-cargo ship. Refitted in 1954, and transferred under MAP in 20-7-63. Used for training midshipmen as well as for carrying military and commercial cargo (4,500 tons). Has one Mk 52 radar gunfire-control system and three Mk 51 gunfire-control systems. Normally carries two LCVP.

HOSPITAL SHIPS

◆ **3 Morona class** Bldr: SIMAI, Iquitos, 1976-77

302 MORONA . . . N. . . . . N. . . . . . .

D: 150 tons (fl) **S:** 12 kts **Dim:** 30.0 × 6.0 × 0.6 **M:** diesels; . . . hp

REMARKS: Serve on the upper Amazon River.

TUGS

◆ **1 ex-U.S. Cherokee-class ocean tug** Bldr: Cramp SB, Philadelphia, Pa.

	Laid down	L	In serv.
123 GUARDIAN RIOS (ex-*Pinto,* ATF 90)	10-8-42	5-1-43	1-4-43

D: 1,235 tons (1,675 fl) **S:** 16.5 kts **Dim:** 62.48 × 11.73 × 4.67
M: 4 G.M. 12-278 diesels, electric drive; 1 prop; 3,000 hp **Electric:** 260 kw
Man: 85 tot.

REMARKS: Transferred in 12-60. Unarmed. Used for salvage and rescue.

SERVICE CRAFT

◆ **2 Selendon-class harbor tugs** Bldr: Ruhrorter, Duisburg, W. Germany (In serv. 1967)

128 OLAYA 129 SELENDON

D: 80 grt **S:** 10 kts **Dim:** 61.3 × 20.3 × 2.3 **M:** 1 diesel; 1 prop; 600 hp

◆ **1 river tug** Bldr: SIMAI, Iquitos (In serv. 1973)

CONTRAESTRE NAVARRO

D: 50 tons

◆ **1 ex-U.S. medium harbor tug** Bldr: Ira S. Bushey, Brooklyn, NY (In serv. 1939)

124 FRANCO (ex-*Tigre,* ex-*Menewa,* YTM 2, ex-*Consultor,* YN 34)

D: 192 tons (fl) **S:** 9 kts **Dim:** 27.73 × 7.01 × 3.35
M: 1 diesel; 1 prop; 805 hp

REMARKS: Purchased 1940 by U.S. Navy for use as a net tender. Transferred in 14-3-47. Has push-bar built across bows for handling barges. Operates in the Upper Amazon Flotilla.

◆ **2 ex-U.S. 174-foot-class yard oilers**

	Bldr	Laid down	L	In serv.
. . . N. . . (ex-YO 221)	Jeffersonville Boat & Mach., Ind.	15-1-45	22-5-45	31-8-45
111 COLAYERAS (ex-YO 171)	RTC Shbldg., Camden, N.J.	18-3-44	20-7-44	15-11-44

D: 1,400 tons (fl) **S:** 10 kts **Dim:** 53.04 × 9.75 × 4.0
M: 2 diesels; 2 prop; 540 hp **Range:** 2,000/8 **Man:** 20 tot.

REMARKS: Ex-YO 221 transferred in 2-75; ex-YO 171 purchased 26-1-81. Cargo: approximately 900 tons (6,570 barrels).

◆ **2 ex-U.S. 174-foot water tankers**

	Bldr	Laid down	L	In serv.
110 MANTILLA (ex-YW 122)	Henry C. Grebe, Chicago, Ill.	29-6-45	22-9-45	17-11-45
. . . N. . . . . . . (ex-YW 128)	Leatham D. Smith, Wisc.	9-4-45	22-5-45	28-7-45

D: 440 tons (1,390 fl) **S:** 7 kts **Dim:** 53.04 × 9.75 × 4.0
M: 1 G.M. diesel; 1 prop; 640 hp **Fuel:** 25 tons **Man:** 23 tot.

REMARKS: No. 110 transferred in 3-63; ex-YW 128 purchased 26-1-81. Cargo: 930 tons.

◆ **2 river-service water tankers**

ABA 113 **D:** 330 tons Bldr: SIMAI, Iquitos (In serv. 1972)

ABA 091 Barge with 800-ton capacity Built: 1972

◆ **1 torpedo retriever** Bldr: Lürssen, Vegesack, W. Germany

ART 322 N. . . (In serv. 1-12-81)

ART 322 P. Voss, 9-81

D: 51.5 tons (65.5 fl) **S:** 19 kts **Dim:** 25.35 (23.47 pp) × 5.62 × 1.68
M: 2 MTU 8V 396 TC 82 diesels; 2 props; 1,590 hp **Range:** 500/15
Fuel: 14 tons **Man:** 9 tot.

REMARKS: Can stow 4 long or 8 short torpedoes on ramp aft.

◆ **1 floating dry dock** Bldr: West Germany (In serv. 1979)

AFD 109

Dim: 195.0 × 42.0 × . . . **Lift capacity:** 15,000 tons

REMARKS: Ordered 13-2-78; first unit lost en route Peru, 1978. Lift capacity can be increased to 18,000 tons by use of extension sections, bringing total length to 225 meters. A new 4,500-ton capacity dock is to be built by SIMA, Callao.

PERU *(continued)*
SERVICE CRAFT *(continued)*

◆ **1 ex-U.S. ARD 2-class floating dry dock** Bldr: Pacific Bridge, Alameda, Cal.

AFD 112 (WY 20, ex-ARD 8) (In serv. 8-43)

Dim: 148.03 × 21.64 × 1.6 (light) **Lift capacity:** 3,500 tons

REMARKS: In service in 1943. Transferred in 2-61; purchased outright 1981.

◆ **1 ex-U.S. AFDL 7-class floating dry dock** Bldr: Foundation Co., Kearny, N.J.

AFD 111 (ex-WY 19, ex-AFDL 33) (In serv. 10-44)

Dim: 87.78 × 19.51 × 0.99 (light) **Lift capacity:** 1,900 tons

REMARKS: In service in 10-44. Transferred in 7-59.

◆ **1 small floating dry dock** Bldr: Thornycroft, Southampton (In serv. 1951)

AFD 108

Dim: 59.13 × 18.7 × . . . **Lift capacity:** 600 tons

REMARKS: Serves the Amazon Flotilla.

◆ **1 ex-U.S. YR 24-class floating workshop** Bldr: DeKom SB, Brooklyn, NY

	Laid down	L	In serv.
RC 105 (ex-YR 59)	3-11-43	22-4-44	24-8-44

D: 520 tons (770 fl) **Dim:** 45.72 × 10.36 × 1.8 **Electric:** 220 kw
Fuel: 75 tons **Man:** 47 tot.

REMARKS: Transferred 8-8-61.

◆ **1 floating crane**

Capacity: 120 tons

REMARKS: Serves at Callao.

COAST GUARD

The Peruvian Coast Guard was established in 1975 and is intended to patrol to the extent of the 200-nautical-mile economic zone.

PATROL BOATS AND CRAFT

◆ **6 Rio Cañete class** Bldr: SIMA, Chimbote (PC 248: SIMA, Callao)

	In serv.		In serv.
PC 243 RIO NEPEÑA	1-12-81	PC 246 RIO HUARMEY	1982
PC 244 RIO TAMBO	1982	PC 247 RIO ZAÑA	12-2-85
PC 245 RIO OCOÑA	1982	PC 248 RIO CAÑETE (ex-8234)	31-3-76

Rio Ocoña (PC 245)—*Rio Tambo* (PC 244) in background U.S. Navy, 1984

D: 296 tons (fl) **S:** 22 kts **Dim:** 50.98 (49.1 pp) × 7.4 × 1.7
A: 1/40-mm AA—1/20-mm AA
M: 4 Bazán/MTU V8V 16/18 TLS diesels; 2 props; 5,640 hp **Electric:** 170 kw
Endurance: 20 days **Range:** 3,000/17 **Man:** 4 officers, 26 men

REMARKS: PC 248 (ex-234), launched 8-10-74 as prototype, has 4 MTU diesels and a 21-kt max. speed. All but PC 248 have steel hulls, aluminum superstructure.

◆ **2 ex-U.S. PGM 71 class**

	Bldr	In serv.
PC 222 RIO SAMA (ex-PGM 78)	Peterson, Sturgeon Bay, Wisc.	9-66
PC 223 RIO CHIRA (ex-PGM 11)	SIMA, Callao	6-72

D: 130 tons (145 fl) **S:** 17 kts **Dim:** 30.8 (30.2 wl) × 6.4 × 1.85
A: 1/40-mm AA—4/20-mm AA (II × 2)—2/12.7-mm mg (I × 2)
Electron Equipt: Radar: 1/Raytheon 1500 Pathfinder
M: 8 G.M. 6-71 diesels; 2 props; 2,200 hp **Range:** 1,000/12 **Man:** 27 tot.

REMARKS: Transferred to the Coast Guard in 1975. *Rio Chira* was built with U.S. aid and equipment.

◆ **4 110-foot class** Bldr: Vosper, Portsmouth

	L		L
PC 224 RIO CHICAWA (ex-*De Los Heroes*)	18-11-64	PC 227 RIO LOCUMBA (ex-*Sanchez Carrion*)	18-2-65
PC 225 RIO PATIVILCA (ex-*Herrera*)	26-10-64	PC 229 RIO VITOR (ex-*Velarde*)	10-7-64

D: 100 tons (130 fl) **S:** 30 kts **Dim:** 33.4 (31.46 wl) × 6.4 × 1.7
A: 2/20-mm AA **Electron Equipt:** Radar: 1/Decca TM 707
M: 2 Napier Deltic T38-37 diesels; 2 props; 6,280 hp
Range: 1,100/15 **Man:** 4 officers, 27 men

REMARKS: All delivered under own power by 10-65. Never fully equipped with armament, although fittings for four 533-mm torpedo tubes were installed in the decks. Air-conditioned. Steel hull, aluminum-alloy superstructure. Transferred to the Coast Guard in 1975 and renamed, their old names going to a new class of naval guided-missile corvettes. Sister *Rio Ica* (228, ex-*Sautillana*) stricken 1982 and *Rio Huaora* (PC 226, ex-*Larrea*) in 1983.

◆ **7 "Anchova" class** Bldr: MacLaren, Niteroi, Brazil (In serv. 1981-82)

PP 230 LA PUNTA, PP 231 CHILLON, PP 232 SANTA, PP 233 MAJES, PP 234 REQUE, PP 235 RIO VIRU, PP 236 RIO LURIN

D: 43 tons (fl) **S:** 25 kts **Dim:** 18.6 × 5.35 × 1.65
A: 2/20-mm AA **M:** 2 G.M. 12V71 TI diesels; 2 props; 1,800 hp

REMARKS: Wooden construction. Chile also operates units of this class.

◆ **3 Rio Zarumilla class** Bldr: Korody Marine, Viareggio, Italy (In serv. 5-9-60)

PC 240 RIO ZARUMILLA, PC 241 RIO TUMBES, PC 242 RIO PIURA

D: 37 tons (fl) **S:** 18 kts **Dim:** 20.0 × 5.2 × 1.1 **Range:** 1,000/14
A: 2/40-mm AA (I × 2) **M:** 2 G.M. 8V71 diesels; 2 props; 1,200 hp

◆ **2 Rio Ramis class**—on Lake Titicaca

PL 290 RIO RAMIS, PL 291 RIO ILAVE

D: 12–14 tons (fl) **S:** . . . **Dim:** . . . × . . . × . . .
A: 1/12.7-mm mg **M:** . . . **Man:** 4 tot.

◆ **3 patrol craft**—on Bolivian border

RIO MANU, RIO INAMBARI, RIO TAMBOPATA

◆ **1 small patrol craft:** RIO LAGATO

PHILIPPINES

PERSONNEL (1983): 1,605 officers, 13,067 enlisted, plus 389 officers and 8,840 enlisted Marines. (*Note:* The Marine Corps has been authorized to grow to 1,039 officers, 14,389 enlisted.)

MERCHANT MARINE (1984): 946 ships—3,441,076 grt
(tankers: 78 ships—867,814 grt)

NAVAL AVIATION: Ten Philippine-built Britten-Norman BN-2 Defender light maritime patrol aircraft and 10 MBB BO-105 helicopters are in service or on order. The Air Force purchased 3 Fokker F-27 Maritime patrol aircraft in 1981.

FUTURE PROGRAMS: In 6-83, plans were announced to acquire two 1,800–2,000-ton frigates using U.S. Foreign Military Sales credits, 50 fast patrol boats, and to establish a "Quick-Reaction Battalion" of 700 officers and men within the Marine Corps. There have been various reports of plans to acquire one or more submarines, possibly from France.

FRIGATES

◆ **1 ex-U.S. Savage class**

	Bldr	Laid down	L	In serv.
PS 4 RAJAH LAKANDULA (ex-*Tran Hung Dao*, ex-*Camp*, DER 251)	Brown SB, Houston	27-1-43	16-4-43	16-9-45

Rajah Lakandula (PS 4)—twin 40-mm AA now fwd of bridge 1977

FRIGATES *(continued)*

D: 1,590 tons (1,850 fl) **S:** 19 kts **Dim:** 93.27 × 11.15 × 4.27
A: 2/76.2-mm DP Mk 34 (I × 2)—2/40-mm AA (II × 1)—4/20-mm AA (II × 2)—1/81-mm mortar combined with 1/12.7-mm mg—2/12.7-mm mg—6/324-mm Mk 32 ASW TT (III × 2)
Electron Equipt: Radar: 1/SPS-10, 1/SPS-28, 1/Mk 34
Sonar: SQS-31
M: 4 Fairbanks-Morse 38D⅛ × 10 diesels; 2 props; 6,080 hp
Electric: 580 kw **Fuel:** 300 tons **Range:** 11,500/11 **Man:** 150 tot.

REMARKS: Transferred to Vietnam 6-1-71; to the Philippines, 5-4-75. Converted to radar picket in the late 1950s, but most electronic warfare gear and ASW ordnance was removed in 1971. Has one Mk 63 and one Mk 51 gunfire-control system.

◆ **4 ex-U.S. Barnegat-class former seaplane tenders** Bldr: Lake Washington SY, Houghton, Wash.

	Laid down	L	In serv.
PS 7 ANDRES BONIFACIO (ex-*Ly Thoung Kiet,* ex-*Chincoteague,* WHEC 375, ex-AVP 24)	23-7-41	15-4-42	12-4-43
PS 8 GREGORIO DE PILAR (ex-*Ngo Kuyen,* ex-*McCulloch,* WHEC 386, ex-*Wachapreague,* AGP 8, ex-AVP 56)	1-2-43	10-7-43	17-5-44
PS 9 DIEGO SILANG (ex-*Tran Quang Khai,* ex-*Bering Strait,* WHEC 382, ex-AVP 34)	7-6-43	15-1-44	19-7-44
PS 10 FRANCISCO DAGAHOY (ex-*Tran Binh Trong,* ex-*Castle Rock,* WHEC 383, ex-AVP 35)	12-7-43	11-3-44	8-10-44

Andres Bonifacio (PS 7)—prior to alterations 1977

D: 1,766 tons (2,800 fl) **S:** 17 kts **Dim:** 95.72 (91.44 wl) × 12.55 × 4.27
A: 1/127-mm DP—4/40-mm AA (II × 1, I × 2)—2/20-mm AA (I × 2)—2/12.7-mm mg—1/Bo-105 helicopter
Electron Equipt: Radar: 1/SPS-53, 1/SPS-29, 1/Mk 26
M: 4 Fairbanks-Morse 38D8⅛ × 10 diesels; 2 props; 6,080 hp
Electric: 600 kw **Fuel:** 400 tons **Range:** 18,000/15 **Man:** 160 tot.

REMARKS: Transferred to U.S. Coast Guard in 1946-48, PS 8 having served as a motor-torpedo-boat tender and the others as seaplane tenders. Transferred to South Vietnam in 1971-72 after extensive overhauls. Escaped from Vietnam 4-75 to Philippines, to which they were formally sold 5-4-76. Two other escapees, ex-*Yakutat* (WHEC 380) and *Cook Inlet* (WHEC 383) were in too poor condition to refit and have been used for cannibalization spares. All received helicopter decks at the 01 level aft in 1978-79; a twin 40-mm mount was added in a tub projecting over the stern, adding 1 meter to the original length. Have Mk 52 GFCS with Mk 26 radar for the 127-mm gun. Two are to be further modernized, with U.S. Harpoon SSM to be added, under the 1985 Budget.

◆ **2 ex-U.S. Cannon class** Bldr: Federal SB & DD Co., Newark, N.J.

	Laid down	L	In serv.
PF 5 DATU SIKATUNA (ex-*Asahi,* ex-*Amick,* DE 168)	30-11-42	27-5-43	26-7-43
PF 6 RAJAH HUMABON (ex-*Hatsuhi,* ex-*Atherton,* DE 169)	14-1-43	27-5-43	29-8-43

D: 1,240 tons (1,620 fl) **S:** 20 kts **Dim:** 93.27 (91.44 wl) × 11.15 × 3.56 (hull)
A: 3/76-mm DP (I × 3)—6/40-mm AA (II × 3)—12/20-mm AA (II × 6)—2/12.7-mm mg (I × 2)—6/Mk 6 d.c. projectors—1/Hedgehog—1/d.c. rack
Electron Equipt: Radar: 1/navigational, 1/Mk 26
Sonar: SQS-17B
M: 4 G.M. 16-278A diesels, electric drive; 2 props; 6,000 hp
Electric: 680 kw **Fuel:** 260 tons **Range:** 11,600/11
Man: 165 tot.

REMARKS: Transferred to Japan on 14-6-55 and stricken 6-75, reverting to U.S. ownership; they were sold to the Philippines 23-12-78 but remained laid up in Japan until towed to South Korea for overhaul in 1979. Both recommissioned 27-2-80. Have one Mk 52 radar GFCS and one Mk 41 range finder for 76.2-mm gun control, plus three Mk 51 Mod. 2 GFCS for the 40-mm guns. Sister *Datu Kalantiaw* (PS 76, ex-*Booth,* DE 170) was grounded in a typhoon 21-9-81 and lost.

CORVETTES

◆ **2 ex-U.S. Auk-class former minesweepers**

	Bldr	Laid down	L	In serv.
PS 69 RIZAL (ex-*Murrelet,* MSF 372)	Savannah Mach. & Foundry, Ga.	24-8-44	29-12-44	21-8-45
PS 70 QUEZON (ex-*Vigilance,* MSF 324)	Associated SB, Seattle, Wash.	28-11-42	5-4-43	28-2-44

Rizal (PS 69)—prior to addition of helicopter deck L. & L. Van Ginderen, 5-65

D: 890 tons (1,250 fl) **S:** 18 kts **Dim:** 67.39 (65.53 wl) × 9.8 × 3.28
A: 1/76.2-mm DP—4/40-mm AA (II × 2)—4/20-mm AA (II × 2)—3/324-mm Mk 32 ASW TT (III × 2)—1/Hedgehog—2/Mk 6 d.c. throwers—2/d.c. racks
Electron Equipt: Radar: 1/SPS-5C
Sonar: SQS-17B
M: 2 G.M. 12-278 (PS 70: 12-278A) diesels, electric drive; 2 props; 3,532 hp
Electric: 360 kw **Fuel:** 216 tons **Man:** 100 tot.

REMARKS: PS 69 transferred 18-6-65, PS 70 on 19-8-67. A small raised helicopter deck has replaced the after 76.2-mm gun.

◆ **7 ex-U.S. PCE 821 and PCER 848 classes**

	Bldr	Laid down	L	In serv.
PS 19 MIGUEL MALVAR (ex-*Ngoc Hoi,* ex-*Brattleboro,* EPCER 852)	A	28-10-43	1-3-44	26-5-44
PS 22 SULTAN KUDARAT (ex-*Dong Da II,* ex-*Crestview,* PCE 895)	B	2-12-42	18-5-43	30-10-44
PS 23 DATU MARIKUDO (ex-*Van Kiep II,* ex-*Amherst,* PCER 853)	A	16-11-43	18-3-44	16-6-44
PS 28 CEBU (ex-PCE 881)	C	11-8-43	10-11-43	31-7-44
PS 29 NEGROS OCCIDENTAL (ex-PCE 885)	C	25-2-44	20-6-44	30-4-45
PS 31 PANGASINAN (ex-PCE 891)	B	28-10-42	24-4-43	15-6-44
PS 32 ILOILO (ex-PCE 897)	B	16-12-42	3-8-43	6-1-45

Bldrs: *A*: Pullman Standard Car Co., Chicago; *B*: Willamette Iron & Steel Corp., Portland, Ore.; *C*: Albina Eng. & Machine Works, Portland, Ore.

D: 903 tons (fl) **S:** 15 kts **Dim:** 56.24 (54.86 wl) × 10.08 × 2.87
A: PS 19-23: 1/76.2-mm DP—2/40-mm AA (I × 2)—8/20-mm AA (II × 1)
PS 28-32: 1/76.2-mm DP—6/40-mm AA (II × 3)—4/20-mm AA (I × 4)
Electron Equipt: Radar: 1/RCA CR 104A
M: 2 G.M. 12-278A diesels; 2 props; 2,000 hp (PS 19, 28, 31: 2 G.M. 12-567A diesels; 2 props; 1,800 hp)
Electric: 240-180 kw **Fuel:** 125 tons **Range:** 9,000/10 **Man:** 100 tot.

REMARKS: PS 28 through PS 32 were transferred 7-48; a fifth, *Leyte* (PS 30, ex-PCE 885), was lost by grounding in 1979. PS 19 through 23 were transferred to South Vietnam on 11-7-66, 29-11-61, and 6-70, and escaped Vietnam in 5-75; they were sold to the Philippines 11-75 (PS 23: 5-4-76). All ASW equipment is now deleted from all units. Ex-PCER and EPCER originally had longer forecastles as rescue ships; they were brought to standard PCE configuration before transfer to South Vietnam. All generally resemble *Magat Salamat,* below.

◆ **1 ex-U.S. Admirable-class former minesweeper** Bldr: Winslow Marine Railway, Seattle, Wash.

	Laid down	L	In serv.
PS 20 MAGAT SALAMAT (ex-*Chi Lang II,* ex-*Gayety,* MSF 239)	14-11-43	19-3-44	23-9-45

D: 650 tons light (905 fl) **S:** 14 kts **Dim:** 56.24 (54.86 wl) × 10.06 × 2.75
A: 1/76.2-mm DP—2/40-mm (I × 2)—8/20-mm AA (II × 4)

CORVETTES *(continued)*

Magat Salamat (PS 20) 1977

Electron Equipt: Radar: 1/RCA CR 104A **Electric:** 280 kw **Fuel:** 140 tons
M: 2 Cooper-Bessemer GSB-8 diesels; 2 props; 1,710 hp

REMARKS: Transferred to Vietnam and escaped to the Philippines 4-75. Acquired by the latter in 11-75.

NOTE: The three South Korean Leopard-class guided-missile patrol boats reported ordered 1980 in the last edition were not, in fact, acquired.

PATROL BOATS

◆ 2 ex-U.S. PC 461-class former submarine chasers

	Bldr	Laid down	L	In serv.
PS 29 NEGROS ORIENTAL ex-E 312, ex-*L'Inconstant*, ex-PC 1171)	L.D. Smith, Sturgeon Bay, Wis.	12-3-43	15-5-43	24-9-43
PS 80 NUEVA VISCAYA (ex-USAF *Altus*, ex-PC 568)	Brown SB, Houston, Tex.	15-9-41	25-4-42	13-7-42

D: 280 tons (450 fl) **S:** 18 kts **Dim:** 52.93 × 7.01 × 2.31 (hull)
A: 1/76.2-mm DP—1/40-mm AA—3 or 5/20-mm AA (I × 3 or 5)
M: 2 G.M. 16-278A diesels; 2 props; 2,880 hp
Electric: 120 kw **Fuel:** 62 tons **Man:** 70 tot.

REMARKS: PS 29 escaped from Cambodia to the Philippines and was acquired by the latter in 1976; she had previously been transferred to France in 1951, then to Cambodia in 1956. PS 80 served the U.S. Air Force 1963-68, transferring to the Philippines in 3-68. Both originally had different diesels, but now have been standardized.

◆ 6 Katapangan class

	Bldr:	In serv.
P 101 KAGITINGAN	W. Müller, Hameln, West Germ.	9-2-79
P 102 BAGONG LAKAS	W. Müller, Hameln, West Germ.	9-2-79
P 103 KATAPANGAN	Cavite NSY	1982
P 104 BAGONG SILANG	Cavite NSY	1982
P 105 GENERAL AMILIO AGUINALDO	Cavite NSY	1984
P 106 N. . .	Cavite NSY	. . .

D: 132 tons (150 fl) **S:** 16 kts **Dim:** 37.0 × 6.2 × 1.7
A: 4/30-mm AA Emerlec (II × 2)—2/12.7-mm mg (I × 2)
M: 2 MTU MB 820 Db1 diesels; 2 props; 2,050 hp

REMARKS: Designed in West Germany. Prototype delivered for trials 11-10-78. Program to build more at Boseco, Bekan, abandoned due to poor performance; intended to reach 28 kts, but obviously underpowereed. P 105, launched 23-6-84, was described as a "missile boat."

◆ 1 ex-U.S. PGM 71 class   Bldr: Peterson Builders, Sturgeon Bay, Wis.

PG 60 BASILAN (ex-*Hon Troc,* ex-PGM 83)

D: 130 tons (145 fl) **S:** 17 kts **Dim:** 30.8 (30.2 wl) × 6.4 × 1.85
A: 1/40-mm AA—4/20-mm AA (II × 2)—4/12.7-mm mg (III × 2)
Electron Equipt: Radar: 1/Raytheon 1500B
M: 8 G.M. 6-71 diesels; 2 props; 2,200 hp **Range:** 1,000/12 **Man:** 27 tot.

REMARKS: In service 4-67. Escaped from Vietnam 4-75, the only one of her class to do so out of 20 transferred; acquired officially by the Philippines 12-76.

◆ 4 ex-U.S. PGM 39 class   Bldr: Tacoma Boat, Tacoma, Wash.

	In serv.
PG 61 AGUSAN (ex-PGM 39)	3-60
PG 62 CATANDUANES (ex-PGM 40)	3-60
PG 63 ROMBLON (ex-PGM 1)	6-60
PG 64 PALAWAN (ex-PGM 42)	6-60

D: 122 tons **S:** 17 kts **Dim:** 30.6 × 6.4 × 2.1 (props)
A: 2/20-mm AA (I × 2) **Electron Equipt:** Radar: 1/Raytheon 1500
M: 2 MTU MB 820 diesels; 2 props; 1,900 hp
Man: 15 tot.

AMPHIBIOUS WARFARE SHIPS

◆ 20 ex-U.S. LST 1 and LST 542-class landing ships

	Bldr	In serv.
LT 54 AGUSAN DEL SUR (ex-*Nha Trang,* ex-*Jerome Cty.*, LST 848)	A	20-1-45
LT 86 CAGAYAN (ex-*Hickman Cty.*, LST 825)	C	8-12-44
LT 87 COTABATO DEL SUR (ex-*Thi Nai,* ex-*Cayuga Cty.*, LST 529)	D	29-2-44
LT 93 MINDORO OCCIDENTAL (ex-T-LST 222)	B	10-9-43
LT 94 SURIGAO DEL NORTE (ex-T-LST 488)	E	24-5-43
LT 95 SURIGAO DEL SUR (ex-T-LST 546)	C	27-3-44
LT 97 ILOCOS NORTE (ex-*Madera Cty.*, LST 905)	F	20-1-45
LT 500 TARLAC (ex-T-LST 47)	F	8-11-43
LT 501 LAGUNA (ex-T-LST 230)	B	3-11-43
LT 502 SAMAR ORIENTAL (ex-T-LST 287)	A	15-12-43
LT 503 LANAO DEL SUR (ex-T-LST 491)	C	3-12-43
LT 504 LANAO DEL NORTE (ex-T-LST 566)	C	29-5-44
LT 505 LEYTE DEL SUR (ex-T-LST 607)	B	24-4-44
LT 506 DAVAO ORIENTAL (ex-*Oosumi,* ex-*Daggett Cty.*, LST 689)	D	2-5-44
LT 507 BENGUET (ex-*Davies Cty.*, T-LST 692)	D	10-5-44
LT 508 AURORA (ex-*Harris Cty.*, T-LST 822)	C	23-11-44
LT 509 CAVITE (ex-*Shimokita,* ex-*Hillsdale Cty.*, LST 835)	A	20-11-44
LT 510 SAMAR DEL NORTE (ex-*Shiretoko,* ex-*Nansemond Cty.*, LST 1064)	G	12-3-45
LT 511 COTABATO DEL NORTE (ex-*Orleans Parrish,* T-LST 1069, ex-MSC 6, ex-LST 1069)	G	31-3-45
LT 512 TAWI-TAWI (ex-T-LST 1072)	G	12-4-45

Bldrs: *A*, American Bridge, Ambridge, Pa.; *B*, Chicago Bridge & Iron Co., Seneca, Ill.; *C*, Missouri Valley Bridge & Iron Co., Evansville, Ind.; *D*, Jeffersonville Boat and Machinery Co., Jeffersonville, Ind.; *E*, Kaiser Co., Richmond, Cal.; *F*, Dravo Corp., Pittsburgh, Pa.; *G*, Bethlehem Steel, Hingham, Mass.

Surigao del Sur (LT 95) G. Arra

D: 1,620 tons (4,080 fl) **S:** 11 kts **Dim:** 99.98 (96.32 wl) × 15.24 × 4.29
A: 7-8/40-mm AA (II × 1 or 2, I × 4-6)—2-4/20-mm AA (ex-T-LST: 6/20-mm AA)
M: 2 G.M. 12-567A diesels (LT 510, 511, 512: 2 G.M. 12-278A); 2 props; 1,700 hp
Electric: 300 kw **Fuel:** 570 tons **Man:** 60-100 tot.

REMARKS: LT 54 and LT 87 escaped from Vietnam (to which they had been transferred in 4-70 and 12-63, respectively) in 4-75; they were officially transferred to the Philippines on 17-11-75. LT 86 and LT 97 were transferred in 11-69. LT 93, LT 94, and LT 95 were transferred unarmed in 7-72 but may since have received guns. LT 500–LT 505, LT 507, LT 508, LT 511, and LT 512 were purchased in 1976, having previously been stricken by the USN and laid up in Japan. LT 506, LT 509, and LT 510 had been transferred to Japan 4-61 and stricken in 1975; they were purchased in 1978. All the LT 500 series were refitted and thoroughly overhauled in Japan, recommissioning in 1978-79. Armament: Some ex-T-LSTs carry only four 20-mm AA (I × 4), while others received a single 40-mm forward after transfer, plus several 20-mm AA. LT 87 has four sets of Welin davits for LCVP landing craft, the others only two; some ex-T-LSTs do not carry LCVPs.

◆ 4 ex-U.S. LSM 1-class landing ships

	Bldr	L	In serv.
LP 41 ISABELA (ex-LSM 463)	Brown SB, Houston	3-2-45	7-3-45
LP 65 BATANES (ex-*Huong Giang,* ex-*Oceanside,* ex-LSM 175)	Charleston Naval SY	3-8-44	25-9-44
LP 66 WESTERN SAMAR (ex-*Hat Giang,* ex-9011, ex-LSM 335)	Pullman, Chicago	10-11-44	9-12-44
LP 68 MINDORO ORIENTAL (ex-LSM 320)	Pullman, Chicago	20-7-44	19-8-44

D: 513 tons (1,095 fl) **S:** 12 kts **Dim:** 620.2 × 10.52 × 12.24
A: 2/40-mm AA (II × 1)—4/20-mm AA (I × 4)
M: 2 G.M. 16-278A (LP 41: Fairbanks-Morse 38D8⅛ × 10) diesels; 2 props; 2,800 hp
Electric: 240 kw **Fuel:** 165 tons **Range:** 5,000/7
Man: 39 tot.

REMARKS: LP 41 transferred 3-61, LP 68 in 4-62. LP 65 and LP 66 escaped from Vietnam (to which they had been transferred in 8-61 and 10-55, respectively, LP 65 having served in the French Navy from 1-54 to 10-55) in 4-75 and were officially transferred on 17-11-75. LP 66 was equipped with hospital facilities in a deckhouse filling much of her tank deck while in Vietnamese service, but retained guns. Ex-*Han Giang,* ex-LSM 110, which also escaped, was transferred also on 17-11-75, but was used for cannibalization.

AMPHIBIOUS WARFARE SHIPS *(continued)*

◆ **3 ex-U.S. LSSL 1-class gunfire-support landing ships**

Bldr: Lawley & Sons, Neponset, Mass. (LS 49: Albina Eng. & Mach., Portland, Ore.)

	L	In serv.
LF 48 Camarines Sur (ex-*Nguyen Duc Bong,* ex-LSSL 129)	13-12-44	31-12-44
LF 49 Sulu (ex-*Nguyen Ngoc Long,* ex-LSSL 96)	6-1-45	24-1-45
LF 50 La Union (ex-*Doan Ngoc Tang,* ex-*Hallebarde,* ex-LSSL 9)	17-8-44	6-9-44

D: 250 tons (387 fl) **S:** 14.4 kts **Dim:** 48.15 × 7.21 × 1.73
A: 1/76-mm DP—4/20-mm AA (II × 2)—4/12.7-mm mg (I × 4)
M: 8 G.M. 6-71 diesels; 2 CP props; 1,320 hp
Electric: 120 kw **Fuel:** 84 tons
Range: 5,000/12

Remarks: These are ex-Vietnamese ships (transferred 1965-66) that took refuge in the Philippines and were acquired by the latter 17-11-75. LF 50 had earlier served in the French (1951-55) and Japanese (1956-64) navies. Four additional ex-Japanese sisters were to have been transferred in 1978, but the sale was canceled.

◆ **3 ex-U.S. LCU 1466-class utility landing craft** Bldr: Japan (In serv. 3-55)

L. . . N. . . . . . . (ex-LCU 2002, ex-LCU 1603)
L. . . N. . . . . . . (ex-LCU 2003, ex-LCU 1604)
L. . . N. . . . . . . (ex-LCU 2005, ex-LCU 1606)

D: 180 tons (347 fl) **S:** 8 kts **Dim:** 35.05 × 10.36 × 1.6 (aft)
A: 2/20-mm AA (I × 2) **M:** 3 G.M. Gray Marine 64YTL diesels; 3 props; 675 hp
Cargo capacity: 167 tons **Man:** 6 men plus 8 troops

Remarks: Built in Japan under the Offshore Procurement Plan; in service 3-55, stricken 1975. Purchased 17-11-75 while laid up, then refitted and recommissioned in 1979.

◆ **9 U.S. LCM(8)-class landing craft**

LCM 257 LCM 258 LCM 260-LCM 266

D: 118 tons (fl) **S:** 9 kts **Dim:** 22.43 × 6.42 × 1.4 (aft)
M: 4 G.M. 6-71 diesels; 2 props; 600 hp **Cargo capacity:** 54 tons

Remarks: Transferred 19-3-75. The similar *Bagong Filipino* (TK 81) and *Dakila* (TK 82), built in the Philippines, have been stricken.

◆ **75 ex-U.S. LCM(6)-class landing craft** (Transferred 1955-75)

D: 56 tons (fl) **S:** 10 kts **Dim:** 17.1 × 4.4 × 1.2 (aft)
M: 2 G.M. Gray Marine 64HN9 diesels; 2 props; 330 hp **Cargo capacity:** 30 tons

◆ **1 (+ . . .) Imelda-class LCVP** Bldr: Navy Yd, Cavite (In serv. 7-85)

D: 8 tons **S:** 13 kts **Dim:** 11.0 × 3.6 × 0.76
M: 1 G.M. 6-71 diesel; 1 prop; 225 hp

Remarks: Glass-reinforced plastic trimaran prototype.

AUXILIARY SHIPS

YACHTS

◆ **1 presidential yacht** Bldr: Vosper, Singapore (In serv. 12-77)

TP 77 Ang Pinuno

D: 150 tons **S:** 28.5 kts **Dim:** 37.9 × 7.2 × 3.8 **Range:** . . . **Man:** . . .
A: None **M:** 3 MTU 12V538 TB91 diesels; 3 props; 7,500 hp

Remarks: Used as a "command ship" for the president. White-painted. Sister *Bataan* is used as a search-and-rescue ship by the Coast Guard.

◆ **1 former transport** Bldr: Ishikawajima, Harima, Japan (In serv. 1959)

TP 777 Ang Pangulo (ex-*The President,* ex-*Roxas,* ex-*Lapu-Lapu*)

Ang Pangulo (TP 777) L. & L. Van Ginderen, 1980

D: 2,230 tons (2,750 fl) **S:** 18 kts **Dim:** 83.84 × 13.01 × 6.4
A: 2/20-mm AA
M: 2 Mitsui-Burmeister & Wain DE 642 VBF 75 diesels; 2 props; 5,000 hp
Electric: 820 kw **Man:** 81 men plus 48 passengers

Remarks: Built as war reparations. Can be converted for use as a troop transport.

TENDERS

◆ **3 ex-U.S. Achelous-class repair ships** Bldr: Chicago Bridge & Iron Co., Seneca, Ill. (AR 67: Bethlehem Steel, Hingham, Mass.)

	L	In serv.
AE 517 Yakal (ex-*Satyr,* ARL 23, ex-LST 852)	13-11-44	24-11-44
AR 67 Kamagong (ex-*Aklan,* ex-*Romulus,* ARL 22, ex-LST 926)	15-11-44	9-12-44
AR 88 Narra (ex-*Krishna,* ARL 38, ex-LST 1149)	25-5-45	3-12-45

D: 3,960 tons (fl) **S:** 11.6 kts **Dim:** 99.98 (96.32 wl) × 15.24 × 3.71
A: 8/40-mm AA (IV × 2)
M: 2 G.M. 12-567A diesels; (AR 67: G.M. 12-278A); 2 props; 1,800 hp
Electric: 420 kw **Fuel:** 620 tons **Man:** 250 tot.

Remarks: AE 517, transferred 24-1-77, may be in use as an ammunition transport, based on the hull number, but was equipped for repair duties on delivery. AR 67 was transferred in 11-61 and AR 88 on 31-10-71. All have a 60-ton capacity A-frame lift boom to port and one 10-ton derrick and one 20-ton derrick.

◆ **2 ex-U.S. LST 542-class small craft tenders**

	Bldr	In serv.
AL 57 Sierra Madre (ex-*Dumagat,* ex-*My Tho,* ex-*Harnett County,* AGP 821, ex-LST 821)	Missouri Valley B & I, Evansville, Ind.	14-11-44
AE 516 Apayao (ex-*Can Tho,* ex-*Garrett County,* AGP 786, ex-LST 786)	Dravo Corp., Pittsburgh, Pa.	28-8-44

D: 1,620 tons (4,080 fl) **S:** 11.6 kts
Dim: 99.98 (96.32 wl) × 15.24 × 4.29 (max.)
A: 8/40-mm AA (II × 2, I × 4)—4/20-mm AA (II × 2)
M: 2 G.M. 12-567A diesels; 2 props; 1,700 hp **Electric:** 500 kw
Fuel: 370 tons **Range:** 19,000/10 **Man:** 160 tot.

Remarks: Converted in the mid-1960s to act as tenders to riverine-warfare craft. Retain bow doors, but much of the tank deck is filled with repair ships and bins for spare parts. Helicopter deck amidships, tripod masts, 10-ton derrick, and enlarged hatch. Transferred to South Vietnam 10-70 and 4-71; both escaped 4-75 and purchased outright on 13-9-77. Different hull numbers (and change of letter-designator and name to AL 57 from AE 57) may indicate new roles.

CARGO TRANSPORTS

◆ **1 ex-U.S Alamosa class** Bldr: Froemming Bros. Inc., Milwaukee, Wis.

TK 90 Mactan (ex-*Kukui,* WAK 186, ex-*Colquitt,* AK 174)

Mactan (TK 90)—with LCM(6) on deck R.A.N. 6-82

D: 4,900 tons (7,450 fl) **S:** 12 kts
Dim: 103.18 (97.54 wl) × 15.24 × 6.43
A: 2/20-mm AA **M:** 1 Nordberg TSM6 diesel; 1 prop; 1,750 hp
Electric: 500 kw **Fuel:** 350 tons **Man:** 85 tot.

Remarks: In service 22-9-45; 6,071 dwt. Built for U.S. Maritime Commission, taken over by the Navy upon completion, then transferred to the U.S. Coast Guard 24-9-45. First platform deck in cargo-hold area converted to personnel accommodations. Transferred to the Philippines 1-3-72 and used as a military transport, supply ship, and lighthouse tender. Purchased outright 1-8-80.

CARGO TRANSPORTS *(continued)*

◆ **3 ex-U.S. Army FS 381 class** Bldr: Ingalls, Pascagoula, Miss. (In serv. 1943-44)

TK 79 Limasawa (ex-*Nettle,* WAK 129, ex-FS 169)
AS 59 Badjao (ex-*Miho,* ex-FS 524)
AS 71 Mangyan (ex-*Nasami,* ex-FS 408)

D: 473 tons light (950 fl) **S:** 13 kts **Dim:** 53.8 (50.27 pp) × 9.75 × 3.05
A: 2/20-mm AA (I × 2) **M:** 2 G.M. 6-278A diesels; 2 props; 1,000 hp
Electric: 225 kw **Cargo capacity:** 345 tons
Fuel: 67 tons **Range:** 4,150/10, 3,700/11 **Man:** . . .

Remarks: *Limasawa* was loaned in 1-68 and purchased outright 31-8-78. The other two were purchased 24-9-76 after having served in the Japanese Navy as an inshore minesweeper depot ship and a mine-countermeasures support ship; they were to be refitted and were recommissioned during 1979. All were to serve as buoy tenders and lighthouse supply ships.

◆ **2 ex-U.S. Army FS 330 class** Bldr: Higgins, Inc., New Orleans (In serv. 1943-44)

TK 45 Lauis Ledge (ex-FS 185) TK 46 Cape Bojeador (ex-FS 203)

Cape Bojeador (TK 46)—in Coast Guard colors G. Arra, 1977

D: 420 tons light (742 fl) **S:** 10 kts **Dim:** 51.77 (48.77 pp) × 9.75 × 2.43
A: 2/20-mm AA (I × 2)
M: 4 Buda-Lanova 6 DHMR-1879 diesels; 2 props; 680 hp
Electric: 225 kw **Fuel:** 18 tons **Range:** 1,370/10 **Man:** . . .

Remarks: TK 45 transferred 11-47; TK 46 transferred 2-50. Can carry up to 50 tons of fuel for a range of 3,830/10. Used as navigational buoy tenders and lighthouse supply ships. Cargo capacity: 150 tons.

◆ **1 ex-Australian motor stores lighter** Bldr: Australia (In serv. 1944)

TK. . . Pearl Bank (ex-U.S. Army LO 4, ex-. . .)

D: 140 tons light (345 fl) **S:** 8 kts **Dim:** 37.26 × 7.47 × 2.07
A: 2/20-mm AA **M:** 2 Fairbanks-Morse 35F8¾ diesels; 2 props; 240 hp
Fuel: 20 tons **Range:** 2,000/6 **Man:** 35 tot.

Remarks: Transferred 1947. Used as a navigational buoy tender and lighthouse supply ship. Cargo capacity: 170 tons

◆ **1 ex-U.S. Admirable-class minesweeper** Bldr: Gulf SB Corp., Madisonville, La.

	Laid down	L	In serv.
TK 21 Mount Samat (ex-*Pagasa,* ex-*Santa Maria,* ex-*Quest,* MSF 281)	24-11-43	16-3-44	25-10-44

Mount Samat (TK 21) G. Arra, 1977

D: 650 tons (945 fl) **S:** 14.8 kts **Dim:** 58.0 (54.86 wl) × 10.06 × 2.97
A: 2/20-mm AA **M:** 2 Cooper-Bessemer GSB-8 diesels; 2 props; 1,710 hp
Electric: 280 kw **Fuel:** 138 tons **Man:** 60 tot.

Remarks: Transferred 2-7-48 and then converted to presidential yacht with considerable additions to superstructure and increased rake to bow. Now primarily used as a lighthouse supply ship. Has 2 navigational radars.

◆ **1 ex-U.S. Coast Guard Balsam-class buoy tender** Bldr: Marine Iron & SB Corp., Duluth, Minn. (In serv. 2-5-44)

TK 89 Kalinga (ex-*Redbud,* WAGL 398, ex-T-AKL 398, ex-AG 398)

Kalinga (TK 89)—in Coast Guard colors 1977

D: 935 tons (1,020 fl) **S:** 13 kts **Dim:** 54.86 × 11.28 × 3.96 **A:** 1/20-mm AA
M: 2 Cooper-Bessemer GSD-8 diesels; electric drive; 1 prop; 1,200 hp
Range: 3,500/7.5 **Man:** 50 tot.

Remarks: Built for U.S. Coast Guard, transferred to the U.S. Navy on 25-3-49 as AG 398, to Military Sealift Command on 10-49 as T-AKL 398, and returned 20-11-70 to the U.S. Coast Guard. Transferred to the Philippines 1-3-72. Has helicopter platform and ice-breaking bow—the latter a useful feature in Philippine waters.

SERVICE CRAFT

TANKERS

◆ **2 ex-U.S. 174-foot YO and YOG-class small tankers** Bldr: R.T.C. SB, Camden, N.J. (YO 78: Puget Sound Naval SY, Washington)

	Laid down	L	In serv.
YO 43 Lake Naujan (ex-YO 173)	17-5-44	30-9-44	22-1-45
YO 78 Lake Buhi (ex-YOG 73)	15-12-43	23-2-44	28-11-44

Lake Naujan (YO 43) G. Arra, 1977

D: 445 tons light (1,420 fl) **S:** 8 kts **Dim:** 53.04 × 10.01 × 4.27
A: 2/20-mm AA (I × 2) **Fuel:** 25 tons **Man:** 23 tot.
M: 2 Union diesels; 2 props; 560 hp (YO 78: 2 G.M. 8-278A diesels; 2 props; 640 hp)

Remarks: YO 43 was transferred in 7-48, and YO 78 (formerly used as a gasoline tanker in 7-67. Ex-U.S. YOG 33 and YOG 80, which escaped from Vietnam, were used for cannibalization spares. Cargo capacity: 985 tons. Sister *Lake Mainit* (YO 35) stricken 1979.

◆ **3 ex-U.S. 174-foot YW-class water tankers** Bldr: L. D. Smith SB, Sturgeon Bay, Wis. (YW 111: Marine Iron & SB Co., Duluth, Minn.)

	Laid down	L	In serv.
YW 33 Lake Boluan (ex-YW 111)	30-9-44	16-12-44	1-8-45
YW 34 Lake Paoay (ex-YW 130)	14-5-45	24-6-45	28-8-45
YW 42 Lake Lanao (ex-YW 125)	18-12-44	7-4-45	16-6-45

D: 440 tons light (1,390 fl) **S:** 8 kts **Dim:** 53.04 × 10.01 × 4.0
A: 2/20-mm AA (I × 2) **M:** 2 G.M. 8-278A diesels; 2 props; 640 hp
Electric: 80 kw **Fuel:** 25 tons **Man:** 23 tot.

Remarks: Transferred YW 33 and YW 34 on 16-7-75 and YW 42 in 7-78. Cargo capacity: 930 tons.

TUGS

◆ **1 ex-U.S. Army tug**

YQ 58 Tiboli (ex-LT 1976)

Remarks: Transferred, 3-76.

◆ **5 ex-U.S. YTL 442 class** Bldr: Everett-Pacific Co., Everett, Wash. (YQ 222: Winslow Marine Railway & SB, Winslow, Wash.)

YQ 222 Igorot (ex-YTL 572)	YQ 226 Tasaday (ex-YTL 425)
YQ 223 Tagbanua (ex-YTL 429)	YQ 271 Agno River (ex-YAS 3, ex-YTL 750)
YQ 225 Ilongot (ex-YTL 427)	

D: 70 tons (80 fl) **S:** 9 kts **Dim:** 20.17 × 5.18 × 1.5
M: 1 Hamilton 685A diesel; 300 hp

Remarks: Built 1944-45. Transferred 7-48, 5-63, 12-69, 8-71, and 11-75—the last from Japan, which had received her from the U.S. in 1-55. The ex-Japanese craft was overhauled and arrived in the Philippines during 1979, sister ex-YAS 4 (ex-YTL 748) having been lost overboard en route.

FLOATING DRY DOCKS

◆ **1 ex-U.S. AFDL** Bldr: V.P. Loftis, Wilmington, N.C. (In serv. 11-44)

YD 205 (ex-AFDL 44, ex-ARDC 11)

Lift Capacity: 2,800 tons **Dim:** 118.6 × 25.6 × 3.1 (light)

Remarks: Transferred, 9-69. Purchased outright 1-8-80.

◆ **3 ex-U.S. AFDL 1 class**

	Bldr	In serv.	Transferred
YD 200 (ex-AFDL 24)	Doullet & Ewin, Mobile, Ala.	1-44	7-48
YD 204 (ex-AFDL 20)	G.D. Auchter, Jacksonville, Fla.	6-44	10-61
YD. . . (ex-AFDL 10)	Chicago Bridge & Iron	12-43	12-78

Lift Capacity: 1,000 tons **Dim:** 60.96 × 19.51 × 1.04 (light)

Remarks: YD 200 transferred 7-48, YD 204 loaned 10-61, purchased 1-8-80; ex-AFDL 10 loaned 12-78.

◆ **2 ex-U.S. Army**

	L	Transferred
YD 201 (ex-AFDL 3681)	1943	5-52
YD 203 (ex-AFDL 3682)	1943	8-55

Lift Capacity: 150 tons **Dim:** 30.63 × 15.83 × 1.0 (light)

FLOATING CRANES

◆ **1 ex-U.S. floating crane**

	In serv.	Transferred
YU 206 (ex-YD 163)	12-5-46	1-71

D: 650 tons (fl) **Dim:** 36.58 × 13.72 × 2.13 **Lift Capacity:** 30 tons

◆ **2 ex-U.S. floating crane**

	In serv.	Transferred
YU 207 (ex-YD 191)	3-52	8-71

D: 920 tons (fl) **Dim:** 36.58 × 18.24 × 2.13 **Lift Capacity:** 60 tons

FLOATING REPAIR BARGES

◆ **1 ex-U.S. Army 230 class**

	L	Transferred
YD 202 (ex-. . .)	1943	7-49

D: 2,100 tons (fl) **Dim:** 64.0 × 12.5 × 3.4 **A:** 2/20-mm AA

BARGES

◆ **1 ex-U.S. YCV 3-class former aircraft transport lighter** Bldr: Pearl Harbor Naval SY (In serv. 25-11-43)

YB 206 (ex-YCV 7)

Dim: 33.53 × 9.14 × . . . **Cargo Capacity:** 250 tons

Remarks: Transferred, 5-63

◆ **2 ex-U.S. Navy barges**

	Transferred
YC 207 (ex-YC 1402)	8-59
YC 301 (ex-YC 1403)	8-71

Dim: 24.38 × 8.73 × 1.22

COAST GUARD

Personnel (1983): 300 officers, 1,700 enlisted men

The size of the Philippine Coast Guard has fluctuated widely since its establishment in the early 1970s. At one time it had responsibility for maintaining navigational aids and included many of the tenders now returned to the Navy. The majority of the patrol craft operated by the Coast Guard have been back under naval control since 1977, leaving only a few small craft and the larger ships described below still under Coast Guard control. In 1982, most small patrol craft in Philippine military service appeared to be under Coast Guard subordination.

PATROL BOATS

◆ **1 Bessang Pass-class search-and-rescue boat** Bldr: Sumidagawa, Tokyo, Japan (In serv. 1976-77)

SAR 100 Tirad Pass

Bessang Pass (SAR 99)—since lost G. Arra, 1977

D: 275 tons (fl) **S:** 30 kts **Dim:** 44.0 × 7.4 × 1.5
A: None **M:** 2 diesels; 2 props; . . . hp **Man:** 32 tot.

Remarks: Sister *Bessang Pass* (SAR 99) ran aground and was lost 9-83. Similar craft constructed for Indian Coast Guard.

◆ **1 search-and-rescue boat** Bldr: Vosper, Singapore (In serv. 12-75)

SAR 77 Bataan

D: 150 tons **S:** 28 kts **Dim:** 37.9 × 7.2 × 3.8
M: 3 MTU 12V538 TB91 diesels; 3 props; 7,500 hp

Remarks: Externally identical to presidential yacht *Ang Pinuno* (TP 77).

PATROL CRAFT

◆ **1 (+ . . .) Mk II design** Bldr: Cavite Navy Yd. (In serv. 7-85)

D: 24.6 tons (fl) **S:** 36 kts **Dim:** 16.7 × 5.0 × 1.3
A: . . . **Electron Equipt:** Radar: 1/. . . nav.
M: 2 MTU 8V396 TB93 diesels; 2 props; 2,400 hp

Remarks: Improved version of following class; glass-reinforced plastic hull.

◆ **25 fiberglass-hulled** Bldr: Marcelo, Manila, 1975-76

PSB 411 through PSB 435

PSB 431 R.A.N., 6-82

D: 15 ton (21.75 fl) **S:** 20 kts **Dim:** 14.07 × 4.32 × 1.04 (1.48 props)
A: 3/12.7-mm mg (II × 1, I × 1) **Electron Equipt:** Radar: 1/LN-66
M: 2 MTU 8V-331 TC80 diesels; 2 props; 1,800 hp
Electric: 7.5 kVA **Range:** 200/36 **Man:** 6 tot.

Remarks: Eighty were ordered 8-75, but of 25 hulls completed during 1975, 15 were destroyed by fire, and the program was terminated. Twin machine-gun mount is recessed into the forecastle. Later examples employ Cummins diesels; craft originally intended to achieve 46 kts(!).

◆ **6 Australian fiberglass-hulled** Bldr: De Havilland Marine, Sydney

PC 326-331 (In serv. 20-11-74 to 8-2-75)

D: 16.5 tons (fl) **S:** 25 kts **Dim:** 14.0 × 4.6 × 1.0
A: 2/12.7-mm mg **M:** 2 Caterpillar D348 diesels; 2 props; 740 hp
Range: 500/12 **Man:** 8 tot.

◆ **20 U.S. Swift Mk III class** Bldr: Sewart Seacraft, Morgan City, Louisiana

PCF 333 through PCF 352 (In serv. 1972-76)

PHILIPPINES *(continued)*
PATROL CRAFT *(continued)*

PCF 335—with Swift Mk II PCF 308 in background G. Arra, 1977

D: 28 tons (36.7 fl) **S:** 30 kts **Dim:** 19.78 × 5.5 × 1.8
A: 2/12.7-mm mg (I × 2)—2/7.6-mm mg (I × 2)
Electron Equipt: Radar: 1/LN-66
M: 3 G.M. 8V71 TI diesels; 3 props; 1,950 hp **Range:** 500/30
Man: 8 tot.

REMARKS: Aluminum construction. Pilothouse offset to starboard. In service 1972-76.

◆ **3 Abra class**

	Bldr	In serv.
FB 83 ABRA	Vosper, Singapore	8-1-70
FB 84 BUKINDON	Cavite NY	1971
FB 85 TABLAS	Cavite NY	1975

D: 40 tons **S:** 25 kts **Dim:** 26.7 × 5.8 × 1.5
A: 2/20-mm AA **M:** 2 MTU diesels; 2 props; 2,400 hp **Man:** 3 officers, 12 men

REMARKS: Wooden hulls, aluminum superstructure. Construction financed by Australia. FB 85 disarmed in 1980.

◆ **12 U.S. Swift Mk I and II class** Bldr: Sewart, Berwick, La.

PCF 300 PCF 301 PCF 306 PCF 307 PCF 309–316

PCF 308—Swift Mk II type (stricken 1979) G. Arra, 1977

D: 17.5 tons (22.1 fl) **S:** 24 kts **Dim:** 15.66 × 4.55 × 1.8 (props)
A: 2/12.7-mm mg (II × 1) **Electron Equipt:** Radar: 1/Raytheon 1500B
M: 2 G.M. 12V71 N diesels; 2 props; 850 hp **Electric:** 6 kw
Range: 400/22 **Man:** 6 tot.

REMARKS: In service 1966-70. PCF 300 and PCF 301, transferred 1966, are Swift Mk I class, 15.3 overall and with flush-decked hulls. All-aluminum construction. PCF 303, PCF 324, PCF 325, and PCF 317 (the last of ferro-concrete construction and used as a yacht) were discarded in 1976; PCF 304, PCF 305, and one other were written off in 1976, and PCF 308 was discarded 1979.

COAST AND GEODETIC SURVEY

The ships listed below are subordinate to the Ministry of Defense and are used for hydrographic survey.

◆ **1 survey ship** Bldr: Ishikawajima Harima, Tokyo

EXPLORER (In serv. 9-2-84)

D: 500 grt **S:** 12 kts **Dim:** 54.50 × 9.40 × 3.80
M: 2 diesels; 2 props; 1,200 hp

◆ **1 survey ship** Bldr: Walkers, Maryborough, Australia (In serv. 1969)

ATYIMBA

D: 611 tons (686 fl) **S:** 11 kts **Dim:** 49.08 (44.3 pp) × 10.14 × 2.74
M: Mirrlees-Blackstone 6-cyl. diesels; 1,620 hp
Electric: 175 kw **Range:** 5,000/8 **Man:** 54 tot.

Atyimba L. & L. Van Ginderen, 1981

◆ **2 Arinya-class coastal survey ships** Bldr: Walkers, Maryborough, Australia

ARINYA (L: 1962) ALUNYA (L: 1964)

D: 245 tons (fl) **S:** 10 kts **Dim:** 30.64 (27.44 pp) × 6.76 × 2.43
M: 2 G.M. 6-71 diesels; 2 props; 336 hp **Man:** 6 officers, 27 men

◆ **1 ex-U.S. Coast & Geodetic Survey ship** Bldr: Lake Washington SY, Houghton, Wash.

	Laid down	In serv.
PATHFINDER (ex-*Pathfinder*, OSS 30, ex-AGS 1)	3-9-42	31-8-43

D: 2,175 tons (fl) **S:** 14 kts **Dim:** 69.9 (63.8 wl) × 11.89 × 4.88
M: 2 sets GT; 2 props; 2,000 hp **Electric:** 145 kw
Boilers: 2 Babcock & Wilcox, 22 kg/cm², 330°C **Fuel:** 340 tons **Man:** 150 tot.

REMARKS: Served in the U.S. Navy during World War II, transferred to the Philippines in the mid-1970s.

POLAND

Polish People's Republic

PERSONNEL (1985): 19,500 total, including 4,100 coast defense personnel

MERCHANT MARINE (1984): 783 ships, 3,267,281 grt (tankers: 24 ships, 237,026 grt)

NAVAL AVIATION: About 40 Mig-17 Fresco and 40 Mig-21 Fishbed fighters and 15 IL-28 Beagle bombers, and about 10 Mi-2 Hoplite, 5 Mi-8 Hip and 10 Mi-4 Hound helicopters. All are of Soviet origin, and all but the Hips are in need of replacement.

SUBMARINES

◆ **3 ex-Soviet Whiskey class**

293 SOKOL 294 KONDOR 295 BIELIK

D: 1,050/1,350 tons **S:** 17/13.5 kts **Dim:** 76.0 × 6.3 × 4.8
A: 6/533-mm TT (4 fwd, 2 aft—14 torpedoes or 28 mines)
Electron Equipt: Radar: 1/Snoop Plate
Sonar: passive array; Tamir 5 MF active
M: 2 Type 37D, 2,000-hp diesels, diesel-electric drive; 2 props; 2,500 hp
Endurance: 40 days **Range:** 6,000/5 snorkel **Man:** 50 tot.

REMARKS: Transferred 1962-65. Sister *Orzel* (292) stricken 30-12-83.

GUIDED-MISSILE DESTROYER

◆ **1 ex-Soviet SAM Kotlin class** (In serv. 1958)

275 WARSZAWA (ex-*Spravedlivyy*)

Warszawa (275) 16th Flot., French Navy, 8-83

GUIDED-MISSILE DESTROYER *(continued)*

Warszawa (275) Polish Navy

D: 2,600 tons (3,500 fl) **S:** 36 kts **Dim:** 126.5 × 13.0 × 4.6 (5.6 sonar)
A: 1/SA-N-1 SAM system (II × 1; 16 missles)—2/130-mm DP (II × 1)—4/45-mm AA (IV × 1)—2/RBU-2500 ASW RL (XVI × 2)—5/533-mm TT (V × 1)—2/d.c. racks (12 d.c.)
Electron Equipt: Radar: 2/RN-231, 1/Head Net A, 1/Sun Visor, 1/Hawk Screech, 2/Peel Group
IFF: 2/Square Head, 1/Salt Pot
Sonar: 1/Pegas MF—EW: . . .
M: 2 sets GT; 2 props; 72,000 hp **Boilers:** 4; 64 kg/cm², 510°C
Electric: 1,400 kw **Range:** 1,050/34; 3,600/18 **Man:** 285 tot.

REMARKS: Transferred in 1970, having completed conversion in 1969. Maintained in immaculate condition. Depth charge racks added early 1980s.

FRIGATES

◆ **0 (+1 + . . .) new design** Bldr: . . .

. . . N. . . (In serv. 1985-86)

D: Approx. 1,100 tons **S:** . . . **Dim:** 81.0 × 10.0 × 3.0
A: . . .
Electron Equipt: . . .
M: CODAG?

REMARKS: NATO temporary nickname: "Balcom 6." First seagoing surface combatant built in Poland since before World War II. Series expected to produce four units.

GUIDED-MISSILE PATROL BOATS

◆ **2 (+ . . .) Soviet Tarantul I class** Bldr: Sridniy Neva SY, Rolpino

434 GORNIK (In serv. 30-12-83) 435 HUTNIK (In serv. 31-3-84)
436 STOCZNIOWIEC (In serv. 1985)

Gornik Polish Navy, 1984

D: 385 tons (455 fl) **S:** 40 kts **Dim:** 56.10 × 10.2 × 2.20 (3.50 props)
A: 4/SS-N-2C SSM (II × 2)—1/76.2-mm DP—1/SA-N-5 point-defense SAM syst. (IV × 1)—2/30-mm gatling AA (I × 2)
Electron Equipt: Radar: 1/Krivach nav., 1/Plank Shave, 1/BASS Tilt
IFF: 1/Square Head, 1/Salt Pot transponder
M: COGOG: 2 NK-12MV, 12,000 hp gas turbines; 2 4,000 hp cruise gas turbines; 2 props; 24,000 hp
Range: 2,300/. . . (1 cruise turbine) **Man:** 38 tot.

REMARKS: Beam is 10.5 m across missile sponsors. Unlike Soviet Navy version, have no EW gear.

◆ **13 Osa-I class**

421–433

D: 185 tons (215 fl) **S:** 36 kts **Dim:** 38.6 × 7.6 × 1.8
A: 4/SS-N-2A Styx SSM (I × 4)—4/30-mm AA (II × 2)

Polish Navy Osa-I 424 1980

Electron Equipt: Radar: 1/Square Tie, 1/Drum Tilt
IFF: 2 Square Head, 1/High Pole B
M: 3 M503A diesels; 3 props; 12,000 hp **Range:** 500/34; 750/25 **Man:** 30 tot.

REMARKS: Built in the U.S.S.R. during the early 1960s, transferred 1966-1967. Two names are known: *Gdynia* (421) and *Darlowo* (430).

TORPEDO BOATS

◆ **8 Wisla class** Bldr: Poland, 1970-74

452 453 454 457 458 459 468 469

Wisla class (496)—old number

D: 68 tons (80 fl) **S:** 50 kts **Dim:** 24.0 × 7.8 × 1.5
A: 2/30-mm AA—4/533-mm TT
Electron Equipt: Radar: 1 Pot Head—IFF: 1/High Pole A
M: 4 M50-F4 diesels; 4 props; 4,800 hp **Range:** 100/50; 500/20 **Man:** 16 tot.

REMARKS: Two units discarded 1983.

PATROL BOATS

◆ **8 Modified Obluze class** Bldr: Oksywie SY, 1970-72

351–358

Modified Obluze-class Zawziety (353) 1975

D: 210 tons (240 fl) **S:** 24 kts **Dim:** 41.0 (39.5 pp) × 6.0 × 2.0 (hull)
A: 4/30-mm AA (II × 2)—4/d.c. racks (2 topside; 2 through stern)
Electron Equipt: Radar: 1/RN-231, 1/Drum Tilt
Sonar: 1/Tamir-11—IFF: 2/Square Head, 1/High Pole
M: 2 Type 40D diesels; 2 props; 5,000 hp **Electric:** 150 kw
Fuel: 25 tons **Man:** 40 tot.

REMARKS: Similar to a larger group in the Polish Border Guard that do *not* have Drum Tilt fire-control radars. Three names are known; *Wyterwaly* (352), *Zawziety* (353), and *Zreczny* (356).

MINE WARFARE SHIPS

◆ **12 Krogulec-class minesweepers** Bldr: Stocznia Gdynska, Gdynia, 1963-67

613 Orlik	617 Czajda	621 Kania
614 Krogulec	618 Albatros	622 Jaskolka
615 Jastrzab	619 Pelikan	623 Zuraw
616 Kormoran	620 Tukan	624 Czapla

Krogulec class—with six 25-mm AA Polish Navy

Krogulec class—with four 23-mm AA aft 1978

D: 450 tons (484 fl) **S:** 18 kts **Dim:** 60.0 (58.0 pp) × 7.6 × 2.3
A: 6/25-mm AA (II × 3)—2/d.c. racks—mines
M: 2 Fiat A-230S diesels; 2 props; 3,740 hp **Range:** 3,200/12
Electron Equipt: Radar: 1/RN-231 **Fuel:** 55 tons
Man: 6 officers, 24 men

Remarks: Some of these ships have four 23-mm rapid-fire AA (II × 2) mounted aft in place of the original four 25-mm AA. Hull numbers currently 625 and up.

◆ **12 Soviet T 43-type minesweepers** Bldr: Stocznia Gdynska, Gdynia, 1957-62

601 Zubr	603 Loz	605 Bizon	607 Rozmak	609 Foka	611 Rys
602 Tur	604 Dzik	606 Bobr	608 Delfin	610 Mors	612 Zbik

D: 520 tons (590 fl) **S:** 14 kts **Dim:** 60.0 × 8.6 × 2.3 (3.5 sonar)
A: 4/37-mm AA (II × 2)—4/25-mm AA (II × 2)—4/14.5-mm mg (II × 2)—2/d.c. projectors—mines
Electron Equipt: Radar: 1/RN-231—Sonar: 1/Tamir-11
IFF: 1/Square Head, 1/High Pole A

Foka (609)—long-hulled version 1978

Zubr (601)—short-hulled version Polish Navy

M: 2 Type 9D diesels; 2 props; 2,200 hp **Electric:** 550 kw
Fuel: 70 tons **Range:** 3,200/10 **Man:** 7 officers, 33 men

Remarks: *Zubr, Tur, Loz,* and *Dzik,* built in the U.S.S.R., are 2 meters shorter and displace 569 tons (fl); they have 8/14.5-mm mg, but no 25-mm AA. *Tur* has been converted into a radar picket, losing the after twin 37-mm AA and all sweep capability in favor of a quadripod mast to support a large radar antenna.

◆ **3 (+ . . .) Notek-class coastal minesweepers** Bldr: Gdynia NSY

630 Goplo (In serv. 2-82) 631 Gardno (In serv. 31-3-84) 632 N. . . (In serv. 1985)

Goplo (630) Polish Navy, 10-84

D: 250 tons (fl) **S:** 12 kts **Dim:** 38.5 × 8.3 × 1.9
A: 2/25-mm AA (II × 2) **M:** 2 diesels; 2 props; . . . hp

Remarks: Glass-reinforced plastic construction. First unit launched 16-4-81.

◆ **2 (+ . . .) Leniwka-class minesweeping boats**

625 626

D: . . . **S:** . . . **Dim:** . . . × . . . × . . .
A: . . . **M:** . . .

Remarks: No details available; first reported 1985.

◆ **23 K 8-class inshore minesweepers** Bldr: Gdansk SY, Poland (In serv. 1953-60)

931–953

Polish Navy K-8-class inshore minesweeper 1977

D: 20 tons (26 fl) **S:** 12 kts **Dim:** 17.0 × 3.2 × 0.8
A: 2/14.5-mm mg (II × 1) **M:** 2 3D6 diesels; 2 props; 600 hp

Remarks: Wooden hulls; simple wire sweeps only. Most in reserve, land-stored. Five have been discarded.

AMPHIBIOUS WARFARE SHIPS

◆ **1 Soviet Polnocny-C-class landing ship** Bldr: Polnocny SY, Gdansk (In serv. 1971)

811 Grunwald

D: 1,150 tons (fl) **S:** 18 kts **Dim:** 81.3 × 10.1 × 2.1
A: 4/30-mm AA (II × 2) — 2/140-mm RL (XVIII × 2)
Electron Equipt: Radar: 1/Drum Tilt, 1/Don 2
IFF: 1/Square Head, 1/High Pole A
M: 2 Type 40D diesels; 2 props; 5,000 hp **Range:** 900/17

◆ **22 Polnocny-A and -B-class landing ships** Bldr: Polnocny SY, Gdansk (In serv. 1964-70)

Balas, Brda, Janow, Lenina, Narwik, Polichno, Rablow, Studziank, Warta, and 13 others — Nos. 801–810, 888–899

Polish Navy Polnocny-A

Polish Navy Polnocny-B 1978

D: A: 770 tons (fl); B: 740 tons (800 fl) **S:** 19 kts
Dim: 73.0 (B: 74.0) × 8.6 × 1.9 **A:** 4/30-mm AA — 2/140-mm RL (XVIII × 2)
Electron Equipt: Radar: 1/RN-231, 1/Drum Tilt
IFF: 1/Square Head, 1/High Pole A
M: 2 Type 40D diesels; 2 props; 5,000 hp
Fuel: 36 tons **Range:** 900/18 **Man:** 35 tot.

Remarks: Polnocny-A has blunt, convex bow form; the "B" version introduced a raked, flared bow to improve seaworthiness. Unlike Soviet Navy units, Polish Polnocnys have a standard armament suit. Cargo: 180 tons vehicles, 130 troops. 801–810 and 890 are Type A; 888, 889 891–899 are Type B. At least one Type A has a high bridge and low-mounted Drum Tilt radar like the "B" version. Some now receiving 2–4 SA-N-5 launchers (IV × 2 or 4), as on Soviet units of the class.

◆ **4 Marabut-class landing craft** (In serv. 1975)

872 873 874 875

Marabut class (872)

D: 60 tons (fl) **S:** 15 kts **Dim:** 21.0 × 4.2 × 1.0
A: 1/14.5-mm mg **M:** 2 diesels; 2 props; . . . hp

Remarks: Glass-reinforced plastic construction.

◆ **15 Eichstaden-class personnel landing craft** (In serv. early 1960s)

857–871

D: 25 tons (fl) **S:** 18 kts **Dim:** 16.6 × 4.0 × 1.7
A: Small arms **M:** 2 3D6 diesels; 2 props; 300 hp **Man:** 3 tot.

Remarks: Cargo: 20 troops. Pointed bow, troops exiting cargo compartment via ramps on sides.

Eichstaden class (866) Polish Navy, 1983

HYDROGRAPHIC SHIPS

◆ **2 modified Fenik class** Bldr: Polnocny SY, Gdansk (In serv. 2-83)

265 Heweliusz 266 Arctowski

Arctowski (266) M.O.D., Bonn, 1984

D: 1,200 tons (fl) **S:** 13 kts **Dim:** 61.30 × 10.80 × 3.27 **Electric:** 675 kVA
Electron Equipt: Radar: 1/RN-231 **Range:** 3,000/10
Man: 5 officers, 23 men
M: 2 Cegielski-Sulzer 6 AL 25/30 diesels; 2 CP props; 1,920 hp; 2 150-kw electric auxiliary drive motors

Remarks: 751 grt, 250 dwt. Able to link via chain drag for clearance surveys. Have a bow-thruster, 4 precision echo-sounders. Compared to Soviet sisters, have forecastle extended nearly to stern, no buoy-handling capability. Civilian sisters *Planeta* (launched 21-5-82) and *Zodiak* (launched 28-8-82) are subordinated to the Maritime Agency, Szczecin. Also sisters in Soviet and East German navies.

◆ **1 Soviet Moma class** Bldr: Polnocny SY, Gdansk (In serv. 1973)

Kopernik

Kopernik — with seismic survey gear streamed 1978

D: 1,260 tons (1,540 fl) **S:** 17 kts **Dim:** 73.3 × 10.8 × 3.8
Electron Equipt: Radar: 2/RN-231
M: 2 Zgoda-Sulzer 6TD48 diesels; 2 CP props; 3,600 hp
Endurance: 35 days **Range:** 8,700/11 **Man:** 56 tot.

Remarks: Sisters in Bulgarian and Yugoslav navies. *Piast*-class salvage ships and *Wodnik*-class training ships are very similar. Two others, the *Nawigator* and *Hydrometr*, serve as intelligence collectors. The *Kopernik* has 35 m² of laboratory deck area and has been modified for use in seismic survey, oil exploration work.

AUXILIARY SHIPS

◆ **3 Moskit-class coastal oilers** Bldr: Poland (In serv. 1971-72)

Z 3 KRAB Z 8 MEDUSA Z 9 SLIMAK

Medusa (Z 8) 1973

D: 1,200 tons (fl) **S:** 10 kts **Dim:** 57.7 (54.0 pp) × 9.5 × 3.4
A: 4/25-mm AA (II × 2) **Electron Equipt:** Radar: 1/RN-231
M: 2 Cegielski-Sulzer diesels; 2 CP props; 850 hp **Man:** 12 tot.

REMARKS: Cargo: 800 tons. Guns occasionally removed.

◆ **3 Type 5-class coastal oilers** (In serv. early 1960s)

Z 5 Z 6 Z 7

D: 625 tons (fl) **S:** 9 kts **Dim:** 44.2 × 6.5 × 3.0
M: 1 diesel; 1 prop; 300 hp **Range:** 1,200/9 **Man:** 16 tot.

REMARKS: Cargo: 280 tons. Can carry 2/25-mm AA (II × 1).

◆ **2 Piast-class salvage ships** Bldr: Polnocny SY, Gdansk

281 PIAST (In serv. 30-11-74) 282 LECH (In serv. 1975)

Piast (281) R. Neth. Navy, 1982

D: 1,560 tons (1,732 fl) **S:** 16.5 kts **Dim:** 73.2 (67.2 pp) × 10.8 × 4.0
Electron Equipt: Radar: 2/RN-231
M: 2 Cegielski-Sulzer 6TD48 diesels; 2 CP props; 3,600 hp **Range:** 3,000/12

REMARKS: Variation of *Moma* design for salvage and rescue duties. Equipped to mount eight 25-mm AA in wartime (II × 4). Carry submarine rescue bell to port, can tow, and have extensive pump and fire-fighting facilities. Sister *Otto von Guericke* is in the East German Navy.

NOTE: A new "salvage tug" named *Gniewko* was reported commissioned 29-8-81; no data available.

◆ **3 Mrovka-class degaussing/deperming tenders** (In serv. 1970-71)

SD 11WRONA SD 12 N. . . . . . . SD 13 N. . . . . . .

SD 12 1980

D: 550 tons (fl) **S:** 9 kts **Dim:** 44.6 × 8.2 × 3.0
M: 1 diesel; 1 prop; 300 hp **Man:** 20 tot.

REMARKS: Provision for 2/25-mm AA (II × 2) on forecastle.

INTELLIGENCE COLLECTORS

◆ **2 modified Moma class** Bldr: Polnocny SY, Gdansk, (In serv. 1975-76)

262 NAWIGATOR 263 HYDROMETR

Hydrometr 1978

REMARKS: Data as for hydrographic ship *Kopernik* above. Crane removed, superstructure lengthened, lattice mainmast as on *Piast* class, two large radomes. Euphemistically described as "navigational training ships." Provision for mounting 8/25-mm AA (II × 4), 2 fwd., 2 aft.

NOTE: B-10 trawler-class intelligence collector *Baltyk* was stricken 12-82.

TRAINING SHIPS

◆ **2 Wodnik class** Bldr: Polnocny SY, Gdansk

251 WODNIK (L: 29-11-75) 252 GRYF (L: 13-3-76)

Gryf (252) Skyfotos, 7-82

D: 1,800 tons (fl) **S:** 16.8 kts **Dim:** 74.0 × 13.0 × 4.2
A: 4/30-mm AA (II × 2)—4/25-mm AA (II × 2)
Electron Equipt: Radar: 2/RN-231, 1/Drum Tilt
M: 2 Cegielski-Sulzer 6TD48 diesels; 2 CP props; 3,600 hp
Range: 7,500/11 **Man:** 60 men + 13 instructors and 87 cadets

REMARKS: Nearly identical to the East German Navy's *Wilhelm Pieck* and similar to the *Luga* and *Oka* in the Soviet Navy. Developed from the *Moma* design. Have latest navigational systems from the West and the U.S.S.R.

◆ **4 Bryza class** Bldr: Wisla SY

	In serv.		In serv.
K 18 BRYZA	1965	712 KADET	19-7-75
711 PODCHORAZY	30-11-74	713 ELEW	8-4-76

D: 147 tons (180 fl) **S:** 10 kts **Dim:** 26.8 × 6.8 × 1.8
Electron Equipt: Radar: 2/RN-231 **M:** 2 diesels; 2 props; 300 hp
Electric: 84 kw **Range:** 1,100/10 **Man:** 11 men, 26 midshipmen

REMARKS: *Bryza,* with a less elaborate superstructure, displaces 167 tons (fl). This class also widely employed by Soviet naval schools and Merchant Marine schools for navigation and seamanship training.

TRAINING SHIPS *(continued)*

Podchorazy (711) 1976

◆ **1 sail-training craft** Bldr: Gdynia SY (In serv. 11-8-82)

Iskra II

D: 341 tons **S:** . . . **Dim:** . . . × . . . × . . .
M: 1 diesel; 1 prop; . . . ; ketch-rigged

Remarks: Can accommodate 40 cadets. The much larger sail-training ship *Dar Mlodziezy,* also completed in 1982, is civilian-subordinated. The old naval sail-training ship *Iskra,* renamed *Iotka,* survives as a youth training craft.

MISCELLANEOUS SERVICE CRAFT

◆ **2 Pajak-class torpedo retrievers** Bldr: Gdynia SY (In serv. 1971)

K 8 Kormoran I K 11 Kormoran II

D: 130 tons (fl) **S:** 21 kts **Dim:** 38.0 × 6.0 × 1.6 **Man:** 18 tot.
A: 2/25-mm AA (II × 1) **M:** 2 M50-F4 diesels; 2 props; 2,400 hp

◆ **2 (+ . . .) Bucha-class harbor tugs** (In serv. 1981-. . .)

H 4 H 7

D: 310 tons (fl) **S:** 11 kts **Dim:** 26.3 (25.4 pp) × 7.0 × 3.0
Electron Equipt: Radar: 1/SRN-206 **Electric:** 76 kw
M: 1 Cegielski-Sulzer 6AL 20/24H diesel; 1 CP prop; 760 hp
Fuel: 20 tons **Man:** 7 tot.

Remarks: Class also built for civil use. Bollard pull: 10 tons

◆ **3 Motyl-class tugs** Bldr: Polnocny SY, Gdansk (In serv. 1962-66)

H 12 H 19 H 20

Motyl-class tug H 20 1974

D: 500 tons (fl) **S:** 12.8 kts **Dim:** 31.6 (28.6 pp) × 8.4 × 3.5
M: 1 Zgoda-Sulzer 5TD48 diesel; 1 prop; 1,500 hp
Electric: 150 kw **Fuel:** 20 tons **Range:** 2,000/12.8 **Man:** 20 tot.

◆ **7 Goliat-class harbor tugs** Bldr: Gdynia SY (In serv. early 1960s)

H 5 H 13–18

D: 150 tons (fl) **S:** 12 kts **Dim:** 21.4 × 6.1 × 2.6 **Man:** 5 tot.
M: 1 Buckau-Wolff 8 NVD 36 diesel; 1 prop; 300 hp **Range:** 300/9

◆ **2-4 K-15-class mooring buoy tenders**

D: 40 tons (fl) **S:** 10 kts **Dim:** 17.8 (15.2 pp) × 4.2 × 1.5
M: 1 diesel; 1 prop; 150 hp **Man:** 5 tot.

◆ **6 R-34-class mooring buoy tenders**

D: 58.5 tons (64.5 fl) **S:** 11 kts **Dim:** 16.8 × 5.5 × 2.4
M: 1 diesel; 1 prop; 300 hp

◆ **1 research submersible** Bldr: Paris Commune SY (In serv. 1982)

Geonur II

D: 34 tons (67 submerged fl) **S:** . . . **Dim:** 9.5 × 4.4 × 3.5 (height)

Remarks: Operated jointly by the Navy and the Institute of Baltic Geodesy. Diving depth: 150 m.

BORDER GUARD (WOP)

PATROL BOATS

◆ **5 Obluze class** Bldr: Oksywie SY (In serv. 1965-68)

321–325

Polish Border Guard Obluze—(old number)

D: 150 tons (fl) **S:** 24 kts **Dim:** 41.0 × 6.0 × 2.1
A: 4/30-mm AA (II × 2)—4 d.c. racks (2 internal)
Electron Equipt: Radar: 1/RN-231
Sonar: Tamir-11
IFF: 1/Square Head, 1/High Pole A
M: 2 Type 40D diesels; 2 props; 5,000 hp

Remarks: Two have no 30-mm AA mount aft. Five additional units with Drum Tilt fire-control radars for the 30-mm AA serve in the Polish Navy.

◆ **9 Gdansk class** Bldr: Oksywie SY (In serv. 1962-64)

311 through 319

Gdansk class 317 1978

D: 180 tons (200 fl) **S:** 18 kts **Dim:** 41.0 × 5.8 × 1.9
A: 2/37-mm AA (I × 2)—2/12.7-mm mg (II × 1)—2 d.c. racks
Electron Equipt: Radar: 1/RN-231
Sonar: Tamir-11
M: 2 diesels; 2 props; 2,400 hp

PATROL CRAFT

◆ **17 Pilica class** Bldr: Poland (In serv. 1973-. . .)

KP 161 to KP 177

Pilica—without torpedo tubes, old number 1977

POLAND *(continued)*
PATROL CRAFT *(continued)*

Pilica—with 2/533-mm TT S. Breyer, 1979

D: 100 tons (fl) **S:** 24 kts **Dim:** 29.2 × 6.0 × 1.4
A: 2/25-mm AA (II × 1)—2/533-mm TT
Electron Equipt: Radar: 1/RN-231 IFF: 1/High Pole A
M: 3 M50-F4 diesels; 3 props; 3,600 hp **Man:** 15 hp

Remarks: All but the first three have had two 533-mm torpedo tubes added.

◆ **12 Wisloka class** Bldr: Poland (In serv. early 1970s)

KP 141–152

Wisloka class S. Breyer, 1979

D: 45 tons (fl) **S:** 14 kts **Dim:** 22.8 × 5.0 × 1.1
A: 2/14.5-mm mg (II × 1) **Electron Equipt:** Radar: 1/navigational
M: 2 diesels; 2 props; 600 hp **Man:** 10 tot.

◆ **21 K-15-class harbor craft** Bldr: Poland (In serv. early 1960s)

KP 108–128

D: 40 tons **S:** 10 kts **Dim:** 17.8 × 4.2 × 1.5
A: Small arms **M:** 1 diesel; 1 prop; 300 hp **Man:** 5 tot.

PORTUGAL

Portuguese Republic

Personnel (1985): 15,555, including 2,600 Marines

Merchant Marine (1984): 359 ships—1,571,007 grt
(tankers: 20 ships—1,028,890 grt)

Naval Aviation: There is no aviation arm *per se,* but eight Air Force Casa 212 Aviocar light transports (four with photo equipment) are equipped for maritime reconnaissance duties. Six ex-Australian P-3B Orions, refurbished by Lockheed, purchased 1985.

SUBMARINES

◆ **3 Daphné class** Bldr: Dubigeon, Normandy

	Laid down	L	In serv.
S 163 Albacora	6-9-65	15-10-66	1-10-67
S 164 Barracuda	19-10-65	24-4-68	4-5-68
S 166 Delfim	14-5-67	23-9-68	1-10-69

Albacora (S 163) G. Gyssels, 10-84

D: 869 surf. f.l./1,043-sub. tons **S:** 13.5/16 kts **Dim:** 57.75 × 6.76 × 4.56
A: 12/550-mm TT (8 fwd, 4 aft, no reloads)
Electron Equipt: Radar: 1/DRUA-31—EW: ARUR, ARUD
Sonar: DUUA-1 active, DSUV passive
M: Diesel-electric propulsion: SEMT-Pielstick 12PA1 diesels (450 kw); 2 props; 1,200 hp
Range: 4,300/7.5 snorkel **Man:** 5 officers, 45 men

Remarks: See remarks on the *Daphné* class in the French section. Sister *Cachalote* (S 165) was purchased by the Pakistani Navy in 1975.

FRIGATES

◆ **0 (+3) MEKO 200 design** Bldrs: Blohm + Voss, Hamburg; Howaldtswerke

	Laid down	L	In serv.
F. . . N. . .	. . .	. . .	. . .
F. . . N. . .	. . .	. . .	. . .
F. . . N. . .	. . .	. . .	. . .

D: 2,000 tons (2,400 fl) **S:** 28 kts **Dim:** 95.00 (88.00 pp) × 11.80 × 3.60 (hull)
A: 8/Harpoon SSM (IV × 2)—1/Mk 29 SAM launcher (VIII × 1; Sea Sparrow missiles)—1/127-mm Mk 45 Mod. 1 DP—2 or 3 CIWS AA gunmounts—6/324-mm Mk 32 ASW TT—1/. . . helicopters
Electron Equipt: Radar:
Sonar: SQS-505
EW:
M: 4 MTU 20V1163 TB93 diesels; 2 CP props; 22,536 hp
Range: 4,000/20 **Fuel:** 380 tons **Electric:** 144 kw **Man:** 123 tot.

Remarks: Similar to Turkish Navy units under construction. Portugal paying only small percent of costs; most borne by NATO partners U.S., West Germany, Canada, and Norway. Ordered 10-85 from consortium of builders plus Thyssen Rheinstall Technik and Ferrostal. Will have U.S.-supplied electronics, plus some Canadian and Norwegian equipment.

◆ **4 Baptiste de Andrade class** Bldr: Bazán, Spain

	Laid down	L	In serv.
F 486 Baptiste De Andrade	1972	3-73	19-11-74
F 487 João Roby	1972	3-6-73	18-3-75
F 488 Afonso Cerqueira	1973	6-10-73	26-6-75
F 489 Oliveira E. Carmo	1973	2-74	2-76

Afonso Cerqueira (F 488) L. & L. Van Ginderen, 1983

Oliveira E. Carmo (F 489) L. & L. Van Ginderen, 3-82

D: 1,252 tons (1,348 fl) **S:** 21 kts **Dim:** 84.59 (81.0 pp) × 10.3 × 3.3
A: 1/100-mm DP, French Model 1968—2/40-mm AA (I × 2)—6/324-mm Mk 32 ASW TT (III × 2)—1/d.c. rack
Electron Equipt: Radar: 1/Decca TM626, 1/Plessey AWS-2, 1/Thomson-CSF Pollux
Sonar: Diodon

FRIGATES *(continued)*

M: 2 OEW-Pielstick 12PC2V400 diesels; 2 props; 10,560 hp
Electric: 1,110 kVA **Range:** 5,900/18 **Man:** 113 tot.

REMARKS: Developed version of the *João Coutinho* class with more modern weapons and electronics. Helicopter platform. Vega GFCS with CSEE Panda optical backup director for 100-mm gun, 2 directors for 40-mm.

◆ **6 João Coutinho class** Bldrs: F 475 to F 477: Blohm + Voss, Germany; F 484 to F 471: Bazán, Spain

	Laid down	L	In serv.
F 475 João Coutinho	9-68	2-5-69	7-3-70
F 476 Jacinto Candido	4-68	16-6-69	10-6-70
F 477 General Pereira D'eca	10-68	26-7-69	10-10-70
F 484 Augusto Castilho	8-68	5-7-69	14-11-70
F 485 Honorio Barreto	7-68	11-4-70	15-4-71
F 471 Antonio Enes	4-68	1-8-69	18-6-71

João Coutinho (F 475) Portuguese Navy

Jacinto Candido (F 476) G. Gyssels, 9-81

D: 1,252 tons (1,401 fl) **S:** 24.4 kts **Dim:** 84.59 (81.0 pp) × 10.30 × 3.30
A: 2/76.2-mm Mk 33 DP (II × 1)—2/40-mm AA (II × 1)—Mk 10 Hedgehog—2/Mk 6 d.c. projectors—2/Mk 9 d.c. racks
Electron Equipt: Radar: 1/Decca TM 626, 1/MLA-1B, 1/SPG-34
Sonar: 1/QCU-2
M: 2 OEW-Pielstick 12PC2V280 diesels; 2 props; 10,560 hp
Electric: 900 kw **Range:** 5,900/8 **Man:** 9 officers, 84 men

REMARKS: Can carry 34 Marines. Have Mk 63 Mod. 21 GFCS for the 76.2-mm mount, Mk 51, Mod. 2 GFCS for the 40-mm. Modernization planned. Carry 1,200 rounds 76.2-mm, 240 Hedgehog projectiles, and up to 84 d.c.

◆ **4 French Commandant Rivière class** Bldr: A.C. de Bretagne, Nantes

	Laid down	L	In serv.
F 480 Comandante João Belo	6-9-65	22-3-66	1-7-67
F 481 Comandante Hermegildo Capelo	13-5-66	29-11-66	26-4-68
F 482 Comandante Roberto Ivens	13-12-66	11-8-67	23-11-68
F 483 Comandante Sacadura Cabral	18-8-67	15-3-68	25-11-69

D: 1,760 tons (2,250 fl) **S:** 25 kts (26.6 max.)
Dim: 103.0 (98.0 pp) × 11.5 × 3.8
A: 3/100-mm DP, Model 1953 (I × 3)—2/40-mm AA (I × 2)—1/305-mm ASW mortar (IV × 1)—6/550-mm ASW TT (III × 2)
Electron Equipt: Radar: 1/Decca RM 316, 1/DRBV-22A, 1/DRBV-50, 1/DRBC-31D
Sonar: 1/DUBA-3, 1/SQS-17A—EW: ARBR-10

Comandante Roberto Ivens (F 482) L. & L. Van Ginderen, 3-85

Comandante João Belo (F 480) L. & L. Van Ginderen, 7-84

M: 4 SEMT-Pielstick diesels; 2 props; 16,000 hp **Electric:** 1,280 kw
Range: 2,300/25; 4,500/15 **Man:** 214 tot.

REMARKS: See remarks on *Commandant Rivière* class in French section. Modernization deferred, but will receive new sonars and EW gear in near future.

◆ **3 U.S. Dealey class** Bldrs: F 472 and F 473: Est. Nav. Lisnave, Lisbon; F 474: Est. Nav. de Viana do Castelo

	Laid down	L	In serv.
F 472 Almirante Pereira Da Silva	14-6-62	2-12-63	20-12-66
F 473 Almirante Gago Coutinho	2-12-63	13-8-65	29-11-67
F 474 Almirante Magalhaes Correa	30-8-63	26-4-65	4-11-68

Almirante Magalhaes Correa (F 474) G. Gyssels, 8-82

D: 1,450 tons (1,950 fl) **S:** 26 kts **Dim:** 95.86 (93.88 wl) × 11.18 × 4.04 (hull)
A: 4/76.2-mm DP (II × 2)—2/375-mm Bofors ASW RL (IV × 2)—6/324-mm Mk 32 ASW TT (III × 2)
Electron Equipt: Radar: 1/Decca RM 316P, 1/978, 1/MLA-1B, 2/Mk 34
Sonar: SQS-30/31/32, DUBA-3A, 1/SQA-10 (VDS)
EW: WLR-1
M: 1 set GT; 1 prop; 20,000 hp **Electric:** 700 kw
Boilers: 2 Foster-Wheeler, 42 kg/cm², 510°C **Fuel:** 360 tons
Range: 1,600/25; 4,400/11 **Man:** 11 officers, 154 men

REMARKS: Funded as U.S. DE 1039, DE 1042, and DE 1046, respectively. Two Mk 63 gunfire-control systems. Search sonars are SQS-30, SQS-31, and SQS-32, respectively, to avoid frequency interference. Two are to be converted to perform 200-n.m. economic zone patrol and search-and rescue duties.

PATROL BOATS

◆ **10 Cacine class** (Launch dates in parentheses)

P 1140 Cacine (1968)
P 1141 Cunene (1968)
P 1142 Mandovi (1968)
P 1143 Rovuma (1968)
P 1144 Quanza (30-5-69)
P 1145 Geba (21-5-69)
P 1146 Zaire (28-11-70)
P 1147 Zambeze (1971)
P 1160 Limpopo (9-4-73)
P 1161 Save (24-10-72)

Mandovi (P 1142) L. & L. Van Ginderen, 1983

Bldrs: P 1140 to 1143: Arsenal do Alfeite; others: Est. Nav. do Mondego

D: 292 tons (310 fl) **S:** 20 kts **Dim:** 44.0 × 7.67 × 2.2
A: 2/40-mm AA (I × 2)—1/20-mm AA—2/d.c. racks
Electron Equipt: Radar: 1/975 **M:** 2 Maybach 12V538 diesels; 2 props; 4,400 hp
Range: 4,400/12 **Man:** 3 officers, 30 men

PATROL BOATS *(continued)*

◆ **4 São Roque-class former minesweepers** Bldr: Estaleiros Navais da C.U.F., Lisbon

	In serv.		In serv.
M 401 São Roque	6-6-56	M 403 Lagoa	10-8-56
M 402 Ribeira Grande	8-2-57	M 404 Rosario	8-2-56

São Roque (M 401) L. & L. Van Ginderen, 1983

D: 394 tons (452 fl) **S:** 15 kts **Dim:** 46.33 (42.69 pp) × 8.75 × 2.5
A: 1/20-mm AA **M:** 2 Mirrlees JVSS-12 diesels; 2 props; 2,500 hp
Fuel: 45 tons **Range:** 2,300/13; 3,000/8 **Man:** 4 officers, 43 men

Remarks: All portable sweep gear offloaded; now used as patrol vessels. Ordered early in 1954 and all launched in 1955. M 401 and M 403 built with U.S. "Offshore" funds as MSC 241 and MSC 242. Similar in appearance to the British "Ton" class. Wooden hulls, fin stabilizers. One 40-mm AA removed in 1972.

PATROL CRAFT

◆ **4 glass-reinforced plastic hulled** Bldr: Cheverton, Cowes, U.K.

Bonanca Mar Chao Mar Eta Surriada

D: 9 tons (fl) **S:** 20 kts **Dim:** 12.0 × 3.6 × 1.0
A: Small arms **Electron Equipt:** Radar: 1/Decca 110
M: 2 Volvo Penta TAMD 66B outdrive diesels; 2 props; 426 hp
Man: 4 tot.

Remarks: First pair delivered 5-82, others in 7-82. Intended to patrol on the Tagus in the Lisbon area.

◆ **6 Albatroz class** Bldr: Arsenal do Alfeite (In serv. 1974-75)

P 1162 Albatroz	P 1164 Andorhina	P 1166 Condor
P 1163 Acor	P 1165 Aguia	P 1167 Cisne

Condor (P 1166) L. & L. Van Ginderen, 1981

D: 45 tons (fl) **S:** 20 kts **Dim:** 23.6 (21.88 pp) × 5.25 × 1.6
A: 1/20-mm AA—2/12.7-mm mg (I × 2)
Electron Equipt: Radar: 1/Kelvin-Hughes 14/9
M: 2 Cummins diesels; 2 props; 1,100 hp **Range:** 450/18; 2,500/12 **Man:** 8 tot.

◆ **1 Dom Aleixo class** Bldr: San Jacintho Aveiro (L: 12-67)

P 1148 Dom Aleixo

Dom Aleixo (P 1148)

D: 62.6 tons (67.7 fl) **S:** 16 tons **Dim:** 25.0 × 5.2 × 1.6
A: 1/20-mm **Electron Equipt:** Radar: Decca RM 316P
M: 2 Cummins diesels; 2 props; 1,600 hp **Man:** 2 officers, 8 men

Remarks: Sister *Dom Jeremias* (A 5202, ex-P 1149) is used as an inshore survey craft.

AMPHIBIOUS WARFARE CRAFT

◆ **2 Bombarda-class landing craft** Bldr: Mondego SY

LDG 201 Bombarda (In serv. 1969) LDG 202 Alabarda (In serv. 1971)
LDG 203 Bacamarte (In serv. 12-85)

Bombarda (LDG 201) 1983

D: 285 tons (635 fl) **S:** 11 kts **Dim:** 59.0 (52.88 pp) × 11.91 × 1.6
M: 2 MTU MD 225 diesels; 2 props; 1,000 hp **Range:** 1,800/8
Man: 2 officers, 18 men

◆ **6 LDM 400-class landing craft** (In serv. 1967)

LDM 406	LDM 420	LDM 422
LDM 418	LDM 421	LDM 423

D: 56 tons (fl) **S:** 9 kts **Dim:** 17.0 × 5.0 × 1.2
A: 1/20-mm **M:** 2 Cummins diesels; 2 props; 450 hp

Remarks: Resemble British LCM(7) class. LDM 424 stricken 1982.

◆ **3 LDM 100-class landing craft** Bldr: Mondego SY (In serv. 1965)

LDM 119 LDM 120 LDM 121

D: 50 tons (fl) **S:** 9 kts **Dim:** 15.25 × 4.37 × 1.17
M: 2 G.M. 6-71 diesels; 2 props; 450 hp **Range:** 130/9

Remarks: U.S. LCM(6) class.

HYDROGRAPHIC SHIPS

◆ **0 (+1) new construction** Bldr: Alfeite Navy Yard

	Laid down	L	In serv.
A. . . N.	. . .	. . .	. . .

D: 1,140 tons (fl) **S:** 15 kts **Dim:** 60.0 × 12.0 × 4.6
M: Diesels: . . . props; 1,700 hp

Remarks: Intended to replace the U.K. "Bay"-class survey ship *Alfonso de Albuquerque* (A 526), stricken 1983. Not yet begun. A second new survey unit is also planned.

◆ **1 ex-U.S. Kellar class** Bldr: Marietta SB Co., Pt. Pleasant, W. Va.

	Laid down	L	In serv.
A 527 Almeida Carvalho (ex-*Kellar,* T-AGS 25)	20-11-62	30-7-64	31-1-69

Almeida Carvalho (A 527) L. & L. Van Ginderen, 1983

D: 1,297 tons (fl) **S:** 13.5 kts **Dim:** 63.50 (58.00 pp) × 11.90 × 4.32
Electron Equipt: 1/RCA CRM-N2A-30, 1/Decca TM 829
M: 2 Caterpillar D-378 diesels, electric drive; 1 prop; 1,000 hp
Fuel: 211 tons **Man:** 5 officers, 25 men

Remarks: Transferred on loan 21-1-72. Similar to U.S. *Robert D. Conrad*-class T-AGOR. Sister *S.P. Lee* is operated by the United States Geological Survey.

◆ **1 inshore survey craft** Bldr: San Jacintho Aveiro (L: 12-67)

A 5202 Dom Jeremias (ex-P 1149)

Remarks: Data as for patrol craft sister *Dom Aleixo.* Retains the 20-mm AA gun.

HYDROGRAPHIC SHIPS *(continued)*

Dom Jeremias (A 5202) L. & L. Van Ginderen, 7-84

AUXILIARY SHIPS

◆ **1 replenishment oiler** Bldr: Est. Nav. de Viana do Castelo

	L	In serv.
A 5206 São Gabriel	1961	3-63

São Gabriel (A 5206)—fueling boom rigged out Portuguese Navy

D: 9,000 tons (14,200 fl) **S:** 17 kts **Dim:** 146.0 (138.0 pp) × 18.22 × 8.0
Electron Equipt: Radar: 1/Decca RM 1226C, 1/Decca RMS 1230C, 1/SPS-6C
M: 1 set Pamtreda GT; 1 prop; 9,500 hp **Boilers:** 2
Range: 6,000/15 **Man:** 9 officers, 93 men

Remarks: 9,854 grt/9,000 dwt. Two liquid- and one solid-store replenishment stations per side. Helicopter platform aft. Former oiler *Sam Bras* is now an accommodations hulk.

◆ **1 lighthouse tender and tug**

	Laid down	L	In serv.
A 54 Schultz Xavier	2-70	1972	14-7-72

Schultz Xavier (A 54) J.-C. Bellonne, 1973

D: 900 tons **S:** 14 kts **Dim:** 56.1 × 10.0 × 3.8
M: 2 diesels; 1 prop; 2,400 hp **Range:** 3,000/12.5
Man: . . .

Remarks: Reported to be in reserve.

◆ **1 sail-training ship** Bldr: Blohm + Voss, Hamburg

	L	In serv.
A 520 Sagres (ex-*Guanabara*, ex-*Albert Leo Schlageter*)	30-10-37	1-2-38

D: 1,725 tons (1,784 fl) **S:** 10.5 kts (18 sail)
Dim: 90.0 (75.90 hull, 70.4 pp) × 11.9 × 5.2
M: 2 M.A.N. diesels; 1 prop; 750 hp
Range: 5,450/7.5 (power) **Man:** 10 officers, 143 men

Remarks: Acquired by U.S. Navy as reparations, 1945; sold to Brazil in 1948 and to Portugal in 1972, commissioning on 2-2-72. Sail area: 2,355 m². Sisters are U.S. Coast Guard *Eagle* and Soviet *Tovarisch.*

Sagres (A 520)

◆ **1 sail-training sloop** (In serv. . . .)

A 5201 Vega (ex-*Arreda*)

D: 60 tons **S:** . . . **Dim:** 19.8 × 4.3 × 2.5

◆ **1 sail-training yacht** (In serv. . . .)

A 5204 Polar (ex-*Anne Linde*)

D: 70 tons **S:** . . . **Dim:** 22.9 × 4.9 × 2.5

SERVICE CRAFT

◆ **1 U.S. 174-foot-class yard oiler** Bldr: Brunswick Marine, Georgia

	Laid down	L	In serv.
UAM 303 Oeiras (ex-BC-3, ex-YO 194)	14-5-45	25-8-45	30-1-46

Oeiras (UAM 303)—in light condition (old number) L. & L. Van Ginderen, 1983

D: 440 tons light (1,390 fl) **S:** 11 kts **Dim:** 53.04 × 9.75 × 3.96
M: 1 G.M. diesel; 1 prop; 800 hp **Electric:** 120 kw
Fuel: 25 tons **Man:** 23 tot.

Remarks: Transferred in 4-62. Cargo: 924 tons.

◆ **2 small yard oilers**

UAM 301 Odeleite UAM 302 Odivelas

Remarks: Cargo: 674 tons; no other data available.

◆ **1 river navigational buoy tender** Bldr: San Jacintho Aveiro

UAM 675 Guia (In serv. . . .)

D: 70 tons **S:** 8.5 kts **Dim:** 22.0 × 7.9 × 2.2
M: 1 Deutz SBA 6M 816U diesel; 1 Schöttel prop; 350 hp—1 Harbor Master 50 F76 maneuvering unit (3.5 kts)

◆ **1 ex-U.S. Army harbor tug**

UAM 614 Nisa (ex-RB 2, ex-ST 1996)

Remarks: Transferred 2-3-62 from U.S. Navy, Sister RB 1 stricken 1984

◆ **1 yacht/tender** Bldr: Halmatic, U.K. (In serv. 10-84)

UAM 901 Alva

D: 6.5 tons (fl) **S:** 20 kts **Dim:** 10.62 (9.37 wl) × 3.50 × 0.84
M: 2 Volvo TAMD 60C diesels; 2 props; 420 hp

Remarks: Glass-reinforced plastic construction. Used as C-in-C's yacht. Carries 12 passengers.

◆ **7 miscellaneous harbor launches**

UAM 907 Coura	UAM 909 Sorraia	UAM 911 Tua
UAM 908 Paiva	UAM 910 Tamega	UAM 912 Vascão
		UAM 913 Zezere

Remarks: Majority intended to ferry personnel in Lisbon area. The craft shown below is from the above group, but names/numbers cannot be correlated.

PORTUGAL *(continued)*
SERVICE CRAFT *(continued)*

ex-YFB 5 L. & L. Van Ginderen, 1983

QATAR

State of Qatar

PERSONNEL (1985): 400 total

MERCHANT MARINE (1984): 61 ships—332,907 grt
(tankers: 4 ships—76,776 grt)

AVIATION: At least 3 SH-3D Sea King helicopters are in service for search-and-rescue duties

GUIDED-MISSILE PATROL BOATS

◆ **3 French Combattante III class** Bldr: CMN, Cherbourg

	Laid down	L	In serv.
Q 01 DAMSAH	6-5-81	17-6-82	10-11-82
Q 02 AL GHARIYAH	26-8-81	23-9-82	10-2-83
Q 03 RBIGAH	27-10-81	22-12-82	11-5-83

D: 395 tons (430 fl) **S:** 38.5 kts
Dim: 56.0 (53.0 pp) × 8.16 × 2.15 hull (2.5 max.)
A: 8/MM 40 Exocet SSM—1/76-mm OTO Melara DP—2/40-mm Breda AA (II × 1)—4/30-mm Emerlec AA (II × 2)
Electron Equipt: Radar: 1/Decca 1226, 1/Thomson-CSF Pollux, 1/Thomson-CSF Castor,
EW: . . . passive, Dagaie chaff RL

Rbigah (Q 03) G. Gyssels, 6-83

M: 4 MTU 20V538 TB93 diesels; 4 props; 19,300 hp **Range:** 2,000/15

REMARKS: Ordered 10-80. Very similar in appearance and equipment to the three Nigerian units of the class. Two CSEE Panda optical gun directors.

PATROL BOATS AND CRAFT

◆ **6 103-foot boats** Bldr: Vosper Thornycroft, Portchester

	In serv.		In serv.
Q 11 BARZAN	13-1-75	Q 14 AL WUSSAIL	28-10-75
Q 12 HWAR	30-4-75	Q 15 FATEH AL KHATAB	22-1-76
Q 13 THAT ASSUARI	3-10-75	Q 16 TARIQ	1-3-76

Fateh Al Khatab (Q 15) L. & L. Van Ginderen, 1976

Damsah (Q 01) CMN, 1982

QATAR *(continued)*
PATROL BOATS AND CRAFT *(continued)*

D: 120 tons **S:** 27 kts **Dim:** 32.4 (31.1 pp) × 6.3 × 1.6
A: 2/30-mm AA (II × 1) — 1/20-mm AA
M: 2 Paxman Valenta 16RP200 diesels; 2 props; 6,250 hp **Man:** 25 tot.

◆ **4 Tracker Mk II class** Bldr: Fairey Allday Marine, Hamble, U.K. (In serv. 1984)

Q 31 Q 32 Q 33 Q 34

Q 32 and a sister L. & L. Van Ginderen, 1984

D: 34 tons (fl) **S:** 24 kts **Dim:** 20.0 × 5.2 × 1.5
A: . . . **Electron Equipt:** Radar: 1/Decca . . . nav.
M: 2 G.M. 12V71 TI diesels; 2 props; 1,300 hp
Range: 650/20 **Man:** 11 tot.

Remarks: Ordered 2-83. Glass-reinforced plastic construction.

◆ **7 P 1200 class** Bldr: Watercraft, Shoreham, U.K. (In serv. 1980)

D: 12.7 tons (fl) **S:** 29 kts **Dim:** 11.9 × 4.1 × 1.1
A: 2/7.62-mm mg (I × 2)
M: 2 Wizeman-Mercedes WM400 diesels; 2 props; 660 hp **Man:** 4 tot.

◆ **2 45-foot craft** Bldr: Vosper/Keith Nelson

D: 13 tons **S:** 26 kts **Dim:** 13.5 × 3.8 × 1.1
A: 1/12.7-mm mg — 2/7.62-mm mg (I × 2)
M: 2 Caterpillar diesels; 2 props; 800 hp **Man:** 6 tot.

◆ **25 Spear-class craft Mk I and Mk II** Bldr: Fairey Marine, Hamble, U.K. (In serv. 1974-77)

Q 71-Q 95

D: 4.3 tons **S:** 26 kts **Dim:** 9.1 × 2.8 × 0.8
A: 3/7.62-mm mg (I × 3) **M:** 2 diesels; 2 props; 290 hp **Man:** 4 tot.

Remarks: First seven delivered 19-6-74 to 2-75; five more ordered 12-75; three more delivered 30-6-75 to 14-7-75. Ten more delivered 4-77.

◆ **2 Interceptor class** Bldr: Fairey Marine, Hamble, U.K. (In serv. 28-11-75)

D: 1.25 tons **S:** 35 kts **Dim:** 7.9 × 2.4 × 0.9
M: 2 Johnson outboards; 270 hp **Range:** 150/30 **Man:** 3 crew + 10 troops

ROMANIA

Socialist Republic of Romania

Personnel (1984): 6,700 men, 900 of whom are in the Border Guard

Merchant Marine (1984): 393 ships — 2,666,820 grt
(tankers: 10 ships — 295,435 grt)

Naval Aviation: Six Soviet Mi-14 Haze A land-based ASW helicopters and several Alouette-III helicopters are in service.

SUBMARINES

Remarks: Romania is known to be attempting to regain its position as a submarine operating power.

DESTROYERS

◆ **1 Muntenia** (In serv. 8-85) Bldr: Mangalia SY No. 2

Muntenia

Remarks: Length: 145 m; no other data available; reported laid down in 1981 and launched by 1983. See addenda for characteristics.

FRIGATES

◆ **3 Tetal class** Bldr: Mangalia SY No. 2

260 N. . . . . . . (In serv. 1983)
. . . N. . . . . . . (In serv. 1983)
. . . N. . . . . . . (In serv. 1985)

D: 1,800 tons (fl) **S:** . . . kts **Dim:** 93.1 × 11.5 × 3.0
A: 4/76.2-mm DP (II × 2) — 4/30-mm AA (II × 2) — 4/. . .-mm ASW TT — 2/RBU-6000 ASW RL (XIII × 2)
Electron Equipt: . . . **M:** . . .

Remarks: "Tetal" is the NATO code name for this class. There is a helicopter platform. First unit laid down 1980. Program slowed by economic problems.

CORVETTES

◆ **3 ex-Soviet Poti class**

V 31 V 32 V 33

V 32 and V 33 — alongside Cosar-class minelayer 274 1982

D: 400 tons (fl) **S:** 38 kts **Dim:** 59.4 × 7.9 × 2.0 (mean)
A: 2/57-mm AA (II × 1) — 2/RBU-2500 ASW RL — 2/533-mm ASW TT (I × 2)
Electron Equipt: Radar: 1/Don 2, 1/Strut Curve, 1/Muff Cob
IFF: 1/High Pole B — EW: 2/Watch Dog
Sonar: Med.-frequency hull-mounted
M: CODAG: 2 M503A diesels (4,000 hp each); 2 GT (20,000 hp each); 2 props
Range: 500/37; 4,500/10 **Man:** 50 tot.

Remarks: Transferred 1970. Have simpler systems than the Soviet units: 533-mm vice 400-mm torpedo tubes. RBU-2500 vice RBU-6000 rocket launchers, etc. Gas turbines force air into tubes abaft the propellers, in a kind of "waterjet" system. The "V" in the pendant number stands for *Vanatore* (chaser).

◆ **4 Democratia-class ex-minesweepers (German M-40 class)** Bldr: Galati (In serv. 1951)

DB 13 Democratia DB 15 Desrobirea
DB 14 Descatusaria DB 16 Dreptatea

D: 643 tons (775 fl) **S:** 17 kts **Dim:** 62.3 × 8.5 × 2.6
A: 5/37-mm AA (II × 2, I × 1) — 4/14.5-mm mg (II × 2) — 2/RBU-1200 ASW RL (V × 2) — mines
Electron Equipt: Radar: 1/Don-2 — Sonar: . . . — IFF: High Pole A
M: 2 diesels; 2 props; 12,400 hp
Boilers: 2 three-drum **Fuel:** 152 tons **Range:** 4,000/10 **Man:** 80 tot.

Remarks: Begun for German Navy as coal burners, launched postwar. Converted to burn fuel oil on completion. Recently modernized with new superstructures, diesel engines in place of the original reciprocating steam plant; minesweeping gear deleted, ASW ordnance updated.

GUIDED-MISSILE PATROL BOATS

◆ **6 ex-Soviet Osa-I class**

194 195 196 197 198 199

D: 185 tons (215 fl) **S:** 36 kts **Dim:** 38.6 × 7.6 × 1.8
A: 4/SS-N-2 missile launchers — 4/30-mm AK-230 AA (II × 2)
Electron Equipt: Radar: 1/Square Tie, 1/Drum Tilt
IFF: 2/Square Head, 1/High Pole B
M: 3 M503A diesels; 3 props; 12,000 hp **Range:** 500/34; 750/25 **Man:** 30 tot.

Remarks: Transferred after 1960.

GUIDED-MISSILE PATROL BOATS *(continued)*

Romanian Osa-I 196 1974

PATROL BOATS

◆ **16 Shanghai-II class** Bldr: Mangalia SY, Romania (In serv. 1973-. . .)

VS 41 to VS 44 VP 20 to VP 28, VP 30, VP 31, VP 35

Shanghai IIs VP 27, 28, 31, and 30 with a service craft 1982

D: 123 tons (135 fl) **S:** 28.5 kts **Dim:** 38.78 × 5.41 × 1.55
A: VS 41 series: 1/37-mm AA—2/14.5-mm mg (II × 1)—2/RBU-1200 ASW RL (V × 2)—VP 20 series: 4/14.5-mm mg (II × 2)
Electron Equipt: Radar: 1/Pot Head
M: 2 M50-F4, 4,200-hp diesels, 2 12D6, 910-hp diesels; 4 props; 4,220 hp
Range: 750/16.5 **Electric:** 39 kw **Endurance:** 7 days **Man:** 36 tot.

REMARKS: Units with VP pendants serve the Border Guard; some, with only two 14.5-mm machine guns and a large deckhouse aft, serve as search-and-rescue boats. VS = *Vanatore de Submarin* (submarine chaser); VP = *Vedette Patrolare* (patrol boat).

◆ **3 ex-Soviet Kronshtadt class** Bldr: U.S.S.R. (In serv. early 1950s)

V 1 V 2 V 3

D: 300 tons (330 fl) **S:** 18 kts **Dim:** 52.1 × 6.5 × 2.2
A: 1/85-mm DP—2/37-mm AA **M:** 3 Type 9D diesels; 3 props; 3,300 hp
Fuel: 20 tons **Range:** 3,500/14 **Man:** 40 tot.

TORPEDO BOATS

◆ **14 (+. . .) Epitrop class** Bldr: Romania (In serv. 1979-. . .)

Epitrop class 1982

D: 215 tons (fl) **S:** 36 kts **Dim:** 38.6 × 7.6 × 1.8
A: 4/30-mm AK-230 AA (II × 2)—4/533-mm TT (I × 4)
Electron Equipt: Radar: 1/Pot Drum, 1/Drum Tilt—IFF: 1/High Pole A
M: 3 M503A diesels; 3 props; 12,000 hp
Range: 500/35; 750/20 **Man:** 28 tot.

REMARKS: Design based on Osa class; "Epitrop" is the NATO nickname for the class. Construction continues, toward an estimated total of 20. Pendant nos. 202–213.

◆ **23 Huchuan-class hydrofoils** Bldr: Dobreta SY, Turnu (1973-. . .)

VT 51 to VT 73

Romanian Huchuan VT 53 1974

D: 39 tons (45 fl) **S:** 50 kts **Dim:** 22.50 × 6.26 (3.80 deck) × 1.15 (1.11 foiling)
A: 4/14.5-mm AA (II × 2)—2/533-mm TT **Man:** 11 tot.
Electron Equipt: 1/Type 756—IFF: 1/High Pole B
M: 3 M50 diesels; 3 props; 3,600 hp **Range:** 500/30 **Electric:** 5.6 kw

REMARKS: Three built in China, remainder in Romania. Two, named *Jupiter* and *Marte*, have had the torpedo tubes and hydrofoils removed and are used as search-and-rescue craft. VT = *Vedette Torpedinare* (torpedo boat).

MINE WARFARE SHIPS

◆ **2 Cosar-class minelayers** Bldr: Romania (In serv. 1980-82)

271 N. . . . . . . 274 N. . . . . . .

Cosar 274 with corvettes Dreptatea (DB 16) and Desrobirea (DB 15) 1982

D: 1,500 tons (fl) **S:** . . . **Dim:** 79.0 × 10.6 × . . .
A: 2/57-mm AA (II × 1)—4/30-mm AA (II × 2)—2/RBU-1200 ASW RL (V × 2)—mines
Electron Equipt: Radar: 1/navigational, 1 Strut Curve, 1/Muff Cob, 1/Drum Tilt
Sonar: . . .
M: Diesels; 2 props; . . . hp

REMARKS: "Cosar" is the NATO nickname. Shares the same hull as the oceanographic research ship *Grigore Antipa.*

◆ **12 ex-Soviet T-301-class minesweepers**

DR 6-9, DR 17-20, DR 26-29

D: 145.8 tons (160 fl) **S:** 12.5 kts **Dim:** 38.0 × 5.1 × 1.6
A: 1/45-mm AA—4/12.7-mm mg (II × 2)—mines
M: 3 6-cyl. diesels; 3 props; 1,440 hp
Fuel: 20 tons **Range:** 2,500/8 **Man:** 32 tot.

REMARKS: Transferred 1956-60. Gradually being disposed of; most probably in reserve or inoperable.

AUXILIARY SHIPS

◆ **1 oceanographic research ship** Bldr: Romania (In serv. 1980)

GRIGORE ANTIPA

D: 1,500 tons (fl) **S:** . . . **Dim:** 79.0 × 10.6 × . . .
M: Diesels; 2 props; . . . hp

REMARKS: Same hull and propulsion system as Cosar-class minelayers above. Carries a small research submersible.

AUXILIARY SHIPS *(continued)*

◆ **2 Croitor-class small combatant tenders** Bldr: Romania (In serv. 1980)

281 N. . . . . . . 283 N. . . . . . .

Croitor class No. 281 1982

Croitor 283—composite photo 1982

D: 3,500 tons (fl) **S:** . . . kts **Dim:** 110.0 × . . . × . . .
A: 2/57-mm AA (II × 1—2/SA-N-5 SAM syst (IV × 2)—4/30-mm AK-230 AA (II × 2)—4/14.5-mm mg (II × 2)—2/RBU-1200 ASW RL (V × 2)
Electron Equipt: Radar: 1/. . . nav., 1/Strut Curve, 1/Muffcob, 1/Drum Tilt
Sonar: . . .—IFF: 1 High Pole A
M: Diesels; 2 props; . . . hp

Remarks: "Croitor" is the NATO nickname. Resembles a smaller edition of the Soviet "Don" class. Helicopter hangar and flight deck aft. Crane forward of bridge tends magazine for torpedoes and missiles. SA-N-5 rack-launchers mounted atop hangar, with ready-service lockers for 8 missiles.

◆ **3 coastal tankers** (In serv. 1971-73)

TM 530 TM . . . TM . . .

D: 1,300 tons (fl) **S:** 10 kts **Dim:** 60.0 × 9.2 × 4.1
A: 1/37-mm AA—2/12.7-mm mg (I × 2)
M: 1 diesel; 1 prop; 600 hp

◆ **1 seagoing rescue tug** Bldr: Romania (In serv. 1984)

Emil Racovita

Remarks: Same hull and propulsion as the Cosar-class minelayers and the oceanographic research ship *Grigore Antipa.*

◆ **2 Soviet Roslavl-class ocean tugs** Bldr: Galati SY (In serv. 1953-54)

RM 101 Viteazul RM. . . Voinicul

D: 750 tons (fl) **S:** 11 kts **Dim:** 44.5 × 9.5 × 3.5
M: Diesel-electric; 2 props; 1,200 hp **Man:** 28 tot.

Remarks: RM = *Remorcher de Mare* (seagoing tug).

Mircea French Navy, 1980

◆ **1 sail-training ship** Bldr: Blohm + Voss, Hamburg

	Laid down	L	In serv.
Mircea	30-4-38	22-9-38	29-3-39

D: 1,630 tons (fl) **S:** 6 kts (10 sail) **Dim:** 81.78 (73.5 hull) × 12.5 × 5.2
M: 1 M.A.N. diesel; 500 hp **Sail area:** 1,750 m²
Man: 20 men + 120 cadets

Remarks: Refitted in Germany, 1966-67.

Note: The training ship *Neptun* serves the Merchant Marine, not the Navy.

◆ **3 ex-French Friponne-class former minesweepers** Bldrs: Lorient and Brest Dockyards (In serv. 1916-17)

NH 111 Stihi (ex-*Mignonne*)
NH 112 Dumitrescu (ex-*Friponne*)
ND 113 Constanta (ex-*Ghiculescu,* ex-*Impatiente*)

Dumitrescu (NH 112)—white-painted, behind yard oiler 131 1982

D: 330 tons (443 fl) **S:** 12 kts **Dim:** 60.9 × 7.0 × 2.5
A: 1/37-mm AA—4/14.5-mm AA (II × 2)—2/RBU-1200 ASW RL (V × 2)
Electron Equipt: Radar: 2/. . . nav.—Sonar: HF, hull-mounted
IFF: 1/High Pole A
M: 2 Sulzer diesels; 2 props; 900 hp
Fuel: 30 tons **Range:** 3,000/10 **Man:** 50 tot.

Remarks: ND 113 used as a headquarters ship, the others as survey ships. Recently modernized with streamlined superstructures, new armament, etc. ND 113 is 57.8 m o.a.

YARDCRAFT

◆ **10 miscellaneous service boats**

SRS 571	SRS 572	SRS 573	SRS 577	SRS 675: harbor tugs
MM 131	MM 132	MM 133	MM 136	MM 137: fuel lighters

◆ **4 diving tenders**

◆ **3 accommodations barges**

Oltul Ialomita Siretul

◆ **6 small floating workshops**

◆ **3 fireboats**

Automatice Electronica Energerica

D: 160 tons (fl) **S:** 12 kts **Dim:** 38.0 × 5.5 × 1.4
M: 2 diesels; 2 props; . . . hp

DANUBE FLOTILLA

◆ **1 (+ . . .) Brutar-class monitor** Bldr: . . . (In serv. 1982)

D: 350–400 tons (fl) **S:** . . . **Dim:** 43.0 × 8.0 × 1.5
A: 1/100-mm tank gun—4/14.5-mm mg (II × 2)—1/122-mm BM-21 RL (XVIII × 1)—mines
M: Diesels; . . . props; . . . hp

Remarks: "Brutar" is the NATO nickname. Very low-lying craft, armored tank turret and machine-gun turrets.

◆ **18 monitors** Bldr: Dulcea SY (In serv. 1973-76)

VB 76 to VB 93

D: 85 tons **S:** 17 kts **Dim:** 32.0 × 4.8 × 0.9
A: 1/85-mm—4/14.5-mm AA (II × 2)—2/81-mm mortars (I × 2)
M: 2 diesels; 2 props; 1,200 hp **Man:** 25 tot.

Remarks: VB = *Vedeta Blindata* (Armored Boat)

◆ **8 VG-class patrol craft** Bldr: Galati (In serv. 1954)

VG 10–VG 17

D: 40 tons (fl) **S:** 18 kts **Dim:** 16.0 × 4.4 × 1.2
A: 1/20-mm AA—1/7.9-mm mg
M: 2 3D12 diesels; 2 props; 600 hp **Man:** 10 men

ROMANIA *(continued)*
DANUBE FLOTILLA *(continued)*

VG class, VG 11 1971

◆ **20 river minesweepers** Bldr: Turnu-Severin SY (In serv. 1975-. . .)

VD 141–VD 160

D: 65 tons (fl) **S:** 18 kts **Dim:** 26.0 × 4.0 × 0.8
A: 4/14.5-mm mg (II × 2)—mines
M: 2 M50 diesels; 2 props; 1,200 hp

Remarks: Replaced the now-discarded Polish TR-40 class.

◆ **9 SM 165-class patrol/utility craft**

SM 161–SM 169

D: 22 tons **S:** 12 kts **Dim:** 12.2 × 3.0 × 0.9

◆ **5 SD 200-class patrol/utility boats**

SD 270 SD 274 SD 275 SD 277 SD 278

◆ **1 Headquarters ship**

Republica

Remarks: A very old side-wheel paddle boat of about 300 tons (fl).

SABAH

State of Sabah (semi-autonomous Malaysian state)

PATROL BOATS

◆ **2 55-foot boats** Bldr: Cheverton, Isle of Wight, U.K. (In serv. 2-75)

Sri Semporna Sri Bangji

D: 50 tons (fl) **S:** 20 kts **Dim:** 16.8 × 4.6 × 0.9
A: 1/12.7-mm mg **M:** 2 diesels; 2 props; 1,200 hp
Range: 300/15 **Man:** 11 tot.

◆ **2 91-foot boats** Bldr: Vosper Thornycroft, Singapore

PX 17 Sri Gumangtong (In serv. 8-4-70) PX 18 Sri Labuan (In serv. 6-4-70)

D: 85 tons (fl) **S:** 29 kts **Dim:** 26.29 × 5.7 × 1.45
A: 2/20-mm AA **M:** 2 Mercedes-Benz MB820Db diesels; 2 props; 2,790 hp
Range: 700/15 **Man:** 15 tot.

Remarks: On detachment from the Royal Malaysian Marine Police.

◆ **1 patrol boat** Bldr: Mengsina Ltd., Singapore (In serv. 3-12-76)

Kuala Bengkoka

D: . . . **S:** . . . **Dim:** 18.3 × . . . × . . .
A: . . . **M:** diesels

◆ **1 103-foot class** Bldr: Vosper Ltd., Portsmouth, U.K.

P 3147 Sri Melaka (L: 25-2-64)

D: 96 tons (109 fl) **S:** 23 kts **Dim:** 31.39 (28.95 pp) × 5.95 × 1.65
A: 2/40-mm AA (I × 2)—2/7.62-mm mg (I × 2)
Electron Equipt: Radar: 1/Decca 1226
M: 2 Mayback MD 655/18 diesels; 2 props; 3,550 hp
Range: 1,660/14 **Man:** 3 officers, 19 men

Remarks: On detachment from Royal Malaysian Navy. Has fin stabilizers.

MISCELLANEOUS UNITS

◆ **1 yacht** Bldr: Vosper Thornycroft, Singapore (In serv. 11-7-71)

Putri Sabah

D: 117 tons **S:** 22 kts **Dim:** 27.3 × 9.5 × 1.65
M: 1 diesel; 1 prop; . . . hp **Man:** 22 tot.

◆ **1 utility landing craft** Bldr: Chung Wah SY, Hong Kong (In serv. 28-1-78)

Gaya II

D: 220 grt **S:** 8 kts **Dim:** . . . × . . . × . . .
M: 2 Caterpillar D3406TA diesels; 2 props; 275 hp

ST. KITTS

State of Saint Christopher-Nevis

Note: Achieved full independence 8-83; the formerly associated island of Anguilla remains a British dependent.

Merchant Marine (1984): 2 ships—556 grt (Anguilla: 14 ships—4,067 grt)

PATROL BOAT

◆ **1 U.S. 110-ft. Commercial Cruiser design** Bldr: Swiftships Inc., Morgan City, Louisiana (In serv. 6-85)

C-253 Stalwart (In serv. 7-85)

Stalwart (C-253) Swiftships, 7-85

D: 99.8 tons (fl) **S:** 24 kts (22 cruise) **Dim:** 33.53 × 7.62 × 2.13
A: 2/12.7-mm mg (I × 2) **Electron Equipt:** Radar: 1/. . . nav.
M: 4 G.M. 12V71TI diesels; 4 props; 2,400 hp
Range: 2,500/15 **Fuel:** 31,608 liters **Man:** . . .

Remarks: Aluminum construction. Acquired with U.S. financial assistance.

POLICE FORCE

◆ **1 Spear class** Bldr: Fairey Marine, U.K. (In serv. 10-9-74)

D: 4.3 tons (fl) **S:** 30 kts **Dim:** 9.1 × 2.8 × 0.8
A: 2/7.62-mm mg (I × 2) **M:** 2 diesels; 2 props; 360 hp
Man: 2 tot.

ST. LUCIA

State of Saint Lucia

Merchant Marine (1984): 7 ships—2,920 grt

COAST GUARD

PATROL CRAFT

◆ **1 U.S. 65-ft Commercial Cruiser design** Bldr: Swiftships, Inc., Morgan City, Louisiana

P-02 Defender (In serv. 3-5-84)

D: 35 tons (fl) **S:** 23 kts **Dim:** 19.96 × 5.59 × 1.52
A: Small arms **Electron Equipt:** Radar: 1/Raytheon 1210
M: 2 G.M. 12V71 TI diesels; 2 props; 1,350 hp **Electric:** 20 kw
Range: 500/18 **Man:** 6 tot.

Remarks: Aluminum construction. Ordered 9-11-83 with U.S. financial aid. Blue hull, white superstructure.

ST. LUCIA *(continued)*
COAST GUARD *(continued)*

Defender (P-02) Swiftships, 5-84

CUSTOMS SERVICE

◆ **1 small craft** Bldr: St. Vincent (In serv. 11-81)

Vigilant

D: 6 tons (fl) **S:** 23 kts **Dim:** 8.2 × 2.4 × . . .
M: 1 Perkins diesel

Remarks: Sister *Helen II* is operated by the police.

Note: Former patrol craft *Helen* sold 1981.

ST. VINCENT

State of Saint Vincent and the Grenadines

Merchant Marine (1984): 49 ships—101,176 grt
(tanker: 1 ship—6,870 grt)

MARINE WING, POLICE FORCE

PATROL BOATS AND CRAFT

Note: One U.S. Swiftships 110-ft. patrol boat is to be acquired with U.S. aid; characteristics as for the St. Kitts unit.

◆ **1 patrol craft** Bldr: Vosper Thornycroft, Portchester (In serv. 23-2-81)

SGV 05 George McIntosh

George McIntosh (SVG 05) L. & L. Van Ginderen, 3-84

D: 70 tons (fl) **S:** 24.5 kts **Dim:** 22.86 × 7.43 × 1.64
A: 1/20-mm AA **M:** 2 Caterpillar 12V D348 TA diesels; 2 props; 1,840 hp
Electric: 24 kw **Range:** 600/21; 1,000/11 **Man:** 3 officers, 8 men

Remarks: Glass-reinforced Nelson-design, glass-reinforced plastic hull.

◆ **2 locally built 8.2-m patrol craft**

SVG 06 Larkai SVG 07 Brighton

Brighton (SVG 07) L. & L. Van Ginderen, 3-84

SAUDI ARABIA

Kingdom of Saudi Arabia

Personnel (1985): 4,200 total (planned: 4,500 by 1987)

Merchant Marine (1984): 422 ships—3,863,272 grt
(tankers: 102 ships—2,103,081 grt)

Naval Aviation: The Saudi Navy has ordered 24 helicopters from S.N.I.A.S., France: 20 SA-365 F/AS Dauphin 2 for ship- and shore-based ASW and ship-attack, and 4 SA-365N Dauphin 2 configured for search-and-rescue duties, with the Omera DRB 32 search radar. The first production SA-365 F/AS flew 2-7-82. First six production units delivered 8-85 (4 SAR, 2 attack); six more to deliver by end-85, 12 in 1986.

SA-365 F/AS Dauphin production version—with 4 AS 15 missiles S.N.A.I.S., 1982

Dauphin 2 helicopter:
Rotor diameter: 13.29 m; fuselage length: 11.41 m; height: 4 m; weight: light: 1,850 kg/max.: 3,900 kg; propulsion: 2 Turbomeca "Arriel" 1C turbines, 710 hp each.
Performance:
Speed: 130 kts max.
Radius of action—100 nautical miles with 4/AS 15; 140 nautical miles with 2/AS 15
Endurance—2 hours with 4/AS 15; 3 hours with 2/AS 15
Armament: 2 or 4 Aerospatiale AS 15 anti-ship missiles or 2 Mk 36 ASW torpedoes.
The AS 15 missile has a range of 15 km, weighs 96 kg, and is 2.16 m long. The helicopter will carry an "Agrion-15" frequency-agile, pulse-doppler radar to provide missile targeting and to permit the helicopter to provide mid-course guidance update information to the ship-launched Otomat Mk 2 ("Erato") missiles.

NAVAL AVIATION *(continued)*

Otomat Mk 2 Erato anti-ship missile:
Length: 4.66 m; range: 90 nautical miles; diameter: 0.40 m (0.46 m rear); weight: 780 kg (210 kg warhead); propulsion: Turbomeca "Arbizon" turbojet, 2 rocket boosters.

GUIDED-MISSILE FRIGATES

◆ 0 (+2) new construction

REMARKS: Planned for acquisition are two larger guided-missile frigates. France has offered the F4000 design, with the U.S. Standard SM1 missile (Mk 13 launcher) and Otomat anti-ship missiles. The U.S. has offered the *Oliver Hazard Perry* (FFG 7) class.

◆ 2 (+2) Al Madinah class

	Bldr	Laid down	L	In serv.
702 AL MADINAH	Arsenal de Lorient	15-10-81	23-4-83	4-1-85
704 HOFOUF	CNIM, La Seyne	14-6-82	24-6-83	31-10-85
706 ABHA	CNIM, La Seyne	7-12-82	23-12-83	3-86
708 TAIF	CNIM, La Seyne	1-3-83	17-3-84	8-86

Hofouf (704) G. Gyssels, 6-85

Al Madinah (702) DCN, 1984

Al Madinah (702) DCAN, 3-4-84

Al Madinah (702) G. Gyssels, 6-85

D: 2,000 tons (2,250 normal, 2,610 fl) **S:** 30 kts
Dim: 115.00 (106.50 pp) × 12.50 wl × 3.40 (4.65 over sonar)
A: 8/Otomat Mk 2 "Erato" SSM (IV × 2)—1/Crotale EDIR SAM syst. (VIII × 1; 26 total missiles)—1/100-mm Compact DP—4/40-mm Breda AA (II × 2)—4 tubes for F17P wire-guided torpedoes—1/Dauphin 2 ASW/anti-ship helicopter
Electron Equipt: Radar: 2/Decca TM 1226, 1/Sea Tiger (DRBV 15), 1/Castor IIC, 1/DRBC-32E (on Crotale launcher); 1/helo control
Sonar: Thomson-CSF TSM 2630 (Diodon) hull-mounted, TSM 2630 (Sorel) VDS
EW: Thomson-CSF DR 4000S intercept syst., Janet jammer, Telegon VI D/F, 2/Dagaie chaff RL
M: 4 SEMT-Pielstick 16 PA 6 BTC diesels/ 2 props; 32,500 hp
Electric: 2,560 kw **Fuel:** 370 tons **Range:** 6,500/18; 8,000/15
Man: 15 officers, 50 petty officers, 114 men

REMARKS: Ordered 10-80 as part of the "Sawari" program, under which France replaced the U.S. Navy as principal naval equipment supplier. Very complex ships, with much new, untried equipment. Have Thomson-CSF TAVITAC computer data system, with 2 Type 15M 125F computers, 6 display consoles, E7000 tactical table; similar to French Navy's SENIT-VI. Retractable fin stabilizers fitted. Alcatel Type DLA torpedo f.c.s.

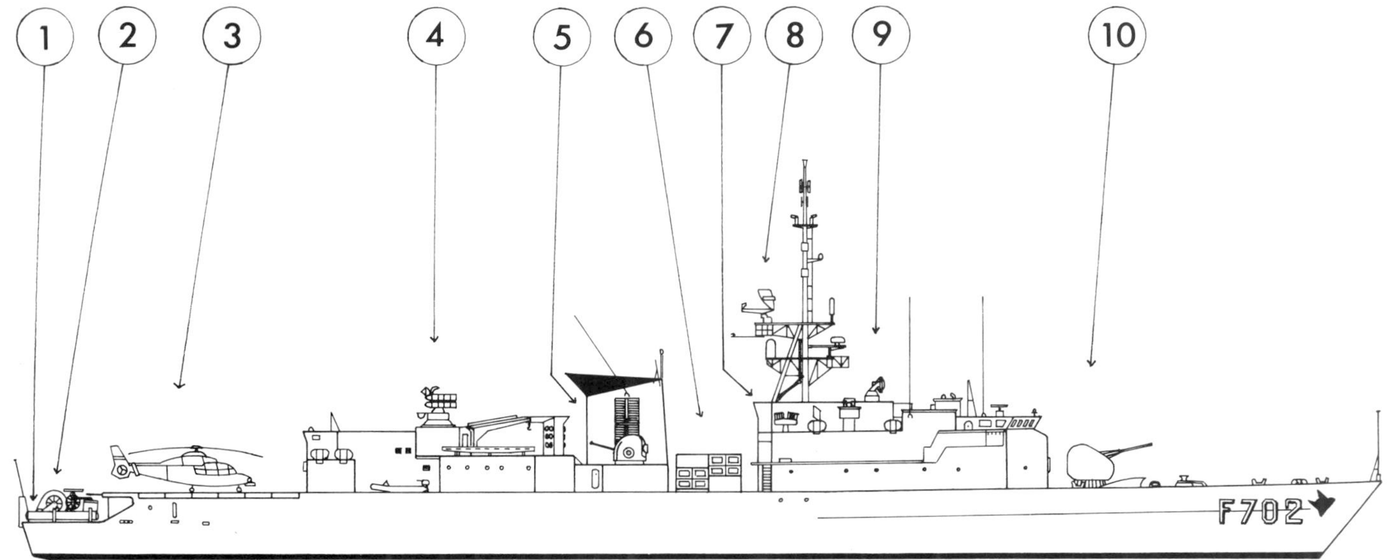

Al Madinah (702) 1. Torpedo tubes 2. Sorel variable depth sonar 3. Dauphin 2 helicopter 4. Crotale EDIR SAM launcher 5. Twin 40-mm Breda AA 6. Otomat SSM launchers 7. Dagaie decoy RL 8. Sea Tiger search radar 9. Castor IIC fire-control radar director 10. 100-mm Compact DP gun

GUIDED-MISSILE FRIGATES *(continued)*

Sorel is a VDS version of the Diodon sonar; both operate at 11, 12, or 13 kHz. There are 4 generator sets of 480 kw and 2 of 320 kw each. Carry 500 rds 100-mm ammunition, 6,300 rds 40-mm. There are two CSEE optical gun directors. There are 13 main watertight bulkheads to the hull.

GUIDED-MISSILE CORVETTES

◆ **4 U.S. PCG class** Bldr: Tacoma Boatbuilding, Tacoma, Wash.

	Laid down	L	In serv.
612 Badr (ex-PCG 1)	30-5-79	26-1-80	28-9-81
614 Al-Yarmook (ex-PCG 2)	13-12-79	13-5-80	10-5-82
616 Hitteen (ex-PCG 3)	19-5-80	5-9-80	12-10-82
618 Tabuk (ex-PCG 4)	22-9-80	18-6-81	10-1-83

Badr (612) G. Arra, 1982

Tabuk (618) G. Arra, 1983

D: 903 tons (1,038 fl) **S:** 30 kts gas turbines, 21 kts diesel
Dim: 74.68 × 9.60 × 2.59
A: 8/Harpoon SSM (IV × 2)—1/76-mm U.S. Mk 75 DP—1/20-mm Vulcan/Phalanx AA—2/20-mm AA (I × 2)—1/81-mm mortar—2/40-mm Mk 19 grenade launchers—6/Mk 32 ASW TT (III × 2)
Electron Equipt: Radar: 1/SPS-55, 1/SPS-40B, 1/Mk 92 fire-control system
Sonar: SQS-56
EW: SLQ-32 (V)1, Mk 36 SRBOC chaff RL (VI × 2)
M: CODOG: 1 G.E. LM-2500 gas turbine (23,000 hp); 2 MTU 12V652 TB91 diesels (3,058 hp tot.); 2 CP props
Electric: 1,200 kw **Man:** 7 officers, 51 men

Remarks: Ordered 30-8-77. Have fin stabilizers. Program completed well behind schedule, with the ships considerably overweight. Have one Mk 24 optical target designator, Mk 309 ASW f.c.s.

GUIDED-MISSILE PATROL BOATS

◆ **9 U.S. PGG class** Bldr: Peterson Builders, Sturgeon Bay, Wisc.

	Laid down	L	In serv.
511 As-Siddiq (ex-PGG 1)	30-9-78	22-9-79	15-12-80
513 Al-Farouq (ex-PGG 2)	12-3-79	17-5-80	22-6-81
515 Abdul-Aziz (ex-PGG 3)	19-10-79	23-8-80	3-9-81
517 Faisal (ex-PGG 4)	4-3-80	15-11-80	23-11-81
519 Khalid (ex-PGG 5)	27-6-80	28-3-81	11-1-82
521 Amr (ex-PGG 6)	21-10-80	13-6-81	21-6-82
523 Tariq (ex-PGG 7)	10-2-81	23-9-81	16-8-82
525 Oqbah (ex-PGG 8)	8-5-81	12-12-81	18-10-82
527 Abu Obaidah (ex-PGG 9)	4-9-81	3-4-82	6-12-82

Amr (521) G. Arra, 1983

Abu Obaidah (527) L. & L. Van Ginderen, 11-82

D: 425 tons (495 fl) **S:** 34 kts gas turbines, 16 kts diesels
Dim: 58.02 × 8.08 × 1.95
A: 4/Harpoon (II × 2)—1/76-mm U.S. Mk 75 DP—1/20-mm Vulcan/Phalanx AA—2/20-mm AA (I × 2)—1/81-mm mortar—2/40-mm Mk 19 grenade launchers
Electron Equipt: Radar: 1/SPS-55, 1/Mk 92 fire-control system
EW: SLQ-32 (V)1, Mk 36 SRBOC chaff RL (VI × 2)
M: CODOG: 1.G.E. gas turbine (23,000 hp); 2 MTU 12V652 TB91 diesels (3,058 hp tot.); 2 CP props
Electric: 800 kw **Range:** 600/30; 2,900/14 **Man:** 5 officers, 33 men

Remarks: Ordered 16-2-77. Fin stabilizers fitted. Delivered behind schedule and considerably over designed displacement. Have one Mk 24 optical target designation transmitter.

TORPEDO BOATS

◆ **3 German Jaguar class (Type 141)** Bldr: Lürssen, Vegesack (In serv. 1969)

Dammam Khabar Maccah

Khabar 1975

D: 170 tons (210 fl) **S:** 40 kts **Dim:** 42.62 × 7.10 × 2.39
A: 2/40-mm AA (I × 2)—4/533-mm TT
M: 4 Maybach 16-cyl. diesels; 4 props; 12,000 hp **Range:** 500/39; 1,000/32
Man: 3 officers, 33 men

Remarks: Refitted 1976 by builders; possibly no longer operable.

MINE WARFARE SHIPS

◆ **4 U.S. MSC 322 class** Bldr: Peterson Builders, Sturgeon Bay, Wisc.

	Laid down	L	In serv.
412 Addiriyah (ex-MSC 322)	12-5-76	20-12-76	6-7-78
414 Al-Quysumah (ex-MSC 323)	24-8-76	26-5-77	15-8-78
416 Al-Wadeeah (ex-MSC 324)	28-12-76	6-9-77	7-9-78
418 Safwa (ex-MSC 325)	5-3-77	7-12-77	20-10-78

MINE WARFARE SHIPS *(continued)*

Al-Quysumah (414) L. & L. Van Ginderen, 8-78

D: 320 tons (407 fl) **S:** 14 kts **Dim:** 46.63 × 8.29 × 4.06 max.
A: 2/20-mm AA Mk 67 (II × 1)
Electron Equipt: Radar: SPS-55—Sonar: SQQ-14
M: 2 Waukesha E1616 diesels; 2 props; 1,200 hp
Electric: 2,150 kw **Man:** 4 officers, 35 men

Remarks: Ordered 30-9-75. Longer than standard U.S. export coastal minesweepers. Wooden construction. Have a 1,750-kw sweep current generator. Used primarily as patrol boats.

AMPHIBIOUS WARFARE CRAFT

◆ **4 U.S. LCU 1646 class** Bldr: Newport SY, Rhode Island (In serv. 1976)

212 Al-Qiaq (ex-SA 310) 216 Al-Ula (ex-SA 312)
214 As-Sulayel (ex-SA 311) 218 Afif (ex-SA 313)

D: 173 tons (403 fl) **S:** 11 kts **Dim:** 41.07 × 9.07 × 2.08
A: 2/20-mm AA (I × 2) **Electron Equipt:** Radar: 1/LN-66
M: 4 G.M. 6-71 diesels; 2 Kort-nozzle props; 900 hp **Cargo:** 168 tons
Electric: 80 kw **Range:** 1,200/10 **Man:** 2 officers, 12 men, 20 passengers

◆ **4 landing craft (LCM)** Bldr: Schlichting Werft, Travemünde, West Germany (In serv. 1982)

201–204

D: 26 tons (light) **S:** . . . **Dim:** 16.5 × 4.0 × . . .
M: 2 diesels; 2 props; . . . hp

◆ **8 U.S. LCM(6)-class landing craft** (4 in serv. 7-77, 4 in serv. 7-80)

D: 24 tons (57.5 fl) **S:** 13 kts **Dim:** 17.07 × 4.37 × 1.14
A: 2/40-mm Mk 19 grenade launchers
M: 2 G.M. 6V71 diesels; 2 props; 450 hp
Range: 130/9 (loaded) **Man:** 5 tot.

Remarks: Cargo: 30 tons or 80 troops. Cargo well: 11.9 × 3.7.

AUXILIARIES

◆ **2 underway replenishment oilers** Bldr: CN la Ciotat, Marseilles

	Laid down	L	In serv.
902 Boraida	13-4-82	22-1-83	29-2-84
904 Yunbou	9-10-83	20-10-84	29-8-85

D: 10,500 tons (trials) **S:** 20.5 kts **Dim:** 135.0 × 18.7 × 7.0
A: 4/40-mm AA (II × 2)—2/Dauphin 2 helicopters
Electron Equipt: Radar: 2/. . . nav.
M: 2 SEMT-Pielstick 14 PC 2.5V400 diesels; 2 CP props; 13,200 hp
Electric: 3,440 kw **Range:** 7,000/17 **Man:** 140 tot. + 55 cadets

Boraida (902) DCN, 1984

Boraida (902) L. & L. Van Ginderen, 8-84

Remarks: Ordered 10-80 as part of the "Sawari" program. Design a reduced version of the French *Durance* class. To act as training ships as well as replenishment vessels. Cargo includes 4,350 tons diesel fuel; 350 tons aviation fuel; 140 tons potable water; 100 tons provisions; 100 tons munitions; and 70 tons spares. One replenishment station per side, plus over-the-stern refueling. Can transfer 1.7-ton solid loads. Have electrical, mechanical, and metal workshops. Endurance: 30 days. Two CSEE Naja directors for the 40-mm AA. The helicopters will be supplied with ASW and anti-ship weapons. 902 left 3-8-84 for Saudi Arabia.

◆ **1 Jetfoil-type hydrofoil royal yacht** Bldr: Boeing, Seattle (In serv. 8-85)

N. . .

D: 115 tons (fl) **S:** 46 kts **Dim:** 27.4 (foils down) × 9.1 × 1.9 hull (5.2 foils down at rest/2.0 foiling)
A: 2/20-mm G.E. Sea Vulcan gatling AA (I × 2)
Electron Equipt: Radar: 1/. . . nav.
M: 2 Allison 501-KF20A gas turbines; 2 Rocketdyne R-20 waterjet pumps; 9,000 hp (7,560 sust.)—2 G.M. 8V92 TI diesels; 2 props; 900 hp for hullborne cruise
Range: 890/40, 1,500/15 (hullborne) **Fuel:** 33 tons **Man:** . . .

Remarks: Aluminum construction. Subcontracted to Boeing by Lockheed. Has a Kollmorgan electro-optical GFCS for the gunmounts. Acts as tender for the larger yachts.

◆ **1 royal yacht** Bldr: Helsingor Vaerft, Denmark (In serv. 12-83)

Abdul Aziz

Abdul Aziz—white with blue funnels Walles Foto, 5-84

D: Approx. 5,200 tons (fl) **S:** 22 kts **Dim:** 147.00 (126.00 pp) × 18.00 × 4.90
M: 2 Lindholmen-Pielstick 12 PC 2-5V400 diesels; 2 props; 15,600 hp
Fuel: 640 tons **Man:** 65 crew, plus 4 royalty, plus 60 passengers

Remarks: Delivered by builders 4-83 to Vosper Shiprepairers, Southampton, for final fitting out and ran post-outfitting trials 15-5-84. Stern ramp leading to vehicle garage. Swimming pool. Helicopter hangar forward. Perhaps the nicest touch: a retractable figurehead, with closure doors in the stem. Presumably supplements the *Al Riyadh,* below.

◆ **1 royal yacht** Bldr: C. Van Lent & Sons, Kaag, Netherlands (In serv. 1-78)

Al Riyadh

D: 670 tons (fl) **S:** 20 kts **Dim:** 64.64 (59.22 pp) × 9.7 × 3.0
A: None **Electron Equipt:** Radar: 1/Decca RM 916
M: 2 MTU 16V956 diesels; 2 props; 5,720 hp **Electric:** 370 kw
Range: 1,750/18 **Man:** 16 tot.

Remarks: Fin stabilizers and Schöttel bow-thruster fitted.

◆ **1 salvage tug** Bldr: Hayashikane, Shimonoseki (In serv. 1978)

13 Jeddah

D: 350 tons **S:** 12 kts **Dim:** 34.4 × . . . × . . . **M:** 2 diesels; 800 hp

◆ **2 U.S. YTB 760 class tugs** (In serv. 15-10-75)

EN 111 Tuwaig (ex-YTB 837) EN 112 Dareen (ex-YTB 838)

D: 291 tons (316 fl) **S:** 12 kts **Dim:** 33.22 × 9.30 × 4.14
A: 2/20-mm AA (I × 2) **Electron Equipt:** Radar: 1/LN-66
M: 2 diesels; 1 prop; 2,000 hp **Electric:** 120 kw
Range: 2,000/10 **Man:** 4 officers, 8 men

Remarks: 25-ton bollard pull. Intended for target towing, firefighting, torpedo recovery, and local patrol duties.

Note: Eleven more tugs in the *Radhwa*-series are government-owned, but not naval.

SAUDI ARABIA *(continued)*

COAST GUARD

PATROL BOAT

◆ **1 U.S. Coast Guard Cape class**

Riyadh

D: 102 tons (fl) **S:** 18 kts **Dim:** 28.95 × 5.8 × 1.55
A: 1/40-mm AA **M:** 4 Cummins VT-12-M-700 diesels; 2 props; 2,324 hp
Electric: 40 kw **Range:** 1,500/12 **Man:** 15 tot.

Remarks: Transferred in 1969.

PATROL CRAFT

◆ **25 Scorpion class** Bldrs: 20 units: Bayerische Schiffsbau, Erlenbach; 5 units: Arminias Werft, Bodenwerder, West Germany (In serv. 1979, except last 10: 28-2-81)

139–164

143 P. Voss, 5-82

D: 33 tons (fl) **S:** 25 kts **Dim:** 17.14 (15.6 pp) × 4.98 × 1.40
A: 2/7.62-mm mg **Electron Equipt:** Radar: 1/Decca RM 914
M: 2 G.M. 12V71 TI diesels; 2 props; 1,300 hp (1,050 sust.)
Range: 200/20 **Man:** 7 tot.

◆ **12 Rapier class** Bldr: Halter Marine, New Orleans, La. (In serv. 1976-77)

127–138

Rapier class Halter Marine, 1976

D: 26 tons (fl) **S:** 28 kts **Dim:** 15.24 × 4.57 × 1.35
A: 2/7.62-mm mg (I × 2) **M:** 1 G.M. 12V71 TI diesels; 2 props; 1,300 hp
Electric: 20 kw **Man:** 1 officer, 8 men

◆ **43 C-80 class** Bldr: Northshore Yacht Yard, U.K. (In serv. 1975-77)

D: 2.8 tons (fl) **S:** 20 kts **Dim:** 8.9 × 2.9 × 0.6 **A:** 1/7.62-mm mg
M: 1 Caterpillar diesel; Castoldi water jet; 210 hp **Man:** 3 tot.

◆ **10 Huntress class** Bldr: Fairey Marine, Hamble, U.K. (In serv. 1976)

D: 4 tons (fl). . . **S:** 20 kts **Dim:** 7.1 × 2.7 × 0.8
A: 1/7.62-mm mg **M:** 1 diesel; 180 hp **Range:** 150/20 **Man:** 4 tot.

◆ **8 SRN.6 Mod. 8 hovercraft** Bldr: British Hovercraft, Cowes (In serv.: 6 in 1981, 2 in 1-82)

D: 17 tons (fl) **S:** 50-55 kts **Dim:** 18.3 × 8.5 × . . .
A: Small arms **Electron Equipt:** Radar: 1/Decca . . .
M: 1 Rolls-Royce Gnome gas turbine; 1 lift fan, 1 airscrew; 1,060 hp

Two Saudi Coast Guard SRN.6 Mod. 8 British Hovercraft, 1981

Remarks: Payload: 6 tons. Endurance: 6 to 11 hours. Carry 1,200 liters fuel internally, plus two 450-l deck tanks.

◆ **16 SRN.6-class hovercraft** Bldr: British Hovercraft, 1970 and 1981

D: 10 tons **S:** 58 kts **Dim:** 14.8 × 7.7 × 4.8 (high) **A:** 1/7.62-mm mg
M: 1 Rolls-Royce Gnome gas turbine; 900 hp

◆ **8 harbor patrol craft** Bldr: Yokohama Yacht, Japan, 1972

D: . . . **S:** 20 kts **Dim:** 10.5 × 3.0 × . . . **M:** 2 diesels; 2 props; 280 hp

Note: There are also several hundred small boats: 200 of 5.1-m length with 40-hp engines and 100 of 4.2-m length with a 20-hp engine.

AUXILIARIES AND SERVICE CRAFT

◆ **1 training ship** Bldr: Bayerische Schiffsbau, Erlenbach, West Germany (In serv. 12-77)

Tebuk

D: 600 tons (750 fl) **S:** 20 kts **Dim:** 60.0 (55.5 pp) × 10.0 × 2.50
Electron Equipt: Radar: 1/Decca TM 1226
M: 2 MTU 16V538 TB81 diesels; 2 props; 5,260 hp (4,800 sust.)
Range: 2,400/18; 3,900/12 **Electric:** 1,040 kVA
Man: 24 crew, plus 36 trainees

◆ **3 small fuel lighters**—27-mm overall

Al Forat Dajlah N. . . . . . .

◆ **2 yachts**

Al Deriyah Promineut

◆ **5 barges**

◆ **4 motor dhows**

SENEGAL

Republic of Senegal

(Note: The "confederation" with the Gambia does not affect military forces.)

Personnel: 650 men

Merchant Marine (1985): 135 ships—44,056 grt
(tankers: 3 ships—3,620 grt)

Naval Aviation: One Canadian de Havilland DHC-6-300M Twin Otter for Maritime patrol.

PATROL BOATS

◆ **0 (+1) Osprey 50 design** Bldr: Fredrikshavn Vaerft, Denmark

	Laid down	L	In serv.
P. . . N. . .	. . .	. . .	. . .

D: 470 tons (fl) **S:** 19 kts **Dim:** 49.90 (45.80 pp) × 10.50 × 3.48
A: 2/40-mm AA—2/20-mm AA (I × 2)—2/12.7-mm mg (I × 2)
Electron Equipt: Radar: . . . **Electric:** 359 kVA
M: 2 Burmeister & Wain 16VL3L-VO diesels; 2 CP props; 4,640 hp
Range: 4,500/16 **Man:** . . .

Remarks: Ordered late 1984. Thornycroft-Giles "short, fat ship" hull. Sisters in Danish and Burmese service. Will probably be used for 200-n.m. economic zone and fisheries patrol.

PATROL BOATS *(continued)*

◆ **1 French PR 72 MS class** Bldr: SFCN, Villeneuve-la-Garenne

	Laid down	L	In serv.
P 773 Njambur	5-80	23-12-80	9-81

Njambur (P 773) SFCN, 1981

D: 381 tons light (451 fl) **S:** 30 kts **Dim:** 58.70 (54.0 pp) × 8.22 × 2.18
A: 2/76-mm OTO Melara Compact (I × 2)—2/20-mm Type F2 AA (I × 2)
Electron Equipt: Radar: 1/Decca 1226
M: 4 AGO 195V16 RVR diesels; 4 props; 12,800 hp
Range: 2,500/16 **Man:** 39 tot. plus 7 passengers

Remarks: Can be equipped later with 4/Exocet SSM. Two CSEE Naja optical GFCS.

◆ **3 PR-48 class** Bldr: SFCN, Villeneuve-la-Garenne

	Laid down	L	In serv.
Saint Louis	20-4-70	5-8-70	1-3-71
Popenguine	12-73	22-3-74	10-8-74
Podor	12-75	20-7-76	13-7-77

Saint Louis 1971

D: 240 tons (avg.) **S:** 23 kts **Dim:** 47.5 (45.5 pp) × 7.1 × 2.5
A: 2/40-mm AA (I × 2)—2/7.62-mm mg (I × 2)
Electron Equipt: Radar: 1/Decca 1226
M: 2 AGO V12 CZSHR diesels; 2 props; 6,240 hp
Range: 2,000/16 **Man:** 3 officers, 22 men

PATROL CRAFT

◆ **3 "Interceptor" class** Bldr: Turbec Ltd., St. Catherine, Canada

Senegal II Siné Saloum II Casamance II

D: 52 tons (62 fl) **S:** 32 kts **Dim:** 26.5 × 5.81 × . . .
A: 2/20-mm AA (I × 2) **Electron Equipt:** Radar: 1/LN-66
M: 2 diesels; 2 props; 2,700 hp

Remarks: In service 2-79, 7-79, and 10-79, respectively. Used for fisheries protection patrol.

Casamance II L. & L. Van Ginderen

AMPHIBIOUS WARFARE SHIPS

◆ **1 (+1) ex-French EDIC-class landing craft** (L: 11-4-58) Bldr (new unit): SFCN, Villeneuve-la-Garenne

Faleme (ex-EDIC 9095) N. . .

D: 250 tons (670 fl) **S:** 8 kts **Dim:** 59.0 × 11.95 × 1.3
A: 2/20-mm AA (I × 2) **M:** 2 MGO diesels; 2 props; 1,000 hp
Range: 1,800/8 **Man:** 16 tot.

Remarks: Transferred 7-1-74. Can carry eleven trucks or five LVT amphibious personnel carriers. Second unit, a possible replacement for the first, ordered, 5-85.

◆ **2 ex-U.S. LCM-6-class landing craft**

Djomboss Douloulou

D: 26 tons (52 fl) **S:** 10 kts **Dim:** 17.1 × 4.4 × 1.2
M: 2 Gray Marine 64 HN9 diesels; 2 props; 330 hp

Remarks: Transferred in 7-68.

AUXILIARY SHIPS

◆ **1 training ship**

Crame Jean (ex-*Raymond Sarr*)

D: 18 tons

Remarks: A former fishing vessel, acquired 1978.

◆ **1 tug**

Ibis

D: 200 tons (fl) **S:** 9 kts **Dim:** 18.4 × 5.7 × 2.5
M: 1 Poyaud diesel; 250 hp **Range:** 1,700/9

Remarks: On loan from the French Navy.

SENEGAL POLICE

PATROL CRAFT

◆ **2 Type DS 01** Bldr: Celayo, Bilbao, Spain (In serv. 1-82)

D: 26 tons (fl) **S:** 20 kts **Dim:** 16.0 (13.3 pp) × 4.8 × 1.6
A: 1/12.7-mm mg **Electron Equipt:** Radar: 1/Decca 110
M: 2 G.M. 5V71 TI diesels; 2 props; 870 hp **Man:** 8 tot.

◆ **4 harbor craft** Bldr: ARESA, Arenys de Mar, Spain (In serv. 1979)

D: 3.5 tons (fl) **S:** 18 kts **Dim:** 8.5 × . . . × . . .

◆ **3 Lance class** Bldr: Fairey Marine, Hamble, U.K. (In serv. 1974-77)

Djibrill Djilor Gorée

D: 15.7 tons **S:** 24 kts **Dim:** 14.8 × 4.7 × 1.3
A: 2/7.62-mm mg (I × 2) **M:** 2 G.M. 8V71 TI diesels; 2 props; 850 hp
Man: 7 tot.

◆ **7 45-foot class** Bldr: Vosper Thornycroft

D: 10 tons (fl) **S:** 25 kts **Dim:** 13.7 × 4.0 × 1.1
A: 1/12.7-mm mg—2/7.62-mm mg (I × 2)
M: 2 diesels; 2 props; 920 hp **Man:** 6 tot.

Remarks: Five sisters discarded.

◆ **2 Huntress class** Bldr: Fairey Marine, Hamble, U.K. (In serv. 1974)

D: 4 tons (fl) **S:** 20 kts **Dim:** 7.1 × 2.7 × 0.8
A: 1/7.62-mm mg **M:** 1 diesel; 180 hp **Man:** 2 tot.

SEYCHELLES

Republic of Seychelles

MERCHANT MARINE (1984): 3 ships — 1,160 grt

NAVAL AVIATION: 1 Britten-Norman BN-42 B/T Maritime Defender for surveillance ordered 1983. Libya donated 2 super Rallye light planes in 1980, and India delivered 2 Chetak (Alouette-III) helicopters in 6-82.

PATROL BOATS AND CRAFT

◆ **1 FPB 42 class** Bldr: C.N. Picchiotti, Viareggio, Italy (In serv. 10-1-83)

505 ANDROMANCHE

Andromanche (505) Picchiotti, 1-83

D: 240 tons (268 fl) **S:** 28 kts **Dim:** 41.80 × 8.00 × 2.50 (props; 1.70 hull)
A: 1/20-mm AA — 2/7.62-mm mg (I × 2)
Electron Equipt: Radar: 2/Furuno. . .
M: 2 Paxman Valenta 16 RP200 CM diesels; 2 props; 6,800 hp (5,700 sust.)
Range: 3,000/16 **Man:** 22 tot.

REMARKS: Ordered 8-10-81. A second unit is planned.

◆ **1 ex-French Sirius-class former minesweeper** Bldr: Seine Maritime (L: 13-6-56)

P. . . TOPAZ (ex-*Croix du Sud,* P 658)

D: 400 tons (440 fl) **S:** 15 kts **Dim:** 46.4 (42.7 pp) × 8.55 × 2.5
A: 1/40-mm AA — 1/20-mm AA **M:** 2 SEMT-Pielstick diesels; 2 props; 2,000 hp
Fuel: 48 tons **Range:** 3,000/10 **Man:** 2 officers, 35 men

REMARKS: Transferred 1979. Minesweeping gear removed.

◆ **2 Soviet Zhuk class**

CONSTANT (In serv. 17-10-81) FORTUNE (In serv. 11-82)

D: 60 tons (fl) **S:** 34 kts **Dim:** 24.0 × 5.0 × 1.8 (props)
A: 4/14.5-mm mg (II × 2) **Electron Equipt:** Radar: 1/Spin Trough
M: 2 M-50 F4 diesels; 2 props; 2,400 hp

◆ **1 glass-reinforced plastic-hulled** Bldr: Tyler, U.K. (In serv. 4-80)

JUNON

D: 40 tons **S:** 26 kts **Dim:** 18.3 × . . . × . . .
M: 2 G.M. diesels; 2 props; 1,040 hp **Range:** 1,000/22

AUXILIARY SHIP

◆ **1 medium landing ship** Bldr: A.C. de la Perrière, France

	Laid down	L	In serv.
5 JUIN	7-4-78	19-9-78	11-1-79

D: 350 tons (855 fl) **S:** 9 kts **Dim:** 58.2 × 11.37 × 1.9
M: 2 Poyaud A12 150M diesels; 2 props; 880 hp **Range:** 2,000/9

REMARKS: Owned by the government but operated in local commercial service. Bow ramp. Cargo: 272 tons.

SIERRA LEONE

Republic of Sierra Leone

PERSONNEL (1985): 45 men

MERCHANT MARINE (1984): 23 ships — 5,573 grt

PATROL CRAFT

◆ **1 Tracker Mk II class** Bldr: Fairey Allday Marine, Hamble, U.K. (In serv. 27-11-82)

PRESIDENT SIOKA STEVENS

D: 31 tons **S:** 29 kts **Dim:** 19.25 × 5.00 × 1.45
A: 1/20-mm AA — 2/7.62-mm mg (I × 2)
Electron Equipt: Radar: 1/Decca 090
M: 2 G.M. 12V71 diesels; 2 props; 1,300 hp **Range:** 650/25 **Man:** 11 tot.

REMARKS: Glass-reinforced plastic construction. Completed 6-12-81, but not placed in service for nearly a year.

NOTE: Three Chinese Shanghai II-class patrol boats delivered in 1976 are no longer in service.

SINGAPORE

Republic of Singapore

PERSONNEL (1985): approximately 3,000 men

MERCHANT MARINE (1984): 825 ships — 6,512,344 grt
(tankers: 149 ships — 2,294,785 grt)

GUIDED-MISSILE PATROL BOATS

NOTE: Some 16–20 U.S. RGM-84A Harpoon anti-ship missiles were ordered in 1985.

◆ **6 FPB 45 class**

	In serv.		In serv.		In serv.
P 76 SEA WOLF	1972	P 78 SEA DRAGON	1974	P 80 SEA HAWK	1975
P 77 SEA LION	1972	P 79 SEA TIGER	1974	P 81 SEA SCORPION	1975

Bldrs: P 76, P 77: Lürssen, Vegesack; others: Singapore SB & Eng., Jurong

Sea Scorpion (P 81) L. & L. Van Ginderen, 3-84

D: 225 tons (252 fl) **S:** 38 kts **Dim:** 44.90 (42.30 wl) × 7.00 × 2.48
A: 5 Gabriel I missiles (III × 1, I × 2) — 1/57-mm AA — 1/40-mm AA
Electron Equipt: Radar: 1/Decca TM 626, 1/H.S.A. WM-28
M: 4 MTU 16V538 diesels; 4 props; 14,400 hp **Range:** 2,000/15 **Man:** 40 tot.

REMARKS: Ordered in 1970. Frequently seen without missiles. Two multiple 57-mm flare launchers on 57-mm mount. Carry 504 rounds 57-mm, 1,008 rounds 40-mm. Intercept equipment on tripod topmast added 1980-81.

PATROL BOATS

◆ **1 (+2) German FPB 57 class** Bldr: Singapore SB & Eng., Jurong

	Laid down	L	In serv.
P. . . N.	6-80	. . .	9-83(?)
P. . . N.	. . .	. . .	. . .
P. . . N.	. . .	. . .	. . .

D: 353 tons normal (398 fl) **S:** 36.5 kts **Dim:** 58.10 (54.40 wl) × 7.62 × 2.83
A: 1/76-mm OTO Melara DP — 2/35-mm Oerlikon GDM-A AA (II × 1)
Electron Equipt: Radar: 1/navigational, 1/H.S.A. WM 28-41
EW: SUSIE-1 passive intercept
M: 4 MTU 16V956 TB91 diesels; 4 props; 18,000 intercept
Electric: 405 kVA **Range:** 700/35 **Man:** 5 officers, 33 men

PATROL BOATS *(continued)*

REMARKS: Three were to be built for Singapore Navy use and three on speculation, for export. Carry 300 rounds 76-mm, 2,750 rounds 35-mm and can be equipped with anti-ship missiles. Program status in doubt; do not appear on fleet lists.

◆ **3 110-foot, "Type A"**

	Bldr	L	In serv.
P 69 INDEPENDENCE	Vosper Thornycroft, Portsmouth	15-7-69	8-7-70
P 70 FREEDOM	Vosper Thornycroft, Singapore	18-11-69	11-1-71
P 72 JUSTICE	Vosper Thornycroft, Singapore	20-6-70	23-4-71

Justice (P 72) L. & L. Van Ginderen, 3-84

D: 100 tons (130 fl) **S:** 30 kts **Dim:** 33.4 (31.46 pp) × 6.4 × 1.71
A: 1/40-mm Bofors AA—1/20-mm Oerlikon AA
Electron Equipt: Radar: 1/Decca TM 626
M: 2 MTU 16V538 diesels; 2 props; 7,200 hp
Electric: 100 kw **Range:** 1,100/15 **Man:** 3 officers, 16 men

REMARKS: Ordered 21-5-68. Two 50-mm flare RL on 40-mm shield sides

◆ **3 110-foot, "Type B"**

	Bldr	L	In serv.
P 71 SOVEREIGNTY	Vosper Thornycroft, Portsmouth	25-11-69	2-71
P 73 DARING	Vosper Thornycroft, Singapore	1970	18-9-71
P 74 DAUNTLESS	Vosper Thornycroft, Singapore	6-5-71	7-71

Sovereignty (P 71) Vosper, 1971

D: 100 tons (130 fl) **S:** 32 kts **Dim:** 33.4 × 6.4 × 1.71
A: 1/76.2-mm Bofors—1/20-mm Oerlikon AA
Electron Equipt: Radar: 1/Decca TM 626, 1/H.S.A. M-26
M: 2 MTU 16V538 diesels; 2 props; 7,200 hp
Range: 1,000/15 **Man:** 3 officers, 16 men

REMARKS: Gun and fire-control system as on the Norwegian *Storm* class. The 76.2-mm is for surface fire only.

◆ **1 British Ford class**

	Bldr	L	In serv.
P 48 PANGLIMA	United Engineers, Singapore	14-1-56	5-56

Panglima (P 48) 1983

D: 119 tons (131 fl) **S:** 14 kts **Dim:** 35.76 × 6.1 × 1.68
A: 1/40-mm AA—1/20-mm AA—2/7.62-mm mg (I × 2)
M: 2 Paxman 12YHAXM diesels; 2 props; 1,000 hp **Fuel:** 15 tons **Man:** 15 tot.

REMARKS: Transferred by Malaysia in 1967 and used for training.

◆ **1 ex-French craft** Bldr: Deggendorfer Werft, West Germany (In serv. 1955)

P 75 ENDEAVOR

D: 184 tons (fl) **S:** 20 kts **Dim:** 40.9 × 7.6 × 2.4 **Range:** 800/8
A: 2/20-mm AA (I × 2) **M:** 2 Maybach diesels; 2 props; 2,000 hp **Man:** 24 tot.

REMARKS: Purchased on 30-9-70. Low freeboard. Used for training and as a diving tender.

PATROL CRAFT

◆ **12 "Swift" class** Bldr: Singapore SB & Eng., Jurong (In serv. 20-10-81)

P 10 SWIFT ARCHER	P 14 SWIFT WARRIOR	P 18 SWIFT CHALLENGER
P 11 SWIFT WARLORD	P 15 SWIFT SWORDSMAN	P 19 SWIFT CAVALIER
P 12 SWIFT LANCER	P 16 SWIFT COMBATANT	P 20 SWIFT CENTURION
P 13 SWIFT KNIGHT	P 17 SWIFT CONQUEROR	P 21 SWIFT CHIEFTAIN

Swift Cavalier (P 19) L. & L. Van Ginderen, 3-84

D: 45.7 tons (fl) **S:** 34 kts (32 sust.)
Dim: 22.7 (20.0 pp) × 6.2 × 1.6 (3.0 props)
A: 1/20-mm AA—2/7.62-mm mg (I × 2)
Electron Equipt: Radar: 1/Decca 1226
M: 2 Deutz 816 diesel; 2 props; 2,880 hp
Range: 960/20 **Man:** 3 officers, 9 men

REMARKS: All commissioned same date; first unit launched 8-6-80. Design based on Australian de Havilland "Capricornica" design. Provision for installing 2 Gabriel SSM.

MINE WARFARE SHIPS

◆ **2 ex-U.S. Redwing-class minesweepers** Bldrs: M 101: Tampa Marine, Tampa, Florida; M 102: Bellingham SY, Bellingham, Washington

	Laid down	L	In serv.
M 101 JUPITER (ex-*Thrasher,* MSC 203)	1-4-54	6-10-54	16-8-55
M 102 MERCURY (ex-*Whippoorwill,* MSC 207)	7-1-54	13-8-54	20-10-55

D: 300 tons (372 fl) **S:** 13 kts **Dim:** 43.0 × 7.95 × 2.55
A: 1/20-mm **Electron Equipt:** Radar: 1/SPS-5—Sonar: UQS-1D
M: 2 G.M. 8-268A diesels; 2 props; 1,200 hp **Fuel:** 40 tons
Range: 2,500/10 **Man:** 39 tot.

REMARKS: Purchased on 5-12-75. Re-armed with new Oerlikon 20-mm AA, 1980.

AMPHIBIOUS WARFARE SHIPS

◆ **5 ex-U.S. LST 542 class**

	Laid down	L	In serv.
L 201 ENDURANCE (ex-*Holmes County,* LST 836)	11-9-44	29-10-44	25-11-44
L 202 EXCELLENCE (ex-T-LST 629)	13-4-44	8-7-44	28-7-44
L 203 INTREPID (ex-T-LST 579)	4-5-44	22-6-44	21-7-44
L 204 RESOLUTION (ex-T-LST 649)	19-7-44	6-10-44	26-10-44
L 205 PERSISTENCE (ex-T-LST 614)	28-1-44	6-5-44	22-5-44

Bldrs: L 201: American Bridge, Pa.; L 202, L 204, L 205, L 206: Chicago Bridge & Iron, Seneca, Ill.; L 203: Missouri Valley Bridge & Iron, Evansville, Ind.

D: 1,653 tons, light (4,080 fl) **S:** 11.6 kts **Dim:** 99.98 (96.32 pp) × 15.24 × 4.29
A: L 201: 5/40-mm AA (I × 5)—others: 1/40-mm AA—all: 2 or more/ 7.62-mm mg
Electron Equipt: Radar: 1/Decca 626 **Electric:** 300 kw **Range:** 19,000/9
M: 2 G.M. 12-567A diesels; 2 props; 1,800 hp **Man:** 120 tot.

REMARKS: Originally numbered A 81 to A 85, L 201 loaned 1-7-71 and purchased 5-12-75; chartered in 1976 for commercial service at which time guns were removed. Others purchased 4-6-76. L 202 has two 40-mm AA (I × 2) forward and a helicopter deck aft. L 204 to 205 in reserve until 1980 when refitting began. All are getting 1/40-mm AA fwd. Three more ex-Military Sealift Command T-LSTs (ex-T-LST 117, ex-T-LST 276, and ex-*Chase County,* T-LST 532) were purchased 4-6-76 but later

SINGAPORE *(continued)*
AMPHIBIOUS WARFARE SHIPS *(continued)*

Persistence (L 205) L. & L. Van Ginderen, 3-83

Endurance (L 201) L. & L. Van Ginderen, 3-83

sold commercially. Sister *Perseverance* (L 206, ex-T-LST 623) is in reserve for spare parts. L 201 has a new aft superstructure.

◆ **2 new-construction landing craft** Bldr: North SY, Singapore (L: 1985)

RPL 60 N. . . . . . RPL 61 N. . . . . . .

D: 151 tons (fl) **S:** . . . **Dim:** 36.0 × . . . × . . . **M:** . . .

◆ **4 Ayer Chawan-class landing craft** Bldr: Vosper Thornycroft, Singapore (In serv. 1968-69)

RPL 54 Ayer Chawan RPL 56 N. . . . . . .
RPL 55 Ayer Merban RPL 57 N. . . . . . .

D: 150 tons (fl) **S:** 10 kts **Dim:** 27.0 × 6.9 × 1.3
M: 2 diesels; 2 props; 650 hp

◆ **2 Brani-class landing craft** Bldr: Australia (In serv. 1955-56)

RPL 41 Brani RPL 42 Berlayer

D: 56 tons (fl) **S:** 9 kts **Dim:** 17.0 × 4.3 × 1.4 **M:** 2 diesels; 2 props; 460 hp

Note: In 5-81 it was announced that a small tanker powered by 2 MWM TBP-6K diesels (2,060 hp) was to be acquired.

MARINE POLICE

PATROL CRAFT

◆ **11 PT 1 class** Bldr: Singapore SB & Eng., Jurong

	Laid down	L	In serv.		Laid down	L	In serv.
PT 1	21-7-83	19-12-83	14-1-84	PT 7	11-10-83	30-5-84	19-6-84
PT 2	25-7-83	6-1-84	17-2-84	PT 8	14-10-83	16-6-84	5-7-84
PT 3	28-7-83	16-1-84	13-3-84	PT 9	21-12-83	4-7-84	1-8-84
PT 4	1-8-83	23-3-84	6-4-84	PT 10	6-1-84	23-7-84	24-8-84
PT 5	15-9-83	23-4-84	15-5-84	PT 11	19-1-84	10-8-84	5-9-84
PT 6	30-9-83	14-5-84	1-6-84				

PT 2 L. & L. Van Ginderen, 7-85

D: 20 tons **S:** 29 kts **Dim:** 14.54 × 4.23 × 1.20 (prop)
A: 1/7.62-mm mg **Electron Equipt:** Radar: 1/Decca . . . nav.
M: 2 M.A.N. D2542 MLE diesels; 2 props; 1,076 hp **Man:** 2–6 tot.

Remarks: Aluminum construction.

◆ **4 PX class** Bldr: Vosper Thornycroft, Singapore (In serv. 1969)

PX 10 PX 11 PX 12 PX 13

D: 80 tons (fl) **S:** 29 kts **Dim:** 26.29 × 5.7 × 1.45 **Range:** 700/15
A: 2/20-mm AA **M:** 12 MTU diesels; 1 props; 2,700 hp **Man:** 15 tot.

◆ **19 PX 14 class** Bldr: Sembawang SY (In serv. 1981)

PX 14–33

D: . . . **S:** 32 kts **Dim:** 11.2 × . . . × . . .
M: 2 MTU diesels; 2 props; 770 hp

◆ **20 PC 32 class** Bldr: Vosper Thornycroft, Singapore (In serv. 1978-79)

PC 32 to PC 51

D: 2 tons (fl) **S:** 35 kts **Dim:** 6.5 × 2.5 × 0.46
A: Small arms **M:** 2 Johnson outboards; 280 hp **Man:** 4 tot.

SOLOMON ISLANDS

Merchant Marine (1984): 26 ships—5,811 grt

PATROL BOATS AND CRAFT

◆ **0 (+1) ASI 315 design** Bldr: Australian SB Ind. (WA), Pty., Ltd., South Coogie, Western Australia (In serv. 1986)

D: 165 tons (fl) **S:** 20 kts (sust.) **Dim:** 31.50 (28.60 wl) × 8.10 × 2.12
A: small arms **Electron Equipt:** Radar: 1/Furuno 1011
M: 2 Caterpillar 3516 diesels; 2 props; 2,400 hp **Endurance:** 10 days
Range: 2,500/12 **Fuel:** 33 tons **Electric:** 120 kw **Man:** 3 officers, 14 men

Remarks: "Pacific Patrol Boat" design winner for Australian foreign aid program. Ordered 5-85.

◆ **1 P-150 class** Bldr: Australian Marine Services Assoc., North Fremantle

02 Savo (ex-*Pioneer*) (In serv. 1987)

Savo (02) L. & L. Van Ginderen, 7-85

D: . . . **S:** 26 kts **Dim:** 25.0 × . . . × . . .
A: . . . **Electron Equipt:** 1/. . . nav. **Range:** 520/20; 1,100/12
M: 2 Caterpillar 3412 V-12 diesels; 2 props, 1,500 hp

Remarks: Glass-reinforced plastic demonstration patrol boat purchased 1984 after Pacific sales tour. Used for fisheries patrol.

◆ **1 Carpentaria class** Bldr: De Havilland Marine, Homebush Bay, Australia

01 Tulagi (In serv. 30-3-79)

D: 27 tons (fl) **S:** 27 kts **Dim:** 16.0 × 5.0 × 1.2 **Man:** 8 tot.
A: 2/7.62-mm mg (I ×2) **Electron Equipt:** Radar: 1/Decca 110
M: 2 G.M. 12V71 TI diesels; 2 props; 1,120 hp **Range:** 700/22

SOLOMON ISLANDS *(continued)*
PATROL BOATS AND CRAFT *(continued)*

Tulagi (01) L. & L. Van Ginderen, 1984

SERVICE CRAFT

◆ **3 27-m landing craft** Bldr: Carpenter Boatyard, Suva (ordered 1980)

LIGOMO III (L: 24-2-81) ULUSAGHE (L: 26-3-81) N. . . . . . . (L: . . .)

D: 195 grt/105 dwt **S:** 9 kts **Dim:** 27.0 × . . . × . . .
M: 2 diesels; 2 props; . . . hp

◆ **2 140-grt oceanographic research craft** Bldr: Murakima (L: 10-8-81)

SOLOMON ATU SOLOMON KARIQUA

SOMALIA

Somali Democratic Republic

PERSONNEL (1985): 700 total

MERCHANT MARINE (1984): 26 ships—28,053 grt

GUIDED-MISSILE PATROL BOATS

◆ **2 ex-Soviet Osa-II class** (transferred 12-75)

Osa-II class—under tow to Somalia 1976

D: 205 tons (240 fl) **S:** 35 kts **Dim:** 38.6 × 7.6 × 2.0
A: 4/SS-N-2 Styx SSM—4/30-mm AA (II × 2)
Electron Equipt: Radar: 2/Square Tie, 1/Drum Tilt
IFF: 2 Square Head, 1/High Pole B
M: 3 M504 diesels; 3 props; 15,000 hp **Range:** 500/34, 750/25 **Man:** 30 tot.

REMARKS: In poor condition.

TORPEDO BOATS

◆ **4 Soviet Mol class**

Somali Mol class—without torpedo tubes 1976

Somali Mol class—with torpedo tubes 1976

D: 170 tons (205 fl) **S:** 38 kts **Dim:** 39.0 × 7.6 × 1.7
A: 4/30-mm AA (II × 2)—4/533-mm TT (I × 4)
Electron Equipt: Radar: 1/Pot Head, 1/Drum Tilt
IFF: 1/Square Head, 1/High Pole B
M: 3 M504 diesels; 3 props; 15,000 hp **Range:** 450/34; 700/20
Man: 25 tot.

REMARKS: New units transferred in 1976. Two did not have torpedo tubes. Boats with tubes are approximately 215 tons (fl), 36 kts max. In marginal operating condition.

NOTE: The last 4 Soviet P-6-class torpedo boats have been discarded.

PATROL BOATS

NOTE: A reported ordering of two Cormoran-class gunboats in 2-84 from Bazán, Cádiz, Spain did not materialize.

◆ **5 ex-Soviet Poluchat-I class** (transferred 1968-69)

D: 80 tons (90 fl) **S:** 18 kts **Dim:** 29.86 × 5.8 × 1.5
A: 2/14.5-mm AA (II × 1)
M: 2 M50 diesels; 2 props; 2,400 hp
Electron Equipt: Radar: 1/Spin Trough
Range: 450/17; 900/10 **Man:** 20 tot.

AMPHIBIOUS WARFARE SHIPS

◆ **1 ex-Soviet Polnocny-A-class landing ship** (transferred 12-76)

D: 770 tons (fl) **S:** 19 kts **Dim:** 73.0 × 8.6 × 1.9
A: 2/25-mm AA (II × 1)—2/140-mm RL (XVII × 2)
Electron Equipt: Radar: 1/Don-2 **Range:** 900/18; 1,500/14
M: 2 diesels; 2 props; 4,000 hp **Cargo:** 180 tons **Man:** 35 tot.

◆ **4 ex-Soviet T-4-class landing craft** (transferred 1968-69)

D: 70 tons (fl) **S:** 10 kts **Dim:** 19.0 × 4.3 × 1.0
M: 2 diesels; 2 props; 600 hp **Man:** 5 tot.

SOUTH AFRICA

Republic of South Africa

PERSONNEL (1985): 6,646, including 763 officers, 4,883 enlisted, and 1,000 conscripts

MERCHANT MARINE (1984): 278 ships—712,220 grt
(tankers: 3 ships—37,597 grt)

NAVAL AVIATION: An Air Force detachment is available to the Navy. 18 Piaggio P166 Albatross aircraft are used for patrol, and 11 Wasp helicopters are available to be embarked on the ships. There are also several Alouette-III helicopters, and Air Force Super Frélon helicopters now can operate from the replenishment ship *Tafelberg*. With the striking of the Shackleton long-range maritime patrol aircraft in 1984 and the arms embargo preventing replacements, a number of C-47 transports equipped with radars have been pressed into service. Two SafAir L-100 Hercules are to be chartered for search-and-rescue and pollution-control duties.

SUBMARINES

◆ **3 French Daphné class** Bldr: Dubigeon, Nantes

	Laid down	L	In serv.
S 97 MARIA VAN RIEBEECK	14-3-68	18-3-69	22-6-70
S 98 EMILY HOBHOUSE	18-11-68	24-10-69	25-1-71
S 99 JOHANNA VAN DER MERWE	24-4-69	21-7-70	21-7-71

SUBMARINES *(continued)*

Maria Van Riebeeck (S 97) S.A.N., 1978

D: 869 surf./1,043 sub. tons **S:** 13/15.5 kts **Dim:** 57.75 × 6.75 × 4.5
A: 12/550-mm TT (8 fwd, 4 aft—no reloads)
Electron Equipt: Radar: DRUA-31—Sonar: DUUA-1 active, . . . passive
M: 2 SEMT-Pielstick 12PA4-135 diesels, 2 450-kw generator sets, electric drive; 2 props; 2,600 hp
Range: 4,300/7.5 (snorkel) **Man:** 6 officers, 41 men

Remarks: See French *Daphné* class. Being modernized with new sonar and combat data systems by Trivetts-UEC, Durban, 1985-86. Two embargoed *Agosta*-class submarines ordered from France in 1975 were sold by France to Pakistan.

FRIGATES

Note: Plans to construct a new 1,400–1,500-ton-frigate design in South Africa have been held in abeyance, due to the embargo on arms-related imports. Details in last edition.

◆ **1 British Whitby class**

	Bldr	Laid down	L	In serv.
F 145 President Pretorius	Yarrow, Scotstoun	21-11-60	28-9-62	4-3-64

President Pretorius (F 145) L. & L. Van Ginderen, 8-85

President Pretorius (F 145)—note stern extension L. & L. Van Ginderen, 8-85

D: 2,250 tons (2,800 fl) **S:** 29 kts **Dim:** 114.00 (100.73 pp) × 12.5 × 5.2 (fl)
A: 2/114-mm Mk 6 DP (II × 1)—2/40-mm AA (I × 2)—6/324-mm Mk 32 ASW TT (III × 2)—1/Mk 10 Limbo mortar (III × 1)—1/Wasp helicopter (Mk 44 torpedoes)
Electron Equipt: Radar: 1 U.K. Type 293M, 1/Thomson-CSF Jupiter, 1/Elsag NA 9C fire-control
Sonar: 1/177, 1/174—EW: UA-8, UA-9 intercept, FH-12 D/F
M: 2 double-reduction GT; 2 props; 30,000 hp **Electric:** 1,140 kw
Boilers: 2 Babcock & Wilcox; 38.7 kg/cm², 454°C **Fuel:** 370 tons
Range: 2,100/26; 4,500/12 **Man:** 13 officers, 190 men

Remarks: Modernized at Simonstown, 1971-77. Jupiter is an export version of the French Navy DRBV-23, L-band radar. Sisters *President Steyn* (F 147) to reserve 1981, stricken 1983; *President Kruger* (F 146) lost in collision with oiler *Tafelberg* 18-2-82.

GUIDED-MISSILE PATROL BOATS

◆ **12 Israeli Reshev ("Minister") class**

	Bldr	L	In serv.
P 1561 Jan Smuts	Israeli SY, Haifa	2-77	9-77
P 1562 P.W. Botha	Israeli SY, Haifa	9-77	12-77
P 1563 Frederick Creswell	Israeli SY, Haifa	1-78	6-78
P 1564 Jim Fouche	Sundock Austral, Durban	9-78	12-78
P 1565 Franz Erasmus	Sundock Austral, Durban	3-79	7-79
P 1566 Oswald Pirow	Sundock Austral, Durban	9-79	4-3-80
P 1567 Hendrik Mentz	Sundock Austral, Durban	26-3-82	11-2-83
P 1568 Kobie Coetzee	Sundock Austral, Durban	3-9-82	11-2-83
P 1569 Magnus Malan	Sundock Austral, Durban	25-11-82	6-83
P 1570 N.	Sundock Austral, Durban	. . .	1983
P 1571 N.	Sundock Austral, Durban	. . .	1984
P 1572 N.	Sundock Austral, Durban	. . .	1984

Jan Smuts (P 1561)—note spherical EW radomes L. & L. Van Ginderen, 8-85

South African Reshev—with 6 Skorpioen S.A.N., 1984

D: 415 tons (450 fl) **S:** 32 kts **Dim:** 58.1 × 7.6 × 2.4
A: 6/Skorpioen SSM (I × 6)—2/76-mm OTO Melara DP (I × 2)—2/20-mm AA (I × 2)—4/12.7-mm mg (II × 2)
Electron Equipt: Radar: 1/Thomson-CSF THD-1040 Neptune, 1/Selenia RTN-10X Orion
EW: Elta MN-53 passive intercept, 4 chaff RL
M: 4 MTU 16V956 diesels; 4 props; 14,000 hp
Range: 1,500/30; 5,000/15 **Man:** 7 officers, 40 men

Remarks: First six ordered 1974. The second six were ordered 15-11-77. Carry 500 rds 76-mm ammunition. Skorpioen is a license-built version of the Israeli Gabriel II anti-ship missile. All named for former Ministers of Defense. The name *Frank Chappel* has also been reported.

PATROL BOATS

◆ **1 former yacht** Bldr: . . . , Italy

P. . . Oryx (ex-*Caroline*)

Remarks: Chartered and refitted 1981 as a patrol ship for duty off the coast of Namibia. No data available.

◆ **1 locally designed** Bldr: . . . , South Africa (In serv. 1976)

P 1558

P 1558—now has twin 20-mm AA aft S.A.N., 1981

D: 80 tons (fl) **S:** . . . **Dim:** 29.5 (27.0 pp) × 5.3 × 1.7
A: 1/40-mm AA—2/20-mm AA (II × 1)—2/12.7-mm mg (I × 2)
Electron Equipt: Radar: 1/Decca 926
M: 2 diesels; 2 props; . . . hp

Remarks: Intended as a prototype for series production for a class that was not built.

PATROL BOATS *(continued)*

◆ 5 British "Ford" class

	Bldr	In serv.
P 3105 Gelderland (ex-*Brayford*)	A. & J. Inglis, Glasgow	30-8-54
P 3120 Nautilus (ex-*Glassford*)	R. Dunstan, Thorne	23-8-55
P 3125 Rijger	Vosper, Portsmouth	1958
P 3126 Haerlem	Vosper, Portsmouth	1959
P 3127 Oosterland	Vosper, Portsmouth	1959

Rijger (P 3125) S.A.N., 1978

Haerlem (P 3126)—white-painted, buff stacks as survey ship S.A.N., 1978

D: 120 tons (160 fl) **S:** 15 kts **Dim:** 35.7 × 6.1 × 2.1
A: 1/40-mm AA **Electron Equipt:** Radar: 1/975
M: 2 Paxman YHAXM diesels; 500 hp each; 1 Foden FD-6 diesel, 100 hp; 3 props
Fuel: 23 tons
Man: 19 tot.

Remarks: P 3126 has been fitted as a hydrographic ship and disarmed. P 3125 and P 3127 still carry two depth-charge racks. P 3120 is manned by the Citizens Force. P 3126 and P 3127 have fin stabilizers.

◆ 4 ex-British "Ton"-class former minesweepers

	Bldr	L
P 1556 Pretoria (ex-*Dunkerton*)	Goole SB Co.	8-3-54
P 1557 Kaapstad (ex-*Hazelton*)	Cook, Welton & Gemmell	6-2-54
P 1559 Walvisbaai (ex-*Packington*)	Harland & Wolff	3-7-58
P 1560 Durban	Camper & Nicholson	12-6-57

Durban (P 1560, ex-M 1499) L. & L. Van Ginderen, 8-85

Remarks: Data as for minesweepers below, except that P 1556 and P 1557 have 2 Mirrlees JVSS-12 diesels of 1,250 hp each. Manned by Citizens Force, having been redesignated 1977-78. Retain most sweep gear and could be used to sweep moored and mechanical mines. All carry Gemini inspection dinghies. P 1556 and P 1557 constitute the Naval Training Command Squadron.

PATROL CRAFT

◆ 24 Namicurra class Bldr: . . . , South Africa (In serv. 1980-81)

Y 1051–Y 1074

Namicurra class S.A.N., 1984

D: 5 tons (fl) **S:** 30 kts **Dim:** 9.0 × . . . × . . .
A: 1/12.7 mm mg—2/7.62-mm mg **M:** 2 diesels **Man:** 4 tot.

Remarks: Radar-equipped, glass-reinforced, plastic-hulled harbor craft, which can be land-transported on trailers.

MINE WARFARE SHIPS

◆ 6 British "Ton"-class minesweepers and minehunters*

	Bldr	L
M 1207 Johannesburg (ex-*Castleton*)	J.S. White	26-8-58
M 1210 Kimberley (ex-*Stratton*)*	Dorset Yacht	29-7-57
M 1212 Port Elizabeth (ex-*Dumbleton*)*	Harland & Wolff	8-11-57
M 1213 Mosselbaai (ex-*Oakington*)*	Harland & Wolff	10-12-58
M 1215 East London (ex-*Chilton*)	Cook, Welton & Gemmell	15-7-57
M 1498 Windhoek	Thornycroft	28-6-57

Johannesburg (M 1207) L. & L. Van Ginderen, 8-85

D: 370 tons (425 fl) **S:** 15 kts (cruising) **Dim:** 46.33 (42.68 pp) × 8.76 × 2.5
A: 1/40-mm AA—1/20-mm AA
Electron Equipt: Radar: 1/978 (*1/1006)—Sonar: (*only): 1/193M
M: 2 Paxman Deltic 18A-7A; 2 props; 3,000 hp **Fuel:** 45 tons
Range: 2,300/13; 3,000/8 **Man:** 27 tot (*36)

Remarks: Four have been redesignated as patrol boats, see above. M 1210, M 1212, and M 1213 have been converted as minehunters, with Type 193M minehunting sonar, Type 1006 radar, two PAP-104 remote-controlled minehunting devices, and mine-disposal diver facilities. All now have enclosed bridges and tripod masts. Single 80-cal 20-mm AA has replaced the twin 70-cal. mount aft.

AUXILIARY SHIPS

◆ 1 British Hecla-class hydrographic ship

	Bldr	Laid down	L	In serv.
A 324 Protea	Yarrow, Scotstoun	20-7-70	14-7-71	23-5-72

D: 2,750 tons (fl) **S:** 15.5 kts **Dim:** 71.6 × 14.9 × 4.6
M: 4 Paxman Ventura diesels; 1 CP prop; 4,800 hp
Fuel: 500 tons **Range:** 12,000/11 **Man:** 123 tot.

Remarks: Ordered 7-11-69. Hull reinforced for navigating in ice. Bow-thruster and anti-roll tanks fitted. Helicopter hangar and flight deck for one Wasp. The "Ford"-class patrol boat *Haerlem* (P 3126) is equipped for inshore survey duties; see above.

AUXILIARY SHIPS *(continued)*

Protea (A 324)—white hull, buff stack S.A.N., 1984

◆ **1 fleet replenishment ship** Bldr: Nakskovs Skibsvaert, Denmark (L: 20-6-58)

A 243 Tafelberg (ex-Danish tanker *Annam*)

Tafelberg (A 243) S.A.N., 1985

D: Approx. 27,000 tons (fl) **S:** 15 kts **Dim:** 170.6 × 21.9 × 9.2
A: 2/40-mm AA (I × 2)—2/20-mm AA (I × 2)
Electron Equipt: 2/. . . nav.
M: 1 Burmeister & Wain diesel; 1 prop; 8,420 hp
Man: 100 tot.

Remarks: 12,499 grt/18,980 dwt (prior to 1984). Purchased and refitted in Durban, 1965-67. Two refueling stations and one solid-stores transfer station per side. Modernized 1983 to 16-7-84, with flight deck amidships, a hangar for two Super Frélon helicopters for search-and-rescue duties, and a hospital facility; one refueling station per side deleted. Now scheduled to operate until 1999.

Note: Plans were announced 22-9-84 to build a "12,600-ton" replenishment oiler at Durban for delivery in 1986(!). The 20-kt ship was to have had helicopters for replenishment and search-and-rescue duties. The ship had not been laid down as of 12-85.

◆ **1 British "Bar"-class net-tender**

	Bldr	Laid down	L	In serv.
P 285 Somerset (ex-*Barcross*)	Blyth Dry Dock	15-4-41	21-10-41	14-4-42

D: 750 tons (960 fl) **S:** 11.7 kts **Dim:** 52.96 × 9.8 × 4.62 (aft)
M: 1 set triple-expansion reciprocating steam; 1 prop; 850 hp
Boilers: 2 **Fuel:** 214 tons **Range:** 3,100/10

Somerset (P 285) S.A.N., 1984

◆ **1 torpedo-recovery and diver-training ship** Bldr: Dorman Long, Durban

P 3148 Fleur (In serv. 3-12-69)

Fleur (P 3148) S.A.N., 1984

D: 220 tons (257 fl) **S:** 14 kts **Dim:** 35.0 × 7.5 × 3.4
M: 2 Paxman-Ventura diesels; 2 props; 1,400 hp
Man: 4 officers, 18 men

Remarks: Ramp at stern for torpedo recovery. Divers' decompression chamber. Refitted by 1981 with fantail area enlarged, new stacks.

◆ **1 training craft** Bldr: Fred Nicholls, Durban (In serv. 1964)

Navigator

D: 75 tons (fl) **S:** 9.5 kts **Dim:** 19.2 × 6.0 × . . .
M: 2 Foden FD-6 diesels; 2 props; 200 hp

Remarks: Wooden-hulled fishing-cutter type. Serves as tender at Naval College, Gordon's Bay.

◆ **1 seagoing tug**

	Bldr	L	In serv.
De Mist	Dorman Long, Durban	21-12-78	12-78

D: 275 grt **S:** 12.5 kts **Dim:** 34.3 (32.3 pp) × 7.8 × 3.4
M: 2 Mirrlees-Blackstone ESL-8-MGR diesels; 2 props; 2,440 hp

◆ **1 large harbor tug**

	Bldr	L	In serv.
De Neys	Globe Engineering, Capetown	7-69	23-7-69

De Neys S.A.N., 1978

SOUTH AFRICA *(continued)*
AUXILIARY SHIPS *(continued)*

D: 282 tons (fl) **S:** 11.5 kts **Dim:** 28.6 (27.0 wl) × 8.1 × 3.6
M: 2 Lister-Blackstone ERS-8-M diesels; 2 Voith-Schneider vertical cycloidal props; 1,268 hp
Man: 10 tot.

REMARKS: 14-ton max. bollard pull.

◆ **1 large harbor tug** Bldr: Globe Engineering, Capetown

DE NOORDE (L: 12-61)

De Noorde S.A.N., 1978

D: 170 grt **S:** 9 kts **Dim:** 34.2 × 8.2 × . . .
M: 2 Lister-Blackstone ERS-8-M diesels; 2 Voith-Schneider vertical cycloidal props; 1,268 hp

◆ **1 catamaran trials craft** (In serv. 4-80)

SHIRLEY T.

REMARKS: A 10.8-m prototype for a 50-m fast combatant design concept.

AIR SEA RESCUE BOATS

◆ **2 Fairey Tracker class** Bldr: Groves & Gutteridge, Cowes, U.K. (In serv. 1973)

P 1554 P 1555

D: 31 tons (fl) **S:** 29 kts **Dim:** 19.25 × 4.98 × 1.45
M: 2 G.M. 12V71 diesels; 2 props; 1,120 hp **Range:** 650/20 **Man:** 11 tot.

◆ **2 German-built** Bldr: Krogerwerft, Rendsburg (In serv. 1961-62)

P 1551 P 1552

P 1551—now has smaller radar S.A.N., 1978

D: 67 tons (73 fl) **S:** 30 kts **Dim:** 28.8 (27.9 pp) × 5.0 × 1.6
A: 1/12.7-mm mg **Electron Equipt:** Radar: 1/. . . nav.
M: 2 Maybach 12-cyl. diesels; 2 props; 3,000 hp **Range:** 600/25 **Man:** 8 tot.

DEPARTMENT OF TRANSPORT

◆ **1 Antarctic survey and supply ship**

	Bldr	Laid down	L	In serv.
AGULHAS	Mitsubishi, Shimonoseki	14-6-77	30-9-77	31-1-78

D: 3,035 dwt **S:** 14 kts **Dim:** 109.2 (100.0 pp) × 18.0 × 5.8
M: 2 Mirrlees-Blackstone K-6 Major diesels; 1 prop; 6,000 hp
Range: 8,200/14 **Man:** 40 crew + 92 scientists/passengers

REMARKS: Manned by the South African Navy. Twin helicopter hangar. Red hull, white upperworks.

SPAIN

Spanish State

PERSONNEL (1985): 52,510, including 5,212 officers, 37,901 men; plus 12,196 Naval Infantry, including 696 officers, and 11,500 enlisted; 9,397 civilians.

MERCHANT MARINE (1984): 2,529 ships—7,004,852 grt (tankers: 110 ships—3,877,230 grt)

WARSHIPS IN SERVICE OR UNDER CONSTRUCTION
AS OF 1 JANUARY 1986

	L	Tons	Main armament
◆ **1 (+1) aircraft carrier**			
1 (+1) PRINCIPE DE ASTURIAS	1982	. . .	4/20-mm 18-22 aircraft
1 INDEPENDENCE	1943	13,000	22/40-mm 20 aircraft
◆ **8 submarines**		Tons (surfaced)	
4 AGOSTA	1981-84	1,490	4/550-mm TT
4 DAPHNÉ	1972-74	870	12/550-mm TT
◆ **10 destroyers**		Tons	
1 ROGER DE LAURIA	1968	3,012	6/127-mm DP, ASW weapons
5 GEARING FRAM-I	1945	2,425	4/127-mm, 1/ASROC system
4 FLETCHER	1942-44	2,080	4 or 5/127-mm, 0 or 6/76.2-mm, ASW weapons
◆ **11 (+5) frigates**			
0 (+5) OLIVER HAZARD PERRY	1984-	2,769	1/76-mm, 1 Standard SAM system, 2 helicopters
6 DESCUBIERTA	1975-79	1,270	1/76-mm, 1/Sea Sparrow
5 BALÉARES	1970-72	3,015	1/127-mm, 1/ASROC system, 1/Standard system, ASW weapons
◆ **4 corvettes**			
4 ATREVIDA	1955-56	977	1/76.2-mm DP, 3/40-mm, ASW weapons

NAVAL AVIATION: Five single-seat AV-8A and two two-seat TAV-8A were delivered in 1976 for service in the *Dedalo;* subsequently, two of the aircraft, named Matador in Spanish service, have been lost. Five more AV-8A were ordered for delivery in 1980-81. In 1985, 9 AV-8A and the 2 TAV-8A were in service, and 12 AV-8B were to be ordered in 1986.

AV-8A Matador on Dedalo

The Arma Aerea de la Armada also operates 12 Agusta-Bell 212 (with SS-12 missiles), 10 Bell 47G, 15 Sikorsky SH-3D/G Sea King (with AS-12 missiles), and 11 Hughes 369-HM (560M) Cayuse helicopters plus 2 Cessna Citations, 2 Piper Comanche and 2 Piper Twin Comanche liaison aircraft. Six U.S. SH-60B Seahawk LAMPS III helicopters were ordered 1983; 12 more may be ordered later. Four of the Sea Kings are to be provided Searchwater air/surface-search radar.

The search-and-rescue service (Servicio de Busqueda y Salvamento) received 3 Fokker F-27 SAR aircraft in 1979 for coastal surveillance; they carry Litton APS-504V radar. Ten AS.332F Super Puma helicopters for rescue duties and 2 as VIP transports were delivered 21-1-84.

The Spanish Air Force performs a maritime surveillance role, using six Lockheed P-3A and four P-3C Orion. Nine Casa C-212 Aerocar with APS-128 radars were delivered 1982-84 for search-and-rescue work.

WEAPONS AND SYSTEMS

Except for naval guns, which are domestically designed and manufactured, most of the weapon systems in use are of American or French make. Twenty-five U.S. Harpoon missiles were ordered 1985 for delivery 1987-90; 55 Harpoons had been delivered earlier. However, an antiaircraft/anti-missile point-defense system of Spanish origin is in de-

WEAPONS AND SYSTEMS *(continued)*

velopment. Called Meroka, it consists of two rows of six 20-mm Oerlikon guns, whose characteristics are:

Length: 120 calibers — Round weight: 320 gr. all-up
Muzzle velocity: 1,200m/sec — Projectile weight: 102 gr.
Maximum rate of fire: 9,000 rounds/minute (per mount)
Maximum effective range: 2,000 m

Meroka uses a Lockheed Electronics AN/PVS-2 Sharpshooter x-band monopulse radar on the mount, with target designation via the search radar and a Selenia PDS-10 TDS console. Current models carry 720 rounds on-mount; later versions will have 2,160 rds.

AIRCRAFT CARRIERS

◆ **1 new construction**

	Bldr	Laid down	L	In serv.
R 11 Principe De Asturias (ex-*Canarias*, ex-*Almirante Carrero Blanco*)	Bazán, el Ferrol	8-10-79	22-5-82	4-87

D: 15,150 tons (fl) **S:** 26.27 kts **Dim:** 195.1 (187.5 pp) × 24.4 (30.0 flight deck) × 6.7
A: 4/Meroka 20-mm gun systems (XII × 4)—20 aircraft (6–8 AV-8B and 12–14 SH-60B or SH-3D/G)

Principe de Asturias (R 11)—at launch — Bazán, 5-82

Electron Equipt: Radar: 1/SPS-55, 1/SPS-52C, 1/SPN-35A air control, 4/PVS-2 f.c.
TACAN: URN-25
EW: Nettunel intercept, Mk 36 Mod. 2 SRBOC chaff (VI × 4)
M: 2 G.E. LM-2500 gas turbines; 1 prop; 46,400 hp (plus 2/800-hp retractable Pleuger auxiliary props, electric drive)
Electric: 7,500 kw **Range:** 6,500/20
Man: 774 total—88–94 officers, 145–153 senior petty officers, 539–542 men

Remarks: Ordered 29-6-77. Design is essentially that of the final version of the U.S. Navy's Sea Control Ship concept, with a 12-degree ski-jump bow added. The flight deck is 175.3 × 29 m and is served by two elevators, one at the extreme aft end. Takeoff pattern angled to starboard. There are 3 Allison 501-K17 gas turbine-driven 2,500-kw generators. Has two pair Denny-Brown fin stabilizers. LINK 11 and LINK 14 data link and U.S. Fleet SATCOMM installed. SPS-52C is to be replaced by SPS-52D later. Has U.S. Prairie/Masker bubbler noise suppression system, SLQ-25 Nixie towed torpedo decoy. Scheduled to commence sea trials 6-86.

◆ **1 ex-U.S. Independence-class light aircraft carrier** — Bldr: New York SB

	Laid down	L	In serv.
R 01 Dedalo (ex-*Cabot*, AVT 3, ex-CVL 28, ex-*Wilmington*, CL 79)	16-3-42	4-4-43	24-7-43

D: 13,000 tons (16,416 fl) **S:** 31 kts (trials)
Dim: 188.35 (182.9 wl) × 21.87 (hull) 31.7 (flight deck) × 7.2 (8.1 max.)
A: 22/40-mm AA (IV × 1, II × 9)—about 20 aircraft, 7 of which are AV-8A
Electron Equipt: Radar: 1/SPS-10, 1/SPS-40A, 1/SPS-8, 1/SPS-6C, 4/Mk 34 fire-control
TACAN: URN-20—EW: WLR-1
M: 4 sets GT; 4 props; 100,000 hp
Boilers: 4 Babcock & Wilcox; 39.8 kg/cm², 454°C **Electric:** 2,400 kw
Fuel: 1,800 tons **Armor:** Partial belt: 37-127 mm **Range:** 7,200/15
Man: 51 officers, 1,049 men

Dedalo (R 01) — Spanish Navy

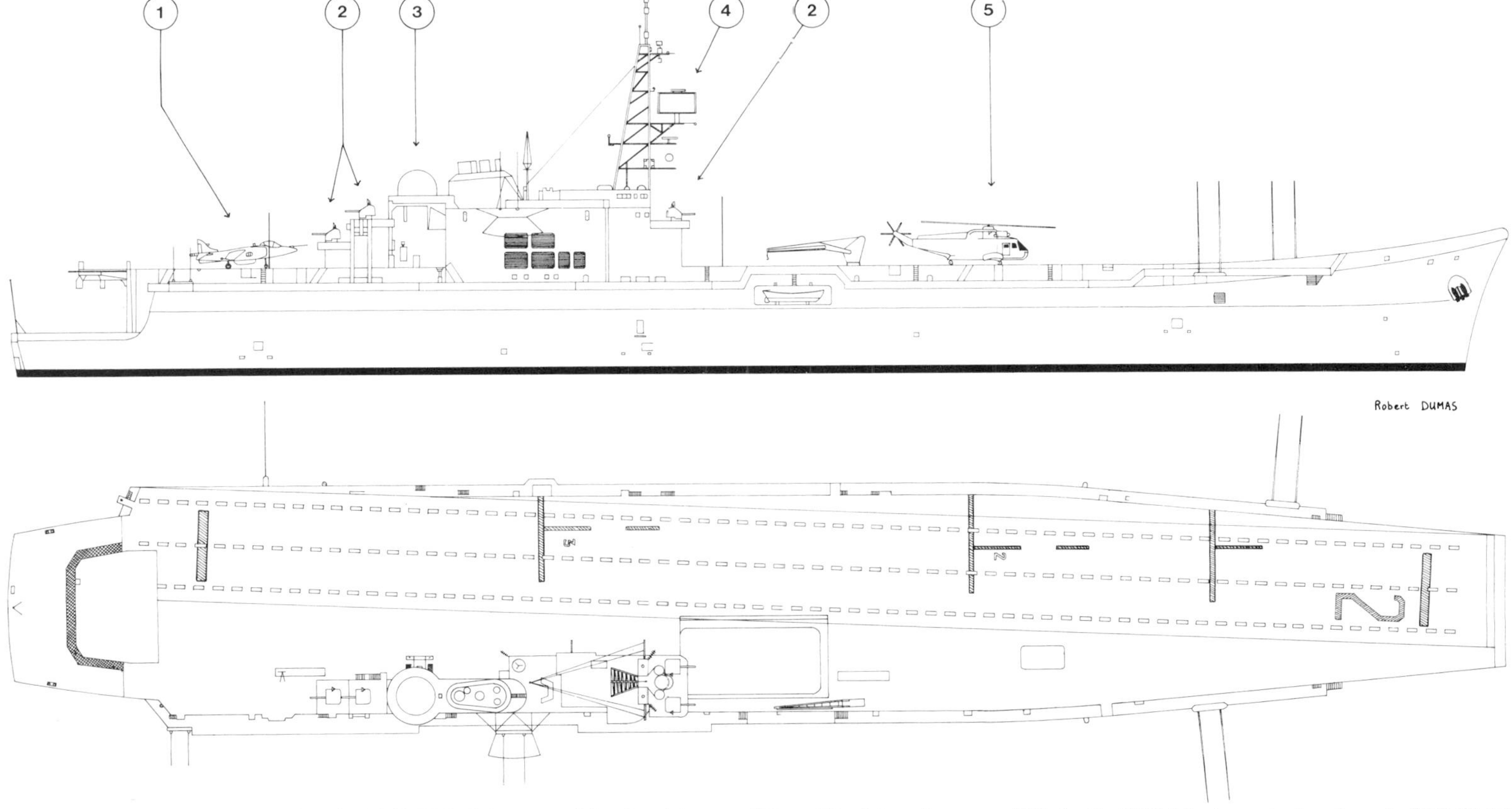

Principe de Asturias 1. Matador V/STOL fighter 2. Meroka AA guns (Note: Final location may differ) 3. SPN-35 air-control radar 4. SPS-52 3-D radar 5. Sea King helicopter

AIRCRAFT CARRIERS *(continued)*

Dedalo (R 01) 16 Flot., French Navy, 1980

REMARKS: Ended service in the U.S. Navy as an aviation transport (AVT 3). Transferred on five-year loan on 30-8-67 and purchased in 12-73. Redesignated from PH (portahelicópteros) to PA (Portaaviones) on 28-9-76, when AV-8A V/STOL fighters were added to her complement. The flight deck is 166.1 × 32.9 m (max.). Two elevators. Four Mk 63 radar gunfire-control systems and seven Mk 51 Mod. 2, optical gunfire control installed. Did not receive SPS-52B radar in place of SPS-8 heightfinder as planned. Forward quad 40-mm AA now removed. She is supposed to be given the Meroka point-defense gun system and will probably be retained even after the completion of *Principe de Asturias.*

SUBMARINES

◆ **0 (+4) "Submarino Biparto" program** Bldr: Bazán, Cartagena

REMARKS: A cooperative design effort between Bazán and DCN/Dubigeon, France, for a diesel-electric hunter-killer submarine, the first of which would be delivered in 1992. Intended to have 70 days' endurance on 210 tons of fuel, the submarines would have four or six TT and carry 20 weapons, including SM 39 Exocet on Sub-Harpoon anti-ship missiles.

◆ **4 Agosta class** Bldr: Bazán, Cartagena

	Laid down	L	In serv.
S 71 GALERNA	5-9-77	5-12-81	17-1-83
S 72 SCIROCO	1978	13-11-82	5-12-83
S 73 MISTRAL	30-5-80	14-11-83	5-6-85
S 74 TRAMONTANA	18-12-81	30-11-84	10-85

Sciroco (S 72) G. Gyssels, 5-84

D: 1,230/1,490/1,750 tons **S:** 12 kts (surf.)/20.5 kts (sub.)
Dim: 67.90 × 6.8 × 5.4
A: 4/550-mm TT (rapid reload—20 F 17, E 18, and L 5 torpedoes)
Electron Equipt: Radar: 1/DRUA-33
Sonar: DUUA-2A, DUUA-2B active, DSUV-22 passive, Elédone intercept
M: 2 SEMT-Pielstick 16 PA4 185 diesel generator sets, 850 kw each; 4,600-hp main engine; 1/23-kw cruising engine; 1 prop
Fuel: 185 tons **Range:** 17.5/1 hr. (sub.); 9,000/10 (snorkel)
Man: 6 officers, 44 men

REMARKS: See also *Agosta* class in section on France. As with the *Daphné* class, being built with French technical assistance. Agreement signed 6-2-74; first two ordered 9-5-75, second pair 29-6-77. Can dive to 300 m. Endurance: 145 days.

◆ **4 French Daphné class** Bldr: Bazán, Cartagena

	Laid down	L	In serv.
S 61 DELFIN	13-8-68	25-3-72	3-5-73
S 62 TONINA	1969	3-10-72	10-7-73
S 63 MARSOPA	19-3-71	15-3-74	12-4-75
S 64 NARVAL	1972	14-12-74	22-11-75

D: 865/1,042 tons **S:** 12.5/15.5 kts **Dim:** 57.78 × 6.75 × 4.60
A: 12/550-m TT (8 fwd, 4 aft)—no reloads
Electron Equipt: Radar: 1/DRUA-31 (with ECM)
Sonar: DUUA-1-ABL active, DSUV passive (see remarks)

Narval (S 64) L. & L. Van Ginderen, 10-84

Delfin (S 61)—in refit, with new sonar dome L. & L. Van Ginderen, 10-84

M: 2 SEMT-Pielstick PA1 450-kw diesel generators; 2 props; 2,000 hp
Man: 6 officers, 41 men

REMARKS: Built with French technical assistance; agreement made on 16-7-66. 300 m. Beginning with S 61, refitting at Cartagena with DUUA-2A forward (retain DUUA-1D aft), DSUV-22 passive sonar and updated torpedo fire-control system; modified units have large bow sonar dome, like French Navy *Daphnés.* S 61 and S 62 have been completed.

NOTE: The two ex-U.S. Navy GUPPY-IIA-class submarines have been stricken: *Isaac Peral* (S 32, ex-*Ronquil,* SS 396) on 2-6-84, and *Narciso Monturial* (S 35, ex-*Jallao,* SS 368) on 31-12-84.

DESTROYERS

NOTE: There are tentative plans to construct two destroyers in the late 1980s, possibly of the U.S. *Spruance* class.

◆ **1 Roger de Lauria class** Bldr: Bazán, el Ferrol, Cartagena

	Laid down	L	Relaunch	In serv.
D 43 MARQUES DE LA ENSENADA	4-9-51	15-7-59	22-2-68	10-9-70

D: 3,012 tons (3,785 fl) **S:** 28 kts (31.5 on trials)
Dim: 116.68 (110.8 pp) × 12.5 × 6.5 (max.)
A: 6/127-mm DP (II × 3)—6/324-mm Mk 32 ASW TT (III × 2)—2/ASW fixed Mk 25 TT for Mk 37 torpedoes
Electron Equipt: Radar: 1/Decca RM 426, 1/SPS-10B, 1/SPS-40, 1 Mk 25, 1/Mk 35
Sonar: 1/SQS-32, 1/SQA-10 VDS—EW: WLR-1
M: 2 sets Rateau-Bretagne GT; 2 props; 60,000 hp **Electric:** 1,900 kw
Boilers: 3 three-drum; 35 kg/cm², 375°C **Fuel:** 673 tons
Range: 4,500/15 **Man:** 20 officers, 235 men

REMARKS: Widened and lengthened during reconstruction after original launching in order to eliminate defects found in the *Oquendo* prototype; completion consequently delayed. U.S. semiautomatic, 38-caliber guns, 1 Mk 37 and 1 Mk 56 radar gun-control system. *Oquendo* was stricken on 2-11-78. Helicopters not currently carried. May receive Meroka 20-mm AA gun system. Badly damaged by a terrorist bomb 2-10-81; repaired at considerable expense, in part by cannibalizing sister *Roger de Lauria* (D 42), which was stricken 15-1-82. Despite being plagued with continued boiler problems, is not scheduled for disposal until the 1990s.

DESTROYERS *(continued)*

Churruca (D 61) VF-102, U.S., Navy, 9-82

◆ **5 ex-U.S. Gearing FRAM-I class**

	Bldr	Laid down	L	In serv.
D 61 Churruca (ex-*Eugene A. Greene,* DD 711)	Federal SB, Newark	17-8-74	18-3-45	8-6-45
D 62 Gravina (ex-*Furse,* DD 882)	Consolidated, Orange, Tex.	23-9-44	9-3-45	10-7-45
D 63 Mendez Nuñez (ex-*O'Hare,* DD 889)	Consolidated, Orange, Tex.	27-1-45	22-6-45	29-11-45
D 64 Langara (ex-*Leary,* DD 879)	Consolidated, Orange, Tex.	11-8-44	20-1-45	7-5-45
D 65 Blas De Lezo (ex-*Noa,* DD 841)	Bath Iron Works	26-3-45	30-7-45	2-11-45

D: 2,425 tons light (3,520 fl) **S:** 31 kts
Dim: 119.02 × 12.45 × 6.4 (sonar) 4.45 (hull)
A: 4/127-mm 38-cal. (II × 2) — 1/ASROC Mk 116 ASW RL (VIII × 1; 17 missiles) — 6/324-mm Mk 32 ASW TT (III × 2)
Electron Equipt: Radar: 1/SPS-10, 1/SPS-29, (D 61, D 62; SPS-40), 1/Mk 25
Sonar: 1/SQS-23 — TACAN: D 65 only; SRN-15
EW: WLR-1, ULQ-6 (not in D 64)
M: GT; 2 props; 60,000 hp **Electric:** 1,100 kw
Boilers: 4 Babcock & Wilcox; 39.8 kg/cm²; 454°C
Fuel: 650 tons **Range:** 2,400/25; 4,800/15 **Man:** 17 officers, 257 men

Remarks: D 61 and D 62 were loaned on 31-8-72, and D 63 to D 65 on 31-10-73. All purchased outright on 17-4-78. D 65 has both her 127-mm mounts forward and no ASROC. Mk 37 fire-control system for guns, Mk 114 ASW f.c.s. Carried Hughes 369 manned helicopter in place of original drones; all but D 65 no longer do so. Scheduled for disposal beginning 1988-89.

◆ **4 ex-U.S. Fletcher class**

	Bldr	Laid down	L	In serv.
D 22 Almirante Ferrandiz ex-*David W. Taylor,* DD 551)	Gulf SB, Orange, Texas	12-6-41	4-7-42	18-9-43
D 23 Almirante Valdes (ex-*Converse,* DD 509)	Bath Iron Works, Me.	23-2-42	30-8-42	20-11-42
D 24 Alcala Galiano (ex-*Jarvis,* DD 799)	Todd, Seattle, Wash.	7-6-43	14-2-44	3-6-44
D 25 Jorge Juan (ex-*McGowan,* DD 678)	Federal SB, Kearny, N.J.	30-6-43	14-11-43	20-12-43

D: 2,850 tons (3,050 fl) **S:** 30-32 kts **Dim:** 114.85 × 12.03 × 5.5
A: D 22: 5/127-mm DP (I × 5) — 6/40-mm AA (II × 3) — 6/20-mm AA (I × 6) — 5/533-mm TT (V × 1) — 2/Mk 11 Hedgehogs — 6/Mk 6 d.c. mortars — 2/d.c. racks
D 23 to D 25: 4/127-mm DP (I × 4) — 6/76.2-mm AA (II × 3) — 5/533-mm TT (V × 1) — 2/Mk 11 Hedgehogs — 4/Mk 6 d.c. mortars (I × 4) — 1/d.c. rack
Electron Equipt: Radar: 1/SPS-10, 1SPS-6C, 2/Mk 25; D 23–25 also: 1/Mk 35, 2/Mk 34
Sonar: SQS-29 series (SQS-4 on D 22)
EW: D 23, 24: BLR-1
M: 2 sets G.E. (D 21, 22: Westinghouse) GT; 2 props; 60,000 hp
Electric: 580 kw **Boilers:** 4 Babcock & Wilcox; 39.8 kg/cm², 454°C
Fuel: 650 tons **Range:** 1,250/32; 4,400/15 **Man:** 17 officers, 273 men

Remarks: D 22 transferred on 15-5-57, D 23 on 1-7-59, D 24 on 3-11-60, and D 25 on 1-12-60. D 22 and 23 have high, "early Fletcher" bridges, the others low bridges. All have one Mk 37 gunfire-control system; D 23 to D 25 also have one Mk 56 and two Mk 63 gunfire-control systems, Mk 5 torpedo director. The quintuple 533-mm TT is being replaced by two triple 324-mm ASW TT mounted on the main deck. All five of these very outdated ships were scheduled to be retired by 1985, but are now being extended, with disposal from 1987-1991. D 22 has been used in fisheries protection duties in the Canary Islands area. Sister *Lepanto* (D 21, ex-*Capps,* DD 550) stricken 12-85.

Lepanto (D 21) — 5/127-mm guns, no EW gear Spanish Navy, 1984

Almirante Valdes (D 23) — 4/127-mm, 6/76.2-mm guns G. Gyssels, 6-83

GUIDED-MISSILE FRIGATES

◆ **0 (+5) U.S. Oliver Hazard Perry class** Bldr: Bazán, El Ferrol

	Laid down	L	In serv.
F 81 Santa Maria (ex-*Navarra*)	22-5-82	24-11-84	1986
F 82 Numanicia (ex-*Niña,* ex-*Murcia*)	11-83	10-85	1987
F 83 Victoria (ex-*Pinta,* ex-*Leon*)	8-84	8-86	1988
F 84 N. . .	. . .	. . .	. . .
F 85 N. . .	. . .	. . .	. . .

D: F 81, 82: 2,769 tons light (3,658 fl); others: 2,851 tons light (3,740 fl)
S: 29 kts **Dim:** 135.64 (F 83–85: 138.80) (125.90 wl) × 13.72 × 4.52 (8.6 max.)
A: 1/Mk 13, Mod. 4 missile launcher (8 Harpoon and 32 Standard SM-1 MR) — 1/76-mm OTO Melara DP — 1 or 2/Meroka 20-mm AA systems — 6/324-mm Mk 32 ASW TT (III × 2) — 2/ASW helicopters
Electron Equipt: Radar: 1/SPS-55, 1/SPS-49, 1/Mk 92 Mod. 2 fire-control system (with STIR) — TACAN: URN-25
Sonar: Raytheon 1160B hull-mounted; SQR-19A TASS
EW: SLQ-32 (V)2; Mk 36 SRBOC RL (VI × 2)

GUIDED-MISSILE FRIGATES *(continued)*

Santa Maria (F 81)—at launch Bazán, 11-84

M: 2 G.E. LM-2500 gas turbines; 1 CP prop; 41,000 hp (2/350-hp electric auxiliary propulsion motors)
Electric: 3,000 kw **Range:** 5,000/18 **Fuel:** 587 tons
Man: 13 officers, 188 men

REMARKS: Although first three officially ordered on 29-6-77, little progress was made until 1981 on construction, the new carrier *Principe de Asturias* taking precedence. Will duplicate U.S. version except for close-defense AA gun system. Sonar essentially the same as the U.S. Navy's SQS-56. First two are "short-hull" version and will have to be back-fitted with longer, raked stern and RAST helicopter deck-handling system to handle SH-60B LAMPS-III helicopters; F 83 and later will get SSQ-28 LAMPS-III date link. Final full-load displacement may top 3,900 tons, as in U.S. units.

◆ **6 Descubierta class**

	Bldr	Laid down	L	In serv.
F 31 DESCUBIERTA	Bazán, Cartagena	16-11-74	8-7-75	18-11-78
F 32 DIANA	Bazán, Cartagena	8-7-75	26-1-76	30-6-79
F 33 INFANTA ELENA	Bazán, Cartagena	26-1-76	14-9-76	12-4-80
F 34 INFANTA CRISTINA	Bazán, Cartagena	14-9-76	19-4-77	24-11-80
F 35 CAZADORA	Bazán, el Ferrol	14-12-77	17-10-78	20-7-81
F 36 VENCEDORA	Bazán, el Ferrol	1-5-78	27-4-79	27-3-82

D: 1,363 tons (1,575 fl) **S:** 26 kts **Dim:** 88.88 (85.8 pp) × 10.4 × 3.9
A: 1/Sea Sparrow SAM system (VIII × 1; 24 missiles)—1/76-mm OTO Melara—2/40-mm AA (I × 2)—1/375-mm Bofors ASW RL (II × 1)—6/324-mm Mk 32 ASW TT (III × 2)

Infanta Elena (F 33) L. & L. Van Ginderen, 10-85

Infanta Cristina (F 34) S. Terzibaschitsch, 1981

Cazadora (F 35) L. & L. Van Ginderen, 10-84

Electron Equipt: Radar: 1/H.S.A. ZW-06/2, 1/H.S.A. DA-05/2, 1/H.S.A. WM 25 fire-control
Sonar: Raytheon 1160B, Raytheon 1167 (VDS, last four)
EW: Elettronica Beta passive system
M: 4 MTU-Bazán 16MA956 TB91 diesels; 2 CP props; 18,000 hp
Electric: 1,810 kw **Fuel:** 250 tons **Range:** 6,100/18
Man: 10 officers, 106 men

REMARKS: Design evolved from the Portuguese Navy's *João Coutinho* class, built by same yard. The first four were ordered on 7-12-73, the others on 25-5-76. Intended to receive 8 Harpoon SSM (IV × 2) between bridge superstructure and Y-shaped stacks, aimed athwartships. All are scheduled to get 1/20-mm Meroka in place of upper 40-mm, and two chaff launchers. Plans call for backfitting Raytheon Type 1167 VDS. Have fin stabilization, plus U.S. Prairie/Masker bubble system to reduce radiated noise below the waterline. Can accommodate thirty troops. Carry 600 rounds 76-mm gun ammunition. Have SEWACO weapons control system. Eight improved units with gas-turbine propulsion (described in previous edition) were to follow; they have been delayed in programming. Sisters *Centinella* (F 37) and *Serviola* (F 38) were sold to Egypt in 1982, prior to completion; another sister has been built for Morocco.

◆ **5 Baleares class** Bldr: Bazán, el Ferrol

	Laid down	L	In serv.
F 71 BALEARES	31-10-68	20-8-70	24-9-73
F 72 ANDALUCIA	2-7-69	30-3-71	23-5-74
F 73 CATALUÑA	20-8-70	3-11-71	16-1-75
F 74 ASTURIAS	30-3-71	13-5-72	2-12-75
F 75 ESTREMADURA	3-11-71	21-11-72	10-11-76

D: 3,015 tons (4,177 fl) **S:** 27/28 kts
Dim: 133.59 (126.5 pp) × 14.33 × 4.6 (7.01 over sonar)
A: 8/Harpoon SSM (IV × 2)—1/Mk 22 guided-missile launcher (16 Standard SM-1 MR)—1/127-mm Mk 42 DP—1/ASROC Mk 116 ASW RL (VIII × 1, plus reloads)—4/324-mm Mk 32 fixed ASW TT (I × 4)—2/fixed Mk 25 ASW TT for Mk 37 torpedoes
Electron Equipt: Radar: 1/Decca 1226, 1/SPS-10, 1/SPS-52A, 1/SPG-51C, 1/SPG-53B—TACAN: SRN-15A
Sonar: 1/SQS-23 (hull), 1/SQS-35V (VDS)
EW: Elsa Mk 1000 passive system
M: 1 set Westinghouse GT; 1 prop; 35,000 hp **Electric:** 3,000 kw
Boilers: 2 Combustion-Engineering; 84 kg/cm², 510°C
Fuel: 750 tons **Man:** 15 officers, 241 men

REMARKS: Built with American aid (agreement of 31-5-66) as U.S. DEG 7 to DEG 11. The Mk 74 missile fire-control system can use both the Mk 73 director (with SPG-51C radar) and Mk 68 director (with SPG-53B) to control two Standard missiles; the Mk 68 is also used to control the 127-mm gun. The ships have the Mk 114 digital ASW computer to control ASROC and ASW-torpedo firing. No less than forty-one ASW torpedoes of the Mk 44/46 and Mk 37 wire-guided types can be accommodated. The Mk 32 torpedo tubes are built into the port and starboard sides of the after superstructure and are oriented to a 45-degree angle outboard of the centerline. The two Mk 25 tubes are built into the stern, facing aft. The Meroka 20-mm AA gun system to be installed on the stern. Fifteen Harpoon missiles were ordered for these ships in 1982. The TRITAN-1 combat data system is being installed during modernizations; F 75 completed 1973, F 72 in works 1985 at el Ferrol.

Asturias (F 74)—prior to refit G. Arra, 1984

GUIDED-MISSILE FRIGATES *(continued)*

Estremadura (F 75)—with 8 Harpoon amidships G. Arra, 1983

CORVETTES

◆ **4 Atrevida class**

	Bldr	Laid down	L	In serv.
PA 61 Atrevida	Bazán, Cartegena	26-6-50	2-12-52	25-4-53
PA 62 Princesa	Bazán, Cartegena	18-3-53	31-3-55	2-10-59
PA 64 Nautilus	Bazán, Cádiz	27-7-53	10-9-56	10-12-59
PA 65 Villa De Bilbao	Bazán, Cádiz	18-3-53	19-2-58	2-9-60

Nautilus (PA 64) L. & L. Van Ginderen, 10-84

D: 977 tons (1,136 fl) **S:** 16-17 kts
Dim: 75.5 (68.0 pp) × 10.2 × 2.64 (4.08 max.)
A: 1/76.2-mm U.S. Mk 26 DP—3/40-mm AA (I × 3)
Electron Equipt: Radar: 1/SPS-5B, 1/Decca . . .
M: 2 Sulzer diesels; 2 props; 3,000 hp
Fuel: 100 tons **Range:** 8,000/10 **Man:** 9 officers, 123 men

Remarks: Tandem machinery arrangement. Electronic equipment and weapons modernized with U.S. aid. Can carry twenty mines. *Diana* (F 63) stricken in 1972. F 61 and F 65 were to be stricken in 1979, but all have been refitted and are now employed in patrolling between Gibraltar and the Canaries. ASW ordnance and sonar removed 1980 when redesignated PA, *Patrullero de Altura.* Have a single lead-computing director for the 40-mm AA; 76.2-mm mount has a rangefinder only. Planned for disposal 1986-91.

PATROL BOATS

◆ **6 Lazaga class** Bldr: P 01: Lürssen, Vegesack; others: Bazán, La Carraca, Cadiz

	L	In serv.		L	In serv.
PC 01 Lazaga	30-9-74	14-6-75	PC 04 Villamil	15-5-75	26-4-77
PC 02 Alsedo	8-1-75	28-2-77	PC 05 Bonifaz	15-5-75	11-7-77
PC 03 Cadarso	8-1-75	10-7-76	PC 06 Recalde	16-10-75	15-12-77

Villamil (PC 04) L. & L. Van Ginderen, 1-85

D: 275 tons (397 fl) **S:** 29.7 kts **Dim:** 57.4 (54.4 pp) × 7.60 × 2.70
A: 1/76-mm OTO Melara DP—1/40-mm Breda-Bofors AA—2/20-mm AA (I × 2)
Electron Equipt: Radar: 1/Raytheon 1620/6, 1/H.S.A. M 22
M: 2 MTU MA-16V956 TB91 diesels; 2 props; 7,780 hp **Electric:** 405 kVA
Fuel: 112 tons **Range:** 2,260/27; 4,200/17 **Man:** 4 officers, 35 men

Remarks: P 01 and P 03 were commissioned with a U.S. Mk 22, 76-mm instead of an OTO Melara 76-mm. Space reserved for addition of six 324-mm Mk 32 ASW torpedo tubes and a small, high-frequency sonar. Carry 300 rounds of 76-mm, 1,472 rounds of 40-mm, and 3,000 rounds of 20-mm. PC = *Patrulleros Cañaneros:* redesignated 1980. PC 03 conducted Meroka sea trials in 1984, with the 12-barreled 20-mm gun in place of the 76-mm mount.

◆ **6 Barcelo class** Bldrs: P 11 Lürssen; others: Bazán, La Carraca, Cádiz

	L	In serv.		L	In serv.
PC 11 Barcelo	6-10-75	26-3-75	PC 14 Ordonez	10-9-76	7-6-77
PC 12 Laya	16-12-75	23-12-76	PC 15 Acevedo	10-9-76	14-7-77
PC 13 Javier Quiroga	16-12-75	1-4-77	PC 16 Candido Perez	3-3-77	25-11-77

Javier Quiroga (PC 13) G. Arra, 1981

D: 110 tons (134 fl) **S:** 36.5 kts **Dim:** 36.2 (43.2 pp) × 5.8 × 1.75 (2.15 props)
A: 1/40-mm Bofors AA—1/20-mm AA—2/12.7-mm mg (I × 2)
Electron Equipt: Radar: 1/Raytheon 1620/6
M: 2 MTU 16V538 TB90 diesels; 2 props; 7,320 hp (6,120 sust.)
Electric: 220 kVA **Fuel:** 18 tons **Range:** 600/33.5; 1,200/16
Man: 3 officers, 16 men

Remarks: Lürssen FPB 36 design. Carry 750 rounds 40-mm, 2,500 rounds 20-mm ammunition.

FISHERIES PATROL BOATS

Note: The following units, designated PVZ—*Patrulleros de Vigilancia de Zona* in 9-80, are operated by the Navy in behalf of the Ministry of Commerce for 200-nautical-mile economic zone patrol.

◆ **10 Anaga class** Bldr: Bazán, San Fernando, Cádiz

	L	In serv.		L	In serv.
PVZ 21 Anaga	14-2-80	30-1-81	PVZ 26 Medas	15-12-80	16-10-81
PVZ 22 Tagomago	14-2-80	30-1-81	PVZ 27 Izaro	15-12-80	9-12-81
PVZ 23 Marola	. . .	4-6-81	PVZ 28 Tabaraca	15-12-80	30-12-81
PVZ 24 Mouro	. . .	14-7-81	PVZ 29 Deva	24-11-81	3-6-82
PVZ 25 Grosa	15-12-80	14-7-81	PVZ 210 Bergantin	24-11-81	30-7-82

D: 296 tons (350 fl) **S:** 20 kts **Dim:** 44.4 (40.0 pp) × 6.6 × 2.6
A: 1/76.12-mm U.S. Mk 22 DP—1/20-mm AA—2/12.7-mm mg (I × 2)
Electron Equipt: Radar: 1/Decca 1226 navigational **Man:** 25 tot.
M: 1 Bazán/MTU 16V956 diesel; 1 prop; 4,800 hp **Range:** 4,000/15

Remarks: Ordered 22-7-78. PVZ 21 laid down 4-79.

FISHERIES PATROL BOATS *(continued)*

Deva (PVZ 29) L. & L. Van Ginderen, 1984

◆ **4 PVZ 31 class** Bldr: Bazán, San Fernando, Cádiz

	L	In serv.
PVZ 31 Conejera (ex-LVE 1)	9-81	31-12-81
PVZ 32 Dragonera (ex-LVE 2)	9-81	31-12-81
PVZ 33 Espalmador (ex-LVE 3)	11-1-82	10-5-82
PVZ 34 Alcanada (ex-LVE 4)	10-2-82	10-5-82

Conejera (PVZ 31) L. & L. Van Ginderen, 10-84

D: 85 tons (fl) **S:** 25 kts **Dim:** 32.15 (30.0 pp) × 5.30 × 1.42
A: 1/20-mm AA — 1/12.7-mm mg
M: 2 Bazán/M.A.N. V8V16/18TLS diesels; 2 props; 2,800 hp
Range: 1,200/15 **Man:** 12 tot.

Remarks: Ordered 1978; first two laid down 20-12-79. Aluminum construction. A planned further six were not built.

Note: The five *Carabo*-class patrol boats (PVZ 12–16) and the single-unit *Aguila* (PVZ . . .) have been returned to customs service duties.

◆ **3 U.S. Adjutant-class former minesweepers**

	Bldr	L	In serv.
PVZ 51 Nalon ex-M 21, ex-MSC 139)	South Coast Co., Newport Beach, Cal.	22-11-52	16-2-54
PVZ 52 Ulla (ex-M 24, ex-MSC 265)	Adams Yacht, Quincy, Mass.	28-1-56	24-7-58
PVZ 54 Turia (ex-M 27, ex-MSC 130)	Hiltebrand DD, Kingston, N.Y.	14-7-54	1-6-55

Remarks: Redesignated 9-80; all portable minesweeping gear removed. Data as for sisters retained as minesweepers. Two others redesignated PVZ have been returned to mine-warfare duties: *Miño* (PVZ 53/M 25) and *Sil* (PVZ 55/M 29).

◆ **1 former trawler** Bldr: Juliana, Gijón (In serv. 1948)

PVZ 11 Salvora (ex-W 32, ex-*Virgen de la Almudena,* ex-*Mendi Eder*)

D: 274 tons (fl) **S:** 11 kts **Dim:** 32.58 × 6.22 × 3.77
A: 1/20-mm AA **M:** 1 Sulzer diesel; 1 prop; 400 hp
Fuel: 25 tons **Man:** 31 tot.

Remarks: Purchased 25-9-54. Redesignated PVZ 11 in 9-80.

◆ **2 former fishing boats**

PVZ 71 Necora PVZ 72 Percebes

D: . . . **S:** . . . **Dim:** . . . × . . . × . . .
A: . . . **M:** . . . **Man:** . . .

Remarks: Acquired 1984. Based at Las Palmas, Canary Islands. No data available.

PATROL CRAFT

◆ **20 PVC 11 class** Bldr: Aresa, Arenys del Mar, Barcelona (In serv. 1978-80)

PVC 11 through PVC 19, PVC 110 through 120

D: 16.9 tons (21.7 fl) **S:** 26 kts **Dim:** 15.90 (13.7 pp) × 4.36 × 1.33
A: 1/12.7-mm mg **Electron Equipt:** Radar: 1/Decca 110
M: 2 Baudouin DNP-8 MIR diesels; 2 props; 768 hp **Electric:** 12 kVA
Fuel: 2.2 tons **Range:** 430/18 **Man:** 2 officers, 4-5 men

Remarks: Formerly LVC 1–LVC 20. Glass-reinforced plastic construction. PVC = *Patrullero Vigilancia Costera.*

PVC 14 P. Voss, 5-82

◆ **1 former customs patrol craft** Bldr: . . . (In serv. . . .)

PVC 41 (ex-*Roquero*)

D: 34 tons (fl) **S:** 14 kts **Dim:** 14.5 × 3.5 × . . .
A: . . . **M:** 2 G.M. diesels; 2 props; 292 hp **Man:** 9 tot.

Remarks: Transferred 1983. Wooden construction.

◆ **1 small patrol craft** Bldr: Aresa del Mar, Barcelona

PVC 31 (ex-V 34) (L: 2-1-75)

D: 14 tons (16.4 fl) **S:** 24 kts **Dim:** 15.7 × 3.9 × 0.7
A: 1/12.7-mm mg **Electron Equipt:** Radar: 1/Decca 110 nav.
M: 2 Cummins 8TV-370-M diesels; 2 props; 740 hp
Range: 500/20 **Man:** 7

Remarks: Was prototype for PVI 11 design; wooden construction.

◆ **1 glass-reinforced plastic patrol craft** Bldr: Viudes, Barcelona

PVC 21 (ex-V 33) (L: 24-3-77)

D: 20.3 tons (25 fl) **S:** 27 kts **Dim:** 16.06 × 4.30 × 0.97
A: 1/12.7-mm mg **Electron Equipt:** Radar: 1/Decca 110
M: 2 M.A.N. D-2542-MTE diesels; 2 props; 1,100 hp
Range: 700/18 **Man:** 9 tot.

◆ **30 PVI 11 class** Bldr: Rodman, Vigo (In serv. 1978-80)

PVI 11 through PVI 19, PVI 110 through PVI 130

PVI 114 L. & L. Van Ginderen, 12-84

D: 3 tons (4.2 fl) **S:** 18 kts **Dim:** 9.0 × 3.1 × 0.8
Range: 120/18 **Man:** 6 tot.
A: 1/7.62-mm mg **M:** 2 Volvo inboard/outboard diesels; 2 props; 240 hp

Remarks: Formerly LVI 1–20, redesignated 9-80. PVI = *Patrullero de Vigilancia Interior.*

◆ **4 PVI 21 class** Bldr: Bazán, La Carraca, Cádiz (In serv. 1963-64)

PVI 21 through PVI 25

PVI 24 P. Voss, 5-82

PATROL CRAFT *(continued)*

D: 17.2 tons (25 fl) **S:** 13 kts **Dim:** 14.04 × 4.57 × 1.0
A: 2/7.62-mm mg (II × 1)
M: 2 Gray Marine 64HN9 diesels; 2 props; 450 hp **Man:** 8 tot.

REMARKS: Copy of U.S. "45-foot picket boat." Formerly LPI 1–5. No radar.

◆ **3 U.S. Coast Guard 83-foot craft** Bldr: Bazán, Cádiz

PAS 11 (In serv. 24-3-65) PAS 12 (In serv. 21-4-65) PAS 13 (In serv. 13-9-65)

PAS 11—with old number 1969

D: 49 tons (63 fl) **S:** 15 kts **Dim:** 25.4 (23.8 pp) × 4.9 × 2.0
A: 1/20-mm AA—2/7.62-mm mg—2 Mk Mousetrap ASW RL (IV × 2)
Electron Equipt: Radar: 1/Decca . . . —Sonar: QCU
M: 2 diesels; 2 props; 800 hp **Man:** 15 tot.

REMARKS: Wooden hull. Based on U.S.C.G. WPB design. PAS = *Patrullero de Antisubmarino.*

◆ **1 river patrol boat** Bldr: Bazán, La Carraca, Cádiz (In serv. 11-1-63)

PVI 01 CABO FRADERA (ex-V 22)

D: 28 tons **S:** 10 kts **Dim:** 17.80 × 4.20 × 0.82 **A:** 2/mg **M:** Diesel; 280 hp

REMARKS: For use on the Miño River, as are the two following craft.

◆ **1 small river patrol craft** Bldr: Cartagena SY (L: 5-5-69)

PVI 31 (ex-V5)

D: 3.1 tons (5 fl) **S:** 7.5 kts **Dim:** 8.3 × 2.7 × 0.8
M: . . . diesel; . . . props; . . . hp **Man:** 7 tot.

◆ **1 small river patrol craft** Bldr: Luarca SY

PVI 32 (ex-V6) (In serv. 10-8-52)

D: 4.5 tons **S:** 7 kts **Dim:** 8.3 × 3.0 × 1.25
M: . . . **Man:** 4 tot.

MINE WARFARE SHIPS

◆ **4 ex-U.S. Aggressive-class minesweepers**

	Bldr	L	In serv.
M 41 GUADALETE (ex-PVZ 41, ex-M 41, ex-*Dynamic,* MSO 432)	Colbert Boatworks, Stockton, Cal.	17-12-52	15-12-53
M 42 GUADALMEDINA (ex-*Pivot,* MSO 463)	Wilmington Boatworks, Wilmington, Cal.	9-1-54	12-7-54
M 43 GUADALQUIVIR (ex-*Persistent,* MSO 491)	Tacoma Boat, Tacoma, Wash.	23-4-55	3-2-56
M 44 GUADIANA (ex-*Vigor,* MSO 473)	Burgess Boat, Manitowoc, Wisc.	24-6-53	8-11-54

Guadalquivir (M 43) L. & L. Van Ginderen, 5-85

D: 665 tons (780 fl) **S:** 14 kts **Dim:** 52.75 × 10.70 × 3.88 (4.2 max.)
A: 2/20-mm AA (II × 1)—2/12.7-mm mg (I × 2)
Electron Equipt: Radar: 1/SPS-5C, 1/Decca TM 626
Sonar: SQQ-14
M: 4 Packard diesels; 2 CP props; 2,280 hp
Range: 2,000/12; 3,000/10 **Man:** 6 officers, 65 men

REMARKS: Modernized 1969-70. Loaned 1-7-71, except M 44 on 4-4-72. All purchased in 8-74. Equipped for mechanical, magnetic, and acoustic sweeping. *Guadelete* (M 41, ex-MSO 432) redesignated PVZ 41 in 9-80, redesigned M 41 late 1981.

◆ **8 ex-U.S. Adjutant, MSC 268* and Redwing**-class minesweepers**

	Bldr	L	In serv.
M 21 JUCAR (ex-M 23, ex-MSC 220)	Bellingham SY, Bellingham, Wash.	24-1-55	22-6-56
M 22 EBRO (ex-M 26, ex-MSC 269)*	Bellingham SY, Bellingham, Wash.	8-11-57	19-12-58
M 23 DUERO (ex-M 28, ex-*Spoonbill,* MSC 202)**	Tampa Marine, Tampa, Fla.	3-8-54	16-6-59
M 24 TAJO (ex-M 30, ex-MSC 287)*	Tampa Marine, Tampa, Fla.	1-5-56	9-7-59
M 25 GENIL (ex-M 31, ex-MSC 279)*	Tacoma Boat, Tacoma, Wash.	8-8-58	11-9-59
M 26 ODIEL (ex-M 32, ex-MSC 288)*	Tampa Marine, Tampa, Fla.	3-9-58	9-10-59
M 27 SIL (ex-PVZ 55, ex-M 29, ex-*Redwing,* MSC 200)**	Tampa Marine, Tampa, Fla.	29-4-54	16-6-59
M 28 MIÑO (ex-PVZ 53, ex-M 25, ex-MSC 266)	Adams Yacht, Quincy, Mass.	14-4-56	25-10-56

Ebro (M 22) L. & L. Van Ginderen, 3-85

Jucar (M 21) Spanish Navy, 1984

D: 355 tons (384 fl) **S:** 12 kts **Dim:** 43.0 (41.5 pp) × 7.95 × 2.55
A: 2/20-mm AA (II × 1) **M:** 2 G.M. 8-268A diesels; 2 props; 1,200 hp
Electron Equipt: Radar: 1/Decca TM 626 or RM 914—Sonar: UQS-1D
Fuel: 40 tons **Range:** 2,500/10 **Man:** 2 officers, 35 men

REMARKS: Originally a group of twelve, transferred under MAP: two in 1954, one in 1955, three in 1956, one in 1958, two in 1959, and three in 1960. *Llobregat* (M 22, ex-MSC 143) was stricken on 4-7-79 after a fire. M 21 and M 23 have a mast well astern of the stack; the others have only a small davit beside the stack. MSC 268-class ships were 43.9 m overall by 8.51 max. beam and had 4 G.M. 6-71 diesels; 2 props; 900 hp. Five sisters were redesignated PVZ in 9-80 and had portable sweep gear removed; two were redesignated minesweepers in 1984: M 27 and M 28.

AMPHIBIOUS WARFARE SHIPS

◆ **2 ex-U.S. Paul Revere-class transports** Bldr: New York SB Corp., Camden, N.J.

	L	In serv.
L 21 Castilla (ex-*Paul Revere,* LPA 248, ex-*Diamond Mariner*)	13-2-54	3-9-58
L 22 Aragón (ex-*Francis Marion,* LPA 249, ex-*Prairie Mariner*)	11-4-53	6-7-61

Castilla (L 21) Spanish Navy, 1984

D: 10,704 light (16,838 fl) **S:** 22.5 kts
Dim: 171.80 (160.94 pp) × 23.24 × 7.32 **A:** 8/76.2-mm Mk 33 DP (II × 4)
Electron Equipt: Radar: 1/LN-66, 1/SPS-10, 1/SPS-12 (L 22: SPS-40)
EW: WLR-1, ULQ-6
M: 1 set G.E. GT; 1 prop; 22,000 hp **Electric:** 2,400 kw
Boilers: 2 Combustion-Eng. (L 22: Foster-Wheeler); 42.3 kg/cm², 467°C
Range: 10,000/22; 17,000/14 **Man:** 28 officers, 424 men + troops: 96 officers, 1,561 men

Remarks: Mariner-class C4-S-1A merchant ships converted to troop transports. LPA 248 by Todd Shipyard, San Diego, and LPA 249 by Bethlehem Steel, Baltimore. Can carry seven LCM(6) and sixteen LCVP. Four Mk 63 gunfire-control systems removed between 1977 and 1978, but intercept and jamming equipment retained. In recent years had served the Naval Reserve Force. Were sold to Spain: L 21 on 17-1-80, and L 22 on 11-7-80. TACAN now removed from L 21.

◆ **1 ex-U.S. Cabildo-class landing ship, dock** Bldr: Philadelphia Navy Yard

	Laid down	L	In serv.
L 31 Galicia (ex-*San Marcos,* LSD 25)	1-9-44	10-1-45	15-4-45

Galicia (L 31)—with old number 1978

D: 4,790 tons (9,375 fl) **S:** 15 kts **Dim:** 139.52 × 21.9 × 5.49 max.
A: 12/40-mm AA (IV × 2., II × 2)
Electron Equipt: Radar: 1/Decca TM 626, 1/SPS-10
M: 2 sets GT; 2 props; 7,000 hp **Boilers:** 2 two-drum, 17.6 kg/cm²
Range: 8,000/15 **Man:** 18 officers, 283 men + 137 troops

Remarks: Loaned 1-7-71 and sold outright 8-74. Well deck is 103.0 × 13.3 m. Platform for three helicopters. Can carry eighteen LCMs with one LCVP nested in each in the well. Cargo capacity: 1,347 tons. Four Mk 51, Mod. 2, lead-computing GFCS (no radar).

◆ **3 ex-U.S. *Terrebone Parish*-class tank landing ships**
Bldrs: L 11 and L 13: Bath Iron Works; L 12: Christy Corp., Sturgeon Bay, Wisc.

	L	In serv.
L 11 Velasco (ex-*Terrebonne Parish,* LST 1156)	9-8-52	21-11-52
L 12 Martin Alvarez (ex-*Wexford County,* LST 1168)	. . .	15-6-54
L 13 Conde del Venadito (ex-*Tom Green County,* LST 1159)	10-7-53	12-9-53

Conde del Venadito (L 13) L. & L. Van Ginderen, 3-84

D: 2,590 tons (6,225 fl) **S:** 13 kts **Dim:** 117.35 × 16.7 × 3.7
A: 6/76.2-mm Mk 33 AA (II × 3)
Electron Equipt: Radar: 1/Decca TM 626, 1/Decca 1229, 2/Mk 34
M: 4 G.M. 16-278A diesels; 2 props; 6,000 hp **Electric:** 600 kw
Fuel: 1,060 tons **Range:** 6,000/9 **Man:** 115 tot.

Remarks: L 11 and L 12 transferred on 29-10-71, and L 13 on 5-1-72. All purchased outright on 1-11-76. Accommodations for 395 troops. Cargo: 2,200 tons. Carry two LCVP to starboard and one LCPL to port. Two Mk 63 radar GFCS.

◆ **3 "Pelicano"-class utility landing craft** Bldr: Bazán, La Carraca, Cádiz

	L	In serv.		L	In serv.
LCT 6	10-11-65	6-12-66	LCT 8	10-11-66	30-12-66
LCT 7	10-2-66	30-12-66			

LCT 6 Spanish Navy, 1984

D: 279 tons (710 fl) **S:** 9.5 kts **Dim:** 59.00 (52.9 pp) × 11.90 × 1.86
A: 2/20-mm AA (I × 2)—2/12.7-mm mg (I × 2)
Electron Equipt: Radar: 1/Decca 404
M: 2 Bazán-M.A.N. R6V16/18 TLS diesels; 2 props; 1,060 hp
Electric: 25 kw **Range:** 1,500/9.5 **Man:** 17 crew + 35 troops

Remarks: In service in 12-66. Cargo: 300 tons. Formerly BDK 6–8. Design based on the French EDIC type.

◆ **2 utility landing craft** Bldr: Bazán, el Ferrol (All in serv. 15-6-59)

LCT 4 (L: 30-4-58) LCT 5 (L: 31-5-58)

D: 302 tons (665 fl) **S:** 8.5 kts **Dim:** 56.6 × 11.57 × 1.7
A: 2/20-mm AA **M:** 2 MGO V8AS diesels; 2 props; 1,000 hp
Range: 1,000/7 **Man:** 1 officer, 19 men

Remarks: Cargo: 300 tons. Formerly BDK 4–5. Similar to the class above. Sister LCT 3 stricken 3-7-84; LCT 4 and LCT 5 to strike 1986.

◆ **2 ex-U.S. LCU 1466-class utility landing craft**
Bldr: Kingston Dry Dock Const. Co., Kingston, N.Y. (L: 4-55)

LCU 11 (ex-LCU 1471) LCU 12 (ex-LCU 1491)

D: 180 tons (347 fl) **S:** 8 kts **Dim:** 35.05 × 10.36 × 1.6
A: 2/20-mm AA **M:** 3 Gray Marine 64YTL diesels; 3 props; 675 hp
Man: 6 crew + 8 troops

Remarks: Transferred in 6-72. Cargo: 160 tons. Formerly LCU 1, 2.

◆ **1 experimental air-cushion vehicle landing craft**
Bldr: Chaconsa, Murcia

VCA 36 (In serv. 1985)

D: 22 tons (36 fl) **S:** 60 kts **Dim:** 25.17 × 11.04 × 9.50 (high)
A: None **Electron Equipt:** . . .
M: 2 Avco-Lycoming gas turbines; 2 airscrew props, 5,000 hp
Range: 150/50 **Electric:** 30 kVA **Man:** 3 crew + 70 troops

Remarks: Ordered 12-82 for the Marine Infantry, who also operate the 400-kg, 6-m, 40-kt trials hovercraft *Furtivo.* VCA 36 will be able to transport 14 tons of cargo or 3 Land Rover trucks, plus 70 troops. There are two centrifugal lift fans. The Navy also operates Chaconsa's VCA-3 hovercraft, a 4-ton test craft completed 1978. Cargo compartment: 18.65 × 2.60 m.

◆ **2 (+ . . .) new-construction landing craft** Bldr: Bazán, San Fernando

LCM 601 (In serv. 28-12-84) LCM 602 (In serv. 1-2-85)

Remarks: No data available.

◆ **6 U.S. LCM(8)-class landing craft** Bldr: Oxnard Boat, Cal. (In serv. 1975)

LCM 81 through LCM 86

LCM 81—with old number 1975

AMPHIBIOUS WARFARE SHIPS *(continued)*

D: 115 tons (fl) **S:** 10 kts **Dim:** 22.7 × 6.55 × 1.83 (aft)
M: 4 G.M. 6-71 diesels; 2 props; 600 hp **Man:** 5 tot.

REMARKS: Transferred 7-75 to 9-75. Formerly E 81–86.

◆ **6 ex-U.S. LCM(6)-class landing craft** Bldr: Lukens Steel, Pa.

LCM 61 through LCM 66

D: 24 tons (57 fl) **S:** 10.2 kts **Dim:** 17.07 × 4.37 × 1.52
M: 2 Gray Marine 64HN9 diesels; 2 props; 330 hp

REMARKS: Transferred on 23-12-74. Cargo: 30 tons

◆ **7 ex-U.S. LCM(3)-class landing craft**

D: 20 tons (50 fl) **S:** 10.2 kts **Dim:** 15.24 × 4.37 × 1.17
M: 2 Gray Marine 64HN9 diesels; 2 props; 330 hp

REMARKS: Transferred in 12-57. Cargo: 25 tons.

◆ **16 ex-U.S. LCP(L)**

D: 10.2 tons (fl) **S:** 19 kts **Dim:** 10.91 × 3.42 × 1.07 (aft)
M: 1 G.M. 8V71N diesel; 1 prop; 350 hp

REMARKS: Transferred in 10-58 and 1971

◆ **49 ex-U.S. LCVP**

D: 13 tons (fl) **S:** 5 kts **Dim:** 11.0 × 3.2 × 1.1 (aft)
M: 1 Gray Marine 64HN9 diesel; 1 prop; 225 hp

NOTE: Above totals reflect landing craft on hand before the transfer of LPA 248 and LPA 249, which retained their nine LCM(6) and eleven LCVP each. Most LCP(L) and LCVP are aboard larger ships.

AUXILIARY SHIPS

◆ **0 (+1) SWATH prototype** Bldr: Bazán, . . .

	Laid down	L	In serv.
. . . N. . .	1985	. . .	. . .

D: . . . **S:** . . . **Dim:** 50.0 × 20.0 × 5.0 **A:** . . . **M:** . . . ; 2 props; . . . hp

REMARKS: SWATH = Small Waterplane Twin Hull, a type of catamaran. Program announced for experimental prototype, financed half by Bazán and half by the Commission on Scientific Research of the Ministry of Education.

◆ **4 Castor-class survey ships** Bldr: Bazán, La Carraca, Cádiz

	L	In serv.		L	In serv.
AH 21 CASTOR	5-11-64	1-12-66	AH 23 ANTARES	5-3-73	21-11-74
AH 22 POLLUX	5-11-64	15-12-66	AH 24 RIGEL	5-3-73	21-11-74

Castor (AH 21) L. & L. Van Ginderen, 7-84

D: 354.5 tons (383.4 fl) **S:** 11.5 kts **Dim:** 38.36 (33.8 pp) × 7.60 × 3.10
Electron Equipt: Radar: 1/Raytheon 1620
M: 1 Echevarria-B & W Alpha 408-26VO diesel; 1 prop; 800 hp
Fuel: 22.5 tons **Range:** 3,000/11.5 **Man:** 38 tot.

REMARKS: Produced in pairs, the later units having full main-deck bulwarks. AH 21 and AH 22 have one Sulzer diesel, one prop, and 720 hp. Have Raydist navigation system, Omega receivers, three echo-sounders, and a Hewlett-Packard 2100A computer. Formerly A 21–24.

NOTE: There are plans to construct a new oceanographic/hydrographic research ship (see addenda).

◆ **2 Malaspina-class hydrographic ships** Bldr: Bazán, La Carraca, Cádiz

	L	In serv.		L	In serv.
AH 31 MALASPINA	14-8-73	21-2-75	AH 32 TOFIÑO	22-12-73	23-4-75

Tofiño (AH 32) G. Arra, 1982

D: 820 tons (1,090 fl) **S:** 15 kts **Dim:** 57.7 (51.4 pp) × 11.7 × 3.64
A: 2/20-mm AA **Electron Equipt:** Radar: 1/Raytheon 1620
M: 2 San Carlos-MWM TbRHS-345-6I diesels; 2 CP props; 2,700 hp
Electric: 780 kVA **Range:** 3,140/14.5; 4,000/12 **Man:** 63 tot.

REMARKS: Have Magnavox satellite navigation system, Omega, Raydist, three echo-sounders, side-scanning mapping sonar Mk 8, and a Hewlett-Packard 2100AC computer. Formerly A 31, 32.

◆ **1 supply ship, ex-merchant refrigerated cargo ship** Bldr: Eriksbergs M/V AB, Göteborg, Sweden (In serv. 5-53)

AT 01 CONTRAMAESTRE CASADO (ex-*Thanasis K.*, ex-*Fortuna Reefer*, ex-*Bonzo*, ex-*Bajamar*, ex-*Leeward Islands*)

Contramaestro Casado (AT 01) J.-C. Bellonne, 3-84

D: Approx. 5,300 tons (fl) **S:** 16 kts **Dim:** 104.20 (96.12 pp) × 14.36 × 6.11
A: None **Electron Equipt:** Radar: 1/Decca 626, 1/Decca TM 1226
M: 1 Eriksberg 7-cyl. heavy-oil diesel; 1 prop; 3,600 hp
Range: 18,600/16 **Fuel:** 727 tons **Electric:** 660 kw **Man:** 72 tot.

REMARKS: 2,272 grt/2,743 refrigerated cargo ship acquired to supply the Canary Islands, commissioned 15-12-82. Four cargo holds. Two 5-ton derricks. Helicopter platform at stern.

◆ **0 (+1) planned new-construction oiler** Bldr: Bazán, . . .

N. . .

D: 13,000 tons (fl) **S:** 20 kts **Dim:** 145.0 × 20.0 × 8.0
A: 2 or 4/Meroka CIWS (XII × 2 or 4) **Electron Equipt:** . . .
M: 1 or 2 Bazán SEMT-Pielstick high-speed diesel; . . . prop; . . . hp
Range: 4,000/20 **Man:** 15 officers, 85 men

REMARKS: A Bazán (not naval) project to replace *Teide.* Would carry 7,000 tons cargo fuel, provisions, ammunition, spares, etc. to service a carrier and a 3- to 5-frigate task force. Not yet ordered.

◆ **1 oiler** Bldr: Bazán, Cartagena

	Laid down	L	In serv.
AP 01 TEIDE	11-11-54	20-6-55	20-10-56

Teide (AP 01)

AUXILIARY SHIPS *(continued)*

D: 2,750 tons (8,030 fl) **S:** 13.5 kts **Dim:** 117.5 × 14.85 × 7.73
A: None **Electron Equipt:** Radar: 1/Decca TM 626
M: 2 diesels; 1 prop; 3,360 hp **Man:** 98 tot.

REMARKS: Fitted for underway refueling, one station each side; can transfer 300 tons/hr. Formerly BP 11. Cargo: 5,350 m³. Normally on charter to state-owned CEPSA oil company for Spain–Canaries service.

◆ **1 netlayer**

	Bldr	L	In serv.
AC 01 CYCLOPE (ex-CR 1, ex-G 6)	Penhoët-Loire, Gran-Quecilly	29-9-54	29-7-55

Cyclope (AC 01)

D: 770 tons (831 fl) **S:** 12 kts **Dim:** 50.45 (44.5 pp) × 10.37 × 3.20
A: 1/40-mm AA—4/20-mm AA (I × 4)
Electron Equipt: Radar: 1/Decca TM 626
M: Diesel-electric propulsion, 2 SEMT-Pielstick PA 1-series diesels, 2/600 generators; 2 prop; 1,600 hp
Range: 5,200/12 **Electric:** 120 kw **Man:** 40 tot.

REMARKS: Same characteristics as the French *Scarabée.* Transferred in 1955 under the U.S. Military Air Program. Named 1982. Refitted 1984; to strike 1987.

◆ **1 submarine rescue, salvage ship, and diving tender** Bldr: Bazán, La Carraca, Cádiz (In serv. 8-8-64)

AS 01 POSEIDÓN (ex BS1, ex-RA 6)

Poseidón (AS 01) G. Gyssels, 6-82

D: 951 tons (1,107 fl) **S:** 15 kts **Dim:** 55.90 (49.80 pp) × 10.00 × 4.80
A: 4/20-mm AA (II × 2) **Electron Equipt:** Radar: 1/Decca TM 626
M: 2 Sulzer diesels; 1 CP prop; 3,200 hp **Range:** 4,640/14 **Man:** 60 tot.

REMARKS: Near sister to AR 44 and AR 45. Can support a frogman group and has a 300-meter-depth rescue bell. Equipped for fire-fighting, towing, and has salvage pumps.

◆ **2 former commercial oilfield support tugs** Bldr: Astilleros Atlantico, Santander (In serv. 1978)

AR 51 MAHÓN (ex-*Circos*) AR 52 LAS PALMAS (ex-*Somiedo*)

D: . . . **S:** 14 kts **Dim:** 41.0 × 11.6 × 5.5
A: 2/12.7-mm mg (I × 2) **Electron Equipt:** Radar: 2/Decca . . .
M: 2 AESA-Sulzer 16 ASV 25/30 diesels; 2 props; 7,744 hp
Range: . . . **Man:** . . .

REMARKS: 700 dwt. Purchased from Compañía Hispano Americana de Offshore SA and commissioned 30-7-81.

Las Palmas (AR 52) P. Voss, 5-82

◆ **2 AR 44-class ocean tugs** Bldr: Bazán, La Carraca, Cádiz

	L	In serv.
AR 42 CADIZ (ex-AR 44, ex-R 4)	20-7-62	25-3-64
AR 43 FERROL (ex-AR 45, ex-R 5)	14-9-62	11-4-64

Ferrol (AR 43)—old number P. Voss, 5-82

D: 951 tons (1,069 fl) **S:** 15 kts **Dim:** 55.9 (49.8 pp) × 10.0 × 4.0
A: 4/20-mm AA (II × 2) **Electron Equipt:** Radar: 1/Decca TM 626
M: 2 Sulzer diesels; 1 CP prop; 3,200 hp **Range:** 4,640/14 **Man:** 49 tot.

REMARKS: Improved version of AR 41 design, similar to AS 01. Can carry and lay twenty-four mines.

◆ **1 royal yacht**

	Bldr	L	In serv.
A 11 AZOR (ex-W 01)	Bazán, el Ferrol	9-6-49	21-7-49

Azor (A 11) J. Taibo, 1970

D: 442 tons (486 fl) **S:** 13.3 kts **Dim:** 46.65 × 7.70 × 3.81
Electron Equipt: Radar: 1/Decca TM 626 **M:** 2 diesels; 2 props; 1,200 hp
Range: 4,000/13 **Man:** 47 tot.

◆ **1 sail-training ship** Bldr: Ast. Echevarrieta, Cádiz

	Laid down	L	In serv.
A 01 JUAN SEBASTIAN DE ELCANO	24-11-25	5-3-27	17-8-28

AUXILIARY SHIPS *(continued)*

Juan Sebastian de Elcano (A 01) Spanish Navy, 1984

D: 3,420 tons (3,754 fl) **S:** 10 kts **Dim:** 94.11 × 13.6 × 6.95
Electron Equipt: Radar: 2/Decca TM 626 **M:** 1 Sulzer diesel; 1 prop; 1,500 hp
Fuel: 230 tons **Range:** 13,000/8 **Man:** 224 men, 80 cadets

REMARKS: Four-masted schooner, 2,467m² sail area. Carries two 37-mm saluting cannon. Also in use is the 10-m, two-masted *Galatea* (in serv. 1941), purchased 1970.

SERVICE CRAFT

◆ **5 navigational training tenders** (In serv. 1982)

AI 01 GUARDIAMARINA BARRUTIA
AI 02 GUARDIAMARINA SALAS
AI 03 GUARDIAMARINA GODINEZ
AI 04 GUARDIAMARINA RULL
AI 05 GUARDIAMARINA CHEREGUINI

D: 90 tons (fl) **S:** 12.5 kts **Dim:** 21.89 × 5.10 × 1.52
A: None **Electron Equipt:** Radar: 1/Halcon 948
M: 2 MTU diesels; 2 props; 800 hp **Range:** 1,000/. . .
Man: . . . crew + 1 intructor and 12–21 cadets

REMARKS: AI 01 in service 14-9-82; AI 04, 05 delivered 6-84. Tenders to the Naval School. Have Magnavox NAVSAT receiver, Decca 21 Navigator. Formerly numbered YE 01–05.

◆ **1 sail-training schooner** (In serv. 1-4-81)

A 21 AROSA

◆ **1 yard oiler** Bldr: Bazán, San Fernando (In serv. 1980)

YPF 21 (ex-PP 6) (In serv. 1980)

D: 523 grt **S:** 10.8 kts **Dim:** 34.0 × 7.0 × 3.0
M: 1 diesel; 1 prop; 600 hp **Cargo:** 300 tons

◆ **1 yard oiler** Bldr: Bazán, San Fernando (In serv. 1980)

YPF 31 (ex-PP 23)

D: 830 grt **S:** 10.7 kts **Dim:** 42.8 × 8.4 × 3.1
M: 1 diesel; 1 prop; 600 hp **Cargo:** . . . tons

◆ **3 YPF 3-class yard oilers** Bldr: Bazán, Cartagena (In serv. 1956-60)

YPF 51 (ex-YPF 3, ex-PP 3)
YPF 52 (ex-YPF 4, ex-PP 4)
YPF 53 (ex-YPF 53, ex-PP 5)

D: 510 grt **S:** 10 kts **Dim:** 37.0 × 6.8 × 3.0
M: 1 diesel; 1 prop; . . . hp

◆ **1 diesel-fuel lighter** Bldr: Bazán, Cartegena (In serv. 1981)

YPG 41

D: 214 grt **S:** 10.7 kts **Dim:** 24.0 × 5.5 × 2.2
M: 1/M.A.N. diesel; 1 prop; 400 hp **Cargo:** 100 tons

◆ **1 diesel-fuel lighter** Bldr: Bazán, Cádiz (In serv. 1980)

YPG 51

D: 520 grt **S:** . . . **Dim:** 34.0 × 7.0 × 2.9
M: 1 diesel; 1 prop; . . . hp **Cargo:** . . .

◆ **3 YPG 21-class diesel-fuel lighters** Bldr: Bazán, Cádiz

YPG 21 (In serv. 1963) YPG 22 (In serv. 1965) YPG 23 (In serv. 1965)

D: 337 grt **S:** 10.7 kts **Dim:** 34.3 × 6.2 × 2.3
M: 1 diesel; 1 prop; 220 hp **Cargo:** 100 tons

◆ **2 YPG 01 class** Bldr: Bazán, el Ferrol

YPT 11 (ex-YPG 01) (In serv. 1956) YPG 13 (ex-YPG 03) (In serv. 1959)

D: 200 grt **S:** 10 kts **Dim:** 34.0 × 6.0 × 2.7
M: 1 diesel; 1 prop; . . . hp **Cargo:** 193 tons

REMARKS: Formerly numbered in the PB series. Sister *YPG 02* stricken 1982.

◆ **1 large water tanker** Bldr: Bazán, San Fernando (In serv. 16-10-81)

AA 41 CONESTABLE ZARAGOZA (ex-AA 32, ex-A 32)

D: 895 tons (fl) **S:** 10.8 kts **Dim:** 48.8 (42.85 pp) × 8.40 × 3.35
M: 1 diesel; 1 prop; 700 hp **Cargo:** 600 tons

◆ **1 large water tanker** Bldr: Bazán, San Fernando (In serv. 1981)

AA 31 MARINERO JARANA (ex-A 31)

D: 535 tons (fl) **S:** 10.8 kts **Dim:** 34.0 × 7.0 × 3.03
M: 1 diesel; 1 prop; 600 hp **Cargo:** 300 tons

◆ **3 A-7-class large water tankers** Bldr: Bazán, La Carraca (all in serv. 6-62)

AA 21 MAQUINISTA MACÍAS (ex-A 9; L: 25-10-58)
AA 22 TORPEDISTA HERNANDEZ (ex-A 10; L: 10-10-58)
AA 23 FOGONERA BAÑOBRE (ex-A 11; L: 5-3-62)

Maquinista Macias (AA 21) L. & L. Van Ginderen, 7-84

D: 610 tons (fl) (ex-A-7, A-8: 706 fl) **S:** 9 kts **Dim:** 44.8 × 7.6 × 3.0
M: 1 diesel; 1 prop; 700 hp **Range:** 1,000/9
Man: 16 tot.

REMARKS: Cargo: 300 tons. Named 1982.

◆ **1 large water tanker** Bldr: Bazán, La Carraca (In serv. 1-4-51)

AA 06 CONTREMAESTRE CASTELLO (ex-A 6)

D: 1,860 tons (fl) **S:** 8 kts **Dim:** 64.05 × 9.60 × 4.80
M: Diesel

NOTE: Water tankers AA 17 and AA 02 stricken 14-7-82 and 2-8-82, respectively.

◆ **3 small water tankers** Bldr: Bazán, Cádiz (In serv. 1965)

YA 01 (ex-AB 1) YA 02 (ex-AB 2) YA 03 (ex-AB 3)

D: 337 grt **S:** 10.7 kts **Dim:** 34.3 × 6.2 × 2.5
M: 1 diesel; 1 prop; 220 hp **Cargo:** 100 tons

◆ **3 gate craft** (In serv. 1959-60)

YPB 01 (ex-PBP 1) YPB 02 (ex-PBP 2) YPB 03 (ex-PBP 3)

D: 140 tons (fl) **Dim:** 22.3 × 8.7 × 0.8 **M:** Non-self-propelled

◆ **4 netlaying barges** (In serv. 1959-60)

YDS 01–02, YDS 04–05 (ex-PR 1,2,4,5)

D: 140 tons **Dim:** 22.3 × 8.7 × 0.8 **M:** Non-self-propelled

REMARKS: Sister YDS 03 stricken 1984.

◆ **4 harbor-defense support tugs** (In serv. 1959-60)

YDS 11 YDS 12 YDS 21 YDS 22

D: . . . **S:** . . . **Dim:** 28.0 × 8.5 × 0.7
M: 1 diesel; 1 prop; . . . hp

REMARKS: Handle the YPB-series gate craft and YDS-series netlaying barges. Sisters YDS 13, 14 stricken 1984.

SPAIN *(continued)*
SERVICE CRAFT *(continued)*

◆ **2 torpedo-recovery craft/harbor minelayers** (In serv. 1961-63)

YTM 11 YTM 16

D: 60 to 190 tons (fl) **S:** . . . **Dim:** . . .

Note: Submarine-support torpedo retrievers YTM 03, 04 stricken 1984.

◆ **7 diving tenders**

YBZ 01 YBZ 03 YBZ 11 Nereida (BXL 10) YBZ 21 Proserpina YBZ 31
YBZ 32 YBZ 61

Remarks: All of 50 tons, self-propelled except YBZ 31, 32. YBZ 21 is a frogman support craft; **D:** 103.5 tons (In serv. 13-4-81). YBZ 61 in serv. 9-9-82.

◆ **6 floating cranes**

YGR 11 Samsón (100 tons capacity) YGR 21, 22, 23 (30 tons capacity)
YGR 31, 33 (15 tons capacity)

◆ **1 floating dry dock:** YDFN 01 (ex-YDF 01)

◆ **2 coastal tugs** Bldr: Bazán, el Ferrol

YRR 21 (ex-YRR 71) (In serv. 10-4-81) YRR 22 (ex-YRR 72) (In serv. 1-6-81)

D: 422 tons (fl) **S:** 12.4 kts **Dim:** 28.0 × 8.0 × 3.8
M: 1 diesel; 1 prop; 1,500 hp

◆ **3 YRR-53-class coastal tugs** Bldr: Bazán, Cartagena (In serv. 1967)

YRR 14 (ex-YRR 53, ex-RR 53) YRR 15 (ex-YRR 54, ex-RR 54)
YRR 16 (ex-YRR 56, ex-RR 56)

D: 227 tons (320 fl) **S:** 12 kts **Dim:** 27.8 × 7.0 × 2.6
M: 1 diesel; 1 prop; 1,400 hp **Man:** 13 tot.

◆ **3 YRR-50-class coastal tugs** Bldr: Bazán, Cartagena (In serv. 1963)

YRR 11 (ex-YRR 31, ex-RR 50) YRR 12 (ex-YRR 32, ex-RR 51)
YRR 13 (ex-YRR 33, ex-RR 52)

D: 205 tons (300 fl) **S:** 10 kts **Dim:** 27.8 × 7.0 × 2.5
M: 1 diesel; 1 prop; 800 hp **Man:** 13 tot.

◆ **2 large harbor tugs** Bldr: Bazán, Cartagena (In serv. 1981)

YRP 11 YRP 12

D: 229 tons (fl) **S:** 11 kts **Dim:** 28.0 × 7.5 × 3.4 **M:** 1 diesel; 1 prop; 950 hp

◆ **1 medium harbor tug** (In serv. 27-12-61)

YRP 41 (ex-RP 40)

D: 150 tons (fl) **S:** 9 kts **Dim:** 21.3 × 5.9 × . . . **M:** 1 diesel; 1 prop; 600 hp

Remarks: In service in 12-61. Former U.S. Army tug.

◆ **11 YRP 01-class small harbor tugs** (In serv. 1965-67)

YRP 01 - YRP 09 YRP 011 - YRP 012

D: 65 tons (fl) **S:** . . . **Dim:** 18.5 × 4.7 × . . . **M:** 1 diesel; 1 prop; 200 hp

Remarks: Sister YRP 010 stricken 1984.

◆ **1 submarine-support push tug** (In serv. 3-11-82)

YRS 01

◆ **1 suction dredge** (In serv. 2-12-81)

YDR 11

◆ **3 miscellaneous launch-type small tugs:** YRP 21 YRP 22 YRP 31

◆ **6 personnel launch/yachts**

QF 11 (ex-LVC 79, ex-*Cynosure*) — ex-patrol craft, ex-yacht
QF 01 through QF 05 — In serv. 1980-81

◆ **1 pontoon barge**

YCFN 01

◆ **37 miscellaneous barges, fuel floats, water barges, etc.** — with hull number prefixes YGC, YGG, YGP, YGT

CUSTOMS SERVICE
(Servicio Especial de Vigilancia Fiscal)

PATROL CRAFT

◆ **1 wooden, 32-meter class** Bldr: Chantiers Navals de l'Estérel, Cannes

Aguila (In serv. 1974)

D: 80 tons (fl) **S:** 30 kts **Dim:** 32.0 × 5.8 × 1.6
A: 1/20-mm AA **Electron Equipt:** Radar: 1/Decca 926
M: 2 MTU 820 diesels; 2,750 hp **Man:** 16 tot.

Aguila L. & L. Van Ginderen, 1981

◆ **3 Aguilucho class** Bldr: J. Roberto Rodriguez, Vigo (In serv. 1973-76)

Aguilucho Gavilan-I Gavilan-II

D: 45 tons (fl) **S:** 30 kts **Dim:** 26.1 × 5.1 × 1.3
A: 1/20-mm AA **M:** 2 MTU 820Db diesels; 2 props; 2,750 hp
Range: 750/30 **Man:** 14 tot.

◆ **3 Albatros class** Bldr: CMN, Cherbourg (In serv. 1968)

Albatros-I Albatros-II Albatros-III

D: 82 tons (fl) **S:** 28 kts **Dim:** 31.8 × 4.7 × 1.7
A: 1/20-mm AA **M:** 2 MTU 820Db diesels; 2 props; 2,750 hp **Man:** 15 tot.

◆ **5 22-meter patrol craft**

Alca Gerifalte Halcon-II Milano Nebli-II

S: 17 kts (*Alca:* 10, *Gerifalte:* 12, *Halcon-II:* 32 kts)

◆ **1 16.5-meter patrol craft:** Colimbo **S:** 20 kts

◆ **13 LVR-clsss patrol craft:** LVR 1 to LVR 13

Dim:: 11.4 × . . . × . . . **S::** 14 kts

SRI LANKA

Republic of Sri Lanka

Personnel (1985): 3,315 men, including 243 officers; plus 491 tot. Volunteer Naval Force, including 64 officers.

Merchant Marine (1984): 93 ships — 745,697 grt (tankers: 12 ships — 259,741 grt)

PATROL BOATS

◆ **. . . class** Bldr: China

Remarks: Four (or five?) patrol boats were ordered 1-85 for delivery late 1985. Class not reported; may be additional units of the Shanghai-II class (see below).

◆ **2 (+3) large patrol boats** Bldr: Colombo DY

	Laid down	L	In serv.
P 601 Jayesagara	5-82	26-5-83	9-12-83
P 602 Sagarawardene	7-82	20-11-83	4-6-84
P 603 N. . .	. . .	. . .	. . .
P 604 N. . .	. . .	. . .	. . .
P 605 N. . .	. . .	. . .	. . .

D: 330 tons (fl) **S:** 15 kts **Dim:** 39.80 × 7.00 × 2.20
A: 2/25-mm AA (II × 1) **M:** 2 M.A.N. 8L 20/27 diesels; 2 props; 2,040 hp
Electric: 220 kw **Man:** 40 tot. **Range:** 3,000/11

Remarks: First two ordered 31-12-81; three more authorized 8-84. Intended as "Offshore patrol boats."

◆ **6 Chinese Shanghai-II class**

Balawitha Jagatha Pakshaka Ramakami Suraya Weeraya

D: 122.5 tons (135 fl) **S:** 28.5 kts **Dim:** 38.78 × 5.41 × 1.55
A: 4/37-mm AA (II × 2) — 4/25-mm AA (II × 2)
Electron Equipt: Radar: 1/Pot Head **Man:** 36 tot.
M: 2 M50-F4, 1,200-hp diesels; 2 12D6, 910-hp diesels; 4 props; 4,220 hp
Range: 750/16.5 **Electric:** 39 kw **Endurance:** 7 days

SRI LANKA *(continued)*
PATROL BOATS *(continued)*

REMARKS: First five transferred in February 1972 and in 1975; *Jagatha* and *Pakshaka* transferred 1980, commissioning 30-11-80. Sister *Daksaya* stricken 1983.

NOTE: The Soviet Mol-class patrol boat *Samudra Devi,* acquired new only in 1975, was stricken 1983.

PATROL CRAFT

◆ **1 (+10 + . . .) Cougar Cat 900 patrol craft** Bldr: Cougar Marine, Netley, U.K.

Cougar Cat 900 prototype Cougar Marine

D: 4.5 tons (fl) **S:** 42 kts **Dim:** 9.20 × 2.89 × 0.78 (0.46 at speed)
A: 1/20-mm AA or several mg
M: 2 Rolls-Royce Sabre diesels; 2 props; 424 hp

REMARKS: First unit purchased 1984 for evaluation in operations from mother ships. Glass-reinforced plastic construction. Ten more ordered 1-85.

◆ **2 (6?) Dvora class** Bldr: Israeli Aircraft Ind. (In serv. 1985)

D: 47 tons (fl) **S:** 36 kts **Dim:** 21.62 × 5.49 × 0.94 (1.82 props)
A: 2/20-mm AA (I × 2)—2/12.7-mm mg (I × 2)
Electron Equipt: Radar: 1/Decca 926
M: 2 MTU 12V331 TC81 diesels; 2 props; 2,720 hp
Range: 700/32 **Electric:** 30 kw **Man:** 8-10 tot.

REMARKS: Reported late 1984; most sources say two, some six. Aluminum construction.

◆ **5 P 445 class** Bldr: Colombo DY

	L	In serv.		L	In serv.
P 445	. . .	20-9-82	P 448	27-8-82	1982
P 446	. . .	17-9-82	P 499	20-9-82	1982
P 447	15-6-82	1982			

D: 40 tons (44 fl) **S:** 22 kts **Dim:** 20.0 (18.3 pp) × 5.1 × 1.3
A: 2/12.7-mm mg (I × 2) **Electron Equipt:** Radar: 1/Decca . . .
M: 2 DDA-G.M. 12V71 TI diesels; 2 props; 1,300 hp
Fuel: 10 tons **Range:** 1,600/14 **Man:** 10 tot.

REMARKS: Improved version of the *Pradeepa* class. Steel construction. Provision for mounting 1/20-mm AA. More may be built.

◆ **6 Pradeepa class** Bldr: Colombo DY, 1976-1981

P 431 PRADEEPA P 432 P 433 P 434 P 435 P 436

D: 40 tons (44 fl) **S:** 19 kts **Dim:** 19.5 × 4.9 × 1.1
A: 2/20-mm AA (I × 2) **M:** 2 G.M. 8V71 TI diesels; 2 props; 800 hp
Range: 1,200/14 **Man:** 10 tot.

◆ **4 craft** Bldr: Colombo DY, 1977-82

P 201 P 202 P 203 P 205

D: 15 tons (22 fl) **S:** 20 kts **Dim:** 13.73 × 3.63 × 0.90
A: 1/12.7-mm mg **Range:** 450/14 **Man:** 1 officer, 5 men
M: 2 G.M. 8V71 TI diesels; 2 props; 800 hp **Fuel:** 2.5 tons **Electric:** 1 kw

REMARKS: Also employed for customs inspection.

◆ **5 Belikawa class** Bldr: Cheverton, Cowes, U.K.

P 421 BELIKAWA P 423 KORAWAKKA P 425 TARAWA
P 422 DIYAKAWA P 424 SERUWA

D: 22 tons (fl) **S:** 23.6 kts **Dim:** 17.0 × 4.5 × 1.2
A: 3/7.62-mm mg **M:** 2 G.M. 8V71 TI diesels; 2 props; 800 hp
Range: 790/18; 1,000/12.2 **Man:** 7 tot.

REMARKS: In service between 4-77 and 10-77. Plastic construction. Originally intended for customs duties but used as patrol craft. The names may have been deleted.

COMMAND MOTHER SHIPS

◆ **3 former "Deckship" container carriers** Bldr: Chung Wah SB & Eng. Co., Ltd., Hong Kong (L: 1976-77; in serv. 9-8-84)

P 714 ABHEETHA (ex-*Carinia*) P 715 EDITHARA (ex-*Francisca*)
P 716 WICKRAMA (ex-*Delicia*)

D: Approx. 2,700 tons **S:** 11 kts **Dim:** 76.66 (71.17 pp) × 17.07 × 3.81 (normal)
A: . . . **Electron Equipt:** Radar: 1/. . . nav.
M: 2 Deutz SBA 12M528 diesels; 2 CP props; 3,000 hp
Range: 5,000/11 **Electric:** 315 kw **Fuel:** 202 tons

REMARKS: Former 1,550 grt/4,318 dwt container carriers with no below-decks cargo capacity and a 30-ton traveling crane. Had a stern ramp to weather deck for vehicle cargo. Purchased 6-84 for use as mother ships for small patrol craft.

◆ **3 former general-cargo ships** Bldr: DeWeal SY, Zaltbommel, the Netherlands (L: . . .)

A 24 MAHWELI (ex- . . .) A 25 LANKA (ex . . .) A 26 KANTHI (ex . . .)

D: . . . **S:** . . . **Dim:** 99.5 × 15.7 × 6.8
A: . . . **Electron Equipt:** Radar: . . .
M: 1 Werkspoor diesel; 1 prop; 3,600 hp
Range: 14,600/. . . **Man:** 37 tot.

REMARKS: Former M/V *Kota Ria* (purchased 6-10-84), *Kota Rukun* (purchased 17-9-84) and one other, of 3,276–3,314 grt/4,360 dwt. Intended to act as mother ships for small patrol craft. Typed "Surveillance Command Tenders," vice "Surveillance Command Ships" for trio above.

SERVICE CRAFT

◆ **1 lighthouse and navigational aids tender** Bldr: Hawker, U.K.

A 501 N. . . . . . . (ex-*Frank Rees*)

D: 57 tons (fl) **S:** . . . **Dim:** 20.0 × 5.5 × 2.0 **M:** 1 Kelvin diesel

REMARKS: Acquired 1-4-76.

◆ **1 coastal tanker:** MAHEWELI

◆ **1 fuel lighter:** MADERA OYA

NOTE: Training for the Ceylonese Navy is carried out aboard the commercial cargo ship LANKA KANTHI, operated by the Ceylon Shipping Corporation.

SUDAN

Democratic Republic of the Sudan

PERSONNEL (1985): 600 men

MERCHANT MARINE (1984): 23 ships—96,134 grt

AVIATION: Two CASA Aviocar C-212 were ordered 6-84 for Maritime Patrol duties.

NOTE: Due to operating conditions and the withdrawal of traditional sources of aid, the material condition of the units of the Sudanese fleet is rapidly declining. A number of patrol craft are no longer operable, and all auxiliaries have been discarded.

In 4-84 Bazán in Spain announced an order for two "Cormoran" guided-missile patrol boats, to be armed with 8 U.S. Harpoon missiles, and six 22-meter patrol craft. Considering the change of Sudanese government in 1985, it is possible that the order may not be carried through to completion.

PATROL BOATS

◆ **0 (+1) U.S. 105-ft Commercial Cruiser** Bldr: Swiftships, Morgan City, Louisiana (In serv. 1985)

N. . .

D: 118 tons (fl) **S:** 32 kts **Dim:** 31.73 × 7.10 × 2.16 (props)
A: . . . **Electron Equipt:** Radar: 1/. . . nav.
M: 2 diesels; 2 props; . . . hp **Man:** 21–24 tot.

REMARKS: Aluminum construction.

◆ **4 El Gihad class** Bldr: Mosor, Yugoslavia (In serv. 1961-62)

PB 1 EL GIHAD PB 3 EL ISTIQLAL
PB 2 EL HORRIYA PB 4 EL SHAAB

El Horriya (PB 2) L.V. Pujo

SUDAN *(continued)*
PATROL BOATS *(continued)*

D: 86 tons (100 fl) **S:** 20 kts **Dim:** 31.4 × 4.9 × 1.45
A: 2/40-mm AA (I × 2) — 2/12.7-mm mg
M: 2 Mercedes Benz diesels; 2 props; 1,820 hp **Range:** 1,200/12 **Man:** 17 tot.

◆ **3 ex-Iranian** Bldr: Abeking & Rasmussen, West Germany (In serv. 1970)

Shekan (ex-*Gohar*) Kader (ex-*Shahpar*) Karari (ex-*Shakram*)

D: 80 tons (fl) **S:** 28 kts **Dim:** 22.9 × 5.0 × 1.8
A: 3/20-mm AA (I × 3) **Electron Equipt:** Radar: 1/Decca 202
M: 2 MTU diesels; 2 props; 2,200 hp **Range:** 1,220/21 **Man:** 3 officers, 16 men

Remarks: Built for the Iranian Navy, transferred to the Iranian Coast Guard in 1975 and to Sudan the same year.

PATROL CRAFT

◆ **4 ex-Iranian 40-foot class** Bldr: Sewart, Morgan City, La. (In serv. 1970)

D: 10 tons (fl) **S:** 39 kts **Dim:** 12.2 × 3.4 × 1.1
A: 1/12.7-mm mg **M:** 2 G.M. 6-71 diesels; 2 props; 600 hp

Remarks: Transferred from the Iranian Coast Guard in 1975. Used for training. One being re-engined, 1984-85.

Note: Five auxiliaries, transferred 1969-70 from Yugoslavia, have been discarded: landing craft *Sobat* and *Dinder,* small oiler *Fashoda,* water tanker *Baraka,* and survey ship *Tirhoga.*

SURINAM
Republic of Surinam

Personnel (1985): 160 total.

Merchant Marine (1985): 25 ships — 15,222 grt (tankers: 1 ship — 208 grt)

Naval Aviation: The Air Force uses four Britten-Norman BN-42 B/T Maritime Defender aircraft for coastal patrol.

PATROL BOATS AND CRAFT

◆ **3 32-meter** Bldr: De Vries, Aalsmeer, Netherlands

S 401 (In serv. 6-11-76) S 402 (In serv. 3-5-77) S 403 (In serv. 1-11-77)

S 403 1980

D: 127 tons (140 fl) **S:** 17.5 kts **Dim:** 32.0 × 6.5 × 1.7
A: 2/40-mm AA (I × 2) — 2/7.62-mm mg (I × 2)
Electron Equipt: Radar: 1/Decca 110
M: 2 Paxman 12 YHCM diesels; 2 props; 2,110 hp **Range:** 1,200/13.5
Man: 15 tot.

◆ **3 22-meter** Bldr: Schöttel, Warmond, the Netherlands

C 301 (In serv. 2-76) C 302 (In serv. 2-76) C 303 (In serv. 11-76)

D: 65 tons (70 fl) **S:** 13.5 kts **Dim:** 22.0 × 4.7 × . . .
A: 1/12.7-mm mg — 2/7.62-mm mg (I × 2)
Electron Equipt: Radar: 1/Decca 110
M: 2 Dorman 8JT diesels; 2 props; 560 hp **Range:** 650/13.5 **Man:** 8 tot.

◆ **3 12.6-meter river patrol craft** Bldr: Schöttel, Warmond, the Netherlands (In serv. 1975)

RP 201 Bahadoer RP 202 Fajablow RP 203 Korangon

D: 15 tons (20 fl) **S:** 14 kts **Dim:** 12.6 × 3.8 × 1.1
A: 1/12.7-mm mg **M:** 1 Dorman 8JT diesel; 280 hp
Range: 350/10 **Man:** 4 tot.

◆ **1 10-meter river patrol craft** Bldr: Schöttel, Warmond, the Netherlands (In serv. 8-75)

D: 10 tons **S:** 14 kts **Dim:** 10.0 × . . . × . . .
A: . . . **M:** 1 Dorman 8JT diesel; 280 hp

SWEDEN
Kingdom of Sweden

Personnel (1985): 3,500 men of the regular navy, including officers, petty officers, enlisted men, and civilians with permanent status, plus 6,200 national service men available for immediate service and 3,500 reserves. Additionally, some 8,000 conscripts receive annual naval training.

Merchant Marine (1984): 679 ships — 3,520,352 grt
(tankers: 109 ships — 1,615,670 grt)

Naval Aviation: 350 men. 32 helicopters: 5 Alouette-II (HKP-2) for training, 10-Agusta Bell 206-A JetRanger (HKP-6), and 17 Vertol 107 (3 HKP-4B for minesweeping and 7 HKP-4C for rescue and ASW, with 6 depth charges or up to 4 Type 422 torpedoes, DUAV-4 dipping sonar). Four of the 17 HKP-4C were transferred from the Air Force in 1984, with three more to follow in 1985-86. A Cessna 404 Titan with a prototype side-looking radar (SLAR) was delivered 6-83, with two more SLAR-equipped aircraft to be acquired by 1987.

HKP-4 (Vertol 107) Royal Swedish Navy

HKP-6 (Agusta Bell 206-A) Royal Swedish Navy

WEAPONS AND SYSTEMS

Most of the electronic equipment in use in the Swedish Navy is of Dutch design (for example, LW-03 air-search radars, H.S.A. fire-control radars), locally manufactured or of wholly Swedish design and construction.

A. Missiles

◆ The U.S. Laser-Hellfire missile is to be procured as the RB-17 for coastal defense service between 1989-95; 25 battalions with RB-17 are to be formed to replace 32 battalions with French wire-guided SS-11 missiles.

WEAPONS AND SYSTEMS *(continued)*

◆ The Saab RB-08A, a surface-to-surface missile based on the CT-30 of the S.N.I.A.S., is in use in the coastal defense batteries.

Length: 5.7 m Wingspan: 3.6 m
Diameter: 0.65 m Weight: 9,000 kg
Max range: 70 nautical miles

◆ The infrared homing Norwegian Penguin Mk 2 missile is in use on board the *Hugin*-class patrol boats, where it is called the RB-12. It has a 120-kg warhead.

Length: 3.0 m Weight: 340 kg
Diameter: 280 mm Speed: Mach 0.7
Wingspan: 1.4 m Max. range: 30 km at an altitude of 60-100 m

◆ The Saab RBS-15 becomes operational in 1985. The missile has a solid rocket booster and a turbojet sustainer. A sea-skimmer, it has a terminal-homing guidance system. The RBS-15F version will be launched from Air Force Viggen jet fighters, and a vertical submerged-launched RBS-17 version may be developed for the *Västergötland*-class submarines.

Length: 4.350 m Weight: 598 kg (770 kg with booster)
Diameter: 0.500 m Speed: Mach 0.8
Wingspan: 0.85 m (folded) Range: 80-100 km at an altitude of 10-20 m
1.4 (extended)

◆ The RBS-70 shoulder-launched SAM entered development in 1983 as a weapon for surface combatants in a version known as the RBS-70 SLM. Range of the IR-homing missile is 5 km, to be extended to 6 km with the Mk II version in the late 1980s.

B. Guns

The Swedish Bofors firm furnishes the guns, the principal ones being:

◆ 57-mm single-barrel automatic SAK 57 Mk 1

Installed on the *Hugin*-class missile boats, the *Spica* and *Spica-II* torpedo boats

Mount weight (without ammunition): 6 tons Elevation: −10°/+75°
Train speed: 55°/sec Max. rate of fire: 200 rounds/min
Elevation speed: 20°/sec

◆ 57-mm single-barrel automatic SAK 57 Mk 2

Entered service aboard *Stockholm* in 1985. Trials with the weapon took place 1981-82 on the *Hugin*-class missile boat *Mjölner.* Also purchased by Canada.

Mount weight: 6 tons Max. rate of fire: 220 rounds/min
Train speed: 55°/sec Shell weight: AA: 5.8 kg (projectile: 2.4 kg)
Elevation: −10°/+85° Surface fire: 6.8 kg
Muzzle velocity: 1,020 m/sec. Range: 14,000 m max. horizontal

Will carry 120 rounds ready service within the low, streamlined gunhouse, automatically loading clips of 20 rounds each.

◆ 40-mm single-barrel semi-automatic L70

World-standard weapon, by Bofors. Mk 2 proximity fuze now offered. A new mounting, the 3.7-ton "Trinity" with 1.025 m/sec muzzle velocity, a 4-km range, and a 330-rpm firing rate; fitted with an integral radar, the "Trinity" fires a 1.1-kg 3-P (Programmed Proximity Prefragmented) round.

C. Torpedoes—FFV Ordnance, Motala

The wire-guided Type 61 is used for anti-surface duties from surface ships and submarines. The weapon entered service in 1977, and is now delivered in the Type 613 version, with a wakeless hydrogen peroxide engine.

Length: 7,025 mm Weight: 1,765 kg Range: 30,000 m
Diameter: 533.4 mm Warhead: 240 kg

The Type 617 is a 6.98-m-long export version weighing 1,850 kg and having a 20,000-m range.

The Type 42 torpedo is wire-guided and has acoustic homing, for use by submarines, surface ships, and aircraft against submarines. It was developed from the similar Type 41, which is still in service. The current Type 422 entered Swedish service in 1983; a reduced-charge warhead is available for peacetime use against intruders. A Type 431, improved ASW torpedo is to enter service in 1987.

Data for the Type 422 include;

Length: 2,600 mm (2,440 mm without wire-guidance attachment)
Diameter: 400 mm Warhead: 50 kg
Weight: 298 kg Range: 20,000 m (10,000 at high speed)

D. ASW Weapons

The Malin small depth charge and Elma harassment device are being procured for helicopter and surface ship use. Elma is a rocket launcher firing 100-mm-dia. charges to ranges of 250–300 m in patterns of 9, 18, 27, or 36 grenades when installed in the normal 4-unit suit. Each grenade weights 4.2 kg and has a shaped-charge warhead. A shallow-water (10-m minimum) version is to enter service in 1986, followed by chaff and IR decoy rounds.

The Bofors 375-mm ASW rocket launcher, no longer in Swedish Navy service, is widely used in foreign navies in 2-, 4-, or 6-tubed versions. Two types of rockets are furnished: the Erika, with ranges from 600–1,600 m and the Nelli, with ranges from 1,600–3,600 m. The SR-375 twin-tubed launcher has a 24-round auto-loading magazine.

E. Sensors

The Ericsson Sea Giraffe series C-band radars are offered for export in various models and provide for air and surface search via two separate channels. The digital, pulse-compression radar is offered at 15–60-kw power with differing antenna gains.

Seven sets of U.S. Klein sidescan high-frequency sonars were purchased in 1984 to assist in locating intruding submarines.

SUBMARINES

◆ 0 (+5) Type 90 Project

REMARKS: The UB 90 is scheduled to replace the *Sjöormen* class, with the first to complete in 1995. No details made public yet, but will probably incorporate Sterling-cycle external-combustion engines in the generator sets.

◆ 0 (+4) Västergötland class (Type A-17) Bldrs: Kockums, Malmö, and Karlskrona

	Laid down	L	In serv.
VGD VÄSTERGÖTLAND	10-1-83	1985	1987
HGD HÄLSINGLAND	1-1-84	1986	1988
SÖD SÖDERMANLAND	. . .	1986	1988
ÖGD ÖSTERGÖTLAND	. . .	1987	1989

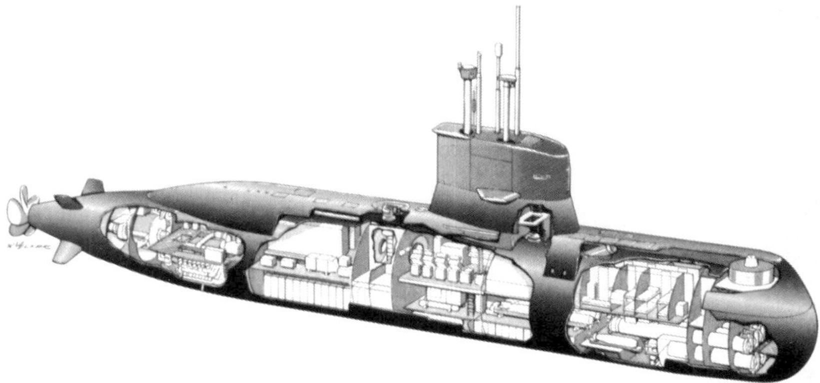

Västergötland—artist's rendering Kockums, 1983

D: 990 tons surf./1,140 sub.) **S:** 12 kts surf./20 kts sub.
Dim: 48.50 × 6.10 × 6.10 (surf.)
A: 4/533-mm TT (8 Type 61B torpedoes or mines)—2/400-mm TT (4 Type 42B torpedoes)—all bow
Electron Equipt: Radar: 1/Terma. . .—Sonar: . . .—EW: . . .
M: 2 Hedemora V12A/15-UG, 1,080-hp diesels; 2 Jeumont-Schneider 760-kw generators; 1 ASEA electric motor; 1/5-bladed prop; 1,800 shp
Man: 17 tot.

REMARKS: Design by Kockums under 17-4-78 contract. Ships ordered 8-12-81, with Kockums building the mid-bodies and Karlskrona building the bows and sterns. May later be equipped with four vertical tubes for RBS-17 anti-ship missiles (a submerged-launch version of the RBS-15) in the sail. The torpedo tubes are arranged with the row of four 533-mm tubes above the two short 400-mm tubes, with separate reload magazine compartments. Very low reserve buoyancy—7%. Bow planes on sail, cruciform stern controls surfaces. Six spare berths for trainees. Tudor lead-acid batteries. Two main watertight compartments. Two periscopes. Will use Ericsson IPS-17 combat data/fire control system.

◆ 3 Näcken (Type A-14) class

	Bldr	Laid down	L	In serv.
NÄK NÄKEN	Kockums, Malmö	11-72	17-4-78	25-4-80
NAJ NAJAD	Karlskrona	9-73	6-12-78	5-12-80
NEP NEPTUN	Kockums, Malmö	3-74	13-8-79	26-6-81

D: 1,030 surf. (fl)/1,125 tons **S:** 20/20 kts **Dim:** 49.5 × 6.1 × 4.1
A: 6/533-mm TT (8 Type 61B torpedoes or mines)—2/400-mm TT (4 Type 42B torpedoes)
M: Diesel-electric: 1 MTU 16V652, 1,800-hp diesel; 1 Jeumont-Schneider generator; 1 5-bladed prop; 1,500 hp
Electric: 150 kw (Scania diesel) **Man:** 5 officers, 14 men

REMARKS: Ordered at the end of 1972. The 168-cell Tudor electric battery installation is mounted on shock absorbers. Single Kollmorgen periscope. An Ericsson IDPS central data system furnishes, in addition to tactical information, data on the main engines; it uses 2 Censor 932 computers. Able to lay mines. Stern planes are x-configuration; bow planes on the sail. *Näcken* and *Neptun* were launched by cranes. Diving depth: 300 m

Näcken (Näk)—with snorkel intake raised Royal Swedish Navy, 1979

SUBMARINES *(continued)*

Näcken (Näk)—abreast *Sjohästen (Shä)* outboard *Alvsborg* (M 02) L. & L. Van Ginderen, 3-82

(500-m collapse). The 533-mm tubes use Type 61 torpedoes, the 400-mm, Type 42. Kockums is developing a "mine-girdle" removable minelaying magazine for this and other Swedish submarine classes.

◆ 5 Sjöormen (Type A-11B) class

	Bldr	Laid down	L	In serv.
SOR SJÖORMEN	Kockums, Malmö	1965	25-1-67	31-7-67
SLE SJÖLEJONET	Kockums, Malmö	1966	29-6-67	16-12-68
SHU SJÖHUNDEN	Kockums, Malmö	1966	21-3-68	25-6-69
SBJ SJÖBJÖRNEN	Karlskrona	1967	6-8-68	28-2-69
SHÄ SJÖHÄSTEN	Karlskrona	1966	9-1-68	15-9-59

Sjölejonet (Sle) L. & L. Van Ginderen, 1981

D: 1,130/1,400 tons **S:** 15/20 kts **Dim:** 50.5 × 6.1 × 5.1
A: 4/533-mm TT (8 Type 61B torpedoes or mines)—2/400-mm TT (4 Type 427 ASW torpedoes)
M: Diesel-electric: 4 Hedemora-Pielstick V12A2 diesel generator groups, 2,100 hp; 1 ASEA electric motor; 1 5-bladed prop; 1,500 hp
Endurance: 21 days **Man:** 7 officers, 11 men

REMARKS: Maximum diving depth 150 meters. Four battery compartments. Stern planes are x-configuration; bow planes on the sail. One unit given turbocharged (vice supercharged) diesels, 1982. Modernized 1984-85 with Ericsson IBS-A17 combat data/fire control system.

◆ 4 Draken (A-11) class

	Bldr	Laid down	L	In serv.
DEL DELFINEN	Karlskrona	1959	7-3-61	7-6-62
NOR NORDKAPAREN	Kockums, Malmö	1959	8-3-60	4-4-62
SPR SPRINGAREN	Kockums, Malmö	1960	21-8-61	7-11-62
VGN VARGEN	Kockums, Malmö	1958	20-5-60	15-11-61

Delfinen (Del)—with *Alvsborg* (M 02) beyond L. & L. Van Ginderen, 3-82

D: 770/835 surf./1,110 tons sub. **S:** 17/20 kts **Dim:** 69.0 × 5.1 × 5.0
A: 4/533-mm TT fwd—12 full-sized torpedoes (see remarks)
M: Diesel-electric: 2 Hedemora-Pielstick 16V-12 PA diesels, 1,660 bhp; 2 electric motors; 1 prop; 1,500 hp
Man: 36 tot.

REMARKS: Snorkel-equipped; 1 periscope. Sisters *Draken* and *Gripen* stricken 1-7-81; the survivors have been modernized. A-17 type will replace them in the late 1980s. Two or three Type 427 torpedoes can fit in each tube, via adapters, using swim-out launching.

◆ 1 2-man midget submarine Bldr: Yugoslavia (In serv. 1-85)

R 2

D: 1.4 tons **S:** 4.4 kts **Dim:** 4.9 × 1.4 × . . .
A: 24-kg total limpet mines
M: Electric motor; 6 hp **Range:** 18/4.4; 23/1.7

REMARKS: Aluminum and Plexiglas hull. Diving depth: 60 m max. Also purchased was a 2-man chariot, R 1, with a range of 8 n.m. at 2.5 kts; the device is 3.7 m long and weighs 145 kg without riders. Both craft are intended to assist in the search for submarine intruders and to act as training targets.

◆ 1 URF-class salvage and rescue submersible Bldr: Kockums, Malmö (L: 8-78)

URF 1

D: 50 tons (surfaced) **S:** 3 kts **Dim:** 13.5 × 4.3 × 2.9

REMARKS: Has a depth capability of 460 meters and can accommodate up to 25 persons rescued from a bottomed submarine. Based at the Naval Diving Center, Berga. Can be towed at up to 10 kts to the scene of an accident. Lock-out capability to support two divers to 300 meters. Pressure hull of HY 130 steel; collapse depth 900 meters. Two projected sisters not built.

NOTE: The *Halland*-class destroyer *Smaland* was stricken 1-7-84; her sister *Halland* has been in reserve since 1982 without refit and is unlikely to see further service.

GUIDED-MISSILE PATROL BOATS

◆ 0 (+4 + 2) Göteborg class (KKV-90 design) Bldr: . . .

	Laid down	L	In serv.
K 21 GÖTEBORG	. . .	. . .	. . .
K 22 GÄVLE	. . .	. . .	. . .
K 23 KALMAR	. . .	. . .	. . .
K 24 SUNDSVALL	. . .	. . .	. . .
K 25 HELSINGBORG	. . .	. . .	. . .
K 26 HÄRNÖSAND	. . .	. . .	. . .

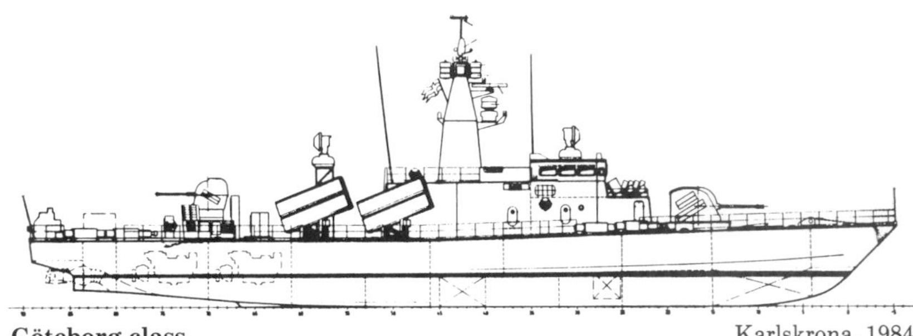

Göteborg class Karlskrona, 1984

D: 355 tons (400 fl) **S:** 35 kts **Dim:** 57.0 (50.0 wl) × 8.0 (7.3 wl) × 1.93
A: 8/RBS-15 SSM (II × 4)—1/57-mm Bofors SAK57 Mk 2 DP—1/40-mm Bofors Trinity AA—8/400-mm ASW TT—4/Elma ASW RL (IX × 4)—mines
Electron Equipt: Radar: 1/. . . nav., 1/Sea Giraffe 50 HC or PEAB Karin, 2/9LV 200 f.c.
Sonar: Simrad SS 304 Spira, Thomson-CSF TSM 2640 Salmon VDS (dismountable)
EW: . . .
M: 3 diesels; 3 KaMeWa waterjets; . . . hp
Range: . . . **Electric:** . . . **Man:** 31 tot.

REMARKS: First four ordered 1-12-85; others to be requested later in 1980s; considered to be "corvettes." An expanded version of the *Stockholm* design, intended to replace the remaining Spica-I missile boats. The Phillips 9LV 400 gunfire control system will use two 9LV 200 Mk 2 radar/optronic directors. Will carry both Type 61 and Type 43-series torpedoes. The decision to construct these ships was placed in abeyance 8-85.

◆ 2 Stockholm class (Spica III/YA-81 design) Bldr: Karlskronavarvet

	Laid down	L	In serv.
K 11 STOCKHOLM	1-8-82	24-8-84	1-3-85
K 12 MALMÖ	14-3-83	21-3-85	10-5-85

D: 290 tons (320 fl) **S:** 32 kts (20 kts on diesels)
Dim: 50.0 (46.6 wl) × 7.5 (6.8 wl) × 1.9 (hull)

GUIDED-MISSILE PATROL BOATS *(continued)*

A: 6–8 RBS-15 SSM (II × 4 or II × 2, I × 1)—1/57-mm Bofors SAK 57 Mk 2 DP—1/40-mm AA—2/533-mm TT—4 Elma ASW RL (IV × 4)—mines
Electron Equipt: Radar: 1/. . . nav., 1/Ericsson Sea Giraffe 50HC, 1/PEAB 9LV 200
Sonar: Simrad SS 304 Spira; Thomson-CSF TSM 2640 Salmon VDS (dismountable)
EW: Saab-Scania EWS-905 intercept; chaff RL
M: CODAG 1 Allison 570KF, 7,170-hp (6,000 sust.) gas turbine; 2 MTU 16V396 TB93 diesels (2,095 hp each); 3 CP props; 11,360 hp
Electric: 648 kw **Range:** . . . **Man:** . . .

Remarks: Considered to be "corvettes." Armament suit interchangeable, the RBS-15 missiles being replaceable by 2 more torpedo tubes, ASW torpedo tubes, and/or mine rails. Have the Ericsson MARIL weapons-control system, with an SRA Censor 932E computer. The 57-mm mount, unlike export versions, can be manned for local control. The 9LV300 gunfire control system incorporates a 9LV200 radar director forward and a 9LV100 optronic director on the aft face of the main mast.

Stockholm (K 11) Karlskrona, 1984

◆ **17 Hugin class** Bldrs: Bergens Mekanske Verksted, Norway (P 154–158 subcontracted to Westermoen, Mandal, Norway)

	L	In serv		L	In serv.
P 150 Jägeren	. . .	8-6-72	P 159 Kaparen	8-8-79	7-8-80
P 151 Hugin	3-6-77	3-7-78	P 160 Väktaren	12-12-79	19-9-80
P 152 Munin	3-10-77	3-7-78	P 161 Snapphanen	18-3-80	14-1-81
P 153 Magne	9-1-78	12-10-78	P 162 Spejaren	13-5-80	21-3-81
P 154 Mode	8-8-78	12-1-79	P 163 Styrbjörn	8-80	26-10-81
P 155 Vale	3-10-78	26-4-79	P 164 Starkodder	1-81	24-8-81
P 156 Vidar	6-3-79	10-8-79	P 165 Tordön	3-2-81	26-10-81
P 157 Mjölner	12-6-79	24-10-79	P 166 Tirfing	17-9-81	21-1-82
P 158 Mysing	18-9-79	14-2-80			

Kaparen (P 159)—with 2 Penguin Mk 2, mines, new EW gear
L. & L. Van Ginderen, 11-83

Hugin (151)—no missiles, 6 mines L. & L. Van Ginderen, 10-84

D: 120 tons (150 fl) **S:** 35 kts **Dim:** 36.53 (33.6 pp) × 6.20 × 1.60
A: 2–6 Penguin Mk 32 (I × 6)—1/57-mm Bofors SAK 57 Mk 1 DP—24 mines or 2/d.c. racks in lieu of missiles—4 Elma ASW RL (IX × 4)
Electron Equipt: Radar: 1/Scanter 009, 1/PEAB 9LV200 Mk 2 system
Sonar: 1/Simrad SQ3D/SF
EW: Saab-Scania EWS-905

Stockholm (K 11) Karlskronavarvet, 1985

GUIDED-MISSILE PATROL BOATS *(continued)*

M: 2 MTU 20V672 TB90 diesels; 2 props; 7,200 hp
Electric: 200 kVA **Range:** 550/35 **Man:** 3 officers, 19 men

REMARKS: Carry 6 Norwegian Penguin Mk 2 (Swedish RB-12) SSM (I × 6), but normally mount only two. P 150 briefly carried 6 Penguin Mk 1. Prototype *Jägaren,* renumbered from P 151, had new engines; those in the others came from discarded *Plejad*-class torpedo boats. Carry 103-mm rocket flare launchers on either side of the 57-mm gunmount. The PEAB 9LV200 Mk 2 fire-control system employs separate search and tracking radars. P 157 carries the prototype SAK 57 Mk 2 57-mm DP gun, but mounted within the original high gunhouse. Saab-Scania EWS-905 "Doughnut" passive intercept EW systems are being added, with the toroidal radome mounted just below the search antenna for the 9LV200 system. Elma 100-mm ASW rocket launchers are being added to all.

◆ **12 Spica-II class** Bldr: Karlskronavarvet and Götaverken

	L	In serv.		L	In serv.
R 131 Nörrkoping	16-11-72	5-11-73	R 137 Umea	13-1-75	15-5-75
R 132 Nynäshamn	24-4-73	8-9-73	R 138 Pitea	12-5-73	13-9-75
R 133 Nortälje	18-9-73	1-8-74	R 139 Lulea	19-8-75	28-11-75
R 134 Varberg	2-2-74	13-6-74	R 140 Halmstad	28-11-75	9-4-76
R 135 Västeras	15-5-74	25-10-74	R 141 Strömstad	26-4-76	13-9-76
R 136 Västervik	2-9-74	15-1-75	R 142 Ystad	3-9-76	10-12-76

Halmstad (R 140)—with 2 RBS-15, 6 TT, EW dome H. Ehlers, 5-84

Umea (R 137)—with 2 RBS-15, 2 TT, 4 Elma RL L. & L. Van Ginderen, 8-85

D: 190 tons (230 fl) **S:** 40.5 kts **Dim:** 43.6 × 7.1 × 1.6 (2.4 props)
A: 2/RBS-115 SSM—6/533-mm TT—4/Elma ASW RL (IX × 4)
Electron Equipt: Radar: 1/Scanter 009, 1/Sea Giraffe 50HC, 1/PEAB 9LV200 Mk 1
EW: Saab-Scania EWS-905 (not in all)
M: 3 Rolls-Royce Proteus gas turbines; 3 props; 12,900 hp
Man: 7 officers, 20 men

REMARKS: All reequipped for the Saab RBS-15 cruise missile during 1982-85. Two missiles are normally carried, plus six 533-mm torpedo tubes for wire-guided Type 61 torpedoes. The fire-control system is an analog version of the digital system used in the *Hugin* class. The gas turbines exhaust through the transom to provide residual thrust. Mines can be substituted for the missiles and the torpedo tubes, the forwardmost of which must be swung out several degrees before firing. All to receive Saab-Scania EWS-905 passive intercept equipment, and the MARIS 880 (SRA) weapons-control system, which permits over-the-horizon targetting data to be received from a helicopter. All have 6 rails for 103-mm rocket radar flares on the 57-mm gunmount.

TORPEDO BOATS

◆ **4 Spica class** (In serv. 1966-68) Bldrs: T 121, 123: Götaverken; others: Karlskronavarvet

	L		L
T 121 Spica	26-4-66	T 125 Vega	7-6-67
T 123 Capella	26-4-66	T 126 Virgo	7-6-67

D: 190 tons (235 fl) **S:** 40 kts **Dim:** 42.5 × 7.3 × 1.6 (2.6 props)
A: 1/57-mm Bofors SAK 57 Mk 1 DP—6/533-mm TT
Electron Equipt: Radar: 1/Scanter 009, 1/H.S.A. M22

Sirius (T 122) Royal Swedish Navy, 1981

M: 3 Bristol-Siddeley Proteus 1274 gas turbines; 3 KaMeWa CP props; 12,720 hp
Electric: 120 kw **Man:** 7 officers, 21 men

REMARKS: Carry four 103-mm (I × 4) and six 57-mm (VI × 1) rocket flare launchers. Mines can be substituted for the torpedo tubes, the forwardmost of which must be swung out several degrees before firing. There are two Rover IS90 gas-turbine generators. No longer scheduled to receive RBS-15 missiles. Sisters *Sirius* (T 122) and *Castor* (T 124) stricken 1-7-85.

PATROL BOATS

◆ **3 Dalerö class** Bldr: Djupriks Varvet, Rönnäng

V 09 Dalerö (In serv. 21-9-84) V 10 Sandhamn (In serv. 5-12-84)
V 11 Osthammar (In serv. 1-3-85)

Dalerö (V 09) Djupviks, 1984

D: 50 tons (fl) **S:** 30 kts **Dim:** 23.40 × 5.10 × 1.05
A: 1/40-mm AA—2/7.62-mm mg (I × 2)—mines
Electron Equipt: Radar: 1/Terma TM 610
M: 2 MTU 8V396 TB83 diesels; 3 props; 2,100 hp
Electric: 60 kw **Man:** 3 officers, 4 men + 3 passengers

REMARKS: Ordered 28-2-83 in lieu of further torpedo-boat-to-patrol-boat conversions.

Lysekil (V 08) L. & L. Van Ginderen, 6-84

PATROL BOATS *(continued)*

◆ **8 Skanör class** Bldr: V 01 – V 04: Kockums, Malmö; others: Naval Dockyard, Stockholm (In serv. 1956–59)

	Conv.		Conv.
V 01 SKANÖR (ex-T 42)	12-76	V 05 ÖREGRUND (ex-T 47)	1-2-83
V 02 SMYGE (ex-T 43)	1977	V 06 SLITE (ex-T 48)	15-4-83
V 03 ARILD (ex-T 45)	1977	V 07 MARSTRAND (ex-T 50)	16-5-83
V 04 VIKEN (ex-T 44)	1977	V 08 LYSEKIL (ex-T 52)	13-6-83

D: 40 tons (44.5 fl) **S:** 27 kts **Dim:** 23.0 × 5.9 × 1.2 (1.4 props)
A: 1/40-mm AA **Electron Equipt:** Radar: 1/Scanter 009
M: 2 MTU 8V396 diesels; 2 props; 1,600 hp

REMARKS: First four converted at Karlskrona 1976-77 for service as surveillance boats; original three gasoline engines replaced for safety and economy. The second batch converted 1981-83 by Djupriks Varvet, with V 05 recommissioning 14-1-83, V 06 on 15-4-83, V 07 on 16-5-83, and V 08 on 13-6-83. Have one six-railed 57-mm rocket flare launcher on the bow. Conversion of four more canceled in favor of building the three *Dalerö*-class patrol boats.

◆ **4 Hanö-class former minesweepers** Bldr: Karlskrona (All in serv. 1954)

V 52 TÄRNÖ (ex-M 52) V 54 STURKÖ (ex-M 54)
V 53 TJURKÖ (ex-M 53) V 55 ORNÖ (ex-M 56)

Ornö (V 55) L. & L. Van Ginderen, 3-82

D: 270 tons **S:** 14.5 kts **Dim:** 42.0 (40.0 pp) × 7.0 × 2.7
A: 2/40-mm AA (I × 2) **Electron Equipt:** Radar: 1/Scanter 009
M: 2 Nohab diesels; 2 props; 910 hp **Man:** 25 tot.

REMARKS: In service since 1954. Redesignated as patrol craft on 1-1-79. Have steel hulls. Renumbered with V-series pendants on 1-1-79. Each has one six-railed 57-mm rocket flare launcher. Two sisters, *Hanö* (V 51) and *Utö* (V 56) stricken 1980.

NOTE: Naval Reserve training patrol craft SVK 11 and SVK 12 were redesignated as minesweeping boats in 1983; patrol craft SVK 1 and SVK 2 were stricken 1983.

MINE WARFARE SHIPS

◆ **1 fleet minelaying/training ship** Bldr: Karlskrona

	Laid down	L	In serv.
M 04 CARLSKRONA (ex-*Karlskrona*)	1980	28-5-80	19-3-82

Carlskrona (M 04)—with revised funnel L. & L. Van Ginderen, 5-85

D: 3,130 tons (3,300 fl) **S:** 20 kts **Dim:** 105.70 (97.50 pp) × 15.2 × 4.00
A: 2/57-mm Bofors DP (I × 2)—2/40-mm Bofors AA (I × 2)—105 mines
Electron Equipt: Radar: 1/Scanter 009, 1/Raytheon . . . , 1/Sea Giraffe HC50, 2/PEAB 9LV200 Mk 2 (9LV400 system)
Sonar: Simrad SQ3D/SF
M: 4 Nohab-Polar F212-D825, 12-cyl. diesels; 2 CP props; 10,560 hp
Electric: 2,570 kVA **Man:** 118 crew + 136 cadets, 46 instructors

REMARKS: Ordered 25-11-77 to replace cadet training ship *Alvsnabben,* which, in the event, expired before her completion. Intended to act as a mine countermeasures ship support tender and submarine torpedo hard target in peacetime, when not conducting the annual Cadet Training Cruise. Hull reinforced below waterline to permit exercise torpedo hits; there are 14 watertight compartments. A bow-thruster is fitted. Has two complete combat information centers (CIC), one duplicating that of a *Hugin* and one duplicating a *Spica-II.* Extensive navigational systems, including Decca Navigator and Omega receivers. Raised helicopter deck above fantail. Name changed to honor the Swedish king. There are 2 lead-computing optical directors to control the 40-mm AA, and 2 radar/optronic 9LV200 Mk 2 directors for the 57-mm guns.

◆ **2 Älvsborg-class minelayers** Bldr: Karlskrona

	Laid down	L	In serv.
M 02 ÄLVSBORG	11-68	11-11-69	10-4-71
M 03 VIBORG	16-10-73	22-1-75	6-2-76

Viborg (M 03) L. & L. Van Ginderen, 8-85

Älvsborg (M 02) L. & L. Van Ginderen, 8-85

D: 2,660 tons (fl) (M 03: 2,450 fl) **S:** 16 kts **Dim:** 92.4 (83.3 pp) × 14.7 × 4.0
A: 3/40-mm AA (I × 3)—300 mines **Electric:** 1,200 kw
Electron Equipt: Radar: 1/Scanter 009, 1/Raytheon . . . , 1/H.S.A. M22 f.c.
M: 2 Nohab-Polar 12-cyl. diesels; 1 CP prop; 4,200 hp **Man:** 97 tot.

REMARKS: M 02 is used as a submarine tender in peacetime and has accommodations for 205 submarine crew members. M 03 is equipped as Flagship, Coastal Fleet, and has accommodations for 158 flag staff. Each has a helicopter deck. Radar suit expanded 1977-78. An intercept array is mounted on the mast just forward of the stack.

◆ **2 (+4 + 2) Landsort (M80)-class coastal minesweeper/hunters**
Bldr: Karlskronavarvet

	Laid down	L	In serv.
M 71 LANDSORT	5-10-81	22-11-82	19-3-84
M 72 ARHOLMA	13-2-82	10-10-84	23-11-84
M 73 KOSTER	1-9-84	. . .	. . .
M 74 KULLEN	1-1-85	. . .	. . .
M 75 VINGA	. . .	. . .	. . .
M 76 VEN	. . .	. . .	. . .

Arholma (M 72) Karlskrona, 1984

D: 310 tons (360 fl) **S:** 15 kts **Dim:** 47.50 (45.00 pp) × 9.60 × 2.30
A: 1/40-mm AA—4/Elma ASW RL (IX × 4)—mines
Electron Equipt: Radar: 1/. . . nav.
Sonar: Thomson-CSF TSM 2022
M: 4 Saab-Scania DSI-14 diesels; 2 Voith-Schneider vertical cycloidal props; 1,440 hp
Electric: 585 kVA **Range:** 2,000/12 **Man:** 7 officers, 32 men

MINE WARFARE SHIPS *(continued)*

REMARKS: Glass-reinforced plastic construction, based on Swedish Coast Guard's TV 171. First pair ordered 25-2-81. Next four ordered 31-1-84; two more planned for 1987-88. PEAB 9LV100 optronic director for the gun. Y-shaped portable mine-rail arrangement, with single laying-point. Computerized integrated navigational/mine system and gun-control system by Philips Elektronikindustier AB (PEAB) in conjunction with Decca-Racal. After the first two, may use the Krupp-Atlas KAE II H sonar with Racal MAINs minehunting control system. Carry 2 SUTEC "Sea Eagle" remote-controlled mine-disposal vehicles, as well as controlling three SAM, glass-reinforced plastic, self-propelled magnetic/acoustic catamaran minesweeping devices.

◆ **5 radio-controlled mine countermeasures craft**

SAM 1 (In serv. 29-3-83) SAM 4 (In serv. 26-5-83)
SAM 2 (In serv. 29-3-83) SAM 5 (In serv. 17-6-83)
SAM 3 (In serv. 26-5-83)

D: 15 tons **S:** 8 kts **Dim:** 18.0 × 6.0 × 0.7 (1.6 prop)
M: 1 Volvo-Penta TAMD 70D diesel; 2 Schöttel shrouded props; 210 hp
Range: 330/7

These craft are also built by Karlskrona: The catamarans also automatically lay swept channel-marking danbuoys. An eventual total of 20 SAMs is planned.

◆ **7 Arkö-class coastal minesweepers**

	L	In serv.		L	In serv.
M 57 Arkö	21-1-57	1958	M 64 Hasslö	1962	1962
M 58 Spårö	1957	1958	M 67 Nämdö	1964	1964
M 61 Styrsö	1961	1962	M 68 Blidö	1964	1964
M 62 Skaftö	1961	1962			

Bldrs: Odd numbers—Karlskrona; even numbers—Hälsingborg

Styrsö (M 61) L. & L. Van Ginderen, 7-85

D: 285 tons (300 fl) **S:** 14.5 kts **Dim:** 44.4 × 7.5 × 2.5 (3.0 prop)
A: 1/40-mm AA **M:** 2 MTU 12V493 diesels; 2 props; 1,000 hp
Man: 25 tot.

REMARKS: Wooden-hulled construction. M 61 through M 68 have a curved rubbing-strake line along the hull side; in earlier ships there are two strakes, paralleling the hull sheer. Have one six-railed 57-mm rocket flare launcher. Sisters *Karlsö* (M 59), *Iggö* (M 60) and *Aspö* (M 63) stricken 1984, *Vinö* (M 65) and *Vallö* (M 66) in 1985.

◆ **3 Gåssten-class inshore minesweepers**

	Bldr	L	In serv.
M 31 Gåssten	Knippla SY	11-72	16-11-73
M 32 Norsten	Hellevikstrands SY	4-73	12-10-73
M 33 Viksten	Karlskrona	18-4-74	1-7-74

Norsten (M 32)—wooden hull L. & L. Van Ginderen, 5-83

Viksten (M 33)—GRP hull L. & L. Van Ginderen, 5-83

D: 120 tons (M 33: 130 tons) **S:** 11 kts **Dim:** 23.0 (M 33: 25.3) × 6.6 × 3.7
A: 1/20-mm AA **M:** 1 diesel; 1 prop; 460 hp

REMARKS: The hull of M 33 is made of glass-reinforced plastic; she was intended to serve as the prototype for a new class of 300-ton, 43-meter coastal minesweepers, which were not built. The other two are built of wood. A 20-mm AA gun has replaced the 40-mm/60-cal. originally carried.

◆ **7 Hisingen-class inshore minesweepers**

	L		L
M 43 Hisingen	1960	M 47 Gillöga	1964
M 44 Blackan	1960	M 48 Rödlöga	1964
M 45 Dämman	1960	M 49 Svartlöga	1964
M 46 Galten	1960		

Hisingen (M 43) H. Ehlers, 4-85

D: 140 tons **S:** 9 kts **Dim:** 22.0 × 6.4 × 1.4
A: 1/20-mm AA **M:** 1 diesel; 1 prop; 380 hp

REMARKS: Wooden-hulled fishing boats. M 47 through M 49 have higher bridges and bluffer bow lines. A 20-mm AA has replaced the original 40-mm/60-cal. AA in all.

◆ **6 M 15-class inshore minesweepers** (All L: 1941)

M 21 through M 26

D: 70 tons **S:** 12-13 kts **Dim:** 27.7 × 5.05 × 1.4 (2.0 props)
A: 1/20-mm AA **M:** Diesels; 1 prop; 320-430 hp **Man:** 10 tot.

REMARKS: Wooden hulls. M 21, M 22, M 25 are used as tenders for mine clearance divers. Sisters M 15 and M 16 were stricken during 1984. See photo next page.

◆ **4 minesweeping boats** (In serv. 1955-56)

SVK 11 (ex-Tv 226) SVK 12 (ex-Tv 228) SVK 13 SVK 14

D: 12 tons **S:** 20 kts **Dim:** 14.0 × 3.4 × 1.2
A: 1/20-mm AA **M:** 1 Volvo Penta diesel; 1 prop; . . . hp

REMARKS: Used for Naval Reserve training. Reclassified from patrol craft in 1983.

MINE WARFARE SHIPS *(continued)*

M 22—note sweep gear and gun deleted, new pole mast atop pilothouse
L. & L. Van Ginderen, 8-85

AUXILIARIES

◆ **1 intelligence collection ship** Bldr: Karlskronavarvet

	Laid down	L	In serv.
A 201 ORION	23-4-82	30-11-83	7-6-84

Orion (A 201) at launch Karlskrona, 1983

D: 1,400 tons (fl) **S:** . . . **Dim:** 61.3 × 11.0 × 4.2
A: None
M: 2 Hedemora V8A/135 diesels; 1 CP prop; 1,840 hp
Man: 35 tot.

REMARKS: Ordered 25-6-81. To last 30 years. Signal collection antennas beneath a large glass-reinforced plastic radome atop full length of the superstructure.

◆ **1 coastal tanker** Bldr: D. W. Kremer Sohn, Elmshorn, West Germany (In serv. 1965)

A 228 BRANNAREN (ex-*Indio*)

D: 857 tons (fl) **S:** 11 kts
Dim: 61.71 (56.76 pp) × 8.6 × 3.57
M: 1 MAK 6 Mu 51 diesel; 1 prop; 800 hp

REMARKS: Eight cargo tanks totaling 1,170 m³. Purchased in 1972.

Brannaren (A 228) Royal Swedish Navy, 1972

◆ **1 submarine rescue and salvage ship** Bldr: . . .

	L	In serv.
A 211 BELOS	15-11-61	29-5-63

Belos (A 211) L. & L. Van Ginderen, 8-85

D: 965 tons (fl) **S:** 13 kts **Dim:** 62.3 × 11.2 × 4.0
M: 2 diesels; 2 props; 1,200 hp

REMARKS: Well-equipped for underwater search: decompression chamber, active rudder, underwater television, and a small helicopter deck. Modernized in 1979-80 to support the URF submarine-rescue submersible.

SERVICE CRAFT

◆ **1 harbor tanker** Bldr: Asiverken, Åmål (In serv. 4-59)

A 229 ELDAREN (ex-*Brotank*)

D: 231 grt/320 dwt **S:** 8 kts **Dim:** 37.22 (34.14 pp) × 6.53 × 2.95
M: 2 Volvo Penta 6-cyl. diesels; 1 CP prop; 420 hp

REMARKS: Purchased 5-81 from commercial service.

◆ **1 water tanker** (L: 1959)

A 217 FRYKEN

D: 307 tons **S:** 10 kts **Dim:** 34.4 (32.0 pp) × 6.1 × 2.9
M: 1 diesel; 1 prop; 370 hp

NOTE: Water tanker *Unden* (A 216) stricken 1983, and provisions lighter *Freja* (A 221) stricken 1984.

◆ **1 torpedo- and missile-recovery craft** Bldr: Lundervarv-Ooverkstads AB, Kramfors

	L	In serv.
A 248 PINGVINEN	26-9-73	3-75

Pingvinen (A 248) L. & L. Van Ginderen, 8-85

D: 191 tons **S:** 13 kts **Dim:** 33.0 × 6.1 × 1.8
M: 2 MTU 12V493 diesels; 2 props; 1,040 hp

REMARKS: Similar to A 247 but has superstructure aft, 2 articulated cranes, and bow bulwarks.

SERVICE CRAFT *(continued)*

◆ **1 torpedo and missile recovery craft** (L: 9-63)

A 247 Pelikanen

Pelikanen (A 247)—with RB-08A missile — Royal Swedish Navy, 1974

D: 130 tons **S:** 15 kts **Dim:** 33.0 × 5.8 × 1.8
M: 2 MTU 12V493 diesels; 2 props; 1,040 hp

◆ **1 torpedo-recovery craft** (L: 1951)

A 246 Hägern

Hägern (A 246) — H. Ehlers, 9-83

D: 50 tons **S:** 10 kts **Dim:** 29.0 × 5.4 × 1.6 **M:** 2 diesels; 2 props; 480 hp

◆ **1 trials craft** (L: 1969)

A 241 Urd (ex-*Capella*)

D: 63 tons (90 fl) **S:** 8 kts **Dim:** 27.0 × 5.6 × 2.8 **M:** 2 diesels; 200 hp

Remarks: Acquired 1970.

◆ **2 mine transport lighters**

	L		L
A 236 Fällaren	1941	A 237 Minören	1940

D: 165 tons **S:** 9 kts **Dim:** 31.5 × 6.1 × 2.1 **M:** 2 diesels; 1 prop; 240 hp

◆ **1 laundry ship** (L: 1961)

A 256 Sigrun

Sigrun (A 256) — Royal Swedish Navy, 1974

D: 250 tons **S:** 11 kts **Dim:** 32.0 × 6.8 × 3.6 **M:** 1 diesel; 1 prop; 320 hp

Remarks: Probably the world's only camouflaged floating laundry, and certainly the fastest.

◆ **1 M 15-class general-purpose tender, former minesweeper** (L: 1941)

A 242 Skuld (ex-M 20)

Skuld (A 242) — F. Jentsch, 8-85

D: 70 tons (fl) **S:** 13 kts **Dim:** 26.0 × 5.0 × 1.4
M: 2 diesels; 2 props; 410 hp

Remarks: Wooden-hulled craft used for mine warfare trials; new deckhouse added abaft original pilothouse. Sisters *Lommen* (A 231, ex-M 17) and *Spoven* (A 232, ex-M 18) stricken 1984.

Note: Five L 51-class stores lighters were stricken in 1983.

◆ **2 stores lighters**

A 341 ATB 1 A 342 ATB 2

ATB 1 (A 341) — G. Gyssels, 1981

Remarks: No data available. Four other small stores lighters were stricken in 1983: *Granatan* (A 345), *Edda* (A 347), *Gerda* (A 349), and ATB 3.

◆ **2 sail-training schooners**

S 01 Gladan (L: 1947) S 02 Falken (L: 1948)

Falken (S 02) — Royal Swedish Navy, 1981

SERVICE CRAFT *(continued)*

D: 220 tons **S:** . . . kts **Dim:** 42.5 (28.3 pp) × 7.27 × 4.2
M: 1 diesel auxiliary; 1 prop; 50-hp; sail area 512 m^2

◆ **2 diving tenders** Bldr: Storebro Bruks AB (In serv. 1980)

D: . . . tons **S:** 24 kts **Dim:** 10.35 × 3.30 × 1.0
Electron Equipt: Radar: 1/Decca 091
M: 2 Volvo Penta TAMD 60 diesels; 2 props; 370 hp

Remarks: Fold-down door at stern. 1.7-ton useful load.

◆ **2 range safety boats** Bldr: Storebro Bruks AB (In serv. 1980)

Remarks: Data as for diving tender version above.

◆ **3 personnel launches** Bldr: Storebro Bruks AB (In serv. 1980)

D: 5.5 tons (fl) **S:** 24 kts **Dim:** 9.30 × 3.30 × 1.0
M: 2 Volvo Penta TAMD 60 diesels; 2 props; 370 hp

Remarks: Builder's Type 31 design; glass-reinforced plastic construction. Can carry 25 men or 6 stretchers.

TUGS

◆ **2 Herkules-class icebreaking tugs**

A 323 Herkules (L: 1969) A 324 Hera (L: 1971)

D: 127 tons **S:** 11.5 kts **Dim:** 21.4 × 6.9 × 3.7
M: Diesels; 615 hp

◆ **2 Achilles-class icebreaking tugs** (L: 1962, 1963)

A 251 Achilles A 252 Ajax

Achilles (A 251) L. & L. Van Ginderen, 2-82

D: 450 tons **S:** 12 kts **Dim:** 35.5 (33.15 pp) × 9.5 × 3.9
M: Diesels; 1,650 hp **Electron Equipt:** Radar: 1 or 2/Decca 1226C

◆ **3 Hermes-class icebreaking tugs** (L: 1953-57)

A 253 Hermes A 321 Hector A 322 Heros

D: 185 tons **S:** 11 kts **Dim:** 24.5 (23.0 pp) × 6.8 × 3.6
M: Diesel; 600 hp

◆ **5 small harbor tugs/tenders** Bldr: Lundevarv (In serv. 1978-79)

A 751–755

D: 42 tons (fl) **S:** 9.5 kts **Dim:** 15.5 × 5.0 × 2.7
M: 1 diesel

Remarks: Can break thin ice. Carry 40 passengers.

◆ **3 miscellaneous small tugs**

A 326 Hebe A 327 Passop A 330 Atlas

Remarks: No data available. Small tugs *Henrik* (A 329) and *Vitsgarn* (A 336) stricken 1983.

Atlas (A 330)—a small push-tug with vertical cycloidal propellers
L. & L. Van Ginderen, 5-81

MINISTRY OF TRANSPORT

ICEBREAKERS

Note: All Swedish icebreakers are owned by the Ministry of Transport, but are manned and administered by the Swedish Navy. In 1984, it was decided to permanently arm all seagoing icebreakers.

◆ **3 Finnish Urho class** Bldr: Wärtsilä, Helsinki, Finland

	Laid down	L	In serv.
Atle	10-5-73	27-11-73	21-10-74
Frej	. . .	3-6-74	30-9-75
Ymer	12-2-76	3-9-76	26-10-77

Frej Wärtsilä, 1975

D: 7,800 tons **S:** 19 kts **Dim:** 104.6 (99.0 pp) × 23.8 × 7.8
A: 4/40-mm AA (I × 4)—3 mine rails
M: 5 Wärtsilä-Pielstick 5,000-bhp diesels; diesel-electric drive; 4 props; 22,000 hp
Man: 16 officers, 38 men

Remarks: Two props forward, two aft. Helicopter platform. All personnel live and normally work above the main deck. Given permanent gun armament, mine rails, and fuel facilities for helicopters: *Frej* in 10-83, others in 1984.

◆ **1 Ale class** Bldr: Wärtsilä, Helsinki, Finland

	L	In serv.
Ale	1-6-73	12-12-73

Ale L. & L. Van Ginderen, 8-82

ICEBREAKERS *(continued)*

D: 1,488 tons **S:** 14 kts **Dim:** 46.0 × 13.0 × 5.0
M: Diesels; 2 props; 4,750 hp **Man:** 21 tot.

REMARKS: Built for service on Lake Vänern in central Sweden, also used for surveying in summer.

◆ **1 modified Tor class** Bldr: Wärtsilä, Helsinki, Finland

	L	In serv.
NJORD	2-10-68	10-69

Njord L. & L. Van Ginderen, 2-85

D: 5,150 tons (5,686 fl) **S:** 18 kts **Dim:** 86.45 (79.45 pp) × 21.18 × 6.9
A: 3/40-mm AA (I × 3)
M: Diesel-electric propulsion: 4 Sulzer 9MH-51 diesels; Stromberg electric motors, 2 fwd (3,400 kw each), 2 aft (2,200 kw each); 4 props; 13,620 hp

◆ **1 Tor class** Bldr: Wärtsilä, Turku, Finland

	L	In serv.
TOR	25-5-63	31-1-64

Tor Wärtsilä

D: 4,980 tons (5,290 fl) **S:** 18 kts **Dim:** 84.4 × 20.42 × 6.2
A: 3/40-mm AA (I × 3)
M: Diesel-electric propulsion, 4 Sulzer 9MH-51 diesels; 4 props; 11,200 hp. Same motors as the *Njord.*

REMARKS: The Finnish *Tarmo* is similar. Two propellers fwd, two aft.

◆ **1 Oden class** Bldr: Sandviken, Helsinki, Finland

	L	In serv.
ODEN	16-10-56	1958

Oden L. & L. Van Ginderen, 3-82

D: 4,950 tons (3,370 light) **S:** 17 kts
Dim: 83.35 (78 pp) × 19.4 × 6.9
M: Diesel-electric; 4 props (2 fwd, 2 aft); 10,500 hp
Fuel: 740 tons **Man:** 75 tot.

REMARKS: Very similar to the Finnish *Voima* and the three Soviet *Kapitan Belousov* class. Can be armed with 4/40-mm AA (I × 4). Refitted 1984-85.

◆ **2 Thule class** Bldr: Karlskrona

	L	In serv.
THULE	10-51	1953

Thule L. & L. Van Ginderen, 3-82

D: 2,280 tons (fl) **S:** 14 kts **Dim:** 57.00 × 16.07 × 5.90
M: 3 diesels, electric drive; 3 props (1 fwd); 4,800 hp **Man:** 43 tot.

REMARKS: A 1980 plan to convert this ship to act as a mine countermeasures support ship was apparently canceled.

◆ **1 harbor icebreaker/navigational aids tender** Bldr: Åsiverken AB

BALTICA (In serv. 1982)

D: 1,238 tons (fl) **S:** 15 kts **Dim:** 54.9 (50.0 pp) × 12.0 × 3.7 (mean)
Electron Equipt: Radar: 1/Decca "Arpa," 1/Decca "Clearscan"
M: 2 Hedemora V16A/12 diesels; 1 CP prop; 3,520 hp
Electric: 1,375 kVA **Fuel:** 140 tons **Man:** 12 tot.

REMARKS: 857 grt/252 nrt. Two 300-hp tunnel side-thrusters. Twelve-ton electrohydraulic crane serving combination buoy hold/workshop. Can tow at 50-ton bollard pull. Capable of operating in light ice conditions. Civilian-manned.

HYDROGRAPHIC SHIPS

NOTE: Swedish hydrographic ships are operated by the Navy, but are owned by the Ministry of Transport. The icebreaker *Ale* also performs survey tasks.

◆ **1 new-construction survey ship** Bldr: Oskarshamns SY

NILS STRÖMKRONA (In serv. 28-6-85)

D: 168 tons (fl) **S:** . . . **Dim:** . . . × . . . × . . .
M: . . .

REMARKS: Built to replace 1894-vintage unit with the same name.

◆ **1 seagoing survey ship** Bldr: Falkenbergs Varvet

	Laid down	L	In serv.
JOHAN NORDENANKAR	1977	1-11-79	1-7-80

D: 2,000 tons (fl) **S:** 15 kts **Dim:** 73.0 (64.0 pp) × 14.0 × 3.8
Electron Equipt: Radar: 1/Raytheon Raycas, 1/Decca . . .
M: 2 Hedemora V16A/12 diesels; 2 KaMeWa CP props; 3,520 hp
Electric: 2,246 kVA **Man:** 66 tot.

REMARKS: Acts as mother ship for nine small survey craft that act in teams. Data collected by the launches are telemetered to the ship and collected via the Krupp-Atlas computer. There are three sets of davits per side, with 3 additional boats in an internal hangar. Ship very maneuverable, with 700-hp drop-down bow-thruster, which can also drive the ship at 4.5 kts, and a Becker KSV flap-rudder; turning radius 150 m. Navigation equipment includes Decca Navigator, Magnavox NAVSAT receiver, Decca Sea Fix, Syledis Ranger, Syledis Miniranger, and 8 echo-sounders. Passive tank stabilization. Helo platform aft. Hull red, superstructure white.

◆ **1 seagoing survey ship** ((L: 14-1-66)

JOHAAN MÅNSSON

D: 977 tons (1,030 fl) **S:** 15 kts **Dim:** 56.0 × 11.0 × 2.6
M: Nohab-Polar diesel; 3,300 hp **Man:** 85 tot.

REMARKS: Survey boats are stowed in a hangar aft and launched/recovered via a ramp.

HYDROGRAPHIC SHIPS *(continued)*

Johann Månsson Royal Swedish Navy, 1975

◆ **1 coastal survey boat** Bldr: Djupviks, Rönnäng (In serv. 10-82)

JACOB HÄGG

D: 130 tons (fl) **S:** 16.5 kts **Dim:** 36.50 × 7.50 × 1.65
M: 4 Saab-Scania DSI-14 diesels; 2 props; 1,684 hp (1,300 sust.)

REMARKS: Aluminum construction. The same builder also delivered a 42-ton, 400-hp hydrographic survey launch in 1953. The former "lead boats" No. 1 and No. 94 were named *Sirius* and *Kompass* in 1982, respectively, and now operate independently.

◆ **2 coastal survey ships**

RAN (L: 1945)

D: 285 tons **S:** 9 kts **Dim:** 30.0 × 7.0 × 2.6
M: 1 diesel; 1 prop; 260 hp **Man:** 37 tot.

ANDERS BURE (ex-*Rali*)

D: 54 tons **S:** 15 kts **Dim:** 24.6 × 5.9 × 2.0
M: 2 diesels; 2 props; . . . hp **Man:** 11 tot.

REMARKS: Former yacht dating from 1968, bought in 1971.

COASTAL ARTILLERY SERVICE

PATROL CRAFT

◆ **17 61 class**

61 to 77

62 H. Ehlers, 4-85

D: 28 tons (30 fl) **S:** 19 kts **Dim:** 21.1 × 4.6 × 1.3
A: 1/20-mm AA **M:** 2 diesels; 2 props; . . . hp
Electron Equipt: Radar: 1/Decca RM914C

REMARKS: Built in two series, nos. 61 to 70 in 1960-61 and nos. 71 to 77 in 1966-67.

NOTE: Single-unit patrol craft V 57 was stricken 1985.

MINELAYERS

◆ **1 (+1 + 8) MUL 20 class** Bldr: Åsiverken, Araal

	L	In serv.		L	In serv.
MUL 20 FURUSUND	16-12-82	10-10-83	MUL 22 N. . .	. . .	. . .
MUL 21 N. . .	. . .	. . .			

D: 225 tons (245 fl) **S:** 11 kts **Dim:** 32.4 (30.0 pp) × 8.4 × 1.8
A: 1/20-mm AA—2/7.62-mm mg (I × 1)—24 tons mines
Electron Equipt: Radar: 1/Decca RM 1226C
M: 2 Saab-Scania GASI-14 diesels (335 hp each), ASEA 300 kVA electric drive; 2 props; 420 hp + 1/125-hp maneuvering prop
Man: 24 tot. (10 peacetime) **Electric:** 73 kw

REMARKS: MUL 20 ordered 23-6-81. An ultimate total of ten is planned.

Furusund (MUL 20) Royal Swedish Navy, 1984

◆ **8 MUL 12-class mine planters** (In serv. 1952-56)

MUL 12 N. . .	MUL 15 N. . .	MUL 18 ÖRESUND
MUL 13 KALMARSUND	MUL 16 N. . .	MUL 19 N. . .
MUL 14 N. . .	MUL 17 N. . .	

Kalmarsund (M 13) H. Ehlers, 4-85

D: 245 tons **S:** 10.5 kts **Dim:** 31.18 (29.0 pp) × 7.62 × 3.1
A: 1/40-mm AA—. . . mines **Electron Equipt:** Radar: 1/Decca RM 1226C
M: 2 Nohab diesels; 2 props; 460 hp

REMARKS: Launched 1952-56. These craft are used for placing and maintaining controlled mine fields. Being given names 1985-86.

◆ **1 coastal mine planter** (L: 1946)

MUL 11

MUL 11 L. & L. Van Ginderen, 10-82

MINELAYERS *(continued)*

D: 200 tons **S:** 10 kts **Dim:** 30.1 (27.0 pp) × 7.21 × 3.65
A: 2/20-mm (I × 2)—mines
M: 2 Atlas diesels; 1 prop; 300 hp

Remarks: Will probably be replaced by MUL 20.

◆ **42 501-class minelaying launches** (L: 1969-71)

501 through 542

502 Royal Swedish Navy, 1981

D: 14 tons (fl) **S:** 14 kts **Dim:** 14.6 × 4.2 × 0.9
A: 12 mines **Electron Equipt:** Radar: 1/Decca RM 914C
M: Diesels **Man:** 7 tot.

Note: The 81 201-series personnel landing craft can also be fitted to lay mines.

◆ **6 small minelaying craft** Bldr: Marinvarvet, Fårösund

1879–1881 (In serv. 4-7-83) 1882–1884 (In serv. 23-1-84)

Remarks: Displace 2.5 tons; no other data available.

LANDING CRAFT

◆ **3 Grim-class utility landing craft** Bldr: Åsiverken

Bore Grim Heimdal

Bore Royal Swedish Navy, 1969

D: 340 tons (fl) **S:** 12 kts **Dim:** 36.0 × 8.5 × 2.6
A: None **M:** 2 diesels; 2 props; 800 hp

Remarks: *Grim* was launched in 1962, *Bore* and *Heimdal* in 1967. Car ferry design; bow hinges upward to permit extending ramp. Can be adapted to lay mines.

◆ **2 Sleipner-class utility landing craft**

Skagul (L: 1960) Sleipner (L: 1959)

D: 335 tons **S:** 10 kts **Dim:** 35.0 × 8.5 × 2.9
A: None **M:** 2 diesels; 2 props; 640 hp

Remarks: Similar to the *Grim* class. Can be adapted to lay mines.

◆ **4 Ane-class utility landing craft** (L: 1943-45)

324 Ane 325 Balder 326 Loke 327 Ring

D: 135 tons **S:** 8.5 kts **Dim:** 28.0 × 8.0 × 1.8 **A:** 1/20-mm AA **M:** 2 diesels

Remarks: Equipped with a bow ramp. Can be adapted to lay mines.

Loke—guns not mounted L. & L. Van Ginderen, 10-82

◆ **9 (+8) vehicle landing craft** Bldr: Djupviks, Tjoern; Oskarhamms; Marinvarvet, Fårösund

601–605, 651–. . .

603 H. Ehlers, 4-85

D: 20 tons (53 fl) **S:** 8-10 kts **Dim:** 21.0 (20.0 pp) × 7.2 × . . .
A: . . . **Electron Equipt:** Radar: 1/Decca RM 914C
M: 2 Saab-Scania DSI-11/40-M20 diesels; 2 Schöttel props; 340 hp
Cargo: 25 tons deck cargo or 30 tons liquid **Man:** . . .

Remarks: The prototype was delivered in 1978; the next 8 were to be delivered 1982-85. No. 603 delivered 2-4-84 by Mariavarvet; Nos. 604, 605 delivered 1-10-84 by Djupviks.

◆ **1 (+ . . .) M 85-class large personnel landing craft** Bldr: Marinvarvet, Fårösund

. . .

M 85 design 1984

D: 55 tons (65 fl) **S:** 20 kts **Dim:** 28.40 (24.00 pp) × 5.60 × 0.80
A: 2 or 3/7.62-mm mg (I × 2 or 3)—mines
Electron Equipt: Radar: 1/. . . nav.
M: 3 Saab-Scania DSI-14 diesels; 3 waterjets; 1,350 hp
Man: 4 crew + 45 troops

LANDING CRAFT *(continued)*

REMARKS: Aluminum prototype replacement design for 201-series. Ordered 27-7-84; laid down 5-12-84. As many as 140 may be built.

◆ **80 201-series large personnel landing craft**

Bldrs: Lundevarv Verkstads and Marinteknik, Oregrund (In serv. 1957-77)

201 through 208; 210 through 276; 280 through 284

201 class L. & L. Van Ginderen, 7-85

281—with mine rails L. & L. Van Ginderen, 5-81

D: 31 tons (fl) **S:** 17 kts **Dim:** 21.4 × 4.2 × 1.3
A: 2 or 3/6.5-mm mg (II × 1, I × 1)—mines
Electron Equipt: Radar: 1/Decca RM 914C
M: 3 Saab-Scania 6 DS 11 diesels; 3 props; 705 hp **Man:** 5 crew, 40 troops

REMARKS: 266 through 269 have Volvo Penta diesels. Early units were 20 meters overall and had three 200-hp diesels. Patrol-boat-like bow opens to permit extension of ramp from troop compartment below decks. Twin machine gun to port, plus single mount aft in some. Mine rails can be laid from the pilothouse over the stern. 210 was re-engined 1984 by Djupviks with 2 Saab-Scania DSI-14 diesels; 2 steerable hydraulic drives; 950 hp; pilot program for a class-wide rehabilitation. 209 was stricken in 1984.

◆ **25 (+ . . .) personnel landing craft**

	L			
370 . . .	1981	**D:** . . . tons	**S:** . . . kts	**M:** 560 hp
337 through 354	1970-73	**D:** 6 tons	**S:** 21 kts	**M:** 225 hp
332 through 336	1967	**D:** 5.4 tons	**S:** 25 kts	**M:** 225 hp
331	1965	**D:** 6 tons	**S:** 20 kts	

333 (332 series) L. & L. Van Ginderen

REMARKS: The prototype of a new series, number 370, was delivered 2-9-81; the craft is powered by two Volvo Penta TAMD 70 diesels. 301 through 330 stricken 1984.

◆ **20 support tenders** Bldr: Djupriks, Tjoern (In serv. 1982-85)

701-705; 751-756, . . .

D: 42 tons **S:** 9.5 kts **Dim:** 15.5 × 5.0 × 2.7
M: 1 diesel; 1 prop; . . . hp

703 H. Ehlers, 4-85

REMARKS: Can be used to transport cargo, personnel, to plant mines or as tugs. Bulwarks at bow open to permit debarking personnel over a beach.

◆ **12 (+ . . .) support tenders**

401-412 (+ . . . ?)

412 L. & L. Van Ginderen, 7-84

REMARKS: Wooden-hulled utility tenders. Number in service not available. Powered by a single diesel; have a Decca RM914C radar.

COAST GUARD

The Swedish Coast Guard, organized in 1638, is primarily concerned with rescue and customs services and with anti-pollution patrol and cleanup. In addition to some 130 boats and craft, it also operates 2 Cessna F337G patrol aircraft with side-looking radar (SLAR), one Cessna 402C (a second is planned), and a chartered helicopter. All boat pendants are prefixed "Tv"—*Tullverket* (Central Customs Office). The Coast Guard is organized into four Regions, with a total of 15 Districts; each District has 2 to 4 stations. All units are painted white and have a narrow red diagonal stripe on each side of the hull. None are armed.

PATROL BOATS AND CRAFT

◆ **2 Tv 171 class** Bldr: Karlskrona

	L	In serv.
Tv 171	11-79	3-9-80
Tv 172	13-9-80	10-81

D: 375 tons (fl) **S:** 20 kts **Dim:** 49.90 (46.00 pp) × 8.52 × 2.40
Electron Equipt: Radar: 2/Decca navigational—Sonar: Simrad Subsea
M: 2 Hedemora V16A/15 diesels; 2 KaMeWa CP props; 4,480 hp
Electric: 340 kVA **Range:** 500/20; 3,000/12 **Man:** 14 tot.

PATROL BOATS AND CRAFT *(continued)*

Tv 172 H. Ehlers, 4-85

Remarks: Class "A" cutters. Tv 171 lengthened by 6 m in 1981; Tv 172 longer as completed. Helicopter platform, bow-thruster. Glass-reinforced plastic sandwich hull construction, originally developed for the not-built M 70-class naval minesweeper. Fire monitor can be replaced by a 40-mm gun, and mine rails can be fitted.

◆ **5 Tv 103 class** Bldr: Djupviks, Tjoern (In serv. 1969-73)

Tv 101 Tv 102 Tv 103 Tv 104 Tv 105

Tv 105 Swedish Coast Guard

D: 53 tons (fl) **S:** 22 kts **Dim:** 26.72 × 5.23 × 1.13
M: 2 MTU 8V331 TC82 diesels; 2 props; 1,866 hp **Electric:** 60 kVA
Fuel: 11 tons **Range:** 1,000/15 **Man:** 6 tot.

Remarks: Class "A" cutters. Aluminum construction. Tv 101: **D:** 50 tons (fl); **Dim:** 24.9 × 5.0 × . . . ; pilothouse farther forward than in others. Three sisters in Liberian Coast Guard.

◆ **8 Tv 271-class** (In serv. 1974-77)

Tv 271 through Tv 278

Tv 275 L. & L. Van Ginderen, 8-82

D: 20 tons (fl) **S:** 20 kts **Dim:** 19.0 × 4.2 × 1.4
M: 2 Volvo Penta TAMD 120A diesels; 2 props; 700 hp
Electric: 46.5 kw **Man:** 5 tot.

Remarks: Alumimum construction. Tv 271, 272: 18.7 × 4.0 × 1.4. Class "B" cutters.

◆ **1 Tv 116-class steel-hulled** (In serv. 1935)

Tv 116

D: 36 tons (fl) **S:** . . . **Dim:** 24.4 × 4.2 × . . . **M:** Diesels

◆ **5 Tv 281-class** Bldr: Djupviks, Tjoern (In serv. 1979-80)

Tv 281 Tv 282 Tv 283 (In serv. 1979-80)
Tv 284 (In serv. 30-1-84) Tv 285 (In serv. 2-5-84)

Tv 284 H. Ehlers, 4-85

D: 37 tons (fl) **S:** . . . **Dim:** 21.0 × 5.0 × . . .
M: 2 diesels; 2 props; . . . hp **Electron Equipt:** 2/Decca . . . nav.

Remarks: Class "B" cutters. Additional units planned. Aluminum construction.

◆ **20 Tv 236-class aluminum-hulled class "D" cutters** (In serv. 1961-72)

Tv 236 through Tv 238, TV 240 through Tv 250, Tv 255 through Tv 261

Tv 256 H. Ehlers, 4-85

D: 17 tons **S:** . . . **Dim:** 16.2 × 3.7 × . . .

◆ **1 Tv 234-class aluminum-hulled, Class "B"** (In serv. 1960)

Tv 234

D: 15 tons (fl) **S:** . . . **Dim:** 15.2 × 3.6 × . . .

◆ **4 Tv 251-class aluminum-hulled, Class "B"** (In serv. 1958-61)

Tv 251 Tv 252 Tv 253 Tv 254

D: 12 tons (fl) **S:** . . . **Dim:** 15.0 × 3.7 × . . .

◆ **3 Tv 220-class**

Tv 220 (In serv. 1954) Tv 230 (In serv. 1957) Tv 232 (In serv. 1957)

D: 12 tons (fl) **S:** 20 kts **Dim:** 14.0 × 3.4 × . . .
M: 1 Volvo Penta diesel; . . . hp

◆ **26 miscellaneous speedboats** (In serv. 1962-79)

Tv 314, 315, 317, 318, 341, 350, 356, 360, 363, 365, 366, 368, 369, 371-374, 381-385, 388-391

◆ **6 inflatable boats** (In serv. 1971-75)

Tv 602, 661–665

◆ **5 iceboats** (In serv. 1965-72)

Tv 801, Tv 804–807—**Dim:** 5.0 × 2.0

POLLUTION-CONTROL SHIPS AND CRAFT

NOTE: Class A anti-pollution units are described as "Depôt Ships"; Class B are "Sea Trucks"; Class C are "Base Ships"; and Class D are catamarans.

◆ **1 Class A** Bldr: Lunde, Ramvik

Tv 06 (L: 24-3-85)

D: 450 tons (fl) **S:** 15 kts **Dim:** 37.35 (33.70 pp) × 8.80 × . . .
M: 2 Cummins KTA-2300M diesels; 2 rudder props; 2,100 hp
Fuel: 30.5 tons **Man:** 6 tot.

REMARKS: Similar to Tv 04 design; ordered 12-84. Also reported as "Tv 010."

◆ **2 Class A** Bldr: Lunde, Ramvik

Tv 04 (In serv. 1980)

Tv 04 H. Ehlers, 4-85

D: 450 tons (fl) **S:** 12 kts **Dim:** 35.5 × 8.0 × 3.0
M: 2 diesels; 2 props; 1,200 hp **Electric:** 224 kVA **Man:** 10 tot.

REMARKS: Helipad on fantail, 200-hp bow-thruster, 30-kt workboat, 80 m^3 oil-containment tanks, 500-m containment boom stowage, oil-spill skimming equipment, fire-fighting gear.

◆ **3 Class A**

	In serv.	D:	Dim:
Tv 01	1971	190 tons (fl)	26.0 × 6.7 × . . .
Tv 02 MÅKLAPPAN	1973	260 tons (fl)	33.0 × 7.2 × . . .
Tv 03	1973	300 tons (fl)	34.0 × 6.6 × . . .

Måklappan (Tv 02)—the only named Coast Guard unit H. Ehlers, 4-85

Tv 03 L. & L. Van Ginderen, 5-82

◆ **2 Tv 050 class, Class B** Bldr: Lunde, Ramvik

Tv 050 (In serv. 20-9-83) Tv 051 (In serv. 6-83)

Tv 050 H. Ehlers, 4-85

D: 340 tons (fl) **S:** . . . **Dim:** 32.6 × 8.5 × . . . **M:** Diesels

REMARKS: Enlarged version of Tv 045 class.

◆ **5 Class B** Bldr: Lunde, Ramvik (In serv. 1980-83)

Tv 045 Tv 046 Tv 047 Tv 048 Tv 049

Tv 048 H. Ehlers, 4-85

D: 133 tons (230 fl) **S:** 11 kts **Dim:** 28.9 (24.80 pp) × 6.5 × 1.9 **Fuel:** 18 tons
M: 2 Saab-Scania DST-11 diesels; 2 props; 540 hp
Electric: 300 kw **Man:** 4 tot.

REMARKS: Resemble landing craft, with bow ramp. 110-m^3 tanks for recovered oil. Hydraulic thrusters fore and aft. Stowage for 800-m oil-spill-containment booms. Endless belt-type oil-recovery device.

◆ **3 Tv 041 class, Class B oil-spill combatting boats** (In serv. 1972)

Tv 041 Tv 042 Tv 043

Tv 042 H. Ehlers, 4-85

D: 70 tons (fl) **S:** . . . **Dim:** 18.4 × 5.4 × . . .

SWEDEN *(continued)*
POLLUTION-CONTROL SHIPS AND CRAFT *(continued)*

◆ **2 miscellaneous Class B oil-spill combatting boats**

	In serv.	D:	Dim:
Tv 044	1976	100 tons (fl)	25.0 × 6.0
Tv 059	1974	22 tons (fl)	

◆ **3 Tv 011 class, Class C**

Tv 011 (In serv. 1974) Tv 012 (In serv. 1970) Tv 014 (In serv. 1971)

D: 50 tons (fl) **S:** . . . **Dim:** 25.0 × 5.1 × . . .

Remarks: Wooden construction.

◆ **1 Tv 015 class, Class C** (In serv. 1971)

Tv 015

D: 140 tons (fl) **S:** . . . **Dim:** 23.0 × 5.5 × . . .

◆ **1 Class D1 catamaran** Bldr: Djupvik, Tjoern (In serv. 8-6-82)

Tv 020

Tv 020 L. & L. Van Ginderen, 2-83

D: 60 tons (fl) **S:** 27 kts **Dim:** 27.6 × 9.2 × 1.5
M: 2 MTU J2V396 TB82 diesels; 2 props; 2,600 hp

Remarks: Drum-type skimmer mounted forward between the hulls can recover up to 40 tons/hr., or a belt-type cleaner can recover 10–20 tons/hr. Design is Norway's Westermoen 88.

◆ **3 miscellaneous Class D2 catamarans**

	In serv.	D:	Dim:
Tv 021	1973	30 tons (fl)	14.0 × 7.0
Tv 022	1973	30 tons (fl)	14.0 × 7.0
Tv 023	1975	30 tons (fl)	16.5 × 7.5

Tv 023—catamaran oil-spill boat H. Ehlers, 4-85

◆ **4 Class E shore cleaning boats** (In serv. 1979-1982)

Tv 0701 Tv 0702 Tv 0703 Tv 0704

D: 9 tons **S:** . . . **Dim:** 9.0 × 3.1 × . . .

Tv 0705—shore cleaning boat (with sister) H. Ehlers, 4-85

◆ **6 miscellaneous Class G oil barges**

	In serv.	D:	Dim:
Tv 061	1974	300 tons (fl)	28.8 × 6.3 × . . .
Tv 062	1975	140 tons (fl)	12.0 × 6.0 × . . .
Tv 063	1974	250 tons (fl)	28.8 × 6.3 × . . .
Tv 064	1981	. . .	. . .
Tv 065	. . .	. . .	. . .
Tv 068	1979	400 tons (fl)	30.6 × 6.8 × . . .
Tv 069	1980	360 tons (fl)	30.6 × 6.7 × . . .

Tv 061—oil barge H. Ehlers, 4-85

Remarks: Tv 065 is a car ferry at Göteborg

◆ **4 Class H small craft** (In serv. 1973-75)

Tv 031–Tv 034

D: 6 tons (fl) **S:** . . . **Dim:** 7.5 × 2.5 × . . .

◆ **1 Class J seasled** (In serv. 1979): Tv 036—Dim: 11.8 × 4.6

◆ **20 miscellaneous Class K workboats** (In serv. 1971-82)

Tv 080–Tv 099

D: 0.8 to 1.0 tons (fl) **S:** . . . **Dim:** 5.8 to 6.5 × 2.4 to 2.7 × . . .

SWITZERLAND

Swiss Confederation

Merchant Marine (1984): 32 ships—319,348 grt (5 tankers—10,065 grt)

SWISS ARMY

PATROL CRAFT

◆ **11 Patrouillenboat 80 class** Bldr: Müller AG, Spiez (In serv. 1981-84)

Antares, Aquarius, Castor, Mars, Orion, Perseus, Pollux, Saturn, Sirius, Venus, Uranus

D: 5.9 tons (fl) **S:** 35 kts **Dim:** 10.7 × 3.3 × 0.9 (0.6 hull)
A: 2/12.7-mm M3 mg (I × 2) **Man:** 6 tot.
M: 2 Volvo Penta AQ 260A gasoline engines; 2 props; 560 hp

Remarks: Glass-reinforced plastic construction, wooden superstructure. Replaced a group of wooden-hulled craft built in 1942.

SWITZERLAND *(continued)*
PATROL CRAFT *(continued)*

P 80 class

SYRIA

Syrian Arab Republic

PERSONNEL (1985): approximately 2,500 total

MERCHANT MARINE (1985): 53 ships—56,156 grt

NAVAL AVIATION: Helicopters: 3 Kamov Ka-25 Hormone-A ASW and 20 Mi-14 Haze-A ASW.

NOTE: Coast-defense batteries of SS C-1b Shaddock and SSC-3 Styx missiles have been transferred from the U.S.S.R. They are mounted on vehicles.

Two Romeo-class submarines delivered 1985; see U.S.S.R. section for characteristics.

FRIGATES

◆ **2 ex-Soviet Petya class**

12 N. . . . . . . 14 N. . . . . . .

Syrian Petya No. 14 6th Flot., French Navy, 10-83

D: 950 tons (1,150 fl) **S:** 29 kts **Dim:** 81.8 (78.00 pp) × 9.2 × 2.97 (mean hull)
A: 4/76.2-mm DP (II × 2)—4/RBU 2500 ASW RL (XVI × 4)—3/533-mm TT (III × 1)—2/d.c. racks—mines
Electron Equipt: 1/Don-2, 1/Strut Curve, 1/Hawk Screech
IFF: 2/Square Head, 1/High Pole B
Sonar: Hull-mounted HF
M: CODAG: 2 gas turbines (15,000 hp each); 1 Type 61V3 diesel (6,000 hp); 3 props; 36,000 hp **Range:** 450/29; 4,800/10 **Man:** 8 officers, 84 men

REMARKS: Transferred: 1975. Standard export version, with triple 533-mm TT substituted for Soviet Navy quintuple 400-mm mount.

CORVETTE

◆ **1 Soviet Natya class**

Syria's Natya (transfer No. 642) 21st Flot., French Navy, 1-85

D: 650 tons (750 fl) **S:** 18 kts **Dim:** 61.0 × 9.8 × 3.0
A: 4/30-mm AK-230 AA (II × 2)—4/25-mm AA (II × 2)
Electron Equipt: Radar: 1/Spin Trough nav., 1/Drum Tilt f.c.
IFF: 2/Square Head interrogators, 1/High Pole A transponder
M: 2 diesels; 2 props; 5,000 hp **Range:** 1,800/16; 5,200/10 **Man:** 60 tot.

REMARKS: Transferred 26-1-85. Not equipped with any of the normal Natya-class seagoing minesweeper mine countermeasures equipment, winches, cranes, etc., nor does she have the standard 2/RBU-1200 ASW rocket launchers or mine rails.

GUIDED-MISSILE PATROL BOATS

◆ **12 ex-Soviet Osa-II class**

Syrian Osa-II 6th Flot., French Navy, 10-83

D: 215 tons (240 fl) **S:** 35 kts **Dim:** 38.6 × 7.6 × 2.0
A: 4/SS-N-2B Styx SSM (I × 4)—4/30-mm AA (II × 2)
Electron Equipt: Radar: 1/Square Tie, 1/Drum Tilt
IFF: 2/Square Head, 1/High Pole B
M: 3 M504 diesels; 3 props; 15,000 hp **Range:** 500/34; 750/25
Man: 28–30 tot.

REMARKS: Two transferred 1978, four in 1979, two in 1982, two in 5-84, two in 1985.

◆ **6 ex-Soviet Osa-I class**

Syrian Osa-I 6th Flot., French Navy, 10-83

D: 180 tons (215 fl) **S:** 36 kts **Dim:** 38.6 × 7.6 × 1.8
A: 4/SS-N-2 Styx (I × 4)—4/30-mm AA (II × 2)
Electron Equipt: Radar: 1/Square Tie, 1/Drum Tilt
IFF: 2/Square Head, 1/High Pole B
M: 3 M503A diesels; 3 props; 12,000 hp **Range:** 500/34 **Man:** 28–30 tot.

REMARKS: Transferred 1966; two were sunk during the Arab-Israeli War, October 1973.

NOTE: Six ex-Soviet Komar-class guided-missile patrol boats deleted due to age and lack of sightings. Eight P-4-class torpedo boats have also been deleted for similar reasons.

SYRIA *(continued)*

PATROL CRAFT

◆ **9 Soviet Zhuk class**

D: 48 tons (60 fl) **S:** 34 kts **Dim:** 24.0 × 5.0 × 1.2 (1.8 props)
A: 4/14.5-mm mg (II × 2)
Electron Equipt: Radar: 1/Spin Trough
IFF: 1/High Pole A
M: 2 M50F-4 diesels; 2 props; 2,400 hp **Fuel:** 10 tons
Range: 700/28; 1,100/15 **Man:** 12 tot.

Remarks: Three delivered 12-83, 3 in 12-84, three in 1-85.

MINE WARFARE UNITS

◆ **1 Soviet T-43-class fleet minesweeper**

504 Yarmouk

D: 500 tons (570 fl) **S:** 14 kts **Dim:** 58.0 × 8.6 × 2.3 (hull)
A: 4/37-mm AA (II × 2) — 8/12.7-mm mg (II × 4) — 2/d.c. mortars — mines
Electron Equipt: Radar: 1/Ball End **M:** 2 Type 9D diesels; 2 props; 2,200 hp
Fuel: 70 tons **Range:** 2,000/14; 3,200/10 **Man:** 75 tot.

Remarks: Transferred 1962; one sister lost in the October 1973 war.

◆ **2 ex-Soviet Vanya-class coastal minesweepers**

D: 210 tons (250 fl) **S:** 16 kts **Dim:** 40.2 × 7.9 × 1.7
A: 2/30-mm AA (II × 1) — mines **Electron Equipt:** Radar: 1/Don-2
M: 2 diesels; 2 props; 2,200 hp **Range:** 1,400/14; 2,400/10 **Man:** 30 tot.

Remarks: Transferred 12-72. Wooden construction; glass-reinforced plastic-sheathed hull.

◆ **2 Soviet Yevgenya class** Bldr: Sredniy Neva SY, Kolpino

D: 80 tons (90 fl) **S:** 11 kts **Dim:** 26.2 × 6.1 × 1.5
A: 2/14.5-mm mg (II × 1) **M:** 2 diesels; 2 props; 600 hp
Electron Equipt: Radar: 1/Spin Trough — IFF: 1/High Pole B
Range: 300/10 **Man:** 10 tot.

Remarks: Transferred 2-85. Glass-reinforced plastic construction. Use television minehunting system to 30-m depths.

AMPHIBIOUS WARFARE SHIPS

◆ **2 Soviet Polnocny-B-class medium landing ships**

D: 800 tons (fl) **S:** 18 kts **Dim:** 74.0 × 8.6 × 2.0
A: 4/30-mm AK-230 AA (II × 2) — 2/140-mm barrage RL (XVIII × 2)
Electron Equipt: Radar: 1/Spin Trough, 1/Drum Tilt
IFF: 1/Square Head, 1/High Pole B
M: 2 diesels; 2 props; 5,000 hp **Range:** 900/18; 1,500/14
Man: 40 crew + 100 troops

Remarks: Transferred from U.S.S.R. 15-1-84 and 2-85. Cargo: about 180 tons. May also have 2 or 4/SA-N-5 point-defense SAM stations (IV × 2 or 4).

AUXILIARIES AND SERVICE CRAFT

◆ **1 Soviet Sekstan-class degaussing tender** (In serv. 1949-55)

D: 400 tons (fl) **S:** 11 kts **Dim:** 41.0 × 9.3 × 4.2
M: 1 diesel; 1 prop; 400 hp **Range:** 1,200/10.5 **Man:** 24 tot.

Remarks: Transferred 12-83. Wooden construction.

◆ **1 Soviet Nyryat-1-class diving tender**

D: 120 tons (fl) **S:** 12 kts **Dim:** 29.0 × 5.0 × 1.7
Electron Equipt: Radar: 1/Spin Trough **M:** 1 diesel; 1 prop; 450 hp
Range: 1,600/10 **Man:** 15 tot.

◆ **3 survey launches** Bldr: ARCOR, La Teste, France (In serv. 1985)

D: . . . **S:** 25 kts **Dim:** 9.80 (8.50 pp) × 3.40 × 0.90
M: 2 Volvo-Penta AQAD-40 diesels; 310 hp **Range:** 300/. . .
Man: 4 tot.

Remarks: Ordered 12-84. Glass-reinforced plastic construction.

TAIWAN

Republic of China

Personnel (1985): 38,000 total Navy, plus 39,000 Marines; 45,000 naval reservists, 35,000 Marine reservists

Merchant Marine (1984): 543 ships — 3,958,418 grt
(tankers: 31 ships — 1,467,344 grt)

Naval Aviation: Eighteen S-2A/E, including 9 ex-U.S.N. delivered late 1985. Twelve Hughes-500 MD/ASW helicopters with ASQ-81(V)2 magnetic anomaly detection (MAD) gear were ordered during 1979 for use from destroyers. The Marines have several light observation aircraft and helicopters.

Warships In Service Or Under Construction
As Of 1 January 1986

	L	Tons (Surfaced)	Main Armament
◆ **2 (+2) submarines**			
0 (+2) Zwaardvis	. . .	2,300	6/533-mm TT
2 GUPPY II	1944-45	1,870	10/533-mm TT
◆ **26 destroyers**		Tons	
12 Gearing FRAM-I	1945-46	2,425	4/127mm, 0-4/40-mm ASW weapons
2 Gearing FRAM-II	1945	2,425	4-6/127-mm, 4-8/40-mm, ASW weapons
2 Allen M. Sumner FRAM-II	1944	2,350	4 or 6/127-mm, SSM, ASW weapons
6 Allen M. Sumner	1943-44	2,200	4 or 6/127-mm, SSM, ASW weapons
4 Fletcher	1942-43	1,680	4-5/127-mm, Sea Chapparal SAM, ASW weapons
◆ **10 frigates**			
1 Rudderow	1943	1,450	2/127-mm, 4/40-mm, ASW weapons
9 Crosley/Charles Lawrence	1943-45	1,680	2/127-mm, 6/40-mm, ASW weapons
◆ **3 corvettes**			
3 Auk	1942-45	890	2/76.2-mm, 4/40-mm, ASW weapons

◆ **50 guided-missile patrol boats**

◆ **13 minesweepers**

◆ **50 amphibious ships and craft**

Note: Almost all ships, weapons, and electronics systems currently in use originated in the United States, the principal exception being the Hsiung Feng anti-ship missile, a copy of the Israeli Aviation Industries' Gabriel II. Although nearly all ships are ex-U.S. Navy units dating to World War II, maintenance has been superb, and many subsystems have been renewed and updated. At the present time, destroyer gunfire-control systems are being upgraded by U.S. contractors, while a locally designed chaff rocket system has been installed on most larger ships. Hull numbers were altered in 1976 and now are not usually worn. The latest known numbers are given, but ships are listed in alphabetical order.

SUBMARINES

◆ **0 (+2) modified Dutch Zwaardvis class** Bldr: Wilton Fijenoord, Schiedam

	Laid down	L	In serv.
. . . N.	12-82	. . .	1986
. . . N.	. . .	. . .	1986

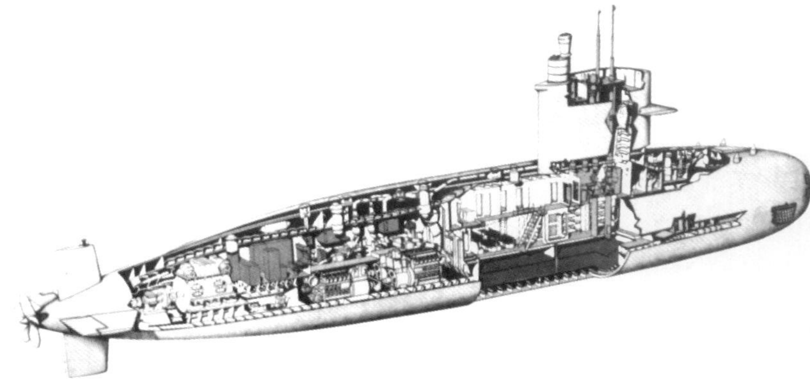

"Sea Dragon" class

D: 2,300 tons surf./2,600 sub. **S:** 11 kts **Dim:** 66.92 × 8.40 × 6.70
A: 6/533-mm TT fwd (28 torpedoes)
Electron Equipt: Radar: 1/Decca . . . — EW: H.S.A. RAPIDS
Sonar: Thomson-CSF Octopus
M: 3 Brons/Stork-Werkspoor 12 ORUB 215 diesels (1,350 hp each); 2/992-kw generator groups, 1 3,800-kw motor; 1 5-bladed prop; 5,100 hp
Fuel: 310 tons **Range:** 10,000/9 (surf.) **Man:** 8 officers, 59 men

Remarks: Ordered late 1980, over mainland China's protests. Design also referred to as "Sea Dragon" class. Highly automated design. "Gipsy" data system, Sperry Mk 29

SUBMARINES *(continued)*

Mod. 2A inertial navigation system. Two 196-cell batteries. Program delayed by shipyard financial problems. Request for 2 more (and option for 5th and 6th) turned down by Dutch government in 1984, due to Chinese pressure.

◆ **2 ex-U.S. GUPPY II class**

	Bldr	Laid down	L	In serv.
736 Hai Shih (ex-*Cutlass,* SS 478)	Portsmouth, NSY	22-7-44	5-11-44	17-3-45
794 Hai Pao (ex-*Tusk,* SS 426)	Cramp SB, Philadelphia	23-8-43	8-7-45	11-4-46

Hai Pao (794)—as *Tusk* 1967

D: 1,517/1,870/2,440 tons **S:** 18/16 kts **Dim:** 93.57 × 8.33 × 5.18
A: 10/533-mm TT (6 fwd, 4 aft)
Electron Equipt: Radar: 1/SS-2
Sonar: BQR-2B, BQS-4C, DUUG-1B
M: Diesel-electric propulsion: 4 Fairbanks-Morse 38D8⅛ diesels; 2 electric motors; 4,610/5,200 hp
Range: 10,000/10 surfaced **Man:** 11 officers, 70 men

Remarks: Transferred 12-4-73 and 18-10-73, for ASW training. Four 126-cell batteries. Source of torpedoes uncertain: may use old Japanese or U.S. Mk 14 World War II-era straight-runners, U.S. Mk 37 or NT-37C homing torpedoes, or U.K. Mk 24 Tigerfish; tubes were welded shut at time of delivery.

DESTROYERS

◆ **12 ex-U.S. Gearing FRAM-I class**

	Bldr	Laid down	L	In serv.
912 Chao Yang (ex-*Hammer,* DD 718)	Federal SB Newark, N.J.	5-4-45	24-11-45	11-7-46
928 Cheng Hua (ex-*Hollister,* D 788)	Todd Pacific SY, Seattle	18-1-45	9-10-45	29-3-46
921 Chien Yang (ex-*James E. Kyes,* DD 787)	Todd Pacific SY, Seattle	27-12-44	4-8-45	8-2-46
978 Han Yang ex-*Herbert J. Thomas,* DD 833)	Bath Iron Wks	30-10-44	25-3-45	29-5-45
915 Kai Yang ex-*Richard B. Anderson,* DD 786	Todd Pacific SY, Seattle	1-12-44	7-7-45	26-10-45
981 Lai Yang (ex-*Leonard F. Mason,* DD 852)	Bethlehem Steel, Quincy	8-6-45	4-1-46	28-6-46
928 Lao Yang (ex-*Shelton,* DD 790)	Todd Pacific SY, Seattle	31-5-45	8-3-46	21-6-46
938 Liao Yang (ex-*Hanson,* DD 832)	Bath Iron Wks	7-10-44	11-3-45	11-5-45
926 Shao Yang (ex-*Hawkins,* DD 873)	Consolidated, Steel, Orange, Tex.	14-5-44	7-10-44	10-2-45
932 Shen Yang (ex-*Power,* DD 839)	Bath Iron Wks	26-2-45	30-6-45	13-9-45
925 Te Yang (ex-*Sarsfield,* DD 837)	Bath Iron Wks	15-1-45	27-5-45	31-7-45
927 Yung Yang (ex-*Johnston,* DD 821)	Consolidated Steel, Orange, Tex.	6-5-45	19-10-45	10-10-46

Liao Yang (wearing 921) L. & L. Van Ginderen, 7-85

Chien Yang wearing 912—note TACAN atop aft mast, chaff RL abaft second stack L. & L. Van Ginderen, 7-85

D: 2,425 tons (3,465-3,540 fl) **S:** 32 kts
Dim: 119.03 (116.74 wl) × 12.52 × 4.61 (6.5 over sonar)
A: 4/127-mm DP (II × 2)—*Han Yang, Kai Yang:* 4/40-mm AA (II × 2); *Chao Yang* and *Yung Yang*: 2/40-mm AA (I × 2)—all: 4 or 6/12.7-mm mg—1/ASROC ASW RL (VIII × 1) (not in *Han Yang, Kai Yang, Chao Yang*)—6/324-mm Mk 32 ASW TT (III × 2)—1/Hughes-500 MD ASW helicopter
Electron Equipt: Radar: 1/SPS-10, 1/SPS-29 (*Chien Yang, Te Yang, Shao Yang, Cheng Hua:* SPS-40), 1/Mk 25
Sonar: SQS-23—TACAN: SRN-15
EW: WLR-1, ULQ-6 in some, 4/chaff RL (XVI × 4)
M: 2 sets G.E. GT; 2 props; 60,000 hp **Electric:** 1,200 kw
Boilers: 4 Babcock & Wilcox; 43.3 kg/cm², 454°C
Fuel: 720 tons **Range:** 1,500/31; 5,800/12 **Man:** 275 tot.

Remarks: *Chien Yang, Lao Yang,* and *Liao Yang* transferred 18-4-73; *Han Yang,* 6-5-74; *Kai Yang,* 10-6-77; *Te Yang, Shen Yang,* 1-10-77; *Lai Yang,* 10-3-78. A ninth unit, *Chao Yang* (ex-*Rowan,* DD 782) was lost 22-8-77 while on tow to Taiwan. Ex-DD 718 and 821 purchased (without ASROC) 27-2-81; ex-DD 788 purchased 3-4-83, ex-DD 873 purchased 17-4-83. *Kai Yang* and *Lao Yang* both have 127-mm twin mounts forward and the Mk 32 ASW torpedo tubes abreast the after stack. *Han Yang* has extra superstructure, as she was converted for NBC-warfare defense trials 1963-64; she has an extra gas-turbine generator to run additional air-conditioning systems. She and *Kai Yang* had no ASROC on transfer and have received two twin 40-mm antiaircraft guns, each with a Mk 51, Mod. 2 director in the ASROC location. In *Chao Yang* and *Yung Yang,* two single Bofors L70, 40-mm AA are mounted on the former ASROC deck. All have Mk 37 gunfire-control radars for the 127-mm guns. New GFCS are to be acquired for all. Hsiung Feng (Israeli Gabriel I) missiles have been added to *Han Yang* and possibly others, in a triple, trainable launcher in lieu of the after 127-mm mount, and most have four multi-tube chaff RL.

◆ **2 ex-U.S. Gearing FRAM-II class**

	Bldr	Laid down	L	In serv.
966 Dang Yang (ex-*Lloyd Thomas,* DD 764)	Bethlehem Steel, San Francisco	26-3-44	5-10-45	21-3-47
907 Fu Yang (ex-*Ernest G. Small,* DD 838)	Bath Iron Works	30-1-45	14-6-45	21-8-45

Fu Yang (907)—now has triple Hsiung Feng launcher aft 1977

D: 2,425 tons (3,477 fl) **S:** 32 kts
Dim: 119.03 (116.74 wl) × 12.52 × 4.61 (6.54 over sonar)
A: 907: 5/Hsiung Feng SSM (III × 1, I × 2)—4/127-mm DP (II × 2)—8/40-mm AA (II × 4)—4/12.7-mm mg (I × 4)—2/Mk 11 Hedgehog—6/324-mm Mk 32 ASW TT (III × 2)—1/d.c. rack
966: 4/127-mm DP (II × 2)—4/40-mm AA (II × 2)—4/12.7-mm mg (I × 4)—1/Mk 15 trainable Hedgehog—6/324-mm Mk 32 ASW TT (III × 2)—1/Hughes-500 ASW helicopter
Electron Equipt: Radar: 907: 1/SPS-58, 1/SPS-37, 2/RCA HR 76
TACAN: URN-6
EW: Argo AR 680/681
966: 1/SPS-10, 1/SPS-6B, 1/Mk 25
EW: WLR-1, WLR-3, ULQ-6
Sonar: SQS-23 series (hull)

DESTROYERS *(continued)*

M: 2 sets G.E. GT; 2 props; 60,000 hp **Electric:** 1,200 kw
Boilers: 4 Babcock & Wilcox; 43.3 kg/cm², 454°C
Fuel: 720 tons **Range:** 1,600/31; 6,100/12 **Man:** 275 tot.

REMARKS: *Dang Yang,* completed as an ASW destroyer (DDE), finished FRAM-I modernization in 11-61 and was transferred to Taiwan on 12-10-72. *Fu Yang,* transferred in 2-71, completed FRAM-II modernization as a radar picket destroyer in 8-61; her SPS-30 height-finder was removed before transfer. Both received 40-mm and 12.7-mm guns in Taiwan. One Mk 37 radar gunfire control for 127-mm, one Mk 51, Mod. 2, optical gunfire control per 40-mm mount. *Fu Yung* acts as fleet flagship and has been modernized like the units below.

◆ **2 ex-U.S. Allen M. Sumner FRAM-II class**

	Bldr	Laid down	L	In serv.
949 Lo Yang (ex-*Taussig,* DD 746)	Bethlehem Steel, Staten I.	30-8-43	25-1-44	20-5-44
954 Nan Yang (ex-*John W. Thomason,* DD 760)	Bethlehem Steel, San Francisco	21-11-43	30-9-44	11-10-45

Lo Yang or Nan Yang *Defense Technology,* 1985

D: 2,350 tons (3,220 fl) **S:** 33 kts **Range:** 1,000/32 **Man:** 275 tot.
Dim: 114.63 (112.52 wl) × 12.52 × 4.4 (5.9 over sonar)
A: 5/Hsiung Feng SSM (III × 1, I × 2)—1/RIM-72C Sea Chaparral point-defense SAM system (VI × 1)—2/127-mm DP (II × 1)—1/76-mm OTO Melara Compact DP—2/40-mm Bofors AA (I × 2)—4/12.7-mm mg (I × 4)—2/Mk 11 Hedgehog ASW mortars (XXIV × 2)—6/324-mm Mk 32 ASW TT (III × 2)—1/Hughes 500 helicopter
Electron Equipt: Radar: 1/SPS-58, 1/SPS-29, 2 RCA HR-76
Sonar: SQS-29 series
EW: Argo AR 680/681, 4 chaff RL—TACAN: SRN-15
M: 2 sets GT; 2 props; 60,000 hp **Electric:** 1,200 kw
Boilers: 4 Babcock & Wilcox; 43.3 kg/cm², 454°C **Fuel:** 500 tons

REMARKS: Both transferred on 6-5-74, having completed FRAM-II modernization in 9-62 and 1-60, respectively. Rebuilt by mid-1985 with "B" 127-mm mount replaced by 76-mm gun, aft 127-mm mount by triple, trainable SSM launcher. The manned Sea Chaparral launcher is at the extreme stern. The Honeywell H930 weapon-control system is supported by two RCA radars mounted on new lattice masts; the old Mk 37 GFCS director is retained without its Mk 25 radar, but with a Kollmorgen electro-optical system added. A similar conversion is probably being effected on some of the larger *Gearing*-class units.

◆ **6 ex-U.S. Allen M. Sumner class**

	Bldr	Laid down	L	In serv.
976 Heng Yang (ex-*Samuel N. Moore,* DD 747)	Bethlehem Steel, Staten Isl.	30-9-43	23-2-44	24-6-44
986 Hsiang Yang (ex-*Brush,* DD 745)	Bethlehem Steel, Staten Isl.	30-7-43	28-12-43	17-4-44
988 Hua Yang (ex-*Bristol,* DD 857)	Bethlehem Steel, San Pedro	5-5-44	29-10-44	17-3-45
972 Huei Yang (ex-*English,* DD 696)	Federal SB, Kearny, N.J.	19-10-43	27-2-44	4-5-44
. . . Po Yang (ex-*Maddox,* DD 731)	Bath Iron Works	28-10-43	19-3-44	2-6-44
944 Yuen Yang (ex-*Haynsworth,* DD 700)	Federal SB, Kearny, N.J.	16-12-43	15-4-44	22-6-44

D: 2,200 tons (3,300 fl) **S:** 33 kts **M:** 2 sets GT; 2 props; 60,000 hp
Dim: 114.63 (112.52 wl) × 12.52 × 4.4 (5.9 over sonar) **Electric:** 1,000 kw
A: *Hsiang Yang, Hua Yang, Yuen Yang:* 5/Hsiung Feng SSM (III × 1, I × 2)—6/127-mm DP (II × 3)—4/40-mm AA (II × 2)—4/12.7-mm mg (I × 4)—2/Mk 11 Hedgehogs—6/324-mm Mk 32 ASW TT (III × 2)—1/d.c. rack
Heng Yang: 6/Hsiung Feng SSM (III × 2)—4/127-mm DP (II × 2)—8/40-mm AA (IV × 1, II × 2)—4/12.7-mm mg (I × 4)—2/Mk 11 Hedgehogs—6/324-mm Mk 32 ASW TT (III × 2)—1/d.c. rack
Huei Yang, Po Yang: 6/127-mm DP (II × 3)—4/76.2-mm DP (II × 2)—4/12.7-mm mg—2/Mk 11 Hedgehogs—6/324-mm Mk 32 ASW TT—1/d.c. rack
Electron Equipt: Radar: 1/SPS-10, 1/SPS-6C (*Po Yang:* SPS-40), 1/Mk 25 (*Huei Yang, Po Yang:* 1/Mk 35 also), Hsiung Feng ships: 1/Orion RTN-10X
Sonar: SQS-29 series EW: WLR-1, 4/chaff RL (XVI × 4)
Boilers: 4 Babcock & Wilcox; 43.3 kg/cm², 454°C
Fuel: 500 tons **Range:** 1,000/32; 4,400/11 **Man:** 275 tot.

REMARKS: *Heng Yang* transferred in 2-70; *Hsiang Yang* and *Hua Yang* on 9-12-69; *Huei Yang* in 9-70; *Po Yang* on 6-7-72; *Yuen Yang* on 12-5-70. All were unmodified units of the class. *Hsiang Yang* had four 76.2-mm DP before Hsuing Feng conversion. Those that have 40-mm antiaircraft guns had them added in Taiwan; each mount has one associated Mk 51, Mod. 2 GFCS. All have Mk 37 radar GFCS for the 127-mm guns; those with 76.2-mm also have one Mk 56 radar GFCS. The Hsiung Feng-equipped units have a Selenia Orion RTN-10X fire-control radar on the after side of the tripod mast.

◆ **4 ex-U.S. Fletcher class**

Bldrs: *An Yang:* Bethlehem Steel, Staten Island; others: Bethlehem, San Francisco

	Laid down	L	In serv.
997 An Yang (ex-*Kimberly,* DD 521)	27-7-42	4-2-43	24-5-43
947 Chiang Yang (ex-*Mullany,* DD 528)	15-1-42	12-10-42	23-4-43
934 Kun Yang (ex-*Yarnell,* DD 541)	5-12-42	25-7-43	30-12-43
908 Kwei Yang (ex-*Twining,* DD 540)	21-11-42	11-7-43	1-2-43

Kwei Yang (908)—alongside *Lao Yang* (928) *Defense Technology,* 1985

D: 2,100 tons (3.036 fl) **S:** 35 kts **Range:** 860/35; 4,700/13 **Man:** 275 tot.
Dim: 114.65 (112.52 wl) × 11.99 × 4.39 (5.38 over sonar)
A: 5/Hsiung Feng SSM (III × 1, I × 2)—2/127-mm DP (I × 2)—1/76-mm OTO Melara DP—1/RIM-72C Sea Chaparral SAM system (VI × 1)—6/324-mm Mk 32 ASW TT (III × 2)—2/Mk 11 Hedgehogs—1/d.c. rack (934 also: 2 mine rails)
Electron Equipt: Radar: 1/SPS-58, 1/SPS-6C, 2/R.C.A. R76C5
Sonar: DD 934, 997: SQS-50; DD 947: SQS-40, DD 956: SQS-41
EW: Argo AR 680/681, 4/chaff RL (XVI × 4)
M: 2 sets GT; 2 props; 60,000 hp **Electric:** 880 kw
Boilers: 4 Babcock & Wilcox; 43.3 kg/cm², 454°C **Fuel:** 512 tons

REMARKS: *An Yang* transferred in 6-67; *Chiang Yang* in 10-71; *Kun Yang* in 6-68; *Kwei Yang* in 10-71. Sea Chaparral is a manned mounting for launching Redeye, heat-seeking, short-range SAMs; it replaced a twin 40-mm antiaircraft mount. SQS-50 is an updated SQS-4; SQS-40 and -41 are updated versions of the SQS-29 and -30. All four have now been modernized with new fire-control systems, two 4-legged lattice masts, and greatly enlarged forward superstructures.

FRIGATES

NOTE: A 3,348-ton, CODOG-powered frigate design prepared for Taiwan by Westinghouse in the U.S. proved too expensive to construct in the numbers necessary to replace Taiwan's aged fleet. Further studies for a more economical design are ongoing.

◆ **1 ex-U.S. Rudderow class** Bldr: Bethlehem Steel, Hingham, Mass.

	Laid down	L	In serv.
959 Tai Yuan (ex-*Riley,* DE 579)	20-10-43	29-12-43	13-3-44

D: 1,450 tons (1,950 fl) **S:** 24 kts **Dim:** 93.27 × 11.24 × 3.43 (4.3 over sonar)
A: 2/12.7-mm DP (I × 2)—4/40-mm AA (I × 2)—4/20-mm AA (I × 4)—1/Mk 11 Hedgehog—6/324-mm Mk 32 ASW TT (III × 2)—2/Mk 9 d.c. racks—mines
Electron Equipt: Radar: 1/SPS-5, 1/SPS-6, 1/Mk 26 fire-control
Sonar: . . .
M: 2 sets G.E. turbo-electric drive; 2 props; 12,000 hp **Electric:** 1,140 kw
Boilers: 2 Foster-Wheeler D-type; 31.7 kg/cm², 399°C
Fuel: 354 tons **Range:** 1,100/24; 5,000/12 **Man:** 200 tot.

REMARKS: Transferred, after modernization, on 10-7-69; purchased outright in 3-74. Has one Mk 52 radar GFCS and two Mk 51, Mod. 2, GFCS. Minelaying capability added in Taiwan.

◆ **9 former high-speed transports**

6 ex-U.S. Crosley class:

	Bldr	Laid down	L	In serv.
838 Fu Shan (ex-*Truxtun,* APD 98, ex-DE 282)	Charleston NY, Charleston, S.C.	13-12-43	9-3-44	3-7-44
854 Hua Shan (ex-*Donald W. Wolf,* APD 129, ex-DE 713)	Defoe SB, Bay City, Mich.	17-4-44	22-7-44	13-4-45

FRIGATES *(continued)*

893 SHOU SHAN (ex-*Kline,* APD 120, ex-DE 687)	Bethlehem Steel, Quincy, Mass.	27-5-44	27-6-44	18-10-44
878 TAI SHAN (ex-*Register,* APD 92, ex-DE 233)	Charleston NY, Charleston, S.C.	27-10-43	20-1-44	11-1-45
615 TIEN SHAN (ex-*Kleinsmith,* APD 134, ex-DE 718)	Defoe SB, Bay City, Mich.	30-8-44	27-1-45	12-6-45
826 YU SHAN (ex-*Kinzer,* APD 91, ex-DE 232)	Charleston NY, Charleston, S.C.	9-9-43	9-12-43	1-11-44

3 ex-U.S. Charles Lawrence class

	Bldr	Laid down	L	In serv.
845 CHUNG SHAN (ex-*Blessman,* APD 48, ex-DE 69)	Bethlehem Steel, Hingham, Mass.	23-3-43	19-6-43	19-9-43
821 LU SHAN (ex-*Bull,* APD 78, ex-DE 693)	Defoe SB, Bay City	14-12-42	25-3-43	12-8-43
834 WEN SHAN (ex-*Gantner,* APD 42, ex-DE 60)	Bethlehem Steel, Hingham, Mass.	21-12-42	17-4-43	23-7-43

Fu Shan (838)—wearing old number *Ships of the World,* 1975

D: 1,680 tons (2,150 fl) **S:** 22 kts **Dim:** 93.27 × 11.24 × 3.96 (hull)
A: 2/127-mm DP (I × 2)—6/40-mm AA (II × 3)—4/20-mm AA (I × 4)—2/Mk 9 d.c. racks—*see also* Remarks
Electron Equipt: Radar: 1/SPS-5, 1/Decca 707; some: 1/Mk 26
Sonar: . . .
M: 2 sets G.E. turbo-electric drive; 2 props; 12,000 hp **Electric:** 1,140 kw
Boilers: 2 Babcock & Wilcox, Foster-Wheeler, or Combustion Engineering; 31.7 kg/cm², 399°C
Fuel: 346 tons **Range:** 1,800/22; 5,000/13 **Man:** 200 crew + 160 troops

REMARKS: *Yu Shan* transferred in 4-62; *Hua Shan* in 5-65; *Fu Shan* and *Shou Shan* in 3-66; *Wen Shan* in 5-66; *Lu Shan* in 8-66; *Tai Shan* in 10-66; *Tien Shan* in 6-67, and *Chung Shan* in 8-67. All were sold outright except *Tien Shan* which, because she was on loan, was not modified by the addition of a second 127-mm mount aft until after her purchase in 1974; the others all received the second gun in lieu of a cargo hold and derrick, beginning about 1970. ASW armaments vary, with *Fu Shan* having two Mk 11 Hedgehogs on her main deck forward and several (but not all) carrying six 324-mm Mk 32 ASW torpedo tubes (III × 2); all have two Mk 9 depth-charge racks, and *Hua Shan* has four *twin* 20-mm antiaircraft guns. Most have only a Mk 51 range finder for 127-mm fire-control forward and a Mk 51 optical gunfire-control system aft, plus three Mk 51, Mod. 2 GFCS for the 40-mm antiaircraft guns. Welin davits are retained amidships, but only two (vice the original four) landing craft are carried, to save topweight. The former *Crosley*-class ships have low navigating bridges, the other ships have high ones. Sisters *Heng Shan* (ex-*Raymond W. Herndon,* APD 121) and *Lung Shan* (ex-*Schmitt,* APD 76) were stricken in 1976, and *Kang Shan* (ex-*George W. Ingram,* APD 43) was stricken in 1978.

CORVETTES

◆ **3 ex-U.S. Auk-class former minesweepers**

	Laid down	L	In serv.
896 CHU YUNG (ex-*Waxwing,* MSF 389)	24-5-44	10-3-45	6-8-45
867 PING JIN (ex-*Steady,* MSF 118)	17-11-41	6-6-42	16-11-42
884 WU SHENG (ex-*Redstart,* MSF 378)	14-6-44	18-10-45	4-4-45

Bldrs: *Wu Sheng:* Savannah Machine & Foundry, Ga; others: American SB, Cleveland, O.

D: 890 tons (1,250 fl) **S:** 18 kts **Dim:** 67.39 (65.53 pp) × 9.8 × 3.3
A: 2/76.2-mm DP (I × 2)—4/40-mm AA (II × 2)—4/20-mm AA (II × 2)—1/Mk 11 Hedgehog—3/324-mm Mk 32 ASW TT (III × 1)—2/Mk 9 d.c. racks
Electron Equipt: Radar: 1/SPS-5
Sonar: SQS-17
M: 2 G.M. 12-278A diesels; 2 props; 3,532 hp
Electric: 360 kw **Fuel:** 216 tons **Man:** 80 tot.

REMARKS: After conversion to corvettes, transferred as follows: *Chu Yung* in 11-65, *Ping Jin* in 3-68, and *Wu Sheng* in 7-65. *Chu Yung* was fitted with mine rails in 1975.

GUIDED-MISSILE PATROL BOATS

NOTE: Unconfirmed reports in mid-1985 indicated that a South African "Minister" (Israeli Sa'ar IV)-class guided-missile patrol boat had been transferred to Taiwan. Negotiations in 1984 to purchase former U.S. Navy *Asheville*-class patrol boats *Asheville* (PG 84), *Marathon* (PG 89), and *Ready* (PG 87) from the Massachusetts Maritime Academy fell through, but decommissioned sisters *Gallup* (PG 85) and *Cannon* (PG 90) may still be transferred from the U.S. government.

◆ **50 Hai Ou class** Bldr: China SB, Kaohsiung (In serv. 1980-. . .)

Hai Ou class

D: 47 tons (fl) **S:** 36 kts **Dim:** 21.62 × 5.49 × 0.94 (1.82 props)
A: 2/Hsiung Feng SSM (I × 2)—2/12.7-mm mg (I × 2) **Electric:** 30 kw
Electron Equipt: Radar: 1/. . . nav., 1/RCA R76 **Man:** 10–12 tot.
M: 2 MTU 12V331 TC81 diesels; 2 props; 2,720 hp **Range:** 700/32

REMARKS: Design evidently based closely on the Israeli Dvora class; name means "Seagull." Have Kollmorgen Mk 35 optical sight, four AV-2 chaff RL (I × 4).

◆ **2 Lung Chiang class and 1 (+5 + . . .) Suikiang class**

	Bldr	In serv.
581 LUNG CHIANG	Tacoma Boatbldg, Tacoma, Wash.	15-5-78
582 N.	China SB, Kaohsiung	1979
583 SUIKIANG	China SB, Kaohsiung	1982
584 N.	China SB, Kaohsiung	1985

First Taiwan-built Lung Chiang on trials—not yet armed Tacoma, 1978

D: 218 tons (250 fl) **S:** 40 kts **Dim:** 50.14 (46.94 pp) × 7.60 × 2.26
A: 4/Hsiung Feng SSM—1/76-mm OTO Melara DP—2/30-mm Emerlec AA (II × 1)—2/12.7-mm mg (I × 2)
Electron Equipt: Radar: 1 navigational 1/RAN 11LX (NA 10 system) (583: see remarks)—EW: 4 AV-2 chaff RL (I × 4)
M: CODOG: 3 G.M. 12V149 TI diesels (3,600 hp), 3 AVCO-Lycoming TF-40A gas turbines; 3 CP props; 15,000 hp
Range: 700/40 (gas turbines), 1,900/30 (3 diesels); 2,700/12 (1 diesel)
Man: 5 officers, 30 men

REMARKS: Design is a variation of Tacoma Boatbuilding (U.S.) PSMM Mk-5 design. The Hsiung Feng missile is a copy of the Israeli Gabriel I. Prototype built in Korea, with follow-on units to be built in Taiwan. Third unit is of revised design, hence new class name; at least 6 are to be built, with the RCA R76C5 fire-control system.

PATROL CRAFT

◆ **2 (+20–24) Vosper design** Bldr: Vosper Pty, Singapore (In serv. 1985)

REMARKS: Prototypes for a cooperative construction program, with the remainder (if built) to be constructed in Taiwan. No data available, except 21 m oa, 40 kts from 2 Stewart & Stevenson 16V92 MTAB diesels, 2,430 hp; **A:** 1/20-mm AA, 2 mg.

◆ **10 or more aluminum-hulled** Bldr: China SB, Kaohsiung

D: 12 tons **S:** 25 kts **Dim:** 15.0 × . . . × . . .
A: 1/40-mm AA **M:** 2 diesels; water-jet drive

REMARKS: Date from 1971. There are believed to be a number of other small patrol craft of Taiwanese construction, for which no details are available.

MINE WARFARE SHIPS

NOTE: New mine countermeasures ships are badly needed to replace the following ships, which have considerably deteriorated. Negotiations with Van der Giessen de Noord in

MINE WARFARE SHIPS *(continued)*

the Netherlands during 1983-84 for six *Alkmaar* ("Tripartite")-class minehunters fell through. Recent reports indicate the possible ordering of two minehunters of the same type ordered by Thailand from Lürssen, Vegesack, West Germany; the ships would have a Krupp-Atlas sonar and carry Gaymarine "Pluto" minehunting, remote-controlled submersibles.

◆ **13 ex-U.S. and ex-Belgian Adjutant, MSC 268*, and MCS 289** classes of coastal minesweepers**

	Bldr	In serv.
. . . Yung An (ex-MSC 123)	. . .	6-55
. . . Yung Chen (ex-*Maaseick,* ex-MSC 78)	Adams Yacht, Quincy, Mass.	7-53
. . . Yung Chi (ex-*Charleroi,* ex-MSC 152)	Hodgdon Bros., Me.	2-54
. . . Yung Ching (ex-*Eakloo,* ex-MSC 101)	Hodgdon Bros., Me.	5-53
. . . Yung Chou (ex-MSC 278)*	Tacoma Boat, Wash.	7-59
. . . Yung Fu (ex-*Diest,* ex-*Macaw,* MSC 77)	Adams Yacht, Quincy, Mass.	5-53
. . . Yung Hsin (ex-MSC 302)**	Dorchester Bldrs., N.J.	3-65
. . . Yung Jen (ex-*St. Nicholas,* ex-MSC 64)	H. B. Nevins, N.Y.	2-54
. . . Yung Ju (ex-MSC 300)**	Tacoma Boat, Wash.	3-65
. . . Yung Lo (ex-MSC 306)**	Dorchester Bldrs., N.J.	4-66
. . . Yung Nien (ex-MSC 277)*	Tacoma Boat, Wash.	5-59
. . . Yung Shan (ex-*Lier,* ex-MSC 63)	H. G. Nevins, N.Y.	7-53
. . . Yung Sui (ex-*Diksmude,* ex-MSC 65)	H. B. Nevins, N.Y.	2-54

Yung Chi—Adjutant class, ex-Belgian, wearing old number 1970

Yung Chou—MSC 268 class, wearing old number 1970

Yung Lo—MSC 289 class, wearing old number 1970

D: 320 tons (378 fl) **S:** 12.5 kts **Dim:** 43.0 (41.5 wl) × 7.95 × 2.55
A: 2/20-mm AA (II × 1)
Electron Equipt: Radar: 1/Decca 45 or 707
Sonar: UQS-1D
M: 2 G.M. 8-268A diesels; 2 props; 1,200 hp (MSC 268 class; 4 G.M. 6-71 diesels; 2 props; 890 hp)
Fuel: 40 tons **Range:** 2,500/12 **Man:** 40 tot.

Remarks: Wooden hulls. All transferred on completion except ex-Belgian ships, transferred in 11-69. Have a variety of configurations, the ex-MSC 258 having a different propulsion scheme and the ex-MSC 289 class having a lower bridge and taller stack. Sister *Yung Ping* (ex-MSC 140) stricken 1982; several others soon to follow.

◆ **1 ex-U.S. minesweeping boat**

MSB 12 (ex-U.S. Navy MSB 4, ex-U.S. Army . . .)

D: 39 tons (fl) **S:** 12 kts **Dim:** 17.5 × 4.6 × 1.25
M: 2 Packard diesels; 2 props; 600 hp **Man:** 6 tot.

Remarks: Built in 1945 and transferred in 12-61. Wooden hull. Sister to South Korean MSB 1.

◆ **8 ex-U.S. minesweeping launches**

MSML 1 MSML 3 MSML 5 MSML 6 MSML 7 MSML 8 MSML 11 MSML 12

D: 24 tons (fl) **S:** 8 kts **Dim:** 15.29 × 3.96 × 1.31
M: 1 diesel; 1 prop, 60 hp **Range:** 800/8 **Man:** 4 tot.

Remarks: Built between 1943 and 1945, and converted from personnel launches before transfer in 3-61. Wooden hulls.

AMPHIBIOUS WARFARE SHIPS

◆ **1 command ship** Bldr: Dravo Corp., Neville I., Pittsburgh, Pa.

	L	In serv.
663 Kao Hsiung (ex-*Chung Hai,* LST 229, ex-*Dukes County,* LST 735)	11-3-44	26-4-44

Kao Hsiung (663)—wearing old number 1968

D: 1,650 tons (4,080 fl) **S:** 11 kts **Dim:** 99.98 × 15.24 × 3.4
A: 8/40-mm AA (II × 2, I × 4)—4/20-mm AA (II × 2)
Electron Equipt: Radar: 1/SPS-10, 1/SPS-12
M: 2 G.M. 12-567A diesels; 2 props; 1,700 hp **Range:** 15,000/9

Remarks: Transferred in 5-57, converted to command ship in 1964, with additional communications gear and radars. Retains bow doors.

◆ **1 ex-U.S. Cabildo-class dock landing ship** Bldr: Gulf SB, Chickasaw, Ala.

	Laid down	L	In serv.
618 Chen Hai (ex-*Fort Marion,* LSD 22)	15-9-44	22-5-45	29-1-46

D: 4,790 tons (9,375 fl) **S:** 15.6 kts **Dim:** 139.52 (138.38 wl) × 22.0 × 5.49
A: 12/40-mm AA (IV × 2, II × 2) **Electron Equipt:** Radar: 1/LN-66, 1/SPS-5
M: 2 sets GT; 2 props; 9,000 hp **Boilers:** 2; 30.6 kg/cm², 393°C
Fuel: 1,758 tons **Range:** 8,000/15 **Man:** 326 crew + several hundred troops

Remarks: Transferred by sale on 15-4-77, having been stricken from the U.S. Navy in 10-74. Modernized under FRAM-II program 12-59 to 4-60. Helicopter platform over 119.5 × 13.4 meter docking well, which can accommodate three LCUs, eighteen LCMs, or thirty-two amphibious armored troop carriers.

Note: *Ashland*-class, dock-landing ship *Chung Cheng* (639, ex-*Tung Hai,* ex-*White Marsh,* LSD 8) was stricken in 1984.

◆ **21 ex-U.S. LST 1 and LST 542-class tank landing ships**

	Bldr	In serv.
. . . Chung Cheng (ex-*Lafayette County,* LST 859)	Chicago B & I, Seneca, Ill.	29-12-44
. . . Chung Chi (ex-LST 1017)	Bethlehem, Fore River, Mass.	12-4-44
. . . Chung Chiang (ex-*San Bernardino County,* LST 1110)	Missouri Valley B & I, Evansville, Ind.	7-3-45
. . . Chung Chien (ex-LST 716)	Jeffersonville B & M, Ind.	18-8-44
. . . Chung Chih (ex-*Sagadohoc County,* LST 1091)	American Br., Ambridge, Pa.	6-4-45
. . . Chung Chuan (ex-LST 1030)	Boston Navy Yd.	19-7-44
619 Chung Fu (ex-*Iron County,* LST 840)	American Br., Ambridge, Pa.	11-12-44
697 Chung Hai (ex-LST 755)	American Br., Ambridge, Pa.	29-7-44
. . . Chung Hsing (ex-LST 557)	Missouri Valley B & I, Evansville, Ind.	5-5-44
. . . Chung Kuang (ex-LST 503)	Jeffersonville B & M, Ind.	14-12-43
691 Chung Lien (ex-LST 1050)	Dravo, Pittsburgh, Pa.	3-4-45
. . . Chung Ming (ex-*Sweetwater County,* LST 1152)	Dravo, Pittsburgh, Pa.	13-4-45
. . . Chung Pang (ex-LST 578)	Missouri Valley B & I, Evansville, Ind.	15-7-44
. . . Chung Sheng (ex-LST(H) 1033)	Chicago B & I, Seneca, Ill.	. . .-4-44
. . . Chung Shu (ex-LST 520)	Chicago B & I, Seneca, Ill.	28-2-44

AMPHIBIOUS WARFARE SHIPS *(continued)*

624 Chung Shun (ex-LST 732)	Dravo, Pittsburgh, Pa.	10-4-44
. . . Chung Suo (ex-*Bradley County,* LST 400)	Newport News SB & DD, Va.	7-1-43
. . . Chung Ting (ex-LST 537)	Missouri Valley B & I, Evansville, Ind.	9-2-44
. . . Chung Wan (ex-LST 535)	Missouri Valley B & I, Evansville, Ind.	4-2-44
. . . Chung Yeh (ex-*Sublette County,* LST 1144)	Chicago B & I, Seneca, Ill.	28-5-45
. . . Chung Yung (ex-LST 574)	Missouri Valley B & I, Evansville, Ind.	26-6-44

Chung Kuang—wearing old number 1969

D: 1,653 tons (4,080 fl) **S:** 11.6 kts **Dim:** 99.98 × 15.24 × 3.4
A: Several: 2/76.2-mm DP (I × 2)—6–8/40-mm AA (II × 2, or I × 2 or 4)—4–8/20-mm AA
M: 2 G.M. 12-567A diesels; 2 props; 1,700 hp **Electric:** 300 kw
Fuel: 569 tons **Range:** 15,000/9 **Man:** 100-125 tot.

Remarks: Six transferred in 1946, two in 1947, *Chung Shu* in 1948, seven in 1958, *Chung Yun* in 1959, *Chung Kuang* in 1960, *Chung Yeh* in 1961, and two subsequently. All extensively rebuilt during the late 1960s, in many cases becoming almost new ships; re-engined at the same time. Most have four pairs of Welin davits, while *Chung Chih, Chung Yung, Chung Sheng,* and *Chung Shu* have six, and *Chung Chien* has two; each pair of davits handles one LCVP. Five or more have two 76.2-mm guns. *Chung Chih* (ex-216, ex-LST 279) was stricken in 1978.

◆ **4 ex-U.S. LSM 1-class medium landing ships**

	Bldr	In serv.
637 Mei Lo (ex-LSM 362)	Brown SB, Houston, Tex.	11-1-45
659 Mei Ping	Brown SB, Houston, Tex.	23-2-45
694 Mei Sung (ex-LSM 457)	Western Pipe & Steel, San Pedro, Cal.	28-3-45
649 Mei Tseng (ex-LSM 431)	Dravo, Wilmington, Del.	25-2-45

Mei Tseng (649)—wearing old number 1969

D: 1,095 tons (fl) **S:** 12.5 kts **Dim:** 62.03 (59.89 wl) × 10.52 × 2.54 (max.)
A: 2/40-mm AA—4 or 8/20 mm AA (I or II × 4)—4/12.7 mm mg (I × 4)
M: *Mei Lo, Mei Ping:* 2 Fairbanks-Morse 38D8⅛ × 10 (others: 2 G.M. 16-278A) diesels; 2 props; 2,800 hp
Electric: 240 kw **Fuel:** 161 tons
Man: 60 tot.

Remarks: *Mei Sung* and *Mei Tseng* transferred in 1946, *Mei Ping* in 11-56, and *Mei Lo* in 5-62.

◆ **6 ex-U.S. LCU 1466-class utility landing craft** Bldr: Ishikawajima, Harima, Japan

. . . Ho Shan (ex-LCU 1596)	. . . Ho Meng (ex-LCU 1599)
. . . Ho Chuan (ex-LCU 1597)	. . . Ho Mou (ex-LCU 1600)
. . . Ho Seng (ex-LCU 1598)	. . . Ho Shou (ex-LCU 1601)

D: 347 tons (fl) **S:** 8 kts **Dim:** 35.08 × 10.36 × 1.6 (max.)
A: 4/20-mm AA (II × 2)
M: 3 Gray Marine 64/65YTL diesels; 3 props; 675 hp
Fuel: 11 tons **Range:** 1,200/6 **Man:** 14 tot.

Remarks: Built under Offshore Procurement Program. In service in 3-55. Cargo: 167 tons.

Ho Mou—wearing old number 1955

◆ **16 ex-U.S. LCU 501 (LCT (6))-class utility landing craft**

	In serv.		In serv.
. . . Ho Chang (ex-LCU 512)	7-9-43	. . . Ho Deng (ex-LCU 1367)	12-10-44
. . . Ho Chao (ex-LCU 1429)	8-12-44	. . . Ho Feng (ex-LCU 1397)	26-10-44
. . . Ho Cheng (ex-LCU 1145)	11-5-44	. . . Ho Hoei (ex-LCU 1218)	25-8-44
. . . Ho Chi (ex-LCU 1212)	16-8-44	. . . Ho Shun (ex-LCU 1225)	4-9-44
. . . Ho Chie (ex-LCU 700)	18-4-44	. . . Ho Teng (ex-LCU 1452)	20-10-44
. . . Ho Chien (ex-LCU 1278)	22-7-44	. . . Ho Tsung (ex-LCU 1213)	17-8-44
. . . Ho Chun (ex-LCU 892)	27-7-44	. . . Ho Yao (ex-LCU 1244)	22-9-44
. . . Ho Chung (ex-LCU 849)	7-8-44	. . . Ho Yung (ex-LCU 1271)	19-8-44

D: 143 tons (309 fl) **S:** 10 kts **Dim:** 36.3 (32.0 wl) × 9.96 × 1.14
A: 2/20-mm AA (I × 2)—2/12.7-mm mg
M: 3 G.M. 6-71 diesels; 3 props; 675 hp **Electric:** 20 kw **Man:** 10 tot.

Remarks: Six transferred between 1946 and 1948, the others between 1958 and 1959.

◆ **several hundred U.S. LCM (3)- and LCM (6)-class landing craft**

Bldrs: U.S. and Taiwan

D: 62 tons (fl) **S:** 9 kts **Dim:** 17.07 × 4.37 × 1.07
A: 1/20-mm AA or 12.7-mm mg in some
M: 2 Gray Marine 64HN9 diesels; 2 props; 450 hp **Range:** 130/9 **Man:** 9 tot.

Remarks: LCM (3) are 56 tons (fl), 15.38 m overall. Cargo: LCM (3): 30 tons, LCM (6): 34 tons.

◆ **about 100 U.S. LCVP class**

D: 13 tons (fl) **S:** 9 kts **Dim:** 10.9 × 3.21 × 1.04
A: 2/7.62-mm mg (I × 2) **M:** 1 Gray Marine 64HN9 diesel; 225 hp
Range: 110/9 **Man:** 3 tot.

Remarks: Most attached to LSTs and former APDs. Wooden construction. Cargo: 36 troops or 4 tons.

HYDROGRAPHIC SHIPS

◆ **1 ex-U.S. C1-M-AV1-class former transport** Bldr: Walter Butler SY, Duluth, Minn.

398 Chiu Hua (ex-*Sgt. George D. Keithley,* T-AGS 35, ex-T-APc 117, ex-*Acorn Knot*)

Chiu Hua—wearing old number 1972

D: 4,100 tons (6,090 fl) **S:** 11.5 kts **Dim:** 103.18 (97.54 wl) × 15.24 × 5.33
A: 1/40-mm AA—2/20-mm AA (I × 2)
M: 1 Nordberg TSM6 diesel; 1 prop; 1,750 hp **Man:** 72 tot.

Remarks: Completed in 1945 as a Maritime Commission cargo ship and taken over by the U.S. Army as a personnel transport. Transferred to the U.S. Navy in 1950 and converted for hydrographic-survey duties in 1966-67. Loaned to Taiwan on 29-3-72 and extended on 19-5-76; purchased outright 1981.

◆ **1 ex-U.S. Sotoyomo-class former auxiliary tug**

Bldr: Gulfport Boiler & Welding Works, Port Arthur, Tex.

	Laid down	L	In serv.
563 Chiu Lien (ex-*Geronimo,* ATA 207)	10-11-44	4-1-45	1-3-45

HYDROGRAPHIC SHIPS *(continued)*

Chiu Lien (563) 1969

D: 835 tons (fl) **S:** 13 kts **Dim:** 43.59 (40.74 wl) × 10.31 × 4.01
A: 1/20-mm AA **M:** 2 G.M. 12-278A diesels, electric drive; 1 prop; 1,500 hp
Electric: 120 kw **Fuel:** 158 tons **Man:** 45 tot.

REMARKS: Transferred in 2-69. Operated for the Institute of Oceanology and equipped with various oceanographic winches and laboratories.

◆ **1 ex-U.S. LSIL 351-class former landing craft**

Bldr: Albina Eng. & Mach. Works, Portland, Ore.

	Laid down	L	In serv.
466 LIEN CHANG (ex-LSIL 1017)	31-1-44	14-3-44	12-4-44

D: 387 tons (fl) **S:** 14.4 kts **Dim:** 48.46 (46.63 wl) × 7.21 × 1.73
A: 1/40-mm AA—4/20-mm AA (I × 4) **M:** 8 G.M. 6-71 diesels; 2 props; 2,320 hp
Fuel: 113 tons **Man:** 40 tot.

REMARKS: Transferred in 5-58. Retains LSIL appearance.

AUXILIARY SHIPS

◆ **1 offshore-island support tanker**

	Bldr	In serv.
512 WAN SHOU	Ujina SB, Hiroshima, Japan	1-11-69

Wan Shou (512) 1970

D: 1,049 tons light (4,150 fl) **S:** 13 kts **Dim:** 86.5 × 16.5 × 5.5
A: 2/40-mm AA (I × 2)—2/20-mm AA (I × 2)
M: 1 diesel; 1 prop; 2,100 hp **Fuel:** 230 tons **Man:** 70 tot.

REMARKS: No underway-replenishment capability. Cargo: 2,600 tons.

◆ **3 ex-U.S. Patapsco-class support tankers** Bldr: Cargill Inc., Savage, Minn.

	Laid down	L	In serv.
. . . CHANG PEI (ex-*Pecatonica,* AOG 57)	6-12-44	17-3-45	28-11-45
. . . HSIN LUNG (ex-*Elkhorn,* AOG 7)	7-9-42	15-5-43	12-2-44
515 LUNG CHUAN (ex-*Endeavor,* ex-*Namakagon,* AOG 53)	1-8-44	4-11-44	10-5-45

Lung Chuan (515)—no armament L. & L. Van Ginderen, 1979

D: 1,850 tons light (4,335 fl) **S:** 14 kts **Dim:** 94.72 (89.0 wl) × 14.78 × 4.78
A: 2/76.2-mm DP (I × 2)—4/20-mm AA (I × 4)
M: 2 G.M. 16-278A diesels; 2 props; 3,300 hp **Electric:** 460 kw
Fuel: 295 tons **Range:** 6,670/10 **Man:** 124 tot.

REMARKS: Former gasoline tankers. Cargo: 2,040 tons. *Chang Pei* transferred on 24-4-61, *Hsin Lung* on 1-7-72, and *Lung Chuan* on 29-6-71 after serving in the New Zealand Navy as Antarctic supply ship since 5-10-62. All used for supplying offshore islands. All purchased outright 19-5-76.

◆ **1 new-construction tender/transport** Bldr: Tsoying Naval SY

525 HAI TU (In serv. 2-85)

Hai Tu fitting out 1984

D: 3,040 tons (fl) **S:** . . . **Dim:** 101.0 × 17.0 × . . .
A: 3/40-mm AA (I × 3) **Electron Equipt:** Radar: 1/. . . nav.
M: 2 diesels; 2 props; . . . hp

REMARKS: Configuration indicates a possible stern docking well for landing craft or small missile boats of the Hai Ou class.

◆ **1 transport**

	Bldr	L	In serv.
522 LING YUEN	Taiwan SB, Keelung	27-1-75	15-8-75

D: 4,000 tons (fl) **S:** . . . **Dim:** 100.2 × 14.6 × 5.0
A: 2/20-mm AA (I × 2)—2/12.7-mm mg (I × 2)
M: 1 6-cylinder diesel; 1 prop; . . . hp **Man:** 55 tot.

REMARKS: 2,510 dwt/3,040 grt. Can carry 500 troops. There is also a slightly smaller Taiwanese-built transport, name not available.

◆ **1 ex-U.S. Achelous-class transport** Bldr: Kaiser Co., Vancouver, Wash.

	Laid down	L	In serv.
520 WU TAI (ex-*Sung Shan,* ex-*Agenor,* ARL 3, ex-LST 490)	24-1-43	3-4-43	20-8-43

D: 4,100 tons (fl) **S:** 11.6 kts **Dim:** 99.98 × 15.24 × 3.4
A: 8/40-mm AA (IV × 2) **M:** 2 G.M. 12-567A diesels; 2 props; 1,800 hp
Electric: 500 kw **Man:** 100 men + 600 troops

REMARKS: Converted to a repair ship while building. Transferred to France in 1951, then to Taiwan on 15-9-57. Converted to transport, 1973-74.

◆ **1 ex-U.S. Army 427-class small transport** Bldr: Higgins, New Orleans, La. (In serv. 21-12-44)

359 YUNG KANG (ex-*Mark,* AKL 12, ex-AG 143, ex-Army FS 214)

Yung Kang (359)—wearing old number 1971

AUXILIARY SHIPS *(continued)*

D: 693 tons (899 fl) **S:** 12 kts **Dim:** 54.86 (52.37 wl) × 9.75 × 3.05
A: 2/20-mm AA (I × 2) **M:** 2 G.M. 6-278A diesels; 2 props; 1,000 hp
Electric: 225 kw **Fuel:** 100 tons **Range:** 4,000/11
Man: 37 tot.

REMARKS: Built as an aircraft maintenance ship for the U.S. Army Air Corps. Transferred to the U.S. Navy on 30-9-47 and to Taiwan on 1-6-71. Sold outright on 19-5-76. Now has intelligence-gathering equipment.

◆ **1 ex-U.S. Amphion-class repair ship** Bldr: Tampa SB, Tampa, Fla.

	Laid	L	In serv.
521 YU TAI (ex-*Cadmus,* AR 14)	30-10-44	5-8-45	23-4-46

Yu Tai (521)—with MARISAT SATCOMM radome L. & L. Van Ginderen, 7-85

D: 7,826 tons light (14,490 fl) **S:** 16.5 kts
Dim: 149.96 (141.73 pp) × 21.18 × 8.38 **Electron Equipt:** Radar: 1/SPS-5
A: 1/127-mm DP—6/40-mm AA (II × 3)
M: 1 set Westinghouse GT; 2 prop; 8,500 hp **Electric:** 3,600 kw
Boilers: 2 Foster-Wheeler D-type; 30.6 kg/cm², 399°C **Fuel:** 2,430 tons
Man: 920 tot.

REMARKS: Transferred on 15-1-74.

◆ **1 ex-U.S. Diver-class salvage ship** Bldr: Basalt Rock Co., Napa, Cal.

	Laid down	L	In serv.
324 TAI HU (ex-*Grapple,* ARS 7)	8-9-42	31-12-42	16-12-43

D: 1,530 tons (1,900 fl) **S:** 14.8 kts **Dim:** 65.08 (63.09 wl) × 11.89 × 4.29
A: 2/20-mm AA (I × 2) **Electron Equipt:** Radar: 1/SPS-53
M: 4 Cooper-Bessemer GSB-8 diesels, electric drive; 2 props; 3,060 hp
Electric: 460 kw **Fuel:** 283 tons **Range:** 9,000/14; 20,000/7 **Man:** 85 tot.

REMARKS: Transferred on 1-12-77.

◆ **4 ex-U.S. Cherokee-, Abnaki-* and Achomawi-**class fleet tugs**

Bldrs: *Ta Tung, Ta Wan:* United Eng., Alameda, Cal.; others: Charleston SB & DD, Charleston, S.C.

	Laid down	L	In serv.
542 TA HAN (ex-*Tawakoni,* ATF 114)*	19-5-43	28-10-43	15-9-44
548 TA TUNG (ex-*Chickasaw,* ATF 83)	14-2-42	23-7-42	4-2-43
550 TA WAN (ex-*Apache,* ATF 67)	8-11-44	8-5-42	12-12-42
551 N. . . . . . . (ex-*Shakori,* ATF 162)**	9-5-45	9-8-45	20-12-45

D: 1,235 tons (1,675 fl) **S:** 15 kts **Dim:** 62.48 (59.44 wl) × 11.73 × 4.67
A: 1/76.2-mm DP—2/12.7-mm mg
M: 4 G.M. 12-278 diesels, electric drive; 1 prop; 3,000 hp **Electric:** 260–400 kw
Fuel: 295 tons **Range:** 6,500/16; 15,000/8 **Man:** 85 tot.

REMARKS: *Ta Tung* transferred 1-66 (sold on 19-5-75), *Ta Wan* on 30-6-74, *Ta Han* on 1-6-78, and ex-ATF 162 on 29-8-80. *Ta Han* has Busch-Sulzer BS-539 diesels and only a small exhaust pipe, and ex-ATF 162 has G.M. 12-278A diesels.

◆ **3 ex-U.S. Sotoyomo-class ocean tugs** Bldr: Levingston SB, Orange, Tex.

	Laid down	L	In serv.
395 TA PENG (ex-*Mohopac,* ATA 196)	24-11-44	21-12-44	6-3-45
357 TA SUEH (ex-*Tonkawa,* ATA 176)	30-1-44	1-3-44	19-8-44
367 TA TENG (ex-*Cahokia,* ATA 186)	16-8-44	18-9-44	24-11-44

D: 435 tons (835 fl) **S:** 13 kts **Dim:** 43.59 (40.74 wl) × 10.31 × 4.01
A: 1/76.2-mm DP—2/20-mm AA (I × 2)
M: 2 G.M. 12-278A diesels, electric drive; 1 prop; 1,500 hp
Electric: 120 kw **Fuel:** 158 tons **Man:** 45 tons

REMARKS: *Ta Peng* transferred on 1-7-71, *Ta Sueh* in 4-62, and *Ta Teng* on 29-3-72 after serving the U.S. Air Force since 1971. *Chiu Lien* is an oceanographic research ship.

SERVICE CRAFT

◆ **1 ex-U.S. 174-foot yard oiler** Bldr: Manitowoc SB, Manitowoc, Wisc.

	Laid down	L	In serv.
504 SZU MING (ex-YO 198)	10-2-45	21-4-45	14-7-45

D: 650 tons (1,595 fl) **S:** 10.5 kts **Dim:** 53.04 × 9.75 × 4.10
A: 1/40-mm AA—5/20-mm AA (I × 5)
M: 1 Union diesel; 1 prop; 560 hp **Man:** 65 tot.

REMARKS: Transferred in 12-49. In reserve.

◆ **6 ex-U.S. Navy YTL 422-class small harbor tugs**

YTL 8 (ex-ST-2002)	YTL 10 (ex-ST-2008)	YTL 12 (ex-YTL 584)
YTL 9 (ex-ST-2004)	YTL 11 (ex-YTL 454)	YTL 14 (ex-YTL 585)

D: 70 tons (80 fl) **S:** 8 kts **Dim:** 20.3 × 5.18 × 2.4
M: 1 diesel; 1 prop; 375 hp

REMARKS: YTL 8 to YTL 10 transferred in 3-62, YTL 11 in 8-63, YTL 12 and YTL 14 in 7-64. First three are former U.S. Army units, built during World War II.

◆ **1 ex-U.S. ARD 12-class floating dry dock** Bldr: Pacific Bridge, Alameda, Cal.

FO WU 6 (ex-*Windsor,* ARD 22)

Dim: 149.86 × 24.69 × 1.73 (light) **Capacity:** 3,500 tons

REMARKS: In service 4-44, transferred on 19-5-76; purchased 1981.

◆ **1 ex-U.S. ARD 2-class floating dry dock** Bldr: Pacific Bridge, Alameda, Cal.

FO WU 5 (ex-ARD 9)

Dim: 148.03 × 21.64 × 1.75 (light) **Capacity:** 3,500 tons

REMARKS: In service 9-43, transferred on 12-1-77; purchased outright 1981.

◆ **2 ex-U.S. floating dry docks** Bldr: V. P. Loftis, Wilmington, N.C.

HAY TAN (ex-AFDL 36) HAN JIH (ex-AFDL 34)

Dim: 73.15 × 19.69 × 1.3 (light) **Capacity:** 1,000 tons

REMARKS: In service 5- and 6-44, transferred in 3-47 and 7-59.

◆ **1 ex-U.S. floating dry dock**

KIM MEN (ex-AFDL 5)

Dim: 60.96 × 19.5 × 1.04 **Capacity:** 1,000 tons

REMARKS: Built in 1944, transferred in 1-48.

CUSTOMS SERVICE

Subordinate to the Ministry of Finance

PATROL SHIPS

◆ **1 or more 75-meter design** Bldr: . . . , Taiwan

REMARKS: A flush-decked design resembling South Korean Coast Guard "Sea Whale" design, but somewhat smaller. Armed with 1/40-mm AA and several 20-mm AA. Diesel-powered.

◆ **2 ex-U.S. Admirable-class former minesweepers**

	Bldr	L	In serv.
HUNG HSING (ex-*Embattle,* MSF 226)	American SB, Lorain, O.	17-9-44	25-4-45
N. . . . . . . (ex -*Improve,* MSF 247)	Savannah Mach., Ga.	26-9-43	29-2-44

D: 945 tons (fl) **S:** 14.8 kts **Dim:** 56.24 × 10.06 × 2.97
A: 2/20-mm AA **M:** 2 Cooper-Bessemer GSB-8 diesels; 2 props; 1,710 hp

REMARKS: Transferred to Taiwan in late 1940s and handed over to the Customs Service in early 1970s.

◆ **3 ex-U.S. PC 461-class submarine chasers**

	Bldr	In serv.
N. . . . . . . (ex-*Tung Kiang,* ex-*Placerville,* PC 1087)	G. Lawley, Neponset, Mass.	22-5-44
N. . . . . . . (ex-*Hsi Kiang,* ex-*Susanville,* PC 1149)	Defoe, Bay City, Mich.	22-6-44
N. . . . . . . (ex-*Pei Kiang,* ex-*Hanford,* PC 1142)	Defoe, Bay City, Mich.	3-6-44

D: 280 tons (450 fl) **S:** 19 kts **Dim:** 52.93 × 7.01 × 2.72
A: 2/20-mm AA (I × 2) **M:** 2 G.M. 16-278A diesels; 2 props; 2,880 hp
Electric: 120 kw **Fuel:** 62 tons **Range:** 6,000/10

REMARKS: Transferred in 7-57 and turned over to the Customs Service in early 1970s.

PATROL CRAFT

◆ **3 aluminum-hulled** Bldr: China SB, Kohsiung

HAI PING (In serv. 28-2-79) HAI AN (In serv. 18-3-79)
HAI CHENG (In serv. 1979)

D: . . . **S:** . . . **Dim:** 26.0 × 5.6 × 2.7
A: . . . **M:** 2 MTU 8V331 TC81 diesels; 2 props; . . . hp

◆ **2 aluminum-hulled** Bldr: Halter Marine, New Orleans (In serv. 1977)

D: 70 tons **S:** . . . **Dim:** 23.77 × . . . × . . . **A:** . . .
M: 2 G.M. diesels; 2 props; . . . hp

TANZANIA

United Republic of Tanzania

PERSONNEL (1985): Approximately 700 men

MERCHANT MARINE (1984): 39 ships — 58,699 grt
(4 tankers — 3,182 grt)

PATROL BOATS

◆ **4 modified North Korean Nampo class**

D: 82 tons (fl) **S:** 40 kts **Dim:** 27.7 × 6.1 × 1.8
A: 4/14.5-mm mg (II × 2) **Electron Equipt:** Radar: 1/Pot Head
M: 4 M50F diesels; 4 props; 4,800 hp **Range:** 375/40 **Man:** 19 tot.

REMARKS: Transferred 1979-81; lack the bow ramp employed on the landing craft version used by North Korea.

◆ **7 Chinese Shanghai-II class**

JW 9861 through JW 9867

JW 9862 1975

D: 122.5 tons (135 fl) **S:** 28.5 kts **Dim:** 38.78 × 5.41 × 1.55
A: 4/37-mm AA (II × 2) — 4/25-mm AA (II × 2)
Electron Equipt: Radar: 1/Pot Head
M: 2 M50F4, 1,200-hp diesels; 2 12D6, 910-hp diesels; 4 props; 4,220 hp
Electric: 39 kw **Endurance:** 7 days **Range:** 750/16.5 **Man:** 36 tot.

REMARKS: Transferred 1970-71.

TORPEDO BOATS

◆ **4 Chinese Huchuan class** Bldr: Hudung SY, Shanghai

JW 9841 through JW 9844

JW 9842 1976

D: 39 tons (45 fl) **S:** 50 kts **Dim:** 22.50 × 3.80 × 1.146
A: 4/14.5-mm mg (II × 2) — 2/533-mm TT (I × 2)
Electron Equipt: Radar: 1/Skin Head **Electric:** 5.6 kw
M: 3 M50 diesels; 3 props; 3,600 hp **Range:** 500/30 **Man:** 11 tot.

REMARKS: Transferred 1975. Unlike Chinese Navy Huchuans, these craft have no hydrofoils. Gunmounts are fore and aft, while on most units of this class both mounts are aft.

COASTAL PATROL CRAFT

◆ **2 East German Schwalbe-class former inshore minesweepers**

ARAKA SALAAM

D: 70 tons (fl) **S:** 14 kts **Dim:** 26.0 × 4.5 × 1.4
A: 2/25-mm AA (II × 2) **M:** 2 diesels; 2 props; 600 hp

REMARKS: Transferred in 1-66 and 1-67. Minesweeping gear removed. No radar.

◆ **4 Chinese Yu Lin-class craft**

D: 9.8 tons (fl) **S:** 25 kts **Dim:** 13.0 × 2.9 × 1.1
A: 2/12.7-mm mg (I × 2) **M:** 1 diesel; 1 prop; 300 hp

REMARKS: Transferred by the Chinese People's Republic in 11-66. These craft operate on Lake Victoria.

◆ **2 aluminum-hulled craft** Bldr: Bayerische Schiffsbau, West Germany, 1967

RAFIKI UHURU

D: 40 tons (fl) **S:** 14 kts **Dim:** 24.0 × 5.0 × 1.3
A: 1/40-mm AA — 2/mg **M:** 2 Caterpillar diesels; 2 props . . . hp

NOTE: The 3 ex-East German, ex-Soviet P-6 class converted torpedo boats and the one ex-Soviet Poluchat-1 class armed torpedo retriever were discarded by 1984.

MISCELLANEOUS UNITS

◆ **1 coastal survey craft** Bldr: Bayerische Schiffsbau, West Germany (In serv. 1979)

UTAFITI

D: 33 tons (fl) **S:** 14 kts **Dim:** 19.05 × . . . × 1.0
Electron Equipt: Radar: 1/Decca 060
M: 2 Caterpillar diesels; 2 props; 456 hp **Range:** 250/12 **Man:** 6 tot.

REMARKS: Has Atlas DESO 10 echo-sounder. Steel hull, aluminum superstructure.

◆ **2 ex-Chinese landing craft for logistics duties**

THAILAND

Kingdom of Thailand

PERSONNEL (1985): Navy: approximately 3,000 officers, 23,000 enlisted total — Marines: 1,000 officers, 19,000 enlisted

MERCHANT MARINE (1985): 225 ships — 517,444 grt
(tankers: 60 ships — 139,850 grt)

NAVAL AVIATION: Available are: 9 Grumman S-2F land-based ASW aircraft; 3 Fokker F-27 Maritime, 8 Nomad Searchwater, and 2 Cessna T-337 Skymaster for maritime surveillance; 2 CL-215 and 2 HU-16 amphibians; 20 C-46 and C-47 transports; 10 Cessna 0-1 Bird Dog observation aircraft; 14 U-17 Skywagon utility aircraft, 2 Lake L-A4 Skimmer training amphibians; and 3 Bell UH-1H and 10 Bell 212 helicopters. Fourteen Marconi Stingray ASW torpedoes were ordered 9-84 for the F-27 Maritimes and for the new U.S.-built corvettes. A fourth Fokker F-27 has been ordered, for delivery mid-1986.

SUBMARINES

NOTE: The Thai Navy planned to order three submarines during 1985. Negotiations have been under way in 1983 with a number of submarine builders, with China (Romeo class), Italy, and West Germany as the leading contenders.

FRIGATES

◆ **1 "Yarrow frigate" class** Bldr: Yarrow, Scotstoun, Glasgow, Scotland

	Laid down	L	In serv.
7 MAKUT RAJAKUMARN	11-1-70	18-11-71	7-5-73

Makut Rajakumarn (7) — prior to modernization R.A.N., 1981

D: 1,650 tons (1,900 fl) **S:** 26 kts (gas turbines)/18 kts (diesel)
Dim: 97.56 (92.99 pp) × 10.97 × 5.5
A: 2/114-mm DP Mk 8 — 2/40-mm AA (I × 2) — 1/Limbo ASW mortar (III × 1) — 2/d.c. projectors, 1/d.c. rack
Electron Equipt: Radar: 1/Decca 626, 1/H.S.A. DA-05, 1/H.S.A. WM-22
Sonar: 1/170B, 1/162, 1/Plessey MS27
M: CODOG: 1 Rolls-Royce Olympus TBM 3B gas turbine (23,125 hp), 1 Crossley-Pielstick 12 PC2 diesel; 2 CP props; 6,000 hp
Electric: 2,200 kw **Range:** 1,000/25; 4,000/18 **Man:** 16 officers, 124 men

FRIGATES *(continued)*

REMARKS: Similar to the Malaysian *Rahmat* but longer and more heavily armed. Highly automated. The WM-22 track-while-scan radar controls the 114-mm guns. Modernized 1984: new air-search radar; Sea Cat missile launcher and director deleted.

◆ 2 ex-U.S. PF 103 class

	Bldr	Laid down	L	In serv.
5 TAPI (ex-PF 107)	American SB, Toledo, Oh.	1-4-70	17-10-70	1-11-71
6 KHIRIRAT (ex-PF 108)	Norfolk SB & DD, Va.	18-2-72	2-6-73	10-8-74

Tapi (5)—as modernized (composite view) 1983

D: 864 tons light (1,143 fl) **S:** 20 kts **Dim:** 84.04 × 10.06 × 3.05 (4.27 sonar)
A: 1/76-mm OTO Melara Compact DP—1/40-mm AA—2/20-mm AA (I × 2)—2/12.7-mm mg (I × 2)—6/324-mm Mk 32 ASW TT (III × 2)—1/Mk 9 d.c. rack
Electron Equipt: Radar: 1/Raytheon navigational, 1/SPS-6, 1/H.S.A. WM-25
Sonar: 1/SQS-17A
M: 2 Fairbanks-Morse 38D8⅛-10 diesels; 2 props; 5,300 hp **Electric:** 750 kw
Fuel: 110 tons **Range:** 2,400/18 **Man:** 15 officers, 135 men

REMARKS: Ordered 27-6-69 and 25-6-71, respectively. Patterned after the Italian-built *Pattimura* class for Indonesia; four sisters built for the Iranian Navy. *Tapi* completed modernization in 1983 with the OTO Melara gun replacing the forward U.S. 76.2-mm mount, a Bofors 40-mm on a raised bandstand replacing the aft 76.2-mm mount, 2 single 20-mm AA replacing the original twin 40-mm mount, and an H.S.A. WM-25 track-while-scan radar director being mounted above the bridge; a Hedgehog ASW mortar was removed. *Khirirat* in modernization 1985-86.

◆ 1 ex-U.S. Cannon class Bldr: Western Pipe and Steel, Los Angeles

	Laid down	L	In serv.
3 PIN KLAO (ex-*Hemminger,* DE 746)	8-5-43	27-12-43	30-5-44

Pin Klao (3) 1980

D: 240 tons (fl) **S:** 20 kts **Dim:** 93.27 (91.44 wl) × 11.15 × 4.3 (sonar)
A: 3/76.2-mm DP Mk 22 (I × 3)—6/40-mm AA (II × 3)—2/12.7-mm mg (I × 2)—1/Mk 10 Hedgehog—6.324-mm Mk 32 ASW TT (III × 2)—8/Mk 6 d.c. projectors—2/Mk 9 d.c. racks
Electron Equipt: Radar: 2/navigational, 1/SC-2, 1/Mk 26, 1/Mk 34
Sonar: . . .
EW: WLR-1
M: 2 G.M. 16-278A diesels, electric drive; 2 props; 6,000 hp **Electric:** 680 kw
Fuel: 260 tons **Range:** 11,500/11 **Man:** 220 tot.

REMARKS: Transferred 7-59; sold outright 6-6-75, at which time the ship underwent extensive overhaul in Guam. Has Mk 52 radar GFCS for 76.2-mm guns, one Mk 63 radar GFCS and two Mk Mod. 2 optical GFCS for the 40-mm guns. To replace *Maeklong* as cadet training ship when corvette *Ratanakosin* is delivered.

◆ 2 ex-U.S. Tacoma class Bldr: Consolidated Steel, Los Angeles

	Laid down	L	In serv.
1 TAHCHIN (ex-*Glendale,* PF 36)	6-4-43	28-5-43	1-10-43
2 PRASAE (ex-*Gallup,* PF 47)	18-8-43	17-9-43	29-2-44

Tahchin 1977

D: 1,430 tons (2,100 fl) **S:** 19 kts **Dim:** 92.63 (87.02 pp) × 11.43 × 4.17 (hull)
A: 3.76.2-mm DP (I × 3)—2/40-mm AA (I × 2)—9/20-mm AA (I × 9)—1/Mk 10 Hedgehog—2/324-mm Mk 32 ASW TT (I × 2)—8/Mk 6 d.c. projectors—2/Mk 9 d.c. racks
Electron Equipt: Radar: 2/. . . nav., 1/SPS-6—Sonar: QCU
M: 2 sets triple-expansion steam; 2 props; 5,500 hp
Boilers: 2, 3-drawn Express; 16.9 kg/cm² **Fuel:** 685 tons
Range: 5,600/16; 7,800/12 **Man:** 180 tot.

REMARKS: Transferred 29-10-57. Both refitted at Guam in the early 1970s. Last active examples of a class that once numbered 100 ships. To be stricken with delivery of the *Ratanakosin*-class corvettes. Both used primarily for training.

CORVETTES

◆ 0 (+2 + 1) PFMM Mk 16 class Bldr: Tacoma Boatbldg., Tacoma, Wash.

	Laid down	L	In serv.
. . . RATANAKOSIN	6-2-84	-85	1986
. . . SUKHOTHAI	26-3-84	-86	1987

D: 840 tons normal (890 fl) **S:** 26 kts **Dim:** 76.82 × 9.55 × 2.44
A: 8/Harpoon SSM (IV × 2)—1/Albatros SAM system (VIII × 1, . . . Aspide missiles)—1/76-mm OTO Melara DP—2/40-mm Breda AA (II × 1)—2/20-mm AA (I × 2)—6/324-mm Mk 32 ASW TT (III × 2)
Electron Equipt: Radar: 1/. . . nav., 1/H.S.A. DA-05, 1/H.S.A. WM-25
Sonar: Krupp-Atlas
EW: Elettronica intercept; Dagaie chaff RL
M: 2 MTU 20V1163 TB83 diesels; 2 props; 14,730 hp

REMARKS: Ordered 9-5-83 for delivery in 1985-86. Enlarged version of Saudi Arabian PCG class. Will have H.S.A. Mini-SADOC weapons control. A third unit may be built in Thailand. Program slowed by builder's financial problems.

GUIDED-MISSILE PATROL BOATS

◆ 3 Ratcharit class Bldr: Breda, Venice, Italy

	L	In serv.
4 RATCHARIT	30-7-78	10-8-79
5 WITTHAYAKOM	2-9-78	12-11-79
6 UDOMET	28-9-78	21-2-80

Ratcharit (4) French Navy, 1980

D: 235 tons light (270 fl) **S:** 36 kts **Dim:** 49.8 (47.25 pp) × 7.5 × 1.68
A: 4/MM 38 Exocet (II × 2)—1/76-mm DP OTO Melara—1/40-mm AA Breda
Electron Equipt: Radar: 1/navigational, 1/H.S.A. M-25
M: 3 MTU MD20 V538 TB91 diesels; 3 CP props; 13,500 hp
Electric: 440 kw **Range:** 650/36; 2,000/15
Man: 7 officers, 38 men

REMARKS: Ordered 23-7-76. Can make 20 kts on two engines.

GUIDED-MISSILE PATROL BOATS *(continued)*

◆ **3 Prabrarapak class** Bldr: Singapore SB & Eng. Co., Jurong, Singapore

	L	In serv.
1 Prabrarapak	29-7-75	28-7-76
2 Hanhak Sattru	28-10-75	6-11-76
3 Suphairin	20-2-76	1-2-77

Hanhak Sattru (2) G. Arra, 1981

D: 224 tons (260 fl) **S:** 41 kts **Dim:** 44.9 × 7.0 × 2.1 (2.46 props)
A: 5/Gabriel-I (III × 1, I × 2)—1/57-mm Bofors AA—1/40-mm Bofors AA
Electron Equipt: Radar: 1/Decca TM 626, 1/H.S.A. WM-28
EW: passive intercept system
M: 4 MTU 16V538 TB92 diesels; 4 props; 14,000 hp **Electric:** 405 kVA
Range: 500/38.5; 1,500/16 **Man:** 40 tot.

Remarks: Similar to the Singapore Navy's Lürssen-designed boats; built under license, 103-mm rocket flare launch rails are mounted on the 57-mm mount.

PATROL BOATS

◆ **4 (+2) PSMM Mk 5 class** Bldr: Ital-Thai SY, Samutprakarn

	Laid down	L	In serv.
4 Sattahip	15-1-82	27-7-83	16-9-83
5 Klongyai	. . .	9-3-84	5-84
6 Takbai	. . .	25-5-84	7-84
7 Katang	. . .	26-10-84	14-10-85
8 Thepa	. . .	. . .	. . .
9 Thai Muang	. . .	. . .	. . .

D: 270 tons (300 fl) **S:** 22 kts **Dim:** 50.14 (47.22 wl) × 7.30 × 1.58 (1.80 props)
A: 1/76.2-mm U.S. Mk 26 DP—1/40-mm AA—2/20-mm AA (I × 2)—2/12.7-mm mg
Electron Equipt: Radar: 1/. . . nav.
M: 2 MTU 16V538 TB91 diesels; 2 props; 6,840 hp
Electric: 420 kw **Fuel:** 80 tons **Range:** 2,500/15 **Man:** 56 tot.

Remarks: First four ordered 9-9-81, others on 27-12-83 and 31-8-84. NA 18 GFCS.

◆ **3 MV 400th design** Bldr: Breda, Puerto Marghera, Venice, Italy

	Laid down	L	In serv.
1 Chonburi	15-8-81	7-6-82	22-2-83
2 Songkhla	15-9-81	6-9-82	12-83
3 Phuket	15-12-81	3-2-83	5-84

Chonburi (1) U.S. Navy, 1983

Songkhla (2) *Ships of the World,* 1983

D: 400 tons (450 fl) **S:** 30 kts **Dim:** 60.40 (57.50 pp) × 8.80 × 1.95
A: 2/76-mm OTO Melara DP—2/40-mm Breda AA (II × 1)
Electron Equipt: Radar: 1/H.S.A. ZW-06, 1/H.S.A. WM-22/61, 1/H.S.A. LIROD
EW: passive intercept, 4/Hycor Mk 135 chaff RL (VI × 4)
M: 2 MTU 20V538 TB92 diesels; 3 CP props; 15,000 hp (12,600 sust.)
Electric: 800 kw **Range:** 900/29; 2,500/18 **Man:** 7 officers, 38 men

Remarks: Ordered 11-79, originally for delivery in 1982, but this slipped considerably. First unit delivered 29-11-82 by shipyard. Able to accommodate anti-ship missiles, but none were to be installed at delivery. Steel hull, aluminum-alloy superstructure. Have LIROD-8 radar optronic GFCS to back up the WM-22/61 system. The chaff system is the same as the U.S. Navy's Mk 36 SRBOC.

◆ **6 (+ . . .) T 93 class** Bldr: Royal Thai Navy Dockyard, Bangkok

T 93 (L: 1973) T 94 (In serv. 16-9-81) T 95 (In serv. 1981)
T 96 (In serv. 1982) T 97 (In serv. 16-9-83) T 98 (In serv. 1984)

T 95 1983

D: 117 tons (125 fl) **S:** 25 kts **Dim:** 34.00 (32.00 wl) × 5.70 × 1.40 (1.65 props)
A: 2/40-mm 60-cal. AA (I × 2)—2/12.7-mm mg (I × 2)
Electron Equipt: Radar: 1/Decca . . .
M: 2 MTU 12V538 TB81 diesels; 2 props; 3,300 hp **Man:** 16 tot.

Remarks: Revised version of T 91 design.

◆ **2 T 91 class** Bldr: Royal Thai Naval Dockyard, Bangkok

T 91 (L: 1965) T 92 (L: 1973)

T 92 G. Arra, 1976

D: 87.5 tons **S:** 25 kts **Dim:** 31.8 × 5.36 × 1.5
A: 2/40-mm AA (I × 2)—2/12.7-mm mg (I × 2) **Electron Equipt:** Radar: 1/Decca . . .
M: 2 MTU diesels; 2 props; 3,300 hp
Range: 770/21 **Man:** 21 tot.

Remarks: T 91 has a longer superstructure and no spray strakes on the hull sides forward, and only one 40-mm AA gun. In refit 1984-85.

PATROL BOATS *(continued)*

◆ **10 ex-U.S. PGM 71 class** Bldr: Peterson Builders, Sturgeon Bay, Wis.

	L	In serv.		L	In serv.
T 11 (ex-PGM 71)	22-5-65	1-2-66	T 16 (ex-PGM 115)	24-4-69	12-2-70
T 12 (ex-PGM 79)	18-12-65	1967	T 17 (ex-PGM 116)	3-6-69	12-2-70
T 13 (ex-PGM 107)	13-4-67	28-8-67	T 18 (ex-PGM 117)	24-6-69	12-2-70
T 14 (ex-PGM 113)	3-6-69	18-8-69	T 19 (ex-PGM 123)	4-5-70	25-12-70
T 15 (ex-PGM 114)	24-6-69	18-8-69	T 20 (ex-PGM 124)	22-6-70	10-70

T 11 G. Arra, 1967

D: 130 tons (144 fl) **S:** 17 kts **Dim:** 30.81 × 6.45 × 2.3
A: 1/40-mm AA—2/20-mm AA (II × 1)—2/12.7-mm mg (I × 2)—1/81-mm mortar
M: 8 G.M. 6-71 diesels; 2 props; 2,040 hp **Range:** 1,000/12 **Man:** 30 tot.

REMARKS: An over-and-under 81-mm mortar/12.7-mm mounting has replaced the original 20-mm AA gun on the fantail.

◆ **3 ex-U.S.C.G. Cape class** Bldr: U.S. Coast Guard, Curtis Bay, Md. (In serv. 1953)

T 81 (ex-CG 13) T 82 (ex-CG 14) T 84 (ex-CG 16)

T 84—with old number 1967

D: 105 tons (fl) **S:** 18 kts **Dim:** 28.95 × 5.8 × 1.55
A: 1/20-mm AA—2/Mk 20 Mousetrap ASW RL—2/d.c. racks
Electron Equipt: Radar: 1/SPN-21
Sonar: QCU
M: 4 Cummins VT-12-M-700 diesels; 2 props; 2,200 hp **Electric:** 40 kw
Fuel: 12 tons **Range:** 2,600/9 **Man:** 15 tot.

REMARKS: Transferred in 1954. Sister T 83 stricken 1982.

◆ **5 ex-U.S. PC 461 class**

	Bldr	L	In serv.
1 SARASIN (ex-PC 495)	Dravo, Pittsburgh	30-12-41	23-4-42
4 PHALI (ex-PC 1185)	Gibbs, Jacksonville, Fla.	27-8-43	24-4-44
5 SUKRIP (ex-PC 1218)	Luders, Stamford, Conn.	24-10-43	29-5-44
6 TONGPLIU (ex-PC 616)	G. Lawley, Neponset, Mass.	4-7-42	19-8-42
7 LIULOM (ex-PC 1253)	Brown, Houston, Tex.	14-10-42	1-4-43

D: 280 tons (450 fl) **S:** 19 kts **Dim:** 52.93 × 7.01 × 2.31 (3.31 sonar)
A: 1/75.2-mm DP—1/40-mm AA—5/20-mm AA (I × 5)—2/324-mm Mk 32 ASW TT (I × 2)—2/Mk 6 d.c. projectors—2 d.c. racks
M: 2 Hoover, Owens, & Rentschler RB-99DA diesels; 2 props; 2,560 hp
Electric: 120 kw **Fuel:** 60 tons **Range:** 6,000/10 **Man:** 62–71 tot.

Tongpliu (6)—outboard the now-stricken *Thayanchon*

REMARKS: In poor condition. Transferred 1947-52. *Sarasin* does not have the two fixed ASW torpedo tubes. *Tongpliu* and *Liulom* have two Fairbanks-Morse 38D8⅛ diesels; 2,880 hp. Sister *Thayanchon* (2, ex-PC 575) stricken 1982; *Longlom* (8, ex-PC 570) in 1984; the others are overdue to follow.

PATROL CRAFT

◆ **0 (+1) Hysacat 18 class** Bldr: Tecnautic, Thailand

REMARKS: 40-ton, 36-kt prototype to deliver late 1986.

◆ **16 T 213 class** Bldr: Ital-Thai Development Co., Bangkok

	In serv.		In serv.
T 213	29-8-80	T 221	16-9-81
T 214	29-8-80	T 222	16-9-81
T 215	29-8-80	T 223	16-9-81
T 216	26-3-81	T 224	19-11-81
T 217	26-3-81	T 225	28-3-84
T 218	26-3-81	T 226	28-3-84
T 219	16-9-81	T 227	1984
T 220	16-9-91	T 228	1984

T 216—alongside T 92 1981

D: 34 tons (fl) **S:** 22 kts (18 sust.) **Dim:** 19.8 × 5.3 × 1.5
A: 1/20-mm AA—1/12.7-mm mg—1/81-mm mortar
Electron Equipt: Radar: 1/Decca 110
M: 2 MTU diesels; 2 props; 1,300 hp **Man:** 1 officer, 7 men

REMARKS: Aluminum construction. Intended for fisheries protection duties.

◆ **12 ex-U.S. Swift Mk II-class inshore patrol craft** Bldr: Swiftships, Morgan City, La.

T 27 through T 35 T 210 through T 212

D: 22.5 tons (fl) **S:** 25 kts **Dim:** 15.64 × 4.14 × 1.06
A: 3/12.7-mm mg (II × 1, and 1 combined with an 81-mm mortar)
Electron Equipt: Radar: 1/Raytheon 1500B **Range:** 400/24
M: 2 G.M. 12V71 N diesels; 2 props; 860 hp **Man:** 1 officer, 7 men

REMARKS: Transferred 1967-75.

◆ **37 ex-U.S. PBR Mk II river patrol boats**

D: 8 tons (fl) **S:** 24 kts **Dim:** 9.73 × 3.53 × 0.6
A: 3/12.7-mm mg (II × 1, I × 1)—1/60-mm mortar
M: 2 Detroit 6V53 N diesels; 2 Jacuzzi waterjets; 430 hp
Range: 150/23 **Man:** 4 tot.

REMARKS: Transferred: 20 in 1966-67; 10 in 1972; 7 in 1973. Employed on upper Mekong River.

◆ **3 ex-U.S. 36-foot RPC class**

T 21 T 22 T 23

D: 10.4 tons (13 fl) **S:** 14 kts **Dim:** 10.9 × 3.15 × 1.0
A: 4/12.7-mm mg (II × 2)—2/7.62-mm mg (I × 2)
M: 2 Gray Marine 64 HN9 diesels; 2 props; 450 hp **Man:** 6 tot.

REMARKS: Transferred 3-67. Survivors of six. Unsuccessful design, supplanted by PBR in the U.S. Navy. Employed on upper Mekong River.

MINE WARFARE SHIPS

◆ **1 mine countermeasures support ship**

	Bldr	L	In serv.
1 Thalang	Bangkok Naval DY	. . .	4-8-80

D: 1,000 tons (fl) **S:** 12 kts **Dim:** 55.7 × 10.0 × 3.1
A: 1/40-mm AA—2/20-mm AA (I × 2)—2/12.7-mm mg (I × 2)—mines
Electron Equipt: Radar: 1/Decca TM 1226
M: 2 MTU diesels; 2 props; 1,310 hp **Man:** 77 tot.

Remarks: Replaces *Rang Kwien* (11), stricken 1979. Designed by Ferostaal, Essen, Germany. Has two 3-ton cranes and carries four sets of spare mine countermeasures equipment for transfer to minesweepers.

◆ **0 (+2 + 2) new-construction minehunters** Bldr: Lürssen, Vegesack

	L	In serv.		L	In serv.
. . . N. . .	. . .	1986	. . . N. . .	. . .	4-87

D: 448 tons (fl) **S:** 16 kts **Dim:** 48.00 (45.50 pp) × 3.30 × 2.56
A: 3/20-mm AA (I × 3)
Electron Equipt: Radar: 1/. . . nav.
Sonar: Krupp-Atlas MNS-80
M: 2 MTU 12V396 TB83-DB51L diesels; 2 props; 2,940 hp
Range: 2,000/12 **Man:** 40 tot.

Remarks: First unit ordered 31-8-84, second (with option for two more) in 6-85. Wooden construction. Will carry two Gaymarine Pluto remote-controlled minehunting and disposal submersibles. May also have a 40-mm AA in addition to the armament listed.

◆ **4 ex-U.S. MSC 289-class minesweepers**

	Bldr	In serv.
5 Ladya (ex-MSC 297)	Peterson, Sturgeon Bay, Wis.	14-12-63
6 Bangkeo (ex-MSC 303)	Dorchester SB, Camden, N.J.	9-7-65
7 Tadindeng (ex-MSC 301)	Tacoma Boat, Wash.	23-8-65
8 Don Chedi (ex-MSC 313)	Peterson, Sturgeon Bay, Wis.	17-9-65

Bangkeo (6) 1967

D: 330 tons (362 fl) **S:** 13 kts **Dim:** 44.32 × 8.29 × 2.6
A: 2/20-mm AA (II × 1)
Electron Equipt: Radar: 1/Decca 707
Sonar: UQS-1D

D: 4 G.M. 6-71 diesels; 2 props; 1,000 hp (880 sust.)
Range: 2,500/10 **Man:** 7 officers, 36 men

Remarks: Transferred on completion. Wooden construction.

◆ **5 ex-U.S. 50-foot motor-launch minesweepers**

MLMS 6 to MLMS 10

D: 21 tons (fl) **S:** 8 kts **Dim:** 15.29 × 4.01 × 1.31
A: Small arms only
M: 1 Navy DB diesel; 1 prop; 50 hp
Range: 150/8 **Man:** 6 tot.

Remarks: Transferred 1963-66. Wooden-hulled former personnel launches, converted before transfer.

AMPHIBIOUS WARFARE SHIPS

◆ **0 (+2 + 4) PS 700** Bldr: Ital-Thai SY, Samatprakarn

	Laid down	L	In serv.
. . . Sichang	. . .	. . .	. . .
. . . N. . .	. . .	. . .	. . .

D: 2,800 tons (fl) **S:** 15 kts **Dim:** 100.00 × 15.65 × 2.6
A: . . . **Electron Equipt:** Radar: . . .
M: 2 diesels; 2 CP props; 5,340 hp
Range: 4,000/14 **Man:** 35 crew + 240 troops

Remarks: Details not certain. Reported to be same design as Libyan *Ibn Ouf* class, to be built under license from Chantiers du Nord et de la Mediterraneé, La Seyne, France. Two units authorized 7-84, with four more planned, to replace World War II-era ex-U.S. units. Displacement also reported as 3,540 tons and engines as 2 MTU 20V1163 TB62 for 10,000 hp, 16 kts, and a range of 7,000 n.m. at 12 kts.

◆ **4 ex-U.S. LST 542-class tank-landing ships**

	Bldr	L	In serv.
2 Chang (ex-*Lincoln Cty.*, LST 898)	Dravo, Pittsburgh	25-11-44	29-12-44
3 Pangan (ex-*Stark Cty.*, LST 1134)	Chicago Br. & Iron, Ind.	16-3-45	7-4-45
4 Lanta (ex-*Stone Cty.*, LST 1141)	Chicago Br. & Iron, Ind.	18-4-45	9-5-45
5 Prathong (ex-*Dodge Cty.*, LST 722)	Jeffersonville Br. & Mach. Co., Ind.	21-8-44	13-9-44

D: 1,625 tons (4,080 fl) **S:** 11 kts **Dim:** 99.98 × 15.24 × 4.36
A: 8/40-mm AA (II × 2, I × 4)
Cargo capacity: 2,100 tons
M: 2 G.M. 12-567A diesels; 1,700 hp

Remarks: The *Chang* was transferred in 8-62, the *Pangan* in 5-66, the *Lanta* on 12-3-70, and the *Prathong* on 17-12-75. The *Chang* has a reinforced bow and waterline, originally intended for arctic navigation.

◆ **3 ex-U.S. LSM 1-class medium landing ships**

Bldrs: Pullman Standard Car Mfg. Co., Chicago (3: Brown SB, Houston, Tex.)

	Laid down	L	In serv.
1 Kut (ex-LSM 338)	17-8-44	5-12-44	10-1-45
2 Phai (ex-LSM 333)	13-7-44	27-10-44	25-11-44
3 Kram (ex-LSM 469)	27-1-45	17-2-45	17-3-45

Kram (3) 1967

D: 743 tons (1,095 fl) **S:** 12.5 kts **Dim:** 62.03 × 10.52 × 2.54
A: 2/40-mm AA (II × 1) (1, 2: 1/40-mm AA)—4/20-mm AA (I × 4)
Electron Equipt: Radar: 1/Raytheon 1500B Pathfinder (3: 1/SPS-5)
M: 2 Fairbanks-Morse 38D8⅛ diesels; 2 props; 2,800 hp
Range: 2,500/12 **Man:** 55 tot.

Remarks: The *Kut* and *Phai* were transferred in 10-46, the *Kram* on 25-5-62. *Kram* has a Mk 51 Mod. 2 optical lead-computing director for the 40-mm guns.

◆ **1 ex-U.S. LCI(M) 351-class infantry-landing ship** Bldr: Commercial Iron Works, Portland, Ore.

	Laid down	L	In serv.
2 Satakut (ex-LSIM 739)	30-1-44	27-2-44	6-3-44

Satakut (2) G. Arra, 1980

D: 231 tons (381 fl) **S:** 14 kts **Dim:** 48.46 × 7.21 × 1.73
A: 1/40-mm AA—4/20-mm AA (I × 4)
Electron Equipt: Radar: 1/Raytheon 1500B
M: 8 G.M. 6-71 diesels; 2 CP props; 1,320 hp
Electric: 40 kw **Fuel:** 113 tons **Man:** 53 tot.

Remarks: Originally one of 60 LCIL (later LSIL) converted to carry three 107-mm chemical mortars, removed before transfer in 5-47. Now used as personnel landing craft. Sister *Prab* (ex-LCI(M) 739) exists as a hulk.

AMPHIBIOUS WARFARE SHIPS *(continued)*

◆ **1 ex-U.S. LSSL 1-class support landing craft** Bldr: Commercial Iron Works, Portland, Ore.

	Laid down	L	In serv.
3 NAKHA (ex-*Himiwari*, ex-LSSL 102)	13-1-45	3-2-45	17-2-45

D: 233 tons (387 fl) **S:** 14 kts **Dim:** 48.16 × 10.52 × 2.54
A: 1/76.2-mm DP Mk 22—4/40-mm AA (II × 2)—4/20-mm AA (I × 4)—4/12.7-mm mg (I × 4)—4/81-mm mortars (I × 4)
Electron Equipt: Radar: 1/Raytheon 1500B Pathfinder
M: 8 G.M. 6-71 diesels; 2 CP props; 1,320 hp **Electric:** 120 kw **Fuel:** 84 tons

REMARKS: Transferred to Japan in 7-59 and to Thailand in 10-66 on return to U.S. control. Used mainly as a tender to small patrol craft.

◆ **4 (+1) Thong Kaeo-class utility landing craft** Bldr: Bangkok Naval DY

7 THONG KAEO (In serv. 23-12-82)
8 THONGLANG (In serv. 19-4-83)
9 WANG NOK (In serv. 16-9-83)
10 WANG NAI (In serv. 11-11-83)
11 N. . .(In serv. . . .)

D: 200 tons (396 fl) **S:** 10 kts **Dim:** 41.0 × 9.0 × 2.1
A: 1/20-mm AA—2/12.7-mm mg (I × 2)
M: 2 G.M. 16V71N diesels; 2 props; 1,400 hp **Range:** 1,200/10
Man: 3 officers, 29 men

REMARKS: Based on U.S. LCU 1626 class. First four ordered 1980, fifth (with 2/20-mm AA) ordered 1984.

◆ **5 ex-U.S. LCU 501-class utility landing craft**

	Bldr	L	In serv.
1 MATAPHON (ex-LCU 1260)	Quincy Barge, Ill.	29-7-44	8-9-44
2 RAWI (ex-LCU 800)	Mt. Vernon Br. Co., Oh.	14-6-44	16-6-44
3 ADANG (ex-LCU 861)	Darby, Kansas City, Kans.	15-2-44	22-2-44
4 PHE TRA (ex-LCU 1089)	Quincy Barge, Ill.	10-5-44	10-6-44
6 TALIBONG (ex-LCU 753)	Quincy Barge, Ill.	30-3-44	10-5-44

D: 134 tons (309 fl) **S:** 10 kts **Dim:** 36.3 × 9.96 × 1.14
A: 4/20-mm AA (II × 2) **M:** 3 G.M. 6-71 diesels; 3 props; 675 hp
Fuel: 10.5 tons **Range:** 1,200/7 **Man:** 10 tot.

REMARKS: Transferred 10-46 to 11-47. Used as logistics transports on the Chao Phraya river. Cargo: 150 tons. Sister *Kolum* (5, ex-LCU 904) stricken 1984.

◆ **24 ex-U.S. LCM(6)-class landing craft**

L 14–16; L 61–68; L 71–78; L 81–82; L 85–87

D: 24 tons (56 fl) **S:** 9 kts **Dim:** 17.11 × 4.27 × 1.17
M: 2 Gray Marine 64 HN 9 diesels; 2 props; 330 hp **Range:** 130/9 **Man:** 5 tot.

REMARKS: Transferred 2-65 to 4-69. Cargo capacity: 34 tons.

◆ **12 ex-U.S. LCVP-class landing craft**

L 51–59; L 510–512

D: 12 tons (fl) **S:** 9 kts **Dim:** 10.9 × 3.21 × 1.04
M: 1 Gray Marine 64 HN 9 diesel; 1 prop; 225 hp
Range: 110/9 **Cargo capacity:** 39 troops

REMARKS: Transferred 3-63. Eight LCVPs are carried aboard the four Thai LSTs.

◆ **3 armored personnel transports** Bldr: Bangkok Dock Co., Ltd. (In serv. 1984)

L 41 L 42 L 43

D: . . . **S:** 25 kts **Dim:** 12.0 × . . . × . . . **M:** 2 Ford Sabre diesels; 2 props; . . . hp

◆ **1 personnel landing craft** Bldr: Royal Thai Navy Dockyard, Bangkok, 11-68

D: 10 tons (fl) **S:** 25 kts **Dim:** 12.0 × 3.0 × 1.0
M: 2 Chrysler diesels; 2 Castoldi model 6 waterjets; . . . hp
Cargo capacity: 35 troops

REMARKS: Built with U.S. aid. Glass-reinforced plastic construction. Additional units may have been constructed.

HYDROGRAPHIC SHIPS

◆ **1 oceanographic and survey ship** Bldr: Bangkok Navy DY

	Laid down	L	In serv.
. . . SUK	27-8-79	16-9-81	3-9-82

D: 1,400 tons (1,526 fl) **S:** 15 kts **Dim:** 62.9 × 11.0 × 4.1
A: 2/20-mm AA (I × 2)—2/7.62-mm mg (I × 2)
M: 2 MTU diesels; 2 props; 2,400 hp **Man:** 58 tot.

◆ **1 navigational buoy tender** Bldr: Royal Thai Naval DY, Bangkok (In serv. 18-1-79)

. . . SURIYA

D: 690 tons light (960 fl) **S:** 12 kts **Dim:** 54.2 (47.3 pp) × 10.0 × 3.0
A: 2/20-mm AA (I × 2) **M:** 2 MTU diesels; 1 prop; 1,310 hp
Electric: 300 kw **Cargo capacity:** 270 tons **Range:** 3,000/12
Man: 14 officers, 46 men

REMARKS: One 10-ton crane.

◆ **1 oceanographic ship** Bldr: C. Melchers, Bremen, W. Germany

	Laid down	L	In serv.
11 CHANDHARA	27-9-60	17-12-60	1961

Chandhara (11) 1966

D: 870 tons (997 fl) **S:** 13 kts **Dim:** 70.0 (61.0 pp) × 10.5 × 3.0
A: 1/40-mm AA—1/20-mm AA **M:** 2 Deutz diesels; 2 props; 1,000 hp
Range: 10,000/12 **Man:** 72 tot.

REMARKS: Built as a training ship.

◆ **2 inshore survey craft** Bldr: Lürssen, Vegesack, West Germany, 1956

D: 96 tons (fl) **S:** 12 kts **Dim:** 29.0 × 5.5 × 1.5
M: 2 diesels; 2 props; . . . hp **Man:** 8 tot.

AUXILIARIES

◆ **1 small underway replenishment oiler**

	Bldr	L	In serv.
2 CHULA	Singapore SY & Eng.	24-9-80	1981

D: 2,000 tons (fl) **S:** 14 kts **Dim:** 67.0 × 9.5 × 4.35 **Man:** 7 officers, 32 men
A: 2/20-mm AA (I × 2) **M:** 2 MTU 12V396 TC62 diesels; 2 props; 2,400 hp

REMARKS: 960 dwt. Cargo: 800 tons, transferred by means of an electrohydraulic boom supporting the hose.

NOTE: Transport *Sichang* (1) was stricken during 1984.

TRAINING SHIPS

◆ **1 ex-British Algerine-class former fleet minesweeper**

Bldr: Redfern Const. Co., Toronto, Canada

	Laid down	L	In serv.
1 PHOSAMTON (ex-*Minstrel*)	27-6-44	5-10-44	9-6-45

Phosamton (1) 1981

D: 1,010 tons (1,300 fl) **S:** 16 kts **Dim:** 68.58 × 10.82 × 3.28
A: 1/102-mm DP—1/40-mm AA—6/20-mm AA (II × 2, I × 2)
Electron Equipt: Radar: 1/Raytheon 1500B Pathfinder, 1/. . . nav.
M: 2 sets triple-expansion steam; 2 props; 2,400 hp
Boilers: 2, 3-drum
Fuel: 235 tons **Range:** 10,000/10 **Man:** 103 tot.

REMARKS: Transferred 4-47. Mechanical minesweeping equipment removed, replaced by a deckhouse to increase accommodations.

◆ **1 Tachin-class former frigate**

Bldr: Uraga Dockyard, Japan

	Laid doqwn	L	In serv.
3 MAEKLONG	24-7-36	27-11-36	6-37

D: 1,400 tons (2,000 fl) **S:** 14 kts **Dim:** 112.5 × 10.5 × 3.2
A: 4/76.2-mm U.S. Mk 22 DP (I × 4)—3/40-mm AA (I × 3)—3/20-mm AA (I × 3)—mines
M: 2 sets triple-expansion reciprocating steam; 2 props; 2,500 hp
Boilers: 2, watertube **Fuel:** 487 tons **Range:** 8,000/12 **Man:** 155 tot.

TRAINING SHIPS *(continued)*

Maeklong (3) R.A.N., 3-82

REMARKS: Sister *Tachin* bombed in 1945 and discarded circa 1950. Formerly carried four 102-mm guns (replaced in 1974) and four 450-mm torpedo tubes (II × 2).

NOTE: Training ship *Bangpakong* (4, ex-Indian *Gandwana*, ex-HMS *Burnet*), the last World War II "Flower"-class corvette in original configuration, was stricken during 1984.

SERVICE CRAFT

◆ **2 Proet-class harbor oilers** Bldr: Royal Thai Navy DY, Bangkok

	In serv.		In serv.
YO 9 PROET	16-1-70	YO 11 SAMED	15-12-70

Samed (11)—while fitting out 1967

D: 360 tons (465 fl) **S:** 9 kts **Dim:** 39.0 (36.6 pp) × 6.1 × 3.1
A: 2/20-mm AA (I × 2) **M:** 1 diesel; 500 hp

◆ **2 provisions transport** Bldr:. . .

AF 7 KLED KEO

Kled Keo (7) 1967

D: 382 tons (450 fl) **S:** 12 kts **Dim:** 46.0 × 7.6 × 4.3
A: 3/20-mm AA (I × 3) **M:** 1 diesel; 600 hp **Man:** 54 tot.

REMARKS: Former trawler. Acquired in 1967.

◆ **1 Charn-class water tanker** Bldr: Bangkok Naval DY

YW 8 CHUANG (L: 14-1-65)

D: 355 tons (485 fl) **S:** 11 kts **Dim:** 42.0 × 7.5 × 3.1
A: 1/20-mm AA **M:** 1 G.M. diesel; 500 hp **Man:** 29 tot..

REMARKS: Near sister *Charn* stricken during 1984.

◆ **2 Rang-class coastal tugs** Bldr: Singapore SB & Eng. (In serv. 9-80)

. . . RANG (L: 12-6-80) . . . RIN (L: 14-6-80)

D: 250 tons (300 fl) **S:** 12 kts **Dim:** 32.3 × 9.0 × . . .
M: 1 MWM TBD 441V/12K diesel; 1 prop; 2,100 hp
Electric: 233 kw **Range:** 1,000/10 **Man:** 16 tot.

REMARKS: Bollard pull: 22 tons

◆ **2 ex-Canadian small harbor tugs** Bldr: Central Bridge Co., Trenton, Ontario (In serv. 1943-44)

YTL 2 KLUENG BADEN YTL 3 MARIN VICHAI

D: 63 grt **S:** 8 kts **Dim:** 19.8 × 5.0 × 1.8 **M:** 1 diesel; 240 hp

REMARKS: Acquired in 1953.

ROYAL THAI MARINE POLICE

This organization performs duties analogous to those of a coast guard and operates a large number of patrol boats and craft. A number of the newer and larger units are listed below. Two "offshore" patrol boats were ordered in 1981 from C.N. Breda, Venice, Italy; no further details announced.

PATROL BOATS AND CRAFT

◆ **2 (+ . . .) new construction** Bldr: Tecnautic, Bangkok (In serv. 1984-. . .)

D: . . . **S:** 27 kts **Dim:** 27.00 × 5.85 × . . .
A: . . . **M:** 3 Isotta-Fraschini diesels; 3 Castoldi 07 waterjets; 2,500 hp

◆ **5 new construction** Bldr: Tecnautic, Bangkok (In serv. 1983)

D: . . . **S:** 26 kts **Dim:** 18.00 × 4.45 × . . .
A: . . . **M:** 2 Isotta-Fraschini diesels; 2 Castoldi 07 waterjets; 1,260 hp

REMARKS: The same yard has also recently built a number of smaller waterjet-driven launches and landing craft for the Royal Thai Marine Police.

◆ **8 aluminum-hulled** Bldr: Captain Co., Thailand (In serv. 1978)

D: 18 tons (fl) **S:** 22 kts **Dim:** 16.5 × 3.8 × . . .
A: 2/12.7-mm mg **M:** 2 Cummins diesels; 400 hp

◆ **3 U.S. Cutlass class** Bldr: Halter Marine, New Orleans, La. (In serv. 1978)

807 PHRA ONG CHAO KHAMROP 808 PICHARN PHOLAKIT 809 RAM INTHRA

Phra Ong Chao Khamrop and sisters—with old numbers Halter, 1978

D: 34 tons (fl) **S:** 25 kts **Dim:** 19.66 × 5.18 × 1.12
A: 2/12.7-mm mg (I × 2) **M:** 2 G.M. 12V71 TI diesels; 2 props; 960 hp
Fuel: 2.7 tons **Man:** 15 tot.

◆ **1 seagoing patrol boat** Bldr: Yokohama Yacht, Japan (In serv. 1975)

1802 DAMRONG RACHANUPHAT (ex-112)

D: 200 grt **S:** 31 kts **Dim:** 37.0 × 6.5 × . . .
A: 1/76.2-mm DP—2/20-mm AA **M:** 4 diesels; 2 props; 2,200 hp

◆ **2 seagoing patrol boats**

1801 N. . . . . . . 1803 N. . . . . . .

1803 1983

D: Approx. 400 tons (fl) **A:** 1/40-mm AA—2/20-mm AA
M: Diesel-powered

NOTE: There are a number of other craft, mostly armed with either one 20-mm antiaircraft or two 12.7-mm machine guns. Most craft are Japanese built.

TOGO

Republic of Togo

Personnel (1985): 200 men

Merchant Marine (1984): 8 ships—29,980 grt

PATROL BOATS

◆ **2 wooden-hulled** Bldr: C. N. de l'Estérel, Cannes, France

Kara (L: 18-5-76) Mono (L: 1976)

Mono French Navy, 12-82

D: 80 tons (fl) **S:** 30 kts **Dim:** 32.0 × 5.8 × 1.5
A: 1/40-mm AA—1/20-mm AA **Electron Equipt:** Radar: 1/Decca 916
M: 2 MTU 12V493 diesels; 2,700 hp **Range:** 1,500/15
Man: 1 officer, 17 men

TONGA

Kingdom of Tonga

Merchant Marine (1984): 20 ships—16,308 grt

MARITIME DEFENSE DIVISION
TONGAN DEFENSE SERVICE

PATROL BOATS AND CRAFT

◆ **0 (+1) ASI 315 design** Bldr: Australian SB Ind. (WA) Pty, Ltd, South Coogie, West Australia

. . . N. . . (In serv. 1987)

D: 165 tons (fl) **S:** 20 kts (sust.) **Dim:** 31.50 (28.60 wl) × 8.10 × 2.12
A: 2/12.7-mm mg (I × 2)
Electron Equipt: Radar: 1/Furuno 1011
M: 2 Caterpillar 3516 diesels; 2 props; 2,400 hp (sust.)
Range: 2,500/12 **Fuel:** 33 tons **Electric:** 120 kw
Endurance: 10 days **Man:** 3 officers, 14 men

Remarks: "Pacific Patrol Boat" design winner for Australian foreign aid program; ordered 5-85. Illustration in Papua New Guinea section.

◆ **2 fiberglass-hulled** Bldr: Brooke Marine, Lowestoft, U.K.

P 101 Ngahau Koula (In serv. 10-3-73) P 102 Ngahau Siliva (In serv. 10-5-74)

D: 15 tons (fl) **S:** 21 kts **Dim:** 13.7 × 4.0 × 1.2
A: 2/12.7-mm mg (I × 2) **Electron Equipt:** Radar: 1/Decca 101
M: 2 Cummins KT2300M diesels; 2 props; 700 hp **Range:** 800/21 **Man:** 7 tot.

AUXILIARIES

◆ **1 Australian-built U.S. LCM (8)-class landing craft** Bldr: North Queensland Eng., Cairns

Late (ex-Australian Army 1057)

D: 34 tons light (116 fl) **S:** 12 kts **Dim:** 22.70 × 6.41 × 1.37
M: 2 G.M. 12V71 diesels; 2 props; 600 hp **Range:** 200/9

Remarks: Transferred to Tongo 1-9-82. Cargo: 55 tons. Has been fitted with a pilot-house and navigational radar.

◆ **1 royal yacht**

Titilupe

Remarks: 10.4-m glass-reinforced plastic craft capable of 8 kts.; also used in patrol work.

TRINIDAD AND TOBAGO

Republic of Trinidad and Tobago

Personnel (1985): 45 officers, 541 men

Merchant Marine (1984): 49 ships—18,969 grt

Naval Aviation: The Coast Guard operates one Twin Beech maritime surveillance aircraft and one Cessna light aircraft. The Air Division of the National Security Forces operates 2 SA.341G Gazelle and 2 Sikorsky S-76 helicopters for surveillance and rescue service.

COAST GUARD

PATROL BOATS AND CRAFT

◆ **2 CG 40 class** Bldr: Karlskrona, Sweden (Both in serv. 6-6-80)

CG 5 Barracuda CG6 Cascadura

Barracuda (CG 5) L. & L. Van Ginderen, 1-84

D: 200 tons (fl) **S:** 31 kts **Dim:** 40.6 × 6.7 × 1.6
A: 1/40-mm Bofors AA—1/20-mm AA
Electron Equipt: Radar: 1/Decca TM 1226
M: 2 Paxman Valenta 16RP200 diesels; 2 props; 8,000 hp
Range: 2,000/15-20 **Man:** 22 tot.

Remarks: Ordered 8-78. Have an optronic GFCS for the 40-mm AA; rescue dinghy carried on stern. 27 kts sustained speed. Have HF and VHF D/F gear.

◆ **4 103-foot** Bldr: Vosper, Portsmouth

	L	In serv.		L	In serv.
CG 1 Trinity	14-4-64	20-2-65	CG 3 Chaguaramas	29-3-71	18-2-72
CG 2 Courland Bay	20-5-64	20-2-65	CG 4 Bucco Reef	1971	18-3-72

Bucco Reef (CG 4) Trinidad & Tobago CG, 1982

D: 96–100 tons (123–125 fl) **S:** 23 kts **Dim:** 31.29 (28.95 pp) × 5.94 × 1.68
A: CG 1 and CG 2: 1/40-mm AA; CG 3 and CG 4: 1/20-mm AA
M: 2 Paxman 12 YJCM Ventura diesels; 2 props; 2,900 hp
Fuel: 18 tons **Range:** 1,800/13.5 **Man:** 3 officers, 14 men

Remarks: Second pair are heavier and have slightly longer range: 2,000/13; their superstructures are broader. All are air-conditioned and have roll-damping fins.

TRINIDAD AND TOBAGO *(continued)*
PATROL BOATS AND CRAFT *(continued)*

◆ **4 Wasp 17-m-class patrol craft** Bldr: W.A. Souter & Sons, Cowes, U.K. (In serv. 27-8-82)

CG 27 Plymouth CG 28 Caroni CG 29 Galeota CG 30 Moruga

Plymouth (CG 27) L. & L. Van Ginderen, 1-84

D: 19.25 tons (fl) **S:** 28 kts (25 sust.) **Dim:** 16.76 (13.90 wl) × 4.20 × 1.40
A: 2/7.62-mm mg (I × 2) **Electron Equipt:** Radar: 1/Decca 150
M: 2 Stevenson-G.M. 8V92 MTI diesels; 2 props; 1,300 hp
Range: 500/18 **Man:** 2 officers, 4-6 men

Remarks: Glass-reinforced plastic construction. Ordered 8-81.

◆ **2 coastal patrol craft** Bldr: Tugs & Lighters, Ltd., Port-of-Spain

CG 01 Naparima (In serv. 15-8-76) CG 25 El Tucuche (In serv. 1977)

D: 20 tons **S:** 20 kts **Dim:** 16.4 × 5.2 × 2.6
M: 2 G.M. 6V71 diesels; 2 props; 460 hp **Man:** 6 tot.

Remarks: Dissimilar craft in appearance. CG 25 is 16.7 m o.a.

◆ **1 fiberglass patrol launch** Bldr: Trinidad (In serv. . . .)

CG 9 Fort Chacon

D: . . . **S:** 27 kts **Dim:** 7.0 × . . . × . . .
M: 1 Caterpillar diesel; . . . hp

◆ **1 sail-training ketch** Bldr: Trinidad, 1966

Hummingbird II

Remarks: 12 meters overall, one 3-cylinder Lister auxiliary diesel.

MARINE POLICE

PATROL CRAFT

◆ **2 Wasp 20-m class** Bldr: W.A. Souter & Sons, Cowes (In serv. 11-82)

N. . . . . . . N. . . . . . .

D: 32 tons (fl) **S:** 36 kts (30 sust.) **Dim:** 20.0 × 5.0 × 1.5
A: 2/7.62-mm mg (I × 2) **Electron Equipt:** Radar: 1/Decca 150
M: 2 G.M. 16V92 TI diesels; 2 props; 2,400 hp
Range: 300/30 **Man:** 2 officers, 4 men

Remarks: Aluminum hulls. Ordered 30-9-81.

◆ **1 fiberglass-hulled** Bldr: Watercraft, Shoreham, U.K. (In serv. 1980)

Sea Dragon

D: 14.9 tons (fl) **S:** 23.5 kts **Dim:** 13.7 × 4.1 × 1.2
A: 2/7.62-mm mg (I × 2) **Electron Equipt:** Radar: 1/Decca 110
M: 2 G.M. 8V92 diesels; 12 props; 700 hp **Range:** 360/20 **Man:** 4 tot.

◆ **2 Sword class** Bldr: Fairey Marine, Hamble, U.K.

Sea Spray (In serv. 1-78) Fox (In serv. 12-78)

D: 15.2 tons (fl) **S:** 28 kts **Dim:** 13.7 × 4.1 × 1.32
A: 1/7.62-mm mg **M:** 2 G.M. 8V71 TI diesels; 2 props; 850 hp
Range: 500/. . . **Man:** 6 tot.

TUNISIA

Republic of Tunisia

Personnel (1985): approx. 2,600 men

Merchant Marine (1984): 63 ships—277,403 grt (tankers: 9 ships—168,719 grt)

FRIGATE

◆ **1 ex-U.S. Savage-class former radar picket** Bldr: Consolidated Steel, Orange, Tex.

	Laid down	L	In serv.
E 7 President Bourguiba (ex-*Thomas J. Gary*, DER 326, ex-DE 326)	15-6-43	21-8-43	27-11-43

President Bourguiba (E 7) French Navy, 7-80

D: 1,590 tons (1,850 fl) **S:** 19 kts **Dim:** 93.27 (91.5 pp) × 11.22 × 4.27
A: 2/76.2-mm DP (I × 2)—2/20-mm AA (I × 2)—6/324-mm ASW TT (III × 2)
Electron Equipt: Radar: 1/SPS-10, 1/SPS-29, 1/Mk 34
Sonar: SQS-29 series
M: 4 Fairbanks-Morse 38D8⅛ × 10 diesels; 2 props; 6,080 hp
Fuel: 310 tons **Electric:** 580 kw **Range:** 11,500/11 **Man:** 160–170 tot.

Remarks: Modified as a radar picket ship in 1957, transferred on 27-10-73. SPS-8 height-finding radar, TACAN, EW, Hedgehog removed about 1968. Has one Mk 63 radar GFCS and one Mk 51 Mod. 2 GFCS for 76.2-mm guns. A replacement is being sought.

GUIDED-MISSILE PATROL BOATS

◆ **3 Combattante III class** Bldr: CMN, Cherbourg

	Laid down	L	In serv.
P 501 La Galite	26-5-82	16-6-83	27-2-85
P 502 Tunis	28-9-82	27-10-83	28-3-85
P 503 Carthage	6-1-83	24-1-84	29-4-85

La Galite (P 501) 35th Flot., French Navy, 5-85

D: 395 tons (425 fl) **S:** 38.5 kts **Dim:** 56.80 (53.00 pp) × 8.16 × 2.15 (2.50 props)
A: 8/MM 40 Exocet SSM (IV × 2)—1/76-mm OTO Melara DP—2/40-mm Breda AA (II × 2)—4/30-mm Oerlikon AA (II × 2)
Electron Equipt: Radar: 1/Castor IIB, 1/Triton S
EW: . . . passive, 1/Dagaie Chaff RL
M: 4 MTU 20V538 TB93 diesels; 4 props; 19,300 hp **Electric:** 405 kVA
Man: 35 tot.

Remarks: Ordered 27-6-81. Have Thomson-CSF Vega II control system for missiles, 76-mm and 40-mm guns; two CSEE Naja optronic directors for the 30-mm AA.

PATROL BOATS AND CRAFT

◆ **3 French P 48 class** Bldr: SFCN, Villeneuve-la-Garenne

	L	In serv.
P 301 Bizerte	20-11-69	10-7-70
P 302 Horria (ex-*Liberty*)	19-2-70	10-70
P 304 Monastir	25-6-74	25-3-75

PATROL BOATS AND CRAFT *(continued)*

Monastir (P 304) G. Gyssels, 10-82

D: 250 tons (fl) **S:** 22 kts **Dim:** 48.0 (45.5 pp) × 7.1 × 2.25
A: 2/40-mm AA (I × 2)—2/20-mm AA (I × 2)—8/SS-12 wire-guided missiles (IV × 2)
Electron Equipt: Radar: 1/Decca TM 1226
M: 2 MGO MB-839 Db diesels; 2 props; 4,000 hp **Range:** 2,000/16
Man: 4 officers, 30 men

Remarks: P 301 lacks the 20-mm AA.

◆ **1 French Le Fougueux class** Bldr: Dubigeon, Nantes (In serv. 12-3-57)

P 303 Sakiet Sidi Youssef (ex-UW 12, ex-PC 1618)

Sakiet Sidi Youssef (P 303) French Navy, 7-80

D: 325 tons (402 fl) **S:** 18.7 kts **Dim:** 53.1 × 6.4 × 2.1 (3.0 max.)
A: 1/40-mm AA—2/20-mm AA (I × 2)—2/Mk 20 Mousetrap ASW RL—2/Mk 9 d.c. racks
Electron Equipt: Radar: 1/DRBN-31
Sonar: DUBA-2
M: 4 SEMT-Pielstick 14 PA17V diesels; 2 CP props; 3,240 hp **Electric:** 60 kw
Fuel: 45 tons **Range:** 3,300/15; 6,350/12 **Man:** 4 officers, 59 men

Remarks: Begun as P 7 for the French Navy, using U.S. "Offshore" funds. Transferred to West Germany and used as a training ship at the Underwater Weapons School. Purchased by Tunisia on 16-6-70. Four depth-charge projectors and Hedgehog removed mid-1970s.

◆ **2 ex-U.S. Adjutant-class former coastal minesweepers**

	Bldr	In serv.
P. . . Hannibal (ex-*Coquelicot,* ex-MSC 48)	Steven Bros., Cal.	10-53
P. . . Sousse (ex-*Marjolaine,* ex-MSC 66)	Harbor Boat, Cal.	4-53

Hannibal J.-C. Bellonne, 1973

D: 300 tons (372 fl) **S:** 13 kts **Dim:** 43.0 (41.5 pp) × 7.95 × 2.55
A: 2/20-mm AA (II × 1) **Electron Equipt:** Radar: 1/DRBN-31
M: 2 G.M. 8-268A diesels; 2 props; 1,200 hp
Fuel: 40 tons **Range:** 2,500/10
Man: 3 officers, 35 men

Remarks: Loaned in 1973 and 1977. Minesweeping gear removed. Used in fisheries-protection duties.

◆ **2 103-foot class** Bldr: Vosper Thornycroft, Portchester, U.K.

	L	In serv.
P 205 Tazarka	19-7-76	27-10-77
P 206 Menzel Bourguiba	19-7-76	27-10-77

D: 100 tons (125 fl) **S:** 27 kts **Dim:** 31.29 (28.95 pp) × 6.02 × 1.98
A: 2/20-mm AA (I × 2) **Electron Equipt:** Radar: 1/Decca 916
M: 2 MTU diesels; 2 props; 4,000 hp **Range:** 1,500/14 **Man:** 24 tot.

◆ **2 Chinese Shanghai-II class** (In serv. 2-5-77)

P 305 Gafsa P 306 Amilcar

Gafsa (P 305) 1978

D: 122.5 tons (135 fl) **S:** 28.5 kts **Dim:** 38.78 × 5.41 × 1.55
A: 4/37-mm AA (II × 2)—4/25-mm AA (II × 2)
Electron Equipt: Radar: 1/. . . nav.
M: 4 MTU 9V331 TC92 diesels; 4 props; 4,260 hp (3,540 sust.)
Range: 800/17 **Man:** 38 tot.

Remarks: Re-engined and refitted at SOLOMENA SY, Bizerte, completing 12-84.

◆ **4 French 32-meter class** Bldr: CN de l'Estérel, Cannes

	In serv.		In serv.
P 201 Istiklal (ex-French VC 11)	1957	P 203 Al Jala	11-63
P 202 Joumhouria	1-61	P 204 Remada	7-67

Istiklal (P 201) 1970

D: 60 tons (82 fl) **S:** 28 kts **Dim:** 31.45 × 5.75 × 1.7
A: 2/20-mm AA (I × 2) **M:** 2 MTU 12V493 diesels; 2 props; 2,700 hp
Range: 1,400/15 **Man:** 3 officers, 14 men

Remarks: Wooden construction. P 201 was launched on 25-5-57 and transferred in 3-59.

◆ **6 French 25-meter class** Bldr: CN de l'Estérel, Cannes (In serv. 1961-63)

V 101 through V 106

V 101 L. & L. Van Ginderen, 1984

D: 38–39 tons **S:** 23 kts **Dim:** 25.0 × 4.75 × 1.25 **Man:** 10 tot.
A: 1/20-mm AA **M:** 2 G.M. 12V71 TI diesels; 2 props; 940 hp **Range:** 900/16

Remarks: V 107 and V 108 were transferred to the Fisheries Administration, disarmed, in 1971, as *Sabeq el Bahr* (T 2) and *Jaouel el Bahr* (T 3).

TUNISIA *(continued)*

AUXILIARY SHIPS

◆ **1 ex-U.S. Sotoyomo-class oceangoing tug**

Bldr: Gulfport Boilers & Welding Works, Port Arthur, Tex.

	Laid down	L	In serv.
. . . Ras Adar (ex-*Zeeland,* ex-*Pan America,* ex-*Ocean Pride,* ex-*Oriana,* ex-BAT 1)	16-3-42	15-8-42	13-12-42

D: 570 tons (835 fl) **S:** 13 kts **Dim:** 43.59 (41.0 pp) × 10.31 × 4.01
A: None **M:** 2 G.M. 12-278A diesels, electric drive; 1 prop; 1,500 hp
Electric: 90 kw **Fuel:** 171 tons **Man:** 45 tot.

Remarks: Built under Lend-Lease, transferred to Great Britain on 22-12-42. Returned and sold commercially in 1946. Purchased for Tunisia from Dutch company in late 1960s. BAT-series had larger superstructure than standard *Sotoyomo* class and were considered to be ocean rescue tugs.

◆ **1 diving tender** (In serv. 1948)

Kerkennah

D: 653 grt **S:** 10 kts **Dim:** 53.95 × 9.75 × 2.75
M: Diesel-electric; . . . props; . . . hp **Man:** 4 officers, 20 men, 4 civilians

TURKEY

Republic of Turkey

Personnel (1985): 45,000 men

Merchant Marine (1984): 776 ships — 3,124,784 grt
(tankers: 93 ships — 1,294,218 grt)

Naval Aviation: A small naval air arm, organized in 1972, consists of 8 S-2A and 12 S-2E Tracker ASW airplanes, 3 AB-204 helicopters, and 9 AB-212 helicopters.

Warships In Service, Authorized, Or Under Construction
As Of 1 January 1986

◆ **17 (+7) submarines**	L	Tons (surfaced)	Main armament
5 (+7) Type 209	1974-81	990	8/533-mm TT
2 Tang	1951	2,100	8/533-mm TT
2 GUPPY III	1945	1,975	10/533-mm TT
7 GUPPY II-A	1943-44	1,848	10/533-mm TT
1 GUPPY I-A	1944	1,870	10/533-mm TT
◆ **14 destroyers**		Tons	
2 Carpenter	1945-46	2,425	2/127-mm 1/ASROC, 6/ASW TT
7 Gearing Fram-I	1944-46	2,425	4/127-mm, 1/ASROC, 6/ASW TT
2 Gearing Fram-II	1945	2,390	4/127-mm, 2/35-mm AA, 1/Hedgehog, 6/ASW TT
1 Allen M. Sumner Fram-II	1944	2,200	6/127-mm 6/ASW TT
1 Robert H. Smith	1944	2,250	6/127-mm, 2/76.2-mm, mines
2 Fletcher	1943	2,050	4/127-mm, 6/76.2-mm, ASW weapons
◆ **4 (+4) frigates**			
0 (+4) Meko 200	. . .	2,000	8/Harpoon SSM, Albatros SAM, 1/127-mm DP, ASW weapons
2 Berk	1971-72	1,450	4/76.2-mm, 6/ASW TT
2 Köln	1959	2,425	2/100-mm, ASW weapons, mines

◆ **53 patrol and torpedo boats**

◆ **48 mine warfare ships and craft**

◆ **51 (+ . . .) seagoing landing ships and craft**

WEAPONS AND SYSTEMS

Most weapons and systems are furnished by the U.S.A., some by West Germany. For characteristics, see the sections on the U.S.A. and Germany, Federal Republic. Twelve Harpoon SSM were ordered in 1981 to supplement existing stocks; Norwegian Penguin Mk 1 missiles are also used. British Sea Skua anti-ship missiles may be purchased for use by AB-212 helicopters.

SUBMARINES

◆ **5 (+7) German Type 209** Bldrs: S 347, S 348, S 349; Howaldtswerke, Kiel; S 350 and later: Gölcük NSY

	Laid down	L	In serv.
S 347 Atilay	1-12-72	23-10-74	23-7-75
S 348 Saldiray	2-1-73	14-2-75	21-10-75
S 349 Batiray	11-6-75	24-10-77	20-7-78
S 350 Yildiray	1-5-76	20-7-77	20-7-81
S 351 Doganay	21-3-80	16-11-83	16-11-84
S 352 Titiray	9-3-81	. . .	. . .
S. . . N. . .	. . .	. . .	. . .

Yildiray (S 350) — with *Ikinci Inönü* (S 333), *Canakkale* (S 341), *Atilay* (S 347), and *Birinci Inönü* (S 346) beyond — H. Ehlers, 3-84

D: 990 tons std./1,180 tons surf./1,290 sub. **S:** 11/22 kts
Dim: 56.10 × 6.20 × 5.50 **A:** 8/533-mm TT fwd (14 torpedoes)
Electron Equipt: Radar: . . .
Sonar: Krupp-Atlas AN526 passive/AN407AS active, DUUX-2 telephone
M: 4 MTU 12V493 TY60 diesels (600 hp each); 4/405-kw generator sets; 1 Siemens electric motor, 5,000 hp
Fuel: 100 tons **Range:** 7,800/8 surf.; 400/4 sub.
Man: 6 officers, 27 men

Remarks: Have H.S.A. M8 torpedo-fire control, two periscopes. A total of 12 are planned, with 8 to be built in Turkey.

◆ **2 ex-U.S. Tang class** Bldr: Portsmouth Naval SY, N.H.

	Laid down	L	In serv.
S 343 Piri Reis (ex-*Tang,* SS 563)	18-4-49	19-6-51	25-10-52
S 344 Hizir Reis (ex-*Gudgeon,* SSAG 567)	20-5-50	11-6-52	21-11-52

Piri Reis (S 343) — L. & L. Van Ginderen, 6-82

D: 1,975/2,600 tons **S:** 15.5/16 kts **Dim:** 87.5 × 8.3 × 5.7
A: 8/533-mm TT (6 fwd, 2 short aft)
Electron Equipt: Radar: 1/BPS-12, 1/ST-3
Sonar: BQS-4, BQG-4 (PUFFS)
M: 3 Fairbanks-Morse 38D8⅛ × 10 diesels; 2 Westinghouse motors; 2 props; 5,600 hp
Range: 7,600/15; 17/9 submerged **Man:** 11 officers, 75 men

Remarks: S 343 leased for five years 8-2-80, ex-SSAG 567 leased 30-9-83. Have Mk 106, Mod. 18, torpedo FCS. Aft tubes can fire Mk 37 torpedoes only.

◆ **2 ex-U.S. GUPPY III class** Bldr: Electric Boat Co., Groton, Conn.

	Laid down	L	In serv.
S 333 Ikinci Inonu (ex-*Corporal,* SS 346)	27-4-44	1-4-45	8-8-45
S 341 Canakkale (ex-*Cobbler,* SS 344)	3-4-44	1-4-45	9-11-45

D: 1,975/2,450 tons **S:** 17.2/14.5 kts **Dim:** 99.52 × 8.23 × 5.18
A: 10/533-mm TT (6 fwd, 4 aft) — 24 torpedoes
Electron Equipt: Radar: 1/SS-2A — Sonar: BQG-4 (PUFFS), BQR-2B
M: 4 G.M. 16-278A diesels (1,625 hp each), diesel-electric drive; 2 props; 6,500/5,200 hp
Range: 10,000–12,000/10; 95/5 (sub.) **Man:** 86 tot.

Remarks: Transferred on 21-11-73. Lengthened by 3.6 meters in 1962 at Philadelphia (S 341) and Charleston (S 333). Two 126-cell batteries. Direct drive on surface.

SUBMARINES *(continued)*

Canakkale (S 341)—showing PUFFS domes, with *Atilay* (S 347) and *Birinci Inönü* (S 346) in background H. Ehlers, 3-84

◆ **7 ex-U.S. GUPPY II-A** Bldrs: S 345: Electric Boat Co., Groton, Conn.; others: Portsmouth NSY

	Laid down	L	In serv.
S 335 Burak Reis (ex-*Sea Fox*, SS 402)	2-11-43	28-3-44	13-6-44
S 336 Murat Reis (ex-*Razorback*, SS 394)	9-9-43	27-1-44	3-4-44
S 337 Oruç Reis (ex-*Pomfret*, SS 391-	17-7-43	27-10-43	19-2-44
S 338 Uluç Ali Reis (ex-*Thornback*, SS 418)	5-4-44	7-7-44	13-10-44
S 340 Cerbe (ex-*Trutta*, SS 421)	22-5-44	18-8-44	16-11-44
S 345 Preveze (ex-*Entemedor*, SS 340)	3-2-44	17-12-44	6-4-45
S 346 Birinci Inönü (ex-*Threadfin*, SS 410)	18-3-44	26-6-44	30-8-44

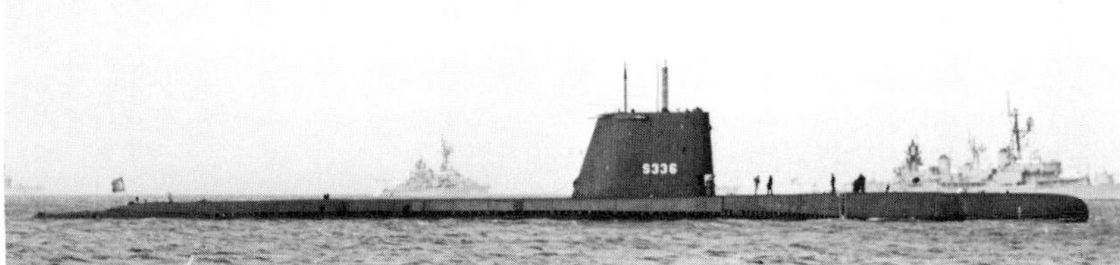

Murat Reis (S 336) H. Ehlers, 3-82

Cerbe (S 340)—showing "stepped" sail, outboard *Burak Reis* (S 335), *Dumlupinar* (S 339), *Murat Reis* (S 336), *Birinci Inönü* (S 346), *Piri Reis* (S 343), and tender *Besaran* (A 582) H. Ehlers, 2-83

D: 1,525/1,848/2,440 tons **S:** 17.4/14 kts, 9.4 snorkel
Dim: 93.36 × 8.32 × 5.04
A: 10/533-mm TT (6 fwd, 4 aft)—24 torpedoes or 40 mines
Electron Equipt: Radar: 1/SS-2A
Sonar: BQR-2B, BQS-4
M: 3 Fairbanks-Morse 38D8⅛ × 10 (S 345: G.M. 16/278A) diesels, electric drive; 2 props; 3,430/5,200 hp
Fuel: 330 tons **Range:** 10,000/10; 95/5 (sub.)
Man: 8–9 officers, 76 men

Remarks: S 335 was transferred in 12-70, S 336 in 11-70, S 337 on 3-5-72, S 338 and S 345 on 24-8-73, S 340 in 6-72, and S 346 on 15-8-73. S 336 and S 338 were at one time while in U.S. service equipped as "hard" targets for ASW training. S 340 is the only operational ex-USN GUPPY to retain the original stepped sail.

◆ **1 ex-U.S. GUPPY I-A class** Bldr: Electric Boat Co., Groton, Conn.

	Laid down	L	In serv.
S 339 Dumlupinar (ex-*Caiman*, SS 323)	1-10-43	30-3-44	17-7-44

D: 1,517/1,870/2,400 tons **S:** 18/15 kts **Dim:** 93.75 × 8.33 × 5.04
A: 10/533-mm TT (6 fwd, 4 aft)—24 torpedoes or 40 mines
Electron Equipt: Radar: 1/SS-2A
Sonar: . . .
M: 4 G.M. 16-278A diesels, diesel-electric direct drive; 2 props; 4,610/5,200 hp
Fuel: 330 tons **Range:** 16,000/10; 95/5 sub. **Man:** 9 officers, 76 men

Dumlupinar (S 339) L. & L. Van Ginderen, 6-82

Remarks: Completed GUPPY I-A conversion in 1951. Transferred 24-8-72. Had been relegated to pierside training duties after collision with a Soviet freighter on 1-9-76 and a fire in 1977, but refitted and recommissioned during 1980. Two 126-cell batteries.

DESTROYERS

◆ **2 ex-U.S. Carpenter class**

	Bldr	Laid down	L	In serv.
D 346 Alcitepe (ex-*Robert A. Owens*, DD 827)	Bath Iron Works, Bath, Maine	29-10-45	15-7-46	5-11-49
D 347 Anitepe (ex-*Gemlik*, ex-*Anitepe*, ex-*Carpenter*, DD 825)	Consolidated Steel, Orange, Tex.	30-7-45	30-12-45	15-12-49

Anitepe (D 347) Pradignac & Leo, 1984

D: 2,425 tons (3,540 fl) **S:** 34 kts **Dim:** 119.03 × 12.52 × 4.61 (6.4 over sonar)
A: 2/127-mm DP (II × 1)—2/76.2-mm Mk 3 DP (II × 1)—2/35-mm Oerlikon AA (II × 1)—1/ASROC ASW RL (VIII × 1, 6 reloads)—6/324-mm Mk 32 ASW TT (III × 2)—1/d.c. rack (9 dlc.)
Electron Equipt: Radar: 1/. . . nav., 2/SPS-10, 1/SPS-40, 1/Mk 35
Sonar: SQS-23
M: 2 sets G.E. GT; 2 props; 60,000 hp **Electric:** 1,200 kw
Boilers: 4 Babcock & Wilcox; 43.3 kg/cm², 454°C **Fuel:** 720 tons
Range: 1,500/31; 5,800/12 **Man:** 14 officers, 260 men

Remarks: D 347 purchased 20-2-81, ex-DD 827 purchased 16-2-82. Name for D 347 changed two weeks after transfer. Variant of the *Gearing* design, originally optimized for ASW. Completed FRAM-I modernizations 1962, retaining high bridges. Have Mk 56 radar GFCS, tripod mast aft, larger hangar superstructure than *Gearing* FRAM-I. Twin 76.2-mm placed on fantail, twin 35-mm forward after transfer, GFCS for the 35-mm mount not identified.

◆ **7 ex-U.S. Gearing FRAM-I class**

	Bldr	Laid down	L	In serv.
D 345 Yucetepe (ex-*Orleck*, DD 886)	Consolidated Steel, Orange, Tex.	18-11-44	12-5-45	15-9-45
D 348 Savastepe (ex-*Meredith*, DD 890)	Consolidated Steel, Orange, Tex.	27-1-45	28-6-45	31-12-45
D 349 Kiliç Ali Paşa (ex-*Robert H. McCard*, DD 822)	Consolidated Steel, Orange, Tex.	26-1-45	9-11-45	26-10-46
D 350 Piyale Paşa (ex-*Fiske*, DD 842)	Bath Iron Wks., Bath, Maine	9-4-45	8-9-45	28-11-45
D 351 M Fevzi Cakmak (ex-*Charles H. Roan*, DD 853)	Bethlehem Steel, Quincy, Mass.	27-9-45	15-3-46	12-9-46
D 352 Gayret (ex-*Eversole*, DD 789)	Todd SY, Seattle, Wash.	28-2-45	8-1-46	10-7-46
D 353 Adatepe (ex-*Forrest Royal*, DD 872)	Bethlehem, Staten Isl., N.Y.	6-6-45	17-1-46	28-6-46

DESTROYERS *(continued)*

Savastepe (D 348)—both 127-mm mounts fwd L. & L. Van Ginderen, 6-82

Piyale Paşa (D 350)—twin 35-mm AA aft L. & L. Van Ginderen, 10-84

Adatepe (D 353)—twin 35-mm mount aft, twin 40-mm fwd H. Ehlers, 4-84

Yucetepe (D 345)—no 35- or 40-mm AA H. Ehlers, 10-84

D: 2,425 tons (3,600 fl) **S:** 32 kts
Dim: 119.03 × 12.49 × 4.56 (6.4 over sonar)
A: 4/127-mm 38 cal. AA (II × 2)—2/40-mm AA (I × 2) (not in D 348-350)—2/35-mm Oerlikon AA (II × 1)—6/324-mm Mk 32 ASW TT (III × 2)—1/ASROC ASW RL (VIII × 1)—1/Mk 9 d.c. rack (9 d.c.)
Electron Equipt: Radar: 1/. . . nav., 1/SPS-10, 1/SPS-40 (D 345, 348–50: SPS-29), 1/Mk 25 (D 351–353: 1/. . . also)
Sonar: SQS-23
EW: WLR-1, WLR-3, ULQ-6 (not in D 348), 2 or 4/chaff RL (XX × 2 or 4)
M: 2 sets GT; 2 props; 60,000 hp **Electric:** 1,200 kw
Boilers: 4 Foster-Wheeler and/or Babcock & Wilcox, 43.3 kg/cm², 454°C
Fuel: 720 tons **Range:** 2,400/25; 4,800/15 **Man:** 14 officers, 260 men

Remarks: D 351 was transferred on 29-9-73, D 352 on 11-7-73, and DD 353 on 27-3-71. All received a twin 40-mm mount just before the bridge (with Mk 51, Mod. 2, optical director) and a twin 35-mm antiaircraft gun on the former DASH drone helicopter deck in the mid-1970s. D 351 has four Babcock & Wilcox boilers, while the other pair have two Babcock & Wilcox and two Foster-Wheeler boilers. All have chaff RL atop former hangar, two saluting guns fwd. GFCS include Mk 37 for 127-mm DP, 1 Mk 51 Mod. 2 for the 40-mm mount, and a radar GFCS (antenna atop after mast). D 348 was purchased 20-3-80 for cannibalization, but was instead refurbished and recommissioned 20-7-81; she has both 127-mm mounts fwd, the twin 35-mm AA on the fantail, no 40-mm AA, and retains the helo deck. D 349 and D 350 were leased for 5 years 5-6-80 and formally recommissioned 30-7-81. Because of their status they were not drastically altered, although one depth-charge rack, the twin 35-mm AA, and chaff RL were added. D 345 purchased 1-10-82, recommissioning 29-3-83; 40-mm and 35-mm AA not added as of late 1984. *McKean* (DD 784), previously damaged in a collision, transferred 1982 for cannibalization.

◆ **1 ex-U.S. Gearing FRAM-II class** Bldr: Bethlehem Steel, San Pedro, Cal.

	Laid down	L	In serv.
D 354 Kocatepe (ex-*Norris*, DD 859)	29-8-44	25-2-45	9-6-45

Kocatepe (D 354) H. Ehlers, 9-84

D: 2,390 tons (3,480 fl) **S:** 32 kts **Dim:** 119.03 × 12.49 × 4.6 (6.54 over sonar)
A: 4/127-mm DP (II × 2)—2/35-mm AA (II × 1)—6/40-mm AA (II × 2, I × 2)—1/Mk 15 trainable Hedgehog—6/324-mm Mk 32 ASW TT (III × 2)—1/Mk 9 d.c. rack
Electron Equipt: Radar: 1/SPS-10, 1/SPS-40, 1/Mk 25, 1/. . . f.c.
Sonar: 1/SQS-23
EW: WLR-1, 2 chaff RL (XX × 2)
M: 2 sets GT; 2 props; 60,000 hp **Electric:** 1,200 kw
Boilers: 4 Babcock & Wilcox; 43.3 kg/cm², 454°C
Fuel: 720 tons **Range:** 2,400/25; 4,800/15 **Man:** 14 officers, 260 men

Remarks: A previous *Kocatepe* (ex-*Harwood*, DD 861) was lost on 21-7-74 when mistakenly bombed by the Turkish Air Force. She was replaced by the *Norris* (DD 859), which had been transferred on 7-7-74 for cannibalization spares. Two single 40-mm AA were mounted on former DASH drone helicopter deck in 1974, and two twin 40-mm AA (with two Mk 51 Mod. 2 directors) added on upper deck between stacks in 1977. Has one Mk 37 radar GFCS. D 354 had a twin Oerlikon 35-mm AA substituted for the two single 40-mm aft and SPS-40 in place of SPS-60 radar in 1980. Sister *Tinaztepe* (D 355) badly damaged in collision 2-5-84 and stricken 1985.

◆ **1 ex-U.S. Allen M. Sumner FRAM-II class** Bldr: Federal SB, Kearney, N.J.

	Laid down	L	In serv.
D 356 Zafer (ex-*Hugh Purvis*, DD 709)	23-5-44	17-12-44	1-3-45

Zafer (D 356) H. Ehlers, 3-84

D: 2,200 tons (3,300 fl) **S:** 33 kts
Dim: 114.76 × 12.49 × 4.39 (5.79 over sonar)
A: 6/127-mm DP (II × 3)—4/40-mm AA (II × 2)—2/35-mm Oerlikon (II × 1)—2/Mk 11 Hedgehogs—6/324-mm Mk 32 ASW TT—1/Mk 9 d.c. rack
Electron Equipt: Radar: 1/. . . nav., 1/SPS-10, 1/SPS-29, 1/Mk 25
Sonar: SQS-29 series
EW: WLR-1, ULQ-6, 2/chaff RL (XX × 2)
M: GT; 2 props; 60,000 hp **Electric:** 1,200 kw
Boilers: 4 Babcock & Wilcox; 43.3 kg/cm², 454°C
Fuel: 650 tons **Range:** 800/32; 4,300/11 **Man:** 15 officers, 260 men

Remarks: Transferred on 15-2-72. In 1977 two twin 40-mm AA with two Mk 52, Mod. 2, optical GFCS for the twin mounts were added amidships; also has Mk 37 radar GFCS for 127-mm DP. Twin 35-mm AA replaced 2 single 40-mm AA on former helicopter flight deck in 1979.

◆ **1 ex-U.S. Robert H. Smith-class destroyer minelayer** Bldr: Bethlehem Steel, San Pedro, Cal.

	Laid down	L	In serv.
DM 357 Muavenet (ex-*Gwin*, MMD 33, ex-DD 772)	31-10-43	9-4-44	30-9-44

DESTROYERS *(continued)*

Muavenet (DM 357) H. Ehlers, 10-84

D: 2,250 tons (3,375 fl) **S:** 34 kts **Dim:** 114.76 × 12.49 × 4.4 (hull)
A: 6/127-mm DP (II × 3)—2/76.2-mm Mk 33 DP (II × 1)—12/40-mm AA (IV × 2; II × 2)—6/324-mm Mk 32 ASW TT (III × 2)—1/Mk 11 Hedgehog ASW Mortars (XXIV × 2)—1/Mk 9 d.c. rack (9 d.c.)
Electron Equipt: Radar: 1. . . nav., 1/SPS-10, 1/SPS-40, 1/Mk 25 f.c., 1/SPG-34 f.c.
Sonar: . . .
EW: LR-1 intercept, 4 decoy RL (XX × 4)
M: 2 sets GT; 2 props; 60,000 hp **Electric:** 900 kw
Boilers: 4 Babcock & Wilcox; 43.3 kg/cm², 454°C
Fuel: 494 tons **Range:** 4,600/15 **Man:** 274 tot.

Remarks: Transferred on 22-10-71 after reactivation and modernization. Fire control includes 1 Mk 37 radar GFCS for 127-mm guns, Mk 63 radar GFCS for the 76.2-mm mount, and two Mk 51, Mod. 2, optical GFCS for 40-mm AA. Mine rails on either side of main deck of what is basically an *Allen M. Sumner*-class destroyer. Survivor of a U.S. Navy class of twelve. Modernized with new radars and armament 1982-83, SPS-40 replacing SPS-6, a twin 76.2-mm mount replacing the after quadruple 40-mm mount, etc.

◆ **2 U.S. Fletcher-class destroyers**

	Bldr	Laid down	L	In serv.
D 340 Istanbul (ex-*Clarence K. Bronson,* DD 668)	Federal SB & DD, Newark, N.J.	9-12-42	18-4-43	11-6-73
D 341 Izmir (ex-*Van Valkenburgh,* DD 656)	Gulf S.B., Corp., Chickasaw, Ala.	15-11-42	19-12-43	2-8-44

D: 2,850 tons normal (3.036 fl) **S:** 32 kts **Dim:** 114.85 × 12.03 × 4.29 (mean)
A: 4/127-mm Mk, 30 DP (I × 4)—6/76.2-mm Mk 33 DP (II × 3)—6/324-mm Mk 32 ASW TT (III × 2)—2/Mk 11 Hedgehog ASW Mortars (XXIV × 2)—1/Mk 9 d.c. racks (9 d.c.)
Electron Equipt: Radar: 1/. . . nav., 1/SPS-10, 1/SPS-6, 1/Mk 25, 2/Mk 34, 1/Mk 35 flc.
Sonar: SQS-29 series—EW: BLR-1, 4 decoy RL (XX × 4)
M: 2 sets geared turbines (D 340: G.E., D 341: Allis-Chalmers); 2 props; 60,000 hp
Boilers: 4 Babcock & Wilcox; 39.8 kg/cm², 454°C **Electric:** 880 kw
Fuel: 650 tons **Range:** 1,260/32; 4,400/15 **Man:** Approx. 20 officers, 275 men

Istanbul (D 340) H. Ehlers, 6-84

Izmir (D 341) H. Ehlers, 10-84

Remarks: Transferred 14-1-67 and 28-2-67, respectively, and *not* stricken in 1982 as reported in the previous edition. Employed as "station ships." Have Mk 37 GFCS for the 127-mm guns, 1 Mk 56 and 2 Mk 63 GFCS for the 76.2-mm guns. Sisters *Izmit* (ex-*Cogswell,* DD 651) scrapped 14-12-84; *Iskenderun* (ex-*Boyd,* DD 544) and *Içel* (ex-*Preston,* DD 795) hulked at Gölcük in late 1984 awaiting scrapping.

FRIGATES

◆ **0 (+4) MEKO 200-class guided-missile frigates**

	Bldr	Laid down	L	In serv.
F 240 Yavuz	Blohm & Voss Hamburg	31-5-85	7-11-85	1987
F. . . N.	Howaldtswerke, Kiel	25-9-85	. . .	. . .
F. . . N.	Gölçük NSY	. . .	. . .	. . .
F. . . N.	Gölçük NSY	. . .	. . .	. . .

D: 2,000 tons (2,784 fl) **S:** 27 kts **Dim:** 95.00 (88.00 pp) × 11.80 × 3.60 (mean hull)
A: 8/Harpoon SSM (IV × 2)—1/Mk 20 SAM launcher (VIII × 1, Sea Sparrow missiles)—1/127-mm Mk 45 Mod. 1 DP—12/25-mm AA (IV × 3, Sea Zenith)—6/324-mm Mk 32 Mod. 5 ASW TT (III × 2)—1/AB 212 helicopter with Sea Skua missiles
Electron Equipt: Radar: 1/nav., 1/Plessey Dolphin, 1/WM-25, 1/STIR
Sonar: SQS-56 hull-mounted—TACAN: . . .
EW: . . . passive, 2/Barricade decoy RL (IX × 2)
M: 4 MTU 20V1163 TB93 diesels; 2 CP props; 22,536 hp
Range: 4,000/20 **Fuel:** 380 tons **Man:** 170 tot. **Electric:** 1,440 kw

Remarks: Ordered 4-83, with Blohm & Voss supplying technical assistance in constructing two in Turkey. The Contraves quadruple 25-mm Sea Guard AA gun system replaced the earlier-proposed single U.S. Vulcan-Phalanx AA. Will have the H.S.A. SEWACO data system and a single Siemens Albis optronic director aft. The air-search radar has also been reported as an H.S.A. DA-08, vice Plessey Dolphin.

◆ **2 Berk class** Bldr: Göçük Naval SY

	Laid down	L	In serv.
D 358 Berk	9-3-67	25-6-71	12-7-72
D 359 Peyk	18-1-68	7-6-72	24-7-75

Peyk (D 359) L. & L. Van Ginderen, 9-83

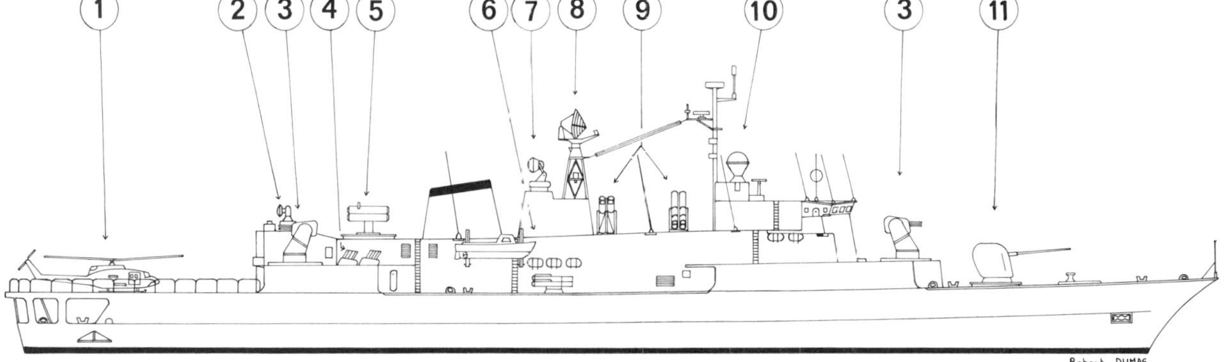

MEKO 200 1. AB-212 helicopter 2. Siemens optronic director 3. Sea Zenith AA 4. decoy RL 5. Mk 29 launcher for Sea Sparrow 6. Mk 32 ASW TT 7. STIR radar f.c. director 8. air-search radar 9. Harpoon missiles 10. WM-25 track-while-scan radar f.c.s. 11. 127-mm DP

FRIGATES *(continued)*

D: 1,450 tons (1,950 fl) **S:** 25 kts **Dim:** 95.15 × 11.82 × 4.4 (5.5 over sonar)
A: 4/76.2-mm DP (II × 2)—2/Mk 11 Hedgehogs—6/324-mm Mk 32 ASW TT (III × 2)—1/Mk 9 d.c. rack
Electron Equipt: Radar: 1/SPS-10, 1/SPS-40, 2/SPG-34
Sonar: 1/SQS-11—EW: WLR-1
M: 4 Fiat-Tosi 16 cyl., 800 rpm, Type 3-016-RSS diesels; 1 prop; 24,000 hp

Remarks: Based on the U.S. *Claud Jones* class, but more heavily armed. Can carry a helicopter but have no hangar. Two Mk 63 GFCS, with the SPG-34 radars mounted on the gunmounts.

◆ **2 ex-German Köln (Type 120) class** Bldr: H.C. Stülcken, Hamburg

	Laid down	L	In serv.
D 360 Gelibolu (ex-*Gazi Osman Paşa*, ex-Karlsruhe, F 223)	15-12-58	24-10-59	15-12-62
D 361 Gemlik (ex-*Emden*, F 221)	15-4-58	21-3-59	24-10-61

Gelibolu (D 360) H. Ehlers, 4-84

Gelibolu (D 360) H. Ehlers, 4-84

D: 2,425 tons (2,970 fl) **S:** 30 kts (20 on diesels)
Dim: 109.83 (105.00 pp) × 10.50 × 4.61
A: 2/100-mm Mod. 1953 DP (I × 2)—6/40-mm AA (II × 2, I × 2)—2/375-mm Bofors ASW RL (IV × 2)—4/533-mm ASW TT (I × 4)—2/d.c. racks (12 d.c.)—up to 82 mines
Electron Equipt: Radar: 1/Kelvin-Hughes 14/9, 1/DA-08, 1/SGR-103, 2/M 44, 1/M 45
Sonar: 1 PAE CWE hull-mounted
EW: . . . intercept, 2 decoy RL (XX × 2)
M: CODAG: 4 M.A.N. 16-cyl., 3,000-hp diesels, 2 Brown-Boveri 13,000-hp gas turbines; 2 CP props; 36,000 hp
Electric: 2,700 kw **Fuel:** 361 tons **Range:** 900/30; 2,900/22
Man: 17 officers, 193 men (in German service)

Remarks: D 360 transferred 28-3-83 at Gölçuk. Ex-*Emden* transferred late 1983. Sister *Köln* may transfer later. Made 33 kts on original trials. Carry 72 rockets for the ASW RL.

GUIDED-MISSILE PATROL BOATS

◆ **6 (+ . . .) German FPB 57-class**

Bldrs: P 340: Lürssen, Vegesack, W. Germany; others: Taskizak NDY, Istanbul

	Laid down	L	In serv.
P 340 Dogan	2-6-75	16-6-76	15-6-77
P 341 Marti	1-7-75	30-6-77	27-7-78
P 342 Tayfun	1-12-75	19-7-79	1980
P 343 Volkan	. . .	11-8-80	1981
P 344 Rüzgar (ex-*Gurbet*)	30-7-81	. . .	1983
P 345 Poyraz	. . .	17-12-84	1985

Dogan (P 340) H. Ehlers, 5-84

D: 353 tons (398 fl) **S:** 36.5 kts **Dim:** 58.1 (54.4 pp) × 7.62 × 2.83
A: 8/Harpoon SSM (IV × 2)—1/76-mm OTO Melara Compact DP—2/35-mm Oerlikon AA (II × 1)—2/7.62-mm mg (I × 2)
Electron Equipt: Radar: 1/Decca 1226, 1/H.S.A. WM-28-41
EW: SUSIE-1 intercept, 2 decoy RL (XX × 2)
M: 4 MTU 16V956 TB91 diesels; 4 props; 18,000 hp (16,000 sust.)
Electric: 405 kVA **Range:** 700/35; 1,600/32.5; 3,300/16
Man: 5 officers, 33 men

Remarks: The 76-mm mount has a local control cupola. Carry 300 rounds 76-mm, 2,750 rounds 35-mm. Steel hulls, aluminum superstructures. Plan continued construction at rate of one per year.

TORPEDO BOATS

◆ **8 Kartal-class guided-missile and torpedo boats** (In serv. 1967-71) Bldr: Lürssen, Vegesack

P 321 Denizkusu	P 324 Kartal	P 328 Simsek
P 322 Atmaca	P 326 Pelikan	P 329 Karsiga
P 323 Sahin	P 327 Albatros	

Sahin (P 323) L. & L. Van Ginderen, 11-83

D: 184 tons (210 fl) **S:** 42 kts **Dim:** 42.8 × 7.14 × 2.21
A: 2/40-mm AA (I × 2)—2/Penguin Mk 1 SSM—2/533-mm TT
Electron Equipt: Radar: 1/Decca 1226
M: 4 MTU 16V538 diesels; 4 props; 12,000 hp
Range: 500/39; 1,000/32 **Man:** 39 tot.

Remarks: Similar to the German *Jaguar* class. Wooden planking; steel and light-metal keel and frames; light-metal superstructure. Can be fitted as fast gunboats or minelayers (four mines). All now carry two Penguin IR-homing anti-ship missiles. Sister *Melten* cut in two by Soviet naval training ship *Khasan* 25-9-85.

◆ **6 ex-West German Zobel class** Bldr: Lürssen, Vegesack (except ex-*Hyäne:* Krogerwerft, Rendsburg)

	Laid down	L	In serv.
P. . . N. . . . . . . (ex-*Gepard*, P 6098)	20-4-61	14-4-62	18-4-63
P. . . N. . . . . . . (ex-*Frettchen*, P 6100)	30-3-62	20-11-62	26-6-63
P. . . N. . . . . . . (ex-*Dachs*, P 6094)	22-11-60	10-6-61	25-9-62
P. . . N. . . . . . . (ex-*Wiesel*, P 6093)	22-8-60	14-3-61	25-6-62
P. . . N. . . . . . . (ex-*Ozelot*, P 6101)	14-4-62	4-2-63	25-10-63
P. . . N. . . . . . . (ex-*Hyäne*, P 6099)	13-7-61	31-3-62	10-5-63

ex-Ozelot (PG 101)—prior to transfer G. Gyssels, 8-83

TORPEDO BOATS *(continued)*

D: 210 tons (230 fl) **S:** 43 kts **Dim:** 42.62 (39.80 pp) × 7.10 × 1.59 (2.20 props)
A: 2/40-mm Bofors AA (I × 2)—2/533-mm TT (2 reloads)
Electron Equipt: Radar: 1/Kelvin-Hughes 14/9, 1/H.S.A. M20-2
EW: . . . intercept
M: 4 MTU 16V538 diesels; 4 props; 12,000 hp **Electric:** 265 kVA
Range: 500/39.5; 740/34.5 **Man:** Approx. 40 tot.

Remarks: Purchased after striking from West German Navy, first three on 14-5-84 and others 8-10-84. Had been modernized with H.S.A. M-20 track-while-scan radar f.c.s. and aft-firing wire-guided torpedoes (Seeal) between 3-8-70 and 16-8-71. Wooden-planked hull on aluminum alloy frame. New names, numbers, and any alterations made by Turkish Navy not reported.

◆ **4 ex-German Jaguar class (Type 140)**

Bldrs: P 330 and P 336: Krögerwerft, Rendsburg; others: Lürssen, Vegesack

	L		L
P 331 Tufan (ex-*Storch*)	16-11-59	P 335 Kalkan (ex-*Löwe*)	8-11-58
P 333 Mizrak (ex-*Häher*)	9-1-60	P 336 Karayel (ex-*Tiger*)	21-4-58

D: 184 tons (210 fl) **S:** 42 kts **Dim:** 42.62 × 7.1 × 2.21 (props)
A: 2/40-mm AA (I × 2)—4/533-mm TT or 2/TT and mines
M: 4 MTU 16V538 diesels; 4 props; 12,000 hp
Range: 500/39; 1,000/32 **Man:** 39 tot.

Remarks: Transferred 1975-76. The *Alk, Iltis,* and *Reiher* were transferred at the same time to be cannibalized for the maintenance of the seven in service. Similar to *Kartal* class but shorter deckhouse with stepped face. Sisters *Firtina* (P 330, ex-*Pelikau*), *Kiliç* (P 332, ex-*Pinguin*), and *Yildiz* (P 334, ex-*Wolf*) stricken 8-6-82; the others will probably go soon.

PATROL BOATS AND CRAFT

◆ **1 German PB 57 class** Bldr: Taskizak Naval DY, Istanbul (In serv. 30-7-76)

P 140 Girne

Girne (P 140) H. Ehlers, 3-83

D: 341 tons (399 fl) **S:** 29.5 kts **Dim:** 58.1 (54.4 pp) × 7.6 × 2.8
A: 2/40-mm AA (I × 2)—2/12.7-mm mg (I × 2)—4/Mk 20 Mousetrap ASW RL—2/d.c. projectors—2/d.c. racks
Electron Equipt: Radar: 2/navigational
M: 2 MTU 16V956 TB91 diesels; 2 props; 9,000 hp **Electric:** 405 kVA
Range: 2,200/28; 4,200/16 **Man:** 3 officers, 27 men

Remarks: Same basic design as the Spanish *Lazaga*-class patrol boats, but with lighter armament. Design by Lürssen. Construction program canceled after one unit. One CSEE Naja optronic GFCS. Single 40-mm Bofors replaced twin 40-mm aft by 1982.

◆ **1 ex-U.S. Asheville class** Bldr: Peterson Builders, Sturgeon Bay, Wisc.

	L	In serv.
P 339 Bora (ex-*Surprise,* PG 97)	15-11-68	24-9-69

Bora (P 339) H. Ehlers, 5-83

D: 225 tons (240 fl) **S:** 40 kts (16 on diesels)
Dim: 50.14 (46.94 pp) × 7.28 × 2.9
A: 1/76.2-mm Mk 34 DP—1/40-mm AA—4/12.7-mm mg (II × 2)
Electron Equipt: Radar: 1/SPS-53, 1/SPG-50
M: CODAG: 1 LM 1500 Mk 7 gas turbine (12,500 hp); 2 Cummins 875V12 diesels (1,450 hp); 2 props
Fuel: 50 tons **Range:** 325/35; 1,700/16 **Man:** 25 tot.

Remarks: Leased on 28-2-73. Mk 63 radar GFCS, with SPG-50 on 76.2-mm gunmount. Sister *Yildirim* (P 338, ex-*Defiance,* PG 95) lost through explosion 11-4-85 near Lesbos.

◆ **12 AB 25 class** Bldrs: Gölçük Naval SY (In serv. 1967-70)

P 1225 AB 25	P 1229 AB 29	P 1233 AB 33
P 1226 AB 26	P 1230 AB 30	P 1234 AB 34
P 1227 AB 27	P 1231 AB 31	P 1235 AB 35
P 1228 AB 28	P 1232 AB 32	P 1236 AB 36

AB 26 L. & L. Van Ginderen, 6-82

D: 150 tons (170 fl) **S:** 22 kts **Dim:** 40.24 × 6.4 × 1.65
A: 1/40-mm AA—1/20-mm AA—2/12.7-mm mg (I × 2)—2/Mk 20 Mousetrap ASW RL—1/d.c. rack
M: SACM-AGO V16CSHR diesels; 2 props; 4,800 hp; 2 cruise diesels; 300 hp

Remarks: Fourteen others are assigned to the Marine Police. Built with French assistance. AB 35 and 36, delivered two years later than others, have a lower hull knuckle forward and bow bulwarks.

◆ **4 ex-U.S. PGM 71 motor gunboats** Bldr: Peterson Builders, Sturgeon Bay, Wisc.

	L	In serv.
P 1221 AB 21 (ex-PGM 104)	4-5-67	8-67
P 1222 AB 22 (ex-PGM 105)	25-5-67	9-67
P 1223 AB 23 (ex-PGM 106)	7-7-67	10-67
P 1224 AB 24 (ex-PGM 108)	14-9-67	5-68

AB 22 1982

D: 104 tons (144 fl) **S:** 17 kts **Dim:** 30.81 × 6.45 × 1.83
A: 1/40-mm AA—4/20-mm AA (II × 2)—2/Mk 22 double Mousetrap ASW RL—2/d.c. racks (4 d.c.)
Electron Equipt: Radar: 1/Raytheon 1500B—Sonar: SQS-17A
M: 8 G.M. 6-71 diesels; 2 props; 2,040 hp **Electric:** 30 kw
Fuel: 16 tons **Range:** 1,000/12 **Man:** 30 tot.

Remarks: Two twin 12.7-mm mg have been removed.

◆ **6 ex-U.S. PC 1638-class antisubmarine patrol boats**

Bldrs: P 116; Gölçük Naval SY; others: Gunderson Bros., Portland, Ore.

	L	In serv.
P 111 Sultan Hisar (ex-PC 1638)	1964	5-64
P 112 Demirhisar (ex-PC 1639)	9-7-64	4-65
P 113 Yarhisar (ex-PC 1640)	14-5-64	9-64
P 114 Akhisar (ex-PC 1641)	14-5-64	12-64
P 115 Sivrihisar (ex-PC 1642)	5-11-64	6-65
P 116 Kochisar (ex-PC 1643)	12-64	7-65

D: 325 tons (477 fl) **S:** 19 kts **Dim:** 52.9 × 7.0 × 3.1 (hull)
A: 1/40-mm AA—4/20-mm AA (II × 2)—1/Mk 15 trainable Hedgehog ASW mortar (XXIV × 1)—4/Mk 6 d.c. projectors—1/Mk 9 d.c. rack (9 d.c.)
Electron Equipt: Radar: 1/Decca 707—Sonar: SQS-17A
M: 2 Alco 16 9 × 10½ T diesels; 2 props; 4,800 hp
Fuel: 60 tons **Range:** 5,000/10 **Man:** 5 officers, 60 men

Remarks: Based on the PC 471 class of World War II.

PATROL BOATS AND CRAFT *(continued)*

Kochisar (P 116) H. Ehlers, 4-83

◆ **4 ex-U.S. Coast Guard 83-foot class** Bldr: U.S.C.G. Yard, Curtis Bay, Md.

P 1209 LS 9 P 1210 LS 10 P 1211 LS 11 P 1212 LS 12

LS 12 (P 1212) H. Ehlers, 15-5-82

D: 63 tons **S:** 18 kts **Dim:** 25.3 × 4.25 × 1.55
A: 1/20-mm AA—2/Mk 20 Mousetrap ASW RL
Electron Equipt: Radar: 1/SO-2—Sonar: QBE-3
M: 4 G.M. 6-71 diesels; 2 props; 900 hp **Man:** 15 tot.

REMARKS: Transferred on 25-6-53. Former Turkish hull numbers P 339, P 308, P 309, and P 310. Wooden hulls.

MINE WARFARE SHIPS

NOTE: The destroyer *Muavenet* (D 357) is also a minelayer when required, and the ex-German *Köln*-class frigates have mine rails.

◆ **1 Danish Falster-class minelayer** Bldr: Frederikshaven Naval DY, Denmark

	Laid down	L	In serv.
N 110 NUSRET (ex-N 108, ex-MMC 16)	1962	1964	16-9-64

Nusret—wearing old number

D: 1,880 tons **S:** 16.5 kts **Dim:** 77.0 (72.5 pp) × 12.8 × 3.4
A: 4/76.2-mm AA Mk 33 (II × 2)—400 mines
Electron Equipt: Radar: 1/navigational, 1/RAN 7S, 2/SPG-34
M: 2 G.M. 16-567D3 diesels; 2 CP props; 4,800 hp
Fuel: 130 tons **Man:** 130 tot.

REMARKS: Paid for by the U.S.A. Two Mk 63 radar GFCS systems.

◆ **1 (+1) Saruçabay-class minelayer/landing ships** Bldr: Taskizak NSY, Istanbul

	Laid down	L	In serv.
NL 123 SARUÇABAY	25-7-80	30-7-81	26-7-84
NL 124 KARAMÜRSEL	26-7-84	26-7-84	. . .

D: 2,600 tons (fl) **S:** 14 kts **Dim:** 92.0 × 14.0 × . . .
A: 4/40-mm AA (II × 2)—4/20-mm AA (II × 2)—50 mines
M: 3 diesels; 3 props; 4,320 hp

REMARKS: Enlarged version of *Cakabey,* with raised forecastle and larger superstructure, helicopter deck aft. Can carry 11 tanks, 12 trucks, and 600 troops. Minelaying ports in stern. Two Mk 51 Mod. 2 lead-computing sights for the 40-mm AA. See photo in addenda.

◆ **1 Cakabey-class minelayer/landing ship** Bldr: Taskizak NSY, Istanbul

	Laid down	L	In serv.
NL 122 ÇAKABEY (ex-L 405)	. . .	3-6-77	25-7-80

D: 1,600 tons **S:** 14 kts **Dim:** 77.3 (74.3 pp) × 12.0 × 2.3
A: 4/40-mm AA (II × 2)—8/20-mm AA (II × 4)—150 mines
M: 3 diesels; 3 props; 4,500 hp

REMARKS: Redesignated as a minelayer/landing ship in 1980. Originally planned as a class of four. As a landing ship, NL 112 can carry 400 troops, 9 U.S. M-48 tanks, and 10 jeeps. Carries two LCVP in davits. Deck cleared forward as a helicopter platform. See photo in addenda.

◆ **2 ex-German, ex-U.S. LST 542-class minelayer/tank landing ships**

Bldrs: L 403: Missouri Valley Bridge & Iron, Evansville, Ind.; L 404: American Bridge Co., Ambridge, Pa.

	Laid down	L	In serv.
NL 120 BAYRAKTAR (ex-L 403, ex-*Bottrop,* ex-*Saline County,* LST 1101)	22-11-44	3-1-45	26-1-45
NL 121 SANCAKTAR (ex-*Bochum,* ex-*Rice County,* LST 1089)	20-12-44	17-2-45	14-3-45

Bayraktar (NL 120) 1983

D: 3,640 tons (4,140 fl) **S:** 11 kts **Dim:** 101.37 × 15.28 × 3.98 (max.)
A: 6/40-mm AA (II × 2, I × 2)—mines **Electric:** 860 kw **Range:** 15,000/9
Electron Equipt: Radar: 1/Kelvin-Hughes 14/9
M: 2 G.M. 16-567A diesels; 2 props; 1,700 hp **Man:** 60 tot.

REMARKS: NL 120 was transferred to West Germany on 6-2-64 and to Turkey on 13-12-72; NL 121 to West Germany on 23-1-64 and to Turkey on 12-12-72. Converted to minelayers while in German service. Six rails on the upper deck, tapering to two at the stern, have been removed, but there remain four rails below decks, exiting through a broadened stern. Four two-ton mine-handling cranes added. Bow doors retained. Redesignated as amphibious ships 1974-75, but again placed in mine warfare category 1980.

◆ **5 minelayers** Bldr: Brown SB, Houston, Tex.

	Laid down	L	In serv.
N 101 MORDOGAN (ex-MMC 11, ex-LSM 484)	17-2-45	10-3-45	15-4-45
N 102 MERIC (ex-MMC 12, ex-LSM 481)	17-2-45	10-3-45	8-4-45
N 103 MARMARIS (ex-MMC 10, ex-LSM 490)	3-3-45	24-3-45	28-4-45
N 104 MERSIN (ex-*Vale,* ex-MMC 13, ex-LSM 492)	28-5-44	22-6-44	4-8-44
N 105 MUREFTE (ex-*Vidar,* ex-MMC 14, ex-MSC 493)	10-3-45	30-3-45	4-5-45

Meric (N 102) L. & L. Van Ginderen, 6-82

D: 743 tons (1,100 fl) **S:** 12.5 kts **Dim:** 62.0 × 10.52 × 2.54
A: 6/40-mm AA (II × 3)—5/20-mm AA (I × 5)—400 mines
Electron Equipt: Radar: 2/navigational
M: 2 G.M. 16-278A diesels; 2 props; 2,800 hp
Fuel: 60 tons **Range:** 2,500/12 **Man:** 70 tot.

REMARKS: Ex-U.S. LSM 1-class medium landing ships. In 10-52 after conversion, the first three were transferred to Turkey, the other two to Norway; the latter were

MINE WARFARE SHIPS *(continued)*

returned to U.S. control in 1960, then reassigned to Turkey. Four booms, two forward, two aft, for the loading of mines. Two minelaying rails. Originally had four twin 40-mm AA and six 20-mm AA. N 104 has two Fairbanks-Morse 38D8⅛ × 10 diesels.

◆ **1 mine-planter** Bldr: Higgins, New Orleans, La. (L: 1958)

N 115 Mehmetcik (ex-YMP 3)

D: 540 tons (fl) **S:** 10 kts **Dim:** 39.62 × 10.67 × 3.05
A: 1/40-mm AA **Electron Equipt:** Radar: 1/Decca 12
M: 2 diesels; 2 props **Man:** 22 tot.

Remarks: Paid for by the U.S. Military Aid Program. Used to place controlled minefields. Gun not normally mounted. See photo in addenda.

◆ **6 ex-German French Mercure-class coastal minesweepers**

Bldr: Amiot (CMN), Cherbourg

	Laid down	L	In serv.
M 520 Karamürsel (ex-*Wörms*)	19-3-58	30-1-60	30-4-60
M 521 Kerempe (ex-*Detmold*)	19-2-58	17-11-59	20-2-60
M 522 Kilimli (ex-*Siegen*)	18-4-58	29-3-60	9-7-60
M 523 Kozlu (ex-*Hameln*)	20-1-58	20-8-59	15-10-59
M 524 Kusadasi (ex-*Vegesack*)	20-12-57	21-5-59	19-9-59
M 525 Kemer (ex-*Passau*)	19-5-58	25-6-60	15-10-60

Kilimli (M 522) L. & L. Van Ginderen, 6-82

D: 366 tons (383 fl) **S:** 14.5 kts **Dim:** 44.62 (42.5 pp) × 8.41 × 2.55
A: 2/20-mm AA (II × 1) **Electric:** 520 kw
Electron Equipt: Radar: 1/Decca 707
M: Mercedes-Benz MB-820 Db diesels; 2 CP props; 4,000 hp **Man:** 40 tot.

Remarks: These ships were built for the German Navy, placed in reserve in 1963, and stricken on 31-12-73. Transferred to Turkey between 6-75 and 10-75, except M 525, in 1979. French sister *Mercure* now a fisheries-protection ship. Wooden construction.

◆ **12 ex-U.S. Adjutant-, MSC 268(*)-, and MSC 289 (**)-class coastal minesweepers**

	L	In serv.
M 507 Seymen (ex-*De Panne,* ex-MSC 131)	. . .	28-10-55
M 508 Selçuk (ex-*Pavot,* ex-MSC 124)	. . .	6-54
M 509 Seyhan (ex-*Renoncule,* ex-MSC 142)	. . .	8-54
M 510 Samsun (ex-MSC 268)*	6-9-57	30-9-58
M 511 Sinop (ex-MSC 270)*	4-1-58	2-59
M 512 Sürmene (ex-MSC 271)*	1958	27-3-59
M 513 Seddul Bahr (ex-MSC 272)*	1958	5-59
M 514 Silifke (ex-MSC 304)**	21-11-64	9-65
M 515 Saros (ex-MSC 305)**	1-5-65	2-66
M 516 Sigaçik (ex-MSC 311)**	12-6-64	6-65
M 517 Sapanca (ex-MSC 312)**	14-9-64	26-7-65
M 518 Sariyer (ex-MSC 315)**	21-4-66	8-9-67

Bldrs: M 507: Hiltebrant DD, Kingston, N.Y.; M 508: Stephen Bros.; M 509: South Coast Co., Newport Beach, Cal.; M 510 to M 513: Bellingham SY, Bellingham, Wash.; M 514, M 515; Dorchester Builders, Dorchester, N.J.; M 516 to M 518: Peterson Builders, Sturgeon Bay, Wisc.

Seyhan (M 509)—Adjutant class L. & L. Van Ginderen, 6-82

Saros (M 515)—MSC 289 class U.S. Navy, 1984

D: 300 tons (392 fl) **S:** 14 kts **Dim:** 43.0 (41.5 pp) × 7.95 × 2.55
A: 2/20-mm AA (II × 1) **M:** 2 G.M. 8/268A diesels; 2 props; 1,200 hp
Range: 2,500/10 **Man:** 4 officers, 34 men

Remarks: M 507 was returned to the U.S.A. by Belgium in 1970, and M 508 and M 509 were returned by France on 23-3-70, then transferred to Turkey. The MSC 268 class have 4 G.M. 6-71 diesels; 2 props; 880 hp. The MSC 289 class have lower superstructure, taller stacks, and 2 Waukesha L-1616 diesels of 600 hp each; **Dim:** 44.32 × 8.29 × 2.55.

◆ **4 ex-Canadian Bay-class coastal minesweepers** Bldr: Davie SB, Lauzon, Quebec

	L		L
M 530 Trabzon (ex-*Gaspé*)	20-5-73	M 532 Tirebolu (ex-*Comax*)	24-4-52
M 531 Terme (ex-*Trinity*)	31-7-53	M 533 Tekirdag (ex-*Ungava*)	12-11-51

Trabzon (M 530)—wearing old number 1969

D: 390 tons (412 fl) **S:** 16 kts **Dim:** 50.0 (46.05 pp) × 9.21 × 2.8
A: 1/40-mm AA **Electron Equipt:** Radar: 1/Sperry Mk 2
M: 2 G.M. 12-278A diesels; 2 props; 2,400 hp **Range:** 4,000/10 **Man:** 44 tot.
Electric: 940-kw sweep/plus 690-kw ship's service **Fuel:** 52 tons

Remarks: Transferred under U.S. Military Aid Program on 19-5-58. Wood-planked skin on steel frame.

◆ **4 ex-U.S. Cape-class inshore minesweepers**

Bldr: Peterson Builders, Sturgeon Bay, Wisc.

	L	In serv.
M 500 Foca (ex-MSI 15)	23-8-66	8-67
M 501 Fethiye (ex-MSI 16)	7-12-66	9-67
M 502 Fatsa (ex-MSI 17)	11-4-67	10-67
M 503 Finike (ex-MSI 18)	11-67	12-67

Foca (M 500) L. & L. Van Ginderen, 6-82

D: 203 tons (239 fl) **S:** 12.5 kts **Dim:** 34.06 × 7.14 × 2.4
A: 1/12.7-mm mg **M:** 4 G.M. 6-71 diesels; 2 props; 960 hp
Electric: 120 kw **Fuel:** 20 tons **Range:** 1,000/9 **Man:** 20 tot.

Remarks: Transferred on completion. Wooden construction.

MINE WARFARE SHIPS *(continued)*

◆ **2 ex-U.S. 64-foot distribution-box minefield tenders**

Y 1148 Samandira L 1   Y 1149 Samandira L 2

D: 72 tons (fl) **S:** 9.5 kts **Dim:** 19.58 × 5.72 × 1.83
A: 1 Gray Marine 64HN9 diesel; 1 prop; 225 hp **Man:** 6 tot.

Remarks: Transferred in 1959.

◆ **9 mine-disposal diving tenders** Bldr: U.K. (In serv. 1942)

P 311 Dalgiç 1 (ex-MTB 1)	P 314 MTB 4	P 318 MTB 8
P 312 Dalgiç 1 (ex-MTB 2)	P 316 MTB 6	P 319 MTB 9
P 313 MTB 3	P 317 MTB 7	P 320 MTB 10

Dalgiç 2 (P 312) H. Ehlers, 7-84

D: 70 tons **S:** 20 kts **Dim:** 21.8 × 4.2 × 2.6
M: 2 diesels; 2,000 hp **A:** 1/12.7-mm mg or 20-mm AA in some

Remarks: First two redesignated diver support boats in 1983.

AMPHIBIOUS WARFARE SHIPS AND CRAFT

Note: The *Cakabey* (NL 112), *Bayraktar* (NL 120), and *Sancaktar* (NL 121), formerly listed as landing ships, are now listed as minelayers; they can still be employed in amphibious landings, as can the new *Saruçabay* (NL 123) class.

◆ **2 ex-U.S. Terrebonne Parish-class tank landing ships**

Bldr: Christy Corp., Sturgeon Bay, Wisc.

	L	In serv.
L 401 Ertugrul (ex-*Windham County,* LST 1170)	22-5-54	15-12-54
L 402 Serdar (ex-*Westchester County,* LST 1167)	18-4-53	10-3-54

Serdar (L 402) H. Ehlers, 5-82

Ç 109 H. Ehlers, 6-84

Ç 137 and a sister H. Ehlers, 7-84

D: 2,590 tons (5,786 fl) **S:** 15 kts **Dim:** 117.35 (112.77 pp) × 17.06 × 5.18
A: 6/76.2-mm DP (II × 3) **Electron Equipt:** Radar: 1/SPS-21, 2/Mk 34
M: 4 G.M. 16-268A diesels; 2 CP props; 6,000 hp **Electric:** 600 kw
Fuel: 874 tons **Man:** 116 crew + 395 troops

Remarks: L 401 transferred in 6-73 and L 402 in 8-74. Cargo: 2,200 tons. Can carry four LCVPs in Welin davits. Two Mk 63 radar GFCS.

◆ **34 (+3 + . . .) Ç 107-class utility landing craft** (In serv. 1966-. . .)

Bldrs: Ç 107 through Ç 138: Gölçük Naval SY; Ç 139–144: Taskizak NDY

Ç 107 through Ç 130; Ç 134; Ç 135; Ç 137–141; Ç 142–144 (L: 25-7-85)

D: 280 tons light (600 fl) **S:** 8.5 kts (loaded) **Dim:** 56.56 × 11.58 × 1.25 (aft)
A: 2/20-mm AA (I × 2)—2/12.7-mm mg (I × 2)
M: 3 G.M. 6-71 diesels; 3 props; 900 hp (675 sust.)
Range: 600/10 (light); 1,100/8

Remarks: Continuing construction program, design based on British LCT(4) design. Also being built for Libya, which received Ç 133 and Ç 134 from Turkish inventory in 12-79, and Ç 131–Ç 133 in 1983. Ç 137 and Ç 138 were launched 21-3-80 and commissioned 20-7-81; Ç 139 through Ç 141 were launched at Taskizak during Aug.-Sept. 1984. Can carry 100 troops and five M-48 tanks. Superstructure configurations vary: Ç 121 and later have mg platform atop pilothouse. Ç 136 lost in storm 30-1-85.

Note: Ex-British LCT(4)-class landing craft Ç 103 stricken 1983.

◆ **14 (+ . . .) utility landing craft** Bldr: Taskizak, Istanbul, 1965-66

Ç 205 through Ç 218

Ç 211 1973

D: 320 tons (405 fl) **S:** 10 kts **Dim:** 44.3 (40.8 wl) × 8.8 × 1.7
A: 2/20-mm AA (I × 2) **M:** 2 G.M. 6-71 diesels; 2 props; 600 hp (450 sust.)

◆ **1 ex-U.S. LCU 501 (LCT (6))-class utility landing craft**

		L	In serv.
Ç 204	Bldr: Pidgeon-Thomas Iron Co., Memphis, Tenn.	9-2-44	16-2-44

Ç 204 L. & L. Van Ginderen, 9-83

D: 143 tons (309 fl) **S:** 8 kts **Dim:** 36.68 × 9.75 × 1.22 (aft)
A: 2/20-mm AA (I × 2) **M:** 3 Gray Marine 64HN9 diesels; 3 props; 675 hp
Electric: 20 kw **Fuel:** 11 tons **Range:** 700/7 **Man:** 12 tot.

Remarks: Transferred in 7-67. Cargo: 150 tons + 8 troops. Sisters Ç 201–Ç 203 stricken 1983.

AMPHIBIOUS WARFARE SHIPS AND CRAFT *(continued)*

◆ **20 U.S. LCM (8)-class landing craft** Bldr: Taskizak NDY, Istanbul (In serv. 1965-66)

Ç 301 through Ç 320

D: 56 tons (113 fl) **S:** 9 kts **Dim:** 22.43 × 6.42 × 1.6
A: 2/12.7-mm mg (I × 2) **M:** 4 G.M. 6-71 diesels; 2 props; 660 hp **Man:** 5 tot.

HYDROGRAPHIC SHIPS

◆ **1 ex-British Catherine-class former minesweeper**

Bldr: Assoc. SB, Lake Washington, Wash.

	Laid down	L	In serv.
A 593 Çandarli (ex-*Frolic*, ex-BAM 29)	5-3-43	20-6-43	18-5-44

Çandarli (A 593) G. Arra, 1972

D: 1,010 tons (1,185 fl) **S:** 18 kts **Dim:** 67.31 × 9.75 × 3.2
A: 1/76.2-mm DP—4/20-mm AA **Electron Equipt:** Radar: 1/Decca 707
M: 4 G.M. 12-278A diesels, electric drive; 2 props; 3,532 hp **Electric:** 360 kw
Fuel: 210 tons **Range:** 3,500/17; 8,500/11 **Man:** 105 tot.

Remarks: Lend-lease version of the U.S. *Auk* class, transferred to Great Britain on completion. Survivor of a group of seven transferred to Turkey in 3-47. Converted later for service as survey ships. Charthouse added between stacks. Sister *Çarşamba* (A 594, ex-*Tattoo*, BAM 32) stricken 1983.

◆ **2 ex-U.S. 52-foot inshore-survey craft** (In serv. 1966)

Y 1221 Mesaha 1 Y 1222 Mesaha 2

D: 31.7 tons (37.6 fl) **S:** 10 kts **Dim:** 15.9 × 4.45 × 1.3
M: 2 G.M. 6-71 diesels; 2 props; 330 hp **Range:** 600/10 **Man:** 10 tot.

AUXILIARY SHIPS

◆ **1 replenishment oiler** Bldr: Gölçük Naval SY, Istanbul (L: 16-11-83)

A 580 Akar

D: Approx. 20,000 tons (fl) **S:** 15 kts **Dim:** 145.1 × 22.8 × . . .
A: 2/76.2-mm DP (I × 2)—2/40-mm AA (I × 2)
M: 1 diesel; 1 prop; 6,500 hp **Man:** 329 tot.

Remarks: 15,000 dwt. Underway replenishment capability.

◆ **1 new-construction transport oiler**

	Bldr	L	In serv.
A 570 Taskizak	Taskizak NDY	28-7-83	1-8-84

Taskizak (A 570)—fitting out H. Ehlers, 5-84

D: Approx. 1,800 tons (fl) **S:** 13 kts **Dim:** . . . × . . . × . . .
A: 1/40-mm AA—2/20-mm AA (I × 2)
M: 1 diesel; 1 prop; 1,400 hp **Man:** 57 tot. **Cargo:** 1,000 dwt

◆ **1 Turkish-designed replenishment oiler** Bldr: Taskizak NDY, Istanbul (L: 7-69)

A 573 Binbaşi Saadettin Gürçan

D: 1,505 tons (4,680 fl) **S:** 16 kts **Dim:** 89.7 × 11.8 × 5.4
A: 1/40-mm AA—2/20-mm AA (I × 2)
M: 4 G.M. 16-567A diesels, electric drive; 2 props; 4,400 hp

Remarks: One liquid-replenishment station on each side. Primarily a tanker. See photo in addenda.

◆ **1 Turkish-designed transport oiler** Bldr: Gölçük NSY, 1964

A 572 Albay Hakki Burak

Albay Hakki Burak (A 572) L. & L. Van Ginderen, 6-82

D: 1,800 tons (3,740 fl) **S:** 16 kts **Dim:** 83.73 × 12.25 × 5.49
A: 2/40-mm AA (I × 2) **Electron Equipt:** Radar: 1/Decca 707
M: 4 G.M. 16-567A diesels, electric drive; 2 props; 4,400 hp **Man:** 88 tot.

Remarks: One liquid-replenishment station on each side. Primarily a transport tanker.

◆ **1 ex-West German Bodensee-class transport oiler** Bldr: Lindenau-Werft, Kiel

	Laid down	L	In serv.
A 575 Inebolu (ex-*Bodensee*, ex-*Unkas*)	24-8-55	19-11-55	11-2-56

Inebolu (A 575)—as the *Bodensee* 1975

D: 1,237 tons (1,840 fl) **S:** 13.5 kts **Dim:** 67.1 (61.2 pp) × 9.84 × 4.27
A: 2/20-mm AA **Electron Equipt:** Radar: 1/Kelvin-Hughes 14/9
M: 1 MAK 6-cyl. diesel; 1 prop; 1,050 hp **Electric:** 238 kVA
Range: 6,240/12 **Man:** 21 tot.

Remarks: Former merchant tanker acquired on 26-3-59 for the West German Navy; transferred to Turkey on 25-8-77. Cargo: 1,231 tons. One replenishment station.

◆ **1 Turkish-designed transport oiler** Bldr: Taskizak NDY, Istanbul

A 571 Yuzbasi Tolünay (ex-*Taskizak*)

Yuzbasi Tolünay (A 571)—with *Pinar*-class water tender Y 1216 alongside H. Ehlers, 3-84

AUXILIARY SHIPS *(continued)*

D: 2,500 tons (3,500 fl) **S:** 14 kts **Dim:** 79.0 × 12.4 × 5.9
A: 2/40-mm AA (I × 2)
M: 2 Atlas-Polar diesels; 2 props; 1,900 hp

REMARKS: Launched on 22-8-50. Has one alongside replenishment station and can replenish over the stern.

◆ **1 ex-U.S. Mettawee-class former gasoline tanker** Bldr: East Coast SY, Bayonne, N.J.

	Laid down	L	In serv.
A 574 AKPINAR (ex-*Chiwaukum,* AOG 26)	2-4-44	5-5-44	22-7-44

D: 700 tons (2,270 fl) **S:** 14 kts **Dim:** 67.21 (64.77 pp) × 11.28 × 3.99
A: 1/76.2-mm DP—1/40-mm AA—2/20-mm AA
M: 1 Fairbanks-Morse 37E16 diesel; 1 prop; 800 hp
Electric: 155 kw **Fuel:** 29 tons

REMARKS: Transferred in 5-48. Cargo: 1,365 tons. Very low freeboard restricts use to sheltered waters.

◆ **2 ex-German Rhein-class tenders**

	Bldr	L	In serv.
A 577 SOKULLU MEHMET PAŞA (ex-*Isar,* A 54)	Blohm + Voss, Hamburg	14-7-62	25-1-64
A 579 CEZAYIRLI GAZI HASAN PAŞA (ex-*Ruhr,* A 64)	Schlieker, Hamburg	18-8-60	2-5-64

Cezayirli Gazi Hasan Paşa (A 579) G. Arra, 1981

D: A 579: 2,370 tons (2,740 fl); A 580: 2,330 tons (2,930 fl)
S: 20 kts (22 trials)
Dim: A 479: 98.18 (92.80 pp) × 11.80 × 3.90
A 580: 98.80 (92.80 pp) × 11.80 × 3.95
A: 2/100-mm Mod. 1953 DP (I × 2)—4/40-mm AA (I × 4)—70 mines
Electron Equipt: Radar: 1/. . . nav., 1/SGR-105, 1/SGR-103, 2/M 45
M: 6 Maybach (A 580: Mercedes-Benz 839Db) diesels (A 580: electric drive); 2 props; 11,400 hp (A 580: 11,000)
Electric: 2,250 hp **Fuel:** 334 tons **Range:** 2,500/16
Man: 98 tot. (accommodations for 40 officers, 170 men)

REMARKS: A 579, transferred on 15-11-76, was built as a Type 401 small combatant tender, but was employed as a training ship in the West German Navy; she continues in this latter role in the Turkish Navy. A 577, transferred on 30-9-82, is configured as a Type 402 mine countermeasures support ship and had been in reserve since 1968. A 579 has CP props. Both have 2 M4 directors for the 100-mm guns.

◆ **2 tenders, ex-West German Angeln-class cargo ships**

Bldr: Ateliers et Chantiers de Bretagne, Nantes, France

	Laid down	L	In serv.
A 586 ÜLKÜ (ex-*Angeln,* ex-*Borée*)	17-5-54	9-10-54	20-1-55
A 588 UMURBEY (ex-*Dithmarschen,* ex-*Hebé*)	20-10-54	7-5-55	17-11-55

D: 2,998 tons (4,089 fl) **S:** 19 kts **Dim:** 90.53 (84.5 pp) × 13.32 × 6.2
A: 2/20-mm AA (I × 2) **M:** 2 SEMT-Pielstick 6-cyl. diesels; 1 prop; 3,000 hp
Electric: 335 kw **Range:** 3,660/15 **Man:** 57 tot.

REMARKS: Former French cargo ships acquired for the West German Navy on 27-11-59 and 19-12-59, respectively. A 586 was transferred to Turkey on 28-3-72 and A 588 on 6-10-76. A 586 is used as a patrol-boat tender and A 588 as a submarine tender. A 588's displacement is 3,098 tons (4,189 fl). Cargo: A 586, 2,665 tons; A 588, 2,670 tons. Six 2.5-ton derricks, three holds.

◆ **1 ex-U.S. Portunus-class patrol-boat tender** Bldr: Bethlehem Steel, Hingham, Mass.

	Laid down	L	In serv.
A 581 ONARAN (ex-*Alecto,* AGP 14, ex-LST 977)	12-12-44	15-1-45	8-2-45

D: 4,100 tons (fl) **S:** 11.6 kts **Dim:** 99.98 × 15.24 × 3.4
A: 8/40-mm AA (IV × 2)—8/20-mm AA (II × 4)
M: 2 G.M. 12-278A diesels; 2 props; 1,800 hp **Electric:** 500 kw
Fuel: 590 tons **Range:** 9,000/9 **Man:** 291 tot.

REMARKS: Transferred in 11-52. Retains bow doors. Superstructure enlarged after transfer.

Onaran (A 581) G. Arra, 1971

◆ **1 ex-U.S. Achelous-class submarine tender** Bldr: Bethlehem Steel, Hingham, Mass.

	Laid down	L	In serv.
A 582 BASARAN (ex-*Patroclus,* ARL 19, ex-LST 955)	22-9-44	22-10-44	13-11-44

REMARKS: Former landing-craft repair ship. Data as for *Onaran,* above, except: **Electric:** 420 kw; **Fuel:** 621 tons. Has less superstructure than *Onaran.*

◆ **1 ex-U.S. Aegir-class submarine tender** Bldr: Ingalls, Pascagoula, Miss.

	Laid down	L	In serv.
A 583 DONATAN (ex-*Anthedon,* AS 24)	1943	15-10-43	15-9-44

Donatan (A 583) L. & L. Van Ginderen, 6-82

D: 16,500 tons (fl) **S:** 18.4 kts (trials) **Dim:** 149.96 (141.73 pp) × 21.18 × 8.23
A: 3/76.2-mm DP (I × 3)—8/40-mm AA (II × 1, I × 6)—8/20-mm AA (I × 8)
M: 1 set Westinghouse GT; 1 prop; 8,500 hp
Boilers: 2 Foster-Wheeler "D"; 37.2 kg/cm², 407°C
Electric: 1,200 kw **Fuel:** 3,045 tons **Man:** 1,460 tot.

REMARKS: Transferred on 7-2-69. Had been in U.S. Navy Reserve Fleet since 21-9-46. Unarmed at transfer. A helicopter platform has been added over the stern. Reported stricken 1985.

◆ **1 ex-U.S. Dixie-class destroyer tender** Bldr: Tampa SB, Tampa, Fla.

	Laid down	L	In serv.
A 576 DERYA (ex-*Piedmont,* AD 17)	1-12-41	7-12-42	5-1-44

Derya (A 576) H. Ehlers, 3-84

D: 9,450 tons light (17,190 fl) **S:** 18 kts **Dim:** 161.70 × 22.33 × 7.80
A: 5/20-mm AA (I × 5) **Electron Equipt:** Radar: 1/LN-66, 1/SPS-10
M: 2 sets GT; 2 props; 11,000 hp **Electric:** 3,600 kw
Fuel: 3,680 tons **Range:** 12,200/12 **Man:** Approx. 1,200 tot.

REMARKS: Transferred by sale 18-10-82 and recommissioned 29-3-83. Modernized early 1960s under FRAM program to serve as repair tender to missile-equipped ships. Extensive workshops, spares capacity. Two 20-ton cranes. Small helicopter deck.

◆ **1 submarine tender** Bldr: A.G. Weser, Bremen (L: 1955)

A 590 ERKIN (ex-*Ege*)

Erkin (A 590) H. Ehlers, 5-84

AUXILIARY SHIPS *(continued)*

D: 6,700 tons (fl) **S:** 16 kts **Dim:** 122.66 (109.86 pp) × 16.57 × 5.79
A: 4/40-mm AA (II × 2) **Electron Equipt:** Radar: 1/. . . nav.
M: 2 M.A.N. diesels; 2 props; 3,620 hp
Electric: 850 kw **Fuel:** 1,380 tons **Range:** 15,950/16 **Man:** 128 tot.

Remarks: Former 6,042 grt passenger-cargo ship. Acquired 1982 and placed in service 1983 to replace former submarine tender of the same name.

◆ **1 ex-U.S. AN 103-class net tender** Bldr: Krögerwerft, Rendsburg, West Germany

	Laid down	L	In serv.
P 305 AG 5 (ex-AN 104)	1960	20-10-60	25-2-61

D: 680 tons (975 fl) **S:** 12.8 kts **Dim:** 52.50 (48.5 hull; 44.6 pp) × 10.6 × 3.70
A: 1/40-mm AA—3/20-mm AA (I × 3)
M: 1 M.A.N. G7V 40/60 diesel; 1 prop; 1,470 hp
Range: 6,500/10.8 **Fuel:** 134 tons **Man:** 5 officers, 45 men

Remarks: Sister to the net layer *Thetis* in the Greek Navy. Built with U.S. Offshore Procurement funds. Carries 1,600 rds. 40-mm, 25,200 rds. 20-mm ammunition.

◆ **1 ex-U.S. AN 93-class net tender** Bldr: Bethlehem Steel, Staten Island, N.Y.

	L	In serv.
P 306 AG 6 (ex-*Cerberus,* ex-AN 93)	5-52	10-11-52

AG 6 (P 306) H. Ehlers, 5-84

D: 780 tons (902 fl) **S:** 12.8 kts **Dim:** 50.29 (44.5 pp) × 10.20 × 3.2
A: 1/76.2-mm DP—4/20-mm AA (I × 4)
M: 2 G.M. 8-268A diesels, electric drive; 1 prop; 1,500 hp
Range: 5,200/12 **Man:** 48 tot.

Remarks: Prototype of a class also built in France and Italy. Transferred to the Netherlands in 12-52 and returned 17-9-70; transferred to Turkey the same day.

◆ **1 ex-U.S. Aloe-class net tender** Bldr: Marietta Mfg. Co., Pt. Pleasant, W. Va.

	Laid down	L	In serv.
P 304 AG 4 (ex-*Larch,* AN 21, ex-YN 16)	18-10-40	2-7-41	13-12-41

AG 4 L. & L. Van Ginderen, 6-82

D: 560 tons (805 fl) **S:** 12.5 kts **Dim:** 49.73 (44.5 wl) × 9.3 × 3.56
A: 1/76.2-mm DP—4/20-mm AA (I × 4)
M: 2 Alco 538-6 diesels, electric drive; 1 prop; 620 hp
Electric: 120 kw **Fuel:** 80 tons **Man:** 48 tot.

Remarks: Transferred in 5-46.

◆ **1 ex-British "Bar"-class net tender** Bldr: Blyth DD & SB Co., U.K.

	Laid down	L	In serv.
P 301 AG 1 (ex-*Barbarian*)	10-6-37	21-10-37	16-4-38

D: 750 tons (1,000 fl) **S:** 11.7 kts **Dim:** 52.96 × 9.8 × 4.62
A: 1/76.2-mm DP **M:** diesels; 1 prop; . . . hp
Range: 3,100/10 **Man:** 32 tot. **Fuel:** 214 tons

Remarks: Transferred in 1947. Sisters *AG 2* (ex-*Barbette*) and *AG 3* (ex-*Barfair*) were stricken in 1975. Original reciprocating steam propulsion plant replaced by diesels in the 1960s.

◆ **1 ex-U.S. Bluebird-class submarine-rescue ship**

Bldr: Charleston SB & DD Co., Charleston, S.C.

	Laid down	L	In serv.
A 584 Kurtaran (ex-*Bluebird,* ASR 19, ex-*Yurok,* ATF 164)	23-6-45	15-2-46	28-5-46

Kurtaran (A 584) H. Ehlers, 5-82

D: 1,294 tons (1,760 fl) **S:** 16 kts **Dim:** 62.48 (59.44) × 12.19 × 4.88
A: 1/76.2-mm DP **M:** 4 G.M. 12-278A diesels, electric drive; 1 prop; 3,000 hp
Electric: 600 kw **Fuel:** 300 tons **Man:** 100 tot.

Remarks: Begun as an *Achomawi*-class fleet tug, but altered while under construction, wooden fenders adding .5 meter to the beam. Carries McCann rescue diving bell and four marker buoys. Transferred on 15-8-50.

◆ **1 ex-U.S. Chanticleer-class submarine-rescue ship**

Bldr: Moore SB & DD Co., Oakland, Cal.

	Laid down	L	In serv.
A 585 Akin (ex-*Greenlet,* ASR 10)	15-10-41	12-7-42	29-5-43

D: 1,770 tons (2,321 fl) **S:** 15 kts **Dim:** 76.61 (73.15 pp) × 12.8 × 4.52
A: 1/40-mm AA—4/20-mm AA (II × 2) **Electron Equipt:** Radar: 1/SPS-5
M: 4 Alco 539 diesels, electric drive; 1 prop; 3,000 hp
Electric: 460 kw **Fuel:** 235 tons **Man:** 85 tot.

Remarks: Loaned on 12-6-70 and purchased outright on 15-2-73. Carries McCann rescue diving bell and four marker buoys.

◆ **1 ex-U.S. Diver-class salvage ship** Bldr: Basalt Rock Co., Napa, Cal.

	Laid down	L	In serv.
A 589 Işin (ex-*Safeguard,* ARS 25)	5-6-43	20-11-43	31-10-44

D: 1,480 tons (1,970 fl) **S:** 14.8 kts **Dim:** 65.08 (63.09 pp) × 12.5 × 4.0
A: 2/20-mm AA (I × 2) **Electric:** 460 kw **Fuel:** 300 tons **Man:** 97 tot.
M: 4 Cooper-Bessermer GSB-8 diesels, electric drive; 2 props; 3,000 hp

Remarks: Purchased on 28-9-79. Wooden fenders add .6 meter to beam. See photo in addenda.

◆ **1 training ship** Bldr: Blohm + Voss, Hamburg, West Germany (L: 28-2-31)

A 578 Savarona (ex-*Gunes Dil*)

Savarona (A 578) J.-C. Bellonne, 1973

AUXILIARY SHIPS *(continued)*

D: 5,750 tons (fl) **S:** 18 kts **Dim:** 123.0 × 16.1 × 5.6
A: 2/75-mm (I × 2)—2/40-mm AA (I × 2)—2/20-mm (I × 2)
Electron Equipt: Radar: 2/Sperry Mk 2
M: 2 sets GT; 2 props; 8,000 hp **Fuel:** 2,100 tons
Boilers: 4 **Range:** 9,000/15 **Man:** 132 crew, 80 midshipmen

REMARKS: A former state yacht converted to a cadet-training ship in 1952. Pendant number not painted on. White hull, buff stacks. Has 75-mm guns for saluting. Seriously damaged by fire 3-10-79.

◆ **1 ex-U.S. Cherokee-class fleet tug** Bldr: United Eng. Co., Alameda, Cal.

	Laid down	L	In serv.
A 587 GAZAL (ex-*Sioux*, ATF 75)	14-2-42	27-5-42	6-12-42

Gazal (A 587) H. Ehlers, 3-84

D: 1,235 tons (1,675 fl) **S:** 16.5 kts **Dim:** 62.48 (59.44 pp) × 11.73 × 4.67
A: 1/76.2-mm DP—2/20-mm AA (I × 2) **Electric:** 260 kw **Fuel:** 300 tons
M: 4 G.M. 12-278 diesels, electric drive; 1 prop; 3,000 hp **Man:** 85 tot.

REMARKS: Transferred on 30-10-72 and purchased outright on 15-8-73. Can be used for salvage. Similar to submarine-rescue ship *Kurtaran* (A 584).

◆ **1 oceanographic survey craft** Bldr: Gölçük NDY (L: 17-11-83)

Y 1251 ÇUBUKTU

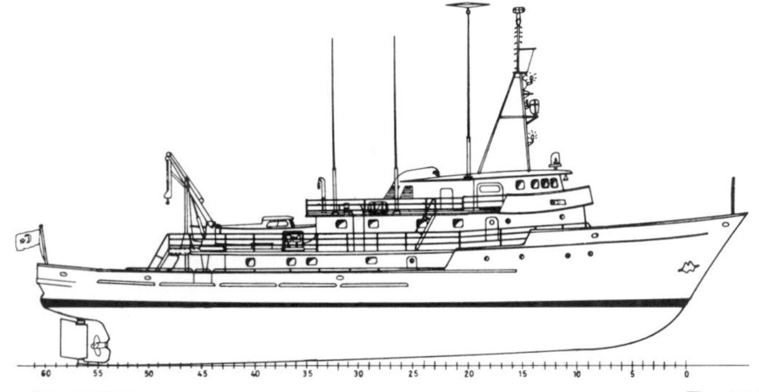

Çubuktu (Y 1251) Turkish Navy

D: 512 tons (600 fl) **S:** . . . **Dim:** 40.4 (36.4 wl) × 9.6 × . . .
M: 1 MWM diesel; 1 CP prop; 820 hp

◆ **3 small yard oilers** Bldr: Taskizak NDY, Istanbul (In serv. 1970s)

Y 1231 H 500 Y 1232 H 501 Y 1233 H 503

D: 300 tons **S:** 11 kts **Dim:** 33.6 × 8.5 × 1.8
M: 1 G.M. 6-71 diesel; 1 prop; 225 hp **Cargo:** 150 tons

REMARKS: See photos of this and other small Turkish Navy tankers in the addenda.

◆ **1 small water tanker** Bldr: Gölçük Naval DY (L: 1979)

Y 1240

D: 850 tons (fl) **S:** 10 kts **Dim:** 51.8 (46.8 pp) × 8.1 × . . .
M: 1 diesel; 1 prop; 480 hp **Cargo:** 530 dwt

◆ **2 Van-class water tankers** Bldr: Gölçük NSY, 1969-70

Y 1208 VAN Y 1209 ULABAT

D: 900 tons (1,250 fl) **S:** 10 kts **Dim:** 53.1 × 9.0 × 3.0
A: 1/20-mm AA **M:** 1 diesel; 1 prop; 650 hp **Cargo:** 700 tons

◆ **1 ex-German FW 1-class water tanker** Bldr: Schichau, Bremerhaven

	Laid down	L	In serv.
Y 1217 SÖGÜT (ex-FW 2)	5-4-63	3-9-63	4-1-64

Sögüt (Y 1217) H. Ehlers, 11-85

D: 598 tons (647 fl) **S:** 9.5 kts **Dim:** 44.03 (41.4 pp) × 7.8 × 2.63
M: 1 MWM 12-cyl. diesel; 1 prop; 230 hp **Electric:** 130 kVA
Fuel: 15 tons **Range:** 2,150/9 **Man:** 12 tot.

REMARKS: Transferred on 3-12-75. Cargo: 343 tons of fresh water.

◆ **4 Pinar-3-class small water tenders** Bldr: Taskizak NDY, Istanbul

Y 1213 PINAR 3 Y 1214 PINAR 4 Y 1215 PINAR 5 Y 1216 PINAR 6

D: 300 tons **S:** 11 kts **Dim:** 33.6 × 8.5 × 1.8
M: 1 G.M. 6-71 diesel; 1 prop; 225 hp **Cargo:** 150 tons

◆ **1 small water tanker** Bldr: Gölcük NDY (In serv. 1958)

Y 1212 PINAR 2

Pinar 2 (Y 1212) H. Ehlers, 5-84

D: 1,300 tons (fl) **S:** 10 kts **Dim:** 51.0 × 8.5 × . . .
A: None **M:** 1 diesel; 1 prop; . . . hp **Man:** 11 tot.

◆ **1 small water tanker** Bldr: Meentzer SY, Neth. (In serv. 1938)

Y 1211 PINAR 1 (ex-*Istanbul*)

D: 490 tons (fl) **S:** . . . **Dim:** . . . × . . . × . . .
M: 1 diesel; 240 hp

◆ **1 small water tanker**

Y 1210 MEHMET KAPTAN

REMARKS: No data available.

◆ **4 Kanarya-class cargo lighters** Bldr: Taskizak NDY, Istanbul (In serv. 1972-74)

Y 1155 KANARYA Y 1156 SARKÖY Y 1157 KARADENIZ ERIGLI Y 1165 ECEABAT

Eceabat (Y 1165) H. Ehlers, 5-84

AUXILIARY SHIPS *(continued)*

D: 823 tons (fl) **S:** 10 kts **Dim:** 50.7 (47.4 pp) × 8.0 × . . .
A: 1/20-mm AA **M:** 1 diesel; 1 prop; 1,440 hp

REMARKS: 500 dwt. Moulded depth: 3.6 m.

◆ **13 Salopa-class stores lighters**

Y 1031–1043 SALOPA 1–13

Salopa 2 (Y 1032) H. Ehlers, 7-84

REMARKS: No data available.

◆ **6 Layter-class lighters**

Y 1011–1016 LAYTER 1–6

◆ **7 pontoon barges**

Y 1061–1067 PANTON 1–7

◆ **2 transport ferries** Bldr: Great Britain, 1940-42

Y 1166 KILYA Y 1168 TUZLA

D: 700 tons (1,102 grt) **S:** 9.5 kts **Dim:** 56.0 × 12.2 × 2.7
A: 1/20-mm AA **M:** 1 set reciprocating steam; 1 prop; 700 hp

REMARKS: Survivors of a class of eleven. Used as personnel and vehicle ferries in the Dardanelles. Ramps at both ends. Can quickly convert to minelayers. Sisters *Lapseki* (Y 1163) and *Erdek* (Y 1164) stricken 1983.

◆ **1 small personnel ferry**

Y 1099 GONCA

◆ **3 vehicle/personnel ferries**

Y 1096 IŞÇI TASITI 1 Y 1097 IŞÇI TASITI 2 Y 1110 IŞÇI TASITI 3

◆ **3 Cephane-class ammunition lighters**

Y 1194 CEPHANE 1 Y 1195 CEPHANE 2 Y 1197 CEPHANE 3

◆ **1 small ammunition lighter**

Y 1196 BEKIRDERE

◆ **7 small danbuoy layers**

Y 1141–1147 SAMANDIRA MOTORU 1–7

◆ **1 training craft, ex-British HDML-class patrol craft** (In serv. 1943-45)

Y 1221 MESAHA 1

D: 46 tons (54 fl) **S:** 11 kts **Dim:** 21.95 × 4.83 × 1.50
M: 2 diesels; 2 props; 320 hp **Range:** 900/10 **Man:** 9 tot.

REMARKS: Wooden construction. Sisters *Mesaha 3* (Y 1223) stricken 1982, *Mesaha* 2 and 4 (Y 1222, Y 1224) in 1985.

◆ **1 training craft, tender to Naval Academy**

Y 1100 TOROS—no further data available. See photo in addenda.

◆ **1 training craft, former minelayer** Bldr: Gölçük NSY (In serv. 1938)

Y 1101 ATAK

D: 350 tons (500 fl) **S:** 13 kts **Dim:** 44.0 × 7.4 × 3.6
M: 1 Atlas-Polar diesel; 1 prop; 1,025 hp

REMARKS: Tender to Naval Academy. See photo in addenda.

◆ **3 ex-U.S. non-self-propelled gate craft** Bldr: Weaver SY, Orange, Texas (In serv. 1960-61)

Y 1201 (ex-YNG 45) Y 1202 (ex-YNG 46) Y 1203 (ex-YNG 47)

D: 325 tons (fl) **Dim:** 33.5 × 10.4 × 1.5

◆ **2 ex-U.S. APL 41-class barracks barges**

	Bldr	L
Y 1204 NAŞIT ÖNGEREN (ex-APL 47)	Puget Sound Bridge & Dredge, Seattle, Wash.	5-1-45
Y 1205 BINBAŞI METIN SÜLÜS (ex-APL 53)	Tampa SB, Tampa, Fla.	3-3-45

D: 2,660 tons (fl) **Dim:** 79.6 × 14.99 × 2.59
Electric: 300 kw **Man:** 650 tot.

REMARKS: Y 1204 was leased in 10-72, Y 1205 in 12-74. Lease extended 1982.

◆ **2 Öncü-class coastal tugs** Bldr: Gölçük NSY (In serv. 1953)

Y 1120 ÖNCÜ Y 1124 ÖNDER

Öncü (Y 1120) L. & L. Van Ginderen, 1980

D: 500 tons **S:** 12 kts **Dim:** 40.0 × 9.1 × 4.0
A: 2/20-mm AA (I × 2) **M:** diesel; 1 prop; . . . hp

REMARKS: Sister Öder (Y 1123) stricken 1971. A new tug, Y 1123, was completed at Taskizak 25-7-85, no data available.

NOTE: Of the three ex-U.S. Army 254-Design tugs, *Kepez* (Y 1119) and Öndev (Y 1128) were stricken in 1983 and *Akbas* (Y 1118) in 1985.

◆ **1 ex-U.S. coastal tug**

Y 1122 KUVVET (ex-. . .)

D: 390 tons **S:** . . . **Dim:** 32.1 × 7.9 × 3.6

REMARKS: Transferred in 2-62.

◆ **1 ex-U.S. Army 320-design small harbor tug**

Y 1134 ERSEN BAYRAK

D: 30 tons **S:** 9 kts **Dim:** 13.8 × 3.9 × 1.6 **M:** 1 diesel; 1 prop; 175 hp

REMARKS: Transferred in 6-71.

◆ **2 Turkish-designed harbor tugs** Bldr: Denizcilik, Bancusi (In serv. 1976)

Y 1130 GÜVEN Y 1132 ATIL

D: 300 grt **S:** . . . **Dim:** 32.8 × 8.9 × . . . **M:** Diesels; 250 hp

REMARKS: Sister *Doğanarslan* (Y 1133) stricken 1984.

◆ **3 ex-U.S. small harbor tugs**

Y 1117 SONDUREN (ex-YTL 751) Y 1129 KUDRET (ex-YTL . . .)
Y 1121 YEDEKCI (ex-YTL 155)

Kudret (Y 1129) H. Ehlers, 5-81

AUXILIARY SHIPS *(continued)*

D: 100 tons (120 fl) **S:** 12 kts **Dim:** 21.34 × 5.89 × 2.21
M: 1 Atlas diesel; 1 prop; 500 hp **Fuel:** 18 tons

REMARKS: Transferred in 5-54 and 11-57.

◆ **18 push tugs** (do not have Y-pendants)

KATIR 1–18

◆ **1 battery-charging craft, ex-U.S. Balao-class submarine** Bldr: Manitowoc SB, Manitowoc, Wisc.

	Laid down	L	In serv.
Y 1243 CERYAN BOTU IV (ex-*Preveze*, ex-*Guitarro*, SS 363)	7-4-43	26-9-43	26-1-44

D: 1,810 tons (fl) **Dim:** 95.0 × 8.31 × 4.65
Electric: 4,700 kw (4 G.M. 16-278A diesels)

REMARKS: Former fleet submarine relegated to harbor service during the mid-1970s. Sisters *Ceryan Botu I* (Y 1240, ex-*Canakkale*, ex-*Bumper*, SS 333), *Ceryan Botu II* (Y 1241, ex-*Inici Inönu*, ex-*Blueback*, SS 326), *Ceryan Botu III* (Y 1242, ex-*Cerbe*, ex-*Hammerhead*, SS 364), and *Ceryan Botu V* (Y 1244, ex-*Piri Reis*, ex-*Mapiro*, SS 376) stricken 1985.

◆ **1 ex-U.S. floating crane** Bldr: Odenback SB, Rochester, N.Y. (In serv. 14-8-51)

Y 1023 ALGARNA III (ex-YD 185)

D: 1,200 tons (fl) **Dim:** 36.6 × 13.7 × 2.7

REMARKS: Transferred in 9-63.

◆ **4 miscellaneous floating cranes**—no data available, except Y 1022: 600-ton lift

Y 1021 ALGARNA I Y 1022 LEVENT Y 1023 ALGARNA Y 1024 TURGUT ALP

◆ **1 dredge**

Y 1029 TARAK—D: 200 tons

◆ **27 miscellaneous service launches**—no data available

Y 1181 through Y 1193, Y 1198, Y 1199 MAVNA 1 through MAVNA 15
Y 1052 TAKIP

Mavna 10 (Y 1190) H. Ehlers, 5-84

◆ **1 ex-U.S. ARD-12-class floating dry dock** Bldr: Pacific Bridge, Alameda, Cal.

Y 1087 (ex-ARD 12) (In serv. 10-43)

Dim: 149.86 × 24.69 × 1.73 (light) **Lift capacity:** 3,500 tons

REMARKS: Launched in 1943 and loaned in 11-71.

◆ **6 miscellaneous floating dry docks**

Y 1081 (16,000-ton capacity) Y 1084 (4,500-ton capacity)
Y 1082 (12,000-ton capacity) Y 1085 (400-ton capacity)
Y 1083 (2,500-ton capacity) Y 1086 (3,000-ton capacity)

REMARKS: Y 1083 was built in Turkey in 1958 with U.S. funds; **Dim:** 116.5 × 26.4 × 9.0 max. These docks are named in sequence *Havuz I* to *Havuz VI.* A new 3-section floating dry dock was completed late in 1980.

◆ **4 miscellaneous officers' yachts**

ACAR HALAS ERSAN GÜL

Acar H. Ehlers, 7-83

REMARKS: Assigned pendant numbers between Y 1088–1092, but do not bear them.

MINISTRY OF THE INTERIOR
COAST GUARD
(SAHIL GÜVENLIK)

PERSONNEL (1985): approx. 5,000 total, headed by a Turkish Navy rear admiral

PATROL BOATS

◆ **0 (+2 + . . .) SAR-37 class**

SG 70 SG 71

REMARKS: First of an enlarged version of the SAR-33 class in service 25-7-85, with second launched the same day at Taskizak NDY. Have higher superstructure than SAR-33, are 37.5 m o.a.

◆ **9 SAR-33 class**

Bldrs: J 61: Abeking & Rasmussen, Lemwerder, West Germany; others: Taskizak NDY, Istanbul (In serv. 1978-. . .)

SG 61–SG 69 (ex-J 61–J 69)

SG 68 and sisters H. Ehlers, 4-84

D: 150 tons (170 fl) **S:** 40 kts **Dim:** 33.00 (29.50 wl) × 8.60 × 1.85
A: 1/40-mm AA—2/76.2-mm mg (I × 2)
M: 3 SACM-AGO V16CSHR diesels; 3 CP props; 12,000 hp
Electric: 300 kw **Fuel:** 18 tons **Range:** 450/35; 1,000/. . . **Man:** 23 tot.

REMARKS: Exact number in service as of 1-86 uncertain. SG 61 was launched on 12-12-77 and SG 62 in 7-78; SG 65 through SG 67 in service 30-7-81. Wedge-shaped hull design of remarkable seaworthiness and steadiness at high speeds in heavy weather. Turkey is also building fourteen units of this class for Libya. The same design can accommodate guns of up to 76-mm bore, missiles, and a propulsion plant of up to twice the power of the above. The 40-mm AA is in a Mk 3 mount.

◆ **14 AB 25 class** Bldr: Taskizak NDY, Istanbul, 1972-78

SG 21–34

SG 33 H. Ehlers, 5-84

D: 170 tons (fl) **S:** 22 kts **Dim:** 40.24 × 6.4 × 1.65
A: 2/40-mm AA (I × 2)—2/12.7-mm mg (I × 2)
M: 2 SACM-AGO V16 CSHR diesels; 2 props; 4,800 hp; 2 cruise diesels; 300 hp

REMARKS: Twelve sisters are operated by the Turkish Navy. Some have one 40-mm AA aft and one 20-mm AA forward. Built with French assistance.

◆ **8 German KW 15 class** Bldr: Schweers, Bardenfleth, West Germany, 1961-62

SG 12–SG 16 SG 18–SG 20

SG 15 H. Ehlers, 5-82

TURKEY *(continued)*
PATROL BOATS *(continued)*

D: 59.5 tons (69.6 fl) **S:** 25 kts **Dim:** 28.9 × 4.7 × 1.42
A: 1/40-mm AA—2/20-mm (I × 2)
M: 2 MTU 12-cyl. diesels; 2 props; 2,000 hp
Fuel: 8 tons **Range:** 1,500/19 **Man:** 15 tot.

◆ **10 ex-U.S. 45-ft Picket Boat class**

SG 41–50

SG 43 H. Ehlers, 4-84

D: 15 tons (fl) **S:** 18 kts **Dim:** 13.94 × 4.17 × 1.10
A: 2/7.62-mm mg (II × 1)
M: 2 Gray Marine 64 HN 9 diesels; 2 props; 450 hp
Range: 200/18 **Man:** 5 tot.

Remarks: Wooden-hulled. Transferred during the 1950s.

◆ **2 miscellaneous small personnel ferries**

SG 101 SG 104

SG 104 H. Ehlers, 4-84

◆ **4 miscellaneous launches**

SG 51–54

◆ **1 utility craft**

SG 102

◆ **1 dispatch boat**

SG 103

U.S.S.R.

Union of Soviet Socialist Republics

Personnel: 463,000, including 177,000 afloat personnel, 70,000 Naval Aviation, 14,000 Coastal Defense, 16,000 Naval Infantry, 57,000 in training, and 129,000 shore support, plus approx. 20,000 civilians manning auxiliaries

Merchant Marine (1984): 7,095 ships—24,492 grt
(tankers: 442 ships—5,368,883 grt)

DISPOSITION OF THE SOVIET FLEET ON 1-10-85
(Submarines and major surface combatants)

	Northern	Baltic	Black Sea	Pacific	Total
Strategic Subs: a) nuclear: Typhoon, Delta I, II, III, IV, Yankee I, II, Hotel III	41			24	65
b) conventional: Golf-II, III, V	2	6		7	15
Cruise-Missile Subs: a) nuclear: Oscar, Papa, Charlie-I, II, Echo-II, Yankee	28			21	49
b) conventional: Juliett	7	3	2	4	16
Torpedo Submarines: a) nuclear: Akula, Mike, Sierra, Alfa, Victor-I, II, III, November, Yankee conv., Echo	51			25	76
b) conventional: Kilo, Tango, Foxtrot, Zulu, Romeo, Whiskey	54	23	24	48	149
Aviation Ships: Kiev, Moskva	1		2	2	5
Guided-Missile Cruisers: Kirov, Kara, Kresta, I, II, Kynda, Slava	9	2	5	12	28
Gun-cruisers: Sverdlov, Mod. Sverdlov	2	2	3	4	11
Guided-Missile Frigates and Destroyers: Udaloy, Sovremennyy, Mod. Kashin, Kashin, Provornyy, Krivak I, II, III, Kanin, SAM, Kotlin, Kildin, Mod. Kildin	23	16	20	25	83
Gun-Destroyers: Mod. Kotlin, Kotlin, Mod. Skoryy, Skoryy	3	7	9	11	30

Warships In Service Or Under Construction As Of 1 January 1986

	L	Tons	Main armament
◆ **0 (+2) aircraft carriers**			
0 (+2) new construction	1985-	50,000(?)	60 aircraft. . . .
◆ **3 (+1) V/STOL carriers**			
3 (+1) Kiev	1972-82	36,000	Missile launchers, guns, helicopters, VTOL aircraft
◆ **374 (+ . . .) submarines**		Tons (surfaced)	
78 (+ . . .) ballistic-missile (63 nuclear):			
4 (+1+) Typhoon (nuclear)	1980-84	. . .	20/SS-N-20, . . . /TT
1 (+3+) Delta-IV (nuclear)	1983-	10,500	16/SS-N-23, 6/TT
14 Delta-III (nuclear)	1975-	10,500	16/SS-N-18, 6/TT
4 Delta-II (nuclear)	1975	10,000	16/SS-N-8, 6/TT
18 Delta-I (nuclear)	1972-75	9,000	12/SS-N-8, 6/TT
1 Yankee-II (nuclear)	1967?	7,900	16/SS-N-6, 6/TT
21 Yankee-I (nuclear)	1967-74	7,900	16/SS-N-6, 6/TT
1 Hotel-III (nuclear)	1965	5,500	3/SS-N-8, 8/TT
1 Golf-V (diesel)	1958-61	2,900	3/SS-N-. . . , 10/TT
1 Golf-III (diesel)	1958-61	2,900	3/SS-N-8, 10/TT
13 Golf-II (diesel)	1958-61	2,900	3/SS-N-5, 10/TT
65 (+) cruise-missile attack (nuclear):			
2 (+ . . .) Oscar (nuclear)	1980-	11,500	24/SS-N-19, 8/TT
1 Papa (nuclear)	1970	6,700	10/SS-N-9, 8/TT
6 Charlie-II (nuclear)	1973-	4,500	8/SS-N-7 or 9, 6/TT
11 Charlie-I (nuclear)	1968-72	4,000	8SS-N-7, 6/TT
1 Yankee (nuclear)	. . .	. . .	12/SS-N-24, 6/TT
28 Echo-II (nuclear)	1960-68	5,000	8/SS-N-3 or SS-N-12, 10/TT
16 Juliett (diesel)	1961-68	3,000	4/SS-N-23, 10/TT
219 (+ . . .) attack: (72 nuclear)			
1 (+ . . .) Akula (nuclear)	1984-	6,800	6/TT
1 (+ . . .) Sierra (nuclear)	1983-	6,000	6/TT
1 (+ . . .) Mike (nuclear)	1983-	7,800	6/TT
6 Alfa (nuclear)	1972-81	2,800	6/TT
21 Victor-III (nuclear)	1978-85	4,800	6/TT
7 Victor-II (nuclear)	1972-77	4,500	6/TT

WARSHIPS *(continued)*

Novorossyisk U.S. Navy, 9-83

	L	Tons	Main armament
16 Victor-I (nuclear)	1967-74	4,300	6/TT
1 (+10) Yankee (nuclear)	1967-74	7,900	6/TT
5 Echo (nuclear)	1060-68	4,500	10/TT
1 (+4) Mod. Hotel (nuclear)	1961	5,000	10/TT
12 November (nuclear)	1958-62	4,500	12/TT
6 (+ . . .) Kilo (diesel)	1980-	2,500	6/TT
19 Tango (diesel)	1972-82	3,000	. . . /SS-N-15, 10/TT
58 Foxtrot (diesel)	1957-74	1,950	10/TT
3 Mod. Golf (diesel)	1958-61	2,300	10/TT
6 Romeo (diesel)	1960	1,330	8/TT
2 Zulu-IV (diesel)	1952-55	1,900	10/TT
53 Whiskey (diesel)	1949-57	1,050	6/TT
12 auxiliary submarines:			
1 Uniform	1982	. . .	. . .
1 Xray	1983	. . .	. . .
2 India (diesel)	1978-79	3,900	. . .
4 Bravo (diesel)	1968-72	2,400	6/TT
1 Lima (diesel)	1979	2,000	. . .
1 Mod. Echo (nuclear)	1960-68	5,000	10/TT
2 Zulu	1952-57	1,900	10/TT

◆ **41 (+3) cruisers**

	L	Tons	Main armament
2 helicopter:			
2 Moskva	1964-66	14,500	2/SA-N-3, 1/SUW-N-1, 14 helicopters*
28 (+3) guided-missile:			
2 (+1) Kirov (nuclear)	1977-81	24,000	20/SS-N-19, 2/SS-N-14, 12/SA-N-6, 2/SA-N-4, 2/100-mm DP, 10/TT, 3 helos
1 (+2) Slava	1979-	10,000	16/SS-N-12, . . . /SA-N-6, 2/SA-N-4, 2/130-mm*
7 Kara	1971-78	8,200	8/SS-N-14, 2/SA-N-3, 4/SA-N-4, 4/76.2-mm DP, 10/TT, 1 helo
10 Kresta-II	1967-76	6,200	8/SS-N-14, 2/SA-N-3, 4/57-mm, 10/TT, 1/helo*
4 Kresta-I	1965-66	6,200	4/SS-N-3, 2/SA-N-1, 4/57-mm, 10/TT, 1/helo*
4 Kynda	1961-65	4,400	8/SS-N-3, 1/SA-N-1, 4/76.2-mm DP, 6/TT*
11 conventional:			
2 Mod. Sverdlov	1950-54	12,900	1/SA-N-4, 6 or 9/152-mm, 12/100-mm DP
9 Sverdlov	1950-60	12,900	12/152-mm, 12/100-mm DP

◆ **66 (+4 + . . .) destroyers**

	L	Tons	Main armament
49 guided-missile:			
7 (+1 + . . .) Udaloy	1978-	6,700	8/SS-N-14, 8/SA-N-9, 2/100-mm DP, 4/30-mm AA, 8/533-mm TT, 2/helos, mines*
5 (+1 + . . .) Sovremenny	1978-	6,700	8/SS-N-22, 2/SA-N-7, 4/130-mm DP, 4/30-mm AA, 4/533-mm TT, 1/helo, mines*
6 Mod. Kashin	1963-72	3,950	4/SS-N-2C, 2/SA-N-1, 4/76.2-mm DP, 5/TT*
12 Kashin	1963-72	3,750	2/SA-N-1, 4/76.2-mm DP, 5/TT*
8 Kanin	1958-60	3,700	1/SA-N-1, 8/57-mm, 10/TT*
3 Mod. Kildin	1958	2,800	4/SS-N-2C, 4/76.2-mm DP, 16/45- or 57-mm AA, 4/TT*
8 Sam Kotlin	1955-57	2,700	1/SA-N-1, 2/130-mm DP, 12/45-mm AA, 5/TT*
17 conventional:			
17 Kotlin and Mod. Kotlin	1954-57	2,600	4/130-mm DP, 16/45-mm AA, 4 or 8/25-mm AA, 5 or 10/TT*

◆ **197 (+ . . .) frigates**

	L	Tons	Main armament
2 Krivak III	1983-	3,000	1/SA-N-4, 1/100-mm, 8 TT*, helo
32 Krivak I, II	1970-	3,100	4/SS-N-14, 2/SA-N-4, 2/100-mm or 4/76.2-mm DP, 8/TT*
1 Koni	1978	1,600	1/SA-N-4, 4/76.2-mm DP*
33 (+ . . .) Grisha-III	1975-	950	1/SA-N-4, 2/57-mm DP, 4/TT*
9 Grisha-II	1974-76	950	4/57-mm DP, 4/TT*
15 Grisha-I	1967-73	950	1/SA-N-4, 2/57-mm DP, 4/TT*
20 Petya-II	1964-69	950	4/76.2-mm DP, 10/TT*
7 Petya-I	1960-63	950	2 or 4/76.2-mm DP, 5/TT*
11 Mod. Petya-I	1960-63	950	4/76.2-mm DP, 5/TT*
1 Mod. Petya-II	1964-69	950	4/76.2-mm DP, 5/TT*
18 Mirka-I, II	1964-66	950	4/76.2-mm DP, 5 or 10/TT*
48 Riga	1951-56	1,260	3/100-mm DP, 2 or 3/TT*

◆ **148 (+ . . .) corvettes**

	L	Tons	Main armament
18 Mirka-I, II	1964-66	950	4/76.2-mm DP, 5 or 10/TT*
48 Riga	1951-56	1,260	3/100-mm DP, 2 or 3/TT*
12 (+ . . .) Tarantul-I, II	1979-	480	4/SS-N-2C, 1/76.2-mm DP
24 (+ . . .) Nanuchka-I, III	1969-	770	6/SS-N-9, 1/SA-N-4, 1/76.2 DP or 2/57-mm AA
14 (+ . . .) Pauk	1979-	480	1/76.2-mm DP, 4/TT*
58 Poti	1960-67	500	2/57-mm DP, 2-4/TT*
6 Ivan Susanin	1975-81	3,400	2/76.2-mm DP
1 Purga	1955	4,500	4/100-mm DP
12 Sorum	1974-. . .	1,210	4/30-mm AA
10 T-58	1956-61	725	4/57-mm DP*
11 T-43	1947-57	500	4/37-mm AA*

* Indicates additional ASW weapons

◆ **173 guided-missile and torpedo units**

◆ **over 275 patrol boats and craft**

◆ **240–260 mine warfare ships and craft**

◆ **73 amphibious warfare ships**

A note to ship class names: The class names used herein are for the most part those used by NATO. Until 1973, Soviet combatants usually did not display names, and thus NATO had devised a series of nicknames based on Russian words (combatants: geographical place names beginning with "K"; small combatants: insects; mine warfare types: diminutives of personal names; amphibious warfare types: reptiles; auxiliaries: rivers). Subsequently, the policy has been to use the actual name of the first ship of a class, as in the West. Often that name is not immediately available, and thus a three-part *interim* nickname is applied. The first syllable denotes the *fleet area* where the class was first identified (BAL = Baltic, BLK = Black Sea, etc), the second syllable indicates the *type* of ship (COM = combatant, SUB = submarine, AUX = auxiliary, etc.), and the

WARSHIPS *(continued)*

third syllable is a roman numeral indicating the order of discovery within a category. Thus, "BAL-COM-III" would be the third new major combatant discovered under construction in the Baltic. As actual names are learned, they replace the temporary nickname. The Soviet Navy itself uses a series of Project Numbers to identify its ships, as in the West German Navy; these are generally not available.

The Soviet Navy has a number of unique ship-type classifications; these are translated, where applicable, in the individual class entries.

WEAPONS AND SYSTEMS

NOTE: All weapon and sensor designations that follow are those assigned by NATO, except where indicated; the Soviet designations are generally unavailable.

A. MISSILES

◆ Ballistic Missiles

NOTE: All have liquid-fuel propulsion, except the SS-N-17 and SS-N-20, which have solid-fuel propulsion.

SS-N-5 Serb (1963)

Range: 900 nautical miles. Single nuclear warhead of about 800 kilotons. Fitted in marines. Can be launched while submerged. Range has been increased from its original 700 nautical miles. Obsolescent but still significant, due to basing of 6 Golf-II in the Baltic.

weight: 16,500 kg — range: 900 nm
length: 13 m — guidance: inertial
diameter: 1.2 m

SS-N-6 (1968)

Range: Initially, 1,300 nautical miles. Nuclear warhead of about 1 megaton in Mod. 1, 2; Mod. 3 has two re-entry vehicles. Fitted in Yankee-I-class nuclear submarines. Can be launched while submerged. 1,850-m CEP (Circular Error Probable).

weight: 18,900 kg — range: Mod. 1—1,300 n.m.
length: 10 m — Mod. 2—1,600 n.m.
diameter: 1.8 m — Mod. 3—1,600 n.m.
guidance: inertial

SS-N-8 Sawfly (1973/77)

Single nuclear warhead of about 1.5 megatons. Fitted in Delta-I and -II nuclear submarines and in the Golf-III experimental submarine. 1,500-m CEP (Circular Error Probable).

weight: 30,000 kg — range: Mod. 1—4,240 n.m.
length: 13 m — Mod. 2—4,950 n.m.
diameter: . . . — guidance: inertial

SS-N-17 (1977)

Single 1-megaton nuclear warhead. First Soviet ballistic missile with solid-fuel propulsion. Aboard the one Yankee-II-class submarine.

weight: . . . — range: 2,000 n.m.
length: 10.6 m — guidance: inertial

SS-N-18 (1978)

Two-stage missile employed on Delta-III class. Three versions: Mod. 1 with three 100-kiloton (KT) re-entry vehicles (RV), Mod. 2 with one 450-KT RV, and Mod. 3 with 7 Multiple Independent Re-entry Vehicles. CEP (Circular Error Probable) estimated at 1,100 n.m.

weight: 34,000 kg — range: Mod. 1—3,530 n.m.
length: 13.6 m — Mod. 2—4,350 n.m.
guidance: inertial — Mod. 3—3,530 n.m.

SS-N-20 (1983)

Three-stage weapon with 6–9 multiple independent re-entry vehicle (MIRV) payload. Range over 4,000 nautical miles. Used by the Typhoon class. CEP estimated at 600 m.

weight: 60,000 kg — range: 4,300 n.m.
length: . . . — guidance: inertial

SS-N-23 (1985)

Three-stage weapon with 7 multiple-independent-re-entry-vehicle (MIRV) payload. Range about 5,000 n.m. Used by Delta IV class. Weight: Approx. 40,000 kg

◆ Surface-to-Surface Cruise Missiles

NOTE: Liquid-fuel propulsion, except for SS-N-7 and 9, which have solid-propellant engines.

SS-N-2 A and B Styx (1958/1964)

Maximum range: 25 nautical miles. Practical range: 16 nautical miles. Liquid propulsion rocket with solid booster. I-band active radar guidance in targeting, with infrared or radar homing in the most recent version, SS-N-2B. Altitude can be preset at 100, 150, 200, 250, or 300 m. 500 kg conventional warhead. Installed in Osa-I and Osa-II guided-missile boats. The SS-N-2B has folding wings.

SS-N-2C (formerly SS-N-11) (1967)

Maximum range: 45 nautical miles. Weight: 2,500 kg; length: 5.8 m; span: 2.8 m. Radar or infrared terminal homing versions. 500 kg warhead. In order to employ fully the over-the-horizon maximum range of the SS-N-2C, it is necessary to have a forward observer. The SS-N-2C is carried by the destroyers of the Modified Kashin and Modified Kildin classes, by the Tarantul guided-missile corvettes, and by the exported Nanuchka-II-class guided-missile corvettes. Length: 6.5 m.

SS-N-3 Shaddock (A: 1962; B: 1962, C: 1960)

Produced in three versions: SS-N-3A for launch by submarines (Juliett and Echo II classes), with inertial guidance, mid-course correction, and active radar terminal homing: SS-N-3B for Kynda- and Kresta I-class cruisers, with similar guidance; and SS-N-3C with inertial-only guidance, possibly still in use from submarines. SS-N-3 is a variant of the SS-C-1 coast-defense missile.

weight: 5,400 kg — span: 5m
warhead: 1,000 kg — range: SS-N-3A/B: 250 n.m.
length: 10.2 m (SS-N-3C 111.8m) — SS-N-3C: 400 n.m.

SS-N-7 Siren (1970)

Maximum range: 35 nautical miles. Conventional warhead. Launched while submerged. Charlie-I-class nuclear-powered attack submarines have eight per ship. 500 kg conventional or nuclear warhead. Weight: 2,900 kg; Length: 7 m.

SS-N-9 (1969)

Inertial guidance, and active radar homing to the target. 500 kg conventional or nuclear warhead. Installed in Nanuchka-I- and III-class guided-missile corvettes and the Sarancha-class hydrofoil. A submerged-launch version is available for the Charlie I- and II and Papa-class submarines. Weight: 3,300 kg; Length: 8.8 m.

SS-N-12 Sandbox (1973)

Maximum range: 300 nautical miles. 1,000 kg conventional or nuclear warhead. Replacing the SS-N-3 on Echo-II-class submarines and is aboard the *Kiev* class and *Slava*-class cruisers.

SS-N-19 (1971)

Maximum range: 300 nautical miles. Conventional or nuclear warhead. Evidently has improved performance characteristics over the SS-N-12 and is carried by the *Kirov*-class cruisers and the Oscar-class nuclear-powered submarine (from which it is submerged-launched).

SS-NX-21 (. . .)

A torpedo-tube-launched weapon similar in concept to the U.S. Tomahawk. Probably intended for submarines, but may be developed for surface ship and air launch as well. Range estimated at 900–1,200 n.m. Speed: Mach 0.7. Will probably become operational by 1986. Probably has a nuclear warhead.

SS-N-22 (1981)

A Mach 2.5 successor to the SS-N-9, but not, to date, used by submarines. Reportedly flies at "sea-skimming" altitudes to a range of 55–68 n.m. Carried by the *Sovremennyy*-class destroyers and some Tarantul II-class missile boats.

SS-N-24 (1985?)

New, large cruise missile. Used in single Yankee-conversion and probably intended for a new class. May be a strategic, vice anti-ship, weapon. Range: circa 1,000 n.m

◆ Surface-to-Air Missiles

SA-N-1 Goa (1961)

Twin-launcher. Range: 20,000 m, interception altitude: 300 to 50,000 feet. Guidance: radar/command. Conventional warhead, 60 kg. Fitted on Kynda and Kresta-I cruisers, as well as on Kashin, Kanin, and Kotlin destroyers. Also has a surface-to-surface capability. Uses Peel Group radar directors. Weight: 400 kg. Sixteen per magazine.

SA-N-3 Goblet (1967)

Twin launcher. Range: 30,000 m, interception altitude: 300 to 80,000 feet. Guidance: radar/command via Head Lights-series radar director. Conventional warhead, 60 kg. Fitted on Kresta-II and Kara cruisers as well as the *Moskva*-class helicopter cruisers. An improved version has a range of 55,000 m and is on the *Kiev*. Goblet has an anti-surface target capability. Weight: 550 kg. Mach 2.5.

SA-N-4 Gecko (1969)

Twin launcher, retracting into a cylindrical magazine holding 20 missiles. Range: 9,000 m, interception altitude: 30 to 10,000 feet. Guidance: radar/command via Pop Group radar director. Conventional warhead. Fitted in Kara and *Kirov* cruisers, two *Sverdlov* cruisers, Krivak guided-missile frigates, Grisha- and Nanuchka-class corvettes, the Sarancha hydrofoil, the landing ship *Ivan Rogov*, and the replenishment ship *Berezina*. Can be used against surface targets. Weight: 190 kg.

SA-N-5 Grail (1974)

Naval version of SA-7 Grail. Fitted on Pauk- and Tarantul-class corvettes, some Osa-class guided-missile patrol boats, landing ships, some minesweepers, and many auxiliaries. Employs either a 4-missile launch rack with operator, or is shoulder-launched, singly. IR-homing, visually aimed. 4.4-km range, 7,800-ft altitude. Weighs 15 kg with launch tube.

SA-N-6 Grumble (1981)

A navalized version of the land-based SA-10. Range 80,000 m or greater, altitudes to 90,000 ft. Employs vertical launch from 8-missile rotating magazines and reportedly uses track-via-missile guidance via the Top Dome radar system. Carried by the *Kirov* and *Slava*-class cruisers. Probably also has an anti-ship capability.

WEAPONS AND SYSTEMS *(continued)*

SA-N-7 Gadfly (1981)

A navalized version of the land-based SA-11, employing single-armed launchers. Mach 3 weapon with 28,000-m range (3,000 minimum) and usable against targets from 100- to 46,000-ft. altitude. Operational on the *Sovremennyy*-class destroyers and the trials destroyer *Provornyy.* Guidance via Front Dome radar tracker/illuminators. Probably has an anti-ship capability.

SA-N-9

A new vertically launched, short-ranged system, probably intended as a successor to SA-N-4. To be carried in groups of 8 in 2-m-diameter launch cylinders aboard the *Udaloy*-class destroyers, and to be fitted in cruiser *Frunze,* carrier *Novorossiysk* and other new construction. Range estimated at 15–16 km and altitude at 40–60,000 ft.

◆ **Air-to-Surface Missiles** (naval use only)

AS 2 Kipper (1961)

Range: 100 nautical miles. Turbojet propulsion. Inertial guidance or automatic pilot with radar homing head. 1,000 kg. Conventional or nuclear warhead. Launched from Badger-C and -G aircraft. Weight: 4,200 kg.

AS 4 Kitchen (1967)

Range: 170 nautical miles. 1,000 conventional or nuclear warhead. Inertial guidance with radar-terminal homing. Mach 3.5. In service on Backfire-B and Blinder-B aircraft. Weight: 6,500 kg.

AS 5 Kelt (1965)

Range: 100 nautical miles. Liquid-fueled rocket propulsion. Inertial or autopilot guidance with J-band radar terminal homing. Conventional and nuclear warheads. In service on Badger-C and -G aircraft. Weight: 4,700 kg.

AS 6 Kingfish (1970)

Range: 150–250 nautical miles. Mach 2.5–3.5. 500 kg. conventional or nuclear warhead. In service on Badger-C and -G aircraft, two on each. Weight: 4,900 kg.

AS 7 (late 1970s)

Range: 6 nautical miles. Mach 1. Tactical weapon. Solid-fuel propulsion. Pencil-beam radar terminal homing. 100 kg. conventional warhead. Used on Forger aircraft.

AS 9 (late 1970s)

Range: 60 nautical miles. Anti-radar missile. Turbojet propulsion; Mach 3.0. Passive homing on electromagnetic radiation. 150 kg. Conventional warhead. In use on Badger, Backfire, and Fitter-C and Fitter-D aircraft.

AS 10 (1980)

Range: 6 nautical miles. Mach 1.0. Solid propulsion. Electro-optical guidance. Conventional warhead of 100 kg. Carried by Fitter-D.

B. GUNS

152-mm dual-purpose

Fitted in triple turrets on *Sverdlov*-class cruisers. Individual barrels can be loaded and elevated separately. Limited AA capability, using barrage fire.

barrel length: 57 calibers
muzzle velocity: 915 m/sec
altitude arc: −5° to +50°
maximum rate of fire: 4 to 5 rds/min/barrel
maximum range: 27,000 m
effective range: 18,000 m
projectile weight: 50 kg
fire control: optical directors with two 8-m base range finders and associated Top Bow ranging radars or local control using 8-m base range finders in each turret and Egg Cup ranging radars atop upper turrets.

130-mm twin, new model dual-purpose

Fully automatic, for surface and aerial targets. Fitted on *Sovremennyy*-class destroyers, *Slava*-class cruisers and *Frunze.* May be mechanically triaxially stabilized. Water-cooled.

barrel length: 70 calibers
muzzle velocity: . . .
are of elevation: −15° to +85°
max. rate of fire: 65 rds/min per mount
max. range: approx. 28,000 m
fire control: Kite Screech radar director or local control by on-mount operator.

130-mm twin dual-purpose

Semi-automatic. Fitted on Kotlin and SAM-Kotlin destroyers. Mechanically triaxially stabilized. Twin mount with electric or hydraulic-electric pointing system.

barrel length: 58 calibers
muzzle velocity: 900 m/sec
arc of elevation: −5° to +80°
maximum rate of fire: 10 rounds/min/barrel
maximum range, surface target: 28,000 m
effective range: surface target: 16,000 to 18,000 m
maximum vertical range: 13,000 m
projectile weight: 27 kg

Fire control: stabilized Wasp Head director, with Sun Visor tracking radar. Egg Cup ranging radar on most mounts.

130-mm twin dual-purpose

Semi-automatic type fitted on *Skoryy*-class destroyers. Obsolescent.

barrel length: 50 calibers
muzzle velocity: 875 m/sec
arc of elevation: −5° to +45°
maximum range: 24,000 m
effective range: 14,000 to 15,000 m
projectile weight: 27 kg
maximum rate of fire: 10 rounds/min/barrel

Fire control: Four Eyes optical director and associated Top Bow or Post Lamp radars.

100-mm twin dual-purpose

Mechanically triaxially stabilized mounts installed on *Sverdlov*-class cruisers.

barrel length: 50 calibers
weight: approx. 40 tons
muzzle velocity: 900 m/sec
effective range, surface target: 10,000 to 12,000 m
arc of elevation: −15° to 85°
maximum rate of fire: 15 rounds/min/barrel
maximum range, surface target: 20,000 m
maximum range, AA fire: 15,000 m
effective range, AA fire: 8,000 to 9,000 m
projectile weight: 16 kg
fire control: Round Top stabilized director with Sun Visor tracking radar and/or associated Top Bow or Post Lamp radars: Egg Cup ranging radar on each mount (being removed) for local surface control.

100-mm automatic dual-purpose

A single-barreled, water-cooled gun in an enclosed mounting found on the cruiser *Kirov, Udaloy*-class destroyers, and Krivak-II-class frigates.

rate of fire: 80 rounds/min
maximum theoretical range: 15,000 m
maximum effective range: 8,000 m
fire control: Kite Screech radar director or local, on-mount control

100-mm single dual-purpose

Gunmount with a shield. Installed on Riga frigates, and Don-class submarine tenders.

barrel length: 56 calibers
muzzle velocity: 850 m/sec
arc of elevation: −5° to +40°
maximum rate of fire: 15 rounds/min
maximum range: 16,000 m
effective range: 10,000 m
projectile weight: 13.5 kg
fire control: stabilized Wasp Head director fitted with Sun Visor radar

85-mm AA

Twin-barreled gunmount on unmodified *Skoryy* destroyers. Obsolescent.

barrel length: 50 calibers
muzzle velocity: 850 m/sec
arc of elevation: −5° to +70°
maximum rate of fire: 10 rounds/min/barrel
maximum range, surface target: 15,000 m
effective range, surface target: 8,000 to 9,000 m
practical maximum range, AA fire: 6,000 m
fire control: Cylinder Head optical director (no radar).

76.2-mm twin dual-purpose

Installed on Kara and Kynda cruisers, Kashin destroyers and Krivak-I, Koni, Petya, and Mirka frigates, *Smol'nyy*-class training ships and *Ivan Susanin*-class icebreakers.

length of barrel: 60 calibers
muzzle velocity: 900 m/sec
maximum rate of fire: 45 rounds/min/barrel
arc of elevation: +80°
fire control: Owl Screech or Hawk Screech radar director
maximum range, AA fire: 10,000 m
effective range, AA fire: 6,000 to 7,000 m
projectile weight: 16 kg

76.2-mm single automatic dual-purpose

Fully automatic, with on-mount crew. Carried by Nanuchka-III, Pauk, and Tarantul-class corvettes, Matka-class guided-missile hydrofoils, and the Slepen-class patrol boat.

rate of fire: 120 rounds/min
theoretical maximum range against surface target: 14,000 m
practical range against aerial target: 6,000 to 7,000 m
fire control: Bass Tilt radar director or local, on-mount control

57-mm twin automatic dual-purpose

This equipment, which appears to be entirely automatic from the ammunition-handling room to the gunmount, is installed on *Moskva,* Kresta-I, and Kresta-II cruisers, Poti and Grisha corvettes, Nanuchka-I guided-missile corvettes, Turya torpedo boats, Ropucha LSTs, Ugra submarine tenders, and the replenishment ship *Berezina.* Now removed from *Boris Chilikin* replenishment ships and *Manych*-class water tankers. Water-cooling system.

length of barrel: 70 calibers
maximum rate of fire: 120 rounds/min/barrel
maximum effective vertical range: 5,000 to 6,000 m
fire control: by Muff Cob or Bass Tilt radar directors

57-mm dual-purpose

Single-barrel gunmount (Mod. *Skoryy* destroyers and some Sasha minesweepers), twin-barrel (several classes), and quadruple on Kanin and Kildin destroyers; in the latter case the guns are mounted in superimposed pairs. Has surface-fire capability.

length of barrel: 70 calibers
muzzle velocity: 900 to 1,000 m/sec
arc of elevation: 0° to +90°
maximum rate of fire: 150 rounds/min/gun
effective vertical range: 4,500 m
fire control by Hawk Screech or Muff Cob radar directors

WEAPONS AND SYSTEMS *(continued)*

Twin 57-mm DP mounts on oiler Berezina

Twin 76.2-mm DP mounts on Krivak-I

SS-N-3b/c Styx launcher on an Osa-II

SS-N-3b/c Styx launcher on a Mod. Kildin

Twin, elevatable SS-N-12 launchers on a Kiev-class carrier

Twin, fixed-elevation SS-N-12 launchers on Slava

Twin 130-mm DP mount on a Sovremennyy

SS-N-2b/c Styx launchers on a Tarantul-II

Quadruple SS-N-3b trainable launcher on a Kynda

Inclined, below-decks SS-N-19 launchers on Kirov

Quadruple SS-N-22 launchers on Sovremennyy

Quadruple, trainable SS-N-14 launchers on Krivak-I and -II

SUW-N-1 launcher and missile on Moskva

RBU-1000 ASW rocket launcher on Sovremennyy

Raised SA-N-4 launcher on a Krivak

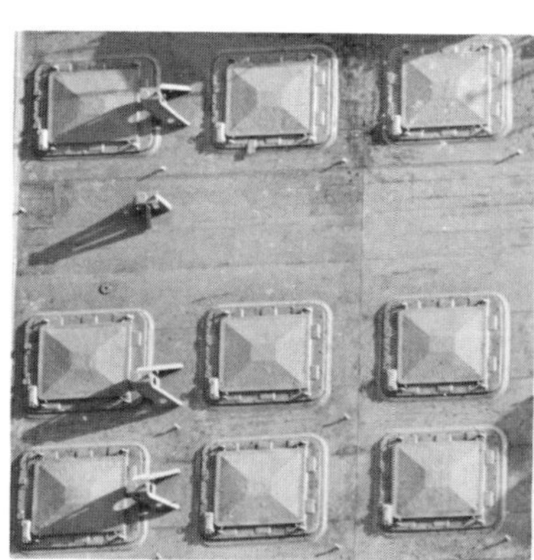

SA-N-6 vertical-launch hatch covers on Kirov

WEAPONS AND SYSTEMS *(continued)*

Twin, reloading SS-N-14 launcher on Kirov

Quadruple, fixed SS-N-14 launchers on Udaloy

RBU-6000 ASW rocket launcher on a Krivak

SA-N-3 launcher with Goblet missile on Moskva

Rotating SA-N-6 vertical launchers on Slava

SA-N-7 single-arm launcher on Sovremennyy

Forward four SA-N-9 vertical-launch positions on Udaloy

Top Pair back-to-back early-warning/3-D antennas on Slava

Top Steer back-to-back early-warning/3-D antennas on Sovremennyy

Top Steer/Top Plate on Osmotritel'nyy

Front Door on the forward side of Slava's tower mast

Big Net early-warning radar antenna on a Kashin

Top Sail (right) and Head Net-C antennas on a Kresta-II

Strut Pair search antenna on Udaloy

Top Plate/Top Mesh on Admiral Zakharov (above Round House TACAN antennas)

Eye Bowl SS-N-14/missile-control radar directors on a Krivak

WEAPONS AND SYSTEMS *(continued)*

Kiev 1. Top Sail 3-D radar 2. Top Knot TACAN radome with High Pole-B IFF transponder atop 3. Top Steer 3-D radar 4. Rum Tub ESM antennas 5. Bell Bash jammer antennas 6. Bell Thump jammer radome 7. Tee Plinth electro-optical device with conical Pert Spring radome just below it 8. Side Globe EW radomes

Kite Screech gun director on Sovremennyy

Pop Group SA-N-4 radar director on a Krivak

Peel Group radar director for SA-N-1, on a Kashin

Front Dome SA-N-7 radar director on Sovremennyy

Top Dome SA-N-6 radar director on Kirov

Two twin AK-230 30-mm AA and their manual ringsight director on a Kanin-class destroyer

76-mm DP gun on a Nanuchka-III corvette

WEAPONS AND SYSTEMS *(continued)*

SS-N-3 cruise-missile tubes in elevated, firing position on a Kresta-I missile cruiser U.S. Navy

A vertical view of the forward missile area on the Kiev-class Novorossiysk, showing the reloading tray arrangements of the 8 SS-N-3 SSM tubes and the blanking plate over where the circular SA-N-4 SAM magazine had been in her earlier sisters. The SUW-N-1 launcher, forward twin 76-mm DP gunmount, and forward SA-N-3 launcher are also visible. French Navy, 1983

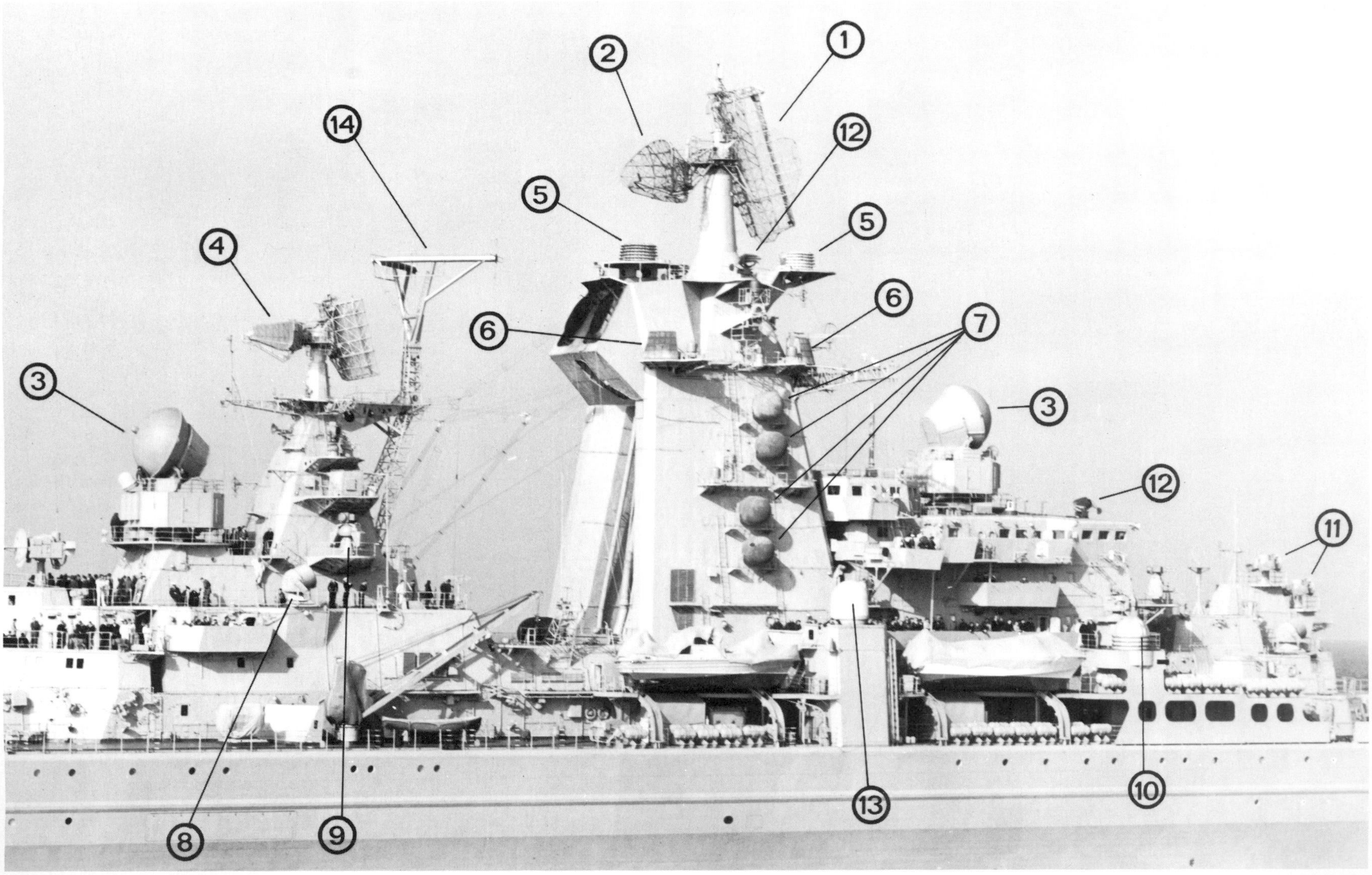

Electronic antennas on the Kirov—1. and 2. Top Pair 3-dimensional long-range air-search radar, comprising Top Sail (1) and Big Net (2) antennas 3. Top Dome SA-N-6 guidance radar 4. Top Steer 3-dimensional air-search radar. 5. Round House helicopter-control/TACAN arrays 6. Rum Tub EW radomes 7. Side Globe EW radomes 8. Bass Tilt 30-mm gatling gun-control radar 9. Tin Man stabilized t.v./IR tracker 10. Bob Tail (in aluminized rubber protective cover) radionavigation sextant (with Pop Group radar for SA-N-4 SAM system just above) 11. Eye Bowl control radars for SS-N-14 ASW cruise missiles 12. Palm Frond surface-search radar 13. Punch Bowl satellite communications antenna radome 14. Vee Tube-C long-range HF communications antenna array

WEAPONS AND SYSTEMS *(continued)*

Towed variable-depth sonar partially deployed from a Krivak-class frigate; the equipment has, in this instance, suffered a casualty to the hoist system.

Helicopter-type dipping sonar being deployed from a Mirka-II-class frigate. Note the circular covers over gas-turbine exhausts and the towed torpedo decoys on deck.

45-mm AA

Quadruple-barreled installations in SAM-Kotlin, Kotlin, and one Mod. Kildin destroyers; single on some Sasha minesweepers. The quadruple-mounted guns are arranged in two superimposed pairs.

length of barrel: 85 calibers
muzzle velocity: 900 m/sec
arc of elevation: 0° to +90°
rate of fire: 300 rounds/min/mount
effective maximum vertical range: 4,000 m
fire control: Hawk Screech radar director (local in Sasha)

37-mm Model 39 AA

Installed in twin-barreled mounts in *Sverdlov* cruisers, *Skoryy* destroyers, Riga frigates, and T-43-class minesweepers.

length of barrel: 60 calibers
muzzle velocity: 900 m/sec
arc of elevation: 0° to +80°?
maximum rate of fire: 160 rounds/min/gun
fire control: on-mount lead-computing sights

30-mm gatling gun AA

This gun is in service on *Kiev*-class carriers, Kara and Kresta-II cruisers, and several other classes. It is installed in mounts similar to those of the 30-mm AA double-barreled automatic guns, and is designed to fire a great number of rounds at an extremely high rate in order to intercept a cruise missile at a comparatively short distance. It has six 30-mm barrels. The often-used designation "ADMG-630" is a NATO nickname, not the Soviet name, which is probably AK-630.

minimum rate of fire: 3,000 rounds/min/mount
fire control: Bass Tilt radar director or remote visual director

30-mm twin automatic AA

Installed in a light mount on several classes of ships—cruisers, destroyers, guided-missile boats, supply ships, etc. Widely exported. Soviet designation: AK-230.

length of barrel: 60 calibers
muzzle velocity: 1,000 m/sec
maximum rate of fire: 1,050 rounds/min/barrel
effective maximum range, AA fire: 2,500 to 3,000 m
fire control: by Drum Tilt radar director or remote optical director.

25-mm twin AA

Found on many ships and made up of two superimposed guns.

length of barrel: 60 calibers
muzzle velocity: 900 m/sec
maximum rate of fire: 150-200 rounds/min/barrel
fire control: on-mount ring sights

C. ANTISUBMARINE WEAPONS

◆ **missiles**

SUW-N-1 system (1967)

Rocket-propelled weapon, installed in *Kiev*-class carriers and *Moskva*-class helicopter cruisers. Maximum range: 16 miles. Nuclear warhead. Unguided solid-fuel rocket based on land-based FROG-7 artillery rocket and often referred to as FRAS-1. There may be a variant with a homing torpedo payload.

SS-N-14 Silex (1974)

A weapon conceptually resembling the Australian Ikara, using a solid-propelled aerodynamic cruise missile that drops a parachute-retarded homing torpedo. Maximum range: 30 nautical miles (4 nautical miles minimum). Carried by *Kirov*, Kara- and Kresta-class cruisers and Krivak-I- and Krivak-II-class frigates. Can also be used against surface ships. Controlled by Head Lights or Eye Bowl radar directors.

SS-N-15 (1972)

ASW missile similar to the U.S. Navy's SUBROC. Maximum range: 21.6 nautical miles. Nuclear warhead. Submerged-launched from submarine torpedo tubes. Carried by Victor I, II, and III and Alfa-class nuclear-powered attack submarines. Also usable against surface targets. Uses a 533-mm torpedo tube.

SS-N-16 (circa 1980)

Derived from the SS-N-15 system but using a homing torpedo payload in lieu of the nuclear depth bomb. Maximum range: 54 nautical miles. Would also be useful against surface targets. Probably requires a large-diameter 650-mm torpedo tube.

◆ **rockets**

NOTE: RBU = *Raketnaya Bombometnaya Ustanovka* (Rocket Depth-charge Launcher)

RBU-6000 (Soviet designation)

Formerly MBU-2500 A. Made up of twelve barrels, approximately 1.600 m in length, arranged in a horseshoe and fired in paired sequence. Vertical automatic loading system, barrel by barrel. Can be trained and elevated. Range: 6,000 m. Installed in *Kiev*-class carriers, *Slava, Kirov, Moskva,* Kynda, Kresta-I, and Kresta-II cruisers, *Udaloy,* Kashin, and Kanin guided-missile destroyers, Krivak frigates, the smaller Mirka and Petya frigates, and the Poti and Grisha corvettes.

RBU-2500 (Soviet designation)

Made up of two horizontal rows of eight barrels each, approximately 1.600 m in length, which can be trained and elevated. Manual reloading. Range: 2,500 m. 21-kg warhead. Carried by Kildin and Mod. Kildin, one SAM Kotlin, most Mod. Kotlin, and all Mod. *Skoryy* destroyers, Riga frigates, Petya-I frigates, and *Smol'nyy* training ships.

RBU-1200 (Soviet designation)

Made up of two horizontal rows of short, superimposed barrels, three on two. Tube diameter: 0.250 m; length: 1.400 m; the 70-kg (34-kg warhead) rocket is somewhat shorter. Range: 1,200 m. Tubes elevate but are fixed in train. Installed in T 58- and Pauk-class corvettes, S.O.-1 patrol boats, and Natya-class minesweepers.

RBU-1000 (Soviet designation)

Made up of six barrels arranged in two vertical rows of three and fired in order, with vertical automatic loading. Trainable. Tube diameter: approx. 0.300 m. Length: approx. 1.800 m. Range: 1,000 m. 90-kg rocket with 55-kg warhead. Installed in Kara, Kresta-I, and Kresta-II cruisers, *Sovremennyy* and Kashin destroyers, and the replenishment ship *Berezina.*

RBU-600 (Soviet designation)

Made up of six barrels, 0.300 m in diameter and 1.500 in length, superimposed in two rows and fired simultaneously. Trainable. Range: 600 m. 90-kg rocket with 55-kg warhead. Used only in Mod. Kotlin destroyers.

◆ **torpedoes**

The Soviet Navy uses 533-mm anti-surface and ASW torpedoes, and short 400-mm ASW homing torpedoes. A larger, probable 650-mm-diameter weapon with a range of around 54 n.m. is also reported to have entered service for submarines, using a wake-homing sensor. Nuclear warheads are apparently widely deployed, especially in submarines, as witness their presence aboard the Whiskey-class submarine that ran aground near Karlskrona Naval Base in Sweden during 10-81.

D. RADARS

NOTE: Designations are NATO code names.

◆ **Navigation**

The most widely used are the I-band Neptune, Ball End, various Don types, and Spin Trough. Don-Kay was placed on most large ships in the 1970s, until it was succeeded by the I-band Palm Frond. Kivach 3 is used on recent small combatants.

◆ **Surface-Search**

Most common on small surface combatants are Square Tie (also used for cruise-missile target-designation), Pot Head, and Pot Drum. Submarines carry Snoop Tray, Snoop Slab, Snoop Plate, or Snoop Pair.

◆ **Long-Range Air-Search**

Cross Bird, still carried by some *Skoryy*-class desroyers. Copy of British World War II Type 291 gear—Soviet name: Gius-2. (P-band, 225-390 mHz).

Head Net-A (C-band, 500–1,000 mHz)

Head Net-B, consisting of 2 Head Net-A antennas, mounted back-to-back in a horizontal plane (found only on Desna-class missile range ships).

Head Net-C, consisting of 2 Head Net-A antennas, mounted back-to-back, one in a horizontal plane, the other inclined. Widely used on cruisers and destroyers.

These radars use a band that gives a 60- to 70-mile detection range on an attack bomber flying at high altitude.

Big Net, a large C-band radar fitted on Kresta-I and a few *Sverdlov* cruisers, and some Kashin destroyers. Its detection range on an aircraft is probably over 100 miles.

Slim Net (E-band), early model radar fitted on some cruisers and destroyers.

Hair Net (E-band, 2-3,000 mHz), early model radar now only on one Riga frigate.

Top Trough (C-band), on some *Sverdlov* cruisers.

Knife Rest A/B (A-band, 0–250 mHz), antenna resembles a large television antenna.

WEAPONS AND SYSTEMS *(continued)*

Strut Curve (F-band, 3–4 mHz), mounted on the Petya and Mirka frigates and Poti and Grisha corvettes.

Strut Pair (F-band), mounted on *Udaloy* class and one Mod. Kildin destroyer. Employs pulse-compression. Antenna essentially two Strut Curve reflectors back-to-back.

Plank Shave (. . . band) on Pauk-class corvettes. An apparent successor to Strut Curve.

High Sieve. Carried by some *Sverdlov* cruisers and *Skoryy* destroyers.

Top Pair (C/F-band), three-dimensional; a Top Sail and a Big Net antenna mounted back-to-back; used on *Kirov.*

Top Plate/Top Mesh, Back-to-back, identical phased-array 3-dimensional radar antenna on *Udalov*-class destroyers *Marshal Vasilevskiy, Admiral Zakharov,* and later.

Top Plate/Top Steer, Back-to-back, 3-dimensional radar antenna using one Top Steer and one Top Plate antenna; on *Sovremennyy*-class destroyer *Osmotritelnyy* and later.

Top Sail (C-band), three-dimensional radar installed in *Kiev, Moskva,* Kresta-II, and Kara cruisers.

Top Steer (F-band), three-dimensional radar found with Top Sail on *Kiev.* Possibly for air-controlling.

◆ **Missile Tracking and Control**

Trap Door, in a retractable mount. Used for SS-N-12 on *Kiev*-class carriers, where it is mounted at the extreme bow; the similar Front Door/Front Piece is used on Echo-II and Juliett submarines for SS-N-3 and SS-N-12.

Peel Group, mounted on Kynda and Kresta-I cruisers as well as Kashin, Kanin, and SAM Kotlin destroyers. Consists of a tracking radar for high altitudes (I-band) and a missile-guidance radar at lower altitudes (E-band). The assembly is made up of two groups of large and small reflectors, in both horizontal and vertical position, with parabolic design. Maximum range approximately 30 to 40 miles. Used for guidance of the Goa missile in the SA-N-1 system.

Head Lights (F-, G-, H-, and D-bands), mounted in *Kiev* carriers and *Moskva,* Kresta-II and Kara cruisers. Similar to the Peel Group with an assembly of tracking radar for the target and guidance radar for the missile. Used for guidance for the Goblet missile of the SA-N-3 system and for the surface-to-underwater missiles of the SS-N-14 system. In several versions, designated "A," "B," and "C."

Scoop Pair (E-band), guidance radar for the Shaddock missile of the SS-N-3 system on board Kynda and Kresta-I cruisers.

Pop Group (F-, H-, and I-bands), missile guidance for the SA-N-4 system.

Eye Bowl (F-band), smaller version of Head Lights, installed in the cruiser *Kirov, Udaloy* destroyers, and Krivak frigates; missile-guidance radar for the SS-N-14 system.

Fan Song E, installed in the *Dzerzhinskiy;* used with the Guideline missile of the SA-N-2 system.

Band Stand, on *Sovremennyy* destroyers, Tarantul-II, and Nanuchka corvettes and the Sarancha hydrofoil, possibly for missile-tracking and control. In large radome.

Top Dome, associated with the SA-N-6 vertically launched SAM system in the cruiser *Kirov.* Employs a 4-m diameter hemispheric radome, fixed in elevation, but mechanically steerable in azimuth. Three smaller dielectric radomes are mounted on the face of its mounting pedestal, and there is also a smaller hemispheric radome below it. Apparently can track multiple targets.

Front Dome, tracker-illuminator associated with the SA-N-7 SAM system in the *Sovremennyy*-class destroyers (with six) and the trials Kashin, *Provornyy* (with eight). Resembles the gun fire-control radar Bass Tilt and is very compact.

Plinth Net, a large parabolic mesh antenna found only in the Kresta-I and Kynda-class cruisers and apparently associated with the SS-N-3 anti-ship missile. May be a data link antenna rather than a radar.

◆ **Gun Fire-Control**

Half Bow, **Post Lamp** } (I-band), mounted on older destroyers: also for torpedo fire control.

Top Bow, 152-mm gun.

Sun Visor, 130-mm DP, 100-mm DP guns; mounted on Round Top or Wasp Head directors.

Hawk Screech, 45-mm and 76.2-mm AA guns; always found in conjunction with back-up optical directors.

Owl Screech, 76.2-mm DP; improved version of Hawk Screech.

Kite Screech, 100-mm and new 130-mm twin DP.

Muff Cob (H-band), for 57-mm AA twin automatic guns. Has t.v. camera attachment.

Egg Cup (E-band), installed in turrets for 152-mm, old twin 130-mm, and old twin 100-mm AA guns

Drum Tilt (H- and I-bands), installed on Osa missile boats and other ships fitted with 30-mm twin-barrel AA.

Bass Tilt (H-band), used with Gatling gun fitted in *Kiev* carriers, Kara and Kresta-II cruisers, and Mod. Kildin destroyers, as well as in Grisha-III corvettes, where it also controls the twin 57-mm, and on Nanuchka-III corvettes and Matka guided-missile hydrofoils, where it also controls the 76.2-mm gun.

E. SONARS

Until the late 1950s, the Soviet Navy showed little interest in antisubmarine warfare or, of course, submarine detection. Most of its ships were equipped with high-frequency sonar (Tamir 11, Pegas, Herkules). New or modernized ships appear to have much-improved sensors.

Medium-frequency hull sonar, on Kresta-II cruisers, Kanin destroyers, Krivak frigates, and Grisha corvettes.

Medium-frequency, towed, variable-depth sonar, on *Kiev* carriers, *Moskva* and Kara cruisers, Mod. Kashin destroyers, and Krivak frigates.

Low-frequency hull sonar, on *Kiev* carriers and *Moskva* cruisers, the cruiser *Kirov* and *Udaloy* destroyers. A low frequency variable-depth sonar is used on the *Kirov* and *Udaloy* classes.

Helicopter dipping sonar, on Mirka frigates, Stenka and Pchela patrol boats, Turya torpedo boats and others. Most diesel submarines still have old equipment (active-passive Herkules, passive Feniks), but nuclear submarines have modern low-frequency sonar and extensive passive hydrophone arrays.

The Soviets are interested in surface-ship-towed passive sonar arrays. There are a number of prototype arrays on surface ships that may be for towed linear hydrophone arrays, and the teardrop-shaped domes on the upper rudder assemblies of Victor III-class, Akula- and Sierra-class submarines may house a towed array, while the Delta-IV and Oscar classes may deploy arrays from a tube at the top of the rudder.

F. ELECTRONIC WARFARE

The increasing number of radomes of every description that can be seen on Soviet ships, especially on the newest and most important types (helicopter and guided-missile cruisers, for example) is an indication of the attention the Soviet Navy gives to electronic warfare. NATO code names for the antenna arrays for intercept or for jamming radars include: Side Globe, Top Hat A and B, Bell Clout, Bell Shroud, Bell Squat, Cage Pot, Watch Dog, and Rum Tub.

Many of the more modern ships are equipped with twin-tubed chaff rocket launchers (*Kiev, Moskva,* Kresta-I and -II, Kara, *Berezina*) or 16-tubed fixed chaff rocket launchers (Mod. Kashin, Krivak-I and -II, Tarantul, Pauk Nanuchka, Matka, etc).

IFF (Identification Friend or Foe) is taken care of by High Pole A and B transponders and by Square Head or other interrogators. The newer Salt Pot A transponders are slowly replacing High Pole A & B. The modern radars have integral IFF interrogation. TACAN systems included the large Top Knot spherical array on the *Kiev*-class carriers, and the various forms of the paired cylindrical Round House array on the *Kirov, Udaloy,* and other classes.

G. COMMUNICATIONS

All Soviet warships are equipped to transmit and receive MF through VHF communications, while submarines have a VLF capability (using towed buoy antennas), and UHF equipment is coming into wider use in surface ships. VHF antennas in use include: Cage Bare, Cage Cone, Cage Stalk, and the older Straight Key. Major warships usually have a Pop Art VHF antenna. Long-range HF communications are handled via the "Vee" series antennas Vee Cone, Vee Tube, or Vee Bars. Fixed arrangements 9-m long with two identical conical components mounted at 70-deg. to each other in the horizontal plane are termed Vee Cone. Vee Tube uses tubular, 8.6-m-long components at 90-deg. separation, and Vee Bars is the nickname for an open-framework arrangement on the *Kiev* class. Submarines rely on VLF, and an ELF station is building.

H. SATELLITES

The Soviets use an ocean surveillance satellite system whose data is transmitted either to ground stations or directly to ships equipped with the SS-N-12 and SS-N-19 cruise-missile systems. The receiving antenna is mounted in a large cylindrical radome termed Punch Bowl. The cruisers *Zhdanov* and *Admiral Senyavin* have two 4.5-m-diameter Big Ball radomes, associated with the *Molniya* and *Raduga* satellite communications systems, although many other ships can apparently receive transmissions from communications and navigational satellites.

V/STOL CARRIERS

NOTE: An over-300-meter-long, nuclear-powered, Western-style, conventional aircraft carrier of about 65,000 tons full-load displacement and equipped with an angled deck and a ski-jump bow is reported to have been launched at Black Sea (formerly: Nosenko) shipyard, Nikolayev late in 1985. Completion about 1989 is expected. A second unit has been laid down.

A flight-deck prototype for the ship has been built at the Crimean naval air base at Saki; some 320-m in length, it incorporates arresting wires, but catapults are not yet installed. Also present are two ski-jump takeoff ramps. Aircraft employed in trials at Saki include the Su-27 Flanker, Su-25 Frogfoot, and the MiG-29 Fulcrum. The actual carrier air group will probably include fixed-wing fighters, V/STOL fighter-bombers, and helicopters. The ship's defensive armament will probably include SA-N-9 vertical-launch SAMs and gatling AA guns.

◆ **3 (+1) Kiev class**

	Bldr	Laid down	L	In serv.
KIEV	Black Sea SY, Nikolayev	9-70	31-12-72	5-75
MINSK	Black Sea SY, Nikolayev	12-72	5-75	2-78
NOVOROSSIYSK	Black Sea SY, Nikolayev	10-75	12-78	9-82
BAKU	Black Sea SY, Nikolayev	1978	3-82	1986

D: 36,000 tons (43,000 fl) **S:** 32 kts
Dim: 273.0 (249.5 wl) × 47.2 (32.70 wl) × 10.0
A: 8/SS-N-12 (II × 4, 16 missiles) — 2/SA-N-3 systems (II × 2; 72 Goblet missiles) — 2/SA-N-4 systems (II × 2, 40 missiles — not in *Novorossiysk, Baku*) — 4/76.2-mm DP (II × 2) — 8/30-mm gatling AA (VI × 8) — 10/533-mm TT (V × 2) — 1/SUW-N-1 ASW RL (II × 1) — 2 RBU-6000 ASW RL (XII × 2) — 14–17/Hormone-A or Helix-A and Hormone-B helicopters — 12–13/Forger A/B VTOL aircraft — *Novorossiysk:* 12/SA-N-9 SAM silos (96 missiles, not yet fitted)

V/STOL CARRIERS *(continued)*

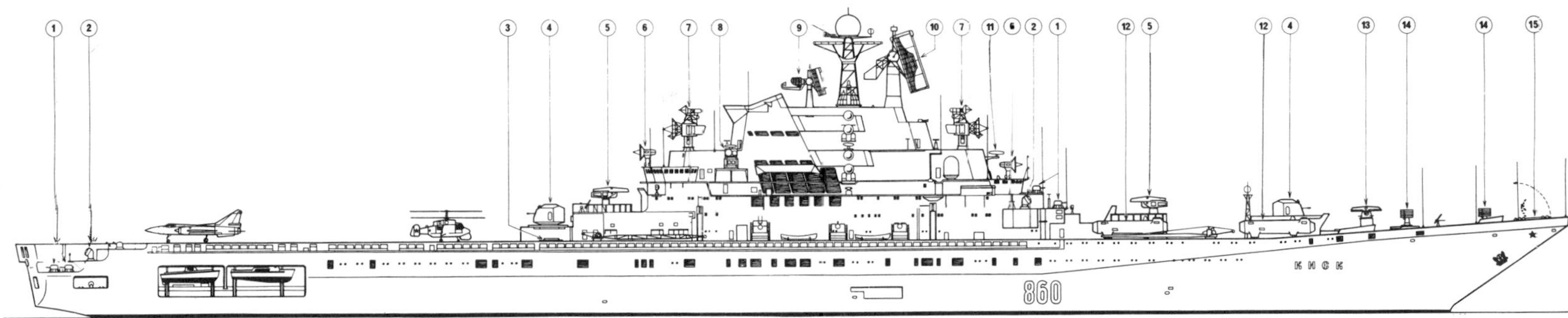

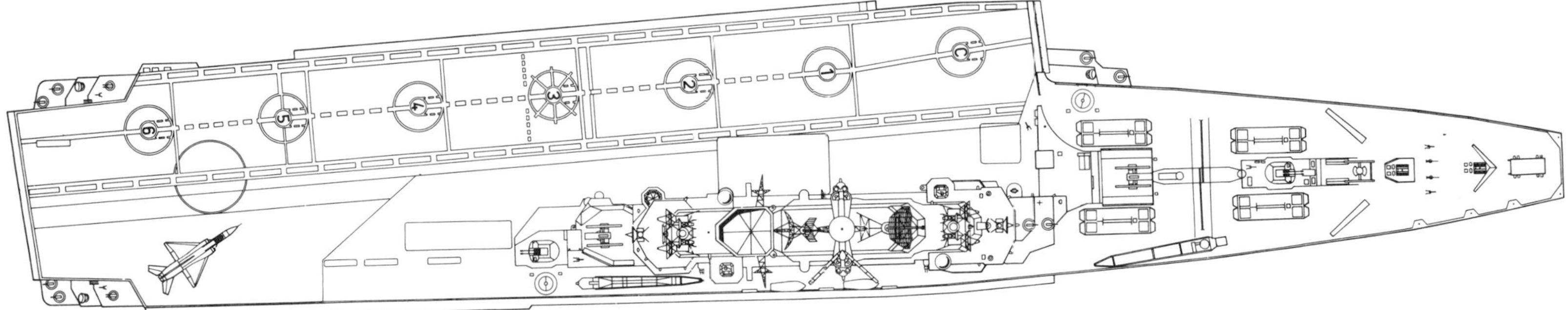

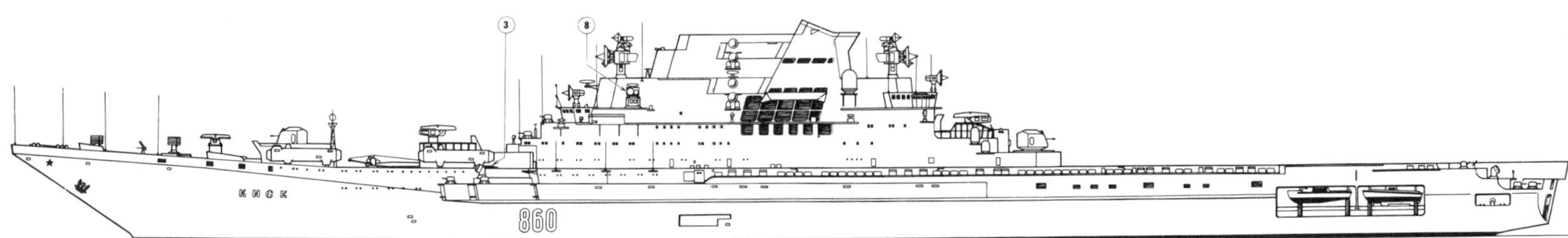

Kiev 1. 30-mm gatling guns 2. Bass Tilt radar 3. SA-N-4 launcher 4. twin 76.2-mm DP mount 5. SA-N-3 launcher 6. Owl Screech radar 7. Head Lights radar 8. Pop Group radar 9. Top Steer radar 10. Top Sail radar 11. Don-2 radar 12. twin launchers for SS-N-12 system 13. SUW-N-1 launcher 14. RBU-6000 15. Trap Door radar
H. Simoni

Note: Plan view shows flight configuration as completed in 1976; the angled-deck centerline stripe is now straight at its forward end, and the after two ammunition elevators have been combined into a single 12.5-m-long lift.

Kiev 16 Flot., French Navy, 5-85

Kiev R. Neth. Navy, 5-85

Novorossiysk—showing wind-baffle arrangement to port of SS-N-12 installation
French Navy, 5-83

V/STOL CARRIERS *(continued)*

Novorossiysk—showing the "black hole" exhaust spray deflector to port of the VDS door in the transom stern and the current arrangement of the flight-deck markings
French Navy, 5-83

Novorossiysk on her first deployment, 5-83. Note absence of SA-N-4 launchers and Side Globe antennas
JMSDF, 1983

Kiev R. Neth. Navy, 1985

Minsk JMSDF, 1984

Novorossiysk French Navy, 1983

Minsk after a 1981-82 refit—with the forward port sponson and flight-deck forward edge rearranged to improve air flow, blast shields added abaft SS-N-12 launchers
JMSDF, 1982

V/STOL CARRIERS *(continued)*

Electron Equipt: Radar: 1/Don Kay, 2/Don-2, 1/Top Sail, 1/Top Steer, 2/Head Lights, 2/Pop Group. 2/Owl Screech, 4/Bass Tilt, 1/Trap Door (*Novorossiysk:* 3 Palm Frond vice Don Kay, Don-2, no Pop Group, plus 2/Strut Pair)
Sonar: 1/low freq., hull-mounted; 1/med.-freq., towed VDS
EW: 8/Side Globe (not in *Novorossiysk*), 4/Top Hat A, 4/Top Hat B, 4/Rum Tub, 2/Bell Clout—2/chaff RL (II × 2)

M: 4 sets GT; 4 props; 200,000 hp **Boilers:** 8 **Fuel:** 7,000 tons
Range: 4,000/31; 13,500/18 **Man:** 1,200 tot.

REMARKS: *General:* The Soviet Navy's designation for the *Kiev* class is *Bolshoy Protolovadochnyy Kreyser* (Large Antisubmarine Cruiser), although the *Minsk* was referred to as a *Taktycheskoye Avionosnyy Kreyser* (Tactical Aircraft-Carrying Cruiser) on her initial deployment. The ships have capabilities for ASW, sea-control, and sea-denial missions. The hull is unusual in having a counter stern that sweeps up several meters above the waterline before meeting the transom. The variable-depth sonar is deployed through doors on the centerline of the transom stern; the black-painted, ribbed recess to port of the VDS housing is a spray deflector to prevent spray from entering air intakes of Forger V/STOL aircraft while landing. For their size and function, the ships carry very small crews. The displacement is still uncertain, with U.S. sources quoting a draft of 8.3 m and a full-load of only 37,100 tons.

Minsk was refitted in 1981-82 at Vladivostok with an extended port forward sponson supporting the 30-mm gatling guns, a rounded leading edge to the flight deck, and a number of blast deflector or wind deflection plates erected on the forecastle abaft the SS-N-12 launchers; all these changes should improve air flow over the flight deck (which has been given an additional V/STOL landing spot) and should prevent sea damage to the guns. The third unit, *Novorossiysk,* has the deflectors and rounded deck edge, but retains the original sponson configuration. *Kiev* entered the Black Sea in 1982 to undergo her first major overhaul and emerged in 1985 with fewer alterations than expected, although air-flow baffles had been added. These ships are hampered by their low freeboard and have a noticeable squat at the stern when moving at higher speeds. There is an enormous bow bulge to accommodate the hull-mounted sonar transducer.

Novorossiysk lacks the SA-N-4 SAM system, instead having blanking plates over what will eventually be SA-N-9 vertical-launch installations abaft the island and forward to port; there are empty director platforms on the superstructure. The ship showed a number of electronics array differences from the first two, including the elimination of the 8-radome Side Globe array and the substitution of six new t.v./electro-optical devices ("Tin Man") for the Tee Plinth devices formerely used.

The ships have a retractable, spherical Bob Tail radio sextant antenna abaft the stack; all have microwave aircraft landing systems.

Aviation installations: The flight deck portion of the upper deck is angled about 4.5° to port of the centerline axis of the ship and is about 185 m long by 20 m wide. To protect against the hot exhaust of the Forger vertical take-off and landing aircraft, it is partially covered with a mosaic of refractory tiles. There are two elevators to the hangar deck: one (19.20 m × 10.35 m) beside the stack; the other (18.50 m × 4.70 m) abaft the island. Four small ammunition elevators are connected by an on-deck rail system. Both *Kiev* and *Novorossiysk* have operated the new Helix A (Ka-27) ASW helicopter.

Armament: The SS-N-12 missiles are launched from four twin, non-trainable elevating tubes. In order to use the full over-the-horizon range of the missiles, a forward-located, target-designation observer platform has to be used. On the *Kiev,* that requirement is met by the Hormone-B, which carries a long-range radar giving a range of 100 nautical miles with the helicopter at an altitude of 4,000 feet. The ship can also use target information relayed by satellite, using the two receiving antennas in the Punch Bowl radomes. There are eight missiles in the launch tubes, plus sixteen reloads raised from a below-decks magazine by a centerline elevator between the launch-tube-sets and aligned with the launchers for loading by a traversing system.

Baku, whose fitting-out period has been more protracted than the others, is reported to incorporate a number of configurational changes, including later radar systems, additional numbers of SS-N-12 launchers, and SA-N-9 vertical-launch SAMs.

HELICOPTER CRUISERS

◆ **2 Moskva class**

	Bldr	Laid down	L	In serv.
MOSKVA	Black Sea SY, Nikolayev	1962	1964	7-67
LENINGRAD	Black Sea SY, Nikolayev	1964	1966	1968

Moskva French Navy, 1979

Leningrad VP-26, U.S. Navy, 5-84

Leningrad U.S. Navy, 5-84

HELICOPTER CRUISERS *(continued)*

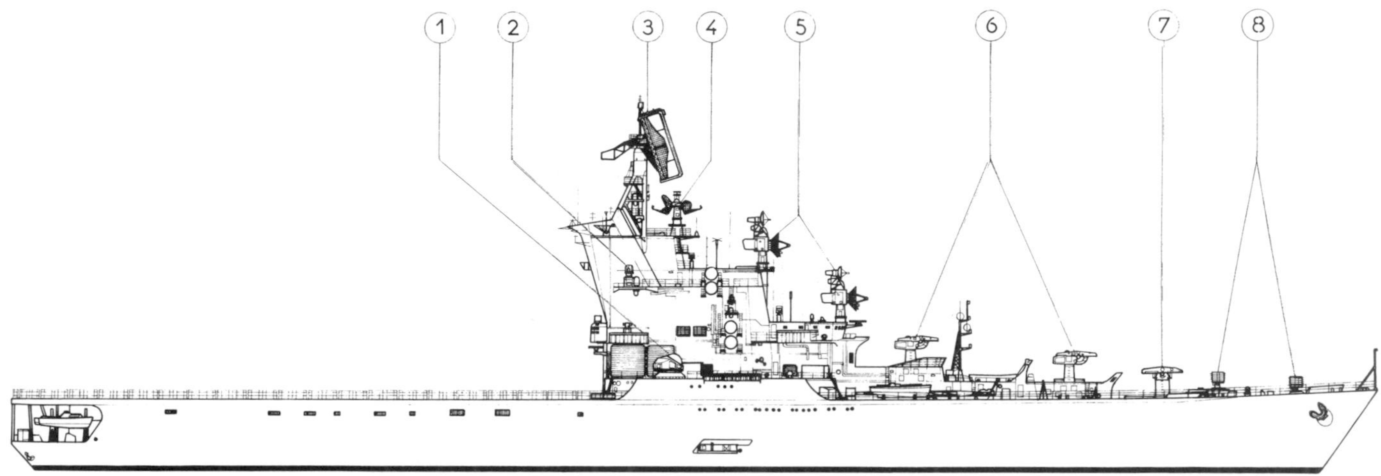

Moskva 1. Twin 57-mm DP mount 2. Muff Cob radar/t.v. gun director 3. Top Sail 3-D radar antenna 4. Head Net-C air-search radar antenna 5. Head Lights missile fire-control radars 6. SA-N-3 launchers 7. SUW-N-1 ASW rocket launcher 8. RBU-6000 ASW rocket launchers L. Gassier

Leningrad—amidships detail U.S. Navy, 6-84

D: 14,500 tons (17,000 fl) **S:** 30 kts **Dim:** 189.0 × 34.1 (flight deck), 26.0 (wl) × 7.6

A: 2/SA-N-3 systems (II × 2; 44 Goblet missiles)—4/57-mm DP (II × 2)—1/SUW-N-1 ASW RL—2/RBU 6000 ASW RL—14 Hormone-A/B/C helicopters

Electron Equipt: Radar: 3/Don-2, 1/Top Sail, 1/Head Net-C, 2/Head Lights, 2/Muff Cob
EW: 8/Side Globe, 2/Top Hat, 8/Misc. Bell-series, 2/chaff RL (II × 2)
Sonar: 1/LF hull-mounted, 1/MF VDS

M: 2 sets GT; 2 props; 100,000 hp **Boilers:** 4

Range: 4,500/29; 14,000/12 **Man:** 850 tot.

Remarks: Soviet type designation: *Protivolodochnyy Kreyser* (Antisubmarine cruiser). Flight deck 86 × 34 m. Hangar beneath flight deck, with small hangar between stack uptakes in superstructure. Two elevators to hangar aft, plus small hangar for two helicopters at forward end of flight deck, between the stack uptakes. The *Moskva* was modified for a time to permit the testing of Yak-38 Forger-A aircraft, which were to go aboard the *Kiev* carriers. Both ships had their ten 533-mm ASW TT removed and the side embrasures plate in during the mid-1970s. Sonar dome is retractable within hull. Fin stabilizers fitted. Have carried Haze-type mine countermeasures helicopters, but cannot hangar them. Hulls trim down about 1 m by the bow, and they are poor sea-boats.

NAVAL AVIATION

Naval aviation, which dates from 1919, is an integral part of the Soviet Navy in which approximately 70,000 men are involved, but its organization and ranks are the same as those of the air forces. Aircraft are part of the four naval fleets (Northern, Baltic, Black Sea, and Pacific) and are under the direct control of the commanders of those fleets. The air arm has some 1,635 aircraft, including:

Tactical:
390 strike bombers: 100 Backfire-B, -C, 250 Badger-C, -G, 40 Blinder-A
135 fighters/fighter-bombers: 60 Forger-A, 75 Fitter-C
Tactical Support:
72 tankers: Badger-A
170 reconnaissance & electronic warfare: 45 Bear-D, 45 Badger-D, -E, -F, -H, -K, -J, . . . Blinder, . . . Hormone-B
465 Antisubmarine Warfare:
205 fixed wing: 60 Bear-F, 50 May, 95 Mail
250 helicopters: 130 Hormone-A, 90 Haze-A, 30 Helix-A
Utility:
400 miscellaneous training, transports, utility helicopters, etc.
Operational aircraft are divided into the four fleets as follows:

	Northern	Baltic	Black Sea	Pacific	Total
Reconnaissance and electronic warfare	55	10	15	60	140
Bombers	70	90	100	130	390
Attack fighters	15	40	0	80	135
Refueling	18	20	14	20	72
ASW (fixed wing)	80	20	25	80	205
Helicopters (all types)	105	50	100	115	370

Note: The Soviet Navy also employs the An-22 Cub transport in a number of variants for intelligence collection, ECM, transport, and research-and-development duties. Il–18 Coots are used as transports, ECM, and ELINT aircraft, and there are a number of utility aircraft and helicopters in service.

COMBAT AIRCRAFT

NATO code name and builder	Mission	Year put in serv.	Max. weight	Wing-span	Length	Engine	Speed max cruising	Operational radius[1]	Armament	Fitted with	Remarks
◆ **FIXED-WING**											
Backfire-B, -C TU-22M (Tupolev)	Reconnaissance and ship attack	1975	121.5 t	34.45 m (26.2 m fully swept)	40.2 m	2 Kuznetsov NK 144 turbojets of 24,000-kg thrust each	Mach. 2.2 at 50,000 ft; Mach 1.3 at 3,000 ft	Supersonic: 3,485/2.250 km with/without refueling Subsonic: 6,300/5,320 km with/without refueling	2/23-mm cannon, 12,000 kg of bombs (nuclear or conventional), on external racks, 1-2 AS 4, AS 6, or AS-9, mines	1 Down Beat navigation and bombing radar; 1 optical bomb sight; 1 Fan Tail tail radar; IFF.	The naval version of Backfire has ECM and ECCM equipment. Has variable-geometry, swept wing Backfire-C has a different air intake configuration Naval units carry no refueling probes.
Blinder-A, -C, -D TU-22 (Tupolev)	A: gravity bomber C: photo reconn D: trainer	1963	85 t	28.8 m	41.7 m	2 Kolesov VD-7 turbojets, 20,000-kg thrust each (14,000-kg thrust without using after burners)	Mach. 1.5 at 36,000 ft	Supersonic speeds: 1,000 km without refueling; 1,600 km with refueling Subsonic speeds: 1,500 km without refueling, 2,000 km with refueling	1/23-mm cannon, 5,000 kg bombs	1 Down Beat navigation radar; 1 Bee Hind tail radar; IFF; 7 cameras	The "C" version is especially configured for maritime reconnaissance. The "D" version is a trainer. Not a very successful design; few in service.

COMBAT AIRCRAFT *(continued)*

COMBAT AIRCRAFT *(cont.)*

NATO code name and builder	Mission	Year put in serv.	Max. weight	Wing-span	Length	Engine	Speed max cruising	Operational radius[1]	Armament	Fitted with	Remarks
Bear-C, -D TU-95 Bear-F TU-142 (Tupolev)	Reconnaissance and electronic warfare	1955	160 t (F: 171 t)	48.5 m (F: 51.1)	47.5 m (F: 49.5)	4 Kuznetsov NK-12MV turboprops of 15,000 hp each; 4 bladed, contrarotating props	500 kts at 25,000 ft 440 kts at sea level	8,000 km without refueling; 9,500 km with refueling	Up to 7/23-mm cannon plus 8,000-kg torpedoes, bombs in Bear-F	Big Bulge A (F: Wet Eye), tail radar; well-equipped with electronic countermeasures.	Bear-F (Tu-142), the ASW version, has sonobuoys, depth charges, and torpedoes; the newest now have a MAD boom.
Badger-A TU-16 (Tupolev)	Aerial refueling	1954	77 t	34.5 m	36.5 m	2 AM-3 M turbojets, 9,550-kg thrust each	540 kts at 22,000 ft 445 kts at sea level	4,800 km	7/23-mm cannon, up to 3,800 kg bombs	1 navigation and bombing radar; 1 tail radar; some electronic warfare equipment.	Wing-tip hose dispensers for refueling. Retains a secondary bombing capability
Badger-C TU-16 (Tupolev)	Ship attack	1960	77 t	34.5 m	36.5 m	2 AM-3 M turbojets, 9,550-kg thrust each	540 kts at 22,000 ft 445 kts at sea level	3,200 km without refueling	6/23-mm cannon, 1 AS-2 Kipper or 2 AS-6 Kingfish	1 Puff Ball Navigation and bombing radar; 1 Doppler radar; 1 Bee Hind tail radar.	
Badger-G TU-16 (Tupolev)	Ship attack	1965	77 t	34.5 m	36.5 m	2 AM-3 M turbojets, 9,550-kg thrust each	540 kts at 22,000 ft 445 kts at sea level	3,200 km without refueling	8/23-mm cannon, 2 AS-5 Kelt or 2 AS-6 Kingfish	1 Short Horn navigation and bombing radar; 1 Doppler radar; 1 Bee Hind tail radar.	
Badger-D, -E, -F, -J TU-16 (Tupolev)	Reconnaissance and electronic warfare	. . .	77 t	34.5 m	36.5 m	2 AM-3 M turbojets, 9,550-kg thrust each	540 kts at 22,000 ft 445 kts at sea level	3,200 km without refueling	6/7/23-mm cannon	1 Puff Ball navigation and bombing radar; electronic warfare equipment; 1 tail radar.	Different versions for ELINT, photo reconnaissance, etc.
Forger-A/B YAK-38 (Yakolev)	A: Ship attack, day interceptor B: 2-seat trainer	1976	9.9 t	7 m	15 m (B: 17.7 m)	1/7,650-kg thrust main engine; 2/3,600-kg lift engines	Mach 1.1 at 36,000 ft	125 nautical miles low-low-low; 240 n.m. low-high-low	16 or 32 rockets, 2/23-mm cannon, 2/AS-7 or AS-10 missiles, or 1,000-kg bombs	Passive warning system; inertial navigation. No radar.	Forger-B, the two-seat training version, is also carried aboard ship. A-version can also carry 2 AA-8 air-to-air missiles. Originally vertical takeoff only, now V/STOL.
Fitter-C, -D SU-20 (Sukhoi)	Ship attack	1976	17 t	14 m (10.5 m swept)	17.6 m	1/Lyulka, AL-21F, 11,000-kg thrust turbojet	Mach 1.8 at 50,000 ft	220 nautical miles low-low-low; 435 n.m. high-low-high	32/57-mm rockets, 2/30-mm cannon, 3,500 kg bombs, nuclear or conventional	Ranging radar; tail warning radar; laser range finder; automatic control	Used by Naval Air Force in Baltic area. Can also carry AA-2 Atoll or AA-8 Aphid air-air or AS-7 or AS-10 air-ground-missiles
May IL-38 (Ilyushin)	ASW	1969	68 t	37.4 m	36.9 m	4 turboprops, 5,200 hp each	380 kts at 30,000 ft 315 kts at sea level	3,000 km, endurance: 12 hours	7,000 kg of bombs, depth charges, torpedoes	Radar, MAD[2], sonobuoys	Il-18 Coot ELINT and ECM aircraft use the same basic airframe. 12-hour endurance.
Mail BE-12 (Beriev)	ASW	1967	30 t	29.7 m	30.2 m	2 AL-20D turboprops, 4,190 hp each	310 kts at 30,000 ft 240 kts at sea level	1,300 km	Bombs, charges, mines	Radar, MAD[2], sonobuoys	Amphibian, but used primarily from land
◆ **HELICOPTERS**											
Haze-A, -B MI 14 (Mil)	A: ASW, B: Mine countermeasures	1976	12 t	rotor diam. 21.3 m	24 m (18.2 fuselage)	2 Isotov TV 3 117A turboshafts, 2,200 hp each	140 kts 122 kts	305 km, endurance: 2.5 hours	Depth bombs or torpedoes: 2,000 kg total	Dipping sonar, towed MAD[2] pod	Land-based; rotors do not fold. Crew of four. B-version tows hydrofoil sled.
Hormone-A, -B, -C KA 25 (Kamov)	A: ASW B: Targeting C: Utility	1967	7.3 t	rotor diam. 16 m	10 m	2 GTD 3 F turboshafts, 905 hp each	120 kts 105 kts	250 km, endurance: 1.5 to 2 hours	Depth charges or torpedoes: 1,000 kg total	Sonobuoys and dipping sonar	Carried on board *Kiev, Moskva,* Kara, and Kresta classes. The B version has a Video Data Link system. C version in various utility configurations, including reconn.
Helix-A, -B, -D KA-27 (Kamov)	A: ASW B: Troop-carrying D: Search-and-rescue	1980	12.6 t	rotor diam. 15.90 m	11.30 m (12.25 folded)	2 Glushevkov TV3 117V turboshafts; 4,450 hp	140 kts 124 kts (with 5,000-kg payload)	400 km, endurance: 2 to 2.5 hours	Depth charges or 2 torpedoes	Sonobuoys and dipping sonar, possible MAD	Civil version, Ka-32 (Helix-C) has lifted 5,000 kg. Helix-B for use on *Ivan Rogov.*
Hip-C MI-8 (Mil)	Transport	1967	12 t	rotor diam. 21.0 m	18.3 m	2 Isetov TV-2-117A turboshafts, 1,500 hp each	125 kts 100 kts	220 km	12 troops, or 4,000 kg cargo		Land-based. Some used for aerial minesweeping.

(1) The operational radius is roughly 60% of the radius given by one-half of the range
(2) MAD = Magnetic Detection

Backfire-B (Tu-22M) naval bomber 1979

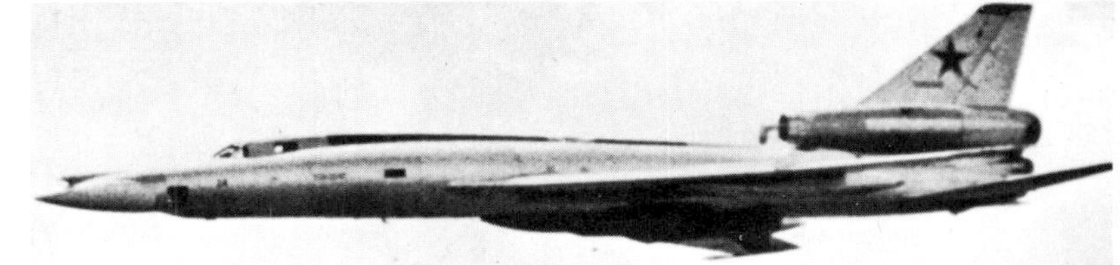

Blinder-A (Tupolev TU-22) U.S. Navy

COMBAT AIRCRAFT *(continued)*

Bear-D (Tu-95)—reconnaissance U.S. Navy, 7-83

Bear-F (Tu-142) long-range ASW aircraft with new MAD boom atop the stabilizer U.S. Navy, 9-83

Badger-A (Tu-16)—tanker, with wingtip drogue system 1972

Badger-E (Tu-16)—ELINT U.S. Navy, 1985

Forger-A (Yak-38), showing flow fences added atop the fuselage 1981

Badger-G (Tu-16)—missile carrier

Forger-B (Yak-38) two-seat training VTOL aircraft 1981

May (Il-38)—ASW aircraft U.S. Navy, 1983

Coot-A (Il-18) intelligence collector 1983

Mail (Be-12)—ASW amphibian—MAD boom protruding aft U.S. Navy, 1984

COMBAT AIRCRAFT *(continued)*

Haze-A (Mi-14) land-based ASW helicopter PH2 P. Soutar, U.S. Navy, 9-83

Hormone-A (Ka-25) ASW helicopter PH2 P. Soutar, U.S. Navy, 9-83

Hormone-B (Ka-25) targeting helicopter U.S. Navy, 1-84

Hip-C (Mi-8) utility helicopter 1981

Hormone-C utility helicopter in SAR configuration French Navy, 1981

Helix-A (Ka-27) ASW helicopter U.S. Navy, 1-84

Helix-D (Ka-27) search-and-rescue helicopter French Navy

SUBMARINES

NOTE: Nuclear-powered submarines are built or modernized in the Severodvinsk (formerly, Molotovsk) Naval Shipyard on the White Sea, near Arkhangelsk; at Komsomolsk-on-Amur in the Far East; in the Gorkiy Shipyard on the Volga; and at the United Admiralty Shipyard in Leningrad (comprising the former Sudomekh and Admiralty Shipyards).

Most modern Soviet submarines have an anechoic hull coating that absorbs the echoes of sonars and thus reduces the intensity of reflected echoes. Reports of exotic propulsion systems, such as magnetohydrodynamic drive, electromagnetic drive, or the use of compliant coatings to improve boundary layer flow, although discussed in the popular press, apparently have yet to find use on an actual operational Soviet submarine class.

BALLISTIC-MISSILE SUBMARINES (NUCLEAR-POWERED)

(Soviet Type: PLARB—*Podvodnaya Lodka Atomnaya Raketnaya Ballisticheskaya* = Nuclear-powered Ballistic Missile Submarine.)

◆ **1 (+3 +) Delta-IV class** Bldr: Severodvinsk SY

Delta-IV class R. Nor. A.F., 1985

D: 10,750 tons (surf.)/13,550 tons (sub.) **S:** 24 kts (sub.)
Dim: 164.0 × 12.0 × 8.7
A: 16/SS-NX-23 ballistic missiles—6/533 or 650-mm TT (bow)
Electron Equipt: Radar: 1/Snoop Tray—Sonar: LF passive/active
M: 2 nuclear reactors, steam turbines; 2/7-bladed props; 50,000 hp
Man: . . .

REMARKS: First unit launched 1-84, operational by 1985; three others in various stages of construction. A further elongation of the early-1960s Yankee design and apparently externally similar to Delta-III. Believed capable of operating under the ice-pack. Distinguishable from Delta-III by possible towed array tube atop rudder and camera housing at aft end of turtledeck.

◆ **4 (+. . .) Typhoon class** Bldr: Severodvinsk SY (L: 9-80, 9-82, 12-83, 1984)

D: 25,000 tons (sub.) **S:** 25 kts (sub.) **Dim:** 170.0 × 25.0 × 13.0 (approx.)
A: 20/SS-N-20 ballistic missiles—. . . /533-mm or 650-mm (torpedoes, SS-N-15/16) TT

Typhoon class M.O.D., U.K., 1984

Typhoon class—pyramidal structures abaft probable communications-buoy hatches abaft sail probably house t.v. cameras M.O.D., U.K., 1984

Electron Equipt: Radar: 1/Snoop Pair—Sonar: LF active/passive
M: 2 330–360 MW nuclear reactors; 2/7-bladed props, . . . hp **Man:** 150 tot.

REMARKS: World's largest submarines. Eight or nine total units expected. Evidently intended to operate beneath the Arctic ice pack, breaking through to launch. The first Typhoon launched two missiles within 15 sec. in 10-82. Design incorporates two parallel pressure hulls within the outer hull, with the massive sail being an additional pressure vessel. Forward location of the missile tubes is unique. The first began trials 6-81, the second in 6-83. Propulsion plant probably generates over 100,000 hp.

◆ **14 Delta-III class** Bldr: Severodvinsk SY

Delta-III class 1982

Delta-III—note communications-buoy hatches on sloped portion of missile turtledeck

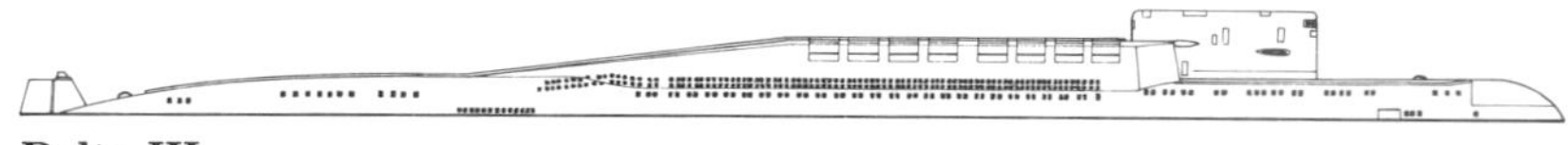

Delta-III

D: 10,500/13,250 tons **S:** 24 kts (sub.) **Dim:** 155.0 × 12.0 × 8.7
A: 16/SS-N-18—6/533-mm TT fwd. (18 torpedoes) **Man:** 120 tot.
Electron Equipt: Radar: 1/Snoop Tray
Sonar: 1/LF active, passive array
M: 2 nuclear reactors, steam turbines; 2/5-bladed props; 50,000 hp

REMARKS: Two went into service in 1975, four in 1976, two in 1977, two in 1978, and three in 1979-81; the 13th was launched 3-4-81, the 14th in 12-81. Has higher "turtle-deck" than Delta-II, to accommodate the longer SS-N-18 tubes. Have towed VLF communications buoys. One is named *60 Let Velikyo Oktyabr.*

BALLISTIC-MISSILE SUBMARINES *(continued)*

◆ **4 Delta-II class** Bldr: Severodvinsk (In serv. 1974-75)

Delta-II

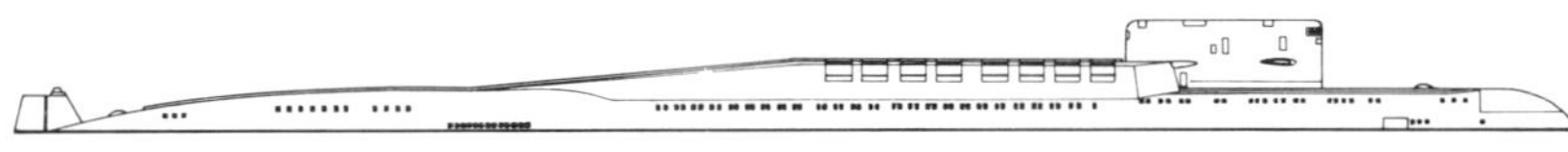

Delta-II

D: 10,000/12,750 tons **S:** 24 kts (sub.) **Dim:** 155.0 × 12.0 × 8.6
A: 16/SS-N-8—6/533-mm TT fwd. (18 torpedoes) **Man:** 120 tot.
Electron Equipt: Radar: 1/Snoop Tray—Sonar: LF active, passive array
M: 2 nuclear reactors, steam turbines; 2/5-bladed props; 50,000 hp

REMARKS: Lengthened version of Delta-I, so as to carry four more SS-N-8.

◆ **18 Delta-I class** Bldrs: Severodvinsk and Komsomolsk, (In serv. 1973-76)

Delta-I class—note stepped casing abaft missile tube area U.S. Navy, 1979

Delta-I class

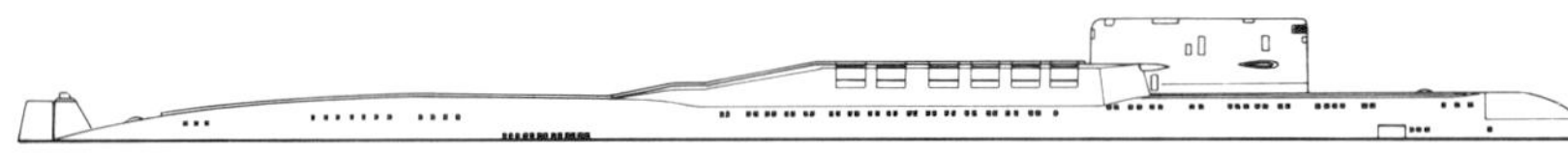

Delta-I

D: 9,000/11,750 tons **S:** 25 kts **Dim:** 140.0 × 12.0 × 8.7
A: 12/SS-N-8—6/533-mm TT fwd. (18 torpedoes)
Electron Equipt: Radar: 1 Snoop Tray
Sonar: 1/LF active, passive arrays
M: 2 nuclear reactors, steam turbines; 2/5-bladed props; 50,000 hp
Man: 120 tot.

REMARKS: One entered service in 1972, four in 1973, six in 1974, two in 1975, two in 1976, and three in 1977. Distinguished from later, longer Delta-II and -III by stepped turtleneck abaft sail.

◆ **1 Yankee-II class** Bldr: Severodvinsk SY (In serv. 1978?)

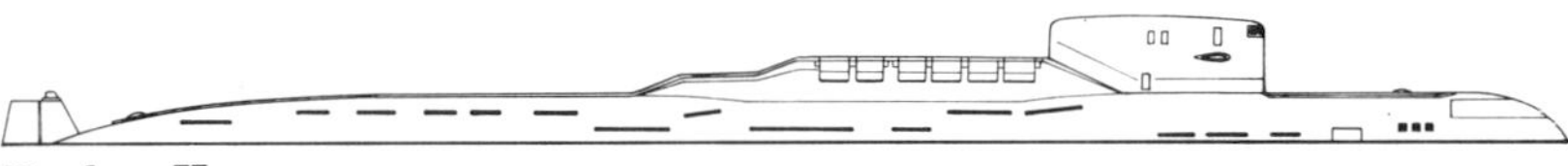

Yankee-II

Yankee-II—distinguishable from Delta-I by sloping forward edge to the missile-tube casing hump 1982

◆ **21 Yankee-I class** Bldrs: Severodvinsk SY and Komsomolsk SY (In serv. 1967-74)

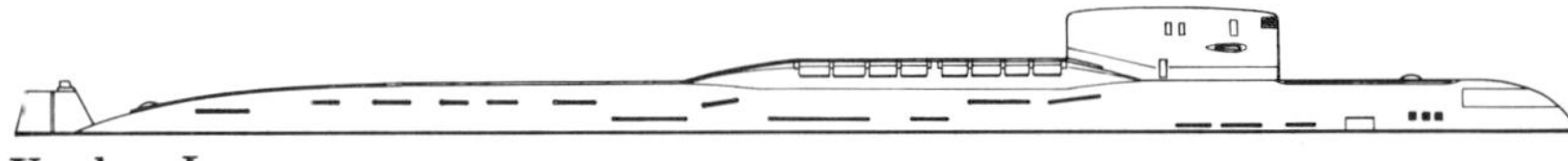

Yankee-I

Yankee-I—with angled forward edge to sail, ESM, D/F, and comms. masts extended, bare metal sonar window U.S. Navy

Yankee class—with painted sonar window, straight forward edge to sail 1982

D: 7,900/9,600 tons **S:** 27 kts **Dim:** 130.0 × 12.0 × 8.8
A: Yankee-I: 16/SS-N-6—6/533-mm TT (18 torpedoes)
Yankee-II: 12/SS-N-17—6/533-mm TT (18 torpedoes)
Electron Equipt: Radar: 1/Snoop Tray
Sonar: 1/LF active, passive arrays
M: 2 nuclear reactors, steam turbines; 2/5-bladed props; 50,000 hp
Man: 120 tot.

REMARKS: In one unit, nicknamed "Yankee-II," SS-N-6 has been replaced by SS-N-17 with twelve tubes. A total of 34 were completed: two in 1967, four in 1968, six in 1969,

BALLISTIC-MISSILE SUBMARINES *(continued)*

eight in 1970, six in 1971, five in 1972, two in 1973, and one in 1974. To date, twelve have had their missile tubes deactivated, in compliance with the U.S.-Soviet SALT agreements; these "de-fanged" Yankees are listed under attack submarines, except for one which has been converted to carry cruise missiles.

◆ **1 Hotel-III class** Bldr: Severodvinsk (In serv. 1965)

D: 5,500/6,400 tons **S:** 20/25 kts **Dim:** 130.0 × 9.0 × 7.0
A: 2/SS-N-8—6/533-mm TT—2/400-mm TT
Electron Equipt: Radar: 1/Snoop Tray
Sonar: 1/MF active, passive arrays
M: 2 nuclear reactors, steam turbines; 2/6-bladed props; 30,000 hp **Man:** 80 tot.

Remarks: Used as trial ship for SS-N-8 missiles. Lengthened during conversion.

Note: All Hotel-II-class nuclear-powered ballistic-missile submarines are believed to have had their SS-N-5 ballistic-missile systems disabled in compliance with SALT requirements. One has been converted as a communications unit, and the others may reappear as attack submarines, although they are quite obsolescent.

BALLISTIC-MISSILE SUBMARINES (DIESEL-POWERED)

(Soviet Type: PLRB = *Podvodnaya Lodka Raketnaya Ballisticheskaya* = Ballistic-Missile Submarine)

◆ **1 Golf-V class**

Remarks: One Golf-II-class submarine has had the original three missile tubes replaced by a single tube for a new missile (possibly SS-N-20) for trials purposes. Other details as for Golf-II class. The single Golf-IV trials conversion for the SS-N-6 missile (6 tubes) has apparently been scrapped.

◆ **1 Golf-III class** Bldr: Severodvinsk SY (In serv. 1958-61)

Golf-III U.S. Navy

D: 2,900/3,300 tons **S:** 12 kts (sub.) **Dim:** 110.0 × 8.5 × 6.6
A: 6/SS-N-8—10/533-mm TT (6 fwd, 4 aft)
Electron Equipt: Radar: 1/Snoop Tray—Sonar: 1/med. freq., passive array
M: 3 diesels; 2,000 hp each, electric drive; 3 props; 5,300 hp (sub.)
Endurance: 70 days **Range:** 9,000/5 **Man:** 87 tot.

Remarks: Converted for trials purposes, early 1970s.

◆ **13 Golf-II class** Bldr: Severodvinsk (In serv. 1958-61)

Golf-II—with VLF comms.-buoy housing near stern (smoke from sail evidently part of a damage-control/salvage exercise) *Ships of the World,* 11-84

Golf-II class—communications-buoy housing abaft sail 1976

D: 2,300/2,700 tons **S:** 12 kts (sub.) **Dim:** 100.0 × 8.5 × 6.6
A: 3/SS-N-5—10/533-mm TT (6 fwd, 4 aft)
M: Diesel-electric drive, 3/2,000-hp diesels; 3 props; 5,300 hp (sub.)
Endurance: 70 days **Range:** 9,000/5 **Man:** 80 tot.

Remarks: These submarines continue to be active, and a number of them have been stationed in the Baltic. The range of the SS-N-5 has been extended from the original 700 nautical miles to 900. All Golf-IIs are conversions from Golf-I. The few remaining unconverted Golf-I-class submarines have been scrapped or converted to other functions.

CRUISE-MISSILE ATTACK SUBMARINES (NUCLEAR-POWERED)

(Soviet Type: PLARK—*Podvodnaya Lodka Atomnaya Reketnaya Krylataya* = Nuclear-Powered Cruise-Missile Submarine)

◆ **2 (+ . . .) Oscar class** Bldr: Severodvinsk SY (In serv. 1982-. . .)

Second Oscar-class unit—note missile-tube doors abreast sail R. Nor. A.F., 1984

Second Oscar-class unit—note buoy housing abaft sail R. Nor. A.F., 1984

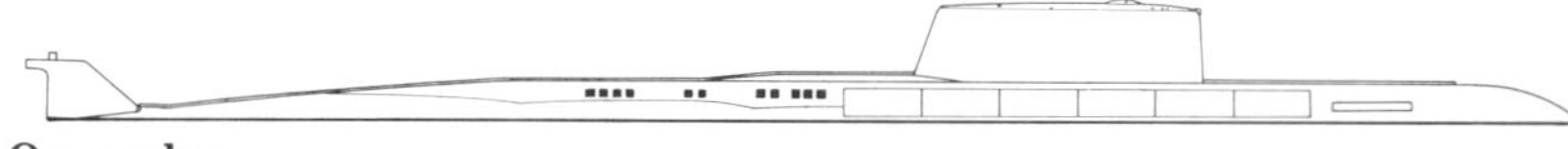

Oscar class

CRUISE-MISSILE ATTACK SUBMARINES *(continued)*

Second Oscar-class unit—snow on deck outlines bow weapons-loading hatch and missile-tube hatch doors R. Nor. A.F., 1984

D: 11,500/14,500 tons **S:** 35 kts (sub.) **Dim:** 150.0 × 18.0 × 11.0
A: 24/SS-N-19 SSM—8/533- or 650-mm TT fwd (24 SS-N-15/16; torpedoes)
Electron Equipt: Radar: . . . —Sonar: 1/LF active, 1/MF active, passive arrays
M: 2 nuclear reactors, steam turbines; 2/7-bladed props; 90,000 hp
Man: . . .

REMARKS: The first was launched in 4-80, the second in 12-82; additional units are expected. The missile tubes are mounted in two rows of twelve, abreast the sail, fixed in elevation at about 40°, with doors opening through the outer hull, as on the Papa and Charlie-I and -II classes. The missiles are launched while the submarine is submerged, presumably using targeting data from a forward observer or from satellite targeting. Six outer hatch doors each cover two tubes. The tubes provide a 3.5-m stand-off between the outer hull and the pressure hull. A towed hydrophone array is dispensed from a tube at the top of the rudder on the second unit.

◆ **1 Papa class** Bldr: Gorkiy SY (In serv. 1970)

D: 6,700/8,000 tons **S:** 39 kts **Dim:** 109.0 × 12.2 × 9.5
A: 10-SS-N-9—6/533-mm TT fwd
M: 2 nuclear reactors, steam turbines; 2/5-bladed props; 60–75,000 hp
Man: 85 tot.

Papa class—note 4 TT, reload hatch, missile-tube covers visible M.O.D., U.K., 1981

REMARKS: May have been a concept prototype. Launched 1968. Missiles launched from submerged condition, apparently against acoustically located targets. Has had two lengthy overhauls and very little active service. May have a titanium pressure hull.

◆ **6 Charlie-II class** Bldr: Gorkiy SY (In serv. 1973-1982)

Charlie-II class U.S. Navy

Charlie-II class—note "collar" at base of sail U.S. Navy, 1979

D: 4,500/5,400 tons **S:** 24 kts (sub.) **Dim:** 102.0 × 10.0 × 8.0
A: 8/SS-N-9—6/533-mm TT fwd. (12 SS-N-15, torpedoes)
Electron Equipt: Radar: 1/Snoop Tray—EW: 1/Brick Spit, 1/Brick Pulp
Sonar: 1/LF active, passive arrays
M: 1 nuclear reactor, steam turbines; 1/5-bladed prop; 15,000 hp **Man:** 110 tot.

REMARKS: All in Northern Fleet. One in service in each of the years 1973, 1974, 1977, 1979, 1980/81, and 1982. The additional 8-m length over the Charlie-I comes between the missile tubes and the sail. Probably can also launch the SS-N-7. Have VLF comms buoy housing abaft the sail.

◆ **11 Charlie-I class** Bldr: Gorkiy SY (In serv. 1968-72)

Charlie-I class—note "collar" added at base of sail 1982

CRUISE-MISSILE ATTACK SUBMARINES *(continued)*

Charlie-I class 2-84

D: 4,000/5,000 tons **S:** 24 kts (sub.) **Dim:** 94.0 × 10.0 × 8.0
A: 8/SS-N-7—6/533-mm TT fwd. (12 SS-N-15, torpedoes)
Electron Equipt: Radar: 1/Snoop Tray—EW: 1/Brick Spit, 1/Brick Pulp
Sonar: 1/LF active, passive arrays
M: 1 nuclear reactor, steam turbines; 1/5-bladed prop; 15,000 hp **Man:** 100 tot.

Remarks: In service at the rate of about two a year between 1968 and 1973. "Collar" structures being added at the forward base of the sail, apparently to smooth water flow. Diving depth: 400 m normal/600 m max. One sank 6-83 in the Pacific; subsequently salvaged.

◆ **1 Yankee-class conversion**

D: 13,650 tons (sub.) **S:** 23 kts (sub.) **Dim:** 153.0 × 12.0 × 9.0
A: 12/SS-N-24 SSM—6/533-mm TT (fwd)
Electron Equipt: Radar: . . . —Sonar: . . .
M: 2 nuclear reactors, steam turbines; 2/5-bladed props; 45,000 hp

Remarks: Converted from a Yankee-I which had her SS-N-6 ballistic-missile system deleted in compliance with SALT. Relaunched 12-82, and apparently operational as trials submarine for the SS-NX-24 cruise-missile system by 1985.

◆ **28 Echo-II class** Bldr: Severodvinsk and Komsomolsk (In serv. 1960-67)

Echo-II with two of the four pairs of SS-N-3 missile tubes elevated
U.S. Navy

Echo-II class

Echo-II class 1974

Echo-II with SS-N-12—note Front Door/Front Piece antenna deployed at forward end of sail, bulge on sail side, and relocated hinge bulge at forward end of the second missile-tube pair 1980

D: 5,000/6,000 tons **S:** 20/23 kts **Dim:** 115.0 × 9.0 × 7.5
A: 8/SS-N-3A or SS-N-12—6/533-mm TT (fwd)—4/400-mm TT (aft)
Electron Equipt: Radar: 1/Snoop Tray, 1/Front Piece, 1/Front Door
Sonar: 1/LF active, passive arrays, including Feniks.
M: 2 nuclear reactors, steam turbines; 2/4-bladed props; 30,000 hp **Man:** 90 tot.

Remarks: Approximately six to date have been modified to launch SS-N-12; they have a bulge on either side of the sail and a bulge at the forward ends of the missile tubes abreast the sail. The Echo-II must be surfaced to launch, the tubes elevating in pairs to fire. The forward part of the sail rotates 180° to expose the Front Door/Front Piece guidance radar. One unit has been converted to an auxiliary function. One Echo-II may be named *Dekabrist.*

CRUISE-MISSILE ATTACK SUBMARINES (DIESEL-POWERED)

(Soviet Type: PLRK = *Podvodnaya Lodka Raketnaya Krylataya* = Cruise-Missile Submarine)

◆ **16 Juliett class** Bldr: Gorkiy SY (In serv. 1961-63)

Juliett class R. Neth. Navy, 1983

Juliett class R. Neth. Navy, 1983

CRUISE-MISSILE ATTACK SUBMARINES *(continued)*

D: 3,000/3,750 tons **S:** 16/8 kts **Dim:** 90.0 × 10.0 × 7.0
A: 4/SS-N-3A — 6/533-mm TT (fwd) — 4/400-mm TT (aft)
Electron Equipt: Radar: 1/Snoop Slab, 1/Front Piece, 1/Front Door
EW: 1/Stop Light
Sonar: 1/MF active, passive arrays
M: 2 diesels, electric drive; 2 props; 5,000 hp
Range: 9,000/7 (snorkel) **Man:** 80 tot.

Remarks: Missiles are in paired tubes, elevating to fire, as on the Echo-II class. Since 1981, six have been based in the Baltic.

Note: The last Whiskey Long Bin cruise-missile submarine is believed to have been discarded during 1985.

ATTACK SUBMARINES (NUCLEAR-POWERED)

(Soviet Type: PLA — *Podvodnaya Lodka Atomnaya* = Nuclear-Powered Submarine)

◆ **1 (+ . . .) Akula class** Bldr: Komsomolsk SY, Komsomolsk-na-Amur

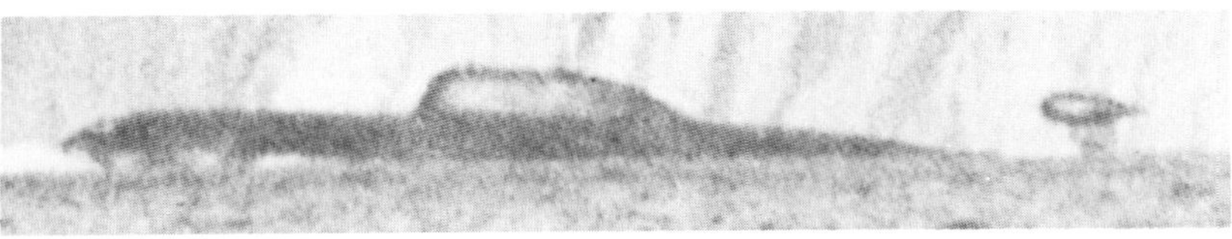

Akula class U.S. Navy, 1984

D: 7,500/10,000 tons **S:** 35 kts **Dim:** 113.0 × 12.0 × . . .
A: 6/650 or 533-mm TT (SS-N-16/21 missiles, torpedoes)
Electron Equipt: Radar: . . .
Sonar: LF active/passive, passive array towed LF linear hydrophone array
M: 2 pressurized water nuclear reactors, steam turbines; 1/7-bladed prop; . . . hp
Man: . . .

Remarks: First unit launched 7-84. Differs from Sierra in having a longer, more streamlined sail. Broader hull than preceding Victor series indicates probable use of "rafted" (sound-isolated) propulsion plant to greatly reduce radiated noise. *Akula* means "shark" in Russian; the NATO nickname was chosen because all the letters of the phonetic alphabet have been used to name recent classes. Steel hull.

◆ **1 (+ . . .) Sierra class** Bldr: Gorkiy SY and, possibly, United Admiralty SY, Leningrad

Sierra class R. Nor. A.F., 1984

Sierra class — detail of flat-topped sail, showing back-to-back radar antenna, with EW array surrounding base of antenna housing R. Nor. A.F., 1984

Sierra class R. Nor. A.F., 1984

ATTACK SUBMARINES *(continued)*

Sierra class—note upper bridge to port, periscope to starboard R. Nor. A.F., 1984

D: 6,000/7,550 tons **S:** 34–36 kts **Dim:** 110.0 × 12.0 × . . .
A: 6/650- and 533-mm TT (SS-N-16/21 missiles/torpedoes)
Electron Equipt: Radar: 1/. . . (back-to-back antennas)
Sonar: LF suite, towed passive hydrophone array
M: 2 pressurized water reactors; 1/7-bladed prop; . . . hp
Man: . . .

REMARKS: First unit launched 7-83 at Gorkiy and transferred via river/canal system to Severodvinsk for completion. Differs from Akula in having a blunter, shorter sail and in lacking a towed communications buoy housing abaft the sail; probably has the same propulsion plant, optimized for radiated noise reduction. May have a titanium hull, if so, this is a successor to the Alfa, while the Akula may be considered as a successor to the Victor-III.

◆ **1 (+ . . .) Mike class** Bldr: Severodvinsk SY

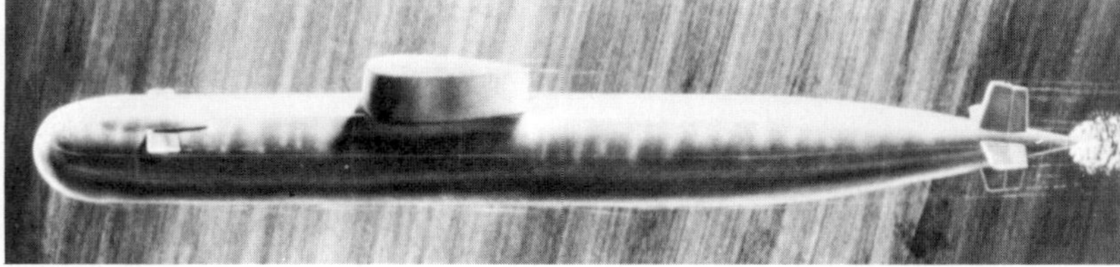

Mike class—artist's rendering U.S. D.O.D., 1984

D: 5,000/7,000 tons **S:** 36–38 kts **Dim:** 122.0 × 12.0 × 9.0
A: 6/650- or 533-mm TT (SS-N-15/16/21 missiles, torpedoes)
Electron Equipt: Radar: . . .
Sonar: LF suite
M: 2 reactors; 1/7-bladed prop; approx. 60,000 hp
Man: . . .

REMARKS: First unit launched 6-83, with a second believed to be under construction. Hull built of titanium, and reactor may employ liquid metal coolant, as in the Alfa-class. Lacks the towed passive linear hydrophone array housing atop the rudder of the Akula, Sierra, and Victor-III classes.

◆ **6 Alfa class** Bldr: Admiralty (Sudomekh) SY, Leningrad, and Severodvinsk SY (In serv. 1979–83)

Alfa-class SSN—note smooth blending of sail to hull U.S. Navy, 1980

Alfa class M.O.D., Norway

D: 2,900/3,680 tons **S:** 43–45 kts (sub.) **Dim:** 81.4 × 9.5 × 7.0
A: 6/533-mm TT (with SS-N-15 missiles, torpedoes)
Electron Equipt: Radar: 1/Snoop Tray—EW: 1/Brick Pulp, 1/Brick Spit, 1/Park Lamp D/F
Sonar: 1/LF active, passive arrays
M: 1 nuclear reactor, steam turbines; 1/7-bladed prop; 45,000 hp
Man: 45 tot.

REMARKS: The prototype, completed 1972, was scrapped about 1974, but the class later entered production as the world's fastest and deepest-diving (over 900 m) combatant submarine. The pressure hull is constructed of titanium, and the ships are highly automated. High speeds are achieved through use of a very "dense" propulsion plant, with safety and accessibility standards much less than those of the West. The reactors use a lead-bismuth mixture as coolant. The second entered active service in 1979.

◆ **21 Victor-III class** Bldrs: Admiralty SY, Leningrad, and Komsomolsk SY (In serv. 1978-85)

Victor-III—showing tandem 8-bladed propeller U.S. Navy, 1983

ATTACK SUBMARINES *(continued)*

Victor-III—note towed linear hydrophone array pod atop the vertical stabilizer

Victor-III—with cylindrical fairing on deck before sail U.S. Navy, 1982

D: 4,800/6,300 tons **S:** 29 kts (sub.) **Dim:** 106.0 × 10.0 × 7.0
A: 6/650- and 533-mm TT (SS-N-15 and/or SS-N-16 missiles, torpedoes)
Electron Equipt: Radar: 1/Snoop Tray—Sonar: 1/LF active, passive arrays
M: 2 reactors, steam turbines; 1/tandem 8-bladed prop; 30,000 hp (plus 2 small props for maneuvering)
Man: 85 tot.

Remarks: Further lengthened over basic Victor-I; distinguished by large teardrop-shaped pod atop vertical stabilizer. The pod houses a towed linear passive hydrophone array. At least one unit has a 10-m fairing on deck forward of the sail. Most employ an unusual 8-bladed propeller, consisting of two tandem 4-bladed props oriented 22.5-deg. apart and co-rotating; others have a standard 7-bladed prop.

◆ **7 Victor-II class** Bldr: Admiralty SY, Leningrad (In serv. 1972-78)

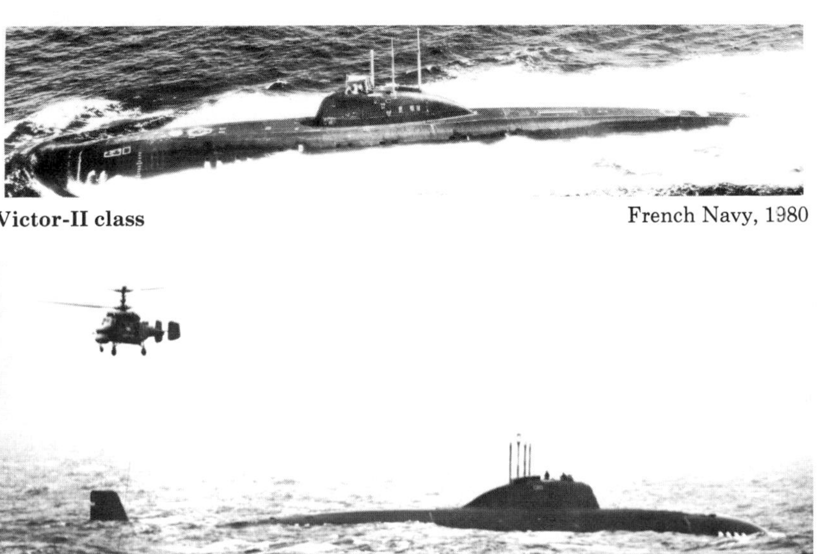

Victor-II class French Navy, 1980

Victor-II class U.S. Navy, 1984

D: 4,500/5,700 tons **S:** 30 kts **Dim:** 100.0 × 10.0 × 7.0
A: 6/533- and 650-mm TT (SS-N-15 and/or SS-N-16 missiles, torpedoes)
M: 2 nuclear reactors, steam turbines; 1/5-bladed prop (plus 2 small props for maneuvering); 30,000 hp
Man: 80 tot.

Remarks: One went into service in each of the years 1972, 1974, and 1975, two in 1976, and one each in 1977 and 1978. Longer than Victor-I, without pronounced hump on forward casing. Have a VLF comms-buoy housing within the casing abaft the sail. Some may have propellers as per the Victor-III class.

◆ **16 Victor-I class** Bldr: Admiralty SY, Leningrad (In serv. 1968-75)

50 Let SSR 15 others

Victor-I class French Navy, 1984

Victor-I class U.S. Navy, 1984

ATTACK SUBMARINES *(continued)*

Victor-I class French Navy, 1984

D: 4,300/5,100 tons **S:** 30 kts **Dim:** 95.0 × 10.0 × 7.0
A: 6/533-mm TT (SS-N-15 missiles, torpedoes)
Electron Equipt: Radar: 1/Snoop Tray—EW: 1/Brick Pulp, 1/Brick Spit
Sonar: 1/LF active passive arrays
M: 2 nuclear reactors, steam turbines; 1/5-bladed prop; 30,000 hp (2 small, 2-bladed props for slow speeds)
Man: 80 tot.

REMARKS: Completed two per year between 1968 and 1975. Diving depth: 600 m max.

◆ **1 (+10) Yankee class** Bldr: Severodvinsk SY and Komsomolsk SY (In serv. 1967-1974)

D: 7,900/10,000 tons **S:** 27 kts **Dim:** 131.0 × 12.0 × 9.0
A: 6/533-mm TT (bow)
Electron Equipt: Radar: 1/Snoop Tray
Sonar: LF suite, passive arrays
M: 2 pressurized water reactors, steam turbines; 2/5-bladed props; 45,000 hp
Man: 80 tot.

REMARKS: These are former ballistic-missile submarines that have had their 16 SS-N-6 tubes disabled in compliance with the U.S.-Soviet SALT agreements. As more Delta-II and Typhoon ballistic-missile submarines are built, more Yankees will receive similar treatment in order to keep the number of submarine-launched ballistic-missile tubes at no more than 950. It is believed that, as the Yankees are relatively new, the Soviet Navy is probably adapting them for some other purpose, probably as attack submarines, or, possibly, as minelayers. The first unit completed alteration and reactivated 1984. One other unit reappeared in 1982, reconfigured to launch cruise missiles.

◆ **5 Echo class** Bldr: Komsomolsk (In serv. 1960-62)

Echo class U.S. Navy, 1975

Echo class—with periscope, Stop Light EW, D/F loop, etc. raised 1978

D: 4,500/5,500 tons **S:** 20/25 kts **Dim:** 110.0 × 9.0 × 7.5
A: 6/533-mm TT (fwd)—4/400-mm TT (aft)
Electron Equipt: Radar: 1/Snoop Tray—Sonar: 1/med. freq.
M: 2 nuclear reactors, steam turbines; 2/5-bladed props; 25,000 hp **Man:** 75 tot.

REMARKS: Former cruise-missile submarines that carried six SS-N-3C. Converted circa 1970-75. One, involved in a casualty 20-8-80, had to be towed to Vladivostok; several men died. All in Pacific Fleet.

◆ **1 (+4) Modified Hotel class** Bldr: Severodvinsk SY (In serv. 1965)

D: 5,000/6,000 tons **S:** 20/25 kts **Dim:** 115.0 × 9.0 × 7.0
A: 6/533-mm TT fwd—4/400-mm TT aft
Electron Equipt: Radar: . . . **Man:** . . .
Sonar: . . .
M: 2 nuclear reactors, steam turbines; 2/6-bladed props; 30,000 hp

REMARKS: Missile tubes removed. The first of these submarines has reportedly been altered to perform the same role as the three Golf-class command-and-communications submarines. The others will probably either emerge similarly reconfigured or altered as straight attack submarines, despite their obsolescence.

◆ **12 November class** Bldr: Severodvinsk SY (In serv. 1958-62)

LENINSKIY KOMSOMOL LENINETS 10 others

November class

D: 4,500/5,300 tons **S:** 30 kts (sub.) **Dim:** 110.0 × 9.0 × 7.7
A: 8/533-mm TT (fwd)—4/400-mm TT (aft)—32 torpedoes or mines
Electron Equipt: Radar: 1/Snoop Tray
Sonar: 1/MF active, passive arrays
M: 2 nuclear reactors, steam turbines; 2 (4- or 6-bladed) props; 30,000 hp
Man: 80 tot.

REMARKS: First unit completed 8-58. One of this class was lost off Cape Finisterre in 4-70. Another was apparently scrapped 1982-83. *Leninskiy Komsomol,* the U.S.S.R.'s first nuclear-powered ship, was commissioned 4-8-58; she later made the Soviet Navy's first trip to the North Pole. Obsolescent.

ATTACK SUBMARINES (DIESEL-POWERED)

(Soviet Type: PL—*Podvodnaya Lodka* = Submarine)

◆ **6 (+. . .) Kilo class** Bldr: Komsomolsk-na-Amur SY, Gorkiy SY, and United Admiralty (Sudomekh) SY, Leningrad (In serv. 1982-. . .)

ATTACK SUBMARINES *(continued)*

Kilo class—note small topside rudder JMSDF, 1984

Kilo class JMSDF, 1984

D: 2,500/3,000 tons **S:** 12/16 kts **Dim:** 70.0 × 9.9 × 6.5
A: 6/533-mm TT (12 torpedoes)—1/SAM system
Electron Equipt: Radar: 1/Snoop Tray—Sonar: LF suite
M: 2 diesels, electric drive; 1/6-bladed prop; . . . hp
Man: approx. 60 tot.

Remarks: Function uncertain; may be intended to replace Whiskey/Romeo-class submarines in the "medium-range" category. First unit launched 9-80, entering service 4-82. The second launched 8-81. Production now seems to be 2 or more per year, with some being for export to such clients as India. Reported to have some form of surface-to-air missile system in the sail. Gorkiy and Leningrad production for export.

◆ **19 Tango Class** Bldr: Gorkiy SY (In serv. 1972-82)

Tango class U.S. Navy, 1-85

Tango-class sail/upper bridge area 1976

Tango class French Navy, 6-84

Tango class U.S. Navy, 1983

D: 3,200/3,900 tons **S:** 20/16 kts **Dim:** 92.0 × 9.0 × 7.0
A: 10/533-mm TT (6 fwd, 4 aft) (SS-N-15 missiles, torpedoes)
Electron Equipt: Radar: 1/Snoop Tray—EW: 1/Brick Pulp, 1/Brick Spit, D/F
Sonar: 1/LF active
M: 3 diesels, electric motors; 3 props; 6,000 hp **Man:** 72 tot.

Remarks: Two entered in 1972, and roughly two per year were built. Hull sheathed in sonar-absorbent rubber compound. Have significantly greater battery capacity then the Foxtrot class.

◆ **58 Foxtrot class** Bldr: Admiralty/Sudomekh SY, Severodvinsk SY (In serv. 1957-68)

Chelyabinskiy Komsomolets	Ul'yanovskiy Komsomolets
Komsomolets Kazakhstana	Vladimirskiy Komsomolets
Kuibishevskiy Komsomolets	Yaroslavskiy Komsomolets
Magnitogorskiy Komsomolets	51 others

Foxtrot class—early limber-hole pattern, with folding HF whip raised 1982

Foxtrot class—later limber-hole pattern U.S. Navy, 3-84

ATTACK SUBMARINES *(continued)*

Foxtrot class—late-construction limber-hole pattern U.S. Navy, 1-79

Globus—a Foxtrot on an oceanographic research cruise
LSPH S. Given, R.A.N., 1981

D: 1,950/2,400 tons **S:** 16/15.5 kts **Dim:** 91.5 × 7.5 × 6.0
A: 10/533-mm TT (6 fwd, 4 aft)—22 torpedoes or 44 mines
Electron Equipt: Radar: 1/Snoop Tray—EW: 1/Stop Light
Sonar: 1/MF active, passive arrays
M: 3 diesels of 2,000 hp, electric motors; 3 props; 5,300 hp (sub.)
Endurance: 70 days **Range:** 11,000/8 (snorkel), 350/2 (sub.)
Man: 8 officers, 70 men

Remarks: Foxtrot is a "long-range" submarine, and the design is a development of that of the Zulu class, with a large bow passive sonar array and a more streamlined sail. When used in oceanographic research service, Foxtrots are given temporary astronomical names; to date *Sirius, Saturn, Yupiter, Regul,* and *Globus* have been applied. Between 1967 and 1983, 17 were built for export at Leningrad: eight to India, six to Libya, and three to Cuba. Several Soviet Navy units have been lost. Early units are approaching obsolescence.

◆ **3 Modified Golf class**

Modified Golf class *Ships of the World,* 5-84

D: 2,300/2,700 tons **S:** 12 kts (sub.) **Dim:** 100.0 × 8.5 × 6.6
A: 10/533-mm TT (6 fwd, 4 aft)
Electron Equipt: Radar: 1/Snoop Tray—EW: 1/Stop Light
Sonar: 1/MF active; passive arrays

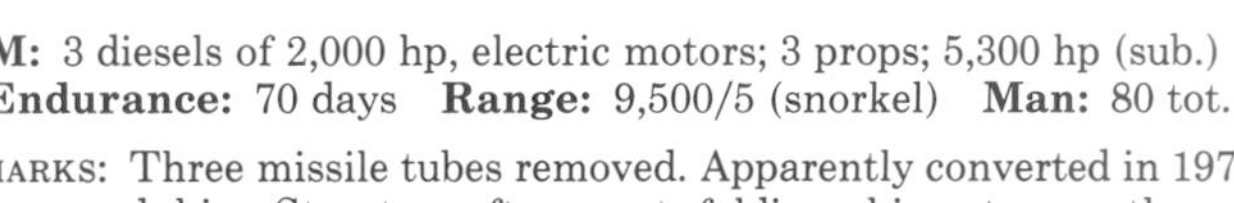

M: 3 diesels of 2,000 hp, electric motors; 3 props; 5,300 hp (sub.)
Endurance: 70 days **Range:** 9,500/5 (snorkel) **Man:** 80 tot.

Remarks: Three missile tubes removed. Apparently converted in 1978 as submersible command ships. Structure aft supports folding whip antennas; there are similar whips on either side of the sail. Sail extension houses VLF buoy antenna. A Hotel nuclear-powered ballistic-missile submarine has received a similar conversion.

◆ **6 Romeo class** Bldr: Baltic SY, Leningrad (In serv. 1957-60)

Romeo class—this unit later transferred to Algeria 1980

D: 1,330/1,700 tons **S:** 15.5/13 kts **Dim:** 77.0 × 6.7 × 4.9
A: 8/533-mm TT (6 fwd, 2 aft)—14 torpedoes or 28 mines
Electron Equipt: Radar: 1/Snoop Plate—EW: 1/Stop Light
Sonar: 1/MF active; passive arrays
M: 2 Type 37D diesels of 2,000 hp, electric motors; 2 props; 3,000 hp (sub.)
Endurance: 45 days **Range:** 7,000/5 (snorkel) **Man:** 56 tot.

Remarks: Diving depth: 270–300 meters. Six transferred to Egypt, two to Bulgaria, two to Algeria, and two to Syria. Also built in China and North Korea. Intended as Whiskey medium-range successor, but only about 20 built. Most have bridge projecting forward from the sail, but one unit (since transferred to Algeria) had the lower portion of the sail extended forward to house a towing hawser drum.

◆ **2 Zulu-IV class** Bldr: Sudomekh SY, Leningrad (In serv. 1952-57)

Zulu-IV class U.S. Navy, 8-84

ATTACK SUBMARINES *(continued)*

D: 1,900/2,350 tons **S:** 18/16 kts **Dim:** 90.0 × 7.5 × 6.0
A: 10/533-mm TT (6 fwd, 4 aft) — 22 torpedoes or 44 mines
Electron Equipt: Radar: 1/Snoop Plate
Sonar: 1/med.-freq.; small passive array
M: 3 Type 37D diesels of 2,000 hp, electric drive; 3 props; 5,300 hp (sub.)
Endurance: 70 days **Range:** 9,500/8 (snorkel) **Man:** 70 tot.

REMARKS: Between 1956 and 1957, several (since scrapped) were converted as Zulu-V ballistic-missile submarines, the world's first of their type; each had two tubes for surface launch of SS-N-4. Sixteen other Zulu-IVs have been scrapped. Earlier configurations (Zulu-I to Zulu-III) had deck guns, AA guns in the sail, and no snorkel; all later updated to Zulu-IV standard. Four additional survivors are in reserve. Two have served in "oceanographic research" roles as *Vega* and *Lira.*

◆ **53 Whiskey class** Bldrs: Baltic SY, Leningrad; Marti SY, Nikolayev; Gorkiy SY; Komsomolsk-na-Amur SY (In serv. 1949-57)

Whiskey class 1977

Whiskey class U.S. Navy, 11-84

D: 1,050/1,350 tons **S:** 17/13.5 kts **Dim:** 76.0 × 6.3 × 4.8
A: 6/533-mm TT (4 fwd, 2 aft) — 12 torpedoes or 24 mines
Electron Equipt: Radar: 1/Snoop Plate
Sonar: 1/Tamir 5 MF active; small passive array
M: 2 Type 37D, 2,000-hp diesels, electric motors; 2 props; 2,500 hp (sub.)
Endurance: 40–45 days **Range:** 6,000/5 (snorkel) **Man:** 50 tot.

REMARKS: Built in prefabricated sections, these strong, uncomplicated boats have proven quite satisfactory. Approximately 236 were built in the U.S.S.R., with China also having built the design. Despite the age, a number remain quite active. Considered to be "medium-range" submarines. Twelve were converted to cruise-missile boats. Four were modified as radar-picket submarines. As many as sixty additional Whiskey-class units are in reserve. Some have been transferred to Bulgaria, Egypt, Poland, Albania, China, and Indonesia. One active Baltic Fleet boat is named *Pskovskiy Komsomolets.*

AUXILIARY SUBMARINES

◆ **1 (+. . .) Uniform class** Bldr: United Admiralty (Sudomekh) SY, Leningrad (L: 6-82)

D: 2,000 tons (sub.) **S:** . . . **Dim:** . . . × . . . × . . .
A: . . . **M:** Nuclear reactor; . . . prop; . . . hp

REMARKS: Apparently intended for research or special operations. The first Soviet single-hulled nuclear-powered submarine.

NOTE: An even smaller nuclear-powered submarine, reportedly similar to the U.S. Navy's NR-1, was launched from the same facility at the end of 1983 and has been designated the Xray class by NATO.

◆ **1 converted Echo-II class**

REMARKS: One Echo-II-class nuclear-powered cruise-missile submarine has been modified for an unknown research purpose. The eight tubes for SS-N-3A missiles have apparently been removed. May be intended for special operations with *Spetsnaz* sabotage swimmers. General data listed earlier otherwise apply.

◆ **1 Lima-class research submarine** Bldr: Admiralty SY, Leningrad (In serv. 1978)

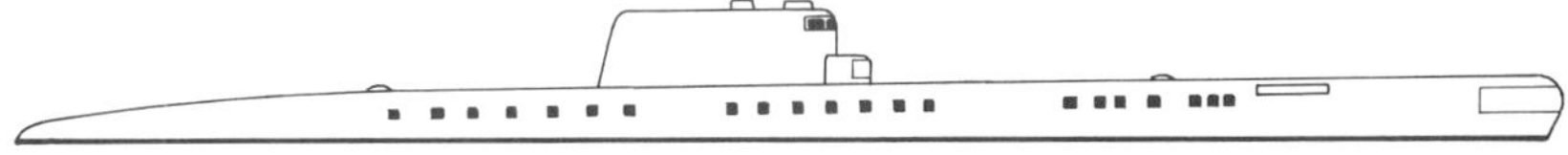

Lima class

D: 2,000/2,450 tons **S:** . . . **Dim:** 86.0 × 9.5 × 7.4
A: None **M:** Diesels, electric drive; . . . props; . . . hp **Man:** . . .

REMARKS: Function not available. Sail, set well aft on unusually bulky hull, has forward extension housing an active sonar transducer and has fixed radar mast.

◆ **2 India-class salvage submarines** Bldr: Komsomolsk-na-Amur SY (In serv. 1979-80)

India class — with two salvage submersibles; note the sail-mounted bow planes 1980

The Northern Fleet India with two salvage submersibles in their docking wells U.S. Navy, 1982

A closer view of one of the 11-meter-long salvage submersibles carried by the India class U.S. Navy, 1982

D: 3,900/4,800 tons **S:** 15/15 **Dim:** 106.0 × 10.0 × . . .
A: Probably none **Electron Equipt:** Radar: . . . — Sonar: 1/med.-freq.; passive arrays
M: . . . diesels, electric motors; 2 props; . . . hp **Man:** . . .

REMARKS: Carry two small salvage/submarine rescue submersibles in wells on after casing. Hull designed for surface cruising. May not have armament, considering function and the narrow hull configuration forward. One unit remains in Pacific, the other transited the Arctic to the Northern Fleet, 1980.

◆ **4 Bravo-class target training submarines** Bldr: Komsomolsk SY, Komsomolsk-na-Amur (In serv. 1968-70)

AUXILIARY SUBMARINES *(continued)*

Bravo class 1975

Bravo class U.S. Navy, 1979

D: 2,400/2,900 tons **S:** 14/16 kts **Dim:** 73.0 × 9.8 × 7.3
A: 6/533-mm TT (fwd)
Electron Equipt: Radar: 1/Snoop Tray—Sonar: 1 passive array
M: Diesel-electric drive; 1 prop; 4,500 hp **Man:** 65 tot.

Remarks: Configured as "hard" targets for torpedo firing training, they may also have a training role and, if indeed armed, could be used as attack subs in wartime.

Note: In addition to the submarines classified as auxiliaries above, a number of units of the combatant classes listed earlier are also employed in research or auxiliary duties. These include Foxtrot- and Zulu-class submarines used in oceanographic research, Whiskey- and Romeo-class submarines used in weapons and sensors development work, the various Golf and Hotel conversions for trials with new ballistic missiles, and the seven Hotel-II- and Golf-II-class submarines altered as command and control submarines.

MINIATURE SUBMARINES (SUBMERSIBLES)

The Soviet Navy possesses a number of small submersibles for clandestine operations by *Spetsnaz* forces. Some are probably similar to the salvage submersibles carried by the India class. Many other small submersibles, Soviet and foreign-built, are used for military and civilian research purposes.

GUIDED-MISSILE CRUISERS (NUCLEAR-POWERED)

◆ **2 (+1) Kirov class** Bldr: Baltic SY, Leningrad

	Laid down	L	In serv.
Kirov	1973	12-77	9-80
Frunze	1-78	23-5-81	8-84
N. . .	. . .	. . .	. . .

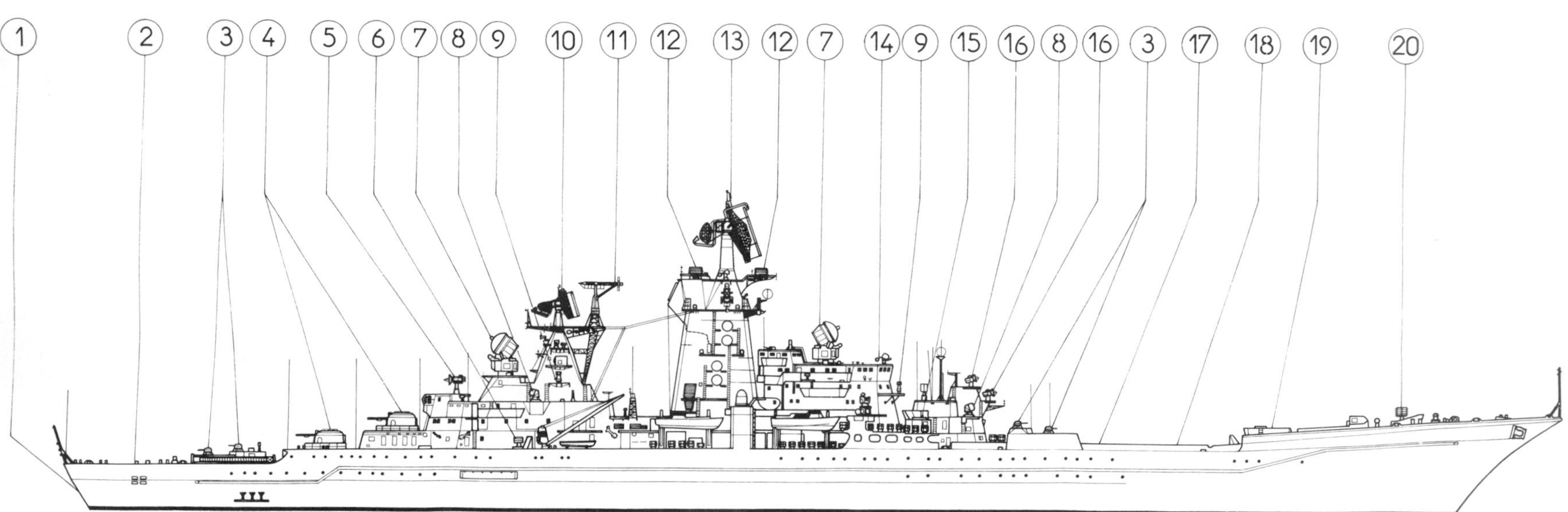

Kirov 1. variable-depth sonar 2. helicopter pad 3. 30-mm gatling AA guns 4. 100-mm DP gunmounts 5. Kite Screech radar director for 100-mm guns 6. RBU-1000 ASW RL 7. Top Dome radar director for SA-N-6 8. Bass Tilt radar director for 30-mm AA 9. Tin Man optronic device 10. Top Steer radar 11. Vee Tube HF comms. antenna 12. Round House TACAN 13. Top Pair 3-D early-warning radar antenna 14. Palm Frond navigational radar 15. SA-N-4 SAM launcher 16. Eye Bowl radar director for SS-N-14 17. SS-N-19 cruise-missile launchers 18. SA-N-6 vertical SAM launch silos 19. twin SS-N-14 ASW/SSM launcher 20. RBU-6000 ASW RL L. Gassier

Frunze 1. variable-depth sonar 2. helicopter pad 3. SA-N-9 vertical-launch SAM silos 4. twin 130-mm DP gunmount 5. 30-mm gatling AA 6. Kite Screech radar director for 130-mm guns 7. RBU-1000 ASW RL 8. Top Dome radar director for SA-N-6 9. Bass Tilt radar director for 30-mm AA 10. Top Steer radar antenna 11. Tin Man optronic device 12. Round House TACAN 13. Top Pair 3-D early-warning radar antenna 14. Big Ball SATCOMM antenna radome 15. Palm Frond navigational radar 16. SA-N-4 SAM launcher 17. Pop Group track-while-scan radar director for SA-N-4 18. SS-N-19 cruise-missile launchers 19. SA-N-6 vertical SAM launch silos 20. RBU-6000 ASW RL L. Gassier

GUIDED-MISSILE CRUISERS *(continued)*

Kirov French Navy, 1984

Kirov French Navy, 1984

Kirov, showing VDS door in stern U.S. Navy, 1984

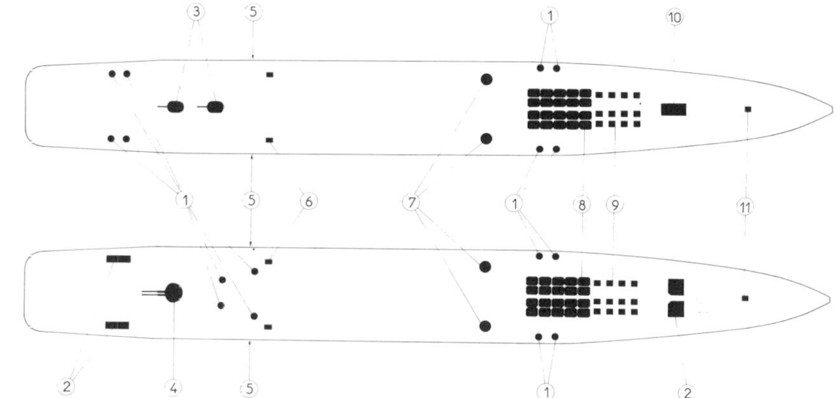

Kirov (top) and Frunze compared 1. 6-barreled 30-mm gatling AA 2. SA-N-9 silos (8 missiles each) 3. 100-mm single-mount DP 4. 130-mm twin-mount DP 5. quintuple torpedo tubes 6. RBU-1000 ASW RL (6-tubed) 7. SA-N-4 twin SAM launchers (20 missiles each) 8. SS-N-19 inclined cruise-missile launch-tube hatches 9. SA-N-6 vertical-launch SAM hatches (8 missiles to each position) 10. RBU-6000 ASW RL (12-tubed)

Frunze, showing twin 130-mm gun aft M.O.D., Bonn, 11-84

D: 24,000 tons (28,000 fl) **S:** 32 kts
Dim: 248.0 (230.0 wl) × 28.0 (24.0 wl) × 8.8
A: *Kirov:* 20/SS-N-19 SSM (20 inclined tubes)—12/SA-N-6 vertical SAM launchers (96 missiles)—2/SA-N-4 SAM syst. (II × 2, 40 missiles)—2/100-mm DP (I × 2)—8/30-mm gatling AA (I × 8)—1/SS-N-14 ASW cruise-missile launcher (II × 1, 14-16 missiles)—10/533-mm TT (V × 2)—1/RBU-6000 ASW RL (XII × 1)—2/RBU-1000 ASW RL (VI × 2)—3/Hormone-A and/or -B helicopters or Helix-A.
Frunze: 20/SS-N-19 SSM (20 inclined tubes)—12/SA-N-6 vertical SAM launchers (96 missiles)—16/SA-N-9 vertical SAM launchers, not yet operational, (128 missiles)—2/SA-N-4 SAM syst. (II × 2, 40 missiles)—2/130-mm DP (II × 1)—8/30-mm gatling AA (I × 8)—10/533-mm TT

GUIDED-MISSILE CRUISERS *(continued)*

Frunze French Navy, 1984

Frunze U.S. Navy, 11-84

(V × 2)—1/RBU-6000 ASW RL (XII × 1)—2/RBU-1000 ASW RL (VI × 2)—2/Helix-A and 1/Hormone-B helicopters

Electron Equipt: *Kirov:* Radar: 3/Palm Frond, 1/Top Pair, 1/Top Steer, 2/Top Dome, 2/Pop Group, 2/Eye Bowl, 1/Kite Screech, 4/Base Tilt, 1/Fly Screen landing aid
IFF: 1/Salt Pot transponder—E/O: 4/Tin Man
Sonar: 1/LF bow-mounted, 1/LF VDS
EW: 8/Side Globe, 4/Rum Tub, 10/Bell-series, 2/chaff RL (II × 2)
TACAN: 2/Round House—SATCOMM: 2/Punch Bowl
Frunze: Radar: 3/Palm Frond, 1/Top Steer, 2/Top Dome, 2/locations for future SA-N-9 f.c., 2/Pop Group, 1/Kite Screech, 4/Bass Tilt, 1/Fly Screen
IFF: . . . —E/O: 4/Tin Man
Sonar: as for *Kirov*
EW: 8/ . . . , 10/Bell-series, 2/chaff RL (II × 2)
TACAN: 2/Round House
SATCOMM: 2/Big Ball, 2/Punch Bowl

M: CONAS: 2 nuclear reactors, 2 oil-fired superheat boilers, steam turbines; 2 props; 150,000 hp

Range: Effectively unlimited **Fuel:** 2,500 tons

Man: Approx. 800 tot.

Remarks:

1. *General:* The *Kirov* is the world's largest "cruiser" and might best be termed a "battlecruiser." The Soviet type-designation applied has been merely RKR—*Raketnyy Kreyser* (Missile Cruiser). The ship is capable of independent operations, due to the virtual autonomy conveyed by the nuclear propulsion system, but it would also make an ideal escort for the forthcoming nuclear-powered carrier. The *Kirov* and *Frunze* differ considerably in armament and sensors, and the third unit, laid down some years later, may differ further still. *Frunze* deployed to the Pacific in 9-10-85, while *Kirov* is in the Northern Fleet.
2. *Hull:* On *Kirov* the high forecastle shelters the reloadable SS-N-14 ASW cruise-missile launcher within a redoubt or cul-de-sac. A long raised strake down either side of the hull acts as an external hull stiffener, as on smaller Soviet warships. The helicopter hangar is beneath the forward portion of the fantail, with an elevator delivering the aircraft to the flight deck. The steeply raked stern has a 9-m broad centerline recess for the VDS installation, whose door when closed is raked forward past the vertical. The screws appear to be mounted unusually far forward. Two solid-stores replenishment stations are fitted: one amidships to port, and one folding station forward to port, abreast the SA-N-6 system; both employ the sliding-stay, constant-tension concept. Oil and water replenishments are handled at stations on either beam abreast the Kite Screech radar. *Frunze*'s forward transfer gear is considerably more compact.
3. *Propulsion:* The two circular reactor access hatches can be seen amidships, just abaft the enormous twin exhaust uptakes for the unusual CONAS (Combined Nuclear and Steam) propulsion system. The steam generated by the reactors is either led to oil-fired superheaters that could theoretically boost the energy output of the steam by 50 to 55% by superheating it; this system would be cut in when maximum speeds were required, and, given the size of the ship, sufficient fuel for global endurance at maximum speed could be accommodated. Alternatively (and more likely), the oil-fired boilers provide steam to completely separate turbines, which are geared to the same drive shafts as the nuclear-supplied turbines. One stack probably serves the oil-fired boilers, while the other serves to ventilate the reactor spaces. Speed on reactors alone (90,000 hp) would be about 24 kts.
4. *Armament:* The launch tubes for the 20 SS-N-19 anti-ship missiles are buried within the hull at a fixed angle of 40–45-degree elevation, in four rows of five, forward of the superstructure. Before these are the 12 vertical launchers for SA-N-6; each has a door, beneath which is a rotating magazine containing 8 missiles. Targeting data, for the SS-N-19, with its 300-nautical-mile maximum range, can come either from a Hormone-B helicopter embarked on the ship, or from satellites, via the Punch Bowl satellite communications antennas on either side of the ship. In *Kirov* only, the SS-N-14 ASW cruise-missile system is the first *reloadable* installation in a Soviet ship, employing a magazine forward of the launcher, buried within the forecastle. The gatling guns are paired and located so as to cover all four quadrants; each pair is served by a Bass Tilt radar director and a manned, optical backup director. *Frunze* has a single twin 130-mm gunmount in place of the two 100-mm mounts and lacks the SS-N-14 system; instead, eight SA-N-9 launchers are buried in the forecastle, while eight more are located in place of the after 30-mm gatling guns, four per side (the gatling guns are mounted on the aft superstructure). The two directors for SA-N-9 were yet to be mounted by 9-85 and are intended to be positioned abaft the Kite Screech aft and between the two Pop Group directors forward; the SA-N-4 installation may be a temporary stopgap.
5. *Electronic equipment:* As might be expected, the communications antenna array is extensive and diverse and includes satellite communications equipment and long-range HF gear. There are four stabilized "Tin Man" electro-optical sensors, covering all four quadrants, as well as smaller remote t.v. cameras. Two Bob Tail radiometric sextant antennas are housed in spherical enclosures. A Fly Screen microwave landing approach radar is mounted on a starboard platform on the after tower mast. The VDS employs a lens-shaped "fish" about 4 m in diameter to house the transducer and has a twin boom-mounted empennage with horizontal and vertical control surfaces. In addition to a low-frequency bow-mounted sonar, there is probably a medium-frequency set for fire-control purposes (including depth determination) for the RBU-series rocket launchers. *Frunze* lacks the large Vee tube HF communications antenna but has port-and-starboard Big Ball SATCOMM antenna radomes; she has a newer model EW suite also.

GUIDED-MISSILE CRUISERS

◆ **1 (+2) Slava class** Bldr: 61 Kommuna SY, Nikolayev

	Laid down	L	In serv.
Slava	1976	1979	1982
N.	1978	1981	1986
N.	1979	1983	1986-87

GUIDED-MISSILE CRUISERS *(continued)*

Slava U.S. Navy, 8-84

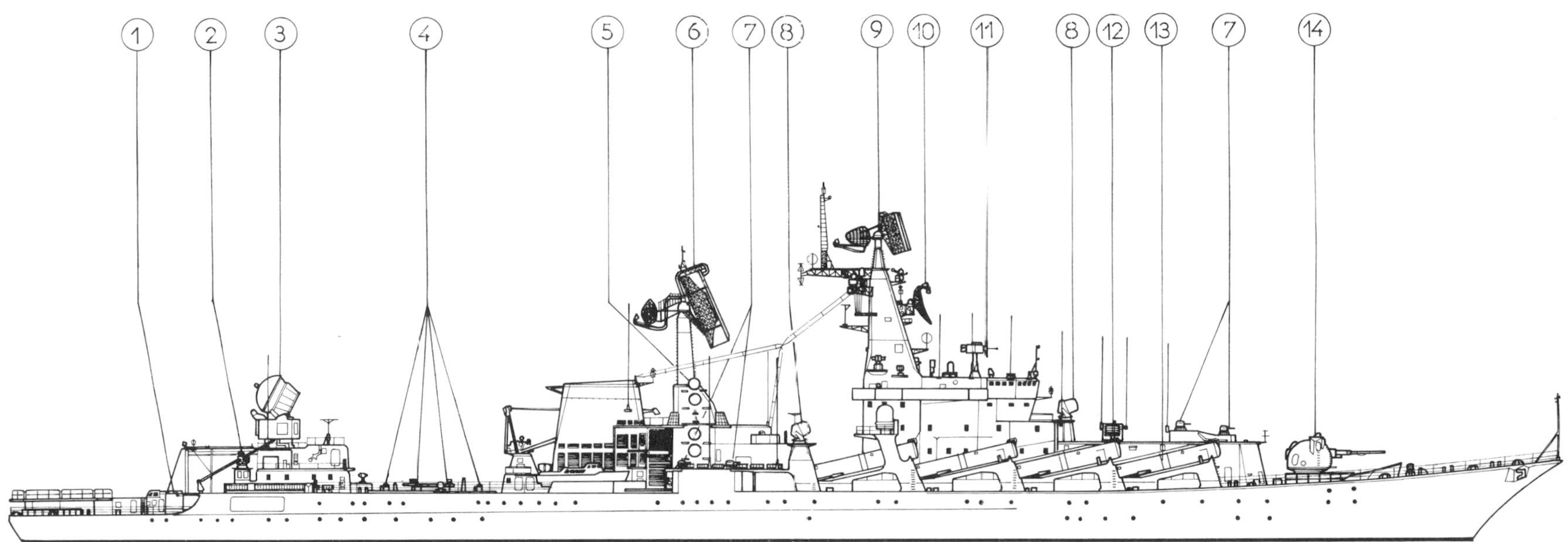

Slava 1. SA-N-4 launchers port and starboard 2. Pop Group radar director for SA-N-4 3. Top Dome radar director for SA-N-6 4. SA-N-6 vertical launchers 5. Side Globe electronic warfare antennas 6. Top Pair 3-D early-warning radar 7. 30-mm gatling AA 8. Bass Tilt radar directors for 30-mm AA 9. Top Steer 3-D air-search radar 10. Front Door/Front Piece tracking radar for SS-N-12 11. Kite Screech fire-control radar for 130-mm DP 12. RBU-6000 ASW RL 13. SS-N-12 anti-ship missile tubes 14. twin 130-mm DP gunmount L. Gassier

Slava, amidships portion—note the boom of the huge boat crane stowed between the paired funnels and the blast deflectors abaft each pair of SS-N-12 cruise-missile launchers U.S. Navy, 1983

GUIDED-MISSILE CRUISERS *(continued)*

Slava U.S. Navy, 1983

Nikolayev U.S. Navy, 7-83

Slava French Navy, 10-83

D: 10,000 tons (12,500 fl) **S:** 32 kts
Dim: 186.0 × 20.3 × 8.0
A: 16/SS-N-12 SSM (II × 8)—8/SA-N-6 vertical launch SAM groups (VIII × 8, 64 missiles)—2/SA-N-4 SAM syst. (II × 2, 40 missiles)—2/130-mm 70-cal. DP (II × 1)—6/30-mm gatling AA (I × 6)—10/533-mm TT (V × 2)—2/RBU-6000 ASW RL (XII × 2)—1/Hormone-B helicopter
Electron Equipt: Radar: 3/Palm Frond, 1/Top Pair, 1/Top Steer, 1/Top Dome, 2/Pop Group, 1/Kite Screech, 3/Bass Tilt, 1/Front Door-Front Piece
EW: 8/Slide Globe, 4/Rum Tub, numerous Bell-series, 2/Chaff RL (II × 2)
Sonar: LF hull mounted, MF VDS
M: 4 gas turbines; 2 props; 120,000 hp **Man:** 720 hp
Range: 2,000/30; 8,800/15

Remarks: *Slava* first deployed from the Black Sea on 15-9-83. Unusual in having considerable equipment that is not the latest of its type in Soviet service, including the main battery, SS-N-12 missile system. There are two Punch Bowl targeting satellite data receivers. Four Tee Plinth electro-optical surveillance devices are installed. Typed *Raketnyy Kreyser* (Missile Cruiser) by the Soviet Navy. Fitted as flagships. *Slava* is attached to the Black Sea Fleet.

Only one Top Dome director is fitted for the SA-N-6 system, limiting its flexibility. The torpedo tubes are mounted behind shutters in the ship's sides, near the stern. Initially referred to by the NATO Code-name "Blk-Com-1" and later, briefly, as the "Krasina" class. The hangar floor is one-half-deck below the flight deck, which is

GUIDED-MISSILE CRUISERS *(continued)*

Slava M.O.D., Bonn, 10-83

reached via an inclined ramp, the helicopter being maneuvered by a chain-haul system.

◆ **7 Kara class** Bldr: 61 Kommuna SY, Nikolayev

	Laid down	L	In serv.
Nikolayev	1969	1971	1973
Ochakov	1970	1972	1975
Kerch	1971	1973	1976
Azov	1972	1974	1977
Petropavlovsk	1973	1975	1978
Tashkent	1975	1976	1979
Tallin	1976	1977	1980

Tallin U.S. Navy, 4-85

Petropavlovsk—with higher hangar, small Round House TACAN radomes, and no RBU-1000 U.S. Navy, 3-82

Tashkent U.S. Navy, 12-84

Petropavlovsk PH1 F. Barbante, U.S.N., 9-83

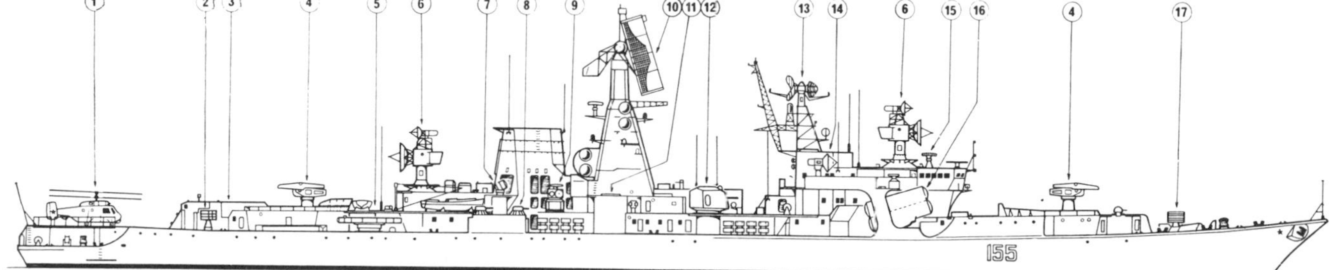

Kara class—Nikolayev 1. Hormone-A helicopter 2. RBU-1000 ASW RL 3. helicopter hangar 4. twin SA-N-3 launcher 5. quintuple 533-mm TT 6. Head Lights SA-N-3/SS-N-14 radar director 7. Bass Tilt 30-mm radar director 8. 30-mm gatling AA guns 9. Pop Group radar director for SA-N-4 10. Top Sail 3-D early-warning radar 11. twin SA-N-4 launcher 12. 76.2-mm DP 13. Head Net-C radar 14. Owl Screech radar director for 76.2-mm 15. Don-Kay nav. radar 16. SS-N-14 ASW/SSM 17. RBU-6000 ASW RL H. Simoni

GUIDED-MISSILE CRUISERS *(continued)*

Tashkent Lts. Mason & Weaver, VF-111, U.S.N., 1984

Petropavlovsk U.S. Navy, 3-82

D: 8,200 tons (9,700 fl) **S:** 34 kts **Dim:** 173.0 × 18.6 × 6.7
A: 8/SS-N-14 (IV × 2, 8 missiles)—2/SA-N-3 systems (II × 2, 44 Goblet missiles)—4/SA-N-4 (II × 2, 40 missiles)—4/76.2-mm DP (II × 2)—4/30-mm gatling AA (I × 4)—10/533-mm TT (V × 2)—2/RBU-6000 ASW RL (XII × 2)—2/RBU-1000 ASW RL (VI × 2)—1/Hormone-A helicopter—see remarks
Electron Equipt: Radar: 1/Don-2 or Palm Frond, 2/Don-Kay, 1/Top Sail, 1/Head Net-C, 2/Head Lights, 2/Pop Group, 2/Owl Screech, 2/Bass Tilt
Sonar: 1/LF hull-mounted, 1/MF VDS
EW: 8/Side Globe, 2/Bell Clout, 2/Bell Slam, 2/Bell Tap (or 4/Rum Tub), 2/chaff RL (II × 2)
IFF: 1/Salt Pot transponder (interrogation by search radars)
M: 4 gas turbines; 2 props; 120,000 hp
Range: 3,000/32; 8,000/15 **Man:** 30 officers, 490 men

Remarks: Soviet type designation: *Bol'shoy Protivolodochnyy Korabl'* (Large Anti-submarine Ship), a type considered to be more in the destroyer than the cruiser category. *Petropavlovsk* has two cylindrical Round House TACAN abreast the helicopter hangar, which is higher than on the other ships; she has no RBU-1000 rocket launchers. She and the *Tashkent* joined the Pacific Fleet in 1979. The *Azov* was a trials ship for SA-N-6 vertically launched surface-to-air missiles and has only one SA-N-3 launcher, forward; a Top Dome missile radar director is mounted aft; the ship has never deployed from the Black Sea. The last three built have incomplete EW suites, having been equipped to take 4 Rum Tub, as on *Petropavlovsk* and *Kerch. Nikolayev* is unique in having Square Head IFF interrogators on either side of the stack. SA-N-3, SA-N-4, and SS-N-14 can also be used against surface targets.

◆ **10 Kresta-II class** Bldr: Zhdanov SY, Leningrad

	L	In serv.		L	In serv.
Kronshtadt	1967	12-69	Admiral Isachenkov	1972	9-74
Admiral Isakov	1968	9-70	Marshal Timoshenko	1973	9-75
Admiral Nakhimov	1969	8-71	Vasily Chapaev	1975	10-16
Admiral Makarov	1970	8-72	Admiral Yumashev	1976	1-78
Marshal Voroshilov	1970	5-73	Admiral Oktyabr'skiy	1971	11-73

Admiral Makarov U.S. Navy

Admiral Isachenkov *Ships of the World,* 1984

Admiral Nakhimov—without Bass Tilt radar directors U.S. Navy, 5-83

GUIDED-MISSILE CRUISERS *(continued)*

Marshal Timoshenko—note enlarged superstructure between bridge and tower mast, Bass Tilt radar directors on bridge wings, above SS-N-14 launchers U.S. Navy, 1982

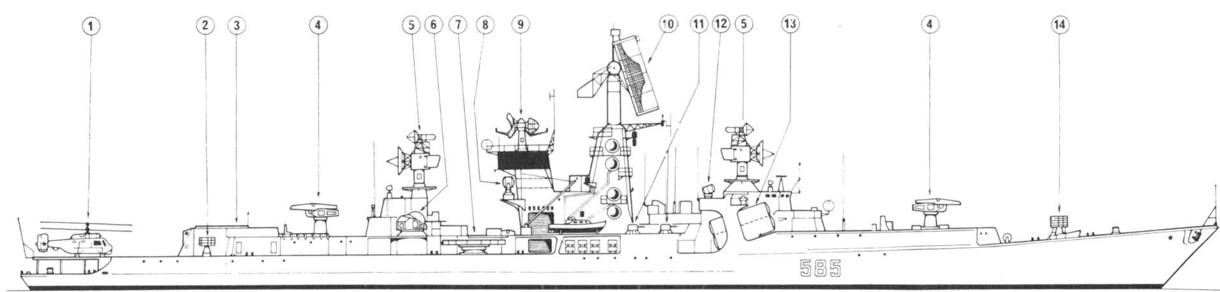

Kresta-II class 1. Hormone-A helicopter 2. RBU-1000 ASW RL 3. helicopter hangar 4. twin SA-N-3 launcher 5. Head Lights SA-N-3/SS-N-14 radar directors 6. twin 57-mm DP 7. quintuple 533-mm TT 8. Muff Cob radar director for 57-mm DP 9. Head Net radar 10. Top Sail 3-D early-warning radar 11. 30-mm gatling AA guns 12. Bass Tilt radar director for 30-mm AA 13. quadruple SS-N-14 launcher 14. RBU-6000 ASW RL H. Simoni
Note: Drawing applies to *Marshal Voroshilov, Admiral Oktyabr'skiy,* and *Admiral Isachenkov.*

D: 6,200 tons (7,700 fl) **S:** 34 kts **Dim:** 159.0 × 17.0 × 6.0 (hull)
A: 8/SS-N-14 (IV × 2, 8 missiles)—2/SA-N-3 systems (II × 2, 44 Goblet missiles)—4/57-mm DP (II × 2)—4/30-mm gatling AA (I × 4)—2/RBU-6000 ASW RL (XII × 2)—2/RBU-1000 ASW RL (VI × 2)—10/533-mm TT (V × 2)—1/Hormone-A helicopter
Electron Equipt: Radar: 1/Don-2, 2/Don-Kay, 1/Top Sail, 1/Head Net-C, 2/Head Lights, 2/Muff Cob, 2/Bass Tilt
Sonar: 1/MF hull-mounted
EW: 8/Side Globe, 1/Bell Clout, 2/Bell Slam, 2/Bell Tap, 2/chaff RL (II × 2)
IFF: 1/High Pole-B, 1/High Pole-A (interrogation by search radars)
M: 2 sets GT: 2 props; 100,000 hp **Boilers:** 4, turbo-pressurized
Fuel: 1,100 tons **Range:** 2,400/32; 10,500/14 **Man:** 380 tot.

Remarks: Soviet type designation: BPK—*Bol'shoy Protivolodochnyy Korabl'* (Large Antisubmarine Ship). The first four units do not have Bass Tilt, and must control their 30-mm AA with lead-computing optical directors only. *Kronshtadt* has earlier versions of the Head Lights control radar for SA-N-3 and SS-N-14. The three final units have larger forward superstructure, the area between the tower foremast and the bridge being filled in by a two-level deckhouse. *Admiral Makarov* has prototype solid-stores equipment to port and prototype underway refueling equipment to starboard. SA-N-3 and SS-N-14 can also be used against surface targets. Have fin stabilizers. The helicopter hangar is one deck lower than the flight deck and is reached by means of an inclined elevator, as on the Kara class.

◆ **4 Kresta-I class** Bldr: Zhdanov SY, Leningrad

	L	In serv.		L	In serv.
Admiral Zozulya	10-65	3-67	Vitse Admiral Drozd	1-67	8-68
Vladivostok	8-66	1-68	Sevastopol	6-67	7-69

Vitse-Admiral Drozd—detail of enlarged superstructure 23 Flot., French Navy, 2-85

D: 6,200 tons (7,600 fl) **S:** 34 kts **Dim:** 155.5 × 17.0 × 6.0 (hull)
A: 4/SS-N-3B (II × 2)—2/SA-N-1 systems (II × 2, 44 Goa missiles)—4/57-mm DP (II × 2)—2/RBU-6000 ASW RL (XI × 2)—2/RBU-1000 ASW RL (VI × 2)—10/533-mm TT (V × 2)—1/Hormone-B helicopter—*Vitse Admiral Drozd:* also 4/30-mm gatling AA (I × 4)

GUIDED-MISSILE CRUISERS *(continued)*

Vitse-Admiral Drozd—with gatling AA guns, Bass Tilt fire-control radars, and enlarged superstructure 1976

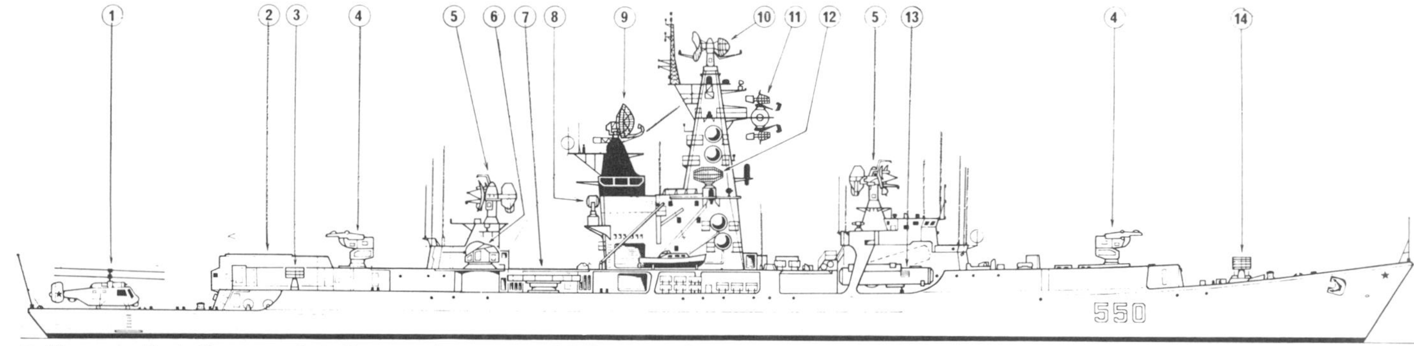

1. Hormone-B helicopter 2. helicopter hangar 3. RBU-1000 ASW RL 4. twin SA-N-1 launcher 5. Peel Group radar director for SA-N-1 6. twin 57-mm DP 7. quintuple 533-mm TT 8. Muff Cob radar director for 57-mm DP 9. Big Net early-warning radar 10. Head Net-C radar 11. Scoop Pair radar for SS-N-3B 12. Plinth Net 13. twin SS-N-3B launcher 14. RBU-6000 ASW RL H. Simoni
Note: Drawing applies to *Admiral Zozulya* and *Vladivostok.*

Admiral Zozulya—with 2 Palm Frond, 1 Don-Kay navigational radars U.S. Navy, 1977

Electron Equipt: Radar: 2/Don-2 or 1/Don-2 and 1/Don-Kay (except *Adm. Zozulya:* 2/Palm Frond, 1/Don Kay), 1/Big Net, 1/Head Net-C, 2/Plinth Net, 1/Scoop Pair, 2/Peel Group, 2/Muff Cob—*Vitse Admiral Drozd:* 2/Bass Tilt also
Sonar: 1/MF, hull-mounted
EW: 8/Side Globe, 1/Bell Clout, 2/Bell Slam, 2/Bell Tap, 2/Bell . . . , 2/chaff RL (II × 2)
IFF: 2/High Pole-B or Salt Pot transponders

M: 2 sets GT; 2 props; 100,000 hp **Boilers:** 4, turbo-pressurized
Fuel: 1,150 tons **Range:** 1,600/34; 7,000/14 **Man:** 380 tot.

Remarks: Soviet type designation: RKR—*Raketnyy Kreyser* (Missile Cruiser). Based on the Kynda class, but has a better-balanced mixture of weapons. The surface-to-surface launchers, fitted on each side of the superstructure, forward under the bridge wings, are elevated to fire, but cannot be trained. No SS-N-3 missile reloads. Installation of gatling guns abaft the Shaddock launchers and construction of a new deckhouse between the gatling guns altered the silhouette of the *Vitse Admiral Drozd* in 1976 (see photos). *Sevastopol* received the new deckhouse, but not the gatling guns or radar, in 1980.

◆ **4 Kynda class** Bldr: Zhdanov SY, Leningrad

	Laid down	L	In serv.
Groznyy	6-59	4-61	6-62
Admiral Fokin	8-60	5-62	8-63
Admiral Golovko	12-60	1962	7-64
Varyag	9-61	6-63	2-65

Groznyy—modernized like *Varyag,* but retaining 2 Head Net A! Has 45-mm saluting cannon mounted atop deckhouse amidships U.S. Navy, 2-83

GUIDED-MISSILE CRUISERS *(continued)*

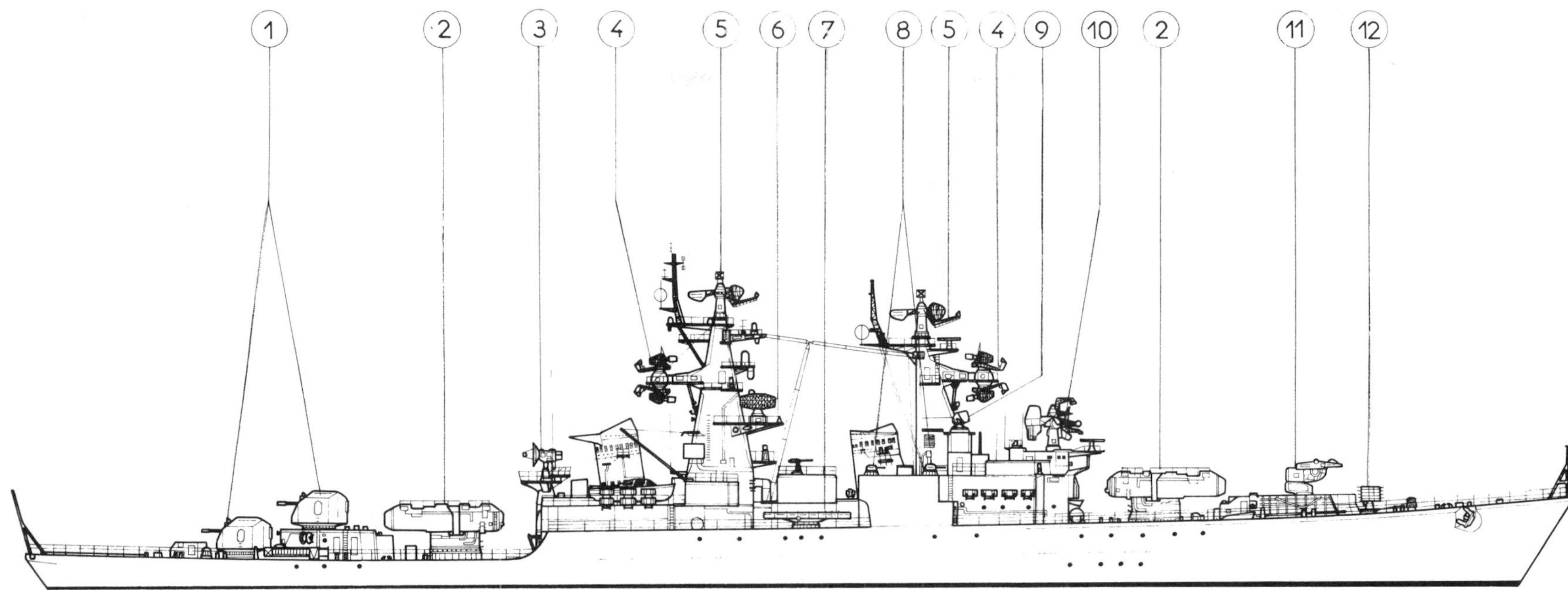

Groznyy 1. twin 76.2-mm DP 2. quadruple SS-N-3B launcher (reloads in adjacent deckhouses) 3. Owl Screech radar director for 76.2-mm DP 4. Scoop Pair radars for SS-N-3B 5. Head Net-A air-search radars 6. Plinth Net antennas 7. triple 533-mm TT 8. 30-mm gatling AA 9. Bass Tilt radar directors for 30-mm AA 10. Peel Group radar director for SA-N-1 11. twin SA-N-1 SAM launcher 12. RBU-6000 ASW RL L. Gassier

Note: Varyag similar, but with Head Net-C, no Plinth Net.

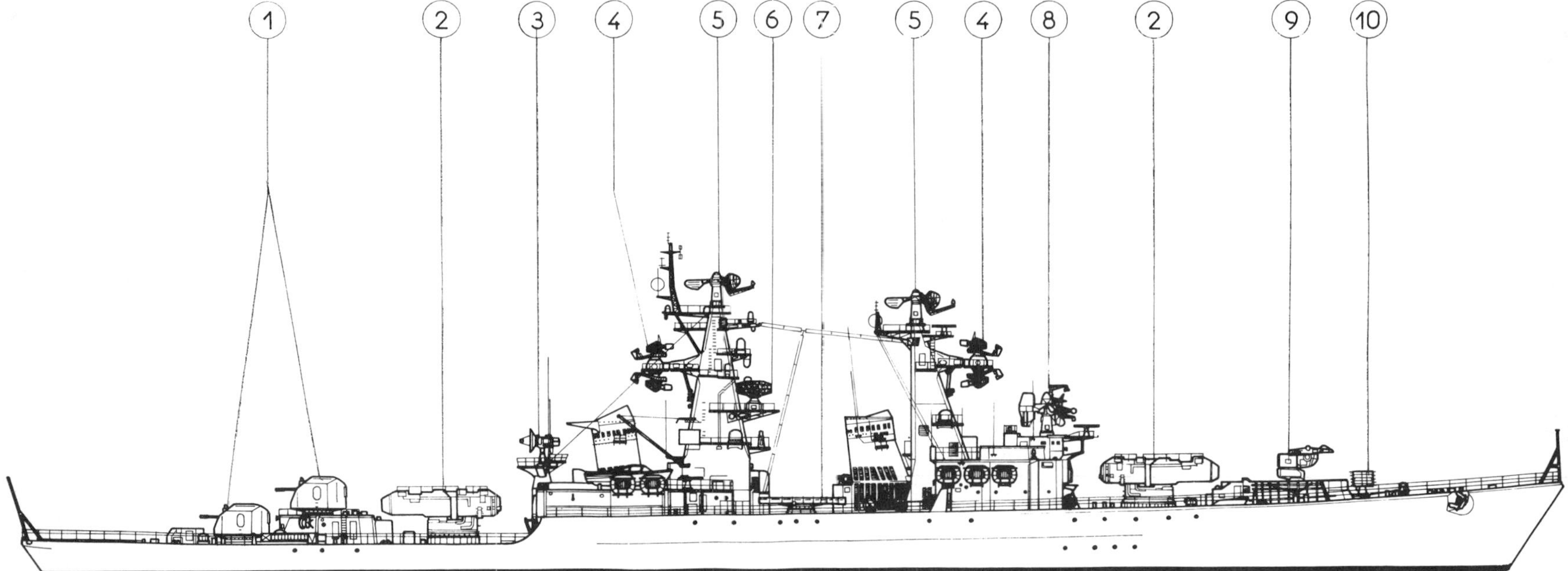

Admiral Golovko 1. twin 76.2-mm DP mounts 2. quadruple SS-N-3B launcher 3. Owl Screech radar director for 76.2-mm DP 4. Scoop Pair radars for SS-N-3B 5. Head Net-A air-search radar antennas 6. Plinth Net antennas 7. triple 533-mm TT 8. Peel Group radar director for SA-N-1 9. twin SA-N-1 launcher 10. RBU-6000 ASW RL L. Gassier

Note: Admiral Fokin similar, but Head Net-C on after mast.

Admiral Fokin—with 1 Head Net-A, 1 Head Net-C, 2 Plinth Net JMSDF, 6-81

GUIDED-MISSILE CRUISERS *(continued)*

Varyag—as modernized, with 4 gatling AA guns and 2 Bass Tilt added, 2 Head Net-C substituted for Head Net-A, and superstructure added between the torpedo-tube mounts; still without Plinth net 1981

Admiral Golovko French Navy, 1978

D: 4,400 tons (5,500 fl) **S:** 34 kts **Dim:** 141.7 (134.0 pp) × 15.8 × 5.3 (hull; 6.1 max.)
A: 8/SS-N-3 (IV × 2, 16 missiles)—1/SA-N-1 SAM system (II × 1, 24 Goa missiles)—4/76.2-mm DP (II × 2)—2/RBU-6000 ASW RL (XII × 2)—6/533-mm TT (III × 2)—*Varyag* and *Groznyy* also: 4/30-mm gatling AA
Electron Equipt: Radar: 2/Don-2 (*Varyag:* 3), 2/Head Net-A or -C, 2/Scoop Pair, 2/Plinth Net (not on *Varyag*), 1/Peel Group, 1/Owl Screech—*Varyag* and *Groznyy* also: 2/Bass Tilt
Sonar: 1/HF, hull-mounted
EW: 2/Guard Dog, 1/Bell Clout, 1/Bell Slam, 1/Bell Tap, 4/Top Hat (varies)
IFF: 2/High Pole-B
M: 2 sets GT; 2 props; 100,000 hp **Boilers:** 4, turbopressurized
Range: 2,000/32; 7,000/14 **Man:** 375 tot.

Remarks: Soviet type designation: RKR—*Raketnyy Kreyser* (Missile Cruiser). Eight Shaddock missiles are loaded in the trainable and elevatable quadruple tubes; reloading from the handling rooms requires some time. *Admiral Fokin* now has one Head Net-A, one Head Net-C, and two Plinth Net; *Groznyy* received two Plinth Net around 1973. *Varyag* received 2 Head Net-C, 2 Plinth Net, 2 Bass Tilt and 4/30-mm gatling AA in 1981, and *Groznyy* received the same treatment during 1980-82. All have a seldom-used helicopter pad on the stern. The function of Plinth Net is uncertain; it may be a data-link antenna for the SS-N-3B missiles, rather than a radar. *Groznyy* joined the Baltic Fleet in 1982. *Admiral Golovko* is in the Black Sea Fleet, and the other two are in the Pacific.

Note: The only *Sverdlov*-class guided-missile cruiser, *Dzerzhinskiy,* was towed home from the Mediterranean in 1979 and has not since deployed; presumed scrapped or hulked. The ship was the only unit to receive the unwieldy SA-N-2 SAM system.

COMMAND CRUISERS

◆ 2 Modified Sverdlov class

	Bldr	Laid down	L	In serv.
Admiral Senyavin	Severodvinsk SY	5-51	9-52	7-54
Zhdanov	Baltic SY, Leningrad	10-49	12-50	1-52

Zhdanov—with triple 152-mm mount aft French Navy, 5-83

Admiral Senyavin—no 152-mm mount aft 1979

For characteristics of hull and machinery, see *Sverdlov*-class light cruisers

A: 6 (*Admiral Senyavin*) or 9/152-mm (III × 2, or 3)—12/100-mm DP (II × 6)—1/SA-N-4 system (II × 1; 40 missiles)—16/37-mm AA—8 (*Zhdanov*) or 16/30-mm AK-230 AA (II × 4 or 8)
Electron Equipt: Radar: 2/Top Bow, 1/Top Trough, 2/Sun Visor, 6/Egg Cup, 1/Pop Group—*Zhdanov:* 2/Drum Tilt—*Admiral Senyavin:* 4/Drum Tilt
EW: None

Remarks: Soviet type designation: KU—*Korabl' Upravleniy* (Command Ship). Both completed modernization in 1972. Excellent long-range communications, including a Vee Cone HF antenna, which can be seen on the after tripod mast, and two Big Ball SATCOMM antenna radomes. The 30-mm guns are divided on each side of the forward stack and, on the *Admiral Senyavin,* on each side of the after deckhouse as well; her two after turrets have been replaced by a hangar and platform for one Hormone helicopter. Both ships have had their mine rails removed. Bag Ball satellite communications antennas were added to both in 1979-81. *Zhdanov* is in the Black Sea Fleet, *Adm. Senyavin* in the Pacific.

COMMAND CRUISERS *(continued)*

Zhdanov U.S. Navy, 5-84

LIGHT CRUISERS

◆ **9 Sverdlov class** Bldrs: A: Baltic SY, Leningrad; B: Marti SY, Nikolayev; C: Severodvinsk SY

	Bldr	Laid down	L	In serv.	Fleet
Admiral Lazarev	A	5-50	10-51	11-52	Pac.
Admiral Ushakov	A	7-50	5-52	8-53	Blk.
Alexandr Nevskiy	B	3-50	6-51	1952	Nor.
Alexandr Suvorov	B	10-50	6-52	1953	Pac.
Dmitriy Pozharskiy	A	9-51	4-53	1953	Pac.
Mikhail Kutuzov	B	1950	5-54	1955	Blk.
Murmansk	C	1952	1955	1955	Nor.
Oktyabrskaya Revolutsiya (ex-*Molotovsk*)	C	1951	1954	9-54	Bal.
Sverdlov	A	7-49	7-50	1951	Bal.

Alexandr Suvorov—modernized, Strut Curve atop foremast French Navy, 3-81

Dmitriy Pozharskiy—note enlarged deckhouse below pilothouse, Big Net air-search radar on after mast-supported deckhouse 1975

D: 12,900 tons (17,200 fl) **S:** 32 kts **Dim:** 210.0 (199.95 pp) × 21.6 × 7.2
A: 12/152-mm (III × 4)—12/100-mm DP (II × 6)—32/37-mm AA (II × 16)—140 mines—*Oktyabrskaya Revolutsiya, Admiral Ushakov, Alexandr Suvorov:* 16/30-mm AA (II × 8) also
Electron Equipt: Radar: 1/Neptune or Don-2, 1/Low Sieve or High Sieve, 1/Big Net or Top Trough, 1/Slim Net, 2/Top Bow, 2/Sun Visor, 8/Egg Cup—Knife Rest in some—ships with 30-mm AA: 4/Drum Tilt also
EW: 2/Watch Dog—IFF: 1/High Pole
Armor: 152-mm turret; 76–100-mm; deck: 25–50 and 50–75-mm; 100-mm; gun shields: 25-mm
M: 2 sets GT; 2 props; 110,000 hp **Boilers:** 6/3-drum; 26 kg/cm², 350°C
Fuel: 3,800 tons **Electric:** 3,500 kw
Range: 2,400/32; 10,000/13.5 **Man:** 70 officers, 940 men

Remarks: Soviet type designation: KR—*Kreyser* (Cruiser). Based on the preceding *Chapayev*-class design, but with armor added. Twenty-four were planned, fourteen put in service between 1951 and 1956; others were laid down, but construction was suspended in 1956 and canceled in 1960. Slight differences in profile, the merging of the forward stack with the bridge structure being noticeable. *Admiral Nakhimov* was scrapped in 1961; *Ordzhonikidze* was transferred to Indonesia in 1962 and has since been scrapped. By 1961 *Dzerhinskiy* (discarded 1979) had been converted to a guided-missile cruiser: two others, *Zhdanov* and *Admiral Senyavin,* completed conversion to command cruisers in 1972. In 1977 *Oktyabrskaya Revolutsiya* completed overhaul,

Admiral Ushakov—modernized version with 16/30-mm AA, 4 Drum Tilt, Knife Rest aft French Navy, 7-82

LIGHT CRUISERS *(continued)*

Alexandr Nevskiy U.S. Navy, 9-83

during which eight twin 30-mm AA and four Drum Tilt radars were added, the Egg Cup radars were removed from her 100-mm mounts, and her bridge was enlarged. Radar suits vary widely. In 1979 the *Admiral Ushakov* and *Alexandr Suvorov* appeared with similar alterations; all three ships have had four of their twin 37-mm AA removed. The Soviets evidently intend to continue this class in operation for some time; the ships provide excellent command facilities, and their powerful gunnery batteries give the U.S.S.R. the world's finest shore-bombardment capability. *Sverdlov* and *Admiral Lazarev* are in reserve, and several unmodernized units are in subsidiary services, such as cadet and gunnery training.

GUIDED-MISSILE DESTROYERS

◆ 7 (+1 + . . .) Udaloy class

	Bldr	Laid down	L	In serv.
Udaloy ("Daring")	Kaliningrad SY	1978	1980	1981
Vitse Admiral Kulakov	Zhdanov SY, Leningrad	1978	1982	4-82
Marshal Vasil'yevskiy	Kaliningrad SY	1979	1981	1983
Admiral Zakharov	Zhdanov SY, Leningrad	1979	4-82	1984
Admiral Spiridonov	Kaliningrad SY	1981	1983	1984
Admiral Tributs	Zhdanov SY, Leningrad	1982	1984	1985
Marshal Shaposhnikov	Zhdanov SY, Leningrad	1983	1985	1985
N.	Kaliningrad SY	1983	1986	. . .

Vitse-Admiral Kulakov French Navy, 5-84

Udaloy—detail showing 100-mm mounts at left, fixed-elevation SS-N-14 mounts (with 45-mm saluting cannon inboard), blank platform atop pilothouse for SA-N-9 SAM system radar director, and electronics arrays. Decks are bare metal in heavily trafficked areas, red-leaded elsewhere, as in most Soviet warships.
R. Neth. Navy, 6-84

Admiral Zakharov—on trials M.O.D., Bonn, 12-83

GUIDED-MISSILE DESTROYERS *(continued)*

Admiral Zakharov—with Cross Sword SA-N-9 control radars added M.O.D., Bonn, 1-85

Vitse-Admiral Kulakov U.S. Navy, 1-84

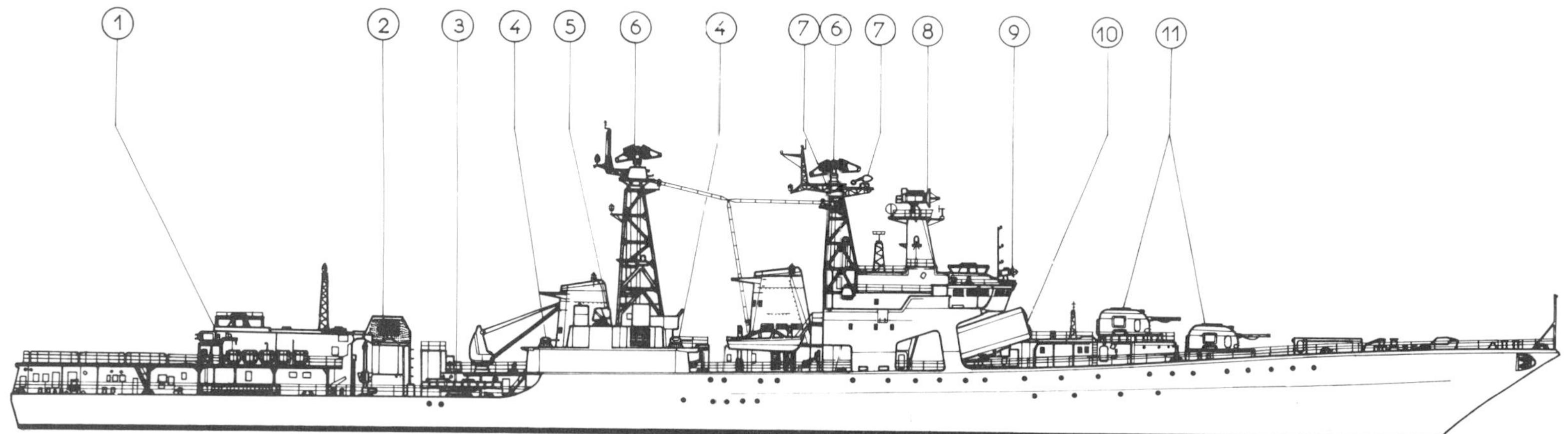

Udaloy 1. helicopter hangar (2 Helix-A) 2. RBU-6000 ASW RL 3. 533-mm ASW TT (IV × 2) 4. 30-mm gatling AA 5. Bass Tilt control radar for 30-mm AA 6. Strut Pair air/surface-search radars 7. Palm Frond navigational/surface-search radars 8. Kite Screech radar gunfire-control director (100-mm guns) 9. Eye Bowl radar directors (SS-N-14 missiles) 10. SS-N-14 missiles (IV × 2) 11. 100-mm DP guns L. Gassier

Note: The SA-N-9 launch groups are located, 2 between the RBU-6000 RL, 2 in the small deckhouse abaft the stores crane, and 4 within the forecastle, forward of the 100-mm gunmounts.

GUIDED-MISSILE DESTROYERS *(continued)*

Marshal Vasil'yevskiy M.O.D., Bonn, 9-83

Udaloy—with two Strut Pair radars at masthead R. Neth. Navy, 6-84

D: 6,200–6,700 tons (8,200 fl) **S:** 34 kts
Dim: 162.0 (150.0 wl) × 19.3 (17.8 wl) × 6.2 (hull)
A: 8/SA-N-9 vertical SAM launchers (VIII × 8; see remarks)—8/SS-N-14 (IV × 2)—2/100-mm DP—4/30-mm gatling AA (I × 4)—2/RBU-6000 ASW RL (XII × 2)—8/533-mm TT (IV × 2)—mines—2/Helix-A ASW helicopters
Electron Equipt: Radar: 3/Palm Frond, *Udaloy, V. Adm. Kulakov:* 2/Strut Pair; others 1/Top Plate/Top Mesh, 2/Eye Bowl, 1/Kite Screech, 2/Cross Sword (late units), 2/Bass Tilt, 1/Fly Screen helo landing control
Sonar: 1/LF bow-mounted, 1/LF VDS
EW: 2/Bell Shroud, 2/Bell Squat, 2/chaff RL (II × 2)
TACAN: 2/Round House—IFF: 1/Salt Pot-B, 1/Salt Pot-C
M: 4 gas turbines; 2 CP props; 120,000 hp
Electric: . . . **Range:** 2,000/33; 5,000/20 **Man:** 300 tot.

Remarks: Formerly carried NATO-nickname BAL-COM-3. Soviet type designation BPK—*Bol'shoy Protivolodochniy Korabl'* (Large Antisubmarine Ship), as the design is obviously primarily intended for ASW. The design is analogous in size and capability to the U.S. *Spruance* class. Provision was made for installation of the SA-N-9 vertically launched SAM system; there are four 2-meter-diameter cover plates on the raised portion of the forecastle, two more disposed athwartships in the small deckhouse between the torpedo tubes, and two arranged fore and aft in the deckhouse between the RBU-6000 ASW RL mounts. Each cylinder can hold perhaps 8 missiles, for a total of 64. There are empty director platforms atop the hangar and atop the bridge. *Admiral Zakharov* was the first ship to actually have the operational system (a probable short-range successor to SA-N-4) installed, with two multi-antenna-equipped radar directors mounted in mid-1984. This is the first BPK design to carry two ASW helicopters. The two hangars are side by side and use inclined elevator ramps to raise the aircraft to the flight deck; the hangar roofs slide forward in two segmented sections to clear the rotors. From the third unit on, the helicopter deck is wider, extending to the sides of the ship. Two Round House TACAN radomes are mounted on yards on the after mast, while the Fly Screen microwave landing-control radar is beside the starboard hangar. The ECM/ESM suit is incomplete, with several empty platforms on the after mast. The sonar suit duplicates that of the nuclear-powered cruiser *Kirov. Marshall Vasil'yevskiy* begins trials 7-83 and *Admiral Zakharov* in 9-83; both have a Top Plate/Top Mesh antenna atop the after mast, with the forward position empty; the early ships lack a height-finding capability. The two twin-barreled chaff RL are located near the bow. *Adm. Spiridonov* to Pacific, 12-85.

◆ **5 (+1 + . . .) Sovremennyy class** Bldr: Zhdanov SY, Leningrad

	Laid down	L	In serv.
Sovremennyy ("Modern")	1976	11-78	1981
Otchayannyy ("Merciless")	1977	8-80	1982
Otlichnyy ("Perfect")	1978	1981	1983
Osmotritel'nyy ("Circumspect")	1979	1982	1984
Bezuprechnyy ("Irreproachable")	1980	1983	7-85
N. . .	1981	1984	1986

Osmotritel'nyy—with unique Top Steer/Top Plate radar M.O.D., Bonn, 7-84

Otchayannyy U.S. Navy, 1-85

Sovremennyy—with hangar retracted. Note rope nets on helo deck as a primitive landing restraint U.S. Navy, 9-83

GUIDED-MISSILE DESTROYERS *(continued)*

Otchayannyy—hangar extended. Note chaff rocket RL at extreme stern, flanking the mine rails. U.S. Navy, 12-84

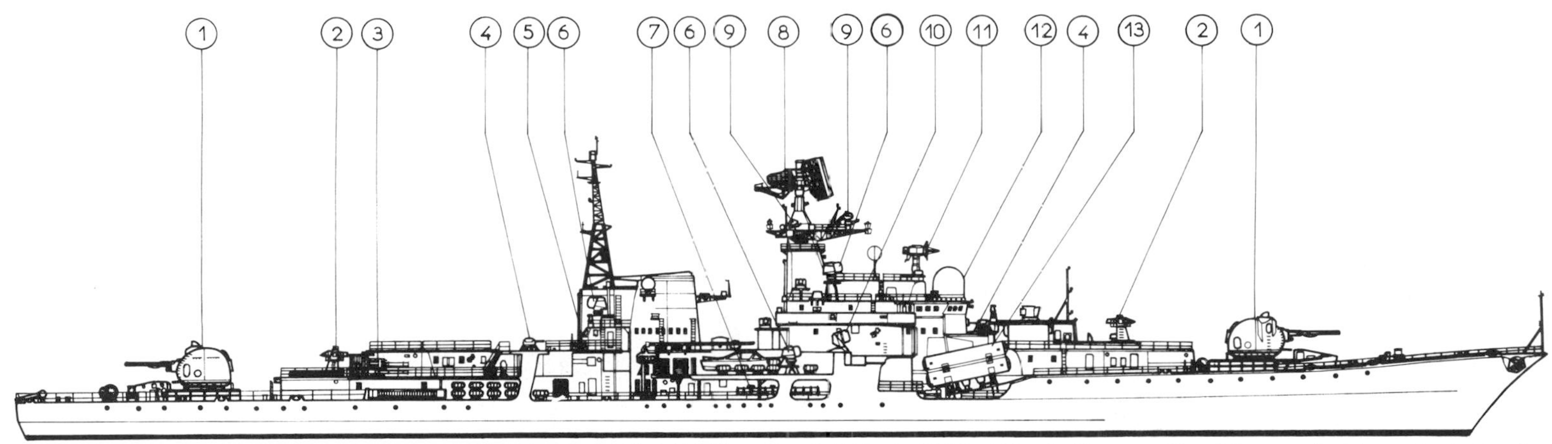

Sovremennyy 1. 130-mm dual-purpose guns (II × 2) 2. SA-N-7 SAM launcher (I × 2) 3. RBU-1000 4. 30-mm gatling AA guns 5. telescoping helicopter hangar (shown in retracted position) 6. Front Dome radar directors for the SA-N-7 system 7. 533-mm TT (II × 2) 8. Top Steer 3-D air-search radar 9. Palm Frond navigational/surface-search radars 10. Bass Tilt radar directors for the 30-mm gatling AA 11. Kite Screech radar director for the 130-mm guns 12. Band Stand radome (SS-N-22 SSM-associated) 13. SS-N-22 SSM (IV × 2) L. Gassier

D: 6,300 tons (7,900 fl) **S:** 34 kts
Dim: 156.0 (145.0 wl) × 17.0 (16.5 wl) × 6.1 (hull)
A: 8/SS-N-22 SSM—2/SA-N-7 SAM systems (I × 2, 40 missiles)—4/130-mm DP (II × 2)—4/30-mm gatling AA (I × 4)—4/533-mm TT (II × 2)—2/RBU-1000 ASW RL (VI × 2)—mines—1/Hormone-B helicopter
Electron Equipt: Radar: 3/Palm Frond, 1/Top Steer (*Osmotritel'nyy:* Top Steer/Top Plate combined), 6/Front Dome, 2/Bass Tilt, 1/Kite Screech, 1/Band Stand
Sonar: 1/MF hull-mounted—Optronic: 1/Squeeze Box
EW: 2/Bell Shroud, 2/Bell Squat, 4/. . . , 2/chaff RL (II × 2)
M: 2 sets GT; 2/4-bladed props; 100,000 hp **Boilers:** 4, turbo-pressurized, 500°C
Range: 2,400/32; 10,500/14 **Man:** 380 tot.

Remarks: Design derived from the Kresta-I and -II series built at the same shipyard; uses same hull form and propulsion. Formerly called the "BAL-COM-2" class by NATO. The class is primarily intended for surface warfare tasks, including anti-ship, shore bombardment, and anti-air defense; the ASW capability is primarily for self-defense. The SS-N-22 anti-ship missile system is probably capable of ranges of not more than 120 nautical miles, as there are no satellite receiving radomes of the Punch Bowl type; the Hormone-B helicopter can provide targeting data for the missiles, and the ships also have the large Band Stand radome associated with missile targeting for the SS-N-9 in the Nanuchka class. There are also two small spherical radomes on the sides of the stack that might be missile-associated. The chaff launchers are at the extreme stern. The 130-mm guns are of a new, fully automatic, water-cooled model, capable of AA or surface fire. The helicopter hangar is partially telescoping, extending aft from the stack structure, and the helicopter facilities are less elaborate than in other contemporary Soviet classes.

◆ **1 Kashin, converted for missile trials** Bldr: Zhdanov SY, Leningrad (In serv. 1964)

Provornyy ("Ferocious")

Provornyy—showing empty SA-N-7 positions forward U.S. Navy, 9-81

GUIDED-MISSILE DESTROYERS *(continued)*

Provornyy—SA-N-7 launcher aft, swathed in canvas U.S. Navy, 9-81

D: 3,750 tons (4,750 fl) **S:** 38 kts **Dim:** 144.0 × 15.8 × 4.8 (hull)
A: 1/SA-N-7 SAM syst. (I × 1, 20 missiles)—4/76.2-mm DP (II × 2)—5/533-mm TT (V × 1)—2/RBU-6000 (XII × 2)—2/RBU-1000 (VI × 2)—mines
Electron Equipt: Radar: 1/Don-2, 2/Don-Kay, 1/Top Steer, 1/Head Net-C, 2/Owl Screech, 8/Front Dome
Sonar: 1/MF, hull-mounted
EW: no intercept arrays, 4/chaff RL (XVI × 4)
M: 4 gas turbines; 2 props; 96,000 hp **Range:** 1,500/35; 4,000/20 **Man:** 300 tot.

REMARKS: Converted during the mid-1970s at a Black Sea shipyard as trials ship for the SA-N-7 SAM system. Both SA-N-1 SAM systems were removed and the superstructure reconfigured as on the Modified Kashin class. An SA-N-7 single-armed launcher was emplaced aft, while provision was made for two more to be added forward. No EW equipment (other than chaff launchers) is installed, but provision has been made for adding 2 Bell Shroud and 2 Bell Squat. With eight SAM directors, the ship has an unusual antiaircraft capability.

◆ 6 Modified Kashin class

	Bldr	In serv.	Conv.
OGNEVOY ("Curtain of Fire")	Zhdanov SY, Leningrad	8-64	2-73
SLAVNYY ("Glorious")	Zhdanov SY, Leningrad	6-66	9-75
STROYNYY ("Harmonious")	61 Kommuna, Nikolayev	1966	1980
SMYSHLENNYY ("Clever")	61 Kommuna, Nikolayev	1968	1974
SMEL'YY ("Daring")	61 Kommuna, Nikolayev	1970	1974
SDERZHANNYY ("Cautious")	61 Kommuna, Nikolayev	1973	. . .

Stroynyy PatRon 11, U.S. Navy, 9-83

Sderzhannyy U.S. Navy, 7-83

Ognevoy French Navy, 1984

Smel'yy L. & L. Van Ginderen, 1981

D: 3,950 tons (4,950 fl) **S:** 35 kts **Dim:** 146.0 × 15.8 × 4.8 (hull)
A: 4/SS-N-2C (I × 4)—2/SA-N-1 SAM syst. (II × 2, 36 Goa missiles)—4/76.2-mm DP (II × 2)—4/30-mm gatling AA (I × 4)—5/533-mm TT (V × I)—2/RBU-6000 ASW RL (XII × 2)
Electron Equipt: Radar: 2/Don-Kay, 1/Head Net-C, 1/Big Net, 2/Peel Group, 2/Owl Screech, 2/Bass Tilt
Sonar: 1/MF, hull-mounted, 1/MF VDS
EW: 2/Bell Squat, 2/Bell Shroud, 4/chaff RL (XVI × 4)
IFF: 1/High Pole-B
M: 4 gas turbines, 2 props; 96,000 hp **Range:** 1,500/35; 4,000/20

REMARKS: Soviet type designation: BPK—*Bol'shoy Protivolodochniy Korabl'* (Large Antisubmarine Ship), having briefly been listed as "Large Missile Ships." Conversions completed from 1973 onward, with *Sderzhannyy* having probably been built to

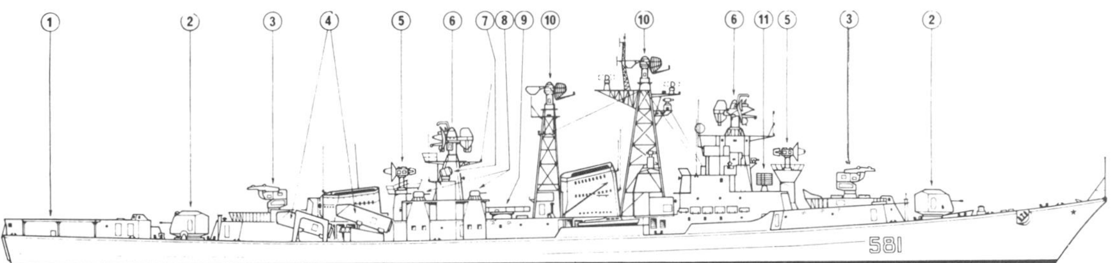

Ognevoy 1. VDS, beneath helo deck 2. twin 76.2-mm DP 3. twin SA-N-1 launcher 4. SS-N-2C 5. Owl Screech radar director for 76.2-mm DP 6. Peel Group radar director for SA-N-1 7. Bass Tilt radar director for 30-mm AA 8. 30-mm gatling AA 9. quintuple 533-mm TT 10. See note 11. RBU-1000 ASW RL
Note: All now have Head Net-C atop foremast and Big Net atop mainmast.

GUIDED-MISSILE DESTROYERS *(continued)*

the new configuration. Hull lengthened by 2 meters, helicopter platform raised above new VDS installation, gatling guns added in place of 2 RBU-1000, new EW gear (not yet fully fitted in all) and radars; *Ognevoy,* the first converted, initially retained original air-search radars, but now has the standard fit.

◆ **12 Kashin class**

Bldrs: *Obraztsovyy, Odarennyy, Steregushchiy:* Zhdanov, Leningrad; others: 61 Kommuna SY, Nikolayev

	In serv.		In serv.
Komsomolets Ukrainyy	2-62	Reshitelnyy ("Decisive")	1-68
Soobrazitel'nyy ("Bright")	9-63	Strogiy ("Severe")	8-68
Obraztsovyy ("Exemplary")	7-65	Smetlivyy ("Intelligent")	9-69
Odarennyy ("Gifted")	9-65	Krasnyy Krym ("Red Crimea")	9-70
Steregushchiy ("Protective")	10-66	Sposobnyy ("Capable")	8-71
Krasnyy Kavkaz ("Red Kavkaz")	1967	Skoryy ("Swift")	8-72

Komsomolets Ukrainyy—2 Head Net-A U.S. Navy, 6-83

Krasnyy Krym—Big Net, Head Net-C U.S. Navy, 10-83

Obraztsovyy—with unique extra EW suite, 2 Head Net-A Skyfotos, 6-84

Odarennyy—a Pacific Fleet Kashin, with 2 Head Net-C, 3 Don-2
PH2 P. Soutar, U.S.N., 9-83

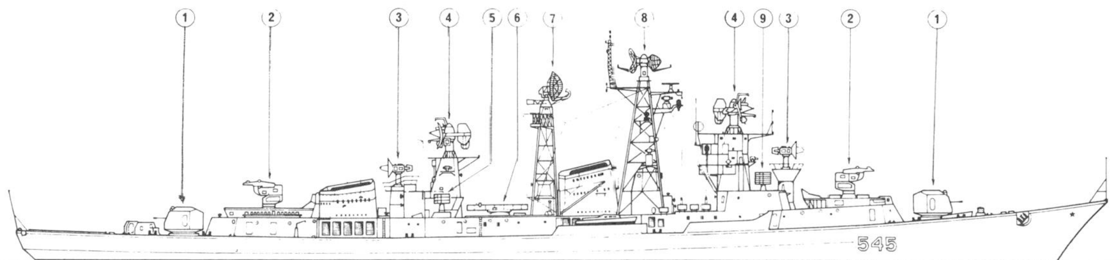

Kashin class 1. twin 76.2-mm DP 2. twin SA-N-1 launcher 3. Owl Screech radar director for 76.2-mm DP 4. Peel Group radar director for SA-N-1 5. RBU-1000 ASW RL 6. quintuple 533-mm TT 7. Big Net radar 8. Head Net-C radar 9. RBU-6000 ASW RL H. Simoni

Sposobnyy—with two Don-Kay navigational radars Lt. McDowell/LCDR Benedict, VF-111, U.S.N., 1983

GUIDED-MISSILE DESTROYERS *(continued)*

Smetlivyy—with Head Net-C atop foremast, Big Net atop mainmast, and two Palm Frond nav. radars French Navy, 9-82

D: 3,750 tons (4,750 fl) **S:** 38 kts **Dim:** 144.0 × 15.8 × 4.8 (hull)
A: 2/SA-N-1 SAM syst. (II × 2, 36 Goa missiles)—4/76.2-mm DP (II × 2)—2/RBU-6000 ASW RL (XII × 2)—2/RBU-1000 ASW RL (VI × 2)—5/533-mm TT (V × I)—mines
Electron Equipt: Radar: 2–3/Don-2 or 2/Don-Kay, or 2/Palm Frond; 2/Head Net-A or 1/Head Net-C and 1/Big Net, (*Odarennyy, Soobrazitel'nny:* 2/Head Net-C), 2/Peel Group, 2/Owl Screech—IFF: 2/High Pole-B or Salt Pot
Sonar: 1/MF, hull-mounted—EW: 2/Watch Dog
M: 4 gas turbines; 2 props; 96,000 hp **Range:** 1,500/36; 4,000/20
Man: 280 tot.

Remarks: Soviet type designation: *Bol'shoy Protivolodochnyy Korabl'* (Large Anti-submarine Ship). One of this class, the *Otvazhnyy,* was sunk 31-8-74 following an explosion: six others have been converted to Modified Kashin configuration and *Provornyy* was converted as SA-N-7 SAM trials ship. All have a helicopter pad on the fantail. The earlier ships carried 2/Head Net-A air-search radars, replaced by two Head Net-C in two ships. *Obraztsovyy* and *Soobrazitel'nyy* have additional Guard Dog EW radomes. The majority are in the Black Sea Fleet.

◆ **8 Kanin class**

	Bldr	In serv.
Gremyashchiy ("Thunderous")	Zhdanov SY, Leningrad	1959
Zhguchiy ("Ardent")	Zhdanov SY, Leningrad	1960
Gordyy ("Proud")	61 Kommuna SY, Nikolayev	1960
Upornyy ("Persistent")	Komsomolsk SY	1960
Derzkiy ("Audacious")	Zhdanov SY, Leningrad	1961
Zorkiy ("Vigilant")	Zhdanov SY, Leningrad	1961
Boykiy ("Valiant")	61 Kommuna SY, Nikolayev	1961
Gnevnyy ("Angry")	61 Kommuna SY, Nikolayev	1961

Gremyashchiy U.S. Navy, 3-82

Zhguchiy French Navy, 1977

D: 3,700 tons (4,750 fl) **S:** 34 kts **Dim:** 139.0 × 15.0 × 5.0 (hull)
A: 1/SA-N-1 system (II × 1, 16 Goa missiles)—8/57-mm AA (IV × 2)—8/30-mm AA (II × 4)—3/RBU-6000 ASW RL (XII × 3)—10/533-mm TT (V × 2)

Electron Equipt: Radar: 2/Don-Kay, 1/Head Net-C, 1/Peel Group, 1/Hawk Screech, 2/Drum Tilt—IFF: 1/High Pole-B
Sonar: 1/MF, hull-mounted—EW: 4/Top Hat, 2/Bell-series
M: 2 sets GT; 2 props; 72,000 hp **Boilers:** 4; 64 kg/cm², 510°C
Range: 1,000/30; 4,500/18 **Man:** 300 tot.

Remarks: Soviet type designation: BPK—*Bol'shoy Protivolodochnyy Korabl'* (Large Antisubmarine Ship). Helicopter platform, but no hangar. Converted from Krupnyy class SS-N-1-equipped "Missile Ships" at Zhdanov SY, Leningrad, except for *Gnevnyy* and *Gordyy,* at Vladivostok in the Far East, 1968-77; bows lengthened to incorporate a bow-mounted sonar and superstructures substantially reconfigured.

◆ **3 Modified Kildin class**

	Bldr	In serv.
Bedovyy ("Daredevilish")	61 Kommuna SY, Nikolayev	1950
Neulovimyy ("Elusive")	Zhdanov SY, Leningrad	1958
Prozorlivyy ("Sagacious")	Zhdanov SY, Leningrad	1959

Bedovyy—with Strut Pair radar, large "Kotlin" stacks U.S. Navy, 8-84

Neulovimyy—small stacks, Head Net-C U.S. Navy, 1985

Prozorlivyy—small stacks, Head Net-C 1982

GUIDED-MISSILE DESTROYERS *(continued)*

D: 2,800 tons (3,700 fl) **S:** 36 kts **Dim:** 126.5 × 13.0 × 4.7 (5.7 sonar)
A: 4/SS-N-2C (I × 4)—4/76.2-mm DP (II × 2)—16/57-mm AA (IV × 4) [except *Bedovyy:* 16/45-mm AA (IV × 4)]—2/RBU-2500 ASW RL (XVI × 2)—4/533-mm TT (II × 2)
Electron Equipt: Radar: 1/Don-2, 1/Head Net-C (*Bedovyy:* Strut Pair), 1/Owl Screech, 2/Hawk Screech
Sonar: 1/HF, hull-mounted (Herkules or Pegas)
EW: 2/Watch Dog—IFF: 1/High Pole-B or Salt Pot
M: 2 sets GT; 2 props; 72,000 hp **Boilers:** 4; 64 kg/cm², 510°C
Electric: 1,400 kw **Range:** 1,000/32; 3,600/18; 4,700/11 **Man:** 300 tot.

Remarks: Soviet type designation: BRK—*Bol'shoy Raketnyy Korabl'* (Large Missile Ship). The *Bedovyy* has broader stacks than her sisters and has Strut Pair radar in place of Head Net-C. Conversions from Kildin configuration completed at Nikolayev, 1973-75. *Prozorlivyy,* launched 30-7-57, is in the Baltic Fleet; the others are in the Black Sea Fleet.

◆ **1 Kildin class**

	Bldr	In serv.
Neuderzhimyy ("Irrepressible")	Komsomol'sk SY, Komsomolsk-na-Amur	1959

Neuderzhimyy U.S. Navy, 6-73

D: 2,600 tons (3,500 fl) **S:** 36 kts **Dim:** 126.5 × 13.0 × 4.6 (5.6 sonar)
A: 1/SS-N-1 (I × 1, 6 Scrubber missiles)—16/57-mm AA (IV × 4)—2/RBU-2500 ASW RL (XVI × 2)—4/533-mm TT (II × 2)
Electron Equipt: Radar: 1/Slim Net, 1/Flat Spin, 1/Top Bow, 2/Hawk Screech, 1/Knife Rest—IFF: 1/High Pole, 2/Square Head
Sonar: 1/HF, hull-mounted—EW: 2/Watch Dog
M: 2 sets GT; 2 props; 72,000 hp **Boilers:** 4; 64 kg/cm², 510°C
Electric: 1,400 kw **Range:** 1,000/34; 3,600/18; 4,700/11 **Man:** 285 tot.

Remarks: Soviet type designation: BRK—*Bol'shoy Raketnyy Korabl'* (Large Missile Ship). The SS-N-1 launcher and reload hangar are aft. Design modified from that of the Kotlin class. Unlikely to be converted, because of age. In the Pacific Fleet, probably in reserve.

◆ **8 SAM Kotlin class** Bldr: Zhdanov SY, Leningrad; (except *Bravyy:* 61 Kommuna SY, Nikolayev; *Vozbuzhdennyy,* Komsomol'sk SY)

	In serv.	Conv.
Skromnyy ("Modest")	1955	1969
Nesokrushimyy ("Invincible")	1956	1967

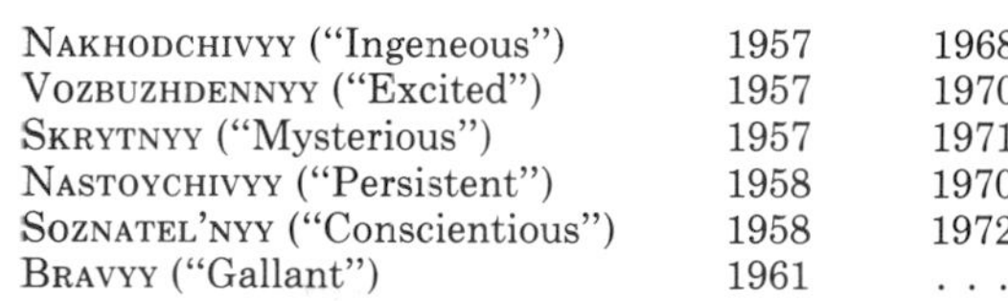

Nakhodchivyy ("Ingeneous")	1957	1968
Vozbuzhdennyy ("Excited")	1957	1970
Skrytnyy ("Mysterious")	1957	1971
Nastoychivyy ("Persistent")	1958	1970
Soznatel'nyy ("Conscientious")	1958	1972
Bravyy ("Gallant")	1961	. . .

Bravyy—conversion prototype, with 12/45-mm AA, Head Net-A, RBU-2500 U.S. Navy, 2-75

Nakhodchivyy—no 30-mm AA U.S. Navy, 5-83

D: 2,700 tons (3,600 fl) **S:** 36 kts **Dim:** 126.5 × 13.0 × 4.6 (avg.)
A: *Bravyy:* 1/SA-N-1 system (II × 1)—2/130-mm DP (II × 1)—12/45-mm AA (IV × 3)—5/533-mm TT (V × 1)—2/RBU-2500 ASW RL (XVI × 2)
Others: 1/SA-N-1 system (II × 1)—2/130-mm DP (II × 1)—4/45-mm AA (IV × 1)—8/30-mm AA (II × 4; not in 3 units)—5/533-mm TT (V × 1)—2/RBU-6000 ASW RL (XII × 2) (*Skromnyy* has RBU-2500, see Remarks)
Electron Equipt: Radar: 1 or 2/Don-2, 1/Head Net-C, 1/Peel Group, 1/Sun Visor, 1/Hawk Screech, 1/Egg Cup, 2/Drum Tilt (not in 4)
Sonar: 1/HF (Herkules or Pegas)
EW: 2/Watch Dog—IFF: 1/High Pole-B
M: 2 sets GT; 2 props; 72,000 hp **Boilers:** 4; 64 kg/cm², 510°C
Electric: 1,400 kw **Range:** 1,000/34; 3,600/18; 4,700/11 **Man:** 300 tot.

Remarks: Soviet type designation: EM—*Eskhadrennyy Minonosets* (Destroyer). *Nesokrushimyy, Skrytnyy, Soznatel'nyy,* and *Vozbuzhdennyy* have eight 30-mm AA (II × 4) in addition to the above, with two Drum Tilt fire-control radars. *Nastoychivyy* has no Egg Cup radar. *Bravyy* has Head Net-A, two extra quadruple 45-mm AA mounts and, as does the *Skromnyy,* RBU-2500 vice RBU-6000. *Bravyy,* which was completed as the SA-N-1 trials ship, was further modified in the mid-1960s with 2 additional 45-mm AA mounts and TT added. Sister *Spravedlivyy* was transferred to Poland in 1970. The SA-N-1 system has 16 Goa missiles.

Vozbuzhdennyy—with 8/30-mm AA, Head Net-C, RBU-6000 U.S. Navy, 7-84

GUIDED-MISSILE DESTROYERS *(continued)*

Soznatel'nyy French Navy, 1-85

DESTROYERS

◆ **17 Kotlin and Modified Kotlin classes** Bldrs: A: Zhdanov SY, Leningrad; B: 61 Kommuna SY, Nikolayev; C: Komsomol'sk-na-Amur

11 Modified Kotlin Class:

	Bldr	In serv.
Svedushchiy ("Experienced")	A	1956
Moskovskiy Komsomolets (ex-*Smyshlennyy*)	A	1956
Burlivyy ("Turbulent")	B	1956
Byvalyy ("Veteran")	B	1956
Vdokhnovennyy ("Inspired")	C	1956
Vzyvayushchiy ("Defiant")	C	1956
Blestyashchiy ("Magnificent")	B	1957
Blagorodnyy ("Noble")	B	1957
Plamennyy ("Fiery")	B	1958
Naporistyy ("Assertive")	B	1958
Vyderzhannyy ("Steadfast")	C	1958

6 Kotlin Class:

	Bldr	In serv.
Speshnyy ("Urgent")	A	1955
Spokoynyy ("Tranquil")	A	1956
Svetlyy ("Luminous")	A	1957
Veskiy ("Imposing")	C	1957
Vliyatelnyy ("Influential")	C	1958
Dalnyvostochnyy Komsomolets (ex-*Vozmushchyennyy*)	C	1958

Moskovskiy Komsomolets—Modified Kotlin with RBU-6000, towed array, no RBU-600 8-80

. . . **Mod. Kotlin with only 4/25-mm AA (II × 2)** U.S. Navy, 6-82

D: 2,600 tons (3,500 fl) **S:** 36 kts **Dim:** 126.5 × 13.0 × 4.6 (5.6 sonar)
A: Kotlin: 4/130-mm DP (II × 2)—16/45-mm AA (IV × 4)—4/25-mm AA (II × 2)—10/533-mm TT (V × 2)—6/BMB-2 d.c. projectors—2/d.c. racks—70 mines
Mod. Kotlin: 4/130-mm DP (II × 2)—16/45-mm AA (IV × 4)—8/25-mm AA (II × 4)—5/533-mm TT (V × 1)—2/RBU-2500 ASW RL (XVI × 2)—2/RBU-600 ASW RL (VI × 2)—70 mines
Electron Equipt: Radar: 1/Neptune or 1 or 2/Don-2, 1/Slim Net, 1/Sun Visor, 2/Hawk Screech, 2/Egg Cup, 1/Post Lamp or Top Bow

Svetlyy—only Kotlin with a helo deck 1977

Vdokhnovennyy—Modified Kotlin with 8/25-mm (II × 4) abreast aft stack 4-79

Sonar: 1/HF (Herkules
EW: 2/Watch Dog—IFF: 1/High Pole, 2/Square Head
M: 2 sets GT; 2 props; 72,000 hp **Boilers:** 4; 64 kg/cm², 510°C
Electric: 1,400 kw **Range:** 1,000/34; 3,600/18, 4,700/11
Man: 36 officers, 300 men

Remarks: Soviet type designation: EM—*Eskhadrennyy Minonosets* (Destroyer). Eleven were modified between 1960 and 1965, receiving two RBU-2500 forward and two RBU-600 in place of their depth-charge equipment, the after bank of five 533-mm TT being removed. Later, most of these ships got eight 25-mm AA (II × 4). The *Moskovskiy Komsomolets* got RBU-6000 forward, nothing aft; in 1978 she received a variable-depth sonar on her stern. Most of those that were not modified received four 25-mm AA (II × 2). *Svetlyy* has a helicopter platform in place of depth-charge gear and thus has no ASW armament. Helicopter decks were removed from the other two ships that had them. Many have had their Egg Cup radars removed. Only about 11 total of both types are active.

◆ **13 Skoryy and 4 Modified Skoryy classes** (In serv. 1949-53)—in reserve

Bldrs: Molotovsk (now Severodvinsk) SY; Zhdanov SY, Leningrad; 61 Kommuna SY, Nikolayev; Komsomol'sk SY, Komsomol'sk-na-Amur

Buynyy—Skoryy class with seven 37-mm AA, no 25-mm AA 7-79

Modified Skoryy class

D: 2,600 tons (3,130 fl) **S:** 34 kts **Dim:** 121.2 (116.5 pp) × 12.0 × 4.5 (hull)
A: Standard: 4/130-mm DP (II × 2)—2/85-mm AA (II × 1)—7 or 8/37-mm AA (I × 7 or II × 4)—4 or 6/25-mm AA (II × 2 or 3—not in 7/37-mm ships)—10/533-mm TT (V × 2)—2/d.c. projectors—2/d.c. racks—50 mines
Modified: 4/130-mm DP (II × 2)—5/57-mm AA (I × 5)—2/RBU-2500 ASW RL (XVI × 2)—5/533-mm TT (V × 1)—50 mines
Electron Equipt: Radar: Standard: 1/High Sieve, 1/Top Bow or Half Bow or Post Lamp, 1/Cross Bird, 1 or 2/Don-2
Modified: 1/Slim Net, 1/Top Bow, 1 or 2/Don-2, 2/Hawk Screech

DESTROYERS *(continued)*

Solidnyy—with 8/37-mm (II × 4), 6/25-mm AA (II × 3) U.S. Navy, 10-80

Sonar: 1/HF (Tamir-5 Pegas)
EW: 2 Watch Dog—IFF: 2/Square Head, 1/High Pole-A
M: 2 sets GT; 2 props; 60,000 hp **Boilers:** 4; 27 kg/cm², 367°C
Electric: 475 kw **Fuel:** 786 tons **Range:** 850/30; 3,000/18
Man: 18 officers, 200 men

Remarks: Soviet type designation: EM—*Eskhadrennyy Minonosets* (Destroyer). Survivors of seventy-two built, derived from prewar *Ognevoy* design. Six early-construction units were modernized around 1960 to *Modified Skoryy* configuration, with improved AAW and ASW equipment and enhanced EW suits. Only those with eight 37-mm AA have been given two or three twin 25-mm AA. Several *Skoryy* class were transferred to Egypt, Poland, and Indonesia. Now of little value, and all believed to be in reserve, with a few periodically activated only for local training duties.

FRIGATES

◆ **2 (+ . . .) Krivak-III class** Bldr: Kamysh Burun SY, Kerch'

Menzhinskiy (In serv. 8-84) Dzerzhinskiy (In serv. 8-85)

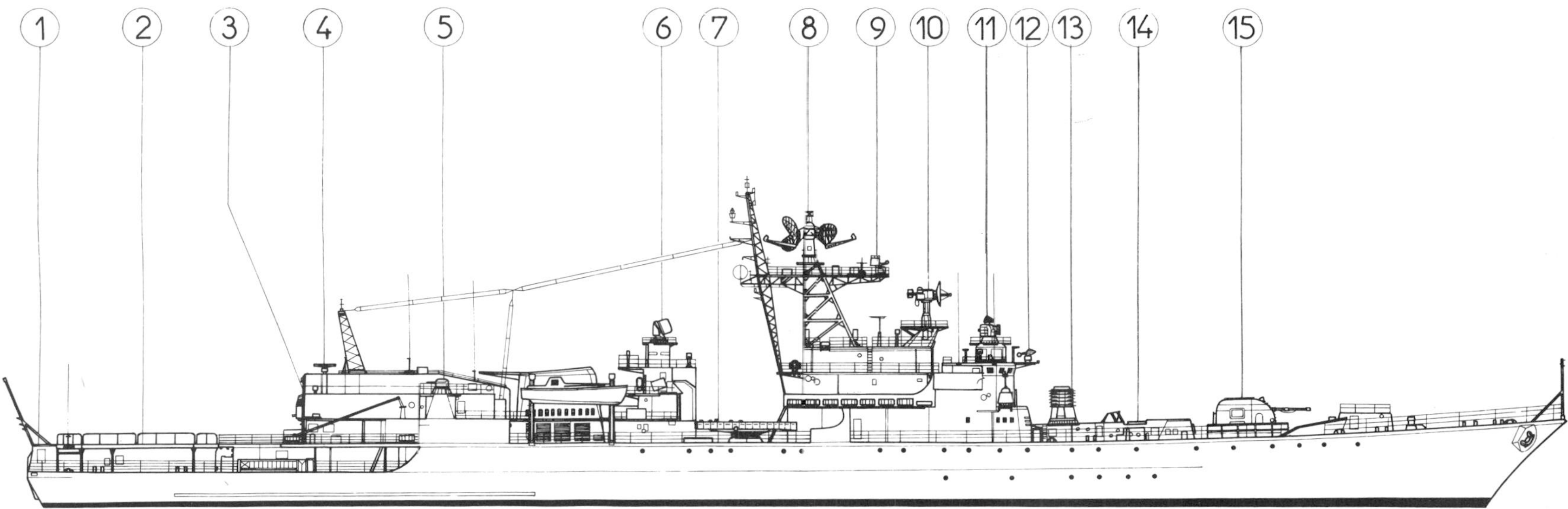

Krivak-III 1. variable-depth sonar housing 2. helicopter deck 3. helicopter hangar 4. Spin Trough radar for helicopter control 5. 30-mm gatling AA 6. Bass Tilt radar director for 30-mm AA 7. quadruple 533-mm TT 8. Head Net-C air-search radar 9. Don-Kay nav. radar 10. Kite Screech radar director for 100-mm gun 11. Pop Group track-while-scan radar for SA-N-4 12. Palm Frond nav. radar 13. RBU-6000 ASW RL 14. twin SA-N-4 launcher 15. 100-mm DP L. Gassier

Menzhinskiy U.S. Navy, 9-84

FRIGATES *(continued)*

Dzerzhinskiy JMSDF, 9-85

Menzhinskiy U.S. Navy, 9-84

D: 3,900 tons (fl) **S:** 32 kts (30 sust.)
Dim: 123.5 (115.4 pp) × 14.1 × 4.5 (hull)
A: 1/SA-N-4 syst. (II × 1) — 1/100-mm automatic DP — 2/30-mm gatling AA (I × 2) — 2/RBU-6000 ASW RL (XII × 2) — 8/533-mm TT — 1/Ka-27 Helix helicopter — mines
Electron Equipt: Radar: 1/Palm Frond, 1/Don-Kay, 1/Don-2, 1/Head Net-C, 1/Pop Group, 1/Kite Screech, 1/Bass Tilt
Sonar: MF hull-mounted, MF VDS
EW: 2/Bell Shroud, 2/Bell Squat, 4/decoy RL (XVI × 4)
IFF: 1/Salt Pot transponder, 1/High Pole-B transponder
M: COGOG: 2 cruise gas turbines of 12,100 hp each/2 high-speed gas turbines of 24,300 hp each; 2 props; 48,600 hp max.
Range: 700/30; 3,900/20 **Man:** 200 tot.

Remarks: Revised version of basic Krivak design for KGB Maritime Border Guard service. Typed PSKR — *Pogranichnyy Storozhevoy Korabl'* (Border Patrol Ship). Named for prominent KGB "heroes." *Menzhinskiy* deployed from the Black Sea 7-9-84, bound for the Pacific, and *Dzerzhinskiy* followed a year later. More probably are building, although the basic design is essentially nearly 20 years old.

The addition of a helicopter facility (with simple deck-transit system) and helicopter weapons reload magazines cost two gunmounts and one SA-N-4 positions aft, while the Krivak-I/II SS-N-14 dual-purpose missile system was replaced by a 100-mm gun, more useful for the mission of these ships. Two 6-barreled gatling guns were added to improve close-in defense. Sensors are not the latest available.

◆ **11 Krivak-II class** Bldr: Kaliningrad SY

	In serv.		In serv.
Rezvyy ("Lively")	1975	Gromkiy ("Thunderous")	1979
Rezkiy ("Brusque")	1976	Gordelivyy ("Trustworthy")	1979
Razitel'nyy ("Wrathful")	1977	R'yanyy ("Spirited")	1980
Grozyashchiy ("Dissuasive")	1977	Revnostnyy ("Roaring")	1980
Neukrotimyy ("Indomitable")	1978	Pytlivyy ("Curious")	1982
Bessmennyy ("Irremoveable")	1978		

Razitel'nyy U.S. Navy, 12-84

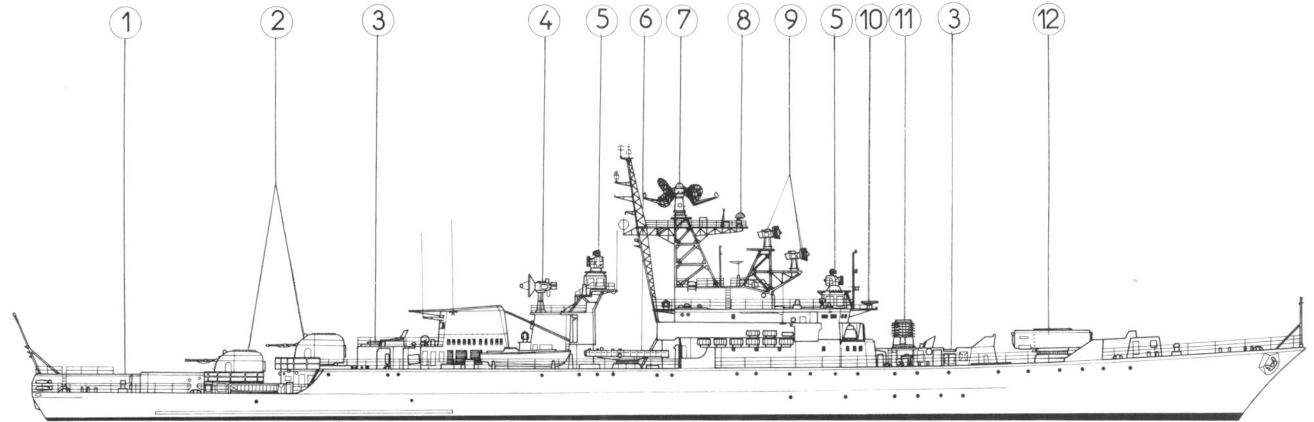

Krivak-II 1. variable-depth sonar housing 2. single 100-mm DP mounts 3. twin SA-N-4 launcher 4. Kite Screech radar director for 100-mm guns 5. Pop Group track-while-scan radar director for SA-N-4 6. quadruple 533-mm TT 7. Head Net-C air-search radar 8. Don-Kay or Palm Frond nav. radar 9. Eye Bowl radar directors for SS-N-14 10. Spin Trough nav. radar 11. RBU-6000 ASW RL 12. quadruple SS-N-14 launcher L. Gassier, 1985

FRIGATES *(continued)*

Razitel'nyy—Don-2 and Palm Frond navigational radars U.S. Navy, 1-85

Pytlivyy French Navy, 4-84

Gromkiy U.S. Navy, 10-83

D: 3,800 tons (fl) **S:** 32 kts (30 sust.) **Dim:** 123.5 × 14.1 × 4.6 (hull)
A: 4/SS-N-14 (IV × 1)—2/SA-N-4 systems (II × 2, 40 missiles)—2/100-mm DP (I × 2)—2/RBU-6000 ASW RL (XII × 2)—8/533-mm TT (IV × 2)—mines
Electron Equipt: Radar: 1/Palm Frond or Don-Kay, 1/Spin Trough or Don-2, 1/Head Net-C, 2/Eye Bowl, 1/Kite Screech, 2 Pop Group
Sonar: 1/MF hull-mounted, 1/MF VDS
EW: 2/Bell Shroud, 2/Bell Squat, 4/decoy RL (XVI × 4)
IFF: 1/High Pole-B or Salt Pot transponder
M: COGOG: 2 cruise gas turbines of 12,100 hp each and 2 high-speed gas turbines of 24,300 hp each; 2 props; 48,600 hp max.
Range: 700/30; 3,900/20 **Man:** 200 tot.

REMARKS: Soviet type designation: SKR—*Storozhevoy Korabl'* (Patrol Ship), formerly BPK—Large Antisubmarine Ship. The VDS housing at the stern is somewhat larger than on the Krivak-Is, but the principal difference is substitution of single 100-mm for twin 76.2-mm guns. The chaff/decoy rocket launchers were moved from the stern to the 01 level, abreast the aft SA-N-4 launcher. *Revostnyy* has four 4-tubed decoy RL mounted between the torpedo tubes, in addition to her normal chaff RL system.

◆ **21 Krivak-I class** Bldrs: A: Zhdanov SY, Leningrad; B: Kaliningrad SY; C: Kamysh-Burun SY, Kerch'

	Bldr	In serv.
BDITEL'NYY ("Vigilant")	B	1970
DOSTOYNYY ("Dignified")	C	1971
BODRYY ("Brave")	B	1971
SVIREPYY ("Ferocious")	B	1971
SIL'NYY ("Powerful")	B	1972
DOBLESTNYY ("Valorous")	C	1972
STOROZHEVOY ("Guarding")	B	1973
RAZUMNYY ("Sensible")	B	1973
RAZYASHCHIY ("Perceptive")	B	1974
DRUZHNYY ("Amicable")	A	1975
DEYATEL'NYY ("Active")	C	1975
ZHARKYY ("Passionate")	B	1975
RETIVYY ("Zealous")	A	1976
LENINGRADSKIY KOMSOMOLETS	A	1976
LETUCHIY ("Flying")	A	1977
BEZZAVETNYY ("Conscientious")	C	1978
PYLKIY ("Ardent")	A	1979
ZADORNYY ("Provocative")	A	1979
BEZUKORIZNENNYY ("Irreproachable")	C	1980
LADNYY ("Friendly")	C	1980
PORYVISTYY ("Impetuous")	C	1982

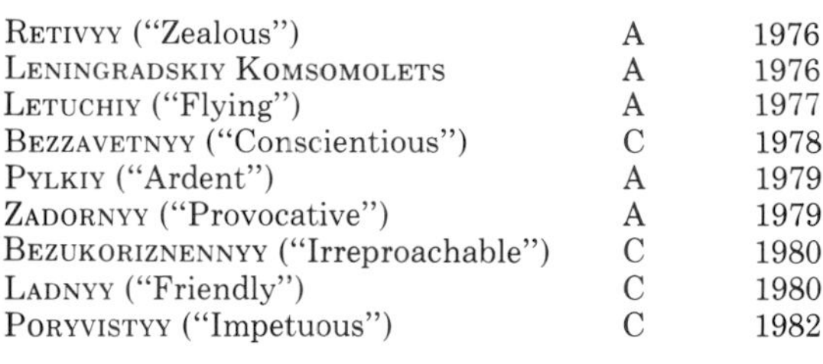

Bezzavetnyy—still without EW suite French Navy, 1984

Sil'nyy—also without EW suite French Navy, 8-84

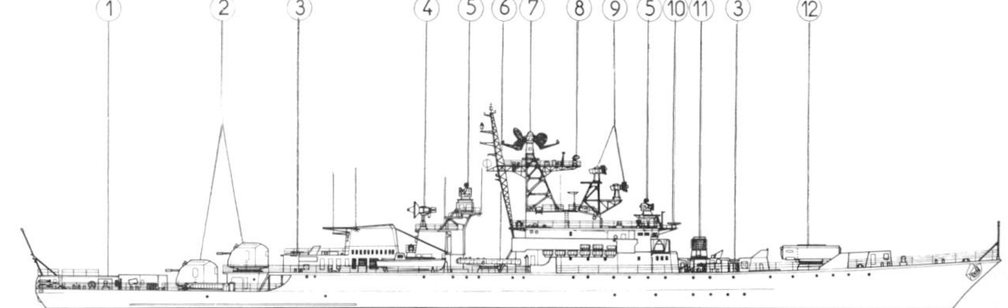

Krivak-I 1. variable-depth sonar housing 2. twin 76.2-mm DP 3. twin SA-N-4 launcher 4. Owl Screech radar director for 76.2-mm DP 5. Pop Group track-while-scan radar directors for SA-N-4 6. quadruple 533-mm TT 7. Head Net-C air-search radar 8. Don-Kay or Palm Frond nav. radar 9. Eye Bowl radar directors for SS-N-14 10. Spin Trough nav. radar 11. RBU-6000 ASW RL 12. quadruple SS-N-14 launcher L. Gassier

FRIGATES *(continued)*

Bezukoriznennyy U.S. Navy, 2-83

Pilkiy—note bow sonar dome, visible beneath the water's surface U.S. Navy, 7-84

Razyashchiy U.S. Navy, 9-83

D: 3,700 tons (fl) **S:** 32 kts (30 sust.) **Dim:** 123.5 × 14.1 × 4.6 (hull)
A: 4/SS-N-14 (IV × 1)—2/SA-N-4 systems (II × 2, 40 missiles)—4/76.2-mm DP (II × 2)—2/RBU-6000 ASW RL (XII × 2)—8/533-mm TT (IV × 2)—mines
Electron Equipt: Radar: 1/Don-2 or Spin Trough, 1/Don-Kay or Palm Frond, 1/Head Net-C, 2/Eye Bowl, 1/Owl Screech, 2/Pop Group
Sonar: 1/MF hull-mounted, 1/MF VDS
EW: 2/Bell Shroud, 2/Bell Squat, 4/chaff launchers (XVI × 4)
IFF: High Pole-B or Salt Pot
M: CODOG: 2 cruise gas turbines of 12,100 hp each and 2 boost gas turbines of 24,300 hp each; 2 props; 48,600 hp max.
Range: 700/30; 3,900/20 **Man:** 200 tot.

REMARKS: Soviet type designation: SKR—*Storozhevoy Korabl'* (Patrol Ship). In 1978 Krivak-I and Krivak-II classes were rerated from BPK (*Bol-shoy Protivolodochnyy Korabl'*—large ASW ship) to SKR (*Storozhevoy Korabl'*—patrol ship), a demotion prompted perhaps by their limited endurance at high speeds, speed, and size. Not all units have the EW gear. *Bodryy* has been equipped with ten 10-tubed chaff RL, *replacing* the original four 16-tubed.

Zadornyy U.S. Navy, 1-85

◆ **1 Koni class** Bldr: Zelenodolsk SY (In serv. circa 1978)

TIMOFEY UL'YANTSEV

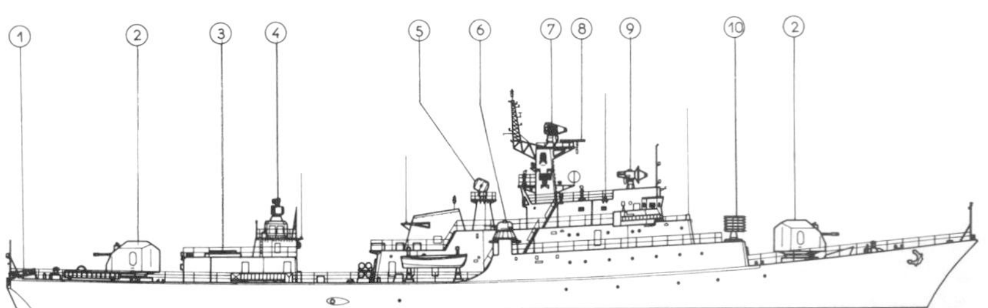

Koni 1. depth-charge racks 2. twin 76.2-mm DP guns 3. twin SA-N-4 SAM launcher 4. Pop Group radar director for SA-N-4 5. Drum Tilt radar director for 30-mm AA 6. twin 30-mm AA 7. Strut Curve surface/air-search radar 8. Don-2 nav. radar 9. Hawk Screech radar director for 76.2-mm guns 10. RBU-6000 ASW RL *Note:* This drawing represents an early-contruction Koni with separate deckhouse aft; the Soviet Navy's unit should be very similar. L. Gassier

FRIGATES *(continued)*

D: 1,900 tons (fl) **S:** 27 kts **Dim:** 95.0 × 12.8 × 4.2 (5.4 max.)
A: 1/SA-N-4 SAM syst. (II × 1, 20 missiles)—4/76.2-mm DP (II × 2)—4/30-mm AK-230 AA—2/RBU-6000 ASW RL (XII × 2)—2/d.c. racks—20 mines
Electron Equipt: Radar: 1/Don-2, 1/Strut Curve, 1/Pop Group, 1/Hawk Screech, 1/Drum Tilt
Sonar: 1/MF hull-mounted
EW: 2/Watch Dog—IFF: 1/High Pole-B
M: CODAG: 1 gas turbine of 15,000 hp, 2 diesels of 7,500 hp; 3 props; 30,000 hp
Range: 1,800/14 **Man:** 110 tot.

REMARKS: One unit of this export SKR—*Storozhevoy Korabl'* (Patrol Ship) design, reportedly with the listed name, has been retained in the Black Sea Fleet for training foreign crews. Only about one Koni per year has been built—all for export—although the design would seem to have been a natural successor for the Riga class. Have a large teardrop-shaped sonar dome. The d.c. racks are bolted to the mine rails. Centerline shaft, powered by the diesel, has controllable-pitch prop. Fin stabilizers. Units have been exported to East Germany, Cuba, Algeria, and Yugoslavia; recent ships have had a continuous after deckhouse and 2 chaff RL (XVI × 2) added.

◆ **33 Grisha-III class** Bldr: Zelenodolsk SY, . . . (In serv. 1975- . . .)

KOMSOMOLETS GRUZIN ORLOVSKIY KOMSOMOLETS KOMSOMOLETS BASHKIRIY
30 others

Grisha-III class PH1 F. Barbante, U.S.N., 9-83

Grisha-III class—Bass Tilt and deckhouse offset to port 7-79

A: 1/SA-N-4 syst. (II × 1, 20 missiles)—2/57-mm DP (II × 1)—1//30-mm gatling AA—2/RBU-6000 ASW RL (XII × 2)—4/533-mm TT (II × 2)—2/d.c. racks (12 d.c.) or mines

REMARKS: See Grisha-I entry for other data. Soviet type designation: MPK—*Malyy Protivolodochnyy Korabl'* (Small Antisubmarine Ship). Construction continues. Bass Tilt, which is atop a small deckhouse to port on the aft superstructure, has been substituted for Muff Cob radar fire control, while a gatling gun has been mounted in the space occupied by Muff Cob in the Grisha-I and -II. Depth-charge racks can be mounted on the aft end of the mine rails. Also built in Soviet Far East. Several Pacific Fleet units serve the KGB Maritime Border Guard; at least one has had an extra boat added to port of the stack, stowed on an 01-level platform. One has 76-mm DP aft, only one RBU-6000 RL, and Strut Pair vice Strut Curve radar.

◆ **9 Grisha-II class** Bldrs: Zelenodolsk SY (In serv. 1974- . . .)

AMETIST IZUMRUD SAFFIR 3 others
BRILLIANT RUBIN ZHEMCHUG

A: 4/57-mm DP (II × 2)—2/RBU-6000 ASW RL (XIII × 2)—4/533-mm TT (II × 2)—2/d.c. racks (12 d.c.) or mines.

REMARKS: See Grisha-I entry for other data. Soviet type designation: PSKR—*Pogranichniy Storozhevoy Korabl'* (Border Patrol Ship). Manned by the KGB Maritime Border Guard. A second twin 57-mm was substituted for SA-N-4 forward, and the Pop Group missile-control radar was not installed. At least one Black Sea Fleet unit has had a boat added to port of the stack, stowed on a new 01-level platform; the after twin 57-mm DP was removed as weight compensation.

Zhemchug—Grisha-II class, 57-mm guns fore and aft 1983

◆ **15 Grisha-I class** Bldrs: Zelenodolsk SY, . . . (In serv. 1968-74)

D: 850 tons (1,100 fl) **S:** 30 kts **Dim:** 71.6 × 9.8 × 3.7
A: 1/SA-N-4 syst. (II × 1, 20 missiles)—2/57-mm DP (II × 1)—2/RBU-6000 ASW RL (XII × 2)—4/533-mm TT (II × 2)—2/d.c. racks (12 d.c.) or mines
Electron Equipt: Radar: 1/Don-2, 1/Strut Curve, 1/Pop Group, 1/Muff Cob (Grisha-III: Bass Tilt)
Sonar: 1/MF hull-mounted, 1/HF dipping
EW: 2/Watch Dog—IFF: 1/High Pole-B, 1/High Pole-A
M: CODAG: 4 diesels; 1/15,000-hp gas turbine; 3 props; 31,000 hp
Range: 450/27; 4,500/10 **Man:** 60 tot.

Grisha-III class—topmast askew U.S. Navy, 7-84

FRIGATES *(continued)*

Remarks: More specialized for ASW than the earlier Petya and Mirka "patrol ships." Russian type designation: MPK—*Malyy Protivolodochnyy Korabl'* (Small Antisubmarine Ship). A plate has been added forward of the Muff Cobb fire-control radar to protect personnel on the bridge from its radiation. The dipping sonar is housed beneath a hump to starboard on the after deckhouse, evidently deploying through the hull bottom.

Unique Grisha-I—with rubbing strake fore and aft of anchor pocket, Square Head IFF interrogator aft U.S. Navy, 2-80

Grisha-I class French Navy, 1977

Grisha-I class French Navy, 1982

◆ **1 Modified Petya-II class**

Modified Petya-II class 7-78

A: 4/76.2-mm DP—2/RBU-6000 ASW RL (XII × 2)—5/400-mm ASW TT (V × 1)—mines

Remarks: Conversion in 1978 similar to Modified Petya-I, but new VDS deckhouse at stern does not extend to the sides of the ship, which permits retention of mine rails. One quintuple ASW torpedo-tube mounting and the d.c. racks have been removed. Apparently experimental, as only one was converted.

◆ **11 Modified Petya-I class** Bldrs: Kaliningrad SY, Komsomol'sk SY (In serv. 1961-64)

Modified Petya-I class—small deckhouse at stern 1980

Modified Petya-I class—standard version U.S. Navy, 8-83

Modified Petya-I—standard configuration L. & L. Van Ginderen, 9-83

Petya-I modified for possible towed-array research 6-80

A: Standard version (see Remarks): 4/76.2-mm DP (II × 2)—2/RBU-2500 RL—5/400-mm ASW TT (V × 1)—1/d.c. rack

A: Others 2/76.2-mm DP (II × 1), 2/RBU-2500 ASW RL (XVI × 2)

Remarks: Conversions began in 1973. Petya-I class altered by the addition of a medium-frequency towed sonar in a new raised stern deckhouse. The designation "Modified Petya I" is also applied to several trials units, one with a very large VDS exposed at the stern (no raised stern); another with a deckhouse abaft the stack and a complex towing array, reels, and winch on her stern; still another with a small, boxlike deckhouse containing a towed sensor at the extreme stern. At least one "standard" Mod. Petya-I has Strut Curve via Slim Net air-search radar. Some have 2/Don-2.

◆ **20 Petya-II class** Bldrs: Kaliningrad SY, Khabarovsk SY (1964-69)

FRIGATES *(continued)*

Petya-II U.S. Navy, 8-83

Petya-II—2/RBU-6000, 10/400-mm TT, Strut Curve 1977

◆ **7 Petya-I class** Bldrs: Kaliningrad SY Khabarovsk SY (In serv. 1961-64)

Petya-I—4/RBU-2500, 5/400-mm TT, Slim Net

D: 950 tons (1,150 fl) **S:** 30 kts **Dim:** 81.8 (78.0 pp) × 9.2 × 2.8 (hull)

A: Petya-I: 4/76.2-mm DP (II × 2)—4/RBU-2500 ASW RL (XVI × 4)—5/400-mm ASW TT (V × 1)—2/d.c. racks—mines
Petya II: 4/76.2-mm DP (II × 2)—2/RBU-6000 ASW RL (XII × 2)—10/400-mm ASW TT (V × 2)—2/d.c. racks—mines

Electron Equipt: Radar: 1/Don-2, 1/Slim Net or Strut Curve, 1/Hawk Screech
Sonar: 1/HF hull-mounted, 1/HF helo dipping sonar (on some)
EW: 2/Watch Dog—IFF: 1/High Pole-B

M: CODAG: 2/15,000 hp gas turbines + 1/6,000-hp Type 61V-3 diesel; 3 props; 36,000 hp

Range: 450/29 (diesel + gas turbine); 1,800/16 (diesel) **Man:** 8 officers, 84 men

Remarks: Soviet type designation: SKR—*Storozhevoy Korabl'* (Patrol Ship). Most carry helicopter dipping sonars in temporary installations amidships. Petya-I has two Square Head IFF interrogators. A version with two RBU-2500 rocket launchers and three 533-mm torpedo tubes (III × 1) was built for export to Ethiopia, India, Syria, and Vietnam, while six standard Petya-IIs were exported from Soviet Navy inventory to Vietnam and Ethiopia during 1983-84. The diesel drives the centerline CP prop and can drive the ships at up to 16 kts. Two small electro-hydraulic maneuvering propellers are mounted at the extreme stern and can produce 3 kts. The teardrop-shaped sonar dome adds 1.5 m to the navigational draft. Some Petya-Is have Slim Net search radars; all Petya-IIs and other Petya Is have Strut Curve. One Black Sea Fleet Petya-I or -II carried a twin SUW-N-1 ASW RL on the bow in place of the gunmount in 1976.

◆ **9 Mirka-I class** Bldr: Kaliningrad SY (In serv. 1964-65)

Mirka-I class—4/RBU-6000, 5/400-mm TT, Slim Net U.S. Navy, 1984

Mirka-I—with dipping sonar cabinet abaft after gunmount, to starboard 5-82

FRIGATES *(continued)*

◆ **9 Mirka-II class** Bldr: Kaliningrad SY (In serv. 1965-66)

IVAN SLADKOV GANGUTETS 7 others

Mirka-II class—with Slim Net and dipping sonar 1977

Mirka-II class—with Strut Curve radar and dipping sonar at stern French Navy, 7-84

D: 950 tons (1,150 fl) **S:** 34 kts **Dim:** 82.4 × 9.2 × 2.9 (hull)
A: Mirka-I: 4/76.2-mm DP (II × 2)—4/RBU-6000 ASW RL (XII × 4)—5/400-mm ASW TT (V × I)—1/d.c. rack
Mirka-II: 4/76.2-mm DP (II × 2)—2/RBU-6000 ASW RL (XII × 2)—10/400-mm ASW TT (V × 2)
Electron Equipt: Radar: 1/Don-2, 1/Slim Net or Strut Curve, 1/Hawk Screech
Sonar: 1/HF hull-mounted—Mirka-II also: 1/dipping
EW: 2/Watch Dog—IFF: 1/High Pole-B, 2/Square Head
M: CODAG: 2/15,000-hp gas turbines + 2/6,000-hp diesels; 2 props in pump-jet tunnels
Range: 500/30 (gas turbine); 4,800/10 (1 diesel) **Man:** 8 officers, 84 men

REMARKS: Soviet type designation: SKR—*Storozhevoy Korabl'* (Patrol Ship). Propulsion system similar in concept to that of the Poti class, using gas turbines to power compressors that inject air into tunnels beneath the ship to produce a jet effect; the diesel-driver propellers are also within the tunnels, while the gas turbine exhaust residual thrust contributes to the overall power. All Mirka-Is have Slim Net, while a few late Mirka-IIs have Strut Curve. All Mirka-IIs have been modernized with a dipping sonar in place of the internal depth-charge rack on the port side of the stern.

◆ **48 Riga class** Bldrs: Yantar SY, Kaliningrad; Khabarovsk SY, Marti SY, Nikolayev (In serv. 1952-58)—14 or more in reserve.

Known names:

ASTRAKHAN'SKIY KOMSOMOLETS
ARKHANGEL'SKIY KOMSOMOLETS
BARS ("Snow Leopard")
BARSUK ("Badger")
BOBR ("Beaver")
BUYVOL ("Buffalo")
BYK ("Bull")
GEPARD ("Cheetah")
GIENA ("Hyena")
KOBCHIK ("Merlin")
KOMSOMOLETS GRUZIY
KOMSOMOLETS LITVIY
KRASNODARSKIY KOMSOMOLETS
KUNITSA ("Martin")
LEOPARD ("Leopard")
LEV ("Lion")
LISA ("Fox")
MEDVED' ("Bear")
PANTERA ("Panther")
RYS (" . . . ")
ROSOMAKHA ("Wolverine")
SHAKAL ("Jackal")
TIGR ("Tiger")
TURMAN (" . . . ")
VOLK ("Wolf")
VORON ("Raven")
YAGUAR ("Jaguar")

Riga class—only one with Bell Series radomes, tall stack cap 1972

Riga class PH2 P. Soutar, U.S.N., 9-83

D: 1,260 tons (1,480 fl) **S:** 30 kts **Dim:** 91.0 × 10.2 × 3.2 (4.4 max.)
A: 3/100-mm DP (I × 3)—4/37-mm AA (II × 2)—4/25-mm AA (II × 2)—2 or 3/533-mm ASW TT (II or III × 1)—2/RBU-2500 ASW RL (XVI × 2)—2/d.c. racks—mines
Electron Equipt: Radar: 1/Neptune or Don-2, 1/Slim Net, 1/Sun Visor
Sonar: 1/HF (Herkules or Pegas)
EW: 2/Watch Dog
IFF: 1/High Pole, 2/Square Head
M: 2 sets GT; 2 props; 20,000 hp **Boilers:** 2; 27 kg/cm², 360°C
Fuel: 230 tons **Electric:** 450 kw
Range: 550/28; 2,000/13 **Man:** 16 officers, 154 men

REMARKS: Soviet type designation: SKR—*Storozhevoy Korabl'* (Patrol Ship). One ship has a Hawk Screech radar director forward and the main gun director aft. Transfers to other countries include Indonesia, Finland, Bulgaria, China, and East Germany. A few reserve examples may retain the original ASW ordnance suit of 1/MBU-600 Hedgehog, 4/BMB-2 d.c. mortars, and 2 d.c. racks. Not all active units have had the two twin 25-mm AA added abreast the stack. Obsolescent.

GUIDED-MISSILE CORVETTES

◆ **10 (+ . . .) Tarantul-II class** Bldr: Sredniy Neva SY, Kolpino; Petrovskiy SY, Leningrad (In serv. 1981- . . .)

Tarantul-II—Band Stand atop bridge, Light Bulb atop mast 1981

Riga class—no 25-mm AA abreast stack, twin TT U.S. Navy, 5-84

GUIDED-MISSILE CORVETTES *(continued)*

Tarantul-II class M.O.D., Bonn, 1982

Electron Equipt: Radar: 1/Kivach, 1/Band Stand, 1/Light Bulb, 1/Bass Tilt

REMARKS: Other data as for Tarantul-I, except that one unit (Tarantul-III?) has 4/SS-N-22 missiles (II × 2) vice SS-N-2C. Light Bulb may be a data link antenna., vice radar.

◆ **2 Tarantul-I class** Bldr: Petrovskiy SY, Leningrad (In serv. 1979- 80)

Tarantul-I class—upper missile-tube doors open M.O.D., Bonn, 1982

Tarantul-I class 1979

D: 480 tons (540 fl) **S:** 36 kts **Dim:** 56.5 (52.5 wl) × 10.5 (9.4 wl) × 2.50
A: 4/SS-N-2C (II × 2)—1/76.2-mm DP—1/SA-N-5 system (IV × 1, . . . Grail missiles)—2/30-mm gatling AA (VI × 2)
Electron Equipt: Radar: 1/Kivach, 1/Bass Tilt, 1/Plank Shave targeting
EW: 4/passive arrays, 2/chaff RL (XVI × 2)
IFF: 1/High Pole, 1/Square Head
M: CODOG or COGOG: 2 NK-12M gas turbines (12,000 hp each), 2 cruise diesels or gas turbines; 2 props; 6,000–8,000 hp
Man: 38 tot. **Range:** 400/36; 2,000/20

REMARKS: Two prototype Tarantul-I retained for trials; others, all for export, have been built at Volodarskiy SY, Rybinsk. Tarantul-II is apparently intended as the successor to the Osa-series, although it is not being built in great numbers.

◆ **6 or 7 (+ . . .) Nanuchka-III class** Bldr: Petrovskiy SY, Leningrad, and Ulis SY, Vladivostok (In serv. 1977- . . .)

Nanuchka class—30-mm gatling gun, 76.2-mm DP aft U.S. Navy, 10-80

Nanuchka-III class—Band Stand on higher pilothouse than Nanuchka-I U.S. Navy, 5-84

D: 770 tons (fl) **S:** 32 kts **Dim:** 59.3 × 12.6 × 2.4
A: 6/SS-N-9 (III × 2)—1/SA-N-4 system (II × 1, 20 missiles)—1/76.2-mm DP—1/30-mm gatling AA (VI × 1) **Range:** 900/30; 2,500/12 (1 engine)
Electron Equipt: Radar: 1/Peel Pair, 1/Band Stand, 1/Bass Tilt
EW: 2/passive arrays, 2/chaff RL (XVI × 2)
IFF: 1/High Pole, 1/Square Head
M: 3 paired M504 diesels; 3 props; 30,000 hp **Man:** 60 tot.

REMARKS: Soviet type designation: MRK—*Malyy Raketnyy Korabl'* (Small Missile Ship). The single 76.2-mm DP was substituted for the twin 57-mm AA aft, the gatling gun is in the position occupied by Muff Cob in the Nanuchka-I, and Bass Tilt is situated atop a new deckhouse abaft the mast. The pilothouse is higher and the superstructure is enlarged. The 30-mm gatling gun is off centerline, to starboard.

◆ **17 Nanuchka-I class** Bldr: Petrovskiy SY, Leningrad (In serv. 1969-76)

BURUN	MOLNIYA	RADUGA	SHTORM	TSIKLON	ZYB'
GRAD	MUSSON	SHKVAL	TAYFUN	ZARNITSA	6 others

Nanuchka-I class—late version U.S. Navy, 5-83

Nanuchka-I class—early version with free-standing missile blast shields French Navy, 1982

D: 770 tons (fl) **S:** 32 kts **Dim:** 59.3 × 12.6 × 2.4
A: 6/SS-N-9 (II × 3)—1/SA-N-4 system (II × 1, 20 missiles)—2/57-mm DP (II × 1)
Electron Equipt: Radar: 1/Peel Pair, 1/Pop Group, 1/Muff Cob, 1/Band Stand
EW: 2/passive arrays, 2/chaff RL (XVI × 2)
IFF: 1/High Pole, 1/Square Head
M: 3 paired M504 diesels; 3 props; 30,000 hp
Range: 900/30; 2,500/12 (1 engine) **Man:** 60 tot.

REMARKS: Soviet type designation: MRK—*Malyy Raketnyy Korabl'* (Small Missile Ship). Named for meteorological phenomena; some of the names above may apply to the Nanuchka-III version. These are reported to be poor sea boats with very unreliable engines. Early units have separate blast shields abaft the SS-N-9 launchers; they have smaller engine air intakes and may employ paired M503 diesels for 24,000 hp total, 30

GUIDED-MISSILE CORVETTES *(continued)*

kts max. Band Stand is associated with target designation for the SS-N-9 missiles. New EW antennas are being added near the top of the mast. The similar Nanuchka-II for export has 4 SS-N-2C missiles.

CORVETTES

◆ **14 or more Pauk class** Bldr: . . . (In serv. 1980– . . .)

KOMSOMOLETS GRUZIN ODESSKIY KOMSOMOLETS 12+ others

Pauk class—KGB unit with low pilothouse U.S. Navy, 1985

Pauk class U.S. Navy, 1984

D: 480 tons (580 fl) **S:** 28-32 kts **Dim:** 58.5 × 9.4 × 2.5
A: 1/76.2-mm DP—1/SA-N-5 SAM syst. (IV × 1, . . . Grail missiles)—1/30-mm gatling AA—2/RBU-1200 ASW RL (V × 2)—4/400-mm ASW TT (I × 4)—2/d.c. racks (12 d.c.)
Electron Equipt: Radar: 1/Spin Trough, 1/air-surface search, 1/Bass Tilt
Sonar: 1/MF hull-mounted, 1/MF dipping
EW: . . . passive arrays; 2/chaff RL (XVI × 2)
M: 2 paired M504 diesels; 2 props; 20,000 hp **Man:** 40 tot.

REMARKS: Built in the Baltic and Pacific areas. Some appear to be operated by the KGB Maritime Border Guard. This class uses same hull as Tarantul-class missile corvette but has ASW armament vice SS-N-2C and an all-diesel propulsion plant vice Tarantul's COGOG/CODOG system. A large housing for a dipping sonar system projects 2 m out from the stern. A new variant noted in 1982 in the Baltic has the pilothouse one half-deck higher. Platforms on the mast are intended to carry EW arrays, while there is a backup optical director for the single gatling AA gun; Bass Tilt can control both the 76-mm and 30-mm guns. The main engines are probably the same twin diesels as used in the Nanuchka class. Probable Soviet designation MPK—*Malyy Protivolodochnyy Korabl'* (Small Antisubmarine Ship), and apparently intended to replace the Poti class

◆ **60 or fewer Poti class** Bldrs: Zelenodolsk SY, poss. others (In serv. 1961-67)

Poti class L. & L. Van Ginderen, 1984

D: 400 tons (fl) **S:** 38 kts **Dim:** 59.4 × 7.9 × 2.0 (hull)
A: 2/57-mm DP (II × 1)—2/RBU-6000 ASW RL (XII × 2)—2 or 4/400-mm TT (I × 2 or 4)
Electron Equipt: Radar: 1/Don-2, 1/Strut Curve, 1/Muff Cob
Sonar: 1/HF hull-mounted, 1/Hormone dipping
EW: 2/Watch Dog—IFF: 1/High Pole-B
M: CODAG: 2 M503A diesels (8,000 hp) + 2 gas turbines (40,000 hp); 2 props
Range: 500/37; 4,500/10 (1 diesel) **Man:** 40 tot.

REMARKS: Soviet type designation: MPK—*Malyy Protivolodochnyy Korabl'* (Small Antisubmarine Ship). Several have old-style open 57-mm AA mounts and two RBU-2500. This class has been exported to Romania and Bulgaria. The two propellers are mounted in thrust tubes of the same length as the poop, which contains the two turbines; the jets exhaust through ports in the stern and also power air compressors that exhaust into the propeller tubes, producing a thrust-jet effect. Slowly being stricken, as Pauk class enters service.

◆ **6 Ivan Susanin-class patrol icebreakers** Bldr: Admiralty SY, Leningrad (In serv. 1975-81)

AYSBERG IMENI XXV SEZDA K.P.S.S. NEVA
DUNAY IMENI XXVI SEZDA K.P.S.S. VOLGA

Imeni XXV Sezda K.P.S.S. 1977

D: 3,400 tons **S:** 14.5 kts **Dim:** 70.0 (62.0 pp) × 18.3 × 6.5
A: 2/76.2-mm DP (II × 1)—2/30-mm gatling AA (I × 2)
Electron Equipt: Radar: 2/Don-Kay, 1/Strut Curve, 1/Owl Screech
IFF: 1/High Pole-B
M: 3 Type 13D100 diesels, electric drive; 2 props; 5,400 hp **Fuel:** 550 tons
Electric: 1,000 kw **Range:** 5,500/12.5; 13,000/9.4 **Man:** 140 tot.

REMARKS: Operated by the KGB Maritime Border Guard in the Pacific area. KGB Type designator: *Pogranichnyy Storozhevoy Korabl'* (Border Patrol Ship). Two sisters, disarmed and painted with black hull and white superstructure, serve as naval auxiliaries: *Ivan Susanin* and *Ruslan.* Have a helicopter deck aft, but no hangar. The gatling AA guns have only lead-computing ringsight directors; Bass Tilt radar directors are not fitted. The Owl Screech radar director controls the 76.2-mm DP mount. *Dunay* and *Neva* also have two positions for hand-launching SA-N-5/SA-7 Grail missiles.

◆ **1 Purga-class patrol icebreaker** Bldr: . . . SY, Leningrad

N. . . (ex-*Purga*) (In serv. 1955)

The Purga-class icebreaker 1983

D: 4,500 tons (fl) **S:** 18 kts **Dim:** 97.5 × 15.2 × 6.4
A: 4/100-mm DP (I × 4)—mines
Electronic Equipt: Radar: 2/Don-2, 1/High Sieve, 1/Strut Curve, 1/Sun Visor-B
EW: 2/Watch Dog—IFF: 2/High Pole
M: 4 diesels; electric drive; 2 props; 8,000 hp **Man:** 250 tot.

REMARKS: Operated by the KGB Maritime Border Guard in the Pacific. Laid down prior to World War II and launched circa 1952. Has a Wasp Head stabilized optical GFCS, with Sun Visor radar. Formerly also carried 8/37-mm AA (II × 4). Riveted construction.

◆ **12 Sorum-class armed tugs** Bldr: Yaroslavl SY (In serv. 1974-)

AMUR KAMCHATKA PRIMORSK YAN BERZIN'
BREST KARELIYA PRIMORYE ZABAYKALYE
CHUKOTKA LADOGA SAKHALIN . . . (065)

CORVETTES *(continued)*

Sakhalin 1975

D: 1,210 tons (1,656 fl) **S:** 14 kts **Dim:** 58.3 × 12.6 × 4.6
A: 4/30-mm AK-230 AA (II × 2)
Electron Equipt: Radar: 2/Don-2—IFF: 1/High Pole-B
M: 2 Type 5-2D42 diesels, electric drive; 1 prop; 1,500 hp
Fuel: 322 tons **Range:** 6,720/13 **Man:** 35 tot.

Remarks: Armed units of a standard naval/commercial seagoing tug, used by KGB Maritime Border Guard for patrol duties. Typed PSKR—*Pogranichnyy Storozhevoy Korabl'* (Border Patrol Ship).

Note: Several Okhtenskiy-class seagoing tugs have also been employed by the KGB Maritime Border Guard, armed with a twin 57-mm gunmount. See later page, under tug version, for details.

◆ **7 T-58-class ex-minesweepers** (In serv. 1957-61)

Irkutskiy Komsomolets
Kaliningradskiy Komsomolets
Komsomolets Latviy
Malakhit
P. Vinogradev
Primorskiy Komsomolets
Sovetskiy Pogranichnik

T-58 class U.S. Navy, 4-83

D: 725 tons (860 fl) **S:** 18 kts **Dim:** 70.0 × 9.1 × 2.5
A: 4/57-mm AA (II × 2)—2/RBU-1200 ASW RL (V × 2)—2/d.c. racks—mines
Electron Equipt: Radar: 1/Spin Trough, 1/Don-2, 1/Muff Cob
Sonar: 1/HF hull mounted
EW: 2/Watch Dog
IFF: 2/Square Head, 1/High Pole-A
M: 2 diesels; 2 props; 4,000 hp **Range:** 2,500/13.5 **Man:** 60 tot.

Remarks: Reclassified SKR—*Storozhevoy Korabl'* (Patrol Ship) in 1978 and portable minesweeping gear offloaded. Some are operated by the KGB Maritime Border Guard as PSKR—*Pogranichnyy Storozhevoy Korabl'* (Border Patrol Ship). Most are in the Pacific Fleet. One has been transferred to Guinea, one to Yemen, and others have been converted as radar pickets, with a Big Net radar aft. (See below.)

◆ **3 T-58-class radar pickets, former minesweepers** (In serv. 1957-61)

T-58-class radar picket—former minesweeper U.S. Navy, 1981

T-58-class radar picket M.O.D., Bonn, 1981

D: 760 tons (880 fl) **S:** 17 kts **Dim:** 70.0 × 9.1 × 2.5
A: 2/57-mm AA (II × 1)—4/30-mm AA (II × 2)—2/SA-N-5 syst. (IV × 2, 16 SA-7 Grail missiles)—2/d.c. racks
Electron Equipt: Radar: 1/Spin Trough, 1/Strut Curve, 1/Big Net, 1/Muff Cob
Sonar: HF hull-mounted—EW: . . .
M: 2 diesels; 2 props; 4,000 hp **Range:** 2,500/13.5 **Man:** 100 tot.

Remarks: First unit conversion completed 1979 at Izhora SY, Leningrad, second in 1981, third around 1983-84. Considering the small number converted, the age of the hulls, and the pace of the program, these ships are probably intended for a specialized range security role, rather than as classical "radar pickets." Naval-operated.

Note: The few remaining T-43 radar picket-class former minesweepers are believed to have been discarded, as none has been sighted since 1976.

◆ **11 T-43 class ex-minesweepers** (In serv. 1947-57)

T-43-class Border Patrol Ship—60-meter version 1981

Remarks: Data as for minesweeper version on later page. Portable minesweeping gear deleted (winch and crane retained). Reclassified during 1970s when transferred to the KGB Maritime Border Guard as PKSR—*Pogranichnyy Storozhevoy Korabl'* (Border Patrol Ship). Operate in the Pacific area. A few have 2/45-mm AA vice 4/37-mm AA.

GUIDED-MISSILE PATROL BOATS

◆ **16 Matka-class semi-hydrofoils** Bldr: Izhora SY, Kolpino (In serv. 1978-81)

Matka class at speed, on foils, with Plank Shave targeting radar

GUIDED-MISSILE PATROL BOATS *(continued)*

Matka class hull-borne—note low freeboard 1979

D: 225 tons (260 fl) **S:** 40 kts **Dim:** 40.0 × 12.0 (7.6 hull) × 2.1 (hull; 3.2 foils)
A: 2/SS-N-2C (I × 2)—1/76.2-mm DP—1/30-mm gatling AA
Electron Equipt: Radar: 1/Cheese Cake, 1/Plank Shave, 1/Bass Tilt
EW: 2/chaff launchers (XVI × 2)
IFF: 1/High Pole-B, 1/Square Head
M: 3 M504 diesels; 3 props; 15,000 hp **Range:** 400/36; 650/25 **Man:** 30 tot.

Remarks: Essentially, a missile-armed version of the Turya-class hydrofoil torpedo boat, with larger superstructure, 76.2-mm gun forward, and missiles and gatling gun aft. Construction proceeded very slowly. Uses Plank Shave targeting radar, larger than Square Tie. Appears to be overloaded, and construction ceased in favor of the Tarantul-series.

◆ **1 Sarancha class** Bldr: Petrovskiy SY, Leningrad (In serv. 1977)

Sarancha class—note two steps to bottom of hydroplane hull

D: 320 tons (fl) **S:** 58 kts
Dim: 53.6 (50.6 foils down hull) × 31.3 (11.0 hull) × 7.3 (2.6 hull)
A: 4/SS-N-9 (II × 2)—1/SA-N-4 syst. (II × 1, 20 missiles)—1/30-mm gatling AA (VI × 1)
Electron Equipt: Radar: 1/Band Stand, 1/Pop Group, 1/Bass Tilt
IFF: 1/Square Head, 1/High Pole-B
M: 2 gas turbines; 4 props; 30,000 hp

Remarks: Too large and complex to be a successor to the Osa class. Essentially a reduced, high-speed Nanuchka. Folding-foil system, with 2 propellers on each of two pods on the after foils. Stepped hydroplane hull bottom. Not a success.

◆ **32 Osa-II class** (In serv. 1966-70)

Amurskiy Komsomolets, Brestskiy Komsomolets, Kaliningradskiy Komsomolets, Kirovskiy Komsomolets, Tambovskiy Komsomolets, 27 others

Osa-II class 1978

Osa-II class—with quadruple SA-N-5 Grail launcher abaft Drum Tilt 1976

D: 215 tons (245 fl) **S:** 35 kts **Dim:** 38.6 × 7.6 × 2.0
A: 4/SS-N-2B/C Styx (I × 4)—4/30-mm AA (II × 2)
Electron Equipt: Radar: 1/Square Tie, 1/Drum Tilt
IFF: 1/High Pole-B, 2/Square Head
M: 3 M504 diesels; 3 props; 15,000 hp **Range:** 500/34; 750/25 **Man:** 30 tot.

Remarks: Soviet type designation: RKA—*Raketnyy Kater* (Missile Cutter). Some units have been given SA-N-5 systems aft. Widely exported during 1970–present, primarily using new-built units. Some reports indicate that they are mediocre sea boats and that the engines (which have been replaced by Western diesels in many transferred units) are very temperamental. Numbers beginning to decline, through foreign transfer and attrition.

◆ **58 Osa-I class** Bldrs: Various (In serv. 1959-66)

Komsomolets Tatariy, Kronshtadtskiy Komsomolets, 56 others

Osa-I class—rib-sided SS-N-2 launchers 1974

Osa-I class—quadruple SA-N-5 launcher abaft Drum Tilt, smooth-sided launchers U.S. Navy, 5-84

D: 185 tons (215 fl) **S:** 36 kts **Dim:** 38.6 × 7.6 × 1.8
A: 4/SS-N-2 Styx (I × 4)—4/30-mm AA (II × 2)—1/SA-N-5 SAM syst. (IV × 1) in some
Electron Equipt: Radar: 1/Square Tie, 1/Drum Tilt
IFF: 1/High Pole-B, 2/Square Head
M: 3 M503A diesels; 3 props; 12,000 hp
Range: 500/34; 750/25 **Man:** 30 tot.

Remarks: Originally built by Petrovskiy SY, Leningrad, but other yards were also involved in the program. Soviet type designation: RKA—*Raketnyy Kater* (Missile Cutter). These small craft can launch their missiles in a Force-4 sea (2-m waves). Many of them have been transferred to other navies. Some have been built as, or converted to, targets. Stenka, Matka, Turya, and Mol (an export torpedo boat, see Somalia) all use Osa hulls and propulsion plants. Diminishing in numbers as some are now over 25 years old.

PATROL BOATS

◆ **4 (+ . . .) Muravey-class hydrofoils** Bldr: (In serv. 1982- . . .)

D: 230 tons (fl) **S:** . . . **Dim:** 38.6 × 7.6 × . . .
A: 1/76.2-mm DP—1/30-mm gatling AA—4/400-mm ASW TT

PATROL BOATS *(continued)*

Electron Equipt: Radar: . . .
Sonar: . . .
M: . . . **Range:** . . . **Man:** . . .

REMARKS: First reported 1983. No further data available. May be KGB Maritime Border Guard-subordinated.

◆ **1 Babochka class** Bldr: . . . (In serv. 1978)

Babochka class 1978

D: 400 tons (fl) **S:** 45 kts **Dim:** 50.0 × 13.0 (8.5 hull) × . . .
A: 8/400-mm ASW TT (IV × 2)—2/30-mm gatling AA (VI × 2)
Electron Equipt: Radar: 1/Don-2, 1/Peel Cone, 1/Bass Tilt
M: CODOG: 2 cruise diesels, 3 gas turbines; 3 props; 30,000 hp (max.)

REMARKS: A prototype ASW hydrofoil with fixed, fully submerged foils fore and aft. The torpedo tubes are mounted, two on two, on either side of the forecastle between the forward gatling gun and the superstructure.

◆ **1 Slepen class** Bldr: Petrovskiy SY, Leningrad (In serv. circa 1969)

D: 205 tons (230 fl) **S:** 36 kts **Dim:** 38.6 × 7.6 × 1.9
A: 1/76.2-mm DP—1/30-mm gatling gun
Electron Equipt: Radar: 1/Don-2, 1/Bass Tilt
EW: 2/passive arrays, 2/chaff RL (XVI × 2)
IFF: 1/High Pole-B, 2/Square Head
M: 3 M504 diesels; 3 props; 15,000 hp **Range:** 500/34; 750/25 **Man:** 30 tot.

REMARKS: Trials craft for systems for small combatants. Twin 57-mm AA replaced by single 76.2-mm DP forward in 1975. Resembles a Matka but does not have missiles or hydrofoils.

◆ **100 or more Stenka class** Bldrs: Petrovskiy SY, Leningrad; . . . (In serv. 1967- . . .)

Stenka class—with new navigational radar U.S. Navy, 11-84

Stenka—with Pot Drum nav. radar L. & L. Van Ginderen, 9-83

D: 170 tons (210 fl) **S:** 36 kts **Dim:** 39.5 × 7.6 × 1.8
A: 4/30-mm AA (II × 2)—4/400-mm ASW TT—2/d.c. racks (12 d.c.)
Electron Equipt: Radar: 1 Pot Drum or . . . , 1/Drum Tilt
Sonar: 1/Hormone-helicopter, dipping
IFF: 1/High Pole-B, 2/Square Head
M: 3 M503A diesels; 3 props; 12,000 hp **Range:** 550/34; 750/25 **Man:** 22 tot.

REMARKS: Soviet type designation: PSKR—*Pogranichnyy Storozhevoy Korabl'* (Border Patrol Ship). Recent units have a new navigational radar vice Pot Drum. Manned by the Maritime Border Guard of the KGB.

NOTE: All remaining S.O.-1-class ASW patrol boats are believed to have been stricken or transferred abroad.

HYDROFOIL TORPEDO BOATS

◆ **31 Turya class** Bldr: Ulis SY, Vladivostok; Srednyy Neva SY, Kolpino (In serv. 1974-79)

Turya class at speed, bow raised on foil

Turya class at low speed, in displacement condition G. Koop, 1984

D: 215 tons (250 fl) **S:** 40 kts
Dim: 39.0 × 7.6 (12.5 over foils) × 2.0 (4.0 over foils)
A: 2/57-mm AA aft (II × 1)—2/25-mm AA (II × 1)—4/533-mm TT (I × 4)
Electron Equipt: Radar: 1/Pot Drum, 1/Muff Cob
Sonar: 1/Hormone-helicopter, dipping
IFF: 1/High Pole-B, 1/Square Head
M: 3 M504 diesels; 3 props; 15,000 hp **Range:** 400/38; 650/25 **Man:** 24 tot.

REMARKS: Fixed hydrofoils forward only; stern planes on water surface. Has Osa-II hull and propulsion. The dipping sonar is housed in a sponson over the starboard quarter. Nine of this class, without dipping sonar, have been delivered to Cuba since 1-79, and others have been exported to Vietnam and Kampuchea.

NOTE: The remaining Shershen-class torpedo boats are believed to have been stricken or transferred abroad.

PATROL CRAFT

◆ **30 or more Zhuk class** Bldr: . . . (In serv. 1975- . . .)

Zhuk class—export version (for the Seychelles), with 4/14.5-mm mg (II × 2)
French Navy, 1983

PATROL CRAFT *(continued)*

D: 48 tons (60 fl) **S:** 34 kts **Dim:** 24.0 × 5.0 × 1.2 (1.8 props)
A: 2/14.5-mm mg (II × 1) **Electron Equipt:** Radar: 1/Spin Trough
M: 2 M50 F-4 diesels; 2 props; 2,400 hp **Fuel:** 10 tons
Range: 700/28; 1,100/15 **Man:** 12 tot.

Remarks: Probably manned by the KGB Border Guard. A large number have been exported, armed with a side-by-side turretted gunmount, as shown in the photo; Soviet units have one (or occasionally two) over-and-under gunmounts.

Note: All units of the Pchela hydrofoil patrol craft class and all Poluchat-I-class patrol craft are believed to have been stricken.

RIVERINE CRAFT

Note: The U.S.S.R. maintains a number of river gunboats on the Lower Danube, on the Amur and Ussuri river systems in the Far East, and possibly elsewhere. In addition to gunboats, the riverine forces have a few support craft, including the administrative craft SSV-10 (ex-PS 10) on the Danube (360 tons, 49 m overall).

SSV-10 (former number)—flagship of the Danube Flotilla, with two 45-mm saluting cannon abreast stack 1972

◆ **15 (+ . . .) Yaz class monitors** Bldr: . . . (In serv. 1981- . . .)

Yaz class

D: Approx. 400 tons (fl) **S:** 14–16 kts **Dim:** 60.0 × . . . × . . .
A: 2/100–120-mm tank guns (I × 2)—2/30-mm gatling AA (I × 2)— . . .
Electron Equipt: Radar: 1/Spin Trough or Kivach, 1/Bass Tilt
M: Diesels; 2 props; . . . hp **Man:** . . .

Remarks: Low-freeboard monitors for the Amur River Flotilla. Also reported in service are 2 Pivyaka-class river monitors and several Vosh-class; no data available.

◆ **81 Shmel-class patrol gunboats** Bldr: . . . (In serv. 1967-74)

Shmel class—RL, armored 25-mm mount aft 4-80

D: 60 tons (fl) **S:** 22 kts **Dim:** 28.3 × 4.6 × 0.9
A: 1/76.2-mm, 48 cal., fwd in a tank turret—2/25-mm AA (II × 1) aft—5/7.62-mm mg (I × 5)—1/122-mm RL (XVIII × 1)—mines
M: 2 M50F-4 diesels; 2 props; 2,400 hp **Range:** 240/20; 600/10 **Man:** 15 tot.

Remarks: Soviet type designation: AKA—*Artilleriyskiy Kater* (Artillery Cutter). Not all these craft have a rocket launcher. An earlier version has a twin machine-gun mount aft that resembles a tank turret. One 7.62-mm is mounted coaxially with the 85-mm gun; the others fire through slits in the sides of the open-topped redoubt forward of the artillery RL. Four transferred to Kampuchea, 1984-85.

MINE WARFARE SHIPS

◆ **3 Alesha-class minelayers** Bldr: . . . (In serv. 1967-69)

Pripet' Vychegda N . . .

Vychegda—the first Alesha 1969

Vychegda JMSDF, 10-85

D: 2,900 tons (3,500 fl) **S:** 17 kts **Dim:** 97.0 × 14.0 × 5.4
A: 4/57-mm (IV × 1)—300 mines
Electron Equipt: Radar: 1/Don-2, 1/Strut Curve, 1/Muff Cob
IFF: 1/High Pole-B
M: 4 diesels; 2 props; 8,000 hp **Range:** 4,000/16; 8,500/8 **Man:** 190 tot.

Remarks: Can also be used as netlayers, minesweeper tenders, and command ships. The second and third ships had two kingposts and booms vice the forward crane.

◆ **1 Natya-II-class fleet minesweeper** Bldr: Sredniy Neva SY, Kolpino (In serv. 1982)

◆ **35 Natya-I-class fleet minesweepers** Bldr: Various (In serv. 1970-1982)

Admiral Pershin	Mashinist	Signal'shchik
Dizelist	Miner	Snayper
Elektrik	Motorist	Turbinist
Kontradmiral Horoshkin	Pulemetchik	Vsevolod Vishnevskiy
Kurskiy Komsomolets (ex-*Navodchik*)	Radist	Zenitchik
	Rulevoy	19 others

Natya class—early unit with gooseneck sweep gear davits U.S. Navy, 8-83

MINE WARFARE SHIPS *(continued)*

Natya-II class—note deckhouse on stern, no 25-mm AA or ASW RL 5-82

Natya-I class—with 2 SA-N-5 systems on superstructure abaft mast, articulated sweep-gear davits U.S. Navy, 10-83

D: 650 tons (750 fl) **S:** 18 kts **Dim:** 61.0 × 9.8 × 3.0
A: 4/30-mm AA (II × 2)—4/25-mm AA (II × 2)—2/RBU-1200 ASW RL (V × 2)—mines
Electron Equipt: Radar: 1/Don-2, 1/Drum Tilt
Sonar: 1/HF
IFF: 1/High Pole-B, 2/Square Head
M: 2 diesels; 2 props; 5,000 hp **Range:** 1,800/16; 5,200/10 **Man:** 60 tot.

Remarks: Soviet type designation: MT—*Morskoy Tral'shchik* (Seagoing Minesweeper). Equipped to serve as ASW escorts. Early units have rigid davits aft; on later units they are articulated. Stem cut back sharply below waterline, as in T-43 and Yurka classes. Aluminum alloy hull. One, designated Natya-II and completed 1982, has a long deckhouse aft, no 25-mm AA or RBU-2500, but does have 2/SA-N-5 systems (IV × 2, 16 SA-7 Grail missiles). Two such SA-N-5 systems have been added to a number of units of the class, just abaft the lattice mast. Some also have an extra navigational radar atop the pilothouse. Current production is for export, with one unit delivered to Syria with no ASW ordnance or minesweeping gear in 1985. Six have been built for India and seven for Libya.

◆ **41 Yurka-class fleet minesweepers** Bldr: . . .

Gafel'
Komsomolets Byelorussiy
Semen Roshal'
Yevgeniy Nikonov
37 others

D: 400 tons (460 fl) **S:** 16 kts **Dim:** 52.0 × 9.3 × 2.0
A: 4/30-mm AA (II × 2)—20 mines
Electron Equipt: Radar: 1 or 2 Don-2, 1/Drum Tilt
Sonar: H/F hull-mounted
IFF: 1/High Pole-B, 2–3/Square Head
M: 2 diesels; 2 props; 4,000 hp **Range:** 2,000/14; 3,200/10
Man: 45-50 tot.

Remarks: Soviet type designation: MT—*Morskoy Tral'shchik* (Seagoing Minesweeper). Aluminum-alloy hull. Four transferred to Egypt in 1969, one to Vietnam in 1979. Several have received 2 SA-N-5 SAM systems (IV × 2, 16 SA-7 Grail missiles).

Yurka class

Yurka with two SA-N-5 launchers, 2 Don-2 radars 9-83

◆ **about 30 T-43-class fleet minesweepers** Bldr: . . . (In serv. 1947-57)

Astrakhanskiy Komsomolets
Ivan Fioletov
Kontradmiral Yurokovskiy
Komsomolets Kalmykiy
Lamine Sadjikaba
Mezhadiy Azizbakov
Nikolay Markin
Sakhalinskiy Komsomolets
Stephan Saumyan

T-43 class—long-hull version 1975

T-43 class—short-hull version 1978

D: 500 tons (590 fl) **S:** 14 kts **Dim:** 60.0 × 8.6 × 2.3
A: 4/37-mm AA (II × 2)—0 or 4/25-mm AA (II × 2)—2/d.c. projectors—mines
Electron Equipt: Radar: 1/Don-2 or Spin Trough, 1/Ball End
Sonar: 1/Tamir-11 (H/F)
IFF: 1/Square Head, 1/High Pole-A
M: 2 Type 9D diesels; 2 props; 2,200 hp **Electric:** 550 kw
Fuel: 70 tons **Range:** 3,200/10 **Man:** 65 tot.

Remarks: Soviet type designation: MT—*Morskoy Tral'shchik* (Seagoing Minesweeper). Many of the T-43 class have been transferred to Poland, Egypt, Algeria, China, etc. The version armed with four 25-mm AA amidships is 60 m long and displaces 590 tons (fl); early units were 58.0 m long, had less hull flare at the stern, and

MINE WARFARE SHIPS *(continued)*

displaced 569 tons (fl). Also built on the T-43 hull were radar pickets, noise-measurement ships, diving tenders, and trials ships. Well over 200 were built. Rapidly being disposed of, with many of the survivors probably in reserve. Eleven are operated by the KGB Border Guard as patrol ships, with sweep gear removed (see under Corvettes).

◆ **45 Sonya-class coastal minesweepers** Bldr: Petrozavodsk SY; Ulis SY, Vladivostok (In serv. 1973- . . .)

Kolomenskiy Komsomolets	Orenburgskiy Komsomolets	41 others
Komsomolets Kirgiziy	Sevastopol'skiy Komsomolets (ex-*Komsomol'skiy Telegraf*)	

Sonya class U.S. Navy, 11-84

Sonya class 1976

D: 380 tons (450 fl) **S:** 15 kts **Dim:** 48.8 × 8.8 × 2.1
A: 2/30-mm AA (II × 1)—2/25-mm AA (II × 1)
Electron Equipt: Radar: 1/Spin Trough
IFF: 1/High Pole-B, 2/Square Head
M: 2 diesels; 2 props; 2,400 hp **Range:** ·1,600/14; 3,000/10 **Man:** 40 tot.

Remarks: Soviet type designation: BT—*Basovyy Tral'shchick* (Base Minesweeper). Wooden hull with plastic sheathing. Two transferred to Cuba, 1980, and two in 1985. Several have received one SA-N-5 SAM system, abaft the boat, to starboard.

◆ **3 Zhenya-class coastal minesweepers** Bldr: . . . (In serv. 1967-1972)

Zhenya class 1974

D: 220 tons (300 fl) **S:** 16 kts **Dim:** 42.4 × 7.9 × 1.8
A: 2/30-mm AA (II × 1) **Electron Equipt:** Radar: 1/Spin Trough
M: 2 diesels; 1 props; 2,400 hp **Range:** 1,400/14 **Man:** 40 tot.

Remarks: Soviet type designation: BT—*Basovyy Tral'shchik* (Base Minesweeper). Glass-reinforced plastic hull. Apparently not successful, as the similar, but larger, wooden-hulled Sonya class went into production instead.

◆ **70 Vanya-class coastal minesweepers** Bldr: . . . (In serv. 1961-73)

Vanya class JMSDF, 1984

D: 200 tons (245 fl) **S:** 14 kts **Dim:** 40.2 × 7.9 × 1.7
A: 2/30-mm AA (II × 1)
Electron Equipt: Radar: 1/Don-2
IFF: 1/High Pole-B, 1/Dead Duck
M: 2 diesels; 2 props; 2,200 hp **Range:** 1,400/14; 2,400/10 **Man:** 30 tot.

Remarks: Soviet type designation: BT—*Basovyy Tral'shchik* (Base Minesweeper). Wooden construction. At least one was built or has been converted as a minehunter, armed with two 25-mm AA (II × 1)—more accurate than 30-mm for mine-disposal—and with one Don-Kay in place of Don-2; has two boats in davits on the fantail. The last half-dozen or so built, classed Vanya-II, are one meter longer, have a larger diesel generator exhaust pipe amidships, and have heavier davits at the stern.

Note: All units of the Sasha-class coastal minesweeper design are believed to have been stricken.

◆ **45 Yevgenya-class inshore minesweepers** Bldr: Svedniy Neva SY, Kolpino (In serv. 1970- . . .)

Yevgenya class M.O.D., Bonn, 1982

D: 80 tons (90 fl) **S:** 11 kts **Dim:** 26.2 × 6.1 × 1.5
A: 2/14.5-mm mg (II × 1) **M:** 2 diesels; 2 props; 600 hp
Electron Equipt: Radar: 1/Spin Trough—IFF: 1/High Pole-B
Range: 300/10 **Man:** 10 tot.

Remarks: Glass-reinforced plastic hull. More built for export than retained by Soviet Navy. Some foreign ships have two 25-mm AA (II × 1). Employs a television minehunting system that dispenses marker buoys to permit later disposal of mines useful to 30-m depths.

◆ **2 Andryusha-class special minesweepers** Bldr: . . . (In serv. 1975-76)

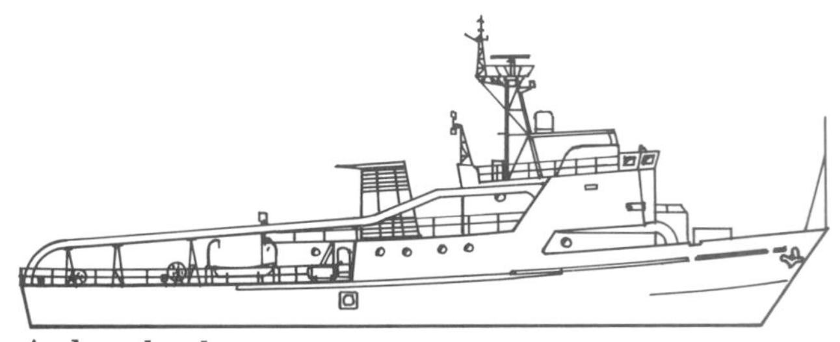

Andryusha class

D: 320 tons (360 fl) **S:** 15 kts **Dim:** 47.8 × 8.5 × 3.0 **A:** None
Electron Equipt: Radar: 1/Spin Trough—IFF: 1/High Pole-B
M: 2 diesels; 2 props; 2,200 hp **Man:** 40 tot.

MINE WARFARE SHIPS *(continued)*

Remarks: Wooden or plastic hulls. Large cable ducts running down both sides indicate probable role in sweeping magnetic mines. Prominent stack for gas-turbine generator; diesel engines exhaust through hull sides. No armament.

◆ **4 Olya-class minesweeping boats** Bldr: . . . (In serv. 1976-)

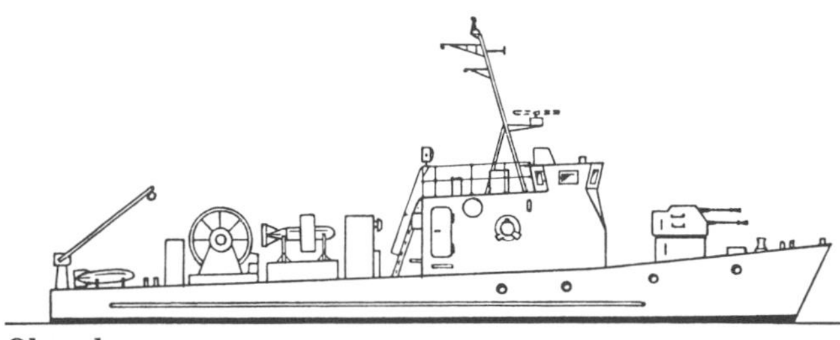

Olya class

D: 44 tons (50 fl) **S:** 18 kts **Dim:** 24.6 × 4.2 × 1.0
A: 2/25-mm AA **Electron Equipt:** Radar: 1/Spin Trough
M: 2 diesels; 2 props; 600 hp **Range:** 500/10 **Man:** 15 tot.

◆ **11 Ilyusha-class minesweeping drones** (In serv. 1970- . . .)

Ilyusha class 1977

D: 80 tons (85 fl) **S:** 12 kts **Dim:** 26.2 × 5.8 × 1.5 **A:** None
Electron Equipt: Radar: 1/Spin Trough—IFF: 1/High Pole-B
M: 1 diesel; 450 hp **Man:** 10 tot.

Remarks: Apparently radio-controlled while operating, but can be manned for transit. Stream sweep arrays through five chocks over stern; may be line-charge mine-disposal laying systems.

◆ **26 K-8-class minesweeping boats** Bldr: Polnocny SY, Gdansk, Poland (In serv. 1954-59)

K-8 class

D: 19.4 tons (26 fl) **S:** 12 kts **Dim:** 16.9 × 3.2 × 0.8
A: 2/14.5-mm mg (II × 1) **Electron Equipt:** None
M: 2 3D6 diesels; 2 props; 300 hp **Range:** 300/9 **Man:** 6 tot.

Remarks: Wooden construction. Tow, but do not carry, wire sweep or self-powered solonoid arrays. Long overdue for replacement.

◆ **25 Polish TR-40-class river minesweepers** Bldr: . . . SY, Poland (1950s)

D: 50 tons (70 fl) **S:** 16 kts **Dim:** 28.0 × 4.1 × 0.70
A: 2/25-mm AA (II × 1)—2/14.5-mm mg (II × 1)—mines
Electron Equipt: Radar: none—IFF: 1/High Pole-A
M: 2 diesels; 2 props; 600 hp **Man:** 16 tot.

Remarks: Wooden construction. Overdue for replacement.

◆ **1 or more Baltika-class auxiliary minesweepers**

Bldr: Leninskaya Kuznitsa SY, Kiev (In serv. 1978- . . .)

D: 210 tons (fl) **S:** 9.5 kts **Dim:** 25.30 (22.00 pp) × 6.80 × 2.45
A: None **Electron Equipt:** Radar: 1/Navigational **Range:** 2,200/9.5
M: 1 ChISP 18/22 diesel; 1 CP prop; 300 hp **Electric:** 25 kw **Man:** 5–10

Remarks: 108 grt/145 nrt. A small stern-haul purse-seiner fishing boat acquired circa 1980-81, apparently for testing the feasibility for rapid conversion of the several hundred civil craft of this class to simple wire-sweep minesweepers in time of war.

◆ **several dozen non-self-propelled mine countermeasures craft**

Towed mine countermeasures craft 1977

Remarks: Apparently a towed equivalent to the Ilyusha class, with an internal cable reel and winch to deploy magnetic sweep arrays or explosive line-charge arrays. Helicopters tow a modified "Volga"-class sports hydrofoil, equipped with noise and electric field generators.

Note: Several Polnocny-class landing ships are equipped to deploy a pair of remote-controlled motor boats that tow line-charge cable to destroy or countermine shallow-water beach obstacle mines; see under amphibious warfare entries.

AMPHIBIOUS WARFARE SHIPS

◆ **2 Ivan Rogov-class landing ships** Bldr: Kaliningrad SY

	L	In serv.
Ivan Rogov	1976	1978
Aleksandr Nikolayev	. . .	11-82

D: 11,000 tons (13,000 fl) **S:** 23 kts **Dim:** 158.0 × 24.0 × 8.2
A: 1/SA-N-4 SAM syst. (II × 1, 20 missiles)—2/76.2-mm DP (II × 1)—*A. Nikolayev* only: 2/SA-N-5 SAM syst. (IV × 2; . . . Grail missiles)—4/30-mm gatling AA (VI × 4)—1/122-mm automatic bombardment RL (XL × 1) for BM-21 rockets—4/Hormone-C or Helix helicopters—3/Lebed air-cushion landing craft

Ivan Rogov—note helo spots, staggered stack locations

Ivan Rogov French Navy, 1979

AMPHIBIOUS WARFARE SHIPS *(continued)*

Aleksandr Nikolayev—vehicles on forward helicopter deck *Ships of the World,* 1-85

Electron Equipt: Radar: 2/Don-Kay (*A. Nikolayev:* Palm Frond), 1/Head Net-C, 1/Owl Screech, 1/Pop Group, 2/Bass Tilt
EW: 2 (*A. Nikolayev:* 3)/Bell Shroud, 2/Bell Squat
IFF: High Pole-B (*A. Nikolayev:* Salt Pot B)

M: 2 gas turbines; 2 props; 50,000 hp

Range: 8,000/20; 12,500/14 **Man:** 200 crew + 550 troops

Remarks: Soviet type designation: BDK—*Bol'shoy Desantnyy Korabl'* (Large Landing Ship). The second unit apparently suffered construction delays. Equipped with bow doors and articulating ramp leading to a vehicle cargo deck in the forward part of the hull, while a stern door provides access to a floodable docking well intended to accommodate up to 3 Lebed air-cushion landing craft or 6 Ondatra-class landing craft. The massive superstructure incorporates a helicopter hangar, with a steep ramp leading downward to a helicopter pad on the foredeck, and doors aft leading to a second helicopter platform over the stern. There are also hydraulically raised ramps leading from the upper deck forward of the superstructure to both the bow doors and the docking well. Capable of transporting an entire naval infantry battalion and its vehicles, including 10 tanks, 30 armored personnel carriers, and trucks. The ability to use helicopters, to beach, and to deploy air-cushion vehicles gives a versatility unmatched by any other amphibious-warfare ship; this is combined with an organic shore-fire-bombardment capability and very extensive command, control, and surveillance facilities. The hull has a pronounced bulb, or beak, projecting forward below the waterline. During 1982-83, both were in the Baltic, with *A. Nikolayev* deploying to the Pacific late 1983. Both have a Squeeze Box optronic device atop the bridge.

◆ **17 Ropucha-class tank landing ships** Bldr: Polnocny SY, Gdansk, Poland (In serv. 1975-78, 1982-84)

Ropucha class—showing stern door French Navy, 9-82

Ropucha class—late version, with curved hances to first superstructure deck; note saluting cannon on deck, abaft empty rocket launcher pedestals. 24 Flot., French Navy, 7-84

AMPHIBIOUS WARFARE SHIPS *(continued)*

Ropucha class U.S. Navy, 5-82

D: 2,200 tons (3,200 fl) **S:** 18 kts **Dim:** 113.0 × 14.0 × 2.9 (aft)
A: 4/57-mm AA (II × 2)—some: 4/SA-N-5 syst. (IV × 4; 32 SA-7 Grail Missiles)
Electron Equipt: Radar: 1/Don-2, 1/Strut Curve, 1/Muff Cob
IFF: 1/High Pole-B
M: 2 diesels; 2 props; 10,000 hp **Range:** 3,500/16
Man: 70 crew + 230 troops

REMARKS: Soviet type designation: BDK—*Bol'shoy Desantnyy Korabl'* (Large Landing Ship). Bow and stern doors permit roll-on/roll-off loading. Cargo capacity: 450 tons; usable deck space: 600 m². The later units have angled hances to the corners of the main-deck superstructure and reinforcing gussets around the forward 57-mm AA platform. Several have received 4/SA-N-5 quadruple launchers for Grail SAMs. Although the class was intended to receive two barrage rocket launchers on the forecastle, none have been installed. One unit was transferred to the People's Democratic Republic of Yemen in 1979. A second series of six identical in nearly all respects to later units of the first, was completed in 1982-84.

◆ **14 Alligator-class tank landing ships** Bldr: Kaliningrad SY (In serv. 1964-77)

ALEKSANDR TORTSEV* | KRYMSKIY KOMSOMOLETS* | SERGEI LAZO
DONETSKIY SHAKHTER* | NIKOLAY FIL'CHENKOV* | TOMSKIY KOMSOMOLETS
ILYA AZAROV* | NIKOLAY VILKOV* | VORONEZHSKIY KOMSOMOLETS
KOMSOMOLETS KARELIYY | NIKOLAY OBYEKOV | 50 LET SHEFSTVA V.L.K.S.M.*
KRASNAYA PRESNYA* | PETR IL'ICHYEV*

D: 3,400 tons (4,700 fl) **S:** 18 kts **Dim:** 112.8 × 15.3 × 4.4 (aft)
A: 2/57-mm AA (II × 1—*N. Fil'chenkov, N. Vilkov* also: 4/25-mm AA (II × 2)—starred units: 1/BM-21, 122-mm RL (XL × 1)
Electron Equipt: Radar: 2/Don-2 and/or Spin Trough
IFF: 1/High Pole-B
M: 2 diesels; 8,000 hp **Range:** 9,000/16; 14,000/10
Man: 75 crew + 300 troops

REMARKS: Soviet type designation: BDK—*Bol'shoy Desantnyy Korabl'* (Large Landing Ship). The design evolved continually during the time these ships were built. They have ramps fore and aft. Their hoisting equipment varies (one or two 5-ton cranes, one 15-ton crane), as does their armament: later ships also have a BM-21, 40-tubed, 140-mm rocket launcher forward for shore bombardment, the last two have four 25-mm AA (II × 2) aft, and some are equipped with 3/SA-N-5 launchers for SA-7 Grail (IV × 3). Cargo capacity is about 600 tons for beaching, twice that in freighting service; can carry about two dozen tanks, plus lighter vehicles on upper decks.

Alligator class—late unit with 122-m rocket launcher forward, 3/SA-N-5 launchers French Navy, 4-83

Voronezhskiy Komsomolets—early unit updated with SA-N-5 U.S. Navy, 2-84

Soviet 140-mm barrage rocket launcher with two clusters of 20 rocket tubes loaded; empty tubes are discarded and two new sets automatically reloaded from below after firing 1981

◆ **40 Polnocny-class medium landing ships** Bldr: Polnocny SY, Gdansk, Poland (In serv. 1961-73)

7 A version:

Polnocny-A—with original low bridge troughs down sides of hull, davits for line-charge towing boats are mounted before the bridge 1977

Polnocny-A—with four SA-N-5 quadruple launchers 1977

AMPHIBIOUS WARFARE SHIPS *(continued)*

D: 770 tons (fl) **S:** 19 kts **Dim:** 73.0 × 8.6 × 1.9 (aft)
A: 2/14.5-mm mg (II × 1) or 2/30-mm AA (II × 1) or none—2/140-mm barrage RL (XVIII × 2)—0–2 or 4/SA-N-5 systems (IV × 0, 2, 4; up to 32 SA-7 Grail)
Electron Equipt: Radar: 1/Spin Trough
IFF: 1/High Pole-A; Some: 1/Square Head
M: 2 diesels; 2 props; 5,000 hp **Range:** 900/18; 1,500/14 **Man:** 35 tot.

24 B version:

Polnocny-B—with high stack and 30-mm AA aft, 4/SA-N-5 launchers 1977

Polnocny-B class—with 4/SA-N-5 systems, no 30-mm aft U.S. Navy, 8-83

Polnocny-B—with side troughs for line charges and two chutes at the stern for launching the tow boats; unit also has four SA-N-5 launchers JMSDF, 8-84

D: 800 tons (fl) **S:** 18 kts **Dim:** 74.0 × 8.6 × 2.0
A: 2 or 4/30-mm AA—2/140-mm barrage RL (XVIII × 2)—4/SA-N-5 systems (IV × 4; 32 SA-7 Grail)
Electron Equipt: Radar: 1/Spin Trough, 1/Drum Tilt
IFF: 1/Square Head, 1/High Pole-B
M: 2 diesels; 2 props; 5,000 hp **Range:** 900/18; 1,500/14
Man: 40 crew + 100 troops

9 C version:

D: 1,150 tons (fl) **S:** 18 kts **Dim:** 81.3 × 10.1 × 2.1
A: 4/30-mm AA (II × 2)—2/140-mm barrage RL (XVIII × 2)—4/SA-N-5 systems (IV × 2, 32 SA-7 Grail missiles)
Electron Equipt: Radar: 1/Spin Trough, 1/Drum Tilt
IFF: 1/Square Head, 1/High Pole-B
M: 2 diesels; 2 props; 5,000 hp **Range:** 1,800/18; 3,000/14
Man: 40 crew, plus 180 troops

Remarks: Soviet type designation: SDK—*Srednyy Desantnyy Korabl'* (Medium Landing Ship). Most have now been equipped with two or four SA-N-5 systems. The Polnocny-Bs that have 30-mm aft have heightened stacks. This class delivered to India, Iraq, Indonesia, Egypt, Angola, etc. Cargo: about 180 tons in A and B, 250 tons in C. "Trough unit" Polnocny-A and -B are line-charge layers for beach-defense minefield clearance; they carry two small remote-controlled motor boats to tow the line charges. "A" version has convex bow form; "B" has concave bow-flare; "C" is longer and has additional accommodations. Numbers of "A"-version declining through strikings, while "B"s continue to be transferred to Soviet clients.

Polnocny-C—longer hull and superstructure French Navy, 10-83

AMPHIBIOUS LANDING CRAFT

◆ **16 Vydra-class utility landing craft** Bldr: U.S.S.R. (In serv. 1967-69)

Vydra class

D: 425 tons (600 fl) **S:** 12 kts **Dim:** 54.9 × 7.6 × 2.0 **A:** None
Electron Equipt: Radar: 1/Spin Trough
IFF: 1/High Pole
M: 2 diesels; 2 props; 800 hp **Range:** 1,900/11.9; 2,700/10
Man: 20 crew, plus 100 troops

◆ **1 (+ . . .) Tsaplya-class air-cushion landing craft** Bldr: . . . (In serv. 1982- . . .)

D: 90 tons (fl) **S:** . . . **Dim:** . . . × . . . × . . .
A: . . . **M:** . . .

Remarks: Class reportedly can carry one amphibious tank plus 80 troops, or 160 troops, or 25 tons of stores. Appears to be a Lebed successor.

◆ **2 (+ . . .) Utenok-class air-cushion vehicles** Bldr: Feodosiya SY (In serv. 1982- . . .)

D: . . . **S:** . . . **Dim:** 26.3 × 13.0 × . . .
A: 4/30-mm AA (II × 2) **M:** . . .

Remarks: Can carry one 45-ton T-72/T-80 tank.

◆ **20 Lebed-class surface-effects landing craft** Bldr: . . .

Lebed class M.O.D., Bonn, 1982

AMPHIBIOUS LANDING CRAFT *(continued)*

Lebed class

D: 85 tons (fl) **S:** 70 kts **Dim:** 24.8 × 10.8 × . . .
A: 2/14.5-mm mg (II × 1) **M:** 3 gas turbines; 2 props **Range:** 100/65; 250/60

REMARKS: Broad bow ramp, ducted props, control cab to starboard, gunmount atop. Can carry one or two PT-76 light tanks or 120 troops or about 45 tons of cargo.

◆ **17 Aist-class surface-effects landing craft** Bldr: Dekabristov SY, Leningrad (In serv. 1971- . . .)

Aist class—on cushion 1978

Aist class—at rest M.O.D., Bonn

D: 250 tons (fl) **S:** 80 kts **Dim:** 47.3 × 17.4 × 0.3
A: 4/30-mm AA (II × 2)
Electron Equipt: Radar: 1/Spin Trough, 1/Drum Tilt
IFF: 1/High Pole-B, 1/Square Head
M: 2 gas turbines; 4 props; 2 lift fans **Range:** 100/65; 350/60

REMARKS: Can carry four PT-76 light tanks or one medium tank and 220 troops. Recent units carry 2/SA-N-5 SAM syst. (IV × 2) and chaff RL (XVI × 2)

◆ **30 Gus-class surface-effects landing craft** (In serv. 1970-74)

Gus class 1970

D: 27.2 tons (fl) **S:** 60 kts **Dim:** 21.3 × 7.1 × 0.2
A: None **M:** 3 gas turbines; 2 props; 1 lift fan; 2,340 hp
Range: 185/50; 200/43

REMARKS: Can carry twenty-four troops. A training version with two pilot positions is also in service.

◆ **16 (+ . . .) Ondatra-class landing craft** (In serv. 1978- . . .)

Ondatra class

D: 90 tons (140 fl) **S:** 10 kts **Dim:** 24.2 × 6.0 × 1.5
A: None **M:** 2 diesels; 2 props; 600 hp **Man:** 4 tot.

REMARKS: Apparently intended as successor to the T-4 class. One carried by *Ivan Rogov* as a tug for Lebed-class air-cushion vehicles. In lieu of Lebed, *Rogov* can carry 6 Ondatra. Cargo well is 15-m × 3.8-m.

◆ **. . . T-4-class landing craft** (In serv. 1954-74)

T-4 class—later, deep-bowed version

D: 70 tons (fl) **S:** 10 kts **Dim:** 19.0 × 4.3 × 1.0
M: 2 diesels; 2 props; 600 hp **Man:** 5 tot.

REMARKS: Built in two versions; later variant with deeper bow could accommodate a medium tank.

SUBMARINE TENDERS

◆ **6 Ugra-class command tenders** Bldr: Black Sea SY, Nikolayev (In serv. 1963-72)

IVAN KOLYSHKIN	IVAN VAKHRAMEEV	VOLGA
IVAN KUCHERENKO	TOBOL	N. . . . . . .

D: 6,750 tons (9,600 fl) **S:** 17 kts **Dim:** 145.0 × 17.7 × 6.4
A: 8/57-mm AA (II × 4)
Electron Equipt: Radar: 1–3 Don-2, 1/Strut Curve, 2/Muff Cob
EW: 4/Watch Dog
IFF: 1/High Pole-B, 1/High Pole-A, 2/Square Head
M: 4 diesels; 2 props; 8,000 hp **Range:** 21,000/10 **Man:** 450 tot.

Ivan Kolyshkin—helicopter hangar aft 1978

SUBMARINE TENDERS *(continued)*

The unnamed Ugra—with 2/SA-N-5 launchers before the stack French Navy, 1-83

Remarks: Soviet type designation: PB—*Plavuchaya Baza* (Floating Base). One modified version was built for India, as *Amba.* The *Ivan Kolyshkin* has a tall helicopter hangar. *Ivan Kucharenko* and *Volga* have a Vee Cone HF communications antenna. Can support eight to twelve submarines at sea with supplies, fuel, provisions, water, and spare torpedoes and can offer repair services. Being backfitted with 2/SA-N-5 syst. (IV × 2, SA-7 Grail missiles). This class and the Don class are frequently used as flagships. One 10-ton and two 6-ton cranes are fitted. Sisters *Gangut* and *Borodino* are configured as training ships for naval officer cadets and do not serve submarines—see Training Ships.

◆ **6 Don-class command tenders** Bldr: Black Sea SY, Nikolayev (In serv. 1958-61)

Dmitriy Galkin, Kamchatskiy Komsomolets, Magomed Gadziev, Fyodor Vidyaev, Magadanskiy Komsomolets, Viktor Kotel'nikov

D: 6,730 tons (9,000 fl) **S:** 17 kts **Dim:** 140.0 × 17.7 × 6.4
A: 4/100-mm AA (I × 4)—4/57-mm AA (II × 2)—see Remarks
Electron Equipt: Radar: 1-2/Don-2, 1/Slim Net, 1/Sun Visor, 2/Hawk Screech—see Remarks
EW: 2/Watch Dog
IFF: 1/High Pole-B, 2/Square Head
M: 4 diesels; 2 props; 8,000 hp **Range:** 21,000/10 **Man:** 450 tot.

Fyodor Vidyaev—Vee Cone communications antenna aft, 8/25-mm AA; Echo-II alongside French Navy, 1981

Magadanskiy Komsomolets—no 100-mm guns, large helo deck JMSDF, 4-83

Dmitriy Galkin—Vee Cone aft, lattice foremast, no 25-mm AA French Navy, 1-84

Viktor Kotel'nikov—helicopter platform aft, 2/100-mm guns forward, Big Ball SATCOMM radomes French Navy, 5-84

Remarks: Soviet type designation: PB—*Plavuchaya Baza* (Floating Base). Can serve as logistic support for a flotilla of eight to twelve submarines. *Viktor Kotel'nikov's* after 100-mm mounts were replaced by a helicopter platform, while the *Magadanskiy Komsomolets* has always had a very large helicopter platform aft and has never carried any 100-mm guns. *Fyodor Vidyaev* has eight 25-mm (II × 4) also, but no Hawk Screech; she and *Dmitriy Galkin* have been fitted with a Vee Cone antenna for long-range communications. A bow lift-hook of 100-ton capacity is fitted, as are one 10-ton, two 5-ton, and two 1-ton cranes. All are used as flagships. One other unit was transferred to Indonesia.

◆ **6 Atrek class** Bldr: Neptunwerft, Rostock, East Germany (In serv. 1955-57)

Atrek, Bakhmut, Evgeniy Osipov, Ayat, Dvina, Murmat

Atrek 1970

D: 3,413 tons (5,386 fl) **S:** 13 kts **Dim:** 102.4 × 14.4 × 5.5
M: 1 triple-expansion engine, 1 exhaust turbine; 1 prop; 2,400 hp
Electron Equipt: Radar: 1/Neptune or Don-2 **Boilers:** 2 **Range:** 6,900/13

Remarks: Soviet type designation: PB—*Plavuchaya Baza* (Floating Base). Modified Kolomna-class cargo ships. Can carry six 37-mm AA (II × 3). Two 5-ton cranes forward. None sighted deployed since early 1970s; believed relegated to harbor service. Can accommodate several hundred submarine crew members.

MISSILE TRANSPORTS

◆ **3 Amga class** Bldr: Krasnoye Sormovo SY, Gorkiy

Amga (In serv. 1973), Vetluga (In serv. 1976), Daugava (In serv. 1981)

Vetluga JMSDF, 1976

Daugava JMSDF, 1981

MISSILE TRANSPORTS *(continued)*

D: 4,500 tons (5,500 fl) **S:** 12 kts **Dim:** 102.0 × 17.7 × 4.4 (see remarks)
A: 4/25-mm AA (II × 2)
Electron Equipt: Radar: 1/Don-2 — IFF: 1/High Pole-B
M: 2 diesels; 2 props; 4,000 hp **Range:** 4,500/12

REMARKS: One 55-ton crane with a reach of 34 meters. Have ice-reinforced hulls. Intended to transport ballistic missiles for strategic submarines. The *Vetluga* is 6-m longer than her sister, and *Daugava* is 113.0 long, displacing 6,200 tons (fl), and has a different crane, with solid sides. *Vetluga* and *Daugava* in Pacific Fleet.

◆ **7 Lama class** Bldr: Black Sea SY, Nikolayev (In serv. 1963-79)

GENERAL RIYABAKOV	PB 868	PM 946	
VORONEZH (PM 872)	PM 150	PM 938	PM. . .

D: 4,500 tons (fl) **S:** 14 kts **Dim:** 112.8 × 14.9 × 4.4
A: 4 or 8/57-mm DP (IV × 1 or 2, or II × 2) — 2 or 4/SA-N-5 SAM syst. (IV × 4, 16 or 32 SA-7 Grail missiles) — *Voronezh* & one other also: 4/25-mm AA (II × 2)
Electron Equipt: Radar: 1/Don-2, 1/Slim Net or Strut Curve, 1 or 2/Hawk Screech or 2/Muff Cob
IFF: 1/High Pole-B, 2/Square Head
M: 2 diesesls; 1 prop; 4,000 hp

REMARKS: PM — *Plavuchaya Masterskaya* (Floating Workshop) and PB — *Plavuchaya Baza* (Floating Base). Vary greatly in equipment. Intended to transport cruise missiles for submarines and surface units. *Voronezh* (PM 872) and one other have larger missile-stowage areas and smaller cranes, and carry two open 57-mm DP (II × 1; one only on *Voronezh*), and four 25-mm AA (II × 2), but have no fire-control radar. These serve Nanuchka-class corvettes and Osa-class patrol boats. Two 20-ton (10-ton on missile-boat tenders) precision cranes. *General Ryabakov,* completed 1979, has an enclosed, automatic 57-mm AA mount and four SA-N-5 systems.

PM-150 — with twin 57-mm DP forward, 2/SA-N-5 launchers abreast stack

General Riyabakov — with twin 57-mm DP, 4/SA-N-5 launchers aft
French Navy, 10-83

◆ **2 Modified Andizhan class** Bldr: Neptunwerft, Rostock, Each Germany (In serv. 1960-61)

VENTA VILYUY

Vilyuy U.S. Navy, 6-83

D: 6,740 tons (fl) **S:** 13.5 kts **Dim:** 104.0 × 14.4 × 6.6
A: None **Man:** 60 tot.
Electron Equipt: Radar: 2/Don-2 — IFF: 1/High Pole-B, 1/Square Head
M: 1 diesel; 1 prop; 1,890 hp **Range:** 6,000/13.5

REMARKS: Converted from cargo ships during the 1970s. Large crane forward, two small cranes and a helicopter deck aft. Forward holds can accommodate ten SS-N-9 missiles and twenty SA-N-1 or SA-N-3. Helicopter pad aft.

◆ **2 MP 6 class** Bldr: Hungary (In serv. 1959-60)

BUREYA KHOPER

Bureya — long forward hatch to missile hold 1982

D: 2,100 tons (fl) **S:** 10.5 kts **Dim:** 74.7 × 11.3 × 4.4
Electron Equipt: Radar: 1/Don-2 **M:** 1 diesel; 1 prop; 1,000 hp
Range: 3,300/9

REMARKS: Former medium landing ships, resembling engines-aft coastal freighters. Bow doors welded shut circa 1960, when they were adapted as cargo vessels. Subsequently modified to transport SS-N-5 ballistic missiles. *Khoper* in the Northern Fleet and *Bureya* in the Pacific.

Voronezh (PM-872) — missile-boat-tender version with forward twin 57-mm DP removed, 2/SA-N-5 added abreast stack U.S. Navy, 5-83

MISSILE TRANSPORTS *(continued)*

◆ **2 Melitopal class** Bldr: . . . , U.S.S.R. (In serv. 1952-55)

INDIRKA FORT SHEVERENKO

D: 1,200 tons (fl) **S:** 11.3 kts **Dim:** 57.6 × 9.0 × 4.3
Electron Equipt: Radar: 1/Don-2 **Range:** 2,500/10.5
M: 1 Type 6DR 30/40 diesel; 1 prop; 600 hp

REMARKS: Converted late 1970s from small, engines-aft coastal cargo vessels. Have one long hold. All cargo-handling gear removed. In Baltic Fleet. Three sisters serve as survey vessels.

NOTE: Muna-class ammunition transports are described on a later page.

REPAIR SHIPS

NOTE: According to the Polish press in 1-85, a new series of "floating repair shops" is to be built at Wisla Shipyard, Gdansk, for the Soviet Navy. No data available.

◆ **2 Malina class** Bldr: Black Sea SY, Nikolayev

PM-63 (In serv. 1984) PM-74 (In serv. 1985)

PM-63 French Navy, 9-84

PM-63 U.S. Navy, 10-84

D: 10,000 tons (fl) **S:** 17 kts **Dim:** 140.0 (126 wl) × 22.0 × 5.0
A: None
Electron Equipt: Radar: 2/Palm Frond—IFF: 1/Salt Pot transponder
M: 4 gas turbines; 1 or 2 props; 60,000 hp **Man:** 260 tot.

REMARKS: PM—*Plavuchaya Masterskaya* (Floating Workshop). Second unit began trials in the spring of 1985. Unusual hull form with no curved surfaces, indicates not intended to move very often. Intended to serve nuclear-powered submarines, as evidenced by the mooring pockets along the hull sides and the two large, specialized reactor recoring cranes. PM-74 to Pacific Fleet, late 1985.

◆ **24 Amur class** Bldr: A. Warski SY, Szczecin, Poland (In serv. 1968-78, 1981-83)

PM-5	PM-34	PM-52	PM-75	PM-129	PM-156
PM-9	PM-37	PM-56	PM-81	PM-138	PM-161
PM-10	PM-40	PM-64	PM-82	PM-139	PM-163
PM-15	PM-49	PM-73	PM-94	PM-140	PM-164

D: 4,000 tons (5,490 fl) **S:** 12 kts **Dim:** 121.7 × 17.0 × 5.1 **A:** None
Electron Equipt: Radar: 1/Don-2
IFF: 1/High Pole-B
M: 2 diesels; 1 prop; 4,000 hp **Range:** 13,200/8
Man: 210 tot., plus up to 210 passengers

REMARKS: PM—*Plavuchaya Masterskaya* (Floating Workshop). Enlarged version of the Oskol class. Two 5-ton cranes. Construction resumed 1980-82, with PM-5 of the new series having a long deckhouse in the forecastle. Early units do not have the passenger facilities. Serve surface-ships and submarines with basic repair facilities and spare parts.

PM-156 Skyfotos, 12-84

PM-82 ("PM" omitted from pendant) R. Neth. Navy, 2-84

PM-82 U.S. Navy, 2-84

REPAIR SHIPS *(continued)*

◆ **12 Oskol class** Bldr: A. Warski SY, Szczecin, Poland (In serv. 1964-67)

PM-2	PM-21	PM-26	PM-51	PM-68	PM-148
PM-20	PM-24	PM-28	PM-62	PM-146	PM-477

PM-21—well-deck Oskol class; twin 12.7-mm mg atop fwd. deckhouse 1981

PM-24—4/25-mm AA aft 16 Flot., French Navy, 10-84

PM-146—flush-decked Oskol class 1970

D: 2,500 tons (3,000 fl) **S:** 12 kts **Dim:** 91.4 × 12.2 × 4.0
Electron Equipt: Radar: 1 or 2/Don-2—IFF: 1/High Pole-A
M: 2 diesels; 1 prop; 4,000 hp **Range:** 9,000/8 **Man:** 60 tot.

Remarks: PM—*Plavuchaya Masterskaya* (Floating Workshop). Most have a well deck forward of the bridge. PM-24 has four 25-mm AA (II × 2); a twin 57-mm gunmount forward was removed between 1980 and 1984. All have one or two 3.4-ton cranes.

◆ **5 Dneper class** Bldr: Black Sea SY, Nikolayev (In serv. 1960-64)

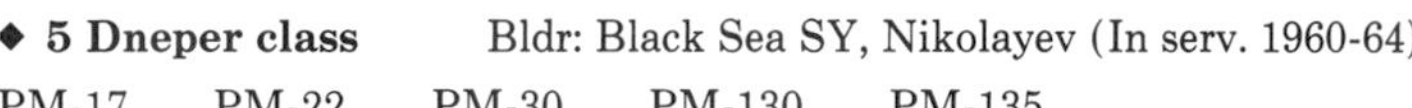

PM-17 PM-22 PM-30 PM-130 PM-135

PM-17 1960

D: 4,500 tons (5,300 fl) **S:** 11 kts **Dim:** 113.3 (100.0 pp) × 16.5 × 4.4
Electron Equipt: Radar: 1/Don or Don-2—IFF: 1/High Pole-A
M: 1 diesel; 2,000 hp **Range:** 6,000/8.3 **Man:** 420 tot.

Remarks: PM—*Plavuchaya Masterskaya* (Floating Workshop). Have one 150-ton bow hoist, one kingpost, and one crane. Equipment varies from ship to ship. PM 130 and 135, the last two units (Modified Dnepr class) are flush-decked. Intended to serve submarines. Can be armed with 2/57-mm AA (II × 1). Not seen since initial delivery voyages.

GENERATOR SHIPS

◆ **4 Tomba class** Bldr: A. Warski SY, Szczecin, Poland (In serv. 1974-76)

ENS-244 ENS-254 ENS-348 ENS-357

ENS-357 L. & L. Van Ginderen, 6-80

D: 4,400 tons (5,800 fl) **S:** 14 kts **Dim:** 107.0 × 17.0 × 5.0
A: None
Electron Equipt: Radar: 1/Don-2—IFF: 1/High Pole-B
M: 1 diesel; 1 prop; 4,500 hp **Range:** 7,000/12 **Man:** 50 tot.

Remarks: ENS—*Elektrostantsiye Nativatel'noye Sudno* (Electric Power Station and Steam-Source Ship). Two stacks and a "mack" on the forecastle, all containing diesel-engine exhausts, while the stack amidships also has the uptake from a large boiler. Two 3-ton cranes.

SUBMARINE RESCUE SHIPS

◆ **1 (+1) El'brus class** Bldr: 61 Kommuna SY, Nikolayev

El'brus (In serv. 1981) N. . . . . . . (In serv. . . . .)

El'brus U.S. Navy, 1-82

SUBMARINE RESCUE SHIPS *(continued)*

El'brus French Navy, 5-84

D: 20,000 tons (fl) **S:** 17 kts **Dim:** 175.0 × 25.0 × 7.5
A: Provision for 4/30-mm gatling AA (I × 4) or 8/30-mm AA (II × 4)
Electron Equipt: Radar: 1/Don-2, 2/Don Kay—IFF: 2/Salt Pot-C
M: 4 diesels; 2 props; . . . hp **Range:** . . . **Man:** 420 tot.

Remarks: Icebreaking hull indicates probable association with the Typhoon program. Large hangar aft of stack holds two or four salvage-and-rescue submersibles, which are moved forward on rails for launching by extendable overhead gantry cranes on either side. Hangar for one Hormone or Helix helicopter, with hangar door dropping to form a ramp leading to the helicopter flight deck. Can lay and retrieve a four-point moor. The 3-ton crane on port quarter has very long folding arm. Has submersible decompression and observation chambers, firefighting equipment. Far and away the world's largest and most elaborate submarine salvage and rescue ship. *El'brus* made one brief deployment in 12-81 to 1-82 and then returned to the Black Sea, not emerging again until 5-84. Second unit reported building 3-83.

◆ **1 Nepa class** Bldr: Black Sea SY, Nikolayev (In serv. 1970)

Karpaty

Karpaty 1971

D: 9,800 tons (fl) **S:** 16 kts **Dim:** 129.5 × 19.2 × 6.4 **A:** None
Electron Equipt: Radar: 2/Don-2—IFF: 1/High Pole-B
M: 2–4 diesels; 2 props; 8,000 hp **Range:** 8,000/14 **Man:** 270 tot.

Remarks: Has a 600-ton lift hook supported by horns extending over the stern, two others beneath the hull. Very large all-purpose salvage ship with submarine-rescue equipment, including several rescue bells and observation chambers.

◆ **8 Prut class** Bldr: Nosenko/Black Sea SY, Nikolayev (In serv. 1960-68)

Altay	Vladimir Trefolev	SS-21	SS-26
Beshtau	Zhiguli	SS-23	SS-83

Zhiguli—tripod foremast, mooring buoys in chutes 1980

SS-21—quadripod foremast, horizontally stowed mooring buoys French Navy, 1981

D: 2,800 tons (3,300 fl) **S:** 20 kts **Dim:** 90.2 × 14.3 × 5.5
Electron Equipt: Radar: 1–2/Don-2 and/or Don
M: 4 diesels; 2 props; 8,000 hp **Range:** 10,000/16 **Man:** 120 tot.

Remarks: SS—*Spasitel'noye Sudno* (Rescue Ship). One derrick, two or three special carriers for rescue chambers, submersible decompression chamber for divers, and salvage observation bells. Four anchor buoys are stowed on inclined racks on the after deck. One unit was armed for a while with four 57-mm AA (IV × 1) controlled by a Muff Cob radar director, long since removed. SS-21, SS-26, SS-86, *Beshtau,* and *Vladimir Trefolev* have quadripod foremasts, smaller mooring buoys; others have tripod foremasts. Sister SS-44 lost during early 1970s.

◆ **11 Modified T-58-class minesweepers** Bldr: . . . (In serv. late 1950s)

Kazbek	Valday	Zangezur	SS-35	SS-47	SS-51
Khibiny	Polkovo	SS-30	SS-40	SS-50	

SS-40 1978

D: 815 tons (930 fl) **S:** 17 kts **Dim:** 71.7 × 9.6 × 2.7
Electron Equipt: Radar: 1/Don-2, 1/Spin Trough or Don or Don-2
Sonar: 1/Tamir—IFF: 1/High Pole-A
M: 2 diesels; 2 props; 4,000 hp **Range:** 2,500/12 **Man:** 60 tot.

Remarks: SS—*Spasitel'noye Sudno* (Rescue Ship). Altered while under construction. Lift rig overhanging the stern to handle divers' gear and submersible decompression chamber. Rescue diving chamber to port, amidships. Can be armed with one 37-mm AA. Sister *Gidrolog* served as an intelligence collector until struck, early 1980s. Another was transferred to India.

FLEET REPLENISHMENT SHIPS

◆ **2 Kaliningrad class** Bldr: Rauma-Repola, Finland

Vyaz'ma (ex-*Katun*) (In serv. 5-83) Argun (ex-*Kallavere*) (In serv. 7-83)

D: 8,700 tons (fl) **S:** 14 kts **Dim:** 115.5 (112.0 pp) × 17.0 × 6.5
A: None **M:** Radar: 1/Okean A, 1/Okean B
M: 1 Russkiy/Burmeister & Wain 5 DKRP 50/110-2 diesel; 1 prop; 3,850 hp
Electric: 805 kw **Range:** 5,000/14 **Man:** 32 tot.

Argun—fueling a Krivak-II moored alongside Lt. Weaver/CLDR Fenzl, VF-111, U.S.N., 5-83

FLEET REPLENISHMENT SHIPS *(continued)*

Vyaz'ma U.S. Navy, 10-83

Remarks: 4,821 grt/5,873 dwt. Last two built of a class that had over two dozen units delivered to the U.S.S.R. Ministry of Fisheries from 1979 to 1982. Originally completed 12-82 and 11-82, respectively. Three liquid replenishment stations (one each side, plus astern); no underway solids replenishment. Carry 5,750 m³ (5,350 tons) liquid cargo in 10 tanks, 80 m³ dry cargo. Two cargo pumps have combined 400 m³/hr capacity. Have a 1,600-ton water ballast capacity.

◆ **1 Berezina class** Bldr: 61 Kommuna SY, Nikolayev (In serv. 1978)

Berezina

Berezina 10-81

Berezina U.S. Navy, 1979

D: 36,000 tons (fl) **S:** 22 kts **Dim:** 212.0 × 26.0 × 10.0
A: 1/SA-N-4 system (II × 1, 20 missiles)—4/57)mm DP (II × 2)—4/30-mm gatling AA (VI × 4)—2/RBU-1000 ASW RL (VI × 2)—2/Hormone helicopters
Electron Equipt: Radar: 1/Don-2, 2/Don-Kay, 1/Strut Curve, 1/Pop Group, 1/Muff Cob, 2/Bass Tilt
Sonar: . . . —IFF: 1/High Pole
EW: 2/chaff RL (II × 2)
M: 2 diesels; 2 props; 54,000 hp **Range:** 12,000/18 **Man:** 600 tot.

Remarks: Soviet type designation: VTR—*Voyenyy Transport* (Military Transport). The largest multipurpose underway replenishment ship yet built for the Soviets and the only one currently to be armed. Can refuel over the stern and from single constant-tension stations on either side, amidships. Solid replenishment is by two sliding-stay, constant-tension transfer rigs on either side. Vertical replenishment is by two specially configured Hormone helicopters hangared in the after superstructure. There are four 10-ton stores-handling cranes to supply ships moored alongside. Cargo: approx. 16,000 tons of fuel oil and diesel fuel, 500 tons fresh water, and 2,000–3,000 tons of provisions, munitions, and combat spares. The very large crew may be accounted for, in part, by a capability to transport crews for spare submarines, for which mooring pockets are provided along the ship's side. No additional units are expected, and *Berezina* has not deployed from the Black Sea in several years.

◆ **6 Boris Chilikin class** Bldr: Baltic SY, Leningrad (In serv. 1971-78)

Boris Butoma | Dnestr | Ivan Bubnov
Boris Chilikin | Genrikh Gasanov | Vladimir Kolyachitskiy

Dnestr U.S. Navy, 12-84

Genrikh Gasanov U.S. Navy, 8-83

Boris Chilikin—with water tanker *Manych* and a Krivak-I frigate alongside U.S. Navy, 9-84

D: 8,700 tons light (24,500 fl) **S:** 17 kts **Dim:** 162.3 × 21.4 × 11.5
A: Removed
Electron Equipt: Radar: 2/Don-Kay—IFF: 1/High Pole-B
M: 1 diesel; 9,600 hp **Range:** 10,000/16.6

Remarks: Soviet type designation: VTR—*Voyenyy Tanker* (Military Tanker). Naval version of the merchant *Velikiy Oktyabr* class. 16,300 dwt. Equipment varies: early units had solid-stores, constant tension-rigs on both sides forward; later units, only to starboard, with liquids to port. All have port and starboard liquid-replenishment stations amidships and can replenish liquids over the stern. Cargo: 13,500 tons liquid (fuel oil, diesel, water); 400 tons ammunition; 400 tons provisions; 400 tons stores. The *Ivan Bubnov* and *Genrikh Gasanov* were completed in merchant colors, without guns, Strut Curve, or Muff Cob; that equipment has now been removed from the other ships, although several retained their gunhouses for a short period.

◆ **4 Dubna class** Bldr: Rauma-Repola, Rauma, Finland

	In serv.		In serv.
Dubna	1974	Pechenga	1978
Irkut	1975	Sventa	1979

Sventa French Navy, 1984

FLEET REPLENISHMENT SHIPS *(continued)*

Dubna—replenishing Kresta-II *Admiral Yumashev* U.S. Navy, 9-83

D: 4,300 tons light (11,100 fl) **S:** 16 kts **Dim:** 130.1 (126.3 pp) × 20.0 × 7.2
A: None **Electron Equipt:** Radar: 2/Don-2
M: 1 Russkiy 8DRPH 23/230, 8-cyl. diesel; 1 prop; 6,000 hp
Electric: 1,485 kVA **Fuel:** 1,056 m³ **Range:** 8,000/15 **Man:** 60 tot.

Remarks: Soviet type designation: VTR—*Voyenyy Tanker* (Military Tanker). 6,022 grt/6,500 dwt. Cargo: 4,364 m³ heavy fuel oil; 2,646 m³ diesel fuel; 140 m³ cargo water; 537 m³ refrigerated provisions; 810 m³ dry stores. Twenty-seven cargo tanks. Can transfer one-ton loads from constant-tension stations forward. Liquid replenishment from one station on port and starboard, amidships, and over the stern. Additional berths for "turnover crews." Original commercial Okean-series radars replaced.

◆ **5 Altay class** Bldr: Rauma-Repola, Rauma, Finland (In serv. 1969-73)

Ilim Izhora Kola Yegorlik Yel'nya

Izhora JMSDF, 1984

D: 2,183 light (2,228 fl) **S:** 14.2 kts **Dim:** 106.0 (97.0 pp) × 15.0 × 6.7
Electron Equipt: Radar: 2/Don-2—IFF: 1/High Pole-A
M: 1 Valmet-Burmeister & Wain BM-550 VTBN-110 diesel; 3,250 hp (2,900 sust.)
Electric: 650 kw **Range:** 8,600/12 **Man:** 60 tot.

Remarks: 3,670 grt/5,045 dwt. All have had an underway replenishment. A-frame kingpost added forward since 1975, permitting them to refuel one ship at a time on either beam. Also able to replenish over stern. Differ in details, heights of masts, etc. More than two dozen sisters in the Soviet merchant marine.

◆ **1 Sofia class** Bldr: U.S.S.R. (In serv. 1969)

Akhtuba (ex-*Khanoi*)

Akhtuba 1976

D: 62,600 tons (fl) **S:** 17 kts **Dim:** 230.6 × 31.0 × 11.8
M: Steam turbine; 1 prop; 19,000 hp **Boilers:** 2
Range: 20,900/17 **Man:** 70 tot.

Remarks: 32,840 grt/49,385 dwt. Largest ship in the Soviet Navy. Carries 44,500 tons of liquid cargo. Can refuel over the stern only; primarily used to refuel other tankers.

◆ **3 Olekhma and Pevek class** Bldr: Rauma-Repola, Rauma, Finland

Olekhma Iman Zolotoi Rog

D: 6,700 tons (fl) **S:** 14 kts **Dim:** 105.0 × 14.8 × 6.8
Electron Equipt: Radar: 1/Don-2 **M:** 1 Burmeister & Wain diesel; 2,900 hp
Range: 7,900/13.6 **Man:** 40 tot.

Remarks: *Zolotoi Rog* belongs to the *Pevek* class. All built in the mid-1960s. 3,300 grt/4,400 dwt. *Olekhma* was modernized in 1978 with A-frame abaft the bridge to permit underway fueling of one ship at a time on either beam. The other two have not

Olekhma—modified for underway replenishment French Navy, 1979

been similarly upgraded. Predecessor to the *Altay* design, but with conventional "three-island" tanker layout. The *Zolotoi Rog* differs only slightly. All can refuel over the stern.

◆ **6 Uda class** Bldr: Vyborg SY (In serv. 1962-64)

Dunay Koida Lena Sheksna Terek Vishera

Sheksna—with two refueling positions amidships French Navy, 5-84

Koida—still with only one bipod refueling kingpost U.S. Navy, 2-84

D: 7,100 tons (fl) **S:** 17 kts **Dim:** 122.0 × 15.8 × 6.3 **A:** Removed
Electron Equipt: Radar: 1/Don, 1/Don-2 (or 2/Don-2)
IFF: High Pole-A
M: 2 diesels; 2 props; 8,000 hp **Range:** 4,000/17 **Man:** 85 tot.

Remarks: Soviet type designation: VTR—*Voyenyy Tanker* (Military Tanker). Equipped to carry eight 57-mm AA (IV × 2), *Dunay, Vishera, Sheksna,* and *Lena* have been equipped with a second A-frame kingpost for liquid replenishment, amidships. Three transferred to Indonesia during the early 1960s.

◆ **3 Kazbek class** Bldr: Admiralty SY, Leningrad, or Kherson SY

Alatyr' Desna Volkhov

Alatyr' 2-84

D: 16,250 tons (fl) **S:** 14 kts **Dim:** 145.5 × 19.24 × 8.5 **A:** None
Electron Equipt: Radar: 2/Don-2—IFF: 1/High Pole-A
M: 2 Russkiy Dizel diesels; 2 props; 4,000 hp **Range:** 18,000/14 **Man:** 46 tot.

Remarks: Soviet type designation: VTR—*Voyenyy Tanker* (Military Tanker). Built in the mid-1950s. 8,230 grt/11,800 dwt. Carry 11,600 tons of fuel. The three naval units can be distinguished from their civilian sisters because they have two tall kingposts and an A-frame kingpost to support fueling hoses before the bridge, and working decks were added over the cargo decks before and abaft the bridge. Merchant units of this class are among those most frequently used to support naval forces.

◆ **1 ex-German, ex-Dutch** Bldr: C. van der Giessen, Krimpen, Netherlands

Polyarnik (ex-*Kärnten*, ex-*Tankboot-I*)

FLEET REPLENISHMENT SHIPS *(continued)*

Polyarnik 1975

D: 12,500 tons (fl) **S:** 17.1 kts **Dim:** 132.1 (125.0 pp) × 16.15 × 7.6
M: 2 Werkspoor 8-cyl. diesels; 2 props; 7,000 hp **Man:** 57 tot.

Remarks: Launched, 3-5-41. War reparations, 30-12-45. Oldest replenishment oiler in any navy. 5,709 grt/6,640 dwt. Liquid cargo 5,600 tons; solid stores and provisions. In the Pacific Fleet.

OILERS

◆ **2 or more Baskunchak class** Bldr: U.S.S.R. (In serv. late 1960s)

Ivan Golubets Ukhta

D: 2,940 tons (fl) **S:** 13.2 kts **Dim:** 83.6 (74.0 pp) × 12.0 × 4.9
Electron Equipt: Radar: 1/Don-2 **M:** 1 Type 8DR 43/61 VI diesel; 2,000 hp
Electric: 325 kw **Fuel:** 124 tons **Range:** 5,000/12.6 **Man:** 30 tot.

Remarks: 1,768 grt/1,660 dwt. Cargo: 1,490 tons (9,993 bbl.). Subordinated to the KGB Maritime Border Guard, in the Pacific area. One sister, *Usedom,* in East German Navy; others in Soviet merchant marine.

◆ **4 Konda class** Bldr: Sweden (In serv. mid 1950s)

Konda Rossoch' Soyana Yakhroma

Yakhroma French Navy, 1981

D: 1,980 tons (fl) **S:** 12 kts **Dim:** 69.0 × 10.0 × 4.3
Electron Equipt: Radar: 1-2/Don-2 and/or Spin Trough
M: 1 diesel; 1,600 hp **Range:** 2,470/10 **Man:** 26 tot.

Remarks: 1,117 grt/1,265 dwt. Can refuel over the stern.

◆ **3 Nercha class** Bldr: Crichton-Vulcan or Valmet, Abo, Finland (In serv. 1952-55)

Klyaz'ma Narva Nercha

Nercha 1967

D: 1,800 tons (fl) **S:** 11.3 kts **Dim:** 63.5 × 10.0 × 4.5
Electron Equipt: Radar: 1/Don **M:** 1 diesel; 1,000 hp
Range: 2,000/10 **Man:** 25 tot.

Remarks: 1,081 grt/1,127 dwt. Can refuel over the stern.

◆ **13 Khobi class** Bldr: Zhdanov SY (In serv. early 1950s)

Cheremshan	Indiga	Khobi	Lovat'	Metan
Orsha	Sasha	Seima	Shelon'	Sos'va
Sysola	Tartu	Tunguska		

D: 1,525 tons (fl) **S:** 12 kts **Dim:** 62.0 × 10.0 × 4.4
Electron Equipt: Radar: 1/Don-2, 1/Spin Trough—IFF: High Pole-A
M: 2 diesels; 2 props; 1,600 hp **Man:** 29 tot.

Lovat' 1978

Remarks: 795 grt/834-915 dwt. Refuel over bows while being towed by receiving ship. *Linda* and one other went to Albania in 1959; others to Indonesia. At least four have been stricken: *Alazan, Baymak, Goryn,* and *Titan.*

◆ **2 ex-German Dora class** Bldr: D. W. Kremer Sohn, Elmshorn (In serv. 1941-43)

Izhma (ex-. . .) Iskra (ex-. . .)

D: 973 tons (fl) **S:** 12 kts **Dim:** 61.0 (56.5 pp) × 9.0 × 2.75
A: None **Electron Equipt:** Radar: . . .
M: 2 M.W.M. 6-cyl. diesels; 2 props; 900 hp **Fuel:** 17.5 tons
Range: 1,200/12 **Man:** 26 tot.

Remarks: Two of a group of four Luftwaffe aviation-fuel tankers—*Dora, Else, Grete,* and *Hanna*—all of which passed into British hands in 5-45 and went to the U.S.S.R. in 1946. The others may also remain in service. 638 grt. Cargo: 331 tons.

◆ **1 ex-German Usedom class** Bldr: Howaldtswerke, Hamburg (In serv. 5-42)

Feolent (ex-*Empire Tegadea,* ex-*Jeverland*) (L: 15-6-38)

D: 5,250 tons (fl) **S:** 15.5 kts **Dim:** 96.16 × 13.8 × 5.56
A: None **Electron Equipt:** Radar: . . .
M: 2 Schichau diesels; 2 props; 3,500 hp **Man:** 64 tot.

Remarks: Completed by Burmeister & Wain. Turned over to Great Britain in 5-45, later to the U.S.S.R. 2,579 grt. Cargo: 2,600 tons of fuel oil. In Black Sea Fleet.

WATER TANKERS

◆ **2 Manych class** Bldr: Vyborg SY

Manych (In serv. 1971) Tagil (In serv. 1977)

Manych U.S. Navy, 1982

Tagil 1983

D: 7,800 tons (fl) **S:** 18 kts **Dim:** 115.8 × 15.8 × 6.7
A: Removed **Electron Equipt:** Radar: 2/Don-Kay; *Manych* also: 2/Muff Cob
M: 2 diesels; 2 props; 9,000 hp **Range:** 11,500/12 **Man:** 90 tot.

Remarks: Originally intended to be small replenishment oilers to carry fuel and solid stores for submarines. Reported in the Soviet press as unsuccessful. *Manych* was assigned as a water tender to support the Mediterranean Squadron. Her four 57-mm guns were removed in 1975. *Tagil* was completed without armament.

WATER TANKERS *(continued)*

◆ **14 Voda class** Bldr: . . . (In serv. 1950s)

Abakan, Sura, MVT-6, MVT-9, MVT-10, MVT-16, MVT-17, MVT-18, MVT-20, MVT-21, MVT-24, MVT-134, MVT-138, MVT-428

Abakan U.S. Navy, 2-84

D: 2,100 tons (3,100 fl) **S:** 12 kts **Dim:** 81.5 × 11.5 × 4.3
Electron Equipt: Radar: 1/Don-2
M: 2 diesels; 2 props; 1,600 hp **Range:** 3,000/10 **Man:** 40 tot.

Remarks: MVT-*Morskoy Vodnyy Tanker* (Seagoing Water Tanker). Several have no working deck over the cargo tank area.

SPECIAL-LIQUIDS TANKERS

◆ **1 Ural class** Bldr: Dalzavod SY, Vladivostok (In serv. 1969)

Ural

Ural 1969

D: 2,600 tons (fl) **S:** 12 kts **Dim:** 90.0 × 10.0 × 3.7
Electron Equipt: Radar: 1/Spin Trough **M:** 2 diesels; 1 prop; 1,200 hp

Remarks: Transports liquid nuclear waste. High freeboard, superstructure aft, traveling crane.

◆ **6 Luza class** Bldr: Sredniy Neva SY, Kolpino (In serv. 1960s)

Alambay, Aragvy, Barguzin, Don, Kana, Selenga

Barguzin 1982

D: 1,900 tons (fl) **S:** 12 kts **Dim:** 62.5 × 10.7 × 4.3
Electron Equipt: Radar: 1/Don-2 **M:** 1 diesel; 1,000 hp **Range:** 2,000/11

Remarks: Carry volatile liquids, probably missile fuel. Three sisters have been stricken: *Oka, Sasima,* and *Yenisey.*

◆ **5 Vala class** (In service: early 1960s)

TNT-11 TNT-12 TNT-19 TNT-29 TNT-. . .

D: 3,100 tons (fl) **S:** 14 kts **Dim:** 76.2 × 12.5 × 5.0
M: 1 diesel; 1,000 hp **Range:** 2,000/11

Remarks: Carry waste liquids from nuclear-propulsion plants. Some carry 2/12.7-mm mg (II × 1).

TNT-12, Vala class

TRANSPORT

◆ **1 Mikhail Kalinin class** Bldr: Mathias Thesen Werft, Wismar, East Germany (In serv. 1963)

Kuban (ex-*Nadezhda Krupskaya*)

Kuban French Navy, 1984

D: 6,400 tons (fl) **S:** 18 kts **Dim:** 122.2 × 16.0 × 5.1
A: None **Electron Equipt:** Radar: 2/Don-2
M: 2 M.A.N. 6-cyl. diesels; 2 props; 8,000 hp
Range: 8,100/17

Remarks: Former passenger-cargo ship used to rotate crews on ships in the Mediterranean Squadron. 5,260 grt/1,354 dwt. Can carry 340 passengers, 1,000 tons of dry cargo.

CARGO SHIPS

Note: Cargo ships are usually referred to as VTR—*Voyenyy Transport* (Military Transport).

◆ **7 (+ . . .) Neon Antonov class** Bldr: . . . (In serv. 1978-. . .)

Irbit, Ivan Asdnev, Ivan Lednev, Mikhail Konovalov, Neon Antonov, Nikolay Sipyagin, Nikolay Starshinkov

Mikhail Konovalov 5-83

D: 5,200 tons (fl) **S:** 16 kts **Dim:** 95.1 × 14.7 × 6.5
Electron Equipt: Radar: 2/Palm Frond—IFF: 1/High Pole-B
A: None (see remarks) **M:** 1 diesel; 1 prop; . . . hp

Remarks: Specialized supply ships for remote garrisons of the KGB Maritime Border Guard in the Pacific area. Carry one or two small landing craft aft. Position for a twin 30-mm AA on the forecastle, two twin 14.5-mm machine guns amidships, and two SA-7 Grail launching positions. *Irbit* is naval-subordinated.

◆ **1 Amguema class** Bldr: U.S.S.R. (In serv. 1975)

Yauza

CARGO SHIPS *(continued)*

Yauza 1976

D: 15,100 tons (fl) **S:** 15 kts **Dim:** 133.1 × 18.9 × 9.1
Electron Equipt: Radar: 2/Don-2—IFF: 1/High Pole-A
M: 4 1,800-hp diesels, electric drive; 1 prop; 7,200 hp **Range:** 10,000/15

Remarks: 7,900 grt/9,045 dwt. Icebreaking passenger-cargo ship. Cargo: 6,600 tons. Numerous merchant sisters.

◆ **4 Yuniy Partizan class** Bldr: Turnu-Severin SY, Romania (In serv. 1975-78)

Pechora Pinega Turgay Ufa

Turgay 11-80

D: 3,947 tons (fl) **S:** 12.9 kts **Dim:** 88.75 (80.25 pp) × 12.8 × 5.2 **A:** None
Electron Equipt: Radar: 1/Don-2—IFF: 1/High Pole-A
M: 1 Sulzer diesel; 1 prop; 2,080 hp **Range:** 4,000/12 **Man:** 25 tot.

Remarks: 2,079 grt/2,150 dwt. Small container ships. Three 10-ton cranes, one of which can be rigged to lift 28 tons. Cargo: 3,200 m³. Originally intended to be able to carry fifty-eight standard cargo containers. Twenty sisters are civilian.

◆ **8 Vytegrales class** Bldr: Zhdanov SY, Leningrad (In serv. 1963-66)

Apsheron (ex-*Tosnales*)
Baskunchak (ex-*Vostok-4*)
Dauriya (ex-*Suzdal*)
Dikson (ex-*Vagales*)
Donbass (ex-*Kirishi*)
Sevan (ex-*Vyborgles*)
Taman' (ex-*Vostok-3*)
Yamal (ex-*Svirles*)

Yamal—with Hormone helicopter on deck 1979

Sevan 1979

D: 9,650 tons (fl) **S:** 16 kts **Dim:** 121.9 × 16.7 × 7.3 **A:** None
Electron Equipt: Radar: 2/Don-2—IFF: 1/High Pole-B **Range:** 7,380/14.5
M: 1 Burmeister & Wain 950 VTBF 110 diesel; 1 prop; 5,200 hp **Man:** 90 tot.

Remarks: Originally built as merchant timber-carriers, then converted as space-event support ships by the addition of more communications facilities and a helicopter platform over the stern—consequently losing access to the after hold. They can carry one Hormone helicopter but have no hangar. Now used as fleet supply ships as well as in space-related activities. *Donbass* has a Big Net air-search radar. A deckhouse over hold number three forward of the superstructure in *Dikson, Taman, Dauriya,* and *Baskunchak.* Seven sisters were converted to serve the Academy of Sciences as satellite-tracking ships.

◆ **9 Keyla class** Bldr: Hungary (In serv. 1960-66)

Mezen' Onega Ponoy Ritsa Teriberka Tuloma Unzha Ussuri Yeruslan

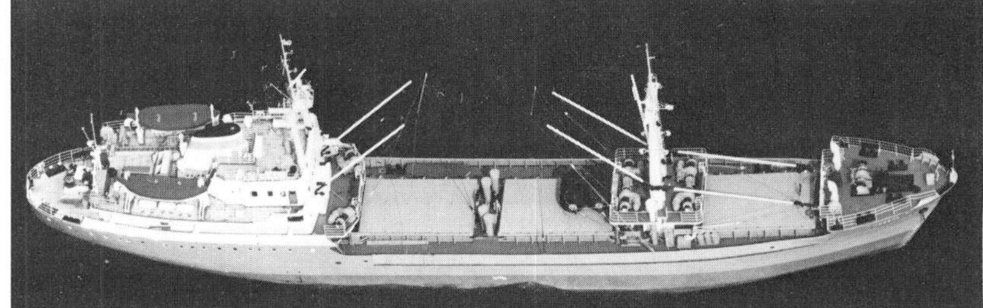
Mezen' U.S. Navy, 2-84

D: 2,000 tons (fl) **S:** 12 kts **Dim:** 78.5 × 10.5 × 4.6
A: None **Electron Equipt:** Radar: 1/Don-2 or Spin Trough
M: 1 diesel; 1 prop; 1,000 hp **Range:** 4,200/10.7 **Man:** 26 tot.

Remarks: 1,296 grt/1,280 dwt. Carry 1,100 tons of cargo. *Ritsa* has a deckhouse over her after hatch and numerous communications antennas, and may collect intelligence.

◆ **3 MP-6-class former landing ships** Bldr: Hungary (In serv. 1959-60)

Bira Irgiz Vologda

D: 2,100 tons (fl) **S:** 12 kts **Dim:** 75.0 × 11.3 × 4.4
M: 1 diesel; 1 prop; 1,000 hp

Remarks: Unsuccessful as landing ships, bow doors welded closed. Sisters *Bureya* and *Khoper* serve as missile transports.

Bira 1975

CARGO SHIPS *(continued)*

◆ **2 Andizhan class** Bldr: Neptunwerft, Rostock, East Germany (In serv. 1959-60)

ONDA POSET

Onda 5-83

D: 6,739 tons (fl) **S:** 13.5 kts **Dim:** 104.2 × 14.4 × 6.6 **M:** 1 diesel; 1,890 hp
A: None **Electron Equipt:** Radar: 1/Don-2 **Range:** 6,000/13.5
Man: 43 tot.

REMARKS: 3,368 grt/4,324 dwt. Cargo: 3,954 tons. Sister *Yemetsk* stricken. Two naval sisters are now missile transports; other sisters are in the merchant service.

◆ **1 Chulym class** Bldr: Szczecin SY, Poland (In serv. 1953-57)

SEVERODONETSK

D: 5,050 tons (fl) **S:** 12 kts **Dim:** 101.9 × 14.6 × 6.0
A: None **Electron Equipt:** Radar: 1/Don-2
M: Reciprocating steam with auxiliary GT; 1 prop; 1,650 hp
Boilers: 2, watertube **Range:** 5,000/11.5 **Man:** 41 tot.

REMARKS: 2,135 grt/3,120 dwt. 2,240 tons of cargo. Sisters *Insar, Kamchatka,* and *Leninsk-Kuznetskiy* stricken.

◆ **1 Donbass class** Bldr: Szczecin SY, Poland (In serv. 1955)

SVIR

D: 7,200 tons (fl) **S:** 12 kts **Dim:** 108.2 × 14.6 × 7.2
A: None **Electron Equipt:** Radar: 1/Neptune
M: Reciprocating steam; 1 prop; 2,300 hp **Boilers:** 2, watertube
Range: 9,800/12

REMARKS: 3,561 grt/4,864 dwt. 3,570 tons of cargo. Originally a coal-burning collier.

◆ **1 Kolomna class** Bldr: Neptunwerft, Rostock (In serv. 1952-54)

SVANETIYA

Svanetiya 1976

D: 6,700 tons (fl) **S:** 13 kts **Dim:** 102.3 × 14.4 × 6.6
Electron Equipt: Radar: 1/Don-2, 1/Neptune
IFF: 1/High Pole-A
M: Reciprocating steam plus GT; 1 prop; 2,450 hp
Range: 6,890/13 **Man:** 44 tot.

REMARKS: 3,758 grt/4,355 dwt. Cargo: 3,634 tons. Coal-burner. *Svanetiya* supports research work. Six sisters serve as *Atrek*-class submarine tenders. Sisters *Kuznetsk, Krasnoarmeysk,* and *Megra* discarded.

◆ **3 Telnovsk class** Bldr: Hungary (In serv. 1949-57)

BUREVESTNIK LAG MANOMETR

D: 1,700 tons (fl) **S:** 11 kts **Dim:** 70.0 × 10.0 × 4.2
M: 1 diesel; 800 hp **Range:** 3,300/9.7 **Man:** 40 tot.

REMARKS: 1,194 grt/1,133 dwt. Several others serve as survey ships. Being discarded.

◆ **up to 5 Khabarovsk class** Bldr: U.S.S.R. (In serv. 1950s)

Khabarovsk class 5-80

D: 650 tons (fl) **S:** 10.4 kts **Dim:** 46.4 × 8.0 × 3.2
A: 2/14.5-mm mg (II × 1) **Range:** 1,600/8
Electron Equipt: Radar: 1 or 2/Spin Trough **M:** 1 diesel; 600 hp

REMARKS: 402 dwt. Used by the KGB Maritime Border Guard in the Far East. Being replaced by the *Antonov* class. Formerly bore numbers in the VTR- . . . series.

PROVISION SHIPS

◆ **8 Mayak class** Bldr: Dnepr SY, Kiev (In serv. 1971-76)

BUZULUK LAMA NEMAN ULMA
ISHIM MIUS RIONI VYTEGRA

Neman 1982

D: 1,050 tons (fl) **S:** 11 kts **Dim:** 54.3 × 9.3 × 3.6
A: None **Electron Equipt:** Radar: 1/Spin Trough
M: 1 diesel; 800 hp **Range:** 9,400/11 **Man:** 29 tot.

REMARKS: 690 grt. Former trawlers. Refrigerated fish holds are used to carry provisions. *Lama* has two lifeboats and lacks bulwarks around the stern. Other naval sisters operate as intelligence-collectors and ASW training ships.

AMMUNITION SHIPS

◆ **10 Muna class** Bldr: Nakhodka SY (In serv. 1960s)

VTR-81 VTR-82 VTR-83 VTR-84 VTR-85
VTR-91 VTR-92 VTR-93 VTR-94 VTR-148

D: 680 tons (fl) **S:** 11 kts **Dim:** 51.0 × 8.5 × 2.7
Electron Equipt: Radar: 1-2/Spin Trough — IFF: 1/High Pole-A
M: 1 diesel; 600 hp **Man:** 40 tot.

REMARKS: When deployed, carry VTR — *Voyenyy Transport* (Military Transport) numbers, but in home waters are listed as MBSS — *Morskaya Barzha Samokhodnaya Sukhogruznaya* (Seagoing Self-Propelled Dry-Cargo Lighter). Specialized transports for torpedoes, surface-to-air missiles, and other munitions; cargo hatch arrangements differ, depending on function.

Muna class VTR-91 — munitions transport version 1982

AMMUNITION SHIPS *(continued)*

Muna class—torpedo transport version 1982

MOORING TENDERS

◆ **10 Sura class** Bldr: Neptunwerft, Rostock, East Germany (In serv. 1965-72, 1976-78)

KIL-1	KIL-21	KIL-23	KIL-29	KIL-32
KIL-2	KIL-22	KIL-27	KIL-31	KIL-33

KIL-32—with salvage submersible on deck amidships PH2 P. Soutar, U.S.N., 9-83

KIL-22—note twin hatches amidships U.S. Navy, 8-83

D: 2,370 tons (3,150 fl) **S:** 13 kts **Dim:** 87.0 (68.0 pp) × 14.8 × 5.0
A: None **Electron Equipt:** Radar: 2/Don-2
M: 4 diesels, electric drive; 2 props; 2,240 hp **Range:** 4,000/10

REMARKS: KIL—*Kilektor* (Mooring Tender). 2,366 grt. 890 tons of cargo in hold amidships. Stern rig, which can lift 60 tons, is used for buoy-handling and salvage. Can also carry several hundred tons of cargo fuel. One has been used to transport two Gus-class amphibious air-cushion personnel landing craft. Mooring buoys are stowed amidships and moved aft for handling by the stern gallows rig via a chain-haul system. The diesel propulsion generator plant is forward.

◆ **10 Neptun class** Bldr: Neptunwerft, Rostock, East Germany (In serv. 1957-60)

KIL-3	KIL-6	KIL-12	KIL-15	KIL-17
KIL-5	KIL-9	KIL-14	KIL-16	KIL-18

D: 700 tons (1,240 fl) **S:** 12 kts **Dim:** 57.3 (46.5 pp) × 11.4 × 3.4
M: 2 triple-expansion; 1,000 hp **Range:** 1,000/11
Man: 41 tot.

REMARKS: KIL—*Kilektor* (Mooring Tender). Most burn coal. 80-ton bow lift for buoy-handling and salvage. Four units deleted 1983; no recent sightings.

Neptun class

CABLE LAYERS

◆ **3 (+2) Emba class** Bldr: Wärtsilä SY, Turku, Finland

EMBA (In serv. 5-80) NEPRYADVA (L: 24-4-81) SETUN (L: 29-4-81)
N . . . (In serv. . . .) N . . . (In serv. . . .)

Setun Wärtsilä, 4-81

D: 2,050 tons (fl) **S:** 11 kts **Dim:** 75.90 (68.50 pp) × 12.60 × 3.10
Electron Equipt: Radar: 1/. . . nav.
M: 2 Wärtsilä Vasa 6R22 diesels; 1 prop; 1,360 hp
Man: 38 tot.

REMARKS: 1,900 grt. Cargo: 300 tons cable. Intended for use in shallow coastal areas, rivers, and harbors. Intended to replace the discarded Kalar class. Have a bow-thruster. Two additional units were ordered from Wärtsilä's Helsinki yard in 1-85; they are to be 86.10-m overall but otherwise similar.

◆ **8 Klazma class** Bldr: Wärtsilä SY, Turku, Finland (In serv. 1962-78)

	In serv.		In serv.		In serv.		In serv.
DONETS	1963	INGURI	1978	TAVDA	1977	YANA	1963
INGUL	1962	KATUN'	1974	TSNA	1968	ZEYA	1970

Ingul—early unit VF-111, U.S Navy, 1985

Tavda—late unit 1979

CABLE LAYERS *(continued)*

D: 6,920 tons (fl) **S:** 14 kts **Dim:** 130.4 (120.0 pp) × 16.0 × 5.75
Electron Equipt: Radar: 2/Don-2
M: 5 1,000-hp Wärtsilä 624TS diesels, electric drive; 2 props; 4,400 hp
Fuel: 250 tons **Range:** 12,000/14 **Man:** 110 tot.

REMARKS: 5,760 grt/3,750 dwt. *Ingul* and *Yana,* the first built, have four 2,436-hp diesels, a longer forecastle, and are 5,645 grt/3,400 dwt (6,810 tons fl). All have ice-strengthened hulls. In the later units, the diesel engines drive five 680-kw generators, which provide power for propulsion and for all auxiliary functions. Soviet type designation: KS-*Kabel'noye Sudno* (Cable Ship). All cable machinery built by Submarine Cables, Ltd., Great Britain. *Katun'* carries 1,850 m³ of cable and displaces 7,885 tons (fl), drawing 5.76 m; she capsized while fitting out. The others have 3 cable tanks totaling 1,600 m³. *Ingul* refitted in Japan 1978, receiving new Dowty paired-wheel cable gear. All have a 500-hp active rudder and a bow-thruster.

◆ **1 Telnovsk class** Bldr: Hungary (In serv. early 1950s)

KS-7

KS-7 1981

D: 1,700 tons (fl) **S:** 11 kts **Dim:** 73.0 × 10.0 × 4.2
M: 1 diesel; 1 prop; 800 hp **Range:** 3,300/9.7

REMARKS: Converted small cargo ship; cable sheaves project 3 m out past bow. In Pacific Fleet.

FLEET TUGS

◆ **2 Neftegaz-class oilfield tug/supply vessels** Bldr: A. Warski SY, Szczecin, Poland

ALEKSEY KORTUNOV (10-83) ILGA (In serv. 4-11-83)

Neftegaz-27—a civilian sister 1984

D: 2,800 tons (fl) **S:** 15 kts **Dim:** 81.5 (71.5 pp) × 16.3 (15.0 wl) × 5.4
A: None **Electron Equipt:** 2/. . . nav.
M: 2 Sulzer-Sgoda diesels; 2 CP props; 7,200 hp
Range: . . . **Fuel:** 533 tons **Man:** 25

REMARKS: 2,372 grt/1,396 dwt. Two of a class of 33 oilfield supply tugs ordered in 1982, the third and fourth to be delivered. Cargo: up to 600 tons dry cargo on deck plus 1,000 m³ liquid cargo. Can act as a tug and has four firefighting water monitors. Has a bow-thruster. Broad, level fantail and round-down stern would permit the ship to be rapidly adapted for minelaying.

◆ **10 Goryn class** Bldr: Rauma-Repola, Finland (In serv. 1977-78, 1982-83)

MB-105 (BAYKALSK) MB-18 (BEREZINSK) MB-119 (BILBINO)
MB-30 MB-31 MB-32 MB-35 MB-36 MB-38 MB-61

D: 2,240 tons (2,600 fl) **S:** 13.5 kts **Dim:** 63.5 × 14.3 × 5.1
Electron Equipt: Radar: 2/Don-2
M: 1 Russkiy Type 67N diesel; 3,500 hp **Range:** . . . **Man:** 40 tot.

REMARKS: Soviet type designation: MB—*Morskoy Buksir* (Seagoing Tug). 1,600 grt. 35-ton pull. For ocean towing, salvage, and fire-fighting. Sister *Bolshevetsk* lost 2-79 off Japan. Later units have a type 671 diesel and produce 43 tons bollard pull. Second series of nine began with MB-30, launched 15-12-81 and ended with MB-108, delivered 9-83. Three others have been redesignated as rescue tugs—SB—*Spastel'noye Buksir*: SB-365 (ex-MB-29), SB-523 (ex-MB-64), and SB-524 (ex-MB-108).

MB-36—second series French Navy, 1983

MB-105—which initially bore the name *Baykalsk* 9-83

◆ **11 (+ . . .) Sorum class** Bldr: Yaroslavl SY, U.S.S.R. (In serv. 1974- . . .)

MB-6	MB-28	MB-115	MB-304
MB-25	MB-58	MB-119	MB-307
MB-26	MB-112	MB-148	

MB-23—a Soviet Navy Sorum 1983

D: 1,210 tons (1,656 fl) **S:** 14 kts **Dim:** 58.3 × 12.6 × 4.6
A: Named units only: 4/30-mm AA (II × 2)
Electron Equipt: Radar: 2/Don-2—IFF: 1/High Pole-B
M: 2 Type 5-2D42 diesels, electric drive; 1 prop; 1,500 hp
Fuel: 322 tons **Range:** 6,720/13 **Man:** 35 tot.

REMARKS: MB means *Morskoy Buksir* (Seagoing Tug). A modified version with larger superstructure and an A-frame kingpost aft is used by the Ministry of Fisheries as a rescue tug, prominently displaying *Spastel'* (Rescue) on the black hull sides; named the *Almaz*-class, it includes *Almaz, Kapitan Beklemishev,* and *Ametist.* Eleven armed versions of the design serve the KGB Maritime Border Guard as patrol ships; see under corvettes on an earlier page.

◆ **51 Okhtenskiy class** Bldr: Petrozavod SY, Leningrad (In serv. 1958-early 1960s)

MB-175—Okhtenskiy class JMSDF, 1985

FLEET TUGS *(continued)*

SB-5—a rescue tug Okhtenskiy

D: 700 tons (950 fl) **S:** 13.3 kts **Dim:** 47.3 × 10.3 × 5.5
Electron Equipt: Radar: 1-2/Don-2 or Spin Trough—IFF: 1/High Pole-A
M: 2 diesels; 1 prop; 1,500 hp **Range:** 7,800/7 **Man:** 40 tot.

REMARKS: Several have two 57-mm AA (II × 1) and are operated by the KGB Maritime Border Guard for use as patrol ships. Units with names are civilian; naval units have MB—*Morskoy Buksir* (Seagoing Tug) or SB—*Spastel'noye Buksir* (Rescue Tug) hull numbers; the latter carry an "unsinkable" lifeboat or divers' workboat to port and are submarine-associated. A total of 63 were built, Soviet name: *Goliat* class.

◆ **9 Roslavl class** Bldr: Riga SY and Repair, and Vano Sturua SY (In serv. 1950s)

MB-69 MB-94 MB-134 MB-145 MB-146 MB-147 3 others

MB-94—Roslavl class 1975

D: 750 tons (fl) **S:** 11 kts **Dim:** 44.5 × 9.5 × 3.5
M: Diesel-electric; 2 props; 1,200 hp **Range:** 6,000/11 **Man:** 28 tot.

REMARKS: All have MB pendants—*Morskoy Buksir* (Seagoing Tug). Distinguished from the Okhtenskiy class by a shorter forecastle, small pilothouse, and single pole mast. Beginning to be discarded.

SALVAGE AND RESCUE SHIPS

◆ **4 Pionier Moskvyy-class salvage ships** Bldr: Vyborg SY

MIKHAIL RUDNITSKIY (In serv. 1979) GIORGIY KOZMIN' (In serv. 1980)
GIORGIY TITOV (In serv. 1983) SAYANIY (In serv. 1984)

Sayaniy—with longer forecastle and poop, additional deckhouse JMSDF, 8-84

Giorgiy Kozmin' PH1 F. Barbante, U.S.N., 9-83

D: 10,000 tons (fl) **S:** 15.4 kts **Dim:** 130.3 (119.0 pp) × 17.3 × 6.93
A: None **Electron Equipt:** Radar: 2/Don-2 **Man:** 120 tot.
M: 1 5DKRN 62/140-3 diesel; 1 prop; 6,100 hp **Electric:** 1,500 kw

REMARKS: Modification of a standard merchant timber-carrier/container-ship design, retaining two holds. The after hold has two superstructure levels built over it, and the small hold forward has been plated over. Retains two 40-ton and two 20-ton booms and has had heavy-cable fairleads cut in the bulwarks fore and aft and a number of boat booms added to starboard. *Titov* has a larger superstructure built over number three hold than do the first two. *Sayaniy*, painted in white and gray, has had the forecastle and poop decks extended, the deckhouse amidships one deck higher, and a two-level deckhouse over the forward hold area: she appears intended for some research role. Equipped with bow- and stern-thrusters and can be attached to a four-point salvage moor. First three carry the ensign of the Naval Salvage and Rescue Service and are named for important developers of research/salvage submersibles. Operate one salvage submersible, stowed in hold number two.

◆ **4 (+2) Sliva-class salvage tugs** Bldr: Rauma-Repola Uusikaupunki SY, Finland

	Laid down	L	In serv.
SB-406	. . .	6-7-83	20-2-84
SB 408	. . .	28-10-83	5-6-84
SB-921	17-8-84	28-12-84	5-7-85
SB-922	31-8-85	3-5-85	. . .

SB-406—exercising fire monitors Rauma-Repola, 1984

SB-408 Rauma-Repola, 1984

D: Approx. 3,300 tons (fl) **S:** 16 kts **Dim:** 69.20 (60.10 pp) × 15.40 × 5.10
Electron Equipt: Radar: 2/. . . nav.
M: 2 SEMT-Pielstick/Russkiy Dizel 6PC 2.5 L400 (TS HN40/46) diesels; 2 CP props; 7,800 hp—bow-thruster
Man: 43 crew + 10 salvage party

REMARKS: 2,050 grt/810 dwt. Ice-reinforced hull. Able to support divers to 60 m. Have four water monitors. One 60- and one 30-ton winch. Unique 350-m floating power cable to support vessels in distress. 5-ton electrohydraulic crane. Second pair ordered 4-84. Two more planned.

SALVAGE AND RESCUE SHIPS *(continued)*

◆ **3 Goryn-class rescue tugs** Bldr: Rauma-Repola, Finland (In serv. 1982-83)

SB-236 (ex-MB-29) SB-523 (ex-MB-64) SB-524 (ex-MB-108)

REMARKS: Data as for tug sisters on earlier page. SB—*Spastel'noye Buksir* (Rescue Tug). Change in designation appears to have been administrative only; no change to characteristics. Several Okhtenskiy class and at least one Roslavl class (SB-46) are also designated as rescue tugs.

◆ **3 Ingul-class salvage tugs** Bldr: United Admiralty SY, Leningrad

PAMIR (In serv. 1975) MASHUK (In serv. 1972) ALATAU (In serv. 1984)

Pamir—in heavy seas, showing bulbous bow 1983

D: 3,200 tons (4,050 fl) **S:** 20 kts **Dim:** 92.8 × 15.4 × 5.8
Electron Equipt: Radar: 2/Don-2
IFF: 1/High Pole-B, 1/Square Head
M: 2 type 58D-4R diesels; 2 props; 9,000 hp
Range: 9,000/18.7 **Man:** 120 tot.

REMARKS: Two sisters, *Yaguar* and *Bars,* in the merchant marine, have 35-man crews, plus bunks for 50 rescued personnel. Very powerful tugs with constant-tension high-line personnel rescue system, salvage pumps, fire-fighting equipment, and complete diving gear, capable of supporting divers to 60-m depths. Have a 94-ton bollard-pull. Large bulbous bow. Photo of *Alatau* in addenda.

◆ **2 Pamir class** Bldr: Gävle, Sweden (In serv. 1958)

AGATAN ALDAN

Aldan French Navy, 1-83

D: 1,443 tons (2,240 fl) **S:** 17.5 kts **Dim:** 78.0 × 12.8 × 4.0
Electron Equipt: Radar: 2/Don-2
M: 2 M.A.N. G10V 40/60 diesels; 2 CP props; 4,200 hp
Range: 15,200/17.5; 21,800/12

REMARKS: 1,443 grt. One 10-ton and two 1.5-ton booms. Carry fixed fire pumps with 2,600 tons/hour capacity and portable pumps with 1,650 tons/hour capacity. Can support divers to a depth of 90 m, and have decompression chambers and powerful air compressors. Two sisters, the *Gidrograf* and *Peleng,* are intelligence collectors. *Agatan* refitted 1981 in Sweden.

◆ **2 Orel class** Bldr: Valmet SY, Turku, Finland

SB 38 SB 43

D: 1,200 tons (1,760 fl) **S:** 15 kts **Dim:** 61.3 × 11.9 × 4.5
Electron Equipt: Radar: 1/Don or Don-2 **Man:** 37 tot.
M: 1 M.A.N. G5Z52/70 diesel; 1,700 hp **Range:** 13,000/13.5

SB-43—Orel class JMSDF, 1985

REMARKS: SB—*Spastel'noye Buksir* (Rescue Tug). Built in the late 1950s. Several civilian sisters, including the *Stremitel'nyy* and *Strogyy,* serve the fishing fleet.

SEAGOING FIRE BOATS

◆ **11 Katun class** Bldr: U.S.S.R. (In serv. 1970- . . .)

PZHS-64 PZHS-96 PZHS-98 PZHS-123
PZHS-124 PZHS-209 PZHS-282 PZHS-. . .
PZHS-. . . PZHS-. . . PZHS-. . .

Katun class

D: 1,016 tons (fl) **S:** 17 kts **Dim:** 62.6 × 10.2 × 3.6
Electron Equipt: Radar: 1/Don-2—IFF: 1/High Pole-B
M: 2 40DM diesels; 2 props; 4,000 hp **Range:** 2,200/16 **Man:** 32 tot.

REMARKS: Originally PDS—*Pozharno-Degazatsionnoye Sudno* (Fire-Fighting and Decontamination Ship); this designation later revised to PZHS—*Pozharnoye Sudno* (Fire-Fighting Ship). Extensive fire-fighting gear, including extendable boom. Powerful pumps. There are several civilian sisters, including the *General Gamidov.* PZHS-64, completed 1981, is the first of a new type, approx. 3-m longer and having an extra level to the superstructure; designated "Katun II" by NATO.

NOTE: See also harbor fireboat entries on page 579.

HOSPITAL SHIPS

◆ **2 Ob' class** Bldr: A. Warski SY, Szczecin, Poland

OB' (In serv. 1980) YENESEY (In serv. 1981)

D: 11,000 tons (fl) **S:** 20 kts **Dim:** 154.0 (142.0 pp) × 20.5 × 5.2
Electron Equipt: Radar: 3/Don-2 **M:** 2 diesels; 2 props; . . . hp
Man: 80 crew + 200 medical personnel

REMARKS: Have civilian crews but carry uniformed naval medical personnel. Have 100 beds, 7 operating rooms. The hangar aft can accommodate a Hormone-C utility

Ob' 5-84

HOSPITAL SHIPS *(continued)*

Yenesey—with Hormone-C SAR helicopter on deck U.S. Navy, 5-84

helicopter. Bow-thrusters fitted. Intended to "provide medical and recreational facilities." There are a physical therapy facility, 2 gymnasiums, 2 pools, a library, and a 100-seat auditorium.

◆ **20 ambulance craft** Bldr: Wisla SY, Poland (In serv. 1978-81)

D: 240 tons (fl) **S:** 11.5 kts **Dim:** 32.7 × 7.4 × 2.0
Electron Equipt: Radar: 1/Mius navigational
M: 2 diesels; 2 props; 570 hp **Man:** 17 tot.

Remarks: Pendant numbers in the SK-600 (SK—*Sanitarnyy Kater* = Clinic Cutter) series. White-painted.

INTELLIGENCE COLLECTORS (AGI)

Note: Many of the Soviet ships of this type, often designated ELINT (electronic intelligence) or SIGINT (signal intelligence) collectors, look like trawlers; others, such as the *Primorye* and and the Bal'zam class are obviously configured for their roles. No pretense is made that the AGIs are anything but intelligence collectors, which detect and analyze radioelectric and electromagnetic signals. Some of them patrol offshore from the home ports of ballistic-missile submarines, others follow Western fleets.

◆ **4 Al'pinist class** Bldr: Yaroslavl SY, U.S.S.R. (In serv. 1981-82)

GS-7 GS-8 GS-19 GS-39

D: 1,202 tons (fl) **S:** 13 kts **Dim:** 53.7 (46.2 pp) × 10.5 × 4.3
Electron Equipt: Radar: 1/Don-2
M: 1 Type 8NVD48-2U diesel; 1 CP prop; 1,320 hp
Fuel: 162 tons **Electric:** 450 kw **Range:** 7,600/13 **Man:** Approx. 50 tot.

Remarks: Selected from a class of several hundred 322-dwt stern-haul trawlers, modified as intelligence collectors, although there are few identifiable intercept antennas. The 218-m³ former fish hold may provide electronics and/or additional accommodations spaces. Have a bow-thruster.

GS-39—Al'pinist class French Navy, 3-81

GS-19—with ELINT "huts" atop pilothouse and fore and aft of the after mast 7-84

◆ **3 Bal'zam class** Bldr: Kaliningrad SY, (In serv. 1980-. . .)

SSV-80 (In serv. 1983) SSV-493 (In serv. 1982) SSV-516 (In serv. 1980)

SSV-80 French Navy, 1985

SSV-493 U.S. Navy, 9-83

D: 5,000 tons (fl) **S:** 22 kts **Dim:** 105.5 × 15.5 × 5.8
A: 1/30-mm gatling AA—2/SA-N-5 syst. (IV × 2, 16 SA-7 Grail missiles)
Electron Equipt: Radar: 2/Don-Kay
M: 2 diesels; 2 props; 9,000 hp **Man:** 200 tot.

INTELLIGENCE COLLECTORS (AGI) *(continued)*

Remarks: SSV—*Sudno Svyazyy* (Communications Vessel). Built-for-the-purpose intelligence-collection-and-processing ships, wholly military in concept. The two spherical radomes probably house satellite transmitting and receiving antennas. There are numerous intercept and direction-finding antenna arrays. Equipped to refuel under way and to transfer solid cargo and personnel via constant-tension rigs on either side of the after mast. There is only a remote "Kolonka" pedestal director for the gatling gun, no radar GFCS. SSV-516 operates in the Atlantic, the other two in the Pacific.

◆ **6 Primor'ye class** Bldr: . . . SY, U.S.S.R. (In serv. . . .)

SSV-591 Kavkaz | SSV-465 Primor'ye | SSV-502 Zakarpat'ye
SSV-590 Krym | SSV-464 Zabaykal'ye | SSV-501 Zaporozh'ye

Kavkaz (SSV-591)—without forward stump mast U.S. Navy, 8-84

Zakarpat'ye (SSV-502)—with new "Christmas tree" intercept array mast amidships U.S. Navy, 1985

D: 2,600 tons (3,700 fl) **S:** 13 kts **Dim:** 84.7 × 14.0 × 5.5
Electron Equipt: Radar: 2/Don-Kay **A:** . . ./SA-N-7 Grail SAM
M: 2 diesels; 1 prop; 2,000 hp **Range:** 12,000/13; 18,000/12 **Man:** 160 tot.

Remarks: Although these ships resemble small passenger liners, they are in fact modified versions of *Mayakovskiy*-class stern-haul factory trawlers. All given SSV—*Sudno Svyazyy* (Communications Vessel) pendants, and names obliterated, 1979–81. Carry hand-held Grail SAMs. SSV-465 has had the aft kingposts and booms removed; SSV-590, -591 have lost the forward stump masts.

◆ **9 Moma class** Bldr: Polnocny SY, Gdansk, Poland (In serv. 1968-74)

SSV-512 Arkhipelag | SSV-. . . Kil'din | SSV-514 Seliger
SSV-. . . Ekvator | SSV-506 Nakhodka | SSV-501 Vega
SSV-472 Il'men | SSV-509 Pelorus | SSV-. . . Yupiter

Nakhodka (SSV-506)—deckhouse atop bridge U.S. Navy, 1983

Seliger (SSV-514)—modernized unit U.S. Navy, 9-83

Ekvator—with 3 ELINT "huts" aft U.S. Navy, 2-84

D: 1,260 tons (1,540 fl) **S:** 17 kts **Dim:** 73.3 × 10.8 × 3.8
Electron Equipt: Radar: 2/Don-2 **Range:** 8,000/11 **Man:** 80–120 tot.
M: 2 Zgoda-Sulzer 6TD48 diesels; 2 CP props; 3,600 hp

Remarks: Ex-survey ships/buoy tenders. The *Yupiter, Il'men, Pelorus,* and *Arkhipelag* have new superstructures in the area forward of the bridge and new masts. *Yupiter* has similar, but less extensive, alterations. The others are much less modified, most having only a few canvas-covered antennas atop the bridge and "vans" for support equipment. Several carry 2/SA-N-5 systems (IV × 2, 16 SA-7 Grail missiles).

◆ **8 Mayak class** Bldr: . . . (In serv. 1967-70)

Aneroyd | Khersones | Kursograf | GS-239
Girorulevoy (GS-536) | Kurs | Ladoga | GS-242

Girorulevoy—circular radome atop bridge U.S. Navy, 7-83

Ladoga—deckhouse added in waist, SA-7 positions fore and aft (*Kurs* similar) French Navy, 6-83

INTELLIGENCE COLLECTORS (AGI) *(continued)*

Khersones—short poop deck extension in waist, with SA-7 positions atop Skyfotos, 11-84

GS-242—submarine Stop Light intercept array atop stack French Navy, 4-83

D: 1,050 tons (fl) **S:** 11 kts **Dim:** 54.2 × 9.3 × 3.6
Electron Equipt: Radar: 1-2/Don-2 and/or Spin Trough
M: 1 8NVD48 diesel; 800 hp **Range:** 9,400/11 **Man:** 60 tot.

Remarks: GS—*Gidrograficheskoye Sudno* (Hydrographic Survey Ship), an interesting euphemism. These ships vary greatly in appearance and equipment carried. Most carry hand-held SA-7 Grail missiles launched from two railed positions fitted either at the bow and stern or atop the deckhouse amidships. *Ladoga* carried 4/14.5-mm mg (II × 2) in 1980, since removed.

◆ **3 Nikolay Zubov class** Bldr: A. Warski, SY, Szczecin, Poland (In serv. 1963-68)

SSV-503 Khariton Laptev SSV-468 Gavril Sarychev
SSV-469 Semyen Chelyushkin

D: 2,200 tons (3,100 fl) **S:** 16.5 kts **Dim:** 90.0 × 13.0 × 4.7
Electron Equipt: Radar: 2/Don-2—IFF: 1/High Pole-B
M: 2 Zgoda 8TD48 diesels; 2 props; 4,800 hp **Range:** 11,000/14 **Man:** 100 tot.

Remarks: Ex-oceanographic ships. Similar to oceanographic sisters, but have a collection of antenna arrays. *Gavril Sarychev* has been extensively reconstructed: her forecastle has been extended to her stern, and an extra deck has been added to her superstructure. All have three launch positions for SA-7 Grail missiles. SSV-469 formerly carried a Strut Curve radar.

Semyen Chelyushkin (SSV-469) French Navy, 9-83

Gavril Sarychev (SSV-468) Phl F. Barbante, U.S.N., 9-83

◆ **2 Pamir class** Bldr: Gävle, Sweden (In serv. 1958)

SSV-480 Gidrograf SSV-477 Peleng (ex-*Pamir*)

Gidrograf (SSV-480) French Navy, 10-82

D: 1,443 tons (2,300 fl) **S:** 17.5 kts **Dim:** 78.0 × 12.8 × 4.0
Electron Equipt: Radar: 2/Don-2
M: 2 M.A.N. G10V 40/60 diesels; 2 CP props; 4,200 hp
Range: 15,200/17.5; 21,000/12 **Man:** 120 tot.

Remarks: Ex-rescue tugs. Both heavily modified: extra deckhouse levels, extended forecastle, numerous collection antenna arrays, etc. Their extremely long endurance makes them invaluable in the Pacific and Indian oceans. Sisters *Agatan* and *Aldan* are salvage ships. Redesignated SSV—*Sudno Svyazyy* (Communications Vessel) in 1979-80. Have three launch positions for SA-7 Grail missiles.

◆ **4 Mirnyy class** Bldr: 61 Kommuna SY, Nikolayev (In serv. circa 1962-64)

Bakan Lotsman Val Vertikal

Vertikal French Navy, 9-82

INTELLIGENCE COLLECTORS (AGI) *(continued)*

D: 850 tons (1,300 fl) **S:** 17.5 kts **Dim:** 63.6 × 9.5 × 4.5
Electron Equipt: Radar: 2/Don-2 **Man:** 60 tot.
M: 4 6-cyl. diesels, electric drive; 1 prop; 4,000 hp **Range:** 18,700/11

REMARKS: Ex-whalers. Differ in detail. Very low freeboard amidships. Have two SA-7 Grail hand-launch positions. All received new deckhouse forward during 1970s.

◆ **15 Okean trawler class** Bldr: East Germany (In serv. 1962-67)

ALIDADA	DEFLEKTOR	LINZA	TEODOLIT
AMPERMETR	EKHOLOT	LOTLIN' (GS-319)	TRAVERS
BAROGRAF	GIDROFON	REDUKTOR	ZOND
BAROMETR	KRENOMETR	REPITER	

Lotlin'—poop deck extended French Navy, 10-82

Teodolit—original, short-poop configuration French Navy, 9-83

D: 700 tons (fl) **S:** 11 kts **Dim:** 50.8 × 8.9 × 3.7
Electron Equipt: Radar: 1-2/Don-2 **M:** 1 diesel; 540 hp
Range: 7,900/11 **Man:** 60 tot.

REMARKS: Ex-trawlers. Appearances vary greatly, many having had their poop deck extended well forward of the bridge superstructure and their port sides plated in. *Barograf* has 4/14.5-mm mg (II × 2), and most have two hand-launch positions for SA-7 Grail missiles.

NOTE: *Dnepr*-class intelligence collectors *Izermetel'* and *Protraktor,* not sighted since 1980, are believed to have been stricken.

OCEANOGRAPHIC-RESEARCH SHIPS

NOTE: The only units included here are those known to be subordinate to the Soviet Navy. There are in addition nearly 300 research ships under the control of civilian agencies, primarily the Ministry of Science and the Ministry of Fisheries. Some of the civilian ships may from time to time perform research in support of military aims, but their purpose is primarily peaceful. All naval units are painted white.

◆ **18 Yug class** Bldr: Polnocny SY, Gdansk, Poland (In serv. 5-78 to 6-9-83)

BRIZ	MARSHAL GELOVANI	STRELETS
DONUZLAY	NIKOLAY MATUSEVICH	STVOR
GALS	PEGAS	TAYGA
GIDROLOG	PERSEY	VIZIR
GORIZONT	PLUTON	YUG
MANGYSHLAK	SENEZH	ZODIAK

D: 2,500 tons (fl) **S:** 15.6 kts **Dim:** 82.50 (75.80 pp) × 13.50 × 3.97
Electron Equipt: Radar: 2/Don-2—IFF: 1/High Pole-B
M: 2 Zgoda-Sulzer 8TD48 diesels; 2 CP props; 4,400 hp (3,600 sust.)
Electric: 1,920 kVA **Fuel:** 343 tons **Endurance:** 40 days **Range:** 9,000/12
Man: 8 officers, 38 men, 20 scientists

Tayga U.S. Navy, 12-84

Marshal Gelovani Skyfotos, 5-84

REMARKS: Deck reinforcements for six 25-mm AA (II × 3). Two 100-kw electric motors for slow-speed operations; 300-hp bow-thruster. Quadrantial davit over stern ramp, with 4-ton lift. Two 5-ton booms and several oceanographic davits. Two Type 727 fiberglass-hulled survey launches. Have 3 echo-sounders, 6 laboratories. Intended to perform all forms of oceanographic research and hydrographic survey duties.

◆ **6 Akademik Krylov class** Bldr: A. Warski SY, Szczecin, Poland (In serv. 1974-79)

ADMIRAL VLADIMIRSKY	IVAN KRUZHENSTERN	LEONID SOBELYEV
AKADEMIK KRYLOV	LEONID DEMIN	MIKHAIL KRUPSKIY

Leonid Sobelyev—pointed stern L. & L. Van Ginderen, 1985

Admiral Vladimirskiy—blunt stern, Post Lamp radars L. & L. Van Ginderen, 2-83

Mikhail Krupskiy—cropped stern, large radome amidships French Navy, 1-83

OCEANOGRAPHIC-RESEARCH SHIPS *(continued)*

D: 6,600 tons (9,100 fl) **S:** 20.4 kts **Dim:** 147.0 × 18.6 × 6.3
Electron Equipt: Radar: 3/Don-2—IFF: 1/High Pole-B
M: 4 diesels; 2 props; 16,000 hp **Endurance:** 90 days
Range: 23,000/15.4 **Man:** 90 tot.

REMARKS: The largest ships of their type in any navy. Equipped with helicopter hangar and flight deck, two survey launches, and twenty-six laboratories totalling 900 m². The *Leonid Demin* and *Mikhail Krupskiy* were delivered in 1978 and 1979, respectively, and because they have pointed sterns, are about 2.5 m longer, as is *Leonid Sobelyev. Admiral Vladimirskiy* carries 2 Post Lamp gun/torpedo fire-control radars, one atop the forward superstructure and one on the foremast—both offset to starboard.

◆ **1 Vladimir Kavrayskiy class** Bldr: Admiralty SY, Leningrad (In serv. 1973)

VLADIMIR KAVRAYSKIY

Vladimir Kavrayskiy 1974

D: 3,900 tons (fl) **S:** 15.4 kts **Dim:** 70.0 × 18.0 × 6.4
M: 3 Type 13D100 diesels, electric drive; 2 props; 4,800 hp
Endurance: 60 days **Range:** 13,900/9.4

REMARKS: Greatly modified version of the *Dobrynya Nikitich* icebreaker class for arctic research. Has helicopter deck but no hangar, a survey launch, nine laboratories, totaling 180 m², one 8-ton crane, two 3-ton booms, and a hold capacity of 200 m³. The *Otto Schmidt,* completed in 1979 and subordinate to the Academy of Sciences, differs in appearance but is of similar design. The civilian research icebreakers *Georgiy Sedov* and *Petr Pakhtusov,* also subordinated to the Academy of Science, are units of the *Dobrynya Nikitich* class with very few external alterations.

◆ **4 Abkhaziya class** Bldr: Mathias Thiesen Werft, Wismar, East Germany (In serv. 1971-73)

ABKHAZIYA ADZHARIYA BASHKIRIYA MOLDAVIYA

Abkhaziya, home-ported at Vladivostok U.S. Navy, 7-84

D: 5,460 tons (7,500 fl) **S:** 21 kts **Dim:** 124.7 × 17.0 × 6.4
Electron Equipt: Radar: 3/Don-2
M: 2 M.A.N. K6Z 57/80 diesels; 2 props; 8,000 hp
Endurance: 60 days **Range:** 20,000/16 **Man:** 85 tot.

REMARKS: Military version of the Academy of Science's *Akademik Kurchatov* class, with helicopter deck, telescoping hangar, Vee Cone communications antenna, stern-mounted A-frame lift gear, two survey launches, and twenty-seven laboratories totaling 460 m².

◆ **8 Nikolay Zubov class** Bldr: A. Warski SY, Szczecin, Poland (In serv. 1963-68)

ALEKSEY CHIRIKOV
ANDREY VIL'KITSKIY
BORIS DAVYDOV
FADDEY BELLINGSGAUZEN
FYODOR LITKE
NIKOLAY ZUBOV
SEMEN DEZHNEV
VASILIY GOLOVNIN

Semen Dezhnev—survey launches deleted U.S. Navy, 7-83

Faddey Bellingsgauzen—late unit with large platform aft J. Jedrlinic, 2-83

D: 2,200 tons (3,020 fl) **S:** 16.5 kts **Dim:** 90.0 × 13.0 × 4.7
Electron Equipt: Radar: 2/Don-2—IFF: 1/High Pole
M: 2 Zgoda-Sulzer 8TD48 diesels 2 props; 4,800 hp
Endurance: 60 days **Range:** 11,000/14 **Man:** 50 tot.

REMARKS: Considerable variation from ship to ship. Can carry four survey launches, but usually have only two. Nine laboratories, totalling 120 m². Two 7-ton and two 5-ton booms, nine .5–1.2-ton oceanographic-equipment davits, 600 m³ capacity total in two holds. The after platform, *not* for helicopters, is larger in the later ships. Three others serve as intelligence collectors.

◆ **1 Nevel'skoy class** Bldr: . . . SY, Nikolayev (In serv. 1962)

NEVEL'SKOY

Nevel'skoy 1983

D: 2,350 tons (fl) **S:** 17 kts **Dim:** 83.8 × 15.2 × 3.8 **Man:** 45 tot.
Electron Equipt: Radar: 2/Don-2 **M:** 2 diesels; 2 props; 4,000 hp
Range: 10,000/11

REMARKS: The only naval oceanographic research ship, other than the *Vladimir Kavrayskiy,* built in the Soviet Union; apparently the prototype for the *Nikolay Zubov* design. In the Pacific Fleet.

◆ **3 Polyus class** Bldr: Neptunwerft, Rostock, East Germany (In serv. 1962-64)

BAYKAL BALKHASH POLYUS

D: 4,560 tons (6,900 fl) **S:** 14.2 kts **Dim:** 111.6 × 14.4 × 6.3
Electron Equipt: Radar: 2/Don-2 (*Balkhash:* 2/Palm Frond)
M: 4 diesels, electric drive; 2 props; 4,000 hp
Endurance: 75 days **Range:** 25,000/12.3

OCEANOGRAPHIC-RESEARCH SHIPS *(continued)*

Balkhash 1983

Polyus French Navy, 2-83

Remarks: Seventeen laboratories, totaling 290 m². *Polyus* has less-extensive superstructure, different mast arrangement.

HYDROGRAPHIC-SURVEY SHIPS

Note: Ships of the Finik, Moma, Biya, Kamenka, and Samara classes are used as hydrographic-survey ships and as navigation tenders, handling buoys, marking channels, etc. They set and retrieve the 2,000 buoys and 4,000 spar buoys that are taken up for the winter months. Most can carry from two to six navigation buoys. In addition, they are equipped to take basic oceanographic and meteorological samplings. The Soviet Navy's Hydrographic Service has the task not only of surveying Soviet and overseas waters, but of maintaining no less than 600 lighthouses, 150 noise beacons, and 8,000 navigation buoys.

◆ **22 Fenik class** Bldr: Polnocny SY, Gdansk, Poland (In serv. 1979-81)

GS-44	GS-260	GS-280	GS-392	GS-400	GS-404
GS-47	GS-270	GS-297	GS-397	GS-401	GS-405
GS-86	GS-272	GS-301	GS-398	GS-402	
GS-87	GS-278	GS-388	GS-399	GS-403	

GS-401 25 Flot., French Navy, 1984

D: 1,200 tons (fl) **S:** 13 kts **Dim:** 61.30 × 11.80 (10.80 wl) × 3.27
Electron Equipt: Radar: 2/Don-2—IFF: 1/High Pole-B
M: 2 Cegielski-Sulzer diesels; 2 CP props; 1,920 hp (plus two 75-kw electric motors for quiet, 6-kt operations)
Electric: 675 kVA **Endurance:** 15 days **Range:** 3,000/13
Man: 5 officers, 23 men

Remarks: GS—*Gidrograficheskoye Sudno* (Hydrographic Vessel). Intended for navigational buoy-tending and survey, for which 4 echo-sounders are fitted. Up to 3 fiberglass 3-dwt utility landing craft can be stowed on the buoy working deck, beneath the 7-ton crane. Bow-thruster of 130 kw fitted. Have hydrological, hydrographic, and cartographic facilities. Also, one built for East Germany and four for Poland (two civilian).

◆ **19 Moma class** Bldr: Polnocny SY, Gdansk, Poland (In serv. 1967-74)

Al'tayr	Artika	Kril'on	Rybachiy (ex-*Odograf*)
Anadyr'	Askol'd	Liman	Sever
Andromeda	Cheleken	Mars	Taymyr
Antares	El'ton	Morzhovets	Zapolar'ye
Antartika	Kolguev	Okean	

Taymyr PH2 P. Soutar, U.S.N., 9-83

Kolguev—with boats disembarked; note auxiliary stack between davits
U.S. Navy, 8-83

Rybachiy—armed unit with deckhouse filling well deck U.S. Navy, 9-83

D: 1,260 tons (1,540 fl) **S:** 17 kts **Dim:** 73.3 × 10.8 × 3.8
Electron Equipt: Radar: 2/Don-2—IFF: 1/High Pole-A
M: 2 Zgoda-Sulzer 6TD48 diesels; 2 CP props; 3,600 hp
Endurance: 35 days **Range:** 8,700/11 **Man:** 56 tot.

Remarks: Carry one survey launch and a 7-ton crane, and have four laboratories, totaling 35 m². The *Rybachiy* (ex-*Odograf*) has a deckhouse in place of the crane and may be involved in oceanographic research; the ship is armed with 4/12.7-mm mg (II × 2) forward and 2/SA-N-5 systems (IV × 2; 32 SA-5 Grail missiles) aft. Sisters in Polish, Bulgarian, and Yugoslav navies. Nine more serve as intelligence collectors.

◆ **14 Biya class** Bldr: Polnocny SY, Gdansk, Poland (In serv. 1972-76)

GS-182	GS-194	GS-202	GS-206	GS-210	GS-269	GS-273
GS-193	GS-198	GS-204	GS-208	GS-214	GS-271	GS-275

D: 750 tons (fl) **S:** 13 kts **Dim:** 55.0 × 9.2 × 2.6
Electron Equipt: Radar: 1/Don-2
M: 2 diesels; 2 CP props; 1,200 hp **Endurance:** 15 days
Range: 4,700/11 **Man:** 25 tot.

Remarks: GS—*Gidrograficheskoye Sudno* (Hydrographic Survey Ship). Similar to Kamenka class, but have longer superstructure and less buoy-handling space; one survey launch; one 5-ton crane. Laboratory space: 15 m². One unit transferred to Guinea-Bissau, another (GS-186) to Cuba in 1980.

HYDROGRAPHIC-SURVEY SHIPS *(continued)*

GS-186—under tow to Cuba; note crane at forecastle break 1980

◆ **10 Kamenka class** Bldr: Polnocny SY, Gdansk, Poland (In serv. 1968-72)

GS-66 GS-107 GS-207
GS-74 GS-108 (ex-*Vernier*) GS-211
GS-82 GS-114 (ex-*Bel'bek*)
GS-103 GS-203

GS-107—note crane in center of working deck 1980

D: 703 tons (fl) **S:** 13.7 kts **Dim:** 53.5 × 9.1 × 2.6
Electron Equipt: Radar: 1/Don-2 **M:** 2 diesels; 2 CP props; 1,765 hp
Range: 4,000/10 **Man:** 40 tot.

Remarks: GS—*Gidrograficheskoye Sudno* (Hydrographic Survey Ship). Similar to Biya class, but have more facilities for stowing and handling buoys. No survey launch. One 5-ton crane. One sister in the East German Navy. One transferred to Cape Verde in 1980.

◆ **15 Samara class** Bldr: Polnocny SY, Gdansk, Poland (In serv. 1962-64)

Azimut Gorizont Rumb (GS-118) Vostok
Deviator Gradus Tropik GS-275 (ex-*Yug*)
Gigrometr Kompas Tura (ex-*Globus*) Zenit
Glubometr Pamyat' Merkuriya Vaygach

D: 1,050 tons (1,276 fl) **S:** 15.5 kts **Dim:** 59.0 × 10.4 × 3.8
Electron Equipt: Radar: 2/Don-2
M: 2 Zgoda 5TD48 diesels; 2 CP props; 3,000 hp **Endurance:** 25 days
Range: 6,200/11 **Man:** 45 tot. (*Tura:* 140 tot.)

Remarks: Have one survey launch and 15 m² of laboratory space. The *Tura* (ex-*Globus*) had her forecastle extended to her superstructure in 1978 and her 7-ton crane removed; able to accommodate 120 personnel, she is used for training. *Deviator* served briefly as an intelligence collector. *Vaygach* has a large deckhouse surrounding the base of the buoy crane.

Pamyat Merkuriya 10-83

Tura—buoy-handling crane removed, forecastle extended 1978

◆ **4 Telnovsk class** Bldr: Hungary (In serv. 1949-57)

Aytodor Sirena Sviyaga Ulyana Gromova

D: 1,300 tons (1,700 fl) **S:** 11 kts **Dim:** 70.0 × 10.0 × 4.2
Electron Equipt: Radar: 1/Neptune, Don, or Don-2
M: 1 Ganz diesel; 800 hp **Range:** 3,300/9.7 **Man:** 50 tot.

Remarks: Similar in most respects to cargo-ship version. All carry one launch; 15 m² of laboratory space. *Ulyana Gromova* has a lengthened poop deck; the similar *Stvor* has been stricken.

◆ **3 Melitopol class** Bldr: U.S.S.R. (In serv. 1952-55)

Mayak Niviler Prizma

D: 1,200 tons (fl) **S:** 11.3 kts **Dim:** 57.6 × 9.0 × 4.3 **Range:** 2,500/10.5
Electron Equipt: Radar: 1/Don **M:** 1 Type 6DR30/40 diesel; 600 hp

Remarks: Converted small, two-hatch cargo ships with few modifications; 673 grt/776 dwt. Carry one survey launch on deck.

◆ **several GPB-480-class inshore-survey craft** Bldr: U.S.S.R. (In serv. 1960s)

GPB-480, GPB-767, etc.

GPB-767—GPB-480 class French Navy, 8-79

D: 120 tons (fl) **S:** 12 kts **Dim:** 29.0 × 5.0 × 1.7
Electron Equipt: Radar: 1/Spin Trough **M:** 1 diesel; 450 hp
Endurance: 10 days **Range:** 1,600/10 **Man:** 15 tot.

Remarks: GPB—*Gidrograficheskoye Pribezhnyy Bot* (Coastal Hydrographic Survey Boat). VM on the diving-tender version stands for *Vodolaznyy Morskoy* (Seagoing Diving Tender). Same hull and propulsion as the Nyryat-I-class diving tenders. The charthouse/laboratory is 6 m², and there are two 1.5-ton derricks. The smaller GPB-710 class is carried aboard the larger survey and oceanographic ships listed above:
D: 7 tons (fl) **S:** 10 kts for 150 nautical miles **Dim:** 11.0 × 3.0 × 0.7.

MISSILE-RANGE INSTRUMENTATION SHIPS

Note: A very large, 260-m missile-range support or space event support ship was reported fitting out at Baltic SY, Leningrad, during 1985; perhaps nearly twice the size of *Marshal Nedelin,* it may be nuclear-powered.

◆ **1 new construction** Bldr: Admiralty SY, Leningrad

Marshal Nedelin (In serv. 1984)

D: 24,000 tons (fl) **S:** 20 kts **Dim:** 213.0 × 27.7 × 7.7
Electron Equipt: Radar: 3/Palm Frond, 1/Strut Pair, 1/Fly Screen (helo control), 1/End Tray (balloon tracking)
IFF: 2/Salt Pot, 1/High Pole transponders
TACAN: 2/Round House
M: 2 gas turbines; 2 props; 54,000 hp
Range: . . . **Man:** 200 tot.

MISSILE-RANGE INSTRUMENTATION SHIPS *(continued)*

Marshal Nedelin French Navy, 10-84

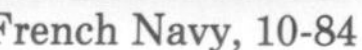

Marshal Nedelin—note 2 covered theodolite tracking camera positions forward
R. Neth. Navy, 10-84

Marshal Nedelin U.S. Navy, 11-84

Remarks: Possibly intended to begin replacement of the aged *Desna-* and *Sibir'*-class range tracking ships, but equipped also to serve in a space tracking and communications role. Tracking antennas include 1/Quad Leaf, 3/Quad Wedge, 4/Quad . . . , and 6 telemetry reception arrays. A large Ship Globe radome conceals a satellite communications antenna. Twin hangars accommodate 2 Ka-27/32 Helix utility helicopters. Hull has a bulbous bow form. Foundations for 6/30-mm gatling AA and 3/Bass Tilt radar directors are present. Has a swimming pool just abaft the stack. Operates in the Pacific Fleet.

◆ **2 Desna class** Bldr: Warnow Werft, Warnemünde (In serv. 1963)

Chazhma (ex-*Dangera*) Chumikan (ex-*Dolgeschtchel'ye*)

D: 14,065 tons (fl) **S:** 15 kts **Dim:** 139.9 × 18.0 × 7.9
Electron Equipt: Radar: 2/Don-2, 1/Head Net-B, 1/Ship Globe (tracking)
EW: 2/Watch Dog
M: 1 M.A.N. diesel; 5,400 hp **Range:** 9,000/13

Remarks: Heavily modified cargo ships. Tracking radar in large dome atop the bridge, with three tracking directors mounted forward. Hormone helicopter with hangar aft. Vee Cone communications antennas atop the stack. Based in the Pacific. Only ships with Head Net-B radar (both reflectors in the same plane).

Chumikan 1981

◆ **4 Sibir' class** Bldr: A. Warski SY, Szczecin, Poland (In serv. 1958)

Chukotka Sakhalin Sibir' Spassk (ex-*Suchan*)

Chukotka—note different superstructures, Big Net radar 1981

Spassk—modified with flush deck, Head Net-C 1981

D: 7,800 tons (fl) **S:** 12 kts **Dim:** 108.2 × 14.6 × 7.2
Electron Equipt: Radar: 2/Don-2, 1/Head Net-C or Big Net, several tracking sets
M: Triple-expansion; 1 props; 2,300 hp **Range:** 11,800/12

Remarks: Converted (circa 1960) Donbass-class cargo ships. Carry Big Net or Head Net-C radar for tracking, and two or three tracking directors forward. Originally, only *Chukotka* was flush-decked; the others had a well deck forward. Now all are flush-decked. All carry one Hormone-C helicopter, but have no hangar. All are in the Pacific Fleet.

NOISE-MEASUREMENT SHIPS

◆ **5 or more Onega class** Bldr: . . . (In serv. 1973- . . .)

GKS-52 GKS-83 GKS-224 GKS-286 SFP-95

GKS-52

D: 1,925 tons (fl) **S:** 20 kts **Dim:** 81.0 × 11.0 × 4.2
Electron Equipt: Radar: 1/Don-2
M: 1 gas turbine; 1 prop; 15,000 hp **Man:** 45 tot.

Remarks: GKS—*Gidroakusticheskoye Kontrol'noye Sudno* (Hydroacoustic Monitoring Ship) and indicates that these ships are successors to the T-43-class noise-monitoring ships. Helicopter deck aft, long forecastle, two pylon masts, and a low stack. SFP—*Sudno Fizicheskiy Poley* (Physical Fields Measuring Vessel)—on SFP-95 indicates different mission and sensors.

◆ **17 Modified T-43 class** Bldr: Various (In serv. mid-1950s)

GKS-11	GKS-14	GKS-17	GKS-20	GKS-23	GKS-42
GKS-12	GKS-15	GKS-18	GKS-21	GKS-24	GKS-45
GKS-13	GKS-16	GKS-19	GKS-22	GKS-26	

GKS-15

D: 500 tons (570 fl) **S:** 14 kts **Dim:** 58.0 × 8.6 × 2.3
Electron Equipt: Radar: 1/Neptune or Spin Trough
IFF: 1/High Pole
M: 2 Type 9D diesels; 2 props; 2,200 hp **Man:** 77 tot.

Remarks: GKS = *Gidroakusticheskoye Kontrol'noye Sudno* (Hydroacoustic Monitoring Ship) and indicates that these ships measure the radiated noise of other ships, including submarines, by laying hydrophone arrays via the numerous small davits they carry aft. One 37-mm AA gun can be installed on the forecastle. At least two (GKS-25, -46) have been stricken.

DEGAUSSING/DEPERMING SHIPS

◆ **1 (+ . . .) Bereza class** Bldr: . . . SY, Poland (In serv. 1985- . . .)

SR-28

D: 2,700 tons (fl) **S:** 15 kts **Dim:** 84.00 (75.80 pp) × 13.50 × 4.0
Electron Equipt: Radar: 1/Kivach—IFF: 1/High Pole-B
M: 2 Zgoda-Sulzer 8TD48 diesels; 2 CP props; 4,400 hp (3,600 sust.)
Electric: . . . **Range:** . . . **Man:** 70 tot.

Remarks: SR = *Sudno Razmagnichivanya* (Deperming Vessel). Design appears to be based on that of the Yug-class oceanographic ship, with the forecastle raised one deck higher. A large crane is fitted aft to handle deperming cables.

◆ **9 (+ . . .) Pelym class** Bldr: . . . (In serv. 1971- . . .)

SR-191 SR-409 7 others

D: 1,300 tons (fl) **S:** 16 kts **Dim:** 65.5 × 11.6 × 3.4
Electron Equipt: Radar: 1/Don-2 **M:** 2 diesels; 2 props; . . . hp
Range: 4,500/12 **Man:** 70 tot.

Remarks: Numbers in the SR—*Sudno Razmagnichivanya* (Deperming Vessel) series. Apparently intended to replace the aged Sekstan and Korall classes. One transferred to Cuba. Late units have a tripod mast aft to support radio antenna wires; early ships had an aerial spreader on the stack.

SR-191 9-83

SR-191 9-83

◆ **1 or more Khabarov class** Bldr: U.S.S.R. (In serv. 1950s)

D: 650 tons (fl) **S:** 10.4 kts **Dim:** 46.4 × 8.0 × 3.3
M: 1 diesel; 1 prop; 600 hp **Range:** 1,600/8

Remarks: Version of the steel-hulled coastal cargo ship design, with large deckhouse over forward hold area.

◆ **up to 20 Sekstan class** Bldr: Finland (In serv. 1949-55)

D: 400 tons (fl) **S:** 11 kts **Dim:** 41.0 × 9.3 × 4.2
M: 1 diesel; 1 prop; 400 hp **Range:** 1,200/10.5 **Man:** 24 tot.

Remarks: Wooden-hulled; built as war reparations. Same hull also used for coastal survey ship and cargo ship versions, now discarded.

ICEBREAKERS

Note: The Soviet Union has far and away the largest and most powerful icebreaker fleet in the world. Its civilian component includes the atomic-powered *Arktika* class, the most powerful of all. The two types, patrol and support, that the navy operates are both based on the same civilian design and are among the very few conventionally driven icebreakers in Soviet service to be designed and built in the U.S.S.R. All other Soviet icebreakers now in service were built in Finland.

◆ **2 Ivan Susanin-class support icebreakers** Bldr: Admiralty SY, Leningrad

Ivan Susanin (In serv. 1974) Ruslan (In serv. 1981)

Ivan Susanin 1983

D: 3,400 tons (fl) **S:** 14.5 kts **Dim:** 70.0 (62.0 pp) × 18.3 × 6.5
Electron Equipt: Radar: 2/Don-Kay—IFF: 1/High Pole-B
M: 3 Type 13D100 diesels, electric drive; 2 props; 5,400 hp **Electric:** 1,000 kw
Fuel: 550 tons **Range:** 5,500/12.5; 13,000/9.4 **Man:** 140 tot.

ICEBREAKERS *(continued)*

Remarks: Based on the *Dobrynya Nikitich* and *Vladimir Kavrayskiy* designs. Sisters *Aysberg, Dunay, Imeni XXV Sezda K.P.S.S., Imeni XXVI Sezda K.P.S.S.* are armed and are operated by the KGB Maritime Border Guard as PSKR—*Pogranichnyy Storozhevoy Korabl'* (Border Patrol Ship). Helicopter deck aft, but no hangar. Both had their guns, Owl Screech and Strut Curve radars removed, were repainted black and white, and are operated as naval icebreakers.

◆ **7 Dobrynya Nikitich-class support icebreakers**

Bldr: Admiralty SY, Leningrad (In serv. 1959-74)

Buran, Dobrynya Nikitich, Il'ya Muromets, Peresvet, Purga, Sadko, Vyuga

Dobrynya Nikitich 1978

D: 2,940 tons (fl) **S:** 14.5 kts **Dim:** 67.7 × 18.3 × 6.1
Electron Equipt: Radar: 1-2/Don-2—IFF: 1/High Pole
M: 3 13D100 diesels, electric drive; 3 props (1 fwd); 5,400 hp
Range: 5,500/12; 13,000/9.4 **Man:** 100 tot.

Remarks: More than twenty of this class were built, the remainder being civilian. *Peresvet, Purga, Sadko,* and *Vyuga* were armed with 2/57-mm AA (II × 1) and 2/25-mm AA (II × 1), now removed. Resemble the *Ivan Susanin* class, but have much less superstructure and an open fantail rigged for ocean towing. Later units do not have a bow propeller but have the same horsepower.

TRAINING SHIPS

◆ **3 Smol'ny class** Bldr: A. Warski SY, Szczecin, Poland (In serv. 1976-78)

Khasan, Perekop, Smol'ny

Khasan Skyfotos, 6-82

Smol'ny J.-C. Bellonne, 1979

D: 8,500 tons (fl) **S:** 20 kts **Dim:** 138.0 × 18.0 × 6.2
A: 4/76.2-mm DP (II × 2)—4/30-mm AA (II × 2)—RBU-2500 ASW RL (XII × 2)
Electron Equipt: Radar: 4/Don-2, 1/Head Net-C, 1/Owl Screech, 1/Drum Tilt
Sonar: 1/M/F, hull-mounted
EW: 2/Watch Dog—IFF: 1/High Pole-B
M: 4 diesels; 2 props; 16,000 hp
Range: 12,000/15 **Man:** 210 crew + 270 cadets

Remarks: Built to relieve the *Sverdlov*-class cruisers that were formerly used for cadet training. Can carry more than 270 cadets. The *Perekop* substitutes one Don-Kay radar for one of the four Don-2s. Carry six rowboats aft for exercising the cadets.

◆ **2 Ugra class** Bldr: Nikolayev (In serv. 1970-71)

Borodino, Gangut

Gangut French Navy, 1982

D: 6,900 tons (9,650 fl) **S:** 17 kts **Dim:** 145.0 × 17.7 × 6.4
A: 8/57-mm AA (II × 4)
Electron Equipt: Radar: 4/Don-2, 1/Strut Curve, 2/Muff Cob
EW: 4/Watch Dog—IFF: 1/High Pole-B
M: 4 diesels; 2 props; 8,000 hp
Range: 21,000/10 **Man:** 300 crew + 400 cadets

Remarks: Soviet type designation: *Uchebnoye Sudno* (Training Ship). Similar to the submarine-tender version, but have accommodations and training facilities in place of workshops, magazines, storerooms, etc. Enlarged after deckhouse incorporates navigation-training space, including numerous duplicate navigator's positions. No helicopter facilities.

◆ **2 Modified Wodnik class** Bldr: Poland (In serv. 1977)

Oka, Luga

Oka 1977

D: 1,500 tons (1,800 fl) **S:** 15 kts **Dim:** 72.0 × 12.0 × 4.0
Electron Equipt: Radar: 3/Don-2
M: 2 Zgoda-Sulzer 6TD48 diesels; 2 CP props; 3,600 hp
Range: 7,500/11 **Man:** 58 men + 90 cadets

Remarks: Used for navigation training. Similar to Polish and East German units of the Wodnik class, but have slightly larger superstructures, pilothouse one deck higher, and are not armed. Based on the Moma design.

◆ **1 or more Mayak class** Bldr: . . . (In serv. 1967-1974)

D: 1,050 tons (fl) **S:** 11 kts **Dim:** 54.2 (50.4 pp) × 9.3 × 3.6
A: 2/25-mm AA (II × 1)—4/RBU-1200 ASW RL (V × 4)—4/400-mm ASW TT (fixed)—2/d.c. racks (6 d.c. each)
Electron Equipt: Radar: 1/Spin Trough—Sonar: HF, hull-mounted
M: 1 Karl Liebnecht 8NVD48 diesel; 1 prop; 800 hp
Range: 9,400/11 **Man:** 60 tot., including students

TRAINING SHIPS *(continued)*

Mayak-class ASW training ship

Remarks: Late-production Mayak hull with basic ASW armament and sensors, apparently converted to provide basic ASW orientation or coastal ASW flotilla proficiency training. ASW RL mounted on forecastle, torpedo tubes in the waist area, depth-charge racks at the stern. The fish-hold area is used for accommodations. Due to low speed, would have little wartime utility.

TRIALS SHIPS AND CRAFT

◆ **1 (or more) Al'pinist class** Bldr: Yaroslavl SY (In serv. . . .)

OS-104

OS-104 JMSDF, 1985

D: 1,200 tons (fl) **S:** 13 kts **Dim:** 53.7 (46.2 pp) × 10.5 × 4.3
Electron Equipt: Radar: 1/Don-2, 1/. . . nav.
M: 1 Type 8NVD48-2U diesel; 1 CP prop; 1,320 hp
Fuel: 162 tons **Electric:** 450 kw **Range:** 7,600/13 **Man:** . . .

Remarks: Modification of a 322-dwt stern-haul trawler. Gallows crane at stern resembles those used to handle submersible decompression chambers on T-58-class submarine rescue ships. Forecastle has been extended aft and supports 2-level deckhouse on starboard side. OS-104 is in the Pacific Fleet.

◆ **5 Potok class** Bldr: . . . (In serv. 1978- . . .)

OS-100 OS-138 OS-145 OS-225 OS-. . .

OS-225

D: 750 tons (860 fl) **S:** 17 kts **Dim:** 71.0 × 9.1 × 2.5
A: 1/533-mm TT, 1/400-mm TT **Electron Equipt:** Radar: 1/Don-2
M: 2 diesels; 2 props; 4,000 hp **Range:** 5,000/12

Remarks: OS—*Opitnoye Sudno* (Experimental Vessel). The design closely resembles the T-58 class, but the forecastle extends well aft. The trainable torpedo tubes are on the bow. A large crane aft is presumably used for retrieval. These ships are probably replacements for Modified T-43-class minesweepers, which had been used in torpedo trials since the 1950s.

◆ **1 or 2 Daldyn class**

Daldyn class 1976

D: 360 tons (fl) **S:** 9 kts **Dim:** 31.7 × 7.2 × 2.8
Electron Equipt: Radar: 1/Spin Trough
M: 1 Type 8NVD 36U diesel; 1 prop; 305 hp **Man:** 15 tot.

Remarks: Modified Kareliya-class purse-seiner, possibly for use in mine countermeasures trials.

◆ **several T-43-class former minesweepers**

T-43-class trials tender 1976

Remarks: Data as for minesweeper version. Some are disarmed former long-hulled minesweepers, while four or more 58-m versions were built as torpedo trials ships.

Note: There are probably a number of additional ships of various classes with OS—*Opitnoye Sudno* (Experimental Vessel)—pendants, either built for the purpose or former combatants or auxiliaries adapted for specific trials duties. The largest was OS-24, the former heavy cruiser *Voroshilov,* since scrapped.

TARGET SERVICE CRAFT

◆ **9 Osa-class target-control boats**

Osa target controller 1974

Remarks: Have Osa hull and propulsion. Used to operate craft shown below by remote control. Carry Square Tie and a High Pole-B IFF transponder. Communications antennas have been enhanced to provide for radio-control.

TARGET SERVICE CRAFT *(continued)*

◆ **8 Modified Osa-class missile targets**

KTs-897, Osa target—with nets strung between the masts 8-80

REMARKS: KTs—*Kontrol'naya Tsel'* (Controlled Target). Have Osa hull and propulsion. Crew departs when ship is in operation. Equipped with radar corner reflectors to strengthen target and two heat-generator chimneys to attract infrared homing missiles.

◆ **14 or more Shelon-class torpedo-retrievers** Bldr: . . . (In serv. 1978- . . .)

Shelon class L. & L. Van Ginderen, 6-85

Shelon variant—no dipping sonar or recovery ramp 1983

D: 270 tons (fl) **S:** 24 kts **Dim:** 41.0 × 6.0 × . . .
Electron Equipt: Radar: 1/Spin Trough
Sonar: 1/helicopter dipping-type
IFF: 1/High Pole-B
M: 2 diesels; 2 props; . . . hp **Man:** 40 tot.

REMARKS: High-speed hull with a covered torpedo-recovery ramp aft. May be replacing the Poluchat-I class.

A new variant of the Shelon-class torpedo retriever design was sighted during 1983 while under tow from the Black Sea to Vladivostok. Unlike earlier units it does not have a slope to the weapons recovery area of the after portion of the deckhouse; it has no hatch in the deckhouse roof and no recovery hatch through the transom stern. The function of the craft, which has a crew of about 30, is unknown.

◆ **up to 40 Poluchat-I-class torpedo-retrievers**

Poluchat-I-class torpedo retriever 1982

D: 90 tons (fl) **S:** 18 kts **Dim:** 29.6 × 6.1 × 1.9
A: 2/14.5-mm AA (II × 1) in some
Electron Equipt: Radar: 1/Spin Trough— IFF: 1/High Pole-A
M: 2 M50 diesels; 2 props; 2,400 hp **Range:** 450/17; 900/10 **Man:** 20 tot.

REMARKS: Carry numbers in the TL—*Torpedolov* (Torpedo-Retriever) series. Built in the 1950s. Recovery ramp aft. Some configured as patrol boats. Many exported abroad. See photo in section on Patrol Craft.

TARGET BARGES

Soviet Navy built-for-the-purpose 107-m target barge, with numerous corner reflectors to enhance radar return U.S. Navy, 7-84

107-m target barge with two heat-generator arrays to attract IR homing missiles G. Koop, 1985

Soviet Navy 64-meter catamaran gunnery target barge G. Koop, 1985

DIVING TENDERS

◆ **8 or more Yelva class** (In serv. 1973- . . .)

VM-268, Yelva class G. Koop, 1985

D: 295 tons (fl) **S:** 12.4 kts **Dim:** 40.9 × 8.0 × 2.1
Electron Equipt: Radar: 1/Spin Trough
M: 2 Type 3D12A diesels; 2 props; 600 hp **Man:** 30 tot.

Remarks: Can support 7 divers at once to 60 m. Have a decompression chamber; some (but not all) also have a submersible decompression chamber. Replaced T-43 minesweepers built for the role. Several exported.

◆ **several Nyryat-1 class** (In serv. late 1950s-mid 1960s)

D: 120 tons (fl) **S:** 12 kts **Dim:** 29.0 × 5.0 × 1.7
Electron Equipt: Radar: 1/Spin Trough
M: 1 diesel; 1 prop; 450 hp **Endurance:** 10 days
Range: 1,600/10 **Man:** 15 tot.

Remarks: Carry VM—*Vodolaznyy Morskoy* (Seagoing Diving Tender)—pendants. Same hull used for GPB-480-class inshore survey craft. Many exported.

◆ **several Nyryat-2 class** (In serv. 1950s)

PO-2 class—Nyryat-2 class similar 1975

D: 50 tons **S:** 9 kts **Dim:** 21.0 × 4.5 × . . .
Electron Equipt: Radar: 1/Spin Trough
M: 1 Type 3D6 diesel; 1 prop; 150 hp **Man:** 10 tot.

Remarks: Uses same hull as PO-2-class utility launch; distinguishable by bulwarks to hull at bow and stern. Hundreds of PO-2 hulls were built; many were exported.

MISCELLANEOUS SERVICE CRAFT

◆ . . . **PZhK-415-class fireboats** Bldr: . . . U.S.S.R. (In serv. 1984- . . .)

D: 320 tons (fl) **S:** 12.5 kfts **Dim:** 36.53 × 7.80 × 2.20
M: 2 Type ZKD 12N-520 diesels; 2 CP props; 1,040 hp
Range: 450/12.5 **Electric:** 400 kw **Man:** 20 tot.

Remarks: Four firefighting water monitors, two with 220 m^3/hr capacity and two of 500 m^3/hr, driven by two 750 m^3/hr diesel-powered pumps. Foam and Freon extinguishing systems. Water curtain to protect boat. Can also be used for towing.

◆ . . . **Pozharney-I-class fireboats** (In serv. 1950s)

D: 180 tons (fl) **S:** 17 kts **Dim:** 35.0 × 6.2 × 2.0
M: 2 Type M50-F1 diesels; 2 props; 1,800 hp

◆ . . . **Prometey-class large harbor tugs** Bldr: Petrozavod SY, Leningrad

D: 319 tons (fl) **S:** 12 kts **Dim:** 29.8 (28.2 pp) × 8.3 × 3.2
M: 2 Type 6D30/50-4 diesels; 2 Kort-nozzle props; 1,200 hp
Electric: 50 kw **Range:** 1,800/12 **Man:** 3–5 tot.

Prometey-class RB-202 1980

Remarks: Built 1970s-80s at Leningrad and Gorokhovets SY; some exported. Also in civil use. Have 14-ton bollard pull, ice-strengthened hull. Over 100 built since 1971.

◆ **26 Sidehole-II-class harbor tugs** Bldr: Petrozavod SY, Leningrad (In serv. 1970s)

D: 197 tons (fl) **S:** 10 kts **Dim:** 24.2 × 7.0 × 3.4
Electron Equipt: Radar: 1/Spin Trough
M: 2 Type 6 CHN25/34 diesels; 2 vertical cycloidal props; 900 hp

Remarks: Soviet class name: *Peredovik.* Also in civil use. Bollard pull: 10.5 tons. Naval units have RB—*Rednyy Buksir* (Roadstead Tug) pendants.

◆ **30 Sidehole-I-class harbor tugs** (In serv. 1960s)

D: 183 tons (fl) **S:** 9 kts **Dim:** 24.4 × 7.0 × 3.3
Electron Equipt: Radar: 1/Spin Trough
M: 2 Type 6 CH25/34 diesels; 2 vertical cycloidal props; 600 hp

◆ . . . **Tugur-class harbor tugs** Bldr: Finland (In serv. 1950s)

D: 300 tons (fl) **S:** 12 kts **Dim:** 30.7 × 7.7 × 2.3
M: 1 set reciprocating steam; 1 prop; 500 hp **Boilers:** 2

Remarks: Originally considered to be seagoing tugs; have MB pendants. Coal-fueled. 214 built.

FUEL-OIL LIGHTERS

◆ . . . **Toplivo-2 class** Bldr: U.S.S.R. and Egypt (In serv. 1958-1975)

D: 466 tons (1,180 tons fl) **S:** 10 kts **Dim:** 54.26 (49.40 pp) × 7.40 × 3.10
Electron Equipt: Radar: 1/Spin Trough
M: 1 Russkiy Dizel 6 DR30/50-5-2 diesel; 1 prop; 600 hp
Electric: 250 kw **Fuel:** 19 tons **Range:** 1,500/10 **Man:** 24 tot.

Remarks: 308 grt/508 dwt. Four cargo tanks, totaling 606 m^3. Built in several versions including fuel-oil lighter, water lighter, and diesel-fuel lighter. Final series built at Alexandria, Egypt, with deliveries terminated by Soviet expulsion. Fully seagoing if required.

◆ . . . **Toplivo-3 class** (In serv. 1950s)

D: 1,300 tons (fl) **S:** 9 kts **Dim:** 53.0 × 10.0 × 3.0
M: 1 diesel; 1 prop; 300 hp

Remarks: Low freeboard, low superstructure harbor craft. There are probably a number of the smaller (450-ton fl) Toplivo-1-class harbor fuel lighters remaining also.

ACCOMMODATIONS BARGES

◆ . . . **Bolva series** Bldr: Valmet Oy, Helsinki, Finland

Myass—Bolva-III class Valmet, 1978

D: 6,500 tons (fl) **Dim:** 110.9 × 13.8 × 2.8 **Man:** 374–394 total berthing

Remarks: First series of 8 Bolva-I built 1960-63, second series of 21 Bolva-II built 1963-72, with hangar-like auditorium built atop superstructure aft. Bolva-III built 1971-. . . , with 34 completed to date, 3 more ordered 1983. Many went to civilian service.

ACCOMMODATIONS BARGES *(continued)*

◆ . . . **Vyn-class** (In serv. 1960s)

D: 3,000 tons (fl) **Dim:** 92.0 × 13.4 × 4.6
Man: Approx. 200

REMARKS: Converted from cargo barges built in Finland in the late 1940s-early 1950s. One was based in Somalia during the mid-1970s. Apparently support submarines, as there is a torpedo-loading hatch. Pendant numbers in the PKZ—*Plavuchiya Kazarma* (Floating Barracks) series.

CIVILIAN SPACE EVENT SUPPORT SHIPS

NOTE: The ships listed below are subordinated to the Academy of Sciences and are primarily intended to provide communications relay services with manned satellites. The large satellite support/tracking ship *Marshal Nedelin,* completed 1983, is a naval unit. The eight naval-subordinated *Vytegrales*-class ships are also used in space event work, as have been several naval Moma- and Samara-class survey ship/buoy tenders.

◆ **4 Kosmonavt Pavel Belyayev class** Bldr: Zhdanov SY, Leningrad

	In serv.	Conv.
KOSMONAVT GEORGIY DOBROVOLSKIY (ex-*Semyon Kosinov*)	1968	1978
KOSMONAVT PAVEL BELYAYEV (ex-*Vytegrales*)	1963	1977
KOSMONAVT VIKTOR PATSEYEV (ex-*Nazar Gubin*)	1968	1978
KOSMONAVT VLADILAV VOLKOV (ex-*Yeniseiles*)	1964	1977

Kosmonavt Viktor Patseyev 9-84

Kosmonavt Vladilav Volkov L. & L. Van Ginderen, 11-83

D: 9,000 tons (fl) **S:** 16 kts **Dim:** 121.8 (113.0 pp) × 16.7 × 7.3
Electron Equipt: Radar: 1/Don-2, 1/Okean, 1/Mod. Kite Screech
M: 1 Bryansk-Burmeister & Wain 950 VTBF 110 diesel; 1 prop; 5,200 hp
Fuel: 350 tons **Range:** 7,400/15 **Man:** 90 tot.

REMARKS: 4,482 grt/2,010 dwt. Like the less-elaborately altered *Borovichi* group, these are conversions from *Vytegrales*-class timber carriers, performed at the building yard. Named for cosmonauts killed on missions. Have large, stabilized "Quad Spring" communications array amidships and three smaller satellite communications arrays. Based in the Baltic.

◆ **1 Kosmonavt Yuriy Gagarin class** Bldr: Baltic SY, Leningrad

KOSMONAVT YURIY GAGARIN (In serv. 12-71)

Kosmonavt Yuriy Gagarin 1983

Kosmonavt Yuriy Gagarin L. & L. Van Ginderen, 7-82

D: 53,500 tons (fl) **S:** 18 kts **Dim:** 231.7 (213.9 pp) × 31.1 × 10.0
Electron Equipt: Radar: 1/Don-Kay, 1/Okean
M: 1 set GT, electric drive; 1 prop; 19,000 hp **Boilers:** 2
Range: 24,000/17.7 **Man:** 160 crew + 180 scientists-technicians

REMARKS: 32,291 grt/31,300 dwt. A *Sofiya*-class tanker hull adapted prior to construction. Has two 27-m-diameter Ship Shell and two 12.5-m-diameter Ship Bowl stabilized communications dishes, 2 Vee Tube HF, and four Quad Ring arrays. Bow- and stern-thrusters. Three swimming pools, 300-seat theater; gymnasium. Endurance: 120 days. Home port: Odessa.

◆ **1 Akademik Sergey Korolev** (In serv. 1970)

Akademik Sergey Korolev French Navy, 4-80

D: 21,465 tons (fl) **S:** 17 kts **Dim:** 181.9 (167.9 pp) × 25.0 × 7.9
Electron Equipt: Radar: 2/Don-Kay
M: 1 Bryansk-Burmeister & Wain diesel; 1 prop; 12,000 hp
Range: 22,500/17 **Man:** 188 crew + 170 scientists-technicians

REMARKS: 17,114 grt/7,067 dwt. Has 80 "laboratories." Space communications antennas include 2 Ship Bowl and 1 Ship Globe and 4 Quad Ring. Based in the Far East.

◆ **1 Kosmonavt Vladimir Komarov class** Bldr: Kherson SY

KOSMONAVT VLADIMIR KOMAROV (ex-*Genichevsk*) (In serv. 1966)

Kosmonavt Vladimir Komarov 1984

D: 17,500 tons (fl) **S:** 17.5 kts **Dim:** 155.7 (146.4 pp) × 22.3 × 8.6
Electron Equipt: Radar: 2/Don-Kay
M: 1 Bryansk-Burmeister & Wain diesel; 1 prop; 9,000 hp
Fuel: 1,656 tons **Range:** 16,700/17.5 **Man:** 254 tot.

REMARKS: 13,935 grt/7,065 dwt. Converted from a *Poltava*-class bulk carrier at Baltic Shipyard, Leningrad, completing in 7-67. Hull amidships replaced by a broader section giving a distinct discontinuity to the lines fore and aft. Space communications antennas include two Ship Globe and 1 Ship Wheel, 2 Quad Ring, and 1 larger multiple yagi array. Two Vee-Cone HF antennas are carried at the mastheads. Based at Odessa.

CIVILIAN SPACE EVENT SUPPORT SHIPS *(continued)*

◆ **4 Borovichi class** Bldr: Zhdanov SY, Leningrad, & Vyborg SY (In serv. 1965-66)

BOROVICHI (ex-*Svirles*) KEGOSTROV (ex-*Taymyr*) MORZHOVETS NEVEL

Borovichi L. & L. Van Ginderen, 3-85

Morzhovets 6-84

D: 7,600 tons (fl) **S:** 15.4 kts **Dim:** 121.9 (113.0 pp) × 16.7 × 4.7
Electron Equipt: Radar: 2/Don-2
M: 1 Bryansk-Burmeister & Wain 950 VTBF 110 diesel; 1 prop; 5,200 hp
Fuel: 325 tons **Range:** 7,400/15 **Man:** 78 tot.

REMARKS: 5,277 grt/1,834 dwt. Space communications antennas include 1 Quint Ring and 4 Quad Ring yagi arrays, and a Vee Cone HF antenna is carried aft. Home-ported in the Baltic. Retain forward cargo hold. Converted 1967 at Zhdanov SY, Leningrad, from *Vytegrales*-class timber carriers.

CIVILIAN SCIENTIFIC RESEARCH SHIPS

The ships listed below are subordinated to a variety of scientific organizations. Many perform military-related research. Major fisheries research ships are presented, but a large number of smaller trawlers of the *Mayak* and similar classes are omitted for reasons of space. Foxtrot-class diesel-powered submarines have also supported civilian research in recent years. Ships are presented in reverse order of class introduction.

◆ **0 (+2) . . . class** Bldr: Rauma-Repola, Savonlinna

	Laid down	L	In serv.
N. . .	. . .	. . .	. . .
N. . .	. . .	. . .	. . .

D: . . . **S:** 11 kts **Dim:** 49.80 (46.40 pp) × 10.50 × 2.00
Electron Equipt: Radar: . . . —Sonar: . . .
M: 2 diesels, electric drive; 2 rudder-props; 1,114 hp
Fuel: 95 tons **Man:** 30 tot.

REMARKS: 920 grt. Ordered 28-2-85. For hydrographic research.

◆ **2 new construction** Bldr: Hollming, Rauma, Finland

	Laid down	L	In serv.
N. . .	. . .	. . .	1986
N. . .	. . .	. . .	1987

D: 6,000 tons **S:** 15 kts **Dim:** . . . (117.10 pp) × 18.20 × 5.90
Electron Equipt: . . .
M: 2 SEMT-Pielstick/Russkiy Dizel 6PC2.5 L400 diesels; 2 CP props; 7,000 hp
Range: . . . **Man:** . . .

REMARKS: Ordered 13-5-85.

◆ **2 Bavenit class** Bldr: Hollming, Rauma, Finland

	Laid down	L	In serv.
BAVENIT	1-2-45	. . .	. . .
N. . .	8-5-85	. . .	. . .

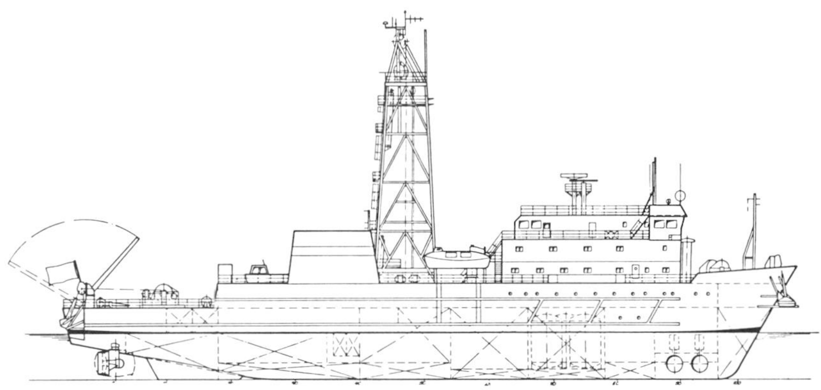

Bavenit Hollming, 1984

D: 5,300 tons **S:** 12.75 kts **Dim:** 85.80 (75.30 pp) × 16.80 × 5.60
Electron Equipt: . . .
M: 4 Russkiy Dizel EG-74 (1,700 hp) diesels, electric drive; 2 Aquamaster rudder-props, 4,000 hp
Range: 8,000/12 **Man:** 65 tot. **Endurance:** 50 days

REMARKS: Ordered 13-4-84 for use by the Far Eastern Academy of Sciences Institute of Thermal Physics. Able to drill to 200-m depths in waters up to 300-m deep, using a 35-m derrick drill support amidships. A-frame trawl gantry at the stern. Ice-reinforced hulls. Two 1,360-hp bow-thrusters plus the two U.S.-supplied Aquamaster, 360-deg.-pivoting props give a dynamic position-keeping capability.

◆ **2 (+7) Type B-93 geophysical research ships** Bldr: Szczecin SY, Szczecin, Poland

	In serv.		In serv.
AKADEMIK FERSMAN	1985	N. . .	. . .
AKADEMIK SHATSKIY	1985	N. . .	. . .
N. . .	. . .	N. . .	. . .
N. . .	. . .	N. . .	. . .
N. . .	. . .		

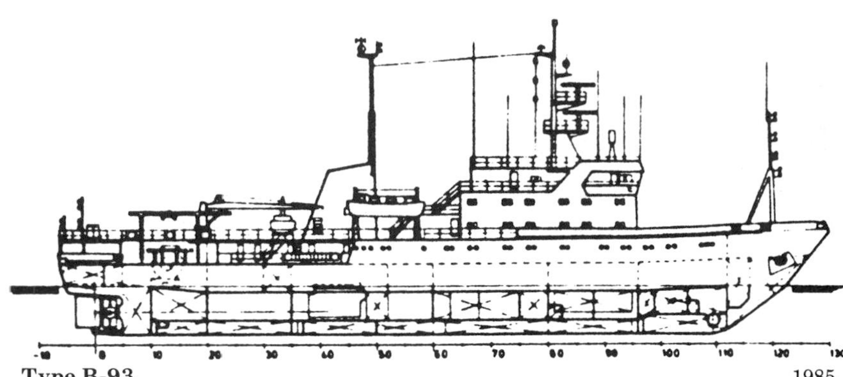

Type B-93 1985

D: Approx. 3,300 tons (fl) **S:** 14.5 kts **Dim:** 81.85 (73.50 pp) × 14.80 × 5.00
Electron Equipt: Radar: 2/. . . nav.—Sonar: 6-km-long seismic array
M: 1 Zgoda-Sulzer 6 ZL 40/48 diesel; 1 Kort-nozzle CP prop; 4,200 hp
Range: 12,000/. . . **Man:** 60 (accommodations)

REMARKS: 1,000 dwt. A series of ships to support the "shelf" research program to search for offshore gas and oil deposits. Ice-strengthened hulls, stern ramp for towing seismic array. Bow-thruster. Geophysical, gravimetric, and chemical laboratories. NAVSAT receiver. First ship launched 24-1-85, second on 19-7-85.

◆ **2 hydrographic echo-sweeping vessels** Bldr: Rauma-Repola, Savonlinna, Finland

	Laid down	L	In serv.
N. . .	9-1-85	. . .	1985
N. . .	24-1-85	. . .	1985

D: 400 tons (fl) **S:** . . . **Dim:** 32.90 × 9.10 × 2.20
M: 2 diesels; 2 props; 590 hp

REMARKS: 50 dwt. Ordered 12-4-84. Intended to operate as a pair, under computerized-control.

CIVILIAN SCIENTIFIC RESEARCH SHIPS *(continued)*

◆ **1 Pulkovskiy Meridian class** Bldr: Chernomorskiy SY, Nikolayev (In serv. 1984)

Akademik Aleksandr Karpenskiy

Akademik Aleksandr Karpenskiy French Navy, 11-84

D: 5,620 tons (fl) **S:** 17 kts **Dim:** 103.10 (94.00 pp) × 16.00 × 5.90
Electron Equipt: Radar: 1/Don-2, 1/Okean
M: 2 Sgoda-Sulzer 6L52511PV diesels; 1 CP prop; 6,900 hp
Range: 7,000/14.5 **Electric:** 450 kw **Man:** Approx. 90 tot.
Fuel: 1,150 tons **Endurance:** 60 days

Remarks: One of a class of two dozen or more stern-haul factory trawlers built since 1974, adopted for fisheries-related oceanographic research.

◆ **6 Akademik Boris Petrov class** Bldr: Hollming, Rauma, Finland

	Laid down	L	In serv.
Akademik Boris Petrov	7-4-83	7-7-83	29-6-84
Akademik M.A. Lavrent'yev	18-8-83	28-10-83	12-10-84
Akademik Nikolai Strakhov	9-11-83	3-2-84	14-5-85
Akademik Oparin	. . .	1-2-85	. . .
Akademik N. . .	. . .	. . .	. . .
Akademik N. . .	. . .	. . .	. . .

Akademik Oparin L. & L. Van Ginderen, 1-86

D: 2,550 tons (fl) **S:** 14.75 kts **Dim:** 75.45 × 14.70 × 4.70
Electron Equipt: Radar: 1/Okean, 1/. . . nav.
M: 2 SEMT-Pielstick/Russkiy Dizel GPC 2.5 L400 diesels; 1 CP prop; 3,500 hp
Range: . . . **Man:** 74 tot.

Remarks: First three ordered 17-6-82 for the Academy of Sciences Vernadskiy Institute for Geochemistry and Analytical Chemistry. Second trio ordered 28-6-84. Intended to conduct geophysical and hydrophysical research worldwide. Bow-thruster; bulbous forefoot to bow. Carry MARISAT SATCOMM system.

◆ **1 geological research catamaran** Bldr: . . . SY, Vladivostok (In serv. 10-83)

Geolog Primor'ye

D: . . . **S:** 9 kts **Dim:** 85.8 (75.3 pp) × 16.8 × 5.6
M: 2 diesels; 2 props; . . . hp—2/1,150-hp bow-thrusters

Remarks: 2,000 dwt. Intended for mineral resources research. Able to 4-point moor.

◆ **10 (+4) Akademik Shuleykin class** Bldr: Laivateollisuus, Turku, Finland

	In serv.
Akademik Shuleykin	1982
Professor Pavel Molchanov	1982
Akademik Shokalskiy	1982
Professor Khromov	1983
Professor Mul'tanovskiy	7-83
Akademik Gamburtsev	20-12-83
Professor Golitsyn	22-2-84
Professor Polshaov	7-4-84
Geolog Dmitriy Nalyvkin	14-2-85
Akademik Aleksandr Sidorenko	18-6-65
N. . .	. . .
N. . .	. . .
N. . .	. . .
N. . .	. . .

Akademik Shokalskiy French Navy, 1-83

D: 2,140 tons (fl) **S:** 14 kts **Dim:** 71.6 (64.3 pp) × 12.8 × 4.8
Electron Equipt: Radar: 1/Okean M, 1/Okean B
M: 2 Gor'kiy Type G-74 diesels; 2 CP props; 3,120 hp **Electric:** 600 kVA
Range: 14,000/12 **Man:** 38 crew + 38 scientists **Endurance:** 50 days

Remarks: 1,800 grt/620 dwt. Academy of Sciences hydrometeorological reporting ships, equipped for cold-weather operations. Home ports: *Shuleykin* at Leningrad, *Shokalskiy* and *Khromov* at Vladivostok, *Molchanov* at Murmansk, and *Mul'tanovskiy* at Leningrad. Second five ordered 1982 for the Ministry of Geology for seismic survey duties; they are of 1,650 grt/600 dwt, draw 4.50 m, and can carry a submersible robot. A third group of four was ordered 1-85. All have a 200-hp bow-thruster.

◆ **1 Akademik Aleksey Kirov class** Bldr: Okean SY, Nikolayev

Akademik Aleksey Kirov (In serv. 1981)

Akademik Aleksey Kirov U.S. Navy, 9-83

D: 9,920 tons (fl) **S:** 16 kts **Dim:** 124.7 (110.0 pp) × 17.5 × 7.2
Electron Equipt: Radar: 1/Okean A, 1/Okean B, 1 Palm Frond
M: 2 Type 58D-6R diesels; 2 CP props; 9,000 hp **Range:** 10,000/16
Electric: 3,600 kw **Man:** 117 crew, 32 scientists

Remarks: 6,358 grt/1,930 dwt. Supports a 13.4-m submersible, hangared amidships, with a large door and internal handling gantry to port. The submersible weighs 10 tons and can dive to 1,500 m. The ship has bow- and stern-thrusters, with a "Zaliv" automated control system. Home-ported at Sevastopol.

◆ **5 modified Al'pinist class** Bldr: Yaroslavl' SY

Rift (In serv. 1982), Diorat (In serv. 1983), Gidrobiolog (In serv. 1983), Diabaz (In serv. 1983), Gidronavt (In serv. 1983)

Rift—with Pisces submersible U.S. Navy, 9-82

D: 1,185 tons (fl) **S:** 12 kts **Dim:** 53.7 × 10.5 × 4.4
Electron Equipt: Radar: 1/Spin Trough
M: 1 Type 8NVD48-2U diesel; 1 CP prop; 1,320 hp
Electric: 778 kw **Range:** 6,900/12 **Man:** 26 crew + 11 scientists

CIVILIAN SCIENTIFIC RESEARCH SHIPS *(continued)*

Remarks: Al'pinist stern-haul trawlers modified while under construction to carry and support a manned submersible beneath a traveling double gantry crane amidships. Employed on oceanography, hydrology, and marine ecology research by the Ministry of Fisheries. Equipped with bow- and stern-thrusters. In late 1983 *Rift,* designed for the Tinro-2 submersible, was carrying the *Argus* submersible and a *Zvak*-4M towed drone submersible. *Diorat* and *Diabaz* are used for geophysical research and have a 15-m drill tower for the 9-ton ZIF-1200 drill in place of the submersible facility.

◆ **3 Vityaz' class** Bldr: Adolf Warski SY, Szczecin, Poland

Vityaz' (In serv. 1981) Akademik A. Nesmeyanov (In serv. 1982)
Akademik Alexandr Vinogradov (In serv. 1983)

Vityaz' French Navy, 3-83

Akademik A. Nesmeyanov U.S. Navy, 7-83

D: 5,700 tons (fl) **S:** 16 kts **Dim:** 110.9 (100.0 pp) × 16.6 × 5.7
Electron Equipt: Radar: 1/Don-2, 1/Okean
M: 2 Zgoda-Sulzer 6ZL140/48 diesels; 2 CP props; 6,500 hp
Electric: 925 kVA **Range:** 16,000/16 **Man:** 61 crew + 65 scientists

Remarks: 4,940 grt/1,790 dwt. Operated by the Academy of Sciences for seabed research, exploring for exploitable natural materials to 10,000-m depths. Have 25 laboratories; 60-day endurance. Carry the *Argus* submersibles: 8 tons, 600-m diving depth, 3-kt. max. speed, crew of 3, with an 8-hour powered endurance. *Vityaz'* also carries a submersible decompression chamber for 3 divers. *Vityaz'* home-ported at Sevastopol, *Nesmeyanov* at Vladivostok.

◆ **1 Akademik Keldysh class** Bldr: Hollming SY, Rauma, Finland

Akademik Mstislav Keldysh (In serv. 12-80)

D: 5,500 (fl) **S:** 16 kts **Dim:** 122.2 × 17.8 × 5.4
M: 4 Wärtsilä Vasa 824TS diesels; 2 props; 5,840 hp
Range: 20,000/165 **Man:** 50 crew + 80 scientists

Remarks: 5,500 grt/1,500 dwt. Operated by the Academy of Sciences for general-purpose oceanography. Has 17 internal laboratories and can carry 4 containerized laboratories. Home-ported at Kaliningrad. Carries a *Pisces*-class research submersible capa-

Akademik Mstislav Keldysh L. & L. Van Ginderen, 3-84

Akademik Mstislav Keldysh L. & L. Van Ginderen, 7-85

ble of descending to 2,000 m with a crew of three. Passive tank anti-rolling system. Bow-thruster and a 360-deg.-rotatable Aquamaster stern propulser.

◆ **1 modified Dobrynya Nikitich class** Bldr: Admiralty SY, Leningrad

Otto Shmidt (In serv. 17-7-79)

D: 2,528 tons (3,600 fl) **S:** 14.8 kts **Dim:** 73.0 (62.0 pp) × 18.0 × 6.6
M: 3 Type 13D100 diesels, electric drive; 2 props; 5,440 hp
Electric: 1,875 kw **Range:** 11,000/14 **Man:** 32 crew + 20 scientists

Remarks: 2,828 grt/1,095 dwt. Operated by the Arctic/Antarctic Institute. Can break 60-cm ice at 2-kt. speeds; 50 days endurance. Has 14 laboratories. The naval research icebreaker *Vladimir Kavrayskiy* has the same hull and propulsion, while two standard units of the *Dobrynya Nikitich* class, *Petr Pakhtusov* and *Georgiy Sedov,* are also employed on research tasks as needed. Endurance: 60 days.

◆ **1 sea-mining research ship** Bldr: . . . , U.S.S.R.

Shelf 1 (In serv. 1976)

D: . . . **S:** 16.5 kts **Dim:** 62.6 × 10.5 × 3.1
M: 2 12-cyl. diesels; 2 props; . . . hp **Range:** . . . **Man:** . . .

Remarks: 669 grt/193 dwt. Built to test ocean-shelf mining techniques to 100-m depths. Has a 5-ton crane.

◆ **1 Antarctic research and supply ship** Bldr: Kherson SY

Mikhail Somov (In serv. 1975)

Mikhail Somov L. & L. Van Ginderen, 1981

D: 5,000 tons (14,000 fl) **S:** 20 kts **Dim:** 133.1 (123.3 pp) × 18.8 × 9.2
Electron Equipt: Radar: 2/Don-2 **M:** 2 diesels, electric drive; 2 props; 7,150 hp
Range: 10,000/16.4 **Man:** 100 tot.

Remarks: 7,714 grt/8,445 dwt. Operated by the Arctic and Antarctic Institute. Essentially an *Amguema*-class icebreaking passenger/cargo ship intended for resupply duties to Soviet research stations in the Antarctic. Commercial sisters, including *Kapitan Myshevskiy* in 1983, are also used for Antarctic resupply.

◆ **18 (+ . . .) Valerian Uryvayev class** Bldr: Khabarovsk SY

	In serv.		In serv.
Chayvo	1982	Poisk	1974
Elm	1982	Professor Fedynskiy	1982
Dalniye Zelentsy*	1978	Rudolf Samoylovich*	1977
Geofizikh	1983	Valerian Uryvayev*	1974
Iskatel'	1977	Vektor	1980
Issledovatel'	1977	Vsevlod Berezkin*	1975
Lev Titov*	1980	Vulkanolog	1976
Modul	1981	Vyacheslav Frolov*	1979
Morskoy Geofizik	1975	Yakov Gakkel*	1975

CIVILIAN SCIENTIFIC RESEARCH SHIPS *(continued)*

Geofizikh—mast aft, large winch on stern French Navy, 2-84

Lev Titov—hydromet version, End Tray amidships L. & L. Van Ginderen, 11-83

D: 1,050 tons (fl) **S:** 11 kts **Dim:** 54.8 × 9.5 × 4.2
Electron Equipt: Radar: 1/Don-2, 1/Okean, 1/End Shield (on 7)
M: 1 Karl Liebnecht diesel; 1 CP prop; 880 hp **Electric:** 450 kw
Range: 10,000/11 **Man:** 40 crew + 12 scientists

REMARKS: 697 grt/350 dwt average. Variously subordinated; those operated for the Institute of Hydrometeorology(*) have an End Shield radiosonde balloon-tracking radar. Others operate for the Arctic and Antarctic Institute or the Academy of Sciences. Have 8 laboratories. Some have twin kingposts at the stern, others a single mast aft, and still others have twin kingposts just abaft the stack. Home-ported: *Berezkin, Zelentsy* at Murmansk; *Titov, Samoylovich* in the Baltic; *Issledovatel', Modul, Vektor, Gakkel* in the Black Sea; *Elm* in the Caspian; remainder in the Far East.

◆ **3 modified Passat-class weather-reporting ships** Bldr: Adolf Warski SY, Szczecin, Poland (In serv. 1971)

ERNST KRENKEL (ex-*Vikhr*) VIKTOR BUGAYEV (ex-*Poriv*)
GEORGIY USHAKOV (ex-*Schkval*)

Georgiy Ushakov L. & L. Van Ginderen, 9-83

D: 4,200 tons (fl) **S:** 16 kts **Dim:** 100.1 (88.4 pp) × 14.8 × 5.1
Electron Equipt: Radar: 2/Don-2, 1/End Tray
M: 2 Cegielski-Sulzer diesels; 2 CP props; 4,800 hp
Electric: 1,089 kw **Fuel:** 652 tons
Range: 15,000/16 **Man:** 110 crew + 63 scientists

REMARKS: 3,311 grt/1,450 dwt. Improved version of the Passat-class hydrometeorological reporting ships. Facilities for launching and tracking radiosonde balloons and rockets. All home-ported in the Black Sea.

◆ **1 shipbuilding techniques trials ship** Bldr: Black Sea SY, Nikolayev

IZUMRUD (In serv. 1970)

Izumrud Ambrose Greenway

D: 5,170 tons (fl) **S:** 14 kts **Dim:** 99.4 (90.0 pp) × 14.0 × 5.4
Electron Equipt: Radar: 1/Don-2, 1/Okean, 1/Low Sieve
M: 4 diesels, electric drive; 1 prop; 4,000 hp
Range: . . . **Man:** 110 crew + 40 scientists

REMARKS: 3,862 grt/2,640 dwt. A modified version of the *Tavriya*-class passenger/cargo ship, built for the Ministry of Shipbuilding for trials with structural concepts, coatings, navigational and communications systems. Portions of the superstructure are made from glass-reinforced plastic.

◆ **19 Dmitriy Ovtsyn class** Bldr: Laivateollisuus SY, Abo, Finland

	In serv.		In serv.
DMITRIY LAPTEV	1970	PROFESSOR BOGOROV*	1976
DMITRIY OVTSYN	1970	PROFESSOR KURENTSOV*	1976
DMITRIY STERLEGOV	1971	PROFESSOR SHTOKMAN*	1979
EDUARD TOLL	1972	PROFESSOR VODYANITSKIY*	1976
FEDOR MATISEN*	1976	SERGEY KRAVKOV	1974
GEORGIY MAKSOMOV*	1977	STEPAN MALYGIN	1970
IVAN KIREYEV*	1977	VALERIAN ALBANOV	1972
NIKOLAY KOLOMEYTSEV	1972	VLADIMIR SUKHOTSKIY	1974
NIKOLAY YEVGENOV	1974	YAKOV SMIRNITSKIY*	1977
PAVEL BASHMAKOV*	1977		

Ivan Kireyev—seismic research L. & L. Van Ginderen, 3-81

Professor Vodyanitskiy L. & L. Van Ginderen, 3-84

D: 1,600 tons (fl) **S:** 14 kts **Dim:** 68.7 (60.0 pp) × 11.9 × 4.1
Electron Equipt: Radar: varies: 2/Don-2, or 1/Okean, or 1/Don, 1/Don-2
M: 1 Humboldt-Klockner-Deutz diesel; 1 CP prop; 2,200 hp
Fuel: 180 tons **Electric:** 595 kw **Range:** 9,700/13.5 **Man:** 42 tot.

REMARKS: 1,134 grt/295 dwt. Ships delivered 1976 and later(*) are considered a second series, but are very similar. Fourteen are subordinated to the Ministry of the Maritime Fleet for hydrographic survey and seismic survey duties, the remainder to the Acad-

CIVILIAN SCIENTIFIC RESEARCH SHIPS *(continued)*

emy of Sciences or to the Hydrometeorological service (units with "Professor" names). *Bogorov* built at Turku.

◆ **23 Agat class** Bldr: . . . (In serv. 1969-79)

Agat	Gidrolog	Monatsit	Tantal
Akvanavt	Granat	Morion	Topaz
Berill	Ilmenit	Pluton	Tsirkon
Borey	Kartesh	Radon	Uran
Brig	Kvarts	Rutil	Yantar
Geotermik	Metan	Shelf	

Shelf L. & L. Van Ginderen, 9-83

D: 350 tons (fl) **S:** 9.5 kts **Dim:** 34.0 × 7.1 × 2.6
Electron Equipt: Radar: 1/navigational
M: 1 Karl Liebnecht 8-cyl. diesel; 1 prop; 300 hp
Electric: 411 kw **Range:** 1,600/9 **Man:** . . .

Remarks: 166 grt/35 dwt. A general-purpose oceanographic tender version of the *Manevrennyy*-class seiner fishing boat. Endurance: 7 days. Subordination about equally divided between the Ministry of Geology, Academy of Sciences, and the Hydrometeorological Institute.

◆ **11 Atlantik-I* and -II-class fisheries research ships** Bldr: Volkswerft, Stralsund, East Germany (In serv. 1968-72)

Alba*	Gerakl'	Professor Mesyatsev
Artemida	Kamenskoye	Shantar
Evrika	Milogradvo	Zond
Fiolent	Professor	

D: 2,240 tons (3,360 fl) **S:** 13.7 kts **Dim:** 82.2 (73.0 pp) × 13.6 × 5.0
Electron Equipt: Radar: 2/Don-2
M: 2 Karl Liebnecht diesels; 2 CP prop; 2,350 hp
Electric: 1,660 kw **Fuel:** 600 tons **Range:** . . . **Man:** 85 tot.

Remarks: Average 2,242 grt/1,025 dwt. Stern-haul factory trawlers adapted for fisheries-related oceanographic research; subordinated to the Ministry of Fisheries. Have a 75-hp bow-thruster.

◆ **6 Passat-class hydrometeorological reporting ships** Bldr: Adolf Warski SY, Szczecin, Poland

	In serv.		In serv.		In serv.
Musson	1968	Volna	1968	Priboy	1969
Passat	1968	Okean	1969	Priliv	1970

Priboy—Vee Cone HF antenna atop foremast L. & L. Van Ginderen, 1984

D: 4,145 tons (fl) **S:** 16 kts **Dim:** 96.9 (88.4 pp) × 13.8 × 5.3
Electron Equipt: Radar: 2/Don-2, 1/End Tray (radiosonde tracker)
M: 2 Cegielski-Sulzer 8TD48 diesels; 2 CP props; 4,800 hp
Electric: 800 kw **Range:** . . .
Man: 50–55 crew + 50–60 scientists and technicians

Remarks: 3,284 grt/1,170 dwt. B-88 design, with 23 laboratory spaces. Have End Tray radiosonde tracking antenna aft and can launch weather balloons and atmospheric probe rockets. 45-day endurance. Subordinated to the Hydrometeorological Institute. Home-ported: Vladivostok, except *Musson, Passat:* Odessa; *Priliv:* Baltic. Vee-series HF antenna atop foremast on *Priboy, Priliv,* and *Okean.*

◆ **1 Sever class** Bldr: Black Sea SY, Nikolayev

Sever (In serv. 1967)

Sever 1982

D: 1,780 tons (2,530 fl) **S:** 13.1 kts **Dim:** 71.0 (64.0 pp) × 13.1 × 5.0
Electron Equipt: Radar: 1/Don-2
M: 3 diesels, electric drive; 1 CP prop; 3,000 hp
Fuel: 350 tons **Range:** 11,000/13 **Man:** 51 tot.

Passat U.S. Navy, 8-83

CIVILIAN SCIENTIFIC RESEARCH SHIPS *(continued)*

REMARKS: 1,940 grt/706 dwt. Operated by the Ministry of Geophysics in geological oceanography studies. Was originally the prototype for a class of stern-haul trawlers, but no others were built. Endurance: 50 days. Operates in the Black Sea.

◆ **1 modified Nereida class** Bldr: Khabarovsk SY

AKADEMIK PETROVSKIY (ex-*Moskovskiy Universitet*) (In serv. 1966)

Akademik Petrovskiy U.S. Navy, 7-81

D: 922 tons (fl) **S:** 11 kts **Dim:** 54.1 (52.8) × 9.3 × 3.7
Electron Equipt: Radar: 1/Don-2, 1/Spin Trough
M: 1 diesel; 1 CP prop; 780 hp
Range: 10,000/11 **Man:** 41 crew + 10 scientists

REMARKS: 577 grt/277 dwt. Operated by Moscow State University for studies in oceanology, hydrobiology, ichthyology, and seismology. Modernized and renamed 1970. Large numbers of this class (unmodified) and the very similar Mayak class perform fisheries research duties.

◆ **7 Akademik Kurchatov class** Bldr: Mathias Thiesen Werft, Wismar, East Germany (In serv. 1966-68)

AKADEMIK KOROLEV	DMITRIY MENDELEYEV
AKADEMIK KURCHATOV	PROFESSOR VIZE
AKADEMIK SHIRSHOV	PROFESSOR ZUBOV
AKADEMIK VERNADSKIY	

Akademik Shirshov—note twin radomes amidships, elaborate tracking radar antenna aft L. & L. Van Ginderen, 1983

Professor Vize—hydrometeorological reporting ship with Vee Bars HF antenna atop foremast L. & L. Van Ginderen, 1-84

Akademik Vernadskiy—scientific unit, with tracking radar removed; note stack-cap U.S. Navy, 7-83

D: 6,986 tons (fl) **S:** 18.3 kts **Dim:** 124.2 (110.0 pp) × 17.0 × 6.1
Electron Equipt: Radar (standard): 2/Don-2, 1 or 2/tracking radars
M: 2 Halberstadt-M.A.N. 6KZ 57/60 diesels; 2 props; 8,000 hp
Fuel: 1,415 tons **Electric:** 1,840 kw
Range: 20,000/18 **Man:** 80 crew + 74 scientists & technicians

REMARKS: 5,460 grt/1,986 dwt. Vary considerably in equipment. *Kurchatov, Vernadskiy,* and *Mendeleyev* subordinate to the Academy of Sciences, the others to the Hydrometeorological Institute. The weather ships originally had radiosonde balloon and rocket launching facilities. End Tray tracking radar, and two theodolite trackers, one of which was a converted naval Wasp Head director (*Shirshov* has two side-by-side tracking radars in radomes amidships and a new type of tracking radar aft, while *Korolev* has had the twin radars, and occasionally the radomes, removed). The other three have a large crane aft for handling oceanographic gear and small submersibles; they also carry one End Tray. The weather ships also have Vee Bars HF antennas atop the foremast. *Korolev* and *Mendeleyev* have an Okean-series navigational radar in lieu of one Don-2. All have two 190-hp bow-thrusters, and a 300-hp Pleuger active rudder. Unlike their naval half-sisters of the *Abkhaziya* class, these ships have *no* helicopter facilities. Home ports: *Korolev, Mendeleyev,* and *Shirshov* at Vladivostok, *Vernadskiy* in the Black Sea, and the others in the Baltic.

◆ **4 Tropik A class** Bldr: V.E.B. Volkswerft, Stralsund, East Germany

	In serv.		In serv.
KALLISTO	1964	PEGAS	1963
NAUKA	1966	RADUGA	1966

Kallisto L. & L. Van Ginderen, 3-83

D: Approx. 3,000 tons (fl) **S:** 12.5 kts **Dim:** 79.8 (71.0 pp) × 13.2 × 5.2
Electron Equipt: Radar: 2/Don-2
M: 2 Karl Liebnecht 8-cyl. diesels; 1 prop; 1,680 hp
Electric: 1,080 kw **Fuel:** 400 tons **Range:** . . .
Man: 42 crew + 29 scientists

REMARKS: 2,435 grt/988 dwt. Former stern-haul factory trawlers. Approximately 70 sisters operate as fishing boats. *Pegas* operates for the Academy of Sciences, *Kallisto* for the Oceanographic Science Research Institute, and the other two for the Ministry of Fisheries.

◆ **2 modified Bologoe-class trawlers** Bldr: Leninskaya Kuznitsa SY, Kiev (In serv. 1963)

AKADEMIK ARCHANGELSKIY YURIY GODIN

D: 580 tons (fl) **S:** 10 kts **Dim:** 43.6 × 7.6 × 3.0
Electron Equipt: Radar: 1/Spin Trough
M: 1 Karl Liebnecht diesel; 1 prop; 450 hp
Range: . . . **Man:** 35 crew + 13 scientists

REMARKS: 416 grt/142 dwt. Greatly modified versions of a standard side-trawler design. Perform seismic and geophysical studies in the Black Sea and Mediterranean under the Ministry of Geology and Geophysics Institute, respectively.

CIVILIAN SCIENTIFIC RESEARCH SHIPS *(continued)*

◆ **1 small research ship** (In serv. 1962)

Professor Kolesnikov

Professor Kolesnikov French Navy, 1984

D: . . . **S:** . . . **Dim:** . . . × . . . × . . .
M: . . .

◆ **1 ex-passenger ship** (In serv. 1961)

Ayu-Dag

Ayu-Dag L. & L. Van Ginderen, 6-83

D: Approx. 1,000 tons (fl) **S:** 13 kts **Dim:** 63.8 × 9.3 × 3.0
M: Diesels; 2 props; . . . hp

Remarks: 1,002 grt. Subordinated to the Academy of Sciences of the Estonian S.S.R. Very little scientific equipment carried.

◆ **1 ex-Norwegian seismic research ship** Bldr: A.M. Liasen SY, Alesund

Shelf II (ex-*Longva*) (In serv. 1962)

D: Approx. 1,400 tons (fl) **S:** 13 kts **Dim:** 63.0 (57.9 pp) × 10.0 × 4.2
Electron Equipt: Radar: 3/navigational
M: 1 Klockner-Humboldt-Deutz diesel; 1 prop; 1,500 hp
Electric: 360 kw **Fuel:** 249 tons **Range:** . . . **Man:** 52 tot.

Remarks: 793 grt. Purchased 1977 for oil exploration. Very elaborately equipped, including data storage computers. Has passive tank stabilization, bow-thruster.

◆ **1 Gromovoy-class former tug** Bldr: Galati SY, Romania

Vladimir Obruchev (In serv. 1959)

D: 900 tons (fl) **S:** 11 kts **Dim:** 45.7 (41.5 pp) × 9.45 × 3.9
Electron Equipt: Radar: 2/Don-2
M: 2 diesels; 1 prop; 1,200 hp **Man:** 33 crew + 11 scientists

Remarks: Employed in seismic research by the Ministry of Geology. Former commercial tug.

◆ **2 converted Fryazino class** Bldr: Crichton-Vulcan, Turku, Finland (In serv. 1956)

Petr Lebedev Sergey Vavilov

Petr Lebedev R. Neth. Navy, 1985

D: 4,800 tons (fl) **S:** 13.5 kts **Dim:** 94.2 (86.7 pp) × 14.0 × 5.7
Electron Equipt: Radar: 1/Okean, 1/Don-2
M: 1 Sulzer 6TD.56 diesel; 1 prop; 2,400 hp
Range: 6,000/13.5 **Man:** 90 tot

Remarks: 3,642 grt/1,675 dwt. Converted for research from cargo ships in 1961; further modified 1966. Perform acoustic research for the Hydroacoustic Institute, Academy of Sciences, in support of naval projects. Invariably work together. Home-ported in the Baltic. Aft stack is a dummy, offset to port.

◆ **11 Mayakovskiy class** Bldr: Black Sea (Nosenko) SY, Nikolayev

	In serv.		In serv.
A.I. Voyeykov	1959	Odissey	1970
Akademik Berg	1963	Persey-III	1968
Akademik Knipovich	1964	Poseidon	1971
Argus	1969	Professor Deryugin	1967
Ekvator	1968	Skif	1969
Ikhtiander	1973		

D: Approx. 3,600 tons (fl) **S:** 13 kts **Dim:** 84.7 (78.1 pp) × 14.0 × 5.7
Electron Equipt: Radar: 2/Don-2
M: 2 Russkiy Dizel diesels; 1 CP prop; 2,000 hp
Electric: 800 kw **Range:** 18,000/12 **Man:** 53 crew + 37 scientists

Remarks: Average 3,220 grt/1,287 dwt. Stern-haul fish-factory trawlers adapted for research purposes. *Voyeykov,* with stern ramp plated up, operates for the Hydrometeorological Institute and has an End Tray radiosonde tracking radar. The remainder support fisheries research for the Ministry of Fisheries. *Odissey* and *Ikhtiander* have a large internal hangar opening through the port side of the hull to launch a *Sever-II* or *Tinro-2* research submersible. *Deryugin, Persey-III, Argus,* and *Poseidon* carry a *Sever-I* submersible, launched via crane. *Skif* and *Ekvator* are essentially unmodified from the fishing-boat version. The six *Primorye*-class intelligence collection ships were built on the same hull.

◆ **1 Mikhail Lomonosov class** Bldr: Neptunwerft, Rostock, East Germany

Mikhail Lomonosov (In serv. 1957)

Mikhail Lomonosov 2-81

D: 5,960 tons (fl) **S:** 13.6 kts **Dim:** 102.4 (95.5 pp) × 14.4 × 6.0
Electron Equipt: Radar: 2/Don-2
M: 1 set reciprocating steam with turbine booster; 1 prop; 2,450 hp
Electric: 746 kw **Fuel:** 780 tons **Boilers:** 2
Range: 11,000/13.6 **Man:** 80 crew + 55 scientists

Remarks: 3,898 grt/2,254 dwt. Altered while under construction as a *Kolomna*-class cargo ship. Operated by the Academy of Sciences, Ukrainian Institute of Oceanology. Has 16 laboratories.

◆ **1 Korall class** Bldr: Laivateollisuus SY, Turku, Finland

Zarya (In serv. 9-52)

D: Approx. 600 tons (fl) **S:** 8 kts **Dim:** 52.5 (42.5 pp) × 9.0 × 3.1
Electron Equipt: Radar: 1/Spin Trough
M: 1 Halberstadt 6NVD36 diesel; 1 prop; 300 hp
Range: 4,000/8 **Man:** 35 crew + 10 scientists

Remarks: 333 grt/78 dwt. One of the last survivors of a large class of wooden-hulled sealer schooners built as war reparations. Several remain in naval service as deperming tenders. *Zarya* has been made as completely non-magnetic as is possible and is used in gravimetric and ocean-current research by the Academy of Sciences. Home-ported at Murmansk. Refitted 1984-85. See photo on the next page.

CIVILIAN ICEBREAKERS

Note: Because of their importance to the Soviet Navy in keeping Arctic sea-lanes open, the Ministry of the Merchant Marine's icebreakers are listed here. There is little doubt that they would come under naval jurisdiction in wartime, and, in fact, the nuclear-powered icebreaker *Leonid Brezhnev* (ex-*Arktika*) was heavily armed during initial sea trials. Naval-subordinated icebreakers are listed in the Soviet Navy section.

CIVILIAN ICEBREAKERS *(continued)*

Zarya L. & L. Van Ginderen, 7-83

NUCLEAR-POWERED ICEBREAKERS

◆ **0 (+2) Taymyr class** Bldr: Wärtsilä, Helsinki/. . . SY, Leningrad

TAYMYR (In serv. 1990) N. . . (In serv. 1991)

Taymyr—artist's rendering Wärtsilä, 1984

D: 20,480 tons (23,460 fl) **S:** 20.5 kts
Dim: 150.00 (136.00 pp) × 30.00 (28.00 wl) × 11.00
Electron Equipt: Radar: 4/. . . nav.
M: 2 pressurized-water reactors, steam turbines, electric drive; 2 props; 74,800 hp
Electric: 11,400 kw (5/2,000 kw turboalternators, 1/1,000-kw diesel set, 2/200-kw diesel sets)
Man: 142 crew + helicopter crew and medical personnel

REMARKS: Ordered 1984 for shallow water work in Arctic estuaries. Reactors to be installed at Leningrad after delivery in 1988 and 1989 from Finland. Will be able to break 2-m thick ice continuously.

◆ **3 (+1) Arktika class** Bldr: Baltic SY, Leningrad

	Laid down	L	In serv.
LEONID BREZHNEV (ex-*Arktika*)	1971	12-72	12-74
SIBIR'	1973	2-76	1977
ROSSIYA	. . .	11-83	11-85
N. . .	11-83	. . .	. . .

D: 19,300 tons light (23,460 fl) **S:** 21 kts (15 kts service)
Dim: 148.0 (136.0 pp) × 30.0 × 11.0
Electron Equipt: Radar: 1/Okean, 1/Don-2, 1/Head Net C
M: 2 pressurized-water reactors, turbogenerators, electric drive; 3 props; 75,000 hp
Electric: 11,400 kw **Man:** 173 tot.

REMARKS: 18,172 grt/4,096 dwt. *Arktika,* renamed 1982, was armed during her trials period with 8/76.2-mm DP (II × 4, controlled by 2/Hawk Screech radar GFCS) and 8/30-mm AA (II × 4, controlled by 2/Drum Tilt radar GFCS) and had an air-search radar; these were removed before the ship left the Baltic. Propulsion power is distributed 37,500 hp on the centerline shaft and 18,750 hp on each of the outboard shafts. Each shaft is driven by two 8,800-kw a.c./8,100-kw d.c. motors. *Rossiya* and the fourth unit have heated waterline ice-strokes and improved, corrosion-resistant hull steel alloys. *Rossiya* began dock trials 8-85. There is a hangar and flight deck for two Helix (Ka-32) ice-reconnaissance helicopters. *Leonid Brezhnev* (as *Arktika*) traveled to the North Pole in 8-77, the first surface ship to do so.

Sibir' *Ships of the World,* 1984

◆ **1 Lenin class** Bldr: Admiralty SY, Leningrad

LENIN (In serv. 20-12-59)

Lenin Sovfoto

D: 15,940 tons light (19,240 fl) **S:** 19.7 kts (18 kts service)
Dim: 134.0 (124.0 pp) × 26.8 × 10.5
M: 2/4-loop pressurized-water reactors, 4/8,200-kw turbogenerators, electric drive; 3/4-bladed props; 39,800 hp
Electric: . . . **Man:** 218 tot.

REMARKS: 14,067 grt/3,849 dwt. The world's first nuclear-powered surface ship. *Lenin* was out of service for many years in the late 1960s and re-emerged with a new reactor plant having only two reactors vice the original three. Helicopter deck and hangar.

SEAGOING ICEBREAKERS

◆ **4 Kapitan Sorokin class** Bldr: Wärtsilä, Helsinki

KAPITAN SOROKIN (In serv. 1977) KAPITAN DRANITSYN (In serv. 1980)
KAPITAN NIKOLAYEV (In serv. 1978) KAPITAN KHLEBNIKOV (In serv. 1981)

D: 10,440 tons light (14,655 fl) **S:** 19 kts (16 kts service)
Dim: 131.9 (122.5 pp) × 26.5 × 8.5
M: 6 Wärtsilä-Sulzer 9ZL 40/48 diesel generator sets, electric drive; 3 props; 22,300 hp
Electric: 4,900 kw **Fuel:** 3,666 tons
Range: 10,700/16 **Man:** 11 officers, 65 crew

REMARKS: 10,609 grt/4,225 dwt. Equipped with the Wärtsilä bubbler system to keep the hull bottom ice-free. Helicopter pad, no hangar. All personnel accommodated in the superstructure. Considered to be "shallow-draft" ships. Equipped to perform salvage and towing operations.

SEAGOING ICEBREAKERS *(continued)*

Kapitan Nikolayev Wärtsilä, 1983

◆ **3 Yermak class** Bldr: Wärtsilä, Helsinki

Yermak (In serv. 4-7-74)
Admiral Makarov (In serv. 6-75)
Krasin (In serv. 2-76)

Admiral Makarov Wärtsilä, 1975

D: 13,280 tons light (20,241 fl) **S:** 19.5 kts
Dim: 135.8 (130.0 pp) × 26.0 × 11.0
M: 9 Wärtsilä-Sulzer 12 ZN 40/48-3,050 diesel generator sets, electric drive; 3/4-bladed props; 36,500 hp
Electric: See remarks **Fuel:** 5,750 tons
Range: 29,300/14 **Man:** 146 tot.

Remarks: 12/231 grt/7,441 dwt. The U.S.S.R.'s most powerful conventional icebreakers. Can break 6-m ice or maintain 2 kts through 1.8-m ice. Have Wärtsilä bubbler system, helicopter pad. Electrical power taken from propulsion generators. *Krasin* refitted 1-84 to 3-84 by Böttcher and Gröning, Hamburg; re-engined.

◆ **5 Moskva class** Bldr: Wärtsilä, Helsinki

Moskva (In serv. 1960)
Leningrad (In serv. 1962)
Kiev (In serv. 1966)
Murmansk (In serv. 1968)
Vladivostok (In serv. 1969)

Kiev Wärtsilä

D: 13,290 tons (15,360 fl) **S:** 18.3 kts **Dim:** 122.1 (112.4 pp) × 24.5 × 10.5
M: 8 Wärtsilä-Sulzer 9MH51, 2,160-kw diesel generator sets, electric drive; 3/4-bladed props; 26,300 hp
Fuel: 5,200 tons **Range:** 20,000/14 **Man:** 116 tot.

Remarks: 9,427 grt/4,221 dwt. Have heeling tanks, capable of shifting 480 tons of water in two minutes. Can carry two ice-reconnaissance helicopters. 60-ton bollard pull towing capacity. *Leningrad* was overhauled at Yokohama in 1969-70 and re-engined.

MEDIUM ICEBREAKERS

◆ **3 Mudyug class** Bldr: Wärtsilä, Helsinki

Mudyug (In serv. 10-82)
Magadan (In serv. 12-82)
Dikson (In serv. 17-3-83)

Mudyug L. & L. Van Ginderen, 7-83

D: 6,138 tons (fl) **S:** 17.45 kts (trials) **Dim:** 92.0 (88.6 hull, 78.5 pp) × 21.4 × 6.5
M: 4 Wärtsilä Vasa 8R32 heavy-oil diesel; 2 CP props; 12,000 hp (9,500 in ice)
Electric: 2,530 kw **Range:** 15,000/16.5 **Man:** 43 tot.

Remarks: Approx. 4,400 grt. Have Wärtsilä air-bubbler system. Intended for use in the Barents, Baltic, and Sea of Okhotsk. Have 917KN bollard pull. Unusual in not employing electric drive.

◆ **14 Dobrynya Nikitich class** Bldr: Admiralty SY, Leningrad

	In serv.		In serv.
Vasiliy Pronchishchev	1961	Semen Chelyushkin	1965
Afanasiy Nikitin	1962	Yuriy Lisyanskiy	1965
Khariton Laptev	1962	Petr Pakhtusov	1966
Vasiliy Poyarkov	1963	Georgiy Sedov	1967
Yerofey Khabarov	1963	Fedor Litke	1970
Ivan Kruzhenshtern	1964	Ivan Moskvitin	1971
Vladimir Rusanov	1964	Semen Dezhnev	1971

Yuriy Lisyanskiy L. & L. Van Ginderen, 7-84

D: 2,675–2,940 tons (fl) **S:** 14.5 kts (12.0 service)
Dim: 67.7 (62.0 pp) × 18.3 × 6.1 **Electron Equipt:** Radar: 1 or 2/Don-2
M: 3 Type 13D100 diesel generator sets; 3/3-bladed props (1 fwd); 5,400 hp
Fuel: 600 tons **Range:** 5,500/12 **Man:** 39 tot.

Remarks: 2,305 grt/1,092 dwt typical. Seven sisters, several of which are armed, serve the Soviet Navy. *Petr Pakhtusov* and *Georgiy Sedov* have been employed on occasional scientific voyages by the Academy of Sciences. The specially built research icebreakers *Otto Schmidt* (civilian) and *Vladimir Kavrayskiy* (naval) are variants of this design, as are the *Ivan Susanin*-class patrol icebreakers. Ships of this class are often used as ocean tugs in summer months.

◆ **3 Kapitan Belousov class** Bldr: Wärtsilä, Helsinki

Kapitan Belousov (In serv. 1954)
Kapitan Voronin (In serv. 1955)
Kapitan Melekhov (In serv. 1956)

MEDIUM ICEBREAKERS *(continued)*

Kapitan Belousov

D: 5,360 tons (fl) **S:** 16.5 kts **Dim:** 83.20 (77.10 pp) × 19.40 × 7.0
M: 6 Wärtsilä diesel generator sets, electric drive; 4 props (2 fwd); 10,600 hp
Fuel: 1,025 tons **Range:** 10,000/14.8 **Man:** 120 tot.

Remarks: 3,377 to 3,710 grt/1,308 to 1,423 dwt. The U.S.S.R.'s first post-W.W. II icebreakers; primarily for harbor and thin-ice work, hence forward-mounted pair of propellers. Can break 1-2-m ice.

RIVER ICEBREAKERS

◆ **8 (+1) Kapitan Yevdokimov class** Bldr: Wärtsilä, Helsinki

Kapitan Yevdokimov (In serv. 31-3-83)	Avraamiy Zavenyagin (In serv. 12-4-84)
Kapitan Babichev (In serv. 30-6-83)	Kapitan Metsayk (In serv. 8-84)
Kapitan Borodkin (In serv. 13-11-83)	Kapitan Demidov (In serv. 22-11-84)
Kapitan Chudinov (In serv. 9-9-83)	N. . .
Kapitan Evdokimov (In serv. 1983)	

Kapitan Evdokimov Wärtsilä, 1984

D: 2,200 tons (fl) **S:** 13.5 kts (12 kts service) **Dim:** 76.5 (. . . pp) × 16.6 × 2.5
M: 4 Wärtsilä Vasa 12V22B, 1,640-hp diesel generator sets, electric drive; 4 props (2 fwd); 5,170 hp
Man: 25 tot.

Remarks: 1,500 grt. Remarkably shallow draft. Intended to clear Arctic rivers. Equipped with Wärtsilä bubbler system and a sewage treatment plant. Ninth ordered 27-6-84.

◆ **6 Kapitan Chechkin class** Bldr: Wärtsilä, Helsinki

	In serv.		In serv.
Kapitan Bukayev	1978	Kapitan Krutov	1978
Kapitan Chadayev	1978	Kapitan Plakhin	1977
Kapitan Chechkin	1977	Kapitan Zarubin	1978

D: 2,240 tons (fl) **S:** 14 kts **Dim:** 77.6 (73.9 pp) × 16.3 × 3.3
M: 3 Wärtsilä diesels, electric drive; 3 props; 6,300 hp
Electric: 330 kw **Range:** . . . **Man:** 28 tot.

Remarks: Approx. 1,600 grt. Capable of breaking 1-meter-thick ice; have air-bubbler system. Service speed 10 kts.

Kapitan Krutov Wärtsilä, 1978

◆ **3 Kapitan M. Izmaylov class** Bldr: Wärtsilä, Helsinki (In serv. 1976)

Kapitan A. Radzhabov	Kapitan M. Izmaylov
Kapitan Kosolabov	

Kapitan A. Radzhabov Wärtsilä, 1976

D: 2,048 tons (fl) **S:** 14 kts **Dim:** 56.3 (52.2 pp) × 16.3 × 4.2
M: 4 Wärtsilä Vasa 824TS diesels, 2/4-bladed props; 5,330 hp
Fuel: 380 tons **Range:** 5,000/14 **Man:** 24 tot.

Remarks: 1,362 grt/354 dwt. Endurance: 15 days.

UNITED ARAB EMIRATES

Personnel (1985): 80 officers, 1,120 men

Merchant Marine (1984): 225 ships—766,493 grt (25 tankers—524,413 grt)

Naval Aviation: Two Britten-Norman BN-2 Islander Maritime Defender ordered 1982 for patrol duties. Abu Dhabi ordered 8 AS-332 Super Puma helicopters with AS 39 Exocet anti-ship missiles in 1983.

Note: Primarily incorporating the former Defense Force Sea Wing of the Abu Dhabi National Defense Force, the UAE Navy was formed on 1 February 1978 as part of the federated forces of Abu Dhabi, Ajman, Dubai, Fujairah, Ras al Khaimah, Sharjah, and Umm al Qaiwan. The merchant marines of these states are also combined into a single administrative unit.

GUIDED-MISSILE PATROL BOATS

◆ **6 TNC-45-class guided-missile boats** Bldr: Lürssen, Vegesack

	In serv.		In serv.
P 4501 Baniyas	11-80	P 4504 Shaheen	4-81
P 4502 Marban	11-80	P 4505 Saqar	6-81
P 4503 Rodqum	4-81	P 4506 Tarif	6-81

UNITED ARAB EMIRATES *(continued)*
GUIDED-MISSILE PATROL BOATS *(continued)*

Rodqum (P 4503) L & L Van Ginderen, 1983

D: 231 tons (259 fl) **S:** 41.5 kts **Dim:** 44.9 (42.3 pp) × 7.0 × 2.46 (prop)
A: 4/MM 40 Exocet (II × 2)—1/76-mm OTO Melara DP—2/40-mm Breda AA (II × 1)—2/76.2-mm mg (I × 2)
Electron Equipt: Radar: 1/Decca TM 1226, 1/PEAB 9LV 200 Mk 2 system
EW: Decca Cutlass RDL-2 passive, 1 Dagaie chaff RL
M: 4 MTU 16V538 TB92 diesels; 4 props; 15,600 hp (13,000 sust.)
Electric: 405 kVA **Range:** 500/38.5; 1,600/16
Man: 5 officers, 27 men

REMARKS: The radar director is equipped with low light-level t.v. and an infrared tracker and has an associated search radar atop the mast. There is a CSEE Panda optical director for the 40-mm mount. Carry 350 rds. 76-mm, 1,800 rds. 40-mm, and 6,000 rds. mg ammunition.

PATROL BOATS AND CRAFT

◆ **6 110-foot class** Bldr: Vosper Thornycroft, Portsmouth, U.K.

	L		L
P 1101 ARDHANA	7-3-75	P 1104 AL GHULIAN	16-9-75
P 1102 ZURARA	13-6-75	P 1105 RADOOM	15-12-75
P 1103 MURBAN	15-9-75	P 1106 GHANADHAH	1-3-76

Ardhana and Zurara 1976

D: 110 tons (140 fl) **S:** 29 kts **Dim:** 33.5 (31.5 pp) × 6.4 × 1.7
A: 2/30-mm BMARC/Oerlikon A32 AA (II × 1)—1/20-mm AA
Electron Equipt: Radar: 1/Decca TM 1226
M: 2 Ruston-Paxman Valenta RP200M diesels; 2 props; 5,400 hp
Range: 1,800/14 **Man:** 26 tot.

◆ **3 Kawkab-class patrol craft** Bldr: Keith Nelson, U.K.

P 561 KAWKAB (In serv. 7-3-69) P 562 THOABAN (In serv. 7-3-69)
P 563 BANIYAS (In serv. 27-12-69)

Kawkab Vosper, 1960

D: 25 tons (32 fl) **S:** 17.52 (15.84 pp) × 4.72 × 1.37
A: 2/20-mm AA (I × 2) **Electron Equipt:** Radar: 1/Decca RM 916
M: 2 Caterpillar diesels; 2 props; 750 hp **Endurance:** 7 days
Electric: 24 kw **Man:** 2 officers, 9 men

REMARKS: Fiberglass hull. Used for coastal patrol, hydrographic surveys, and surveillance of petroleum leases. Designed by Keith Nelson, a division of Vosper. Freshwater evaporator provides 900 liters daily.

SERVICE CRAFT

◆ **1 repair tender** Bldr: Singapore Slipway

BARRACUDA (In serv. 6-83)

D: . . . **S:** . . . **Dim:** 58.0 × . . . × . . .
M: 2 Ruston-Paxman RKCM diesels; 2 props; 6,000 hp

◆ **2 workboats** Bldr: Cheverton, Cowes, U.K. (In serv. 1975)

A 271 A 272

D: 3.3 tons **S:** 8 kts **Dim:** 8.2 × 2.7 × 0.8
M: 1 Lister-Blackstone RMW3 diesel; 150 hp

REMARKS: Glass-reinforced plastic construction.

COAST GUARD

REMARKS: The Coast Guard operates under the Ministry of the Interior.

PATROL CRAFT

◆ **9 45-ft MK-II class** Bldr: Watercraft, Ltd., U.K. (In serv. 1982-83)

D: 10 tons (fl) **S:** 26 kts **Dim:** 13.90 × 4.26 × 1.14
A: 1/7.62-mm mg **Electron Equipt:** Radar: . . .
M: 2 M.A.N. D2542 MLE diesels; 2 props; 1,300 hp **Man:** 5 tot.

REMARKS: Glass-reinforced plastic construction. Ordered 2-82.

◆ **17 P 1200 class** Bldr: Watercraft, Ltd., U.K. (In serv. 1979-81)

D: 10 tons (fl) **S:** 29 kts **Dim:** 11.90 (10.16 wl) × 4.08 × 1.06
A: 2/7.62-mm mg (I × 2) **M:** 2 MTU diesels; 2 props; 800 hp
Range: 300/20 **Man:** 4 tot.

REMARKS: Glass-reinforced plastic hulls. First ten delivered 1979-80; seven more ordered, 1980.

◆ **6 Dhafeer-class patrol craft** Bldr: Keith Nelson, Bembridge, U.K.

	L	In serv.		L	In serv.
P 401 DHAFEER	2-68	1-7-68	P 404 DURGHAM	9-68	7-6-69
P 402 GHADUNFAR	5-68	1-7-68	P 405 TIMSAH	9-68	7-6-69
P 403 HAZZA	5-68	1-7-68	P 406 MURAYJIB	2-70	7-7-70

D: 10 tons **S:** 19 kts **Dim:** 12.5 × 3.65 × 1.1
A: 2/7.62-mm mg (I × 2) **M:** 2 Cummins diesels; 2 props; 370 hp
Range: 15/18; 350/15 **Man:** 1 officer, 5 men

REMARKS: Subordinate to Marine Police. Fiberglass hull.

◆ **6 Spear-class police patrol craft** Bldr: Fairey Marine, Hamble, U.K.

D: 10 tons **S:** 26 kts **Dim:** 9.1 × 2.75 × 0.84
A: 2/12.7-mm mg **M:** 2 Perkins T 6-354 diesels; 2 props; 580 hp **Man:** 3 tot.

REMARKS: In service in 8-74, 9-74, and 1-75. Fiberglass hull.

◆ **5 P-77A customs patrol craft** Bldr: Camcraft, New Orleans, La. (In serv. 9-75)

No. 21 through No. 25

D: 70 tons (fl) **S:** 25 kts **Dim:** 23.4 × 5.5 × 1.5 **A:** 2/20-mm AA (I × 2)
M: 2 G.M. 12V 71T diesels; 2 props; 1,400 hp **Range:** 750/25

◆ **2 50-foot customs patrol craft** Bldr: Cheverton, Cowes, U.K. (In serv. 2-75)

AL SHAHEEN AL AQAB

D: 20 tons **S:** 23 kts **Dim:** 15.2 × 4.3 × 1.4
A: 1/7.62-mm mg **M:** 2 G.M. diesels; 2 props; 850 hp
Range: 1,000/20 **Man:** 8 tot.

U.S.A.

PERSONNEL (9-85): Navy: 571,300 active (70,973 officers, 495,802 enlisted, 4,525 midshipmen), plus 106,194 selected reserve, 14,257 TAR active-duty reservists; Marines: 198,025 active (20,145 officers, 177,850 enlisted), plus 41,919 selected reserve (3,381 officers, 38,538 enlisted) and 56,062 inactive reserve (3,647 officers, 48,415 enlisted); civilians: 356,500 total.

Merchant Marine (1984): 6,441 ships — 19,291,868 grt
(tankers: 323 ships — 8,205,818 grt)

Naval Program

The table lists new construction programs for fiscal years 1984 through 1990. The annual five-year program has fluctuated drastically for many years and, because of changing political pressures, cannot be relied on as an accurate projection of what will actually be proposed, let alone authorized and appropriated by the Congress. It is nonetheless given here as the best available forecast; it will probably be reduced.

SHIPBUILDING PROGRAM 1984–1991

	Authorized			Proposed				
New construction:	FY84	FY85	FY86	FY87	FY88	FY89	FY90	FY91
SSBN, *Ohio*	1	1	1	1	1	1	1	1
SSN, *Los Angeles*	3	4	4	4	3	3	4	1
SSN-21	—	—	—	—	—	1	—	2
CG, *Ticonderoga*	3	3	3	2	2	2	2	—
DDG, *Arleigh Burke*	—	1	—	3	3	3	3	5
LSD, *Whidbey Isl.*	1	2	2	—	—	—	—	—
LSD, LSD-41 var.	—	—	—	—	1	1	1	1
LHD, *Wasp*	1	—	1	—	1	1	—	1
MCM, *Avenger*	3	4	2*	3	3	—	—	—
MSH, *Cardinal*	1	—	4	4	4	4	—	—
T-AO, *H.S. Kaiser*	2	3	2	2	2	2	2	2
T-AGOS	—	2	2	3†	3	2	2	2
AE, AE-36	—	—	—	—	1	—	2	2
AOE, AOE-6	—	—	—	1	—	1	1	1
AGOR	—	—	—	1	—	—	2	3
ARS	—	—	—	—	—	—	—	1
Total	15	20	21	24	24	21	20	22
Major Conversions/ SLEP/reactivations:								
CV SLEP	—	1	—	—	1	—	—	1
LPD SLEP	—	—	—	—	—	1	3	3
BB, *Iowa*	1	—	1	—	—	—	—	—
AO-177 stretch	—	—	—	1	1	1	2	—
T-ACS conv.	1	2	3	2	2	2	—	—
	2	3	4	3	4	4	5	4

* Navy requested 4, Congress authorized 3, then funded 2.
† One each in FY 87, 88 to be new design, both in FY 89, 90, 91.

Marine Corps

Created in 1775, the Marine Corps has three missions:
— to seize and/or defend advanced bases as needed for the operations of the fleet
— to furnish security detachments on board ships and at land bases
— to carry out any other operations that the president of the United States may assign.

The third mission permits the corps to be used in operations that are not purely naval (e.g., Belleau Wood in 1918 and Vietnam in the 1960s and 1970s).

Its total strength of about 198,025 men and women forms three Marine Amphibious Force (MAF) divisions (one stationed in Okinawa/Japan, two in the United States), each of 32,600 men, and three air wings, organized under two Fleet Marine Forces (FMF). These last also maintain heavy support elements for the divisions. A fourth division-wing team constitutes a reserve cadre. Each MAF has 70 tanks, 280 aircraft, 340 helicopters, and 100 artillery batteries attached.

The Marine Corps has approximately 400 fighter and attack aircraft (A-4M, A-6, AV-8A/C, F-4), 600 assault and utility helicopters, more than 500 tanks, and some 450 amphibious landing vehicles.

The major operational unit is the Marine Amphibious Force (MAF), which consists of one division, one air wing, and Fleet Marine Forces augmentation, for a total of about 58,000 Marines, plus about 26,300 naval personnel aboard ships, etc.

Amphibious ships currently in service do not permit the rapid overseas deployment of MAFs, but only of two Marine Amphibious Brigades (MAB). A MAB consists of one Regimental Landing Team, a strong unit with two or more battalion landing teams of about 822 men each; one mixed air group of 110 fighter, attack fixed-wing aircraft and 120 helicopters, 15 tanks and 30 artillery batteries, and some augmentation from the Fleet Marine Force, for a total of about 15,500 men. The smallest assault unit is the Marine Amphibious Unit (MAU), with a landing team, air squadrons, and support personnel, totaling 2,500, and has 5 tanks, 6 aircraft, 30 helicopters, and 5 artillery batteries.

Special Forces

Consisting of 1,700 men in 1985, the 6 SEAL Teams were divided into 41 platoons. By 1990 the force is to grow to 2,700 men in 7 teams/70 platoons, all capable of aerial or seaborne insertion.

The Naval Reserve Force

Naval Reserve Force ships have cadre crews of regular naval personnel, with reserve augmentation personnel constituting up to two-thirds of the total crew assigned. As of 30-9-85, the Force included: 1 destroyer, 11 frigates, 18 ocean minesweepers, 2 tank landing ships, 2 salvage ships, 4 Special Boat Units, 16 Mobile Inshore Undersea Warfare Units, 17 Mobile Construction Battalions, and 6 Cargo-Handling Battalions. Naval Reserve Force Air Wings will consist of 51 aircraft squadrons: 4 fighter, 6 attack, 2 light photographic, 2 carrier air early warning, 2 tactical electronic warfare, 2 aerial refueling, 13 patrol squadrons (organized into 2 patrol wings), 1 helicopter wing (4 ASW squadrons, 1 combat support squadron, and 2 light attack squadrons), 1 tactical support wing (with 11 logistical support squadrons), and 2 fleet composite squadrons. Also incorporated in the Naval Reserve program will be 2,100 other units supporting 35 programs to augment Regular Navy staffs in wartime.

The Military Sealift Command

The Military Sealift Command (MSC) operates or charters ships in support of the United States Navy. Headed by an active-duty U.S. Navy flag officer, its ships are manned primarily by civilians, either civil service or contract employees. The ships of the MSC are listed in a separate section, after naval units.

Warships In Active Service, Under Construction, Or Appropriated As Of 1 January 1986

	L	Std. Tons	Main armament
◆ 14 (+3) attack carriers			
0 (+3) Theodore Roosevelt (CVN)	1984-89	82,000	88-90 aircraft, 3/Sea Sparrow
3 Nimitz (CVN)	1972-80	81,600	88-90 aircraft, 3/Sea Sparrow
1 Enterprise (CVN)	1960	75,700	88-90 aircraft, 2/Sea Sparrow
1 John F. Kennedy (CV)	1967	61,000	88-90 aircraft, 3/Sea Sparrow
3 Kitty Hawk (CV)	1960-64	60,100	88 aircraft, 2-3/Sea Sparrow
4 Forrestal (CV)	1954-58	59,600	88 aircraft, 2/Sea Sparrow
2 Midway (CV)	1945-46	51,000	65 aircraft, 0 or 2/Sea Sparrow
◆ 12 (+2) amphibious assault helicopter carriers			
0 (+2) Wasp (LHD)	1987	28,000	2/Sea Sparrow, up to 42 a/c
5 Tarawa (LHA)	1972-78	28,000	3/127-mm DP, 2/Sea Sparrow, 19 or 30 helicopters
7 Iwo Jima (LPH)	1960-69	17,000	4/76.2-mm, 2/Sea Sparrow, 28 helicopters
◆ 36 (+6) nuclear-powered ballistic-missile submarines			
		(surfaced)	
6 (+6) Ohio (SSBN)	1979-	15,750	24/Trident, 4/TT
30 Lafayette (SSBN)	1962-66	7,250	16/Poseidon or Trident, 4/TT
◆ 96 (+19) nuclear-powered attack submarines			
33 (+19) Los Angeles	1973-	6,000	4/TT
1 Glenard P. Lipscomb	1973	5,813	4/TT
37 Sturgeon	1966-74	3,640	4/TT
1 Narwhal	1967	4,550	4/TT
13 Permit	1961-66	3,526	4/TT
1 Tullibee	1960	2,317	4/TT
2 Ethan Allen	1960-62	6,300	4/TT
5 Skipjack	1958-60	3,075	6/TT
2 Skate	1957-58	2,570	8/TT
1 Seawolf	1955	3,765	6/TT
◆ 4 diesel/electric-powered attack submarines			
3 Barbel	1958-59	2,146	6/TT
1 Darter	1956	1,720	8/TT
◆ 2 (+2) battleships			
2 (+2) Iowa	1942-44	46,100	32 Tomahawk, 16 Harpoon, 9/406-mm, 12/127-mm DP, 4/20-mm Vulcan/Phalanx AA, 3 helicopters
◆ 30 (+16) cruisers			
9 nuclear-powered		Tons	
4 Virginia (CGN)	1974-78	10,400	2/missile launchers, 8/Tomahawk, 8/Harpoon, 2/127-mm DP, 6/ASW TT
2 California (CGN)	1971-72	10,400	2/missile launchers, 8/Harpoon, 2/127-mm DP, ASROC, 4/ASW TT
1 Truxtun (CGN)	1964	8,600	1/missile launcher, 8/Harpoon, 1/127-mm DP, 4/ASW TT
1 Bainbridge (CGN)	1961	8,600	2/missile launchers, 8/Harpoon, ASROC, 6/ASW TT
1 Long Beach (CGN)	1959	15,500	2/missile launchers, 8/Tomahawk 8/Harpoon, ASROC, 6/ASW TT

WARSHIPS IN ACTIVE SERVICE *(continued)*

18 (+16) conventional:			
3 (+16) Ticonderoga	1981-	7,400	2/missile launchers, 8/Harpoon, 2/127-mm DP, 6/ASW TT, 1/helicopter
9 Belknap (CG)	1963-65	6,570	1/missile launcher, 8/Harpoon, 1/127-mm DP, 6/ASW TT, 1/helicopter
9 Leahy (CG)	1961-63	6,070	2/missile launchers, 8/Harpoon, ASROC, 6/ASW TT

◆ **69 (+1) destroyers**

0 (+1) Arleigh Burke	1988-	6,500	2/VLS missile groups, 8/Harpoon, 1/127-mm DP, 6/ASW TT
4 Kidd	1979-80	8,140	2/missile launchers, 2/127-mm DP, 6/ASW TT, 1/helicopter
31 Spruance	1973-81	5,830	1/Sea Sparrow, 8/Harpoon, 2/127-mm DP, ASROC, 6/ASW TT, 1/helicopter
23 Charles F. Adams	1959-63	3,370	1/missile launcher, Harpoon, 2/127-mm DP, ASROC, 6/ASW TT
10 Coontz	1958-60	4,700	1/missile launcher, 8/Harpoon, 1/127-mm DP, ASROC, 6/ASW TT
1 Forrest Sherman	1955-58	2,780	3/127-mm DP, 6/ASW TT

◆ **111 (+5) frigates**

46 (+5) Oliver Hazard Perry	1976-	2,997	1/missile launcher, Harpoon, 1/76-mm, 6/ASW TT, 1/helicopter
46 Knox	1966-73	3,011	0 or 1/Sea Sparrow, Harpoon, 1/127-mm DP, ASROC, 4/ASW TT, 1/helicopter
6 Brooke	1963-66	2,643	1/missile launcher, 1/127-mm DP, ASROC, 6/ASW TT, 1/helicopter
10 Garcia	1963-65	2,624	2/127-mm DP, ASROC, 6/ASW TT, 1/helicopter
1 Glover	1965	2,650	1/127-mm DP, ASROC, 6/ASW TT
2 Bronstein	1962	2,360	2/76.2-mm DP, ASROC, 6/ASW TT

◆ **6 guided-missile patrol hydrofoils**

◆ **21 (+14) mine countermeasures ships**

◆ **51 (+7) amphibious warfare ships (plus helicopter carriers above)**

WEAPONS AND SYSTEMS

A. MISSILES

◆ **fleet ballistic missiles**

Poseidon C-3 (UGM 73A) — Lockheed

Length: 10.4 m
Diameter: 1.8 m
Weight: 29.48 tons at launch
Propulsion: solid propellant, two stages
Guidance: inertial
Range: 2,500 or 3,200 nautical miles
Warhead: 14 warheads with independent and controllable trajectory, each of 50 kt (MIRV) to 2,500 nautical miles or 10 of 50 kt to 3,200 nautical miles. Some warheads have been "uploaded" to increase destructive force.

Trident-1 C-4 (UGM-96A) — Lockheed

Operational in 1978. Designed for the *Ohio*-class SSBNs, which carry 24, and for 12 *Lafayette* and *Benjamin Franklin* SSBNs, which carry 16. A total of 630 is programmed, 150 for operational testing. The first eight *Ohio*-class SSBNs will slowly convert to the later D-5, from 1-91 to 1999. Seventy-two procured FY 83, 52 approved FY 84, the final year of production requests.

Length: 10.4
Weight: 31.75 tons at launch
Propulsion: solid propellant, three stages
Guidance: Inertial
Range: 4,350 nautical miles
Warhead: 8 MIRV of 100 kt, Mk 4

The Mk 500 Evader MARV (Maneuverable Re-entry Vehicle) with six 100-kt warheads was developed by Lockheed, with procurement commencing in 1980.

Trident-2 D-5 — Lockheed

In development for deployment in the late 1980s in the Pacific Fleet, and 1992 in the Atlantic. First ship to carry will be SSBN 734. First 27 to be requested under FY 87.

Length: 13.9 m
Weight: 57.15 at launch
Propulsion: solid propellant, three stages
Range: 6,000 nautical miles with 122-m circular point of error (CEP)
Warhead: 14 MIRV of 150 kt each or 7 MARV (Maneuverable Re-entry Vehicles) of 300 kt each. Initially will use same Mk 12A re-entry vehicles as the land-based Minuteman III and Peacemaker (MX), with 475-kt W87 warheads.

◆ **surface-to-surface missiles**

Tomahawk (BGM-109) — General Dynamics

Two versions are projected, strategic and tactical. The anti-ship tactical version was to become fully operational in 3-84, and the conventional land-attack version is to enter service in 9-85. Planned procurement is for 3,994 total missiles, with 2,600 potential launchers: submarines (using torpedo tubes or special vertical launch tubes), surface ships (using 4-missile armored box launchers or vertical launch cells), and aircraft. Fifty-one procured FY 83, 124 approved FY 84, 180 in FY 85, 249 in FY 86.

Length: 6.17 m
Diameter: 0.52 m
Weight: 1,542 kg at launch (1,816 kg encapsulated for submarine launch)
Propulsion: solid booster, turbojet sustainer
Strategic version: 1,400 nautical miles range, operating at an altitude between 15 and 100 meters, at a speed of Mach 0.7. For launching from submarines, the weapon will be fired from torpedo tubes in a special container, jettisoned on leaving the water. Nuclear or conventional warhead. Guidance: TAINS (Tercom-Aided Inertial Navigation System) using preprogrammed data plus TERCOM (Terrain Contour Matching). By 30-9-86, there will be 14 surface ships and 30 attack submarines equipped for Tomahawk.
Tactical version: 250 nautical miles range, thus requiring an external means of target designation. Warhead weight up to 454 kg, conventional. Guidance: inertial, with active radar and anti-radiation homing.

Tomahawk variant designations are:		Navy procurement goal:
BGM-109A:	land-attack, nuclear warhead	758
BGM-109B:	anti-ship	593
BGM-109C:	land-attack, conventional	2,643*
BGM-109D:	land-attack, bomblets	0
BGM-109E:	anti-ship	0
BGM-109F:	land-attack, anti-airfield	560
BGM-109G:	ground-launched, nuclear (GLCM)	0
AGM-109C:	MRASM proposal, terrain follower	0
AGM-109I:	MRASM proposal, infrared seeker	0
AGM-109H:	MRASM proposal, bomblets	0

* 1486 Block IIA with Bullpup warheads, 1,157 Block IIB with bomblet payloads.
There are also sub-variants for ship or submarine launch.

Harpoon (RGM-84A) — McDonnell Douglas

An all-weather cruise missile that can be launched by aircraft, surface ships, or submarines. A total of 281 surface ships and submarines are programmed to receive it. As of 9-82, there were 162 ships, 34 submarines, and 78 P-3 aircraft equipped to launch Harpoon. By 2-85, some 1,148 ship-launched variants had been delivered toward a force goal of 1,876. Under FY 82, 240 were procured, with 221 approved under FY 83, 315 in FY 84, 354 in FY 85, 395 in FY 86, and 153 planned for FY 87.

Length: 4,628 m ship-launched/3.848 m air-launched
Diameter: 0.343 m — Wingspan: 0.914 m
Weight: 681 kg from canister, 680 kg from SAM launcher or 653 kg from ASROC launcher (with booster)
Propulsion: CAE-JA02 turbojet, with a rocket booster added to the ship- and submarine-launched versions
Speed: Mach 0.85
Guidance: inertial, then active homing on J band in the final trajectory
Range: 70 nautical miles (85 n.m. in Block I missiles with improved JP-10 fuel)
Warhead: 227 kg

AGM-84 is the 526-kg, air-dropped version, which does not require a solid rocket booster, and **UGM-84** is the submarine version. The submarine version is shrouded and is launched from the torpedo tubes while submerged. In order to reach the maximum range, it is necessary to use targeting systems external to the launching unit—helicopters, for example. The AGM-84 will be carried by A-6E, P-3B and P-3C and Air Force B-52 (12 each) aircraft. The U.S. Air Force acquired 85 undelivered Iranian AGM-84 in 8-84.

◆ **surface-to-air missiles** (*Note:* Standard and Sea Sparrow can also be used against surface ships)

Standard SM-1 MR (RIM-66B) — General Dynamics

Single-stage missile, replaced Tartar.

Length: 4.47 m
Diameter: 0.34 m
Weight: 625 kg
Guidance: semi-active homing
Range: 25 nautical miles, 150–60,000 ft

System comprises Mk 11 twin launcher or Mk 13 single launcher with a vertical ready-service magazine containing 40 missiles (on the FFG 1 class: Mk 22 with 16 missiles), a computer, an air-search radar, a three-dimensional SPS-39, SPS-48, or SPS-52 radar, and SPG-51 guidance radars. A series of missiles of approximately the same size as the first RIM 24 Mod. 0 (U.S. military designation) but with constantly improved propulsion, miniaturization of components, and improved missile flight profile. Acceptance trials with the Block 6 variant (digital computer, monopulse radar) were carried out 3-83. 650 approved under FY 83.

MISSILES *(continued)*

Standard SM-2 MR (RIM-66C)—General Dynamics

Single-stage missile for use with Aegis-equipped ships. Initial procurement of 30 in FY 80. 150 approved under FY 83, 846 in FY 86.

Length: 4.70 m
Diameter: 0.34 m
Weight: 706 kg (Block II missiles)
Guidance: semi-active homing, with mid-course guidance capability, inertial reference, and improved ECCM
Range: more than 25 nautical miles

Standard SM-1 ER (RIM-67)—General Dynamics

Two-stage missile that replaced the Terrier family. "Block II" series (1,095 ordered under FY 82, 375 under FY 83) to get increased intercept altitude, greater warhead lethality, and improved jam resistance.

Length: 7.98 m
Diameter: 0.34 m (booster diameter: 0.46 m)
Weight: 1,306 kg
Guidance: semi-active homing
Range: 30–40 nautical miles

Standard SM-2 ER (RIM-67B)—General Dynamics

Two-stage missile to replace Talos. Will be employed in ships with Mk 10 or Mk 26 launch systems, and later in vertical launchers. A nuclear warhead option is under development. Initial procurement of 55 in FY 80. 470 authorized under FY 86.

Length: 7.98 m
Diameter: 0.34 m (booster diameter: 0.46 m)
Weight: 1,442 kg
Guidance: semi-active homing, with mid-course guidance capability, inertial reference, and improved ECCM
Range: 75–90 nautical miles

NOTE: A number of the superannuated RIM-2 Terrier missiles with nuclear warheads will be retained in inventory until the nuclear warhead SM-2 Standard is available. Under FY 84, funds were appropriated for 1,190 Standard missiles of all types, with 1,380 under FY 85 and 1,316 in FY 86.

Sea Sparrow (RIM-7)—Raytheon

Known at first as BPDMS (Basic Point Defense Missile System). The 50 initial installations employed RIM-7E-5 fixed-fin missiles launched from the eight-celled Mk 25 launcher and controlled by the Mk 115 radar-equipped fire-control system. These are being replaced by the Mk 15 Vulcan/Phalanx 20-mm gatling gun system, beginning in 1982. A lightweight launcher, Mk 29, employing eight RIM-7F folding-fin missiles and the Mk 91 radar fire-control system, is now in use. In Europe this later system, IPDMS (Independent Point Defense Missile System), is also known as NATO Sea Sparrow and was first tested in the *Downes* (FF 1070). The RIM-7M version now being procured uses a blast-fragmentation warhead vice the earlier RIM-7H's expanding rod variety and has a monopulse radar; 1,593 were ordered in FY 82-83. 314 RIM-7M authorized under FY 85.

Length: 3.657 m   Weight: 204 kg
Diameter: 0.20 m   Range: 8 nautical miles

Aegis (ex-Advanced Surface Missile-System—ASMS)

Development began 1964. A fire-control system based on the AN/SPY-1 "billboard" fixed-array radar to provide 360° coverage. Employs SM-2 MR missiles to simultaneously attack a number of targets under the most adverse electronic countermeasures conditions, including targets at extremely low altitude. Three clusters of four AN/UYK-7 computer systems direct all functions automatically: the detection and tracking of the closing targets, data distribution for target evaluation and designation through pre-programmed information retained in the system, integration of radar and other information sources in the ship, and the selection of missiles and distribution of fire.

The Mk 26 twin launcher, which can also handle the ASROC ASW surface-to-surface missiles, is used. The various types of missiles are stowed vertically in ready-service magazines below the launcher. The Aegis system underwent trials in the *Norton Sound* beginning in 1974 and became operational in CG 47 in 1983. The Martin-Marietta Mk 41 vertical-launch system is being developed to follow the Mk 26. Trials commenced in late 1981 on *Norton Sound*, with first operational employment to be in CG 52; it will be able to accept Tomahawk and vertical-launch ASROC missiles as well.

RAM (Rolling Airframe Missile) (XRIM-116A)—General Dynamics

A point-defense system intended to replace or supplement Sea Sparrow. Will use a 127-mm missile that employs slow spinning for stability (hence the name). Guidance is by dual-mode anti-radiation and/or infrared proportional navigation homing, and either a Mk 31 21-missile launcher, or modified Mk 29 Sea Sparrow-type launchers may be used as the launcher. The 21-missile launcher uses the Phalanx mounting, while the version for use in the Mk 29 launcher would put 5 missiles into each of two cells of the 8-celled launcher. A lightweight, 8–10 round launcher is under development for Denmark. The missile homes on active radiation from the target until it picks up an infrared target signature and employs the current Stinger seeker in conjunction with Sidewinder fuzes, warheads, and rocket motors. The 21-missile launch installation weighs 4,977 kg above deck, 800 kg below. Target designation will be by the Mk 23 TAS system in U.S. Navy ships. Being developed under a 7-76 agreement by the U.S., Denmark, and West Germany, with introduction into U.S. Navy service planned for late 1980s. First 30 built under FY 85.

Under FY 86, 117 initial production missiles were authorized for the U.S. Navy, with another 130–150 to be built for West Germany, which will produce the missiles itself by the RAM System GmbH consortium (Messerschmidt, AEG-Telefunken, RTG).

Length: 2.794 m
Diameter: 127 mm
Weight: 70.9 kg
Speed: Mach 2+

NOTE: The Marine Corps employs the shoulder-launched infrared-homing General Dynamics FIM-92A Stinger SAM with troops and the deployable MIM-23B I-Hawk (Improved Hawk) SAM battery for airfield and strong point defense. Under FY 84, 1,205 Stinger and 360 I-Hawk missiles were authorized for procurement, with 2,360 Stinger authorized in FY 85 and 3,439 requested under FY 86. Stinger is also deployed aboard a number of Navy ships:

Length: 1.52 m   Warhead: 3 kg (proximity fuze)
Diameter: .07 m   Speed: Mach 2.0
Weight: 15.1 kg

◆ **antisubmarine warfare missiles**

ASROC (RUR-5A)—Honeywell

A solid-fuel rocket used with a parachute-retarded Mk 46 torpedo. Range is regulated by the combustion time of the rocket motor. Rocket-torpedo separation is timed. The Mk 112 launcher carries eight rockets that can be trained together and elevated in pairs. Fire control is made up of a computer linked with an SQS-23, SQS-26, or SQS-53 sonar.

Length: 4.42 m   Range: 9,200 m
Diameter: 0.324 m   Warhead: Mk 46 Mod. 1 torpedo or Mk 17 nuclear depth bomb
Weight: 454 kg

On *Knox*-class frigates the ASROC launcher was modified to permit the launching of Standard SSM missiles (later, Harpoon) in place of two ASW weapons. On older installations, loading is slow because the rockets have to be manually transferred from the magazines. However, on later *Brooke*- and *Garcia*-class and all *Knox*-class frigates, a hoist transfers the rocket from a magazine below the bridge for semiautomatic loading, while in the *Spruance* class the missiles are reloaded vertically. Some 12,000 ASROC rounds were procured between 1960 and 1970, when production ceased.

ASROC is launched from the Mk 10 missile launchers in the CG 26 and CGN 35 classes and from the Mk 26 launchers in the CGN 38 and CG 47 classes. A vertical-launch ASROC is under development for use with Mk 41 launchers in CG 52 and later *Ticonderoga*-class cruisers and in DDG 51-class destroyers. With booster attached, the weapon will be 5.08 m long, 0.358 m in diameter, and will weigh about 750 kg.

SUBROC (UUM-44A-2)

Introduced in 1962 as a submarine torpedo tube-launched ASW weapon with a nuclear depth-bomb payload, SUBROC was to be phased out because of the age of its solid-fueled rocket motors and because its analog fire-control system was incompatible with the Mk 117 Mod. 3 digital fire-control systems installed or backfitted in U.S. Navy submarines. However, in 1983, Congress authorized funds to alter the fire-control systems.

Weight: 1,816 kg   Propulsion: two-stage solid-fuel rocket
Length: 6.40 m   Range: 30 nautical miles
Diameter: .533 m   Guidance: inertial

SOW (Sea Lance)

A replacement for SUBROC, designated the ASW SOW (Stand-Off Weapon), was canceled in 1981 in favor of an abortive program to produce a *single* weapon to replace both SUBROC and ASROC. That having predictably proven impracticable, the programs were again separated in 1982. The new SOW will be launched from SSN 688-class submarines operating at down to 80 percent of their test depths. Plans call for acquisition of 2,400 weapons, with either nuclear or conventional warheads, and with operational deliveries commencing about 1991.

Length: 6.25 m   Range: 1056 nautical miles
Diameter: .533 m   Guidance: inertial in flight
Weight: 1,406 kg

◆ **air-to-surface missiles**

NOTE: In the early stages of development is a 7 to 15 n.m. "fire-and-forget" ground attack weapon to enter service circa 2000: AIWS—Advanced Interdiction Weapon System.

PENGUIN Mk 2 Mod. 7 (AGM-. . .)—Kongsberg/Grumman

Initially tested for the U.S. Navy in 1982-83 as a surfaced-launched weapon, Penguin is being developed for firing by SH-60B LAMPS-III helicopters. Range is being extended, the wings are being made foldable, and the infrared homing seeker is being improved. Only 272 are planned for procurement, to be carried aboard 35 FFG 7 frigates and 20 DD 963 destroyers. If procurement goes forth, about 130 helicopters will be modified to carry the missile.

Weight: 1,202 kg   Warhead: Bullpup Mk 19
Range: 15+ n.m.

Other data approximately as for the Norwegian Navy version.

Skipper (AGM-123A)—Aerojet General

Skipper is essentially a Mk 83, 1,000-lb bomb, equipped with a Paveway II infrared seeker and guidance head and a Shrike (AGM-45) solid rocket motor. Developed by the

MISSILES *(continued)*

Naval Weapons Station, China Lake, Cal., it offers a very low unit price ($20,000/weapon) and reasonable accuracy. Some 2,500 were to be acquired during FY 84.

Maverick (AGM-65E and AGM-65F) — Hughes

Developed from the Air Force AGM-65D, the AGM-65E is a laser-designated, air-launched missile for the Marine Corps, while the AGM-65F version for the Navy will use infrared homing. Both have the same 136-kg penetrator, blast-fragment warhead. For use by A-7 and A/F-18 aircraft and, later, the A-6E. Rapid escalation of price initially forced scaling back of procurement; 90 were procured under FY 83 and 165 were bought under FY 84. In FY 85 600 were authorized, while under FY 86, 1,500 AGM-65E and 195 AGM-65F were authorized.

Weight: E: 208.8 kg/F: 307 kg — Span: 0.72 m
Length: 2.49 m — Propulsion: solid-fuel rocket
Diameter: 0.305 m — Range: 50 nautical miles

Standard-ARM (AGM-78) — General Dynamics

Air-launched version of Standard that homes on electromagnetic radiation. More versatile than Shrike. No longer in production.

Length: 4.57 m — Warhead: 97.6 kg
Range: 35 nautical miles — Weight: 624.2 kg

Shrike (AGM-45) — Texas Instruments

An anti-radar missile. No longer in production.

Length: 3.048 m — Propulsion: solid-propellant rocket motor
Diameter: 0.2 m — Range: 12,000 to 16,000 m
Weight: 117 kg — Speed: Mach 2
Wingspan: 0.914 m

Walleye I and II (AGM-62) — Martin-Marietta/Hughes

Glide bomb guided by television. Uses Mk 82 or Paveway II bomb.

Length: I: 3.5 m; II: 4.0 m — Range: I: 16 nautical miles; II: 35 nautical miles
Diameter: 0.325 m
Weight: I: 511 kg; II: 1,090 kg — Warhead: conventional—I: 373 kg; II: 908 kg
Wingspan: 1.16 m

Harpoon (AGM-84)

See under surface-to-surface missiles.

HARM (AGM-88A) — Texas Instruments

HARM (High-Speed Anti-Radiation Missile) will be employed by A-7E, A-6E, FA-18, and U.S. Air Force F-4E Wild Weasel aircraft to suppress or destroy ground defenses. Will replace the obsolescent Shrike. Production of 5,000 was scheduled to start in 1982, with 160 authorized in FY 83, 381 in FY 84, 813 in FY 85 and 904 under FY 86.

Length: 4.17 m — Propulsion: solid-propellant, low-smoke rocket
Diameter: 0.253 m — Guidance: homes on electromagnetic radiation
Weight: 360 kg — Range: . . .
Span: 1.13 m — Speed: Mach 2.0+

TOW-2 (MGM-71) — Hughes

Wire-guided, helicopter- or ground-launched anti-tank weapon that uses optical sight and tube launcher. TOW = Tube-launched, Optically-guided, Wire-controlled. 2,200 approved under FY 84, 4,782 ITOW-2 under FY 86.

Length: 1.174 m — Span: 1.14 m
Weight: 18.9 kg — Propulsion: solid-propellant rocket
Diameter: .152 m — Warhead: 3.6 kg hollow, shaped-charge
Range: 2.3 nautical miles at Mach 1.0

ITOW (Improved TOW) weighs 19.1 kg, ITOW-2 weighs 21.5 kg.

NOTE: The Marine Corps uses TOW from AH-1T helicopters and from land, with each division now programmed to have 144 launchers. The Marines also employ the AGM-114A Hellfire anti-tank missiles and the lightweight M82 LAW, the latter being phased out. Some 219 Hellfire were authorized under FY 84, 438 under FY 85, and 1,500 in FY 86.

Length: 1.727 m or 1.778 m (imaging IR version)
Diameter: 0.1778 m (span: 0.3262 m)
Weight: 45.7 to 47.88 kg

Hellfire has three variants: Laser-designated, RF/IR (Radio-Frequency Infrared), and IRIS (Imaging Infrared).

◆ **air-to-air missiles**

Sparrow III (AIM 7F,M) — Raytheon

The AIM-7F entered service in 1976 with a continuous-rod warhead. AIM-7M, the current version, entered service in 1983 with a blast/fragmentation warhead, active fuze, and improved seeker. In FY 85, 936 were authorized for procurement.

Length: 3.65 m — Guidance: semi-active homing
Diameter: 0.203 m — Speed: Mach 2.5
Weight: 227 kg — Range: 26,000 m
Propulsion: solid-fuel rocket — Warhead: 27 kg, proximity fuse

Sidewinder (AIM-9H, L, M) — Raytheon

Over 110,000 Sidewinder missiles have been built. The AIM-9L version uses an active optical fuze and has a guidance system permitting all-angle attacks. The AIM-9M version supplanted the -9L in production in 1981 and has improved capabilities against countermeasures and against targets seen against warm backgrounds. Only 500 AIM-9 L/M were authorized under FY 83, 350 under FY 84, none in FY 85, and 1,850 (for all services) under FY 86. "Sidearm" is a program to convert early-model AIM-9C missiles for anti-radiation homing; conversion of 885 was authorized under FY 86.

Length: 2.90 m — Propulsion: solid-fueled rocket
Diameter: 0.127 m — Guidance: infrared homing
Wingspan: 0.61 m — Speed: Mach 2.5
Weight: 84.4 kg — Range: 12 nautical miles

PHOENIX (AIM-54A, C) — Hughes

AIM-54A ceased production in 1980 after only 2,500 had been built for the U.S. and, unfortunately, Iran. The first 30 pilot-production AIM-54C were delivered 10-81, with 60 more to follow. Scheduled to enter service 1983-84. Only 90 procured under FY 83, rising to 265 under FY 84; in FY 85 only 265 were authorized, with 265 again in FY 86.

Length: 3.96 — Weight: 453 kg
Diameter: 0.380 m — Propulsion: solid-fueled rocket
Wingspan: 0.914 m — Range: about 120 km
Warhead: 60.3 kg (continuous rod)

AMRAAM (AIM-120A) — Hughes and Raytheon

AMRAAM (Advanced Medium-Range Air-to-Air Missile) is intended to replace the AIM-7F Sparrow. In development; first firings in 1985. The AIM-120B will have infrared homing added, and the AIM-120C will have improved aerodynamic performance. 90 developmental missiles requested under FY 86 for Navy and Air Force.

Length: 3.65 m — Warhead: 22.7 kg
Diameter: 0.178 m — Range: over 74 km
Weight: 151.5 kg
Guidance: inertial mid-course, active terminal homing

B. GUNS

406-mm, Model 1936

Fitted in 1,700-ton triple turrets in *Iowa*-class battleships. Requires a crew of 77 men per mount, plus 30–36 men in the magazine. In 1981, 15,500 high-capacity, 3,200 armor-piercing, and 2,300 B, L, & P rounds were available, with 12,500 full-service and 12,600 reduced-charge sets remaining. Armor-piercing rounds can penetrate 9 m of reinforced concrete. Reworked powder has produced very high accuracy.

Length: 50 calibers
Muzzle velocity: armor-piercing: 739 m/sec.; high-cap: 902 m/sec.
Rate of fire: 2 rounds/minute/barrel
Maximum range: armor-piercing shell: 36,700 m; high-capacity shell: 38,000 m
Weight of projectile: armor-piercing shell: 1,226 kg; high-capacity shell; 863 kg
Cartridge bags: 6 per charge, 50-kg or 24-kg reduced-charge
Fire control: Mk 38 director with Mk 13 radar

203-mm Mk 16 Mod. 0

Automatic weapon fitted in 451-ton triple turrets on *Des Moines*-class cruisers.

Length: 55 calibers
Muzzle velocity: 900 m/second
Arc of elevation: −5° to +41°
Rate of fire: 10 rounds/min/barrel
Maximum range: armor-piercing shell: 27,500 m; high-capacity shell: 28,670 m
Weight of projectile: armor-piercing shell: 152 kg; high-capacity shell: 113 kg
Fire control: Mk 54 director with Mk 13 radar

127-mm, twin barrel, Mk 12 Mod. 1

Semiautomatic, dual-purpose gun fitted in the Mk 32 series mounts of the *Iowa*-class battleships and *Des Moines*-class cruisers. 720,000 rounds of 127-mm ammunition for these and the single "5-inch/38" mounts below remained available in 1981.

Length: 38 calibers
Muzzle velocity: 792 m/sec
Elevation: −15° to +85°
Rate of fire: 18 rounds/minute/barrel with a well-trained crew
Maximum range on a surface target: 16,500 m
Maximum effective range on a ship target: 12,000 to 13,000 m
Maximum range in antiaircraft fire: 11,400 m
Maximum effective range in antiaircraft fire: 8,000 m
Weight of projectile: 25 kg
Fire control: Mk 37 director with Mk 25 radar; Mk 56 director with Mk 35 radar in a few ships

127-mm, Mk 30

Single mounting, weighing 20.4 tons, enclosed Mk 30 series mountings on FFG 1, FF 1040, and CGN 9 classes. Other data as for twin mounting.

127-mm, Mk 42

Single-barrel, dual-purpose gun fitted on ships built in the 1950s and 1960s. Most mounts converted to Mk 42 Mod. 10 configuration. An SAL (Semi-Active Laser-guided projectile) is being developed for these and the Mk 45 gun. Trials at sea commenced in

GUNS *(continued)*

Briscoe (DD 977) in 1981. The round is 1.548 m long, weighs 47.49 kg, and is similar in concept to the U.S. Army's Copperhead weapon.

Length: 54 calibers
Muzzle velocity: 810 m/second
Mount weight: 65.8 tons, mod. 10: 63.9 tons
Arc of elevation: −5° to +80°
Rate of elevation: 80°/second
Rate of fire: 20 rounds/minute
Weight of projectile: 32 kg
Range: 23,700 m horizontal/14,840 vertical
Rate of train: 50°/second
Fire control: Mk 68 system with SPG-53 radar in most ships
Personnel: 13 men, with 2 in mount

Loading entirely automatic from two ammunition drums in the handling room up to the loading tray by means of a rotating hoist. Each drum contains twenty rounds. The rate of fire can be maintained for only one minute, inasmuch as it is necessary to reload the drums. Firing rate reduced from original 40 r.p.m. for safety.

127-mm Mk 45—Northern Ordnance/FMC

Single-barrel mount fitted on *Ticonderoga-*, *California-*, and *Virginia*-class cruisers, *Spruance-*, *Kidd-*, and *Arleigh Burke*-class destroyers, and *Tarawa*-class amphibious assault ships. The Mod. 1 version permits rapid switching from one type of ammunition to another. A laser-guided projectile is in development.

Length: 54 calibers
Muzzle velocity: 810 m/second
Mount weight: 21.7 tons
Arc of elevation: −5° to +65°
Rate of fire: 16 to 20 rounds/minute
Range: 23,700 m horizontal/14,840 vertical
Fire control: Mk 86 GFCS with SPQ-9 search radar: SPG-60 tracking radar
Personnel: none on mount; 6 in handling room to reload ammunition drums

76.2-mm, Mk 22

Automatic dual-purpose gun in single (Mk 34) or twin (Mk 33) mounts, Mk 27 twin mounts in CA 134 and CA 139. Thoroughly obsolescent.

Length: 50 calibers
Mount weight: 15 tons. Mk 33 open mount
Weight of projectile: 3.2 kg
Rate of fire: 45 rounds/minute/barrel
Maximum range: 12,840 m horizontal/8,950 vertical
Fire control: Mk 56 system with Mk 35 radar or none in active ships

76.2-mm, Mk 21

Obsolescent. Single-fire, dual-purpose gun on two auxiliaries and some Coast Guard ships. Mk 26 mount.

Length: 50 calibers
Mount weight: 4.2 tons
Weight of projectile: 3.2 kg
Rate of fire: 20 rounds/minute
Maximum range: 12,840 horizontal/8,950 vertical
Fire control: ring sight only

76-mm, Mk 75—Northern Ordnance/FMC and OTO Melara

Single-barrel, license-built version of OTO Melara Compact, tested in the frigate *Talbot* and used in PHM and FFG 7 classes and Coast Guard *Bear*-class cutters; to backfit in Coast Guard ships. 1985 order to OTO Melara vice U.S. licensee, Northern Ordnance.

Length: 62 calibers
Mount weight: 6.2 tons
Weight of projectile: 6.4 kg
Rate of fire: 85 rounds/minute
Maximum range: 19,200 m horizontal/11,900 m vertical
Fire control: Mk 92 radar system
Personnel: 4 below decks

40-mm, Mk 19 Mod. 3

Strictly speaking not a gun, but rather a lightweight rapid-fire grenade launcher in portable tripod-legged mountings. Found aboard auxiliaries and Coast Guard ships.

Range: 2,195 m; rate of fire: 300 r.p.m.

25-mm Mk 88 (M 242 Bushmaster)—Hughes Helicopter

A "chain gun," using linked Oerlikon M790 ammunition. For use on Mk III patrol boats, the new SWCM and later LSD 42-class landing ships.

Length: 2.74 m overall
Weight: 109 kg (gun)
Rate of fire: single-shot, 100, or 200 r.p.m.
Fire control: ring sight

20-mm, Mk 16 Mod. 5

Single-barrel Mk 67 or Mk 68 mounting in small combatants, amphibious ships, and auxiliaries.

Length: 80 calibers
Mount weight: . . .
Rate of fire: 800 rounds/minute
Maximum range: 3,000 m horizontal
Fire control: ring sights on mount
Weight of projectile: 0.34 kg

20-mm Mk 10

Single-barrel, license-built Oerlikon mounting in minesweepers and auxiliaries.

Length: 70 calibers
Mount weight: 318–500 kg
Rate of fire: 450 rounds/minute
Maximum range: 4,390 m horizontal/3,050 m vertical
Fire control: ring sights on mount

20-mm, Mk 15 Mod. O Block 0 CIWS (Close-In Weapon System)—General Dynamics (G. E. gun)

Vulcan/Phalanx "Close-in" system designed to destroy missiles. It consists of a multibarrel, M61A1 20-mm gun with a very high rate of fire, which is co-mounted with two radars, one of which follows the target and the other the projectile stream. A computer furnishes necessary corrections for train and elevation so that the two radar targets coincide, bringing heavy fire to bear on the target. 672 units programmed to be fitted to U.S. ships. Only 989 rds. in Block O magazine. The first production unit completed 9-8-79 and was installed, with two others, in *America* (CV 66) on 17-4-80. An improved "Block I" version with more rounds on mount and a higher rate of fire will enter service in late 1986—three years late. Uses Mk 149 rounds with depleted uranium sub-caliber penetrators, although tungsten rounds are furnished for export. Later versions may use a 4-barreled GAU-10, 30-mm gatling gun or a 5- or 7-barreled 25-mm gatling gun.

Mount weight: 5.4 tons
Rate of fire: 3,000 rounds/minute
Maximum range: 1,486 m horizontal

C. TORPEDOES

◆ submarine torpedoes

Mk 48 Mod. 1, Mod. 3, and Mod. 4

Entered service 1972. Can be launched from a submarine against a surface target or a submarine. No surface ships are currently equipped to launch Mk 48, although that capability was originally intended. A total of 3,059 Mk 48s were procured through 1980, plus 56 for Australia and 92 for the Netherlands; 144 additional for the U.S. Navy were appropriated under FY 80 and again in FY 81 through FY 84. FY 85 was the last year of production, with 108 authorized.

Length: 5.84 m
Diameter: 0.533 m
Weight: 633 kg
Speed: 55 kts
Propulsion: 500 hp Otto-cycle swashplate engine
Depth: Up to 760 m

Can be launched with its own active-passive or acoustic homing system or with a wire-guidance system. High speed (40 knots) and long run duration (50,000 m). An improvement program, ADCAP (Added Capability) is being instituted, with the first twenty-two conversion kits requested under FY 80. The first "Near-Term Update" Mk 48 Mod. 4 torpedo was delivered 12-80. ADCAP will enter service in 1986, with the first 30 having been authorized under FY 85 and 123 authorized under FY 86.

◆ surface-launched torpedoes

Mk 46 Mod. 1, 2, and 5—Honeywell

ASW torpedo using liquid fuel (Otto fuel), and twin, counter-rotating props. Entered service 1963. Active-passive guidance. Launched from Mk 32 ASW torpedo tubes or as payload for the ASROC ASW missile system.

Length: 2.60 m (4.50 with ASROC booster)
Diameter: 0.324 m
Weight: 232.4 kg
Warhead: 45.4 kg HE

The Mk 46 Mod. 1 and Mod. 2 are being upgraded to Mod. 6 NEARTIP (Near-Term Improvement Program) status with improved acoustic homing system and countermeasures resistance. Under FY 80, 576 conversion kits were requested, and 1,128 more were requested under FY 82; ultimately, some 2,700 torpedoes will be updated. The Mk 46 Mod. 4 is the payload for the Captor mine. 570 *new* Mk 46 Mod. 5 torpedoes were ordered from Honeywell in 1980, 440 under FY 83, and 1,200 under FY 84, 1,565 authorized FY 85, and 500 in FY 86. Production now planned to continue into the early 1990s.

Mk 50 ALWT—Honeywell

The ALWT (Advanced Lightweight Torpedo) is being developed as a replacement for the Mk 46 series and will be supplied in surface-launched and air-droppable configurations. It will be roughly the same weight as the Mk 46 and of the same dimensions, but will be deeper-diving (over 600 m), faster (over 40 knots), and have better homing and counter-countermeasures capabilities. Due to continuing program delays, will not be operational before the early 1990s. Weight: 362 kg; length: 2.93 m.

NT-37E—Honeywell

Remanufactured and greatly improved Mk 37 homing torpedoes available for export, but not used by U.S. Navy. Propelled by a 90-hp Otto-fuel motor.

Length: 3,467 m
Diameter: 0.483 m
Weight: . . .
Speed: 35 kts
Range: 18,000 m
Warhead: 148 kg HE

◆ aircraft torpedoes

Mk 46 Mod. 0

Similar to the surface-launched weapon, but equipped with a retarding parachute, solid vice liquid propellant, and does not have a straight run-out before commencing helical search. Will be replaced by the ALWT.

D. MINES

Mk 52 Mod. 1, 2, 3, 5, 6

Air-dropped. All 2.75-m long by 338-mm diameter (840 mm over fins). All carry 270 kg HBX explosive. Mod. 1 is an acoustic mine, weight: 542.5 kg. Mod. 2 is a magnetic influence version, weight: 568 kg. Mod. 3 is a dual-pressure/magnetic influence version, weight: 572.5 kg. Mod. 5 is an acoustic/magnetic influence version, weight: 570.7 kg. Mod. 6 is a pressure/acoustic/magnetic influence version, weight: 546 kg. All are bottom mines for depths of up to 47 m (Mod. 2: 183 m) and can be carried by U.S.A.F. B-52D and H bombers as well as Navy aircraft.

Mk 55 Mod. 2, 3, 5, 6, 7

Air-dropped bottom mines. All 2.89 kg long by .592 m diameter (1.03 m over fins) and carry 577 kg HBX-1 explosive. Versions: Mod. 2: magnetic influence, weight: 989 kg; Mod. 3: pressure/magnetic influence, weight: 994 kg; Mod. 5: acoustic/magnetic influence, weight: 994 kg; Mod. 6: pressure/acoustic/magnetic, weight 997 kg; Mod. 7: dual-channel magnetic influence, weight: 996 kg. All can be laid in 46-m-deep water, except Mod. 2, 7: 183 m. Can also be laid by surface ships, using portable rails.

Mk 56 Mod. 0

Aircraft-dropped moored mine. 996-kg. 3.51 m long by 592-mm diameter (1.06 over fins). Total-field magnetic influence exploder. Carries 577-kg HBX-3 explosive. Depth: 350 m.

Mk 57 Mod. 0

Submarine-laid moored mine. 1,012 kg, 3.07 long by 510-mm diameter. Carries 935 kg HBX-3 explosive. Depth: 250 m

Mk 60 Captor (enCAPsulated TORpedo)

Submarine-laid or aircraft-dropped. Uses Mk 46 Mod. 4 acoustic-homing torpedo payload. Primarily ASW in function. 908 kg, 3.66 m long by 324-mm diameter. 44.5-kg warhead. In development since 1961 but still not fully reliable. 260 requested under FY 80 in first major operational buy, with 500 approved under FY 83, 300 under FY 84, 300 under FY 85 and 150 (unrequested) under FY 86. Mod 1 conversion kit gives improved target detection.

Mk 65 Quickstrike

Submarine-launched, 3.25 m long. 1,000 on order 1985.

Mk 67 SLMM (Submarine-Launched Mobile Mine)

Converted Mk 37 Mod. 0 torpedo. 754 kg, 4.09 m long by 483-mm diameter. Bottom mine. Remains in development.

DST-36 Quickstrike series (Mods. 0-5)

Aircraft-dropped bottom mine. Converted from 500-lb (227 kg) Mk 82 standard aircraft bomb. Magnetic. 87-kg H-6 explosive charge. Over 4,000 procured.

DST-40 Quickstrike series (Mods. 0-5)

Aircraft-dropped bottom mine. Converted from 1,000-lb (454-kg) Mk 83 standard aircraft bomb. Magnetic.

DST-41 Quickstrike series (Mods. 0-5)

Aircraft-dropped bottom mine. Converted from 2,000-lb (908-kg) Mk 84 bomb. Magnetic or magnetic/seismic influence. 3.83 m long. Minelaying: no surface ships are capable of minelaying. Naval aircraft of the S-3, P-3, A-6, and A-7 types are capable of laying mines, as are some 80 operational Air Force B-52D bombers. Theoretically, any U.S. Navy submarine can lay mines from its torpedo tubes.

E. RADARS

Radars for active ships are:

◆ surface-search and navigation

SPS-10: C-band, Mods. B through F in service. Primary surface-search set before the introduction of SPS-55. Being replaced by SPS-67.

SPS-53: X-band. Navigational set for large ships and for MSOs, auxiliaries, and Coast Guard ships.

SPS-55: X-band, slotted waveguide antenna. On *Spruance*-class destroyers and FFG 7 frigates, etc.

SPS-59: Official designation for the LN-66 navigational radar.

SPS-63: X-band. U.S. version of the Italian 3RM-20N for use on the *Pegasus*-class hydrofoils.

SPS-64: X-band. Used by USCG in several versions and being introduced into the USN for auxiliaries and minesweepers, etc., in the SPS-64(V)9 version. Raytheon.

SPS-67: C-band. A solid-state replacement for the SPS-10, using same antenna. Also has an ultra-short pulse mode for navigation. First use on refitted *Long Beach* (CGN 9) in 1982.

Also in use are the small navigational radar sets LN-66, SPS-51, SPS-57, SPS-59, SPS-60, SPS-64, and SPS-66, all X-band and most using slotted-waveguide antennas.

BPS-4, 11, 14, 15: X-band. Submarine search, navigational, and fire-control radars. Mounted on telescoping masts.

◆ two-dimensional air-search

SPS-6: L-band. Obsolescent; used only on *Thomaston* (LSD 28) class.

SPS-29: P-band. On some of the older DDGs and DDs. Same antenna as SPS-37 and SPS-43A.

SPS-37: On some CVs, CGs, and DDGs. SPS-37A used long SPS-43A antenna. Pulse-compression version of SPS-29.

SPS-40: B-band. The most widely used air-search radar. Range against medium bombers: 150–180 miles. Earlier "A" models being modernized to SPS-40D. P-band pulse-compression.

SPS-43: SPS-43A with large antenna. Being replaced in aircraft carriers by SPS-49; SPS-43 with small antenna on missile cruisers, also being replaced by SPS-49.

SPS-49: Aboard FFG 7-class and others. S-band.

SPS-58/65: L(D)-band, pulse-doppler. Combined air surface-search radar, now uses modified SPS-10 antenna; used for low-altitude defense. Some 51 sets procured. Used in carriers; being replaced by Mk 23 TAS.

◆ three-dimensional air-search

SPS-39: S-band. Mod. A uses same antenna as SPS-52. In some DDGs: E-band. SPS-52 is a version developed to interface directly with the NTDS data system.

SPS-48A: Mounted on CG classes. Frequency-scanning system.

SPS-48C, E: Electronic frequency scanning in elevation, improved SPS-48A. E version has doubled power, armored antenna, reduced side-lobe level, adaptive energy beam management, solid-state transmitter.

SPS-52C: S-band improvements on SPS-39. Electronic frequency scanning in elevation.

SPY-1A: S-band. Aegis system. Obtaining a directional effect by dipole radiation to secure an electronic sweep, it has four fixed aerials that provide instant 360° coverage. Long-range air-search, target-tracking, and missile-guidance. SPY-1B, with reduced side lobes to enter service 1988; SPY-1C developed for possible use on carriers; lighter-weight SPY-1D in development for DDG 51 program.

◆ fire-control

Mk 13: 3-cm wavelength. Ranging set for Mk 38 director on *Iowa*-class battleships and on Mk 34 director on CA 134 and CA 139.

Mk 25: X-band. Mounted on Mk 37 GFCS directors on CA, BB. Dish antenna.

Mk 35: 3-cm wavelength. Mounted on Mk 56 GFCS director for 127-mm and 76.2-mm guns. On older FFGs and FFs. Removed from auxiliaries. Dish antenna.

Mk 91: Technically, the fire-control *system* for the Sea Sparrow SAM system, used with the Mk 29 lightweight launcher. Either one (Mod. 0) or two (Mod. 1) radar directors per launcher. Uses Mk 57 Mod. 2 radar.

Mk 92/94: U.S Navy adaptation of Dutch H.S.A. (Hollandse Signaal Apparaaten) WM-20 series track-while-scan gun/missile fire-control system. Used in FFG 7, PHM 1, and the Coast Guard's new WMEC classes. Antennas mounted in egg-shaped radome. Combined with STIR (modified SPG-60) antenna in FFG-7 class. Improvement program in FFG 7 to end Phase I in 1984. Phase II CORT will further update system.

Mk 115: Technically the fire-control *system* for Sea Sparrow when launched from the Mk 25 heavy launcher. Older than Mk 91 and being phased out.

SPQ-9: X-band, track-while-scan special surface-search and weapons-control for use with Mk 86 GFCS. Antenna mounted in spherical radome. Range: 36 km.

SPG-51B, C, D: Standard MR illuminator-tracker; used with Mk 74 missile fire-control system.

SPG-53: Mounted on Mk 68 GFCS director on CG, DDG, and DD with 127-mm Mk 42 guns.

SPG-55A, B: Standard ER illuminator-tracker; used with Mk 76 missile fire-control system.

SPG-60: Standard MR X-band, 4-horn monopulse, pulse-doppler illuminator-tracker with Mk 74 missile fire-control system in later CGN classes; also illuminates for guns in conjunction with Mk 86 GFCS. STIR version, used on FFG 7 class, is modified for use with Mk 92 Mod. 2 missile/gun control system. STIR = Separate Tracking & Illumination Radar. Can track Mach 3.0 targets to 183 km. Has a co-mounted t.v. tracker.

SPG-62: Standard SM-2 illuminator; used with Aegis system in CG 47 class. Slaved to SPY-1 radar.

TAS/Mk 23: D-band. Technically a Target Acquisition System, employing a rapidly rotating, stabilized linear array antenna in conjunction with a UYK-20 computer to counter high- and low-angle aircraft and cruise-missile attacks. Range 20 n.m. on small missiles to 90 n.m. on aircraft. Mod. 0 on *Downes* (FF 1070) in 1975, Mod. 1 being added to *Spruance* (DD 963) class, Mod. 2 (with UYA-4 console) on *Sacramento* class, beginning with AOE 3 in 4-80. Can track 54 targets simultaneously.

RADARS *(continued)*

◆ **carrier-controlled approach systems**

SPN-6: Formerly installed on aircraft carriers but now limited to AVT 16 and some LPH. Antenna in large radome.

SPN-10: Aircraft landing aid, incorporating a radar set to determine aircraft position relative to the carrier. Antennas are two small conical dishes; SPN-10 remained on 5 ships in 1985 as the radar associated with the ACLS (Automatic Carrier Landing System) and CCA (Carrier-Controlled Approach) systems. Being replaced by SPN-42, which is less bulky. Other carrier aircraft landing aid/radar systems include SPN-41, SPN-43, and SPN-44. SPN-46 is to be added beginning in 1986 for use with Automatic Carrier Landing System.

F. COUNTERMEASURES SYSTEMS

◆ **electronic systems, surface ships**

WLR-1: Radar warning array in older ships. Being updated to WLR-1H (7-18 gHz).

WLR-3: Radar warning and signal collection — also in some submarines.

WLR-8: Radar warning system for the SSN 688 class, and (V)4 version in one carrier.

ULQ-6: Deception repeater/jammer in cruisers, destroyers — being replaced by SLQ-32(V)3 in high-value ships.

WLR-11: Radar warning system.

SLQ-17: Jammer array for carriers; creates false target.

SLQ-29: The combined WLR-8/SLQ-17 package.

SLQ-32(V)1: Radar warning (H- , I- , J-bands) for auxiliaries and amphibious ships (to be on 113 ships).

SLQ-32(V)2: Radar warning (B–J bands) for newer destroyers and frigates — replaces WLR-1 where fitted (to be on 107 ships).

SLQ-32(V)3: Radar warning (B–J bands) *and* jamming/spoofing (H–J bands) for cruisers, DDG 37 class, and major amphibious ships (to be on 64 ships).

SLQ-33: A Ship-Towed Acoustic Deception Device.

SLQ-34 OUTBOARD: An intelligence collection system.

◆ **electronic systems, submarines**

BLQ-3, 4, 5, 8: Acoustic jamming system

BLR-1-10, 13-15: Radar warning systems; BLR-14 also launches countermeasures.

WLR-9: Sonar detection system.

WLR-10: Radar warning receiver.

◆ **physical countermeasures systems**

T-Mk 6 Fanfare: Mechanical towed anti-torpedo noisemaker — obsolescent.

SLQ-25 Nixie: Towed torpedo countermeasure/noisemaker, to replace T-Mk 6 — 180 sets procured.

Chaffroc: Two-celled (8-rocket) launcher for modified Zuni chaff-deploying rockets — obsolescent.

Mk 33 RBOC: Rapid-Blooming Overboard Chaff launcher — replaced by Mk 36.

Mk 36 SRBOC: Super-RBOC — Mod. 1 with two 6-tubed mortars for ships under 140 m; Mod. 2 with four 6-tubed mortars for ships over 140 m. All use Mk 182 chaff-dispensing cartridges, which climb to 244 m. "Torch" infrared decoy being developed for use with Mk 36 SRBOC, and the NATO Sea Gnat rocket chaff dispenser may be adopted.

Mk 70 MOSS: Mobile Submarine Simulator — small torpedo-like device for launch by *Ohio*-class SSBNs.

G. SONARS

◆ **on surface ships**

SQQ-14: High-frequency, minehunting, and classification set in retractable-transducer array on MSOs. A towed version, SQQ-35, is in development.

SQQ-23: PAIR (Performance and Integration Refit). Modified SQS-23 using two transducer domes (except in CGN 9 and CG 16 classes: one dome); also in 4 DDG 2, 2 DDG 37 class.

SQQ-28: LAMPS-III helicopter data-link processing system.

SQQ-30: Minehunting sonar developed by General Electric for use on mine countermeasures ships; used only on MCM 1-8, MSH 1.

SQQ-32: Raytheon/Thomson-CSF sonar to replace SQQ-30 in later units of the MCM 1 class and for the MSH 1 class. Separate detection and classification transducers lowered through well and towed well below the hull. Uses two UYK-44 computers.

SQQ-89: Suite integrating the SQR-19 towed array, SQS-52B hull-mounted sonar, Mk 116 Underwater Fire Control System, SQQ-28 processor, and UYQ-28 SIMAS (Sonar In-Mode Assessment System) for CG 56 and later, and for DDG 51. Trials in DD 980 late 1985.

SQR-15: Developmental passive towed array, in FF 1037 and some FF 1040-class frigates.

SQR-17: Passive shipboard classification device for processing data transmitted to CG 26, DD 963, F 1040, 1052, and FFG 7-class ships via LAMPS-I helicopters from various sonobuoys. Uses SKR-4 link receiver, AKT-22 link, ARR-75 sonobuoy receiver.

SQR-18A: TACTAS (Tactical Towed Acoustic Sensor). For use on FF 1052 class equipped with SQS-35 VDS; array attaches to VDS towed body. Normal cable length is 1,706 m; towed at depths up to 366 m; array is 82.6-mm diameter. Latest version, SQR-18(v)1 with 730-m cable is aboard 35 FF 1052-class ships; uses 8 modular hydrophone sections. SQR-18A(v) uses SQR-19 towing rig for the non-VDS-equipped units of the FF 1052 class.

SQR-19: Improved TACTAS for use on CG 47, DD 963, and FFG 7 classes; to be deployed through port in stern. Still in development.

SQS-23: Bow- or hull-mounted low-frequency, active-passive. In CV 66, CGN 25, some CG, older DDG, and D 931 classes.

SQS-26: Bow-mounted, low-frequency set, in various versions. In older CGN, CG 26, FFG 1, FF 1037, FF 1040, FF 1052, FF 1098 classes.

SQS-35: Independent, variable-depth, towed, active-passive. In some DD 931 class, most FF 1052 class.

SQS-38: Hull-mounted SQS-35 for USCG cutters.

SQS-53: SQS-26 with digital computer interface, for use with Mk 116 UWFCS (Underwater Fire Control System) on DD 963, DDG 993, CG 47 classes. SQS-53B (General Electric/Hughes) has multiple target tracking and classification aids, weapons checkout routines, UYK-44 imbedded computers, UYQ-21 display, UYS-1 signal processor, a 60-percent reduction in required manning, 2,000-hour mean time between failures, and a 30-minute mean time to repair.

SQS-56: Raytheon 1160B commercial active-passive, hull-mounted, medium-frequency set; used on FFG 7 class.

SQS-58: Raytheon. In development. No data available.

UQQ-2 SURTASS: SURveillance Towed-Array Sonar System, for use in the *Stalwart* (T-AGOS 1) class. Trails 1,830-m passive hydrophone array at about 3 knots.

◆ **on submarines**

BQQ-4: PUFFS (Passive Underwater Fire Control). Three-fin arrays, on SSN 597, SS 574, SS 563 classes.

BQQ-2: Active-passive system on SSN 594 class, SSN 597, SSN 637 class, SSN 671, SSN 685. Incorporates BPR-7 conformed hydrophone array and BQS-6 spherical hydrophone array. Being upgraded to BQQ-5 in most ships.

BQQ-5: Active-passive system on the SSN 688 class; being backfitted in SSN 594 and SSN 637 classes. Incorporates BQS-11, 12, or 13 spherical bow hydrophone array. BQQ-5C has expanded DIFAR reception.

BQQ-6: Passive-only version of the BQQ-5 system, for SSBN 626 class; has 944 hydrophone transducers mounted on a sphere.

BQQ-9: Towed array signal processing system for BQR-15; Rockwell.

BQR-15: Towed, passive array for SSN 608, SSN 616 classes. Incorporates BQR-23 signal processor.

BQR-19: Active, short-range, navigational set for SSGNs. Raytheon.

BQR-21: DIMUS (Digital Multi-Beam Steering). Passive array for SSBNs.

BQR-23: STASS (Submarine Towed Array Sonar System). Used with BQR-25 in SSN 688, SSBN 726 classes. Current version: BQR-23A.

BQR-24: Raytheon; processor, used with BQR-21.

BQR-25: See BQR-23.

BQS-4: Active/passive set in older SSN, SS.

BQS-14, 20: Under-ice and mine-avoidance, high-frequency set, mostly on later SSNs. Part of the BQQ-2, -5, -6 systems.

BQS-13: Raytheon. Active set.

BQS-15: Under-ice set tailored to the requirements of the SSN 688 class.

SUBACS: In development. "Basic" version is suite for later SSN 688-class SSNs. To use UYS-1 signal processor, USH-26 signal recorder, UYK-20A data processor. Passive arrays plus SADS (Submarine Active Detection Sonar) and towed passive array.

◆ **on helicopters**

AQS-13: Dipping sonar used on SH-3 Sea King series.

AQS-14: Mine countermeasures set used by MH/CH-53D helicopters.

H. PROCESSING OF TACTICAL DATA

The NTDS (Naval Tactical Data system) uses digital calculators (AN/UYK-20 and AN/UYK-7) to give an overall picture of a tactical situation — air, surface, and

PROCESSING OF TACTICAL DATA *(continued)*

underwater—and enables the commander to employ the means necessary to oppose the enemy. Excellent automatic data transmission systems (Link-11 and Link-14) permit the exchange of tactical information with similarly equipped ships and aircraft carrying the ATDS (P-3C Orion and S-3A Viking) and amphibious landing forces equipped with NTDS.

Nearly all ships are equipped to receive SATCOMM (Satellite Communications) messages, while most can send ultra-high-frequency messages via satellite, and 31 can send super-high-frequency messages. The Tactical Flag Command Center (TFCC) is being backfitted into 13 CV/CVN, 2 LCC, and 5 CG. It employs USQ-81(v) computer-generated displays in an integrated 6.2-m × 6.2-m display space.

NUCLEAR-POWERED AIRCRAFT CARRIERS

◆ **0 (+3) improved Nimitz class** Bldr: Newport News SB & DD

	Program	Laid down	L	In serv.
CVN 71 Theodore Roosevelt	FY 80	31-10-81	27-10-84	27-10-86
CVN 72 Abraham Lincoln	FY 83	3-11-84	9-87	12-89
CVN 73 George Washington	FY 83	8-86	9-89	12-91

Theodore Roosevelt (CVN 71)—note lack of any catapult bridle horns at bow or from angled deck W. Donko, 7-85

Theodore Roosevelt (CVN 71)—fitting out L. & L. Van Ginderen, 7-85

D: 73,973 tons light (96,300–96,836 fl) **S:** 30+ kts
Dim: 332.85 (317.0 pp) × 40.85 (flight deck: 78.33) × 11.71
A: 3/Mk 29 launchers (VIII × 3) for Sea Sparrow—4/20-mm Mk 15 CIWS gatling AA—86 aircraft, including 20 F-14, 18 F/A-18, 5 EA-6B, 20 A-6E, 5 E-2C, 10/S-3A, and 8/SH-3D

Electron Equipt: Radar: 1/LN-66 nav., SPS-64 nav., 1/SPS-67(v), 1/SPS-48E, 1/SPS-49, 1/SPS-65, 1/SPN-41, 1/SPN-43A, 1/SPN-44, SPN-45, 3/Mk 91 Mod. 1 (6 directors)
EW: WRL-1H, WLR-8, SLQ-17, Mk 36 SRBOC chaff RL (VI × 4)
TACAN: URN-25

M: 2 A4W/A1G pressurized-water reactors (42.3 kg/cm²), 4 sets GT; 4 props; 280,000 hp
Electric: 64,000 kw + 8,000-kw emergency power from 4 diesel sets
Man: 6,286 tot. (203 officers, 3,205 men crew + 366 officers, 2,512 men air group).

Remarks: CVN 71 authorized under FY 80; had been repeatedly delayed in favor of conventionally powered designs of inferior capabilities. Won out over both an administration-sponsored 62,427-ton (fl) paper CVV design and a compromise 82,561-ton repeat *John F. Kennedy* (CV 67) design.

The hangar will have 7.6 m clear height. The angled deck will be 237.7 m long and will be equipped with four arrester wires and a Mk 7 Mod. 3 barrier, as well as four C 13 Mod. 1 catapults (92.1 m long), and four elevators (21.3 × 1.58 m, 47-ton capacity). An aviation payload of some 14,909 tons will be carried, and the aviation ordnance magazines will hold 1,954 tons. Aviation fuel capacity will be about 9,000 tons. Kevlar armor will be fitted over vital spaces, and hull-protection arrangements have been improved. Other data under the *Nimitz* class will generally apply. CVN 72 and 73 will have new, lower-pressure catapults and SPN-46 landing aids.

◆ **3 Nimitz class (SCB 102 Type)** Bldr: Newport News SB & DD

	Program	Laid down	L	In serv.
CVN 68 Nimitz	FY 67	22-6-68	13-5-72	3-5-75
CVN 69 Dwight D. Eisenhower	FY 70	15-8-70	11-10-75	18-10-77
CVN 70 Carl Vinson	FY 74	11-10-75	15-3-80	13-3-82

Authorized: CVN 68 in FY 67, CVN 69 in FY 71, CVN 70 in FY 74.

Carl Vinson (CVN 70) L. & L. Van Ginderen, 12-84

Nimitz (CVN 68) G. Gyssels, 2-85

Nimitz (CVN 68)—post 1983-84 refit CO USS *Nimitz*, 6-84

NUCLEAR-POWERED AIRCRAFT CARRIERS *(continued)*

Carl Vinson (CVN 70) Pradignac & Leo, 1983

Carl Vinson (CVN 70) G. Arra, 10-84

Dwight D. Eisenhower (CVN 69) G. Gyssels, 2-85

Dwight D. Eisenhower (CVN 69)—still with SPS-43 G. Gyssels, 2-85

D: 70,916 tons light; 81,600 standard (91,700 fl) **S:** 30+ kts
Dim: 327.0 (over catapult bridle retrieval horns: 332.8, pp: 317.0) × 40.85 (flight deck: 77.11, max.: 89.4) × 11.3
A: 86 airplanes and helicopters: 20 F-14, 18 F/A-18, 5 EA-6B, 20 A-6E, 5 E-2C, 10 S-3, 8 SH-3D—3/Mk 29 launchers (VIII × 3) for Sea Sparrow—3 (CVN 70: 4)/20-mm Mk 15 CIWS
Electron Equipt: Radar: 1/LN-66, 1/SPS-10F, 1/SPS-49, 1/SPS-48B, 1/SPN-41, 2/SPN-42, 1/SPN-43A, 1/SPN-44, 3/Mk 115 (6 directors), 1/Mk 23 TAS
EW: WLR-1H, WLR-8, SLQ-17, Mk 36 SRBOC chaff (VI × 4)
TACAN: URN-25
M: 2 G.E. A4W/A1G pressurized-water reactors, 4 sets GT; 4 props; 280,000 hp
Electric: 64,000 kw + 8,000 kw emergency power from 4 diesel sets
Man: 6,286 tot. (569 officers, 3,091 crew, plus aviation personnel: (304 officers, 2,322 men)

Remarks: CV 68, 69 in Atlantic, CV 70 in Pacific, where CV 70 is to transfer. Carry 90% more aviation fuel and 50% more ammunition than the *Forrestal* class. ASCAC (Antisubmarine Classification and Analysis Center) permits instant sharing of target data between the carrier, its ASW aircraft, and escorting ships. *Nimitz* in refit 6-83 to 9-84; *Eisenhower* in refit 28-10-85 to 4-87.

Electronics: SPS-49 replaced SPS-43A in CVN 68 and CVN 70 in 1983, and in CVN 69 in 1986. Carry OE-82 satellite communications antennas and have full NTDS installations. The Mk 23 TAS is being added to improve defense against low-fliers and cruise missiles.

Armament: *Carl Vinson* completed with three Mk 29 launchers (VIII × 3) for Sea Sparrow, six directors for the missile (3 Mk 91 Mod. 1 FCS), and four Mk 15 CIWS (Vulcan/Phalanx) gatling AA guns. The others have been similarly refitted, but will have only three Vulcan/Phalanx.

Armor: Decks and hull are of extra-strong, high-tensile steel to limit the impact of semi-armor-piercing bombs. Apart from the longitudinal bulkheads, there are twenty-three watertight transverse bulkheads (more than 2,000 compartments) and ten firewall bulkheads. Foam devices for fire-fighting are very well developed, and pumping equipment is excellent, a 15° list being correctable in 20 minutes. Thirty damage-control teams are available at all times. *Nimitz*-class ships can withstand three times the severe pounding taken by the *Essex*-class aircraft carriers in 1944-45, and they can take impacts and shock waves in the same proportion. They are being equipped with Kevlar armor over vital spaces during refits.

Machinery: The cores of these ships are expected to last 13 years (CVN 70: 15) in normal usage, for a cruising distance of 800,000 to 1,000,000 miles. The evaporators can produce 1,520 tons of fresh water per day.

Aircraft-handling installations: There are four side elevators: two forward, one aft of the island to starboard, and one on the stern to port. There are also four C13 Mod. 1 steam catapults, 94.5 m long. CVN 69 and 70 have only the forward starboard bridle retrieval horn, because most aircraft in service do not require the bridle for launching. The 15,134 m³ total aviation magazine spaces can hold 1,954 tons of aviation ordnance, and the total aviation-associated payload is on the order of 15,000 tons. The hangar is 7.8 meters high and can accommodate only 35–40% of the aircraft aboard. The angled part of the flight deck is 237.7 meters long and has four Mk 14 arrester wires and a barrier to halt aircraft (to be changed to 3 wires, 1 net). Sufficient aviation fuel for 16 days' operations is carried. CVN 69 has the prototype AVCARS (Augmented Visual Carrier Aircraft Recovery System); the production version entered service 1984.

◆ **1 Enterprise class (SCB 160 type)**—FY 58 Program

	Bldr	Laid down	L	In serv.
CVN 65 Enterprise	Newport News SB & DD	4-2-58	24-9-60	25-11-61

Authorized: FY 58

D: 73,500 tons light (90,970 fl) **S:** 33 kts
Dim: 335.75 (over catapult bridle horn: 342.3, wl: 317.0) × 40.54 (flight deck: 78.4) × 11.9
A: 86 airplanes and helicopters: 20 F-14, 18 F/A-18, 5 EA-6B, 20 A-6E, 5 E-2C, 10 S-3A, 8 SH-3A—2/Mk 29 launchers (VIII × 2) for Sea Sparrow—3/20-mm Mk 15 CIWS gatling AA (I × 3)
Electron Equipt: Radar: 1/LN-66, 1/SPS-65, 1/SPS-48C, 1/SPS-49, 1/SPN-41, 1/SPN-42, 1/SPN-35A, 1/SPN-44, 2/Mk 91 Mod. 1 (4 directors)

Enterprise (CVN 65) G. Arra, 8-85

NUCLEAR-POWERED AIRCRAFT CARRIERS *(continued)*

Enterprise (CVN 65) G. Arra, 8-85

Enterprise (CVN 65)—rebuilt island, starboard side, with SPS-49 and SPS-48C radars atop superstructure, SPS-10F and SPN-35A on mast

G. Arra, 8-85

EW: WLR-1, WLR-8, WLR-11, SLQ-17(v)4, Mk 36 SRBOC chaff RL (VI × 4)
TACAN: URN-25

M: 8 Westinghouse A2W reactors, supplying 32 Foster-Wheeler heat exchangers; 4 sets Westinghouse GT; 4 props; 280,000 hp
Electric: 40,000 kw + 8,000 kw emergency
Man: 462 officers, 5,102 men (including 304/2,323 aviation personnel)

Enterprise (CVN 65) G. Arra, 8-85

Remarks: Began what was to have been a two-year overhaul at Puget Sound NSY 15-1-79, during which the radar and other electronics suites were extensively renovated; completed 11-81. The SPS-32 and SPS-33 "billboard" radar arrays were removed, as was the "beehive" dome atop the blockhouse superstructure. A new mast, resembling that on the *Nimitz,* was installed atop the superstructure. SPS-48C and SPS-49 are mounted atop the island. There are four C13 Mod. 1 steam catapults and four elevators—one on the port side of the angled deck, three to starboard—two of which are forward of and one abaft the island. Elevators are steel and alloy and weigh 105 tons; 26 m long, 16 m wide, lift 45 tons. The hangar is 7.62 m high and the flight deck is more than 20,000 m². Carries half again as much aviation fuel as the *Forrestal* class (8,500 tons), which permits 12 days of intensive aerial operations without replenishment. Carries fuel oil to replenish other ships. Has NTDS and ASCAC (Antisubmarine Classification and Analysis Center) and will receive TFCC (Tactical Flag Communications Center). A third Mk 29 Sea Sparrow SAM launcher and the Mk 23 TAS radar are to be added during the next major overhaul in the early 1990s. Air group to be updated to 20 F-14, 20 F/A-18, 20 A-6E/KA-6D, 5 EA-6B, 5 E-2C, 10 S-3, 6SH-3H.

CONVENTIONAL AIRCRAFT CARRIERS

◆ **1 John F. Kennedy class (SCB 127C type)** Bldr: Newport News SB & DD

	Program	Laid down	L	In serv.
CV 67 John F. Kennedy	FY 63	22-10-64	27-5-67	7-9-68

D: 59,200 tons light (80,940 fl) **S:** 32 kts
Dim: 320.34 (301.8 wl) × 39.17 (flight deck: 81.38, max. 82.30) × 11.13
A: 78 aircraft: 24 F-14, 24 A-6E, 4 KA-6D, 5 EA-6B, 5 E-2C, 10 S-3A, 6 SH-3H—3/Mk 29 launchers (VIII × 3) for Sea Sparrow—3/20-mm Mk 15 CIWS (I × 3)
Electron Equipt: Radar: 1/LN-66, 1/SPS-10F, 1/SPS-49, 1/SPS-48C, 1/SPN-35, 1/SPN-41, 2/SPN-42, 1/SPN-43A, 1/SPN-44, 3/Mk 91 Mod. 1 (6 directors), 1 Mk 23 TAS
EW: WLR-1, WLR-3, WLR-11, SLQ-26, SLQ-17, Mk 36 SRBOC RL (III × 4)
TACAN: URN-25
M: 4 sets G.E. GT; 4 props; 280,000 hp
Boilers: 8 Foster-Wheeler; 83.4 kg/cm², 520°C **Electric:** 17,000 kw
Man: 535 officers, 5,224 men (including aviation personnel)

Remarks: Operates in the Atlantic Fleet. Four side elevators, three to starboard (two forward of and one abaft the island) and one on the port quarter. Completely automatic landing system, permitting all-weather operation. Four arrester wires and a

John F. Kennedy (CV 67) L. & L. Van Ginderen, 5-84

CONVENTIONAL AIRCRAFT CARRIERS *(continued)*

John F. Kennedy (CV 67) G. Arra, 1984

John F. Kennedy (CV 67)—note Chaffroc RL, 2 Sea Sparrow directors, island with canted stack French Navy, 6-82

barrier on the 227-m angled flight deck. Three 90-m C13 and one 94.5-m C13-1 catapults. Has PLAT, which facilitates the control of launching and recovery operations. Stack angled to starboard. The 11,808-m² aviation-ordnance magazine can accommodate 1,250 tons of ammunition. Carries 5,919 tons of aviation fuel. Equipped to carry SQS-23 sonar in bow dome, but it was not installed. SPS-49 replaced SPS-43A in 1979-80, and SPS-58 was deleted. Obsolescent Chaffroc chaff RL replaced with Mk 36 SRBOC (VI × 4), during 10-84 to 10-85 refit, when two additional Mk 15 CIWS and the Mk 23 TAS radar were also added.

◆ **3 Kitty Hawk class (SCB 127A and SCB 127B types)**

	Bldr	Laid down	L	In serv.
CV 63 Kitty Hawk	New York SB	27-12-56	21-5-60	29-4-61
CV 64 Constellation	Brooklyn NSY	14-9-57	8-10-60	27-10-61
CV 66 America	Newport News SB	9-1-61	1-2-64	23-1-65

Authorized: CV 63 in FY 56, CV 64 in FY 57, CV 66 in FY 61

D: 60,100 tons (82,200 fl; CV 66: 79,700) **S:** 33 kts
Dim: 318.8 (CV 66: 319.25) (301.76 pp) × 39.62 (flight deck: 76.81) × 11.4 (CV 66: 11.3)
A: 86 aircraft: 24 F-14, 12 A-6E, 24 A-7E, 4 KA-6D, 4 EA-6B, 10 S-3A, 4 E-2C, 6 SH-3H—3/Mk 29 (CV 63: 2) launchers (VIII × 2 or 3) for Sea Sparrow—3/20-mm Mk 15 CIWS gatling AA (I × 3)

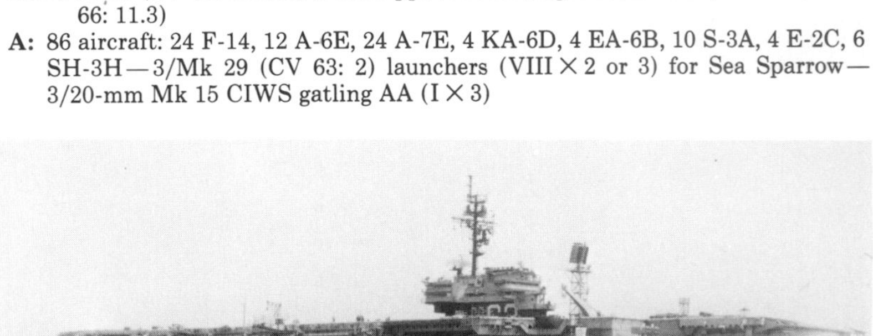

Kitty Hawk (CV 63) W. Donko, 7-85

America (CV 66) L. & L. Van Ginderen, 10-84

America (CV 66) L. & L. Van Ginderen, 9-85

America (CV 66) L. & L. Van Ginderen, 9-85

CONVENTIONAL AIRCRAFT CARRIERS *(continued)*

Kitty Hawk (CV 63) G. Arra, 10-83

America (CV 66) Pradignac & Leo, 9-84

CONVENTIONAL AIRCRAFT CARRIERS *(continued)*

Electron Equipt: Radar: 1/LN-66, 1/SPS-10F, 1/SPS-48C, 1/SPN-35, 1/SPN-41, 2/SPN-42, 1/SPN-43A, 2 or 3/Mk 91 Mod. 1 (4 or 6 directors)
EW: SLQ-29 (WLR-8 + SLQ-17); WLR-1H, WLR-11, Mk 36 SRBOC RL (VI × 4)
TACAN: URN-25

M: 4 sets Westinghouse GT; 4 props; 280,000 hp **Fuel:** 7,800 tons
Boilers: 8 Foster-Wheeler; 83.4 kg/cm², 520°C **Range:** 4,000/30; 8,000/20
Man: Approx. 5,400: 137 officers, 2,765 men + air group: 290 officers, 2,200 men
Electric: 15,000 kw (CV 66: 18,000 kw)

Remarks: These ships are a great improvement over the *Forrestal* class, on which they are based, and have one significant difference: three elevators on the starboard side, two forward of and one abaft the island, and one to port, abaft the angled flight deck. Aircraft can be landed and catapulted simultaneously, a difficult operation on the earlier ships. Four C13 steam catapults, except on CV 66, on which one is of the longer C13-1 type. Carry 5,882 tons of aviation fuel. CV 66 was the first ship to receive the Mk 15 CIWS, in 4-80. CV 63 has only two Mk 29 launchers for Sea Sparrow. CV 64 retained two Mk 10 twin launchers for Terrier HT missiles and two SPQ-55B radar directors until 12-82 to 2-84 refit at Bremerton. CV 66 was the first to have a special integrated CIC and airborne ASW control center (ASCAC). CV 66 had an SQS-23 bow sonar until 1981. CV 63 is to enter SLEP (Service Life Extension Program) 11-87, emerging in 5-90 with new catapult rotary engines, Mk 7 Mod. 3 arrester gear (3 wires), SPN-46 landing-aid radar, SPS-48E and SPS-49(V) upgrade air-search radars, updated NTDS (Naval Tactical Data System), a torpedo decoy system, the WQN-1 "channel-finder" sonar, upgraded EW equipment, and the Mk 23 TAS low-altitude radar added. CV 64 is to undergo a similar SLEP from 12-89 to 6-92. CV 66 is not scheduled for SLEP until 1994-96, but will receive Mk 23 TAS during regular overhaul in the late 1980s.

Air groups being modified, with 18 A/F-18 replacing the 24 A-7E, the number of F-14 being reduced to 20. CV 63 and CV 64 are in the Pacific, CV 66 in the Atlantic Fleet.

◆ 4 Forrestal class (CV 59: SCB 80 type, CV 60 to CV 62: SCB 80M type)

	Bldr	Laid down	L	In serv.
CV 59 Forrestal	Newport News SB & DD	14-7-52	11-12-54	1-10-55
CV 60 Saratoga	Brooklyn NSY	16-12-52	8-10-55	14-4-56
CV 61 Ranger	Newport News SB & DD	2-8-54	29-9-54	10-8-57
CV 62 Independence	Brooklyn NSY	1-7-55	6-6-58	10-1-59

Authorized: CV 59 in FY 52, CV 60 in FY 53, CV 61 in FY 54, CV 62 in FY 55

Ranger (CV 61)—post-overhaul, with Mk 23 TAS on mast USS Ranger, 6-85

Ranger (CV 61)—note sponsons forward G. Arra, 1-86

Forrestal (CV 59)—at conclusion of SLEP—Mk 14 CIWS not yet added G. Arra, 5-85

Independence (CV 62)—prior to SLEP L. & L. Van Ginderen, 3-84

Saratoga (CV 60) PH3 L. Hilley, USN, 4-84

Saratoga (CV 60)—bow view G. Gyssels, 6-84

CONVENTIONAL AIRCRAFT CARRIERS *(continued)*

Saratoga (CV 60)—post-SLEP modernization

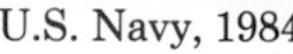

U.S. Navy, 1984

Independence (CV 62)—stern view L. & L. Van Ginderen, 5-84

D: CV 59, 60: 59,600 tons (78,200 fl); CV 61, 62: 60,000 tons (79,200 fl) **S:** 33 kts
Dim: CV 59: 331.0; CV 60: 324.0; CV 61: 326.4; CV 62: 326.1 (319.13 flight deck, 301.8 wl) × 39.63 (CV 59, 60: 76.3; CV 61, 62: 82.3 max.) × 11.3
A: 86 aircraft: 20 F-14, 20 F/A-18, 16 A-6E, 4 KA-6D, 5 EA-6B, 10 S-3A, 5 E-2C, 6 SH-3H—2 Mk 29 (CV 60, 62: 3) launchers (VIII × 2 or 3) for Sea Sparrow—3/20-mm Mk 15 CIWS gatling AA (I × 3)
Electron Equipt: Radar: 1/LN-66, 1/SPS-10, 1/SPS-49, 1/SPS-48C, 1/SPN-35, 1/SPN-41, 2/SPN-42, 1/SPN-43A, 2 or 3/Mk 91 Mod. 1 (4 or 6 directors); CV 61 also: Mk 23 TAS
EW: WLR-1, WLR-3, WLR-11, SLQ-26, Mk 36 SRBOC chaff RL (VI × 4)
TACAN: URN-25
M: 4 sets G.E. or Westinghouse GT; 4 props; CV 59: 260,000 hp, others: 280,000 hp
Boilers: 8 Babcock & Wilcox; CV 59: 41.7 kg/cm², other: 83.4 kg/cm², 520°C
Fuel: 7,800 tons **Range:** 4,000/30; 8,000/20
Man: Approx. 4,940: 145 officers, 2,645 enlisted + air group: 290 officers, 3,100 enlisted.

Remarks: CV 61 in Pacific Fleet, others in the Atlantic. Hangar is 7.6 m high and 234–240 m long. Four side elevators (15.95 × 18.9). Deck angled at 8°. Armored flight deck. Four-cable arresting gear. CV 59 and CV 60 have two Mk-C7 (75 m) and two Mk-C11 (65 m) steam catapults; the others have four Mk-C7. Carry 5,880 tons of aviation fuel. CV 59 has three rudders and four propellers, the two outboard being five-bladed, the two inboard, four-bladed. Deck protection and internal compartmentation are extensive (1,200 watertight compartments). Two longitudinal bulkheads are fitted from keel to waterline from stem to stern; there are transverse bulkheads about every 10 meters. Air groups evolving as F/A-18 replaced A-7E; earlier ships carried 24 F-14, 12 A-6E, 24 A-7E. CV 61 carries: 24 F-14, 28 A-6E/KA-6D, 10 S-3, 6 SH-3H, 5 E-2C, and 5 EA-6B.

CV 60 received first SLEP (Service Life Extension Program) modernization, beginning 1-10-80 at Philadelphia Navy yard, completing 2-83 (but boiler defects kept her inoperative until 18-11-83). CV 59 SLEP from 21-3-83 to 20-5-85; CV 62 planned 18-4-85 to 8-87. *Ranger* not scheduled for SLEP until 1-92 to 5-94, but did get extensive overhaul at Puget Sound NSY 5-84 to 6-85, when improved evaporators, Halon and aqueous film firefighting systems, Mk 23 TAS, and 3 Mk 15 CIWS were added. All will ultimately be armed with three Mk 29 Sea Sparrow launchers, each with two directors, three Mk 15 CIWS Vulcan/Phalanx gatling guns, and the Mk 23 TAS low-altitude radar. All catapults will be replaced with longer and more powerful C13s. The ships will get Kevlar armor, improved data systems, the Tactical Flag

CONVENTIONAL AIRCRAFT CARRIERS *(continued)*

Saratoga (CV 60)—SPS-49 on platform abreast stack, SPS-48 atop bridge, 2 Mk 91 directors, one above the other, separate platforms for Mk 15 CIWS and SRBOC
G. Gyssels, 6-84

Command Center, and more habitability. All originally carried eight 127-mm/54, Mk 42 guns. CV 61 relinquished her last two guns in 1977, later than her sisters did, and retains her forward gun sponsons. Stacks raised 3 m in CV 59 and 62.

◆ **2 Midway class** Bldr: Newport News SB & DD

	Laid down	L	In serv.
CV 41 Midway	27-10-43	20-3-45	10-9-45
CV 43 Coral Sea	10-7-44	2-4-46	1-10-47

D: CV 41: 53,400 tons light (67,000 fl)—CV 43: 48,000 tons (65,200 fl) **S:** 33 kts
Dim: CV 41: 306.78 (274.32 wl) × 55.78 (36.88 wl) × 10.97
CV 43: 306.00 (274.32 wl) × 47.55 (36.38 wl) × 10.67
A: 76 aircraft—48 F/A-18, 10 A-6E, 4 KA-6D, 4 EA-6B, 4 E-2C, 6 SH-3H—CV 41: 2/Mk 25 launchers (VII × 2) for Sea Sparrow—2/20-mm Mk 15 CIWS AA (I × 2)—CV 43: 3/20-mm Mk 15 CIWS

Electron Equipt: Radar: CV 41: 1/LN-66, 1/SPS-65, 1/SPS-49, 1/SPS-48C, 2/SPN-42, 1/SPN-44, 2/Mk 115; CV 43: 1/LN-66, 1/SPS-67, 1/SPS-49, 1/SPS-48C, 1/SPN-41, 2/SPN-42, 1/SPN-43A
EW: WLR-1, WLR-10, WLR-11, Mk 36 SRBOC chaff RL (VI × 4)
TACAN: URN-25

Midway (CV 41) G. Arra, 1984

Midway (CV 41) L. & L. Van Ginderen, 9-84

Coral Sea (CV 43)—post-refit, with Mk 15 CIWS recessed for protection, new radars
G. Arra, 2-85

Midway (CV 41)—with F-4, A-7, EA-6B, A-6E, E-2C, and SH-3H aircraft on deck *Ships of the World,* 9-84

CONVENTIONAL AIRCRAFT CARRIERS *(continued)*

M: 4 sets Westinghouse GT; 4 props; 212,000 hp **Electric:** 11,700 kw
Boilers: 12 Babcock & Wilcox; 41.7 kg/cm², 454°C
Man: CV 41: 402 officers, 4,278 enlisted (including aviation personnel)
CV 43: 411 officers, 4,320 enlisted (including aviation personnel)

REMARKS: CV 43 transferred to the East Coast 1983 and was modernized at Norfolk for service up to 1992, when she will replace *Lexington* (AVT-16) as training carrier; re-entered service 29-1-85, but was damaged in collision 11-4-85, losing 11 m of the bow; repaired by 7-85. CV 41, home-ported at Yokosuka, Japan, is having larger bulges added 1985-86 to improve stability and is to be retained in service to the end of the century. Sister *Franklin D. Roosevelt* (CV 42) was stricken on 1-10-72. Machinery and ships' bottoms very similar to the *Iowa*-class battleships.

Two side elevators to starboard, one forward of and one abaft the island; one side elevator to port abaft the angled flight deck. CV 41 has a considerably larger flight deck than does CV 43. CV 41 has two C13 steam catapults (both forward) and three arrester wires on the angled deck. CV 43 retains three C11-1 steam catapults. CV 43 carried the listed air group in 1985, CV 41 will carry the same on completion of refit in 1986.

Refits: From 1954 to 1963, the ships underwent several overhauls: angled flight deck installed; flight deck lengthened; hydraulic catapults replaced with steam ones; side armor removed and "bulges" added. Reinforced arresting gear and barriers installed; centerline elevators replaced with side ones; aviation fuel capacity increased. In October 1967 CV 41 began another major overhaul and returned to service in 1-70. Her angled flight deck was extended to port; her three elevators were enlarged; her forward port elevator was moved aft; her catapults were replaced by more powerful ones; and all her electronic equipment was replaced. In 1979-80, during short overhauls at Yokosuka, CV 41's radar suit was updated and the Tactical Flag Command Center was added. CV 43 was overhauled 11-78 to 10-79 at Puget Sound NSY, where her catapults were brought up to C13 capability.

RESERVE AIRCRAFT CARRIERS

◆ **4 Essex,* and Hancock† class** (all in reserve)

	Bldr	Laid down	L	In serv.
CVS 12 HORNET*	Newport News SB	3-8-42	29-8-43	29-11-43
CVS 20 BENNINGTON*	New York NSY	15-12-42	26-2-44	6-8-44
CVA 31 BON HOMME RICHARD†	New York NSY	1-2-43	29-4-44	26-11-44
CV 34 ORISKANY†	New York NSY	1-5-44	13-10-45	25-9-50

Bennington (CVS 20)—Essex class U.S. Navy, 1967

Oriskany (CV 34)—in reserve at Bremerton G. Arra, 10-85

D: Approx. 33,000 tons (40,600 to 41,900 fl) **S:** 30+ kts
Dim: 274.01 (CVS 38: 270.97) (249.9 wl) × 31.39 (CV 34: 32.46) (flight deck: approx. 58.5 × 9.45)
A: 4/127-mm DP (I × 4), except CV 34: 2/127-mm DP (I × 2)
Electron Equipt: Radar: 1/SPS-10, 1/SPS-30, 1/SPS-43A (CVS 11, CV 34: SPS-37), 1/SPN-10, 1/SPN-43, 1-2/Mk 25, 0-4 Mk 35
Sonar: CVS only: SQS-23 (bow-mounted)
TACAN: URN-6 or URN-20

M: Westinghouse GT; 4 props; 150,000 hp
Boilers: 8 Babcock & Wilcox; 41.7 kg/cm², 454°C **Electric:** 7,000 kw
Fuel: 6,750 tons **Range:** 18,000/12 **Man:** None

REMARKS: All in Category "C" reserve, all berthed at Bremerton, Washington. CV 34 was placed in reserve on 30-9-76; recommissioning (to cost approx. $510 million), to take 28–34 months, proposed by Reagan Administration for FY 82 but was turned down by Congress. Sister *Intrepid* (CVS 11) stricken 27-4-81 and transferred to New York City as a memorial; *Shangri La* (CVS 38) stricken 15-7-82, had been placed in reserve 30-7-71. *Lexington* (formerly CVT 16) was redesignated AVT 16 on 1-7-78 and is used for training in deck landing; see entry in auxiliary section. CVS 12 was decommissioned on 15-1-70, CVS 20 on 30-6-69, and CVA 31 on 2-7-71. CVS 12 and CVS 20 retain their Mk-H8 hydraulic catapults; the others have C8 steam catapults. All have three elevators: one on the centerline between the catapults, one at the forward end of the angled deck, and one (vertically stowable) to starboard, abaft the island. Four arrester wires. CV 34 has two Mk 37 gun directors. The others have one Mk 37 and two or three Mk 56 directors.

NAVAL AND MARINE CORPS AVIATION

Aviation is an integral part of the U.S. Navy and Marine Corps. There were approximately 6,083 aircraft assigned on 1-1-85:

134 strike fighters	148 air early warning	1,156 jet trainers
878 fighters	138 transports	1,437 helicopters
1,284 attack aircraft	60 aerial refueling	6 special mission
168 shipboard ASW	94 observation	39 drones
427 patrol	114 utility	

Some 36 basic fixed-wing aircraft designs (in 99 different sub-variants) and 8 basic helicopter designs (in 34 sub-variants) are flown.

The U.S. Air Force has programmed conversion of two 15-aircraft B-52G squadrons (one for each coast) for sea control duties. The B-52G will carry up to 12 Harpoon missiles externally and 8 internally and will have a 2,000 n.m. combat radius with 2 hrs. on station.

Air squadrons are designated by an alphanumerical system, the letter prefixes for the principal squadron types being ("X" denotes various models in aircraft type listings):

Navy:

HC	Helicopter Combat Support (CH-46)
HM	Helicopter Mine Countermeasures (RH-53D, MH-53E)
HS	Helicopter Antisubmarine (SH-3)
HSL	Light Helicopter Antisubmarine (SH-2)
HT	Helicopter Training (TH-57X, UH-1E, TH-1L)
VAL	Light Attack (A-7)
VAM	Medium Attack (A-6, KA-6)
VAQ	Tactical Electronic Warfare (EA-6B)
VAW	Carrier Airborne Early Warning (E-2C)
VC	Fleet Composite (utility aircraft)
VF	Fighter (F-4, F-14, F-18)
VFP	Light Photographic (RF-8G)
VP	Patrol (P-3)
VQ	Fleet Air Reconnaissance (EP-3, EA-3B), also: Communications Support (EC-130)
VR	Fleet Logistics Support (C-9, C-130, C-131, etc.)
VRC	Fleet Logistics Support-COD (Carrier Onboard Delivery) (C-1A, C-2A)
VRF	Aircraft Ferry
VS	Air Antisubmarine (S-3A)
VT	Training (TA-4J, T-28, T-2C, T-39D, T-44A)
VX	Air Test and Evaluation
VXE	Antarctic Development (LC-130F, UH-1)
VXN	Oceanographic Development (RP-3A/D)

Marine Corps:

HMA	Marine Attack Helicopter (AH-1)
HMH	Marine Heavy Helicopter (CH-53)
HML	Marine Light Helicopter (UH-1X)
HMM	Marine Medium Helicopter (CH-46)
VMA	Marine Attack (A-4X, A-6E, AV-8X)
VMAQ	Marine Electronic Warfare (EA-6B)
VMFA	Marine Fighter-Attack (F-4, F/A-18)
VMFP	Marine Photo Reconnaissance (RF-4B)
VMGR	Marine Refueler-Transport (KC-130F)
VMO	Marine Observation (OV-10)

◆ **Naval Aviation 1985**

Navy first-line combat squadrons include:
3 fighter-attack with F/A-18 Hornets
24 fighter with F-14 Tomcats and F-4 Phantom-IIs
22 light attack with A-7E Corsair-IIs
12 heavy attack with A-6E and KA-6D Intruders
9 tactical electronic warfare with EA-6B Prowlers
12 carrier airborne early warning with E-2B/C Hawkeyes
24 patrol with P-3B/C Orions
11 antisubmarine with S-3A Vikings

NAVAL AND MARINE CORPS AVIATION *(continued)*

12 helicopter antisubmarine with SH-3H Sea Kings and SH-60B Seahawks
6 light helicopter antisubmarine with SH-2F Seasprites

Naval Reserve Force combat squadrons include:
4 fighter with F-4N/S Phantom-IIs
6 light attack with A-7B/E Corsair-IIs
2 tactical electronic warfare with EA-6A Prowlers
2 carrier airborne early warning with E-2B/C Hawkeyes
13 patrol with P-3A/B Orions
2 carrier refueling with KA-3B Skywarriors
4 helicopter antisubmarine with SH-3D Sea Kings
1 light photographic with RF-8G Crusaders

The combination of all the aircraft on board an aircraft carrier is called a Carrier Air Wing (CAW), whose composition varies according to the carrier's mission. There are three basic types of air wing: one to project power or support landing operations; one to control the sea, with emphasis on antisubmarine warfare and the protection of ships; and one to perform the two previously mentioned missions at the same time.

◆ Marine Corps Aviation

The Marines operate a considerable air force, with all aircraft procured and "owned" by the Navy. U.S.M.C. aircraft are intended to operate principally from amphibious-warfare ships, but squadrons of attack, reconnaissance, and electronic-warfare aircraft frequently operate from carriers as well. The air complement in 1984 was:

Tactical Fixed-Wing Squadrons
30 Squadrons

Type	Number
Fighter (F-4N, F/A-18A)	144
All Weather Attack (A-6E)	50
Light Attack (AV-8, A-4M)	120
ECM (EA-6B)	15
Reconnaissance (RF-4B)	21
Tanker (KC-130)	40
TAC(A) (OV-10)	29

Land Force Aviation Squadrons
29 Squadrons

Type	Number
Heavy Lift (CH-53D/E)	128
Medium Lift (CH-46D/E)	180
Attack (AH-1J/T)	72
Utility (UH-1)	72
Observer	36

Fixed-Wing Training Squadrons
4 Squadrons

Type	Number
Fighter (F-4)	27
All Weather Attack (A-6)	15
Light Attack (A-4)	37

Land Force Aviation Training
3 Squadrons

Type	Number
Heavy Lift (CH-53)	32
Medium Lift (CH-46)	20
Attack (AH-1T)	12
Utility (UH-1)	8

Base and Command Support
1 Squadron

Type	Number
VP-3A	1
C-9	2
CT-39	5
UC-12	12
HH-46	12
H-1	4

NAVY AIRCRAFT PROCUREMENT PLAN FY 87

	FY 84	FY 85	FY 86	FY 87	FY 88	FY 89	FY 90
A-6E/F (Intruder)	6	6	11	11	12	18	24
EA-6B (Prowler)	6	6	12	12	12	12	12
F-14A/D (Tomcat)	24	24	18	15	12	18	24
F/A-18A (Hornet)	84	84	84	120	132	132	163
AV-8B (Harrier)	27	32	46	42	42	42	42
SH-2F (Seasprite)	6	6	6	6	—	—	—
CH-53E (Super Stallion)	11	10	4	4	4	4	4
MH-53E (Sea Dragon)	—	—	10	10	10	10	8
SH-60B (Seahawk)	24	24	18	17	6	6	6
SH-60F	—	—	—	7	24	30	30
UH-60A	—	2	4	—	—	3	3
VH-60	—	9	—	—	—	—	—
P-3C (Orion)	5	9	9	9	8	8	8
RP-3D (Orion)	—	—	—	—	1	1	1
MV-22A (Osprey)	—	—	—	—	—	18	42
E-2C (Hawkeye)	6	6	6	6	6	6	6
C-9B (Skytrain II)	8	4	—	—	—	—	—
UC-12B/CX	—	12	12	12	—	—	—
C-2A (Greyhound)	6	8	8	9	—	—	—
T-34C (Mentor)	—	—	38	—	—	—	—
T-44A (King Air)	—	—	—	—	—	—	15
T-45A (Goshawk)	—	—	—	—	12	24	24
TH-57 (Sea Ranger)	21	36	—	—	—	—	—
E-6A	—	—	2	3	3	3	3
KC-130T (Hercules)	2	2	—	—	—	—	—
F-16N	4	10	12	—	—	—	—
C-2 Kfir (lease)	—	12	13	—	—	—	—
Boeing 707 FEWSG	1	—	—	—	—	—	—

◆ Aircraft Losses

Operational loss rates remain high, largely because of the intense tempo of U.S. Navy flight operations. In 1982, 88 aircraft were lost, while in 1983, 87 were lost. In 1984 the number lost fell to 69: 1/F/A-18, 4/F-4, 4/F-14A, 7/A-6, 3/EA-6B, 13/A-7, 4/A-4, 9/TA-4, 1/AV-8, 2/T-2, 1/T-34, 1/T-44, 1/H-1, 4/H-2, 2/H-3, 2/H-46, and 4/H-53.

◆ Aircraft Designations

Besides the name given to an aircraft — Phantom, Intruder, Orion, etc. — each type is designated by a group of letters and figures divided by a hyphen and made up in the following manner:

1. The letter immediately preceding the hyphen indicates the principal mission:

A — attack	P — patrol
B — bomber	S — antisubmarine
C — cargo/transport	T — training
E — airborne early warning	U — utility
F — fighter	V — VTOL/STOL, vertical or short takeoff and landing
K — tanker, inflight refueling	X — research
O — observation	

2. The figure that comes immediately after the hyphen is the design sequence number. When a letter follows this figure, its position in the alphabet indicates that the aircraft is the first, second, third, etc. modification to the original design.

Example: A-4E = an attack aircraft, the fourth attack plane design, the fifth modification.

3. When an aircraft is assigned to duty that is not its principal mission, a second letter precedes the letter of that mission (see para. 1 above):

A — attack	M — missile carrier or mine-countermeasures
C — cargo/transport	Q — drone aircraft
D — direction or control of drones, aircraft, or missiles	R — reconnaissance
	S — antisubmarine
E — special electronic installation	T — trainer
H — search and rescue	U — utility, general service
K — tanker, inflight, refueling	V — staff
L — cold weather; for arctic regions	W — weather, meteorology

4. A third prefixed letter in front of an aircraft's designation means:

G — permanently grounded	X — experimental
J — temporary special test	Y — prototype
N — permanent special test	Z — planning

CURRENT U.S. NAVY MARINE CORPS
AIRCRAFT DESIGNATIONS

◆ Attack

A-3 SKYWARRIOR:

EA-3B	ECM mission equipment
KA-3B	Tanker
ERA-3B	FEW support group configuration
TA-3B	Bombardier/navigator training version
VA-3B	High-speed personnel transport

A-4 SKYHAWK:

A-4E	J-52, basic attack
A-4F	A-4E with improved systems
EA-4F	ECM version of TA-4F
TA-4F	Two-place training version
TA-4J	Advanced training version of TA-4F
A-4M	Uprated engine and improved system
OA-4M	TA-4F modified to TACA configuration

A-6 INTRUDER:

EA-6A	ECM mission equipment
EA-6B	ECM mission
KA-6D	A-6A configured as tanker
A-6E	A-6A with improved systems

A-7 CORSAIR II:

A-7B	A-7A with improved engine
A-7C	Advanced weapon delivery system
TA-7C	A-7B/C modified to two-place trainer
A-7E	A-7B with TF-41 and improved weapons systems

F/A-18 HORNET:

F/A-18A	First-line fighter/attack aircraft
TF/A-18A	Two-place trainer version

AV-8 HARRIER:

AV-8A	Single-place, attack
TAV-8A	Two-place trainer version
AV-8B	Major redesign, improved capability
AV-8C	AV-8A reworked, modernized

◆ Fighters

F-4 PHANTOM:

QF-4B	F-4B target drone
RF-4B	Photoreconnaissance
F-4J	Improved systems and engines
EF-4J	EW version

NAVAL AND MARINE CORPS AVIATION *(continued)*

F-4N Converted/Improved F-4B
F-4S F-4J modified for extended life

F-5 TIGER II:
F-5E Adversary aircraft
F-5F Two-place version

F-8 CRUSADER:
RF-8G Photoreconnaissance

F-14 TOMCAT:
F-14A Front-line fighter aircraft, TF-30
F-14D Improved systems

F-16 FIGHTING FALCON:
F-16N Adversary aircraft

F-21 KFIR:
F-21A Adversary aircraft

◆ **Utility**

OV-10 BRONCO:
OV-10A COIN/LARA twin turboprop
OV-10D Night gunship

◆ **Patrol**

P-3 ORION
P-3A Land-based ASW, T56-A-10W engine
EP-3A Electronic reconnaissance configuration
RP-3A Special T&E and ocean research
VP-3A Personnel transport
P-3B P-3A with T56-A-14 engines
EP-3B Electronic reconnaissance
P-3C Improved avionics systems
RP-3D Configured for Project Magnet
EP-3E Electronic reconnaissance

◆ **Cargo Transport**

C-1 TRADER:
C-1A COD transport, twin engines, piston R-1820s

C-2 GREYHOUND:
C-2A Carrier logistics

C-9 SKYTRAIN II:
C-9B Commercial DC-9

C-12 SUPER KING AIR:
UC-12B Passenger logistics

C-130 HERCULES:
C-130F Turboprop logistics transport
KC-130F Tactical tanker/cargo transport
LC-130F Polar use, ski/wheel gear
EC-130G TACAMO
EC-130Q Improved TACAMO
KC-130R Improved tanker
LC-130R Improved polar version
KC-130T Improved avionics, tanker capabilities

C-131 SAMARITAN:
C-131F Convair 340 cargo version
C-131G Convair 440 cargo version
C-131H Modified turboprop

◆ **Antisubmarine Warfare**

S-3 VIKING:
S-3A Carrier-based ASW aircraft
US-3A Utility version
S-3B Improved avionics

◆ **Airborne Early Warning**

E-2 HAWKEYE:
TE-2A Training version
TE-2B Training only
E-2B AEW aircraft, carrier-based
E-2C Improved system

◆ **Trainers**

T-2 BUCKEYE:
T-2B Two-engine jet trainer, J60 engines
T-2C J85 engines

C-4 ACADEME/GULFSTREAM:
TC-4C Bombardier/navigator trainer, prop

T-34 MENTOR:
T-34B Primary trainer, single-engine, piston 0-470-4 engine
T-34C Improved systems, PT6A-25 turboprop

T-39 SABRELINER:
T-39D Pilot/NFO trainer, jet
CT-39E Rapid response airlift
CT-39G Modified CT-39E, lengthened fuselage

T-44 KING AIR:
T-44A Advanced multiengine trainer

T-45 GOSHAWK:
T-45A Advanced jet trainer

◆ **Tilt-Wing Aircraft (JVX)**

V-22 OSPREY:
MV-22A Marine Corps Transport

◆ **Airborne Mine Countermeasures**

H-53 SEA STALLION/SUPER STALLION:
RH-53D Sea Stallion, twin-engine, AMCM, logistics (see HELICOPTERS)
MH-53E Sea Dragon, three-engines, AMCM version of the CH-53E

◆ **Helicopters**

UH-1 IROQUOIS/HUEY:
UH-1E Single rotor, T53-L-11 engine
HH-1K T53-L-13 engine, similar to UH-1E, orange paint
TH-1L Trainer, UH-1E armor/armament deleted, T53-L-13 engine
UH-1L Utility, UH-1E, T53-L-13 engine
UH-1M T53-L-13 engine
UH-1N Special transport, twin-engine T400-CP-400
VH-1N Executive version

AH-1 SEA COBRA:
AH-1G Attack version, T53-L-13 engine
AH-1J USMC avionics, T400-CP-400 engine
AH-1T Modified AH-1J, T400-WV-402 engine

H-2 SEASPRITE:
SH-2F LAMPS MK 1 sea-based ASW

H-3 SEA KING:
HH-3A Search and rescue, T58-GE-8 engines
SH-3A Sea-based ASW, amphibious, twin-engine
UH-3A Utility
VH-3A Executive transport
SH-3D SH-3A with T58-GE-10 engines
VH-3D Executive transport
SH-3G Improved SH-3A, sea-based ASW and logistics
SH-3H SH-3G for sea-based ASW/ASMD, T58-GE-10 engines

H-46 SEA KNIGHT:
HH-46A CH/UH-46A with improved systems
UH-46A Utility version
CH-46D Improved engines, T58-GE-10 engines
UH-46D Utility version, T58-GE-10 engines
CH-46E Improved engines, T58-GE-16 engines
CH-46F CH-46D with instrument panel changes

H-53 SEA STALLION:
CH-53A Two-engine assault helicopter, T64-GE-6B engines
CH-53D Improved engines, T64-GE-413 engines
RH-53D AMCM

H-53E SUPER STALLION:
CH-53E Three-engine
MH-53E AMCM version of CH-53E, larger fuel tanks

H-57 SEA RANGER:
TH-57A Trainer
TH-57C Advanced Instrument Trainer

SH-60 SEAHAWK:
SH-60B Sea-based LAMPS MK III ASW
SH-60F Carrier-based, dipping–sonar
UH-60 Combat SAR
VH-60 VIP transport

F/A-18 Hornet fighter bombers McDonnell Douglas, 1981

NAVAL AND MARINE CORPS AVIATION *(continued)*

F/F-14 Tomcat, all-weather fighter U.S. Navy, 9-83

F/F-14s of VF-33 aboard CV 66 L. & L. Van Ginderen, 9-85

F-4S—U.S. Marines McDonnell Douglas, 1-82

Four A-6E Intruder heavy attack aircraft—with Mk 82 bombs
Grumman, 1981

AV-8A Harrier attack aircraft (Marine Corps) 1971

AV-8B Harrier attack aircraft (Marine Corps) McDonnell Douglas, 10-82

A-4F Skyhawk attack aircraft of VT-43 S. Terzibaschitsch, 4-84

ERA-3B Skywarrior—one of 12 EW "Whales," shadowing a Tu-95 Bear D
U.S. Navy, 9-83

A-7E Corsair light attack aircraft U.S. Navy, 1982

RF-8G Crusader reconnaissance aircraft (Naval Reserve)

NAVAL AND MARINE CORPS AVIATION *(continued)*

P-3C Orion patrol aircraft PH1 W. Wickham, USN, 1980

C-2A Greyhound COD (Carrier On-board Delivery) aircraft 1981

SH-3A Viking ASW aircraft French Navy, 1981

Bronco observation/attack/OV-10 utility aircraft, USMC
PH2 C. Griffin, USN, 9-80

SH-3H Sea King ASW helicopter W. Donko, 7-84

SH-2F Sea Sprite LAMPS-I ASW helicopter Kaman, 1982

CH-46E Sea Knight transport helicopter S. Terzibaschitsch, 4-84

SH-60B Seahawk LAMPS-III ASW helicopter Sikorsky, 1980

EA-6B Prowler electronics warfare aircraft—low-visibility paint
Grumman, 1981

NAVAL AND MARINE CORPS AVIATION *(continued)*

E-2C Hawkeye early-warning aircraft Grumman, 1976

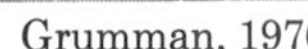

AH-1 Sea Cobra with Sidearm trials missile, USMC S. Wyatt, USN, 10-81

PRINCIPAL COMBAT AIRCRAFT

Class, builder	Mission	Wingspan in m	Length in m	Height in m	Weight in kg	Engine	Max speed Mach/knots	Ceiling in feet	1) Ferry range (nautical miles) 2) Combat radius (nautical miles) 3) Range (hours)
SHIP-BASED FIXED WING:									
F/A-18A Hornet (McDonnell Douglas)	Multirole fighter (Navy)	11.43	17.07	4.67	10,437 (empty) 32,150 (max.)	2 G.E. F404-GE-400 6,800-kg thrust each	M 1.8	49,400	1,600 450 with 1,814 kg payload 3
	Armament: 5,900 kg of conventional or nuclear bombs; 2/Sidewinder; 4/Sparrow-III; 1/20-mm M61A1 cannon. APG-65 radar; FLIR pod being added.								
	REMARKS: 154 in service 1-1-86; 84 building. Uses a microprocessor to control the various weapons. A two-seat TF-18 is also being built at about 5/yr. Procurement of at least 1,377 planned. First USMC squadron operational 7-1-83; first USN squadron 10-83; first of 10 planned Naval Reserve squadrons in 1984.								
F-14A/D Tomcat (Grumman)	Two-man all-weather fighter with variable-geometry wing	19.53/ 11.63	18.85	4.88	28,236 (18,186 empty) (F-14D: 32,865 max.)	2 P&W TF30-P-414A 9,480-kg thrust each, with afterburners	M 2.34	60,000	2,000 500 2.50 to 3
	Armament: 1/20-mm M61A1 Vulcan gun; 2/Phoenix, 2/Sidewinder and 2/Sparrow missiles or 3,856 kg of Sparrow and Sidewinder missiles of bombs, including nuclear bombs, AWG-9 radar. Three in each squadron fitted for TARPS photo-reconnaissance pod.								
	REMARKS: 428 in service 1-1-86; 18 building. Primarily an interceptor. Max. landing speed: 120 knots. The F-14D, using the G.E. F110-GE100 engine, a digitized version of the AWG-9 radar, and other avionics improvements, is slated to supplant the F-14A in production under FY 1988. The FY 87 increment of F-14s will use the new engine and remain typed F-14A; 40 earlier F-14A may be backfitted.								
F-4 N/S Phantom (McDonnell Douglas)	All-weather fighter (Navy) fighter-bomber (Marine Corps)	11.71	17.75	4.96	24,767 (12,700 empty)	2 G.E. J79-GE-8 10B 8,120-kg thrust each, with afterburners (RF-4B: G,E,J,N: 79-GE-8)	M 2.2	51,800–55,000	2,300 900 2.25
	Armament: 4/Sparrow III and 4/Sidewinder missiles (standard weapons) or 6/Sparrow III or 7,258 kg of missiles, rockets, or bombs: 18/340-kg, 15/309-kg, 11/454-kg bombs; 7/smoke bombs; 11/napalm bombs; 4/Bullpup missiles; 15/air-to-surface rocket pods.								
	REMARKS: Several versions: J, N, S, and RF-4B (reconnaissance). Max. landing speed: 140 knots. 235 F-4B/J upgraded to F-4N or S with slats, new avionics, etc. RF-4B to get G.E. J79-G.E.-10B smokeless engines. Used operationally only on CV 41 & CV 43. Four Reserve squadrons fly F-4N/S.								
A-4M Skyhawk (McDonnell Douglas)	Attack (Navy Reserve and Marine Corps)	8.38	12.50	4.57	10,904 (4,747 empty)	1 P&W J52-P-408A 5,080-kg thrust	504 kts (sea level) 537 kts (10,000 ft)	33,250	2,055 150 at 396 kt. 2.12
	Armament: 2/20-mm Mk 12 guns; 2,950 kg (12 MU 81) bombs, rockets. To be equipped with Maverick missiles.								
	REMARKS: Nonfolding wings. Several versions: A-4E & M remain in active Marine squadrons, but Navy use is by Reserves and in support duties. Final units built 1979, after 25 years' production. A-4M has large hump on spine, for electronics. About 260 two-seat TA-4F and J trainers also in use, as well as several dozen specialized aircraft.								
A-6E Intruder (Grumman)	All-weather attack (Navy and Marine Corps)	16.15	16.67	4.92	27,392 (11,627 empty)	2 P&W J52-P8A/8B 4,218-kg thrust each	594 kts	52,700	2,400 320 at 400 kt . . .
	Armament: 18,000 pounds of conventional or nuclear bombs, rockets, etc. Examples of ordnance: 46/250-pound, 30/450-pound, 15/900-pound, 4/2,000-pound bombs; 13 pods with 247 rockets; 52/Zuni rockets; 4/Sidewinder or 4/Bullpup missiles. Now being equipped for Harpoon, HARM, Maverick, Sidewinder, and Walleye. APQ-156 radar.								
	REMARKS: Approx. 353 in service 1-1-86. KA-6D tanker versions, conversions of A-6A/E, carry 30,000 lb. fuel for transfer; 53 now operational. A-6E getting TRAM (Target Recognition-Attack Multisensor); 45 had it by 1981, all were to have it by 1984. Synthetic aperture radar being developed for A-6E, which will also get a Sidewinder launch capability for self-defense, and Harpoon. A-6F version desired by Navy for production in 1989 would have STOL capability, improved avionics, and self-defense: 27,553 kg max. t.o. weight, 2 G.E. 404-400D engines for Mach 0.84 and a max. altitude of 38,740 ft; combat radius: 600+ n.m.								

NAVAL AND MARINE CORPS AVIATION *(continued)*

Class, builder	Mission	Wingspan in m	Length in m	Height in m	Weight in kg	Engine	Max speed Mach/knots	Ceiling in feet	1) Ferry range (nautical miles) 2) Combat radius (nautical miles) 3) Range (hours)
A-7E Corsair II (Ling-Temco-Vought)	Attack	11.80	14.06	4.90	17,278 (8,973 empty)	1 Allison TF41-A-2 6,800-kg thrust	553 kts (sea level)	33,500	2,800 425 at 460 kt. 2.25

Armament: 1/20-mm M61A1 Vulcan gun; up to 6,800 kg bombs, rockets, or missiles, according to the mission and the target distance. Examples of weapons: 24/113-kg Mk 81 bombs; 4/Zuni rockets; 28/2.75-inch rockets; 1/Shrike missile and 1/Walleye guided bomb; 12/Snakeye bombs; 2/Shrike missiles; 2/907-kg bombs. Normally carry two Sidewinder AAM for defense. Have APQ-126 attack radar. APR-43 warning syst. (to be replaced by ALR-45F).

Remarks: A-7E is the only version in use on carriers; earlier A-7E with P&W TF30-P-408 engines are used by the Reserves. 81 TA-7C two-seat trainers converted from single-seat B&C models, with 43 getting TF-41 engines in place of TF30-P-408; ETA-7C electronics aircraft are also being re-engined 1985-86. A-7E getting capability to launch HARM missiles, plus FLIR sensor being added.

Class, builder	Mission	Wingspan in m	Length in m	Height in m	Weight in kg	Engine	Max speed Mach/knots	Ceiling in feet	1) Ferry range 2) Combat radius 3) Range (hours)
AV-8C Harrier (McDonnell Douglas)	Attack (Marine Corps)	7.70	13.87	3.43	VTOL: 7,938 STOL: 10,109	1 Rolls-Royce Pegasus F402-RR-404A	640 kts	50,000	2,000 VTOL: 160; STOL: 500 1

Armament: 2/30-mm guns; bombs, rockets, etc. to a total of 2,700 kg. Can carry two Sidewinder AAM for defense.

Remarks: Eight two-seat TAV-8A and 108 single-seat AV-8A were acquired. High loss rate through accidents; only about 45 left by end 1985. Surviving AV-8A aircraft were upgraded to AV-8C with ALE-39 chaff/flare dispensers, APR-43 and ALR-45F threat warning systems.

Class, builder	Mission	Wingspan in m	Length in m	Height in m	Weight in kg	Engine	Max speed Mach/knots	Ceiling in feet	1) Ferry range 2) Combat radius 3) Range (hours)
AV-8B Harrier (Mc Donnell Douglas)	Attack (Marine Corps)	9.22	14.10	3.53	VTOL: 8,720 STOL: 13,492	1 Rolls-Royce Pegasus F402-RR-406 9,751-kg thrust	650 kts; 585 kts at sea level (Mach 0.91/0.86)	50,000	2,460 VTOL: 100+ STOL: 300 1

Armament: 2/30-mm guns; 2/Sidewinder AAM, and 14/227-kg or 6/454-kg bombs or 4/Maverick ASM. No radar.

Remarks: Plan eight 20-plane squadrons, 334 tot. aircraft (34 being 2-seat TAV-8B); 33 were flying by mid-1985. First AV-8B squadron operational 6/85, with first of four AV-8B developmental aircraft flying 10-81. Twenty operational aircraft in service by 1-1-86.

Class, builder	Mission	Wingspan in m	Length in m	Height in m	Weight in kg	Engine	Max speed Mach/knots	Ceiling in feet	1) Ferry range 2) Combat radius 3) Range (hours)
S-3A Viking (Lockheed)	ASW	20.93	16.26	6.94	23,853 (12,160 empty)	2 G.E. TF34-GE-400 4,210-kg thrust each	Max: 450 kts Cruise: 350 kts Patrol: 210 kts	40,000	3,000 1,150 9

Armament: 60/sonobuoys, 4/Mk 32 bombs; 4/Mk 57 depth charges; 4/Mk 53 depth charges or 4/Mk 53 mines or 4/Mk 46 torpedoes. APS-116 radar. ASQ-81(V)1 magnetic anomaly detector (MAD).

Remarks: Fitted with a Univac AYK-10 digital computer to apply the information from the sensors on board. Four-man crew. 180 built; conversions include six US-3A COD aircraft for Indian Ocean deployments and one KS-3A serial refueler. Some 140 of the 160 S-3A survivors were to be updated to S-3B, at the rate of 3/month, beginning 4/87. Will receive WSIP (Weapon & Sensor Improvement Program) with APS-137(V)1 synthetic aperture radar, Harpoon launch capability, new Auxiliary Power Unit (APU), ALE-40 ECM dispenser. Program currently behind schedule, however.

Class, builder	Mission	Wingspan in m	Length in m	Height in m	Weight in kg	Engine	Max speed Mach/knots	Ceiling in feet	1) Ferry range 2) Combat radius 3) Range (hours)
RF-8G Crusader (Ling-Temco-Vought)	Photo recon- naissance	10.87	16.61	4.80	12,620 (7,619 empty)	1 P&W J57-P420 8,165-kg thrust with afterburner (5,190 kg without)	854 kts	51,800	. . . 640 2

Armament: None.

Remarks: Five RF-8G are retained as the only carrier-operated photo-reconnaissance aircraft owned by the Navy; all are very old, but have been refurbished. Flown only by Naval Reserve squadrons. Carry ALR-45, ALR-50, and ALE-26 countermeasures gear.

Class, builder	Mission	Wingspan in m	Length in m	Height in m	Weight in kg	Engine	Max speed Mach/knots	Ceiling in feet	1) Ferry range 2) Combat radius 3) Range (hours)
E-2C Hawkeye (Grumman)	Airborne early warning and air control	24.58	17.56	5.59	23,810 (17,091 empty)	1 Allison T56-A-425 turboprops, 4,591 shp each	315 kts (270 kts, cruise)	30,800	1,525 . . . 6

Remarks: APS-125 radar in 7.32-m circular, rotating radome. ESM-equipped. Five-man crew. By 1-1-86 a total of 76 E-2C were available, 6/yr. built. Can track 600+ air and surface targets in a 250 n.m. radius and control 25 simultaneous intercepts; to be improved by TRAC-A (Total Radiation Aperture Control Antenna) radar to reduce side-lobes. First reserve squadron received in 1984. Beginning with FY 86, uprated T56-A-427 engines to be used. A dozen earlier E-2B remain for training.

Class, builder	Mission	Wingspan in m	Length in m	Height in m	Weight in kg	Engine	Max speed Mach/knots	Ceiling in feet	1) Ferry range 2) Combat radius 3) Range (hours)
EA-6B Prowler (Grumman)	Electronics warfare	16.15	18.11	4.95	27,392 (12,185 empty)	2 P&W J52-P-408, 5,080-kg thrust each	520 kts (410 kts, cruise)	34,400	2,400 710 . . .

Remarks: ECM version of A-6 Intruder; four-man crew. APS-130 radar. Five ALQ-99F jammer rods beneath wings and fuselage. 76 in service 1-1-86; 15 operated by USMC. Two-seat Naval Reserve and Marine Corps Reserve EA-6A Intruders carry five ALQ-31B jammer pods and can alternatively be used as an attack aircraft, with up to 8,160 kg of ordnance; 27 were built, of which about 20 remain. Both aircraft are distinguished from the standard A-6E by a large, streamlined electronics-equipment pod atop the vertical stabilizer. See also remarks under A-6E.

Class, builder	Mission	Wingspan in m	Length in m	Height in m	Weight in kg	Engine	Max speed Mach/knots	Ceiling in feet	1) Ferry range 2) Combat radius 3) Range (hours)
EA-3B Skywarrior (McDonnell Douglas)	Electronics warfare	22.11	23.28	6.94	35,380 (18,685 empty)	2 P&W J57-P-10 5,625-kg thrust each	556 kts (400 kts, cruise)	41,300	5,000 1,100 6

Remarks: Badly need replacement; none planned. KA-3B is used by Reserves for flight refueling. RA-3B and ERA-3B are used for reconnaissance. There is also one VA-3B transport.

Class, builder	Mission	Wingspan in m	Length in m	Height in m	Weight in kg	Engine	Max speed Mach/knots	Ceiling in feet	1) Ferry range 2) Combat radius 3) Range (hours)
P-3C Orion (Lockheed)	Maritime patrol and ASW	30.37 (P-3C Update IV and P-3B: 31-13)	35.61	10.28	62,994 (27,892 empty)	4 Allison T56-A-14 turboprops, 4,910 hp each	405 kts (209 kts patrol)	34,000	4,500 2,380 patrol 14.5

Armament: 6/908-kg mines; 2/Mk 101 nuclear depth charges; 4/Mk 46 torpedoes; 87/sonobuoys, 4/Harpoon anti-ship missiles, etc. Weapons vary. Can carry a total of 7,700 kg of disposable ordnance and sensors. APS-115 radar. ASQ-81(v)1 magnetic anomaly detector (MAD), ASQ-114 digital computer, P-3C has AAS-36 FLIR gear. 63 to receive 4 Harpoon stations under FY 83 budget.

Remarks: In service 1-1-85: 151 P-3A flown by Reserves, 124 P-3B (Reserves plus 3 active squadrons), 233 P-3C (19 squadrons), 12 EP-3. Crews of up to 15 men. The P-C is fitted with an A-NEW central operations module built around the ASQ-114 miniaturized computer and with an Air Tactical Data System. ASQ-10 magnetic anomaly detector (MAD), APS-115 radar, electronics countermeasures carried. EP-3B/E are for electronics warfare, RP-3A/D are for research, and WP-3D perform weather reconnaissance. P-3C are expected to last 28 years each. Total built for USN through 1985: 157 P-3A, 124 P-3B, 233 P-3C, 1 RP-3D, 2 WP-3D. Over 30 converted to EP-3A/B/E. RP-3A, VP-3A and CP-3A. Also over 70 to date for overseas customers FY 84 aircraft are Update III, with new sonobuoy communications. Adaptive-Controlled Phased Array antennas; Update IV will have new wingtip EW antennas.

NAVAL AND MARINE CORPS AVIATION *(continued)*

Class, builder	Mission	Wingspan in m	Length in m	Height in m	Weight in kg	Engine	Max speed Mach/knots	Ceiling in feet	1) Ferry range (nautical miles) 2) Combat radius (nautical miles) 3) Range (hours)
C-1A Trader (Grumman)	Carrier Onboard Delivery (COD)	21.23	22.80	4.98	12,247	2 Wright R1820-82 piston; 1,525 hp each	242 kts	22,000	965 at 145 kts . . . . . .

Remarks: Despite advanced obsolescence, retained until more C-2A can be built. Cargo version of out-of-service S-2 Tracker ASW aircraft. Two-man crew plus 9 passengers. Cargo capacity: 1,589 kg. Some 40 C-1A remained in service as of 7-83.

Class, builder	Mission	Wingspan in m	Length in m	Height in m	Weight in kg	Engine	Max speed Mach/knots	Ceiling in feet	1) Ferry range (nautical miles) 2) Combat radius (nautical miles) 3) Range (hours)
C-2A Greyhound (Grumman)	Carrier Onboard Delivery (COD)	24.57	17.27	4.85	24,668 (14,175 empty)	2 Allison T56-A-8A turboshaft; 4,050 shp each	old: 296 kts new: 343 kts (257 kts, cruise)	28,800 (33,800 new units)	1,490 at 260 kt.

Remarks: Variant of E-2 Hawkeye with large-diameter fuselage. Twelve of the original series remain, with 39 more delivering 8/yr 1985-89; may order 6 more. Three-man crew plus 32 passengers or 20 litter patients or 3,724 kg cargo. Stern ramp for loading, provision for aerial refueling. New aircraft use T-56-A-425 engines. Payload: 5,535 kg.

Class, builder	Mission	Wingspan in m	Length in m	Height in m	Weight in kg	Engine	Max speed Mach/knots	Ceiling in feet	1) Ferry range (nautical miles) 2) Combat radius (nautical miles) 3) Range (hours)
MV-22A Osprey (Boeing-Bell)	Troop-carrier/ SAR (Marines)	14.17 (11.58 rotor dia.)	17.32	6.14 (5.28 folded)	24,943 (max.)	Allison 501-MBOC turboshaft; 6,000 shp each	380 kts (cruise)	32,000	1,200 range (1,814 kg cargo) 2,500 max.

Remarks: To enter service 1991 with Marines, 1992 with Navy. USMC plans 552 aircraft, Navy about 50 for SAR duties. To carry 24 troops 200 n.m. at 3,000 ft. Up to 4,535 kg external load. SAR version is to rescue 4 persons at up to 460 n.m. radius. Planned 12.7-mm nose gun deleted. First flight planned for 1987.

HELICOPTERS:

Class, builder	Mission	Diameter (rotor)	Length (overall)	Height	Weight in kg	Engine	Max. speed in knots	Ceiling in feet	1) Mission range (nautical miles) 2) Ferry range (nautical miles) 3) Endurance (hours)
SH-3D, G, H Sea King (Sikorsky)	ASW	18.9	22.16 (16.70, fuselage)	5.13	9,300 (5,302 empty)	2 G.E. T58-GE-10 turboshaft, 1,400 shp each	144 118, cruise	10,800	625 . . . 4.50

Armament: Two Mk 46 torpedoes, sonobuoys.

Remarks: Four-man crew. On CV aircraft carriers or land-based; can be carried on *Spruance*-class DD. SH-3H is a multipurpose version of the SH-3G utility model. Fitted with AQS-13 dipping sonar. AQS-81(V)2 MAD. SH-3G models updating to SH-3H standard, carry APS-24 radar. Planned to replace with SH-60F. Eleven USMC VH-3A/D serve the Presidential Flight, and there are also several UH-3A in service. 98 SH-3H were in service as of 1-1-84; 26 SH-3D were to convert to "H" model, with deliveries beginning 1986.

Class, builder	Mission	Diameter (rotor)	Length (overall)	Height	Weight in kg	Engine	Max. speed in knots	Ceiling in feet	1) Mission range (nautical miles) 2) Ferry range (nautical miles) 3) Endurance (hours)
SH-2F Sea Sprite LAMPS-I (Kaman)	ASW	13.42	16.04 (11.69 fuselage)	4.73	5,806 (3,154 empty)	2 G.E. T58-GE-8F turboshaft, 1,350 hp each	143 130, cruise	22,500	445 . . . 2.50

Armament: 15/DIFAR and DICASS sonobuoys, 2/Mk 46 AWS torpedoes, 8 smoke markers. ASQ-81(V)2 MAD (Magnetic Anomaly Detector), LN-66 radar, ALR-66 ESM, ARR-75 sonobuoy dispenser fitted.

Remarks: Found on FF, DD, and CG types. 106 in service 1-1-86. Until 1983, all were conversions of UH-2 Sea Sprite utility helicopters. Reintroduced into production, with 42 new aircraft approved in FY 83 to FY 87 to serve in ASW ships not getting SH-60B. First *new* SH-2F delivered 12-8-83. 24 older SH-2F to Reserve squadrons to replace SH-3D.

Class, builder	Mission	Diameter (rotor)	Length (overall)	Height	Weight in kg	Engine	Max. speed in knots	Ceiling in feet	1) Mission range (nautical miles) 2) Ferry range (nautical miles) 3) Endurance (hours)
SH-60B Seahawk LAMPS-III (Sikorsky)	ASW	16.36	19.76 (15.24, fuselage)	5.23	9,435	2 G.E. T700-GE-401 turboshaft, . . . 1,723 max. hp each (1,543 hp cont.)	130 kts	. . .	150 . . . 1.3

Armament: 25/sonobuoys; 2/Mk 46 ASW torpedoes.

Remarks: 204 sought, 93 of which to be in service by 10-88. APS-124 radar, ASQ-811(V)2 MAD, 25 SSQ-53 DIFAR and SSQ-60 DICASS active sonobuoys. ALQ-142 ESM. Highly automated; all sensors display on ship which controls the helicopter. 42 SH-60F with ASQ-13F dipping sonars version sought to begin replacement of carrier-based SH-3G/H. Congress required 6 UH-60 version for combat search and rescue in FY 85-86. Nine VH-60 in FY 86 for Presidential Flight. 44 SH-60B in service 1-1-86.

Class, builder	Mission	Diameter (rotor)	Length (overall)	Height	Weight in kg	Engine	Max. speed in knots	Ceiling in feet	1) Mission range (nautical miles) 2) Ferry range (nautical miles) 3) Endurance (hours)
CH-46 HH-46A, D, E Sea Knight (Boeing Vertol)	Troop-carrying assault (Marine Corps)	15.56	25.72 (13.67 fuselage)	5.08	10,438 (5,947 empty)	2 G.E. T58-GE-10 turboshaft, 1,450 shp each CH-46E: 2 G.E. T58-GE10, 1,870 shp each	144	14,000	206 774 . . .

Remarks: Can carry 18 fully equipped troops. The cargo version (HH-46A) is Navy-subordinated and is usually assigned to vertical-replenishment duties in modern underway replenishment ships. Can carry 1,360 kg of cargo internally or 4,536 kg in a sling beneath. CH-46E is updated (1977) version with automatic navigation system and armored seats; all earlier CH-46D will be modernized. Glass-reinforced plastic rotors being substituted and infrared jamming equipment being added. Over 300 in service, all models. USMC reorganizing from 13 squadrons of 18 CH-46E to 15 squadrons of 12 helos each in 1985.

Class, builder	Mission	Diameter (rotor)	Length (overall)	Height	Weight in kg	Engine	Max. speed in knots	Ceiling in feet	1) Mission range (nautical miles) 2) Ferry range (nautical miles) 3) Endurance (hours)
CH-53 A, D, RH-53D Sea Stallion (Sikorsky)	Navy RH-53D: Minesweeping Marine Corps CH-53A, D: Assault transport	22.04	26.92 (20.48, fuselage)	7.59	19,050 (10,718 empty)	2 G.E. T 64-GE-413 turboshaft, 2,925 hp each	170 150 cruise	21,000	540 886 3.50

Remarks: CH-53A and D can carry 38 fully equipped troops or 24 occupied stretchers with 4 hospital corpsmen or 4 tons of freight (2 Hawk missiles, for example). The RH-53D version is equipped for serial minesweeping and has T64-GE-415 engines, 2/12.7-mm machine guns, and points for towing Mk 103 cutters, Mk 104 magnetic minesweeping arrays, Mk 105 hydrofoil sled, MK 106 acoustic sweep array, SPU-1 shallow-water sweep rig, and AQS-14 minehunting sonar; 23 RH-53D remained by 1985; 16 USMC CH-53 have provision for mine countermeasures towing. 12 CH-53A traded to Israel for loan of 14 F-21A.

Class, builder	Mission	Diameter (rotor)	Length (overall)	Height	Weight in kg	Engine	Max. speed in knots	Ceiling in feet	1) Mission range (nautical miles) 2) Ferry range (nautical miles) 3) Endurance (hours)
CH-53E Super Stallion MH-53E Sea Dragon (Sikorsky)	Troop-carrying assault (Marines) Heavy lift (Navy)	24.08	30.20 (22.35, fuselage)	8.44	31,638 (14,910 empty)	3 G.E. T64-GE-416 turboshaft; 4,380 max. shp each (3,695 shp cont.)	170 150 cruise	18,500	230 with 8,630 kg; 50 with 14,500 kg cargo; 1,000 . . .

Remarks: CH-53E can carry 56 troops or 14,500 kg cargo. Three-man crew. Seven-bladed main rotor. 35th CH-53E rebuilt under FY 80 budget as MH-53E minesweeper prototype, delivered 1983. First MH-53E requested under FY 84. Navy use for CH-53E is for cargo, aircraft-recovery, and heavy lift. 85 CH-53E delivered by 1985. Plan total of 194 CH-53E/31 MH-53E, but production FY 86-89 mostly MH-version. MH-53 has enlarged side sponsons holding 4,478 lbs fuel and has a cable winch with 137-m cable, exerting a 13.6-ton pull; tows the ALQ-166 mine countermeasures sled, day or night. 78 CH-53E/2 MH-53E in service 1-1-86.

NAVAL AND MARINE CORPS AVIATION *(continued)*

Class, builder	Mission	Diameter (rotor)	Length (overall)	Height	Weight in kg	Engine	Max. speed in knots	Ceiling in feet	1) Mission range (nautical miles) 2) Ferry range (nautical miles) 3) Endurance (hours)
UH-1E/N Iroquois (Bell)	Assault (Marine Corps)	14.70	17.47 (12.93, fuselage)	4.39	4,763 (2,517 empty)	2 Pratt & Whitney PT6 turboshaft, 900 shp each	110	15,000	250 / . . . / 2
	Armament: 2/7.62-mm machine guns and rockets.								
	REMARKS: Can carry 16 troops. UH-1N replaced earlier UH-1E, which had 1 Lycoming T53 turboshaft of 1,100 shp. Navy uses UH-1E and TH-1L for utility and training duties.								
AH-1J, T Sea Cobra (Bell)	Attack (Marine Corps)	13.42	16.27 (13,60, fuselage)	4.17	4,536 3,000 empty	2 Pratt & Whitney T400-WV-402 turboshaft; 1,970 hp each	180	10,500	360 / . . . / 2
	Armament: 1/20-mm XM-197 gatling gun, plus 76/2.75-in rockets or 2/7.62-mm minigun, Hellfire and Sidearm missiles (AH-1T also: TOW anti-tank missiles).								
	REMARKS: AH-1W Super Cobra in production, 22 each authorized FY 85, FY 86: T-700 engine, 1,700 kg (vice 680 kg) payload, 120 kts at 6,349 kg gross with 8 Hellfire missiles. Plan update of all 46 remaining earlier AH-1T with same engines.								

Also in service with Navy and Marine Corps aviation are 13 F-5E/F and 20 OA-4M aircraft for "Top Gun" training to simulate Soviet aircraft, about 20 OV-10A and 18 OV-10D twin-engine observation/attack aircraft for the Marines (all OV-10A converting to OV-10D under FY 83, with engine upgrade, laser designator), 27 C-9B transports (military DC-9) for the Marines and Naval Reserve, C-130 Hercules (in C-130, LC-130 arctic, DC-130 drone control, and EC-130 TACAMO communications versions), C-131F, G, and H Samaritan transports, T-2C Buckeye jet trainers, T-34B/C student trainers, T-38A Talon jet test-pilot trainers, T-39D Sabreliner flight-officer trainers (and CT-39E/G light transport versions), T-44A Pegasus twin-engine trainers, and TH-57A helicopter trainers.

Two EC-130Q TACAMO aircraft delivered 1984 (with the USC-13(V) trailing wire communications system) were the last of their type, with production planned to switch to the E-6A (Boeing 707 variant), of which 14 are scheduled to fly by 1991. The E-6A will fly a 14 hour, Mach 0.75 mission to a range of about 6,000 n.m. The max. takeoff weight will be 155,102 kg.

The T-45 Goshawk (British Aviation Hawk variant) series of trainers from McDonnell Douglas was planned to include 54 T-45B land-only and 253 F-45A carrier-capable aircraft; first T-45B flight 1987, first T-45A a year later. Congress canceled T-45B in late 1983. In the interim, 15 stored T-2B Buckeye jet trainers were reactivated in 1982.

Fifteen Cessna Citation II corporate jets were leased 5-83 as the T-47A for flight-officer navigational training, with initial deliveries late in 1984; Emerson APQ-159 radar added. For adversary training, Congress authorized 4 new aircraft in FY 84, 8 in FY 85, and 12 in FY 86; these will be a stripped version of the Air Force Fighting Falcon, as the F-16N. As an interim measure, 12 Israeli early model Kfir fighters were leased for 3 years as F-21As, arriving beginning in 4-85; a second squadron of 13 to be leased 1986 for Marine adversary training.

T-34C Mentor trainer Beech Aircraft

T-44A King Air trainer Beech Aircraft

EC-130G Hercules TACAMO communications aircraft PH2 W. Harvey, USN, 1977

T-2C Buckeye advanced trainer PHCS L. Ramage, USN, 8-78

CH-53E Super Stallion W. Donko, 7-85

F-21A Kfir adversary trainer U.S. Navy, 10-85

NAVAL AND MARINE CORPS AVIATION *(continued)*

C-9B Skytrain II transport McDonnell Douglas, 1973

NUCLEAR-POWERED BALLISTIC-MISSILE SUBMARINES

◆ **7 (+6 + 5 + . . .) Ohio class (SCB 304 design)** Bldr: General Dynamics, Groton, Conn. (SSBN 726–737)

	Program	Laid down	L	In serv.
SSBN 726 Ohio	FY 74	10-4-76	7-4-79	11-11-81
SSBN 727 Michigan	FY 75	4-4-77	26-4-80	11-9-82
SSBN 728 Florida	FY 75	9-6-77	14-11-81	8-6-83
SSBN 729 Georgia	FY 76	7-4-79	6-11-82	11-2-84
SSBN 730 Henry M. Jackson (ex-*Rhode Island*)	FY 77	19-1-81	15-10-83	6-10-84
SSBN 731 Alabama	FY 78	27-8-81	19-5-84	25-5-85
SSBN 732 Alaska	FY 78	9-3-83	12-1-85	25-1-86
SSBN 733 Nevada	FY 80	8-8-83	14-9-85	10-86
SSBN 734 N.	FY 81	. . .	11-86	12-88
SSBN 735 N.	FY 83	. . .	1987	8-89
SSBN 736 N.	FY 84	. . .	1988	1990
SSBN 737 N.	FY 85	. . .	. . .	1-91
SSBN 738 N.	FY 86	. . .	. . .	12-91
SSBN 739 N.	FY 87	. . .	. . .	12-92
SSBN 740 N.	FY 88	. . .	. . .	12-93
SSBN 741 N.	FY 89	. . .	. . .	12-94
SSBN 742 N.	FY 90	. . .	. . .	12-95

D: 16,764/18,750 tons **S:** 20+ kts (sub.) **Dim:** 170.69 × 12.80 × 11.13 (surf.)
A: 24/Trident-C-4 missiles—4/533-mm Mk 68 TT
Electron Equipt: Radar: BPS-15A—EW: WLR-8(V)
Sonar: BQQ-6, BQS-13, BQS-15, BQR-15, BQR-19
M: 1 G.E. S8G natural circulation pressurized-water reactor; turboeduction drive; 1 prop; 60,000 hp
Endurance: 70 days **Man:** 15 officers, 145 men (2 crews)

Remarks: SSBN 726 ran first trials 17-6-81 and was delivered 3 years late. Program now on schedule. The availability of this class as a whole is to be 66 percent, using a planned schedule of 70-day patrols, followed by 25-day refit periods, and with a 12-month overhaul every nine years. Each ship has two crews. None ordered under FY 79 because of program delays and cost overruns. Ordering of SSBN 734 was deferred to 7-1-82 due to contract disputes between the Navy and General Dynamics.

Able to submerge to 300 meters. Carry two Mk 2 SINS (Ship's Inertial Navigational System) and have navigational satellite receivers. Mk 98 digital computer missile-fire-control system and Mk 118 torpedo-fire-control system are installed. SSBN 734 and later will have Trident D-5 as built. All have 1 Kollmorgen Type 152 and 1 Type 82 periscopes.

SSBN 726 made her first operational deployment 1-10-82 to 10-12-82, having fired her first missile on 17-1-82. The first eight will be based at Bangor, Washington; later units are to base at King's Bar, Georgia. SSBN 732 began sea trials 18-9-85.

Michigan (SSBN 727) Gen. Dynamics, 9-82

Florida (SSBN 728) Gen. Dynamics, 6-83

Alabama (SSBN 731) Gen. Dynamics, 5-85

Henry M. Jackson (SSBN 730) Gen. Dynamics, 10-84

NUCLEAR-POWERED BALLISTIC-MISSILE SUBMARINES *(continued)*

◆ **30 Lafayette class (SCB 216 and SCB 216A types)**

	Bldr	Laid down	L	In serv.
SSBN 616 Lafayette	Gen. Dynamics	17-1-61	8-5-62	23-4-63
SSBN 617 Alexander Hamilton	Gen. Dynamics	26-6-61	18-8-62	27-6-63
SSBN 619 Andrew Jackson	Mare Island NSY	26-4-61	15-9-62	3-7-63
SSBN 620 John Adams	Portsmouth, NSY	19-5-61	12-1-63	12-5-64
SSBN 622 James Monroe	Newport News	31-7-61	4-8-62	7-12-63
SSBN 623 Nathan Hale	Gen. Dynamics	2-10-61	12-1-63	23-11-63
SSBN 624 Woodrow Wilson	Mare Island NSY	13-9-61	22-2-63	27-12-63
SSBN 625 Henry Clay	Newport News	23-10-61	30-11-62	20-2-64
SSBN 626 Daniel Webster	Gen. Dynamics	23-12-61	27-4-63	9-4-64
SSBN 627 James Madison*	Newport News	5-3-62	15-3-63	28-7-64
SSBN 628 Tecumseh	Gen. Dynamics	1-6-62	22-6-63	29-5-64
SSBN 629 Daniel Boone*	Mare Island NSY	6-2-62	22-6-63	23-4-64
SSBN 630 John C. Calhoun*	Newport News	4-6-62	22-6-63	15-9-64
SSBN 631 Ulysses S. Grant	Gen. Dynamics	18-8-62	2-11-63	17-7-64
SSBN 632 Von Steuben*	Newport News	4-9-62	18-10-63	30-9-64
SSBN 633 Casimir Pulaski*	Gen. Dynamics	12-1-63	1-2-64	14-8-64
SSBN 634 Stonewall Jackson*	Mare Island NSY	4-7-62	30-11-63	26-8-64
SSBN 636 Nathanael Greene	Portsmouth NSY	21-5-62	12-5-64	19-12-64
SSBN 640 Benjamin Franklin*	Gen. Dynamics	25-5-63	5-12-64	22-10-65
SSBN 641 Simon Bolivar*	Newport News	17-4-63	22-8-64	29-10-65
SSBN 642 Kamehameha	Mare Island NSY	2-5-63	16-1-65	10-12-65
SSBN 643 George Bancroft*	Gen. Dynamics	24-8-63	20-3-65	22-1-66
SSBN 644 Lewis and Clark	Newport News	29-7-63	21-11-64	22-12-65
SSBN 645 James K. Polk	Gen. Dynamics	23-11-63	22-5-65	16-4-66
SSBN 654 George C. Marshall	Newport News	2-3-64	21-5-65	29-4-66
SSBN 655 Henry L. Stimson*	Gen. Dynamics	4-4-64	13-11-65	20-8-66
SSBN 656 George Washington Carver	Newport News	24-8-64	14-8-65	15-6-66
SSBN 657 Francis Scott Key*	Gen. Dynamics	5-12-64	23-4-66	3-12-66
SSBN 658 Mariano G. Vallejo*	Mare Island NSY	7-7-64	23-10-65	16-12-66
SSBN 659 Will Rogers	Gen. Dynamics	20-3-65	21-7-66	1-4-67

Authorized: SSBN 616 to SSBN 626 in FY 61, SBN 627 to SSBN 636 in FY 62, SSBN 640 to SSBN 645 in FY 63, and SSBN 654 to SSBN 659 in FY 64

D: 7,350/8,250 tons **S:** 15/25 kts **Dim:** 129.54 × 10.05 × 9.0
A: 16/Poseidon or Trident-1 missiles—4/533-mm TT (fwd)
Electron Equipt: Radar: BPS-11A or BPS-15
Sonar: BQR-7, BQR-15, BQR-19, BQR-21, BQS-4
M: 1 Westinghouse SW5 pressurized-water reactor; 1/7-bladed prop; 15,000 hp
Endurance: 68 days **Man:** 13–14 officers, 129–133 men

Remarks: The 12 units marked with an asterisk received Trident-1 missiles by 12-82. SSBN 640 and following units have quieter propulsion machinery and are officially designated the *Benjamin Franklin* class. Three Mk 2 SINS were installed during conversion. Submersion depth for all is more than 300 meters. Mk 88 missile-fire-control system and Mk 113 torpedo-fire-control system fitted. Conversion of both classes from Polaris A-3 to Poseidon missiles was completed between 1970 and 1977. Funds were requested each year thereafter through FY 82. SSBN 657 commenced the first Trident-1 operational patrol on 20-10-79. All Trident-1 (C-4) units are to be home-ported at King's Bay, Georgia, and all ships in both classes belong to the Atlantic Fleet. They operate on a schedule of 68-day patrols, followed by 32-day refit periods; every six years a 16-month yard period is requested, giving an overall force availability of 55 percent. Each ship has two crews. SSBN 641 and two others are now on a nine-year operational/overhaul cycle. *Sam Rayburn* (SSBN 635) began deactivation of her missile system 16-9-85, preparatory to striking 9-86; she is to be converted to an immobile engineering training craft. *Andrew Jackson* (SSBN 619) and *Nathan Hale* (SSBN 623) are to be deactivated about 5-86 as SALT II compensation when *Nevada* (SSBN 733) begins sea trials.

Andrew Jackson (SSBN 619) P. Voss, 3-83

George Bancroft (SSBN 643) G. Arra, 1984

Woodrow Wilson (SSBN 624) G. Arra, 8-85

NUCLEAR-POWERED ATTACK SUBMARINES

◆ **0 (+0 + 1 + . . .) Seawolf ("SSN 21") class**

	Bldr	Laid down	L	In serv.
SSN. . . Seawolf	. . .	. . .	. . .	1995

Seawolf submerged—artist's rendering W. Lupien/U.S. Navy, 1985

Seawolf surfaced in an icepack—artist's impression W. Lupien/U.S. Navy, 1985

NUCLEAR-POWERED ATTACK SUBMARINES *(continued)*

D: 9,150 tons (sub.) **S:** 35 kts (sub.) **Dim:** 99.37 × 12.19 × 10.94
A: 8/TT (fwd: SOW, Tomahawk, Harpoon missiles, Mk 48 torpedoes, mines)
Electron Equipt: Radar: . . .
Sonar: SUBACS suite, Wide-aperture passive array
M: 1 pressurized-water reactor, . . . drive; 1 prop; 60,000 hp
Man: Approx. 15 officers, 134 enlisted

REMARKS: First unit to be requested under FY 89. General Dynamics and Newport News SB & DD competing for initial unit design. Will offer significant improvements in speed, quietness, weapons load, sonar processing, etc. over *Los Angeles* class, to continue U.S. lead over Soviet submarine technology.

Submarine will have smaller length-to-beam ratio to improve maneuverability. Retractable bow planes and six stern fins will be carried. A small wedge at the base of the forward edge of the sail will improve hydrodynamic flow. Propeller will be of pump-jet design.

◆ **33 (+19 + 6) Los Angeles class (SCB 303 type)**

	Bldr	Laid down	L	In serv.
SSN 688 Los Angeles	Newport News	8-1-72	6-4-74	13-11-76
SSN 689 Baton Rouge	Newport News	18-11-72	18-4-75	25-6-77
SSN 690 Philadelphia	Gen. Dynamics	12-8-72	19-10-74	25-6-77
SSN 691 Memphis	Newport News	23-6-73	3-4-76	17-12-77
SSN 692 Omaha	Gen. Dynamics	27-1-73	21-2-76	11-3-78
SSN 693 Cincinnati	Newport News	6-4-74	19-2-76	10-6-78
SSN 694 Groton	Gen. Dynamics	3-8-73	9-10-76	8-7-78
SSN 695 Birmingham	Newport News	26-4-75	15-10-77	20-12-78
SSN 696 New York City	Gen. Dynamics	15-12-73	18-6-77	10-3-79
SSN 697 Indianapolis	Gen. Dynamics	19-10-74	30-7-77	5-1-80
SSN 698 Bremerton	Gen. Dynamics	8-5-76	22-7-78	28-3-81
SSN 699 Jacksonville	Gen. Dynamics	21-2-76	18-11-78	16-5-81
SSN 700 Dallas	Gen. Dynamics	9-10-76	28-4-79	18-7-81
SSN 701 La Jolla	Gen. Dynamics	16-10-76	11-8-79	24-10-81
SSN 702 Phoenix	Gen. Dynamics	30-7-77	18-12-79	19-12-81
SSN 703 Boston	Gen. Dynamics	11-8-78	19-4-80	30-1-82
SSN 704 Baltimore	Gen. Dynamics	21-5-79	18-12-80	24-7-82
SSN 705 City of Corpus Christi	Gen. Dynamics	4-9-79	25-4-81	8-1-83
SSN 706 Albuquerque	Gen. Dynamics	27-12-79	13-3-82	21-5-83
SSN 707 Portsmouth	Gen. Dynamics	8-5-80	18-9-82	1-10-83
SSN 708 Minneapolis-Saint Paul	Gen. Dynamics	20-1-81	19-3-83	10-3-84
SSN 709 Hyman G. Rickover	Gen. Dynamics	23-7-81	27-8-83	21-7-84
SSN 710 Augusta	Gen. Dynamics	1-4-82	21-1-84	19-1-85
SSN 711 San Francisco	Newport News	26-5-77	27-10-79	24-4-81
SSN 712 Atlanta	Newport News	17-8-78	16-8-80	6-3-82
SSN 713 Houston	Newport News	29-1-79	21-3-81	25-9-82
SSN 714 Norfolk	Newport News	1-8-79	31-10-81	21-5-83
SSN 715 Buffalo	Newport News	25-1-80	8-5-82	5-11-83
SSN 716 Salt Lake City	Newport News	26-8-80	16-10-82	12-5-84
SSN 717 Olympia	Newport News	31-3-81	30-4-83	17-11-84
SSN 718 Honolulu	Newport News	10-11-81	24-9-83	6-7-85
SSN 719 Providence	Gen. Dynamics	30-9-82	4-8-84	27-7-85
SSN 720 Pittsburgh	Gen. Dynamics	9-4-83	8-12-84	23-11-85
SSN 721 Chicago	Newport News	5-1-83	13-10-84	8-86
SSN 722 Key West	Newport News	6-7-83	20-7-85	1-87
SSN 723 Oklahoma City	Newport News	4-1-84	-2-11-85	3-87
SSN 724 Louisville	Gen. Dynamics	24-9-84	14-12-85	1987
SSN 725 Helena	Gen. Dynamics	28-3-85	28-6-86	1987
SSN 750 Newport News	Newport News	3-3-84	29-3-86	1987
SSN 751 San Juan	Gen. Dynamics	3-8-85	11-86	1987
SSN 752 Springfield	Gen. Dynamics	12-85	3-87	1988
SSN 753 N.	Newport News	22-4-85	3-87	5-88
SSN 754 N.	Gen. Dynamics	4-86	7-87	7-88
SSN 755 N.	Gen. Dynamics	9-86	12-87	12-88
SSN 756 N.	Newport News	4-86	. . .	6-89
SSN 757 N.	Gen. Dynamics	3-87	. . .	7-89
SSN 758 N.	Newport News	9-86	. . .	1989
SSN 759 N.	Newport News	1-87	. . .	1990
SSN 760 N.	. . .	. . .	. . .	1990
SSN 761 N.	. . .	. . .	. . .	1990
SSN 762 N.	. . .	. . .	. . .	1990
SSN 763 N.	. . .	. . .	. . .	1990
SSN 764 N.	. . .	. . .	. . .	. . .
SSN 765 N.	. . .	. . .	. . .	. . .
SSN 766 N.	. . .	. . .	. . .	. . .
SSN 768 N.	. . .	. . .	. . .	. . .
SSN 769 N.	. . .	. . .	. . .	. . .
SSN 770 N.	. . .	. . .	. . .	. . .

Authorized: SSN 688 to SSN 690 in FY 70, SSN 691 to SSN 694 in FY 71, SSN 695 to SSN 700 in FY 72, SSN 701 to SSN 705 in FY 73, SSN 706 to SSN 710 in FY 74, SSN 711 to SSN 713 in FY 75, SSN 714 to SSN 715 in FY 76, SSN 716 to SSN 718 in FY 77, SSN 719 in FY 78, SSN 720 in FY 79, SSN 721 to SSN 722 in FY 80, SSN 723 to SSN 724 in FY 81, SSN 725 and 750 in FY 82, SSN 751 to SSN 752 in FY 83, SSN 753 to SSN 755 in FY 84, SSN 756 to SSN 759 in FY 85, SSN 760 to SSN 763 in FY 86. Requested: SSN 764 to SSN 767 in FY 87. Planned: 3 in FY 88, FY 89, 4 in FY 90, 1 in FY 91.

D: 6,080/6,927 tons **S:** 30+ kts. (sub.) **Dim:** 109.73 × 10.06 × 9.75
A: SSN 719 and later: 12/vertical tubes for Tomahawk—all: 4/533-mm TT Mk 67 (amidships) for Tomahawk, Harpoon, Mk 48 torpedoes, mines, etc. (22 reloads)
Electron Equipt: Radar: 1/BPS-15A
EW: BRD-7 direction finder, WLR-8(V)2, WLR-12
Sonar: 1/BQQ-5A(V)1, BQS-15, BQR-15 (SSN 751: SUBACS)

Salt Lake City (SSN 716) U.S. Navy, 5-84

Indianapolis (SSN 697)—note BQR-15 towed array fairing down starboard side
ABPH M. Russell, R.A.N., 1-85

Hyman G. Rickover (SSN 709)—on trials Gen. Dynamics, 4-84

Groton (SSN 694) L. & L. Van Ginderen, 9-85

NUCLEAR-POWERED ATTACK SUBMARINES *(continued)*

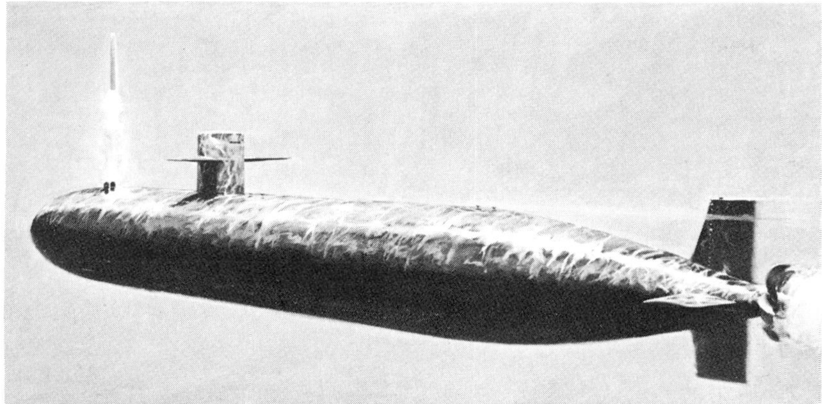

Providence (SSN 719)—with vertical-launch Tomahawk—artist's rendering
Gen. Dynamics, 1983

M: G.E. S6G reactor, 2 GT; 1/7-bladed prop; 35,000 hp
Man: 12 officers, 115 men

REMARKS: SSN 719 and later are receiving twelve vertical-launch tubes for Tomahawk cruise missiles, located between the forward end of the pressure hull and the spherical array for the BQQ-5 bow sonar; SSN 751 and later will have bow-mounted vice sail-mounted diving planes and will have the first-generation SUBACS (Submarine Advanced Combat System) integrated sonar/weapons-control suit from I.B.M. All carry a UYK-7 general-purpose computer and have WSC-3 satellite comms. gear. One Mk 2 optical and one Sperry Mk 18 multi-function periscope fitted. Mk 113 Mod. 10 torpedo-fire-control in SSN 688 to SSN 699, Mk 117 in later units to be backfitted in all. Under FY 83, the Mk 117 f.c.s. is being modified to permit launching SUBROC missiles. Will carry ASW SOW when available in the early 1990s. Harpoon began to be carried in 1978. SSN 688–720 will carry 8 Tomahawk cruise missiles, later units will have 20. Maximum diving depth is 450 m. Described as the finest ASW platforms now afloat. Bow is of fiberglass as a streamlined cover over the spherical BQQ-5-A(V)1 sonar array. There are two SINS, to be replaced by the ESGN (Electrically Suspended Gyro Navigator). All have one Fairbanks-Morse 38D8⅛ diesel generator set and batteries for emergency propulsion. The BLD-1 electromagnetic interferometer is being added, beginning 1985. The reactor core is expected to last 10–13 years between refuelings. SSN 694 traveled around the world submerged 4-4-80 to 8-10-80. SSN 701 was the first of the class to be equipped to launch Tomahawk missiles from the torpedo tubes, in 1983; SSN 712 first *operational* sub with Tomahawk, 30-11-83.

◆ **1 Glenard P. Lipscomb class**

	Bldr	Laid down	L	In serv.
SSN 685 GLENARD P. LIPSCOMB	Gen. Dynamics	5-6-71	4-8-73	21-12-74

Authorized: FY 68

Glenard P. Lipscomb (SSN 685) G. Gyssels, 11-85

D: 5,813 standard/6,480 tons (sub.) **S:** 25 kts **Dim:** 111.3 × 9.7 × 8.8
A: 4/533-mm TT (amidships) **Man:** 14 officers, 98 men
Electron Equipt: Radar: BPS-15—Sonar: BQQ-5, BQS-14
M: 1 Westinghouse S5WA, natural circulation reactor, G.E. turboelectric drive; 1 prop; . . . hp

REMARKS: This TEDS (Turbo-Electric Drive Submarine) was an effort to make an exceptionally quiet submarine at the expense of some speed. Most other equipment is similar to the *Sturgeon* class. During 3-81 to 7-82 overhaul, was equipped to launch Harpoon, with BQQ-5 vice BQQ-2 sonar, and Mk 117 torpedo-fire-control vice Mk 113 Mod. 8; problems with the turbogenerator system kept the ship in the yard into early 1985. Will carry up to 8 Tomahawk cruise missiles.

◆ **37 Sturgeon class (SCB 188A and SCB 188M types)**

	Bldr	Laid down	L	In serv.
SSN 637 STURGEON	Gen. Dynamics	10-8-63	26-2-66	3-3-67
SSN 638 WHALE	Gen. Dynamics	27-5-64	14-10-66	12-10-68
SSN 639 TAUTOG	Ingalls SB	27-1-64	15-4-67	17-8-68
SSN 646 GRAYLING	Portsmouth NSY	12-5-64	22-6-67	11-10-69
SSN 647 POGY	New York SB	4-5-64	3-6-67	15-5-71
SSN 648 ASPRO	Ingalls SB	23-11-64	29-11-67	20-2-69
SSN 649 SUNFISH	Gen. Dynamics	15-1-65	14-10-66	15-3-69
SSN 650 PARGO	Gen. Dynamics	3-6-64	17-9-66	1-5-68
SSN 651 QUEENFISH	Newport News	11-5-64	25-2-66	6-12-66
SSN 652 PUFFER	Ingalls SB	8-2-65	30-3-68	9-8-69
SSN 653 RAY	Newport News	1-4-65	21-6-66	12-4-67
SSN 660 SANDLANCE	Portsmouth NSY	15-1-65	11-11-69	25-9-71
SSN 661 LAPON	Newport News	26-7-65	16-12-66	14-12-67
SSN 662 GURNARD	Mare Island NSY	22-12-64	20-5-67	6-12-68
SSN 663 HAMMERHEAD	Newport News	29-11-65	14-4-67	28-6-68
SSN 664 SEA DEVIL	Newport News	12-4-66	5-10-67	30-1-69
SSN 665 GUITARRO	Mare Island NSY	9-12-65	27-7-68	9-9-72
SSN 666 HAWKBILL	Mare Island NSY	12-9-66	12-4-69	4-2-71
SSN 667 BERGALL	Gen. Dynamics	16-4-66	17-2-69	13-3-69
SSN 668 SPADEFISH	Newport News	21-12-66	15-5-68	14-8-69
SSN 669 SEAHORSE	Gen. Dynamics	13-8-66	15-6-68	19-9-69
SSN 670 FINBACK	Newport News	26-6-67	7-12-68	4-2-70
SSN 672 PINTADO	Mare Island NSY	27-10-67	16-8-69	11-9-71
SSN 673 FLYING FISH	Gen. Dynamics	30-6-67	17-5-69	29-4-70
SSN 674 TREPANG	Gen. Dynamics	28-10-67	27-9-69	14-8-70
SSN 675 BLUEFISH	Gen. Dynamics	13-3-68	10-1-70	8-1-71
SSN 676 BILLFISH	Gen. Dynamics	20-9-68	1-5-70	12-3-71
SSN 677 DRUM	Mare Island NSY	20-8-68	23-5-70	15-4-72
SSN 678 ARCHERFISH	Gen. Dynamics	19-6-69	16-1-71	24-12-71
SSN 679 SILVERSIDES	Gen. Dynamics	13-12-69	4-6-71	5-5-72
SSN 680 WILLIAM H. BATES (ex-*Redfish*)	Ingalls SB	4-8-69	12-71	5-5-73
SSN 681 BATFISH	Gen. Dynamics	9-2-70	9-10-71	1-9-72
SSN 682 TUNNY	Ingalls SB	22-5-70	10-6-72	26-1-74
SSN 683 PARCHE	Ingalls SB	10-12-70	12-72	17-8-74
SSN 684 CAVALLA	Gen. Dynamics	4-6-70	19-2-72	9-2-73
SSN 686 MENDEL RIVERS	Newport News	26-6-71	2-6-73	1-2-75
SSN 687 RICHARD B. RUSSELL	Newport News	19-10-71	12-1-74	16-8-75

Authorized: SSN 637 to SSN 639 in FY 62, SSN 646 to SSN 653 in FY 63, SSN 660 to SSN 664 in FY 64, SSN 665 to SSN 670 in FY 65, SSN 672 to SSN 677 in FY 66, SSN 678 to SSN 682 in FY 67, SSN 683 and SSN 684 in FY 68, SSN 686 and SSN 687 in FY 69

D: 4,250/4,780 tons (SSN 678 and later, plus modernized units: 4,460/4,960)
S: 15/30 kts **Man:** 12 officers, 95 men
Dim: 89.0 (SSN 678 and later and 19 refitted units: 92.1) × 9.65 × 8.8
A: 4/533-mm TT (amidships for 15 Mk 48 torpedoes, 4/Harpoon, and 4/SUBROC—up to 8 Tomahawk in lieu of other weapons)
Electron Equipt: Radar: 1/BPS-14 or 15—EW: WLR-4 intercept

William H. Bates (SSN 680) with DSRV Avalon G. Arra, 1985

Puffer (SSN 652) LSPH E. Pitman, R.A.N., 1985

NUCLEAR-POWERED ATTACK SUBMARINES *(continued)*

Pintado (SSN 672)—note fairing running the length of the hull on the port side for housing the towed sonar array G. Arra, 12-84

Silversides (SSN 679)—with aftward sail extension L. & L. Van Ginderen, 5-84

Sonar: BQQ-2 (with BQS-6 active/BQR-7 passive) or BQQ-5, BQS-8, SSN 637 to SSN 664: BQS-12; others: BQS-13

M: 1 Westinghouse S5W2 pressurized-water reactor, 2 G.E. or de Laval GT; 1 prop; 20,000 hp

Remarks: The construction contract of SSN 647 with New York Shipbuilding, Camden, N.J., was canceled in 4-67, and completion of the ship was given to Ingalls, Pascagoula, Miss. Completion of SSN 665 was delayed twenty-eight months after ship sank while fitting out. The Mk 113 torpedo-fire-control system is being replaced by Mk 117 to permit Harpoon launching. SSN 678 and later units (SCB 188M) were lengthened to permit installation of BQQ-5 sonar suit. Diving planes are 11.6 wide. Maximum depth is about 400 m. The 70-megawatt S5W reactor plant operates at 160 kg/cm², has two primary steam loops and two steam generators to supply steam to the two steam turbines. Original core life was 5,000 hours. SSN 666, SSN 672, and others have been modified to carry a DSRV (salvage submarine), which can be launched and recovered while submerged. The after hatch is so constructed that people can be transferred between the two ships while submerged. Since 1978, SSN 679 and 687 have an aftward extension to the lower portion of the sail to accommodate a towed communications array. Class expected to serve 30 years each. SSN 665 conducted the initial Tomahawk missile trials. SSN 680 has a low, forward extension to the sail. SSN 684 has been equipped to carry a cylindrical device associated with swimmers. Will be receiving ESGN (Electronically Suspended Gyro Navigator) in lieu of SINS.

◆ **1 Narwhal class (SCB 245)**

	Bldr	Laid down	L	In serv.
SSN 671 Narwhal	Gen. Dynamics	17-1-66	9-9-67	12-7-69

Authorized: FY 64

D: 5,284/5,830 tons **S:** 20/25 kts **Dim:** 96.0 × 11.5 × 7.9

A: 4/533-mm TT (amidships, for Mk 48 torp., Harpoon, up to 8 Tomahawk)

Electron Equipt: Radar: BPS-14—EW: WLR-8
Sonar: BQQ-5 BQS-8

M: 1 G.E. S5G reactor, 2 GT; 1 prop; 17,000 hp **Man:** 12 officers, 108 men

Remarks: Prototype seagoing reactor designed to study the cooling of the S5G reactor by natural circulation, thus eliminating circulation pumps and their noise. In most other respects, essentially a lengthened *Sturgeon.* Original BQQ-2 sonar suit and Mk 113 Mod. 6 fire-control system replaced by Mk 117 f.c.s. and BQQ-5.

Narwhal (SSN 671) J.-C. Bellonne, 1-83

Narwhal (SSN 671) G. Arra, 1982

◆ **13 Permit class (SSN 594 to SSN 612 and SSN 621 are SCB 188 type, SN 613 to SSN 615 are SCB 188M type)**

	Bldr	Laid down	L	In serv.
SSN 594 Permit	Mare Island NSY	16-7-59	1-7-61	29-5-62
SSN 595 Plunger	Mare Island NSY	2-3-60	9-12-61	21-11-62
SSN 596 Barb (ex-*Pollack*)	Ingalls SB	9-11-59	12-2-62	24-8-63
SSN 603 Pollack (ex-*Barb*)	New York SB	14-3-60	17-3-62	26-5-64
SSN 604 Haddo	New York SB	9-9-60	18-8-62	16-12-64
SSN 605 Jack	Portsmouth NSY	16-9-60	24-4-63	31-3-67
SSN 606 Tinosa	Portsmouth, NSY	24-11-59	9-12-61	17-10-64
SSN 607 Dace	Ingalls SB	6-6-60	18-8-62	4-4-64
SSN 612 Guardfish	New York SB	28-2-61	15-5-65	20-12-66
SSN 613 Flasher	Gen. Dynamics	14-4-61	22-6-63	22-7-66
SSN 614 Greenling	Gen. Dynamics	15-8-61	4-4-64	3-11-67
SSN 615 Gato	Gen. Dynamics	15-12-61	14-5-64	25-1-68
SSN 621 Haddock	Ingalls SB	24-4-61	21-5-66	22-12-67

Authorized: SSN 594 to SSN 596 in FY 58, SSN 603 to SSN 607 in FY 59, SSN 612 to SSN 615 in FY 60, SSN 621 in FY 61

Barb (SSN 596) G. Arra, 12-84

NUCLEAR-POWERED ATTACK SUBMARINES *(continued)*

Guardfish (SSN 612)—note towed array fairing down port side of hull G. Arra, 1983

Pollack (SSN 603) G. Arra, 1983

SSN 594 to SSN 604, SSN 606 to SSN 612, and SSN 621:

D: 3,780/4,465 tons **Dim:** 84.88 × 9.65 × 8.80

SSN 605:

D: 4,000/4,467 tons **Dim:** 90.65 × 9.65 × 8.80

SSN 613 to SSN 615:

D: 4,250/4,770 tons **Dim:** 89.1 × 9.65 × 8.80
S: 15/30 kts **A:** 4/533-mm TT (amidships) **Man:** 12 officers, 94 men
Electron Equipt: Radar: BPS-15, BPS-5 or 9—EW: WLR-1
Sonar: BQQ-3 (BQS-11 active/BQR-7 passive), BQS-14
M: 1 Westinghouse S5W reactor; 2 G.E. or de Laval GT; 1 prop; 15,000 hp

Remarks: Sister *Thresher* (SSN 593) was lost 10-4-63. SSN 605 has contrarotating props with a contrarotating turbine and no reduction gearing. SSN 613 to SSN 615 have longer and taller sails (6.1 m long vice 4.2 or 4.6 in other ships), heavier machinery, and had safety features built in that were later backfitted in the others. The BQR-7 spherical array is in the bow, necessitating placement of the tubes abreast the sail. These ships are fitted to carry Harpoon, and received Mk 117 torpedo-fire-control systems in place of Mk 113. SSN 594 conducted Harpoon trials during 1976. All are scheduled to receive the BQQ-5 sonar suit during refits. SSN 621 ran trials in 7-79 for the Sperry PASRAN (passive-ranging) sonar system, which is similar to the exported "Micro Puffs" concept, but with an array of six larger hydrophones.

◆ 2 Ethan Allen class (SCB 180 type) former ballistic-missile submarines

	Bldr	Laid down	L	In serv.
SSN 609 Sam Houston	Newport News	28-12-59	2-2-61	6-3-62
SSN 611 John Marshall	Newport News	4-4-60	15-7-61	21-5-62

Authorized: FY 59

Thomas Jefferson (SSN 618) as SSBN 618 PH1 A. Legare, USN, 6-76

D: 6,930/7,880 tons **S:** 15/20 kts **Dim:** 124.96 × 10.05 × 9.0
A: 4/533-mm TT (fwd)—up to 67 swimmers
Electron Equipt: Radar: BPS-9—Sonar: BQR-7, BQR-15, BQR-19, BQS-4
M: 1 Westinghouse SW5 pressurized-water reactor, GT; 1/7-bladed prop; 15,000 hp
Man: 13 officers, 111 men

Remarks: Survivors of a class of five: first U.S. submarines designed from the outset to launch ballistic missiles. Retained Polaris A-3 missiles until redesignated SSN: SSBN 609 on 10-11-80; SSBN 611 on 1-5-81 at conclusion of final Polaris cruises. Modified by 1984 for further service as SSNs. Beginning with SSN 608 in 1-82 and followed by SSN 609 and 610 in FY 83 and the others in FY 84, cement ballast filled the 16 missile tubes, one of the two Mk 2 Mod. 3 SINS (Ship's Inertial Navigation Systems) was removed, and the Mk 84 missile-control system was depleted. Formerly had two complete crews; complement reduced as SSNs. Deeper-diving (300 m +) than SSN 598 class. Both in Pacific Fleet. Converted beginning 10-84 to carry up to 67 SEAL swimmers at Puget Sound Naval SY.

Sisters *Ethan Allen* (SSN 608) deactivated 30-9-82 and decommissioned 31-3-83; *Thomas A. Edison* (SSN 610) deactivated 30-9-83 for decommissioning 15-1-84, *Thomas Jefferson* (SSN 618) deactivated beginning 1-6-84 for decommissioning 24-1-85—all three in storage for later disposal.

Note: The two remaining *George Washington*-class SSNs (ex-SSBN) have been decommissioned to storage for ultimate scrapping: *George Washington* (SSN 598) on 24-1-85 and *Patrick Henry* (SSN 599) on 3-2-85.

◆ 1 Tullibee class (SCB 178 type)

	Bldr	Laid down	L	In serv.
SSN 597 Tullibee	Gen. Dynamics	26-5-58	27-4-60	9-11-60

Authorized: FY 58

Tullibee (SSN 597)—PUFFS domes now removed U.S. Navy, 1975

D: 2,336/2,607 tons **S:** 15/20 kts **Dim:** 83.15 × 7.31 × 6.1
A: 4/533-mm Mk 64 TT (amidships)
Electron Equipt: Radar: 1/BPS-9—EW: WLR-1
Sonar: BQQ-3 (BQS-12 active/BQR-7 passive)
M: 1 Combustion Engineering S2C reactor, turboelectric propulsion; 1 prop; 2,500 hp
Man: 6 officers, 50 men

Remarks: The torpedo tubes have a 10° angle from the centerline. PUFFS hydrophones were mounted in three fins along the top of the hull. Mk 112 Mod. 1 torpedo-fire-control system. Active in Atlantic Fleet, but considered to be second-line.

Note: The one-of-a-kind nuclear-powered submarines *Halibut* (SSN 587, ex-SSGN 587) and *Triton* (SSN 586, ex-SSRN-586), in reserve since 30-6-76 and 3-5-69, respectively, have for all intents and purposes been discarded, although they remain in storage for ultimate scrapping.

◆ 5 Skipjack class (SCB 154 type)

	Bldr	Laid down	L	In serv.
SSN 585 Skipjack	Gen. Dynamics	29-5-56	26-5-58	15-4-59
SSN 588 Scamp	Mare Island, NSY	23-1-59	8-10-60	5-6-61
SSN 590 Sculpin	Ingalls	3-2-58	31-3-60	1-6-61
SSN 591 Shark	Newport News SB	24-2-56	16-3-60	9-2-61
SSN 592 Snook	Ingalls	7-4-58	31-10-60	24-10-61

Authorized: SSN 585 in FY 56, SSN 558 and SSN 590 to SSN 592 in FY 57

D: 3,080/3,500 tons **S:** 15/30 kts **Dim:** 76.8 × 9.75 × 8.5
A: 6/533-mm TT (fwd) **Man:** 9 officers, 85 men
Electron Equipt: Radar: BPS-12—Sonar: Modified BQS-4, BQR-2, SQS-49
M: 1 Westinghouse S5W reactor; SSN 585; 2 Westinghouse GT, others: 2 G.E. G.T.; 1 prop; 15,000 hp

Remarks: The reactor compartment takes up 6.10 m. Between the reactor and the propeller, all engine fittings are duplicated (two heat exchangers, two pressurized-water coolers; two groups of turbines, two groups of turbo generators). In case of emergency, submerged propulsion can take over by means of two electric motors linked directly on the propeller shaft and feeding off two electric batteries or two small diesel generators. Better hull form than later SSNs. Still considered first-line subma-

NUCLEAR-POWERED ATTACK SUBMARINES *(continued)*

Sculpin (SSN 590) G. Gyssels, 4-84

rines. Mk 101 Mod. 17 torpedo-fire-control system. Sister *Scorpion* (SSN 589) disappeared in the Atlantic about 27-5-68.

◆ **2 Skate class (SCB 121 type)**

	Bldr	Laid down	L	In serv.
SSN 579 Swordfish	Portsmouth NSY	25-1-56	27-8-57	15-9-58
SSN 583 Sargo	Mare Island NSY	21-2-56	10-10-57	1-10-58

Authorized: SSN 579 in FY 55, SSN 583 in FY 56

Sargo (SSN 583) L. & L. Van Ginderen, 8-84

D: 2,570/2,860 tons **S:** 15/19 kts **Dim:** 81.4 × 7.62 × 6.1
A: 8/533-mm TT (6 fwd, 2 aft)
Electron Equipt: Radar: BPS-12—Sonar: BQR-2, SQS-49
M: 1 Westinghouse reactor—S3W in SSN 578 and SSN 583, S4W in SSN 579 and SSN 584; 2 GT; 2 props; 13,200 hp
Man: 9 officers, 86 men

Remarks: SSN 578 passed under the North Pole twice (8-58), coming to the surface nine times while in ice-capped waters during this cruise. She ran 120,862 miles in 39 months with her first core. Mk 101 Mod. 19 torpedo-fire-control system. Now considered second-line submarines. *Seadragon* (SSN 584) began deactivation 30-9-83 for decommissioning to reserve 12-6-84; *Skate* (SSN 578) stood down late in 1985 for decommissioning 3-8-85—both placed in storage for ultimate scrapping.

◆ **1 Seawolf class (SCB 64A type)**

	Bldr	Laid down	L	In serv.
SSN 575 Seawolf	Gen. Dynamics	15-9-53	21-7-55	30-3-57

Authorized: FY 53

Seawolf (SSN 575)—note side-thrusters fore and aft U.S. Navy, 1977

D: 4,400/4,970 tons **S:** 20/20 kts **Dim:** 102.87 × 8.45 × 6.7
A: 6/533-mm TT (fwd) **Man:** 11 officers, 90 men
M: 1 Westinghouse S2WA reactor; 2 GT; 2 props; 15,000 hp
Electron Equipt: Radar: BPS-15—EW: WLR-1
Sonar: BQR-4, SQS-51

Remarks: The original propulsion plant, which was by an S2G reactor with sodium cooling, did not prove satisfactory and was replaced by an S2WA. Four side-thrusters, two forward and two aft, have been added to the casing above the pressure hull for precision maneuvering while submerged, and foundations have been added at the stern to permit a DSRV to be carried and to mate with the after rescue hatch. Mk 101 Mod. 8 torpedo-fire-control system. Now considered a second-line submarine; to decommission during 1986.

Note: The *Nautilus* (SSN 571), the world's first nuclear-powered ship, was placed in technical reserve on 30-9-79 and formally decommissioned 3-3-80. She was stripped of her reactor plant and towed in 1985 to Groton, Connecticut, where she serves as a monument to the technical achievements of the U.S. submarine service and Adm. H.G. Rickover, her dauntless creator.

CONVENTIONAL SUBMARINES

◆ **3 Barbel class (SCB 150 type)**

	Bldr	Laid down	L	In serv.
SS 580 Barbel	Portsmouth NSY	18-5-56	19-7-58	17-1-59
SS 581 Blueback	Ingalls	15-4-57	16-5-59	15-10-59
SS 582 Bonefish	New York SB	3-6-57	22-11-58	9-7-59

Authorized: FY 56

Bonefish (SS 582) L. & L. Van Ginderen, 9-84

Blueback (SS 581) G. Arra, 1985

D: 1,740/2,146/2,640 tons **S:** 12/25 kts **Dim:** 66.75 × 8.84 × 5.8
A: 6/533-mm TT (fwd)
Electron Equipt: Radar: BPS-12—Sonar: BQR-2, SQS-49
EW: WLR-1
M: 3 1,600-hp Fairbanks-Morse 38D8⅛ × 10 diesels, 1 Westinghouse electric motor; 1 prop; 3,150 hp
Man: 8 officers, 70 men

Remarks: Teardrop hull design. Diving planes were moved to the sail structure in 1961-62. Dutch *Zwaardvis* class based on this design. Mk 101 Mod. 20 torpedo-fire-control system. Last conventional submarines built for the U.S. Navy. SS 582 transferred to the Atlantic Fleet in 1982, the only U.S. Navy diesel-powered submarine in that area.

◆ **1 Darter class (SCB 116 type)**

	Bldr	Laid down	L	In serv.
SS 576 Darter	Electric Boat Co.	10-11-54	28-5-56	26-10-56

Authorized: FY 54

D: 1,590/1,975/2,250 tons **S:** 16/20 tons **Dim:** 81.68 × 8.23 × 5.8
A: 8/533-mm TT (6 fwd, 2 aft)
Electron Equipt: Radar: 1/BPS-12—EW: WLR-1
Sonar: BQS-4, BQG-4 (PUFFS), BQR-4
M: 3 Fairbanks-Morse 38D8⅛ × 10 diesels, 2 Westinghouse motors; 2 props; 3,200 hp
Man: 8 officers, 75 men

CONVENTIONAL SUBMARINES *(continued)*

Darter (SS 576) G. Arra, 1-80

Remarks: Very similar to the ultimate configuration of the *Tang* class. Mk 106 Mod. 11 torpedo-fire-control system. Home-ported as Sasebo, Japan, in 3-79. To have been stricken in 9-79, but has been retained in service. Collided with merchant ship 18-6-85 but not badly damaged. Near-sister *Kusseh* (ex-*Trout,* SS 566) of the similar *Tang* class transferred to Iran 19-12-79 and later abandoned, remains in storage in good condition at Philadelphia Naval SY; sister *Wahoo* (ex-SS 565), stricken 27-6-80, was towed away for scrap 4-85.

Note: The research submarine *Dolphin* (AGSS 555) is described later, with auxiliary ships.

BATTLESHIPS

◆ **2 (+2) Iowa class**

	Bldr	Laid down	L	In serv.	Recomm.
BB 61 Iowa	New York NSY	27-6-40	27-8-42	22-2-43	28-4-84
BB 62 New Jersey	Philadelphia NSY	16-9-40	7-12-42	23-5-43	28-12-82
BB 63 Missouri	New York NSY	6-1-41	29-1-44	11-6-44	10-5-86
BB 64 Wisconsin	Philadelphia NSY	25-1-41	7-12-43	16-4-44	1-89

D: 46,177 tons light (57,353 fl) **S:** 33 kts (30.5 sust.)
Dim: 270.57 (262.13 pp) × 33.00 × 11.02
A: 32/Tomahawk (IV × 8)—16 Harpoon (IV × 4)—9/406-mm (III × 3)—12/127-mm DP (II × 6)—4/20-mm Mk 15 CIWS gatling AA (I × 4)—up to 4 helicopters

Iowa (BB 61) G. Arra, 1984

New Jersey (BB 62) G. Arra, 1983

New Jersey (BB 62) Pradignac & Leo, 1983

Iowa (BB 61)—midships superstructure G. Arra, 1984

New Jersey (BB 62) G. Arra, 1983

BATTLESHIPS *(continued)*

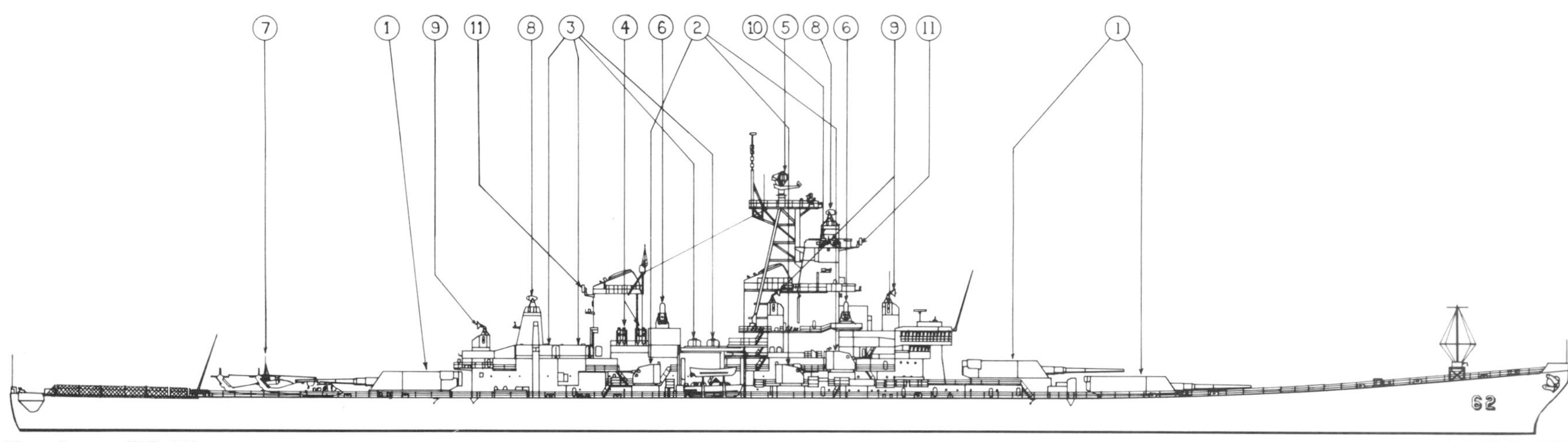

New Jersey (BB 62) A.D. Baker III

1. 406-mm triple turret 2. 127-mm twin DP 3. Tomahawk box-launcher (IV × 8) 4. Harpoon canister launcher (IV × 4) 5. SPS-49 radar 6. Mk 15 20-mm gatling CIWS 7. Helicopter parking area 8. Mk 38 GFCS (with Mk 13 radar) 9. Mk 37 GFCS (with Mk 25 radar) 10. SLQ-32 EW gear 11. OE-82 SATCOMM antennas

Iowa (BB 61) Ingalls SB, 4-84

Electron Equipt: Radar: 1/LN-66, 1/SPS-67, (BB 62: SPS-10F), 1/SPS-49, 2/Mk 13, 4/Mk 25
TACAN: URN-25
EW: SLQ-32(V)3, Mk 36 SRBOC chaff RL (VI × 8)
M: 4 sets G.E. GT; 4 props; 212,000 hp **Electric:** 10,500 kw
Boilers: 8 Babcock & Wilcox; 44.6 kg/cm², 454°C **Fuel:** 8,800 tons
Armor: Belt: 307-mm, tapering to 41-mm (343-mm abreast prop shafts)
Main turrets: 432-mm face/184-mm top/305-mm back
Barbettes: 295-mm max.
Decks: 3 armored (152-mm second deck)
Conning tower: 440-mm (184-mm top)
Range: 5,000/30; 14,800/20
Man: BB 62: 74 officers, 1,471 men; BB 61: 67 officers, 1,459 men

Remarks: BB 62, reactivated 6-4-68 for Vietnam service and decommissioned again 17-12-69, was towed from the Bremerton, Washington, mothball facility on 27-7-81, arriving 8-6-81 at Long Beach Naval Shipyard. Congress voted $326 mil. under FY 82 to modernize the ship with new radars and gear, Tomahawk and Harpoon cruise missiles, upgraded communications gear (including the WSC-3 SATCOMM system), seven new 125-ton/hr. air-conditioning plants, provision for Link-11 data link (but not NTDS), and conversion of the boilers to burn distillate fuel (which cut endurance by approx. 10 percent). Further modifications ("Phase II") are no longer planned. Funds were authorized in FY 82 for work on BB 61 at Avondale SY, New Orleans, and Ingalls, Pascagoula. BB 63, towed to Long Beach Naval SY, began reactivation 1-10-84. Funds to reactivate B 64 were authorized under FY 86, with work to take place 1-87 to 1-89. These ships act in autonomous battle groups, augmenting carrier forces on carrying out independent assignments.

The helicopter facilities include increased parking area to accommodate up to four helicopters, but there is no hangar; some maintenance facilities, a control cab, fuel tankage, and a glide-path indicator were added. The Tomahawk missiles are in eight elevating armored box launchers, while the Harpoons are placed abreast the after stack in the standard fixed 4-missile canister arrangement. BB 62 successfully launched her first land-attack Tomahawk on 10-5-83 and deployed with eight aboard in 6-83.

The 406-mm guns are controlled by two Mk 38 radar (Mk 13) GFCS and one Mk 40 director, while four Mk 37 GFCS (with Mk 25 radar) will be retained for the 127-mm guns. BB 62's six Mk 56 AA GFCS were replaced by the Vulcan/Phalanx (Mk 15 CIWS) gatling guns and 8 Super RBOC chaff launchers. While in reserve, BB 61 retained 6 Mk 56 and 2 Mk 63 GFCS, and BB 63 had 6 Mk 57 and 2 Mk 63 GFCS; BB 64 had all light AA GFCS removed when decommissioned in 1958. As activated have WRN-5A NAVSAT, Omega, and other modern navigational systems.

NUCLEAR-POWERED GUIDED-MISSILE CRUISERS

◆ 4 Virginia class

	Bldr	Laid down	L	In serv.
CGN 38 Virginia	Newport News SB	19-8-72	14-12-74	11-9-76
CGN 39 Texas	Newport News SB	18-8-73	9-8-75	10-9-77
CGN 40 Mississippi	Newport News SB	22-2-75	31-7-76	5-8-78
CGN 41 Arkansas	Newport News SB	17-1-77	21-10-78	18-10-80

Authorized: CGN 38 in FY 70, CGN 39 in FY 71, CGN 40 in FY 72, and CGN 41 in FY 75

D: 10,400 tons light (11,300 fl) **S:** 30+ kts
Dim: 177.3 × 19.2 × 9.6 (sonar; 7.4 hull)
A: 8/Harpoon SSM (IV × 2)—2/Mk 26 launchers (II × 2; 68 total Standard SM-1 MR surface-to-air and ASROC ASW missiles)—2/127-mm Mk 45 DP (I × 2)—CGN 38, 40: 2/20-mm Mk 15 CIWS gatling AA (I × 2) all: 4/12.7-mm mg (I × 4)—6/324-mm Mk 32 ASW TT (III × 2, Mk 46 torpedoes)—1/SH-2F LAMPS-II ASW helicopter (CGN 41 also 8/Tomahawk SSM (IV × 2)

NUCLEAR-POWERED GUIDED-MISSILE CRUISERS *(continued)*

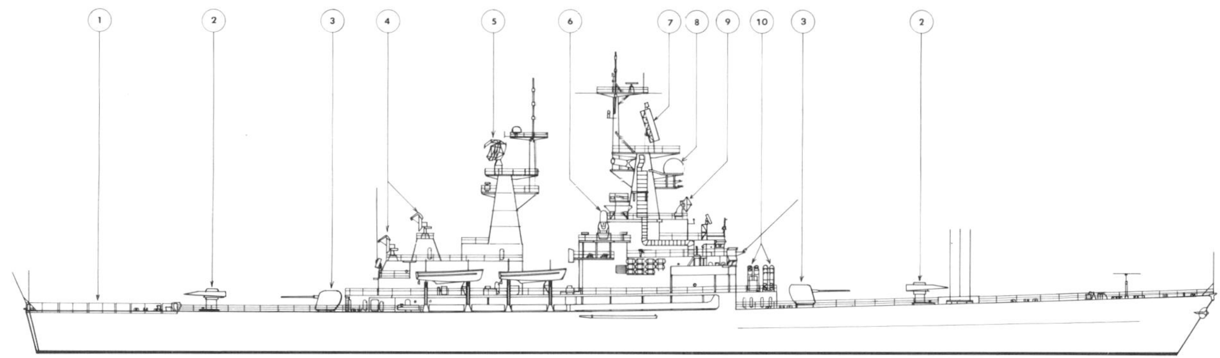

Virginia (CGN 38) A.D. Baker III

1. Helicopter flight deck (over hangar) 2. Mk 26 guided-missile launcher 3. 127-mm Mk 45 gun 4. SPG-51D radar missile directors 5. SPS-40B air-search radar 6. Mk 15 CIWS, 20-mm Vulcan/Phalanx AA(*Note*: Should be shown one deck higher, with SLQ-32 array mounted in the lower position.) 7. SPS-48B 3-D air-search radar 8. SPG-9A gun-control radar 9. SPG-60D missile/gun-control radar 10. Harpoon anti-ship missiles (IV × 2)

Texas (CGN 39)—note large platforms abreast foremast for future addition of Vulcan/Phalanx LCDR G. Moe/Ltjg R. Dickerson, USN, 1983

Mississippi (CGN 40)—with Mk 15 CIWS Pradignac & Leo, 2-85

Texas (CGN 39) Pradignac & Leo, 1984

Arkansas (CGN 41)—with Tomahawk box-launchers aft G. Arra, 7-85

Electron Equipt: Radar: 1/LN-66, 1/SPS-55, 1/SPS-40B, 1/SPS-48A, 2/SPG-51D, 1/SPQ-9A, 1/SPG-60D
Sonar: 1/SQS-53A
TACAN: CGN 40: URN-20, SRN-15; CGN 41: URN-25
EW: SLQ-32(V)3, Mk 36 SRBOC chaff RL (VI × 4)

M: 2 G.E. D2G reactors; 2 props; 70,000 hp **Man:** 38 officers, 490 men

Remarks: These ships are expected to operate for 10 years on one nuclear fueling. The Standard SM-1 MR antiaircraft missiles, stowed vertically, will be replaced by SM-2-MR, and the ships are intended to receive the "New Threat Upgrade" combat system improvements. Eventually, the ships will carry eight Tomahawk cruise missiles in two armored box-launchers. A hangar is fitted beneath the fantail, the helicopter being raised to the main deck by elevator. These ships are no longer scheduled to carry UH-60B LAMPS-III helicopters. CGN 40 and 41 have SPS-48C vice 48A. All have WSC-3 SATCOMM and NTDS data system. The missile-fire-control system is Mk 74; ASW fire control is Mk 116; and the GFCS is Mk 86 Mod. 5. SQS-53A sonar is a

NUCLEAR-POWERED GUIDED-MISSILE CRUISERS *(continued)*

greatly improved version of SQS-26. Kevlar plastic armor is being added over vital topside and magazine spaces during sequential overhauls scheduled from FY 82 to FY 86. Mk 16 CIWS is being added on an 05 level platform, with the SLQ-32(V)3 arrays being moved down to the platform originally intended for the guns; this prevents electronic interference. CGN 41, with Tomahawk, lost helicopter capability.

◆ **2 California class (SCB 241.65 type)**

	Bldr	Laid down	L	In serv.
CGN 36 California	Newport News SB	23-1-70	22-9-71	16-2-74
CGN 37 South Carolina	Newport News SB	1-12-70	1-7-72	25-1-75

Authorized: CGN 36 in FY 67, CGN 37 in FY 68

California (CGN 36)—superstructure G. Arra, 1984

South Carolina (CGN 37)—with Mk 15 CIWS G. Gyssels, 1985

California (CGN 36)—note Harpoon launchers just forward of aft 127-mm gun G. Arra, 1984

California (CGN 36)—with Mk 15 CIWS ABPH M. Russell, R.A.N., 7-85

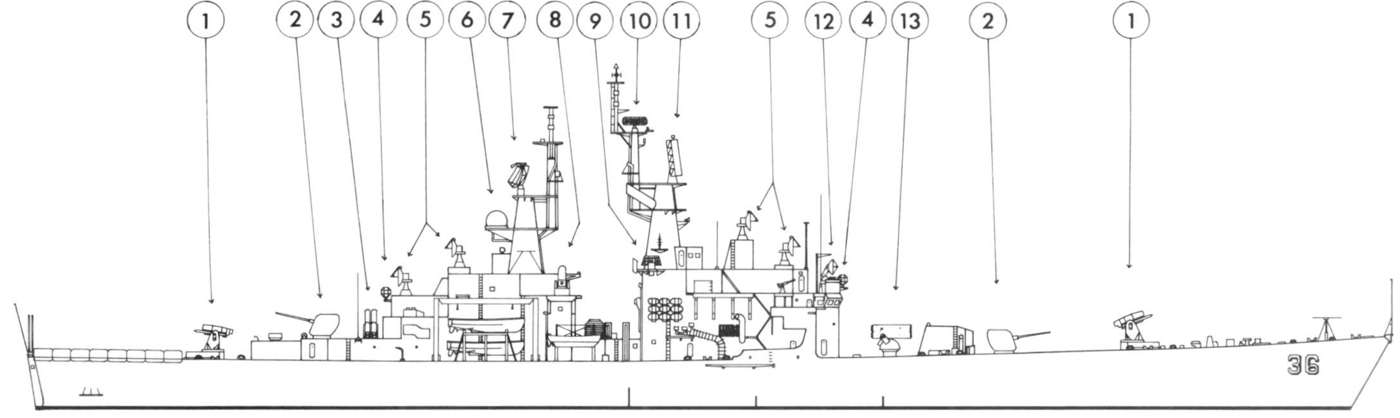

California Robert Dumas

1. MK 13 Standard SM-1 MR SAM launchers 2. 127-mm Mk 45 DP 3. Harpoon SSM canister launchers (IV × 2) 4. UHF satellite communications antennas 5. SPG-51D radar directors 6. SPQ-9A gun f.c. radar 7. SPS-40 air-search radar 8. 20-mm Mk 15 CIWS gatling AA 9. SLQ-32(V)3 EW antenna 10. SPS-10 surface-search radar 11. SPS-48C 3-D air-search radar antenna 12. SPG-60D gun f.c. radar director 13. ASROC ASW RL

NUCLEAR-POWERED GUIDED-MISSILE CRUISERS *(continued)*

D: 9,676 tons light (10,530 fl) **S:** 30+ kts
Dim: 181.66 × 18.6 × 9.6 (sonar: 7.4 hull) **Man:** 28 officers, 512 men
A: 8/Harpoon SSM (IV × 2)—2/Mk 13 launchers (I × 2; 80 Standard SM-1 MR missiles)—2/127-mm Mk 45 DP (I × 2)—2/20-mm Mk 15 CIWS AA (I × 2)—4/12.7-mm mg (I × 4)—1/Mk 116 ASROC ASW RL (VIII × 1)—4/324-mm Mk 32 ASW TT (II × 2)
Electron Equipt: Radar: 1/LN-66, 1/SPS-10, 1/SPS-40B, 1/SPS-48C, 4/SPG-51D, 1/SPQ-9A, 1/SPG-60
Sonar: 1/SQS-26CX—TACAN: URN-25
EW: SLQ-32(V)3, Mk 36 SRBOC chaff RL (VI × 4)
M: 2 G.E. D2G pressurized-water reactors, 2 GT; 2 props; 70,000 hp

REMARKS: Each Mk 13 launcher magazine holds 40 vertically stowed missiles, and the ASROC system includes automatic reloading from a magazine on deck, forward of the launcher. Both will eventually get Tomahawk in two 4-missile box launchers. They have no helicopter hangar. Weapons are controlled by the Mk 11 Mod. 3 direction system, handling two Mk 74 Mod. 2 missile fire-control systems and Mk 86 Mod. 3 gunfire-control system. ASW fire is controlled by a Mk 114 system. Both have WSC-3 SATCOMM and NTDS data system. Kevlar plastic armor will be added over vital spaces in overhauls scheduled for 1986 and 1987. Eventually, SPS-67 will replace SPS-10, and SPS-49 the SPS-40B. Both will receive the NTU (New Threat Upgrade) modernization.

◆ **1 Truxtun class (SCB 222 type)**

	Bldr	Program	Laid down	L	In serv.
CGN 35 TRUXTUN	New York SB, Camden, N.J.	FY 62	17-6-63	19-12-64	27-5-67

Truxtun (CGN 35)—2 Mk 15 CIWS added J. Zeitlhofer, 7-84

D: 8,000 tons light (8,800 fl) **S:** 30+ kts
Dim: 171.91 × 17.67 × 9.5 (sonar, 7.3 hull)
A: 8/Harpoon (IV × 2)—1/Mk 10 launcher (II × 1, for 40 Standard SM-1 ER and 20 ASROC missiles)—1/127-mm Mk 42, 54-cal. DP—2/20-mm Mk 15 CIWS AA (I × 2)—4/12.7-mm mg (I × 4)—4/324-mm Mk 32 ASW TT (II × 2)—1/SH-2F LAMPS-II ASW helicopter
Electron Equipt: Radar: 1/LN-66, 1/SPS-67, 1/SPS-40D, 1/SPS-48C, 1/SPG-53F, 2/SPG-55B
Sonar: 1/SQS-26BX—TACAN: URN-25
EW: WLR-1, SLQ-32(V)3, Mk 36 SRBOC chaff RL (VI × 4)
M: 2 G.E. D2G pressurized-water reactors, 2 sets GT; 2 props; 70,000 hp
Electric: 14,500 kw **Man:** 36 officers, 530 men

REMARKS: During 4-10-82 to 4-84 received two Vulcan/Phalanx Mk 15 CIWS 20-mm AA, new TACAN, and EW suite. Eight Harpoon SSM (IV × 2) replaced 2/76.2-mm DP in 1980. Two Mk 25 torpedo tubes at stern removed. Eventually will carry the SM-2 ER SAM and will receive the NTU (New Threat Upgrade) modernization. The magazine has 3/20-missile horizontal drums. Has flag accommodations for six officers and twelve enlisted in addition to crew. Mk 76 Mod. 6 missile-control system. Mk 68 fire-control system for the 127-mm gun. Has Mk 14 weapon direction system, WSC-3 SATCOMM, and NTDS data system. Mk 114 ASW fire-control system. The fixed Mk 32 ASW TT are mounted within the superstructure.

◆ **1 Bainbridge class**

	Bldr	Program	Laid down	L	In serv.
CGN 25 BAINBRIDGE	Bethlehem Steel, Quincy	FY 59	5-59	15-4-61	6-10-62

D: 8,000 tons light (9,100 fl) **S:** 30+ kts
Dim: 172.21 (167.65 wl) × 17.57 × 9.5 (sonar, 7.3 hull) **Electric:** 14,500 kw
A: 8/Harpoon SSM (IV × 2)—4/Mk 10 launchers (II × 2; 80 Standard SM-2 ER missiles)—2/20-mm Mk 15 CIWS gatling AA (I × 2)—4/12.7-mm mg (I × 4)—1/Mk 116/ASROC ASW RL (VIII × 1)—6/324-mm Mk 32 ASW TT (III × 2)

Bainbridge (CGN 25)—new radars, Mk 15 CIWS added J. Zeitlhofer, 8-85

Bainbridge (CGN 25) G. Arra, 8-85

Electron Equipt: Radar: 1/LN-66, 1/SPS-67, 1/SPS-48C, 1/SPS-49, 4/SPG-55B
Sonar: 1/SQQ-23—TACAN: URN-25
EW: WLR-1, SLQ-32(V)3, Mk 36 SRBOC (VI × 6)
M: 2 G.E. D2G reactors, 2 GT; 2 props; 70,000 hp **Man:** 42 officers, 500 men

REMARKS: In refit-modernization at Puget Sound NSY from 6-74 to 9-76 to improve AAW; refit completed at San Diego in 4-77. Obsolete 76.2-mm DP removed, temporarily replaced by two 20-mm AA, 1978-79. Two quadruple Harpoon canister launch groups replaced the 20-mm AA during 1979, those to port firing forward and those to starboard firing aft. Large deckhouse added aft to house NTDS data system. Two Mk 15 Vulcan/Phalanx 20-mm AA added during 10-83 to 4-85 refit; SPS-37 replaced by SPS-49, SLQ-32(V)3 ECM/ESM and Mk 36 RBOC chaff-flare system added and missile system updated to launch standard SM-2 ER. Helicopter platform but no hangar. Mk 111 ASW fire-control system, two Mk 76 missile fire-control systems. Mk 14 weapons direction system. Has flag accommodations for 6 officers, 12 men.

◆ **1 Long Beach class (SCB 169 type)**

	Bldr	Program	Laid down	L	In serv.
CGN 9 LONG BEACH	Bethlehem Steel, (Quincy)	FY 57	2-12-57	14-7-59	9-9-61

D: 15,100 tons light (17,100 fl) **S:** 30.5 kts **Dim:** 219.75 × 22.35 × 9.45 (over sonar)
A: 8/Tomahawk SSM (IV × 2)—16/Harpoon SSM (IV × 2)—1/Mk 10 Mod. 0 and 1/Mk 10 Mod. 1 launcher (II × 2, 120 Standard SM-2 ER missiles)—2/127-mm 38-cal. DP (I × 2)—2/20-mm Mk 15 CIWS AA (I × 2)—1/Mk 116 ASROC ASW RL (VIII × 1)—6/324-mm ASW TT (III × 2)
Electron Equipt: Radar: 1/LN-66, 1/SPS-67, 1/SPS-48C, 1/SPS-49, 4/SPG-55D, 2/Mk 35
Sonar: SQQ-23 PAIR (single-dome)—TACAN: URN-25
EW: SLQ-32(V)3, Mk 36 SRBOC chaff RL (VI × 4)

Long Beach (CGN 9)—with Tomahawk box-launchers aft G. Arra, 12-85

NUCLEAR-POWERED GUIDED-MISSILE CRUISERS *(continued)*

Long Beach (CGN 9) POPHOT S. Given, R.A.N., 6-84

M: 2 Westinghouse C1W pressurized-water reactors, 8 Foster-Wheeler heat exchangers, 2 sets G.E. GT; 2 props; 80,000 hp
Electric: 17,000 kw
Man: 86 officers, 1,076 men, + flag group: 10 officers, 58 men

REMARKS: The first U.S. surface ship to have nuclear propulsion. Original number was CLGN 160, then CGN 160. Originally intended to carry Regulus-II cruise missiles and eight Polaris ballistic missiles. Under FY 77, Congress appropriated long-lead funds to equip the ship with Aegis radar/fire-control system, since it is planned to operate the ship into the twenty-first century; the radical modernization plans were, however, canceled in 12-76.

Long Beach entered Puget Sound NSY 6-10-80 for a less-extensive two-year modernization period. The Mk 12 launch system aft for Talos missiles (deactivated in 1978) was stripped out in 1979, and the pedestals on the after superstructure that formerly supported SPG-49B Talos missile-direction radars carry the two Mk 15 CIWS (Vulcan/Phalanx) gatling AA guns. Harpoon canister clusters, arranged to fire athwartships, were situated abaft the superstructure, which is surmounted by a tall lattice mast to support the antenna for the SPS-49 air-search radar. The "billboard" fixed-array antennas on the blockhouse-style forward superstructure were removed, and the forward superstructure received 44-mm aluminum armor. Radar foundations and waveguides also were armored. SPS-48C replaced SPS-12 on the foremast. The obsolescent Mk 30, 127-mm, dual-purpose guns and their two equally aged Mk 56 directors (Mk 35 radars) were retained, as were the original ASW weapons and the forward missile-launching arrangements. No helicopter hangar was provided, only a pad on the stern. The Mk 10 Mod. 0 launcher for Standard missiles has two magazine drums, each holding 20 missiles; the Mk 10 Mod. 1 in the upper position has four magazine drums. Standard SM-2 ER has been substituted for SM-1 ER. The *Long Beach* will continue to have flagship facilities (10 officers, 58 men), and extensive satellite-communications facilities are provided. The Tactical Flag Command Center (TFCC) will be added at her next overhaul, as will additional protective armor. Armored box-launchers for Tomahawk SSM replaced the Harpoon SSMs in 1985; the Harpoon canister launchers were relocated atop the after superstructure.

GUIDED-MISSILE CRUISERS

◆ 4 (+ 15 + 8) Ticonderoga class

	Bldr	Laid down	L	In serv.
CG 47 TICONDEROGA	Ingalls, Pascagoula	21-1-80	25-4-81	22-1-83
CG 48 YORKTOWN	Ingalls, Pascagoula	19-10-81	17-1-83	4-7-84
CG 49 VINCENNES	Ingalls, Pascagoula	20-10-82	14-1-84	6-7-85
CG 50 VALLEY FORGE	Ingalls, Pascagoula	14-4-83	23-6-84	18-1-86
CG 51 THOMAS S. GATES	Bath Iron Works	23-8-84	14-12-85	1-87
CG 52 BUNKER HILL	Ingalls, Pascagoula	11-1-84	11-3-85	8-86
CG 53 MOBILE BAY	Ingalls, Pascagoula	5-6-84	10-85	2-87
CG 54 ANTIETAM	Ingalls, Pascagoula	15-11-84	2-86	7-87
CG 55 LEYTE GULF	Ingalls, Pascagoula	18-3-85	6-86	11-87
CG 56 SAN JACINTO	Ingalls, Pascagoula	22-7-85	10-86	3-88
CG 57 LAKE CHAMPLAIN	Ingalls, Pascagoula	2-86	4-87	6-88
CG 58 N.	Bath Iron Works	-86	1-87	6-88
CG 59 N.	Ingalls, Pascagoula	6-86	9-87	1-89
CG 60 N.	Bath Iron Works	. . .	. . .	3-89
CG 61 N.	Bath Iron Works	. . .	. . .	7-89
CG 62 N.	Ingalls, Pascagoula	. . .	. . .	10-89
CG 63 N.	Bath Iron Works	. . .	. . .	. . .
CG 64 N.	Bath Iron Works	. . .	. . .	. . .
CG 65 N.	Ingalls, Pascagoula	. . .	. . .	. . .
CG 66 N.	. . .	. . .	. . .	. . .
CG 67 N.	. . .	. . .	. . .	. . .
CG 68 N.	. . .	. . .	. . .	. . .
CG 69 N.	. . .	. . .	. . .	. . .
CG 70 N.	. . .	. . .	. . .	. . .
CG 71 N.	. . .	. . .	. . .	. . .
CG 72 N.	. . .	. . .	. . .	. . .
CG 73 N.	. . .	. . .	. . .	. . .

Authorized: CG 47 in FY 78, CG 48 in FY 80, CG 49–50 in FY 81, CG 51–53 in FY 82, CG 54–56 in FY 83, CG 57–59 in FY 84, CG 60–62 in FY 85, CG 63–65 in FY 86; planned: 2/yr. through CG 73 in FY 90

D: 7,260 tons light (9,530 fl; CG 49: 9,400; CG 52: 9,500 fl)
S: 30+ kts **Dim:** 172.5 (162.4 wl) × 16.76 × 6.52 (9.57 over sonar)
A: CG 47–51: 2/Mk 26 Mod. 1 launchers (II × 2; 68 Standard SM-2 MR and 20 ASROC) — 8/Harpoon SSM (IV × 2) — 2/127-mm Mk 45 DP (I × 2) — 2/20-mm Mk 15 CIWS AA (I × 2) — 4/12.7-mm mg (I × 4) — 6/324-mm Mk 32 ASW TT (III × 2) — 1 or 2/SH-2F LAMPS-I (CG 49-51: SH-60B LAMPS-III) ASW helicopters
CG 52–73: 2/Mk 41 Mod. 0 vertical launch groups (122 missiles: Standard SM-2 MR, Tomahawk, and ASROC — no ASROC in CG 52–55) — 2/127-mm Mk 45 Mod. 1 DP (I × 2) — 2/20-mm Mk 15 CIWS

GUIDED-MISSILE CRUISERS *(continued)*

Yorktown (CG 48)—on initial sea trials Ingalls SB, 17-1-84

Vincennes (CG 49)—note lighter tripod masts and lower superstructure amidships than on CG 47 and CG 48

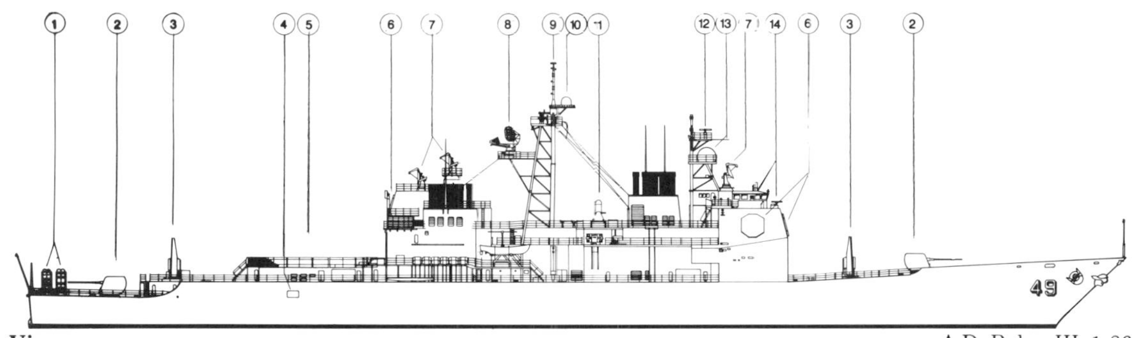

Vincennes A.D. Baker III, 1-86

1. Harpoon SSM 2. 127-mm Mk 45 DP 3. Mk 26 GMLS 4. Mk 32 ASW TT (behind shutters) 5. helicopter deck 6. AN/SPY-1A radar 7. AN/SPG-62 illuminator 8. AN/SPS-49(V)6 radar 9. AN/URN-25 TACAN 10. AN/SQQ-28 LAMPS antenna 11. 20-mm Mk 15 CIWS 12. AN/SPS-55 radar 13. AN/SPQ-9 radar director 14. AN/SPS-64 radar

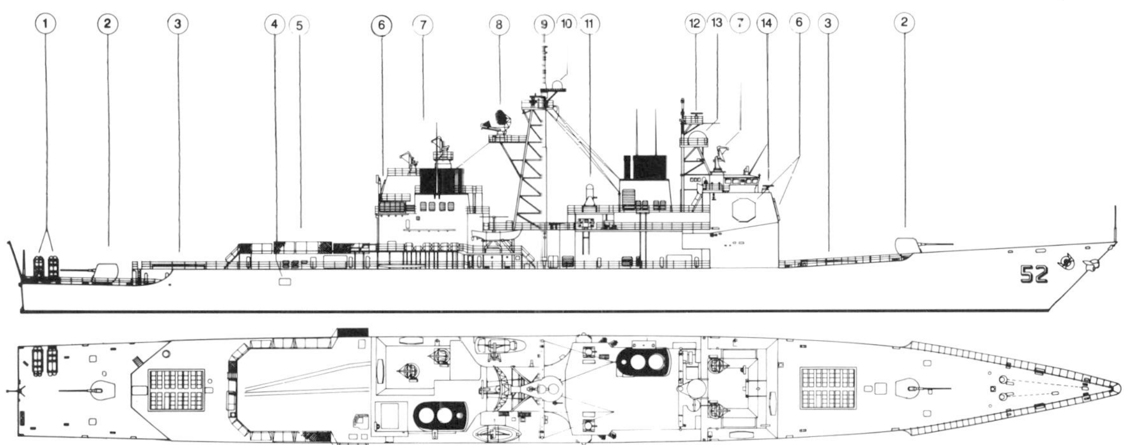

Bunker Hill (CG 52) A.D. Baker III

1. Harpoon SSM 2. 127-mm Mk 45 DP 3. Mk 41 Mod. 0 vertical launch 4. Mk 32 ASW TT (behind shutters) 5. helicopter deck 6. AN/SPY-1A radar 7. AN/SPG-62 illuminator 8. AN/SPS-49(V)6 radar 9. AN/URN-25 TACAN 10. AN/SQQ-28 LAMPS antenna 11. 20-mm Mk 15 CIWS 12. AN/SPS-55 radar 13. AN/SPQ-9 radar director 14. AN/SPS-64 radar

GUIDED-MISSILE CRUISERS *(continued)*

Valley Forge (CG 50)

Ingalls SB, 10-85

Bunker Hill (CG 52)—note tripod after mast, vertical launchers, reduced superstructure amidships V. Piecyk/RCA, 11-83

Ticonderoga (CG 47) L. & L. Van Ginderen, 9-85

Vincennes (CG 49) Ingalls SB, 1985

AA (I × 2)—6/324-mm Mk 32 Mod. 14 ASW TT (III × 2)—1 or 2/SH-60B LAMPS-III ASW helicopters

Electron Equipt: Radar: 1/SPS-53 (CG 49–73: SPS-64), 1/SPS-55, 1/SPS-49(V)6, 1/SPY-1A (CG 59–73: SPY-1B), 4/SPG-62, 1/SPQ-9A

Sonar: CG 47–55: SQS-53A (CG 54, 55: SQR-19 also); CG 56–73: SQQ-89 (SQS-53B, SQR-19)

TACAN: SRN-25—IFF: UPX-29 interrogator

EW: SLQ-32(V)3, Mk 36 SRBOC chaff RL (VI × 4)

M: 4.G.E. LM-2500 gas turbines; 2/5-bladed CP props; 86,000 hp (80,000 normal)

Electric: 7,500 kw **Fuel:** 2,000 tons **Range:** 6,000/20

Man: 33 officers, 329 men

Remarks: Greatly revised version of the *Spruance*-class destroyer, using same hull and propulsion but incorporating the Aegis Mk 7 weapon system (SPY-1A phased-array radar, four missile illuminator radars, Mk 26 missile-launch system, etc.). Designa-

GUIDED-MISSILE CRUISERS *(continued)*

tion changed from DDG to CG in late 1979. A total of 27 to be built. Named for battles and campaigns, except for CG 51, named for a former Secretary of Defense and of the Navy.

Each Mk 26 Mod. 1 missile-launcher magazine holds 44 missiles, the forward magazine holding the 20 ASROC. The Mk 86 fire-control system for the 127-mm guns provides no AA capability in this class, as no SPG-60 radar is carried. The R.C.A.-built Aegis Mk 7 Mod. 2 system, which uses 12 UYK-7 and 1 UYK-20 computers, uses the four fixed faces of the SPY-1A radar to detect and track up to several hundred targets simultaneously; the four illuminators are slaved to the system and can, through time-share switching, serve more than a dozen missiles in the air at once; the Mk 99 missile fire-control *system* uses 4 Mk 80 *illuminator-directors* with SPG-62 *radars.* The UPX-29 IFF circular antenna array is carried on the mainmast. The Harpoon missiles are in an exposed position at the extreme stern. Bow bulwarks were required to keep decks dry, as draft was increased about one meter over that of the original *Spruance* design. No fin stabilization is fitted. CG 48's keel was "laid" at Yorktown, Virginia, by President Reagan as part of the ceremonies commemorating the defeat of the British there in 1781; actual structural work commenced 12-81 at Pascagoula, Mississippi.

Modifications to accept newly developed equipments are to be phased in, with the Ingalls yard intended to receive the building contract for the first ship of each new block:

- Block 0: CG 47, 48: Basic Aegis Mk 7 system, with SPY-1A, Weapons Control System Mk 1, Standard SM-2 MR Block 1 missiles, the Mk 116 Mod. 4 ASW fire-control system, and the SH-2F LAMPS-I ASW helicopter.
- Block 1: CG 49–51: The RAST haul-down and deck-maneuvering system is added for SH-60B LAMPS-III helicopters, Standard SM-2 MR Block 2 missiles are carried, Aegis has improved data displays, and the EW suit is enhanced. Both masts tripods vice quadripods.
- Block 2: CG 52–55: The Mk 40 Mod. 0 vertical-launch system is substituted for the Mk 26 twin-armed launchers, vertical-launch Tomahawk capability is added, as is an improved LINK II data-link system. As vertical-launch ASROC will not be ready in time, these ships will not receive a launch capability until early 1990s refits. Congress mandated the omission of SPS-49 radars and the SQQ-28 LAMPS-III data link in CG 54–56, but gave permission in 5-84 to add the equipment. CG 54 and 55 will have stand-alone SQR-19 linear towed passive sonar arrays.
- Block 3: CG 56 will introduce the SQQ-89 integrated ASW suite, with SQQ-53B hull-mounted sonar, SQR-19 towed array, and the Mk 116 Mod. 6 ASW fire-control system.
- Block 4: CG 59 and later: The lighter SPY-1B radar, with improved radiating characteristics, is substituted for SPY-1A, and new computers (UYK-44) will be employed, along with improved displays.

There have been a number of ill-informed criticisms of this class, which is nonetheless *the* most capable AAW platform in any navy. The ships are not unstable, although quite cramped, and have sufficient stability margin to operate at up to 10,200 tons full load. CG 47 and 48 carry a small amount of lead ballast, but later units will not. The final programmed ship, CG 73, should be delivered in 1994. All carry up to 36 Mk 46 ASW torpedoes.

◆ **9 Belknap class (SCB 212 type)**

	Bldr	Laid down	L	In serv.
CG 26 Belknap	Bath Iron Works	5-2-62	20-7-63	7-11-64
CG 27 Josephus Daniels	Bath Iron Works	23-4-62	2-12-63	8-5-65
CG 28 Wainwright	Bath Iron Works	2-7-62	25-4-64	8-1-66
CG 29 Jouett	Puget Sound NSY	25-9-62	30-6-64	3-12-66
CG 30 Horne	San Francisco NSY	12-9-62	30-10-64	15-4-67
CG 31 Sterett	Puget Sound NSY	25-9-62	30-6-64	8-4-67
CG 32 Wiliam H. Standley	Bath Iron Works	29-7-63	19-12-64	9-7-66
CG 33 Fox	Todd SY, San Pedro	15-1-63	21-11-64	28-5-66
CG 34 Biddle	Bath Iron Works	9-12-63	2-7-65	21-1-67

Authorized: Three in FY 61 and six in FY 62

Josephus Daniels (CG 27) L. & L. Van Ginderen, 8-85

Biddle (CG 34)—with broader 04 level deckhouse than sisters, SPS-40 radar G. Gyssels, 6-84

Wainwright (CG 28) G. Arra, 1984

William H. Standley (CG 32) G. Arra, 10-85

Jouett (CG 29)—amidships area G. Arra, 1984

GUIDED-MISSILE CRUISERS *(continued)*

D: 5,340 light/6,570 std. tons (8,065 fl; CG 26: 8,575) **S:** 33 kts
Dim: 166.72 × 16.76 × 5.9 (8.8 over sonar)
A: 8/Harpoon SSM (IV × 2)—1/Mk 10 Mod. 7 launcher (II × 1, 40 Standard SM-2 ER and 20 ASROC missiles)—1/127-mm Mk 42 DP (aft)—2/20-mm Mk 15 CIWS AA (I × 2)—4/12.7-mm mg (I × 4)—6/324-mm Mk 32 ASW TT (III × 2; 18 Mk 46 torpedoes)—1/SH-2D Sea Sprite LAMPS-I helicopter
Electron Equipt: Radar: 1/LN-66, 1/SPS-10F or SPS-67, 1/SPS-49(V)3 (except CG 31–34: SPS-40), 1/SPS-48C, 2/SPG-55D, 1/SPG-53A
Sonar: 1/SQS-26BX (CG 26: SQS-53A, CG 27: SQS-26AXR)
TACAN: SRN-6 or URN-25
EW: SLQ-32(V)3, Mk 36 SRBOC chaff RL (VI × 4)
M: 2 sets GT; 2/6-bladed props; 85,000 hp
Boilers: CG 24, CG 28, CG 32, CG 34: 4 Foster-Wheeler; others: 4 Combustion Engineering; 84 kg/cm², 520°C
Electric: 6,800 kw **Range:** 2,500/30; 8,000/14
Man: 31 officers, 461 men + flag group: 6 officers, 12 enlisted

Remarks: Formerly typed DLG; classified CG on 1-7-75. CG 26, severely damaged in collision with CV 67 in Mediterranean in November 1975, was out of commission for repairs at Philadelphia until 10-5-80. She had her 76.2-mm guns replaced by 8 Harpoon SSM, received SPS-48C and SPS-49 radar, SM-2 MR missiles, the SLQ-25 Nixie towed torpedo decoy system, improved electronics (including NTDS Mod. 4) and communications gear, and SQS-53A sonar and is now officially considered to be a separate class. In a further refit, from 7-85 to 7-86, the ship is being equipped as 6th Fleet Flagship, with enhanced communications and staff accommodations at the expense of the helicopter hanger. CG 31 was the first to lose her 76.2-mm, in 1976, to make way for eight Harpoon ASM (IV × 2), now also carried by the others (firing forward to port, aft to starboard). By 1983, all but CG 31 had the Mk 15 gatling CIWS. CG 28 has been used as trials ship for SM-2 ER, now carried by all units of the class. The 127-mm gun is controlled by a Mk 68 radar GFCS. Mk 114 (CG 26: Mk 116) ASW fire-control system, one Mk 11 (CG 26: Mk 14) weapon-direction system, and two Mk 76 Mod. 9 missile fire-control systems. These ships will not receive the SH-60B LAMPS-III ASW helicopter. CG 26, 28, 30, and 31 are scheduled to receive the Tactical Flag Command Center in 1983-85. All will eventually have the SPS-10F replaced by SPS-67, and the SPS-48 updated to SPS-48E; the SYS-2 weapon-control system will be added. Several have enhanced electronics warfare suites, with additional equipment over the SLQ-32(V)3 fit. All are scheduled to receive the NTU (New Threat Upgrade) modernization, with Weapons Direction System Mk 14 and missile tracking set SYR-1 during refits from 1986 to the early 1990s.

◆ **9 Leahy class (SCB 172 type)**

	Bldr	Laid down	L	In serv.
CG 16 Leahy	Bath Iron Works	3-12-59	1-7-61	4-8-62
CG 17 Harry E. Yarnell	Bath Iron Works	31-5-60	9-12-61	2-2-63
CG 18 Worden	Bath Iron Works	19-9-60	2-6-62	3-8-63
CG 19 Dale	New York SB	6-9-60	28-7-62	23-11-63
CG 20 Richmond K. Turner	New York SB	9-1-61	6-4-63	13-6-64
CG 21 Gridley	Puget Sound SB & DD Co.	15-7-60	31-7-61	25-5-63
CG 22 England	Todd SY, Los Angeles	4-10-60	6-3-62	7-12-63
CG 23 Halsey	San Francisco NSY	26-8-60	15-1-62	20-7-63
CG 24 Reeves	Puget Sound NSY	1-7-60	12-5-62	15-5-64

Authorized: 3 in FY 58, 6 in FY 59

Worden (CG 18) LSPH E. Pitman, R.A.N., 7-85

Harry E. Yarnell (CG 17)—CIWS, SPS-43 radar, and SLQ-32 EW suite with Harpoon, Vulcan/Phalanx L. & L. Van Ginderen, 3-84

Reeves (CG 24) LSPH E. Pitman, R.A.N., 9-85

Gridley (CG 21)—enlarged superstructure amidships G. Arra, 11-85

Leahy (CG 16) LSPH E. Pitman, R.A.N., 4-85

D: 6,070 tons (8,200 fl) **S:** 33 kts **Dim:** 162.46 × 16.15 × 5.9 (7.9 over sonar)
A: 8/Harpoon SSM (IV × 2)—2/Mk 10 launchers (II × 2, 80 Standard SM-2 ER missiles)—2/20-mm Mk 15 CIWS AA (I × 2)—4/12.7-mm mg (I × 4)—1/Mk 116/ASROC ASW RL (VIII × 2)—6/324-mm Mk 32 ASW TT (III × 2)
Electron Equipt: Radar: 1/LN-66, 1/SPS-10F or SPS-67, 1/SPS-49(V)3, (CG 20, 24: SPS-37), 1/SPS-48A, 4/SPG-55B
Sonar: SQS-23 (CG 17: SQQ-23B PAIR, single-dome)
TACAN: SRN-6 or URN-25
EW: SLQ-32(V)3, Mk 36 SRBOC chaff RL (VI × 4) (CG 21, 23, 24: WLR-1, WLR-3 also)
M: CG 16 to CG 19: 2 sets G.E., CG 20 to CG 22: 2 sets de Laval, CG 23 and CG 24: 2 sets Allis Chalmers GT; 2/5-bladed props; 85,000 hp
Boilers: CG 16 to CG 20: 4 Babcock & Wilcox; others: 4 Combustion Engineering; 84 kg/cm², 520°C
Electric: 6,800 kw **Fuel:** 1,800 tons **Range:** 2,500/30; 8,000/14
Man: 27–31 officers, 366–376 men + flag group: 6 officers, 12 men

Remarks: These are former DLGs, classified CG on 1-7-75. During overhauls 1967-72, the *Leahy*-class ships received an advanced version of the Mk 76 missile fire-control system, permitting firing of Standard SM-1 ER missiles. CG 16 was the first to complete this overhaul and returned to active service on 17-8-68. All had received SM-2 ER missile capability by 1985. The four 76.2-mm (II × 2) guns have been removed from all, and their gun tubs are used as locations for Harpoon missile launchers. Like CGN 25, these ships are, unfortunately, completely devoid of larger gun armament. There are no reloads for the ASROC system. CG 19 received SPS-49 in place of SPS-43 in 1976; the others were similarly re-equipped, and all now have the

GUIDED-MISSILE CRUISERS *(continued)*

SLQ-32 (V)3 EW system, with CG 21 and CG 24 also retaining the older WLR-1 and WLR-3 equipment, updated. Mk 76 missile fire-control system, with 4 SPG-55B radar trackers/illuminators. Mk 114 ASW fire control, Mk 14 weapons-control system. All have NTDS data system and WSC-3 SATCOMM equipment.

NOTE: The *Albany*-class guided-missile cruiser *Albany* (CG 10, ex-CA 123), in reserve since 29-8-80, was stricken 30-6-85 for possible museum use; sister *Chicago* (CG 11, ex-CA 136) was stricken 31-1-84. *Galveston*-class guided-missile cruiser *Oklahoma City* (CG 5, ex-CL 91), stricken 15-12-79 but retained in partial preservation at Bremerton, is to be used as a museum or as a target.

HEAVY CRUISERS

◆ **2 Des Moines class** — In reserve

	Bldr	Laid down	L	In serv.
CA 134 DES MOINES	Bethlehem, Fore River	28-5-45	27-9-46	16-11-48
CA 139 SALEM	Bethlehem, Fore River	4-7-45	25-3-47	14-5-49

The stricken *Newport News* (ex-CA 148) moored outboard *Des Moines* (CA 134) and *Salem* (CA 139) at Philadelphia Naval Shipyard — A.D. Baker, 8-84

D: 17,225 tons (21,470 fl) **S:** 32 kts **Dim:** 218.42 (213.36 wl) × 22.96 × 7.5
A: 9/203-mm (III × 3) — 12/127-mm DP (II × 6) — 20–22/76.2-mm DP (II × 10 or 11)
Electron Equipt: Radar: 1/SG-6, 1/SPS-8, 1/SPS-6C (CA 139: SPS-12), 2/Mk 13, 4/Mk 25, 4/Mk 35 (CA 139: 2/Mk 34 also)
TACAN: URN-6
M: 4 sets GT; 4 props; 120,000 hp **Electric:** 7,700 kw
Boilers: 4 Babcock & Wilcox; 43.9 kg/cm², 454°C
Armor: Belt: 102–152-mm; Upper deck: 25-mm; Lower deck: 85-mm; Turrets: 203-mm face, 95-mm sides, 102-mm roof; Barbettes: 160-mm; Conning Tower: 102–160-mm; Steering Room: 96–160-mm
Fuel: 2,600 tons **Range:** 8,000/15 **Man:** 105 officers, 1,745 men (wartime)

REMARKS: CA 139 to reserve on 30-1-59, CA 134 on 14-7-61, both at Philadelphia. Sister *Newport News* (CA 148), in reserve since 27-6-75, was stricken on 30-6-78 but has remained at Philadelphia as a possible source of spares. CA 134 has ten twin 76.2-mm Mk 34 DP mounts, her sister has eleven. Each has two Mk 54 directors (with Mk 13 radar) for the 203-mm guns, four Mk 37 fire-control systems for the 127-mm guns, and four Mk 56 and Mk 63 fire-control systems for the 76.2-mm guns. Magazines can carry 1,350 rounds 203-mm, 6,060 rounds 127-mm, 12,000 rounds 76.2-mm. All radar antennas have been removed for storage. To be retained for possible reactivation as naval gunfire support ships; are in excellent condition but have badly outdated electronics.

GUIDED-MISSILE DESTROYERS

◆ **0 (+1 + 6282) Arleigh Burke class**

	Bldr	Laid down	L	In serv.
DDG 51 ARLEIGH BURKE	Bath Iron Wks.	14-12-87	21-8-88	10-89
DDG 52 N. . .	. . .	. . .	. . .	. . .
DDG 53 N. . .	. . .	. . .	. . .	. . .
DDG 54 N. . .	. . .	. . .	. . .	. . .

Authorized: DDG 51 in FY 85; programmed: 3/yr FY 87–FY 90, 5/yr thereafter

D: 6,609 tons light (8,300 fl) **S:** 30+ kts
Dim: 153.77 (142.03 wl) × 20.40 (18.0 wl) × 6.09 (9.32 over sonar)
A: 2 Mk 41 Mod. 0 vertical-launch groups (1/64-cell, 1/32-cell; 90 Standard SM-2 MR Block 2, ASROC and Tomahawk missiles) — 8/Harpoon SSM (IV × 2) — 1/127-mm Mk 45 Mod. 1 DP — 2/20-mm Mk 15 CIWS AA (I × 2) — 6/324-mm Mk 32 ASW TT (III × 2)
Electron Equipt: Radar: 1/SPS-64, 1/SPS-67, 1/SPY-1D, 3/SPG-62
Sonar: SQS-53C, SQR-19 towed array

Arleigh Burke (DDG 51) — late 1984 concept — V. Piecyk/RCA, 11-84

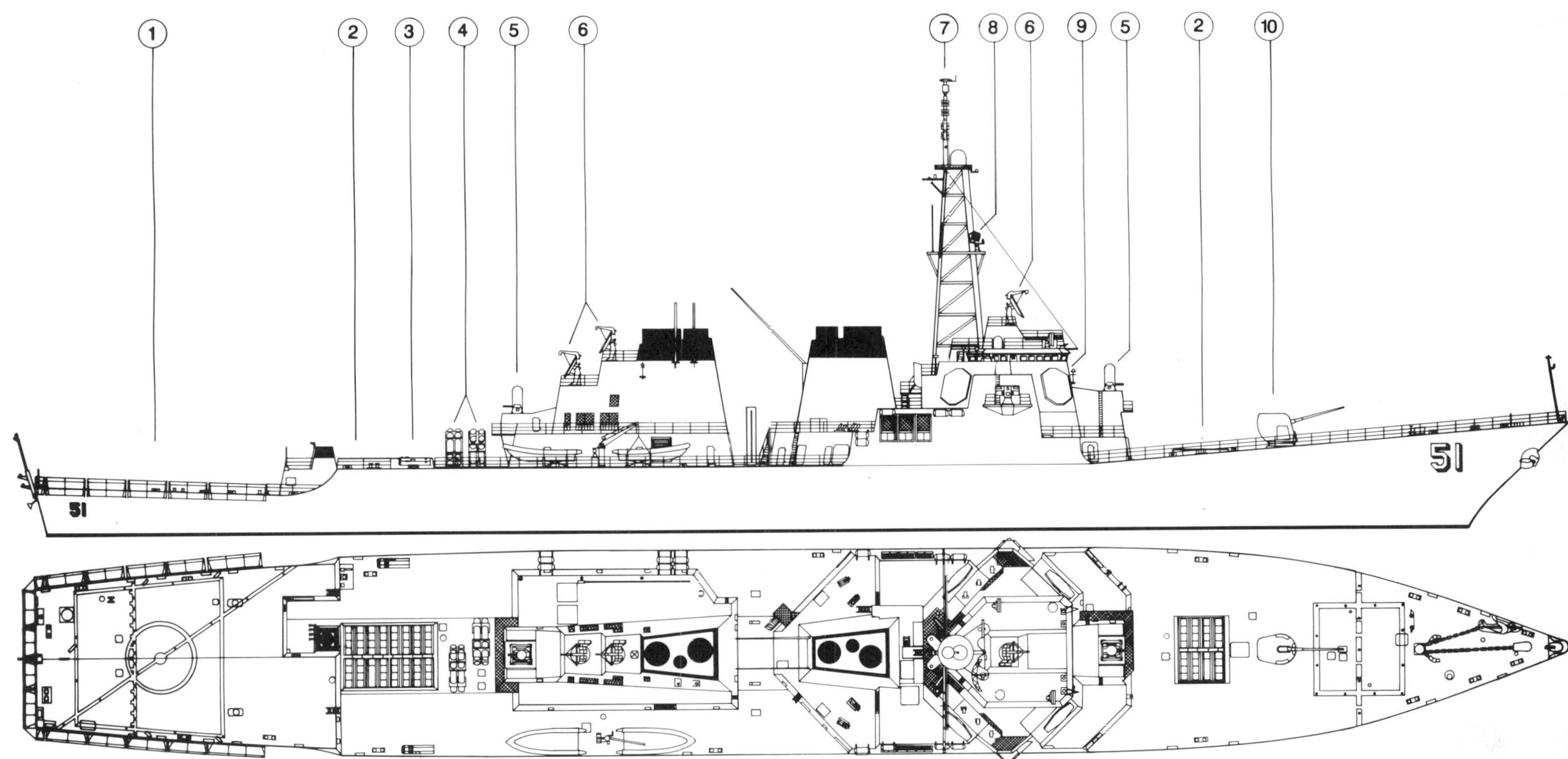

A.D. Baker

Arleigh Burke (DDG 51)
1. helicopter deck 2. Mk 41 vertical-launch missile system (VLS) 3. Mk 32 triple ASW TT 4. Harpoon SSM 5. Mk 15 CIWS 20-mm AA 6. SPG-62 radars for Mk 99 illuminator system 7. URN-25 TACAN 8. SPS-67 radar (SPS-64 to port) 9. SPY-1D radar 10. 127-mm Mk 45 DP

GUIDED-MISSILE DESTROYERS *(continued)*

Arleigh Burke (DDG 51)—design model

RCA, 4-85

Arleigh Burke (DDG 51)—design model RCA, 4-85

Arleigh Burke (DDG 51)—design model RCA, 4-85

EW: SLQ-32(V)2, Mk 36 SRBOC chaff RL (VI × 4)
TACAN: URN-25—IFF: UPX-29

M: 4 G.E. LM-2500-30 gas turbines; 2/5-bladed CP props; 100,000 hp
Electric: 7,500 kw
Fuel: . . . **Range:** 4,400/20 **Man:** 303 tot. (23 officers, 280 men)

Remarks: This design, overly long in development, is intended to provide a general-purpose destroyer capable of carrying out its assignments in the threat environment of the 1990s and beyond. The ships will have steel superstructures and the first comprehensive CBR protection system in a U.S. Navy ship. Over 130 tons of armor will be used for vital spaces. Congress has forced development of the RACER (Rankine-Cycle Energy Recovery) system, to provide cruising power by using the waste heat from one of the gas turbines to generate about 8,000 propulsion horsepower; it will not be incorporated until at least the 10th ship and may not be used at all. With or without RACER, the ships will have considerably reduced endurance as compared to other recent USN destroyers. The hull form is unusually broad in relation to length; fin stabilizers are not planned.

The flight deck will accept the SH-60B/F Seahawk helicopter, and the SQQ-28 LAMPS-III data-link/control system will be installed. The SLQ-25 Nixie towed torpedo decoy system will be carried.

The Aegis SPY-1D will have all four faces mounted on the forward superstructure; the system will employ 5 UYK-43B computers, and the Combat Information Center will be below the main deck. The gun will be controlled by the Mk 160 Mod. 4 GFCS (which uses radar input data from the SPS-67 or SPY-1D); the planned Mk 121 Mod. 0 Seafire t.v./laser/infrared director has been canceled but may be replaced by a less-costly system. The gun will have no AA capability and will be furnished with a probable 600 rounds of ammunition. The Standard SM-2 MR Block 2 missiles will be controlled by the Aegis system, using the three Mk 80 illuminators for terminal designation only. The Mk 116 Mod. 7 ASW f.c.s. will be carried. WSC-3 satellite communications and Links 11 and 14 will be fitted.

It is planned to have two or three shipyards participate in the *Arleigh Burke*-class program, with at least the first 29 ships to be built to the design described above. The first unit will cost about $1.1 billion FY 83 dollars, with follow-up ships tightly constrained to not more than $700 million each. The contract for the first unit was signed 2-4-85.

◆ **4 Kidd class** Bldr: Ingalls, Pascagoula Authorized: FY 79 Supplemental

	Laid down	L	In serv.
DDG 993 Kidd (ex-*Kouroush*)	26-6-78	11-8-79	27-6-81
DDG 994 Callaghan (ex-*Daryush*)	23-10-78	1-12-79	29-8-81
DDG 995 Scott (ex-*Nader*)	12-2-79	1-3-80	24-10-81
DDG 996 Chandler (ex-*Andushirvan*)	7-5-79	24-5-80	13-3-82

Chandler (DDG 996) LSPH E. Pitman, R.A.N., 6-84

GUIDED-MISSILE DESTROYERS *(continued)*

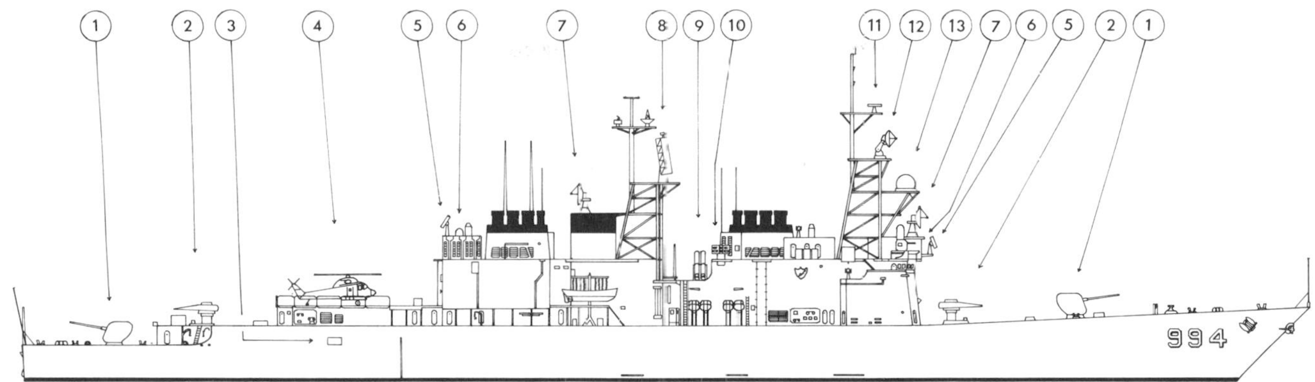

Kidd (DDG 993) Robert Dumas

1. 127-mm Mk 45 DP gun 2. Mk 26 guided-missile launcher 3. ports for Mk 32 ASW TT (III × 2) 4. SH-2F helicopter 5. OE-82 UHF SATCOMM antennas 6. Mk 15 CIWS 7. SPG-51D missile-control radar 8. SPS-48C 3-D radar 9. Harpoon SSM (IV × 2) 10. SLQ-32(V)2 array 11. SPS-55 radar 12. SPG-60 radar gun director 13. SPQ-9A radar gun director

Kidd (DDG 993) G. Arra, 1982

Callaghan (DDG 994)—with Mk 15 CIWS, URN-25 TACAN G. Arra, 10-85

Scott (DDG 995) L. & L. Van Ginderen, 6-84

D: 9,574 tons (fl) **S:** 30+ kts
Dim: 171.7 (161.23 wl) × 16.76 × 7.01 (10.06 over sonar)
A: 1/Mk 26 Mod. 3 and 1/Mk 26 Mod. 4 launcher (II × 2, 52 Standard SM-1 MR and 16 ASROC missiles)—8/Harpoon SSM (IV × 2)—2/127-mm Mk 45 DP (I × 2)—2/20-mm Mk 15 CIWS AA (I × 2)—4/12.7-mm mg (I × 4)—6/324-mm Mk 32 ASW TT (III × 2; 24 torpedoes)—1/SH-SF LAMPS-I ASW helicopter
Electron Equipt: Radar: 1/SPS-53, 1/SPS-55, 1/SPS-48C, 2/SPG-51D, 1/SPG-60, 1/SPQ-9A
Sonar: SQS-53A—TACAN: URN-25
EW: SLQ-32(V)2, Mk 36 SRBOC chaff RL (VI × 4)
M: 4 G.E. LM-2500 gas turbines; 2/5-bladed CP props; 86,000 hp
Electric: 6,000 kw **Range:** 3,300/30; 6,000/20 **Man:** 32 officers, 332 men

Remarks: The original order for these superb ships placed with the U.S. Navy by Iran in 1974 was for six; two were canceled before the order to Ingalls Shipbuilding for the remaining four was issued on 23-3-78. DDG 993 and DG 994 were canceled by the new Iranian government on 3-2-79, and the other pair shortly thereafter. Their completion for the U.S. Navy was authorized by the U.S. Congress under a Fiscal 1979 Supplementary Appropriation Act. At approximately $510 million each, they represented a considerable bargain. The first two were to have been numbered DD 995 and DD 996; the new numbers do not fit in USN hull-numbering sequence for guided-missile destroyers.

The capability to control Standard SM-2 MR missiles will be backfitted at a later date, and the ships are planned to receive the NTU (New Threat Upgrade) modernization. Two Mk 74 missile fire-control systems (with SPG-55D radar tracker/illuminators) are carried, as well as the Mk 86 Mod. 5 gunfire-control system, which uses the SPQ-9A radar for surface fire and the SPG-60 for AA (the latter can also be used as a missile illuminator). The ASROC missiles are carried in the larger Mk 26 Mod. 1 missile-launch system's magazine, which is aft; the Mk 116 underwater battery fire-control system is carried. SLQ-25 Nixie towed anti-torpedo decoys are fitted; the ships were not intended to have the SQR-19A TACTASS towed passive sonar array, but it may be backfitted later. During post-commissioning yard periods, URN-25 TACAN replaced URN-20, Harpoon was added amidships, and two Vulcan/Phalanx MK 15 CIWS were installed.

These ships were given better air-intake filter systems than the U.S. *Spruance* class has, in order to handle the dust and sand prevailing in Iranian operating areas. They also have greater air-conditioning capacity. These features should make them invaluable for duties in the Indian Ocean. The Iranian Navy planned to type them as cruisers. Full-load displacement has grown by over 1,000 tons above the original plan, partly as a result of additional Kevlar and aluminum-alloy armor being added.

◆ **23 Charles F. Adams class (SCB 155 type) (modified ships*)**

	Bldr	Laid down	L	In serv.
DDG 2 Charles F. Adams	Bath Iron Works	16-6-58	8-9-59	10-9-60
DDG 3 John King	Bath Iron Works	25-8-58	30-1-60	4-2-61
DDG 4 Lawrence	New York SB	27-10-58	27-2-60	6-1-62
DDG 5 Claude V. Ricketts (ex-*Biddle*)	New York SB	18-5-59	16-4-60	5-5-62
DDG 6 Barney	New York SB	18-8-59	10-12-60	11-8-62
DDG 7 Henry B. Wilson	Defoe SB	28-2-58	22-4-59	17-12-60
DDG 8 Lynde McCormick	Defoe SB	4-4-58	9-9-60	3-6-61
DDG 9 Towers	Todd, Seattle	1-4-58	23-4-59	24-6-61
DDG 10 Sampson	Bath Iron Works	2-3-59	9-9-60	24-6-61
DDG 11 Sellers	Bath Iron Works	3-8-59	9-9-60	28-10-61
DDG 12 Robison	Defoe SB	23-4-59	27-4-60	9-12-61
DDG 13 Hoel	Defoe SB	1-6-59	4-8-60	16-6-62
DDG 14 Buchanan	Todd, Seattle	23-4-59	11-5-60	7-2-62
DDG 15 Berkeley	New York SB	1-6-60	29-7-61	15-12-62
DDG 16 Joseph Strauss	New York SB	27-12-60	9-12-61	20-4-63
DDG 17 Conyngham	New York SB	1-5-61	19-5-62	13-7-63
DDG 18 Semmes	Avondale SY	18-8-60	20-5-61	10-12-62
DDG 19 Tattnall*	Avondale SY	14-11-60	26-8-61	13-4-63
DDG 20 Goldsborough*	Puget Sound SB & DD	3-1-61	15-12-61	9-11-63
DDG 21 Cochrane	Puget Sound SB & DD	31-7-61	18-7-62	21-3-64
DDG 22 Benjamin Stoddert*	Puget Sound SB & DD	11-6-62	8-1-63	12-9-64
DDG 23 Richard E. Byrd	Todd, Seattle	12-4-61	6-2-62	7-3-64
DDG 24 Waddell	Todd, Seattle	6-2-62	26-2-63	28-8-64

Authorized: 8 in FY 57, 5 in FY 58, 5 in FY 59, 3 in FY 60, and 2 in FY 61

GUIDED-MISSILE DESTROYERS *(continued)*

Tattnall (DDG 19)—modernized, with Mk 86 GFCS and other new electronics, but with no ASROC reload magazine G. Arra, 2-85

Robison (DDG 12)—Mk 11 launcher, SPS-40 radar, SLQ-32(V)2 EW, old TACAN G. Arra, 1984

Berkeley (DDG 15)—note two helicopter "VERTREP" areas outlined aft on deck G. Arra, 1984

Richard E. Byrd (DDG 23)—Mk 13 launcher, SPS-40 radar, ASROC reload magazine, bow anchor, SLQ-32(V)2 EW L. & L. Van Ginderen, 3-85

Cochrane (DDG 21)—with old TACAN, SLQ-32(V)2 EW, SPS 40, and 2 navigational radars LSPH E. Pitman, R.A.N., 9-85

D: 3,570 tons light (4,825 fl) **S:** 31.5 kts
Dim: 133.19 (128.0 wl) × 14.32 × 6.1 (8.3 over sonar)
A: 1/Mk 11 twin missile launcher or, beginning with DDG 15, 1/Mk 13 single launcher (4–6 Harpoon and 34–36 Standard SM-1 MR missiles)—2/127-mm Mk 42 DP (I × 2)—4/12.7 mm mg (I × 4)—1/Mk 116 ASROC ASW RL (VIII × 1; 8 or 12 missiles)—6/324-mm Mk 32 ASW TT (III × 2)
Electron Equipt: Radar: 1/SPS-10F, 1/SPS-40B/D, 1/SPS-52B, 2/SPG-51C, 1/SPG-53A (DDG 19, 20, 22: 1/LN-66, 1/SPS-10D, 1/SPS-40D, 1/SPS-52C, 1/SPQ-9A, 2/SPG-51D, 1/SPG-60)
Sonar: SQQ-23A or 1/SQS-23A (hull-mounted in DDG 2 to DDG 19: bow-mounted in DDG 20 to DDG 24)
EW: SLQ-32(V)2, SLQ-20, Mk 36 SRBOC (VI × 4)
TACAN: URN-25 or SRN-6

M: 2 sets GT; 2 props; 70,000 hp **Electric:** 2,200 kw (DDG 19, 20, 22; 3,000 kw)
Boilers: 4; 84 kg/cm², 520°C **Fuel:** 900 tons
Range: 1,600/30; 6,000/14 **Man:** 20–24 officers, 319–330 men

Remarks: Sisters DDG 25, DDG 26, and DDG 27, built at the Defoe Shipbuilding Company, Bay City, Michigan, were ordered by Australia; DDG 28, DDG 29, and DDG 30 were built at Bath Iron Works for the West German Navy. Ships with bow-mounted sonars have stem-mounted anchors. Many have been backfitted with an ASROC ASW missile reload magazine (with 4 missiles) beside the forward stack, to starboard. It was planned to give these ships a badly needed modernization, beginning with DDG 3 under FY 80. Costs rose enormously, and the program was cut to ten, permitting them to operate for another fifteen to twenty years. Congressional reluctance to spend $221 million per ship (then equal to the cost of a new FFG 7-class frigate) forced cancellation of even the reduced program.

The full modernization program was finally cut to only three ships: DDG 19, 20, and 22. DDG 19 underwent conversion 31-8-81 to 28-11-82 at Philadelphia; DDG 20 and 22 converted at Pearl Harbor 4-83 to 7-84 and 4-84 to 8-85. Changes include: replacement of the Mk 68 GFCS with Mk 86 Mod. 8 (with 1/SPQ-9A and 1/SPG-60 radar); SLQ-32(V)2, SLQ-20, and Mk 36 SRBOC replacing the original suite; the original missile f.c.s. replaced by Mk 74 Mod. 4, with the Weapons Direction System Mk 13 Mod. 4 replacing the original Mk 4; the addition of the SYS-1 data system with UYA-4 NTDS; upgrading the search radar suite to: 1/LN-66, 1/SPS-10D, 1/SPS-40D, and SPS-52C; improving the communications suite; and increasing the output of the four generator sets to 750 kw each. The ships can direct 3 Standard missiles simultaneously, using the SPG-60 and the two SPG-51D tracker/illuminators.

The non-conversion ships are also being upgraded during regular overhauls: SPS-40 has replaced the SPS-37 originally fitted to the first 13 ships in at least 8 units to date; SLQ-32(V)2 is replacing the WLR-1F and ULQ-6B suite, and Mk 36 SRBOC chaff launchers are being added; URN-25 lightweight TACAN is replacing SRN-6; the Mk 68 GFCS is receiving a digital computer system in DDG 4–6, 8–12, 15, 18, and 21; SPS-39A radars have been replaced by SPS-52B in nearly all, and other improvements are being made to the communications suites. Only four ships have the SQQ-23 sonar.

In ships with Mk 11 launchers, 4 Harpoons are carried; in Mk 13-equipped ships, 6 are carried. Several carry one or more small navigational radars.

◆ 10 Coontz class (SCB 142/149 type)

	Bldr	Laid down	L	In serv.
DDG 37 Farragut (ex-DLG 6)	Bethlehem Steel (Quincy)	3-6-57	18-7-58	12-10-60
DDG 38 Luce (ex-DLG 7)	Bethlehem Steel (Quincy)	1-10-57	11-12-58	20-5-61
DDG 39 Macdonough (ex-DLG 8)	Bethlehem Steel (Quincy)	15-4-58	9-7-59	4-11-61
DDG 40 Coontz (ex-DLG 9)	Puget Sound NSY	1-3-57	6-12-58	15-7-60

GUIDED-MISSILE DESTROYERS *(continued)*

DDG 41 King (ex-DLG 10)	Puget Sound NSY	1-3-57	6-12-58	17-11-60
DDG 42 Mahan (ex-DLG 11)	San Francisco NSY	31-7-57	7-10-59	25-8-60
DDG 43 Dahlgren (ex-DLG 12)	Philadelphia NSY	1-3-58	16-3-60	8-4-61
DDG 44 William V. Pratt (ex-DLG 13)	Philadelphia NSY	1-3-58	16-3-60	4-11-61
DDG 45 Dewey (ex-DLG 14)	Bath Iron Works	10-8-57	30-11-58	7-12-59
DDG 46 Preble (ex-DLG 15)	Bath Iron Works	16-12-57	23-5-59	9-5-60

Authorized: DDG 37 to 42 in FY 57, DDG 43 to 46 in FY 57

Mahan (DDG 42)—New Threat Upgrade trials ship, with SPS-48E radar, SM-2 ER missiles, etc. G. Arra, 8-84

Dahlgren (DDG 43) Pradignac & Leo, 1982

Macdonough (DDG 39)—with SLQ-32, but still with SPS-37 G. Arra, 8-85

Coontz (DDG 40) G. Arra, 1984

D: 4,700 tons (5,960–6,150 fl) **S:** 34 kts **Dim:** 156.21 × 16.0 × 7.6 (max.)
A: 8/Harpoon SSM (IV × 2)—1/Mk 10 Mod. 0 twin launcher (II × 1, 40 Standard SM-1 ER missiles)—1/127-mm Mk 42 automatic DP—4/12.7-mm mg (I × 4)—1/ASROC ASW RL (VIII × 1)—6/324-mm ASW TT (III × 2)
Electron Equipt: Radar: 1/SPS-53 or Raytheon 2900, 1/SPS-10B, 1/SPS-49, 1/SPS-48C (48E in DDG 42), 2/SPG-55B, 1/SPG-53A
Sonar: SQS-23 PAIR
TACAN: SRN-6
EW: SLQ-32(V)2, Mk 36 SRBOC (VI × 4)
M: DDG 37 to 39, DDG 45: 2 sets de Laval GT; others: 2 sets Allis-Chalmers GT; 2 props; 85,000 hp
Boilers: 4 Foster-Wheeler (Babcock & Wilcox in DDG 40 to DDG 46); 84 kg/cm², 520°C
Electric: 4,000 kw **Fuel:** 900 tons **Range:** 1,500/30; 6,000/14
Man: 21 officers, 356 men + flag group: 7 officers, 12 men

Remarks: These are the only *destroyers* with Standard SM-1 ER. Reclassified DDG from DLG 6 to DLG 15 in 1975. All modernized between 1970 and 1977 with Standard SM-1 ER missiles, NTDS (fitted earlier in DDG 40, DDG 41), SPS-48 radar, etc.; four 76.2-mm DP (II × 2) removed and Harpoon launchers installed in their former locations (firing forward to port, aft to starboard). DDG 37, the first to be modernized, received an ASROC reload magazine forward of the bridge and a taller after mast; to save weight and cost, the others were not similarly equipped. Missile fire control is Mk 76. A Mk 68 fire-control system is carried for the 127-mm gun. DDG 40 carried two Vulcan gatling guns (*not* Phalanx) in 1975. DDG 41 conducted Mk 15 CIWS Vulcan/Phalanx 20-mm gatling AA sea trials in 1973-74, before she was modernized; however, the ships will not receive two Vulcan/Phalanx, due to their age, space, and weight problems. Mk 111 Mod. 8 ASW fire-control systems and satellite-communications antenna systems in all units. The SQQ-23A PAIR sonar installed uses two separate domes. Helicopter landing pad on stern. The SPS-49 2-D air-search radar had replaced SPS-37 and the SLQ-32(V)2 EW system had replaced WLR-1, WLR-11, and ULQ-6B in nearly all by 1985.

DDG 42 is trials ship for the NTU (New Threat Upgrade) refit, with the SPS-48E 3-D radar, SPS-49(V)5 2-D radar, the SYS-2 IADT (Integrated Automatic Target Detection and Tracking) computerized action information system, Weapons Direction System Mk 14, and Standard SM-2 ER Block 2 missiles. The suite will not be backfitted to the others.

Note: Of the four *Decatur*-class guided-missile destroyers, *Parsons* (DDG 33, ex-DD 949), decommissioned 19-11-82, was stricken 15-5-84 and *John Paul Jones* (DDG 32, ex-DD 932), decommissioned 15-12-82, was stricken 30-11-85. *Decatur* (DDG 31, ex-DD 936), decommissioned 30-6-83, and *Somers* (DDG 34, ex-DD 947), decommissioned 19-11-82, remained on the Navy List at the end of 1985, awaiting striking and cannibalization.

DESTROYERS

◆ **31 Spruance class (SCN 275 type)** Bldr: Ingalls SB, Pascagoula, Miss. (Litton Industries)

	Laid down	L	In serv.
DD 963 Spruance	17-11-72	10-11-73	20-9-75
DD 964 Paul F. Foster	6-2-73	23-2-74	21-2-76
DD 965 Kinkaid	19-4-73	25-5-74	10-7-76
DD 966 Hewitt	23-7-73	24-8-74	25-9-76
DD 967 Elliot	15-10-73	19-12-74	22-1-76
DD 968 Arthur W. Radford	14-1-74	1-3-75	16-4-77
DD 969 Peterson	29-4-74	21-6-75	9-7-77
DD 970 Caron	1-7-74	24-6-75	1-10-77
DD 971 David R. Ray	23-9-74	23-8-75	19-11-77
DD 972 Oldendorf	27-12-74	21-10-75	4-3-78
DD 973 John Young	17-2-75	7-2-76	20-5-78
DD 974 Comte De Grasse	4-4-75	26-3-76	5-8-78
DD 975 O'Brien	9-5-75	8-7-76	3-12-77
DD 976 Merrill	16-6-75	1-9-76	11-3-78
DD 977 Briscoe	21-7-75	15-12-76	3-6-78
DD 978 Stump	25-8-75	29-1-77	19-8-78
DD 979 Conolly	29-9-75	19-2-77	14-10-78
DD 980 Moosbrugger	3-11-75	23-7-77	16-12-78
DD 981 John Hancock	16-1-76	29-10-77	10-3-79
DD 982 Nicholson	20-2-76	11-11-77	12-5-79
DD 983 John Rodgers	12-8-76	25-2-78	14-7-79
DD 984 Leftwich	12-11-76	8-4-78	25-8-79

DESTROYERS *(continued)*

DD 985 Cushing	2-2-77	17-6-78	22-9-79
DD 986 Harry W. Hill	1-4-77	10-8-78	10-11-79
DD 987 O'Bannon	24-6-77	25-9-78	1-12-79
DD 988 Thorn	29-8-77	22-11-78	12-1-80
DD 989 Deyo	14-10-77	20-1-79	22-3-80
DD 990 Ingersoll	5-12-77	10-3-79	12-4-80
DD 991 Fife	6-3-78	1-5-79	31-5-80
DD 992 Fletcher	24-4-78	16-6-79	12-7-80
DD 997 Hayler	20-10-80	2-3-82	5-3-83

Authorized: D 963–965 in FY 70, DD 966–971 in FY 71, DD 972–978 in FY 72, DD 979–985 in FY 74, Dd 986–992 in FY 75, DD 997 in FY 78

David R. Ray (DD 971)—prototype RAM launcher on starboard quarter, WLR-1 *and* SLQ-32 EW arrays, TAS Mk 23 and Mk 15 CIWS added G. Arra, 1-85

John Young (DD 973)—still with old TACAN, but with Mk 15 CIWS and Mk 23 TAS added L. & L. Van Ginderen, 3-85

John Hancock (DD 981)—Mk 23 TAS and two Mk 15 CIWS added, URN-25 TACAN replaced SRN-6 Ingalls SB, 8-85

Peterson (DD 969)—note ports for Nixie decoy in stern L. & L. Van Ginderen, 10-85

Oldendorf (DD 972) LSPH E. Pitman, R.A.N., 9-85

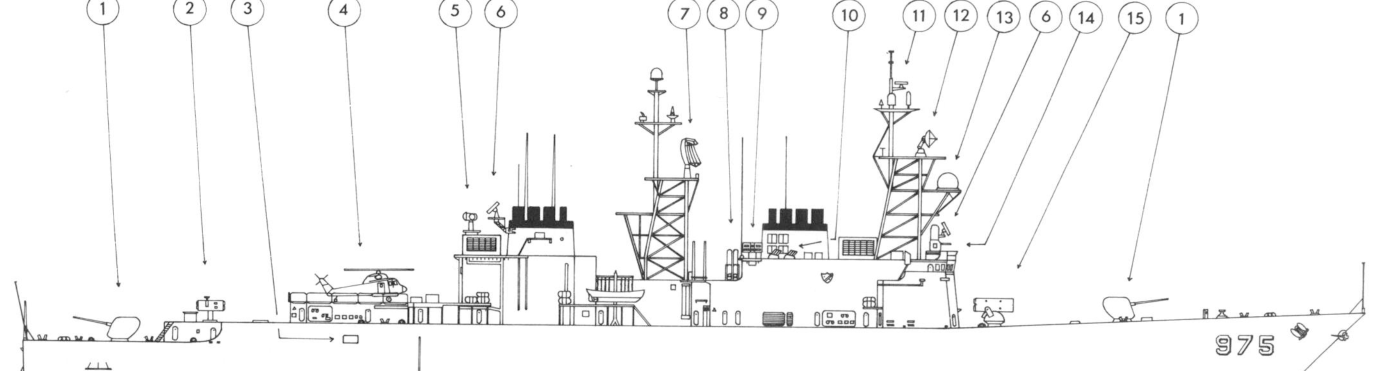

O'Brien (DD 975) Robert Dumas
1. 127-mm Mk 45 DP 2. Octuple Mk 29 Sea Sparrow launcher 3. Shutters over triple Mk 32 ASW TT 4. SH-2F LAMPS-I helicopter 5. radar director for Mk 91 Mod. 0 Sea Sparrow 6. OE-82 UHF SATCOMM antenna 7. SPS-40 air-search radar 8. quadruple Harpoon canister launcher mounting 9. SLQ-32(V)2 EW array 10. Mk 137 launchers for Mk 36 Super RBOC decoy system 11. SPS-55 surface-search radar 12. SPG-60 radar gun director 13. SPQ-9A radar gun director radome 14. Mk 15 CIWS 20-mm gatling AA 15. Mk 112 ASROC ASW missile launcher

DESTROYERS *(continued)*

Comte de Grasse (DD 974)—with two 4-round Tomahawk ABL flanking the ASROC launcher — Ingalls SB, 1985

John Rodgers (DD 983)—post-overhaul, with Tomahawk ABL abreast ASROC, D/F ESM array atop foremast, no Mk 15 CIWS — Ingalls SB, 1985

Moosbrugger (DD 980)—SQQ-89 trials ship, with SSQ-28 LAMPS-III helo data link antenna radome on foremast platform — Ingalls SB, 9-85

Cushing (DD 985) — L. & L. Van Ginderen, 10-84

D: 5,916 tons light (8,040 fl) **S:** 32.5 kts
Dim: 171.68 (o.a.) (161.25 pp) × 16.76 × 5.79 (8.84 over sonar)
A: 8/Harpoon SSM (IV × 2)—1/Mk 29 launcher (VIII × 1, 24 Sea Sparrow)—2/127-mm Mk 45 DP (I × 2)—2/20-mm Mk 15 CIWS (I ×2)—4/12.7-mm mg (I × 4)—1/Mk 116 ASROC ASW RL (VIII × 1, 24)—6/324-mm Mk 32 ASW TT (III × 2; 18 Mk 46 torpedoes)—1/SH-2F LAMPS-I (DD 989: SH-60B LAMPS-III) ASW helicopter
Electron Equipt: Radar: 1/SPS-55, 1/SPS-40 B/C/D (DD 997: SPS-49) 1/SPQ-9A, 1/SPG-60, 1/Mk 91 Mod. 0; Mk 23 TAS in 14 or more ships
Sonar: 1/SQS-53A (DD 980: SQS-53B and SQR-19 TASS)
TACAN: URN-25 or URN-20
EW: SLQ-32(V)2, Mk 36 SRBOC chaff RL (VI × 4); DD 971, 975: WLR-1 also
M: 4 G.E. LM-2500 gas turbines; 2 CP props; 86,000 hp (80,000 sust.)
Electric: 6,000 kw **Fuel:** 1,650 tons
Range: 3,300/30; 6,000/20; 8,000/17 **Man:** 18 officers, 232 men (296 tot. accom.)

Remarks: Largest post-World War II U.S. destroyer program, and the first non-SAM destroyers ordered since the 1950s. DD 997 intended by Congress *to be of an* "air-capable" design, with enlarged hangar for 4 ASW helicopters, but costs rose to the point that the ship was ordered 29-9-79 as a nearly standard version of the class. The basic *Spruance* hull and propulsion plant have also served as the basis for the *Kidd* (DDG 993) and *Ticonderoga* (CG 47, ex-DDG 47) designs. DD 981 carries her name across the stern in script, duplicating the signature of the first signer of the Declaration of Independence. Displacements have risen considerably as equipment has been added; they were originally intended to displace under 7,000 tons full load.

The propulsion machinery is very silent. Prairie-Masker bubbler systems are installed to enhance quietness. On each of the two shafts, two General Electric LM-2500 gas turbines are coupled to a reduction gear. Each shaft turns a controllable-pitch propeller (5.1 m in diameter, 168 rpm at 30 knots). Electric power is furnished by three Allison 501-K17 gas turbines, each powering one 2,000-kw alternator and mounted in separate compartments. Full speed can be reached from 12 knots in only 53 seconds. All propulsion machinery is under the control of a single operator in a central control station (CCS). 30 knots was considerably exceeded on trials. Endurance can be extended greatly by using one engine on one shaft for cruising. The plant has been very successful, except for the exhaust-gas auxiliary boilers. The mean time between overhauls for the LM-2500 gas turbines has been extended to 9,000 hours. DD 997 has the Litton automated engine control system prototype for the DDG 51 class.

The hull form was designed to minimize rolling and pitching; there are no fin stabilizers. Habitability received particular attention, living spaces being divided by bulkheads and intended for no more than six men each, with a recreational area and good sanitary facilities. The crew is small for a ship the size of the *Spruance* class, because all the machinery and systems have advanced automation.

The armament is being augmented by the installation of two Mk 15 CIWS, but only half the class were equipped by early 1985. ASW is handled by a Mk 116 fire-control system. The Mk 32 torpedo tubes are standard triple trainable mountings, fired through doors in the ships' sides. The Mk 91 Mod. 0 fire-control system for Sea Sparrow uses a single radar director. The Mk 86 Mod. 3 fire-control system for the 127-mm guns uses the SPG-60 radar for AA and the SPQ-9A for surface fire. Magazines hold 1,200 rounds 127-mm. The ASROC reload missiles are stowed vertically, directly beneath the launcher. Kevlar plastic armor is to be added inside vital spaces, beginning with four ships under FY 81; the entire class was to be equipped by 1986. Nine ships (including DD 976 in FY 83, DD 974, 979, 983 in FY 84, DD 984, 985, 989 in FY 85) are currently funded to receive 8 Tomahawk cruise missiles (IV × 2); box-launcher firing trials were carried out on DD 976 in 1-81 and later, while first operational installation was in DD 974 in late 1984. In 1985-86 DD 963 and 990 are receiving Mk 41 Mod. 0 vertical-launch groups in place of the ASROC launcher; the 32-cell group will hold up to 30 Tomahawk and, later, vertical-launch ASROC missiles. At some future date it may be possible to launch Standard SM-2 MR missiles as well, with the missiles to be controlled by an accompanying Aegis-equipped ship. DD 964, 966, and 991 are to receive the vertical group in 1986-87. DD 977 has had the GFCS modified to Mk 86 Mod. 10 (with a UYK-7 computer in place of the Mk 152 computer, Mk 113 display consoles, new fuze-setters, etc.) to conduct trials with semi-active laser-guided projectiles. DD 976 was also used in 1981 for trials with the General Electric EX-83, 30-mm gatling gun system, which uses a GAU-8 heavy gun and was to carry out trials with an extended-range version of Sea Sparrow. Planned backfitting of the Mk 71, 203-mm gun in the forward position was canceled in 1978 when development of that excellent weapon was unfortunately canceled. DD 971 carries a prototype EX-41 RAM point-defense missile launcher on the starboard quarter.

DESTROYERS *(continued)*

Eight ships will receive Tomahawk in two armored box launchers, with DD 974, 976, and 983 equipped by end-1985; the remainder will get VLS, beginning with DD 963 in 1986.

All ships of the class are scheduled to receive the Hughes Mk 23 TAS (Target Aquisition System), which uses a high-rpm radar mounted on an aft-projecting platform on the mainmast to detect low-flying, high-speed missiles and aircraft. The SPS-55 surface-search radar has been moved to a new, higher platform on the foremast. Plans still call for the addition of the SQR-19 TACTASS (Tactical Towed-Array Sonar System), but its introduction has been delayed; DD 980 commenced trials fall 1985 with the integrated SQQ-89 sonar system, incorporating the SQS-53B active bow sonar and the SQR-19 TACTASS array. DD 966 carried the SQR-15 TASS on a WestPac tour during 1985. All have the SLQ-25 Nixie torpedo decoy system. Early units were given the WLR-1 EW system as an interim installation until SLQ-32(V)2 was available; at least two ships (DD 971, 975) now have *both.* DD 974 carries the prototype SSQ-74 ICADS (Integrated Cover and Deception System). RAST deck-haul systems are being added (beginning with DD 989 in 4-85) to permit handling the SH-60B LAMPS-III ASW helicopter; SQQ-28 data link equipment will also be added. Half the class had received TAS by late 1985. DD 976 has WSN-5 SINS.

◆ 11 Forrest Sherman and Hull classes (SCB 240 type)

NOTE: All in reserve, except DD 946.

6 ASW refits (1967–71) (SCB 221 modernization)

	Bldr	Laid down	L	In serv.
DD 937 DAVIS	Bethlehem, Quincy	1-2-55	28-3-56	28-2-57
DD 940 MANLEY	Bath Iron Works	10-2-55	12-4-56	1-2-57
DD 941 DUPONT	Bath Iron Works	11-5-55	8-9-56	1-7-57
DD 943 BLANDY	Bethlehem, Quincy	29-12-55	19-12-56	8-11-57
DD 948 MORTON	Ingalls, Pascagoula	4-3-57	23-5-58	26-5-59
DD 950 RICHARD S. EDWARDS	Puget Sound SB & DD	20-12-56	21-9-57	5-2-59

5 unmodified:

	Bldr	Laid down	L	In serv.
DD 931 FORREST SHERMAN	Boston NSY	27-10-53	5-2-55	9-11-55
DD 942 BIGELOW	Bath Iron Works	6-7-55	2-2-57	8-11-57
DD 944 MULLINIX	Bethlehem, Quincy	5-4-56	18-3-57	7-3-58
DD 946 EDSON	Bath Iron Works	3-12-56	1-1-58	7-11-58
DD 951 TURNER JOY	Puget Sound SB & DD	30-9-57	5-5-58	3-8-59

Authorized: DD 931 FY 55, DD 937 in FY 54, DD 940–944 in FY 55, others in FY 56

D: 2,780–2,850 tons (4,050–4,090 fl) **S:** 32.5 kts
Dim: 127.51 (DD 945 to DD 951: 127.4) × 13.7 × 6.1
A: ASW refits: 2/127-mm Mk 42 DP (I × 2)—1/Mk 116 ASROC ASW RL (VIII × 1)—6/324-mm Mk 32 ASW TT (III × 2)
Others: 3/127-mm Mk 42 DP (I × 3)—6/324-mm Mk 32 ASW TT (III × 2)
Electron Equipt: Radar: 1/SPS-10, 1/SPS-40, (DD 937, DD 942, DD 946, DD 951: SPS-29), 1/SPG-53A, 1/Mk 35
Sonar: SQS-23D; ASW refits: SQS-35 VDS also
EW: WLR-1, WLR-3, ULQ-6
TACAN: DD 946, 951: SRN-6

Edson (DD 946)—the only active unit — L. & L. Van Ginderen, 8-84

Mullinix (DD 944)—unmodified, outboard the ASW conversion *Dupont* (DD 941) at Philadelphia NSY — A.D. Baker, 8-84

Richard S. Edwards (DD 950)—ASW version — G. Gyssels, 9-81

Turner Joy (DD 951)—unmodified, while active — L. & L. Van Ginderen, 1980

M: 2 sets G.E. (DD 931, Westinghouse) GT; 2 props; 70,000 hp
Boilers: DD 937, DD 943, DD 944, DD 948: 4 Foster-Wheeler; Others: 4 Babcock & Wilcox; 84 kg/cm², 520°C
Fuel: 750 tons **Range:** 4,500/20
Man: ASW refits: 19 officers, 287 men; others: 13 officers, 275 men

REMARKS: All in reserve, except DD 946, assigned to the Naval Reserve Force for reserve training and as a training ship for the Officer Candidate School, Newport. Being retained as potential gunfire support ships. From DD 937 on, the bows are somewhat higher than DD 931 and DD 933, while DD 945 and later were considered a separate class by reason of their different bow design. Four of the same series were rebuilt as DDGs. There are two radar gunfire-control systems, Mk 68 forward and Mk 56 aft (positions reversed in DD 931 and DD 944). ASW refits have Mk 114 ASW-fire-control systems, the others Mk 105. All Hedgehog and depth charges removed in early 1970s. Originally had four 76.2-mm DP (II × 2), but they were removed from all by 1978. There is an ASROC reload magazine just forward of the launcher on the ASW conversion units.

Decommissioned to reserve: DD 931, DD 942 and DD 943 on 5-11-82; DD 948 and DD 951 on 22-11-82; DD 950 on 15-12-82; DD 937 on 20-12-82; DD 940, and DD 941 on 4-3-83; and DD 944 on 11-8-83. Ex-*Barry* (DD 933), decommissioned 5-11-82 and struck 31-1-83, is on exhibition at the Washington, D.C., Navy Yard. Sister *Jonas Ingram* (DD 938), decommissioned 4-3-83 and stricken 15-6-83, was stripped of armament and radars for use as engineering equipment test hulk at Philadelphia NSY; *Hull* (DD 945), decommissioned 11-7-83, was stricken 15-10-83 for eventual use as a target.

NAVAL RESERVE FORCE FRIGATES

Twenty-four *Oliver Hazard Perry-* and *Knox-*class frigates are programmed for the Naval Reserve Force, transferring from the active fleet between 1982 and 1988. In addition, three Reserve Force Squadrons of SH-2F LAMPS-1 helicopters are being formed to supply aircraft for the ships, HSL 84 in FY 1984, HSL 75 in FY 1985, and another in FY 1986. The dates of transfer to the Naval Reserve Force are:

MILLER (FF 1091)	17-1-82	SAMUEL ELIOT MORISON (FFG 13)	6-86
LANG (FF 1060)	17-1-82	SIDES (FFG 14)	8-86
GRAY (FF 1054)	15-7-82	ESTOCIN (FFG 15)	9-86
VALDEZ (FF 1096)	14-8-82	JOHN A. MOORE (FFG 19)	1-87
BLAKELEY (FF 1072)	11-6-83	ANTRIM (FFG 20)	1-87
PATTERSON (FF 1061)	15-6-83	LEWIS B. PULLER (FFG 23)	1-87
DUNCAN (FFG 10)	13-1-84	ROARK (FF 1053)	6-87
OLIVER HAZARD PERRY (FFG 7)	31-5-84	FLATLEY (FFG 21)	11-87
CLIFTON SPRAGUE (FFG 16)	31-8-84	TISDALE (FFG 27)	1-88
WADSWORTH (FFG 9)	30-6-85	FAHRION (FFG 22)	1-88
CLARK (FFG 11)	30-9-85	COPELAND (FFG 25)	1-88
GEORGE PHILIP (FFG 12)	18-1-86	MEYERKORD (FF 1058)	1-88

GUIDED-MISSILE FRIGATES

◆ 48 (+3) Oliver Hazard Perry class (SCN 207/2081 type)

	Bldr	Laid down	L	In serv.
FFG 7 OLIVER HAZARD PERRY	Bath Iron Works	6-12-75	9-25-76	30-11-77
FFG 8 MCINERNEY	Bath Iron Works	16-1-78	4-11-78	15-12-79
FFG 9 WADSWORTH	Todd, San Pedro	13-7-77	29-7-78	28-2-80
FFG 10 DUNCAN	Todd, Seattle	29-4-77	1-3-78	24-5-80

GUIDED-MISSILE FRIGATES *(continued)*

FFG 11 Clark	Bath Iron Works	17-7-78	24-3-79	17-5-80
FFG 12 George Philip	Todd, San Pedro	14-12-77	16-12-78	18-11-80
FFG 13 Samuel Eliot Morison	Bath Iron Works	4-12-78	14-7-79	11-10-80
FFG 14 Sides	Todd, San Pedro	7-8-78	19-5-79	30-5-81
FFG 15 Estocin	Bath Iron Works	2-4-79	3-11-79	10-1-81
FFG 16 Clifton Sprague	Bath Iron Works	30-7-79	16-2-80	21-3-81
FFG 19 John A. Moore	Todd, San Pedro	19-12-78	20-10-79	14-11-81
FFG 20 Antrim	Todd, Seattle	21-6-78	27-3-79	26-9-81
FFG 21 Flatley	Bath Iron Works	13-11-79	15-5-80	20-6-81
FFG 22 Fahrion	Todd, Seattle	1-12-78	24-8-79	16-1-82
FFG 23 Lewis B. Puller	Todd, San Pedro	23-5-79	15-3-80	17-4-82
FFG 24 Jack Williams	Bath Iron Works	25-2-80	30-8-80	19-9-81
FFG 25 Copeland	Todd, San Pedro	24-10-79	26-7-80	7-8-82
FFG 26 Gallery	Bath Iron Works	17-5-80	20-12-80	5-12-81
FFG 27 Mahlon S. Tisdale	Todd, San Pedro	19-3-80	7-2-81	13-11-82
FFG 28 Boone	Todd, Seattle	27-3-79	16-1-80	15-5-82
FFG 29 Stephen W. Groves	Bath Iron Works	16-9-80	4-4-81	17-4-82
FFG 30 Reid	Todd, San Pedro	8-10-80	27-6-81	19-2-83
FFG 31 Stark	Todd, Seattle	24-8-79	30-5-80	23-10-82
FFG 32 John L. Hall	Bath Iron Works	5-1-81	24-7-81	26-6-82
FFG 33 Jarrett	Todd, San Pedro	11-2-81	17-10-81	2-7-83
FFG 34 Aubrey Fitch	Bath Iron Works	10-4-81	17-10-81	9-10-82
FFG 36 Underwood	Bath Iron Works	30-7-81	6-2-82	29-1-83
FFG 37 Crommelin	Todd, Seattle	30-5-80	1-7-81	18-6-83
FFG 38 Curts	Todd, San Pedro	1-7-81	6-3-82	8-10-83
FFG 39 Doyle	Bath Iron Works	16-11-81	22-5-82	21-5-83
FFG 40 Halyburton	Todd, Seattle	26-9-80	13-10-81	7-1-84
FFG 41 McCluskey	Todd, San Pedro	21-10-81	18-9-82	10-12-83
FFG 42 Kalkring	Bath Iron Works	19-2-82	18-9-82	20-8-83
FFG 43 Thach	Todd, San Pedro	6-3-82	18-12-82	17-3-84
FFG 45 De Wert	Bath Iron Works	14-6-82	18-12-82	19-11-83
FFG 46 Rentz	Todd, San Pedro	18-9-82	16-7-83	30-6-84
FFG 47 Nicholas	Bath Iron Works	27-9-82	23-4-83	10-3-84
FFG 48 Vandegrift	Todd, Seattle	13-10-81	15-10-82	24-11-84
FFG 49 Robert E. Beadley	Bath Iron Works	28-12-82	13-8-83	11-8-84
FFG 50 Taylor	Bath Iron Works	5-5-83	5-11-83	1-12-84
FFG 51 Gary	Todd, San Pedro	18-12-82	19-11-83	17-11-84
FFG 52 Carr	Todd, Seattle	26-3-82	26-2-83	27-7-85
FFG 53 Hawes	Bath Iron Works	22-8-83	17-2-84	9-2-85
FFG 54 Ford	Todd, San Pedro	16-7-83	23-6-84	29-6-85
FFG 55 Elrod	Bath Iron Works	14-11-83	12-5-84	6-7-85
FFG 56 Simpson	Bath Iron Works	27-2-84	31-8-84	9-11-85
FFG 57 Reuben James	Todd, San Pedro	10-9-83	8-2-85	22-3-86
FFG 58 Samuel B. Roberts	Bath Iron Works	21-5-84	8-12-84	12-4-86
FFG 59 Kauffman	Bath Iron Works	8-4-85	29-3-86	3-87
FFG 60 Rodney M. Davis	Todd, San Pedro	8-2-85	11-1-86	12-86
FFG 61 Ingraham	Todd, San Pedro	12-86	11-87	12-88

Authorized: FFG 7 in FY 73, FFG 8–10 in FY 75, FFG 11–16 in FY 76, FFG 19–26 in FY 77, FFG 27–34 in FY 78, FFG 36–43 in FY 79, FFG 45–49 in FY 80, FFG 50–55 in FY 81, FFG 56–58 in FY 82, FFG 59, 60 in FY 83, FFG 61 in FY 84.

D: 2,769 tons light (3,658 fl); FFG 8, 36–61: 3,010 tons light (3,900 fl)
S: 29 kts (30.6 trials)
Dim: 135.64; FFG 8, 36–58: 138.80 (125.9 wl) × 13.72 × 5.7 (8.6 max.)
A: 1/Mk 13 Mod. 4 launcher (4 Harpoon and 36 Standard SM-1 MR missiles)—1/76-mm Mk 75 DP; FFG 8, 13, 19, 23, 25, 27–61: 1/20-mm Mk 15 CIWS—

Aubrey Fitch (FFG 34)—short hull profile L. & L. Van Ginderen, 7-84

Simpson (FFG 56) Bath Iron Wks./R. Farr, 9-85

Rentz (FFG 46)—at speed J. Graham/Todd SY, 4-8

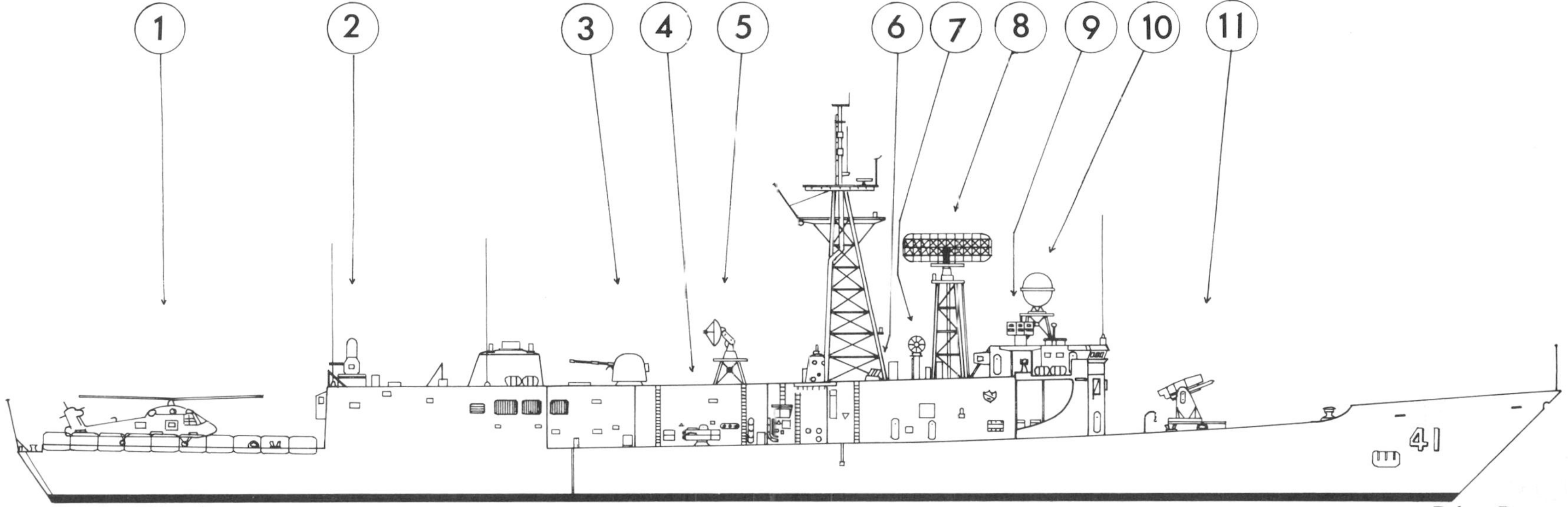

McCluskey (FFG 41) Robert Dumas

1. SH-2F LAMPS-I helicopter 2. Mk 15 CIWS 3. 76-mm Mk 75 DP 4. Mk 32 triple ASW TT 5. STIR f.c. radar 6. Mk 137 RL for Mk 36 SRBOC system 7. OE-82 UHF SATCOMM antennas 8. SPS-49 air-search radar 9. SLQ-32 EW array 10. Mk 92 f.c.s. radome 11. Mk 13 launcher

GUIDED-MISSILE FRIGATES *(continued)*

Sides (FFG 14) Lt.jg M. Higgins/Lt. J. Chartrand, USN, 1983

Thach (FFG 43)—long hull profile Todd SY, 10-84

Mahlon S. Tisdale (FFG 27)—short stern profile G. Arra, 1984

Stark (FFG 31)—short LAMPS-I stern, rubbing strakes on sides for Great Lakes cruise L. & L. Van Ginderen, 6-85

Robert E. Bradley (FFG 49)—Mk 15 CIWS, long stern, no RAST G. Arra, 1984

6/324-mm ASW TT (III × 2)—1/SH-2F LAMPS-I (FFG 8, 36–61: 2/SH-60B LAMPS-III) ASW helicopters

Electron Equipt: Radar: 1/SPS-55, 1/ SPS-49(V)2, 1/Mk 92 Mod. 4, 1/STIR (SPG-60 Mod.)
Sonar: 1/SQS-56—TACAN: URN-25
EW: SLQ-32(V)2, Mk 36 SRBOC chaff RL (VI × 2)

M: 2 G.E. LM-2500 gas turbines; 1 5.5-m diameter CP, 5-bladed prop; 41,000 hp (40,000 sust.)—2 drop-down propulsors; 700 hp

Electric: 3,000 kw **Fuel:** 587 tons + 64 tons helicopter fuel

Range: 4,200/20; 5,000/18 **Man:** 17 officers, 15 chief petty officers, 183 men

Remarks: Although these ships were intended to operate the LAMPS-III ASW helicopter, FFG 7–35 (less FFG 8) lack the equipment necessary to handle them and will retain LAMPS-I. Beginning with the FY 79 ships (FFG 36 and later), helicopter support equipment is aboard on completion: fin stabilizers, RAST (Recovery Assistance, Securing, and Traversing System, not fitted as completed until FFG 50), and other systems. The RAST system permits helicopter launch and recovery with the ship rolling through 28 degrees and pitching 5 degrees. The equipment was first installed in *McInerney* (FFG 8), which was reconstructed, completing 12-2-81 at Bath Iron Works, to act as LAMPS-III/SH-60B Sea Hawk helicopter trials ship; the stern was lengthened by 2.2 m (the extension being slightly lower than the flight deck, to accommodate mooring equipment) by changing the rake of the stern. FFG 26 conducted fin stabilizer trials in 1982. These ships were supposed to have received SQR-19 TACTASS equipment, beginning with FFG 36, and SQR-18A to be backfitted in earlier units; however, delays in development left *none* of the ships with the gear into 1985. The Mk 15 CIWS (Close-In Weapon System) 20-mm Vulcan/Phalanx was to be backfitted into all by 1988. Two Mk 24 optical target designators (mounted in tubs atop the pilothouse) were not fitted to the ships as completed until FFG 27 and have been backfitted in the earlier ships. FFG 7 was originally numbered PF 109. Speed on one turbine is 25 knots; the auxiliary power system uses two retractable pods located well forward and can drive the ships at up to 6 knots. The Mk 92 Mod. 4 fire-control system controls missile and 76-mm gunfire; it uses a STIR (modified SPG-60) antenna and a U.S.-built version of the Hollandse Signaal Apparaaten WM-28 radar forward, and can track four separate targets. The Mk 92 system is programmed for three stages of improvement; the first, given trials in FFG 29 in 1983, was to be backfitted to all by 10-84 as the "Near-Term Improvement," along with Standard SM-1 MR Block 6 missiles. Phase two (Mk 92 CORT) began trials in FFG 15 in 5-86. The Mk 75 gun is a license-built version of the OTO Melara Compact. A Mk 13 weapons-direction system is fitted. The only ship-launched ASW ordnance is the Mk 46 torpedoes in the two triple torpedo tubes. These ships are particularly well protected against splinter and fragmentation damage, with 19-mm aluminum-alloy armor over magazine spaces, 16-mm steel over the main engine-control room, and 19-mm Kevlar plastic armor over vital electronics and command spaces.

Original complement was planned at 17 officers, 167 men, which was found to be too many officers but far too few enlisted men to run and maintain the ships. Therefore,

GUIDED-MISSILE FRIGATES *(continued)*

FFG 19 and up are fitted with 30 additional enlisted bunks, with the others to be backfitted.

FFG 17, 18, 35, and 44 of this class were built by Todd, Seattle, for Australia, which is building two more in-country. Spain is building five.

The Navy had hoped to phase out construction of this class with the FY 83 ships, FFG 59 and 60, but Congress authorized (but did not fully fund) FFG 61 in FY 84; FFG 61 was initially mandated to have the as yet unbuilt and untested Sperry Phase-III update to the Mk 92 f.c.s., adding four fixed phased-array radar panels (two facing the after quadrants on a mast platform and two covering the forward quadrants atop the bridge). Instead, the ship will have the "Phase-II" Mk 92 Mod. 6 f.c.s.

Already possessing a "surplus" of frigates, the U.S. Navy has no immediate plans for new construction in this category.

◆ **6 Brooke class (SCR 199B type)**

	Bldr	Laid down	L	In serv.
FFG 1 Brooke	Lockheed, Seattle	10-12-62	19-7-63	12-3-66
FFG 2 Ramsey	Lockheed, Seattle	4-2-63	15-10-63	3-6-67
FFG 3 Schofield	Lockheed, Seattle	15-4-63	7-12-63	11-5-68
FFG 4 Talbot	Bath Iron Works	4-5-64	6-1-66	2-4-67
FFG 5 Richard L. Page	Bath Iron Works	4-1-65	4-4-66	5-8-67
FFG 6 Julius A. Furer	Bath Iron Works	12-7-65	22-7-66	11-11-67

Authorized: FFG 1–3 in FY 62, FFG 4–6 in FY 63

Brooke (FFG 1)—no ASROC reloads L. & L. Van Ginderen, 10-85

Julius A. Furer (FFG 3)—ASROC reload version G. Arra, 8-85

Talbot (FFG 4) R. Scheina, 7-84

D: 2,643 tons (3,600 fl) **S:** 27.2 kts
Dim: 126.33 (121.9 wl) × 13.47 × 7.9 (over sonar)
A: 1/Mk 22 launcher (I × 1, 16 Standard SM-1 MR missiles)—1/127-mm 38-cal. DP—1/Mk 116 ASROC ASW RL (VIII × 1)—6/324-mm Mk 32 ASW TT (III × 2)—1/SH-2F LAMPS-I ASW helicopter
Electron Equipt: Radar: 1/LN-66, 1/SPS-10F, 1/SPS-52B, 1/SPG-51C, 1/Mk 35
Sonar: 1/SQS-26BX—TACAN: SRN-15
EW: SLQ-32(V)2, Mk 36 SRBOC chaff RL (VI × 2)
M: 1 set Westinghouse (FFG 4 to FFG 6: G.E.) GT; 1 prop; 35,000 hp
Boilers: 2 Foster-Wheeler; 84 kg/cm², 510°C **Electric:** 2,000 kw
Fuel: 600 tons **Range:** 4,000/20 **Man:** 16 officers, 250 men

Remarks: Differ from the *Garcia* class in having their aft 127-mm gun replaced by a missile launcher. Excellent sea-keeping qualities. Anti-rolling stabilizers. The hangar, which was enlarged for the SH-2 LAMPS-I helicopter, is telescoping, as on the *Knox* class. FFG 4 through FFG 6 have an ASROC reload magazine with 8 missiles. FFG 4 was used as an experimental ship for the weapons and systems of the *Oliver Hazard Perry* (FFG 7), but was restored to standard configuration. A Mk 56 Mod. 43 radar gunfire-control system is carried, while the missile system is Mk 74 Mod. 6; Mk 4 Mod. 2 weapons-direction system is fitted, as is the Mk 114 ASW-control system. These ships are not scheduled to receive Harpoon SSM or the Mk 15 CIWS 20-mm gatling gun, but they are getting the SLQ-32(V)2 intercept array in place of the original WLR-1, WLR-3 and ULQ-6 suite. FFG 6 has SQS-26AXR sonar.

FRIGATES

◆ **46 Knox class (SCN 199C, 200 and 200-65 types)**

	Bldr	Laid down	L	In serv.
FF 1052 Knox	Todd, Seattle	5-10-65	19-11-66	12-4-69
FF 1053 Roark	Todd, Seattle	2-2-66	24-4-67	22-11-69
FF 1054 Gray	Todd, Seattle	19-11-66	3-10-67	4-4-70
FF 1055 Hepburn	Todd, San Pedro	1-6-66	25-3-67	3-7-69
FF 1056 Connole	Avondale SY	23-3-67	20-7-68	30-8-69
FF 1057 Rathburne	Lockheed, Seattle	8-1-68	2-5-69	16-5-70
FF 1058 Meyerkord	Todd, San Pedro	1-9-66	15-7-67	28-11-69
FF 1059 William S. Sims	Avondale SY	10-4-67	4-1-69	3-1-70
FF 1060 Lang	Tod, San Pedro	25-3-67	17-2-68	28-3-70
FF 1061 Patterson	Avondale SY	12-10-67	3-5-69	14-3-70
FF 1062 Whipple	Todd, Seattle	24-4-67	12-4-68	22-8-70
FF 1063 Reasoner	Lockheed, Seattle	6-1-69	1-8-70	31-1-71
FF 1064 Lockwood	Todd, Seattle	3-11-67	5-9-68	5-12-70
FF 1065 Stein	Lockheed, Seattle	1-6-70	19-12-70	8-1-72
FF 1066 Marvin Shields	Todd, Seattle	12-4-68	23-10-69	10-4-71
FF 1067 Francis Hammond	Todd, San Pedro	15-7-67	11-5-68	25-7-70
FF 1068 Vreeland	Avondale SY	20-3-68	14-6-69	13-6-70
FF 1069 Bagley	Lockheed, Seattle	22-9-70	24-4-71	6-5-72
FF 1070 Downes	Todd, Seattle	5-9-68	13-12-69	28-8-71
FF 1071 Badger	Todd, San Pedro	17-2-68	7-12-68	1-12-70
FF 1072 Blakely	Avondale SY	3-6-68	23-8-69	18-7-70
FF 1073 Robert E. Peary (ex-*Conolly*)	Lockheed, Seattle	20-12-70	23-6-71	23-9-72
FF 1074 Harold E. Holt	Todd, San Pedro	11-5-68	3-5-69	26-3-71
FF 1075 Trippe	Avondale SY	29-7-68	1-11-69	19-9-70
FF 1076 Fanning	Todd, San Pedro	7-12-68	24-1-70	23-7-71
FF 1077 Ouellet	Avondale SY	15-1-69	17-1-70	12-12-70
FF 1078 Joseph Hewes	Avondale SY	15-5-69	7-3-70	24-4-71
FF 1079 Bowen	Avondale SY	11-7-69	2-5-70	22-5-71
FF 1080 Paul	Avondale SY	12-9-69	20-6-70	14-8-71
FF 1081 Aylwin	Avondale SY	13-11-69	29-8-70	18-9-71
FF 1082 Elmer Montgomery	Avondale SY	23-1-70	21-11-70	30-10-71
FF 1083 Cook	Avondale SY	20-3-70	23-1-71	18-12-71
FF 1084 McCandless	Avondale SY	4-6-70	20-3-71	18-3-72
FF 1085 Donald B. Beary	Avondale SY	24-7-70	22-5-71	22-7-72
FF 1086 Brewton	Avondale SY	2-10-70	24-7-71	8-7-72
FF 1087 Kirk	Avondale SY	4-12-70	25-9-71	9-9-72
FF 1088 Barbey	Avondale SY	5-2-71	4-12-71	11-11-72
FF 1089 Jesse L. Brown	Avondale SY	8-4-71	18-3-72	17-2-73
FF 1090 Ainsworth	Avondale SY	11-6-71	15-4-72	31-3-73
FF 1091 Miller	Avondale SY	6-8-71	3-6-72	30-6-73
FF 1092 Thomas C. Hart	Avondale SY	8-10-71	12-8-72	28-7-73
FF 1093 Capodanno	Avondale SY	12-10-71	21-10-72	17-11-73
FF 1094 Pharris	Avondale SY	11-2-72	16-12-72	26-1-74
FF 1095 Truett	Avondale SY	27-4-72	3-2-73	1-6-74
FF 1096 Valdez	Avondale SY	30-6-72	24-3-73	27-7-74
FF 1097 Moinester	Avondale SY	25-8-72	12-7-73	2-11-74

Authorized: 10 in FY 64, 16 in FY 65, 10 in FY 66, 10 in FY 67

Downes (FF 1070)—Mk 15 CIWS aft, no bow bulwarks, WLR-1 and SLQ-32 EW gear G. Arra, 1984

FRIGATES *(continued)*

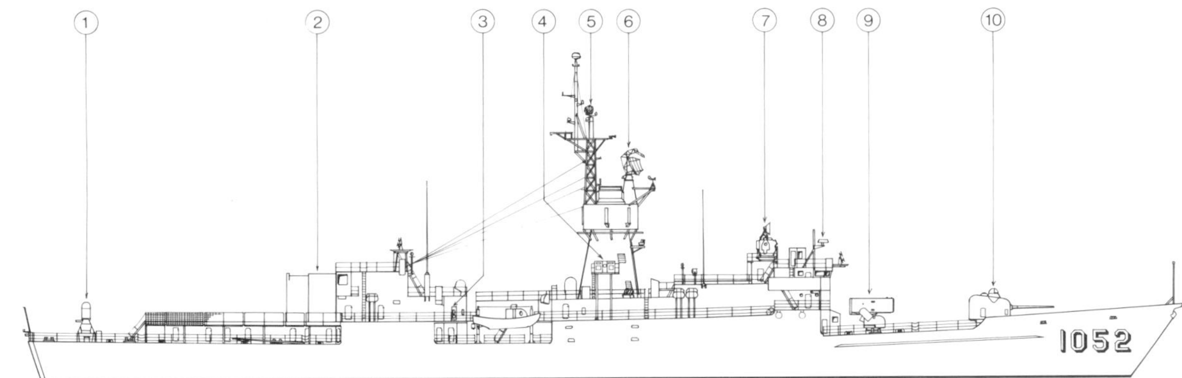

Knox (FF 1052) A.D. Baker III

1. Mk 15 CIWS (20-mm Vulcan/Phalanx) AA 2. Telescoping hangar for LAMPS-I helicopter 3. Mk 32 ASW TT (II × 2) 4. SLQ-32(V)2 EW 5. SPS-10 surface-search radar 6. SPS-40 air-search radar 7. Mk 68 GFCS 8. navigational radar 9. Mk 116 ASROC ASW RL (VIII × 1) 10. 127-mm 54-cal. Mk 42 DP gun

McCandless (FF 1084)—no bow bulwarks, Mk 15 CIWS aft
L. & L. Van Ginderen, 7-85

Aylwin (FF 1081)—with Mk 15 CIWS aft, bow bulwarks G. Arra, 8-85

Kirk (FF 1087)—*Pollack* (SSN 603) alongside. Note WLR-1 *and* SLQ-32 EW gear, SH-2F helo, Mk 15 CIWS G. Arra, 3-85

Vreeland (FF 1068)—VDS door in stern Pradignac & Leo, 9-84

Capodanno (FF 1093) R. Farr/Bath Iron Wks., 1984

FRIGATES *(continued)*

Bagley(FF 1069) G. Arra, 7-85

D: 3,066 tons light (4,250 fl) **S:** 27+ kts
Dim: 133.59 (126.5 wl) × 14.33 × 4.60 (7.55 over sonar)—see remarks
A: 4/Harpoon SSM (using Mk 116 ASROC launcher system)—1/127-mm Mk 42 DP—1/20-mm Mk 15 CIWS *or* 1/Mk 25 BPDMS Sea Sparrow launcher (VIII × 1)—1/Mk 116 ASROC system (VIII × 1)—4/324-mm Mk 32 fixed ASW TT—1/SH-2 LAMPS-I ASW helicopter
Electron Equipt: Radar: 1/LN-66, 1/SPS-10, 1/SPS-40B, 1SPG-53
Sonar: 1/SQS-26CX, SQS-35(V) VDS (except FF 1053 to FF 1055, FF 1057 to FF 1062, FF 1072, FF 1077), SQR-18A(V)1 TACTASS on VDS ships
EW: SLQ-32(V)1 or 32(V)2, Mk 36 SRBOC chaff RL (VI × 2)
TACAN: SRN-15
M: 1 set Westinghouse GT; 1 prop; 35,000 hp **Electric:** 3,000 kw
Boilers: 2 Babcock & Wilcox or Foster-Wheeler; 84 kg/cm², 510°C
Fuel: 750 tons **Range:** 4,300/20 **Man:** 20 officers, 255 men

Remarks: An additional ten ships of the FY 68 program (FF 1098 to FF 1107) were canceled. Bow bulwarks and a spray strake were being added forward to reduce deck wetness, a problem in this class, but funding shortages curtailed the program before all were altered; the addition extends length overall to approx. 134.0 m. The ASROC system has an automatic reloading magazine beneath the bridge; it is also used to stow Harpoon missiles, which are launched from the port pair of eight launcher cells (FF 1091 first to receive Harpoon, 1976). FF 1084 to FF 1097 did not receive a Mk 25 BPDMS launcher for Sea Sparrow. FF 1070 has been used as NATO Sea Sparrow trials ship; she carried a Mk 29 NATO Sea Sparrow launcher and the two-director Mk 91 Mod. 1 fire-control system, later reduced to one director (Mk 91 Mod. 0 system); FF 1070 also carried the Hughes Mk 23 Mod. 0 TAS (Target Acquisition System) in place of the SPS-40 radar; these systems were removed during her 1983 refit. The ASW torpedo tubes are fixed, in the forward end of the hangar superstructure, aimed outboard at an angle of 45°. The Mk 25 BPDMS (Basic Point Defense Missile System) launcher for Sea Sparrow is being *replaced* by a 20-mm Mk 15 CIWS, Vulcan/Phalanx gatling AA system, beginning with FF 1087 in 1982; by 10-83 13 ships had the gun, and all 46 will have it by 1990. Beginning with twelve ships under FY 80, the SQS-35 towed VDS transducer body and hoist was modified to permit towing the SQR-18A TACTASS. FF 1088 also has acted as a trials ship and had a controllable-pitch prop; the large inflatable radome atop her hangar has been removed. All carry a Mk 68 gunfire-control system with SPG-53A, D, or F radar. All are receiving SRN-15 TACAN sets during overhauls, and SPS-67 will replace SPS-10 later in the 1980s. SLQ-32(V)1 (later upgraded to (V)2) is replacing WLR-1C as the EW suit; some (FF 1064, 1067, 1070, 1087, etc.) have *both.* A few ships retain LN-66 navigational radars and all have two OE-82 satellite-communications antennas for the WSC-3 system. Ships with Sea Sparrow have a single Mk 115 missile-fire-control system (Mk 71 director). All have Mk 114 ASW fire-control system. FF 1078 to FF 1097 have a TEAM (SM-5) computer system for the continual monitoring of the ship's electronic equipment. Anti-rolling fin stabilizers fitted in all. Prairie-Masker bubble system fitted to hulls and propellers to reduce radiated noise. All are to receive the ASW TDS (ASW Tactical Data System) beginning FY 83. Six serve the Naval Reserve Force, with two more to follow; see the names and dates on page 640. Non-VDS ships to get SQR-18A(V)2 TACTASS; trials in FF 1077, 1983.

◆ **1 former experimental escort ship (SCB 198 type)**

	Bldr	Laid down	L	In serv.
FF 1098 Glover (ex-AGFF 1, ex-AGDE 1, ex-AG 163)	Bath Iron Works	29-7-63	17-4-65	13-11-65

Authorized: FY 61

Glover (FF 1098)—note raised stern for VDS L. & L. Van Ginderen, 5-84

D: 2,700 tons (3,630 fl) **S:** 27 kts
Dim: 126.33 (121.9 wl) × 13.47 × 7.9 (over sonar)
A: 1/127-mm 38-cal. DP—1/Mk 116 ASROC ASW RL (VIII × 1)—6/324-mm Mk 32 ASW TT (III × 2)
Electron Equipt: Radar: 1/SPS-10, 1/SPS-40, 1/Mk 35
Sonar: SQS-26AXR, SQS-35 VDS
EW: WLR-1, ULQ-6, 2/Mk 33 RBOC chaff
M: 1 set Westinghouse GT; 1 prop; 35,000 hp **Electric:** 2,000 kw
Boilers: 2 Foster-Wheeler; 83.4 kg/cm², 510°C **Man:** 15 officers, 218 men
Range: 4,000/20 **Fuel:** 600 tons

Remarks: Redesignated from AGFF on 1-10-79 because she now conducts operational cruises. "FF 1098" was previously used for a later-canceled *Knox*-class frigate; this is the first instance of a previously allocated hull number being reused. Basically a *Garcia*-class ship with identical hull form, but with a pump-jet propeller and the after 127-mm gun omitted to provide accommodations for civilian technicians. Extreme stern raised during installations of SQS-35 VDS. No ASROC reload magazine.

◆ **10 Garcia class (SCB 199A type)**

	Bldr	Laid down	L	In serv.
FF 1040 Garcia	Bethlehem, San Francisco	16-10-62	31-10-63	21-12-64
FF 1041 Bradley	Bethlehem, San Francisco	17-1-63	26-3-64	15-5-65
FF 1043 Edward McDonnell	Avondale SY	1-4-63	15-2-64	15-2-65
FF 1044 Brumby	Avondale SY	1-8-63	6-6-64	5-8-65
FF 1045 Davidson	Avondale SY	20-9-63	3-10-64	7-12-65
FF 1047 Voge	Defoe SB, Michigan	21-11-63	4-2-65	25-11-66
FF 1048 Sample	Lockheed, Seattle	19-7-63	28-4-64	23-3-68
FF 1049 Koelsh	Defoe SB, Michigan	19-2-64	8-6-65	10-6-67
FF 1050 Albert David	Lockheed, Seattle	29-4-64	19-12-64	19-10-68
FF 1051 O'Callahan	Defoe SB, Michigan	19-2-64	20-10-65	13-7-68

Authorized: 2 in FY 61, 3 in FY 62, 5 in FY 63

Garcia (FF 1040)—no ASROC reload magazine G. Arra, 8-85

Bradley (FF 1041) G. Arra, 9-85

Albert David (FF 1050)—ASROC reloads, but no LAMPS capability G. Arra, 5-85

FRIGATES *(continued)*

D: 2,624 tons (3,400–3,560 fl) **S:** 27 kts
Dim: 126.33 (121.9 wl) × 13.47 × 7.9 (over sonar)
A: 2/127-mm 38-cal. DP (I × 2)—1/ASROC ASW RL (VIII × 1)—6/324-mm Mk 32 ASW TT (III × 2)—1/SH-2 LAMPS-I ASW helicopter (except FF 1040, 1043, 1048, 1050)
Electron Equipt: Radar: 1/LN-66, 1/SPS-10, 1/SPS-40, 1/Mk 35
Sonar: FF 1040–1045: SQS-26BX; others: SQS-26AXR; FF 1040, 1043 also: SQR-15 TACTASS
EW: WLR-1, WLR-3, ULQ-6
TACAN: SRN-15 in LAMPS-I ships
M: 1 set G.E. GT; 1 prop; 35,000 **Electric:** 2,000 kw
Boilers: 2 Foster-Wheeler; 83.4 kg/cm², 510°C **Range:** 4,000/20
Fuel: 600 tons **Man:** 18 officers, 250 men

REMARKS: Anti-rolling stabilizers fitted. FF 1047 and FF 1049 have a special ASW NTDS. The boilers are vertical and have turbopressurized combustion. Hangar enlarged for SH-2F LAMPS-I helicopter, 1972-75, except for FF 1048 and FF 1050, which carried the BQR-15 towed passive linear hydrophone array on their sterns until 1982; FF 1040 and 1043, which have the enlarged hangar, carry BQR-15 *instead* of helicopters. Gunfire control is by a Mk 56 radar director, and the Mk 114 ASW fire-control system is installed. FF 1047 and later have an ASROC reload magazine beneath the bridge. Twin Mk 25 torpedo tubes at the stern have been removed from the ships that had them. FF 1041 carried Mk 25 Sea Sparrow launcher in 1967-68 for trials. Although these are relatively recent ships, there are no plans to modernize their obsolescent gun systems or to add Harpoon or modern EW gear.

◆ **2 Bronstein class**

	Bldr	Laid down	L	In serv.
FF 1037 BRONSTEIN	Avondale SY	16-5-61	31-5-62	16-6-63
FF 1038 MCCLOY	Avondale SY	15-9-61	9-6-62	21-10-63

McCloy (FF 1038) Pradignac & Leo, 1984

Bronstein (FF 1037) L. & L. Van Ginderen, 3-84

D: 2,000 tons (2,650 fl) **S:** 26 kts **Dim:** 113.23 × 12.34 × 7.0
A: 2/76.2-mm Mk 33 (II × 1)—1/Mk 116 ASROC ASW RL (VIII × 1)—6/324-mm Mk 32 ASW TT (III × 2)
Electron Equipt: Radar: 1/LN-66, 1/SPS-10, 1/SPS-40, 1/Mk 35
Sonar: 1/SQS-26AXR, 1/SQR-15 TASS (not in FF 1037)
EW: WLR-1, WLR-3, ULQ-6
M: 1 set de Laval GT; 1 prop; 20,000 hp **Fuel:** 480 tons
Boilers: 2 Foster-Wheeler; 42.2 kg/cm², 440°C **Man:** 13 officers, 197 men

REMARKS: Only remaining U.S. frigates with 76.2-mm guns, controlled by a Mk 56 radar director. Single 76.2-mm aft replaced by SQR-15 TASS towed passive hydrophone array sonar. Have Mk 114 Mod. 7 ASW fire-control system. No ASROC reload magazine. TASS towed array gear removed from FF 1037 circa 1981; port boat and davits removed from both.

GUIDED-MISSILE PATROL BOATS

◆ **6 PHM (Patrol Hydrofoil Missile) class (SCB 602 type)**

	Bldr	Laid down	L	In serv.
PHM 1 PEGASUS (ex-*Delphinus*)	Boeing, Seattle	10-5-73	9-11-74	9-7-77
PHM 2 HERCULES	Boeing, Seattle	12-9-80	13-4-82	12-3-83
PHM 3 TAURUS	Boeing, Seattle	30-1-79	8-5-81	7-10-81
PHM 4 AQUILA	Boeing, Seattle	10-7-79	16-9-81	19-12-81
PHM 5 ARIES	Boeing, Seattle	7-1-80	11-81	18-9-82
PHM 6 GEMINI	Boeing, Seattle	13-5-80	17-2-82	12-3-83

Authorized: 2 in FY 73, 4 in FY 75

Hercules (PHM 2) Boeing Marine, 1982

Aquila (PHM 4)—with foils raised L. & L. Van Ginderen, 1984

Aries (PHM 5) Boeing Marine, 1983

GUIDED-MISSILE PATROL BOATS *(continued)*

D: 198 tons light (241 fl, except PHM 1: 235 fl) **S:** 50 kts (11 on diesel)
Dim: 40.5 (44.7 with foils retracted; 36.00 wl) × 8.6 (14.5 over aft foils) × 7.1 (1.9 with foils retracted)/2.7 foilborne
A: 8 Harpoon SSM (IV × 2)—1/76-mm Mk 75 DP (OTO Melara Compact)
Electron Equipt: Radar: 1/SPS-63, 1/Mk 92 Mod. 1 fire-control system
EW: SLR-20, Mk 34 RBOC chaff RL (VI × 2)
M: CODOG: 1 G.E. LM-2500 PB 102 gas turbine; 1 Aerojet AJW-18800-1 water jet; 16,000–19,416 hp; 2 MTU 8V331 TC81, 815 hp diesels; 2 Aerojet AJW-800-1 water jets; 1,340 hp
Electric: 405 kVA **Range:** 600/40; 1,200+/11
Fuel: 50 tons **Man:** 4 officers, 17 men

Remarks: PHM 2 originally authorized under FY 73 and laid down on 30-5-74; her construction was suspended in 8-75, when 40.9 percent complete, but a new hull was laid down 12-9-80 with FY 76 funds. Originally projected as a class of thirty, also to be built by or for other NATO nations, but the additional cost over that of conventional missile craft with similar capabilities was prohibitive, and the U.S. Navy's interest in the type waned. PHM 1 began her protracted trials on 2-25-75. PHM 2 through PHM 6 were canceled on 15-4-77, then reinstated on 14-8-77 at the insistence of Congress, the contract going to Boeing on 20-10-77. PHM 1's gas turbine develops 16,000 hp; on the others 19,416 hp is possible, with the water jet pumping some 341,000 liters/min. at full speed; 55 kts was achieved on trials. Two AIResearch ME 831-800 gas turbines power the two generators. The Mk 92 Mod. 1 fire-control system is an Americanized version of the Hollandse Signaal Apparaaten WM-28 system. PHM 1 has the earlier Mk 94 Mod. 1 variant. SPS-63 is an Americanized version of the Italian SMA 3TM 20-H radar. It was planned at one time to carry eight reload Harpoons, for a total of sixteen. Magazine capacity 400 rds. 76-mm. PHM 6 didn't receive her armament or Mk 92 f.c.s. until 9-83. These craft are extraordinarily steady weapons platforms. All are being backfitted with the SSQ-87(V) collision-avoidance and tracking system. Based at Key West, Florida, as PHM Squadron 2; they are supported by 7 officers and 181 men, working from 73 mobile vans.

Note: Approval to strike the last 2 of 17 *Asheville*-class gunboats, *Gallup* (PG 85) and *Canon* (PG 90) was granted 12-84; both had been stricken 31-1-77 but restored to the Navy List 17-7-81 and are stored at Bremerton. Sisters *Beacon* (PG 99) and *Green Bay* (PG 101), stricken 1-4-77, remain in storage at Little Creek, Va., for possible foreign sale.

PATROL CRAFT

Note: The former "Multi-Mission Patrol Boat" (PBM) program has been officially redesignated "Special Warfare Craft, Medium (SWCM) and is now described with amphibious warfare units on a later page.

◆ **3 Sea Spectre PB Mk-IV class** Bldr: Atlantic Marine, Ft. George Island, Fla. (In serv. 17-12-85)

D: . . . **S:** . . . **Dim:** 20.72 × 5.50 × . . .
A: . . . **Electron Equipt:** 1/. . . nav.
M: 3 G.M. 8V71 TI diesels; 3 props; 1,950 hp
Range: . . . **Man:** . . .

Remarks: Approved under FY 85 for Canal Zone service. Essentially a lengthened version of the PB Mk-III below. Aluminum construction.

◆ **17 Sea Spectre PB Mk-III class** Bldr: Peterson Bldrs. (In serv. 1975-79)

D: 28 tons (36.7 fl) **S:** 30 kts **Dim:** 19.78 × 5.5 × 1.8
A: 1/40-mm AA or 1-2/25-mm Mk 88 AA (I × 1 or 2)—2/12.7-mm mg (I × 2)—1/81-mm mortar/12.7-mm mg combination (see remarks)
Electron Equipt: Radar: 1/. . . nav.
M: 3 G.M. 8V71 TI diesels; 3 props; 1,950 hp
Range: 500/30 **Man:** 1 officer, 4 men

Remarks: Thirteen operate with active fleet Special Boat Units, 4 with Naval Reservists. Winner in competition with Mk-I. Sisters were built for Iran and the Philippines. One was used as trials craft for Norwegian Penguin Mk II missiles in 1981-82, with four missiles mounted on the stern. The 40-mm weapon is in a special, stabilized mounting.

PB Mk-III class—with 12.7-mm mg fore and aft, 81-mm mortar amidships L. & L. Van Ginderen, 6-83

PB Mk-III—with stabilized 40-mm AA forward, 2/12.7-mm mg G. Arra, 1983

◆ **2 PB Mk-I class** Bldr: Sewart Seacraft, Berwick, La. (In serv. 1973)

PB Mk-I class—disarmed as a pilot boat G. Arra, 1985

D: 27 tons (36.3 fl) **S:** 20 kts **Dim:** 19.78 × 5.25 × 1.37
A: 2/20-mm AA (II × 1)—4/12.7-mm mg—1/81-mm mortar/12.7-mm mg combination (now removed)
M: 2 G.M. 12V71 diesels; 2 props; 1,200 hp
Range: 30/26 **Man:** 2 officers, 6 men

◆ **2 PCF Mk-II class** Bldr: Swiftships, Morgan City, La. (In serv. 1967-68)

◆ **3 PCF Mk-I** Bldr: Swiftships (In serv. 7-65 to 7-66)

PCF Mk-I class (PCF 67)

D: 17.5 tons (22.5 fl) **S:** 22 kts **Dim:** 15.3 (Mk-II: 15.66) × 4.55 × 1.1
A: 1/81-mm mortar/12.7-mm mg combination—2/12.7-mm mg
Electron Equipt: Radar: 1/Raytheon 1500B **Range:** 400/22 **Man:** 6 tot.
M: 2 G.M. 12V71 TI diesels; 2 props; 850 hp **Electric:** 6 kw

Remarks: Survivors of some 125 built. Aluminum alloy construction. Used for Naval Reserve training by Special Boat Unit SBU 22 at New Orleans. Mk-II added a low forecastle.

RIVERINE WARFARE CRAFT

◆ **32 PBR (Patrol Boat, Riverine) Mk-II** Bldr: Uniflite, Bellingham, Wash. (In serv. 12-81 to 8-83)

RIVERINE WARFARE CRAFT *(continued)*

PBR Mk-II class U.S. Navy, 1974

D: 8.9 tons (fl) **S:** 24 kts **Dim:** 9.73 × 3.53 × 0.81
A: 3/12.7-mm mg (II × 1, I × 1)—1/60-mm mortar
Electron Equipt: Radar: 1/Raytheon 1900
M: 2 G.M. 6V53N diesels; 2 Jacuzzi water jets; 430 hp
Range: 150/23 **Man:** 4 tot.

Remarks: Fiberglass hull, plastic armor. Used for Naval Reserve training by Special Boat Units. Some recent export versions of this class have G.M. 6V53T engines, for 550 hp and speeds of 30 kts. Three delivered 1982 had G.M. 4-53N diesels.

MINE WARFARE SHIPS

Note: In addition to the ships and craft listed below, there are also 23 RH-53D minesweeping helicopters in service, and 16 Marine Corps CH-53D that can be used to tow sweep gear; 56 MH-53E minesweeping helicopters are programmed. Except for MSO 443, MSO 448, and MSO 490, all minesweepers are assigned to the Naval Reserve Force.

◆ 0 (+5 + 12) MSH 1-class coastal minehunters

	Bldr	Laid down	L	In serv.
MSH 1 Cardinal	Bell-Halter, New Orleans	13-2-86	. . .	2-88
MSH 2 N.	. . .	. . .	. . .	1988
MSH 3 N.	. . .	. . .	. . .	1988
MSH 4 N.	. . .	. . .	. . .	1989
MSH 5 N.	. . .	. . .	. . .	1989

Programmed: MSH 1 in FY 84, MSH 2–5 in FY 86.
Programmed: 4/yr in FY 87–89.

D: 440 tons (fl) **S:** 14 kts **Dim:** 57.60 × 11.89 × 4.04 (0.76 on cushion)
A: 2/12.7-mm mg (I × 2)
Electron Equipt: Radar: SPS-64(V)9—Sonar: SQQ-32
M: 2 Isotta-Fraschini ID36 SS6V-AM diesels; 2/5-bladed props; 1,160 hp (2 Isotta-Fraschini ID36 SS8V-AM diesels for lift fans; 1,650 hp)—1/180-hp retractable ducted prop; 2/180-hp hydraulic motors to drive main props
Range: . . . **Endurance:** 5 days **Electric:** 900 kw **Man:** 4 officers, 37 men

Cardinal (MSH 1)—artist's rendering J. Carr/Bell-Halter, 1983

Remarks: Winner in design contest contracted 15-4-83. Uses Swedish Karlskrona-developed foam core glass-reinforced plastic construction for much of the catamaran hull structure. Basic concept is a rigid-sidewall air-cushion vehicle, with rubber seals fore and aft to capture the air bubble. Two of the three 300-kw generators will be powered by the lift engines, the third by an additional ID36-series diesel. A Honeywell SLQ-48 MNS (Mine Neutralization System) remote-controlled submersible will be carried. The ships, all to be named for "state birds," are to be operated by the Naval Reserve Force and based in U.S. commercial ports—an interesting operational concept, considering the complexity of the design.

MSH 1 was authorized in FY 84 and ordered 26-11-84, with options to build the next eight. MSH 2–5 were authorized under FY 86. Future programming uncertain, as it is intended to "second-source" to another yard to keep down acquisition costs. The data above are not final; displacement has grown considerably, and congressional pressures may mandate a change of engines in later units.

◆ 0 (+11 + 3) MCM 1-class oceangoing minesweeper/minehunters

	Bldr	Laid down	L	In serv.
MCM 1 Avenger	Peterson Bldrs	3-6-83	15-6-85	10-86
MCM 2 Defender	Marinette	1-12-83	7-86	1987
MCM 3 Sentry	Peterson Bldrs	8-10-84	8-86	9-87
MCM 4 Champion	Marinette	28-6-84	9-86	1988
MCM 5 Guardian	Peterson Bldrs	8-5-85	10-86	1988
MCM 6 N.	. . .	. . .	. . .	. . .
MCM 7 N.	. . .	. . .	. . .	. . .
MCM 8 N.	. . .	. . .	. . .	. . .
MCM 9 N.	. . .	. . .	. . .	. . .
MCM 10 N.	. . .	. . .	. . .	. . .
MCM 11 N.	. . .	. . .	. . .	. . .

Authorized: MCM 1 in FY 82, MCM 2 in FY 83, MCM 3–MCM 5 in FY 84, MCM 6–9 in FY 85, MCM 10–11 in FY 86. Programmed: MCM 12–14 in FY88.

Avenger (MCM 1)—artist's rendering U.S. Navy, 1982

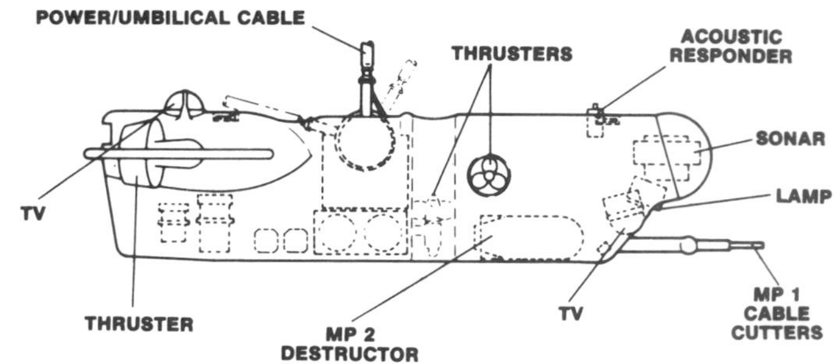

An/SOQ-48 Mine Neutralization System Honeywell

D: 1,312 tons (fl) **S:** 14 kts **Dim:** 68.37 (64.9 wl) × 11.89 × 3.50 (hull)
A: 2/12.7-mm mg (I × 2)
M: MCM 1–2: MCM 3–9: 4 Isotta-Fraschini ID36 SS6V-AM diesels; 2 CP props; 2,600 hp—1/350-hp Omnithruster; 4 Waukesha L-1616 diesels; 2 CP props; 2,280 hp—1/350-hp Omnithruster;
Electron Equipt: Radar: 1/SPS-55
Sonar: SQQ-30 (MCM 6 and later: SQQ-32), WQN-1 Channel Finder
Electric: 1,128 kw **Range:** . . . **Man:** 5 officers, 67 men

Remarks: To be operated by the Naval Reserve Force. First unit was ordered 29-6-82. Wooden-hulled, with fiberglass superstructure. Will be able to sweep deep-moored

MINE WARFARE SHIPS *(continued)*

mines to 180 m as well as sweeping magnetic and acoustic mines. Will have two Honeywell SLQ-48 MNS (Mine Neutralization System), a remote-controlled mine-hunting and destruction device 3.8 m long by .9 m high, weighing 1,136 kg; powered by two 15-hp hydraulic motors for 6-kt speeds, it will have 1,524 m of control cable. Will carry the SSN-2 precision navigation system and/or the Decca-Racal Hyper-Fix precision radio navaid system. Three additional diesels of the same type as the main engines each drive a 376-kw generator.

The wooden hull employs four glued layers of 127-mm planking over 254-mm × 457-mm frames spaced at 1.07-m intervals. All structural members are built up from thinner materials, using phenol/resorcinal glue. The hull had to be lengthened by about 1.8 m after construction had begun, due to stability problems. The first unit was also delayed by design problems and the discovery that the main engines rotated opposite to the gear boxes.

This program has been fraught with major delays and cost increases. Contracts to build the FY 85 quartet had not been let by 3-86, and Congress cut the 4 requested for FY 86 authorization to 2. Congress also stipulated that MCM 10 and later must have U.S.-made diesels.

◆ 2 Acme-class oceangoing minesweepers

Bldr: Frank L. Sample, Jr., Boothbay Harbor, Maine

	Laid down	L	In serv.
MSO 509 Adroit	18-11-54	20-8-55	4-3-57
MSO 511 Affray	24-8-55	18-12-56	8-8-58

Adroit (MSO 509) L. & L. Van Ginderen, 4-82

D: 682 tons light (818 fl) **S:** 14 kts **Dim:** 52.73 × 10.97 × 4.3
A: 2/12.7-mm mg (I × 2)
Electron Equipt: Radar: 1/SPS-53—Sonar: SQQ-14
M: 4 Packard 1D-1700 diesels; 2 CP props; 2,280 hp **Fuel:** 47 tons
Range: 3,000/10 **Man:** 8 officers, 37 men + 4 officers, 33 men Reserves

Remarks: Similar to the *Aggressive* class below, but slightly larger and originally equipped as Mine Division flagships. Not modernized. At 28-29 years of age, they are the U.S. Navy's newest minesweepers. In Naval Reserve Force.

◆ 19 Aggressive class oceangoing minesweepers

	Bldr	Laid down	L	In serv.
MSO 427 Constant	Fulton SY	16-8-51	14-2-53	8-9-54
MSO 433 Engage	Colberg Boat Wks	7-11-51	18-6-53	29-6-54
MSO 437 Enhance	Martinolich SB	12-7-52	11-10-52	16-4-55
MSO 438 Esteem	Martinolich SB	1-9-52	20-12-52	10-9-55
MSO 439 Excel	Higgins, New Orleans	4-2-53	25-9-53	24-2-55
MSO 440 Exploit	Higgins, New Orleans	28-12-51	10-4-53	31-3-54
MSO 441 Exultant	Higgins, New Orleans	22-5-52	6-6-53	22-6-54
MSO 442 Fearless	Higgins, New Orleans	23-7-52	17-7-53	22-9-54
MSO 443 Fidelity	Higgins, New Orleans	15-12-52	21-8-53	19-1-55
MSO 446 Fortify	Seattle, SB & DD	30-11-51	14-2-53	16-7-54
MSO 448 Illusive	Martinolich SB	23-10-51	12-7-52	14-11-53
MSO 449 Impervious	Martinolich SB	18-11-51	29-8-52	15-7-54
MSO 455 Implicit	Wilmington Boat Wks.	29-10-51	1-8-53	10-3-54
MSO 456 Inflict	Wilmington Boat Wks.	29-10-51	6-10-53	11-5-54
MSO 464 Pluck	Wilmington Boat Wks.	31-3-52	6-2-54	11-8-54
MSO 488 Conquest	J. M. Martinac	26-3-53	20-5-54	20-7-55
MSO 489 Gallant	J. M. Martinac	21-5-53	4-6-54	14-9-55
MSO 490 Leader	J. M. Martinac	22-9-53	15-9-54	16-11-55
MSO 492 Pledge	J. M. Martinac	24-6-54	20-7-55	20-4-56

D: 716 tons light (853 fl) **S:** 14 kts **Dim:** 52.42 × 10.97 × 4.2
A: 2/12.7-mm mg (I × 2) **Range:** 2,400/10
Electron Equipt: Radar: SPS-53E or L—Sonar: SQQ-14
M: 4 Waukesha L-1616 diesels; 2 CP props; 2,400 hp **Fuel:** 48 tons
Man: 8 officers, 70 men (Naval Reserve Force ships: 3 officers, 36 men + 3 officers and 44 men Reserves.

Fearless (MSO 442) G. Arra, 1982

Leader (MSO 490)—Regular Navy unit G. Gyssels, 8-83

Remarks: Wooden construction; nonmagnetic, stainless-steel machinery. Except for MSO 443, MSO 448, and MSO 490, which are employed in experimental mine-warfare-related duties, all are operated for the Naval Reserve Force. Ninety-three of the MSO 421 to MSO 508 classes were built; many transferred abroad. Hoist machinery for the SQQ-14 minehunting sonar occupies the position of the former 40-mm AA gun. Twelve of the *Aggressive* class were re-engined with Waukesha diesels; the remainder (MSO 427, 439, 440, 455, 464, 489, and 492) retained Packard 1D1700 diesels, totaling 2,280 hp; those ships displace 684 tons light, 762 full load. *All* the survivors were given very thorough rehabilitations during the early to mid-1970s, receiving semi-enclosed bridges, enlarged superstructures abaft the bridge, SQQ-14 minehunting sonars, new communications gear, and upgraded accommodations. The SPS-53 radars are to be replaced by SPS-64(V)9.

In 1975 MSO 440 was equipped with the prototype SSN-2 precise-navigation system for the new MCM class, and in 1980 MSO 443 conducted trials with the prototype SQQ-30 sonar being developed for the MCM 1 class.

MINESWEEPING BOATS

◆ 1 MSB 29 class Bldr: Trumpy, Annapolis (In serv. 1954)

MSB 29 G. Arra, 7-84

MINESWEEPING BOATS *(continued)*

D: 80 tons (fl) **S:** 12 kts **Dim:** 25.0 × 5.8 × 1.7
A: 1/12.7-mm mg **Electron Equipt:** Radar: 1/Raytheon 1900
M: 2 Packard 2D850 diesels; 2 props; 600 hp **Man:** 2 officers, 9 men

REMARKS: Enlarged MSB 5; only one built. Based at Charleston.

◆ **6 MSB 5 class**

MSB 15, MSB 16, MSB 25, MSB 28, MSB 41, MSB 51

MSB 16 G. Arra, 1984

D: 30 tons light (44 fl) **S:** 12 kts **Dim:** 17.45 × 4.83 × 1.2
A: 1/12.7-mm mg **Electron Equipt:** Radar: 1/Raytheon 1900
M: 2 Packard 2D850 diesels; 2 props; 600 hp **Man:** 6 tot.

REMARKS: Survivors of a class of forty-seven built between 1952 and 1956. Wooden hulls; nonmagnetic machinery. Two Garrett diesel sweep generator sets, except MSB 25: 2 Boeing 502 gas turbine sets. All based at Charleston. Former MSB 7, 13, 17, 35, and 50 were rerated as training craft for the Surface Warfare Officers' School, San Diego, and were to be replaced by ex-YP 654-class training boats late in 1985 and stricken.

◆ **2 (+15) COOP (Craft of Opportunity Program) conversions from wooden-hulled training craft**

	Bldr	L	In serv.	To COOP
CT - 4 (ex-YP 659)	Stephens Bros., Stockton, Cal.	3-58	7-58	9-85
CT - 5 (ex-YP 660)	Stephens Bros., Stockton, Cal.	3-58	8-58	11-85

D: 60 tons (fl) **S:** 13.3 kts **Dim:** 24.51 × 5.72 × 1.60
Electron Equipt: Radar: 1/SPS-53—Sonar: towed side-scan array
M: 4 G.M. 6-71 diesels; 2 props; 590 hp **Man:** 9 tot.

REMARKS: CT stands for COOP Trainer. Conversions from YP 654–675 series wooden-hulled training craft built for the Naval Academy, Annapolis, and the Naval Officer Candidate School, Newport, Rhode Island: two in 1985, four more in 1986, three in 1987, and remainder in 1988. The after deckhouse is being removed, handling gear for a towed precision side-scan sonar added at the stern, and ballast added. Six to convert under FY 86. Each will have four, rotating, 9-man Naval Reserve Force crews, the idea being that three crews will take over previously designated civilian craft in wartime. All will operate on the U.S. East and Gulf coasts. See photo in addenda.

◆ **5 COOP conversions from miscellaneous craft**

CT 1 (ex-*Ida Green*) CT 2 (ex-*Tiki*) CT 3 (ex-*Scheherezade*)
CT. . . (ex-. . .) CT. . . (ex-. . .)

CT 3 U.S. Navy, 1985

REMARKS: Conversion from commercial fishing craft captured while running drugs. All to operate on U.S. West Coast. CT 3, placed in service 28-6-85, is a former shrimp boat 30.8 m o.a. Some 66 additional legitimate commercial craft are to be identified for wartime use by the Naval Reserve crews of these units. In peacetime, the 9-man crews will conduct detailed bottom obstacle surveys. The COOP prototype, MSSB 1 (ex-*Robin Gail* II), has been discarded.

AMPHIBIOUS WARFARE SHIPS

◆ **2 Blue Ridge-class amphibious command ships (SCN 400-65 type)**

	Bldr	Laid down	L	In serv.
LCC 19 BLUE RIDGE	Philadelphia NSY	27-2-67	4-1-69	14-11-70
LCC 20 MOUNT WHITNEY	Newport News SB & DD	8-1-69	8-1-70	16-1-71

Authorized: FY 65 and FY 66

Blue Ridge (LCC 19)—with Mk 15 CIWS fore and aft *Ships of the World*, 1985

Mt. Whitney (LCC 20) Skyfotos, 7-83

D: 19,290 tons (fl) **S:** 21.5 kts
Dim: 189.0 (176.8 wl) × 32.9 (25.0 wl) × 7.5 (8.8 max.)
A: 4/76.2-mm DP (II × 2)—2/Mk 25 BPDMS for Sea Sparrow (VIII × 2)
Electron Equipt: Radar: 1/LN-66, 1/SPS-10, 1/SPS-48, 1/SPS-40, 2/Mk 115
EW: SLQ-32(V)3, Mk 36 SRBOC chaff RL (IV × 4)
TACAN: SRN-6
M: 1 set G.E. GT; 1 prop; 22,000 hp **Fuel:** 2,800 tons
Boilers: 2 Foster-Wheeler; 42.3 kg/cm^2, 467°C **Range:** 13,000/16
Man: 41 officers, 734 men + flag group: 200 officers, 500 men + 150 troops

REMARKS: LCC 19 is the flagship of the Seventh Fleet; LCC 20 is the flagship of the Second Fleet. These ships have a good cruising speed (20 knots) and excellent satellite communications and analysis systems: ACIS (Amphibious Command Information System); NIPS (Naval Intelligence Processing System); NTDS, and photographic laboratories and document-publication facilities. Three LCP, two LCVP landing craft, and one 10-m personnel launch are carried in Welin davits. No helicopter hangar, but they do have a landing pad at the stern. Same machinery and basic hull form as the *Iwo Jima*-class LPH. Air-conditioned; fin stabilizers. Two Mk 56 fire-control systems for the 76.2-mm guns deleted in 1978; two Mk 115 fire-control systems for Sea Sparrow retained. Kevlar plastic armor to be added, as will be the Tactical Flag Command Center. LCC 19 received Mk 15 CIWS in 1985, with stern sponson and bow bulwarks lengthening the ship some 5 m. overall.

◆ **0 (+2 + 8 or 9) Wasp-class helicopter/dock landing ships**

	Bldr	Laid down	L	In serv.
LHD 1 WASP	Ingalls, Pascagoula	30-5-85	8-87	31-3-89
LHD 2 ESSEX	. . .	. . .	. . .	6-91
LHD 3 N.	. . .	. . .	. . .	3-92

Authorized: LHD 1 in FY 84, LHD 2 in FY 86. Programmed: LHD 3 in FY 88, LHD 4 in FY 89, LHD 5 in FY 91.

D: 25,800 tons light (40,533 fl) **S:** 24 kts
Dim: 257.30 (237.14 wl) × 42.67 (32.31 wl) × 8.13

AMPHIBIOUS WARFARE SHIPS *(continued)*

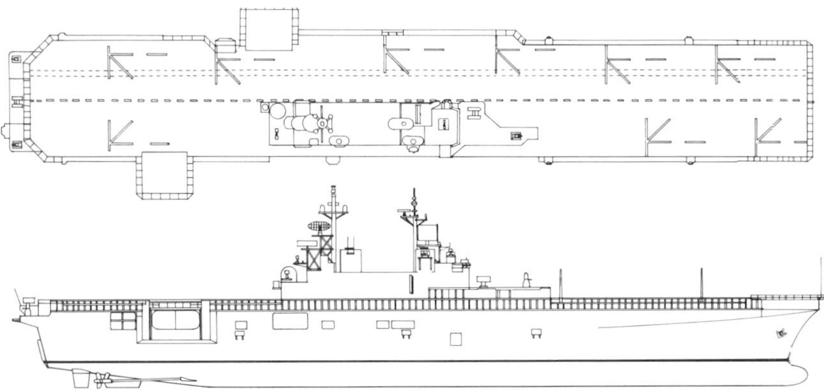

Wasp (LHD 1) A.D. Baker III, 12-83

Wasp (LHD 1)—artist's rendering Ingalls SB/Hamalrath, 1982

A: Assault mode: 42/CH-46 (or fewer CH-53) helicopters and 6/AV-8B Harriers; carrier mode: 20/AV-8B Harriers and 4–6/SH-60B ASW helicopters—2/Mod. Mk 29 launchers for 6 Sea Sparrow (XVI × 2)—3/20-mm Mk 15 CIWS AA (I × 3) 8/12.7-mm mg (I × 8)

Electron Equipt: Radar: 1/SPS-64(V)9, 1/SPS-67, 1/SPS-49(V)5, 1/SPS-52C, 1/Mk 23 TAS, 2/Mk 57 Mod. 2 (on Mk 91 f.c.s.), 1/SPN-35A, 1/SPN-43B
EW: SLQ-32(V)3, Mk 36 SRBOC (VI × 4 or 8)

M: 2 sets GT: 2 props; 77,000 hp (71,000 sust.) **Fuel:** 6,200 tons

Boilers: 2; 49.3 kg/cm², 482°C **Electric:** 14,600 kw

Range: 9,500/20 **Man:** 98 officers, 61 chief petty officers, 921 men, plus 1,873 troops (+200 additional emergency troops accom.)

REMARKS: Design based on that of the LHA 1 class, but intended to be convertible from an assault ship to an ASW ship with Harrier V/STOL fighters for ground assault. Because of the desire to maximize the number of deck spots, no ski-jump V/STOL ramp will be fitted. Differences from the LHA 1 include: use of an LSD/LPD-type lowering stern gate, vice the sectional, rising gate of the LHA; provision for three LCAC in a single-bay, narrower docking well (which can alternatively hold up to 12 LCM(6)); using larger 34-ton elevators, with the stern elevator relocated to starboard; internal stowage for ship's boats; a bulbous forefoot to the bow; a squared-off flight deck forward (made possible by the omission of the 127-mm guns); using HY 100 steel to construct the stronger flight deck; additional cargo elevators; a lower, narrower, and longer island; provision of 3 hospitals, totaling 600 beds; a narrower vehicle ramp to the flight deck; and better ballistic protection. They will have 2,127 m² of vehicle parking space and 3,087 m³ of dry cargo space. Some 1,232 tons of JP-5 aviation fuel and about 50 tons of vehicle fuel will be carried. The SYS-2(V)3 data system will control defensive weapons. An additional 200 troops can be carried in an emergency.

◆ **5 Tarawa-class amphibious assault ships (SCB 410 type)** Bldr: Ingalls SB, Litton Ind., Pascagoula, Miss.

	Laid down	L	In serv.
LHA 1 TARAWA	15-11-71	1-12-73	29-5-76
LHA 2 SAIPAN	21-7-72	18-7-74	15-10-77
LHA 3 BELLEAU WOOD (ex-*Philippine Sea*)	5-3-73	11-4-77	23-9-78
LHA 4 NASSAU (ex-*Leyte Gulf*)	13-8-73	21-1-78	28-7-79
LHA 5 PELELIU (ex-*Da Nang*, ex-*Khe Sanh*)	12-11-76	25-11-78	3-5-80

Authorized: 1 in FY 69, 2 in FY 70, 2 in FY 71

Saipan (LHA 2)—with MK 15 CIWS on deckhouse in place of forward Sea Sparrow launcher Pradignac & Leo, 3-85

Nassau (LHA 4)—with CIWS just before bridge, and fwd Sea Sparrow retained Maritime Photographic, 10-85

Nassau (LHA 4)—showing stern door opening aft to hangar, and port elevator in stowed position L. & L. Van Ginderen, 10-85

Belleau Wood (LHA 3) LSPH S. Given, R.A.N., 5-84

Tarawa (LHA 1) G. Arra, 1984

AMPHIBIOUS WARFARE SHIPS *(continued)*

D: 25,120 tons light (39,400 fl) **S:** 24 kts
Dim: 254.20 (237.14 pp) × 40.23 (32.31 wl) × 7.92
A: 2 (except LHA 2: 1)/Mk 25 Sea Sparrow launchers (VIII × 2)—3/127-mm 54-cal. Mk 45 DP (I × 3)—LHA 2, 4: 1/20-mm Mk 15 CIWS—all: 6/20-mm Mk 67 AA (I × 6)—typical: 16/CH-46, 6/CH-53 and 4/UH-1 helicopters (maximum: 38 CH-46 equivalents)
Electron Equipt: Radar: 1/SPS-53, 1/SPS-10F, 1/SPS-40B, 1/SPS-52B, 1/SPN-35, 1/SPG-60, 1/SPQ-9A, 2/Mk 115
EW: LHA 1, 2: SLQ-32(V)3; others: WLR-1; all: 4/Mk 36 SRBOC chaff (VI × 4)
TACAN: URN-20; (LHA 1, 2: URN-25)
M: 2 sets Westinghouse GT; 2 props; 77,000 hp (70,000 sust.); 900-hp bow-thruster
Electric: 14,600 kw (4 × 2,500 kw, 2 × 2,000 kw, 4 × 150 kw)
Boilers: 2 Combustion Engineering V2M-VS; 49.3 kg/cm², 482°C
Fuel: 5,900 tons
Range: 10,000/20 **Man:** 94 officers, 920 men + 1,924 troops

REMARKS: The LHA is a multipurpose assault transport, a combination of LPH and LPD. It has the general profile of an aircraft carrier, with its superstructure to starboard, flight deck, helicopter elevators to port (folding) and aft, and an 80 × 23.4-m well deck for landing craft (up to four LCU 1610 class). Two LCM(6) and two LCP are stowed on deck. Vehicle stowage garage forward of docking well totals 3,134 m², and the palletized cargo holds total 3,311 m³. Carry approx. 1,200 tons JP-5 fuel for helicopters. The boilers are the largest ever installed in a U.S. Navy ship; the propulsion plant is highly automated. Communications systems include satellite antennas and a large, long-range, high-frequency, log-periodic array. LHA-4 carried 20 AV-8A Harrier V/STOL attack fighters as well as transport helicopters during a 1981 exercise. Very complete 300-bed hospital and mortuary facilities are fitted. All troops have bunks. Completely air-conditioned. Four additional units were canceled in 1971. The 127-mm guns are aboard primarily to provide shore fire support, but can also be used for AA; they are controlled by a Mk 86 Mod. 4 fire-control system with SPQ-9A radar for surface fire, SPG-60 for AA,, and two unmanned electro-optical backup directors. Each Mk 25 Sea Sparrow launcher has an associated Mk 115 radar fire-control system with Mk 71 directors. All scheduled to receive two 20-mm Vulcan/Phalanx gatling AA and SLQ-32(V)3 in place of their present EW systems; in LHA 2, the single CIWS fitted to date has *replaced* the forward Sea Sparrow launcher, while in LHA 4, the CIWS is mounted abaft the missile launcher. Kevlar plastic armor added to all 1982-85. A bulbous forefoot (as on the *Wasp*-class LHD) is to be backfitted to improve endurance, and one 127-mm gun is to be removed to make room for a second Mk 15 CIWS.

AMPHIBIOUS ASSAULT HELICOPTER CARRIERS

◆ 7 Iwo Jima class (SCB 157, LPH 12: SCB 401-66)

	Bldr	Laid down	L	In serv.
LPH 2 Iwo Jima	Puget Sound NSY	2-4-59	17-9-60	26-8-61
LPH 3 Okinawa	Philadelphia NSY	1-4-60	14-8-61	14-4-62
LPH 7 Guadalcanal	Philadelphia NSY	1-9-61	16-3-63	20-7-63
LPH 9 Guam	Philadelphia NSY	15-11-62	22-8-64	16-1-65
LPH 10 Tripoli	Ingalls, Pascagoula	15-6-64	31-7-65	6-8-66
LPH 11 New Orleans	Philadelphia NSY	1-3-66	3-2-68	16-11-68
LPH 12 Inchon	Ingalls, Pascagoula	8-4-68	24-5-69	20-6-70

Authorized: 1 each year in FY 59-63, FY 65, FY 66

D: 11,000 tons light (17,515-18,300 fl) **S:** 23 kts
Dim: 183.6 (169.5 wl) × 31.7 (25.5 wl) × 7.9 (hull)
A: 4/76.2-mm DP (II × 2)—2/Mk 25 Sea Sparrow launchers (VIII × 2)—2/20-mm Mk 15 CIWS (I × 2)—20-24/CH-46 helicopters—4/CH-53 heavy helicopters—4/UH-1 utility or AH-1 attack helicopters

Inchon (LPH 12)—with CIWS *and* Sea Sparrow launcher on port quarter, LCVP in davits, no SPN-35 L. Grazioli, 9-84

Okinawa (LPH 3)—with MH-53E minesweeping helicopters, CIWS in lieu of both Sea Sparrow launchers G. Arra, 6-84

Guadalcanal (LPH 7)—SPN-35 abaft island, CIWs added on sponsons G. Arra, 10-85

Okinawa (LPH 3) LSPH E. Pitman, R.A.N., 9-85

Electron Equipt: Radar: 1/LN-66, 1/SPS-10, 1/SPS-40, 1/SPN-35 (not in LPH 12), SPN-43
EW: SLQ-32(V)3 (except LPH 10: WLR-1) Mk 36 SRBOC chaff RL (VI × 4)
TACAN: SRN-6 or URN-25
M: 1 set GT; 1 prop; 23,000 hp **Electric:** 6,500
Boilers: 4 Combustion Engineering (LPH 9: Babcock & Wilcox); 42.3 kg/cm², 467°C
Man: 47 officers, 605 men + 190 officers, 1,900 troops

REMARKS: The ships can also act as carriers for RH-53 minesweeping helicopters or for AV-8B Harriers. One folding side elevator forward, to port; one to starboard, aft of the island; 70-m hangar. Excellent medical facilities (300 beds). LPH 9 has an ASCAC (Air-Surface Classification and Analysis Center). LPH 12, to a slightly different design, carries two LCVP in davits. Two Mk 63 GFCS removed. LPH 2, 3, 7, and 12 had 2 Mk 15 CIWS added by 1985; initially CIWS replaced the Sea Sparrow launchers, but now it is being mounted (as in LPH 12), one on a sponson on the port quarter and one on a sponson forward, to starboard. Two Sea Sparrow launchers and two twin 76.2-mm gunmounts being retained in all.

AMPHIBIOUS TRANSPORTS, DOCK

◆ 11 Austin class (SCB 187B type)

	Bldr	Laid down	L	In serv.
LPD 4 Austin	New York NSY	4-2-63	27-6-64	6-2-55
LPD 5 Ogden	New York NSY	4-2-63	27-6-64	19-6-65
LPD 6 Duluth	New York NSY	18-12-63	14-8-65	18-12-65
LPD 7 Cleveland	Ingalls, Pascagoula	30-11-64	7-5-66	21-4-67

AMPHIBIOUS TRANSPORTS, DOCK *(continued)*

LPD 8 Dubuque	Ingalls, Pascagoula	25-1-65	6-8-66	1-9-67
LPD 9 Denver	Lockheed SB, Seattle	7-2-64	23-1-65	26-10-68
LPD 10 Juneau	Lockheed SB, Seattle	23-1-65	12-2-66	12-7-69
LPD 12 Shreveport	Lockheed SB, Seattle	27-12-65	25-10-66	12-2-70
LPD 13 Nashville	Lockheed SB, Seattle	14-3-66	7-10-67	14-2-70
LPD 14 Trenton	Lockheed SB, Seattle	8-8-66	3-8-68	6-3-71
LPD 15 Ponce	Lockheed SB, Seattle	31-10-66	20-5-70	10-7-71

Authorized: 3 in FY 62, 4 in FY 63, 3 in FY 64, 2 in FY 65

Ponce (LPD 15)—non-flagship, with 2 Mk 15 CIWS L. & L. Van Ginderen, 3-84

Nashville (LPD 13)—flagship version, with 2 Mk 15 CIWS Pradignac & Leo, 3-85

Duluth (LPD 6)—non-flagship version, still with WLR-1 G. Arra, 8-85

Ogden (LPD 5)—showing stern door G. Arra, 10-85

Cleveland (LPD 7) LSPH E. Pitman, R.A.N., 9-85

D: 11,050 tons (16,550–17,595 fl) **S:** 21 kts
Dim: 173.4 × 25.6 (hull) × 7.0-7.2
A: 4/76.2-mm DP (II × 2)—LPD 12, 13, 15: 2/20-mm Mk 15 CIWS (I × 2)
Electron Equipt: Radar: 1/LN-66, 1/SPS-10, 1/SPS-40
EW: SLQ-32(V)1 (LPD 6: WLR-1); all: Mk 36 SRBOC chaff RL (VI × 4)
TACAN: SRN-6 or URN-25
M: 2 sets de Laval GT; 2 props; 24,000 hp
Boilers: 2 Foster-Wheeler (LPD 5, LPD 12: Babcock & Wilcox), 42.3 kg/cm², 467°C
M: 24 officers, 373 men (+90 staff in LPD 7 to LPD 13) + 930 troops (840 in LPD 7 to LPD 13)

Remarks: Lengthened version of the *Raleigh* class. Combination LSD and assault transports; well deck 120 × 15.24; helicopter platform. Either one LCU and three LCM(6) or nine LCM(6) or four LCM(8) or twenty-eight LVT can be carried in the well deck. Six cranes, one 8.15-ton elevator, two forklifts. Up to six CH-46 helicopters can be carried for brief periods, but the small, telescoping hangar can accommodate only one utility helicopter. LPD 7 to LPD 13 are fitted for flagship duty and have one additional superstructure deck. All have lost their one Mk 56 and two Mk 63 gunfire control, leaving the 76.2-mm guns locally controlled. Two twin 76.2-mm DP removed 1977-78 (port fwd, stbd aft). Two 20-mm Mk 15 CIWS Vulcan/Phalanx AA being added, as well as four Mk 36 SRBOC chaff launchers and the SLQ-32(V)1 EW system. Sister *Coronado* (LPD 11) redesignated AGF 11, 1-10-80. These ships are programmed to receive a SLEP (Service Life Extension Program) modernization, now delayed to FY 89–93, to extend their service lives by 10–15 years. Will be able to support one LCAC, CH-46 helicopters, and will receive SPS-67 in place of SPS-10, new pumps and compressors, and increased vehicle and cargo space.

◆ **2 Raleigh class**

	Bldr	Laid down	L	In serv.
LPD 1 Raleigh	New York NSY	23-6-60	17-3-62	8-9-62
LPD 2 Vancouver	New York NSY	19-11-60	15-9-62	11-5-63

Authorized: FY 59 and FY 60

Raleigh (LPD 1) L. & L. Van Ginderen, 3-84

D: 8,276 tons ight (14,650 fl) **S:** 21 kts
Dim: 159.0 (152.4 wl) × 25.60 (hull) × 6.7

AMPHIBIOUS TRANSPORTS, DOCK *(continued)*

A: 6/76.2-mm DP (II × 3)
Electron Equipt: Radar: 1/LN-66, 1/SPS-10, 1/SPS-40—TACAN: SRN-6
EW: SLQ-32(V)1, Mk 36 SRBOC chaff RL (VI × 4)
M: 2 de Laval GT; 2 props; 24,000 hp **Electric:** 3,600 kw
Boilers: 2 Babcock & Wilcox; 40.8 kg/cm², 467°C
Man: 30 officers, 460 men + 930 troops

Remarks: Sister *La Salle* (LPD 3), modified as flagship for CoMideastFor in the Indian Ocean and reclassified AGF 3, had an additional superstructure deck like LPD 7 to LPD 13. Docking well, 51.2 × 15.2 m, is shorter than on *Austin* class. Emphasis in LPD is on personnel capacity, in LSD on dock capacity; the flight deck, which forms the top of the well deck, can handle up to six CH-46 helicopters; there is no hangar. The port, fwd twin 76.2-mm gunmount and all fire-control systems were removed 1977-78. These ships are not planned to receive SLEP modernization.

DOCK LANDING SHIPS

◆ 0 (+0 + 3 + . . .) LSD 49 class

	Bldr	Laid down	L	In serv.
LSD 49	. . .	. . .	. . .	circa 1994

Remarks: Essentially a cargo variant of the *Whidbey Island* class, with well-deck space for only two LCAC, and an increase in vehicle and cargo capacity. will displace about 16,600 tcns (fl) and carry 504 troops; other data as for LSD 41. First unit programmed for FY 89, with one per year thereafter, but as LSD 41 class is cheaper, it may continue in procurement.

◆ 2 (+6) Whidbey Island class

	Bldr	Laid down	L	In serv.
LSD 41 Whidbey Island	Lockheed, Seattle	4-8-81	10-6-83	9-2-85
LSD 42 Germantown	Lockheed, Seattle	5-8-82	29-6-84	8-2-86
LSD 43 Fort McHenry	Lockheed, Seattle	10-6-83	1-2-86	6-87
LSD 44 N.	Avondale SY	5-86	6-87	7-88
LSD 45 N.	Avondale SY	10-86	. . .	12-88
LSD 46 N.	Avondale SY	. . .	. . .	5-89
LSD 47 N.	Avondale SY	. . .	. . .	1990
LSD 48 N.	Avondale SY	. . .	. . .	1990

Authorized: LSD 41 in FY 81, LSD 42 in FY 82, LSD 43 in FY 83, LSD 44 in FY 84, LSD 45, 46 in FY 85, LSD 47, 48 in FY 86.

D: 11,274 tons (15,165 fl) **S:** 22 kts **Dim:** 185.80(176.80 wl) × 25.60 × 5.84
A: 2/20-mm Mk 15 CIWS AA (I × 2)—2/20-mm AA Mk 67 (I × 2)—8/12.7-mm mg (I × 8)
Electron Equipt: Radar: 1/LN-66, 1/SPS-67, 1/SPS-49—TACAN: URN-25
EW: SLQ-32(V)1, Mk 36 SRBOC chaff RL (VI × 4)
M: 4 Colt-Pielstick 16 PC2.5V400 diesels; 2 CP props; 41,600 hp (33,000 sust.)
Electric: 9,200 kw **Man:** 24 officers, 391 men + 504 troops (including 166 staff)
Fuel: 2,000 tons **Range:** Approx. 8,000/20

Remarks: The design was originally to have been a near-repeat of the LSD 36 class, but a requirement to be able to hold four LCAC (Air-Cushion Landing Craft) in the docking well, which measures 134.0 × 15.24 m clear, necessitated the change. The helicopter deck is raised above the docking well (which can also hold 21 LCM(6) or 3 LCU or 64 LVTP) in order to provide all-around ventilation for the gas turbine-engined LCACs. There are two landing spots for up to CH-53-sized helicopters but no hangar facilities. Forward of the docking well is 1,214 m² of vehicle parking space and 149 m³ of palletized cargo. Carry 90 tons JP-5 fuel for helicopters. Carry one LCM(6), two LCPL Mk-II, and one LCVP on deck, handled by one 20-ton and one 60-ton crane. The FY 85 and later ships will have the Mk 88 Mod. 0 Bushmaster 25-mm gun in place of the 20-mm Mk 67 AA.

Whidbey Island (LSD 41) Lockheed, 9-84

Whidbey Island (LSD 41) Lockheed, 9-84

Whidbey Island (LSD 41) Lockheed, 9-84

DOCK LANDING SHIPS *(continued)*

Germantown (LSD 42)—fitting out G. Arra, 10-85

◆ **5 Anchorage class (SCN 404-65 and 66 types)**

	Bldr	Laid down	L	In serv.
LSD 36 Anchorage	Ingalls, Pascagoula	13-3-67	5-5-68	15-3-69
LSD 37 Portland	Gen'l Dynamics, Quincy	21-9-67	20-12-69	3-10-70
LSD 38 Pensacola	Gen'l Dynamics, Quincy	12-3-69	11-7-70	27-3-71
LSD 39 Mount Vernon	Gen'l Dynamics, Quincy	29-1-70	17-4-71	13-5-72
LSD 40 Fort Fisher	Gen'l Dynamics, Quincy	15-7-70	22-4-72	12-9-72

Authorized: 1 in FY 65, 3 in FY 66, 1 in FY 67

Pensacola (LSD 38)—open 76.2-mm gunmounts, SLQ-32, 2 CIWS G. Arra, 10-85

Fort Fisher (LSD 40)—enclosed gunmounts LSPH E. Pitman, R.A.N., 9-85

D: 8,600 tons light (14,000 fl) **S:** 22 kts
Dim: 168.66 (162.8 wl) × 25.9 × 5.6(6.1 max.)
A: 6/76.2-mm DP (II × 3)—LSD 38: 2/20-mm Mk 15 CIWS (I × 2)
Electron Equipt: Radar: 1/LN-66, 1/SPS-10, 1/SPS-40
EW: SLQ-32(V)1, Mk 36 SRBOC chaff RL (VI × 4)
M: 2 sets de Laval GT; 2 props; 24,000 hp
Boilers: 2 foster-Wheeler (LSD 36: Combustion Eng.); 42.3 kg/cm², 467°C
Fuel: 2,750 tons **Man:** 20 officers, 430 men + 338 troops

Remarks: Carry assault landing craft in the well deck (113.28 × 15.24); can accommodate 3 LCU or 15 LCM(6) or 8 LCM(8) or 50 LVT. One or two LCM(6) stowed on deck, handled by the two 50-ton cranes. Have 1,115 m² of vehicle parking space forward of the docking well. The helicopter deck is removable; 90 tons JP-5 fuel carried for helicopters. The starboard forward twin 76.2-mm removed to allow later mounting of two 20-mm Mk 15 CIWS (one to go aft). Mk 56 and Mk 63 directors removed in 1977.

◆ **8 Thomaston class (SCB 75 type)** Bldr: Ingalls, Pascagoula, Miss.

	Laid down	L	In serv.	To Reserve
LSD 28 Thomaston	3-3-53	9-2-54	17-9-54	5-9-84
LSD 29 Plymouth Rock	5-5-53	7-5-54	29-11-54	30-9-83
LSD 30 Fort Snelling	17-8-53	16-7-54	24-1-55	28-9-84
LSD 31 Point Defiance	23-11-53	28-9-54	31-3-55	30-9-83
LSD 32 Spiegel Grove*	7-9-54	10-11-55	8-6-56	...
LSD 33 Alamo*	11-10-54	20-1-56	24-8-56	...
LSD 34 Hermitage*	11-4-55	12-6-56	14-12-56	...
LSD 35 Monticello	6-6-55	10-8-56	29-3-57	1-10-85

Authorized: 4 in FY 52, 2 in FY 54, 2 in FY 55—*Active

Hermitage (LSD 34)—with Mk 15 CIWS G. Arra, 10-85

Alamo (LSD 33) G. Arra, 1984

D: 6,880 tons (12,150 fl) **S:** 22.5 kts **Dim:** 155.45 × 25.6 × 5.4 (5.8 max.)
A: 6/76.2-mm DP (II × 3)—LSD 34 also: 2/20-mm Mk 15 CIWS (I × 2)
Electron Equipt: Radar: 1/LN-66, 1/SPS-10, 1/SPS-6
M: 2 sets G.E. GT; 2 props; 24,000 hp **Range:** 10,000/20
Boilers: 2 Babcock & Wilcox, 40.8 kg/cm² pressure
Fuel: 1,390 tons **Man:** 20 officers, 385 men + 318 troops

Remarks: Portable helicopter platform. Can carry 3 LCU, 18 LCM(6), or 9 LCM(8) in 119.2 × 14.6 well deck, with 975 m² of vehicle parking space forward of the docking well. Two 50-ton cranes. Originally had 16 76.2-mm DP (II × 8). Now have one mount forward to starboard, and two amidships. Two Mk 56 and Mk 63 gunfire-control systems removed in 1977. Last active ships with SPS-6 air-search radar. To be replaced by new LSD 41 class. Being decommissioned to National Defense Reserve Fleet for retention for possible emergency mobilization.

TANK LANDING SHIPS

◆ **20 Newport class (SCN 405-66 type)**

Bldrs: LST 1179: Philadelphia NSY; others: National Steel SB, San Diego

	Laid down	L	In serv.
LST 1179 Newport	1-11-66	3-2-68	7-6-69
LST 1180 Manitowoc	1-2-67	4-6-69	24-1-70

TANK LANDING SHIPS *(continued)*

LST 1181 Sumter	14-11-67	13-12-69	20-6-70
LST 1182 Fresno	16-12-67	28-9-68	22-11-69
LST 1183 Peoria	22-2-68	23-11-68	21-2-70
LST 1184 Frederick	13-4-68	8-3-69	11-4-70
LST 1185 Schenectady	2-8-68	24-5-69	13-6-70
LST 1186 Cayuga	28-9-68	12-7-69	8-8-70
LST 1187 Tuscaloosa	23-11-68	6-9-69	24-10-70
LST 1188 Saginaw	24-5-69	7-2-70	23-1-71
LST 1189 San Bernardino	12-7-69	28-3-70	27-3-71
LST 1190 Boulder*	6-9-69	22-5-70	4-6-71
LST 1191 Racine*	13-12-69	15-8-70	9-7-71
LST 1192 Spartanburg County	7-2-70	11-11-70	1-9-71
LST 1193 Fairfax County	28-3-70	19-12-70	16-10-71
LST 1194 La Moure County	22-5-70	13-2-71	18-12-71
LST 1195 Barbour County	15-8-70	15-5-71	12-2-72
LST 1196 Harlan County	7-11-70	24-7-71	8-4-72
LST 1197 Barnstable County	19-12-70	2-10--71	27-5-72
LST 1198 Bristol County	13-2-71	4-12-71	5-8-72

Authorized: 1 in FY 65, 8 in FY 66, 11 in FY 67—*Naval Reserve Force

D: 4,973 tons light (8,450 fl) **S:** 22 kts (20 sust.)
Dim: 159.2 (171.3 over horns) × 21.18 × 5.3 (aft) × 1.80 (fwd)
A: 4/76.2-mm DP (II ×2)—LST 1179, 1180, 1181, 1192, 1194 also: 1/20-mm Mk 15 CIWS
Electron Equipt: Radar: 1/LN-66, 1/SPS-10—see remarks

La Moure County (LST 1194)—with CIWS atop pilothouse G. Arra, 10-84

Saginaw (LST 1188) Skyfotos, 3-83

Spartanburg County (LST 1192)—with CIWS atop pilothouse, causeway pontoon sections along sides, aft Pradignac & Leo, 3-85

Bristol County (LST 1198) G. Arra, 1984

M: 6 Alco 16-251 (LST 1179 to LST 1181: G.M. 16-645-E5) diesels; 2 CP props; 16,500 hp
Fuel: 1,750 tons **Man:** 12 officers, 174 men + 20/411 troops

Remarks: LST 1190 transferred to the Naval Reserve Force 1-12-80 and LST 1191 on 15-1-81. Can carry 500 tons of cargo on 1,765 m² of deck space, and up to 431 troops (386 normal). A side-thruster propeller forward helps when marrying to a causeway. There is a mobile aluminum ramp forward (34 tons), which is linked to the tank deck by a second ramp. These ramps can carry 75 tons. Aft is a helicopter platform and a stern door for loading and unloading vehicles. Four pontoon causeway sections can be carried on the hull sides. Mk 63 radar gunfire-control systems removed 1977-78. SLQ-32(V)1 and chaff RL are *not* planned. LST 1179 has *two* navigational radars. Some receiving 1 Mk 15 CIWS 20-mm gatling AA atop pilothouse in an interim installation; still plan to carry 2 CIWS and delete 76.2-mm guns.

Note: Three surviving *DeSoto County* tank landing ships have been in the National Defense Reserve Fleet since 1972: *Suffolk County* (LST 1173), *Wood County* (LST 1178), and *Lorain County* (LST 1177).

AMPHIBIOUS CARGO SHIPS

◆ **5 Charleston class**

	Bldr	Laid down	L	In serv.
LKA 113 Charleston	Newport News	5-12-66	2-12-67	14-12-68
LKA 114 Durham	Newport News	10-7-67	29-3-68	24-5-69
LKA 115 Mobile	Newport News	15-1-68	19-10-68	29-9-69
LKA 116 St. Louis	Newport News	3-4-68	4-1-69	22-11-69
LKA 117 El Paso	Newport News	22-10-68	17-5-69	17-1-70

Authorized: 4 in FY 65, 1 in FY 66

Charleston (LKA 113) G. Gyssels, 3-84

Durham (LKA 114) G. Arra, 1984

D: 10,000 tons (18,600 fl) **S:** 20 kts
Dim: 175.6 (167.6 wl) × 18.9 × 8.5 (max.)
A: 6/76.2-mm DP (II × 3)
Electron Equipt: Radar: 1/LN-66, 1/SPS-10
EW: SLQ-32(V)1, Mk 36 SRBOC chaff RL (VI × 2)
M: 1 set Westinghous GT; 1 prop; 22,000 hp
Boilers: 2 Combustion Engineering; 42.2 kg/cm², 443°C
Fuel: 2,400 tons **Man:** 25 officers, 366 men + 15 officers, 211 troops

Remarks: All but LKA 116 transferred to the Naval Reserve Force, LKA 113 on 21-11-79, LKA 114 on 1-10-79, LKA 115 on 1-9-80, and LKA 117 on 1-3-81. Returned to Regular Navy: LKA 113 on 13-2-83, LKA 114 on 1-10-82, LKA 115 on 1-7-83 and LKA 117 on 1-10-82. Air-conditioned. Machinery control is automatic. Helicopter

AMPHIBIOUS CARGO SHIPS *(continued)*

platform. Fittings include two 70-ton heavy-lift booms, two 40-ton booms, and eight 15-ton booms. Normally carry four LCM(8), five LCM(6), two LCVP, and two LCP. Two Mk 56 radar gunfire-control systems and one twin 76.2-mm gunmount removed 1977-78; to receive two 20-mm Vulcan/Phalanx AA, but not until late 1980s.

NOTE: The *Mariner*-class amphibious cargo ship *Tulare* (LKA 112) was stricken on 1-8-81 and is retained in the National Defense Reserve Fleet by the Maritime Administration.

UTILITY LANDING CRAFT

◆ **38(+2) LCU 1610 class (SCB 149, 149B, and 406 types)** Bldrs: See remarks (In serv. 6-59 to 12-71, except LCU 1680, 81: 9-86)

LCU 1616	LCU 1629 to 1635	ASDV 1 (ex-LCU 1621)
LCU 1617	LCU 1643 to LCU 1646	ASDV 2 (ex-LCU 1623)
LCU 1619	LCU 1648 to LCU 1666	ASDV 3 (ex-LCU 1628)
LCU 1624	LCU 1680	
LCU 1627	LCU 1681	

LCU 1649 L. & L. Van Ginderen, 3-84

LCU 1641—minelaying workboat at Charleston, So. Carolina; note crane to port, rail over stern G. Arra, 1984

ASDV 1 (ASDV 2, 3 similar)—midships area decked over G. Arra, 1984

D: 190 tons (390 fl) **S:** 11 kts **Dim:** 41.07 × 9.07 × 2.08
A: 2/12.7-mm mg (I × 2) **Electron Equipt:** Radar: 1/navigational
M: 4 G.M. 6-71 diesels; 2 Kort-nozzle props; 1,200 hp
Fuel: 13 tons **Range:** 1,200/11 **Man:** 6 men + 8 troops

REMARKS: LCU 1616–1619, LCU 1623, LCU 1624 delivered 6-59 to 9-60 by Gunderson Bros., Portland, Oregon; LCU 1621, 1626, 1629, and 1630 delivered 6-60 to 1968 by Southern Shipbuilding, Slidell, La.; LCU 1627, 1628, 1631–1635 built by General Ship & Eng. Wks., East Boston, Mass.; LCU 1643–1645 delivered 8-67 to 1969 by Marinette Marine, Marinette, Wisc.; LCU 1646–1666 delivered 1969-70 by Defoe SB, Bay City, Wisc.; LCU 1667–1670 built by General Ship & Eng. Wks.; LCU 1680, 81 ordered 10-85 from Moss Point Marine, Escatanapa, Miss., for delivery 9-86 to Naval Reserve Force units. The similar, aluminum-hulled LCU 1637 is now a seagoing training device at Roosevelt Roads, Puerto Rico. Missing numbers have either been redesignated as yard craft (YFU—see later pages) or transferred to the U.S. Army (LCU 1667–1679). LCU 1621 has vertical cycloidal propellers. Cargo capacity is 143 tons; cargo space, 30.5 × 5.5 m. Usually unarmed; can be equipped with an LN-66 or other small navigation radar. Minor differences as construction progressed: five others serve as workboats: LCU 1613, 1614, 1637, 1641, 1647; of these, three have been designated as ASDV (Auxiliary Swimmer Delivery Vehicle) and assigned to Special Boat Unit 22; they have a crew of 13 and carry a decompression chamber. Twelve of these extremely useful craft are to be given a Service Life Extension Program (SLEP) modernization.

◆ **1 LCU 1466 class (SCB 25 type)**

LCU 1473 (In serv. 5-55)

D: 180 tons (347 fl) **S:** 8 kts **Dim:** 35.08 × 10.36 × 1.6(aft)
M: 3 Gray Marine 64YTL diesels; 3 props; 675 hp **Electric:** 40 kw
Fuel: 11 tons **Range:** 1,200/6 **Man:** 6 men + 8 troops

REMARKS: Built between 1953 and 1958. Can carry 167 tons. Engines and bridge aft. Improved version of LCU 501 class. Missing numbers have been either transferred, sunk, or converted to service craft (YFU). LCU 1473 is operated by the Naval Reserve Force at Buffalo, NY (to be replaced 1986 by a new unit); two sisters, LCU 1564 and LCU 1578, are classified as utility boats, but have not been redesignated YFU. A number of additional units of the class are operated by the U.S. Army. LCU 501 (ex-LCT(6))-class landing craft LCU 1232 (ex-YFU 67) survives at Subic Bay: 134 tons (349 fl).

MINOR LANDING CRAFT

◆ **3(+30 +56) LCAC class** Bldr: Bell Aerospace/Textron-Halter Marine and Lockheed SB, Pascagoula, Mississippi

Authorized: 3 in FY 82, 3 in FY 83, 6 in FY 84, 9 in FY 85, 12 in FY 86
Programmed: 9 each in FY 88-91

LCAC 1 Bell Aerospace Textron, 12-84

LCAC 1 Bell Aerospace Textron, 12-84

D: 88 tons light (200 fl) **S:** 54 kts (40 when loaded)
Dim: 26.8 (24.7 hull) × 14.3 (13.4 hull) × 0.87 (at rest)
A: None **Electron Equipt:** Radar: 1/navigational
M: 4 Avco TF40B gas turbines (2 for lift); 2 shrouded airscrews; 12,444 hp
Fuel: 6.2 tons **Range:** 223/48; 200/40(loaded **Man:** 4 crew + 24 troops

REMARKS: Design derived from that of the JEFF-B prototype. Original program for 101 or more has been cut to 90 total. Cargo capacity: 60 tons normal/75 overload. To be carried by the LSD 41, LPD 17, LHD 1, and LHA 1 classes. Bow ramp is 8.8 m wide, stern ramp 4.6 m. The deck has 168-m² parking area. First unit launched 2-5-84 and placed in service 24-12-84; second unit launched 18-1-85 and delivered 19-7-85. First 12 by Bell-Halter, numbers 13-14 ordered 10-85 from Lockheed, with orders for 7 other FY 85 units delayed. Prototype has experienced numerous design and reliability problems. LCAC 1–6 to operate as ACU 5 from Camp Pendleton, Cal., in 1986, LCAC 7–12 as ACU 4 from Little Creek, Va., in 1988.

MINOR LANDING CRAFT *(continued)*

◆ **23(+15) LCM(8) Mk 4 class** (In serv. 1967-79; 1985-86)

◆ **54 LCM(8) Mk 3 class** (In serv. 1953-55)

◆ **25 LCM(8) Mk-2 class** (In serv. 1967-69)

LCM(8) Mk-2 class 16 of ACU 2—note mounts for 2/12.7-mm mg abreast pilot-house L. & L. Van Ginderen, 3-84

D: 34 tons light (121 fl) **S:** 12 kts **Dim:** 22.43 × 6.40 × 1.40 (aft)
M: 4 G.M. 6-71 diesels; 2 props; 590 hp **Range:** 150/12

REMARKS: Began building in 1969. Aluminum version of LCM(8) Mk 1. Cargo: 58 tons. Some have two G.M. 12V71 diesels. Ten were to be built under FY 82 for use aboard the new T-AKX maritime prepositioning ships; canceled. Eight were ordered from Marine Power Co., Seattle, under FY 83; 10 authorized (some for T-AKX) under FY 84; 3 authorized under FY 85. Ten ordered 10-85 from Twin City shipyards.

◆ **6 LCM(8) Mk 1 class** (In serv. 1954)

LCM(8) Mod. 1 class of ACU 2 L. & L. Van Ginderen, 3-82

D: 56 tons light (116 fl) **S:** 9 kts **Dim:** 22.43 × 6.42 × 1.57
M: 4 G.M. 6-71 diesels; 2 props; 620 hp **Range:** 140/9

REMARKS: Built between 1949 and 1976. Cargo: 54 tons. U.S. Army also uses large numbers of this type.

◆ **approx. 106 LCM(6) class**

LCM(6)—rigged as push tug and beach retrieval craft G. Gyssels, 1982

Standard LCM(6)—attached to Naval Air Base, San Diego W. Donko, 7-84

D: 24 tons (56 fl) **S:** 10 kts **Dim:** 17.07 × 4.37 × 1.17 (aft)
M: 2 Gray Marine 64HN9 (G.M. V71 on Mk-3) diesels; 2 props; 330 hp
Range: 130/10

REMARKS: Designed during World War II and built between 1952 and 1980. Many used in utility roles. Cargo: 30 tons. Two new examples requested under FY 85 for delivery 1-86. Majority (67) in service are Mk-3, delivered 1977-80; another 36 are Mk-2, delivered 1960-71.

◆ **136 LCVP Mk-7 class** (In serv. 1966-69)

D: 13 tons(fl) **S:** 9 kts **Dim:** 10.90 × 3.21 × 1.04 (aft)
M: 1 Gray Marine 64HN9 diesel; 225 hp **Range:** 110/9

REMARKS: Glass-reinforced plastic hulls. Can carry 36 troops or 3.5 tons cargo.

◆ **131 LCPL Mk-12 class**

D: 13 tons (fl) **S:** 19 kts **Dim:** 10.98 × 3.97 × 1.13
Electron Equipt: Radar: 1/LN-66
M: 1 G.M. 8V71 TI diesel; 350-425 hp **Range:** 150/. . . **Man:** 3 crew + 17 passengers

REMARKS: Plastic construction. For use as control craft. Carried abroad LHA, LPD, LSD, LST classes, etc. Total includes 75 LCP(L) Mk-12 ordered from Watercraft America, Edgewater, Fla., in 30-6-83, with 23 more on option; first delivered 8-84 and last by 9-85. Earlier Mk-12 delivered 9-81 to 4-84. In FY 85, 48 more planned for ordering, plus 50 in FY 86 and 16 in FY 87-88, for an eventual total of 214.

◆ **88 LCPL Mk-11** (In serv. 1960-67)

◆ **33 LCPL Mk-4** (In serv. 1968-71)

REMARKS: Generally similar to LCPL Mk-12, except steel construction. Mk-11 employs G.M. 6121T diesel, 350 hp. All Mk-11 and Mk-4 to be replaced by Mk-12 by 1988.

◆ **2 amphibious warfare warping tugs** Bldr: Campbell Machine Wks., San Diego, Cal. (In serv. 4-70)

LWT 1 LWT 2

D: 61 tons light **S:** 9 kts **Dim:** 25.9 × 6.7 × 2.1
M: 2 G.M. 8V71 diesels; 2 steerable props; 420 hp **Man:** 6 tot.

REMARKS: Aluminum construction, intended for handling causeway sections and ship-to-beach fuel lines. Series production not pursued.

◆ **5 powered causeway section side-loadable warping tugs**

SLWT 1-5 (In serv. 1969)

D: 81.5 tons (light) **S:** 9.5 kts **Dim:** 27.61 × 6.48 × 0.81
M: 2 G.M. 8V71 TI diesels; 2 Peerless centrifugal waterjet pumps; 850 hp

REMARKS: Essentially standard Navy "lighted pontoon" barges with a built-in waterjet propulsion section. Intended for vehicle or container offloading for larger ships and for deploying the Amphibious Assault Fuel Supply Facility to a beachhead.

SPECIAL WARFARE CRAFT

◆ **0(+1 + 18) Special Warfare Craft, Medium (SWCM)** Bldr: R.M.I., National City, Cal.

	Laid down	L	In serv.
SWCM 1	. . .	1-86	. . .

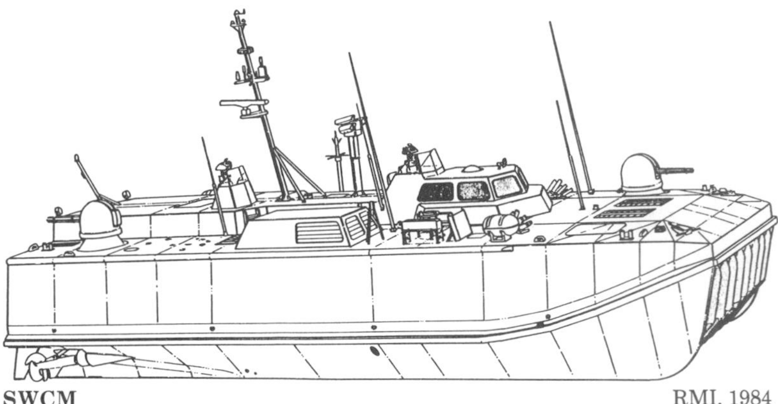

SWCM RMI, 1984

D: 83 tons light (115 fl) **S:** 35 kts
Dim: 23.93 × 10.67 × 1.50 (0.60 on cushion)
A: 2/25-mm Sea Vulcan gatling AA—Stinger hand-held SAMs
Electron Equipt: Radar: 1/SPS-64(V)9
EW: Argo AR700-1 intercept, Mk 34 RBOC RL (VI × 2)
M: 2 G.M. Allison 16V149 TI diesels; 2 props, 3,600 hp—2 G.M. 8V92 TA diesel lift fan engines; 680 hp
Range: . . . **Man:** 3 officers, 6 men + 16 special forces troops

SPECIAL WARFARE CRAFT *(continued)*

Remarks: Originally typed PBM—Patrol Boat, Multimission. Intended to support Navy SEAL special forces teams. Prototype ordered 10-5-85. Plan nine for each coast, plus one for training. Lift engines power six lift fans. Rigid sidewall air-cushion vehicle, with flexible rubber seals at bow and stern. Will have a Magnavox optronic sensor based on the H.S.A. LIOD. Three additional units in FY 86, followed by 6 each in FY 87 and FY 88 and three in FY 89; however, program delays in design stage have slowed progress.

◆ **70 SWCL "Seafox" class** Bldr: Uniflite, Bellingham, Wash. (In serv. 1980-83)

Seafox U.S. Navy, 1980

D: 11.3 tons (fl) **S:** 30+ kts **Dim:** 11.0 × 3.0 × 0.84
A: Small arms **Electron Equipt:** Radar: 1/LN-66
M: 2 G.M. 6V-92 TA diesels; 2 props; 930 hp **Man:** 3 tot.

Remarks: Glass-reinforced plastic construction. SWCL = Special Warfare Craft, Light. Intended for use by SEAL Team commandos; can stow a rubber raft. Have secure voice communications gear, IFF, night-vision equipment, and an echo-sounder.

◆ **22 Mini-ATC class** Bldr: Sewart Seacraft, Berwick, La. (In serv. 1972-73)

Mini-ATC Sewart Seacraft, 2-72

D: 9.3 tons light (13 fl) **S:** 28.5 kts **Dim:** 10.97 × 3.89 × 0.30
A: Up to 4/12.7-mm mg (I × 4)—1/40-mm Mk 19 grenade launcher—1/M60 mortar
M: 2 G.M. 8V53N diesels; 2 Jacuzzi 14YJ waterjets; 566 hp
Range: 37/28
Man: 2 crew + 15 troops

Remarks: Aluminum construction. Rectangular platform; bow ramp. Seven weapon-mounting positions. Can carry an LN-66 radar. Very quiet in operation. All operated by Naval Reserve Force Special Boat Units.

Note: SEAL teams also operate 4-man Mk-7, 6-man Mk-8, and 2-man Mk-9 swimmer delivery submersibles.

AUXILIARY SHIPS

Note: This section includes only ships that are subordinate to the U.S. Navy proper. Ships assigned to the civilian-manned Military Sealift Command are listed separately in a following section. Below, ships are listed alphabetically by their U.S. Navy type designation, i.e., AD, AF, AG, etc.

◆ **6 Samuel Gompers-class destroyer tenders (SCB 244 type)**

Bldrs: AD 37 and AD 38, Puget Sound NSY; AD 41 to AD 44, National Steel, San Diego

	Laid down	L	In serv.
AD 37 Samuel Gompers	9-7-64	14-5-66	1-7-67
AD 38 Puget Sound	15-2-65	16-9-66	27-4-68
AD 41 Yellowstone	27-6-77	27-1-79	28-6-80
AD 42 Acadia	14-2-78	28-7-79	6-6-81
AD 43 Cape Cod	27-1-79	2-8-80	17-4-82
AD 44 Shenandoah	2-8-80	6-2-82	17-12-83

Authorized: 1 in FY 64, 1 in FY 65, 1 in FY 75, 1 in FY 76, 1 in FY 77, 1 in FY 79

Samuel Gompers (AD 37) L. & L. Van Ginderen, 3-83

Puget Sound (AD 38)—when 6th Fleet flagship, with special SATCOMM antenna atop lattice mast, URN-25 TACAN atop foremast L. & L. Van Ginderen, 7-84

Shenandoah (AD 44) L. & L. Van Ginderen, 5-84

D: AD 37, 38: 13,600 tons light (20,500 fl); AD 41–44: 13,318 tons light (20,224 fl)
S: 20 kts **Dim:** 196.29 × 25.91 × 6.86
A: AD 37, 38: 4/20-mm AA (I × 4); others: 2/20-mm AA (I × 2); all: 2/40-mm Mk 19 grenade launchers
Electron Equipt: Radar: 1/LN-66, 1/SPS-10—TACAN: AD 41: URN-25
M: 1 set de Laval GT; 1 prop; 20,000 hp **Electric:** 12,000 kw
Boilers: 2 Combustion Engineering; 43.6 kg/cm², 462°C
Man: AD 37, 38: 43 officers, 1,233 men; AD 41–44: 87 officers, 1,508 men

Remarks: Similar to *L. Y. Spear*-class submarine tenders; AD 41 and later considered a separate class (SCB 700 type) and have facilities to carry and overhaul LM-2500 gas turbines, being tailored to support DD 963, DDG 993, and FFG 7-class ships. All have helo deck aft, no hangar (except AD 38). Maintenance ships for guided-missile cruisers and destroyers. Two 30-ton cranes; two 3.5-ton traveling cranes. Excellent workshops for electronic equipment and surface-to-air missiles. Carry 60,000 different types of repair parts in 65 storerooms totaling 1,795 m³. Originally planned to carry Sea Sparrow in AD 41 and later. One 127-mm DP removed from AD 38 in 1979. AD 38 became 6th Fleet flagship in 7-80, having received an extra mast to support a special SATCOMM antenna (all have the standard WSC-3 SATCOMM installation, with two OE-82 drum-shaped antennas); relieved by *Coronado* (AGF 11) in 8-85.

◆ **1 Klondike-class destroyer tender—in reserve**

	Bldr	Laid down	L	In serv.
AD 24 Everglades	Los Angeles SB	26-6-44	28-1-45	25-5-51

D: 8,165 tons (14,700 fl) **S:** 18 kts **Dim:** 149.96 (141.73 pp) × 21.25 × 8.3
A: None **Electron Equipt:** Radar: 1/SPS-10
M: 1 set Westinghouse GT; 1 prop; 8,500 hp **Electric:** 3,600 kw
Boilers: 2 Foster-Wheeler; 30.6 kg/cm², 393°C
Fuel: 2,415 tons **Man:** 800–918 tot.

AUXILIARY SHIPS *(continued)*

Everglades (AD 24)—in reserve A.D. Baker, 8-84

REMARKS: In reserve, used as an accommodations ship at Philadelphia. Built on C-3 cargo hull. Helicopter deck; hangar for DASH.

◆ **3 Dixie-class destroyer tenders**

	Bldr	Laid down	L	In serv.
AD 15 PRAIRIE	New York SB	7-12-38	9-12-39	5-8-40
AD 18 SIERRA	Tampa SB	31-12-41	23-2-43	20-3-44
AD 19 YOSEMITE	Tampa SB	19-1-42	16-5-43	25-3-44

Prairie (AD 15) L. & L. Van Ginderen, 9-84

D: 9,450 tons (17,190 fl) **S:** 18 kts **Dim:** 161.7 × 22.33 × 7.8
A: 4/20-mm AA (I × 4) **Electron Equipt:** Radar: 1/LN-66 1/SPS-10
M: 2 sets GT; 2 props; 11,000 hp **Electric:** 4,100 kw
Boilers: 4 Babcock & Wilcox; 28.4 kg/cm², 382°C
Fuel: 3,680 tons **Range:** 12,200/12
Man: 37 officers, 893 men

REMARKS: The design of these support ships goes back to pre-1939 programs. Modernized under the FRAM program from 1959 to 1963 to serve as maintenance vessels for guided-missile ships, they have workshops, spare parts for missiles, and two 20-ton rotating cranes. Helicopter deck. 127-mm guns removed 1974-75. Sisters *Dixie* (AD 14) struck 15-6-82 for scrap, *Piedmont* (AD 17) struck 30-9-82; sold to Turkey 18-10-82.

◆ **0 (+0 + 5) new-construction ammunition ships**

	Bldr	Laid down	L	In serv.
AE 36 N.	. . .	. . .	. . .	. . .

Programmed: 1 in FY 88, 2 each in FY 90, 91

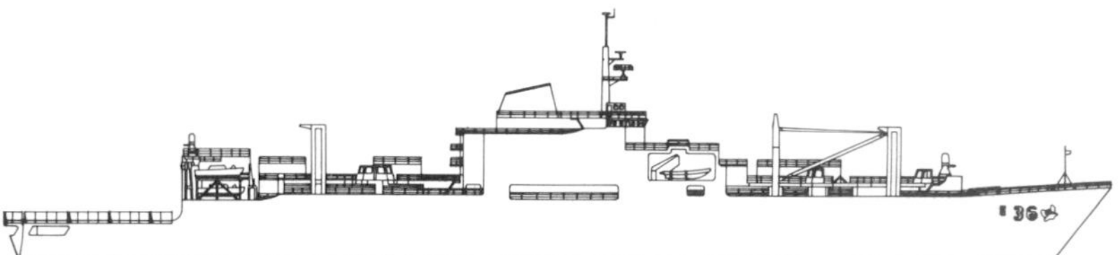
AE 36 class—provisional sketch A. D. Baker III, 1985

D: 22,790 tons (fl) **S:** 20 kts **Dim:** 175.9 × 26.8 × 8.5
A: 2/20-mm Mk 15 CIWS AA (I × 2)—2/25-mm Mk 88 AA (I × 2)—1 or 2/UH-46 helicopters
Electron Equipt: Radar: 1/SPS-64(V)9, 1/SPS-67—TACAN: URN-25
EW: SLQ-32(V)1, Mk 36 SRBOC (VI × 2)
M: 1 or 2 G.E. LM-2500 gas turbines or diesels; 1 CP prop; 25,000 hp
Man: 30 officers, 420 men **Range:** 10,000/20

REMARKS: Intended to replace AE 21–25. Construction authorization requests delayed from FY 86 by fiscal constraints. Will carry 6,000 tons ammunition and other cargo and will have a helicopter hangar and flight deck.

◆ **7 Kilauea-class ammunition ships (SCB 703 type)**

	Bldr	Laid down	L	In serv.
AE 27 BUTTE	Gen. Dynamics	21-7-66	9-8-67	14-12-68
AE 28 SANTA BARBARA	Bethlehem, Sparrows Pt	20-12-66	23-1-68	11-7-70
AE 29 MOUNT HOOD	Bethlehem Sparrows Pt	8-5-67	17-7-68	1-5-71
AE 32 FLINT	Ingalls, Pascagoula	4-8-69	9-11-70	20-11-71
AE 33 SHASTA	Ingalls, Pascagoula	10-11-69	3-4-71	26-2-72
AE 34 MOUNT BAKER	Ingalls, Pascagoula	10-5-70	23-10-71	22-7-72
AE 35 KISKA	Ingalls, Pascagoula	4-8-71	11-3-72	16-12-72

Authorized: 2 in FY 65, 2 in FY 66, 2 in FY 67, 2 in FY 68

D: 9,338 tons light (19,937 fl) **S:** 20 kts **Dim:** 171.9 × 24.7 × 8.5
A: 4/76.2-mm DP (II × 2)—AE 32–35: 2/20-mm Mk 15 CIWS AA (I × 2)—all: 2/UH-46 helicopters
Electron Equipt: Radar: 1/LN-66, 1/SPS-10—TACAN: URN-25
EW: SLQ-32(V)1, Mk 36 SRBOC chaff RL (VI × 2)
M: 1 set G.E. GT; 1 prop; 22,000 hp **Electric:** 5,500 kw
Boilers: 3 Foster-Wheeler; 42.3 kg/cm², 467°C **Man:** 28 officers, 373 men

Shasta (AE 33)—with Mk 15 CIWS added W. Donko, 7-84

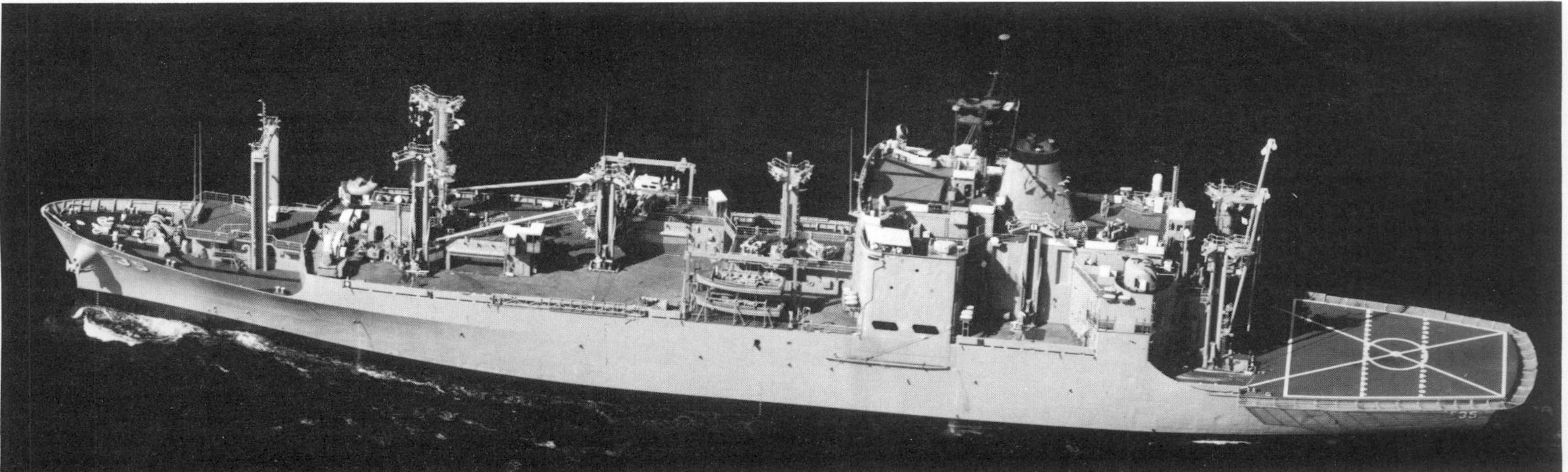
Kiska (AE 35)—with Mk 15 CIWS to port fwd., and to starboard amidships VF-111. U.S. Navy, 10-84

AUXILIARY SHIPS *(continued)*

Remarks: Sister *Kilauea* (AE 26) disarmed and transferred to Military Sealift Command 1-10-80. Sophisticated FAST rapid-replenishment system. Twin hangar and flight deck aft. Two twin 76.2-mm mounts and both Mk 56 directors removed; two 20-mm Vulcan/Phalanx AA amidships to be added to AE 32–35. Mk 36 SRBOC chaff-flare launchers to be added to all. AE 32 and later have a larger bulbous forefoot to the bow. Carry cargo fuel for transfer, as well as ammunition. Several solid transfer rigs deactivated to reduce crew size.

◆ **3 Nitro-class ammunition ships (SCB 114A type)** Bldr: Bethlehem Steel Corp., Sparrows Point, Md.

	Laid down	L	In serv.
AE 23 Nitro	20-5-57	26-6-58	1-5-59
AE 24 Pyro	21-10-57	5-11-58	24-7-59
AE 25 Haleakala	10-3-58	17-2-59	3-11-59

Nitro (AE 23)—open gunmounts G. Gyssels, 5-85

Pyro (AE 24)—with enclosed gun houses G. Arra, 1984

D: 13,990 tons (17,450 fl) **S:** 20 kts **Dim:** 156.1 × 22.0 × 8.8
A: 4/76.2-mm DP (II × 2)—4/12.7-mm mg (I × 4)
Electron Equipt: Radar: 1/LN-66, 1/SPS-10
M: 1 set Bethlehem GT; 1 prop; 16,000 hp
Boilers: 2 Combustion Eng.; 43.9 kg/cm², 454°C **Man:** 17 officers, 312 men

Remarks: All had landing platforms for cargo helicopters added aft during the 1960s. Mk 63 gun directors removed, 1977-78. SPS-6 radar removed. AE 24 transferred to Naval Reserve Force 1-9-80 but returned to regular Navy 1-1-82. AE 24 and 25 have enclosed gun houses. Planned to receive SLQ-32(V)1 and Mk 36 SRBOC EW equipment, but had not by 1985.

◆ **2 Suribachi-class ammunition ships (SCB 114 type)** Bldr: Bethlehem Steel Corp., Sparrows Point, Md.

	Laid down	L	In serv.
AE 21 Suribachi	16-5-55	3-5-56	30-3-57
AE 22 Mauna Kea	31-1-55	2-11-55	17-11-56

Mauna Kea (AE 22)—note gun arrangement on forecastle
L. & L. Van Ginderen, 10-84

D: 14,000 tons (17,000 fl) **S:** 21 kts **Dim:** 156.1 × 22.0 × 8.8
A: 4/76.2-mm DP (II × 2)
Electron Equipt: Radar: 1/LN-66, SPS-10
EW: SLQ-32(V)1, Mk 36 SRBOC chaff RL (VI × 2)
M: 1 set GT; 1 prop; 16,000 hp **Boilers:** 2 Combustion Eng.; 42.2 kg/cm², 440°C
Electric: 12,550 kw **Man:** 17 officers, 312 men

Remarks: SPS-6 radar removed. Gunmounts superfiring, whereas AE 23 to AE 25 have them side by side. Mk 63 gunfire-control systems removed, 1977-78. AE 22 conducted minelaying trials with Mk 55 aircraft mines laid from portable rails during 1983.

◆ **7 Mars-class combat stores ships (SCB 208 type)** Bldr: National Steel & SB Co., San Diego

	Laid down	L	In serv.
AFS 1 Mars	5-5-62	15-6-63	21-12-63
AFS 2 Sylvania	18-8-62	10-8-63	11-7-64
AFS 3 Niagara Falls	22-5-65	25-3-66	29-4-67
AFS 4 White Plains	2-10-65	23-7-66	23-11-68
AFS 5 Concord	26-3-66	17-12-66	27-11-68
AFS 6 San Diego	11-3-67	13-4-68	24-5-69
AFS 7 San Jose	8-3-69	13-12-69	23-10-70

White Plains (AFS 4)—with Mk 15 CIWS abreast stack
LSPH E. Pitman, R.A.N., 7-85

San Jose (AFS 7) LSPH E. Pitman, R.A.N., 7-85

Authorized: 1 in FY 61, 1 in FY 62, 1 in FY 64, 2 in FY 65, 1 in FY 66, 1 in FY 67

D: 9,200 tons light (16,070 fl) **S:** 20 kts **Dim:** 177.08 (161.54 pp) × 24.08 × 7.32
A: 4/76.2-mm DP (II × 2)—AFS 4: 2/20-mm Mk 15 CIWS (I × 2)—all: 2/UH-46 helicopters
Electron Equipt: Radar: 1/LN-66, 1/SPS-10—TACAN: SRN-6
EW: SLQ-32(V)1, Mk 36 SRBOC chaff RL (VI × 2)
M: 1 set de Laval (AFS 6: Westinghouse) GT; 1 prop; 22,000 hp **Electric:** 4,800 kw
Boilers: 3 Babcock & Wilcox; 40.8 kg/cm², 440°C **Man:** 45 officers, 441 men

Remarks: Helicopter platform and hangar. Four M-shaped cargo masts with constant-tension equipment; transfer from the supply ship to the receiving ship takes 90 seconds. Five holds (1 and 5 for spare parts, 3 and 4 for provisions, 2 for aviation parts) have only two hatches. Eleven hoists, which raise up to 5.5 tons, link the decks; several others feed into the helicopter area. Ten loading areas (five on each side) and palletized cargo help in the control of replenishment. There are four refrigerated compartments, and three for the storage of dried provisions. Some 25,000 types of spare parts are divided between 40,000 bins and racks and are accounted for by five data-processing machines. 16,597 m³ total stores volume. Quarters air-conditioned. Draw 2.7 m more aft than forward. One boiler always in reserve. SPS-40 radar, Mk 56 fire-control directors and two twin 76.2-mm mounts amidships removed. Two Vulcan/Phalanx are to be added during the late 1980s/early 1990s. Remaining twin gunmounts on the forecastle are enclosed.

Note: Three ex-Royal Fleet Auxiliaries of the "Ness" class are operated by the Military Sealift Command as T-AFS 8, 9, and 10 and are described on a later page.

AUXILIARY SHIPS *(continued)*

◆ **1 former salvage ship** Bldr: Sun Ship, Chester, Pa.

AG 193 (ex-*Hughes Glomar Explorer*) (In serv. 7-73)

AG 193—as *Hughes Glomar Explorer* U.S. Navy

D: 63,300 tons (fl) **S:** 10.8 kts **Dim:** 188.6 (169.8 pp) × 35.3 × 14.3
M: 5 Nordberg 16-cyl. diesels; 6 G.E. electric motors, 2 props; 13,200 hp—6 side-thrusters
Man: 178 tot.

REMARKS: Built for the Central Intelligence Agency for the sole purpose of recovering a sunken Soviet Golf-class ballistic-missile submarine; given the "cover" role as a deep-sea mining ship (for which she was also useable) by the titular owners, the Summa Corporation. Transferred to Navy ownership in 9-76 and laid up at Suisun Bay, California, was chartered in June 1978 for thirteen months by Global Marine Corporation for deep-water mineral exploration. In late 1979 it was announced that she would be placed at the disposal of the National Science Foundation and would embark on a ten-year research program as a deep-sea drilling ship for the Ocean Marine Drilling Program. When conversion was completed, the ship would have been able to drill to depths of 6,100 meters beneath the sea floor while operating in 4,000–5,500 meters of water. The project was unfortunately not funded, and AG 193 was returned to the Navy 25-4-80 and transferred to the Maritime Administration for mothballing at Suisun Bay, California. The ship's associated support barge was reacquired from the Environmental Protection Agency in 10-82 and laid up.

◆ **1 auxiliary deep-submergence support ship** Bldr: Maryland SB & DD

	L	In serv.
AGDS 2 POINT LOMA (ex-*Point Barrow,* T-AKD 1)	25-5-57	28-2-58

Point Loma (AGDS 2)—note radomes near bow G. Arra, 1984

D: 8,000 tons light (12,430 fl) **S:** 12 kts **Dim:** 150.0 (144.8 pp) × 22.6 × 5.8
Electron Equipt: Radar: 1/SPS-53, 1/SPS-10
M: 2 sets Westinghouse GT; 2 props; 3,000 hp
Boilers: 2 Foster-Wheeler; 32 kg/cm², 400°C
Range: 8,800/10 **Man:** 11 officers, 111 men

REMARKS: Maritime Commission S2-ST-23A design. Built for Arctic supply and configured like a landing ship, dock (LSD). Served in MSC until 28-9-72, when placed in reserve. Transferred to the Navy on 28-2-74, renamed, renumbered, and reactivated as a tender for deep-submergence vehicles, recommissioning 30-4-75. Operates from San Diego in support of the Trident SSBN program; 4 "Golf Ball" spherical antennas on white-painted deckhouses on bow. Crew has 5 women officers, 25% enlisted women. Carries 275 tons of gasoline as flotation liquid for submersibles. Two cranes. Second stack added for diesel-generator exhausts.

◆ **1 Austin-class auxiliary command ship, ex-amphibious transport, dock**

	Bldr	Laid down	L	In serv.
AGF 11 CORONADO (ex-LPD 11)	Lockheed SB, Seattle	3-5-65	30-7-66	23-5-70

Coronado (AGF 11)— now painted gray L. & L. Van Ginderen, 7-83

D: 11,050 tons (17,000 fl) **S:** 21 kts **Dim:** 173.4 × 25.6 (hull) × 7.2
A: 4/76.2-mm DP (II × 2)—2/20-mm Mk 15 CIWS (I × 2)
Electron Equipt: Radar: 1/LN-66, 1/SPS-10, 1/SPS-40—TACAN: URN-20
EW: SLQ-32(V)2, Mk 36 SRBOC chaff RL (VI × 2)
M: 2 sets de Laval GT; 2 props; 24,000 hp
Boilers: 2 Foster-Wheeler; 42.3 kg/cm², 467°C
Man: 27 officers, 446 men + staff: 120 officers, 47 men

REMARKS: Redesignated AGF on 1-10-80, initially only as a temporary relief for *La Salle* (AGF 3), but now retained in a command ship role. Communications enhanced over that of rest of class, but otherwise not as extensively altered as AGF 3. Replaced *Puget Sound* (AD 38) as flagship, Sixth Fleet, 8-85 to 6-86. Other remarks under *Austin* class pertain.

◆ **1 Raleigh-class auxiliary command ship**

	Bldr	Laid down	L	In serv.
AGF 3 LA SALLE (ex-LPD 3)	New York NSY	2-4-62	3-8-63	22-2-64

Authorized: FY 61

La Salle (AGF 3)—white-painted G. Arra, 1983

D: 8,040 tons light (14,650 fl) **S:** 21 kts **Dim:** 158.4 (155.4 wl) × 25.6 × 6.4
A: 4/76.2-mm DP (II × 2)—2/20-mm Mk 15 CIWS gatling AA (I × 2)
Electron Equipt: Radar: 1/LN-66, 1/SPS-10, 1/SPS-40—TACAN: URN-25
EW: SLQ-32(V)2, WLR-1, Mk 36 SRBOC chaff RL (VI × 4)
M: 2 sets de Laval GT; 2 props; 24,000 hp
Boilers: 2 Babcock & Wilcox; 42.2 kg/cm², 467°C **Electric:** 3,600 kw
Man: 18 officers, 369 men + flag staff: 12 officers, 47 men

REMARKS: Ex-landing platform, dock (LPD). Since redesignated 1-7-72 employed as flagship of Commander, Middle East Force. Painted white. Well deck used for ship's boats. Helicopter hangar for one SH-3 built on flight deck, to port, with shelter for ceremonial activities to starboard. One Mk 56 and two Mk 63 gunfire-control systems removed 1977-78; lost one gunmount but gained two 20-mm Mk 15 CIWS during major overhaul commencing 27-1-81; resumed flagship duty 13-3-83. A large parabolic dish SATCOMM antenna is mounted on the first mast platform.

◆ **1 Dolphin class (SCB 207 type) research submarine**

	Bldr	Laid down	L	In serv.
AGSS 555 DOLPHIN	Portsmouth NSY	9-11-62	8-6-68	17-8-69

Authorized: FY 61

Dolphin (AGSS 555) G. Arra, 3-85

AUXILIARY SHIPS *(continued)*

D: 860/950 tons **S:** 7.5/10 or 15 (see Remarks) **Dim:** 50.29 × 5.92 × 4.9
Electron Equipt: Sonar: BQS-15, bow passive array, towed array, BQR-2
M: Diesel-electric, 2 G.M. 12V71 diesels; 1 prop; 1,650 hp
Endurance: 14 days (12 hours sub.)
Man: 3 officers, 26 men, 5 scientists

Remarks: The pressure hull is a perfect cylinder, 5.49 m in diameter, strongly braced and closed at the forward and after ends by two hemispheric bulkheads. Used for deep-diving tests as well as acoustic and oceanographic experiments. Single torpedo tube removed in 1970. Scientific payload of 12 tons. Using two 165 cell, 250-volt, lead-acid batteries, 10 knots can be reached when submerged; when silver-zinc batteries are substituted, the speed is 15 knots. Very quiet machinery. Has four mini-computers for scientific-data processing. Several scientific, passive multihydrophone arrays are fitted at the bow, and acoustic arrays can be towed at up to 4,000 feet behind the craft. Most support is shore-based. Home-ported at San Diego. Has a portable SPS-53 radar for surface navigation.

◆ **1 hospital ship—in reserve**

	Bldr	Laid down	L	In serv.
AH 17 Sanctuary	Sun SB & DD	. . .	15-8-44	20-6-45

Sanctuary (AH 17) U.S. Navy, 1974

D: 11,141 tons (15,400 fl) **S:** 18.3 kts **Dim:** 158.5 (151.18 pp) × 21.79 × 7.32
Electron Equipt: Radar: 1/SPS-53, 1/SPS-10B
M: 1 set G.E. GT; 1 prop; 9,000 hp **Electric:** 2,400 kw
Boilers: 2 Babcock & Wilcox, 31.7 kg/cm², 396°C
Fuel: 2,055 tons **Man:** 70 officers, 460 men

Remarks: In reserve. Survivor of a class of six; built on C4-S-B2 cargo-ship hull. Converted 15-12-71 to 18-11-72 as a dependent support ship for service at Piraeus, Greece. Has 74-bed hospital that can be expanded to 300. In addition to medical facilities, had stores, entertainment facilities, etc. Could carry 50 officers and 120 enlisted medical personnel. Change in government in Greece canceled plan; decommissioned 28-3-74, having not filled intended purpose. Probably soon to be discarded.

Note: Two new hospital-ship conversions, *Mercy* (T-AH 19) and *Comfort* (T-AH 20) are described in the Military Sealift Command section.

◆ **5 Cimarron-class oilers (SCB 379 type)**

	Bldr	Laid down	L	In serv.
AO 177 Cimarron	Avondale SY	18-5-78	28-4-79	10-1-81
AO 178 Monongahela	Avondale SY	15-8-78	4-8-79	5-9-81
AO 179 Merrimack	Avondale SY	16-7-79	17-5-80	14-11-81
AO 180 Willamette	Avondale SY	4-8-80	18-7-81	18-12-82
AO 186 Platte	Avondale SY	2-2-81	30-1-82	16-4-83

D: 27,500 tons (fl) **S:** 20 kts
Dim: 180.29 (167.64 pp) × 25.33 × 10.16 (11.35 prop)
A: AO 180, 186: 2/20-mm Mk 15 CIWS (I × 2)

Monongahela (AO 178) L. & L. Van Ginderen, 7-84

Merrimack (AO 179) L. & L. Van Ginderen, 3-84

Platte (AO 186)—with 2 Mk 15 CIWS G. Arra, 1984

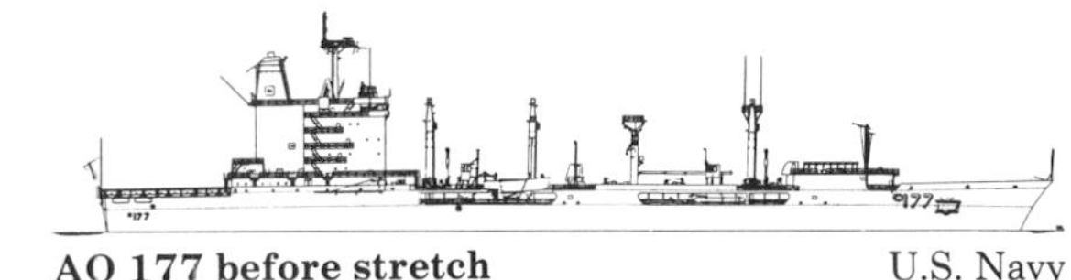

AO 177 before stretch U.S. Navy

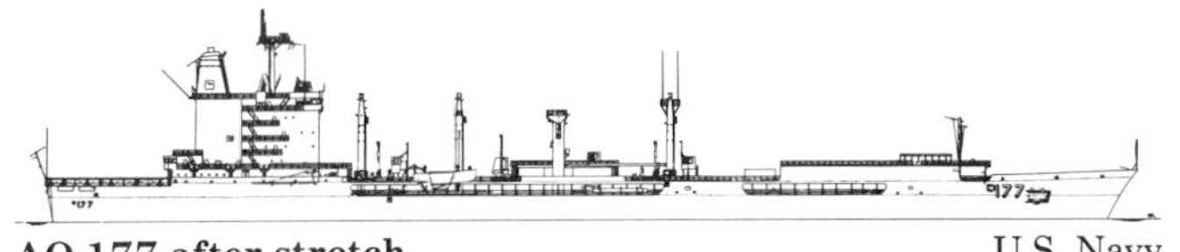

AO 177 after stretch U.S. Navy

Electron Equipt: Radar: 1/LN-66, 1/SPS-55 (AO 180, 186: SPS-10B)
M: 1 set GT; 1 prop; 24,000 hp **Electric:** 8,250 kw
Boilers: 2 Combustion Engineering; 42.25 kg/cm², 454°C
Man: 11 officers, 124 men (225 tot. accommodations)

Remarks: Carry 72,000 barrels fuel oil, 48,000 barrels JP-5 gas turbine fuel, and can replenish ships while making 15 knots. Also carry 98 m³ dry stores and 3 refrigerated stores containers. There is a helicopter platform aft. Four constant-tension replenishment stations to port, three to starboard. Able to transfer 408,000 liters of fuel oil and 245,000 liters JP-5 per hour. No additional units planned; subsequent oilers will be under Military Sealift Command control. Although these are high-value targets, no chaff or SLQ-32 systems are installed.

These ships are scheduled to be lengthened; one each year in FY 87-89 and two in FY 90. Subsequent to "jumboizing," they will displace 37,866 tons (fl) on a draft of 10.16 m, and length will be 215.95 m overall. Speed will drop to 19.4 kts. Cargo capacity will be 183,000 barrels fuel oil/JP-5, 401 m³ feedwater, 397 m³ potable water, 205 m³ dry stores, and 8 refrigerated stores containers. Accommodations will be increased to 235, Mk 15 CIWS will be added to AO 177–179; SLQ-32(V)1 and Mk 36 SRBOC EW equipment will be added, as will SLQ-25 Nixie towed torpedo decoys. A new-design propeller and rudder will be fitted, and underway transfer capability will be enhanced.

◆ **3 Ashtabula-class oilers (SCB 244 jumbo type)—1 in reserve***
Bldr: Bethlehem Steel, Sparrows Point, Md.

	L	In serv.
AO 51 Ashtabula*	22-5-43	7-8-43
AO 98 Caloosahatchee	6-7-45	3-12-45
AO 99 Canisteo	2-6-45	10-10-45

Canisteo (AO 99) L. & L. Van Ginderen, 8-84

AUXILIARY SHIPS *(continued)*

Caloosahatchee (AO 98)—in light condition W. Donko, 7-85

D: 36,500 tons (fl) **S:** 18 kts **Dim:** 196.3 × 22.9 × 9.6
A: 2/76.2-mm Mk 26 DP (I × 2)
Electron Equipt: Radar: 1/Raytheon 1650/6x, 1/SPS-10
M: 1 set GT; 2 props; 13,500 hp **Range:** 16,000/11
Boilers: 4 Foster-Wheeler "K"; 31.7 kg/cm², 399°C **Man:** 20 officers, 350 men

REMARKS: Lengthened 27 m by insertion of new mid-body during 1960s. Two 76.2-mm removed, 1977-78, along with one Mk 52 and two Mk 51 GFCS. Carry 143,000 barrels of fuel, 175 tons of ammunition, and 100 tons of provisions. No helicopter deck. Last World War II-built oilers in regular naval service; both in Atlantic. AO 51 decommissioned 30-9-82 to National Defense Reserve Fleet.

◆ **0 (+0 + 4) new-construction fast combat support ships**

	Bldr	Laid down	L	In serv.
AOE 6 SUPPLY	...	...	...	...
AOE 7 N.	...	...	...	...
AOE 8 N.	...	...	...	...
AOE 9 N.	...	...	...	...

Programmed AOE 6 in FY 87, AOE 7 in FY 89, AOE 8 in FY 90, AOE 9 in FY 91

AOE 6—artist's concept T. Freeman/U.S. Navy, 1985

D: 48,500 tons (fl) **S:** 26 kts **Dim:** 230.1 × 32.6 × 11.89
A: 1/Mk 29 launcher (XVI × 1, Sea Sparrow and RAM missiles)—2/20-mm Mk 15 CIWS (I × 2)—2/25-mm Mk 88 AA (I × 2)—3 helicopters
Electron Equipt: Radar: 1/SPS-64(V)9, 1/SPS-67, 1/Mk 23 TAS, 1/Mk 91 f.c.s. (2 directors)
EW: SLQ-32(V)3, Mk 36 SRBOC chaff RL (VI × 4)
TACAN: URN-25
M: 4 G.E.LM-2500 gas turbines; 2 props; 100,000 hp
Electric: . . . **Man:** 35 officers, 625 men (accommodations)

REMARKS: Modified version of the AOE 1 class with better protective systems. Cargo: 156,000 bbl liquid, plus 2,450 tons dry stores.

◆ **4 Sacramento-class fast combat support ships (SCB 196 type)**

	Bldr	Laid down	L	In serv.
AOE 1 SACRAMENTO	Puget Sound NSY	30-6-61	14-9-63	14-3-64
AOE 2 CAMDEN	New York SB	17-2-64	29-5-65	1-4-67
AOE 3 SEATTLE	Puget Sound NSY	1-10-65	2-3-68	5-4-69
AOE 4 DETROIT	Puget Sound NSY	29-11-66	21-6-69	28-3-70

Authorized: 1 in FY 61, 1 in FY 63, 1 in FY 65, 1 in FY 66

Camden (AOE 2)—Mk 15 CIWS aft USS *Ranger*, 10-83

Seattle (AOE 3)—with Mk 23 TAS on foremast, SLQ-32 EW G. Gyssels, 6-84

D: 18,700 tons light (53,600 fl) **S:** 26 kts **Dim:** 241.4 (215.8 pp) × 32.9 × 11.6
A: 1/Mk 29 launcher for Sea Sparrow (VIII × 1)—2/20-mm Mk 15 CIWS (I × 2)—2/UH-46 helicopters
Electron Equipt: Radar: 1/SPS-53, 1/SPS-10 (AOE 1 and 2: 1/SPS-40 also), 1/Mk 91 Mod. 1, AOE 3: Mk 23 TAS
EW: AOE 1, 2, 4: WLR-1, WLR-3; AOE 3: SLQ-32(V)3, Mk 36 SRBOC chaff RL (III × 4)
TACAN: URN-20 (AOE 3, 4: URN-25)
M: G.E. GT; 2 props; 100,000 hp
Boilers: 4 Combustion Engineering, 42.2 kg/cm², 480°C
Range: 10,000/17 **Man:** 33 officers, 567 men

REMARKS: Sea Sparrow launcher and Mk 91 Mod. 1 control system with two directors replaced two twin 76.2-mm DP forward; two Mk 56 GFCS removed. The two remaining 76.2-mm gunmounts aft replaced by two 20-mm Mk 15 CIWS Vulcan/Phalanx. The SLQ-32(V)3 ECM will replace WLR-1, and Mk 36 SRBOC chaff rocket system is being added. AOE 3 was the first to get the Mk 23 TAS Mod. 2 (Target Acquisition System), which in these ships will be a stand-alone system employing the UYA-4 computer. Carry 177,000 barrels fuel plus 2,150 tons ammunition, 750 tons provisions. Helicopter hangar and flight deck for 2–3 UH-46 Sea Knight vertical-replenishment helicopters. Turbines in AOE 1 and AOE 2 are from battleship *Kentucky* (BB 66). AOE 1, 2 in Pacific; other pair in Atlantic. A fifth unit was canceled. AOR 2 is testing the "standard Navy UNREP" suite, with new winches, rams, ram-tensioners and control booths.

◆ **7 Wichita-class replenishment oilers (SCB 707 type)** Bldr: General Dynamics, Quincy, Mass.

	Laid down	L	In serv.
AOR 1 WICHITA	18-6-66	18-3-68	7-6-69
AOR 2 MILWAUKEE	29-11-66	17-1-69	1-11-69
AOR 3 KANSAS CITY	20-4-68	28-6-69	6-6-70
AOR 4 SAVANNAH	22-1-69	25-4-70	5-12-70
AOR 5 WABASH	21-1-70	6-2-71	20-11-71
AOR 6 KALAMAZOO	28-10-70	11-11-72	11-8-73
AOR 7 ROANOKE	19-1-74	7-12-74	30-10-76

Authorized: 2 in FY 66, 2 in FY 67, 2 in FY 68, 1 in FY 73

D: 12,500 tons light (41,350 fl) **S:** 20 kts **Dim:** 200.9 × 29.3 × 10.1
A: AOR 1: unarmed—AOR 2: 4/20-mm AA (I × 4)—AOR 3: 1/Mk 29 launcher (VIII × 1, Sea Sparrow missiles)—AOR 4-7: 1/Mk 29 launcher (VIII × 1)—2/Mk 15 CIWS gatling AA (I × 2)

Kansas City (AOR 3)—Sea Sparrow, but no CIWS LSPH E. Pitman, R.A.N., 9-85

AUXILIARY SHIPS *(continued)*

Roanoke (AOR 7)—Sea Sparrow launcher abaft stack, missile directors atop lattice towers, UH-46 helicopter VF-111, U.S. Navy, 8-84

Savannah (AOR 4)—with Mk 15 CIWS and SLQ-32 EW gear G. Arra, 1984

Electron Equipt: Radar: 1/LN-66 or SPS-53, 1/SPS-10, Sea Sparrow ships: 2/Mk 91 Mod. 1 (2 directors)
EW: Mk 36 SRBOC chaff RL (VI × 4)—AOR 4 also: SLQ-32(V)3
TACAN: URN-25 (AOR 2, 3, 7: SRN-15)
M: G.E. GT; 2 props; 32,000 shp
Boilers: 3 Foster-Wheler; 43.3 kg/cm², 454°C **Electric:** 8,000 kw
Range: 6,500/20; 10,000/17 **Man:** 20 officers, 363-420 men

Remarks: Carry 175,000 barrels fuel (90,000 distillate fuel), 600 tons ammunition, 575 tons provisions. All except AOR 7 originally had no hangars flanking stack and had 4/76.2-mm DP. Several carried interim armaments of 2 or 4 single 20-mm AA after hangars were added. SLQ-32(V)3 will be added. As with AOE 1 class, they are eventually to get the Mk 23 Mod. 2 TAS (Target Acquisition System) radar with associated UYA-4 computerized data system. The two Mk 76 radar directors for the Mk 91 Mod. 1 missile fire-control system are mounted atop tall lattice towers just forward of the stack. There are four stations for liquid transfer and two for solid transfer to port, three liquid and two solid to starboard; all have constant-tension devices. AOR 2 used in minelaying trials 1983, using Mk 55 mines and portable rails.

◆ **4 Vulcan-class repair ships**

	Bldr	Laid down	L	In serv.
AR 5 Vulcan	New York SB	26-12-39	14-12-40	16-6-41
AR 6 Ajax	Los Angeles SB & DD	7-5-41	22-8-42	30-10-42
AR 7 Hector	Los Angeles SB & DD	28-7-41	11-11-42	7-2-44
AR 8 Jason	Los Angeles SB & DD	9-3-42	3-4-43	19-6-44

Hector (AR 7) G. Arra, 1984

D: 9,325 tons (16,245 fl) **S:** 19.2 kts **Dim:** 161.37 (158.5 pp) × 22.35 × 7.11
A: 4/20-mm AA (I × 4) **Electron Equipt:** Radar: 1/CRP 1500, 1/SPS-10
M: 2 sets GT; 2 props; 11,535 hp **Electric:** 4,500 kw
Boilers: 4 Babcock & Wilcox; 28.2 kg/cm², 382°C
Fuel: 3,800 tons **Range:** 18,000/12 **Man:** 41 officers, 979 men

Remarks: Very elaborately equipped repair facilities. Four 127-mm DP (I × 4) removed from all. *Jason,* typed ARH 1 (heavy hull-repair ship), was redesignated as AR 8 in 1957. AR 8 badly damaged in collision with AO 186, 2-86.

◆ **1 Achelous-class small repair ship** Bldr: Bethlehem Steel, Hingham, Mass.

	Laid down	L	In serv.	Recomm.
ARL 24 Sphinx (ex-LST 963)	20-10-44	18-11-44	12-12-44	26-7-85

Sphinx (ARL 24) U.S. Navy, 7-85

D: 3,960 tons (fl) **S:** 11.6 kts **Dim:** 99.98 (96.32 wl) × 15.24 × 3.71
A: 8/40-mm Mk 2 AA (IV × 2)—4/Stinger SAM launch positions—6/12.7-mm mg (I × 6)
Electron Equipt: Radar: 1/SPS-10—TACAN: URN-25
EW: Intercept and D/F arrays
M: 2 G.M. 12-278A diesels; 2 props; 1,800 hp **Electric:** 520 kw
Fuel: 620 tons **Man:** . . .

Remarks: Recommissioned after extensive alterations that took over three times the period required to build her during World War II. Equipped for duties off Central America, with new communications and intercept arrays, helicopter deck amidships. Has two obsolete Mk 51 Mod. 2 lead-computing optical directors for the antiquated 40-mm gunmounts. Retains a 25-ton boom forward and carries two LCVP in Welin davits abreast enlarged after superstructure. Sister *Indra* (ARL 37, ex-LST 1147) was stricken 1-12-77 but has since been retained at Norfolk as an accommodations hulk.

◆ **2 (+2) ARS 50-class salvage ships** Bldr: Peterson Bldrs., Sturgeon Bay, Wisc.

	Laid down	L	In serv.
ARS 50 Safeguard	8-11-82	12-11-83	17-8-85
ARS 51 Grasp	2-5-83	23-4-84	14-12-85
ARS 52 Salvor	16-9-83	28-7-84	6-86
ARS 53 Grapple	25-4-84	8-12-84	8-86

Authorized: 1 in FY 81, 2 in FY 82, 1 in FY 83

D: 2,300 tons light (2,880 fl) **S:** 13.5 kts **Dim:** 77.72 (73.15 wl) × 15.54 × 4.72
A: 2/12.7-mm mg (I × 2) **Electron Equipt:** Radar: 1/SPS-55
M: 4 Caterpillar diesels, geared drive; 2 CP Kort-nozzle props; 4,200 hp
Electric: 2,250 kw **Range:** 8,000/12 **Man:** 6 officers, 97 men

AUXILIARY SHIPS *(continued)*

Safeguard (ARS 50)—on trials U.S. Navy, 5-85

Grasp (ARS 51)—on trials U.S. Navy, 8-85

Grasp (ARS 51)—on trials U.S. Navy, 8-85

Remarks: First unit ordered 1981, with option for four more from same shipyard; fifth ship deleted from program by Congress, but may be built under FY 91. Design developed from ARS 38. Have 54-ton open-ocean bollard pull and, using beach extraction gear, are able to exert 360-ton pull. Have 500-hp bow-thruster. 30-ton boom aft, 5-ton forward. Able to dead-lift 150 tons over bow or stern. Cargo hold 596 m³. Able to support hard-hat divers to 58-m and SCUBA divers; decompression chamber fitted. Up to 25 percent of crew may be women; 12 extra berths to be fitted. Three foam firefighting monitors. Program far behind schedule.

◆ **7 Diver*- and Bolster-class salvage ships** Bldr: Basalt Rock Co., Napa, Calif.

	Laid down	L	In serv.	To reserve
ARS 8 Preserver*	26-10-42	1-4-43	11-1-44	30-9-86
ARS 38 Bolster	20-7-44	23-12-44	1-5-45	active
ARS 39 Conserver	10-8-44	27-1-45	9-6-45	30-9-86
ARS 40 Hoist	13-9-44	31-3-45	21-7-45	. . .
ARS 41 Opportune	13-9-44	31-3-45	5-10-45	. . .
ARS 42 Reclaimer	11-11-44	25-6-45	20-12-45	. . .
ARS 43 Recovery	6-1-45	4-8-45	15-5-46	. . .

Opportune (ARS 41)—2 OE-82 SATCOMM antennas above pilothouse G. Gyssels, 9-83

D: 1,530 tons (1,970 fl), ARS 38 to ARS 43: 2,045 (fl) **S:** 14.8 kts
Dim: 65.1 × 12.5 (ARS 38 to ARS 43: 13.4) × 4.0
A: 2/20-mm AA (I × 2)—2/12.7-mm mg (I × 2)
Electron Equipt: Radar: 1/SPS-53 (ARS 40, 41, 43: SPS-10), ARS-43: 1/Raytheon 3400 also
M: 4 Cooper-Bessemer GSB-8 or Caterpillar D399 diesels, electric drive; 2 props; 3,060 hp (2,440 sust.)
Electric: 460 kw **Fuel:** 300 tons **Range:** 9,000/14; 20,000/7
Man: 6 officers, 77 men (ARS 38–43: 7 officers, 98 men)

Remarks: Equipped for diver support, salvage, and towing. ARS 38, ARS 39, and ARS 42 re-engined with Caterpillar diesels. ARS 8 transferred to Naval Reserve Force 1-11-79 and ARS 38 on 30-6-83. *Escape* (ARS 6) reactivated from Maritime Administration reserve and transferred to Coast Guard 4-12-80. *Clamp* (ARS 33) stricken 1963 to MARAD reserve fleet; reacquired 1973, but not reactivated and again stricken. *Curb* (ARS 21 and *Gear* (ARS 34) stricken and sold 30-4-81. All except ARS 38 and ARS 43 are to be decommissioned on completion of the ARS 50 class.

◆ **5 L. Y. Spear-class submarine tenders (SCB 702 and 737 types)**

	Bldr	Laid down	L	In serv.
AS 36 L. Y. Spear	Gen. Dynamics, Quincy	5-5-66	7-9-67	28-2-70
AS 37 Dixon	Gen. Dynamics, Quincy	7-9-67	20-6-70	7-8-71
AS 39 Emory S. Land	Lockheed SB, Seattle	2-3-76	4-5-77	7-7-79
AS 40 Frank Cable	Lockheed SB, Seattle	2-3-76	14-1-78	5-2-80
AS 41 McKee	Lockheed SB, Seattle	14-1-78	16-2-80	15-8-81

Authorized: 1 in FY 65, 1 in FY 66, 1 in FY 72, 1 in FY 73, 1 in FY 77

D: AS 36, 37: 12,770 tons light (23,493 fl); AS 39–41: 711 tons light (22,560 fl)
S: 20 kts (18 sust.) **Dim:** 196.29 × 25.91 × 7.77 **A:** 4/20-mm AA (I × 4)
Electron Equipt: Radar: 1/. . . nav., 1/SPS-10
M: 1 set de Laval GT; 1 prop; 20,000 hp **Electric:** 11,000 kw
Boilers: 2 Combustion Engineering; 43.6 kg/cm², 462°C
Man: AS 36 and AS 37: 51 officers, 1,029 men
AS 29 to AS 41: 50 officers, 1,108 men + flag staff: 75 officers, 44 men

Remarks: Provide support to up to 12 submarines with up to 4 alongside at once. AS 39 to AS 41 having been specifically tailored to the needs of the *Los Angeles* class. One 30-ton crane and two 5-ton traveling cranes. Have a total of 53 specialized repair shops. Medical facilities include operating room, 23-bed ward, and dental clinic. AS 39 and later also carry 2/40-mm Mk 19 grenade launchers. Helicopter deck, but no

McKee (AS 41) U.S. Navy, 1981

AUXILIARY SHIPS *(continued)*

Emory S. Land (AS 39) G. Arra, 1984

hangar. AS 37 equipped to support Tomahawk cruise missiles. AS 36 and AS 37 have General Electric turbines and Foster-Wheeler boilers. No longer planned to fit Vulcan/Phalanx or Sea Sparrow in later ships. Two 127-mm DP (I × 2) removed from AS 36 and AS 37. AS 38 (FY 69) canceled 27-3-69. No other submarine tenders currently programmed.

◆ **2 Simon Lake-class submarine tenders (SCB 238 type)**

	Bldr	Laid down	L	In serv.
AS 33 Simon Lake	Puget Sount NSY	7-1-63	8-2-64	7-11-64
AS 34 Canopus	Ingalls, Pascagoula	2-3-64	12-2-65	4-11-65

Authorized: 1 in FY 63, 1 in FY 64

Simon Lake (AS 33) G. Arra, 8-85

D: 12,000 tons [AS 33: 19,934 (fl), AS 34: 21,089 (fl)] **S:** 18 kts
Dim: 196.2 × 25.9 × 8.7 **A:** 4/76.2-mm DP (II × 2)
Electron Equipt: Radar: 1/SPS-10 **M:** de Laval GT; 1 prop; 20,000 hp
Electric: 11,000 kw **Boilers:** 2 Combustion Engineering; 43.6 kg/cm², 462°C
Man: 60 officers, 1,206 men

Remarks: Specifically equipped to support nuclear-powered, ballistic-missile submarines, with 16 missiles stowed vertically amidships. Converted to carry Poseidon missiles, 1969-71. Both are to serve Trident-equipped SSBNs; AS 33 converted under FY 78, and AS 34 converted 1984-85 and has been given new cranes. Sister AS 35 canceled on 3-12-64. Two 30-ton cranes and four 5-ton traveling cranes. Helicopter deck aft, but no hangar. Two Mk 63 fire-control systems for guns removed.

◆ **2 Hunley-class submarine tenders (SCB 194 type)**

	Bldr	Laid down	L	In serv.
AS 31 Hunley	Newport News SB	28-11-60	28-9-61	16-6-62
AS 32 Holland	Ingalls, Pascagoula	5-3-62	19-1-63	7-9-63

Authorized: 1 in FY 60, 1 in FY 62

Hunley (AS 31) L. & L. Van Ginderen, 5-82

D: 11,000 tons light (19,819 fl) **S:** 19 kts **Dim:** 182.6 × 25.3 × 7.4
A: 4/20-mm AA (I × 4) **Electron Equipt:** Radar: 1/LN-66, 1/SPS-10
M: 10 Fairbanks-Morse 38D⅛ diesels, electric drive; 1 prop; 15,000 hp
Electric: 12,000 kw **Man:** 60 officers, 1,206 men

Remarks: Intended to support SSBNs; converted to carry Poseidon missiles, 1973-75. Air-conditioned. Helicopter platform. Original 32.5-ton rotating hammerhead gantry crane removed around 1970 and replaced by two 30-ton cranes.

◆ **1 Proteus-class submarine tender (SCB 190 conversion type)** Bldr: Moore SB & DD, Oakland, Cal.

	Laid down	L	In serv.	Conv.
AS 19 Proteus	15-9-41	12-11-42	31-1-44	8-7-60

Proteus (AS 19) LSPH E. Pitman, R.A.N., 9-84

D: 14,195 tons (20,295 fl) **S:** 15.4 kts **Dim:** 175.1 (171.9 wl) × 27.3 × 8.4
A: 4/20-mm AA (I × 4) **Electron Equipt:** Radar: 1/LN-66, 1/SPS-10
M: 8 G.M. 16-248 diesels, electric drive; 2 props, 11,520 hp
Electric : 5,000 kw **Range:** 26,000/10 **Man:** 57 officers, 1,119 men

Remarks: Lengthened 13.4 m, 1959-60, as the first SSBN tender, carrying Polaris missiles in the new section, handled by an extendable gantry crane. Superstructure enlarged over that of former sisters in the *Fulton* class. Served the *George Washington* and *Ethan Allen* class SSBNs in the Pacific: often stationed at Diego Garcia since 1981 as a general-purpose tender.

◆ **3 Fulton-class submarine tenders— 1 in reserve***

	Bldr	Laid down	L	In serv.
AS 11 Fulton	Mare Island NSY	19-7-39	27-12-40	12-9-41
AS 12 Sperry*	Mare Island NSY	1-2-41	17-12-41	1-5-42
AS 18 Orion	Moore SB, Oakland	31-7-41	14-10-42	30-9-43

Orion (AS 18)—with new cranes C. Martinelli, 10-84

D: 9,734 tons (12,215 fl) **S:** 15.4 kts **Dim:** 161.4 × 22.3 × 7.8
A: 4/20-mm AA (I × 4) **Electron Equipt:** Radar: 1/LN-66, 1/SPS-10
M: 8 G.M. 16-248 diesels, electric drive; 2 props; 11,200 hp **Electric:** 2,300 kw
Fuel: 3,760 tons **Range:** 32,000/15 **Man:** 57 officers, 1,217 men

Remarks: All received FRAM-II modernization and can support nuclear submarines. Foundry can cast pieces up to 250 kg. Two 20-ton rotating cranes are fitted. AS 12 decommissioned to reserve 30-9-82. Sisters *Bushnell* (AS 15) stricken 15-11-80 and sunk 3-6-83 as a torpedo target; *Howard W. Gilmore* (AS 16) decommissioned 30-9-80 and struck 1-12-80; *Nereus* (AS 17), long in reserve, was stricken by 30-9-82.

◆ **2 Pigeon-class submarine-rescue ships (SCB 721 type)** Bldr: Alabama DD & SB, Mobile

	Laid down	L	In serv.
ASR 21 Pigeon	17-7-68	13-8-69	28-4-73
ASR 22 Ortolan	22-8-68	10-9-69	14-7-73

Authorized: 1 in FY 67, 1 in FY 68

D: 3,411 tons (4,570 fl) **S:** 15 kts **Dim:** 76.5 × 26.2 × 6.5
A: 2/20-mm AA (I × 2) **Electron Equipt:** Radar: 1/SPS-53, 1/. . . nav.
M: 4 Alco high-speed diesels; 2 props; 6,000 hp **Range:** 8,500/13
Man: 10 officers, 89 men + DSRV crew: 4 officers, 20 men

Remarks: The catamaran hulls (7.92-m beam) are separated by 10.36 m. Diving bells and other salvage equipment are lowered between the two hulls by a moving crane. The ships can carry two small DSRV (Deep Submergence Rescue Vehicle) subma-

AUXILIARY SHIPS *(continued)*

Pigeon (ASR 21) L. & L. Van Ginderen, 10-84

Ortolan (ASR 22) G. Arra, 1984

rines, but the only two DSRV built are land-stored in fly-away status. Excellent lowering and handling equipment for up to 60 tons; divers to 260 m. Carry Mk 2 Mod. 1 saturation diving gear. Helicopter platform aft spans both hulls. Not considered to be successful ships, being overly complex and difficult to maneuver. ASR 21 has an LN-66 navigational radar, ASR 22 a Raytheon set.

◆ **4 Chanticleer-class submarine-rescue ships** Bldr: Savannah Machine Foundry (ASR 9: Moore SB & DD, Oakland)

	Laid down	L	In serv.
ASR 9 Florikan	30-9-41	14-6-42	5-4-43
ASR 13 Kittiwake	5-1-45	10-7-45	18-7-46
ASR 14 Petrel	26-2-45	29-9-45	24-9-46
ASR 15 Sunbird	2-4-45	3-4-46	28-1-47

Florikan (ASR 9)—SATCOMM antennas flanking foremast G. Arra, 5-85

D: 1,670 tons (2,015 fl) **S:** 14.9 kts **Dim:** 76.7 × 13.4 × 4.9
A: 2/20-mm AA (I × 2) **Electron Equipt:** Radar: 1/SPS-53
M: 4 G.M. 12-278A diesels, electric drive; 1 prop; 3,000 hp
Electric: 460 kw **Man:** 10 officers, 89 men

Remarks: Carry a McCann rescue bell aft. All equipped for helium/oxygen diving. ASR 9 has Alco Model 539 diesels. All have sonar and underwater communications equipment. No plans to replace these elderly units before mid-1990s.

◆ **5 Abnaki and Achomawi*-class fleet ocean tugs—all in reserve**

	Bldr	L	In serv.	To reserve
ATF 105 Moctabi	Charleston SB & DD	25-3-44	25-7-44	30-9-85
ATF 110 Quapaw	United Eng., Alameda	15-5-43	6-5-44	30-8-85
ATF 113 Takelma	United Eng., Alameda	18-9-43	3-8-44	30-9-83
ATF 159 Paiute*	Charleston SB & DD	4-6-45	27-8-45	23-8-85
ATF 160 Papago*	Charleston SB & DD	21-6-45	3-10-45	28-6-85

Takelma (ATF 113) USS *Ranger,* 9-83

D: 1,235 tons (1,640 fl) **S:** 16.2 kts **Dim:** 62.48 (59.44 pp) × 11.73 × 4.67
A: None **M:** 4 Caterpillar D399 diesels, electric drive; 1 prop; 3,000 hp
Electric: 400 kw **Range:** 6,500/16; 15,000/8
Man: 5 officers, 60 men + Reserves: 3 officers, 25 men

Remarks: All now in National Defense Reserve Fleet, on Navy List. Developed from pre-World War II *Apache* class. ATF 105, ATF 110, and ATF 113 originally had four Busch-Sulzer BS-539 diesels and a small-diameter funnel; the others had G.M. 12-278A diesels and a large funnel. Have a 150-ton pull capability to salvage beached vessels, carry 640-m 53-mm steel towing cable, plus 730-m nylon towing line. Five sisters serve in the U.S. Coast Guard, and the class can be found in many of the world's navies.

Ten sisters in the National Defense Reserve Fleet are to be discarded or otherwise used: of the *Cherokee* class, *Seneca* (ATF 91) is to become an immobile engineering trials craft at Annapolis, while *Chippewa* (ATF 69), *Hopi* (ATF 71), *Moreno* (ATF 87), *Narragansett* (ATF 88), and *Wenatchee* (ATF 118) are to be discarded, as are *Atakapa* (ATF 149), *Mosopelea* (ATF 158), and *Achomawi* (ATF 148) of the *Achomawi* class. *Tenino* (ATF 115) is in use as a salvage training hulk.

Note: The three serving units of the *Sotoyomo*-class auxiliary ocean tugs in the National Defense Reserve Fleet, *Accokeek* (ATA 181), *Navigator* (ATA 203), and *Keywadin* (ATA 213) are to be used as salvage training hulks.

◆ **3 Edenton-class salvage and rescue ships** Bldr: Brooke Marine, Lowestoft, U.K.

Authorized: 1 in FY 66; 2 in FY 67

	Laid down	L	In serv.
ATS 1 Edenton	1-4-67	15-5-68	23-1-71
ATS 2 Beaufort	19-2-68	20-12-68	22-1-72
ATS 3 Brunswick	5-6-68	14-11-69	19-12-72

Edenton (ATS 1) L. & L. Van Ginderen, 6-85

D: 2,650 tons (3,200 fl) **S:** 16 kts **Dim:** 88.0 (80.5 pp) × 1.53 × 4.6
A: 2/20-mm AA (I × 2) **Electron Equipt:** Radar: 1/SPS-53, 1/Raytheon . . . nav.
M: 4 Paxman 12 YLCM (900 rpm) diesels; 2 Escher-Wyss CP props; 6,000 hp
Electric: 1,200 kw **Range:** 10,000/13 **Man:** 7 officers, 106 men

AUXILIARY SHIPS *(continued)*

Remarks: ATS 4 (FY 72) and ATS 5 (FY 73) canceled in favor of *Powhatan* class T-ATF. Can tow ships up to AOE 1-class size. 272-ton dead lift over the bow. 20-ton crane aft; 10-ton boom forward. Can conduct dives to 260 m. Powerful pumps and complete fire-fighting equipment. Equipped with bow-thruster.

◆ **1 Currituck-class guided-missile ship** Bldr: Los Angeles SB & DD Co., San Pedro

	Laid down	L	In serv.
AVM 1 Norton Sound (ex-AV 11)	7-9-42	28-11-43	8-1-45

Norton Sound (AVM 1)—showing SPY-1 Aegis radar installation G. Arra, 7-79

D: 10,310 tons light (15,590 fl) **S:** 19 kts
Dim: 164.72 (158.5 wl) × 21.11 × 7.16
A: 1/Mk 26 Mod. 0 launcher (II × 1, 24 Standard SM-1/2 MR missiles)—16/EX-41 VLS cells (see remarks)
Electron Equipt: Radar: 1/SPS-53, 1/SPS-10, 1/SPS-40, 1/SPY-1A, 1/SPG-62
TACAN: SRN-6
M: 2 sets Allis-Chalmers GT; 2 props; 12,000 hp **Electric:** 5,625 kw
Boilers: 4 Babcock & Wilcox Express; 28.2 kg/cm², 366°C
Fuel: 2,300 tons **Man:** 35 officers, 460 men

Remarks: Ex-seaplane tender. Has served as a guided-missile trials ship since 1948. The prototype Aegis system was installed in 1975, with only forward, starboard "face" of the SPY-1A phased-array radar operational. SPS-40 replaced the unique, large-antenna SPS-52 variant radar in 1975. Helicopter landing pad between Mk 26 launcher and hangar. Refitted by Ingalls, Pascagoula, 1981, with 16-cell Martin-Marietta EX-41 VLS (Vertical Launching System) recessed into forecastle. Three of the cells are required for a telescoping replenishment-at-sea boom, leaving 13 cells for Standard, Harpoon, and Tomahawk missiles. Firing trials began 12-81. A new, longer, production version of the EX-41 (Mk 41 Mod. 1) was installed during 1983.

◆ **1 Intrepid-class auxiliary-training aircraft carrier**

	Bldr	Laid down	L	In serv.
AVT 16 Lexington	Bethlehem, Quincy	16-7-41	25-9-42	17-2-43

Lexington (AVT 16)—arriving at Philadelphia for overhaul G. Arra, 10-84

D: Approx. 33,000 tons (42,550 fl) **S:** 30 + kts
Dim: 270.97 (249.94 wl) × 31.39 (58.5 flight deck) × 9.4
A: Removed (no aircraft permanently assigned)
Electron Equipt: Radar: 1/SPS-10, 1/SPS-12, 1/SPN-35, 1/SPN-43
TACAN: URN-20
M: 4 sets Westinghouse GT; 4 props; 150,000 hp
Boilers: 8 Babcock & Wilcox; 41.7 kg/cm², 454°C **Electric:** 7,000 kw
Fuel: 6,750 tons **Range:** 18,000/12 **Man:** 75 officers, 1,365 men

Remarks: Employed in deck-landing training at Pensacola, Fla. Was to have been stricken in FY 80 and replaced by the *Coral Sea* (CV 43), but has been extended in service through FY 90. On 29-12-68 her number changed from CVS 16 to CVT 16; changed to AVT 16 on 15-7-78. Has two Type C11 Mod. 1 steam catapults, three elevators (one centerline forward; one at the forward end of the angled deck; and one to starboard, abaft the island), and four Mk 7 arrester wires. Flight deck composed of 76-mm-thick Douglas fir planking. All guns and fire-control equipment removed. Completed major overhaul 5-80; received a 12-month overhaul beginning 10-84.

UNCLASSIFIED MISCELLANEOUS SHIPS

◆ **1 Trident missile-firing simulator barge**

IX 512 (ex-U.S. Army BD 6651)—acquired 1-9-83

Remarks: Works with YD 244. No characteristics available.

Note: IX 511 (ex-LST 399) was stricken 15-6-85 for use as a target.

◆ **1 explosives damage-control barge** Bldr: Norfolk NSY (In serv. 1942)

IX 509 (ex-*Underwater Test Barge No. 1,* ex-YC. . .)

IX 509 W. Donko, 7-84

D: 3,000 tons (fl) **Dim:** 56.1 × . . . × 3.7

Remarks: Operated for the Naval Ships Research and Development Center. Reclassified IX 509 on 1-12-79. Has a 60-ton crane.

◆ **1 satellite navigation systems trials craft**

IX 508 (ex-LCU 1618) Bldr: Gunderson Bros., Portland, Ore. (In serv. 1959)

IX 508 G. Arra, 1984

D: 190 tons (390 fl) **S:** 11 kts **Dim:** 41.07 × 9.07 × 2.08
M: 4 G.M. 6-71 diesels; 2 Kort-nozzle props; 1,200 hp
Fuel: 13 tons **Range:** 1,200/11 **Man:** . . .

Remarks: Adapted 1978 for Naval Ocean Science Center, San Diego, to conduct trials with NAVSTAR global positioning system. Reclassified IX from LCU 1-12-79.

◆ **2 Admiral W.S. Benson-class barracks ships** Bldr: Bethlehem Steel, Alameda, Cal.

	L	In serv.
IX 507 General Hugh J. Gaffey (ex TAP 121, ex-*Admiral W.L. Capps,* AP 121)	. . .	18-9-44
IX 510 General William O. Darby (ex-TAP 127, ex-*Admiral W.S. Sims,* AP 127)	4-6-45	27-9-45

D: 12,657 tons light (22,574 fl) **S:** 19 kts
Dim: 185.6 (174.65 pp) × 23.01 × 8.05
M: 2 sets G.E. GT, electric drive; 2 props; 18,000 hp **Electric:** 2,875 kw
Boilers: 4 Combustion Engineering "D," 42.3 kg/cm², 449°C
Fuel: 4,037 tons **Man:** Berthing for 499 officers, 1,577 men

Remarks: Former troop transport transferred to the Army in 1946, reacquired by the Navy on 1-3-50 for MSC (then MSTS). Stricken on 9-1-69 and transferred to Maritime Commission Reserve Fleet. Partially reactivated and redesignated IX 507 on 1-11-78 for service at Bremerton NSY, Washington, as berthing ship for crew of CVN 65, then undergoing overhaul. IX 510 reclassified 10-81 and towed from James River, Virginia, to Norfolk Naval Shipyard; placed in service 1-7-82. Propulsion plants not reactivated.

UNCLASSIFIED MISCELLANEOUS SHIPS *(continued)*

General William O. Darby (IX 510) W. Donko, 7-83

◆ **1 YFU 71-class trials tender** Bldr: Pacific Coast Eng. Co., Alameda, Cal.

IX 506 (ex-YFU 82) (In serv. 10-68)

IX 506 G. Arra, 5-83

D: 220 tons (380 fl) **S:** 8 kts **Dim:** 38.1 × 10.97 × 2.29 **Electric:** 120 kw
M: 4 G.M. 6-71 diesels; 2 props; 1,000 hp **Man:** 2 officers, 10 men

Remarks: Ex-harbor utility craft. Reclassified on 1-4-78 for service with Naval Ocean Systems Center, San Diego, to replace IX 505 (ex-YTM 759). Former barge YFN 816 is used as a work platform with this unit.

◆ **3 Benewah-class barracks ships** Bldr: Boston NSY

	Laid down	L	In serv.
IX 502 Mercer (ex-APB 39)	25-8-44	17-11-44	19-9-45
IX 503 Nueces (ex-APB 40)	2-1-45	6-5-45	30-11-45
IX 504 Echols (ex-APB 37)	6-45	30-7-45	1-1-47

Mercer (IX 502) W. Donko, 7-85

D: 2,189 tons light (3,640 fl) **S:** 10 kts **Dim:** 100.0 × 15.2 × 3.4
M: 2 G.M. 12-267 ATL diesels; 2 props; 1,600 hp **Electric:** 500 kw
Man: (when operational): 13 officers, 180 men + 26 officers, 1,200 troops

Remarks: IX 502 and IX 503 recommissioned 1968 for service in Vietnam, placed back in reserve 1969-71; activated again in 1-11-75 as barracks ships at Puget Sound NSY. IX 504, in reserve since completion in 1947, activated 1-2-76 as a barracks ship for *Ohio*-class SSBN crews at General Dynamics, Groton. Propulsion plant inactivated. Eight 40-mm AA (IV × 2) removed.

◆ **1 test range support ship (ex-LSMR)** Bldr: Brown SB, Houston

	Laid down	L	In serv.
IX 501 Elk River (ex-LSMR 501)	24-3-45	21-4-45	27-5-45

D: 1,280 tons (fl) **S:** 11 kts **Dim:** 70.0 × 15.2 × 2.8
Electron Equipt: Radar: 1/LN-66 **Electric:** 440 kw
M: 2 G.M. 16-278A diesels; 2 props; 2,880 hp **Man:** 25 men + 20 technicians

Elk River (IX 501) G. Arra, 1983

Remarks: Former fire-support rocket ship converted 1967-68 at Avondale Shipyards, Westwego, Louisiana, to act as support ship at the San Clemente Island Range for the Navy deep-submergence diving program. 2.4-m bulges were added to her hull sides and a center well cut for lowering equipment through the hull. The well is straddled by a 65-ton traveling gantry crane. Thrusters added to allow accurate dynamic mooring. Tests diving procedures, equipment, and small diving vehicles.

◆ **1 sonar test barge**

IX 310 (no name)

Remarks: Actually, two barges moored in Lake Seneca, New York; subordinated to the Naval Underwater Sound Laboratory, Newport, Rhode Island. In service in 1971. IX 309, *Monob One,* is now numbered YAG 61.

◆ **1 U.S. Army FS 381-class torpedo-trials ship**

	Bldr	In serv.
IX 308 New Bedford (ex-AKL 17, ex-FS 289)	Martinolich SB, San Diego, Cal.	3-45

D: 526 tons light (940 fl) **S:** 13 kts **Dim:** 54.10 (50.29 wl) × 9.75 × 3.05
A: 1/533-mm TT—3/324-mm Mk 32 ASW TT (III × 1)
M: 2 G.M. 6-278A diesels; 2 props; 1,000 hp
Electric: 225 kw **Fuel:** 67 tons **Range:** 3,200/11 **Man:** 24 accomm.

Remarks: Operated by the Coast Guard for the Army during World War II; transferred to the Navy as a cargo ship on 1-3-50. Converted as a torpedo-trials ship in 1963. Operated by the Naval Torpedo Station, Keyport, Washington. Carries the CURV remote-controlled underwater recovery vehicle.

◆ **1 U.S. Army FS 330DC-class torpedo-trials ship**

	Bldr	In serv.
IX 306 (ex-FS 221)	Higgins Industries, New Orleans	1-45

D: 460 tons (906 fl) **S:** 12 kts **Dim:** 54.81 × 9.75 × 4.32
A: 1/533)mm TT—3/324-mm Mk 32 ASW TT (III × 1)
M: 2 Enterprise diesels; 2 props; 800 hp **Electric:** 225 kw **Fuel:** 62 tons

Remarks: Employed by the Army as a cargo ship until transferred to the Navy on 1-1-69 as a torpedo- and general-experimentation trials ship for the Naval Underwater Weapons Research and Engineering Center, Newport, R.I., at the Atlantic Underwater Test and Evaluation Center (AUTEC) in the Bahamas. Naval and civilian crew. Painted white with blue bow; torpedo-tube exits on starboard bow.

◆ **1 ocean construction platform** Bldr: Missouri Valley Br. & Iron, Ind.

	Laid down	L	In serv.
Seacon (ex-YFNB 33)	16-1-45	22-3-45	25-10-45

D: 2,780 tons (fl) **S:** 7 kts **Dim:** 79.25 × 14.63 × 2.9
M: 1 G.M. 12-71 diesel, 2 G.M. 6-71 diesels; 3 Voith-Schneider 14E/87 vertical cycloidal props; 1,020 hp
Electric: 575 kw **Man:** 50 tot.

Remarks: A large covered barge belonging to the Navy and used by NASA for transporting rockets, the *Seacon* was converted 1974-76 by Norfolk SB & Dry Dock Co. to serve as a seagoing work ship for the Navy Ocean Engineering and Construction Project Office. Intended to be towed at up to 11 knots to work locations and then to use own propulsion for precision maneuvering. Can be used to lay cable, can moor in 200-m water, and has open work deck 40 × 14 aft. Unique in having no ship or yard-craft number.

◆ **1 sail frigate relic** Bldr: Hart's SY, Boston, Mass.

Constitution (ex-IX 21) (L: 21-10-1797)

D: 2,200 tons **S:** 13 kts (sail) **Dim:** 53.4 (hull) × 13.7 × 6.1
A: 30/24 pdr.—16/18-pdr carronade—10/12-pdr (nominal)
Man: 2 officers, 47 men

Remarks: Remains in commission. Wooden construction. First went to sea 22-7-1798. Three masts: 28.7, 31.7, and 24.7 m high. Remains docked at former Boston Navy Yard except for twice-yearly "turnaround" to prevent warpage. Designated IX 21 from 8-12-41 to 1-9-75, and briefly bore name *Old Constitution* from 1917 to 1925.

UNCLASSIFIED MISCELLANEOUS SHIPS *(continued)*

Constitution L. & L. Van Ginderen, 9-83

EXPERIMENTAL CRAFT

◆ **1 BH 110-class Rigid Sidewall Surface Effect Trials craft**

	Bldr	L	In serv.
SES-200 (ex-USCG *Dorado,* WSES 1)	Bell-Halter, New Orleans	12-78	2-79

SES-200 Bell-Halter, 9-82

D: 128 tons light (210 fl) **S:** 28–32 kts
Dim: 48.76 × 11.89 × 2.40 at rest/1.70 on cushion
Electron Equipt: Radar: 2/Decca navigational
M: 2 G.M. 16V149 TI diesels for propulsion; 2 CP props; 3,200 hp, 2 G.M. 8V92 TI diesels for lift; 2 centrifugal fans; 990 hp
Electric: 60 kw **Range:** 300–500/35 on cushion; 2,500/23
Man: 2 officers, 18 men, 3 civilian technicians **Fuel:** 59.6 tons

Remarks: Designed by Bell Aerospace-Textron and built by Halter Marine in a jointly financed effort. Leased 1-80 for one month by U.S. Coast Guard and then again for a longer trials period in 1981, commencing with a six-month joint USN/USCG operational evaluation from Key West. In early 1982 the ship came under U.S. Navy control and had accommodations for 14 additional personnel added. Placed in service 24-9-82. Functions by trapping a fan-generated air bubble between the rigid sidewalls and rubber seals at bow and stern. Assigned to David Taylor Naval Ship Research and Development Center. Conducted trials for U.S. Coast Guard late 1984.

◆ **1 space-vehicle booster recovery ship** Bldr: Bishop Marine Service (In serv. 1966)

RSB 1 (ex-*A.B. Wood II*)

RSB 1 U.S. Navy

D: 291 tons (fl) **S:** 13 kts **Dim:** 47.85 × 10.97 × 3.35
M: 2 diesels; 2 props; 1,530 hp **Man:** 5 (civilians)

Remarks: Operated by civilian contractor for Naval Surface Warfare Center, Fort Lauderdale, Fla. Used to recover space-vehicle boosters. Has a bow-thruster and a 35-ton telescoping crane.

◆ **1 propulsion trials craft**

Jupiter II

Jupiter II U.S. Navy, 9-80

Remarks: Jupiter II is a 19.8-m workboat operated by the Naval Ships Research and Development Center, Annapolis, Md. On 23-9-80 the gas-turbine-powered craft began trials with a 300-kw superconducting electric propulsion motor, producing 6–7 kt speeds. A 2,250-kw superconducting motor was to be substituted late in 1981.

◆ **1 SWATH (Small Waterplane Area, Twin-Hull) prototype**

SSP 1 Kaimalino Bldr: U.S. Coast Guard, Curtis Bay, Md. (L: 7-3-73)

Kaimalino (SSP 1) U.S. Navy, 1980

D: 228 tons (fl) **S:** 22 kts **Dim:** 26.92 × 12.99 × 4.65
Electron Equipt: Radar: 1/LN-66 (SPS-59)

EXPERIMENTAL CRAFT *(continued)*

M: CODOG 2 G.E. T64-6B gas turbines, chain drive; 2 CP props; 5,000 hp—or: 2 G.M. 6-71 diesels, 2 hydraulic motors; 160 hp
Electric: 78 kw **Range:** 450/17; 1,500/5 **Man:** 15 max.

Remarks: Catamaran hull with cigar-shaped flotation pontoons. Helicopter deck. Operated by the Naval Ocean Systems Center, Hawaii Laboratory. The SWATH concept shows great promise as an economical, high-performance/high endurance ASW ship, but has been hampered in its development by a lack of funding. *Kaimalino* has been used in torpedo-firing trials and as a weapons-recovery craft. Planned stretch to 600 tons (fl) not carried out, due to costs, although material was assembled 1982 for the conversion.

◆ **2 Asheville-class engineering-trials ships** Bldr: Tacoma Boat

	In serv.
Athena I (ex-*Chehalis,* PG 94)	11-8-69
Athena II (ex-*Grand Rapids,* PG 98)	9-5-70

Athena I (foreground) and Athena II—yellow hulls, white superstructure
David Taylor Model Basin, 1980

D: 225 tons (250 fl) **S:** 40 kts **Dim:** 50.14 × 7.28 × 2.9
M: CODOG: 1 G.E. 7LM-1500-PE 102 LM-1500 gas turbine (12,500 hp), 2 Cummins VT12-875M diesels (1,400 hp); 2 CP props
Electric: 200 kw **Fuel:** 50 tons **Range:** 325/37; 2,400/14

Remarks: These craft are regarded as equipment, and therefore do not have USN hull numbers. Operate from Panama City, Florida, for the Naval Ships Research and Development Center, Carderock. Have civilian crews and are disarmed. *Athena I* reclassified on 21-8-75, *Athena II* on 1-10-77. Have a 10-ton instrumentation payload. Both can carry a 14.9-m², portable, glass-reinforced plastic laboratory on the stern, and *Athena* I has a permanent 18.6-m² lab added forward. *Douglas* (PG 100) was to have been converted to *Athena III* in FY 83; lack of funds canceled project and ship discarded 12-84.

◆ **1 hydrofoil research craft** Bldr: Boeing/Martinac, Tacoma, Washington

	Laid down	L	In serv.
High Point (ex-PCH 1)	27-2-61	17-8-62	15-8-63

High Point (PCH 1)—ashore, auxiliary propeller lowered W. Donko, 7-83

D: 110 tons (fl) **S:** 48 kts **Dim:** 35.0 × 9.4 × 1.8 (5.2, foils extended)
M: 2 Bristol-Siddeley/Rolls-Royce Proteus gas turbines; 4 props (paired, counter-rotating); 6,200 hp—2 Packard 2D850 diesels; 1 prop; 600 hp for hull-borne drive (12 kts)
Man: 1 officer, 12 men

Remarks: Officially stricken 30-9-79, but retained as "floating equipment" for experimental purposes at Bremerton, Wash. Foils retract vertically: single forward set is steerable, while after pair each have a nacelle with a propeller at each end. A 40-mm AA and 4/324-mm Mk 32 ASW TT (I × 4, fixed) have been removed. Used for high-speed Harpoon SSM launch trials in 1973-74. On loan to Boeing during 1984-85.

◆ **1 Cove-class former inshore minesweeper** Bldr: Bethlehem SY, Bellingham, Wash.

	Laid down	L	In serv.
MSI 2 Cape	1-5-57	5-4-58	27-2-59

Cape (MSI 2) 1959

D: 200 tons (240 fl) **S:** 12 kts **Dim:** 34.1 × 7.1 × 3.0
M: 2 G.M. diesels; 2 props; 650 hp **Man:** . . . (civilians)

Remarks: Wooden construction; sweep gear removed. MSI 2 has been operated by the Applied Physics Laboratory of Johns Hopkins University since 31-7-70. Sister *Cove* (MSI 1) is now classed as floating property and operates at San Diego for the Naval Ocean Systems Center. Sisters operate as minesweepers in the Iranian and Turkish navies.

DEEP-SUBMERGENCE RESEARCH CRAFT

◆ **1 nuclear research submarine for deep diving**

	Bldr	Laid down	L	In serv.
NR-1	Electric Boat Co.	10-6-67	25-1-69	27-10-69

Authorized: FY 66

NR-1 U.S. Navy

D: 372 tons surfaced/700 submerged **S:** 4.6/3.6 kts **Dim:** 41.78 × 3.81 × 4.57
M: 1 pressurized-water reactor, turboelectric drive; 2 props
Man: 2 officers, 3 men, 2 scientists

Remarks: Project approved 18-4-65. Fitted for all oceanographic missions, military and civilian, and for bottom salvage. Thick cylindrical hull. Wheels for moving on ocean bottom. A very successful vehicle, but cost three times the original estimate. No periscope, uses television cameras. Four ducted maneuvering thrusters. Can dive to over 800 m. Operated by Submarine Squadron 17, Bangor, Washington, since 1-84.

◆ **2 DSRV class** Bldr: Lockheed Missile & Space Co., Sunnyvale, Calif.

	In serv.	Accepted
DSRV 1 Mystic	6-8-71	4-11-77
DSRV 2 Avalon	28-7-72	1-1-78

D: 30.5 tons **S:** 4.5 kts **Dim:** 15.0 × 2.5 × 3.28 (high)
M: 1 electric motor; 1 shrouded-pivoting prop; 15 hp
Man: 4 tot. + 24 recued men

Remarks: The DSRVs are intended to: operate at a maximum depth of 1,500 m; stand pressure equal to 2,750 m; dive and rise at 30 m a minute; make a maximum speed of 5 knots while submerged; remain submerged for 30 hours at 3 knots; maintain station in a 1-knot current; and operate all machinery even while submerged at a 45° angle. DSRVs can bring to the surface as many as 24 men at one time. Motor, powered by a silver-zinc battery, turns a regular propulsion propeller and two thrusters, one for-

DEEP-SUBMERGENCE RESEARCH CRAFT (*continued*)

ward and one aft, which can be positioned to permit a close approach to a sunken object. Their size and weight were determined by the possible need to airlift them in an Air Force Starlifter (Lockheed C-141A) cargo plane. Additional equipment, especially a truck transport for the DSRV, would be carried in a second Starlifter. In addition, SSNs have received the equipment necessary to fasten a DSRV to their decks and carry it at 15 knots. The SSN will serve as a base for the DSRV while it awaits the arrival of a *Pigeon*-class rescue ship (ASR). Hull consists of two HY-140 steel spheres surrounded by a fiberglass outer hull. One received a potassium superoxide (KO_2) breathing system in 1982, providing 480 man hours submerged endurance. A cost overrun of nearly 1,500 percent prevented the procurement of any more DSRVs. Twelve were originally planned. Names were assigned in 1977. Photo in addenda.

◆ **2 Turtle class** Bldr: General Dynamics, Groton, Conn.

DSV 3 TURTLE (ex-*Autec-I*) DSV 4 SEA CLIFF (ex-*Autec-II*)

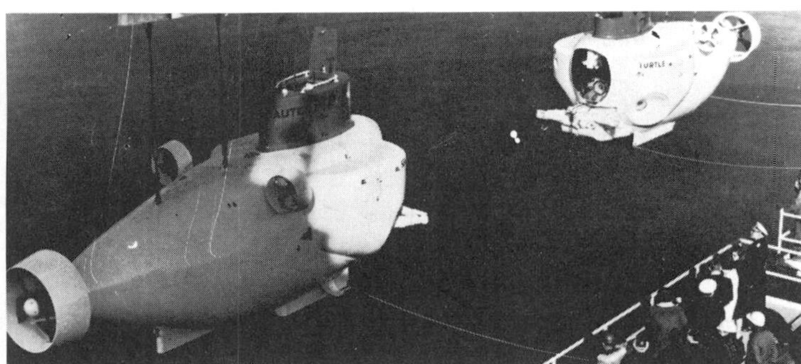

Sea Cliff and Turtle—at "launch" 1968

D: 21 tons (*Sea Cliff:* 29) **S:** 2 kts **Dim:** 7.9 (Sea Cliff: 9.4) × 2.4 (3.7 over thrusters)
M: 1 electric motor; 1 prop; 2 thrusters **Man:** 2 men + 1 scientist
Endurance: 16 hrs.

REMARKS: Launched on 11-12-68. Could originally descend to 1,980 m. Spherical pressure hull of HY-100 steel. The *Turtle* was modified in 1979 to descend to 3,660 meters, and the *Sea Cliff* received a titanium pressure sphere in 1981-84, permitting 6,100-m descents. Air transportable. Fitted with external manipulator arms. Eight hours' endurance at 1 knot. Operated by Submarine Development Group 1, San Diego. *Sea Cliff* dove to 6,096 m on 10-3-85, supported by *Point Loma* (AGDS 1). *Turtle* had a serious fire 17-8-84 and was still in repair at end-1985. Three craft are usually supported by the chartered R.V. *Lulu,* a 230-ton, 32.0 × 15.0 m catamaran.

◆ **1 Alvin class** Bldr: General Mills, Minneapolis, Minn. (In serv. 1965)

DSV 2 ALVIN

D: 16 tons **S:** 2 kts **Dim:** 6.9 × 2.4 × . . .
M: Electric motors; 1 prop; 2 thrusters **Man:** 1 man + 2 scientists

REMARKS: Operated by civilian Woods Hole Oceangraphic Institute on contract to the Navy. Sank on 16-10-68, but raised, repaired, and returned to service in 11-72. Single titanium pressure sphere permits descents to 4,000 m. Supported by the Woods Hole Institute research ship *Atlantis II. Trieste II* (DSV 1) was stricken 1-4-85. *Nemo* (DSV 5) is a remote-controlled vehicle, now on display at the Naval Ocean Science Center, San Diego.

SERVICE CRAFT

NOTE: The force still consists largely of craft built during World War II. The units marked with an asterisk are non-self-propelled.

◆ **1 former West German floating dry dock*** Bldr: Seebeckwerft AG, Bremerhaven

AFDB 8 MACHINIST (In serv. 1980)

Lift Capacity: 39,300 tons **Dim:** 251.46 (285.31 on blocks) × 53.54 (42.77 between wingwalls) × 10.0 over blocks (flooded)

REMARKS: Purchased from builder 5-8-85 and towed to the Philippines for service at Subic Bay, to arrive 3-86. Has two 7.5-ton traveling cranes.

◆ **3 AFDB large auxiliary floating dry docks***

	Bldr	In serv.	Capacity (tons)
AFDB 2	Mare Island NSY	4-44	30,000
AFDB 4	Mare Island NSY	8-44	55,000
AFDB 7 LOS ALAMOS	Mare Island NSY	3-45	31,000

REMARKS: AFDB 2 was originally a 10-section, 90,000-ton-capacity dock. Sections C, D, H, and I of AFDB 2 are active at Subic Bay, with the remainder in reserve at Pearl Harbor. The others were originally all 7-section docks. AFDB 4 is in reserve, while sections C, E, and G of ADFB 7 are active at Holy Loch, Scotland, in support of SSBNs; sections A and B are in reserve. *Artisan* (AFDB 1) was placed on sale in 1983. AFDB 3, long in reserve, was transferred to the state of Maine in 1982 for use by Bath Iron Works at Portland; AFDB 5 was transferred to the city of Port Arthur, Texas, in 1984 and leased to Todd Shipyards.

◆ **3 AFDL small auxiliary floating docks***

	Bldr	In serv.	Capacity (tons)
AFDL 6 DYNAMIC	Chicago Bridge & Iron	3-44	1,000
AFDL 23 ADEPT	G.D. Auchter	12-44	1,900
AFDL 25 UNDAUNTED	. . .	1944	1,000

REMARKS: All one-piece docks. *Diligence* (AFDL 48), built of concrete, and the only postwar unit, was commercially leased 23-3-80. *Reliance* (AFDL 47) had been reacquired 18-1-81 from Maritime Commission reserve, but was returned 12-8-81. Seven additional units (AFDL 12, 15, 16, 21, 22, 29, 40) are leased to commercial shipbuilders and ship repairers; AFDL 37, 38, and 45, long on lease, were sold outright 1-10-81; AFDL 8 was stricken 1-12-81 and sunk as a fishing reef; AFDL 2 was stricken 15-11-81, AFDL 9 was stricken 15-7-82, AFDL 19 and 41 sold 4-83, *Endeavor* (AFDL 1) stricken 1985. AFDL 25 re-acquired 6-84, refitted, and towed to Guantánamo Bay 9-84. AFDL 6 and 25 are 61.0 m by 19.5 m; AFDL 23 is 87.8 × 19.5 m.

◆ **6 AFDM medium auxiliary floating dry docks*** Bldr: Everett Pacific

(AFDM 8: Chicago Bridge & Iron, AFDM 14: Pollock-Stockton SB, Cal.)

	In serv.		In serv.
AFDM 5 RESOURCEFUL (ex-YPD 21)	2-43	AFDM 8 RICHLAND (ex-YFD 63)	12-44
AFDM 6 COMPETENT (ex-YFD 62)	6-44	AFDM 10 RESOLUTE (ex-. . .)	1945
AFDM 7 SUSTAIN (ex-YFD 63)	1-45	AFDM 14 STEADFAST (ex-YFD 71)	7-45

Sustain (AFDM 7)—with YD 214 alongside J. Jedrlinic, 1980

REMARKS: All active and of 18,000-ton capacity. 189.6 × 37.8 m, except AFDM 14: 14,000 tons, 182.3 × 36.0 m. AFDM 14 reclassified 1-2-83. AFDM 7 overhauled 1983. AFDM 1–3, 9 are on commercial lease.

◆ **17 APL barracks craft***

APL 2, 4, 5, 15, 18, 19, 29, 31, 32, 34, 42, 43, 45, 50, 54, 57, 58

APL 45 W. Donko, 7-84

REMARKS: Built 1944-45. All active. 2,600 tons (fl), 79.6 × 15.0 × 2.6. Can accommodate 6 officers and 680 men. Have 300-kw generator capacity.

◆ **2 ARD auxiliary repair dry docks*** Bldr: Pacific Bridge, Alameda, Cal.

ARD 5 WATERFORD (In serv. 6-42) ARD 30 SAN ONOFRE (In serv. 8-44)

San Onofre (ARD 30)—*Dixon* (AS 37) in background L. & L. Van Ginderen, 5-82

SERVICE CRAFT *(continued)*

Remarks: Both active, 3,500-ton capacity. Sisters *West Milton* (ARD 7) to Maritime Commission for lay-up 16-7-81, ARD 24 stricken 15-1-80.

◆ **2 Shippingport-class submarine support docks***

	Bldr	In serv.
ARDM 4 Shippingport	Bethlehem Steel, Sparrows Pt., Md.	1979
ARDM 5 Arco	Todd Pacific, Seattle	2-86

Shippingport (ARDM 4)—with special pier facilities U.S. Navy, 1979

Capacity: 7,800 tons (8,400 emergency)
Dim: 150.0 × 29.3 × 16.6 (max.)

Remarks: Intended to support *Los Angeles*-class submarines. Length of blocks: 118 m. 20.7 m clear height inside. Require shore support. Have 2/25-ton cranes. ARDM = Medium Support Dock. ARDM 5 ordered 13-10-82. First floating dry docks built for U.S. Navy since World War II. ARDM 5 laid down 25-7-83, launched 14-12-84. Have accommodations for 12.

◆ **3 ARD 12-class submarine support docks*** Bldr: Pacific Bridge, Alameda, Cal.

	In serv.
ARDM 1 Oak Ridge (ex-ARD 19)	3-44
ARDM 2 Alamagordo (ex-ARD 26)	6-44
ARDM 3 Endurance (ex-ARD 18)	2-44

Capacity: 3,500 tons **Dim:** 149.4 × 24.7

Remarks: Converted from ARD auxiliary repair docks to service nuclear submarines. One end has a pointed, ship-type bow to permit towing. ARDM 1 refit completed 6-85.

◆ **1 YAG miscellaneous auxiliary yard craft** (In serv. 1966)

YAG 62 Deer Island

Deer Island (YAG 62) MAR, Inc., 1983

D: . . . **S:** 10.5 kts **Dim:** 36.58 × 8.53 × 2.13
M: 2 diesels; 2 props; . . . hp **Electron Equipt:** Radar: 2/. . . nav.
Range: 6,200/10.5 **Man:** 20 crew and scientists.

Remarks: 172 grt/117 nrt, former oilfield supply tug placed on Navy List 15-3-83 and operated for David Taylor Naval Ship Research and Development Center from Port Everglades, Fla., by MAR Inc. for sound-quieting trials.

◆ **1 YAG miscellaneous auxiliary yard craft** Bldr: Zenith Dredge Co., Duluth, Minn.

	Laid down	L	In serv.
YAG 61 Monob One (ex-IX 309, ex-YW 87)	1-12-42	3-4-43	11-11-43

Monob One (YAG 61)—yellow hull, masts, white superstructure U.S. Navy, 12-80

D: 1,390 tons (fl) **S:** 11 kts **Dim:** 53.0 × 10.1 × 4.8
M: 1 Caterpillar diesel; 1 prop; 850 hp **Range:** 2,500/9

Remarks: Redesignated from IX 309 on 1-7-70. Former water lighter modified in 1959 to support the ballistic-missile submarine silencing program. Based at Port Canaveral, Fla., and operated by the David Taylor Naval Ships Research and Development Center, Carderock, Md., Acoustic Trials Detachment. Has four laboratories, totaling 279 m². To be replaced in 1988-89 by *Hayes* (T-AG 195, ex-T-AGOR 16).

◆ **227 (+20 + 16) YC open lighters***

YC 306–1571

YC 1433, pushed by Anoka (YTB 810) J. Jedrlinic, 1984

Remarks: Built 1915–83. Five are in reserve. YC 1517 to YC 1522 built 1976-77, YC 1523–1527 built 1978-79, YC 1528–1551 built 1979-83. Three authorized under FY 82 budget. Current design is YC 1554 class, of which six were authorized FY 83, 14 authorized FY 84, and 11 in FY 85, and 2 in FY 86, are programmed: 250 tons light (660 fl); 33.53 × 9.75 × 1.98 (max.). YC 1458 was stricken 15-6-82, YC 1515 stricken 1-8-82. YC 1386 sold 15-10-82. YC 1542 sold 1-2-83. Ex-YD 89 reclassified YC 1553 on 1-6-83; YFN 1214 reclassified YC 1552 on 15-3-83; YC 1530 reclassified a camel, 1-6-24; YC 1546 reclassified floating equipment 6-84; YC 1435 stricken 6-85.

◆ **1 YCF car float***

YCF 16 (In serv. 25-1-42)

Remarks: 45.72 × 10.21; used to transport railroad cars. Active.

◆ **5 (+0 + 1) YCV aircraft transportation lighters***

YCV 8 (In serv. 4-3-44)
YCV 10 (In serv. 21-8-44)
YCV 11 (In serv. 6-10-44)
YCV 16 (In serv. 29-8-45)
YCV 17 (In serv. 7-89)

Remarks: 2,480 tons (fl); 28.96 × 9.14; 80-ton capacity. All active. YCV 17 to be requested FY 88

◆ **56 YD floating cranes***

Remarks: Built 1913-70s. All active. YD 171, ex-German, has largest capacity: 350 tons: refitted 1984-85, built 1941 by Demag, Bremerhaven (62.5 × 33.5 × 114.0 high, uses 3,560 m wire rope!). Most U.S. Navy YD are rectangular barges. Typical data: 1,630 tons (fl), 42.7 × 21.3, 90–100 tons capacity. One new YD authorized FY 82, 3 in FY 83, 5 in FY 84, 3 under FY 85: 2 in FY 86 and 3 each programmed for FY 87-88, 1,650 tons (fl); 54.4 × 24.4 × 2.0. YD 149, 154, 181, 189, 231, 241 stricken 15-1-85; all but YD 189 were in reserve. YD 88 stricken 1-9-85. YD 145 stricken 15-1-86.

SERVICE CRAFT *(continued)*

◆ **3 YDT diving tenders**

YDT 14 PHOEBUS (ex YF 294), YDT 15 SUITLAND (ex-YF 336): 600 tons, 40.4 × 9.1, 1 Union diesel: 600 hp (In serv. 10-12-42 and 16-6-43, respectively)
YDT 16* TOM O'MALLEY (ex-YFNB 43): 2,000 tons (fl), 79.6 × 14.6

REMARKS: YDT 3 (ex-YFNG 1) stricken 1984.

◆ **2 YF covered lighters, YF 852 class**

	Bldr	L	In serv.
YF 866 KODIAK	Missouri Valley Bridge & Iron	26-10-45	17-11-45
YF 885 KEYPORT	Defoe SB	19-5-45	4-8-45

D: 300 tons light (505 fl) **S:** 10 kts **Dim:** 40.5 × 9.1 × 2.7
M: 2 G.M. diesels; 2 props; 1,000 hp **Electric:** 120 kw **Fuel:** 40 tons

REMARKS: YF 885 active at Torpedo Testing Station, Keyport, Washington, with **A:** 3/324-mm Mk 32 ASW TT; has "omnithruster" bow-thruster. YF 866 in reserve. Sister YF 862 stricken from reserve 15-2-85.

◆ **6 YFB ferryboats**

YFB 83 Bldr: John H. Mathis Co., Camden, N.J. (In serv. 4-49)

D: 500 tons (fl) **S:** 8.5 kts **Dim:** 49.4 × 17.7
M: 2 diesels **Cargo:** 500 passengers, 38 vehicles

YFB 87 Bldr: Western Boat (In serv. 5-70)

D: 773 tons (fl) **Dim:** 54.9 × 18 **M:** 2 diesels

YFB 88 to YFB 91 (ex-LCU 1646, ex-LCU 1638 to LCU 1640)

D: 390 tons (fl) **S:** 10 kts **Dim:** 41.0 × 9.0
M: 4 G.M. diesels; 2 props; 1,200 hp

REMARKS: Built 1965–69. Modified 1969-70. All active.

◆ **155 (+8) YFN covered lighters***

YFN 862–1264

YFN 979 (misnumbered on side) S. Terzibaschitsch, 4-84

REMARKS: Built 1940–84. 153 active. Majority are 685 tons (fl), 33.5 × 9.8. Large rectangular deckhouse. Nine YFN 1254 class authorized under FY 81 (11 actually built), 6 approved under FY 85, 2 under FY 86: 260 tons light (660 fl); 33.53 × 9.75 × 2.23 m; have a small deckhouse; will be delivered 4-86 to 10-86. YFN stricken, 15-1-86.

◆ **13 YFNB large covered lighters***

YFNB 5, 8, 25, 30, 31, 32, 34, 36, 37, 39, 41, 42, 47 (ex-YRR9)

YFNB 24—now stricken 1969

REMARKS: Built 1945. All active. All 831 tons light (2,780 fl), 79.2 × 14.6 × 2.9. YFNB 47 reclassified 11-83. YFNB 4, on loan to Maritime Administration since 1980, transferred permanently 1-6-85.

◆ **2 YFND dry-dock companion craft***

YFDN 5 (ex-YFN 268; in serv. 3-2-41) YFND 29 (ex-YFN 974; in serv. 28-8-45)

REMARKS: 590 tons (fl), 33.53 × 9.75, converted YFN. YFND 5 in reserve.

◆ **14 YFNX special-purpose lighters***

YFNX 4, 7, 15, 20, 22–26, 30–33

REMARKS: All active except YFNX 7. Most converted YFN. Delivered 1942–70. YFNX 30 (200 tons light; 34.0 × 10.0 × 1.7 m) at Naval Ocean Science Center, San Diego, supports the remote-controlled submersible CURV II. YFNX 4–24 are 33.5 m × 10.0 × 1.7 m; YFNX 25, 26 are 38.4 × 10.0. Several have maneuvering propulsion systems.

◆ **YFP floating power barges***

YFP 3 (ex-YC 1114) YFP 11 (ex-YFN 1207) YFP 12 (ex-YFN 1216)

REMARKS: 33.5 × 9.7-m. YFP 12 in reserve. Completed: YFD 3 in 4-45, other two in 1965.

YFP 14 INDUCTANCE (ex-Army BD 6235)

REMARKS: Built 1943-45. Transferred 1-10-77.

NOTE: Refrigerated cargo lighter YFR 888 stricken 15-2-85.

◆ **4 YFRN refrigerated cargo lighters***

YFRN 385 (ex-YF 385) YFRN 412 (ex-YF 412) YFRN 997 (ex-YF997)
YFRN 1235 (ex-U.S. Army BR 6435)

REMARKS: Built 1943-45. All in reserve. Most 45.7 × 10.4. Sisters YFRN 1256 and 1257 stricken 3-84.

◆ **4 YFRT covered lighter range tenders**

	Bldr	Laid down	L	In serv.
YFRT 287	Norfolk NSY	2-41	5-41	7-41
YFRT 451	Basalt Rock Co., Napa, Cal.	2-44	7-44	10-44
YFRT 520	Erie Concrete & Steel, Erie, Pa.	10-42	3-43	8-43
YFRT 523	Erie Concrete & Steel, Erie, Pa.	3-45	8-45	9-45

D: 650 tons (fl) **S:** 9.5 kts **Dim:** 40.5 × 9.1 × 2.7
A: 3/324-mm Mk 32 ASW TT
M: 2 Union (YFRT 287: Cooper-Bessemer) diesels; 600–1,000 hp

REMARKS: Torpedo trials craft. YFRT 287 built as such, rest converted from YFR. Sister YFRT 418 stricken 2-84. To be replaced late 1980s by new-construction YTT.

◆ **11 YFU harbor utility craft**

YFU 50 (ex-LCU 1486): see LCU 1466 class data; in reserve

YFU 74, YFU 75, YFU 79, YFU 81 (1967-68): Sisters to IX 506 (ex-YFU 82). All in reserve. Delivered 1967-68. Sisters YFU 71, 72, 76, 77 to Dept. of the Interior, 1-12-84.
YFU 83, YFU 91 (ex-LCU 1608), YFU 94 (ex-LCU 1488), YFU 97 (ex LCU 1611), YFU 100 (ex-LCU 1610), YFU 102 (ex-LCU 1642). All LCU 1610 class converted, except YFU 83, built for purpose and YFU 94, in reserve. Built 1955-68 by Pacific Coast Engineering Co., Alameda, Cal. YFU 98 (ex-LCU 1615) and YFU 101 (ex-LCU 1612) stricken 1-86. YFU 79 converting to Helicopter Landing Trainer (HLT 1) by Bender SB; to deliver 3-86.

YFU 100—in standard LCU configuration R. Scheina, 7-84

YFU 91—sides cut down, superstructure heightened L. & L. Van Ginderen, 1984

◆ **3 YGN garbage lighters***

YGN 80, 81, 83 Bldr: Zidel, Portland, Ore. (In serv. 1970-71)

REMARKS: All active. 309 tons light (855 fl), 37.8 × 10.7 rectangular barges. Have hopper-type bottoms to permit dumping at sea. YGN 70 and 82, redesignated as "equipment" 1-84, remain available also.

SERVICE CRAFT *(continued)*

◆ **2 YHLC salvage lift craft, heavy***

YHLC 1 Crilley YHLC 2 Crandall

Crilley (YHLC 1)—outboard *Crandall* (YHLC 2) J. Jedrlinic, 1980

Remarks: Ex-*Hiev* and ex-*Griep* purchased from Germany for Vietnam War duties. Built in 1940s. In the James River Maritime Commission reserve fleet since 9-76, but remain Navy property.

◆ **5 YM dredge**

YM 17 YM 32 YM 33 YM 35 YM 38

Remarks: Characteristics vary. YM 32 and YM 33 in reserve. YM 17 (500 tons) in service 1934; YM 33, 35, in service 1970, are only 13.1 m and 21.3 m overall, respectively.

◆ **2 YNG gate craft***

YNG 11 YNG 17

Remarks: Built 1941 to tend harbor-defense nets. **D:** 225 tons (fl); **Dim:** 33.5 × 10.5.

◆ **1 YO 46-class fuel-oil lighter**—in reserve Bldr: Lake Superior SB, Superior, Wisc.

YO 47 Casing Head (In serv. 11-42)

D: 950 tons (2,660 fl) **S:** 10 kts **Dim:** 71.6 × 11.3 × 4.6 **Cargo:** 1, 350 tons
M: 2 Enterprise diesels; 820 hp. **Electric:** 280 kw **Man:** 34 tot.

◆ **9 YO 43† and YO 65 class** Bldr: Jeffersonville Boat & Machine Co., Jeffersonville, Ind. (except: YO 129: Smith SY, Pensacola, Fla.; YO 203: Manitowoc SB, Manitowoc, Wisc.; YO 241: John H. Mathis, Camden, N.J.)

	In serv.		In serv.		In serv.
YO 129	4-44	YO 224	10-45	YO 241†	10-43
YO 203	8-45	YO 225	10-45	(ex-YOG 5)	
YO 220	8-45	YO 228	11-45		
YO 223	9-45	YO 230	12-45		

YO 203 G. Arra, 11-85

D: 440 tons light (1,390 fl) **S:** 9 kts **Dim:** 53.04 × 9.75 × 3.96
M: 1 G.M. (see remarks) diesel; 1 prop, 640 hp **Electric:** 80 kw

Remarks: Cargo is 900 tons/6,570 bbl. YO 129 has a Union diesel, 560 hp; YO 241 has a Fairbanks-Morse diesel, 480 hp. YO 228 and YO 241 are in reserve. Sisters YO 106 stricken 12-83, YO 200 stricken 7-83, YO 264 stricken 15-11-85. Same basic design as 53.04-mm YOG and YW.

◆ **1 YO 153 class** Bldr: Ira S. Bushey, Brooklyn, N.Y.—In reserve

YO 153 (In serv. 7-43)

D: 370 tons light (1,095 fl) **S:** 10 kts **Dim:** 47.63 × 9.32 × 3.66
M: 1 Fairbanks-Morse diesel; 1 prop; 525 hp **Electric:** 39 kw

Remarks: Cargo: 660 tons/6,071 bbl. In reserve.

YO 153—in reserve at Philadelphia, with 5 reserve YO/YOG/YW A.D. Baker, 8-84

◆ **7 YOG . . . gasoline lighters** Bldrs: RTC SB, Camden, N.J. (except: YOG 78, 79: Puget Sound NSY; YOG 68: George Lawley & Sons, Neponset, Mass.)

YOG 58, YOG 68, YOG 78, YOG 79, YOG 88, YOG 93, YOG 196 (ex-YO 196) (In serv. 1945-46)

YOG 88 W. Donko, 7-83

D: 440 tons light (1,390 fl) **Dim:** 53.04 × 9.75 × 3.96
M: 1 G.M. diesel; 1 prop; 640 hp **Electric:** 80 kw

Remarks: Four in reserve. Carry about 950 tons aviaton fuel. YOG 58 has a Union diesel.

◆ **13 YOGN gasoline barges***

YOGN 8, 9, 10, 26, 110, 111, 113, 114, 115, 122, 123, 124, 125

Remarks: Built 1943-71. All active. Carry aviation fuel. All 1,270–1,360 tons (fl), approx. 50 × 10.7 m.

◆ **47 (+3) YON fuel-oil barges**

Remarks: Most built 1942-76. 46 active. Typical unit: 1,445 tons (fl); 50.3 × 12.0 × 2.7. YON 305, 306 built under FY 80. YON 255 and later (30 units) were built 1964-76. Five are ex-U.S. Army, including YON 305, 306, transferred 7-79. YON 235 is ex-YW 73. Can carry a variety of fuels. Three YON 307 requested under FY 87: 1,600 tons (fl); 56.0 × 10.7 × 3.0.

◆ **12 YOS oil-storage barges***

YOS 8, 10–12, 15–17, 20, 21, 24, 28 (ex-YC 707), 33 (ex-YSR 46), 34

Remarks: Built 1944-65. All active. Ten: 100 tons light; 24.4 × 10.4; others: 140 tons light; 33.5 × 10.4. YOS 34 (ex-Army OB61-2) acquired 1-9-79. Two new YOS requested under FY 87: 725 tons (fl).

◆ **7 (+20) YP 676-class patrol craft/training tenders** Bldrs: YP676–682: Peterson, Bldrs., Sturgeon Bay, Wisc.; others: Marinette SB., Marinette, Wisc.

	Laid down	L	In serv.		Laid down	L	In serv.
YP 676	7-4-83	9-4-84	14-11-84	YP 681	29-10-84	1-6-85	9-95
YP 677	10-10-83	23-6-84	5-12-84	YP 682	7-1-85	8-85	10-85
YP 678	15-12-83	3-11-84	5-85	YP 683	23-7-85	30-4-86	8-86
YP 679	18-4-84	11-12-84	7-85	YP 684	9-85	29-8-85	. . .
YP 680	2-7-84	23-3-85	29-7-85	YP 685	10-85	8-10-85	. . .

SERVICE CRAFT *(continued)*

YP 686	27-1-86	. . .	. . .	YP 691	. . .	. . .	. . .
YP 687	3-86	. . .	. . .	YP 692	. . .	. . .	. . .
YP 688	4-86	. . .	. . .	YP 693	. . .	. . .	. . .
YP 689	5-86	. . .	. . .	YP 694	. . .	. . .	. . .
YP 690	6-86	. . .	. . .	YP 695	. . .	. . .	10-87

YP 677 L. & L. Van Ginderen, 12-84

YP 678 L. & L. Van Ginderen, 5-85

D: 172.4 tons (fl) **S:** 12 kts **Dim:** 32.91 (30.99 pp) × 7.30 × 1.75
Electric Equipt: Radar: 1/. . . nav.
M: 2 G.M. 12 V71N diesels; 2 props; 875 hp **Electric:** 100 kw
Man: 2 officers, 4 men, 24 midshipmen

Remarks: Wooden construction boats to replace YP 654 class. YP 676 ordered 15-10-82; YP 677–682 ordered 25-5-83; YP 683–695 ordered 12-6-84; YP 696–702 on 13-9-85.

◆ **17 YP patrol craft** In serv. 2-58 to 11-79 Bldrs: YP 654–663, 666: Stephens Bros., Stockton, Cal; YP 664, 665: Elizabeth City SY, Elizabeth City, N.C.; others: Peterson Bldrs., Sturgeon Bay, Wisc.

YP 654, 657, 662–666, 668–675

YP 658 (now a COOP trainer) G. Arra, 1982

D: 60 tons (71 fl) **S:** 13.3 kts **Dim:** 24.51 × 5.72 × 1.6
M: 2 G.M. 6-71 diesels; 2 props; 590 hp **Electric:** 20 kw
Man: 2 officers, 8 men, 24 midshipmen

Remarks: Wooden construction. Seven used for navigation and maneuvering training at Naval Academy, Annapolis, and rest at Naval Officer Candidate School, Newport. Not armed. YP 655 fitted for oceanographic training at Naval Academy. Sisters YP 659 and YP 660 were transferred to the COOP minehunting program in 9-85 and 11-85. Fifteen others are to become COOP craft in FY 86-88. YP 655, 656, and 667 were retyped as "boats" during 8-85 and transferred to the Surface Warfare Officers' School, San Diego.

◆ **5 YPD floating pile drivers***

YPD 37, 41, 42, 45 (ex-YC 1498), 46 (ex-YFNB 35)

Remarks: Built 1943-65. YPD 42 in reserve. Most built on standard 24.4 × 10.4 barge hulls, except YPD 6: 79.6 × 14.6; 2,700 tons (fl)

◆ **27 YR floating workshops***

YR 9, 25–27, 29, 36, 44, 46, 50, 60–65, 68, 70, 73, 76–78, 83 (ex-YRL 5), 84-88

YR 26 1969

Remarks: Built 1941-45. Twenty-one active. Most 520 tons light (770 fl); 46.6 × 10.7 × 1.8. Differ in equipment.

◆ **5 YRB repair and berthing barges***

YR 1 (ex-YFN 258), 2, 22 (ex-YC 1079), 25 (ex-YFN 298), 29 (ex-YRST 5)

Remarks: All 33.5 × 9.1. Built 1940-45. Support submarines.

◆ **38 YRBM repair, berthing, and messing barges***

YRBM 1–6, 8, 9, 11–15, 20, 23–46

YRBM 31 Marinette Marine, 10-80

YRBM 15 W. Donko, 7-84

SERVICE CRAFT *(continued)*

Remarks: Built 1955-83. All active; support submarines and ships in overhaul. Marinette SB constructed YRBM 31 to YRBM 46 during 1979-83: 688 tons; 44.5 × 14.0 × 1.3; accommodations for 26 officers, 231 men. Have office, workshop, eating, and recreation spaces, 96-seat training theater, galley, etc. YRBM 23–30, also by Marinette (In serv. 8-70 to 6-71) of similar dimensions, but 585-tons (fl). YRBM 20 is 2,700 tons, 79.6 × 14.6; remainder are approx. 310 tons (fl), 33.5 × 10.4.

◆ **4 YRDH floating dry dock workshops, hull***

YRDH 1 (ex-YR 55), 2 (ex-YR 56), 6, 7 (In serv. 1943-44)

Remarks: YRDH 6 active. 770 tons (fl), 46.6 × 10.7 × 1.8.

◆ **4 YRDM floating dry-dock workshops, machinery***

YRDM 1 (ex-YR 52), 2 (ex-YR 53), 5, 7 (In serv. 1943-44)

Remarks: YRDM 5 active. 770 tons (fl), 46.6 × 10.7 × 1.8.

◆ **12 YRR radiological repair barges***

YRR 1 (ex-YR 49)
YRR 2 (ex-YR 74)
YRR 3 (ex-YFN 333)
YRR 4 (ex-YFN 685)
YRR 5 (ex-YRDM 8)
YRR 6 (ex-YR 39)
YRR 7 (ex-YR 31)
YRR 10 (ex-YR 79)
YRR 11 (ex-YRDH 3)
YRR 12 ex-YRDH 4)
YRR 13 (ex-YRDM 3)
YRR 14 (ex-YRDM 4)

Remarks: In serv. 1937-45; all active. All converted from other barge-hulled functions: 770 tons (fl), 46.6 × 10.7 × 1.8. Sister YRR 9 reclassified YFND 47 in 11-83.

◆ **3 YRST salvage-craft tender***

YRST 1 (ex-YDT 11) YRST 2 (ex-YDT 12) YRST 6 (ex-YFNX 10)

Remarks: In serv. 1945; all active. YRST 3 and YRST 5 stricken 4-84. YRST 1, 2 are 2,700 tons (fl), 79.6 × 14.6; YRST 6 is 670 tons (fl), 33.5 × 10.7. All are rectangular barges.

◆ **4 YSD seaplane wrecking derricks**

YSD 39, 53, 63, 74 (In serv. 1944)

YSD 53 M. Curtin, 11-85

D: 240 tons (276 fl) **S:** 10 kts **Dim:** 31.7 × 9.5 × 1.2
M: 2 Superior diesels; 2 props; 320 hp

Remarks: All active. Employed as 10-ton capacity, self-propelled cranes. Sister YSD 15 stricken 4-84.

◆ **20 YSR sludge-removal barges***

Remarks: Built 1932-46. Eighteen active. Most either 24.4 × 9.8 or 33.5 × 10.4. YSR 39 stricken 8-85, YSR 17 stricken late 1985; both to other U.S. government agencies.

◆ **81 YTB large harbor tugs (SCB 147/147A type)** Bldrs: YTB 752, 753: Christy Corp., Sturgeon Bay, Wisc.; YTB 756–759, 763–766, 799–802: Southern SB Corp., Slidell, La.; YTB 760–761: Jakobson SY, Oyster Bay. New York; YTB 762: Commercial Iron Wks., Portland, Ore.; YTB 767–771: Mobile Ship Repair, Mobile, Ala.; YTB 774–798, 816-836: Marinette Marine Corp., Marinette, Wisc.; YTB 803–815: Peterson Bldrs, Sturgeon Bay, Wisc.

YTB 752 Edenshaw
YTB 753 Marin
YTB 756 Pontiac
YTB 757 Oshkosh
YTB 758 Paducah
YTB 759 Bogalusa
YTB 760 Natick
YTB 761 Ottumwa
YTB 762 Tuscumbia
YTB 763 Muskegon
YTB 764 Mishawaka
YTB 765 Okmulgee
YTB 766 Wapakoneta
YTB 767 Apalachicola
YTB 783 Redwing
YTB 784 Kalispell
YTB 785 Winnemucca
YTB 786 Tonkawa
YTB 787 Kittanning
YTB 788 Wapato
YTB 789 Tomahawk
YTB 790 Menominee
YTB 791 Marinette
YTB 792 Antigo
YTB 793 Piqua
YTB 794 Mandan
YTB 795 Ketchikan
YTB 796 Saco
YTB 810 Anoka
YTB 811 Houma
YTB 812 Accomac
YTB 813 Poughkeepsie
YTB 814 Waxahatchie
YTB 815 Neodesha
YTB 816 Campti
YTB 817 Hyannis
YTB 818 Mecosta
YTB 819 Iuka
YTB 820 Wanamassa
YTB 821 Tontogany
YTB 822 Pawhuska
YTB 823 Canonchet
YTB 768 Arcata
YTB 769 Chesaning
YTB 770 Dahlonega
YTB 771 Keokuk
YTB 774 Nashua
YTB 775 Wauwatosa
YTB 776 Weehawken
YTB 777 Nogales
YTB 778 Apopka
YTB 779 Manhattan
YTB 780 Saugus
YTB 781 Niantic
YTB 782 Manistee
YTB 797 Tamaqua
YTB 798 Opelika
YTB 799 Natchitoches
YTB 800 Eufaula
YTB 801 Palatka
YTB 802 Cheraw
YTB 803 Nanticoke
YTB 804 Ahoskie
YTB 805 Ocala
YTB 806 Tuskegee
YTB 807 Massapequa
YTB 808 Wenatchee
YTB 809 Agawan
YTB 824 Santaquin
YTB 825 Wathena
YTB 826 Washtuena
YTB 827 Chetek
YTB 828 Catahecassa
YTB 829 Metacom
YTB 830 Pushmataha
YTB 831 Dekanawida
YTB 832 Petalesharo
YTB 833 Shabonee
YTB 834 Newagen
YTB 835 Skenandoa
YTB 836 Pokagon

Wathena (YTB 825) L. & L. Van Ginderen, 9-84

D: 286 tons (356 fl) **S:** 12.5 kts **Dim:** 33.05 × 9.3 × 4.14
M: 1 Fairbanks-Morse $38D8\frac{1}{8}$ × 12 diesel; 1 prop; 2,000 hp
Electric: 120 kw **Fuel:** . . . **Range:** 2,000/12 **Man:** 12 tot.

Remarks: Built 1959-70. YTB 752 to YTB 759 have a less-streamlined superstructure, and are considered a separate class (SCB 147 type); YTB 752, 753 have Alco diesels. All active. Minor differences in displacement between units by different builders. Three also built for Saudi Arabia.

Note: Planned procurement of 28 YTB 839 tugs of 3–4,000 hp was canceled 1984 in favor of contracting for tug services from private industry. The result will be lower overall costs and a diminished requirement for military personnel. Nearly all surviving active YTL and YTM-type tugs were stricken during 1985 (dates below) as a result of the same decision, and the surviving reserve fleet units will probably be discarded during 1986.

◆ **1 YTL 422 class small harbor tug** Bldr: Robert Jacob, City Isl., N.Y.

YTL 602 (In serv. 10-45)

D: 70 tons (80 fl) **S:** 8 kts **Dim:** 20.1 × 5.5 × 2.4
M: 1 Hoover, Owens, Rentschler diesel; 375 hp **Man:** 4 tot.

Remarks: Survivor of several hundred YTL 422 class; many still in foreign navies. A few others remain in Navy use, retyped as craft. Sisters YTL 588 stricken 15-1-85, YTL 422, 438, 439, 583 stricken 15-2-85; YTL 434 stricken 30-9-85.

◆ **1 YTM 138-class medium harbor tug** Bldr: Pacific Coast Eng., Alameda, Cal.

YTM 189 Nepanet (In serv. 4-43)

D: 260 tons (310 fl) **S:** 12 kts **Dim:** 30.8 × 8.5 × 3.4
M: 1 Enterprise diesel; 1 prop; 820 hp **Man:** 19 tot.

Remarks: In reserve. Sister *Dekaury* (TYM 178) stricken 30-9-85.

◆ **4 YTM 174-class medium harbor tugs** Bldr: Gulfport SB, Port Arthur, Tex.

YTM 359 Pawtucket (In serv. 3-43)
YTM 381 Chepanoc (In serv. 8-44)
YTM 382 Coatopa (In serv. 8-44)
YTM 383 Cochali (In serv. 8-44)

D: 210 tons (320 fl) **S:** 12 kts **Dim:** 31.1 × 7.6 × 3.0
M: 2 G.M. diesels; 1 prop; 820 hp **Man:** 15 tot.

Remarks: In reserve. Sisters *Chanagi* (YTM 380) stricken 30-9-85, *Dekanisora* (YTM 252) on 31-12-85.

◆ **2 YTM 265-class medium harbor tugs** Bldr: Birchfield Boiler, Tacoma, Wash.

YTM 265 Hiawatha (In serv. 11-42) YTM 268 Red Cloud (In serv. 3-43)

D: 230 tons (310 fl) **S:** 12 kts **Dim:** 30.5 × 8.5 × 3.0
M: 1 Enterprise diesel; 1 prop; 820 hp **Man:** 14 tot.

Remarks: Both in reserve.

◆ **3 YTM 364-class medium harbor tugs**

YTM 364 Sassaba (In serv. 9-44)
YTM 406 Kittaton (In serv. 1-45)
YTM 398 Natahki (In serv. 4-45)

D: 260 tons (310 fl) **S:** 10.5 kts **Dim:** 30.8 × 8.5 × 3.4
M: 2 Fairbanks-Morse diesels; 1 prop; 820 hp **Man:** 14 tot.

Remarks: Sisters *Numa* (YTM 399) stricken 15-1-85; *Yanegua* (YTM 397), *Otokomi* (YTM 400). *Coshecton* (YTM 404), *Cusseta* (YTM 405), *Porobago* (YTM 413) and

SERVICE CRAFT *(continued)*

Secota (YTM 415) stricken 30-9-85; *Winamac* (YTM 394), *Wingina* (YTM 395) and *Taconnet* (YTM 417) stricken 31-12-85. Survivors in reserve.

◆ **5 YTM 518 class**

YTM 534 Nadli (In serv. 7-45)
YTM 544 Yatanocas (In serv. 12-45)
YTM 545 Accohanoc (In serv. 12-45)
YTM 546 Takos (In serv. 10-45)
YTM 549 Migadan (In serv. 1-46)

D: 260 tons (310 fl) **S:** 11 kts **Dim:** 30.8 × 8.5 × 3.3
M: 2 G.M. diesels; 1 prop; 820 hp **Man:** 8 tot.

Remarks: YTM 544, 545, and 549 are active; other two in reserve. Sisters *Nabigwon* (YTM 521), *Wahaka* (YTM 526), *Nahoke* (YTM 536), *Chegodega* (YTM 542), *Matunak* (YTM 548), *Acoma* (YTM 701), *Arawak* (YTM 702), and *Moratoc* (YTM 704) stricken 30-9-85; *Yanaba* (YTM 547) stricken 31-12-85.

◆ **1 ex-U.S. Army tug**

YTM 750 Hackensack (ex-Army LT 2089)

D: 470 tons (fl) **S:** 12 kts **Dim:** 32.6 × 8.0 × 4.5
M: 2 diesels; 1 prop; 1,200 hp

Remarks: Active.

◆ **2 YTM 760-class medium harbor tugs** Bldr: Jakobson SY, Oyster Bay, N.Y.

YTM 760 Mascoutah (ex-YTB 772) YTM 761 Menasha (ex-YTB 773)

Mascoutah (YTM 760)—with old number PH3 E. Pichette, 1964

D: 200 tons (fl) **S:** 12 kts **Dim:** 25.9 × 7.3 × 3.4 **Man:** 8 tot.
M: 2 G.M. 6-71 diesels; 2 Voith-Schneider vertical cycloidal props; 450 hp

Remarks: Built 1965-66. The U.S. Navy's only cycloidal-prop tugs. Both active.

◆ **2 YTM 764-class medium harbor tugs**

YTM 768 Apohola (ex-YTB 502) (In serv. 1-46)
YTM 776 Hiamonee (ex-YTB 513) (In serv. 11-45)

D: 260 tons (350 fl) **S:** 11 kts **Dim:** 30.8 × 8.5 × 3.7
M: 2 Enterprise diesels; 1 prop; 1,270 hp
Man: 8 tot.

Remarks: Sisters *Mimac* (YTM 770, ex-YTB 507) stricken 31-12-55; *Pocasset* (YTM 779, ex-YTB 516) stricken 30-9-85. Survivors in reserve.

Note: A large number of converted LCM(6) landing craft have been converted for use as push-tugs for local use, in place of YTLs.

◆ **0 (+1 + 1) torpedo trials craft** Bldr: . . .

	Laid down	L	In serv.
YTT 8 N. . .	. . .	. . .	. . .
YTT 9 N. . . .	. . .	. . .	. . .

D: 1,030 tons light (1,270 fl) **S:** 11 kts **Dim:** 64.62 (60.35 pp) × 12.07 × 3.20
A: 2/533-mm TT (submerged)—3/324-mm Mk 32 ASW TT (III × 1)
Electron Equipt: Radar: 1/SPS-64(V)9
M: 2 diesels, electric drive; 2 props; 2,500 hp—1/350-hp omnidirectional bow-thruster
Range: 1,800/11 **Fuel:** 85 tons **Man:** 32 crew + 12 technicians
Electric: 2,500 kw

Remarks: Intended to replace YAG and YFRT currently used for torpedo trials. First unit was in FY 86 Budget as a YFRT but was rejected by Congress; now in FY 87. Will have crane amidships to recover torpedoes and to handle sensor arrays and recovery equipment. Will have batteries to permit quiet operations. Will test Mk 48 ADCAP, Mk 46 and Mk 50 ASW torpedoes.

◆ **7 YW water barges**

	Bldr	L	In serv.
YW 83	John H. Mathis, Camden, N.J.	7-43	3-44
YW 86	Zenith Dredge Co., Duluth, Minn.	4-43	8-43
YW 98	George Lawley & Son, Neponset, Mass.	9-45	11-45
YW 101	Mare Island NSY, Cal.	5-44	12-44
YW 113	Marine Iron & SB, Duluth, Minn.	. . .	1944
YW 126	Leatham D. Smith, Sturgeon Bay, Wisc.	1945	1945
YW 127	Leatham D. Smith, Sturgeon Bay, Wisc.	5-45	7-45

D: 1,282 tons (fl) **S:** 8 kts **Dim:** 53.0 × 9.7 × 4.6 **Man:** 22 tot.
M: 1 G.M. 8-2784 (YW 86: Fairbanks-Morse) diesel; 1 prop; 560 hp

Remarks: Cargo: 930 tons water. YW 113, 127 active; others in reserve. Same basic design as YO and YOG classes. Sisters YW 123 stricken 15-2-84; YW 108 stricken 15-10-85 (to Kings Pt. Maritime Academy).

◆ **6 YWN water barges***

YWN 70, 71, 78, 79, 82, 156

Remarks: Built 1944-45. All but YWN 79 active; 220 tons light (1,270 fl); 50.3 × 10.7 × 2.4. YWN 147 stricken 7-85.

Note: In addition to the above yard and service craft, all of which have hull numbers and are carried on the Navy List, there are more than 3,000 small craft that are listed as property, including ships' boats and such diverse craft as the Naval Academy's large fleet of sailing craft. Among the larger of those listed as property are the two classes of torpedo retrievers and one presidential yacht listed below.

◆ **5 (+3 + . . .) new construction** Bldr: Marinette Marine, Wisc.

New torpedo retriever TWR 823 L. & L. Van Ginderen, 12-85

D: 174 tons (fl) **S:** 16 kts **Dim:** 36.58 × 7.62 × 3.65 **Range:** 1,700/16
Electron Equipt: Radar: 1/LN-66
M: 2 Caterpillar D 399 diesels; 2 props; 2,350 hp **Man:** 1 officer, 14 men
Electric: 128 kw **Fuel:** 28 tons **Endurance:** 7 days

Remarks: First five ordered 8-7-83 for delivery 15-12-84 to 15-3-85; three more ordered 10-83, all for delivery 7-85; two ordered 2-85 for delivery 6-86. However, program is far behind schedule, and first not accepted until 11-85; four more accepted 12-85. Stern ramp and electro-hydraulic crane aft. Can carry 14 Mk 48 torpedoes. Have 43.7 tons permanent ballast! Congress halted further procurement, 1985.

◆ **7 modified patrol-boat-design torpedo retrievers** Bldr: Peterson Bldrs., Sturgeon Bay, Wisc. (In serv. 1969-70)

TWR 3 G. Arra, 8-85

D: 110 tons light (165 fl) **S:** 18 kts **Dim:** 31.1 × 6.4 × 2.4 **Fuel:** 7 tons
Electron Equipt: Radar: 1/LN-66
M: 2 G.M. 12V-149 diesels; 2 props; 1,350 hp **Range:** 1,920/10 **Man:** 15 tot.

Remarks: Design based on PGM 59-class patrol boat. Ramp at stern. Stowage for 17 tons of recovered ordnance. Given unofficial retriever dog names, list unavailable. There are also a number of 19.8-m torpedo retrievers based on a patrol-craft design; the same design has also been built as an air/sea rescue boat.

Note: Also in use are six 19.8-m torpedo retrievers delivered 10-67 to 11-68 (35 tons, 2 G.M. 12V71 diesels), 17 21.9-m retrievers delivered 1958-66 and displacing 58 tons, and six 25.9-m craft. The 21.9 and 25.9-m units were to be replaced by the new 36.58-m class. See addenda for photos.

SERVICE CRAFT *(continued)*

NOTE: As a measure of the number of U.S. Navy craft, as of 1-85, some 383 units were on order: 33/7.32-m Explosive Ordance Disposal Boats, 4/7.32-m Boom-Handling Boats, 6/10.05-m Utility Boats, 5/17.07-m Target Boats, 30/10.05-m Personnel Boats, 52/15.42-m Work Boats, 23/12.9-m Utility Boats, 22/12.19-m Personnel Boats, 12/15.24-m Utility Boats, 102/7.92-m Motor Whale Boats, 15/6.70-m Utility Boats, 64/5.49-m Utility Boats, and 15/5.49-m Target Boats.

◆ **1 presidential yacht** Bldr: Mathias Yacht & SB Co., Camden, NJ

SEQUOIA (ex-AG 23) (L: 1925)

Sequoia U.S. Navy, 1966

D: 105 tons (fl) **S:** 12 kts **Dim:** 31.70 (30.18 pp) × 5.54 × 1.37
M: 2 diesels; 2 props; 400 hp

REMARKS: Wooden-hulled craft purchased from private owner as presidential yacht on 31-3-31. Served as Secretary of the Navy's yacht 3-36 to 1969 when again used as presidential yacht until sold during Carter Administration, 1977. Re-acquired mid-1985 as donation from private owners. Based at Washington, D.C., and listed as a "craft."

MILITARY SEALIFT COMMAND

This organization was founded in 1949 as the Military Sea Transportation Service, and given its current name on 1-8-70. It is headed by a flag officer of the U.S. Navy. Its ships, which are not armed, are considered to be noncommissioned, and are manned by civilians (either government civil servants or contract personnel). They are described below in the order of their hull type numbers. The prefix "T" is appended to the hull numbers of its ships.

In the following pages the government-owned units are listed and described in alphabetical order by ship type. Then chartered ships are described, in particular the ships of the Forward Deployment Logistics Force, the Near-Term Prepositioning Force, and, finally, the other ships on charter for cargo, tanker, scientific support, and fleet services duties.

NOTE: MSC ships are painted gray (AGOR/AGS: white) and have blue and gold-yellow stack bands. Fleet support replenishment ships operated by MSC began to carry their hull numbers during late 1979; other MSC ships do *not* display hull numbers.

AMMUNITION SHIP (T-AE)

◆ **1 Kilauea class**

	Bldr	Laid down	L	In serv.
T-AE 26 KILAUEA	Gen'l Dynamics, Quincy	10-3-66	9-8-67	10-8-68

Kilauea (T-AE 26) LSPH E. Pitman, R.A.N., 9-85

D: 17,937 tons (fl) **S:** 20 kts **Dim:** 171.9 × 24.7 × 8.5
Electron Equipt: Radar: 1/navigational, 1/SPS-10—TACAN: URN-25
M: 1 set G.E. GT; 1 prop; 22,000 hp **Man:** 121 MSC crew, 67 Navy
Boilers: 3 Foster-Wheeler; 42.3 kg/cm², 467°C **Fuel:** 2,612 tons

REMARKS: 8,593 dwt. Transferred to MSC 1-10-80; six sisters remain in Navy. Can carry about 6,500 tons of munitions and has a hangar and flight deck for two UH-46 replenishment helicopters. Can also refuel ships, using forward, starboard station. Navy personnel perform ammunition handling and operate the communications and helicopter. Superstructure filled in on starboard side to increase accommodations space.

STORES SHIPS (T-AF)

◆ **1 Rigel class**

	Bldr	L	In serv.
T-AF 58 RIGEL	Ingalls, Pascagoula	15-3-55	2-9-55

Rigel (T-AF 58) L. & L. Van Ginderen, 6-83

D: 9,696 tons light (15,540 fl) **S:** 20 kts **Dim:** 153.0 × 22.0 × 8.8
Electron Equipt: Radar: 1/SPS-10, 1/Raytheon 1650/CX
M: 1 set G.E. GT; 1 prop; 16,000 hp
Boilers: 2 Combustion Engineering; 42.2 kg/cm², 440°C
Range: 11,000/18 **Man:** 16 officers, 97 men MSC, + 67 Navy

REMARKS: 10,781 grt/8,112 dwt. Twelve 10-ton booms. Cargo: 5,975 m³ dry, 5,400 m³ refrigerated. Transferred to MSC 23-6-75 and disarmed. Provides fleet support. Satellite communications equipment carried.

COMBAT STORES SHIPS (T-AFS)

◆ **3 British Lyness-class combat stores ships** Bldrs: Swan Hunter & Wigham Richardson, Wallsend-on-Tyne, U.K.

	Laid down	L	In serv.
T-AFS 8 SIRIUS (ex-*Lyness*)	4-65	7-4-66	22-12-66
T-AFS 9 SPICA (ex-*Tarbatness*)	4-66	22-2-67	10-8-67
T-AFS 10 SATURN (ex-*Stromness*)	10-65	16-9-66	21-3-67

Sirius (T-AFS 8)—with hangar L. & L. Van Ginderen, 10-85

Spica (T-AFS 9) Lt. D. Frasier/Lt. jg D. Winkowski, USN, 1983

D: 9,010 tons light (16,792 fl) **S:** 19 kts
Dim: 159.52 (149.35 pp) × 22.0 × 7.77
Electron Equipt: Radar: 1/Kelvin-Hughes 14/9, 1/Kelvin Hughes 14/12
TACAN: T-AFS 8, 10: URN-25
M: 1 Sulzer 8RD76 diesel; 1 prop; 12,700 hp **Electric:** 3,575 kw
Fuel: 1,310 tons heavy oil, 264 tons diesel
Range: 11,000/19; 27,500/12 **Man:** 130 MSC, 17 Navy

COMBAT STORES SHIPS (T-AFS) *(continued)*

Remarks: T-AFS 8 was leased from Great Britain on 12-1-81 for one year for use in the Mediterranean and was to be purchased outright 30-1-82; T-AFS 9, which had been in reserve at Gibraltar, was leased 30-9-81 and was purchased 30-9-82. An agreement to purchase T-AFS 10 was made on 27-1-83, and the ship arrived at Bayonne, New Jersey, 4-83 awaiting purchase under the FY 84 budget, 13-12-83; T-AFS 10 was modernized under FY 85 with improved helicopter facilities, improved communications, five STREAM transfer stations, an automated data facility, and conversion to use U.S. Navy fuel. T-AFS 8 completed a similar upgrading 1-10-83; both can accommodate 2 UH-46 helicopters. 12,358 grt/4,744 nrt. Helicopter deck aft 33.5 × 18.3. Have four holds, with 15 levels, 8 stores elevators. Total cargo volume: 12,234 m³ (8,313 m³ dry stores, 3,921 m³ refrigerated/frozen). Cranes: 1/25-ton, 2/12.5-ton, 1/12-ton, and 2/5-ton. Carry 40,000 different repair parts and can support 15,000 men at sea for one month. Accommodations for 193 total. Very successful, comfortable ships—a useful bargain.

MISCELLANEOUS RESEARCH SHIPS (T-AG)

◆ **1 sound trials ship (SCB 762 type)** Bldr: Todd SY, Seattle

	Laid down	L	In serv.
T-AG 195 Hayes (ex-T-AGOR 16)	12-11-69	2-7-70	21-7-71

Hayes (T-AG 195)—before conversion L. & L. Van Ginderen, 6-83

D: 3,860 tons (fl) **S:** 12 kts **Dim:** 75.10 (67.06 pp) × 22.86 × 6.70
Electron Equipt: Radar: 1/Raytheon TM 1650/6X, 1/Raytheon TM 1660/125
Sonar: TUMS towed sound-measurement array
M: . . . diesels, electric drive; 2 props; . . . hp
Endurance: 30 days **Range:** 6,000/12 **Man:** 10 officers, 26 men, MSC crew + 29 technicians

Remarks: Catamaran, with each hull of 7.3 m. Being converted as sound trials vessel under FY 86 Budget to replace *Monob One* (YAG 61), with completion scheduled for 1989. Will transport, deploy, and retrieve acoustic arrays in support of the Submarine Noise Reduction Program. Will be reengined, with original 4 high-speed diesels driving controllable-pitch props being replaced by a diesel-electric plant. Had been laid up since 1982 and was transferred from the Oceanographer of the Navy to the David Taylor Naval Ships Research and Development Center's control in 1983 awaiting the FY 86 conversion. Was not a success as a research platform, suffering from excessive pitching.

◆ **1 Vanguard class** Bldr: Marine Ship Corp., Sausalito, Cal.

	L	In serv.
T-AG 194 Vanguard (ex-T-AGM 19, ex-*Muscle Shoals*, ex-*Mission San Fernando*, T-AO 122)	23-11-43	21-10-47

Vanguard (T-AG 194) L. & L. Van Ginderen, 2-84

D: 21,478 tons (fl) **S:** 16 kts **Dim:** 181.4 × 22.9 × 7.6
Electron Equipt: Radar: 1/Raytheon 1650/9X, 1/Raytheon 1660/12S
M: 1 set G.E. GT, electric drive; 1 prop; 8,700 hp
Boilers: 2 Babcock & Wilcox "D"; 42.3 kg/cm², 440°C
Range: 27,000 n.m./16 **Fuel:** 3,995 tons **Man:** 19 officers/179 men

Remarks: 16,060 grt/16,255 dwt.; *Vanguard* was converted 1964-66 from a T2-SE-A2-type tanker to a tracking and communications ship to support NASA manned space flights. Reclassified 30-9-80 as T-AG 194 while under conversion to replace *Compass Island* (AG 153) as ballistic-missile submarine navigational system trials ship for the Navy Strategic Systems Project Office. Conversion commenced 1-4-80 at Todd Shipyard, San Pedro, Cal. Appearance similar to *Redstone* (T-AGM 20) but without tracking radars. Has a MARISAT satellite communications facility. Trials with a ring-laser gyro for navigation began 4-85.

Note: The experimental auxiliary *Kingsport* (T-AG 164; ex-*Kingsport Victory*, AK 239) was deactivated 5-84 and approved for disposal late in 1985.

RANGE INSTRUMENTATION SHIPS (T-AGM)

◆ **1 Mariner class**

	Bldr	L	In serv.
T-AGM 23 Observation Island (ex-AG 154, ex-YAG 53, ex-*Empire State Mariner*)	New York SB, Camden, N.J.	15-8-53	5-12-53

Observation Island (T-AGM 23) MSC, 9-85

D: 16,076 tons (fl) **S:** 20 kts **Dim:** 171.6 × 23.27 × 9.1
Electron Equipt: Radar: 1/Raytheon 1650/9X, 1/Raytheon 1660/12S, 1/SPQ-11
M: 1 set G.E. GT; 1 prop; 22,000 hp
Boilers: 2 Combustion Engineering, 42.3 kg/cm², 467°C
Fuel: 2,652 tons **Range:** 17,000,13 **Man:** 78 civilians + 60–65 technicians

Remarks: Former ballistic-missile trials ship. Acquired by the Navy on 10-9-56; used for Polaris and Poseidon missile trials until placed in reserve on 29-9-72. Reclassified T-AGM 23 on 1-5-79. Converted between 7-79 and 4-81 to carry Cobra Judy (SPQ-11) missile-tracking, phased-array radar aft. Two large parabolic collection antennas in geodesic radomes atop bridge. Operated for the U.S. Air Force in the Pacific. Painted white. Refitted 1-84 to 8-84 by Northwest Marine, Portland, Ore., with a new foremast, heightened stacks, 3 new turbogenerator sets, new deckhouses, 2 new evaporators, and upgraded electronics (including adding an X-band tracking radar).

◆ **1 converted Haskell-class attack transport** Bldr: Permanente Metals, Richmond, Cal.

	L	In serv.
T-AGM 22 Range Sentinel (ex-*Sherburne*, APA 205)	10-7-44	20-9-44

Range Sentinel (T-AGM 22) MSC, 1979

D: 11,860 tons (fl) **S:** 15.5 kts **Dim:** 138.7 × 18.9 × 8.8
Electron Equipt: Radar: 1/Raytheon TM 1650/9X, 1/Raytheon TM 1660/12S, 1/SPQ-7, 3/other tracking
M: 1 set GT; 1 prop; 8,500 hp

RANGE INSTRUMENTATION SHIPS *(continued)*

Boilers: 2 Combustion Engineering, 37 kg/cm², 399°C **Fuel:** 1,197 tons
Range: 10,000/15.5 **Man:** 14 officers, 54 men, 27 technicians

REMARKS: 8,306 grt/5,301 dwt. Converted between 10-69 and 14-10-71 as support ship for the Poseidon (and later, Trident) program. Reclassified T-AGM 22 on 14-10-71. VC2-S-AP 5 Victory-type hull and propulsion. Operates from Port Canaveral, Florida, for the Atlantic Test Range.

◆ **1 Vanguard class** Bldr: Marine Ship, Sausalito, Cal.

	In serv.
T-AGM 20 REDSTONE (ex-*Johnstown*, ex-*Mission de Pala*, AO 114)	22-4-44

Redstone (T-AGM 20) MSC, 1983

D: 16,800 tons light (24,700 fl) **S:** 16 kts **Dim:** 181.4 × 22.9 × 7.6
Electron Equipt: Radar: 1/Raytheon 1650/9X, 1/Raytheon 1660/12S
M: 1 set G.E. GT, electric drive; 1 prop; 8,700 hp
Boilers: 2 Babcock & Wilcox "D," 42.3 kg/cm², 440°C
Fuel: 3,995 tons **Range:** 27,000/16 **Man:** 19 officers, 71 men, 108 technicians

REMARKS: 16,060 grt/16,255 dwt. Former T2-SE-A2-type tanker converted 1964-66 to serve as tracking and communications ship for NASA manned space flights; 22 meters added amidships. Sister *Mercury* (T-AGM 21) stricken in 1969 after very little use, and sister *Vanguard* (T-AGM 19) redesignated T-AG in 1980. Two tracking radars, two large communications dish antennas, now all mounted in geodesic plastic radomes.

NOTE: *General H. H. Arnold* (T-AGM 9) was stricken and placed in the Maritime Commission National Defense Reserve Fleet on 23-2-82 and sold for scrap 25-10-82. Sister *General Hoyt S. Vandenberg* (T-AGM 10) was transferred to the MARAD NDRF on 8-2-83 and remains in storage in the James River in Virginia.

OCEANOGRAPHIC RESEARCH SHIPS (T-AGOR)

NOTE: *All* naval-owned oceanographic research ships are listed here, for convenience sake; those without "T" before their hull numbers are operated by private organizations, generally on naval-related research programs. A new oceanographic ship for transfer to an academic agency is included in the FY 87 Budget request.

◆ **2 Gyre class (SCB 734 type)** Bldr: Halter Marine, New Orleans

	Laid down	L	In serv.
AGOR 21 GYRE	9-10-72	7-6-73	14-11-73
AGOR 22 MOANA WAVE	9-10-72	23-6-73	16-1-74

Moana Wave (AGOR 22)—prior to lengthening L. & L. Van Ginderen, 1984

D: 950 tons (1,190 fl) **S:** 12.5 kts **Dim:** 53.14 × 11.05 × 3.05
M: 2 Caterpillar diesels; 2 CP props; 1,700 hp (plus 170-hp retractable maneuvering prop)
Range: 8,000/. . . **Endurance:** 40 days
Man: 10 crew plus 19 scientists (AGOR 22: 15 crew plus 13 scientists)

REMARKS: On completion, assigned to Texas A&M University and University of Hawaii, respectively. Modified oil-field supply ships using modular equipment vans on long, open fantail. AGOR 22 has conducted trials 1979-84 with the satellite communications and towed passive sonar equipment for the T-AGOS program, under contract to the Naval Electronics Command (NAVELEX); the SATCOMM antenna was mounted on a platform between the ship's paired stacks. In 1984-85, the ship was lengthened to 62.24 by Halter Marine at Mobile, Ala., and given a lengthened permanent deckhouse laboratory aft, plus facilities for two portable lab modules.

◆ **2 Melville class (SCB 710 type)** Bldr: Defoe SB, Bay City, Mich.

	Laid down	L	In serv.
AGOR 14 MELVILLE	12-7-67	10-7-68	27-8-69
AGOR 15 KNORR	9-8-67	21-8-68	14-1-70

Melville (AGOR 14)—blue hull, white superstructure L. & L. Van Ginderen, 5-82

D: 1,915 tons (2,080 fl) **S:** 12.5 kts **Dim:** 74.7 (67.0 pp) × 14.1 × 4.6
M: 2 Enterprise diesels; Voith-Schneider cycloidal props; 2,500 hp
Range: 10,000/12 **Man:** 9 officers, 16 men, 25 researchers

REMARKS: Operated for the Office of Naval Research, AGOR 14 by Scripps Institute, AGOR 15 by Woods Hole Oceanographic Institution. One vertical cycloidal propeller forward, larger unit aft; intended for precise maneuvering but, because mechanical rather than electric drive was used, have proven troublesome. AGOR 19 and AGOR 20 of this class were therefore canceled. AGOR 15 located the wreck of RMS *Titanic* on 1-9-85, using a new remote-controlled submersible.

◆ **6 Robert D. Conrad class (SCB 185 and 710* types)**

	Bldr	L	In serv.
AGOR 3 ROBERT D. CONRAD	Gibbs, Jacksonville	26-5-62	29-11-62
T-AGOR 7 LYNCH	Marinette, Wisc.	17-3-65	27-3-65
AGOR 9 THOMAS G. THOMPSON	Marinette, Wisc.	18-7-64	24-8-65
AGOR 10 THOMAS WASHINGTON	Marinette, Wisc.	1-8-64	27-9-65
T-AGOR 12 DE STEIGUER*	N.W. Marine, Portland	3-6-66	28-2-69
T-AGOR 13 BARTLETT*	N.W. Marine, Portland	24-5-66	31-3-69

D: 1,088 tons light (1,410 fl) **S:** 13.5 kts
Dim: 63.7 (59.7 pp) × 11.4 × 4.9 (6.3 m max.)
Electron Equipt: Radar: MSC units: 1/Raytheon 1650/SX, 1/Raytheon 1660/12S
M: 2 Caterpillar D-378 (T-AGOR 7–13: Cummins) diesels, electric drive; 1 prop; 1,000 hp
Electric: 850 kw **Fuel:** 211 tons
Range: 9,000/12 **Man:** 11 officers, 17 men, 15 researchers

Lynch (T-AGOR 7)—MARISAT radome added L. & L. Van Ginderen, 8-84

OCEANOGRAPHIC RESEARCH SHIPS *(continued)*

Thomas Washington (AGOR 10)—long forecastle, less superstructure (number no longer carried) 1965

Remarks: All civilian crews; 3 under Navy control, 3 under MSC. Assigned: AGOR 3: Lamont Geophysical Lab., Columbia U.; T-AGOR 7: MSC for Oceanographer of the Navy; AGOR 9: U. of Washington for Navy; AGOR 10: Scripps Inst. Of Oceanography; T-AGOR 12 and T-AGOR 13: MSC for Oceanographer of the Navy. Vary in details and paint (see photos). *Sands* (T-AGOR 6) on loan to Brazil: *Charles H. Davis* (T-AGOR 5) to New Zealand; *James M. Gillis* (AGOR 4), in reserve since 18-3-81, was leased to Mexico 15-6-83. Large stack contains 620-hp gas-turbine generator set used to drive main shaft at speed up to 6.5 kts for experiments requiring "quiet" conditions. Also have retractable electric bow-thruster/propulsor, which provides up to 4.5 kts. AGOR 3 has a wide aperture array, multi-channel seismic system. AGOR 10 carries the Sea Beam bottom contour mapping system. AGOR 3, 9, and 10 were modernized 1981-84 with new oceanographic winches and cables to work to 4–5,000-m depths.

◆ **2 Eltanin class** Bldr: Avondale Marine, New Orleans, La.

	L	In serv.
AGOR 8 Eltanin (ex-*Islas Orcadas*, Q9, ex-*Eltanin*, T-AGOR 8)	. . .	7-3-58
T-AGOR 11 Mizar (ex-T-AK 272)	7-10-57	22-11-57

Mizar (T-AGOR 11)—new superstructure amidships, foremast struck G. Arra, 1982

D: 2,040 tons light (3,750 fl) **S:** 13 kts **Dim:** 81.1 × 15.8 × 6.9
Electron Equipt: Radar: T-AGOR 11: Raytheon TM 1650/6X, 1/Raytheon TM 1660/12S
M: 4 Alco diesels, Westinghouse motors; 2 props; 3,200 hp
Fuel: 675 tons **Range:** 14,000/12 **Man:** 11 officers, 30 men, 15 technicians

Remarks: 2,486 grt/1,850 dwt. Former sisters to *Mirfak* (T-AK 271). Reclassified AGOR on 15-4-64. T-AGOR 11 operates for the Naval Electronics Command. Icebreaker hull; covered well on centerline for lowering equipment. AGOR 8 loaned to Argentina in 12-73 as *Islas Orcadas,* returned 1-8-79 and laid up at Norfolk Virginia.

Note: Also owned by the U.S. Navy but operated by civilian research organizations are the following small units: *Hoh* and *Onar,* operated by the University of Washington; *Edgerton,* operated by the Massachusetts Institute of Technology; a 16-m former buoy tender operated by the Massachusetts Maritime Academy; a 20-meter workboat operated by the University of Rhode Island; and an LCM(6)-class landing craft, operated by the University of Florida. YP 655, operated by the U.S. Naval Academy, is also equipped for oceanographic research.

OCEAN SURVEILLANCE SHIPS (T-AGOS)

◆ **0 (+1 + 9) SWATH T-AGOS** Bldr: . . .

	Laid down	L	In serv.
T-AGOS 17 N.	. . .	. . .	. . .
T-AGOS 21 N.	. . .	. . .	. . .
T-AGOS 22 N.	. . .	. . .	. . .
T-AGOS 23 N.	. . .	. . .	. . .

Authorized: T-AGOS 17 in FY 87. Programmed: T-AGOS 21–23 in FY 88, 2/yr in FY 89, 90, 91

D: 3,300–4,300 tons (fl) **S:** . . . **Dim:** . . . × . . . × . . .
Electron Equipt: Radar: 2/. . . nav.—Sonar: UQQ-2 SURTASS
M: Diesels; 2 props; . . . hp **Range:** . . . **Man:** . . .

Remarks: First SWATH (Small Waterplane Twin-Hull) T-AGOS requested FY 86 for operational capability by 1990-91. Design provides excellent stability in heavy seas—a necessity in higher latitudes. Design not fixed by early 1986.

◆ **7 (+12) Stalwart class** Bldr: T-AGOS 1–12: Tacoma Boat, Tacoma, Wash.; 13–14: Halter Marine, Moss Point, Miss.

	Laid down	L	In serv.
T-AGOS 1 Stalwart	3-11-82	11-7-83	9-4-84
T-AGOS 2 Contender	1-10-82	20-12-83	29-7-84
T-AGOS 3 Vindicator	14-4-83	1-6-84	20-11-84
T-AGOS 4 Triumph	3-1-84	7-9-84	19-2-85
T-AGOS 5 Assurance	31-5-84	20- . . .	1-5-85
T-AGOS 6 Persistent	28-9-84	6-4-85	14-8-85
T-AGOS 7 Indomitable	30-11-84	16-7-85	2-12-85
T-AGOS 8 Prevail	13-3-85	7-12-85	3-86
T-AGOS 9 Assertive	30-7-85	. . .	. . .
T-AGOS 10 Invincible	8-11-85	. . .	. . .
T-AGOS 11 Audacious (ex-*Dauntless*)	. . .	. . .	. . .
T-AGOS 12 Bold (ex-*Vigorous*)	. . .	. . .	. . .
T-AGOS 13 Adventurous	19-12-85	. . .	1988
T-AGOS 14 Worthy	2-86	. . .	1988
T-AGOS 15 N.	. . .	. . .	. . .
T-AGOS 16 N.	. . .	. . .	. . .
T-AGOS 18 N.	. . .	. . .	. . .
T-AGOS 19 N.	. . .	. . .	. . .
T-AGOS 20 N.			

Authorized: T-AGOS 1 and 2 in FY 79, T-AGOS 3 in FY 80, T-AGOS 4–8 in FY 81, T-AGOS 9–12 in FY 82, T-AGOS 13, 14 in FY 85, T-AGOS 15, 16 in FY 86; Programmed: T-AGOS 18, 19, 20 in FY 87

Vindicator (T-AGOS 3) MSC 1985

Stalwart (T-AGOS 1) L. & L. Van Ginderen, 10-85

D: 1,600 tons light (2,285 fl) **S:** 11 kts **Dim:** 68.28 (62.1 wl) × 13.10 × 4.57
Electron Equipt: Radar: 2/navigational—Sonar: UQQ-2 SURTASS
M: 4 Caterpillar-Kato D-348B 800-hp diesels, G.E. electric drive; 2/4-bladed props; 2,200 hp (1,600 hp sust.)—550-hp bow-thruster
Electric: 1,500 kVA **Range:** 3,000/11 plus 6,480/3 **Endurance:** 98 days
Man: 8 officers, 11 men contract crew, 7 RCA technicians

Remarks: The first three T-AGOS were contracted for 26-9-80. AN/UQQ-2 SURTASS (SURveillance Towed Array Sensor) is an 1,829-m linear, hydrophone array deployed over the ship's stern in a flexible, neutrally buoyant cable; the output from the SURTASS will be instantaneously relayed to shore monitoring stations via WSC-6 satellite communications, and the on-board technicians are primarily for maintenance and backup. Main-engine motor/generator sets also supply ship's-service power; there is a 250-kw emergency generator. Will have passive roll stabilization. Intended to conduct

OCEAN SURVEILLANCE SHIPS *(continued)*

60–90-day patrols and to be at sea 292 days per year. T-AGOS 13 and later have 3 more berths and more space per man; T-AGOS 13, 14 ordered 4-6-85, with option to build through T-AGOS 18.

First 12 to be operated under 1-2-85 contract with Sea Mobility Div., Falcon Contractors; contract duration 4 years, 8 months, with six to base on each coast at Pearl Harbor and Little Creek, Va. Technicians supplied by RCA on contract. Tacoma Boat's bankruptcy late 1985 will further delay an already much-delayed program; work ceased 14-2-86 on unlaunched T-AGOS 9–12.

SURVEYING SHIPS (T-AGS)

◆ **0 (+2) Maury class** Bldr: Bethlehem SY, Sparrows, Point, Maryland

	Laid down	L	In serv.
T-AGS 39 MAURY	...	...	28-12-87
T-AGS 40 TANNER	...	...	28-4-88

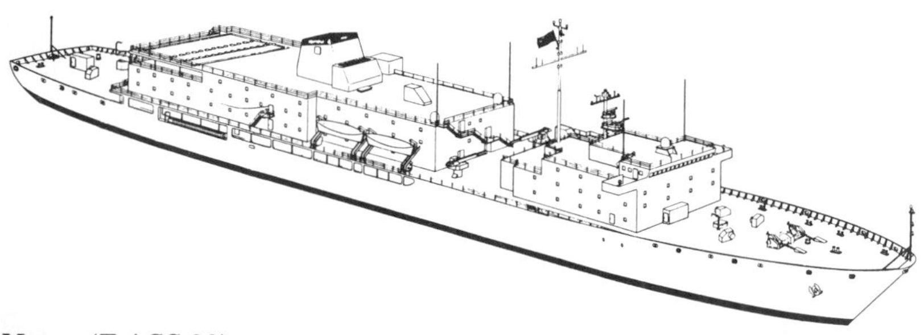

Maury (T-AGS 39) U.S. Navy, 6-85

D: 8,810 tons light (15,821 fl) **S:** 21 kts
Dim: 152.35 (140.84 pp; 145.09 wl) × 21.95 × 9.30
A: None
Electron Equipt: Radar: 2/. . . nav.—Sonar: SQN-17
M: 2 Transamerica Delaual R5-V16 Enterprise diesels; 1 CP prop; 25,000 hp
Range: 17,800/20 **Fuel:** 3,200 tons
Electric: . . . **Man:** 56 MSC crew; 3 naval officers, 29 naval men, 20 scientists

REMARKS: Ordered 28-6-85 under FY 85 funding. Replaced a program to convert two C3-S-33a cargo ships (*Lake* and *Scan*) from the Navy/Marad Ready Reserve Force. Intended as replacements for *Bowditch* (T-AGS 21) and *Dutton* (T-AGS 22) in support of SSBN operations through sea-floor charting and gravimetric mapping. Hull volume largely voids except for engineering spaces. Will carry up to 7,339 tons of water ballast. SQN-17 BOTOSS (BOttom TOpography Survey System) will map to depths of 7,300 m.

◆ **1 converted cargo ship (C4-SA type)** Bldr: National Steel, San Diego, Cal.

	L	In serv.
T-AGS 38 H.H. Hess (ex-*Canada Mail*)	3-65	16-1-78

H.H. Hess (T-AGS 38) MSC, 1982

D: 13,520 tons light (21,250 fl) **S:** 21 kts
Dim: 171.8 (160.93 pp) × 23.16 × 9.6
Electron Equipt: Radar: 1/Raytheon TM 1650/6X, 1/Raytheon TM 1660/12S
M: 1 set G.E. GT; 1 prop; 19,250 hp **Electric:** 1,400 kw
Boilers: 2 Foster-Wheeler, 43.3 kg/cm², 457°C
Fuel: 3,178 tons **Range:** 14,000/20 **Man:** 30 MSC crew, 74 Navy

REMARKS: Mariner-type passenger-cargo ship acquired from the Maritime Administration on 9-7-76 for conversion to replace the *Michelson* (T-AGS 23) in the SSBN navigational support program. Retains original six cargo holds, but most cargo booms removed. Converted at National Steel and SB, San Diego, 3-77 to 1-78.

◆ **2 Chauvenet class (SCB 723 type)** Bldr: Upper Clyde SB, Glasgow, U.K.

	Laid down	L	In serv.
T-AGS 29 CHAUVENET	24-5-67	13-5-68	13-11-70
T-AGS 32 HARKNESS	30-6-67	12-6-68	29-1-71

D: 3,040 tons (4,330 fl) **S:** 15 kts **Dim:** 119.8 (101.8 pp) × 16.5 × 4.9
Electron Equipt: Radar: 1/Raytheon TM 1650/6X, 1/Raytheon TM 1660/12S
M: 2 Alco diesels, Westinghouse motor; 1 CP prop; 3,600 hp
Electric: 1,500 kw **Endurance:** 90 days **Fuel:** 824 tons **Range:** 15,000/12
Man: MSC: 13 officers, 56 men + Navy: 6 officers, 49 men + 12 civilian scientists

Harkness (T-AGS 32) G. Arra, 1983

REMARKS: 2,890 grt/1,030 dwt. Very complete navigation and communications systems. Can carry four small survey launches; hangar and flight deck for two helicopters. Operated for the Oceanographer of the Navy; 61–76 naval personnel aboard in 1985.

◆ **4 Silas Bent class (SCB 226, 725*, and 728† types)**

	Bldr	L	In serv.
T-AGS 26 SILAS BENT	American SB, Lorain	16-5-64	23-7-65
T-AGS 27 KANE	Christy, Sturgeon Bay	20-11-65	19-5-67
T-AGS 33 WILKES*	Defoe, Bay City, Mich.	31-7-69	28-6-71
T-AGS 34 WYMAN†	Defoe, Bay City, Mich.	30-10-69	3-11-71

Silas Bent (T-AGS 26) G. Arra, 10-85

D: 1,790 to 1,935 tons (2,420 to 2,596 fl) **S:** 15 kts
Dim: 86.9 (80.8 pp) × 14.6 × 4.6
Electron Equipt: Radar: 1/Raytheon RM 1650/9X, 1/Raytheon TM 1660/12S
M: 2 Alco diesels, Westinghouse or G.E. motor; 1 CP prop; 3,600 hp (plus 350-hp bow-thruster)
Electric: 960 kw **Fuel:** 461 tons **Range:** 14,000/15
Man: 12 officers, 35 men, 30 scientists

REMARKS: Operated for Oceanographer of the Navy. T-AGS 34, used in support of the strategic missile programs, is equipped with the Sperry SQN-17 BOTOSS (BOttom TOpography Survey System) for mapping depths to 7,300 m; the system consists of two planar transducer arrays and an HP 2100 computer, which averages the results of four separate passes through an area. Have MARISAT satellite communications equipment.

◆ **2 Bowditch class** Bldr: Oregon SB, Portland, South Coast Co.

	L	Conv.
T-AGS 21 BOWDITCH (ex-*South Bend Victory*)	30-6-45	8-10-48
T-AGS 22 DUTTON (ex-*Tuskegee Victory*)	8-5-45	30-9-58

Bowditch (T-AGS 21) L. & L. Van Ginderen, 6-84

D: 4,700 tons light (13,050 fl) **S:** 16.5 kts
Dim: 138.76 (133.05 pp) × 18.98 × 7.62
Electron Equipt: Radar: 1/Raytheon TM 1650/9X, 1/Raytheon TM 1660/12S
M: 1 set GT; 1 prop; 8,500 hp
Boilers: 2 Combustion Engineering; 37 kg/cm², 399°C
Electric: 1,260 kw **Fuel:** 2,824 tons
Range: 20,000/16.5 **Man:** 14 officers, 47 men, 15 scientists

SURVEYING SHIPS *(continued)*

Remarks: 7,783 grt/8,350 dwt. Victory-class cargo ships converted to support the SSBN program. Used for sea-floor charting and magnetic mapping. Sister *Michelson* (T-AGS 23) stricken in 1975. To be replaced by T-AGS 39 and 40.

HOSPITAL SHIPS (T-AH)

◆ **0 (+2) converted San Clemente-class merchant tankers** Bldr: National Steel, San Diago, Cal.

	L	Conv. start	In serv.
T-AH 19 Mercy (ex-*Worth*)	1976	20-7-84	7-86
T-AH 20 Comfort (ex-*Rose City*)	1976	2-4-85	12-86

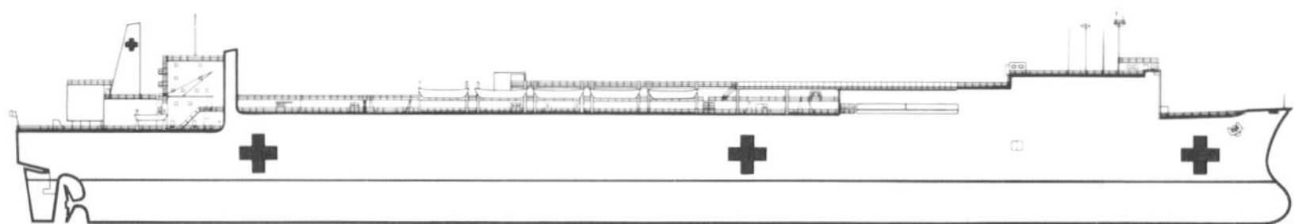

Mercy (T-AH 19) U.S. Navy

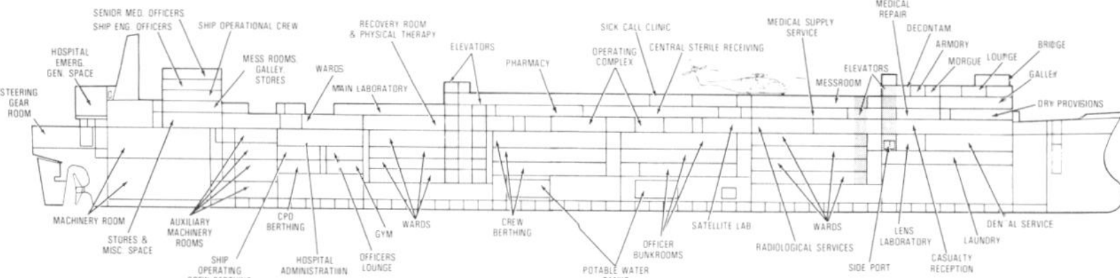

Mercy (T-AH 19)—interval arrangements U.S. Navy

Mercy (T-AH 19)—under conversion W. Donko, 7-85

D: 24,712 tons light (69,320 fl) **S:** 17.5 kts
Dim: 272.49 (260.61 pp) × 32.23 × 9.98
Electron Equipt: Radar: 2/. . . nav.
M: 1 set steam turbines; 1 prop; 24,500 hp
Boilers: 2/. . . **Fuel:** 5,747 tons **Range:** 13,420/17.5
Man: 14 officers, 154 men MSC, 1,207 Navy staff + 1,000 patients

Remarks: Builder contracted 29-6-83 to convert Apex Marine's tanker *Worth* to a hospital ship with FY 83 funds; T-AH 20's conversion ordered from same yard 16-12-83 with FY 84 funds. Were originally 44,875 grt/91,849 dwt.

The entire midships area has been altered to provide a large helicopter deck, accommodations, and boat stowage. Have 12 operating rooms, 4 X-ray rooms, an 80-bed intensive-care unit, a burn-care facility, and a 50-bed reception/triage area. Of the 1,508 accommodations for naval personnel, there will be 259 officers, 31 chief petty officers, and 530 enlisted, augmented in emergencies by 372 naval medical support personnel; also aboard will be 14 communications specialists. One will be kept on each U.S. coast, on 5-days' steaming notice, and they will be used about 7 days per year on exercises. In port, they will be maintained by the MSC crew and a small civilian contract crew. Fresh water tankage for 1,525 tons will be carried, plus two 278-ton/day distilling plants. Much of the displacement will be sea-water ballast.

CARGO SHIPS (T-AK)

◆ **1 Northern Light class (C2-S-33a type)** Bldr: Sun SB & DD Co., Chester, Pa.

	In serv.	In USN
T-AK 286 Vega (ex-*Bay*, ex-*Mormacbay*)	14-10-60	15-10-81

D: 16,363 tons (fl) **S:** 19 kts **Dim:** 148.15 (139.59 pp) × 20.72 × 8.68
Electron Equipt: Radar: 1/Raytheon TM 1650/6X, 1/Raytheon TM 1660/12S
M: 1 set G.E. GT; 1 prop; 11,000 hp (15,700 emergency) **Electric:** 1,275 kw
Boilers: 2 Combustion Engineering 43.3 kg/cm², 457°C
Fuel: 3,056 tons **Range:** 14,000/18 **Man:** 68 MSC crew plus 7 naval

Vega (T-AK 286) G. Arra, 8-85

Remarks: T-AK 286 (originally to have been renamed *King's Bay*) acquired 29-4-81 and placed on the Navy List on 15-10-81, recommissioned 18-3-83 after being converted to transport 16 Trident ballistic missiles in vertical cells in place of No. 3 hold. Former 9,260 grt/12,500 dwt cargo ship acquired from Maritime Administration's National Defense Reserve Fleet.

Sisters *Northern Light* (T-AK 284, ex-*Cove*, ex-*Mormaccove*) and *Southern Cross* (T-AK 285, ex-*Trade*, ex-*Mormactrade*) were deactivated 9-84 and 12-84, respectively, and transferred to the Maritime Administration-administered Ready Reserve Force, although remaining as Navy property. Both were configured as general cargo ships. Funds were requested in FY 85 to convert sister *Cape* as a ballistic-missile transport (T-AK 295) but were denied by Congress; *Cape* and sisters *Lake* and *Scan* (which were to have been converted as survey ships T-AGS 39 and 40) are also in the Ready Reserve Force.

Note: Former attack cargo ship *Wyandot* (T-AK 283, ex-AKA 92), in reserve since 5-3-76, was stricken 31-1-86, as was the *Alchiba*-class heavy-lift cargo ship *Marine Fiddler* (T-AK 267), also long in reserve.

◆ **2 Norwalk class**
Bldr: Oregon SB, Portland (T-AK 281: Permanente, Richmond, Calif.)

	L	Conv.
T-AK 280 Furman (ex-*Furman Victory*)	18-5-45	7-10-64
T-AK 282 Marshfield (ex-*Marshfield Victory*)	15-5-44	28-5-70

Marshfield (T-AK 282) G. Arra, 1984

D: 6,700 tons light (11,150 fl) **S:** 16.5 kts
Dim: 138.76 (133.05 pp) × 18.90 × 7.32
Electron Equipt: Radar: 1/Raytheon TM 1650/6X, 1/Raytheon 1660/12S
M: 1 set GT; 1 prop; 8,500 hp **Boilers:** 2; 37 kg/cm², 399°C
Fuel: 2,824 tons **Range:** 20,000/16.5
Man: T-AK 280: 35 tot. MSC; T-AK 282: 14 officers, 57 men MSC, plus 7 Navy

Remarks: 7,491 grt/9,649 dwt. In T-AK 282, hold No. 3 accommodates 16 vertically stowed Poseidon or Polaris SLBMs to support SSBN activities. Has MARISAT SATCOMM system. Carries torpedoes, submarine spares, etc.; also carries 18,000 barrels cargo fuel (7,566 bbl diesel/10,434 bbl fuel oil). 40-ton cargo booms. Small Navy security detachment aboard. T-AK 280, originally converted like T-AK 282, was to have been stricken 20-9-81, but was instead reserved for conversion to a cable transporter for the Naval Electronics Command. Contracted to Atlantic Drydock Co., Jacksonville, Fla., on 17-11-82, the ship had all winches and cargo booms removed, as well as the refrigeration equipment deleted; completed 20-4-83, she now has a crew of only 35.

Sister *Norwalk* (T-AK 279) was stricken 1-8-79 and *Victoria* (T-AK 281) was transferred to the Maritime Commission for long-term layup on 18-1-84; stricken 31-1-86.

CARGO SHIPS *(continued)*

◆ 1 Eltanin-class Arctic service

	Bldr	L	In serv.
T-AK 271 MIRFAK	Avondale Marine, New Orleans, La.	5-8-57	30-12-57

Mirfak—while active U.S. Navy, 1970

D: 2,022 tons light (4,800 fl) **S:** 13 kts **Dim:** 81.1 × 15.8 × 7.0
Electron Equipt: Radar: 1/Raytheon TM 1650/6X, 1/Raytheon TM 1660/12S
M: 4 Alco diesels, Westinghouse electric drive; 2 props; 2,700 hp
Fuel: 612 tons **Range:** 14,000/13 **Man:** 48 tot.

REMARKS: 2,486 grt/1,850 dwt. Maritime Administration C1-ME2-13a Type, intended for Arctic operations and having an icebreaker hull form. Cargo: 2,634 m³ dry/227 m³ refrigerated. Deactivated 11-12-79 and transferred to the Maritime Administration; remains Navy property and is laid up in the James River, in Virginia. Sisters *Eltanin* (AGOR 8, ex-AK 270) and *Mizar* (T-AGOR 11) were converted to serve as oceanographic research ships.

NOTE: In addition to the above-listed Navy-owned ships, the Military Sealift Command charters a number of general cargo ships, both for the Near-Term Prepositioning Force and for general cargo transport. The ships on charter as of late 1985 are listed at the end of this section with other chartered units. The Reagan Administration is also attempting to enlarge the pool of cargo ships readily available for national emergencies by rehabilitating suitable vessels in the Maritime Commission National Defense Reserve Fleet; these ships are to be activatable in 5 or 10 days and are identified as part of the Ready Reserve Force (RRF), ultimately to include some 116 ships. On 11-10-85 there were 59 cargo ships and 7 tankers in the RRF.

VEHICLE CARGO SHIPS (T-AKR)

◆ 7 (+1) SL-7-class container cargo ships

	Bldr	In serv.	In Navy	AKR conv.
T-AKR 287 ALGOL (ex-*Sea-Land Exchange*)	Rotterdamse DDM, Rotterdam	5-73	13-10-81	19-6-84
T-AKR 288 BELLATRIX (ex-*Sea-Land Trade*)	Rheinstahl Nord-seewerke, Emden	12-73	13-10-81	10-9-84
T-AKR 289 DENEBOLA (ex-*Sea-Land Resource*)	Rotterdamse DDM, Rotterdam	12-73	27-10-81	10-85
T-AKR 290 POLLUX (ex-*Sea-Land Market*)	A.G. Weser, Bremen	9-73	16-11-81	3-86
T-AKR 291 ALTAIR (ex-*Sea-Land Finance*)	Rheinstahl Nord-seewerke, Emden	9-73	5-1-82	13-11-85
T-AKR 292 REGULUS (ex-*Sea-Land Commerce*)	A.G. Weser, Bremen	3-73	27-10-81	28-8-85
T-AKR 293 CAPELLA (ex-*Sea-Land McLean*)	Rotterdamse DDM, Rotterdam	10-72	16-4-82	1-7-84
T-AKR 294 ANTARES (ex-*Sea-Land Galloway*)	A.G. Weser, Bremen	9-72	16-4-82	12-7-84

D: 55,355 tons (fl) **S:** 33 kts **Dim:** 288.38 (268.37 pp) × 32.16 × 11.13
M: 2 sets G.E. MST-19 GT; 2 props; 120,000 hp **Electric:** 7,500 kw
Boilers: 2 Foster-Wheeler; 61.6 kg/cm², 507°C **Fuel:** 8,500 tons
Range: 7,000/23 **Man:** 62 max.

REMARKS: 48,525 grt/24,270 dwt (varies). Six acquired under FY 81 and two under FY 82, with the original intent of extensively converting them to serve as T-AKR, "Roll-on/Roll-off" vehicle cargo ships for the Rapid Deployment Force. Instead, under FY 82 Congress mandated that four be given a "partial" Ro/Ro conversion and the other four be given only a "mini-modification." This has since been changed to give all the same modification, T-AKR 287, 288, 293, and 294 under FY 82 and the others under FY 84. The conversions were performed by: T-AKR 287, 288, 292: National Steel, San Diego; T-AKR 289 and 293: Pennsylvania SB, Chester, Pa.; and the others by Avondale SY, Westwego, La. The ships were given T-AK hull numbers when purchased; these were changed to T-AKR without changing the actual numbers assigned, first two on 10-9-82, others on 1-11-83.

Algol (T-AKR 287) L. & L. Van Ginderen, 9-84

Antares (T-AKR 294) L. & L. Van Ginderen, 1-86

Capella (T-AKR 293) MSC, 7-84

The ships were originally tailored to transport up to 1,086 nonstandard *35-ft.* containers (standard cargo containers are either 20 or 40 feet in length); 4,000 containers were purchased along with the first six ships. These ships proved expensive to operate for the former merchant owner, and their sophisticated propulsion plants have not been overly reliable. Up to 9,484 tons of salt-water ballast can be carried.

On completion three are to be maintained crewed, ready for sea on each coast, with the other two to be placed on 5 days' notice in the Ready Reserve Force. Conversion entailed filling in the amidships portion to produce a multi-deck vehicle cargo area and helicopter hangar totaling 12,170 m² on 5 decks (can accommodate up to 120 UH-1 helicopters or 183 M-1 tanks). This is topped by a flight deck of 3,252 m² with a twin 35-ton crane plumbing two hatches interrupting the forward half. The stern provides 1,719 m² of vehicle parking, as well as cargo space for 8 "Seashed" containerized vehicle stowage or 46/20-ft. containers; it is served by a twin 50-ton crane. There are vehicle access ramps amidships, port and starboard. Operated on contract by original owners, SeaLand Service, Inc.

◆ 2 Maine (C7-S-95a-type) class Bldr: Bath Iron Wks., Maine

	L	In serv.
T-AKR 10 MERCURY (ex-*Illinois*, ex-*Arizona*)	7-76	1977
T-AKR 11 JUPITER (ex-*Lipscomb Lykes*, ex-*Arizona*)	1-11-75	14-5-76

D: 14,222 tons light (33.765 fl) **S:** 23 kts (sust.)
Dim: 208.71 (195.07 pp) × 31.09 × 9.78
Electron Equipt: Radar: 1/Raytheon TM 1650/6X, 1/Raytheon TM 1660/12S
M: 2 sets G.E. GT; 2 props; 37,000 hp **Electric:** 4,000 kw
Boilers: 2 Babcock & Wilcox; 77.5 kg/cm² **Fuel:** 3,394 tons
Range: 10,000/23 **Man:** 41 tot. MSC

VEHICLE CARGO SHIPS *(continued)*

Jupiter (T-AKR 11) MSC, 1982

REMARKS: 13,156 grt/19,172 dwt. T-AKR 10 long-term chartered 14-4-80 and T-AKR 11 on 7-5-80. Have MSC contract crews, as part of the Near-Term Prepositioning Force at Diego Garcia; owners: T-AKR 10: Lykes Brothers; T-AKR 11: Wilmington Trust Bank. Capable of carrying container, as well as vehicle, cargo and can land helicopters amidships on upper deck; can also transport 728 tons liquid cargo. Two 15-ton cranes (paired) forward. A 7.3-m-wide by 24.4-m stern ramp is fitted, and there are two side-loading doors also. Total bale cargo volume is 56,640 m³; vehicle cargo deck space is 16,258 m². Plans to acquire two more ships of this class and to enlarge and modify T-AKR 10 and 11 were abandoned.

NOTE: *Meteor* (T-AKR 9) was deactivated and placed in the Ready Reserve Force in 9-85. The similar *Comet* (T-AKR 7) was transferred to the Maritime Commission Ready Reserve Force 3-85, both remain Navy property.

REPLENISHMENT OILERS

◆ **0 (+9 + 10 + . . .) Henry J. Kaiser class** Bldr: A: Avondale SY, Westwego, La.; B: PennShip, Chester, Pa.

	Bldr	Budget	Laid down	L	In serv.
T-AO 187 HENRY J. KAISER	A	FY 82	22-8-84	5-10-85	9-86
T-AO 188 JOSHUA HUMPHREYS	A	FY 83	17-27-84	22-2-86	1-87
T-AO 189 JOHN LENTHALL	A	FY 84	15-7-85	8-86	5-87
T-AO 190 ANDREW J. HIGGINS	A	FY 84	21-11-85	11-86	9-87
T-AO 191 N.	B	FY 85	. . .	. . .	1989
T-AO 192 N.	B	FY 85	. . .	. . .	1989
T-AO 193 N.	A	FY 85	. . .	. . .	1988
T-AO 194 N.	A	FY 86	. . .	. . .	. . .
T-AO 195 N.	A	FY 86	. . .	. . .	. . .
T-AO 196 N.	. . .	. . .	. . .	. . .	. . .
T-AO 197 N.	. . .	. . .	. . .	. . .	. . .

D: 9,500 tons light (40,700 fl) **S:** 20 kts (sust.)
Dim: 206.50 (198.10 pp) × 29.72 × 10.67
A: Provision for 2/20-mm Mk 15 CIWS (I × 2)
Electron Equipt: Radar: 2/navigational **Electric:** 10,600 kw
M: 2 Colt-Pielstick 10 PC4.2V diesels; 2 CP props; 32,540 hp
Range: 6,000/20 **Man:** 95 MSC crew, plus 21 Navy (137 berths)

REMARKS: 26,500 dwt. Cargo: 180,000 bbl liquid (86,400 bbl fuel oil; 54,000 bbl JP-5; 39,600 convertible; plus 327 tons feedwater, 390 tons potable water), plus dry cargo and eight 20-ft. provisions containers. Initially intended to be an MSC variant of the *Cimarron* class, designed to merchant standards, but the design has since grown. Will be equipped for underway replenishment of liquids and solids. Helicopter deck aft, no hangar. Design contract to George Sharp, Inc., 11-7-80. A total of at least 20, to replace all earlier MSC-manned replenishment oilers, is planned, but building program has been scaled back from 4/yr to 2/yr. Five alongside fueling stations (3 to port), 1 solid transfer station per side. The engines for the first two were built by Alsthom in France. Have an CGEE-Alsthom integrated auxiliary electric drive system for low speeds, driving either or both props. Will have the SLQ-25 Nixie torpedo system but no EW gear.

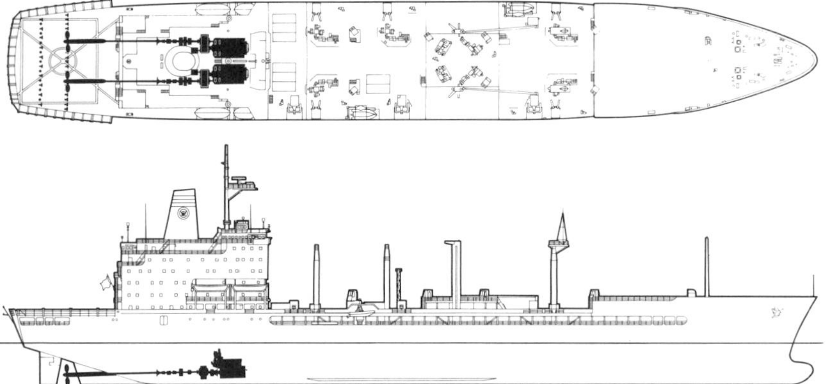

T-AO 187—plan view and side elevation Colt-Pielstick, 1984

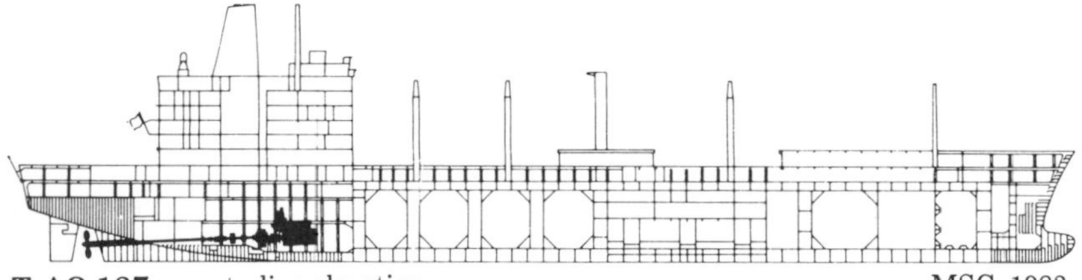

T-AO 187—centerline elevation MSC, 1983

Henry J. Kaiser (T-AO 187)—artist's rendering MSC, 1984

◆ **6 Neosho class (SCB 82 type)**
Bldr: New York SB, Camden, N.J. (T-AO 143: Bethlehem, Quincy, Mass.)

	L	In serv.	To MSC
T-AO 143 NEOSHO	10-11-53	24-9-54	25-5-78
T-AO 144 MISSISSINEWA	12-6-54	18-1-55	15-11-76
T-AO 145 HASSAYAMPA	12-9-54	19-4-55	17-8-78
T-AO 146 KAWISHWI	11-12-54	6-7-55	1-10-79
T-AO 147 TRUCKEE	10-3-55	23-11-55	30-1-80
T-AO 148 PONCHATOULA	9-7-55	12-1-56	5-9-80

D: 19,533 tons light (36,840 fl) **S:** 20 kts
Dim: 199.65 (195.07 wl) × 26.21 × 10.67
Electron Equipt: Radar: 1/SPS-10, 1/Raytheon TM 1650/6X or 12X
M: 2 sets G.E. GT; 2 props; 28,000 hp **Electric:** 1,500 kw
Boilers: 2 Babcock & Wilcox; 42.2 kg/cm², 357°C
Fuel: 5,000 tons **Man:** 21 officers, 105 men MSC + 21 Navy

REMARKS: 19,553 grt/36,840 dwt. Carry 180,000 bbl. liquid cargo (approx. 23,600 tons). Helicopter platform aft in all but T-AO 145, 146 and T-AO 148. Operated by MSC as underway-replenishment ships for Navy. Transferred to MSC as a cost-saving measure (Navy crew was 360 total). Masting and superstructures differ in detail.

Ponchatoula (T-AO 148) L. & L. Van Ginderen, 9-84

Ponchatoula (T-AO 148) LSPH S. Given, R.A.N., 5-84

REPLENISHMENT OILERS *(continued)*

Hassayampa (T-AO 145) LSPH E. Pitman, R.A.N., 4-85

◆ **5 Mispillion class (jumboized T3-S2-A3 type)** Bldr: Sun SB, Chester, Pa.

	L	In serv.	To MSC
T-AO 105 Mispillion	10-8-45	29-12-45	26-7-73
T-AO 106 Navasota	30-8-45	27-2-46	13-8-75
T-AO 107 Passumpsic	31-10-45	1-4-46	24-7-73
T-AO 108 Pawcatuck	19-2-46	10-5-46	15-7-75
T-AO 109 Waccamaw	30-3-46	25-6-46	24-2-75

Mispillion (T-AO 105) G. Arra, 1984

Waccamaw (T-AO 109) U.S. Navy, 1984

D: 9,486 tons light (35,090 fl) **S:** 16 kts **Dim:** 196.9 × 22.9 × 10.8
Electron Equipt: Radar: 1/SPS-10, 1/Raytheon TM 1650/6X
M: 2 sets Westinghouse GT; 2 props; 13,500 hp
Boilers: 4 Babcock & Wilcox; 32.7 kg/cm², 393°C
Fuel: 2,205 tons **Man:** 23 officers, 85 men MSC, plus 21 Navy

Remarks: 19,294 grt/23,250 dwt. Cargo: 107,000 bbl. fuel oil, diesel, etc. plus dry cargo. Fleet support units transferred from the Navy and intended for underway replenishment. Had four single 76.2-mm guns, but now disarmed. Helicopter deck forward. Replenishment station forward of bridge removed around 1980. All lengthened 28.3 m during the mid-1960s. T-AO 105 scheduled to be deactivated FY 81, but was retained in active service.

◆ **2 Cimarron class (T3-S2-A1 type)** Bldr: Bethlehem, Sparrows Point, Md. — in reserve.

	L	In serv.	To MSC
T-AO 57 Marias	21-12-43	12-2-44	2-10-73
T-AO 62 Taluga	10-7-44	25-8-44	4-5-72

D: 24,450 tons (fl) **S:** 18 kts **Dim:** 168.56 × 22.86 × 10.1
Electron Equipt: Radar: 1/SPS-10, 1/Raytheon 1650/9X
M: 2 sets GT; 2 props; 13,500 hp **Electric:** 950 kw
Boilers: 4 Foster-Wheeler; 31.7 kg/cm², 399°C **Range:** 10,000/15
Fuel: 2,205 tons **Man:** 20 officers, 85 men MSC, plus 16 Navy

Remarks: 12,000 grt/18,400 dwt. Cargo: 87,000 bbl. fuel oil, diesel, etc. Fleet support ships intended for underway replenishment. Deactivated and placed in National Defense Reserve Fleet (on Navy List), T-AO 57 on 22-11-82 and T-AO 62 on 21-11-83. Foreign sale of T-AO 57 no longer planned.

Marias (T-AO 57) 1975

TRANSPORT OILERS (T-AOT)

Note: The four Falcon Lines freighting tankers chartered in 1974 and given U.S. Navy hull numbers have been returned to their owners: *Neches* (T-AOT 183, ex-*Falcon Duchess*) on 30-9-83, *Columbia* (T-AOT 182, ex-*Falcon Lady*), *Hudson* (T-AOT 184, ex-*Falcon Princess*), and *Susquehanna* (T-AOT 185, ex-*Falcon Countess*) during 1984. The single-unit tanker *Potomac* (T-AOT 181, ex-*Shenandoah*, ex-*Potomac*, T-AO 150) was placed in the MARAD-administered Ready Reserve Force on 5-3-84, still under Navy ownership.

◆ **9 Sealift class** Bldrs: First four: Todd, Los Angeles; others: Bath Iron Works

	L	In serv.
T-AOT 168 Sealift Pacific	13-10-73	14-8-74
T-AOT 169 Sealift Arabian Sea	26-1-74	6-5-75
T-AOT 170 Sealift China Sea	20-4-74	9-5-75
T-AOT 171 Sealift Indian Ocean	27-7-74	29-8-74
T-AOT 172 Sealift Atlantic	26-1-74	26-8-74
T-AOT 173 Sealift Mediterranean	9-3-74	6-11-74
T-AOT 174 Sealift Caribbean	8-6-74	10-2-75
T-AOT 175 Sealift Arctic	31-8-74	22-5-75
T-AOT 176 Sealift Antarctic	26-10-74	1-8-75

Sealift Antarctic (T-AO 176) — MARISAT radome atop bridge
L. & L. Van Ginderen, 10-85

TRANSPORT OILERS *(continued)*

D: 33,000 tons (fl) **S:** 16 kts
Dim: 178.92 (170.80 pp) × 25.61 × 10.50
Electron Equipt: Radar: 1/Raytheon TM 1650/6X, 1/Raytheon TM 1645
M: 2 Colt-Pielstick, 14PC-2V400 14-cyl., 520-rpm diesels; 1 CP prop; 14,000 hp
Electric: 2,600 kw **Fuel:** 3,440 tons
Range: 12,000/16 **Man:** 9 officers, 17 men, 2 cadets (contract crew)

REMARKS: 17,157 grt/27,217 dwt (vary slightly). Cargo: 225,154 barrels fuel oil, diesel, etc. Equipped with bow-thruster. MSC chartered these ships for twenty years and has a commercial contractor operating them; current owner is the Irving Trust Co., New York. All redesignated T-AOT on 30-9-78. These ships may be altered to permit them to conduct underway alongside liquid replenishment. A five-year operating contract for these ships was signed with Marine Transport Lines, Secaucus, N.J., in 3-85.

NOTE: *American Explorer* (T-AOT 165) was placed in the MARAD-administered Ready Reserve Force in 6-84, still under Navy ownership.

◆ **2 Maumee class (T5-S-12A type)**

	Bldr	Laid down	L	In serv.
T-AOT 149 MAUMEE	Ingalls SB	8-3-55	16-2-56	12-12-56
T-AOT 152 YUKON	Ingalls SB	16-5-55	16-3-56	17-5-57

Yukon (T-AOT 152) L. & L. Van Ginderen, 6-83

D: 32,000 tons (fl) **S:** 18 kts **Dim:** 189.0 × 25.5 × 9.8
Electron Equipt: Radar: 1/Raytheon TM 1650/6X, 1/Raytheon TM 1660/12S
M: 1 set GT; 1 prop; 20,460 hp **Boilers:** 2 Combustion Engineering
Fuel: 4,321 tons **Range:** 18,000/18 **Man:** 11 officers, 20 men MSC

REMARKS: 15,626 grt/26,943 dwt. Cargo: 187,000 bbl fuel oil, diesel, etc. plus 878 m³ dry cargo. T-AOT 149 has ice-reinforced bow. Sister *Potomac* (T-AO 150, now T-AOT 181) rebuilt to different design. All retyped T-AOT on 30-9-78. Sister *Shoshone* (T-AOT 151) was placed in the MARAD-administered Ready Reserve Force in 6-84, still under Navy ownership.

◆ **1 Mission class (T2-SE-A2 type)** Bldr: Marineship, Sausalito, Calif.—in reserve

	Laid down	L	In serv.
T-AOT 134 MISSION SANTA YNEZ	9-9-43	19-12-43	13-3-44

D: 5,730 tons light (22,380 fl) **S:** 16.5 kts **Dim:** 159.7 (153.3 pp) × 20.7 × 9.4
M: 1 set G.E. GT, electric drive; 1 prop; 10,000 hp **Electric:** 1,120 kw
Boilers: 2 Babcock & Wilcox; 42.2 kg/cm², 441°C
Fuel: 1,375 tons **Range:** 13,000/14.5 **Man:** 52 tot.

REMARKS: 10,461 grt/17,056 dwt. Acquired by the Navy on 22-10-47. Cargo: 16,500 tons liquid (approx. 134,000 bbl). In National Defense Reserve Fleet at Suisun Bay, Cal., since 6-3-75. Retyped T-AOT on 30-9-78.

◆ **1 Suamico class (T2-SE-A1 type)** Bldr: Sun SB & DD, Chester, Pa.—in reserve

	Laid down	L	In serv.
T-AOT 75 SAUGATUCK (ex-*Newton*)	16-9-42	7-7-42	19-2-43

D: 5,782 tons light (21,880 fl) **S:** 15 kts **Dim:** 159.7 (153.3 pp) × 20.7 × 9.4
M: 1 set G.E. GT, electric drive; 1 prop; 8,250 hp (T-AOT 67 and T-AOT 75: 1 set Westinghouse GT, electric drive; 1 prop; 6,600 hp)
Electric: 1,100–1,160 kw **Boilers:** 2 Babcock & Wilcox 42.2 kg/cm², 441°C
Fuel: 1,375 tons **Range:** 13,000/14.5 **Man:** 52 tot.

REMARKS: 10,296 grt/16,500 dwt. Sisters *Tallulah* (T-AOT 50, ex-*Valley Forge*), *Cache* (T-AOT 67, ex-*Stillwater*), *Millicoma* (T-AOT 73, ex-*Conestoga*, ex-*King's Mountain*), and *Schuylkill* (T-AOT 76, ex-*Louisburg*) were approved for disposal in 31-1-86. Taken over by the Navy while under construction and completed as a fleet oiler. Transferred to MSTS (later MSC) in 1949 and operated with civilian crews until placed in the Maritime Administration's National Defense Reserve Fleet between 1972 and 1975. Cargo: 141,000 bbl. Reclassified T-AOT on 30-9-78.

NOTE: The *Alatna*-class gasoline tankers, *Alatna* (T-AOG 81) and *Chattahoochee* (T-AOG 82) were laid up in Japan in 1984 as part of the MARAD-administered Ready Reserve Fleet. *Tonti*-class gasoline tanker *Nodaway* (T-AOG 78, ex-*Tarcoola*) was laid up at Pearl Harbor in 1984 in similar circumstances; all three remain Navy property. Their functions were replaced by two chartered tug/barge combinations.

TRANSPORTS

NOTE: The transports listed below are maintained in the Maritime Administration's reserve fleet, but remain the Navy's property, earmarked for the MSC, should the requirement arise. Most were placed in reserve in 1969 and 1970. Of the three *Barrett*-class transports, *Barrett* (AP 196) has been on loan to the New York State Maritime Academy since 5-9-73, *Geiger* (AP 197), on loan to the Massachusetts Maritime Academy in 12-2-80, was damaged by fire in 1981 and was returned to the Maritime Commission for disposal, and was replaced by *Upshur* (AP 198).

◆ **4 Admiral class (P2-S2-R1 type)** Bldr: Bethlehem, Alameda, Cal.—in reserve

	L	In serv.
AP 122 GENERAL ALEXANDER M. PATCH (ex-*Admiral R.E. Coontz*)	22-4-44	21-11-44
AP 123 GENERAL SIMON B. BUCKNER (ex-*Admiral E.W. Eberle*)	14-6-44	24-1-45
AP 125 GENERAL NELSON M. WALKER (ex-*Admiral H.T. Mayo*)	26-11-44	24-4-45
AP 126 GENERAL MAURICE ROSE (ex-*Admiral Hugh Rodman*)	25-2-45	10-7-45

D: 12,657 tons light (22,574 fl) **S:** 19 kts
Dim: 185.6 (174.65 wl) × 23.01 × 8.07
Fuel: 3,877 tons **Range:** 15,000/19
M: 2 sets G.E. GT, electric drive; 2 props; 18,000 hp **Electric:** 2,000 kw
Boilers: 4 Combustion Engineering "D," 42.2 kg/cm², 449°C
Man: 319 tot.

REMARKS: 16,039 grt/9,944 dwt. All operated by the Army Transportation Service until 1-3-50, when transferred to MSTS (later MSC). Active into the late 1960s. Can carry 1,757 troops, 2,889 m³ dry cargo. *Hugh J. Gaffey* (T-AP 121) redesignated IX 507 on 1-11-78 and used as a barracks ship. *General William O. Darby* (AP 127) reactivated as barracks ship (IX 510) in 10-81 (see pg. 669). *General Nelson M. Walker* (AP 125) donated 25-1-81 to Life International for conversion as a civilian hospital ship, but remained laid up in the James River, on the Navy List in 1983. All could originally carry 5,100 troops. Two others stricken. For appearance, see IX 510.

◆ **3 General class (P2-S2-R2 type)** Bldr: Federal SB & DD, Kearny, N.J.—in reserve

	L	In serv.
AP 110 GENERAL JOHN POPE	21-3-43	5-8-43
AP 117 GENERAL W. H. GORDON	7-5-44	29-6-44
AP 119 GENERAL WILLIAM WEIGEL (ex-*General C. H. Barth*)	3-9-44	6-1-45

General W.H. Gordon (AP 117)—in Maritime Commission James River reserve fleet J. Jedrlinic, 5-80

D: 11,450 tons light (20,700 fl) **S:** 21 kts **Dim:** 189.77 × 23.01 × 7.77
M: 2 sets de Laval GT; 2 props; 17,000 hp **Electric:** 1,600 kw
Boilers: 4 Foster-Wheeler "D," 32.7 kg/cm², 407°C
Fuel: 3,043 tons **Range:** 11,000/19
Man: . . .

REMARKS: T-AP 110: 17,927 grt/7,479 dwt; others vary. Can carry from 2,154 to 3,825 passengers or troops. Also remaining in Maritime Commission custody are sisters *Gen. A.E. Anderson* (ex-AP 111), *Gen. W.A. Mann* (ex-AP 112), *Gen. William Mitchell* (ex-AP 114), and *Gen. J.C. Breckenridge* (ex-AP 176); these, plus three Navy-owned units, are likely to be disposed of shortly.

CABLE SHIPS (T-ARC)

◆ **1 new construction** Bldr: National Steel, San Diego, Calif.

	Laid down	L	In serv.
T-ARC 7 ZEUS	1-6-81	9-10-82	19-3-84

Authorized: FY 79

Zeus (T-ARC 7)—on trials L. & L. Van Ginderen, 7-85

CABLE SHIPS *(continued)*

D: 8,297 tons light (14,225 fl) **S:** 15.8 kts **Dim:** 153.2 (138.4 pp) × 22.3 × 7.3
Electron Equipt: Radar: 2/navigational
M: 5 G.M. EMD 20-cyl., 3,600-hp diesels, electric drive; 2 CP props; 12,500 hp
Range: 10,000/15 **Fuel:** 1,816 tons **Electric:** 3,500 kw
Man: 88 MSC crew, 8 Navy, 32 civilian technicians, 38 spare berths

Remarks: 3,750 dwt. Ordered 17-8-79 to replace T-ARC. Plans to request a second have been canceled. Has passive tank roll stabilization, two 1,200-hp funnel bow-thrusters forward and two aft. Cable capacity is 1,170 m^3 coiled (about 590 n.m.) plus 1,004 m^3 spare capacity (506 n.m.), and up to 3,117 tons of cable repeaters can be stowed. Will be able to conduct acoustic, hydrographic, and bathymetric surveys. The five main engines also provide for the ship's-service generators; there is also a 500-kw emergency generator. Painted white.

◆ **2 Neptune class (S3-S2-BP1 type)** Bldr: Pusey & Jones, Wilmington, Del.

	L	In serv.
T-ARC 2 Neptune (ex-*Wm. H. G. Bullard*)	1945	1-6-53
T-ARC 6 Albert J. Meyer	1945	13-5-63

Albert J. Meyer (T-ARC 6)—note heavy bow sheaves and OE-82 SATCOMM antennas L. & L. Van Ginderen, 10-85

D: 5,818 tons light (8,510 fl; T-ARC 2: 8,625 fl) **S:** 13 kts
Dim: 112.8 (98.1 pp) × 14.3 × 7.6
Electron Equipt: Radar: 1/Raytheon TM 1650/6X, 1/Raytheon TM 1660/12S
M: 4 G.E. diesels, electric drive; 2 props; 4,000 hp
Fuel: 980 tons (T-ARC 6: 1,129 tons) **Range:** 10,000/13
Man: 16 officers, 58 men MSC, 18 technicians

Remarks: T-ARC 2: 3,929 grt/2,000 dwt; T-ARC 6: 4,012 grt/4,332 dwt. Differ in detail, with T-ARC 6 being flush-decked. T-ARC 2 was in Army reserve from 1946-52, then in U.S. Navy, and was transferred to MSC 8-11-73. T-ARC 6 transferred from Army on 18-9-63. Both have been extensively modernized, including the replacement of the original Skinner Uniflow reciprocating steam plants with diesel-electric machinery: T-ARC 2 from 2-80 to 10-82 and T-ARC 6 from 3-78 to 5-80. Both have a 1,000-hp tunnel thruster forward. Cable capacity is nominally 1,240 m^3 (about 625 nautical miles), and they can carry 2,020 tons of cable repeaters. T-ARC 2 had a helicopter deck; removed during modernization.

Note: *Aeclus*-class cable ship *Aeolus* (T-ARC 3, ex-*Turandot,* AKA 47) was stricken from the Navy List 28-3-85 and transferred to the Maritime Administration for disposal.

FLEET TUGS

◆ **7 Powhatan class** Bldr: Marinette Marine, Wisc.

	Laid down	L	In serv.
T-ATF 166 Powhatan	30-9-76	24-6-78	15-6-79
T-ATF 167 Narragansett	5-5-77	28-11-78	9-1-79
T-ATF 168 Catawba	14-12-77	12-5-79	28-5-80
T-ATF 169 Navajo	14-12-77	20-12-79	13-6-80
T-ATF 170 Mohawk	22-3-79	5-4-80	16-10-80
T-ATF 171 Sioux	22-3-79	30-10-80	12-5-81
T-ATF 172 Apache	22-3-79	20-12-80	30-7-81

Authorized: 1 in FY 75, 3 in FY 76, 3 in FY 78

D: 2,000 tons (2,260 fl) **S:** 15 kts **Dim:** 73.2 (68.88 pp) × 12.8 × 4.6
Electron Equipt: Radar: 1/Raytheon TM 1660/12S, 1/SPS-53
M: 2 G.M. EMD 20-645X7 diesels, electric drive; 2 Kort-nozzle props; 4,500 hp (3,600 sust.)
Electric: 1,200 kw **Fuel:** 600 tons **Range:** 10,000/13
Man: 6 officers, 14 men + Navy communications team

Remarks: Modified oilfield-supply-boat design built to merchant marine specifications. If required, could mount two 20-mm AA (I × 2) and two 12.7-mm machine guns (I × 2). Five were requested under FY 78, three approved. Have a 300-hp bow-thruster and one 10-ton electrohydraulic crane. Can carry the Mk 1 Mod. 1, 90-ton deep-diving

Navajo (T-ATF 169)—note bow anchor slot L. & L. Van Ginderen, 10-84

Apache (T-ATF 172) G. Arra, 12-85

support module on the stern and can support a 20-man Navy salvage team. Have a 60-ton bollard-pull capacity. Foam firefighting equipment. Hull has unusual double-chine configuration. Electrohydraulic 10-ton crane.

MILITARY SEALIFT COMMAND
CHARTERED FLEET

The following section describes those MSC-controlled ships on long-term charter, beginning with the 13 units intended for the Afloat Prepositioning Force (formerly the Rapid Deployment Logistics Force).

AFLOAT PREPOSITIONING FORCE (Formerly "Rapid Deployment Force")

◆ **3 (+2) 2nd Lt John P. Bobo class Maritime Prepositioning Ships**
Bldr: General Dynamics, Quincy

	Laid down	L	In serv.
2nd Lt John P. Bobo	16-9-83	19-1-85	14-2-85
Pfc Dewayne F. Williams	16-9-83	18-5-85	6-6-85
1st Lt Baldomero Lopez	3-84	26-10-85	23-11-85
1st Lt Jack Lummus	6-84	22-2-86	3-86
Sgt William R. Button	11-84	5-86	6-86

D: 22,700 tons light (41,700 fl) **S:** 18.8 kts (trials); 17.7 kts sustained
Dim: 205.18 (187.32 pp/199.00 wl) × 32.16 × 8.99

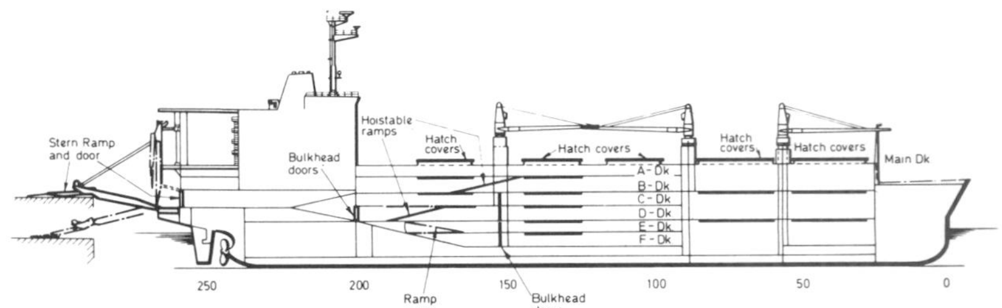

2nd Lt John P. Bobo Navire, 3-83

AFLOAT PREPOSITIONING FORCE *(continued)*

2nd Lt. John P. Bobo Gen. Dynamics, 2-85

2nd Lt. John P. Bobo D. Price, 3-85

Electron Equipt: Radar: 2/navigational
M: 2 Stork Werkspoor 18TM410V diesels; 1 prop; 26,400 hp
Electric: 7,850 kw **Range:** 11,107/17.7 **Fuel:** 3,080 tons
Man: 30 contractor crew, 7 MSC crew, 7 Navy, 25 maintenance crew + 102 troops

Remarks: 44,543 grt/26,523 dwt (22,700 cargo dwt)/14,461 nrt. First two contracted for on 17-8-82, others on 14-1-83. Intended to transport material needed for ¼ of one Marine Assault Battalion. Will be operated by the builder's crews. In addition to listed personnel, will have 102 temporary berths. Cargo capacity includes up to 522 standard 20-ft. vans (350 for ammunition, 110 general stores, 30 with fuel drums, and 32 refrigerated), plus 14,000 m² of roll-on/roll-off vehicle capacity to carry up to 1,400 vehicles. A Navire stern slewing ramp provides access to the six vehicle decks and can either discharge 60-ton vehicles to a pier or amphibious vehicles of up to 23 tons directly into the water; the stern door is 11 × 4.55 m. The upper deck will be used to stow 2 LCM(8) landing craft, 6 unpowered causeway sections, 4 powered causeway sections, a warping tug, 4 pipe trailers and 16 hose reels. The ships will carry 5,764.6 m³ (1,523,000 gallons) of transferable bulk fuel, plus 2,039 55-gallon drums and will also transport 307 m³ of potable water. Five 39-ton pedestal cranes are fitted, with two sets being paired, and there is a large helicopter deck at the stern. A 1,000-hp bow-thruster is fitted. Unloading rates: all vehicles and ⅛ cargo at a pier in 12 hrs; all cargo at a pier in 3 days; all cargo while moored out in 5 days; there is a 4-point mooring system. Operated on expected 25-year charter by American Overseas Marine. *Bobo* is in MPS Squadron One; rest will form MPS Squadron 3 in 10-86.

◆ **5 Cpl Louis J. Hauge, Jr. class** Bldr: Odense SY, Lindo, Denmark

	In serv.	Acq.	Conv. by	In serv.
Cpl Louis J. Hauge, Jr. (ex-*Estelle Maersk*)	10-79	3-1-83	Bethlehem SY, Baltimore, Md.	7-9-84
Pfc William B. Baugh (ex-*Eleo Maersk*)	4-79	17-1-83	Bethlehem SY, Beaumont, Tx.	29-10-84
Pfc James Anderson, Jr. (ex-*Emma Maersk*)	6-79	31-10-83	Bethlehem SY, Baltimore, Md.	26-3-85
1st Lt Alex Bonnyman (ex-*Emelie Maersk*)	1-80	30-1-84	Bethlehem SY, Beaumont, Tx.	26-9-85
Pvt Harry Fisher (ex-*Evelyn Maersk*)	4-80	2-4-83	Bethlehem SY, Baltimore, Md.	12-9-85

Cpl. Louis J. Hauge, Jr. Bethlehem Steel, 1985

PFC James Anderson, Jr. G. Arra, 10-85

D: 28,249 tons light (46,484 fl) **S:** 18.5 kts (17.2 sust.)
Dim: 230.25 (215.00 pp) × 27.48 × 10.02
Electron Equipt: Radar: 2/navigational **Fuel:** 3,228 tons
M: 1 Sulzer 7RND 76M, 7-cyl. diesel; 1 prop; 16,800 hp
Electric: 4,250 kw **Range:** 10,800/17.2
Man: 30 contractor and 7 MSC crew, Navy, 30 maintenance crew + 80 troops

Remarks: Operated by Maersk Lines on long-term charter. Carry ⅙ of the vehicles, equipment, and supplies to outfit a Marine Assault Battalion. Transport up to 413 containers (280 ammunition, 86 general cargo, 23 drummed fuel, 24 refrigerated), plus providing 11,369 m² vehicle cargo space. There are 4/30-ton and 2/36-ton pedestal cranes, side-loading vehicle ports amidships, and a Navire slewing ramp has been added aft, beneath a helicopter deck. There are 8 cargo hatches, and three vehicle parking decks. Liquid cargo includes 4,920 m³ transferable vehicle fuel, 504 m³ potable water, and 2,252 m³ of lube oil. There is a bow-thruster. First 3 ordered 17-8-82, others on 14-1-83. All five are part of Maritime Prepositioning Ship Squadron 2, operating in the Western Pacific. *Bonnyman* originally to be named *Ist Lt. Alexander Bonnyman, Jr.*

◆ **3 SGT Matej Kocak class** Bldr: Sun Shpbldg., Chester, Pa.

	In serv.	Converted by	In serv.
Sgt Matej Kocak (ex-*John D. Waterman*)	14-3-81	National Steel, San Diego	5-10-84
Pfc Eugene A. Obregon (ex-*Thomas Heywood*)	11-82	National Steel, San Diego	15-1-85
Maj Stephen W. Pless (ex-*Charles Carroll*)	3-83	National Steel, San Diego	1-5-85

D: 15,000 tons light (38,500 fl) **S:** 20.9 kts
Dim: 210.46 (195.07 pp) × 32.16 × 10.06
Electron Equipt: Radar: 2/navigational
M: 2 sets G.E. GT; 1/6-bladed prop; 32,000 hp **Boilers:** 2; . . .
Fuel: 3,450 tons (+ 300 tons diesel) **Range:** 13,000/20.9
Man: 85 crew, 7 MSC crew, 8 Navy, 25 maintenance crew

Sgt. Matej Kocak MSC, 10-84

AFLOAT PREPOSITIONING FORCE *(continued)*

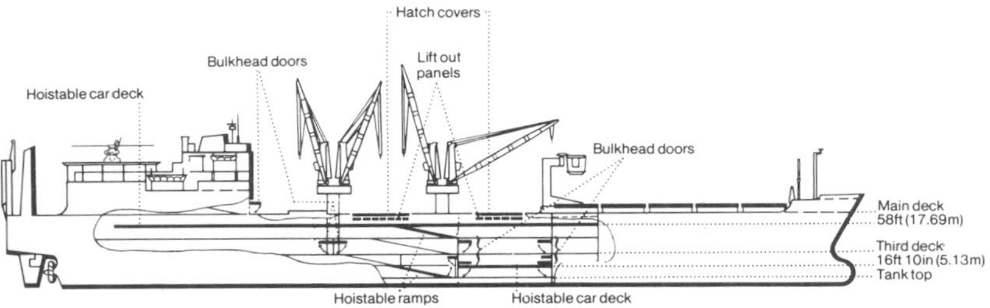

Sgt. Matej Kocak class Navire, 1982

Maj. Stephen W. Pless—with 20-ft. containers forward, pontoon sections and an LCM(8) on deck amidships MSC, 5-85

REMARKS: 25,426 grt/22,910 dwt. First two contracted for on 17-8-82, third on 14-1-83 with Waterman Steamship Co. as operator. Intended to transport ¼ of the vehicles, fuel, supplies, and provisions to support a Marine Assault Battalion. Will carry 213 ammunition containers, 150 "Lo/Lo" containers, 10 general cargo containers, 32 drummed fuel containers, and 32 refrigerated containers, plus a large number of vehicles and cargo fuel and water. Not lengthened during conversion, but helicopter deck and ramp added. Have paired 50-ton and paired 35-ton portal cranes and retain a traveling container gantry forward. Owned by various investment consortia. All operated from U.S. East Coast as MPS Squadron 1.

GENERAL CARGO SHIPS

◆ **1 Antarctic support ship** Bldr: . . . , West Germany (In serv. 1-80)

GREEN WAVE (ex-*Woerman Mira*)

D: . . . **S:** 17 kts **Dim:** 154.5 × 21.3 × 7.6
M: Diesels **Range:** 11,000/17 **Fuel:** 7,725 tons
Man: . . .

REMARKS: 9,521 grt/12,487 dwt. Charted 8-84 for 4 to 5 years from Central Gulf Lines to act as Antarctic supply ship in place of *Southern Cross* (T-AK 285). Has ice-strengthened hull, long hatches for container or break-bulk cargo. Six 25-ton cranes, four of which can be ganged to lift up to 80 tons from holds 3 and 4.

◆ **1 C5-78 Type Combination Cargo ship** Bldr: Ingalls SY, Pascagoula

	In serv.	Chartered	To
ROVER (ex-*American Rover*, ex-*Defiance*, ex-*Mormacsea*)	4-69	6-3-82	6-3-87

Rapid L. & L. Van Ginderen, 5-84

D: 27,980 tons (fl) **S:** 23.6 kts **Dim:** 183.33 (170.69 pp) × 27.43 × 10.39
Electron Equipt: Radar: 2/navigational
M: 2 sets G.E. GT; 1 prop; 30,000 hp **Boilers:** 2 Combustion Eng.; 74 kg/cm²
Fuel: 2,790 tons **Electric:** 3,000 kw **Range:** 12,000/23.6

REMARKS: 11,757 grt/15,694 dwt. Chartered from Central Gulf Lines. Cargo: 70 standard containers, plus 33,814 m³ dry cargo volume. Stern door for vehicle cargo, seven hatches. Sister *Rapid* off-charter 12-85.

◆ **2 Maritime Commission C4-S-69 Type** Bldr: Avondale SY, Westwego, La.

	In serv.	Chartered	To
AMERICAN TITAN (ex-*Colorado*)	9-68	29-7-81	14-9-86
AMERICAN TROJAN* (ex-*Montana*)	1-69	1-12-81	23-12-86

* Near-Term Prepositioning Force

American Spitfire at Diego Garcia MSC, 1982

D: 21,617 tons (fl) **S:** 23 kts **Dim:** 176.48 (165.96 pp) × 24.99 × 9.78
M: 2 sets G.E. GT; 1 prop; 24,000 hp **Boilers:** 2 Babcock & Wilcox
Electric: 2,000 kw **Fuel:** 2,658 tons **Range:** 12,000/23
Man: 36 tot.

REMARKS: 13,053 grt/13,074 dwt. Cargo: 21,665 m³ bale dry cargo/1,133 m³ refrigerated. Can carry standard shipping containers and can also accommodate 7,000 bbl liquid cargo. Seven cargo holds. Cranes: one 70-ton, eight 20-tcn, eight 10-ton, eight 5-ton. Charters from United States Lines, have an option for extension into 1986. Gray-painted, MARISAT terminals added, extra cargo containers even-stacked on superstructure. Sister *American Spitfire* off-charter 12-85.

◆ **3 Maritime Commission C4-S-66 type** Bldr: Avondale SY, Westwego, La.

	In serv.	Chartered	To
ELIZABETH LYKES*	1-66	1983	5-88
LETITIA LYKES*	1-68	23-5-83	23-5-88
LOUISE LYKES	1965	5-84	5-88

* Near-Term Prepositioning Force

D: 21,840 tons (fl) **S:** 20 kts **Dim:** 164.59 (156.94 pp) × 23.16 × 9.96
Electron Equipt: Radar: 1/navigational **Electric:** 1,500 kw
M: 2 sets de Laval or Westinghouse GT; 1 prop; 15,500 hp
Boilers: 2 Foster-Wheeler; 49 kg/cm² **Fuel:** 2,753 tons
Range: 12,000/20

REMARKS: 10,723 grt/14,662 dwt. Chartered from Lykes Brothers Lines. Cargo: 21,240 m³ bale, plus 4,000 bbl liquid. Six hatches; one 80-ton Stülcken boom, 20 smaller capacity. *Letitia Lykes* carries the 1,000-bed "Navy Rapidly Deployable Medical Facility," replacing the Army portable medical facility carried by *Gulf Trader* at Diego Garcia on 30-6-83. Thirteen sister ships are in the Ready Reserve Force.

◆ **1 Maritime Commission C5-S-75 class** Bldr: . . . (In serv. 1-68)

PRESIDENT ADAMS

D: . . . **S:** 20.8 kts **Dim:** 184.4 × 25.0 × 10.7
M: GT; 1 prop; . . . hp **Range:** 14,000/20 **Fuel:** 3,570 tons
Man: . . .

REMARKS: 15,949 grt/22,208 dwt. Chartered 1984 from American President Lines for the Near-Term Prepositioning Force, but later used in ocean transportation.

◆ **2 Maritime Commission C4-S-64 class** Bldr: . . .

SANTA ADELA (In serv. 1-66) SANTA JUANA (In serv. 1-66)

D: . . . **S:** 20.8 kts **Dim:** 165.8 × 22.9 × 9.8
M: GT; 1 prop; . . . hp **Range:** 7,000/20 **Fuel:** 2,354 tons
Man: . . .

REMARKS: 11,039 grt/13,695 dwt. Chartered 1984 from Vessel Charters, Inc. and Prudential Lines. Have 19,400 m³ dry cargo capacity plus 481 m³ refrigerated cargo and 9,000 bbl liquid cargo.

◆ **1 Maritime Commission C4-S-58 type** Bldr: Ingalls SB, Pascagoula

	In serv.	Chartered	To
DAWN (ex-. . .)	6-63	3-5-80	3-5-88

Dawn L. & L. Van Ginderen, 9-84

GENERAL CARGO SHIPS *(continued)*

D: 17,379 tons (fl) **S:** 20 kts **Dim:** 174.35 (164.90 pp) × 22.86 × 9.40
Electron Equipt: Radar: . . .
M: 2 sets G.E. GT; 1 prop; 18,150 hp **Boilers:** 2 Foster-Wheeler; 49 kg/cm²
Electric: 1,800 kw **Fuel:** 3,353 tons **Range:** 17,000/20

REMARKS: 11,309 grt/12,728 dwt. Chartered from Central Gulf Lines; extended 5-84. Cargo: 17,841 m³ dry bale cargo, plus 821 m³ refrigerated and 8,000 bbl liquid cargo.

FLOAT-ON/FLOAT-OFF CARGO SHIPS

◆ **1 converted tanker** Bldr: Eriksbergs Mek. Verkstads, Gothenburg, Sweden (In serv. 17-9-75)

AMERICAN CORMORANT (ex-*Ferncarrier*, ex-*Kollbris*)

American Cormorant—as *Ferncarrier*, with a drilling rig as cargo
Dyvi Heavy Lift, 1982

D: . . . **S:** 15 kts **Dim:** 225.06 (213.90 pp) × 41.15 × 9.96 (20.05 flooded)
M: 1 Eriksberg/Burmeister & Wain 10K84EF 10-cyl., 114-rpm diesel; 1 prop; 25,000 hp (19,700 under owner's restrictions
Range: 23,700/13 **Electric:** 3,360 kw **Endurance:** 76 days

REMARKS: 47,500 dwt. Former 135,900-dwt tanker converted to a heavy-lift float-on/float-off cargo ship in 1982. Capacity: 45,000 tons on the 120-m × 42-m, 4,870-m² midbody cargo deck created by removing the upper portions of the cargo tanks and reducing original length by 55 m. Chartered 10-85 for 18 mos. to test "flo-flo" utility for Military Sealift Command missions.

VEHICLE CARGO SHIPS

◆ **1 Finneagle class** Bldr: Kockums, Mälmo, Sweden

	In serv.	Chartered	To
AMERICAN EAGLE (ex-*Zenit Eagle*, ex-*Finneagle*)	20-2-81	6-83	. . .

American Eagle L. & L. Van Ginderen, 4-85

D: . . . **S:** 19.5 kts **Dim:** 194.00 (180.80 pp) × 28.00 × 9.00
Electron Equipt: Radar: 2/navigational
M: 2 Cegielski-Sulzer 6RND68M diesels; 1 prop; 21,500 hp
Electric: . . . **Fuel:** 2,850 tons **Range:** 16,000/19

REMARKS: 15,700 grt/20,404 dwt. Chartered 6-83 for U.S.-Europe service. Versatile design capable of transporting up to 1,040 standard 20-ft. cargo vans or vehicles, with 10,500 m³ parking space for the latter. Has two side-by-side stern ramps, two bow-thrusters. Can carry up to 8,500 tons salt-water ballast.

◆ **1 former German vehicle cargo ship** Bldr: Howaldtswerke, Kiel

	In serv.	Chartered	To
LYRA* (ex-*Reichenfels*)	30-9-77	27-5-81	. . .

* In Near-Term Prepositioning Force

Lyra R.A.N., 1982

D: 9,870 tons light (24,555 fl) **S:** 21 kts
Dim: 193.32 (178.00 pp) × 27.00 × 8.61
Electron Equipt: Radar: 1/Decca RM 1229, 1/Decca TM-S 1230
M: 12 M.A.N. 9L52/55A diesels; 1 CP prop; 18,990 hp (sust.)—2 Lips 1,200-hp bow-thrusters
Electric: 4,590 kw **Fuel:** 2,579 tons **Range:** 27,000/18 **Man:** 49 tot.

REMARKS: 12,160 grt/14,591 dwt. Chartered from Lykes Bros., along with the similar *Cygnus* (ex-*Rabenfels*); both had been purchased from the defunct Hansa Lines on 19-1-81. *Lyra* has an articulated slewing stern ramp capable of supporting 160 tons. Vehicle cargo can also enter via two 4.65 × 4.20 side ports. 316 20-ft or 156 40-ft cargo containers can be stowed on deck, while below decks can accommodate the equivalent of 180 40-ft wheeled trailers. A portable ramp is used between the first and second vehicle decks, and there are two 80-ton vehicle elevators serving the inner bottom. Can carry up to 6,500 tons of water ballast.

◆ **1 former German vehicle cargo ship** Bldr: Sasebo Heavy Industries, Japan

	L	In serv.	Chartered	To
CYGNUS (ex-*Rabenfels*)	30-3-77	8-7-77	28-3-81	. . .

Cygnus G. Gyssels, 9-83

D: 26,455 tons (fl) **S:** 21.4 kts (trials)
Dim: 193.21 (178.00 pp) × 27.00 × 9.12
Electron Equipt: Radar: 1/Decca RM 1229, 1/Decca TM-S 1230
M: 2 Kawasaki-M.A.N. 9L 52/5A diesels; 1 CP prop; 18,980 hp
Electric: 4,200 kw **Fuel:** 3,060 tons
Range: 21,600/19.2 **Man:** 49 tot.

REMARKS: 13,098 grt/14,935 dwt. Chartered from Lykes Brothers, who had purchased her from Hansa Lines 19-1-81. Can carry 522 standard 20-ft containers, plus 236 40-ft trailers, the latter in the 42,277 m³ of vehicle space. Has two 1,200-hp bow-thrusters, 160-ton capacity Navire slewing, articulated ramp aft (door 11.2-m wide × 7.5 m high) and two 40-ton capacity side ports. Used in service between U.S. and Europe.

◆ **1 Admiral Wm. M. Callaghan class** Bldr: Sun SB & DD Co., Chester, Pa.

	L	In serv.	Chartered	To
ADMIRAL WM. M. CALLAGHAN	17-10-67	12-67	12-67	. . .

Adm. Wm. M. Callaghan L. & L. Van Ginderen, 9-85

VEHICLE CARGO SHIPS *(continued)*

D: 26,573 tons (fl) **S:** 26 kts **Dim:** 211.61 (193.12 pp) × 28.00 × 8.86
Electron Equipt: Radar: 1/navigational
M: 2 G.E. LM 2500 gas turbines; 2 props; 40,000 hp **Electric:** 1,500 kw
Fuel: 4,421 tons **Range:** 6,000/25 **Man:** 33 tot.

Remarks: 24,471 grt/13,500 dwt. Built for U.S. Navy service, as the earliest example of the current "Build-and-Charter" concept; owned by Sunexport Holdings. Original Pratt & Whitney FT-4 gas turbines replaced 12-77 by LM 2500 engines; used as trials ship for LM 2500 engine life extension and fuel economy improvements. Has stern ramp and four side-loading ports for up to 750 vehicles, on 15,607 m² of parking area. Unusual for a "Ro-Ro" in having full set of cargo booms: 2 of 120-tons capacity and 12 of 5–10 tons; flush hatches permit access to 38,515 m³ of cargo space. Used on U.S.-Europe service.

CARGO BARGE CARRIERS

◆ **2 Maritime Commission C9-S-81D Type** Bldr: Avondale SY, Westwego, La.

	In serv.	Chartered	To
Green Island* (ex-*George Wythe,* ex-*Green Island*)	2-75	17-9-82	17-9-87
Green Valley* (ex-. . .)	1-74	2-84	2-86

* In the Near-Term Prepositioning Force

Green Island J. Jedrlinic, 1980

D: 62,314 tons (fl) **S:** 22 kts **Dim:** 272.29 (243.03 pp) × 30.48 × 12.44
Electron Equipt: Radar: 2/navigational
M: 2 sets de Laval GT; 1 prop; 32,000 hp **Electric:** 4,000 kw
Boilers: 2 Combustion Eng.; 75.7 kg/cm² **Fuel:** 5,800 tons
Range: 15,000/22 **Man:** 32 tot

Remarks: 32,278 grt/46,152 dwt. Chartered from Central Gulf Lines. Unlike many LASH ships, do not have a container-handling capability. Can carry 89 standard LASH barges, loaded and unloaded by a 455-ton capacity traveling crane. Carry a small tug to move the barges.

◆ **2 Maritime Commission C8-S-81b-Type lighter carriers**

Bldr: Avondale SY, Westwego, La.

	In serv.	Chartered	To
American Veteran* (ex-. . .)	1-73	12-4-84	12-4-86
Green Harbour (ex-*Austral Rainbow,*	5-72	27-10-81	27-10-86
ex-*China Bear*)	5-72	27-10-81	27-10-86

* In Near-Term Prepositioning Force

Green Harbour (as Austral Rainbow) L. & L. Van Ginderen, 8-80

D: 44,606 tons (fl) **S:** 22.5 kts **Dim:** 249.94 (220.68 pp) × 30.48 × 10.70
M: 1 set de Laval GT; 1 prop; 32,000 hp **Boilers:** 2 Babcock & Wilcox
Electric: 4,500 kw **Fuel:** 5,500 tons (10,427 max.) **Range:** 13,000/22.5

Remarks: 26,456 grt/29,820 dwt. Converted from cargo-barge-only carriers to container or barge carriers by owners, prior to lease. Can carry up to 71 cargo barges or 840 (*Austral Rainbow:* 1,004) standard cargo containers, handled by a 30-ton traveling crane. The traveling barge crane can lift 446 ton. Also have two 5-ton cranes. Both are carrying palletized munitions, the largest such explosive cargo ever carried by individual ships.

BULK CARRIERS

Note: To support the U.S. "Solid Fuels" program, using U.S. coal for energy at U.S. overseas military installations, one or more bulk carriers are normally on voyage or short-term charter. As of 10-85, the 14,310 grt/25,541 dwt *Overseas Harriette* and *Overseas Marilyn* were on charter.

TANKERS

◆ **3 (+2) Paul Buck (T-5) class** Bldr: American SB, Tampa, Fla.

	Laid down	L	In serv.
Paul Buck (ex-*Ocean Champion*)	26-12-83	11-84	7-6-85
Gus W. Darnell (ex-*Ocean Freedom*)	6-2-84	10-8-85	11-9-85
Samuel L. Cobb (ex-*Ocean Triumph*)	. . .	. . .	11-11-85
Richard G. Matthieson (ex-*Ocean Spirit*)	. . .	. . .	10-2-86
Lawrence H. Gianella (ex-*Ocean Star*)	. . .	. . .	12-5-86

Gus W. Darnell American SB, 9-85

D: 9,000 tons light (39,624 fl) **S:** 16 kts **Dim:** 187.45 × 27.43 × 10.36
Electron Equipt: Radar: 1/. . . nav. **Electric:** 3,400 kw
M: 1 Mitsubishi or Ishikawajima-Sulzer 5RTA-76 diesel; 1 prop; 15,300 hp
Range: 12,000/16 **Fuel:** 1,675 tons **Man:** 23 tot.

Remarks: 19,037 grt/30,150 dwt. First two contracted for with Ocean Carriers, Houston, Texas, on 30-9-82, and other three ordered 24-4-83. Operated by Trinidad Corp., Philadelphia, Pa. Some sections of the ships built at Nashville, Tenn., for later joining to the main body, and the forebodies were subcontracted to Avondale SY. Ice-strengthened hulls. Engines in first two built by Mitsubishi; others by Ishikawajima-Harima Heavy Industries. Cargo: 240,000 bbl. Chartered for five years. Intended to replace T-AOT 149–152, 165, and 181.

◆ **2 Falcon Leader class** Bldr: Bath Iron Works

	Laid down	L	In serv.
Falcon Leader*	7-6-82	26-2-83	19-9-83
Falcon Champion	. . .	10-9-83	19-1-84

* In the Near-Term Prepositioning Force

Falcon Leader Skyfotos, 9-83

D: 42,369 tons (fl) **S:** 16 kts **Dim:** 203.0 (194.8 pp) × 25.6 × 10.97
M: 2 de Laval Enterprise RV16 diesels; 1 prop; 14,720 hp (11,500 sust.)
Fuel: 3,321 tons **Range:** 27,000/16 **Man:** . . .

Remarks: 17,735 grt/33,870 dwt. Maritime Commission T6-M-136A design. Ordered 19-1-81 for Falcon Sea Transport Co. for 5-year charter to MSC. Cargo: 225,000 bbl. *Falcon Leader* replaced *Neches* (T-AOT 183).

TANKERS *(continued)*

◆ **1 New York Sun class** Bldr: Sun SB, Chester, Pa.

	Laid down	L	In serv.
New York Sun	23-3-78	22-7-79	1-81

New York Sun J. Jedrlinic, 1981

D: 40,062 tons (fl) **S:** 15.5 kts **Dim:** 186.50 (176.78 pp) × 27.43 × 11.27
M: 1 Mitsubishi-Sulzer, 122-rpm 6 RND 76M diesel; 1 prop; 14,200 hp (sust.)
Fuel: 10,213 tons **Range:** 12,000/15.5

Remarks: 19,000 grt/33,000 dwt. Operated by Sun Transport Cargo: 247,781 bbl. First U.S. ship to be powered by a low-speed diesel in 50 years. Late note: off charter 1-86.

◆ **3 Maritime Commission T6-M-98 type** Bldr: . . .

Courier (ex-*Zapata Courier*) (In serv. 1-77)
Ranger (ex-*Zapata Ranger*) (In serv. 1-76)
Rover (ex-*Zapata Rover*) (In serv. 1-77)

Rover L. & L. Van Ginderen, 10-83

D: . . . **S:** 16 kts **Dim:** 216.7 × 25.6 × 11.3
M: Diesels; 1 prop; . . . hp **Range:** 12,000/16 **Fuel:** 3,416 tons

Remarks: 21,572 grt/35,100 dwt. Cargo: 308,000 bbl. Chartered from Ogden Transport and operated by Ocean Carriers.

◆ **3 Overseas class** Bldr: Bethlehem Steel, Sparrows Point, Md.

	In serv.	Chartered	To
Overseas Alice*	1-68	8-82	8-87
Overseas Valdez* (ex-*Overseas Audrey*)	1-68	8-82	8-87
Overseas Vivian*	1-69	8-82	8-87

* In the Near-Term Prepositioning Force

Overseas Alice Skyfotos, 2-83

D: 46,273 tons (fl) **S:** 16.25 kts **Dim:** 201.23 (192.03 pp) × 27.49 × 11.17
M: 2 sets G.E. GT; 1 prop; 15,000 hp **Boilers:** 2 . . .
Electric: 1,200 kw **Fuel:** 2,845 tons **Range:** 13,000/16 **Man:** . . .

Remarks: 20,879 grt/38,421 dwt. Cargo: 336,000 bbl. Have 25 cargo tanks. Chartered from Overseas Bulk Tank Corporation (*Overseas Alice:* Inter-Continental Bulk Tankers) and operated by Maritime Overseas Corp.

◆ **1 Japanese-built** Bldr: Kasado SY, Kudamatsu

Knight (ex-. . .) (In serv. 1-58)

D: . . . **S:** 17 kts **Dim:** 201.5 (175.01 pp) × 27.4 × 11.01
M: 1 set GT; 1 prop; . . . hp **Boilers:** 2/. . .
Range: 14,000/17 **Fuel:** 2,871 tons

Remarks: 20,025 grt/34,723 dwt. Cargo: 275,000 bbl. Chartered 6-85 from Heavy Lift Inc.

◆ **1 Maritime Commission T2-SE-A1 class** Bldr: Sun SB, Chester, Pa.

	L	In serv.	Chartered	To
Texas Trader (ex-*Texaco South Carolina*, ex-*South Carolina*, ex-*Diamond Island*)	11-44	12-44	11-80	11-85

Texas Trader J. Jedrlinic, 12-80

D: 33,946 tons (fl) **S:** 14.5 kts **Dim:** 193.2 × 22.6 × 10
M: 1 set G.E. GT, electric drive; 1 prop; 10,000 hp
Boilers: 2 Combustion Engineering; 42 kg/cm², 44°C
Fuel: 2,017 tons **Range:** 12,000/14.5

Remarks: 15,129 grt/27,500 dwt. Chartered from American Trading Transportation Co. Cargo: 237,000 bbl. Stretched from original 159.6-m length in 1969 by Newport News SB & DD.

Note: The Military Sealift Command also voyage-charters tankers as needed to meet fuel and liquid cargo commitments around the world. As of 10-85, there were two U.S. registry tankers in this status: *Chablis* (30,806 dwt) and *Mormacstar* (38,300 dwt); see last edition for further details. Also under MSC control are tankers used to support the U.S. Strategic Petroleum Reserve; however, in late 1985, no tankers were on charter for that purpose.

◆ **1 coastal tanker** Bldr: . . .

Bravado (In serv. 1-77)

D: . . . **S:** 12.5 kts **Dim:** 92.7 × 14.6 × 6.7
M: 1 diesel; 1 prop; . . . hp **Range:** 6,000/12 **Fuel:** 250 tons

Remarks: 2,110 grt/4,330 dwt. Cargo: 28,000 bbl. Chartered from Sealift, Inc. and operated by Ocean Carriers in the Western Pacific in place of three MSC-owned T-AOG since 1984. Also on charter for the same purpose in the Pacific area are the combination articulated tug/barges *Kings Challenger/Barge Hanna 4002* and *Seneca/Barge 255.*

READY RESERVE FORCE

The Ready Reserve Force (RRF) is a group of vessels maintained within the National Defense Reserve Fleet (NDRF) by the Maritime Administration (MARAD) in 5- 10- or 20-day readiness status. RRF ships are activated by a Navy (Military Sealift Command) request to MARAD. Selected ships are exercised periodically. Acquisition and maintenance of the RRF ships are funded by the Navy, which retains ownership of former naval units included in the fleet. As of 12-85 there were 73 ships in the RRF, most of them maintained at NDRF anchorages at Beaumont, Texas, Suisun Bay, California, and in the James River, Virginia. In addition to these ships, there are approximately 135 units in the NDRF that could be activated given longer notice. The RRF is scheduled to grow to 116 ships by the late 1980s.

ROLL-ON/ROLL-OFF CARGO SHIPS

◆ **5 former Barber Line ships**

	Bldr	In serv.
Cape Decision (ex-*Tombara*)	Eriksberg, Göteborg	30-8-73
Cape Diamond (ex-*Tricolor*)	Ch. de France, Donkerque	9-72
Cape Domingo (ex-*Tarago*)	Ch. de France, Donkerque	1-73
Cape Douglas (ex-*Lalandia*)	Eriksberg, Göteborg	22-2-73
Cape Ducato (ex-*Berenduna*)	Eriksberg, Göteborg	9-72

D: 35,173 tons (fl) **S:** 22 kts **Dim:** 207.34 (193.24 pp) × 29.57 × 9.59
Electron Equipt: Radar: 2/Raytheon . . . **Electric:** 4,180 kw
M: 3 SEMT-Pielstick 18PC2V diesels; 1 CP prop; 22,860 hp **Man:** 36 tot.

Remarks: 13,887 grt/21,500–23,725 dwt. Five-deck vehicle cargo ships acquired 1-85 and "reflagged" (safety features upgraded to U.S. Coast Guard standards by Bethlehem Steel, Sparrows Point, Md.). Delivered for storage in the James River, Virginia. Work began 3-85 for completion by 11-85. 1,500-hp bow/1,000-hp stern thrusters; 65-ton stern ramp. 1,327 containers/52,863 m³ bale capacity. Photo in addenda.

◆ **1 Meteor class (C4-ST-67a type)** Bldr: Puget Sound Bridge & DD

	Laid down	L	In serv.
Meteor (T-AKR 9, ex-*Sea Lift*, ex-LSV 9)	19-5-64	18-4-64	25-5-67

ROLL-ON/ROLL-OFF CARGO SHIPS *(continued)*

Meteor (T-AKR 9) L. & L. Van Ginderen, 1984

D: 9,154 tons light (21,480 fl) **S:** 22 kts **Dim:** 164.7 × 25.5 × 8.8
Electron Equipt: Radar: 1/Raytheon TM 1650/6X, 1/Raytheon TM 1660/12S
M: 1 set GT; 2 props; 19,400 hp **Boilers:** 2; 52.8 kg/cm², 471°C
Range: 10,000/20 **Man:** 56 tot. MSC

Remarks: 16,467 grt/12,326 dwt. Cargo: 10,200 tons: 26,819 m³ vehicle parking volume (7,896 m² deck space). Stern and four side ramps for Ro-Ro loading/unloading. Can carry 12 passengers. Authorized as T-AK 278, completed as T-LSV 9, retyped T-AKR 14-8-69. Renamed 12-9-75. Assigned to Rapid Deployment Force 4-80–6-81. Placed in Ready Reserve Force 9-85.

◆ **1 Maritime Administration C3-ST-14A type**

	Bldr	Laid down	L	In serv.
Comet (T-AKR 7)	Sun SB & DD, Chester, Pa.	15-5-56	31-7-57	27-1-58

Comet (T-AKR 7) L. & L. Van Ginderen, 9-82

D: 8,175 tons light (18,286 fl) **S:** 18 kts **Dim:** 152.1 × 23.8 × 8.9
Electron Equipt: Radar: 1/Raytheon TM 1650/6X, 1/Raytheon TM 1660/12S
M: 1 set G.E. GT; 1 props; 13,200 hp **Fuel:** 2,423 tons **Range:** 12,000/18
Boilers: 2 Babcock & Wilcox; 43.3 kg/cm³, 454°C
Man: 16 officers, 40 men MSC

Remarks: 13,792 grt/10,111 dwt. Cargo: 7,350 tons: more than 700 military vehicles in holds totaling 19,370 m³ volume (7.525 m² deck space). Side and stern ramps. Denny-Brown fin stabilizers. Authorized as T-AK 269, changed to T-LSV 7 on 1-6-63, then to T-AKR 7 on 1-1-69. Remains Navy property; placed in the Maritime Administration RRF in 3-85.

AIRCRAFT MAINTENANCE SHIPS

◆ **2 converted Maritime Administration C5-S-78a, "Seabridge" type**
Bldr: . . .

	In serv.	Conversion
T-AVB 3 Wright (ex-*Young America*)	1970	14-12-84 to 3-86
T-AVB 4 Curtiss (ex-*Great Republic*)	1969	. . . 9-86

D: 23,872 tons (fl) **S:** 23.6 kts **Dim:** 183.2 × 27.4 × 9.0
Electron Equipt: Radar: 2/. . . nav.
M: 2 sets GT; 1 prop; 30,000 hp **Boilers:** 2; . . . **Fuel:** 2,904 tons
Range: 12,000/23.6 **Man:** 2 officers, 39 men + 25 officers, 300 Marines

Remarks: Roll-on/Roll-off vehicle cargo and container carriers being converted by Todd SY, Galveston, Texas, to transport the men and equipment vans of a Marine Intermediate Maintenance Activity in support of aircraft deployed ashore. Additional accommodations built on aft and helicopter deck added over former forward hold. Will still be able to carry 664 standard 20-ft containers and 14,000 bbl liquid cargo. Intended to revert to cargo-carrying role after delivering the aviation support personnel and equipment. Will be maintained in the RRF (but not strictly part of it), being broken out for exercises.

Wright (T-AVB 3)—artist's concept S. Holt/MSC, 1983

AUXILIARY CRANE SHIPS (T-ACS)

◆ **2 (+1) Maritime Administration C6-S-1qd class** Bldr: National Steel, San Diego, Cal.

	In serv.	Conv.
T-ACS 1 Keystone State (ex-*President Harrison*)	1-66	5-84
T-ACS 2 Gem State (ex-*President Monroe*)	1965	10-85
T-ACS 3 Grand Canyon State (ex-*President Polk*)	1-65	9-86

Keystone State MSC, 6-84

D: 28,660 tons (fl) **S:** 20 kts **Dim:** 203.82 (192.95 pp) × 23.22 × 10.06
Electron Equipt: Radar: 2/. . . nav. **Electric:** 4,780 kw
M: 2 sets G.E. GT; 1 prop; 19,250 hp **Boilers:** 2; . . .
Range: 13,000/20 **Fuel:** 3,450 tons **Man:** 18 officers, 71 men

Remarks: 17,128 grt/13,600 dwt. Cargo: 303 20-ft containers. "T-ACS" is an authorization number and not an official U.S. Navy hull number designation. Conversion of T-ACS 1 by Bay SB, Sturgeon Bay, Wisc., took place under FY 83 funding; ordered 18-3-83. T-ACS 1 (FY 84) began conversion 9-10-84 by Continental Marine, San Francisco. T-ACS 3's conversion was authorized under FY 85, but had not been contracted for by 10-85. T-ACS 4–6 were authorized under FY 86 and will be of a different class; two per year additional conversions are programmed FY 87-89 for a total of 12.

In T-ACS 1–3, the original cargo-handling gear was replaced by three sets of twin 30-ton cranes mounted on the starboard side. The T-ACS is expected to unload its own container cargo and then unload containers from non-self-sustaining container carriers at the rate of about 300 containers per day; the cranes have a 33-m reach. Additional generator capacity (3,280 kw) was added. In wartime, or during peacetime exercises, the ships will operate under MSC control, with contractor crews; they will be maintained as part of the MARAD-administered Ready Reserve Force. All will carry state nicknames in place of their previous names.

CARGO BARGE CARRIERS

◆ **1 Maritime Commission C8-S-81b type lighter carrier**

Bldr: Avondale SY, Westwego, La.

Austral Lightning (ex-*Lash España*) (In serv. 4-71)

Austral Lightning—with mixed barge and container cargo, at Diego Garcia MSC, 1982

CARGO BARGE CARRIERS *(continued)*

D: 44,606 tons (fl) **S:** 22.5 kts **Dim:** 249.94 (220.68 pp) × 30.48 × 10.70
M: 1 set de Laval GT; 1 prop; 32,000 hp **Boilers:** 2 Babcock & Wilcox
Electric: 4,500 kw **Fuel:** 5,500 tons (10,427 max.) **Range:** 13,000/22.5

Remarks: 26,456 grt/29,820 dwt. LASH-ship, converted from cargo barge-only carrier to container or barge carrier. Can carry up to 71 cargo barges or 840 standard cargo containers, handled by a 30-ton traveling crane. The traveling barge crane can lift 446 tons. Also has two 5-ton cranes. Formerly chartered for the Near-Term Prepositioning Force, for which two sisters will operate. The larger C9-S-81 LASH ships *Benjamin Harrison* and *Edward Rutledge* are in the NDRF at Beaumont, Texas.

GENERAL CARGO SHIPS

◆ **3 Maritime Administration C3-S-76a type** Bldr: . . . (In serv. 1968)

Del Monte Del Valle Del Viento

D: . . . **S:** 18.6 kts **Dim:** 159.1 × 21.3 × 9.4
M: 2 sets GT; 1 prop; 11,700 hp **Boilers:** 2/. . .
Range: 15,000/18.6 **Fuel:** 2,175 tons

Remarks: 10,396 grt/13,039 dwt. Cargo: 17,077 m³ bale dry cargo, 1,246 m³ refrigerated cargo, 11,000 bbl liquid. Six holds. One 75-ton boom, . . . smaller. All laid up at Beaumont, Texas.

◆ **6 Maritime Administration C4-S-65a class** Bldr: . . .

Santa Barbara (In serv. 1967) Santa Elena (In serv. 1967)
Santa Clara (In serv. 1966) Santa Isabel (In serv. 1967)
Sante Cruz (In serv 1966) Santa Lucia (In serv. 1966)

D: . . . **S:** 20 kts **Dim:** 170.7 × 24.7 × 9.1
M: 2 sets GT; 1 prop; 14,000 hp **Boilers:** 2/. . .
Range: 12,000/20 **Fuel:** 2,287 tons

Remarks: 9,322 grt (*S. Cruz, S. Lucia:* 9,313)/12,472–12,693 dwt. Cargo: 20,872 m³ bale dry cargo, plus 7,000 bbl liquid. Can carry 12 passengers. *Santa Isabel* has a 150-ton heavy-lift boom; the others have a 70-ton boom. Seven holds. All laid up in the James River, Virginia.

◆ **5 Maritime Administration C4-S-66 type** Bldr: Avondale SY, Westwego, La.

	In serv.
Cape Blanco (ex-*Mason Lykes*)	9-66
Cape Bon (ex-*Velma Lykes*)	1-67
Cape Borda (ex-*Howell Lykes*)	1-67
Cape Bover (ex-*Frederick Lykes*)	1-67
Cape Breton (ex-*Dolly Turman*)	5-67

Cape Breton (as Dolly Turman) Airfoto, 1981

D: 21,840 tons (fl) **S:** 20 kts **Dim:** 164.59 (156.94 pp) × 23.16 × 9.96
Electron Equipt: Radar: 1/nav. **Electric:** 1,500 kw
M: 2 sets de Laval or Westinghouse GT; 1 prop; 15,500 hp
Boilers: 2 Foster-Wheeler; 49 km/cm² **Fuel:** 2,753 tons **Range:** 12,000/20

Remarks: 10,723 grt/14,662 dwt. Break-bulk ships purchased from Lykes Brothers Lines for $21,250,000 in 1-85. Cargo: 21,240 m³ bale plus 4,000 bbl liquid. Six hatches; one 80-ton heavy-lift boom, 20 smaller.

◆ **18 Maritime Administration C3-S-37c type** Bldr: . . . (In serv. 1963-64)

Cape Ann (ex-. . .)
Cape Alexander (ex-. . .)
Cape Archway (ex-. . .)
Cape Alava (ex-. . .)
Cape Avinof (ex-. . .)
Cape Canaveral (ex-*Allison Lykes*)
Cape Canso (ex-*Aimee Lykes*)
Cape Carthage (ex-*Margaret Lykes*)
Cape Catoche (ex-*Christopher Lykes*)
Cape Chalmers (ex-*Adabelle Lykes*)
Cape Charles (ex-*Charlotte Lykes*)
Cape Clear (ex-*Mayo Lykes*)
Cape Cod (ex-*Sheldon Lykes*)
Gulf Banker
Gulf Farmer
Gulf Merchant
Gulf Shipper
Gulf Trader

Cape Alava W. Donko, 7-85

D: . . . **S:** 18.0 kts **Dim:** 150.8 × 21.0 × 9.75
Electron Equipt: Radar: 1/. . . nav.
M: 2 sets GT; 1 prop; 11,000 hp **Boilers:** 2/. . .
Range: 17,000/18 **Fuel:** 2,827 tons

Remarks: 9,296 grt/12,684 dwt. Cargo: 16,000 m³ dry bale, plus 8,000 bbl liquid. Five cargo holds; 1/60-ton boom, 20 others.

◆ **3 Maritime Administration C4-S-57a type** Bldr: . . . (In serv. 1963)

Pioneer Commander Pioneer Contractor Pioneer Crusader

D: . . . **S:** 21.0 kts **Dim:** 171.0 × 22.9 × 9.8
M: 2 sets GT; 1 prop; 19,500 hp **Boilers:** 2; . . .
Range: 12,000/21 **Fuel:** 2,538 tons

Remarks: 11,164 grt/13,535 dwt (varies slightly). Cargo: 18,210 m³ bale dry cargo, 1,246 m³ refrigerated, 8,000 bbl liquid. Six holds. One 70-ton boom, . . . smaller. All stored at Beaumont, Texas.

◆ **1 Maritime Administration C4-S-1u type** Bldr: . . .

Santa Ana (In serv. 1963)

D: . . . **S:** 20.0 kts **Dim:** 172.2 × 23.2 × 9.8
M: 2 sets GT; 1 prop; 19,200 hp **Boilers:** 2; . . .
Range: 14,000/20 **Fuel:** 3,266 tons

Remarks: 12,724 grt/14,376 dwt. Cargo: 19,059 m³ bale dry cargo, 1,104 m³ refrigerated, 17,000 bbl liquid; can also carry 12 passengers. Has 6 holds; one 60-ton boom, . . . smaller. Stored at Beaumont, Texas.

◆ **1 Maritime Commission C4-S-1u type** Bldr: . . .

California (In serv. 1962)

D: . . . **S:** 20.0 kts **Dim:** 172.2 × 23.2 × 9.8
M: 2 sets GT; 1 prop; 19,200 hp **Boilers:** 2; . . .
Range: 14,000/20 **Fuel:** 3,266 tons

Remarks: 12,693 grt/14,349 dwt. Cargo: 19,059 m³ bale dry cargo; 1,104 m³ refrigerated cargo; 17,000 bbl liquid; 12 passengers. Six holds; 1/60-ton boom; several smaller. Stored at Naval Supply Center, Oakland, Cal.

◆ **2 Maritime Administration C3-S-46a type** Bldr: National Steel, San Diego

Banner (In serv. 1961) Courier (In serv. 1962)

Builder (sister in NDRF) L. & L. Van Ginderen, 1-84

D: 19,400 tons (fl) **S:** 18.5 kts **Dim:** 150.26 (143.26 pp) × 22.25 × 9.32
Electron Equipt: Radar: 2/. . . nav.
M: 2 sets G.E. GT; 1 prop; 13,750 hp **Boilers:** 2 Babcock & Wilcox; 53 kg/cm²
Range: 13,000/18.5 (*Courier:* 9,000)
Fuel: 3,280 tons (*Courier:* 1,333 tons) **Electric:** 1,400 kw

GENERAL CARGO SHIPS *(continued)*

REMARKS: *Banner:* 10,659 grt/12,629 dwt; *Courier:* 11,000 grt/12,705 dwt. Cargo: *Banner:* 18,776 m³ bale dry cargo, 708 m³ refrigerated, 12,000 bbl liquid; *Courier:* 20,277 m³ bale dry cargo; 12,000 bbl liquid. Six holds; one 60-ton boom, 18 smaller, plus 2 cranes. *Courier* altered to carry containers. In James River, Virginia, with non-RRF sisters *Builder* and *Commerce;* sister *Buyer* is in NDRF at Beaumont, Texas.

◆ **1 Maritime Administration C4-S-1Q type** Bldr: . . .

PRESIDENT (In serv. 1961)

D: . . . **S:** 20.0 kts **Dim:** 171.9 × 23.2 × 9.6
M: 2 sets GT; 1 prop; 17,500 hp **Boilers:** 2; . . .
Range: 14,000/20 **Fuel:** 3,211 tons

REMARKS: 13,265 grt/14,244 dwt. Cargo: 14,840 m³ bale dry cargo, 736 m³ refrigerated, 10,000 bbl liquid, 12 passengers. Partially configured for carrying containers. Seven holds. Stored at Suisun Bay, Cal., with non-RRF sister, *Lincoln.*

◆ **5 Maritime Administration C3-S-33a type**

Bldr: Sun SB & DD Co., Chester, Pa., and Todd SY, San Pedro, Cal.

	In serv.
LAKE (ex-*Mormaclake*)	1961
NORTHERN LIGHT (T-AK 285, ex-*Cove,* ex-*Mormaccove*)	1961
PRIDE (ex-*Mormacpride*)	1960
SCAN (ex-*Mormacscan*)	1961
SOUTHERN CROSS (T-AK 286, ex-*Trade,* ex-*Mormactrade*)	1962

Southern Cross (as T-AK 285) G. Gyssels, 6-83

Lake (with Scan beyond) A.D. Baker, 8-84

D: 18,365 tons (fl) **S:** 19 kts **Dim:** 148.15 (139.59 pp) × 20.72 × 8.68
Electron Equipt: Radar: ex-T-AK: 1/Raytheon TM 1650/6X, 1/Raytheon TM 1650/12S; others: 1/. . . nav.
M: 1 set G.E. GT; 1 prop; 12,100 hp (15,700 emergency/11,000 normal)
Boilers: 2 Combustion Engineering; 43.3 kg/cm², 457°C
Fuel: 2,556 (T-AK: 3,064) **Range:** 14,000/18
Electric: 1,275 kw **Man:** 68 togt.

REMARKS: 9,260 grt/12,500 dwt. Cargo: 16,992 m³ bale dry cargo and 1,333 m³ refrigerated cargo, 20,000 bbl liquid cargo. Have 5 holds, plus 10 deep tanks for liquids. One 75-ton, 8/10-ton, and 10/5-ton cargo booms. Accommodations for 12 passengers. *Lake* and *Scan,* stored at Philadelphia NSY, were to have been converted into survey ships T-AGS 39 and 40; *Northern Light* was acquired for the U.S. Navy Military Sealift Command 22-4-80 and laid up in the RRF 9-84, while *Southern Cross,* acquired 30-4-80 for MSC, was laid up after refit in 2-85.

◆ **4 Maritime Administration C3-S-38a type** Bldr: . . .

ADVENTURER (In serv. 1960) AIDE (In serv. 1961)
AGENT (In serv. 1961) AMBASSADOR (In serv. 1960)

D: . . . **S:** 18.5 kts **Dim:** 150.27 × 22.25 × 8.53
Electron Equipt: Radar: 1/. . . nav.
M: 1 set GT; 1 prop; 13,000 hp **Boilers:** 2; . . .
Range: 13,000/18.5 **Fuel:** 2,230 tons

REMARKS: 7,848 grt/10,986–11,089 dwt. Cargo: 16,284 m³ bale dry plus 9,000 bbl liquid. Can carry 12 passengers. Have 5 holds. All stored in the James River, Virginia.

Adventurer—in refit for RRF L. & L. Van Ginderen, 5-84

◆ **1 Maritime Administration C4-S-1H "Mariner" type** Bldr: . . .

CRACKER STATE MARINER (In serv. 1954)

D: . . . **S:** 20.0 kts **Dim:** 171.80 (160.94 pp) × 23.24 × 9.45
M: 1 set G.E. GT; 1 prop; 22,000 hp **Boilers:** 2; 42.3 kg/cm², 467°C
Range: 18,000/20 **Fuel:** 3,808 tons

REMARKS: 9,069 grt/13,409 dwt. Cargo: 17,898 m³ bale dry cargo, 821 m³ refrigerated, 23,000 bbl liquid, 12 passengers. Has six holds. Stored in James River, Virginia, with non-RRF sisters *Old Dominion Mariner* and *Lone Star Mariner;* sister *Hoosier Mariner* is in the NDRF at Beaumont, Texas.

◆ **3 Maritime Administration VC2-S-AP2 "Victory" type**

AMERICAN VICTORY (ex-*Carthage,* AG 185; in serv. 6-45)
CATAWBA VICTORY (In serv. 7-45) HATTIESBURG VICTORY (in serv. 9-45)

D: Approx. 13,000 ft **S:** 16.5 kts **Dim:** 138.76 (133.05 pp) × 18.90 × 8.53
M: 1 set cross-compount GT; 1 prop; 6,600 hp
Boilers: 2; 37 kg/cm², 399°C **Fuel:** 2,881 tons **Range:** 24,000/16.5

REMARKS: 7,637 grt/10,681 dwt. Cargo: 12,829 m³ bale dry cargo. Five holds; one 50-ton boom, 14/5-ton booms. Classic "Victory" ship used in trials 1984-85 to determine continued utility of the 103 remaining ships of this design in the NDRF. *Catawba* and *American Victory* are in the James River with 38 sisters; *Hattiesburg Victory* is at Beaumont, Texas with 18 sisters, and 44 are at Suisun Bay, Cal.

◆ **3 Seatrain-type former T2-SE-A2 tankers** Bldr: Marinship Corp., Sausalito, Cal.

	In serv.	Location
MAINE (ex-*Seatrain Maine,* ex-*Tomahawk*)	4-44	James R.
OHIO (ex-*Seatrain Ohio,* ex-*Mission San Jose*)	1-44	Beaumont
WASHINGTON (ex-*Seatrain Washington,* ex-*Mission San Diego*)	4-44	Beaumont

Washington MSC, 1980

D: . . . **S:** 16.5 kts **Dim:** 170.66 (164.3 pp) × 20.70 × 8.22
M: 1 set G.E. GT, electric drive; 1 prop; 10,000 hp **Electric:** 1,120 kw
Boilers: 2 Babcock & Wilcox; 42.2 kg/cm², 441°C
Range: 12,000/16 **Fuel:** 2,438 tons **Man:** . . .

REMARKS: *Maine:* 8,025 grt/12,249 dwt; *Ohio:* 8,047 grt/12,293 dwt; *Washington:* 8,039 grt/12,292 dwt. Converted to carry containers, railway cars, and vehicles by Maryland SB & DD, Baltimore, for Hudson Waterways Corp. 1966-67, using portions of various tankers plus a new mid-body; ex-original names above are those of the propulsion sections. Can also carry aircraft. Sisters *Florida* and *Puerto Rico* are also in National Defense Reserve Fleet, but not in RRF.

TANKERS

◆ **1 Potomac class** Bldr: Ingalls SB, Pascagoula, Miss.

	Laid down	In serv.
Potomac (T-AOT 181, ex-*Shenandoah,* ex-*Potomac,* T-AO 150)	9-6-55	1-57/14-12-64

Potomac (T-AOT 181)—with MARISAT radome J. Jedrlinic, 12-79

D: 35,000 tons (fl) **S:** 18 kts **Dim:** 189.0 × 25.5 × 10.4
Electron Equipt: Radar: 1/Raytheon RM 1650/6X, 1/Raytheon 1660/12S
M: 1 set GT; 1 prop; 20,460 hp **Boilers:** 2
Fuel: 4,321 tons **Range:** 18,000/18 **Man:** 11 officers, 20 men MSC

Remarks: 15,739 grt/26,040 dwt. Carries 200,000 bbl fuel plus 878 m³ dry cargo. Originally belonging to the *Maumee* class, she was heavily damaged in 1961; only her stern was salvaged. Rebuilt by Sun SB & DD, Chester, Pa., and operated on charter to MSC as the *Shenandoah* from 1964 until purchased on 12-1-76. Reclassified T-AOT on 30-9-78. Placed in RRF at Suisun Bay on 5-3-84. Briefly used for trials with the prototype "Product Transfer System," a 4-mile floating offshore pipeline for bringing fuels to a beachhead.

◆ **1 American Explorer class (T5-S-RM2A type)** Bldr: Ingalls SB, Pascagoula, Miss.

	Laid down	L	In serv.
American Explorer (T-AOT 165)	9-7-57	11-5-58	27-10-59

American Explorer (T-AOT 165) L. & L. Van Ginderen, 4-81

D: 8,400 tons light (31,300 fl) **S:** 20 kts **Dim:** 187.5 × 24.4 × 9.8
Electron Equipt: Radar: 1/Raytheon TM 1650/6X, 1/Raytheon TM 1660/12S
M: 1 set GT; 1 prop; 22,000 hp **Boilers:** 2 Babcock & Wilcox
Fuel: 3,482 tons **Range:** 14,000/20 **Man:** 11 officers, 20 men MSC

Remarks: 14,984 grt/22,908 dwt. Cargo: 174,000 bbl fuel oil, diesel, etc. plus 878 m³ dry cargo. Operated by commercial firm. Retyped AOT on 30-9-78. Deactivated to RRF 6-84 at Beaumont, Texas.

◆ **1 Maumee class (Maritime Administration T5-S-12a type)**

	Bldr	Laid down	L	In serv.
Shoshone (T-AOT 151)	Sun SB, Chester, Pa.	15-8-55	17-1-57	15-4-57

D: 32,000 tons (fl) **S:** 18 kts **Dim:** 189.0 × 25.5 × 9.8
Electron Equipt: Radar: 1/Raytheon TM 1650/6X, 1/Raytheon TM 1660/12S
M: 1 set GT; 1 prop; 20,460 hp **Boilers:** 2 Combustion Engineering
Fuel: 4,321 tons **Range:** 18,000/18 **Man:** 11 officers, 20 men MSC

Remarks: 15,626 grt/26,943 dwt. Cargo: 187,000 bbl fuel oil, diesel, etc. plus 878 m³ dry cargo. T-AOT 149 has ice-reinforced bow. Sister *Potomac* (T-AO 150, now T-AOT 181) rebuilt to different design. All retyped T-AOT on 30-9-78. Attached to the Near-Term Rapid Deployment Force on 30-9-83, but deactivated to the RRF at Suisun Bay 6-84. Two sisters remain in Military Sealift Service.

◆ **1 stretched Maritime Administration T2-SE-A1 type**

Bldr: Sun SB, Chester, Pa.

Chancellorsville (L: 10-43)

D: . . . **S:** 14.5 kts **Dim:** 178.31 (171.91 pp) × 24.46 × 10.06
M: 1 set G.E. GT, electric drive; 1 prop; 7,240 hp (6,000 sust.)
Boilers: 2 Babcock & Wilcox; 42.2 kg/cm², 441°C
Range: 12,000/14.5 **Fuel:** 11,485 tons **Electric:** 1,160 kw

Remarks: 14,445 grt/25,194 dwt. Cargo: 205,000 bbl liquid, 425 m³ bale dry cargo. Stretched with new midbody built by Mitsubishi, Yokohama, by Todd SY, Alameda, Cal., completing 7-61. Stored at Beaumont, Texas.

GASOLINE TANKERS

◆ **2 Alatna class (T1-MET-24a type)** Bldr: Bethlehem Steel, Staten I., N.Y.

	L	In serv.
Alatna (T-AOG 81)	6-9-56	7-57
Chattahoochee (T-AOG 82)	4-12-56	22-10-57

Chattahoochee (T-AOG 82) L. & L. Van Ginderen, 12-83

D: 5,720 tons (fl) **S:** 12 kts **Dim:** 92.0 × 18.6 × 7.0
M: 4 Alco diesels, Westinghouse electric motors; 2 props; 4,000 hp
Fuel: 535 tons **Range:** 5,760/10 **Man:** 51 tot.

Remarks: 3,459 grt/4,933 dwt. Icebreaker-type hulls; originally intended as Arctic/Antarctic support ships. Cargo: 30,000 bbls light petroleum products. Both placed in the Maritime Administration's reserve fleet on 8-8-72; reactivation began 28-11-79 at National Steel, San Diego. Returned to service to replace T-AOG 77 and T-AOG 79, T-AOG 81 on 3-2-82 and T-AOG 82 on 11-1-82. Received new diesel engines. Small helicopter deck aft. Laid up 1984 in Japan as part of the RRF when replaced by chartered tug/barge combinations.

◆ **1 Tonti class (T1-M-BT2 type)** Bldr: Todd SY, Houston, Texas

	Laid down	L	In serv.
Nodaway (T-AOG 78, ex-*Tarcoola*)	19-2-42	15-5-45	11-9-50

D: 2,060 tons light (5,984 fl) **S:** 10 kts **Dim:** 99.1 × 14.7 × 5.9
Electron Equipt: Radar: 1/Raytheon 1660, 1/R.C.A. CRM-N1C-75
M: 2 Nordberg diesels; 1 prop; 1,400 hp **Electric:** 515 kw
Fuel: 154 tons **Range:** 5,500/10 **Man:** 11 officers, 34 men MSC

Remarks: 3,160 grt/3,933 dwt. Cargo: 31,284 bbl light fuels (diesel, JP-5, gasoline). Laid up 1984 at Pearl Harbor as part of the RRF.

UNITED STATES COAST GUARD

Personnel (1-85): 5,181 officers, 1,448 warrant officers, 31,316 enlisted and 728 cadets, plus 5,729 civilians, 16,000 Reserves, and 40,000 Coast Guard Auxiliary

GENERAL

The Revenue Marine, which was created in 1790, became the Coast Guard on 28 January 1915 by act of Congress. Until 1 April 1967 the Coast Guard was part of the Department of the Treasury; at that time it was transferred to the Department of Transportation. The act that created the service calls for it to operate in time of crisis under the control of the Navy. The principal responsibilities of the Coast Guard are:
—preparation and training for combat in cooperation with the Navy;
—enforcement of the laws of the sea and the policing of navigation;
—control of territorial waters, suppression of smuggling, and policing and assisting the fishing industry;
—surveillance of the coasts and protection of access to ports and bases;
—search and rescue at sea, including transocean air routes;
—manning and maintaining aids to navigation: lighthouses, beacons, buoys, and Loran stations (46,000 in all);
—control of piloting and the investigation of accidents at sea;
—control of the safety and seaworthiness aspects of shipbuilding;
—international ice patrols (keeping track of drifting icebergs);
—protection of offshore oil installations;
—pollution control and protection of the environment;
—meteorologic, oceanographic, and hydrographic surveying.

ORGANIZATION

The Coast Guard is divided into two main components, one for the Pacific and one for the Atlantic. Each of these area commands is headed by a rear admiral. The Coast Guard is further divided into twelve Coast Guard Districts in order to fulfill its responsibilities along the U.S. coastline (more than 10,000 nautical miles, not including Hawaii).

A four-star admiral heads the Coast Guard. He is appointed for four years and is assisted by a general staff. The commandant reports to the Secretary of Transportation and not the Joint Chiefs of Staff.

COMPOSITION OF THE FLEET

Coast Guard patrol ships have their names preceded by USCGC (United States Coast Guard Cutter). Cutters and patrol craft are white, icebreakers have red hulls, buoy tenders, black. All ships and craft carry a diagonal red stripe and the USCG shield on the hull.

As of 1-86 the in-service, seagoing USCG fleet was composed of the following:

- **15 high-endurance cutters** (WHEC):
  - 12 *Hamilton* class, 3,050 tons (fl)
  - 1 *Casco* class, 2,505 tons (fl)
  - 2 *Secretary* class, 2,656 tons (fl)
- **33 medium-endurance cutters** (WMEC) from 935 to 1,745 tons (fl)
- **5 icebreakers** (WAGB)
- **3 air-cushion patrol boats** (WSES)
- **79 patrol craft** (WPB), 105 tons (fl) and 66 to 69 tons (fl)
- **43 seagoing buoy tenders** (WLB and WLM)
- **43 inland, river, and construction buoy tenders** (WLI, WLR, WLIC)
- **25 tugs** (WTGB, WYTM, and WYTL)
- **1 officer training ship** (WIX)
- **2 reserve training ship** (WTR)
- **approximately 2,000 small boats under 20 m length**

AVIATION

As of 1-4-85, the Coast Guard had 65 fixed-wing aircraft, which included:

- 23 HC-130 Hercules long-range search-and-rescue aircraft (2 HC-130B, 1 HC-130E, 20 HC-130H)
- 41 HU-25 Guardian patrol aircraft
- 1 Grumman VC-4A Gulfstream-I as a personnel transport
- 1 Grumman VC-11A Gulfstream-II as a personnel transport

Helicopters in use included:

- 4 HH-65A Dolphin for rescue duties (with 86 to follow) (22 delivered by 1-86)
- 31 HH-3F Pelican for rescue duties (with 6 more in storage)
- 64 HH-52A Sea Guard for rescue duties (with 1 more in storaga)

In 6-79, ninety Aérospatiale SA-366N SRR (Short-Range Recovery) helicopters were ordered from France under the USCG designation HH-65A Dolphin; these will replace the HH-52A helicopters. The first HH-65A Dolphin was to deliver in 9-82, with all 90 to be in service by early 1986, but the first was not accepted until 19-11-84; deliveries were to take place at 1/month into 1985, then rise to 2/month.

Although chronically short of funding, the Coast Guard is studying the acquisition of up to 40 HH-60 Seahawk helicopters to replace the HH-3F Pelican; these would be for land-based service and would have manually folding rotor blades. Additional NC-130H long-range SAR aircraft are programmed, and a non-rigid airship is to be leased for trials. Five additional HC-130H approved under FY 86.

HU-25A Guardian — Aerojet General, 1983

USCG HC-130H-7 — Lockheed

USCG HH-52A Sea Guard — USCG

PRINCIPAL U.S. COAST GUARD AIRCRAFT

Class, builder	Mission	Wingspan in m	Length in m	Height in m	Weight in kg	Engines	Max speed knots	Ceiling in feet	Radius (nautical miles)
FIXED-WING HC-130 B/E/H[1] Hercules (Lockheed)	SAR/cargo/personnel transport (Dates apply to HC-130H)	40.42	29.80	11.66	33,397 empty, 49,780 loaded, 70,300 max.	4 Allison T 56-A-15 turboprops; 4,508 shp (4,061 sust.) each	302 kts (287 cruise)	25,000	3,734 ferry, 2,517 with max. payload at 5,000 ft.
HU-25[2] Guardian (Dassault/ Grumman)	SAR	16.30	17.15	5.32	8,618 empty 9,476 loaded; 14,515 max.	2 Garrett AiResearch ATF3-6-2C turbofans; 2,512 kg thrust each	461 kts (40,000 ft); 150 kts (search)	40,000	2,250 SAR
HELICOPTERS:	Mission	Rotor diameter (m)	Length overall (m)	Height in m	Weight in kg	Engines	Max speed in knots	Ceiling in feet	
HH-3F Pelican (Sikorsky)	SAR/ transport	18.90	22.25	5.51	10,000 max.	2 G.E. T58-GE-5 turboshafts; 1,500 shp each	141 kts (109 cruise)	11,400	400
HH-52A Sea Guard (Sikorsky)	SAR	16.17	13.87	4.88	2,306 empty; 3,674 max.	1 G.E. T58-GE-8B turboshaft; 1,250 shp	95 kts (85 cruise)	11,200	475 ferry, 150 SAR radius
HH-65A Dolphin (Aérospatiale)	SAR	11.94	11.43	3.99	1,900 empty; 3,992 max.	2 Avco Lycoming LTS 101-750A-1[3] turboshafts; 680 hp each (646 sust.)	175 kts (145 cruise; 128 SAR)	7,150	420 ferry (4.1 hr mission)

[1] Five HC-130H delivered 1984 with T56-A-7 engines; 4 delivered 1985 with T56-A-15 turboprops and provision for APS-134 radar.
[2] Trials 1983-84 with Aerojet General "Aireye" Surveillance System: APA-131 Side-looking radar (SLAR), Low-light tv (LLTV), RS-18C infrared/ultraviolet linescanner, KS-87B camera.
[3] Later units may receive uprated LTS 101-750A-3 engines.

AVIATION *(continued)*

HH-65A Dolphin USCG

USCG HH-3F Pelican USCG

HIGH-ENDURANCE CUTTERS

◆ 12 Hamilton class (378-ft class)

Bldr: Avondale SY, Westwego, La.

	Laid down	L	In serv.
WHEC 715 Hamilton	1-65	18-12-65	20-2-67
WHEC 716 Dallas	7-2-66	1-10-66	1-10-67
WHEC 717 Mellon	25-7-66	11-2-67	22-12-67
WHEC 718 Chase	15-10-66	20-5-67	1-3-68
WHEC 719 Boutwell	12-12-66	17-6-67	14-6-68
WHEC 720 Sherman	13-2-67	23-9-67	23-8-68
WHEC 721 Gallatin	17-4-67	18-11-67	20-12-68
WHEC 722 Morgenthau	17-7-67	10-2-68	14-2-69
WHEC 723 Rush	23-10-67	16-11-68	3-7-69
WHEC 724 Munro	18-2-70	5-12-70	10-9-71
WHEC 725 Jarvis	9-9-70	24-4-71	30-12-71
WHEC 726 Midgett	5-4-71	4-9-71	17-3-72

D: 2,716 tons (3,050 fl) **S:** 29 kts
Dim: 115.37 (106.68 pp) × 13.06 × 4.27 (6.2 over sonar)
A: 1/127-mm 38-cal. DP—2/20-mm AA (I × 2)—4/12.7-mm mg (I × 4)—2/40-mm Mk 64 grenade launchers (I × 2)—6/324-mm Mk 32 ASW TT (III × 2)
Electron Equipt: Radar: 2/SPS-64(V)6 navigational surface-search, 1/SPS-29D air-search, 1/Mk 35
Sonar: SQS-38—EW: WLR-1, WLR-3

Chase (WHEC 718) L. & L. Van Ginderen, 6-84

Gallatin (WHEC 721)—EW van on helicopter deck L. & L. Van Ginderen, 6-83

Munro (WHEC 724) U.S. Navy, 9-83

M: CODOG: 2 Fairbanks-Morse 38TD8⅛, 12-cyl. diesels, 3,500 hp each; 2 Pratt & Whitney FT4-A6 gas turbines, 18,000 hp each; 2 CP props; 36,000 hp—350-hp retractable bow propeller
Electric: 1,500 kw **Fuel:** 800 tons
Range: 2,400/29; 9,600/19 (gas turbines); 14,000/11 (diesel)
Endurance: 45 days **Man:** 15 officers, 140 men

Remarks: Helicopter platform, 26.82 × 12.2. Living spaces air-conditioned. Laboratories for weather and oceanographic research. Welded hull; aluminum superstructure. Named after early Secretaries of the Treasury and Coast Guard heroes. Thirty-six planned, only twelve built. Mk 56 radar gunfire-control director and Mk 309 ASW fire-control system installed. For FY 85 through FY 88, modernizations will include: replacing the 127-mm gun and Mk 56 gunfire-control system with a 76-mm Mk 75 (OTO Melara Compact) gun and Mk 92 radar gunfire-control system, replacing the SPS-29D radar with SPS-40B, replacing the WLR-1 EW system with SLQ-32 and the Mk 36 SRBOC chaff system, and adding satellite communications gear; provision will be made to carry the LAMPS-I ASW helicopter and one 20-mm Mk 15 CIWS gatling AA gun. Eight are to be modified by Todd SY, Seattle, and the others by Bath Iron Works, Maine; the first ship was to enter the yards in 10-85 for delivery spring 1987, and the last will complete by 3-90. The grenade launchers have replaced the 81-mm mortars formerly carried. The helicopter hangars have been blanked off. SQS-38 is a hull-mounted version of the Navy's SQS-35 variable-depth sonar. WHEC 716–723 have synchronizing clutches; the final three have synchro-self-shifting (SSS) clutches.

◆ 2 Secretary class (327-ft class)

	Bldr	Laid down	L	In serv.
WHEC 35 Ingham	Philadelphia NSY	1-5-35	3-6-36	6-11-36
WHEC 37 Taney	Philadelphia NSY	1-5-35	3-6-36	24-10-36

Taney (WHEC 37)—extra deckhouse atop bridge French Navy, 6-81

D: 2,397 tons (2,656 fl) **S:** 19.8 kts **Dim:** 99.67 (93.88 wl) × 12.55 × 4.57
A: 1/127-mm 38-cal. DP—2/12.7-mm mg (I × 2)—2/40-mm Mk 64 grenade launchers (I × 2)
Electron Equipt: Radar: 1/SPS-64(V)1, 1/SPS-64(V)6

HIGH-ENDURANCE CUTTERS *(continued)*

M: 2 sets Westinghouse GT; 2 props; 6,200 hp
Boilers: 2 Babcock & Wilcox; 28.2 kg/cm² **Fuel:** 572 tons
Range: 4,000/19.8; 8,000/10.5 **Man:** 13 officers, 124 men

REMARKS: Despite great age, comfortable and highly reliable ships. WHEC 37 is the last active survivor of the 7-12-41 Pearl Harbor attack. Has a weather balloon inflation hangar just abaft the stack. All gunfire-control and ASW equipment removed, and SPS-29D air-search radars removed 1981-82. WSR-S1 weather removed from WHEC 37 in 1980. Sister *Spencer* (WHEC 36) was sold late 1981; *Campbell* (WHEC 32) stricken 1-4-82; *Bibb* (WHEC 31) stricken 30-7-85; *Duane* (WHEC 33) stricken 1-8-85; *Ingham* (WHEC 35) was scheduled to strike 12-85, but remained in service into 1-86. *Taney* scheduled to strike 5-86 after nearly 50 years' service.

◆ **1 Casco class (311-ft class)** Bldr: Associated SB, Seattle

	Laid down	L	In serv.
WHEC 379 UNIMAK (ex-WTR, ex-WHEC, ex-AVP 31)	12-2-42	27-5-43	31-12-43

Unimak (WHEC 379) L. & L. Van Ginderen, 6-81

D: 1,766 tons (2,505 fl) **S:** 17 kts **Dim:** 94.7 (91.5 pp) × 12.52 × 3.65
A: 1/127-mm 38-cal. DP—4/12.7-mm mg (I × 4)—2/40-mm Mk 64 grenade launchers (I × 2)
Electron Equipt: Radar: 1/SPS-64(V)1, 1/SPS-64(V)6
M: 4 Fairbanks-Morse 38D8⅛ diesels; 2 props; 6,080 hp **Electric:** 600 kw
Fuel: 400 tons **Range:** 8,000/17; 20,000/10 **Man:** 12 officers, 77 men

REMARKS: The last of a series of small seaplane tenders (AVP), eighteen of which were transferred to the Coast Guard, 1947-48; seven were given to South Vietnam beginning in 1970, and eight have been taken out of service since 1968. WHEC 379 was a training ship from 11-69 until placed in reserve on 30-5-75. She was recommissioned on 15-8-77 for patrol duties in the 200-nautical-mile economic zone. Gunfire-control and ASW systems have been removed. Likely to be decommissioned during 1986.

MEDIUM-ENDURANCE CUTTERS

◆ **5 (+8) Bear class (270-ft class)** Bldr: WMEC 901–904: Tacoma Boatbuilding, Tacoma, Wash.; WMEC 905–913: Robert E. Direcktor, Middletown, Rhode Isl.

	Laid down	L	In serv.
WMEC 901 BEAR	23-8-79	25-9-80	4-2-83
WMEC 902 TAMPA	3-4-80	19-3-81	16-3-84
WMEC 903 HARRIET LANE	15-10-80	6-2-82	20-9-84
WMEC 904 NORTHLAND	9-4-81	7-5-82	17-12-84
WMEC 905 SPENCER (ex-*Seneca*)	26-6-82	17-4-84	23-12-85
WMEC 906 SENECA (ex-*Pickering*)	16-9-82	17-4-84	5-86
WMEC 907 ESCANABA	1-4-83	6-2-85	9-86
WMEC 908 TAHOMA (ex-*Legare*)	28-6-83	6-2-85	1-87
WMEC 909 CAMPBELL (ex-*Argus*)	10-8-84	11-85	5-87
WMEC 910 THETIS (ex-*Tahoma*)	24-8-84	11-85	9-87
WMEC 911 FORWARD (ex-*Erie*)	1-86	6-86	1-88
WMEC 912 LEGARE (ex-*McCulloch*)	1-86	6-86	5-88
WMEC 913 MOHAWK (ex-*Ewing*)	2-86	1-87	9-88

Authorized: 2 in FY 77, 2 in FY 78, in FY 79, 3 in FY 80, 1 in FY 81, 3 in FY 82.

D: 1,200 tons light (1.780 fl) **S:** 19.5 kts **Dim:** 82.3 (77.7 wl) × 11.58 × 4.11
A: 1/76-mm Mk 75 DP—2/12.7-mm mg (I × 2)—2/40-mm Mk 19 grenade launchers (I × 2)—1/HH-52A or HH-65A helicopter
Electron Equipt: Radar: 1/SPS-64(V)1, 1/SPS-64(V)6, 1/Mk 92 fire-control
Sonar: Provision for SQR-19A TASS
EW: SLQ-32(V)1, Mk 36 SRBOC chaff RL (VI × 2)
TACAN: URN-25
M: 2 Alco Model 251, 18-cyl. diesels; 2 CP props; 7,000 hp **Electric:** 1,350 kw
Range: 4,080/18.5; 7,680/15; 10,250/12 **Man:** 11 officers, 89 men

Bear (WHEC 901)—hangar extended USCG, 3-83

Bear (WMEC 901)—hangar retracted USCG, 3-83

Northland (WMEC 904) G. Arra, 12-85

REMARKS: Names have been altered since original listing. Program has suffered numerous delays; first ship was to have completed 31-12-80. WMEC 905–913 originally ordered from Tacoma in 8-80, but lawsuit caused reassignment to R.E. Direcktor, 17-1-81. The latter initially lacked the facilities to build the ships. Intended to be able to act as ASW escorts in wartime. No hull-mounted sonar or on-board ASW weapons. Space and weight reserved for Mk 15 CIWS 20-mm gatling AA gun and two quadruple Harpoon missile-launch canisters. Satellite-communications system will be carried. Can carry van-mounted towed passive sonar array on fantail. Telescoping hangar, provision for fin stabilization. Have six light weapons mountings capable of accepting 12.7-mm mg or 40-mm Mk 19 grenade launchers. Reportedly overloaded and very uncomfortable ships in a seaway; 76-mm gun raised .76 m to reduce damage. Have accommodations for up to 17 officers, 123 men.

◆ **16 Reliance class (210-ft A* and 210-ft B class)**

	Bldr	L	In serv.
WTR 615 RELIANCE*	1	25-5-63	20-6-24
WMEC 616 DILIGENCE*	1	20-7-63	26-8-64
WMEC 617 VIGILANT*	1	24-12-63	3-10-64
WMEC 618 ACTIVE*	2	31-7-65	17-9-66
WMEC 619 CONFIDENCE*	3	8-5-65	19-2-66
WMEC 620 RESOLUTE	3	30-4-66	8-12-66
WMEC 621 VALIANT	4	14-1-67	28-10-67
WMEC 622 COURAGEOUS	4	18-5-67	10-4-68

MEDIUM-ENDURANCE CUTTERS *(continued)*

WMEC 623 Steadfast	4	24-6-67	25-9-68
WMEC 624 Dauntless	4	21-10-67	10-6-68
WMEC 625 Venturous	4	11-11-67	16-8-68
WMEC 626 Dependable	4	16-3-68	27-11-68
WMEC 627 Vigorous	4	4-5-68	2-5-69
WMEC 628 Durable	3	29-4-67	8-12-67
WMEC 629 Decisive	3	14-12-67	23-8-68
WMEC 630 Alert	3	19-10-68	4-8-69

Bldrs: 1. Todd Shipyards — 2. Christy Corp., Sturgeon Bay, Wis. — 3. Coast Guard SY, Curtis Bay, Md. — 4. American SB, Lorain, Ohio.

Diligence (WTR 616) L. & L. Van Ginderen, 1-84

Resolute (WMEC 620) G. Arra, 8-85

D: 759 tons (993* or 1,007 fl) **S:** 18 kts **Dim:** 64.16 (60.96 pp) × 10.36 × 3.2
A: 1/76.2-mm Mk 22 DP — 4/12.7-mm mg (I × 4) — 2/40-mm Mk 64 grenade launchers (I × 2) — 1/HH-52A helicopter
Electron Equipt: Radar: 2/SPS-64(V)1 **Endurance:** 21 days
M: 2 Alco 251B 16-cyl. diesels, 2,500 hp each; 2 CP props; (WTR 615 to WMEC 619: 2 Cooper-Bessemer FVBM12-T diesels, 1,500 hp each; 2 CP props; 3,000 hp
Electric: 500 kw **Range:** 2,700/18; 6,100/14 (*2,100/18; 6,100/13)
Man: 8 officers, 54 men

Remarks: WTR 615 replaced WHEC 379 as reserve training cutter in 1974; she retains full WMEC capabilities. No hangar. Designed to operate up to 500 miles off the coast. High superstructure permits 360-degree visibility. Can tow a 10,000-ton ship. Air-conditioned.

WTR 615 – WMEC 619 originally had CODAG propulsion, with two Solar Saturn T-100s gas turbines providing an additional 2,000 hp; the turbines have been removed. These five ships are being re-engined and otherwise updated by the U.S. Coast Guard Yard, Curtis Bay with Alco 251B engines like their sisters. The remaining ships are to be refitted by private yards beginning in 3-86. Crews are to be enlarged to 86 total, provisions capacities enlarged, and exhausts are to be rearranged; displacements will rise to over 1,300 tons on completion.

◆ **3 Diver class (213-ft class)** Bldr: Basalt Rock Co., Napa, Calif.

	Laid down	L	In serv.
WMEC 6 Escape (ex-ARS 6)	24-8-42	22-11-42	20-11-43
WMEC 167 Acushnet (ex-WAGO 167, ex-WAT 167, ex-*Shackle,* ARS 9)	26-10-42	1-4-43	6-2-44
WMEC 168 Yocona (ex-WAT 168, ex-*Seize,* ARS 26)	28-9-43	8-4-44	3-11-44

D: 1,246 tons (1,745 fl) **S:** 15.5 kts **Dim:** 65.08 (63.09 wl) × 12.5 × 4.57
A: None **Electron Equipt:** Radar: 2/SPS-64(V)1 **Electric:** 460 kw
M: 4 Cooper-Bessemer GSB-8 diesels, electric drive; 2 props; 3,000 hp
Fuel: 300 tons **Range:** 9,000/15.5; 20,000/7 **Man:** 7 officers, 65 men

Remarks: Former salvage ships; WMEC 167, 168 taken over from the Navy in 1946. WMEC 167 served as WAGO 167 from 1968 to 1978, then retyped WMEC. WMEC 6, reactivated from reserve and transferred on loan from U.S. Navy 4-12-80, has a mainmast. Maximum sustained speed is 13 kts.

Escape (WMEC 6) G. Arra, 8-85

◆ **1 Storis class (230-ft class)** Bldr; Toledo SB, Toledo, Ohio

	Laid down	L	In serv.
WMEC 38 Storis (ex-*Eskimo*)	14-7-41	4-4-42	30-9-42

Storis (WMEC 38) 1971

D: 1,296 tons light (1,916 fl) **S:** 14 kts **Dim:** 70.1 × 13.1 × 4.6
A: 1/76.2-mm Mk 22 DP — 4/12.7-mm mg (I × 4)
Electron Equipt: Radar: 2/SPS-64
M: 3 Fairbanks-Morse 38D8⅛ diesels, electric drive; 1 prop; 1,800 hp
Fuel: 330 tons **Range:** 12,000/14; 22,000/8 **Man:** 10 officers, 96 men

Remarks: Rated as WAG until 1966, and WAGB until 1-7-72, when she was retyped WMEC. Resembles a *Balsam*-class buoy tender, but is larger. Has an icebreaker hull, but is no longer considered capable of acting as such. Based at Kodiak, Alaska.

◆ **5 Cherokee and Achomawi* class (205-ft class)**

	Bldr	Laid down	L	In serv.
WMEC 76 Ute (ex-T-ATF 76)	United Eng., Alameda	27-2-42	24-6-42	31-12-42
WMEC 85 Lipan (ex-T-ATF 85)	United Eng., Alameda	30-5-42	17-9-42	29-4-43
WMEC 153 Chilula* (ex-ATF 153)	Charleston SB	13-7-44	1-12-44	5-4-45
WMEC 165 Cherokee (ex-ATF 66)	Bethlehem, Staten I.	23-12-38	10-11-39	26-4-40
WMEC 166 Tamaroa (ex-*Zuni,* ATF 95)	Commercial Iron Works, Portland, Oregon	8-3-43	13-7-43	9-10-43

D: 1,217 tons (1,731 fl) **S:** 16.2 kts **Dim:** 62.48 (59.44 pp) × 11.73 × 5.18
A: 1/76.2-mm Mk 22 DP **Electron Equipt:** Radar: 2/SPS-64
M: 4 G.M. 12-278 diesels, electric drive; 1 prop; 3,000 hp **Electric:** 260 kw
Fuel: 315 tons **Range:** 6,500/16.2; 15,000/8 **Man:** 6 officers, 65 men

Remarks: WMEC 165 and WMEC 166 were the first and last of their numerous group to be built; WMEC 153 is one of a later version that has similar appearance, but her diesels are G.M. 12-278A. WMEC 153, 165, and 166 are former U.S. Navy fleet tugs loaned to the Coast Guard in 1946 and transferred outright on 1-6-69; WMEC 76 and 85 were transferred on 30-9-80 and then towed from San Francisco to Curtis Bay, Md., for refits; they have no 76.2-mm guns. WMEC 76, 85 refitted 12-84 to 7-85 by Atlantic Dry Dock, Ft. George, Florida.

MEDIUM-ENDURANCE CUTTERS *(continued)*

Tamaroa (WMEC 166) J. Jedrlinic, 1982

◆ **3 Balsam class (180-ft.) former seagoing buoy tenders** Bldr: Marine Iron & SB, Duluth, Minn.

	Laid down	L	In serv.
WMEC 292 Clover (ex-WLB 292)	3-12-41	25-4-42	8-11-42
WMEC 295 Evergreen (ex-WAGO 295, ex-WLB 295)	15-4-42	3-7-42	30-4-43
WMEC 300 Citrus (ex-WLB 300)	29-4-42	15-8-42	30-5-43

Evergreen (WMEC 295) G. Arra, 6-85

Citrus (WMEC 300) F. Zeitlhofer, 7-85

Remarks: WMEC 292 reclassified 6-79 to replace *Modoc* (WMEC 194), and WMEC 300 reclassified 2-80 to replace *Comanche* (WMEC 202). Data as for buoy tender sisters on later page. WMEC 300, stationed at Coos Bay, Oregon, has had her hull strengthened for icebreaking. WMEC 292 based at Eureka, Cal. WMEC 295, converted as an oceanographic research ship and redesignated WAGO 295 in 2-73, was redesignated WMEC 295 on 1-5-83. Armament for all is 2/40-mm grenade launchers (I × 2) and 2/12.7-mm mg. All three were proposed for decommissioning in 1982 but remain in service.

ICEBREAKERS

◆ **0 (+2) new-construction polar icebreakers**

Remarks: Congress authorized commencement of studies for a new polar icebreaker class to replace WAGB 281 and 282 in FY 85. Construction funding to be requested in FY 88. A third is desired. Will be 15,000 tons (fl), 137.16 m o.a.

◆ **2 Polar Star class (399-ft class)** Bldr: Lockheed SB, Seattle

	Laid down	L	In serv.
WAGB 10 Polar Star	15-5-72	17-11-73	19-1-76
WAGB 11 Polar Sea	27-11-73	24-6-75	23-2-78

D: 10,430 tons (13,190 fl) **S:** 18 kts **Dim:** 121.91 (102.78 pp) × 25.45 × 1.14
Electron Equipt: Radar: 2/SPS-64—TACAN: SRN-15

Polar Star (WAGB 10) L. & L. Van Ginderen, 1983

Polar Star (WAGB 10) G. Arra, 11-85

M: CODAG: 6 Alco 16V251 diesels, 3,000 hp each; 3 Pratt & Whitney FT-4A12 gas turbines, 25,000 hp each, down-rated; electric drive; 3 CP props; 66,000 hp
Fuel: 3,555 tons **Range:** 16,000/18; 28,275/13
Man: 13 officers, 125 men, 10 scientists, 15 helicopter detachment

Remarks: No additional units planned. Carry two HH-52A helicopters, painted red. Can break 2-meter ice at 3 knots, 6.4-meter ice maximum. Propulsion plant completely cross-connected and automatic. Two 15-ton cranes. Four 20-mm AA (I × 4) and two 40-mm Mk 64 grenade launchers (I × 2) can be installed. Both home-ported at Seattle.

◆ **1 Glacier class (310-ft class)** Bldr: Ingalls SB, Pascagoula, Miss.

	Laid down	L	In serv.
WAGB 4 Glacier	3-8-53	27-8-54	27-5-55

Glacier (WAGB 4)—SPS-6 radar since removed 1972

D: 6,406 tons (8,775 fl) **S:** 17.6 kts **Dim:** 94.5 (88.4 pp) × 22.6 × 8.8
A: 2/40-mm Mk 64 grenade launchers (I × 2) 2/12.7-mm mg—2/HH-52A helicopters
Electron Equipt: Radar: 2/SPS-64
M: Diesel-electric propulsion; 10 Fairbanks-Morse 38D8⅛ diesels and 2 Westinghouse electric motor-generators; 21,000 hp

ICEBREAKERS *(continued)*

Range: 12,000/17.6; 29,000/12 **Man:** 14 officers, 183 men

Remarks: Built for the U.S. Navy and transferred to the Coast Guard on 1-7-66. Two 12.5-ton cranes. Based at Long Beach, Cal. Originally had 2/127-mm (I × 2) and 6/76.2-mm (II × 3) guns. Was to have been stricken in 1992 but may be modernized and retained.

◆ **2 Wind class (269-ft class)** Bldr: Western Pipe & Steel, San Pedro, Calif.

	Laid down	L	In serv.
WAGB 281 Westwind (ex-AGB 6, ex-*Severniy Polyus*)	24-8-42	31-3-43	18-9-44
WAGB 282 Northwind	10-7-44	22-2-45	28-7-45

Northwind (WAGB 282) H. Serig, 7-84

D: 3,500 tons (6,515 fl) **S:** 16 kts **Dim:** 81.99 (76.2 pp) × 19.36 × 8.84
Electron Equipt: Radar: 2/SPS-64
M: 4 Enterprise diesels, electric drive; 2 props; 10,000 hp **Fuel:** 2,200 tons
Electric: 400 kw **Range:** 16,000/16; 38,000/10.5 **Man:** 14 officers, 100 men

Remarks: Can make way in 2.7-m ice. Double hull entirely welded. Telescoping hangar for one HH-52A helicopter. Both reengined 1973-75. Two 12.5-ton cranes. WAGB 281 was in the Soviet Navy from 31-3-45 to 6-12-51.

WAGB 281, damaged by ice in 1984, is laid up at Mobile, Ala., awaiting repair funding. WAGB 282, which is based at Wilmington, North Carolina, is to be refitted under FY 86.

◆ **1 Mackinaw class (290-ft class)** Bldr: Toledo SB, Toledo, Ohio

	Laid down	L	In serv.
WAGB 83 Mackinaw (ex-*Manitowoc*)	20-3-43	4-3-44	20-12-44

Mackinaw (WAGB 83) USCG, . . .

D: 3,049 tons (5,252 fl) **S:** 18.7 kts **Dim:** 88.39 × 22.66 × 5.79
Electron Equipt: Radar: 2/SPS-64 **Electric:** 1,260 kw
M: 4 Fairbanks-Morse 38D8⅛ diesels, electric drive; 3 props (2 aft, 1 fwd); 10,000 hp
Range: 10,000/18.7; 41,000/9 **Man:** 10 officers, 97 men

Remarks: Built for use on the Great Lakes. Helicopter platform. Fitted with two 12-ton cranes. Can break 1.2-m solid ice. Overhauled 1982 at Bay SB, Sturgeon Bay, Wisc.; cranes aft removed and some fuel tankage converted to ballast tanks.

PATROL BOATS

◆ **0 (+0+. . .) SWATH design**

SWATH Patrol Boat USCG, 1985

D: 600 tons (fl) **S:** 20 kts **Dim:** 42.4 × 18.3 × 4.4
A: 2/12.7-mm mg (I × 2)—2/40-mm Mk 19 grenade launchers
Electron Equipt: Radar: 1/SPS-64
M: 2 diesels; 2 CP props; approx. 8,000 hp **Range:** 3,300/12–14
Endurance: 10 days **Man:** 30 tot.

Remarks: Design effort commenced 12-82 for a SWATH (Small Waterplane Area, Twin Hull) patrol boat now planned to be ordered under FY 86. A larger, oceangoing SWATH program has been shelved. The lower pontoon hulls will be 36.5-m long, with a 3.0 m diameter. The helicopter deck will accommodate an HH-65A Dolphin. There will be fin pitch and role stabilizers.

◆ **3 (+13) "Island" (110-ft) class** Bldr: Bollinger Machine Ship & SY, Lockport, Louisiana

	In serv.		In serv.
WPB 1301 Farallon	21-2-86	WPB 1309 Aquidneck	1986
WPB 1302 Manitou	28-2-86	WPB 1310 Mustang	1986
WPB 1303 Matagorda	3-86	WPB 1311 Naushon	1986
WPB 1304 Maui	4-86	WPB 1312 Sanibel	1986
WPB 1305 Monhegan	1986	WPB 1313 Edisto	1987
WPB 1306 Nunivak	1986	WPB 1314 Sapelo	1987
WPB 1307 Ocracoke	1986	WPB 1315 Matinicus	1987
WPB 1308 Vashon	1986	WPB 1316 Nantucket	1987

Farallon (WPB 1301) Bollinger, 9-85

Farallon (WPB 1301) USCG, 9-85

PATROL BOATS *(continued)*

D: 136 tons normal (161 fl) **S:** 29.7 kts **Dim:** 33.53 × 6.40 × 2.23
A: 1/20-mm AA—2/40-mm Mk 19 grenade launchers
Electron Equipt: Radar: 1/SPS-64(V)
M: 2 Paxman Valenta 16 RP200 CM diesels; 2 props; 5,760 hp
Electric: 198 kw **Range:** 1,882 nm (26 kts × 24 hrs + 13.1 kts × 96 hrs)
Man: 2 officers, 2 CPO, 12 men

REMARKS: Fifteen ordered 8-84; 16th ordered 3-5-85 in place of earlier winner Marine Power & Equipment, Seattle, Washington, whose contract was successfully contested by Bollinger. Modified Vosper-Thornycroft design, with increased tophamper. Steel hull, aluminum deck and superstructure. Fin stabilizers fitted. Carry LORAN-C and Omega receivers, IFF transponder, and SQN-18 echo-sounder. Engines governor-limited to 2,880 hp each from nominal max. 4,000 hp. First delivered 23-8-85 for trials; others were to follow at 45-day intervals. Sixteen additional patrol boats authorized under FY 86.

◆ **3 Bell 110 surface-effect patrol boats**
Bldr: Bell-Halter, Inc., New Orleans

WSES 2 SEA HAWK (In serv. 16-10-82)
WSES 3 SHEARWATER (In serv. 16-10-82)
WSES 3 PETREL (In serv. 18-6-83)

Sea Hawk (WSES 2) and Shearwater (WSES 3) Bell Aerospace, 10-82

D: 110 tons (160 fl) **S:** 35 kts (designed; now make about 18 kts)
Dim: 33.53 × 11.89 × 2.36 at rest/1.37 on cushion **Man:** 2 officers, 16 men
A: 2/12.7-mm mg (I × 2) **Electron Equipt:** Radar: 2/Decca 914
M: 2 G.M. 16V149 TI diesels for propulsion; 2 CP props; 3,200 hp; 2 G.M. 8V92 TI diesels for lift; 2 certrifugal; 990 hp
Electric: 60 kw **Range:** 300–500/35; 1,500/23 on cushion

REMARKS: Ordered 6-82 after the very successful trials with *Dorado* (WSES 1), now in U.S. Navy service. Rigid sidewall design, with rubber seal bags fore and aft. Aluminum construction. Based at Key West on anti-drug patrol and intercept duties. Extra equipment has greatly lowered performance; vibration problems have caused redesign of skirt vents.

PATROL CRAFT

◆ **22 95-ft Cape class** Bldr: Coast Guard Yard, Curtis Bay, Md., 1953-59

WPB 95300 CAPE SMALL
WPB 95302 CAPE HIGGON
WPB 95303 CAPE UPRIGHT
WPB 95304 CAPE GULL
WPB 95305 CAPE HATTERAS
WPB 95306 CAPE GEORGE
WPB 95307 CAPE CURRENT
WPB 95309 CAPE CARTER
WPB 95310 CAPE WASH
WPB 95311 CAPE HEDGE
WPB 95312 CAPE KNOX
WPB 95313 CAPE MORGAN
WPB 93516 CAPE FOX
WPB 95317 CAPE JELLISON
WPB 95319 CAPE ROMAIN
WPB 95320 CAPE STARR
WPB 95321 CAPE CROSS
WPB 95322 CAPE HORN
WPB 95324 CAPE SHOALWATER
WPB 95326 CAPE CORWIN
WPB 95328 CAPE HENLOPEN
WPB 95332 CAPE YORK

Cape Corwin (WPB 95326) USCG, 1983

D: 83 tons (105 fl) **S:** 18 kts (cruising, fl) **Dim:** 28.96 × 6.1 × 1.55
A: 2/12.7-mm mg(I × 2)—2/40-mm Mk 64 grenade launchers (I × 2)
Electron Equipt: Radar: 1/SPS-64(V)1 **Electric:** 40 kw
M: 4 Cummins VT-12-M-700 diesels; 2 props; 2,324 hp **Endurance:** 5 days
Range: WPB 95300 to WPB 95311: 460/20; 2,600/9; WPB 95312 to WPB 95320: 460/20; 3,000/9; WPB 95321 to WPB 95332: 500/20; 2,800/9

REMARKS: Two transferred to Haiti (1956), two to Ethiopia (1958), four to Thailand, and one to Saudi Arabia. Nine were given to South Korea (1969-70). Several others have been scrapped. The survivors were reengined and rehabilitated, 1977-81, in lieu of building thirty new WPBs. Sister *Cape Coral* (WPB 95301) stricken 6-6-83, *Cape Strait* (WPB 95308) in 1-83, *Cape Newhagen* (WPB 95318) in 9-82, and *Cape Fairweather* (WPB 95314) 4-3-85.

◆ **53 83-ft Point Class** Bldr: Coast Guard Yard, Curtis Bay, Md. (except WPB 82345 to WPB 83249: J. Martinac SB, Tacoma, Wash.)

In serv: WPB 82302 to WPB 82314: 1960-61; WPB 82318 to WPH 82370: 1961-67; WPB 82371 to WPB 82379: 1970

WPB 82302 POINT HOPE
WPB 82311 POINT VERDE
WPB 82312 POINT SWIFT
WPB 82314 POINT THATCHER
WPB 82318 POINT HERRON
WPB 82332 POINT ROBERTS
WPB 82333 POINT HIGHLAND
WPB 82334 POINT LEDGE
WPB 82335 POINT COUNTESS
WPB 82336 POINT GLASS
WPB 82337 POINT DIVIDE
WPB 82338 POINT BRIDGE
WPB 82339 POINT CHICO
WPB 82340 POINT BATAN
WPB 82341 POINT LOOKOUT
WPB 82342 POINT BAKER
WPB 82343 POINT WELLS
WPB 82344 POINT ESTERO
WPB 82345 POINT JUDITH
WPB 82346 POINT ARENA
WPB 82347 POINT BONITA
WPB 82348 POINT BARROW
WPB 82349 POINT SPENCER
WPB 82350 POINT FRANKLIN
WPB 82351 POINT BENNETT
WPB 82352 POINT SAL
WPB 82353 POINT MONROE
WPB 82354 POINT EVANS
WPB 82355 POINT HANNON
WPB 82356 POINT FRANCIS
WPB 82357 POINT HURON
WPB 82358 POINT STUART
WPB 82359 POINT STEELE
WPB 82360 POINT WINSLOW
WPB 82361 POINT CHARLES
WPB 82362 POINT BROWN
WPB 82363 POINT NOWELL
WPB 82364 POINT WHITEHORN
WPB 82365 POINT TURNER
WPB 82366 POINT LOBOS
WPB 82367 POINT KNOLL
WPB 82368 POINT WARDE
WPB 82369 POINT HEYER
WPB 82370 POINT RICHMOND
WPB 82371 POINT BARNES
WPB 82372 POINT BROWER
WPB 82373 POINT CAMDEN
WPB 82374 POINT CARREW
WPB 82375 POINT DORAN
WPB 82376 POINT HARRIS
WPB 82377 POINT HOBART
WPB 82378 POINT JACKSON
WPB 82379 POINT MARTIN

Point Huron (WPB 82357) L. & L. Van Ginderen, 6-83

D: 64 tons (66-69 fl) **S:** 23.7 kts (*see* Remarks) **Dim:** 25.3 × 5.23 × 1.95
A: 2/12.7-mm mg (I × 2)—2/40-mm Mk 64 grenade launchers (I × 2)
Electron Equipt: Radar: 1/SPS-64(V)1
M: 2 Cummins VT-12-M diesels; 2 props; 1,690 hp **Fuel:** 5.7 tons
Range: 460/23.7; 1,400–1,500/8-9 **Man:** 1 officer, 7 men

REMARKS: Hull in mild steel. High-speed diesels controlled from the bridge. The heavier WPB 82371 and later make 22.6 knots, and have a range of 320/22.6; 1,200/8. WPB 82314 had two gas turbines with 1,000 hp (27-knot potential) and controllable-pitch propellers, but was reequipped with diesels. Well-equipped for salvage and towing. Beginning in 6-65, 26 others were sent to Vietnam; transferred 1969-70.

TRAINING CUTTER

◆ **1 Horst Wessel class** Bldr: Blohm + Voss, Hamburg, Germany

	L	In serv.
WIX 327 EAGLE (ex-*Horst Wessel*)	13-6-36	1-46

D: 1,435 tons light (1,732 fl) **S:** 18 kts **Dim:** 89.9 (70.4 wl) × 11.9 × 5.2
Electron Equipt: Radar: 1/SPS-64(V)1
M: 1 Caterpillar D-399, V-16 diesel; 1 prop; 1,000 hp (10.5 kts); 2,355 m² sail area
Electric: 450 kw **Range:** 5,450/7.5 (diesel)
Man: 19 officers, 46 men, 180 cadets

TRAINING CUTTER *(continued)*

Eagle (WIX 327) 1977

Remarks: Training ship at the Coast Guard Academy, New London. Sisters operate in the Brazilian Navy and Soviet merchant marine. Re-engined and extensively overhauled at the U.S. Coast Guard Yard, Curtis Bay. Has 390 tons fixed ballast.

Note: *Reliance:* (WTR 615, ex-WMEC 615) acts as training cutter for Coast Guard reserve personnel. Four small training tenders, T1 through T4, are used at the Coast Guard Academy for navigational and maneuvering training.

BUOY TENDERS, SEAGOING

◆ **30 Balsam class** Bldrs: WLB 297: U.S. Coast Guard Yard, Curtis, Bay, Md.; others: A: Marine Iron SB Co.; B: Duluth Iron & SB Co.; C: Zenith Dredge Co. — all of Duluth, Minn.

	Bldr	Laid down	L	In serv.
WLB 277 Cowslip*	A	16-9-41	11-4-42	17-10-42
WLB 290 Gentian*	B	3-10-41	23-5-42	3-11-43
WLB 291 Laurel†	B	17-4-42	4-8-42	24-11-42
WLB 296 Sorrel*	B	26-5-42	28-9-42	15-4-43
WLB 297 Ironwood‡		2-11-42	16-3-43	4-8-43
WLB 301 Conifer*	A	6-7-42	3-11-42	1-7-43
WLB 302 Madrona*	B	6-7-42	11-11-42	30-5-43
WLB 305 Mesquite‡	A	20-8-42	14-11-42	27-8-43
WLB 306 Buttonwood†	A	5-10-42	30-11-42	24-9-43
WLB 307 Planetree†	A	4-12-42	20-3-43	4-11-43
WLB 308 Papaw†	A	16-11-42	19-2-43	12-10-43
WLB 309 Sweetgum	A	21-2-43	15-4-43	20-11-43
WLB 388 Basswood†	A	21-3-43	20-5-43	12-1-44
WLB 389 Bittersweet	B	16-9-43	11-11-43	11-5-44
WLB 390 Blackhaw†	A	16-4-43	18-6-43	17-2-44
WLB 392 Bramble‡	B	2-8-43	23-10-43	22-4-44
WLB 393 Firebrush	B	12-11-43	3-2-44	20-7-44
WLB 394 Hornbeam‡	A	19-6-43	14-8-43	14-4-44
WLB 395 Iris†	B	10-12-43	18-5-43	11-8-44
WLB 396 Mallow†	B	10-10-43	9-12-43	6-6-44
WLB 397 Mariposa‡	B	25-10-43	14-1-44	1-7-44
WLB 399 Sagebrush†	B	15-7-43	30-9-43	1-4-44
WLB 400 Salvia	B	24-6-43	15-9-43	19-2-44
WLB 401 Sassafras	A	16-8-43	5-10-43	23-5-44
WLB 402 Sedge‡	A	6-10-43	27-11-43	5-7-44
WLB 403 Spar‡	A	13-9-43	2-11-43	12-6-44
WLB 404 Sundew‡	A	29-11-43	8-2-44	24-8-44
WLB 405 Sweetbrier‡	A	3-11-43	30-12-43	26-7-44
WLB 406 Acacia (ex-*Thistle*)‡	B	16-1-44	7-4-44	1-9-44
WLB 407 Woodbrush‡	B	4-2-44	28-4-44	22-9-44

* has received Service Life Extension overhaul
† has received austere renovation
‡ has received major renovation

D: 935 tons (1,025 fl) **S:** 12.8–13 kts **Dim:** 54.9 × 11.3 × 4.0
A: WLB 297, 389, 401, 402, 405: 2/20-mm AA (I × 2)
Electron Equipt: Radar: 1/SPS-64(V)1
M: 2 diesels, electric drive; 1 prop; WLB 277 to WLB 302: 1,000 hp; WLB 297, WLB 305 to WLB 407: 1,200 hp. WLB 404: 1,800 hp (*see* Remarks)
Range: Most: 4,600/12–18: 14,000/7.4; WLB 297, WLB 306 to WLB 308, WLB 388, WLB 390, WLB 396, WLB 401: 8,000/12; 23,500/7.5; WLB 305, WLB 392, WLB 406, WLB 407: 10,500/13; 31,000/7.5
Fuel: Varies **Man:** 7 officers, 45 men **Electric:** 400 kw

Remarks: *Evergreen* (WLB 295) converted to oceanographic research ship and now used as a patrol ship. WLB 296, WLB 390, WLB 392, WLB 402, WLB 403, and WLB 404 have strengthened hulls for icebreaking, but all have icebreaker hull form. All have 20-ton derrick. These ships have been, or are being, modernized, and have rebuilt G.E. EMD 8-645E6A engines and propulsion motors, improved habitability, hydraulic cargo-handling gear, and bow-thrusters. *Blackthorn* (WLB 391) rammed and sunk 28-1-80, replaced by *Cowslip* (WLB 277), which was previously stricken 23-3-73, sold 1976, repurchased 19-1-81, and recommissioned 9-11-81. *Clover* (WLB 292) redesignated WMEC in 2-80, *Citrus* (WLB 300) redesignated WMEC in 6-79. WLB 404 has a maximum speed of 15 knots. Modernized ships have greater endurance. A total of 14 are planned to receive Service Life Extension, including WLB 290 and 296, completed 1983, WLB 277, completed 25-6-84, and WLB 301 and 302, completed in 1985.

Mallow (WLB 396) D. Westerberg, USCG, 1984

Laurel (WLB 291) G. Arra, 7-85

BUOY TENDERS, COASTAL

◆ **5 Red class (157-ft class)** Bldr: Coast Guard Yard, Curtis Bay, Md.

WLM 685 Red Wood
WLM 686 Red Beech
WLM 687 Red Birch
WLM 688 Red Cedar
WLM 689 Red Oak

Red Cedar (WLM 688) G. Arra, 1976

D: 471 tons (512 fl) **S:** 12 kts **Dim:** 47.9 × 10.1 × 1.9
M: 2 diesels; 2 CP props; 1,800 hp
Range: 2,248/12.8; 3,055/11.6
Man: 4 officers, 27 men

Remarks: WLM 685 and WLM 686 completed in 1964, WLM 687 in 1965, WLM 688 in 1970, and WLM 689 in 1971. Can break light ice. Have 10-ton derrick, and a bow-thruster.

◆ **6 White class (133-ft class)**

WLM 540 White Sumac
WLM 543 White Holly
WLM 544 White Sage
WLM 545 White Heath
WLM 546 White Lupine
WLM 547 White Pine

D: 435 tons (600 fl) **S:** 9.8 kts **Dim:** 40.5 × 9.4 × 2.7
M: 2 Union diesels; 2 props; 600 hp **Range:** 2,100/9.8; 4,500/5.1
Electric: 90 kw **Fuel:** 40 tons **Man:** 1 officer, 20 men

Remarks: WLM 540 completed in 1943, WLM 542 and WLM 543 in 1944; others in 1942. Former U.S. Navy YF (covered lighter, self-propelled). One 10-ton boom. Sister *White Bush* (WLM 542) stricken 16-9-85.

BUOY TENDERS, COASTAL *(continued)*

White Sage (WLM 544) 1976

◆ **1 Hollyhock class (175-ft class)** Bldr: Moore DD Co., Oakland, Cal.

WLM 212 Fir (In serv. 1-10-40)

Fir (WLM 212) 1974

D: 825 tons (986 fl) **S:** 12 kts **Dim:** 53.4 × 10.4 × 3.7
M: 2 diesels; 2 props; 1,350 hp **Electron Equipt:** Radar: 1/SPS-64(V)1
Range: 5,650/12; 8,675/7.5 **Man:** 5 officers, 35 men

Remarks: Redesignated from WLB to WLM on 1-1-65. Has a 20-ton boom. Sisters *Hollyhock* (WLM 220) and *Walnut* (WLM 252) stricken 31-3-82 and 15-6-82, respectively.

BUOY TENDERS, INLAND

◆ **1 (+ . . .) Tern (80-ft.) class** Bldr: . . .

80801 Tern (In serv. 1982)

D: 135 tons (168 normal fl) **S:** 10 kts **Dim:** 24.6 × 7.0 × 1.45
Electron Equipt: Radar: 1/. . . navigational
M: 2 diesels; 2 right-angle hydraulic drive props; 470 hp — 1/125 hp 360-degree rotating bow-thruster
Fuel: 53 tons

Remarks: Prototype for a new class. Can carry and lay buoys of up to 35 tons weight. Considered a "boat," hence no WLI number.

◆ **1 Buckthorn class** (In serv. 1963)

WLI 642 Buckthorn

D: 200 tons (fl) **S:** 11.9 kts **Dim:** 30.5 × 7.3 × 1.2
M: 2 diesels; 2 props; 600 hp **Range:** 1,300/11.9; 2,000/7.3
Man: 1 officer, 13 men

Remarks: Bow rectangular at main deck. Has one 5-ton boom. Based on the Great Lakes.

◆ **2 Bayberry class (65400 class)** (In serv. 1954)

WLI 65400 Bayberry WLI 65401 Elderberry

D: 68 tons (fl) **S:** 11.3 kts **Dim:** 19.8 × 5.2 × 1.2
M: 2 diesels; 2 props; 400 hp **Range:** 800/11.3; 1,700/6 **Man:** 5 tot.

◆ **2 Blackberry class (65300 class)** (In serv. 1946)

WLI 65303 Blackberry WLI 65304 Chokeberry

D: 68 tons (fl) **S:** 9 kts **Dim:** 19.8 × 5.2 × 1.2
M: 1 diesel; 1 prop; 220 hp **Range:** 700/9; 1,500/5 **Man:** 5 tot.

◆ **1 Cosmos class (100-ft class)** Bldr: Burchfield Boiler Co., Tacoma, Wash.

	Laid down	L	In serv.
WLI 313 Bluebell	20-3-44	28-9-44	24-3-45

D: 178 tons (fl) **S:** 10.5 kts **Dim:** 30.5 × 7.3 × 1.5
M: 2 diesels; 2 props; 600 hp **Range:** 1,400/10.5; 2,700/7

Remarks: Four sisters retyped WLIC on 1-10-79.

BUOY TENDERS, RIVER

◆ **0 (+1) new-construction 75 ft.**

Remarks: One new unit requested under FY 86 Budget to act as push-tug for an aids-to-navigation barge on the Arkansas River.

◆ **9 Gasconade class (75-ft class)**

	In serv.		In serv.
WLR 75401 Gasconade	1964	WLR 75406 Kickapoo	1969
WLR 75402 Muskingum	1965	WLR 75407 Kanawha	1969
WLR 75403 Wyaconda	1965	WLR 75408 Patoka	1970
WLR 75404 Chippewa	1965	WLR 75409 Chena	1970
WLR 75405 Cheyenne	1966		

Gasconade (WLR 75401) — with CGB 90008, a 27.4-m buoy barge USCG, 6-83

D: 141 tons (fl) **S:** 7.6-8.7 kts **Dim:** 22.9 × 6.7 × 1.2
M: 2 diesels; 2 props; 600 hp **Range:** 1,600/7.6; 3,100/6.5
Man: 12 tot.

Remarks: Flat-ended, barge-like hulls. WLR 75401 and WLR 75405 have associated buoy barges, which they push; they also have slightly larger crews. One 1-ton crane. All operate on the Mississippi River and its tributaries.

◆ **6 Ouachita class (65-ft class)**

WLR 65501 Ouachita WLR 65503 Obion WLR 65505 Osage
WLR 65502 Cimarron WLR 65504 Scioto WLR 65506 Sangamon

Cimarron (WLR 65502) — with CGB 90009, a 27.4-m buoy barge USCG, 12-83

D: 130–143 tons (fl) **S:** 10 kts **Dim:** 20.1 × 6.4 × 1.5
M: 2 diesels; 2 props; 600 hp **Range:** 1,700/10.5; 3,500/6 **Man:** 10 tot.

Remarks: WLR 65501 and WLR 65502 completed in 1960, others in 1962. WLR 65504 has an associated push-type buoy barge with a 3-ton crane, and a larger crew. All have a 3-ton crane aboard. Operate on the Mississippi River and its tributaries.

◆ **1 Sumac class (115-ft class)** Bldr: Peterson & Haecker, Blair, Nebraska

WLR 311 Sumac (In serv. 11-11-44)

D: 404 tons (478 fl) **S:** 10.6 kts **Dim:** 35.1 × 9.1 × 1.8
M: 3 Fairbanks-Morse diesels; 3 props; 2,250 hp
Range: 5,000/10.6; 11,600/5 **Man:** 1 officer, 22 men

BUOY TENDERS, RIVER *(continued)*

Sumac (WLR 311)—with work barge USCG, 3-85

◆ **1 Lantana class (80-ft class)** Bldr: Peterson & Haecker, Blair, Nebraska

WLR 80310 LANTANA (In serv. 6-11-43)

D: 235 tons (fl) **S:** 10 kts **Dim:** 24.3 × 9.1 × 1.8
M: 3 diesels; 3 props; 945 hp **Range:** 5,000/10 **Man:** 1 officer, 19 men

◆ **1 Dogwood class (114-ft class)** Bldr: Dubuque Boat & Boiler Wks., Iowa

WLR 259 DOGWOOD (In serv. 17-9-41)

D: 230 tons (310 fl) **S:** 11 kts **Dim:** 34.8 × 7.9 × 1.2
M: 2 diesels; 2 props; 800 hp
Range: 1,300/11; 2,800/5.5 **Man:** 1 officer, 20 men

CONSTRUCTION TENDERS, INLAND

◆ **4 Pamlico class (160-ft class)** Bldr: Coast Guard Yard, Curtis Bay, Md.

	In serv.		In serv.
WLIC 800 PAMLICO	1966	WLIC 803 KENNEBEC	1977
WLIC 801 HUDSON	1966	WLIC 804 SAGINAW	1977

Pamlico (WLIC 800) 1976

D: 413 tons (459 fl) **S:** 11.5 kts **Dim:** 49.1 × 9.1 × 1.2
Electron Equipt: Radar: 1/Raytheon 1900
M: 2 Cummins D379, 8-cyl. diesels; 2 props; 1,000 hp
Range: 1,400/11; 2,200/6.5 **Man:** 1 officer, 13 men

REMARKS: Design combines capabilities of the *Anvil* class and their associated equipment barges. One 9-ton crane.

◆ **10 Anvil class (75-ft class)** (In serv. 1962-65)

WLIC 75301 ANVIL
WLIC 75302 HAMMER
WLIC 75303 SLEDGE
WLIC 75304 MALLET
WLIC 75305 VISE
WLIC 75306 CLAMP
WLIC 75307 WEDGE
WLIC 75308 SPIKE
WLIC 75309 HATCHET
WLIC 75310 AXE

D: 145 tons (fl) **S:** 9.1 kts **Dim:** 22.9 × 6.7 × 1.2
M: 2 diesels; 2 props; 600 hp **Range:** 2,200/5 **Man:** 0 or 1 officer, 9 men

REMARKS: All except *Anvil* and *Mallet* have an associated push-type barge with a 9-ton crane. WLIC 75306 to WLIC 75310 are 23.2 m overall and can make 9.4 knots.

◆ **3 Cosmos class (100-ft class)** Bldr: Dubuque Boat & Boiler, Dubuque, Iowa

	L	In serv.		L	In serv.
WLIC 293 COSMOS	11-11-42	5-12-42	WLIC 315 SMILAX	18-8-44	1-11-44
WLIC 298 RAMBLER	6-5-43	26-5-43	WLIC 316 PRIMROSE	18-8-44	23-10-44

D: 178 tons (fl) **S:** 10.5 kts **Dim:** 30.5 × 7.3 × 1.5
Electron Equipt: Radar: 1/Raytheon 1900 **M:** 2 diesels; 2 props; 600 hp
Range: 1,400/10.5; 2,700/7 **Man:** 1 officer, 14 men

REMARKS: Reclassified from WLI on 1-10-79. Sister *Bluebell* remains typed WLI (WLI 313). WLIC 293 and WLIC 298 have associated construction barges, while WLIC 316 has a pile driver on her bow. All have a 5-ton crane. Sister *Cosmos* (WLIC 293) stricken 1985.

Primrose (WLIC 316)—with non-standard pile driver USCG, 5-81

ICEBREAKING TUGS

◆ **8 (+1 + 1) Katmai Bay class (140-ft class)** Bldr: Tacoma Boatbuilding, Tacoma, Wash., except WTGB 107, 109: Bay City Marine, Tacoma, Wash.

	Laid down	L	In serv.
WTGB 101 KATMAI BAY	7-11-77	8-4-78	8-1-79
WTGB 102 BRISTOL BAY	13-2-78	22-7-78	5-4-79
WTGB 103 MOBIL BAY	13-2-78	11-11-78	6-5-79
WTGB 104 BISCAYNE BAY	29-8-78	3-2-79	8-12-79
WTGB 105 NEAH BAY	6-8-79	. . .	18-8-80
WTGB 106 MORO BAY	6-8-79	. . .	25-1-80
WTGB 107 PENOBSCOT BAY	1-7-83	27-7-84	2-1-85
WTGB 108 THUNDER BAY	20-7-84	15-8-85	4-11-85
WTGB 109 STURGEON BAY	7-86	. . .	6-86
WTGB 110 N.	. . .	. . .	. . .

Authorized: 1 in FY 76, 3 in FY 77, 2 in FY 78, 1 in FY 81.

Katmai Bay (WTGB 101) L. & L. Van Ginderen, 5-85

Biscayne Bay (WTGB 104) L. & L. Van Ginderen, 6-85

ICEBREAKING TUGS *(continued)*

D: 662 tons (fl) **S:** 14.7 kts **Dim:** 42.67 (39.62 pp) × 11.43 × 3.66
Electron Equipt: Radar: 1/SPS-64(V)1
M: 2 Fairbanks-Morse 38D8⅛ diesels, Westinghouse electric drive; 1 prop; 2,500 hp
Electric: 250 kw **Range:** 1,800/14.7; 4,000/12
Fuel: 71 tons **Man:** 3 officers, 14 men

Remarks: Displace 673 tons in fresh water. Reclassified from WYTM on 5-2-79. WTGB 101–105 operate on the Great Lakes. Can break 76-mm ice. Have portable bubble-generator system housed in a removable deckhouse on the fantail. Two fire-fighting monitors atop the pilothouse, which provides near 360-degree viewing. One 2-ton crane handles a 4.9-m plastic workboat. Initially intended to replace the older WYTMs in service. WTGB 109 authorized FY 86 using Navy funds; at least one more planned.

WTGB 102 operates with a 45.72 × 18.29 × 3.05 former jackup barge converted 11-84 by Bay SB, Sturgeon Bay, Wisc., for a 2-year experimental program on the Great Lakes. A 300-hp Schöttel vertical cycloidal bow-thruster prop, powered by a G.M. 8V92 diesel was added to the barge, as was a 10-ton 21.3-m extendable boom, to permit the craft to act as an aids-to-navigation tender.

HARBOR TUGS, MEDIUM

◆ **5 110-ft class**

Bldr: Ira S. Bushey, Brooklyn, N.Y. (except WYTM 60: Coast Guard Yard, Curtis Bay, Md.)

	In serv.		In serv.
WYTM 60 Manitou	15-3-43	WYTM 96 Chinook	24-3-44
WYTM 73 Mohican	29-2-44	WYTM 98 Snohomish	2-5-44
WYTM 93 Raritan	11-4-39		

Chinook (WYTM 96) USCG, 1977

D: 370 tons (384 fl) **S:** 11.2 kts **Dim:** 33.54 × 8.29 × 3.51
Electron Equipt: Radar: 1/SPS-64(V)1 or Raytheon 1900
M: 2 G.M. or Ingersoll-Rand 8-cyl. diesels, electric drive; 1 prop; 1,000 hp
Range: 1,845/11.2; 4,000/8 **Man:** 1 officer, 19 men

Remarks: *Arundel* (WYTM 90) stricken 30-4-82; *Yankton* (WYTM 72) and *Mahoning* (WYTM 91) stricken 10-84. *Sauk* (WYTM 99) stricken 5-85, *Apalachee* (WYTM 71) stricken 4-11-85. WYTM 98 scheduled to strike 4-86, and WYTM 96 in 7-86.

HARBOR TUGS, SMALL

◆ **14 65-ft class** (In serv. 1961-67)

WYTL 65601 Capstan	WYTL 65606 Catenary	WYTL 65611 Line
WYTL 65602 Chock	WYTL 65607 Bridle	WYTL 65612 Wire
WYTL 65603 Swivel	WYTL 65608 Pendant	WYTL 65614 Bollard
WYTL 65604 Tackle	WYTL 65609 Shackle	WYTL 65615 Cleat
WYTL 65605 Towline	WYTL 65610 Hawser	

Capstan (WYTL 65601) R. Scheina, 1979

D: 72 tons (fl) **S:** 9.8 (first 6: 10.5) **Dim:** 19.8 × 5.8 × 2.1
Electron Equipt: Radar: 1/Raytheon 1900 **M:** 1 diesel; 1 prop; 400 hp
Range: 850/9.8; 2,700/5.8 (WYTL 65601 to WYTL 65606: 3,600/6.8; 8,900/10.5)
Man: 10 tot.

Remarks: Sister *Bitt* (WYTL 65613) stricken 10-4-82. All serve on U.S. East Coast.

Note: The two remaining U.S. Coast Guard lightships have been stricken, *Lightship I* (WLV 612) on 29-3-85, and *Lightship II* (WLV 613) in late 1984.

FERRIES

Note: The following three ships are not commissioned cutters of the U.S. Coast Guard, but are under Coast Guard control. Their status is "in service" and they are civilian-manned. Former U.S. Army units, they operate from Governors Island in New York Harbor.

Lt. Samuel S. Cours (In serv. 1956) Pvt. Nicholas Minue (In serv. 1956)

D: 869 tons **S:** 12 kts **Dim:** 54.9 × 18.9 × 3.0
M: Diesel-electric drive; . . . props; 1,000 hp

The Tides (In serv. 1946)

The Tides J. Jedrlinic, 1981

D: 774 tons (l) **S:** 12 kts **Dim:** 56.4 × 16.8 × 2.7
M: Diesel-electric drive; . . . props; 1,350 hp

SMALL CRAFT

The U.S. Coast Guard operates some 2,000 small craft, including over 1,000 under 7.62-m classified as UTL (Utility Boat, Light). No central registry of their numbers is maintained, their administration being the responsibility of the stations to which they are attached. All carry five-digit serial numbers, the first two digits of which denote the craft's length in feet. Two 16.8-m buoy boats were authorized under FY 84. Typical units in several numerically important classes are shown on the following pages.

◆ **250 41-ft Utility Boats** Bldr: USCG Yard, Curtis Bay, Md. (In serv. 1971-83)

41407 W. Donko, 7-85

D: 12.8 tons (fl) **S:** 22–26 kts **Dim:** 12.40 × 4.11 × 1.22
Electron Equipt: Radar: 1/Raytheon 1900
M: 1 Cummins V903M (280-hp) or VT903M (320-hp) diesel; 1 prop

Remarks: Prototype delivered 1971; between 1973-1982 some 249 more followed. Aluminum construction. Hull numbers start with 41300.

◆ **365 30-ft Utility Boat Mk III Type**

D: 6 tons (fl) **S:** 25 kts **Dim:** 9.14 × 2.31 × 0.86
Electron Equipt: Radar: 1/Raytheon 1900
M: 1 Cummins VT8-370M (270 hp) or UT6-250M (280 hp) diesel; 1 prop

Remarks: Glass-reinforced plastic construction.

SMALL CRAFT *(continued)*

32305—30-ft Utility Boat Mk III L. & L. Van Ginderen, 5-84

◆ **20 55-ft-class Aids-to-Navigation Boats**

D: 28.8 tons (fl) **S:** 22 kts **Dim:** 17.68 × 5.18 × 1.52
M: 1 G.M. 12 V71 TI diesel; 1 prop; 540 hp

REMARKS: Aluminum construction.

◆ **. . . 45-ft-class Aids-to-Navigation Boats**

Powered by a single G.M. 6-71 diesel, the 45-ft. buoy-tender class handles small navigational buoys with a hydraulically powered quadrantial derrick over the bow. Number 45312 has a Raytheon 1900 radar C. Dragonette, 1980

◆ **50 (+. . .) 21-ft Aids-to-Navigation Boats** Bldr: MonArk, Monticello, Ark. (In serv. 1981-. . .)

21-ft. Aids-to-Navigation Boat MonArk, 1985

D: 1.59 tons light (3.17 fl) **S:** 30 kts **Dim:** 6.50 × 2.44 × 0.36 (hull)
M: 1 gasoline engine; 1 prop; 228 hp

REMARKS: Aluminum construction, design based on builder's 21-V, deep-Vee hull design. Can be mounted on a trailer for land transport.

◆ **. . . 44-ft Motor Lifeboat class** Bldr: USCG Yard, Curtis Bay, Md.

44-ft. Motor Lifeboat 44350 R. Scheina, 8-84

D: 16 tons (fl) **S:** 15 kts **Dim:** 13.06 × 3.86 × 0.93
Electron Equipt: Radar: 1/. . . nav. **Man:** 3 tot.
M: 2 G.M. 6-71 diesels; 2 props; 360 hp **Range:** 150/12 **Fuel:** 1.2 tons

REMARKS: "Unsinkable" design, built during the 1960s. Fifty or more in service. Also built for Canadian Coast Guard, under license.

◆ **. . . 30-ft Surf Rescue Boats**

30-ft. Surf Rescue Boat 30201 USCG, 10-79

D: 4.6 tons (fl) **S:** 28 kts **Dim:** 9.25 × 2.84 × 1.09
M: 1 G.M. GV92T diesel; 1 prop; 375 hp

A 20-ft outdrive-powered, glass-reinforced, plastic-hulled local patrol craft, Number 201511, is a standard Penn Van pleasure craft adapted for Coast Guard requirements A.D. Baker, 7-76

NATIONAL OCEANIC AND ATMOSPHERIC ADMINISTRATION
U.S. DEPARTMENT OF COMMERCE

PERSONNEL: 350 commissioned officers, approx. 2,250 civilians

NOAA operates a fleet of 23 research ships divided into the two categories of Research and Survey. Headquartered in Rockville, Maryland, and commanded by a rear admiral, it has its major maritime facilities at the Atlantic Marine Center in Norfolk, Virginia, and the Pacific Marine Center in Seattle, Washington.

Hulls and superstructures are white, masts and stacks buff. Hull numbers appear on either side (preceded by "R" for research or "S" for Survey) above the letters "NOAA." The front digit in the 3-digit hull number is the NOAA class (i.e., size) number for the ship, determined from the gross tonnage and horsepower. The ships are described below in descending size order.

Funding shortages for oceanographic research have resulted in plans to lay up many of NOAA's ships during 1986, as noted in the listings.

OCEANOGRAPHIC RESEARCH SHIPS

◆ **2 Oceanographer class** Bldr: Aerojet-General SY, Jacksonville, Fla.

	L	In serv.	Base
R 101 OCEANOGRAPHER	4-64	7-66	Seattle (laid up)
R 102 DISCOVERER	10-64	4-67	Seattle

Discoverer (R 102) NOAA, 1985

D: 4,033 tons (fl) **S:** 15 kts (sust.) **Dim:** 92.4 × 15.8 × 6.0
M: 2 Westinghouse 1,150 diesel generator sets, 2 Westinghouse motors; 2/4-bladed props; 5,000 hp
Range: 12,250/15 **Fuel:** 937 tons **Electric:** 1,200 kw
Man: R 101: 14 NOAA officers; 6 licensed officers; 57 crew, 30 scientists
R 102: 13 NOAA officers, 6 licensed officers, 60 crew, 24 scientists

REMARKS: 3,701 grt/1,095 n.t. Both carry PDP 11/34 data-processing computers. R 101 has a large weather radar aft; both have two navigational radars. Endurance is 34 days. Laboratories include chemistry, wet and dry oceanographic, meteorological, gravimetric, and photographic. A computerized data recording and processing system is installed. There are several precision oceanographic winches. A 400-hp bow-thruster is fitted. R 102 received the Seabeam, 12-kHz multi-beam bathymetric mapping sonar, INMARSAT SATCOMM system for dataline transmission and the TI-410 Global Position Indicator in 1985; she has an underwater observation chamber.

◆ **1 Researcher class** Bldr: American Shpbldg., Toledo, Ohio

	Launched	In serv.	Base
R 103 RESEARCHER	10-68	10-70	Miami

Researcher (R 103)—showing helicopter pad aft NOAA

D: 2,963 tons (fl) **S:** 12.5 kts (sust.) **Dim:** 84.8 × 15.5 × 5.6
M: 2 Alco diesels; 2 CP props; 3,200 hp
Range: 10,800/12.5 **Fuel:** 568 tons **Electric:** 1,500 kw
Man: 13 NOAA officers, 5 licensed officers, 50 crew, 14 scientists

REMARKS: 2,802 grt/946 nrt. Bow dome for sonars and echo-sounders, five laboratories, 5 oceanographic winches. PDP 11/34 computerized data system. Endurance: 36 days. Has a 450-hp Pleuger retractable bow-thruster. Receiving INMARSAT and Global Position Indicator, Seabeam multi-beam mapping sonar in 1986. Carries seismic profile compressors. Has a helicopter deck and a stern ramp.

◆ **1 Miller Freeman class** Bldr: American Shipbldg., Lorain, Ohio

	L	In serv.	Base
R 223 MILLER FREEMAN	1967	1974	Seattle

Miller Freeman (R 223)—note portable van beside stack NOAA

D: 1,920 tons (fl) **S:** 14 kts (sust.) **Dim:** 66.0 × 12.5 × 6.1
M: 1 G.M. diesel; 1 CP prop; 2,200 hp **Electric:** 700 kw
Range: 13,800/14 **Fuel:** 450 tons
Man: 7 NOAA officers, 4 licensed officers, 30 crew, 11 scientists

REMARKS: 1,515 grt/680 nrt. Conducts fisheries and living marine resources research. Endurance: 41 days. Chemical, wet oceanographic, fish processing, utility labs. Fish-finder sonars, several echo-sounders. Lowerable stabilization centerboard increases draft to 9.3 m. Has a stern trawl ramp and net-handling gallows. 400 hp Schöttel lowerable bow-thruster. Planned to lay up at Seattle in 1986.

◆ **1 Oregon II class** Bldr: Ingalls SB, Pascagoula, Miss.

	L	In serv.	Base
R 332 OREGON II	2-67	8-67	Pascagoula

Oregon II (R 332) NOAA

D: 952 tons **S:** 12 kts (sust.) **Dim:** 51.8 × 10.4 × 4.3
M: 2 Fairbanks-Morse diesels; 1 CP prop; 1,600 hp
Range: 9,500/12 **Fuel:** 255 tons **Electric:** 400 kw
Man: 6 licensed officers, 10 crew, 6 scientists

REMARKS: 703 grt/228 nrt. Conducts fisheries and living marine resource research in the Gulf of Mexico, Caribbean, South Atlantic, and Southeast U.S. Atlantic Coast. Endurance: 33 days. Has 2 trawls, 1 hydrographic and 1 bathythermographic winches, five laboratories.

◆ **1 Albatross IV class** Bldr: Southern SB, Slidell, Louisiana

	L	In serv	Base
R 342 ALBATROSS IV	4-62	5-63	Woods Hole, Mass.

OCEANOGRAPHIC RESEARCH SHIPS *(continued)*

Albatros IV NOAA

D: 1,089 tons (fl) **S:** 12 kts (sust.) **Dim:** 57.0 × 10.0 × 4.9
M: 2 Caterpillar diesels; 1 Kort-nozzle CP prop; 1,130 hp
Range: 4,300/12 **Fuel:** 150 tons **Electric:** 450 kw
Man: 7 NOAA officers, 15 crew, 15 scientists

Remarks: 931 grt/300 nrt. Conducts fisheries and living marine resources research off the U.S. Northeast Atlantic Coast. Has wet and dry oceanographic, photographic, biological, plankton, and electronics laboratories, four scientific winches, vertical fish-finding sonar, and deep- and shallow-water echo-sounders. There is a 125-hp bow-thruster. Endurance: 15 days. Planned to be laid up during 1986.

◆ **1 Townsend Cromwell class** Bldr: J. Ray McDermott Co., Morgan City, La.

	L	In serv.	Base
R 443 Townsend Cromwell	7-63	7-63	Honolulu

Townsend Cromwell (R 443) NOAA

D: 652 tons (fl) **S:** 11.5 kts (sust.) **Dim:** 49.7 × 10.0 × 3.9
M: 2 White-Superior diesels; 2 CP props; 800 hp **Electric:** 350 kw
Range: 8,300/11.5 **Fuel:** 132 tons
Man: 4 NOAA officers, 3 licensed officers, 10 crew, 9 scientists

Remarks: 564 grt/384 nrt. Conducts fisheries and living marine resources research off the Hawaiian Islands and in the Central Pacific. Has a single oceanographic laboratory and an underwater bow observation chamber. Endurance: 30 days. Taken over by NOAA 6-75.

◆ **1 David Starr Jordan class** Bldr: Christy Corp., Sturgeon Bay, Wisc.

	L	In serv.	Base
R 444 David Starr Jordan	12-64	1-66	San Diego, Cal.

David Starr Jordan (R 444) NOAA

D: 993 tons (fl) **S:** 11.5 kts (sust.) **Dim:** 52.1 × 11.2 × 3.8 (4.8 over sonar)
M: 2 White-Superior diesels; 2 CP props; 1,086 hp
Electric: 400 kw **Fuel:** 180 tons **Range:** 8,560/11.5
Man: 6 licensed officers, 10 crew, 13 scientists

Remarks: 873 grt/262 nrt. Conducts fisheries and living marine resources research off U.S., Central, and South American Pacific coasts. Physical and biological oceanography, chemical and photographic labs. Has a retractable fish-finding sonar, a vertical fish-finder, and several echo-sounders. Schöttel retractable bow-thruster of 200 hp. Endurance: 31 days. Has an underwater observation chamber at the bow. Planned to be laid up during 1986.

◆ **1 Delaware II class** Bldr: South Portland Engineering Corp., South Portland, Maine

	L	In serv.	Base
R 445 Delaware II	12-67	10-68	Woods Hole, Mass.

Delaware II NOAA

D: 758 tons (fl) **S:** 11.5 kts (sust.) **Dim:** 47.2 × 9.2 × 4.5
M: 1 G.M. diesel; 1 prop; 1,230 hp **Electric:** 300 kw
Fuel: 132 tons **Range:** 6,600/11.5
Man: 6 licensed officers, 9 crew, 9 scientists

Remarks: 483 grt/231 nrt. Conducts fisheries and living marine resources research off U.S. Atlantic coast. Two oceanographic labs, fish-finding sonars, stern net ramp. Endurance: 24 days. Planned to be laid up, 1986.

◆ **1 Chapman class** Bldr: Bender SB & Repair Co., Washington

	L	In serv.	Base
R 446 Chapman	12-79	7-80	Pascagoula, Miss. (laidup)

Chapman (R 446) NOAA

D: 520 tons (fl) **S:** 11 kts (sust.) **Dim:** 38.7 × 9.1 × 4.3
M: 1 Caterpillar D 399 diesel; 1 CP prop; 1,250 hp **Electric:** 420 kw
Fuel: 126 tons **Range:** 6,000/11
Man: 3 NOAA officers, 1 licensed officer, 7 crew, 6 scientists

Remarks: 427 grt/290 nrt. Conducts fisheries and living marine resources research off the Pacific Northwest and Alaskan coasts. Has a fish-processing and a dry laboratory. Stern-haul trawler with a 150-hp Omnithruster bow-mounted waterjet. Laid up 1984 for two years or more.

◆ **1 John N. Cobb class** Bldr: Western Boatbldg., Tacoma, Wash.

	L	In serv.	Base
R 552 John N. Cobb	1-50	2-50	Seattle

D: 250 tons (fl) **S:** 9.3 kts (sust.) **Dim:** 28.3 × 7.9 × 3.3
M: 1 Fairbanks-Morse diesel; 1 prop; 325 hp **Electric:** 60 kw
Range: 2,900/9.3 **Fuel:** 25 tons **Man:** 4 licensed officers, 4 crew, 4 scientists

Remarks: 185 grt/78 nrt. Conducts fisheries and living marine resources research off Southeast Alaska and U.S. Pacific Northwest coasts. Has a single laboratory. Endurance: 13 days. Planned to be laid up, 1986.

OCEANOGRAPHIC RESEARCH SHIPS *(continued)*

John N. Cobb (R 552) NOAA

◆ **1 Murre II class** Bldr: U.S. Army

	L	In serv.	Base
R 663 Murre II	1943	. . .	Juneau, Alaska

Murre II NOAA

D: 295 tons (fl) **S:** 8 kts **Dim:** 26.1 × 8.2 × 2.3
M: 2 Caterpillar diesels; 2 props; 330 hp **Electric:** 32 kw
Fuel: 15 tons **Range:** 1,500/8 **Man:** 2 licensed officers, 1 crew, 5 scientists

Remarks: 189 grt/95 nrt. Conducts fisheries research and cargo shipment duties in Southeast Alaskan waters. Former wooden-hulled Army powered barge. One chemical and one biological laboratory. Has a 2-ton cargo boom for deck cargo. Endurance: 8 days. Planned to be laid up, 1986.

SURVEY SHIPS

◆ **1 Surveyor class** Bldr: National Steel & SB, San Diego, Cal.

	L	In serv.	Base
S 132 Surveyor	4-59	4-60	Seattle

Surveyor (S 132) NOAA

D: 3,440 tons (fl) **S:** 15 kts (sust.) **Dim:** 89.0 × 14.0 × 5.9
M: 2 sets de Laval GT; 1 prop; 3,200 hp **Electric:** 800 kw
Boilers: 2 Combustion Engineering; 32.7 kg/cm², 385°C
Fuel: 785 tons **Range:** 13,680 n.m./15
Man: 12 NOAA officers, 6 licensed officers, 58 crew, 16 scientists

Remarks: 2,653 grt/682 nrt. Has PDP 11/34 data-processing computer, seismic reflection profile compressors, wet and dry oceanography, gravimetric, and photographic laboratories, extensive navigational equipment, deep and shallow echo-sounders, stabilized mapping sonar system, Hydroplot data-processing system, seismic reflection profile compressors, and a small helicopter platform. Carries 3/11-m wooden survey launches, an ex-U.S. Navy LCVP, and 2/7.9-m motor whaleboats. Has a 200-hp electric auxiliary propulsion motor aft. Endurance: 38 days. Received Seabeam 12-kHz, 9,000-m multi-beam mapping sonar in 1985.

◆ **3 Mt. Mitchell class** Bldr: Aerojet-General SY, Jacksonville, Fla.

	L	In serv.	Base
S 220 Fairweather	3-67	10-68	Seattle
S 221 Rainier	3-67	10-68	Seattle
S 222 Mt. Mitchell	11-66	3-68	Norfolk

Fairweather (S 220) NOAA

D: 1,800 tons (fl) **S:** 13 kts **Dim:** 70.4 × 12.8 × 4.2
M: 2 G.M. diesels; 2 CP props; 2,400 hp **Electric:** 600 kw
Fuel: 353 tons **Range:** 7,000/13
Man: 12 NOAA officers, 5 licensed officers, 52 crew, 4 scientists

Remarks: 1,591 grt/578 nrt. Have an oceanographic laboratory, Hydroplot data-processing system (also carried in two of the 3 or 4 8.8-m survey boats aboard), several echo-sounders, and an oceanographic winch. In addition to the survey launches, carry 2 motor whaleboats and 3 Boston Whaler utility boats. Have a 200-hp bow-thruster. Endurance: 22 days.

◆ **2 Peirce class** Bldr: Marietta Mfg. Co., Pt. Pleasant, West Va.

	L	In serv.	Base
S 328 Peirce	10-62	5-63	Norfolk
S 329 Whiting	11-62	7-63	Norfolk

SURVEY SHIPS *(continued)*

Peirce (S 328) NOAA, 1985

D: 907 tons (fl) **S:** 12 kts (sust.) **Dim:** 49.7 × 10.1 × 3.4
M: 2 G.M. diesels; 2 CP props; 1,600 hp **Electric:** 440 kw
Fuel: 138 tons **Range:** 5,700/12
Man: 8 NOAA officers, 3 licensed officers, 30 crew, 2 scientists

REMARKS: 696 grt/151 nrt. Have the Hydroplot data system to record hydrographic data; also fitted to the two 8.8-m survey launches. Have deep, shallow, and hydrographic survey echo-sounders. Work on the U.S. Atlantic Coast, Gulf of Mexico, and U.S. Caribbean possessions; *Peirce* also operates in the Great Lakes. Endurance: 20 days. Planned to lay up S 329 in 1986.

◆ **2 McArthur class** Bldr: Norfolk SB & DD, Norfolk, Va.

	L	In serv.	Base
S 330 McARTHUR	11-65	12-66	Seattle
S 331 DAVIDSON	5-66	3-67	Seattle

McArthur (S 330) NOAA, 1985

D: 995 tons (fl) **S:** 12 kts (sust.) **Dim:** 53.3 × 11.6 × 3.7
M: 2 G.M. diesels; 2 CP props; 1,600 hp **Electric:** 440 kw **Fuel:** 186 tons
Range: 6,000/12 **Man:** 8 NOAA officers, 3 licensed officers, 27 crew, 2 scientists

REMARKS: 854 grt/207 nrt. S 330 primarily performs seawater circulatory studies, and S 331 performs hydrographic surveys; both operate off the U.S. Pacific Coast, and in Alaskan coastal waters. S 331 has the Hydroplot data-recording system, while S 330 uses the same system's PDP 11/34 computer to record current data. S 331 has the Bathymetric Swath Survey System, a stabilized, 22-beam 600-m depth mapping sonar. S 330 planned to be laid up 1986. Endurance: 17 days.

◆ **1 Ferrell class** Bldr: Zigler SY, Jennings, La.

	L	In serv.	Base
S 492 FERRELL	4-68	6-68	Norfolk

D: 360 tons (fl) **S:** 10 kts (sust.) **Dim:** 40.5 × 9.8 × 2.5
M: 2 Caterpillar diesels; 2 props; 750 hp **Electric:** 300 kw
Fuel: 46 tons **Range:** 2,200/10
Man: 5 NOAA officers, 2 licensed officers, 12 crew

Ferrell (S 492) NOAA, 1985

REMARKS: 349 grt/86 nrt. Has a PDP 11/34 data-processing computer. Conducts coastal and estuarine seawater circulation studies off the U.S. East Coast and Gulf of Mexico. Has an electronics laboratory and a small oceanographic laboratory, and carries an 8.5-m workboat. Has a 100-hp bow-thruster. Computerized data-recording system. Endurance: 9 days. Planned to lay up, 1986.

◆ **2 Rude class** Bldr: Jakobson SY, Oyster Bay, N.Y.

	L	In serv.	Base
S 590 RUDE	8-66	3-67	Norfolk
S 591 HECK	8-66	3-67	Norfolk

Heck (S 591) NOAA

D: 220 tons (fl) **S:** 10 kts (sust.) **Dim:** 27.4 × 6.7 × 2.2
M: 2 Cummins diesels; 2 Kort-nozzle props; 800 hp **Electric:** 120 kw
Fuel: 12 tons **Range:** 800/10
Man: 3 NOAA officers, 1 licensed officer, 7 crew

REMARKS: 150 grt/42 nrt. Work together in making wire drag surveys off U.S. Atlantic and Gulf Coasts. Have side-scan sonars and computerized data storage. Equipped with two 70-hp hydraulic auxiliary drives. Endurance: 3 days.

NOTE: U.S. Navy sludge-removal barge YSR 29 was transferred to NOAA 8-85 for use as an underwater habitat support barge. Completed 12-45, the craft displaces 160 tons light (360 fl) and measures 24.4 × 9.8. It will be equipped with a centerline "moon pool."

U.S. ARMY

The U.S. Army's fleet is divided into units (primarily dredges) operated by the Corps of Engineers, and landing craft and logistics support craft operated by the Corps of

U.S.A. *(continued)*
U.S. ARMY *(continued)*

Transportation. Units belonging to the latter are numerous but almost entirely obsolescent, while a new construction program has been thwarted by lack of congressional support and by contractual litigation. Principal Corps of Transportation units are listed below.

◆ **1 Design 5002 Beach Discharge Lighter (Medium Landing Ship)**
Bldr: National Steel, San Diego, Cal.

Lt. Col. John D. Page (In serv. 11-58)

D: 1,548 tons light (4,126 fl) **S:** 10 kts **Dim:** 103.09 × 19.83 × 4.17 (max)
M: 2 Fairbanks-Morse diesels; 2 vertical cycloidal props; 2,400 hp
Electric: 525 kw **Range:** 7,776/9 **Man:** 49 crew + 200 passengers

Remarks: A large, open-deck vehicle ferry, intended to mate with U.S. Navy's vehicle cargo ship *Comet* (T-AKR 7). Only one built of a projected large class. Cargo: 600 tons landing, 2,200 tons max. 1,395 m² deck space. Beaching displacement is 2,340 tons.

◆ **0 (+4) Vehicle Landing Ships** Bldr: . . .

D: . . . **S:** 12 kts **Dim:** 83.0 × 18.3 × . . .
M: . . . **Range:** 5,500/12

Remarks: Ordered 8-85 from Norfolk SB, Norfolk, Va., but contract canceled 10-85 over ambiguities in the original bid package. If reordered, will be able to transport 2,000 tons vehicle cargo or 11,000 bbl liquids. Army had hoped to order up to 24 units of this size, to replace the current LCU fleet.

◆ **13 U.S. Navy LCU 1646-class Utility Landing Craft** (In serv. 1976-78)

LCU 1675 L. & L. Van Ginderen, 7-79

Remarks: Data as for U.S. Navy sisters. Retain former U.S. Navy hull numbers and now bear names commemorating Army battles.

◆ **43 U.S. Navy LCU 1466-class Utility Landing Craft** (In serv. 1954)

LCU 1547 L. & L. Van Ginderen, 6-83

D: 180 tons light (347 fl) **S:** 8 kts **Dim:** 35.08 × 10.36 × 1.6 (aft)
M: 3 Gray Marine 64 YTL diesels; 3 props; 675 hp **Electric:** 40 kw
Fuel: 11 tons **Range:** 1,200/6 (700/7 loaded) **Man:** 11 tot.

Remarks: Despite age, in good condition, with some kept in land storage. Some 35 are to be rehabilitated for further service.

◆ **about 120 U.S. Navy LCM(8)-class landing craft** (In serv. 1954-72)

Remarks: Data as for U.S. Navy version. About 30 manned by Army Reserves, 37 by National Guard forces, with another 30 in storage.

◆ **20 (+10) LACV-30 air-cushion vehicles** Bldr: Bell Aerospace-Textron (In serv. 1982-87)

Remarks: 30-ton payload amphibious air-cushion vehicle for LOTS (Logistics Over the Shore) operations. 26 were to be in service by mid-1986, all by 1987. Can carry 2/20-ft MILVAN containers at 35 kts. Craft can be transported by trailer, rail, aircraft, or aboard ships. Also in use are about 65 LARC XV, 30 LARC LX, and 25 LARC 5 wheeled amphibious transport vehicles.

Note: In addition to the above, the Corps of Transportation operates 30 65-ft and 30 100-ft tugs, 160 barges in 36.6-, 33.5-, and 24.7-m lengths, 12 36.6-m liquid cargo barges, 5 13.7-m liquid cargo barges, 3 refrigerated barges, 20 floating DeLong piers, 26 floating cranes, and a variety of small craft. Three small coastal freighters are also in service. Army new-construction plans called for 2 large tugs, 3 medium tugs, 2 workboats, and 3 DeLong piers to be ordered with FY 85 funds.

LACV in action L. & L. Van Ginderen, 6-83

Army small harbor tug ST-2124 with 36.6-m barge BC-6461
L. & L. Van Ginderen, 5-85

URUGUAY

ORIENTAL REPUBLIC OF URUGUAY

Personnel (1985): 4,400, including 500 officers, 2,900 enlisted, and 1,000 Marines

Merchant Marine (1984): 89 ships — 190,309 grt
(tankers: 6 ships — 94,933 grt)

Naval Aviation: Fixed-wing assets include 3 S-2G Tracker ASW patrol aircraft delivered 1982-83, 9 T-28 Fennec light attack aircraft, 3 Beech TC-45H utility trainer/light transports, a Beech King Air 200 Maritime Patrol aircraft, and 3 Beech T-34C-1 turbo-trainers. Helicopters include one Bell 222, 2 Bell 476, and 2 Sikorsky SH-34C. The Air Force operates one Embraer EMB 110B Bandeirante and 4 Casa 212 Aviacar for coastal patrol

Note: The scheduled 1983 acquisition of the destroyer ex-*William C. Lawe* (DD 763) from the United States was canceled by Uruguay.

FRIGATES

◆ **1 ex-U.S. Dealey class** Bldr: Bath Iron Works, Me.

	Laid down	L	In serv.
DE 3 18 Julio (ex-*Dealey,* DE 1006)	15-10-52	8-11-53	3-6-54

D: 1,450 tons (1,914 fl) **S:** 25 kts **Dim:** 95.86 × 11.2 × 4.04 (5.27 over sonar)
A: 4/76.2-mm DP (II × 2) — 6/324-mm Mk 32 ASW TT — 1/d.c. rack

18 de Julio (DE 3) L. & L. Van Ginderen, 1975

FRIGATES *(continued)*

Electron Equipt: Radar: 2/. . . nav., 1/SPS-6E, 2/SPG-34
Sonar: 1/SQS-29 series—EW: WLR-1
M: 1 set de Laval GT; 1 prop; 20,000 hp
Boilers: 2 Foster-Wheeler "D"; 42 kg/cm², 510°C
Fuel: 360 tons **Range:** 4,400/11 **Man:** 11 officers, 150 men

REMARKS: First and least-modified of her class and also the last survivor. Two Mk 63 GFCS. New superstructure added abreast the stack. Purchased on 28-7-72. Refitted 1979-80 in Brazil, original SPS-5D surface-search radar replaced by two commercial navigational radars.

◆ **2 ex-U.S. Cannon class** Bldr: Federal SB & DD, Newark, N.J.

	Laid down	L	In serv.
DE 1 URUGUAY (ex-*Baron,* DE 166)	30-11-42	9-5-43	5-7-43
DE 2 ARTIGAS (ex-*Bronstein,* DE 189)	26-8-43	14-11-43	13-12-43

Uruguay (DE 1) *Ships of the World,* 1985

D: 1,240 tons light (1,900 fl) **S:** 19 kts **Dim:** 93.27 × 11.15 × 3.56 (hull)
A: 3/76.2-mm DP (I × 3)—2/40-mm AA (II × 1)—3/20-mm AA (I × 3)—1/Mk 11 Hedgehog
Electron Equipt: Radar: 1/SPS-5, 1/SPS-6C (not in DE 1), 1/navigational
Sonar: SQS-4 series
M: 4 G.M. 16-278A diesels, electric drive; 2 props; 6,000 hp
Electric: 680 kw **Fuel:** 315 tons **Rnage:** 8,300/14 **Man:** 160 tot.

REMARKS: DE 1 was transferred in 5-52 and DE 2 in 3-52. Modernized in late 1960s with new radars. No radar fire control, but do have Mk 51 range-finder for 76.2-mm guns and Mk 51 Mod. 2 lead-computing director for 40-mm AA. DE 1 does not have stub mainmast and has had the SPS-6C radar removed. Both have had single 20-mm AA added. Depth-charge equipment had been removed by 1985, and both are in marginal operating condition.

CORVETTE

◆ **1 ex-U.S. Auk-class former minesweeper**

Bldr: Defoe Boiler & Machine Works, Bay City, Mich.

	Laid down	L	In serv.
4 COMANDANTE PEDRO CAMPBELL (ex-MS 31, ex-*Chickadee,* MSF 59)	21-8-41	20-7-42	9-11-42

Comandante Pedro Campbell (4)—outboard *18 de Julio* (DE 3) *Ships of the World,* 1985

D: 890 tons (1,250 fl) **S:** 18 kts **Dim:** 67.41 (65.53 wl) × 9.78 × 3.28
A: 1/76.2-mm DP—4/40-mm AA (II × 2)—8/20-mm AA (II × 4)
Electron Equipt: Radar: 1/navigational
M: 4 Alco 539 diesels, electric drive; 2 props; 3,118 hp
Electric: 300 kw **Man:** 105 tot.

REMARKS: Transferred on 18-8-66 and purchased on 18-8-76. All minesweeping equipment removed; has no ASW capability. Minesweeping winch used for towing.

PATROL BOATS

◆ **3 French Vigilante class** Bldr: CMN, Cherbourg

	Laid down	L	In serv.
5 15 DE NOVIEMBRE	6-12-79	16-10-80	25-3-81
6 25 DE AGOSTO	6-2-80	11-2-80	25-3-81
7 COMODORO COE	16-5-80	27-1-81	25-3-81

15 de Noviembre (5)—on trials CMN, 1981

D: 166 tons (190 fl) **S:** 28 kts **Dim:** 41.15 (28.00 pp) × 6.80 × 2.5 (1.50 hull)
A: 1/40-mm AA
Electron Equipt: Radar: 1/Decca TM 1226C, 1/Decca 1229
M: 2 MTU 12V538 TB91 diesels; 2 props; 5,400 hp
Range: 2,400/15 **Man:** 5 officers, 22 men

REMARKS: Ordered 1978. CSEE Panda optronic GFCS for the 40-mm gun, which has a fiberglass cover to the mount. All commissioned day of departure under own power to Uruguay from Cherbourg. Twin 20-mm AA planned aft, not mounted.

◆ **1 ex-U.S, Adjutant-class former minesweeper**

Bldr: National Steel SB, San Diego, Cal.

	In serv.
13 RIO NEGRO (ex-MS 32, ex-*Marguerite,* ex-MSC 94)	3-54

Rio Negro (13)—old number, most minesweeping gear now removed

D: 300 tons (372 fl) **S:** 13 kts **Dim:** 43.0 (41.5 pp) × 7.95 × 2.95
A: 2/20-mm AA (II × 1)
Electron Equipt: Radar: 1/DRBN-31—Sonar: UQS-1D
M: 2 G.M. 8-268A diesels; 2 props; 1,200 hp
Range: 2,500/10 **Man:** 38 tot.

REMARKS: On completion, transferred to France, then to Uruguay on 10-11-69. Wooden construction. Most minesweeping equipment, including sweep winch and cable drum, now removed.

PATROL CRAFT

◆ **1 U.S. 85-foot commercial cruiser** Bldr: Sewart Seacraft, Morgan City, La.

PR 12 PAYSANDU (L: 11-68)

D: 43.5 tons (54 fl) **S:** 22 kts **Dim:** 25.91 × 5.69 × 2.1
A: 3/12.7-mm mg (I × 3) **Electron Equipt:** Radar: 1/Raytheon 1500B
M: 2 G.M. 16V71N diesels; 2 props; 1,400 hp **Electric:** 40 kw
Range: 800/21 **Man:** 8 tot.

REMARKS: Built under U.S. Military Assistance Program. Aluminum construction.

PATROL CRAFT *(continued)*

◆ **1 ex-German FL-9 class** Bldr: Krögerwerft, Rendsburg (In serv. 1955)

PR 11 Carmelo

D: 67 tons (73 fl) **S:** 30 kts **Dim:** 28.8 (27.9 pp) × 5.0 × 1.6
A: 1/20-mm AA **Electron Equipt:** Radar: 1/Decca 12
M: 2 Maybach 12-cyl. diesels; 2 props; 3,000 hp **Range:** 600/25 **Man:** 8 tot.

Remarks: One of five sisters built as air-sea-rescue craft for the British Royal Air Force. Taken over by Uruguayan Navy in 1964. Wooden construction.

◆ **1 ex-U.S. 63-foot AVR class**

PR 10 Colonia (L: 4-7-44)

D: 25 tons (34 fl) **S:** 28 kts **Dim:** 19.3 × 4.67 × 1.22
A: 4/12.7-mm mg (II × 2)
M: 2 Hall-Scott Defender V-12 gasoline engines; 2 props; 1,260 hp
Fuel: 4.3 tons **Range:** 450/25; 600/15 **Man:** 8 tot.

Remarks: Former air-sea-rescue boat, transferred in about 1945. Wooden construction. No radar.

AMPHIBIOUS WARFARE CRAFT

◆ **2 LD 45-class landing craft** Bldr: Naval SY, Paysandu

LD 45 LD 46

D: 31.4 tons **S:** 10.5 kts **Dim:** 17.50 × 7.0 × 0.8
M: 2 G.M. 6V71 diesels; 2 props; 272 hp

Remarks: LD 45 laid down 12-79. Referred to as Type 5-06.

◆ **2 LD 43-class landing craft** Bldr: Naval SY, Montevideo

LD 43 (In serv. 26-7-78) LD 44 (In serv. 1979)

D: 13 tons (fl) **S:** 9 kts **Dim:** 10.85 × 3.50 × 0.70
M: 1 G.M. 6-71 diesel; 1 prop; 140 hp **Range:** 580/9

Remarks: Up to four more may have been completed 1979-81. Can carry five tons cargo.

◆ **1 small landing craft** Bldr: Mapell S.A. (In serv. . . .)

LD 42

D: 12 tons **S:** 6 kts **Dim:** 12.0 × 3.4 × 1.1
M: 2 British G.M. Bedford 330 diesels; 2 props; 192 hp

◆ **2 U.S. LCM(6)-class landing craft**

LD 40 LD 41

D: 24 tons (57 fl) **S:** 10 kts **Dim:** 17.07 × 4.37 × 1.17
M: 2 Gray Marine 64HN9 diesels; 2 props; 450 hp **Range:** 130/9

Remarks: LD 40 and LD 41 were leased in 10-72; lease extended 1982. Cargo: 30 tons.

HYDROGRAPHIC SHIPS

◆ **1 Paysandu-class former patrol boat** Bldr: CNR, Ancona

14 Salto (ex-GS 24) (L: 11-8-35)

D: 150 tons (180 fl) **S:** 17 kts **Dim:** 42.1 × 5.8 × 1.58
M: 2 Krupp-Germania diesels; 2 props; 1,000 hp
Range: 4,000/10 **Man:** 26 tot.

Remarks: Survivor of a class of three, placed on present duties as a survey craft and navigational-buoy tender in 1972.

AUXILIARY SHIPS

◆ **1 supertanker** Bldr: Kawasaki, Kobe, Japan, 1975

27 Juan A. Lavalleja (ex-*Solfonn*)

D: 145,000 tons (fl) **S:** 15.5 kts **Dim:** 273.0 × 44.1 × 15.7
M: 2 sets GT; 1 prop; 24,500 hp **Boilers:** 2 **Man:** . . .

Remarks: 131,633 dwt, 68,931 grt. Literally, the world's largest naval ship, by a wide margin. Laid up by Norwegian owner on 13-10-75, when she was completed. Purchased by Uruguay on 13-1-77 for use by ANCAP, the state petroleum monopoly, in commercial service with a naval crew. No underway replenishment capability. Grounded 28-12-80 off Arzew, Algeria; refloated 17-2-81 and repaired in France.

◆ **1 tanker** Bldr: Bazán, Spain, 1971

28 Presidente Rivera (L: 20-5-71)

D: 36,000 tons (fl) **S:** 16.5 kts **Dim:** 194.0 (191.0 pp) × 25.4 × 9.8
M: 1 diesel; 1 prop; 15,300 hp **Man:** 58 tot.

Remarks: 31,885 dwt, 19,656 grt. Used in commercial service, with a naval crew, by ANCAP, the state petroleum monopoly. Late note: sold 1-86.

◆ **1 transport, former merchant cargo ship**

	Bldr	In serv.
29 Presidente Oribe (ex-Danish *Catrina*)	Frederikshavn, Denmark	1966

D: 1,153 tons **S:** 10 kts **Dim:** 54.2 × 9.6 × 3.3
M: 1 Burmeister & Wain diesel; 1 prop; 520 hp

Remarks: Ran aground while in merchant service 11-78 and salvaged by Uruguayan Navy; purchased from British insurance company and commissioned 19-8-80.

◆ **1 ex-U.S. Cohoes-class salvage ship** Bldr: Commercial Ironworks, Portland, Ore.

	Laid down	L	In serv.
AM 25 Huracán (ex-*Nahant,* AN 83, ex-YN 102)	31-3-45	30-6-45	24-8-45

Huracán (AM 25) L. & L. Van Ginderen, 1979

D: 650 tons (855 fl) **S:** 12.3 kts **Dim:** 51.36 (44.5 pp) × 10.31 × 3.3
A: Removed **Electron Equipt:** Radar: 1/SPS-5
M: 2 Busch-Sulzer BS539 diesels, electric drive; 1 prop; 1,200 hp **Man:** 48 tot.

Remarks: Former netlayer. Transferred in 12-68. A decompression chamber for divers is carried.

◆ **1 miscellaneous service tender** Bldr: . . . , Glasgow, Scotland

AM 26 Vanguardia (ex-*Balizador*) (In serv. 1908)

D: 95 tons **S:** 12 kts **Dim:** . . . × . . . × . . .
M: 1 set triple-expansion reciprocating steam; 1 prop; 200 hp

Remarks: Employed on hydrographic survey duties; white hull, buff upper works.

Note: A craft named *Oyarvide* is also in naval service, function and characteristics not available. A 15-m tender, 71 (ex-PS 1), is used as a tug.

◆ **1 sail-training ship**

	Bldr	In serv.
20 Capitan Miranda (ex-GS 20)	Soc. Española de Construcción Naval, Matagorda, Cádiz, Spain	1930

Capitan Miranda (20)—number not borne 1980

URUGUAY *(continued)*
AUXILIARY SHIPS *(continued)*

D: 516 tons (550 fl) **S:** 11 kts **Dim:** 54.6 (61.0 bowspirit/45.0 pp) × 8.4 × 3.2
Electron Equipt: Radar: 1/Decca TM 1226C
M: 1 M.A.N. diesel; 1 prop; 500 hp **Fuel:** 45 tons **Man:** 49 tot.

Remarks: Originally built as a hydrographic survey ship. Refitted and rigged as a three-masted schooner for cadet training, recommissioning 1978.

COAST GUARD
(PREFECTURA MARITIMA)

The Uruguayan Coast Guard has 100 officers and about 1,900 enlisted men. Primarily intended for a shore-based coast watch and port police function, it does operate three 13-m patrol boats, three 9-m patrol craft, and a number of outboard-motor-powered semi-inflatable rubber boats; all have pendant numbers beginning with PM, PS, etc.

VANUATU

Personnel: . . .

Merchant Marine: 21 ships — 89,591 grt (1 tanker — 2,999 tons)

PATROL BOATS

◆ **0 (+1) Australian ASI 315 class** Bldr: Australian SB Industries, South Coogie, Western Australia (In serv. 1987)

N. . .

D: 165 tons (fl) **S:** 20 kts **Dim:** 31.5 (28.6 wl) × 8.1 × 2.12
A: . . . **Electron Equipt:** Radar: 1/Furuno 1011
M: 2 Caterpillar 3516 diesels; 2 props; . . . hp **Electric:** . . .
Range: 2,500/12 **Fuel:** 33 tons **Man:** 3 officers, 14 men

Remarks: Provided by Australian foreign aid. Sisters being built for other Southwest Pacific nations. See illustration under Papua New Guinea.

◆ **1 patrol boat, former yacht**

Mala (In serv. . . .)

Mala L. & L. Van Ginderen, 5-85

Remarks: No data available.

VENEZUELA

Republic of Venezuela

Personnel: (1985): 7,500 men, including 4,000 marines

Merchant Marine (1984): 250 ships — 1,003,381 grt
(tankers: 26 ships — 562,072 grt)

Naval Aviation: The small naval aviation component operates 4 Casa 212A Aviocar, one de Havilland Dash-7, and one transport, 2 Beech King Air 98 light and one Turbo Commander transports, one Cessna 337 liaison aircraft, and twelve Agusta-Bell AB-212 helicopters.

The newly established Coast Guard operates four HU-16A Albatross amphibians for maritime surveillance, as well as four Casa C-212 light transports.

SUBMARINES

◆ **2 German Type 209** Bldr: Howaldtswerke, Kiel

	Laid down	L	In serv.
S-31 Sabalo	2-5-73	1-17-75	6-8-76
S-32 Carite	1-8-73	6-11-75	11-3-77

Sabalo (S-31) Howaldtswerke, 1979

D: 990/1,290 tons **S:** 11/22 kts **Dim:** 56.10 × 6.20 × 5.50
A: 8/533-mm TT — 14 U.S. Mk 37 and West German SST-4 torpedoes
M: Diesel-electric propulsion: 4 MTU Type 12V492 Tb90, 600-hp diesels; 4/405-kw generators; Siemens electric motor; 5,000 hp
Fuel: 100 tons **Range:** 7,800/8 surf.; 400/4 sub. **Man:** 5 officers, 26 men

Remarks: Ordered 1971: S 31 damaged by fire in 1979, overhauled at Kiel. A planned second pair were apparently not ordered. S-32 refitted by builder 1984.

◆ **1 ex-U.S. GUPPY II**

	Bldr	Laid down	L	In serv.
SS-22 Picua (ex-*Grenadier,* SS 525)	Boston Naval SY	8-2-44	15-12-44	10-2-51

Picua (S-22) R. Scheina, 7-84

D: 2,040/2,420 tons **S:** 18/16 kts **Dim:** 93.57 × 8.33 × 5.18
A: 10/533-mm TT (6 fwd, 4 aft) **Electron Equipt:** Radar: 1/SS-2 — Sonar: BQR-2
M: Fairbanks-Morse 38D8⅛ diesels, electric drive; 2 props; 4,160 hp **Man:** 82 tot.

Remarks: Purchased 15-5-73. Unusual in having been *completed* as a GUPPY II. Four 126-cell batteries. Sister *Tiburon* (S 21, ex-*Cubera,* SS 347) stricken 1979. S-22 was overhauled at Punta Belgrano Naval SY, Argentina, from 1979 to 7-81, but is in marginal operating condition. To be refitted for further service.

GUIDED-MISSILE FRIGATES

◆ **6 Italian Lupo class** Bldr: CNR, Riva Trigoso and Ancona(*), Italy

	Laid down	L	In serv.
F-21 Mariscal Sucre	4-10-77	28-9-78	14-7-80
F-22 Almirante Brion	26-1-78	22-2-79	7-3-81
F-23 General Urdaneta*	23-1-78	23-3-79	8-8-81
F-24 General Soublette	26-8-78	4-1-80	4-12-81
F-25 General Salom*	7-11-78	13-1-80	3-4-82
F-26 Almirante José M. Garcia (ex-*General José Felix Ribas*)	21-8-79	4-10-80	30-7-82

D: 2,213 tons (2,525 fl) **S:** 35 kts (20.5 on diesels)
Dim: 112.8 (106.0 pp) × 11.98 × 3.84 (hull)
A: 8/Otomat Mk II SSM (I × 8) — 1/Albatros SAM system (VIII × 1, 8 Aspide missiles) — 1/127-mm OTO Melara DP — 4/40-mm Breda Dardo AA (II × 2) — 6/324-mm Mk 32 ASW TT (III × 2, for A244 torpedoes) — 1/AB-212 ASW helicopter

General Urdaneta (F-23) — AB 212 helo on deck R. Scheina, 7-84

GUIDED-MISSILE FRIGATES *(continued)*

Almirante José M. Garcia (F-26)—on trials G. Arra, 1981

Electron Equipt: Radar: 1/3RM-20 navigational, 1/RAN-11/X air and surface search, 1/RAN-10S air search, 2/Orion RTN-10X, 2/Orion RTN-20X—TACAN: SRN-15A
Sonar: Edo 610E—EW: Lambda-F, 2/SCLAR chaff RL (XX × 2)
M: CODOG: 2 Fiat G.E. LM-2500 gas turbines, 25,000 hp each; 2 GMT A230-2M diesels, 3,900 hp each; 2 CP props
Electric: 3,120 kw **Range:** 900/35; 1,050/31.7; 5,500/16 **Man:** 185 tot.

REMARKS: Ordered 24-10-75. Fin stabilizers fitted. Gun (127-mm) and missile fire control by two Elsag NA-10 Mod. 0 systems. The Albatros system uses Aspide missiles, a re-engineered version of NATO Sea Sparrow. Each twin 40-mm Dardo system antiaircraft mount has an associated RTN-20X radar director. All weapons controlled by a Selenia IPN-10 computerized data system. Fixed, nontelescopic hangar. Near-sisters in the Iraqi, Italian, and Peruvian navies.

NOTE: The two surviving *Almirante Clemente*-class frigates have been transferred to the Coast Guard.

AMPHIBIOUS WARFARE SHIPS

◆ **4 tank landing ships** Bldr: Korea-Tacoma SY, Masan, S. Korea

	L	In serv.		L	In serv.
T-61 CAPAÑA	25-3-83	21-6-84	T-63 GOAJIRA	. . .	11-84
T-62 ESEQUIBO	25-3-83	21-6-84	T-64 LOS LLANOS	. . .	11-84

Capaña (T-61)—without armament G. Gyssels, 2-85

D: 1,800 tons light (3,770 fl) **S:** 15 kts **Dim:** 104.0 × 15.4 × 3.0 (4.2 max.)
A: 3/40-mm AA (I × 3)—2/20-mm AA (I × 2)
Electron Equipt: Radar: . . .
M: 2 diesels; 2 props; 5,600 hp **Electric:** 750 kw
Range: 7,500/13 **Man:** 13 officers, 104 men + troops: 10 officers, 192 men

REMARKS: Ordered 8-82. Cargo: 1,800 tons maximum, 690 tons beaching load. Improved version of U.S. WW II-era LST. Have an elevator to the upper deck and a 50-ton tank turntable on the tank deck. Sisters in the Indonesian Navy. T-61, 62 arrived 10-84 in Venezuela, T-63 in 12-84, and T-64 early in 1985; all delivered without armament. Have a helicopter deck aft.

◆ **1 ex-U.S. Terrebonne Parish-class landing ship**

Bldr: Ingalls, Pascagoula

	Laid down	L	In serv.
T-51 AMAZONAS (ex-*Vernon County*, LST 1161)	14-4-52	1952	1954

Amazonas (T-51) 1977

D: 2,590 tons (5,786 fl) **S:** 13 kts **Dim:** 117.35 × 16.76 × 5.18
A: 6/76.2-mm DP (II × 3) **Electric:** 600 kw
Electron Equipt: 1/Decca navigational, 1/SPS-21, 2/SPG-34
M: 4 G.M. 16-278A diesels; 2 CP props; 6,000 hp **Man:** 116 tot.
Range: 6,000/9 **Fuel:** 1,060 tons

REMARKS: Loaned 29-6-73, purchased outright 30-12-77. Cargo: 2,200 tons vehicles and stores, 395 troops. Two Mk 63 radar GFCS. Normally carries 2 LCVPs. Went aground 6-8-80 at St. Lucia in a hurricane but was salvaged. To be refitted.

NOTE: The U.S. *Achelous*-class former light repair ship, *Guyana* (T-31, ex-*Quirinas*, ARL 39, ex-LST 1151) was stricken 22-8-84. The U.S. LSM 1-class medium landing ship *Los Frailes* (T-23, ex-LSM 544) was stricken after a fire, 21-6-84.

◆ **2 utility landing craft** Bldr: Swiftships, Morgan City, La. (In serv. 1984)

T-71 MARGARITA (In serv. 1-84) T-72 LA ORCHILA (In serv. 5-84)

Margarita (T-71) Swiftships, 3-84

D: 428 tons (fl) **S:** 13 kts **Dim:** 39.62 × 10.97 × 1.30
A: None **Electron Equipt:** Radar: 1/. . . nav.
M: 2 G.M. Detroit Diesel 16V149 N diesels; 2 props; 1,800 hp
Range: 2,500/10 **Fuel:** 64 tons **Man:** 4 officers, 17 men

REMARKS: Aluminum construction. Cargo: vehicles, supplies, up to 108 tons fuel and 149 tons water. Bow ramp, 15-ton crane on bow. Carries 156 tons ballast. Intended for coastal and riverine use. Four more planned.

◆ **12 U.S. LCVP-class landing craft** Bldr: Dianca, Puerto Cabello, 1976-77

D: 12 tons (fl) **S:** 9 kts **Dim:** 10.9 × 3.2 × 1.0
M: 1 diesel; 1 prop; 225 hp **Range:** 110/9

REMARKS: Follow design of U.S.-built LCVP. Several other LCVP and LCPL transferred with U.S. Navy ships probably also survive.

AUXILIARY SHIPS

◆ **1 ex-U.S. Cohoes-class survey ship** Bldr: Commercial Iron Works, Portland Ore.

	Laid down	L	In serv.
H-11 PUERTO SANTO (ex-*Marietta*, AN 82, ex-YN 101)	17-2-45	27-4-45	25-6-45

D: 650 tons (855 fl) **S:** 12 kts **Dim:** 48.2 (44.5 wl) × 10.3 × 3.6
A: 3/20-mm AA
M: 2 Busch-Sulzer BS 539 diesels, electric drive; 1 prop; 1,500 hp
Electric: 240 kw **Fuel:** 110 tons **Man:** 46 tot.

REMARKS: Ex-net tender. Transferred 1-61 under Military Aid Program; purchased outright 30-12-77. Converted for use as a hydrographic survey ship in 1962 by U.S. Coast Guard Yard, Curtis Bay, Md. Original bow horns removed, reducing overall length from 51.4 meters. Retains 12-ton boom forward. Bridge superstructure raised one deck. A replacement, to be named *Francisco de Miranda*, entered the planning stage in 5-84.

◆ **2 Gabriela-class survey craft**

Bldr: Abeking & Rasmussen, Lemwerder, West Germany

	Laid down	L	In serv.
P-119 GABRIELA	10-3-73	29-11-73	5-2-74
P-121 LELY	28-5-73	12-12-73	7-2-74

AUXILIARY SHIPS *(continued)*

D: 90 tons (fl) **S:** 20 kts **Dim:** 27.0 × 5.6 × 1.5
M: 2 MTU diesels; 2 props; 2,300 hp **Man:** 16 tot.

REMARKS: Civilian-manned.

◆ **1 former merchant ship** Bldr: . . .

T. . . PUERTO CABELLO (ex-*Sierra Nevada*)

D: . . . **S:** . . . **Dim:** . . . × . . . × . . .
M: . . .

REMARKS: Acquired late 1985 for use as a naval transport to replace *Las Aves;* no data yet available.

◆ **1 Maracaibo-class cargo ship** Bldr: Canadian Vickers, Montreal (In serv. 1953)

T-42 VALENCIA (ex-*Ciudad de Valencia*)

D: Approx. 8,100 tons (fl) **S:** 15 kts **Dim:** 128.15 × 16.76 × 6.78
M: 1 Nordberg diesel; 1 prop; 4,275 hp
Man: 7 officers, 50 men

REMARKS: 4,297 grt/5,885 dwt. Transferred from State Shipping Co. in 1977. Five cargo holds. Additional superstructure added on stern to increase accommodations. Refitted 1982 at Port Everglades, Florida.

NOTE: The fleet tugs of the U.S. *Achomawi* class have been transferred to the Coast Guard. The small transport-cum-presidential yacht *Las Aves* (T-11) was stricken during 1983.

◆ **1 sail-training ship** Bldr: Ast. Celeya, Bilbao, Spain

	Laid down	L	In serv.
SIMÓN BOLÍVAR	5-6-79	21-9-79	14-8-80

Simón Bolívar P. Roullet, 1981

D: 1,200 tons (fl) **S:** 10.5 kts **Dim:** 82.5 (58.5 pp) × 10.6 × 4.2
M: 1 G.M. 12V149 diesel; 1 prop; 750 hp
Man: 17 officers, 75 men, 18 instructors, 84 cadets

REMARKS: 934 grt. Sister to Ecuadorian *Guayas.* Three-masted bark; sail area: 1,650 m². Ordered 7-78.

SERVICE CRAFT

◆ **1 large harbor tug** Bldr: Dianca, Puerto Cabello, 1978

C-142

D: . . . **S:** . . . **Dim:** . . . × . . . × . . .
M: 2 Werkspoor diesels; 2 props; 1,600 hp

REMARKS: Ordered 1973. Used for Navy by Dianca SY. Three sisters operated by Ministry of Communications: C-139, C-140, C-141.

◆ **1 ex-U.S. medium harbor tug** Bldr: Ramsey & Sons, New Orleans, La.

R-11 FERNANDO GOMEZ (ex-*Dudley,* YTM 744)

D: 161 tons **S:** 15 kts **Dim:** 24.5 × 5.8 × 2.4
A: 2/12.7-mm mg (I × 2) **M:** 1 Clark 6-cyl. diesel; 1 prop; 380 hp
Man: 10 tot.

REMARKS: Built 1938. Acquired by U.S. Navy 1-42; sold to Venezuela 1-47.

◆ **1 ex-U.S. floating repair barge** Bldr: Mare Isl. NSY, Cal. (L: 30-5-43)

. . . (ex-YR 48)

D: 520 tons (770 fl) **Dim:** 46.6 × 13.1 × 2.1
Electric: 220 kw **Fuel:** 75 tons **Man:** 46 tot.

REMARKS: Leased 7-61; purchased outright 30-12-77.

◆ **1 floating crane—Capacity:** 40 tons

◆ **1 small service craft** Bldr: Ast. Lago Maracaibo (In serv. 5-80)

ANGU-01

◆ **3 service launches** Bldr: American SB & Design, Miami, Fla.

MTC-6 (In serv. 31-10-83) MTC-7 (In serv. 15-12-83) MTC-8 (In serv. 26-2-84)

D: 4.8 tons (fl) **S:** 32 kts **Dim:** 10.06 (9.19 pp) × 3.35 × 0.76
M: 2 G.M. diesels; 2 props; 550 hp **Range:** 450/. . .

REMARKS: Glass-reinforced plastic construction.

VENEZUELAN COAST GUARD

The Venezuelan Coast Guard was established in 8-82 to patrol the 200-nautical-mile economic zone. Initially operating only four Cessna 210 light aircraft, it has now received a number of former Venezuelan Navy vessels, as well as four CASA Aviacar maritime-patrol-configured light transports, four former naval HU-16 Albatross amphibians, and six former naval S-2E Tracker aircraft (the latter discarded 2-85). The Coast Guard is headquartered at Puerto Cabello under the Ministry of the Navy and is commanded by a rear admiral.

FRIGATES

◆ **2 Almirante Clemente class** Bldr: Ansaldo, Livorno

	Laid down	L	In serv.
F-11 GENERAL JOSÉ TRINIDAD MORAN	5-5-54	12-12-54	1956
F-12 ALMIRANTE CLEMENTE	5-5-54	12-12-54	1956

Almirante Clemente (F-12)—refitting at Genoa C. Martinelli, 1984

D: 1,300 tons (1,500 fl) **S:** 22 kts **Dim:** 97.6 × 10.84 × 2.6
A: 2/76-mm OTO Melara DP (I × 2)—2/40-mm AA (II × 2)—6/324-mm Ilas-3 ASW TT (III × 2)
Electron Equipt: Radar: 1/Decca 1226, 1/Plessey AWS-2, 1/Orion RTN-10X
Sonar: Plessey MS-26
M: 2 G.M.T. 16-645E7CA diesels; 2 props; 6,000 hp **Range:** . . . **Fuel:** 350 tons
Man: 12 officers, 150 men

REMARKS: Survivors of a class of six: *General José de Austria* stricken 1976, *General José Garcia* stricken 1977, and *General Juan José Flores* and *Almirante Brion* stricken 1978. Both were extensively refitted by Cammell Laird, Birkenhead, from 1968 to 1975-76 (much delay caused by financial and labor problems). New radars, sonar, and armament fitted, with OTO Melara Compact mounts replacing the original four 102-mm dual-purpose (II × 2). Have NA-10 GFCS for the 76-mm guns and a lead-computing sight for the 40-mm AA mount. When new, could make 32 knots. Very lightly built, with much use of aluminum alloy. Denny-Brown fin stabilizers. Being re-engined by C.N.R., Genoa, Italy, with diesels 10-84 to 27-7-85 and transferred to the new Coast Guard.

PATROL BOATS

◆ **6 Constitución class** Bldr: Vosper Thornycroft, Portsmouth, U.K.

	Laid down	L	In serv.
P-11 CONSTITUCIÓN	1-73	1-6-73	16-8-74
P-12 FEDERACIÓN	8-73	26-2-74	25-3-75
P-13 INDEPENDENCIA	2-73	24-7-73	20-9-74
P-14 LIBERTAD	9-73	5-3-74	12-6-75
P-15 PATRIA	3-73	27-9-73	9-1-75
P-16 VICTORIA	3-73	3-9-74	22-9-75

D: 150 tons (170 fl) **S:** 31 kts **Dim:** 36.88 (33.53 wl) × 7.16 × 1.73
A: P-11, P-13, P-15: 1/76-mm OTO Melara Compact
P-12, P-14, P-16: 2/Otomat Mk I SSM (I × 2)—1/40-mm AA
Electron Equipt: 1/SPQ-2D; P-11, P-13, P-15: 1/Orion RTN-10X also
M: 2 MTU MD 16V538 TB90 diesels; 1 prop; 7,080 max. hp/5,900 sust. hp
Electric: 250 kw **Range:** 1,350/16 **Man:** 3 officers, 14 men

REMARKS: Ordered 4-72. All equipped with Vosper fin stabilizers. New hull numbers assigned 1978. Maximum sustained speed is 27 knots. NA-10 Mod. 1 GFCS in 76-mm gun-equipped boats. Transferred from the Navy, 1983. All to be refitted.

PATROL BOATS *(continued)*

Federación (P-12)—missile version

Constitución (P-11)—76-mm gun version Vosper, 1975

◆ **2 ex-U.S. Achomawi-class fleet tugs** Bldr: Charleston SB & DD, S.C.

	Laid down	L	In serv.
R-21 Felipe Larrazabel (ex-*Utina,* ATF 163)	6-6-45	31-8-45	30-1-46
R-23 Miguel Rodriguez (ex-*Salinin,* ATF 161)	13-4-45	20-7-45	11-9-45

Miguel Rodriguez (R-23) L. & L. Van Ginderen, 5-81

D: 1,235 tons (1,675 fl) **S:** 16.5 kts **Dim:** 62.48 (59.44) × 11.74 × 4.67
A: R-21 only: 1/76.2-mm DP **Electron Equipt:** Radar: 1/SPS-53
M: 4 G.M. 16-278A diesels, electric drive; 1 prop; 3,000 hp
Electric: 400 kw **Fuel:** 300 tons **Range:** 7,000/15 **Man:** 85 tot.

Remarks: R-21 loaned 3-9-71; purchased outright 30-12-77. R-23 purchased 1-9-78. Sister *Antonio Picardi* (R-22, ex-*Nipmuc,* AFT 157), ran aground and was lost 12-4-82. R-21 and R-23 transferred to Coast Guard in 1983, where they are used in patrol duties.

Note: Former trawler LG-12 was commissioned for Coast Guard use as a patrol boat in early 1984; no data available. A widely reported order for five Picchiotti of Italy 41.8-m patrol boats has not yet materialized.

NATIONAL GUARD

PATROL CRAFT

◆ **12 42-ft design** Bldr: MonArk Workboats, Monticello, Ark., U.S.A.

	In serv.		In serv.
B-8421 Rio Arauca II	2-7-84	B-8427 Rio Sarare	4-9-84
B-8422 Rio Catatumbo II	2-7-84	B-8428 Rio Uribante	4-9-84
B-8423 Rio Apure II	1-8-84	B-8429 Rio Cinaruco	1-11-84
B-8424 Rio Nearo II	1-8-84	B-8430 Rio Icabara	1-11-84
B-8425 Rio Meta II	30-8-84	B-8431 Rio Guarico II	-84
B-8426 Rio Portuguesa II	30-8-84	B-8432 Rio Yaracuy	-84

Rio Catatumbo II (B-8422) MonArk, 7-84

D: 15 tons (fl) **S:** 28 kts **Dim:** 13.03 (12.55 pp) × 4.47 × 1.17
A: 3/12.7-mm mg **Electron Equipt:** Radar: 1/Raytheon 1900
M: 2 G.M. Detroit Diesel 8V92 T diesels; 2 props; 1,100 hp
Range: 600/. . . **Electric:** 10.5 kw **Man:** 4 tot.

Remarks: Aluminum construction. For river and lake patrol. Replace 12 French-built craft delivered 1970-77.

◆ **10 21-ft design** Bldr: MonArk Workboats, Monticello, Ark., U.S.A.

A-6901 Lago 1	A-7918 Rio Cabriales	A-7921 Rio Tuy
A-6902 Lago 2	A-7919 Rio Chama	A-7929 Rio Manati
A-6903 Lago 3	A-7920 Rio Caribe	A-8223 Rio Goaigoaza
A-6904 Lago 4		

21-ft. design—outboard motors not fitted MonArk, 1984

D: 1.25 tons (fl) **S:** 30 kts **Dim:** 6.02 × 2.36 × 0.33
A: 1/12.7-mm mg **Man:** 4 tot.
M: 2 Evinrude gasoline outboard motors; 230 hp

Remarks: Aluminum construction. For river and lake patrol. Equipped with push-knees to act as pusher tugs.

◆ **15 18-ft chase boat design** Bldr: MonArk Workboats, Monticello, Ark., U.S.A. (In serv. 11-1-85)

D: 0.5 tons (fl) **S:** 30 kts **Dim:** 5.48 × 2.08 × 0.15
A: 1/12.7-mm mg **Man:** 4 tot.
M: 1 Evinrude gasoline outboard motor; 140 hp

Remarks: Aluminum construction.

VENEZUELA *(continued)*
PATROL CRAFT *(continued)*

18-ft. chase boat MonArk, 1985

◆ **12 U.S. design** Bldr: Robert E. Direcktor SY, Mamaroneck, N.Y.

A-8201 Punta Peret	A-8207 Punta Ballena
A-8202 Punta Mulato	A-8208 Punta Macuro
A-8203 Punta Barima	A-8209 Punta Mariusa
A-8204 Punta Mosquito	A-8210 Punta Moron
A-8205 Punta Playa	A-8211 Punta Macoya
A-8206 Punta Mulatos	A-8212 Punta Cardon

"Punta" class—ramp stern version F. Nakajima/Direcktor SY, 1984

D: Approx. 50 tons (fl) **S:** 28.5 kts **Dim:** 23.44 × 4.88 × . . .
A: . . . **Electron Equipt:** Radar: 1/Furuno . . . **Electric:** 60 kw
M: 2 G.M. 12V92M TI diesels; 2 props; 1,950 hp **Range:** 1,100/22 **Man:** 10 tot.

Remarks: First six ordered 1980, delivered 8-82; second six ordered 1982 and delivered by 10-84. Aluminum construction. Of the first increment, three have a small helicopter platform aft, and three have ramps for landing small vehicles.

Note: The National Guard is also acquiring numbers of 11.6-m "Batalla del Lago" and 8.5-m "General José Antonio Piez"-class glass-reinforced plastic-hulled patrol craft built in Venezuela by Yamaha Fibra, C.A. Numbers built and characteristics are unavailable.

◆ **21 Rio Orinoco class** Bldr: C 87-96: INMA, La Spezia; others: Dianca, Puerto Cabello (In serv. 1974-78)

C-87 Rio Orinoco	C-94 Rio San Juan	C-132 Rio . . . .
C-88 Rio Ventuari	C-95 Rio Tucuyo	C-133 Rio . . . .
C-89 Rio Caparo	C-96 Rio Turbio	C-134 Rio . . . .
C-90 Rio Venamo	C-128 Rio Guaicaipuro	C-135 Rio . . . .
C-91 Rio Torres	C-129 Rio Tamanco	C-136 Rio . . . .
C-92 Rio Escalente	C-130 Rio Manaure	C-137 Rio . . . .
C-93 Rio Limon	C-131 Rio Ara	C-138 Rio . . . .

D: 65 tons (fl) **S:** 31 kts **Dim:** 28.3 × 4.8 × 1.5
A: 1/12.7-mm mg **M:** 2 MTU 12V 493 TY diesels; 2 props; 2,200 hp
Range: 500/. . . **Man:** 8 tot.

Remarks: Wooden construction.

◆ **17 U.S. Enforcer class** Bldr: Bertram Yacht, Miami, Fla.

Remarks: Four of the 11.6-m version delivered 1978, ten more in 1980. One 14.0-m version and two 13.4-m version delivered 1980. All have outdrive motors and glass-reinforced plastic hulls. **A:** Small arms.

VIETNAM

Socialist Republic of Vietnam

Personnel (1985): Approx. 6,000 total

Merchant Marine (1984): 119 ships—278,899 grt
(tankers: 13 ships—37,361 grt)

Note: The following listings include ships known to have been in North Vietnamese service in 1975, those units left behind in South Vietnam that did not escape the communist victory, and a number of ships known to have been turned over to Vietnam by the Soviet Union since 1975. The operability of much of the former U.S. equipment is questionable, but several of the larger units have been seen at sea. New ships names are not known.

Naval Aviation: Three Soviet Beriev Be-12 Mail antisubmarine patrol amphibians were delivered in 1981 for coastal surveillance duties, and there may be up to 10 Mi-4 helicopters.

FRIGATES

◆ **5 ex-Soviet Petya-II class**

HQ 08 HQ 09 HQ. . . HQ. . . HQ. . .

Petya II of the Vietnamese Navy U.S. Navy, 7-79

D: 950 tons (1,150 fl) **S:** 30 kts **Dim:** 82.3 × 9.1 × 3.2
A: 4/76.2-mm DP (II × 2)—3/533-mm TT (III × 2)—4/RBU-2500 ASW RL (XVI × 4)—2/d.c. racks—mines
Electron Equipt: Radar: 1/Don-2, 1/Strut Curve, 1/Hawk Screech
Sonar: 1/high frequency—EW: 2/Watch Dog
M: CODAG: 2 gas turbines, 15,000 hp each; 1 diesel, 6,000 hp; 3 props
Range: 4,000/10 (diesel); 500/30 (CODAG) **Man:** 80–90 tot.

Remarks: Of the same export version as has been transferred to India and Syria. Two transferred 12-78, two transferred 1-83, one transferred 12-84; the last three had 2/RBU 6000 ASW RL and 5/400-mm ASW TT (V × 1).

◆ **1 ex-U.S. Savage-class former radar picket**

Bldr: Consolidated Steel Corp., Orange, Texas

	Laid down	L	In serv.
HQ 03 Dai Ky (ex-*Tran Khahn Du*, ex-*Forster*, DER 334)	31-8-43	13-11-43	25-1-44

D: 1,590 (1,850 fl) **S:** 20 kts **Dim:** 93.3 (91.4 wl) × 11.2 × 4.3 (hull)
A: 2/76.2-mm DP (I × 2)—1/81-mm mortar—2/127-mm mg (I × 2)
Electron Equipt: Radar: 1/SPS-10, 1/SPS-29, 1/SPG-34
Sonar: SQS-29 series
M: 4 Fairbanks-Morse 38D8⅛ diesels; 2 props; 6,000 hp **Electric:** 580 kw
Fuel: 310 tons **Range:** 10,000/15 **Man:** Approx. 170 tot.

Remarks: Transferred to South Vietnam 25-9-71. Was in overhaul at Saigon in 1975 and has been reactivated by the new government. Mk 63 radar GFCS forward, Mk 51 Mod. 2 optical GFCS aft. Additional AA guns probably added.

◆ **1 ex-U.S. Barnegat class** Bldr: Lake Washington SY, Houghton, Wash.

	Laid down	L	In serv.
HQ 06 N. . . . . . . (ex-*Tham Ngu Lao*, ex-U.S.C.G. *Absecon*, WHEC 374, ex-AVP 23)	23-7-41	8-3-42	28-1-43

D: 1,766 tons (2,800 fl) **S:** 18 kts **Dim:** 94.7 (91.4 wl) × 12.5 × 4.1
A: 1/127-mm 38-cal. DP—2/81-mm mortars (I × 2)
Electron Equipt: Radar: 1/SPS-21, 1/SPS-29, 1/Mk 26
M: 4 Fairbanks-Morse 38D8⅛ diesels; 2 props; 6,080 hp **Electric:** 600 kw
Fuel: 26 tons **Range:** 20,000/10
Man: Approx. 200 tot.

Remarks: Transferred to South Vietnam in 1971, having served in the U.S. Coast Guard since 1948. Believed to have been made operational by Vietnam. Has probably had 37-mm AA added to armament and reportedly has been equipped with 2 SS-N-2A Styx missiles removed from a stricken Komar-class unit.

CORVETTES

◆ **2 ex-U.S. Admirable-class former fleet minesweepers**

	Bldr	Laid down	L	In serv.
HQ. . . (ex-*Ky Hoa*, ex-*Sentry*, MSF 299)	Winslow Marine Railway, Winslow, Wash.	16-5-43	15-8-43	30-5-44
HQ-07 (ex-*Ha Hoi*, ex-*Prowess*, IX 305, ex-MSF 280)	Gulf SB, Chickasaw, La.	15-9-43	17-2-44	27-9-44

D: 650 tons (945 fl) **S:** 14.8 kts **Dim:** 56.2 (54.9 wl) × 10.1 × 3.0
A: 2/57-mm AA (II × 1)—2/37-mm AA (I × 2)—6/23-mm AA (II × 3)
Electron Equipt: Radar: 1/SPS-53

CORVETTES *(continued)*

M: 2 Cooper-Bessemer GSB-8 diesels; 1,710 hp **Electric:** 280 kw
Man: Approx. 80 tot.

REMARKS: Transferred to South Vietnam 8-62 and 6-70, respectively. All minesweeping gear removed before transfer, and antisubmarine warfare gear removed during overhauls in early 1970s. At least one, now numbered HG 07, is operational, rearmed with Soviet or Chinese weapons.

GUIDED-MISSILE PATROL BOATS

◆ **8 Soviet Osa-II class**

D: 215 tons (245 fl) **S:** 35 kts **Dim:** 38.6 × 7.6 × 2.0
A: 4/SS-N-2B Styx (I × 4)—4/30-mm AA (II × 2)
Electron Equipt: Radar: 1/Square Tie, 1/Drum Tilt
IFF: 2/Square Head, 1/High Pole B
M: 3 M-504 diesels; 3 props; 15,000 hp
Range: 500/34; 750/25 **Man:** 30 tot.

REMARKS: Transferred: 2 in 10-79, 2 in 9-80, 2 in 11-80, and 2 in 2-81.

TORPEDO BOATS

◆ **16 Soviet Shershen class**

Shershen, with torpedo tubes, under tow to Vietnam U.S. Navy, 9-79

D: 135 tons (170 fl) **S:** 45 kts **Dim:** 34.7 × 6.7 × 1.5
A: 4/30-mm AA (II × 2)—4/533-mm TT—2/d.c. racks (12 d.c.)
Electron Equipt: Radar: 1/Pot Drum, 1/Drum Tilt—IFF: 1/High Pole A, 1-2/Square Head
M: 3 M503A diesels; 2 props; 12,000 hp **Range:** 460/42; 850/30 **Man:** 19 tot.

REMARKS: Transferred: 2 (without torpedo tubes) on 16-4-79, 2 on 12-9-79, 2 in 8-80, 2 in 10-80, 2 in 1981 and 4 in 6-83.

PATROL BOATS

◆ **2 Soviet Turya-class semi-hydrofoils** Bldr: Ulis SY, Vladivostok

D: 210 tons (245 fl) **S:** 40 kts **Dim:** 39.0 × 7.6 (12.5 over foils) × 2.0 (4.0 over foils)
A: 2/57-mm DP aft (II × 1)—2/25-mm AA fwd. (II × 1)
Electron Equipt: Radar: 1/Pot Drum, 1/Muff Cob
IFF: 1/High Pole B, 1/Square Head
M: 3 M504 diesels; 3 props; 15,000 hp **Range:** 400/38; 650/25 **Man:** 24 tot.

REMARKS: One transferred 5-84, the second in 11-84; neither had torpedo tubes or the standard helicopter-type dipping sonar.

◆ **6 Soviet Zhuk class**

D: 48 tons (60 fl) **S:** 34 kts **Dim:** 24.0 × 5.0 × 1.2
A: 4/14.5-mm AA (II × 2) **Electron Equipt:** Radar: 1/Spin Trough
M: 2 M50-F diesels; 2 props; 2,400 hp
Range: 700/28; 1,100/15 **Man:** 12 tot.

REMARKS: Transferred: 3 in 1978, 3 in 1979, and one in 5-85.

◆ **up to 17 PGM 59 and PGM 71 class**

Bldrs: ex-PGM 59 to ex-PGM 63: J. M. Martinac SB, Seattle, Wash.; ex-PGM 64 to ex-PGM 69: Marinette Marine, Marinette, Wisc.; others: Peterson Bldrs., Sturgeon Bay, Wisc. (In serv. 1963-67)

ex-HQ 600 ex-PHU DU (ex-PGM 64)
ex-HQ 601 ex-TIEN MOI (ex-PGM 65)
ex-HQ 602 ex-MINH HOA (ex-PGM 66)
ex-HQ 603 ex-KIEN VANG (ex-PGM 67)
ex-HQ 606 ex-MAY RUT (ex-PGM 59)
ex-HQ 607 ex-NAM DU (ex-PGM 61)
ex-HQ 608 ex-HOA LU (ex-PGM 62)
ex-HQ 609 ex-TO YEN (ex-PGM 63)
ex-HQ 610 ex-DINH HAI (ex-PGM 69)
ex-HQ 611 ex-TRUONG SA (ex-PGM 70)
ex-HQ 612 ex-THAI BINH (ex-PGM 72)
ex-HQ 613 ex-THI TU (ex-PGM 73)
ex-HQ 614 ex-SONG TU (ex-PGM 74)
ex-HQ 615 ex-TAT SA (ex-PGM 80)
ex-HQ 616 ex-HOANG SA (ex-PGM 82)
ex-HQ 617 ex-PHU QUI (ex-PGM 81)
ex-HQ 619 ex-THO CHAU (ex-PGM 91)

D: 102 tons light (142 fl) **S:** 17 kts **Dim:** 30.81 × 6.45 × 2.3
A: 1/40-mm AA—4/20-mm AA (II × 2)—4/12.7-mm mg (II × 2)

ex-Dinh Hai (HQ 610) 1967

M: ex-PGM 59 to ex-PGM 70: 2 Mercedes Benz MB 820 Db diesels; 2 props; 1,900 hp
ex-PGM 71 to ex-PGM 91: 8 G.M. 6-71 diesels; 2 props; 2,040 hp
Electric: 30 kw **Fuel:** 16 tons **Range:** 1,000/17 **Man:** 30 tot.

◆ **8 ex-Soviet S.O.-1 class**

D: 190 tons (215 fl) **S:** 28 kts **Dim:** 42.0 × 6.1 × 1.9
A: 4/25-mm AA (II × 2)—4/RBU-1200 ASW RL (V × 4)—2/d.c. racks (24 d.c.)—mines
Electron Equipt: Radar: 1/Pot Head—Sonar: 1/high frequency
M: 3 Type 40D diesels; 3 props; 7,500 hp **Range:** 1,100/13 **Man:** 30 tot.

REMARKS: Transferred: 2 in 3-80, 2 in 9-80, 2 in 5-81, and 2 in 9-83. An earlier increment transferred in 1960-66 have all been discarded.

◆ **8 ex-Chinese Shanghai-II class**

D: 122.5 tons normal (134.8 fl) **S:** 28.5 kts **Dim:** 38.78 × 5.41 × 1.55 hull
A: 4/37-mm AA (II × 2)—4/25-mm AA (II × 2)
Electron Equipt: Radar: Skin Head
M: 2 M50-F4, 1,200-hp diesels, 2 12D6, 900-hp diesels; 4 props; 4,220 hp
Range: 750/16.5 **Electric:** 39 kw **Endurance:** 7 days **Man:** 36 tot.

REMARKS: Transferred: four in 1966 and four in 1968. Probably in very poor condition.

◆ **up to 26 ex-U.S. Coast Guard Point class** Bldr: Coast Guard Yard, Curtis Bay, Md. (In serv. late 1950s)

ex-HQ 700 ex-LE PHUOC DUI (ex-*Pt. Garnet,* WPB 82310)
ex-HQ 701 ex-LE VAN NGA (ex-*Pt. League,* WPB 82304)
ex-HQ 702 ex-HUYNH VAN CU (ex-*Pt. Clear,* WPB 82315)
ex-HQ 703 ex-NGUYEN DAO (ex-*Pt. Gammon,* WPB 82328)
ex-HQ 704 ex-DAO THUC (ex-*Pt. Comfort,* WPB 82317)
ex-HQ 705 ex-LE NGOC THAN (ex-*Pt. Ellis,* WPB 82330)
ex-HQ 706 ex-NGUYEN NGOC THACH (ex-*Pt. Slocum,* WPB 82313)
ex-HQ 707 ex-DANG VAN HOANH (ex-*Pt. Hudson,* WPB 82322)
ex-HQ 708 ex-LE DINH HUNG (ex-*Pt. White,* WPB 82308)
ex-HQ 709 ex-THUONG TIEN (ex-*Pt. Dume,* WPB 82325)
ex-HQ 710 ex-PHAM NGOC CHAU (ex-*Pt. Arden,* WPB 82309)
ex-HQ 711 ex-DAO VAN DANG (ex-*Pt. Glover,* WPB 82307)
ex-HQ 712 ex-LE DGOC AN (ex-*Pt. Jefferson,* WPB 82306)
ex-HQ 713 ex-HUYNH VAN NGAN (ex-*Pt. Kennedy,* WPB 82320)
ex-HQ 714 ex-TRAN LO (ex-*Pt. Young,* WPB 82303)
ex-HQ 715 ex-BUI VIET THANH (ex-*Pt. Partridge,* WPB 82305)
ex-HQ 716 ex-NGUYEN AN (ex-*Pt. Caution* WPB 82301)
ex-HQ 717 ex-NGUYEN HAN (ex-*Pt. Welcome,* WPB 82329)
ex-HQ 718 ex-NGO VAN QUYEN (ex-*Pt. Banks,* WPB 82327)
ex-HQ 719 ex-VAN DIEN (ex-*Pt. Lomas,* WPB 82321)
ex-HQ 720 ex-HO DANG LA (ex-*Pt. Grace,* WPB 82323)
ex-HQ 721 ex-DAM THOAJ (ex-*Pt. Mast,* WPB 82316)
ex-HQ 722 ex-HUYNH BO (ex-*Pt. Grey,* WPB 82324)
ex-HQ 723 ex-NGUYEN KIM HUNG (ex-*Pt. Orient,* WPB 82319)
ex-HQ 724 ex-HO DUY (ex-*Pt. Cypress,* WPB 82326)
ex-HQ 725 ex-TROUNG BA (ex-*Pt. Maromec,* WPB 82331)

ex-Ngo Van Quyen (HQ 718) 1969

PATROL BOATS *(continued)*

D: 64 tons (67 fl) **S:** 23.7 kts **Dim:** 25.3 × 5.23 × 1.95
A: 1/81-mm mortar combined with 12.7-mm mg—4/12.7-mm mg (I × 4)
M: 2 Cummins VT-12-M-700 diesels; 2 props; 1,600 hp
Fuel: 5.7 tons **Range:** 460/23.7; 1,400/8 **Man:** 12 tot.

REMARKS: Had been operating in Vietnamese waters with U.S. Coast Guard crews when transferred to South Vietnam in 1969-70. Probably rearmed, if operational.

PATROL CRAFT

◆ **2 ex-Soviet PO 2 class**

D: 50 tons (fl) **S:** 9 kts **Dim:** 21.0 × 4.5 × . . .
A: 1/12.7-mm mg **M:** 1 diesel; 1 prop; 150 hp

REMARKS: Transferred 2-80. Utility craft also useable as a tug or, with appropriate equipment, a diving tender.

◆ **2 ex-East German Bremse class**

D: 25 tons **S:** 14 kts **Dim:** 23.0 × 5.0 × 1.1
A: . . . **M:** 2 diesels; 2 props; 600 hp

REMARKS: Transferred late 1970s. Intended for patrol in sheltered waters and inland waterways.

◆ **up to 107 ex-U.S. Swift Mk-1 and Mk-2 class** Bldr: Swiftships Inc., Morgan City, La. (In serv. 1968-70)

D: 19 tons (fl—Mk-2: 19.2) **S:** 25 kts
Dim: Mk-1: 15.28 × 3.99 × 1.07; Mk-2: 15.64 × 4.14 × 1.07
A: 1/81-mm mortar combined with 12.7-mm mg—2/12.7-mm mg (II × 1)
M: 2 G.M. 12V71N diesels; 2 props; 860 hp **Range:** 400/24 **Man:** 6 tot.

REMARKS: Transferred on completion. Most believed still serviceable. Most (approx. 90) were of the Mk-I variety, without forecastle.

RIVERINE WARFARE CRAFT

◆ **up to 9 ex-U.S. CCB (command and control boat) class** (In serv. 1969-70)

CCB class 1967

D: 160 tons light (75.5 fl) **S:** 8.5 kts **Dim:** 18.29 × 5.33 × 1.0
A: 1/20-mm AA—1/12.7-mm mg—2/7.62-mm mg (I × 2)—1/60-mm mortar
M: 2 Gray Marine 64HN9 diesels; 2 props; 450 hp
Range: 160/8 **Man:** 11 tot.

REMARKS: Equipped with communications facility in well, occupied by 105-mm mortar in otherwise similar LCM monitor class. Can tow disabled craft. Some had three 20-mm AA (I × 3) with an ASPB-type turret forward.

◆ **up to 60 ex-U.S. ASPB (assault support patrol boat) class** (In serv. 1969-70)

D: 30 tons light (38 fl) **S:** 14 kts **Dim:** 15.3 × 5.32 × 1.22
A: 2/20-mm AA (I × 2)—2/76.2-mm mg (I × 2)—2/40-mm grenade launchers
M: 2 G.M. 12V71N diesels; 2 props; 1,050 hp
Range: 200/10 **Man:** 5 tot.

REMARKS: Two armored turrets with interchangeable armaments of one 20-mm AA, two 12.7-mm mg, or two 40-mm grenade launchers (or a combination thereof). A few had an 81-mm mortar aft in an open well.

◆ **up to 42 ex-U.S. monitor Mk-V class** (In serv. 1969-70)

D: 60.3 tons light (75.5 fl) **S:** 8.5 kts **Dim:** 18.29 × 5.33 × 1.0
A: 2/20-mm AA (I × 2)—2/12.7-mm mg (I × 2)—4/7.62-mm mg—1/81-mm mortar
M: 2 Gray Marine 64HN9 diesels; 2 props; 450 hp
Range: 160/8 **Man:** 11 tot.

REMARKS: Originally built as monitors, rather than converted as the class below. A few had a turret-mounted 105-mm howitzer in place of the bow 20-mm turret and 81-mm mortar in well. All had screen and "venetian-blind-like" bar armor to break up projectiles. Towing rig on stern of most.

Monitor Mk-V class 1967

◆ **up to 22 ex-U.S. converted LCM(6) monitors**

D: 75 tons (fl) **S:** 8 kts **Dim:** 18.29 × 5.2 × 1.0
A: 1/40-mm AA (in some)—1/20-mm AA—2/12.7-mm mg (I × 2)—1/81-mm mortar (or 2 M10-8 flame throwers)
M: 2 Gray Marine 64HN9 diesels; 2 props; 450 hp
Man: 10 tot.

REMARKS: Converted from LCM(6)-class landing craft. Transferred 1964-67.

◆ **up to 60 ex-U.S. ATC (armored troop carriers) class**

ATC class—note bar armor 1967

D: 55.8 tons light (70 fl) **S:** 8.5 kts **Dim:** 17.09 × 5.33 × 3.0
A: 1/20-mm AA—2/12.7-mm mg (I × 2)—2-6/7.62-mm mg (I × 2-6)—2/40-mm grenade launchers (I × 2)
M: 2 Gray Marine 64HN9 diesels; 2 props; 450 hp **Man:** 7 tot.

REMARKS: Transferred 1969. Converted LCM(6)-class landing craft. Can carry up to 40 troops. Bow ramp. Bar armor on hull and superstructure, bullet-proof awning over troop space. A few had a small helicopter platform in place of awning. Others were configured for refueling with 4,500-liter tank in the cargo well. Four CSB (combat salvage boat) versions of the LCM(6) design were also left in Vietnam, having been transferred 1969-70.

◆ **up to 293 ex-U.S. PBR (patrol boat, riverine) Mk-II class** Bldr: Uniflite, Bellingham, Wash. (In serv. 1968-70)

D: 6.7 tons light (8 fl) **S:** 24 kts **Dim:** 9.73 × 3.53 × 0.6
A: 3/12.7-mm mg (II × 1, I × 1)—1/60-mm mortar
M: 2 G.M. 6V53N diesels; 2 Jacuzzi water jets; 430 hp
Range: 150/23 **Man:** 4 tot.

MINE WARFARE SHIPS AND CRAFT

◆ **1 ex-Soviet Yurka-class fleet minesweeper**

D: 400 tons (460 fl) **S:** 18 kts **Dim:** 52.0 × 9.3 × 2.0
Electron Equipt: Radar: 1/Don-2, 1/Drum Tilt
IFF: 3/Square Head, 1/High Pole B
M: 2 diesels; 2 props; 4,000 hp **Man:** 45 tot.

REMARKS: Transferred 12-79. Aluminum alloy hull.

◆ **2 Soviet Yevgenya-class inshore minesweepers** Bldr: Svedniy Neva SY, Kolpino

D: 80 tons (90 fl) **S:** 11 kts **Dim:** 26.2 × 6.1 × 1.5
A: 2/14.5-mm mg (II × 1) **Electron Equipt:** Radar: 1/Spin Trough
M: 2 diesels; 2 props; 660 hp **Range:** 300/10 **Man:** 10 tot.

REMARKS: Delivered to Cam Ranh Bay 11-84. Glass-reinforced plastic hull. Employ a television minehunting system that dispenses marker buoys to permit later disposal of the mines; useful to 30-m depths.

MINE WARFARE SHIPS AND CRAFT *(continued)*

◆ **5 ex-Soviet K-8-class minesweeping boats**

D: 26 tons (fl) **S:** 12 kts **Dim:** 16.9 × 3.2 × 0.8
A: 2/14.5-mm mg (II × 1) **M:** 2 6D12 diesels; 2 props; 300 hp **Man:** 6 tot.

REMARKS: Transferred 10-80. Wooden construction, built in Poland in the late-1950s. No radar.

◆ **up to 8 ex-U.S. MSB-5-class minesweeping boats** (In serv. 1952-56)

D: 30 tons (42 fl) **S:** 12 kts **Dim:** 17.45 × 4.83 × 1.32
A: Several 12.7-mm mg **M:** 2 Packard 2D850 diesels; 2 props; 600 hp
Fuel: 15.8 tons **Man:** 6 tot.

REMARKS: Transferred 1970. Wooden construction. Two sweep-current generators; capable of sweeping magnetic, contact, and acoustic mines.

◆ **up to 8 ex-U.S. MSR (minesweeper, riverine) class** (In serv. 1970)

D: 30 tons light (38 fl) **S:** 14 kts **Dim:** 15.3 × 5.32 × 1.22
A: 2/12.7-mm mg (II × 1) — 1/7.62-mm mg — 1/60-mm mortar
M: 2 G.M. 12V71N diesels; 2 props; 1,050 hp
Range: 200/10 **Man:** 5 tot.

REMARKS: A minesweeping version of the ASPB class. Some were equipped with a pipe frame projecting ahead of the craft to explode contact mines. Others had four 88.9-mm rocket launch tubes mounted on the twin machine gun turret on the bow. One or two 40-mm grenade launchers could also be carried.

◆ **up to 8 ex-U.S. MSM (minesweeping monitor) river minesweepers**

D: 70 tons (fl) **S:** 8.5 kts **Dim:** 17.09 × 5.33 × 3.1
A: 2/20-mm AA (I × 2) — 1/12.7-mm mg — 2/40-mm grenade launchers
M: 2 G.M. 64HN9 diesels; 2 props; 450 hp **Man:** 5 tot.

REMARKS: Converted LCM(6)-class landing craft, transferred in 1970. Not all had the 20-mm AA. Bar armor fitted to sides. Retained bow ramp. Could sweep mechanical and acoustic mines.

AMPHIBIOUS WARFARE SHIPS

◆ **3 ex-Soviet Polnocny-B medium landing ships** Bldr: Polnocny SY, Gdansk, Poland

D: 770 tons (fl) **S:** 18 kts **Dim:** 72.5 × 8.4 × 1.8
A: 2 or 4/30-mm AA (I or II × 2) — 2/140-mm barrage RL (XVIII × 2)
Electron Equipt: Radar: 1/Spin Trough, 1/Drum Tilt
M: 2 40D diesels; 2 props; 5,000 hp

REMARKS: Transferred: 1 in 5-79, 1 in 11-79, and 1 in 2-80.

◆ **3 ex-U.S. LST 1- and LST 542-class tank landing ships**

	Bldr	Laid down	L	In serv.
ex-HQ 501 ex-DA NANG (ex-*Maricopa County,* LST 938)	Bethlehem, Hingham, Mass.	12-7-44	15-8-44	9-9-44
ex-HQ 503 ex-VUNG TAU (ex-*Coconino County,* LST 603)	Chicago B & I, Seneca, Ill.	10-12-43	15-4-44	15-5-44
ex-HQ 504 ex-QUI NHON (ex-*Bullock County,* LST 509)	Jeffersonville B & M, Ind.	7-10-43	23-11-43	8-1-44

D: 1,623 tons light (4,080 fl) **S:** 11.6 kts **Dim:** 99.98 × 15.24 × 4.29
Electron Equipt: Radar: 1/SPS-53
M: 2 G.M. 12-567A (ex-HQ 501: G.M. 12-278A) diesels; 2 props; 1,700 hp
Electric: 300 kw **Fuel:** 590 tons **Range:** 6,000/9 (loaded)
Man: Approx. 100 tot.

REMARKS: Transferred to South Vietnam 7-62, 7-69, and 4-70, respectively. All believed to be operational; probably rearmed with Soviet-supplied weapons. Several of the ex-U.S. LSTs may have been transferred to Vietnam by China, at least one configured as a fuel tanker.

◆ **4 ex-U.S. LSM 1-class medium landing ships**

	Bldr	Laid down	L	In serv.
ex-HQ 401 ex-HAN GIANG (ex-Fr. LSM 9012, ex-LSM 110)	Brown SB, Houston	7-10-44	28-10-44	25-11-44
ex-HQ 403 ex-NINH GIANG (ex-LSM 85)	Brown SB, Houston	22-8-44	15-9-44	12-10-44
ex-HQ 405 ex-TIEN GIANG (ex-LSM 313)	Pullman Car, Chicago	16-3-44	24-5-44	25-6-44
ex-HQ 406 ex-HAU GIANG (ex-LSM 276)	Federal SB, Newark, N.J.	11-8-44	20-9-44	16-10-44

D: 520 tons light (1,095 fl) **S:** 12.5 kts **Dim:** 62.03 × 10.52 × 2.54
A: 2/40-mm AA (II × 1) — 4 or 5/20-mm AA (I × 4 or 5) — 4/12.7-mm mg (I × 4)
M: 2 Fairbanks-Morse 38D8⅛ diesels (ex-HQ 406: G.M. 278A); 2 props; 2,880 hp
Fuel: 160 tons **Range:** 4,900/12
Man: Approx. 70 tot.

REMARKS: Transferred to South Vietnam 10-55 (after service in French Navy), 10-56, 6-62, and 3-63, respectively. Ex-HQ 401 had been converted for hospital ship duties.

Ex-HQ 401 as a hospital ship U.S. Navy, 1967

◆ **up to 14 ex-U.S. LCU 1466-class utility landing craft**

ex-LCU 1475	ex-LCU 1485	ex-LCU 1502
ex-LCU 1479	ex-LCU 1493	ex-LCU 1594
ex-LCU 1480	ex-LCU 1494	ex-LCU 1595
ex-LCU 1481	ex-LCU 1498	ex-YFU 90 (ex-LCU 1582)
ex-LCU 1484	ex-LCU 1501	

D: 367 tons (fl) **S:** 8 kts **Dim:** 35.14 × 10.36 × 1.5
A: 4/20-mm AA (II × 2) **M:** 3 Gray Marine 64YTL diesels; 3 props; 675 hp
Fuel: 11 tons **Range:** 1,200/6 **Man:** 14 tot.

REMARKS: Transferred 1954-70 (ex-YFU 90 in 7-71). Cargo: 167 tons.

◆ **1 ex-U.S. LCU 501 (LCT(6))-class utility landing craft** Bldr: Bison SB, Buffalo, N.Y.

ex-LCU 1221 (L: 27-8-44)

D: 143 tons light (309 fl) **S:** 8 kts **Dim:** 36.42 × 9.75 × 1.3
A: 4/20-mm AA (II × 2) **M:** 3 Gray Marine 64HN9 diesels; 3 props; 675 hp
Fuel: 11 tons **Range:** 1,200/7 **Man:** 13 tot.

REMARKS: Transferred to South Vietnam 11-55. Cargo: 150 tons. Three half-sisters converted as salvage lift craft were also left behind in 1975; ex-YLLC 1 (ex-LCU 1348), ex-YLLC 3 (ex-YFU 33, ex-LCU 1195), and ex-YLLC 5 (ex-YFU 2, ex-LCU 529).

NOTE: Eighty-four U.S. LCM(6), 38 LCM(8), 40 LCVP, and several LCP-type landing craft were also abandoned; many have probably been returned to service.

◆ **12 or more ex-Soviet T4-class landing craft**

D: 35 tons (93 fl) **S:** 10 kts **Dim:** 19.9 × 5.6 × 1.4
M: 2 3D6 diesels; 2 props; 600 hp **Range:** 6,500/10

REMARKS: Transferred 1979 and later.

AUXILIARIES AND SERVICE CRAFT

◆ **1 ex-Soviet Kamenka-class hydrographic survey ship/buoy tender**

Bldr: Polnocny SY, Gdansk, Poland

D: 703 tons (fl) **S:** 13.7 kts **Dim:** 53.5 × 9.1 × 2.6
Electron Equipt: Radar: 1/Don-2
M: 2 diesels; 2 CP props; 1,765 hp **Range:** 4,000/10

REMARKS: Transferred 12-79. One 5-ton buoy crane.

◆ **3 ex-U.S. 174-foot-class gasoline tankers**

Bldr: George Lawley & Sons, Neponset, Mass. (ex-YOG 56: R.T.C. SB, Camden, N.J.)

	Laid down	L	In serv.
ex-HQ 472 (ex-YOG 67)	26-1-45	17-3-45	4-5-45
ex-HQ 473 (ex-YOG 71)	11-6-45	24-7-45	27-8-45
ex-HQ 475 (ex-YOG 56)	17-5-44	30-9-44	19-2-45

D: 440 tons light (1,390 fl) **S:** 11 kts **Dim:** 53.04 (51.2 pp) × 9.75 × 3.94
A: 2/20-mm AA (I × 2)
M: 1 G.M. diesel (ex-YOG 56: Union diesel); 1 prop; 640 hp (ex-YOG 56: 540 hp)
Electric: 80 kw **Fuel:** 25 tons **Cargo:** 860 tons **Man:** 23 tot.

REMARKS: Transferred to South Vietnam in 7-67, 3-70, and 6-72. Employed in transporting diesel fuel.

◆ **1 ex-U.S. 174-foot-class water tanker** Bldr: Nav. Mec. Castellamare, Italy (In serv. 1956)

ex-HQ 9118 (ex-YW 152)

D: 1,250 tons (fl) **S:** 9 kts **Dim:** 54.4 × 9.8 × 4.3
A: 2/20-mm AA (I × 2)
M: 1 Ansaldo diesel; 1 prop; 600 hp **Man:** 23 tot.

REMARKS: Built with U.S. funds for South Vietnam under the Offshore Procurement Program.

◆ **3 ex-U.S. Cholocco-class medium harbor tugs** Bldr: Commercial Iron Wks, Portland, Ore.

VIETNAM *(continued)*
AUXILIARIES AND SERVICE CRAFT *(continued)*

	In serv.
Ex-HQ 9550 (ex-*Poknoket,* YTM 762, ex-YTB 517)	25-1-46
Ex-HQ 9551 (ex-*Hombro,* YTM 769, ex-YTB 508)	7-7-45
Ex-HQ 9552 (ex-*Nootka,* YTM 771, ex-YTB 506)	8-11-45

D: 260 tons (350 fl) **S:** 11 kts **Dim:** 30.8 × 8.5 × 3.7
M: 2 Enterprise diesels; 1 prop; 1,270 hp **Man:** 8 tot.

Remarks: Reclassified YTM from YTB in 1966; transferred to South Vietnam 1971.

◆ **up to 9 ex-U.S. YTL-type small harbor tugs**

ex-YTL 152	ex-YTL 245	ex-YTL 456
ex-YTL 200	ex-YTL 423	ex-YTL 457
ex-YTL 206	ex-YTL 452	ex-YTL 586

D: 70 tons (80 fl) **S:** 10 kts **Dim:** 20.16 × 5.18 × 2.44
M: 1 Hoover-Owens-Rentschler diesel; 1 prop; 300 hp
Electric: 40 kw **Fuel:** 7 tons **Man:** 4 tot.

Remarks: Built 1941-45. Four transferred to South Vietnam in 1955-56, two in 1969, and two in 1971.

◆ **2 ex-U.S. Navy repair barges (non-self-propelled)**

Ex-HQ 9601 (ex-YR 24) Ex-HQ 9611 (ex-YR 71)

D: 520 tons light (770 fl) **Dim:** 46.6 × 10.7 × 1.8

◆ **4 ex-U.S. Navy repair, berthing, and messing barge (non-self-propelled)**

Ex-HQ 9610 (ex-YRBM 17) Ex-HQ 9613 (ex-YRBM 21)
Ex-HQ 9612 (ex-YRBM 16) Ex-HQ-. . . (ex-YRBM 18)

D: 236 tons (310 fl) **Dim:** 34.1 × 11.0 × 0.9

Remarks: Completed 1964-65. Ex-HQ 9613 is 498 tons (585 fl); 44.5 × 14.0 × 0.9 and was completed in 1970.

◆ **2 ex-U.S. Navy barracks craft (non-self-propelled)**

Ex-HQ 9050 (ex-APL 26) Ex-HQ 9051 (ex-APL 27)

D: 1,300 tons (2,580 fl) **Dim:** 79.6 × 15.0 × 2.6

Remarks: Completed 1944-45.

◆ **1 ex-U.S. Navy refrigerated lighter** Bldr: Defoe SB, Bay City, Mich.

Ex-HQ 490 (ex-YFR 889) (In serv. 1945)

D: 300 tons (660 fl) **S:** 10 kts **Dim:** 40.5 × 9.1 × 2.7
M: 2 G.M. diesels; 1 prop; 1,000 hp **Fuel:** 30 tons **Cargo:** 300 tons

Remarks: Coastal cargo ship, transferred 1971.

◆ **2 ex-U.S. Navy large covered lighters**

Ex-YFNB 18 Ex-YFNB 28

D: 700 tons (2,700 fl) **Dim:** 79.6 × 14.6 × 4.0

Remarks: Ex-HQ numbers not available. Transferred 1971. Cargo: 2,000 tons.

◆ **8 ex-U.S. Navy open lighters**

Ex-YC 791, 797, 806, 807, 1108, 1320, 1414, 1415

Remarks: Ex YC 791, 1108, and 1320 displace 190 tons light/690 fl, others are 130 tons light/630 fl (33.5 × 9.8 × 2.4). Transferred around 1971.

◆ **2 ex-U.S. Navy floating cranes**

ex-HQ 9650 (ex-YD 230) Ex-HQ 9651 (ex-YD 195)

◆ **2 ex-U.S. floating drydocks** (In serv. 1944)

Ex-HQ 9600 (ex-AFDL 13) Ex-HQ 9604 (ex-AFDL 22)

Remarks: Ex-HQ 9600 has a capacity of 1,000 tons and is 61.0 × 19.5. Ex-HQ 6904 has a capacity of 1,900 tons and is 87.8 × 19.5. Both were left behind in 1975.

◆ **1 ex-U.S. water barge (non-self-propelled)**

ex-HQ 9113 (ex-YWN 153)

D: 220 tons (1,270 fl) **Dim:** 36.6 × 10.1 × 2.4 **Cargo:** 1,050 tons

Note: In addition to the ships and craft listed above, the Vietnamese Navy undoubtedly employs many smaller craft ("junks") in patrol and logistics duties. Cargo ships of up to several hundred deadweight tons capacity were built in North Vietnamese shipyards during the Vietnamese War for infiltration purposes; many of these armed craft may still be in military service.

VIRGIN ISLANDS

British Virgin Islands

ROYAL VIRGIN ISLANDS POLICE FORCE

◆ **1 patrol craft** Bldr: Brooke Marine, Lowestoft, U.K. (In serv. 1975)

Virgin Clipper

D: 15 tons (fl) **S:** 22 kts **Dim:** 12.2 × 3.7 × 0.6
A: 1/7.62-mm mg **Electron Equipt:** Radar: 1/Decca 101
M: 2 Caterpillar diesels; 2 props; 370 hp **Man:** 4 tot.

◆ **2 Sea Eagle-class launches** Bldr: Coloso Boat Co. (In serv. 1980)

D: . . . **S:** . . . **Dim:** 7.0 × . . . × . . .
M: 2 Evinrude outboard engines; 110 hp

WESTERN SAMOA

PATROL BOAT

◆ **0 (+1) Australian ASI 315 class** Bldr: Australian SB Industries, South Coogie, Western Australia (In serv. 1987)

D: 165 tons (fl) **S:** 20 kts **Dim:** 31.5 (28.6 wl) × 8.1 × 2.12
A: . . . **Electron Equipt:** Radar: 1/Furuno 1011
M: 2 Caterpillar 3516 diesels; 2 props; . . . hp **Electric:** . . .
Fuel: 33 tons **Range:** 2,500/12 **Man:** 3 officers, 14 men

Remarks: Provided by Australian foreign aid. Sisters being built for other Southwest Pacific nations. See illustration under Papua New Guinea.

YEMEN

People's Democratic Republic of Yemen (South Yemen)

Personnel (1985): About 1,000 total

Merchant Marine (1984): 28 ships — 12,495 grt (1 tanker — 1,886 grt)

Note: A number of naval units were lost during the 1-86 coup.

CORVETTE

◆ **1 ex-Soviet T-58 class**

D: 750 tons (860 fl) **S:** 18 kts **Dim:** 70.0 × 9.1 × 2.5
A: 4/57-mm AA (II × 2) — 2/RBU-1200 ASW RL (V × 2) — 2/d.c. racks — mines
Electron Equipt: Radar: 1/Don-2, 1/Muff Cob
Sonar: 1/high frequency
M: 2 diesels; 2 props; 4,000 hp **Range:** 2,500/13.5 **Man:** Approx. 60 tot.

Remarks: Former minesweeper. Built in the late 1950s, transferred 1978. Minesweeping equipment entirely deleted. Believed probably inoperable by 1984.

GUIDED-MISSILE PATROL BOATS

◆ **8 ex-Soviet OSA-II class**

D: 210 tons (240 fl) **S:** 35 kts **Dim:** 38.6 × 7.6 × 2.0
A: 4/SS-N-2B Styx SSM (I × 4) — 4/30-mm AA (II × 2)
Electron Equipt: Radar: 1/Square Tie, 1/Drum Tilt
M: 3 M504 diesels; 3 props; 15,000 hp
Range: 500/34; 750/25 **Man:** 30 tot.

Remarks: Transferred: 2 in 2-79 to 4-79, 3 in 1-80, 1 in 12-80, 1 in 2-83, 1 in 9-83.

TORPEDO BOATS

◆ **2 Soviet MOL class**

D: 170 tons (210 fl) **S:** 40 kts **Dim:** 38.6 × 7.6 × 1.8
A: 4/30-mm AA (II × 2) — 4/533-mm TT
Electron Equipt: Radar: 1/Pot Drum, 1/Drum Tilt
M: 3 M503 diesels; 3 props; 12,000 hp
Range: 450/34; 700/20 **Man:** 30 tot.

Remarks: Transferred 1978. Design based on Osa-class guided-missile patrol boat. Sisters in Somali Navy.

YEMEN (SOUTH) *(continued)*

PATROL BOATS

◆ **2 ex-Soviet Zhuk class**

D: 44 tons (60 fl) **S:** 34 kts **Dim:** 24.0 × 5.0 × 1.2
A: 2/14.5-mm mg (II × 1) **Electron Equipt:** Radar: 1/Spin Trough
M: 2 M50 diesels; 2 props; 2,400 hp **Range:** 700/28; 1,100/15 **Man:** 12 tot.

Remarks: Transferred in 2-75.

AMPHIBIOUS WARFARE SHIPS

◆ **1 ex-Soviet Ropucha class** Bldr: Polnocny SY, Gdansk, Poland

South Yemen's Ropucha 3-81

D: 2,200 tons (3,200 fl) **S:** 18 kts **Dim:** 113.0 × 14.0 × 2.9 (aft)
A: 4.57-mm AA (II × 2)
Electron Equipt: Radar: 1/Don-2, 1/Strut Curve, 1/Muff Cob
IFF: 1/High Pole B
M: 2 diesels; 2 props; 10,000 hp **Range:** 3,500/16 **Man:** 70 crew + 230 troops

Remarks: Transferred 1980. By far the largest unit in South Yemen's service.

◆ **4 ex-Soviet Polnocny-B-class medium landing ships**

Bldr: Polnocny SY, Gdansk, Poland

D: 800 tons (fl) **S:** 19 kts **Dim:** 74.0 × 8.6 × 2.0
A: 2 or 4/30-mm AA (II × 1)—2/140-mm barraga RL (XVIII × 2)—4/SA-N-5 systems
Electron Equipt: Radar: 1/Spin Trough, 1/Drum Tilt
IFF: 1/Square Head, 1/High Pole B
M: 2 diesels; 2 props; 4,000 hp
Range: 900/18; 1,500/14 **Man:** 40 crew + 100 troops

Remarks: Two delivered 8-73, one in 7-77 and one in 1979.

◆ **5 ex-Soviet T-4-class landing craft**

D: 35 tons light (93 fl) **S:** 10 kts **Dim:** 19.9 × 5.6 × 1.4
M: 2 Type 3D6 diesels; 2 props; 600 hp **Range:** 1,500/10

Remarks: Transferred: 3 in 11-70, 2 in 1982. Resemble U.S. LCM(6) class.

MINISTRY OF THE INTERIOR

◆ **5 Tracker-2 class** Bldr: Fairey Marine, U.K.

D: 31 tons (fl) **S:** 29 kts **Dim:** 19.25 × 4.98 × 1.45
A: 1/20-mm AA **M:** 2 MTU 8V331 TC diesels; 2 props; 2,200 hp
Range: 650/25 **Man:** 11 tot.

Remarks: Ordered 8-77; delivered 1977-78. Used in customs duties.

◆ **4 Spear class** Bldr: Fairey Marine, U.K.

D: 4.5 tons (fl) **S:** 26 kts **Dim:** 9.1 × 2.8 × 0.8
A: 3/7.62-mm mg **M:** 2 diesels; 2 props; 290 hp

Remarks: Three delivered 20-9-75; fourth during 1978. Used in customs duties. Glass-reinforced plastic construction.

◆ **1 Interceptor class** Bldr: Fairey Marine, U.K.

Remarks: Catamaran with two 135-hp outboard motors, can carry eight 25-man life rafts, and intended for rescue duties. Overall: 7.6 meters.

YEMEN

YEMEN ARAB REPUBLIC (North Yemen)

Personnel (1985): Approximately 200 men, plus 250 naval port police

Merchant Marine (1984): 10 ships—3,203 grt

GUIDED-MISSILE PATROL BOATS

◆ **2 ex-Soviet OSA-II class**

D: 210 tons (240 fl) **S:** 35 kts **Dim:** 38.6 × 7.6 × 2.0
A: 4/SS-N-2B Styx SSM (I × 4)—4/30-mm AA (II × 2)
Electron Equipt: Radar: 1/Square Tie, 1/Drum Tilt
M: 3 M504 diesels; 3 props; 15,000 hp **Range:** 500/34; 750/25 **Man:** 30 tot.

Remarks: Delivered 20-5-82.

PATROL BOATS

◆ **3 Broadsword class** Bldr: Halter Marine, New Orleans, La. (In serv. 1978)

200 Sana'a 300 13th June 400 25th September

13th June 1981

D: 90 tons (fl) **S:** 28 kts **Dim:** 32.0 × 6.3 × 1.9
A: 2/23-mm AA (II × 1)—2/14.5-mm mg (II × 1)—2/12.7-mm mg (I × 2)
Electron Equipt: Radar: 1/Decca 914
M: 3 G.M. 16V71 TI diesels; 3 props; 1,400 hp **Electric:** 120 kw
Fuel: 16.3 tons **Man:** 14 tot.

Remarks: Ordered 1977. Armament, added after delivery, is of Soviet origin.

◆ **4 Soviet Zhuk class**

D: 48 tons (60 fl) **S:** 34 kts **Dim:** 24.6 × 5.2 × 1.2
A: 4/14.5-mm mg (II × 2) **Electron Equipt:** Radar: 1/Spin Trough
M: 2/M50F diesels; 2 props; 2,400 hp **Range:** 700/28; 1,100/15 **Man:** 12 tot.

Remarks: Two transferred 1978, two in 1980. Unlike other units of this class, the North Yemeni units have their twin machine guns in enclosed gun houses with hemispherical covers.

MINE COUNTERMEASURES CRAFT

◆ **2 Soviet Yevgenya class**

D: 80 tons (90 fl) **S:** 11 kts **Dim:** 26.2 × 6.1 × 1.5
A: 2/14.5 or 25-mm AA (II × 1) **Electron Equipt:** Radar: 1/Spin Trough
M: 2 diesels; 2 props; 600 hp **Range:** 300/10 **Man:** 10 tot.

Remarks: Delivered 5-82. Glass-reinforced plastic construction. Export Yevgenyas normally have a twin 25-mm AA mount; uncertain in this instance.

AMPHIBIOUS WARFARE

◆ **2 Soviet Ondatra-class landing craft**

D: 90 tons (140 fl) **S:** 10 kts **Dim:** 24.2 × 6.0 × 1.5
A: None **M:** 2 diesels; 2 props; 600 hp **Man:** 4 tot.

Remarks: Transferred 1-83. Cargo well 15.0 × 3.8 m; bow ramp. Replaced two T-4-class landing craft transferred around 1970.

YUGOSLAVIA

SOCIALIST FEDERAL REPUBLIC OF YUGOSLAVIA

Personnel (1985): 1,500 officers, 11,600 men (2,300 in Coast Defense Force)

Merchant Marine (1984): 480 ships—2,681,879 grt
(tankers: 23 ships—230,880 grt)

Naval Aviation: One squadron of 8 Soviet Ka-25 Hormone ASW helicopters, two Canadian DHC-2 Beaver STOL light transports, four Canadian CL 215 amphibians, and several license-built French SA 341H Gazelle (Partizan) helicopters may enter naval service.

The Air Force has a "Naval Cooperation Regiment," equipped with 50 RT-33 reconnaissance, MiG-21 fighter, and Jastreb attack aircraft.

SUBMARINES (P = *Podnornica*)

◆ **2 Sava-class submarines** Bldr: Split SY

	Laid down	L	In serv.
P 831 Sava	1975	1977	1978
P 832 Drava	1977	1982	1982

Drava *Front,* 1-83

D: 770/964 tons **S:** 16 kts (sub.) **Dim:** 55.8 × 5.05 × . . .
A: 6/533-mm TT—10 torpedoes or 20 mines **Endurance:** 28 days
M: Diesel-electric; 1 prop; 2,400 hp **Man:** 35 tot.

Remarks: Maximum diving depth: 300 meters. Resemble the Heroj class, but are smaller.

◆ **2 Heroj class** Bldr: Uljanik SY, Pula

	Laid down	L	In serv.
P 822 Junak	1966	1968	1969
P 823 Uskok	1968	1-70	1970

Junak (P 822) French Navy, 1982

Uskok (P 823) 1984

D: 1,068/1,170/1,350 tons **S:** 16/10 kts **Dim:** 64.0 × 7.2 × 5.0
A: 6/533-mm TT (fwd) **M:** 2 diesels, electric motors; 1 prop; 2,400 hp
Range: 9,700/8 **Man:** 36 tot.

Remarks: Sister *Heroj* (821) stricken 1982 after an accident.

◆ **2 Sutjeska class** Bldr: Uljanik SY, Pula

	Laid down	L	In serv.
P 811 Sutjeska	1957	28-9-58	9-60
P 812 Neretva	1957	1959	1962

Neretva (P 812)—now has bulbous bow G. Arra, 1969

D: 700/820/945 tons **S:** 14/9 kts **Dim:** 60.0 × 4.8 × 4.8
A: 6/533-mm TT (4 fwd, 2 aft; 8 torpedoes)
M: 2 Sulzer diesels, electric motors; 1,800 hp
Range: 4,400/8.6 **Man:** 38 tot.

Remarks: First submarines built in Yugoslavia. New bow sonar arrays added during the early 1970s.

MIDGET SUBMARINES

◆ **2 Type M100 or Una class** Bldr: . . .

D: 90 tons surfaced/100 sub. **S:** 8.5/11.0 kts **Dim:** 18.0 × 3.7 × 2.50
A: 6 mines or 6 swimmer delivery vehicles, Type R1
M: Diesel-electric propulsion

Remarks: First unit completed 5-5-85. The second may be destined for Libya. Surfaced displacement also given as 76 tons. Type R1 swimmer delivery chariots weigh 145 kg, are 3.7-m long by 0.52 beam, and have a range of 8 n.m. at 3 kts.

◆ **2 or more Type R2, Mala-class swimmer delivery vehicles**

Mala (R 2) class 1984

D: 1.4 tons **S:** 4.4 kts **Dim:** 4.90 × 1.22 × 1.32 (1.70 fins)
A: 2/50-kg mines **Range:** 23/3.7
M: 1 electric motor; 1 prop; 6 hp **Man:** 2 tot.

Remarks: Diving depth: 60 m.

FRIGATES (VPB—*Velici Patrolni Brod*—Large Patrol Ship)

◆ **0 (+2) new construction** Bldr: Tito SY, Kraljevica

	Laid down	L	In serv.
VPB 33 Kotor	1981	29-5-84	1986
VPB 34 N.	. . .	. . .	. . .

Kotor (VPB 33)—artist's concept 1984

D: 1,850 tons (fl) **S:** 27 kts **Dim:** 96.7 (92.0 wl) × 11.2 × 3.55 (5.80 over sonar)
A: . . . **Electron Equipt:** Radar: . . . —Sonar: . . .
M: CODAG: 2 SEMT-Pielstick 12 PA6V280 diesels (4,800 hp each), 1 Soviet gas turbine (15,000 hp); 3 props (CP outboard); 24,600 hp
Electric: 1,350 kw **Man:** Approx. 90 tot.

Remarks: These ships will apparently be a modification of the design for two similar training frigates recently built for Indonesia and Iraq and may have similar armament (4 anti-ship missiles, 1/57-mm Bofors DP, several 40-mm AA, etc.). The main propulsion diesels were ordered in 6-80 (two to be built under license in Yugoslavia), and the first was delivered 31-3-81; the propulsion concept duplicates the arrangement in the Koni class.

◆ **2 Soviet Koni class** Bldr: Zelenodolsk SY

VPB 31 Split (In serv. 4-80) VPB 32 Koper (In serv. 19-2-83)

D: 1,900 tons (fl) **S:** 30 kts **Dim:** 95.0 × 12.8 × 4.2 (5.4 over sonar)
A: 4/SS-N-2C Styx SSM (I × 4)—1/SA-N-4 SAM syst. (II × 1, 20 Gecko missiles)—4/76.2-mm DP (II × 2)—4/30-mm AA (II × 2)—2/RBU-6000 ASW RL (XII × 2)—2/d.c. racks (12 d.c.)—mines
Electron Equipt: Radar: 1/Don-2, 1/Strut Curve, 1/Prop Group, 1/Hawk Screech, 1/Drum Tilt
Sonar: 1/med. freq., hull-mounted

Split (VPB 31)—with Styx missiles 1983

M: CODAG: 1 15,00-hp gas turbine, 2 diesels; 3 props; 30,000 hp **Range:** 1,800/14
Man: 110 tot.

Remarks: New-construction units. Sisters in the Algerian, East German, Cuban, and Soviet navies. *Koper* received Styx missiles during 1984-85; they were added to *Split* during 1982. *Koper* arrived in Yugoslavia on 5-12-83.

CORVETTES (PBR = *Patrolni Brod*)

◆ **2 Mornar class** Bldr: Tito SY, Kraljevica

	Laid down	L	In serv.
PBR 551 Mornar	1957	1958	10-9-59
PBR 552 Borac	1964	1965	1965

Borac (PBR 552) 1973

D: 330 tons (430 fl) **S:** 24 kts **Dim:** 51.8 × 6.97 × 3.1 (2.0 hull)
A: 2/40-mm AA (I × 2)—2/20-mm AA (I × 2)—4/RBU-1200 ASW RL (V × 4)—2/Mk 6 d.c. projectors—2/Mk 9 d.c. racks
Electron Equipt: Radar: 1/Decca 45—Sonar: 1/Tamir-11
M: 3 Werkspoor diesels; 3 props; 7,500 hp **Fuel:** 55 tons
Range: 660/24; 3,000/12 **Man:** 60 tot.

Remarks: Modernized 1970-73 at Sava Kovacevic Naval Yard, Tivat. Original two 76.2-mm DP guns, two older-model 40-mm AA, and Mousetrap ASW rocket launchers replaced by new Bofors guns and Soviet ASW rocket launchers.

◆ **1 French Le Fougueux class** Bldr: F.C. Méditerranée, Le Havre

	Laid down	L	In serv.
PBR 581 Udarnik (ex-P 6, ex-PC 1615)	1954	21-12-54	1-56

Udarnik (PBR 581) H. Ehlers, 4-84

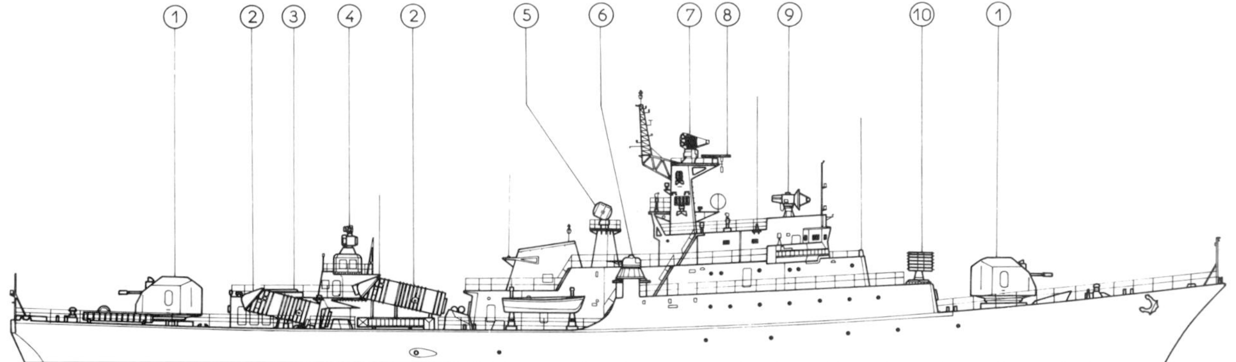

Yugoslav Koni class L. Gassier
1. twin 76.2-mm DP 2. launchers for SS-N-2C 3. launcher/magazine for SA-N-4 SAM system 4. Pop Group radar director for SA-N-4 5. Drum Tilt radar director for 30-mm AA 6. twin 30-mm AA 7. Strut Curve air/surface-search radar 8. Don-2 navigational/surface-search radar 9. Hawk Screech radar director for the 76.2-mm guns 10. RBU-6000 ASW RL (XII × 2)

CORVETTES *(continued)*

D: 329 tons (409 fl) **S:** 18.7 kts **Dim:** 53.10 (50.9 wl) × 7.3 × 3.0 (2.1 hull)
A: 1/40-mm AA—2/20-mm AA (I × 2)—1/RBU 1200 ASW RL (V × 1)—2/d.c. racks
Electron Equipt: Radar: 1/DRBN-30—Sonar: 1/DUBA-2
M: 4 SEMT-Pielstick PA17V diesels; 2 props; 3,240 hp **Electric:** 120 kw
Fuel: 45 tons **Range:** 3,300/15; 6,350/12 **Man:** 62 tot.

Remarks: Built with U.S. Offshore Procurement Funds as U.S. PC 1615; transferred on completion. One sister in the Tunisian Navy. Engines can produce 3,840 hp for brief periods. Armament revised by 4-84

GUIDED-MISSILE PATROL BOATS (RT = *Raketni Topovnjača*)

◆ **1 (+9?) Type 400, Kobra class** Bldr: Tito SY, Kraljevica

D: 385 tons (525 fl) **S:** 34 kts **Dim:** 54.80 (51.88 pp) × 8.96 (8.16 wl) × 2.46
A: 4/SS-N-2C Styx SSM—1/76-mm OTO Melara DP—2/40-mm Breda Dardo AA (II × 1)—8/20-mm AA (IV × 2)
M: 4 MTU 20V538 TB92 diesels; 4 props; 14,000 hp
Range: . . . **Endurance:** 15 days **Man:** . . .

Remarks: A missile "corvette" class intended to begin replacement of the elderly OSA-I class. Also reported as being built for Libya. Chaff rocket launchers will be mounted on the sides of the 76-mm mount. First unit may have been completed 1985.

◆ **6 Rade Končar class** Bldr: Tito SY, Kraljevica

	L	In serv.
RT 401 Rade Končar	15-10-76	4-77
RT 402 Vlado Četkovič	28-8-77	1977
RT 403 Ramiz Sadiku	1978	10-9-78
RT 404 Hasan Zahirovič Lasa	1979	11-79
RT 405 Jordan Nikolov-Orce	1979	1979
RT 406 Ante Banina	1979	12-79

Rade Končar (RT 401) 1977

Rade Končar (RT 401) 1977

D: 242 tons (. . . fl) **S:** 39 kts (27 sust.) **Dim:** 45.0 × 8.0 × 1.8 (2.5 props)
A: 2/SS-N-2B Styx SSM—2/57-mm Bofors DP (I × 2)
Electron Equipt: 1/Decca 1226—1/9LV200 system
M: CODAG: 2 Rolls-Royce Proteus gas turbines, 4,500 hp each; 2 MTU 20V538 TB 92 diesels, 3,600 hp each; 4 CP props; 16,200 hp
Range: 880/23; 1,650/15 **Man:** 5 officers, 10 petty officers, 15 men
Electric: 300 kVA

Remarks: Of Yugoslav design, using Swedish (Svensk Phillips) fire control and guns and Soviet missiles; RT 401 has 9LV200 Mk I, later ships have 9LV200 Mk II. Have a Soviet Square Head IFF interrogator. Styx missiles chosen over the Exocet originally planned, probably for economic reasons. Steel hull, aluminum superstructure. Have NBC warfare protection. Endurance: 7 days

◆ **10 ex-Soviet OSA-I class** (RC = *Raketni Čamac*)

RC 301 Mitar Acev
RC 302 Vlado Bagat
RC 303 Petar Drapšin
RC 304 Steven Filipovič
RC 305 Velimir Škorpik
RC 306 Nikola Martinovič
RC 307 Josip Mazar
RC 308 Karlo Rojc
RC 309 Franc Rozman-Stane
RC 310 Zikaca Jovanovič-Španac

Mitar Acev (RC 301)

D: 185 tons (215 fl) **S:** 35 kts **Dim:** 38.6 × 7.6 × 1.8
A: 4/SS-N-2 Styx SSM—4/30-mm AA (II × 2)
Electron Equipt: Radar: 1/Square Tie, 1/Drum Tilt
IFF: 1/High Pole B, 2/Square Head
M: 3 M503A diesels; 3 props; 12,000 hp **Range:** 500/34; 750/25 **Man:** 25 tot.

Remarks: Transferred 1965-69. Reported to be showing their age.

TORPEDO BOATS (TČ = *Torpedni Čamac*)

◆ **14 Soviet Shershen class** Bldrs: 4 in USSR; others: Tito SY, Kraljevica (In serv. 1966-71)

TČ 211 Topčider
TČ 212 N. . . . . . .
TČ 213 Proleter
TČ 214 Pionir
TČ 215 Ivan
TČ 216 Jadran
TČ 217 Kornat
TČ 218 N. . . . . . .
TČ 219 N. . . . . . .
TČ 220 Crvena Zvijezda
TČ 221 Biokovak
TČ 222 Partizan-II
TČ 223 N. . . . . . .
TČ 224 N. . . . . . .

Biokovak (TC 221) 1980

D: 150 tons (180 fl) **S:** 45 kts **Dim:** 34.0 × 7.2 × 1.5
A: 4/30-mm AA (II × 2)—4/533-mm TT—mines
Electron Equipt: Radar: 1/Pot Drum, 1/Drum Tilt
Sonar: 1/High Pole B, 1/Square Head
M: 3 M503A diesels; 3 props; 12,000 hp **Range:** 450/34; 700/20 **Man:** 22 tot.

Remarks: Ten built in Yugoslavia under license, after four were transferred in 1965. Unlike Soviet units, have no depth-charge racks. Other known names: *Partizan, Pionir II, Strjelco, Sloga, Napredak.*

PATROL BOATS (PČ = *Patrolni Čamac*)

◆ **. . . Type 80 class** Bldr: . . .

Type 80 class (without 20-mm AA) 1984

PATROL BOATS *(continued)*

D: 80 tons **S:** 32 kts (26 sust.) **Dim:** 27.35 × 6.55 × 1.15 (2.20 props)
A: 1/40-mm AA—4/20-mm AA (IV × 1)
Electron Equipt: Radar: 1/. . . nav. **Man:** 17 tot.
M: 3 diesels; 3 props; 4,350 hp **Range:** 400/25 **Endurance:** 5 days

Remarks: Reduced edition of Mirna design; offered for foreign sale. Has four illumination/chaff RL on foredeck.

◆ **10 Type 240 Mirna class** (In serv. 1981-82)

PČ 171 Biokovo, PČ 172 Pohorse, PČ 173 Koprivnik, PČ 174 Učka, PČ 175 Brmec, PČ 176 Mukos, PČ 177 N. . . . . . ., PČ 178 Kosmaj, PČ 179 N. . . . . . ., PČ 180 N. . . . . . .

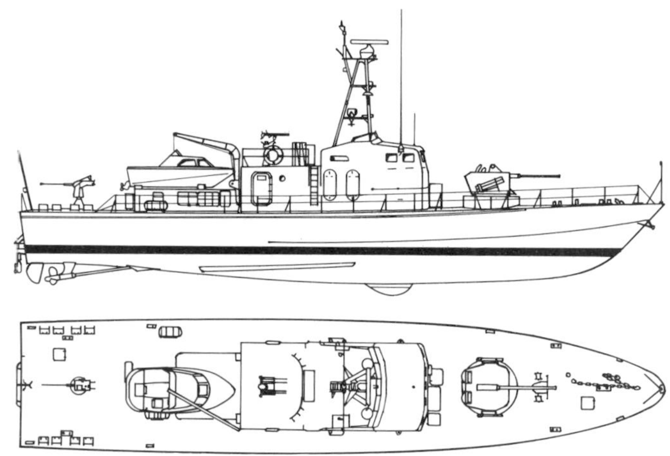

Mirna-class patrol boat

D: 120 tons (. . . fl) **S:** 30 kts **Dim:** 32.00 × 6.68 × 1.60 (2.30 max.)
A: 1/40-mm Bofors L70 AA—1/20-mm AA—8/Type MDB-MT3 d.c.
Electron Equipt: Radar: 1/. . . nav.—Sonar: high freq. set
M: 2 SEMT-Pielstick 12 PA4 200GDS diesels; 2 props; 6,000 hp—electric motors for low speeds (6 kts)
Electric: . . . **Range:** 400/20 **Man:** 3 officers, 4 petty officers, 12 men

Remarks: The first 10 propulsion diesels were ordered in 1979, for license production in Yugoslavia. Endurance at 20 kts can be increased to 530 n.m. in emergencies. Peacetime endurance is four days, wartime: 8 days. Have 4-rail chaff launcher amidships. There are 4 chaff or illumination rocket rails on the sides of the 40-mm AA.

◆ **7 Type 131 coastal patrol craft** Bldr: Trogir SY (In serv. 1965-68)

PČ 132 Kalnik, PČ 133 Velebit, PČ 134 Grandičar, PČ 135 Grudnik, PČ 136 Romanija, PČ 137 Kamenar, PČ 140 Kožuf

Grudnik (PC 135)

D: 85 tons (120 fl) **S:** 22 kts **Dim:** 32.0 × 5.5 × 2.5
A: 6/20-mm Hispano Suiza HS831 AA (III × 2)
Electron Equipt: Radar: 1/Kelvin-Hughes 14/9
M: 2 MTU MB820 Db diesels; 2 props; 1,600 hp

Remarks: May serve in the Maritime Border Brigade, an organization similar to a coast guard. Sisters *Cer* (PČ 138) and *Durmitor* transferred to Malta 31-3-82. Several others have been scrapped: Type 80 class appears intended as their replacements.

PATROL CRAFT

◆ . . . **Type 20 coastal and riverine**

D: 55 tons **S:** 16 kts **Dim:** 21.78 (20.06 wl) × 5.29 × 1.20
A: 2/20-mm AA (I × 2)—mines **Electron Equipt:** Radar: 1/Decca 110
M: 2 diesels; 2 props; 1,156 hp **Range:** 200/15 **Man:** 10 tot.

Remarks: Hull numbers in the 200-series.

◆ . . . **Type 18 coastal and riverine**

Type 18 patrol craft 1984

D: 29 tons (fl) **S:** 20 kts **Dim:** 18.70 × 3.60 × 0.90 mean
A: 2/20-mm AA (I × 2)—9/7.62-mm light mg (I × 9)
Electron Equipt: Radar: 1/Decca 110
M: 2 diesels; 2 props; 752 hp **Range:** 480/17
Man: 9 crew + 40 troops

Remarks: Intended for patrol, troop transport, and logistic support duties, with up to 4 tons of cargo

◆ . . . **Type 16 coastal and riverine**

Type 16 patrol craft 1984

D: 23 tons (fl) **S:** 15 kts **Dim:** 17.00 × 3.60 × 0.85 mean
A: 1/20-mm AA—7/7.62-mm light mg (I × 9)
Electron Equipt: Radar: 1/Decca 110

PATROL CRAFT *(continued)*

M: 2 diesels; 2 props; 464 hp **Range:** 340/15
Man: 7 crew + 30 troops or frogmen

REMARKS: Intended for patrol, troop transport, and logistic support duties, with up to 3 tons of cargo.

◆ **5 or more Type 15-class riverine and lake**

PČ 15-1 through PČ 15-5

PČ 15-5 and two sisters 1984

D: 19.5 tons (fl) **S:** 16 kts **Dim:** 16.87 × 3.90 × 0.65 (0.70 props)
A: 1/20-mm AA—2/7.62-mm mg (I × 2) **Electron Equipt:** Radar: 1/Decca 110
M: 2 diesels; 2 props; 330 hp **Range:** 160/12 **Man:** 6 tot.

MINE WARFARE SHIPS (M = *Minolovac*)

◆ **4 French Sirius-class coastal minesweepers**

Bldrs: M 161: Mali Losinj SY, Yugoslavia; others: A Normand, Le Havre, France

	In serv.
M 151 VUKOV KLANAC (ex-*Hrabri*, ex-MSC 229)	9-57
M 152 PODGORA (ex-*Smeli*, ex-MSC 230)	9-57
M 153 BLITVENICA (ex-*Slobodni*, ex-MSC 231)	9-57
M 161 GRADAC (ex-*Snazhi*)	1960

D: 400 tons (440 fl) **S:** 15 kts (sweeping: 11.5)
Dim: 46.4 (42.7 pp) × 8.55 × 2.5
A: 2/20-mm AA (II × 2)
Electron Equipt: Radar: 1/DRBN-30—Sonar: Plessey 193M
M: 2 SEMT-Pielstick 16 PA1-175 diesels; 2 props; 2,000 hp **Electric:** 375 kw
Fuel: 48 tons **Range:** 3,000/10 **Man:** 40 tot.

REMARKS: First three built with U.S. Offshore Procurement funds. Wooden-planked hulls on metal framing. Equipped with Plessey 193M minehunting sonar, French PAP-104 remote-controlled minehunting/disposal submersibles, and Decca Hifix precision navigation systems, commencing 1981.

◆ **4 British "Ham"-class minesweepers** Bldr: Yugoslavia (In serv. 1964-66)

M 141 N. . . . . . . (ex-MSI 98)	M 143 IZ (ex-MSI 100)
M 142 BRSEC (ex-MSI 99)	M 144 OLIB (ex-MSI 101)

D: 123 tons (164 fl) **S:** 14 kts **Dim:** 32.43 × 6.45 × 1.7
A: 1/40-mm **Electron Equipt:** Radar: 1/Decca 45
M: 2 Paxman YHAXM diesels; 2 props; 1,100 hp **Fuel:** 15 tons
Range: 1,500/12; 2,000/9 **Man:** 22 tot.

REMARKS: Built under U.S. Offshore Procurement Program. Composite construction: wooden planking over a metal-framed hull

◆ **6 117-class inshore minesweepers** Bldr: Yugoslavia, 1966-68

ML 117 ML 118 ML 119 ML 121 ML 122 ML 123

D: 120 tons (131 fl) **S:** 12 kts **Dim:** 30.0 × 5.5 × 1.5
A: 1/20-mm AA—2/12.7-mm mg (I × 2) **Electron Equipt:** Radar: 1/Decca 45
M: 2 G.M. diesels; 1,000 hp **Man:** 25 tot.

REMARKS: Also used for coastal patrol

◆ **7 Nestin-class Type 50 river minesweepers** Bldr: Brodotehnika, Belgrade (In serv. 1976-80)

	L		L
M 331 NESTIN	20-12-75	M 335 VUČEDOL	1979
M 332 MOTAJICA	18-12-76	M 336 DJERDAP	1980
M 333 BELEGIS	1-77	M 337 PANONSKO MORE	1980
M 334 BOSUT	1978		

D: 68 tons (78 fl) **S:** 12 kts **Dim:** 27.00 × 6.50 × 1.05 (1.15 max.)
A: 5/20-mm AA (III × 1, I × 2)—24 small mines
Electron Equipt: Radar: 1/Decca 101
M: 2 diesels; 2 props; 520 hp **Range:** 864/10.8 **Man:** 17 tot.

REMARKS: M 331 launched 20-12-75, M 332 launched 18-12-76, and M 333 launched 1-77. Hull of light metal alloy. Sweep gear includes Type PEAM magnetic and acoustic sweep, Type AEL-1 explosive sweep, and Types MDL-1 and MDL-2 mechanical sweeps. Two illumination chaff rocket launchers are fitted. Used on the Danube. Three also built for Iraq.

Nestin (M 331) 1978

AMPHIBIOUS WARFARE SHIPS

NOTE: The new Type PO multipurpose transports can also be used as landing ships.

◆ **17 DTM 211-class landing craft** Bldr: Yugoslavia (In serv. 1950s)

DTM 212, 213, 215, 216, 219, 221, 223, 224, 225, 226, 228, 229, 232, 233, 234, 237, GOLOR

DTM 213 L. & L. Van Ginderen, 6-84

D: 240 tons (410 fl) **S:** 10.3 kts **Dim:** 49.8 × 8.6 × 1.6 (2.1 max.)
A: 3/20-mm AA (III × 1) **M:** 3 Gray Marine 64HN9 diesels; 3 props; 625 hp
Range: 500/9.3 **Man:** 27 tot.

REMARKS: DTM = *Desantni Tenkonosac.* Near-duplicates of the World War II German MFP-D class. Nearly all have been equipped with 1-m-wide hull sponsons, extending beam to 8.6 meters and providing space for two mine rails with a total capacity of up to 100 small mines. Bow ramp. Can carry 140 tons of vehicles or 200 men. Seven additional units have been discarded. Unit now named *Golor* is probably considered an auxiliary.

◆ **4 DTM 401 class** (In serv. 1950s)

D: 227 tons (350 fl) **S:** 10.3 kts **Dim:** 46.5 × 6.5 × 1.3 (max.)
A: 5/20-mm AA (III × 1, I × 2)—2/mortars
M: 3 G.M. 64HN9 diesels; 3 props; 678 hp **Range:** 500/9

REMARKS: Similar to the DTM 211 class; used on the Danube River. No mine sponsons.

◆ **22 601-class (Type 21) landing craft** Bldr: Gleben SY, Vela Luka, Korčula (In serv. 1976-77)

DSC 601 to DSC 622

D: 32 tons (fl) **S:** 23.5 kts **Dim:** 21.20 × 4.84 × 1.07 (1.58 props)
A: 1/20-mm AA **Electron Equipt:** Radar: 1/Decca 101 **Man:** 6 crew
M: 1 MTU 12V331 TC 81 diesel; 2 props; 1,450 hp **Range:** 320/22

REMARKS: DSC = *Desantni Jurišni Čamac.* Glass-reinforced plastic construction. Bow ramp. Can carry 40 troops or 6 tons in 32 m² cargo area. Offered for export also.

◆ **. . . Type 11 vehicle/personnel landing craft**

D: 4.8 tons (fl) **S:** 23 kts **Dim:** 11.30 × 3.00 × 0.30

Type 11 1984

AMPHIBIOUS WARFARE SHIPS *(continued)*

M: 2 diesels; 2 waterjets *or* 2 outdrives; . . . hp **Range:** 100/15 **Man:** 2

Remarks: Glass-reinforced plastic construction. Can carry two jeeps or a squad of troops. Have a small navigational radar.

AUXILIARY SHIPS

◆ **1 Soviet Moma-class hydrographic ship** Bldr: Gdansk, Poland, 1971

PH 33 Andrija Mohorovičič

Andrija Mohorovičič (PH 33) 1971

D: 1,260 tons (1,540 fl) **S:** 17 kts **Dim:** 73.3 × 10.8 × 3.8
Electron Equipt: Radar: 1/Don-2 **Man:** 56 tot.
M: 2 Zgoda-Sulzer 6TD48 diesels; 2 CP props; 3,600 hp **Range:** 8,700/11

Remarks: Transferred in 1972. Carries one survey launch. Five-ton crane for navigational buoy handling. Four laboratories totaling 35 m^2 deck space. Used for oceanographic research, hydrographic surveys, and buoy tending.

◆ **1 submarine rescue and salvage ship** Bldr: Tito SY, Belgrade (In serv. 10-9-76)

PS 12 Spasilac

D: 1,590 tons (fl) **S:** 13.4 kts **Dim:** 55.50 × 12.00 × 3.84 (4.34 max.)
A: 10/20-mm AA (IV × 2, I × 2) **Electric:** 540 kVA
Electron Equipt: Radar: 1/. . . nav.—Sonar: . . .
M: 2 diesels; 2 Kort-nozzle props; 4,340 hp **Range:** 4,000/13.4 **Man:** 53 tot. (72 accom.)

Remarks: Resembles an oilfield supply vessel; low freeboard aft. Sister *Aka* is in the Iraqi Navy, and another has been sold to Libya. Equipped for underwater cutting and welding, towing, carrying up to 250 tons deck cargo, transferring 490 tons cargo fuel, 48 tons cargo water and 5 tons lube oil. Also capable of salvage lifting, firefighting, and other salvage tasks. Can support divers to 300 m with a 3-section decompression chamber. Also has capability to support a small rescue submersible. Has a bow-thruster and can lay a 4-point moor.

◆ **1 salvage ship** Bldr: Howaldtswerke, Kiel (In serv. 1929)

PS 11 (ex-*Spasilac*)

D: 740 tons **S:** 14.5 kts **Dim:** 53.6 × 8.8 × 4.0
M: 1 set triple-expansion reciprocating steam; 1 prop; 2,000 hp **Boilers:** 2

Remarks: Not scrapped as previously reported when new *Spasilac* completed in 1976.

◆ **1 cadet-training ship** Bldr: Ansaldo, Genoa (In serv. 1938)

Galeb (ex-*Kuchuk*, ex-*Ramb III*)

Galeb L. & L. Van Ginderen, 8-83

D: 5,182 tons (5,700 fl) **S:** 16 kts **Dim:** 121.2 (116.9 pp) × 15.2 × 5.6
A: 4/40-mm AA (I × 4)—8/20-mm AA (IV × 2)
M: 2 Burmeister & Wain diesels; 2 props; 7,200 hp **Range:** 20,000/16

Remarks: Begun as a commercial banana carrier; used as an auxiliary cruiser and minelayer by the Italian Navy during World War II. Ceded to Yugoslavia after the war. Has been used as the presidential yacht, but is mostly used as a cadet-training ship. Retains old German quadruple 20-mm AA mounts; may still be useable as a minelayer.

◆ **1 missile-boat tender and command ship** Bldr: . . . , Yugoslavia (In serv. 1956)

Vis

D: 510 tons (680 fl) **S:** 17 kts **Dim:** 57.0 × 8.5 × 3.5
A: 1/40-mm AA—2/20-mm AA (I × 2) **M:** 2 diesels; 2 props; 1,900 hp

Remarks: Resembles a yacht; primarily an administrative flagship.

◆ **1 topsail training schooner** Bldr: Blohm + Voss, Hamburg (In serv. 1932)

Jadran

Jadran Yugoslav Navy

D: 720 tons (800 fl) **S:** (14.5 sail/9.5 diesel) kts **Dim:** 60.0 × 8.8 × 4.2
M: 12 Linke-Hoffman diesel; 375 hp **Sail area:** 933 m^2

Remarks: Accommodations for 100 cadets and 20 instructors.

◆ **1 riverine command ship** Bldr: Bordotehnika, Belgrade

36 Sabač (In serv. 1985)

Sabač (34)—at launch *Front,* 1985

D: Approx. 200 tons (fl) **S:** . . . **Dim:** . . . × . . . × . . .
A: . . . **Electron Equipt:** Radar: 1/Decca 110
M: 2 diesels; 2 props; . . . hp **Range:** . . . **Man:** . . .

Remarks: Intended to replace Danube River Flotilla flagship *Kozara.* Patrol-boat-type hull, with superstructure set well aft.

◆ **1 riverine command ship** Bldr: Linzer Schiffswerft, Austria (In serv. 1940)

Kozara (ex-U.S. *Oregon*, ex-German *Brünhild*)

D: 535 tons (693 fl) **S:** 12.4 kts **Dim:** 67.0 × 9.5 × 1.4
A: 9/20-mm AA (III × 3) **Fuel:** 44 tons
M: 2 Deutz RV6M545 diesels; 2 props; 800 hp

Remarks: Taken over by U.S. in immediate postwar period, then turned over to Yugoslavia. Used as a floating hotel until 1960, when taken over by the navy. In 1962 recommissioned as flagship of the Danube River Flotilla. Painted blue and white and home-ported at Bosanka Gradiška. May have been stricken 1985 on completion of *Sabač.*

YUGOSLAVIA *(continued)*

SERVICE CRAFT

◆ **4 PN 13-class fuel tankers** Bldr: Yugoslavia (In serv. 1955-56)

PN 13 PN 14 PN 15 PN 16

D: 420 tons (650 fl) **S:** 7 kts **Dim:** 43.2 × 7.0 × 4.2
M: 1 Burmeister & Wain diesel; 1 prop; 300 hp **Range:** 1,500/7
Cargo: 300 tons

Remarks: Sister PN 17 transferred to Sudan in 1969. PN = *Pomoćni Naftonosac.*

◆ **2 PN 24-class fuel tankers** Bldr: Split SY (In serv. early 1950s)

PN 24 PN 25

D: 300 tons (430 fl) **S:** 7 kts **Dim:** 46.4 × 7.2 × 3.2
M: 1 Burmeister & Wain diesel; 1 prop; 300 hp

◆ **4 PT 71-class cargo lighters** Bldr: Split SY (In serv. 1950s)

PT 71 PT 72 PT 73 PT 74

D: 310 tons (428 fl) **S:** 7 kts **Dim:** 43.1 × 7.2 × 4.85
M: 1 Burmeister & Wain diesel; 1 prop; 300 hp

Remarks: PT = *Pomoćni Transporter.*

◆ **6 PT 61-class cargo lighters** Bldr: Pula and Sibenik SYs (In serv. 1951-59)

PT 61 PT 62 PT 63 PT 64 PT 65 PT 66

D: 695 tons (fl) **S:** 7 kts **Dim:** 46.4 × 7.2 × 3.2
M: 1 Burmeister & Wain diesel; 1 prop; 300 hp

◆ **1 or more Type PO multipurpose transports** Bldr: . . .

PO 91 PO . . .

PO 91—with bow visor open, ramp extended 1984

D: 600 tons (860 fl) **S:** 16 kts (sust.) **Dim:** 58.20 × 11.00 × 2.75 (mean)
A: 1/40-mm AA—8/20-mm (IV × 2) **Electron Equipt:** Radar: 1/. . . nav.
M: 2 diesels; 2 CP props; 3,480 hp **Range:** 1,500/16
Man: 43 crew + 150 fully equipped troops, 6 vehicle drivers **Endurance:** 10 days

Remarks: Intended to supply combatants with missiles, torpedoes, mines, and other ordnance, using two slewing cranes on upper deck. Continuous cargo deck can accommodate up to 6 tanks; has a visor-type bow and extendable bow ramp.

◆ **5 PO 52-class ammunition lighters** Bldr: Split SY, 1950s

PO 52 PO 53 PO 54 PO 55 PO 56

D: 695 tons (fl) **S:** 7 kts **Dim:** 46.4 × 7.2 × 3.2
M: 1 Burmeister & Wain diesel; 1 prop; 300 hp

Remarks: PO = *Ponoćni Oružar.*

◆ **1 water tanker** Bldr: Yugoslavia (In serv. 1950s)

PV 16

D: 200 tons (600 fl) **S:** 7.5 kts **Dim:** 44.0 × 7.9 × 3.2
M: 1 diesel; 1 prop; 300 hp
Range: 1,500/7.5

Remarks: Cargo: 380 tons. PV = *Pomoćni Vodonosac.*

◆ **4 PR 37-class coastal tugs** (In serv. 1950s)

PR 37 PR 38 PR 39 PR 40

D: 550 tons (fl) **S:** 11 kts **Dim:** 32.0 × 8.0 × 5.0
M: Diesels

Remarks: Originally reciprocating steam-propelled; recently re-engined with diesels. PR = *Pomorski Remorker.*

◆ **8 LR 67-class harbor tugs** (In serv. 1960s)

LR 67 LR 68 LR 69 LR 70 LR 71 LR 72 LR 73 LR 74

Remarks: LR = *Lučki Remorker.*

◆ **. . . diving tenders and utility transports**

Diving tender version 1984

D: 43–46 tons (fl) **S:** 12 kts **Dim:** 20.50 × 4.50 × 1.42
A: 2/20-mm AA (I × 2) **Electron Equipt:** Radar: 1/Decca 101
M: 2 diesels; 2 props; 304 hp **Range:** 400/12
Man: Diving tender: 6 crew + 4 divers; transport: 60 crew + 70 troops

Remarks: Diving tender displaces 46 tons (fl). Wooden construction. Transport version has 55 m³ for 15 tons cargo in lieu of the 70 troops. Armament is not usually aboard.

ZAIRE

REPUBLIC OF ZAIRE

Personnel (1985): Approx. 900 officers and men, plus 600 marines

Merchant Marine (1984): 33 ships—84,720 grt

PATROL CRAFT

◆ **up to 25 Arcoa class** Bldr: Arcoa SY, France (In serv. 1975-81)

Remarks: Original 12 ordered in 7-74; 14 more delivered by 11-80, another 15 delivered 1981; no other data available. For use on lakes and rivers.

◆ **6 ex-U.S. Swift Mk-II class** Bldr: Swiftships, Morgan City, La. (In serv. 1971)

D: 19.2 tons (fl) **S:** 25 kts **Dim:** 15.64 × 4.14 × 1.07
A: 6/12.7-mm mg (II × 1, I × 4)
M: 2 G.M. 12V71N diesels; 2 props; 860 hp **Range:** 400/24
Man: 12 tot.

Remarks: Used on inland lakes. Aluminum construction. In poor condition.

Note: There are a number of additional small riverine patrol and logistics support craft. Three North Korean-built torpedo boats delivered 1974, and four Chinese Shanghai-II-class patrol boats delivered 1976-78 are no longer in service.

ZANZIBAR

Although part of the United Republic of Tanzania, Zanzibar has internal autonomy and its own armed forces.

◆ **4 patrol craft** Bldr: Vosper Thornycroft, U.K.

D: 70 tons **S:** 24.5 kts **Dim:** 22.9 × 6.0 × 1.5
A: 2/20-mm AA (I × 2) **M:** 2 diesels; 2 props; 1,840 hp
Range: 800/20 **Man:** 11 tot.

Remarks: The first two units were delivered 6-7-73, the last two in 1974. Glass-reinforced plastic construction; Keith Nelson design.

INDEX OF SHIPS

All ships are indexed by their full names, e.g., Almirante Guillermo Brown.

L

M

NAME	Pages

ADDENDA

Through 31 January 1986

ALGERIA

License options to build three additional Brooke Marine 37.5-m ("Kebir")-class patrol boats for the Coast Guard were purchased 11-85; 346, the fourth Mers-el-Kebir-built unit of the design, was delivered 10-11-85.

ARGENTINA

NAVAL AVIATION: Delivery of 12 ex-Israeli A-4 Skyhawks had not occurred as of 12-85. Israeli Aircraft Industries is to deliver a Boeing 707 equipped for maritime surveillance during 1986.

MEKO 140 A16-class frigate *Espora* (P 4) was commissioned 5-7-85. Submarine *San Juan* (S 34) was accepted 18-11-85 and left for Argentina shortly thereafter; she may be delivered later to another navy. In general, Argentine naval steaming hours have been sharply curtailed, and readiness has suffered greatly.

AUSTRALIA

15,536 personnel were authorized for naval service in 1985-86.

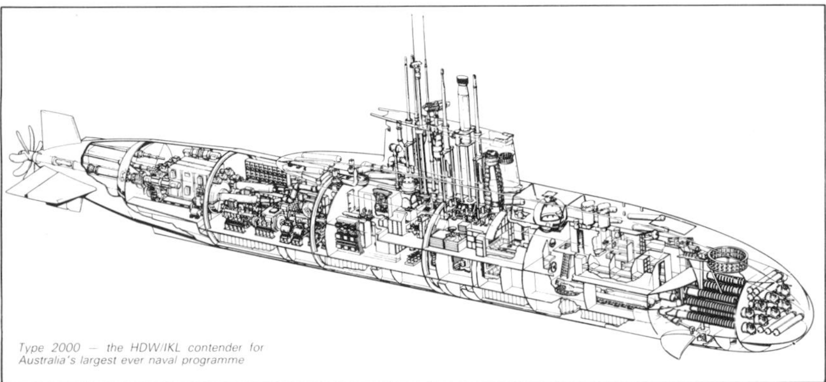

HDW's entry in the R.A.N. submarine program

Future R.A.N. frigates will be of a new design, not a variant of the U.S. FFG 7 class. Patrol boat *Wollongong* (P 206) grounded 31-5-85 in Bass Strait; has been salvaged and re-entered service 11-85, minus her cruising engine. *Attack*-class patrol boat *Assail* (P 89) transferred to Indonesia 18-10-85. Landing craft *Balikpapan* (L 126), *Labuan* (L 128), *Tarakan* (L 129, on 4-1-85), and *Wewak* (L 130, on 16-8-85) are in land-storage reserve; *Brunei* (L 127) and *Betano* (L 133) have been refitted as inshore survey craft, to operate with *Flinders* (A 312) and her survey launch, *Bramble*. Replenishment oiler *Success* (AOR 304) began sea trials 11-85. Tender *Banks* (AG 244) has served as reservist training ship in Darwin since 18-10-85.

BAHRAIN

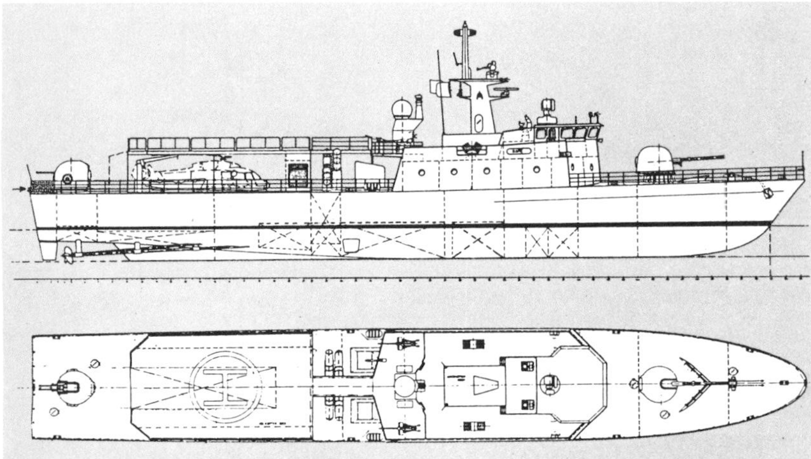

Type 62-001 missile corvette — Lürssen, 1985

Two additional TNC-45-class missile boats reported ordered 6-85.

BANGLADESH

Nirbhoy, commissioned 1-12-85, is a probable Chinese "Hainan"-class submarine chaser. Two Chinese Type 069 landing craft were deliver 1984 for use as survey craft:

A 581 DARSHAK A 582 TALLESHI

Khadem (A 721) — Chinese Dinghai class — 1984

D: 83 tons (fl) **S:** 11.5 kts (light) **Dim:** 24.1 × 5.2 × 1.1
M: 2 Type 12V150 diesels; 2 props; 600 hp

BELGIUM

The surviving riverine patrol boats are *Meuse* (P 903, in serv. 20-8-53, guardship at Antwerp) and *Liberation* (P 902, used for recruiting and public relations). Boëlwurf, Temse, is building a 20-kt fisheries patrol craft for delivery during 1986. Minehunter *Aster* (M 915) was placed in service 16-12-85.

Aster (M 915) — L. & L. Van Ginderen, 12-85

BOLIVIA

Aluminum-hulled patrol craft *Santa Cruz de la Sierra* (PR 51) was delivered 1985 by Hope/Progessive Shipbuilding, Houma, Louisiana, and traveled to Bolivia under her own power:

Santa Cruz de la Sierra (PR 51) — Hope, 1985

D: . . . **S:** . . . **Dim:** 20.4 × . . . × . . .
A: 1/20-mm AA **M:** 2 G.M. diesels; 2 props; . . . hp
Electron Equipt: Radar 1/Furuno . . .

BRAZIL

Naval Aviation: In 10-85, it was announced that 6 AS.332 Super Puma helicopters and additional Esquilo (AS.350) helicopters are to be acquired. *Sixteen* used Bell 206B JetRanger helicopters were acquired for pilot training, 3-85.

Submarine *Tupi* laid down 8-3-85 by Howaldtswerke for delivery 1988; a second German-built unit is to deliver 1989, and *three* are to be built in Brazil. Frigate *Jaceguary* laid down 15-10-84 for launch 6-86 and delivery 4-88; the seventh through twelfth ships of this class are to carry Brazilian-developed Barracuda anti-ship missiles and Avibras SSA-N-1 surface-to-air missiles (units 3 and 4 had still not been ordered by end 1985). The four Mk 10 ASW frigates are to be backfitted with 4/Exocet SSM each; all six Mk 10 will get Plessey Shield decoy RL. U.S. *Sotoyomo*-class patrol tugs *Tritão* (R 21), *Tridente* (R 22), and *Triunfo* (R 23) are to be replaced by three oil-field supply tugs built by ESTENAVE at Manaos and acquired from PETROBRAZ in 1985; a helicopter deck will be fitted.

Porto Esperanca, the first of three planned gunboats for the Paraguay River was laid down at the Rio de Janeiro Naval Arsenal 14-1-85; two others are to be ordered in 1986 and 1987 from private yards:

D: 270 tons (380 ft) **S:** 12 kts **Dim:** 49.33 (45.57 pp) × 8.45 × 1.40
A: . . .
M: . . . **Man:** 8 officers, 54 men

Remarks: Will have a helicopter deck and carry 2 LCVP landing craft.

Buoy tender H 21 is named *Sirius.* Impounded U.S. fishing boats *Sea Horse* and *Condor* have been adapted as buoy tenders, while ex-*Night Hawk* is used as a yacht. Sail yacht *Cisne Branco* is in naval service. Buoy tender *Tenente Boanerges* (H . . .) was completed 1985.

CANADA

Frigate *Halifax* (FFH 330) laid down 8-85. The submarine replacement program has slipped several years, with deliveries now planned for 1995-97 vice 1992-94. Not all "Tribal"-class destroyers may receive the TRUMP modernization. The six *St. Laurent*-class frigates will be decommissioned 1986-87, with *Fraser, Skeena,* and *Ottawa* to be refitted (as will be the harbor training hulk *St. Croix,* at Halifax since 1973).

Coast Guard: Light icebreaker *Walter E. Foster* stricken 10-7-85 after boiler "collapse." *Edward Cornwallis* to strike 1986. Icebreaker *Norman McLeod Rogers* re-engined with two Ruston HP16 RKC diesels (8,000 hp total) from 7-11-83 to 14-9-84; gas turbines removed, crew now 78. New Type 1100 icebreakers *Sir William Alexander* and *Edward Cornwallis* will have buoy derricks stepped from a kingpost forward, vice stepped on the face of the bridge, as in their sisters. Type 1000 icebreaker *Simon Fraser* has been refitted for search-and-rescue duties. *Narwhal* (Type 1100) to complete refit 2-86. Type 600 SAR cutter *Mary Hichens* in Coast Guard service 19-4-85. Small rescue craft *Sterne* (Type 100), based in the Laurentian region, entered service 1985; originally to have been named *L'Oie Blanche.*

Samuel Risley (Type 1050)—Coast guard L. & L. Van Ginderen, 8-85

Department of Fisheries and Oceans patrol ship *Leonard J. Cowley* entered service 8-5-85.

Leonard J. Cowley West Coast Manley, 1985

CHILE

Cruiser ex-*Chacabuco* (ex-*Prat,* ex-*Nashville,* C 243) towed to Taiwan for scrap, 1985. Only *two* ex-Israeli *Reshev*-class missile boats have been delivered. BATRAL-type landing ship *Chacabuco* (AP 93) launched 16-7-85. Small harbor tanker *Aquila* (AP 48, ex-*Australgas*), built in Denmark, is in naval use:

D: 397 tons (fl) **S:** 10 kts **Dim:** 51.3 × 8.7 × 4.2
M: Diesels **Range:** 6,000/10

CHINA

The air-dropped version of the HY-2 anti-ship missile (Chinese Styx copy) is referred to as the C801 and is officially stated to have a range of 95–100 km, a speed of Mach 0.9 and a length of 7.38 m; two can be carried by Badger aircraft. Jianghu-class frigates remain in production; they and the two Jiangdong-class frigates are powered by two SEMT-Pielstick 12PA6 diesels. Five G.E. LM-2500 gas turbines have been ordered from the U.S. A prototype submarine-launched cruise missile was reportedly launched from land early in 10-85. A guided-missile frigate (probably a Jianghu-class unit) was launched 28-12-85 at Shanghai. Three of the 20 remaining Super Frélon helicopters are to be converted for ASW duties.

COSTA RICA

65-ft. patrol boat FP 657 Swiftships, 4-85

Also delivered to Costa Rica during 1985 were two 10.36-m and one 12.80-m patrol craft from Swiftships, Inc., Morgan City, Louisiana.

CUBA

Four Soviet Stenka-class patrol boats were delivered during 1985, two in March and two in August; they differed from the standard Soviet model in lacking all ASW equipment, including the 4/400-mm ASW TT. A fourth Sonya-class minesweeper was delivered 12-85. The 3,600 grt/5,631 dwt merchant tanker *Las Guasimas,* delivered 1978 by Niigata, Japan, is equipped for underway alongside refueling:

D: Approx. 8,300 tons (fl) **S:** 12.75 kts **Dim:** 106.99 (100.01 pp) × 14.84 × 6.99
M: 1 diesel; 1 CP prop; 4,000 hp **Fuel:** 862 tons **Electric:** 900 kw

DENMARK

Three of Norway's Type 207, *Kobben*-class submarines are to be purchased for delivery 1987-89, after refit. Both *Peder Skram*-class frigates are to be reduced to reserve during 1986. Fisheries protection frigate *Vaedderen* has been equipped with a large, inflated radome atop her mast. The contract for the first "Standard-Flex" patrol boat (plus an option for six more) was signed with Aalborg Vaerft on 27-7-85; the first hull and the hull mold will be built by Karlskronavarvet. The prototype, to be armed with a new 76-mm OTO Melara "Super-Rapid" gun, is to be delivered by mid-1987 (the hull was begun 15-8-85 for delivery to Aalborg in 6-86) and will be powered by a G.E. LM 500 gas turbine and two diesels driving three shafts.

A new class of fisheries protection frigates to replace the *Hvidbjørnen* class was being designed by Y-ARD early in 1986 under contract to the Danish Navy. The ships will displace over 1,970 tons and will carry a 76-mm gun and a helicopter.

DJIBOUTI

Moussa Ali, the first of two PLASCOA patrol craft, was completed 8-6-85.

ECUADOR

Halter Marine, New Orleans, is building several small patrol craft for delivery 1986.

Neville Boatyard, Louisiana, is reported to be building two 15-m patrol craft, with a further four to be built in Ecuador with U.S. technical assistance.

EGYPT

Two "Tripartite"/*Alkmaar*-class minehunters were ordered from Van der Giessen de Noord, the Netherlands, on 6-3-85.

EL SALVADOR

GC-11, with 2/12.7-mm mg Swiftships, 6-85

Six 10.97-m riverine patrol craft are to be delivered by Lantana Boatyard, Lantana, Florida, in mid-1986; see photo and data under Honduras entry in addenda for appearance and characteristics.

ETHIOPIA

A Soviet Turya-class semi-hydrofoil torpedo boat was delivered during 2-85, apparently without dipping sonar equipment.

FIJI

No final decision had been announced by end-1985 as to whether to proceed with indigenous patrol boat construction or to accept an Australian Government offer of four "Pacific Patrol Boats" of the type being built for Papua New Guinea.

FINLAND

The second *Helsinki*-class guided-missile boat, *Turku* (61) was delivered 1-6-85 and the third, *Oulu* (62) on 1-10-85; both have two twin 23-mm AA (vice *Helsinki*'s one), Argo EW gear, a DataSaab EOS-400 optronic fire-control system, and a revised pilothouse window configuration. The Coast Guard ordered three Agusta-Bell AB 212 helicopters for SAR duties in 1985. A second "Karhu II" icebreaker was ordered from Wärtsilä late in 1985.

FRANCE

Latest data on the nuclear-powered aircraft carrier *Richelieu,* officially ordered 23-1-86:

D: 34,000 tons normal (36,000 fl) **S:** 28 kts (trials speed)
Dim: 261.50 (238.00 pp) × 64.36 (31.50 wl) × 8.50
A: 35–40/fixed-wing aircraft and helicopters—2/SAAM vertical-launch SAM groups (40–48 missiles)—2/SADRAL point-defense SAM
Electron Equipt: Radar: 2/Decca . . . nav., 1 DRBJ 11B, 1/DRBV 15C, 1/DRBV 27, 1/ . . . SAAM f.c., 1/DABJ 113
EW: ARBR 17, ARBB 33, 4/Sagaie decoy RL
IR: DIBV 10 *Vampir*
M: 2 Type K15, 150-mw pressurized water reactors; double-reduction geared steam turbines; 2/4-bladed props; 83,000 hp
Electric: 15,400 kw (6/2,000 kw turbo-alternators, 4/850 kw diesel sets)
Man: 1,150 ship's company + 550 air group

Remarks: The angled deck will be 195-m long, at an angle of 8.5-deg. The two 75-m steam catapults will be of the U.S. Type C13 vice C7. There will be three deck arrester wires and a barrier. The two elevators will be of 40-ton capacity, vice 50-tons. The *Syracuse II* satellite communications system will be fitted.

Carriers *Clemenceau* (R 98) and *Foch* (R 99) are receiving two Sagaie decoy RL as part of their modernizations, as are the two *Suffren*-class guided-missile destroyers. The P 400-class patrol boat *La Tapageuse* (P 691) was laid down 13-8-85.

Aconit (D 609)—after modernization French Navy, 1985

The fourth *Rubis*-class submarine (S 604) has been named *Émeraude;* the fifth may be named *Perle.*

A second commercial oiler for Indian Ocean freighting service under charter to the French Ministry of Defense was reported to have been ordered late 1985. Data, as for the initial unit:

D: 32,000 tons (fl) **S:** 14.5 kts **Dim:** 178.00 (165.02 pp) × 27.50 × 15.30
M: 1 SOCATRA-Burmeister & Wain 6L-67 GBE diesel; 1 prop; 11, 110 hp

Remarks: Will be capable of alongside underway liquid replenishment.

Orion (M 645) L. & L. Van Ginderen, 12-85

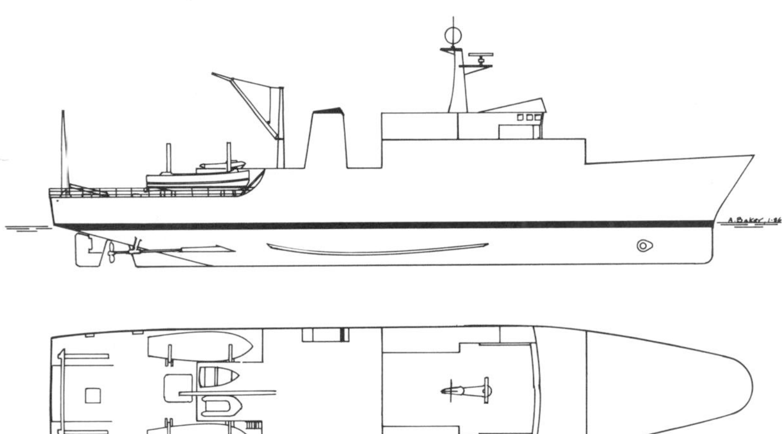

La Pérouse (A 791) A. Baker, 1-86

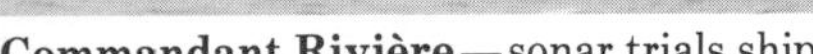

Commandant Rivière—sonar trials ship French Navy, 12-85

EAST GERMANY

A third Tarantul-I-class guided-missile corvette was delivered during 1985.

Albin Kobis—Tarantul-I class 1984

WEST GERMANY

The first of the two Type 122 frigates ordered during 1985 is to be named *Augsberg,* vice *Braunschweig.* Former *Zobel*-class torpedo boat *Hermelin* (P 6095) has been renamed *Kor-Z* as a Type 740 target craft.

Landing craft LCM 15 has been retyped as an auxiliary and renumbered A 1408. Small electronics intercept craft *Holnis* has been renumbered A 836. Two Type 442 intelligence-collection ships are to replace the three Type 442/422 units now in use:

◆ **0 (+2) Type 442 intelligence collectors** Bldr: Flensberger SB

	Laid Down	L	In Serv.
A. . . N. . .	. . .	. . .	. . .
A. . . N. . .	. . .	. . .	. . .

D: 2,400 tons (fl) **S:** . . . **Dim:** 83.5 × 14.6 × . . . (9.4 moulded depth)
M: Diesels: . . . **Man:** 40 tot.

Remarks: Will have three crews for the two ships.
Harbor tanker *Borkum* (Y 824) remains in service:

◆ **1 Class 763 harbor oiler** Bldr: Flenderwerke, Lübeck

	L	In serv.
Y 824 Borkum (ex-A 54, ex U.S.N. 105, ex-*Borkum*)	25-3-36	19-5-36

Borkum (Y 824) H. Ehlers, 9-85

D: 268 tons (light) **S:** 8 kts **Dim:** 37.52 (34.50 pp) × 7.60 × 3.60 (max.)
Electron Equipt: Radar: 1/ . . . nav. **Electric:** 24 kw
M: 1 8-cyl. MWM diesel; 1 prop; 150 hp **Man:** 6 tot.

Remarks: Served U.S. Navy 1954 until recommissioned in Bundesmarine 1-11-56. Stationed at Wilhelmshaven. Cargo: 286 tons.

Two additional KW 15 (Type 369) rescue tenders remain in service: H 11 (Y 857, ex-FL 5) and H 13 (Y 859, ex-FL 7). KFK-class wooden-hulled tender KW 3 (Y 829) remains in service as a radio calibration craft at Wilhelmshaven. Net tender trials craft SP 1 has been renumbered A 837 (ex-Y 837):

SP 1 (A 837) H. Ehlers, 9-85

GREAT BRITAIN

Carrier *Ark Royal* (R 07) does not carry the twin 30-mm AA shown in the drawing in the text; *Invincible* to refit 4-86 to 7-88 at Devonport to *Ark Royal* standard, with 12-deg. ramp. *Trafalgar*-class submarine *Triumph* (S . . .) was ordered 12-85 from Vickers. Three *Upholder*-class diesel submarines were ordered 12-85 from Cammell-Laird, Birkenhead. *Oberon*-class submarines are receiving the MEL Manta EW suite. The three additional "Duke" (Type 23)-class frigates to have been ordered by the end of 1985 (including the second unit, which was to have been built by Swan Hunter) have been delayed until 6-86. *Cornwall* (F 99) of the Type 22 Batch 3 class was launched 14-10-85. *Yarmouth* (F 101) of the *Rothesay* class reported due for disposal 1986.

Data for the P.2000-class training patrol craft should read:

D: 38 tons (43 fl) **S:** 22.5 kts **Dim:** 20.80 (18.00 pp) × 5.80 × 1.50
A: None **Electron Equipt:** Radar: 1/Decca AC 1216C
M: 2 Perkins CV M800T diesels; 2 props; 1,590 hp (1,380 sust.)
Range: 330/20; 500/15 **Electric:** 62 kVA **Man:** 11 tot.

Remarks: *Example* (P 153) delivered 13-8-85 to Royal Naval Auxiliary Service, as was *Explorer* (P 154) on 6-9-85. *Archer* (P 264) launched 25-6-85, delivered 9-8-85, and commissioned 13-8-85. *Biter* (P 270) delivered 23-8-85, and *Blazer* (P 279) delivered 12-9-85—all to the RNR.

Turbulent (S 87) G. Arra, 8-85

Sandown (M . . .), first of the "Single-Role Mine Hunter" type, was ordered 28-8-85 from Vosper-Thornycroft for delivery 3-89:

D: less than 500 tons (fl) **S:** 13 kts **Dim:** 52.50 (50.00 pp) × 9.50 × 2.10
A: 1/30-mm Rarden AA
Electron Equipt: Radar: . . .—Sonar: Type 2093
M: 2 Paxman Valenta RP 200E 1500 diesels; 2 vertical cycloidal props; 3,000 hp—bow-thruster
Range: 3,500/12 **Electric:** 750 kw **Man:** 7 officers, 33 men

Remarks: Will travel at up to 6.5 kts on auxiliary electric drive while minehunting.

Itchen (M 2009)—"River" class M. Louagie, 8-85

New landing ship *Sir Galahad* will be powered by two Mirrlees-Blackstone 9K Major Mk 3 diesels; 2 props; 13,320 hp. Armament will be: 2/40-mm AA (I × 2), 2/20-mm AA (I × 2). *Sir Lamorak* (L 3532) was sold commercially 11-85 as *Merchant Trader. Sir Tristram* (L 3505) re-entered service 9-10-85 after repair, modernization, and lengthening; the mast and superstructure were revised, and a Chinook helicopter can now land amidships.

Sir Tristram (L 3505)—as rebuilt L. & L. Van Ginderen, 10-85

Survey ship *Herald* (A . . .) was launched 14-11-85.

◆ **1 chartered stern trawler** Bldr: Goole SB & Repairing, Goole

Arctic Freebooter: (In serv. 2-66)

D: . . . **S:** . . . **Dim:** 67.79 (64.62 wl) × 12.63 × . . .
Electron Equipt: Radar: . . .
M: 1 6-cyl., 4-stroke Mirrlees National diesel; 1 CP prop; 2,380 hp
Man: . . .

Remarks: Chartered from Boyd Line fall 1985 to replace chartered trawler *Northella* as submarine escort at Faslane. Also used to observe Soviet intelligence collectors off U.K. coast.

Chartered trawler Northella L. & L. Van Ginderen, 11-85

Northella, chartered 10-83 for navigational training and submarine security duties in the Clyde area, transferred to Portsmouth late in 1985:

D: 1,238 grt **S:** 16.5 kts **Dim:** 70.2 (65.2 pp) × 12.6 × 4.9
M: 1 Mirrlees-Blackstone KMR-7 Major diesel; 1 CP prop; 3,246 hp

Seagoing tug *Confident* (A 290) was stricken by end 1985.

The Royal Air Force's Marine Branch was to be disestablished 31-3-86, with the following craft to be retained by the government and operated and maintained by James Fisher, Ltd., in their former roles: *Seal* (5000), *Seagull* (5001), *Spitfire* (4000), *Halifax* (4003), *Hampden* (4004), *Hurricane* (4006), *Lancaster* (4006), *Wellington* (4007), and 1300-series rescue pinnaces 1374, 1387, 1389, 1390, and 1392. *Sunderland* (4001) and *Stirling* (4002) were transferred to the Royal Navy at Gibraltar on 29-8-85 as HMS *Hart* and *Cormorant,* respectively.

Spitfire (4000) L. & L. Van Ginderen, 7-85

GREECE

Training ship *Aris* (A 74) has a top speed of 17.8 kts (15 sust.) and has a crew of 21 officers, 34 petty officers and warrants, and 60 men, plus up to 359 cadets. A 1986 refit will provide a new CIC and full helicopter facilities (including reactivating the hangar) for an Alouette-III or AB 212 helicopter.

HONDURAS

A third Lantana 32-m patrol boat is under construction, for delivery 6-86; it will be powered by 3 G.M. 16V92 TI diesels. Armament includes a G.E. 20-mm Sea Vulcan gatling gun, which will be backfitted to the other two craft. Eight river patrol craft were delivered 3-2-86 from Lantana Boatyard, Lantana, Florida:

Lantana 11-m patrol craft Lantana, 1-86

D: 8.16 tons (fl) **S:** 26 kts (22 sust.) **Dim:** 11.00 (10.06 wl) × 3.05 × 0.53
A: 2/12.7-mm mg (I × 2)—2/7.62-mm mg (I × 2)
M: 2 Caterpillar 3208 TA diesels; 2 props; 630 hp
Endurance: 5 days **Man:** 5 tot.

Remarks: Aluminum construction with Dupont Kevlar armor. Sisters building for El Salvador.

INDIA

Eight additional Sea King helicopters were ordered 7-85, for a total of 20. Cruiser *Mysore,* out of service for many years, officially stricken 29-8-85. Frigate *Ganga* commissioned 1-1-86. Landing craft L 37 launched by Goa SY, 22-7-85.

INDONESIA

Australian *Attack*-class patrol boat *Assail* is to be delivered 1986 as *Sigurot* (8. . .). The two *Lerici*-class minehunters are to be delivered 8-87 and 3-86.

Teluk Ende (517)—with helicopter hangar, enlarged superstructure R.A.N., 1982

IRAQ

Frigate *Al Qadissiya* (F 17) was launched 6-85.

ISRAEL

A program to construct two 117.0 × 17.0 × 2.1-m tank landing ships to carry 12 tanks, 14 armored personnel carriers, 250 troops, and two helicopters each was canceled during 1985.

ITALY

Small carrier *Giuseppe Garibaldi* (C 551) was delivered 31-7-85 and commissioned 30-9-85, but will not be fully operational until 1987. The government gave permission for a program to acquire V/STOL fixed-wing aircraft for the ship on 6-8-85.

Giuseppe Garibaldi (C 551) Italian Navy, 1985

Latest data for the *Animoso*-class guided-missile destroyers:

D: 5,300 tons (fl) **S:** 31.5 kts **Dim:** 135.60 × 16.10 × . . .
A: 8/Otomat Mk 2/Teseo SSM (II × 4)—1/Mk 13 SAM launcher (40 standard SM-1 MR)—1/Albatros SAM syst. (VIII × 1, . . . Aspide missiles)—1/127-mm 54-cal. OTO Melara DP—3/76-mm OTO Melara Super Rapid DP (I × 3)—6/324-mm ILAS-3 ASW TT (III × 2)—2/AB-212 ASW helicopters (EH.101 later)
Electron Equipt: Radar: 1/MM/SPS-703 nav., 1/MM/SPS-702 surf.-search, 1/MM/SPS-768 air-search, 1/SPS-52 3-D, 2/SPG-51, 1/RTN-30X Dardo
Sonar: . . . bow-mounted, . . . VDS
EW: . . . intercept, 4/ . . . chaff RL
M: CODOG: 2 LM-2500 gas turbines (27,500 hp each), 2 GMT BL230-20 DVM diesels (6,300 hp each); 2 CP props; 12,600/55,000 hp
Man: 400

The "Super-Rapid" version of the OTO Melara 76-mm gun will be installed on the corvettes of the *Minerva* class. *Minerva* and *Urania* were laid down 3-85 and 4-85, respectively, at Riva Trigoso. Landing ship *San Giorgio* (L 9892) was laid down 1-7-85 for launch in fall 1986; sister *San Marco* laid down 9-85 for launch 6-87.

Maestrale (F 570) G. Arra, 8-85

Milazzo (M 5552)—Lerici class G. Arra, 7-85

Quarto (A 5314) G. Arra, 7-85

Pietro Cavezzale (A 5301) G. Arra, 7-85

Anteo (A 5309) G. Arra, 7-85

Five offshore patrol vessels are to be ordered during 1986 as part of a new Navy-operated fisheries and economic resources patrol force:

◆ **5 Cassiopeia class**

	Bldr	Laid Down	L	In serv.
. . . Cassiopeia	. . .	. . .	. . .	. . .
. . . Libra	. . .	. . .	. . .	. . .
. . . Orione	. . .	. . .	. . .	. . .
. . . Spica	. . .	. . .	. . .	. . .
. . . Vega	. . .	. . .	. . .	. . .

D: 1,002 tons (1,361 fl) **S:** 19+ kts **Dim:** 73.2 (68.0 pp) × 11.6 (11.4 wl) × 3.6
A: 1/76-mm DP— . . . —1/helicopter
Electron Equipt: Radar: . . .
EW: intercept gear
M: 2 diesels; 2 props; 6,400 hp **Electric:** . . .
Range: 5,000/15 **Fuel:** 165 tons **Man:** . . .

Remarks: Intended to operate in up to Sea State 5-6. Equipped for rescue, firefighting, and supply duties. The 76-mm guns will replace older OTO Melara "Allargate" models, removed from discarded warships. There will be a telescopic helicopter hangar and a 22-m × 8-m flight deck, with fuel for 90 hours of aircraft operations.

IVORY COAST

The acquisition of two 65-m patrol boats is planned.

JAMAICA

Paul Bogle (P 8), a "Guardian"-class patrol boat, was completed by Lantana Boatyard, Lantana, Florida on 26-9-85:

D: 93 tons (fl) **S:** Over 30 kts **Dim:** 32.31 × 6.25 × 1.24 (2.13 props)
A: 1/20-mm AA—2/12.7-mm mg (I × 2)
Electron Equipt: Radar: 2/Furuno . . . nav.
M: 3 MTU 396 TB92 diesels; 3 props; 3,600 hp **Electric:** 100 kw
Endurance: 7 days **Man:** 4 officers, 16 men

Remarks: Originally to have been named *Cape George.* Aluminum construction. Two G.M. 4-71 generator sets.
Patrol boat *Fort Charles* (P 7) overhauled 1985–86 by Atlantic Marine, Florida.

Paul Bogle (P 8) Lantana, 9-85

JAPAN

Approved under the FY 86 Budget were one 3,400-ton destroyer (DDK 138), one 1,900-ton frigate (DE 229-new design), one 2,400-ton *Yushio*-class submarine (SS 583), two 440-ton minesweepers (MSC 668, 669), one 2,200-ton training support ship (ATS 4202), one 420-ton landing craft (LCU), two 260-ton tugs (YT 68, 69), and a 12-ton self-propelled lighter (YF). Aircraft approved were 10 P-3C Orion, one US-1A rescue amphibian, 13 HSS-2B Sea King ASW helicopters, four MH-53E minesweeping helicopters, one KM-2 Kai basic trainer, and one TC-90 instrument trainer.

The 1986-90 aviation procurement plan calls for 50 P-3C Orion, 36 SH-60J Sea Hawk ASW helicopters, 30 HSS-2B Sea King ASW helicopters, 12 MH-53E Sea Dragon minesweeping helicopters, 3 Shin Meiwa US-1 SAR amphibians, and 3 Learjet 36A jet trainers. Previous orders through 1985 include 49 P-3C (21 in service by 1985), 2 SH-60J, 54 HSS-2B, 10 US-1, and 2 Learjet 36A.

Maritime Safety Agency medium-endurance cutter PM 11 was launched 20-8-85 and delivered 11-85.

SOUTH KOREA

Seoul (952)—Ulsan class 1985

Paek Ku 58 (PGM 358)—with 4 Harpoon 1985

KUWAIT

On 25-7-85, Azimut SY, Torino, Italy, delivered glass-reinforced plastic Customs Service patrol craft *Jamarek I* and *II*:

D: 26 tons (fl) **S:** 28 kts **Dim:** 18.40 (15.50 pp) × 5.10 × 0.93
M: 2 MAN D2842-LE diesels; 2 props; 1,520 hp **Fuel:** 3.75 tons

A larger Customs Service craft was ordered from Azimut in 6-85:

D: 30 tons (fl) **S:** 27 kts **Dim:** 20.00 × 5.10 × 1.50
M: 2 MAN D2842-LE diesels; 2 props; 1,560 hp

LIBYA

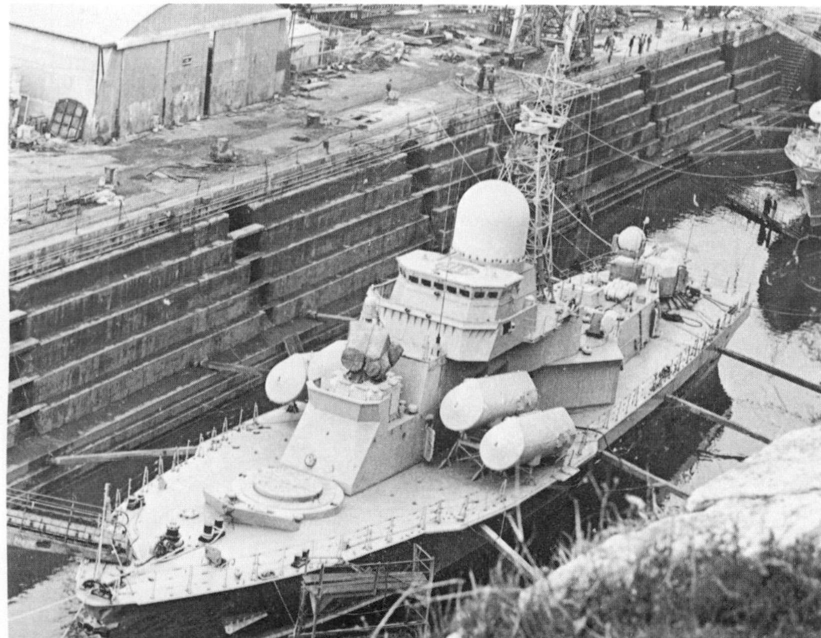

Tariq Ibn Ziyad (416) and sister in dry dock at Malta—a fourth Nanuchka-II was delivered during 9-85 L. & L. Van Ginderen, 1985

MADAGASCAR

A former French Navy EDIC landing craft was transferred 28-9-85 and named *Aina Vao Vao.*

MALAYSIA

The possibility of acquiring submarines was under study during 1985. The *Lerici*-class minehunters have been renumbered M 11–14. They were commissioned together 11-12-85 and were to leave Italy on 19-1-86, for arrival in home waters around 28-3-86.

Jerai (M 12)—with 40-mm AA forward G. Arra, 7-85

Jerai (M 12)—PAP 104 stowed aft G. Arra, 7-85

MOROCCO

Three austere versions of the Spanish *Lazaga* class for 200-n.m. economic zone patrol were ordered from Bazán 2-10-85, with an option for three more:

D: 300 tons (. . . fl) **S:** 22 kts **Dim:** 58.1 (54.4 pp) × 7.60 × 2.70
A: 1/40-mm AA—2/20-mm AA (I × 2)
Electron Equipt: 1/ . . . nav.
M: 2 diesels; 2 props; . . . hp **Range:** 3,290/12

NETHERLANDS

Submarine *Dolfijn* (S 808), stricken 1-2-85, sold for scrap 22-7-85. The second increment of four "M" (*De Zeven Provincen*)-class frigates was officially ordered 1-8-85. Ten "Goalkeeper" 30-mm CIWS were ordered 12-85 for installation in the *Kortenaer* class. Three landing craft were ordered 6-85 from Schöttel at Warmond, presumably follow-on units of the L 9530 group. Former destroyer *Gelderland* (D 811), static training ship, has had her radar antennas replaced; former minesweeper *Grypskerk* (M 826) still exists as a training hulk.

Jacob Van Heemskerck (F 812) Maritime Photographic, 10-85

L 9532—new landing craft L. & L. Van Ginderen, 9-85

RP 16—National Police Force L. & L. Van Ginderen, 9-85

NEW ZEALAND

Frigate *Wellington* (F 69) has a range of 6,500 n.m. at 12 kts after modernization, through the addition of 220 tons additional fuel tankage (**D:** 3,184 tons fl); she is now equipped with the Graseby G 750 hull-mounted sonar.

NIGERIA

The Coast Guard took delivery of P 215, the first of two MillSpeed P/20 patrol boats from Van Mill Marine Service, Hardinxveld-Giessendam, the Netherlands:

D: 45 tons (fl) **S:** 35+ kts **Dim:** 20.20(18.00 wl) × 5.30 × 1.75
A: 1/20-mm AA—2/7.62-mm mg (I × 2) **Electron Equipt:** Radar: . . . nav.
M: 3 G.M. 12V71 TI diesels; 3 props; 2,100 hp
Range: 950/25; 1,200/11 **Man:** 2 officers, 10 men

REMARKS: Glass-reinforced plastic construction.
Two P.2000 patrol boats have been ordered from Watercraft, Ltd. for delivery 3-86:

D: 45 tons (fl) **S:** 30 kts **Dim:** 21.80 (19.00 wl) × 5.80 × 1.50
A: . . . **Electron Equipt:** Radar: 1/ . . . nav.
M: 2 MTU 8V396 TB93 diesels; 2 props; 2,600 hp (2,176 sust.)

REMARKS: Glass-reinforced plastic construction. Hulls 1-m longer than standard P.2000. May be intended for the Marine Police.

NORWAY

Three Type 207, *Kobben*-class submarines are to be refurbished for sale to Denmark, delivering 1987–89. The generators in the new Type 210 submarines will be powered by two MTU 16V652 MB diesels.

OMAN

A fourth "Province"-class guided-missile patrol boat was ordered 12-85 from Vosper-Thornycroft for delivery late 1988/early 1989; the unit will be equipped like the second and third Omani examples of the class. The Royal Omani Coast Guard reportedly ordered two 8.5-m glass-reinforced plastic patrol craft from Gulf Crafts, Ajman, UAE, in 1985; two 140-hp Evinrude outboard motors give 40-kt speeds.

PAPUA NEW GUINEA

The order for four 31.5-m patrol boats from Australia was placed 31-10-85.

PERU

Former U.K. "Colonies"-class cruiser *Colonel Bolegnesi* was towed to Taiwan for scrap 8-85. Two additional *Friesland*-class destroyers may be discarded during 1986–87, reducing the total to four.

PORTUGAL

The contract for three MEKO 200 frigates was signed with the Howaldtswerke-Blohm + Voss consortium on 11-12-85. Platform data will be generally similar to the quartet building for Turkey, but U.S., Canadian, and Norwegian electronics and armament equipment will be fitted.

SOUTH AFRICA

According to an official statement by the Chief of Naval Operations, South African Navy, the following units may have to be decommissioned to effect necessary economies: frigate *President Pretorius,* the five "Ford"-class units, net tender *Somerset,* and the just extensively refitted oiler/search-and-rescue ship *Tafelberg.*

SPAIN

Bazán, San Fernando launched P 53, the first of two "Cormorant"-class patrol boats built on speculation, on 15-10-85; no customer has been announced:

D: 357 tons (fl) **S:** 32 kts **Dim:** 52.02 × 7.54 × 1.87
A: . . . **Electron Equipt:** . . .
M: 3 Bazán-MTU MA16V956 TB91 diesels; 3 (1 CP) props; 11,250 hp
Range: 2,000/15.5 **Man:** 30 tot.

REMARKS: Rumored sale to Somalia did not materialize.
A design for a new oceanographic ship has been prepared by Bazán; if built, the ship will be paid for by the Ministry of Foreign Affairs, but operated by the Navy.

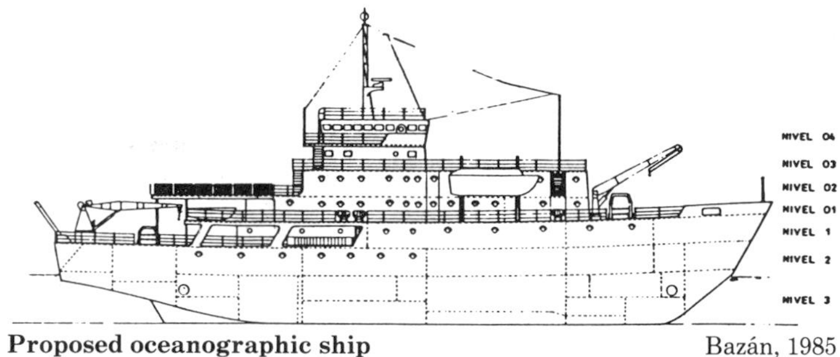

Proposed oceanographic ship Bazán, 1985

D: 2,600 tons (light) **S:** 15 kts **Dim:** 67.00 (pp) × 14.00 × 4.80
M: 3,600-bhp diesel generator plant, electric drive; 1 prop; 2,700 hp (bow- and stern-thrusters)

REMARKS: Icebreaker bow for Antarctic duties. Helicopter deck, but no hangar. Endurance of 100 days. Diver-support to 200 m. Total 330 m² laboratory space.

SRI LANKA

Two landing craft were ordered from Vosper PTY, Singapore, during 1985:

D: 200 tons **S:** 8 kts **Dim:** 30.00 × 8.00 × 1.50
M: 2 Caterpillar 3408TA diesels; 2 props; 1,524 hp
Range: 1,800/8 **Man:** . . .

The last two of ten follow-on orders for the Cougar CAT 900 patrol craft were delivered 10-85.

TAIWAN

Nine additional S-2E Tracker ASW aircraft were delivered from surplus U.S. stocks late in 1985. The prototype patrol boat delivered during 1985 from Vosper PTY, Singapore, has the following characteristics:

D: . . . **S:** 40 kts **Dim:** 21.0 × . . . × . . .
A: 1/20-mm AA—2/12.7-mm mg (I × 2)
M: 2 G.M.-Stewart & Stevenson 16V92M TAB diesels; 2 props; 2,400 hp

Transport Tai Hu (525) *Military Technology,* 1985

THAILAND

Frigate *Makut Rajakumarn* received a Krupp-Atlas DSQS-21B sonar in place of the original U.K.-built suite during 1985 repairs after a gas-turbine fire. PSMM Mk 5-class patrol boat *Katang* (7) reported commissioned 14-10-85.

TURKEY

Additional photo coverage, courtesy Dipl.-Ing. Hartmut Ehlers and L. & L. Van Ginderen:

Ikinei Inonu (533)—GUPPY-III class H. Ehlers, 1-85

Savestepe (D 348)—with quadruple decoy RL atop pilothouse and hangar (IV × 4)
L. & L. Van Ginderen, 11-85

Mehmetcik (N 115)—mineplanter H. Ehlers, 6-83

Sarucabey (NL 123) H. Ehlers, 1984

Cakabey (NL 122) H. Ehlers, 4-84

Işin (A 589) H. Ehlers, 5-83

Binbaşi Saadettin Gürçon (A 573) H. Ehlers, 1-85

USSR

Delta-II ballistic-missile submarine U.S. Navy, 1985

Admiral Yumashev (Kresta-II class) U.S. Navy, 1985

Osmotritel'nyy (Sovremennyy class) en route to the Pacific
PHC J. Kristoffersen, USN, 10-85

Imeni XXV Sezda K.P.S.S.—*Ivan Susanin* class KGB patrol icebreaker
U.S. Navy, 1985

Frunze (Kirov class) en route to the Pacific U.S. Navy, 10-85

Alatau—the third naval Ingul-class rescue ship U.S. Navy, 11-85

Dauriya—Vytegrales-class fleet support ship, with deckhouse over third hold and tracking radars above the bridge U.S. Navy, 1985

USA

A new "low-cost torpedo" is to be developed for submarine use against lower-value targets. It is hoped that the weapons will cost about one-tenth the price of a Mk 48 ADCAP weapon. Speed is estimated at 35 kts for 3 nautical miles.

LCAC-2, leading LCAC-1 Bell-Halter, 1985

Arkansas (CGN 41)—with two Tomahawk armored box launchers replacing the helicopter facility at the stern. White rectangles on deck fore and aft mark helicopter vertical replenishment hovering areas. G. Arra, 10-85

CT 4—the first YP training craft to be redesignated a COOP mine-disposal training craft G. Arra, 9-85

Side-loading warping tug, with portable deckhouse, winch, and two diesel outdrives G. Arra, 1985

Avalon (DSRV 2)—Deep Submergence Rescue Vehicle, aboard submarine *William H. Bates* (SSN 680) G. Arra, 1985

Arco (ARDM 5)—fitting out at Seattle G. Arra, 10-85

65-foot torpedo retriever 4 G. Arra, 8-85

D: 34.8 tons (35.2 fl) **S:** 18.7 kts **Dim:** 19.80 × 5.25 × 1.17
M: 2 G.M. 12V71 diesels; 2 props; 1,008 hp (800 sust.)
Range: 280/18 **Electric:** 10 kw **Man:** 6 tot.

REMARKS: Aluminum construction. Can recover up to 5 tons of weapons. There are also utility boat and personnel boat versions of this design, with the latter having a low deckhouse aft.

72-foot torpedo retriever Mk 2 G. Arra, 10-85

D: 53 tons (fl) **S:** 18 kts **Dim:** 22.17 × 5.18 × 1.68
M: 2 diesels; 2 props; 1,000 hp **Range:** 450/18 **Man:** 6 tot.

REMARKS: Wooden construction. Can carry up to 10.8 tons of weapons retrieved via a stern ramp. Obsolescent, to be replaced by new Marinette-built units. Craft in photo above modified to a non-torpedo retrieval role.

Retriever (DR 1) G. Arra, 9-85

D: 125 tons (fl) **S:** 22 kts **Dim:** 30.02 × 7.92 × 2.13
M: 4 G.M. diesels; 4 props; . . . hp **Man:** 1 officer, 17 men

REMARKS: Former PT 109, launched 7-8-50 by Electric Boat, Groton, Ct. Later named *Guardian* for Secret Service use as chase boat for presidential yacht. Used at Little Creek, Va., since 12-74 as a drone target control and recovery craft. Aluminum construction.

Chaparral (TWR 7) G. Arra, 10-85

REMARKS: Employed at San Diego. One of two 85-foot torpedo retrievers completed in 1976 by Tacoma Boat.

Henry J. Kaiser (T-AO 187)—shortly after launch U.S. Navy, 10-85

Louise Lykes—Military Sealift Command charter G. Arra, 3-85

During January 1986, the Navy purchased an additional 13 merchant ships for the Maritime Administration-controlled Ready Reserve Force. These included roll-on/roll-off vehicle cargo ships *Paralla* (1971, American Automar), *Lipscomb Lykes, Charles Lykes* (both 1976, Lykes Brothers Steamship Co.); *Barber Tonsberg, Barber Priam,* and *Barber Taif* (all 1979, Barber Steamship); lighter-aboard-ship (LASH) barge carriers *Delta Mar* (1973), *Delta Sud* (1973), *Delta Norte* (1973), and *Delta Caribe* (1971—all United States Lines); and Sea Bee barge carriers *Almerica Lykes* (1972), *Doctor Lykes* (1972), and *Tillie Lykes* (1973—all Lykes Brothers Steamship Co). The ships with corporate names will probably be renamed in the MARAD "Cape" series during their layup overhauls.

Cape Domingo—Ready Reserve Force Ro-Ro MSC, 12-85

LATE ADDENDA

Through 28 February 1986

AUSTRALIA

Fleet replenishment ship *Success* (AOR 304) scheduled to commission 15-4-86.

BRAZIL

Two *Inhaúma*-class frigates were ordered 1-12-85 from Verolme Brazil, Porto Alegre.

CANADA

Coast Guard: Construction of at least two Type 1000 ice-capable buoy tenders and one Type 900 navigational aids tender is to begin in 1987–88. *Samuel Risley* (Type 1050) entered service 5-85. *Martha L. Black* (Type 1100) entered service in 8-85 and sister *George R. Pearkes* in 11-85. Type 800 small navigational aids tenders *Île des Barques* and *Partridge Island* entered service 9-85, while the similar "Type F" tenders *Île Saint Ours* and *Caribou Isle* completed later in the year. Current search-and-rescue craft programs include three Type 100 craft to replace *Osprey* and *Bittern,* two Type 200 ice-strengthened rescue craft, two Type 300 self-righting lifeboats, *Cap Goelands* and *Souris,* completed 1985 by Hike Metal, Wheatley, Ont., and to replace *Spume,* a Type 400, Kevlar-hulled boat is being built: 22.74 (19.00 wl) × 6.12 × 1.50. Large icebreakers *John A. Macdonald* and *Louis S. St. Laurent* are to be given life-extension overhauls, including new engines and a new bow shape in the latter. Rescue cutter *Alert* is also to be modernized, while *Sir Humphrey Gilbert, Simon Fraser,* and *Narwhal* were undergoing modernization 1985–86; *Fraser* has been reconfigured for search and rescue, with additional lifeboats but losing her hangar. A very large arctic icebreaker is again being contemplated, at the possible expense of naval programs.

CHILE

A new transport to replace *Aquiles* was ordered 4-10-85 from ASMAR, Talcahuano, and will also be named *Aquiles:*

D: 4,500 tons (fl) **S:** 19 kts **Dim:** 97.0 × 17.0 × 6.0
A: . . .
M: Diesels **Man:** 80 tot., plus 250 troops

Remarks: Two holds, served by one electric crane. Helicopter deck. Will be convertible as a hospital ship for disaster relief.

CHINA

A program to construct British Cougar Marine 14-m patrol craft in China, using Cougar-supplied moulds has commenced. The craft will be powered by two Soviet-design M50-series diesels, for 2,400 hp and very high maximum speeds. The moulds for the glass-reinforced plastic boats are to be delivered 8-86.

GREAT BRITAIN

"County"-class guided-missile destroyer *Glamorgan* (D 19), frigates *Leander* (F 109), *Galatea* (F 18), and *Yarmouth* (F 101), *Oberon*-class submarines *Orpheus* (S 11) and *Oberon* (S 09), "Ton"-class minehunter *Bildeston* (M 1110) and sister minesweepers *Alfriston* (M 1103), *Bickington* (M 1109), *Hodgeston* (M 1146), *Walkerton* (M 1188), and *Stubbington* (M 1204), and survey ship *Hydra* (A 144) are to be decommissioned during 1986; some of the mine countermeasures units and *Hydra* will be maintained in reserve, the remainder stricken.

INDIA

One Sea King Mk 42 helicopter was lost 1-86.

INDONESIA

Netherlands Navy *Van Speijk*-class frigate *Tjerk Hiddes* (F 804) will be transferred 1-10-86, followed by *Van Speijk* (F 802) on 1-11-86, per a 10-2-86 agreement; options were also taken to purchase sisters *Van Galen* (F 803) and *Van Nes* (F 805), for delivery in 11-87 and 2-88.

NETHERLANDS

Jacob Van Heemskerck (F 812) commissioned 15-1-86. *Hellevoetsluis* (M 859) launched 13-12-85. Two (and possibly four) *Van Speijk*-class frigates to transfer to Indonesia (see above).

SAUDI ARABIA

Two 27-m patrol boats, possibly for the Coast Guard, were ordered late in 1985 from Abeking & Rasmussen, Lemwerder, West Germany.

SOUTH AFRICA

Agulhas—naval-manned research ship — L. & L. Van Ginderen, 1-86

USA

Characteristics for the new Coast Guard icebreaker, to be delivered 1992, include:

D: 15,951 tons (fl) **S:** . . . **Dim:** 137.47 × 26.82 × 9.94
A: 2/12.7-mm mg (I × 1)—helicopters
M: 4 medium-speed diesels, electric drive; 2 props; 30,000 hp
Endurance: 80 days **Man:** 124 men plus 30 scientists

Remarks: To be capable of breaking 1.4-m ice at 3 kts continuously. To replace "Wind" class.